ROBERT NORTH S.J.

ELENCHUS OF BIBLICA

1991

EDITRICE PONTIFICIO ISTITUTO BIBLICO
ROMA 1994

ROBERT NORTH S.J.

ELENCHUS OF BIBLICA

1991

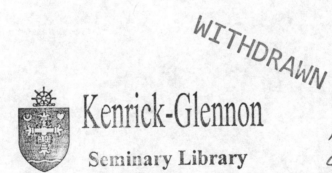
EDITRICE PONTIFICIO ISTITUTO BIBLICO
ROMA 1994

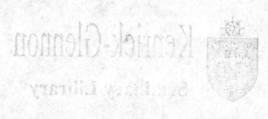

Editrice Pontificio Istituto Biblico
Piazza della Pilotta, 35 - 00187 Roma

Why does our Elenchus come so late? (mid-1994 for 1991)

In a way the question is a transitory one, since we live in expectation of the day when the biblical sciences will have available on-line service for publications of a few days or weeks previous, from a computer-bank, as has been the case for medical and legal research for many years already.

Meanwhile it may be of use to describe the procedure by which this Elenchus is compiled, which will show also how the delay is in some ways an advantage, at least for the printed volumes in series.

The compiler has a little booklet of some 1200 periodical titles, indicating their collocation in some nearby library and the date of the last issue excerpted. Already in 1991 was begun the process of taking down some titles from the available 1991 issues, some 100 items per day along with earlier titles not yet done. No more could be excerpted per day because of the urgent needs of editing and proofreading earlier volumes already in an advanced stage.

Thus only toward the end of 1992 were some 15,000 titles available, enough to begin the editing process. This consists in subdividing the random titles into their categories (indicated 'synoptically' on the two following pages), then alphabetizing the items within each category. Then for each item a search had to be made, in order to indicate whether it had appeared in a preceding volume and where. And with each title had to be inserted the necessary style-indications for the printer.

Meanwhile through late 1992 and most of 1993 other 1991 titles continued to be gathered. Actually many 1991 issues arrive only in 1992, and surprisingly many also only in 1993. Almost all of these can be inserted (with greater or less difficulty) into the editing-process, right up through the correction of the first or even final proofs.

Thus this volume, properly for 1991, contains most publications dated 1991 but actually published perhaps much later. It contains also all the materials from volumes dated '1991s', i.e. begun in 1991 but continuing also in 1992; and some later reviews of books dated 1991.

The procedure described above for periodicals is roughly the same for *books* published in 1991 (or earlier, but not yet noted), especially the many *Festschrifts* and *Acta* of scholarly meetings, of which the individual articles have to be excerpted as far as possible. For other books, we rely chiefly on the book-reviews; though many titles also are taken down directly from libraries in which they are displayed.

The proofreading operations for the 1991 volume take up almost all the compiler's time from September 1993 through March 1994. It must be admitted that this toil, and also the compilation of the Index, would go much faster if divided among many helpers: but it must also be noted that many errors can be eliminated when a single person checks every item as many as ten times within the continuing editing process.

So, until the on-line computer is available, your 1992 volume is worth the longer wait.

Index systematicus – Contents

**Production-costs of this volume were aided by a grant
from the Catholic Biblical Association of America**

AA	Ann Arbor	Lp	Leipzig
Amst	Amsterdam	Lv(N)	Leuven (L-Neuve)
B	Berlin	M/Mi	Madrid/Milano
Ba/BA	Basel/Buenos Aires	Mkn/Mp	Maryknoll/Minneapolis
Barc	Barcelona	Mü	München
Bo/Bru	Bologna/Brussel	N	Napoli
CasM	Casale Monferrato	ND	NotreDame IN
CinB	Cinisello Balsamo	Neuk	Neukirchen/Verlag
C	Cambridge, England	NHv	New Haven
CM	Cambridge, Mass.	Nv	Nashville
Ch	Chicago	NY	New York
ColMn	Collegeville MN	Ox	Oxford
Da: Wiss	Darmstadt, WissBuchg	P/Pd	Paris/Paderborn
DG	Downers Grove IL	Ph	Philadelphia
Dü	Düsseldorf	R/Rg	Roma/Regensburg
E	Edinburgh	S/Sdr	Salamanca/Santander
ENJ	EnglewoodCliffs NJ	SF	San Francisco
F	Firenze	Shf	Sheffield
FrB/FrS	Freiburg-Br/Schw	Sto	Stockholm
Fra	Frankfurt/M	Stu	Stuttgart
Gö	Göttingen	T/TA	Torino/Tel Aviv
GR	Grand Rapids MI	Tü	Tübingen
Gü	Gütersloh	U/W	Uppsala/Wien
Ha	Hamburg	WL	Winona Lake IN
Heid	Heidelberg	Wmr	Warminster
Hmw	Harmondsworth	Wsb	Wiesbaden
J	Jerusalem	Wsh	Washington
K	København	Wsz	Warszawa
L	London	Wu/Wü	Wuppertal/Würzburg
LA	Los Angeles	Zu	Zürich

Price of books

is herein rounded off in view of inflation
and for conciseness

Thus $13 even where the cited source has $12.95
(less often £20 for 19.90; DM 40 for 39,80)

Acronyms: Periodica - Series (small). *8 fig.* = ISSN; *10 fig.* = ISBN; *6/7* = DissA.

🅐: *arabice,* in Arabic.

AAS: Acta Apostolicae Sedis; Vaticano. 0001-5199.

AASOR: Annual of the American Schools of Oriental Research; CM.

Abh: Abhandlungen Gö Lp Mü etc.; ➤ DOG / DPV.

AbhChrJüDial: Abhandlungen zum christlich-jüdischen Dialog; Mü, Kaiser.

AbrNahr: Abr-Nahrain; Lv, Peeters.

AcAANorv: Acta ad archaeologiam et artium historiam; R, Inst. Norv.

AcArchLov: Acta archaeologica Lovaniensia; Lv.

Acme; Mi, Fac. Lett. Filos. 0001-494X.

AcNum: Acta Numismatica; Barc. 0211-8386.

Act: Actes/Acta (Congrès, Colloque).

ActAntH: Acta Antiqua; Budapest.

Acta PIB: Acta Pontificii Instituti Biblici: Roma.

ActArchH/K: Acta Archaeologica; Hungarica, Budapest. 0001-5210 / København. 0065-101X.

ActClasSAfr: Acta Classica; Pretoria. 0065-1141.

ActIran: Acta Iranica; Téhéran/Leiden.

ActOrH/K: Acta Orientalia: Budapest. 0044-5975 / K (Soc. Or. Danica, Norveigica). 0001-6438.

ActPraeh: Acta Praehistorica/Archaeol.; B.

ActSum: Acta Sumerologica; Hiroshima Univ., Linguistics. 0387-8082.

ActuBbg: Actualidad Bibliográfica; Barcelona. 0211-4143.

ADAJ: Annual of the Department of Antiquities, Jordan; 'Amman.

ADPF: Association pour la diffusion de la pensée française; Paris ➤ RCiv.

Aeg: Aegyptus; Milano. 0001-9046.

ÄgAbh: Ägyptologische Abhandlungen; Wb.

ÄgAT: Ägypten und Altes Testament; Wiesbaden. 0720-9061.

AegHelv: Aegyptiaca Helvetica: Basel Univ. Äg. Sem. (Univ. Genève).

ÄgLev: Ägypten und Levante; Wien. 1015-5014.

AEM: Archives Épistolaires de Mari.

ÄthF: Äthiopische Forschungen; Stu.

AevA: Aevum Antiquum; Mi, Univ. Cattolica/ViPe.

Aevum; Milano [anche Univ. Catt.].

AfER: African Ecclesial Review; Eldoret, Kenya.

AfJB: African Journal of Biblical Studies; Ibadan.

AfO: Archiv für Orientforschung; Graz.

AfTJ: Africa Theological Journal; Arusha, Tanzania. 0856-0048.

AGJU: Arbeiten zur Geschichte Antik. Judentums und des Urchristentums; Leiden.

AIBL: Académie des Inscriptions et Belles-Lettres; P ➤ CRAI. – **AIEMA** ➤ BMosA.

AION [-Clas]: Annali (dell')Istituto Universitario Orientale [Classico] di Napoli ➤ ArchStorAnt.

AIPHOS: Annuaire de l'Institut de Philologie et d'Histoire Orientales et Slaves; Bru.

AJA: American Journal of Archaeology; Princeton NJ. 0002-9114.

AJS: Association for Jewish Studies Review; CM 0364-0094.

Akkadica; Bruxelles/Brussel.

al.: et alii, and other(s).

Alexandria, cosmology; GR. (1,1991).

ALGHJ: Arbeiten zur Literatur und Geschichte des hellenistischen Judentums; Leiden.

Al-Kibt, The Copts, die Kopten; Ha.

Altertum (Das); Berlin. 0002-6646.

AltOrF: Altorientalische Forschungen; Berlin. 0232-8461.

AmBapQ: American Baptist Quarterly; Valley Forge PA. 0015-8992.

AmBenR: American Benedictine Review; Richardton ND. 0002-7650.

Ambrosius, bollettino liturgico; Milano. 0392-5757.

America; NY. 0002-7049.

AmHR: American Historical Rev.; NY.

AmJAncH: American Journal of Ancient History; CM.

AmJPg: American Journal of Philology; Baltimore. 0002-9475.

AmJTPh: American Journal of Theology and Philosophy; W. Lafayette IN.

AmMessianJ: The American Messianic Jew; Ph.

AmNumM: American Numismatic Society Museum Notes; NY.

AmPhTr: Transactions of the American Philosophical Society; Ph.

AmstCah: Amsterdamse cahiers voor exegese/bijbelse theologie; Kampen.

AmstMed ➤ Mededelingen.

AmStPapyr: American Studies in Papyrology; NHv.

AnalPapyr: Analecta Papyrologica; Messina. (1,1989).

AnáMnesis: teología, Dominicos; México. (3,1991).

AnArStorAnt: Annali di Archeologia e Storia Antica.

AnASyr: Annales Archéologiques Arabes Syriennes; Damas.

Anatolica; Istanbul. 0066-1554.

AnatSt: Anatolian Studies; London.

AnAug: Analecta Augustiniana; R.

ANaut: Archaeonautica; P. 0154-1854.

AnBib: Analecta Biblica. Investigationes scientificae in res biblicas; R. 0066-135X.

AnBoll: Analecta Bollandiana; Bruxelles. 0003-2468.

AnBritAth: Annual of the British School at Athens; London.

AnCalas: Analecta Calasanctiana; Salamanca. 0569-9789.

AnCÉtRel: Annales du Centre d'Études des Religions; Bru.

AncHB: Ancient History Bulletin; Calgary/Chicago. 0835-3638.

AnChile: Anales de la Facultad de Teolog'a; Santiago, Univ. Católica.

AnchorB[D] [Dict]: Anchor Bible; NY.

AncHRes: Ancient History Resources for Teachers; Sydney. 0310-5814.

AnCist: Analecta Cisterciensia; Roma. 0003-2476.

AnClas: Annales Universitatis, sectio classica; Budapest.

AnClémOchr: Annuaire de l'Académie de théologie 'Ochrida'; Sofya.

AnCracov: Analecta Cracoviensia (Polish Theol. Soc.); Kraków. 0209-0864.

AncSoc: Ancient Society. Katholieke Universiteit; Leuven. 0066-1619.

AncW: Ancient World; Ch. 0160-9645.

AndrUnS: Andrews University Seminary Studies; Berrien Springs, Mich. 0003-2980.

AnÉCS: Annales Économies Sociétés Civilisations; P. 0395-2649.

AnEgBbg: Annual Egyptological Bibliography; Leiden.

AnÉPH: Annuaire ➤ ÉPHÉ.

AnÉth: Annales d'Éthiopie; Addis-Ababa.

AnFac: Let: Annali della facoltà di lettere, Univ. (Bari/Cagliari/Perugia).

— **Ling/T:** Annal(es) Facultat(is); linguarum, theologiae.

AnFg: Anuario de Filología; Barc.

Ang: Angelicum; Roma. 0003-3081.

AnglTR: Anglican Theological Review; Evanston IL. 0003-3286.

AnGreg: Analecta (Pont. Univ.) Gregoriana; Roma. 0066-1376.

AnHArt: Annales d'histoire de l'art et d'archéologie: Bru.

AnHConc: Annuarium Historiae Conciliorum; Paderborn.

ANilM: Archéologie du Nil Moyen; Lille. 0299-8130.

AnItNum: Annali (dell')Istituto Italiano di Numismatica; Roma.

AnJapB: Annual of the Japanese Biblical Institute; Tokyo ❶ ➤ Sei-Ron.

AnLetN: Annali della Facoltà di lettere e filosofia dell'Univ.; Napoli.

AnLovBOr: Analecta Lovaniensia Biblica et Orientalia; Lv.

AnnTh: Annales Theologici; Roma.

AnOr: Analecta Orientalia: Roma.

AnOrdBas: Analecta Ordinis S. Basilii Magni; Roma.

AnPg: L'Année Philologique; P. ➤ 858.

AnPisa: Annali della Scuola Normale Superiore; Pisa.

AnPraem: Analecta Praemonstratensia; Averbode.

AnRIM: Annual Review of the Royal Inscriptions of Mesopotamia Project; Toronto. 0822-2525.

AnRSocSR: Annual Review of the Social Sciences of Religion; The Hague. 0066-2062.

ANRW: Aufstieg und Niedergang der römischen Welt ➤ 659.

AnSacTar: Analecta Sacra Tarraconensia; Barcelona.

AnSemClas: Annali del Seminario di Studi del Mondo Classico; N, Univ.

AnStoEseg: Annali di Storia dell'Esegesi; Bologna. 1120-4001.

AntAb: Antike und Abendland; Berlin. 0003-5696.

AntAfr: Antiquités africaines; Paris. 0066-4871.
AntClas: L'Antiquité Classique; Bru.
AntClCr: Antichità classica e cristiana; Brescia.
Anthropos; 1. Fribourg/Suisse. 0003-5572. / [2. Famiglia; Roma].
Anthropotes; Roma, Città Nuova.
AntiqJ: Antiquaries Journal; London. 0003-5815.
Antiquity; Gloucester. 0003-5982.
Ant/ka: Ⓖ Anthropologiká: Thessaloniki.
AntKu: Antike Kunst; Basel. 0003-5688.
Anton: Antonianum; Roma. 0003-6064.
AntRArch: Antiqua, Rivista d'Archeologia e d'Architettura; Roma.
AnTVal: Anales de Teología, Universidad de Valencia.
AntWelt: Antike Welt; Feldmeilen.
Anvil, Anglican Ev. theol.; Bramcote, Nottingham. 0003-6226.
AnzAltW: Anzeiger für die Altertumswissenschaft; Innsbruck. 0003-6293.
AnzW: Anzeiger der österreichischen Akademie; Wien. 0378-8652.
AOAT: Alter Orient und Altes Testament: Kevelaer/Neukirchen.
AOtt: Univ. München, Arbeiten zu Text und Sprache im AT; St. Ottilien.
Apollonia: Afro-Hellenic studies; Johannesburg, Rand Afrikaans Univ.
Appoint; Montréal. (25,1992).
ArabArchEp: Arabian Archaeology and Epigraphy; K. 0905-7916.
Aram: Oxford.
Arasaradi, journal of theological reflection: Tamilnadu, Madurai (3/2, 1990).
ArBegG: Archiv für Begriffsgeschichte (Mainz, Akad.); Bonn.
ArbGTL: Arbeiten zur Geschichte und Theologie des Luthertums, NF; B.
ArbKiG: Arbeiten zur Kirchengeschichte; B.
ArbNTJud: Arbeiten zum NT und zum Judentum; Frankfurt/M. 0170-8856.
ArbNtTextf: Arbeiten zur Neutestamentlichen Textforschung; B/NY.
ArbT: Arbeiten zur Theologie (Calwer); Stu.
ArCalc: Archeologia e calcolatori; F, Univ. Siena [1 (1990) 88-7814-072-4].
ARCE → J[News]AmEg.
Archaeología; Wsz. 0066-605X.
Archaeology; Boston. 0003-8113.

Archaeometry; L. 0003-813X.
ArchAnz: Archäologischer Anzeiger; Berlin. 0003-8105.
ArchAth: Ⓖ Archaiología; Athēna.
ArchBbg: Archäologische Bibliographie zu JbDAI; Berlin.
ArchClasR: Archeologia Classica; Roma. 0391-8165.
Archeo, attualità del passato; Milano.
Archéologia; (ex-Paris) Dijon, Faton. 0570-6270 → Dossiers.
ArchEph: Ⓖ Archaiologikē Ephēmeris; Athēnai.
ArchInf: Archäologische Informationen; Bonn.
ArchMIran: Archäologische Mitteilungen aus Iran, N.F.; Berlin.
ArchNews: Archaeological News; Tallahassee FL. 0194-3413.
ArchRCamb: Archaeological Reviews from Cambridge (Eng.). 0261-4332.
ArchRep: Archaeological Reports; Wmr, British Sch. Athens. 0570-6084.
ArchStorAnt: [= a *third* AION] Archeologia e Storia Antica; Napoli, Univ. Ist. Or./Cl. 0393-070X.
Arctos, Acta Philologica Fennica; Helsinki. 0570-734X.
ArEspArq: Archivo Español de Arqueología; Madrid. 0066-6742.
ARET/S: Archivi Reali di Ebla, Testi/Studi; Roma, Univ.
Arethusa; Buffalo NY. 0004-0975.
ArFrancHist: Archivum Franciscanum Historicum; Grottaferrata.
ArGlottIt: Archivio Glottologico Italiano; Firenze. 0004-0207.
ArHPont: Archivum Historiae Pontificiae; Roma.
ArKulturg: Archiv für Kulturgeschichte; Köln. 0003-9233.
ArLtgW: Archiv für Liturgiewissenschaft; Regensburg. 0066-6386.
ArOr: Archiv Orientální; Praha. 0044-8699.
ArPapF: Archiv für Papyrusforschung; Leipzig. 0066-6459.
ArRefG: Archiv für Reformationsgeschichte; Gütersloh.
ArSSocRel: Archives de Sciences Sociales des Religions; Paris.
ArTGran: Archivo Teológico Granadino; Granada. 0210-1629.

ArztC: Arzt und Christ; Salzburg.

ASAE: Annales du Service des Antiquités de l'Égypte; Le Caire.

AsbTJ: Asbury Theological Journal; Wilmore, KY.

AshlandTJ: ... Theological J. (Ohio).

AsiaJT: Asia Journal of Theology; Bangalore. (1,1992).

ASOR: American Schools of Oriental Research; CM (diss.: Dissertation Series).

Asprenas... Scienze Teologiche; Napoli.

At[AcBol/Tor/Tosc]: Atti [dell'Accademia... di Bologna / di Torino / Toscana].

ATANT: Abhandlungen zur Theologie des Alten & Neuen Testaments; Zürich.

ATD: Das Alte Testament Deutsch. Neues Göttinger Bibelwerk; Gö.

AteDial: Ateismo e Dialogo; Vaticano.

AtenRom: Atene e Roma; Firenze. 0004-6493.

Athenaeum: Letteratura e Storia dell'antichità; Pavia.

`Atiqot; J, Dept. Ant.; from 20 (1991) Eng. + ❺. 0066-488X.

AtKap: Ateneum Kapłańskie; Włocławek. 0208-9041.

ATLA: American Theological Library Association; Menuchen, NJ.

Atualização; Belo Horizonte, MG.

AuCAfr: Au cœur de l'Afrique; Burundi.

AugL: Augustinus-Lexikon ➤ 660.

AugLv: Augustiniana; Leuven.

AugM: Augustinus; Madrid.

AugR: Augustinianum; Roma.

AugSt: Augustinian Studies; Villanova PA.

AulaO: Aula Orientalis; Barc.

AusgF: Ausgrabungen und Funde; B.

AustinSB: Austin (TX) Sem. Bulletin.

AustralasCR: Australasian Catholic Record; Sydney. 0727-3215.

AustralBR: Australian Biblical Review; Melbourne.

AVA: ➤ BeitAVgA.

BA: Biblical Archaeologist; CM. 0006-0895.

Babel (translation); Budapest, Akad.

BaBernSt: Basler und Berner Studien zur hist./systematischen Theologie; Bern.

Babesch: Bulletin Antieke Beschaving; Haag. 0165-9367.

BaghMit: Baghdader Mitteilungen DAI; Berlin.

BAH: Bibliothèque Archéologique et Historique (IFA-Beyrouth).

BAngIsr: Bulletin of the Anglo-Israel Archaeological Soc.; L. 0266-2442.

BangTF: Bangalore Theological Forum.

BaptQ: Baptist [Historical Soc.] Quarterly; Oxford. 0005-576X.

BArchAlg: Bulletin d'Archéologie Algérienne; Alger.

BarIlAn: Bar-Ilan Annual; Ramat-Gan. 0067-4109.

BAR: British Archaeology Reports; Ox.

BAR-W: Biblical Archaeology Review; Washington. 0098-9444.

BArte: Bollettino d'Arte; Roma.

BAsEsp[Or/Eg]: Boletín de la Asociación Española de Orientalistas / de Egiptología (2, 1990); Madrid.

BASOR: Bulletin of the American Schools of Oriental Research; Atlanta. 0003-097X.

BASP: Bulletin, American Society of Papyrologists; NY. 0003-1186.

BAusPrax: Biblische Auslegung für die Praxis; Stuttgart.

Bazmaveb (Pazmavep; Armenian); Venezia.

BBArchäom: Berliner Beiträge zur Archäometrie; Berlin. 0344-5098.

BBB: ➤ BiBasB & BoBB.

BbbOr: Bibbia e Oriente; Bornato BS.

BBelgRom: Bulletin de l'Institut Historique Belge; R. 0073-8530.

Bbg: Bibliographia/-y.

BBRes: Bulletin for Biblical Research; Annandale NY. (1,1991).

BBudé: Bulletin de l'Association G. Budé; Paris.

BBVO: Berliner Beiträge zum Vorderen Orient: Berlin, Reimer.

BCanadB: Bulletin Canadian Society of Biblical Studies; Ottawa.

BCanMedit: Bulletin of the Canad. Mediterranean Institute ➤ BMes.

BCentPrei: Bollettino del Centro Camuno di Studi Preistorici; Brescia. 0057-2168.

BCentProt: Bulletin du Centre Protestant d'Études; Genève.

BCH: Bulletin de Correspondance Hellénique; Paris. 0007-4217.

BCILL: Bibliothèque des Cahiers de l'Institut de Linguistique; Lv/P.

BCNH-T: Bibliothèque Copte de Nag Hammadi -Textes; Québec.

BEcuT: Bulletin of ecumenical theology; Enugu, Nigeria.

BeerSheva: ❻ Annual: Bible/ANE; J.

BÉF: Bibliothèque des Écoles françaises d'Athènes et de Rome; R. ➤ MÉF.

BEgS: Bulletin of the Egyptological Seminar; NY.

BeitATJ: Beiträge zur Erforschung des Alten Testaments und des Antiken Judentums; Bern. 0722-0790.

BeitAVgArch: Beiträge zur allgemeinen und vergleichenden Archäologie; München, Beck.

BeitBExT: Beiträge zur biblischen Exegese und Theologie [ipsi: BET]; Frankfurt/M.

BeitEvT: Beiträge zur evangelischen Theologie; München.

BeitGbEx: Beiträge zur Geschichte der biblischen Exegese; Tübingen.

BeitHistT: Beiträge zur Historischen Theologie; Tübingen.

BeitNam: Beiträge zur Namenforschung N. F.; Heid. 0005-8114.

BeitÖkT: Beiträge zur ökumenischen Theologie; München, Schöningh. 0067-5172.

BeitRelT: Beiträge zur Religionstheologie; Wien-Mödling.

BeitSudan: Beiträge zur Sudanforschung; Wien, Univ.

Belleten (Türk Tarih Kurumu); Ankara.

Benedictina; Roma.

Berytus (Amer. Univ. Beirut); K.

BethM: ❻ Beth Mikra; Jerusalem. 0005-979X.

BÉtOr: Bulletin d'Études Orientales; Damas, IFAO.

BFaCLyon: Bulletin des Facultés Catholiques; Lyon. 0180-5282.

Bib ➤ Biblica; Roma. 0006-0887.

BibAfr: La Bible en Afrique [francophone]; Lomé, Togo.

BiBasB: Biblische Basis Bücher; Kevelaer/ Stuttgart.

BiBeit: Biblische Beiträge, Schweizerisches Kath. Bibelwerk; Fribourg.

BibFe: Biblia y Fe; M. 0210-5209.

BibIll: Biblical Illustrator; Nv.

BibKonf: Biblische Konfrontationen; Stu.

Bible Bhashyam: Kottayam. 0970-2288.

Biblica: commentarii Pontificii Instituti Biblici; Roma. 0006-0887.

Biblos 1. Coimbra; 2. Wien.

BibNot: Biblische Notizen; Bamberg. 0178-2967.

BibOrPont: Biblica et Orientalia, Pontificio Istituto Biblico; Roma.

BibTB: Biblical Theology Bulletin; St. Bonaventure NY. 0146-1079.

BibTSt: Biblisch-Theologische Studien; Neukirchen-Vluyn. 0930-4800.

BibUnt: Biblische Untersuchungen; Regensburg.

BIFAO: Bulletin de l'Institut Français d'Archéologie Orientale; Le Caire. 0255-0962.

Bijd: Bijdragen, Filosofie en Theologie; Nijmegen. 0006-2278.

BijH: Bijbels Handboek; Kampen = World of the Bible; GR ➤ 661.

BiKi: Bibel und Kirche; Stuttgart. 0006-0623.

BInfWsz: Bulletin d'Information de l'Académie de Théologie Catholique; Warszawa. 0137-7000.

BInstArch: Bulletin of the Institute of Archaeology; London. 0076-0722.

BIP[Br]: Books in Print, U.S., annual; NY, Bowker [British, L, Whitaker]; fr./it./dt.

BiRes: Biblical Research; Chicago. 0067-6535.

Biserica ... Ortodoxă; București.

BIstFGrec: Bollettino dell'Istituto di Filologia Greca, Univ. Padova; R.

Bits and bytes review; Whitefish MT. 0891-2955.

BJG: Bulletin of Judaeo-Greek Studies; Cambridge Univ.

BJRyL: Bulletin of the John Rylands Library; Manchester. 0301-102X.

BKAT: Biblischer Kommentar AT; Neuk.

BL: Book List, The Society for Old Testament Study. 0309-0892.

BLCéramÉg: Bulletin de liaison ... céramique égyptienne; Le Caire, IFAO. 0255-0903.

BLitEc [Chr]: Bulletin de Littérature Ecclésiastique [Chronique]. Toulouse. 0007-4322 [0495-9396].

BLtg: Bibel und Liturgie; Wien-Klosterneuburg. 0006-064X.

BMB: Bulletin du Musée de Beyrouth.

BMeijiG: Bulletin Christian Research Institute Meiji Gakuin Univ.; Tokyo.

BMes: Bulletin, the Society for Mesopotamian Studies; Toronto.

BMosA [ipsi **AIEMA**]: Bulletin, étude mosaïque antique; P. 0761-8808.

BO: Bibliotheca Orientalis; Leiden. 0006-1913.

BoBB: Bonner Biblische Beiträge; Königstein.

Bobolanum, teologia; Wsz. 0867-3330.

BogSmot: Bogoslovska Smotra; Zagreb. 0352-3101.

BogVest: Bogoslovni Vestnik; Ljubljana.

BonnJb: Bonner Jahrbücher.

Boreas [1. Uppsala, series]; 2. Münster, Archäologie. 0344-810X.

BProtF: Bulletin de la Société de l'Histoire du Protestantisme Français; Paris.

BR: Bible Review; Wsh. 8755-6316.

BRefB: Bulletin, Reformation Biblical Studies: Fort Wayne.

BritJREd: British Journal of Religious Education; London.

BRöG: Bericht der Römisch-Germanischen Kommission DAI; Mainz. 0341-9312.

BrownJudSt/StRel: Brown Judaic Studies / Studies in Religion; Atlanta.

BS: Bibliotheca Sacra; Dallas, TX. 0006-1921.

BSAA: Boletín, Seminario Estudios Arte y Arqueología; Valladolid.

BSAC: Bulletin de la Société d'Archéologie Copte; Le Caire.

BSeptCog: Bulletin of the International Organization for Septuagint and Cognate Studies; ND.

BSignR: Bulletin Signalétique, religions; Paris. 0180-9296.

BSLP: Bulletin de la Société de Linguistique; Paris.

BSNAm: Biblical Scholarship in North America; Atlanta, SBL.

BSNEJap ➤ Oriento.

BSO: Bulletin of the School of Oriental and African Studies; London. 0041-977X.

BSoc[Fr]Ég: Bulletin de la Société [Française] d'Égyptologie; Genève [Paris].

BSoGgIt: Bollettino della Società Geografica Italiana; R. 0037-8755.

BSpade: Bible and Spade; Ballston NY.

BStLat: Bollettino di Studi Latini; N.

BSumAg: Bulletin on Sumerian Agriculture; Cambridge. 0267-0658.

Bt: Bibliotheca/-que.

BTAfr: Bulletin de Théologie Africaine; Kinshasa.

BTAM: Bulletin de Théologie Ancienne et Médiévale; Lv. ➤ RTAM.

BtEscB/EstB: Biblioteca Escuela Bíblica; M / de Estudios Bíblicos, Salamanca.

BtETL: Bibliotheca, ETL; Leuven.

BThemT: Bibliothek Themen der Theologie; Stuttgart.

BtHumRef: Bibliotheca Humanistica et Reformatorica; Nieuwkoop, de Graaf.

BtHumRen: Bibliothèque d'Humanisme et Renaissance; Genève/Paris.

BtMesop: Bibliotheca Mesopotamica; Malibu CA.

BToday: The Bible Today; Collegeville MN. 0006-0836.

BTrans: The Bible Translator [Technical/ Practical]; Stu. 0260-0943.

BtScRel: Biblioteca di Scienze religiose; Roma, Salesiana.

BTSt: Biblisch-theologische Studien (ex-Biblische Studien); Neukirchen.

BtStor: Biblioteca di storia e storiografia dei tempi biblici; Brescia.

BTT: Bible de tous les temps; Paris.

BtTPaid: Biblioteca Teologica; Brescia.

BTZ: Berliner Theologische Zeitschrift; Berlin. 0724-6137.

BuBbgB: Bulletin de Bibliographie Biblique; Lausanne.

BudCSt: Buddhist-Christian Studies; Honolulu, Univ. 0882-0945.

Burgense; Burgos. 0521-8195.

BurHist: Buried History; Melbourne. 0007-6260.

BVieChr: Bible et Vie Chrétienne; P.

BViewp: Biblical Viewpoint; Greenville SC, Jones Univ. 0006-0925.

BW: Beiträge zur Wissenschaft vom Alten und Neuen Testament; Stuttgart.

BySlav: Byzantinoslavica; Praha. 0007-7712.

ByZ: Byzantinische Zeitschrift; München. 0007-7704.

Ⓖ Byzantina; Thessaloniki.

Byzantion; Bruxelles.

ByzFor: Byzantinische Forschungen; Amsterdam.

BZ: Biblische Zeitschrift; Paderborn. 0006-2014.

BZA[N]W: Beihefte zur ➤ ZAW [ZNW].

CAD: [Chicago] Assyrian Dictionary; Glückstadt. ➤ 9273.

CADIR: Centre pour l'Analyse du Discours Religieux; Lyon ➤ SémBib.

CAH: Cambridge Ancient History[2]; Cambridge Univ. ➤ 662.

CahArchéol: Cahiers Archéologiques; Paris.

CahCMéd: Cahiers de Civilisation Médiévale; Poitiers.

CahDAFI: Cahiers de la Délégation Archéologique Française en Iran; Paris. 0765-104X.

CahÉv: Cahiers Évangile; Paris. 0222-8741.

CahHist: Cahiers d'Histoire; Lyon.

CahIntSymb: Cahiers Internationaux de Symbolique; Mons, Belgique.

CahLV: Cahiers voor Levensverdieping; Averbode.

CahRechScRel: Cahiers de Recherche en Sciences de la Religion; Québec.

CahSpIgn: Cahiers de spiritualité ignatienne; Québec.

CahSubaq: Cahiers d'archéologie subaquatique; Fréjus. (10,1991).

CahTrB: Cahiers de traduction biblique; Pierrefitte France. 0755-1371.

CahTun: Les Cahiers (de la Faculté des Lettres) de Tunisie; Tunis.

CalvaryB: Calvary Baptist Theological Journal; Lansdale PA. 8756-0429.

CalvinT: Calvin Theological Journal; Grand Rapids MI. 0008-1795.

CalwTMg: Calwer Theologische Monographien (A: Biblisch); Stuttgart.

CamArch: Cambridge (Eng.) Archaeological Journal. 0959-7743. (1,1991).

CamCW: Cambridge Commentary on Writings of the Jewish and Christian World.

CanadCR: Canadian Catholic Review; Saskatoon.

Carmel: Tilburg.

Carmelus: Roma. 0008-6673.

Carthage Conservation Bulletin; Tunis.

Carthaginensia; Murcia, Inst. Teol. 0213-4381.

CathCris: Catholicism in crisis; ND.

CathHR: Catholic Historical Review; Wsh. 0008-8080.

Catholica (Moehler-Institut, Paderborn); Münster.

Catholicisme: Paris ➤ 664.

Catholic Studies, Tokyo ➤ Katorikku.

CathTR: Catholic Theological Review; Clayton/Hong Kong.

CathTSocAmPr: ➤ PrCTSAm [AnCTS].

CATSS: Computer assisted tools for Septuagint studies: Atlanta ➤ SBL.

CBQ: Catholic Biblical Quarterly; Washington, DC. 0008-7912.

CC: La Civiltà Cattolica; R. 0009-8167.

CCGraec/Lat/Med: Corpus Christianorum, series graeca / latina / continuatio mediaev.; Turnhout.

CdÉ: Chronique d'Égypte; Bruxelles.

CEB: Commentaire évangelique de la Bible; Vaux/Seine ➤ Édifac.

Center Journal; Notre Dame.

CERDAC: (Atti) Centro di Ricerca e Documentazione Classica; Milano.

CERDIC: Centre d'échanges et de recherches sur la diffusion et l'inculturation du christianisme.

CETÉDOC: Centre de Traitement Électronique des Documents; Lv.

CGL: Coptic Gnostic Library ➤ NHS.

CGMG: Christlicher Glaube in moderner Gesellschaft; FrB.

ChCu: Church and Culture; Vatican.

CHermProt: Centre d'Herméneutique Protestante.

ChH: Church History; Indiatlantic FL.

CHH: Center for Hermeneutical Studies in Hellenistic & Modern Culture; Berkeley.

Chiea [ChAfC]: Nairobi, Catholic Higher Institute of Eastern Africa.

CHIran: Cambridge History of Iran.

Chiron: Geschichte, Epigraphie; München.

CHistEI: ❶ Cathedra, History of Eretz-Israel; Jerusalem.

CHist-J: Jerusalem Cathedra.

CHJud: Cambridge History of Judaism ➤ 665.

Chm: Churchman 1. (Anglican); London: 0009-661X / 2. (Humanistic); St. Petersburg FL: 0009-6628.

ChrCent: Christian Century; Chicago.

Christus; 1. Paris; 2. México.

ChrJRel: Christian Jewish Relations; L.

ChrNIsr: Christian News from Israel; Jerusalem.

ChrOost: Het Christelijk Oosten; Nijmegen.

ChrSchR: Christian Scholar's Review; Houston TX.

ChrT: Christianity Today; Carol Stream IL. 0009-5761.

ChSt: Chicago Studies; Mundelein IL.

Church: NY, Nat. Pastoral Life.

ChuT: Church & Theology; L. (6,1986).

ChWoman: The Church Woman; NY. 0009-6598.

CistSt: Cistercian Studies; ed. Getsemani KY; pub. Chimay, Belgium.

Citeaux; Achel, Belgium. 0009-7497.

Cithara: Judaeo-Christian Tradition; St. Bonaventure (NY) Univ.

CiTom: Ciencia Tomista; S. 0210-0398.

CiuD: Ciudad de Dios; M. 0009-7756.

CivClCr: Civiltà classica e cristiana; Genova. 0392-8632.

CiVit: Città di Vita; Firenze. [0]009-7632.

Claret: Claretianum; Roma.

ClasA: [formerly California Studies in] Classical Antiquity; Berkeley.

ClasB: Classical Bulletin; Ch. 0009-8137 (ᴱAsbury Coll., Wilmore KY).

ClasJ: Classical Journal; Greenville SC. 0009-8353.

ClasMed: Classica et Mediaevalia; København. 0106-5815.

ClasOutl: The Classical Outlook; Ch [ed. Miami Univ. OH]. 0009-8361.

ClasPg: Classical Philology; Chicago. 0009-8361.

ClasQ: Classical Quarterly NS; Oxford. 0009-8388.

ClasR: Classical Review NS; Oxford. 0009-840X.

ClasWo: Classical World; Pittsburgh. 0009-8148.

CLehre: Die Christenlehre; Berlin.

Clio, studi storici; N.

CMatArch: Contributi e materiali di archeologia orientale; Roma, Univ.

CNRS: Conseil National de Recherche Scientifique; Paris.

CogF: Cogitatio Fidei; Paris.

ColcCist: Collectanea Cisterciensia; Forges, Belgique.

ColcFranc: Collectanea Franciscana; Roma. 0010-0749.

ColcT: Collectanea Theologica; Warszawa. 0137-6985.

ColcTFu: Collectanea theol. Univ. Fujen = *Shenhsileh Lunchi*; Taipei.

CollatVL: Collationes, Vlaams... Theologie en Pastoraal; Gent.

Colloquium; Auckland, Sydney.

ColStFen: Collezione di Studi Fenici; Roma, Univ.

Commentary; NY. 0010-2601.

CommBras: Communio Brasiliensis: Rio de Janeiro.

CommND: Communio USA; Notre Dame. 0094-2065.

CommRevue: Communio [various languages, not related to **ComSev**]: revue catholique internationale; Paris.

CommStrum: Communio, strumento internazionale per un lavoro teologico; Milano.

Communio deutsch ➤ **IkaZ.**

ComOT: Commentaar op het Oude Testament. Kampen.

CompHum: Computers and the Humanities; Osprey FL. 0010-4817.

CompNT: Compendium rerum Iudaicarum ad NT; Assen.

Compostellanum; Santiago de Compostela.

ComRatisbNT: Comentario de Ratisbona; Barc.

ComSev: Communio; Sevilla. 0010-3705.

ComSpirAT/NT: Commenti spirituali dell'Antico / Nuovo Testamento; Roma.

ComTeolNT: Commentario Teologico del NT; Brescia.

ComViat: Communio Viatorum; Praha. 0010-7133. Suspended 33 (1990).

ConBib: Coniectanea Biblica OT/NT; Malmö.

Conc: Concilium, variis linguis; Paris, E, M... [deutsch = ➤ IZT].

ConcordJ: Concordia Journal; St. Louis. 0145-7233.

ConcordTQ: Concordia Theological Quarterly; Fort Wayne.

ConsJud: Conservative Judaism; NY. 0010-6542.

Contacts/Orthodoxe, de théologie et spiritualité; P. 0045-8325.

Continuum; NY. (1,1991).
ContrIstStorAnt: Contributi dell'Istituto di Storia Antica; Milano, Univ. Catt.
Coptologia [also for Egyptology]: Thunder Bay ONT, Lakehead Univ.
CouStR: Council for the Study of Religion Bulletin; Macon GA, Mercer Univ.
CovQ: Covenant Quarterly; Chicago.
CRAI: Comptes rendus de l'Académie des Inscriptions et Belles-Lettres; P.
Cretan Studies; Amst.
CRIPEL ➤ SocUÉg.
CriswT: Criswell Theological Review; Dallas.
Criterio; Buenos Aires. 0011-1473,
CritRR: Critical Review of Books in Religion: Atlanta.
CrkvaSv: Crkva u Svijetu; Split.
CrNSt: Cristianesimo nella Storia; Bologna. 0393-3598.
CroatC: Croatica Christiana; Zagreb.
CrossC: Cross Currents; West Nyack NJ. 0011-1953.
Crux: Vancouver. 0011-2186.
CSCO: Corpus Scriptorum Christianorum Orientalium; Lv. 0070-0401.
CScrN: Corpus Sacrae Scripturae Neerlandicae Medii Aevi; Leiden.
CuadFgClás: Cuadernos de Filología Clásica; M, Univ.
CuadTeol: Cuadernos de Teología; Buenos Aires.
CuadTrad: Cuadernos de Traducción y Interpretación; Barc.
CuBíb: Cultura Bíblica; M: AFEBE. 0211-2493.
CuesT: Cuestiones Teológicas; Medellín.
CuH: Culture and History; K.
CurrTMiss: Currents in Theology and Mission; St. Louis. 0098-2113.
CyrMeth: Cyrillomethodianum; Thessaloniki.
D: director: 1. (in Indice etiam *auctor*) Dissertationis; 2. Congressus, *etc.*
DAFI: Délégation Archéologique Française en Iran (Mém); Paris.
DAI: Deutsches Archäologisches Institut; Rom (nobis utilissimum), *al.* ➤ Mi(tt).
DanTTs: Dansk Teologisk Tidsskrift; København.
DanVMed/Skr: Dansk. Videnskabornes Selskap, Hist./Fil. Meddelelser / Skriften; K.

DBS [= SDB].
DECR: Department for External Church Relations of the Moscow Patriarchate: Moskva.
DeltChr: Deltion tes christianikēs archaiologikēs hetaireias: Athēna.
DeltVM: ⊚ Deltío vivlikôn meletôn, Bulletin Études Bibliques; Athēnai.
DHGE: Dictionnaire d'Histoire et de Géographie Ecclésiastiques; P ➤ 667.
Diakonia; Mainz/Wien. 0341-9592; Stu.
DialArch: Dialoghi di Archeologia; Mi.
DiálEcum: Diálogo Ecuménico; Salamanca. 0210-2870.
DialHA: Dialogues d'Histoire ancienne; Besançon. 18,1 (1992): 2-251-60475-8.
Dialog; Minneapolis. 0012-2033.
DialR: Dialog der Religionen. (1,1991).
DialTP: Diálogo teológico; El Paso TX.
DictSpir: Dictionnaire de Spiritualité; Paris ➤ 668.
Didascalia; Rosario ARG.
Didaskalia; Lisboa.
DielB: Dielheimer Blätter zum Alten Testament [ipsi DBAT]; Heid.
Dionysius: Halifax. 0705-1085.
Direction; Fresno CA.
DiscEg: Discussions in Egyptology; Oxford. 0268-3083.
Disciple, the (Disciples of Christ); St. Louis. 0092-8372.
DissA: Dissertation Abstracts International; AA/L. -A [= US *etc.*]: 0419-4209 [C = Europe. 0307-6075].
DissHRel: Dissertationes ad historiam religionum (supp. Numen); Leiden.
Divinitas, Pont. Acad. Theol. Rom. (Lateranensis); Vaticano. 0012-4222.
DivThom: Divus Thomas; Bologna. 0012-4257.
DizTF: Dizionario di Teologia Fondamentale ➤ 669.
DJD: Discoveries in the Judaean Desert; Oxford.
DLZ: Deutsche Literaturzeitung; Berlin. 0012-043X.
DMA: Dictionary of the Middle Ages; NY ➤ 670.
DocCath: Documentation Catholique; Paris.
DoctCom: Doctor Communis; Vaticano.

DoctLife: Doctrine and Life; Dublin.
DOG: Deutsche Orient-Gesellschaft: B.
DosB: Les dossiers de la Bible; P.
DossHA: Histoire et archéologie, les dossiers; Dijon.
DowR: Downside Review; Bath. 0012-5806.
DPA: Dizionario patristico e di antichità cristiane; Casale Monferrato ➤ 671.
DrevVost: ❻ Drevnij Vostok; Moskva.
DrewG: The Drew [Theological School] Gateway; Madison NJ.
DumbO: Dumbarton Oaks Papers; CM. 0070-7546.
DutchMgA: Dutch Monographs in Ancient History and Archaeology; Amst.
E: editor, Herausgeber, *a cura di.*
EAfJE: East African Journal of Evangelical Theology; Machakos, Kenya.
EAsJT: East Asia Journal of Theology [combining NE & SE AJT]; Tokyo. 0217-3859.
EAPast: East Asian Pastoral Review; Manila. 0040-0564.
ÉchMClas: Échos du Monde Classique/Classical Views; Calgary. 0012-9356.
ÉchSM: Les Échos de Saint-Maurice; Valais, Abbaye.
EcOr: Ecclesia Orans; R, Anselm.
ÉcoutBib: Écouter la Bible; Paris.
EcuR: Ecumenical Review; Geneva. 0013-0790.
EDIFAC: Éditions de la Faculté libre de Théologie Évangélique; Vaux/Seine.
EfMex: Efemerides Mexicana; Tlalpan.
Egb: Ergänzungsband.
ÉglT: Église et Théologie; Ottawa.
EgVO: Egitto e Vicino Oriente; Pisa.
ÉHRel: Études d'histoire des religions.
Eikasmós, Quaderni di Filologia Classica; Bologna, Univ.
Einz: Einzelband.
EkK [Vor]: Evangelischer-katholischer Kommentar zum NT; Z/Köln; Neukirchen-Vluyn ['Vorarbeiten'].
EkkT: ❼ Ekklēsía kaì Theología; L. Elenchos, ... pensiero antico; Napoli.
Elliniká; ❼ Thessaloniki.
Emerita: (lingüística clásica); M.
Emmanuel: St. Meinrads IN/NY. 0013-6719.

Enc. Biblica ➤ EnṣMiqr.
EncHebr: ❹ Encyclopaedia Hebraica; J/TA.
Enchoria, Demotistik/Koptologie; Wsb.
EncIran: Encyclopaedia Iranica; L.
EncIslam: Encyclopédie de l'Islam. Nouvelle édition [+ Eng]; Leiden/P ➤ 672.
EncKat: Encyklopedia Katolicka; Lublin.
Encounter (theol.); Indianapolis.
EncRel: (1) ᴱ*Eliade* M., The encyclopedia of religion; NY ➤ 674; (2) Enciclopedia delle Religioni; Firenze.
EncTF: Enciclopedia di Teologia Fondamentale; Genova ➤ 675.
EnṣMiqr: ❹ *Enṣiqlopediya miqrā'it,* Encyclopaedia Biblica; Jerusalem.
Entschluss: Wien. 0017-4602.
EnzMär: Enzyklopädie des Märchens; B.
EOL: Ex Oriente Lux ➤ 1.Jb/2. Phoenix.
Eos, ... philologia; Wsz. 0012-7825.
EpAnat: Epigraphica anatolica; Bonn.
ÉPHÉ[H/R]: École Pratique des Hautes-Études, Annuaire [Hist.-Pg. / Sc. Rel.]; Paris.
EpHetVyz: ❼ Ephēmeris tēs Hetaireías Vyzantinōn Spoudōn; Athēnai.
EphLtg: Ephemerides Liturgicae; R.
EphMar: Ephemerides Mariologicae; Madrid.
ÉPR: Études préliminaires aux religions orientales dans l'Empire romain; Leiden.
Eranos[/Jb]: Acta Philologica Suecana; Uppsala / Jahrbuch; Fra.
ErbAuf: Erbe und Auftrag; Beuron.
ErfTSt/Schr: Erfurter Theologische Studien/ Schriften.
ErIsr: Eretz-Israel; J. 0071-108X.
ErtFor: Ertrag der Forschung; Darmstadt, Wissenschaftliche Buchg. 0174-0695.
EscrVedat: Escritos del Vedat; Valencia. 0210-3133.
EsprVie: Esprit et Vie: 1. [< Ami du Clergé]; Langres; 2. Chambray.
EstAgust: Estudio Agustiniano; Valladolid. 0425-340X.
EstBíb: Estudios Bíblicos; Madrid. 0014-1437.
EstDeusto: Estudios de (Universidad) Deusto; Madrid. 0423-4847.
EstE: Estudios Eclesiásticos; Madrid. 0210-1610.
EstFranc: Estudios Franciscanos; Barcelona.

EstJos: Estudios Josefinos; Valladolid.

EstLul: Estudios Lulianos; Mallorca.

EstMar: Estudios Marianos; Madrid.

EstTrin: Estudios Trinitarios; Salamanca.

EstudosB: Estudos Bíblicos; Petrópolis.

ÉtBN: Études Bibliques, Nouvelle Série; Paris. 0760-3541.

ÉtClas: Les études classiques; Namur. 0014-200X.

ÉtFranc: Études Franciscaines; Blois.

ETL: Ephemerides Theologicae Lovanienses; Leuven. 0013-9513. ➤ **Bt.**

ÉtPapyr: Études [Société Égyptienne] de Papyrologie; Le Caire.

ÉtPgHist: Études de Philologie et d'Histoire; Genève, Droz.

ÉTRel: Études Théologiques et Religieuses; Montpellier. 0014-2239.

ÉtTrav: Études et Travaux; Varsovie.

Études; Paris. 0014-1941.

Euhemer (❷ hist. rel.); Wsz. 0014-2298

EuntDoc: Euntes Docete; Roma.

EurHS: Europäische Hochschulschriften / Publ. Universitaires Européennes; Fra.

EurJT: The European journal of theology: Edinburgh. (1,1991).

Evangel; Edinburgh. 0265-4547.

EvErz: Der evangelische Erzieher; Frankfurt/M. 0014-3413.

EvJ: Evangelical Journal; Myerstown.

EvKL: Evangelisches Kirchenlexikon; ➤ 676.

EvKom: Evangelische Kommentare; Stuttgart. 0300-4236.

EvQ[RT]: Evangelical Quarterly [Review of Theology]; Exeter.

EvT: Evangelische Theologie, NS; München. 0014-3502.

EWest: East and West; 1. L / 2. R.

EWSp: Encyclopedia of World Spirituality; NY/L.

ExAud: Ex auditu; Princeton. 0883-0053.

ExcSIsr: Excavations and Surveys in Israel < Ḥadašot; J. 0334-1607.

ExGG: Exegetical guide to the Greek NT; GR.

Expedition; Ph. 0014-4738.

Explor [sic]; Evanston. 0362-0876.

ExpTim: The Expository Times; Edinburgh. 0014-5246.

ExWNT (Eng.) ➤ 699.

F&R: Faith and Reason; Front Royal VA. 0098-5449.

FascBíb: Fascículos bíblicos; Madrid.

Faventia: clásica; Barc. 0210-7570.

fg./fil.: filologia/co, filosofia/co.

FgNt: Filologia neotestamentaria; Córdoba, Univ. 0214-2996.

FidH: Fides et Historia; Longview TX.

FilT: Filosofia e teologia; Napoli.

FoiTemps: La Foi et le Temps. NS; Tournai.

FoiVie: Foi et Vie; Paris. 0015-5357.

FolArch: Folia Archaeologica; Budapest. 0133-2023.

FolOr: Folia Orientalia, Polska Akademia Nauk; Kraków. 0015-5675.

Fondamenti; Brescia, Paideia.

ForBib: Forschung zur Bibel; Wü/Stu.

ForBMusB: Forschungen und Berichte, Staatliche Museen zu Berlin.

ForGLProt: Forschungen zur Geschichte und Lehre des Protestantismus; Mü.

ForJüdChrDial: Forschungen zum jüdisch-christlichen Dialog; Neuk.

ForKiDG: Forschungen zur Kirchen- und Dogmengeschichte; Gö.

Fornvännen; Lund. 0015-7813.

ForSystÖ: Forschungen zur Systematischen & Ökumenischen Theologie; Gö.

ForTLing: Forum Theologiae Linguisticae; Bonn.

Fortunatae; revista canaria de filología; Tenerife. (1,1991).

Forum [= Foundations & Facets]; Bonner MT. 0883-4970.

ForumKT: Forum Katholische Theologie; Münster. 0178-1626.

FOTLit: Forms of OT Literature; GR, Eerdmans.

FraJudBei: Frankfurter Judaistische Beiträge: Fra.

FranBog: Franciscanum, ciencias del espíritu; Bogotá. 0120-1468.

FrancSt: Franciscan Studies; St. Bonaventure, NY. 0080-5459.

FranzSt: Franziskanische Studien; Pd.

FraTSt: Frankfurter Theologische Studien; Fra, S. Georgen.

FreibRu: Freiburger Rundbrief. ... christlich-jüdische Begegnung; FrB.

FreibTSt: Freiburger Theologische Studien; Freiburg/Br.

FreibZ: Freiburger Zeitschrift für Philosophie und Theologie; Fribourg.

FRL: Forschungen zur Religion und Literatur des Alten und NTs; Gö.

FutUo: Il futuro dell'uomo; Firenze, Assoc. Teilhard. 0390-217X.

Ⓖ *Graece*; title/text in Greek.

GCS: Die Griechischen Christlichen Schriftsteller der ersten Jahrhunderte; B.

GdT: Giornale di Teologia; Brescia.

GeistL: Geist und Leben; Würzburg. 0016-5921.

Genava (archéologie, hist. art); Genève. 0072-0585.

GenLing: General Linguistics; University Park PA. 0016-6553.

Georgica: Jena/Tbilissi. 0232-4490.

GerefTTs: Gereformeerd Theologisch Tijdschrift; Kampen. 0016-8610.

Gerión, revista de Historia Antigua; Madrid, Univ. 0213-0181.

GGA: Göttingische Gelehrte Anzeigen; Göttingen. 0017-1549.

GItFg: Giornale italiano di filologia; Napoli. 0017-0461.

GLA/NT: Grande Lessico dell'A/NT (< TWA/NT); Brescia → 677.

GLÉCS: (Comptes rendus) Groupe Linguistique d'Études Chamito-Sémitiques; Paris.

GLern: Glaube und Lernen; Gö.

GLeven: Geest en leven; Eindhoven.

Glotta: griech.-lat.; Gö. 0017-1298.

Gnomon; München. 0017-1417.

GöMiszÄg: Göttinger Miszellen ... zur ägyptologischen Diskussion; Göttingen. 0344-385X.

GöOrFor: Göttinger Orientforschungen; Würzburg.

GöTArb: Göttinger Theologische Arbeiten; Göttingen.

GraceTJ: Grace Theological Journal; Winona Lake IN. 0198-666X.

GraecChrPrim: Graecitas Christianorum Primaeva; Nijmegen, van den Vegt.

Grail, ecumenical quarterly; Waterloo.

GreeceR: Greece and Rome; Oxford.

Greg[LA/Inf.]: Gregorianum; R, Pontificia Universitas Gregoriana [Liber Annualis / Informationes PUG].

GrOrTR: Greek Orthodox Theological Review; Boston. 0017-3894.

GrRByz: Greek, Roman and Byzantine Studies; CM. 0017-3916.

GrSinal: Grande Sinal; Petrópolis.

Gymn: Gymnasium; Heid. 0342-5231.

Ⓗ *(Neo-)hebraice*; (modern) Hebrew.

HaBeiA: Hamburger Beiträge zur Archäologie. 0341-3152.

HABES: Heidelberger Althistorische Beiträge und Epigraphische Studien: Stu.

Ḥadašôt arkeologiyôt Ⓗ [News]; J.

HalleB: Hallesche Beiträge zur Orientwissenschaft; Halle. 0233-2205.

Hamdard Islamicus [research]; Pakistan. 0250-7196.

Handes Amsorya [armen.]; Wien.

HarvSemMon/Mus: Harvard Semitic Monographs / Museum Series; CM.

HarvStClasPg: Harvard Studies in Classical Philology; CM.

HarvTR: The Harvard Theological Review; CM. 0017-8160.

HbAltW: Handbuch der Altertumswissenschaft; München.

HbAT/NT: Handbuch zum Alten/Neuen Testament; Tübingen.

HbDG: Handbuch der Dogmengeschichte; Freiburg/B.

HbDTG: Handbuch der Dogmen- und Theologiegeschichte; Göttingen.

HbFT: Handbuch der Fundamentaltheologie; FrB → 678.

HbOr: Handbuch der Orientalistik; Leiden.

HbRelG: Handbuch der Religionsgeschichte; Göttingen.

HbRwG: Handbuch Religionswissenschaftlicher Grundbegriffe; Stuttgart.

HDienst: Heiliger Dienst; Salzburg. 0017-9620.

HebAnR: Hebrew Annual Review; Columbus, Ohio State Univ.

HebSt: Hebrew Studies; Madison WI. 0146-4094.

Hekima; Nairobi.

Helikon (Tradizione e Cultura Classica, Univ. Messina); Roma.

Helinium; Stockholm.

Hellenika; Bochum. 0018-0084; → *Ell.*

Helmantica; Salamanca, Univ.

Henceforth; Lenox MA.

Henoch (ebraismo): Torino (Univ.).

Hephaistos, Theorie / Praxis Arch.; Ha.

HerdKor: Herder-Korrespondenz; Freiburg/Br. 0018-0645.

HerdTKom, NT: Herders Theologischer Kommentar zum NT; FrB.

Heresis; Carcassonne. 0758-3737.

Hermathena; Dublin. 0018-0750.

Hermes; Wiesbaden. 0018-0777.

HermUnT: Hermeneutische Untersuchungen zur Theologie; Tü. 0440-7180.

HervTS: Hervormde Teologiese Studies; Pretoria.

Hesperia: 1. (American School, Athens); Princeton. 0018-098X. -2. Roma. (1,1990).

Hethitica. Travaux édités; Lv.

HeythJ: Heythrop Journal; London. 0018-1196.

HistJb: Historisches Jahrbuch; Mü.

Historia; 1. Baden-Baden: 0018-2311; 2. Santiago/Chile, Univ. Católica.

HistRel: History of Religions; Chicago. 0018-2710.

HLand[S]: Das Heilige Land (Deutscher Verein) Köln [(Schw. Verein); Luzern].

Hokhma; Lausanne. 0379-7465.

HolyL: Holy Land: J, OFM. 0333-4851 ➤ **TerraS.**

Homoousios; Buenos Aires.

HomP: Homiletic and Pastoral Review; New York. 0018-4268.

HomRel: Homo religiosus (histoire des religions); Louvain-la-Neuve.

HorBibT: Horizons in Biblical Theology; Pittsburgh. 0195-9085.

Horizons (College Theology Society); Villanova PA. 0360-9669.

Hsientai Hsüehyüan (= Universitas); Taipei.

HSprF: Historische Sprachforschung; Göttingen. 0935-3518.

HUC|A: Hebrew Union College [+ Jewish Institute of Religion] Annual; Cincinnati.

Humanitas; 1. Brescia; 2. Tucuman.

HumT: Humanística e Teologia; Porto.

HWomenRel: History of women religious, news and notes; St. Paul MN.

Hypom: Hypomnemata; Göttingen, VR.

HZ: Historische Zeitschrift; München. 0018-2613.

IBMiss: International Bulletin of Missionary Research; Mp.

ICC: International Critical Commentary; Edinburgh.

IClasSt: Illinois Classical Studies; Urbana. 0363-1923.

IFA|O|: Institut Français d'Archéologie (Orientale, Le Caire / Beyrouth).

IglV: Iglesia Viva; Valencia/Madrid.

IkaZ: Internationale Katholische Zeitschrift [= Communio]; Rodenkirchen. 0341-8693.

IkiZ: Internationale kirchliche Zeitschrift; Bern. 0020-9252.

Immanuel (ecumenical); J. 0302-8127.

InBeitKultW/SprW/TS: Innsbrucker Beiträge zur Kulturwissenschaft / Sprachwissenschaft / Theologische Studien.

Index Jewish Studies ➤ **RAMBI.**

IndIranJ: Indo-Iranian Journal; (Canberra-) Leiden. 0019-7246.

IndJT: Indian Journal of Theology; Serampore.

IndMissR: Indian Missiological Review; Shillong.

IndogF: Indogermanische Forschungen; Berlin. 0019-7262.

IndTSt: Indian Theological Studies; Bangalore, St. Peter's.

InfPUG ➤ Gregoriana; R.

Interp: Interpretation; Richmond VA. 0020-9643.

IntJNaut: International Journal of Nautical Archaeology L/NY. 0305-7445.

IntJPhR: International Journal for the Philosophy of Religion; Haag.

IntJSport: International Journal of the history of sport; London.

IntRMiss: International Review of Mission; London. 0020-8582.

Iran; London. 0578-6967.

IrAnt: Iranica Antiqua; Leiden.

Iraq; London. 0021-0889.

IrBSt: Irish Biblical Studies; Belfast. 0268-6112.

Irén: Irénikon; Chevetogne. 0021-0978.

IrTQ: Irish Theological Quarterly; Maynooth. 0021-1400.

Islam, Der: Berlin. 0021-1818.

Islamochristiana; Roma, Pontificio Istituto di Studi Arabi. 0392-7288.

IsrEJ: Israel Exploration Journal; Jerusalem. 0021-2059.

IsrJBot/Zool: Israel Journal of Botany 0021-213X / Zoology 0021-2210: J.

IsrLawR: Israel Law Review; Jerusalem. 0021-2237.

IsrMusJ: Israel Museum Journal; Jerusalem.

IsrNumJ[SocB]: Israel Numismatic Journal, J [Society Bulletin: TA].

IsrOrSt: Israel Oriental Studies; Tel Aviv. Istina; Paris. 0021-2423.

Italoellenika, rivista di cultura greco-moderna; Napoli. (2,1989).

IVRA (Jura); Napoli.

IZBG → 778: Internationale Zeitschriftenschau für Bibelwissenschaft und Grenzgebiete; Pd. 0074-9745.

IZT: Internationale Zeitschrift für Theologie [= Concilium deutsch].

JAAR: Journal, American Academy of Religion; Atlanta. 0002-7189.

JACiv: Journal of Ancient Civilizations: Chang-chun, Jilin (4, 1989).

JAfAL: Journal of Afroasiatic Languages; Leiden. 0894-9824 (3,1991).

J[News]AmEg: Journal [Newsletter] of the American Research Center in Egypt [ARCE]; Winona Lake IN.

JAmScAff: Journal of the American Scientific Affiliation (evang.); Ipswich MA. 0003-0988.

JANES: Journal of the Ancient Near Eastern Society; NY, Jewish Theol. Sem. 0010-2016.

JanLing[Pract]: Janua Linguarum [Series Practica]; Haag / Paris.

JAOS: Journal of the American Oriental Society; NHv. 0003-0279.

JapJRelSt: Japanese Journal of Religious Studies; Nagoya.

JapRel: Japanese Religions; Tokyo.

JArchSc: Journal of Archaeological Science; London/New York.

JAs: Journal Asiatique; P. 0021-762X.

JAsAf: Journal of Asian and African Studies; Toronto / Leiden.

Jb: Jahrbuch [Heid, Mainz...]; Jaarbericht.

JbAC: Jahrbuch für Antike und Christentum; Münster im Westfalen.

JbBerlMus: Jahrbücher der Berliner Museen; Berlin.

JbBTh: Jahrbuch für biblische Theologie; Neukirchen.

JbEOL: Jaarbericht van het Vooraziatisch-Egyptisch Genootschap Ex Oriente Lux; Leiden.

JBEq: Journal of Biblical Equality; Lakewood CO.

JbEvHL: Jahrbuch des Deutschen Evangelischen Instituts für Altertumswissenschaft des Heiligen Landes; Firth.

JBL: Journal of Biblical Literature; Atlanta. 0021-9231.

JBlackT: Journal of Black Theology; Atteridgeville SAf.

JbLtgH: Jahrbuch für Liturgik und Hymnologie; Kassel.

JbNumG: Jahrbuch für Numismatik und Geldgeschichte; Regensburg.

JbÖsByz: Jahrbuch der Österreichischen Byzantinistik; W. 0378-8660.

JBQ: Jewish Bible Quarterly (< Dor le-Dor); Jerusalem. 0792-3910.

JChrB: Journal of the Christian Brethren Research Fellowship; Wellington NZ.

JChrEd: Journal of Christian Education; Sydney. 0021-9657.

JCS: Journal of Cuneiform Studies; CM. 0022-0256.

JDharma: Journal of Dharma; Bangalore.

JdU: Judentum und Umwelt; Frankfurt/M.

JEA: Journal of Egyptian Archaeology; London. 0307-5133.

JEcuSt: Journal of Ecumenical Studies; Ph, Temple Univ. 0022-0558.

Jeevadhara; Alleppey, Kerala.

JEH: Journal of Ecclesiastical History; Cambridge. 0022-0469.

JEmpirT: Journal of empirical theology; Kampen.

JerónMg: Institución S. Jerónimo, estudios y monografías; Valencia.

JESHO: Journal of Economic and Social History of the Orient; Leiden.

JEvTS: Journal of the Evangelical Theological Society; Wheaton IL.

JewishH: Jewish History; Leiden. 0334-701X.

JFemR: Journal of Feminist Studies in Religion; Chico CA. 8755-4178.

JFiel: Journal of Field Archaeology; Boston, Univ. 0093-4690.

JGlass: Journal of Glass Studies; Corning, NY. 0075-4250.

JGraceEv: Journal of the Grace Evangelical Society; Roanoke TX (4,1991).

JHistId: Journal of the History of Ideas; Ph, Temple Univ. 0022-5037.

JHMR: Judaica, Hermeneutics, Mysticism, and Religion; Albany, SUNY.

JhÖsA: Jahreshefte des Österreichischen Archäologischen Institutes; Wien. 0078-3579.

JHS: Journal of Hellenic Studies; London. 0075-4269.

JIndEur: Journal of Indo-European Studies; Hattiesburg, Miss.

JIntdenom: Journal, Interdenominational Theological Center; Atlanta.

JIntdis: Journal of the Society for Interdisciplinary History; CM, MIT.

JJC: Jésus et Jésus-Christ; Paris.

JJS: Journal of Jewish Studies; Oxford. 0022-2097.

JJurPap: Journal of Juristic Papyrology; Warszawa.

JLawA: Jewish Law Annual (Oxford).

JMeditArch: Journal of Mediterranean Archeol.; Sheffield. 0952-7648.

JMedvRenSt: Journal of Medieval & Renaissance Studies; Durham NC.

JMoscPatr: [Engl.] Journal of the Moscow Patriarchate; Moscow.

JNES: Journal of Near Eastern Studies; Chicago, Univ. 0022-2968.

JNWS: Journal of Northwest Semitic Languages; Leiden.

JPersp: Jerusalem perspective.

JPrehRel: Journal of Prehistoric Religion; Göteborg. 0283-8486.

JPseud: Journal for the Study of the Pseudepigrapha; Sheffield. 0951-8207.

JPsy&C/Jud/T: Journal of Psychology & Christianity; Farmington Hills MI. 0733-4273 / ... & Judaism; NY / ... & Theology; Rosemead CA.

JQR: Jewish Quarterly Review (Ph, Dropsie Univ.); WL. 0021-6682.

JRArch: Journal of Roman Archaeology; AA.

JRAS: Journal of the Royal Asiatic Society; London.

JRefJud: Journal of Reform Judaism; NY. 0149-712X.

JRel: Journal of Religion; Chicago. 0022-4189.

JRelAf: Journal of Religion in Africa; Leiden. 0022-4200.

JRelEth: Journal of Religion and Ethics; ND (ᴱRutgers). 0384-9694.

JRelHealth: The Journal of Religion and Health; New York.

JRelHist: Journal of Religious History; Sydney, Univ. 0022-4227.

JRelPsyR: Journal of Religion and Psychical Research; Bloomfield CT.

JRelSt: Journal of Religious Studies; Cleveland.

JRelTht: Journal of Religious Thought; Washington DC.

JRit: Journal of ritual studies; Pittsburgh/Waterloo ON.

JRMilit: Journal of Roman Military Equipment Studies; Newcastle. 0961-3684 (1,1990).

JRomArch: Journal of Roman Archaeology: Ann Arbor MI (4,1991).

JRPot: Journal of Roman Pottery Studies: Oxford.

JRS: Journal of Roman Studies; London. 0075-4358.

JSArm: Journal of the Society for Armenian Studies; LA.

JSav: Journal des Savants: Paris.

JScStR: Journal for the Scientific Study of Religion; NHv. 0021-8294.

JSemant: Journal of Semantics; Oxford. 0167-5133.

JSemit: Journal for Semitics / Tydskrif vir Semitistiek; Pretoria, Unisa.

JSHZ: Jüdische Schriften aus hellenistischer und römischer Zeit; Gütersloh.

JSS: Journal of Semitic Studies; Manchester. 0022-4480.

JSStEg: Journal of the Society for the Study of Egyptian Antiquities [ipsi SSEA]; Toronto. 0383-9753.

JSt[HL]JTht: Jerusalem Studies in [Hebrew literature] Jewish Thought; J.

JStJud: Journal for the Study of Judaism in the Persian, Hellenistic, & Roman Periods; Leiden. 0047-2212.

JStNT/OT: Journal for the Study of NT/OT; Sheffield, Univ. 0142-064X/0309-0892. **Supp.** 0143-5108/ 0309-0787.

JStRel: Journal for the study of religion [formerly Religion in Southern Africa]; Pietermaritzburg, Natal.

JTS: Journal of Theological Studies; Oxford/London. 0022-5185.

JTSAfr: Journal of Theology for Southern Africa; Rondebosch.

Judaica; Zürich. 0022-572X.
Judaism; NY. 0022-5762.
JudTSt: Judaistische Texte und Studien; Hildesheim.
JWarb: Journal of the Warburg and Courtauld Institutes; London.
JwHist: Jewish History; Haifa.
JWomen&R: Journal of Women and Religion; Berkeley.
JyskR ➤ **RJysk.**
Kadmos; Berlin. 0022-7498.
Kairos 1. (Religionswiss.); Salzburg. 0022-7757. - 2. Guatemala 1014-9341.
Karawane (Die); Ludwigsburg.
Karthago (archéologie africaine); P.
KAT: Kommentar zum AT: Gütersloh.
KatBlät: Katechetische Blätter; Mü.
KatKenk: Katorikku Kenkyu < Shingaku; Tokyo, Sophia. 0387-3005.
KBW: Katholisches Bibelwerk; Stu [bzw. Österreich, Schweiz].
KeK: Kritisch-exegetischer Kommentar über das NT; Göttingen.
KerDo: Kerygma und Dogma; Göttingen. 0023-0707.
KerkT: Kerk en Theologie; Wageningen. 0165-2346.
Kernos, religion grecque; Liège.
Kerux; Escondido CA. 0888-8513.
Kerygma (on Indian missions); Ottawa. 0023-0693.
KGaku: ❶ Kirisutokyo Gaku (Christian Studies); Tokyo, 0387-6810.
KingsTR: King's College Theological Review; London.
KirSef: ❷ Kiryat Sefer, Bibliographical Quarterly; Jerusalem, Nat.-Univ. Libr. 0023-1851. ➤ Rambi.
KIsr: Kirche und Israel, theologische Zeitschrift; Neukirchen. 0179-7239.
KkKS: Konfessionskundliche und Kontroverstheologische Studien; Paderborn.
KkMat: Konfessionskundliches Institut, Materialdienst; Bensheim.
KleinÄgTexte: Kleine ägyptische Texte; Würzburg.
Kler: ❸ Klēronomia; Thessaloniki.
Klio; Berlin. 0075-6334.
KLK: Katholisches Leben und Kirchenreform im Zeitalter der Glaubensspaltung; Münster.
KölnFG: Kölner Jahrbuch für Vor- und Frühgeschichte; B. 0075-6512.

KomBeiANT: Kommentare und Beiträge zum Alten und N.T.; Düsseldorf.
Kratylos (Sprachwissenschaft); Wsb.
KřestR [TPřil]: Křest'anská revue [Theologická Příloha]; Praha.
KTB/KUB: Keilschrifttexte/urkunden aus Boghazköi; B, Mann/Akademie.
Ktema; Strasbourg, CEDEX.
KuGAW: Kulturgeschichte der Antiken Welt; Mainz.
KvinnerA: Kvinner i arkeologi i Norge; Bergen, Historisk Museum.
KZg: Kirchliche Zeitgeschichte; Gö.
LA: Liber Annuus; J. 0081-8933. ➤ SBF.
Labeo, diritto romano; N. 0023-6462.
LAeg: Lingua aegyptia, Journal of Egyptian language studies; Gö/LA. (1,1991).
Landas: Journal of Loyola School of Theology; Manila,
Language; Baltimore. 0097-8507.
LAPO: Littératures Anciennes du Proche-Orient; Paris, Cerf. 0459-5831.
Lateranum; R, Pont. Univ. Lateranense.
Latomus (Ét. latines); Bru. 0023-8856.
Laur: Laurentianum; R. 0023-902X.
LavalTP: Laval Théologique et Philosophique; Québec.
Laverna, Wirtschafts- und Sozialgeschichte; St. Katharinen. 0938-5835.
LDiv: Lectio Divina; Paris, Cerf.
LebSeels: Lebendige Seelsorge; Wü/FrB.
LebZeug: Lebendiges Zeugnis; Paderborn. 0023-9941.
Lěšonénu (Hebrew Language); J.
Levant (archeology); London.
LexÄg: Lexikon der Ägyptologie; Wsb ➤ 680.
LexMA: Lexikon des Mittelalters; Mü/Z ➤ 681.
LexTQ: Lexington [KY] Theological Quarterly. 0024-1628.
LFrühJ: Literatur und Religion des Frühjudentums; Wü/Gü.
LGB: Lexikon des Gesamten Buchwesens²; Stu ➤ 749.
LIAO: Lettre d'Information Archéologie Orientale; Valbonne, CNRS. 0750-6279.
LIMC: Lexicon iconographicum mythologiae classicae; Z. ➤ 750.
LimnOc: Limnology & Oceanography; AA.

LinceiR/Scavi/BClas: Accademia Nazionale dei Lincei. Rendiconti / Notizie degli Scavi / Bollettino Classico. 0391-8270: Roma.
LingBib: Linguistica Biblica; Bonn. 0342-0884.
Lire la Bible; P, Cerf. 0588-2257.
Listening: Romeoville IL.
LitCu: Literary currents in biblical interpretation; Louisville.
LitLComp: Literary and Linguistic Computing; Ox. 0268-1145.
LitTOx: Literature and theology; Ox.
LivLight: The Living Light (US Cath. Conf.); Huntington. 0024-5275.
LivWord: Living Word; Alwaye, Kerala.
LoB: Leggere oggi la Bibbia; Brescia, Queriniana.
LogosPh: Logos, philos.; Santa Clara.
Logotherapie; Bremen.
LOrA: Langues orientales anciennes; Lv. 0987-7738.
LPastB: Lettura pastorale della Bibbia: Bo.
LStClas: London studies in classical philology [8, Corolla Londiniensis 1]; Amst.
LtgJb: Liturgisches Jahrbuch; Münster/Wf.
Lucentum; prehistoria, arqueología e historia antigua; Alicante, Univ.
LumenK: Lumen; København.
LumenVr: Lumen; Vitoria.
LumièreV: Lumière et Vie; Lyon. 0024-7359.
Luther [Jb]; Ha. 0340-6210. - [Gö].
LuthMon: Lutherische Monatshefte; Hamburg. 0024-7618.
LuthTJ: Lutheran Theological Journal; North Adelaide, S. Australia.
LuthTKi: Lutherische Theologie und Kirche; Oberursel. 0170-3846.
LuxB: Lux Biblica; R, Ist. B. Evangelico (1,1990).
LVitae: Lumen Vitae; Bru. 0024-7324.
LvSt: Louvain Studies.
Ⓜ magyar: *hungarice*, en hongrois.
ᴹ: *mentio, de eo*; author commented upon.
Maarav; WL. 0149-5712.
MadMitt [B/F]: DAI Madrider Mitteilungen [Beiträge/Forschungen]; Mainz.
MAGA: Mitteilungen zur Alten Geschichte und Archäologie; B.
Maia (letterature classiche); Messina. 0025-0538.

MaimS: Maimonidean Studies; NY, Yeshiva Univ./KTAV (1,1990).
MaisD: Maison-Dieu; P. 0025-0937.
Manresa (espiritualidad ignaciana); Azpeitia-Guipúzcoa.
Manuscripta; St. Louis.
Mara: tijdschrift voor feminisme en theologie.
MarbTSt: Marburger Theologische Studien; Marburg.
MARI: Mari, Annales de Recherches Interdisciplinaires; Paris.
Marianum; Roma.
MariolSt: Mariologische Studien; Essen.
MarŠipri; Boston, Baghdad ASOR.
MarSt: Marian Studies; Washington.
Masaq, al-, Arabo-Islamic Mediterranean studies; Leeds (1,1988).
Masca: Museum Applied Science Center for Archaeology Journal; Ph.
MasSt: (SBL) Masoretic Studies; Atlanta.
MastJ: Master's Seminary Journal; Sun Valley, CA (1,1990).
MatDClas: Materiali e discussioni per l'analisi dei testi classici; Pisa. 0392-6338.
MatKonfInst: Materialdienst des konfessionskundlichen Instituts; Bensheim.
MatPomWykBib: Materiały pomocznicze do wykładów z biblistyki; Lublin.
Mayéutica; Marcilla (Navarra).
MDOG: Mitteilungen der Deutschen Orientgesellschaft; B. 0342-118X.
Meander: Wsz Akad. 0025-6285.
Med: Mededelingen [Amst,]; Meddelander.
MeditArch: Mediterranean Archaeology; Sydney. 1030-8482.
MeditHR: Mediterranean historical review Tel Aviv Univ.; L. 0951-8967.
MeditQ: Mediterranean Quarterly; Durham NC.
MedvHum: Mediaevalia & Humanistica (Denton, N. Texas U.); Totowa.
MedvSt: Mediaeval Studies; Toronto. 0076-5872.
MÉF-A [= **MélÉcFrR**]: Mélanges de l'École Française de Rome/Athènes, Antiquité. 0223-5102.
MélSR: Mélanges de Science Religieuse; Lille.
Mém: Mémoires ⇥ AIBL ... AcSc, T...
Menora: Jahrbuch deutsch-jüdische Geschichte; Mü. (1,1990).

MenQR: Mennonite Quarterly Review; Goshen, Ind.

Mensaje; Chile.

Meroit: Meroitic Newsletter / Bulletin d'informations méroitiques: Paris, CNRS.

MESA: Middle East Studies Association (Bulletin); Tucson, Univ. AZ.

MesCiv: Mesopotamian Civilization; WL.

MesopK: Mesopotamia: København.

MesopT: Mesopotamia; T (pub. F).

Mesorot [Language-tradition researches]; Jerusalem.

MESt: Middle Eastern Studies; L.

MetB: Metropolitan Museum Bulletin; New York. 0026-1521.

MethT: Method and theory in the study of religion; Toronto.

Mêtis, Anthropologie grecque; P.

Mg: Monograph (-ie, -fia); ➤ CBQ, SBL, SNTS.

MgANE: Monographs on the Ancient Near East; 1. Leiden; 2. Malibu.

MGraz: Mitteilungen der archäologischen Gesellschaft; Graz.

MgStB: Monographien und Studienbücher; Wu/Giessen.

MHT: Materialien zu einem hethitischen Thesaurus; Heidelberg.

MiDAI-A/K/M/R: Mitteilungen des Deutschen Archäologischen Instituts: Athen / Kairo / Madrid / Rom 0342-1287.

MidAmJT: Mid-America Journal of Theology: Orange City, Iowa.

Mid-Stream, Disciples of Christ; Indianapolis. – Midstream (Jewish); NY. 0026-332X.

Mikael; Paraná, Arg. (Seminario).

MilltSt: Milltown Studies (philosophy, theology); Dublin. 0332-1428.

Minerva: 1. filología clásica; Valladolid; 2. (incorporating Archaeology Today); L (1,1990).

Minos (Filología Egea); Salamanca. 0544-3733.

MiscCom: Miscelánea Comillas, estudios históricos; M. 0210-9522.

MiscFranc: Miscellanea Francescana; Roma (OFM Conv.).

Mishkan, a theological forum on Jewish evangelism; Jerusalem.

MissHisp: Missionalia hispanica; Madrid, CSIC Inst. E. Flores.

Missiology; Scottdale PA.

Mitt: Mitteilungen [Gö Septuaginta; Berliner Museen ...]; ➤ MiDAI.

Mnemosyne, Bibliotheca Classica Batava [+ Supplements]; Leiden.

ModChm: Modern Churchman; Leominster, Herf.

ModJud: Modern Judaism; Baltimore.

ModT: Modern Theology; Oxford.

MonSt: Monastic Studies; Montreal. 0026-9190.

MondeB: Le Monde de la Bible: 1. P. 0154-9049. – 2. Genève.

Monde Copte, Le: 0399-905X.

Month; London. 0027-0172.

Moralia; Madrid.

MsME: Manuscripts of the Middle East; Leiden. 0920-0401.

MSVO: Materialien zu den frühen Schriftzeugnissen des Vorderen Orients: B.

MüÄgSt: Münchener Ägyptologische Studien; München/Berlin.

MüBeit[T]PapR: Münchener Beiträge zur [Theologie] Papyruskunde und antiken Rechtsgeschichte; München.

MünstHand: Münsterische Beiträge zur Antiken Handelsgeschichte; St. Katharinen. 0722-4532.

MüStSprW: Münchener Studien zur Sprachwissenschaft; Mü. ➤ AOtt.

MüTZ: Münchener Theologische Zeitschrift; St. Ottilien. 0580-1400.

Mus: Le Muséon; LvN. 0771-6494.

MusHelv: Museum Helveticum; Basel.

MUSJ: Mélanges de l'Université Saint-Joseph (rediviva); Beyrouth [51 (1990): 2-7214-5000-X].

MusTusc: Museum Tusculanum; København. 0107-8062.

MuzTA: ✪ Muzeon Ha-Areṣ NS; TA.

NABU: Nouvelles assyriologiques brèves et utilitaires; 0989-5671.

NachGö: Nachrichten der Akademie der Wissenschaften; Göttingen.

NarAzAfr: ✪ Narody: Peoples of Asia and Africa; Moskva.

NatGeog: National Geographic; Washington. 0027-9358.

NatGrac: Naturaleza y Gracia; S.

NBL: Neues Bibel-Lexikon; Z ➤ 682.

NBlackfr: New Blackfriars; London. 0028-4289.

NCent: The New Century Bible Commentary (reedited); Edinburgh / GR.

NChrIsr: Nouvelles Chrétiennes d'Israël: Jérusalem.

NDizTB: Nuovo Dizionario Teol.B ➤ 683.

NduitsGT: Nederduits-Gereformeerde Teologiese Tydskrif; Kaapstad. 0028-2006.

NedTTs: Nederlands Theologisch Tijdschrift; Wageningen. 0028-212X.

Neotestamentica; Pretoria; NTWerk.

Nestor, Classical Antiquity, Indiana Univ.; Bloomington. 0028-2812.

NesTR: Near East School of Theology Review; Beirut.

News: Newsletter: Anat[olian Studies; NHv]; Targ[umic and Cognate Studies; Toronto]; ASOR [Baltimore]; Ug[aritic Studies; Calgary]; ➤ JAmEg.

NewTR: New theology review: Ch. 0896-4297.

NHC: Nag Hammadi Codices, Egypt UAR Facsimile edition; Leiden.

NHL/S: Nag Hammadi Library in English / Studies; Leiden.

NHLW: Neues Handbuch der Literaturwissenschaft: Wsb, Athenaion.

Nicolaus (teol. ecumenico-patristica); Bari.

NICOT: New International Commentary OT; Grand Rapids, Eerdmans.

NigJT: The Nigerian Journal of Theology; Owerri.

NIGT: New International Greek Testament Commentary; Exeter/GR.

NJBC: New Jerome Biblical Commentary ➤ 1686.

NOrb: NT & Orbis Antiquus; FrS/Gö.

NorJ: Nordisk Judaistik.

NorTTs: Norsk Teologisk Tidsskrift; Oslo. 0029-2176.

NoTr: Notes on Translation; Dallas.

NOxR: New Oxford Review; Berkeley.

NRT: Nouvelle Revue Théologique; Tournai. 0029-4845.

NS [NF]: Nova series, nouvelle série.

NSys: Neue Zeitschrift für systematische Theologie und Religionsphilosophie; Berlin. 0028-3517.

NT: Novum Testamentum; Leiden. 0048-1009.

NTAbh: Neutestamentliche Abhandlungen. [N.F.]; Münster.

NTAbs: New Testament Abstracts; CM. 0028-6877.

NTDt: Das Neue Testament deutsch; Gö.

NTS: New Testament Studies; C.

NTTools: Leiden. 0077-8842.

NubChr: Nubia Christiana; Wsz.

Nubica; Köln (1,1990).

NumC: Numismatic Chronicle; London. 0078-2696.

Numen (History of Religions); Leiden.

Numisma; Madrid. 0029-0015.

NumZ: Numismatische Zeitschrift; Wien. 0250-7838.

NuovaUm: Nuova Umanità; Roma.

NVFr/Z: Nova et Vetera; 1. Fribourg, Suisse. / 2. Zamora.

NZMissW: Neue Zeitschrift für Missionswissenschaft; Beckenried, Schweiz. 0028-3495. ➤ **NSys.**

ObnŽiv: Obnovljeni Život; Zagreb.

OBO: Orbis Biblicus et Orientalis: FrS/Gö.

OEIL: Office d'édition et d'impression du livre; Paris.

ÖkRu: Ökumenische Rundschau; Stuttgart. 0029-8654.

ÖkTbKom, NT: Ökumenischer Taschenbuchkommentar; Gütersloh / Würzburg.

ÖsterrBibSt: Österreichische Biblische Studien; Klosterneuburg.

Offa, ... Frühgeschichte; Neumünster. 0078-3714.

Ohio ➤ **JRelSt:** Cleveland.

OIAc/P/C: Oriental Institute Acquisitions / Publications / Communications; Ch.

OikBud: Oikumene, historia; Budapest.

Olivo (El), diálogo jud.-cr.: Madrid.

OLZ: Orientalistische Literaturzeitung; Berlin. 0030-5383.

OMRO: Oudheidkundige Mededelingen, Rijksmuseum Oudheden; Leiden.

OneInC: One in Christ (Catholic Ecumenical); Turvey, Bedfordshire.

OnsGErf: Ons Geestelijk Erf; Antwerpen. ➤ **GLeven.**

OpAth/Rom: Opuscula Atheniensia / Romana; Swedish Inst.

OPTAT: Occasional Papers in Translation and Textlinguistics: Dallas.

Opus, storia economica (Siena); R.

Or: ➤ Orientalia; Roma.

OraLab: Ora et Labora; Roriz, Portugal.

OrAnt[Coll]: Oriens Antiquus [Collectio]; Roma.

OrBibLov: Orientalia et Biblica Lovaniensia; Lv.

OrChr: Oriens Christianus; Wsb.

OrChrPer[An]: Orientalia Christiana Periodica [Analecta]; R, Pontificium Inst. Orientalium Stud. 0030-5375.

OrExp: L'Orient express, informations archéologiques. (1,1991).

OrGand: Orientalia Gandensia; Gent.

Orientalia (Ancient Near East); Rome, Pontifical Biblical Institute. 0030-5367.

Orientierung; Zürich. 0030-5502.

Orient-Japan: Orient, Near Eastern Studies Annual; Tokyo. 0743-3851; cf. ❹ Oriento. 0030-5219.

Origins; Washington Catholic Conference. 0093-609X.

OrJog: Orientasi, Annual ... Philosophy and Theology; Jogjakarta.

OrLovPer[An]: Orientalia Lovaniensia Periodica [Analecta]; Lv. 0085-4522.

OrMod: Oriente Moderno; Napoli. 0030-5472.

OrOcc: Oriente-Occidente. Buenos Aires, Univ. Salvador.

OrPast: Orientamenti Pastorali; Roma.

Orpheus: 1. Catania; 2. -Thracia; Sofya (1,1990).

OrSuec: Orientalia Suecana; Uppsala.

OrtBuc: Ortodoxia; Bucureşti.

OrthF: Orthodoxes Forum; München.

OrTrad: Oral Tradition; Columbia. MO.

OrVars: Orientalia Varsoviensia; Wsz. 0860-5785.

OstkSt: Ostkirchliche Studien; Würzburg. 0030-6487.

OTAbs: Old Testament Abstracts; Washington. 0364-8591.

OTEssays: Old Testament essays; Pretoria. 1010-9919.

OTS: Oudtestamentische Studiën; Leiden. 0169-9555.

OTWerkSuidA: Die Ou Testamentiese Werkgemeenskap Suid-Afrika; Pretoria.

OvBTh: Overtures to Biblical Theology; Philadelphia.

Overview; Ch St. Thomas More Asn.

OxJArch: Oxford Journal of Archaeology; Ox. 0262-5253.

℗: *polonice,* in Polish.

p./pa./pl.: page(s)/paperback/plate(s).

PAAR: Proceedings of the American Academy for Jewish Research; Ph.

Pacifica: Australian theological studies; Melbourne Brunswick East.

PacTR: Pacific theological review: SanAnselmo, SF Theol.Sem.

Palaeohistoria; Haarlem.

PalCl: Palestra del Clero; Rovigo.

PaléOr: Paléorient; Paris.

PalSb: ❽ Palestinski Sbornik; Leningrad.

PapBritSR: Papers of the British School at Rome; London.

PAPS: Proceedings of the American Philosophical Society; Philadelphia.

PapTAbh: Papyrologische Texte und Abhandlungen; Bonn, Habelt.

PapyrolColon: Papyrologica Coloniensia; Opladen. 0078-9410.

Parabola; New York.

Paradigms; Louisville KY.

ParOr: Parole de l'Orient; Kaslik.

ParPass: Parola del Passato; Napoli. 0031-2355.

ParSpV: Parola, Spirito e Vita; Bologna.

ParVi: Parole di Vita; T-Leumann.

PasT: Pastoraltheologie; Göttingen.

PastScP: Pastoral / Sciences pastorales; psych.sociol.théol.; Ottawa.

Patr&M: Patristica et Mediaevalia; BA.

PatrMedRen: Proceedings of the Patristic, Mediaeval and Renaissance Conference; Villanova PA.

PatrStudT: Patristische Studien und Texte; B. 0553-4003.

PBtScB: Petite bibliothèque des sciences bibliques; Paris, Desclée.

PenséeC: La Pensée Catholique; P.

PEQ: Palestine Exploration Quarterly; London. 0031-0328.

PerAz: Peredneaziatskij Sbornik; Moskva.

Persica: Leiden.

PerspRelSt: Perspectives in Religious Studies (Baptist); Danville VA.

PerspT: Perspectiva Teológica; Belo Horizonte.

Pg/Ph: philolog-/philosoph-.

PgOrTb: Philologia Orientalis; Tbilisi.

Phase; Barcelona.
PhilipSa: Philippiniana Sacra; Manila.
Philologus; B. 0031-7985.
Phoenix; Toronto. 0031-8299.
PhoenixEOL; Leiden. 0031-8329.
Phronema: Greek Orthodox; Sydney.
Phronesis; Assen. 0031-8868.
Pneuma, Pentecostal; Pasadena.
PoinT: Le Point Théologique; P.
Polin: Polish-Jewish Studies; Oxford.
PontAcc, R/Mem: Atti della Pontificia Accademia Romana di Archeologia, Rendiconti/Memorie; Vaticano.
PrPeo [< *CleR*]: Priests and People; L.
PracArch: Prace Archeologiczne; Kraków, Univ. 0083-4300.
PraehZ: Praehistorische Zeitschrift; Berlin. 0079-4848.
PrakT: Praktische theologie; Zwolle.
PraktArch: ⊕ Praktika, Archeology Society Athens.
PrCambPg: Proceedings of the Cambridge Philological Soc. 0068-6735.
PrCTSAm: Proceedings Catholic Theological Society of America; Villanova.
PredikOT/NT: De Prediking van het OT / van het NT; Nijkerk.
Premislia Christiana; Przemyśl.
Presbyteri; Trento.
Presbyterion; St. Louis.
PresPast: Presenza Pastorale; Roma.
PrêtreP: Prêtre et Pasteur; Montréal. 0385-8307.
Priest (The); Washington.
PrincSemB: Princeton Seminary Bulletin; Princeton NJ.
PrIrB: Proceedings of the Irish Biblical Association; Dublin.
Prism; St. Paul MN.
ProbHistChr: Problèmes de l'Histoire du Christianisme; Bruxelles, Univ.
ProcClas: Proceedings of the Classical Association; London.
ProcCom: Proclamation Commentaries; Ph.
ProcGLM: Proceedings of the Eastern Great Lakes and Midwest Bible Societies; Buffalo.
ProcIsrAc: Proceedings of the Israel Academy of Sciences & Humanities; Jerusalem.
Prooftexts; Baltimore.
PrOrChr: Proche-Orient Chrétien; Jérusalem. 0032-9622.

Prot: Protestantesimo; R. 0033-1767.
Proyección (mundo actual); Granada.
ProySal: Proyecto Centro Salesiano de Estudios; Buenos Aires.
PrPg/PrehS: Proceedings of the Philological/Prehistoric Society; Cambridge.
PrSemArab: Proceedings of the Seminar for Arabian Studies; London.
Prudentia (Hellenistic, Roman); Auckland.
PrzOr[Tom/Pow]: Przegląd Orientalistyczny, Wsz: [Tomisticzny; Wsz / Powszechny, Kraków].
PT: Philosophy/Theology: Milwaukee, Marquette Univ.
PubTNEsp: Publicaciones de la Facultad Teológica del Norte de España; Burgos.
PUF: Presses Universitaires de France; P.
Qadm: Qadmoniot ⊕ Quarterly of Dept. of Antiquities; Jerusalem.
Qardom, ⊕ mensuel pour la connaissance du pays; Jerusalem, Ariel.
QDisp: Quaestiones Disputatae; FrB.
Qedem: Monographs of the Institute of Archaeology: Jerusalem.
QLtg: Questions Liturgiques; Lv.
QRMin: Quarterly Review [for] Ministry; Nv. 0270-9287.
QuadCatan / Chieti: Quaderni, Catania / Chieti; Univ.
QuadSemant: Quaderni di Semantica; Bologna.
QuadSemit: Quaderni di Semitistica; Firenze.
QuadUrb: Quaderni Urbinati di Cultura Classica; Urbino. 0033-4987.
Quaerendo (Low Countries: Manuscripts and Printed Books); Amst.
QuatreF: Les quatre fleuves: Paris.
QüestVidaCr: Qüestions de Vida Cristiana; Montserrat.
QumC: Qumran Chronicle; Kraków.
⊕: *russice,* in Russian.
R: *recensio,* book-review(er).
RAC: Reallexikon für Antike und Christentum; Stuttgart → 684.
Radiocarbon; NHv, Yale. 0033-8222.
RAfrT: Revue Africaine de Théologie; Kinshasa/Limete.
RAg: Revista Agustiniana; Calahorra.
RAMBI: Rešimat Ma'amarim bemadda'ê ha-Yahedût, Index of articles on Jewish Studies; J. 0073-5817.

RaMIsr: Rassegna mensile di Israel; Roma. 0033-9792.
RArchéol: Revue Archéologique; Paris. 0035-0737.
RArchéom: Revue d'Archéométrie; Rennes.
RArtLv: Revue des Archéologues et Historiens d'Art; Lv. 0080-2530.
RasArch: Rassegna di archeologia; F (9,1990).
RasEtiop: Rassegna di Studi Etiopici; R/N.
RAss: Revue d'Assyriologie et d'Archéologie Orientale; Paris.
RasT: Rassegna di Teologia; Roma [ᴱNapoli]. 0034-9644.
RazF: Razón y Fe; M. 0034-0235.
RB: Revue Biblique; J/P. 0035-0907.
RBén: Revue Bénédictine; Maredsous. 0035-0893.
RBgNum: Revue Belge de Numismatique et Sigillographie; Bruxelles.
RBgPg: Revue Belge de Philologie et d'Histoire; Bru. 0035-0818.
RBBras: Revista Bíblica Brasileira; Fortaleza.
RBíbArg: Revista Bíblica; Buenos Aires. 0034-7078.
RCatalT: Revista Catalana de Teología; Barcelona, St. Pacià.
RCiv: Éditions Recherche sur les Civilisations [Mém(oires) 0291-1655]; P ➤ ADPF.
RClerIt: Rivista del Clero Italiano; Milano. 0042-7586.
RCuClaMed: Rivista di Cultura Classica e Medioevale; R. 0080-3251.
RÉAnc: Revue des Études Anciennes; Bordeaux. 0035-2004.
RÉArmén: Revue des Études Arméniennes. 0080-2549.
RÉAug: Revue des Études Augustiniennes; Paris. 0035-2012.
REB: 1. Revista Eclesiástica Brasileira; Petrópolis. 2. ➤ RNEB.
RÉByz: Revue des Études Byzantines; Paris.
RECAM: Regional Epigraphic Catalogues of Asia Minor [AnSt].
RechAug: Recherches Augustiniennes; Paris. 0035-2021.
RechSR: Recherches de Science Religieuse; Paris. 0034-1258.

RecTrPO: Recueil de travaux, Proche-Orient ancien; Montréal.
RefEgy: Református Egyház; Budapest. 0324-475X.
ReferSR: Reference Services Review; Dearborn MI, Univ.
RefF: Reformiertes Forum; Zürich.
RefGStT: Reformationsgeschichtliche Studien und Texten: Münster.
RefJ: The Reformed Journal; Grand Rapids. 0486-252X.
Reformatio; Zürich. 0034-3021.
RefR: Reformed Review; New Brunswick NJ / Holland MI. 0034-3072.
RefTR: Reformed Theological Review; Hawthorn, Australia. 0034-3072.
RefW: Reformed World; Geneva. 0034-3056.
RÉG: Revue des Études Grecques; Paris. 0035-2039.
RÉgp: Revue d'Égyptologie; Paris.
RÉJ: Revue des Études Juives; Paris. 0035-2055.
RÉLat: Revue des Études Latines; P.
RelCult: Religión y Cultura; M.
RelEdn: Religious Education (biblical; Jewish-sponsored); NHv.
Religion [... and Religions]; Lancaster. 0048-721X.
RelIntL: Religion and Intellectual Life; New Rochelle. 0741-0549.
RelPBeit: Religionspädagogische Beiträge; Kaarst.
RelSoc: Religion and Society; B/Haag.
RelSt: Religious Studies; Cambridge. 0034-4125.
RelStR: Religious Studies Review; Macon GA. 0319-485X.
RelStT: Religious Studies and Theology; Edmonton. 0829-2922.
RelTAbs: Religious and Theological Abstracts; Myerstown, Pa.
RelTrad: Religious Traditions; Brisbane. 0156-1650.
RencAssInt: Rencontre Assyriologique Internationale, Compte-Rendu.
RencChrJ: Rencontre Chrétiens et Juifs; Paris. 0233-5579.
Renovatio: 1. Zeitschrift für das interdisziplinäre Gespräch; Köln: 2. (teologia); Genova.
RepCyp: Report of the Department of Antiquities of Cyprus; Nicosia.

RépertAA: Répertoire d'art et d'archéologie; Paris. 0080-0953.
REPPAL: Revue d'Études Phéniciennes-Puniques et des Antiquités Libyques; Tunis.
REspir: Revista de Espiritualidad; San Sebastián.
ResPLit: Res Publica Litterarum; Kansas.
RestQ: Restoration Quarterly; Abilene TX.
Résurrection, bimestriel catholique d'actualité et de formation.
RET: Revista Española de Teología; Madrid.
RÉtGC: Revue des Études Géorgiennes et Caucasiennes; Paris. 0373-1537 [< Bedi Kartlisa].
RevCuBíb: Revista de Cultura Bíblica; São Paulo.
RevSR: Revue des Sciences Religieuses; Strasbourg. 0035-2217.
RExp: Review and Expositor; Louisville. 0034-6373.
RFgIC: Rivista di Filologia e di Istruzione Classica; Torino. 0035-6220.
RgStTh: Regensburger Studien zur Theologie; Fra/Bern, Lang.
RgVV: Religionsgeschichtliche Versuche und Vorarbeiten; B/NY, de Gruyter.
RHDroit: Revue historique de Droit français et étranger; Paris.
RHE: Revue d'Histoire Ecclésiastique; Louvain. 0035-2381.
RheinMus: Rheinisches Museum für Philologie; Frankfurt. 0035-449X.
Rhetorik [Jb]; Stu / Bad Cannstatt.
RHist: Revue Historique; Paris.
RHPR: Revue d'Histoire et de Philosophie Religieuses; Strasbourg. 0035-2403.
RHR: Revue de l'Histoire des Religions; Paris. 0035-1423.
RHS ⇒ RUntHö; RU ⇒ ZPrax.
RHText: Revue d'Histoire des Textes; Paris. 0373-6075.
Ribla: Revista de interpretación bíblica latinoamericana; San José CR.
RIC: Répertoire bibliographique des institutions chrétiennes; Strasbourg ⇒ 6,1063.
RICathP: Revue de l'Institut Catholique de Paris. 0294-4308

RicStoB: Ricerche storico bibliche; Bologna. 0394-980X.
RicStorSocRel: Ricerche di Storia Sociale e Religiosa; Roma.
RIDA: Revue Internationale des Droits de l'Antiquité; Bruxelles.
RIMA ⇒ AnRIM.
RINASA: Rivista Ist. Nazionale di Archeologia e Storia dell'Arte; Roma.
RitFg: Rivista italiana di Filologia Classica.
RItNum: Rivista Italiana di Numismatica e scienze affini; Milano.
RivArCr: Rivista di Archeologia Cristiana; Città/Vaticano. 0035-6042.
RivArV: Rivista di Archeologia, Univ. Venezia; Roma.
RivAscM: Rivista di Ascetica e Mistica; Roma.
RivB: Rivista Biblica Italiana; Bologna, Dehoniane. 0393-4853.
RivLtg: Rivista di Liturgia; T-Leumann.
RivPastLtg: Rivista di Pastorale Liturgica; Brescia. 0035-6395.
RivScR: Rivista di Scienze Religiose; Molfetta.
RivStoLR: Rivista di Storia e Letteratura Religiosa; F. 0035-6573.
RivStorA: Rivista Storica dell'Antichità; Bologna. 0300-340X.
RivVSp: Rivista di Vita Spirituale; Roma. 0035-6638.
RJysk: Religionsvidenskapeligt Tidsskrift (Jysk/Jutland); Aarhus. 0108-1993.
RLA: Reallexikon der Assyriologie & vorderasiatischen Archäologie; B ⇒ 685.
RLatAmT: Revista Latinoamericana de Teología; El Salvador.
RNEB: revision of New English Bible ⇒ 1630.
RNouv: La Revue Nouvelle; Bruxelles. 0035-3809.
RNum: Revue Numismatique; Paris.
RoczOr: Rocznik Orientalistyczny; Warszawa. 0080-3545.
RoczTK: Roczniki Teologiczno-Kanoniczne; Lublin. 0035-7723.
RömQ: Römische Quartalschrift für Christliche Altertumskunde...; Freiburg/Br. 0035-7812.
RomOrth: Romanian Orthodox Church News, French Version [sic]; Bucureşti.

RossArkh: Rossijskaja Arkheologija [➤ SovArch] after 1992/2: Moskva.
RPg: Revue de Philologie, de Littérature et d'Histoire anciennes; Paris, Klincksieck. 0035-1652.
RQum: Revue de Qumrân; P. 0035-1725.
RRéf: Revue Réformée; Saint-Germain-en-Laye.
RRel: Review for Religious; St. Louis. 0034-639X.
RRelRes: Review of Religious Research; New York. 0034-673X.
RRns: The Review of Religions; Wsh. 0743-5622.
RSO: Rivista degli Studi Orientali; Roma. 0392-4869.
RSPT: Revue des Sciences Philosophiques et Théologiques; [Le Saulchoir] Paris. 0035-2209.
RStFen: Rivista di Studi Fenici: R.
RSzem: Református Szemle; Budapest.
RTAM: Recherches de Théologie Ancienne et Médiévale; Louvain. 0034-1266. ➤ BTAM.
RTBat: Revista Teológica (Sem. Batista); Rio de Janeiro.
RThom: Revue Thomiste; Toulouse/Bru. 0035-4295.
RTLim: Revista Teológica; Lima.
RTLv: Revue théologique de Louvain. 0080-2654.
RTPhil: Revue de Théologie et de Philosophie; Épalinges. 0035-1784.
RuBi: Ruch Biblijny i Liturgiczny; Kraków. 0209-0872.
RUntHö: Religionsunterricht an höheren Schulen; Dü. (**RU** ➤ **ZPrax**).
RVidEspir: Revista de vida espiritual; Bogotá.
RZaïrTP: Revue Zaïroise de Théologie Protestante.
SAA[B]: State Archives of Assyria [Bulletin]; Helsinki.
SacEr: Sacris Erudiri; Steenbrugge.
Saeculum; FrB/Mü. 0080-5319.
Sales: Salesianum; Roma. 0036-3502.
Salm: Salmanticensis; S. 0036-3537.
SalT: Sal Terrae; Sdr. 0211-4569.
Sandalion (Sassari); R, Herder.
SAOC: Studies in Ancient Oriental Civilization: Ch, Univ. 0081-7554. ➤ **OI.**

Sap: Sapienza; Napoli. 0036-4711.
SapCro: La Sapienza della Croce; R.
sb.: subscription; price for members.
SbBrno: Sborník praci filozoficke fakulty; Brno, Univ.
SBF Anal/Pub [min]: Studii Biblici Franciscani: Analecta / Publicationes series maior 0081-8971 [minor]; Jerusalem. ➤ LA.
SBL [AramSt / Mg / Diss / GRR / MasSt / NAm / SemP / TexTr]: Society of Biblical Literature: Aramaic Studies / Monograph Series / Dissertation Series / Graeco-Roman Religion / Masoretic Studies / Biblical Scholarship in North America / Seminar Papers 0145-2711 / Texts and Translations. ➤ **JBL; CATSS; CritRR.**
SBS [KBW]: Stuttgarter Bibelstudien; Stuttgart, Katholisches Bibelwerk.
ScandJOT: Scandinavian Journal of the Old Testament; Aarhus.
ScAnt: Scienze dell'Antichità; storia archeologia antropologia; Roma (3s,1989s).
ScEsp: Science et Esprit; Montréal. 0316-5345.
SCHN: Studia ad Corpus Hellenisticum NT; Leiden.
Schönberger Hefte; Fra.
Scholars Choice; Richmond VA.
SChr: Sources Chrétiennes; P. 0750-1978.
SCompass: Social Compass, revue internat. sociologie de la religion: Lv.
ScotBEv: The Scottish Bulletin of Evangelical Theology; E. 0265-4539.
ScotJT: Scottish Journal of Theology; Edinburgh. 0036-9306.
ScotR: Scottish Journal of Religious Studies; Stirling. 0143-8301.
ScrCiv: Scrittura [scrivere] e Civiltà; T.
ScrClasIsr: Scripta Classica Israelica; J.
ScriptB: Scripture Bulletin; London. 0036-9780.
Scriptorium; Bruxelles. 0036-9772.
ScripTPamp: Scripta theologica; Pamplona, Univ. Navarra. 0036-9764.
Scriptura; Stellenbosch. 0254-1807.
ScriptVict: Scriptorium Victoriense; Vitoria, España.
ScuolC: La Scuola Cattolica; Venegono Inferiore, Varese. 0036-9810.
SDB [= DBS]: Supplément au Dictionnaire de la Bible; Paris ➤ 686.

SDH: Studia et documenta historiae et iuris; Roma, Pont. Univ. Lateran.
SecC: The Second Century; Malibu CA. 0276-7899.
Sefarad; Madrid. 0037-0894.
SEG: Supplementum epigraphicum graecum; Withoorn.
Segmenten; Amsterdam, Vrije Univ.
SelT: Selecciones de Teología; Barc.
SémBib: Sémiotique et Bible; Lyon ➤ CADIR. 0154-6902.
Semeia (Biblical Criticism) [Supplements]; Atlanta. 0095-571X.
Seminarios; Salamanca.
Seminarium; Roma.
Seminary Review; Cincinnati.
Semiotica; Amsterdam. 0037-1998.
Semitica; Paris. 0085-6037.
Semitics; Pretoria. 0256-6044.
Sens; juifs et chrétiens; Paris.
SeptCogSt: ➤ B[ulletin].
Servitium; CasM (ᴱBergamo).
SEST: South-Eastern [Baptist] Seminary Studies; Wake Forest NC.
Sevārtham; Ranchi.
Sève = Église aujourd'hui; P. 0223-5854.
SFulg: Scripta Fulgentina; Murcia. (1,1991s).
SGErm: ❻ Soobščeniya gosudarstvennovo Ermitaža, Reports of the State Hermitage Museum; Leningrad. 0432-1501.
ShinKen: ❹ *Shinyaku Kenkyū,* Studia Textus Novi Testamenti; Osaka.
ShMišpat: Shnaton ha-Mišpaṭ ha-Ivri, Annual of Jewish Law.
ShnatM: ❺ Shnaton la-Mikra (Annual, Biblical and ANE Studies); TA.
SicArch: Sicilia archaeologica; Trapani.
SicGym: Siculorum Gymnasium; Catania.
Sidra, a journal for the study of Rabbinic literature; Ramat-Gan.
SIMA: Studies in Mediterranean Archaeology; Göteborg.
SixtC: The Sixteenth Century Journal; St. Louis (Kirksville). 0361-0160.
SkK: Stuttgarter kleiner Kommentar.
SkrifK: Skrif en Kerk; Pretoria, Univ.
SMEA: Studi Micenei ed Egeo-Anatolici (Incunabula Graeca); Roma.

SMSR: Studi e Materiali di Storia delle religioni: Roma.
SNTS (Mg.): Studiorum Novi Testamenti Societas (Monograph Series); Cambridge.
SNTU-A/B: Studien zum NT und seiner Umwelt; Linz [Periodica / Series].
SocAnRel: Sociological analysis (sociology of religion); Chicago.
SocUÉg: Sociétés Urbaines en Égypte et au Soudan; Lille.
SocWB: The Social World of Biblical Antiquity; Sheffield.
Soundings; Nashville. 0585-5462.
SovArch: ❻ [Sovyet/] ➤ Rossijskaja Arkheologija; Moskva. 0038-5034.
Speculum (Medieval Studies); CM. 0038-7134.
SPg: Studia Philologica. 0585-5462.
SpirC, SpirNC: La Spiritualità cristiana / non-cristiana; R ➤ 5,907.
Spiritus; Paris. 0038-7665.
SpirLife: Spiritual Life; Washington. 0038-7630.
Sprache; Wien. 0038-8467.
SR: Studies in Religion / Sciences Religieuses; Waterloo, Ont. 0008-4298.
SSEA ➤ JSStEg.
ST: (Vaticano) Studi e Testi.
ST: Studia Theologica; K. 0039-338X.
StAäK: Studien zur altägyptischen Kultur; Hamburg. 0340-2215.
StAChron: Studies in Ancient Chronology; London. 0952-4765.
Stadion, Geschichte des Sports; Sankt Augustin. 0178-4029.
StAns: Studia Anselmiana; Roma.
StANT: Studien zum Alten und Neuen Testament; München.
StAntCr: Studi di Antichità Cristiana; Città del Vaticano.
Star: St. Thomas Academy for Research; Bangalore.
Stauròs, Bollettino trimestrale sulla teologia della Croce; Pescara.
StBEC: Studies in the Bible and Early Christianity; Lewiston NY.
StBEx: Studies in Bible and Exegesis; Ramat-Gan.
StBib: Dehon/Paid/Leiden: Studi Biblici; Bo, Dehoniane / Brescia, Paideia / Studia Biblica; Leiden.
StBoğT: Studien zu den Boğazköy-Texten; Wiesbaden.

STBuc: Studii Teologice; Bucureşti.

StCatt: Studi cattolici; Mi. 0039-2901.

StCEth: Studies in Christian Ethics; Edinburgh. 0953-9468.

StChrAnt: Studies in Christian Antiquity; Wsh.

StChrJud: Studies in Christianity and Judaism; Waterloo ON.

StClasBuc: Studii Clasice; Bucureşti.

StClasOr: Studi Classici e Orientali; R.

StCompRel: Studies in Comparative Religion; Bedfont. 0039-3622.

StDelitzsch: Studia Delitzschiana (ᴱMünster); Stuttgart. 0585-5071.

StEbl: Studi Eblaiti; Roma, Univ.

StEcum: Studi Ecumenici; Verona. 0393-3687.

StEgPun: Studi di Egittologia e di Antichità Puniche (Univ. Bo.); Pisa.

StEpL: Studi Epigrafici e Linguistici sul Vicino Oriente antico; Verona.

STEv: Studi di Teologia dell'Istituto Biblico Evangelico; Padova.

StFormSp: Studies in Formative Spirituality; Pittsburgh, Duquesne Univ.

StGnes: Studia Gnesnensia; Gniezno.

StHistANE: Studies in the history of the ancient Near East; Leiden. 0169-9024.

StHJewishP: Studies in the History of the Jewish People; Haifa.

StHPhRel: Studies in the History and Philosophy of Religion; CM.

StHRel [= Numen Suppl.] Studies in the History of Religions; Leiden.

StIran: Studia Iranica; Leiden. 0772-7852.

StIsVArh: Studii şi cercetări de Istorie Veche şi arheologie; Bucureşti. 0039-4009.

StItFgC: Studi Italiani di Filologia Classica; Firenze. 0039-2987.

StiZt: Stimmen der Zeit; FrB. 0039-1492.

StJudLA: Studies in Judaism in Late Antiquity; Leiden. 0169-961X.

StLatIt: Studi Latini e Italiani: R, Univ. (5,1991).

StLeg: Studium Legionense; León.

StLtg: Studia Liturgica; Nieuwendam.

StLuke: St. Luke's Journal of Theology; Sewanee TN.

StMiss: Studia Missionalia, Annual; Rome, Gregorian Univ.

StMor: Studia Moralia; R, Alphonsianum. 0081-6736.

StNT: Studien zum Neuen Testament; Gütersloh; **STNT** ➤ Shin-Ken.

StNW: Studies of the NT and its World; E.

StOr: Studia Orientalia; Helsinki, Societas Orientalis Fennica. 0039-3282.

StOrL: Studi Orientali e Linguistici; Bologna, Univ. Ist. Glottologia.

StOrRel: Studies in Oriental Religions; Wiesbaden.

StOvet: Studium Ovetense; Oviedo.

StPatav: Studia Patavina; Padova. 0039-3304.

StPatrist: Studia Patristica; Berlin.

StPhilonAn: Studia Philonica Annual; Atlanta.

StPostB: Studia Post-Biblica; Leiden.

StPrace: Studia i Prace = Études, Wsz. Streven: 1. cultureel; Antwerpen. 0039-2324; 2. S.J., Amst.

StRicOrCr: Studi e Ricerche dell'Oriente Cristiano; Roma.

StRom: Studi Romani; Roma. Stromata (< Ciencia y Fe); San Miguel, Argentina. 0049-2353.

StRz: Studia Religioznawcze (Filozofii i Socjologii); Wsz, Univ.

StSemLgLing: Studies in Semitic Language and Linguistics; Leiden.

StSp (Dehoniane) ➤ 6,854*.

StSpG (Borla) ➤ 6,855.

StTNeunz: Studien zur Theologie und Geistesgeschichte des Neunzehnten Jh.; Göttingen.

StudiaBT: Studia Biblica et Theologica; Pasadena CA. 0094-2022. Studies; Dublin. 0039-3495.

StudiesBT: Studies in Biblical Theology; L. Studium; 1. Madrid; 2. R – 0039-4130.

StVTPseud: Studia in Veteris Testamenti Pseudepigrapha; Leiden.

STWsz: Studia theologica Varsaviensia; Warszawa.

SubsBPont: Subsidia Biblica; R, Pontifical Biblical Institute.

SudanTB: Sudan Texts Bulletin; Ulster, Univ. 0143-6554. Sumer (Archaeology-History in the Arab World); Baghdad, Dir. Ant.

SUNT: Studien zur Umwelt des NTs; Gö.

SUNY: State University of New York; Albany etc.

Supp.: Supplement → NT, JStOT, SEG.
Supplément, Le: autrefois 'de VSp'; P.
SvEx: Svensk Exegetisk Årsbok; U.
SVlad: St. Vladimir's Theological Quarterly; Tuckahoe NY. 0036-3227.
SvTKv: Svensk Teologisk Kvartalskrift; Lund.
SWJT: Southwestern Journal of Theology; Fort Worth. 0038-4828.
Symbolae (graec-lat.); Oslo. 0039-7679.
Symbolon: 1. Ba/Stu; 2. Köln.
Synaxe; annuale, Catania.
Syria (Art Oriental, Archéologie); Paris, IFA Beyrouth.
SyrMesSt: Syro-Mesopotamian Studies (Monograph Journals); Malibu CA.
Szb: Sitzungsberichte [Univ.], phil.-hist. Klasse (Bayr.). Mü. 0342-5991.
Szolgalat Ⓦ ['Dienst']; Eisenstadt, Ös.
Ⓣ: *lingua turca,* Turkish; – ᵀtranslator.
Tablet; London. 0039-8837.
TAik: Teologinen Aikakauskirja / Teologisk Tidskrift; Helsinki.
TaiwJT: Taiwan [Presbyterian Sem.] Journal of Theology; Taipei.
TAJ: Tel Aviv [Univ.] Journal of the Institute of Archaeology. 0334-4355.
TAn: Theology Annual; Hongkong.
ṬanṭurYb: Ecumenical Institute for Theological Research Yearbook; J.
TANZ: Texte und Arbeiten zum neutestamentlichen Zeitalter; Tü.
TArb: Theologische Arbeiten; Stu/B.
Tarbiẓ ❶ (Jewish Studies); Jerusalem, Hebr. Univ. 0334-3650.
TArg: Teología; Buenos Aires.
Target, translation studies; Amst.
TAth: ❸ Theología; Athēnai.
TAVO: Tübinger Atlas zum Vorderen Orient [Beih(efte)]: Wiesbaden.
TBeit: Theologische Beiträge; Wu.
TBer: Theologische Berichte: Z/Köln.
TBraga: Theologica; Braga.
TBud: Teologia; Budapest, Ac. Cath.
TBüch: Theologische Bücherei. (Neudrukke und Berichte 20. Jdt.); München.
TCN: Theological College of Northern Nigeria Bulletin; Bukuru.
TContext[o]: Theology in Context; Aachen 8,1 (1991). 0176-1439 = Teología in Contexto 1,1 (1991). 0938-3468 = **TKontext,** Theologie im Kontext 12,1 (1991). 0724-1628.

TDeusto: Teología-Deusto; Bilbao/M.
TDienst: Theologie und Dienst; Wu.
TDig: Theology Digest; St. Louis. 0040-5728.
TDNT: Theological Dictionary of the NT [< TWNT]; Grand Rapids → 5,811.
TDocStA: Testi e documenti per lo studio dell'Antichità; Milano, Cisalpino.
TDOT: Theological Dictionary of the Old Testament [< TWAT] GR → 689.
TEdn: Theological Education; Vandalia, Ohio.
TEdr: Theological Educator; New Orleans.
TEFS: Theological Education [Materials for Africa, Asia, Caribbean] Fund, Study Guide; London.
Téléma (réflexion et créativité chrétiennes en Afrique); Kinshasa-Gombe.
Teocomunicação.
Teresianum; Roma.
TerraS / TerreS: Terra Santa: 0040-3784. / La Terre Sainte; J (Custodia OFM). → **HolyL.**
TEspir: Teología Espiritual; Valencia.
TEuph: Transeuphratène [Syrie perse]; P.
TEV: Today's English Version (Good News for Modern Man); L, Collins.
TEvca: Theologia Evangelica; Pretoria, Univ. S. Africa.
TExH: Theologische Existenz heute; Mü.
Text; The Hague. 0165-4888.
TextEstCisn: Textos y Estudios 'Cardenal Cisneros'; Madrid, Cons.Sup.Inv.
TextPatLtg: Textus patristici et liturgici; Regensburg, Pustet.
Textus, Annual of the Hebrew Univ. Bible Project; J. 0082-3767.
TFor: Theologische Forschung; Ha.
TGegw: Theologie der Gegenwart in Auswahl; Münster, Regensberg-V.
TGʟ: Theologie und Glaube; Pd.
THandkNT: Theologischer Handkommentar zum NT; Berlin.
THAT: Theologisches Handwörterbuch zum AT; München. → 1,908.
Themelios; London. 0307-8388.
Theokratia, Jahrbuch des Institutum Delitzschianum; Leiden/Köln.
Theológos, Ho; Fac. Teol. Palermo.
THist: Théologie Historique; P. 0563-4253.
This World; NY.
Thomist, The; Wsh. 0040-6325.

Thought; NY, Fordham. 0040-6457.
TierraN: Tierra Nueva.
Tikkun; Oakland CA.
TimLitS: Times Literary Supplement; L.
TItSett: Teologia; Brescia (Fac. teol. Italia settentrionale).
T-Iusi: Teología, Instituto Universitario Seminario Interdioc.; Caracas.
TJb: Theologisches Jahrbuch; Leipzig.
TKontext: Theologie im Kontext; Aachen. 0724-1682. ➤ **TContext[o]**.
TLond: Theology; London. 0040-571X.
TLZ: Theologische Literaturzeitung; Berlin. 0040-5671.
TolkNT: Tolkning [commentarius] av Nya Testamentet; Stockholm.
TopO: Topoi Orient-Occident; Lyon. (1,1991).
TorJT: Toronto Journal of Theology.
TPast: Theologie en pastoraat; Zwolle.
TPhil: Theologie und Philosophie; Freiburg/Br. 0040-5655.
TPQ: Theologisch-praktische Quartalschrift; Linz, Ös. 0040-5663.
TPract: Theologia Practica; München/Hamburg. 0720-9525.
TR: Theologische Revue; Münster. 0040-568X.
TradErn: Tradition und Erneuerung (religiös-liberales Judentum); Bern.
Traditio; Bronx NY, Fordham Univ.
Tradition, orthodox Jewish; NY.
TRE: Theologische Realenzyklopädie; Berlin ➤ 690.
TRef: Theologia Reformata; Woerden.
TRevNE: ➤ NesTR.
TRicScR: Testi e ricerche di scienze religiose; Brescia.
TrierTZ: Trierer Theologische Zeitschrift; Trier. 0041-2945.
TrinJ: Trinity Journal; Deerfield IL. 0360-3032.
TrinSemR: Trinity Seminary Review; Columbus.
TrinT: Trinity theological journal; Singapore.
TrinUn [St/Mg] Rel: Trinity University Studies in Religion, San Antonio.
Tripod; Hong Kong.
TRu: Theologische Rundschau; Tübingen. 0040-5698.
TS: Theological Studies; Baltimore. 0040-5639.

TsGesch: Tijdschrift voor Geschiedenis; Groningen.
TsLtg: Tijdschrift voor Liturgie; Lv.
TStAJud: Texte und Studien zum Antiken Judentum; Tübingen. 0721-8753.
TsTKi: Tidsskrift for Teologi og Kirke; Oslo. 0040-7194.
TsTNijm (ipsi **TvT**)**:** Tijdschrift voor Theologie; Nijmegen. 0168-9959.
TStR: Texts and Studies in Religion; Lewiston NY.
TSzem: Theologiai Szemle; Budapest. 0133-7599.
TTod: Theology Today; Princeton. 0040-5736.
TU: Texte und Untersuchungen, Geschichte der altchristlichen Literatur; Berlin.
Tü [ÄgBei] ThS: Tübinger [Ägyptologische Beiträge; Bonn, Habelt] Theologische Studien; Mainz, Grünewald.
[Tü]TQ: [Tübinger] Theologische Quartalschrift; Mü. 0342-1430.
TürkArk: Türk Arkeoloji dergisi; Ankara.
TUmAT: Texte aus der Umwelt des ATs; Gütersloh ➤ 691.
TVers: Theologische Versuche; Berlin. 0437-3014.
TViat: Theologia Viatorum; SAfr.
TVida: Teología y Vida; Santiago, Chile. 0049-3449.
TWAT: Theologisches Wörterbuch zum Alten Testament; Stu ➤ 692.
TWiss: Theologische Wissenschaft, Sammelwerk für Studium und Beruf; Stu.
TWNT: Theologisches Wörterbuch zum NT; Stuttgart (➤ GLNT; TDNT).
TXav: Theologica Xaveriana; Bogotá.
TxK: Texte und Kontexte (Exegese); Stuttgart.
Tyche, Beiträge zur alten Geschichte, Papyrologie und Epigraphik; Wien.
Tychique (Chemin Neuf); Lyon.
TyndB: Tyndale Bulletin; Cambridge.
TZBas: Theologische Zeitschrift; Basel. 0040-5741.
UF: Ugarit-Forschungen; Kevelaer/ Neukirchen. 0342-2356.
Universitas; 1. Stuttgart. 0041-9079; 2. Bogotá. 0041-9060.
UnivT: Universale Teologica; Brescia.
UnSa: Una Sancta: 1. Augsburg-Meitingen; 2. Brooklyn.

UnSemQ: Union Seminary Quarterly Review; New York.

UPA: University Press of America; Wsh/ Lanham MD.

Update [religious trends]; Aarhus.

URM: Ultimate Reality and Meaning; Toronto.

VAeg: Varia Aegyptiaca; San Antonio. 0887-4026.

VBGed: Verklaring van een Bijbelgedeelte; Kampen.

VChrét: Vie Chrétienne; P. 0767-3221.

VComRel: La vie des communautés religieuses; Montréal.

VDI: ❻ Vestnik Drevnej Istorii; Moskva. 0321-0391.

Veleia, (pre-) historia, filología clásicas; Vitoria-Gasteiz, Univ. P. Vasco.

Verbum; 1. SVD; R; - 2. Nancy.

Veritas; Porto Alegre, Univ. Católica.

VerkF: Verkündigung und Forschung; München. 0342-2410.

VerVid: Verdad y Vida; M. 0042-3718.

VestB: Vestigia Biblica; Hamburg.

VetChr: Vetera Christianorum; Bari.

Vidyajyoti (Theology); Ranchi.

VieCons: La Vie Consacrée; P/Bru.

VigChr: Vigiliae Christianae; Leiden. 0042-6032.

ViMon: Vita Monastica; Arezzo.

ViPe: Vita e Pensiero: Mi, S. Cuore.

VisLang: Visible Language; Cleveland.

VisRel: Visible Religion, annual for iconography; Leiden. 0169-5606.

VitaCons: Vita Consacrata; Milano.

VivH: Vivens Homo, scienze rel.; F.

VizVrem: ❻ Vizantijskij Vremennik; Moskva. 0136-7358.

VO: Vicino Oriente; Roma.

Vocation; Paris.

VoxEvca: Vox Evangelica; London. 0263-6786.

VoxEvi: Vox Evangelii; Buenos Aires.

VoxRef: Vox Reformata; Geelong, Australia.

VoxTh: Vox Theologica; Assen.

VSp: La Vie Spirituelle; Paris. 0042-4935; ➤ **Supplément.** 0083-5859.

VT: Vetus Testamentum; Leiden. 0042-4935.

WDienst: Wort und Dienst; Bielefeld. 0342-3085.

WegFor: Wege der Forschung; Da, Wiss.

WeltOr: Welt des Orients; Göttingen. 0043-2547.

WesleyTJ: Wesleyan Theological Journal; Marion IN. 0092-4245.

WestTJ: Westminster Theological Journal; Philadelphia. 0043-4388.

WEvent: Word + Event; Stuttgart.

WienerSt: Wiener Studien; Wien.

WisLu: Wisconsin Lutheran Quarterly; Mequon. (88,1991).

Wiss: Wissenschaftliche Buchhandlung; Da.

WissPrax: Wissenschaft und Praxis in Kirche und Gesellschaft; Göttingen.

WissWeish: Wissenschaft und Weisheit; Mü-Gladbach. 0043-678X.

WM: Wissenschaftliche Monographien zum Alten/Neuen Testament; Neukirchen.

WoAnt: Wort und Antwort; Mainz.

Word and Spirit; Still River MA.

WorldArch: World Archaeology; Henley.

World Spirituality ➤ EWSp.

Worship; St. John's Abbey, Collegeville, Minn. 0043-9414.

WrocST: Wrocławskie Studia Teologiczne / Colloquium Salutis; Wrocław. 0239-7714.

WUNT: Wissenschaftliche Untersuchungen zum NT; Tübingen.

WVDOG: Wissenschaftliche Veröffentlichungen der Deutschen Orient-Gesellschaft; Berlin.

WWorld: Word and World; St. Paul.

WZ: Wissenschaftliche Zeitschrift [... Univ.].

WZKM: Wiener Zeitschrift für die Kunde des Morgenlandes; Wien. 0084-0076.

Xilotl, revista nicaraguense de teología.

YaleClas: Yale Classical Studies; NHv.

Yuval: Studies of the Jewish Music Research Centre [incl. Psalms]; Jerusalem.

ZäSpr: Zeitschrift für Ägyptische Sprache und Altertumskunde; Berlin. 0044-216X.

ZAHeb: Zeitschrift für Althebraistik; Stuttgart. 0932-4461.

ZAss: Zeitschrift für Assyriologie & Vorderasiatische Archäologie; Berlin. 0048-5299.

ZAW: Zeitschrift für die Alttestamentliche Wissenschaft; Berlin. 0044-2526.

ZDialekT: Zeitschrift für dialektische Theologie; Kampen.

ZDMG: Zeitschrift der Deutschen Morgenländischen Gesellschaft; Wiesbaden.

ZDPV: Zeitschrift des Deutschen Palästina-Vereins; Stu. 0012-1169.

ZeichZt: Die Zeichen der Zeit, Evangelische Monatschrift; Berlin.

Zeitwende (Die neue Furche); Gü.

ZeKUL: Zeszyty Naukowe Katolickiego Uniw. Lubelskiego; Lublin. 0044-4405.

Zephyrus; Salamanca. 0514-7336.

ZEthnol: Zeitschrift für Ethnologie; Braunschweig. 0044-2666.

ZEvEthik: Zeitschrift für Evangelische Ethik; Gütersloh. 0044-2674.

ZfArch: Zeitschrift für Archäologie: Berlin. 0044-233X.

ZfG: Zeitschrift für Geschichtswissenschaft; Berlin. 0044-2828.

ZGPred: Zeitschrift für Gottesdienst und Predigt; Gütersloh.

Zion: ✡; Jerusalem. 0044-4758.

ZIT: Zeitschriften Inhaltsdienst Theologie; Tübingen. 0340-8361.

ZKG: Zeitschrift für Kirchengeschichte; Stuttgart. 0044-2985.

ZkT: Zeitschrift für katholische Theologie; Innsbruck. 0044-2895.

ZMissRW: Zeitschrift für Missionswissenschaft und Religionswissenschaft; Münster. 0044-3123.

ZNW: Zeitschrift für die Neutestamentliche Wissenschaft & Kunde des Alten Christentums; B. 0044-2615.

ZPapEp: Zeitschrift für Papyrologie und Epigraphik; Bonn. 0084-5388.

ZPraxRU: Zeitschrift für die Praxis des Religionsunterrichts; Stuttgart.

ZRGg: Zeitschrift für Religions- und Geistesgeschichte; Köln. 0044-3441.

ZSavR: Zeitschrift der Savigny-Stiftung (Romanistische) Rechtsgeschichte: Weimar. 0323-4096.

ZSprW: Zeitschrift für Sprachwissenschaft; Göttingen. 0721-9067.

ZTK: Zeitschrift für Theologie und Kirche; Tübingen. 0513-9147.

Zwingliana; Zürich.

Zygon; Winter Park FL. 0591-2385.

| I. Bibliographica |

A1   *Opera collecta* .1 **Festschriften,** memorials.

1 Collected essays: CBQ 53 (1991) 158-168. 514-532. 728-732; – *Epp* E. J. *al.*, JBL 110 (1991) 365-371. 557-562; – *Langlamet* F., Recueils et Mélanges: RB 98 (1991) 293-9. 449-474. – AJS 16 (1991) 253-271. – AnzAltW 44,3 (1991) 129-147 (5 Festschriften); – RHE 86 (1991) 76*. 311*, concentration de Festschriften; – Sammelschriften: LuJb 57 (1990) p. 318-322; 58 (1991) p. 144-8.

2 *a)* **IJbF:** Internationale Jahresbibliographie der Festschriften [8 (1987) 1 & 9 (1989) ➤ 6,2b], ᴱ**Zeller** Otto & Wolfram, 10. Osnabrück 1990, Dietrich. 692 + 995 + 453 p.

— *b)* **Danton** J. Periam, *Anderson* Ottilia C., Index to Festschriften in librarianship. NY 1970. [DLZ 113,1].

3 ABRAMOWICZÓWNIA Zofia: Collectanea classica Thorunensis 9. Toruń 1987, Univ. [AnPg 60, p. 871].

4 ABRAMSKY Chimen: Jewish History, ᴱ**Rapoport-Albert** Ada, *Zipperstein* Steven J. L 1988, Halban. xi-700 p.; portr. 1-82001-519-3. 30 art., (post–) medioev.; 2 infra. – ᴿAJS 16 (1991) 253s (titles sans pp.).

4* ALBERT Karl: Probleme philosophischer Mystik, 70. Gb., EJain Elenor, *al.* St. Augustin 1991, Academia. 362 p.; Bibliog. 353-362. DM 58,50 [TR 88,348, some tit.pp.] 2 infra ➤ 4133*ab*.

5 AMALORPAVADASS D. S. mem.: Third World theologies in dialogue, EChandran J. Russell. Bangalore 1991, EATWOT. 212 p. [TContexto 2/2,136, G. *Evers*].

6 AMIRAN David, Eretz-Israel 22 (1991), EAviram Joseph, *Shachar* Arie. x + 41* + ❻16 + 227 p.; bibliog. viii-x + ❻ 12-16; portr. $40. 26 art.; 5 infra. [RB 99,587, only two items; NRT 114,777, X. *Jacques*; OLZ 87,400, G. *Pfeifer*].

7 AMPE Albert [➤ 5,10], Spiritualia neerlandica, ECockx-Indestege E., *al.* = OnsGErf 63,2-4 (1989) 119-416; 64,1-3 (1990) 1-275 [ETL 67,10*].
ANSELM (St.) College, Manchester NH centennial 1989/91 ➤ 470.

8 ARETIN Karl O. von: Deutschland und Europa in der Neuzeit, 65. Gb., EMelville R., *al.*: Mainz Eur. Gesch. (Universal–) 134. Stu 1988, Steiner. I. xxii-521 p. [LuJb 57 (1990) p. 322 with indication of three items there cited].

9 ARSLAN Ermanno A.: Monetazione, EMartini Rodolfo, *Vismara* Novella; I. greca e greco-imperiale; II. romana; III. tardoantica, medioevale e moderna: Glaux 7. Mi 1991, Ennerre. I. XVII-258 p.; 53 pl.; bibliog. p. 1-8; II. p. 261-580; 76 fig.: pl. 54-98; III. 585-877; pl. 99-141. 12 + 12 + 17 art.; 5 infra.

10 ❺ Athens National and Capodistrian University 1837-1987: May 2-5, 1987, Anniversary celebrations. 326 p. – RTAth 62 (1991) 584-6 (E. A. *Theodorou*: ❺ no authors listed).

11 AUBENQUE Pierre: Herméneutique et ontologie, EBrague Rémi, *Courtine* Jean-François: Épiméthée. P 1990, PUF. xxi-388 p. [AnPg 61, p. 728; dépouillé].

12 BAELZ Peter: The weight of glory; a vision and practice for Christian faith; the future of liberal theology, EHardy D. W., *Sedgwick* P. H. E 1991, Clark. 316 p. £20 [TR 87,435; JTS 43,367, J. *Macquarrie*]. 0-567-09579-7. 25 art. – RExpTim 103 (1991s) 185s (M. *Camroux*).

13 BAETKE Walter: 80 Gb... Weimar 1966, Böhlau. 391 p.; 12 pl.; portr. 30 art.; 5 infra.

14 BAGATTI Bellarmino [Camillo], 11.XI.1905 – 17.X.1990: Padre ~ , francescano, sacerdote, archeologo, ENiccacci Alviero, *al.*; SBF Museum 9. J 1991, Custodia Terra Santa / Prov. Toscana O.F.M. 175 p.; ill.; 15-52 bibliog. (G. *Bottini*, 723 items; 128-131 su lui); 53-77 scavi; poi testimonianze ecc. (non art.).

BALIL ILLANA A. mem. [I. 1990 ➤ 6,9] II. Mosaicos romanos 1990 ➤ a628.

14* BALOG P. mem.: IsrNumJ 10 (1988s).

15 BAMMEL Ernst: Templum amicitiae, essays on the Second Temple, 67th b., EHorbury William: JStNT supp 48. Sheffield 1991, Academic. 519 p.; portr.; bibliog. 477-484. £45. 1-85075-272-7. – *Bammel* C. P., Law and temple in ORIGEN 273-7; + 19 art. infra. – [CBQ 54,822, G. R. *Koester*, tit. pp.; RHPR 72,195, C. *Grappe*, themes sans pp.; ÉTRel 67,116, É. *Cuvillier*; JTS 43,567-573, R. J. *McKelvey*]; – RTR 87 (1991) 162 (tit. pp.).

16 BAPTISTAE: '...Lebenn nach der Ler Jhesu... Das sind aber wir!', Berner Täufer und Prädikanten im Gespräch. Gedenkband 450-Jr. Täuferdisputation Bern 1538. Bern c. 1990, Schw. Verein für Täufergeschiche. 208 p. Fs 42. – RTZBas 47 (1991) 89 (H. *Jecker*).

17 BARTHÉLEMY Dominique: Tradition of the text, 70th b., ENorton Gerard J., *Pisano* Stephen: OBO 109. FrS/Gö 1991, Univ/VR. xi-310 p. Fs 84. –

3-7278-0761-X / 3-525-53742-5. 19 art.; infra. [BL 92,46, S. P. *Brock*; ZAW 104, 312 & TR 87,425 & RB 99,588, tit. pp.].

18 BASTIAENSEN Antoon A. R.: Eulogia, 65ᵉ aniv., ᴱ**Bartelink** G.J.M., *al.*: Instrumenta patristica 24. Steenbrugge/Haag 1991, Sint Pietersabdij/ Nijhoff. xviii-497 p.; 2 pl. bibliog. vii-xviii. Fb 3500. [TR 88,164, tit. pp.; RHE 87,787, J. *Doignon*; JEH 43,636, C. P. *Bammel*; JTS 43,648, H. *Chadwick*; N. B. **not** = ᶠBartelink, ᴱBastiaensen, Centesimus annus: InstrPatr 19, 1989 ↠ 5,17] – 36 art., 25 infra.

19 BAYER Oswald: Aufmerksam aufs Wort, 50. Gb. ᴱ**Dieter** Theo. Tü 1989, auct. 219 p. [LuJb 58, p. 145, indicating 3 cited items].

20 *a*) BECKER U.: Lernen für eine bewohnbare Erde; Bildung und Erneuerung im ökumenischen Horizont, 60 Gb., ᴱ**Johannsen** F., *Noormann* H. Gü 1990, Mohn. 374 p. DM 68. 3-579-01766-7. – ᴿTsTNijm 31 (1991) 213 (T. *Bratting*).

– *b*) BEDNARSKI A. F. [Wojciech], 80° compleanno: Angelicum 68,4 (1991); 449-456 laudatio (Edward *Kaczynski*, Eng.); 457-467 (B. *Mazur*).

– *c*) BEHRENS Peter 19.VII.1931-11.II.1989, Gedenkschrift: Ägypten im Afro-Orientalischen Kontext; Aufsätze zur Archäologie, Geschichte und Sprache eines unbegrenzten Raumes, ᴱ**Mendel** Daniela, *Claudi* Ulrike: Afrik.Arbeitspapiere, Sondernummer. Köln 1991, Inst. Afrikanistik. 439 p.; Bibliog. 13-15. 0178-725X. 29 art.; 3 infra.

21 BENNETT Emmett L.ᴶ, Texts, tablets and scribes; studies in Mycenaean epigraphy and economy, ᴱ**Olivier** J. P., *Palaima* T. G.: Minos supp. 10. S 1988, Univ. S/Pais Vasco. – ᴿEmerita 59 (1991) 375-7 (F. *Aura Jorro*).

22 BENOÎT André: 70ᵉ: *a*) RHPR 71/1 (1991) 127 p.; portr.; bibliog. p. 121-3.

– *b*) Lectures anciennes de la Bible: BibPatr cah. 1. Strasbourg 1987, Centre d'Analyse et de Documentation Patristiques. 330 p. – ᴿZKG 102 (1991) 113s (W. A. *Bienert*: pp.ohne Titel). ↠ 1592*.

23 *a*) BERNAND Étienne: Mélanges, ᴱ**Fick** N., *Carrière* J.-C.: AnnLBesançon 444. P 1991, BLettres. xii-410 p. [RÉAnc 94,474, R. S. *Bagnall*; RÉG 104,680; CdÉ 67,383, J. *Bingen*].

– *b*) BÉRUBÉ Camille, O.F.M. Cap.: Études de philosophie et théologie médiévales, 80ᵉ anniv., ᴱ**Criscuolo** V. R 1991, Ist. Storico Cappuccini. 527 p. [ColcFran 62,685, E. *Ponzalli*]. – ᴿMiscFran 91 (1991) 501-3 (O. *Todisco*). [RHE 87,220*].

– *c*) BESUTTI Giuseppe M., O.S.M.: Virgo liber Verbi, ᴱ**Calabuig** Ignazio M. R 1991, Marianum. xvi-733 p. [TR 88,425; ScripTPamp 24,1112, J. L. *Bastero*]. – ᴿMarianum 53 (1991) 680s (A. *Bossard*).

– *d*) BISKOW Per: Florilegium patristicum. Delsbo 1991, Sahlin & D. 259 p., ill. [TR 88,429].

24 BLANCO FREIJEIRO Antonio: Estudios de geografía y de historia 3. M 1989, Univ. Complutense. 479 p.; ill. [AnPg 61, p. 729, dépouillé].

25 BLÁZQUEZ MARTÍNEZ José: Arte, sociedad, economía y religión durante el Bajo Imperio y la Antigüedad Tardía, 65 años, ᴱ**González Blanco** Antonino *al.*: Antigüedad y cristianismo 8. Murcia 1991, Univ. 582 p.; portr.; ill.; bibliog. 571-582 (*Conde Guerri* Elena). $50. 0214-7165. 32 art.

26 BLOCH Marc aujourd'hui; histoire comparée et sciences sociales, ᴱ**Atsma** H., *Burgière* A. P 1990, ÉPHÉS. 454 p. [RHE 86,256*].

27 BLOCH Peter: 65. Gb. [Kunst]; ᴱ**Krohm** Hartmut, *Theuerkauff* Christian. Mainz 1990, von Zabern. xviii-420 p.; ill.; portr.; biobibliog. xi-xviii, 3-8053-1120-6. 43 art., 3 infra.

28 BOENDERMAKER J. P.: Voor de achtste dag; het Oude Testament in de eredienst, 65. Verjaardag. ᴱ**Horst** K. van der, *al.* Kampen 1990,

Kok. 342 p. *f* 40. 90-242-2280-X. – ᴿDielB 27 (1991) 281s (B. J. *Diebner*); TsTNijm 31 (1991) 440 (A. *Scheer*).

29 BOCKMÜHL Klaus mem.: Gott lieben und seine Gebote halten, ᴱBockmuehl Markus! Giessen 1991, Brunnen. 365 p.; 356-365 Bibliog. DM 42 [TR 88,161].

30 BONNARD Pierre, La mémoire et le temps; Mélanges offerts à ~, ᴱMarguerat Daniel, *Zumstein* Jean: MondeB 23. Genève 1991, Labor et Fides. 323 p.; portr. 2-8309-0631-4. 21 art., infra. [TR 88,162, tit. pp.; ÉTRel 67,115, É. *Cuvillier*; RHPR 72,193, C. *Grappe*, titres sans pp.; RTPhil 124,358, Muriel *Schmid*].

31 BORGEN Peder: Context: 60. År, ᴱBøckman Peter W., *Kristiansen* R. E.: Relieff 24. Trondheim 1988, Tapir. 238 p. [TsTKi 61 (1990) 154]. — N. B. ᶠBøCKMAN P. is Relieff 23, 1987 → 4,15.

32 BOVINI Giuseppe † 1975: Studi in Memoria di ~ : Bt Felix Ravenna 6. Ravenna 1989. 798 p.; ill. – ᴿRivArCr 67 (1991) 498-505 (Maria Gabriella *Zanotti*).
Braga Sé dedicação 1090-1990 congreso → 475.

33 BRUMBAUGH Roger S.: Plato, time and education, ᴱHendley Brian P. Albany 1987, SUNY. 326 p. [AnPg 61, p. 729, dépouillé].

34 CALDERONE Salvatore: Hestiasis I-II, Studi di tarda antichità: Studi tardoantichi Is. Messina 1966 (1988), Sicania. L-385 p.; 435 p.; portr. [AnPg 60, p. 872].

35 CAMERON James H.: Humanism and reform; the Church in Europe, England, and Scotland 1400-1643, ᴱKirk J.: StChH Subsidia 8. Ox 1991, Blackwell. xvi-443 p.; 1 fig.; 1 pl. [RHE 87,52*].
CAMPS Arnulf: Popular religion, congress 1990/91 → 480.

36 CANFORA Giovanni, O.M.I., 70° compleanno: RivB 39,2 (1991) 'alcuni studi; altri nel prossimo numero'.
CARMIGNAC Jean, Mogilany 1989/91 → 420.

37 Cause dei Santi: Miscellanea in occasione del IV centenario della Congregazione per le ~ (1588-1988) [metà della Congregazione dei Riti fino al 1969]. Vaticano 1988. iv-450 p. [177-209, *Eszer* A., 211-220 *Giunchi* G., sui miracoli]. – ᴿGregorianum 72 (1991) 590-2 (P. *Gumpel*); RHE 87 (1991) 207s (R. *Aubert*); Teresianum 42 (1991) 361s (M. *Caprioli*).

38 CHENU Marie-Dominique: Hommage = RSPT 75,3 (1991) 361-504; présent. **Congar** Y.: 6 art. sur Chenu.

38* CIECHANOWIECKI Andrzej: Curia maior; studia z dziejów kultury, ᴱGieysztor G. Wsz 1990, Château royal. – ᴿRHE 86 (1991) 614-6 (R. *Szmydki*).

39 CLASSEN Carl Joachim: Memoria rerum veterum; neue Beiträge zur antiken Historiographie und alten Geschichte, 60. Gb., ᴱAx Wilhelm: Palingenesia 32. Stu 1990, Steiner. 216 p.; portr. 3-515-05598-3. 8 art., 3 infra.

40 CLÈRE Jacques Jean [7.IX.1906-30.V.1989]. Mélanges: Cahiers... Papyrologie / Égyptologie 13. Lille 1991, Univ. 147 p.; 20 pl.; 13-16 biog., *Edwards* I.E.S. 0153-5021. 18 art.; 6 infra.

41 *a*) COBB John B.: Theology and the University, ᴱGriffin David R., *Hough* Joseph C.ᴶ. Albany 1991, SUNY. viii-276 p.; bibliog. p. 243-265. $49.50 [RelStR 18,126, P. *Hodgson*; TDig 38,384; TR 87,434, tit. pp.].

— *b*) CRANMER Thomas: Essays in commemoration of the 500th anniversary of his birth [Durham-linked authors], ᴱJohnson Margot. Durham 1990, Turnstone. xiii-103 p. £13. 0-946-10508-1. – ᴿExpTim 102 (1990s) 281

(P. N. *Brooks*; severe except for G. BONNER; hardly a 'stimulating mosaic'); Worship 65 (1991) 475-8 (L. L. *Mitchell*).
— *c*) CZAPKIEWICZ Andrzej memorial, I.: Folia Orientalia 28 (1991). 205 p.; portr.; biobibliog. 5-12 (E. *Górska*). 14 art., mostly on Arabic; 5 infra.
— *d*) DAVID Marcel: Convergences. Quimper 1991, Calligrammes. 508 p. [RHE 87,220*].
DEGRASSI Attilio mem., Epigrafia 1991 ⇒ 583.
42 DEMMER Nikolaus: Ethische Theorie praktisch; der fundamental-moral-theologische Ansatz in sozialethischer Entfaltung, 60. Gb., ᴱFurger Franz, *al*.: Inst.Chr.Soz.-Wiss. 23. Münster 1991, Aschendorff. 311 p.; Bibliog. p. 305-9. 17 art. DM 57 [TR 87,436, tit. pp.].
43 DERCHAIN Philippe: Religion und Philosophie im Alten Ägypten, 65. Gb., ᴱVerhoeven Ursula, *Graefe* Erhart: OrLovAn 39. Lv 1991, Univ/Peeters. xiii-412 p.; ill.; bibliog. p. 1-10 (*Götte* Karin). 90-6831-337-1. 32 art., 28 infra.
43* *a*) DICKSON Martin B.: Intellectual studies on Islam, ᴱMarzaoui Michel M., *Moreen* Vera B. Salt Lake City 1990, Utah Univ. 276 p.; 4 pl. $40. 13 art. [RelStR 18, 244, W. *Smyth*].
— *b*) DIETZFELBINGER Chr., Schritte zur Freiheit, ᴱGrosshennig S., *al*. Tü 1989 [BibNot 57,7n].
44 DIMIER Anselme: Mélanges, ᴱChauvin B., I. L'homme, l'oeuvre. Pupillin 1987. 506 p.; 106 fig. F 600. 2-904690-06-9. [⇒ 5,48; II. 1986! III. 1983]. – ᴿColcCist 51 (1989) 101-7 (F. de *Place*, aussi II, 48,324; III ᴿ*Bouton* J., 45,155).
44* DÖRNER Friedrich K.: Studien zum antiken Kleinasien, 80. Gb.: Asia Minor Studien 3. Bonn 1991, Habelt. viii-151 p.; 17 pl. 3-7749-2508-9 [OIAc 2,17, noᴱ].
45 DOLLEY Michael mem. [1944-1983], ᴱBlackburn M.A.S. Leicester 1986, Univ. 315-360 bibliog. (R. H. *Thompson*). [AnPg 61, p. 734].
45* DOWEY Edward A.ᴶ, Probing the Reformed tradition, ᴱMcKee Elsie A., *Armstrong* Brian G. Louisville c. 1990, W-Knox. 464 p. $28 [JEH 43,343, D. W. *Bebbington*]. – ᴿAmerica 165 (1991) 101 (G. M. *Rosell*).
46 DRIEHAUS Jürgen [23.VII.1927-29.XII.1986], Gedenkschrift für ~, ᴱAndraschko Frank M., *Teegen* Wolf-Rüdiger. Mainz 1990, von Zabern. XII-381 p.; 126 fig.; 40 pl. + 1 color.; p. XI-XXI biobibliog. 3-8053-1133-8. 27 art., 3 infra.
46* EHRLICH Ernst L.: Israel und Kirche heute, Beiträge zum christlich-jüdischen Dialog, 70. Gb., ᴱMarcus M., *Stegemann* E., *Zenger* E. FrB 1991, Herder. 439 p.; portr.; Bibliog. p. 432-9. DM 78. [TLZ 117, 334, G. *Begrich*; TR 88,82, tit. pp.; TsTNijm 32,438, K. *Waaijman*; TüTQ 172,61, W. *Gross*]. 16 art.; 7 infra.
47 ENGELHARDT Paulus: Versöhnung; Versuche zu ihrer Geschichte und Zukunft, ᴱEggensperger Thomas, *al*.: Walberberger Studien, Philos. 8. Mainz 1991, Grünewald. 268 p.; Bibliog. p. 253-260. DM 41 [TR 87,425; TsTNijm 32,210, H.-E. *Mertens*; ZkT 114,104, K. *Neufeld*].
47* ENGEMANN Josef: Tesserae, 65. Gb., ᴱDassmann E.: JbAC Egb 18. Münster 1991, Aschendorff. x-419 p.; portr.; 64 pl.; Bibliog. p. vii-x. 3-402-08537-2; pa.-6-4. 32 art.; infra. [NRT 114,927, N. *Plumat*].
48 ERLICH Victor: Russian formalism; a retrospective glance, ᴱJackson Robert L., *Rudy* Stephen: Yale Russian & East European. NHv 1985, Univ. xiii-304 p. 0-936586-06-0. 21 art.; 2 infra.
48* ESENÇ Tevfik † 1982: Revue des Études Géorgiennes et Caucasiennes 6s (1990s). 0373-1537.

49 ESTEVE FORRIOL José: Homenatge, ᴱRoca Ismael, *Sanchis* Jorge L. Valencia 1990, Univ. 179 p.; ill [AnPg 61, p. 729, dépouillé].

50 FABRICIUS Cajus, mem. † 12.II.1990: Greek and Latin studies, ᴱTeodorsson Sven-Tage: AcGöteborg, St gr./lat. 54. Göteborg 1990, Univ. 265 p. Sk 100. 91-7346-228-4 [AntClas 61,785, L. De *Lennoy*: titres]. − ᴿWienerSt 104 (1991) 286 (H. *Schwabl*).

51 FALATURI Abdoldjavad, Gottes ist der Orient, Gottes ist der Okzident, 65. Gb., ᴱTworuschka Udo: KöVeröffRelG 21. Wien 1991, Böhlau. xvi-650 p. DM 98 pa. [TR 87,337; TLZ 117,655, H. *Klautke*].

52 FASOLA Umberto Maria: Quaeritur inventus colitur [→ 5,56: non 'invenitur'], miscellanea in onore di Padre ~, ᴱPergola Philippe, *Bisconti* Fabrizio: Studi 40. R 1989, Pontificio Istituto di Archeologia Cristiana. I. 398 p.; portr.; bibliog. 11-19 (*Casti* G. B.); II. p. 405-830. 23 + 24 art.; 4 infra.

54 FLUSSER David: The New Testament and Christian-Jewish dialogue, ᴱLowe Malcolm = Immanuel 24s (1990). 317 p.; bibliog. 292-305. 0302-8127. 17 art., infra [RB 100,290, tit. pp.].

55 FOSSIER Lucie: (I) À propos des Actes d'évêques, ᴱParisse M.: Actes des Évêques de France. Nancy 1991, Univ. 324 p.; 1 fig.; 1 facsim. [RHE 87,16*].

55* — (II) L'écrit dans la société médiévale; divers aspects de sa pratique du XIᵉ au XVᵉ siècle, ᴱBourlet Caroline, *Dufour* Annie. P 1991, CNRS/IRHT. 300 p. [RHE 87,799, B.-M. *Tock*].

56 FOX Marvin: From ancient Israel to modern Judaism; Intellect in quest of understanding [I. → 6,47*], ᴱNeusner Jacob, *al.*: BrownJudSt 159.173. 174.175. Atlanta 1989, Scholars. I. xxiv-292 p.; II. xxiv-315 p.; III. xxiv-254 p.; IV. xxiv-235 p. 1-55540-335-2; -41-7; -42-5; -43-3 [CritRR 5,527, tit. pp.]. 56 art.; 28 infra.

57 FREND W.H.C.: Early Christianity; origin and evolution to AD 600, ᴱHazlett Ian. L 1991, SPCK. xvi-335 p.; map. £15. 0-281-04476-7. − ᴿJEH 42 (1991) 635s (E. D. *Hunt*); NBlackf 72 (1991) 542-4 (A. *Meredith*); TLond 94 (1991) 364s (G. *Gould*).

57* FRIES H., Gelähmte Ökumene; was jetzt noch zu tun ist, 80. Gb., ᴱKoch Kurt. FrB 1991, Herder. 237 p. DM 29,80 [TLZ 117,727-730, H. *Krüger*].

58 FROEHLICH Karlfried: Biblical hermeneutics in historical perspective, 60th b., ᴱBurrows M.S., *Rorem* P. GR 1991, Eerdmans. xxi-367 p.; bibliog. p. 350-4. $25. 0-8028-3693-3 [BL 92,143; ChrCent 109,849, W. *Stegner*]; TR 88,340, tit. pp.; TTod 49,426, W. *Sundberg*]. 20 art., 16 infra.

59 FÜGLISTER Notker O.S.B.: Ein Gott, eine Offenbarung; Beiträge zur biblischen Exegese, Theologie und Spiritualität, 60 Gb., ᴱReiterer Friedrich V. Wü 1991, Echter. 619 p. 3-429-01363-1 [TR 88,425, some tit. pp.; NTAbs 36,101; RivB 40,117, A. *Bonora*]. 25 art.; 17 infra. − ᴿErbeAuf 67 (1991) 325 (S. *Petzolt*); OTAbs 14 (1991) 347 (C. T. *Begg*: OT tit. pp.).

60 FUHRMANN Horst: Papsttum, Kirche und Recht im Mittelalter, 65. Gb., ᴱMordek Hubert. Tü 1991, Niemeyer. vi-420 p. DM 174 [TR 87,429, tit. pp.].

GARBRECHT Günther: Wasserbau 1987 → 638.

61 GARELLI Paul: Marchands, diplomates et empereurs; études sur la civilisation mésopotamienne, ᴱCharpin D., *Joannès* F. P 1991, RCiv. 439 p.; ill.; portr.; bibliog. p. 7-10. F 240. 2-86538-214-8. 29 art.; 19 infra.

62 GARITTE Gérard [1914-1990]: Byzantion 61,2 (1991) 315-529; phot.; 315-321, présent. *Mossay* J.

62* GARRETT James L.: The people of God; essays on the Believers' Church, 65th b., EBasden Paul, *Dockery* David S. Nv 1991, Broadman. 367 p. $20/12. 0-8054-6023-3. 25 art. [NTAbs 36,127 mentions six]. – RSWJT 34,3 (1991s) 35 (B. *Hunt*).

63 GASSMANN Günther: Gemeinsamer Glaube und Strukturen der Gemeinschaft; Erfahrungen, Überlegungen, Perspektiven, 60. Gb., EMeyer Harding. Fra 1991, Lembeck. 221 p.; Bibliog. p. 209-220. DM 48. 14 art.; 2 infra [TR 87,435 tit. pp.].

64 GEYER Hans-Georg: Wahrheit und Versöhnung; theologische und philosophische Beiträge zur Gotteslehre, EKorsch Dietrich, *Ruddies* Hartmut. Gü 1989, Mohn. 279 p. DM 68. 3-579-00272-4 [TsTNijm 32,106, H. *Häring*]. – RActuBbg 28 (1991) 174 (J. *Boada*).

65 GINER SORIA Maria Concepción: Stephanion [➔ 5,67], ECodoñer C., *al.*: Acta Salmanticensia, Fg. 200. S 1988, Univ. 254 p. – RFaventia 11,2 (1989) 199-201 (J. *Gómez Pallarès*).

65* GIOVANNI DELLA CROCE s. † 1591: Angelicum 68,3 (1991) 291-444; 5 art. [+ 1 in fasc. 4].

66 GOETERS Johann F. G.: Standfester Glaube, 65. Gb. EFaulenbach Heiner: Verein Rhein.KG 100. Köln 1991, Rheinland. ix-490 p.; Bibliog. 451-9 [TR 88,164].

67 GOLUB Ivan: Homo imago et amicus Dei, miscellanea in honorem ~ , 60. nat., EPerić Ratko: Collectanea Croatico-Hieronymiana de Urbe 4. R 1991, Pontificium Collegium Croaticum S. Hieronymi. xiv-710 p.; portr.; (color.) ill.; 1-26 biobibliog. (A. *Tamarut*, *al.*) 53 art.; 7 infra.

67* GOTTWALD Norman K.: The Bible and the politics of exegesis, 65th b., EJobling D., *al.* Cleveland 1991, Pilgrim. xvii-360 p. $25. 0-8298-0913-9. 21 art. [NTAbs 36,410, topics].

68 GRACIOTTI Sante: Filologia e letteratura nei paesi slavi, E(Brogi) **Bercoff** Giovanna, *al.* R 1990, Carucci. xvi-966 p.; portr.; bibliog. ix-xiv. 88-85116-21-3. 81 art. (all on Slavic), 3 infra.

68* Graz Univ. Inst. Geschichte 125. Jahr-Jubiläum, Geschichtsforschung in Graz, EEbner H., *al.* Graz 1990, Univ. 530 p. [RHE 87,169*].

69 a) GREEN Peter: Classical bearings; interpreting ancient history and culture. L 1989, Thames & H. 328 p. [AnPg 61, p. 734].

— b) GREENBERG Joseph H.: Studies in typology and diachrony, 75th b., ECroft William, *al.*: Typological Studies in Language 20. Amst/Ph 1990, Benjamins. xxxiii-243 p. *f* 125; pa. *f* 50 [Kratylos 37, 14, P. *Sgall*].

70 GRUIJS A.: Codex in context; studies over codicologie, kartuizergeschiedenis en laatmiddelecuws geestesleven, EBacker C. de, *al.* 1985 ➔ 4,57; *f* 60.25. – ROnsGErf 65 (1991) 287s (J. de *Grauwe*).

71 HABERLAND Elke: 65 Gb. = Paideuma 37 (1991) 1-203; portr. Stu 1991, Steiner. 0078-7809. Afrikanische Anthropologie.

72 HAHN Ferdinand: Anfänge der Christologie, 65. Gb., EBreytenbach Cilliers, *Paulsen* Henning. Gö 1991, VR. 492 p.; Bibliog. 473-493 (*Hoegen-Ruhls* Christina). 3-525-58157-2. 28 art.; infra [ZkT 114,208, R. *Oberforcher*]. – RNT 33 (1991) 373s (M. de *Jonge*); TR 87 (1991) 163 (tit. pp.) & 453s (H. *Giesen*).

72* HARNONCOURT Philipp: Sursum corda; Variationen zu einem liturgischen Motiv, 60. Gb., ERenhart Erich, *Schnider* Andreas. Graz 1991, Akad. 496 p.; ill [TR 88,351, some tit. pp.] ➔ 4181. – RTAth 62 (1991) 903s (E. A. *Theodorou* ⊖).

73 HAVER Jozef Van: Liber amicorum, 65e verjaardag, ERoeck A., *al.* Bru 1991, Comm. Volkskunde. 612 p.; ill. [RHE 87,52*].

74 HEITGER Marian: Gefährdung der Bildung — Gefährdung des Menschen; Perspektiven verantworteter Pädagogik, 60 Gb., ᴱBreinbauer Ines M., *Langer* Michael. W 1987, Böhlau. 348 p. - ᴿZkT 113 (1991) 117s (H. *Pissarek-Hudelist*).
Helsinki Univ. 350th Anniv. 1990/1 ➤ 447, ᴱ*Luomanen*.

75 HERRMANN Siegfried: Prophetie und geschichtliche Wirklichkeit im alten Israel, 65. Gb., ᴱ**Liwak** Rüdiger, *Wagner* Siegfried. Stu 1991, Kohlhammer. 476 p.; ill.; Bibliog. 469-475. 3-17-011314-3. [TR 88,161, tit. pp.; BL 93,17, R. *Mason*; TüTQ 172,149, W. *Gross*]. 32 art.; infra.

76 HILGERT Earle: Heirs of the Septuagint; PHILO, Hellenistic Judaism and Early Christianity, ᴱ**Runia** David T., *al.*; BrownJudSt 230 = StPhilonAn 3. Atlanta 1991, Scholars. 397 p.; portr.; bibliog. (of Philo). 1-55540-625-4. 20 art.; infra.

77 HOFTIJZER J.: Studies in Hebrew and Aramaic syntax, 65th b., ᴱ**Jongeling** K., *al.*: StSemLLing 17. Leiden 1991, Brill. xvi-219 p.; portr.; bibliog. xi-xvi. 90-04-09520-9 [RB 100,127 & ZAW 104,463, tit. pp.; BL 93,154, J. C. L. *Gibson*]. 16 art., infra.

78 HRUBY Kurt: zum 70. Gb. = Judaica 47,1s (1991). 119 p.; p. 116-9, ausgewählte Bibliog.

79 HÜBENER Wolfgang: Archäologischer Befund und historische Deutung, 65 Gb., ᴱ**Lüdtke** Hartwig, *al.*: Hammaburg NF 9. Neumünster 1989, Wachholtz. 348 p.; ill.; Bibliog. 11-16. 3-529-01357-9. 28 art. (Nord-Europa). ➤ b863.

80 HUIE Wade P.: Preaching in and out of season, ᴱ**Long** Thomas G., *McCarter* Neely D. Louisville 1990, W-Knox. 129 p. $10. 9 art. - ᴿInterpretation 45 (1991) 303 (P. H. *Biddle*: fresher than most).

81 HYMAN Arthur: [I. 1989 ➤ 6,86]; II. A straight path; studies in medieval philosophy and culture, ᴱ**Link-Salinger** Ruth. Wsh 1988, Catholic Univ. xiv-310 p. 22 art. [Henoch 14,342, Caterina *Rigo*]. - ᴿAJS 16 (1991) 264s (titles sans pp.).

82 JACOBS Louis: A traditional quest, ᴱ**Cohn-Sherbok** Dan: JStOT supp 114. Sheffield 1991, JStOT. 233 p.; portr.; bibliog. 217-226. £35. 1-85075-279-6. 13 art.; 8 infra. [RB 99,455, tit. pp.; BL 92,10, S. C. *Reif*; JSS 37,112, N. *Solomon*].

83 JEWETT Paul K.: Perspectives on Christology, ᴱ**Shuster** M., *Muller* R. GR 1991, Zondervan. xxvii-302 p.; portr. $15 pa. 0-310-39731-6. [NTAbs 36,285] 15 art.

84 JONES Philip: City and countryside in late medieval and Renaissance Italy, ᴱ**Dean** T., *Wickham* C. L 1990, Hambledon. xv-199 p. - ᴿNuova Rivista Storica 75 (1991) 463-6 (M. *Lunari*) [RHE 87,152*].

85 *a*) JORISSEN Hans, Mit dem Rücken zur Transzendentaltheologie; theologische Passagen, zum 65. Gb., ᴱ**Hoeps** Reinhard, *Rüster* Thomas: Bonner Dogm. St. 10. Wü 1991, Echter. 286 p.; Bibliog. p. 277-282. DM 39. 13 art. [TR 87,434, tit. pp.], 2 infra.
— *b*) JOURNET Charles né 1891: NVFr 66,4 (1991). 188 p.; phot.; bibliog. p. 183-8. 13 art., 4 infra.
— *c*) KAISER Werner: 65. Gb., ᴱ**Gb.**, MiDAI 47 (1991). xv-434 p.; portr.; 63 pl. Bibliog. p. xi-xv. 3-8053-1205-9. 49 art., 16 infra.
— *d*) KAUFMAN Gordon K., Theology at the end of modernity, ᴱ**Davaney** Sheila G. Ph 1991, Trinity. xii-276 p. $25. 13 art., 4 infra [TR 88,346, tp].

86 KENNEDY George A., Persuasive artistry; studies in New Testament rhetoric, ᴱ**Watson** Duane F.: JStNT supp 50. Sheffield 1991, Academic. 390 p.; portr. £40. 1-85075-284-2 [TR 88,339 & CBQ 54,830, F. W. *Bur-*

nett: tit. pp.; ÉTRel 67,117, E. *Cuvillier*]. 17 art., infra. – ᴿExpTim 103 (1991s) 119 (I. H. *Jones*).

86* KNOCH Otto Bernhard: Die Freude an Gott — unsere Kraft, 65. Gb., ᴱ**Degenhardt** Johannes J., Erzb. [*Bek* Eleonore, *Sitarz* Eugen]. Stu 1991, KBW. Plures infra.

87 KOCH Klaus: Ernten, was man sät, 65. Gb., ᴱ**Daniels** Dwight R., *Glessmer* Uwe, *Bösel* Martin. Neuk 1991, Neuk.-V. xi-595 p.; Bibliog. p. 583-595. DM 98. 3-7887-1402-6. ➤ 6,2387. [TR 88,73, tit. pp.; ZAW 104,445, H. C. *Schmitt*, 522 tit. pp.; GerefTTs 92,193, N. A. *Schuman*]. 30 art., infra.

88 KOEHLER Theodore: Mater fidei et fidelium, 80th b.: Marian Library Studies [12.]23. Dayton [1985–] 1991, Univ. 818 p. [TR 88,74].

89 KOSTELECKY Alfred: Pax et iustitia, 70. Gb., ᴱ**Kaluza** Hans-W., *al.* B 1990, Duncker & H. 651 p. DM 248. 3-428-06879-3. – ᴿActuBbg 28 (1991) 191 (A. *Borràs*).

90 *a*) KRAUS Fritz R. 21.III.1910-19.I.1991: BO 48,3s (1991) only 331-5 portr., biobibliog. (M. *Stol*).

— *b*) KUNZE Horst: Von der Wirkung des Buches, 80. Gb., ᴱ*Krause* Friedhilde. B 1990, Staatsbibliothek. 251 p.; ill. DM 30 [RHE 87,220*; DLZ 113,1, K.-H. *Jägelt*].

— *c*) LAARHOVEN J.C.P.A.: Kerk in beraad, ᴱ**Ackermans** Gian, *al.* Nijmegen 1991, Kath. Univ. Faculteit der Godgeleerdheid. 336 p. [RHE 87,453, M. *Cloet*, contenu sans tit. pp.].

91 LECLERCQ Jean: S. BERNARD, neuvième centenaire 1090-1990: ColcCist 52,1-4 (1990). 344 p. 18 art., sur les rapports de Bernard avec d'autres saints, et ➤ g428*, influence sur LUTHER.

92 LEÓN Luis de: Homenaje a Fray ∼ , 1527-1591, IV centenario de su muerte: *a*) RivAg 32,97 (1991) 1-522; 31,94 (1990) 1-278, Bibliografía, *Lazcano González* Rafael [RHE 87, p. 292] 6 art., 2 infra. – *b*) CiuD 204,2s (1991) 319-995. 21 art., 3 infra.

LEROY Maurice mém.: Le souverain à Byzance, colloque 1990/1 ➤ 636a.

93 LESLAU Wolf; Semitic Studies, 85th b., ᴱ**Kaye** Alan S. I-II. Wsb 1991, Harrassowitz.

94 LEVI Doro: Eumeneia, ᴱ**Carinci** F. R 1990. 190s, bibliog. [Sileno 17,358].

94* LINDBECK George: Theology and dialogue, essays in conversation with [in honor of] ∼ , ᴱ**Marshall** Bruce D. ND 1990, Univ. xi-302 p. $30. 0-268-01873-1 [TDig 38,384].

95 Ljubljana 1919-1989, Zbornik ob sedemdesetletnici teološke fakultete, ᴱ**Valenčič** Rafko: BogVest 50,1 (1990). 190 p.

95* LONERGAN Bernard: Religion and Culture, ᴱ**Fallon** Timothy P., *Riley* Philip B., Albany 1987, SUNY. x-395 p.; portr. 0-88706-289-X. 24 art., 3 infra.

96 *a*) LUPI, Joseph: Veterum exempla, essays in honor of mgr. prof. emeritus ∼ , ᴱ**Borg** Vincent: MelT supp 1. Malta 1991. 194 p. [BL 92,8].

— *b*) LYON Bryce: Law, custom, and the social fabric in medieval Europe, ᴱ**Bachrach** B. S., *Nicholas* D.: Studies in Medieval Culture 28. Kalamazoo 1990, Western Michigan Univ. – ᴿRHist 286 (1991) 465s (R. *Fossier*). [RHE 87,221*].

97 MARIOTTI Scevola: Dicti studiosus. Urbino 1990, Quattro-Venti. 426 p.; 8 pl. – ᴿRFgIC 119 (1991) 540s (Rossella *Bianchi*: dai suoi allievi).

97* MAY Georg: Fides et ius, 65. Gb., ᴱ**Aymans** Winfried, *al.*, Rg 1991, Pustet. 639 p.; Bibliog. 603-636 (Anna *Egler*). DM 98. 3-7917-1290-X [TR 88, 319: ius canonicum, tit. pp. Analysen]. 29 art., ➤ 8112*.

98 MAYER Augustinus Kard., O.S.B.: In unum congregati, 80. Gb., ^EHaering Stephan. Metten 1991, Abtei. 604 p.; Bibliog. p. 593-8. DM 98/78 [TR 87,435]. ^RErbAuf 67 (1991) 485 (T. *Burger*).

98* MEKHITARIAN Arpag, 80e anniv.: CdÉ 66,131s (1991).

99 MESTERS Carlos, 60 años: Métodos para ler a Bíblia = EstudosB 32 (1991) 106 p.

100 METZLER Josef: Ecclesiae memoria, Miscellanea in onore del R. P. ~ O.M.I.; Prefetto dell'Archivio Segreto Vaticano, ^EHENKEL W. R 1991, Herder. 495 p.; portr. bibliog. p. 482-495, *Della Torre* Giacomo [RHE 87,885, J. *Pirotta*; TR 88,432, some mission-history titles; NRT 114.925, J. *Masson*]. – ^RClaretianum 31 (1991) 157s (S. M. *González Silva*).

101 MEULEMAN G. E., Cultuur als partner van de theologie. Kampen 1990, Kok. 224 p. 90-242-5178-8. – ^RTsTNijm 31 (1991) 304s (M. van den *Nieuwenhuizen*).

102 *a*) MEYER Hans Philipp: Glaube — Bekenntnis — Kirchenrecht, 70. Gb., ^EBesier Gerhard, *Lohse* Eduard. Hannover 1989, LVH. 300 p. [LuJb 58, p. 147, with indication of 9 items there cited].

— *b*) MEYER Paul W.: Faith and history; ^ECosgrove Charles H., *Johnson* E. Elizabeth. Atlanta 1991, Scholars. viii-377 p. $50; sb. $35. 1-55540-383-2. 22 art. [TDig 39,160; incl. *Cullmann, Harrelson, Meeks, Minear,* E. *Schweizer*...].

— *c*) MIKASA Takahito, prince: Near Eastern Studies, 75th. b., ^EMori Masao: B. Mid-East in Japan 5. Wsb 1991, Harrassowitz. 500 + p. 34 art.; 12 infra [OT 5: ZAW 104, 453]. 3-447-03139-5.

— *d*) MIKAT Paul: Staat, Kirche, Wissenschaft in einer pluralistischen Gesellschaft, 65. Gb. ^ESchwab Dieter, *al.* B 1989, Duncker & H. 899 p. – ^RHistJb 111 (1991) 195-200 (A. von *Campenhausen*).

103 MOLTMANN-WENDEL Elisabeth: Mit allen Sinnen glauben; feministische Theologie unterwegs, 65. Gb., ^EPissarek-Hudelist H., *Schottroff* Luise: Tb Siebenstern 532. Gü 1991, Mohn. 249 p.; ill. [TR 88, 161; TLZ 117,659, U. *Gerber*; TsTNijm 32,426, C. *Halkes*].

103* MONACO Giusto: Studi di filologia classica I-IV: Palermo 1991, Univ. xvi-1840 p.; bibliog. xiii-xvi [BStLat 22, 100, Valeria *Viparelli*; CivClasCr 13,216, A. *Della Casa*].

104 MONTERO DIAZ Santiago: Gerión Anejos 2. M 1989, Univ. Complutense. 459 p.; ill. [AnPg 61, p. 730, dépouillé].

105 MÜHLENBROCK Georg: Du führst mich hinaus ins Weite; Erfahrungen im Glauben — Zugänge zum priesterlichen Dienst, ^EHillenbrand Karl, *Kehl* Medard. Wü 1991, Echter. 456 p. DM 58 [TR 87,249].

106 MÜLLER C. Detlef. G.: Nubia et Or. chr. [AnPg 59,15537]. 1988. ➤ 5,e489.

107 MÜLLER Hans Martin: Zur Freiheit befreit, Predigten über Rechtfertigung, 60. Gb., ^EBeutel Albrecht, *Drehsen* Volker. Tü 1989, Katzmann. 241 p. DM 28 [TPQ 140, 203, W. *Blasig*].

108 Müller [–WIENER, I ➤ 6,127] Wolfgang: II. Et exaltavit humiles, 60. Gb., ^EConrad J. Saarbrücken 1991, Thinnes & N. 184 p.; ill. DM 29,80 [RHE 86,311*].

109 MUNIER W.A.J., Munire ecclesiam; opstellen over 'gewone gelovigen', ^ELaarhoven J. van: 70 verjaardag; Werken 13. Maastricht 1990, Limburg.-Geschieden-Oudheidkundig Genootschap. 378 p.; bibliog. 11-25. *f* 55. 90-71581-04-7 [TR 87,523]. 22 art. – ^RTsTNijm 31 (1991) 198 (C. *Brakkee* mentions only post-Reformation details).

110 *a*) NEUSER Wilhelm, 65. Gb.: CALVIN, Erbe und Auftrag ᴱSpijker Willem van 't. Kampen 1991, Kok. xi-430 p.; 411-428, Bibliog. *f*79,50 [TR 88,167, tit. pp.; JEH 43,687, A. *McGrath*; RHE 87,908, J.-T. *Gilmont*].
— *b*) NEWMAN after a hundred years, ᴱKer Ian, *Hill* Alan G. Ox 1990, UP. xvi-472 p. 22 art. – ᴿCathHR 77 (1991) 316-8 (R. J. *Schiefen*).
— *c*) NIJENHUIS W.: Gericht verleden, ᴱJong C. de. Leiden 1991, Groen. 269 p.; ill [TR 88,249].

111 O'MEARA John: From Augustine to Eriugena, essays on Neoplatonism and Christianity, ᴱMartin F. X., *Richmond* J. A. Wsh 1991, Catholic University of America. xxi-190 p.; portr.; biobibliog. ix-xx. 0-8132-0732-0. 15 art.; 6 infra.

112 OVERBOSCH W. G.: Het nodige overbodige, 70ᵉ verjaardag, ᴱ*Besten* A. C. den, *al.* Kampen 1989, Kok. 185 p. *f*27.50. 90-24207-89-4. 26 auteurs. [NedTTs 45,151].

113 PARATORE Ettore, ottuagenario: Abruzzo 23-28. Chieti 1990, Vecchio Faggio. 880 p.; 3 fig.; 18 pl.; 3 maps. Lit. 160.000. 88-7113-064-2. – ᴿJRS 81 (1991) 252 (D. W. *Rathbone*).

114 PARLASCA Klaus: Das antike Rom und der Osten, 65. Gb., ᴱBörker Christoph, *Donderer* Michael: ErlangerF 56. Erlangen 1990, Univ. 237 p.; 41 pl.

115 PARRINDER Geoffrey: Turning points in religious studies, ᴱKing Ursula. E 1990, Clark. x-330 p. £20. 0-567-09564-9. 28 art. – ᴿExpTim 103 (1991s) 27 (P. D. *Bishop*); Month 252 (1991) 210s (M. *Barnes*); Numen 38 (1991) 274 (J. *Waardenburg*).

116 PARRY Milman memorial: Comparative research on oral traditions, ᴱFoley John M. Columbus 1987, Slavica. 597 p. $30 [ClasR 40, p. 1, J. B. *Hainsworth*: no paper on Parry, Homer, or formulae!].

117 PIEGSA Joachim; Natur und Gnade; die christozentrisch-pneumatische Grundgestalt der christlichen Sittlichkeitslehre, 60. Gb. ᴱDobisch Hubert: MorTStud, syst. 16. St. Ottilien 1990, EOS. 254 p. DM 68 [TR 86,436].

118 PIÉRARD Christiane: Annales du Cercle Archéologique de Mons 74 (1990) xxx-313 p. Fb 1150. 12 art.; biobibliog. *Bruwier* Marinette [RHE 86, p. 489, J.-P. *Hendrickx*].

118* PINCKAERS Servais: Novitas et veritas vitae; aux sources du renouveau de la morale chrétienne, 65° anniv., ᴱPinto de Oliveira C.-J.: ÉtÉthChr 37. FrS/P 1991, Univ./Cerf. xi-233 p. Fs 19 [TR 88,260, tit. pp.; NRT 114,262, L. *Volpe*].

119 PLOIER Eduard: Zwischenrufe, 60. Gb., ᴱFeichtbeuer Hubert, *al.*, Linz 1990, Veritas. 448 p. DM 59. – ᴿTPQ 139 (1991) 114s (J. *Hörmandinger*).

120 *a*) PÖSCHL Viktor: Musik und Dichtung, 80. Gb., ᴱAlbrecht Michael, *Schubert* Werner: QStudMusikG 23. Fra 1990, Lang. 528 p. [AnPg 51, p. 732, dépouillé].
— *b*) POTOTSCHNIG Franz: Scientia canonum, 65. Gb., ᴱPaarhammer Hans, *Rinnerthaler* Alfred. Mü 1991, Kovar. 588 p.; Bibliog. p. 12-15. DM 78 [TR 88,173, tit. pp.].
— *c*) Pro Oriente, 25 Jahre 1989, ein Laboratorium für die Einheit, ᴱKirch-schläger K. *Stirnemann* A.: Pro Oriente 13. Innsbruck 1991, Tyrolia. 428 p.; 4 fig. Sch. 480 [NRT 114, 127, A. *Harvengt*].

121 RAMAROSON Léonard: Ta parole est ma joie; mélanges bibliques. Am-batoroka-Antananarivo 1991, Inst. Sup. Théologie. 147 p.; bibliog. 6-11 (J. L. *Peter*), biog. 13-19 (B. *Laurent*). [NTAbs 36,417] 12 art., 10 infra.

122 RAMÍREZ DULANTO Santiago O.P. († 1967): centenario de nacimiento: CiTom 118,2 (1991) p. 209-380; portr. [filosofia].

123 RASCHINI Maria Adelaide: Responsabilità della cultura. L'Aquila 1990,
Japadre. 322 p. – ᴿSapienza 44 (1991) 104-6 (P. *Colonnello*).
124 RASCO Emilio: Luca-Atti, 70° compleanno, ᴱ**Marconi** Gilberto, *O'Collins*
Gerald: Commenti e studi biblici NS. Assisi 1991, Cittadella. 334 p.;
bibliog. 5-7. 88-308-0490-8, 13 art., infra [CC 143/2,618, M. *Simone*;
Teres 43,543, V. *Pasquetto*].
124* RASMUSSEN Niels K. † 1987: Fountain of life; in memory of ~ O.P.;
ᴱ**Austin** Gerard. Wsh 1991, Pastoral. ix-249 p.; incl. bibliog. $25 pa. 0-
912405-85-6 [TDig 39,263: for a distinguished Denmark-born liturgist, on
the focus of tradition; RSPT 76,174s, P.-M. *Gy*, tit. pp.].
125 RATSCHOW Carl Heinz: 80 Gb. = NSys 33,2 (1991).
126 RICHTER Wolfgang: Text, Methode und Grammatik, 65. Gb., ᴱ**Gross**
Walter, *al.* St. Ottilien 1991, EOS. xii-606 p.; portr. 3-88096-675-3. 32
art., infra [RB 100,124 & TR 88,249, tit. pp.].
126* RIES Julien, Manichaica selecta; 70th b., ᴱ**Tongerloo** A. van, *Gieversen*
S.: Manichean Studies 1. Lv/Lund 1991, Int.Ass.Manich.St./Center Hist.
Rel. 402 p. [Revue Philosophique de Louvain 90, 218-221, L. *Rizzerio*:
RHE 87,252*].
127 ROSENMEYER Thomas G., Cabinet of the Muses; essays on classical and
comparative literature, 70th b., ᴱ**Griffith** Mark, *Mastronarde* Donald J.:
SBL Homage. Atlanta 1989, Scholars. xiii-402 p.; portr.; bibliog. xi-xiii.
1-55540-408-1; pa. –9-X. 26 art.
128 ROUGÉ Jean, Navires et commerces de la Méditerranée antique,
ᴱ**Roman** Y., *Tchernia* A.: Cah. Hist. 33,3s (1988) p. 243-510; biobibliog.
243-253. 18 art. 4 infra [< ᴿBStLat 21 (1991) 85-87 (Lietta *De Salvo*)].
129 St. Andrews St. Mary's 450th anniversary: In divers manners; a St.
Mary's miscellany, ᴱ**Shaw** D.W.D. St Andrews 1990, St. Mary's. 245 p.
£5.50. 0-9516136-0-X [ExpTim 102,383].
130 SANDERS Gabriel: Aevvm inter vtrvmqve, ᴱ**Uytfanghe** Marc Van, *Demeulenaere* Roland: Instrumenta Patristica 23. Steenbrugge 1991, S. Pie-
tersabdij. xli-537 p.; portr.; ill.; bibliog. xvii-xli (D. *Pikhaus*). [RHE
87,52*; TR 88,341, tit. pp.; NRT 114,925, S. *Hilaire*; RÉLat 70,416,
J.-C. *Richard*]. 42 art.; 6 infra.
131 SAWYER Peter H.: People and places in Northern Europe 500-1600,
ᴱ**Wood** I., *Lund* N. Woodbridge 1991, Boydell & B. xxii-248 p. [RHE
87,223* < EngHR 107,380, J. *Blair*].
131* [Bellincioni] SCARPAT Maria, mem.: Tradizione dell'antico nelle letterature e nelle arti d'Occidente: La civiltà delle scritture 10. R 1990, Bulzoni.
xvi-663 p.; portr.; ill. [AnPg 61, p. 728].
132 SCHAUF Heribert, Gedenkschrift: Geist und Kirche; Studien zur Theologie
im Umfeld der beiden Vatikanischen Konzilien; ᴱ**Hammans** Herbert, *al.* Pd
1991 [TR 87,343, tit. pp.; TsTNijm 32,328, P. van *Leeuwen*]. ➤ 7522.
133 SCHLETTE Heinz R.: Konkrete Humanität; Studien zur praktischen Philosophie und Religionsphilosophie, 60. Gb., ᴱ**Brosseder** Johannes. Fra
1991, Knecht. 486 p. DM 168 [TR 88,161].
134 SCHMITT Erich Ludwig: Deutscher Wortschatz, lexikologische Studien,
80. Gb., ᴱ**Munske** Horst H. B/NY 1988, de Gruyter. xxxi-927 p. [LuJb
57 (1990) p. 321, with indication of three items there cited].
135 *a)* SCHNEIDER Gerhard: Der Treue Gottes trauen; Beiträge zum Werk des
Lukas, ᴱ**Bussmann** Claus, *Radl* Walter. FrB 1991, Herder. 400 p. DM 64
[RB 99,452 & TLZ 117,339 & TR 87,426, tit. pp.; NTAbs 36,116; RivB
40,118, A. *Bonora*; TGL 82,367, K. *Backhaus*; TPQ 140,186, A. *Fuchs*].
3-451-21680-9.

— b) SCHNEIDER Theodor. Auf seiner Spur; ein Werkstattbuch, 60. Gb.,
  EMoos Alois. Dü 1990, Patmos. 451 p.; Bibliog. p. 434-442. DM 54 [TR
  88,337].
— c) SCHROEDER David: The Church as theological community, EHuebner
  Harry. Winnepeg 1990, CMBC. xvi-313 p.
— d) SCHRÖER Henning: Praktisch-theologische Hermeneutik; Ansätze —
  Anregungen — Aufgaben; 60. Gb., EZillessen Dietrich, al. Rheinbach-Merzbach 1991, CMZ. xiv-574 p.; 3 fig. DM 38 pa. [TLZ 117, 816,
  H. Hollenstein].
— e) SCHULMAN Alan R.: Bulletin of the Egyptological Seminar 10 (NY
  1989s). – 178 p.; portr.; ill.; 8-13 bibliog. (Guzman Diane).
— f) SEDOS (Servizio di Documentazione e Studi, Rome-based center of 72
  Catholic mission societies), 25 years: Trends in Mission; toward the third
  millennium, EJenkinson William, O'Sullivan Helene. Mkn 1991, Orbis.
  xx-419 p. $27. 0-88344-766-5. 48 art. [TDig 39,190].
136 SICHERL Martin, Philophronema, 75 Gb., EHarlfinger D.: StGKAlt 1/4.
  Pd 1990, Schöningh. 389 p. – RArTGran 53 (1990) 415s (A. Segovia).
136* SIEVERS Angelika: Pilgrimage in world religions, 75 b., EBhardwaj S. M.,
  Rinschede G.: [Univ. Eichstätt] Geographia Religionum 4. B 1988,
  Reimer. 200 p.; ill. DM 38 [NRT 114, 287, J. Masson].
137 SINGER Hans-Rudolf: Festgabe 65. Gb. 6. April 1990, EForstner Martin.
  Fra 1991, Lang.
138 SMET Joachim: The land of Carmel, EChandler Paul, Egan J. R 1991,
  Inst. Carmelitanum. 497 p.; 1 fig. [RHE 87,158*; TR 88,425]. – RGregorianum 73 (1992) 765s (M. Ruiz Jurado).
139 SMITH Huston: Fragments of infinity; essays in religion and philosophy,
  ESharma Arvind. Bridport UK 1991, Prism. xx-301 p. [RelStR 18, 214,
  C. Chapple].
140 SMYTH-FLORENTIN Françoise: Lectio difficilior probabilior? L'exégèse
  comme expérience de décloisonnement, ERömer Thomas: DielBL Beih 11.
  Heid 1991, Wiss.-theol. Seminar. xxi-335 p.; bibliog. 329-331 [ZAW 104,
  153, tit. pp.]. – 22 art., infra. – RDielB 27 (1991) 297-9 (B. J. Diebner:
  tit. pp.); OTAbs 14 (1991) 347s (C. T. Begg: 15 tit. pp.).
141 SOGGIN J. Alberto: Storia e tradizioni di Israele, EGarrone Daniele, Israel
  Felice. Brescia 1991, Paideia. xlvi-310 p.; portr.; bibliog. xix-xlvi. 88-
  394-0467-8. 24 art.; infra [TR 88,513 & ZAW 104,311, tit. pp.; BL 92,13,
  A. Gelston; ExpTim 103,299, R. J. Coggins].
142 SOLMSEN Friedrich, mem.: Illinois Classical Studies 16,1s (1991). 402 p.
143 STAMM J.J. (80. Gb.): Onomata, EXella P. = StEpL 8 (1991). Verona
  1991, Essedue. 244 p. 88-85697-37-2 [BL 92,141, W.G.E. Watson: im-
  proved quality and 100 more pages at same price as StEpL 7].
144 STAMPFLI Hans R.: Beiträge zur Archäozoologie, Archäologie, Anthropologie, Geologie und Paläontologie, ESchibler Jörg, al. Basel 1990,
  Helbing & L. xviii-325 p.; ill., portr.; Bibliog. x-xiii. 3-7190-1068-6. 29
  art., 1 infra.
145 STARCKY Jean mémorial: I. textes et études qumraniens, EPuech Émile,
  Garcia Martinez Florentino, RQum 15,57s (1991). vii-314; phot.;
  biobibliog. 1-20 (Puech). F 620 [II. p. 321-480: 7 tit.; F 310].
146 STEINMETZ Peter: Pratum Saraviense, 65. Gb., EGörler Waldemar, Koster
  Severin: Palingenesia [0552-9638] 30. Stu 1990, Steiner. 221 p. portr.;
  Bibliog. 217-221 (Horst Walter). 3-515-05582-7 [RÉLat 70,419s, Jacqueline
  Fabre]. 13 art.; 3 infra. – RArTGran 54 (1991) 468 (A. S. Muñoz: some
  classical titles); ClasR 41 (1991) 272s (N. Horsfall).

147 STIBBE Conrad M., Stips votiva, ᴱGnade Marijke. Amst 1991, Univ. A.
Pierson Museum. xv-264 p.; portr.; ill.; bibliog. xi-xv. 90-71211-19-3. 35
art.; 4 infra.

148 a) STIMPFLE Josef: (I) Im Dienst des Evangeliums. 1988, Donauwörth.
928 p. DM 86 [ScripTPamp 24,1110, D. Ramos-Lissón]. – ᴿDivinitas 34
(1990) 187-191 (W. Imkamp.).
— b) (II) Kirche im Kommen, Fs für Bischof ~, ᴱKleindienst Eugen. Fra
1991, Propyläen. 640 p. DM 48. [TR 87,249].
— c) (III) Sendung und Dienst im bischöflichen Amt, 75. Gb., ᴱZiegenaus A.,
al.: Theol. Fak. Augsburg. St. Ottilien 1991, EOS. vi-398 p. DM 68 [RHE
86,311*]. – ᴿForumKT 7 (1991) 312-6 (J. Rief).

149 STOTT John: a) AD 2000 and beyond; a mission agenda, 70th b. ᴱSamuel
V., Sugden C. Ox 1991, Regnum. xii-167 p.; portr. 1-870345-09-6. – b)
One Gospel — many clothes; Anglicans and the decade of evangelism,
ᴱWright Chris, Sugden Chris. ... 1990, Regnum. 190 p. [IntRMiss 81,613,
M. L. Kretzmann].

149* STRAUB Johannes: Studien zur Geschichte der römischen Spätantike,
ᴱChrysos Evangelos. (Hg. Fourlas Athanasios). Athen 1989, Pelasgos.
266 p. 960-7137-01-9. 13 art.; 2 infra.

150 TADMOR Hayim: Ah, Assyria...! Studies in Assyrian history and
Ancient Near Eastern historiography: ᴱCogan Mordachai, Eph'al Israel:
ScrHieros 33. J 1991, Hebrew Univ. 347 p.; portr.; maps; bibl. p. 341-7.
$33. 0080-8369 [BO 48,985; BL 92,10, D. J. Wiseman]. 30 art., infra.

151 TALLEY Thomas J.: Time and community, ᴱAlexander J. Neil. Wsh 1990,
Pastoral. xi-338 p. $35. 18 art. on liturgy, 2 infra [TR 87,440 & Speculum
67,511: tit. pp.; RSPT 76,172, P. Gy]. – ᴿWorship 65 (1991) 378-381 (D.
Tripp).

152 THEODOROU Evangelos: Axíes kai politismós. Athenai 1991. xxxvii-
432 p. – ᴿTAth 62 (1991) 413s (P. B. Paschos, tit. pp.).

153 THEOPHANU Kaiserin: Begegnung des Ostens und Westens um die Wende
des ersten Jahrtausends, 1000. Todesjahr, ᴱEuw A. von, Schreiner P.:
Schnütgen-Museum. Köln 1991, Stadt. 422 p.; 436 p.; ill. [RHE 86,317*].

154 THOMPSON Dorothy B.: The coroplast's art; Greek terracottas of the
Hellenistic world, 90th b. (exhibition Princeton, SUNY New Paltz art
gallery, al. 1990), ᴱUhlenbrock Jaimee P. New Rochelle NY 1990,
Caratzas. 175 p.; ill. 0-89241-496-0; pa. -5-2. 12 essays + catalog,
52 fig.

154* TORRANCE James: Christ in our place; the humanity of God for the
reconciliation of the world, ᴱHart T., Thimell D. Exeter/Pittsburgh 1989,
Paternoster/Pickwick. 387 p. £15. 0-85364-504-3 / 1-55635-009-0 [NTAbs
36,101].

155 TRAPP Damasus: Via AUGUSTINI, Augustine and the later Middle Ages,
Renaissance, and Reformation, ᴱOberman Heiko A., James Frank A.:
Studies in Medieval and Reformation Thought 48. Leiden 1991, Brill.
vii-242 p.; portr.; bibliog. 221-6. 10 art. [NRT 114,297, R Escol; JEH
43,682, E. Cameron; TR 87,341, tit. pp.], 3 infra ➤ g624.

156 TRAUBE Ludwig, Gedenkschrift: Lateinische Kultur im VIII. Jahrhundert,
ᴱLehner Albert, Berschin Walther. St. Ottilien 1989, EOS. 251 p.; ill.
3-88096-695-8. [AnBoll 110, 189, R. Gidding, tit. pp.; 'en 1889 Traube
inaugurait l'enseignement de la philologie latine du moyen âge').

156* TURNER Harold W.: Exploring new religious movements, ᴱWalls A. F.,
Shenk Wilbert R. Elkhart IN 1990, Mission Focus. vi-215 p. – ᴿMis-
siology 19 (1991) 101 (B. Fargher).

157 URMSON J.O.: Human agency; language, duty and value, EDancy J. al.
Stanford 1988, Univ. 308 p. $35. – RNBlackf 72 (1991) 349s (A. R. White).
158 VANSTEENKISTE Clemente J.; Littera, sensus, sententia; studi in onore del
Prof. ~ O.P., ELobado A. Mi 1991, Univ. S. Thomae in Urbe. 707 p.
Lit. 75.000 [ActuBbg 29,49, E. Forment; DocCom 45,300, D. Vibrac]. –
RDivThom 94 (1991) 182s (L. Elders).
159 VEREECKE Louis [I. StMor 28,1A (1990) 245 p.; p. 330-602 biobibliog 7-23
(S. Majorano) ➤ 6,182*] II. Historia memoria futuri, 70ᵉ anniv. présent.
Rossano Pietro [= StMor 29 (1991) 137-143]: QM 5. R 1991, Lateran
Univ. 516 p. [Gregorianum 72,159s, J. T. Bretzke; NRT 114,263, L. Volpe;
TR 88,83, tit. pp.].
160 VISCHER Lukas: Ökumenische Theologie in den Herausforderungen der
Gegenwart, 65. Gb., E(Bredull) Gerschwiler Karin, al. Gö 1991, Vandenhoeck & R. 463 p.; portr.; Bibliog. 429-454 (Karrer A., al.). 3-525-
56114-8. 25 art.; 10 infra. [TR 88,347, some tit. pp.].
161 VÖGTLE Anton: Salz der Erde — Licht der Welt; exegetische Studien zum
Matthäusevangelium, 80. Gb., EOberlinner Lorenz, Fiedler Peter. Stu
1991, KBW. 432 p. DM 66 [TR 87 (1991) 162s, tit. pp., NTAbs 36,114;
Salesianum 54,159, J. J. Bartolomé].
162 VREDEBREGT Ben: Uitzien naar God; perspectieven aan de secularisatie
voorbij, EHoutepen A.W.J., Steendam H. Haag 1989, Meinema. 120 p.
f 21,90. 90-211-3540-X. – RTsTNijm 31 (1991) 109 (P. A. van Gennip).
162* WAGGONER Nancy N., mem.: Mnemata, EMetcalf W. E., NY 1991,
American Numismatic Soc. 115 p.; 21 pl. [AntClas 61,552, F. de Callatay;
RÉAnc 94,478, F. Planet]. – RRHist 283,1 (1992) 181s (J. P. Callu).
163 WAGNER Siegfried: Gottesvolk, Beiträge zu einem Thema biblischer
Theologie, 60. Gb., EMeinhold Arndt, Lux Rüdiger. B 1991, Ev.-V. 247 p.
DM 69. [JbBT 7,415, W. Kraus; RB 99,760s, tit. pp.] 3-374-00978-6. 14
art.; infra.
164 a) WALLIS Gerhard: Überlieferung und Geschichte, 65. Gb., EObst H.
Halle 1990.
— b) WANDRUSZKA Mario: Wege in der Sprachwissenschaft; 44 autobio-
graphische Berichte, EGauger Hans-Martin, Pöckl Wolfgang: TüBeitLing
362. Tü 1991, Narr. 259 p. DM 68 [Kratylos 37, 178, Rüdiger Schmitt:
apparently uninfluenced by the similar 1980 'First Person Singular',
EDavis B., O'Cain R.].
— c) WARD W. R.: Protestant evangelicalism; Britain, Ireland, Germany and
America, c. 1750 – c. 1950, ERobbins Keith: Ecclesiastical History Soc.,
Subs 7. Ox 1991, Blackwell. xii-367 p. $64. 0-631-17818-X [TDig 38,374].
— d) WATANABE Morimichi: Nicholas of CUSA in search of God and
wisdom, EChristianson Gerald, Izbicki Thomas M.: StHChrTht 45. Leiden
1991, Brill. xvi-298 p. f 140 [TR 88, 170, some tit. pp.].
165 WEGENAST Klaus: Klassiker der Religionspädagogik, 60. Gb., ESchröer
Henning, Zillessen Dietrich. Fra 1989, Diesterweg. 304 p. DM 42. –
RTLZ 116 (1991) 17-20 (G. Stächel: die katholischen 'Klassiker' interessieren nicht; auch die 'Belobigung' A. EXELERS stimmt eher de-
pressiv).
165* WEISHEIPL James A., O.P., 1923-1984, mem.: Philosophy and the God of
Abraham, ELong R. James: Papers in Mediaeval Studies 12. Toronto
1991, Pont. Inst. Medv. St. x-296 p. $31. 0-88844-812-0 [TDig 39,181]. 18
art.
166 WILKS Michael: The Church and sovereignty, c. 590-1918, EWood Diana:
StChH subsidia 9. Ox 1991, Blackwell. xx-513 p. portr. £37.50 [TR 88,164].

167 WINDEKENS Albert Joris van, mem.: Studia etymologica indoeuropea, ᴱIsebaert L.: OrLovAn 45. Lv 1991, Univ. xv-343 p.; ix-xii bibliog. depuis 1980. 90-6831-378-9. ... art.; plures infra.

168 WOLLASCH Joachim: Vinculum societatis, 60. Gb., ᴱNelske Franz, *al.* Sigmaringen 1991, Glock. x-352 p.; Bibliog. 326-331. DM 98 [TR 88,165 tit. pp.; RHE 87,796, U. *Meyer*]. 11 art.

169 YARSHATER Ehsan: Iranica varia: Acta Iranica 30 (3/16), Leiden 1990, Brill. – ᴿVDI 198 (1991) 209-215 (M. A. *Dandamayev* ⊕ also on ᶠASMUSSEN).

169* ZIMMERMANN Harald: Ex ipsis rerum documentis; Beiträge zur Mediävistik, 65. Gb. ᴱHerbers Klaus, *al.* Sigmaringen 1991, Thorbecke. xiv-664 p. DM 148. [BeiNam 27,428s, H. *Jakobs*; CathHR 78,437, B. *Tierney*; JEH 43,676, Jane E. *Sayers*].

170 ZUMSTEIN Jean: Johannes-Studien; Interdisziplinäre Zugänge zum Johannes-Evangelium, ᴱRose Martin: Univ. Neuchâtel, 16. Z 1991, Theol.-V. 207 p.; ill. 3-290-10143-6. 9 art.; infra. [NTAbs 36,109].

A1.2 Miscellanea *unius* auctoris.

Ackroyd Peter R., The Chronicler in his age [3 inedita + reprints 1967-88]: JStOT supp. 101, 1991 → 2604.

171 Adinolfi Marco, Ellenismo e Bibbia; saggi storici ed esegetici. R 1991, Dehoniane. 200 p. 88-396-0375-1 [NTAbs 36,288]. Ineditum 4. Sogni di S. Paolo, Atti 16 ... 27, p. 59-72; + 5 reprints.

172 Aleshire Sara B., Asklepios at Athens; epigraphic and prosopographic essays on the Athenian healing cults. Amst 1991, Gieben. xii-257 p., 13 pl. 90-5063-068-5. 9 art., prosopography.

173 *a)* Alston W. P., Epistemic justification; essays in the theory of knowledge [since 1970]. Ithaca NY 1989, Cornell Univ. xi-354 p. – ᴿScripTPamp 23 (1991) 1084s (P. *Conesa*).

— *b)* Alves Rubem A., The poet, the warrior, the prophet [1990 Cadbury Lectures]. L 1990, SCM. 148 p. 0-334-02475-7 [ScotJT 44,547]. – ᴿTLond 94 (1991) 386s (D. *Scott*: a joy, but hard to say what it is about).

— *c)* Amargier P., Un âge d'or du monachisme; Saint-Victor de Marseille (990-1090). Marseille 1991, Tacussel. 194 p. F 120. 29 reprints. [NRT 114,606, A. *Toubeau*].

— *d)* BALDINGER Kurt, Die Faszination der Sprachwissenschaft, Ausgewählte Aufsätze 70. Gb., ᴱStraka Georges, *Pfister* Max. Tü 1990 Niemeyer. xvi-1034 p.; portr. DM 430 [Kratylos 37, 97, C. *Schmitt*].

174 Barbieri Guido, Scritti minori, pref. *Panciera* Silvio. R 1988, Univ. 506 p.; 33 fig.; bibliog. (*Leone* Elvira, *Licordari* Antonio). – ᴿRivArCr (1991) 198-201 (A. R. *Felle*).

175 BAYER Karl, Das Angebot der Antike; humanistische Aufsätze zum altsprachlichen Unterricht, 70. Gb. ᴱMaier Friedrich, *Westphalen* Klaus. Bamberg 1990, Buchner. 202 p.; Bibliog. 199-202 [AnPg 61, p. 733].

176 Beardslee William A., Margins of belonging; essays on the New Testament and theology; AAR 58. Atlanta 1991, Scholars. ix-246 p. 1-55540-468-5. 16 art.

177 Beld A. van den, Is geloof een deugd? [8 reprint] Studies over God, deugd en het eeuwige leven. Baarn 1990, Ten Have. 175 p. *f* 29,50. 90-259-4443-4. – ᴿTsTNijm 31 (1991) 108s (J. *Dijkman*).

178 Bethge Eberhard, Erstes Gebot und Zeitgeschichte; Aufsätze und Reden 1980-1990. Mü 1991, Kaiser. 248 p. DM 48 pa. 23 art. [JBL 110,565].

179 **Blázquez** R., Tradición y esperanza [9 art.]: BtS 113. S 1989, Univ.
217 p. – ᴿArTGran 53 (1990) 339s (E. *Barón*).

179* **Blumhardt** Johann C. Ausgewählte Schriften [c. 1840-80], ᴱ*Bruder* O.,
²ʳᵉᵛ*Bittner* W. J.; 1. Schriftauslegung; 2. Verkündigung; 3. Seelsorge.
Giessen 1991, Brunnen, *al.* xxiii-342 p.; portr. / xvi-338 p. / xiii-336 p. DM
59 pa. [TLZ 117, 684, P. *Schicketanz*].

180 **Boer** P.A.H. de, [24] Selected studies in OT exegesis, ᴱ*Duin* C. van: OTS
27. Leiden 1991, Brill. ix-146 p.; portr. 90-04-09342-7. 24 art. – ᴿDielB 27
(1991) 275s (B. J. *Diebner*); ZAW 103 (1991) 445 (H.-C. *Schmitt*: tit. pp.).

181 **Boff** Leonardo, Faith on the edge; religion and marginalized existence
[essays gathered 1978 & 1980]. SF 1989, Harper & R. 212 p. $20. – ᴿJRel
71 (1991) 451 (R. *Haight*).

182 **Bottéro** Jean, *a)* La Mésopotamie; l'écriture, la raison et les dieux
(reprints) 1987 ⮕ 4,194; – *b)* Mesopotamia, la scrittura, la mentalità e gli
dèi, ᵀ*Matthiae* Claudia: Saggi 744. T 1991, Einaudi. xxxvi-351 p.; 36 fig.
in centro. 88-06-12264-9.

183 **Bouchard** G., La scritta del Pilato; meditazioni bibliche [1961-89, + 6 art.;
da riviste evangeliche]. T 1989, Claudiana. 212 p. Lit. 19.000. – ᴿProtestantesimo 46 (1991) 149 (A. *Comba*).

184 *a)* **Bougerol** Jacques G., S. BONAVENTURE; études sur les sources de sa
pensée: CS 306. Northampton 1989, Variorum. viii-302 p. £39. 0-
86078-254-9. – ᴿJEH 42 (1991) 516s (J. *Dunbabin*).

— *b)* **Boulad** Henri, All is grace; God and the mystery of time. L/Ph 1991,
SCM/Trinity. 154 p. £10. 0-334-01876-5. – ᴿExpTim 103 (1991s) 30 (J.
Polkinghorne).

— *c)* **Braudel** F., Écrits sur l'histoire, 2. 1967-1983. P 1990, Arthaud. 307 p.;
ill. [RHE 87,220*].

— *d)* **Braun** Karl: Aus Liebe der Kirche; [seine] Predigten und Ansprachen,
60. Gb. ᴱ*Scybold* M. Eichstätt 1990, Brönner & D. 154 p. – ᴿForumKT
7 (1991) 140s (A. *Ziegenaus*).

185 **Brico** Rex, Af en toe een oase; gesprekken met profeten, prelaten en
andere wegbereiders, 1972-1987. Kampen 1988, Kok. 285 p. *f* 34. –
ᴿBijdragen 52 (1991) 104s (J. G. *Hahn*: een begnadigd journalist).

186 **Brueggemann** Walter, Interpretation and obedience; from faithful reading
to faithful living. Mp 1991, Fortress. x-325 p. $15 pa. 0-8006-2478-5
[TDig 39,53; TLZ 117,595, W. *Popkes*].

187 **Bynum** Caroline W., Fragmentation and redemption; essays on gender
and the human body in mediaeval religion [over 6 years]. NY 1991, Zone.
426 p.; 44 fig. $25. – ᴿTS 52 (1991) 554s (Margaret R. *Miles*).

188 **Chadwick** Henry, Heresy and orthodoxy in the early Church. Aldershot
1991, Variorum. xii-322 p. £45 [TR 88,165; RÉAug 38,197s, J.-N. *Guinot*].

Chevallier Max-Alain, Souffle de Dieu; le Saint-Esprit dans le NT [I-II
1978-90 ⮕ 58,8329; 6,7556], III. Études [6 reprints + 1 inédit]; préf. *Aletti*
J.: PoinT 55 1991 ⮕ 7523 [RB 99,454, tit. pp.].

190 **Clark** Grahame, Economic prehistory, [32 1942-5] papers on archaeology.
C 1989, Univ. xviii-638 p.; ill. £50. 0-521-34481-6. – ᴿBInstArch 27
(1990) 171-3 (P. M. *Christie*).

191 **Clive** John, Not by fact alone; essays on the writing and reading of
history. NY 1989, Knopf. xiv-334 p. – ᴿHistTheor 30 (1991) 106-112
(Doris S. *Goldstein*).

192 **Cohn-Sherbok** Dan, Rabbinic perspectives on the New Testament [10
reprints]: StBeC 28. Lewiston NY 1990, Mellen. 126 p. $50. 0-88946-
689-0 [TDig 38,352].

193 **Collins** Raymond F., These things have been written; studies on the Fourth Gospel [12 reprints]: Louvain theological and pastoral mg 2. Lv/GR 1991, Peeters/Eerdmans. xiii-277 p. $20 pa. /0-8028-0561-2 [TDig 39,58].

193* **Corbato** Carlo, [21] Scritti di letteratura greca: Univ. Antich. 6. Trieste 1991, Bernardi. xv-420 p. 88-85873-03-0.

194 **Dahl** Nils A., Jesus the Christ, the historical origins of Christological doctrine (7 reprints + 2 inedita], ᴱ*Juel* Donald. Mp 1991, Fortress. 249 p. $25. 0-8006-3458-0 [TDig 39,57; RB 99,453, tit. pp.].

195 **Delorme** Jean, Au risque de la parole; lire les Évangiles [6 textes]: Parole de Dieu. P 1991, Seuil. 248 p. F 130. 2-02-013518-3 [NTAbs 36,262].

197 **Dubois** Jacques, † 8.XII-1991, Martyrologes; de l'Usuard au martyrologe romain, [ses] articles, 70ᵉ anniv.; préf. *Fleury* Michel. Abbeville 1990, Paillart. 246 p. F 250 [RHE 87,455, E. *Palazzo*].

197* **Ebach** Jürgen, Theologische Reden, mit denen man keinen Staat machen kann [Gn 1s...]: SWI ausser Reihe 4. Bochum 1989, SWI. 179 p. [TLZ 117,99, T. *Mickel*].

198 **Ellis** E. Earle, The OT in early Christianity; canon and interpretation in the light of modern research: WUNT 54. Tü 1991, Mohr. xiii-188 p. DM 78. 3-16-145660-2 [organized reprints: JBL 110,567; NTAbs 36,102; CritRR 5, 86-88, J. J. *Collins*: useful, but holds the Church followed an existing Hebrew canon different from the Septuagint]. – ᴿArTGran 54 (1991) 367 (A. *Segovia*).

198* **Erickson** John H., The challenge of our past; studies in Orthodox canon law and church history. Crestwood NY 1991, St. Vladimir. 174 p. $11. 0-88141-086-1 [TDig 39,260].

199 **Fee** Gordon D., Gospel and Spirit; issues in New Testament hermeneutics [8 reprints]. Peabody MA 1991, Hendrickson. xiv-143 p. $10 pa. 0-943575-78-8 [NTAbs 36,253; BtS 142,496, D. L. *Bock*]. 2 infra.

199* **Filoramo** Giovanni, Il risveglio della gnosi ovvero diventare dio: Quadrante 33. R 1990, Laterza. 235 p. – ᴿRivStorLR 27 (1991) 523-6 (P. A. *Gramaglia*).

200 **Fohrer** Georg, Studien zum Alten Testament (1966-1988) [last of the series of 5]; mitsamt Bibliographie G. Fohrer 1991, p. 170-186: BZAW 196. B 1991, de Gruyter. vii-186 p. DM 104. 3-11-012819-5. [BL 92,13; RB 99,446 & CBQ 55,185, R. *Gnuse*: tit. pp.; BZ 36,288, J. *Scharbert*]. 10 reprints; 3 infra + 3 vermutlich inedita, infra ⇒ 1428. – ᴿExpTim 103 (1991s) 247 (R. *Coggins*).

201 **García de Haro** Ramón (art. 20 años), Cristo, fundamento de la moral; los conceptos básicos de la vida moral en la perspectiva cristiana. Barc 1990, EIUNSA. 190 p. – ᴿAnnTh 5 (1991) 431-5 (C. *Bermúdez*).

202 **Garlan** Y., Guerre et économie en Grèce ancienne [⇒ 6,g740... half = revised reprints]: Textes à l'appui. P 1989, Découverte. 226 p. F 98. – ᴿJHS 111 (1991) 244s (J. F. *Lazenby*: 'not my kind of history').

202* **Geffré** C., Passion de l'homme, passion de Dieu [38 homélies + 6 art.]. P 1991, Cerf. 253 p.; 12 fig. F 100 [NRT 114,461].

203 **Gerl** Hanna-Barbara, Die bekannte Unbekannte [10 Art.], Frauen-Bilder in der Kultur- und Geistesgeschichte. Mainz 1988, Grünewald. 160 p. DM 24,80. – ᴿTLZ 116 (1991) 928-930 (Susanne *Heine*).

204 *a)* **Gese** Hartmut, Alttestamentliche Studien. [I. 1974; II.] Tü 1991, Mohr. viii-307 p. DM 118 [BL 92,14; RB 99,446, tit. pp.]. 3-16-145739-0; pa. -699-8. 1 ineditum + 15 reprints; 6 infra. – ᴿExpTim 103 (1991s) 298 (R. *Coggins*); TR 87 (1991) 465s (C. *Dohmen*).

— *b*) **Gigante** Marcello, Classico e mediazione; contributi alla storia della filologia antica [reprints]: Studi Superiori N 15-70. R 1989, Nuova Italia Scientifica. 243 p. Lit. 34.000. – ᴿClasR 41 (1991) 214s (H. *Lloyd-Jones*).

— *c*) **Gilkey** Langdon B., Through the tempest; theological voyages in a pluralistic culture [15 art. 1975-88], ᴱ*Pool* Jeff B. Mp 1991, Fortress. xx-252 p. $15 pa. 0-8006-2484-X [TDig 39,264].

— *d*) **Goetz** George, Philosophie und Judentum; Vorträge und Aufsätze aus den Jahren 1924-1968, ᴱ*Goetz* H., *Haag*, C. Brunner-Instituut. Husum 1991, Hansa. 218 p. DM 17,80 [TLZ 117,929, U. *Kern*].

205 **Goldhill** Simon, The poet's voice; essays on poetics and Greek literature. C 1991, Univ. xi-369 p. 0-521-39062-1; pa. -570-4.

206 **Goldstein** Jonathan A., Semites, Iranians, Greeks and Romans [11 art. 1966-88]: BrownJudSt 217. Atlanta 1990, Scholars. x-257 p. 1-55540-512-6. – ᴿOTAbs 14 (1991) 339s (C. T. *Begg*: tit. pp. date).

207 **Gollwitzer** Helmut, *a*) Auch das Denken darf dienen; Aufsätze zu Theologie und Geistesgeschichte, I, ᴱ*Marquardt* Friedrich-W. – *b*) ... dass Gerechtigkeit und Friede sich küssen; Aufsätze zur politischen Ethik I., ᴱ*Pangritz* Andreas: Ausgewählte Werke 8.4 [aus 10], Tb 45. Mü 1988, Kaiser. 427 p. / 246 p. [LuJb 58,145, indicating eight cited items].

208 *a*) **Griffiths** J. Gwyn, Atlantis and Egypt, with other selected essays. Cardiff 1991, Univ. Wales. xiv-329 p. 0-7083-1071-0 [OIAc 1 (1991) 17; excerpted there; NTAbs 36,293].

— *b*) **Gunton** Colin E., The promise of trinitarian theology. E 1991, Clark. xii-188 p. $33. – ᴿHorizons 19 (1992) 321s (J. A. *Bracken*).

— *c*) **Hamman** A. G., Études patristiques; méthodologie, liturgie, histoire, théologie [33 reprints depuis 1951]: THist 85. P 1991, Beauchesne. 474 p. F 150 [NRT 114,765, V. *Roisel*; RSPT 76,617, G. M. de *Durand*; Teresianum 43,530, M. *Diego Sánchez*].

210 *a*) **Hartshorne** Charles, Wisdom as moderation; a philosophy of the Middle Way: SUNY ph. Albany 1987, SUNY. xi-157 p. 10 essays. – ᴿTPhil 66 (1991) 135s (F. *Ricken*).

— *b*) **Heras** H., [Jesuit guru † 14.XII.1955; 13] Indological studies, ᴱ*Anderson* Bernard, *Correia-Afonso* John. New Delhi 1990, Promilla / Heras Institute. xiv-207 p. rs. 250. – ᴿBSO 54 (1991) 441s (A.D.H. *Bivar*).

— *c*) **Heymel** M., Zur Verherrlichung Israels; Vorträge und Predigten [➤ 6,245]. Fra 1990, Lang. 204 p. Fs 26. 3-631-42793-X [BL 92,106, R. A. *Mason*: Christian apologetic].

— *d*) **Hoerber** R. G., Studies in the NT [13 + 22 Concordia Journal editorials]. Cleveland 1991, Biblion. xviii-114 p. $12 pa. 0-9620063-5-1 [NTAbs 36,254]. – ᴿRExp 89 (1992) 417s (G. *Feagin*, not enthusiastic).

211 **Holtz** Traugott, Geschichte und Theologie des Urchristentums; Gesammelte Aufsätze, ᴱ*Reinmuth* Eckart, *Wolff* Christian: WUNT 57. Tü 1991, Mohr. x-492. 3-16-145763-3. 28 reprints; 10 infra [RB 100,129, tit. pp.; BZ 36,283, R. *Schnackenburg*; TR 87,340; NTAbs 36,103; TLZ 117,656-9, U. *Wilckens*]. – ᴿArTGran 54 (1991) 371 (A. *Segovia*).

211* **Hooker** Morna D., From Adam to Christ; essays on Paul. C 1990, Univ. 224 p. $49.50. 0-521-343178. – ᴿTLond 94 (1991) 463s (Clare *Dryry*).

212 **Horst** Pieter van der, Essays on the Jewish world of early Christianity [not = 6,250]: NOrb 14. FrS/Gö 1990, Univ./VR. 269 p. Fs 68. 3-7278-0683-4 / 3-525-53915-0. [RB 99,762, tit. pp.] 14 art., 2 infra.

212* **Houlden** J. L., Bible and belief [12 art.]. L 1991, SPCK. xi-174 p. £11. 0-281-04546-1 [NTAbs 36,254].

213 **Isaac** Glynn † 1985, The archaeology of human origins, ᴱ*Isaac* Barbara. C 1990, Univ. $59.50. 0-521-36573-2. – ᴿJField 18 (1991) 224-230 (J.F. *O'Connell*).

214 **Jagersma** H., Tekst en interpretatie; studies over gestalten, teksten, verhalen en geschiedenis in het Oude Testament. Nijkerk 1990, Callenbach. 131 p. Fb 690. – ᴿCollatVL 21 (1991) 316 (H. *Hoet*).

215 **Jonge** Marinus De, Jewish eschatology, early Christian Christology and the Testaments of the Twelve Patriarchs: NT supp 63. Leiden 1991, Brill. xix-242 p.; portr.; bibliog. 314-326.   90-04-09326-5 [BL 92,123s, C.J.A. *Hickling*; CBQ 54,600, J. R. *Mueller*; CiuD 205,753, J. *Gutiérrez*; ETL 68, 165, J. *Neirynck*; RB 99,449, tit. pp.] 20 art.; 6 infra.

216 *a*) **Jüngel** Eberhard, Wertlose Wahrheit; zur Identität und Relevanz des christlichen Glaubens: TErört 3 / BeitEvT 107. Mü 1990, Kaiser. xiv-405 p. DM 89. 3-459-01866-6. – ᴿTGL 81 (1991) 489s (G. *Fuchs*); TsTNijm 31 (1991) 205 (W. *Logister*: 'Onder een prikkelende titel ... 20 art. vooral uit de jaren tachtig').

— *b*) **Kannengiesser** Charles, ARIUS and ATHANASIUS, two Alexandrian theologians: CS 353. Aldershot 1991, Variorum. xiv-330 p. [RHE 87,559, A. de *Halleux*].

— *c*) **Kassel** Rudolf, Kleine Schriften, ᴱ*Nesselrath* Heinz-G., B 1991, de Gruyter. xii-704 p. DM 358 [Eikasmos 3,369, E. *Degani*]. – ᴿRÉG 105 (1992) 264 (J. *Irigoin*).

217 **Kaufmann** Franz-Xaver, Religion und Modernität; sozialwissenschaftliche Perspektiven [10 art. 1984-8]. Tü 1989, Mohr. 286 p. DM 58. 3-16-545530-9 [TLZ 117, 113, F. *Wagner*]. – ᴿActuBbg 28 (1991) 172 (J. *Boada*).

217* **Kertelge** K., Grundthemen paulinischer Theologie. FrB 1991, Herder [NTAbs 36,122; RivB 40,369, R. *Penna*; TvT 32,196, J. *Smit*; GeistL 65,156].

218 **Koch** Klaus, Spuren des hebräischen Denkens; Beiträge zur alttestamentlichen Theologie, Ges.Aufs. 1, ᴱ*Janowski* B., *Krausc* M. [12 Art. 1952-90; Band 2 erwartet]. Neuk 1991. ix-312 p. DM 90. 3-7887-1343-7 [ZAW 104,152, tit. pp.; TLZ 117,667, S. *Herrmann*]. – ᴿErbAuf 67 (1991) 324s (R. *Dietzfelbinger*); TsTNijm 31 (1991) 426 (J. *Holman*).

219 **Koch** Kurt, Aufbruch statt Resignation; Stichworte zu einem engagierten Christentum [Ges. Aufs.]. Z 1990, Benziger. 336 p. Fs 38,80. – ᴿTPQ 139 (1991) 330 (J. *Hörmandinger*).

220 **KOLPING** Adolf [80. Gb.], Kirche — die komplexe Wirklichkeit; eine Auswahl von Aufsätzen (1928-78). Münster 1989, Regensberg. 309 p. DM 36 [TR 88, 134, J. *Schumacher*].

221 **Kraus** Hans-Joachim, Rückkehr zu Israel; Beiträge zum christlich-jüdischen Dialog [17 reprints 1952-89 + 2 inedita]. Neuk 1991. vii-368 p. DM 88. 3-7887-1356-9 [ZAW 104, 298, tit. pp.; inedita infra].

221* **Küng** Hans, Die Hoffnung bewahren; Schriften zur Reform der Kirche. Einsiedeln 1990, Benziger. 232 p. Fs 28,20. 3-545-24067-2. – ᴿTLZ 116 (1991) 607s (H. *Kirchner*).

222 *a*) **Langmuir** Gavin I., Toward a definition of anti-Semitism [3 inedita, 11 reprints]. Berkeley 1991, Univ. California. x-427 p. $45. [RelStR 18, 72, R. C. *Stacey*; TS 53,349, J. *Bernauer*].

— *b*) **Lapide** Pinchas, Jesus, das Geld und der Weltfrieden: Siebenstern 1435. Gü 1991, Mohn. 155 p. DM 26,80. 3-579-01435-8. 17 art. [NTAbs 36,283].

— *c*) **Lenel** Otto, Gesammelte Schriften, ᴱ*Behrends* Okko, *d'Ippolito* Federico, I 1876-1889: Antiqua 52. N 1990, Jovene. 568 p. [AnPg 61, p. 735].

— *d*) **Lincoln** Bruce, Death, war, and sacrifice; studies in ideology and practice [6 inedita + 14]. Ch 1991, Univ. xxi-289 p. $55; pa. $22. 0-

22648199-9; -200-6 [TDig 39,173, W. C. *Heiser*: Wendy DONAGER made him do it].

223 **Livrea** Enrico, Studia hellenistica Is: Papyrologica Florentina 21. F 1991, Gonnelli. xiii-317 p.; p. 319-644; X pl.

223* **Lloyd-Jones** Hugh, *a*) Greek comedy, Hellenistic literature, Greek religion, and miscellanea; academic papers. Ox 1990, Clarendon. x-424 p. 0-19-814745-7. 38 art. – *b*) Greek in a cold climate [title of p. 220-233 + 30 other reprints]. L 1991, Duckworth. vi-236 p. 0-7156-2358-3 [ClasR 42,421, W. G. *Arnott*].

224 **Lohfink** Norbert, Studien zum Deuteronomium und zur deuteronomistischen Literatur I. 1976-90; II.: SBAufs 8. 12. Stu 1991, KBW. 392 p. 303 p. DM 49 (II). 3-460-06081-6; -121-9. [BL 92,77, A.D.H. *Mayes*, high praise; JBL 111,739, T. F. *Fretheim*, 8 & RB 100,128,12: tit. pp.; TLZ 116,592; ZAW 104,449, H. C. *Schmitt*]. 13 + 13 art., infra.

225 **Lord** A. B. †, Epic singers and oral tradition. Ithaca NY 1991, Cornell Univ. xii-362 p. $36.50; pa. $13 [RelStR 18, 139, J. P. *Hershbell*]. – RClasR 42 (1992) 320s (W. *McLeod*).

226 **Lubac** Henri de, Théologie dans l'histoire [1. 1990 ➤ 6,266]; 2. Questions disputées et résistance au nazisme: Théologie. P 1990, D-Brouwer. 424 p. F 175. – RZkT 113 (1991) 110s (K. H. *Neufeld*).

227 **MacMullen** Ramsay, Changes in the Roman Empire; essays in the ordinary. Princeton 1990, Univ. xiv-399 p.; 2 fig.; 9 pl. 0-691-03601-2. 24 art. (20 reprinted); 2 infra.

228 **Madison** G. B., The hermeneutics of postmodernity; figures and themes [reprints; 2 ined.]. 1988 ➤ 4,a882: RJRel 71 (1991) 276 (M. I. *Wallace*).

229 **Mansfeld** Jaap, Studies in later Greek philosophy and Gnosticism [1972-88]. L 1989, Variorum. x-234 p. [AnPg 61, p. 735].

230 **Marcovich** Miroslav, Studies in Greek poetry: ILCL supp. 1. Atlanta 1991, Scholars. ix-249 p. 1-55540-603-3. 46 art.

231 **Mastrocinque** Attilio, Lucio Giunio Bruto; ricerche di storia, religione e diritto della repubblica romana: Univ. Trento. Trento 1988, La Reclame. 293 p. Lit. 70.000. – RAmJPg 112 (1991) 407-9 (J. *Linderski*).

232 **Mathisen** Ralph W., [25] Studies in the history, literature and society of late antiquity. Amst 1991, Hakkert. xvi-449 p.; 3 maps. 90-256-0983-X.

233 **Meer** C. van der, Afscheid van het leven; 20 jaar denken over sterven en dood [reprints]. Kampen 1990, Kok. 222 p. *f* 29,90. 90-242-4861-2. – RTsTNijm 31 (1991) 113s (W.J.M. van *Haaren*).

234 **Mélèze-Modrzejewski** Joseph, L'Égypte ptolémaïque (Aspects institutionnels) [5 reprints]. P 1991, Univ. I Panthéon-Sorbonne. 123 p. [OIAc 1,21 excerpted].

235 *a*) **Michalowski** Kazimierz, Opera minora I. Wsz 1990, Państwowe Naukowe. 891 p. 83-01-03045-3. – RRuBi 44 (1991) 157s (J. *Chmiel*).

— *b*) **Mitchell** Leonel L., Worship; initiation and the churches [essays since 1960, revised]. Wsh 1991, Pastoral. viii-217 p. $13. 0-912405-84-8 [TDig 39,276].

— *c*) **Möhler** Johann A. [Stenographie *Lösch* Stephan] Nachgelassene Schriften, 2 Exegetische Vorlesungen, E*Reinhardt* Rudolf (*Rieger* Reinhold): KkSt 3. Pd 1990, Bonifatius. 440 p. DM 108. – RMüTZ 42 (1991) 189s (G. L. *Müller*).

236 **Moioli** Giovanni, Scritti sul prete [20 sin dal 1965]: Quodlibet 1. Mi 1990, Glossa. 327 p. Lit. 48.000. – RETL 67 (1991) 474 (A. de *Halleux*); ScuolC 119 (1991) 3-36 (T. *Citrini*, + p. 37-44, ancora due inediti del M.); Teresianum 42 (1991) 631s (M. *Caprioli*).

237 **Momigliano** Arnaldo, Die Juden in der alten Welt, [T]*Kempter* Martina [cf.
➤ 3,260; 4,232]: KlKultWB 5. B 1988, Wagenbach. 93 p. DM 21. – [R]HZ
252 (1991) 141-3 (Helga *Botermann*).

238 **Moretti** Luigi, Tra epigrafia e storia; scritti scelti e annotati. R 1990.
432 p.; 24 fig. [AntClas 61,531s, Marie-T. *Raepsaet-Charlier*; Gnomon
62,259, P. *Hermann*]. – [R]RivArCr 67 (1991) 202-8 (A. E. *Felle*).

239 **Moscati** Sabatino, Passeggiate nel tempo [ristampi sugli eventi più no-
tevoli dell'archeologia 1988s]. Novara 1990, De Agostini. 320 p.; 48 fig.
Lit. 32.000. – [R]Archeo 65 (1990) 127 (S. F. *Bondì*).

240 **Müller** Hans-Peter, Mythos-Kerygma-Wahrheit; Gesammelte Aufsätze
zum AT in seiner Umwelt und zur biblischen Theologie: BZAW 200. B
1991, de Gruyter. xiv-319 p. 3-11-012885-3. [BL 92,19, J. R. *Porter*; RB
99,587 & ZAW 104,303, tit. pp.] 11 art. + 1 ineditum, infra.

241 **Müller** Karlheinz, Studien zur frühjüdischen Apokalyptik: SBAufs
11. Stu 1991 KBW. 335 p. DM 48 [TR 88,426]. 3-460-06111-1. 6 art.,
2 infra.

241* **MURPHY** Francis X., ['Rynne X'.], Patristic heritage in the Renaissance
and the modern world, republished for his 75th b., [E]*Shaifer* Norman. Old
Tappan NY 1990, Shepherd. vii-237 p. $15 [TR 88,255]. – [R]Jeevadhara 20
(1990) 329 (J. B. *Chethimattam*).

242 **Mussner** Franz, Dieses Geschlecht wird nicht vergehen; Judentum und
Kirche. FrB 1991, Herder. 185 p. DM 46. 3-451-22305-8 [RB 99,454,
tit. pp.]. – [R]TGL 81 (1991) 392 (J. *Ernst*).

242* **Nagy** Gregory, Greek mythology and poetics [1973-85]: Myth and
Poetics 2. Ithaca NY 1990, Cornell Univ. xi-363 p. $35 [Maia 44,123s,
Nicoletta *Marini*]. – [R]ClasR 41 (1991) 87-89 (S. *Goldhill*).

243 **Neirynck** Frans, Evangelica II, 1982-1991, [E]*Segbroeck* F. Van: BtETL 99.
Lv 1991, Univ. xiv-874 p. Fb 2800. [RB 99,451, tit. pp.; ÉTRel 67,461, E.
Cuvillier; FgNt 5,213, S. E. *Porter*]. 40 art. 1982-91 (29 in Eng.) [I was
1982; 14 art. 1966-75 + 29, 1976-81].

243* **Neusner** J., The city of God in Judaism and other comparative and
methodological studies: SFL StHistJud 23. Atlanta 1991, Scholars.
xii-353 p. $75. 1-55540-586-X [NTAbs 36,297].

244 **Ochoa Sanz** Xavier [1.XII.1923-22.III.89]: Miscellanea [in onore] del prof.
~, [E]*Basso* mons. Michele. Vaticano 1990. 474 p. – [R]TEspir 35 (1991)
325s (A. *Bernal Palacios*: derecho).

245 **Painter** John, The quest for the Messiah; the history, literature and
theology of the Johannine community [14 art., half expanded reprints]. E
1991, Clark. xiv-425 p. £20. 0-567-09592-4 [RB 99,611, B. *McConvery*:
papers reordered 'toward a commentary', sans tit. pp.].

245* **Pannenberg** Wolfhart, Metaphysics and the idea of God. E 1990, Clark.
xiv-170 p. £15. – [R]TLond 94 (1991) 208s (D. A. *Pailin*: 3 + 1 ineditum).

246 **Papathomopoulos** Manolis, Varia philologica et papyrologica [24 art.
1961-86, français sauf 2 Eng., 3 ⑥]. Jannina 1990. 303 p. – [R]RÉG 104
(1991) 594 (G. *Husson*).

247 **Penna** Romano, L'apostolo Paolo; studi di esegesi e teologia [30 reprints,
20 anni, rev.: Lateranum 58,609, ipse]: Parola di Dio 2/12. CinB 1991,
Paoline. 712 p. Lit. 40.000. 88-215-2323-3 [infra ➤ 5285; 5415].

248 **Pinckaers** Servais, L'èvangile et la morale [art. de 20 ans]: Ét.Éth. Chr.
29. FrS/P 1990, Univ./Cerf. 292 p. – [R]StMor 29 (1991) 484-8 (R. *Gallagher*).

248* **Pixner** Birgil, Wege des Messias und Stätten der Urkirche; Jesus und das
Judenchristentum im Licht neuer archäologischer Erkenntnisse [25 art.],

ᴱ*Riesner* R. Giesen 1991, Brunnen. 435 p.; 80 fig.; 7 pl. DM 48. 3-7655-9802-X [NTAbs 36,300].

249 **Power** David N., Worship, culture and theology [reprints]. Wsh 1990, Pastoral/Columba. xii-283 p. $12. 0-912405-77-5 / 1-85607-922-0 [TDig 39,79: Catholic Univ. teacher]. – ᴿExpTim 103 (1991s) 254 (G. S. *Wakefield*: can help Protestants to 'learn liturgy from reformed Rome' — but recommends some return from Vatican II).

250 **Pugliese Carratelli** Giovanni, Tra Cadmo e Orfeo; contributi alla storia civile e religiosa dei Greci d'Occidente: Collezione TSt Stor. Bo 1991, Mulino. 490 p. 88-15-02692-4. 37 art., → u2.9.

250* **Ratzinger** Joseph, Zur Gemeinschaft gerufen; Kirche heute verstehen [5 Vorträge]. FrB 1991, Herder. 158 p. DM 22.80. – ᴿMüTZ 42 (1991) 416-8 (G. L. *Müller*).

251 **Raubitschek** A. E., The school of Hellas; essays on Greek history, archaeology, and literature; ᴱ*Obbink* Dirk, *Vander Waerdt* Paul. Ox 1991, UP. 384 p. $45 [JAAR 59,884].

251* **Rawson** Elizabeth [† 1988], Roman culture and society; collected papers. Ox 1991, UP. x-615; portr. £70 [GreeceR 39,102, T. E. J. *Wiedemann*].

252 **Rendtorff** Rolf, Kanon und Theologie; Vorarbeiten zu einer Theologie des ATs [12 reprints 1981-90 teils < Eng.; + 6 inedita]. Neuk 1991. x-198 p. DM 50. 3-7887-1382-8 [ZAW 104,306, tit. pp.] 3 inedita + 1 infra.

Reumann John, Variety and unity in NT thought 1991 → 3797.

254 **Rosenthal** Franz, Muslim intellectual and social history [collected essays 1; (2 will be the Greek heritage; 3. his whole bibliography)]. Aldershot 1990, Variorum. x-326 p. £39. 0-86078-257-3. – ᴿBO 48 (1991) 929-931 (Remke *Kruk*).

255 **Rostagno** Sergio, Teologia e società; saggi sull'impegno etico. T 1989, Claudiana. 168 p. Lit. 22.000. – ᴿRasT 32 (1991) 214 (G. *Mattai*).

256 **Sabbe** Maurits, Studia neotestamentica, collected essays: BtETL 98. Lv 1991, Univ. xvi-573 p.; bibliog. xiii-xv. Fb 2000. 18 art. [RB 100,130, tit. pp.; NRT 115,905, X. *Jacques*; REH 87,886, C. *Focant*].

256* **Sacchi** Paolo, L'apocalittica giudaica e la sua storia [12 art.]: BtCuRel 66. Brescia 1990, Paideia. 374 p. Lit. 47.000. 88-394-0446-5 [NTAbs 36,141]. – ÉTRel 67,101, Jeanne-M. *Léonard*].

257 **Sánchez Ruipérez** Martín, Opuscula selecta ... zur griechischen und indogermanischen Sprachwissenschaft, ᴱ*García-Ramón* José L.; InnsbSprW 58. Innsbruck 1989, Univ. xv-332 p. [AnPg 61, p. 737].

257* **Schäfer** Rolf, Gotteslehre und kirchliche Praxis; [15 1968-88] Ausgewählte Aufsätze, ᴱ*Köpf* U., *Rittner* R. Tü 1991, Mohr. vi-345 p. DM 34 [TLZ 117,860, E. *Sturm*].

258 **Schenker** Adrian, Text und Sinn im Alten Testament; textgeschichtliche und bibeltheologische Studien: OBO 103. FrS/Gö 1991, Univ/VR. 302 p. Fs 75. 3-7278-0730-X / 3-525-53735-2. 1 ineditum + 13 art.; 6 infra [RB 99,447 & ZAW 104,308 & CBQ 55,205, B. C. *Ollenburger*: tit. pp.; AustralBR 40,72, R. *Boid*; BZ 36,289, J. *Scharbert*; TZBas 48,293, E. *Kellenberger*]. – ᴿOTAbs 14 (1991) 349s (C. T. *Begg*: tit. pp. date); RHPR 71 (1991) 227 (J.-G. *Heintz*); RivB 39 (1991) 353-5 (A. *Bonora*).

259 **Schmeemann** Alexander, Liturgy and tradition; theological reflections, ᴱ*Fisch* Thomas. Crestwood NY 1990, St. Vladimir. 157 p. $7 [RelStR 18,125, D. *Hester*].

260 **Schneemelcher** Wilhelm, Reden und Aufsätze; Beiträge zur Kirchengeschichte und zum ökumenischen Gespräch. Tü 1991, Mohr. 263 p. [NTAbs 36,142; TR 87,252; TLZ 117,950, J. *Rogge*].

261 **Schrader** Franz, Stadt, Kloster und Seelsorge, Beiträge zur ~ –geschichte im Raum der mittelalterlichen Bistümer Magdeburg und Halberstadt, gesammelte Aufsätze: Studien zur katholischen Bistums- und Klostergeschichte 29. Lp 1988, St. Benno. x-359 p. [LuJb 57 (1990) p.319 with indication of two articles there cited].

262 **Schuon** Frithjof, To have a center. Bloomington IN 1990, World Wisdom. vii-184 p. $12 [RelStR 18,219, H. L. *Carrigan*: uneven but good on 'integral anthropology'].

262* **Segal** Robert A., Religion and the social sciences; [13 1976-87] essays on the confrontation: BrownStR 3. Atlanta 1989, Scholars. 184 p. $44. – RZygon 26 (1991) 436-9 (W. E. *Paden*).

263 **Sesboüé** Bernard, Pour une théologie oecuménique; église et sacrements; Eucharistie et ministères; la Vierge Marie: CogF 100. P 1990, Cerf. 424 p. F 189 [MaisD 187,143, N. *Derrey*; TLZ 117,952, K.-H. *Neufeld*; RTLv 23,498]. – REsprVie 101 (1991) 319s (P. *Jay*); ETL 67 (1991) 181s (A. de *Halleux*: 2 inedita sur 20); ÉTRel 66 (1991) 623-5 (A. *Gounelle*; deçu); NRT 113 (1991) 579s (R. *Escol*); RSPT 75 (1991) 542s.

264 **Smend** Rudolf, Gesammelte Studien 3. Epochen der Bibelkritik: BeitEvT 109. Mü 1991, Kaiser. 254 p. DM 98 [BL 92,23, TR 87,425]. 3-459-01885-2. P. 43-62, [Robert] LOWTH in Deutschland, ineditum; also ined. 11-32; 12 other art.

264* **Speyer** Wolfgang, Frühes Christentum im antiken Strahlungsfeld; ausgewählte Aufsätze: WUNT 50. Tü 1989, Mohr. 531 p. [GrazBeit 18,303, J. B. *Bauer*]. – RClasR 41 (1991) 248s (H. *Chadwick*).

265 *a*) **Stone** M. E., Selected studies in pseudepigrapha and apocrypha...: StVTPseud 9. Leiden 1991, Brill. *f*200. 90-04-09343-5 [RB 99,450, tit. pp.].

— *b*) **Strasburger** Hermann, Studien zur Alten Geschichte, E*Schmitthenner* Walter, *Zoepfel* Renate, 3: Collectanea 42/3. Hildesheim 1990, Olms. 562 p. [GrazBeit 18,280, H. *Grassl*].

— *c*) **Studer** Basil, Dominus salvator; Studien zur Christologie und Exegese der Kirchenväter: StudAnselm. R 1991, Benedictina. 551 p. Lit. 82.000. [TR 88,429].

266 **Sydow** Jürgen, Cum omni mensura et ratione, Ausgewählte Aufsätze, Festgabe 70. Gb., E*Maurer* Helmut. Sigmaringen 1991, Thorbecke. xiv-406 p. DM 78 [TR 87,252].

266* **Talley** Thomas J., Worship; reforming tradition [8 reprints + 2 inedita]. Wsh 1990, Pastoral. ix-255 p. $12. – RWorship 65 (1991) 378s (D. *Tripp*).

267 **Tedeschi** John. The prosecution of heresy; collected studies on the Inquisition in early modern Italy: MedRenTSt. Binghamton 1991, SUNY. xxii-417 p. $25 [RelStR 18,235, R. *Kolb*: moderate].

268 **Thadden** Rudolf von, Weltliche Kirchengeschichte; ausgewählte Aufsätze. Gö 1989, Vandenhoeck & R. 219 p. [LuJb 58, p.148, with indication of three items there cited].

269 **Theissen** Gerd, The open door; variations on Biblical themes [25 sermons → 6,1495], T*Bowden* John. L/Mp 1991, SCM/Fortress. xii-191 p. £10 [BL 92,113, C.J.A. *Hickling*; NRT 114,944, A. *Toubeau*]. 0-334-02510-9. – RExpTim 103 (1991s) 35s (C. S. *Rodd*: appealing).

270 **Treves** Marco †, Conjectures sur la Bible [< VT, JBL, RQum, *al.*]. Les Sables-d'Olonne 1990, Pinson. 350 p. [BL 92,24, R. N. *Whybray*].

271 **Vernant** Jean-Pierre, Mortals and immortals; collected essays. TE*Zeitlin* Froma I. (mostly 1980-90; partly from L'individu, la mort, l'amour, P 1989; 6 on death, + 13). Princeton 1991, Univ. ix-341 p. 0-691-06831-3.

272 **Veyne** Paul, La société romaine. P 1991, Seuil [Masses Ouvrières 445, 106, F. *Dumortier*].
273 **Voegelin** Eric, Ordnung, Bewusstsein, Geschichte — späte Schriften, eine Auswahl, [E]*Opitz* Peter J. Stu 1988, Klett-Cotta. – [R]ZRGg 43 (1991) 378s (J. *Gebhardt*).
274 **Volkov** Shulamit, Jüdisches Leben [10 reprints]. Mü 1990, Beck. 233 p. DM 40. 3-406-34761-4. – [R]ActuBbg 28 (1991) 239s (J. *Boada*).
275 **Waldenfels** Hans, Begegnung der Religionen [20 art. 1967-90]: Theologische Versuche I. Begegnung Kontextdialog 1. Bonn 1990, Borengässer. xi-377 p. DM 44. 3-923946-18-X [TContext 10/2,105, G. *Evers*]. – [R]ArTGran 54 (1991) 419 (A. *Segovia*); TsTNijm 31 (1991) 335 (H. *Stoks*); ZkT 113 (1991) 316s (K. H. *Neufeld*).
276 **Weinstein** Fred, History and theory after the Fall. Ch 1990, Univ. x-205 p. – [R]HistTheor 30 (1991) 339-347 (P. *Pomper*).
276* **Weiser** A., Studien zu Christsein und Kirche: SBAufs 9. Stu 1990, KBW. 373 p. DM 39 pa. 3-460-06091-3. [NTAbs 36,260: 19 art., topics sans tit. pp.].
277 **Westbrook** Raymond, Property and the family in biblical law [2 inedita + 5 reprints]: JStOT supp. 113. Sheffield 1991, Academic. 177 p. £39.50; pa. £22.50. 1-85075-271-0. [OIAc 1,27; excerpted].
278 **Wilder** Amos N., The Bible and the literary critic [4 inedita + 7 reprints from the (and his) 80s]. Mp 1991, Fortress. xiv-186 p. $13. 0-8006-2436-X [CritRR 5,533, tit. pp.; TDig 38,389; RelStR 18,141, C. *Bernas*]. – [R]ExpTim 103 (1991s) 151 (J.I.H. *McDonald*: Wilder is 'exercised by the notion that literary critics such as ALTER, FRYE, and KERMODE [and CROSSAN] may confine the transcendental flow of scripture within the lock-gates of their own presuppositions'); TTod 48 (1991s) 501 (N. R. *Peterson*).
278* **Wilson** Bryan R., The social dimensions of sectarianism; sects and new religious movements in contemporary society [organized reprints]. Ox 1990, Clarendon. xii-299 p. $59. [TS 53,171, J. A. *Coleman*].
279 **Wirsching** Johannes, Glaube im Widerstreit; ausgewählte Aufsätze und Vorträge: Kontexte 4. Fra 1988, Lang. 219 p. [LuJb 58, p. 148, with indication of six items there cited].
280 **Wlosok** Antonie, Res humanae, res divinae; Kleine Schriften, [E]*Heck* Eberhard, *Schmidt* Ernst A.: Biblióthek KlasAltW NF 2/84. Heid 1990, Winter. 550 p.; bibliog. p. 9-14. 3-533-04303-7; pa. –2-9. 25 art.; 5 infra. – [R]Faventia 12s (1990s) 496s (J. *Velaza*).
281 **Wolf** George, Lexical and historical contributions on the biblical and rabbinic Passover. NY 1991. ix-206 p. 66 art. Eng. (some with ✡ titles); 5 infra; many others on Seder [Helmantica 43,463, S. *García-Jalón*].
282 **Wolter** Allan B., [13 essays, 40 years], [E]*Adams* M., The philosophical theology of John Duns SCOTUS. Ithaca 1990, Cornell Univ. ix-356 p. $47.50. – [R]TS 52 (1991) 555-7 (J. M. *McDermott*).
283 **Yardeni** Myriam, Anti-Jewish mentalities in early modern Europe [< 1969-89 French/Hebrew]. Lanham MD 1990, UPA. xv-297 p. $34.50. – [R]CathHR 77 (1991) 695 (R. A. *Schneider*).
284 **Zumstein** Jean, Miettes exégétiques: MondeB. Genève 1991, Labor et Fides. 421 p. 2-8309-0638-1 [RB 100,132, tit. pp.; NRT 115,906, X. *Jacques*].

A1.3   *Plurium compilationes* **biblicae.**

284* [E]**Aguirre Monasterio** Rafael, Pedro en la Iglesia primitiva: CuadJer 23. Estella 1991, VDivino. 258 p.

285 EAlmog Shmuel, *Heyd* Michael, ❺ Chosen people, elect nation, and universal mission. J 1991, Shazar. 326 p. [RelStR 18,37, M. *Kellner*].
286 EAlonso Schökel Luis, *Artola* Antonio M., La Palabra de Dios en la historia de los hombres; commentario temático a la Constitución 'Dei Verbum' del Vaticano II 1965: = 'comentario 1969 actualizado', p. 18; omet. 244-265 F. G. *Martínez*; 700-723 J. P. *Richard*, traducciones; 724-751 F. *Pastor*, ahora J. M. *Sánchez Caro*, Escritura y teologia 607-620]. Bilbao 1991, Deusto/Mensajero. 702 p. 84-271-1676-4 [BL 92,93, R. *Hammer*]. – RGregorianum 72 (1991) 802 (J. *Wicks*: some bibliography omissions: de LA POTTERIE on Scripture in the Spirit in 4 languages).
287 **Alonso Schökel** Luis, coord.: [p. 155-222], *a*) Emaús y Manresa; Biblia y Ejercicios. R 1991, Centrum Ignatium Spiritualitatis. – *b*) Pregare con Ignazio; Bibbia ed Esercizi Spirituali: Bibbia e Preghiera 8. R 1991, Apost. Preghiera.
288 EAnderson Gary A., *Olyan* Saul M., Priesthood and cult in ancient Israel [8 invited papers, infra]: JStoT supp 125. Sheffield 1991, Academic. 217 p. £27.50; pa. £20. 1-85075-322-9.
290 EBassler Jouette M., Pauline theology, I. Thes Php Gal Phm. Mp 1991, Fortress. xiv-289 p. $30 [CBQ 54,201].
291 EBauckham Richard, *al.*, [(? deutsch) *Thiede* C. P.] Jesus 2000, die faszinierendste Gestalt der Geschichte; damals, heute, morgen [1989]T. Wu 1991 Brockhaus. 239 p. DM 50. RTR 87 (1991) 445 (H. *Giesen*: 30 Autoren aus 8 Ländern; 'eine konservative Linie, die nicht mit dem heutigen Forschungsstand übereinstimmt').
291* EBernal Restrepo Sergio, Teologia e dottrina sociale; il dialogo ecclesiale in un mondo che cambia [seminario interdisciplinare Pont. Univ. Gregoriana 1989s, 100º anniv. Rerum Novarum]. CasM 1991, Piemme. 100 p. Lit. 15.000. 88-384-1584-6. 5 art.; ➤ 8413.
292 EBianchi Enzo, *al.*, *a*) La libertà: ParSpV 23. Bo 1991, Dehoniane. 331 p. Lit. 17.000. 19 art., infra. – *b*) [At 6,7] 'La parola del Signore cresceva' [in sé, non solo nel numero degli accettanti]: ParSpV 24 (1991). 286 p. Lit. 17.000. 17 art., infra.
292* EBlack David A., *Dockery* David S., NT criticism and interpretation. GR 1991, Zondervan. 619 p. $18 pa. 0-310-51911-X [NTAbs 36,101].
293 *a*) **Bovon** François, *al.*, La fable apocryphe² [4-6 Esdras, Apocalypse de Pierre, Actes de Pilate/André...]: Le champ des apocryphes 2. Turnhout 1991, Brepols. 300 + 14 p.; 28 fig. [RB 99,590, tit. pp.; RHE 87,440, † L. *Leloir*].
— *b*) EBradshaw Paul F. [➤ 474], *Hoffman* Lawrence A., The changing face of Jewish and Christian worship in North America: Two Liturgical Traditions 2. ND 1991, Univ. xiii-271 p. 0-268-00784-5.
— *c*) EBurger C. W., *al.*, Riglyne vir prediking oor vrede: Woord teen die lig B-3 [Guidelines for preaching on peace: Word against (the background of) the light; 30 biblical passages]. Cape Town 1990, Kerk-U. 318 p. – RNeotestamentica 25 (1991) 446s (I. A. *Nell*).
— *d*) ECamps A., Oecumenische inleiding in de Missiologie; teksten en contexten van het wereldchristendom. Kampen 1990, Kok. 525 p. *f* 99 [NedTTs 44,346].
294 ECharlesworth James H., Jesus' Jewishness; exploring the place of Jesus within early Judaism [ten reprints]. Ph/NY 1991, Interfaith/Crossroad. 288 p. 23 fig. $25. 0-8245-1061-5 [RB 99, 763s, tit. pp.; TDig 39,67]. 3 infra.
295 EClines David J. A., *Eskenazi* Tamara C., Telling Queen Michal's story; an experiment in comparative interpretation: JStoT supp 119. Sheffield

1991, Academic. 301 p. £35; sb. £27.50. 1-85075-299-0 [OIAc 1 (1991) 14; excerpted]. 6 inedita, infra + 22 reprints.

295* ᴱCrockett W. V., *Sigountos* J. G., Through no fault of their own? The fate of those who have never heard. GR 1991, Baker. 278 p. $16 pa. 0-8010-2562-1. 21 art. [*Pinnock* C., Acts 4,12; *Bock* D., Acts 17,16-34; *Moo* D., Rom 2: < NTAbs 36,281].

296 ᴱCuldaut Francine, *al.*, À la naissance de la Parole chrétienne; tradition et écritures au deuxième siècle: CahÉv supp 77. P 1991, Cerf. 204 p. F 90. – ᴿEsprVie 101 (1991) 688 (E. *Cothenet*).

297 ᴱDesreumaux A., *Schmidt* F., Moïse géographe 1988 ⇒ 5,e823 [11 essays: Jubilees, EGERIA, INDICOPLEUSTES ...]: ᴿBL (1991) 108 (S. P. *Brock*).

298 ᴱDonfried Karl P., The Romans debate²ʳᵉᵛ [¹1977: adding 4 (Eng.) inedita and 24 p. introd.]. Peabody MA 1991, Hendrickson. lxxii-372 p. $20. 0-943575-42-7. [J *Fitzmyer*, J. *Murphy-O'Connor*, V. P. *Furnish*, K. *Stendahl* commend this availability of the major studies in a single volume].

299 ᴱDufft Gottfried, Gottes Weisungen; von der Gültigkeit der Zehn Gebote. Stu 1991, Quell. 96 p. DM 12,80 [JBL 110,567]. 10 art.

300 Escravidão e escravos na Bíblia / A mulher na Bíblia: EstudosB 18.20s. Petròpolis 1988s, Vozes. 72/80/8ç p. – ᴿBrotéria 132 (1991) 89 (F. *Pires Lopes*).

302 ᴱFlothkötter Hermann, *Nacke* Bernhard, Das Judentum — eine Wurzel des Christlichen; neue Perspektiven des Miteinander. Wü 1990, Echter. 224 p. DM 29. – ᴿZkT 113 (1991) 309s (R. *Oberforcher*).

303 Friedman Mordechai A., ⊕ Studies in Judaica: Teʻuda 7. TA 1991, Univ. Rosenberg School. xxv-449 p. + XXV Eng. summaries. 18 art.; 4 biblical infra [RB 99,758, tit. pp.; VT 42,564, Maria *Pollack*].

304 ᴱGranat Wincenty, *Kopeć* Edward, Jesus Chrystus — historia i tajemnica.² Lublin 1988, KUL. 619 p. – ᴿColcT 60,2 (1990) 191s (J. *Królikowski*).

305 ᴱGray Donald, The Word in season; essays by members of the Joint Liturgical Group on the use of the Bible in liturgy. Norwich 1988, Canterbury. 141 p. £6. – ᴿScotJT 44 (1991) 270s (D. J. *Kennedy*: calendaric differences unresolved).

305* ᴱGreenspahn Frederick E., Essential papers on Israel and the Ancient Near East: EssP JewishSt. NY 1991, NYU. xix-464 p. 0-8147-3037-X. 17 art., incl. *Malamat* A., Mari 153-75; *Fritz* V., Temple 116-128; *Weinfeld* M., Covenant 69-102; *Cazelles* H., Hebrews 269-293; *Greenberg* M., Criminal law 333-352; *Gwaltney* W. C., Lamentations 242-265; *Würthwein* E., Eg/OT Wisdom 129-149; *Moran* W., Love of God Dt 103-115; *Smith* M., theology 49-65; *Saggs* W. history 17-48; *Talmon* S., Comparative method 381-419.

ᴱGunn David M., Narrative and novella in Samuel ... GRESSMANN H. al. 1906/91 ⇒ 2462.

307 ᴱHartin P. J., *Petzer* J. H., Text and interpretation; new approches to the criticism of the NT [continuation of ᶠMETZGER B., South African perspective 1986 ⇒ 2,72]: NTToolsSt 15. Leiden 1991, Brill. viii-326 p. 90-04-094016-6 [TR 88,339 & CritRR 5,521: tit. pp.; NRT 114,740, X. *Jacques*; NT 34,402s, J. K. *Elliott*; NTAbs 36,102]. 16 art.; infra.

309 ᴱHundert G. D., Essential Papers on Hasidism; origins to present: EssP JewishSt NYU 1991. xi-546 p.; 2 maps. $75; pa. $31.50 [RHE 86,121*].

310 Janowski Bernd, *Welker* Michael, present. Altes Testament und Christlicher Glaube: JbBT 6. Neuk 1991, NV. x-372 p. 3-7887-1385-2. 18 art.; infra.

311 ᴱJobling David, *Moore* Stephen D., Poststructuralism as exegesis: Semeia 54. Atlanta 1991, Scholars. IX-255 p. 10 art., infra; p. 239-255, *Detweiler* D., 'Overliving'.

312 ᴱKloppenborg John S., [with *Vaage* L. p. 1-14], Early Christianity and Jesus: Semeia 55. Atlanta 1991, Scholars. viii-265 p. 8 art., infra [p. 213-223-235-243, responses, *Tuckett* C. M., *Attridge* H. W., *Crossan* J. D.].

313 ᴱKudasiewicz J., Biblia w nauczaniu chrześciańskim [... in Christian education]. Lublin 1991, KUL. 416 p. [AtKap 118,350].

314 ᴱLach Jan, Studia z biblistyki 6. Wsz 1991, Akad. Teol. Katolickiej. 318 p.

316 **Lentzen-Deis** Fritzleo [p. 13-45], *al.*, Jesús en la reflexión exegética y co-munitaria; la exégesis y la lectura de la Biblia en grupos: Evangelio y Cultura 1. Bogotá 1990, Paulinas. 184 p. 958-607-510-9. 3 *al.* art., infra.

317 ᴱLevine Amy-Jill, 'Women like this'; new perspectives on Jewish women in the Greco-Roman world: SBL Early Judaism 01. Atlanta 1991, Scholars. xvii-260 p. $25; sb/pa. $16. 1-55540-462-6; –3-4. [RB 99, 589 & TR 88,425 & CritRR 5,524: tit. pp.]. 11 art., infra.

319 **Maraval** P., présent., Figures du Nouveau Testament chez les Pères [= models; tandis que le Cah. 2, 1989 'Figures de l'AT' étaient des types]: CahBPatr 3. Strasbourg 1991, Centre Doc.Patr. 234 p. F 135. 2-906805-02-5. 11 art.

319* ᴱMartin Jochen, *Quint* Barbara, Christentum und antike Gesellschaft: WegFor 649. Da 1990, Wiss. vi-479 p. DM 89, sb. 69 [Gymnasium 99,56-58, M. *Wolter*; ZkT 114,226, R. *Oberforcher*].

320 ᴱMeinhold Arndt, *Lux* Rüdiger, Gottesvolk; Beiträge zu einem Thema biblischer Theologie. B 1991, Ev.-V. 248 p. DM 69. [NTAbs 36,284]. 14 art.

321 ᴱMüller Hans-Peter [p. 1-30; 114-155; 400-422], Babylonien und Israel; historische, religiöse und sprachliche Beziehungen: WegF 633. Da 1991, Wiss. vii-544 p.; Bibliog. 495ss (*Doherty* Timothy J. G.) DM 128. 3-534-09554-5. 18 art., infra (1 ineditum → 9640).

321* ᴱOchs Peter, Understanding the rabbinic mind; essays on the hermeneutic of Max KADUSHIN: SFlorida StHJud 14. Atlanta 1990, Scholars. xxvii-247 p. 1-55540-544-4.

322 ᴱOtto Eckart [p. 9-27; p. 63-87, Ethik], Bibel und Christentum im Orient; Studien zur Einführung der Reihe [:] Orientalia Biblica et Christiana 1. Glückstadt 1991, Augustin. 87 p. DM 48. 3-87030-150-3 [BL 92,21, M. A. *Knibb*]. → 9407.

323 ᴱPacomio Luciano (p. 5-16; p. 12, I. de *la Potterie* 'curatore del volume' → 1033*). L'esegesi cristiana oggi [6 saggi 1928-89]. CasM 1991, Piemme. 285 p. Lit. 40.000. 88-384-1638-9 [RivB 40,379, C. *Ghidelli*].

324 ᴱPorter Stanley E. [p. 11-38], The language of the New Testament; classic essays [DEISSMANN A., MOULTON J., TORREY C., BLACK M., FITZMYER J., *al.*]: JStNT supp. 60. Sheffield 1991, Academic. 238 p. £27.50; pa. £20. 1-85075-325-3 [RB 99,765, tit. pp.; TDig 69,272].

324* ᴱPrickett Stephen, Reading the text; biblical criticism and literary theory [6 inedita]. Ox 1991, Blackwell. vi-354 p. 0-631-16012-4.

325 *a)* **Quinzio** S. *al.* Israele e le genti [< RasT 1980-90]: RdT books 2. R 1991, AVE. 180 p. Lit. 18.000 [RB 99,454, tit. pp.]. 6 art.; 3 infra.

— *b)* ᴱRaffelt Albert, Begegnung mit Jesus? Was die historisch-kritische Methode leistet: Freiburger Akademieschriften 1. Dü 1991, Patmos. 86 p. DM 14,80 [TR 88,387, H. *Giesen*: teils gegen DREWERMANN].

— c) ᴱRapoport-Albert A, [9] Essays on Jewish historiography [= Hist-TheorBeih 27, 1988 + *Neusner* J., 2 items]. Atlanta 1991, Scholars. 190 p. $70. 1-55540-561-4 [NTAbs 36,302].

ᴱRestrepo Sergio B., Teologia e dottrina sociale 1989/91 → 291*.

326 ᴱReumann John, The promise and practice of biblical theology. Mp 1991, Fortress. x-214 p. 0-8006-2495-5 [RB 99,760, tit. pp.].

327* *Rossano* P., *al.*, Attualità della Lettera ai Romani: Guidati dallo Spirito 25. R 1989, AVE. 115 p. Lit. 13.000 pa. [NTAbs 36,124].

328 ᴱSchäfer G. K., *Strohm* T., Diakonie — biblische Grundlagen und Orientierungen. Heid 1990, Heid.-VA. 67-93, *Crüsemann* F., Das AT als Grundlage der Diakonie [ZAW 104,145].

329 ᴱScott Jamie, *Sampson-Housley* Paul, Sacred places and profane spaces; essays in the geographics of Judaism, Christianity, and Islam. NY 1991, Greenwood. 216 p. $43 [TDig 39,186].

330 ᴱSugirtharajah R. S., Voices from the margin; interpreting the Bible in the Third World. Mkn 1991, Orbis. ix-454 p. $20 pa. 0-88344-770-3 [CBQ 54,828s, Alice L. *Laffey*, tit. pp.; NTAbs 36,106].

332 ᴱWallis Gerhard, [cf. → 4,328] Erfüllung und Erwartung; Studien zur Prophetie auf dem Weg vom Alten zum Neuen Testament. B 1990, Ev.-VA. 180 p. DM 24.80. 6 art. [TR 87,524, tit. pp.; ZAW 104,445, H.-C. *Schmitt*].

333 a) ᴱWansbrough Henry, Jesus and the oral Gospel tradition [*Aune* D., *al.*]; 1989/91 → 460*b*.

— b) ᴱWarner Martin, The Bible as rhetoric; studies in biblical persuasion and credibility: Warwick Studies in Philosophy and Literature. L 1990, Routledge. x-236 p. 0-415-08617-8; pa. -4409-X. 11 art.

334 ᴱWiederkehr Dietrich, Wie geschieht Tradition? Überlieferung im Lebensprozess der Kirche: QDisp 133. FrB 1991, Herder. 176 p. – ᴿMiscFranc 91 (1991) 522s (J. *Imbach*).

334* ᴱYounger K. Lawsonᴶ, *Hallo* William W., *Batto* Bernard F., The biblical canon in comparative perspective: Scripture in Context 4. Lewiston NY 1991, Mellen. xv-328 p. 0-7734-9648-3 [RB 100,453, tit. pp.].

A1.4 *Plurium compilationes* theologicae.

335 ᴱAhlers Reinhild, *Krämer* Peter, Das Bleibende im Wandel; theologische Beiträge zum Schisma von Marcel LEFÈBVRE. Pd 1990, Bonifatius. 148 p. DM 24,80. – ᴿTLZ 116 (1991) 154s (H. *Kirchner*).

335* ᴱAman Kenneth, Border regions of faith; an anthology of religion and social change. Mkn 1987, Orbis. 528 p. – ᴿTGL 81 (1991) 130-3 (Kossi J. *Tossou*).

336 ᴱAnderson Gerald H., *al.*, Mission in the 1990s [17 reprints < IntBMissRes]. GR/NHv 1991, Eerdmans / Overseas Ministries Study Center. 80 p. $11. 0-8028-0542-6 [TDig 39,74].

337 ᴱAntón Angel, L'ecclesiologia del dopo-concilio; acquisizioni e problemi [4 art. ecclesiologia; 4 mariologia]: Teologia. R 1989 [TR 87,435, 'Angel A.' some tit. pp.].

338 a) ᴱBannach Klaus, *Rommel* Kurt, Religiöse Strömungen unserer Zeit; eine Einführung und Orientierung. Stu 1991, Quell. 202 p. DM 19,80. 35 art. [TLZ 117,260, J. *Sudbrack*].

— b) ᴱBecher J., Women, religion and sexuality; studies on impact of religious teaching on women [ONU/WCC depuis 1980]. Geneva 1990, WCC. xii-265 p. Fs 25 [NRT 114,451, A. *Harvengt*].

— c) EBecker Hansjakob, Gottesdienst, Kirche, Gesellschaft; interdisziplinäre und ökumenische Standortsbestimmungen nach 25 Jahren Liturgiereform: Pietas Liturgica 5. St. Ottilien 1991, EOS. xv-542 p.; ill. DM 98 [TR 88,175, tit. pp.]. 26 art.

339 EBeinert Wolfgang (p. 15-50), Nicht wie die Schriftgelehrten; Theologie — eine Chance für die Verkündigung [13-29, Ritt, Bibelauslegung in der pastoralen Praxis]. Rg 1990, Pustet. 150 p. DM 24,80. 3-451-02131-5. 2 other art. – RZkT 113 (1991) 355s (K. H. Neufeld).

340 a) EBerger Teresa, Gerhards Albert, Liturgie und Frauenfrage; ein Beitrag zur Frauenforschung aus Liturgiewissenschaftlicher Sicht: Pietas Liturgica 7. St. Ottilien 1990, EOS. ix-674 p. DM 68. [30 Aut. TR 88,140, B. Kranemann]. – RTGL 81 (1991) 413s (W. Beinert).

— b) EBernhardt Reinhold, Horizontüberschreitungen; die pluralistische Theologie der Religionen [Hick J., Ruether R. Smith W. C., Knitter P., al.]. Gü 1991, Mohn. 251 p. DM 278 [TR 88,258 tit. pp.]. 3-579-00276-7.

— c) EBertsch Ludwig, Was der Geist den Gemeinden sagt; Bausteine einer Ekklesiologie der Ostkirchen: Theologie der Dritten Welt 15. FrB 1991, Herder. 214 p. DM 38 pa. [TLZ 117,697].

— d) EBesier Gerhard, Wolf Stephan, Pfarrer, Christen und Katholiken; das Ministerium für Staatssicherheit der ehemaligen DDR und die Kirchen: Hist.T.St. 19/20.Jh. Neuk 1991, Neuk.-V. x-867 p. [TLZ 117,641].

— e) EBockenforde Ernst-Wolfgang, Shils Edward. Jews and Christians in a pluralistic world. L 1991, Weidenfeld. xv-191 p. £25 [TR 88,347].

341 a) EBørresen Kari E., Image of God and gender models in Judaeo-Christian tradition. Oslo 1991, Solum [US Humanities Int.]. 281 p. $40. 82-560-0741-9 [TDig 39,268].

— b) EBrauer Jerald C., The lively experiment [MEAD S. E., 1963 ➤ 5,133] continued. Macon GA 1988, Mercer Univ. 250 p. $19. 0-86554-290-2. – RRExp 88 (1991) 279s (B. J. Leonard).

— c) EBrown David, NEWMAN, a man for our time. L 1990, SPCK. 168 p. £6 [Studies 80/91,88].

— d) EByrne Lavinia, The hidden tradition; women's spiritual writings rediscovered. L 1991, SPCK. 198 p. £13. 0-281-04519-4 [ScotJT 44,549].

342 ECameron Nigel, The power and weakness of God: ScotBEvT special. 4. ... Rutherford. 140 p. £8 pa [Int 45,109, sans date].

342* EChampion F., Hervieu-Léger D., De l'émotion en religion; renouveaux et traditions. P 1990, Centurion. 253 p. F 125 [NRT 114,286, J. Scheuer].

343 a) EChirban John T., Health and faith; medical, psychological and religious dimensions. Lanham MD 1991, UPA. vi-145 p. $34.50; pa. $17.50 [CBQ 54,401].

— b) ECleary Edward L., Born of the poor [... CELAM Medellin 1968, Pueblo 1979]. ND 1990, Univ. 210 p. $24. – RMissiology 19 (1991) 355 (J. C. Anderson).

— c) ECoffele Gianfranco, Tonelli Riccardo, Verso una spiritualità laicale e giovanile. R 1989, LAS. 302 p. Lit. 30.000. – RAngelicum 68 (1991) 556s (R. D'Andrea).

345 ECohen Jeremy, Essential papers on Judaism and Christianity in conflict, from late antiquity to the Reformation. NYU 1991. 578-xiv p. – [CritRR 5,516, tit. pp.; RHE 87,156-8, Bat-Sheva Albert].

345* *a*) ^E**Cohn-Sherbok** Dan, The sayings of Moses; – *b*) ^E**Linzey** Andrew, ... of Jesus → 3611; – *c*) ^E**Parrinder** Geoffrey, ... of the Buddha; – *d*) ^E**Robinson** Neal, ... of Muhammad. L 1991, Duckworth. £5 each. – ^RTablet 245 (1991) 1285 (N. *Braybrooke*).

346 Communio (ital. ^E**Guerriero** E., Mi 1991, Jaca): **115.** La vita eterna; – **116.** L'unità nella Chiesa universale; il ministero del Papa; – **117.** Cento anni dalla Rerum Novarum; nuove frontiere della questione sociale; – **118.** Il peccato originale; – **119.** Beati gli afflitti; – **120.** 'Solo l'amore è credibile'; H.U. v. BALTHASAR, una teología dagli spazi illimitati. c. 130 p., Lit. 18.000 ciascuno. > franç.; Eng. (ND); IkaZ deutsch.

347 Concilium (English now L,SCM and Ph, Trinity) 1991: **1.** ^E*Beuken* Wim, *al.*, The Bible and its readers; **2.** ^E*Collins* Mary, *Power* David N., The pastoral care of the sick; – **3.** ^E*Cahill* Lisa S., *Mieth* D., Aging; – **4.** ^E*Metz* J. B., *Schillebeeckx* E., No heaven without earth [ecology]; – **5.** ^E*Coleman* J., *Baum* G., Rerum novarum, 100 years of Catholic social teaching; – **6.** ^E*Carr* Anne, *Schüssler Fiorenza* Elisabeth, The special nature of women? – c. 124 p. each. 0010-5236.

348 Concilium 1991: éd. française, P.-Beauchesne: **233.** La Bible et ses lecteurs, ^E*Beuken* W., *al.*; – **234.** Le service pastoral des malades, ^E*Collins* Mary, *Power* David; – **235.** Le grand âge [vieillesse], ^E*Cahill* Lisa S., *Mieth* D.; – **236.** Pas de ciel sans la terre; théologie et écologie, ^E*Metz* J. B., *Schillebeeckx* É.; – **237.** Cent ans d'enseignement social catholique, ^E*Coleman* J., *Baum* G.; – **238.** La femme a-t-elle une nature spéciale?; ^E*Carr* A., *Schüssler Fiorenza* E. c. 160 p. F 70 chaque. Éditions semblables español etc.; deutsch = IZT.

348* ^E**Coon** Lynda L., *al.*, That gentle strength; historical perspectives on women in Christianity. Charlottesville 1990, Univ. Virginia. 267 p. $35; pa. $15. 13 art. [RelStR 18,333, D. A. *Johnson*: very fine].

349 *a*) ^E**Coreth** Emerich, *al.*, Christliche Philosophie im katholischen Denken des 19. und 20. Jahrhunderts, 1. Neue Ansätze im 19. Jh.; 2. Ruckgriff auf scholastisches Erbe; 3. Moderne Strömungen im 20. Jh. Graz 1987-88-90, Styria. 799 p.; 870 p.; 919 p. Sch 770+980+980 [TR 88,70, H. *Verweyen*].

— *b*) ^E**Curran** Charles E., *McCormick* Richard A., Natural law and theology: Readings in moral theology 7. NY 1991, Paulist. vi-465 p. $15. 0-8091-3179-X [TDig 39,277]. 18 reprints.

350 *a*) ^E**Dierkens** Alain, Apparitions et miracles [... valoriser la spécificité des créations artistiques et des phénomènes dits mystiques]: ProbHistRel 2. Bru 1991, Univ. 192 p. Fb 795 [RHE 87,438, J. *Daoust*: érudit, plein d'intérêt].

— *b*) ^E**Doré** J., Introduction à l'étude de la théologie I: Le Christianisme et la foi chrétienne. P 1991, Desclée. 662 p. F 289 [NRT 114,897, R. *Escol*: premier des trois tomes à compléter le Manuel en dix volumes].

— *c*) ^E**Ebenbauer** Alfred, *al.*, Die Juden in ihrer mittelalterlichen Umwelt. W 1991, Böhlau. 320 p.; ill. DM 68 [TR 88,253].

351 *a*) ^E**Engel** Lothar, *Werner* Dietrich, Ökumenische Perspektiven theologischer Ausbildung: ÖkRu Beih 60. Fra 1990, Lembeck. 231 p. DM 28. – ^RTLZ 116 (1991) 948s (H. *Krüger*).

— *b*) Epistēmonikē parousía Hestías theológōn Chálkēs ⊕ ... scholarly presence of the Chalkis theological Hestía (in Athens), 2. Athenai 1991. 520 p. – ^RTAth 62 (1991) 901s (E. A. *Theodorou* ⊕).

— *c*) Essais de théologie pratique; l'institution et le transmettre; UER: PoinT 49. P 1988, Beauchesne. 210 p. – ^RScEsp 43 (1991) 130s (G. *Raymond*:

LAFON P., créativité et invention risquée pour accéder à l'Écriture; BEAUCHAMP P., 'Livre institué').

352 ᴱ**Feldman** Emanuel, *Wolowelsky* Joel B., The conversion crisis; essays from the pages of tradition [on conversions to Judaism, including one essay by Abraham *Carmel* † 1982, the first Roman Catholic priest in 1000 years to convert to Judaism]. Brooklyn 1990; KTAV. 105 p. $9. 0-88125-334-0. – ᴿExpTim 103 (1991s) 88 (C. *Middleburgh*: rigid Orthodox; and except for M. *Angel*, contemptuous of Progressive Judaism).

353 ᴱ**Fornet-Betancourt** Raul, Verhindert der Glaube die Wirtschaft? Theologie und Ökonomie in Lateinamerika: Theologie der Dritten Welt 16. FrB 1991, Herder. 189 p. DM 32 pa. [TR 88,327, J. *Wiemeyer*].

353* **Forrester** Duncan B., Theology and practice. 1990, Epworth. 130 p. £6,50 pa. – ᴿTLond 94 (1991) 148s (J. *Woodward*: competent but unexciting essays).

354 ᴱ**Gerardi** Renzo, La creazione, Dio, il cosmo, l'uomo. R 1990, Studium. 270 p. Lit. 18.000. – ᴿProtestantesimo 46 (1991) 328s (P. *Ribet*).

355 ᴱ**Glaz** Maxine, *Stevenson* Jeanne, Women in travail and transition; a new pastoral care. Mp 1991, Fortress. 225 p. 0-8006-2420-3 [ScotJT 44,552].

356 ᴱ**Graf** Friedrich W., Profile des neuzeitlichen Protestantismus, 1. Aufklärung — Idealismus – Vormärz: Siebenstern 1430. Gü 1990, Mohn. 329 p. DM 39,80. 3-579-01430-7 [TLZ 117,368s, M. *Greschat*]. – ᴿTsT-Nijm 31 (1991) 102s (N. *Schreurs*: STORR, PAULUS, DAUB, NITZSCH ...; niet BAUR, STRAUSS).

Grudem Wayne, sometimes given as first editor, ➤ 375, ᴱ**Piper** J.

357 ᴱ**Guerrière** Daniel, Phenomenology of the truth proper to religion [... HEIDEGGER, RICOEUR, DERRIDA ...]. Albany 1990, SUNY. vii-324 p. $59,50: pa. $20 [RelStR 18,218, R. B. *Williams*].

357* *Hänggi* Anton, al., [ᴱ**Schlemmer** Karl, Tagung Passau Okt. 1990], Gemeinsame Liturgie in getrennten Kirchen?: QDisp 132. FrB 1991, Herder. 136 p.

358 a) ᴱ**Hastings** Adrian, Modern Catholicism; Vatican II and after. L/NY 1991, SPCK/Oxford-UP. 473 p. $30. /0-19-520657-6 [TDig 38,370]. – ᴿEstE 66 (1991) 252s (M. *Alcalá*); Month 252 (1991) 339s (P. *McPartlan*); NBlackf 72 (1991) 352-4 (A. *Kee*).

— b) ᴱ**Heimbrock** Hans-Günter, *Boudewijnse* H. Barbara, Current studies on rituals; perspectives for the psychology of religion: IntPsyR 2. Amst 1990, Rodopi. 197 p. *f* 60. 11 Dutch and 5 other authors [TLZ 117,698, N.-P. *Moritzen*].

— c) ᴱ**Herms** Eilert, Gesellschaft gestalten [16 reprints 1979-91]; Beiträge zur evangelischen Sozialtethik. Tü 1991, Mohr. 408 p. DM 59 pa. [TLZ 117,721-8, M. *Honecker*].

— d) ᴱ**Hillenbrand** Karl, Priester heute; Anfragen, Aufgaben, Anregungen [DREWERMANN E.]. Wü 1990, Echter. 256 p. DM 29 [TR 88,237, H. *Werners*].

359 a) ᴱ**Holloway** Richard [Anglican bishop of Edinburgh], Who needs feminism? L 1991, SPCK. £8. – ᴿTablet 245 (1991) 1055 (Monica *Furlong*: a new and potent phase in the defense of feminism, notably P. SHELDRAKE's recollections of 'power over and fear of' women in his Jesuit training).

— b) ᴱ**Hünermann** Peter, *Mieth* Dietmar, Streitgespräch über Theologie und Lehramt; die Instruktion über die kirchliche Berufung der Theologen in der Diskussion. Fra 1991, Knecht. 243 p. DM 26. 3-7820-0624-0 [TsTNijm 32,303, W. *Logister*]. – ᴿTGL 81 (1991) 495s (W. *Beinert*: RATZINGER und KASPER erlaubten nicht den Abdruck ihrer Erklärungen).

— c) ᴱJost R., *Kubera* U., Befreiung hat viele Farben. Gü c. 1991, Mohn.
— d) ᴱKeeble N. H., John BUNYAN; conventicle and Parnassus, tercentenary essays. Ox 1988, Clarendon. x-278 p. £30. – ᴿEvQ 63 (1991) 363s (A. G. *Newell*).
— e) ᴱKer I., *Hill* Alan G., Newman after 100 years [22 art.]. Ox 1990, Clarendon. xvi-470 p. [NRT 114,932, P. *Evrard*]. 0-19-012891-6.
360 ᴱKlos Frank W. *al.*, Lutherans and the challenge of religious pluralism. Mp 1990, Augsburg. viii-197 p. [RelStR 18,131, Peggy *Starkey*].
360* ᴱKochanek Hermann, Die verdrängte Freiheit; Fundamentalismus in den Kirchen. FrB 1991, Herder. 280 p. DM 39 pa. [NRT 114,623, A. *Toubeau*]. – ᴿTGL 81 (1991) 484s (W. *Beinert*).
361 **Kranenbourg** Reender, *Verburch* Hugo S., *al.*, Reincarnatie — een veelzijdig perspectief? Kampen 1988, Kok Agora. 190 p. ƒ 24,75. ᴿBijdragen 52 (1991) 109s (W. G. *Tillmans*).
362 ᴱKselman Thomas, Belief in history; innovative approaches to European and American religion. ND 1991, Univ. x-309 p. $36. [Horizons 19,137, Maureen A. *Tilley*; CathHR 78,260, J. *Hennesey*].
363 a) ᴱLangevin Gilles, *Pirro* Raphaël, Le Christ et les cultures dans le monde et dans l'histoire [interviews Radio-Canada 3]. Montréal 1991, Bellarmin. 400 p. – ᴿScEsp 43 (1991) 217-225 (R. *Latourelle*: 'à propos de l'inculturation').
— b) ᴱLeonard Bill J., Becoming Christian; dimensions of spiritual formation. Louisville 1990, Westminster/Knox. 213 p. $16. 0-664-25119-6. – ᴿRExp 88,2 (1991) 220s (C. *Davis*: laudable Louisville Baptist faculty collaboration).
— c) ᴱLoth Wilfried, Deutscher Katholizismus im Umbruch zur Moderne: Konfession und Gesellschaft 3. Stu 1991, Kohlhammer. 284 p. DM 44 [TR 88,431, tit. pp.].
364 ᴱMackey James P., An introduction to Celtic Christianity [including PELAGIUS by M. F. *Nicholson*]. E 1989, Clark. 440 p. $35 [RelStR 18,143, S. *Duffy*].
364* ᴱMcManners John, The Oxford illustrated history of Christianity [19 authors]. Ox 1990, UP. xi-724 p.; 318 fig + 32 colour. – ᴿChrCent 108 (1981) 336s (R. T. *Handy*); TLond 94 (1991) 227s (M. *Morrill*: high class; one-fourth devoted to outside-Europe since 1800).
365 ᴱMaduro Otto, Judaism, Christianity, and liberation; an agenda for dialogue [ten answers to his two questions]. Mkn 1991, Orbis. viii-152 p. $15. 0-88344-693-6 [Horizons 19,339s, D. M. *Bossman*; TDig 39,68].
366 ᴱMarshall Sherrin, Women in Reformation and Counter-Reformation Europe; private and public worlds. Bloomington 1989, Indiana Univ. 215 p. [RelStR 18,66, J. L. *Farthing*: good].
367 ᴱMay Melanie A., Women and Church; the challenge of ecumenical solidarity in an age of alienation: NCC Faith & Order. GR/NY 1991, Eerdmans/Friendship. xxiii-197 p. $11. 0-8028-0552-3 / NY 0-337-00235-6 [TDig 38,390; RelStR 18,220, P. C. *Phan*].
367* ᴱMeynell Hugo A., Grace, politics and desire; essays on AUGUSTINE. Calgary 1990, Univ. x-193 p. $20. 11 art., 5 infra. [TR 88,253, tit. pp.].
368 ᴱMoll Helmut, The Church and women, a compendium. SF 1988, Ignatius. 273 p. – ᴿAnnTh 4 (1990) 217-221 (E. *Juliá*).
369 ᴱMoyser George, Politics and religion in the modern world. NY 1991, Routledge. 294 p. $50 [JAAR 59,883].

370 ᴱMüller Karl, Ist Christus der einzige Weg zum Heil?: Miss.Pr.Sem. Bonn- S.Augustin 40. Nettetal 1991, Steyler. 199 p. DM 38; – p. 67-88, biblische Sicht, *Hahn* Viktor [TR 87,344, tit. pp.].

371 ᴱMulvey Michael, Priests of the future; formation and communionᵀ. NY 1991, New City. 123 p. $8 [CBQ 53,536].

371* ᴱNicholls David, *Kerr* Fergus, J. H. NEWMAN; reason, rhetoric and romanticism. Bristol 1991, Classic. 257 p. £25 [TR 88,79].

372 ᴱNicolin Friedhelm, *Pöggeler* Otto, Hegel-Studien [5 aus den 7 über Religionsphilosophie] Band 24. Bonn 1989, Bouvier. 343 p. DM 98 pa. ᴿZkT 113 (1991) 453-5 (W. *Kern*).

373 ᴱNiewiadomski Josef, Verweigerte Mündigkeit? Politische Kultur und die Kirche: Theol. Trends 2, Thaur 1989, Giesriegel. 220 p. Fs 26,20. 3-85395-131-7.

375 ᴱPiper John, *Grudem* Wayne, Recovering biblical manhood and womanhood; a response to evangelical feminism. Wheaton IL 1991, Crossway. xxviii-29 + 566 p. 0-89107-586-0. 26 art., 16 infra. [JBL 110,567, ᴱGrudem]. – ᴿTrinJ 12 (1991) 221-4 (W. L. *Kynes*).

376 *a*) ᴱRauch Albert, *Imhof* Paul, Das Dienstamt der Einheit in der Kirche; Primat, Patriarchat, Papsttum: Koinonia 9. St. Ottilien 1991, EOS. 505 p. DM 38 [TR 88,435, some tit. pp.].

— *b*) ᴱRichardson James T., *al.*, The Satanism scare: Social Institutions and Social Change. NY 1991, Aldine de Gruyter [a division of Walter de Gruyter]. vi-320 p. DM 98; pa. DM 49. 0-202-30378-0; –9-9 [TDig 39,285].

— *c*) ᴱRichter Klemens, Eheschliessung — mehr als ein rechtlich Ding?: QDisp 120. FrB 1989, Herder. 180 p. 3-451-02120-X. 11 art.

— *d*) ᴱRichter Klemens, Das Konzil war erst der Anfang; die Bedeutung des II. Vatikanums für Theologie und Kirche. Mainz 1991, Grünewald. 245 p. – ᴿNatGrac 38 (1991) 405 (A. *Villalmonte*).

377 *a*) ᴱRobertson Roland, *Garrett* William R., Religion and global order: Religion and the Political Order 4. NY 1991, Paragon. 322 p. $30 [JAAR 59,884].

— *b*) ᴱRoest Crollius Arij A., Effective inculturation and ethnic identity: Inculturation 9. R 1991, Pont. Univ. Gregoriana. xi-127 p. Lit. 20.000.

— *c*) ᴱRosenblatt Marie-Eloise, Where can we find her? Searching for women's identity in the new Church. NY 1991, Paulist. iv-166 p. $13 [Horizons 19,330, Mary A. *O'Neill*].

378 ᴱRothschild Fritz A., Jewish perspectives on Christianity. NY 1990, Crossroad. x-363 p. $30 [Horizons 19,175, Susannah *Heschel*].

379 ᴱSchüssler Fiorenza Francis, *Galvin* John P., Systematic Theology; Roman Catholic perspectives. Mp 1991, Fortress. xv-336 p.; xv-384 p. $22 each, $40 both [Horizons 19,109]. – ᴿExpTim 103 (1991s) 249s (R. *Butterworth*: separate essays by a strong scholarly team on the Catholic rethinking called for by Vatican II).

380 Séminaires et esprit missionnaire: Bulletin de Saint-Sulpice 17. P 1991. 364 p.; 25 auteurs [NRT 114,470].

381 ᴱSheridan E. F. The social teaching of the Canadian Catholic bishops, I. Do justice; 2. Love kindness. Sherbrook / Toronto 1987/1991, Paulines/ Jesuit Centre for Social Faith & Justice. 470 p.; 560 p. $18 + 20. 2-89039-113-2; -469-7 [TDig 39,58].

382 ᴱSoskice Janet M., After Eve; women, theology and the Christian tradition. L 1990, Collins/Pickering. £6 pa. 0-551-02039-3. 10 inedita. ᴿMonth 252 (1991) 434 (P. *Gallagher*, chiefly on P. FIDDES on BARTH); NBlackf 72 (1991) 455s (R. *Woods*).

383 ᴱStaudinger Hugo, (*Schlüter* Johannes), Die Glaubwürdigkeit der Offenbarung und die Krise der modernen Welt; Überlegungen zu einer trinitarischen Metaphysik [18 Autoren]: Pd Deutsches Institut für Bildung und Wissen. Stu 1987, Burg. 268 p. – ᴿZkT 113 (1991) 99s (E. *Coreth*).

383* ᴱStrahm Doris, *Strobel* Regula, Vom Verlangen nach Heilwerden; Christologie in feministisch-theologischer Sicht. Fr 1991, Exodus. 240 p. DM 32,30. 13 art. [TR 88,347 tit. pp.] 5 infra.

384 ᴱSykes Stephen W. (bp.). Sacrifice and redemption; Durham essays in theology. C 1991, Univ. xi-339 p. £35. 0-521-34033-0. 17 art.; infra [BL 92,113, R. J. *Coggins*].

384* ᴱTennis H. B., *al.*, Kerstening van christenen; de verhouding van geestelijken en leken in de hoge middeleeuwen. Amst 1991, Rodopi. 163 p. *f* 39,50 [TR 88,78].

385 *a*) ᴱTrompf G. W., Cargo cults and millenarian movements; transoceanic comparisons of new religious movements. B/NY 1990, M. de Gruyter. xvii-456 p. DM 168 [RelStR 18,37, D. *Owen*: 10 art., mostly Australian, often fascinating].

— *b*) ᴱViladesau Richard, *Mass* Mark S., Foundations of theological study; a sourcebook [67 brief selections from classic or outstanding authors, in six categories]. NY 1991, Paulist. xxi-319 p. $15 pa. 0-8091-3381-8 [TDig 39,292].

— *c*) ᴱWacker Marie-Theres, *Zenger* Erich, Der eine Gott und die Göttin; Gottesvorstellungen des biblischen Israel im Horizont feministischer Theologie: QDisp 135. FrB 1991, Herder. 192 p. 3-451-02135-8. 7 art.

386 *a*) ᴱWegener H., *al.*, Frauen fordern eine gerechte Sprache: Siebenstern 484. Gü 1990, Mohn. 160 p. DM 24,80. 3-579-00484-0. – ᴿTsTNijm 31 (1991) 438 (C. *Halkes*: PRAETORIUS L., 'Der kleine Unterschied zwischen Mutter und Retorte').

— *b*) ᴱWilliams Oliver F., *al.*, The making of an economic vision; JOHN PAUL II's 'On social concern'. Lanham MD 1991, UPA. xvi-378 p.; $57.75. [TR 88,349, tit. pp.].

387 ᴱWohlmuth Josef, Katholische Theologie heute; eine Einführung in das Studium. Wü 1990, Echter. 378 p. DM 29. 3-429-01284-8. – ᴿCarthaginensia 7 (1991) 520 (J. *García H.*); TLZ 116 (1991) 262s (Roija *Weidhas*).

387* ᴱZillesse Dietrich, Praktisch-theologische Hermeneutik; Ansätze, Anregungen, Aufgaben [... SCHLEIERMACHER, RICOEUR]. Rheinbach-Merzbach 1991, CMZ. xiv-574 p. DM 38 [TR 88,436, many tit. pp.].

A1.5 *Plurium compilationes* **philologicae** *vel* **archaeologicae.**

388 ᴱAssmann Aleida, Weisheit: Archäologie der literarischen Kommunikation 3. Mü 1991, Fink. 571 p. 3-7705-2655-5. 39 art.; 5 infra.

388* ᴱBinder G., Kunst und Bildersprache: Saeculum Augustum 3. [2. 1988 ⇸ 6,473]: WegFo 632. Da 1991, Wiss. 431 p.; 56 pl. 3-534-08949-9.

389 ᴱClassen Carl J., Die klassische Altertumswissenschaft an der Georg-August-Universität Göttingen, eine Ringvorlesung zu ihrer Geschichte: Gö Univ-Schr A-14. Gö 1989, Vandenhoeck & R. 248 p. 36 fig. DM 52. 3-525-35845-8. – ᴿJRS 81 (1991) 250s (T. *Wiedemann*).

390 ᴱConkey Margaret W., *Hastorf* Christine A., The uses of style in archaeology: New Directions in Archaeology. C 1990, Univ. ix-124 p.

392 ᴱFaraone Christopher A., *Obbink* Dirk, Magika hiera; Ancient Greek magic and religion. NY 1991. Oxford-UP. xiii-298 p. 0-19-504450-9. 10 art.; 3 infra.

393 ^E**Frielingsdorf** Karl, *Kehl* Medard, Ganz und heil; unterschiedliche Wege zur 'Selbstverwirklichung'. Wü 1990, Echter, 228 p.; 10 fig. DM 29. – ^RTR 87 (1991) 500-2 (K. *Thomas*: New Age, ROGERS, JUNG, FRANKL ...).

394 ^E**Gero** Joan M., *Conkey* Margaret W., Engendering archaeology; women and prehistory: Social Archaeology. Ox 1991, Blackwell. xiii-418 p. 0-631-16505-3 [OIAc F91,9 with titles sans pp. of the 15 art.]: *Spector* Janet D., What this awl means; *Gero/Wright* R., Women's roles in stone tool / pottery production ...

395 ^E**Giardina** A., L'uomo romano. Bari 1989, Laterza. xix-417 p. – ^RArcheo 65 (1990) 128s (S. *Moscati*); Faventia 12s (1990s) 472-7 (J. *Gómez Pallarès*).

396 ^E**Griffin** M., *Barnes* H., Philosophia togata; essays on philosophy and Roman society. Ox 1989, Clarendon. viii-302 p. £30. 0-19-814884-4. – ^RJRS 81 (1991) 177s (Catherine *Osborne*).

397 ^E**Grousset** René, *al.*, L'âme de l'Iran. P 1990, A. Michel. 268 p. F 98. – ^RÉtudes 347 (1991) 284 (H. *Loucel*).

398 ^E**Guilaine** J., Pour une archéologie agraire; à la croisée des sciences de l'homme et de la nature. P 1991, A. Colin. 576 p.; 176 pl. + 24 color. F 470. ➤ e511.

399 ^E**Helleman** Wendy E., [p. 11-30; 31-51 on *Basil*] Christianity and the classics; the acceptance of a heritage: Christian Studies Today. Lanham MD 1990, UPA. 219 p. $17.75. 9 other art. [TR 87,526, tit. pp.].

400 **Lamb** Sydney M., *Mitchell* E. Douglas, Sprung from some common source; investigations into the prehistory of languages. Stanford 1991, Univ. xii-411 p. 0-8047-1897-0 [OIAc 1,19, sans excerpts].

400* **Le Roy Ladurie** Emmanuel, *al.*, Pharaonen-Dämmerung; Wiedergeburt des Alten Ägypten. Strasbourg 1990, DNA. 240 p. 2-7165-0259-5 [OIAc 2,22, excerpted].

401 ^E**McIntyre** C. T., *Perry* M., TOYNBEE; reappraisals. Toronto 1989, Univ. viii-254 p. – ^RSR 20 (1991) 250s (E. J. *Furcha*: no indication of whether it was a meeting).

401* ^E**Marschall** Wolfgang, Klassiker der Kulturanthropologie, von MONTAIGNE bis Margaret MEAD. Mü 1990, Beck. 379 p.; 17 fig. DM 58 [TLZ 117,624, C. *Frey*].

402 ^E**Mikasa** Takahito, prince, & *Omura* Sachihiro, Essays on Ancient Anatolian and Syrian studies in the 2d and 1st millennium B.C.: BME Culture Center in Japan 4. Wsb 1991, Harrassowitz. vii-212 p. 3-447-03138-7. Japan Keban Dam salvage project, Kaman-Kalehöyük p. 62-86, *Mikami* Tsugio & Omura; + 8 art. [OLZ 87,150, H. *Klengel*]. – ^RJNES 50 (1991) 76 (G. *Beckman*: KAMMENHUBER on horse-training ignores Marburg school, OTTEN, CARRUBA, NEU).

404 ^E**Pinsky** Valerie, *Wylie* Alison, Critical traditions in contemporary archaeology; essays in the philosophy, history, and socio-politics of archaeology: New directions in archaeology. C 1990, Univ. ix-160 p.; ill. £27.50. 0-521-32109-3. – ^RBInstArch 27 (1990) 236s (M. *Patton*).

405 ^E**Pomeroy** Sarah B., Women's history and ancient history. Chapel Hill 1991, Univ. N. Carolina. ix-317 p. 0-8078-4310-5 [OIAc 1,22; excerpted].

406 ^E**Raffaelli** Renato, Rappresentazioni della morte [5 art.; *Mainoldi* Carla, Sonno e morte in Grecia antica ... frères inséparables]. Urbino 1987, Quattroventi. 255 p.; 8 pl. – ^RRÉG 104 (1991) 608s (Hélène *Cassimatis*).

407 ^E**Rast** Walter E. (*Zeiger* Marion), Preliminary reports of ASOR sponsored excavations [1990 ➤ 6,500], 1982-89: BASOR supp. 27. Baltimore 1991, Johns Hopkins Univ. vi-154 p.; maps. 6 art., infra.

407* ᴱReardon B. P. [19] Collected ancient Greek novels. Berkeley 1989, Univ. California. viii-837 p. $75; pa. $25 [SecC 9,119, R. I. *Pervo*].

408 **Schiffer** Michael B., Archaeological Method and Theory [continuation of 'Advances in ...' 1978-87]. Tucson 1989, Univ. Arizona. 285 p.; 17 fig. $35. ISSN 1043-1691. – ᴿJField 18 (1991) 523-6 (T. G. *Baugh*: K. KVAMME best).

408* ᴱSinor Denis, The Cambridge History of Early Inner Asia. C 1990, Univ. x-518 p. [OLZ 87,117].

409 ᴱSordi Marta, L'impero romano-cristiano; problemi politici, religiosi, culturali: Cultura e attualità 3. R 1991, Coletti. 216 p. – ᴿVetChr 28 (1991) 216 (D. *Lassandro*).

409* ᴱTraugott Elizabeth C., *Heine* Bernd, Approaches to grammaticalization [I. ...] 2: Typological Studies in Language 19.2. Amst/Ph 1991, Benjamins. → 9058.

410 ᴱVian Paolo, Speculum Mundi; Roma centro internazionale di ricerche umanistiche; Unione int. degli Istituti di Archeologia, Storia e Storia dell'Arte in Rome, intr. *Pallottino* Massimo. R 1991, Presidenza del Consiglio, Dip. Informazione. 937 p.; ill.

410* ᴱWiehn Erhard R., Juden in der Soziologie; eine öffentliche Vortragsreihe, Univ. Konstanz 1989, Hartung-G. 351 p. – ᴿZRGg 43 (1991) 282s (A. *Silbermann*).

411 ᴱWodak Ruth, Language, power and ideology; studies in political discourse: Critical theory; interdisciplinary approaches to language, discourse and ideology 7. Amst/Ph 1989, Benjamins. xx-388 p. – ᴿRBgPg 69 (1991) 651-5. (J. *Reighard*).

A2 **Acta** *congressuum* .1 **biblica** [*Notitiae*, reports → Y7.2].

412 ᴱAlexander Loveday, [p. 11-18] Images of empire [biblical colloquium, Sheffield March 1990]: JStOT supp 122. Sheffield 1991, Academic. 316 p. £35; pa. £26, 1-85075-312-1 [CBQ 55,191, D. J. *Harrington*, tit. pp.; GreeceR 39,241, T. *Wiedemann* & 249, P. *Walcot*]. 13 art.; infra.

413 L'Apocalyptique [session de rentrée 1990]: Travaux et Conférences du Centre Sèvres 23. P 1991, Média-Sèvres. 217 p. [Masses Ouvrières 445, 102, J.-M. *Carrière*].

414 ᴱAssaf David, Proceedings of the Tenth World Congress of Jewish Studies, Aug. 18-24, 1989: B. History of the Jewish People [→ 6,508]; C. Jewish Thought; D. Jewish languages. J 1990, World Union. – ᴿJStJud 22 (1991) 185-18 (M. *Mach*); OTAbs 14 (1991) 345-7 (C. T. *Begg*: vol. A → 6,507: tit. pp. in English).

415 *a*) ᴱBaarda T. *al.*, Jodendom en vroeg christendom; continuiteit en discontinuiteit: StNTConventus. Kampen 1991, Kok. 191 p. *f*47. 90-242-3058-6 [CritRR 5,515, tit. pp.]. – ᴿJStJud 22 (1991) 254s (A. S. van der *Woude*).

— *b*) ᴱBackus Irena, [Colloque 1988 → 4,470]: Studies in Medieval and Reformation Thought 40. Leiden 1988, Brill. lxxxv-619 p. *f*216. – ᴿJTS 42 (1991) 766-8 (D. F. *Wright*).

— *c*) ᴱBackus Irena, *Higman* F., Théorie et pratique de l'exégèse. Genève 1990 → 6,511 [JTS 42,768; K. *Hagen* on commentaries].

— *d*) ᴱBalch David L., The social history of the Matthean community [in Roman Syria, SMU Oct. 1989]; cross-disciplinary approaches. Mp 1991, Augsburg-Fortress. xxiii-286 p. 0-8006-2445-9 [RB 99, 765, tit. pp.].

416 **Ballis** Giovanni coord., Il mondo dell'uomo nascosto; le beatitudini [conferenze Roma s. R. Bellarmino 1990s]: Le Spighe. R 1991, Borla. 167 p. Lit. 18.000. 88-263-0894-2. 9 art., infra.

416* ᴱ**Bassler** Jouette M., Pauline theology, I. Thessalonians, Philippians, Galatians, Philemon [SBL consultation 1986-8; 19 contributors, incl. P. *Achtemeier*, J. L. *Martyn*, J. D. G. *Dunn*, Pheme *Perkins*]. Mp 1991, Fortress. xiv-289 p. $30. 0-8006-2488-2 [TDig 39,181].

417 ᴱ**Beutler** Johannes, *Fortna* Robert T., The shepherd discourse of John 10 and its context [SNTS meetings, Trondheim 1985, Atlanta 1986]: SNTS mg 67. C 1991, Univ. x-173 p. $34.50. 0-521-39211-X [TDig 39,83]. – ᴿExpTim 103 (1991s) 25 (S. S. *Smalley*); TR 87 (1991) 283s (B. *Kowalski*).

418 BIBLIA: Giuseppe o l'uomo dai doppi destini; Seminario invernale, Loreto 26-28 gen. 1990. Settimello Fi 1991, Biblia. 6 art., infra.

419 ᴱ**Bori** Pier Cesare, Atti del 7º Seminario di 'Studi sulla letteratura esegetica cristiana e giudaica antica', Sacrofano, 18-20 ottobre 1989: AnStoEseg 7,2 (1990) 373-703.

420 CARMIGNAC Jean: Mogilany 1989 [cf. 1987 → 6,539*], Papers on the Dead Sea Scrolls offered in memory of ~, ᴱ**Kapera** Zdzisław J. Kraków 1991, Enigma. I (in press: biobibliog.; 16 art.); II. 14 art., infra, $28 each; pa. $18.

421 ᴱ**Carreira das Neves** J., *Collado Bertomeu* V., *Vilar Hueso* V., III simposio bíblico español (I Luso-espanhol) [17-20 sept. 1989]. Valencia/ Lisboa 1991, Fundación Bíblica Española. 762 p. 84-86067-48-0. 52 art.; infra [portug. también → 422].

422 — Luso-Spanish Biblical Symposium, Lisbon Sept. 17-20 1989 [Portuguese papers, also in Spanish Acta] = Didaskalia 20,1 (1990). 240 p. $40.

422* ᴱ**Cecolin** R., Dall'esegesi all'ermeneutica attraverso la celebrazione; Bibbia e liturgia 1 [simposi S. Giustina, Padova 1987s]: Caro salutis cardo 6. Padova 1991, Messaggero. 331 p. Lit. 30.000. [Asprenas 39, 457s, A. *Petti*].

423 **Ceresa-Gastaldo** Aldo, present., Lingua e stile del Vangelo di Giovanni [seminari D.AR.FI.CL.ET 1989s]: Pubbl. 140. Genova 1991, Univ. 155 p. 0225-0852. 5 art., infra.

424 ᴱ**Cohen** Shaye J. D., *Greenstein* Edward L., The state of Jewish studies [1987 NY conference]. NY/Detroit 1990, Jewish Theol. Sem. / Wayne State Univ. 279 p. $35; pa. $19. [RelStR 18, 152, M. S. *Jaffee*].

425 ᴱ**Collins** John J., *Charlesworth* James H., Mysteries and revelations; apocalyptic studies since the Uppsala Colloquium [1979: Anaheim Nov. 19, 1989]: JPseud supp. 9. Sheffield 1991, Academic. 172 p. £22.50; pa. £18.75. 1-85075-299-0. 8 art.; 5 infra.

426 ᴱ**Cox** Claude E., Congress 7 of the international organization for Septuagint and Cognate Studies, Leuven 1989. Atlanta 1991, Scholars. xxxi-459 p.; ill. 1-55540-647-5 [RB 99,758s & TLZ 117,677 tit. pp.; BL 92,45, A. G. *Auld*; TDig 39,268]. 25 of the 27 papers infra.

426* ᴱ**Dal Covolo** Enrico [p. 7-17], Lo studio dei Padri oggi: BtScR 96. R 1991, LAS. 234 p. Lit. 30.000. [TR 88,252, tit. pp.] 8 art., 5 al. infra → e975.

427 ᴱ**Davies** Philip R., [11-19, Sociology and the Second Temple; SBL consultation], Second Temple studies I. Persian period: JStOT supp. 117. Sheffield 1991, Academic. 192 p. 1-85075-315-6. 10 art., infra. [BL 92,11, J. R. *Bartlett*; RB 99,761 & ZAW 104,309, tit. pp.]. – ᴿExpTim 103 (1991s) 343 (R. *Mason*: research in too early a stage to be authoritative).

427* ᴱDíaz Esteban Fernando, Abraham IBN EZRA y su tiempo / and his age; Proceedings of the international symposium, Madrid, Tudela, Toledo, 1-8 febrero 1989. M 1990, As. Esp. Orientalistas. 396 p.; 8 pl. + 11 color. [TLZ 117,424]. – ᴿSefarad 51 (1991) 460-4 (M. *Gómez Aranda*).

428 ᴱEdelman Diana V., [p. 13-25] The fabric of history; text, artifact and Israel's past [SBL/ASOR symposium 1989]: JStOT supp. 127. Sheffield 1991, Academic. 1-85075-324-5. [BL 92,143].

428* ᴱEdelman Diana, Toward a consensus on the emergence of Israel in Canaan [SBL-ASOR section, New Orleans, 18.XI.1990]: ScandJOT 5,2 (1991) 1-116.

429 ᴱEmerton J. A., [IOSOT] Congress volume, Leuven 1989 [27 Aug.-1 Sept.]: VT supp. 43. Leiden 1991, Brill. vii-398 p. 90-04-09398-2. 23 art., infra. [TR 88,426, tit. pp.].

430 ᴱEnroth-Voitila Anne-Marit, *Myllykoski* Matti, Alkukirkko ja juutalaisuus: Suomen Eksegeettisen Seuran Julkaisuja 53. Helsinki 1991, Kirjapaino Raamattutalo. 182 p. 951-9217-08-8 [no word in German or English].

431 ᴱEskenazi Tamara C., *Harrington* Daniel J., *Shea* William H., The Sabbath in Jewish and Christian traditions [conference Denver, May 1989]. NY 1991, Crossroad. xvi-272 p. $29.50. 0-8245-1093-3 [TDig 39,186].

433 ᴱFelder Cain H., Stony the road we trod; African American biblical interpretation [Black professors' Collegeville meetings 1986-9]. Mp 1991, Fortress. xii-260 p.; map. 0-8006-2501-3 [CritRR 5,519, tit. pp.; NRT 114,629, J. *Masson*]. 11 art.; infra.

434 ᴱFrankel Jonathan, Jews and messianism in the modern era; metaphor and meaning [symposium Hebrew University, Jerusalem, 10 essays; + 10 others, + 76ᴿ + recent dissertations]: Studies in Contemporary Jewry, an annual, 7. Ox 1991, UP. xv-439 p. [TDig 39,171].

435 [ᴱGowan Donald E.] 'I believe in God ... maker of heaven and earth' [Princeton consultation Oct. 12-14, 1990]: HorBT 12,2 (1990). v-96 p.

436 ᴱHalpern Baruch, *Hobson* Deborah W., Law and ideology in monarchic Israel [1986s York Univ. seminar]: JStOT supp. 124. Sheffield 1991, Academic. 235 p. £60; sb. £35. 1-85075-323-7 [RB 100,129, tit. pp.]; Halpern p. 11-107; + 2 infra.

437 ᴱHengel Martin, *Heckel* Ulrich, Paulus und das antike Judentum; Tübingen-Durham-Symposium im Gedenken an den 50. Todestag Adolf SCHLATTERS (1938): WUNT 58. Tü 1991, Mohr. xiii-475 p. DM 248 [TR 88,163, tit. pp.]. 3-16-145795-1. 11 art.; infra.

438 ᴱHengel Martin, *Schwemer* Anna Maria, [p. 1-19], Königsherrschaft Gottes und himmlischer Kult im Judentum, Urchristentum und in der hellenistischen Welt [Symposion Tü 1986s über *Newsom* C. 1985, *Camponovo* O. 1984 ...]: WUNT 55. Tü 1991, Mohr. 495 p. DM 278. 3-16-145667-X. 11 art.; infra. – ᴿTR 87 (1991) 468-470 (D. *Zeller*); 425 tit. pp. [also RB 99,763].

439 ᴱHentschel Georg, *Zenger* Erich, Lehrerin der Gerechtigkeit [kath. Tagung Erfurt 1988 über Weisheit Salomos]: ErfurtTSchr 19. Lp 1991, St. Benno 182 p. 3-7462-0539-5. – ᴿOTAbs 14 (1991) 340s (R. E. *Murphy*; subjects sans tit. pp.).

440 ᴱHoftijzer Jacob, *Kooij* G. Van der, The Balaam text from DeirʿAlla reevaluated; proceedings of the international symposium held at Leiden 21-24 August 1989. Leiden 1991, Brill. xi-324 p. 90-04-09317-6. 20 art.; infra.

441 ᴱHolzner Johann, *Zeilinger* Udo, Die Bibel im Verständnis der Gegenwartsliteratur [Symposium Innsbruck Okt. 1988]. St. Pölten 1988, Niederöst.-P. 166 p. Sch 248 pa. – ᴿZkT 113 (1991) 86-88 (R. *Frick-Pöder*).

441* ᴱJames Eric, A last eccentric; symposium concerning F. A. SIMPSON [plus selections from him]. L 1991, Christian Action. 220 p. £15. 0-901500-39-9 [ExpTim 103,62].

442 ᴱJaspert Bernd, Bibel und Mythos; fünfzig Jahre nach Rudolf BULTMANNS Entmythologisierungsprogramm. [Hofgeismar, 15.-16. Apr. 1991]. Gö 1991, Vandenhoeck & R. 128 p. 3-525-33577-6. 5 art.

443 ᴱKedar B. Z., *Dothan* Trude, *Safrai* Shmuel, *Peraqim / Mišḥar*, Commerce in Palestine throughout the ages, Studies [J Seminar 1980]: J 1990, YadBenZvi / Isr. Expl. Soc. v-337 p.; ill. šeq. 46. 22 art., 13 infra. – ᴿIsrEJ 41 (1991) 306s (A. *Kempinski*: tit., pp.).

444 ᴱKlimkeit Hans-Joachim, Biblische und ausserbiblische Spruchweisheit, Tagung Basel 26.-29.1988: StOrRel 20. Wsb 1991, Harrassowitz. viii-146 p. 3-447-03150-6. 8 art.; 6 infra.

444* ᴱLiberti Vittorio, Ricchezza e povertà nella Bibbia: Corso XI, Studio biblico Aquilano (1989). R 1991, Dehoniane. xiv-260 p. Lit. 30.000. 88-396-0378-6. 10 art.; infra.

445 ᴱLipiński E., Phoenicia and the Bible [Conference 15-16. III. 1990]: StPhoen 11 / OrLovAn 44. Lv 1991, Univ./Peeters. ix-244 p.; ill. 90-6831-377-0. 13 art.; infra.

446 ᴱLovering Eugene A., Seminar papers, SBL 127th annual meeting, Kansas City Nov. 23-26, 1991: SBLSemP 30. Atlanta 1991, Scholars. ix-839 p. 1-55540-624-6. 52 art., infra.

447 ᴱLuomanen Petri, Luke-Acts, Scandinavian perspectives. Publ. 54. Helsinki/Gö 1991, Finnish Exeg.Soc./VR. 194 p. DM 58 [TR 88,163 & RB 99,453, tit. pp.]. – ᴿExpTim 103 (1991s) 153s (I. H. *Marshall*).

448 *a)* ᴱMarc'hadour Germain, Le lexique chrétien; permanences et avatars [Colloque]: CCLLR 4. Angers 1989, Univ. Ouest. iii-195 p. – ᴿScripTPamp 23 (1991) 712s (A. *Viciano*).

— *b)* ᴱMiller Donald G., Christology and Incarnation; papers from the North Park Symposium on theological interpretation of Scripture, Ch Oct. 18-20, 1991: ExAud 7 (1991) 105 p.

449 ᴱMor Menachem, Eretz Israel; Israel and the Jewish Diaspora, mutual relations; Ist Klutznick symposium, Oct. 9-10, 1989 [Omaha Creighton Univ.]: StJewishCiv 1. Lanham MD 1991, UPA. 242 p. $19.75. 14 art.; 2 biblical, infra. [NTAbs 36,138].

450 ᴱNeyrey Jerome H., The social world of Luke-Acts; models for interpretation ['The Context Group', Chicago seminar since 1986]. Peabody MA 1991, Hendrickson. xviii-436 p. $20. 0-943575-48-6. 13 art.; infra. [RB 99,590 & CritRR 5,530: tit. pp.].

451 ᴱPadovese Luigi, Atti del I simposio di Efeso su S. Giovanni Apostolo [Efeso 7-9.V.1990]: Turchia, la Chiesa e la sua storia: Cappuccini Parma. R 1991, Antonianum, Ist. Francescano di Spiritualità. 151 p. 10 art.; 7 infra.

ᴱPeláez del Rosal Jesús, Sobre la vida y obra de MAIMONIDES, congreso Córdoba 1985/91 → a41.

452 Pesce Mauro, present.; Atti dell'VIII seminario di 'Studi sulla letteratura esegetica cristiana e giudaica antica', Trani 10-12 ott. 1990: AnStoEseg 8,2 (1991), 349-705.

453 ᴱPiñero Antonio, Orígenes del cristianismo; antecedentes y primeros pasos [curso de verano, Madrid Univ. Complutense, Almería ag. 1989].

Córdoba 1991, Almendro. 476 p. 84-86077-95-8. 15 art., infra. – ᴿFg-Nt 4 (1991) 235-7 (J. *Peláez*).

453* ᴱReumann John, The promise and practice of biblical theology [5 guest + 5 faculty lectures for Philadelphia Lutheran Theological Seminary 125th anniversary]. Mp 1991, Fortress. $13 pa. 0-8006-2495-5 [TDig 39,183: the 5 guest topics].

454 *a*) ᴱRichardson Peter, *Westerholm* Stephen, Law in religious communities in the Roman period; the debate over Torah and Nomos in post-biblical Judaism and early Christianity: StChrJud 4. Waterloo 1991, W. Laurier Univ. x-164 p. $20. 0-88920-201-X [CBQ 55,202, M. *McNamara*, tit. pp.; JBL 110,569]. 5 art.

— *b*) ᴱRosenblatt Jason P., *Sitterson* Joseph C.ᴶ, 'Not in heaven'; coherence and complexity in biblical narrative [< conference on 'The Bible and contemporary literary theory', Georgetown Univ., Wsh April 28-29, 1989]: StBLit. Bloomington 1991, Indiana Univ. 262 p. $40; pa. $15. 0-253-35036-0 (-20678-2). 10 art., infra. [RB 99,759s, tit. pp.].

— *c*) ᴱSchmid Hans H., *Mehlhausen* Hans H., Sola Scriptura; das reformatorische Schriftprinzip in der säkularen Welt [VI. Europäischer Theologenkongress (Ev. DDR) 24.-28. Sept. 1990]: WissGesTheol. Gü 1991, Mohn. 374 p. 3-579-00179-5 [TsTNijm 32,106, G. P. *Hartvelt*]. 26 art.; 22 infra.

455 *a*) ᴱSchultz Hans-Joachim, *Speigl* Jakob, Bild und Symbol, glaubens-stiftende Impulse [Symposium Würzburg für Ök. Konz. VII. 1987]. Wü 1988, Echter. 208 p.; ill. DM 30. – ᴿBijdragen 52 (1991) 108 (W. G. *Tillmans*).

— *b*) ᴱShanks Hershel, The Dead Sea Scrolls after forty years [symposium Oct. 1990, Smithsonian Wsh.]. Wsh 1991, Biblical Archaeological Soc. x-85 p.; 4 pl.; map. $8 pa. [NTAbs 36,302].

— *c*) ᴱSharon Moshe, The Holy Land in history and thought ... international conference on relations to the world outside it, Johannesburg 1986: Samson Chair 1. Leiden 1988. XIV-291 p. ƒ98. 90-04-08855-5. 23 art. – ᴿZDMG 141 (1991) 171s (G. *Wanke*: tit. pp.).

456 ᴱSollamo Raija, Paimentolaisten uskonnosta kirkkolaitokseksi [Helsinki 1988]: Suomen Eksegeettisen Seuran Julkaisuja 55. Helsinki 1991, Vammalan Kirjapaino Oy. [viii-] 133 p. 951-9217-10-X. 10 art.; no word in German or English.

457 SOTS bulletin for 1991: **66th** winter meeting, L 2-4.I.1991: *Gelston* A., presidential address, Universalism in 2-Is; – *Snaith* J., An ascetic Qohelet in Syriac writers?; – *Lieu* Judith, Can Sarah be saved?; – *Gray* M. D., Ps. xvi.15; did the children of Israel get what they asked for?; – *Millard* A. R., Lv and the Late Bronze Age; – *Coggins* R. J., The minor prophets; one book or twelve; – *Gibson* J. C. L., Thoughts on revising Davidson's Hebrew Syntax. — **67th** summer meeting, Durham 16-19.VII.1991 with OT Werkgezelschap on 'Texts and Versions': *Dirksen* P. B., Peshitta and textual criticism; – *Hajnal* Piroska, Gn 1-3 in Greek Jewish lit.; – *Goulder* M. D., The exegesis of Gn 1-3 in the NT; – *Alexander* P. S., Gn 1 in rabbinic lit.; – *Solomon* N., Gn and modern Judaism; – *Emmerson* Grace I., Gn 1-3 in feminist interpretation; – *Vermes* G., Gn 1-3 pre-Mishnah; – *Koster* M. D., Peshitta revisited; – *Smelik* K., Manasseh 2K 21, 2 Chr 33; – *Lane* D., Text, scholar and Church; Leiden Peshitta; – *Kooij* A. van der, The story of David and Goliath; the early history of its text 1 Sam 17; – *Becking* B., Jeremiah's Book of Consolation, Masoretic and Old Greek; – *Gordon* R. P., Dialogue and disputation in the Targum to the Prophets.

458 ᴱTalmon Shemaryahu, Jewish civilization in the Hellenistic-Roman period [workshop Jerusalem 1986]: JPseud 10. Sheffield 1991, Academic. 269 p. £30; pa. £22.50. 1-85075-320-2. 15 art., infra [RB 99,761s, tit. pp.; BL 92,131, L. L. *Grabbe*]. – ᴿExpTim 103 (1991s) 343 (R. *Mason*).

459 ᴿTamani Giuliano [p. 9-27; 195-201], *Vivian* Angelo [215-226], Manoscritti, frammenti e libri ebraici nell'Italia dei secoli XV-XVI: Atti del VII Congresso Internazionale: Associazione Italiana per lo studio del giudaismo 7. R 1991, Carucci. 259 p. 88-85116-14-0. 18 art., 3 *al*. infra.

460 *a*) ᴱTollet Daniel, Politique et religion dans le Judaïsme ancien et médiéval [Sorbonne-IV 1987]: Relais 7. P 1989, Desclée. 370 p. – ᴿScEsp 43 (1991) 122-5 (J.-J. *Lavoie*).

— *b*) ᴱWansbrough Henry, Jesus and the oral gospel tradition [Dublin 1989 + Gazzada, Italy 1990]: JStNT supp. 64. Sheffield 1991, JStOT. $70; sb. $52.50. 1-85075-329-6 [TDig 39,269: 14 art.; author + topic or title; RB 99,764, tit. pp.].

A2.3   **Acta congressuum theologica** [reports ➔ Y7.4].

461 AGOSTINO d'Ippona, De moribus ecclesiae catholicae et de moribus Manichaeorum; De quantitate animae [Acta, Pavía]: Lectio Augustini 7. Palermo 1991. 213 p. – ᴿScripTPamp 23 (1991) 1075s (A. *Viciano*: autores sin tit. pp.).

462 ᴱAlberigo Giuseppe, *a*) Christian unity; the council of Ferrara-Florence 1438/39-1989 [symposium Florence 1989]: BtETL 97. Lv 1991, Univ./ Peeters. 680 p. Fb 3000. [NRT 114, 121, L. J. *Renard*].

— *b*) Chiese italiane e Concilio; esperienze pastorali nella chiesa italiana tra Pio XII e Paolo VI [Bologna ott. 1986]. Genova 1988, Marietti. 321 p. Lit. 40.000 pa. – ᴿEngHR 106 (1991) 1065s (P. *Hebblethwaite*).

463 ᴱAlici Luigi, Interiorità e intenzionalità in S. AGOSTINO, I-II Seminario Perugia: StEphAug 32. R 1990, Inst. Patristicum Augustinianum. 207 p. Lit. 45.000 [TR 87,527; RHE 87,255* < RFilosNeoS 54 (1991) 475-8 (G. *Marchetti*)].

463* ᴱAmirtham Samuel, *Pryor* Robin, Resources for spiritual formation in theological education; the invitation to the feast of life [1989 Yogyakarta consultation]. Geneva c. 1991, WCC. vii-249 p. $11 [TDig 39,184].

464 ᴱAngelini Giuseppe, Il prete; identità del ministero e oggettività della fede [colloquio febb. 1990]: Disputatio 2. Mi 1990, Glossa. 235 p. Lit. 30.000. – ᴿETL 67 (1991) 187 (A. de *Halleux*).

465 ᴱAssmann Hugo, *al*., René GIRARD como teólogo da libertação; um diálogo sobre ídolos e sacrifícios [Piracicaba SP, 25-29. VI. 1990]. Petrópolis/Piracicaba 1991, Vozes/UNIMEP. 332 p. – ᴿREB 51 (1991) 743-5 (*Jung Mo Sung*).

465* ᴱAssmann J., *Sundermeier* T., Das Fest und das Heilige; religiöse Kontrapunkte zur Alltagswelt [Tagung Heidelberg Feb. 1988]: Studien zum Verstehen fremder Religionen 1. Gü 1991, Mohn. 253 p. DM 78. 3-57901-783-7 [BL 92,99, J. R. *Porter*: M. *Klinghardt* good on Sabbath; R. *Rendtorff* disappointing on 'theology (mostly calendars) of feast']. 15 art.; 2 infra.

466 ᴱAufrecht Walter E., Concepts and methods in religious studies, Univ. Lethbridge seminar: RelStT 9,2s (1989) 7s (-63); p. 47-54, *Grimes* John, The contribution of the study of Scripture to the study of theology.

467 ᴱBeinert Wolfgang [Dogma], Glaube als Zustimmung; zur Interpretation kirchlicher Rezeptionsvorgänge [kath. Tagung. Berlin 1988]: QDisp

131. FrB 1991, Herder. 168 p. (H. J. *Pottmeyer*, fundamental theology; 2 *al.*) [RelStR 18, 43, J. R. *Sachs*].

468 **Bein Ricco** Elena, Dio e la storia (Valdesi, Torre Pellice 27. VIII. 1988). T 1989, Claudiana. 134 p. Lit. 15.000. – ᴿHumBr 46 (1991) 143 (A. *Biazzi*).

469 ᴱ**Bernard** C. A., L'antropologia dei Maestri spirituali, simposio Univ. Gregoriana Ist. Spiritualità Roma 25 apr.-1 mag. 1989. Mi 1991, Paoline. 379 p. – ᴿAsprenas 38 (1991) 397-9 (B. *Forte*).

470 ᴱ**Berthold** George, Faith seeking understanding; learning and the Catholic tradition: St. Anselm College Centennial [Apr. 20-23, 1989]. Manchester NH 1991. [viii-] 274 p. $9 [RHE 86,349*; TTod 49,448, C. E. *Curran*]. 0-96-29547-0-5. 24 art., 4 infra.

470* **Blondeau** Anne-Marie, *Schipper* Kristofer, Essais sur le rituel, Colloque du centenaire ÉPHÉR: BtÉPHÉR 92.95. Lv/P 1988-90, Peeters. I. xiii-210 p.; II. xvii-236 p. 90-6831-122-0; -302-9.

471 ᴱ**Böhme** Wolfgang, *Sudbrack* Josef, Der Christ von morgen — ein Mystiker? [Tagung Bad Herrenalb Dez. 1988]. Wü/Stu 1989, Echter/ Steinkopf. 136 p. DM 16,80. – ᴿTPQ 39 (1991) 328s (J. *Weismayer*).

473 ᴱ**Bolle** Pierre, *Godel* Jean, Spiritualité, théologie et résistance; Yves de MONTCHEUIL, théologien au maquis du Vercors [colloque S.-Hugues-de-Biviers 27-29 sept. 1984]. Grenoble 1987, Univ. 381 p. – [RHE 87, 227-9, A. *Dantoing*].

ᴱ**Bost** Hubert, Genèse et enjeux de la laïcité 1990 → 7853.

474 ᴱ**Bradshaw** Paul F. [→ 293*b*], *Hoffman* Lawrence A., The making of Jewish and Christian worship; two liturgical traditions, I [Notre Dame conference 1988]. ND 1991, Univ. x-211 p. $25. 0-268-01207-5 [TDig 39,73]. 8 art.

475 Braga, IX Centenário da dedicação da Sé, Congreso internacional, Actas I-III. Braga 1990, Univ. Católica. 783 p.; 688 p.; 366 p.; ill.; 28 maps. [RHE 86,224*]. – ᴿRHE 87 (1991) 166s (Ana Maria *Jorge*).

475* ᴱ**Brecht** Martin, Martin LUTHER und das Bischofsamt [Seminar Oslo 1988]. Stu 1990, Calwer. 145 p. DM 48 [TLZ 117, 199, G. *Heintze*].

476 *a*) ᴱ**Bresch** Carsten, *al.*, Kann man Gott aus der Natur erkennen? Evolution als Offenbarung [Symposium 1989]: QDisp 125. FrB 1990, Herder. 175 p. – ᴿTLZ 116 (1991) 688-690 (H.-H. *Jenssen*).

— *b*) ᴱ**Brovelli** F., *Citrini* T., La spiritualità del prete diocesano, Atti dei seminari e convegni di studio 1979-1989. Mi 1990, Glossa. 475 p. – ᴿTeresianum 42 (1991) 632s (M. *Caprioli*).

— *c*) ᴱ**Brown** David, NEWMAN, a man for our time [7 Oxford lectures]. L 1990, SPCK. 168 p. £6. 0-281-04486-4. – ᴿExpTim 103 (1991s) 31 [C. S. *Rodd*].

477 ᴱ**Bryant** M. Darrol, Pluralism, tolerance and dialogue: six studies [Waterloo ongoing colloquium]. Waterloo ON 1989, Univ. x-150 p. – ᴿSR 20 (1991) 238-240 (Marilyn F. *Nefsky*).

477* ᴱ**Burgess** Joseph A., In search of Christian unity; basic consensus / basic differences [1987 conference La Ceiba, Puerto Rico]. Mp 1991, Fortress. vii-259 p. $15 pa. 0-8006-2302-9 [TDig 39,170]. – ᴿExpTim 103 (1991s) 250 (J. A. *Newton*).

478 ᴱ**Cahill** P. Joseph, RelStT Research Asn, 3d annual meeting, Red Deer, Alberta, May 3, 1990: RelStT 9,1 (1989!) 7-26.

479 ᴱ**Calder** William M.ᴵᴵᴵ, The Cambridge ritualists reconsidered; proceedings of the first Oldfather [-professorship financed] Conference, Urbana-Champaign Apr. 27-30, 1989: ILCL supp. 2. Atlanta 1991, Scholars. xii-295 p. 1-55540-605-X. 14 art.; 6 infra.

480 ᴱ**Camps** A., *al.*, Œcumenische inleiding in de missiologie; teksten en konteksten van het wereldchristendom [Werkgroep Docenten Missiologie]. Kampen 1988, Kok. 525 p. – ᴿRTLv 22 (1991) 421s (C. *Soetens*: fera date).
— *b*) ᶠCᴀᴍᴘs Arnulf: Popular religion, liberation and contextual theology; congress Jan. 2-7, 1990, Nijmegen, ᴱ**Nieuwenhove** Jacques van: Kerk en Theologie in Context 8. Kampen 1991, Kok. vii-254 p. ƒ49 [TR 88,344, some tit. pp.].
— *c*) ᴱ**Carrasco** Juan A., San José en el siglo XVIII; Actas del Quinto Simpósion internacional (México, 17-24 septiembre 1989): EstJos septiembre 1989): EstJos 45, 88s (1991) 878 p. 49 art., 4 'S. Escr.', infra.
481 **Castiau** C., présent., Monothéisme et Trinité: Fac. S. Louis colloque: Publ. 52. Bru 1991, Fac. Univ. S. Louis. 145 p. 2-8028-0078-7. 5 art.; 3 infra.
482 Les Chrétiens et l'Économie; colloque de l'Association française d'histoire religieuse contemporaine. P 1991, Centurion. 248 p. – ᴿEsprVie 101 (1991) 683-5 (F. *Mabille*).
483 ᴱ**Chrostowski** Waldemar, Materiały z II Sympozjum teologicznego 'Kościół a Żydzi [the Church and the Jews] i Judaizm', Akad. Teol. Kat. Wsz 3-4. IV. 1990: ColcT 61,3 (1991) 5-9 presentation; 137-140 Eng. summary; 55-70 in Poland (further 37-53, *Sherwin* Byron L.; 71-79, *Krajewski* Stanisław); in England, *Solomon* Norman, 11-35.
484 ᴱ**Cipriani** Settimio, Nuove frontiere dell'etica economica [convegno Napoli maggio 1989]. R 1990, Ave. 200 p. Lit. 20.000. – ᴿCC 142 (1991,3) 102-4 (F. *Cultrera*).
485 ᴱ**Clarke** Andrew D., *Winter* Bruce W., One God, one Lord in a world of religious pluralism: Conference July 1991. C 1991, Tyndale House. 192 p. + indexes. £10. 0-9518-3560-2 [TyndB 42,317 adv.] 10 art., infra.
485* ᴱ**Cohn-Sherbok** Dan, The Canterbury papers [17 lectures at Kent Univ.] ... 1990, Bellew. 242 p. £13. 0-947792-49-X. – ᴿExpTim 102 (1990s) 348 (D. *Forrester*: skimpy); TLond 94 (1991) 230s (Susan F. *Parsons*: some of the lectures already published).
486 ᴱ**Cooke** Bernard J., The papacy and the Church in the US [Holy Cross College conference]. NY 1989, Paulist. 220 p. $11 pa. [Horizons 19, 144, Sally Ann *McReynolds*].
487 ᴱ**Decot** Rolf, *Vinke* Rainer, Zum Gedenken an Joseph Lᴏʀᴛᴢ (1887-1975); Beiträge zur Reformationsgeschichte und Ökumene: Eur.Rel.-G. Mainz, Beiheft 30. Stu 1989, Steiner. viii-396 p. 3-515-05159-7. – ᴿGregorianum 72 (1991) 381-3 (J. *Wicks*: Lortz's Die Reformation in Deutschland 1939s, translated c. 1970 in French, Italian, English, Spanish, marks turning-point in Catholic attitudes to Protestantism).
487* ᴱ**DeWitt** Calvin B., The environment and the Christian; what does the New Testament say about the environment? [Au Sable institute forum]. GR 1991, Baker. 156 p. $8 pa. – ᴿGraceTJ 12,1 (1991) 153s (R. A. *Young*).
488 ᴱ**Dierkens** A., Apparitions et miracles [Bruxelles, mai 1991 ⇒ 350a]: ProbHistRel fasc. 2. Bru 1991 Univ. Inst. Rel./Laïcité. 191 p. Fb 775.
488* Dios es Padre: Semanas 25. S 1991, Secr. Trinitario. 341 p. [NRT 114,898, R. *Escol*].
489 ᴱ**D'Onorio** Joël-Benoît, La laïcité au défi de la modernité; Actes du Xᵉ colloque national de juristes catholiques, Paris 11-12 nov. 1989; préf. *Poupard* card. Paul. P 1990, Téqui. 247 p. F 110. 2-85244-989-7. – ᴿGregorianum 72 (1991) 188s (J. *Joblin*); RTLv 22 (1991) 275 (R. *Guelluy*).

490 ᴱd'Onorio Joël-Benoît, La liberté religieuse dans le monde, analyse
doctrinale et politique; Actes du colloque international 21-22.IV.1989,
Aix-en-Provence. P 1991, Univ. 341 p. [NRT 114,445, T. *Toubeau*; RHE
87, 299s, G. *Thils*]. – ᴿRTLv 22 (1991) 275 (R. *Guelluy*).

490* ᴱDouglas J. D., Proclaim Christ until he comes [Manila 1989, called
'Lausanne II']. Mp 1990, World Wide. 463 p. $13 pa. – ᴿMissiology 19
(1991) 349s (R. *Bassham*).

491 D'Sa Francis X., *al.*, The future of God [7th conference, Assisi
1-7.V.1990]: Dialogue & Alliance 5,2 (1991) 4-9 (-22).

491* ᴱDucret Roland, *al.*, Christianisme et modernité, colloque T.-More:
ScHumRel. P 1990, Cerf. 328 p. [RThom 92,855, G. *Narcisse*]. –
ᴿRHPR 71 (1991) 481s (G. *Vahanian*).

492 ᴱEickelman Dale F., *Piscatori* James, Muslim travellers; pilgrimage,
migration, and the religious imagination [conference on Movement and
Exchange in Muslim societies]: Comparative Studies on Muslim Societies.
Berkeley 1990, Univ. California. xxii-281 p. $15. [RelStR 18,75, A. *Nanji*].

493 ᴱEllem Elizabeth W., The Church made whole; National Conference on
women in the Uniting Church in Australia 1991 [Melbourne 1990].
Melbourne 1990, Lowell. 209 p. A$17. – ᴿAustralasCR 68 (1991) 381s
(Marie *Farrell*); Pacifica 4 (1991) 243s (E. *White*).

494 L'Europa dei secoli XI e XII fra novità e tradizione; sviluppi di una
cultura; Atti della Xᵃ settimana internazionale di studio, Mendola, 25-29
agosto 1986: MiscMedv 12. Mi 1989, ViPe. xxxi-421 p.; 24 fig.; 6 facsim.
Lit. 80.000. [RHE 87,57*].

494* ᴱFelici Sergio, La mariologia nella catechesi dei Padri (età postnicena),
Pont. Inst. Altioris Latinitatis 10-11 marzo 1989: BtScRel 95. R 1991,
LAS. 324 p. – ᴿMarianum 53 (1991) 268-271 (E. *dal Covolo*).

495 Les fonctions des saints dans le monde occidental (IIIᵉ-XIIIᵉ s.): Actes du colloque, Rome 27-29 oct. 1988, Univ./Éc.Franç.: Coll.Éc.
Franç. 149. R 1991, École française. iv-551 p. [RHE 87,95*; TR 88,
436, tit. pp.].

496 ᴱFurcha E. J., Truth and tolerance; papers from the 1989 international
symposium: ARC Supp. 4. Montréal 1990, McGill Univ. 184 p. C$ 15.
0-7717-0220-5. – ᴿÉTRel 66 (1991) 297 (H. *Bost* : stresses role of various
Protestantisms).

496* ᴱGaleota Gustavo, Roberto BELLARMINO, arcivescovo di Capua, teo-
logo e pastore della Riforma cattolica [28 sett.-2 ott. 1988], Capua 1990,
Ist. Sup. Sc. Rel. 929 p. (2 vol.) [NTAbs 36,305]. – ᴿTS 52 (1991) 748-750
(J. P. *Donnelly*).

497 ᴱGioia Mario, [in dialogo con *Bernard* Charles-André], Teologia spirituale; temi e problemi [Napoli fac. S. Luigi 1-2.V.1990]: Saggi 29. R
1991, A.V.E. 293 p. Lit. 32.000. 10 art.

498 ᶠGOESER Robert L.: Lutheran confessional theology faces the 21st
century, Pacific Lutheran Theological Seminary conference, Berkeley
1990, ᴱGold Victor, *Peters* Ted: CurrTM 18,1 (1991) 2-44; 6-11 Goeser,
LUTHER, word of God, language, and art.

498* González Montes A., present., 'El Espíritu Santo como coherencia viva';
ponencias de la VI Asamblea de la Societas Oecumenica Europea (Dublin,
23-29.VIII.1990): Diálogo Ecuménico 26,86 (S 1991) 423-6 (-550) [< ZIT
92,120].

499 ᴱGordan Paulus, Im Anfang schuf Gott Himmel und Erde (Vorlesungen
der Salzburger Hochschulwochen 23.VII-4.VIII.1990). Graz 1991, Styria.
248 p. DM 35 [TR 87,161].

500 ᴱGrane Leif ... *Horby* Kai, Die dänische Reformation vor ihrem internationalen Hintergrund: ForKDGesch 46. Gö 1990, VR. [TR 86,343].

501 Grech Prosper, *al.*, Alle radici della mistica cristiana, Convegni di S. Spirito 5. Palermo 1989, Augustinus. 113 p. Lit. 14.000. – ᴿRTLv 22 (1991) 87s (A. de *Halleux*).

501* GREGORIO Magno e il suo tempo, con ÉcFrR 9-12 mai 1990: StEphAug 33s. R 1991, Inst. Patr. Aug. I. Studi storici 314 p.; II. questioni letterarie e dottrinali. Lit. 125.000. I. p. 5-25, *Clark* F. [TR 88,429, tit. pp.].

502 Greisch Jean, présent., Penser la religion; recherches en philosophie de la religion: Philosophie 13. P 1991, Beauchesne. 430 p. F 180 [TR 87,346, tit. pp.].

503 ᴱGreive Wolfgang, *Niemann* Raul, Neu glauben? Religionsvielfalt und neue religiöse Strömungen als Herausforderung an das Christentum [Tagung Loccum]. Gü 1990, Mohn. 180 p. – ᴿTZBas 47 (1991) 92s (W. *Neidhardt*; p. 92 & ind. Neidhart).

504 ᴱGuerriero Elio, *Tarsia* Antonio, L'ombra di Dio; l'Ineffabile e i suoi nomi: Primo convegno teologico Ed. Paoline, CinB 15-17.VI.1990. CinB 1991, Paoline. [AcPIB 9/8,658]. Lit. 22.000. 88-215-2151-6. 8 art.; 3 infra. [VivH 3,422: *Forte* B., *La Potterie* I. de, *Mancini* I., *al.*].

505 ᴱHamesse Jacqueline, *Murille-Samaran* Colette, Le travail au Moyen-Âge, une approche interdisciplinaire; Actes du Colloque international de Louvain-la-Neuve 21-23 mai. 1987. LvN 1990, Inst. Ét. Médiévales. 440 p. – ᴿScripTPamp 23 (1991) 688-690 (M. *Lluch-Baixauli*).

506 ᴱHamnett Ian, Religious pluralism and unbelief [Bristol meeting]. L 1990, Routledge. vii-279 p. £30. – ᴿNBlackf 72 (1991) 249s (W. S. F. *Pickering*: attempts no correlation).

507 ᴱHayes Victor C., Identity issues and world religions; selected proceedings [27 short papers out of the 281, Sydney 1985] of the fifteenth congress of the International Association for the History of Religions. Bedford Park SA 1986, Australian Asn. HR. vii-293 p. $20 [RelStR 18,37, C. *Ernst*].

508 ᴱHebblethwaite Brian, *Henderson* Edward, Divine action; studies inspired by the philosophical theology of Austin FARRER [Louisiana State Univ. 1986, Fourth Conference]. E 1990, Clark. 281 p. $40. – ᴿTTod 48 (1991s) 348.350.352 (J. U. *Lewis*).

509 HEIDEGGER: ᴱBraun H. J., Martin Heidegger und der christliche Glaube [Symposium 100. Gb. Zürich, Ev. Hochschule]. Z 1990, Theol.-V. 159 p. 3-290-10115-0. – ᴿTsTNijm 31 (1991) 202s (P. *Leenhouwers*).

509* — ᴱPöltner Günther, Auf der Spur des Heiligen; HEIDEGGERS Beitrag zur Gottesfrage. Wien 1991, Böhlau. 108 p. DM 42 [TR 87,346, tit. pp.].

510 ᴱHeim S. Mark, Faith to creed, consultation Oct. 25-27, 1989, Waltham MA; ecumenical perspectives on the affirmation of the apostolic faith in the fourth century: NCC Faith and Order. GR 1991, Eerdmans. xxiii-206 p. $14. 0-8028-0551-5 [TDig 39,59]. 10 art.

511 ᴱHerzog Frederick, *Groscurth* Reinhard, Anfragen und Dokumente aus der United Church of Christ (USA). Neuk 1989, Neuk.-V. 176 p. [EvT 51,202 → 8077*].

512 ᴱHeuclin J., Mentalités religieuses et révolution française: Lille 12-13 mai 1989: MélSR 48,1s (1991) 130 p.

513 Heusch Luc de, *al.*, Religion et tabou sexuel [colloque Bru 4-5.X.1990, Univ. Libre, Inst. Religions et Laïcité]: ProbHistRel 1. Bru 1990, Univ. 159 p. [RHE 87,246s, P. *Vandermeersch*].

514 ᴱHick John, *Meltzer* Edmund S., Three faiths — one God; a Jewish, Christian, Muslim encounter [Claremont March 1985]. Albany 1989, SUNY. xiv-240 p. $50; pa. $15 [RelStR 18,38, J. T. *Pawlikowski*].

515 ᴱHummel Gert, New creation or eternal now? Is there an eschatology in Paul TILLICH's work? 3d international symposium, Frankfurt 1990: TBt Töpelmann 54. B/NY 1991, de Gruyter. 243 p. DM 98 [TR 88,344, tit. pp.] 14 art., 3 infra.

515* ᴱJeanrond Werner C., Radical pluralism and truth; David TRACY and the hermeneutics of religion. NY 1991, Crossroad. xxvii-296 p.; 286-293, Tracy bibliog., *Webb* Stephen H. $34.50 [TR 88,346, some tit. pp.] 6 infra.

516 ᴱJenkins Arthur H., J. H. NEWMAN and modernism [Tenth Newman-Conference, Birmingham 1983]: IntNSt 14. Sigmaringendorf 1990, Glock & L. 190 p. DM 60 [TR 87,431, tit. pp.; TLZ 117,74, J. *Mann*]. 12 art., 4 infra.

516* ᴱJha Makhan, Social anthropology of pilgrimage [1988 Zagreb symposium]. New Delhi 1991, Inter-India [Columbia MO, South Asia books, $50]. 372 p.; 14 pl. 20 art. [RelStR 18,213, D. L. *Halbernan*].

517 ᴱKhoury Adel T., *Muth* Ludwig, Glauben durch Lesen? Für eine christliche Lesekultur [Ringvorlesung Münster 1989]: QDisp 128. FrB 1990, Herder. 152 p. DM 46. – ᴿTsTNijm 31 (1991) 105 (F. *Maas*); ZkT 113 (1991) 498-500 (U. *Zeilinger*).

518 ᴱKnitter Paul F., Pluralism and oppression; theology in world perspective [LA meeting 1988]: CTS Annual 34. Lanham MD 1988, UPA. xii-278 p. $45.50; pa. $27.25. 0-8191-7904-3; -5-1 [TDig 38,373 with alternative 0-8091-]. 15 art.; R. *Panikkar*, E. *Dussel*, al.

518* ᴱKoehler T. A., Proceedings of the 38th National Convention of the Mariological Society of America, Washington 1-2.VI.1987: Marian Studies 38. Dayton 1987, Marian Library. – ᴿTLZ 116 (1991) 155s (H. J. E. *Beintker*).

519 ᴱKohlschein Franz, Aufklärungskatholizismus und Liturgie; Reformentwürfe für die Feier von Taufe, Firmung, Busse, Trauung und Krankensalbung [Kolloquium Bamberg 1986, 'Aufgeklärte Ritualien']: Pietas Liturgica 6. St. Ottilien 1989, EOS. 238 p. DM 49. – ᴿTLZ 116 (1991) 151-3 (H. *Reifenberg*).

520 [*Ladrière* Jean, *al.*] Christianisme et modernité; Actes du colloque [sept. 1987] Centre Thomas More, Lyon-Arbresle: Sciences humaines et religions. P 1990, Cerf. 322 p. – ᴿEsprVie 101 (1991) 468-471 (J. *Milet*).

521 ᴱLago Alba L. [627-631 sumario, Absoluto y verdad en la historia], V Jornadas de teología fundamental, Granada 12-15 junio 1991: CiTom 118 (1991) 437-626.

521* ᴱLangevin G., *Pirro* Raphaël, Le Christ et les cultures dans le monde et l'histoire [Radio-Canada 1987]. Montréal 1991, Bellarmin. 401 p. [NRT 114,900, P. *Evrard*].

522 ᴱLilienfeld F. von, *Ritter* A. M., Einheit der Kirche in vorkonstantinischer Zeit: Patristische Arbeitsgemeinschaft, Bern 2.-4.I.1985: Oikonomia 25. Erlangen 1989, Lehrstuhl chr. Ostens. vii-165 p. [RHE 87,53*].

522* Llamas E., La Sociedad Mariológica de España; cincuenta años de historia [Zaragoza 9.X.1940 - (44º) 12-15.VIII.1990]: EstMar 56 (1991) 25-40 (41-51, *Diez Merino* L., Biblia; -451, al.).

523 ᴱMaccarrone Michele, Il primato del vescovo di Roma nel primo millennio, ricerche e testimonianze; Atti del Symposium storico-teologico Roma 9-13 ott. 1989: Atti e Documenti 4. Vaticano 1991, Editrice. xi-782 p. 88-209-1706-4. 18 art.; 3 infra.

524 **McDonnell** Kilian, *Montague* George T. [➤ h74] Fanning the flame; what does baptism in the Holy Spirit have to do with Christian initiation? [Catholic Charismatic 'Heart of the Church consultation', Techny IL May 6-11, 1990]. 30 p. $2. 0-8146-5013-9.

524* ^E**McInerny** Ralph, The Catholic woman: Wethersfield Inst. NY Sept. 28, 1990. SF 1991, Ignatius $ 10. 0-89870-369-7 [TDig 39,154].

525 ^E**Magesa** Laurenti, The prophetic role of the Church in Tanzania today, symposium of five papers [Moshi Apr. 1990]: Spearhead 115. Eldoret 1991, Gaba. 94 p. – ^RTContext 8,2 (1991) 137 (H. *Janssen*).

526 **Manna** Salvatore, present., Conciliarità e autorità nella Chiesa; Atti VIII colloquio cattolico-ortodosso 25-27.V.1989 Bari: Nicolaus 18,1s (1991) 5-13 (-304).

527 Marie mère de Dieu, Rencontre spirituelle et théologique 1988. Venasque 1989, Carmel. 330 p.; 75-89, *La Potterie* I. de; 103-131, *Quacquarelli* A.; 39-72, *Goedt* M. de (Annunciation as beginning of the New Covenant); 32-46, *Ponnau* D., (it happened that the mother of Jesus was Jewish). – ^RColcT 61,2 (1991) 191-3 (S. C. *Napiórkowski*, ❷).

529 ^E**Massaut** Jean-Pierre, Colloque érasmien de Liège, commémoration du 450e anniversaire de la mort d'Érasme: Univ. Bt. ph/lett 247. P 1987, BLettres. x-313 p. [LuJb 57 (1990) p. 321, with indication of 8 articles there cited].

530 ^E**Mensen** Bernhard, Die Schöpfung in den Religionen [St. Augustin Akademie 1989s]: Völker und Kulturen 13. Nettetal 1990, Steyler. 111 p. DM 24. [TR 88,157, G. *Risse*]. – ^RForumKT 7 (1991) 320 (A. *Ziegenaus*).

531 ^E**Mercado** Leonardo N., *Knight* James J., Mission and dialogue; theory and practice [Tagaytay symposium 1-7.XII.1988]. Manila 1989, Divine Word. x-249 p. – ^RVerbumSVD 32 (1991) 105-9 (O. *Gächter*).

532 ^E**Meslin** Michel, Maître et disciples dans les traditions religieuses; Actes du Colloque, Paris-Sorbonne Centre HistCompRel 15-16 avril 1988: Patrimoines HistRel. P 1990, Cerf. 230 p. F 99. 2-204-04157-2. – ^RNumen 38 (1991) 276s (P. *Antes*); RHPR 71 (1991) 343s (P. *François*).

533 ^E**Meyuhas Ginio** Alisa, Jews, Christians, and Muslims in the Mediterranean world after 1492 = MeditHR 6/2 (1991). 296 p. 17 art.; 4 infra.

534 ^E**Militello** Cettina, Donne e ministero; un dibattito ecumenico [Palermo 17-19.XI.1989]. R 1991, Dehoniane [RasT 32,188].

535 **Miola** Gabriele, present., Atti del Convegno su 'Giustizia e violenza' [Fermo, serie d'incontri 1991s]: Firmana, quaderni di teologia e pastorale [1]. 100 p.

535* ^E**Moingt** Joseph, [p. 162-5, 391-400] Un corps pour l'Église [11e Colloque Chantilly 28-30.VI.1990]: RechSR 79,2 (1991) 162-252.325-400.

536 **Molette** Charles, *al.*, Le mystère de Marie et la femme aujourd'hui; 47e Session de la Société Française d'Études Mariales. Blois 1-6 sept. 1990. P 1991, Médiaspaul. 192 p. F 150. – ^REsprVie 101 (1991) 589-592 (B. *Billet*).

536* ^E**Molette** C., Marie, mythe ou modèle pour la femme d'aujourdhui, 46e session, Soc. Française d'Études Mariales, N. D. du Laus. P 1990, OEIL. 101 p. F 100. [NRT 114,466].

537 *a*) El Monasterio como centro de producción cultural; tercer seminario sobre el Monacato (Aguilar del Campo 1-5 agosto 1989: Codex Aquilarensis 3 (1990) 7-124. – ^RRivStoLR 27 (1991) 340-3 (Rita *Lizzi*).
— *b*) Monothéisme et Trinité; Publ. 52. Bru 1991, Fac. Univ. S.-Louis. 145 p.

— c) ᴱMontgomery John W., Evidence for faith; deciding the God question: Cornell Symposium, Ithaca NY 29 Aug.-7 Sept. 1986. Dallas 1991, Probe (distr. Word). 366 p. $15. 0-945241-15-1 [TDig 39,260].

— d) Müller Karl, Prawdzik Werner, Ist Christus der einzige Weg zum Heil? [Studienwoche Juni 1990, Missionspriesterseminar S. Aug.]: Veröff. 40. Nettetal 1991, Steyler. 199 p. DM 35. – ᴿTGL 81 (1991) 490-3 (W. Sosna).

538 ᴱNipkow Karl E., Praktische Theologie und Kultur der Gegenwart; ein internationaler Dialog. Gü 1991, Mohn. 202 p.; DM 42 pa. 10 art.

539 ᴱOlupona Jacob E., African traditional religions in contemporary society [Nairobi Sept. 10-14, 1987]. NY 1991, Paragon. 204 p. $13. 14 art. [TR 87,530, tit. pp.]. D'Onorio ➤ 489.

540 Oroz Reta José, San AGUSTÌN en Oxford (3.º), X Congreso internacional de estudios patristicos [< Ox 1987, Peeters, 5 vol.],ᵀ AugM 36, 140-3 (1991) 1-364. 35 art., 11 infra.

541 ᴱPalaver Wolfgang, Centesimo anno; 100 Jahre katholische Soziallehre, Bilanz und Ausblick.: Theologische Trends 4. Thaur 1991, Kulturverlag. 355 p. DM 35. [TR 87,349]. 14 art.

541* Palaver Wolfgang, editor, Williams James G., executive secretary, Newsletter of the Colloquium on Violence and Religion [Stanford meeting, May 16-18 1991, SCHWAGER Raymond, president], semiannual from September (announced June 21) 1991.

542 Pérez Jiménez Lázaro, present., Congreso Nacional de teología a los 25 años del Concilio Vaticano II [23-25.IV.1990, México, Univ. Pont.]; EfMex 9,2 (1991) 153-316.

543 a) ᴱPiolanti A., Atti del IX Congresso Tomistico internazionale, Roma 24-29.VI.1990: Studi Tomistici 41s. Vaticano 1991, Editrice (Pont. Accad. S. Tommaso). 362 p.; 380 p. Lit. 45.000 ciascuno. – ᴿRasT 32 (1991) 433s (A. Orazzo).

— b) ᴱPirotte J., Derroitte H., Églises et santé dans le Tiers Monde, hier et aujourd'hui [Centre Lebbe, LvN 19-21.X.1989]: Studies in Christian Mission 5. Leiden 1991, Brill. xxi-176 p.; 4 fig. 95 f [NRT 114,590, G. Menin]. 90-04-09470-9.

— c) ᴱPizzolato L. F., 'De libero arbitrio' di AGOSTINO d'Ippona: settimana pavese 6. Palermo 1990, Augustinus. 87 p. Lit. 15000. 4 art. – ᴿRÉAnc 93 (1991) 425-7 (P. Mattei).

544 ᴱPotestà G. L., Il profetismo gioachimita tra Quattrocento e Cinquecento; Atti III Congresso, S. Giovanni in Fiore, 17-21 sett. 1989: Opere Strum 3. Genova 1991, Marietti. 520 p.; 16 pl. [RHE 87,86*].

545 Poulain Gaston mgr., présent., Synode de Rome 1990, La formation des prêtres: Documents de l'Église. P 1991, Centurion/Cerf. 335 p. – ᴿEspr-Vie 101 (1991) 129-131 (C. Bouchaud).

546 [Poulat E. al.] Nouveaux enjeux de la laïcité, Colloque. 1990. – ᴿHerdKor 44 (1990) 394 (K. Nientiedt).

547 ᴱPrabhakar M. E., Towards a Dalit theology [Madras Dec. 1986, 14 art.; Guntur 1986, 9 art.]. New Delhi 1988, ISPCK/CDLM. 185 p. rs 40. – ᴿArasaradi 3,1 (1990) 53-55 (D. Chellappa).

548 ᴱPrawdzik Werner, Wirklichkeit und Theologie; theologische Versuche und pastorale Impulse aus der Weltkirche [Studienwoche Bonn-St. Augustin 1987]: Missionspriesterseminar Veröff 36. Nettetal 1988, Steyler. 164 p. DM 35. – ᴿZkT 113 (1991) 319s (H. B. Meyer).

Il prete; identità del ministero e oggettività della fede [Atti Fac. T. Italia Settentrionale 20-21.II.1990]: Disputatio 2, 1990 ➤ 464.

549 *a*) ᴱ**Prinzing** Günter, *Simon* Dieter, Fest und Alltag in Byzanz. Mü 1990, Beck. 226 p.; 3 fig. – ᴿEllinika 41 (1990) 422-5 (L. *Maksimović*, franç.).
— *b*) ᴱ**Puthanangady** Paul, Emerging India and the Word of God [Bangalore 4-8.III.1991: 25 years 'Dei Verbum']. Bangalore 1991, National Biblical Catechetical and Liturgical Centre. 626 p. [TContexto 2/1, 129, G. *Evers*].
— *c*) **Raquez** Olivier, present., Amore del bello; studi sulla Filocalia; Atti del Simposio internaz. Pont. Collegio Greco, Roma nov. 1989. Magnano ᴠᴄ 1991, Qiqayon. c. 290 p. Lit. 30.000. – [Asprenas 39,113, L. *Fatica*].

550 *a*) Rɪᴄœᴜʀ Paul, Les Métamorphoses de la raison herméneutique; Actes du colloque de Cerisy-la-Salle 1-11 août 1988, ᴱ**Greisch** J., *Kearney* R. P 1991, Cerf. 413 p. F 175. 2-204-04308-7 [BL 92,15, R. P. *Carroll*].
— *b*) ᴱ**Ries** Julien, *Limet* Henri, Anges et démons; colloque Liège et LvN 25-26 nov. 1987: Homo Religiosus 14. Lv 1989, Centre Hist. Rel. 466 p. ⟶ 5,728 [RHPR 71 (1991) 245].
— *c*) ᴱ**Robertson** Roland, *Garrett* William R., Religion and global order [New Era conference]: Religion and the political order 4. NY 1991, Paragon. 322 p. $30; pa. $15. 0-89226-090-4; -1-2 [TDig 39,183]. 15 art.

551 ᴱ**Röckle** G., Diakonische Kirche; Sendung — Dienst — Leitung; Versuche einer theologischen Orientierung [Diakonat, Berlin 1989]. Neuk 1990. 185 p. DM 24,80. 3-7887-1325-9. – ᴿTsTNijm 31 (1991) 110s (E. *Henau*).

552 **Rondot** P., présent., Les chrétiens du monde arabe; problématiques actuelles et enjeux: colloque C. M. A., Paris sept. 1987. P 19... Maisonneuve & L. 160 p. – ᴿRThom 91 (1991) 169s (J. *Jomier*: plaidoirie adaptée ?).

552* ᴱ**Roof** Wade C., World Order and religion [Amherst ᴍᴀ 1989]: Religion-Culture-Society. Albany 1991, ꜱᴜɴʏ. 320 p. $59.50; pa. $20. 0-7914-0739-X; -40-3. 14 art. [TDig 39,295].

553 *a*) **Rosa** M. present., Città italiane del 1500 tra Riforma e Controriforma [Atti del Congresso internazionale Lucca 1983]. Lucca 1988, Fazzi. 366 p. – ᴿRHPR 71 (1991) 388s (A. *Moda*).
— *b*) Rᴏꜱᴍɪɴɪ Antonio: Filosofia e ascesi nel pensiero di ∼, Convegno Trento 5-7 dic. 1988: BtRosmini 2. Brescia 1991, Morcelliana. 397 p. Lit. 50.000 [TR 88,255].

554 *a*) ᴱ**Rütte** Hans von, Bäuerliche Frömmigkeit und kommunale Reformation: Schw. Historikertag 23.X.1987, Bern: Itinera 8. Ba 1988, Schwabe. 122 p. Fs 28 pa. – ᴿTZBas 47 (1991) 88 (K. *Hammer*).
— *b*) ᴱ**Rusch** William G., A commentary on 'Ecumenism; the vision of the ᴇʟᴄᴀ'. Mp 1990, Augsburg. 159 p. $7 [TR 88,83].
— *c*) ᴱ**Sánchez Gil** F. V., *Martínez Fresneda* F., De la América española a la América americana; Actas del simposio América V Centenario: Publ. 4. Murcia 1991, Inst. Teol. Franciscano. 196 p. [NRT 114,621, P. *Evrard*].

555 ᴱ**Sargent** Michael G., De cella in seculum; religious and secular life and devotion in late medieval England [conference for 8th centenary of Carthusian Hᴜɢʜ of Avalon consecrated bishop]. C 1989, Brewer. xiii-244 p.; 24 pl. £45. – ᴿJTS 42 (1991) 382-4 (Alexandra *Barratt*).

556 ᴱ**Sartori** Luigi, Comunicazione e ritualità; la celebrazione liturgica alla verifica delle leggi della comunicazione [Padova O.S.B. 1984s]: Caro Salutis Cardo 4. Padova 1988, Messaggero. 357 p. Lit. 30.000 pa. [TR 88,318, R. *Kaczynski*].

557 *a*) ᴱ**Schlette** Friedrich, *Kaufmann* Dieter, Religion und Kult in ur- und frühgeschichtlicher Zeit, 13. Tagung, Halle 4.-6.XI.1985. B 1989, Akademie. 304 p. 3-05-000662-5. 29 art., 2 infra.

— b) ᴱSchmidtke Dietrich, 'Minnichlichiu gotes erkennusse'; Studien zur frühen abendländischen Mystik; Symposium Heidelberg 16.I.1989: Mystik 1/7. Stu 1990, Frommann-Holzboog. 163 p. DM 48. [TR 88, 34-36, Hildegard *Koller*].

— c) ᴱScicolone Ildebrando, La celebrazione del triduo pasquale; anamnesis e mimesis; Atti del III Congresso Internazionale di Liturgia, Roma 3-13.V.1988: StudAnselm 102 / AnalLtg 14. R 1991, Studia Anselmiana. 308 p.; 19 pl. Lit. 70.000 [TR 88,439, tit. pp.].

— d) La spiritualità mariana della Chiesa alla luce dell'Enciclica 'Redemptoris Mater' [XXIX Settimana Spiritualità 21-25 febb. 1988]: Fiamma viva 29. R 1988, Teresianum. 199 p. – ᴿMarianum 52 (1990) 441-3 (P. *Sartor*).

558 ᴱStickler A. M., *al.*, Studi Gregoriani 13 [int. Konferenz Salerno Mai 1986]. R 1989, LAS(alesianum). xi-433 p.; 8 pl. [TLZ 117,849, J. *Irmscher*].

559 ᴱStrolz Maria Katharina, *Binder* Margarete, John H. NEWMAN, lover of truth: Symposium Rome 26-28 April 1990. R 1990, Pont. Univ. Urbaniana. 174 p. Lit. 30.000 [TR 87,529]. – ᴿForumKT 7 (1991) 221-3 (L. *Govaert*).

560 ᴱSwidler Leonard, *al.*, Bursting the bonds? A Jewish-Christian dialogue on Jesus and Paul [Temple Univ. dialogues 1980-6]: Faith Meets Faith. Mkn 1990, Orbis. viii-224 p. $35; pa. $17 [CBQ 54,591, tit. pp.]. – ᴿColcT 61,3 (1991) 196-8 (W. *Chrostowski*, **Ө**); Worship 65 (1991) 550-2 (D. M. *Bossman*).

560* ᴱTaylor William D., Internationalizing missionary training; a global perspective [11 papers from July 1989 Manila consultation + 12 others]. Exeter/GR 1992, Paternoster/Baker. xiv-286 p. $20. 0-8010-8903-4 [TDig 39,268].

561 a) Theological workshop on priestly vocation, Fujen Catholic University, Taipei Nov. 29 - Dec. 1, 1990 **Ⓒ** = ColcFuJen 87 (1991) 7-162.

— b) Théologie africaine, bilan et perspectives, 17ᵉ Sém. Théologique, Kinshasa 2-8.IV.1989. Kinshasa 1990, Fac. Catholiques. 441 p. [NRT 114, 592, J. *Masson*].

— c) ᴱThiemann Ronald F., The legacy of H. Richard NIEBUHR [1894-1962; Harvard Sept. 1988; 4 art. + responses]: HarvTSt 36. Mp 1991, Fortress. ix-148 p. $14. 0-8006-7084-1 [TDig 39,172].

— d) ᴱTragan P. R., Alle origini del battesimo; Atti dell'VIII convegno di teologia sacramentaria, Roma 9-11.III.1989: StudAns 106. R 1991, S. Anselmo. 296 p, [TR 88,339, tit. pp.].

562 [ᴱTriacca A. M., *Pistoia* A.], Liturgie, éthique et peuple de Dieu, S. Serge 37ᵉ semaine, 1990. R 1991, Liturgiche. 320 p. Lit. 50.000 [Salesianum 54,596s, A. *Cuva*]. – ᴿEsprVie 101 (1991) 652-4 (P. *Rouillard*: analyses sans pp.).

563 ᴱTriacca Achille M., [p. 67-103], Il mistero del Sangue di Cristo e la catechesi; Atti del IV Convegno Pastorale, Roma 27-30 dic. 1990: Sangue e Vita 9. R 1991, Pia Unione P. Sangue. 619 p.; ill.; map. Lit. 35.000. P. 17-35, *Vanhoye* Albert, Catechesi biblica e sangue di Cristo; p. 37-65, *Dal Covolo* Enrico, Catechesi patristica e sangue di Cristo; + 22 al.

564 ᴱUllrich Lothar, Aspekte eines christlichen Menschenbildes: Erfurter Theologische Woche 1989: ErfTSchr 21. Lp 1990, Benno. 123 p. 3-7462-0602-2. - 9 art., 5 infra.

564* ᴱUtz Arthur F., Die katholische Soziallehre und die Wirtschafts-ordnung: Humanum. Trier 1991, Paulinus. 384 p. DM 36,80. [TR 88, 173, tit. pp.]. 12 art.

565 ᴱVattioni Francesco, Sangue e antropologia nella teologia medievale; Atti della VII Settimana, Roma 22 nov. - 2 dic. 1989: Centro Studi Sanguis Christi 7. R 1991, Pia Unione P. Sangue. I. Bibbia-Giudaismo, 417 p.; 11 art.; 7 infra. - II. p. 419-1081, 32 art.; 6 infra. - III. p. 1083-1858, 18 art.; 1 infra (1791-1858, indici vol. 1-7). Lit. 100.000.

566 ᴱVesey Godfrey, The philosophy in Christianity [Cambridge Royal Institute of Philosophy lectures 1988s]. C 1989, Univ. xvi-244 p. – ᴿScripTPamp 23 (1991) 1044 (F. Conesa).

566* ᴱViaud P., Les religions et la guerre; judaïsme, christianisme, Islam [représentatifs 'réunis' par le Secrétariat de la Défense de France]: Recherches morales. P 1991, Cerf. 578 p. F 145. [NRT 114,600, L. Volpe].

567 Wahrheit und Geschichtlichkeit: Salzburg 1988, 1989 ᴱHorst U. ➤ 6,628; 3-491-77782-8: ᴿTsTNijm 31 (1991) 105 (P. Valkenberg).

568 a) ᴱWeder H., Gerechtigkeit, Friede, Bewahrung der Schöpfung; Überlegungen ['Kursus' der Z Universitätstheologen 1989s]. Z 1990, Theol-V. 181 p. Fs 28. 3-290-10114-2 [TLZ 117,20, J. Ziemer]. – ᴿTsTNijm 31 (1991) 306s (T. Brattinga).

— b) ᴱWerbick Jürgen, Offenbarungsspruch und fundamentalistische Versuchung [Kolloquium Siegen 1989]: QDisp 129. FrB 1991, Herder. 245 p. DM 49 pa. 3-451-02129-3. 6 art. – ᴿTGL 81 (1991) 485s (W. Beinert).

— c) ᴱWestphal M., Signes de l'Esprit: WCC Septième Assemblée, Canberra 7-20 févr. 1991. Genève 1991, WCC. viii-442 p. Fs 35 [NRT 114,771, A. Harvengt].

— d) ᴱYovel Yirmiyahu, God and nature; SPINOZA's metaphysics; 1st Jerusalem Conference, Ethica 1: Spinoza by 2000, 1. Leiden 1991, Brill. xiii-253 p. ƒ 125 [TR 88,433, tit. pp.].

A2.5 *Acta philologica et historica* [reports ➤ Y7.6].

569 Actes de l'association pour l'encouragement des études grecques 1990s: RÉG 104,2 (1991) ix-L.

570 **Argyriou** Asterios, présent., Byzance après Byzance, 5º symposion byzantinon 19-21 nov. 1987 = ByzF 17 (1991) 1-163.

571 ᴱ**Baxter** P.T.W., *Fardon* Richard, Voice, genre, text; anthropological essays in Africa and beyond [< 'Texts in Action', Manchester workshop, April 1990] = BJRyL 73,3 (1991). 234 p. 13 art.

572 ᴱ**Bergenholtz** Henning, *Mugdan* Joachim, Lexikographie und Grammatik, Akten des Essener Kolloquiums 28.-30.VI.1984. Tü 1985, Niemeyer. 403 p. DM 124. – ᴿIndogF 95 (1990) 241-5 (H. Sauer).

573 ᴱ**Berti** Fede, Dionysos, mito e mistero; Atti del Convegno internazionale Comacchio 3-5 nov. 1989. Ferrara 1991, Liberty. 444 p. Lit. 60.000. 29 art., 2 infra.

574 ᴱ**Binder** Gerhard, *Effe* Bernd, Mythos; erzählende Weltdeutung im Spannungsfeld von Ritual, Geschichte und Rationalität: Bochumer Altertumsw. Colloquium 2. Trier 1990, Wiss. 223 p.

575 **Binder** G., *Effe* B., Tod und Jenseits im Altertum; Bochumer Altertumsw. Colloq 6. Trier 1991, 'WVT'. 249 p., 6 phot. DM 36. 3-922031-89-7 [ZAW 104,312].

576 ᴱ**Blänsdorf** Jürgen, Theater und Gesellschaft im Imperium Romanum [Symposium Mainz, Univ. Nov. 1987]: Mainzer ForDramaT 4. Tü 1990, Francke. 276 p.

577 Byzantines: Congrès 18ᵉ internationale des études ~ : ❸ Rus' mešdu vostokom i zapadnom: Kuľtura i obščestvo, X-XVII vv, (Russland zu

Orient und Occident, Kultur und Gesellschaft, alles ⑬) Moskva 8-15 avgusta 1991. Moskva 1991 I. 314 p.; II. 347 p.; III. 253 p.

578 ᴱ**Calvo Martínez** Tomás, *Ávila Crespo* Remedios, Paul RICŒUR, Los caminos de la interpretación; Actas del Symposium internac. Granada 23-27 nov. 1987, ᵀ*García Rúa* José L. AutTT-Fil 37. Barc 1991, Anthropos. 447 p. 84-7658-315-X. 16 art., 3 infra.

579 ᴱ[Radici] **Colace** Paola, *Caccamo Caltabiano* Maria, Atti del I Seminario di Studi sui Lessici tecnici greci e latini (Messina, 8-10 marzo 1990) Atti Accad. f/a 66 supp. 1 (1990). Messina 1991, Accademia Peloritana dei Pericolanti. 400 p.; ill. 24 art.; 6 infra.

580 ᴱ**Coleman** Robert, New studies in Latin linguistics; selected papers, 4th international colloquium, Cambridge April 1987: StLangComp 21. Amst 1991, Benjamins. x-478 p. 90-272-3024-2. 29 art., 4 infra.

581 ᴱ**Croisille** J. M., Alejandro Magno, modelo de los emperadores romanos; Actes du IVᵉ colloque de la SIEN [Soc. Internat. d'Études Néroniennes], Madrid 1987: Coll. Latomus 209. Bru 1990. 398 p. – ᴿBStLat 21 (1991) 368-371 (Eugenia *Mastellone*).

582 ᴱ**Danielewicz** Jerzy, Lirica greca e latina: Convegno di Studi Polacco-Italiano, Poznań 2-5 maggio 1990: AION-clas. 12 (1990) 309 p. 18 art., → g296*.

583 DEGRASSI Attilio mém.: Epigrafia; Actes du Colloque international d'épigraphie latine, Rome 27-28 mai 1988, ᴱ**Piétri** C. Coll. ÉcFr 143. R 1991, Univ. x-760 p. 2-7283-0221-5. 24 art., 2 infra.

584 Deutscher Altphilologenverband, Kongress Hamburg 17.-21. April 1990, I-II-III: Gymnasium 98, 2.3.5 (1991) 97-176. 193-254. 385-482.

584* **Díaz y Díaz** M. C., present., Actas del VIIIº coloquio del Comité internacional de paleografía latina, Madrid-Toledo 29.IX.-1.X.1987: Estudios y ensayos 6. Madrid 1990, Joyas bibliográficas. 242 p.; ill. [RHE 87,175*].

585 ᴱ**D'Ippolito** Gennaro, *Gallo* Italo, Strutture formali dei 'Moralia' di PLUTARCO; Atti del III Convegno plutarcheo, Palermo 3-5 maggio 1989. N 1991, D'Auria. 514 p. 88-7092-044-5. 34 art.; 2 infra.

586 ᴱ**Doeser** M. C., *Musschenga* A. W., De werkelijkheid van de wetenschappen [VU Studiegroep]: Bezinningscentrum V.U. 16. Kampen 1989, Kok. 199 p. ƒ32,50. 90-24248-58-2. 11 art.; *Kuitert* H. 'meta-theologische toetsing'. – ᴿNedTTs 45 (1991) 75-77 (A. F. *Sanders*).

587 ᴱ**Étienne** Roland, *Le Dinahet* Marie-Thérèse, L'espace sacrificiel dans les civilisations méditerranéennes de l'antiquité; Actes du colloque tenu à la Maison de l'Orient, Lyon, 4-7 juin 1988: Univ. Bt Reinach 2/5. P 1991, de Boccard. 346 p. 2-9505633-0-9. 38 art., 3 infra.

587* ᴱ**Falkner** Thomas M., *de Luce* Judith, Old age in Greek and Latin literature [3 U.S. conferences 1985s]. Albany 1989, SUNY. xv-260 p. $49.50; pa. $17. – ᴿClasR 41 (1991) 93-95 (J. G. F. *Powell*).

588 ᴱ**Fossey** John M., (*Morin* Jacques) International congress on the Hellenic diaspora, from antiquity to modern times, 1. Montréal 17-22.IV.1988 / Athens 26-30.IV.1988: Univ. McGill Mg 10,1s. Amst 1991, Gieben. I to 1453, xvii-294 p.; II, xv-508 p. 90-5063-060-X. 22 art.; 8 infra.

589 ᴱ**Fossier** Lucie, *Irigoin* Jean, Déchiffrer les écritures effacées; Actes de la Table ronde organisée par l'Institut de Recherche et d'Histoire des Textes (Paris, mai 1981). P 1990, CNRS. – ᴿRÉG 104 (1991) 622s (P. *Cauderlier*).

590 ᴱ**Geertman** H., *Jong* J. J. de, Munus non ingratum; proceedings of the international symposium on VITRUVIUS 'De architectura' and the Hel-

lenistic and Republican architecture: Babesch supp. 2. Leiden 1989. 239 p.; ill. ƒ135. 91-72821-01-7. 23 art. – ᴿJRS 81 (1991) 210s (E. V. *Thomas*).

590* ᴱ**Genet** J.-P., L'historiographie médiévale en Europe; Actes du colloque, Univ. Paris I, Centre Hist.-Jurid. 29.III.-1.IV.1989. P 1991, CNRS. 342 p.; 3 maps. [RHE 87,168*].

591 *a*) ᴱ**Godman** Peter, *Murray* Oswyn, Latin poetry and the classical tradition; essays in medieval and renaissance literature: London Warburg Inst., Dec. 1988. Ox 1990, Clarendon. xi-243 p. – ᴿRFgIC 119 (1991) 486-493 (H. D. *Jocelyn*; very severe; a handsome volume but badly proofread and of vague goals. – J. M. ZIOLSKOWSKI divides views about **inspiration** expressed by medieval Latin poets into those which refer to God, Jordan River, or some saint; and those which invoke Muses, Bacchus, or mental disturbance).

— *b*) ᴱ**Goyon** Jean-Claude, *al.*, L'idéologie du pouvoir monarchique dans l'Antiquité; Actes du Colloque, Soc. Prof. Hist. Anc. Univ., Lyon/Vienne 26-28 juin 1989. P 1991, de Boccard. 115 p. 2-909142-01-9 [OIAc 2,20].

— *c*) ᴱ**Güttgemanns** Erhardt, [p. 7-21; 39-70] Das Phänomen der 'Simulation'; Beiträge zu einem semiotischen Kolloquium [Bonn 1989]: Forum Theologiae Linguisticae 17. Bonn 1991, Linguistica Biblica. 276 p.; ill. DM 29. 3-87797-017-6. 14 art.; 10 infra.

— *d*) ᴱ**Harlfinger** Dieter, *Prato* Giancarlo, Paleografia e codicologia greca; Atti del II Colloquio Internazionale, Berlino-Wolfenbüttel 17-21 ottobre 1983. Alessandria 1991, Orso. I. 579 p.; 34 art. II. 258 p.; 21 art. 88-7694-034-0 both.

— *e*) ᴱ**Harmatta** J., Proceedings of the XVIIIth International Congress of the Committee Eirene, Budapest, Sept. 1988, section I-II, IV, VI: ActAntH 33,1-4 (1990-2) 411 p.

— *f*) Heidelberg Univ. Seminar für Alte Geschichte 100-j. Jubiläumsvorträge, Vom frühen Griechentum bis zur römischen Kaiserzeit, ᴱ**Alföldy** Geza: HABES 6. Stu 1989, Steiner. vi-108 p.; 12 pl. – ᴿGerión 8 (1990) 299s (J. *Martínez-Pinna*).

592 HÉRODOTE et les peuples non grecs [ᴱ*Reverdin* Olivier]; EntrAntClas 35 (22-26.VIII.1988). Genève 1990, Hardt. 350 p. [RÉG 104,679]. 9 art.; 3 infra.

593 ᴱ**Herzfeld** Michael, *Melazzo* Lucio, Semiotic theory and practice; proceedings IASS 3d, Palermo 1984. B 1988, Mouton de Gruyter. 2 vol. – ᴿSemiotica 87 (1991) 119-146 (Susan *Petrilli*, 'For a semiotic narration of semiotics').

594 *a*) ᴱ**Hörandner** Wolfram, *Trapp* Erich, Lexicographica byzantina; Beiträge zum Symposion zur byzantinischen Lexikographie (Wien, 1-4.III.1989): ByzVindobonensia 20. W 1991, Österr. Akad.

— *b*) ᴱ**Kahil** Lilly, *Linant de Bellefonds* Pascale, Religion, Mythologie, Iconographie: Actes du Colloque international Rome mai 1989: MÉF-Ant 103 (1991) 7-306. = R 1991, École Française. 324 p.

— *c*) [**Kefer** Michel, *al.*, présent.] Universals of Language [réunion Anvers 1986]: Belgian Journal of Linguistics 4 (1989). 193 p. Fb 844. – ᴿBSLP 85 (1990) 15s (X. *Mignot*).

— *d*) Klassische Archäologie: Akten des XIII. internationalen Kongresses für ~, Berlin 1988, DAI. Mainz 1990, von Zabern. xviii-700 p.; 95 pl., 5 foldouts. [RArchéol 92,396, C. *Le Roy*].

595 ᴱ**Leander Touati** Anne-Marie, *al.*, Munuscula Romana, Lund papers 1-2.X.1988 for re-opening of Swedish Institute in Rome: Acta Svenska

Inst. 8,17. Sto 1991, Åström. 138 p.; ill. 91-7042-139-0. 14 art.; 2 infra.

596 ᴱLordkipanidzé Otar, *Lévêque* Pierre, Le Pont-Euxin vu par les Grecs; sources écrites et archéologie; Symposium de Vani (Colchide) sept.-oct. 1987: Annales Besançon 427, Hist. Anc. 100. P 1990, BLettres. 348 p.

596* ᴱMurray Oswyn, *Price* Simon, The Greek city, from Homer to Alexander [4 inedita + 10 from 1986s Ancient History Seminar]. Ox 1991, Clarendon. xv-372 p.; ill. £18. 0-19-814791-0.

597 ᴱNicosia Salvatore, La traduzione dei testi classici; teoria, prassi, storia; Atti del Convegno di Palermo [Univ., etc.] 6-9 aprile 1988. N 1991, D'Auria. 383 p. Lit. 160.000. 88-7092-071-2. 26 art.; 3 infra.

597* ᴱPérez Jiménez Aurelio, *Cerro Calderón* Gonzalo del, Estudios sobre Plutarco, obra y tradición; Actas del I Symposion Español, Fuengirola 1988. Málaga 1990, Univ. 289 p. pt. 2000. 84-7496-187-4. 31 art.

598 ᴱPetrikovitz H. von, [*Rosén* Haiim B., Palästina, *al.*] Die Sprachen im römischen Reich der Kaiserzeit, Kolloquium 8.-10.IV.1974, Bonn Landesmuseum: BonnJbb Beih 40. Köln 1990, Rheinland (Bonn, Habelt). viii-367 p. 3-7927-0431-5. – ᴿBO 48 (1991) 836s (F. T. *Gignac*, nothing on why now).

599 ᴱPotter Paul, *al.*, La maladie et les malades dans la Collection Hippocratique; Actes du VIᵉ colloque international hippocratique. Québec 1990, Spinx. 465 p. – ᴿRÉG 104 (1991) 288-290 (L. *Villard*: 'Spinx'; tit. pp.).

600 ᴱRawson Beryl, Marriage, divorce, and children in ancient Rome: Canberra Humanities Research 1988. Ox 1991, Clarendon. xii-252 p.; 8 pl. 0-19-814918-2. 9 art., 2 infra.

600* Realtà e idea della storia, V convegno culturale con l'Enciclopedia Italiana, Roma 25-27.I.1991: Studium 87 (1991) 773-977.

601 ᴱRich John, *Wallace-Hadrill* Andrew, City and country in the ancient world: Leicester-Nottingham 1986-8 seminars: StAncSoc 2. L 1991, Routledge. xviii-305 p.; 18 maps, 5 plans. £35. 0-415-01974-5 [JRS 81,261]. 11 art., 5 infra. – ᴿGreeceR 38 (1991) 229s (W. H. *Manning*).

602 ᴱSaid Suzanne, Hellenismos; quelques jalons pour une histoire de l'identité grecque: Colloque de Strasbourg 25-27.IX.1989: Centre Recherche PrOr-Grèce 11. Leiden 1991, Brill. 402 p. 90-04-09379-6. 21 art.; 7 infra.

603 ᴱSenner Wayne M., The origins of writing [1984 Arizona State Univ. exhibit: *Green* M. Sumerian; *Fischer* H. Eg.; *Cross* F. Canaanite...]. Lincoln 1989, Univ. Nebraska. ii-245 p.; 94 fig.; 27 pl. – ᴿPhoenix 44 (Toronto 1990) 385-8 (H. *Konishi*).

604 ᴱSetaioli Aldo, Seneca e la cultura [Convegno Univ. Perugia 1989]. N 1991, Ed. Scientifiche. 137 p. – ᴿBStLat 21 (1991) 64s (Antonella *Borgo*).

605 Société des études latines, Compte-rendu des séances de 1991: RÉLat 69 (1991) 1-23; IX-XXIX liste des membres.

605* ᴱSordi Marta, 'Dulce et decorum est pro patria mori'; la morte in combattimento nell'antichità [< seminario Univ. Catt.]: Ist. Stor. Ant. 16. Mi 1990, ViPe. viii-293 p. Lit. 46.000. 88-343-0347-4 [AntClas 61, 497s, P. *Lévêque*].

606 ᴱThélamon F., Sociabilité, pouvoirs et société [Grèce ancienne], Actes du colloque de Rouen, 24-26 nov. 1983: Publ. 110. Rouen 1987, Univ. 654 p. – ᴿRÉAnc 92 (1990) 422-4 (E. *Deniaux*).

606* ᴱToaff Ariel, *Schwarzfuchs* Simon, The Mediterranean and the Jews; banking, finance and international trade (XVI-XVIII centuries) [1984

conference]. Ramat-Gan 1989, Bar-Ilan. 307p. 16 art. – RJQR 81 (1990s) 462s (W. C. *Jordan*).
607 ETomić Olga Mišeska, [p. 1-10], Markedness in synchrony and diachrony [only part from Ohred 1986, Soc. Linguistica Europea]: TrendsLingSM 39. B 1989, Mouton de Gruyter. x-411p. 3-1101-1780-0. 19 art.; 2 infra.
608 Traina A. present. [p. 11-13], LUCREZIO; l'atomo e la parola; colloquio Bologna 26 gen. 1989: Quad. Bt. Umanist. 3. Bo 1990, Coop. Univ. 109 p. Lit. 20.000. 4 art. [Gymnasium 99, 92, R. *Glei*].
609 EUglione Renato, La donna nel mondo antico [I, 21-23.IV.1986: 1987 ➤ 4,699] II, Torino 19-20 Aprile 1988. T 1989, Assessorato alla Cultura. 276 p. – ROrpheus 11 (1990) 404-7 (Vincenza *Milazzo*).
610 EWalker Susan, *Cameron* A., The Greek renaissance in the Roman Empire; papers from the tenth British Museum classical colloquium: Bulletin supp. 55. L 1989, Institute of Classical Studies. 225 p.; 73 pl. – RAJA 95 (1991) 357s (G. W. *Bowersock*): RÉG 104 (1991) 434 (P. *Gauthier*, with indication of 11 items).
611 Zinko C., Akten der 13. Österreichischen Linguistentagung, Graz 25.-27. Oktober 1985: Arb. Verg. Sprachw. I. Graz 1988, Leykam. 338p. DM 58,60. – RIndogF 96 (1991) 238-240 (K. H. *Schmidt*: mit einigen von 1983).

A2.7 *Acta* **orientalistica.**

612 [Allen James P., *al.*] Religion and philosophy in ancient Egypt [Yale symposium 1988]: YaleEg 3. NHv 1989, Eg. Seminar. viii-160 p. 0-912532-18-1. – RBO 48 (1991) 771-4 (L. *Kákosy*).
613 EBottema S., *Entjes-Nieborg* G., *Zeist* W. Van, Man's role in the shaping of the Eastern Mediterranean landscape: INQUA/BAI Symposium Groningen 6-9.III.1989. Rotterdam 1990, Balkema. x-349 p. 90-6191-138-9.
613* Church and State in the Christian East; IXth Congress of the Society for the Law of the Oriental Churches, Kavala, Sept. 17-24, 1989: Kanon 10 (W 1991) c. 250 p. [ZIT 91,685, tit. pp.].
614 ECohen M. R., *Udovitch* A.I., Jews among Arabs; contacts and boundaries [colloquium Princeton 1986]. Princeton 1989, Darwin. 140 p. 6 art. – RHenoch 13 (1991) 380s (R. *Tottoli*).
616 EEndesfelder Erika, [p. 5-61] Probleme der frühen Gesellschaftsentwicklung im Alten Ägypten: Heidelberg-Prague co-meetings. B 1991, Univ. 168 p.; maps. 3-86175-004-X. 3 al. art.
617 EGodlewski Włodzimierz, Coptic studies; Acts of Third International Congress, Warsaw 20-25 August 1984. Wsz 1990, PWN. 506 p. 83-01-07663-1 [OIAc 1,17; excerpted].
618 E[Morigi] Govi Cristiana, *al.*, L'Egitto fuori dell'Egitto; dalla riscoperta all'egittologia; Atti del Convegno internazionale Bologna 26-29 marzo 1990. Bo 1991, Clueb. ix-460 p. 38 art., plures infra.
619 EKlengel Horst, *Sundermann* Werner, Ägypten, Vorderasien, Turfan; Probleme der Edition und Bearbeitung altorientalischer Handschriften; Tagung Berlin, Mai 1987: SchrGKuAO 23. B 1991, Akademie. 178 p.; XXIV pl., mostly portraits. 3-05-000922-5.
619* EKraatz Martin, *al.*, Das Bildnis in der Kunst des Orients [colloquia Marburg 1984, Würzburg 1985]: AbhKundeMorgL 50. Stu 1990, Steiner. 309 p. DM 190. [18 art.; 9-16, Kraatz, 'Religionswissenschaftliche Bemerkungen zur Porträtierbarkeit von "Gott und Göttern" ']. – RBSO 54 (1991) 595s (Christa *Paula*).

620 ᴱLoprieno Antonio, Proceedings of the second international conference
on Egyptian grammar (Crossroads II), Los Angeles, October 17-20, 1990:
Lingua Aegyptia 1. Gö 1991, Univ. Sem.Äg./Kopt. vii-445 p. 20 art.,
plures infra.

621 [ᴱMeyer L. De] Mésopotamie et Élam; Actes de la XXXVIème Rencontre
Assyriologique Internationale, Gand 10-14 juillet 1989. Ghent 1991,
Univ. Mesopotamian History and Env. 1. xi-222 p.; ill. 22 art.; plures
infra.

621* ᴱOberhammer Gerhard, Beiträge zur Hermeneutik indischer und abend-
ländischer Religionstraditionen; Arbeitsdokumentation eines Symposiums:
Szb ph/h 573. Wien 1991, Österr. Akad. 256 p. DM 98 [TR 88,257: 9
art., tit. pp.].

622 ᴱReinink G. J., Vanstiphout H. L. J., Dispute poems and dialogues in the
ancient and mediaeval Near East; forms and types of literary debates in
Semitic and related literatures [symposium Groningen 15-17 Mar. 1989]:
OrLovAn 42. Lv 1991, Univ. Dep. Orientalistiek. xx-244 p. 90-6831-
341-X [OIAc 1,23, excerpted]. 14 art.; 6 pre-medieval, infra.

623 ᴱSchoske Sylvia, Geschichte, Verwaltungs- und Wirtschaftsgeschichte,
Rechtsgeschichte, Nachbarkulturen; Akten des vierten internationalen
Ägyptologen-Kongresses, München 1985: StAäKu Beih 4. Hamburg
1991, Buske. vii-367 p.; 10 pl. 3-87118-904 [OIAc 1,24, excerpted].

624 — Sesto [6th etc.] Congresso internazionale di Egittologia, Abstracts of
papers, Turin 1-8 Sept. 1991. T 1991, IAE. 464 p. [OIAc 1,18].

625 ᴱShafer Byron E., Religion in ancient Egypt; gods, myths and personal
practice: Ithaca NY 1991, Cornell Univ. xiv-217 p. $38.50; pa. $13.50.
0-8014-9786-8; -2550-6 [BO 48,984].

625* ᴱYücel Yaşar, ❶ XIᵉ assemblée scientifique de la Société d'histoire
turque, 5-9 Sept. 1990: Belleten 54,211 (1990) 907-1282.

A2.9 Acta archaeologica [reports ➤ Y7.8].

626 ᴱAbu Assaf Ali, al., International Colloquium — Ebla; the history and
archeology of the Idlib Mohafazat, Idlib 25-28 Sept. 1989 = AnASyr 40
(1990). 16 art. + 11 ◉.

627 ᴱAcquaro E., al., Atti del II Congresso internazionale di Studi Fenici e
Punici, Roma 9-14 nov. 1987: StFen 30. R 1991, Cons. Naz. Ric. 440 p.;
p. 441-895; p. 897-1314. 138 art.; 13 infra.

627* AIA: Archaeological Institute of America, 92d annual meeting, abstracts
of papers: AJA 95 (1991) 290-338; 338s index (some 200 authors; only a
few infra).

628 BALIL ILLANA Alberto mem.: Mosaicos romanos; Estudios sobre iconografía; Actas del homenaje, Guadalajara 27-28.IV.1990. Guadalajara
(Mex.) 1990, Museo. 215 p.; ill. 7 art., 2 infra.

629 ᴱBarker Graeme, Lloyd John, Roman landscapes; archaeological survey
in the Mediterranean region [1988 Rome British school conference on
agriculture]: Mg 2. L 1991, British School at Rome. xvi-240 p.; 101 fig.
£22. 0-904152-16-2. – ᴿAntiquity 65 (1991) 1010s (A. M. Snodgrass).

630 Baurain C., al., Lire et écrire en Méditerranée; Actes du Colloque de
Liège, 15-18 nov. 1989, Groupe interuniv. phén/pun: Coll.ÉtClas 6.
Namur 1991, Soc. ÉtClas. xvii-742 p. 2-87037-166-7. 42 art., 31 infra.

630* ᴱBirks Hilary H., al., The cultural landscape; past, present, and future
[centenary conference of Bergen Univ. Botanical Institute 1986]. C 1988,
Univ. 521 p.; 225 fig. – ᴿAJA 95 (1991) 165 (D. Gilbertson: a gem).

631 ᴱ**Bommelaer** Jean-François, Le dessin d'architecture dans les sociétés antiques; Actes du Colloque de Strasbourg, 26-28 janvier 1984: Univ. Travaux PrOrGrèce 8. Leiden 1985, Brill. 344 p., ill., maps. 25 art.; 8 infra.

632 ᴱ**Castrén** Paavo, Ancient technology, symposium Finnish Institute at Athens, Apr. 1987. Helsinki 1990, Tekniikan Museo. 87 p.; ill. 951-95233-4-0. 5 art.; 4 infra.

632* ᴱ**Cauvin** Marie-Claire, Rites et rythmes agraires; séminaire de recherches: Lyon, Travaux Maison de l'Orient 20. P 1991, de Boccard. 156 p. 2-903264-49-X [OIAc 2,16, excerpted].

633 ᴱ**Chevallier** R., Archéologie de la vigne et du vin [Colloque Paris, École normale supérieure, 28-29 mai 1988]: Caesarodunum 24. P 1990, de Boccard. 259 p. 3 infra; le reste sur la France. – ᴿBStLat 21 (1991) 378-382 (Claudia *Neri*).

634 ᴱ**Çilingiroğlu** Altan, *French* David H., Anatolian Iron Ages; Proceedings of the Second Colloquium, Izmir 4-8 May 1987: British Institute of Ankara Mg 13. Ox 1991, Oxbow. xxviii-164 p. 0-946897-38-7. 11 art.; 4 infra.

634* ᴱ**Clark** Geoffrey A., Perspectives on the past; theoretical biases in Mediterranean hunter-gatherer research. Ph 1991, Univ. Pennsylvania. xix-538 p. 0-8122-8190-X [OIAc 2,16, excerpted].

635 ᴱ**Davies** W. V., Egypt and Africa; Nubia from prehistory to Islam [symposium for exposition at new gallery]. L 1991, British Museum/Eg.Expl.Soc. x-320 p.; 16 pl.; maps. 0-7141-0962-2. 30 art.; 2 infra.

636 *a*) ᴱ**Dierkens** Alain, *Sansterre* Jean-Marie, Le souverain à Byzance et en Occident du VIIIᵉ au Xᵉ siècle, Actes du colloque international Inst. Hautes Études de Belgique / Univ. Libre de Bruxelles (27-28 avril 1990) [Hommage à la mémoire de Maurice Lᴇʀᴏʏ]: Byzantion 61,1 (1991) 312 p.; portr.

— *b*) ᴱ**Djindjian** François, *Ducasse* H., Data processing and mathematics applied to archaeology: European postgraduate course 3 (1983): PACT 16 (1987). 472 p. Fb 4000. 0257-8727. 26 art.; 2 infra.

— *c*) ᴱ**Ehrenreich** Robert M., Metals in society; theory beyond analysis [Society for American Archaeology, New Orleans, April 1991]: Masca 8,2 (1991) 92 p. 9 art.

— *d*) ᴱ**Elayi** J., *Sapin* J., [*Briend* J., *al.*] La Syrie-Palestine à l'époque perse; pouvoirs locaux et organisation du territoire: Actes du Colloque international, Inst. Protestant de Théologie de Paris, 29-31 mars 1989: Transeuphratène 2s. P 1990, Gabalda, 219 p.; 197 p. 2-85021-043-9; -4-7. 13 + 12 art.; 8 infra.

637 ᴱ**Gale** N. H., Bronze Age trade in the Mediterranean: Oxford conference Dec. 1989: StMeditArch 90. Jonsered 1991, Åström. v-398 p., ill. 91-7081-003-6. 21 art., infra.

638 Gᴀʀʙʀᴇᴄʜᴛ Günther: Wasserbau in der Geschichte, Kolloquium zu ehren ∼ : Mitt. Leichtweiss Inst. Braunschweig 1987, Techn. Univ. [AnPg 61, p. 729, dépouillé].

639 **Garwood** Paul, *al.*, Sacred and profane; proceedings of a conference on archaeology, ritual and religion, Oxford 1989: Mg 32. Ox 1991, Committee for Archaeology. xvii-171 p. £18. 0-947816-32-1 [Antiquity 66, 566, M. P. *Pearson*]. 15 art.; 2 infra.

639* ᴱ**Glumac** Peter D., Recent trends in archaeometallurgical research [Society for American Archaeology, Las Vegas 1990]: Masca 8,1 (1991). 7 art. ➔ b548*.

640 ᴱ**Guineau** Bernard (*Reynaud* Denise), Pigments et colorants de l'antiquité et du Moyen Âge; teinture, peinture, enluminure, études historiques et physico-chémiques: Colloque CNRS. P 1990, CNRS. 375 p., ill. 2-222-04401-4.

641 ᴱ**Gunter** Ann C., [p. 9-17] Investigating artistic environments in the Ancient Near East: Sackler Gallery 1988 Symposium. Wsh 1990, Smithsonian. xiv-153 p.; ill. 0-299-97070-1. 10 art., infra.

641* ᴱ**Hägg** Robin, *Nordquist* Gullog C., Celebrations of death and divinity in the Bronze Age Argolid (ᶠPERSSON A.): Proceedings of the Sixth International Symposium at the Swedish Institute of Athens, 11-13 June, 1988: Skrifta 4.40. Sto 1990, Åström. 296 p.; 278 fig. Sk 400. 91-7916-021-2. – ᴿClasR 41 (1991) 436-9 (R. A. *Tomlinson*).

642 ᴱ**Hardy** D. A., *al.*, Thera and the Aegean world 3: Proceedings of the 3d Int. Congress Santorini 3-9 Sept. 1989; 1. Archaeology; 2. Earth sciences; 3. Chronology. L 1991, Thera Foundation. 512 p., 356 fig.; 488 p., 271 fig., 8 pl.; 240 p., 122 fig. £350 all 3. 0-9506133-4-7; -5-5; -6-3. – ᴿAntiquity 65 (1991) 998-1001 (S. *Sherratt*).

643 **Herrmann** Bernd, *al.*, Energieflüsse in prähistorischen/historischen Siedlungen und Gemeinschaften [Tagung Göttingen 11.-13.VII.1990]: Saeculum 42,3s (1991) 218-224 (-348).

643* ᴱ**Holland** Thomas A., Publications of the Oriental Institute 1906-1991; exploring the history and civilization of the Near East: OIC 26. Ch 1991, Univ. xv-126 p. 0-918986-77-X [OIAc 2,21, excerpted].

644 **Holst** J., *al.*, Die deutschen Ausgrabungen in Karthago: [ᴱ*Rakob* F.] Karthago, DAI-Tunis. Mainz 1991, von Zabern. x-279 p.; 112 fig.; volume of 41 plans + iv-21 p. DM 198. 3-8053-0985-6 [JRS 81,255].

645 ᴱ**Hornung** Erik, Zum Bild Ägyptens im Mittelalter und in der Renaissance [Basel 7.VI. 1986]: OBO 96. FrS/Gö 1990. Fs 64 [RB 98,298, tit. pp.].

645* ᴱ**Karageorghis** Vassos, The civilizations of the Aegean and their diffusion in Cyprus and the Eastern Mediterranean, 2000-600 B.C.: Proceedings of an International Symposium, Pierides Foundation Museum 1839-1989 (18-24.IX). Larnaca 1991, Pierides-F. 144 p., XXX pl. 9983-560-52-5 [RB 99,756, tit. pp.].

646 ᴱ**Kellens** Jean, La religion iranienne à l'époque achéménide: Actes du Colloque de Liège, 11 déc. 1987: IrAnt supp. 5. Gent 1991. 135 p. 90-6831-329-0 [OIAc 1,19; excerpted].

647 ᴱ**Kerner** Susanne, The Near East in antiquity; German contributions to the archaeology of Jordan, Palestine, Syria, Lebanon and Egypt [Amman Goethe-Inst. lectures 1988s]. Amman 1990, Kutba. 110 p. [OIAc 1,19; excerpted].

647* **Laiou** Angeliki E., present., Symposium on the Byzantine family and household, May 1989: DumbO 44 (1990) 97-226. 11 art., 2 infra.

648 **Lepelley** C., introd., [*Lancel* S., *al.*], Carthage et son territoire dans l'antiquité: Histoire et archéologie de l'Afrique du Nord, IV colloque 1 [113ᵉ Congrès national des sociétés savantes, Strasbourg 5-9 avril] 1988. P 1990, Comité Hist. Scient. 257 p.; ill.; maps. F 250. 2-7355-0201-5 [JRS 81,256].

648* ᴱ**Maniatis** Y., Archaeometry; proceedings of the 25th international symposium [Athens 1986]. Amst 1989, Elsevier. xi-718 p.; 258 fig. *f* 280. – ᴿAJA 95 (1991) 540s (J. M. *Weinstein*).

649 *a*) ᴱ**Mastroroberto** M., Archeologia e botanica; Atti Pompeii 7-9 aprile 1989: Soprintendenza Mg 2. R 1990, Bretschneider. 117 p.; 3 fig.; 10 pl. + 10 color. Lit. 80,000. 88-7062-682-2 [JRS 81,255].

— b) ᴱMessenber Phyllis M., The ethics of collecting; cultural property, whose culture? whose property? [Minneapolis 1986 conference with invited additions]. Albuquerque 1989, Univ. N. Mexico. xxvi-266 p. $32.50. – ᴿAJA 95 (1991) 342-4 (O. W. *Muscarella*).

— c) ᴿMohen J. P., *Eluère* C., Découverte du métal; Colloque international P 1989: Millénaires, dossier 2. P 1991, Picard. 448 p. 2-7084-0404-1 [BSAA 58,537-542, J. *Fernández Manzano*].

— d) ᴱMusti D., *al.*, La transizione dal Miceneo all'Alto Arcaismo, dal palazzo alla città; Atti del Convegno Internazionale Roma 14-19 marzo 1988: Mg.Sc.Umane. R 1991, Cons.Naz.Ricerche. 629 p. 43 art.; 5 infra.

650 ᴱPailler Jean-Marie, Actualité de l'antiquité [Colloque Toulouse-Le Mirail déc. 1985]: Archéologie. P 1989, CNRS. 275 p. F 190. 2-222-04339-5 [ÉTRel 66,106].

651 [Perlès Catherine, présent., / *Tixier* J., Cogitations non conclusives] 25 ans d'études technologiques en préhistoire, bilan et perspectives; Actes des rencontres 18-19-20 octobre 1990, CNRS/Ville d'Antibes. Juan-les-Pins 1991, APDCA. 397 p. F 220. 2-904-110-14-3. 31 art., 2 infra.

651* ᴱPini Ingo (Hg.), *Müller* Walter (Red.), Corpus der minoischen und mykenischen Siegel Beih. 3, 3. Int. Siegel-Symposium 1.-7.IX.1985. B 1989, Mann. vii-353 p. – ᴿGnomon 63 (1991) 620-6 (W. *Schiering*).

652 ᴱPury Albert de, Histoire et conscience dans les civilisations du Proche-Orient ancien; Actes du Colloque de Cartigny 1986: CEPOA Cah 5. Genève/Lv 1990, Univ. Centre d'Étude du Proche-Orient Ancien/Peeters. 90-6831-216-2 [OIAc 1,23, excerpted].

653 Quaegebeur J., organizer, Ritual and Sacrifice in the Ancient Near East: international conference, Leuven 17-20.IV.1991 [announced in Biblica 71,590].

655 ᴱRowell R. M., *Barbour* R. J., Archaeological wood — properties, chemistry, and preservation [Symposium LA 1988]: Advance Series 225. Wsh 1990, American Chemical Soc. 472 p.; 105 fig., 115 phot. $80. 0-8412-1623-1. – ᴿJField 18 (1991) 249-250 (J. A. *Spriggs*).

656 a) ᴱSchlette Friedrich, *Kaufmann* Dieter, Religion und Kult in ur- und frühgeschichtlicher Zeit, Halle 4.-6. Nov. 1985. B 1989, Akademie. 304 p.; 68 fig. 3-05-000662-5. – ᴿAcPraeh 22 (1990) 195-9 (S. *Hansen*); Fornvännen 86 (1991) 213s (Berta *Stjernquist*).

— b) ᴱSigaut François, *Fournier* Dominique, La préparation alimentaire des céréales, Table Ronde Ravello, 11-14 avril 1988: PACT 26 (1991). 136 p. Fb 1400. 0257-8727. 9 art.

— c) ᴱSlater William A., Dining in a classical context [symposium Hamilton ᴼᴺ, McMaster Univ. Sept. 1989]. AA 1991, Univ. Michigan. 217 p. 27 + 36 + 8 fig. 0-472-10194-3. 11 art., mostly on literary descriptions like 'betrothal symposium', 'war and symposium'; little about food.

— d) Vetters Hermann, *Kandler* Manfred, Akten des 14. Internationalen Limeskongresses 1986 in Carnuntum: Der Römische Limes in Österreich 36. W 1990, Österr. Akad.

657 ᴱWalsh John, *Papageorghiou* Athanasios, Chalcolithic Cyprus [Getty Museum Feb. 1990; also published separately there]: BASOR 282s, 1991. 12 art.

657* ᴱWarner Rex L., Rescue archaeology, proceedings of the second New World conference [Dallas 1984]. Dallas 1987, Southern Methodist Univ. xxx-231 p. – ᴿAJA 95 (1991) 539s (R. J. *Elia*).

658 ᶠWATERBOLK Harm T., Archeologie en landschap, symposium 19-
20.X.1987, ᴱBierma Mette, *al.* Groningen 1988. 206 p.; ill.

A3 *Opera consultationis* – **Reference works** .1 *plurium* **separately** *infra.*

659 **ANRW:** Aufstieg und Niedergang der Römischen Welt, 2., ᴱHaase
Wolfgang [➤ 6,828]: 33,3ss, Sprache und Literatur... traian. frühhadrian.
Zeit, 1991: p. 1651-2382. 2385-3259. 3263-3959. / 36,4 (1990), Epiku-
reismus... Orphica p. 2257-3243. B: de Gruyter. 3-11-012541-2; -716-4;
-793-8 / -441-6. – ᴿAnzAltW 44 (1991) 51-67 (J. B. *Bauer,* 25,1-6); ÉtClas
59 (1991) 90s.369 (A. *Wankenne,* 33,1s.4); GreeceR 38 (1991) 253s (T.
Wiedemann: 33,2); Gymnasium 98 (1991) 561-4 (F. *Bömer,* 18,3; 33,2.4);
Irénikon 64 (1991) 303-5 (E. *Lanne,* 25/5s).
660 **AugL:** Augustinus-Lexikon, ᴱMayer Cornelius: I,4, 1990 ➤ 6,829: ᴿÉt-
Clas 59 (1991) 92 (P.-A. *Deproost,* 1/3); JEH 42 (1991) 150 (H. *Chadwick,*
1/4); Klio 73 (1991) 707s (F. *Winkelmann,* 1/3); TPhil 66 (1991) 249s (H. J.
Sieben, 1/4); TüTQ 171 (1991) 137-9 (H. J. *Vogt,* 1/4); VigChr 45 (1991)
376-387 (J. van *Oort* 1,1-4).
661 **BijH:** World of the OT, Bible Handbook 2, ᴱWoude A. van der,
ᵀWoudstra Sierd 1989 ➤ 5,880; 6,830: ᴿCBQ 53 (1991) 124-6 (D. H.
Little).
662 **CAH²** [4, 1988 ➤ 6,831; 8, 1989 ➤ 6,832] 7/2 The Rise of Rome to 220
B.C., ᴱWalbank F. W., *al.* C 1989, Univ. xvii-811 p. £55. – ᴿÉtClas 59
(1991) 98 (A. *Wankenne*) & 99 (G. *Defossé*); GreeceR 38 (1991) 102 (T.
Wiedemann, 7/2; 8); JRS 81 (1991) 157-163 (R. *Sallery,* 7/2; 8); AmJPg
112 (1991) 403-7 (G. K. *Sams, al.*).
664 Catholicisme — hier, aujourd'hui, demain, ᴱMathon G., *al.* [XII, 54, 1988
➤ 5,882; 6,833; volume entier XII, 55-58 Propriété-Rites 1990]. – XIII, 59s
col. 1-256, Rites-Sacerd., F 66; 257-512, -S. Germain; F 82. P 1991, Letouzey & Â. 3-7063-0182-1 (vol. XIII). – ᴿNRT 114 (1992) 455 (L.-J.
Renard, 58s); RHE 86 (1991) 590s (R. *Aubert,* 56-58); ÉTRel 66 (1991)
157s (A. *Gounelle,* 56s: 'Rembrandt' ignore le vrai rapport avec CALVIN);
RThom 91 (1991) 679 (B. *Montagnes*).
665 **CHJud:** The Cambridge History of Judaism, 2. The Hellenistic age,
ᴱDavies W. D., *Finkelstein* L., 1989: £65; ➤ 5,884; 6,835: ᴿBL (1991)
35s (J. R. *Bartlett*); ClasR 41 (1991) 422-4 (J. *Geiger:* inferior to
SCHÜRER-VERMES); ÉTRel 66 (1991) 283s (Jeanne-Marie *Léonard,* 2);
JStJud 22 (1991) 259-264 (A. S. van der *Woude,* 2: detailed analyses);
Salesianum 53 (1991) 178 (R. *Vicent,* 2).
666 **CHLC:** The Cambridge history of literary criticism, ᴱKennedy George
A., I 1989 ➤ 5,942; 6,909; $44.50: ᴿRelStR 17 (1991) 256 (A. T. *Kraabel*).
667 **DHGE:** Dictionnaire d'Histoire et de Géographie Ecclésiastiques, ᴱAu-
bert R., XXIV, 138, 1990 ➤ 6,836. – ᴿEsprVie 101 (1991) 379-384 (G. de
Pasquier, 126-138); RHE 86 (1991) 234-240 (H. *Silvestre,* 23s, 136ss).
668 **DictSpir:** Dictionnaire de Spiritualité, ᴱRayez A., *al.* [XIV, 92-94, 1989
➤ 5,886] 96-98, Taborin-Thiers. P 1991, Beauchesne. col. 1-704. 2-7010-
1208-2. – XV,99-101, 1991. – ᴿIrénikon 64 (1991) 308s (E. *Lanne,* 99ss);
Marianum 52 (1990) 439-441; 53 (1991) 294-6 (L. *Gambero,* 92-94 & 95-98);
NRT 113 (1991) 931s (L.-J. *Renard,* 99-101); OrChrPer 56 (1990) 214-
6. 470-2 (V. *Poggi,* 92-98); RThom 91 (1991) 679 (B. *Montagnes,* 96-101).
669 **DizTF:** Dizionario di Teologia Fondamentale, ᴱLatourelle R., *Fisichella*
R. 1990 ➤ 6,837*: ᴿGregorianum 72 (1991) 403-5 (R. *Fisichella*); PrzPow
272,2 (1991) 364s (J. *Kulisz*); STEv 3 (1991) 266s (P. *Bolognesi*).

670 **DMA:** Dictionary of the Middle Ages, ᴱ**Strayer** Joseph R. [12, 1989
→ 6,838]: 13, index: ᴿSpeculum 66 (1991) 147-9 (C. T. *Wood*, 6-13).

671 *a*) **DPA:** Dizionario patristico e di antichità cristiane, ᴱ**Di Berardino**
Angelo [1-3. → 4,793; 6,838*], 3. Atlante patristico, indices. Genova
1988, Marietti. vii-417 p.; 275 fig. + 51 color.; 44 maps. Lit. 100.000 [TR
88,295s, H. R. *Seeliger*: letzte Präzision fehlt].

— *b*) ᴱ**Di Berardino** Angelo [1-3, 1983-8 → 4,793; 6,838*], Dictionnaire
encyclopédique du christianisme ancien, ᵀᴱ*Vial* François, 1990 → 6,839:
ᴿÉtClas 59 (1991) 182s (F.-X. *Druet*, 1); RÉG 104 (1991) 306s (P. *Nautin*:
useful but not perfect); RTLv 22 (1991) 530-2 (J. *Ponthot*).

— *c*) Encyclopedia of the Early Church, ᵀ*Walford* Adrian; additions *Frend*
W. H. C. NY 1991, Oxford-UP. ... v-1130 p. $175. 0-19-520-892-7.

— *d*) Diccionario patristico y de la antigüedad cristiana: Verdad e imagen 97s.
S 1991s, Sígueme. xxvii-1138 p.; p. 1139-2300 [OLZ 87,374, J. *Irmscher*].

672 **EncIslam:** Encyclopedia of Islam², ᴱ**Bosworth** C. E., *al.* [VII. 115s, 1990
→ 6,840] 117s, 1991.

673 — EncIslam, ᴱ**Donzel** E. van, Index to vols 1-6 and to the supplement
fasc. 1-6. Leiden 1991, Brill.

674 **EncRel:** Encyclopedia of Religion, ᴱ**Eliade** M., 1987 → 2,585 ... 6,841.

675 **EncTF:** Enciclopedia di Teologia Fondamentale, ᴿ**Ruggieri** Giuseppe, I.
1987 → 4,797; 6,843.

676 **EvKL:** Evangelisches Kirchenlexikon, ᴱ**Fahlbusch** E., II (1987) → 5,894;
6,844; – III (Lfg. 7) (1990) 480 col., Lachen-MAKirchG [RelStR 18,
218]: ᴿActuBbg 28 (1991) 168s (J. *Boada*, 2); EcuR 41 (1991) 282 (G.
Wenz, 1s: finds 'emphatically traditional academic German scholarship' at
variance with 'evangelical universality'); Henoch 13 (1991) 233-5 (J. A.
Soggin, 1s); LuJb 58 (1991) 124-6 (H. *Junghans*, 2); TPQ 139 (1991) 431
(R. *Zinnhobler*, III/7: Laientätigkeiten, Lateinamerika ...); TsTNijm 31
(1991) 94 (Bärbel de *Groot-Kopetzky*, 2/6).

ExWNT, ᴱ**Balz** H., *Schneider* G., → 699, Exegetical Dictionary of the NT
1990.

677 **GLNT:** Grande Lessico del Nuovo Testamento [< TWNT, ᴱ**Kittel** G.],
ᵀ**Montagnini** Felice, *al.*, 15, 1988 → 6,845: ᴿNRT 113 (1991) 751s (X.
Jacques).

678 **HbFT:** Handbuch der Fundamentaltheologie 1-4, ᴱ**Kern** Walter, *al.*,
1985-8 → 1,898 ... 6,846: ᴿTPhil 66 (1991) 286-8 (P. *Knauer*, 4).

680 **LexÄg:** Lexikon der Ägyptologie, ᴱ**Helck** W. [Indices, Lfg. 52 → 6,848:
ᴿWZKM 78 (1988) 226-233 (E. *Winter*, vol. 4-6).

681 **LexMA** [→ 6,849], Lexikon des Mittelalters, ᴱ**Giertz** Gernot: V: [1
Hiera-Huntingdon; 2, Hunyadi-Insekten] 3. Insert-Isabella, col. 449-672;
4. Isagoge-Kämpfer, col. 673-896; 5. Kanal-Kietz, col. 897-1120: 1990;
3-7608-8843-7; -4-5; 5-3. – Lfg. 8, Kümmel-Leeuwarden, col. 1569-1792.
Mü 1991, Artemis. 3-7608-8848-4. – ᴿBogVest 50 (1990) 336-9 (M.
Smolik, 1-4); DLZ 112 (1991) 749-751 (J. *Irmscher*, 3s); HZ 253 (1991)
717 (E. *Bashof*, 4); OnsGErf 65 (1991) 286s (J. *Andriessen*, 3/7-10; 4/1-4);
TAth 61 (1990) 326s (K. G. *Bonis*, 4/8ss).

682 **NBL:** Neues Bibel-Lexikon, ᴱ**Görg** Manfred, *Lang* Bernhard [I. (Lfg. 5,
Fleisch-Gymnasium 1991, col. 681-695; DM 38) → 6,850], II, Lfg. 6,
Haar-Herr. Z 1991, Benziger. 128 col. DM 38. – ᴿTLZ 116 (1991) 652-4
(R. *Stahl*, I. Lfg. 2-4); ZkT 113 (1991) 77s (J. M. *Oesch*: Fasz. 2s, drei
Jahre nach 1., anstatt 2-3 pro Jahr wie geplant).

683 **NDizTB** [→ 4,806 ... 6,851]ᵀ, Nuevo diccionario de teología bíblica,
ᴱ**Rossano** P., *al.*, 1990 → 6,852: ᴿBrotéria 133 (1991) 358 (T. *Ribeiro*):

Carthaginensia 7 (1991) 499 (F. *Martínez Fresneda*); CommSev 24 (1991) 102s (M. de *Burgos*).

684 **RAC:** Reallexikon für Antike und Christentum, ᴱ**Dassmann** Ernst [XV,116 –Hispania 1990 ➤ 6,853]: 117-121, –Hoffnung col. 641-1262 [RHE 96,262*]; Stu 1991, Hiersemann; ᴿJTS 42 (1991) 301-312 (C. P. *Bammel*, 97-104).

685 **RLA:** Reallexikon der Assyriologie, ᴱ**Edzard** Dietz O., *al.*, 7 (1990) ➤ 6,853*: ᴿBO 48 (1991) 153s (W. W. *Hallo*, 7/3s, chiefly HAAS/ BOTTÉRO Magie).

686 **SDB:** Supplément au Dictionnaire de la Bible, ᴱ**Briend** Jacques, *Cothenet* Édouard [XI,63, 1990 ➤ 6,854]: XI,64A-65, Samuel-Sarepta, col. 1057-1420. P 1990, Letouzey & Â. 2-7063-0016-3 (vol. XI).

687 **StSp:** Storia della Spiritualità, ᴱ**Barbaglio** G. 1988 ➤ 6,854*.

688 **StSpG:** Storia della Spiritualità, ᴱ**Grossi** V. [1989 ➤ 5,909] ➤ 6,855.

689 **TDOT:** Theological dictionary of the Old Testament [ᴱ**Ringgren** H., *al.* ➤ 692], ᵀ*Green* David E., 6, 1990 ➤ 6,856: ᴿGraceTJ 12,1 (1991) 120-2 (T. J. *Finley*, 6).

690 **TRE:** Theologische Realenzyklopädie, ᴱ**Müller** Gerhard, *al.* [19s, 1990 ➤ 6,857]: 21. Leonardo da Vinci - Malachias von Armagh. B/NY 1991, de Gruyter. 806 p. 3-11-012-952-3; ᴿBL (1991) 20 (R. N. *Whybray*, 19, & p. 23 on Register 1-17); CC 142 (1991,2) 471-8 (C. *Capizzi*, 17-20); CiuD 203 (1990) 240 & 747 (J. M. *Ozaeta*, 18s); DLZ 112 (1991) 87-90 & 368-370 (G. *Wendelborn*, 16; 19); ÉTRel 66 (1991) 156s & 625s (B. *Reymond*, 18-20); JEH 42 (1991) 463s (O. *Chadwick*); NRT 113 (1991) 299s & 932 (L.-J. *Renard*, 19s); Protestantesimo 46 (1991) 209 (J. A. *Soggin*, 20); RHPR 71 (1991) 492s (A. *Birmelé*, 18s); SvTKv 37 (1991) 103-5 (B. *Hägglund*, 18); TPQ 139 (1991) 211 & 430s (G. *Bachl*, 18ss); TR 87 (1991) 367-370 & 459-462 (R. *Bäumer*, 19s).

691 **TUmAT:** Texte aus der Umwelt des Alten Testaments [3/1, 1990 ➤ 6,858]: 2/6, Assmann J., *al.*, Religiöse Texte, Lieder und Gebete II. Gü 1991, Mohn. S. 785-938. DM 108. 3-579-00071-3 [BL 92,120, W. G. *Lambert*]. – ᴿHenoch 13 (1991) 99s & 365s (J. A. *Soggin*: vol. 1, testi legali e storici; 2. sarà religiosi, 3. sapienziali).

692 **TWAT:** Theologisches Wörterbuch zum Alten Testament, ᴱ**Fabry** H., *Ringgren* H. [VII,5, 1990 ➤ 6,859 (no new fascicle in 1991)]: ᴿNRT 113 (1991) 103s (J.-L. *Ska*, 6/11; 7/1s); RTLv 22 (1991) 77s (P.-M. *Bogaert*, 6; 7,1).

A3.3   *Opera consultationis* **biblica** *non excerpta infra* – **not subindexed.**

693 **Ashkenasi** Shmuel, *Jarden* Dov, ❻ *Oṣar rašê tᵉbot*, Thesaurus of Hebrew abbreviations. J 1991, Kiryat Sefer. 600 col. 765-17-0203-6 [OIAc 2,13].

694 **Bellinger** Gerhard, Dictionnaire illustré de la Bible 1990 ➤ 6,861: ᴿÉt-Clas 59 (1991) 182 (A. *Wankenne*).

695 **Blain** E. P., The illustrated Bible handbook 1987 ➤ 4,823: ᴿRelStT 10,2 (1990) 105s (A. A. *Trites*).

696 ᴱ**Brown** Colin, O novo dicionario internacional de teologia do Novo Testamento [1975 ...], ᵀ*Chown* Gordon, ᴱ*Zabatiero* J. E. P. São Paulo 1981-3, Vida Nova. 4 vol. – ᴿRCuBíb 14,55s (1990) 164-7 (J. M. *Terra*).

697 ᴱ**Butler** T. C., Holman Bible dictionary. Nv 1991, Holman. 1488 p.; 600 color phot.; 39 color maps. $40. 1-55819-053-8 [NTAbs 36,251].

698 **Coggins** R. J., *Houlden* J. L., A dictionary of biblical interpretation 1990 ➤ 6,865: ᴿColcT 61,3 (1991) 201-4 (M. *Wojciechowski*, ❻); CritRR 4

(1991) 74-76 (K.R. *Crim*); HeythJ 32 (1991) 77-79 (R.E. *Brown*); Interpretation 45 (1991) 428.430 (C. *Bernas*: stresses what went on through the centuries); PrzPow 827s (1990) 230-2 (W. *Chrostowski*, ❷); RExp 88 (1991) 285 (W.L. *Hendricks*); ScotJT 44 (1991) 541s (H. *Anderson*: 'a whole new ball game'); TrinJ 12 (1991) 241-3.

699 **ExWNT:** ᴱ**Balz** H., *Schneider* G., Exegetical dictionary of the NT,ᵀ [1. Aarōn-Enōch 1978 ➤ 60,880 ... 1,894 and single items there 1990 ➤ 6, 868]; 2. *ex-opsōnion*. GR 1991, Eerdmans. xxiv-555 p. 0-8028-2410-2 [NTAbs 36,249]. – ᴿExpTim 102 (1990s) 344s (D. *Bill*: '2½ cheers'); Neotestamentica 25 (1991) 189s (A.H. *Snyman*); NewTR 4,3 (1991) 97s (Barbara E. *Reid*); STEv 3 (1991) 267s (P. *Guccini*); TS 52 (1991) 144s (J.A. *Fitzmyer*).

700 ᴱ**Galbiati** E. [*Grollenberg* L. + *Corswant* W.], Dizionario enciclopedico della Bibbia e del mondo biblico 1986 ➤ 2,622*; 3,908: ᴿEstE 66 (1991) 351-3 (J. *Alonso Díaz*).

701 **Gerritzen** Ch., Lexikon der Bibel. Elville 1990, Bechtermünz. 512 p. 3-927117-51-X. – ᴿRuBi 44 (1991) 78 (J. *Łach*).

702 **Girard** André-Marie, Dictionnaire de la Bible: Bouquins. P 1989, Laffont. 1500 p. F 150. – ᴿEsprVie 101 (1991) 491s (C. *Jean-Nesmy*).

703 **Mills** Watson E., Mercer dictionary of the Bible 1990 ➤ 6,879: ᴿCritRR 4 (1991) 76s (K.R. *Crim*); Interpretation 45 (1991) 428 (J.S. *Siker*: worthy Baptist challenge to Harper's 1985; has more items on extracanonical texts and current theological issues); RExp 88,3 (1991) 261s (J.L. *Blevins*).

704 **Monloubou** Louis, Diccionario bíblico compendiado [1989 ➤ 5,955]. Valencia 1991, Edicep. 267 p. – ᴿSFulg 1 (1991s) 166s (J.M. *García*).

705 **Müller** F.-G., Lessico della scienza biblica: LoB 3.11, 1990 ➤ 6,880: ᴿAsprenas 38 (1991) 105s (A. *Rolla*).

706 **Negev** Avraham, *a*) The archaeological encyclopedia of the Holy Land³ [¹1982 ²ʳᵉᵛ1986: BAR-W 17/3,8]; – *b*) Archäologisches Bibel-Lexikon [1986], ᵀᴱ*Rosenthal-Heginbottom* Renate, *Zwickel* W. Stu-Neuhausen 1991, Hänssler. xiii-520 p.; 58 color. phot. 3-7751-1685-0 [+ 189 p. Begleitbuch 'Die Suche nach Eden': ZAW 104,291, H.-C. *Schmitt*].

707 ᴱ**Rienecker** Fritz, Lexikon der Bibel [2d special ed. = 19 ed. of 1960 work.]. Wu/Z 1991, Brockhaus/Gondrom. 1597 p. + index; 96 pl. Wu 3-417-24585-0 / Z 3-8112-4868-3.

708 ᴱ**Shamir** I., *Shavit* J., Encyclopedie van de joodse geschiedenis [Eng. 1987], ᵀ*Endedijk* H.C. Kampen/Turnhout 1989, Kok/Brepols. 284 p. ƒ99. 90-24232-51-1. – ᴿNedTTs 45 (1991) 151s (P.W. van der *Horst*).

709 **Waldram** J., Encyclopedie van de bijbel. Baarn 1990, Tirion. 279 p. ƒ34,50. 90-5121-178-3. – ᴿTsTNijm 31 (1991) 190 (J. *Negenman*: no Ebla).

A3.5   *Opera consultationis* **theologica** *non excerpta infra.*

710 ᴱ**Ancilli** Ermanno, Dizionario enciclopedico di spiritualità²ʳᵉᵛ [¹1975]. R 1990, Città Nuova. 2,734 p. (3 vol.) Lit. 280.000. – ᴿCC 142 (1991,1) 434s (G. *Mucci*); ScripTPamp 23 (1991) 745s (J.L. *Illanes*).

711 **Assfalg** Julius, *Krüger* Paul, Petit dictionnaire de l'Orient chrétien [1975], ᵀ*Longton* Joseph. Turnhout 1991, Brepols. xxxiii-551 p.; 25 fig.; xvi pl.; 7 maps. 2-503-50062-5.

712 ᴱ**Atiya** Aziz S., The Coptic encyclopedia. NY 1991, Macmillan. 8 vol. 0-02-897025-X [2, 382-9, *Bourguet* P. du, *al.*, Biblical subjects in Coptic art.].

713 ᴱBäumer Remigius, *Scheffczyk* Leo, Marienlexikon [I-II 1988s ➤ 4,819
... 6,889] III. Greco-Laib. St. Ottilien 1991, EOS. 704 p. DM 148. –
ᴿMarianum 53 (1991) 296-8 (L. *Gambero*, 2); TR 87 (1991) 462-4 (H.
Vorgrimler, 1-3).

714 ᴱ**Beinert** Wolfgang, Diccionarío de teología dogmática [1987 ➤ 3,884]ᵀ.
Barc 1990, Herder. 803 p. pt. 6132. 84-254-1668-X: ᴿActuBbg 28
(1991) 194s (J. *Boada*); ScripTPamp 23 (1991) 313-9 (L. F. *Mateo-Seco*).

715 **Brugués** Jean-Louis, Dictionnaire de morale catholique. Chambray-les-
Tours 1991, CID. 478 p. F 250. – ᴿDivThom 94 (1991) 168-170 (Y.
Poutet); RThom 91 (1991) 685-7 (S. T. *Pinckaers*).

716 ᴱ**Bubolz** Georg, Religionslexikon; Kompaktwissen für Schüler und junge
Erwachsene. Fra 1990, Cornelsen. 367 p. DM 29,80. – ᴿTGL 81 (1991)
387 (W. *Beinert*).

717 ᴱ**Cancik** H., *al.*, Handbuch religionswissenschaftlicher Grundbegriffe, 2.
Apokalyptik–Gesch. 1990 ➤ 6,893: ᴿTüTQ 171 (1991) 70-73 (M. *Seckler*).

718 ᴱ**Canobbio** G., Piccolo lessico di teologia 1989 ➤ 6,894: ᴿRasT 32
(1991) 107 (N. *Galantino*).

718* **Cohn-Sherbok** Dan, A dictionary of Judaism and Christianity. Ph
1991, Trinity. ix-181 p. $16 pa. 1-56338-030-7 [NTAbs 36,252].

719 **Cully** I. & K., Harper's encyclopedia of religious education 1990
➤ 6,897: ᴿAndrUnS (1990) 256s (G. R. *Knight*); Interpretation 45 (1991)
436.8 (Carol L. *Hess*: K. Cully had a similar volume with Westminster
1963); RExp 88,2 (1991) 238 (T. *Lines*).

720 ᴱ**Douglas** J. D., New 20th century encyclopedia of religious knowledge
[¹1955, ᴱ*Loetscher* Lefferts A. < Schaff-Herzog 1886]. GR 1991, Baker.
xv-896 p. $40. 0-8010-3002-1. – ᴿTDig 38 (1991) 284 (W. C. *Heiser*:
two-thirds of the articles are new and Catholics are included).

721 ᴱ**Eicher** Peter, Diccionario de conceptos teológicos 1990 ➤ 6,904:
ᴿAugM 35 (1990) 400s (P. *Merino*); BibFe 16 (1990) 154 (A. *Salas*);
TVida 32 (1991) 248s (M. *Barrios V.*).

722 **Eliade** Mircea, *Couliano* Ioan P., Handbuch der Religionen, ᵀ*Ronte*
L., *al.* Z 1991, Artemis. 366 p. DM 68. – ᴿTGL 81 (1991) 387s (W.
Beinert).

723 ᴱ**Ferguson** Everett, The encyclopedia of early Christianity 1990 ➤ 6,907:
ᴿGraceTJ 11 (1990) 256s (J. E. *McGoldrick*: conservative-Protestant
bypassed); JEH 42 (1991) 333 (G. *Bonner*); Mid-Stream 30 (1991) 290-2
(Agnes *Cunningham*); RExp 88 (1991) 464s (E. G. *Hinson*).

724 **Fink** Peter E., The new dictionary of sacramental worship. Dublin/
ColMn 1990, Gill, & M./Liturgical. 1352 p. £50. 0-7171-1718-9/-. –
ᴿExpTim 102 (1990s) 243s [C. S. *Rodd*: a momentous production]; Month
252 (1991) 74s (J. *McDade*); Studies 80 (1991) 330s (G. E. *Thiessen*).

725 **Gasper** Hans, *al.*, Lexikon der Sekten, Sondergruppen und Weltan-
schauungen; Fakten, Hintergründe, Klärungen³. FrB 1991, Herder.
605 p. DM 98. 3-451-21408-3. – ᴿZkT 113 (1991) 320 (R. *Pacik*).

726 **Guiley** Rosemary E., Harper's encyclopedia of mystical and paranormal
experience. SF 1991, Harper. xiii-666 p. $36. 0-06-250365-0 [TDig 39,
166: 500 items, enjoyable reading].

727 ᴱ**Kazhdan** Alexander P., *al.*, The Oxford [/Dumbarton Oaks] dictionary of
Byzantium. Ox 1991, Univ. I. li-728 p.; II. xxvi, p. 729-1473; III. xxxi,
p. 1445-2232; 125 fig. $275. 0-19-504652-8. – ᴿBAR-W 17,5 (1991) 6
(R. J. *Schork*); TDig 38 (1991) 286 (W. C. *Heiser*: 5200 entries, 127 contributors; 125 fig.).

728 **Kelly** John N. D., Grande dizionario illustrato dei Papi. CasM 1989, Piemme. 815 p. [1986 ⇥ 2,630; deutsch 1988 ⇥ 4,845]. – RCC 142 (1991,1) 209s (G. *Caprile*: l'autore anglicano presiede ai rapporti con la Chiesa cattolica; la traduzione è presentata come anche revisione, per la quale sono aggiunti altri suggerimenti).

729 EKomonchak J. A., *al.*, New dictionary of theology 1987 ⇥ 3,923 ... 6,912: RPrPeo 4 (1990) 456s (M. Cecily *Boulding*).

730 ELippy Charles H., *Williams* Peter W., Encyclopedia of the American religious experience 1988 ⇥ 4,853; 6,915: RCritRR 3 (1990) 299-302 (M. G. *Toulouse*); RelStR 17 (1991) 112-4 (J. C. *Brauer*: What is an encyclopedia? Why is this one not alphabetical? and other reserves) & 115.117-9 (W. R. *Hutchison*: magnificent).

731 ELipsitz Edmond Y., World Jewish directory [largely bibliographical orientation]. Downsview ON 1991, JESL Educational. vi-267 p. [2 vol.] $55 + 4. 0-9691-2647-6 [TDig 39,90].

732 **McManners** John, The Oxford illustrated history of Christianity. Ox 1990, UP. xi-724 p. £25. – RHorizons 18 (1991) 319s (G. *Macy*); Month 252 (1991) 166 (M. *Walsh*).

733 **Mennonna** Antonio R., Il piccolo glossario del cristianesimo. R 1991, Dehoniane. xiv-451 p. 88-396-0832-4.

734 **Midali** M., *Tonelli* R., Dizionario di pastorale giovanile. T-Leumann 1989, LDC. 1162 p. Lit. 90.000. – RCC 142 (1991,2) 511s (P. *Vanzan*).

735 **Mondin** Battista, *a)* Dizionario enciclopedico di filosofia, teologia e morale. Mi 1989, Massimo. 855 p. Lit. 90.000. – RCC 142 (1991,1) 319 (P. *Valori*); – *b)* Dizionario enciclopedico del pensiero di San Tommaso d'AQUINO. Bo 1991, Studio Domenicano. 688 p. Lit. 80.000 [TR 88,430].

736 ENyssen Wilhelm, *Wiertz* Paul [⇥ 6,918], *al.*, Handbuch der Ostkirchenkunde² rev [¹1971]. Dü 1984-9, Patmos. xxxiv-392 p.; xx-273 p.; ill. je DM 49,80 [TLZ 117,551, H.-D. *Döpmann*].

737 **O'Collins** Gerald, *Farrugia* Edward G., A concise dictionary of theology. NY 1991, Paulist. 268 p. $12. 0-8091-3235-4 [NRT 114,581, R. *Escol*].

738 **Pannet** Robert †, *Bevaud* Georges, *Margerie* Bertrand de, Dictionnaire marial. Chambray-les-Tours 1991, C.L.D. 190 p. F 165. – REsprVie 101 (1991) 559 (G.-M. *Oury*).

739 **Parrinder** Geoffrey, A dictionary of religious and spiritual quotations. L/NY 1990, Routledge/Simon & S. 218 p. £15. 0-415-04128-7. – RExpTim 102 (1990s) 319 [C. S. *Rodd*].

740 EPoupard P., Grande dizionario delle religioni 1988 ⇥ 4,865b; 5,960; ²1990 [Cittadella + Piemme]: RProtestantesimo 46 (1991) 239s (B. *Corsani*).

741 EReid Daniel G., *al.*, Dictionary of Christianity in America 1990 ⇥ 6,922; 1305 p.; 2400 art., 1500 biographical. – RInterpretation 45 (1991) 204.206 (H. M. *Goodpasture*).

742 ERotter H., *Virt* G., Neues Lexikon der christlichen Moral 1990 ⇥ 6,923: RTPQ 139 (1991) 330s (K. *Hörmann*).

743 EStravinskas Peter M. J., Our Sunday Visitor's Catholic encyclopedia. Huntington IN 1191. 1007 p. $30. 0-87973-457-4 [TDig 38,372].

744 ETerrer T., Catholic mission history and the 500th anniversary of Christopher Columbus' arrival; a time for mourning and for celebrating: Mission Studies 9/1 (1992) 7-23 (-107) [< TR 88,256].

745 **Tröger** Sigrid & Karl-Wolfgang, Kirchenlexikon; christliche Kirchen, Freikirchen und Gemeinschaften im Überblick. Mü 1990, Beck. 254 p. DM 34. – ᴿTPQ 139 (1991) 429s (R. *Zinnhobler*: sehr nützlich).

A3.6   *Opera consultationis* **philologica** *et generalia.*

746 ᴱ**Bright** William, International encyclopedia of linguistics. NY 1991, Oxford-UP. xvi-429 p.; viii-440 p.; viii-456 p.; viii-482 p. 0-19-505196-3 [OIAc 1,13; excerpted].

747 **Crystal** David, The Cambridge encyclopedia of language. C 1991, UP. £15 pa. 0-521-42443-7. – ᴿMonth 252 (1991) 542s (P. *Hackett*).

ᴱ**Kahil** Lilly, *Linant de Bellefonds* Pascal, Religion, mythologie, iconographie 1991 ➔ 594*b*. **LIMC** ➔ 750.

749 **LGB:** Lexikon des gesamten Buchwesens, ᴱ**Corsten** Severin, *al.* [II,18, 1990 ➔ 6,933] III. Fotochemographische Verfahren [bis] Institut für Buchmarkt-Forschung. Stu 1991, Hiersemann. vii-631 p. 3-7772-9136-6 (-2527-7 ganzes Werk). p. 308-312, *Corsten*, GUTENBERG; p. 351-270, *Milde* W., *al.*, Handschrift [...-en(handel usw.)].

750 **LIMC:** Lexikon iconographicum mythologiae classicae, ᴱ**Kahil** Lilly, V 1990 ➔ 6,934*: ᴿAnzAltW 44 (1991) 248-250 (H. *Walter*); Archaiognosia 6 (1990) 195-202 (M. *Tiverios,* 4 ⓖ).

751 ᴱ**Lissner** Annaliese, *Süssmuth* Rita, *Walter* Karin, Frauenlexikon; Traditionen, Fakten, Perspektiven². FrB 1988, Herder [➔ 4,854; ²1989 ➔ 5,952]. 623 p. DM 69. 3-451-20977-2 [TR 88,285, Eva *Schmetterer,* Ursula *Waldingbrett*].

752 **Robbins** Vernon K., Ancient quotes and anecdotes 1989 ➔ 5,963 [not V. E.]: ᴿInterpretation 45 (1991) 326 (D. B. *Gowler*: 1750 *chreiai,* stories with punch-line, from SBL 1975 Gospels Pronouncement Story group); RB 98 (1991) 308s (J. *Murphy-O'Connor,* entertaining at least).

753 ᴱ**Schröpfer** J., Wörterbuch der vergleichenden Bezeichnungslehre (Onomasiologie) I,1-8. Heid 1979-89, Winter. cxxvi-514 p. DM 304. – ᴿGymnasium 98 (1991) 189s (R. *Schmitt*).

754 **Wessel** Klaus, *Restle* Marcell, Reallexikon zur byzantinischen Kunst IV, Lfg. 29-32, Konstantinopel-Kreta. Stu 1990; Hiersemann. col. 641-1236; 97 fig. [TLZ 117,291, K. *Onasch*; 116 (1991) 630s, Lfg. 26ss].

A3.8   *Opera consultationis* **archaeologica** *et* **geographica.**

755 ᴱ**Bonte** Pierre, *Izard* Michel, *al.*, Dictionnaire de l'ethnologie et de l'anthropologie. P 1991, PUF. xii-755 p. 2-13-043383-9.

756 **Bunson** Margaret, The encyclopedia of ancient Egypt. NY 1991, Facts on file. xv-291 p. 0-8160-2093-0.

757 **Henze** Dietmar, Encyklopädie der Entdecker und Erforscher der Erde III,14, McNair-Moskwitin. Graz 1991, Akademische DV. 127 p. DM 98 [DLZ 113,16, K.-R. *Biermann*].

758 ᴱ**Matthiae** Paolo, Archéo, l'encyclopédie de l'archéologie; à la recherche des civilizations disparues, 3. Proche-Orient. Bru 1987, Atlas. 320 p. 2-7312-0503-2 [OIAc 1,20].

759 ᴱ**Mostyn** Trevor, *Hourani* Albert, The Cambridge Encyclopedia of the Middle East and North Africa 1988 ➔ 6,948: ᴿJAOS 111 (1991) 200s (J. R. *Clark*: more an introductory textbook than an encyclopedia, *but* too heavy for a textbook and more suited to a reference library, *but* should be read through).

760 **Whitehouse** Ruth D., Dizionario di archeologia. Mi 1989, Sugarco.
635 p. Lit. 65.000. – RArcheo 62 (1990) 127 (S. *Moscati*).
761 E**Yarshater** Ehsan, Encyclopaedia Iranica [➤ 3,949... 6,951] Ātaš –
Bayhaqī. Costa Mesa/L 1989, Routledge-KP/Mazda. xxix-896 p. – V,3,
Central Asia –češtīya; p. 225-336; 0-939214-70-9; VI,4, –Chinese-Iranian,
p. 337-348; -71-7; V,4, –čirdad, p. 449-560, -72-5; V,6, –Class System, p.
561-672; -73-3 [OIAc 1,27; 2,29]. – RArOr 59 (1991) 406-9 (M. *Shaki*, 2s);
BSO 54 (1991) 171-8 (W. *Jessup*: much longer than EncIslam and with
some better articles, but selection capricious); Gnomon 63 (1991) 64 (J.
Wiesehöfer, 1-3); JAOS 111 (1991) 152s (F. *Daftary*, 3); VDI 198 (1991)
203-9 (I. N. *Medvedskaya*).

A4 **Bibliographiae**, computers .1 **biblicae.**

762 *Aletti* Jean-Noël, Bulletin d'exégèse du NT; bulletin paulinien: RechSR
79 (1991) 37-56; 25 livres.
AnPg 'Testamenta' [= NT] ➤ 858.
763 **BL:** Society for Old Testament Study, Book List (for 1991). 1992. Retiring
editor, **Auld** E. Graeme; incoming editor **Grabbe** Lester L. [his address for
books for review: Hull, Univ., HU6 7RX, England].
764 Bibliografia biblica latino-americana 1990, vol. 3. São Bernardo do
Campo 1991, Vozes. 379 p.
765 *Bori* Pier Cesare, *Perrone* Lorenzo, Una bibliografia generale di Storia
dell'Interpretazione Biblica: AnStoEseg 7 (1990) 345-366 . 725-767; 8
(1991) 305-335 . 721-771 [295-303, *Pesce* Mauro, Rassegna di storia
dell'esegesi].
766 **Bourquin** David R., First century Palestinian Judaism, a bibliography of
works in English: StJudaica 6. San Bernardino 1990, Borgo. 104 p. $20;
pa. $10. 0-89370-373-7; -473-3 [NTAbs 36,133; TDig 39,51].
767 *Brauer* Bernd, *al.*, Bibliographische Dokumentation; lexikalisches und
grammatisches Material: ZAHeb 4 (1991) 95-114 [115-7, *Loersch* Sigrid,
Neu entdeckte Texte] 194-209 [210-2, *Lichtenberger* H., Neuveröffent-
lichungen aus den Qumranfunden; 213-235, *Dahmen* Ulrich, Nachträge
zur Qumran-Konkordanz (*Kuhn* K. 1963 *al.*)].
768 Chiwriter (Version 3.16) Greek, Hebrew, Arabic edition. San José 1990,
Horstmann Software. £110. – RScotJT 44 (1991) 280s (I. R. *Torrance*:
serious rival to Multi-Lingual Scholar; operation described in detail).
769 CRAIGIE Peter C.: Addendum to the [1988F] bibliography: JStOT 51
(1991) 115-7 (Rebecca G. S. *Idestrom*, J. G. *Taylor*).
770 *Delcor* Mathias, Chronique de l'AT [... SÁENZ-BADILLOS A.]: BLitEc 92
(1991) 277-284.
771 Dissertation Abstracts – A [mostly in English] seems to have introduced
the category 'Religion: Biblical Studies' for the first time in 52/4 (1991s) p.
1371-5; though as many equally biblical titles are still found under
'Theology' etc. p. 1381-99.
772 **Evans** Craig A., Life of Jesus research, an annotated bibliography:
NTTools 13. Leiden 1989, Brill. xiii-207 p. 90-04-09180-7.
773 **Fitzmyer** Joseph A., An introductory bibliography for the study of
Scripture[3]: SubsBPont 3, 1990 ➤ 6,968: RETL 67 (1991) 162s (F. *Neirynck*, franç.: adds some 40 titles, and warns that the *Concordantia
polyglotta* which he still assumes published from a 1980 announcement
has been *annulée*); RB 98 (1991) 463-5 (J. *Murphy-O'Connor*: high praise,
also for DSS[2] 1990).

774 *Gotenburg* Erwin, Bibelwissenschaft [Theologische Bibliographie]: TR 87 (1991) 73-76 [-88]. 101-4 [-176]. 249-252 [-264]. 337-340 [-352]. 425-7 [-440]. 523-5 [-536]. — A priceless resource for this *Elenchus*.

775 *Harrington* Daniel J., [32] Books on the Bible: America 164 (1991) 126-134.

776 *Heintz* Jean-Georges, Chronique d'AT; ancien Orient et Israël antique; des textes sémitiques aux traditions prophétiques en période d'exil: RHPR 71 (1991) 183-226; p. 186-9, une dizaine de publications sur le centenaire de l'École Biblique de Jérusalem.

777 **Hupper** William G., An index to English periodical literature on OT-ANE 1987s ➤ 3,966... 6,974: ᴿJNES 50 (1991) 61s (R. D. *Biggs*: a single dedicated individual using simply file-cards); JQR 82 (1991s) 511-4 (C. *Cohen* notes only ten errors in the Hebrew, 8 repeated).

778 *Kelly* Joseph F., A catalogue of early medieval Hiberno-Latin Bible commentaries II: Traditio 45 (1989s) 393-434.

Lindboe Inger M., Women in the New Testament; a select bibliography [717 items] 1990 ➤ 8821.

779 **mac-Bible;** software for Bible study and research on the Macintosh; RSV text disks and Greek NT (UBS 3) text disks. GR 1990, Zondervan. $100 (NIV, KJV, NRSV also available at same price) / $175 (Hebrew also available at same price). – ᴿBibTB 21 (1991) 76 (B. B. *Scott*).

780 — [**Mounce** William D., manual] macBible version 2.3 [computer disks] GR 1991, Zondervan. [manual xxi-220 p.] Hebrew $200; Greek $200; NRSV $130, apocr. $90. – ᴿOTAbs 14 (1991) 235s (A. A. *Di Lella*: operates twice as fast as Version 2).

781 *Piñero* Antonio, New Testament philology bulletin 7/8 : FgNt 4 (1991) 85-114 / 229-244 [117-121 Libros recibidos, comentos; 253-8 *Godoy* Rufino].

Purvis James D., Jerusalem bibliography II, 1991 ➤ d336.

782 **Reinhardt** K., *Santiago-Otero* H., Biblioteca bíblica ibérica medieval, I. Nomenclator de autores medievales hispánicos: MedvHum 1, 1986 ➤ 3,980: ᴿCrNSt 12 (1991) 197s (J. *Leclercq*, aussi sur 2-3).

783 ᴱ**Sæbø** Magne (*Brekelmans* Chris, *Haran* Menahem), Hebrew Bible / Old Testament, the history of its interpretation; Oslo 1991, HBOT Project. I. **Stordalen** Terje, General bibliography. x-250 p.

784 South Africa NT society members & addresses: Neotestamentica 25 (1991) 449-455.

785 *Stuhlmueller* Carroll, The Bible in review, OT 120 books [*Senior* Donald, NT 100 books]: BToday 28 (1990) 51-55. 117-120. 185-8. 246-9. 309-317 [55-59. 121-4. 189-191. 250-3. 380]; Audio-Visuals in Review, *Hang* F. 254s; *Cannon* Kathleen, 385s.

786 *a*) *Wanke* Gunther, Zeitschriftenschau [Bücherschau, *Schmitt* H.C.]: ZAW 103 (1991) 124-146. 275-290. 424-442 [147-173. 290-314. 443-465]. – ZNW 82 (1991) 138-141. 280-2.

A4.2 *Bibliographiae* **theologicae.**

787 ᴱ**Anestidis** Adamantios S., ☉ *Bibliographia tēs theologías kai ton boēthētikōn*... 1983: Hellēnikē Theologikē Bibliographia 7. Athenai 1990, Univ. xliv-882 p.

788 *Arató* Pál, Bibliographia historiae pontificiae: ArHPont 28 (1990) 431-718.

789 Augustinianum 31,1 (Roma 1991), 5-192: Index I-XXX (1961-1990).

790 *Baudry* Gérard-Henry,   Bulletin teilhardien; répertoire international des thèses consacrées à TEILHARD de Chardin: MélSR 48 (1991) 173-185.

791 *Benzerath* Martín,   Bibliographie sélective de morale: StMor [27,2 (1989) fasc. entier] 28 (1990) 281-334; 29 (1991) 163-266.

792 E*Bertuletti* Angelo, *al.*,   I problemi metodologici della teologia sulle Riviste del 1990: TItSett 16 (1991) 316-397 [336-345, Teologia e Scrittura].

793 Bibliographikon Deltíon [Theology, largely Scripture, articles in alphabetical order of author]: TAth 61 (1990) 859-883 / 62 (1991) 874-900.

794 *Bonino* Serge-Thomas,   Thomistica: RThom 91 (1991) 315-328.

795 *Boudaroua* Joël,   Liturgie d'hier et d'aujourd'hui: RThom 91 (1991) 335-343.

796 *Boudens* R., *al.*,   Elenchus bibliographicus 1990:   ETL 67,2s (1991) 639* p.; 11643 items; S.Scr. p. 130*-316*.

797 *Bourgeois* Henri,   Bulletin de théologie sacramentaire: RechSR 79 (1991) 133-156; 23 livres.

798 *Briend* Jacques, (*Carrière* Jean-Marie),   Bulletin d'exégèse de l'Ancien Testament: RechSR 79 (1991) 261-290; 35 livres.

799 BRINKTRINE Johannes [1889-1965]: Eine bibliographische Erinnerung an ~: TGL 81 (1991) 121-8 (W. *Koch*).

800 Bulletin bibliographique: périodiques/ouvrages: ArchivScSocRel 67,2 (1989) 211-229 / 231-344; 68,2 (1989) 181-192 / 193-312; 70 (1990) 209-226 / 227-322; 72 (1990) 213-223 / 225-311; 74 (1991) 203-216 / 217-309; 75 (1991) 191-210 / 211-315.

801 **Capon** Cornelia,   Hans Urs von BALTHASAR; Bibliographie 1925-1990. Einsiedeln 1990, Johannes.   174 p.   DM 32.   3-89411-029-5. – RGregorianum 72 (1991) 581 (R. *Fisichella*: 'tutte le pagine dell'Indice sono errate').

802 E**Carman** John, *Juergensmeyer* Mark,   A bibliographic guide to the comparative study of ethics.   C 1991, Univ.   viii-811 p. $100 [TR 88,172].

802* CHAUSSY Yves, 1912... Bío-bibliografía: StMonast 33 (Montserrat 1991) 145-151 (A. *Linage Conde*).

803 *Cirillo* Antonio,   La teologia e il teologo in recenti scritti: AnnTh 4 (1990) 309-332; 5 (1991) 351-386.

804 **CritRR**: Critical review of books in religion [1989s → 6,1006] vol. 4, E**Epp** Eldon J.   Atlanta 1991, Scholars.   vii-525 p.   0894-8860.

805 CURRAN Charles E.,   Bibliography 1961-90; thirty years of Catholic moral theology: Horizons 18 (1991) 265-278 (T. W. *O'Brien*).

806 DAHL Nils A.,   A bibliography of his writings, **Hansen** Karstein M. Oslo 1991, Univ. Theol. Bibliog. 3.   112 p.   82-991913-3-5 [NTAbs 36,102].

807 **Deitrick** Bernard E.,   A basic book list for church libraries⁴ [¹1977]: CSLA.   Portland OR 1991, Church and Synagogue Library Asn.   17 p. $6 + 1.   0-915324-32-6 [TDig 39,57].

808 Dissertations in Religion: RelStR 17 (1991) 190-5, completed; 280-287, in progress.

809 *Doré* Joseph,   Bulletin de théologie fondamentale: RechSR 79 (1991) 99-132; 33 livres.

810 *Dubois* Jean-Daniel, Chronique patristique VII: ÉTRel 66 (1991) 243-260.

811 *Elm* Kaspar,   Sechzig Jahre Wichmann-Jahrbuch [der Diözesangeschichte Berlin] (1930 bis 1990) [und die neuen Aufgaben, die sich die Neue Folge gestellt hat]: Wichmann-Jb NF 1 = 30s (1990s)... [< TR 88,391, F. *Schrader*].

812 Études Théologiques et Religieuses, Tables et index 1976-1990 (à part). 1991.   178 p.   F 50 [ÉTRel 66,16].

813 ᴱ*Gliściński* Jan, ❷ Biuletyn patrystyczny; – *b*) ᴱ*Marcol* Alojzy, ...
     moralny; – *c*) ᴱ*Kubik* Władysław, ... katechyzny; – *d*) ... ᴱ*Weron* Euge-
     niusz, ... laikatu; – *e*) ᴱ*Gorski* Jan, ... misjonologiczno-religioznawczy; – *f*)
     ᴱ*Nadolski* Bogusław, ... liturgiczny: ColcT 61 (1991) 1,101-6. 2,93-102 .
     3,141-153 . 4,119-128 / 2,103-118 . 3,155-171 . 4,129-144 / 1,187-218 .
     2,135-151 . 3,155-171 . 4,145-158 / 1,119-132; 2,153-164 . 4,159-170 /
     4,171-186 / 1,89-100 . 2,119-134 . 3,173-190.
814 — ColcT 60 (1990) ❷ Patrystyczny: *Obrycki* Kazimierz 1,125-134;
     Gliściński Jan 2,147-157; 4,109-118; Liturgiczny: *Nadolski* Boguslaw
     1,63-74; 2,67-80; 3,110-134; Moralny: *Marcol* Alojzy 3,135-164; 4,95-104;
     Katechetyczny: *Kubik* Władysław 1,75-94; 2,81-108; 4,119-132; Teologii
     Laikatu: *Weron* Eugeniusz 1,95-108; 2,107-126; 4,133-146; Misjolo-
     giczno-religioznawczy: *Kowalak* Władysław 109-124; Socjologii Religii,
     Kamiński Ryszard, 2,127-146; 3,165-179.
815 *Graça Perição* Maria da, Bibliografia mariana portuguesa dos séculos
     XVII e XVIII: Didaskalia 20,2 (1990) 249-462 [p. 273-6, 'Tratados teo-
     lógicos' nada bíblico].
816 *a)* *Gy* Pierre-Marie, Bulletin de liturgie; – *b*) *Jossua* Jean-Pierre, Bulletin
     de théologie littéraire: RSPT 75 (1991) 129-143 (144-7, *Palazzo* E., sur
     Gy) / 301-320.
817 Habilitationen / Dissertationen im akademischen Jahr 1990/91: TR 87
     (1991) 511-522.
818 HAENDLER Otto (1890-1981), Bibliographie: TLZ 116 (1991) 950-7
     (Kerstin *Voigt*).
819 *Haverals* M., Bibliographie: RHE 86 (1991) 1*-253* . 255*-551*; 7451
     items + recensions & index.
820 **Heiser** W. Charles, Theology Digest book survey 38 (1991) 45-94 .
     147-196 . 249-295 . 345-393: of constant helpfulness infra.
820* **Hillerbrand** Hans J., Anabaptist bibliography, 1520-1630²ʳᵉᵛ. St. Louis
     1991, Center for Reformation Research. xxii-590 p. $75. 0-910345-03-1
     [TDig 39,169, W. C. *Heiser*: 6113 items, double the size of ¹1962].
821 HÖFFNER Joseph, Schriftenverzeichnis 1984-8, ᴱ**Weyand** Winfried.
     Köln 1989, Diözes. xiii-100 p. [TLZ 116,268].
822 Index international des dissertations doctorales en théologie et en droit
     canonique présentées en 1990: RTLv 22 (1991) 568-648; 571-582 index
     par Institut scientifique; 582-5 index de noms de personnes *cités* (non
     auteurs ou directeurs). 899 items (some repeated under various num-
     bers): largely included (with gratitude) in our Elenchus 6 (for 1990,
     published 1993).
823 HOLTZ Traugott, 60. Gb.: Bibliographie: TLZ 116 (1991) 553-8 (Bettina
     Stephan, K.-W. *Niebuhr*).
824 Islamochristiana, Index général 1 (1975) – 15 (1989). R 1991, Pont. Ist.
     di Studi Arabi. 65 p. + ❹ 7.
825 Istina, Tables des tomes 1 à XXXV, années 1954-1990: Istina 35 (1990)
     353-448.
826 JAVELLI Chrysostomus O.P. (ca. 1470-1538): Angelicum 68 (1991) 109-
     121 (M. *Tavuzzi*).
827 *Junghans* Helmar, *al.*, Lutherbibliographie 1990/1991: LuJb 57 (1990)
     316-373; 1106 items / 58 (1991) 142-210; 1318 items.
828 JUNGHANS Helmar, 60. Gb., Bibliographie: TLZ 116 (1991) 775-796 (M.
     Beyer, 481 items).
829 KIESOW Ernst R., Bibliographie 65. Gb.: TLZ 116 (1991) 76-79, 109
     items (F.-H. *Beyer*).

830 ᴱ*Kraft* Robert A., Offline; computer assisted research for religious studies 33: CouSR 19,4 (1990) 105-111; 20,4 (1991) 73-78. 101-3 ...
831 Louvain Studies, Index 1-16 (1966-1991): LvSt 16 (1991) 355-381.
832 LUDOLPHY Ingetraut, 70. Gb. Bibliographie: TLZ 116 (1991) 234-9; 122 items (G. *Müller*).
833 **Magnuson** Norris A., *Travis* William G., American evangelism; an annotated bibliography. W. Cornwall CT 1990, Locust Hill. xix-495 p. $45 [TR 88,83].
834 MAIER Hans, Bibliographie 1950-1990, **Jonas** G., *Mooser* A. FrB 1991, Herder. 61 p. DM 9,80 [TLZ 117,259].
835 *Marlé* René, Bulletin de théologie protestante: RechSR 79 (1991) 57-84; 45 livres.
836 *Monachino* Vincenzo, Alle origini di 'Archivum Historiae Pontificiae': ArHPont 28 (1990) 9-22.
837 **Mills** Watson E., Religious Studies Review Index 1-15 (1974-89). Macon GA 1992, Mercer Univ. $35; pa. $20 [RelStR 18,42 adv.].
838 *Montagnes* Bernard, Chronique d'histoire religieuse [ᴱMAYER J. 6 et 12, 1990; LAGRANGE ᴱGilbert; *al.*, plusieurs infra]: RThom 91 (1991) 666-680.
839 MONTINI Giovanni B., arcivescovo di Milano (1955-1963) [= Paulus VI]; bibliografia: Salesianum 53 (1991) 521-560 (T. *Kadziński*).
839* **Moreno Ortega** R., Teología narrativa (reseña bibliográfica 1970-1990): Moralia 13 (M 1991) 413-430 [< ZIT 92,49].
840 **Neuhauser** Hanns P., Internationale Bibliographie 'Liturgische Bücher; eine Auswahl ... Art-historical and liturgical science literature'. Mü 1991, Saur. xxii-147 p. [TR 88,221, K. *Richter*].
841 ONASCH, Karl, Bibliographie: TLZ 116 (1991) 632.
841* OURY Guy, 1929 ..., bibliografía: StMonast 33 (1991) 389-404 (A. *Linage Conde*).
842 Pelas revistas: REB 51 (1991) 250-6. 523-8. 762-8. 1028-1034.
843 *Segovia* Augusto, Boletin de historia de la teología en el período 1500-1800: ArTGran 53 (1990) 245-290 / 54 (1991) 325-350.
Sieben Hermann J., Kirchenväterhomilien ... NT; Repertorium 1991 ⟶ 1598.
845 Significant ecumenical journals, table of contents [of each, but reprinted without page numbers] / Bibliographia œcumenica: EcuR 41 (1991) 153-7. 289-295. 381-5. 490-4 / 158-160. 296-9. 386s. 495-7.
846 **Starkey** Edward D., Judaism and Christianity; a guide to the reference literature: Reference Sources in the Humanities. Englewood CO 1991, Libraries Unlimited. xiv-256 p. $42. 0-87287-533-4 [TDig 38,291].
847 **Stein** Gordon, God pro and con; a bibliography of atheism. NY 1990, Garland. xv-531 p. $65 [TR 88,170].
848 ŠUŠTARJA Alojzja, Bibliografija nadškofa: BogVest 50 (1990) 301-8 (A. *Štrukelj*).
849 *Tarragon* J.-M. de, [*al.*], Revue biblique [+ 38 autres Revues]: ⟶ 664, Catholicisme XII,57 (1990) 1156 [1155-1174].
850 *Thomist*: Index 51-55 (1987-91): Thomist 55 (1991) 657-697.
851 *Tretter* H., Bibliographie: OstkSt 39 (1990) 78-104. 230-280. 353-382; 40 (1991) 89-112. 233-260. 350-382.
852 **Troxell** Kay, Resources in sacred dance [and 'movement in relation to religion']; annotated bibliography from Christian and Jewish traditions²ʳᵉᵛ [¹1986]. Stow OH 1991, Sacred Dance Guild. 300 items. $10 + $2.50. 0-96231-371-8 [TDig 39,81].
853 *Vallin* Pierre, Bulletin d'ecclésiologie: RechSR 79 (1991) 85-98; 13 livres.

854 WÄCHTER Ludwig, Bibliographie 70. Gb.: TLZ 117 (1992) 957-963 (R. Golling).
855 **Walsh** Michael, The Tablet 1840-1990, a commemorative history. L 1990, Tablet. xii-84 p.; 15 fig. £5. 0-9516162-0-X. – ᴿDoctLife 41 (1991) 161s (T. Arnold); JEH 42 (1991) 342 (E. Norman).
856 ᴱ**Wenhardt** Franz, Handbuch der katholisch-theologischen Bibliotheken³ʳᵉᵛ [180, German, by city]; Hodick Erich, Büchereien: Arbeitsgemeinschaft KTB Veröff. 4. Mü 1991, Saur. 175 p. $85. 3-598-10919-9 [TDig 39,46].

A4.3   *Bibliographiae* **philologicae** *et* **generales.**

857 ᴱ**Affeldt** Werner, *Nolte* Cordula, *al.*, Frauen im Frühmittelalter [nicht = 6,715]; eine ausgewählte, kommentierte Bibliographie. Fra 1990, Lang. xviii-711 p.; map. DM 169 [TR 88,298, Gisela *Muschiol*].
858 **AnPg**: L'année philologique, ᴱ**Ernst** Juliette, *al.* [59 pour 1988 (1990) ⇥ 6,1098] 60 pour 1989 (1991). xxxvii-977 p.; 'Testamenta' (= NT) p. 336-359.
Arlen Shelley, HARRISON-MURRAY bibliog. 1990 ⇥ a595.
860 Bibliographische Beilage: Gnomon 63 (1991) 1, *1-36 . 37-88 . 89-128 . 129-168*; – p. 81-90, 1991 zu erwartende Neuerscheinungen.
861 *Chaniotis* Angelos, Epigraphic bulletin for Greek religion: Kernos 4 (1991) 287-311.
862 **Chastagnol** André, *al.*, L'année épigraphique (... romaine), 1988. P 1991, PUF. 390 p.; 1147 items (0056-2348) 2-13-043570-X. – ᴿRÉLat 67 (1989) 392s (P. *Grimal* sur 1986).
863 *Chénier* Paul, Author index 26-35, NS 1-10, 1982-1991: ÉchMClas 35 (1991) 389-416.
865 *Cockshaw* Pierre, *Manning* Eugène, *al.*, Bulletin codicologique: Scriptorium 44 (1990) 1*-112* . 113*-294*; 45 (1991) 1*-104* . 105*-200*.
866 *Cupaiolo* Giovanni, Notiziario bibliografico [in ordine alfabetico degli autori antichi]: BStLat 21 (1991) 249-290 . 443-465 [139-247 . 383-442, Rassegna delle Riviste].
867 *Dierse* U., *Scholz* G., Register der Bände 1 bis 30: ArBegG whole volume 31 (1988). Bonn 1991, Bouvier. 198 p. 0003-8946. Not by authors or titles, only by topics, first German then Greek.
868 *Duval* Noël, *al.*, Chronique d'antiquité tardive et de christianisme ancien et médiéval (1991): RÉAnc 92 (1990!) 347-398 [91 (1989) 121-150].
869 École nationale des chartes; positions des thèses. P 1991, École des chartes. 232 p. [RHE 86,14*].
870 *Gauthier* P., *al.*, Bulletin épigraphique: RÉG 103 (1990) 435-616.
871 *Gioia* Louis L., Bibliography of editions and translations in progress: Speculum 66 (1991) 261-8.
872 Helmantica 42, 127ss (1991) 289 p.: Indices generales I-XL (1950-1989) – 129* (1991) Suplemento bibliográfico p. 301-432.
872* ᴱ*Hohlweg* A., *Papademetriou* H., Bibliog. ByZ 83 (1991) 516-760.
873 **Kaske** R. E., *al.*, Medieval Christian literary imagery; a guide to interpretation: Medieval Bibliographies 11. Toronto 1988, Univ. xxiv-247 p. $35; pa. $16. – ᴿSpeculum 66 (1991) 176 (G. H. *Brown*).
874 *Modrzejewski* Joseph, Papyrologie documentaire 1985-8: JJurPap 21 (1991) 105-265.
875 Periodical literature: CathHR 77 (1991) 154-171 . 361-371 . 564-576 . 742-753.

876 *Pirenne-Delforge* Vinciane, *al.*,   Revue des Revues [Actes de Colloques]: Kernos 4 (1991) 353-364 [348s].

877 RICŒUR Paul,   Bibliographie, compléments [au livre 1985]:   Revue Philosophique de Louvain 89 (1991) 243-288 [< RSPT 75,685].

878 *Russo* François,   Bibliothèque de France et autres bibliothèques: Études 374 (1991) 201-9.

879 **Saenger** Paul,   A catalogue of the pre-1500 Western manuscript books of the Newberry Library. Ch 1989, Univ. xxvii-260 p.; (color.) ill. [Bibles de la collection Probasco]. – ᴿRHE 86 (1991) 513 (L. *Reynhout*).

880 SCHÜTZEICHEL Rudolf,   Bibliographie, ᴱMeineke Eckhard; Vorw. *Bergmann* Rolf: Germanistische Bibliothek 6.   Heid 1991, Winter. 104 p. – ᴿBeiNam 26 (1991) 395s (G. *Lohse*).

881 Scripta academica; thèses de l'Université d'Uppsala, année scolaire 1988/89. Uppsala c. 1990, Univ. 16 p. 0280-5324.

882 **Sinkewicz** Robert E.,   Manuscript listings for the authors of classical and late antiquity: Greek index project series 3. Toronto 1990, Pont. Inst. Mediaeval Studies. vi-49 p.; 6 microfiches. – ᴿRÉG 104 (1991) 276-8 (J. *Irigoin*).

883 *Skarsten* Roald,   Some applications of computers to the study of ancient Greek texts; a progress report: Symbolae Osloenses 66 (1991) 203-220.

884 Vestnik Drevnej Istorii index 1986-90: VDI 199 (1991) 191-212.

885 WILAMOWITZ-MOELLENDORFF Ulrich von,   Bibliography 1867-1990 [= *Hiller* F., *Klaffenbach* G. revised], ᴱArmstrong M., *al.* Hildesheim 1991, Weidemann. xi-165 p. 3-615-00062-6 [OIAc 2,13].

886 *Wolff* Hartmut, *al.*,   Aus Zeitschriften und Sammelbänden [periodical articles gathered by general topics under chronological periods]: HZ 252 (1991) 220-255 . 487-518 . 752-783; 253 (1991) 238-272 . 514-548 . 798-830.

A4.4 *Bibliographiae* **orientalisticae.**

887 *Acquaro* E., *al.*,   Bibliografia 19: RStFen 18 (1990) 235-266; 19 (1991) 243-276.

888 **Balcani** Carla, *al.*,   Bibliografia metodica / Testi recentemente pubblicati: Aegypta 71 (1991) 315-374, indice 375-380 / 243-279.

888* *Brock* S. P.,   Syriac studies 1981-1985, a classified bibliography: ParOr 14 (1987) 289-... [< ZIT 92,136].

889 *Deller* K., *Klengel* H.,   Keilschriftbibliographie 50 (1988-9): Orientalia 60 (1991) 1*-145* [p. 43* lesen Guman für Giunan N° 678 & Ind.].

890 **Desreumaux** Alain, *Briquel-Chatonnet* F.,   Répertoire des bibliothèques et des catalogues de manuscrits syriaques (Documents, études et répertoires publiés par l'Institut de Recherches et d'Histoire des Textes). P 1991, CNRS. 285 p. – ᴿRHE 86 (1991) 519s (A. de *Halleux*); RHPR 71 (1991) 366 (P. *Maraval*).

891 **Geiberger** Michaela,   Internationaler Katalog der Themen von Magisterarbeiten und Dissertationen in der Ägyptologie, pref. *Simpson* W. K. B 1990, International Association of Egyptologists. ii-57 p. [OIAc 1,17].

892 *Gilliot* Claude,   Bulletin d'Islamologie et des études arabes: RSPT 75 (1991) 613-649.

893 ᴱ**Jones** Charles E.,   [➤ 896] Pirradziš, [bibliographical] bulletin of Achaemenian studies 3 (Aug. 1991). 12 p.

894 *List* Harald,   Arabistische Dissertationen an der Ca' Foscari in Venedig: WZKM 78 (1988) 75-85.

895 *Neumann* Hans,   Forschungen zur altorientalischen Geschichte in der DDR (1980-1990):   AltOrF 18 (1991) 346-370.
896 *a)* **OIAc**: [new (periodical) form of] Oriental Institute Research Archives Acquisitions List, N° 1 (Aug. Sept. Oct. 1991), ᴱ**Jones** Charles E.   Ch 1991, Univ. Or. Inst. 202 p.; of which only 10-28 are the new books as in the previous format; and pp. 48-162 give titles only, without pp., of 2001 periodical-articles; then book reviews. – *b)* Oriental Institute Research Archives Acquisitions list, with an indexed list of essays, articles and reviews, ᴱ**Jones** Charles E., *al.*, 2 (1991s) 13-32 new books; p. 45-177, 2279 articles, regrettably unusable without pages; p. 179-197, books reviewed.
897 ᴱ**Orlandi** Tito,   Coptic Bibliography VII, 1989. – ᴿBO 48 (1991) 847s (L. S. B. *MacCoull*: now on large-page 'microfiches').
898 *Thissen* Heinz-Josef,   Demotische Literaturübersicht 18:   Enchoria 18 (1991) 153-174.
899 **Woods** John E., *Woodworth* Mark, TAQWIM, an Islamic calendar converter [computer program]. Ch 1989, Univ. Center for ME studies. $30. – ᴿJAOS 111 (1991) 203 (Jeannette *Wakin* praises; it shows Arab-Persian and Julian-Gregorian dates back to 4713 B.C., but she says nothing about Near East or classic world history).
900 **Zonhoven** L. M. J., *al.*,   Annual Egyptological bibliography 40 for 1986. Leiden 1991, Int. Asn. Egyptologists / Ned.Inst.Nab.Oosten. ix-272 p. 90-72147-07-3 [OIAc 1,28].

A4.5   *Bibliographiae* **archaeologicae.**

901 Acta Numismatica 20 (1990) 247-271: Index Vols. 11-20 (1981-1990).
902 Archäologische Dissertationen [50; nur 3 infra]: ArchAnz (1991) 145-9.
902* Archéologia: Répertoire des articles parus 1 (1964) - 263 (1990) par sites, périodes, sujets, méthodes: 72 p. après 266 (1991). F 20.
903 *Bauer* Johannes B.,   Christliche Antike, 7. Forschungsbericht: AnzAltW 44 (1991) 1-72.
904 *Calmeyer* Peter,   Archäologische Bibliographie 1989/1990:   ArchMIran 23 (1990) 325-341; 24 (1991) 287-301.
905 *Decker* Wolfgang, *al.*,   Jahresbibliographie zum Sport im Altertum 1990: Nikephoros 3 (1990) 235-259.
906 *Homès-Fredericq* Denyse, *Tanret* Michel,   Conspectus librorum: Akkadica 66 (1990) 64-67; 67, 46-49; 68, 36-40; 69, 31-38; 70, 41-44 / 72 (1991) 41-45; 73, 40-49; 74s, 75-79 [56-65, Tanret, Informatica].
   Martin Geoffrey T., [Post-] Amarna bibliography 1991 → d898.
907 *Metzger* Henri,   Bulletin archéologique: RÉG 103 (1990) 617-668.
908 *Müller* Walter W.,   Südarabien im Altertum; ausgewählte und kommentierte Bibliographie (1988s): AfO 36s (1989s) 375-389.
909 NAUMANN Rudolf,   Schriften-Verzeichnis 80. Gb.   Bonn 1990, Habelt. 30 p.; ill.
910 *Parker* A. J., *Kapitän* G.,   Periodical Notes: IntJNaut 20 (1991) 73-76.
911 **Parry** Donald W., *al.*,   A bibliography on temples of the Ancient Near East and the Mediterranean world arranged by subject and author: ANE TSt 9. Lewiston 1991, Mellen. xi-311 p. 0-7734-9775-7 [OIAc Ap 91,10].
912 *a) Sapin* J., [bibliog.] Archéologie; – *b) Lemaire* A.,   Épigraphie; – *c) Elayi* J., *Lemaire* A.,   Numismatique: TEuph 4 (1991) [83-102] 103-111 / 113-8 / 119-132 [133-145 AT, signées].
913 *a) Saporetti* Claudio, [*al.*],   Informatica ed Assiriologia; – *b) Bresciani* Edda, [*al.*],   Informatica ed Egittologia a Pisa; – *c) Avanzini* Alessandra,

Progetto per un lessico sudarabico antico: Geo-Archeologia (1990,1) 11-23 [-58] / 61-78; 17 fig. [79-105] / 109-115.
914 *Symonds* R. P., Roman pottery bibliography: JRPot 4 (1991) 83-120; 121-3, index of waretypes, *Perrin* J.
915 *Taracha* Piotr, Materials for the bibliography of classical [antycznej] archaeology in Poland for the years 1986-1987: ArchWsz 41 (1990) 129-157.
916 *Vseviov* L. M., Soviet works on archaeology 1988, bibliographical index: SovArch (1990,4) 271-288.

| **II. Introductio** |

B1   *Introductio* .1   *tota vel VT* – **Whole Bible or OT.**

916* *Addinall* Peter, The Bible and history: ExpTim 102 (1990s) 328-332.
917 ᴱ**Anderson** Bernhard W., The Books of the Bible I-II 1989 ➤ 5,377: ᴿJAOS 111 (1991) 385s (A. *Cooper*: New Jerome gives double the information at half the price).
918 **Arenhoevel** Diego, Introduzione all'AT 1989 ➤ 6,1154: ᴿAntonianum 66 (1991) 583 (M. *Nobile*); Laurentianum 32 (1991) 299s (F. *Raurell*).
919 **Barth** Christoph † [ᴱ*Bromiley* Geoffrey W., from almost-complete English shortened from Indonesian original] God with us; a theological introduction to the Old Testament. GR 1991, Eerdmans. x-403 p. $30. 0-8028-3680-1 [OTAbs 14,335].
920 ᴱ**Avis** Paul, The threshold of theology 1988 ➤ 4,338; 5,7127: ᴿScotJT 44 (1991) 490-2 (S. *Williams*: 'According to the publisher's condemnation', presumably for commendation: ... OT J. *Rogerson*, NT B. *Lindars, al.*).
921 **Bartlett** John R., The Bible, faith and evidence; a critical inquiry into the nature of biblical history. L 1990, British Museum. 272 p. £20. 0-7141-1717-X. – ᴿExpTim 102 (1990s) 375 (C. S. *Rodd* praises, while noting anomalies, other than that of publication by a museum).
922 **Barucq** A., *al.*, ᵀᴱ*Borgonovo* G., Scritti dell'Antico VO e fonti bibliche 1988 ➤ 4,1052: ᴿProtestantesimo 46 (1991) 211 (P. *Ribet*).
923 **Beasley** James R., *al.*, An introduction to the Bible. Nv 1991, Abingdon. 496 p. $25. 0-687-19493-8 [NTAbs 36,250].
924 **Boadt** Lawrence, Reading the OT, an introduction 1984 ➤ 1,1172... 4,1055: ᴿBA 54 (1991) 218s (-234 'has the best coverage of archaeology' and costs least, of the 17 similar books here reviewed by V. H. *Matthews* & J. C. *Moyer*).
 Brett M. G., Biblical criticism in crisis? The impact of the [CHILDS B.] canonical approach on OT studies 1991 ➤ 1425b.
925 ᴱ**Brooks** Roger, *Collins* John J., Hebrew Bible or OT? 1980/90 ➤ 6,519*: ᴿTTod 48 (1991s) 89s. 92 (W. *Brueggemann*).
926 **Campbell** A. F., Study companion to OT 1989 ➤ 6,1159: ᴿBL (1991) 67 (R. J. *Coggins*: pruning would help); Interpretation 45 (1991) 305 (M. J. *Haar*); NewTR 4,1 (1991) 77s (Dianne *Bergant*).
927 **Charpentier** Étienne, Para ler el A/NT 1986 ➤ 2,793: ᴿBrotéria 132 (1991) 478 (P. de *Sales Baptista*).
928 **Coggins** R., Introducing the OT 1990 ➤ 6,1161: ᴿMonth 252 (1991) 255 (Jennifer *Dines*).
929 **Comte** Fernand, Les livres sacrés [de l'humanité; surtout AT-NT]: Compacts. P 1990, Bordas. 256 p. – ᴿÉtudes 375 (1991) 140 (J. *Thomas*).

930 **Crenshaw** James L., Old Testament story and faith; a literary and theological introduction. Peabody MA 1991, Hendrickson. viii-472 p. $20. 0-943575-91-5.
931 *Crowe* J., How the Bible came about — O.T. and N.T.: Melanesian Journal of Theology 6,1 (1990) 7-16 [< NTAbs 36,1].
932 **Duggan** Michael, The consuming fire; a Christian introduction to the Old Testament. SF 1991, Ignatius. 670 p. $30. 0-89870-376-X [TDig 39,259].
933 **Freedman** David N., The unity of the Hebrew Bible [3 lectures AA March 1988]. AA 1991, Univ. Michigan. x-125 p. 0-472-10245-1.
934 **Gottwald** Norman K., Introdução socioliterária à Biblia Hebraica [➔ 5,1144], ᵀ*Alvarez* Anacleto: Biblia e sociologia. São Paulo 1988, Paulinas. 651 p. 85-05-00774-3). – ᴿPerspT 22 (1990) 241s (J. *Vitório*).
935 *a)* ᴱ**Greenberg** M., ❻ *Paršanût*... Jewish biblical exegesis; – *b)* ᴱ**Rabin** C., ❻ *Targumê miqra*... Bible translations; – *c)* **Licht** Y. S., ❻ *Mô'adê Yiśra'el*... Feasts and calendars. Reprints from *Enṣiqlopedia Miqrait.* J 1983/4/8, Bialik. 138 p.; 189 p.; 227 p. – ᴿHenoch 12 (1990) 368s (B. *Chiesa*).
936 **Henrichsen** Walter, *Jackson* Gayle, Studying, interpreting, and applying the Bible. GR 1990, Zondervan-Youth. 352 p. $13. 0-310-37781-1.
937 **Hill** A. E., *Walton* J. H., A survey of the Old Testament. GR 1991, Zondervan. xviii-461 p. $23. 0-310-51600-5 [BL 92,74, B. P. *Robinson*].
938 *Kaiser* Otto, [*Strecker* Georg], Literaturgeschichte, biblische, AT [NT]: ➔ 690, TRE 21 (1991) 306-337 [338-358].
939 **Laffey** Alíce, *a)* An introduction to the OT; a feminist perspective 1988 ➔ 4,1075 ... 6,1172: ᴿCCurr 40 (1990s) 131s (Mary *Curtin*: scarcely seen as Jewish books); RRel 49 (1990) 633-5 (Kay *O'Neil*: wholly meritorious); – [=] *b)* Wives, harlots and concubines SPCK 1990 ➔ 6,1173: ᴿTLond 94 (1991) 215s (Sue *Gillingham*).
940 **Lambiasi** Francesco, La Bibbia, introduzione generale [non = 1985, ᵀespañol 1988 ➔ 6,1174]: Manuali di Base 1. CasM 1991, Piemme. 128 p.
941 **Mannucci** Valerio, Bibbia come Parola di Dio; introd. gen. ²1981, ⁶1986 ➔ 62,1157 ... español 1985 ➔ 1,1195: ᴿColcT 60,4 (1990) 169-171 (J. *Warzecha*, ❷).
942 **Matthews** Victor H., *Benjamin* Don C., Old Testament parallels; laws and stories from the Ancient Near East. NY 1991, Paulist. vi-276 p.; ill.; maps. $15. 0-8091-3182-X [BAR-W 17/1,4; BL 92,119, W. G. *Lambert*: ANET simplified and by biblical book]. ➔ 958 infra.
943 **Mertens** Heinrich A., Manual de la Biblia [²1984]ᵀ, 1989 ➔ 6,1176: ᴿAugM 35 (1990) 395 (P. *Merino*); Carthaginensia 7 (1991) 251 (R. *Sanz Valdivieso*); CiTom 118 (1991) 186 (J. *Huarte*); Iter 2 (1991) 151s (J.-P. *Wyssenbach*).
944 ᴱ**Mulder** M., *Sysling* H., Mikra 1988 ➔ 4,317 ... 6,1177: ᴿJAOS 111 (1991) 274-6 (J. A. *Sanders*: KASHER's task 'ominous'); JPseud 7 (1990) 122-6 (Carol *Newsom*); JStNT 41 (1991) 128 (David E. *Orton*); NedTTs 45 (1991) 152s (A. van der *Kooij*); TR 87 (1991) 10s (E. *Zenger*); VT 41 (1991) 503s (H. *Williamson*); ZkT 113 (1991) 80-82 (R. *Oberforcher*: Bibliographie betont englischsprachige Literatur).
945 **Ohler** Annemarie, Studying the OT, from tradition to canon 1985 ➔ 1,1198 ... 6,1178*: ᴿOTAbs 14 (1991) 103 (J. R. *Spencer*).
946 **Olst** Evert H. van, The Bible and liturgy [i. the liturgical structure of the Bible, p. 1-46; ... iii. some anthropological assumptions, p. 95-134 ...], ᵀ*Vriend* John. GR 1991, Eerdmans. xii-159 p. 0-8028-0306-7.

947 **Pilch** J. J.,   Introducing the cultural context of the Old Testament: Hear the word! 1. NY 1991, Paulist. 0-8091-3271-0 [BL 92,145]. → 3548* NT.

948 *Raurell* Frederico,   El antiguo próximo oriente y la tradición bíblica (conferencia Univ. Roma 15.I.1991): EstFranc 92 (1991) 535-554.

949 **Ravasi** Gianfranco,   Antico Testamento, introduzione.   CasM 1991, Piemme.   272 p. Lit. 28.000. – ^RMiscFranc 91 (1991) 519s (M. *Holc*); NRT 113 (1991) 903s (J.-L. *Ska*).

950 **Rendtorff** Rolf,   Introduzione all'AT; storia, vita sociale e letteratura d'Israele in epoca biblica 1990 → 6,1180:   ^RAntonianum 66 (1991) 436s (M. *Nobile*); Henoch 13 (1991) 235-8 (P. *Sacchi*); ScEsp 43 (1991) 246s (P.-É. *Langevin*).

951 **Rogerson** John, *Davies* Philip,   The Old Testament world 1989 → 5,1163; 6,1181:   ^RNBlackf 31 (1990) 562s (T. *Axe*); RelStT 10,2 (1990) 98-101 (H. D. *Maier*); ScotJT 44 (1991) 109s (S. B. *Dawes*: clear but with 20 + 'spelling mistakes').

952 ^E**Sanchez Caro** J. M., *al.*,   Introducción al estudio de la Biblia; I. La Biblia en su entorno 1990 → 6,370*; II. Biblia y palabra de Dios, ^E**Artola** A. 1989 → 5,1447; 6,1502 [infra → 7067]:   ^RCiuD 203 (1991) 487-9 (J. *Gutierrez*, 1); ComSev 24 (1991) 101s (M. de *Burgos*); NRT 113 (1991) 902s (J.-L. *Ska*, 1); RB 98 (1991) 618-624 (J. *Loza*, castellano); RET 51 (1991) 510-3 (P. *Barrado Fernández*, 2); RivB 39 (1991) 344s (A. *Bonora*); TLZ 116 (1991) 649-652 (W. *Nagel*, 2).

953 **Schultz** Samuel J.,   The Old Testament speaks; a complete survey of OT history and literature⁴. SF 1990, Harper & R.   440 p. $25 [Int 45,224]. – ^RGraceTJ 11 (1990) 235-7 (R. L. *Giese*: conservative-historical).

954 **Schmidt** Werner,   Old Testament introduction [Einführung ¹1979 ⁴1989 → 5,1166]. NY c. 1990, Crossroad.   368 p. $17 pa. [Int 45,224].

955 **Silver** Daniel J., *zal*,   The story of Scripture; from oral tradition to the written word. NY 1990, Basic.   302 p. $23.   0-465-08205-X. – ^RRExp 88,3 (1991) 264 (J. D. W. *Watts*).

956 **Smend** Rudolf,   Entstehung des ATs⁴ [= ¹1978], 1989 → 6,1183: ^RCBQ 53 (1991) 483 (R. *Gnuse*: 1970-80 bibliography added but not incorporated into the discussion).

957 **Soggin** J. Alberto,   Introduction to the OT³ [Italian ¹1968s, ⁴1987 'no page unchanged'], new ^T*Bowden* John [¹1974] 1989 → 5,1170; 6,1184: ^RCBQ 53 (1991) 483s (A. A. *DiLella*); PerspRelSt 18 (1991) 181s (K. M. *Craig*).

958 **Walton** J. H.,   [→ 942 supra] Ancient Israelite literature ... parallels 1989 → 6,1186:   ^RBL (1991) 101 (D. J. *Wiseman*); ZAW 103 (1991) 461 (H.-C. *Schmitt*).

B1.2   **'Invitations' to Bible or OT.**

959 **Allen** Steve,   On the Bible, religion and morality.   Buffalo NY c. 1991, Prometheus. – ^RAmerica 164 (1991) 424-6 (W. J. *O'Malley*).

960 **Avril** A. C., *Lenhardt* P.,   La lettura ebraica della Scrittura, con antologia di testi rabbinici, ^{TE}*Mello* Alberto.   Magnano VC 1984, Qiqajon. 122 p. Lit. 7.000. – ^RBenedictina 38 (1991) 226-230 (G. *Anelli*).

961 **Barbiere** Flavio,   La Bibbia senza segreti 1988 → 6,1188:   ^RScuolaC 119 (1991) 417s (A. *Ghisalberti*: severo).

962 **Barton** John,   What is the Bible? L 1991, SPCK.   vi-169 p. £5. 0-281-04538-3 [NTAbs 36,249; BL 92,61, J. G. *Snaith*].

963 **Beauchamp** Paul, Leggere la sacra Scrittura oggi; con quale spirito accostarsi alla Bibbia [Parler d'Écritures saintes 1987]: Sorgenti di vita 19, 1990 → 6,1192: ᴿRivB 39 (1991) 54-56 (G. *De Virgilio*).

964 **Brown** R.E., Responses to 101 questions on the Bible 1990 → 6,1194: ᴿTTod 42 (1991s) 261 (Carolyn *Osiek*).

965 **Burke** D., Genesis to Jesus; making sense of the Old Testament. Leicester 1991, Frameworks. 96 p. £3.25. 0-85111-219-6 [BL 92,103, B.P. *Robinson*: every second statement questionable].

966 **Carroll** R.P., Wolf in the sheepfold; the Bible as a problem for Christianity. L 1991, SPCK. xi-159 p. £10. 0-381-04525-9 [NTAbs 36, 251: 'ecclesiastical captivity' and other problems].

967 **Cronk** George, The message of the Bible; an orthodox Christian perspective. Crestwood NY 1990 = 1982, St. Vladimir. 293 p. 0-913836-94-X.

968 **Deissler** Alfons, Gehen mit Gott; Leittexte aus dem Alten Testament: StuTb 5. Stu 1991, KBW. 128 p. 3-460-11105-8.

969 *Domeris* W.R., Reading the Bible against the grain [MOSALA J.]: Scriptura 37 (1991) 68-81.

970 (Lane) **Fox** Robin, The unauthorized version; truth and fiction in the Bible. L 1991, Viking. 478 p. 0-670-82412-7 [BL 92,144].

971 **Hanegraaff** J., Met de Torah is het begonnen, I. Oecumenische inleiding in het OT; II. De voortgang van het Woord in Tenach en Septuagint 1988s → 5,1193 [-graaf]: ᴿBijdragen 52 (1991) 95s (E. *Eynikel*).

972 **Hanson** R. & A., The Bible without illusions 1989 → 5,1194: ᴿInterpretation 45 (1991) 76.80 (P.J. *Culbertson*: prejudiced attack on fundamentalism).

973 **Hövelmann** Hartmut, Kernstellen der Lutherbibel; eine Anleitung zum Schriftverständnis: TArbB 5. Bielefeld 1989, Luther. 394 p. DM 58. – ᴿLuJb 58 (1991) 129-132 (H. *Junghans*); TLZ 116 (1991) 493-5 (M. *Brecht*).

973* **Junco** Garza C., 'Escucha, Israel...' Aproximación a la Sagrada Escritura. Mex 1990, Claveria. vii-371 p. 968-442-170-2 [NTAbs 36,103, also on two cognate volumes].

974 **Kaiser** W.C., [73] Hard sayings of OT. L 1991, Hodder & S. 259 p. £8. 0-340-54617-4 [BL 92,107, R. *Davidson*: his conservatism makes them hard].

975 ᴱ**Klopfenstein** M. *al.*, Mitte der Schrift? ...jüdisch-chr. Gespräch 1985/7 → 3,549; 4,1120: ᴿTGL 81 (1991) 231s (J. *Gamberoni*).

976 **Lohfink** Norbert, Unsere neuen Fragen und das AT, wiederentdeckte Lebensweisung 1988 → 5,301: ᴿColcT 60,1 (1990) 159-163 (J.W. *Roslon*).

977 **Lys** Daniel, Treize énigmes de l'AT 1988 → 4,1125; 5,1206: ᴿVT 41 (1991) 494 (R.P. *Gordon*).

978 **Magonet** J., A rabbi's Bible [...approach]. L 1991, SCM. x-178 p. £9.50. 0-334-02506-0 [BL 92,126, S.C. *Reif*: fresh, thoughtful].

979 **Maiberger** Paul, Das Alte Testament in seinen grossen Gestalten. Mainz 1990, Grünewald. 220 p. DM 36. – ᴿBiKi 46 (1991) 135s (Kalle *Schmitz*).

980 **Manara** Amilcare, I segreti della Bibbia e il mistero di Dio in videocassetta. Mi 1991, Cinehollywood. 6 videocassette.

980* Il messaggio della Bibbia [Ox 1988]ᵀ. T-Leumann 1990, LDC. 256 p.; ill. Lit. 42.000. 88-01-13964-0. – ᴿCC 142 (1991,3) 450 (G. *Giachi*).

981 **Mesters** Carlos, Defenseless flower, a new reading of the Bible 1989 → 6,1215: ᴿCritRR 4 (1991) 482-4 (D.L. *Smith*); HorBT 13 (1991) 79-81

(L.W. *Countryman*); TLond 94 (1991) 64s (D. *Cohn-Sherbok*, also on ROWLAND & CORNER).

982 *Murray* Donal, The biblical apostolate in today's world: DocLife 41 (1991) 507-516.

983 **Oden** Robert A., The Bible without theology 1987 → 3,269 ... 6,1218: RCurrTMiss 18 (1991) 222s (E. F. *Campbell*: 'theology' meaning apologetics).

983* ERadday Yehuda T., *Brenner* Athalya, On humour and the comic in the Bible 1990 → 6,367: RCBQ 55,201, R, C. *Culley*, tit. pp.; ExpTim 102 (1990s) 315 (G. S. *Rodd*: CARROLL holds no real humour; BRENNER's claim of Ct as *wasf* parody was seen by some students to import obscenity).

984 **Rohr** Richard, EMartos Joseph, Das entfesselte Buch; die Lebenskraft des ATs TEbert Andreas. FrB 1990, Herder. 188 p. DM 24,80 [TPQ 140,191, Roswitha *Unfried*].

984* *Russell* E. A., Some reflections on humour in Scripture and otherwise: IrBSt 13 (1991) 199-210.

985 **Schottroff** Luise & Willy, Die kostbare Liebe zum Leben; biblische Inspirationen: Tb 104. Mü 1991, Kaiser. 142 p. DM 19,80 [TR 88,73].

986 **Springer** Bernhard, Was uns Verheissen ist; Wege zum biblischen Glauben [< Sendboten/Antonius]: HTb 1670. FrB 1990, Herder. 256 p. DM 14,90 [TPQ 140,196, J. *Hörmandinger*].

986* **Stott** John, La Bibbia, libro per oggi.T. Perugia 1989, Patmos. 114 p. – RSTEv 2 (1990) 233 (G. *Freri*).

987 **Stuhlmueller** Carroll, New paths through the OT 1989 → 5,1220; 6,1229: RCarthaginensia 7 (1991) 505 (R. *Sanz Valdivieso*); CBQ 53 (1991) 311 (X. J. *Harris*); OTAbs 14 (1991) 106 (W. T. *Miller*).

988 **Subilia** Vittorio, La Parola che brucia: Meditazioni bibliche. T 1991, Claudiana. 176 p. Lit. 19.000.

989 *Trublet* Jacques, Quand l'AT invite à la remémoire: Christus 37 (P 1990) 190-203.

990 EWest Delno C., † *Kling* August, The Libro de las profecías of Christopher COLUMBUS [his view of himself as missionary and crusader; a notebook of his personal Bible studies, in Latin with English on facing pages]. Gainesville 1991, Univ. Florida. x-274 p. $50. 0-8130-1054-3 [TDig 38,366].

B1.3 *Paedagogia biblica* – **Bible-teaching techniques.**

991 **Berg** Horst K., Ein Wort wie Feuer; Wege lebendiger Bibelauslegung: HbBibUnt 1. Mü/Stu 1991, Kösel/Calwer. 488 p. DM 48 [TLZ 117, 732, Gisela *Kittel*]. – RArTGran 54 (1991) 351s (A. *Segovia*); ErbAuf 40 (1991) 484 (B. *Schwank*).

992 **Hill** Robert C., Breaking the bread of the Word; principles of teaching Scripture: SubsBPont 15. R 1991, Pontificio Istituto Biblico. xiv-185 p. Lit. 22.500. 88-7653-596-9 [TDig 39,168].

993 **Kellner** Gerhard, Das Verstehen biblischer Texte im Kindes- und Jugendalter: kath. Diss. Augsburg 1991, DPaul. – TR 87 (1991) 515.

994 *Pelletier* Anne-Marie, La Bible comme mémoire culturelle; un enseignement à inventer: Études 374 (1991) 381-393.

995 *Plessis* J. G. du, Teaching biblical studies creatively; a theological perspective: Scriptura 34 (1990) 28-37 [1-11, *Lategan* B. C.; 12-27, *Toit* I. du; 38-47, *Vosloo* W.: < NTAbs 36,4].

996 *Pyle* M.W., The international children's Bible; a Bible even a child [age 8-9] can read: RestQ 33 (1991) 87-96 [< NTAbs 36,14].

997 *Scharer* Matthias, Wie das Wort Gottes konkret wird; die Bibel in der Katechese: TPQ 139 (1991) 284-295 [289s, Ein Seitenblick; die Bibel in der Katechese Lateinamerikas ...].

998 **Schinzer** Reinhard, Spielräume in der Bibel... in Gruppen 1989 → 6,1243: ^RZkT 113 (1991) 96s (H.-A. *Pissarek*^J).

999 *Schmidt* Günter B., Bleibende Spannungen; Religionspädagogik in den 80er Jahren: TRu 55 (1990) 424-472.

1000 **Schoneveld** Jacobus, Die Bibel in der israelischen Erziehung; eine Studie über Zugänge zur Hebräischen Bibel und zum Bibelunterricht in der israelischen pädagogischen Literatur [Eng. 1987], ^T*Olmesdahl* R. Neuk 1987, Neuk.-V. x-255 p. DM 50. – ^RTLZ 116 (1991) 274s (G. *Begrich*).

1001 *Smit* J.A., New avenues; the dialogical nature and method of Bible instruction: Scriptura 38 (1991) 39-59 [< NTAbs 36,155].

1002 *Wcela* Emil A., Who do you say that they are? Reflections on the biblical audience today [... Gallup poll; CBA presidential address, ND 13.VIII.1990]: CBQ 53 (1991) 1-17.

1003 **Weber** Hans-Ruedi, *a)* Experiments with Bible study² [¹1981; it. 1989 → 5,1653]. Geneva 1989, WCC. ix-319 p.

— *b)* Esperimenti di studio biblico. T 1989, Claudiana. 240 p. – ^RSTEv 2 (1990) 233s (P. *Finch*).

B2.1 **Hermeneutica.**

1004 *a) Abel* Olivier, Qu'est-ce que s'orienter dans l'interprétation?; – *b) Bonnard* Pierre, Qui cherche trouve... le sens; – c*) Ruff* Pierre-Yves, Texte et ruse; la non-origine principielle du fait littéraire: → 140, ^FSMYTH-FLORENTIN Françoise 1991, 1-15 / 271-6 / 277-290.

1005 *Abesamis* Carlos H., Some paradigms in re-reading the Bible in a Third World setting: Mission Studies 7,1 (1990) 21-34; ^{TE}*Messa* Joseph: SelT 30 (1991) 243-250.

1006 **Addinall** Peter, Philosophy and biblical interpretation; a study in nineteenth-century conflict. C 1991, Univ. 330 p. £35. 0-521-40423-1 [ScotJT 44,547].

1007 **Alter** Robert, I piaceri della lettura; il testo liberato. Mi 1990, Leonardo. 253 p. – ^RRivB 39 (1991) 43-48 (G. *Ravasi*).

1007* *a) Alter* Robert, Biblical imperatives and literary play; – *b) Levinson* Bernard B., The right chorale; from the poetics to the hermeneutics of the Hebrew Bible; – c*) Sanders* James A., The integrity of biblical pluralism: → 454*b*, Not in heaven 1989/91, 13-27 . 226s / 129-153 . 241-7 / 154-169 . 247-9.

1008 *Barr* James, Literality: Faith and Philosophy 6 (1989) 412-428 [< BS 148 (1991) 118s (B.B. *Miller*)].

1009 **Barr** James, Sémantique du langage biblique 1988 → 4,1177: ^RRTPhil 121 (1989) 337 (J.-C. *Margot*).

1010 **Bori** Pier Cesare, L'interpretazione infinita; l'ermeneutica cristiana antica e le sue trasformazioni: Saggi 236, 1987 → 4,a862: ^RCrNSt 11 (1990) 636s (G. *Ruggieri*).

1011 **Bori** Pier Cesare, L'interprétation infinie; l'herméneutique chrétienne ancienne et ses transformations [1987 → 4,a862], ^T*Vial* François: Passages. P 1991, Cerf. 148 p. F 120 [BL 92,101, N. *de Lange*]. 2-204-04156-4. – ^REsprVie 101 (1991) 566s (É. *Cothenet*).

1011* *Chico* Gabriel, Valor hermenéutico del Midrash: CommSev 24 (1991) 3-18.

1012 **Cowley** Roger W., Ethiopian biblical interpretation 1988 ➤ 4,1186; 6,1259: ᴿBijdragen 52 (1991) 332s (M. *Parmentier*, Eng.); JTS 42 (1991) 276-281 (M. A. *Knibb*).

1013 **D'Ambrosio** Marcellino G., Henri de LUBAC and the recovery of the traditional hermeneutic: diss. Catholic Univ., ᴰ*Dulles* A. Wsh 1991. 405 p. 91-23092. – DissA 52 (1991s) 964-A.

1014 *Deist* F. E., Objektiewe Skriftuitleg?: HervTSt 47 (1991) 367-385 [< NTAbs 36,150; subtitle 'Marginal notes to the interpretation of Scripture in the Dutch Reformed Church'].

1015 *a) Díaz Mateos* Manuel, The Word in history; – *b) Viladesau* Richard, The cultural linguistics model for theology; a critical evaluation; – *c) Chethimattam* John B., The Christian hermeneusis and other religions; – *d) Verstraaten* J., Christian approach to other religions from a sociologist's perspective: Jeevadhara 21 (1991) 391-5 / 371-9 / 339-364 / 380-3.

1015* **Dicenso** James J., Hermeneutics and the disclosure of truth; a study in the work of HEIDEGGER, GADAMER, and RICŒUR. Charlottesville 1990, Univ. Virginia. 208 p. $32.50. 0-8139-1249-0. – ᴿSWJT 34,1 (1991s) 78 (B. K. *Putt*).

1016 **Fishbane** Michael, Garments of Torah 1989 ➤ 5,259; 6,1266: ᴿJRel 71 (1991) 568s (R. L. *Cohn*).

1017 **Fortin-Melkevik** Anne, Pour une théorie rationnelle de l'herméneutique en théologie: diss. ᴰ*Geffré* C., Inst.Cath./Sorbonne. P 1991. 389 p. – RICathP 41, 214-8; RTLv 23, p. 536.

1018 **Früchtel** Ursula, (*Büscher* Hans-Werner), Mit der Bibel Symbole entdecken. Gö 1991, Vandenhoeck & R. 573 p.; 14 fig.; 40 pl. 3-525-61106-4.

1019 **Genette** Gérard, Figuras III [1972, ya importante para MÍNGUEZ D. 1976, BALAGUER V. 1990, CAMPOS A. 1991],ᵀ. Barc 1989, Lumen. 338 p. – ᴿScripTPamp 23 (1991) 690-2 (J. M. *Casciaro*: alternativa a GREIMAS).

1020 *Gese* Hartmut, *a)* Hermeneutische Grundsätze der Exegese biblischer Texte [< ᴱ*Gunneweg*, Standort 1985/6, 43-62]; – *b)* Der auszulegende Text [< TüTQ 167 (1987) 252-265]: ➤ 204, At. Studien 1991, 249-265 / 266-282.

1021 *Gnilka* Joachim, La historia de los efectos, acceso a la comprensión de la Biblía [< MüTZ 40 (1989) 51-62], ᵀᴱ*Giménez* Joseph: SelT 30 (1991) 233-240.

1022 **Graham** W. A., Beyond the written word 1987 ➤ 4,1200 ... 6,1270: ᴿJRel 71 (1991) 129s (R. C. *Martin*).

1023 *a) Greisch* Jean, Herméneutique et philosophie pratique; bulletin de philosophie; – *b) Courcier* Jacques, Herméneutique, sciences et Écritures; bulletin de philosophie des sciences: RSPT 75 (1991) 97-128 / 257-300.

1024 *Griffin* Philip, Some admonitions of J. H. NEWMAN regarding the correct use of Scripture in the quest for revealed truth [i. acknowledge the evidence of tradition; ii. discover what is implicit in Scripture; iii. interpret Scripture in accordance with its nature]: AnnTh 5 (1991) 301-326.

1025 **Gruenler** R. G., Meaning and understanding; the philosophical framework for biblical interpretation: FoundBInt 2. GR 1991, Zondervan. 223 p. 0-310-40931-4 [NTAbs 36,102].

1026 *a) Hardmeier* Christof, Hermeneutik und Grammatik; zum Zusammenhang von Sprachbeschreibung und Textwahrnehmung; – *b) Hassl-*

berger Bernhard, Dialog mit der Bibel; methodische Fragestellungen in der theologischen Erwachsenenbildung: → 126, ^FRICHTER W., Text 1991, 119-140 / 141-154.

1027 **Jeanrond** Werner G., Theological hermeneutics; development and significance. NY 1991, Crossroad. xv-220 p. $23.   0-8245-1117-4 [TDig 39,269; NTAbs 36,255].

1027* *a) Jeanrond* Werner G., Biblical criticism and theology; toward a new biblical theology; – *b) Geffré* Claude, Toward a hermeneutics of inter-religious dialogue; – *c) Ogden* Schubert M., Problems in the case for a pluralistic theology of religions; – *d) Baum* Gregory, Radical pluralism and liberation theology; – *e) Ruether* Rosemary R., Feminist hermeneutics; scriptural authority and religious experience; the case of the Imago Dei and gender equality; – *f) Neusner* Jacob, Another path to truth; from ritual to theology in Judaism: → 515*, D. Tracy and the hermeneutics of religion 1991, 38-48 / 250-269 / 270-285 / 1-17 / 95-106 / 161-175.

1028 *Kaiser* Walter C., Hermeneutics and the theological task: TrinJ 12,1 (1991) 3-14.

1029 *Keown* Gerald L., Biblical criticism and the hermeneutical task: RExp 88 (1991) 85-92.

1030 *Körtner* Ulrich H. J., Lector in Biblia; Schriftauslegung zwischen Rezeptionsästhetik und vierfachem Schriftsinn: WDienst 21 (1991) 215-233.

1031 **Kuen** A., Comment interpréter la Bible. St-Légier 1991, Emmaüs. 321 p. Fs 24.   2-8287-0042-9 [NTAbs 36,255].

1032 **Kuhatschek** Jack, Taking the guesswork out of applying the Bible. DG 1990, InterVarsity. 163 p. $8. – ^RBS 148 (1991) 245 (R. B. *Zuck*: needed).

1033 **Laks** André, *Neschke* Ada, La naissance du paradigme herméneutique: CahPg. Lille 1990, Presses Univ. 396 p. – ^RRÉG 104 (1991) 595s (L. *Dubois*: grands noms de la 'philogie' d'Allemagne depuis 1800).

1033* *La Potterie* Ignace de, *a)* L'esegesi biblica scienza della fede, ^T*Tosolini* Fabricio; – *b)* Il Concilio Vaticano II e la Bibbia, ^T*Costantini* V. M.: → 323, L'esegesi cristiana oggi 1991, 127-165 / 19-42.

1034 *Laurenzi* Maria Cristina, Perché la Scrittura? La lettera biblica come fatto etico: RasT 32 (1991) 233-255.

1034* *Letis* Theodore, Brevard CHILDS and the Protestant dogmaticians; a window to a new paradigm of biblical interpretation: Churchman 105 (L 1991) 261-... [< ZIT 92,71].

1035 *a) Longman* Tremper^{III}, What I mean by historical-grammatical exegesis; why I am not a literalist; – *b) Johnson* Elliott E., What I mean by historical-grammatical interpretation and how that differs from spiritual interpretation [Dispensationalist approach]: GraceTJ 11 (1990) 137-155 / 157-169.

1036 *Loose* D., L'interprétation des interprétations ou la théologie de la métaphore: SémBib 63 (1991) 34-40.

1037 **McGehee** M. D., God's word expressed in human words; the Bible's literary forms. ColMn 1991, Liturgical. 103 p. $8 pa. 0-8146-2009-4.

1038 ^E**McKim** Donald K., A guide to contemporary hermeneutics 1986 → 2,258 ... 6,1295: ^RJDharma 15 (1990) 83 (sr. *Thaijasa*).

1039 *a) Marques Gonçalves* Manuel, A noemática bíblica em Sebastião BARRADAS (1543-1615); – *b) Carreira das Neves* Joaquim, A Bíblia como história frente ao esoterismo; – *c) Coelho Matías* José, Manuel de Sá, precursor do método histórico-crítico: → 421, Luso-Esp 1989/91, 543-573

/ 575-595 / 609-626 = 422, Didaskalia 20 (1990) 93-123 / 167-187 / 125-142.

1040 *a) Mesters* Carlos, A Bíblia lê a Bíblia — sobre o fenómeno de releitura dentro da Bíblia; – *b) Faria Jacia de Freitas Silva* José B. da, Leitura bíblica através de símbolos e imagens: ↦ 99, ᶠMESTERS, EstudosB 32 (1991) 39-45 / 27-32.

1040* **Molina Palma** M. A., La interpretación de la Escritura en el Espíritu ᴰ1987 ↦ 6,1302: ᴿAugM 34 (1989) 404s (J. A. *Galindo*).

1041 **Morgan** R., *(Barton* J.), Biblical interpretation 1988 ↦ 4,1231 ... 6,1304: ᴿAnStoEseg 8 (1991) 711s (M. *Pesce*); JStNT 41 (1991) 127 (D. L. *Baker*); JTS 42 (1991) 285-7 (I. H. *Jones*).

1042 **Murtonen** A., Reality and the Bible; prolegomena to a multidimensional interpretation. Melbourne 1991, auct. vii-223 p. [ZAW 104,452, H.-C. *Schmitt*].

1043 *a) Myers* William H., The hermeneutical dilemma of the African American biblical student; – *b) Shannon* David T., 'An ante-bellum sermon'; a resource for an African American hermeneutic: ↦ 433, Stony the road 1986/91, 40-56 / 98-123.

1044 *a) Osiek* Carolyn, Literal meaning and allegory; – *b) Reid* Barbara E., Once upon a time... [parables]; – *c) Trigg* Joseph W., The legacy of ORIGEN; – *d) Hoppe* Leslie J., The Bible tells me so: BToday 29 (1991) 261-6 / 267-272 / 273-8 / 279-283.

1045 **Panagopoulos** Ioannis, Ⓖ The interpretation of Holy Scripture in the Church of the Fathers, I. Athenai 1990. 394 p. 960-7006-63-1. – ᴿTAth 61 (1990) 885s (E. A. *Theodorou*, Ⓖ).

1046 *Peinado-Muñoz* Miguel, Criterios hermenéuticos de Jaime PÉREZ de Valencia: ↦ 421, Luso-Esp 1989/91, 667-672.

1047 *a) Petitdemange* Guy, Récit biblique et détresse du présent [+ ᵀ*García Rúa* J.]; – *b) Rubio Ferreres* José M., Lenguaje religioso y hermenéutica filosófica; – *c) Pérez de Tudela y Velasco* Jorge, Desvelamiento y revelación, el círculo hermenéutico en Paul RICŒUR: ↦ 578, Caminos 1987/91, 247-260 [261-274] / 219-240 (275s.241s réponses) / 369-383.

1048 *Pharantos* (Farados) Megas, Ⓖ *Biblikē theología* [T. KONTIDIS, Biblike hermeneutike... hermeneutic method of Farados, DeltioVM 9 (1990) 60-69]: TAth 61 (1990) 588-606; Eng. 906 title given as 'Hermeneutic a-theology': against this Jesuit priest's rejection of theological presuppositions of Orthodox and Roman Catholic systematic theology].

1049 **Pleitner** Henning, Das Ende der liberalen Hermeneutik am Beispiel Albert SCHWEITZERS: Diss. Heidelberg 1991, ᴰ*Berger.* – TR 87 (1991) 518.

1050 **Prichard** Rebecca B., Genre, metaphor and theology; the interpretation of form and content in theological texts: diss. Graduate Theological Union, ᴰ*Reist* B. Berkeley 1990, – RTLv 23,537.

1051 *a) Quadrato* Renato, 'Interpretatio' e 'iuris processus'; – *b) Marotta Mannino* Beatrice, Gli Instituta di Giunilio; alcuni aspetti esegetici: ↦ 452, AnStoEseg 8,2 (1990/1) 351-362 / 405-419.

1052 *a) Ratzinger* Joseph, L'interpretazione biblica in conflitto, ᵀ*Benazzi* Natale; – *b) Bianchi* Enzo, La lettura spirituale della Scrittura oggi; – *c) Colombo* Giuseppe, Intorno all' 'esegesi scientifica': ↦ 323, ᴱ*Pacomio* L., L'esegesi 1991, 93-125 / 215-277 / 169-214.

1053 **Rieger** Reinhold, Interpretation und Wissen; zur philosophischen Begründung der Hermeneutik bei F. SCHLEIERMACHER und ihrem geschichtlichen Hintergrund: S.-Archiv 6. B 1988, de Gruyter. ix-361 p. DM 105. – ᴿBijdragen 52 (1991) 111s (H. J. *Adriaanse*).

1054 **Rödszus-Hecker** Marika, Der buchstäbliche Zungensinn; eine Studie zur Metaphernsynthese vom Wort der Schrift: ev. Diss. ᴰ*Timm* H. München 1991s. – RTLv 23, p. 537.

1055 **Rothen** Bernhard, Die Klarheit der Schrift, I: M. LUTHER; die wiederentdeckten Grundlagen. Gö 1990, Vandenhoeck & R. 262 p. DM 38. – ᴿLuJb 58 (1991) 132s (H. *Junghans*); TLZ 116 (1991) 746-8 (U. *Dietzfelbinger*).

1056 *Stevens* B., Les deux sources de l'herméneutique: RPhilLv 87 (1989) 504-515.

1056* **Tate** W. Randolph, Biblical interpretation, an integrated approach. Peabody MA 1991, Hendrickson. xxi-226 p. 0-943575-50-8.

1057 ᴱ**Thoma** Clemens, *Wyschogrod* Michael, Understanding Scripture 1984/7 ➤ 3,570; 4,1255: ᴿBZ 35 (1991) 117s (J. *Maier*).

1058 *Wackenheim* Charles, Les textes normatifs à l'épreuve de l'interprétation [comme Mt 9,37s (ouvriers pour la moisson), Mt 12,47 (frères de Jésus) indûment restreints par l'exégèse catholique]: RevSR 65 (1991) 94-108.

1059 *Ward* G., Biblical narrative and the theology of metonymy: ModT 7,4 (1991) 335-349 [< NTAbs 36,9].

1059* *White* Erin, Between suspicion and hope; Paul RICŒUR's vital hermeneutic: LitTOx 5 (1991) 311-... [< ZIT 91,570].

1060 **Whitman** J., Allegory; dynamics 1987 ➤ 4,1260 ... 6,1325: ᴿCrNSt 12 (1991) 191-3 (J. *Leclercq*).

Young Frances, The art of performance; towards a theology of Holy Scripture 1990 ➤ 1673.

B2.2 **Structuralismus biblicus** (generalior ➤ J9.4).

1061 *a*) *Detweiler* Robert, *Robbins* Vernon K., From New Criticism to Poststructuralism; twentieth-century hermeneutics; – *b*) *Hart* Kevin, The poetics of the negative: ➤ 324*, Reading the text 1991, 225-280 / 281-340.

1062 **Frank** Manfred, What is [post-deconstructionist] Neostructuralism? Mp 1989, Univ. Minnesota. 482 p. $45; pa. $20. – ᴿTTod 48 (1991s) 123s (D. *Allen*).

1063 **Milne** Pamela J., V. PROPP and the study of structure in Hebrew biblical narrative 1988 ➤ 3,1309 ... 6,1332: ᴿJTS 42 (1991) 623s (J. W. *Rogerson*).

1064 **Patte** Daniel, The religious dimensions of biblical texts; GREIMAS's structural semantics and biblical exegesis: SBL SS. Atlanta 1990, Scholars. xi-293 p. $32; sb./pa. $21. – ᴿCritRR 4 (1991) 95 (F. W. *Burnett*: best to date on Greimas).

1065 *Steenekamp* N. J. S., *Aarde* A. G. van, Dekonstruktie en Bybelse hermeneutiek: HervTSt 47 (1991) 473-486 [< NTAbs 36,156].

B2.4 *Analysis* **narrationis** *biblicae* (generalior ➤ J9.6).

1066 *Aletti* Jean-Noel, L'approccio narrativo applicato alla Bibbia; stato della questione e proposte, ᵀ*Pistone* R.: RivB 39 (1991) 257-275; Eng. 275s.

1067 **Alter** Robert, L'arte della narrativa biblica 1990 ➤ 6,1336: ᴿCC 142 (1991,3) 448s (V. *Fusco*); RivB 39 (1991) 43-46 . 48-52 (G. *Ravasi*: raccolta riveduta di articoli da Commentary, Poetics Today e Critical Inquiry).

1067* *Alter* Robert, Putting together biblical narrative: → 127, ᶠROSEN-MEYER T., Cabinet of the Muses 1989, 117-129.

1068 **Bar-Efrat** Shimon, Narrative art in the Bible: BLit 17 / JStOT supp 70, 1989 → 5,1312; 6,1337: ᴿCBQ 53 (1991) 456s (J. S. *Coolidge*); RB 98 (1991) 303-7 (F. *Langlamet*); VT 41 (1991) 371 (R. P. *Gordon*).

1069 ᴱ**Bühler** P., *Habermacher* J.-F., La narration; quand le récit devient communication 1983/8 → 4,a911 ... 6,1338: ᴿRTPhil 123 (1991) 213-220 (Corina *Combet-Galland*).

1070 **Culbertson** Diana, The poetics of revelation; recognition and the narrative tradition: Studies in American Biblical Hermeneutics 4, 1989 → 6,1340: ᴿCritRR 4 (1991) 64-66 (J. L. *Staley*).

1071 **Dennis** Trevor, Lo and behold! The power of Old Testament storytelling. L 1991, SPCK. 164 p. £9. 0-281-04491-0. – ᴿExpTim 102 (1990s) 376 (J. G. *Snaith*); TLond 94 (1991) 462s (P. R. *Davies*).

1072 **Ellingsen** Mark, The integrity of biblical narrative; story in theology and proclamation 1990 → 6,1341: ᴿInterpretation 45 (1991) 434.6 (J. D. *Kuenzel*).

1073 **Funk** Robert W., The poetics of biblical narrative [only NT] 1988 → 4,1273 ... 6,1344: ᴿCBQ 53 (1991) 134-6 (Elizabeth S. *Malbon*); CritRR 4 (1991) 85-87 (Adele *Berlin*); JTS 42 (1991) 619s (J. I. H. *McDonald*).

1074 *Garsiel* Moshe, ❻ Ways of metonymic and metaphorical description in biblical narrative: Biqqurot wᵉ-Pišrot 23 (c. 1991) 5-40.

1075 **Kort** Wesley A., Story, text, and Scripture; literary interests in biblical narrative 1988 → 4,1276 ... 6,1347: ᴿCritRR 4 (1991) 93-95 (B. *Britt*); ModT 7 (1990s) 488-490 (D. *Rhoads*); HeythJ 32 (1991) 254s (B. L. *Horne*).

McGrath Alister, The genesis of doctrine [... as interpretation of narrative]. 1990 → 7128.

1077 **Payne** Michael W., The Bible as 'poem'; reconsidering RICŒUR; from symbol to metaphor to narrative, the poetic functions of religious language in the philosophy of Paul Ricœur: diss. Westminster Theol.Sem., ᴰ*Knudsen* R. 1989. 460 p. 91-22223. – DissA 52 (1991s) 1789-A.

1078 *Polak* Frank, ❻ Epic formulae in biblical narrative and the origins of ancient Hebrew prose: → 303, Teuda 7 (1991) 9-53; Eng. VIIs.

1079 **Powell** Mark A., What is narrative criticism?: GuidesBSch, 1990 → 6,1349: ᴿCurrTMiss 18 (1991) 380s (Lynn A. *Kauppi*).

ᴱ**Rosenblatt** Jason P., *Sitterson* Joseph C.ᴶ, 'Not in heaven'; coherence and complexity in biblical narrative: StBibLit, 1991 → 454b.

1081 **Ska** J. L., 'Our fathers have told us'; introduction to the analysis of Hebrew narratives: SubsBPont 13, 1990 → 6,1352: ᴿÉTRel 66 (1991) 591 (Danielle *Ellul*); NRT 113 (1991) 423s (X. *Jacques*).

1082 *Ska* Jean Louis, Narrativa ed esegesi biblica: CC 142 (1991,3) 219-230.

1083 **Vanhoozer** Kevin J., Biblical narrative in the philosophy of Paul RICŒUR 1990 → 6,1356: ᴿBL (1991) 99 (D. J. A. *Clines*: lucid, appreciative); ÉTRel 66 (1991) 466s (J.-P. *Gabus*); EvQ 63 (1991) 355-7 (A. C. *Thiselton*); LavalTP 47 (1991) 436-9 (R. *Martinez*); TsTNijm 31 (1991) 333 (J. Van den *Hengel*).

1083* *Ward* Graham, Biblical narrative and the theology of metonymy: ModT 7 (Ox 1990s) 335-350 [< ZIT 91,604].

1084 **Wedekind** Klaus, Generating narratives; interrelations of knowledge, text variants, and [examples from Africa] Cushitic focus strategies: TrLing

StMg 52. B/NY 1990, Mouton de Gruyter. xi-727 p. 3-11-012141-7 /
US 0-89925-595-7.

B2.6 *Critica reactionis lectoris* – **Reader-response criticism.**

1085 *a*) *Beaugrande* Robert de, *al.*, Meaning, metaphor, and imagery in
audience response; 'lawless and incertain thought'? – *b*) *Patry* Richard,
Ménard Nathan, Relations entre composantes informatives (rhématiques)
et typologie des textes; une étude exploratoire; – *c*) *Potter* Rosanne G.,
Pragmatic research on reader responses to literature with an emphasis on
gender and reader responses: RBgPg 69,3 ('Decoder le texte' 1991) 539-
554 / 576-598 / 599-617.

1086 *a*) *Conrad* Edgar, The Bible and the reader [*Franzmann* Majella, re-
sponse]; – *b*) *Patterson* Sue, Word, Words and World: Colloquium 23,2
(Sydney 1991) 49-56 [57s] / 71-84 [< ZIT 91,409].

1087 **McKnight** Edgar V., Post-modern use of the Bible; the emergence of
reader-oriented criticism 1988 ⇒ 5,1340; 6,1358: ᴿAndrUnS 28 (1990)
265-7 (J. *Paulien*); HorBT 12,2 (1990) 101-3 (N. *Elliott*).

1088 *Meyer* Ben F., Mises en question de la méthode historico-critique pour
le texte et le lecteur: ᵀ*Divault* André: ⇒ 348, Concilium 233 (P 1991)
13-25.

B3 *Interpretatio ecclesiastica* .1 **Bible and Church.**

1089 *Allen* Roger Van, The Charles CURRAN case: Horizons 18 (1991)
59-62.

1090 *Barr* J., *a*) 'Fundamentalism' and evangelical scholarship [*France* R.]:
Anvil 8 (1991) 141-152 [< NTAbs 36,2]; – *b*) Fundamentalism — a
challenge to the Church: QRMin 11,2 (1991) 30-39.

1091 **Barton** John, People of the book? The authority of the Bible in
Christianity (Bampton Lectures 1988) 1988 ⇒ 4,1294 … 6,1365: ᴿEvQ 63
(1991) 278-280 (I. H. *Marshall*).

1092 *Beinert* Wolfgang, Die Rezeption und ihre Bedeutung für Leben und
Lehre der Kirche: Catholica 44 (1990) 91-118.

1093 **Boone** Kathleen J., The Bible tells them so ᴰ1989 ⇒ 5,1351; 6,1367:
ᴿCritRR 4 (1991) 283-5 (D. S. *Ferguson*).

1093* **Bradley** Robert, The [Trent] Roman catechism in the catechetical
tradition of the Church [Diss. ᴰ*Duroux*]. Lanham MD 1990, UPA.
230 p. [ScEspr 44,106-8, B. de *Margerie*].

1094 *Burggraeve* Roger, De taak van het kerkelijk Leerambt in ethische
aangelegenheden: CollatVL 21 (1991) 159-182.

1095 **Burke** Cormac, *a*) Autoridad y libertad en la Iglesia. M 1988, Rialp. –
b) Autorità e libertà nella Chiesa. Mi 1989, Ares. 288 p. – ᴿAnnTh 4
(1990) 221-3 (A. *Cirillo*).

1096 **Carlen** Claudia, Papal pronouncements; a guide, 1740-1978; I. Benedict
XIV to Paul VI; II. Paul VI to John Paul I. AA 1990, Pierian. xxiii-
433 p.; vi + p. 435-957. $195 [CBQ 53,534].

1097 *Claramunt Llácer* Francisco, La relación entre la Sagrada Escritura y la
Iglesia en la relación 'de sacro canone et de ejus sensibus' de Domingo de
SOTO, con el texto inédito de la misma: AnVal 4 (1990) 63-106.

1098 ᴱ**Cohen** Norman, The fundamentalist phenomenon 1990 ⇒ 6,591: ᴿRExp
88 (1991) 278 (B. J. *Leonard*).

1099 *Colombo* Giuseppe, Magistero e teologia: TItSett 16 (1991) 291-305.

1100 *Comollo* Adriano, Il dissenso religioso in DANTE: Archivum Romanicum Bt 1/235. F 1990, Olschki. 153 p. [TR 88,78].

1101 **Curran** Charles E., Catholic higher education, theology, and academic freedom. ND 1990, Univ. 272 p. $28 [RelStR 18,44, J. E. *Thiel*]. – ᴿAmerica 164 (1991) 19-22 (Lisa S. *Cahill*); CritRR 4 (1991) 289-291 (D. *Wright*).

1102 *Duddy* Marie, 'Liberation' in religious education; the application of LONERGAN [... to Vatican 1988 document]: MilltSt 24 (1989) 113-141.

1103 Les évêques de France, Catéchisme pour adultes; l'alliance de Dieu avec les hommes. P 1991, Centurion + 12! 456 p. F 99. – ᴿÉtudes 375 (1991) 255-261 (G. *Adler*, sans un seul nom de vrai 'auteur').

1104 — *Bagot* Jean-Pierre, Le catéchisme pour adultes [Épiscopat français 1991] mis en perspective historique: RechSR 79 (1991) 401-413, traite non de ses idées doctrinales mais de son fonctionnement.

1105 *Extremeño* Claudio G., La vocación eclesial del teólogo: Studium 31 (M 1991) 3-26.

1106 *Falise* Michel (recteur Univ. Cath. Lille), Rome et les Universités catholiques [document sept. 1990 bien accueilli parce que fruit d'un 'dialogue réussi']: Études 374 (1991) 687-695.

1106* *Feldkaemper* Ludger, Reflection on biblical-pastoral ministry: EAPast 27 (1990) 294-304.

1107 *Fisher* David H., We have met the enemy, and he is us; reflections on liberal anxieties about fundamentalism: AnglTR 73 (1991) 26-37.

1108 *Franco* Ricardo, ¿Fundamentalismo católico?: Proyección 37 (1990) 251-270.

1109 *Fuchs* Josef, The magisterium and moral theology [< FreibZ 36 (1989) 395-407], ᵀᴱ*Day* Martin: TDig 38 (1991) 103-7.

1110 *Gaboriau* Florent, Progrès de la théologie; à quelles conditions?: TNouv. P 1991, FAC. 268 p. F 165 [TR 88,170].

1111 **Gaillardetz** Richard, The development of theologies of the ordinary universal magisterium from 1840 to 1990: diss. ᴰ*O'Meara* T. Notre Dame 1991. – RelStR 18,171; RTLv 23,565.

1112 *González Faus* José I., Evangelización e Iglesia / e inquisición: RLat-AmT 23 (1991) 231-251 / 191-210 = RCatalT 16 (1991) 121-139; Eng. 139.

1113 *Greeley* Andrew M., The Catholic imagination and the Catholic university: America 164 (1991) 285-8.

1114 a) *Guardini* Romano, Sacra Scrittura e scienza della fede [1929], ᵀ*Tosto* Luciano B.; – b) *Ratzinger* Joseph card., L'interpretazione biblica in conflitto (problemi del fondamento ed orientamento dell'esegesi contemporanea: → 323, L'esegesi 1991, 45-91 / 93-125.

1115 *Gudorf* Christine, Le magistère et la Bible; expérience nord-américaine, ᵀ*Divault* André: → 348, Concilium 233 (P 1991) 107-120.

1116 *Häring* Bernhard, The loyalty of the critic [... the Church should be self-critical, with no more secrecy than necessary]: TDig 38 (1991) 309-312 [ᵀᴱ*Asen* B. A. < TGegw 33 (1990) 65-70, Die Loyalität der Kritik].

1117 *Hasler* Victor, Bibelglaube und biblischer Glaube; Erwägungen zum evangelikalen Fundamentalismus: TZBas 47 (1991) 136-147.

1118 **Heckel** Martin, Die theologischen Fakultäten im weltlichen Verfassungsstaat: JusEccl 31. Tü 1986, Mohr. xxvi-416 p. DM 68 [TR 88,225, J. *Listl*].

1119 a) *Henkys* Jürgen, Sola Scriptura im gegenwärtigen kirchlichen Handeln; – b) *Schultze* Harald, Sola scriptura im Bereich von kirchenleitenden Handeln: → 558, Sola Scr. 1990/1, 79-98 / 107-115.

1120 *Herrera* Aceves, Hechos y palabras en la revelación y en la Iglesia:
➤ 542, EfMex 9,2 (1991) 289-313.
1121 *a) Höslinger* Norbert W., 25. Jahre Dei Verbum; – *b) Scharbert* Josef,
Das II Vat. und das AT; – *c) Schnackenburg* Rudolf, Dei Verbum und
die neutestamentliche Exegese: BiKi 45 (1990) 174-8 / 179-186 / 187-192.
1122 *a) Hollerbach* Alexander, Aktuelle Fragen aus dem Recht der Theologischen Fakultäten; – *b) Kaufmann* Franz-Xaver, Theologie zwischen
Kirche und Universität; – *c) Baumgartner* Hans-Michael, Von der
Königin der Wissenschaften zu ihrem Narren? Bemerkungen zur Frage,
warum Theologie zur Universität unserer Tage gehört; – *d) Wirsching*
Johannes, Evangelische Theologie an der Universität — Anmerkungen
und Überlegungen; — *e) Hünermann* Peter, Die Theologie und die universitas litterarum — eine historische und systematische Reflexion im
Ausgang vom II. Vaticanum: TüTQ 171 (1991) 251-264 / 265-277 /
278-299 / 299-316 / 316-329 [247-250, *Kasper* W., 241-6, *Seckler* M.].
1123 *a) Hoogen* T. van den, WKTN [Werkgenootschap van Katholieke
Theologen in Nederland] over kerkelijke democratisering en de vaticaanse
instructie over de rol van theologen; – *b) Cornille* Catherine, Colloquium
over de universaliteit van het Christendom [Lv 21-22.II]: TsTNijm 31
(1991) 183-5-6.
1124 **Icenogle** Gareth W., Biblical, theological and integrative foundations for
small group ministry: diss. Fuller Theol. Sem., *ᴰAnderson* R. Pasadena
1990. 263 p. 92-08154. – DissA 52 (1991s) 3630-A.
1125 [*Kasper* Walter, *al.* ➤ 6,1398] Commissio theologica internationalis, De
interpretatione dogmatum [oct. 1989]: Gregorianum 72 (1991) 5-37.
1126 **Kasper** Walter, Wahrheit und Freiheit; die 'Erklärung über die Religionsfreiheit' des II. Vat.: Szb Heid ph/h 1988/4. Heid 1988, Winter.
41 p. – ᴿZKG 102 (1991) 426-8 (W. *Huber*).
1127 — *Izquierdo* César, El dogma y su interpretación [ᴱ*Kasper* W. 1990]:
ScripTPamp 23 (1991) 893-919.
1128 *Keenan* James F., Compelling assent; magisterium, conscience and oaths:
IrTQ 57 (1991) 209-227.
1129 **Kelly** George A., Keeping the Church Catholic with John Paul II. NY
1990, Doubleday. 300 p. – ᴿEcuR 41 (1991) 486s (C. *Angell*: against
theologians more American than Catholic, puts prohibition of altar-girls
on same level as belief in the Trinity).
1130 ᴱ**Kern** Walter, Die Theologie und das Lehramt [Tagung Januar 1981 ...
Fall KÜNG]: QDisp 91, 1982 ➤ 63,538; 64,1334: ᴿTPQ 139 (1991) 212s
(A. *Riedl*).
1131 ᴱ**Kienzler** Klaus, Der neue Fundamentalismus; Reifung oder Gefahr für
Gesellschaft und Religion?: Bayern Kath.Akad. Dü 1990, Patmos. 124 p.
DM 26,80. 3-491-77794-1. – ᴿTLZ 116 (1991) 585s (K.-W. *Tröger*).
1132 *a) Klein* Aloys, Verbindliches Lehren — Gegenwärtige Bemühungen in
den Reformatorischen Kirchen; – *b) Löser* Wernes, ... in der katholischen
Kirche: Catholica 44 (1990) 119-130 / 187-202.
1133 *Knauer* Peter, *a)* Das kirchliche Lehramt und der Beistand des Heiligen
Geistes [Instructio 24.V.1990]; – *b)* Der neue kirchliche Amtseid: StiZt
208 (1990) 661-673 / 93-101.
1134 *Komonchak* Joseph A., *a)* NEWMAN's infallible instincts; the argument
for elbowroom: Commonweal 117 (1990) 445-8. – *b)* The Magisterium
and theologians: ChSt 29 (1990) 307-329.
1135 *Kosch* Daniel, Schriftauslegung als 'Seele der Theologie'; Exegese im
Geist des Konzils [RATZINGER J., QDisp ...]: FreibZ 38 (1991) 205-233.

1136 **La Potterie** Ignace de, Il Vaticano II e la Bibbia, ᵀ*Costantini* V. M. Sessa Aurunca 1991. 36 p.

1137 *Lefebvre* Marcel, Quelle est la mission du théologien?: ÉglT 22 (1991) 177-192.

1138 **Longfield** Bradley J., The Presbyterian controversy; fundamentalists, modernists, and moderates. NY 1990, Oxford-UP. 333 p. $34.50 [Rel-StR 18,161, J. R. *Stone*].

1139 *McGovern* Thomas, Magisterium, Scripture and Catholic exegetes: HomP 91,10 (1991) 11-19; 91,11 (1991) 24-32.71.

1140 *McSwain* Larry L., Anatomy of the [1979] Southern Baptist Convention institutional crisis: RExp 88 (1991) 25-35 [9-23, *Ammermann* Nancy T.; 37-65, *al.*; p. 5, *Culpepper* R. A., In 1990 'Moderate leaders gave up hope of electing a moderate president and began to search for ways to continue to be Baptist without capitulating to the entrenched fundamentalist leadership'].

1141 **Marsden** George M., Reforming fundamentalism... Fuller 1987 ➤ 3,1348 ... 6,1407: ᴿHeythJ 32 (1991) 151s (B. *Aspinwall*).

1142 **Marsden** George M., Understanding fundamentalism and evangelicalism. GR 1991, Eerdmans. x-208 p. $13 pa. 0-8028-0539-6 [TDig 39,73, focuses J. G. MACHEN].

1143 **Mercer** Floyd J., Keeping the vision; a course in historic Baptist discipleship in response to the ascendency [sic] of fundamentalism in the Southern Baptist Convention with reference to John BUNYAN's 'Pilgrim's Progress': diss. Princeton Theol. Sem. 1991. 196 p. 91-33842. – DissA 52 (1991s) 2181-A.

1144 *Mesters* Carlos, *a*) La Biblia en la nueva evangelización, ᵀ*Gispert-Sauch* Ana: Páginas 16,107 (1991) 63-77; – *b*) 'Seht, ich mache alles neu'; die Bibel in der Neuevangelisierung: BiKi 46 (1991) 2-22.

1145 *a*) *Mesters* Carlos, 'Listening to what the Spirit is saying to the churches'; popular interpretation of the Bible in Brazil; – *b*) *Gudorf* Christine E. [➤ 1115], The Magisterium and the Bible; North American experience: ➤ 347, Concilium (1991,1) 100-111 / 79-90.

1146 *Meyer* Thomas, Fundamentalismus; Aufstand gegen die Moderne 1989 ➤ 5,1394; 3-499-12414-9: ᴿNumen 38 (1991) 128-133 (H. G. *Kippenberg*, also on four cognate works).

1147 *Müller* Gerhard L., Was ist kirchlicher Gehorsam? Zur Ausübung von Autorität in der Kirche: Catholica 44 (1990) 26-48.

1148 *Murray* Robert, La Iglesia docente y la Iglesia pensante [< Month 23 (1990) 310-318], ᵀᴱ*Ferrer Pi* Pedro: SelT 30 (1991) 207-214.

1149 *a*) *Narchison* J. Rosario, Understanding Christian fundamentalism through American evangelicalism; – *b*) *O'Connell* Colin, A Heideggerian analysis of fundamentalism; – *c*) *Lourdusamy* Stan, Religious fundamentalism as political weapon; socio-economic and political factors: JDharma 15 (1990) 95-113 / 114-124 / 125-134.

1150 ᴱ**Neuhaus** R., Biblical interpretation in crisis; the RATZINGER conference 1989 ➤ 6,m203: ᴿRB 98 (1991) 443-8 (P. *Grelot*); RRel 50 (1991) 467s (C. *Bernas*).

1151 — *Frankemölle* Hubert, Schriftauslegung im Widerstreit: BiKi 45 (1990) 200-4.

1152 *Neuner* Peter, Die Warnungen sind berechtigt; zur Diskussion über den 'katholischen Fundamentalismus': HerdKorr 45 (1991) 422-7.

1153 **Newbigin** Lesslie, Truth to tell; the Gospel as public truth [Holland MI Osterhaven Lectures: our culture has driven a wedge between liberals and fundamentalists]. GR/Geneva 1991, Eerdmans/WCC. $7 pa. 0-8028-0607-4 [TDig 39,278].

1154 **Nichols** Aidan, The shape of Catholic theology. Collegeville MN 1991, Liturgical. 374 p. $15 [RelStR 18,43, J. R. *Sachs*: skirts the real issues].

1155 ᴱ**Niewiadomski** Józef, Verweigerte Mündigkeit? Politische Kultur und die Kirche: Theologische Trends 2, 1989 ➤ 6,1416: ᴿTLZ 116 (1991) 58 (tit. pp.).

1156 **Noll** Mark A., Between faith and criticism; evangelicals, scholarship, and the Bible: SBL Confessional Perspectives. Leicester/GR 1991, Apollos/Baker. xii-271 p. £15. 0-85111-425-3.

1157 *Noort* Edward, Fundamentalismus in Exegese und Archäologie; eine Problemanzeige: ➤ 310, JbBT 6 (1991) 311-331.

1158 *a*) *O'Collins* Gerald, 'Dei Verbum' and biblical scholarship; – *b*) *Konstan* David, The use of the Bible within the Church: ScripB 21 (1991) 2-7 / 8-14.

1159 **Örsy** Ladislas, The Church learning and teaching 1987 ➤ 4,1346... 6,1419: ᴿETL 67 (1991) 457s (J. E. *Vercruysse*).

1159* *a*) *Oldfield* John S., Il fondamentalismo in un'ottica evangelica, ᵀ*Castellina* Paolo; – *b*) *Piccirillo* Gianfranco, Fondamentalismo e mass-media in Italia; – *c*) *Finch* Paul, Aspetti psicologici del fondamentalismo; – *d*) *Sartori* Luigi, Esiste un fondamentalismo cattolico?: STEv 2 (1990) 131-149 / 158-166 / 167-174 / 175-182.

1160 **O'Meara** Thomas F., Fundamentalism; a Catholic perspective 1990 ➤ 6,1422: ᴿHorizons 18 (1991) 330s (W. E. *McConville*); RelStR 17 (1991) 149 (J. R. *Sachs*); StVlad 35 (1991) 87s (J. *Gros*).

1161 *Parvis* Paul, Guardian angels and carrotburgers; two views of the role of the Magisterium [NEWMAN, RATZINGER]: NBlackf 71 (1990) 368-376.

1162 ᴱ**Penaskovic** Richard, Theology and authority; maintaining a tradition of tension 1987 ➤ 4,401: ᴿRelStT 9,1 (1989) 47-49 (B. P. *Toombs*).

1163 Précis of official Catholic teaching on... *a*) faith, revelation and the Bible; – *b*) Christ our Lord, true God and true man; – *c*) eight others to come. Wsh 1991, Catholics Committed to Support the Pope. xii-108 p.; xii-189 p. $5.50 each [TDig 39,55].

1164 **Principe** Walter H., Faith, history and cultures; stability and change in Church teachings: Père Marquette Theology Lecture 1991. Milwaukee 1991, Marquette Univ. 63 p. $8. 0-87462-546-7 [TDig 39,79].

1165 **Rausch** Thomas P., Authority and leadership in the Church 1989 ➤ 5,8112: ᴿThomist 55 (1991) 165-8 (Susan K. *Wood*).

1166 ᴱ**Reese** T. J., The universal catechism reader 1990 ➤ 6,1429: ᴿAmerica 165 (1991) 75s (W. C. *McFadden*); LvSt 16 (1991) 186-9 (H. *Lombaerts*: Scripture use by Mary C. *Boys*).

1167 **Rheinbay** Georg, Das ordentliche Lehramt in der Kirche; die Konzeption Papst PIUS' XII und das Modell Karl RAHNERS im Vergleich [Diss.]: TrierTSt 46. Trier 1988, Paulinus. iv-298 p. DM 75. – ᴿTGL 81 (1991) 396-8 (W. *Beinert*); ZkT 113 (1991) 65-70 (A. *Batlogg*: hauptsächlich ein Fallbeispiel).

1168 **Riesebrodt** Martin, Fundamentalismus als patriarchalische Protestbewegung; Amerikanische Protestanten (1911-28) und iranische Schriften (1961-79) im Vergleich. Tü 1990, Mohr. viii-298 p. DM 98. – ᴿTGL 81 (1991) 230s (W. *Beinert*).

1169 *Ruland* Vernon, The Vatican's loyalty oath; vouching for fidelity again & again & again: Commonweal 117 (1990) 710-2.

1170 *a) Sala* Giovanni B., Fehlbare Lehraussagen unter dem Bestand des Heiligen Geistes? Zum ordentlichen Lehramt in der Kirche; – *b) Scheffczyk* Leo, Das Problem der Aufhebung der Lehrverurteilungen: ForumKT 7 (1991) 1-20 / 38-60.

1171 *Sánchez Mielgo* Gerardo, La Sagrada Escritura en la vida de la Iglesia (a la luz de la 'Dei Verbum' del Concilio Vaticano II): TEspir 35 (1991) 157-200.

1172 **Scharr** Peter, Consensus fidelium; zur Unfehlbarkeit der Kirche aus der Perspektive einer Konsenstheorie der Wahrheit: Diss. FrB 1991, ᴰ*Greshake* G. 300 p. – TR 87 (1991) 517; RTLv 23, p. 566.

1173 **Schultze** Harald, Verantwortung für Freiheit und Bindung kirchlicher Lehre im Dialog mit den Denkvoraussetzungen seit der Aufklärung: Hab.-Diss. Halle-Wittenberg 1991, ᴰ*Winkler.* – TR 87 (1991) 512.

1174 *Schulz* Winfried, Konsens und Widerspruch als rechtserhebliches Handeln in der Kirche? — Kanonistische Erwägungen zur Rezeptionsproblematik: TGL 81 (1991) 339-354.

1175 **Schulze-Berndt** Hermann, Wenn die Kirche Stellung nimmt: Absichten, Erfahrungen, Beispiele. Wü 1990, Echter. 142 p. DM 24,80. – ᴿZkT 113 (1991) 495s (A. *Batlogg*: deutsche 'bischöfliche Stellungnahmen'; kaum etwas über Theologenkommissionen, Laien, Ausländer).

1176 **Segundo** Juan Luis, El dogma que libera; fe, revelación y magisterio dogmático: Presencia teologica 53. Sdr 1989, Sal Terrae. 406 p. – ᴿPerspT 22 (1990) 382-5 (A. T. *Murad*).

1177 **Silva** Moisés, Has the Church misread the Bible? 1987 ⇥ 3,1365; 4,1351: ᴿEvQ 63 (1991) 351s (C. *Gempf*); STEv 3 (1991) 132s (J. *Terino*).

1178 **Spong** John S., Rescuing the Bible from fundamentalism [...J. FALWELL]. L 1991, Harper Collins. £6. – ᴿTablet 245 (1991) 1858 (G. *O'Collins*).

1179 *Sullivan* Francis A., The theologian's ecclesial vocation and the 1990 CDF instruction: TS 52 (1991) 51-68.

1180 ᴱ**Swidler** Leonard, *O'Brien* Herbert, A Catholic Bill of Rights [support from 1983 Canon Law for 32 rights also formulated in 1983]. KC 1988, Sheed & W. 187 p. $9 [RelStR 18,219, P. C. *Phan*: just talk unless fines are imposed on unconforming ecclesiastics].

1180* *Taber* Douglass ᴶ, Pierre d'AILLY and the teaching authority of the theologian: ChH 59 (1990) 163-174.

1181 Teologi in rivolta [ma eseguendo Pio XII, 'mancherebbe qualcosa del corpo vivo della Chiesa se la sua vita non fosse alimentata dall'opinione pubblica di sacerdoti e laici' (p. 191)]; i testi e i documenti integrali della 'contestazione nella Chiesa'. R 1990, Logos. 196 p. Lit. 22.000. – ᴿRasT 32 (1991) 437 (B. *Marra*).

1182 **Thiel** John E., Imagination and authority; theological authorship in the modern tradition. Mp 1991, Fortress. xii-228 p. $25 [TR 88,434].

1183 *Thiel* John E., The theologian in the eyes of the magisterium [RATZINGER 1990]: HeythJ 32 (1991) 383-7.

1184 **Thils** Gustave, *Schneider* Theodor, Glaubensbekenntnis und Treueid; Klarstellungen zu den 'neuen' römischen Formeln für kirchliche Amtsträger. Mainz 1990, Grünewald. 143 p. DM 19,80 pa. – ᴿZkT 113 (1991) 324 (K. H. *Neufeld*).

1185 *Thils* G., La spécificité de l'enseignement supérieur catholique [Jean-Paul II, Les universités catholiques 1980 [ᴱ*Falise* M. P (1990) Centurion. 51 p.; DocCath 87 (1990) 934-945]: ETL 67 (1991) 188-195.

1186 *a*) *Thornhill* John, Fundamentalism, an important contemporary categorization; – *b*) *O'Farrell* Patrick, ... an historico-contemporary meditation; – *c*) *O'Leary* Humphrey, The LEFEBVRE movement: AustralasCR 67,4 ('Fundamentalism' 1990) 387-9 / 390-3 / 401-412.

1187 *a*) *Tihon* Paul, La liberté de la foi comme principe d'ecclésialité; – *b*) *Valdrini* Patrick, Le statut de l'opinion publique dans l'Église et le droit canonique; l'impossible contrôle: → 535*, RechSR 79,3 (1991) 353-369 / 371-390; Eng. 323s.

1188 *Toolan* David S., A disagreeable bunch in the bark of Peter [... RATZINGER: theologians are not to be seen or heard in the public media]: America 164 (1991) 76s.

1189 *Topping* Richard R., The anti-foundationalist challenge to evangelical apologetics: EvQ 63 (1991) 45-60.

1190 ᴱ**Ubaldi** M., Vocazione ecclesiale del teologo; testo integrale dell'omonima Istruzione, pref. RATZINGER J. R 1990, Logos. 116 p. Lit. 14.000. – ᴿRasT 32 (1991) 437s (B. *Marra*).

1191 *Vereecke* Louis, Magistère et théologie du XIIIᵉ au XVIIᵉ siècle; esquisse historique: StMor 29 (1991) 27-58; Eng. 59.

1192 *a*) *Villegas* M. Beltrán, La Evangelización en la Biblia; – *b*) *Noemi* C. Juan, Presupuestos bíblicos de la evangelización: TVida 32,1s ('Quinto centenario, reflexiones histórico-teológicas' 1991) 5-19 / 125-140.

1193 *Wicks* Jared, Biblical criticism criticized [RATZINGER's 'lively, nuanced' German in QDisp 117,1989 shows also the importance of G. LINDBECK's response; but the English ᴱ*Neuhaus* R., 'plodding, wooden translation with forty errors' adds important contributions of R. E. *Brown* and P. T. *Stallworth* not in the German]: Gregorianum 72 (1991) 117-128.

1194 ᴱ**Werbick** J., Offenbarungsanspruch und fundamentalistische Versuchung: QDisp 129. FrB 1991, Herder. 245 p. DM 49. 3-451-02129-3 → 568*b* [BL 92,114, R. J. *Coggins*; 6 art.; *Peek-Horn* M. on Gn 28,10-22].

1195 *Wilkes* Paul, The hands that would shape our souls [the 56,000 students of 200 U.S. seminaries are not fitting themselves to cope with our moral chaos]: Atlantic Monthly (Dec. 1990) 56-88 [< BS 148 (1991) 366-8 (K. O. *Gangel*: his pessimism does not hold for evangelical seminaries)].

1196 **zu Eltz** Johannes, Lehrstuhlbesetzung und Beanstandung am Fachbereich Katholische Theologie der Universität Mainz. Mainz 1988, Bischöf. Stuhl. 151 p. DM 30. – ᴿTLZ 116 (1991) 153s (K. *Schwarz*: neueres über das Nihil-Obstat-Problem, W. WEBER, H. FLATTEN).

B3.2   *Homiletica* – **The Bible in preaching.**

1197 **Achtemeier** Elizabeth, Preaching from the OT 1989 → 6,1449*: ᴿInterpretation 45 (1991) 189-191 (W. H. *Willimon*); JRel 71 (1991) 257s (W. L. *Michel*).

1198 **Andrae** Christian, Ferdinand Christian BAUR als Prediger, exemplarische Interpretation zu seinem handschriftlichen Predigtnanlass: ev. Diss. Tübingen, ᴰ*Rössler* D. 1991. 324+127 p. – TLZ 117,712s; RTLv 23, p. 552.

1198* **Bailey** R., Jesus [→ 6,1450] / Paul the preacher. Nv 1990/1, Broadman. /130 p. /0-8054-6035-7 [NTAbs 36,272].

1199 **Barth** Karl, Homiletics [1932s, fuller notes than in 1963 The preaching of the Gospel], ᵀ*Bromiley* Geoffrey W., *Daniels* Donald E. Louisville 1991, W-Knox. 136 p. $11. 0-664-25158-7 [TDig 39,149].

1200 *Bartlett* D. L., Preaching at the margins: Affirmation 4,1 (Richmond 1991) 41-53 [< NTAbs 36,69].

1201 *a)* *Bartlett* David L., Story and history; narratives and claims [in preaching]; – *b)* *Rogers* John B.[J], 'The foolishness of preaching'; – *c)* *Theiss* Norman, Preaching for public life; – *d)* *Van Seters* Arthur, The problematic of preaching in the Third Millennium: Interpretation 45 (1991) 229-240 / 241-252 / 253-266 / 267-280.

1202 *Baugh* Steven M., KITTEL [TDNT] and biblical theology [-preaching]: Kerux 3,2 (1988) 36-45.

1203 **Best** Ernest, From text to sermon² 1988 ➤ 4,1362...6,1452: ᴿEvQ 63 (1991) 78-81 (B. W. *Fong*).

1204 ᴱ**Biddle** Perry H., Preaching the lectionary; a workbook for Year C. Louisville 1991, W-Knox. 334 p. $39 [CBQ 54,201].

1205 **Bieritz** K.-H. + 14 *al.*, Handbuch der Predigt. B 1990, Ev.-V. 624 p. – ᴿTLZ 116 (1991) 861-3 (C. *Münchow*).

1206 *a)* *Boyd* James O., Biblical theology in the study and the pulpit; – *b)* *Dennison* James T.[J], What is biblical theology? [Vos G.]; – *c)* *Semel* Lawrence, The Church and proclamation: Kerux 2,1 (1987) 3-19 / 33-41 / 1,1 (1986) 37-47.

1207 **Brueggemann** Walter, Finally comes the poet 1989 ➤ 6,1454: ᴿInterpretation 45 (1991) 73s (R. N. *Boyce*: the book itself disproves his 'poetry not instruction'); NewTR 4,1 (1991) 79s (C. *Stuhlmueller*).

1207* **Burger** C. W., *al.*, Sermon guides... Easter, Ascension, Pentecost. GR 1988, Eerdmans. x-284 p. 0-8028-0283-4. – ᴿVidyajyoti 55 (1991) 72 (P. M. *Meagher*).

1208 *Chandran* Russell, John 20,21 [sermon for the consecration of a bishop]: Arasaradi 3/2 (1990) 26-33.

1209 **Clark** Neville, Preaching in context; word, worship and the people of God. ...1991, K. Mayhew. 94 p. £7. 0-86209-174-8. – ᴿExpTim 103,2 2d-top choice (1991s) 34s (C. S. *Rodd*).

1210 ᴱ**Cox** James W., Best sermons [2. 1989 ➤ 5,1426] 3. SF 1990, Harper. 281 p. $17.65. 0-06-06160-5. – ᴿRExp 88 (1991) 447 (J. R. *Rodman*).

1211 **Denecke** Axel, Gotteswort als Menschenwort; Karl BARTHS Predigtpraxis — Quelle seiner Theologie [Hab.-Diss. Marburg]. Hannover 1989, Luth. Vgh. 321 p. DM 37. – ᴿTLZ 116 (1991) 146-8 (H. *Genest*).

1212 *Dennison* Charles G., Preaching and application; a review [GREIDANUS S. 1989]: Kerux 4,3 (1989) 44-52.

1213 **Drewermann** Eugen, *a)* Leben, das dem Tod entwächst; Predigten zur Passions- und Osterzeit, ᴱ*Marz* B. – *b)* Zwischen Staub und Sternen; Predigten im Jahreskreis. Dü 1991, Patmos. 301 p.; DM 40 / 237 p.; DM 35. – *c)* Was uns Zukunft gibt; vom Reichtum des Lebens, ᴱ*Heller* A. [< Christ in der Gegenwart]. Olten 1991, Walter. 229 p. DM 32. – ᴿTGL 81 (1991) 506s (K. *Hollmann*).

1214 ᴱ**Farmer** David A., *Hunter* Edwina, And blessed is she; sermons by women 1990 ➤ 6,1462: ᴿRExp 88 (1991) 492s (Karen E. *Smith*); TS 52 (1991) 399 (W. J. *Burghardt*).

1215 *a)* *Ferry* Patrick, Martin LUTHER on preaching; – *b)* *Posset* Franz, BERNARD of Clairvaux as Luther's source: ConcordTQ 54 (1990) 265-280 / 281-... [< ZIT 91,338].

1216 **Gaddy** C. Welton, Turning the heart; [for rather] secular university sermons. Macon 1990, Mercer Univ. 179 p. $25. – ᴿInterpretation 45 (1991) 304s (H. B. *Adams*).

1217 **Gradwohl** Roland, Bibelauslegungen aus jüdischen Quellen... Predigt-texte 1-4, 1986-9 → 6,1466: ᴿTLZ 116 (1991) 24-26 (C. *Hinz*).

1218 *Gräb* Wilhelm, Das Schriftprinzip in der Predigt der Gegenwart: → 558, Sola Scriptura 1990/1, 319-334.

1219 **Greidanus** Sidney, The modern preacher and the ancient text 1988 → 5,1432; 6,1468: ᴿTrinJ 11 (1990) 237s (D. L. *Larsen*).

1220 *a) Hamesse* Jacqueline, La prédication universitaire; éloquence sacrée, éloquence profane?; – *b) Zier* Mark A., Preaching by distinction; Petrus COMESTOR and the communication of the Gospel: EphLtg 105 (1991) 283-300 / 301-329.

1221 **Hermelink** Jan, Die homiletische Situation; Varianten empirischer Homiletik nach 1945: Diss. Heidelberg 1991, ᴰ*Rau*. – TR 87 (1991) 518.

1222 *Leimgruber* Stephan, Neuere Ansätze in der Homiletik: StiZt 208 (1990) 635-641.

1223 **Long** Thomas C., Preaching and the literary forms of the Bible 1989 → 5,1435; 6,1477: ᴿRExp 88 (1991) 119s (C. A. *Loscalzo*).

1224 **McComiskey** Thomas E., Reading Scripture in public; a guide for preachers and lay readers. GR 1991, Baker. 196 p. $8. 0-8010-6278-0 [TDig 39,174].

1225 *Marshall* I. Howard, Preaching from the New Testament [1991 Finlayson lecture]: ScotBEvT 9 (1991) 104-7.

1226 *McEvenue* Sean, *a)* Uses and abuses of the Bible in liturgy and preaching: → 347, Concilium (1991,1) 91-99; – *b)* Emploi et abus de la Bible en liturgie et dans la prédication; ᵀ*Divault* André: → 348, Concilium 233 (P 1991) 121-131.

1226* *Meagher* P. M., The word of life [Sunday sermons]: Vidyajyoti 55 (1991) 47-54 and every issue through p. 706-713.

1227 **Olivar** Alexandre, La predicación cristiana antigua: BHerd/tf 189. Barc 1991, Herder. 997 p. 84-254-1715-5. – ᴿActuBbg 28 (1991) 213 (J. *Boada*); ArTGran 54 (1991) 433s (A. *Segovia*); RCatalT 16 (1991) 208-212 (A. *Franquesa*).

1228 *a)* ᴱ**Outler** Albert C., *Heitzenrater* Richard P., John WESLEY's sermons, an anthology; – *b)* **Outler**, J. Wesley's sermons, an introduction. Nv 1991, Abingdon. 572 p.; $20 / 107 p.; $8. 0-687-20495-X; -6-8 [TDig 39,293].

1229 **Peurifoy** Robert C., Proclamation and explanation; an integrated approach to the teaching and preaching of the Bible: diss. Drew, ᴰ*Newton* J. Madison NJ 1991. 131 p. 92-13397. – DissA 52 (1991s) 4363-A.

1230 **Saperstein** Marc, Jewish preaching 1989 → 6,1489: ᴿSpeculum 66 (1991) 695-7 (N. *Roth*: some interesting comparisons to Christian preaching).

1230* *a) Senior* Donald, Scripture and homiletics; what the Bible can teach the preacher; – *b) Hilkert* Mary Catherine, Preaching and theology; rethinking the relationship: Worship 65 (1991) 386-398 / 398-409.

1231 *Sensing* T. R., Imitating the genre of parable in today's pulpit: RestQ 33 (1991) 193-207 [< NTAbs 36,173].

1232 *Surya* Prakash P., Sermon preparation; biblical preaching, methodological issues and perspectives: BangalTFor 23,3 (1991) 25-37 [< NTAbs 36,156].

1233 *Warren* Timothy S., A paradigm for preaching: BS 148 (1991) 463-486.

1234 *a) Waznak* Robert P.,   Like a story; an update on narrative preaching; –
   b) Parachini Patricia,   Preaching to children: NewTR 4,2 (1991) 93-100
   [3,70-81] / 4,3 (1991) 64-69.
Williamson C., *Allen* R.,   Interpreting difficult texts; anti-Judaism and
   Christian preaching 1989 ➤ a235.

B3.3   *Inerrantia, inspiratio* – **Authority of the Bible.**

E**Artola** Antonio M. (*Alonso Schökel* L.) Palabra de Dios ➤ 952.
1235 **Avant** John P.J,   The relationship of changing views of the inspiration
   and authority of Scripture to evangelism and church growth... United
   Methodist, Southern Baptist: diss. SW Baptist theol. sem. 1990, 416 p.
   91-15398. – DissA 52 (1991s) 187-A.
1236 *Burkhardt* Helmut,   Inspiration der Schrift auch weisheitliche Perso-
   nalinterpretation [i. Inspirationslehre in der neueren Theologie; ii. Zur
   Inspirationslehre PHILOS von Alexandrien]: TZBas 47 (1991) 214-225.
1237 *Campbell* Ted A.,   Scripture as an authority in relation to other
   authorities; a Wesleyan evangelical perspective: QRMin 11,3 (1991)
   33-40.
1238 **Conn** Harvie M.,   Inerrancy and hermeneutic; a tradition, a challenge, a
   debate 1988 ➤ 5,388:   RCritRR 3 (1990) 65s (E.J. *Epp*).
1239 *Culbertson* P.,   The authority of Scripture in the Episcopal Church:
   StLuke 34 spec. (1991) 20-37 [< NTAbs 36,3].
1240 *a) Frerichs* Ernest S.,   The role of inspiration relative to other ex-
   planations of the formation of the Hebrew Bible; – *b) Pesce* Mauro,   The
   transformation of a religious document; from early Christian writings to
   canon, T*Leech* Patrick, ➤ 56, FFOX M. 1 (1991) 59-67 / 133-148.
1241 **Fuss** M.,   Buddhavaçana and Dei Verbum; a phenomenological and
   theological comparison of Scriptural inspiration in the Saddharmapun-
   darika Sutra and in the Christian tradition: Indological 3. Leiden 1991,
   Brill.   xvi-479 p. 240 f. [NRT 114,597, J. *Masson*].
1242 *Hart* D.G.,   A reconsideration of biblical inerrancy and the [1920ss
   MACHEN J.; ARMSTRONG W.] Princeton Theology's alliance with fundamentalism: ChrSchR 20 (1991) 362-375 [NTAbs 36,5].
1243 **Hogan** Frances,   Can you trust the Bible? L 1991, Darton-LT.   iv-
   219 p.   0-232-51904-8.
1244 **Jedock** Darrell,   The Church's Bible; its contemporary authority 1989
   ➤ 5,1380*; 6,1517:   RCritRR 4 (1991) 91-93 (D.S. *Cunningham*); Interpretation 45 (1991) 206.208 (D.L. *Bartlett*).
1245 *a) Johnston* Robert K.,   Biblical authority and hermeneutics; the growing
   evangelical dialogue; – *b) Brooks* James A.,   The text of the New
   Testament and biblical authority; – *c) Newport* John P.,   Southern
   Baptists and the Bible; seeking a balanced perspective: SWJT 34,2
   (1991s) 22-30 / 13-21 / 31-43.
1245* *McEvenue* Sean,   The spiritual authority of the Bible: ➤ 95*,
   FLONERGAN B., 1987, 205-219.
1246 *Martin* François, L'inspiration des Écritures: SémBib 63 (1991) 18-33;
   64 (1991) 15-34.
1246* *Neusner* Jacob,   Holy writing; the social setting: MethTStR 3,1 (Toronto 1991) 84-99 [< ZIT 92,139].
1247 *Piñero* Antonio,   A Mediterranean view of prophetic inspiration; on
   the concept of inspiration in the Liber Antiquitatum Biblicarum by
   Pseudo-PHILO: MeditHR 6 (1991) 5-34.

1248 *Reese* James M., † [intended CBA presidential address], ᴱ*Dailey* Thomas F., Inspiration; toward a sociosemiotic definition: BibTB 21 (1991) 4-12.

1249 *Smit* D. J., Wat beteken 'die Bybel sè'? [What does 'the Bible says' mean? A typology of reader constructs]: HervTSt 47,1 (1991) 167-185 [< NTAbs 36,9].

1250 **Warnke** Christof, Die Bibel ist nicht vom Himmel gefallen; 55 theologische Informationen: GEP-Buch. Stu 1990, Steinkopf. 62 p. [TLZ 116,654].

1251 **Weeks** Noel, The sufficiency of Scripture. E 1988, Banner of Truth. 309 p. £10. 0-85151-523-1. – ᴿScotBEvT 9 (1991) 145s (C. M. *Cameron*).

1252 *a) Wright* N. T., How can the Bible be authoritative? [1989 Laing Lecture]; – *b) Gempf* Conrad, Two opinions about exegesis: VoxEvca 21 (1991) 7-32 / 81-87.

B3.4 **Traditio.**

1253 *Anselmetto* Claudio, Rivelazione privata e tradizione nell'epistolario di CIPRIANO: AugR 30 (1990) 279-312.

1254 *Arens* Werner, Tradition und Wertewandel; Versuch einer Orientierung in der Massengesellschaft: TGL 81 (1991) 161-176.

1255 *Boumis* Panagiotis I., Die authentische Überlieferung der Kirche, das Kriterium der Orthodoxie: OstkSt 40 (1991) 38-48.

1256 **Boyer** Pascal, Tradition as truth and communication; a cognitive description of traditional discourse. C 1990, Univ. 143 p. $39.50. 0-521-37417-0. – ᴿNumen 38 (1991) 261-5 (E. T. *Lawson*).

1257 **Bunnenberg** Johannes, Lebendige Treue zum Ursprung... Traditionsverständnis CONGARs 1989 ➤ 5,1474; 6,1531: ᴿRTLv 22 (1991) 413-5 (J. *Famerée*).

1258 ᴱ**Clover** F. M., *Humphreys* R. S., Tradition and innovation in late antiquity 1984/9 ➤ 5,781: ᴿJAOS 111 (1991) 397s (I. *Shahîd*).

1259 *Duprey* Pierre, Schrift, Tradition und Kirche: ➤ 63, ᶠGASSMANN G., Gemeinsamer Glaube 1991, 50-57.

1260 **Hanegraaff** J., Met de Torah is het begonnen, 3. Rondom de mondelinge Traditie. Nijkerk 1990, Callenbach. *f* 54,50. 90-266-0219-7. – ᴿTsTNijm 31 (1991) 191 (J. *Holman*) [vol. 2 was 30 (1989) 86].

1261 ᶠHANSON Richard P. C., Scripture, tradition and reason, ᴱ**Drewery** B., *Bauckham* R. 1988 ➤ 4,60; 6,1535: ᴿEvQ 63 (1991) 71-78 (M. *Partridge*); NBlackf 72 (1991) 253-6 (A. *Nichols*).

1262 **Hintzen** Georg, Die Selbstbezeugung des Wortes Gottes; Gedanken zu Schrift, Tradition und kirchlichem Lehramt: Catholica 44 (1990) 1-25.

1263 **Kelber** Werner, Tradition orale et Écriture, préf. *Ong* Walter J. [Oral and Written Gospel 1983 ➤ 64,4877], ᵀ*Prignaud* J.: LDiv 145. P 1991, Cerf. 332 p. F 200. 2-204-04246-3.

1264 *Navone* John, A tradição na história da comunidade: Brotéria 132 (1991) 453-463.

1265 *Treanor* Oliver, Scripture, tradition and the local church: PrPeo 5 (1991) 92-97.

B3.5 **Canon.**

1266 *Aune* D. E., On the origins of the 'Council of Javneh' myth: JBL 110 (1991) 491-3.

1267 *Beckwith* R.T., A modern theory of the OT canon: VT 41 (1991) 385-395.
1267* **Bovon** François (p. 107-138), *Koester* Helmut (p. 23-106; names reversed on cover), Genèse de l'écriture chrétienne: Mémoires premières. Turnhout 1991, Brepols. 139 p. 2-503-50044-7.
1268 *a) Cazelles* Henri, L'unité canonique des Saintes Écritures; – *b) Dupuy* Bernard, Réception des Écritures et fixation du canon; recherches et perspectives nouvelles: Istina 36 (1991) 160-181 / 131-159.
1269 *Diebner* Bernd J., Anmerkungen zur hermeneutischen Funktion des 'Exils' für das Verständnis des Kanons der Biblia Hebraica (TNK): DielB 26 (1989s) 173-182.
   Ellis E. Earle, The Old Testament in early Christianity; canon and interpretation in the light of modern research[2rev]: WUNT 54, 1991 ➤ 198.
1270 *Falk* Z., ⊕ 'The holy writings defile the hands': Sinai 106 (1990s) 94s [< JStJud 22,318].
1271 **Gisel** Pierre, Croyance incarnée; tradition – écriture – canon – dogme: Lieux théologiques 9, 1986 ➤ 3,1450; 4,1440: ᴿBijdragen 52 (1991) 225 (H. *Rikhof*: 'fundamental theology themes').
1271* *Hallo* William W., The concept of canonicity in cuneiform and biblical literature; ➤ 334, ᴱYOUNGER K., Biblical canon 1991 ...
1272 *a) Koch* Klaus, Rezeptionsgeschichte als notwendige Voraussetzung einer biblischen Theologie – oder: Protestantische Verlegenheit angesichts der Geschichtlichkeit des Kanons; – *b) Paulsen* Henning, Sola Scriptura und das Kanonproblem; – *c) Wenz* Günther, Das Schriftprinzip im gegenwärtigen ökumenischen Dialog zwischen den Reformationskirchen und der römisch-katholischen Kirche; eine Problemskizze: ➤ 454c, Sola Scr. 1990/1, 143-155 / 61-78 / 304-316.
1273 *Kraemer* David, The formation of rabbinic canon; authority and boundaries: JBL 110 (1991) 613-630.
1274 *Linebarger* M., History meets theology; three recent books about the canon [BRUCE F., METZGER B., MCDONALD L.]: Crux 27,3 (Vancouver 1991) 34-37 [< NTAbs 36,147].
1275 **McDonald** Lee M., The formation of the Christian biblical canon 1988 ➤ 4,1446; 5,1480: ᴿRExp 88,3 (1991) 262-4 (C. L. *Scalise*: should have omitted the whole first chapter misunderstanding CHILDS).
1276 **Meade** David G., Pseudonymity and canon: WUNT 39, 1986 ➤ 2,1040 ... 5,1481: ᴿScripTPamp 23 (1991) 1073s (J. M. *Casciaro*).
1277 **Metzger** Bruce M., The canon of the NT 1987 ➤ 3,1456 ... 5,1482: ᴿAsburyTJ 46,1 (1991) 119-121 (D. R. *Bauer*); CiuD 203 (1990) 736s (J. *Gutierrez*; SvTKv 66 (1990) 33s (B. *Gerhardsson*).
1278 **Morgan** Donn F., Between text and community; the 'Writings' in canonical interpretation 1990 ➤ 6,1564*: ᴿBL (1991) 118 (R. P. *Carroll*); CritRR 4 (1991) 151-3 (Dianne *Bergant*: canon study); Interpretation 45 (1991) 420 (K. H. *Richards*); RExp 88,3 (1991) 265 (J. D. W. *Watts*: shows value of J. SANDERS); TTod 48 (1991s) 114s (C. R. *Seitz*).
1279 *Müller* M., Hebraica sive graeca veritas; the Jewish Bible at the time of the NT and the Christian Bible: ScandJOT (1989/2) 55-71 [= DanTTs 51 (1988) 220-237 < JStJud 22,307].
1280 *Oakes* Edward T., The canon of Scripture in postmodern aesthetics: CommND 17 ('Christianity and the question of postmodernity' 1990) 261-280.
1280* *Piñero* A., *a)* Cómo y por qué se formó el Nuevo Testamento; el canon neotestamentario; – *b)* Epílogo: ➤ 453, Orígenes del cristianismo 1989/91, 339-397 / 401-454.

1281 **Rendtorff** Rolf, *a)* Zur Bedeutung des Kanons für eine Theologie des ATs [< ᶠ*Kraus* H.-J. 1983, 3-11]; – *b)* Nach vierzig Jahren; vier Jahrzehnte selbsterlebte alttestamentliche Wissenschaft in Heidelberg und anderswo [ineditum]: ➤ 252, Kanon 1991, 54-63 / 29-39.

1282 *Sanders* James A., Stability and fluidity in text and canon: ➤ 17, ᶠBARTHÉLEMY D., Tradition 1991, 203-217.

1283 *Sawyer* M. James, Evangelicals and the canon of the NT: GraceTJ 11 (1990) 29-52.

1284 *Skarsaune* Oskar, From books to testimonies; remarks on the transmission of the Old Testament in the early Church: ➤ 54, ᶠFLUSSER D., Immanuel 24s (1990) 207-219.

1285 **Steck** Odil Hannes, Der Abschluss der Prophetie im Alten Testament; ein Versuch zur Frage des Kanons: BibTSt 17. Neuk 1991, Neuk. V. 198 p. 3-7887-1380-1 [ZAW 104,310s, H. C. *Schmitt*].

1286 *Stone* Michael E., Armenian canon lists V – anonymous texts: Harv-TR 83 (1990) 141-161.

1286* **Stuhlhofer** Franz, Der Gebrauch der Bibel von Jesus bis EUSEB... Kanongeschichte 1988 ➤ 4,1461; 5,1494: ᴿOrChrPer 57 (1991) 225s (E. G. *Farrugia*).

1287 ᴱ**Théobald** C., Le Canon des Écritures 1990 ➤ 6,557*: ᴿCarthaginensia 7 (1991) 502 (R. *Sanz V.*); Salesianum 53 (1991) 579 (R. *Vicent*).

1288 **Vasholz** Robert J., The OT canon in the OT Church; the internal rationale for OT canonicity 1990 ➤ 6,1573: ᴿGraceTJ 11 (1990) 237s (R. *Spender*).

1290 **Ziegenaus** A., Kanon...: HbDG 1/3a 1990 ➤ 6,1575: ᴿNRT 113 (1991) 422 (X. *Jacques*); ScripTPamp 23 (1991) 706 (A. *Viciano*); TPhil 66 (1991) 580s (H. *Engel*).

1291 *Ziegler* Thierry, Un regard neuf sur la formation du canon: ➤ 22, ᶠBENOÎT A., RHPR 71 (1991) 45-59; Eng. 125.

B4   *Interpretatio humanistica* – .1 **The Bible and man,** health, toil, age.

1292 **Alonso Schökel** Luis, Esperanza; meditaciones bíblicas para la tercera edad: El Pozo de Siquem 45. Sdr 1991, Sal Terrae. 310 p. 84-293-0890-3. – ᴿCarthaginensia 7 (1991) 544s (F. *Oliver Alcón*); REspir 50 (1991) 304 (S. *Castro*).

1293 **Alonso Schökel** Luis, In the autumn of life; biblical meditations on hope for the elderly. Middlegreen 1991, St. Paul. 191 p. 0-85439-375-7.

1294 *Álvarez Barredo* M., La queja del hombre ante Dios: Carthaginensia 7 (1991) 19-42; Eng. iii.

1295 *Cotterell* F. Peter, Disaster and disorder; the human predicament [... Rom 7,15-18; Qoh 1-4; 12; Jn 9,2]: VoxEvca 21 (1991) 89-105.

1296 *Dobberahn* Friedrich E., *Marschner* Walter, 'Sou cidadão de que país? Sou herói de qual história?' — Os 'meninos e meninas de rua' hoje e no Antigo Testamento: EstudosB 27 ('Os marginalizados' 1990) 9-19.

1296* **Franklin** William R., *Shaw* Joseph M., The case for Christian humanism ['strong and caring interest for human beings as such']. GR 1991, Eerdmans. 270 p. £19 pa. – ᴿGraceTJ 12,1 (1991) 141s (M. E. *Travers*: follow-up to 'Readings in Christian humanism', firmly distinct from secular humanism).

1297 *Guelluy* Robert, La souffrance; approches spirituelles: RTLv 22 (1991) 185-201; Eng. 303.

1298 a) *Hempel* Johannes, Die Heilige Schrift im Alltag der Menschen; – b) *Honecker* Martin, Sola Scriptura im Gereich sozialethischer Entscheidungen; – c) *Petzoldt* Matthias, Sola scriptura – brauchbares Prinzip zur Rechenschaft über den Glauben? → 454c, ᴱ*Schmid* H., Sola Scriptura 1990/1, 13-17 / 130-140 / 292-303.

1299 *Hossfeld* Frank-Lothar, Graue Panther im Alten Testament? – Das Alter in der Bibel: ArztC 36 (1990) 1-11.

1300 **Kysar** Robert, Called to care; biblical images for social ministry. Mp 1991, Fortress. ix-165 p. 0-8006-2470-X [NRT 114,309].

1301 *Langkammer* Hugolin, ❷ Biblische Grundlagen einer christlichen Spiritualität der Ruhe: RoczTK 34,1 (1991 für 1987) 57-70; deutsch 71.

1302 **McDermott** John, a) The Bible on human suffering. Middlegreen 1990, St. Paul. 155 p.; – b) La sofferenza umana nella Bibbia: PiccBtT 9. R 1990, Dehoniane. 200 p. Lit. 18.000. 88-396-0316-6. – ᴿGregorianum 72 (1991) 197 (*ipse*); TPhil 66 (1991) 579s (V. *Maraldi*).

1303 *Mannucci* Valerio, Teologia biblica del lavoro; a dieci anni dalla 'Laborem exercens': RasT 32 (1991) 443-468.

1304 a) *Martin-Achard* Robert [→ 2089], Perspectives bibliques sur la vieillesse; 'Abraham était vieux... et le Seigneur l'avait béni'; – b) *Lieth* Elisabeth von der, 'Un autre te nouera la ceinture et te conduira là où tu ne voudrais pas' (Jn 21,18), ᵀ*Guého* Marie-Thérèse: → 348, Concilium 235 (P 1991) 33-41 / 51-59.

1305 *Muir* Ian, Un regard biblique sur l'homme et ses 'trésors', sur l'homme à la recherche de son identité, sur l'homme qui entre dans le 'quotidien' de la vie en pérennité: FoiVie 90,2 (1991) 55-64 (-76, discussion).

1306 **Pattison** Stephen, A critique of pastoral care. L 1988, SCM. 210 p. £9. – ᴿScotJT 44 (1991) 398-400 (J. I. H. *McDonald*: chapter on 'The Bible in pastoral care' could have been enriched by reader-response theory).

1307 *Swindoll* Charles R., Stress fractures; biblical splints for everyday pressures [compilation of 13 of his booklets]. Portland OR 1990, Multnomah. 273 p. $11. – ᴿBS 148 (1991) 252s (R. A. *Pyne*).

1308 *Underwood* Ralph L., Scripture; the substance of pastoral care: QRMin 11,4 (1991) 33-46.

B4.2 *Femina, familia;* Woman in the Bible [→ H8.8s].

1309 *Annandale* J., Die rol van die godsdiens in die lewe [Leben] van die Israelitiese en Babiloniese vrou [dissent from TOORN K. van der 1987]: OTEssays 4 (1991) 415-424 [< ZAW 104,436].

1310 **Archer** Léonie J., Her price... the Jewish woman in Graeco-Roman Palestine ᴰ1990 → 6,1590: ᴿJTS 42 (1990) 641-3 (Carol *Meyers*: noteworthy features 'mitigated' by flaws); TLZ 116 (1991) 344s (W. *Herrmann*).

1311 **Aynard** Laure, La Bible au féminin; de l'ancienne tradition à un christianisme hellénisé: LDiv 138. P 1990, Cerf. 326 p. F 170. – ᴿZkT 113 (1991) 95s (H.-A. *Pissarek*ᴶ: the positive comes from Israel's pure traditions, the negative from Hellenism, p. 309).

1312 **Badinter** Elisabeth, The unopposite sex; the end of the gender battle, ᵀ*Wright* Barbara. NY 1989, Harper & R. 279 p. $22.50. – ᴿSWJT 34,2 (1991s) 76 (G. *Greenfield*: overlooks biblical message).

1313 ᴱ**Bal** Mieke, Anti-covenant 1989 → 5,625; 6,1593: ᴿCritRR 4 (1991) 119-121 (Gale A. *Yee*); OTAbs 14 (1991) 215s (W. T. *Miller*).

1314 *Boyarin* Daniel, Reading androcentrism against the grain; women, sex and Torah-study: Poetics Today 12 (Duke Univ. 1991) 29-53.

1315 **Darr** K.P.,   Far more precious than jewels; perspectives on biblical women [Ruth, Sarah, Hagar, Esther]: Gender and the Biblical Tradition. Louisville 1991, W-Knox. 223 p. $16.   0-664-25107-2 [BL 92,104, G.I. *Emmerson*; NTAbs 36,291; TDig 39,156].

1316 ᴱ**Day** Peggy L.,   Gender and difference in ancient Israel 1989 → 5,391; 6,1603: ᴿBA 54 (1991) 179 (Claudia V. *Camp*); BibTB 21 (1991) 119 (J.M. *Ford*); BL (1991) 108 (G.I. *Emmerson*); Horizons 18 (1991) 315 (Celia *Deutsch*); ScotJT 44 (1991) 544s (Gillian *Muddiman*); TorJT 7 (1991) 102-4 (Irene *Nowell*).

1317 **Engelken** Karen,   Frauen im alten Israel: BW 130, ᴰ1990 → 6,1606: ᴿExpTim 102 (1990s) 301s (R.J. *Coggins*); TLZ 116 (1991) 180-4 (Gerda *Weiler*: Korrektur Zeilen 18-30 p.319); TPQ 139 (1991) 319 (Irmtraud *Fischer*: Mangel an kritischer Sichtweise); TüTQ 171 (1991) 69s (W. *Gross*); ZkT 113 (1991) 92s (R. *Frick-Pöder*).

1318 **Frankiel** Tamar,   The voice of Sarah; feminine spirituality and traditional Judaism. SF 1990, Harper. xv-140 p. $19. 0-06-063016-7. – ᴿOT-Abs 14 (1991) 138 (Irene *Nowell*).

1319 **Grassi** Joseph A.,   Children's liberation; a biblical perspective.   ColMn 1991, Liturgical. 128 p. $6.

1320 ᴱ**Greenberg** Simon,   The ordination of women as rabbis.   NY 1988, Jewish Theol. Sem. viii-225 p. – ᴿRHR 208 (1991) 107s (S. *Schwarzfuchs*).

1321 **Hack** C.,   Een verrukkelijke zwakte; het vrouwelijke in het denken van Emmanuel LEVINAS.   Kampen/Kapellen 1990, Kok/Pelckmans. 143 p. *f* 19,90.   90-242-7652-7 / 90-289-1348-3. – ᴿTsTNijm 31 (1991) 446s (Hedwig Meyer *Wilmes*).

1322 **Jeansonne** Sharon P.,   The women of Genesis; from Sarah to Potiphar's wife 1990 → 6,1612; $10: ᴿBL (1991) 80 (G.I. *Emmerson*); CritRR 4 (1991) 146-8 (J.R. *King*); Interpretation 45 (1991) 416 (J.M. *Bracke*).

1323 **Lacocque** André,   The feminine unconventional 1990 → 6,1614: ᴿCurr-TMiss 18 (1991) 220.222 (E.F. *Campbell*); TS 52 (1991) 355 (Alice L. *Laffey*).

1324 ᴱ**Lesko** Barbara S., Women's earliest records... Egypt, Asia 1989 → 5, 851; 6,1615: ᴿJAOS 111 (1991) 642-4 (Susan T. *Hollis*); JESHO 34 (1991) 234-8 (E. *Woestenburg*: more successfully unified than Rencontre 23).

1325 **Ljung** Inger,   Silence or suppression; attitudes towards women in the OT: Acta U, Women in religion 2.   Stockholm 1989, Almqvist & W. 159 p. Sk 113. – ᴿNRT 113 (1991) 96s (J.-L. *Ska*); RHPR 71 (1991) 230s (P. de *Robert*).

1326 *Luke* K., Women and politics in ancient Israel: Jeevadhara 21 (1991) 133-149.

1327 **Maillot** Alphonse,   Ève, ma mère; étude sur la femme dans l'AT 1989 → 5,1538; 6,1619: ᴿCritRR 4 (1991) 490 (K.A. *Farmer*); ÉTRel 66 (1991) 433 (D. *Bourguet*: deux regrets); OTAbs 14 (1991) 101s (C.T. *Begg*).

1328 *Meier* Samuel A.,   Women [as scribes and messengers in Israel and Mesopotamia] and communication in the Ancient Near East: JAOS 111 (1991) 540-7.

1329 **Méroz** Christiane,   Donne dell'Antico Testamento; Sara – Agar – Rebecca – Rachele – Lia: Bibbia per tutti.   Assisi 1991, Cittadella. 182 p. Lit. 15.000.

1330 *a*) *Meyers* Carol L.,   Of drums and damsels; women's performance in ancient Israel; – *b*) *Lesko* Barbara S.,   Women's monumental mark on ancient Egypt: BA 54 (1991) 16-27 / 4-15; ill.; cover photo, Omaha

Joslyn Museum Amenirdis I, who shared rule for 13 years in 25th dynasty [*Meyers'* rejoinder on female hegemony and Gary *Rendsburg* on purple dyeing: BA (53,142; 98) 54,2 (1991) inside back cover].

1331 *a*) *Nash* Kathleen S., A promise partially fulfilled; home and family in the Pentateuch; – *b*) *Maloney* Elliott C., 'We have given up everything to follow you'; the family and homelessness in the Synoptic Gospels; – *c*) *Mindling* Joseph, Home is where your family is; St. Paul on homecoming: BToday 29 (1991) 197-204 / 210-214 / 215-9.

1332 *a*) *Nowell* Irene, Roles of women in the Old Testament; – *b*) *Hoppe* Leslie, The Bible on women; patterns of interpretation; – *c*) *Aschlimann* Sylvia A., A new look at women of old; – *d*) *Stuhlmueller* Carroll, The women of Genesis; – *e*) *Bergant* Dianne, Might Job have been a feminist?: BToday 28,6 (1990) 364-8 / 330-5 / 353-7 / 347-352 / 336-341.

1333 **Ochs** Vanessa, Words on fire; one woman's journey into the sacred [... Torah]. NY 1990, Harcourt-BJ. $23. – [R]CCurr 41 (1991s) 417-420 (G. *Comstock*).

1334 **Pardes** Ilana, Countertraditions in the Bible; a feminist approach. CM 1991, Harvard Univ. $30 [JBL 111,162 adv.].

1335 *Piper* John, A vision of biblical complementarity; manhood and womanhood defined according to the Bible: ➤ 375, Recovering 1991, 31-59 (-92). 474-9.

1336 **Plaskow** Judith, Standing again at Sinai; Judaism from a feminist perspective 1990 ➤ 6,1625: [R]Horizons 18 (1991) 182s (Alice L. *Laffey*); JRel 71 (1991) 633 (D. *Novak*: discourse or proclamation?); Paradigms 7,2 (1991s) 37s (K. Jane *Buchanan*).

1337 *Schmitt* John J., Israel and Zion – two gendered images; biblical speech traditions and their contemporary neglect: Horizons 18 (1991) 18-32.

Schmitt Pantel Pauline, Storia delle donne in occidente; l'antichità 1990 ➤ b182.

1338 *Umansky* Ellen M., Finding God; women in the Jewish tradition: CCurr 41 (1991s) 521-537.

1339 **Wegner** Judith R., Chattel or person... Mishnah 1988 ➤ 4,b177; 6,1632: [R]JJS 42 (1991) 274-280 (Naomi *Granot*).

1340 **Weiler** Gerda, Das Matriarchat im Alten Israel 1989 ➤ 6,1633: [R]ZkT 113 (1991) 90-92 (R. *Frick-Pöder*).

1340* — *Laut* Renate, Interpretation und Willkur in feministisch-theologischer Literatur, ein Exempel (WEILER Gerda, Das Matriarchat 1989): ZRGg 43 (1991) 360-4.

1341 **Wöller** H., Vom Vater verwundet; Töchter der Bibel: Tabus des Christentums. Stu 1991, Kreuz. 137 p. DM 19.80. 3-7831-1073-6 [BL 92,114, R. J. *Coggins*].

B4.4 *Exegesis litteraria* – **The Bible itself as literature.**

1341* *Adam* Albrecht, Ein Schriftsteller als Träger göttlicher Botschaft? Vom Anspruch und Selbstverständnis biblischer und ausserbiblischer Literatur: LuthTK 15 (1991) 90-105 [< ZIT 91,642].

1342 [E]**Alter** R., *Kermode* K., The literary guide to the Bible: 1987 ➤ 3,324... 6,1636: [R]Kerux 4,2 (1989) 42-44 (J. T. *Dennison*, unfavoring); WZKM 79 (1989) 309-315 (S. *Segert*, Eng.).

1342* **Frye** Northrop [† I.1991], Words with power; being a second study of the Bible and literature. NY 1991, Harcourt-BJ. 342 p. $35. – [R]America 164 (1991) 382-4 (W. A. *Kort*).

1343 **Jasper** David, The study of literature and religion, an introduction. Mp 1989, Augsburg Fortress. 160 p. $13. 0-8006-2325-8. – RHeythJ 32 (1991) 548-550 (W. D. *Lindsey*).

1344 **Josipovici** Gabriel, The book of God; a response to the Bible 1988 → 4,1073 ... 6,1643: EExpTim 103,5 top choice (1991s) 129 (C. S. *Rodd*: pre-paperback missed among the 600 books he gets each year); JBL 110 (1991) 323-5 (M. *Fishbane*); JRel 71 (1991) 634 (R. *Clifford*: good except on Paul).

1344* **Lawton** D., Faith, text and history; the Bible in English [aims to disturb the polarization of religious and literary uses of the Bible]. NY 1990, Harvester Wheatsheaf. x-203 p. £35. 0-7450-0569-1; pa. -1033-4 [BL 92,17: D. J. A. *Clines* does not share praise of S. PRICKETT and N. FRYE; rambling; clear, but for those who know nothing of biblical scholarship].

1345 **Longman** TremperIII, Literary approaches to biblical interpretation 1987 → 4,1529: REvQ 63 (1991) 353s (C. *Gempf*).

1346 E**Olshen** Barry N., *Feldman* Yael S., Approaches to teaching the Hebrew Bible as literature in translation: Approaches to teaching world literature. NY 1989, Modern Language Asn. x-156 p. $32; pa. $17.50. – RCritRR 4 (1991) 153s (J. S. *Ackerman*).

1347 **Prickett** Stephen, *Barnes* Robert, The Bible [...influence on English literature]: Landmarks of world literature. C 1991 Univ. xii-141 p. £20; pa. £7. 0-521-36569-4; -759-X [BL 92,85, W. G. E. *Watson*]. – RExpTim 103,4 (1991s) 98s (C. S. *Rodd* considers important chiefly as raising the question of how the project might have been better handled).

1348 **Rosenberg** David, A poet's Bible; rediscovering the voices of the original text. NY 1991, Hyperion. xxvii-410 p. $23. 1-56282-988-2.

1349 **Ryken** Leland, Words of delight; a literary introduction to the Bible 1987 → 3,1202 ... 6,1649: RKerux 6,1 (1991) 45-49 (R. A. *Riesen*).

1349* *Schmidt* Johann M., Die Bibel als Weltliteratur; zur Formgeschichte der ganzen Bibel – ein hermeneutischer und didaktischer Versuch: → 87, FKOCH K., Ernten 1991, 561-582.

B4.5 Influxus biblicus in litteraturam profanam, *generalia*.

1350 *Biggs* Frederick M., The fourfold division of souls; the Old English 'Christ III' and the insular homiletic tradition: Traditio 45 (Fordham 1989s) 35-51.

1351 **Blondel** Jacques, Bible et littérature anglaise — de l'Écriture souveraine à la création littéraire: Astraea 3. Montpellier 1990, Univ. – RFoiVie 90,1 (1991) 106-8 (Dominique *Millet*: 20 études, en partie déjà publiées).

1352 **Buzard** Ina L., Romanticism and biblical poetics: diss. Columbia. NY 1991. 345 p. 91-27826. – DissA 52 (1991s) 1317-A.

1353 *Castelli* Ferdinando, Scrittori moderni dinanzi alla parabola del Figliol Prodigo [→ 1380; 4555s]: CC 142 (1991,2) 457-470.

1354 *Chrząstowska* Bożena, ❺ Les paradoxes de la présence de la Bible dans la littérature contemporaine: PrzTow 272,1 (1991) 72-90; franç. 91.

1355 **Clark** Joanna J., Jews and Judaism in Polish romantic literature: diss. Pennsylvania, DAlter Jane. Ph 1990. 247 p. 91-12548. – DissA 52 (1991s) 155s-A.

1356 **Damrosch** LeopoldJ, God's plot and men's stories; studies in the fictional imagination from Milton to Fielding 1985 → 6,1639: REvQ 63 (1991) 83-85 (A. G. *Newell*).

1357 *Dinwiddy* Hugh, Biblical usage and abusage in Kenyan writing: JRelAf 19 (1989) 27-47.

1358 *a*) *Donnelly* Doris, Divine folly; being religious and the exercise of humor; – *b*) *Eckardt* Roy A., Divine incongruity; comedy and tragedy in a post-holocaust world; – *c*) *McTavish* John, John UPDIKE and the funny theologian: TTod 48 (1991s) 385-398 / 399-412 / 413-425.

1359 **Fiddes** Paul S., Freedom and limit; a dialogue between literature and Christian doctrine [... Gn 1-3]. NY 1991, St. Martin's. 269 p. $60. 0-312-06814-X [TDig 39,261].

1360 **Finkelstein** Bluma, L'écrivain juif et les Évangiles: Essais. P 1991, Beauchesne. 148 p. F 150. 2-7010-1226-0. – REsprVie 101 (1991) 567s (É. *Cothenet*: une certaine réhabilitation romanesque de Judas chez E. FLEG et E. WIESEL; p. 20 dénonce CHOURAQUI).

1361 **Hansen** Elaine T., The Solomon complex; reading wisdom in Old English poetry: McMaster OE texts 5. Toronto 1988, Univ. ix-228 p. $40. – RSpeculum 66 (1991) 886-8 (T. A. *Shippey*: 15 poems, claimed to be a cohesive 'wisdom' genre; no other relevance to Solomon or biblical Wisdom-books indicated).

1362 **Lobet** Marcel, L'Esprit ou la lettre. (Belgique) 1990, Les Éperonniers. 240 p. – REsprVie 101 (1991) 225-235 (C. *Jean-Nesmy*, 'Le salut par l'écriture'; malgré les titres du livre et de la récension, il s'agit des écrivains récents).

1363 **Mastag** Horst D., The transformations of Job in modern German literature: diss. Univ. of British Columbia, DStenberg P., 1991. 259 p. 0-315-63962-8 [DANN 63962]. – DissA 52 (1991s) 3615s-A.

1364 **Mayne** Heather J., Biblical paradigms in four twentieth century African-American novels: diss. Stanford 1991, DDrake Sandra. 191 p. 92-05682. – DissA 52 (1991s) 3284-A.

1365 *Morey* James H., Adam and Judas in the Old English Christ and Satan: StPg 87 (1990) 397-409.

1366 *Nunes Carreira* José, Cervos/as, pastores e bailarinas; tres motivos veterotestamentários da lírica galaico-portuguesa: → 421, Luso-Esp 1989/ 91, 627-637 = 422, Didaskalia 19 (1989) 143-153.

1367 **Pifano** P., Tra teologia e letteratura; inquietudine e ricerca del sacro negli scrittori contemporanei. Mi 1990, EP. 279 p. Lit. 22.000. – RRasT 32 (1991) 106s (F. *Giunchedi*: ... Giobbe).

1368 ERosenberg D., Congregation; Jewish writers read the Hebrew Bible 1987 → 4,1543; 6,1670: RCCurr 40 (1990s) 566s (D. *Xiques*).

1369 *Schmidt* Joël, Écriture protestante, écriture du Protestantisme? [... comme 'littérature catholique' dans les manuels]: FoiVie 90,1 (1991) 49-71.

1370 **Wright** T. R., Theology and literature 1988 → 4,1532: RCritRR 4 (1991) 72-74 (K. A. *Richardson*).

B4.6 *Singuli auctores* – **Bible-influence on individual authors.**

1371 BLAKE: **Boutang** Pierre, William Blake, manichéen et visionnaire. P 1990, La Différence. 316 p. F 138. – RÉtudes 374 (1991) 269s (J. *Mambrino*: ouvrage inquisition-bûcher sur ses excellentes traductions d'il y a vingt ans).

1372 *Steenburg* David, [Blake W.] Chaos at the marriage of heaven and hell: HarvTR 84 (1991) 447-466.

1373 **Yogev** Michael, Covenant of the Word; the Bible in William Blake's late prophetic poems: diss. Washington, ᴰ*Adams* H. Seattle 1991. 280 p. 92-03321. – DissA 52 (1991s) 2938-A.

1374 BULGAKOV: *Schwab* Claude, Le figuratif de la Passion chez Michel Boulgakov et Iouri DOMBROVSKI [période stalinienne]: FoiVie 90,5 = CahB 30 (1991) 59-67.

1375 BUNYAN: **Richey** Robert A., The Puritan doctrine of sanctification; constructions of the saints' final and complete perseverance as mirrored in Bunyan's 'The Pilgrim's Progress': diss. Mid-Western Baptist Theol. Sem. 1990. 258 p. 91-18484. – DissA 52 (1991s) 194-A. ➤ g669*.

1376 CHRISTOPHERSON: ᴱ**Upton** Christopher, John Christopherson, Iephte; William GOLDINGHAM, Herodes: Renaissance Latin drama in England 2/7. Hildesheim 1989, Olms. iv-125 p. DM 74. – ᴿClasR 41 (1991) 270s (G. *Eatough*: uncommunicated enthusiasm).

1377 DANTE: **Pelikan** Jaroslav, Eternal feminine; three theological allegories in Dante's Paradiso. New Brunswick 1990, Rutgers. xii-144 p. $32; pa. $14. – ᴿTS 52 (1991) 588s (L. M. *LaFavia*).

1378 DICKENS: **Piret** Michael J., Charles Dicken's 'Children's New Testament'; an introduction, annotated edition, and critical discussion: diss. Michigan, ᴰ*Hornback* B. AA 1991. 261 p. 92-08623. – DissA 52 (1991s) 3613-A.

1379 DÜRRENMATT: *Bühler* Pierre, Le grotesque de la grâce; motifs bibliques dans l'œuvre de Dürrenmatt [† 1990]: FoiVie 90,5 = CahB 30 (1991) 93-102.

1380 GIDE: *Pelletier* Anne-Marie, Métamorphoses littéraires d'une parabole; 'Le fils prodigue' selon Gide, RILKE et KAFKA: FoiVie 90,5 = CahB 30 (1991) 21-32.

1381 **Roggenkamp-Kaufmann** Antje, Der Protestant André Gide und die Bibel: Diss. ᴰ*Strecker* G., Göttingen 1991. – RTLv 23, p. 560.

1382 GREENE: *Terrier* Samuel, Was Graham Greene a Donatist?: TTod 48 (1991s) 436-443.

1383 KEROUAC: *Pérès* Jacques-Noël, La croix, un jalon sur la route de Jack Kerouac [1922-1969]: FoiVie 90,5 = CahB 30 (1991) 69-80.

1384 LANGLAND William: **Kerby-Fulton** Kathryn, Reformist apocalypticism and 'Piers Plowman': StMedLit 7: ᴿJEH 42 (1991) 664 (J. *Simpson*); JTS 42 (1991) 758-760 (Gloria *Cigman*); RHE 86 (1991) 262 (D. *Bradley*).

1385 **Scase** Wendy, 'Piers plowman' and the new anticlericalism [➤ 5,g986*]: Cambridge Studies in Medieval Literature 5. C 1989, Univ. xx-249 p. $44.50. – ᴿJTS 42 (1991) 377s (Gloria *Cigman*); RHE 86 (1991) 262 (D. *Bradley*).

1386 MELVILLE: *Sachs* Viola, Moby Dick: or, The Whale [sic, indeed 'Wale' in the title] et l'Écriture Biblique: FoiVie 90,5 = CahB 30 (1991) 81-92.

1387 MILTON: *Fishman* Sylvia B., Paradise lost as a midrash on the biblical bride of God: ➤ 56, ᶠFOX M., 4 (1991) 87-103.

1388 **Schwartz** Reginald, Remembering... in Paradise Lost 1988 ➤ 5,1598*: ᴿCritRR 4 (1991) 70-72 (D. R. *Dickson*).

1389 PATIENCE: *Nicholson* R. H., [Middle English] Patience; reading the Prophetia Jonae: MedHum 16 (1988) 97-115.

1390 PEARL: *Stanbury* Sarah, Pearl and the idea of Jerusalem: MedHum 16 (1988) 117-131.

1391 SHAKESPEARE: **Milward** Peter, Biblical influences in Shakespeare's great tragedies. Bloomington 1987, Indiana Univ. xvi-208 p. – ᴿEvQ 63 (1991) 364s (A. G. *Newell*).

1392 **Shaheen** Naseeb, Biblical references in Shakespeare's tragedies. Newark 1987, Univ. Delaware. 245 p. £22.50. – ᴿEvQ 63 (1991) 365-7 (A. G. *Newell*).
Woods Deane J., Statius/Apocalypse ᴰ1990 ➤ 5060.
1393 Stryjkowski: *Sobolewska* Anna, **❾** Le triptyque biblique de Julian Stryjkowski: PrzPow 269,827s (1990) 160-176; franç. 176.
1394 Thoreau: *Bori* Pier Cesare, 'Sacred Scriptures or Bibles of mankind' in *Walden* by Henry David Thoreau: ➤ 56, ᶠFox M. 4 (1991) 105-114.

B4.7 *Interpretatio* **athea, materialistica, psychiatrica.**

1395 *Biser* Eugen, Der Protagonist der Angstüberwindung [Baudler G., Erlösung vom Stiergott 1989]: StiZt 208 (1990) 427-9.
1396 *Clark* David K., Interpreting the biblical words for the self: JPsy&T 18 (1990) 309-317 [< zit 91,316].
1397 *Dourley* John P., The Jung, Buber, White exchanges; exercises in futility: SR 20 (1991) 299-309.

1398 Drewermann Eugen, La parole qui guérit, ᵀ*Bagot* J.-P. P 1991, Cerf. 329 p. F 160. 2-204-04300-1. – ᴿEsprVie 101 (1991) 522s (L. *Walter*: polémique simplifiée empêche d'entendre les questions valables); Études 374 (1991) 715 (J. *Thomas*); NRT 113 (1991) 795s (A. *Toubeau*); RHPR 71 (1991) 255s (B. *Kaempf*: quintessence de sa pensée importante, dans un style journalistique).
1399 **Drewermann** Eugen, Was uns Zukunft gibt. Olten c. 1990, Walter. 232 p. DM 32 [TPQ 139,180].
1400 **Drewermann** Eugen, Worte für ein unentdecktes Land, ᴱ*Walter* Karin. FrB 1990, Herder. 128 p. DM 12,80. – ᴱErbAuf 67 (1991) 151 (Renate *Fütterer*).
1401 **Drewermann** Eugen, *Jeziorowski* Jürgen, Gespräche über die Angst: Siebenstern 1296. Gü 1991, Mohn. 122 p. DM 14,80 [TLZ 117,382, G. M. *Martin*].
1402 — ᴱ**Eicher** Peter, Der Klerikerstreit... E. Drewermann. Mü 1990, Kösel. 368 p. – ᴿTPhil 66 (1991) 304-8 (J. *Splett*).
1403 — **Fehrenbacher** Gregor, Drewermann verstehen; eine kritische Hinführung. Olten 1991, Walter. 290 p. DM 27,80. 3-530-21021-8. – ᴿHerd-Korr 45 (1991) 489 (K. *Nientiedt*).
1404 — ᴱ**Görres** Albert, *Kasper* Walter, Tiefenpsychologische Deutung des Glaubens? Anfragen an E. Drewermann: QDisp 113, ²1988 ➤ 4,305... 6,1698: ᴱRTLv 22 (1990) 268 (P. *Weber*).
1404* — *a)* Hoppe K. D., Kleriker, Kirche und Psychanalyse; – *b)* Schneider-Harprecht C., Psychoanalytische Bibelauslegung; – *c)* Krauss I., Ingeborg *Bachmann* Malina, ...eine Interpretation: WegMensch 43 (Gö 1991) 306-316 / 323-334 / 361-... [< zit 91,685].
1405 — **Marcheselli-Casale** C., Il caso Drewermann; psicologia del profondo, un nuovo metodo per leggere la Bibbia? CasM 1991, Piemme. 326 p. Lit. 32.000. 88-384-1639-7 [NRT 114,452, A. *Toubeau*].
1406 — *Martin* Gerhard M., Zur neueren Religionspsychologie [Drewermann E., Theissen G. ...]: TRu 56 (1991) 280-295.
1407 — *Morandi* Franco, Il caso Drewermann teologo e psicoanalista: CiVit 46 (1991) 571-580.

1408 — *a*) *Scippa* Vincenzo, Parola che salva, parola che guarisce; Drewermann e l'interpretazione simbolica della Bibbia: Asprenas 38 (1991) 232-242; – *b*) *Wanner* Ulrich, Eugen Drewermanns Priestertum der Persönlichkeit: LuthMon 30 (1991) 535-7 [< ZIT 91,779].

1409 FREUD: **Gay** P., A godless Jew, Freud 1987 → 4,1587... 6,1706: ᴿZygon 26 (1991) 432-5 (R. A. *Segal*).
1410 **Gay** Peter, Un Juif sans Dieu; Freud, l'athéisme et la naissance de la psychanalyse. P 1989, PUF. 176 p. F 98. – ᴿÉtudes 347 (1991) 854s (F. *Courel*).
1411 — **Forsyth** James, Freud, JUNG and Christianity. Ottawa 1989, Univ. viii-185 p. – ᴿSR 20 (1991) 370s (G. *Havers*).
1412 — **Frieden** Ken, Freud's dream of interpretation [... and Talmud Berakot]. Albany 1990, SUNY. 159 p. – ᴿJudaica 46 (1990) 245 (S. *Hurwitz*).
1413 — *Goodnick* Benjamin, Jacob Freud's dedication to his son [Sigmund]; a reevaluation: JQR 82 (1991s) 329-360.
1414 — **Rice** Emanuel, Freud and Moses; the long journey home. Albany 1990, SUNY. 266 p. $49.50; pa. $17. – ᴿJAAR 55 (1991) 862-4 (V. P. *Gay*).
1415 — **Yerushalmi** Yosef H., Freud's Moses; Judaism terminable and interminable. NHv 1991, Yale Univ. 159 p. $25 [JAAR 59,886].
1415* **Fromm** Erich, You shall be as gods; a radical interpretation of the Old Testament and its tradition. NY 1991 = 1966, Holt. [x-] 241 p. 0-8050-1605-8.
Gibert Pierre, Le récit biblique de rêve... confrontation analytique 1990 → 2063.
1416 **Kahn** Judith, The Hebrew Bible as a journey through consciousness: diss. Union Institute 1991. 522 p. 92-01078. – DissA 52 (1991s) 3966-A.
1417 JUNG: **Nehb** Tilman, Die Bedeutung des Bösen in der Tiefenpsychologie von Carl Gustav Jung und die Bedeutung des Dämonischen in der Theologie von Paul TILLICH: Diss. Tübingen 1990. 496 p. – TLZ 117,953.
1418 — ᴱMoore Robert L., *Meckel* Daniel S., Jung and Christianity in dialogue [first of four volumes]. NY 1990, Paulist. ix-266 p. 13. – ᴿCurrTMiss 18 (1991) 368 (J. C. *Rochelle*).
1419 *Myers* David G., Steering between the extremes; on being a Christian scholar within psychology: ChrSchR 20 (1991) 376-383 [< ZIT 91,484].
1419* **Oates** Wayne E., Temptation; a biblical and psychological approach. Louisville 1991, W-Knox. 109 p. $10 pa. [Horizons 19,343, N. J. *Rigali*].
1420 **Pfister** Oskar, [9] Scritti su psicoanalisi e cura d'anime [1909-1942], ᵀᴱ*Ossicini* A., *Bernet* W. R 1990, Kappa. 317 p. – ᴿProtestantesimo 46 (1991) 130-5 (E. *Genre*).
1420* *Pitzele* Peter A., The psychodrama of the Bible; mirror and window of soul: RelEdn 86 (Ch 1991) 562-571 [< ZIT 92,59].
1421 *Ponzo* Ezio, Le discutibili certezze psicologiche di Heribert MÜHLEN [Problema dell'essere e morte di Dio 1969]: Protestantesimo 46 (1991) 201-4.
1422 *Schmitz* Stefan, Tiefenpsychologie in Theologie: → 85, ᶠJORISSEN H., Mit dem Rücken 1991, 45-59.

B5 **Methodus exegetica.**

1423 *Banon* David, Exégèse biblique et philosophie: ÉTPhil 66 (1991) 489-504.

1424 **Beattie** D. R. G., First steps in biblical criticism 1988 ➤ 4,1608 ... 6,1716: ᴿBL (1991) 64 (W. J. *Houston*).

1425 *a*) **Brekelmans** C., *Vervenne* M., Continuing questions in OT method and theology²ʳᵉᵛ 1989 ➤ 5,383: ᴿColcT 61,4 (1991) 201-4 (W. *Chrostowski,* ❷).

— *b*) **Brett** Mark G., Biblical criticism in crisis? The impact of the canonical approach [diss. Sheffield ᴰ*Rogerson* J.]. C 1991, Univ. xiii-237 p. £30. 0-521-40119-4 [ZAW 104,293, H.-C. *Schmitt*]. – ᴿExpTim 103 (1991s) 119s (W. *Moberly*: should put an end to CHILDS' being regarded as an oddity in Britain, though it has nothing on NT as Canon nor enough on Childs' practical goals).

— *c*) *Campbell* Antony F., Past history and present text; the clash of classical and post-critical approaches to biblical text: AustralBR 39 (1991) 1-18 [< ZIT 92,238].

1426 *a*) *Colombo* Giuseppe, Intorno all' 'esegesi scientifica'; – *b*) *Bianchi* Enzo, La lettura spirituale della Scrittura oggi: ➤ 323, L'esegesi 1991, 169-214 / 215-277.

1427 *Elders* Léon, La méthode en exégèse biblique d'après saint Thomas d'AQUIN: DivThom 93 (1990) 225-242.

1428 *Fohrer* Georg, *a*) Christliche Fehldeutungen der hebräischen Bibel; – *b*) Auslegung des ATs — einige Hinweise für Nichtexegeten; – *c*) Die prophetische Botschaft und der heutige Mensch: ➤ 200, Studien zum AT V (1991) 160-6 / 151-9 / 132-150.

1429 **Fohrer** Georg, *al.*, Exegese des Alten Testaments; Einführung in die Methodik: Uni-Tb 267. Heid 1989, Quelle & M. [¹1973]. 229 p. 3-494-02165-1 [-024-8].

1430 *Girardet* Giorgio, La dimensione orale della comunicazione biblica: Protestantesimo 46 (1991) 116-127.

1430* *a*) *Görg* Manfred, Kontrastive Exegese — Für den Widerstreit in der Schriftauslegung; – *b*) *Peek-Horn* Margret, Warum haftet dem Alten Testament ein Makel des Uneigentlichen an?: RuHöh 34 (1991) 213-226 / 227-233 [< ZIT 91,684].

1431 **Grafton** Anthony, Forgers and critics; creativity and duplicity in western scholarship. Princeton 1990, Univ. x-157 p. $15 [RelStR 18,143, T. F. X. *Noble*: an intellectual feast: forgery, and not merely its detection, is akin to criticism, and begets awareness of anachronism].

1432 **Guillemette** Pierre, *Brisebois* Mireille, Introduzione ai metodi storico-critici 1990 ➤ 6,1726: ᴿProtestantesimo 46 (1991) 211s (L. *De Lorenzi*); Teresianum 42 (1991) 347s (V. *Pasquetto*).

1433 *a*) *Hughes* J. J., Beyond word processing; – *b*) *Scrimgeour* A. D., The computer as a tool for research and communication in religious studies: CritRR 3 (1990) 1-43 / 45-59 [< NTAbs 35,148s].

1434 *La Potterie* Ignace de, *a*) L'esegesi biblica, scienza della fede; – *b*) Il Concilio Vaticano Ii e la Bibbia: ➤ 323, ᴱ*Pacomio* L., L'esegesi 1991, 127-165 / 19-42.

1435 **Lentzen-Deis** Fritzleo, *al.*, Avances metodológicos de la exégesis para la praxis de hoy: Evangelio y cultura 2. Bogotá 1990, Paulinas. 139 p. 958-607-509-5.

1435* *Le Roux* J. H., Oor paradigmas en progressie in die teologie [VORSTER V., LATEGAN B., AARDE A., van]: SkrifKerk 12 (1991) 276-291.

1436 **Linnemann** Eta, Historical criticism of the Bible; methodology or ideology [Wissenschaft oder Meinung? 1986], ᵀ*Yarbrough* Robert W., 1990 ➤ 5,1730: ᴿGraceTJ 11 (1990) 246-8 (J. *Blair*: university equals pagan).

1437 **Lord** Albert B., Epic singers and oral tradition: Myth and Poetics. Ithaca NY 1991, Cornell Univ. xiv-262 p. 0-8014-2472-0; pa. -9717-1.

1438 *a) Meijering* Reinhard P., 'Sola Scriptura' und die historische Kritik; – *b) Baur* Jörg, Sola Scriptura – historisches Erbe und bleibende Bedeutung; – *c) Beintker* Michael, Anmerkungen zur Kategorie der Texttreue: → 454c, Sola Scr. 1990/1, 44-60 / 19-43 / 281-291.

1439 *Meyer* Ben F., The challenges of text and reader to the historical-critical method: → 347, Concilium (1991,1) 3-12.

1440 **Meynet** Roland, L'analyse rhétorique 1989 → 5,1642; 6,1731: ᴿBL (1991) 86 (R.P. *Carroll*: simple and concrete); Gregorianum 72 (1991) 567s (E. *Farahian*); NRT 113 (1991) 104s (Y. *Simoens*).

1440* *O'Grady* John F., Biblical methodologies: ChSt 29 (1990) 87-99.

1441 **Patrick** D., *Scult* A., Rhetoric and biblical interpretation: JStOT supp. 82 / BLit 26, 1990 → 6,1736: ᴿBL (1991) 90 (R.P. *Carroll*); ÉTRel 66 (1991) 433s (J. *Rennes*); JTS 42 (1991) 177s (Meg *Davies*); TLZ 116 (1991) 497-9 (W. *Herrmann*).

1442 *Patte* Daniel, Greimassian semiotic analysis of texts and its application to biblical studies ['De Jésus et des femmes' 1987]: Semiotica 82 (1990) 305-312.

1443 *a) Robinson* Bernard, Whither Catholic biblical studies?; – *b) Wijngaards* John, On planning Scripture studies; – *c) Fuller* R.C., The Catholic Biblical Association of Great Britain: PrPeo 4 (1991) 278-281 / 270-7 / 251-4.

1444 *Rogerson* John W., Exegese als Literaturwissenschaft, revisited [Rɪᴄʜ-ᴛᴇʀ's rigorous program 1971, implemented withous parallel]: → 126, ᶠRɪᴄʜᴛᴇʀ W., Text 1991, 379-386.

1445 *Sander-Gaiser* M., Frühe jüdische und christliche Mnemotechnik — ein pädagogischer Beitrag zum Thema 'Auswendiglernen': Rosch Pina 8 (Mülheim 1990) 3-22 [10 (1990), *Butting* K., *al.*, Zeit für Kohelet; < Judaica 46,252].

1446 *Schmidt* Ludwig, [*Merk* Otto], Literaturkritik AT [NT]: → 690, TRE 21 (1991) 211-222 [-233]; 233-306 *al.*, Literatur und Religion.

1447 *Schottroff* Luise, Sozialgeschichtliche Bibelauslegung: Junge Kirche 52,1 (Bremen 1991) 32-34 [< ZIT 91,81].

1448 **Stenger** Werner, † 7.VI.1990, Los métodos de la exégesis bíblica [Biblische Methodenlehre 1987 → 3,1617], ᵀ*Ruiz Garrido* C.: BtTeol 14. Barc 1990, Herder. 357 p. – ᴿCarthaginensia 7 (1991) 501s (R. *Sanz Valdivieso*); Iter 2 (1990) 128s (J.P. *Wyssenbach*); NatGrac 38 (1991) 390s (F. *Ramos*); RazF 223 (1991) 551 (M. *Matos*); Salmanticensis 38 (1991) 369s (G. *Pérez*); ScripTPamp 23 (1991) 351-6 (J.M. *Casciaro*).

1449 ᴱ**Uffenheimer** Benjamin, *Reventlow* Henning, Creative biblical exegesis; Christian and Jewish hermeneutics through the centuries 1984/7 → 4,505 ... 6,1742: ᴿBZ 35 (1991) 111s (J. *Scharbert*); JTS 42 (1991) 288s (I.H. *Jones*).

1450 *Zumstein* Jean, Croire et comprendre [exégèse entre savante et pieuse]: ÉTRel 66 (1991) 329-343.

III. Critica Textus, Versiones

D1 **Textual Criticism.**

1451 **Avrin** Leila, Scribes, script and books; the book arts from antiquity to the Renaissance. Ch 1991, American Library Asn. xxxii-356 p.; 35 fig.; 308 pl.; 7 maps. 0-7123-0245-X.

1452 **Beit-Arié** M., *al.*, ❻ Specimens of mediaeval Hebrew scripts, I. Oriental and Yemenite manuscripts 1987 → 4,1655; 5,1657:   ᴿHenoch 12 (1990) 393s (G. *Tamani*).

1453 ᴱ**Brandis** Tilo, *Becker* Peter J., Glanz alter Buchkunst; mittelalterliche Handschriften der Staatsbibliothek Preussischer Kulturbesitz Berlin [125 Farbphotos mit kurzer Erklärung]: Kataloge 33. Wsb 1988, Reichert. 272 p. DM 58. – ᴿSpeculum 66 (1991) 386s (J. J. G. *Alexander*).

1454 *Brennecke* Hanns C., LUCIAN von Antiochien [... Bibelrezeption]: → 690, TRE 21 (1991) 474-9.

1455 *Brubaker* Leslie, The introduction of painted initials in Byzantium: Scriptorium 45 (1991) 22-46.

1456 **Capasso** Mario, Manuale di papirologia ercolanese. N 1991, Congedo. 340 p.; 75 fig.; XVI pl. – ᴿAegyptus 71 (1991) 299-302 (Orsolina *Montevecchi*).

1457 **Carrez** Maurice, Manuscrits et langues de la Bible, du papyrus aux Bibles imprimées²ʳᵉᵛ [¹1983]; préf. *Grelot* P. P 1991, Soc. Biblique Française. 116 p. F 70. – ᴿEsprVie 101 (1991) 564 (É. *Cothenet*).

1458 ᴱ**Cavallo** Guglielmo, Le biblioteche nel mondo antico e medievale 1988 → 5,533*b*:   ᴿAugM 35 (1990) 215s (J. *Oroz*); Scriptorium 44 (Bru 1990) 132-6 (F. *Gasparri*).

1459 ᴱ**Cavallo** Guglielmo, Le strade del testo, 1984/7 → 5,533*a*; 6,1764:   ᴿLatomus 50 (1991) 757s (L. *Reynhout*).

1460 **Comfort** Philip W., Early manuscripts and modern translations of the NT. L 1990, Tyndale. $20. 0-8423-0766-4. – ᴿAndrUnS 29 (1991) 83-85 (S. *Kubo*); JTS 42 (1991) 282-5 (P. *Ellingworth*).

1461 **D'Amico** John F. † 1987, Theory and practice in Renaissance textual criticism: Beatus RHENANUS [1485-1547; first biographer of ERASMUS] between conjecture and history. Berkeley 1988, Univ. California. 310 p. $38. – ᴿCritRR 4 (1991) 478-480 (T. P. *Letis*); Speculum 66 (1991) 145-7 (C. L. *Stinger*).

1462 *Dorandi* Tiziano, Den Autoren über die Schulter geschaut; Arbeitsweise und Autographie bei den antiken Schriftstellern: ZPapEp 87 (1991) 11-23.

1463 *Elliott* J. Keith, Textkritik heute [Gastvorlesung Leipzig 1986]: ZNW 82 (1991) 34-41.

1464 *Fälschungen* im Mittelalter 1986/8 → 4,1662*... 6,1775:   ᴿHZ 253 (1991) 422-8 (H. *Müller*); ZKG 102 (1991) 116-8 (T. *Vogtherr*).

1465 *Gallo* Italo, Greek and Latin papyrology [1983] ᵀ1986 → 2,1167 ... 6,1778:   ᴿMnemosyne 44 (1991) 509-512 (F. A. J. *Hoogendijk*).

1466 ᴱ**Gamillscheg** E., *Harlfinger* D., Repertorium der griechischen Kopisten 800-1600 [I. England 1981] IIA. Handschriften aus Bibliotheken Frankreichs, Verzeichnis der Kopisten; B. (**Hunger** H.) Paläographische Charakteristika; C. Tafeln 1989 → 6,1779:   ᴿByZ 83 (1991) 480-2 (J. *Irigoin*); Ellinika 42 (1991) 202-4 (A. *Sakellaridou-Sotiroudi*); Klio 73 (1991) 711s (K. *Treu*); Scriptorium 44 (Bru 1990) 132s (J. *Irigoin*).

1467 ᴱ**Grant** John N., Editing Greek and Latin texts 1987/9 → 6,738:   ᴿClasR 41 (1991) 208-210 (N. G. *Wilson*).

1468 ᴱ**Griffiths** Jeremy, *Pearsall* Derek, Book production and publishing in Britain, 1373-1475: Studies in Publishing and Printing History. C 1989, Univ. xix-463 p.; 64 fig. $69.50. 15 art., one on 'the religious orders' [*Doyle* A. I., 109-123]. – ᴿSpeculum 66 (1991) 961, tit. pp.

1469 *Guineau* B., *Vezin* J., Nouvelles méthodes d'analyse des pigments et des colorants employés pour la décoration des livres manuscrits [... Corbie 12ᵉ s.]: → 584*, Paleografia latina 1987/90, 83-94.

1470 *Heiligenthal* Roman, LAGARDE, Paul Anton de (1827-1891): ➤ 690, TRE 20 (1990) 375-8.

1471 ᴱ**Hoogendijk** Francisca, *Minnen* P. van, Papyri, ostraca, parchments and waxed tablets in the Leiden Papyrological Institute (P.L.Bat 25): Pap-LugdunoB 25. Leiden 1991, Brill. xiv-317 p.; XLIII pl. 90-04-09339-7.

1472 *Horak* Ulrike, Fälschungen auf Papyrus, Pergament, Papier und Ostraka: Tyche 6 (1991) 91-98; pl. 4-8.

1473 **Hunger** Herbert, Schreiben und lesen in Byzanz; die byzantinische Buchkultur 1989 ➤ 5,1673; 6,1790: ᴿAnzAltW 44 (1991) 98-103 (W. *Neuhauser*).

1473* *Jacobs* L. D., Die tekstkritiek van die Nuwe Testament (1): Die huidige metodologiese situasie: SkrifKerk 12 (1991) 259-275 [< NTAbs 36,312].

1474 *Lama* Mariachiara, Aspetti di tecnica libraria ad Ossirinco; copie letterarie su rotoli documentari: Aegyptus 71 (1991) 55-120.

1475 **Lemaire** Jacques, Introduction à la codicologie 1989 ➤ 5,1675; 6,1795: ᴿLatomus 50 (1991) 449s (A. *Martin*); ScripTPamp 23 (1991) 1078 (M. *Lluch-Baixauli*).

1476 *Lopik* T. van, Tekstkritiek; telt het wegen of weegt het tellen? ['counts the weight or weighs the count'; Eng. 136 'counting or weighing of manuscripts'; on de JONGE 1988]: NedTTs 45 (1991) 101-6.

1477 **Martin** Ernest L., *a)* The original Bible restored. 332 p. $15; – *b)* The star that astonished the world. 224 p. $15; – *c)* Secrets of Golgotha; the forgotten history of Christ's crucifixion. 280 p. $15. Pasadena c. 1990, Center for Biblical Studies [BAR-W 17/6,19 adv.].

1478 **Mazal** Otto, Paläographie und Paläotypie; zur Geschichte der Schrift im Zeitalter der Inkunabeln: Bibliothek des Buchwesens 8. Stu 1984, Hiersemann. viii-404 p.; 140 fig. – ᴿAnzAltW 44 (1991) 106-9 (W. *Neuhauser*).

1479 **Mazzotta** O., Monaci e libri greci nel Salento medioevale: Scriptorium 2. Novoli 1989, Bibliotheca Minima. xvi-125 p.; 48 fig.; 2 maps. Lit. 30.000 [RHE 86,12*].

1480 **Montevecchi** Orsolina, La papirologia² [= 1973, ristampa corretta con addenda]. Mi 1988, ViPe. 822 p. Lit. 78.000. 88-343-6910-6. – ᴿSalesianum 53 (1991) 170s (R. *Sabin*).

1481 **Narkiss** Bezalel, Hebrew illuminated manuscripts in the British Isles, 1. Spanish and Portuguese 1982 ➤ 64,1721; 65,1476: ᴿJQR 82 (1991s) 188-190 (Evelyn M. *Cohen*).

1482 *Nida* Eugene A., Textual criticism and entropy: ➤ 17, ꟳBARTHÉLEMY D., Tradition 1991, 122-8.

1483 *Paci* D., Iscrizioni cristiane in manoscritti: ➤ 130, ꟳSANDERS G., Aevum 1991, 301-6.

1484 *Papazoglu* George K., A supplementary catalogue of the manuscripts of the Dionysiou Monastery of Mt. Athos [items 805-1064]: TAth 61 (1990) 443-505.

1485 **Pestman** P. W., The new papyrological primer⁵ [¹1940 was by M. *David* and B. A. van *Groningen*, = Eng. ²1946]. Leiden 1990, Brill. 318 p. 90-04-09348-6. – ᴿOrChrPer 57 (1991) 460s (J. *O'Callaghan*).

1486 *Robinson* James M., Handling future manuscript discoveries [< Claremont OccP 23]: BA 54 (1991) 235-240.

1487 *Rothschild* Jean-Pierre, Listes de livres hébreux en Italie; nouveaux documents pour une typologie: RHText 19 (1989) 291-334; index 334-9, plusieurs Bibles et livres particuliers.

1488 **Ruiz García** E., Manual de codicología. S/M 1988, Fund. Ruipé-rez/Piramide. 432 p. 16 pl. pt 2650 [Quaerendo 20,236s, J. *Gumberts*: RHE 86,17*].
1489 *Samely* Alexander, The interpreted text; among the [23 ft. shelf of] Hebrew manuscripts of the J. R. U. Library: BJRyL 73,2 (1991) 1-20.
1490 **Seider** Richard, Paläographie der griechischen Papyri 3/1, 1990 ➤ 6, 1816; DM 480: ᴿCdÉ 65 (1990) 365s (A. *Martin*).
1491 *a) Sermoneta* Giuseppe, Le pergamene ebraiche negli Archivi di Stato; consuntivo di una prima indagine; – *b) Richler* Benjamin, The con-tribution of the Italian parchment fragments to the history of medieval rabbinic literature and booklore; – *c) Chiesa* Bruno, Un testimone della traduzione araba del Pentateuco di SAADIA Gaon: ➤ 459, Manoscritti 1988/91, 29-40 / 41-50 / 203-
1492 *Sève* Michel, Sur la taille des rayonnages [size of the shelves] dans les bibliothèques antiques: RPg 64 (1990) 173-9.
1493 *Soetermeer* F. P. W., À propos d'une famille de copistes; quelques remarques sur la librairie à Bologne aux XIIIᵉ et XIVᵉ siècles: StMedv 30 (1989) 425-478 [< RSPT 75,172].
1494 *Supino* Martini P., Storia della scrittura e storia del libro nell'Alto Medioevo: Anuario de Estudios Medievales 21 (Barc 1991) 387-403 [< RHE 87,176*].
1495 *Tamani* Giuliano, Un'insolita grafia in manoscritti ebraici sefarditi del sec. XIII: Henoch 12 (1990) 323-330 + 14 pl.; Eng. 345.
1496 **Yakerson** S. M., Hebrew incunabula ... Moscow, Leningrad 1988 ➤ 5, 1691: ᴿHenoch 12 (1990) 394s (G. *Tamani*).
1497 **Zerdoun** Bat-Yehouda Monique, Les papiers filigranés médiévaux; essai de méthodologie descriptive: Bibliologia 7s. Turnhout 1989, Bre-pols. 142 p.; p. 143-270; ill. – ᴿScriptorium 45 (1991) 131s (Mo-nique-Cécile *Garand*).

D2.1   *Biblia hebraica,* **Hebrew text.**

1498 *Anglada* Ángel, Unas notas de crítica textual sobre nombres hebreos en PACIANO de Barcelona [... Reginensis 331 maintains the Hebrew names of Pacian's text in their genuine form]: Emerita 59,1 (1991) 155-182.
1499 *Cassuto* Philippe, Qerê-Ketiv et Massora Magna dans le manuscrit B 19a: Text 15 (1990) 85-118.
1500 **Deist** F. E., Witnesses to the OT; introducing OT textual criti-cism: LitOT 5. Pretoria 1988, NG Kerk. viii-225 p. [JBL 111,512, J. R. *Davila*].
1501 *Margain* J., Samaritain (Pentateuque): ➤ 686, SDB XI,63s (1990) 762-773.
1502 *Ognibeni* B., Libri ebraici a Piacenza, incunaboli e cinquecentine: Bollettino Storico Piacentino 86 (1991) 129-142; 1 fig. [< RHE 86,262*].
1503* *Ortega Monasterio* María Teresa, Editing the Masoretic Index of the Cairo Codex: Sefarad 51 (1991) 447-451.
1503 *Penkower* Jordan S., [Dt 34,9-12] ➊ A Pentateuch fragment from the tenth century attributed to Moses Ben-Asher (Ms Firkowicz B 188): Tarbiz 60 (1990s) 355-369 + 3 photos; Eng. II-III.
1504 ᴱRevell E. J., VIII congress, International Organization for Masoretic Studies 1988/90 ➤ 6,551: ᴿBL (1991) 154 (J. *Barr*).
1505 **Richter** Wolfgang, Biblia hebraica transcripta 1-3, mit Satzeinteilungen und ... tiberisch-masoretischen Autoritäten, Gn, Ex-Lv, Nm-Dt.: Mü

Univ. AOtt 33.   St. Ottilien 1991, EOS.   viii-485 p.; v-629 p.; v-701 p.
DM 58 + 68 + 78 [ZAW 104,307].   3-88096-533-1; -82-X; -83-8.

1506 **Róth** Ernst, *Striedl* Hans, Hebräische Handschriften ... in Deutschland 6, 1984 → 65,1478:   ᴿJAOS 111 (1991) 646s (I. O. *Lehman*).

1507 **Róth** E., *Prijs* L.,   Hebräische Handschriften 1-B, Fra-Univ.   Stu 1991, Steiner [ZAW 104,307, J. *Maier*].

1508 **Tov** E., ❹ *Biqqoret* ... The textual criticism of the Bible, an introduction. J 1989, Biblical Encyclopaedia Library 4.   24-326 p. – ᴿZAW 103 (1991) 311 (J. *Maier*).

1509 *Tov* Emanuel,   Hebrew biblical manuscripts from the Judaean Desert; their contribution to textual citicism: → 458, Jewish-Hellenistic 1986/91, 107-137.

1510 *a*) *Tov* Emanuel,   The original shape of the biblical text; – *b*) *Díez Merino* L.,   Fidelity and editorial work in the Complutensian Targum tradition: → 429, IOSOT 1989/91, 345-359 / 360-382.

1510* *Valle* C. del,   Dos nuevos incunables hebreos españoles y su censo [Haftarot Gn 28,15 ... Dt 28,54; Yôrê deʿâ de J. ben Ašer 1270?-1340]: Sefarad 51 (1991) 199-202; 453, dos rectificaciones (*Offenberg* A. K.).

1511 *a*) *Waard* Jan de,   The interim and final HOTTP [Hebrew Old Testament Text Project] reports and the translator; a preliminary investigation; – *b*) *Ognibeni* Bruno,   La collezione massoretica *oklah* wᵉ-*oklah*: → 17, ᶠBARTHÉLEMY D., Tradition 1991, 277-284 / 156-183.

1512 *Weil-Guény* Anne-Marie,   Les manuscrits bibliques de la Bibliothèque Universitaire de Bologne: Henoch 13 (1991) 287-317: four partial Hebrew Bibles from San Domenico and five from San Salvatore.

1513 **Widawsli** Lea, ❹ The *paseg* in the Hebrew Bible; occurrences in medieval manuscripts, characteristics and relation to the accentuation system: diss. Bar-Ilan.   Ramat-Gan 1991. 395 + 39 p. – RTLv 23, p. 541.

D2.2   **Targum.**

1514 *Böhl* F.,   Der erweiterte Vergleich im Targum: FraJudBeit 18 (1990) 23-43 [< JStJud 22,266].

1515 *Chrostowski* Waldemar, ❺ The Palestinian Targums to the Pentateuch: ColcT 61,2 (1991) 33-46; Eng. 46.

1516 *Díez Merino* L.,   Los discípulos de la Escuela Targúmica de la Universidad de Barcelona; investigadores de dicha Escuela de Estudios Arameos: Henoch 13 (1991) 65-92.

1517 *Díez Merino* Luis,   Los Tiqqune Soferim en la tradición targúmica: → 17, ᶠBARTHÉLEMY D., Tradition 1991, 18-44.

1518 *Garr* W. Randall,   **ay > a* in Targum Onqelos: JAOS 111 (1991) 712-9.

1519 **Goshen-Gottstein** Moshe, (*Kasher* Rimon), ❹ Fragments of lost Targumim 1983 → 64,1733;   65,1491 ... :   ᴿZDMG 141 (1991) 400s (P. *Schäfer*).

1520 **Grossfeld** Bernard, Targum Onqelos to Gn / Ex / LvNm / Dt 1988 → 4,1701 ... 6,1844*b*: ᴿCBQ 53 (1991) 102-5 (B. M. *Cook*: should render *memra* for what it is, three different possibilities besides 'word' — buts hould not render the same Aramaic word differently in different verses).

1521 *Hayward* Robert,   Pirqe de Rabbi Eliezer and Targum Pseudo-Jonathan: JJS 42 (1991) 215-246.

1522 **Klein** M. L.,   Geniza ... Targum to Pentateuch 1986 → 2,1298 ... 6,1846: ᴿCiuD 203 (1991) 233-5 (J. *Gutiérrez*).

1523 **Levine** Etan, Aramaic... Bible: BZAW 174, 1988 ➤ 4,1706... 6,1848:
ᴿAJS 16 (1991) 211-4 (B. *Grossfeld*: some notable typos); BO 48 (1991)
638-644 (J. *Cook*); BZ 35 (1991) 309s (J. *Maier*).
1524 *a)* **Mangan** Celine, The Targum of Job; – *b)* *Healey* John F., ... of
Proverbs; – *c)* *Knobel* Peter S., The Targum of Qohelet: Glazier Aramaic
Bible 15. Collegeville MN 1991, Liturgical. v-94 p.; viii-65 p.; vii-60 p.
0-8146-5490-8 [RelStR 18,240, J. A. *Lund*]. – ᴿOTAbs 14 (1991) 364
(R. E. *Murphy*).
1525 **Naumann** Paul, Targum – Brücke zwischen den Testamenten, 1. Tar-
gum-Synopse ausgewählter Texte aus den palästinischen Pentateuch-
Targumen. Konstanz 1991, Christliche VA. 200 p. DM 30 [TLZ 117,
403, L. *Wächter*: ZAW 104,161, U. *Becker*].
1526 *Shinan* Avigdor, Echoes from ancient synagogues; vocatives and 'emendations' in the Aramaic targums to the Pentateuch: JQR 81 (1990s) 353-364.

D3.1 *Textus graecus* – **Greek NT.**

1527 **Aland** Kurt & Barbara, The text of the NT² [¹1987] 1989 ➤ 3,1667...
6,1875: ᴿAndrUnS 29 (1991) 73-76 (J. *Paulien* assesses earlier criticisms);
Neotestamentica 25 (1991) 182s (J. H. *Petzer*); TrinJ 12 (1991) 231-3
(D. S. *Huffman*); Vidyajyoti 55 (1991) 55s (P. M. *Meagher*).
1528 **Comfort** Philip W., Early manuscripts and modern translations of the
NT 1990 ➤ 6,1852: ᴿBTrans 42 (1991) 343-5 (J. K. *Elliott*); CritRR 4
(1991) 184s (T. C. *Geer*).
1529 **Elliott** J. K., A bibliography of Greek NT manuscripts 1989 ➤ 5,1738...
6,1865: ᴿActuBbg 28 (1991) 71s (J. *O'Callaghan*); CBQ 53 (1991) 131-3
(A. *Cody*); FgNt 4 (1991) 76s (también J. *O'Callaghan*).
1530 *a)* *Jonge* H. J. de, Die tekstvorm in een oecumenische kerkbijbel; – *b)*
Bruggen J. van, De mondige bijbellezer en de tekst van het Nieuwe
Testament: Met andere woorden; kwartaalblad van het Nederlands
Bijbelgenootschap 7,4 (1988) 3-5 . 11/6-10 . 12 [< NedTTs 45,101].
1531 ᴱ**Letis** T. P., The majority text; essays and reviews in the continuing
debate 1987 ➤ 4,1722 [(? also) GR, Institute for Biblical Textual Studies]:
ᴿNeotestamentica 25 (1991) 184s (J. H. *Petzer*).
1532 *Parker* T. C., Scripture is tradition: TLond 94 (1991) 11-17.
1533 **Pelusi** Simonetta, Novum Testamentum Bosniacum Marcianum Cod.
Or. 227 (= 168): Helios 3. Padova 1991, Programma. 405 p. (99-386
ms. phot.).
1533* *Petzer* J. H., *a)* Westerse teks, Alexandrynse teks en die oorspronklike
teks van die Nuwe Testament; is daar 'n oplossing vir die probleem?:
HervTSt 47 (1991) 950-967; – *b)* Eclecticism and the text of the NT:
➤ 3756, Text 1991, 47-62.
1534 **Sturz** Harry A., The Byzantine text-type; New Testament textual
criticism. Nv 1984, Nelson. 305 p. – ᴿTAth 61 (1990) 894-6 (G. C. *Papademetriou*, Eng.: recommends highly).
1535 *Synnes* M., Hvilken tekst er best? Nestle-Aland contra Majoritetstekst:
TeolKirk 62 (1991) 161-171 [< NTAbs 36,158].
1536 [*Vaganay* Léon] **Amphoux** Christian-Bernard, An introduction to NT
textual criticism²ʳᵉᵛ, ᵀ*Heimerdinger* Jenny. C 1991, Univ. xxiv-227. £11.
0-321-36433-7; pa. -42493-3.
1537 *Wallace* Daniel B., *a)* The majority text and the original text; are they
identical? : BS 148 (1991) 151-169: – *b)* Inspiration, preservation, and
New Testament textual criticism: GraceTJ 12,1 (1991) 21-50.

1538 *Wevers* John W., THEODORET's *Quaest* and the Byzantine text: Henoch 13 (1991) 29-64; ital. 64.

1539 **Wisselink** William F., Assimilation as a criterion for the establishment
of the text... MtMkLk ᴰ1989 ➤ 5,1570: ᴿJBL 110 (1991) 158s (M. W.
Holmes); NT 33 (1991) 179s (J. K. *Elliott*: as a dissertation satisfactory).

D3.2   *Versiones graecae* – **VT, Septuaginta etc.**

1540 **Dorival** G., *Harl* M., *Munnich* O., La bible grecque des Septante 1988
➤ 4,1732... 6,1883: ᴿRivB 39 (1991) 83-85 (Anna *Passoni Dell'Acqua*);
Salesianum 53 (1991) 179s (M. *Cimosa*: nuovo SWETE); ZkT 113 (1991)
72-74 (J. M. *Oesch*).

1541 *Dorival* Gilles, La Bible des Septante; 70 ou 72 traducteurs?: ➤ 17,
ᶠBARTHÉLEMY D., Tradition 1991, 45-62.

1542 *Goldstein* Jonathan A., The message of Aristeas to Philocrates...: obey
the Torah, venerate the temple of Jerusalem, but speak Greek; put your
hopes in the Ptolemaic dynasty: ➤ 449, Eretz/Diaspora 1988/91, ...

1543 *a) Harl* Marguerite, Le renouvellement du lexique des 'Septante' d'après
le témoignage des recensions, revisions et commentaires grecs anciens; – *b)*
Jenkins R. C., Colophons of the Syrohexapla and the Textgeschichte of
the recensions of Origen; – *c) Muraoka* Takamitsu, Hebrew hapax le-
gomena and Septuagint lexicography; – *d) Sollamo* Raija, The pleonastic
use of the pronoun in the Greek Pentateuch: ➤ 426, Septuagint 7,
1989/91, 239-259 / 261-277 / 205-222 / 75-85.

1544 **Hastoupis** A. H., ⊖ The ancient Greek translations of the OT: WissZ =
Epistēmonikē Epeteris 28. Athenai 1989, Univ. p. 77-135. – ᴿTAth 62
(1991) 589s (P. *Simotas*).

1545 **Haverling** Gerd, Studies on SYMMACHUS' language and style: StGL-
Goth 49. Göteborg 1988, Univ. 295 p. 91-7346-208-X.

1546 *Lust* Johan, De Septuaginta; de Bijbel van de Christenen?: CollatVL
21 (1991) 230-249.

1547 *Lust* J., Translation-Greek and lexicography of the Septuagint [Mel-
bourne Symposium]: ETL 67 (1991) 69-72.

1548 **Olofsson** Staffan, The LXX version / God is my rock 1990 ➤ 6,1887:
ᴿJJS 42 (1991) 263-6 (Alison *Salvesén*).

1549 **Parker** D. C., Codex Bezae ᴰLeiden. 1990. – ᴿTsTNijm 31 (1991) 91.

1549* *Pazzini* Massimo, La trascrizione dell'ebraico nella versione di TEO-
DOZIONE: LA 41 (1991) 201-222; Eng. 491.

1550 **Sailhamer** J. H., The translational techniques of the Greek Septuagint
for the Hebrew verbs and participles in Psalms 3-41: StBibGreek 2. NY
1991, Lang. xiv-225 p. $45. 0-8204-1030-6 [NTAbs 36,141].

1551 **Salvesen** Alison, SYMMACHUS in the Pentateuch [diss. Oxford 1988]:
JSS Mg 15. Manchester 1991, Univ. xviii-329 p. £30. 0-9516124-2-5 [BL
92,47, J. M. *Dines*; ZAW 104,456, H.-C. *Schmitt*].

1552 *a) Seeligmann* Isaac L., Problems and perspectives in modern Septuagint research [= JbEOL 7 (1940) 359-390], ᵀ*Seeligmann* Judith; – *b)*
Greenspoon Leonard J., Recensions, revision, rabbinics; D. BARTHÉLEMY
and early developments in the Greek traditions: Text 15 (1990) 169-232 /
153-167; ⊕ 10/11s.

Tov E., Greek minor prophets... Nahal Hever 1990 ➤ 3380.

1553 *a) Tov* Emanuel, The CATSS project — a progress report; – *b) Mar-
quis* Galen, The CATSS-base; computer-assisted tools for Septuagint
study for all — transcript of a demonstration; – *c) Bajard* Jean, *Poswick*

R.-Ferdinand, Aspects statistiques des rapports entre la Septante et le texte massorétique: ➤426, Septuagint 7, 1989/91, 157-163 / 165-203 / 123-156.

D4 Versiones orientales.

1554 *Amersfoort* J. van, TATIANUS en de Nederlanden; de invloed van het Diatessaron op enige Middelnederlandse levens van Jezus: NedTTs 45 (1991) 34-45; Eng. 60.

1555 ᴱDirksen P.B., *Mulder* M.J., The Peshitta 1985/8 ➤4,480... 6,1897: ᴿJBL 110 (1991) 150-2 (J.A. *Lund*).

1556 **Falla** Terry C., Key to the Peshitta Gospels 1. (all words beginning with the first four Syriac letters): NTTools 14. Leiden 1991, Brill. xi-136 + 21 p. ƒ110. 90-04-09354-0. – ᴿExpTim 103 (1991s) 56 (J.G. *Snaith*); Muséon 104 (1991) 391s (A. de *Halleux*).

1557 *Hunt* Lucy-Anne, The Syriac Buchanan Bible in Cambridge; book-illumination in Syria, Cilicia and Jerusalem in the later twelfth century: OrChrPer 57 (1991) 331-369; fig. 2-42.

1558 *Isḥaq* Yusif M., ❹ The Syriac translation of Holy Scripture known to the Peshitta: Aram 1 (1989) 318-327.

1559 **Isteero** Albert, 'Abdullāh Muslim IBN QUTAYBA's biblical quotations and their sources; an inquiry into the earliest existing Aramaic Bible translations: diss. Johns Hopkins. Baltimore 1991. 289 p. 91-13683. – DissA 51 (1990s) 4140-A.

1560 *Joosten* Jan, *a*) West Aramaic elements in the Old Syriac and Peshitta Gospels: JBL 110 (1991) 271-289; – *b*) The OT quotations in the Old Syriac and Peshitta Gospels; a contribution to the study of the Diatessaron: Text 15 (1990) 55-78; ❺ 8.

1561 ᴱLane D.J., Leviticus, Numeri (*Hayman* A.P.), Deuteronomium (*Vliet* W.M. van) [+ Josue, *Erbes* J.E.]: VTSyriaca II/1b. Leiden 1991, Brill. xxix-79 p.; xxiv-111 p.; xxiv-99 p.; xix-65 p. ƒ240 [ZAW 104,464].

1562 *Luke* K., Tatian's diatessaron: IndJT [24 (1987) 201-219] 27 (1990) 175-191 [MARMARDJI 1936 Arabic ed. called by C. PETERS 'Gipfel von Unmethode'].

1563 **Lyon** Jeffrey P., Syriac Gospel translations; a comparison of the languages and translation method used in the Old Syriac, the Diatessaron, and the Peshitto: diss. UCLA, ᴰ*Segert* S., 1991. 388 p. 92-06710. – DissA 52 (1991s) 3320-A.

1564 **Bouvarel-Boudhors** Anne, Catalogue des fragments coptes, I. bibliques 1987 ➤ 4,1753 ... 6,1901: ᴿJEA 77 (1991) 233 (M. *Green*).

1565 ᴱDiebner B.J., *Kasser* R., Hamburger Papyrus Bil. 1., Die alttestamentlichen Texte des Papyrus Bilinguis I [Ct-Lam copt.; Eces gr.-copt.] 1989 ➤ 5,1765: ᴿBiblica 72 (1991) 418-421 (M. *Smith*); JTS 42 (1991) 320-5 (K.H. *Kuhn*); Muséon 104 (1991) 206-8 (C. *Detienne*); NRT 113 (1991) 98s (J.-L. *Ska*); RTLv 22 (1991) 67-69 (P.-M. *Bogaert*).

Schenke H., Apg 1-15 koptisch 1991 ➤ 4638.

1566 **Schmitz** F.-J., *Mink* G., Liste der koptischen Handschriften... SahEv 2 [1,1989 ➤ 6,1905], 1/2 ArbNTTf 15. B 1991, de Gruyter. xii + p. 451-1279 [NTAbs 36,111]. – ᴿArTGran 54 (1991) 374 (A. *Torres*); CBQ

53 (1991) 504s (L. S. B. *MacCoull*, 2/1: adds some details about seven 'inaccessible' items).

Isaac E., The Ethiopic history of Joseph 1990 ➤ 2119.
Zuurmond Rochus, NT aethiopice ... Mark 1989 ➤ 4277.

1568 **Minassian** Martiros, Le texte du Nouveau Testament et l'arménien classique; 1. Divergences textuelles des évangiles arméniens; 2. Les mots composés du NT; 3. Examen d'une critique de l'arménien classique. Genève 1990, Fond. Ghoukassiantz. 221 p.
1569 *Bailey* Kenneth, Early Arabic New Testaments of Mt. Sinai and the task of exegesis: NESTR 12 (1991) 45-62.

1570 **Griepentrog** Wolfgang, Synopse der gotischen Evangelientexte: MüSt-SpW Beih 14, 1988 ➤ 4,1764; DM 22,80: ᴿKratylos 36 (1991) 202s (P. *Scardigli*).

D5 Versiones latinae.

1571 *Andreu* F., Il teatino A. AGELLIO e la Volgata Sistina: Regnum Dei 45 (1989) 105-144 [< RHE 86,38*].
Bergren Theodore A., A Latin-Greek index of the Vulgate NT (SCHMOLLER equivalents) 1991 ➤ 1674.
1572 **Bischoff** Bernhard, Latin palaeography; antiquity and Middle Ages [1979 ²1986], ᵀ1990, Univ./Medieval Academy of Ireland ➤ 6,1915: ᴿClasR 41 (1991) 206-8 (B. C. *Barker-Benfield*); JRS 81 (1991) 251s (M. *Gibson*); Speculum 56 (1991) 121s (B. *Ross*).
1573 **Buonocore** Marco, Codices Vaticani latini 9734-9782: 1988 ➤ 4,1767 ['Amatiani']: ᴿGnomon 63 (1991) 599-604 (H. *Walter*).
1573* **Bux** Nicola, Codici liturgici latini di Terra Santa: SBF Museum, 8. Fasano BR(indisi) 1990, Schena. 147 p.; ill. – ᴿLA 41 (1991) 483 (J. P. *Gumbert*).
1574 **Cardon** Bert, *al.*, Typologische taferelen uit het leven van Jezus, a manuscript from the Gold Scrolls Group (Bruges ca. 1440) in the Pierpont Morgan library NY, Ms Morgan 649: Corpus of Illuminated Manuscripts from the Low Countries [ᴱ*Smeyers* Maurits]. Lv 1985, Peeters. 207 p.; 48 fig. + 2 color. [RHE 87,486, R. Van *Schoute*].
1575 *Chapman* Gretel, The Floreffe Bible [1153-6] revisited: Manuscripta 35 (1991) 96-132 + 7 fig.
1576 *Euw* Anton von, Ein fehlendes Blatt im franko-sächsischen Evangeliar Cod. 14 der Kölner Dombibliothek: ➤ 27, ᶠBLOCH P. 1990, 1-8; 6 fig.
1577 ᴱ**Gryson** R., *Bogaert* P.-M., Recherches sur l'histoire de la Bible latine 1987 ➤ 3,544; 6,1925: ᴿBijdragen 52 (1991) 216s (M. *Parmentier*, Eng.: 'historie'; a many-splendoured workshop).
1578 **Henderson** George, From Darrow to Kells; the insular gospel-books. 650-800. L 1987, Thames & H. – ᴿEngHR 106 (1991) 147-9 (A. P. *Smyth*).
1579 **Kross** Renata (Kommentarband), Der Goslarer Evangeliar: Codices selecti 91. Graz 1991, Akad. 258 p.; 118 p. DM 8000 (Komm. nur DM 185). – ᴿErbAuf 67 (1991) 495s (Ursula *Wolf*).

1580 *Kuapiński* R., La Bible de Plock; son manuscrit à la lumière des recherches récentes: Studia Plockie 18 (1990) 237-256 [RHE 87,178*, langue non indiquée].

1581 ᵀᴱ**Labriola** Albert C., *Smeltz* John W., The Bible of the poor = Biblia pauperum, facsimile of British Library C.9 d.2: 1990 → 6,1930: ᴿLvSt 16 (1991) 269s (R. F. *Collins*: in places pre-critical); Manuscripta 35/1 (1991) 66 (Joan A. *Range*); RelStR 17 (1991) 367 (D. R. *Janz*); TS 52 (1991) 589s (Kathleen M. *Irwin*: title unfortunate, dates only from 18th century).

1582 ᴱ**Lindsay** Wallace M., Palaeographia latina 1-6 [= St. Andrews Univ. Publ. 14.16.19s.23.28]. Hildesheim 1989, Olms. 1. 1922, 64 p.; 2,1923, 84 p.; 3. 1924, 66 p.; 4,1925, 85 p.; 5. 1927, 78 p.; 6. 1989, 68 p.; all plus foldouts. 3-487-05308-X.

1583 *Muir* Bernard J., Watching the Exeter Book scribe copy Old English and Latin texts: Manuscripta 35,1 (1991) 3-15 + 7 pl.

1584 *Parker* T. C., Unequally yoked; the present state of the Codex Bobbiensis [Turin Old Latin gospel]: JTS 42 (1991) 581-8.

1585 *Platelle* H., L'évangéliaire de Saint-Mihiel, une nouvelle mise au point par le professeur Ulrich KUDER: MélSR 48 (1991) 231-5.

1586 **Powitz** Gerhardt, Die Frankfurter Gutenberg-Bibel; ein Beitrag zum Buchwesen des 15. Jhrts.: FraBtSchr 3. Fra 1990, Klostermann. 144 p. 'DEM' 28. – ᴿRHE 87 (1991) 272 (J.-F. *Gilmont*).

1587 *Stevick* Robert D., A geometer's art; the full-page illuminations in St. Gallen Stiftsbibliothek Cod. Sang. 51, an insular Gospels book of the vIIIth century: Scriptorium 44 (Bru 1990) 161-192; pl. 17-20.

1588 ᴱ*Zatelli* Ida, La Bibbia a stampa da GUTENBERG a Bodoni: Biblioteca Medicea Laurenziana. F 1991, Biblia. 22 p.

D5.5 *Citationes apud Patres* — the Patristic Bible.

1589 Biblia patristica [4,1987 → 4,1787]; 5. *Basile* de Césarée, *Grégoire* de Nazianze, *Grégoire* de Nysse, *Amphiloque* d'Iconium. P 1991, CNRS centre patr. 409 p. F 230 [< RHE 87,30*]. – ᴿZKG 102 (1991) 114 (W. A. *Bienert*, 4).

1590 ᴱ**Bloch** Denise, *Schlafer* Jacqueline, Catalogue général des manuscrits latins, 7: Nº 3776 à 3835, Homéliaires. P 1988, Bibliothèque Nationale. xx-476 p. F 500. – ᴿRHE 86 (1991) 125s (M. *Haverals*).

1591 **Brooks** James A., The New Testament text of GREGORY of Nyssa [diss. Oxford; close to the Byzantine text]: SBL NT in the Greek Fathers 2. Atlanta 1991, Scholars. xi-267 p. $35; sb./pa. $23. 1-55540-580-1; -1-9 [TDig 39,53].

1592 — **Drobner** H. R., Bibelindex... GREGORS von Nyssa 1988 → 5,g802; 6,k217: ᴿZKG 102 (1991) 114s (W. A. *Bienert*).

1593 **Bux** Nicola, Codici liturgici latini di Terra Santa: SBF Museum 8. ... 1990, Schena. 148 p. (testo italiano e inglese), 112 (color.) ill. – ᴿSMSR 57 (1991) 172-5 (Alessandra *Acconci*).

1593* [*Dorival* Gilles, on pagan references to Septuagint, etc.] in Lectures anciennes de la Bible: Cahiers de Biblia Patristica 1. Strasbourg 1987, Centre Patristique. – ᴿJTS 41 (1990) 230s (Frances M. *Young*: some authors and subjects, sans tit. pp.).

1594 *Kelly* J. F., A catalogue of early medieval Hiberno-Latin commentaries [NT]: Traditio [44 (1988) 537-571] 45 (1989s) 393-434.

1595 ᵀᴱ**Leloir** Louis, Saint EPHREM, Commentaire de l'Évangile Concordant; texte syriaque (Manuscrit C. Beatty 709), folios additionnels: C. Beatty Mg 8. Leuven 1990, Peeters. xxiii-157 p. 90-6831-327-4.

1596 ᴱLowe E.A.,   The Bobbio missal; a Gallican mass-book (MS. Paris.
Lat. 13346), 1920 + (Wilmart André, al.) Notes and studies, 1924: H.
Bradshaw publ. 58+61. Rochester NY 1991, Boydell. xi-198-v-159 p.
$90. 1-870252-00-4 [TDig 39,151].

1597 Peressotti Giuseppe, Letture dei Padri della Chiesa nei breviari del
medioevo; analisi e confronto tra alcuni manoscritti di tradizione
aquileiese e di quella romana: diss. Anselmianum N° 146, ᴰDinell J. R
1990, Pont. Athenaeum S. Anselmi. 214 p.

1598 Sieben Hermann J., Kirchenväterhomilien zum Neuen Testament; ein
Repertorium der Textausgaben und Übersetzungen; Anhang, Kommentare: InstrPatr 22. Haag/Steenbrugge 1991, Nijhoff/Sint-Pietersabdij.
202 p. Fb 1950. – ᴿRHE 86 (1991) 472 (A. de Halleux).

Visonà Giuseppe, Citazioni patristiche e critica testuale neotestamentaria; il
caso di Lc 12,49: AnBib 125, 1990 ➤ 4548.

D6   Versiones modernae   .1   romanicae, romance.

1600 ᴱBogaert Pierre-M., (Cannuyer Christian, al.), Les Bibles en français;
histoire illustrée du moyen âge à nos jours. Turnhout 1991, Brepols.
279 p.; ill. [RHE 87,27*]. 2-503-50059-5.

1601 Chédozeau Bernard, La Bible et la liturgie en français; l'Église tridentine
et les traductions bibliques et liturgiques 1990 ➤ 6,1945; F 195: ᴿEspr-
Vie 101 (1991) 27-29 (É. Cothenet); RBén 101 (1991) 195s (P.-M.
Bogaert); RThom 91 (1991) 672s (B. Montagnes, Ché- en titre, Che- en
texte: oblige à réviser bon nombre d'idées reçues); RTLv 22 (1991) 232-5
(aussi P.-M. Bogaert).

1602 Delforge F., La Bible en France et dans la Francophonie; histoire,
traduction, diffusion: La France au fil des siècles. P/Villiers-le-Bel 1991,
Publisud/Soc.Biblique Française. 383 p.; 25 facsim.; map. F 208 [RHE
87,27*].

1603 Engammare M., Cinquante ans de revision de la traduction biblique
d'Olivétan; les Bibles réformées genevoises en français au XVIᵉ siècle:
BibHumRen 53 (1991) 347-377; 5 fig. [< RHE 86,279*].

1604 ᵀLemaître de Sacy, La Bible [17ᵉ s.], présent. Sellier Philippe: Bouquins.
P 1990, Laffont. 1740 p. F 170. – ᴿEsprVie 101 (1991) 491s (C. Jean-
Nesmy).

1605 Amigo Espada Lorenzo, Biblias en romance y Biblias en ladino;
evolución de un sistema de traducción: CiuD 203 (1990) 111-142.

1606 Cerni Ricardo, AT interlineal hebraico-español I. Pentateuco. Terrasa
1990, Clie. 873 p. 84-7645-397-3. – ᴿEstE 66 (1991) 362s (A. Var-
gas-Machuca).

1607 Nuevo Testamento with NIV on facing pages. GR 1991, Zondervan.
xii-520 p. 0-310-90834-5 [NTAbs 36,257].

1608 Pepoli Carlo, L'Evangeli secònd S. Mattì: Bt Dialettale Bolognese 2.
Bo 1991 [= L 1862], Santarini. 189 p.; ill.

D6.2   Versiones anglicae — English Bible translations.

1609 Cassirer Heinz W., God's new Covenant; a New Testament translation
1989 ➤ 6,1811: ᴿAndrUnS 29 (1991) 79-81 (S. Kubo); BTrans 42 (1991)

144s [R. B. *Bratcher* regrets that he would not 'conform to the fashion of this present world' (Rom 12,2) regarding inclusive language]; Vidyajyoti 55 (1991) 173 (P. M. *Meagher*).

1609* **CEV:** *Doty* S., The Contemporary English Version, a review [less careful exegesis than NIV]: NotTr 5,4 (1991) 48-55 [< NTAbs 36,316, plus similar items].

1610 **Chamberlin** William J., Catalogue of English Bible translations; a classified bibliography of versions and editions, including books, parts, and Old and New Testament Apocrypha and apocryphal books: Bibliographies and Index in Religious Studies 21. NY 1991, Greenwood. xliii-898 p. $125 [NTAbs 36,410]. 0-313-28041-X.

1611 Christian community Bible, Manila 1988 → 6,1957: ᴿIndTSt 27 (1990) 194-6 (L. *Legrand*: beautifully produced and on the whole sound; aggressive rather than ecumenical).

1612 *Collins* Raymond F., Éditions récentes de la Bible en anglais; traits et tendances [26 de la Bible entière + 25 NT, depuis RSV 1952]: RTLv 22 (1991) 226-231.

1613 **Gaus** A., The unvarnished New Testament [translation]. GR 1991, Phanes. 508 p. $25; pa. $15. 0-933999-98-4; -9-2 [NTAbs 36,254].

1614 *Greenspoon* Leonard, It's all Greek to me; the Septuagint in modern English versions of the Bible: → 426, Septuagint 7, 1989/91, 1-21.

1615 ᴱ*Hayford* J. W., *al.*, The Spirit-filled life Bible [King James with notes]. Nv 1991, Nelson. lii-2154 p.; 55 maps. $35. 0-8407-1800-4 [NTAbs 36,258].

1616 **Hogue** W. M., An Authorized Bible for Americans: Anglican and Episcopal History 60 (Austin 1991) 361-382 [< NTAbs 36,161].

1617 **Kim Taejin**, The particle *pa* in the West-Saxon gospels; a discourse-level analysis: diss. Georgia, ᴰ*Klein* J. 1990. 237 p. 91-18146. – DissA 52 (1991s) 525-A.

Lawton D., The Bible in English 1990 → 1344*.

1618 **Lewis** Jack P., The English Bible from KJV to NIV, a history and evaluation² [¹1981]. GR 1991, Baker. 512 p. $22 pa. 0-8010-5666-7 [TDig 39,173].

1619 *Metzger* Bruce M., Recent translations; a survey and evaluation: SWJT 34,2 (1991s) 5-12.

1620 **NAB:** ᴱ**Senior** Donald, Catholic Study Bible 1990 → 6,2039: ᴿHorizons 18 (1991) 313 (Dolores L. *Greeley*: uniquely useful).

1621 **NIV: Verbrugge** Verlyn D., The NIV topical study Bible. L 1989, Hodder & S. xvii-1461 p. + (concordance) 153 p.; 12 maps with finder. 0-340-53778-7.

1622 **NRSV:** The New Revised Standard Bible [eliminating masculine pronouns for common gender and even sometimes for God]. Nv 1990, Holman. – ᴿBTrans 42 (1991) 337-341 (R. L. *Omanson*); RExp 88 (1991) 451s (J. L. *Blevins*); TLond 94 (1991) 357-360 (A. E. *Harvey*: Prov 10,5 'child' for 'son' hardly fits).

1623 — *Kubo Sakae*, The new Revised Standard Version: AndrUnS 29 (1991) 61-69.

1623* — *Lewis* Jack P., Minor prophets in the NRSV: RestQ 33 (1991) 129-140 [< ZIT 91,645].

1624 — *Mendham* P., The new standard?: St Mark's Review 142 (Canberra 1990) 34-37 [37s, *Saunders* R. on gender; *al.* 143 (1990) 34-36: < NTAbs 36,161s].

1625 — *Scholer* D. M., The NRSV: Covenant Quarterly 79,10 (Ch 1990) 12-15 [< NTAbs 36,14].

1626 — **Metzger** Bruce M., *al.*, The making of the New Revised Standard Version of the Bible. GR 1991, Eerdmans. viii-92 p.; group picture. 0-8028-0620-1.
1626* — **Metzger** Bruce M., NRSV exhaustive concordance. Nv 1991, Nelson. xii + 1434 + 90 + 59 + 219 p. 0-8407-6800-1.
1627 — ᴱ**Metzger** Bruce M., *Murphy* Roland E., The New Oxford Annotated Bible with the [NRSV] apocryphal/deuterocanonical books. NY 1991, Oxford-UP. xxxvi-436 p.; maps.
1628 — *Duke* R., Public worship and the use of the NRSV: Prism 6,1 (St. Paul 1991) 37-52 [< NTAbs 36,12: aloud often better than RSV]; further p. 21-28 (*Harrelson* W.), 29-36 (*Throckmorton* B.].
1629 **Orlinsky** Harry M., *Bratcher* Robert G., A history of Bible translation and the North American contribution: SBL BScholNAm 17. Atlanta 1991, Scholars. xv-359 p. $45; sb./pa. $30.
1630 **RNEB:** ᴱ**McHardy** W. D., The Revised [New²] English Bible with the Apocrypha 1989 ↝ 5,1820; 6,1975: ᴿEvQ 63 (1991) 254-7 (H. P. *Scanlin*); JSS 36 (1991) 150-3 (F. F. *Bruce*); OTAbs 14 (1991) 104 (T. P. *McCreesh*); PrPeo 5 (1991) 32s (B. *Robinson*); SWJT 34,3 (1991s) 34s (A. *Fasol*: 'fewer creative translations than NEB and far fewer then NRSV').
1631 — **Coleman** Roger, New light and truth; the making of the Revised English Bible 1989 ↝ 6,1976: ᴿNT 33 (1991) 182-5 (J. K. *Elliott*, also on RNEB itself).
1633 **Robertson** E. H., Makers of the English Bible. 1990, Lutterworth. 222 p. £8 [BL 92,23]. – ᴿTLond 94 (1991) 360s (D. *Coggan*: like BRUCE, an introduction to the many works on that subject).
1634 **Shaw** Susan J., A religious history of Julia Evelina SMITH's 1876 translation of the Holy Bible: diss. Drew, ᴰ*Rowe* K. 1991. 353 p. 91-29316. – DissA 52 (1991s) 1383-A; RelStR 18,174.

D6.3 *Versiones germanicae* — **Deutsche Bibelübersetzungen.**

1635 *Bauer* E., Heinrich HALLER O.Cart. als Bibelübersetzer: AnCart 63 [1990] 212-9.
1636 Das Neue Testament in der deutschen Übersetzung von Martin LUTHER, Studienausgabe I. Text mit Holzschnitten 1545; II. Entstehungsvarianten, Glossar. Stu 1989, Reclam. 380 p. – ᴿBeiNam 26 (1991) 79s (E. *Meineke*).
1637 Hoffnung für alle; das NT. Basel 1991, Brunnen. 373 p. DM 3,90 pa. 3-7655-5839-7 [NTAbs 36,254].
1638 *Masser* A., Die lateinisch-althochdeutsche TATIAN-bilingue des Cod. Sang. 56: NachGö (1991,3) 83-127; 12 facsim. [< RHE 87,40*].
1639 *Rothen* Bernhard, Der Hang zur frommen Lüge; Die Gute Nachricht als Beispiel einer kritiklosen natürlichen Theologie: KerDo 37 (1991) 280-305; Eng. 305s, 'The inclination to the pious lie; a modern "translation" of the Bible as example of uncritical natural theology'.
1640 **Schröder** Ingrid, Die Bugenhagenbibel; Untersuchungen zur Übersetzung und Textgeschichte des Pentateuchs [< Diss. Göttingen]: MDtsF 105. Köln 1991, Böhlau. 479 p. DM 68 [TR 88,255].
1641 **Steurer** Rita M., Das AT, Interlinearübersetzung hebräisch-deutsch 1. Gn-Dt. Neuhausen 1989, Hänssler. xv-1277 p. DM 128. – ᴿTüTQ 171 (1991) 226s (W. *Gross*: an enterprise like this requires more careful execution).
1642 **Stier** Fridolin, Das Neue Testament, ᴱ*Beck* Eleanore *al.* 1989 ↝ 6,1988: ᴿTPQ 139 (1991) 324 (C. *Niemand*); ZkT 113 (1991) 306s (A. *Batlogg*).

1643 — a) *Biser* Eugen, Die Botschaft — hörbar gemacht; zu Fridolin STIERS Übersetzung des NTs; – b) *Kuschel* Karl-Josef, F. Stier als Theologe und Sprachkunstler: StiZt 208 (1990) 135s / 687-702.
1644 **Strohm** Stefan, *al.*, Deutsche Bibeldrucke 1466-1600: Bibelsammlung Landes-Bt. Stu 2/1. Stu-Bad Cannstatt 1987, Frommann-Holzboog. lvi-480 p. DM 720. – ᴿTLZ 116 (1991) 495-7 (M. *Petzoldt*).

D6.4 Versiones nordicae *et variae.*

1645 **Astås** Reidar, An Old Norse biblical compilation; studies in Stjórn ['History Bible']: AmerUnivSt 7/109. NY 1991, Lang. ix-251 p. [RHE 87,191*]. 0-8204-1585-5.
1646 Tre bibelböcker [Gen Prov Jer] i översättning av [Svenska] Bibelkommissionen. Helsingborg 1991, Atlantis. 368 p.; 2 maps. 91-7486-971-X [BL 92,59, G. W. *Anderson*].
1647 *Kyas* Vladimir, Quomodo prologus in bibliam palaeobohemicam ortus sit: → 68, ᶠGRACIOTTI S. 1990, 25-27.
1648 *Rozman* Francè, Translating the Bible (in Slovene): BogVest 50 (1990) 427-442; Eng. 441.
1649 **Saydon** P. P., Bibbja II (Maltese) [I/I 1977 NT; 1982 OT historical books], all the rest, ᴱ*Attard* Carmel. Malta 1990, Museum [BL 92,56, A. *Abela*: Maltese more Semitic than now spoken]
1649* *Shelke* Christopher, Die Bibel in Marathi: NZMissW 47 (1991) 119-127.

D7 *Problemata vertentis* — Bible translation techniques.

1650 *Aejmelaeus* Anneli, Translation technique and the intention of the translator: → 426, Septuagint 7, 1989/90, 23-36.
1650* *Austin* Michael R., The curse of the metaphysical capital: ExpTim 103 (1991s) 104-107 [capitalizing words like Lamb, Son of Man, and especially Spirit is a misleading editorial comment]: cf. p. 109, *Rodd*'s comment on *Hamilton*'s Genesis 1,2 'Spirit [with capital] runs the risk of superimposing trinitarian concepts on Gen 1 that are not necessarily present'.
1651 *Barnwell* K. Procedures for preparing Scriptures for publication: NotTr 4,2 (1990) 38-44 (also 2-37); cognate 5,3 (1991) 23-50, B. *Bradley* [< NTAbs 36,315s].
1651* ᴱ**Beer** Jeanette, Medieval translators and their craft: Studies in Medieval Culture 25. Kalamazoo 1989, Western Michigan Univ. [x-] 428 p. 0-918720-95-8. 15 art.; 2 infra.
1652 *Bons* Eberhard, Die Übersetzung der Bibel: BiKi 45 (1990) 193-9.
1653 *Borutti* Silvana, Traduction et connaissance: RTPhil 123 (1991) 369-393; Eng. 457.
1654 *Buth* Randall, The meturgeman: 'and' or 'but' — so what?: Jerusalem Perspective 4,2 (1991) 13-15.
1655 a) *Carena* Carlo, I turbamenti di San GEROLAMO; – b) *Salanitro* Giovanni, Traduzioni e critica testuale; – c) *Siedl* Suitbertus H., Quid sit versio?: → 597, Traduzione 1988/91, 207-219 / 231-6 / 355-363.
1656 ᴱ**Contamine** Geneviève, Traduction et traducteurs au Moyen Âge 1986/9 → 6,727*a: ᴿRÉByz 49 (1991) 322s (A. *Failler*).
1657 a) *Ellington* John, Wit and humor [the Bible's own: puns, irony...] in Bible translation; – b) *Bascom* Robert A., Recognizing the otherness of the text; avoiding accommodation in translation: BTrans 42 (1991) 301-313 / 314-325.

1658 **Greenstein** Edward L.,   Essays on biblical method and translation 1989
➤ 5,269; 6,2004:   ᴿCritRR 4 (1991) 87-89 (J. S. *Kaminsky*).

1659 ᴱ**Hamesse** Jacqueline, *Fattori* Marta, Rencontres... Traductions et
traducteurs 1989/90 ➤ 6,727*b: ᴿScripTPamp 23 (1991) 1093s (M.
Lluch-Baixauli).

1660 **Howsam** Leslie,   Cheap Bibles; nineteenth-century publishing and the
British and Foreign Bible Society: Studies in Publishing and Printing
History. C 1991, Univ. xviii-245 p.; 18 fig. 0-521-39339-6.

1660* *Janowitz* Naomi, The rhetoric of translation; three early perspectives
on translating Torah: HarvTR 84 (1991) 129-140.

1661 ᴱ**Krawutschke** Peter W., Translation and interpreter training 1989
➤ 6,351 wrongly Krawutscke and index wrongly Krawutsche.

1661* *McKerras* R., Don't put out the fire: NotTr 5,2 (1991) 1-20 [< NTAbs
36,317: striving for accuracy makes for dullness or even distortion].

1662 **Margot** Jean-Claude, Traducir sin traicionar 1987 ➤ 5,1858: ᴿRTLim
25 (1991) 492s (J. *Picasso*).

1662* *Mavrofides* S., ☺ The corrective translation of the Hebrew Bible: DeltioVM 10,2 (1991) 5-14.

1663 *Meurer* Siegfried, Die Notwendigkeit ökumenischer Bibelübersetzungen
und ihre Grenzen: ➤ 75, ᶠHERRMANN S., Prophetie 1991, 263-9.

1664 *Ott* W., Section-titles in printed Scripture: NotTr 4,3 (Dallas 1990)
34-49 [< NTAbs 36,14].

1665 *Prickett* S., The changing Bible [translations betray theological pre-
suppositions]: LitTOx 5 (1991) 322-7 [< NTAbs 36,161].

1666 *a*) *Salevsky* Heidemarie, Theory of Bible translation and general theory
of translation; – *b*) *Corro* Anicia del, The use of figurative language; – *c*)
Nida Eugene A., Paradoxes of translation; – *d*) *Larson* Mildred L.,
Indigenizing the translation process [*Kenyoro* Musimbi]; – *e*) *Luzbetak*
Louis, Roman Catholics, Bible societies, and Bible translation: BTrans
42 (1991) 101-114 / 114-127 [April 1991 special issue 2A exceptionally
paginated] (2-)5-27 / (25-) 27-34 [47-56] / 41-47.

1667 *Schenker* Adrian, Was übersetzen wir? Fragen zur Textbasis, die sich
aus der Textkritik ergeben [< ᴱ*Gnilka* J., Übersetzung der Bibel 1985,
65-80]: ➤ 258, Text 1991, 247-262.

1668 **Smalley** William A., Translation as mission; Bible translation in the
modern missionary movement: Modern Mission Era. Macon GA 1991,
Mercer Univ. xiii-297 p. $20.65 [TR 88,80]. – ᴿCathHR 77 (1991) 663-5
(A. A. *Di Lella*: fascinating).

1669 *Smith* Jill, Footnotes and glossaries: BTrans 42 (1991) 414-420.

1670 *Toivanen* Aarne, A Bible translation as the communicator of alien
culture: Temenos 26 (Helsinki 1990) 129-138 [< zIT 91,403].

1671 *Ugang* Hermogenes, *Soesilo* Daud, Are honorific terms of address
necessary in the Indonesian Bible?: BTrans 42 (1991) 442-7.

1672 *Waard* Jan de, Traduction et altération; l'interprète en quête de fidélité:
RHPR 71 (1991) 151-168; Eng. 269.

1673 **Young** Frances, The art of performance; towards a [pre-translation] theology of Holy Scripture. L 1990, Darton-LT. ix-198 p. £10. 0-232-
51779-7. – ᴿBTrans 42 (1991) 147 (P. *Ellingworth*).

D8 *Concordantiae, lexica specialia* – **Specialized dictionaries, synopses.**

1674 **Bergren** Theodore A., A Latin-Greek index of the Vulgate NT [i.e. each
Greek word of *Schmoller* A., Handkonkordanz ³1989 listed alphabetically

under Vulgate equivalent], with an index of Latin equivalences characteristic of 'African' and 'European' Old Latin versions of the NT: SBL Resources 26. Atlanta 1991, Scholars. xiii-207 p. [NTAbs 36,250]. 1-55540-614-9.

1675 [*Bertinetti* Giovanni, 'worked on' [8]1957; the only author mentioned in the history of this pre-[2]1893 work], Chiave Biblica ossia Concordanza della Sacra Scrittura compilata sulla versione riveduta[9]. T 1991, Claudiana. [viii-] 753 p.

1676 [E]**Clapp** P. S., *Friberg* B. & T., Analytical concordance of the Greek NT, I. Lexical focus [alphabetical but subdivided into grammatical forms]; 2. Grammatical focus: Greek NT Library 2s. GR 1991, Baker. xxxiii-2619 p.; xii-2215 p. $95 each. 0-8010-2548-6; -9-4 [NTAbs 36,252].

1677 Itifaki ya Biblia [Konkordanz zur (Swahili-) Bibel]. Dodoma 1990, Central Tanganyika Press. 776 p. [TLZ 117,101, Irmtraud *Herms*].

1678 **Kohlenberger** John R[III], The NRSV concordance unabridged, including the apocryphal [i.e., only] deuterocanonical books. GR 1991, Zondervan. xvi-1483 + 76 (particles) + 53 (footnotes) + 76 (topics). 0-310-53910-2 [BL 92,14s, A. G. *Auld*].

1679 *Lang* M. H. de, Jean GERSON's Harmony of the Gospels [Monotessaron] (1420): Ned/Dutch Review of Church History 71 (Leiden 1991) 37-49 [< NTAbs 36,166: used AUGUSTINE's De consensu; not at all TATIAN].

Metzger Bruce: NRSV exhaustive concordance 1991 → 1626*.

1680 **Rinaldi** Giancarlo, Biblia gentium 1989 → 5,1872; 6,2028: [R]AugR 30 (1990) 489s (M. *Simonetti*); Bijdragen 52 (1991) 445 (M. *Parmentier*, Eng.: a unique achievement, showing massive toil; though most of the quotations come from Celsus, Porphyry, Julian; and the best or latest editions are not always used; nor DI BERARDINO); BStLat 21 (1991) 71s (A. V. *Nazzaro*); ColcT 60,3 (1990) 184-8 (J. *Gliściński*, ❷); Tarbiz 60 (1990s) 451-467 (D. *Rokéaḥ* ❸; Eng. VII-VIII).

IV. → K1	V. Exegesis generalis VT vel cum NT

D9   **Commentaries on the whole Bible or OT.**

Annotated Study Bibles: NAB → 1620; NIV → 1621; NRSV → 1627 [RNEB → 1992].

1681 *a*) [E]**Bergant** Dianne, *Karris* R. J., Collegeville Bible Commentary 1989 → 5,1876; 6,2031: [R]PrPeo 4 (1990) 202s (R. *Duckworth*); StMonast 33 (1991) 171s (R. *Ribera-Mariné*).

— *b*) [E]**Criswell** W. A., *al.*, The believer's study Bible (New King James). Nv 1991, Nelson. xxii-1987 p.; (195 p. concordance); 57 maps. $35 [NTAbs 36,409].

— *c*) [E]**Douglas** J. D., [NT, [E]*Comfort* P. W.] New commentary on the whole Bible [< *Jamieson* R. †1880, *Fausset* A. †1910, *Brown* D. †1897]. Wheaton IL 1990, Tyndale. xiii-813 p. $25. 0-8423-4731-3 [NTAbs 36,411].

1682 **Federici** T., Per conoscere Lui 1987 → 3,216...6,2033: [R]Antonianum 66 (1991) 446 (T. *Larrañaga*, ciclo B).

1683 [E]**Gaebelin** Frank E., The Expositor's Bible commentary with NIV, 5. Psalms [to] Song of Songs. GR 1991, Zondervan. xvi-1244 p. $35. 0-310-36470-1 [TDig 39,59: eleventh of the 12 volumes to appear].

1684 **Longman** Tremper[III], Old Testament commentary survey. GR 1991, Baker. 160 p. $11. 0-8010-5670-5 [BL 92,18, R. A. *Mason*: appreciative but humorously unsatisfied].
1685 **ᴱMays** James L., Harper's Bible Commentary 1988 → 4,1895 ... 6,2035: ᴿJAOS 111 (1991) 186s (F. L. *Moriarty*); PrzPow 831 (1990) 330-4 (W. *Chrostowski*, also on Harper's Bible Dictionary 1985).
1686 **NJBC:** New Jerome Biblical Commentary, ᴱ**Brown** R. E., *al.*, 1989 → 5,384; 6,2036: ᴿBijdragen 52 (1991) 437s (J. *Lambrecht*); Horizons 18 (1991) 143s (G. S. *Sloyan*); IndTSt 27 (1990) 351s (M. D. *Ambrose*, brief); LavalTP 47 (1991) 286 (P.-É. *Langevin*); Month 252 (1991) 113s (J. *Ashton*); PrPeo 5 (1991) 33-35 (R. *Robinson*); RB 98 (1991) 134-6-7 (G. J. *Norton*, OT; J. *Murphy-O'Connor*, NT); ZkT 113 (1991) 85 (G. *Fischer*: in 12 Zeilen, wie ungefähr für 13 AT-Bücher).
1687 **Owens** John J., Analytical key to the OT, 1. Gn-Jos 1990 → 6,2038: ᴿAndrUnS 29 (1991) 182s (J. B. *Doukhan*); GraceTJ 11 (1990) 232s (J. L. *Crawford*); RelStR 17 (1991) 345 (W. Lee *Humphreys*: caution); VT 41 (1991) 512 (Judith M. *Hadley*: refers to page where BDB *begins* a word instead of to the *relevant* page).
1688 **Owens** John J., Analytical key to the OT 3. Ezra - Song of Solomon. GR 1991, Baker. xi-660 p. $40. 0-8010-6715-4 [TDig 39,77].
1689 **Quinzio** Sergio, Un commento alla Bibbia[2] [[1]1972-6]: Saggi NS 5. Mi 1991, Adelphi. 820 p. Lit. 60,000. 88-459-0864-X.

VI. Libri historici VT

E1 **Pentateuchus, Torah** .1 *Textus, commentarii.*

1690 **Boorer** Suzanne, The promise of the land [Ex 13,5 ...] as oath; a key to the formation of the Pentateuch [Diss. Emory, ᴰ*Tucker* G. Atlanta 1991. 519 p. 91-27579. – DissA 52 (1991s) 1386-A; RelStR 18,172; RTLv 23, p. 538; OIAc 2,15]: BZAW 205. B 1992, de Gruyter. xv-470 p.
1691 ᵀᴱ**Davis** Avrohom, The Metsudah Chumash, a new linear translation, with RAŠI, ᵀ*Kleinkaufman* Avrohom. Hoboken 1991 Ktav. I. Bereishis. ix-575 p. $27.50. 0-88125-389-8 [BL 92,53, S. C. *Reif*; TDig 39,254].
1692 **Finkel** Avraham Y., The great Torah commentators. Northvale NJ 1990, Aronson. xi-256 p. 0-87668-841-5.
1693 **Kraus Reggiani** C., La creazione: FILONE, La filosofia mosaica ... 1987 → (4,a984) 5,1893; 6,2045*: ᴿAugM 35 (1990) 201s (J. *Oroz*); CiuD 203 (1991) 497s (J. *Gutiérrez*).
1694 **Malbim** (Meir Loeb ben Jehiel Michael), Ha-Torah ve-ha-Mitzvah (commentary on the Pentateuch, the Mekhilta, Sifra and Sifrei). TA 1978. I. 828 p.; II. p. 829-1743.
1695 ᴱ**Shavel** H., ḤIZZEKUNI (Ḥezekiah ben Manoah) on the Torah. J 1987, Mosad Kook. 650 p.

E1 *Pentateuchus* .2 **Introductio; Fontes JEDP.**

1696 *Ausín* Santiago, La composición del Pentateuco; estado actual de la investigación crítica: ScripTPamp 23 (1991) 171-183.
1697 **Berge** Kåre, Die Zeit des Jahwisten; ein Beitrag zur Datierung jahwistischer Vätertexte [ᴰ1985, ᴰ*Bjørndalen* A.]: BZAW 186, 1990 → 6,2048: ᴿJBL 110 (1991) 501-3 (J. *Van Seters*: grounds for exciting

debate); TLZ 116 (1991) 174-6 (M. *Rose*); ZAW 103 (1991) 293 (H.-C. *Schmitt*).

1698 ᴱ**Bloom** H., text ᵀ*Rosenberg* D., The book of J, 1990 ➤ 6,2055: ᴿCCurr 41 (1991s) 410-3 (Y. *Gitay*); CritRR 4 (1991) 126s (R. E. *Friedman*: 'an unfortunate step in Bloom's career'; omits much that is J, includes much that is not); RExp 88 (1991) 453s (J. D. W. *Watts*); TTod 48 (1991s) 234 . 236 . 238 . 240 (W. *Brueggemann*).

1699 **Coote** Robert B., In defense of revolution; the Elohist history. Mp 1991, Fortress. x-150 p. $11. 0-8006-2496-3 [TDig 39,155].

1700 **Coote** R., *Ord* D., [➤ 1757] The Bible's first history [J] 1989 ➤ 6,2049: ᴿInterpretation 45 (1991) 73 (R. G. *Boling*); ScotJT 44 (1991) 403s (M. C. *Tower*: clear, but final 'implications' could have been more systematic; and *mal'ak* not rendered 'genie').

1701 **Levin** Christoph, Der Jahwist: ev. Hab-Diss. Göttingen 1991, ᴰ*Smend* R. – TR 87 (1991) 512.

1702 **Paran** Meir, ❹ Forms of the priestly style in the Pentateuch, intr. *Haran* M., 1989 ➤ 6,2053: ᴿJBL 110 (1991) 503s (F. E. *Greenspahn*: at least will preclude continuing to call P 'dry; legalistic').

1703 ᴱ**Pury** Albert de, Le Pentateuque en question 1987/9 ➤ 5,601; 6,2053 [ed. 2 corrigée. Genève 1991, Labor et Fides. 421 p. Fs 60] : ᴿAntonianum 65 (1990) 661s (M. *Nobile*); EstudosB 30 (1991) 74-78 (L. *Garmus*); Henoch 13 (1991) 101-8 (P. *Sacchi*); RTLv 22 (1991) 78s (P.-M. *Bogaert*); Salesianum 53 (1991) 589s (M. *Cimosa*); ScripTPamp 23 (1991) 705s (S. *Ausín*).

1704 **Ska** Jean Louis, Un nouveau Wellhausen? [BLUM E. (1984) 1990, Studien zur Komposition des Pentateuch ➤ 2133]: Biblica 72 (1991) 253-263.

1705 **Wenham** G. J., Method in Pentateuchal source criticism: VT 41 (1991) 84-109.

E1.3 *Pentateuchus,* **themata.**

1706 *Dozeman* Thomas B., The institutional setting of the late formulation of the Pentateuch in the work of John VAN SETERS: ➤ 446, SBL Sem 30 (1991) 253-263 (264s, Van Seters).

1707 *a) García López* Félix, Dalla Torah al Pentateuco; – *b) Boschi* Bernardo G., Origini della Torah e Pentateuco; – *c) Prato* Gian Luigi, L'esclusivismo jahwista alle origini storico-religiose della Torah; – *d) Cardellini* Innocenzo, Dalla Legge alla Torah, una ipotesi di studio; – *e) Garbini* Giovanni, Torah e Mosè; – *f) Vivian* Angelo, Il concetto di Legge nel Rotolo del Tempio: RicStoBib 3,1 (1991) 11-36 / 27-40 / 41-55 / 57-81 / 63-96 / 97-114.

1708 *Gordon* Robert P., Compositeness, conflation and the Pentateuch [TIGAY J. 1985]: JStOT 51 (1991) 57-69.

1709 **Gorman** Frank H., Ideology of ritual... P: JStOT supp. 91, ᴰ1990 ➤ 6,2059: RÉTRel 66 (1991) 272s (Françoise *Smyth*); Interpretation 45 (1991) 418 (T. W. *Mann*); JTS 42 (1991) 626s (G. J. *Wenham*).

1710 **Hallo** William W., The book of the people [chiefly the five introductory essays to his Torah 1974-83]: BrownJudSt 225. Atlanta 1991, Scholars. x-220 p. $60; sb. $40. 1-55540-591-6 [TDig 39,167].

1711 **Halpern** Baruch, The first historians 1988 ➤ 4,d139 ... 6,2062: ᴿJNES 50 (1991) 215-7 (N. P. *Lemche*: the biblical historians tried to write history, but it was far removed from what actually happened); JQR 82 (1991s) 550-4 (R. *Polzin*).

1712 **Honigwachs** Y., The unity of Torah; a commentary on the organization and purpose of the five books, I. J/NY 1991, Feldheim. 350 p. 0-87306-802-5 [BL 92,74, S. C. *Reif*].

1713 **Köckert** Matthias, Leben vor Gott; Studien zum Verständnis des Gesetzes in der deuteronomischen und priesterlichen Literatur des Alten Testaments: Hab.-Diss. Jena 1991, ᴰ*Smend* R. – TR 87 (1991) 512.

1714 **Mann** Thomas W., The book of the Torah; the narrative integrity of the Pentateuch 1988 ➤ 4,1928; 6,2068: ᴿCBQ 53 (1991) 110s (M. F. *Fischer*).

1715 **Metzler** Ed., Discovering Mosaistics; introduction to the scientific study of the law of Moses and Mosaical antiquity. Herborn 1990, Baalschem. 224 p. 3-924448-08-6. – ᴿBO 48 (1991) 879s (J. A. *Soggin*: weird).

1716 *a) Nicholson* E. W., The Pentateuch in recent research; a time for caution; – *b) Schmidt* Werner H., Elementare Erwägungen zur Quellenscheidung im Pentateuch; – *c) Blum* Erhard, Gibt es die Endgestalt des Pentateuch?; – *d) Van Seters* John, The so-called Deuteronomic redaction of the Pentateuch?: ➤ 429, IOSOT 1989/91, 10-23 / 22-45 / 46-57 / 58-77.

1717 *Osten-Sacken* Peter von der, 'Tora des Mose vom Sinai'; Pentateuchstruktur und rabbinisches Toraverständnis: ➤ 78, ᶠHRUBY K., Judaica 47,1 (1991) 8-11.

1718 **Weber** Reinhard, Eusebes logismos; Studien zum Verständnis und zur Funktion der Thora im hellenistischen Judentum: ev. Hab.-Diss. Göttingen, ᴰ*Stegemann*, 1991. – TR 87 (1991) 312.

1719 *Wevers* John W., The Göttingen Pentateuch; some post-partem [partum? Exodus now finished] Pentateuch: ➤ 426, Septuagint 7, 1989/91, 51-60.

    E1.4 **Genesis;** *textus, commentarii.*

1720 **Baldwin** Joyce G., The message of Genesis 12-50; from Abraham to Joseph: The Bible Speaks Today. Leicester/DG 1986, Inter-Varsity. 224 p. 0-85110-759-1/US 0-87784-298-1.

1721 **Cattani** L., RASHI, Commento alla Genesi 1985 ➤ 1,1948: ᴿProtestantesimo 46 (1991) 326s (J. A. *Soggin*).

1722 **Dattler** Frederico, Génesis, texto e comentário 1984 ➤ 1,1951: ᴿRCuBíb 13,51s (1989) 170-3 (J. *Salvador*).

1723 **Díez Macho** Alejandro, Targum palaestinense ... Jonathan / hisp., 1. Genesis 1988 ➤ 6,2080: ᴿBZ 35 (1991) 303 (J. *Maier*: monumental).

1724 ᵀᴱ**Fox** Everett, Genesis and Exodus, a new English rendition, with commentary and notes. NY c. 1990, Schocken. 457 p. $17 pa. [Interp 45,333].

1725 **Hamilton** Victor P., The Book of Genesis, chapters 1-17: NICOT, 1990 ➤ 6,2082*: ᴿAsbTJ 46,2 (1991) 91-93 (J. N. *Oswalt*); ExpTim 103 (1991s) 109 (C. S. *Rodd*: 'loosening of conservative rigidities', unlike Robertson's Nicot Nahum ?with Jonah); RExp 88 (1991) 452 (J. D. W. *Watts*: evangelical, important); SWJT 34,3 (1991s) 36 (D. G. *Kent*).

1726 ᵀᴱ**Harl** Marguerite, La Genèse ... Septante 1986 ➤ 2,1384* ... 5,1921: ᴿTAth 62 (1991) 904-7 (P. *Simotas*, Ⓖ).

1726* *McAllister* Patricia A., Apocryphal narrative elements in the Genesis of the Middle Low German Historienbibel Helmstedt 611.1: ➤ 1651*, Medieval Translators 1988, 81-92.

1727 **Neusner** Jacob, Confronting creation; how Judaism reads Genesis; an anthology of Genesis Rabbah. Columbia 1991, Univ. S. Carolina. xii-385 p. $25. 0-87249-732-1 [NTAbs 36,138].

1728 **Petit** Françoise, [➤ 2,1388 Catenae 1986] La Chaîne sur la Genèse, édition intégrale: Traditio Exegetica Graeca 1. Lv 1991, Peeters. – I, ch. 1 à 3, xxxvii (+ 3 facsim.) – 340 p. 90-6831-375-4. – ᴿVizVrem 51 (1990) 228-230 (A. I. *Sidorov* Ⓑ: 1986).

1728* *Reinhardt* Klaus, La Expositio in Genesim de fray Luis de León a la luz del manuscrito 19 de la Biblioteca capitular de Palencia: ➤ 92, ᶠLEÓN L. de, CiuD 204 (1991) 937-945.

1729 **Soggin** J. Alberto, Genesi: CommStoEseg 1/1. Genova 1991, Marietti. I. 221 p. 88-211-6720-8.

1730 ᵀᴱ**Strickman** H. N., *Silver* A. M., IBN EZRA's commentary on ... Genesis 1988 ➤ 6,2047 (Vol. 1): ᴿBL (1991) 79 (S. C. *Reif*: useful though U. SIMON's latest work not included).

1731 ᵀᴱ**Teske** Roland J., Saint AUGUSTINE on Genesis; two books on Genesis against the Manichees and On the literal interpretation of Genesis, an unfinished book: Fathers 84. Wsh 1991, Catholic University of America. xiii-198 p. $28. 0-8132-0084-9 [TDig 39,47]. – ᴿAugSt 22 (1991) 223-230 (R. J. *O'Connell*).

1732 ᵀᴱ**Townsend** John T., Midrash Tanhuma, I. [Lectionary readings from] Genesis. Hoboken 1989, KTAV. xvii-334 p. $39.50. – ᴿAnglTR 73 (1991) 205-7 (P. *Culbertson*).

1733 **Westermann** C., Genesis [1850 pages reduced to 338], ᵀ*Green* D. 1987 ➤ 3,1906 ... 6,2095: ᴿScripB 21 (1991) 17s (A. *Graffy*).

1734 **Westermann** Claus, Genesi [sintesi], ᵀ*Riccio* A. CasM 1990, Piemme. 342 p. Lit. 50.000. – ᴿProtestantesimo 46 (1991) 212s (D. *Garrone*).

E1.5   *Genesis, themata.*

1735 **Baruk** Henri, Le message des patriarches hébreux. 1990. – ᴿRÉJ 150 (1991) 455s (Élisabeth *Couteau*).

1736 **Brisman** Leslie, The voice of Jacob; on the composition of Gen 1990 ➤ 6,2098: ᴿJRel 71 (1991) 427 (M. C. *Douglas*).

1737 **Erffa** Hans M. von, Ikonologie der Genesis I, 1989 ➤ 6,2099: ᴿJTS 42 (1991) 289-297 (B. *Murdoch*); TLZ 116 (1991) 133s (W. *Wischmeyer*).

1738 **Fokkelman** Jan P., Narrative art in Genesis; specimens of stylistic and structural analysis² [¹1975]: Biblical Seminar 12. Sheffield 1991, Academic. xvi-244 p. £15. 1-85075-311-3.

1739 **Jong** Saskia de, Onvruchtbare moeders; een feministische lezing van Genesis. Boxtel/Brugge ᴰ1989, KBS/Tabor. 110 p. ƒ19,90. 90-6173-454-1 / 90-6597-284-6. – ᴿBijdragen 52 (1991) 453 (W. *Straatman*); TsTNijm 31 (1991) 426s (C. *Halkes*).

1740 *a*) *Kselman* H., The book of Genesis; a decade of scholarly research; – *b*) *Santmire* H. Paul, The Genesis creation narratives reconsidered; themes for a global age; – *c*) *Mann* Thomas W., 'All the families of the earth'; the theological unity of Genesis: Interpretation 45 (1991) 380-392 / 366-379 / 341-353.

1741 **Michaud** Robert, Los Patriarcas, historia y teología³ [¹1976], ᵀ*Asurmendi Ruiz* Jesús M.: Buena noticia 2. Estella 1991, VDivino. 244 p. 84-7151-096-0.

1742 **Portnoy** Stephen, *Petersen* David L., Statistical differences among documentary sources [RADDAY Y., Gn. Authorship Study 1985]: JStOT 50 (1991) 3-14 [checked by MANOVA, does not disprove J-E distinction].

1743 **Rendsburg** G. A.,   The redaction of Genesis 1986 ➤ 2,1412 ... 6,2105:
  RWeltOr 22 (1991) 170s (T. *Podella*: based on FISHBANE, SASSON,
  CASSUTO and SARNA).
1744 **Rogerson** J., Genesis 1-11: OT Guides. Sheffield 1991, JStOT. 87 p. £6.
  1-85075-274-5 [BL 92,87, R. *Davidson*].
1745 *Şimmudi* Joseph, ❷ The uses of *mubla'ot* in the chapters of Genesis:
  BethM 36,126 (1990s) 235-249. [*mubla'* means 'mingled', 'incidental' and
  mubla'ah 'enclave'].
1746 **Steinmetz** Devora, From father to son; kinship, conflict, and continuity
  in Genesis: Luterary currents in biblical interpretation. Louisville 1991,
  W-Knox. 223 p. $16 [TR 88,162]. 0-664-25116-1.
1747 TE**Thoma** Clemens, *Lauer* Simon, Die Gleichnisse der Rabbinen II.
  Von der Erschaffung der Welt bis zum Tod Abrahams, Bereschit Rabba
  1-63: Judaica et Christiana 13. Bern 1991, P. Lang. 426 p. 3-261-
  04396-2.
1747* *Thoma* C., Die jüdisch-christliche Sicht der Schöpfung: ➤ 530,
  Schöpfung 1989/90, 9-20.
1748 **Thompson** Thomas L., The origin tradition [Gn & Ex 1-23] 1987
  ➤ 3,1917 ... 6,2107: RBZ 35 (1991) 285-7 (J. *Scharbert*: faces current
  exegesis superficially).
1749 E**Vanetti** Pietro, Genesi: Fumetti d'Arte. Mi 1990. 199 p. Lit. 32.500.
  – RCC 142 (1991,1) 632 (C. *Giachi*).
1750 **White** Hugh C., Narration and discourse in the Book of Genesis. C
  1991, Univ. XIII-312 p. £35 [TR 88,74; ZAW 104,315, H. C. *Schmitt*].
  0-521-39020-6. – RExpTim 103 (1991s) 23 (G. *Lloyd Jones*: structuralism;
  difficult but rewarding).
1751 E**Williams** Michael E., The storyteller's companion to the Bible, 1.
  Genesis. Nv 1991, Abingdon. 201 p. $11 [CBQ 54,206].
1752 **Wright** Logan S., Reported speech in Hebrew narrative; a typology and
  analysis of texts in the book of Genesis: diss. Emory, D*Buss* M. Atlanta
  1991. 486 p. 91-27632. – DissA 52 (1991s) 1375-A; RelStR 18,173; RTLv
  23, p. 541.

          E1.6   **Creatio,** *Genesis 1s.*

1752* **Anderson** B., Creation versus chaos [= 1967 + Cosmic dimension, lectures 1987]. Ph 1987, Fortress. 210 p. – RRelStT 9,2s (1989) 85-87 (Donna R. *Runnels*).
1753 **Atkinson** David, The message of Gn 1-11, the dawn of creation:
  The Bible Speaks Today. Leicester/DG 1990, Inter-Varsity. 190 p.
  0-85110-676-5 / US 0-8308-1229-6. – RGraceTJ 12,1 (1991, not 1992
  as top of page) 119 (D. B. *DeYoung*); RSWJT 34,3 (1991s) 35s (B.
  Heflin).
1754 *Bolewski* Jacek, ❷ The Ignatian dimension of the truth about creation:
  Bobolanum 2 (1991) 111-148; franç. 159.
1755 **Bonora** A., La creazione, Dio, il cosmo, l'uomo: Coscienza. R 1990,
  Studium. 162 p. – RScripTPamp 23 (1991) 1061s (J. *Morales*: 'Borona',
  también p. 755; ometido p. 159).
1756 *Bucher* Gérard, Retour à la Genèse [... réactualiser un mythe?]: RHPR
  71 (1991) 297-308; Eng. 421.
1757 **Coote** Robert B. [➤ 1699s], *Ord* David R., In the beginning; creation
  and the Priestly history. Mp 1991, Fortress. x-182 p. $13. 0-8006-
  2527-7 [TDig 39,155].

1758 *Deist* Ferdinand, Genesis 1-11; oppression and liberation: JTSAf 73 (1990) 3-11 [biblical anthropology a needed frame for use of exodus in liberation theology].

1759 **Eberlein** Karl, Gott der Schöpfer – Israels Gott...: BErfAJ 1989 ➤ 2,1423 ... 5,1960: RColcT 61,1 (1991) 161-3 (W. *Chrostowski* ❷).

1760 *a) Green* Garrett, Myth, history, and imagination; the creation narratives in Bible and theology; – *b) Ollenburger* Ben C., We believe in God... maker of heaven and earth; metaphor, Scripture, and theology; ➤ 435, HorBT 12,2 (1990) 19-38 / 64-96.

1761 *Herrmann* W., [Gn 14; Ps 19; Amos...] Wann wurde Jahwe zum Schöpfer der Welt?: UF 23 (1991) 165-180.

1762 *a) McFague* Sallie, Cosmology and Christianity; implications of the common creation story for theology; – *b) Gustafson* James M., Theological anthropology and the human sciences; – *c) Schüssler Fiorenza* Francis, The crisis of hermeneutics and Christian theology; – *d) Maimela* Simon S., Black theology and the quest for a God of liberation: ➤ 85*d*, FKAUFMAN G., 19-40 / 61-77 / 117-140 / 141-159.

1763 *McVey* Kathleen E., The use of Stoic cosmogony in THEOPHILUS of Antioch's Hexaemeron: ➤ 58, FFROEHLICH K. 1991, 32-58.

1764 *Maranesi* P., La 'triplex veritas' BONAVENTURIANA di Hexaëmeron IV-V 22 e riunificazione del sapere cristiano: ColcFr 61 (1991) 149-176 [< RHE 86,296*].

1765 *Monloubou* L., Sens biblique de la création: EsprVie 101 (1991) 170-3 [< BLitEc 1991].

1766 *Morrone* Fortunato, 'La creazione; tra teologia e filosofia' [Catanzaro 23-26.IX.1991]: RasT ForumATI 32 (1991) 526-531.

1767 **Naldini** Mario, BASILIO di Cesarea, Sulla Genesi (Omelie sull'Esamerone) 1990 ➤ 6,2126; 88-04-33074-0. – RMaia 43 (1991) 233 (A. *Ceresa-Gastaldo*).

1768 — *Romano* Roberto, Per la fortuna dell'Hexahemeron di Basilio: StTardAnt 8 (1989) 245-253.

1769 *Peinado Muñoz* Miguel, Génesis y Ecología [... lectura ecológica del Génesis]: EstE 66 (1991) 397-414.

1770 **Roh Se Young,** Creation and redemption in Priestly theology: diss. Drew. Madison NJ 1991. 257 p. 92-13375. – DissA 52 (1991s) 4366-A.

1771 *Samuelson* Norbert M., MAIMONIDES' doctrine of creation: HarvTR 84 (1991) 249-271.

1772 *a) Samuelson* Norbert M., Creation in medieval philosophical, rabbinic commentaries; – *b) Fishbane* Michael, Some forms of divine appearance in ancient Jewish thought: ➤ 56, FFOX M. 2 (1991) 231-259 / 261-270.

1773 **Savasta** Carmelo, Forme e strutture in Genesi I-II: Proposte, 1988 ➤ 5,1975; 6,2132: RRB 98 (1991) 459s (J. *Loza*: remarques intéressantes d'un amateur avoué).

1774 *Schmid* Hans H., Anspruch und Grenze der Verantwortung; eine Betrachtung zur jahwistischen Urgeschichte: ➤ 163, FWAGNER S., Gottesvolk 1991, 136-142.

1775 *Schwartz* Dov, ❺ The fourteenth-century neoplatonic trend in Jewish doctrine of creation: Tarbiz 60 (1990s) 593-623; Eng. IV.

1776 **Schwarz** Hans, Die biblische Urgeschichte; Gottes Traum von Mensch und Welt 1989 ➤ 5,1976; 6,2134: RColcT 60,2 (1990) 178-182 (J.W. *Roslon*, ❷).

1777 *Simoens* Yves, La création selon l'Écriture: Christus 37 (P 1990) 290-303.

1778 *Thoma* C., Die jüdisch-christliche Sicht der Schöpfung: → 530, [E]*Mensen* B., Die Schöpfung in den Religionen [... Islam, Hindu, China] 1989/90, 9-20 [*al.*].

1779 **Trigo** P., Creation and history. Mkn 1991, Orbis. xix-267 p. $40; pa. $17. 0-88344-737-1; -6-3 [NTAbs 36,145].

1780 **Vannier** Marie-Anne, 'Creatio', 'conversio', 'formatio' chez saint AUGUSTIN: Paradosis 31. FrS 1991, Univ. xxxviii-238 p. [TR 88,341]. 2-8271-0544-6.

1781 *Vannier* Marie-Anne, Aspects de l'idée de création chez S. AUGUSTIN: RevSR 65 (1991) 213-225.

1782 *a*) *Vannier* Marie-Anne, El papel del hexamerón en la interpretación agustiniana de la creación; – *b*) *Putney* Richard H., La cosmogonia agustiniana en la biblia de san Huberto; – *c*) *Teske* Roland J., El Homo spiritualis en el De Genesi contra Manichaeos; – *d*) *Lee* Arthur R., Revisión de la taxonomía numérica; John GRIFFITH, el análisis cladístico y las Quaestiones in Heptateuchum de san AGUSTÍN: → 540, AugM 36 (1991) 343-355 / 213-221; 1 pl. / 305-310 / 163-171 [todos [T]*Oroz* J.].

Walker-Jones A., Alternative cosmogonies in the Psalms [D]1991 → 2794.

1783 *Welker* Michael, *a*) Was ist 'Schöpfung'? — Genesis 1 und 2 neu gelesen: EvT 51 (1991) 208-224; – *b*) What is creation? Rereading Genesis 1 and 2: TTod 48 (1991s) 56-71.

1784 **Alexandre** Monique, Le commencement du livre Genèse I-V; la version grecque de la Septante et sa réception: Christianisme Antique 3, 1988 → 4, 1976 (5,1952); 6,2139: [R]CrNSt 12 (1991) 177s (A. *Schenker*); ÉTRel 66 (1991) 583 (C.-B. *Amphoux*); Gregorianum 72 (1991) 765-8 (G. L. *Prato*); TPhil 66 (1991) 595s (H. J. *Sieben*).

1785 *Bovati* Pietro, Significare la vita; riflessioni sul capitolo primo della Genesi: → 6,633*, La responsabilità ecologica 1990, 111-136.

1786 *Brett* Mark G., Motives and intentions in Genesis 1: JTS 42 (1991) 1-16.

1787 *Bourguet* Daniel, Les premiers versets de la Genèse: ÉTRel 66 (1991) 169-181.

1788 **Brown** William P., Structure, role, and ideology in the Hebrew and Greek texts of Genesis 1:1-2:3: diss. Emory, [D]*Newsom* Carol. Atlanta 1991. 495 p. 92-04807. – DissA 52 (1991s) 3318s-A; RelStR 18,172 & RTLv 23, p. 538, title 'Ideological and textual-critical readings of the early versions of Gn 1:1-2:3'.

1789 *Cerbelaud* Dominique, La citation 'hébraïque' de la Démonstration d'IRÉNÉE (Dém. 43), [Gn 1,1 mentionne 'Fils de Dieu']; une proposition: Muséon 104 (1991) 221-234.

1790 *Morris* Thomas V., [Gen 1,1] The metaphysical doctrine of creation: AsburyTJ 46,1 (1991) 95-112.

1791 *Verbeke* G., The Bible's first sentence in GREGORY of Nyssa's view: → 81, [F]HYMAN A. 1988 ...

1792 *Simon* Heinrich, Die Interpretation der Begriffe Tohu und Bohu: Kairos 30s (1988s) 64-68 [< ZIT 91,629].

1793 **Tsumura** David T., The earth and the waters in Genesis 1 and 2, 1989 → 5,1978; 6,2141: [R]CBQ 53 (1991) 312s (J. E. *Rybolt*); JBL 110 (1991) 136-8 (G. A. *Rendsburg*); RB 98 (1991) 458s (J. *Loza*).

1794 *Zatelli* Ida, Astrology and the worship of the stars in the Bible: ZAW 103 (1991) 86-99.

1795 *Marin* Marcello,   [Gen 1,5] Nomen quasi notamen; una nota su AuG.
Gen. litt. impf. 6,26 [1. ... metodica dell'interpretazione letterale]:   VetChr
28 (1991) 267-275.

1796 *MacCoull* L. S. B. [De opificio mundi on Gen 1,6s] Philoponus on Egypt:
ByzF 17 (1991) 167-172.

1797 *Rottzoll* Dirk U., Die Vorbedingungen für Gottes grosse 'Ausei-
nander-Schöpfung'; eine vornehmlich syntaktische Untersuchung zum
Prolog des priesterlichen Schöpfungsberichts (Gen 1,11);   BZ 35 (1991)
247-256.

1798 *Matthews* Victor H., *Benjamin* Don C., [Gn 1,26] The divine assembly:
BToday 29 (1991) 157-162.

Gen. 1,26: imago Dei:

1799 *Bray* Gerald,   The significance of God's image in man [since D. CLINES'
1967 preference of Near East influences to theological tradition]: TyndB
42 (1991) 195-225.

1799* *Clanton* Jann A., In whose image?   L/NY 1991, SCM/Crossroad.
vii-135 p. £7.   0-334-02080-8. – RExpTim 103 (1991s) 92 (Nicola *Slee*:
effect our gendered images of God have on our psychological wellbeing).

1800 *Dolby Múgica* Maria del Carmen,   El hombre como imagen de Dios en
la especulación AGUSTINIANA: AugM 34 (1989) 119-154.

1801 **Golub** Ivan,   Imago Dei; der Mensch als Bild Gottes — Gottespräsenz
und Gottesdarstellung (Gen. 1,26-27 und verwandte Texte); Versuch eines
neuen theologischen Zugangs zu einem alten Problem: Theologisches
Südosteuropaseminar [ERitter A. M.] Egb 3. Heidelberg 1991, Univ.
[viii-] 82 p.

1802 — *Babić* Mile,   Božja Slika u TEODORETA Cirskog i Ivana GOLUBA:
→ 67, FGOLUB I., 1991, 114-130 (croat.); 131 ital.: Theodoret explained
'image', ignored 'likeness'; Golub explained them separately (Čovjek slika
Božja 1968); 'annullare la differenza significa annientare la vita'.

1803 *Børresen* K. E., *a*) God's image, man's image? Patristic interpretation of
Gen. i,27 and 1 Cor. xi,7; – *b*) God's image; is woman excluded?
Medieval interpretations of Gen i,27 and 1 Cor. xi,7:   → 472, Image/
gender 1991, 188-207 / 208-227.

1804 *Costa Freitas* Manuel B. da,   À imagem e semelhança de Deus; um tema
de antropologia AGOSTINIANA: Didaskalia 19 (Simposio Lisboa 12-14.XI.
1987/1989) 21-34.

1805 *Douglas* J. D.,   The image of God in women as seen by LUTHER and
CALVIN: → 472, Image/gender 1991, 228-257.

1806 *a*) *Frame* John M.,   Men and women in the image of God; – *b*) *Ortlund*
Raymond C.J,   Male-female equality and male headship: → 375, Recovering 1991, 225-232. 506-8 / 95-112. 479-483.

1807 *Grözinger* K. E.,   Der Mensch als Ebenbild Gottes — im Wandel der
jüdischen Tradition: NorJud 10 (1989) 315 [< JStJud 22,315].

1808 *Hentschel* Georg,   Der Mensch als Bild Gottes: → 564, Erfurter 1989/90,
10-19.

1809 **Hughes** Philip E.,   The true image; the origin and destiny of man in
Christ 1989 → 6,1174:   RScotJT 44 (1991) 401-3 (T. *Hart*).

1810 *Kaiser* Otto,   Der Mensch, Gottes Ebenbild und Statthalter auf Erden:
→ 125, FRATSCHOW C., NSys 33 (1991) 99-111.

1811 *Lamau* Marie-Louise,   L'homme à l'image de Dieu chez les théologiens
et spirituels du XIIème siècle: MélSR 48 (1991) 203-214.

1812 *a*) *Sherwin* Byron L., The human body and the image of God; – *b*) *Cunningham* Adrian, Psychoanalytic approaches to biblical narrative (Genesis 1-4): ➤ 82, ᶠJACOBS L. 1991, 75-85 / 113-132.
1813 **Smith** Robert S., In the image of God. ... 1988, Yuganta. $10 pa. – ᴿCCur 41 (1991s) 269-271 (J. D. *Ryan*).
1814 *Teske* Roland J., The image and likeness of God in St. AUGUSTINE's De Genesi ad litteram liber imperfectus: AugR 30 (1990) 441-451.
1815 **Cohen** Jeremy, [Gn 1,28] 'Be fertile ... and master it'; the ancient and medieval career of a biblical text 1989 ➤ 5,1992: ᴿAmHR 96 (1991) 824 (G. T. *Armstrong*); CathHR 77 (1991) 658s (Caroline W. *Bynum*).
1816 *Foex* Pierre, La bénédiction [Gn 1,28; 9,1-7; 12,1-3; Luc 2,13s; 24,50], l'accompagnement [Ps 139], la substitution [Jn 10,11-16; Gn 4]: FoiVie 90,2 (1991) 89-103.
1817 *Junod* Éric, Une interprétation originale de Genèse 1,28 indûment attribuée à ORIGÈNE (Pap. bibl. Univ. Giss. Inv. 30): ➤ 22, ᶠBENOÎT A., RHPR 71 (1991) 11-31.

E1.7   *Genesis 1s:*   **Bible and myth** [➤ M3.5].

1818 ᴱ**Audretsch** Jürgen, *Mainzer* Klaus, Vom Anfang der Welt; Wissenschaft, Philosophie, Religion, Mythos [Konstanz Univ. 1987s]. Mü 1989, Beck. 228 p.; 49 fig. – ᴿTPhil 66 (1991) 141-3 (P. *Erbrich*).
1819 **Beltz** Walter, Gott und die Götter; biblische Mythologie: Dokumentation Essayistik. B 1990, Aufbau. 323 p. 3-351-00976-3 [OIAc 1,12].
1820 *Currid* John D., An examination of the Egyptian background of the Genesis cosmogony: BZ 35 (1991) 18-40.
1821 **Dalley** Stephanie, Myths from Mesopotamia; creation, the Flood, Gilgamesh and others 1989 ➤ 5,1997; 6,2175: ᴿBO 48 (1991) 852s (M. E. *Vogelzang*); BSO 54 (1991) 145s (A. R. *George* notes several regrettable mistranslations); ClasR 41 (1991) 113-5 (W. G. *Lambert*: rather from Sumerian area); CritRR 4 (1991) 108s (J. R. *Davila*).
1822 **Diakonoff** I. M., ❻ *Archaičeskie* ... Ancient myths of East and West. Moskva 1990, Nauka. 246 p.; Eng. 244-6. 5-02-017016-X [OIAc 1,14].
1823 *a*) *Hermann* W., Jahwe und sein Kampf gegen das Meer: ➤ 163, ᶠWAGNER G. 1990, 111-9. – *b*) *Erikson* G., Alam och Adapa: SvTKv 66 (1990) 122-8.
1824 **Hutter** Manfred, Altorientalische Vorstellungen von der Unterwelt ... Nergal & Ereškigal: OBO 63, 1985 ➤ 1,2058.a687 ... 6,2178: ᴿHenoch 13 (1991) 93-99 (L. *Cagni*: acribia).
1825 **Isermann** G., Revitalisierung der Mythen? Gegen den Missbrauch alter Geschichten für neue Interessen [echte Mythen sind polytheistisch ...]: Vorlagen NF 10. Hannover 1990, Luth.VH. 144 p. DM 12,80 [ZAW 104,151].
1826 **Kramer** S. N., *Maier* J., Myths of Enki 1989 ➤ 5,2007: ᴿCritRR 4 (1991) 107s (J. R. *Davila*).
1827 **Kuwabara** Toshikazu, The nether world in Sumero-Akkadian literature: diss. Univ./GTU, ᴰ*Kilmer* Anne D. Berkeley 1991. 212 p. 91-26308. – DissA 52 (1991s) 1385-A; RelStR 18,173.
1828 *a*) *Maag* Victor, Alttestamentliche Anthropogonie in ihrem Verhältnis zur altorientalischen Mythologie [< Asiatische Studien 9 (1955) 15-44 = Kultur, Ges. Aufs. 1980, 60-89]; – *b*) *Lambert* Wilfred G., A new look at the Babylonian background of Genesis [< JTS 16 (1965) 287-300]; – *c*) *Müller* Hans-P., Mythische Elemente in der jahwistischen Schöpfungs-

erzählung [< ZTK 69 (1972) 259-289]: → 321, WegF 633 (1991) 6393 / 94-113 / 114-153.

1829 *Müller* Hans Peter, Eine neue babylonische Menschenschöpfungserzählung im Licht keilschriftlicher und biblischer Parallelen — Zur Wirklichkeitsauffassung im Mythos [< Orientalia 58 (1989) 61-85]: → 240, Mythos 1991, 43-67.

1830 ᴱ**Niditch** Susan, Text and ... folklore [1989 Amherst] 1990 → 6,2183: ᴿInterpretation 45 (1991) 420.2 (J.S. *Ackerman*); JQR 82 (1991s) 230-2 (Pamela J. *Milne*, also on Underdogs).

1830* *Pascual* Enrique, Estructura generativa del mito de Génesis 1: RET 51 (1991) 501-5.

1831 *Staudinger* Hugo, Mythos und Geschichte; Überlegungen zur historisch-kritischen Exegese: ForumKT 7 (1991) 161-174.

1832 a) *Uehlinger* Christoph, Der Mythos vom Drachenkampf; ein biblisches Feindbild und seine Geschichte; - b) *Meyer* Ivo, Feindbilder; - c) *Godar* Anastasia B., Fremdheit zwischen Angst und Faszination, die 'fremde Frau': BiKi 46 (1991) 66-72; 5 fig. / 55-59 / 60-65.

1832* **Worthen** Thomas D., The myth of replacement; stars, gods, and order in the universe. Tucson 1991, Univ. Arizona. xii-318 p. 0-8165-1200-0 [OIAc 2,29].

E1.8 *Gen 1s, Jos 10,13 ...:* **The Bible, the Church, and Science.**

1833 **Ambrose** Edmund J. [biologist], The mirror of creation: Theology and Science at the Frontiers of Knowledge 11, 1990 → 6,2191: ᴿScripTPamp 23 (1991) 1062 (J. *Morales*); TS 52 (1991) 393 (F.R. *Haig*).

1834 *Arcidiacono* Salvatore, DARWINISMO e ominazione: CiVit 46 (1991) 285-296.

1835 **Aviezer** Nathan [Bar-Ilan physics prof.], In the beginning 1990 → 6,2193: ᴿGraceTJ 11 (1990) 98-100 (D.B. *De Young*: unsuccessful).

1836 **Banner** Michael C., The justification of science and the rationality of religious belief 1990 → 6,2194: ᴿJAAR 59 (1991) 389-392 (H. *Rolston*); JTS 42 (1991) 808-810 (R. *Trigg*); TLond 94 (1991) 71s (P. *Byrne*); Zygon 27 (1992) 221-4 (P. *Clayton*).

1837 **Barbour** Ian, Religion in an age of science 1990 → 6,2195: ᴿAmerica 164 (1991) 603s (M.J. *Himes*, also on two cognate works); AndrUnS 29 (1991) 78s (J.T. *Baldwin*); AnglTR 73 (1991) 351-3 (S. *Paradise*); CCurr 41 (1991s) 559s (F.B. *Burnham*); Interpretation 45 (1991) 438 (R. *Hutchinson*); JTS 42 (1991) 810-4 (A. *Peacocke*); RelStR 17 (1991) 237 (P.C. *Hodgson*); RRel 50 (1991) 941s (R.A. *Brungs*); TS 52 (1991) 168s (J.F. *Salmon*).

1838 **Battistini** A., Introduzione a GALILEI: Gli Scrittori 9. Bari 1989, Laterza. 194 p. - ᴿAnStoEseg 8 (1991) 709 (M. *Pesce*).

1839 **Beale** G., Evolution and a creator? Lancaster UK 1991, Clinical. x-90 p. £10 [TS 52,601].

1840 **Berra** Tim, Evolution and the myth of creationism. SF c.1990, Stanford Univ. 198 p. $29.50 [Interp 45,109].

1841 **Bird** Wendell R., The Origin of Species revisited [→ 6,2201]; the theories of evolution and of abrupt appearance. NY 1989, Philosophical. 551 p.; 563 p. - ᴿTPhil 66 (1991) 143s (P. *Erbrich*).

1842 **Birx** H. James, Interpreting evolution; DARWIN and TEILHARD de Chardin. Buffalo 1991, Prometheus. 326 p. $30. 0-87975-636-5 [TDig 39,50].

1843 **Blackwell** Richard J., GALILEO, BELLARMINE, and the Bible. ND 1991, Univ. x-291 p. $30. 0-268-01024-2 [TDig 38,150]. – ^RAmerica 165 (1991) 76s (R. L. *Spaeth*).

1844 **Blanc** Marcel, Les héritiers de DARWIN; l'évolution en mutation. P 1990, Seuil. 272 p. F 120. – ^RÉtudes 374 (1991) 127s (J.-M. *Moretti*).

1845 *Borasi* Carlo, Sulla 'visione cosmica' di TEILHARD de Chardin; considerazioni sul paradigma evoluzionistico tra teologia e scienza: Asprenas 38 (1991) 491-504.

1846 **Brooke** John H., Science and religion; some historical perspectives. C 1991, Univ. 422 p. £27.50; pa. £11. 0-521-23961-3; pa.-8374-4. – ^RExpTim 103,4 co-starred at top (1991s) 97s (C. S. *Rodd*).

1847 *Burnham* Frederic B., Maker of heaven and earth; a perspective of contemporary science: → 435, HorBT 12,2 (1990) 1-18.

1847* **Cantor** Geoffrey, Michael FARADAY, Sandemanian [or Glasite, Scots Christian sect] and scientist. L 1991, Macmillan. 359 p. £40. 0-333-55077-3. – ^RExpTim 103 (1991s) 128 (C. S. *Rodd*: how a good shy man sought to follow his Master).

1848 *Carroll* William E., GALILEO and the Inquisition: NBlackf 71 (1990) 185-193.

1849 **Carvin** Walter, Creation and scientific explanation 1988 → 4,2067 (index 'Carwin'): ^RScotJT 44 (1991) 100-2 (A. *Thomson*).

1850 **Clayton** Philip, Explanation from physics to theology; an essay in rationality and religion 1989 → 5,2034; 6,2206: ^RSWJT 34,1 (1991s) 79 (B. K. *Putt*).

1851 **Clouser** Roy A., The myth of religious neutrality; an essay on the hidden role of religious belief in theories [about math, physics, economics, as well as sociology, politics, art]. ND 1991, Univ. xii-330 p. $40; pa. $19. 0-268-01390-X; -9-3 [TDig 39,256].

1852 *Coyne* George V., Religione e scienza; tradizione e attualità: CC 142 (1991,4) 585-592 = ℗, ^T*Matusiak* Maria M.: PrzPow 854 (1992) 81-91.

1853 **Croft** L. R., How life began. Welwyn 1988, Evangelical. 176 p. £5. 0-85234-254-3. – ^REvangel 8,3 (1990) 23 (J. B. *Arthur*: a bit too reactionary against DARWINISM).

1854 *Daecke* Sigurd M., Naturgesetz und Judentum im Denken Albert EINSTEINS: EvKomm 24 (1991) 642-5 [< ZIT 91,772].

1855 **Desmond** Adrian, *Moore* James, DARWIN. L 1991, M. Joseph. £20. – ^RTablet 245 (1991) 1252 (R. *Webs*: hero-worship).

1856 **Drees** Willem B., Beyond the big bang; quantum cosmologies and God, ^D1990 → 5,2039; 6,2215: ^RTS 52 (1991) 584-6 (C. L. *Currie*).

1857 **Ecker** Ronald L., Dictionary of science and creationism. Buffalo 1990, Prometheus. vii-262 p. – ^RScripTPamp 23 (1991) 1061 (J. *Morales*).

1857* **Ellul** Jacques, The technological bluff [1986], ^T*Bromiley* Geoffrey W. GR 1990, Eerdmans. 418 p. $25. 0-8028-3678-X. – ^RExpTim 103 (1991s) 126 (Sue *Birchmore*: too sweepingly hollow 'brave new world').

1858 **Finocchiaro** Maurice A., The Galileo affair 1989 → 5,2041; 6,2220: ^RRHE 86 (1991) 516 (R. *Aubert*).

1859 *Finocchiaro* M. A., *a*) Aspetti metodologici della condanna galileiana: Intersezioni 4 (1984) 503-532; – *b*) The methodological background to GALILEO's trial, in ^E*Wallace* W. A., Reinterpreting Galileo (StPhilHistP 15; Wsh 1986) 241-272. – ^RAnStoEseg 8 (1991) 296-9 (M. *Pesce*).

1860 **Gans** Eric, Science and faith; the anthropology of revelation. c. 1990, Bowman & L. 129 p. $39.50 [Interp 45,222].

1861 *Gismondi* Gualberto, Faith, science, religion in post-modern culture: Antonianum 66 (1991) 227-264; español 227.

1862 **Gould** Stefen J., La vie est belle; les surprises de l'évolution, ᵀ*Blanc* Marcel. P 1991, Seuil. 400 p. F 150. – ᴿÉtudes 375 (1991) 261-3 (J.-M. *Moretti*).

1863 *Grossmann* Sigrid, 'Vom Anfang der Welt an ist der Materie ein lebendiges Lebenselement beigegeben'; von der All-Lebendigkeit der Schöpfung bei Friedrich C. OETINGER: Zeitwende 62 (Karlsruhe 1991) 93-99 [< ZIT 91,287].

1864 **Guitton** Jean, *Bogdanov* Grichka & Igor, Dieu et la science. P 1991, Grasset. 195 p. – ᴿEsprVie 101 (1991) 479 (J. *Crépin*) & 541-3 (P. *Jay*: la science est inachevée et inachevable); Études 375 (1991) 693s (M. de *Heaulme*); RCatalT 16 (1991) 219s (F. *Nicolau*).

1865 **Hawking** Stephen, A brief history of time. 1989, Bantam. 160 p. $9 [→ 6,2222 *ab*]. – ᴿAmerica 164 (1991) 95-97 (R. J. *Russell*).

1865* *Honner* John, A new [quantum mechanics] ontology: Incarnation, Eucharist, Resurrection, and physics: Pacifica 4 (1991) 15-50.

1866 **Isak** Rainer, Evolutionismus und Theologie; eine Auseinandersetzung mit dem teleologischen Denken Robert SPAEMANNS und Reinhard LÖWS mit einem Ausblick auf die zielgerichtete Deutung der Evolution bei Carsten BRESCH: Diss. FrB 1991, ᴰ*Greshake* G. 440 p. – TR 87 (1991) 517; RTLv 23, p. 569 (ᴰ*Riedlinger* H.).

1867 **Israel** Martin, Creation, the consummation of the world. L 1989, Collins Fount. 141 p. £3. – ᴿPrPeo 4 (1990) 77 (P. E. *Hodgson*: an Anglican priest on faith/science).

1868 **Jaki** Stanley L., The purpose of it all. ... c. 1990, Scottish Academic. £9.50. – ᴿDowR 109 (1991) 309-311 (D. *O'Keeffe*: DARWIN's inability to see design, p. 149); Tablet 245 (1991) 1028s (P. *Hodgson*: immense learning).

1869 **Jaki** Stanley L., Pierre DUHEM [† 1916], homme de science et de foi [Uneasy genius]ᵀ: Scientifiques et croyants 4. P 1990, Beauchesne. 275 p. F 150. 2-7010-1224-4. – ᴿRHPR 71 (1991) 485 (G. *Siegwalt*).

1870 *Jaki* Stanley L., NEWMAN and evolution: DowR 109 (1991) 16-34.

1871 **Johnson** Michael R., Genesis, geology and catastrophism; a critique of creationist science and biblical literalism 1988 → 5,2065: ᴿBL (1991) 112 (B. P. *Robinson*).

1871* **Kaiser** Christopher B., Creation and the history of science. GR 1991, Eerdmans. 316 p. $18 pa. – ᴿGraceTJ 12,1 (1991) 142-4 (D. B. *DeYoung*).

1872 **Liderbach** Daniel, The numinous universe 1989 → 6,2236: ᴿNewTR 4,1 (1991) 88s (G. A. *Reisch*).

1873 **Lima-de-Faria** Antonio, Evolution without selection; form and function by autoevolution. Amst 1988, Elsevier. 372 p.; 132 fig. – ᴿTPhil 66 (1991) 139-141 (P. *Erbrich*).

1874 *Lonchamp* Jean-Pierre, Le principe anthropique [... l'univers est-il ce qu'il est pour rendre possible l'apparition de l'homme?]: Études 437 (1991) 493-502.

1875 *Magnin* Thierry, *al.*, Recherche de l'unité des contradictoires dans l'activité scientifique et dans celle du théologien: MélSR 48 (1991) 153-8.

1876 *Maldamé* Jean-Michel, Dire la Création à la lumière des sciences de l'Univers: BLitEc 92 (1991) 93-106; Eng. 105 'Telling of creation...'.

1877 *a*) *Maldamé* Jean-Michel, Cosmologie, cosmogenèse, religiosités cosmiques; principes teihhardiens de discernement; – *b*) *Dupleix* André, TEILHARD et les théologiens; – *c*) *Carles* Jules, Teilhard, 50 ans après; du

groupe à l'individu: BLitEc 92 (1991) 31-42; Eng. 42 / 13-29; Eng. 30
'Teilhard versus theologians' / 5-11; Eng. 11.

1878 — **King** Thomas M., TEILHARD de Chardin. Wilmington 1988, Glazier.
184 p. $11. – ᴿRRel 49 (1990) 629s (J. M. *Ballweg*).

1879 — **Pageau** Yvon, [TEILHARD P.], Le phénomène humain et l'évolution.
P 1990, Méridien. 520 p. – ᴿÉtudes 374 (1991) 704 (J. M. *Moretti*).

1880 ᴱ**Mangum** John M., The new faith-science debate 1987/9 → 5,702;
6,2240: ᴿAndrUnS 28 (1990) 264s (A. J. *Greig*); NewTR 4,1 (1991) 86s
(G. A. *Reisch*); RelStT 10,1 (1990) 53-55 (C. B. *O'Connell*); SWJT 34,1
(1991s) 79 (S. *Lemke*).

1881 *Martin* R. N. D., The trouble with authority; the GALILEO affair and
one of its historians [DUHEM P.]: ModT 7 (Ox 1991) 269-280 [< ZIT
91,454].

1882 **Mitchell** Ralph G., EINSTEIN and Christ; a new approach to the defence
of the Christian religion 1987 → 4,2110: ᴿScotJT 43 (1990) 516-8 (J. C.
Puddefoot: enjoyable despite oversimplified science and Catholic piety).

1883 *Mooney* Christopher F., Theology and science; a new commitment to
dialogue: TS 52 (1991) 289-329.

1884 *Morandini* Simone, Scienza e teologia in dialogo; il concetto di modello:
VivH 2 (1991) 69-95.

1885 ᴱ**Mott** Nevill, Can scientists believe? L 1991, James & James. £21. –
ᴿTablet 245 (1991) 1178s (J. *Cornwell*, also on BARBOUR I. and
PEACOCKE A.).

1886 ᴱ**Müller** Hans-Peter, Was ist Wahrheit? [evolutionäre Erkenntnis-
theorie, Ringvorlesung Münster]: 1989 → 5,495: ᴿTLZ 116 (1991) 53s (B.
Hildebrandt).

1887 *Müller* Helmut, Wie hältst Du's mit der Evolution? Zur Gretchenfrage
des Religionslehrers: ForumKT 7 (1991) 120-7.

1888 *a*) *Odenwald* Sten F., A modern look at the origin of the universe; – *b*)
Bowker J. W., Cosmology, religion, and society: Zygon 25 (1990) 25-45 /
7-23.

1889 **Ostovich** Stephen T., Reason in history; theology and science as
community activities [diss. ᴰ*Lamb* M.]: AAR 71. Atlanta 1990, Scholars.
xi-277 p. $23, pa./sb. $15. – ᴿCritRR 4 (1991) 420-2 (B. L. *Whitney*); TS
52 (1991) 757-9 (J. A. *Colombo*).

1890 **Paul** I., Knowledge of God; CALVIN, EINSTEIN and POLANYI 1987
→ 4,2117; 6,2247: ᴿHeythJ 32 (1991) 123s (H. *Meynell*).

1891 **Peacock** Roy E., A brief history of eternity [to HAWKING S., A brief
history of time 1988 → 1865 supra]. Wheaton IL 1990, Crossway. 160 p.
$8. – ᴿBS 148 (1991) 494 (F. R. *Howe*).

1892 **Peacocke** Arthur, Theology for a scientific age; being and becoming,
natural and divine. Ox 1990, Blackwell. x-221 p. $40. – ᴿCCurr 41
(1991s) 415-7 (Nancey *Murphy*); JTS 42 (1991) 814-9 (D. A. *Pailin*); LvSt
16 (1991) 265-7 (H. E. *Mertens*); TLond 94 (1991) 391s (J. C. *Puddefoot*);
Zygon 27 (1992) 350-2 (T. *Peters*).

1893 *a*) *Peacocke* Arthur [profile, bibliog.]; – *b*) *Russell* Robert J., The
theological scientific vision of A. Peacocke: Zygon 26 (1991) 455-493.
527-546 / 505-517 [495-503, *Eaves* Lindon; 519-525, *Nelson* James S.].

1893* *Pesce* Mauro, Momenti della ricezione dell'ermeneutica biblica galileiana e della Lettera a Cristina nel XVII secolo: AnStoEseg 8 (1991)
55-104.

1894 *Peters* Karl E., Empirical theology in the light of science: Zygon 27
(1992) 297-325.

1895 **Peters** Ted, Cosmos as creation; theology and science in consonance. Nv 1989, Abingdon. 288 p. $13 pa. – ᴿCritRR 4 (1991) 422-4 (P. *Clayton*).

1896 a) *Plantinga* Lavin, [*Pun* Pattie, *McMullin* Ernan, responses]; – b) *Van Till* Howard J., When faith and reason cooperate: ChrSchR 21,1 (1991) 8-32 . 80s [46-54 . 55-79] / 31-45 [< ᴢɪᴛ 92,3].

1897 **Polkinghorne** John, Reason and reality; the relationship between science and theology. L 1991, SPCK. 119 p. £7. 0-281-04487-2. – ᴿExpTim 102,11 1st choice (1990s) 321s (C. S. *Rodd*: excellent, yet ultimately wants to see Gen 1-11 both as fiction and as normative for theology); Month 252 (1991) 254s (G. J. *Hughes*).

1898 **Polkinghorne** J., Science and creation; the search for understanding 1988 ➤ 5,2085; 6,2250: ᴿPrzPow 271 (1991) 167-9 (M. *Heller* ❾).

1899 **Polkinghorne** J., Science and Providence 1989 ➤ 5,2086; 6,2251; ᴿZygon 25 (1990) 504-7 (J. C. *Eccles*).

1900 — *Avis* Paul, Apologist from the world of science, John ᴘᴏʟ-ᴋɪɴɢʜᴏʀɴᴇ FRS: ScotJT 43 (1990) 485-502: takes some risks which would scare ʙᴀʀᴛʜ.

1901 **Poythress** Vern S., Science and hermeneutics 1988 ➤ 4,2128 ... 6,2252: ᴿEvQ 63 (1991) 354s (C. *Gempf*).

1902 *Putrament* Aleksandra, ❾ Niepotrzebny spór [ᴢᴀʙᴏʀsᴋɪ W., ᴅᴀʀ-ᴡɪɴɪᴢᴍ w obec rozumu i nauki]: PrzPow 268, 824 (1990) 276-285.

1903 *Reich* K. Helmut, The relation between science and theology; the case for complementarity revisited: Zygon 25 (1990) 369-390.

1904 **Reichholf** Josef H., Das Rätsel der Menschwerdung; die Entstehung des Menschen im Wechselspiel mit der Natur. Stu 1990, Deutsche Ver-lagsanstalt. 280 p. – ᴿTPhil 66 (1991) 144s (R. *Koltermann*).

1905 **Reichholf** Josef, L'émergence de l'homme, ᵀ*Étoré* Jeanne. P 1991, Flammarion. 360 p. F 130. – ᴿÉtudes 348 (1991) 126 (J.-M. *Moretti*).

1906 **Riaza Morales** J. M., El comienzo del mundo, 1. El hombre, la vida y la tierra; sus orígenes a la luz de los avances cientᶜficos actuales. M 1984, BAC. xxviii-500 p.; 12 pl. – ᴿAntonianum 66 (1991) 161s (T. *Larrañaga*).

1907 **Ritvo** Lucille B., ᴅᴀʀᴡɪɴ's influence on ꜰʀᴇᴜᴅ; a tale of two sciences. NHv 1990, Yale Univ. xii-267 p. $30. – ᴿAmHR 96 (1991) 1501s (J. C. *Burnham*).

1907* **Roberts** John H., ᴅᴀʀᴡɪɴɪsᴍ and the divine 1988 ➤ 4,2133; ... 6,2257: ᴿChH 59 (1990) 114s (W. J. *Wilkins*).

1908 **Rothschild** Richard C., The emerging religion of science. NY 1989, Praeger. 176 p. $35. – ᴿCritRR 4 (1991) 424-6 (J. R. *Sibley*).

1909 **Ruse** Michael, The Darwinian paradigm; essays on its history, phi-losophy and religious implications. L 1989, Routledge. 299 p. $25. – ᴿZygon 25 (1990) 497-504 (D. J. *Hull*, also on two cognate Ruse books).

1910 ᴱ**Scheffczyk** Leo, Evolution, Probleme und neue Aspekte ihrer Theorie: Grenzfragen. Fr 1991, Alber. 248 p. DM 68 [TLZ 117,934, U. *Gerber*].

1911 *Schöpf* Hans-Georg, ɴᴇᴡᴛᴏɴ zwischen Physik und Theologie: NSys 33 (1991) 262-281; Eng. 281.

1912 **Sherrard** Philip, The rape of man and nature; an enquiry into the origins and consequences of modern science. ... 1991, Golganooza. £6. – ᴿPrPeo 5 (1991) 475s (M. *Atkins*).

1913 **Stanesby** Derek, Science, reason, and religion 1988 = 1985 ➤ 5,2100; 6,2265: ᴿRelStR 17 (1991) 140 (Nancey *Murphy*).

1914 **Thompson** Ross, Holy ground, the spirituality of matter. L 1990, SPCK. viii-280 p. £10 pa. – ᴿTLond 94 (1991) 389s (A. *Louth*).

1915 **Thomson** Alexander, Tradition and authority in science and theology
1987 ➤ 4,2148: ᴿScotJT 43 (1990) 512-4 (J. C. *Puddefoot*: falls just short
of greatness; applies POLANYI but not to Catholic ecclesiology).
1916 *Tornos* Andrés, Teología y orígen del hombre: EstE 66 (1991) 415-440.
1917 **Torrance** Thomas F., Science théologique [1969], ᵀ*Lacoste* Jean-Yves.
P 1990, PUF. 410 p. F 260. – ᴿRHPR 71 (1991) 484 (G. *Vahanian*,
aussi sur son Reality and scientific theology 1985); RTLv 22 (1991) 253s
(R. *Guelluy*).
1917* **Trusted** Jennifer, Physics and metaphysics — Theories in space and
time. L 1991, Routledge. xii-210 p. £30. 0-415-05948-8. – ᴿExpTim 103
(1991s) 124s (J. *Polkinghorne*: 'no physics without metaphysics' or possibly
even religion).
1918 **Van Till** Howard J., *al.*, Portraits of creation; biblical and scientific
perspectives on the world's formation. GR 1990, Eerdmans. 285 p. $15.
– ᴿBS 148 (1991) 494-6 (F. R. *Howe*: unacceptable); GraceTJ 11 (1990)
119s (D. B. *De Young*: defense of Calvin Sem. 'theistic evolution' which
has disturbed the 'constituents'); SWJT 34,1 (1991s) 71 (R. L. *Smith*);
TTod 48 (1991s) 80. 82 (D. W. *Musser*: best since L. GILKEY 1959).
1918* *Vinck* Dominique, Science, foi et société aujourd'hui: LVitae 46
(1991) 29-40.
1919 *Wright* John H., Theology, philosophy and the natural sciences [PRO-
VINE W. 1988]: TS 52 (1991) 651-668 [669-688, *Rigby* P. *al.*].
1920 *Życiński* Józef, ❷ Le Dieu de HAWKING et le Logos chrétien: PrzPow
267/823 (1990) 399-416; franç. 416.

E1.9 *Peccatum originale,* **The Sin of Eden,** *Genesis 2-3.*

1921 *Batto* Bernard F., Paradise reexamined: ➤ 334*, ᴱ*Younger* L., Biblical
canon 1991, ...
1922 *Baudler* Georg, Der Baum in der Mitte des Gartens; historisch-sym-
bolische Bibelauslegung am Beispiel der Sündenfall-Erzählung (Gen
3,1-24): KatBlätt 116 (Mü 1991) 415-7 [< ZIT 91,466].
1923 *Baudry* Gérard-Henry, L'hypothèse de l'Adam métahistorique; réflexions
sur la théorie de LÉONARD [A., Les raisons de croire 1987]: MélSR 48
(1991) 215-230.
1924 [*Baudry* Gérard-Henry, Le péché originel à Vatican II], *Monloubou*
Louis, Le mal — Dieu — la Bible: EsprVie 101 (1991) 668-672.
1925 **Bolewski** Jacek, Reiner Anfang; Dialektik der Erbsünde in marianischer
Perspektive nach Karl RAHNER: kath. Diss. Fra St.-Georgen 1991, ᴰ*Kunz*
E. 296 p. – TR 87 (1991) 517, RTLv 23, p. 568 ('Der reine Anfang', 1990).
1926 **Chiesa** Bruno, Creazione e caduta dell'uomo nell'esegesi giudeo-araba
medievale: StBPaid 85, 1989 ➤ 5,2131: ᴿCC 142 (1991,2) 95-97 (G. L.
Prato); Helmantica 42,129* (1991) 400s (S. *Garcʿa-Jalón*); RivB 39
(1991) 76-78 (M. *Perani*).
1927 **Clines** David J. A., What does Eve do to help? 1990 ➤ 6,213: ᴿÉTRel
66 (1991) 431 (D. *Lys*); Interpretation 45 (1991) 416.418 (Phyllis A. *Bird*:
makes 'authority' per se male).
1928 *Coninck* Frédéric de, Une lecture de la société à partir de la triade
Création, Chute, Rédemption: RRéf 42,2 (1991) 31-42 [< ZIT 91,218].
1928* *Coyle* Kathleen, A theological reflection on Genesis 3: EAPast 27
(1990) 40-58.
1929 **Day** Peggy L., An Adversary in heaven; Satan in the Hebrew Bible:
HarvSemMg 43, 1988 ➤ 4,2167; 6,2295: ᴿBO 48 (1991) 621-4 (G.

Wanke); JSS 36 (1991) 156-8 (J. *Day*); RelStT 10,2 (1990) 110-2 (S. *Slater*); Syria 67 (1990) 530 (A. *Caquot*); VT 41 (1991) 374 (R. P. *Gordon*).

1930 *Deist* Ferdinand, The nature and origin of evil; Old Testament perspectives and their theological consequences [*Abrahams* S. P., response]: JTSAf 76 (1991) 71-81 [82-85; < ZIT 91,708].

1931 *Delumeau* Jean, Le paradis terrestre se trouvait à l'Équateur?: CRAI (1991) 135-144.

1932 **Deurloo** Karel, De mens als raadsel en geheim; verhalende antropologie in Genesis 2-4, 1989 ➤ 5,2134; 90-259-4380-2: ᴿOTAbs 14 (1991) 220 (C. T. *Begg*).

1933 **Dohmen** Christoph, Schöpfung und Tod... Gen 2/3: SBB 17, 1988 ➤ 4,2169... 6,2297: ᴿBiblica 72 (1991) 107-111 (J. *Vermeylen*); BiKi 45 (1990) 58s (F. J. *Stendebach*); BZ 35 (1991) 125s (J. *Scharbert*).

1934 **Forsyth** N., The old enemy; Satan and the combat myth 1987 ➤ 3,2095... 5,2137: ᴿBL (1991) 110 (R.P.R. *Murray*: 'paperback reprint after only two years').

1935 **Fox** Matthew, *a*) Original blessing, a primer in creation spirituality 1983 ➤ 65,1725; – *b*) Der grosse Segen; umarmt von der Schöpfung; eine spirituelle Reise auf vier Pfaden durch sechsundzwanzig Themen mit zwei Fragen, ᵀ*Wichmann* Jörg; Vorw. *Rohr* Richard. Mü 1991, Claudius. 384 p. DM 36 [TR 88, 305, Barbara *Hallensleben*].

1936 *a*) *Fragomeni* Richard N., Wrestling with the angels; Satan and the struggle with evil; – *b*) *Hickey* John, Pastoral responses to the phenomenon of Satanism in America today; – *c*) *Schreiter* Robert J., Traveling the occult underworld: NewTR 4,3 (1991) 28-38 / 16-27 / 6-15.

1937 *Fulkerson* Mary M., Sexism as original sin; developing a theacentric discourse [SAIVING V.; DALY M., RUETHER R....]: JAAR 59 (1991) 653-675.

1938 **Garrett** Susan R., The demise of the devil... Luke 1989 ➤ 5,5036*; 6,2303*: ᴿBibTB 21 (1991) 167s (N. *Elliott*); CBQ 53 (1991) 495s (C. H. *Talbert*); Interpretation 45 (1991) 312.314 (J. A. *Darr*); JBL 110 (1991) 532-4 (R. J. *Pervo*); Neotestamentica 25 (1991) 175-7 (P. J. *Hartin*); ScriptTPamp 23 (1991) 709s (J. *Morales*).

1939 **Gestrich** Christof, *a*) Die Wiederkehr des Glanzes in der Welt; die christliche Lehre von der Sünde und ihrer Vergebung in gegenwärtiger Verantwortung. Tü 1989. – *b*) Sprache, Sünde und Wort Gottes: Bijdragen 52 (1991) 185-199; Eng. 199s, against view (KANT, SCHILLER, HEGEL) that human freedom begins with the first sin in Gn. 3.

1940 *Grossi* Vittorino, L'auctoritas di AGOSTINO nella dottrina del 'peccatum originis' da Cartagine (418) a Trento (1546): AugR 31 (1991) 329-360.

1941 *Hardt* Michael, Erbsünde — was heisst das eigentlich?: StiZt 208 (1990) 775-783.

1942 **Hauke** Manfred, Heilsverlust in Adam; Stationen griechischer Erbsündenlehre, IRENÄUS — Kappadozier: kath. Hab.-Diss. Augsburg 1991, ᴰ*Ziegenaus*. – TR 87 (1991) 511.

1943 **Hoping** Helmut, Freiheit im Widerspruch; eine Untersuchung der Erbsündenlehre im Ausgang von Immanuel KANT: kath. Diss. ᴰ*Hünermann* P. – Tübingen 1989; InnsbTSt 30, 1990. – RTLv 23, p. 569.

1944 *Kemeny* Paul C., Peter ABELARD; an examination of his doctrine on original sin: JRelHist 16 (1990s) 374-386.

1945 *Köttke* Horst, Bilder vom Teufel: CLehre 44 (1991) 416-420 [< ZIT 91,819].

1946 **Konya** Alex, Demons [mostly NT]. Schaumberg IL 1990, Regular Baptist. 151 p. $11. – ᴿBS 148 (1991) 239s (R. P. *Lightner*).

1947 **Kowalski** Aleksander, Perfezione e giustizia di Adamo nel Liber Graduum: OrChrAn 237, 1989 → 5,2148; 6,2316: ᴿAugR 30 (1990) 502-5 (A. *Camplani*); OrChr 75 (1991) 267 (M. van *Esbroeck*).

1947* *Kreppold* Guido, Zum Thema Erbsünde: Lebendige Katechese 13,2 (Taufkatechese 1991) 111-4 [< ZIT 92,57].

1948 **Leisch-Kiesl** Monika M., Eva in Kunst und Theologie des Früh-christentums und Mittelalters; zur Bedeutung 'Evas' für die Anthropologie der Frau: kath. Diss. Salzburg 1991, ᴰ*Bach*. – TR 87 (1991) 514.

1949 **Levison** John R., Portraits of Adam in early Judaism 1988 → 4,2192; 6,2320: ᴿHeythJ 32 (1991) 404s (Margaret *Barker*).

1950 **Manaranche** André, Adam, où es-tu? Le péché originel: Lumière Vérité 1991 → 6,2324: ᴿEsprVie 101 (1991) 545-7 (P. *Jay*).

1951 **Marconcini** Benito, *al.*, Angeli e demoni; il dramma della storia tra il bene e il male: Corso di teologia sistematica 11. Bo 1991, Dehoniane. 429 p. [VivH 3,433s].

1952 *Margerie* Bertrand de, Le péché des origines, à la lumière de la justice originale, du magistère récent et du jugement final: RThom 91 (1991) 624-650.

1953 *Mary* Corona, Woman in creation story: Jeevadhara 21 (1991) 96-106.

1954 ᴱ**Mora** George, Witches, devils, and doctors in the Renaissance; Johann WEYER, De praestigiis daemonum [1563 'one of the ten most important books of all time', FREUD], ᵀ*Shea* John: MedRenTSt 73. Binghamton 1991, SUNY. xcii-790 p. $33 [RelStR 18,149, D. R. *Janz*].

1955 **Marlière** F., *a*) Et leurs yeux ... *b*) Et ils virent 1989s → 6,2325*ab*; ᴿDivThom 94 (1991) 194s (L. *Elders*, pas enthousiaste).

1956 **Nielsen** K., Satan, den fortabte søn? [Satan, the prodigal son? biblical and pseudepigraphical conceptions of Satan as one of the sons of God]. Fredriksberg 1991, Anis. 162 p. Dk 168. 87-7457-11-7 ... [BL 92,81, K. *Jeppesen*].

1957 *a*) *Oberman* Heiko A., LUTHER and the devil; – *b*) *Edwards* Mark O.ᴶ, Luther and the servants of Satan; – *c*) *Jenson* Robert W., Evil as person: Lutheran Theological Seminary Bulletin 69,1 (Gettysburg PA 1989), 48 p. [LuJb 57 (1990) p. 320].

1958 *Olivier* Hannes, Die mensbeeld in die skeppingsverhale van Genesis: JSem 1 (Pretoria 1989) 70-87 [< OTAbs 14,286].

1959 **Pagels** Elaine, Adam, Eve, and the serpent 1988 → 4,2203 ... 6,2329: ᴿHorizons 18 (1991) 147s (Mary Ann *Donovan*); JEH 42 (1991) 294s (Christine *Trevett:* fresh).

1960 *Pagels* Elaine, The social history of Satan, the 'intimate enemy'; a preliminary sketch: HarvTR 84 (1891) 105-128.

1961 *Park* William, Why Eve? [attack not on woman but on polytheistic religion]: StVlad 35 (1991) 127-135.

1962 *Rapisarda* Grazia, Cielo e terra, angeli e demoni nell'esegesi biblica di CROMAZIO di Aquileia: → 452, AnStoEseg 8,2 (1990/1) 615-630.

1962* *Ravasi* Gianfranco, All'ombra dell'albero della conoscenza del bene e del male; note ermeneutiche su Genesi 2-3: → 346, Communio 118 (1991) 25-35.

1963 *Renwart* Léon, Péché d'Adam, péché du monde: NRT 113 (1991) 535-542.

1964 *Resnick* Irven M., ODO of Tournai's De peccato originali and the problem of original sin: Medieval Philosophy and Theology Annual 1 (ND 1991) ... [TDig 39,275].

1966 *Rodrigues da Cruz* Eduardo, O moral e o trágico no mito de Adão: REB 51 (1991) 120-130.

1967 *Rouillard* Philippe, [Gen 1-3; Mt 19,1-10; Eph 5,21-33] Liturgie et théologie du mariage; une approche nouvelle: EsprVie 101 (1991) 273-283.

1968 *Săndulescu* Gheorghe, Invâtâtura Sfîntului GRIGORIE de Nyssa despre căderea omumui şi păcatul originar: STBuc 39,1s (1987) 61-83.

1969 ^E**Scherer** Siegfried, Die Suche nach Eden; Wege zur alternativen Deutung der menschlichen Frühgeschichte. Stu-Neuhausen 1991, Hänssler. 189 p.; ill.; maps. 3-7751-1677-X.

1970 **Schönborn** C., *al.*, Zur kirchlichen Erbsündenlehre; Stellungnahmen zu einer brennenden Frage: Kriterien 87. Fr 1991, Johannes. 102 p. [NRT 114, 899, L. *Renwart*].

1971 **Schüngel-Straumann** Helen, Die Frau am Anfang, Eva und die Folgen 1989 ➤ 6,2345: ^RTR 87 (1991) 370s (E. *Zenger*); ZkT 113 (1991) 93-95 (H.-A. *Pissarek*^J).

1972 ^E**Schwaiger** Georg, Teufelsglaube und Hexenprozesse: B-Reihe 337, 1987 ➤ 3,2120: ^RArKulturG 72 (1990) 465s (P. *Blum*).

1973 **Stewart** Charles, Demons and the devil; moral imagination in modern Greek culture. Princeton 1991, Univ. 330 p. [JAAR 59,891].

1974 *Teske* Roland J., St. AUGUSTINE's view of the original human condition in De Genesi contra Manichaeos: AugSt 22 (1991) 141-156.

1975 **Testa** Emanuele, La legge del progresso organico ... monogenismo: SBF Anal 25, 1987 ➤ 3,2075 ... 6,2351: ^RETL 67 (1991) 183-5 (A. *Vanneste*: érudition remarquable).

1976 **Thomas** Pascal, Le diable, oui ou non? 1989 ➤ 5,2183: ^RScEsp 43 (1991) 361s (G. *Novotný*).

1977 **Toorn** K. van der, Sin and sanction in Israel and Mesopotamia 1985 ➤ 1,2242 ... 6,2352: ^RBASOR 284 (1991) 93a (D. P. *Wright*); WeltOr 22 (1991) 166-170 (Brigitte *Groneberg*).

1978 *Turner* J. Munsey, Adam and Eve and a talking snake: ExpTim 102 (1991s) 16-18.

1979 *Vanneste* A., La nouvelle théologie du péché originel [VILLALMONTE A. de, 'changed more radically in these 25 years than in the 15 preceding centuries']: ETL 67 (1991) 249-277.

1980 *Villalmonte* Alejandro, Voluntad salvífica universal y pecado original [defense of his 1978 Pecado original], respuesta al prof. Alfred VANNESTE [ETL 56 (1980) 139-146]: EstFranc 92 (1991) 1-24.

1981 *Villalmonte* Alejandro, El problema del mal y el pecado original en san AGUSTÍN: NatGrac 38 (1991) 235-263.

1982 *Wagener* Kenneth C., Repentant Eve, perfected Adam; conversion in the Acts of Andrew: ➤ 446, SBL Sem 30 (1991) 348-356.

1983 **Wallace** Howard N., The Eden narrative: HarvSemMg 32, 1985 ➤ 1,2243 ... 6,2356: ^RJJS 42 (1991) 123s (J. *Hughes*).

1984 *Ward* John O., Satan and his persecutors [MOORE R. 1987; KELLY H. 1985]: JRelHist 16 (1990s) 217-220.

1985 **Wenisch** Bernhard, Satanismus; schwarze Messen — Dämonenglaube — Hexenkulte. Mainz/Stu 1988, Grünewald/Quell. 151 p. DM 22,80. – ^RTLZ 116 (1991) 817-9 (H. *Seidl:* im Titel 'Sanatismus'; gegenwärtig auftretend).

1986 *a) Wölbert* Karl-Josef, Der Mythos vom Teufel oder: Woher kommt das Böse?; – *b) Niehl* Franz W., Der gedruckte Teufel; Literatur- und Medienübersicht: ZPraxRU 21 (Stu 1991) 147-150/151-... [< ZIT 91,827].

1987 **Wolde** Ellen J. van, A semiotic analysis of Genesis 2-3; a semiotic theory and method of analysis applied to the story of the Garden of Eden [diss. Nijmegen, ᴰ*Nelis* J.]: StSemNeerl 25, 1989 ➤ 6,2357 [BL 92,96, R.P. *Carroll:* 'first fruit of study with Umberto ECO at Bologna and at the Pontificium Institutum Biblicum in Rome']: ᴿNedTTs 45 (1991) 244s (N. *Tromp*).

1988 **Zimmerman** Anthony F., Original sin; where doctrine meets science. NY 1990, Vantage. 264 p. – ᴿVerbumSVD 32 (1991) 336 (H. *Dumont*).

1989 *Tosatti* Teodora, Gen 2,4ss; storia di un nome non dato: Protestantesimo 46 (1991) 301-8.

1990 *Meier* Samuel A., Linguistic clues on the date and Canaanite origin of Genesis 2:23-24: CBQ 53 (1991) 18-24.

1991 *Diebner* Bernd, *Zot* [Gn 2,23*a*] Anmerkungen zur Identität der Urmutter: DielB 26 (1989s) 15-31 [81-92, Rückkehr des *arôn* nach 'Israel'].

1992 *a) Hre Kio* Stephen, The problem of cultural adjustment; understanding and translating Genesis 2,24; – *b) Sembiring* M.K., Biblical kinship terms and their translation into the Karo language: BTrans 42 (1991) 210-7/217-225.

1993 *Müller* Hans-Peter, Drei Deutungen des Todes; Genesis 3, der Mythos von Adapa und die Sage von Gilgamesch: ➤ 310, JbBT 6 (1991) 117-134.

1994 *Lewis* Jack P., The woman's seed (Gen 3:15) [the Fathers should have compared Gen 16,10 Hagar and 24,60 Rebecca]: JEvTS 34 (1991) 299-319 [< NTAbs 36,236].

1995 *Schmitt* John J., Like Eve, like Adam; *mšl* in Gen 3,16: Biblica 72 (1991) 1-22; franç. 22.

E2.1 **Cain et Abel;** *gigantes, longaevi; Genesis 4s.*

1996 *Bovati* Pietro, Violenza e giustizia nell'AT, 1. La violenza nei racconti di origine [Gn 4,1-16...]; 2. La violenza nella storia (secondo la tradizione deuteronomista): ➤ 535, Firmana 1 (1991s) 7-36.

1997 *Nazzaro* Antonio V., Ambrosiana IV. Su Cain 1.3,11-4,12: StTardAnt 8 (1989) 255-269.

1998 *Vermeylen* Jacques, La descendance de Caïn et la descendance d'Abel (Gen 4,17-26 + 5,28b-29): ZAW 103 (1991) 175-193.

1999 *Wolde* Ellen van, The story of Cain and Abel; a narrative study: JStOT 52 (1991) 25-41.

2000 *Hess* Richard S., [Gn 4,18-23; 5,25-33] Lamech in the genealogies of Genesis: BBRes 1 (1991) 21-25.

2001 *Cole* Timothy J., [Gen 5,21-24] Enoch, a man who walked with God: BS 148 (1991) 288-297.

E2.2 *Diluvium,* **The Flood;** Gilgameš (Atraḫasis); **Genesis 6...**

2002 **Bailey** L.R., Noah 1989 ➤ 5,2216; 6,2377: ᴿCritRR 4 (1991) 118s (H.T.C. *Sun*).

2003 **Blanc** Yannick, Enquête sur la mort de Gilgamesh. P 1991, Felin. 133 p. [OIAc 2,14].

2004 **Cazeaux** J., La trame et la chaîne 2. Le cycle de Noé dans PHILON d'Alexandrie: ArbLGJ 20, 1989 ➤ 5,2217: ᴿBL (1991) 133 (C.J.A. *Hickling*).

2004* *Cornick* David, [Gn 6] The ways of God: ExpTim 103 (1991s) 146s.
2005 ᴱ**Dundes** Alan, The flood myth 1988 ➤ 4,2246... 6,2379: ᴿBZ 35 (1991) 114s (J. *Scharbert*).
2006 *Edzard* Dietz O., Zahlen, zählen und messen im Gilgameš-Epos: ➤ 126, ꜰRɪᴄʜᴛᴇʀ W., Text 1991, 57-66.
2007 *Holloway* Steven W., What ship goes there? The Flood narratives in the Gilgamesh Epic and Genesis considered in light of Ancient Near Eastern temple ideology: ZAW 103 (1991) 328-355.
2008 ᴱ**Kovacs** Maureen G., The epic of Gilgamesh 1989 ➤ 5,2224: ᴿAnOr 59 (1991) 329s (B. *Hruška*).
2009 **Künzler** Nicolas, Le déluge; l'avenir est à la promesse: CahB 2. Aubonne 1990, Moulin. 34 p. [RHPR 71,231]. – ᴿÉTRel 66 (1991) 583s (D. *Lys*).
2010 *Lambert* Wilfred G., *a*) Three new pieces of Atra-ḫasis; – *b*) Another trick of Enki?: ➤ 61, ꜰGᴀʀᴇʟʟɪ P., Marchands 1991, 411-4 [*Groneberg* Brigitte 398-410] / 415-420.
2010* *Müller* Hans-P., Gilgamesch-Epos und AT: 87, ꜰKᴏᴄʜ K., Ernten 1991, 75-99.
2011 *Moran* William L., Ovid's *blanda voluptas* and the humanization of Enkidu: JNES 50 (1991) 121-7.
2012 *Noegel* Scott B., A Janus parallelism in the Gilgamesh flood story: AcSum 13 (1991) 419-421.
2013 **Schweizer** Andreas, Der Held und die Göttin; eine religionspsychologische Deutung des Gilgamesch-Epos: ev. Diss. Zürich 1991, ᴰ*Bernet*. – TR 87 (1991) 515.
2013* *Selvanayagam* Israel, Floating Ark and shipwreck; contrary biblical models for multi-faith context and Christian living: AsiaJT 5 (1991) 338-345 [< ᴢɪᴛ 91,558].
2014 *Soden* W. von., Der Urmensch im Atramḫasis-Mythos: ➤ 621, Rencontre 36, 1989/91, 47-51.
2015 *Zuurmond* Rochus, The flood according to Enoch in early Christian literature: ➤ 446, SBL Sem 30 (1991) 766-772.

2016 *Müller* Hans-P., [Gn 6,5]. Die Motive für die Sintflut; die hermeneutische Funktion des Mythos und seiner Analyse [< ZAW 97 (1985) 295-316]: ➤ 240, Mythos 1991, 88-109.
2017 **Oberforcher** Robert, Die Flutprologe als Kompositionsschlüssel der biblischen Urgeschichte [ᴰ1977] 1981 ➤ 62,2422... 65,1955: ᴿRB 98 (1991) 460s (J. *Loza* excuse le retard).
2018 **Pio** Joseph-Régis, L'épopée de Gilgamesh; poème. P 1989, Edifra. 149 p.; ill (Dabdoub R.). 2-904070-33-8 [OIAc 1,22].
2019 *Fernández Marcos* Natalio, [Gn 6] Las medidas del arca de Noé en la exégesis de Aʀɪᴀs Mᴏɴᴛᴀɴᴏ: ➤ 421, Luso-Esp 1989/91, 737-743; 1 fig.
2020 *Zipor* Moshe A., A note on Genesis VI 13 [*m* for *ny*]: VT 41 (1991) 366-9.
2021 *Steiner* Richard C., [Gen 8,4] The mountains of Ararat, Mount Lubar and *hār ha-qedim*: JJS 42 (1991) 247-9.
2022 *Lust* John, 'For man shall his blood be shed'; Gen 9:6 in Hebrew and in Greek: ➤ 17, ꜰBᴀʀᴛʜᴇ́ʟᴇᴍʏ D., Tradition 1991, 91-102.
2023 *Zincone* Sergio, Il tema del sangue nel commento di Bᴇᴅᴀ a Gen 9,4-6: ➤ 565, Sangue 1989/91, 951-960.

2024 **Müller** Klaus, Tora für die Völker, die noachidischen Gebote im Beziehungsfeld zwischen Judentum und Christentum: Diss. ᴰRitschl D. Heidelberg 1991. – RTLv 23, p. 541.

2025 *Nodes* D. J., [Gen 9,12-17] Noah's rainbow in early Jewish and Christian exegesis: AmBenR 42 (1991) 236-250.

2026 a) *Felder* Cain H., [Gen 9, 18-27] Race, racism, and the biblical narratives; – b) *Copher* Charles B., The Black presence in the OT; – c) *Bailey* Randall C., Beyond identification; the use of Africans in OT poetry and narratives: ➤ 433, Stony the road 1986/91, 127-145 / 146-164 / 165-184.

2027 *Maier* Johann, Zu ethnographisch-geographischen Überlieferungen über Japhetiten (Gen 10,2-4) im frühen Judentum: Henoch 13 (1991) 157-194; Eng. 194 (tells what texts he used but nothing of his conclusions).

2028 *Tsirkin* Yu. B., [Gn 10,5] Japhet's progeny and the Phoenicians; ᵀChristonogova A.: ➤ 445, Phoenicians 1990/1, 117-134.

2029 *Ayaso Martínez* José Ramón, Etnografía judía en la Alta Edad Media; la lista de las naciones del Sefer Yosippon: ➤ 421, Luso-Esp 1989/91, 697-717.

2030 *Derrida* Jacques, Des tours dc Babel [English by *Graham* Joseph F., < Differences in translation, Cornell 1985]: ➤ 211, Semeia 54 (1991) 3-34; 1 fig.

2031 **Marty** François, [Gn 11] La bénédiction de Babel 1990 ➤ 6,2401: ᴿÉTRel 66 (1991) 306 (J. *Ansaldi*: magistral: langage créateur d'humanité).

2032 *Scarpat* Giuseppe, La Torre di Babele in FILONE [(?Terap. ?conf.) 183] e nella Sapienza (Sap 10,5): RivB 39 (1991) 167-173.

2033 *Schöttler* Heinz-Günther, Turmbaumenschheit oder Abrahamskindschaft — Genesis 11,1-9 aus historisch-kritischer Sicht: PraxRU 21,1 (Stu 1991) 12-15 (–35, al. < ZIT 91,188].

2034 a) *Soggin* J. Alberto, Der Turmbau zu Babel; – b) *Willi* Thomas, Die Funktion der Schlusssequenzen in der Komposition der jahwistischen Urgeschichte: ➤ 75, ꜰHERRMANN S., Prophetie 1991, 371-5 / 429-444.

2035 *Stoevesandt* Hinrich, Die eine Menschheit und die vielen Völker; die biblische Erzählung vom Turmbau zu Babel: KerDo 37 (1991) 44-61; Eng. 61.

2036 **Uehlinger** Christoph, Weltreich und 'eine Rede', Gn 11: OBO 101, 1990 ➤ 5,2238; 6,2403: ᴿTüTQ 171 (1991) 135-7 (W. *Gross*).

E2.3   **Patriarchae, Abraham;** *Genesis 12s.*

2037 **Abela** A., Themes of Abraham ..., Gn 11-25, ᴰ1989 ➤ 6,2404: ᴿAntonianum 66 (1991) 585s (M. *Nobile*).

2038 *Abela* Anthony, Redactional structuring within the Abraham narrative [... as a unit] in Genesis: ➤ 96, ꜰLUPI J., Veterum exempla 1991, 35-82.

2038* *Breuning* Wilhelm, Mit dem Stamm Abrahams geistlich verbunden: ➤ 46*, ꜰEHRLICH E. 1991, 22-34.

2039 *Gese* Hartmut, a) [Gen 11-25] Die Komposition der Abrahamserzählung [unveröffentlicht]; – b) Die dreifache Gestaltwerdung des ATs [< ᴱKlopfenstein M., Mitte der Schrift? 1987, 299-328]: ➤ 204, At. Studien 1991, 29-51 / 1-28.

2040 **Hansen** G. Walter, Abraham in Galatians 1989 [diss. 1985 Toronto]: ᴿJBL 110 (1991) 353-5 (J. S. *Siker*).

2041 *a) Heide* Albert van der, The call of Abraham as read by Jews and Christians; – *b) Stemberger* Günter, The treatment of the Bible in Judaism: ➤ 347, Concilium (1991,1) 13-26 / 37-46.

2042 *Decena* H., [Gen 12s] Un estudio sobre la promesa-alianza a Abrahán: Mayéutica 17,43 (1991) 39-64 [< NTAbs 36,233].

2043 **Fonseca Pires** João Paulo, Paz y pecado en los relatos patriarcales: diss. ᴰ*Varo Pineda* F. Pamplona 1991. – RTLv 23, p. 539.

2044 *La Hurd* Carol S., One God, one Father; Abraham in Judaism, Christianity, and Islam: Dialog 29 (1990) 17-24 [< TLZ 116,344].

2045 *Sauer* Georg, Abraham — tragende Gestalt der Frömmigkeit? [Eɪᴄʜʀᴏᴅᴛ W. 100 Gb. 1.VIII.1990]: TZBas 47 (1991) 291-8.

2046 ꟳScʜᴀʀʙᴇʀᴛ Josef, Die Väter Israels, ᴱ*Görg* Manfred 1989 ➤ 5,169: ᴿTAth 12 (1991) 185-7 (P. *Simotas*).

2047 **Scriba** Albrecht, Die Geschichte des Motivkomplexes Theophanie; seine Elemente, Einbindung in Geschehensablaufe und Verwendungsweisen in altisraelitischer, frühjüdischer und frühchristlicher Literatur: ev. Diss. ᴰ*Brandenburger* E. Mainz 1991. – RTLv 23, p. 546.

2048 **Siker** Jeffrey S., Disinheriting the Jews; Abraham in early Christian controversy. Louisville 1991, W-Knox. 296 p. $19 pa. [CBQ 54,206].

2049 *Steinberg* Naomi, [Gn 11,27 - 36,43] Alliance or descent? The function of marriage in Genesis: JStOT 51 (1991) 45-55.

2050 *Segal* Eliezer, [Gen 11,29], Sarah and Ishak; method and message in midrashic tradition: JQR 82 (1991s) 417-429.

2051 *a) Beuken* Wim, [Gn 11,31 ...] De trektocht van Abraham; – *b) Beentjes* Panc, Partner — partij — paniek; de bijbelse notie 'Verbond' en zijn problemen: CollatVʟ 21 (1991) 271-286 / 287-300.

2052 *Heide* Albert van der, [Gn 12] La vocation d'Abraham, ᵀ*Braat* Anne: ➤ 348, Concilium 233 (P 1991) 27-42.

2053 *Firestone* Reuven, [Gen 12, 10-20 ...] Difficulties in keeping a beautiful wife; the legend of Abraham and Sarah in Jewish and Islamic tradition: JJS 42 (1991) 196-214.

E2.4 **Melchisedech, Sodoma;** *Genesis 14.*

2054 *Cockerill* Gareth L., Melchizedek or 'King of Righteousness'? [< diss. Richmond]: EvQ 63 (1991) 305-312.

2055 *Dubois* Jean-Daniel, Une exégèse manichéenne de Genèse 14?: ➤ 140, ꟳSᴍʏᴛʜ-Fʟᴏʀᴇɴᴛɪɴ F. 1991, 263-267.

2056 **Gammie** John G., Melchizedek; an exegetical study of Genesis 14 and the Psalter; diss. Edinburgh 1962! 326 p. BRD-91773. – DissA 52 (1991s) 951-A.

2057 *Scharbert* Josef, 'Gesegnet sei Abram vom höchsten Gott'; zu Gen 14,19 und ähnlichen Stellen im AT: ➤ 126, ꟳRɪᴄʜᴛᴇʀ W., Text 1991, 387-401.

E2.5 **The Covenant** (alliance, Bund); *Foedus, Genesis 15 ...*

2058 **Ha** John, Genesis 15, BZAW 181, ᴰ1989 ➤ 5,2272; 6,2424: ᴿBLitEc 92 (1991) 56s (M. *Delcor*); BO 48 (1991) 624-6 (J. *Van Seters*); CBQ 53 (1991) 470s (J. I. *Hunt*: nicely executed and beautifully printed); Henoch 13 (1991) 108s (P. *Sacchi* does not agree that its authorship is shown exceptional); JBL 110 (1991) 505-7 (D. *Carr* compares with Mᴏʟʟᴇ); Syria 67 (1990) 756 (A. *Caquot*).

2059 **Kalluveettil** Paul, Declaration and covenant: AnBib 88, ᴰ1982 ➤ 63, 2298 ... 1,2308: ᴿBZ 35 (1991) 283s (H.-C. *Schmitt*).

2060 **Kreuzer** Siegfried, Die Frühgeschichte Israels: BZAW 181, 1989 ➤ 5,2274; 6,2425: ᴿWeltOr 22 (1991) 159-162 (E. *Blum*).

2061 **Mölle** H., Genesis 15: ForBi 62, 1988 ➤ 4,2309; 6,2426: ᴿZAW 103 (1991) 304 (H.-C. *Schmitt*).

2062 *Römer* Thomas, Gen 15 und Gen 17; Beobachtungen und Anfragen zu einem Dogma der 'neueren' und 'neuesten' Pentateuchkritik: DielB 26 (1989s) 32-47.

2063 **Gilbert** Pierre, Le récit biblique de rêve; essai de confrontation analytique. Lyon 1990, Profac. 134 p. 2-85317-041-1. – ᴿRHPR 71 (1991) 195 (B. *Kaempf*, sous rubrique 'Théologie pratique').

2064 **Hendricks** Lois L., Discovering my biblical dream heritage [i.e. dreams in the OT]. San Jose 1989, Resource. 197 p. $10. 0-89390-144-X. – ᴿRExp 88 (1991) 100s (D. S. *Hunsicker*: valuable, balanced).

2065 *Sutherland* D. Dixon, Gen. 15.6 and early Christian struggles over election: ScotJT 44 (1991) 443-456.

2066 **Firestone** Reuven, Journeys in holy lands; the evolution of the Abraham-Ishmael legends in Islamic exegesis 1990 ➤ 6,3433: ᴿJAOS 111 (1991) 799s (Vera B. *Moreen*).

2066* *Janzen* J. Gerald, Hagar in Paul's eyes [... Gal 3,28] and in the eyes of Yahweh (Genesis 16); a study in horizons: HorBT 13 (1991) 1-22.

2067 *Waters* John W., [Gen 16,1-6; 21,8-21] Who was Hagar?: ➤ 433, Stony the road 1986/91, 187-205.

2068 **Williams** Delores S., A study of the analogous relation between African-American women's experience and Hagar's experience and the challenge posed to Black Liberation theology: diss. Union, ᴰ*Driver* T. NY 1990. – RelStR 18,172.

2069 *Brueggemann* Walter, Genesis 17:1-22 [Sarah & heir], expository: Interpretation 45 (1991) 55-59.

2070 *Roshwald* Mordecai, [Gn 18,23-32] Un diálogo entre el hombre y Dios [< ScotJT 42 (1989) 145-165], ᵀᴱ*Messa* Josep: SelT 30 (1991) 21-29.

2071 **Mulder** M. J., Sodom en Gomorra, een verhaal van dode steden: Exegetische Studies 4, 1988 ➤ 5,2286: ᴿBijdragen 52 (1991) 328 (M. *Parmentier*).

2072 **Letellier** Robert I., Day in Mamre, night in Sodom; Abraham, Lot and the judge of all the earth; the structure, language and symbolism of Genesis 18 and 19 considered as a literary unit: diss. Pont. Univ. Gregoriana, ᴰ*Conroy* C. Rome 1991. 363 p.; extr. Nᵒ 3723, 117 p. – RTLv 23, p. 539 [< DissA-C].

2073 **Miller** William T., [Gn 18; 22]. Mysterious encounters at Mamre and Jabbok 1984 ➤ 65,2002 ... 6,2439: ᴿJAAR 59 (1991) 411-3 (Mary C. *Callaway*).

2074 *Husser* Jean-Marie, Le songe comme procédé littéraire; à propos de Gn 20: RevSR 65 (1991) 157-172.

2075 *Sarna* Nahum M., Genesis 21,33; a study in the development of a biblical text and its rabbinic transformation: ➤ 56, ᶠFox M. 1 (1991) 69-75.

2076 *a) Jesus e Silva* Maria de, O poço concentra a vida e marca os acontecimentos (Gn 21,25); – *b) 'Sandra'* + 3 *al*, As parteiras; 'as mulheres hebréias são cheias de vida!' (Ex 1,15-22); – *c) 'Béqui'* + 4 *al.*,

Pesquisa preliminar sobre Raab (Js 2,1-21; 6,17-25): EstudosB 29 ('A mulher na sociedade tribal', 1991) 91-95 / 33-39 / 40-53.

E2.6   **The 'Aqedâ;**   *Isaac, Genesis 22 ...*

2077 *Ackerman* Susan, The deception of Isaac, Jacob's dream at Bethel, and incubation on an animal skin: ➤ 288, Priesthood 1991, 92-120.

2078 *Davis* Ellen F., Self-consciousness and conversation; reading Genesis 22: BBRes 1 (1991) 27-40.

2079 *Rodd* C.S., [Gn 22, 1-18] What kind of God is this?: ExpTim 103 (1991s) 18s.

2080 *Roshwald* Mordecai, [Gn 22] The meaning of faith: ModT 7 (1990s) 381-401.

2080* *Trible* Phyllis, Genesis 22, the sacrifice of Sarah: ➤ 454b, Not in heaven 1989/91, 170-191, 249-253.

2081 **Tschuggnall** Peter, Das Abraham-Opfer als Glaubensparadox; bibeltheologischer Befund, literarische Rezeption, KIERKEGAARDS Deutung [Diss. Innsbruck 1989, ᴰKern W., ➤ 6,2449]: EurHS 23/399. Bern 1990, Lang. 208 p. Fs 53. 3-631-42835-0. – ᴿRHPR 71 (1991) 217-9 (J.-G. *Heintz*); TsTNijm 31 (1991) 331s (M. van den *Nieuwenhuizen*).

2082 *Vetter* D., Die Bindung Jizchaks; das sprachliche Werk — 'ein mit den Lippen geschlossener Bund': ➤ 6,96, ᶠKHOURY A.T., 60 Gb., 'Ihr alle aber seid Brüder', ᴱHagemann L., *Pulsfort* E. [Wü 1990, Echter] 263-284 [ZAW 104,151].

2083 *Wilfong* Marsha M., Genesis 22, 1-18: Interpretation 45 (1991) 393-6.

2084 *Kalimi* Isaac, [Gn 22,21; 2 Chr 3,1] The land of Moriah, Mount Moriah, and the site of Solomon's Temple in biblical historiography: HarvTR 83 (1990) 345-362.

2085 *Davila* James R., The name of God at Moriah; an unpublished fragment from 4QGenExodᵃ [Lᴙ M YᴙˤH]: JBL 110 (1991) 577-582; 1 fig.

2086 *Bejaoui* Fathi, L'intervention divine et le sacrifice d'Abraham sur la sigillée africaine; deux coupes inédites de Tunisie: RivArCr 67 (1991) 325-336; 10 fig.

2086* *Schmid* Herbert, Die Gestalt des Isaak; ihr Verhältnis zur Abraham- und Jakobtradition: ErtFor 274. Da 1991, Wiss. vi-122 p. DM 26,80 [TR 88,426].

2087 *Sternberg* Meier, [Gn 23,2-6 Macpelah] Double cave, double talk; the indirections of biblical dialogue: ➤ 454b, Not in heaven 1989/91, 28-57. 227-231.

2088 *a) Tavares* António A. [Gen 23,3], Instituições dos Hititas em Hebron no contexto do Medio Oriente, – *b) Coelho Dias* Geraldo J.A., Filisteus em Canaã, uma cultura desaparecida?; – *c) Carreira das Neves* Joaquim, A Bíblia como história frente ao esoterismo: ➤ 422, Didaskalia 20,1 (1989/90) 189-197 / 199-210 / 167-187.

2089 *Martin-Achard* Robert [➤ 1304a], Biblical perspectives on aging... Gen 24,1: ➤ 347, Concilium (1991,3) 31-38.

E2.7   **Jacob and Esau;**   ladder-dream; *Jacob, somnium, Genesis 25 ...*

2090 *Nazor* Anica, [Gn 25,8] *Još...* (Croatian) An apocryphal Glagolithic text about Abraham's death (with facsimile): ➤ 68, ᶠGRACIOTTI S. 1990, 55-63.

2091 *Clifford* Richard J., Genesis 25:19-34 [Isaac's marriage], expository: Interpretation 45 (1991) 397-401.

2092 **Hendel** Ronald S., The epic of... Jacob ᴰ1987 ➤ 5,2308; 6,2460: ᴿJTS
42 (1991) 153s (R. N. *Whybray*); Syria 67 (1990) 217 (A. *Caquot*).

2093 *Pury* Albert de, Le cycle de Jacob comme légende autonome des origines
d'Israël: ➤ 429, IOSOT 1989/91, 78-96.

2094 *Feld* Helmut, Jakob der Lügner, zur Auslegung von Gn 25,31 und
27,19.24 im 16. Jahrhundert [Kolloquium Bibelexegese 16.Jh. Genf Sept.
1988]: LuJb 58 (1991) 43-63.

2095 *Snijders* L. A., Genesis 27, het bedrog van Jakob [*Tal* Justus (?), De
zegen van Jakob 1950]: NedTTs 45 (1991) 183-192; Eng. 241.

2096 **Dicou** B., [Gn 27s] Jakob en Esau, Israël en Edom; Israël tegenover de
volken in de verhalen over Jakob en Esau in Genesis en in de grote
profetieën over Edom [diss. Amsterdam]. Vorburg 1990, Publivorm.
vii-299 p. 90-6495-225-6. – ᴿBL (1991) 71 (J. A. *Emerton*); ZAW 103
(1991) 295 (H.-C. *Schmitt*).

2097 *Abegunde* Solomon O., [Gen 27,33-37] Curses and blessings in Genesis in
the light of the extension of personality [JOHNSON A., One and Many]:
BTrans 42 (1991) 242-7.

2098 *Joosten* Jan, The syntax of *habarākāh 'aḥat hî' lakā 'ābî* (Gen. 27: 38aa):
JSS 36 (1991) 207-221.

2099 *Dennison* William D., Bethel, house of God; Genesis 28:10-22: Kerux
2,3 (1987) 23-30.

2100 *Husser* Jean-Marie, Les métamorphoses d'un songe; critique littéraire de
Genèse 28, 10-22: RB 98 (1991) 321-342; Eng. 321.

2101 *Whartenby* Thomas J., Gn 28:10-22 [Jacob's ladder], expository: Interpretation 45 (1991) 402-5.

2101* *Berlin* Adele, [Gn 29 Rachel; 1 Sam 19,13 Michal] Literary exegesis of
biblical narrative, between poetics and hermeneutics: ➤ 454*b*, Not in
heaven 1989/91, 120-8 . 239-241.

2102 *a*) *Diebner* Bernd J., Rachels Niederkunft bei Bethlehem und die
jüdische Vereinnahmung der israelitischen Königstradition, I; – *b*) *Nauerth*
Claudia, Rahel und Maria auf dem Wege nach Bethlehem: DielB 26
(1989s) 48-57 / 58-69.

E2.8 **Jacob's wrestling; the Angels;** *lucta, Angelus/mal'ak Gn 31* ...

2103 *Cunchillos* J. L., [*mal'ak*] 'El encargado o comisionado'; recorrido por
los senderos de la exégesis; de la filología a las instituciones; de lo profano
a lo religioso, de la historia de las religiones a la teología: ➤ 421,
Luso-Esp 1989/91, 83-94.

2104 *Fass* E., How the angels do serve: Judaism 40 (1991) 281-9 [< NTAbs
36,86].

2105 *García Cordero* Maximiliano, El ministerio de los ángeles en los escritos
del Nuevo Testamento: CiTom 118 (1991) 3-40.

2106 **Meier** S. A., Messenger [*mal'ak / mar sipri*] 1989 ➤ 5,1230*; 6,2487:
ᴿBO 48 (1991) 602s (D. *Pardee*); ZAW 103 (1991) 303 (I. *Kottsieper*).

2107 *Plathow* Michael, Engel — ein Modethema? Gedankensplitter zu einer
theologischen Herausforderung heute: Deutsches Pfarrerblatt 91 (Essen
1991) 233-6 [< ᴢɪᴛ 91,461].

2108 ᴱ**Ries** Julien, (*Limet* Henri), Anges et démons: Homo Religiosus 14,
1987/9 ➤ 550*b*: ᴿGregorianum 72 (1991) 577s (J. *Galot*); RHPR 71
(1991) 245s (M. *Scopello*).

2109 *Schneider* Alfred, [Ps 91,11; Ef 3,10] 'Er befiehlt seinen Engeln': ObnŽiv
46 (1991) 325-334 (croat.); 334 deutsch.

2110 **Vorgrimler** Herbert, Wiederkehr der Engel; ein altes Thema neu durchdacht. Kevelaer 1991, Butzon & B. 120 p. DM 20. 3-7666-9752-8. – RErbAuf 47 (1991) 486 (U. J. *Plaga*).

2111 *Klein* Ralph W., [Gn 32s] Celebrating and sharing the gift; reflections on Jacob, Israel's ancestor: CurrTMiss 18 (1991) 263-272.

2112 **Massenet** Michel, [Gn 32] Jacob ou la fraude: Parole présente. P 1991, Cerf. 144 p. – RRTLv 22 (1991) 532 (P.-M. *Bogaert*).

2113 **Sheres** Ita, [Gn 34] Dinah's rebellion, a biblical parable for our time 1990 → 6,2491: RCurrTMiss 18 (1991) 300 (R. W. *Klein*); NewTR 4,3 (1991) 92s (Dianne *Bergant*).

2113* *Fewell* Danna N., *Gunn* David M., Tapping the balance; STERNBERG'S Reader and the rape of Dinah [Poetics 1985]: JBL 110 (1991) 193-211.

2114 *Rose* Martin, L'itinérance du Iacobus pentateuchus; réflexions sur Genèse 35,1-15: → 140, FSMYTH-FLORENTIN F., 1991, 113-126.

2115 *Châtillon* J., † 29.IX.1988, [Gn 35,18] Le De duodecim patriarchis ou Beniamin minor de RICHARD de Saint-Victor; description et essai de classification des manuscrits: RHTextes 21 (1991) 159-236 (237-242, *Hasenohr* Geneviève).

2116 *Kronholm* Tryggve, Holy adultery; the interpretation of the story of Judah and Tamar (Gen 38) in the genuine hymns of EPHRAEM Syrus (ca. 306-373): OrSuec 40 (1991) 149-163.

2117 **Neeb** John H.C., Genesis 38:12; the function of a biblical text in early Jewish and Christian communities: diss. St. Michael, DWalters S. Toronto 1991. 308 p. – RTLv 23, p. 541.

E2.9   **Joseph;** Jacob's blessings; *Genesis 37; 39-50.*

2118 *Amit* Yaira, ❿ The repeated situation; a poetic princip[le] in the modeling of the Joseph narrative: → 303, Teuda 7 (1991) 55-66; Eng. IX.

2119 *Isaac* E., The Ethiopic History of Joseph, translation with introduction and notes: JPseud 6 (1990) 3-125.

2120 **Longacre** Robert E., Joseph 1989 → 5,2334; 6,2505: RCBQ 53 (1991) 292-4 (N. *Winther-Nielsen*); SWJT 34,1 (1991s) 72 (D. *Hays*).

2121 *a) Rossi de Gasperis* Francesco, Giuseppe, il fratello saggio, panorama sapienziale del ciclo di Giuseppe; – *b) Garrone* Danièle, La storia di Giuseppe, un approccio esegetico; – *c) Laras* Giuseppe, Il midrash su Giuseppe; – *d) Roccati* Alessandro, Ambientazione egiziana delle storie di Giuseppe e racconti romanzati paralleli; – *e) Flores d'Arcais* Francesco, La storia di Giuseppe in Thomas MANN: → 418, Biblia gen. 1990, 73-108 / 111-139 / 9-33 / 143-151 / 37-70.

2122 **Schweizer** Harald, Die Josefsgeschichte, Konstituierung des Textes: Textwissenschaft/Informatik 4. Tü 1991, Francke. x-358 p.; v-203 p. 3-7720-1953-6 [OIAc 1,24].

2123 *Marconi* Nazzareno, Contributi per una lettura unitaria di Gen 37: RivB 39 (1991) 277-303; Eng. 303.

2124 *Voitila* Anssi, La technique de traduction du Yiqtol (imparfait hébreu) dans l'Histoire de Joseph grecque (Gen 37.39-50): → 426, Septuagint 7, 1989/91, 223-237.

2125 **Da Silva** Aldina, Une lecture de la théologie de Genèse 37-50 à la lumière de la symbolique des vêtements et des rêves: diss. DMyre A. Montréal 1991. 307 p. – RTLv 23, p. 538.

2126 **Kugel** James L., [Gn 39,1] In Potiphar's house [first half]; the interpretive life of biblical texts [other half] 1990 → 6,2504: ᴿParadigms 7,2 (1991s) 39 (T. *Linafelt*).

2127 *Teugels* G., [Gen 39,1-20; *ṣaddîq*] De kuise Jozef; de receptie van een bijbels model: NedTTs 45 (1991) 193-203; Eng. 241.

2128 *Zurro Rodríguez* Eduardo, El hapax *'abrēk* (Gn 41,43): EstB 49 (1991) 265-9 [gobernador].

2129 *Gnuse* Robert, The Jewish dream interpreter in a foreign court; the recurring use of a theme in Jewish literature: JPseud 7 (1990) 29-35.

2130 *Vattioni* Francesco, Genesi 45,17 [*be'îr*], carri o animali?: Henoch 13 (1991) 151-6; Eng. 156 [*poreîon* in papyri can be animal as well as wagon or ship].

2130* *Pautasso* L. G., Neofiti's reversal of the motif of the 'wandering Jews' in Genesis 47:21: Sefarad 51 (1991) 115-142; español 143.

2131 a) *Tábet* M. A., Las cuestiones de Isaac ABRABANEL al Gn 49,1-28 (el Testamento de Jacob); – b) *Alonso-Fontela* Carlos, Utilización del comentario a los profetas posteriores de D. Isaac Abravanel en la Universidad Complutense: → 421, Luso-Esp 1989/91, 679-687 / 673-8.

E3.1   **Exodus event and theme;** *textus, commentarii.*

2132 ᴱ**Bloom** Harold, Modern critical interpretations [Gn 1986 → 4, 1961; Gospels 1988 → 5,379]: Exodus. NY 1987, Chelsea. 143 p. 0-87754-909-5. – ᴿRExp 88 (1991) 453 (J.D.W. *Watts*: series to include 100 titles; literary, not theological; refreshing for the teacher who has become over-familiar with the Bible story).

2133 **Blum** Erhard, [Ex 1-14] Studien zur Komposition des Pentateuch: BZAW 189, 1990 → 6,2527: ᴿArTGran 54 (1991) 353-6 (A. *Torres*); Biblica 72 (1991) 253-263 (J.-L. *Ska*); Henoch 13 (1991) 366s (J. A. *Soggin*); TüTQ 171 (1991) 132s (W. *Gross*); ZAW 103 (1991) 148 (H.-C. *Schmitt*).

2134 *Dijkstra* M., Verdreven, vrijgelaten of gevlucht? De overlevering van de Exodus in nieuw historisch perspectief: NedTTs 45 (1991) 1-15; Eng. 60.

2135 **Drazin** I., Targum Onkelos to Exodus; an English translation of the text with analysis and commentary. Hoboken/Denver 1990, KTAV/Univ. Center for Judaic Studies. xiii-383 p. $59.50. 0-88125-342-1 [BL 92,45, R. P. *Gordon*].

2136 *Eslinger* Lyle, Freedom or knowledge? Perspective and purpose in the Exodus narrative (Exodus 1-15): JStOT 52 (1991) 43-60.

2137 **Fretheim** Terence E., Exodus: Interpretation comm. Louisville 1991, Knox. vii-321 p. $22. 0-8042-3102-8 [TDig 39,60]. – ᴿHorBT 13 (1991) 179s (L. *Meyer*); TTod 48 (1991s) 362.364 (S. A. *Reed*).

2138 ᵀᴱ**Giron-Blanc** Luis-Fernando, Midrás Éxodo Rabbah 1, 1989 → 5,2353; 6,2536: ᴿCritRR 4 (1991) 357s (J. *Neusner:* good but unusable for lack of reference system).

2139 *Giroud* Jean-Claude, Figures et organisation de l'espace dans le livre de l'Exode; problèmes et perspectives: SémBib 62 (1991) 21-33.

2140 EZECHIEL, Exagoge: ᴱ**Holladay** C. R., Fragments... Ezek.Trag. 1989 → 5,b678: ᴿZAW 103 (1991) 298 (I. *Kottsieper*).

2141 — *Collins* Nina L., Ezekiel, the author of the Exagoge; his calendar [day began at dawn] and home [Egypt, probably Alexandria]: JStJud 22 (1991) 201-211 [< NTAbs 36,232].

2142 **Houtman** C., Exodus I-II [to 19,25], 1989 ➤ 5,2356; 6,2339: ᴿBO 48 (1991) 883-5 (J.W. *Wevers*: one of the best; starts with 145 pages on the 51 Hebrew roots commonest in Exodus, and on numerals, names, fauna, flora ...); RB 98 (1991) 461s (J. *Loza* ajoute à 96,632 de J.-M. *Rousée* que 'l'information est incontestablement plus complète que celle des autres grands commentaires de l'Exode que nous connaissions').

2143 **Isabelle de la Source** sr., Moïse: Lire la Bible avec les Pères 2, 1990 ➤ 6,2539*: ᴿEsprVie 101 (1991) 432 (É. *Cothenet*).

2143* *Johnson* Dan G., The relation of history and story in the Exodus tradition: JRelSt 17 (Cleveland 1989) 146-157 [< ʑɪᴛ 91,764].

2144 **Johnstone** W., Exodus: OT Guides 1990 ➤ 6,2540: ᴿBL (1991) 80 (W.J. *Houston*); VT 41 (1991) 249s (J.A. *Emerton* queries Dtr influence); ZAW 103 (1991) 157 (H.-C. *Schmitt*).

2145 *Kitchen* Kenneth A., Israel seen from Egypt; understanding the biblical text from visuals and methodology: TyndB 42 (1991) 113-126: use time-honored pictures and parallels with caution.

2146 **Le Boulluec** A., *Sandevoir* P., La Bible d'Alexandrie 2., L'Exode 1989 ➤ 6,2541: ᴿNedTTs 45 (1991) 252s (P.W. van der *Horst*); RÉG 103 (1991) 349 (A. *Wartelle*); Salesianum 53 (1991) 182s (M. *Cimosa*); VT 41 (1991) 255 (J.A. *Emerton* claims a Festschrift should not be cited as such).

2147 *a) Levenson* John D., Exodus and liberation; – *b) Brueggemann* Walter [Ex 1 ...]. A Gospel language of pain and possibility: HorBT 13 (1991) 134-174 / 95-133.

2147* **Magnante** Antonio, La teologia dell'Esodo nei Salmi: diss. ᴰ*Federici* T. R 1991, Pont. Univ. Urbaniana. 391 p.

2148 **Martini** Carlo M., ☉ Ludu mój, wyjdż z Egiptu [rekolekcja Mediolan 1982]. Kraków 1990, Apost. Modlitwy. 135 p. – ᴿPrzPow 830 (1990) 171-3 (A. *Rekiel*).

2149 **Peters** Melvin K.H., A critical edition of the Coptic (Bohairic) Pentateuch, 2. Exodus 1986 ➤ 2,1733; 5,1766: ᴿBO 48 (1991) 539-543 (P. *Luisier*).

Poniży Bogdan, ☉ Reinterpretation of Exodus in the Book of Wisdom²ʳᵉᵛ 1991 ➤ 3085.

2150 **Sarna** Nahum M., Exodus; the traditional Hebrew text with the new JPS translation: JPS Torah Commentary. Ph 1991, Jewish Publication Society. xxv-278 p. 0-8276-0327-4.

2151 **Schmidt** Werner H., Exodus 1-6: BK 1988 ➤ 4,2429; 6,2550*: ᴿZkT 113 (1991) 78s (R. *Oberforcher*: nach 14 Jahren, noch ohne Einführung).

2152 ᴱ**Sierra** S., Rᴀsʜɪ, Esodo 1988 ➤ 5,2367; 6,2551: ᴿAntonianum 66 (1991) 159-161 (M. *Nobile*).

2153 **Stiebing** W.H., Out of the desert? 1989 ➤ 5,2369; 6,2553: ᴿBL (1991) 41s (G.I. *Davies*: sound, archeological; discusses even Vᴇʟɪᴋᴏᴠsᴋʏ; but not much on patriarchal traditions or *apiru*); CBQ 53 (1991) 133s (J.L. *Sullivan*); JRel 71 (1991) 571s (W.G. *Dever*); PerspRelSt 18 (1991) 182-5 (E. *Rowell*).

2153* *a) Virgulin* Stefano, Rilettura aggadica dell'Esodo nei Salmi; – *b) Mello* Alberto, La figura di Mosè nei profeti e nei Salmi; – *c) Rochettes* Jaqueline des, Il Targum rilegge Mosè; – *d) Marconcini* Benito, Rilettura e profezia dell'esodo nel Secondo-Isaia; – *e) Priotto* Michelangelo, Attualità e interpellazione nella rilettura dell'Esodo in Sapienza: ➤ 292*b*, ParSpV 24 (1991) 43-56 / 57-80 / 95-109 / 17-29 / 81-93.

2154 **Wevers** J.W., Notes on the Greek text of Exodus: SBL SeptCog 30, 1990 ➤ 6,2555: ᴿETL 67 (1991) 148-150 (J. *Lust*); JSS 36 (1991) 337-9 (A. *Salvesen*); JStJud 22 (1991) 153-5 (A. *Hilhorst*).

2155 **Wevers** J.W. (*Quast* U.) Exodus: Septuaginta 2/1. Gö 1991, VR. 474 p. DM 254; sb. 216. 3-525-53431-0; p. 467-474, Abweichung von BROOKE-MACLEAN [ZAW 104,458].

2156 *Wevers* John W., The lectionary texts of Exodus: ➤ 17, ᶠBARTHÉLEMY D., Tradition 1991, 293-300.

2157 **Wittenberg** Gunther H., I have heard the cry of my people; a study guide to Exodus 1-15: Bible in Context 1. Hilton SAf 1991, Pietermaritzburg Cluster. [x–] 77 p. R 10 [CBQ 54,406].

2158 *Wolska-Conus* Wanda, La 'Topographie chrétienne' de COSMAS Indicopleustès; hypothèses sur quelques thèmes de son illustration: RÉByz 48 (1990) 155-191; 19 fig. p. 170-186, illustration de l'Exode.

2159 **Zakovitch** Yair, 'And you shall tell your son...' The concept of the Exodus in the Bible. J 1991, Magnes. 144 p. $20. 965-223-780-9.

E3.2 Moyses – Pharaoh, Goshen – *Exodus 1 ...*

2160 *a*) **Alonso Schökel** Luis, *Gutiérrez* Guillermo, La missione di Mosè, meditazioni bibliche [1989 ➤ 5,2372]: Bibbia e Preghiera 7. R 1991, Apost. Preghiera. 176 p. Lit. 15.000. 88-7357-086-0.

— *b*) *Balout* Lionel, *al.* La momie de Ramsès II 1985 ➤ 4,2442.h275; 5,2375: ᴿCdÉ 66 (1991) 190-2 (I. *Morimoto*).

— *c*) *Bimson* John J., Merneptah's Israel and recent theories of Israelite origins: JStOT 49 (1991) 3-29.

2161 **Coats** George W., Moses 1988 ➤ 4,2448 ... 6,2561: ᴿBZ 35 (1991) 290-2 (J. *Scharbert*, auch über AURELIUS E.).

2162 *Feldman* Louis H., JOSEPHUS' portrait of Moses: JQR 82 (1991s) 285-328.

2163 *Hafemann* Scott J., Moses in the apocrypha and pseudepigrapha; a survey: JPseud 7 (1990) 79-104.

2164 **Martini** Carlo M., Through Moses to Jesus 1988 ➤ 4,2460: ᴿRRel 49 (1990) 627s (M. Catherine *Smith*).

2165 **Mélèze-Modrzejewski** J., Les Juifs d'Égypte, de Ramsès II à Hadrien: Néréides. P 1991, Errance. 216 p. 2-87772-048-9 [RB 99, 750, C. *Saulnier*].

2166 ᴱ**Musurillo** H., GREGORII Nysseni De vita Moysis: Inst. Clas. Harvard., Opera 7/1. Leiden 1991 Brill. £61.50. [NRT 114, 763, V. *Roisel*].

2167 (*Alexandre* S.) *Rossi* Luiz, Espiritualidade dos hebreus versus espiritualidade do Faraó: EstudosB 30 ('Conflitos de espiritualidade na Bíblia' 1991) 26-31.

2168 *Heller* Jan, [Ex 1,14; 5,6-19] Ziegel oder Steine: ➤ 75, ᶠHERRMANN S., Prophetie 1991, 165-170.

2169 *Willi-Plein* Ina, Ort und literarische Funktion der Geburtsgeschichte des Mose: VT 41 (1991) 110-8.

E3.3 Nomen divinum, Tetragrammaton; *Exodus 3,14 ...* Plagues.

2170 **Fischer** Georg, Jahwe unser Gott ... Ex 3s: OBO 91, ᴰ1989 ➤ 5,2390; 6,2599: ᴿBiblica 72 (1991) 404-410 (M. *Vervenne*); CBQ 53 (1991) 467s

(T. B. *Dozeman*: excellent); CC 142 (1991,3) 209 (G. L. *Prato*); JBL 110 (1991) 330s (S. *Lasine*); RivB 39 (1991) 90s (A. *Bonora*).

2171 *Croatto* J. Severino, Die Relecture des Jahwe-Namens; hermeneutische Überlegungen zu Ex 3,1-15 und 6,2-13 [< RIBL 4 (1989) 7-14], ᵀ*Kessler* R.: EvT 51 (1991) 39-49.

2172 *Muriankari* Athul, [Ex 3,4]. A view of God from the Bible: Bible Bhashyam 17 (1991) 60-64.

2173 *Hess* Richard S., The divine name Yahweh in Late Bronze Age sources?: UF 23 (1991) 181-8.

2174 *Arranz* Miguel, Une traduction du tétragramme divin dans quelques textes liturgiques slaves: ➤ 67, ᶠGᴏʟᴜʙ I., 1991, 497-504; croat. 504.

2175 *a) Royse* James R., Pʜɪʟᴏ, *kýrios*, and the Tetragrammaton; – *b) Terian* Abraham, Strange interpolations in the text of Philo; the case of Quaestiones in Exodum: ➤ 76, ᶠHɪʟɢᴇʀᴛ E., StPhilonAn 3 (1991) 167-183 / 320-7.

2176 *Eissfeldt* Otto, Gottesnamen in Personennamen als Symbole menschlicher Qualitäten: ➤ 12, ᶠBᴀᴇʟᴢ W. 1966, 110-7.

2176* *Klawek* Aleksy † 1969, *a)* Les noms hébraïques 'Jahveh' et 'Elohim'; – *b)* The name Jahveh in the light of most recent discussions: FolOr 27 (Kraków 1990) 5-9 / 11s.

2177 **Norin** Stig I. L., Sein Name ... Jhw-Personennamen 1986 ➤ 2,1783; 3,2347: ᴿJNES 50 (1991) 142s (D. *Pardee*).

2178 *Pritz* Ray, The divine name in the Hebrew New Testament: Jerusalem Perspective 4,2 (1991) 10-13.

2179 **Mettinger** Tryggve N. D., In search of God; the meaning and message of the everlasting names 1988 ➤ 4,2477 ... 6,2607: ᴿBA 54 (1991) 57s (H. D. *Hummel*); BTrans 42 (1991) 150-2 (K. de *Blois*); BZ 35 (1991) 303s (H. *Niehr*); RB 98 (1991) 279-285 (J. *Loza*); SWJT 34,1 (1991s) 68s (D. G. *Kent*); VT 41 (1991) 499s (J. A. *Emerton*).

2180 *a) Knauf* Ernst A., Dushara und Shai' al-Qaum; Yahwe und Baal; Dieu: ➤ 140, ᶠSᴍʏᴛʜ-Fʟᴏʀᴇɴᴛɪɴ F. 1991, 19-29.

— *b) Rösel* Martin, Die Übersetzung der Gottesbezeichnungen in der Genesis-Septuaginta: ➤ 87, ᶠKᴏᴄʜ K., Ernten 1991, 357-377.

— *c) Saracino* Francesco, Sull''interpretatio graeca' del Nome di Dio: ➤ 292*b*, ParSpV 24 (1991) 227-235.

2181 *Schreiner* Josef, Soll man Ex 3,14 als unbedingtes Heilswort übersetzen?: ➤ 86* ᶠKɴᴏᴄʜ O., Freude 1991, 37-46.

2182 *Floss* Johannes P., 'Ich bin mein Name'; die Identität von Gottes Ich und Gottes Namen nach Ex 3,14: ➤ 126, ᶠRɪᴄʜᴛᴇʀ W., Text 1991, 67-80.

2183 *Shankman* Ray, The cut that unites; word as covenant in Exodus 4:24-26: CCurr 41 (1991s) 168-178.

2184 **Grünwaldt** Klaus, Beschneidung, Passa und Sabbat in der Priesterschrift: Diss. ᴰ*Seebass* H. Bonn 1991s. – RTLv 23, p. 539.

2184* *Walkenhorst* Karl H., Gotteserfahrung und Gotteskenntnis im Sinne der priesterlichen Redaktion von Ex 7-14: ➤ 59, ᶠFüɢʟɪsᴛᴇʀ N., 1991, 373-397.

2185 **Schmidt** Ludwig, Beobachtungen zu der Plagenerzählung in Exodus VII 14 - XI 10: StB 4, 1990 ➤ 6,2624: ᴿJBL 110 (1991) 706-8 (T. B. *Dozeman*); OTAbs 14 (1991) 108 (C. T. *Begg*); RB 98 (1991) 462s (J. *Loza*); ZAW 103 (1991) 169 (H.-C. *Schmitt*).

2186 *Fretheim* Terence E., The plagues as ecological signs of historical disaster: JBL 110 (1991) 385-396.

E3.4 *Pascha, sanguis, sacrificium:* **Passover, blood, sacrifice,** *Ex 11 ...*

2187 *Halperin* Bilhah, ✪ Character of Pesaḥ in the biblical period: BethM 36,127 (1990s) 343-351.

2188 *Wolf* George, *a*) Till what time was the Paschal sacrifice eaten according to the book of Jubilees [... JOSEPHUS and Mishnah]?; – *b*) From festival of unleavened bread to festival of pesach; why and when was the name changed: 281, Lexical/Passover 1991, 25-27 [–30] / 32-44 [45s].

2188* *López Álvarez* Ana María, *Palomero Plaza* Santiago, Un 'reposte-ro' de Pesaḥ del Museo Sefardi de Toledo: Sefarad 51 (1991) 163-172; 3 fig.

2189 *Kreuzer* Siegfried, Zur Priorität und Auslegungsgeschichte von Exodus 12,40 MT; die chronologische Interpretation des Ägyptenaufenthalts in der judäischen, samaritanischen und alexandrinischen Exegese: ZAW 103 (1991) 252-8.

2190 **Bauer** Uwe F. W., *Kol ...* All diese Worte; Impulse zur Schriftauslegung aus Amsterdam, expliziert an der Schilfmeererzählung in Exodus 13,17 -14,31 [Diss. Amst 1982, ᴰ*Deurloo* K., TsTNijm 32,85]: EurHS 23/442. Fra 1991, Lang. 378 p. 3-631-44373-0.

2191 *Olyan* Saul M., [Exod 14,11-14] The Israelites debate their options at the Sea of Reeds; LAB 10:3, its parallels, and Pseudo-PHILO's ideology and background: JBL 110 (1991) 75-91.

2192 *Hall* Thomas N., [Ex 14,21; Jos 3,13-20; I Enoch 89,23-27; 4 Ezra 13,44-47]. The reversal of the Jordan in Vercelli homily 16 and in Old English literature: Traditio 45 (Fordham 1989s) 53-86.

2192* *Bulas* Ryszarda, ✪ The passage across the Red Sea in the synagogue in Dura Europos (the mid-third century) as *akedah* of the Jewish nation: Roczniki Humanistyczne 39s,4 (1991s) 5-15; 2 fig.; Eng. 15s.

2193 **Brenner** Martin L., The song of the sea: Ex 15,1-21 [Diss. Angelicum, ᴰ*Zerafa* P., R 1988]: BZAW 195. B 1991, de Gruyter. viii-193 p. DM 88. 3-11-012340-1. – ᴿExpTim 103 (1991s) 82 (J. *Day*); TüTQ 171 (1991) 227s (W. *Gross*).

2194 *Niehr* Herbert, [Ex 15,26] JHWH als Arzt; Herkunft und Geschichte einer alttestamentlichen Gottesprädikation [*šalôm*; *r*ᵉ*pa'îm* und phönizische Heilsgötter]: BZ 35 (1991) 3-17; p. 17: our knowledge of medicine in Israel is too skimpy to warrant [*Seybold* K., *al.*] the view that YHWH's role left no room for human physicians.

2195 *Ahuviyah* Avraham, ✪ 'Six days you shall gather (manna)' [Ex 16,26]: BethM 36,126 (1990s) 226-9.

2196 **Schart** Aaron, Mose und Israel im Konflikt ... OBO 98, 1990 → 6,2647: ᴿErbAuf 67 (1991) 239 (E. *Dietzfelbinger*); ETL 67 (1991) 150s (J. *Lust*, Eng.); JBL 110 (1991) 709-711 (D. T. *Olson*); TüTQ 171 (1991) 134s (W. *Gross*).

2197 *Römer* Thomas, Exode et anti-Exode; la nostalgie de l'Égypte dans les traditions du désert: → 140, ᶠSMYTH-FLORENTIN F., 1991, 155-172.

2198 **Dozeman** Thomas B., God on the mountain ... Ex 19-24: SBL Mg 37, 1989 → 5,2420; 6,2650: ᴿBiblica 72 (1991) 263-8 (E. *Blum*); CBQ 53 (1991) 281s (R. J. *Clifford*); JBL 110 (1991) 507-9 (H.T.C. *Sun*: promotes RENDTORFF); JQR 82 (1991s) 583-5 (J. *Van Seters*: unconvinced); JRel 71 (1991) 426s (D. T. *Olson*).

2198* *Rendtorff* Rolf, Der Text in seiner Endgestalt; Überlegungen zu Exodus 19: ➤ 87, ᶠKOCH K., Ernten 1991, 459-470.

E3.5 Decalogus, *Ex 20* = *Dt 5; Ex 21ss;* Ancient Near East Law.

2199 **Ben-Chorin** S., De Tien Woorden [Die Tafele des Bundes 1987]ᵀ. Baarn 1988, Ten Have. 184 p. ƒ32,50. 90-259-4374-8. – ᴿNedTTs 45 (1991) 256 (P. van der *Horst*).

2200 *Branden* A. Van den, Le décalogue: BbbOr 33 (1991) 93-124.

2201 ᴱ**Dales** R. C., *King* E. B., [➤ 2254] GROSSETESTE Robert, De decem mandatis: Auctores Britannici Medii Aevi 10, 1987 ➤ 3,2889; 5,2426: ᴿSalesianum 53 (1991) 190s (P. T. *Stella*).

2202 — *McEvoy* James, Robert Grosseteste on the Ten Commandments: RTAM 58 (1991) 167-205 (-212, text and sources).

2203 **Harrelson** Walter, Os dez mandamientos e os direitos humanos, ᵀ*Mesquitella* Carlos T. 1987 ➤ 6,2656: ᴿPerspT 22 (1990) 242-5 (J. *Vitório*).

2204 **Loza** J., Las palabras de Yahve... Decalogo 1989 ➤ 5,2434: ᴿBL (1991) 84 (J. R. *Porter*: admirably judicious); CBQ 53 (1991) 678s (R. H. *McGrath*: not merely the only Spanish treatment available); NRT 113 (1991) 97s (J.-L. *Ska*).

2205 **Mesters** Carlos, Befreit – gebunden; die 10 Gebote, das Bundesbuch 1989 ➤ 6,2658*: ᴿBiKi 45 (1990) 56 (M. *Helsper*); NZMissW 47 (1991) 316 (G. *Schelbert*); ZMissRW 75 (1991) 242-5 (L. *Schwienhorst-Schönberger*).

2206 *a) Muszyński* Henryk bp., ❷ 'Dix paroles simples de Dieu' appelées 'Dix commandements'; – *b) Bajda* Jerzy, ❷ Tu ne tueras pas: AtKap 117,495s (1991) 221-233 / 251-261.

2207 **Peters** Albrecht, Kommentar zu LUTHERS Katechismen, I. Die zehn Gebote [II. Das Apostolikum], ᴱ*Seebass* G. Gö 1990 [1991], Vandenhoeck & R. 325 p. [266 p.] je DM 38 [TLZ 117, 285, B. *Hägglund*]. – ᴿRHPR 71 (1991) 392 (M. *Arnold*).

2208 **Renaud** Bernard, La théophanie du Sinaï, Ex 19-24; exégèse et théologie: CahRB 30. P 1991, Gabalda. 219 p. 2-85021-049-8.

2209 *Arendt* Rudolph, [Ex 20,2s] Det første bud: DaTTs 54 (1991) 161-182 [< ZAW 104,269].

2210 ᴱ**Dohmen** Christoph, *Sternberg* Thomas, '... kein Bildnis machen'; Kunst und Theologie im Gespräch² 1987 ➤ 3,395; 4,2528: ᴿTGL 81 (1991) 242s (J. *Gamberoni*).

2211 **Prigent** Pierre, Le Judaïsme et l'image: TStAJ 24,1990 ➤ 6,2665: ᴿFoiVie 90,2 (1991) 117 (P. *François*); RHPR 71 (1991) 265s (*ipse*); RivArCr 67 (1991) 475-7 (Anna *Campese Simone*).

2212 *Veijola* Timo, [Ex 20,7] Das dritte Gebot (Namenverbot) im Lichte einer ägyptischen Parallele: ZAW 103 (1991) 1-17.

2213 **Peli** Pinchas H., [Ex 20,8] The Jewish Sabbath; a renewed encounter. NY 1991, Schocken. 173 p. $12 pa. [JAAR 59,89].
  ᴱ**Eskenazi** Tamara C., *al.*, The Sabbath in Jewish and Christian traditions 1989/91 ➤ 431.

2214 **Robinson** Gnana, The origin and development of the OT sabbath; a comprehensive exegetical approach; BeitBExT 21, ᴰ1988 ➤ 4,2538; 6,2671: ᴿBO 48 (1991) 880-2 (E. *Jenni*, unconvinced).

2215 **Spier** Erich, Der Sabbat [p. 11-80, in der Geschichte Israels]: Das Judentum 1, 1989 ➤ 5,2449; 6,2672: ᴿTLZ 116 (1991) 504s (A. *Strobel*); ZRGg 43 (1991) 374s (A. *Silbermann*).

2216 *Cazelles* Henri, Histoire et institutions dans la place et la composition d'Ex 20,22 - 23,19: ➤ 75, ᶠHᴇʀʀᴍᴀɴɴ S., Prophetie 1991, 52-64.

2217 *a*) *Magonet* Jonathan, Ownership and autonomy; elements of composition in the 'Book of the Covenant'; – *b*) *Cohn-Sherbok* Dan, Law in reform Judaism: ➤ 82, ᶠJᴀᴄᴏʙs L. 1991, 154-167 / 168-179.

2218 **Osumi** Yuichi, Die Kompositionsgeschichte des Bundesbuches Exodus 20,22b - 23,33 [Diss. Bethel ᴰ*Crüsemann* F. 1989 ➤ 5,2455]: OBO 105. FrS/Gö 1991, Univ./VR. 273 p. DM 110 [TR 87,426]. 3-7278-0744-X / VR 3-525-53738-7.

2219 **Otto** Eckart, Rechtsgeschichte... Ešnunna/Bundesbuch: OBO 85, 1989 ➤ 5,2456; 6,2676: ᴿArTGran 54 (1991) 377s (J. L. *Sicre*); Biblica 72 (1991) 113-6 (R. *Scoralick*); WeltOr 22 (1991) 163-6 (G. *Cardascia*).

2220 **Schwienhorst-Schönberger** Ludger, Das Bundesbuch...: BZAW 188, 1990 ➤ 6,2675: ᴿBiblica 72 (1991) 556-9 (A. *Schenker*); RechSR 79 (1991) 267s (J. *Briend*); TüTQ 171 (1991) 67-69 (W. *Gross*).

2221 *Otto* Eckart, *a*) Vom Profanrecht zum Gottesrecht; das Bundesbuch [Sᴄʜᴡɪᴇɴʜᴏʀsᴛ-Sᴄʜöɴʙᴇʀɢᴇʀ L. 1990]: TRu 56 (1991) 421-7; – *b*) Zur Geschichte des Talions im Alten Orient und Israel: ➤ 87, ᶠKᴏᴄʜ K., Ernten 1991, 101-130.

2222 **Sprinkle** Joe M., A literary approach to biblical law; Exodus 20:22 - 23:19: diss. HUC, ᴰ*Brichto* H. Cincinnati 1991. 493 p. 91-23418. – DissA 52 (1991s) 955-A.

2223 *Cavassa* Ernesto, 'No dejaré de oír su clamor' (Ex. 22,23): Páginas 15,101 (1990) 41-47.

2224 **Barbiero** Gianni, L'asino del nemico; rinuncia alla vendetta e amore del nemico nella legislazione dell'AT (Es 23,4-5; Dt 22,1-4; Lv 19,17-19) [diss. Frankfurt St. Georgen 1988, ᴰ*Lohfink* N.]: AnBib 128. R 1991, Pontificio Istituto Biblico. vii-418 p. 88-7653-128-9. – ᴿHenoch 13 (1991) 368-371 (P. *Sacchi*: molto importante).

2225 *Ben-Barak* Zafrira, Trials for treason against the king in Israel and the Near East: RIDA 38 (1991) 11-37.

2226 **Dorff** E., *Rosett* A., A living tree 1988 ➤ 5,2468; 6,2689: ᴿJAAR 59 (1991) 164-6 (D. *Ellenson*).

2227 **Falk** Ze'ev W., Religious law and ethics; studies in biblical and rabbinical theonomy. J 1991, Mesharim. [x-] 221 p. 965-313-000-5.

2228 ᴱ**Firmage** Edwin B., Religion and Law 1985/90 ➤ 6,526: ᴿBL (1991) 109 (J. F. A. *Sawyer*).

2229 *Fretheim* Terence E., The reclamation of creation; redemption and law in Exodus: Interpretation 45 (1991) 354-365.

2230 **Gordis** R., Dynamics of Jewish Law 1990 ➤ 6,a200: ᴿAJS 16 (1991) 214-8 (S. *Morell*).

2231 **Houten** Christiana van, The alien in Israelite law; a study of the changing legal status of strangers in ancient Israel [Diss. Notre Dame]: JStOT supp. 107. Sheffield 1991, JStOT. 200 p. £25 [TR 88,162]. 1-85075-317-2.

2232 ᴱ**Lindars** B., Law and religion 1985/8 ➤ 5,588: – ᴿScotJT 44 (1991) 400 (P. S. *Cameron*).

2233 *Lohfink* Norbert, Poverty in the laws of the Ancient Near East and of the Bible: TS 52 (1991) 34-50.
2234 *a) Mainelli* Helen K., Aliens in our midst; their place in OT law codes; – *b) Laffey* Alice, Strangers and sojourners; – *c) Pilch* John J., 'Visiting strangers' and 'resident aliens': BToday 29 (1991) 205-9 / 330-335 / 357-361.
2235 **Otto** Eckart, Körperverletzungen in den Keilschriftrechten und im AT; Studien zum Rechtstransfer im AT: AOAT 226. Neuk/Kevelaer 1991 Neuk-V./Butzon & B. 227 p. 3-7887-1372-0 / 3-7666-9725-0 [OIAc F91,17].
2236 [E]**Patrick** D., Thinking biblical law 1989 ➤ 5,596: [R]JAOS 111 (1991) 818-820 (M. *Greenberg*).
2236* *Peckham* Brian, The function of the law in the development of Israel's prophetic traditions: ➤ 436, Law 1986/91, JStOT sup 124, 108-146.
2237 *a) Ska* Jean Louis, Ricchezza e povertà nell'esperienza e la legislazione dell'Esodo; – *b) Cimosa* Mario, La ricchezza è una benedizione e la povertà una maledizione; la prospettiva del Deuteronomio; – *c) Fabris* Rinaldo, La scelta dei poveri nella prospettiva biblica: ➤ 444*, Ricchezza 1991, 19-40 / 41-63 / 1-17.
2238 *Weingart* A., Éthique et droit dans la tradition du judaïsme: RHDroit 68 (1990) 463-470 [< RSPT 75,532].
2239 **Westbrook** Raymond, Studies in biblical and cuneiform law 1988 ➤ 4,2568 ... 6,2699: [R]BO 48 (1991) 409-437 (W. F. *Leemans*).
Westbrook R., Property and the family in biblical law 1991 ➤ 277.

2240 *Abusch* Tzvi, 'He should continue to bear the penalty of that case'; some observations on Codex Ḫammurabi §§3-4 and §13: ➤ 56, [F]Fox M. 1 (1991) 77-96.
2240* — *a) Klengel* Horst, Hammurapi von Babylon; neue Informationen aus dem Schriftzeugnis seiner Zeit; – *b) Gordon* Cyrus H., New directions in the study of ancient Middle Eastern cultures: ➤ 102c, [F]Prince Mikasa 1991, 179-191 / 53-65.
2241 *Allam* S., Sur l'ordalie en Égypte pharaonique: JESHO 34 (1991) 361-3.
2242 **Cruz-Uribe** Eugene, Saite and Persian demotic cattle documents; a study in legal forms and principles in ancient Egypt: AmStPap 26, 1985 ➤ 1,e762: [R]WZKM 79 (1989) 255-8 (G. *Vittmann*).
2243 **Johns** C. H. W., The relations between the laws of Babylonia and the laws of the Hebrew peoples (Schweich Lectures 1912). Mü 1980, Kraus. xv-96 p. 3-601-00512-3.
2244 **Malul** Meir, Studies in Mesopotamian legal symbolism [D]1988 ➤ 4,2852: [R]BO 48 (1991) 157-9 (R. *Haase*); OLZ 86 (1991) 287-290 (G. *Ries*).
2245 *Malul* Meir, On nails and pins in Old Babylonian legal praxis [pinning to a wall was form of promulgation]: AcSum 13 (1991) 237-248.
Matthews V., *Benjamin* D., OT parallels; laws and stories from the Ancient Near East 1991 ➤ 942.
2246 *Otto* Eckart, *a)* [pilfering wife] Die Rechtsintention des Paragraphen 6 der Tafel A des mittelassyrischen Kodex in Tradition und Redaktion: UF 23 (1991) 307-314; – *b)* Auf dem Weg zu einer altorientalischen Rechtsgeschichte [THÉODORIDÈS A. *al.* 1988]: BO 48 (1991) 5-13.
2247 *Passoni dell'Acqua* Anna, Prassi greca e costume egiziano nel negozio giuridico di una donna ebrea di Alessandria: Aegyptus 70 (1990) 123-

172 [p. 144-150, La schiavitù per debiti nell'ambiente ebraico; la legislazione biblica; p. 150 s, il NT].

2248 *a) Stol* Martin, Eine Prozessurkunde über 'falsches Zeugnis'; – *b) Lackenbacher* Sylvie, Un contrat d'adoption et fraternité: ➤ 61, [F]GA-RELLI P., Marchands 1991, 333-340 / 341-4.

2249 **Stone** Elizabeth C., *Owen* David I., Adoption in Old-Babylonian Nippur and the archive of Mannum-mešu-lişşur: Mesopotamian Civilizations 3. WL 1991, Eisenbrauns. x-149 p.; 12 facsim.; 63 pl. 0-931464-53-6 [OIAc 1,25].

2250 **Westbrook** Raymond, Old Babylonian marriage laws: AfO Beih 23, 1988 ➤ 4,2592; 5,2490: [R]BO 48 (1991) 567-574 (M. van de *Mieroop*).

2251 *Westbrook* Raymond, The phrase 'his heart is satisfied' in ancient Near Eastern legal sources: JAOS 111 (1991) 219-224.

2252 **Yaron** Reuven, The laws of Eshnunna[2rev] [[1]c.1970] 1988 ➤ 5,2492; [non 2429: 6,2714]: [R]BL (1991) 133 (B. S. *Jackson*).

2253 *Zéman* François, Le statut de la femme en Mésopotamie d'après les sources juridiques: ScEsp 43 (1991) 69-86.

E3.6 **Cultus,** *Exodus 24-40.*

2254 [E]**Dales** Richard C., *King* Edward R. [➤ 2201], Robert GROSSETESTE, De cessatione legalium [part of De incarnatione showing that the OT ritual laws but not the Decalogue are replaced]: Auctores Britannici Medii Aevi 7. Ox 1986, Clarendon. xxx-215 p. £25 [RHE 87,470, R. *Hissette*].

2255 *a) Lemche* Niels P., The development of the Israelite religion in the light of recent studies on the early history of Israel; – *b) Nelson* R. D., The role of the priesthood in the Deuteronomistic history; – *c) Toorn* Karel van der, The Babylonian New Year festival; new insights from the cuneiform texts and their bearing on OT study: ➤ 429, IOSOT 1989/91, 97-115 / 132-147 / 331-344.

2256 **Koester** Craig, The dwelling of God... [diss. [D]*Brown* R. E.]: CBQ Mg 22, 1989 ➤ 5,2500; 6,2719: [R]CritRR 4 (1991) 366-8 (G. E. *Sterling*); Salesianum 53 (1991) 181 (R. *Vicent*).

2257 **Utzschneider** H., Das Heiligtum: OBO 77, 1988 ➤ 4,2604... 6,2716: [R]BZ 35 (1991) 304-6 (J. *Scharbert*).

2258 **Zwickel** Wolfgang, Räucherkult...: OBO 97, [D]1990 ➤ 6,2721: [R]TüTQ 171 (1991) 69 (W. *Gross*); ZAW 103 (1991) 313 (H.-C. *Schmitt*).

2259 *Brown* Cheryl A., [Ex 24,5-11...] The peace-offerings (*š[e]lāmîm*) and Pauline soteriology: ➤ 54, [F]FLUSSER D., Immanuel 24s (1990) 59-76.

2260 *Hatton* Howard, [Ex 26,15-19] The projections on the frames of the tabernacle: BTrans 42 (1991) 205-9; 2 fig.

2261 *Hendrix* Ralph E., A literary structural analysis of the Golden-Calf episode in Exodus 32:1–33:6: AndrUnS 28 (1990) 211-7.

2262 *Krašovec* Jože, The breaking and renewing of the Covenant in Ex 32-34 (in Slovene): BogVest 50 (1990) 197-216; Eng. 214.

2263 *Baumann* Rolf, Das Stierbild und der bildlose Jahwe: ZPraxRU 21,1 (1991) 8-12 [1-7, *al.*; < ZIT 91,188].

2264 *Joosten* J., The syntax of *zeh Mošeh* (Ex 32,1.23): ZAW 103 (1991) 412-5.

2265 *Hempelmann* Heinzpeter, Was ein Gott heisst (Ex 32,7-14): TBeit 22 (Wu 1991) 57-60 [< ZIT 91,221].

2265* *Raitt* Thomas M., [Ex 34,6s ...: varying reasons given in OT texts] Why does God forgive?: HorBT 13 (1991) 38-58.

E3.7 Leviticus.

2266 *Avery-Peck* Alan J., Max KADUSHIN as exegete; the conceptual commentary to Leviticus Rabbah: ⇒ 321*, *Ochs*/KADUSHIN 1990, 73-93.

2266* **Demarest** Gary W., Leviticus: Communicator's comm. 3. Dallas 1990, Word. 286 p. 0-8499-0408-0.

2267 *Kruse* Heinz, The rationale of the Old Testament sacrifice: KatKenk 29 (1990) 187-210 [< OTAbs 14,248].

Lane D. J. *al.,* Peshitta Lev Nm Dt ⇒ 1561.

2268 **Levine** Baruch A., Leviticus: JPS Torah comm. 1989 ⇒ 5,2516: RCrit-RR 4 (1991) 148-150 (D. P. *Wright*).

2269 Midrash Rabbah ha-Mevoar, Leviticus [E*Steinberger* Avraham I., *al.*]. J 1991, Institute Midrash Rabbah.

2270 **Milgrom** Jacob, Leviticus 1-16: AnchorB 3. NY 1991, Doubleday. 1136 p. $42. 0-385-11434-6 [UF 23,451].

2271 **Neusner** J., Sifra in perspective; the documentary comparison of the Midrashim of ancient Judaism: BrownJudSt. Atlanta 1988, Scholars. 277 p. $40. 1-55540-232-1. – RJAAR 59 (1991) 849-852 (A. J. *Avery-Peck*).

2272 **Neusner** J., Uniting the dual Torah; Sifra and the problem of the Mishnah. C 1990, Univ. xii-233 p. £32.50. 0-521-38125-8 [BL 92,128, P. R. *Davies*: how Sifra differs from Sifré or Leviticus Rabbah].

2273 *Neusner* Jacob, (*Chilton* Bruce D.), Uncleanness; a moral or an ontological category in the early centuries A.D. ?: BBRes 1 (1991) 63-80 (-88).

2274 *Pérez Fernández* Miguel, Los *mešalim* del Midras Sifra [Lev]: EstB 49 (1991) 149-163.

2275 *Seebass* Horst, Levi/Leviten: ⇒ 690, TRE 21 (1991) 36-40.

2276 *Visotzky* R. L., Anti-Christian polemic in Leviticus Rabbah, AmerAcad Jewish Res 56 (1990) 83-100 [< NTAbs 36,92].

2277 **Anderson** Gary A., [Lv 1s] Sacrifices 1987 ⇒ 3,2476 ... 6,2742: RBO 48 (1991) 619s (H. *Jagersma*); Syria 67 (1990) 216 (A. *Caquot*).

2278 *Stoebe* Hans Joachim, Schicksal erkennen – Schuld bekennen; Gedanken im Anschluss an Lev 5, V. 17-19: ⇒ 75, FHERRMANN S., Prophetie 1991, 385-397.

2278* *a) Milgrom* Jacob, The consecration of the priests; a literary comparison of Leviticus 8 and Exodus 29; – *b) Steck* Odil H., Aufbauprobleme in der Priesterschrift: ⇒ 87, FKOCH K., Ernten 1991, 273-286 / 287-308.

2279 **Kiuchi** N., [Lev 10 ...] The purification offering 1988 ⇒ 4,2624; 5,2521: RBZ 35 (1991) 119s (K. *Grünwald*).

2280 *Milgrom* Jacob, [Lev 11] ⊕ Two Priestly terms, *šeqes* and *ṭāmē'*: Tarbiz 60 (1990s) 423-8; Eng. V.

2281 *a) Milgrom* Jacob, The composition of Leviticus, chapter 11; – *b) Wright* David P., The spectrum of priestly impurity [Lev 11-16; Nm 19]; – *c) Schwartz* Baruch J., The prohibitions concerning the 'eating' of blood in Leviticus 17: ⇒ 288, Priesthood 1991, 183-191 / 150-182 / 34-66.

2282 **Carelsen** Hermanus L., Leviticus 13 and 14, a model for the interpretation of Old Testamentical lawtexts [in Afrikaans]: diss. Pretoria 1991, ᴰ*Prinsloo* W. S. – DissA 52 (1991s) 4373-A.

2283 *Whitekettle* Richard, Leviticus 15,18 reconsidered; chiasm, spatial structure and the body: JStOT 49 (1991) 31-45.

2284 *Deiana* Giovanni, Il *kippur* nei testi dell'AT: ➤ 565, Sangue 1989/91, 13-177.

2285 *McLean* Bradley H., [Lv 16] The interpretation of the Levitical sin-offering and the scapegoat: SR 20 (1991) 345-356.

2286 *Moor* J. C. de, *Sanders* P., [Lv 16] An Ugaritic expiation ritual and its OT parallels: UF 23 (1991) 283-300.

2287 *a) Olmo Lete* G. del, [Lv 16] El sacrificio de expiación nacional en Ugarit (KTU 1,40 y par.); – *b) Vincent* R., Les festes jueves en el Liber Antiquitatum Biblicarum, context literari i interpretació: ➤ 5,594, Paraula 1985/9, 46-56 / 74-85 [< OTAbs 14,334].

2288 *Zipor* Moshé A., Notes sur les chapitres XIX à XXII du Lévitique dans la Bible d'Alexandrie: ETL 67 (1991) 328-337.

2289 **Mathys** Hans-Peter, [Lv 19,18] 'Liebe deinen Nächsten wie dich selbst' ...: OBO 71, 1986 ➤ 2,1895 ... 5,2530: ᴿTR 87 (1991) 373-5 (L. *Schwienhorst-Schönberger*).

2290 *Stahl* R., Erlassjahr und Sabbatjahr – Möglichkeiten wirtschaftlichen Verhaltens heute?: Kirchliche Hochschule Forschungsstelle Judentum 3 (Lp c. 1991) 1-22 [< ZAW 104,274].

2291 *Wittenberg* Gunther H., [Lv 25 ...] The significance of land in the Old Testament: JTSAf 77 (1991) 58-60 [< ZIT 92,75].

2292 **Wright** C., God's people in God's land [ᴰ1977] 1990 ➤ 6,2762: ᴿÉTRel 66 (1991) 587s (Françoise *Smyth*); ExpTim 103 (1991s) 131 (C. S. *Rodd*: meanwhile author of the important Living as the People of God); TTod 48 (1991s) 352.354 (J. M. *Hamilton*).

2292* *a) Glessmer* Uwe, Der 364-Tage-Kalender und die Sabbatstruktur seiner Schaltungen in ihrer Bedeutung für den Kult; – *b) Ebach* Jürgen, Über 'Freiheit' und 'Heimat'; Aspekte der *mᵉnuḥâ*: ➤ 87, ᶠKOCH K., Ernten 1991, 379-398 / 495-518.

2293 *Welten* Peter, [Lv 25,10], Erklärt dieses fünfzigste Jahr für heilig; Entwurf und Wirklichkeit des Sabbatjahres: BTZ 8 (1991) 121-8.

2293* *Robinson* Gnana, [Lv 25,10] Das Jobeljahr, die Lösung einer sozial-ökonomischen Krise des Volkes Gottes: ➤ 87, ᶠKOCH K., Ernten 1991, 471-494.

2294 *Chilton* Bruce, [Lv 25,23-28] The *gô'ēl* in ancient Israel; theological reflections on an Israelite institution: BBRes 1 (1991) 3-19.

2295 *Martin* A.-G., [Lv 26,34s; Rom 8,18-25; Gn 2,1-4] Le repos de la création: RRéf 42,3 (1991) 11-17 [< NTAbs 36,74].

2296 **Berlinerblau** Jacques D., [Lv 27] The Israelite vow and the so-called 'popular religion'; a sociological and philological investigation: diss. NYU 1991, ᴰ*Levine* B. 442 p. 91-34642. – DissA 52 (1991s) 2243-A.

E3.8   *Numeri;*   **Numbers, Balaam.**

2297 **Boschi** Bernardo G., Numeri; versione, introduzione, note: Nuovissima Versione 4. R 1983, Paoline. 263 p. 88-215-0531-6.

2298 **Ingalls** Alan D., The literary unity of the Book of Numbers: diss. Dallas Theol. Sem. 1991. 253 p. 92-14485. – DissA 52 (1991s) 4366-A: 'While the

book's order seems strange to the modern Western mind, Numbers is by
no means the literary jumble it is purported to be'.
2299 **Jagersma** H., Numeri [I. 1983 ➤ 64,2557; II. 1988 ➤ 4,2651] III,
c. 25-36: PredikingOT. Nijkerk 1990, Callenbach. 204 p. ƒ71,50;
sb. 64,50. 90-266-0231-6 [BL 92,74, J. W. *Rogerson*].
2301 **Licht** Jacob, ❿ A commentary on the Book of Numbers XI-XXI: Perry
Foundation. J 1991, Magnes. xv-253 p. $15 [TR 88,425]. 965-223-760-4.
2302 ᵀᴱ**Pérez Fernández** Miguel, Midrás Sifre Números 1989 ➤ 5,2538;
6,2770: ᴿBL (1991) 142 (C. T. R. *Hayward*); CritRR 4 (1991) 376-9 (J.
Neusner: reliable despite improvable method); NRT 113 (1991) 103 (J.-L.
Ska).
2303 *Pérez Fernández* Miguel, Parábolas rabínicas; el *mašal* midrásico o el
mašal como recurso hermenéutico para abrir la Escritura (ensayo sobre
los mešalim de Midrás Sifré Números): Scripta Fulgentina 1 (Murcia
1991s) 5-55.
2304 *Pérez Fernández* Miguel, El reino de la Escritura (Sobre los principios
hermenéuticos de R. YISMAEL en el Midrás Sifre Números): ➤ 421,
Luso-Esp 1989/91, 489-495.

2305 *Milgrom* Jacob, [Nm 6,14...] The *hattā't*; a rite of passage?: RB [96
(1989) 27-48, *Marx* A.] 98 (1991) 120-4; franç. 120.
2306 *Yardeni* Ada, [Nm 6,24-26] Remarks on the priestly blessing on two
ancient amulets from Jerusalem: VT 41 (1991) 176-191; 2 fig.
2307 **Hickcox** Alice M., Between redemption and promise; literary-theological readings in Numbers 11-21: diss. Emory, ᴰ*Gunn* D. Atlanta 1991.
160 p. 92-04813. – DissA 52 (1991s) 3319-A; RelStR 18,173 & RTLv 23,
p. 539 omit from title 'Between r. & promise'.
2308 **Ris** Gerard, Mozes en de profeten; verklaring van Numeri 11,35-12,1-16
vanuit de rabbijnse geschriften. Kampen 1990, Kok. 101 p. ƒ19,50 [TR
87,523].
2309 *Zobel* Hans-J., [Ex 15-18, Num 10-31] Die Zeit der Wüstenwanderung
Israels im Lichte prophetischer Texte: VT 41 (1991) 192-202.
2310 *Knohl* Israel, The sin offering law in the 'Holiness School' (Numbers
15,22-31): ➤ 288, Priesthood 1991, 192-203.
2311 *Milgrom* Jacob, ❿ Two notes on Numbers 15:22-31 and its purpose:
Tarbiz 60 (1990s) 429 only (Eng. V) [431-3, *Knohl* Israel, on Milgrom's
view of these verses].
2311* *McNamara* Martin, Early exegesis in the Palestinian Targum (Neofiti)
Numbers Chapter 21: SUNT A-16 (1991) 127-150 [< ZIT 92,309].
2312 *Hoogsteen* T., The bronze serpent history; Nm 21:1-9; 2 Kgs 18:1-8; Jn
3:14s: Kerux 2,3 (1987) 10-15.

2313 **Hackett** Jo Ann, The Balaam text from Deir'Alla 1984 ➤ 65,2375...
6,2784: ᴿJNES 50 (1991) 139-142 (D. *Pardee*).
2314 *Hilger* Georg, Biblische Eseleien; Bibelarbeit mit Num 22,21-35, die
Eselin des Bileam: KatBlätt 116 (Mü 1991) 858-863 [< ZIT 91,823].
2315 **Moore** Michael S., The Balaam traditions; their character and
development: SBL diss. (Drew) 113, 1990 ➤ 6,2790: ᴿJBL 110 (1991)
703-6 (G. J. *Hamilton*).
2316 *a*) *Puech* Émile, Approches paléographiques de l'inscription sur plâtre
de Deir'Alla; – *b*) *Kooij* G. van der, Book and script at Deir'Alla; –

c) *Dijkstra* M., response: ➤ 534, Balaam text 1989/91, 221-238 / 239-262 / 263-270.
2317 a) *Weippert* Manfred, The Balaam text from Deir'Allā and the study of the OT [response *Dijkstra* M.]; – b) *Lemaire* André, Les inscriptions sur plâtre de Deir'Alla et leur signification historique et culturelle; – c) *Levine* Baruch A., The plaster inscriptions from Deir'Alla; general interpretation [response *Hackett* J. A.]: ➤ 534, Balaam text 1989/91, 151-184 [206-217] / 33-57 / 58-72 [73-84].
2318 *Zeron* A., [Num 22-24] Pseudo-PHILONIC parallels to the inscriptions of Deir'Alla: VT 41 (1991) 186-191.
2319 *Boudreau* George R., [Num 25, 1-18 ...] A study of the traditio-historical development of the Baal of Peor tradition: diss. Emory, ᴰ*Miller* J. M. Atlanta 1991. 387 p. 91-27581. – DissA 52 (1991s) 2171-A.
2320 *Sly* Dorothy, Changes in the perception of the offence in Numbers 25:1: ProcGLM 11 (1991) 200-9.

E3.9   Liber Deuteronomii.

2320* *Bonora* Antonio, Il Deuteronomio come scuola della Parola: ➤ 292a, ParSpV 24 (1991) 7-16.
2321 **Cairns** Ian, Word and presence; a commentary on the Book of Deuteronomy: IntTCom. GR/E 1991, Eerdmans/Handsell. x-309 p. $19.
2322 **Calvin** John, Sermons on Deuteronomy, ᵀ*Golding* A. 1987 ➤ 6,2800; £37; 0-85151-511-8: ᴿEvangel 8,3 (1990) 21 (T. *Baxter*).
2323 **Chingota** Felix L. B., The use of the concept of fear in Deuteronomy to denote the relationship between God and Israel: diss. ᴰ*Johnstone* W. Aberdeen 1991. 359 p. – RTLv 23, p. 538.
2324 **Chong Chee Min** Eric, The deuteronomistic historian's use of the Transjordanian traditions; history and symbol: diss. ᴰ*Coggins* R. London 1991. 244 p. – RTLv 23, p. 538 [DissA 53,184-A; 282 p.; BRDX-95657].
2324* **Clements** R. E., Deuteronomy: OTGuides 1989 ➤ 5,2572: ᴿEvQ 63 (1991) 343 (J. G. *McConville*).
2325 ᵀᴱ**Cortes** Enric, *Martínez* Teresa, Sifre Deuteronomio; commentario tannaitico I, Pisqa 1-160, 1989 ➤ 6,2802: ᴿLaurentianum 32 (1991) 429-433 (Madeleine *Taradach*); Salesianum 53 (1991) 186s (R. *Vicent*).
2326 *Eshel* Esther, 4QDt – a text that has undergone harmonistic editing: HUCA 62 (1991) 117-152+2 pl.
2326* **Fraade** Steven D., From tradition to commentary; Torah and its interpretation in the Midrash Sifre to Deuteronomy. Albany 1991, SUNY. xviii-343 p. 0-7914-0495-1.
2327 a) *Kramer* Pedro, O órfão e a viúva no livro do Deuteronômio; – b) *Pinzetta* Inácio, Um projeto de defesa aos estrangeiros; a proposta do Deuteronômio; – c) *Kilpp* Nelson, Deficientes físicos no Antigo Testamento: EstudosB 27 (1990) 20-28 / 29-37 / 38-46.
2328 **Labuschagne** C. J., Deuteronomium [I. 1957 ➤ 5,2577]; II [12-26]: PredikOT. Nijkerk 1990. Callenbach. 320+77 p. ƒ99.50; sb. 89,50. 90-266-0246-4. – ᴿBL (1991) 57 (J. W. *Rogerson*: judicious and sensitive); TR 87 (1991) 97-102 (T. *Gommans*, 1s); TsTNijm 31 (1991) 324 (A. *Schoors*); VT 41 (1991) 254s (A. van der *Kooij*).
2329 *Lohfink* Norbert, a) Das Deuteronomium [Urmanuskript > IDB Supp. (1976) 229-232]; – b) Gott im Buch Dt [< BtETL 41 (1976) 101-125]; – c) Die Gattung der 'Historischen Kurzgeschichte' in den letzten Jahren von Juda und in der Zeit des babylonischen Exils [< ZAW 90 (1978) 319-347];

– *d*) Kerygmata des deuteronomistischen Geschichtswerkes [< ᶠ*Wolff*
H. W. 1981, 87-100]: → 224, SBAufs 12 (1991) 15-24 / 25-53 / 55-86 /
125-142.

2330 **Miller** Patrick D., Deuteronomy: Interpretation Comm. 1990 → 6,2810:
ᴿAsburyTJ 46,1 (1991) 113s (P. D. *Hall*); TTod 48 (1991s) 366.368.370
(J. A. *Sanders*); TS 52 (1991) 775 (S. *McEvenue*).

2331 **Payne** David F., Deuteronomy: Daily Study Bible 1985 → 1,2646*;
4,2695: ᴿRExp 88,3 (1991) 264s (T. G. *Smothers*: 'the devotional approach has both benefits and dangers').

2332 **Pressler** Carolyn Jo, The views of women found in the Deuteronomistic
family laws: Diss. Princeton 1991, ᴰ*Sakenfeld* Katherine D. iii-214 p.
91-27011. – OIAc 2,25.

2333 **Regt** L. J. de, Parametric... Dt 1-30 ᴰ1988 → 4,2696... 6,2816: ᴿJAOS
111 (1991) 365s (H. V. *Parunak*); OLZ 86 (1991) 520s (R. *Stahl*).

2334 *Regt* L. J. de, Word order in different clause types in Deuteronomy
1-30: → 77, ᶠHOFTIJZER J. 1991, 152-172.

2335 **Römer** Thomas, Israels Väter; Untersuchungen zur Väterthematik im
Deuteronomium und in der deuteronomistischen Tradition: OBO 99,1990
→ 6,2817: ᴿArTGran 54 (1991) 383s (J. L. *Sicre*); ETL 67 (1991) 151s (J.
Lust, Eng.); ÉTRel 66 (1991) 425s (Françoise *Smyth*); JBL 111 (1992) 125s
(W. *Roth*); TR 87 (1991) 102-4 (H. *Seebass*); ZAW 103 (1991) 307 (H.-C.
Schmitt).

2336 — **Lohfink** Norbert, Die Väter Israels in Deuteronomium [gegen RÖ-
MER, aber mit Römers Stellungnahme p. 111-123]: OBO 111. FrS/Gö
1991, Univ./VR. x-135 p. 3-7278-0778-4 / VR 3-525-53744-1.

2337 **Weinfeld** Moshe, Deuteronomy: AnchorB 5. NY 1991, Doubleday. I
(1-11) xv-458 p. $34. 0-385-17593-0 [BL 92,59, R. E. *Clements*: tries
perhaps too hard to be open to other views while defending his own].

_____

2338 *Lohfink* Norbert, Dt 1,6-3,29 / 4,1-40 / 5 / 16,18-18,22 / 26,5-9 /
26,17-19 / 28,69- 32,47 [< Biblica, BZ, TPhil, ZkT, *al.*] → 224a, SBAufs 8
(1990) 15-44.45-51 / 167-191 / 193-209.363-378 / 305-323 / 263-290.
291-303 / 211-261 / 53-82.

2339 **Knapp** P., Dt 4, 1987 → 3,2564... 6,2826: ᴿVT 41 (1991) 253s (G. I.
Davies).

2340 *a*) *Amsler* Samuel, 'Un seul et même YHWH'; pour un sens diachronique
de Dt 6,4b; – *b*) *Ricœur* Paul, D'un Testament à l'autre; essai d'herméneutique biblique; – *c*) *Bouttier* Michel, La parole et les mots: → 30,
ᶠBONNARD P., Mémoire 1991, 289-297 / 299-309 / 311-7.

2341 *a*) *Bonora* Antonio, La libertà di scelta in Dt 11,22-28 e 30,15-20; – *b*)
Manicardi Luciano, L'esperienza dell'esodo; liberati per servire; – *c*)
Garrone Daniele, Alleanza e libertà; – *d*) *Virgulin* Stefano, Le istituzioni
della libertà; – *e*) *Rochettes* Jacqueline des, Torah e libertà: → 292a,
ParSpV 23 (1991) 49-60 / 9-33 / 35-48 / 61-72 / 73-87.

2342 **Achenbach** Reinhard, Israel zwischen Verheissung und Gebot; literarkri-
tische Untersuchungen zu Deuteronomium 5-11 [ev. Diss. Göttingen 1989,
ᴰ*Perlitt* L.]: EurHS 23/422. Fra 1991, Lang. ix-442 p. Fs 99 [ZAW 104,
289, H.-C. *Schmitt*].

2343 **Braulik** George, *a*) Die deuteronomischen Gesetze und der Dekalog;
Studien zum Aufbau von Dt 12-26 [2 reprints + Dt 22,13-26,16]: SBS 145.
Stu 1991, KBW. 124 p. DM 36 [RB 100,287, tit. pp.; ZAW 104, 443,

H.-C. *Schmitt*].   3-460-04451-9. – *b*) Die Funktion von Siebengruppie-
rungen im Endtext des Deuteronomiums: ➤ 59, ᶠFÜGLISTER N., 1991,
37-50.

2344 **Langer** Gerhard, Von Gott erwählt – Jerusalem; die Rezeption von Dtn
12 im frühen Judentum: ÖsBSt 8, 1989 ➤ 5,2590; 6,2832: ᴿBiblica 72
(1991) 111s (M. *Weinfeld*); CBQ 53 (1991) 475s (P. L. *Redditt*); JBL 110
(1991) 510s (M. S. *Moore*).

2345 **Levinson** Bernard M., The hermeneutics of innovation; the impact of
centralization upon the structure, sequence, and reformulation of legal
material in Deuteronomy: diss. Brandeis. Boston 1991. 498 p. 91-29763. –
DissA 52 (1991s) 1780-A.

2346 *Lohfink* Norbert, *a*) [Dt 12] Die Bundesurkunde des Königs Josias
(Eine Frage an die Deuteronomiumsforschung) [< Biblica 44 (1963)
261-288 . 461-498]; – *b*) [Dt 1,37... 31,2-67] Die deuteronomistische
Darstellung des Übergangs der Führung Israels von Moses auf Josue;
ein Beitrag zur alttestamentlichen Theologie des Amtes [< Scholastik 37
(1962) 32-44]; – *c*) Bundestheologie im AT; zum gleichnamigen Buch von
Lothar Perlitt [ineditum]: ➤ 224*a*, SBAufs 8 (1990) 99-165 / 83-97 /
325-361.

2347 *Lohfink* Norbert, Dt 12,1 (Gn 15,18) / 12,14 / 17,16 (Hos 11,5): ➤ 224*b*,
SBAufs 12 (1991) 229-256. 287-292 (257-285) / 147-177 / 143-5.

2348 *a*) *Tov* Emanuel, Deut 12 and 11QTemple LII-LIII; a contrastive
analysis; – *b*) *Weinfeld* M., God versus Moses in the Temple Scroll, — 'I
do not speak on my own authority but on God's authority' (Sifrei Deut.
sec. 5; John 12,48f): ➤ 145, ᶠSTARCKY J., RQum 15 (1991) 169-173 /
175-180.

2349 **Hughes** Harry W., Divine purpose in Deuteronomic polity; theological
implications of the 'motive' clauses expressing purpose or result in
chapters 13-26 of Deuteronomy: diss. Union Theol. Sem., Richmond
1990. 286 p. 91-21696. – DissA 52 (1991s) 966-A.

2350 *Dion* Paul E., Deuteronomy 13; the suppression of alien religious
propaganda in Israel during the Late Monarchical era: ➤ 436, *Halpern* B.,
Law 1987/91, 147-216.

2351 *Lindenberger* James M., How much for a Hebrew slave? The meaning
of *mišneh* in Deut 15:18:   JBL 110 (1991) 479-482.

2352 *Otto* Eckart, Soziale Verantwortung und Reinheit des Landes; zur
Redaktion der kasuistischen Rechtssätze in Deuteronomium 19-25: ➤ 75,
ᶠHERRMANN S., Prophetie 1991, 290-306.

2353 **Pressler** Carolyn J., [Dt 21-25] The view of women found in the
Deuteronomic family laws: diss. ᴰ*Sakenfeld* Katharine D. Princeton
1991. 222 p. 91-27011. – DissA 52 (1991s) 1374-A; RelStR 18,173.

2354 *Segal* Eliezer, [Dt 22,6] Justice, mercy and a bird's nest: JJS 42 (1991)
176-195.

2355 **Lenchak** Timothy A., A rhetorical-critical and theological study of Dt
29-30: Diss. 6954, Pont. Univ. Gregoriana, ᴰ*Conroy* C. R 1991s. – Inf-
PUG 24/122,28.

2356 *Harl* Marguerite, Le péché irrémissible de l'idolâtre arrogant; Dt
29,19-20 dans la Septante et chez d'autres témoins: ➤ 17, ᶠBARTHÉLEMY
D., Tradition 1991, 63-78.

2357 *a*) *Cortès* E., L'elecció d'Israel a Sifre Dt 32,9 (312); – *b*) *Mas* J.,
Tendències antimonárquiques en l'obra deuteronomística: ➤ 5,594,
Paraula 1985/9, 65-73 / 40-45 [< OTAbs 14,334].

2358 **Axelsson** Lars E., [Dt 33,2] The Lord rose up from Seir 1987 ➤ 3,2592; 4,2728: ᴿJNES 50 (1991) 217-9 (Diana *Edelman*).

E4.1 *Deuteronomista; Origo Israelis in Canaan;* **Liber Josue.**

2359 **Arx** U. von, Studien zur Geschichte des alttestamentlichen Zwölfersymbolismus, I. Fragen im Horizont der Amphiktyoniehypothese von Martin NOTH: EurHS 23/197. Fra 1990, Lang. 583 p. £42. 3-261-04250-8. – ᴿExpTim 102 (1990s) 345s (R. *Coggins*: NT prof but widely read in this area; indispensable evidence though without conclusions); LA 41 (1991) 560s (E. *Cortese*); TsTNijm 31 (1991) 427s (A. *Schoors*); VT 41 (1991) 369s (J. A. *Emerton*).

2360 **Burgmann** Hans, Der 'Sitz im Leben' in den Josuafluchtexten, in 4 Q 379 22 II und 4 Q Testimonia: Qumranica Mogilanensia 1. Kraków 1990, 'Secesja'. 61 p.

2361 *Cangh* Jean-Marie van, Les origines d'Israël et de la foi monothéiste; apports de l'archéologie et de la critique littéraire: RTLv 22 (1991) 305-326; Eng. 455.

2362 **Coote** Robert B., Early Israel, a new horizon 1990 ➤ 6,2852: ᴿBA 54 (1991) 176s (D. *Edelman*); ExpTim 102 (1990s) 375s (J. R. *Bartlett*).

2363 **Coote** R. B., *Whitelam* K. W., Emergence of early Israel 1987 ➤ 3,2595... 6,2851: ᴿBZ 35 (1991) 281s (D. *Kinet*); JNES 50 (1991) 299-302 (Diana *Edelman*).

2364 *Duhaime* Jean, Religion et société dans l'Israël pre-monarchique selon Norman K. GOTTWALD: ScEsp 43 (1991) 161-174.

2365 **Dus** Jan, Israelitische Vorfahren — Vasallen palästinischer Stadtstaaten? Revisionsbedürftigkeit der Landnahmehypothese von Albrecht ALT: EurHS 23/404. Fra 1991, Lang. ii-118 p. DM 39. 3-631-42974-6 [TLZ 117,826, U. *Hübner*, severe; ZAW 104, 444, H.-C. *Schmitt*: unconvincing]. – ᴿLA 41 (1991) 568s (P. *Kaswalder*).

2366 **Finkelstein** Israel, The archaeology of the Israelite settlement 1988 ➤ 4,2733.e629... 6,2853.d921: ᴿJQR 81 (1990s) 471-4 (A. *Mazar*); REB 51 (1991) 989-991 (F. E. *Dobberahn*); Syria 67 (1990) 529s (H. de *Contenson*).

2367 **Frick** F., Formation of... Israel 1985 ➤ 1,2799*... 5,2614: ᴿETL 67 (1991) 135-9 (M. *Vervenne*, Eng.).

2368 *Geus* C. H. J. de, Nieuwe gegevens over het oudste Israel [FINKELSTEIN I. 1988] PhoenixEOL 37,2 (1991) 32-41; 2 maps.

2369 *Gnuse* Robert, Israelite settlement of Canaan; a peaceful internal process: BibTB 21 (1991) 56-66. 109-117.

2370 **Kelm** George L., Escape to conflict; a biblical and archaeological approach to the Hebrew Exodus and settlement in Canaan: Fort Worth 1991, IAR. 290 p. $17 pa. – ᴿSWJT 34,2 (1991s) 52s (B. *Heflin*).

2371 ᴱ**Laperrousaz** E.-M., La protohistoire d'Israël; de l'exode à la monarchie. P 1990, Cerf. 343 p. F 170. 2-204-04138-9 [BL 91,38, A. *Mayes*]. – ᴿNRT 113 (1991) 576-8 (J.-L. *Ska*).

2372 **Lemche** N. P., Early Israel; anthropological and historical studies on the Israelite society before the monarchy: VTSup 37, 1985 ➤ 2,1955... 6,2859: ᴿBO 48 (1991) 616-9 (J. W. *Rogerson*); NedTTs 45 (1991) 62s (K. A. D. *Smelik*).

2373 *a) Lemche* Niels P., Sociology, text and religion as key factors in understanding the emergence of Israel in Canaan; – *b) Ahlström* Gösta W., The origin of Israel in Palestine; – *c) Coote* Robert B., Early Israel; –

d) Finkelstein Israel, The emergence of Israel in Canaan; consensus, mainstream and dispute; – *e) Whitelam* Keith W., Between history and literature; the social production of Israel's traditions of origin: → 428*, ScandJOT (1991,2, 'Toward a consensus on the emergence of Israel in Canaan') 7-18 / 19-34 / 35-46 / 47-59 / 60-74.

2374 *Luria* B. Z., ⊕ Origins of the Hebrews: BethM 36,127 (1990s) 289-298.

2375 *Waltke* Bruce K., The date of the conquest [c. 1400; peasant revolt, infiltration, and 2-phase, all diverge too radically from the Bible]: WestTJ 52 (1990) 181-200 [< BS 148 (1991) 233s (R. D. *Ibach*)].

2376 *Zertal* Adam, Israel enters Canaan; following the pottery trail [GOTTWALD N. etc.]: BAR-W 17,5 (1991) 28-47; (color.) ill. (+ Trek of the tribes p. 48s. 75).

2377 **Görg** Manfred, Josua: NEchter 26. Wü 1991, Echter. 115 p. DM 28 3-429-01398-4 [ZAW 104, 446, H.-C. *Schmitt*].

2378 *Habel* Norman, Conquest and dispossession; justice, Joshua, and land rights: Pacifica 4 (1991) 76-92 [< OTAbs 14,295].

2379 **Hamlin** E. J., Inheriting the land (Joshua) 1983 → 64,2645 ... 1,2616: RScotJT 44 (1991) 107-9 (S. B. *Dawes,* spelling 'Hamilton', comparing also six other IntTC volumes with parallel Daily Study Bible, which is not surpassed even by the three praised: 'Hamilton', Gowan's Gn 1-11, and Brueggemann's Jer 1-25).

2380 **Hauch** Gerhard, Text and contexts; a literary reading of the conquest narrative (Joshua 1-11): diss. DOlson D. Princeton 1991. 392 p. 91-27012. – DissA 52 (1991s) 1373-A; RelStR 18,173 'Texts and ...'.

2381 **Huffman** John A., Joshua: Communicator's comm. 6. Waco 1986, Word. 282 p. 0-8499-0411-0.

2382 **Koorevaar** H. J., De opbouw van het boek Jozua, D1990 → 6,2868: RETL 67 (1991) 418s (E. *Eynikel* comparos CORTESE E.); ZAW 103 (1991) 452 (H.-C. *Schmitt*).

2383 **Martínez Borobio** E., Targum Jonatan 1. Josué – Jueces: TEstCisn 46, 1989 → 4,2814.2750; 5,2628: RBO 48 (1991) 644s (B. *Grossfeld*); Sefarad 51 (1991) 207-9 (J. *Ribera*).

2384 **Mitchell** Gordon, The role of the nations in the book of Joshua: Diss. Heidelberg 1991, DRendtorff R. – TR 87 (1991) 518.

2385 **Noth** Martin, The Deuteronomistic history[2]: JStOT supp. 15. Sheffield 1991, Academic. 156 p. £20; pa. £16.

2386 **O'Brien** M. A., The Deuteronomic History hypothesis; a reassessment [diss. Melbourne 1987]: OBO 92, 1989 → 5,2608; 6,2869: RArTGran 53 (1990) 293-5 (J. L. *Sicre*); CBQ 53 (1991) 680s (R. M. *Arnold*: underpins rather than challenges NOTH); Henoch 12 (1990) 380-5 (P. *Sacchi*: documentatissima); JBL 110 (1991) 138-141 (S. L. *McKenzie*); VT 41 (1991) 508s (H. *Williamson*).

2387 **Ottosson** Magnus, Josuaboken, en programskrift für davidisk restauration: AcU, bibl.1. Sto 1991, Almqvist & W. 300 p. Sk 174. 91-554-2782-0 [TLZ 117, 902, H. *Ringgren*; ZAW 104, 453s, H.-C. *Schmitt*]. – ROrSuec 40 (1991) 295-7 (T. *Kronholm*).

2388 *Stone* Lawson G., Ethical and apologetic tendencies in the redaction of the book of Joshua: CBQ 53 (1991) 25-36: moves away from the early Holy War tradition.

2389 **Wiesel** Elie, Vijf bijbelse persoonlijkheden; Jozua, Elia, Saul, Jeremia, Jona. Hilversum 1990, Gooi & S. 123 p. Fb 480. – ᴿCollatVʟ 21 (1991) 215s (Anne-Marie van *Schoors*).

2390 *Deurloo* Karel A., Spiel und Verweis auf Torah-Worte in Jos 2-6; 9: DielB 26 (1989s) 70-80.

2391 **Felber** Anneliese, Ecclesia ex gentibus congregata; die Deutung der Rahabepisode (Jos 2) in der Patristik: Diss. Graz 1991, ᴰ*Bauer* J.-B. 200 p. – TR 87 (1991) 513 ('et gentibus', 'Zahab'); RTLv 23, p. 548.

2392 *Spila* Seppo, The Septuagint version of Joshua 3-4: ➤ 426, Septuaginta 7, 1989/91, 63-74.

2393 **Fahr** Heinz, *Glessmer* Uwe, Jordandurchzug und Beschneidung als Zurechtweisung in einem Targum zu Josua 5 (Edition des Ms T.-S. B 13,12): OrBibChr 3. Glückstadt 1991, Augustin. 162 p.; ill. 3-87030-152-X [BL 92,143].

2394 *Eshel* H. [Jos 6,26] The historical background of the pesher interpreting Joshua's curse on the rebuilder of Jericho: ➤ 145, ᶠStARCKY J., RQum 15 (1991s) 409-420.

2395 *Stec* D. M., [Jos 7,21] The mantle hidden by Achan: VT 41 (1991) 356-9.

2396 **Younger** K. Lawson, [Jos 9-12] Ancient conquest accounts; a study in ANE and biblical history writing: JStOT supp 98, 1990 ➤ 6,b404: ᴿÉTRel 66 (1991) 273s (Françoise *Smyth*); JTS 42 (1991) 627s (G. *Auld*).

2397 *Fischer* Danielle, Jean CALVIN, Congrégation sur Josué 11 (Sept. 1563), première éd.: FreibZ 38 (1991) 351-367.

2398 **Cortese** Enzo, Josua 13-21; ein priesterschriftlicher Abschnitt im deuteronomistischen Geschichtswerk [Hab/D Wien]: OBO 94. FrS/Gö 1990, Univ./VR. Fs 34. 3-7278-0661-3 / VR 3-525-53724-7. – ᴿBL (1991) 70 (A. G. *Auld*: strident defense of his ᴰ1972, Terra di Canaan); JBL 110 (1991) 711-3 (S. L. *McKenzie*: will have to be considered even if not widely accepted).

2399 *Kallai* Zechariah, (Jos 16,1s) Beth-El-Luz and Beth-Aven: ➤ 75, ᶠHERR-MANN S., Prophetie 1991, 171-188.

2400 *Govrin* Yehuda, [Jos 19,2] The Naḥal Yatir site – Moladah in the inheritance of the tribe of Simeon?: 'Atiqot 20 (1991) 178s; ❶ 13*-23*.

2401 *Auld* A. Graeme, The cities in Joshua 21; the contribution of textual criticism: Text 15 (1990) 141-152; ❶10.

2402 *Reed* Stephen A., A puzzling Masoretic note in Joshua 21:35: Text 15 (1990) 77-83.

2403 *a) Brekelmans* C., Joshua xxiv; its place and function [presidential address IOSOT 1989]; – *b) Weippert* Helga, Geschichten und Geschichte; Verheissung und Erfüllung im deuteronomistischen Geschichtswerk: ➤ 429, IOSOT 1989/91, 1-9; phot. / 116-131.

2404 **Koopmans** W. I., Joshua 24 as poetic narrative: JStOT supp 93, 1990 ➤ 6,2880: ᴿBL (1991) 82 (B. *Lindars*: what is the difference between 'poetic narrative' and 'solemn, measured' – and redacted – prose?).

2405 *Edelman* Diana, Are the kings of the Amorites 'swept away' in Jos XXIV 12?: VT 41 (1991) 279-286.

E4.2 *Liber Judicum:* **Richter, Judges.**

2406 *Bartelmus* Rüdiger, Forschung am Richterbuch seit Martin NOTH: TRu 56 (1991) 221-259.

2406* *Bayley* Raymond, Which is the best commentary? 14. Judges [SOGGIN, without the evasions of many articles in this series]: ExpTim 103 (1991s) 136-8.

2407 **Davis** Dale R., Such a great salvation; expositions of the Book of Judges: Expositor's Guide to the Historical Books. GR 1990, Baker. 224 p. $12. 0-8010-2996-1. – RBS 148 (1991) 123s (T. L. *Constable*).

2408 **Hamlin** E. John, Judges; at risk in the Promised Land: IntTheolComm 1990 ⮀ 6,2887: RGraceTJ 11 (1990) 230-2 (J. L. *Crawford*).

2408* *Kaswalder* P., I giudici di Israele [sia 'maggiori' che 'minori' negati da LEMCHE N. contro RÖSEL H.; bilancio]: LA 41 (1991) 9-40; Eng. 489.

2409 **Klein** Lillian R., Triumph of irony 1988 ⮀ 4,2763 ... 6,2888: RAsburyTJ 46,1 (1991) 115-7 (L. G. *Stone*: 'sad that such an important subject has recived such poor treatment in such a distinguished series'); JSS 36 (1991) 153-5 (B. *Lindars*: irritatingly absurd literal translations).

2410 *Trebolle Barrera* J., Édition préliminaire de 4QJuges[b]; contribution des manuscrits qumraniens des Juges à l'étude textuelle et littéraire du livre: ⮀ 145, FSTARCKY J., RQum 15 (1991) 79-100; pl. 5.

2410* *Viganò* Lorenzo, Judges at Ebla [*di-ku₅* in ARCHI A., ARES 1 (1988) 205-306; but often *da-núm, da-nu*]: LA 41 (1991) 303-310.

2411 **Webb** Barry G., The book of Judges, an integrated reading: JStOT supp 46, 1987 ⮀ 3,2638 ... 6,3891: RAsburyTJ 46,1 (1991) 117-9 (L. G. *Stone*).

2412 *Szwarc* Ursula, ❷ The literary composition of Jg. 1: RoczTK 36,1 (1989) 5-15; Eng. 15.

2413 **Eslinger** Lyle, Into the hands of the living God [Jg 2; 1 Sam 12; 2 Kgs 17 narratology] 1989 ⮀ 5,1316; 6,1343: RCBQ 53 (1991) 465-7 (L. J. *Hoppe*: really a rejection of NOTH's Deuteronomist, and pointless polemic against all historico-critical analysis of Jos-Kgs); ETL 67 (1991) 417s (J. *Lust*, Eng.); Interpretation 45 (1991) 307s (M. *Hillmer*); JBL 110 (1991) 141s (R. D. *Nelson*); JTS 42 (1991) 160-2 (H. *Mowvley*: claim of unified narrative, not successive dtr recensions); VT 41 (1991) 485-8 (R. H. *O'Connell*, 'great orations' of dtr).

2414 *Williams* Jay G., The structure of Judges 2,6-16,31: JStOT 49 (1991) 77-85.

2415 *Brettler* Marc, [Jg 3,12-30] Never the twain shall meet? The Ehud story as history and literature: HUCA 62 (1991) 285-304.

2416 *Ogden* Graham S., The special features of a story; a study of Judges 3:12-30: BTrans 42 (1991) 408-414.

2417 *Knauf* Ernst A., Eglon and Ophrah; two toponymic notes on the Book of Judges [3,12s; 6,11]: JStOT 51 (1991) 25-44.

2418 *Barré* Michael L., The meaning of *pršdn* in Judges III 22 [excrement]: VT 41 (1991) 1-11.

2419 **Bal** Mieke, [Jg 4] Murder and difference... Sisera 1988 ⮀ 4,2772 ... 6,2894: RRelStR 17 (1991) 1-10 (D. *Jobling*, also on her Lethal love and Death & dissymmetry).

2420 *Bal* Mieke, Murder and difference; uncanny sites in an uncanny world: LitTOx 5,1 (1991) 11-19 [< ZIT 91,211].

2421 *Matthews* Victor H., Hospitality and hostility in Judges 4: BibTB 21 (1991) 13-21.

2422 *Younger* K. Lawson, Heads! Tails! Or the whole coin? Contextual method and intertextual analysis, Judges 4 and 5: → 334*, ^E*Younger*, Biblical canon 1991 ...

2423 **Gill** Deborah M., The female prophet; gender and leadership in the biblical tradition: diss. Fuller Theol. Sem., ^D*Martin* R. Pasadena 1991. 315 p. 91-35883. – DissA 52 (1991s) 3970-A.

2424 *Scippa* Vincenzo, Giaele, una donna forte dell'Antico Testamento; analisi strutturale di Gdc 5,23-27 e 4,17-23: RivB 39 (1991) 385-421; Eng. 421s.

2425 **Gibert** P., [Jg 6-8] Vérité historique... Gédéon/HÉRODOTE 1990 → 6, 2901: ^RCritRR 4 (1991) 138s (B. O. *Long*); ÉTRel 66 (1991) 274s (Françoise *Smyth*); NRT 113 (1991) 575s (J.-L. *Ska*).

2426 *Légasse* Simon, Le cycle de Gédéon (Juges 6-8) d'après l'ancienne littérature juive: BLitEc 92 (1991) 163-180. 243-257; Eng. 180.258.

2427 *Pury* Albert de, Le raid de Gédeon (Juges 6,25-32) et l'histoire de l'exclusivisme yahwiste: → 140, ^FSMYTH-FLORENTIN F. 1991, 173-205.

2428 **Tanner** James P., Textual patterning in biblical Hebrew narratives; a case study in Judges 6-8: diss. Texas, ^D*Liebowitz* H. A. Austin 1990, 293 p. 91-16989. – DissA 52 (1991s) 195-A.

2429 *a) Thiel* Winfried, [Jdc 8,4-17; 1 Reg 12,25; Gen 32,31] Pnuël im Alten Testament; – *b) Schunck* Klaus-Dietrich, Falsche Richter im Richterbuch: → 75, ^FHERRMANN S., Prophetie 1991, 398-414; 8 fig. / 364-370.

2430 *Bekkum* Wout J. Van, Observations on the Hebrew debate in medieval Europe [mostly attributed to objects like trees as in Jg 9,8-15]: → 622, Dispute poems 1989/91, 77-90.

2430* *Melzger* Martin, Zeder, Weinstock und Weltenbaum: → 87, ^FKOCH K., Ernten 1991, 197-229.

2431 **Roberts** Samuel P., [Jg 11] Content and form within the Jephthah narrative; a literary-historical investigation: diss. Southern Baptist Theol. Sem., ^D*Smothers* T. 1991. 269 p. 92-10180. – DissA 52 (1991s) 3633-A.

2432 **Trible** Phyllis, Verhalen van verschrikking 1986 → 6,2906: ^RBijdragen 52 (1991) 96 (Anne-Francine *Van Gogh*).

2433 **Kaswalder** P. A., La disputa diplomatica... Gdc 11,12-28: SBF Anal 29, 1990 → 6,2908: ^RBL (1991) 37 (J. R. *Porter*: a strong case); Salesianum 53 (1991) 586 (R. *Vicent*); ZAW 103 (1991) 158 (J. A. *Soggin*: wichtig).

2434 **Bader** Winfried, [Ri 13-16] Simson bei Delila; computerlinguistische Interpretation des Textes Ri 13-16 [kath. Diss. ^D*Schweizer* H. Tübingen 1989. – RTLv 23, p. 537]: Textw/Informatik 3. Tü 1991, Francke. x-468 p. DM 136 [ZAW 104,442, M. *Witte*].

2435 *Greene* Mark, Enigma variations; aspects of the Samson story, Judges 13-16: VoxEvca 21 (1991) 53-79.

2436 **Amit** Yairah, ⊕ [Jg 17s] *Polemos smwi* in the story of the conquest of Dan: BethM 36,126 (1990s) 267-278.

2437 **Cross** Diane H., The post-structuralist literary theory of Roland BARTHES applied to Judges 19-21, the rape of the Levite's concubine: diss. Golden Gate Baptist Theol. Sem. 1991, ^D*Eakins* J. 232 p. 91-28062. – DissA 52 (1991s) 1372-A.

E4.3 **Liber Ruth,** *'V Rotuli'*, the Five Scrolls.

2438 **Atkinson** David, The message of Ruth; the Wings of Refuge: The Bible Speaks Today. Leicester/DG 1989, Inter-Varsity. 128 p. 0-85110-740-0 / US 0-87784-294-9.

2439 **Barber** Cyril J.,   Ruth, a story of God's grace.   Neptune NJ 1989 =
1983 [Moody < periodicals], Loizeaux.   198 p. – ᴿGraceTJ 11 (1990) 229s
(J. J. *Lawlor*).

2440 *Black* James,   Ruth in the dark; folktale, law and creative ambiguity in
the Old Testament: LitTOx 5,1 (1991) 20-36 [< zıт 91,211].

2441 *Dumortier* F.,   Ruth: → 664, Catholicisme XIII, 95 (1991) 221-3.

2442 **Fewell** Diana N., *Gunn* David M.,   Compromising redemption; relating
characters in the Book of Ruth: Literary currents in biblical interp., 1990
→ 6,2920;   ᴿÉTRel 66 (1991) 428s (P. *Lys*); RelStR 17 (1991) 350 (W. L.
Humphreys).

2443 *Grant* Reg,   Literary structure in the Book of Ruth: BS 148 (1991)
424-442.

2444 *Hallaire* Jacques,   Un jeu de structures dans le Livre de Ruth: NRT 113
(1991) 708-727.

2445 **Hubbard** Robert L.,   The book of Ruth: NIntComm 1988 → 4,2793* ...
6,2923:   ᴿBiblica 72 (1991) 566-9 (E. *Zenger*: wichtig, informativ,
hilfreich); HeythJ 32 (1991) 544s (P. W. *Coxon*).

2446 **Martin** R. A., *al.,*   Syntactical concordance to the correlated Greek and
Hebrew text of Ruth: Computer Bible 30AB.   ... 1988s, Biblical Research
Associates. I. 277 p.; II. 209 p.   0-935106-26-X; -30-8.

2447 *Nicol* George G.,   Neglected books of the Bible, 2. Ruth: ExpTim 102
(1990s) 272-4.

2448 **Neusner** Jacob,   The Midrash compilations of the sixth and seventh
centuries; an introduction to the rhetorical, logical, and topical program,
3. Ruth Rabbah: BrownJudSt 189 [cf. 183, also 1989 → 6,2929.a219].
xx-157 p. [RelStR 18, 156, J. T. *Townsend*].

2449 **Sasson** Jack M., Ruth 1989 → 5,2698 ... 6,2931:   ᴿBZ 35 (1991) 127s (J.
Scharbert, auch über HUBBARD R.).

2450 **Waard** Jan de, *Nida* Eugene A.,   A translator's handbook on the Book
of Ruth² [¹1973]: Helps for Translators.   NY 1991, United Bible
Societies.   ix-110 p. $8.   0-8267-0108-6.

2451 **Zenger** Eric,   Das Buch Ruth: Z BK AT 8, 1986 → 3,2664 ... 6,2935:
ᴿCBQ 53 (1991) 313s (P. R. *House*: anti-Hasmonean composition dubious).

2452 *Benjamin* Don C.,   [Ruth 1,1-22; Lk 18,1-8] The persistent widow:
BToday 28 (1990) 213-9.

2453 *Bernstein* Moshe J.,   [Ruth 3; 4,11s]   Two multivalent readings in the
Ruth narrative: JStOT 50 (1991) 15-26.

2454 *Jones* Stuart,   The redeemer of Ruth [4:1-22]: Kerux 3,3 (1988) 15-20.

E4.4   **1-2 Samuel.**

2455 **Anderson** A. A.,   2 Samuel: Word Comm. 11, 1989 → 5,2704; 6,2939:
ᴿCBQ 53 (1991) 278 (P. D. *Miscall*); CritRR 4 (1991) 116-8 (R. G.
Bowman); EvQ 63 (1991) 257-9 (T. D. *Alexander*); JTS 42 (1991) 162s
(R. P. *Gordon*); ScotJT 44 (1991) 545s (S. B. *Dawes*).

2456 **Baldwin** Joyce,   1 & 2 Samuel: Tyndale OT comm. 1988 → 4,2806 ...
6,2940:   ᴿEvQ 63 (1991) 63-66 (H. G. M. *Williamson,* also on six Tyndale
minor prophets).

2457 **Brueggemann** Walter,   First and Second Samuel: Interpretation comm.
1990 → 6,2941:   ᴿCritRR 4 (1991) 127s (R. W. *Klein*); HorBT 13 (1991)
83s (E. J. *Hamlin*); RelStR 17 (1991) 350 (C. *Bernas*: extremely readable);

TS 52 (1991) 349s (J. C. *Endres*); TTod 48 (1991s) 108. 110 (Deborah K. *Dees*).

2458 **Campbell** Antony F., Of prophets and kings...: CBQ Mg 17, 1986 ➤ 2,2012 ... 5,2709: ᴿRB 98 (1991) 142s (F. *Langlamet*).

2458* *Campbell* Antony F. [1 Sam 4-6; 2 Sam 6] OT narrative as theology: Pacifica 4 (1991) 165-180.

2459 *Caquot* A., Samuel (Livres de): ➤ 686, SDB XI, 64 (1991) 1048-1098.

2460 **Chafin** Kenneth L., 1,2 Samuel: Communicator's Comm. 8 [ᴱ*Ogilvie* L.]. Dallas 1989, Word Books. 404 p. 0-8499-0413-7. – ᴿTLZ 116 (1991) 178-180 (H. J. *Stoebe*).

2461 **Fernández Marcos** N., *Busto Saiz* J. R., 1-2 Samuel antioqueno: Est-Cisn 50, 1989 ➤ 5,2711; 6,2943: ᴿJJS 42 (1991) 130s (S. *Brock*); JStJud 22 (1991) 134-6 (A. *Hilhorst*); RÉG 104 (1991) 668 (P. *Nautin*).

2462 *Gressmann* Hugo, *al.* , Narrative and novella in Samuel [1906-1923]; ᴱ*Gunn* David M. JStOT supp. 116, Historic Texts 9. Sheffield 1991, Almond. 1-85075-281-8 [BL 91,158]. – ᴿETL 67 (1991) 419s (J. *Lust*).

2463 *Hastoupis* Athanasios, ⊕ The books of I and II Samuel: TAth 61 (1990) 96-119; Eng. 903.

2464 **Martini** Carlo M., Samuel, profeta religioso y civil [CasM 1990], ᵀ*Ortiz García* Alfonso: Servidores y testigos 51. Sdr 1991, Sal Terrae. 159 p. 84-293-0907-1.

2465 **Mommer** Peter, Samuel, Geschichte und Überlieferung [Diss. Marburg 1990 ᴰ*Boecker* W.]: WM 65. Neuk 1991, Neuk.-V. vii-248 p. DM 68. 3-7887-1381-X [ZAW 104, 154, H. C. *Schmitt*].

2466 **Morano Rodríguez** Ciríaca, Glosas... vulgatas españoles, 1-2 Samuel: EstCisn 48, 1989 ➤ 5,2716; 6,2948: ᴿClasR 41 (1991) 243s (J. N. *Birdsall*); JJS 42 (1991) 131s (S. *Brock*); Muséon 104 (1991) 205s (J.-C. *Haelewyck*).

2467 **Polzin** R., Samuel and the Deuteronomist II, 1 Sm 1989 ➤ 5,2719; 6,2951: ᴿJAAR 59 (1991) 193-7 (H. C. *White*); JQR 82 (1991s) 461-482 (L. *Eslinger*); JRel 70 (1990) 625s (M. Z. *Brettler*: enjoyable).

2468 ᴱ**Vogüé** A. de, GRÉGOIRE, Roís [1 Sam 1s]: SChr 351, 1989 ➤ 6,2954: ᴿBLitEx 92 (1991) 59 (H. *Crouzel*); DowR 109 (1991) 231-4 (Petra *Boëx*).

2469 **Wonneberger** Reinhard, Redaktion; Studien zur Textforschung im AT, entwickelt am Beispiel der Samuel-Überlieferung: ev. Hab.-Diss. Mainz 1991. – TR 87 (1991) 512.

2470 *a)* **Zijl** (= Zyl) A. H. van, 1 Samuel, Deel I-II, 1988s ➤ 4,2823; 5,2725: ᴿBL (1991) 62 (J. A. *Emerton*); CBQ 53 (1991) 685s (C. T. *Begg*, 2: some inadequacies of bibliography and 'helps to preaching').
– *b)* *Rendtorff* Rolf, Die Geburt des Retters; Beobachtungen zur Jugend-geschichte Samuels im Rahmen der literarischen Komposition: ➤ 252, Kanon 1991, 132-140 (ineditum).
– *c)* *Benedict* Hans-Jürgen, Hannas Lobgesang; Bibelarbeit über 1. Samuel 2. 1-10: Junge Kirche 52 (Bremen 1991) 462-4 [< ᴢɪᴛ 91,569].
– *d)* *Spina* Frank A., A prophet's 'pregnant pause'; Samuel's silence in the Ark narrative (1 Sam. 4:1-7:2): HorBT 13 (1991) 59-73.

E4.5 *1 Sam 7 ... Initia potestatis regiae,* **Origins of kingship.**

2471 *a)* *Boggio* Giovanni, I poveri di ᴊʜᴡʜ nei Salmi; – *b)* *Soggin* J. Alberto, Il re d'Israele difensore dei poveri: ➤ 444*, Ricchezza 1989/91, 81-107 / 65-79.

2472 **Brettler** Marc Z.,   God is king...: JStOT supp 76, D1989 ➤ 5,2733;
6,2968: RCBQ 53 (1991) 660-2 (L.F. *Asma*); ÉTRel 66 (1991) 279s (D.
Lys); Interpretation 45 (1991) 310 (W. *Soll*); JAOS 111 (1991) 820s (B.
Halpern); JSS 36 (1991) 332-4 (B. *Lindars*); TLZ 116 (1991) 819s (H.
Spieckermann).

2473 *Conrad* Joachim,   Überlegungen zu Bedeutung und Beurteilung der
Kritik an Königtum und Staat innerhalb des Alten Testaments: ➤ 163,
FWAGNER S., Gottesvolk 1991, 91-97.

2474 EGaley J.C.,   Kingship and kings. Chur 1990, Harwood. v-280 p. $54.
3-7186-5066-5 [BL 92,105, N. *Wyatt* on *Caquot* A, ancient Israel].

2474* *Jensen* Hans J.L.,   The fall of the king: ScandJOT 5,1 (1991) 121-147,
not about Saul.

2475 **Kluger** Rivkah S.,   Psiche e Bibbia [Z 1974] TVentura Milka. F 1991, La
Giuntina. 143 p. 88-85943-59-4. p. 49-84 Re Saul e lo spirito di Dio;
85-136 La regina di Saba nella Bibbia e nella leggenda.

2476 **Noth** Martin, Gott, König, Volk im Alten Testament; eine methodologische Auseinandersetzung mit einer gegenwärtigen Forschungs-
richtung [< ZTK 47 (1950) 157-191 = GesSt 1² (1960) 188-229]: ➤ 321,
WegF 633 (1991) 157-197.

2477 *Nunes Carreira* José,   Charisma und Institution; zur Verfassung des
Königtums in Israel und Juda: ➤ 75, FHERRMANN S., Prophetie 1991,
39-51.

Polish David, Give us a king... Jewish sovereignty 1989 ➤ e945*.

2478 *Savignac* Jean de,   La royauté en Israël [... Égypte, Mésopotamie]:
ÉTRel 66 (1991) 413-7.

2479 **Weisman** Zev, ❸ People and king in biblical *mišpaṭ*. TA 1991, Meuḥad.
224 p. – RZion 56 (1991) 447-450 (Yair *Zakovitch*).

2480 **Wénin** André, Samuel et l'instauration de la monarchie (1S 1-12) 1988
➤ 4,2839 ... 6,2981: RCarthaginensia 7 (1991) 255s (R. *Sanz Valdivieso*).

2481 *Walters* Stanley D., Saul of Gibeon: JStOT 52 (1991) 61-76.

2482 **Edelman** Diana V., King Saul in the historiography of Judah: JStOT
supp 121. Sheffield 1991, JStOT. 347 p. £40; pa. £30. [TR 88,426].
1-85075-321-0.

2483 **Berges** Ulrich, Die Verwerfung Sauls: ForBi 61, D1989 ➤ 6,2985:
RArTGran 53 (1990) 291s (A.S. *Muñoz*); BO 48 (1991) 886s (K.A.D.
Smelik); CBQ 53 (1991) 95s (R.D. *Nelson*); ColcT 61,2 (1991) 179s (J.
Łach, ❸); OTAbs 14 (1991) 109s (W. *Roth*).

2483* *Berges* Ulrich, Lectura pragmática de 1 Sm 12: RTLim 25 (1991)
368-388.

2484 **Long** V. Philips, The reign and rejection of King Saul D1989 ➤ 5,2738:
RBL (1991) 83 (A.G. *Auld*); CritRR 4 (1991) 150s (L. *Eslinger*).

2485 *Hunter* J.H., Deconstruction and the OT; an evaluation of 'context'
with reference to 1 Samuel 9:2: OTEssays 4 (1991) 362-372.

2486 *Zalewski* Saul, ❸ [1 Sam 10,26s] Contempt of the sons of Belial for Saul
and his reaction: BethM 36,127 (1990s) 299-322.

E4.6   *1 Sam 16 ... 2 Sam: Accessio Davidis,*   **David's Rise.**

Dassmann Ernst, Zu den Davidzyklen im Apollonkloster von Bawit 1991
➤ b998*c.

2487 **Elazar** Daniel J., Dealing with fundamental regime change; the biblical paradigm of the transition from tribal federation to federal monarchy under David: ➤ 56, FFOX M. 1 (1991) 97-129.

2488 **Flanagan** James W., David's... hologram 1988 ➤ 4,2855 ... 6,2990: RBZ 35 (1991) 280s (D. *Kinet*); ETL 67 (1991) 139-142 (M. *Vervenne*, Eng.); HeythJ 32 (1991) 388s (J.F.A. *Sawyer*).

2489 **Martini** Carlo M., David et le Christ, retraite ignatienne, TDerouau W.: Chrétiens d'aujourd'hui 6. Namur 1991, Culture et vérité. 187 p. [ScEspr 44, 229s, C.R. *Nadeau*].

2490 *Millet-Gérard* Dominique, Le prêtre, le pécheur et le poète; méditation claudélienne sur le roi David: FoiVie 90,5 = CahB 30 (1991) 43-58.

2491 a) *Schwartz* Regina M., The histories of David; biblical scholarship and biblical stories; – b) *Nohrnberg* James C., Princely characters [Joseph/ David]: ➤ 454*b*, Not in heaven 1989/91, 192-210 . 253s / 58-97 . 231-9.

2492 *Schwartz* Regina M., Adultery in the house of David; the metanarrative of biblical scholarship and the narratives of the Bible: ➤ 311, Semeia 54 (1991) 35-55.

2493 **Urbina** Pedro A., David, el Rey: MCBiog 2. M 1990, Palabra. 360 p. pt. 1350. 84-7118-679-9. – RActuBbg 28 (1991) 102 (F. de P. *Solá*).

2494 **Veijola** Timo, David 1990 ➤ 6,315: RErbAuf 67 (1991) 148 (R. *Dietzfelbinger*); TLZ 116 (1991) 734-7 (Eva *Osswald*).

2495 **Nelson** William B., 1 Samuel 16-18 and 19: 8-10; a traditio-historical study: diss. Harvard. CM 1991, 209 p. 91-32093. – DissA 52 (1991s) 1775-A.

2496 *Salibi* Kamal, The 'Goliath' problem [1 Sam 16s; 2 Sam 21,19: Elhanan slew Oregim, a Bethlehemite in Gittim]; NESTR 12 (1991) 3-13.

2497 *Joosten* Jan, 1 Samuel XVI 6,7 in the Peshitta version: VT 41 (1991) 226-233.

2498 *Trebolle* Julio, The story of David and Goliath (1 Sam 17-18); textual variants and literary composition: BSeptCog 23 (1990) 16-30 [< ZIT 91,360].

2499 *Ḥemiel* Ḥ., ⊕ What [of] Aaron the priest between the kings Saul and David?: BethM 36,126 (1990s) 190-211.

2500 *Philonenko* Marc, Humilitas et superbia [= David & Goliath]; note sur la Psychomachie de Prudence: ➤ 22, FBENOÎT A., RHPR 71 (1991) 115-9; 1 fig.

2501 **Segal** Lore, The story of King Saul and King David. NY 1991, Schocken. 123 p. $20 [JAAR 59,885].

2502 a) *Eskenazi* Tamara C., [1 Sam 18,12-29; 2 Sam 6,12-23], Michal in Hebrew sources; – b) *Kapelovitz* Abbey P., Michal, a vessel for the desires of others; – c) *Miscall* Peter D., Michal and her sisters; – d) *Polzin* Robert, A multivoiced look at the Michal narratives: ➤ 295, Michal 1991, 157-174 / 207-223 / 246-260 / 261-9.

2503 *Simotas* Panagiotis N., ⊖ David, self-exiled in the land of the Philistines: TAth 62 (1991) 294-311; Eng. 929.

2504 *Coggins* Richard, [1 Sam 28; 1 Kgs 20] On kings and disguises: JStOT 50 (1991) 55-62.

2505 *Collins* Nina L., The start of the pre-exilic calendar day of David and the Amalekites; a note on 1 Samuel XXX 17: VT 41 (1991) 203-210.

2506 *Littlewood* A.R., Michael PSELLUS and the witch of Endor: JÖsByz 40 (1990) 225-231 [< RHE 87,40*].

2507 ᴱSimonetti Manlio, ORIGENE, EUSTAZIO, GREGORIO di Nissa, La maga di Endor: BtPatr 15, 1988 ➤ 5,2770: ᴿAnStoEseg 8 (1991) 300s (M. *Pesce*).

2508 *a*) *Clines* David J.A., The story of Michal, wife of David, in its sequential unfolding: – *b*) *Bowman* Richard G., The fortune of King David / the fate of Queen Michal; a literary critical analysis of 2 Samuel 1-8: ➤ 295, Michal 1991, 129-140 / 97-120.

2509 **Kleven** Terence J., Hebrew style and narrative sequence in 2 Samuel 1-7: diss. McMaster 1990, ᴰ*Combs* A. 497 p. 0-315-60664-9 (DANN-60664). – DissA 52 (1991s) 3633-A; RTLv 23, p. 539.

2510 *Kleven* Terence, Reading Hebrew poetry; David's lament over Saul and Jonathan (2 Sam 1:17-27): ProcGLM 11 (1991) 51-65.

2511 **Fokkelman** J.P., Narrative art [1. 1981 ➤ 63,2962*a*; – 2. 1986 ➤ 2,2042] 3. Throne and city [2 Sam 2-8 & 21-24] ➤ 6,3008: ᴿExpTim 103 (1991s) 23 (R. *Coggins*: subtleties doubtfully intended by the narrator); JNES 50 (1991) 221s (D. *Pardee*, 2: some good ideas far too badly worked out); NedTTs 45 (1991) 242-4 (K. S. D. *Smelik*, 1s).

2512 **Gelander** Shamai, David and his God; religious ideas as reflected in biblical historiography and literature: Jerusalem Biblical Studies 5. J 1991, Simor. 202 p. 965-242-007-7 [OIAc 2,19].

2513 *Dennison* James T.ᴶ, A King and a cripple; 2 Sam 4:4; 9:1-11; 16:1-4; 19:16,17,24-30: Kerux 1,2 (1986) 18-26.

2514 **Floss** Johannes P., David und Jerusalem ... 2 Sam 5,6-9: AOtt 30, 1987. – ᴿBZ 35 (1991) 123-5 (W. *Thiel*); OTAbs 14 (1990) 110 (C. T. *Begg*); VT 41 (1991) 376 (R. P. *Gordon*); ZkT 113 (1991) 76s (J. M. *Oesch*).

2514* *a*) *Janowski* Bernd, Keruben und Zion; Thesen zur Entstehung der Zionstradition; – *b*) *Kraus* Hans-Joachim, Tore der Gerechtigkeit: ➤ 87, ꟳKOCH K., Ernten 1991, 231-264 / 265-272.

2515 **Ollenburger** B. C., Zion 1987 ➤ 3,2718 ... 6,3012: ᴿVT 41 (1991) 510s (J. A. *Emerton*).

2516 **Seow Choon Leong,** [2 Sam 6,14; 1 Sam 4,3; 7,2; Ps 132] Myth, drama, and the politics of David's dance: HarvSemMg 44, 1989 ➤ 5,2777: ᴿCBQ 53 (1991) 308-310 (M. S. *Smith*); JBL 110 (1991) 142-4 (S. A. *Meier*).

2517 **Jones** Gwilym H., [2 Sam 7; 12; 1 Kgs] The Nathan narratives: JStOT supp 80. Sheffield 1990, JStOT. 196 p. £25. 1-85075-225-7. – ᴿBL (1991) 81 (A. *Mayes*); CBQ 53 (1991) 656-8 (P. D. *Miscall*).

2517* *Soggin* J. A., [2 Sam 9 ...] Gedanken zur Vor- und Frühgeschichte Altisraels und -Judas: ➤ 102*c*, ꟳPrince MIKASA 1991, 383-392.

2518 *a*) *Ishida* Tomoo, [2 Sam 9 ...] The succession narrative and Esarhaddon's apology; a comparison; – *b*) *Kramer* S. N., Solomon and Šulgi, a comparative portrait; – *c*) *Oded* Bustenay, [2 Kgs 18,25 ...] 'The command of the god' as a reason for going to war in the Assyrian royal inscriptions; – *d*) *Machinist* Peter, The question of distinctiveness in ancient Israel; an essay: ➤ 150, ꟳTADMOR H., Ah Assyria, 1991, 166-173 / 189-195 [294-313, *Klein* J. on Šulgi] / 223-230 / 196-212.

2519 **Bailey** Randall C., David in love and war ... 2 Sam 10-12: JStOT supp 75, ᴰ1990 ➤ 6,3019: ᴿCBQ 53 (1991) 656-8 (P. D. *Miscall*); JTS 42 (1991) 453 (A. A. *Anderson*).

2520 *Niehr* Herbert, Ein unerkannter Text zur Nekromantie in Israel; Bemerkungen zum religionsgeschichtlichen Hintergrund von 2 Sam 12,16a: UF 23 (1991) 301-6.

2521 **Bar-Efrat** Shimon, Narrative art in the bible, [sample 2 Sam 13], [T]*Shefer-Vanson* D.: JStOT supp. 70, 1989 ⇥ 5,1312: [R]ETL 67 (1991) 415 (J. *Lust*).

2522 *Dennison* James T.[J], The rape of Tamar, 2 Samuel 13: Kerux 3,2 (1988) 27-35.

2523 *Kaske* R.E. †, Amnon and Thamar on a misericord in Hereford cathedral: Traditio 45 (Fordham 1989s) 1-6+4 pl.

2524 *Wesselius* J.W., De wijze vrouwen in 2 Samuel 14 en 20: NedTTs 45 (1991) 89-100; Eng. 138.

2525 *Lewis* Theodore J., The ancestral estate (*nah^alat Elohim*) in 2 Samuel 14:16: JBL 110 (1991) 597-612.

2526 *Dieterlé* Christiane, *Monsarrat* Violaine, Famine, guerre et peste en 2 Samuel 21-24: ⇥ 139, [F]SMYTH-FLORENTIN F. 1991, 207-220.

2526* *Wiseman* Donald J., [...2 Sam 21,17, 'the lamp of Israel'] Light from the East: ⇥ 102c, [F]Prince MIKASA 1991, 485-490.

2527 *Weinfeld* Moshe, [2 Sam 24] ❶ The census of Mari, Israel, and Rome [*tēbibtum* and also Roman *lustrum* show census accompanied by expiatory ritual]: Zion 56 (1991) 233-7; Eng. XXI.

E4.7 *Libri Regum;* Solomon, Temple: 1 Kings...

2528 *Halpern* Baruch, *Vanderhooft* David S., The editions of Kings in the 7th-6th centuries B.C.E.: HUCA 62 (1991) 179-244.

2529 *Dreher* Carlos A., Das tributäre Königtum in Israel unter Salomo [< RIBL 5s (1990) 14-24], [T]*Reimer* H.: EvT 51 (1991) 49-60.

2530 *Dumortier* F., Rois (Livras des): ⇥ 664, Catholicisme XIII, 59 (1991) 61-66.

2531 *Hastoupis* Athanasios P., ❺ The books of I and II Kings: TAth 61 (1991) 345-379; Eng. 905.

2532 **Hobbs** T.R., 1,2 Kings: Word **Themes**. Dallas 1989, Word. viii-104 p. $10. – [R]CBQ 53 (1991) 288 (P.J. *Griffin*); GraceTJ 11 (1990) 102 (R. *Patterson*); ScripB 21 (1991) 26s (R. *Duckworth*).

2533 **Long** Burke O., 2 Kings: FOTLit 10. GR 1991, Eerdmans. xiii-324 p. 0-8028-0535-3.

2534 **McKenzie** S.L., The trouble with kings; the composition of the Book of Kings in the Deuteronomistic history: VT supp 42. Leiden 1991, Brill. xii-183 p. *f* 98 [ZAW 104, 301, H.-C. *Schmitt*]

2535 **Mulder** M.J., Koningen I (I,1-7): CommentaarOT, 1987 ⇥ 4,2904; 5,2793: [R]NedTTs 45 (1991) 246-8 (M.D. *Koster*).

2535* **Rice** Gene, 1 Kings; nations under God: InternatTheolComm., 1990 ⇥ 6,3035; $11 pa.: [R]GraceTJ 12,1 (1991) 129-131 (J.I. *Lawlor*: product of team-taught exegetical preaching classes).

2536 *a) Spottorno* Victoria, The Lucianic text of Kings in the New Testament; – *b) Trebolle* Julio, The text-critical use of the Septuagint in the Books of Kings: ⇥ 426, Septuagint 7, 1989/91, 279-284 / 285-299.

2537 *Brettler* Marc, The structure of 1 Kings 1-11: JStOT 49 (1991) 87-97.

2538 *Garsiel* Moshe, Puns upon names as a literary device in 1 Kings 1-2: Biblica 72 (1991) 379-386.

2539 *Frisch* Amos, Structure and its significance; the narrative of Solomon's reign (1 Kings 1-12.24): JStOT 51 (1991) 3-14; 15-21 response, *Parker* Kim I.; 22-24 rejoinder.

2540 *Koopmans* W.T., The testament of David in 1 Kings II 1-10: VT 41 (1991) 429-449.
2541 *Millard* A.R., [1 Kgs 2,3-15] Texts and archaeology; weighing the evidence; the case for King Solomon: PEQ 123 (1991) 19-27 [28-31, response by *Miller* J.M., Solomon, international potentate or local king?; 117s, Millard rejoinder].
2542 *Lefebvre* Philippe, [3 Kingdoms 4,12...] Salomon et Bacchus: ↠ 426, Septuagint 7, 1989/91, 313-323.
2543 *Jobling* David, [1 Kgs 5,13] 'Forced labor'; Solomon's golden age and the question of literary representation: ↠ 311, Semeia 54 (1991) 57-76.

Templum, 1 Reg 6s:

2544 *Adler* Stephen J., The Temple Mount in court; will Israel's supreme court prove the destruction of ancient remains?: BAR-W 17,5 (1991) 60-68. 72.
2545 **Barker** Margaret, The gate of Heaven; the history and symbolism of the Temple in Jerusalem. L 1991, SPCK. ix-198 p. £11. 0-281-04510-0 [NTAbs 36,127]. – RExpTim 103 (1991s) 52 (J.F. *Healey*).
2546 **Chalvon-Demersay** Guy, Le symbolisme du Temple et le Nouveau Temple: diss. Inst. Cath. DCazelles H. Paris 1991. 459 p. – RTLv 23, p. 542.
2547 *Diebner* Bernd J., Gottes Welt, Moses Zelt und das salomonische Heiligtum: ↠ 140, FSMYTH-FLORENTIN F., 1991, 127-154; 2 fig.
2548 *Görg* Manfred, Die 'ehernen Säulen' (1 Reg 7,15) und die 'eiserne Säule' (Jer 1,18); ein Beitrag zur Säulenmetaphorik im AT: ↠ 75, FHERRMANN S., Prophetie 1991, 134-154.
2549 *Knauf* Ernst A., [1 Kgs 7,46] King Solomon's copper supply ↠ 445, Phoenicia 1990/1, 167-186.
Lumpkin W., Temple in Apocalypse and Qumran D1991 ↠ 5041.
2550 *Sporty* Lawrence D., The location of the holy house of Herod's temple; evidence from the post-destruction period [...farther north]: BA 54 (1991) 28-35 continuing 53 (1990).
Renwick David, Paul, the Temple, and the presence of God 1991 ↠ 5238.

2550* *a) Ishida* Tomoo, [2 Sam 12:24s] The role of Nathan the Prophet in the episode of Solomon's birth; – *b) Ikeda* Yutaka, [1 K 9,28] King Solomon and his Red Sea trade: ↠ 102c, FPrince MIKASA 1991, 133-8 / 113-128+3 fig.; map.
2551 **Beyer** Rolf, [1 Kön 10,1-12] Die Königin von Saba, Engel und Dämon 1987 ²1988 ↠ 4,2927... 6,3055: RTRu 56 (1991) 446s (R. *Warland*); ZKG 102 (1991) 104-6 (W.A. *Schulze*).
2552 **Vanoni** Gottfried, Literarkritik... 1 Kön 11s: AOtt 21, 1984 ↠ 65,2487 ... 3,2779: RJNES 50 (1991) 224-6 (D. *Pardee*: admirable volume of an interesting series).
2553 *Cohen* Matty, Maqṭîrôt ûmᵉzabbᵉḥôt lē'lōhêhen (1 Rois XI 8b): VT 41 (1991) 332-341: 'encensoirs et autels pour leurs dieux'.
2554 *Willis* Timothy M., The text of 1 Kings 11:43-12:3: CBQ 53 (1991) 37-44.
2555 *Vattioni* Francesco, 3(1) Re 12,10; 2 Par (Cr) 10,10 e TEODORETO di Ciro: AugR 31 (1991) 475-482.
2556 *Auneau* J., Roboam: ↠ 664, Catholicisme XIII, 59 (1991) 28s.
2557 **Barnes** William H., Studies in the chronology of the Divided Monarchy of Israel [D1986]: HarvSemMg 48. Atlanta 1991, Scholars. xiv-186 p. $30; pa./sb. $20.

2558 **Hayes** John H., *Hooker* Paul K., A new chronology for the kings 1988
➤ 4,2931 ... 6,3058: ᴿBZ 35 (1991) 299s (W. *Thiel*); Henoch 12,3 (1990)
378s (B. *Chiesa*); RivB 39 (1991) 92s (A. *Bonora*); VT 41 (1991) 246
(G. I. *Davies*).

2559 *McFall* Leslie, A translation guide to the chronological data in Kings
and Chronicles: Bibliotheca Sacra 148 (1991) 3-45.

2560 *Frisch* Amos, *Wa-ᵗᵃnîtem* (1 Reg 12,7): an ambiguity and its function in
the context: ZAW 103 (1991) 415-8.

2561 *Deboys* David G., 1 Kings XIII — a 'new criterion' reconsidered: VT
[39 (1989) 31-43 (D. Van *Winkle*)] 41 (1991) 210s.

2562 *Jones* Stuart R., Samaritan hospitality; 1 Kings 13: Kerux 2,3 (1987)
16-22.

E4.8   *1 Regum 17-22: Elias,*   **Elijah.**

Brodie T., Elijah/Luke 1990 ➤ 6,3063: in ᴱ*Richard* E. **6,551*** not 369.
2562* **Hauser** A., *Gregory* R., [1 Kgs 17-19] From Carmel ... Elijah 1990
➤ 6,3068: ᴿÉTRel 66 (1991) 275s (Françoise *Smyth*).

2563 *Leloir* Louis, Élie et Jean le Baptiste; leur message aux moines et
moniales d'aujourd'hui: ColcCist 53 (1991) 123-145. 195-215.

2564 *Masson* Michel, L'expérience mystique du prophète Élie, *qol dᵉmama
daqqa* [not a faint noise but absolute silence]: RHR 208 (1991) 243-271;
Eng. 243.

2565 *Thiel* Winfried, Deuteronomistische Redaktionsarbeit in den Elia-Erzäh-
lungen: ➤ 429, IOSOT 1989/91, 148-171.

2566 *Catastini* Alessandro, Un'applicazione dello *iudicium* in filologia veterotestamentaria (1 Re 17,20-22): ➤ 565, Sangue 1989/91, 219-224.

2568 *Balzer* H. R. [1 Kgs 18; 20; 2 Kgs 18s] My God and your idols; political
rivalry between human representatives of the divine in the OT: OTEssays
4 (1991) 257-271 [< ZAW 104, 436].

2569 *Robinson* Bernard P., Elijah at Horeb, 1 Kings 19:1-18; a coherent
narrative: RB 98 (1991) 513-536; franç. 513.

2570 *Wagner* Siegfried, Elia am Horeb; methodologische und theologische
Überlegungen zu 1 Reg 19: ➤ 75 ᶠHERRMANN S., Prophetie 1991,
415-424.

2571 *Martin-Achard* Robert, La vigne de Naboth (1 Rois 21) d'après des
études récentes: ÉTRel 66 (1991) 1-16.

2572 *Matthews* Victor H., The king's call to justice [1 Kgs 21 ...; 'the king is
above the law ... the only restraint upon his conduct was appeal to divine
justice', WHITELAM K.]: BZ 35 (1991) 204-216.

2573 *Poulssen* Niek, Wijngaard en tuin; twee sporen in 1 Kon 21,1-29:
Bijdragen 52 (1991) 405-427; Eng. 427, Vineyard and garden, two
threads.

2573* **Ziolkowski** Jan M., Jezebel, a Norman Latin poem of the early
eleventh century: Humana Civilitas 10. NY 1989, P. Lang. xiv-226 p.;
12 pl. $33. – ᴿLatomus 50 (1991) 883s (K. *Bate*).

2574 *Dorp* Jaap van, Als Josafat nach Samarien kam (1 Kön 22. 2b): DielB
26 (1989s) 93-101.

E4.9   **2 Reg 1 ...** *Elisaeus* ... Ezechias, Josias.

2575 **Cogan** M., *Tadmor* H., II Kings: AnchorB 11, 1988 ➤ 4,2952 ... 6,3077:
ᴿBijdragen 52 (1991) 207 (E. *Eynikel*, Eng.: archeology pushed).

2576 **Moore** Rick D., God saves; lessons from the Elisha stories: JStOT supp 95, 1990 ➤ 6,3081: ᴿÉTRel 66 (1991) 585s (J.-P. *Sternberger*).

2577 **Reinhold** G. G. G., Die Beziehungen Israels zu den altaramäischen Staaten in der israelitisch-jüdischen Königszeit [Diss. Fra ➤ 5,2843]: EurHS 23/365. Fra 1990, Lang. 586 p. Fs 82. 3-631-42010-2. – ᴿExpTim 102 (1990s) 303s (R. J. *Coggins*); TLZ 116 (1991) 903-5 (D. *Vieweger*).

2578 *Schröer* Henning, Leseerfahrung mit 2 Kön 2,19-22: EvErz 43 (Fra 1991) 226-8 [< ᴢɪᴛ 91,537].

2579 *Asurmendi* Jesús, [2 Re 3,4-27; 6,8-7,20] Las guerras de Eliseo como relatos ficticios: ➤ 421, Luso-Esp 1989/91, 185-201.

2580 *Conroy* Charles, Riflessioni metodologiche su recenti studi della pericopa di Naaman (2 Re 5), ᵀ*Corsani* Maria C.: ➤ 124, ᶠRASCO E., Luca-Atti 1991, 46-71.

2581 *Lasine* Stuart, Jehoram and the cannibal mothers (2 Kgs 6.24-33); Solomon's judgment in an inverted world: JStOT 50 (1991) 27-53.

2582 *Lemaire* André, [2 Rois 8,8 + 22 fois] Hazaël de Damas, roi d'Aram: ➤ 61, ᶠGARELLI P., Marchands 1991, 91-108.

2583 **Lowery** Richard H., The reforming kings; cult and society in First Temple Judah [diss. Yale]: JStOT supp 120. Sheffield 1991, JStOT. 236 p. £27.50 [TR 88,162]. 1-85075-318-0.

2584 *a) Diakonoff* I. M., [2 Kgs 17,5] '*Arê Miday*, the cities of the Medes; – *b) Eph'al* Israel, 'The Samarian(s)' in Assyrian sources; – *c) Garelli* Paul, The achievement of Tilgath-pileser III; novelty or continuity; – *d) Na'aman* Nadav, Forced participation in alliances in the course of the Assyrian campaigns to the west; – *e) Zadok* Ran, Elements of Aramaean pre-history: ➤ 150, ᶠTADMOR H., Ah, Assyria 1991, 13-20 / 36-45 / 46-51 / 80-98 / 104-117.

2585 *Luria* B. Z., [2 Kgs 17,7-18] Between Judah and Israel: BethM 36,126 (1990s) 230-4.

2586 *Frevel* Christian, Vom Schreiben Gottes; Literarkritik, Komposition und Auslegung von 2 Kön 17,34-40: Biblica 72 (1991) 23-48; franç. 48.

2587 **Camp** Ludger, Hiskija... 2 Kön 18-20: ᴰ1990 ➤ 5,2866; 6,3095: ᴿBiblica 72 (1991) 268-272 (B. *Renaud*); JBL 110 (1991) 713-5 (G. N. *Knoppers* disagrees but admits well founded); JTS 42 (1991) 164-6 (A. D. H. *Mayes*); TLZ 116 (1991) 346-8 (H. *Reventlow*).

2588 *Greenfield* Jonas C., [2 Kgs 18,26; Yariris' knowing '4 scripts, 12 languages' (Carchemish Luwian)] Of scribes, scripts and languages: ➤ 630, Phoinikeia 1989/91, 173-185.

2588* *Tadmor* Hayim, [... 2 Kgs 18,26] On the role of Aramaic in the Assyrian Empire: ➤ 102*c*, ᶠPrince MIKASA 1991, 419-423.

2589 *Ehrlich* Carl S., Coalition politics in eighth century ʙ.ᴄ.ᴇ. Palestine; the Philistines and the Syro-Ephraimite war: ZDPV 107 (1991) 48-58.

2590 **Provan** I. W., Hezekiah and the... Deuteronomistic history: BZAW 172, 1988 ➤ 4,2979... 6,3098: ᴿBZ 35 (1991) 297s (W. *Thiel*); Henoch 13 (1991) 242-4 (A. *Catastini*); RechSR 79 (1991) 269s (J. *Briend*).

2591 **Vera Chamaza** G. W., [2 Re 18,13-20,19] Hizkijjahu ᴰ1988 ➤ [2,2135*] 4,2980: ᴿBL (1991), 99 (J. R. *Porter*: over-subtle).

2592 *Yurco* Frank J., The Shabaka-Shebitku coregency and the supposed second campaign of Sennacherib against Judah; a critical assessment: JBL 110 (1991) 35-45.

2593 *a) Gonçalves* Francolino J., Senaquerib na Palestina e a tradição bíblica; – *b) Caramelo* Francisco, As divisões da sociedade de Judá por ocasião da queda de Jerusalém: → 422, Didaskalia 20,1 (1990) 5-32 / 33-41 = 421, Luso-Español 1989/91, 203-230 / 231-9.

2594 *Clements* Ronald E., The prophecies of Isaiah to Hezekiah concerning Sennacherib, 2 Kings 19,21-34 ‖ Isa. 37.22-35: → 75, FHERRMANN S., 1991, 63-78.

2595 **Hayes** John H. *Kuan* Jeffrey K., The final years of Samaria (730-720 B.C.): Biblica 72 (1991) 153-181; Eng. 181.

2596 *Ben Zvi* Eliud, The account of the reign of Manasseh in II Reg. 21,1-18 and the redactional history of the Book of Kings: ZAW 103 (1991) 355-374.

2596* *Halpern* B., Jerusalem and the lineages in the seventh century BCE; kinship and the rise of individual moral liability: → 436, Law 1986/91, JStOT supp 124, 11-91; bibliog 91-107.

2597 *Lohfink* Norbert, *a)* Die Kultreform Joschijas von Juda; 2 Kön 22-23 als religionsgeschichtliche Quelle [Urmanuskript > FCROSS F., 1987, 459-475]; – *b)* Zur neueren Diskussion über 2 Kön 22-23 [< BtETL 68 (1985) 24-48]: → 224*b*, SBAufs 12 (1991) 209-227 / 179-207.

2598 *Na'aman* N., The kingdom of Judah under Josia: TAJ 18 (1991) 3-71 [< ZAW 104,282].

2599 **Tagliacarne** Pierfelice, 'Keiner war wie er' [2 Kön 23,25, Josias]... 2 Kön 22s [kath. Diss. München 1987]: AOtt 31, 1989 → 5,2870: RBL (1991) 97 (G. H. *Jones*); JBL 110 (1991) 716-8 (M. H. *Floyd*); OTAbs 14 (1990) 111 (C. T. *Begg*); RivB 39 (1991) 241-6 (R. P. *Merendino*).

2600 *Washburn* David L., [2 Kgs 22,1-23,30; 2 Chr 34s] Perspective and purpose; understanding the Josiah story: TrinJ 12 (1991) 59-78.

2601 *Brettler* Marc, 2 Kings 24:13-14 as history [despoiling of Temple 597 (or 586 as STADE)]: CBQ 53 (1991) 541.

2602 *Galil* Gershon, *a)* The Babylonian calendar and the chronology of the last kings of Judah: Biblica 72 (1991) 367-378. – *b)* A new look at the chronology of the last kings of Judah: Zion 56 (1991) 5-19; Eng. V.

E5.1   *Chronicorum libri* – **The books of Chronicles.**

2603 *Abadie* P., Bulletin; Chroniques et Esdras/Néhémie: TEuph 4 (1991) 141-5 [133-140, *Römer* T., AT].

2604 **Ackroyd** Peter R., The Chronicler in his age: JStOT supp. 101. Sheffield 1991, JStOT. 397 p. £40. [TR 88,162]. 1-85075-254-0. – RETL 67 (1991) 422s (J. *Lust*). ExpTim 103 (1991s) 151 (R. *Mason*: essays since 1960, but hardly dated).

2605 **Cavedo** R., 1-2 Cronache Esdra e Neemia: LoB 1.9s. Brescia 1991, Queriniana. 108 p. Lit. 12.000. 88-399-1560-5. – RNRT 113 (1991) 907s (J.-L. *Ska*).

2606 **De Vries** Simon J., 1&2 Chronicles: FOTLit 11, 1989 → 5,2880; 6,3116: RBL (1991) 71 (R. J. *Coggins*: series has become more ponderous since Roland MURPHY started it off in 1980); CritRR 4 (1991) 128-130 (R. S. *Duke*).

2607 **Duke** Rodney S., The persuasive appeal of the Chronicler: JStOT supp 88, 1990 → 6,3119: RAndrUnS 29 (1991) 170s (J. W. *Wright*).

2608 *Fernández Marcos* Natalio, The Antiochian text in I-II Chronicles: → 426, Septuagint 7, 1989/91, 301-311.

2609 **Gard** Daniel L., Warfare in Chronicles: diss. DBlenkinsopp J. Notre Dame 1991. 370 p. 92-07289. – DissA 52 (1991s) 3319-A.

2610 **Graham** Matt P., Utilization of 1-2 Chr..., ᴰ1990 ➤ 6,3120: ᴿCritRR
4 (1991) 139s (J. W. *Wright*); ETL 67 (1991) 422 (J. *Lust*); Interpretation
45 (1991) 308 (J. C. *VanderKam*).

2611 **Japhet** Sara, The ideology of the Book of Chronicles and its place in
biblical thought [< diss. Hebrew Univ.]: BeitErfAJ 9, 1989 ➤ 5,2884 ...
6,3122: ᴿBL (1991) 79 (G. H. *Jones*: ACKROYD and WILLIAMSON not
noted); TsTNijm 31 (1991) 192 (N. *Tromp* notes the claim of p. 23 that
C's YHWH 450 t. as LXX has been replaced by redactor's Elohim; Adonai
is avoided because identical with tetragrammaton; 'En zijn twee formules
identiek in betekenis wanneer ze verwisselbaar zijn?'); VT 41 (1991) 379
(J. A. *Emerton*).

2612 **Kegler** Jürgen, *Matthias* Augustin, Synopse zum chronistischen Ge-
schichtswerk²ʳᵉᵛ [¹1984 ➤ 65,2539]: BeitErfAJ 1. Fra 1991, Lang.
241 p. 3-631-43384-0. – ᴿLA 41 (1991) 559s (E. *Cortese*).

2613 **Mason** Rex A., Preaching the tradition; homily and hermeneutics after
the Exile [corrects von RAD's 'Levitical sermons' of Chr] 1990 ➤ 6,3125:
ᴿBiblica 72 (1991) 563-6 (J. *Becker*); BL (1991) 85 (A. *Phillips*:
important); JTS 42 (1991) 634-6 (E. M. *Meyers*); OTAbs 14 (1991) 113
(C. T. *Begg*); VT 41 (1991) 496s (H. *Williamson*).

2614 **Ruffing** Andreas, Jahwekriegstexte der Chronikbücher; Untersuchungen
zu ihrer Form, Sprache und theologischen Bedeutung im Rahmen der
chronistischen Geschichtsdarstellung: kath. Diss. Bochum 1991, ᴰ*Berg* –
TR 87 (1991) 516: (> Stu KBW, 'Jahwekrieg als Weltmetapher') RTLv
23, p. 540.

2615 *Sugimoto* Tomotoshi, The Chronicler's technique in quoting Samuel-
Kings: AnJapB 16 (1990) 30-70 [< TLZ 116,826].

2616 **Willi** Thomas, Chronik: BK AT 24 Lfg. 1 (1,1-2,2 + teils 2,3-4,43).
Neuk 1991, Neuk-V. 80 p. DM 30 [ZAW 104, 293, H. C. *Schmitt*].

2617 **Kartveit** Magnar, Motive und Schichten der Landtheologie in 1 Chronik
1-9 [< Diss. Uppsala, ᴰ*Carlson* R.]: ConBib OT 28, 1989 ➤ 5,2895;
6,3130: ᴿJBL 110 (1991) 338-340 (G. N. *Knoppers*).

2618 **Oeming** M., Das wahre Israel; die 'genealogische Vorhalle' 1 Chr 1-9:
BW 128, ᴰ1990 ➤ 6,3131: ᴿBL (1991) 89 (H. G. M. *Williamson*: a major
contribution, defending Chronicler's own arrangement); Henoch 13 (1991)
374s (J. A. *Soggin*); ZAW 103 (1991) 305 (H.-C. *Schmitt*).

2619 *Edelman* Diana, The Manassite genealogy in 1 Chronicles 7:14-19; form
and source: CBQ 53 (1991) 179-201.

2620 *Na'aman* Nadav, [1 Chr 7,20-40] Sources and redaction in the
Chronicler's genealogies of Asher and Ephraim: JStOT 49 (1991) 99-111.

2621 **Snyman** Gert F., [1 Chr 15,25-16,43] Biblical hermeneutics and
reception theory; the authority of biblical texts and the Chronicler's
interpretation of the sacred story of the Ark: diss. ᴰ*Deist* F. Pretoria
1991. 324 p. – OTEssays 4 (1991) 447s; RTLv 23, p. 540.

2622 *Nel* H. W., And who is David? [Chronicles describes him in terms
tacitly drawn from Nehemiah]: JSemit 3 (1991) 144-155.

2623 *Wright* John W., The legacy of David in Chronicles; the narrative
function of 1 Chronicles 23-27: JBL 110 (1991) 229-242.

2624 *Williamson* H. G. M., The Temple in the books of Chronicles: ➤ 15,
ᶠBAMMEL E. 1991, 15-31.

2625 *Runnalls* Donna, [1 Chr 26,18] The *parwār*; a place of ritual separation?:
VT 41 (1991) 324-331.

2626 *Estes* Daniel J.,   Metaphorical sojourning in 1 Chronicles 29:15:   CBQ 53 (1991) 45-49.
2627 *Knoppers* Gary N., [2 Chr 17-20] Reform and regression; the Chronicler's presentation of Jehoshaphat: Biblica 72 (1991) 500-524; franç. 524.
2628 **Strübind** Kim, Tradition als Interpretation; die Josaphat-Rezeption in den Chronikbüchern als Beitrag zur Theologie des Chronisten [Diss. Kirchliche Hochschule Berlin 1991, ᴰ*Welten* ➤ 6,3144; TR 87 (1991) 515]: BZAW 201. B/NY 1991, de Gruyter. xiii-220 p. DM 98. 3-1101-2791-1 [BL 92,93, H. G. M. *Williamson*].
2629 *Frevel* Christian, [2 Chr 33,7; 1 Chr 10,10] Die Elimination der Göttin aus dem Weltbild des Chronisten: ZAW 103 (1991) 263-271.
2630 *Schniedewind* William M., [2 Chr 33,11-13] The source citations of Manasseh; King Manasseh in history and homily: VT 41 (1991) 450-461 : mirror of the exile and restoration of all Israel, as R. *Mosis*, H. *Williamson*.

E5.4   *Esdrae libri* [etiam 3-5] – **Ezra, Nehemiah**.

2631 **Becker** Joachim, Ezra-Nehemiah: NEchter 25, 1990 ➤ 6,3147: ᴿBL (1991) 52 (H. G. M. *Williamson*); OTAbs 14 (1991) 113 (C. T. *Begg*); TAth 62 (1991) 907-910 (P. *Simotas* Ⓖ).
2632 **Blenkinsopp** Joseph, Ezra-Nehemiah 1988 ➤ 4,3032; 6,3148:   ᴿCarthaginensia 7 (1991) 257 (R. *Sanz Valdivieso*); HeythJ 32 (1991) 391s (B. P. *Robinson*: spirited defense of Chronicler).
2632* a) *Daniels* Dwight R., The composition of the Ezra-Nehemiah narrative; – b) *Talmon* Shemaryahu, Esra-Nehemia, Historiographie oder Theologie?: ➤ 87, ᶠKOCH K., Ernten 1991, 311-328 / 329-356.
2633 *Dion* Paul E., The civic-and-temple community of Persian period Judaea; neglected insights from Eastern Europe: JNES 50 (1991) 281-7.
2634 **Eskenazi** Tamara C., In an age of prose ... EzN 1988 ➤ 4,3036... 6,3150: ᴿCBQ 53 (1991) 97s (Alice L. *Laffey*: dissertation but readable).
2635 a) *Grabbe* Lester L., Reconstructing history from the book of Ezra; – b) *Smith* Daniel L., The politics of Ezra; sociological indicators of postexilic Judaean society; – c) *Hoglund* Kenneth, The Achaemenid context; – d) *Blenkinsopp* Joseph, Temple and society in Achaemenid Judah; – e) *Halligan* John M., Nehemiah 5; by way of a response to Hoglund and Smith: ➤ 427, 2d Temple I (1991) 98-106 / 73-97 / 54-72 / 33-53 / 146-153.
2636 **Hausmann** Jutta, Israels Rest: BW 124,1987 ➤ 3,2869 ... 6,3153: ᴿTR 87 (1991) 277-9 (W. *Werner*).
2637 a) *Japhet* Sarah, 'History' and 'literature' in the Persian period; the restoration of the Temple; – b) *Artzi* Pinhas, Aššur-uballit and the Suṭians; – c) *Weinfeld* Moshe, Semiramis; her name and her origin: ➤ 150, ᶠTADMOR H., Ah Assyria 1991, 174-188 / 254-7 / 99-103.
2638 a) *Japhet* Sara, The relationship between Chronicles and Ezra-Nehemiah; – b) *Pohlmann* K.-F., Zur Frage von Korrespondenzen und Divergenzen zwischen Chronikbüchern und dem Esra-Nehemia-Buch: ➤ 429, IOSOT 1989/91, 298-313 / 314-330.
2639 *Kooij* Arie van der, Zur Frage des Anfangs des 1. Esrabuches [G = Vlg 3.]: ZAW 103 (1991) 239-252.
2640 **Smith** Daniel L., The religion of the landless; the social context of the Babylonian Exile 1989 ➤ 5,2923.g366; 6,g690: ᴿBibTB 21 (1991) 129s (R. *Gnuse*); Interpretation 45 (1991) 76 (W. *Brueggemann*); JBL 110 (1991) 336-8 (Carol *Meyers*); OTAbs 14 (1991) 105 (D. B. *Sharp*).

2641 **Sorgwe** Felisi, The canonical shape of Ezra-Nehemiah and its theological and hermeneutical implications: diss. Baylor 1991, *DCresson* B. 224 p. 92-14715. – DissA 52 (1991s) 4367-A.

2642 **Stone** Michael E., *Satran* David, Emerging Judaism; studies in the fourth and third centuries B.C.E. 1989 → 5,421: RGregorianum 72 (1991) 141s (G. L. *Prato*); TorJT 7 (1991) 107-9 (D. J. *Reimer*).

2643 **Throntveit** Mark A., Ezra-Nehemiah: Interpretation comm. Louisville 1991, Knox. xiii-129 p. $17.

2644 *Williamson* H. G. M., Ezra and Nehemiah in the light of the texts from Persepolis: BBRes 1 (1991) 41-61.

2644* a) *Zertal* A., The Pahwah of Samaria (northern Israel) during the Persian period; types of settlement, economy, history and new discoveries; – b) *Lemaire* A., Populations et territoires de Palestine à l'époque perse; – c) *Lipiński* E., Géographie linguistique de la Transeuphratène à l'époque achéménide; – d) *Calmeyer* P., Die sogenannte Fünfte Satrapie bei HERODOT: TEuph 3 (1989/90) 9-16 + 15 fig. / 31-73 + 1 map / 95-107 / 109-127; 5 fig.; pl. VIII-X; franç. 111.

2645 **Sack** Ronald H., Images of Nebuchadnezzar; the emergence of a legend. Selinsgrove/L 1991, Susquehanna Univ./Assoc. Univ. 143 p. 0-945636-35-0.

2646 *Bianchi* Francesco, Zorobabele re di Giuda: Henoch 13 (1991) 133-149; Eng. 150 [bypassed in biblical Ezra reworking of Esdras-a; Hag-Zc use royal names 'branch', 'servant', 'seal'].

2647 *Luria* B. Z., ❺ a) Judah in the days of return from exile [Ezra 2,1; Neh 7,6]: BethM 36,127 (1990s) 368-376; – b) ❺ What befell Zerubbabel [after the Temple ...]: BethM 36,126 (1990s) 185-9.

2647* *Japhet* Sara, The Temple in the Restoration period; reality and ideology: UnSemQ 44 (1991) 195-(?) 252 [< zit 91,656].

2648 *Margalith* Othniel, [Ezra 4,3] The political background of Zerubbabel's mission and the Samaritan schism: VT 41 (1991) 312-323 [321-3 *'am ha-areṣ*].

2649 *Kooij* Arie van der, On the ending of the book of 1 Esdras: → 426, Septuagint 7, 1989/90, 37-49.

2650 *Green* Alberto R. W., The date of Nehemiah; a reexamination: AndrUnS 28 (1990) 195-209.

2651 *Homerski* Józef, ❺ Nehemiah as a lay religious reformer: RoczTK 36,1 (1989) 17-28; Eng. 28.

2652 *Abadie* P., [Neh 2,20 ...] Sanballat: → 686, SDB XI,64 (1991) 1098-1104.

2653 *Bailey* Nicholas A., Nehemiah 3: 1-32; an intersection of the text and the topography; PEQ 122 (1990) 34-40; map.

2654 *Wahl* Otto, Grundelemente eines festlichen Wortgottesdienstes nach Neh 8,1-12: → 86*, FKNOCH O., Freude 1991, 47-59.

2655 a) *Kooij* Arie van der, Nehemiah 8:8 and the question of the 'Targum'-tradition; – b) *Schenker* Adrian, La relation d'Esdras-A^ au texte masorétique d'Esdras-Néhémie: → 17, FBARTHÉLEMY D., Tradition 1991, 79-90 / 218-248.

2656 *Rendsburg* Gary A., The northern origin of Nehemiah 9: Biblica 72 (1991) 348-366; franç. 366.

2657 *Chrostowski* Waldemar,   ℗ An examination of conscience by God's people as exemplified in Neh 9,6-37:   ColcT 60,4 (1990) 5-16; Eng. 16s.
2658 *a) VanderKam* James C., [Neh 12] Jewish high priests of the Persian period; is the list complete?; – *b) Anderson* Gary A., The praise of God as a cultic event: ➤ 288, Priesthood 1991, 67-91 / 15-33.

2659 **Bergren** T. A.,   Fifth Ezra 1990 ➤ 6,3167:   ᴿETL 67 (1991) 156s (J. *Lust*); JSS 36 (1991) 339-342 (T. H. *Lim*); NT 33 (1991) 285-7 (J. K. *Elliott*).
2660 *Mędala* Stanisław,   Le Quatrième Livre d'Esdras et les textes qoumrâniens: ➤ 420, Mogilany 1989-II, 197-205. ➤ 9788*b*.
2661 *O'Neill* J. C., The desolate house and the new kingdom of Jerusalem; Jewish oracles of Ezra in 2 Esdras 1-2: ➤ 15, ꟳBAMMEL E., Templum 1991, 226-236
2662 **Stone** M., Fourth Ezra: Hermeneia 1990 ➤ 6,3168:   ᴿExpTim 103 (1991s) 107s (C. S. *Rodd*: a major work of scholarship, not for beginners; excludes '5-6 Ezra', additions in ch. 1s and 15s); TS 52 (1991) 546-8 (*Brown*: splendid).

E5.5   **Libri Tobiae, Judith, Esther.**

2663 *Bow* Beverly, *Nickelsburg* George W. E.,   Patriarchy with a twist; men and women in Tobit: ➤ 329, Women like this 1991, 127-143.
2664 **Marinoni** Maria Carla,   La versione valdese del libro di Tobia: Biblioteca della ricerca traduttologica 20.   Fasano 1986, Schena.   108 p.; 2 pl. – ᴿRBgPg 69 (1991) 817-9 (R. *Schlösser*).
2665 *Stolper* Matthew W.,   Tobits in reverse; more Babylonians in Ecbatana: ArchMIran 23 (1990) 161-176, Achemenid legal texts, facsmile-transliteration-translation-comment: Darius II 416, Artaxerxes I 435.
2666 *Bertrand* Daniel A.,   'Un bâton de vieillesse', à propos de Tobit 5,23 et 10,4 (Vulgate) [remonte a GRÉGOIRE de Nazianze]: ➤ 22, ꟳBENOIT A., RHPR 71 (1991) 33-37.

2667 **Elder** Lynda B.,   Transformations in the Judith mythos; a feminist critical analysis: diss. Florida State, ᴰ*Priest* J.   1991.   530 p. 92-02297. – DissA 52 (1991s) 2955-A.
2668 **Labouérie** Guy [amiral au Golfe],   Judith espérance d'Israël; une femme contre le totalitarisme.   P 1991, Centurion.   148 p. – ᴿÉtudes 375 (1991) 569 (J. *Thomas*: 'Mais la paix à quel prix?'); RTLv 22 (1991) 532 (P.-M. *Bogaert*).
2669 **Ploeg** J. P. M. van der,   The [Syriac, 1734 Indian manuscript] Book of Judith: Moran 'Etho 3. Kottayam 1991, St. Ephrem Ecumenical Research Inst. 53 + 38 p. [BL 92,47, S. P. *Brock*].

2670 *Bal* Mieke, [Esther] Lots of writing: ➤ 311, Semeia 54 (1991) 77-102.
2671 **Börner-Klein** Dagmar,   Eine babylonische Auslegung der Ester-Geschichte; der Midrasch in Megilla 10b-17a: JudUmw 30.   Fra 1991, Lang. [x-] 292 p. $59.   3-631-43489-8 [NTAbs 36,289].

2672 **Fox** Michael V.,   Character and ideology in the Book of Esther: StPersOT. Columbia 1991, Univ. South Carolina. xv-317 p. $33. 0-87249-757-7.
2673 **Fox** Michael V.,   The redaction of the books of Esther; on reading composite texts: SBL Mg 40.   Atlanta 1991, Scholars.   x-195 p. $30; pa. $19 [TLZ 117, 742, A. *Meinhold*]. 1-55540-444-8 [-3-X].
2674 *Fox* Michael V.,   The alpha text of the Greek Esther: Text 15 (1990) 27-54.
2675 **Grossfeld** Bernard,   The two Targums of Esther: Aramaic Bible 18. E/ColMn 1991, Clark/Liturgical.   xiv-237 p.   0-567-09495-8 / 0-8146-5454-1 [NTAbs 36,293].
2676 *Haelewyck* Jean-Claude,   La version latine du livre d'Esther dans le 'Monacensis' 6239: RBén 101 (1991) 7-27.
2677 *McBride* William T.,   Esther passes; chiasm, lex talio, and money in the book of Esther: → 454*b*, Not in heaven 1989/91, 211-223. 254-260.
2678 *Milik* J.T.,   Les modèles araméens du livre d'Esther dans la Grotte 4 de Qumran: → 145, FSTARCKY J., RQum 15 (1991s) 321-399 + pl. I-VII.
2679 *Clines* David J.A.,   [Est 2,5] In quest of the historical Mordecai: VT 41 (1991) 129-136 [220-6, *Horbury* William, The name Mardochaeus in a Ptolemaic inscription].
2680 *Wiebe* John M.,   Esther 4:14: 'Will relief and deliverance arise for the Jews from another place?': CBQ 53 (1991) 409-415.

E5.8   *Machabaeorum libri,* 1-2 [-4] Maccabees.

2681 *Annandale-Potgieter* Joan,   The High Priests in I Maccabees and in the writings of JOSEPHUS: → 426, Septuagint 7, 1989/91, 393-429.
2682 **Bar-Kochva** Bezalel,   Judas Maccabaeus; the Jewish struggle against the Seleucids 1989 → 5,2960; 6,3197: RAmHR 96 (1991) 850s (S.J.D. *Cohen*); Tarbiz 60 (1990s) 443-450 (D.R. *Schwartz,* ✪; Eng. VI-VII).
2683 **Bickerman** Elias J.,   Gli Ebrei in età greca, TTroiani L.: TSt. Bo 1991, Mulino. 430 p. Lit. 46.000. 88-15-03240-1 [Antonianum 67,145, M. *Nobile*].
2684 TEBrodersen Kai,   APPIANS Abriss der Seleukidengeschichte (Syriake 45,232 - 70,369). ArbAG 1. Mü 1989, Univ. 256 p. DM 49 pa. – RClasR 41 (1991) 319s (A. *Erskine*).
2685 *a*) *Fischer* Thomas,   Hasmoneans and Seleucids; aspects of war and policy in the second and first centuries B.C.E.; – *b*) *Mélèze-Modrzejewski* Joseph,   L'image du Juif dans la pensée grecque vers 300 avant notre ère: [cf. → 6,3202]; → 6,540, Greece/Israel 1985/90, 3-19 / 105-118.
2686 *Goldstein* Jonathan A.,   *a*) How the authors of I and II Maccabees treated the 'messianic' promises; – *b*) Jewish acceptance and rejection of Hellenism (1981): → 206, Semites 1990, 221-250 / 1-32.
2687 *Grabbe* Lester L.,   Maccabean chronology; 167-164 or 168-165 BCE: JBL 110 (1991) 59-74.
2688 **Harrington** Daniel J.,   The Maccabean revolt 1988 → 4,3092 ... 6,3203: RTorJT 7 (1991) 116s (S. *Mason*).
2689 **Kampen** John,   Hasideans... Pharisaism; 1-2 Mcb 1988 → 4,3093 ... 6,3206: RJSS 36 (1991) 161-4 (G.J. *Brooke*); RelStT 10,2 (1990) 117-9 (W. *Braun*).
2690 *Kasher* Aryeh,   The changes in manpower and ethnic composition of the Hasmonaean army (167-63 BCE): JQR 81 (1990s) 325-352.
2691 *Mandell* Sara R.,   Did the Maccabees believe that they had a valid treaty with Rome?: CBQ 53 (1991) 202-220.

2692 **Martola** Nils,   Capture and liberation ... 1 Mcb 1984 ➤ 65,2594 ...
3,2923: ᴿCBQ 53 (1991) 294s (N. *McEleney*).
2693 *Moda* Aldo, Libri dei Maccabei: BbbOr 33 (1991) 15-30.
2694 *Piejko* Francis, Antiochus III and Ptolemy son of Thraseas; the
inscripton of Hefzibah [Bet-Šean] reconsidered [found 1960; IsrEJ 16
(1966) 54-70, *Landau* Y.]: AntClas 60 (1991) 245-259; 2 phot.
2695 *Rappaport* Uriel, ❽ The Hasmonean state and Hellenism: Tarbiz 60
(1990s) 477-503; Eng. I.
2696 *Sandelin* K.-G., Dragning till hednisk kult bland [attraction to pagan cult
among] Judar under hellenistisk tid och tidlig kejsartid: NorJud 10 (1989)
27-38 [< JStJud 22,315].
2697 **Saulnier** Christiane, A revolta dos Macabeus 1987 ➤ 6,3208: ᴿPerspT
22 (1990) 245-7 (J. *Vitório*).
2698 *Schunck* Klaus-Dietrich, Makkabäer/-bücher: ➤ 690, TRE 21 (1991)
736-745.
2699 *Schwartz* Joshua, *Spanies* Joseph, On Mattathias and the desert of
Samaria: RB 98 (1991) 252-271; map p. 259; franç. p. 252.
2700 *Schwartz* Seth, Israel and the nations roundabout; 1 Maccabees and
the Hasmonean expansion: JJS 42 (1991) 16-38.
2701 **Sievers** Joseph, The Hasmoneans and their supporters [diss. Columbia
NY 1981] 1990 ➤ 6,3210: ᴿJStJud 22 (1991) 285s (A. S. van der *Woude*).

2702 *Delcor* Mathias, L'éloge des Romains d'après 1 Mac 8:   Henoch 13
(1991) 19-28; ital. 28.
2703 *a) Donner* Herbert, Der verlässliche Prophet; Betrachtungen zu 1 Makk
14,41ff und zu Ps 110; – *b) Fischer* Thomas, [2 Makk 3,4 - 4,2] Heliodor
im Tempel zu Jerusalem — ein 'hellenistischer' Aspekt der 'frommen
Legende': ➤ 75, ᶠHERRMANN S., Prophetie 1991, 89-98 / 122-133.
2704 *Geller* M. J., [2 Mcb 4,7] New information on Antiochus IV from
Babylonian astronomical diaries: BSO 54 (1991) 1-4.
2705 **Henten** J. W. van, [2/4 Mcb, Diss 1986 ➤ 2,2211*], *al.*, Die Entstehung
der jüdischen Martyrologie 1989 ➤ 5,a99; 6,533: ᴿNumen 38 (1991) 142
(M. *Niehoff*).
2706 *Jonge* Marinus de, Jesus' death for others and the death of the Maccabean martyrs [ᶠ*Klijn* A., 1988, 142-151]: ➤ 215, GesAufs 1991, 125-134.
2707 *Young* Robin D., [2 Mcb 6,7 - 7,42] The 'woman with the soul of
Abraham'; traditions about the mother of the Maccabean martyrs: ➤ 329,
Women like this 1991, 67-81.

2708 **Klauck** Hans-Josef, 4. Makkabäerbuch: JSHZ 3, 1989 ➤ 5,2979: ᴿTLZ
116 (1991) 656s (W. *Wiefel*).
2709 *Weber* Reinhard, Eusébeia und logismós; zum philosophischen Hintergrund von 4. Makkabäer: JStJud 22 (1991) 212-234.

> **VII. Libri didactici VT**

E6.1   *Poesis .1 metrica*, **Biblical versification.**

2710 **Alonso Schökel** Luis, A manual of Hebrew poetics: SubsBPont 11, 1988
➤ 4,3103 ... 6,3223: ᴿBTrans 42 (1991) 341s (W. D. *Reyburn*); HeythJ 32

(1991) 255 (J. *Mulrooney*); JQR 81 (1990s) 481 (P. J. *Raabe*); SvEx 56 (1991) 121-3 (L. O. *Eriksson*).

2711 **Alonso Schökel** Luis, Manuale di poetica ebraica 1989 ➤ 5,2982; 6,3224: ᴿCC 142 (1991,1) 519s (G. L. *Prato*).

2712 **Alter** R., The art of biblical poetry 1985 (Clark 1990) 1,2978 ... 6,3225: ᴿTLond 94 (1991) 144s (T. *Dennis*).

2713 **Berlin** Adele Biblical poetry through medieval Jewish eyes [diss. Uppsala, ᴰ*Kronholm* T., 1990]: StBibLit. Bloomington 1991, Indiana Univ. xix-205 p. $30. 91-554-2518-6.

2714 **Fisch** Ronald, Poetry with a purpose 1988 ➤ 4,3115 ... 6,3233: ᴿJQR 82 (1991s) 227-9 (B. O. *Long*); JTS 42 (1991) 620-2 (J. W. *Rogerson*: 'really distinguished in design and execution').

2715 **Grossberg** Daniel, Centripetal and centrifugal structures in biblical poetry [Ps 120-134; Ct; Lam]: SBL Mg 39, 1989 ➤ 5,2990; 6,3238: ᴿCBQ 53 (1991) 667-9 (A. R. *Ceresko*: sensitive and convincing, but too many typos and no index); ETL 67 (1991) 153 (W. A. M. *Beuken*).

Lattke Michael, Hymnus; Materialen zu einer Geschichte der antiken Hymnologie: NOrb 19, 1991 ➤ 8219.

2717 *Long* Burke O., The 'new' biblical poetics of ALTER [R. 1981] and STERNBERG [M. 1985]: JStOT 51 (1991) 71-84.

2718 **Meer** W. van der, *Moor* J. C. de, The structural analysis of biblical and Canaanite poetry: JStOT supp 74, 1988 ➤ 5,410; 6,3241: ᴿBO 48 (1991) 882s (W. S. *Prinsloo*); JSS 36 (1991) 195-9 (J. F. *Healey*).

2719 **Rousseau** François, La poétique fondamentale. 1989.

2720 *Trublet* Jacques, La poétique des Psaumes: LumièreV 40,202 (1991) 55-73.

2721 **Wagner** Ewald, Grundzüge der klassischen arabischen Dichtung 1987 ➤ 6,9495: ᴿWZKM 79 (1989) 276-9 (A. A. *Ambros*).

2722 **Zurro** Eduardo, Procedimientos iterativos en la poesía ugarítica y hebrea [diss. R 1985]: BOrPont 43, 1987 ➤ 3,2947 ... 6,3246: ᴿCBQ 53 (1991) 486-8 (M. P. *O'Connor* supplies an analytic summation which, though itself dense, he feels needed to appreciate the book's usefulness); OrAnt 28 (1989) 158 (J. A. *Soggin*); OTAbs 14 (1991) 353 (Mark R. *Smith*).

E6.2   Psalmi, textus.

2723 **Ammassari** A., Salterio di Pietro 1987 ➤ 3,2949 ... 6,3247: ᴿETL 67 (1991) 153s (J.-C. *Haelewyck*).

2724 *Dodwell* C. R., The final copy of the Utrecht Psalter and its relationship with the Utrecht and Eadwine Psalters (Paris B. N. Lat 8846), ca. 1170-1190: Scriptorium 44 (Bru 1990) 21-53; pl. 1-9.

2725 **Eggenberger** Christoph, Psalterium aureum Sancti Galli; mittelalterliche Psalterillustration im Kloster St. Gallen. Sigmaringen 1987, Thorbecke. 211 p.; 204 (color.) pl. DM 112. – ᴿSpeculum 66 (1991) 629-631 (L. *Nees*).

2726 *Gołębiewski* Marian, ➌ Les versions grecques et latines du Psautier: ColcT 60,4 (1990) 19-44; franç. 44.

2727 **Hiebert** Robert J. V., The 'Syrohexaplaric' Psalter [diss. Toronto, ᴰ*Pietersma* A.]: SBL SeptCog 27, 1989 ➤ 5,3005: ᴿCBQ 53 (1991) 669s (D. *Bundy*); CritRR 4 (1991) 144-6 (B. A. *Taylor*: good); ZAW 103 (1991) 156 (H.-C. *Schmitt*).

2728 *Pietersma* A., Articulation in the Greek Psalms; the evidence of Papyrus Bodmer xxiv: ➤ 17, ᶠBARTHÉLEMY D., Tradition 1991, 184-202.

2729 *Pulsiano* Phillip, Old English glossed psalters; editions versus manuscripts: Manuscripta 35 (1991) 75-95.

2729* The revised Psalms of the New American Bible. NY 1991, Catholic Book. 287 p. $5 [TS 53,602].

2730 *Rondeau* Marie-Joseph, Un témoin méconnu de la chaîne 'athanasio'-évagrienne sur les Psaumes, le Vindobonensis Theol. gr. 298: RHText 19 (1989) 351-367; pl. X-XI [< RHE 87,178*].

2730* *St. Jacques* Raymond C., The Middle English Glossed Prose Psalter and its French source: → 1651*, Medieval Translators 1989, 135-154.

2731 *Simons* Walter, Beguines and psalters [OLIVER J. 1988]: OnsGErf 65 (1991) 23-30.

2732 *a) Tournay* Raymond-Jacques, À propos du 'Psautier de Jérusalem'; – *b) Higman* Francis, 'Chantez au Seigneur' nouveau cantique; le Psautier de Genève au XVIᵉ siècle: LumièreV 40, 202 (1991) 41-53 / 25-39.

2733 **Wagenaar** Christofoor, Het boek der Psalmen naar de Septuagint: Schrift en Liturgie 12. Bonheiden 1988, Abdij Bethlehem. 447 p. ƒ 66,25. 90-71837-11-4. – ᴿBijdragen 52 (1991) 207 (M. *Parmentier*).

E6.3 Psalmi, introductio.

2734 *Burger* J., Wysheidskriteria vir die klassifikasie van psalms as wysheidspsalms: HervTS 47 (1991) 213-230 [< OTAbs 14,301].

2735 **Day** J., Psalms: OT Guides 1990 → 6,3257: ᴿVT 41 (1991) 489s (W. *Horbury*).

2736 **Gerstenberger** E., Psalms I: FOTLit 14, 1988 → 4,3117 ... 6,3258: ᴿHeythJ 32 (1991) 389s (R. *Althann*); Interpretation 45 (1991) 74s (D. C. *Hopkins*).

2737 *Gier* J. de, MARNIX' levenserk, De Psalmen Davids: TRef 34,1 (Woerden 1991) 54 ... [< ZIT 91,220].

2738 *Koenen* Klaus, *Maśkil* – 'Wechselgesang'; eine neue Deutung zu einem Begriff der Psalmenüberschriften: ZAW 103 (1991) 109-112.

2739 *Marín Heredia* F., Los cinco libros del Salterio: Carthaginensia 7 (1991) 3-17; Eng. iii.

2740 *Mays* James L., A question of identity; the threefold hermeneutic of psalmody: AsburyTJ 46,1 (1991) 87-94.

2741 *Monloubou* L., Psaumes: → 664, Catholicisme XII, 55 (1990) 176-192 (-6).

2742 **Neveu** Louis, Au pas des Psaumes; lecture organique à trois voix [1. 1988; 2. 1990; not a liturgical reading implied by rubric of → 6,3328], III: CahLLitR 7. Angers 1991, Univ. Cath. Ouest. 216 p. F 145. – ᴿCBQ 53 (1991) 479s (D. *Launderville*: a procrustean bed; claims to find in *each* psalm three composition-phases called 'voices': i. a base; ii. a homogeneous complement; iii. a marginal supplement; volume 1 of the 4 starts with 40 selected psalms).

2743 **Raabe** Paul R., Psalm structures; a study of psalms with refrains: JStOT supp. 104. Sheffield 1990, JStOT. 240 p. £25. [RB 99, 456, R. J. *Tournay*].

2744 *Ribera-Mariné*, 'El llibre de les lloances'; estudi redaccional del salteri: RCatalT 16 (1991) 1-19.

2745 **Seybold** Klaus, Die Psalmen, eine Einführung²ʳᵉᵛ [¹1986]: Urban-Tb 382. Stu 1991, Kohlhammer. 216 p.; 40 fig. 3-17-011122-1.

2746 **Seybold** Klaus, Introducing the Psalms [1986 → 2,2257], ᵀ*Dunphy* R. G., 1990 → 6,3261: ᴿBL (1991) 95 (J. H. *Eaton*: adds 'ten pages on Scots and English versions').

2747 **Simon** Uriel, Four approaches to the Book of Psalms; from Saadiah Gaon [; 2. Karaite; 3. Moses ibn Giqatilah;] to Abraham Ibn Ezra, T*Schramm* Lenn J.: SUNY series in Judaica; hermeneutics, mysticism, and religion. Albany 1990. xii-364 p. $73.50; pa. $25. 0-7914-0241-X; -2-8 [TDig 38,380].

2748 *Smith* Mark S., The Levitical compilation of the Psalter: ZAW 103 (1991) 258-261.

2749 **Trèves** M., The dates of the Psalms 1988 ➜ 4,3149; 5,3020: RNedTTs 45 (1991) 246-8 (B. *Becking*).

2750 *Waltke* Bruce K., Superscripts, postscripts, or both?: JBL 110 (1991) 583-596.

2751 *Walton* John H., Psalms, a cantata about the Davidic covenant: JEvTS 34 (1991) 21-32 [< ZIT 91, 415].

E6.4 Psalmi, commentarii.

2752 **Bellinger** W.H.J, Psalms; reading and studying the book of praises. Peabody MA 1990, Hendrickson. 160 p. $10. 0-943575-35-4. – RRExp 88 (1991) 455-9 (M. E. *Tate*, also on DAY J., SEYBOLD K. Eng.); SWJT 34,1 (1991s) 69s (D. G. *Kent*).

2753 **Bratcher** R. G., *Reyburn* W. D., A translator's handbook on the Book of Psalms. NY 1991, United Bible Societies. xi-1219 p. $20 pa. 0-8267-0118-3. – ROTAbs 14 (1991) 359 (C. T. *Begg*).

2754 **Bryn** Einar *al.*, Fortolkning til Salmenes bok II. Oslo 1987, Nye Luther F. / Lunde. – RTsTKi 60 (1989) 141s (Solfrid *Storøy*).

2755 **Curti** C., Eusebiana I., In Psalmos 1987 ➜ 5,249; 6,3265: RMélSR 48 (1991) 187s (M. *Spanneut*).

2756 E**Daur** Klaus-D., ARNOBII iunioris Commentarii in Psalmos: CChrSL 25, 1990 ➜ 6,3266; Fb 3550: RAugR 31 (1991) 488-490 (B. *Studer*); NRT 113 (1991) 595s (H. *Harvengt*); RFgIC 119 (1991) 378 (M. *Simonetti*).

2757 — Simonetti Manlio, [Due note su testi di AGOSTINO e] ARNOBIO il Giovane, Commentarii in Psalmos: RFgIC 119 (1991) [319-] 324-9.

2758 **Dorival** Gilles, Les chaînes exégétiques grecques sur les Psaumes; contribution à l'étude d'une forme littéraire [1. 1986 ➜ 3,2984], 2: Spicilegium Sacrum Lovaniense [43] 44. Lv 1989, Peeters. 327 p.; 383 p. 90-6831-059-3; -300-0.

2759 **Feuer** Avrohom C., Sepher Tehilim, Les psaumes I (1-30), T*Ittah Ta*mar: La Bible commentée. P 1990, Colbo. liv-368 p. – RRÉJ 150 (1991) 456s (G. *Nahon*); RTPhil 123 (1991) 454s (J. *Borel*).

2760 St. GREGORY, The xii-th cent. Psalter commentary in French for Laurette d'Alsace [Ps 1-50]: TDiss 29. L 1990, Modern Humanities Research Asn. xiii-388 p.; xiii-340 p. £56. – RMAev 60 (1991) 315s (W. *Rothwell*) [< RHE 87,44*].

2760* **Kinzig** W., In search of ASTERIUS... on Psalms D1990 ➜ 6,3269: RVigChr 45 (1991) 194-203 (K.-H. *Uthemann*); 388-398, Kinzig rejoinder.

2761 **Kraus** H. J., Psalms 1988s ➜ 5,3026; 6,3270: RCBQ 53 (1991) 474 (R. E. *Murphy*); Interpretation 45 (1991) 195 (J. L. *Mays*).

2761* **Nielsen** Eduard, 31 udvalgte salmer fra Det gamle Testamente 1990 ➜ 6,3271: Ferderksberg 1990, ANIS. 135 p. 87-7457-098-6. – RSvEx 56 (1991) 126-8 (L. O. *Eriksson*).

2762 **Prinzivalli** Emanuela, DIDIMO il cieco e l'interpretazione dei Salmi 1988 ➜ 4,3160: RBLitEc 92 (1991) 61s (H. *Crouzel*).

2762* **Tate** Marvin E., Psalms 51-100: Word Comm. 1990 ➤ 6,3264*b*: [R]Exp-Tim 103 (1991s) 108s (C.S. *Rodd*: 'competent'; notes that the Word Comm. is 'modelled' on BK, of which KRAUS's commentary now in English is indispensable).

2763 *VanGemeren* Willem A., Psalms: ➤ 1683, Expositor's Bible Commentary 5, 1991; p. 1-880.

2764 [TE]**Walsh** P.G., CASSIODORUS, Explanation of the Psalms, I (1-50): Ancient Christian Writers 51. NY/... 1991, Paulist/Gracewing. 618 p. £19. 0-8091-0441-5. – [R]ExpTim 103 (1991s) 24 (V. *Eaton*: seeing Christ everywhere).

2765 **Westermann** Claus, Salmi, generi ed esegesi [1984], [T]1990 ➤ 6,3263: [R]CC 142 (1991,4) 626 (G.L. *Prato*).

2766 **Westermann** C., The living Psalms 1989 ➤ 6,3280: [R]JRel 71 (1991) 256s (J. *Kaminsky*); PrPeo 5 (1991) 163s (R. *Duckworth*); Vidyajyoti 55 (1991) 208s (P.M. *Meagher*, also on H.-J. KRAUS, 1985).

2767 **Zenger** Erich, Ich will die Morgenröte wecken; [25] Psalmenauslegungen. FrB 1991, Herder. 268 p. DM 34. [NRT 114, 939, A. *Harvengt*].

E6.5 Psalmi, themata.

2768 *Alonso Schökel* Luis, El lenguaje psicológico de los Salmos: ➤ 421, Luso-Esp 1989/91, 257-266.

2769 *Beaucamp* Évode, Le salut dans les Psaumes; LumièreV 40,202 (1991) 93-105.

2770 **Broyles** Craig C., The conflict of faith and experience in the Psalms; a form-critical and theological study: JStOT Supp 52, [D]1989 ➤ 6,3286: [R]CBQ 53 (1991) 159s (P.D. *Miller*); EvQ 63 (1991) 259s (T.D. *Alexander*); Henoch 13 (1991) 371s (J.A. *Soggin*); JQR 82 (1991s) 191-3 (Ellen F. *Davis*); ScripB 21 (1991) 18s (T. *Collins*); VT 41 (1991) 373 (H.G.M. *Williamson*).

2771 **Brueggemann** Walter, Abiding astonishment; Psalms, modernity, and the making of history: Literary Currents in Biblical Interpretation. Louisville 1991, W-Knox. 94 p. 0-664-25134-X.

2772 *Brueggemann* Walter, Bounded by obedience and praise; the Psalms as canon: JStOT 50 (1991) 63-92.

2773 *Cahill* Michael, The Psalm citations in an early Irish (?) commentary on Mark; text type and provenance: RBén 101 (1991) 257-267.

2774 *Doignon* J., L'interprétation romaine de la formule in tituli inscriptione dans les Traités sur les Psaumes d'HILAIRE de Poitiers: ➤ 130, [F]SANDERS G., Aevum 1991, 121-5.

2774* *Dominic* A. Paul, Springs of justice in the Psalms: EAPast 28 (1991) 270-291.

2775 **Grantson** Emmanuel F.Y., Death in the individual psalms of lament; an exegetical study with implications for theology and mission: diss. Lutheran School of Theology. [Ch] 1991. 410 p. 91-29532. – DissA 52 (1991s) 1372s-A.

2776 *Hobbs* T. Raymond, *Jackson* B. Kenneth, The enemy in the Psalms: BibTB 21 (1991) 22-29.

2777 **Israel** Martin, A light on the path; an exploration of integrity through the Psalms. L 1990, Darton-LT. 150 p. £8. 0-232-51900-5. – [R]ExpTim 102 (1990s) 377 (A. *Curtis*: a very Christian approach); Month 252 (1991) 342s (Jennifer *Dines*).

2778 **Jauss** Hannelore,   Tor der Hoffnung;   Vergleichsformen und ihre Funktion in der Sprache der Psalmen [Diss. Tübingen 1987, ᴰ*Rüger* H.]: EurHS 23/412.   Fra 1991, Lang.   xxviii-330 p.   3-631-42892-8. – ᴿLA 41 (1991) 557s (E, *Cortese*).

2779 **Kraus** Hans-Joachim,   Teologia dei Salmi, ᵀᴱ*Gianotto* Claudio 1989 ➤ 5,3061:   ᴿAntonianum 65 (1990) 662s (M. *Nobile*); CC 142 (1991,2) 297s (G. L. *Prato*).

2779* *a) Langer* Gerhard,   Zum Problem des Umgangs mit Macht am Beispiel der Psalmen; – *b) Schreiner* Josef,   Gottes verfügen durch 'Geben' und 'Nehmen' in der Sicht der Psalmen: ➤ 59, ᶠFÜGLISTER N., 1991, 165-187 / 307-331

2780 *Lindon* Thomas,   Oríkì òrìsà; the Yoruba prayer of praise: JRelAf 20 (1990) 205-224.

2781 *Markschies* Christoph,   'Ich aber vertraue auf dich, Herr!' – Vertrauensäusserungen als Grundmotiv in den Klageliedern des Einzelnen: ZAW 103 (1991) 386-398.

2781* *Mathias* Dietmar,   Das 'Gottesvolk' in der Sicht der Geschichtssummarien des Psalters: ➤ 163, ᶠWAGNER S.,   Gottesvolk 1991, 193-208.

2782 *a) Mays* James L.,   'In a vision'; the portrayal of the Messiah in the Psalms; – *b) Klein* Ralph W.,   Christology and Incarnation; fulfillment and radical reinterpretation of the OT prophets; – *c) Kelly* Balmer H., Word of promise; the Incarnation in the OT: ➤ 448*, Ex Auditu 7 (1991) 1-8 / 9-17 / 19-27.

2782* *Noel* Virginia L.,   Reflexiones agustinianas sobre el amor en las Enarrationes in Psalmos, ᵀ*Oroz* J.:   ➤ 540, AugM 36 (1991) 185-190.

2783 **Paciorek** Piotr, ☻ Pismo Święte ... L'Écriture Sainte comme règle de foi et de moralité dans l'Église d'après les 'Enarrationes in Psalmos' de saint AUGUSTIN: diss. ᴰ*Drączkowski* F.   Lublin 1991. 236 p. – RTLv 23, p. 549.

2784 *Raabe* Paul R., [➤ 2743] Deliberate ambiguity [... pun] in the Psalter: JBL 110 (1991) 213-227.

2785 **Rasmussen** Tarald,   Inimici Ecclesiae; das ekklesiologische Feindbild in LUTHERS 'Dictata super psalterium' (1513-1515) im Horizont der theologischen Tradition: StMedRefTht 44.   Leiden 1989, Brill.   x-242 p. ƒ120 [TLZ 117, 200-3, J. *Rogge*].

2786 **Rendsburg** Gary A.,   Linguistic evidence for the northern origin of selected psalms 1990 ➤ 6,3306:   ᴿJSS 36 (1991) 334s (M. *Goulder*: claims to isolate 'N-Israel' from Judahite usage).

2787 **Sailhamer** John H.,   The translational techniques of the Greek Septuagint for the Hebrew verbs and participles in Psalms 3-41: Studies in Biblical Greek 2.   NY 1991, P. Lang. [XIV-] 225 p.   0-8204-1030-6.

2788 **Sidebottom** Dorothy M.,   Zion and the Psalms; a re-examination of the Zion tradition and its relation to the Psalms: diss. ᴰ*Curtis* A.   Manchester 1991. – RTLv 23, p. 540.

2789 **Sperling** Uwe,   'Das theophanische Jahwe-Überlegenheitslied'; Forschungsbericht und gattungskritische Untersuchung der sogenannten Zionlieder [Diss. FrB 1991, ᴰ*Deissler* A.   402 p. – TR 87 (1991) 517; RTLv 23, p. 540]: EurHS 23/426.   Fra 1991, Lang.   472 p. Fs 35 [TR 88,426].

2790 **Spieckermann** Hermann,   Heilsgegenwart; eine Theologie der Psalmen: FRL 148, ᴰ1989 ➤ 5,3072; 6,3308:   ᴿBiKi 46 (1991) 134s (F.J. *Stendebach*); TGL 81 (1991) 233-5 (J. *Gamberoni*); TLZ 116 (1991) 350-2 (H. *Seidel*); ZkT 113 (1991) 79s (R. *Oberforcher*: Neuansatz hinter wenig aussagekräftigem Titel).

2791 *a) Stummer* Friedrich, Die Psalmengattungen im Lichte der altorientalischen Hymnenliteratur [< Journal of the Society of Oriental Research (? JAOS) 8 (1924) 123-134]; – *b) Begrich* Joachim, Die Vertrauensäusserungen im israelitischen Klagelied des Einzelnen und in seinem babylonischen Gegenstück [< ZAW 46 (1928) 221-260 = GesSt 1964, 168-216]; – *c) Gerstenberger* Erhard S., Der bittende Mensch; Schlussbetrachtung [< WM 51, 1980, p. 161-9]: ➤ 321, WegF 633 (1991) 303-315 / 316-371 / 372-380.

2792 *Veissière* Michel, Guillaume BRIÇONNET [évêque de Meaux; Correspondance 1521-4] et les Psaumes: RSPT 75 (1991) 235-248; Eng. 249.

2793 *Vian* Giovanni M., Ancora sull'antologia esegetica ai Salmi del Laudano greco 42: AnStoEseg [6 (1989) 125-149] 8,2 (1990/1) 589-597.

2794 **Walker-Jones** Arthur W., Alternative cosmogonies in the Psalms: diss. ᴰ*Miller* P. Princeton 1991. 220 p. 91-27020. – DissA 52 (1991s) 1375-A; RTLv 23, p. 540.

E6.6 *Psalmi: oratio, liturgia*; **Psalms as prayer.**

2795 **Aejmelaeus** Anneli, The traditional prayer in the Psalms: BZAW 167, 1986 ➤ 2,2295 ... 4,3203: ᴿCBQ 53 (1991) 376s (W. L. *Humphreys*).

2796 **Arminjon** B., Sur la lyre à dix cordes 1990 ➤ 6,3215: ᴿÉtudes 375 (1991) 283s (F. *Evain*).

2797 **Asensio** Félix, La oración en los Salmos; la antítesis 'justo-impio': FacTNEsp 56. Burgos 1991, Aldecoa. 205 p. pt 1250 [TR 88,162]. 84-7009-236-0. – ᴿNRT 113 (1991) 910 (J.-L. *Ska*).

2798 *a) Berrouard* Marie-François, Saint AUGUSTIN et la prière chrétienne des Psaumes; – *b) Motte* Dominique, L'homme des psaumes [qui prie]; LumièreV 40, 202 (1991) 107-121 / 123-140.

2799 **Brueggemann** Walter, Israel's praise 1988 ➤ 4,3205 ... 6,3319: ᴿRRel 49 (1990) 941-3 (V. P. *Branick*).

2800 **Carrarini** S., Salmi d'oggi; condivisione e contemplazione diventano preghiera di un credente² [¹1985]: Solco 1. Verona 1991, Mazziana. 285 p. Lit. 14.000 [NRT 114, 459, A. *Toubeau*]. – ᴿSapienza 44 (1991) 344s (A. *Cavadi*).

2801 **Cimosa** Mario, Il vocabolario della preghiera nella traduzione greca (LXX) dei Salmi: EphLtg 105 (1991) 89-119.

2802 **Gilbert** Maurice, *a)* Les louanges du Seigneur; commentaire pastoral et spirituel des psaumes du dimanche et des fêtes. P/LvN 1991, AELF/ Edime. F 199. 542 p. 2-87217-22-7. – *b)* Ogni vivente dia lode al Signore; commento dei Salmi delle domeniche e delle feste, I. Avvento, Natale, 2-9 per annum ecc., ᵀ*Ronchitelli* Domenico: Bibbia e Preghiera 9. R 1991 Apost. Preghiera. I. 298 p.; II. 296 p.; III. 415 p. Lit. 24.000 ciascuno. 88-7357-000-0; -104-2; -111-5.

2803 **Goulder** Michael, The prayers of David (Psalms 51-72): Studies in the Psalter 2 / JStOT supp 102, 1990 ➤ 6,3332: ᴿBL (1991) 75 (J. C. L. *Gibson* favors the combating of invented 'Sitzen' im Leben). ETL 67 (1991) 155s (W. A. M. *Beuken*).

2804 **McPolin** James, Los Salmos como oraciones de los pobres: RLatAmT 23 (1991) 169-190.

2805 **Perrin** Xavier, Imprécations du Psautier et prière chrétienne aujourd'hui: RThom 91 (1991) 68-94 [122 verses from 22 Psalms out of 3527 verses in all, have been omitted from Breviary, including 136,3-9; 139,10-12; entire Ps 57; 82; 108: justifiably].

2806 **Quesson** Noël, The spirit of the Psalms; a guide for reading and praying fifty of the most beloved Psalms with Israel, with Jesus and with the present moment, ᵀᴱ*Curtin* Marie-France. NY 1990, Paulist. iii-260 p. $15. 0-8091-3199-4 [TDig 38,374: 3 successive readings for each Psalm].

2807 **Sanguinetti Montero** Alberto, Gratuidad y respuesta del hombre a Dios; estudio en las 'Enarrationes in Psalmos' de San AGUSTIN: diss. ᴰ*Marangoni* V. Montevideo 1983, Ist. Teológico Soler. xx-239 p.

2809 **Smith** Mark S., Psalms, the divine journey 1987 ➤ 3,2039 ... 6,3332: ᴿRelStT 10,2 (1990) 92s (A. H. *Konkel*).

2810 **Tagliabue** Fortunato, I salmi, poesia di sempre; con laudario. CasM 1987, Piemme. 254 p. – ᴿScripTPamp 23 (1991) 1048s (C. *Basevi*: piadosas licencias poéticas).

2811 **Tournay** Raymond J., Voir et entendre Dieu avec les Psaumes 1988 ➤ 4,3222 ... 6,3335: ᴿColcT 60,1 (1990) 163-7 (T. *Brzegowy*, ❷).

2812 **Tournay** Raymond J., Seeing and hearing God with the Psalms; the prophetic liturgy of the Second Temple in Jerusalem [1988 ➤ 4,3222], ᵀ*Crowley* J. Edward: JStOT supp 118. Sheffield 1991, Academic. £30; pa. £22.50. 1-85075-313-X.

2813 *Urbina* Pedro A., Los salmos de David en la 'Subida del Monte Carmelo': ScripTPamp 23 (1991) 939-959.

2814 **Vincent** Monique, S. AUGUSTIN maître de prière, d'apres les En. in Ps.: THist 84, 1990 ➤ 6,3338: ᴿRThom 91 (1991) 495s (X. *Perrin*); TPhil 66 (1991) 589s (H. J. *Sieben*).

2815 *Woolfenden* Graham, The Psalms in Jewish and early Christian worship: PrPeo 4 (1990) 309-314.

E6.7 *Psalmi: versiculi* – **Psalms by number and verse**

2816 *Botha* P. J., The junction of the two ways; the structure and theology of Psalm 1: OTEssays 4 (1991) 381-396 [< ZAW 104,436].

2817 *Sedgwick* Colin J., The message of the psalmists, 7. The two ways, Ps 1: ExpTim 102 (1990s) 274s.

2818 *Tagliacarne* Pierfelice, Grammatik und Poetik; Überlegungen zur Indetermination in Psalm I: ➤ 126, ᶠRICHTER W., Text 1991, 549-559.

2819 ᴱ**Schreiner** Josef, Beiträge... Ps 2&22: ForBi 60, 1988 ➤4,3226; 5,3098: ᴿBO 48 (1991) 896s (W. S. *Prinsloo*: a major contribution); ColcT 60,2 (1990) 182-6 (J. W. *Roslon*, ❷); ScripTPamp 23 (1991) 370s (K. *Limburg*).

2820 *Culley* Robert C., Psalm 3; content, comfort and coherence: ➤ 126, ᶠRICHTER W., Text 1991) 29-39.

2821 *Lohfink* Norbert, Ps 7,2-6 — vom Löwen gejagt: ➤ 86* ᶠKNOCH O., Freude 1991, 60-67.

2822 *Ogden* Graham S., Translating Psalm 10,11 [belongs with the following]: BTrans 42 (1991) 231-3.

2823 *Auffret* Pierre, 'Qui donnera depuis Sion le Salut d'Israël?' Étude structurelle des Psaumes 14 et 53: BZ 35 (1991) 217-230.

2823* *Sedgwick* Colin J., The message of the Psalmists 10. The man of integrity, Ps 15: ExpTim 103 (1991s) 147s.

2824 **Steingrimsson** Sigurdur Ö., Tor der Gerechtigkeit... Ps 15; 24,3-5; Jes 33,14-16: ÀOtt 22, 1984 ➤ 65,2724 ... 2,2321: ᴿJNES 50 (1991) 226-8 (D. *Pardee*: below the standard of the series).

2825 *Mindling* Joseph A., Hope for a felicitous afterlife in Psalms 16, 49 and 73: Laurentianum 32 (1991) 305-369.

2826 *Cohen* M., *'Aššûrênû 'attâ s^ebabûnî* (Q *s^ebābûnû*) (Psaume XVII 11A): VT 41 (1991) 137-144.

2827 *Tronina* Antoni, ❷ Theophanie im Gewitter, Ps 18,8-16: RoczTK 34,1 (1991 für 1987) 27-36; deutsch 37.

2827* *Knierim* Rolf P., On the theology of Psalm 19: ⇥ 87, ^FKOCH K., Ernten 1991, 439-458.

2828 *Heinz* Andreas, Der Psalm vom guten Hirten (Ps 23) in der erneuerten Messliturgie: TrierTZ 100 (1991) 289-306 [243-288; *al.*, 'Pastor-bonus'– Pastoral].

2828* *Steingrimsson* Sigurdur Ö., Der priesterliche Anteil; Bedeutung und Aussageabsicht in Psalm 23: ⇥ 126, ^FRICHTER W., Text 1991, 483-519.

2829 *Hohlfeld* Winfried, 'Die Erde ist des Herrn und die darauf wohnen'; Bibelarbeit zu Psalm 24,1-6: Diakonie (Stu 1991,6) 326-9 [< ZIT 92,53].

2830 *Lohfink* Norbert, [Ps 25] *a*) Covenant, Torah and pilgrimage of the nations to Mount Zion: Service Documentation Judéo-Chrétienne 24,2s (1991) 31-3 [< ZAW 104,281]; – *b*) Lexeme und Lexemgruppen in Ps 25; ein Beitrag zur Technik der Gattungsbestimmung und der Feststellung literarischer Abhängigkeiten: ⇥ 126, ^FRICHTER W., Text 1991, 271-295. – *c*) [Ps 25; Jer 31,31; Mi 4] Der neue Bund und die Völker: KIsr 6 (1991) 115-133. – *d*) Einige Beobachtungen zu Psalm 26: ⇥ 59, ^FFÜGLISTER N., Ein Gott 1991, 189-204.

2831 *Tronina* Antoni, ❷ Le milieu cananéen du Psaume 29: RoczTK 36,1 (1989) 29-41; franç. 42.

2832 **Kloos** Carola, [Ps 29; Ex 15] YHWH's combat with the sea 1986 ⇥ 2,2333 ... 6,3368: ^RCBQ 53 (1991) 472-4 (C. L. *Seow*).

2833 *Basevi* Claudio, El Salmo 29; algunas observaciones filológicas sobre el texto hebreo y griego: ScripTPamp 22 (1990) 13-47 [< OTAbs 14,303].

2834 **Eriksson** LarsOlov, 'Come, children, listen to me!' Psalm 34 in the Hebrew Bible and in early Christian writings: ConBib OT 32. Uppsala 1991, Almqvist & W. [vi–] 216 p. Sk 164. 91-22-01464-0.

2835 *Naor* Menahem, ❹ Ps 34, textual research: BethM 36,127 (1990s) 377-381.

2836 ^E**Prinzivalli** Emanuela, ORIGENE, Omelie sui Salmi XXXVI - XXXVII - XXXVIII: BtPatr 18. F 1991, Nardini. 510 p. 88-404-2020-7.

2837 *Prinzivalli* Emanuela, 'Vinea spiritalis intellegentiae'; l'interpretazione omiletica dei Salmi in ORIGENE; un'indagine a partire dalle omelie sui Salmi 36, 37, 38: AnStoEseg 7,2 (1989/90) 397-416.

2838 **Paulus** R., Paschasius RADBERTUS, Expositio in Psalmum XLIV: CCMed 94. Turnhout 1991, Brepols. xvii-126 p., 1 pl. Fb 1855 [CETEDOC Instr. Lex. 69, 39 p. + 3 microfiches, Fb 1325: < RHE 87,40*].

2839 *Baudoz* Jean-François, 'Elohim, de nos oreilles nous l'avons entendu ...'; étude des versets 2-9 du Psaume 44: NRT 113 (1991) 25-46.

2840 *Auffret* Pierre, L'ensemble des trois psaumes 46, 47 et 48; étude structurelle: ScEsp 43 (1991) 339-348 [41 (1989) 323-341 & 42 (1990) 61-75. 305-324, les trois à part]. N. B. P. Auffret a fait imprimer et circuler (25.V.93) une bibliographie de 101 numéros de ses Études structurelles avec une Table dans l'ordre de ces 101 psaumes à la fin.

2841 *Rosendal* Bent, 'Gott ist aufgestiegen'; zur Geschichte der Interpretation von Psalm 47: ScandJOT 5,1 (1991) 148-154.

2842 *Scharbert* Josef, Das historische Umfeld von Psalm 48: ⇥ 59, ^FFÜGLISTER N., 1991, 291-306.

2843 **Keefer** Sarah L., Psalm-poem and Psalter-glosses; the Latin and Old English Psalter-text background to 'Kentish psalm 50': AmerUnivSt 7/95. NY 1991, Lang. x-177 p. 0-8204-1479-4.

2843* *Hossfeld* Frank L., Ps. 50 und die Verkündigung des Gottesrechts:
  ↠ 59, ᶠFÜGLISTER N., Ein Gott 1991, 83-101.

2844 *Auffret* Pierre, 'Sacrifie à Dieu un sacrifice d'action de grâce'; étude
  structurelle du Psaume 50: ↠ 41*, ᶠCZAPKIEWICZ A., FolOr 28 (1991)
  135-155.

2845 *Monloubou* Louis, Les Psaumes poèmes de croyants; Ps 51: EsprVie 101
  (1991) 686s.

2846 *Schützeichel* Heribert, Ein Grundkurs des Glaubens; CALVINS Auslegung
  des 51. Psalms: Catholica 40 (1990) 203-217.

2846* *Sedgwick* Colin J., A man and his sin; Ps 51: ExpTim 103 (1991s)
  176-8.

2847 *Herrmann* Wolfram, Duo augmina emendantia [Sara, Ps 54,14... in
  Qumran Gn-Apokr; Drachen Ug.]: VT 41 (1991) 342s [344-7, ein Brief
  von MOWINCKEL].

2848 *Alonso-Schökel* Luis, [Ps 55; 58] Giustizia e violenza nella preghiera
  d'Israele: ↠ 535, Firmana 1 (1991s) 37-50.

2848* ᴱ**Deun** P. Van, MAXIMI Confessoris opuscula exegetica duo [In Ps 59;
  Expositio Orationis Dominicae]: CCSGr 23. Turnhout 1991, Brepols.
  clxxii-135 p. Fb 4300. – ᴿNRT 113 (1991) 596s (A. *Harvengt*).

2849 *Blackburn* Bill, Psalm 71, expository: RExp 88,3 (1991) 241-5.

2850 *Carrière* J.-M., Le Ps 72 est-il un psaume messianique?: Biblica 72
  (1991) 49-69; Eng. 69: as social idealism, yes.

2850* *Cortese* Enzo, Salmo 72: che Messia? per quali poveri?: LA 41 (1991)
  41-60; Eng. 489.

2851 *Feininger* Bernd, [ᴰ1991 ↠ 113,8], 'Denk ich an Gott, muss ich seufzen'
  Ps 77,4: BiKi 46 (1991) 152-8.

2852 **Dorner** Christoph, Summa et caput totius pietatis; das Hauptgebot in
  der Verkündigung des 81. Psalms: Diss. Graz 1991, ᴰ*Marböck* J. – TR 87
  (1991) 513; RTLv 23, p. 538.

2853 *Salters* R. B., Psalm 82,1 and the Septuagint: ZAW 103 (1991)
  225-239.

2854 *Sedgwick* Colin J., The message of the Psalmists, 9. The prayer of a
  happy man, Ps 84: ExpTim 102 (1990s) 371-3.

2855 *Rokay* Zoltan, Die Datierung des Psalms 85: ZkT 113 (1991) 52-61.

2855* *Stadelmann* Andreas, Psalm 87 (86) – theologischer Gehalt und gesellschaftliche Wirkung: ↠ 59, ᶠFÜGLISTER N., 1991, 333-356.

2856 *Füglister* Notker, Psalm lxxxviii; der Rätsel Lösung?: ↠ 429, IOSOT
  1989/91, 264-297.

2857 *Illman* Karl-Johan, Psalm 88 — a lamentation without answer: Scand-
  JOT 5,1 (1991) 112-120.

2857* *Zenger* Erich, Israel und Kirche im gemeinsamen Gottesbund; Beobachtungen zum theologischen Problem des 4. Psalmenbuchs [Ps 90-106]:
  ↠ 46*, ᶠEHRLICH E. 1991, 236-255.

2858 *Schlicht* Matthias, Überlieferung und Theologie von Luthers Vorlesung
  über Psalm 90: Diss. ᴰ*Lohse* B. Hamburg 1991s. – RTLv 23, p. 552.

2858* *Auffret* Pierre, Yahvé règne; étude structurelle du Psaume 93: ZAW
  103 (1991) 101-9.

2859 *Irsigler* Hubert, Thronbesteigung in Psalm 93? Der Textverlauf als
  Prozess syntaktischer und semantischer Interpretation: ↠ 126, ᶠRICHTER
  W., Text 1991, 155-190.

2859* *Mosis* Rudolf, 'Ströme erheben, Jahwe, ihr Tosen...' Betrachtungen zu
  Ps 93: ↠ 59, ᶠFÜGLISTER N. 1991, 223-255.

2860 *Tarazi* Paul N., An exegesis of Psalm 93: StVlad 35 (1991) 137-148.

2861 **Scoralick** Ruth, Trishagion ... Ps 99: SBS 138, 1989 ⮕ 5,3144; 6,3398: ᴿCBQ 53 (1991) 481s (J. *Limburg*); JBL 110 (1991) 519s (J. A. *Durlesser*); ZkT 113 (1991) 88s (R. *Frick-Pöder*).

2862 *Willis* T. M., 'So great is his steadfast love'; a rhetorical analysis of Psalm 103: Biblica 72 (1991) 525-537.

2863 *Dion* Paul E., ʏʜᴡʜ as storm-god and sun-god; the double legacy of Egypt and Canaan as reflected in Psalm 104: ZAW 103 (1991) 43-71.

2864 *Monloubou* Louis, Les psaumes, poèmes de croyants; Ps 107: EsprVie 101 (1991) 607s.

2865 *Booij* Th., Psalm CX, 'Rule in the midst of your foes': VT 41 (1991) 396-407.

2865* *Kilian* R., Relecture in Ps 110; ⮕ 148c, ᶠSᴛɪᴍᴘꜰʟᴇ J., Sendung 1991, 285-302.

2866 *Sterk* Jan P. ['neither a native English speaker nor a poet'], An attempt at translating a Psalm [110]: BTrans 42 (1991) 437-442.

2867 **Neri** U., Interpretaciones hebreas del Hallel de Pascua (Salmos 113-118) [ital],ᵀ. Bilbao 1989, D-Brouwer. 226 p. – ᴿCiuD 203 (1991) 237s (J. *Gutiérrez*).

2868 *Pinto León* Adolfo, Salmo 114; constricciones — tropos — convergencias: EfMex 9 (1991) 97-113.

2869 ᴱMilhau Marc, Hɪʟᴀɪʀᴇ, Ps 118: SChr 344.347, 1988 ⮕ 4,3309 ... 6,3413: ᴿLatomus 50 (1991) 190-2 (J. *Oroz Reta*); RTPhil 123 (1991) 338 (É. *Junod*).

2870 **Soll** Will, Psalm 119; matrix, form and setting [diss. Vanderbilt 1982, ᴰ*Harrelson* W.]: CBQ Mg 23. Wsh 1991, CBA. 192 p. 0-915170-22-1. – ᴿArTGran 54 (1991) 388 (A. *Segovia*); LA 41 (1991) 558s (E. *Cortese*).

2870* *Cody* Aelred, Psalm 120 (119), 7: ⮕ 59, ᶠFüɢʟɪsᴛᴇʀ N., Ein Gott 1991, 51-64.

2871 *Viviers* Hendrik, [Afrikaans]. A text immanent study on the coherence of the *ma'ᵃlôt*-psalms [120-134]: diss. ᴰ*Prinsloo* W. Pretoria 1991. – DissA 52 (1991s) 2183-A.

2872 *Estes* Daniel J., Like arrows in the hand of a warrior (Psalm CXXVII): VT 41 (1991) 304-311.

2872* *Keel* Othmar, Psalm 127, ein Lobpreis auf Den, der Schlaf und Kinder gibt: ⮕ 59, ᶠFüɢʟɪsᴛᴇʀ N., Ein Gott 1991, 155-163.

2873 **Hartberger** Brigit, 'An den Wassern von Babylonien', Ps 137 / Jer 51: BoBB 63, 1986 ⮕ 4,3319 ... 6,3421: ᴿBO 48 (1991) 632-4 (T. *Booij*).

2874 **Ribera-Mariné** Ramón, La tercera colección de salmos davídicos (Sl 138-145); redacción y tradición: diss. Pont. Ist. Biblico, ᴰ*Simian-Yofre* Horacio. R 1991. – AcPIB 9/8, 684 & 733; RTLv 23, p. 539.

2875 *Jeyaraj* Jesudason B., An exposition of Psalm 146; God's rule or Lord's rule: Arasaradi 4,1 (1991) 15-23.

2876 *Vanoni* Gottfried, Zur Bedeutung der althebräischen Konjunktion wᵉ – am Beispiel von Psalm 149,6: ⮕ 126, ᶠRɪᴄʜᴛᴇʀ W., Text 1991, 561-578.

E7.1 **Job**, *textus, commentarii.*

2877 **Clines** David J. A., Job 1-20: Word Comm. 17, 1989 ⮕ 5,3173; 6,3430: ᴿAndrUnS 29 (1991) 169s (G. *Christo*); AsbTJ 46,2 (1991) 93-95 (G. I. *Miller*); Biblica 72 (1991) 411-8 (J. E. *Hartley*); BibTB 21 (1991) 118s (J. B. *Burns*); BL (1991) 55s (J. C. *Gibson*: quite marvellous achievement, warts and all); BS 148 (1991) 370 (R. B. *Zuck*: indispensable despite disagreements); Interpretation 45 (1991) 196 (R. E. *Murphy*: 'an incredible

53-p. bibliography'); JTS 42 (1991) 166-8 (J. *Job:* one commentary on Job has appeared every 18 months since 1527; ROWLEY thought DHORME's best but maybe he surpassed it; Clines claimed FOHRER's but again his may surpass it); ScripB 21 (1991) 27s (T. *Dennis:* excellent); SWJT 34 (1991s) 69 (H. B. *Hunt:* best ever).

2878 **Good** Edwin M., In turns of tempest 1990 ➤ 6,3432: ᴿExpTim 103 (1991s) 111 (C. S. *Rodd* notes that of the 18 commentaries he here evaluates, this is the only one 'that stands on its own' not in a series; and is thus the only one not written to support existing convictions); TS 52 (1991) 541s (Dianne *Bergant*).

2879 ᵀᴱ**Goodman** L. E., SAADIAH Job 1988 ➤ 5,3178; 6, 3433: ᴿCritRR 4 (1991) 389-391 (M. D. *Yaffe*).

2880 **Gutiérrez** G., Von Gott sprechen... Ijob 1988 ➤ 5,3198: ᴿForumKT 6 (1990) 149s (Sabine *Düren*: subjektiv; zweifelhafte Theorien; Vergewaltigung des Schrifttextes).

2881 **Hagedorn** U. & D., J. CHRYSOSTOMUS, Komm. zu Hiob: PatrTSt 35, 1990 ➤ 6,3435*a*: ᴿArTGran 54 (1991) 394s (A. *Segovia*); TPhil 66 (1991) 248s (H. J. *Sieben*).

2882 **Hartley** John F., The Book of Job: NICOT 1988 ➤ 4,3327... 6,3436: ᴿAndrUnS 28 (1990) 263s (G. *Christo*); HeythJ 32 (1991) 390s (J. *Eaton* compares to COX D.).

2883 **Mangan** Céline, The Targum of Job (*al.* Prov. Qoh. infra]: Aramaic Bible 15. E/ColMn 1991, Clark / Liturgical. 98 p. [+ 65 p. + 60 p.] 0-567-09477-4.

2884 **Nakazawa** K., Yobuki, tr. comm. Tokyo 1991, Shinkyo Shuppanshu. 204 p. Y 2200 [BL 92,54].

2885 ᴱ**Sorlin** Henri, CHRYSOSTOME sur Job: SChr 346.348, 1988 ➤ 4,3337... 6,3439: ᴿScEsp 43 (1991) 125s (L. *Sabourin*).

2886 ᵀ**Luzzato** Amos, Il libro di Giobbe; introd. *Trevi* Mario: Univ. Economica, classici 2020. Mi 1991, Feltrinelli. 155 p. Lit. 8.000. 88-07-82020-X.

E7.2   *Job: themata,* **Topics**... *Versiculi,* **Verse-numbers.**

2887 **Atkinson** David, The message of Job; suffering and grace: The Bible Speaks Today. Leicester 1991, Inter-Varsity. 188 p. 0-85110-956-X / US 0-8308-1230-X.

2888 **Caesar** Lael O., Character in Job: diss. Wisconsin, ᴰ*Fox* M. Madison 1991. 369 p. 92-07548. – DissA 52 (1991s) 3951s-A.

2888* *Coggi* R., La prova morale dell'immortalità dell'anima nel commento di S. TOMMASO al libro di Giobbe: SacDoc 35 (1990) 612-9 [< ZIT 92,232].

2889 *Collins* Brendan, Wisdom in JUNG's Answer to Job [1953: only 1% of his 10,000 published pages, but it raised a storm]: BibTB 21 (1991) 97-101.

2890 *Cox* Claude, Vocabulary for wrongdoing and forgiveness in the Greek translations of Job: Text 15 (1990) 119-130.

2891 **Cox** Dermot, Man's anger and God's silence; the book of Job [... an interpretative key]. Slough 1990, St. Paul. 144 p. – ᴿMilltSt 27 (1991) 152-4 (S. *Goan*).

2892 **Dell** Katharine J., The book of Job as sceptical literature [diss. Oxford 1988 ➤ 5,3190; ᴰ*Barton* J.]: BZAW 197. B 1991, de Gruyter. x-259 p. DM 104. 3-1101-2554-4 [ZAW 104, 293, H.-C. *Schmitt*].

2893 *Dittrich* William F., [Job] An experience of developing relationship: BToday 29 (1991) 169-173.

2894 **García-Moreno** A., Sentido del dolor en Job [más generalmente: Juan de PINEDA 1558-1638 y su época]. Toledo 1990, S. Ildefonso. 190 p. – ᴿAngelicum 68 (1991) 583s (J. *García Trapiello*).

2895 **Girard** René, Hiob — ein Weg aus der Gewalt [La route antique 1985 → 3,3161]. Z 1990, Benziger, 214 p. DM 32. – ᴿTPhil 66 (1991) 242 (P. *Knauer*); TPQ 139 (1991) 318s (J. *Janda*).

2896 **Hagedorn** Ursula & Dieter, Nachlese zu den Fragmenten der jüngeren griechischen Übersetzer des Buches Hiob: NachGö 1991/10. Gö 1991, Vandenhoeck & R. 37 p.

2897 *Haiman-Weitzmann* Anita, Pierre LEROUX [1797-1871] and the Book of Job [which he translated, finding in it confirmation of his socialism]: → 4, ᶠABRAMSKY C. 1988, 369-377.

2898 *Hoffman* [page-headings Hoffmann] Yair, Ancient Near Eastern literary conventions and the restoration of the Book of Job: ZAW 103 (1991) 399-411.

2899 ᴱ**Jagersma** H., Job, studies over en rondom en bijbelboek 1989/90 → 6,538: ᴿTsTNijm 31 (1991) 96 (E. van *Wolde:* subjects without tit. pp.).

2900 *Kaiser* Otto, Ijob's Abrechnung mit den Freunden: BiKi 46 (1991) 159-164 [186-8, *Klehr* F.-J., Tagung Weingarten 2.-3. III. 1991; 190s, *Kurz* P.K., zu STIER F.].

2901 **Loades** A.L., KANT and Job's Comforters 1985 → 4,k228*: ᴿCritRR 3 (1990) 394-6 (R. *Meerbote*).

2901* **Maggioni** Bruno, Giobbe e Qohelet; la contestazione sapienziale nella Bibbia: Bibbia per tutti. Assisi 1989, Cittadella. 111 p.

2902 **Martini** Carlo M., Wer in der Prüfung bei mir bleibt; von Ijob zu Jesus [1990 → 6,3458], ᵀ*Gerberich* M. FrB 1991, Herder. 158 p. DM 24,80 [TLZ 117, 119].

2903 *a) Müller* Hans-Peter, Keilschriftliche Parallelen zum biblischen Hiobbuch; Möglichkeit und Grenze des Vergleichs [< Orientalia 47 (1978) 360-375]; – *b) Stamm* Johann J., Die Theodizee in Babylon und Israel [< JbEOL 9 (1944) 99-107]: → 321, WegF 633 (1991) 400-419 / 383-399.

2904 **Penchansky** David, The betrayal of God; ideological conflict in Job: Lit. Currents in Bibl. Interp. 1990 → 6,3463: Louisville 1990, Westminster / Knox. 124 p. $12. 0-664-25132-3. – ᴿBL (1991) 90 (J.C.L. *Gibson*); BS 148 (1991) 501 (R.B. *Zuck:* good questions, hasty answers); ÉTRel 66 (1991) 429s (D. *Lys*); ExpTim 102 (1990s) 345 (J. *Eaton*); GraceTJ 11 (1990) 234s (R.L. *Giese*); Paradigms 7,2 (1991s) 38 (T. *Linafelt*).

2905 **Perdue** Leo G., Wisdom in revolt; metaphorical theology in the Book of Job: JStOT supp 112/BLit 29. Sheffield 1991, Almond [US, Cornell Univ.]. 296 p. $52.50. 1-85075-283-4 [TDig 39,78].

2906 *Quillo* Ronald, Naked am I; psychological perspectives on the unity of the book of Job: PerspRelSt 18 (1991) 213-222.

2907 **Reiser** W., Hiob; ein Rebell bekommt Recht. Stu 1991, Quell. 208 p. DM 30. 3-7918-4422-2 [NTAbs 36, 305].

2908 **Ronen** Miriam, The Hebrew Apologia; Job in the light of Socrates. diss. NYU 1991, ᴰ*Levine* B. 238 p. 91-24760. – DissA 52 (1991s) 908-A.

2908* *San José Lera* Javier, Fray Diego de ZUÑIGA y fray Luis de León frente al Libro de Job: → 92*, ᶠLEÓN, CiuD 204 (1991) 967-983.

2909 *Strong* David, The promise of technology versus God's promise in Job: TTod 48 (1991s) 170-181.

2910 **Theobald** Gerd, Hiobs Prozess und Gottes Gericht; die poetische Theodizee des Welttheaters: Diss. Heidelberg 1991, ᴰ*Timm* H. 351 p. – TR 87 (1991) 519; RTLv 23, p. 573.

2911 *Tomasoni* Francesco, Giobbe modello di fede razionale in KANT (Questioni di confine, ᵀ*Desideri* F. 1990): HumBr 46 (1991) 267-9.

2912 **Unen** Chaim van, Job, dwarsligger of verbondsgenoot? Een nieuwe kijk op een oud boek 1987 ➤ 4,3375; 5,3216: ᴿBijdragen 52 (1991) 207s (Kathleen *Maenhaut*).

2913 *Vincent* Monique, El libro de Job en la predicación de san AGUSTÍN, ᵀ*Oroz* J.: ➤ 540, AugM 36 (1991) 355-360.

2914 *Wiener* Claudia, Beobachtungen zur Überlieferung von GREGORS 'Moralia in Job' im späten achten Jahrhundert in Würzburg und Freiburg: WüDiözBl 53 (1991) 5-14 [< ZIT 92,107].

2915 **Wilcox** John T., The bitterness of Job 1989 ➤ 5,3219 ... 6,3470: ᴿCrit-RR 4 (1991) 160s (J. G. *Janzen:* among the best).

2916 *a)* *Wittenberg* G. H., Job the farmer; the Judean *'am ha-areṣ* and the wisdom movement [did not originate at the court]; – *b)* *Scheffler* E., JUNG's Answer to Job; an appraisal: OTEssays 4 (1991) 151-170/327-341 [< ZAW 104, 435].

2917 **Zuckerman** Bruce, Job the silent; a study in historical counterpoint. NY 1991, Oxford-UP. 294 p. £26 [TR 88,162]. 0-19-505896-8. – ᴿExpTim 103 (1991s) 182 (R. *Coggins:* 'Job as parody' — an elusive figure of speech).

———

2918 *Rensburg* J. F. J. van, Wise men saying things by asking questions; the function of the interrogative in Job 3 to 14: OTEssays 4 (1991) 227-247 [< ZAW 104,436].

2919 **Cotter** David W., A study of Job 4-5 in the light of contemporary literary theory [diss. Pont. Univ. Gregoriana, ᴰ*Cox* D., Rome 1989]: SBL diss. 124. Atlanta 1990, Scholars. xi-259 p. $45; sb./pa. $30.

2920 *Burns* John B., The šwṭ lšwn [lash of the tongue] in Job 5,21a as metaphor and irony: BZ 35 (1991) 93-96.

2921 *Swanepoel* M. G., Job 12 – an (other) anticipation of the Voice from the Whirlwind?: OTEssays 4 (1991) 192-205 [< ZAW 104,435].

2922 *Burns* John B., The mythological background to Job 18,5-6 [turns attention from SARNA's 1963 Ugarit back to Mesopotamia]: BbbOr 33 (1991) 129-140.

2923 *Ebach* Jürgen, Die 'Schrift' in Hiob 19,23: ➤ 75, ᶠHERRMANN S., Prophetie 1991, 99-121.

2924 *Althann* R., [Job 19,25-27; 29,18] Job and the idea of the beatific after-life: OTEssays 4 (1991) 316-326 [< ZAW 104,436].

2925 *Cox* Claude, Job's concluding soliloquy, chh. 29-31: ➤ 426, Septuagint 7, 1989/91, 325-339.

2926 **Mende** Theresia, Durch Leiden zur Vollendung, die Elihureden im Buch Ijob [32-37: Diss. Trier 1989, ᴰ*Haag* E.]: TrierTSt 49. Trier 1990, Paulinus. ix-469 p. DM 115 [TR 87,523].

2927 **Wahl** Harald, Der gerechte Schöpfer, eine Auslegung der Elihureden, Hiob 32-37: Diss. ᴰ*Kaiser* O. Marburg 1991s. – RTLv 23, p. 540.

2928 *Calati* Benedetto, Die Juden im Denken GREGORS des Grossen; Bemerkungen zu Moralia in Job 35,26, [ML 76,763], ᵀ*Cunz* Martin: ➤ 78, ᶠHRUBY K., Judaica 47,1 (1991) 31-37.

2929 *Schneider* Thomas, Hiob 38 und die demotische Weisheit (Papyrus Insinger 24): TZBas 47 (1991) 108-124.

2930 *Miller* James E., Structure and meaning of the animal discourse in the theophany of Job (38,39-39,30): ZAW 103 (1991) 418-421.

2931 a) *Nel* P.J., [Job 40s] Cosmos and chaos; a reappraisal of the divine discourses in the book of Job; – b) *Oosthuizen* M.J., – Divine insecurity and Joban heroism; a reading of the narrative framework of Job: OTEssays 4 (1991) 206-226/295-315 [< ZAW 104, 436].

2931* *Gradl* Felix, Ijobs Begegnung mit Gott; Anmerkungen zu Ijob 40,6-8.9-14: ➤ 59, ᶠFÜGLISTER N., Ein Gott, 65-82.

2932 *O'Connor* Daniel J., The cunning hand; repetitions in Job 42:7,8: IrTQ 57 (1991) 14-25.

2933 *Porter* Stanley E., The message of the Book of Job; Job 42:7b as key to interpretation?: EvQ 63 (1991) 291-304.

E7.3 *Canticum Canticorum*, Song of Songs, Das Hohelied, *textus, comm.*

2934 **Alonso Schökel** L., Il Cantico dei Cantici; la dignità dell'amore, ᶠ*Costacurta* Bruna 1990 ➤ 6,3493: ᴿNRT 113 (1991) 134 (A. *Toubeau*); Protestantesimo 46 (1991) 213 (J.A. *Soggin*); RivB 39 (1991) 89 (A. *Bonora:* splendido, malgrado qualche licenza poetica nella traduzione).

2935 **Alonso Schökel** Luis, Steh auf, meine Freundin, meine Schöne, und komm; Gedanken zum Hohenlied [1990 ➤ 6,3492]. Mü 1991, Neue Stadt. 134 p. [AcPIB 9/8, 652].

2937 **Crociani** Lamberto, APPONII, In Canticum Canticorum explanationes libri VI; tradizione del testo, fonti, liturgia, teologia: diss. S. Anselmo, n. 151, ᴰ*Chupungco* A. R 1990, Pont. Ateneo S. Anselmo. iv-161 p. (extr.).

2938 **Deckers-Dys** M., *a)* Hooglied: Belichting. Boxtel/Brugge 1989, KBS/Tabor, 160 p. Fb 920. – *b)* [➤ 2958] semiotische Analyse ᴰ1991, Utrecht. ᴿCollatVL 21 (1991) 440-2 (F. *Lefevre*).

Diebner B., *Kasser* R., Hamburg Pap. (copt.) Ct Lam Eces 1989 ➤ 1565.

2939 **Dönzl** Franz, Braut und Bräutigam; die Auslegung des Canticum durch GREGOR von Nyssa: Diss. ᴰ*Brox* N. Regensburg 1991. 543 p. – RTLv 23, p. 548.

2940 ᵀᴱ**Falchini** Cecilia, GUGLIELMO di S. Thierry, Commento al Cantico dei Cantici: Padri Occidentali Medievali. Magnano VC 1991, Qiqajon. 336 p. 88-85227-31-7.

2941 **Falk** Marcia, Song of Songs 1990 ➤ 6,3498*: ᴿHorizons 18 (1991) 314 (Alice L. *Laffey*).

2942 *Font* F., Fray Luis de LEÓN y el 'Cantar de los Cantares': ➤ 92, ᶠLuis de LEÓN, RAg 32 (1991) 63-78.

2943 **Girón-Blanc** Luis Fernando, Midrás, Cantar de los Cantares Rabbá: BtMidrásica SJerónimo 11. Estella 1991, VDivino. 355 p.

2944 **Hamburger** Jeffrey F., The Rothschild Canticles; art and mysticism in Flanders and the Rhineland circa 1300: Publ. Hist. Art. NHv 1990, Yale Univ. xii-336 p.; 225 fig. + 12 color. pl. $50. 0-300-04308-2 [TDig 39,167].

2945 **Heinevetter** Hans-J., 'Komm...' Das Hohelied als programmatische Komposition: BoBB 69, 1988 ➤ 5,3242*; 6,3500: ᴿJBL 110 (1991) 332-6 (Francis *Landy* rates above even impressive *Keel* O. and *Tournay* R.); RelStR 17 (1991) 355 (J.L. *Crenshaw*); TPhil 66 (1991) 573 (H. *Engel*).

2946 **Kamin** Sarah, *Saltman* Avrom, Secundum Salomonem 1989 ➤ 5,3243; 6,3501: ᴿAJS 16 (1991) 173-8 (Y. *Thompson*); BL (1991) 82 (P.W. *Coxon:* the Latin Christian author avowedly adapts Rashi, with drastic plastic surgery); RHE 86 (1991) 135s (P.-M. *Bogaert*).

2947 **Keel** Othmar, Das Hohelied: Z BK 18, 1986 ⟶ 2,2438 ... 6,3502: ᴿCBQ
53 (1991) 105-7 (Elizabeth F. *Huwiler*: good but not much in dialogue
with other commentators especially non-German); VT 41 (1991) 252 (J. A.
Emerton).

2948 *Kellner* Menachem, 'Introduction to the commentary on Song of Songs
composed by the sage Levi BEN GERSHOM' – an annotated translation:
⟶ 56, ᶠFOX M. 2 (1991) 187-205.

2948* *Kinlaw* Dennis F., Song of Songs: ⟶ 1683, Expositor's Bible commentary 5 (1991) 1199-1244.

2949 *Manns* Frédéric, Le Targum du Cantique des Cantiques; introduction et traduction du codex Vatican Urbinati I: LA 41 (1991) 223-301;
Eng. 491.

2949* *Marcos Sánchez* María Mercedes, *Sánchez Zamarreño* Antonio, Fray
Luis y su 'Exposición del Cantar de los Cantares'; por las rutas de su
vocación literaria: ⟶ 42*, ᶠLEÓN L. de, CiuD 204 (1991) 765-784.

2950 ᵀᴱ**Moreschini** Claudio, GREGORIO di Nissa, Omelie sul Cantico 1988
⟶ 5,3246; 6,3507: ᴿAugR 30 (1990) 216s (E. *Peretto*).

2950* **Müller** Susanne, 'Fervorem discamus amoris'; das Hohelied und seine
Auslegung bei GREGOR dem Grossen [Diss. FrB 1991, ᴰ*Frank* K. S. 287 p.
– TR 87 (1991) 517; RTLv 23, p. 550]: DissTh 46. St. Ottilien 1991, EOS.
viii-238 p. DM 32 [TR 88,253].

2951 **Murphy** Roland E., Song of Songs: Hermeneia comm. Mp 1990, Fortress. xxii-235 p. £20. 0-8006-6026-9. – ᴿExpTim 103 (1991s) 107 (C. S.
Rodd: more rounded exposition than POPE's massive AnchorB); Vidyajyoti 55 (1991) 605s (J. *Raja*).

2952 **Neusner** Jacob, Song of Songs Rabbah, an analytical translation:
Brown JudSt 197s. Atlanta 1989, Scholars. xii-250 p.; xvi-257 p.;
$57 + $55 [RelStR 18,241, H. *Fox* + 190, also 1989 Midrash 6th-7th c.
SSRabbah].

2953 *Riedlinger* H., Hohelied, das (Auslegung): ⟶ 681, LexMA 5 (1990) 79-81.

2954 **Robertson** Joel B., The Syriac version(s) of the Song of Songs: diss.
UCLA, ᴰ*Segert* S. 1991. 361 p. 92-07717. – DissA 52 (1991s) 3619-A.

2955 **Rozelaar** Marc, Het Hooglied. Kampen 1988, Kok. 148 p. ƒ 34,50. 90-
242-3055-1. – ᴿNedTTs 45 (1991) 64s (M. J. *Mulder*).

E7.4 **Canticum,** *themata, versiculi.*

2956 *Alonso Schökel* Luis, Come leggere il 'Cantico dei Cantici'? VConsacr
27 (1991) 260-266.

2957 **Brenner** Athalya, Song of Songs: OTGuides 1989 ⟶ 5,3253; 6,3514:
ᴿÉTRel 66 (1991) 111s (D. *Lys*).

2958 **Deckersdijs** M., Begeerte in bijbelse liefdespoëzie; een semiotische
analyse van het Hooglied: kath. diss. Utrecht, ᴰ*Tromp* N. Kampen 1991,
Kok. 315 p. 90-242-3160-4. – TsTNijm 31 (1991) 321; [Deckers-Dijs]
RTLv 23, p. 538.

2959 **Elliott** sr. M. Timothea, The literary unity of the Canticle: EurUnivS
23/371, ᴰ1989 ⟶ 5,3259; 6,3520: ᴿBiblica 72 (1991) 570-2 (F. *Landy*); BL
(1991) 72 (P. W. *Coxon*: skilful and meticulous defense of unity under-
estimates possible powers of skilful compilers); Helmantica 42, 129* (1991)
393s (S. *García-Jalón*); ZAW 103 (1991) 152 (H.-C. *Schmitt*).

2960 *Feuillet* André, La double insertion du Cantique des Cantiques dans la
vie de la communauté chrétienne et dans la tradition religieuse de l'Ancien
Testament: Divinitas 35 (1991) 3-18.

2961 *Jeffreys* Elizabeth, The Song of Songs and twelfth-century Byzantium: Prudentia 23 (1991) 36-54.

2962 **Mariaselvam** A., Song...Tamil: AnBib 118, ᴰ1988 ➤ 4,3425...6,3526: ᴿVT 41 (1991) 255s (Christine M. *Frost*).

2963 **Matter** Ann E., The voice of my beloved; the Song of Songs in western medieval Christianity 1990 ➤ 6,3528: ᴿHorizons 18 (1991) 320s (E. *Dreyer*); JTS 42 (1991) 376s (G. R. *Evans:* not bad, just ordinary); Manuscripta 35/1 (1991) 60 (B. A. *Asen*); RExp 88,2 (1991) 224 (E. G. *Hinson*); RHPR 71 (1991) 383s (W. *Fick*).

2963* *Niccacci* Alviero, Cantico dei Cantici e canti d'amore egiziani: LA 41 (1991) 61-85; Eng. 489.

2964 **Pelletier** Anne-Marie, Lectures du Ct...: AnBib 121, 1989 ➤ 5,3264; 6,3532: ᴿCBQ 53 (1991) 117s (R. E. *Murphy* is puzzled); CC 142 (1991,4) 317-9 (G. L. *Prato*).

2965 — *Sonnet* Jean-Pierre, 'Figures (anciennes et nouvelles) du lecteur'; du Cantique des Cantiques au Livre entier; à propos d'un ouvrage récent [PELLETIER A.-M., AnBib 121, 1988]: NRT 113 (1991) 75-86.

2966 *Pigeon* M., Les 'larmes' dans le Commentaire du Cantique des Cantiques de Robert de TOMBELAINE: ColcCist 51 (1989) 310-6.

2967 **Raurell** F., El Càntic... segles XII-XIII, 1990 ➤ 6,3535: ᴿEstFranc 92 (1991) 320-2 (J. *Llimona,* en catalán).

2968 *Saxer* Victor, Marie Madeleine dans le commentaire d'HIPPOLYTE sur le Cantique des Cantiques: RBén 101 (1991) 219-239.

———

2969 *Nunes Carreira* José, [Ct 2,7; 4,16; 6,11...] Cervos/as, pastoras e bailarinas; três motivos veterotestamentários de lírica galaico-portuguesa: ➤ 422, Didaskalia 20,1 (1989/90) 143-153.

2969* *Schweizer* Harald, Erkennen und lieben; zur Semantik und Pragmatik der Modalitäten am Beispiel von Hld 4: ➤ 126, ᶠRICHTER W., Text 1991, 423-444.

2970 *Loretz* Oswald, Cant 4,8 auf dem Hintergrund ugaritischer und assyrischer Beschreibungen des Libanons und Antilibanons: ➤ 87, ᶠKOCH K., Ernten 1991, 131-141.

2970* *Barbiero* Gianni, L'ultimo canto dell'amata (Ct 7,10*b* – 8,7); saggio di lettura 'metaforica': Salesianum 53 (1991) 631-648.

2971 *Wirt* Scherwood Eliot, Some new thoughts about the Song of Solomon: JEvTS 33 (1990) 433-6 [< ZIT 91,268].

E7.5   *Libri sapientiales* – **Wisdom literature.**

2971* *a*) *Assmann* Jan, Magische Weisheit; Wissensformen im ägyptischen Kosmotheismus; – *b*) *Wilcke* Claus, Göttliche und menschliche Weisheit im alten Orient: ➤ 388, Weisheit 1991, 241-257 / 259-270.

2972 *Ben-Shammai* Haggai, ⊕ New fragments from the Arabic original of Mivḥar ha-Peninim [IBN-GABIROL, ethical aphorisms]: Tarbiz 60 (1990s) 577-591; Eng. IV.

2973 ᵀᴱ**Berger** Klaus, Die Weisheitsschrift aus der Kairoer Geniza [➤ 3002] 1989 ➤ 6,3546*a*: ᴿJBL 110 (1991) 148-150 (J. J. *Collins*).

2974 *Berger* Klaus, Die Bedeutung der wiederentdeckten Weisheitsschrift aus der Kairoer Geniza für das Alte Testament: ZAW 103 (1991) 113-121 [= NTS ➤ 6,3546*b*].

2975 *Bernard-Weil* E., Le couple biblique *ḥokma-bina* (sagesse-intelligence) du point de vue de l'épistémologie des systèmes: FoiVie 90,3s (1991) 55-85.

2976 ᴱ**Berndt** Rainer, ANDREAE de S. Victore, Expositiones historicae in libros Salomonis: Opera 3, CCMed 53-B. Turnhout 1991, Brepols. xxviii-149 p. [RHE 86,295*] (54 p.; 5 microfiches).

2977 **Blenkinsopp** J., Wisdom and law in the OT 1983 ⇥ 64,3250... 2,2466: ᴿRelStT 9,1 (1989) 27s (K. I. *Parker*).

2978 **Brunner** Hellmut, Die Weisheitsbücher der Ägypter; Lehren für das Leben. Z 1991, Artemis. 527 p. DM 58. 3-7608-3683-6. – ᴿErbAuf 67 (1991) 488 (T. *Hogg*).

2979 **Cimosa** M., Temi di Sapienza biblica: PiccBT 8, 1989 ⇥ 6,3277 ['8.5.'?]: ᴿAsprenas 38 (1991) 107s (V. *Scippa*).

2980 **Clements** Ronald E., Wisdom in a changing world [Bailey Lectures 1989] 1990 ⇥ 6,3548: ᴿNewTR 4,1 (1991) 80s (Dianne *Bergant*).

2981 **Davidson** Robert, Wisdom and worship [Cadbury lectures 1989] 1990 ⇥ 6,3550: ᴿBL (1991) 107 (A. *Gelston*); OTAbs 14 (1991) 225 (C. T. *Begg*); RelStR 17 (1991) 353 [J. L. *Crenshaw:* a healthy skepticism (especially about life beyond Sheol in some psalms and Job 19,26) contrasting with self-confidence of Ps 32-34 and Job's friends]; TLond 94 (1991) 304s (D. F. *Murray*).

2982 **de Mello** Anthony, La preghiera della rana; saggezza popolare dell'oriente. Mi 1989, EF. 372 p. Lit. 16.000. – ᴿRasT 32 (1991) 108s (L. *Borriello*).

2983 *Dietrich* Manfried, Der Dialog zwischen Šūpē-amēli und seinem 'Vater'; die Tradition babylonischer Weisheitssprüche im Westen: UF 23 (1991) 33-68 (69-74, *Keydana* Götz, Die hethitische Version).

2984 **Eaton** John, The contemplative face of Old Testament wisdom [comparing China, Japan, India] 1990 ⇥ 6,3350*: ᴿRelStR 17 (1991) 353 (J. L. *Crenshaw*).

2985 ᴱ**Gilbert** Maurice, La sagesse de l'AT²ʳᵉᵛ 1990 ⇥ 6,3551: ᴿNRT 113 (1991) 906 (J.-L. *Ska*).

2986 **Grundmann** Walter † 1976, [Nachlass; ein kleiner Ausschnitt schon in ꟲ*Schürmann* H. 1978, 1-7]. Weisheit im Horizont des Reiches Gottes; Erwägungen zur Christusbotschaft und zum Christusverständnis im Lichte der Weisheit in Israel 1988 ⇥ 5,3248: ᴿTR 87 (1991) 281 (D. *Zeller:* trotz allem, nützlich).

2987 *Hill* Robert C., The perspective of wisdom [... beyond von RAD's 'slightly tinged with the pallor of (too narrow) theological reflexion']: ScripB 21 (1991) 16-20.

2988 *a) Jasnow* Richard, A demotic wisdom papyrus in the Ashmolean Museum (P. Ashm. 1984, 77 Verso); – *b) Hagedorn* Dieter, P. Ashm. 1984, 77 Rekto [seltsamerweise aus Theben]: Enchoria 18 (1991) 43-54; pl. 9-11 / 37-42.

2989 *a) Kaniarakath* G., Biblical proverbs and Malayalam proverbs; a comparative study; – *b) Kalluveettil* Paul, Biblical proverbs; genres and features; – *c) Manickam* Thomas, Proverbs in Indian religious culture: Jeevadhara 20 (1990) 95-104 / 120-132 / 105-119.

2990 *a) Klimkeit* Hans-Joachim, 'Gerechtigkeit' in der persischen Spruchweisheit; – *b) Klaes* Norbert, Indische Spruchweisheit und das Verständnis von *dharma*; – *c) Sundermeier* Theo, Weisheit in den afrikanischen Religionen: ⇥ 444, Spruchweisheit 1988/91, 69-84 / 85-101 / 117-134.

2991 **Kottsieper** Ingo, Die Sprache der Aḥiqarsprüche [Diss. Marburg 1989]: BZAW 194, 1990 ➤ 6,3563: ᴿArTGran 54 (1991) 463-6 (A. *Torres*); TLZ 116 (1991) 733s (K. *Beyer*).

2991* a) *Lang* Bernhard, Klugheit als Ethos und Weisheit als Beruf; zur Lebenslehre im AT; – b) *Theissen* Gerd, Weisheit als Mittel sozialer Abgrenzung und Öffnung; – c) *Alster* Bernd, Väterliche Weisheit in Mesopotamien: ➤ 388, ᴱ*Assmann* A., Weisheit 177-192 / 193-204 / 103-115.

2992 **Lips** Hermann von, Weisheitliche Traditionen im NT 1990 ➤ 6,3564: ᴿTR 87 (1991) 12-16 (K.-G. *Sandelin*).

2993 a) *Luck* Ulrich, Weisheitsüberlieferungen vom ANT; – b) *Brunner* Hellmut, Die menschliche Willensfreiheit und ihre Grenze in ägyptischen Lebenslehren; – c) *Stolz* Fritz, Von der Weisheit zur Spekulation: ➤ 444, Spruchweisheit 1988/91, 7-31 / 32-46 / 47-66.

2994 a) *Masenya* M.J., In the school of wisdom; an interpretation of some OT proverbs in a Northern Sotho context; – b) *Le Roux* J.H., The study of wisdom literature in south Africa: OTEssays 4 (1991) 171-191 / 342-361 [< ZAW 104,435].

2995 **Mieder** Wolfgang, International proverb scholarship, an annotated bibliography [1982], Supp. 1 (1800-1981). NY 1990, Garland. xvii-436 p. $54. – ᴿDLZ 112 (1991) 619s (H.M. *Militz*).

2996 *Monloubou* L., Sagesse: ➤ 664, Catholicisme XIII, 96 (1991) 436-9 (-442, de *Salomon*).

2997 **Murphy** Roland E., The tree of life 1990 ➤ 6,3567: ᴿSWJT 34,2 (1991s) 72 (H.B. *Hunt*).

2998 [Ney] *Pereira* Brasil, A escravidão nos Sapienciais; RevCuB 49s (1989) 46-60; español ᴱ*Bueno* Alexis: SelT 30 (1991) 98.

2999 **Preuss** Horst D., Einführung... Weisheitsliteratur 1987 ➤ 3,3244; 5,3297: ᴿCBQ 53 (1991) 304s (G. *Matties:* 'he rarely agrees with other scholars').

3000 **Römer** Thomas, La Sagesse dans l'AT. Aubonne 1991, Moulin. 30 p. ᴿEsprVie 101 (1991) 271 (L. *Monloubou:* louange); ÉTRel 66 (1991) 427s (D. *Lys*).

3002 **Rüger** Hans Peter † 2.X.1990, aet. 57, Die Weisheitsschrift aus der Kairoer Geniza; Text, Übersetzung und philologischer Kommentar: WUNT 53. Tü 1991, Mohr. ix-276 p.; portr. [BL 92,88, A.P. *Hayman:* transcription more accurate than in K. BERGER's book of identical title, ➤ 2973 above, which is otherwise more usable]. – ᴿArTGran 54 (1991) 385s (J. *Vilchez*).

3003 **Schneider** Theo, The sharpening of wisdom; Old Testament proverbs in translation: diss. ᴰ*Burden* J. Pretoria 1991. 199 p. – RTLv 23, p. 540.

3004 a) *Toorn* Karel Van der, The Ancient Near Eastern literary dialogue as a vehicle of critical reflection; – b) *Bottéro* Jean, La 'tenson' [dispute poétique du Moyen-Âge, p. 8] et la réflexion sur les choses en Mésopotamie; – c) *Vogelzang* Marianna E., Some questions about the Akkadian disputes; – d) *Vanstiphout* Herman L.J., Lore, learning and levity in the Sumerian disputations; a matter of form, or substance?: ➤ 622, Dispute poems 1989/91, 59-75 / 7-22 / 47-57 / 23-46.

3005 *Trublet* Jacques, Le corpus sapientiel et le Psautier; approche informatique du lexique: ➤ 429, IOSOT 1989/91, 248-263.

3006 ᴱ**Leutzsch** Ernst L. von, *Schneidewin* Friedrich W., (*Latte* Kurt, Supp.), Corpus paroemiographorum graecorum [...paroemia I. PLUTARCHUS; 6

items with original pagination]. Hildesheim 1991 = 1887, Olms-Weidmann. 3-487-00086-5.

E7.6 **Proverbiorum liber**, *themata, versiculi.*

3007 **Bonora** Antonio, Proverbi-Sapienza; sapere e felicità: LoB 1.14. Brescia
1990, Queriniana. 134 p. Lit. 15.000. – ᴿAsprenas 38 (1991) 391-3 (A.
Rolla).

3008 *Cook* Johann, Hellenistic influence in the Septuagint book of Proverbs:
→ 426, Septuagint 7, 1989/91, 341-353.

3009 **Farmer** Kathleen A., Who knows what is good? a commentary
on the books of Proverbs and Ecclesiastes: IntTheolComm. E/GR
1991, Handsel/Eerdmans. xii-120 p. $16. / 0-8028-0161-7 [TDig 39,59].
ᴿGraceTJ 12,1 (1991) 126s (R. D. *Spender*).

3010 ᵀᴱ**Géhin** Paul, ÉVAGRE, Scholies aux Proverbes: SChr 340, 1987 → 3,
3254... 6,3583: ᴿChH 59 (1990) 387s (J. W. *Trigg*); RevSR 65 (1991)
396 (Mariette *Canévet:* imprécisions de méthode).

3011 *Girardi* Mario, BASILIO di Cesarea esegeta dei Proverbi: VetChr 28
(1991) 25-60.

3012 **Hubbard** David A., Proverbs: Communicator's Comm. 15a, 1989 → 5,
3312; 0-8499-0421-8: ᴿTLZ 116 (1991) 422s (W. *Herrmann*).

3013 *Knobel* Peter S., The Targum of Proverbs [with **Mangan** C., of Job
→ 2883]: Aramaic Bible 15. ColMn 1991, Liturgical. 65 p. [$65].

3014 **Meinhold** Arndt, Die Sprüche, Kommentar [Hab-Diss. Leipzig 1991,
ᴰ*Wagner*. – TR 87 (1991) 512]: I 1-15, II 16-31: Z BK 16. Z 1991,
Theol.-V. VIII-262 p.; p. 263-542. je DM 34 [ZAW 104, 450, H.-C.
Schmitt].

3015 **Michaud** Robert, Proverbi e Giobbe: Parole di Vita. Mi 1990, Àncora.
155 p. Lit. 15.000. – ᴿBenedictina 38 (1991) 221-3 (P. M. *Pierini*).

3016 *Ross* Allen P., Proverbs: → 1683, Expositor's Bible Commentary 5 (1991)
881-1134.

3017 **Boström** Lennart, The God of the Sages ... Prov.: ConBib OT 29, 1990
→ 6,3578: ᴿBiblica 72 (1991) 272-6 (R. N. *Whybray*); BibTB 21 (1991)
166 (Betty Jane *Lillie*); JTS 42 (1991) 628-630 (J. L. *Crenshaw*); ST 45,1
(1991) 75s (ipse); TLZ 116 (1991) 418-421 (A. *Meinhold*); TZBas
47 (1991) 565s (E. *Kellenberger:* zurückhaltend mit 'Ordnung', nicht im
weisheitlichen Vokabular; weniger mit 'Transzendenz'); VT 41 (1991) 372
(R. H. *O'Connell*); ZAW 103 (1991) 149 (H. *Wahl*).

3018 **Krispenz-Pichler** Jutta, Spruchkompositionen im Buch Proverbia [ev.
Diss. München 1987]: EurHS 23/349, 1989 → 5,3315; 6,3585: ᴿBijdragen
52 (1991) 208s (P. C. *Beentjes*); RelStR 17 (1991) 254 (J. L. *Crenshaw*);
ZAW 103 (1991) 301 (M. *Witte*).

3019 **Steiert** Franz-Josef, Die Weisheit Israels — ein Fremdkörper im AT?
eine Untersuchung zum Buch der Sprüche auf dem Hintergrund der
ägyptischen Weisheitslehre 1988s → 5,3303]: FreibTSt 143, ᴰ1990 → 6,
3573: ᴿExpTim 102 (1990s) 302 (R. J. *Coggins*); NRT 113 (1991) 911s
(J.-L. *Ska*); TLZ 116 (1991) 657-660 (H. D. *Preuss*); ZAW 103 (1991) 458
(K.E.D. *Römheld*).

3020 *Vermeylen* Jacques, La femme étrangère dans le livre des Proverbes:
→ 140, ᶠSMYTH-FLORENTIN F., 1991, 207-220.

3021 **Whybray** R. N., Wealth and poverty in the Book of Proverbs: JStOT supp. 99, 1990 ➤ 6,3591: ᴿExpTim 102 (1990s) 277 (C. S. *Rodd*); JTS 42 (1991) 631s (J. *Job*); TLZ 116 (1991) 737 (G. *Sauer*).

3022 *Blenkinsopp* Joseph, The social context of the 'outsider woman' in Proverbs 1-9: Biblica 72 (1991) 457-473; franç. 473.

3023 **Burns** Camilla, The heroine with a thousand faces; woman wisdom in Proverbs 1-9: diss. Graduate Theological Union, ᴰ*Morgan* Donn F. Berkeley 1991. iv-199 p. 91-12328. – OIAc 1,13.

3024 **Pardee** Dennis, Ugaritic ... Prov 2: VT supp 39, 1988 ➤ 4,3490 ... 6,3595: ᴿCBQ 53 (1991) 115-7 (L. *Boadt*: a workbook, leaves us awaiting more).

3025 *O'Connell* Robert H., Proverbs VII 16-17; a case of fatal deception in a 'woman and the window' type-scene: VT 41 (1991) 235-241.

3026 **Rogers** Cleon L. ᴵᴵᴵ, An exegetical and theological study of Proverbs 8: diss. Dallas Theol. Sem. 1991, ᴰ*Glenn* D. 430 p. 92-14489. – DissA 52 (1991s) 4366-A.

3027 *a) Davis* William C., The claims of wisdom in Proverbs 8:1-36; – *b)* *Baugh* Steven M., Wisdom and folly: Kerux 3,1 (1988) 20-32 / 33-39.

3028 **Westermann** Claus, Forschungsgeschichte zur Weisheitsliteratur 1950-1990: ArbT 71. Stu 1991, Calwer. 51 p. DM 22 pa. 3-7668-0789-7 [BL 92, 95, R. N. *Whybray*: really only on Prov 10-22; 25-29; but also before 1950, since Eɪssfeʟᴅᴛ 1913]. – ᴿOTAbs 14 (1991) 352s (R. E. *Murphy*: 'God-talk' not as theology but in everyday experience).

3029 **Westermann** Claus, [Prov 10-22; 25-29] Würzeln der Weisheit; die ältesten Sprüche Israels und anderer Völker 1990 ➤ 6,3597: ᴿOTAbs 14 (1991) 116s (C. T. *Begg*).

3030 **McCreesh** Thomas P., Biblical sound and sense; poetic sound patterns in Proverbs 10-29 [diss. Catholic Univ.; Wsh 1981]: JStOT supp 128. Sheffield 1991, Academic. 164 p. 1-85075-326-1 [OIAc 2,23].

3031 *Hildebrandt* Ted, Proverbial strings; cohesion in Proverbs 10: GraceTJ 11 (1990) 171-185.

3032 **Cottini** Valentino, [Prov 12,28 ... 24,19] La vita futura nel libro dei Proverbi; contributo alla storia dell'esegesi: SBF Anal 20, 1984 ➤ 65,2930: ᴿHenoch 12 (1990) 385s (B. *Chiesa*).

3033 *Franzmann* Majella, The wheel in Proverbs XX 26 and Ode of Solomon XXIII 11-16: VT 41 (1991) 171-3.

3034 **Römheld** Diethard, Wege der Weisheit ... Prov 22 ...: BZAW 184, ᴰ1989 ➤ 6,3600*: ᴿBL (1991) 93 (J. H. *Eaton*); BLitEc 92 (1991) 147 (M. *Delcor*); BO 48 (1991) 459-465 (H. W. *Fischer-Elfert*); CBQ 53 (1991) 306 (R. E. *Murphy*); RHPR 71 (1991) 207 (J.-G. *Heintz*); ScripTpamp 23 (1991) 369s (K. *Limburg*); TLZ 116 (1991) 660-2 (Jutta *Körner*).

3035 *Bonora* Antonio, Quale ideale di società secondo Pr 22,1-16?: RivB 39 (1991) 145-156.

3036 **Goutsch** Darlene R., 'The words of the wise'; a canonical critical study of Proverbs 22:17 to 24: 22: diss. Golden Gate Baptist Theol. Sem., ᴰ*Cate* R. 250 p. 91-28063. – DissA 52 (1991s) 2955-A.

3037 **Dinzolele** Nzambi Philippe, Proverbes bibliques et proverbes kongo; étude comparative de Proverbia 25-29 et quelques proverbes kongo: kath. Diss. Tübingen 1991, ᴰ*Gross*. – TR 87 (1991) 522.

3038 **Snell** Daniel C., The most obscure verse in Proverbs; Proverbs XXVI 10: VT 41 (1991) 350-6: 'A great one makes a fool of everyone, but a drunkard is a fool (even) of passers-by'.

3039 **Liew Sow-Pheng,** The social and literary context of Proverbs 28-29 [... for instruction of kingship]: diss. Westminster Theol. Sem. 1991. 396 p. 91-25468. – DissA 52 (1991s) 1373s-A; OIAc 2,22.

3040 *Rüterswörden* Udo, Es gibt keinen Exegeten in einem gesetzlosen Land (Prov 29,18 LXX); Erwägungen zum Thema, Der Prophet und die Thora: ➤ 75, FHERRMANN S., Prophetie 1991, 326-347.

3041 *Luke* K., The ideal wife (Prv 31: 10-31): Jeevadhara 21 (1991) 118-132.

3042 *Fernández Tejero* Emilia, [Prov 31,10-15...] ¿'Esposa' o perfecta casada? Dos personajes femeninos en la exégesis de Fray Luis de LEÓN: ➤ 421, Luso-Esp 1989/91, 719-730.

E7.7   *Ecclesiastes –* **Qohelet,** *themata, versiculi.*

3043 *Amigo Espada* Lorenzo, Las glosas de Mosé ARRAGUEL de Guadalajara al Eclesiastés: ➤ 421, Luso-Esp 1989/91, 649-665.

3044 **De Gregorio** Domenico, Gli insegnamenti teologici di S. GREGORIO di Agrigento nel suo 'Commento all'Ecclesiaste' 1989 ➤ 6,3612: RCC 142 (1991,1) 100 (C. *Capizzi*).

3045 **Diego Sánchez** Manuel, El comentario al Eclesiastés de DÍDIMO Alejandrino; exégesis y espiritualidad [dis. DSimonetti M.]: StTh 9. R 1991, Teresianum/Univ. Lateran./Inst. Patr. Aug. 308 p. 88-85317-01-4. RArTGran 54 (1991) 395s (J. *Vilchez*: de Toura en Egipto en 1941); Teresianum 42 (1991) 653-5 (F. *Vega Santoveña*).

3046 **Habermann** Willi, Alles Seifenblasen; der Prediger Salomo schwäbisch. Stu 1989, Steinkopf. 60 p. DM 12,80. – RErbAuf 67 (1991) 147 (Elisabeth *Bitter*).

3047 *Healy* John F., The Targum of Qoheleth [with **Magnan** C., of Job ➤ 2883]: Aramaic Bible 15. ColMn 1991, Liturgical. 60 p. [$65].

3048 **Jarick** John, GREGORY Thaumaturgos' paraphrase of Ecclesiastes [diss. Melbourne]: SBL SeptCog 29, 1990 ➤ 6,3624: RBL (1991) 47 (R. B. *Salters*).

3049 *Jarick* John, AQUILA's Koheleth: Text 15 (1990) 131-9.

3050 TELeanza Sandro, GREGORIO di Nissa, Omelie sull'Ecclesiaste: TPatr 86, 1990 ➤ 6,3629a: RAsprenas 38 (1991) 252s (L. *Fatica*).

3051 *Wright* J. Stafford, Ecclesiastes: ➤ 1683, Expositor's Bible commentary 5 (1991) 1135-1197.

3052 **Zafrani** Haim, *Caquot* André, La version arabe de la Bible de SA'ADYA Gaon, L'Ecclésiaste 1989 ➤ 6,3647: RRÉJ 150 (1991) 444-8 (D. *Gimaret*).

3053 **Byargeon** Ricky W., The significance of the *eyn ṭôb* concept in Qoheleth's challenge of the wisdom tradition: diss. SWBaptist Theol. Sem. 1991. 214 p. 91-35748. – DissA 52 (1991s) 2588-A.

3054 *Delsman* W. C., Die Inkongruenz im Buch Qoheleth: ➤ 77, FHOFTIJZER J., 1991, 27-37.

3055 **Fox** Michael V., Qohelet and his contradictions: JStOT supp. 71, 1989 ➤ 5,1337; 6,3618: RCBQ 53 (1991) 284-6 (A. G. *Wright*); Henoch 13 (1991) 110-2 (P. *Sacchi*: fa riflettere, non chiude il problema).

3056 **Fredericks** Daniel C., Qoheleth's language; re-evaluating its nature and date 1988 ➤ 4,3520... 6,3619: RCBQ 53 (1991) 99s (J. A. *Gladson*); JAOS 111 (1991) 821-4 (J. R. *Davila*).

3057 **Harrison** C. Robert[J], Qoheleth in socio-historical perspective: diss. Duke, [D]*Crenshaw* J. Durham NC 1991. 412 p. 91-27512. – DissA 52 (1991s) 2170-A; RelStR 18,173.

3058 *Klopfenstein* Martin A., Kohelet und die Freude am Dasein: TZBas 47 (1991) 97-107.

3059 **Lange** Armin, Weisheit und Torheit bei Kohelet und in seiner Umwelt: EurHS 23/433. Fra 1991, Lang. vi-196 p. [TR 88,162].

3060 *Mateo Seco* Lucas F., *Ho eúkairos thánatos*; consideraciones en torno a la muerte en las Homilías al Eclesiastés de GREGORIO de Nisa: Scrip-TPamp 23 (1991) 921-937.

3061 **Michaud** R., Qohélet y el helenismo 1988 ➤ 5,3349: [R]EfMex 9 (1991) 396 (F. *Nieto*).

3062 **Michel** Diethelm, Untersuchungen zur Eigenart des Buches Qohelet: BZAW 183, 1989 ➤ 5,3350; 6,3633: [R]Bijdragen 52 (1991) 209 (P. C. *Beentjes*); BO 48 (1991) 897-9 (J. A. *Loader*: careless, not updated); CBQ 53 (1991) 679s (J. F. *Craghan* queries only reliance on 1-3,15 as a unit and fundamental); NedTTs 45 (1991) 142s (P. B. *Dirksen*); OLZ 86 (1991) 399-402 (O. *Loretz*); RechSR 79 (1991) 282s (J. *Briend*); RB 98 (1991) 301s (R. J. *Tournay*); RelStR 17 (1991) 355 (J. L. *Crenshaw*, valuable spinoff of his ErtFor 258); Syria 67 (1990) 757s (M. *Delcor*).

3063 *a) Michel* Diethelm, Kohelet und die Krise der Weisheit / Probleme der Koheletauslegung heute / Zur Philosophie Kohelets [7,1-10] / Gott bei Kohelet – *b) Lohfink* Norbert, 'Freu dich, junger Mann...' (Koh 11,9-12,8) / Das 'Prokilometron', Kohelet und Menippos von Gadara / Von Windhauch: BiKi 45 (1990) 2-6.6-11.21-25 .32-36 / Lohfink 12-18. 19.26-31.

3064 *Murphy* Roland E., *a)* On translating Ecclesiastes [text-transmission satisfactory, but New Jewish Version gives 'meaning uncertain' for 14 phrases]: CBQ 53 (1991) 571-9; – *b)* Qoheleth and theology?: BibTB 21 (1991) 30-33.

3065 **Schubert** Mathias, Schöpfungstheologie bei Kohelet [< Diss. Lp 1986]: BeitErfAJ 15, 1989 ➤ 5,3356; 6,3641: [R]BL (1991) 120 (R. B. *Salters*); RelStR 17 (1991) 355 (J. L. *Crenshaw*).

3066 **Whybray** R. N., Ecclesiastes: OTGuides, 1989 ➤ 5,3365: [R]CBQ 53 (1991) 464-6 (J. A. *Gladson*, also on his NCent comm, and with updating from *Fredericks* D.); EvQ 63 (1991) 343s (J. G. *McConville*: 3d cent.; clear and persuasive); ÉTRel 66 (1991) 112s (D. *Lys*).

3067 *Zuck* Roy B., God and man in Ecclesiastes: BS 148 (1991) 46-56.

3068 *Loretz* Oswald, *a)* Anfänge jüdischer Philosophie nach Qohelet 1.1-11 und 3,1-15; – *b)* 'Frau' und griechisch-jüdische Philosophie im Buch Qohelet (7.23-8.1 und 9.6-10): UF 23 (1991) 223-244 / 245-264.

3069 *Fischer* Alexander, Beobachtungen zur Komposition von Kohelet 1,1-3,15: ZAW 103 (1991) 72-86.

3070 *Min Young-Jin*, How do the rivers flow? (Ecclesiastes 1.7): BTrans 42 (1991) 226-231.

3071 *a) Verheij* Arian, Paradise retrieved; on Qohelet 2.4-6; – *b) Hayman* A. P., Qohelet and the book of creation; – *c) Fredericks* Daniel C., Life's storms and structural unity in Qoh 11.1-12.8: JStOT 50 (1991) 113-5 / 93-113 / 52 (1991) 95-114.

3071* *Whybray* R. N., 'A time to be born and a time to die'; some observations on Ecclesiastes 3:2-8: ➤ 102c, [F]Prince MIKASA 1991, 469-483.

3072 *Bosson* Nathalie, [prière sur Qoh 5-7; Sir 8-11] Un palimpseste du musée copte du Caire: Muséon 104 (1991) 5-37 + X pl.

3073 *Davis* Barry C., Ecclesiastes 12:1-8 – Death, an impetus for life: BS 148 (1991) 298-318.

3074 *Vogels* Walter, Performance vaine et performance saine chez Qohélet: NRT 113 (1991) 363-385.

E7.8   *Liber Sapientiae* – **Wisdom of Solomon.**

3075 ᴱHentschel Georg, *Zenger* Erich, Lehrerin der Gerechtigkeit, Studien zum Buch der Weisheit: ErfurtTSchr 19. Lp 1991, Benno. 182 p. 3-7462-0539-5. 6 art., infra.

3076 **Larcher** C., Le Livre de la Sagesse 1-3, 1983/4/5 ➤ 64,3332... 1,3385: ᴿTorJT 7 (1991) 94 (M. *Kolarcik*, also on AnchorB).

3077 ᴱ**Scarpat** Giuseppe, Libro della Sapienza 1, 1989 ➤ 5,3377: ᴿAntonianum 66 (1991) 584s (M. *Nobile*); BL (1991) 93s (P. R. *Davies*); BStLat 21 (1991) 69-71 (A. V. *Nazzaro*); ÉtClas 59 (1991) 351s (X. *Jacques*); Helmantica 42, 129* (1991) 394s (S. *García-Jalón*); Maia 43 (1991) 247s (Paola *Graffigna*); Protestantesimo 46 (1991) 213s (J. A. *Soggin*); RTLv 22 (1991) 80s (J. *Vermeylen*).

3078 **Schmitt** Armin, Weisheit: NEchter 23, 1989 ➤ 5,3379; 6,3659: ᴿTPQ 139 (1991) 317s (H. *Engel*).

3079 **Thiele** Walter, Sapientia Salomonis: VLat Beuron 11 [1977-85 ➤ 6,3660] 7s, Sap 13,1-18,18 p. 481-560 / 18,18 - Schluss, p. 561-598; 1984s: ᴿTR 87 (1991) 11s (G. D. *Kilpatrick* †, ᵀ*Woestmann* Annegret).

3080 **Kolarcik** Michael, The ambiguity of death in the Book of Wisdom 1-6; a study of literary structure and interpretation [diss. Pont. Ist. Biblico, ᴰ*Gilbert* M., Roma 1989 ➤ 5,3381]: AnBib 127. R 1991, Biblico. xii-208 p. 88-7653-127-0.

3081 *Seeley* David, Narrative, the righteous man and the philosopher; an analysis of the story of the *díkaios* in Wisdom 1-5: JPseud 7 (1990) 55-78.

3081* *a*) *Engel* Helmut, Weish 1,11d/7,22-8,1; – *b*) *Werner* Wolfgang 'Denn Gerechtigkeit ist unsterblich'; Schöpfung. Tod und Unvergänglichkeit nach Weish 1,11-15 und 2,21-24 ➤ 3075 supra: Lehrerin 1991, 62-66. 67-102 / 26-61.

3082 *Schmitt* Armin, Komposition, Tradition und zeitgeschichtlicher Hintergrund in Weish 1,16-2,24 und 4,20-5,23: ➤ 126, ᶠRICHTER W., Text 1991, 403-421.

3082* *Busto Saiz* José Ramón, The meaning of Wisdom 2:9a: ➤ 426, Septuagint 7, 1989/91, 355-9.

3083 *Marin* Marcello, [Sap 6,26; Mt 11,25] I fedeli 'chiamati alla sapienza' secondo AGOSTINO: VetChr 28 (1991) 61-75.

3083* *Haag* Ernst, 'Die Weisheit ist nur eine und vermag doch alles' ... Weish 11s: ➤ 3075, Lehrerin 1991, 103-155.

3084 *Schwenk* Udo, Textauslegung innerhalb des Septuaginta-Kanons; Sapientia Salomonis 10-19 als Beispiel für die Auslegung des Buches Genesis, Exodus 1-15 und Teile der Wüstentradition: ev. Diss. München 1991, ᴰ*Baltzer*. – TR 87 (1991) 520.

3085 **Poniży** Bogdan, ❷ De reinterpretatione Exodi in libro Sapientiae²ʳᵉᵛ [¹1988 ➤ 4,3553]: Pont. Fac. Theol. Posnaniae Studia et Textus 8. Poznań 1991, Św. Wojciecha. 165 p. 83-7015-220-1.

3085* *a*) *Görg* Manfred, Die Religionskritik in Weish 13,1s; – *b*) *Marböck* Johannes, ... Weish 18,5-19,22: ➤ 3075, Lehrerin 1991, 13-25 / 156-178.

E7.9   *Ecclesiasticus, Siracides;* **Wisdom of Jesus Sirach.**

3086 **Bohlen** Reinhold, Die Ehrung der Eltern bei Ben Sira; Studien zur Motivation und Interpretation eines Familienethischen Grundwerts in frühhellenistischer Zeit [Hab-Diss. FrB 1991, ᴰ*Ruppert*. – TR 87 (1991) 512]: TrierTSt 61. Trier 1991, Paulinus. 434 p. DM 96 [TR 88,162]. 3-7902-1279-2.

3087 *a*) [Brasil] *Pereira* Ney, A mulher no Sirácida; – *b*) *Kloppenburg* Bonaventura, A mulher na vida e missão da Igreja: RCuBíb 13,53s (A mulher na Igreja 1989) 128-142 / 46-48 [*al.* gran parte de outras revistas].

3088 *Camp* Claudia V., Understanding a patriarchy; women in second century Jerusalem through the eyes of Ben Sira: ➤ 329, Women like this 1991, 1-39.

3089 **Nelson** Milward D., Syriac... Ben-Sira 1988 ➤ 4,3564 ... 6,3671: ᴿJAOS 111 (1991) 663s (B. A. *Taylor*); JSS 36 (1991) 164-7 (R. J. *Owens*).

3090 *Orlinsky* Harry M., Some terms in the prologue to Ben Sira and the Hebrew Canon: JBL 110 (1991) 483-490.

3091 *Reiterer* F. V., *a*) Die Stellung Ben Siras zur Arbeit; Notizen zu einem kaum berücksichtigten Thema sirazidischer Lehre: ➤ 59, ᶠFÜGLISTER N., Ein Gott 1991, 257-289; – *b*) Markierte und nicht markierte direkte Objekte bei Ben Sira; präliminaria zur Untersuchung der Hebraizität Siras anhand der Verben mit *et*-Verwendung: ➤ 126, ᶠRICHTER W., Text (1991) 359-378.

3092 *Roth* Wolfgang, Sirach, the first graded curriculum: BToday 29 (1991) 298-302.

3093 **Sanders** J. T., Ben Sira and demotic wisdom 1983 ➤ 64,2347 ... 3,3327: ᴿTorJT 7 (1991) 92s (M. *Kolarcik*, also on AnchorB).

3094 **Skehan** Patrick W. †, *Di Lella* Alexander A., The wisdom of Ben Sira: AnchorB 39, 1987 ➤ 3,3329 ... 6,3674: ᴿCarthaginensia 7 (1991) 507s (R. *Sanz Valdivieso*); Gregorianum 72 (1991) 561-5 (G. L. *Prato*).

3095 **Thiele** Walter, Ecclesiasticus: VLat Beuron 11 [1s 1988 ➤ 4,3568; 3, 1989 ➤ 5,3394], 4. Ecus 1,3-3,31. FrB 1989, Herder. p. 161-240. 3-451-00426-7. – ᴿBL (1991) 50 (J. *Barr*); JTS 42 (1991) 179-181 (J. K. *Elliott*).

3096 ᵀᴱ**Vannini** M., M. ECKHART, Commento all'Ecclesiastico. F 1990, Nardoni. 120 p. Lit. 15.000. 88-404-2404-0. – ᴿHumBr 46 (1991) 483s (G. *Colombi*).

3097 **Wright** Benjamin G., No small difference 1989 ➤ 5,3395; 6,3676: ᴿCBQ 53 (1991) 686-8 (J. L. *Trafton*: chiefly and not adequately statistical); TLZ 116 (1991) 28s (G. *Sauer*).

3098 *Calduch Benages* Nuria, La sabiduría y la prueba en Sir 4,11-19: EstB 49 (1991) 25-48; Eng. 25.

3099 *Fogliata* Mateus, A figura do pastor e do rebanho em Eclo 18,13: RCuBíb 14,55s (1990) 68-75.

3100 *a*) *Hayward* R., [Sir 24 ...] Sacrifice and world order; some observations on Ben Sira's attitude to the Temple service; – *b*) *Jones* D. R., Sacrifice and holiness: ➤ 384, Sacrifice 1991, 22-34 / 9-21.

3101 **Strotmann** Angelika, 'Mein Vater bist du!' Sir 51,10; zur Bedeutung der Vaterschaft Gottes in kanonischen und nichtkanonischen frühjüdischen

Schriften [Diss. Fra 1990 → 7064 infra]: FraTSt 39. Fra 1991, Knecht.
xvi-408 p. DM 68 [TR 87,337].

VIII. Libri prophetici VT

E8.1 **Prophetismus.**

3102 **Alonso Schökel** Luis, *Gutiérrez* Guillermo, Mensajes de profetas; meditaciones bíblicas: El Pozo de Siquem 47. Sdr 1991, Sal Terrae. 183 p.
84-293-0912-8.

3103 **Asurmendi** Jesús, O profetismo, das origens à época moderna [El
profetismo 1987 → 4,3780], ᵀ*Fraga de Alineida* S. Estella. São Paulo 1988,
Paulinas. 151 p. – ᴿPerspT 21 (1989) 139 (J. *Vitório*).

3104 **Beaucamp** Évode, Los profetas de Israel o el drama de una alianza 1988
= 1956 → 5,3410; 6,3688: ᴿProyección 37 (1990) 61 (J. L. *Sicre*).

3105 *Ben-Shammai* Haggai, ❹ SAADYA's Introduction to Isaiah as an
Introduction to the Books of the Prophets: Tarbiz 60 (1990s) 371-404;
Eng. III-IV.

3105* **Bretón** S., Vocación y mision ᴰ1987 → 3,3350 ... 6,3693: ᴿETL 67
(1991) 152s (E. *Eynikel*); RAg 30 (1989) 273 (S. *Sabugal*).

3106 *Cahill* Michael, The oracles against the nations [in all OT prophets except Hosea]; synthesis and analysis for today: LvSt 16 (1991)
121-136.

3107 **Catastini** A., Profeti e tradizione: Seminari di Orientalistica. Pisa 1990,
Gardini. x-151 p. [ZAW 104, 293, H.-C. *Schmitt*].

3108 *a) Cryer* Frederick H., Der Prophet und der Magier; Bemerkungen anhand einer überholten Diskussion; – *b) Liwak* Rüdiger, Die
altorientalischen Grossmächte in der Metaphorik der Prophetie; – *c)
Malamat* Abraham, The secret council and prophetic involvement in
Mari and Israel; – *d) Schmidt* Werner H., 'Prophetie und Wirklichkeit',
ein Gespräch mit S. HERRMANN: → 75, ᶠHERRMANN S., Prophetie 1991,
79-88 / 206-230 / 231-6 / 348-363.

3109 **Dearmann** J.A., Property rights in the ... prophets ᴰ1988 → 4,3595 ...
6,3700: ᴿJAOS 111 (1991) 644s (B.A. *Levine*); JQR 82 (1991s) 485-7
(Susan *Ackerman*).

3109* *a) Herrmann* Siegfried, Zwischen Intellekt und Charisma; eine Auseinandersetzung mit K. Kochs 'Profeten'; – *b) Schmidt* W.H., Zu-
kunftsgewissheit und 'nachlaufende Erkenntnis' – ein Gespräch mit K.
Koch: → 87, ᶠKOCH K., Ernten 1991, 145-159 / 161-181.

3110 *Jemielity* Thomas, The prophetic character; good, heroic and naive:
LitTOx 5,1 (1991) 37-48 [< ZIT 91,211].

3111 **Lightner** Robert P., The last days handbook; a comprehensive guide to
understanding the different views of prophecy; who believes what about
prophecy and why. Nv 1990, Nelson. 223 p. – ᴿGraceTJ 11 (1990) 244-6
(M. *Brubacher*).

3112 *Lipiński* E., Profetisme en waarzeggerij: PhoenixEOL 37,2 (1991) 5-11.

3113 **Lohfink** Norbert, I profeti ieri e oggi³ [¹1967]: GdT 16. Brescia 1990,
Queriniana. 95 p. Lit. 12.000. [ZAW 104, 154].

3114 *Lowden* J., Illuminated prophet books 1988 → 4,3613: ᴿSpeculum 66
(1991) 437-440 (H. *Maguire*: insights of wide application).

3115 **Miller** J.W., Meet the prophets 1987 → 3,3378 ... 6,3714: ᴿLvSt 16
(1991) 270s (J. *Lust*).

3116 **Overholt** Thomas, Channels of prophecy; the social dynamics of prophetic activity 1989 ➤ 5,3438; 6,3717: ᴿBA 54 (1991) 120 (R. D. *Haak*); BibTB 21 (1991) 126 (R. *Gnuse*); BL (1991) 40 (A. G. *Auld*); CBQ 53 (1991) 301-3 (D. L. *Smith*); JAAR 59 (1991) 852-5 (J. *Paper*); NewTR 4,1 (1991) 104s (C. *Stuhlmueller*); OTAbs 14 (1991) 118 (L. *Boadt*).

3116* *Peckham* Brian, The function of the Law in the development of Israel's prophetic tradition: ➤ 436, ᴱ*Halpern* B., Law 1987/91, 108-146.

3117 *Petersen* David L., Israelite prophecy; change versus continuity: ➤ 429, IOSOT 1989/91, 190-203.

3117* *Rendtorff* Rolf, Der Ort der Prophetie in einer Theologie des ATs [< Eng. SBL Wien 1990, unveröffentlicht]: ➤ 252, Kanon 1991, 64-71.

3118 **Renker** Alwin, Propheten — das Gewissen Israels 1990 ➤ 6,3723: ᴿOTAbs 14 (1991) 228 (M. P. *Graham:* secondary school text); ZkT 113 (1991) 472-4 (A. H. *Pissarek*).

3119 **Rofé** Alexander, The prophetical stories 1988 ➤ 4,3829 ... 6,3725: ᴿJQR 82 (1991s) 507-510 (M. *Brettler*).

3120 **Rofé** Alexander, Storie di profeti; la narrativa sui profeti nella Bibbia ebraica; generi letterari e storia, ᵀᴱ*Borbone* Pier G.: BtStoB 8. Brescia 1991, Paideia. 270 p. Lit. 38.000. 88-394-0461-9. – ᴿIrénikon 64 (1991) 139 (E. *Lanne*); OTAbs 14 (1991) 348 (C. T. *Begg*).

3121 **Schneider** Christoph, Die innerprophetische Auseinandersetzung des Alten Testaments als Krisis des Jahweglaubens; zur Frage der sogenannten falschen Prophetie: Diss. Kirchliche Hochschule Leipzig 1991, ᴰ*Herrmann*. – TR 87 (1991) 519.

3122 *Schoen* Edward L., The roles of predictions in science and religion: IntJPhilosR 29 (1991) 1-31 [< TR 87,170].

3123 **Sicre** José Luis, *al.*, La Iglesia y los Profetas: En torno al NT 5, 1989 ➤ 5,3447; 6,3730: ᴿCBQ 53 (1991) 665s (C. *Bernas*).

3124 *Simian-Yofre* Horacio, Povertà, ricchezza e ingiustizia nel pensiero profetico: ➤ 444*, Ricchezza 1991, 109-134.

3125 *a) Soden* Wolfram von, Verkündigung des Gotteswillens durch prophetisches Wort in den altbabylonischen Briefen aus Mari [< WeltOr 1 (1947-52) 397-403 = BibelAO, BZAW 162 (1985) 19-31]; – *b) Nötscher* Friedrich, Prophetie im Umkreis des Alten Israel [< BZ 10 (1966) 161-197]: ➤ 321, WegF 633 (1991) 201-213 / 214-258.

3126 **Stacey** W. D., Prophetic drama in the OT. L 1990, Epworth. x-310 p. £12.50. 0-7162-0470-3. – ᴿBL (1991) 96 (R. P. *Carroll*); TLond 94 (1991) 305s (R. *Mason*: 'drama' is Wheeler ROBINSON's 1927 'symbolism').

3127 *Stuhlmueller* Carroll, Prophetic-mystic and social justice; an exploration: *a)* [... reflections, *Viviano* Pauline A.; response, *Klein* Ralph W.]: BiRes 36 (1991) 35-60 [61-68, 69-73]; – *b)* ScripB 21 (1991) 2-15.

3128 **Tidiman** Brian, L'analyse rhétorique et l'exégèse des écrits prophétiques de l'Ancien Testament: prot. diss. Strasbourg 1991. 210 p. – RTLv 23, p. 540.

3129 **Vogels** Walter, Les Prophètes; L'Horizon du croyant. Ottawa 1990, Univ. S.-Paul. 165 p. – ᴿEsprVie 101 (1991) 272 (L. *Monloubou*: il est permis de rester sceptique).

3130 **Westermann** Claus, Prophetische Heilsworte im AT: FRL 145, 1987 ➤ 3,3398 ... 6,3741: ᴿCBQ 53 (1991) 127-9 (G. M. *Tucker*: undeniably important but frustratingly undocumented).

3131 **Westermann** Claus, Prophetic oracles of salvation in the Old Testament [1987 ➤ 3,3398], ᵀ*Crim* Keith. 283 p. $19 pa. 0-664-25239-7 [TDig 39,294].

3132 **Westermann** Claus, Basic forms of prophetic speech [1960], ᵀ*White* Hugh C. Louisville 1991 = 1967, W-Knox. xvi-222 p. $19 pa. 0-664-25244-3 [TDig 39,294].

E8.2 **Proto-Isaias,** *textus, commentarii.*

3133 ᴱ**Gryson** Roger, Esaias [5. 1990 ➤ 6,3749], 6. Isa 14,13 - 22,5; 7. 22,5-26,20; 8. 26,20-30,15: VLat Beuron 12. FrB 1991, Herder. p. 401-480. 481-560. 561-640. [RHE 86,279*]. – ᴿRHE 86 (1991) 463s (P.-M. *Bogaert*, 4-6).

3134 **Hayes** J. H., *Irvine* S. A., Isaiah 1987 ➤ 4,3656 ... 6,3752: ᴿBO 48 (1991) 887-890 (W. *Dietrich*: 'Spätfrucht des Historismus' outside VERMEYLEN's broad spectrum: a whole book as the prophet's ipsissima vox); BZ 35 (1991) 284s (H. *Seebass*: These eindrucksvoll); CritRR 4 (1991) 142-4 (J. *Jensen*: strained defense of authenticity); JQR 81 (1990s) 491-3 (C. R. *Seitz*); RelStT 10,1 (1990) 64-66 (G. J. *Hamilton,* also on Hayes' Amos).

3135 **Jacob** Edmond, Ésaïe 1-12: CommAT 8a, 1987 ➤ 3,3403 ... 6,3754: ᴿSalesianum 53 (1991) 585s (M. *Cimosa*).

3136 **Jay** Pierre, L'exégèse de S. JÉRÔME ... Isaïe 1985 ➤ 1,3467 ... 5,3468: ᴿAugM 34 (1989) 186-8 (J. *Oroz*); ZkT 113 (1991) 74s (J. M. *Oesch*).

3137 **Kilian** Rudolf, Jesaja 1-12: NEchter 17, 1986 ➤ 2,2627 ... 6,3755: ᴿSalesianum 53 (1991) 586s (M. *Cimosa* commenda l'Excursus sull'Emmanuele).

3138 **Montagnini** Felice, Isaia 1-39; l'occhio del profeta sugli eventi della storia: LoB 1.18. Brescia 1990, Queriniana. 134 p. Lit. 15.000. – ᴿHumBr 46 (1991) 474 (A. *Bonora*); NRT 113 (1991) 912 (J.-L. *Ska*); RivB 39 (1991) 53s (B. *Marconcini*).

3139 **Ribera Florit** Josep, El Targum de Isaías ... : BiblMidrásica 6, 1988 ➤ 4,3663 ... 6,3739: ᴿBL (1991) 429 (C.T.R. *Hayward*: important contributions like CHILTON B. overlooked).

3140 **Werlitz** Jürgen, Gericht und Heil in Jesaja 1-39; Studien zur literarkritischen Methode: kath. Diss. Augsburg 1991, ᴰ*Kilian*. – TR 87 (1991) 515.

3141 **Widyapranawa** S. H., The Lord is savior ... Isa 1-39: ➤ 6,3762: ᴿGrace-TJ 12,1 (1991) 134-6 (M. A. *Grisanti*); RelStR 18 (1991) 137 (M. A. *Sweeney*: oversimplified; egregious errors); SWJT 34,1 (1991s) 70 (H. B. *Hunt*: 16-vol. series aimed to reflect a more universal view of the Scriptures, largely by non-western scholars but well aware of the issues).

3142 **Wildberger** Hans, Isaiah 1-12: Continental commentaries. Mp 1991, Fortress.

E8.3 [Proto-] **Isaias 1-39,** *themata, versiculi.*

3143 **Conrad** Edgar W., Reading Isaiah [reader reaction, contemporary literary theory: structural wholeness of the book]: OvBT. Mp 1991, Fortress. xiv-185 p. $13 pa. 0-8006-1560-3 [TDig 93,56].

3144 **Deck** Ulrike, Die Berichtsbotschaft Jesajas; Charakter und Begründung: Diss. FrB 1991, ᴰ*Ruppert*. – TR 87 (1991) 517; [*Deck* Scholastica, RTLv 23, p. 538 und TR 88,162]: ForBi 67. Wü 1991, Echter. ix-310 p.

3144* *Irsigler* Hubert, Gott als König in Berufung und Verkündigung Jesajas: ➤ 59, ᶠFÜGLISTER N, Ein Gott 1991, 127-157.

3145 **McMichael** Steven, Was Jesus of Nazareth the Messiah? Alfonso de ESPINA's argument against the Jews based on his commentary on the

Book of Isaiah in the 'Fortalitium Fidei' (c. 1464); an edition, translation and commentary: diss. Pont. Univ. Gregoriana, [D]*Dupuis* J. R 1991s. [InfPUG (May 92) 10].

3146 *Miscall* Peter D., Isaiah; the labyrinth of images: ↠ 311, Semeia 54 (1991) 103-121.

3147 **Nielsen** Kristen, [1-Is] There is hope for a tree [[D]1985, [T]*Crowley* Christine & Frederick]: JStOT supp 65, 1989 ↠ 5,3491; 6,3768: [R]CBQ 53 (1991) 112-4 (K. M. *Craig*); JQR 82 (1991s) 545-7 (J. *Magonet*); JTS 42 (1991) 168s (R. E. *Clements*); OrSuec 40 (1991) 291-5 (G. *Avraham*).

3148 **Paściak** Józef, ❷ Izajasz wieszczem (poet of) Chrystusa: Attende lectioni 12. Katowice 1987, Św. Jacka. 152 p. – [R]ColcT 60,1 (1990) 169s (J. *Królikowski*, ❷).

3149 *Rendtorff* Rolf, The book of Isaiah, a complex unity; synchronic and diachronic reading: ↠ 446, SBL Sem 30 (1991) 8-20.

3150 [E]**Vermeylen** J., Book of Isaiah 1987/9 ↠ 5,614; 6,3771: [R]Bijdragen 52 (1991) 209s (P. C. *Beentjes*); JTS 42 (1991) 632s (R. E. *Clements*); RechSR 79 (1991) 273-5 (J.-M. *Carrière*).

3151 **Watts** John D. W., Isaiah: Word **Themes** 1989 ↠ 5,3481 [**comm.** 1985 ↠ 2,2632; 6,3772]: [R]CBQ 53 (1991) 126s (C. *Stuhlmueller*); EvQ 63 (1991) 344s (J. G. *McConville*).

3152 *Watts* John D. W., Reading Isaiah in a new time: RExp 88,2 (1991) 131-6.

3153 *Worgul* John E., The quatrain in Isaianic poetry [examples from Is 1-20]: GraceTJ 11 (1990) 187-204.

3154 **Gitay** Yehoshua, Isaiah and his audience; the structure and meaning of Isaiah 1-12: StSemNeerl 30. Assen 1991, Van Gorcum. xi-283 p. *f* 49,50. 90-232-2493-0 [BL 92,71, R. E. *Clements*].

3155 **Sweeney** Marvin A., Isa 1-4: BZAW 171, 1988 ↠ 4,3679 ... 6,3776: [R]BZ 35 (1991) 293s (J. *Becker*).

3156 *Dennison* James T., A tale of two cities; Isaiah and worship, Isaiah 1:1-31; 6:1-8: Kerux 4,2 (1989) 33-41.

3157 *Cate* Robert L., We need to be saved (Isaiah 1:1-2; 5:1-2; 6:1-13): RExp 88,2 (1991) 137-152.

3158 *Ben Zvi* Ehud, Isaiah 1,4-9, Isaiah, and the events of 701 BCE in Judah: ScandJOT 5,1 (1991) 95-111.

3159 *Haag* Ernst, Sündenvergebung und neuer Anfang; zur Übersetzung und Auslegung von Jes 1,18: ↠ 86*; [F]KNOCH O., 1991, 68-80.

3160 **Bartelt** Andrew H., Style and structure in prophetic rhetoric; Isaiah 2-12: diss. Michigan, [D]*Freedman* D. N. AA 1991. 441 p. 91-23976. – DissA 52 (1991s) 935-A.

3161 *Maas* R., [Isa 2,2-5] Instruction from Zion; Jesus as the 'globalization' of Torah: LivLight 28,1 (Wsh 1991) 69-79 [< NTAbs 36,220].

3162 *Belardi* W., [Isa 5,2; Mt 21,33] La 'torre' nelle parabole bibliche della vigna [*migdal* piuttosto 'incastellatura (per il frantoio), palmento' (means rather winepress-frame or millstone)]: [F]GABRIELI Francesco, 80° compleanno, [E]**Raini** R. (R 1984, Univ.) 61-71 [< Henoch 12 (1990) 375, B. *Chiesa*, con altri tit. pp. di 'questa imponente Festschrift'].

3163 **Wagner** Renate, Textexegese als Strukturanalyse... Jes 6,1-11 [Diss. Aachen, [D]*Floss* J.]: Mü Univ. AOtt 32, 1989 ↠ 5,3510: [R]BL (1991) 100 (G. I. *Davies:* '3d generation' of W. RICHTER methods); CritRR 4 (1991)

156-8 (M. A. *Sweeney*); ᴿTLZ 116 (1991) 108-110 (Jutta *Körner*); ZAW 103 (1991) 460 (H.-C. *Schmitt*).

3164 *Gowan* Donald E., Isaiah 6,1-8, expository: Interpretation 45 (1991) 172-6.

3165 **Spinks** Bryan, Isa 6,3 The sanctus in the Eucharistic prayer. C 1991, Univ. 260 p. £30. 0-521-39307-8. – ᴿExpTim 103 (1991s) 131 (G. *Tellini*: OT and Judaism usages first examined in context).

3166 *Beale* G. K., Isaiah VI 9-13; a retributive taunt against idolatry: VT 41 (1991) 257-278.

3167 **Evans** Craig A., To see and not perceive, Is 6,9s ...: JStOT supp 64, 1989 → 5,3512: ᴿBijdragen 52 (1991) 438 (A. van *Wieringen*); CBQ 53 (1991) 666s (D. G. *Johnson*); CritRR 4 (1991) 80-83 (B. *Chilton*); EvQ 63 (1991) 264s (K. E. *Brower*); JTS 42 (1991) 264-6 (Mary Ann *Beavis*); NedTTs 45 (1991) 334s (P. B. *Dirksen*); SWJT 34,3 (1991s) 37s (B. *Heflin*).

3168 *Szwarc* Urszula, ❷ The sense of Isa 6,10*b* in the light of the Synoptics [Mt 13,10-17 ...]: RoczTK 34,1 (1991 für 1987) 39-46; deutsch 46.

3169 **Irvine** Stuart A., Isaiah, Ahaz and the Syro-Ephraimite crisis: SBL diss 123, 1990 → 6,3783: ᴿBiblica 72 (1991) 560-3 (J. *Asurmendi*, castellano); BL (1991) 79 (W. J. *Houston*).

3170 *Haag* Ernst, Das Immanuelzeichen in Jesaja 7: TrierTZ 100 (1991) 3-22.

3171 *Reymond* Robert L., Who is the '*almâ* of Isaiah 7:14?: Presbyterion 15 (St. Louis 1989) 1-15 [< OTAbs 14,310].

3172 *Rösel* Martin, Die Jungfrauengeburt des endzeitlichen Immanuel; Jesaja 7 in der Übersetzung der Septuaginta: → 310, JbBT 6 (1991) 135-151.

3173 **Salij** Jacek, ❷ *Tajemnica*... The mystery of Emmanuel today. Poznań 1989, W Drodze. 111 p. – ᴿColcT 61,2 (1991) 201-3 (J. *Królikowski*, ❷).

3174 *a*) *Poe* Harry L., Isaiah 8:5-15, expository; – *b*) *Oswalt* John, God's determination to redeem his people (Isaiah 9:1-7; 11:1-11; 26:1-9; 35:1-10): RExp 88,2 (1991) 189-193 / 153-165.

3175 *Wegner* Paul D., Another look at Isaiah VIII 23*b*: VT 41 (1991) 481-4.

3175* *Roberts* J. J. M., The translation of Isa 11:10 and the syntax of the temporal expression wa-yᵉhî ba-yôm ha-hû': → 102*c*, ꜰPrince MIKASA 1991, 363-370.

3176 **Gosse** B., Isa 13s: OBO 78, 1988 → 4,3691 ... 6,3793: ᴿBZ 35 (1991) 306s (J. *Hausmann*).

3177 *Witt* Douglas A., The houses plundered, the women raped; the use of Isaiah 13 in Zechariah 14:1-11: ProcGLM 11 (1991) 66-74.

3178 *Gryson* Roger, Saint JÉRÔME traducteur d'Isaïe; réflexions sur le texte d'Isaïe 14,18-21 dans la Vulgate et dans l'In Esaiam: Muséon 104 (1991) 57-72.

3179 *Fudji* Edmond, Yahvé, Assur et les nations; Isaïe 14,24-27: Masses Ouvrières 438 (1991) 49-58.

3180 *Gosse* Bernard, Isaïe 14,28-32 et les traditions sur Isaïe d'Isaïe 36-39 et Isaïe 20,1-6: BZ 35 (1991) 97s.

3181 *Easterly* Ellis, Is Mesha's *Qrḥḥ* mentioned in Isaiah XV 2?: VT 41 (1991) 215-9.

3182 *Willis* Timothy M., Yahweh's Elders (Isa 24,23): senior officials of the divine court: ZAW 103 (1991) 375-385.

3183 *Redditt* Paul L., Isaiah 26, expository RExp 88,2 (1991) 195-9.

3184 *Fouts* David M., A suggestion for Isaiah XXVI 16: VT 41 (1991) 472-5.

3185 *Dennison* James T.ᴶ, The righteous king — the just kingdom, Isaiah 32:1-3: Kerux 5,3 (1990) 29-38.

3186 *Beuken* Willem A. M., Jesaja 33 als Spiegeltext im Jesajabuch: ETL 67 (1991) 5-35; Eng. 35.

3187 *Weis* Richard D., Angels, altars, and angles of vision; the case of *Ar'ellîm* in Isaiah 33:7: ➤ 17, ᶠBARTHÉLEMY D., 1991, 285-292.
3188 *Tanghe* Vincent, Der Schriftgelehrte in Jes 34,16-17: ETL 67 (1991) 338-345.
3189 **Seitz** Christopher R., Zion's final destiny; the development of the Book of Isaiah; a reassessment of Isaiah 36-39 [Hezekiah-narrative pivotal to Isaiah's growth]. Mp 1991, Fortress. xii-228 p. $25. 0-8006-2504-8 [TDig 39,286].

E8.4   **Deutero-Isaias 40-52:** *commentarii, themata, versiculi.*

3190 **Barstad** H.M., A way in the wilderness, 2-Ex 2-Is 1989 ➤ 6,3804: ᴿJSS 36 (1991) 155s (B. *Lindars*).
3191 **Beaucamp** Évode, Livre de la consolation d'Israël, Is XL-LV: Lire la Bible 93. P 1991, Cerf. 255 p. F 95. 2-204-04370-2 [NRT 114,940, L.J. *Renard*].
3192 **Farfan Navarro** Enrique, El desierto transformado; una imagen deuteroisaiana de regeneración (con particular referencia a Is 41,17-20): diss. Pont. Ist. Biblico, ᴰ*Simian-Yofre* H. R 1991. - AcPIB 9/7, 579.621; Biblica 72,145; RTLv 23, p. 538.
3193 **Greggs** Gilbert A., Priesthood, prophecy and apocalyptic; a study of the prophetic texts of the Restoration: diss. Yale, ᴰ*Wilson* R. NHv 1991. - RelStR 18,173.
3194 **Grimm** Werner, *Dittert* Kurt, Deuterojesaja; Deutung — Wirkung — Gegenwart: Calwer BKomm. Stu 1990, Calwer. 496 p. + Übersetzung 'Das Trostbuch Gottes' 96 p. DM 98. 3-7668-3051-1; –0-3. - ᴿOTAbs 14 (1991) 230 (C.T. *Begg*); ZAW 103 (1991) 448 (H.C. *Schmitt*).
3195 *Hamlin* E. John, Deutero-Isaiah's interpretation of the Exodus in the Babylonian twilight: ProcGLM 11 (1991) 75-80.
3196 **Hessler** Eva, Das Heilsdrama Jes 40-55, 1988 ➤ 5,3541; 6,3811: ᴿBO 48 (1991) 890-3 (P. *Höffken*: Irrweg); VT 41 (1991) 247 (H.G.M. *Williamson*).
3197 *a*) *Kelley* Page H., Doing it God's way [Isaiah 40:1-20; 45:8-25; 52:13 - 54; 55:1-13]; – *b*) *Drinkard* Joel F., Isaiah 44:24 - 45:13: RExp 88,2 (1991) 167-176 / 201-4.
3198 *Kida* Kinichi, The prophet, the Servant, and Cyrus in the prophecies of Second Isaiah: AnJapB 16 (1990) 3-29 [< TLZ 116,826].
3199 **Kratz** Reinhard G., Kyros im Deuterojesajabuch; redaktionsgeschichtliche Untersuchungen zur Entstehung und Theologie von Jes 40-55 [ev. Hab.-Diss. Zürich 1991, - TR 87 (1991) 511]: ForschAT 1. Tü 1991, Mohr. x-254 p. DM 148. 3-16-145757-9.
3200 **Leene** H., De vroegere en de nieuwe dingen bij Deuterojesaja ᴰ1987 ➤ 5,3544; 6,3814: ᴿBZ 35 (1991) 287s (J. *Becker*); VT 41 (1991) 382 (G.I. *Davies*).
3201 **Matheus** Frank, Singt dem Herrn ein neues Lied; die Hymnen Deuterojesajas [< diss. Heidelberg, ᴰ*Rendtorff* R.]: SBS 141. Stu 1990, KBW. 192 p.; foldout. DM 37,80 pa. [RelStR 18,226, M.A. *Sweeney*].
3202 *Melugin* Roy F., The Servant, God's call, and the structure of Isaiah 40-48: ➤ 446, SBL Sem 30 (1991) 21-30.
3203 *Ruppert* Lothar, Die Disputationsworte bei Deuterojesaja in neuem religionsgeschichtlichem Licht: ➤ 75, ᶠHERRMANN S., Prophetie 1991, 317-325.
3204 **Trever** John C., The contributions of Second Isaiah [34s; 40-66] to the semantic development of Hebrew words: diss. Yale. NHv 1943. 241 p. 91-28420. - DissA 52 (1991s) 1776-A; OIAc 2,28.

3205 **Wilson** A. The nations in Dt-Isa ᴰ1986 ➤ 3,3478; 6,3818: ᴿBL (1991) 103 (A. *Gelston*: interesting, unusual).

3206 *Korpal* M.C.A., Soldering in Isaiah 40: 19-20 and 1 Kings 6.21: UF 23 (1991) 219-222.

3207 *Dion* Paul E., The structure of Isaiah 42,10-17 as approached through versification and the distribution of poetic devices: JStOT 49 (1991) 113-124.

3207* *Baldauf* Borghild, Jes 42, 18-25; Gottes tauber und blinder Knecht: ➤ 59, ᶠFÜGLISTER N., Ein Gott 1991, 13-36.

3208 *Dempsey* Deirdre A., A note on Isaiah XLIII 9: VT 41 (1991) 212-5.

3208* *Heintz* Jean-Georges, Lectio difficilior; l'oracle d'Ésaïe 43/14-15 et son arrière-plan spatial et thématique: ➤ 140, ᶠSMYTH-FLORENTIN F. 1991, 61-85.

3209 *Franke* Chris A., The function of the satiric lament over Babylon in Second Isaiah (XLVII): VT 41 (1991) 408-418.

3209* *Vanoni* Gottfried, 'Die Tora im Herzen' (Jes 51,7) oder, Über das Vergleichen: ➤ 59, ᶠFÜGLISTER N., 1991, 357-371.

3210 *Terian* Abraham, The hunting imagery in Isaiah LI 20a: VT 41 (1991) 464-471.

3211 *Inks* David, Come out of Babylon; Isaiah 52:11: Kerux 6,1 (1991) 32-44.

E8.5 *Isaiae 53ss, Carmina Servi YHWH:* **Servant-Songs.**

3212 *a)* *Ellis* Robert R., The remarkable Suffering Servant of Isaiah 40-55; – *b)* *Ellis* E. Earle, Isaiah in the New Testament; – *c)* *Taylor* Larry, The Holy One of Israel is Savior; theological themes in Isaiah; – *d)* *Prince* Robert, Isaiah, the man and his book: SWJT 34,1 (1991s) 20-30 / 31-35 / 13-19 / 5-8.

3213 *Gosse* Bernard, Isaïe 52,13 –53,12 et [= modifie le pessimisme d'] Isaïe 6: RB 98 (1991) 537-543.

Jones B., Suffering Servant in Rev ᴰ1990 ➤ 5036.

3214 *Kilian* R., Anmerkungen zur Bedeutung von *mišpāṭ* im ersten Gottesknechtslied: ➤ 86*, ᶠKNOCH O., Freude 1991, 81-88.

3215 **Koenig** Jean, Oracles / exil 1988 ➤ 4,3713 ... 6,3838: ᴿAfO 36s (1989s) 184s (W. von *Soden*); BO 48 (1991) 635-7 (W.A.M. *Beuken*); RTPhil 123 (1991) 453s (T. *Römer*).

3216 *Lourenço* João, Targum de Is 52,13 - 53,12; presupuestos históricos e processos literários: ➤ 422, Didaskalia 20,1 (1989/90) 155-166 = 421, Luso-Esp 529-540.

3217 **Mettinger** T.N.D., Farewell to the Servant 1983 ➤ 64,3525 ... 5,3563: ᴿBO 48 (1991) 626-632 (J. A. *Emerton*: not yet).

3218 *Varo* Francisco, El siervo sufriente (Is 52,13 - 53,12) en la exégesis hebrea, según Don Isaac ABRABANEL): ➤ 421, Luso-Esp 1989/91, 597-608.

3219 *a)* *Wurz* Heinrich, Zu den Gottesknechtliedern; – *b)* *Marböck* Johannes, König, Kind und Knecht; zum Weg messianischer Hoffnung im Alten Testament: ➤ 6,171, ᶠSTÖGER Alois, Exeget 1990, 171-181 / 103-112.

3220 **Glassner** Gottfried [ᴰPaul Anton], Jesaja 54, Vision eines auf Verheissung gegründeten Jerusalem [kath. Diss. Salzburg 1991, ᴰ*Füglister N.* –

TR 87 (1991) 514. ➤ 6,3843]: ÖsBSt 11. Klosterneuburg 1991, ÖstKBW. ix-278 p. Sch 262. 3-85396-082-0.

E8.6   [Trito-] Isaias 56-66.

3221 **Beuken** W.A.M., Jesaja III-AB 1989 ➤ 6,3843: ᴿBiblica 72 (1991) 276-280 (A. *Schoors*); Bijdragen 52 (1991) 439s (O. H. *Steck*).

3222 *Höffken* Peter, Tritojesaja in redaktionsgeschichtlicher Sicht [SEKINE S. 1989; KOENEN K. 1990]: BO 48 (1991) 736-742.

3223 **Koenen** Klaus, Ethik und Eschatologie im Tritojesajabuch... WM 62, ᴰ1990 ➤ 6,3847: ᴿTLZ 116 (1991) 26-28 (R. *Stahl*).

3224 **Sekine** Seizo, Die tritojesajanische Sammlung...: BZAW 175, ᴰ1989 ➤ 5,3574; 6,3848: ᴿCBQ 53 (1991) 121-3 (B. C. *Ollenburger*); NedTTs 45 (1991) 145s (W.A.M. *Beuken*).

3225 **Steck** Odil Hannes, Studien zu Tritojesaja: BZAW 203. Berlin 1991, de Gruyter. xiv-294 p. 3-11-013434-9. 9 reprints + these 5 inedita: 119-139, Zu jüngsten Untersuchungen von Jes 60-62; – 143-166, Jes 62,10-12 als Abschluss eines Grossjesajabuches; – 192-213, Zu jüngsten Untersuchungen von Jes 56,9-59,21; 63,16; – 229-265, Zu jüngsten Untersuchungen von Jes 56,1-8; 63,7-66,24; – 269-277, Anschlussprobleme einer redaktionellen Entstehung von Tritojesaja.

3226 *Stachowiak* Lech, ℗ Das Volk Gottes in der nachexilischen Zeit nach Jes. 56,1-12: RoczTK 34,1 (1991 für 1987) 5-12; deutsch 12.

3227 **Langer** Birgit, Gott als 'Licht'...Jes 60,1-3: ÖsBS 7,1989 ➤ 5,3580; 6,3852: ᴿAfO 36s (1989s) 185-7 (W. von *Soden*); BiKi 45 (1990) 56-58 (C. *Uehlinger*); CBQ 53 (1991) 675s (A. J. *Everson*).

3228 *Bratcher* Margaret D., Salvation achieved (Isaiah 61:1-7; 62:1-7; 65:17-66:2): RExp 88,2 (1991) 177-188. N. B. Fascicle 3 unaccountably begins again with p. 175, so that the pages 177-266 must be referred either to fasc. 2 or to fasc. 3.

3229 *Fischer* Irmtraud, Wo ist Jahwe? Das Volksklagelied Jes 63,7-64,11 als Ausdruck des Ringens um eine gebrochene Beziehung [Diss. 1988]: SBS 19, 1989 ➤ 5,3583; 6,3857 [auch 4284, falsch 'Wo ist Jesus']: ᴿTLZ 116 (1991) 588s (E,-J. *Waschke*); TPQ 139 (1991) 317 (J. M. *Oesch*); ZAW 103 (1991) 296 (H.-C. *Schmitt*, Titel falsch bei uns in ➤ 6,4284).

3230 *Beuken* W.A.M., Isaiah chapters lxv-lxvi; Trito-Isaiah and the closure of the book of Isaiah: ➤ 429, IOSOT 1989/91, 204-221.

E8.7   Jeremias.

3231 *Archer* Gleason L., The relationship between the Septuagint translation and the Massoretic Text in Jeremiah: TrinJ 12 (1991) 139-150.

3232 **Brueggemann** Walter, To pluck...Jer 1-25, 1988 ➤ 4,3746... 6,3862: ᴿCBQ 53 (1991) 460s (C. F. *Mariottini*).

3233 **Brueggemann** Walter, To build, to plant; a commentary on Jeremiah 26-52: International Theological Comm. GR/E 1991, Eerdmans/Handsel. xi-298 p. $16. 0-8028-0600-7/– [TDig 39,152].

3234 **Clements** R. E., Jeremiah: Interpretation Comm. 1988 ➤ 4,3749; 6,3864: ᴿCBQ 53 (1991) 280s (J. M. *Berridge*).

3235 **Holladay** W. L., Jeremiah II: Hermeneia comm. 1989 ➤ 5,3591; 6,3867 (not 'Jeremias'): ᴿBS 148 (1991) 371s (E. H. *Merrill*: a standard, despite qualms); CBQ 53 (1991) 672-4 (J. R. *Lundbom*); Gregorianum 72 (1991)

565-7 (C. *Conroy*); TLZ 116 (1991) 266-9 (W. *Thiel*); TorJT 7 (1991) 112-4 (Kathleen M. *O'Connor*); Vidyajyoti 55 (1991) 535-8 (P. M. *Meagher* compares with CARROLL).

3236 **Kidner** Derek, The message of Jeremiah; against wind and tide: The Bible Speaks Today 1987 → 4,3758: ᴿRelStR 17 (1991) 61 (H. W. *Lay*).

3237 *a) Lust* Johan, Messianism and the Greek version of Jeremiah; – *b) Cowe* S. Peter, The Armenian version of the Epistle of Jeremiah; parent text and translation technique: → 426, Septuagint 7, 1989/91, 87-122 / 373-391.

3238 *Moynihan* R., The manuscript tradition of the Super Hieremiam and the Venetian editions of the early xvith cent.: → 544, Profetismo gioachimita 1989/91, 129-137.

3239 *Quacquarelli* Antonio, Il genere omiletico in ORIGENE; le Omelie su Geremia: → 452, AnStoEseg 8,2 (1990/1) 507-517.

3240 *Ribera Florit* Josep, Algunos aspectos doctrinales característicos del Targum de Jeremías: → 421, Luso-Esp 1989/91, 521-527.

3241 **Soderlund** S., The Greek text of Jeremiah: JStOT supp 47, 1985 → 2, 2741 ... 6,3873: ᴿNedTTs 45 (1991) 63s (A. van der *Kooij*).

3242 *Weippert* Helga, Hieremias quadruplex; vier neue Kommentare zum Jeremiabuch [CARROLL R., HOLLADAY W., MCKANE W.; HERRMANN S.]: TR 87 (1991) 177-188.

3243 *Ausín* Santiago, La palabra y la persona del profeta (Sobre el doble texto de Jeremías): → 421, Luso-Esp 1989/91, 171-184.

3244 **Bak Dong Hyun,** Klagender Gott ...: BZAW 193, 1990 → 6,3876: ᴿOLZ 87 (1992) 402-4 (G. *Begrich*).

Beyerlin Walter, Reflexe der Amosvisionen im Jeremiabuch 1989 → 3413.

3245 **Carroll** R. P., Jeremiah: OTGuides, 1989 → 5,3602; 6,3879: ᴿCBQ 53 (1991) 462 (D. F. *Morgan*).

3246 **Graupner** A., Auftrag und Geschick des Propheten Jeremia; literarische Eigenart, Herkunft und Intention der vordeuteronomistischen Prosa im Jeremiabuch [ev. Diss. Bonn, ᴰ*Schmidt* W.]: BTSt 15. Neuk 1991. 202 p. [ZAW 104,295, G. *Wanke*]. 3-7887-1364-X.

3247 *Herrmann* Siegfried, Der Beitrag des Jeremiabuches zur biblischen Theologie: → 163, ᶠWAGNER S., Gottesvolk 1991, 156-174.

3248 *Lundbom* Jack R., Jeremiah and the break-away from authority preaching: SvEx 56 (1991) 7-28.

3249 *McConville* J. Gordon, Jeremiah, prophet and book: TyndB 42 (1991) 80-95.

3250 *Mendecki* Norbert, Ezechielische Redaktion des Buches Jeremia?: BZ 35 (1991) 242-7.

3251 **Odashima** Taro, Heilsworte: BW 125, ᴰ1989 → 5,3616; 6,3884: ᴿCBQ 53 (1991) 114s (C. T. *Begg*).

3252 *Reynolds* Blair, CALVIN's exegesis of Jeremiah and Micah; use or abuse of Scripture?: ProcGLM 11 (1991) 81-91.

3253 **Seitz** Christopher R., Theology in conflict; reactions to the Exile in the book of Jeremiah: BZAW 176, ᴰ1989 → 5,1622; 6,3886: ᴿÉTRel 66 (1991) 276s (T. *Römer*); JBL 110 (1991) 513-5 (W. L. *Holladay*); NedTTs 45 (1991) 335-7 (B. *Becking*); RechSR 79 (1991) 276s (J. *Briend*); Syria 67 (1990) 756s (M. *Delcor*); TR 87 (1991) 189-192 (H. *Weippert*).

3254 *Stipp* Hermann-Josef, w'=hayā für nichtiterative Vergangenheit? Zu syntaktischen Modernisierungen im masoretischen Jeremiabuch: → 126, ᶠRICHTER W., Text 1991, 521-547.

3255 **Strobel** A., Geremia... LamBar; Cordoglio per Gerusalemme 1989
→ 5,3596: ᴿClaretianum 31 (1991) 374s (J. *Sánchez Bosch*).

3256 **Unterman** Jeremiah, From repentance to redemption; Jeremiah's
thought in transition 1987 → 3,3543 ... 6,3888: ᴿBZ 35 (1991) 121-3
(W. *Thiel*).

3257 **Wilcox** Brian K., Rejection of the word of Yahweh and judgment in the
book of Jeremiah: diss. Baptist Theol. Sem. ᴰ*Smith* B. K. New Orleans
1990. 165 p. 91-17899. – DissA 52 (1991s) 186-A.

3258 *Lundbom* Jack R., Rhetorical structures in Jeremiah I: ZAW 103 (1991)
193-210.

3259 **Cloete** Walter T. W., Versification and syntax in Jeremiah 2-25...:
SBL diss 117, 1989 → 5,3634; 6,3891: ᴿCBQ 53 (1991) 663s (J. A.
Lundbom).

3260 *Hardmeier* Christof, Die Redekomposition Jer 2-6; eine ultimative
Verwarnung Jerusalems im Kontext des Zidkijaaufstandes: WDienst 21
(1991) 11-42 [< ZIT 91,791].

3261 **Biddle** Mark E., A redaction history of Jeremiah 2:1-4: [diss. Zurich
1988, ᴰ*Schmid* H.] 1990 → 6,3890: ᴿJBL 110 (1991) 515-7 (J. R.
Lundbom); OTAbs 14 (1991) 120 (C. T. *Begg*: product of a complex
development all posterior to the person of Jeremiah); RelStR 17 (1991)
350 (M.A. *Sweeney*); TLZ 116 (1991) 104-6 (W. *Thiel*); ZAW 103 (1991)
148 (G. *Wanke*).

3262 *Wal* A.J.O. van der, Jeremiah II 31; a proposal: VT 41 (1991) 360-5:
'Such a generation you are; hear the word of the Lord'.

3263 *Hess* Richard S., Hiphil forms of QWR in Jeremiah VI 7: VT 41 (1991)
347-350.

3264 **O'Connor** Kathleen M., [Jer 11-20] Confessions of Jeremiah 1988
→ 4,3784 ... 6,3901: ᴿSWJT 34,1 (1991s) 70s (D. G. *Kent*).

3265 **Pohlmann** K.-F., Die Ferne Gottes... Konf. Jer: BZAW 179, 1989
→ 5,3647; 6,3902: ᴿRivB 39 (1991) 351-3 (A. *Bonora*).

3266 **Mottu** H., Geremia [11 ...] una protesta 1990 → 6,3900: ᴿRivB 39 (1991)
348-351 (B. *Marconcini*).

3267 *Hubmann* Franz D., Jeremia 13,1-11; Zweimal Euphrat retour oder wie
man einen Propheten fertigmacht; → 59, ᶠFÜGLISTER N. 1991, 103-126.

3268 *Gitay* Yehoshua, [Jer 14] Rhetorical criticism and the prophetic
discourse: → 86, ᶠKENNEDY G., Persuasive 1991, 13-24.

3269 *a) Metzger* Martin, 'Thron der Herrlichkeit', ein Beitrag zur Inter-
pretation von Jeremia 17,12f; – *b) Odashima* Taro, Zu einem verborgenen
'Weitblick' im Jeremiabuch — Beobachtungen zu Jer 4,3; – *c) Rofé*
Alexander, The name YHWH SEBA'OT and the shorter recension of
Jeremiah: → 75, ᶠHERRMANN S., Prophetie 1991, 237-262 / 270-289 /
307-316.

3270 *Gosse* Bernard, [Jer 23,7s; 31,31 ...] La nouvelle alliance et les promesses
d'avenir se référant à David dans les livres de Jérémie, Ézéchiel et Isaïe:
VT 41 (1991) 419-428.

3271 *Wessels* W. J., Jeremiah 24:1-10 as a pronouncement of hope: OTEssays
4 (1991) 397-407 [< ZAW 104,436].

3272 *Fischer* Georg, Jer 25 und die Fremdvölkersprüche; Unterschiede
zwischen hebräischem und griechischem Text: Biblica 72 (1991) 474-499;
franç. 499.

3273 *Smelik* Klaas A. D., Jeremia 26 als literarische Komposition: DielB 26 (1989s) 102-124.

3274 **Stipp** Hermann-Josef, Jeremia und die judäische Nobilität; Studien zur Textentwicklung von Jer 26,36-43 und 45 als Beitrag zur Geschichte Jeremias, seines Buches und der deuteronomistischen Bewegung: kath. Hab.-Diss. Tübingen 1991, ᴰ*Gross*. – TR 87 (1991) 513.

3275 *Dotan* Aron, ❻ Jer 29:17 [*šo'arim* not 'dirty' but 'at the gate']: ➤ 303, Teuda 7 (1991) 67-73, Eng. IXs.

3276 **Bozak** Barbara A., Life 'anew'; a literary-theological study of Jer. 30-31 [diss. Pont. Gregorian Univ., ᴰ*Conroy* C., Rome 1988 ➤ 4,3795]: AnBib 122. R 1991, Pont. Ist. Biblico. xviii-196 p. 88-7653-1223-X [BL 92,64, R. P. *Carroll*: excellent, surpasses BÖHMER and BRACKE].

3277 *Lohfink* Norbert, a) Der junge Jeremia als Propagandist und Poet; zum Grundstock von Jer 30-31 [< BtETL 54 (1981) 351-368]; – b) Die Gotteswortverschachtelung in Jer 30-31 [< ᶠ*Schreiner* J., Künder 1982, 105-119]: ➤ 224b, SBAufs 12 (1991) 87-105 / 107-123.

3278 *Zatelli* Ida, [Jer 31,15-17] The Rachel's lament in the Targum and other ancient Jewish interpretations: RivB 39 (1991) 477-490.

3279 *Schenker* Adrian, a) Die Tafel des Herzens; eine Studie über Anthropologie und Gnade im Denken des Propheten Jeremia im Zusammenhang mit Jer 31,31-34 [< Vierteljahresschrift für Heilpädagogik 48 (1979) 236-250]; – b) Unwiderrufliche Umkehr und neuer Bund; Vergleich zwischen der Wiederherstellung Israels in Dt 4,25-31; 30,1-14 und dem neuen Bund in Jer 31,31-34 [< FreibZ 27 (1980) 93-106]: ➤ 258, Text 1991, 68-81 / 83-96.

3279* *Rendtorff* Rolf, [Jer 31,31] Was ist neu am 'Neuen Bunde? [< Eng.; unveröffentlicht]: ➤ 252, Kanon 1991, 185-195.

3280 *Carrière* Jean-Marie, Une prière d'espérance; Jérémie 32,16-25: Masses Ouvrières 435 (1991) 49-63.

3281 *Bartelmus* Rüdiger, [Jer 32,33] *haškem wᵉ-lammed* — die 'Unermüdlichkeitsformel' und die Etymologie von *hiškîm*, oder 'Hat engagiertes Leben etwas mit dem Beladen von Kamelen zu tun?': ➤ 126, ᶠRICHTER W., Text 1991, 17-27.

3282 a) *Bogaert* Pierre-Maurice, Urtext, text court et relecture; Jérémie xxxiii 14-26 TM et ses préparations; – b) *Carroll* Robert P., Arguing about Jeremiah; recent studies and the nature of a prophetic book: ➤ 429, IOSOT 1989/91, 236-247 / 222-235.

3283 *Fortuna* Mariola, The ideal of nomadic life in Jeremiah 35 (the Rechabites): ➤ 314, Biblistyka 6 (1991) 5s. 255-316; Eng. 317s.

3284 **Hardmeier** Christof, Prophetie im Streit vor dem Untergang Judas; Erzählkommunikative Studien zur Entstehungssituation der Jesaja- und Jeremiaerzählungen in 2 Reg 18-20 und Jer 37-40: BZAW 187, 1990 ➤ 6,3916: ᴿBL (1991) 77 (R. E. *Clements*); JBL 110 (1991) 511-3 (C. R. *Seitz*: 'a certain clever appeal'); OLZ 86 (1991) 521-6 (H.-J. *Stoebe*); RechSR 79 (1991) 277-9 (J. *Briend*); RHPR 71 (1991) 319s (J.-G. *Heintz*).

3284* *Callaway* Mary C., Telling the truth and telling stories; an analysis of Jeremiah 37-38: UnSemQ 44 (1991) 253-266 [< ZIT 91,656].

3285 *Keown* Gerald L., Jeremiah 40:1-6, expository: RExp 88 (1991) 69-72.

3286 *Brueggemann* Walter, [Jer 42; 50 ... Dan 4] At the mercy of Babylon; a subversive rereading of the empire [SBL presidential address, New Orleans 17.XI.1990]: JBL 110 (1991) 3-22.

3287 *a) Bogaert* Pierre-Maurice, Les trois formes de Jérémie 52 (MT, LXX et VL); *b) Tov* Emmanuel, 4QJer^C (4Q72): → 17, ^FBARTHÉLEMY D., Tradition 1991, 1-17/249-276; pl. I-VII.

E8.8 Lamentationes, *Threni;* Baruch.

3288 *Krašovec* Jože, Self-accusation of Jerusalem in Lamentations: (Slovene): BogVest 50 (1990) 357-365; Eng. 364.

3289 **Mayoral López** Juan Antonio, Sufrimiento y esperanza en Lamentaciones: diss. Pont. Univ. Gregoriana, ^DConroy C., N° 6954 teol. – InfPUG 24,122 (1992) 28.

3290 **Provan** Iain W., Lamentations (RSV): New Century Bible Comm. L/GR 1991, Marshall Pickering / Eerdmans. xviii-142 p. $15 pa. -/0-8028-0547-7 [TDig 39,183].

3291 **Paulus** Beda, Pascasii RADBERTI Expositio in Lamentationes Hieremiae libri quinque: CCMed 85. Turnhout 1988, Brepols. XX-375 p. – ^RScriptorium 45 (1991) 140s (J.-P. *Bouhot*).

3292 **Westermann** Claus, Die Klagelieder 1990 → 6,3924: ^RTLZ 116 (1991) 110s (D. *Vieweger*); ZAW 103 (1991) 173 (H. *Wahl*).

3293 *Provan* Iain W., Past, present and future in Lamentations III 52-66; the case for a precative perfect re-examined: VT 41 (1991) 164-175.

3294 *Wolff* Christian, Irdisches und himmlisches Jerusalem; die Heilshoffnung in den Paralipomena Jeremiae: ZNW 82 (1991) 147-158.

3294* *Riaud* Jean, Paralipomena Jeremiae prophetae [deutsch, 1986]: FolOr 27 (1990) 25-41.

3295 *Martin* Raymond, The syntax criticism of Baruch: → 426, Septuagint 7, 1989/91, 361-371.

3296 **Willett** Tom W., Eschatology in the theodicies of 2 Baruch and 4 Ezra: JPseud supp 4, 1989 → 5,3677; 6,3930: ^RCBQ 53 (1991) 512s (R. D. *Chesnutt*); JBL 110 (1991) 343 (M. E. *Stone*).

3297 *Bohak* Gideon, Greek-Hebrew gematrias in 3 Baruch and in Revelation: JPseud 7 (1990) 119-121.

E8.9 Ezechiel: *textus, commentarii; themata, versiculi.*

3298 **Becker** J., *Fenz* A. Kurt, Ezechiele / Daniele [1971-4], ^T1989 → 5,3679: ^RAsprenas 38 (1991) 244 (V. *Scippa*).

3299 **Blenkinsopp** J., Ezekiel: Interpretation comm. 1990 → 6,3934: ^RBL (1991) 53s (P. W. *Joyce*).

3300 ^TEBorret Maurice, ORIGÈNE, Homélies sur Ézéchiel: SChr 352, 1989 → 5,3680; 6,3935: ^RHelmantica 42 sup (1991) 320 (María *Jiménez*); RHE 86 (1991) 351s (R. *Gryson*); RTPhil 123 (1991) 336s (E. *Junod*); TLZ 116 (1991) 518s (K. *Treu*).

3301 **Maarsingh** B., Ezechiël II [16-32]: PredikOT 1988 → 4,3832 ... 6,3939: ^RNedTTs 45 (1991) 67s (M. *Dijkstra*).

3302 ^TEMorel Charles, GRÉGOIRE le Grand, Homélies sur Ézéchiel II: SChr 360, 1990 → 6,3940: ^RRHE 86 (1991) 353 (R. *Gryson*: index confus).

3303 **Vawter** Bruce, *Hoppe* Leslie J., A new heart; a commentary on the book of Ezekiel: IntTC. GR/E 1991, Eerdmans/Handsel. xi-218 p. $16 [TR 87,337]. 0-8028-0331-8/. – ^RGraceTJ 12,1 (1991) 131-4 (R. *Patterson*:

evangelicals won't accept); HorBT 13 (1991) 181s (Margaret *Odell*, severe on Vawter).

3304 **Auffarth** Christoph, Der drohende Untergang; 'Schöpfung' in Mythos und Ritual im Alten Orient und in Griechenland am Beispiel der Odyssee und des Ezechielbuches: RelGVersV 39. B 1991 de Gruyter. xviii-655 p. 3-11-012640-0.

3305 **Bodi** Daniel, The book of Ezekiel and the poem of Erra [diss. Union (NY) 1987]: OBO 104. FrS/Gö 1991, Univ./VR 324 p. Fs 78. – RArTGran 54 (1991) 356s (J. L. *Sicre*); ExpTim 103 (1991s) 152 (R. P. *Carroll*: interesting but technical).

3306 **Davis** Ellen F., Swallowing ... Ezek D1989 ➤ 5,3692; 6,3943: RCBQ 53 (1991) 462s (R. W. *Klein*); JBL 110 (1991) 144-6 (D. J. *Block*); JTS 42 (1991) 169-172 (P. *Joyce*).

3307 **Fechter** Friedrich, Bewältigung der Katastrophe; Untersuchungen zu ausgewählten Fremdvölkersprüchen im Ezechielbuch: ev. Diss. Erlangen-N 1991, DWanke G. – TR 87 (1991) 517; RTLv 23, p. 539 ('18.VII.1992').

3308 **Hals** Ronald M., Ezekiel: FOTLit 19, 1989 ➤ 5,3693: RBL (1991) 76 (P. W. *Joyce*); CritRR 4 (1991) 140-2 (L. C. *Allen*); RelStR 17 (1991) 351 (D. J. *Block*).

3309 **Hamilton** Peter C., Theological implications of the divine title Adonai Yehovah in Ezekiel: diss. SW Baptist Theol. Sem. Fort Worth 1990. 222 p. 91-15303. – DissA 52 (1991s) 191-A.

3310 **Krüger** Thomas, Geschichtskonzepte im Ez: BZAW 180, D1989 ➤ 5, 3696; 6,3948: RBijdragen 52 (1991) 97s (P. C. *Beentjes*); BO 48 (1991) 893-5 (B. *Maarsingh*: wissenschaftlich ausgezeichnet); CBQ 53 (1991) 107s (W. E. *Lemke*: difficult reading); RechSR 79 (1991) 279s (J. *Briend*: Ébauches d'histoire); TLZ 116 (1991) 900-3 (M. *Köckert*).

3311 ELust J., Ezekiel 1985/6 ➤ 2,384 ... 5,3697: RColcT 61,1 (1991) 163-5 (W. *Chrostowski* ❷).

3312 *Pons* Jacques † 1989, Ezéchiel a-t-il été un prophète intercesseur?: ÉTRel 66 (1991) 17-21.

3313 **Rooker** M. F., Biblical Hebrew in transition; the language of the book of Ezekiel: JStOT supp. 90, D1990 ➤ 6,3950: RBL (1991) 155 (J.F.A. *Sawyer*); ETL 67 (1991) 424 (J. *Lust*); ÉTRel 66 (1991) 110 (Françoise *Smyth*); JJS 42 (1991) 124-6 (E. *Qimron*); ZAW 103 (1991) 308 (H. W. *Hoffmann*).

3314 **Setodzo** Frédéric Kokou, Conscience prophétique et critique sociale dans le Livre d'Ézéchiel: prot. diss. DHeintz J. Strasbourg 1991. 286 p. – RTLv 23, p. 540.

3315 *Daoust* J., Les exilés juifs 'au bord des fleuves de Babylonie' [*Tassin* Claude, *al.*, MondeB 71, 1991]: EsprVie 101 (1991) 644s.

3316 **Halperin** David, [Ezek 1] Faces of the chariot 1988 ➤ 4,3825; 6,3954: RJAOS 111 (1991) 130-3 (A. F. *Segal*); JQR 81 (1990s) 496-500 (E. R. *Wolfson*); RTPhil 123 (1991) 334 (J. *Borel*).

3317 *Barthélemy* Dominique, Trois problèmes posés par le texte massorétique de Éz 7,11*b* et 19,9: Text 15 (1990) 1-25.

3318 **Ohnesorge** Stefan, Jahwe gestaltet sein Volk neu; zur Sicht der Zukunft
Israels nach Ez 11,14-21; 20,1-44; 36,16-38; 37,1-14.15-28 [Diss. Würzburg
➤ 6,3959]: ForBi 64. Wü 1991, Echter. xii-457 p. DM 56 [TR 87,250].
3-429-01353-4. − RETL 67 (1991) 424-6 (J. *Lust*: 'continues H. SIMIAN'
1974, F. HOSSFELD 1977).

3319 *Chrostowski* Waldemar, ❷ The evolution of the meaning of the biblical
text; the Aramaic version of Ezek 16: ColcT 61,1 (1991) 63-79; Eng. 79s.

3320 **Galambush** Julia, [Ezek 16; 23] Jerusalem in the Book of Ezekiel; the city
as Yahweh's wife: diss. Emory, DHayes J. Atlanta 1991. 315 p. 91-27594.
− DissA 52 (1991s) 1372-A; RelStR 18,172; RTLv 23, p. 539.

3320* *Monari* Luciano, Ez 16 e le tradizioni di Israele: ➤ 292b, ParSpV 24
(1991) 31-42.

3321 *Zipor* Moshe A., Ezechiel 16,7: ZAW 103 (1991) 99s.

3322 *Kennedy* James M., Hebrew *pithon peh* in the book of Ezekiel [16,63;
29,21]: VT 41 (1991) 233-5.

3323 **Joyce** Paul, [Ezek 18,31; 36,26] Divine initiative and human response
in Ezekiel: JStOT supp 51, 1989 ➤ 5,3694; 6,3946: RBijdragen 52 (1991)
98s (P. C. *Beentjes*); ÉTRel 66 (1991) 109 (D. *Lys*: Ezek on individual
responsibility is neither innovative nor preeminent).

3324 **Sedlmeier** Franz, Studien zu ... Ezech 20: SBB 21, D1990 ➤ 6,3966:
RColcT 61,2 (1991) 181-5 (W. *Chrostowski*, ❷).

3325 *a) Greenberg* Moshe, Nebuchadnezzar and the parting of the ways;
Ezek 21:26-27; − *b) Liverani* Mario, The trade network of Tyre according to Ezek. 27; − *c) Elat* Moshe, Phoenician overland trade within
the Mesopotamian empires: ➤ 150, FTADMOR H., Ah, Assyria 1991,
267-272 / 65-79 / 21-35.

3326 *Block* Daniel I., Ezekiel's boiling cauldron; a form-critical solution to
Ezekiel XXIV 1-14: VT 41 (1991) 12-37.

3327 *Morla Asensio* Víctor, [Ez 24] Aspectos forenses de la terminología de la
colera en el AT [*ham, ap* ...]: ➤ 421, Luso-Esp 1989/91, 241-256.

3328 *Jeppesen* Knud, [Ezek 28,2.14] You are a cherub, but no God!:
ScandJOT 5,1 (1991) 83-94.

3329 *Bogaert* Pierre-Maurice, Le Chérub de Tyr (Ez 28,14.16) et l'hippocampe
de ses monnaies: ➤ 75, FHERRMANN S., Prophetie 1991, 29-38.

3330 **Mori** A., ❶ *Seisho no* − Concentric structure in the Bible (1) OT [Ezek
34,1-6]. Tokyo 1991, Yorudansha. 186 p. Y 2300 [BL 92,142, D. T.
Tsumura].

E9.1   **Apocalyptica VT.**

3331 **Cerutti** Maria Vittoria, Antropologia [iranica vista dai Greci] e
apocalittica [nel tardo giudaismo]: Storia delle Religioni 7. R 1990,
Bretschneider. 194 p. 88-7062-706-3.

3332 *a) Collins* John J., Genre, ideology and social movements in Jewish
apocalyticism; − *b) Boccaccini* Gabriele, Jewish apocalyptic tradition; the
contribution of Italian scholarship; − *c) Stone* Michael E., On reading an
apocalypse: ➤ 425, Mysteries 1989/91, 11-32 / 33-50 / 65-78.

3333 EHellholm David, Apocalypticism in the Mediterranean world and the
Near East 1979/²1989 ➤ 5,3723; 6,3977: RGregorianum 72 (1991) 369s
(D. *Cox*); JTS 42 (1991) 185-7 (C. C. *Rowland*, also on FMARTYN 1989);
RTLv 22 (1991) 246s (J. *Ponthot*).

3334 EKappler Claude, *al.*, Apocalypses et voyages dans l'au-delà 1987
➤ 3,3625; 4,3866: RBZ 35 (1991) 120s (J. *Maier*).

3335 **Marconcini** B., Apocalittica 1985 ➤ 3,3627; 6,3980: RHenoch 13 (1991) 376s (Liliana *Rosso Ubigli*).

3336 *Müller* Karlheinz, *a*) Die frühjudische Apokalyptik [< TRE 3 (1978) 202-251]; – *b*) Die Ansätze der Apokalyptik [< EMaier J., Lit. Rel. Früh-J. 1973, 31-42]: ➤ 241, Studien 1991, 35-193 / 19-33.

3337 *Pöhlmann* Wolfgang, Beobachtungen zur jüdisch-christlichen Apokalyptik und zur apokalyptischen Geschichtsdeutung im Dritten Reich: KerDo 37 (1991) 160-171.

3338 **Russell** David S., L'apocalittica giudaica (200 a. C. – 100 d. C.) [1964 ³1980]: BtTeol 23. Brescia 1991, Paideia. 549 p. Lit. 78.000. 88-394-0472-4.

3339 **Sacchi** Paolo, L'apocalittica giudaica e la sua storia: BtCuRel 55, 1990 ➤ 6,3984: RAntonianum 66 (1991) 158s (M. *Nobile*); Protestantesimo 46 (1991) 74 (J. A. *Soggin*).

E9.2 **Daniel:** *textus, commentarii; themata, versiculi.*

3340 *Ben-Shammai* Haggai, Fragments of Daniel al-QŪMISĪ's commentary on the book of Daniel as a historical source [< ❻Šalem 3 (1981) 295-307T]: Henoch 13 (1991) 259-274; text 275-8, translated (T. *Mann* c. 1920 revised) 278-281; ital. 281.

3341 **Ferguson** Sinclair B., Daniel: Communicator's comm. 19. Waco 1988, Word [publisher, as ➤ 5,3748, but not 'Themes' (nor 'Word Comm.')]. 252 p. 0-8499-0425-0.

3342 **Goldingay** J. E., Daniel: Word comm 30, 1989 ➤ 4,3880; 6,3990: RAndrUnS 29 (1991) 91-93 (G. *Pfandl*).

3342* **Phillips** John, *Vines* Jerry, Exploring the book of Daniel. Neptune NJ 1990, Loizeaux. 290 p. – RGraceTJ 12,1 (1991) 127-9 (J. I. *Lawlor*: the 'Exploring' series includes ten volumes by Phillips and two by Vines).

3343 **Russell** D. S., Daniel, an active volcano 1989 ➤ 5,3741: RInterpretation 45 (1991) 75s (A. J. *Everson*).

3344 **Wit** Hans de, Libro de Daniel, una relectura desde América Latina. Santiago de Chile 1990, Rehue. 248 p. – RIter 2 (1991) 152-4 (E. *Frades*).

3345 *Zier* M. A., The medieval Latin interpretation of Daniel; antecedents in ANDREW of St. Victor: RTAM 58 (1991) 43-78 [< RHE 86,294*].

3346 **Azzam** Jean, Daniel ou le déchiffrement d'une souffrance devenue excessive: diss. Pont. Ist. Biblico, DVanni U. R 1991. – AcPIB 9/8, 684 & 728s; RTLv 23, p. 537.

3347 *Davies* Philip R., [Dan 6 not focused] Daniel in the lions' den: ➤ 412, Images of empire 1990/1, 160-178.

3348 **Ferch** Arthur J., Daniel on solid ground [for Adventists, neither a commentary nor a homily...]. Wsh 1988, Review & Herald. 95 p. $10. – RAndrUnS 28 (1990) 258s (J. *Doukhan*).

3349 *Gese* Hartmut, *a*) Das Geschichtsbild des Danielbuches und Ägypten [< FBrunner H. 1983, 139-154]; – *b*) Die Bedeutung der Krise unter Antiochus IV. Epiphanes für die Apokalyptik des Danielbuches [< ZTK 80 (1983) 373-388]; – *c*) Die Weisheit, der Menschensohn und die Ursprünge der Christologie als konsequente Entfaltung der biblischen Theologie [< SvEx 44 (1979) 77-114]: ➤ 204, At. Studien 1991, 189-201 / 202-217 / 218-248.

3350 **Goldingay** J., Daniel: Word **themes** 1989 ⇥ 6,3997: ᴿBL (1991) 74 (P. R. *Davies*: nothing not in his comm. ⇥ 3342 supra).

3351 *Koch* Klaus, Weltgeschichte und Gottesreich im Danielbuch und die iranischen Parallelen: ⇥ 75, ᶠHERRMANN S., Prophetie 1991, 189-205.

3352 **Kratz** Reimbard G., Translatio imperii; Untersuchungen zu den aramäischen Danielerzählungen und ihrem theologiegeschichtlichen Umfeld [Diss. Zürich 1987, ᴰ*Steck* O.]: WM 63. Neuk 1991. xii-324 p. DM 96 [ZAW 104,297s, H. C. *Schmitt*]. 3-7887-1322-4.

3353 *Miller* James E., The redaction of Daniel: JStOT 52 (1991) 115-124.

3354 **Mills** Lawrence H., [† 1918] Avesta eschatology, compared with the books of Daniel and Revelations; being supplementary to Zarathushtra, PHILO, the Achaemenids and Israel. NY 1977 = 1908, AMS. vii-85 p. portr. 0-404-12816-5.

3355 *Müller* Karlheinz, *a)* Der Menschensohn im Danielzyklus [< ᶠ*Vögtle* A. Jesus 1975, 37-80]; – *b)* Menschensohn und Messias [< BZ 16 (1972) 161-187; 17 (1973) 52-66]: ⇥ 241, Studien 1991, 229-278 / 279-322.

3356 **Reid** Stephen B., Enoch and Daniel: BIBAL mg 2, ᴰ1989 ⇥ 6,4002: ᴿCBQ 53 (1991) 118s (G. W. *Buchanan*).

3357 *Vermes* Geza, JOSEPHUS' treatment of the Book of Daniel: JJS 42 (1991) 149-166.

3358 **Fewell** Danna N., Circle of sovereignty... Dan 1-6, 1988 ⇥ 4,3887 ... 6,4003 [not 'circles']: ᴿCBQ 53 (1991) 283s (M. S. *Moore*); CritRR 4 (1991) 131-3 (W. L. *Humphreys*); EvQ 63 (1991) 170s (R.W.L. *Moberly*); TLZ 116 (1991) 23s (K. *Koch*).

3359 **Wenthe** Dean O., The Old Greek translation of Daniel 1-6: diss. ᴰ*Ulrich* E. ND 1991. 286 p. 91-33244. – DissA 52 (1991s) 2172-A; RTLv 23, p. 541 (RelStR 18,174 'translations').

3360 *Gutwirth* E., Daniel 1/4 y las 'Ansiedades del Cortesano': ⇥ 421, Luso-Esp 1989/91, 639-648.

3361 *Steiner* Richard C., [Dan 2,12] Meaninglessness, meaningfulness, and super-meaningfulness in Scripture; an analysis of the controversy surrounding Dan 2:12 in the Middle Ages: JQR 82 (1991s) 431-449.

3362 *Rundgren* Frithiof, [Dan 2,14 *rab-ṭabbāḥayyā*]. A loan translation in Daniel; Old Syriac *daxša*: OrSuec 40 (1991) 220-225.

3363 *Margain* J., Le livre de Daniel [3-5]; commentaire philologique du texte araméen: LOrA 3 (1991) 163-182.

3364 *Avalos* Hector I., The comedic functions of the numerations of officials and instruments in Daniel 3: CBQ 53 (1991) 580-8.

3365 *Brottier* Laurence, 'Et la fournaise devint source'; l'épisode des trois jeunes gens dans la fournaise (Dan. 3) lu par Jean CHRYSOSTOME: RHPR 71 (1991) 309-327; Eng. 421.

3366 *D'Angela* Cosimo, Presunta scena dei tre giovani ebrei nella fornace su un frammento di sigillata africana da Canosa: ⇥ 52, ᶠFASOLA U., 1989, 177-183, 4 fig.

3367 *Wolters* Al, *a)* The riddle of the scales in Daniel 5: HUCA 62 (1991) 155-177; – *b)* Untying the king's knot; physiology and wordplay in Daniel 5: JBL 110 (1991) 117-122.

3368 *Brewer* David I., Mene mene teqel uparsin; Daniel 5,25 in cuneiform: TyndB 42 (1991) 310-6.

3369 *Willi-Plein* Ina, Daniel 6 und die persische Diaspora: ⇥ 78, ᶠHRUBY K., Judaica 47,1 (1991) 12-21.

3370 **Jeansonne** Sharon P., Old Greek Dan 7-12: 1988 → 4,3900 ... 6,4013: ᴿBS 148 (1991) 247s (R. A. *Taylor*).

3371 **Nuñez** Samuel, The vision of Daniel 8; interpretations from 1700 to 1900: ᴰ1989 → 6,4020: ᴿBL (1991) 89 (P. W. *Coxon*: dense footnotes like Rowley's).

3372 *Gese* Hartmut, [Dan 12,7] Die dreieinhalb Jahre des Danielbuches; → 87, ᶠKoch K., Ernten 1991, 399-421.

3373 *Raurell* Frederic, La 'doxa' del vident en Dn-LXX 12,13: RCatalT 16 (1991) 21-38; Eng 38.

E9.3   *Prophetae minores,* **Dōdekaprophētōn ... Hosea, Joel.**

3374 **Buske** Thomas, Der Christus absconditus in der Predigt der Kleinen Propheten; Studie zu Luthers alttestamentlicher Schriftauslegung. Neustadt/Aisch 1991, Schmidt. 158 p.; ill. DM 48,50 [TR 88,166].

3375 **Chisholm** Robert B.ᴶ, Interpreting the Minor Prophets. GR 1990, Zondervan. 308 p. + index. $15 pa. – ᴿGraceTJ 12,1 (1991) 122-6 (B. L. *Woodard*).

3376 **Gelston** A., The Peshiṭta of the Twelve Prophets 1987 → 3,3674 ... 6,4029: ᴿBS 148 (1991) 124s (R. A. *Taylor*).

3377 **House** P. R., Unity of the Twelve 1990 → 6,4030: ᴿÉTRel 66 (1991) 586s (D. *Lys*); Henoch 13 (1991) 373s (Ariella *Boffi*); JTS 42 (1991) 173-5 (R. *Mason*: lacks logic and academic rigour).

3378 **Nogalski** James, Redactional layers and intentions uniting the writings of the Book of the Twelve: ev. Diss. Zürich 1991, ᴰSteck. – TR 87 (1991) 515.

3379 *Puech* Émile, Les fragments non identifiés de 8 Kh[ever] XIIgr et le manuscrit grec des douze petits prophètes: RB 98 (1991) 161-9; 3 fig.

3380 **Tov** E., *al.*, Greek Minor Prophets scroll ... DJD 8, 1990 → 6,4033: ᴿBAR-W 17,2 (1991) 4s (H. *Shanks*); BZ 35 (1991) 276-8 (K. *Müller*); CdÉ 65 (1990) 244 (A. *Martin*); CurrTMiss 18 (1991) 52 (R. W. *Klein*); JSS 36 (1991) 158-161 (N. *Fernández Marcos*: Barthélemy confirmed); JTS 42 (1991) 175-7 (H.F.D. *Sparks* notes 7 occurrences of *kaige* not in the usual LXX).

3381 **Andeberhan** W. Tensae, Commentari etiopici sul libro del profeta Osea; edizione critica di mss. inediti, principi ermeneutici, temi teologici: diss. Pont. Univ. Gregoriana, ᴰConroy C. R 1991. 316 p. – RTLv 23, p. 537 [> DissA-C].

3382 **Beeby** H. D., Hosea, Grace abounding 1989 → 5,3786; 6,4035: ᴿCBQ 53 (1991) 659s (J. D. *Newsome*); GraceTJ 11 (1990) 100s (R. D. *Spender*); HorBT 12,2 (1990) 104s (D. *Mosser*).

3383 **Borbone** Pier Giorgio, Il libro del profeta Osea, edizione critica del testo ebraico ᴰ1990 → 6,4036: ᴿBLitEc 92 (1991) 282s (M. *Delcor*).

3384 **Daniels** Dwight R., Hosea and salvation history; the early traditions of Israel in the prophecy of Hosea [Diss. Hamburg 1987, ᴰKoch K.]: BZAW 191. B 1990, de Gruyter. [ix-] 148 p. 3-11-042143-3. – ᴿExpTim 102 (1990s) 276 (G. *Lloyd Jones*).

3385 **Doorly** William J., Prophet of love; understanding the Book of Hosea. NY 1991, Paulist. iv-138 p. $9. 0-8091-3241-9 [TDig 39,157].

3386 *Feuillet* André, Aux origines de la mystique nuptiale du Cantique des Cantiques; le prophète Osée: Divinitas 35 (1991) 107-113.

3387 **Light** Gary W., Theory-constitutive metaphor and its development in the book of Hosea: diss. Southern Baptist Theol. Sem., ᴰ*Watts* J. 1991. 234 p. 91-31509. – DissA 52 (1991s) 1775-A.

3388 **Naumann** Thomas, Hoseas Erben; Strukturen der Nachinterpretation im Buch Hosea [< Diss. Halle]: BW 131. Stu 1991, Kohlhammer. 198 p. DM 69 [TR 88,162]. 3-1701-1579-0.

3389 **Neef** Hans-Dieter, Die Heilstraditionen / Hosea 1987 → 3,3683 ... 6,4044: ᴿVT 41 (1991) 505s (G. I. *Davies*).

3391 **Ogilvie** Lloyd J., Hosea, Joel, Amos, Obadiah, Jonah: Communicator's comm. 20. Dallas 1990, Word Publisher. xiv-436 p. 0-8499-0426-9.

3392 *Pisano* Stephen, Egypt in the Septuagint text of Hosea [8 of the 13 occurrences systematically modified]: → 17, ᶠBARTHÉLEMY D., Tradition 1991, 301-8.

3393 *Pixley* Jorge, Hosea, ein neuer Lesungsvorschlag aus Mittelamerika [< RIBLa 1 (1988) 67-86], ᵀ*Kessler* R.: EvT 51 (1991) 60-81.

3394 **Stacey** W. D., Prophetic drama in the OT. L 1990, Epworth. x-310 p. £12.50. 0-7162-0470-3. – ᴿTsTNijm 31 (1991) 324 (A. van *Wieringen*).

3395 **Stuart** Douglas, Hosea-Jonah: Word **Themes** 1989 → 5,3795: ᴿCBQ 53 (1991) 310s (J. C. *Kesterson*); EvQ 63 (1991) 346s (J. G. *McConville*); GraceTJ 11 (1990) 103s (R. *Patterson*).

3396 **Yee** Gale A., Composition and tradition in Hosea 1987 → 3,3684 ... 6,4047: ᴿJQR 82 (1981s) 488-490 (F. I. *Andersen*).

3397 *Rallis* Irene K., [Hos 2] Nuptial imagery in the book of Hosea; Israel as the bride of Yahweh: StVlad 34 (1990) 197-219.

3398 **Nissinen** Martti, Prophetie, Redaktion und Fortschreibung im Lichte von Hosea 4 und 11 [Diss. Helsinki, ᴰ*Veijola*ᵀ]; AOAT 251. Kevelaer/ Neuk 1991, Buxton & B. / Neuk. V. XI-406 p. 3-7666-9744-7 / 3-7887-9744-7 [ZAW 104,453, O. *Kaiser*]; – ᴿUF 22 (1990!) 512 (O. *Loretz*).

3399 *Reventlow* Henning, Zeitgeschichtliche Exegese prophetischer Texte? Über die Grenzen eines methodischen Zuganges zum AT (am Beispiel von Hos 5,8-14): → 75, ᶠHERRMANN S., Prophetie 1991, 155-164.

3400 *Kuan* Jeffrey K., Hosea 9.13 and JOSEPHUS, Ant. IX, 277-287: PEQ 123 (1991) 103-8.

3401 *Ausín* Santiago, La tradición de Jacob en Oseas 12: EstB 49 (1991) 5-23; Eng. 5.

3402 *Whitt* William D., The Jacob traditions in Hosea and their relation to Genesis; ZAW 103 (1991) 18-43.

3402* *Gese* Hartmut, *a*) Jakob und Mose; Hosea 12:3-14 als einheitlicher Text [< ᶠ*Lebram* J. 1986, 38-47]; – *b*) Der auszulegende Text [< TüTQ 107 (1987) 252-265]; – *c*) Hermeneutische Grundsätze der Exegese biblischer Texte [< ᴱ*Gunneweg*, Standort 1985/6, 43-62]: → 204a, Altt. St. 1991, 84-93 / 266-282 / 249-265.

3403 *Fuller* Russell, A critical note on Hosea 12:10 and 13:4 [4QXII^C agrees with LXX against MT on 13,4]: RB 98 (1991) 341-357.

3404 *Vos* Geerhardus, [Hosea 14,8]. The wonderful tree: Kerux 6,2 (1991) 3-22.

3405 **Bergler** S., Joel als Schriftinterpret 1988 → 4,3938; 5,3815: ᴿBL (1991) 65s (R. E. *Clements*).

3406 **Boggio** Giovanni, Gioele – Baruc – Abdia – Aggeo – Zaccaria – Malachia; gli ultimi profeti: LoB 1.26. Brescia 1991, Queriniana. 133 p. Lit. 15.000. 88-399-1576-1.

3407 **Finley** Thomas J., Joel, Amos, Obadiah: Wycliffe Comm. Ch 1990, Moody. 417 p. $26. 0-8024-9262-2. – ᴿRExp 88 (1991) 460s (J.D.W. *Watts*).
3408 *Hastoupis* Athanasios, Ⓖ The book of Joel / Naum / Sophonias / Zacharias: TAth 62 (1991) 66-76 / 278-285 / 417-426 / 601-620; Eng. 929s.
3409 **Hubbard** D. A., Joel and Amos: Tyndale OT comm. Leicester 1989, Inter-Varsity. 245 p. – ᴿEvQ 63 (1991) 260-2 (H.G.M. *Williamson*); ScripB 21 (1991) 25s (W.G.E. *Watson*).
3410 **Meer** Willem van der, Oude woorden ... Joël ᴰ1989 → 5,3821; 6,4057: ᴿCBQ 53 (1991) 296s (W. A. *Vogels*); NedTTs 45 (1991) 140s (B. *Becking*).
3410* *Barbaglio* Giuseppe, La profezia di Gioele riletta in Atti: → 292*b*, ParSpV 24 (1991) 165-177.
3411 **Simkins** Ronald, Yahweh's activity in history and nature in the book of Joel [< diss. The day of the locusts, ᴰCross F., Chicago 1990 → 6, 4061]: ANE TSt 10. Lewiston ɴʏ 1991, Mellen. xii-322 p. 0-7734-9683-1 [OIAc 1,25].

E9.4 Amos.

3412 **Andersen** F. I., *Freedman* D. N., Amos 1989 → 5,3827; 6,4064: ᴿAndr-UnS 29 (1991) 76-78 (D. R. *Clark*); AsbTJ 46,2 (1991) 95-98 (D. L. *Thompson*); BTrans 42 (1991) 340s (H. P. *Scanlin*); Carthaginensia 7 (1991) 506 (R. *Sanz Valdivieso*); CBQ 53 (1991) 653-5 (H. *Gossai*); Claretianum 31 (1991) 364 (J. *Sánchez Bosch*); ÉTRel 66 (1991) 110s (D. *Lys*); Interpretation 45 (1991) 194s (J. D. *Newsome*); JBL 110 (1991) 517-9 (J. J. *Jackson*); NRT 113 (1991) 99s (J.-L. *Ska*); RechSR 79 (1991) 270s (J.-M. *Carrière*); TLZ 116 (1991) 20-22 (E. *Otto*); ZAW 103 (1991) 146 (G. *Wanke*).
3413 **Beyerlin** Walter, Reflexe der Amosvisionen im Jeremiabuch: OBO 93, 1989 → 5,3829: ᴿTLZ 116 (1991) 176-8 (W. *Thiel*).
3414 *Bulkeley* Tim, The long and the short of it: [ANDERSEN-FREEDMAN and HAYES on] Amos: JStOT 51 (1991) 119-121.
3415 *Dempster* Stephen, The Lord is his name; a study of the distribution of the names and titles of God in the book of Amos: RB 98 (1991) 170-189; franç, 170.
3416 **Doorly** William, Prophet of justice... Amos 1989 → 5,2832; $6: ᴿBL (1991) 72 (A. G. *Auld*: crystal clear); CBQ 53 (1991) 665 (C. *Bernas*); NewTR 4,3 (1991) 95 (M. *Trainor*).
3417 *Freedman* David N., Confrontations in the Book of Amos: PrincSemB 11 (1990) 240-252 [< ZIT 91,145].
3418 **Hasel** Gerhard F., Understanding the book of Amos; basic issues in current interpretations. GR 1991, Baker. 171 p. (bibliog. 46 p.). $11 pa. 0-8010-4353-0 [TDig 39,168].
3419 *Hasel* Gerhard F., The alleged 'No' of Amos and Amos' eschatology: AndrUnS 29 (1991) 3-18.
3420 **Hayes** J. H., Amos 1988 → 4,3954; 6,4068: ᴿBL (1991) 78 (B. P. *Robinson*); CBQ 53 (1991) 471s (Kathleen S. *Nash*); Vidyajyoti 55 (1991) 539-541 (P. M. *Meagher*, also on his Isa).
3421 **King** Philip J., Amos, Hosea, Micah — an archaeological commentary 1988 → 4,3956 ... 6,4071: ᴿRelStT 9,2s (1989) 81 (W. E. *Aufrecht*: superb).
3422 *Köckert* Matthias, Jahwe, Israel und das Land bei den Propheten Amos und Hosea: → 163, ᶠWAGNER S. 1991, 43-74.

3423 **Mowvley** Harry, The books of Amos and Hosea: Epworth (REB!) Commentaries. L 1991, Epworth). xix-168 p. £7.50. 0-7126-0475-4. – ᴿTsTNijm 31 (1991) 427 (A. *Schoors*).

3424 *Müller* Hans-Peter, Ein Paradigma zur Theorie der Alttestamentlichen Wissenschaft; Amos, seine Epigonen und Interpreten: → 125, ᶠRATSCHOW C., NSyst 33 (1991) 112-138; Eng. 138.

3425 **Paul** Shalom M., Amos, a commentary: Hermeneia, ᴱ*Cross* Frank M. Mp 1991, Fortress. xxvii-409 p. 0-8006-6023-4.

3426 *Pfeifer* Gerhard, *a*) Jahwe als Schöpfer der Welt und Herr ihrer Mächte in der Verkündigung des Propheten Amos: VT 41 (1991) 475-481; – *b*) Über den Unterschied zwischen Schriftstellern des zwanzigsten Jahrhunderts nach und des ersten Jahrtausends vor Christus, zur Entstehung des Amosbuches: VT 41 (1991) 123-7.

3427 **Polley** Max E., Amos and the Davidic empire; a socio-historical approach 1989 → 5,3841; 6,4073: ᴿCBQ 53 (1991) 682s (K.C. *Hanson*); JRel 70 (1990) 626s (R.B. *Coote*); ZAW 103 (1991) 167 (H.-C. *Schmitt*).

3428 **Rösel** H.N. ☉ Amos... 1990 'Ach'. 316 p. [ZAW 104,307].

3429 **Rosenbaum** Stanley N., Amos [government-official] of Israel, a new interpretation. Macon GA 1990, Mercer. xii-129 p. $25. – ᴿCritRR 4 (1991) 135s (M.E. *Bidlle*).

3430 **Schwantes** M., Das Land kann seine Worte nicht ertragen; Meditationen zu Amos [1987]ᵀ: Tb 105. Mü 1991, Kaiser. 186 p. DM 24 [ZAW 104,457, H.-C. *Schmitt*].

3431 *Smith* Gary V., Continuity and discontinuity in Amos' use of tradition: JEvTS 34 (1991) 33-42 [< ZAW 104,270].

3432 *Witaszek* Gabriel, ☉ Amos z Tekoa... prophet of the future: RuBi 44 (1991) 18-25.

3433 *Aerathedathu* Thomas, The social teaching of Amos [I–] II: Indian Journal of Spirituality 4,2 (1991) 149-...

3434 **Fleischer** Gunther, [Amos 2,6...] Von Menschenverkäufern... Amos: BoBB 74, ᴰ1989 → 5,3834: ᴿBiblica 72 (1991) 410-2 (P. *Bovati*); CritRR 4 (1991) 133-5 (M.E. *Biddle*); TR 87 (1991) 466-8 (R. *Kessler*); TüTQ 171 (1991) 66s (W. *Gross*).

3435 **Block** David M., Samuel TERRIEN's 'The elusive presence' [1978] as reflected in the Day of the Lord in Amos, Joel, and Zephaniah: diss. SW Baptist Theol. Sem. 1990. 234 p. 91-15300. – DissA 52 (1991s) 189-A.

3436 *Schmitt* John J., [Am 5,2; Jer 31,4] The virgin of Israel; referent and use of the phrase in Amos and Jeremiah: CBQ 53 (1991) 365-387: not Israel itself but the two capital cities, Samaria in Amos and Jerusalem in Jeremiah.

3437 *Kaimakis* Dimitris, [Amos 5,18...] ☉ The Lord's Day for the prophets of the OT: Epistemonike Epeteris Thessalonikis 29 (1988) 207-289 [< TAth 61 (1990) 527s, P. *Simotas*].

3438 *Baltzer* Klaus, Bild und Wort; Erwägungen zu der Vision des Amos in Am 7,7-9: → 126, ᶠRICHTER W., Text 1991, 11-16.

3439 **Hobbs** A.G.W., [Am 7,10-17; Is Mi] The communication of the prophetic message in pre-exilic Israel [PETERSEN D., WILSON R., social science techniques]: diss. Kent. Canterbury 1990. 434 p. BRDX-93732. – DissA 52 (1991s) 2174-A.

3440 *Jeremias* Jörg, Am 8,4-7 — ein Kommentar zu 2,6 f: → 126, ᶠRICHTER W., Text 1991, 205-220.

3441 *Olyan* Saul M., The oaths of Amos 8.14: ➤ 288, Priesthood 1991, 121-149.

E9.5 **Jonas.**

da **Silva** Celso P., *ḥamas*/Jonas ᴰ1991 ➤ 3451.
3442 **Golka** Friedemann W., Jona: Calwer BKomm. Stu 1991, Calwer. 108 p. [ZAW 104,295, H.C. *Schmitt*]. 3-7668-3115-7.
3443 *Ḥemiel* Ḥayyim Y., ✪ Judgment and mercy in the book of Jonah: BethM 36,127 (1990s) 323-334.
3444 *Jürgens* Anne, Warum erzählt der Verfasser des Jonabuches eine so übertriebene Geschichte von der Umkehr Ninives?: RUntHöh 34,1 (Dü 1991) 44-48 [< ZIT 91,252].
3445 **LaCocque** André, *Lacocque* Pierre E., Jonah 1990 ➤ 6,4096: ᴿJTS 42 (1991) 172s (Meg *Davies*); RelStR 17 (1991) 352 (W. Lee *Humphreys* spella only André 'LaCocque' but says they are father and son).
3446 *Mendes de Castro* J., Versão medieval do livro de Jonas: Didaskalia 19 (1989) 181-189.
3447 *Mulrooney* Joseph, The spiritual pilgrimage of Jonah: BToday 29 (1991) 163-8.
3448 **Potgieter** Johan H., 'n Narratologiese ondersoek van die boek Jona: HervTSt supp 3. Pretoria 1991, Nederduitsch Hervormde Kerk. 131 p. $20. 0-9583208-1-0.
3449 **Sasson** Jack M., Jonah: AnchorB 248, 1990 ➤ 6,4102: ᴿHorBT 13 (1991) 77s (M. E. *Biddle*).
3450 *a) Schwantes* Milton, Jonas — 'Os ninivitas creram em Deus'; – *b) Jesus* José P.T. de, Evangelização e resistência — uma leitura de Daniel 1; – *c) Bailão* Marcos P., Evangelizar é criar uma nova sociedade — a formação da nação Israel como anúncio do Reino de Deus; – *d) Tomita* Luiza E., A autoridade das mulheres na evangelização primitiva; – *e) Santin* Jandir, O evangelista-trabalhador; – *f) Nogueira* Paulo A. de S., Apocalíptico sim! alienado não: EstudosB 31 (1991) 27-34 / 35-46 / 18-26 / 47-58 / 59-70 / 71-78.
3451 **Silva** Celso P. da, Implicações do vocábulo *ḥāmās* na leitura do livro de Jonas: diss. Angelicum, ᴰ*Boschi* B. R 1991. 290 p. – RTLv 23,538.
3452 *a) Woodard* Branson L. [not Woodward as Contents and page-headings], The book of Jonah and biblical tragedy; – *b) Patterson* Richard, A literary look at Nahum, Habakkuk, and Zephaniah: GraceTJ 11 (1990) 3-16 / 17-27.
3453 *Barré* Michael L., Jonah 2,9 and the structure of Jonah's prayer: Biblica 72 (1991) 237-248.

E9.6 *Michaeas,* **Micah.**

3454 **Alfaro** Juan J., Justice and loyalty... Micah: IntTC, 1989 ➤ 5,3880; 6,4110: ᴿCBQ 53 (1991) 94s (A. J. *Petrotta*: especially valuable as making ALONSO-SICRE 1980 available); ExpTim 103 (1991s) 110 (C. S. *Rodd*: to avoid becoming quickly dated, Alfaro rarely brings out relevance to present-day situations, expressed with more passion by WOLFF now in English; Rodd praises also WIDYAPRANAWA and BEEBY though calling the series 'idiosyncratic'); RelStR 17 (1991) 352 (D. *Carr*).
3455 **Hagstrom** David G., The coherence of the book of Micah ᴰ1988 ➤ 4,4002; 6,4111: ᴿJQR 82 (1991s) 530s (Y. *Gitay*).

3456 *Hardmeier* Christof, Die Propheten Micha und Jesaja im Spiegel von Jeremia xxvi und 2 Regum xviii-xx; zur Prophetie-Rezeption in der nach-josijanischen Zeit: → 429, IOSOT 1989/91, 172-189.

3457 **Mason** Rex, Micah, Nahum, Obadiah: OTGuides. Sheffield 1991, JStOT for SOTS. 116 p. £6. 1-85075-702-X [BL 92,80, R. B. *Salters*].

3458 **Miller** Dane E., Micah and its literary environment; rhetorical critical case studies: diss. Arizona, D*Ackerman* S. 1991. 244 p. 91-23491. – DissA 52 (1991s) 955-A.

3459 **Otto** Eckart, Techniken der Rechtssatzredaktion israelitischer Rechtsbücher in der Redaktion des Prophetenbuches Micha: ScandJOT 5,2 (1991) 119-150.

3460 **Petrotta** Anthony J., Lexis ludens; wordplay and the Book of Micah [diss. Sheffield, D*Clines* D.]; AmerUnivSt 7/105. NY 1991, P. Lang. [xii-] 166 p. 0-8204-1539-1 [BL 92,145].

3461 **Renaud** Bernard, Michée – Sophonie – Nahum: Sources Bibliques 1987 → 3,3740... 6,4113: RRB 98 (1991) 143s (R. J. *Tournay*).

3462 **Schibler** Daniel, Le livre de Michée: CommÉv 11, 1989 → 5,3885; 6,4115: RNRT 113 (1991) 101 (J.-L. *Ska*).

3463 **Schuman** N. A., Micha: VBGed 1989 → 5,3886: RNedTTs 45 (1991) 245 (J. A. *Wagenaar*); TsTNijm 31 (1991) 192 (A. *Schoors*).

3464 **Stansell** Gary, Micah & Isaiah D1988 → 4,4010; 6,4118: RJQR 82 (1991s) 215-7 (Y. *Gitay*).

3465 **Wal** Adri van der, Micah... bibliography 1990 → 6,4121: RCBQ 53 (1991) 684s (A. J. *Petrotta* adds six peripheral items).

3466 **Wolff** H. W., Micah: Augsburg Continental Comm. 1990 → 6,4123: RInterpretation 45 (1991) 307s (D. G. *Hagstrom*).

3467 **Niccacci** Alviero, Un profeta tra oppressori e oppressi... Mi 2: SBF Anal 27, 1989 → 5,2889: RAntonianum 66 (1991) 155s (M. *Nobile*); BL (1991) 88 (W.G.E. *Watson*: superb).

E9.7 *Abdias, Sophonias*... **Obadiah, Zephaniah, Nahum.**

3468 *Clark* David J., Obadiah reconsidered: BTrans 42 (1991) 236-338.

3469 **Ben Zvi** Ehud, A historical-critical study of the Book of Zephaniah: BZAW 198. B D1991, de Gruyter. xii-390 p. 3-11-012837-3 [ZAW 104, 292, H. C. *Schmitt*].

3470 *Gorgulho* Gilberto, Zefanja und die historische Bedeutung der Armen [< RIBLa 3 (1989) 26-35], T*Reimer* H.: EvT 51 (1991) 81-92.

3471 **House** Paul R., Zephaniah, a prophetic drama 1988 → 4,4026... 6,4129: RHeythJ 32 (1991) 392s (J. *Eaton*); VT 41 (1991) 248s (R. P. *Gordon*).

3472 **Spreafico** Ambrogio, Sofonia: CommStoEseg AT 38. Genova 1991, Marietti. 256 p. 88-211-8041-7.

3473 *Sweeney* Marvin A., A form-critical reassessment of the Book of Zephaniah: CBQ 53 (1991) 388-408.

3474 **Weigl** Michael P., Option für die Armen; eine Untersuchung zur Theologie des Buches Zefanja: kath. Diss. Wien 1991, D*Braulik* G. – TR 87 (1991) 514, RTLv 23, p. 540.

3475 **Bonora** Antonio, Nahum Sof Abacuc Lam: LoB 1.25, 1989 → 5,3910; 6,4134: RSalesianum 53 (1991) 766 (M. *Cimosa*: '1984').

3476 **Clark** David J., *Hatton* Edward A., A translator's handbook on the books of Nahum, Habakkuk, and Zephaniah 1989 → 5,3912; 6,4136: RCBQ 53 (1991) 662s (M. A. *Sweeney*).

3477 **Roberts** Jimmy Jack McBee, Nahum, Habakkuk, and Zephaniah; a commentary. Louisville 1991, W-Knox. 223 p. $20. 0-664-21937-3 [TDig 39,185].

3478 **Robertson** O. Palmer, Books of Nahum Habakkuk Zephaniah: NICOT 1990 → 6,4138: RAndrUnS 29 (1991) 185-7 (G. F. *Hasel*); STEv 3 (1991) 130s (G. *Emetti*).

3479 *Williams* D. T., The acrostic of Nahum [1,2-8]; call of the prophet: OTEssays 4 (1991) 248-256 [< ZAW 104,436].

E9.8   *Habacuc,* **Habakkuk.**

3480 **Balancin** Euclides M., *Storniolo* Ivo, Como ler o livro de Habacuc. São Paulo 1991, Paulinas. 48 p. [REB 51,1020].

3481 **Barsotti** Divo, Meditazione su Abacuc: Bibbia e Liturgia 35. Brescia 1991, Queriniana. 61 p. 88-399-1635-0.

3482 **Feltes** Heinz, Die Gattung des Habakukkommentar von Qumran (1QpHab), eine Studie zum frühen jüdischen Midrasch [Diss. Bochum 1984]: ForBi 58, 1986 → 2,8137 ... 5,a15: RPhil 66 (1991) 243 (H. *Engel*).

3483 **Haak** R. D., Habakkuk [Diss. Ch 1986, DAhlström G.]: VTSup 44, Leiden 1991, Brill. VIII-180 p. *f* 100 [ZAW 104,447, Ulrike *Schorn*].

3484 *Sweeney* Marvin A., Structure, genre, and intent of the book of Habakkuk: VT 41 (1991) 63-83.

3485 *Tsumura* David T., Ugaritic poetry and Habakkuk: TyndB 40,1 (1989) 24-48.

3486 *Floyd* Michael H., Prophetic complaints about the fulfillment of oracles in Habakkuk 1:2-17 and Jeremiah 15:10-18: JBL 110 (1991) 397-418.

E9.9   *Aggaeus,* **Haggai** – *Zacharias,* **Zechariah** – *Malachias,* **Malachi.**

3487 **Bauer** Lutz, Das Haggai-Sacharja-Maleachi-Korpus und Aspekte seiner ökonomischen Theorie: Diss. Bethel, DCrüsemann F. Bielefeld 1991. 364 p. – RTLv 23, p. 537.

3488 *Hastoupis* Athanasios P., ⊙ The book of Haggai: TAth 61 (1990) 553-565; Eng. 906.

3489 **Meyers** C. & E., Haggai, Zechariah 1-8: AnchorB 25 B, 1987 → 3,3781 ... 6,4145: RVT 41 (1991) 500s (J. A. *Emerton*).

3490 *Petersen* David L., The Temple in Persian period prophetic texts: BibTB 21 (1991) 88-96.

3491 *a) Petersen* David L., The Temple in Persian period prophetic texts; – *b) Carroll* Robert P., Textual strategies and ideology in the Second Temple period: – *c)* responses, *Bedford* Peter R., *Horsley* Richard A., *Jobling* David: → 427, Second Temple I (1991) 125-144 / 108-124 / 154-163-175-182.

3492 *Unger* Tim, Noch einmal; Haggais unreines Volk [2,15-19]: ZAW 103 (1991) 210-225.

3492* *Kline* Meredith G., *a)* The structure of the Book of Zechariah: JEvTS 34 (1991) 179-194 [< ZIT 91,563]. – *b)* [Zech 1,13-17] How long?: Kerux [6,1 (1991) 16-31] 6,2 (1991) 23-42.

3493 *VanderKam* James C., Joshua the high priest and the interpretation of Zechariah 3: CBQ 53 (1991) 553-570.

3494 *Freund* Joseph, ❺ [Zech 9,7] 'As *allup* in Judah, and Eqron as Jebusite': BethM 36,127 (1990s) 335-342.

3495 *Raurell* F., *a*) Els LXX com a mediacío teológica per al Nou Testament (Za xi i xii); – *b*) Dinamisme interpretatiu a l'interior dels textos bíblics; tensió entre diversitat i unitat: ⇥ 5,594, Paraula 1985/9, 32-39 / 7-31 [< OTAbs 14,334].

3496 **Witt** Douglas A., Zechariah 12-14; its origins, growth and theological significance: diss. Vanderbilt, ᴰ*Harrelson* W. Nv 1991. 194 p. 91-25325. – DissA 52 (1991s) 956-A; RelStR 18,173.

3497 **Hugenberger** Gordon P., Marriage as a covenant; a study of biblical law and ethics governing marriage developed from the perspective of Malachi: diss. British Awards Council 1991. 468 p. BRDX-95350. – DissA 52 (1991s) 4366-A.

3498 *Meinhold* Arndt, Zustand und Zukunft des Gottesvolkes im Maleachibuch: ⇥ 163, ꟳ*Wagner* S., Gottesvolk 1991, 175-192.

3499 **O'Brien** Julia M., Priest and Levite in Malachi [four current theses rejected]. Atlanta 1990, Scholars. xiv-164 p. $23; pa./sb. $15. 1-55540-438-3; –9-1 [TDig 38,371].

3500 *Fuller* Russell, Text-critical problems in Malachi 2:10-16: JBL 110 (1991) 47-57 (phot. from 4QXiiᵃ).

3501 *Homerski* Józef, [Mal 2,17...] ❺ Der Tag des Herrn beim Propheten Maleachi: RoczTK 34,1 (1991 für 1987) 13-24; deutsch 25.

3502 *Jones* David C., Malachi on divorce: Presbyterion 15 (St. Louis 1989) 16-22 [< OTAbs 14,320].

IX. NT Exegesis generalis

F1.1 **New Testament Introduction.**

3503 ᴱ**Baarlink** H., Inleiding tot het NT 1989 ⇥ 6,4165: ᴿNedTTs 45 (1991) 148s (M. de *Jonge*).

3504 **Baldermann** I., Der Himmel ist offen; Jesus aus Nazareth, eine Hoffnung für heute. Mü/Neuk 1991, Kösel. 229 p. DM 26,80. 3-466-36194-X / 3-7887-1387-9 [NTAbs 36,261].

3505 **Barrett** C.K., Texte zur Umwelt des NTs² [1987], ᵀ*Thornton* Claus-Jürgen: Uni-Tb 1591. Tü 1991, Mohr. XXXIV-413 p. DM 40. 3-16-145619-X [NTAbs 36,288].

3505* *a*) *Ben Ami* Shlomo, Palestina en el primer siglo de la era común; – *b*) *Puente Ojea* Gonzalo, La evolución ideológica dentro del Nuevo Testamento; – *c*) *Shavit* Yaakob, ¿Ex Qumran lux? Notas históricas y literarias sobre los manuscritos del mar Muerto y los orígenes del cristianismo: ⇥ 453, Orígenes 1989/91, 15-34 / 325-337 / 135-174.

3506 **Berger** Klaus, Hermeneutik des NTs 1988 ⇥ 4,4076; 5,3954: ᴿTRu 56 (1991) 306-313 (H. *Weder*: kritisch?).

3507 **Berger** Klaus, Historische Psychologie des Neuen Testaments: SBS 146s. Stu 1991, KBW. 303 p. 3-460-04461-6.

3508 *a*) *Bovon* François, L'éthique des premiers chrétiens, entre la mémoire et l'oubli; – *b*) *Weder* Hans, Le souvenir évangélique; réflexions néotestamentaires sur la présence du passé; – *c*) *Légasse* Simon, 'Scribes et pharisiens'; de l'anamnèse à Jésus; – d) *Marguerat* Daniel, Jésus et la Loi dans la mémoire des premiers chrétiens: ➤ 30, ᶠBONNARD P., La mémoire et le temps 1991, 17-30 / 31-46 / 47-53 / 55-74.

3509 *Chance* J. Bradley, Fiction in ancient biography; an approach to a sensitive issue in Gospel interpretation: PerspRelSt 18 (1991) 125-142.

3510 **Chiarazzo** Rosario, Introduzione al Nuovo Testamento: Manuali di Base 3. CasM 1991, Piemme. 208 p. Lit. 15.000. 88-384-1703-2.

3511 The complete biblical library [apparently only NT; no data on authors or sources]. Springfield MO c. 1990, World Library Press. 16 volumes, $30 each [BAR-W 17/6,43 adv].

3512 **Court** J. M. & K. M., The New Testament world 1990 ➤ 6,4175: ᴿBA 54 (1991) 117s (W. *Willis* compares with ᴱFERGUSON 1987); ÉTRel 66 (1991) 127s (E. *Cuvillier*: 'John-Kathleen'); NRT 113 (1991) 752 (X. *Jacques*: introduction, not geography); TLond 94 (1991) 146s (J.L. *North*, W.E. *Sproston*).

3513 **Culbertson** Philip L., What is left to believe in Jesus after the scholars have done with him?: JEcuSt 28,1 (Ph 1991) 1-17 [< ZIT 92,407].

3514 **Davids** P. H., More hard sayings of the NT [72, after *Bruce* F. 1983 Jesus and *Brauch* M. 1989 Paul]. DG 1991, InterVarsity. 312 p. $11. 0-8308-1747-6 [NTAbs 36,252].

Delorme Jean, Au risque de la Parole; lire les Évangiles 1991 ➤ 195.

3516 ᴱ**Doré** Joseph, Sur l'identité chrétienne 1990 ➤ 6,404: ᴿEsprVie 101 (1991) 44, répétée 137 (P. *Daubercies*).

3517 **Ebeling** Gerhard, Evangelische Evangelienauslegung; eine Untersuchung zu LUTHERS Hermeneutik³ʳᵉᵛ [¹1942, ²1962]. Tü 1991, Mohr. viii-560 p. 3-16-145665-3.

3518 **Epp** E., *MacRae* G., NT and its modern interpreters 1989 ➤ 5,394; 6,4180: ᴿInterpretation 45 (1991) 80 (D. L. *Barr*).

3519 **Fausti** Silvano, Ricorda e racconta il Vangelo. Mi 1990, Àncora. 560 p. Lit. 45.000. – ᴿCiVit 46 (1991) 216 (Duccia *Camiciotti*); Vidyajyoti 55 (1991) 534s (P. M. *Meagher*, also on R. E. BROWN's 101 QQ).

3520 **Ferguson** E., Backgrounds of early Christianity 1987 ➤ 3,3817... 6,4181: ᴿRelStT 10,2 (1990) 101s (B. *Przybylski*).

3521 **[Fernández] Ramos** Felipe, El Nuevo Testamento I-II, 1988s ➤ 6,4182: ᴿCiTom 118 (1991) 187 (J. *Huarte*); EfMex 9 (1991) 123s (J. A. *Díaz Pérez*); RTLim 25 (1991) 493s (M. *Díaz Mateos*); SFulg 1 (1991s) 166s (J. M. *García*).

3522 **Freed** Edwin D., The NT, a critical introduction² [¹c. 1985]. Belmont CA 1991, Wadsworth. xvii-462 p.; ill. 0-534-13872-1 [NTAbs 35 (1991) 93].

3523 **Freyne** Sean, The world of the New Testament: NTMessage 2. Dublin 1988, Veritas [= 1980, Glazier]. xxi-199 p.; maps. 0-89453-123-9.

3524 *Gill* A., Contemporary study of the Gospels, I. Theological analysis: StMark's Review 147 (Canberra 1991) 11-20 [< NTAbs 36,322].

3525 **Goodenough** [Erwin R.] on the beginnings of Christianity [11 art. 1925-68 (+) Paul and the Hellenization of Christianity], ᴱ*Kraabel* A. T.: BrownJudSt 212. Atlanta 1990, Scholars. xxv-187 p. $55; sb. $35. 1-55540-403-7 [TDig 39,165].

3525* **Grant** Patrick, Reading the NT 1989 ➤ 5,3966; 6,4185: ᴿCritRR 4 (1991) 193-5 (D. L. *Barr*: provocative and literary); NBlackf 71 (1990) 254s (R. *Finn*).

3526 **Grelot** P. (*Dumais* M.), Homélies sur l'Écriture à l'époque apostolique² Intr.NT 8, 1989 ➤ 5,g657; 6,k27 [avec Pères Apostoliques, mais surtout Cor Rom Heb]: ᴿCBQ 53 (1991) 702s (J. G. *Lodge*).

Grelot Pierre, Introduction à la Bible, (Liturgie), NT 9 1991 ➤ 8207.

3526* **Guthrie** D., NT introduction⁴ 1990 ➤ 6,4187*: ᴿTLZ 116 (1991) 596s (J. *Roloff*).

3527 *Heiligenthal* Roman, Erforschung des NTs; Tendenzen und Entwicklungen in den letzten Jahren: DtPfarrbl 91 (1991) 309-311 [< TLZ 117,437].

3528 *Holtz* Traugott, Jesus-Überlieferung und Briefliteratur; zur Frage des Ortes der Jesus-Überlieferung in der frühen Gemeinde [< WZHalle 34,1 (1985) 103-112]: ➤ 211, Geschichte 1991, 17-30.

3529 **Horsley** G.H.R., New documents 5 (essays), 1989 ➤ 5,401: ᴿRB 98 (1991) 607-615 (J. *Taylor*).

3531 **Horst** P. W. van der, *Mussies* G., Studies in the Hellenistic background of the NT 1990 ➤ 6,4191: ᴿSecC 8 (1991) 125-7 (J. N. *Bailey*).

3532 **Jantsch** Johanna, Die Entstehung des Christentums bei A. von HARNACK und E. MEYER ᴰ1990 ➤ 6,4192: ᴿRHE 86 (1991) 190 (A. de *Halleux*); TLZ 116 (1991) 921-3 (G. *Wendelborn*).

3533 *Kea* Perry V., Dan VIA as NT critic in the existentialist mode: Persp-RelSt 18 (1991) 249 ...

3534 **Kemmer** Alfons, Das NT, Einführung für Laien² [¹1976]: Tb 1728, 1990 ➤ 6,4196 (³): ᴿRuBi 44 (1991) 79 (S. *Pisarek*).

ᴱ**Kertelge** K., Metaphorik und Mythos im NT: QDisp 126, 1989/90 ➤ 4049.

3535 **Köster** H., Introducción al NT 1988 ➤ 5,3977; 6,4198: ᴿEfMex 9 (1991) 132-5 (R. *López*).

3536 **Koester** H. [1960], *Bovon* F., Genèse de l'écriture [= littérature] chrétienne: Memoires premières. Turnhout 1991, Brépols. 138 p. [ÉTRel 67, 112, E. *Cuvillier*]. – ᴿÉtudes 348 (1991) 137 (J.-N. *Aletti*).

3537 *Lagarde* Claude, Pour raconter l'évangile dans l'homélie et la catéchèse. P 1991, Centurion. 194 p. F 120. – ᴿÉtudes 375 (1991) 282 (R. *Marlé*).

3538 *Leonardi* Giovanni, Le prime comunità cristiane e i loro scritti. R 1988, Paoline. 239 p. – ᴿTeresianum 42 (1991) 355s (V. *Pasquetto*).

3539 [*Léthel* F.-M., présent.], L'Évangile de Jésus... Venasque 1990 ➤ 6,542: ᴿAngelicum 68 (1991) 579s (S. *Jurić*).

3540 *a) Levison* John R., Did the Spirit inspire rhetoric? An exploration of George KENNEDY's definition of early Christian rhetoric; – *b) Robbins* Vernon K., Writing as a rhetorical act in PLUTARCH and the Gospels; – *c) Vinson* Richard B., A comparative study of the use of enthymemes in the Synoptic Gospels; – *d) Pogoloff* Stephen M., ISOCRATES and contemporary hermeneutics: ➤ 86, ᶠKENNEDY G., Persuasive 1990, 25-40 / 142-168 / 119-141 / 338-362.

3541 **Lohse** Eduard, Die Entstehung des Neuen Testaments⁵ʳᵉᵛ [¹1972]: Theologische Wissenschaft 4. Stu 1991, Kohlhammer. 159 p. 3-17-011355-0.

3542 **McConnell** D. R., A different Gospel; a historical and biblical analysis of the modern faith movement. Peabody MA 1991 = 1988, Hendrickson. xix-195 p. 0-913573-78-7.

3543 ᴱ**Martin** Francis, Narrative parallels to the NT 1988 ➤ 6,4207: ᴿCBQ 53 (1991) 500 (R. I. *Pervo*: 555 parallels; 50 OT, 173 rabbinic, 293 Hellenistic).

3544 **Meyer** Ben F., Critical realism and the NT 1989 ➤ 5,319: ᴿJTS 42 (1991) 267-270 (E. *McKnight*); TorJT 7 (1991) 100s (M. *Vertin*: 'good will comes first but suspicion has its uses').

3545 **Neill** S., ²*Wright* T., The interpretation of the NT 1861-1986: 1988 ➤ 4,4103 ... 6,4212: ᴿAnStoEseg 8 (1991) 712-4 (M. *Pesce*); ScripB 21 (1991) 20s (M. *McNamara*).

3546 **Penna** Romano, Letture ... Saggi esegetici sui quattro Vangeli 1989 ➤ 5,3992; 6,4216: ᴿBenedictina 38 (1991) 223-6 (P. M. *Pierini*: ricco, un po' stenografico).

3547 **Perkins** Pheme, Reading the NT² 1988 ➤ 4,4104; 6,4217: ᴿRelStT 10,2 (1990) 81-83 (Mary Ann *Beavis* compares HARRIS S.).

3548 *Perrone* Lorenzo, Le Quaestiones evangelicae di EUSEBIO di Cesarea; alle origini di un genere letterario: ➤ 419, AnStoEseg 7,2 (1989/90) 417-435.

3548* **Pilch** John J., Introducing the cultural context of the [Old ➤ 947] New Testament: Hear the Word! 2. NY 1991, Paulist. xiv-254 p. 0-8091-3272-9.

3549 *a) Piñero* Antonio, El marco religioso del cristianismo primitivo; I.; – *b) Montserrat Torrents* José, II.: ➤ 453, Orígenes 1989/91, 37-66 / 67-80.

3549* **Ralph** Margaret N., Discovering the first century Church [I. Gospels c. 1990; II.] The Acts of the Apostles, Letters of Paul and the Book of Revelation: Discovering the Living Word 2. NY 1991, Paulist. vii-329 p.; 9 maps. $13. 0-8091-3254-0 [NTAbs (35,245) 36,278].

3550 **Rebell** W., Zum neuen Leben gerufen; kommunikative Gemeindepraxis im frühen Christentum [Mk: family of God; Mt: brothers and sisters; Lk: place for social justice; also Jn Paul...]: Tb 88. Mü 1990, Kaiser. 223 p. DM 19,80. 3-459-01869-0. – ᴿTsTNijm 31 (1991) 326 (A. van *Schaik*).

3551 *Roloff* Jürgen, Neutestamentliche Einleitungswissenschaft; Tendenzen und Entwicklungen: TRu 55 (1990) 385-423.

3552 **Russell** D. S., Poles apart; the Gospel in creative tension 1990 ➤ 6,4221: ᴿExpTim 103 (1991s) 60 (R. *Lunt*: good).

3553 *Sanders* E. P., Jesus, his religious 'type': Reflections (NHv 1992) 4-12 [< NTAbs 36,326].

3554 **Schierse** Franz J., Introduzione al NT 1987 ➤ 3,3849; 6,4224: ᴿTeresianum 42 (1991) 356s (V. *Pasquetto*).

3555 **Schneiders** Sandra M., The revelatory text; interpreting the NT as Sacred Scripture. SF 1991, Harper. xvi-206 p. 0-06-067097-5 [TDig 39,285].

3555* ᵀᴱ**Schröder** Heinrich O., P. Aelius ARISTIDES, Heilige Berichte: Wiss-KommGrLS. Heid 1986, Winter. 150 p. 3-533-03698-7; pa. –7-9.

3556 **Schweizer** Eduard, Theologische Einleitung in das NT: NTD Egb 2, 1988 ➤ 5,3997; 6,4225: ᴿBLtg 63 (1990) 250 (F. *Kogler*); TR 87 (1991) 375-7 (O. B. *Knoch*).

3557 ᴱ**Sevrin** J.-M., NT ... Réception: BtETL 86, 1986/9 ➤ 5,606; 6,4227: ᴿJTS 42 (1991) 693-5 (Frances M. *Young*).

3559 **Stein** Robert H., Difficult passages in the NT [= 1988 + 1985 + 1988]. GR 1990, Baker. 392 p. – ᴿGrace TJ 11 (1990) 109s (D. R. *Rickards*).

3560 **Weil** Simone, Intimations of Christianity among the ancient Greeks [< Source 1952 + Intimations 1951],ᵀ. L 1987 = 1957, Ark paperbacks. vii-208 p. 0-7448-0059-5.

3560* *Young* Norman, Word and Church in the NT: OneInC 25 (1989) 311-322.

F1.2 *Origo Evangeliorum,* **the Origin of the Gospels.**

3561 **Baird** J. A., A comparative analysis of the Gospel genre; the Synoptic mode and its uniqueness: StBeC 24. Lewiston NY 1991, Mellen. iv-166 p. $60. 0-7734-9460-X [NTAbs 36,418].

3562 *Barnette* Henlee H., *al.,* The glorious Gospel: SWJT 34,3 (1991s) 4-7 (-32).

3563 *Brownson* J. V., What is 'the Gospel'?: RefR 45,2 (1991) 85-106 [< NTAbs 36,382].

3564 ᴱCeresa-Gastaldo A., Storia e preistoria dei Vangeli 1988 ➤ 5,572: ᴿLatomus 50 (1991) 475-7 (J. Gijsel).

3565 Collin Matthieu, Pourquoi Jésus n'a-t-il rien écrit?: Notre Histoire 72 (nov. 1990) [EsprVie 101 (1991) 246s (J. Daoust)].

3566 Frankemölle Hubert, Evangelium; Begriff und Gattung 1988 ➤ 4,4125; 6,4241: ᴿTR 87 (1991) 377s (I. Broer).

3567 Grelot P., L'origine dei Vangeli, controversia con J. CARMIGNAC 1989 ➤ 6,4245: ᴿAngelicum 68 (1991) 576s (S. Jurić); Divinitas 35 (1991) 195 (T. Stramare).

3568 Hultgren A.J., The Gospel and the Gospel traditions in early Christianity: WWorld 11,1 (1991) 23-28 [< NTAbs 35,194].

3569 Kealy Seán P., Gospel studies since 1970 (2): IrTQ 57 (1991) 93-104.

3570 Koester Helmut, Ancient Christian gospels [... (pre-)NT] 1990 ➤ 6,4246: ᴿExpTim 102 (1990s) 315 (W.G. Morrice); Salmanticensis 38 (1991) 241-3 (R. Trevijano); TsTNijm 31 (1991) 326s (B. Dehandschutter).

3571 Merkel Helmut, La pluralità dei Vangeli [... Padri dei primi quattro secoli], ᵀᴱToso Giovanni. T 1990, SEI. xxxii-182 p. Lit. 35.000. – ᴿCC 142 (1991,3) 449s (A. Ferrua).

3572 O'Grady John F., The four Gospels and the Jesus tradition 1989 ➤ 5,4015; 6,4247: ᴿCarthaginensia 7 (1991) 514s (R. Sanz Valdivieso).

Pikaza X., El evangelio 1990 ➤ 3921.

3574 Powell J. Enoch, The genesis of the Gospel: JStNT 42 (1991) 5-16.

3575 Stanton Graham N., The Gospels and Jesus: [10-vol.] Oxford Bible Series, 1989 ➤ 5,4016; 6,4252: ᴿAndrUnS 29 (1991) 187s (H. Weiss); CBQ 53 (1991) 508s (P. Zilonka).

3576 ᴱStuhlmacher Peter, The Gospel and the gospels [1982 Tübingen symposium 1983 ➤ 64,428], ᵀ. GR 1991, Eerdmans. xxviii-412 p. $35. 0-8028-3688-7 [TDig 39,63].

F1.3 Historicitas, chronologia Evangeliorum.

3577 [Funk R.], The Jesus seminar; voting records [1544: 1985-91] sorted by gospel, chapter, and verse; Forum FF 6,1 (1990) 3-55 [< NTAbs 36,167].

3578 Grelot P., Las palabras de Jesucristo 1988 ➤ 4,4140... 6,4260: ᴿScripTPamp 23 (1991) 709 (J. M. Casciaro).

3579 Kee Howard C., What can we know about Jesus?: [also ed.] Understanding Jesus today, 1990 ➤ 6,4262*: ᴿNBlackf 72 (1991) 501s (K. Grayston: also on J. RICHES, Pheme PERKINS, D. TIEDE in the series).

3580 Kulisz Józef, ⊕ Jesus in the light of history. Wsz 1989, Akad. Teol. Katolickiej. 68 p. – ᴿPrzPow 268, 824 (1990) 467-471 (H. Seweryniak); RuBi 44 (1991) 80s (J. Królikowski).

3581 O'Neill J.C., The lost written records of Jesus' words and deeds behind our records: JTS 42 (1991) 483-503.

3582 Robinson J.A.T., Wann entstand das NT? [⁴1981] 1986 ➤ 2,3051... 4,4150: ᴿTPhil 66 (1991) 243s (H. Engel).

3583 Spila Arnaldo, Storia di Gesù. [Vaticano, aggiunto] 1991. 480 p. Lit. 30.000. – ᴿEsprVie 101 (1991) 323-jaune (M. Noirot: une nouvelle chronologie, nombre de conjectures).

3584 Stuhlhofer Franz, Jesus und seine Schüler; Wie zuverlässig wurden Jesu Worte überliefert?: ABC-Team. Giessen 1991, Brunnen. 110 p. 3-7655-3930-9.

3585 Wenham John, Redating Matthew, Mark and Luke; a fresh assault on the Synoptic Problem. L 1991, Hodder & S. xix-319 p. £15;

pa. £10. 0-340-54619-0 pa. – ᴿDowR 109 (1991) 230s (A. G. *Murray*); ExpTim 102 (1990s) 377 (Meg *Davies*: eight contentions, altogether unacceptable); NBlackf 72 (1991) 502s (H. *Wansbrough*).

F1.4 *Jesus historicus* – **The human Jesus.**

3586 **Alt** Franz, Jesus, der erste neue Mann 1989 ➜ 6,4267: ᴿActuBbg 28 (1991) 35-41 (J. *Boada*: 'nada más que un hombre').
3587 **Alt** F., Jezus — de eerste nieuwe man [DBR TV 'Report']. Baarn 1990, Ten Have. 169 p. Fb 585. – ᴿCollatVL 21 (1991) 216s (J. De *Kesel*).
3588 *Boada* Josep, Jesús de Nazaret; aspectos sistemáticos, exegéticos, históricos y filosóficos: ActuBbg 28 (1991) 5-58 [9 libros, infra].
3589 **Boers** Hendrikus, Who was Jesus? 1989 ➜ 5,4037; 6,4268: ᴿCBQ 53 (1991) 129s (G. W. *Buchanan* gives title as 'Who was Jesus? The historical and synoptic gospels' and cites p. 119 'matter of curse' and without page-number 'The significance of Jesus was not to be found in her person').
3590 **Bordoni** Marcello, Gesù di Nazaret; presenza, memoria, attesa 1988 ➜ 5,4038.7484; 6,4269: ᴿGregorianum 72 (1991) 155-7 (J. *Dupuis*).
3591 **Borg** Marcus J., Jesus, a new vision 1987 ➜ 4,4155 ... 6,4270: ᴿCurrTMiss 18 (1991) 128-130 (E. *Krentz* compares with HORSLEY R. A. 1987).
3592 *Borg* Marcus J., Portraits of Jesus in contemporary North American scholarship: HarvTR 84 (1991) 1-22.
3593 **Castellano** D., *al.*, Eutanasia del cattolicesimo? Considerazioni sul 'nuovo cristianesimo' gnostico di Rinaldo FABRIS [... Gesù 1983]. N 1990, Ed. Scientifiche. 119 p. – ᴿSapienza 44 (1981) 95s (G. *Turco*).
3594 **Chabert** Yvette, *Philibert* Roger, Jésus Christ: JC tout simplement. P 1991, Éd. Ouvrières. – ᴿMasses Ouvrières 440 (1991) 96s (J.-P. *Lemonon*).
3595 **Coulot** Claude, Jésus et le disciple; étude sur l'autorité messianique de Jésus: ÉtBN 8, ᴰ1987 ➜ 3,3917 ... 6,4277: ᴿCiuD 203 (1990) 738s (J. *Gutiérrez*); EsprVie 101 (1991) 235-9 (L. *Walter*).
3596 **Crossan** John D., The historical Jesus; the life of a Mediterranean Jewish peasant. SF/E 1991, HarperCollins/Clark. xxxiv-507 p. $30. 0-06-061607-5/– [NTAbs 36,420]. – ᴿChrCent 108 (1991) 1194-1204 (an abridged selection and his answers to questions).
3597 **Cunningham** Philip A., Jesus and the evangelists ... synoptic 1988 ➜ 4,4166 ... 6,4280: ᴿScripTPamp 23 (1991) 710s (J. M. *Casciaro*).
3598 **Dimont** M. I., Appointment in Jerusalem; a search for the historical Jesus. NY 1991, St. Martin's. xiv-194 p. $18. 0-312-06291-5 [NTAbs 36,262].
3598* **Dingayan** Luna L., Towards a Christology of struggle; a proposal for understanding the Christ: CTC Bulletin 10,1 (Hong Kong 1991) 15-34 [< TContexto 2/1,112].
3599 **Flood** E., The Jesus story. KC 1991, Sheed & W. vi-120 p. $8 pa. 1-55612-404-X [NTAbs 35,240].
3600 **Gnilka** Joachim, Jesus von Nazaret, Botschaft und Geschichte 1990 ➜ 6,4289; 3-451-21989-1: ᴿAnnTh 4 (1990) 435 (B. *Estrada*); ExpTim 102 (1990s) 266 (E. *Best*); TGL 81 (1991) 389-391 (J. *Ernst*); TLZ 117 (1992) 122-4 (J. *Becker*); TsTNijm 31 (1991) 325s (A. van *Schaik*).
3601 *Gubler* M.-L., Das faszinierende Ärgernis Jesus: Diakonia 22 (W 1991) 379-387 [< NTAbs 36,168].
3602 **Gutiérrez Cuervo** Rafael, Cristo hombre perfecto; el seguimiento de Cristo como compromiso con la justicia en las obras de José GONZÁLEZ

FAUS: diss. Pont. Univ. Gregoriana N° 6942, ᴰ*Demmer* K. – InfPUG 24/122, 28.

3603 **Harrington** Wilfrid J., The Jesus story. ColMn/Dublin 1991, Liturgical/Columba. 168 p. $10. 0-8146-5709-0 / 0-948183-93-4 [NTAbs 36,109].

3604 **Herbst** Karl, Der wirkliche Jesus; das total andere Gottesbild; Vorw. *Alt* F. Olten 1988, Walter. 295 p. 3-530-34551-2. – ᴿActuBbg 28 (1991) 50-53 (J. *Boada*: subjetivo más que real).

3605 **Hill** B., Jesus the Christ; contemporary perspectives. Mystic CT 1991, Twenty-Third. x-308 p. $15. 0-89622-492-9 [NTAbs 36,264].

3606 *Holtz* Traugott, *a*) Kenntnis von Jesus und Kenntnis Jesu; eine Skizze zum Verhältnis zwischen historisch-philologischer Erkenntnis und historisch-theologischem Verständnis [< TLZ 104 (1979) 1-12]; – *b*) Jesus-Überlieferung und Briefliteratur; zur Frage des Ortes der Jesus-Überlieferung in der frühen Gemeinde [< WZtsHalle 34 (1985) 103-112]: ➤ 211, Geschichte 1991, 3-16 / 17-30.

3607 **Hurth** Elisabeth, In his name; comparative studies in the quest for the historical Jesus; Life of Jesus research in Germany and America [Diss. Boston Univ. 1988]: Eur UnivSt 23/367, 1989 ➤ 5,4062; 6,4295: ᴿCritRR 4 (1991) 205-7 (J. *Reumann*).

3608 **Kähler** Martin, The so-called historical Jesus and the historic biblical Christ [1896] ᵀᴱ*Braaten* Carl E. Ph 1988, Fortress. 152 p. – ᴿNeotestamentica 25 (1991) 180s (B. A. du *Toit*: justified, as Tillich for 1960s republication).

3609 *Kelly* Tony, The historical Jesus and human subjectivity; a response to John MEIER [TS 51 (1990) 3-24 (=) NJBC]: Pacifica 4 (1991) 202-228.

3610 ᴱ**Lentzen-Deis** Fritzleo, Images of Jesus; contributions to biblical method, ᵀ*Pascual* H., pref. *Grail* Pearl G. Bangalore 1989, St. Paul. – ᴿJDharma 15 (1990) 278s (G. *Kaniarakath*).

3611 **Linzey** Andrew, The sayings of Jesus. L 1991, Duckworth. 64 p. £5. 0-7156-2364-8. – ᴿExpTim 103 (1991s) 155s (P. D. *Bishop*: best in the series he edited on Sayings of the Great Religious Leaders). ➤ 345*.

3612 **McCulloh** Gerald W., Christ's person and life-work in the theology of A. RITSCHL, with special attention to the Munus Triplex. Lanham MD 1990, UPA. iv-228 p. $40.25. – ᴿJTS 42 (1991) 785-7 (J. *Draper*: outdated).

Macquarrie John, Jesus Christ in modern thought 1990 ➤ 7479.

3614 **Marguerat** Daniel, L'homme qui venait de Nazareth; ce qu'on peut aujourd'hui savoir de Jésus. Aubonne 1991, Moulin. 122 p. – ᴿEsprVie 101 (1991) 564s (É. *Cothenet*); ÉTRel 66 (1991) 441s (E. *Cuvillier*).

3615 **Mazzillo** G., Gesù e la sua prassi di pace: Percorsi. Molfetta 1990, Meridiana. 140 p. Lit. 20.000. – ᴿAsprenas 38 (1991) 116-8 (P. *Incoronato*); RasT 32 (1991) 106 (G. *Mattai*: 'biografia teologica' continuando sua Teologia come prassi di pace); RivB 39 (1991) 355-7 (R. *Fabris*: 'di carattere cristologico').

3615* *Meier* John P., Reflections on Jesus-of-History research today [first publication of the original version abridged as 'Jesus among the historians' in NYTimes Sunday Book Review (Dec. 21, 1986) 1.16-18]: ➤ 294, Jesus' Jewishness 1991, 84-107.

3616 *Meyer* Ben F., Jesus' scenario of the future: DowR 109 (1991) 1-15.

3617 ᴱ**Miguez Bonino** J., Faces of Jesus; Latin-American Christologies 1984 ➤ 65,348 ... 3,7070: ᴿLvSt 14 (1989) 394s (H.-E. *Mertens*).

3618 [➤ 8236] *a*) *Moore* Sebastian, Jesus the liberator of desire; – *b*) *Dunne* John S., The ways of desire [GIRARD mimesis not mentioned, but claimed

p. 435 to be followed]: CCurr 40,4 ['The liberation of desire' 1990s] 477-498 (= DownR 1990) / 437-456.

3619 *Panimolle* Salvatore A., Il ministero pubblico di Gesù nel Dialogo con Trifone di GIUSTINO: AugR 31 (1991) 277-307; follows chiefly Mt.

3620 **Patin** Alain, Celui qu'on appelle Jésus: Foi Vivante 259. P 1990, Ouvrières. 184 p. – ᴿEsprVie 101 (1991) 159 (L. *Barbey*: pour un milieu jociste, bien; réserves).

3621 **Pikaza** Xabier, El Evangelio I. Vida y pascua de Jesús 1990 → 6,4316: ᴿBiFe 17,49 (1991) 141s (A. *Salas*); CiTom 118 (1991) 416 (A.O.); NatGrac 38 (1991) 403s (M. *González del Blanco*).

3622 *Riesner* Rainer, Moderne Jesus-Bilder [ALT F. 1989, nicht historisch; THEISSEN G. 1986] und der Christus der Evangelien: TBeit 22 (1991) 320-331 [< NTAbs 36,169].

3623 **Roux** J.-P., Jésus 1989 → 6,4322; 2-213-02377-8: ᴿÉTRel 66 (1991) 596s (C.-B. *Amphoux*: déplaisant, agressif).

3624 **Ruckstuhl** Eugen, Jesus im Horizont der Evangelien: SBAufs NT 3, 1988 → 4,4203; DM 39: ᴿTR 87 (1991) 451-3 (H. *Giesen*, detailliert; etwas weniger über STUHLMACHER P. 1988).

3625 **Santos Ferreira** José M. dos, Jesus Cristo luz e sentido da solidão [solitudo] do homem [diss. R, Pont. Univ. Gregoriana, ᴰ*Latourelle* R.]. Lisboa 1990, Rei dos Livros. 344 p. – ᴿDidaskalia 19 (1989) 267-271 (B. de *Margerie*, franç.).

3626 *a*) **Sauer** Jürgen R., Rückkehr des Heils; eine Untersuchung zum Problem der 'ethischen Radikalismen' des historischen Jesus: ev. Diss. Göttingen, ᴰ*Stegemann* 1991. – TR 87 (1991) 517. – *b*) Rückkehr und Vollendung des Heils; eine Untersuchung zu den ethischen Radikalismen Jesu [Diss. Göttingen 1990, ᴰ*Stegemann* H.]: Theorie und Forschung 133. Rg 1991, Roderer. xii-1009 p. DM 168. 3-89073-512-6 [NTAbs 36,269].

3627 **Schillebeeckx** E., Jesus in our western cultures; mysticism, ethics and politics 1987 → 3,3959 [not 3059 as → 5,4084]: ᴿLvSt 16 (1991) 183-5 (H.-E. *Mertens*).

3628 **Schwager** Raymund, Dem Netz des Jägers entronnen; das Jesusdrama nacherzählt. Mü 1991, Kösel. 204 p. DM 30. – ᴿTR 87 (1991) 448 (H. *Giesen*: 'das Leben Jesu im Spiegel des ATs').

3629 **Segundo** Juan Luis, An evolutionary approach to Jesus of Nazareth 1989 → 5,7441: ᴿRExp 88 (1991) 483 (Molly *Marshall-Green*).

3630 **Segundo** Juan Luis, La historia perdida y recuperada de Jesús de Nazaret, de los sinópticos a Pablo: Presencia teologica. Sdr c. 1991, Sal Terrae. 672 p. pt. 2400 [RazF 224 dic. adv.].

3631 **Selby** G. R., Jesus, Aramaic & Greek. Doncaster 1990, Brynmill. v-120 p. £12. 0-907839-40-1 [NTAbs 36,270]. – ᴿExpTim 102 (1990s) 279 (H. *Guite*: Jesus spoke also Greek; exuberant against BURNEY, SCHILLEBEECKX ...).

3632 *Sugirtharajah* R. S., 'What do men say remains of me?' Current Jesus research and Third World Christologies: AsiaJT 5,2 (1991) 331-7 [< NTAbs 36,19].

3633 **Theissen** Gerd, L'ombre du Galiléen 1989 → 5,4092; 6,4330*b*: ᴿChristus 37 (P 1990) 206 (C. *Flipo*).

3634 **Theissen** Gerd, L'ombra del Galileo, romanzo storico 1990 → 5,4093; 6,4330: ᴿCC 142 (1991,2) 403s (V. *Fusco*); HumBr 46 (1991) 303s (F. *Montagnini*).

3635 **Theissen** G., La sombra del galileo 1988 ³1990 → 4,4217; 5,4093: ᴿRazF 222 (1990) 119 (J. *García Pérez*).

3636 **Tomić** Celestin, Isus iz Nazareta prorok [prophet] i Krist; Isusovo javno djelovanje [public life] (Mt 3-20; Mk 1-10; Lk 3,1 - 19,27; Iv 1,19 - 11,54]: Povijest spasenja [history of salvation] 11. Zagreb 1991, Provincijalat hrvatskih franjevaca konventualaca. 357 p.   ↠ 3710.

3637 *Verhoeven* Paul, Christ the man [for film]: The Fourth R 4,1 (Sonoma CA 1991) 5-8 (9-11-13-14, *Hoover* R., *Chilton* B., *Dewey* A., responses).

3638 *Vorster* W. S., *a)* Jesus the Galilean; – *b)* Jesus; eschatological prophet and/or wisdom teacher: HervTSt 47 (1991) 121-135 / 526-542 [< NTAbs 36,19.169].

Wessels Anton, Images of Jesus; how Jesus is perceived and portrayed in non-European cultures 1990 ↠ 3748.

3640 *Wink* Walter, Jesus and the domination system [... economic equality; women ... Students writing a paragraph on Jesus tend to stress what they themselves would like to be, as SCHWEITZER's Quest showed]: ↠ 446, SBL Sem 30 (1991) 265-286.

3641 *Wojciechowski* Michał, ✪ Czynności symboliczne Jezusa [The symbolic actions of Jesus, ᴰ1986 ↠ 6,4330* (wrongly in F4.3, ↠ 3,3532; 5,4727)]: 314, Studia z Biblistyki 6. Wsz 1991, Akad. Teol. Katolickiej. 253 p.; Eng. 245-253 [NTAbs 36,429].

3642 **Zöhrer** Josef, Der Glaube an die Freiheit und der historische Jesus; eine Untersuchung der Philosophie Karl JASPERS' unter christologischem Aspekt [< kath. Diss. Regensburg]: RgStT 35. Fra 1986, Lang. vi-192 p. – ᴿTLZ 116 (1991) 452s (M. *Petzoldt* bekam sein Exemplar erst 1989).

F1.5   *Jesus et Israel* – **Jesus the Jew.**

3642* *Betz* Hans-Dieter, WELLHAUSEN's dictum 'Jesus was not a Christian, but a Jew' in light of present scholarship [Mowinckel lecture, Oslo 1990]: ST 45 (1991) 83-110.

3643 *Betz* Otto, Das Alte Testament; Jesu Bibel, unsere Bibel: Lutherische Kirche in der Welt 38 (Erlangen 1991) 13-26 [< ZIT 91,625].

3644 **Calimani** Riccardo, Gesù ebreo: Orizzonti della Storia. Mi 1990, Rusconi. 471 p. Lit. 38.000. 88-18-88017-9 [NTAbs 35,379]. – ᴿStPatav 38 (1991) 151-164 (G. *Leonardi*: against his view that Jesus was a pious, perhaps Zealot, Jew and not a Christian, we can hold he was the first Christian) [< NTAbs 36,18].

3645 **Casey** Maurice, From Jewish prophet to Gentile God. C 1991, J. Clark. 197 p. £22.50. 0-227-67920-2 [ScotJT 44,549].

3646 **Charlesworth** James H., Jesus within Judaism 1988 ↠ 4,4225 ... 6,4337: ᴿBAR-W 17,1 (1991) 4.6 (A. *Saldarini*); RelStT 10,2 (1990) 96-98 (T. L. *Donaldson*).

3646* *Charlesworth* James H., The foreground of Christian origins and the commencement of Jesus research in the 1980s [< PrIrB 10 (1986) 40-54 + PrincSemB 6 (1985) 221-230]: ↠ 294, Jesus' Jewishness 1991, 63-84.

3647 **Chilton** Bruce, Profiles of a rabbi; synoptic opportunities in reading about Jesus: BrownJudSt 177, 1989 ↠ 5,4410: ᴿAbrNahrain 29 (1991) 135-8 (J. *Painter*): CritRR 4 (1991) 178-180 (W. R. *Stegner*).

3648 **Chouraqui** Bernard, Jésus, le rabbi de Nazareth [... 'les Évangiles sont une bombe jetée par un fou d'Israël sur la réalité irréelle pour la faire exploser ...']. P c.1991, Différence. – ᴿFoiVie 90,6 (1991) 98 (B. *Chavannes*).

3649 *Dautzenberg* Gerhard, Jesus und die Tora: Orientierung 55 (1991) 229-232.243-6.

3650 **Dunn** J.D.G., The partings of the ways between Christianity and Judaism and their significance for the character of Christianity [1990 Rome Gregorian lectures]. L/Ph 1991, SCM/Trinity. xvi-368 p. $30. 0-334-02508-7 / 1-56338-022-6 [NTAbs 36,361].

3651 **Finkelstein** B., L'écrivain juif et les évangiles. P 1991, Beauchesne. 148 p. F 150 [TS 52,600].

3652 **Flusser** David, Het christendom, een joodse religie [1990 ➤ 6,4345], T. Baarn 1991, Ten Have. 170 p. *f* 30. – RCollatVL 21 (1991) 427s (H. *Hoet*).

3653 *Fossum* Jarl, The new religionsgeschichtliche Schule; the quest for Jewish Christology: ➤ 446, SBL Sem 30 (1991) 638-646.

3654 *Frankemölle* Hubert, ❷ Das Urchristentum als Reformjudentum? Jesus und Paulus als Juden, TZałęski Jan [Akad. Wsz. 27.III.1990]: ColcT 61,1 (1991) 5-21; deutsch 21.

3655 **Freyne** Seán, Galilee, Jesus and the Gospels 1988 ➤ 4,4238...6,4346: RJBL 110 (1991) 155-8 (W.M. *Swartley*); RelStT 9,2 (1989) 107s (J.S. *Kloppenborg*); RB 98 (1991) 309-311 (J. *Murphy-O'Connor*).

3656 *Harrington* Daniel J., 'Jesus, the son of David, the son of Abraham...'; Christology and Second Temple Judaism: IrTQ 57 (1991) 185-195.

3657 **Hengel** M., *Markschies* C., 'Hellenization' of Judaea 1989 ➤ 6,4351: RZAW 103 (1991) 298 (O. *Kaiser*).

3658 **Hooker** Morna D., Continuity and discontinuity; early Christianity in its Jewish setting 1986 ➤ 2,3138...6,4353: RJJS 42 (1991) 268s (C.R.A. *Murray-Jones*).

3659 **Horsley** Richard A., Jesus and the spiral of violence 1987 ➤ 3,3995 ...5,4126: RJQR 82 (1991s) 534s (M. *Goodman*).

3660 *Johnson* L.T., A marginal Mediterranean Jewish peasant [MEIER J., CROSSAN J.]: Commonweal 119 (1992) 24-26.

3661 **Jonsson** Jakob, Humour and irony in NT/Talmud [= D1965] 1985 ➤ 1,4013; 3,3997: RRelStT 10,2 (1990) 69-72 (W.O. *McCready*: NT influenced Talmud).

3662 **Karrer** Martin, Der Gesalbte; die Grundlagen des Christustitels [Hab.-Diss. Erlangen]: FRL 151. Gö 1991, Vandenhoeck & R. 482 p. DM 138. 3-525-53833-2. – RTR 87 (1991) 456-8 (H. *Giesen*: häufigstes Prädikat im NT, erst jetzt untersucht).

3663 **Landsman** Salcia, Jesus und die Juden, oder Die Folgen einer Verstrickung 1989 ➤ 5,4130: RBiKi 46 (1991) 138-140 (O.B. *Knoch*).

3664 **Lee** Bernard J., The Galilean Jewishness of Jesus 1988 ➤ 4,4250; 6,4381: RHorizons 18 (1991) 144-6 (Elizabeth *Bellefontaine*); RB 98 (1991) 211s (J. *Murphy-O'Connor*: there is nothing good to say); RelStT 10,2 (1990) 109s (J.S. *Kloppenborg*).

Luckert Karl W., Egyptian light and Hebrew fire...roots of Christendom 1991 ➤ a806.

3665 **Maccoby** Hyam, Judaism in the first century; issues in religious studies. 1989, Sheldon. 136 p. £5. – RNBlackf 71 (1990) 412-4 (Meg *Davies* compares with CHARLESWORTH).

3666 **Marquardt** Friedrich-W., Das christliche Bekenntnis zu Jesus, dem Juden; eine Christologie II. Mü 1991, Kaiser. 400 p. DM 96 [TR 87,347].

3666* *Massonnet* J., Sanhédrin: ➤ 686, SDB 11,65 (1991) 1353-1413.

3667 **Meier** John P., A marginal Jew; rethinking the historical Jesus, 1. The roots of the problem and the person: AnchorB RefLibrary. NY 1991,

Doubleday.   xii-484 p. $25.   0-385-26425-9 [TDig 39,177; RB 99,781, J. *Murphy-O'Connor*: 'most significant event in the history of 20th century Catholic biblical studies'; unjustified preference of Lk infancy]. – [R]NYTimes Book Review (Dec. 22, 1991) 3,23 (M. *Goodman*) [< NTAbs 36,169].

3668 **Murphy** F. J., The religious world of Jesus; an introduction to Second Temple Palestinian Judaism. Nv 1991, Abingdon. 406 p. 0-687-36049-8 [NTAbs 36,138].

3669 *Murray* Gregory, *a*) Jesus and the feasts of the Jews; – *b*) The Gospels and history: DowR 109 (1991) 217-225 / 290-6.

3670 **Neusner** Jacob, Judaism and Christianity in the age of Constantine 1987 → 3,4011 ... 6,4371: [R]HeythJ 32 (1991) 135s (T. D. *Barnes*); JQR 82 (1991s) 185-7 (W. *Adler*).

3671 **Neusner** Jacob, Il giudaismo nei primi secoli del cristianesimo [1984] 1989 → 5,4140; 6,4372: [R]RivB 39 (1991) 74-76 (M. *Perani*); Salesianum 53 (1991) 184s (M. *Cimosa*).

3673 **Neusner** Jacob,   Jews and Christians; the myth of a common tradition.   L/Ph 1991, SCM/Trinity.   159 p.   £10.50.   0-334-02465-X. – [R]CurrTMiss 18 (1991) 298 (J. C. *Rochelle*); ExpTim 103 (1991s) 55 (M. *Braybrooke*).

3674 *Neusner* Jacob,   Mr Sanders' Pharisees and mine; a response to E. P. SANDERS, Jewish Law from Jesus to the Mishnah [1990: 'mere anecdotes and episodes with reference to the Gospels']:   ScotJT 44 (1991) 73-95.

3675 *Newport* Kenneth G. C., The Pharisees in Judaism prior to A.D. 70: AndrUnS 29 (1991) 127-137.

3676 *Oberforcher* R., Jesus von Nazareth und die Vielfalt der religiösen Landschaft Palästinas: → 373, Mündigkeit 1989, 155-177.

3677 *Odumuyiwa* E. Ade, A historical note on Christianity and Jewish culture (AD 29-70): AsiaJT 5 (1991) 286-295 [< ZIT 91,558].

3678 **Oegema** G. S., De messiance verwachtingen ten tijde van Jezus; een inleiding in die messiaanse verwachtingen en bewegingen gedurende de hellenistisch-romeinse tijd. Baarn 1991, Ten Have. 214 p. f 39,50 [TR 88,77].

3679 *Pelletier* Marcel, Les pharisiens; histoire d'un parti méconnu: Lire la Bible 86, 1990 → 6,4377: [R]ArTGran 54 (1991) 378-380 (P. *Contreras*); CBQ 53 (1991) 303s (D. J. *Harrington*: he calls the movement 'pharisianisme' in the hope of avoiding 'pharisaic' connotations); ÉTRel 66 (1991) 286s (Jeanne-M. *Léonard*); FoiVie 90,1 (1991) 99s (P. *Giniewski*: pernicieux).

3680 **Perelmuter** Hayim G., Siblings; rabbinic Judaism and early Christianity at their beginnings 1989 → 5,4146; 6,4378: [R]CBQ 53 (1991) 504 (E. J. *Fischer*: admirable); Horizons 18 (1991) 316s (J. S. *Siker*); JRel 71 (1991) 457s (J. T. *Townsend*: midrashic in contrast to scholarly NEUSNER); NewTR 4,1 (1991) 107s (A. *Milavec*); RivB 39 (1991) 246-8 (Anna *Passoni dell'Acqua*); Salesianum 53 (1991) 186 (R. *Vicent*).

3680* *a*) Piñero Antonio, La herencia de la Biblia hebrea; – *b*) *García Martínez* Florentino, ¿La apocalíptica judía como matriz de la teología cristiana? [elementos, *Piñero*]; – *c*) *Peláez* Jesús, Jesús y el reino de Dios; las comunidades primitivas, el judeo-cristianismo; – *d*) *Oppenheimer* Aharon, Sectas judías en tiempos de Jesús; fariseos, saduceos, los 'amme ha-'aretz: → 453, Orígenes 1989/91, 83-98 / 177-199 [201-218] / 221-281 / 123-134.

3681 *Poorthuis* M.J.H.M., De joodse groeperingen ten tijde van Jezus; oorsprong, inhoud en relatie tot Jezus: Oecumenereeks 892-d. 's-Hertogenbosch 1989, Willibrordvereniging. 48 p. *f* 6,50. 90-7036-555-3 [TsTNijm 31,116].

3682 *Riches* J.K., Apocalyptic – strangely relevant [... to Jesus' teaching, partly as BULTMANN]: ➤ 15, ᶠBAMMEL E., Templum 1991, 236-263.

3682* **Røsaeg** Nils A., Jesus from Galilee and political power; a socio-historical investigation [diss. Oslo 1991]. Oslo 1990, Teol. Menighetsfakultet. 587 + 236 p. – ST 46,72.

3683 **Rothschild** Fritz A., Jewish perspectives on Christianity; the views of BAECK, BUBER, ROSENZWEIG, HERBERG and HESCHEL. NY 1990, Crossroad. 320 p. $27.50. 0-8245-0937-4. – ᴿTS 52 (1991) 579-581 (D. J. *Moore*).

3684 **Russell** David S., Dal primo giudaismo alla Chiesa delle origini [1986], ᵀ*Portino* Margherita, ᴱ*Montagnini* Felice: StBPaid 96. Brescia 1991, Paideia. 195 p. 88-394-0458-9.

3685 *a*) *Safrai* Shmuel, The Jewish cultural nature of Galilee in the first century; – *b*) *Safrai* Ze'ev, The origins of reading the Aramaic Targum in the synagogue: ➤ 54, ᶠFLUSSER D., Immanuel 24s (1990) 147-186 / 187-193.

3686 *Safrai* Shmuel, Spoken/literary languages in the time of Jesus [chiefly Hebrew!]: Jerusalem Perspective 4,1 (1991) 3-8.13 [supported by 9-11, *Pileggi* David, The Bar-Kochva letters] 4,2 (1991) 3-9.

3687 *Sand* Alexander, Ist Jesus der Messias? oder sollen wir auf einen anderen warten?: Renovatio 47 (Köln 1991) 229-243 [< ZIT 92,18].

3688 **Sanders** E. P., Jewish law from Jesus to the Mishnah 1990 ➤ 6,295: ᴿJStJud 22 (1991) 274-283 (P. J. *Tomson*); TLond 94 (1991) 308s (A. *Chester*).

3689 *Schäfer* Peter, Der vorrabbinische Pharisäismus: ➤ 437, Paulus 1988/91, 125-172 (–5).

3690 **Schelkle** Karl H., Israele nel Nuovo Testamento [1985], ᵀ*Panini* Marisa, ᴱ*Soffritti* Omero: StBPaid 95. Brescia 1991, Paideia. 204 p. 88-394-0457-0.

3691 *Schwartz* G.P., As if Jesus and the Pharisees were developing similarly and simultaneously: NewTR 4,4 (1991) 63-77.

3692 *Segal* A.F., Studying Judaism with Christian sources: UnSemQ 44 (1991) 267-286 [< NTAbs 36,174].

3693 *Sievers* Joseph, Chi erano i farisei? Un nuovo approccio a un problema antico: NuovaUm 12 (1991) 53-68 [< AcPIB 9/8, 660].

3694 **Stegner** W.R., Narrative theology in early Jewish Christianity 1989 ➤ 6,9882: ᴿAsburyTJ 46,1 (1991) 125-7 (M.A. *Powell*); CritRR 4 (1991) 233s (H.C. *Waetjen*).

3695 **Swidler** Leonard, Der umstrittene Jesus. Stu 1991, Quell. 143 p. DM 24,80 pa. – ᴿTR 87 (1991) 443 (H. *Giesen*: 'Jesus der Jude; ein Heilbringer unter vielen').

3696 **Tresmontant** C., The Hebrew Christ 1989 ➤ 5,4156: ᴿCritRR 4 (1991) 247-9 (J. R. *Michaels*).

3697 *Trocmé* Étienne, Les Juifs d'après le NT: FoiVie 90,6 = CahÉtJuives 24 (1991) 3-22.

3698 **Wilson** Marvin R., Our father Abraham; Jewish roots of the Christian faith 1989 ➤ 5,4160; 6,4389: ᴿGraceTJ 11 (1990) 126-8 (R. L. *Giese*); Horizons 18 (1991) 167-171 (J. S. *Siker*).

3699 **Zeitlin** Irving M., Jesus and the Judaism of his time 1988 ⇥ 4,4278
...6,4390: ᴿHeythJ 32 (1991) 396s (N. *King*).

3700 **Stern** David H., The Jewish New Testament. J/Clarksville MD 1989,
Jewish NT Publications. 965-359-003-0. – ᴿBTrans 42 (1991) 146s (R. G.
Bratcher, dubious).

F1.6 *Jesus in Ecclesia* – **The Church Jesus.**

3701 **Booth** Roger P., Contrasts — Gospel evidence and Christian beliefs,
1990 ⇥ 6,4393 (Paget!). viii-256 p. £11. 0-9515220-0-0. – ᴿExpTim 102
(1990s) 316 (B. G. *Powley*: the author, with degrees in law and theology,
holds Jesus' view especially of resurrection influenced by his belief in
Satan and demons; the 'appearances' were hallucinations...); JStJud 22
(1991) 121-3 (J.D.M. *Derrett*).

3702 **Edlinger** Franz, War Jesus ein 'Rechter' oder ein 'Linker'? Die Kirche
auf dem Weg zwischen Fundamentalismus und Befreiungstheologie. Bad
Sauerbrunn 1991, Tau. 116 p. DM 19,80 [TR 87,347].

3703 **Helm** Thomas E., The Christian religion; an introduction. ENJ 1991,
Prentice-Hall. xiii-273 p. [RelStR 18,59, R. F. *Wilson*].

3704 **Kay** James F., Christ our contemporary; Rudolf BULTMANN's Christus
praesens [in Church proclamation] in retrospect and prospect: diss. Union,
ᴰ*Morse* C. NY 1991. 322 p. 91-28445. – DissA 52 (1991s) 1391-A; RelStR
18,171.

3705 **Köhler** U., Jesus der Befreier, von Religion, Magie und Ideologie. Fra
1990, Haag & H. 183 p. DM 22. 3-89228-500-4 [NTAbs 36,265].

3706 *Marchesi* Giovanni, Da Gesù alla Chiesa; la chiamata del nuovo popolo
di Dio [... il Gesù storico ha voluto fondare una chiesa? e questa cor-
risponde all'intenzione?]: CC 142 (1991,4) 553-566.

3707 *a)* [Martins] *Terra* João E., Aspectos bíblicos da unidade e diversidade
na Igreja; – *b) Nogueira* M. Celina, Bases bíblicas da 'Evangelii
nuntiandi': RCuBíb 14,55s ('Evangelho e Igreja' 1990) 3-43 / 81-86.

3708 *a) Salado* Domingo, Jesucristo, sacramento de Dios para los hombres; –
b) Martínez Felicísimo, Dios, liberador de todos los hombres: TEspir 35
(1991) 357-382 / 395-418.

3709 **Schneider** Diethelm, Theorien des Übergangs ⇥ 5,g360 [einer von Jesu
immer mehr entfernten Kirche]: EurHS 23/355. Fra ᴰ1989, Lang. 359 p.
DM 71. 3-631-41478-1. – ᴿActuBbg 28 (1991) 183s (J. *Boada*).

3710 **Tomic** Celestin [⇥ 3636], Isus iz Nazareta – Bog z nama (God with us).
Zagreb 1990, prov. Franciscan. 270 p. – ᴿBogVest 50 (1990) 463-5 (F.
Rozman).

3711 **Wéber** Édouard-Henri, Le Christ selon S. T. d'AQUIN: JJC 35, 1988
⇥ 6,7485: ᴿDivinitas 35 (1991) 96-98 (D. *Vibrac*).

F1.7 *Jesus 'anormalis':* **to atheists, psychoanalysts, romance ...**

3712 **Breech** James, Jesus and postmodernism 1989 ⇥ 5,4175: ᴿCBQ 53 (1991)
316 (A.K.M. *Adam*: against M.C. TAYLOR 'God is death' and J.D. CROS-
SAN 'Jesus offers no final security'); CritRR 4 (1991) 175-7 (S.D. *Moore*).

3713 **Bruce** Frederick F., Ausserbiblische Zeugnisse über Jesus und das frühe
Christentum [1974], ᵀᴱ*Güting* Eberhard. Giessen 1991, Brunnen. 190 p.
DM 29 [RHE 86,312*]. 3-7655-9366-4.

3714 **Bruce** F.F., Gesù visto dai contemporanei 1989 ➤ 6,4402*: ᴿScuolC 118 (1990) 275s (F. *Baj*).

3715 **Camacho** Haroldo S., A synthesis of MOLTMANN's archetypal Christology with JUNG's God-image archetype; a theological psychology for pastoral counseling and psychotherapy: diss. ᴰ*Schurman* P. Claremont 1991. 209 p. 91-35028. – DissA 52 (1991s) 2176-A.

3716 **Castelli** Ferdinando, Volti di Gesù nella letteratura moderna. CinB 1987-90, Paoline. 584 p.; 628 p. Lit. 28.000 + 30.000. – ᴿCC 142 (1991,1) 93s (B. *Papàsogli*).

3717 **Cottret** Bernard, Le Christ des lumières; Jésus de NEWTON à VOLTAIRE (1680-1760): Jésus depuis Jésus. P 1990, Cerf. x-187 p.; 4 pl. F 152. – ᴿÉTRel 66 (1991) 134s (H. *Bost*); NRT 113 (1991) 609 (P. *Evrard*); RHPR 71 (1991) 401s (M. *Arnold*).

3718 *a*) *Crossan* John D., Open healing and open eating; Jesus as a Jewish Cynic?; – *b*) *White* John L., Jesus as actant; – *c*) *Collins* Adela Y., Jesus the prophet: BiRes 36 (1991) 6-18 / 19-29 / 30-34.

3719 **Dart** John, The Jesus of heresy and history... NH [= ²The laughing savior] 1988 ➤ 4,4305; 5,4179: ᴿChH 59 (1990) 389-391 (R.M. *Grant*).

3720 **Downing** F. Gerald, Christ and the Cynics; Jesus and other radical preachers in first-century tradition: JStOT manual 4, 1988 ➤ 4,4306... 6,4409: ᴿCurrTMiss 18 (1991) 127 (E. *Krentz*: not a book with an argument, but a collection of citations); HeythJ 32 (1991) 259s (J.D.M. *Derrett*).

3721 **Fox** Matthew, The coming of the cosmic Christ 1988 ➤ 4,8510... 6,4414: ᴿHorizons 18 (1991) 172s (Dolores *Greeley*).

3722 **Grant** Jacquelyn, White women's Christ and black women's Jesus 1989 ➤ 5,4187: ᴿHorizons 18 (1991) 164 (Barbara H. *Andolsen*).

3723 **Grelot** Pierre, Un Jésus de comédie² [= ¹1989 + Un Paul de farce: MESSADIÉ Gérard 1989s & 1991], lecture critique de trois livres récents. P 1991, Cerf. 141 p. F 50. 2-204-04430-X. – ᴿBLitEc 92 (1991) 292s (S. *Légasse*); EsprVie 101 (1991) 532s (L. *Walter*: certains regretteront la véhémence du redoutable polémiste).

3724 *Hilberath* Bernd J., Traum von einem Mann oder Gottes Weg zum Menschen? [ALT F.]: StiZt 208 (1990) 180-192.

3725 **Kamel** Hisham S., Christ in Arabic literature: diss. Fuller, ᴰ*Woodberry* D. Pasadena 1991. 221 p. 91-26151. – DissA 52 (1991s) 1370-A.

3726 **Keenan** J.P., The meaning of Christ; a Mahāyāna theology: Faith meets Faith. Mkn 1989, Orbis. viii-312 p. $30; pa. $17. – ᴿETL 67 (1991) 467s (E. *Brito*); Missiology 19 (1991) 237s (M.G. *Fonner*); NRT 113 (1991) 288 (J. *Masson*); RelStR 17 (1991) 149 (R.J. *Corless*).

3727 **Klatt** Norbert, Lebte Jesus in Indien?; eine religionsgeschichtliche Klärung. Gö 1988, Wallstein. 176 p. DM 24,80. – ᴿOLZ 86 (1991) 571-4 (M. *Kraatz*).

3728 *a*) *Krüggeler* Michael, Der verschwindende und sich wandelnde Jesus; eine soziologische Miniatur der Empirie des heutigen Jesus-Bildes; – *b*) *Biser* Eugen, Zur Neuentdeckung Jesu im heutigen Glaubensbewusstsein; – *c*) *Fuchs* Gotthard, Der arme Jesus und der Reichtum der Wissenden; negative Christologie und moderne Gnosis; – *d*) *Burrichter* Rita, Jesus in der modernen Kunst — eine Herausforderung für Theologie und Kirche; – *e*) *Valentin* Friederike, Jesus-Bilder der evangelikalen und pfingstlichen Bewegungen: Diakonia 22 (Mainz 1991) 365-372 / 373-8 / 388-399 / 400-2 / 411-4 [< ZIT 91,748].

3729 *LeBorgne* Michel, Le Christ à l'écran: FoiVie 90,5 = CahB 30 (1991) 103-110.

3730 *Marchesi* Giovanni, Il Cristo dei filosofi; è possibile una cristologia filosofica? [TILLIETTE X. ➤ 3744.]: CC 142 (1991,2) 571-583.

3731 **Messadié** M. G., L'homme qui devint Dieu 1989; 2. Sources 1989 ➤ 5,4199: RRCatalT 16 (1991) 207s (M. *Taradach*, aussi sur Saül).

3732 **Pappas** P. C., Jesus' tomb in India; the debate on his death and resurrection. Berkeley CA 1991, Asian Humanities. xi-202 p. $14. 0-89581-946-5 [NTAbs 36,267: by a professor of history at WV Tech.].

3733 **Pelphrey** Bryant, Christ our mother; JULIAN of Norwich. Wilmington 1989, Glazier. 271 p. – RRRel 49 (1990) 631s (Wendy M. *Wright*).

3734 **Rhodes** Ron, The counterfeit Christ of the New Age movement. GR 1990, Baker. 255 p. $12. 0-8010-7757-5 [TDig 38,377].

3735 **Risse** G., Gott ist Christus ... im Koran; Diss. Bonn 1989 ➤ 5,4204: RArTGran 54 (1991) 414s (A. *Segovia*); NZMissW 46 (1990) 220s (L. *Hagemann*); OrChr 75 (1991) 276s (M. van *Esbroeck*); TPQ 139 (1991) 340 (K. *Prenner*); TR 87 (1991) 159s (A. T. *Khoury*: Verdienst mehr für Dogmengeschichte als für Islamwissenschaft); Verbum SVD 32 (1991) 102-5 (J. *Henninger*).

3736 **Robinson** Neal, Christ in Islam and Christianity; the representation of Jesus in the Qur'ān and the classical Muslim commentaries. Basingstoke/Albany 1991, Macmillan/SUNY. £40 / $19 pa. [RHE 87,252*; TDig 39,185: 0-7914-0558-3; –9–1].

3737 *Rocheman* Lionel, Évangile(s) et histoire; à propos de 'L'invention de Jésus' de Bernard DUBOURG: Les Nouveaux Cahiers 98 (P 1989) 30-36 [< Judaica 46,63].

3738 *Saouma* R., Le Christ-époux chez BERNARD de Clairvaux et la Dame dans le 'fin'amore' des troubadours: StMedv 30 (1989) 533-566 [< RSPT 75,533].

3739 **Saramago** José, O Evangelho segundo Jesus Cristo ['... um simples romance, não um ensaio teológico romano']. São Paulo 1991, Schwarcz. 446 p. – RREB 51 (1991) 1006-8 (E. *Ferreira Alves*).

3740 **Savignano** Armando, Il Cristo di UNAMUNO, con una antologia di testi: GdT 194. Brescia 1990, Queriniana. 138 p. Lit. 15.000. – RETL 67 (1991) 466s (E. *Brito*); HumBr 46 (1991) 644 (V. *Liccaro*).

3741 **Schiwy** Günther, Der kosmische Christus ['mein Traum'; TEILHARD ...]; Spuren Gottes ins Neue Zeitalter. Mü 1990, Kösel. 176 p. – RZkT 113 (1991) 313s (K. H. *Neufeld*: eigenwillig, verwirrend).

3742 Der schwarze Christus [franç.], TFaymonville U., EBertsch Ludwig: Theologie der dritten Welt 12. FrB 1989, Herder. 206 p. DM 34. – RTLZ 116 (1991) 635s (S. *Krügel*).

3743 **Sheaffer** R., The making of the Messiah; Christianity and resentment [Jesus illegitimate deceiver]. Buffalo 1991, Prometheus. 192 p. $20. 0-87975-691-8 [NTAbs 36,278].

3744 **Tilliette** X., Le Christ de la philosophie 1990 ➤ 6,7548: REtudes 347 (1991) 856s (G. *Petitdemange*); TS 52 (1991) 752s (T. F. *O'Meara*). ➤ 3730 supra.

3745 **Tilliette** Xavier, Filosofi davanti a Cristo, TESansonetti Giuliano: Testi 5. Brescia 1989, Queriniana. 534 p. Lit. 55.000. 88-399-1105-7. – RActuBbg 28 (1991) 53s (J. *Boada*).

3746 **Wedel** Ezzelino von, Als Jesus sich Gott ausdachte; die unerwiderte Liebe zum Vater: Tabus des Christentums. Stu 1990, Kreuz. 143 p. 3-7831-1011-4. – RActuBbg 28 (1991) 188s (J. *Boada*: some real exegesis and Christology, along with some fantasy which wins out).

3747 *Weiss-Deaux* Solange, Jésus de Montréal, flagrant délit d'Évangile: ÉTRel 66 (1991) 545-563.

3748 **Wessels** Anton, Images of Jesus; how Jesus is perceived and portrayed in non-European cultures, [T]*Vriend* John. L/Ph 1990, SCM/Trinity. ix-195 p. £10.50. 0-334-00697-X. – [R]ExpTim 103 (1991s) 30 (G. *Parrinder*); TLond 94 (1991) 295s (R. S. *Sugirtharajah*); Worship 65 (1991) 472-4 (W. J. *Cahoy*).

3749 *Zahniser* A. H. Mathias, The Word of God and the apostleship of 'Īsā; a narrative analysis of āl 'Imrān (3): 33-62: JSS 36 (1991) 77-112.

F2.1   *Exegesis creativa* – innovative methods.

3750 **Bash** A., How to study the New Testament; six simple steps [= Stepping into Bible study 1988]. GR 1990, Zondervan. 72 p. $4. 0-310-52951-4 [NTAbs 36,249].

3751 *Botha* J. Eugene, *a)* Style in the NT; the need for serious reconsideration: JStNT 43 (1991) 71-87; – *b)* Speech act theory and NT exegesis: HervTSt 47 (1991) 294-303 [< NTAbs 36,150].

3752 **Cole** Thomas, The origins of rhetoric in ancient Greece. Baltimore 1991, Johns Hopkins Univ. [xvi–] 191 p. [p. 178, n. 17-22 omitted; furnished separately]. 0-8018-4055-4.

3753 **Egger** Wilhelm, Methodenlehre zum NT 1987 → 3,4096 ... 6,4442: [R]ColcT 61,1 (1991) 165-7 (R. *Bartnicki*, ❷); Salesianum 53 (1991) 581s (J. J. *Bartolomé*).

3754 **Egger** Wilhelm, Metodologia del NT 1990 → 6,4443: [R]Letture 46 (1991) 281s (G. *Ravasi*).

3755 **Ginn** Jeffery B., The re-shaping of the demythologizing hermeneutic; an examination of approaches to selected post-Bultmannians [... S. OGDEN]. Diss. Mid-America Baptist Theol. Sem. 1990. 189 p. 91-18483. – DissA 52 (1991s) 185-A.

[E]**Hartin** Patrick J., *Petzer* J. H., Text and interpretation; new approaches in the criticism of the New Testament: NT Tools 15 1991 → 307; 16 art., infra; in continuation of [F]METZGER → 2,72.

3757 *Hobbel* Anne Jarand, Hermeneutics in Talmud, Midrash and the New Testament: → 54, [F]FLUSSER D., Immanuel 24s (1990) 132-146.

3758 **Lentzen-Deis** Fritzleo, Un día en Cafarnaún; nuevos métodos en la exégesis bíblica; esbozo de un comentario. México 1991, Clavería. 60 p. [AcPIB 9/8,656].

3759 **Mack** Burton L., Rhetoric and the NT 1990 → 6,4446: [R]Biblica 72 (1991) 116-9 (D. F. *Watson*); CBQ 53 (1991) 714s (F. W. *Burnett*); CritRR 4 (1991) 211s (A. J. *Dewey*).

3760 *Moloney* Francis J., Narrative criticism of the Gospels: Pacifica 4 (1991) 181-201.

3761 **Moore** Stephen D., Literary criticism and the Gospels; the theoretical challenge 1989 → 5,4229; 6,4447: [R]CBQ 53 (1991) 711-3 (R. M. *Fowler*); JAAR 59 (1991) 186-9 (W. A. *Beardslee*: contrasts O'TOOLE and TANNEHILL methods); JBL 110 (1991) 152-5 (J. A. *Darr*); JTS 42 (1991) 647-9 (D. *Jasper*); TLond 94 (1991) 218s (J. *Court*); TorJT 7 (1991) 122-4 (S. *Brown*).

3762 **Mouson** Jean †, Initiation à la lecture critique des Évangiles: Cah. 4. Charleroi 1990, Faculté Ouverte Religion et Laïcité. 212 p. – [R]RTLv 22 (1991) 405s (J. *Ponthot*).

3763 **Muñoz-León** D., Deras targúmico y Nt 1987 ⇒ 3,4009.1610... 5,4230:
ᴿCiuD 203 (1991) 235s (J. *Gutièrrez*); Marianum 53 (1991) 657-660 (M. *Masini*).

3764 **Patte** Daniel, Structural exegesis for NT critics: GuidesBS. Mp 1990,
Fortress. x-134 p. – ᴿCBQ 53 (1991) 714 (F. W. *Burnett*); CritRR 4 (1991) 211-3 (A. J. *Dewey*).

3765 *Schulz* Hans-Joachim, 'Historisch-kritische' Evangelieninterpretation und 'formgeschichtliche' Überlieferungskritik; ökumenische Chance oder Rückfall in die Zeit der Aufklärung?: MüTZ 42 (1991) 15-43. 323-349.

3766 *Söding* Thomas, Was tut sich in der neutestamentlichen Exegese? Ein Überblick zu Themen, Methoden und Problemstellungen: HerdKorr 45 (1991) 524-9.

3767 *a) Villiers* P.G.R. de, The end of hermeneutics? On New Testament studies and postmodernism; – *b) Craffert* P.F., Towards an interdisciplinary definition of the social-scientific interpretation of the NT: Neotestamentica 25,1 (1991) 145-156 / 123-144.

3767* *a) Vorster* W.S., Historical criticism through the eyes of a historian; – *b) Plessis* J.G. du, Speech act theory and NT interpretation with special reference to G. N. LEECH's pragmatic principles / Fundamentalism as methodological principle; – *c) Draper* J.A., 'For the Kingdom is inside of you and it is outside of you'; contextual exegesis in South Africa: ⇒ 307, Text 1991, 15-43 / 129-142. 201-213 / 235-257.

F2.2   *Unitas VT-NT:* **The Unity of the Two Testaments.**

3768 **Alonso Schökel** Luis, [Dt; Gen 28,10] Cómo puede leer el Antiguo Testamento un cristiano de hoy: Cómo leer el AT. M 1991, Fund. S. María. 30 p. 84-348-3429-X.

3769 **Baker** David L., Two testaments, one Bible; a study of the theological relationship between the Old and New Testaments²ʳᵉᵛ [¹1976]. Leicester 1991, Apollos. 302 p. £15. 0-85111-422-9.

3770 **Beauchamp** Paul, L'un et l'autre Testament, 2. Accomplir les écritures 1990 ⇒ 6,4555; 2-02911-424-0: ᴿBL (1991) 64 (R. J. *Coggins*: still true what was said of the first volume, 'how different a tradition from Anglo-Saxon empiricism'); ExpTim 102 (1990s) 302s (also R. J. *Coggins*); RB 98 (1991) 272-9 (F. *Langlamet*: respectfully dismayed); RechSR 79 (1991) 253-260 (A.-M. *Pelletier*: his *parrhesía* blends the most extreme modernity with an essential fidelity); RevSR 65 (1991) 136s (B. *Renaud*); RThom 91 (1991) 651-665 (J.-M. *Maldamé*); TLZ 116 (1991) 345s (J.P.M. van der *Ploeg*: 'ein eigenes genre littéraire... sein Hauptwert liegt in den theologischen Betrachtungen'); TS 52 (1991) 350-2 (P. J. *Cahill*).

3771 **Begrich** Gerhard, Das evangelische Zeugnis des Alten Testaments im Festkreis des Kirchenjahres: Hab.-Diss. Berlin 1991, ᴰ*Schreiner*. – TR 87 (1991) 511.

3772 [Pinto] **Cardoso** Arnaldo, Da Antiga à Nova Aliança; relações entre o Antigo e o Novo Testamento em Sebastião BARRADAS (1543-1615) [diss. FrB 1985]. Lisboa 1987, Inst. Nac. Inv. 538 p. – ᴿDidaskalia 19 (1989) 271s (B. de *Margerie*).

3773 **Clowney** Edmund P., The unfolding mystery; discovering Christ in the Old Testament. Colorado Springs 1988, Navpress. 202 p. $8 pa. 0-8910-9259-5. – ᴿKerux 5,2 (1990) 32-36 (L. *Semel*).

Ellis E. Earle, The OT in early Christianity; canon and interpretation in the light of modern research [revised reprints]: WUNT 54. Mohr 1991 ⇒ 198.

3775 **Feuillet** A., L'accomplissement des Prophéties, ou Les annonces convergentes du Sauveur messianique dans l'AT et leur réalisation dans le NT: BtThéol. P 1991, Desclée. 181 p. – ᴿEsprVie 101 (1991) 524s (L. *Walter*: defend souvent des positions conservatrices, par indépendance d'esprit; 'au lecteur de faire preuve d'une semblable indépendance envers cet ouvrage, et les autres').

3776 **Gese** Hartmut, Sulla teologia biblica [... esempi di rapporto fra ANT; Zur BT ¹1977 ³1989 ➤ 5,265],ᵀ: BtCuRel. Brescia 1989, Paideia. 285 p. Lit. 30.000. – ᴿProtestantesimo 46 (1991) 240 (B. *Corsani*).

3777 *a) Görg* Manfred, Christentum und Altes Testament; – *b) Schmid* Hans Heinrich, Alttestamentliche Voraussetzungen neutestamentlicher Christologie; – *c) Fuchs* Ottmar, Die Herausforderungen Israels an die spirituelle und soziale Praxis der Christen; – *d) Koch* Klaus, Der doppelte Ausgang des Alten Testamentes in Judentum und Christentum: ➤ 310, JbBT 6 (1991) 5-31 / 33-45 / 89-113 / 215-242.

3778 *Goossens* André, HetOT in de Liturgie: CollatVL 21 (1991) 397-416.

3779 **Gravgaard** Anne-Mette, Inscriptions of Old Testament prophecies in Byzantine churches; a catalogue: Opuscula Byzantina et Neograeca 1. K 1979, Museum Tusculanum. 112 p.

Grelot P., *Dumais* M., Homélies sur l'Écriture à l'époque apostolique [relecture de l'AT, aussi dans le NT] 1989 ➤ 3526.

3780 **Grollenberg** Luc, Onverwachte Messias 1987 ➤ 4,4370: ᴿNedTTs 43 (1989) 246 (J. *Tromp*).

3781 **Guinot** J.-N. [typologie], *al.*, Figures de l'AT chez les Pères: Biblia Patristica Cah 2. Strasbourg 1989, Centre d'Analyse. – ᴿJTS 42 (1991) 705-7 (Frances M. *Young*).

3782 **Heyer** C. J. den, Een Bijbel – twee Testamenten; de plaats van Israel in een bijbelse theologie. Kampen 1990, Kok. 75 p. Fb 298. – ᴿCollatVL 21 (1991) 315 (J. De *Kesel*).

3783 *Holtz* Traugott, *a)* Zur Interpretation des ATs im NT [< TLZ 99 (1974) 19-32]; – *b)* Das AT und das Bekenntnis der frühen Gemeinde zu Jesus Christus [< ᶠ*Trilling* W., Christus bezeugen 1989, 55-66]; – *c)* Überlegungen zur Geschichte des Urchristentums [< TLZ 100 (1975) 321-332]: ➤ 211, Geschichte 1991, 75-91 / 92-105 / 31-44.

3784 *Hübner* Hans, Intertextualität — die hermeneutische Strategie des Paulus; zu einem neuen Versuch der theologischen Rezeption des Alten Testaments im Neuen [HAYS R., Echoes 1989]: TLZ 116 (1991) 881-898.

3785 *a) Jensen* Joseph, The OT in the NT and in the Liturgy; – *b) Stockhausen* Carol K., Paul the exegete: BToday 28 (1990) 207-212 / 196-202.

3786 **Jonge** Marinus de, Jesus, the Servant-Messiah. NHv 1991, Yale Univ. viii-115 p. $16 [CBQ 53,736].

Kimball C., OT in Luke ᴰ1991 ➤ 4508.

3787 *Knights* C. H., [2 Tim 3,14 – 4,8] Why bother with the Old Testament?: ExpTim 103 (1991s) 45-47.

3788 *Kraus* H.-J., *a)* Das Reich Gottes zuerst! Von den Wurzeln des Evangeliums im AT; – *b)* Tora und Volksnomos [inedita]: ➤ 221, Rückkehr 1991, 121-145 / 223-236.

3789 ᶠLINDARS B., It is written; Scripture citing Scripture, ᴱ**Carson** D. 1988 ➤ 4,97 ... 6,4564: ᴿEvQ 63 (1991) 178-183 (R. B. *Edwards*).

3790 *Mulder* Martin J., Iets over de relatie tussen Oude en Nieuwe Testament: CollatVL 21 (1991) 301-314.

Naumann Paul, Targum, Brücke zwischen den Testamenten I, 1991 ➤ 1525.

3791 **Neusner** Jacob, Christian faith and the Bible of Judaism; the Judaic encounter with Scripture 1987 ➤ 4,4255; 5,4137: ᴿRExp 88 (1991) 267 (T. G. *Smothers*).

3792 *a) Nowell* Irene, Typology, a method of interpretation; – *b) Torvend* Samuel, Jesus, cleft rock and saving river; – *c) Burns* Rita J., Jesus and the bronze serpent: BToday 28 (1990) 70-76 / 77-83 / 84-89.

3793 *a) Quinzio* Sergio, La redenzione messianica nell'ebraismo e nel cristianesimo; – *b) Di Sante* Carmine, L'Antica e la Nuova Alleanza; il rapporto tra i due Testamenti; – *c) Ravasi* Gianfranco, Missione e universalismo nell'AT: ➤ 325*a*, Israele/Genti 1991, 31-51 / 53-71 / 89-128.

Schuchard B., OT in NT ᴰ1991 ➤ 4842.

3794 **Villegas** Guillermo V., The OT as a Christian book [GRELOT P., MCKENZIE J., ALONSO SCHÖKEL L.] ᴰ1988 ➤ 4,4383; 5,4271: ᴿBibTB 21 (1991) 40 (J. F. *Craghan*); BZ 35 (1991) 288-290 (H. D. *Preuss*).

3795 **Zenger** Erich, Das erste Testament; die jüdische Bibel und die Christen. Dü 1991, Patmos. 208 p. 3-491-72247-0.

F2.3 *Unitas interna* – NT – **Internal unity.**

3796 **Dunn** James D.G., Unity and diversity in the NT² 1990 ➤ 6,4577: ᴿCurrTMiss 18 (1991) 223s (D. *Rhoads*); JTS 42 (1991) 692s (Clare *Drury*).

3797 **Reumann** John, Variety and unity in New Testament thought: Oxford Bible Series. Ox 1991, UP. xiv-330 p. 0-19-826202-9; pa. -4-3. – ᴿExpTim 103 (1991s) 183 (E. *Franklin*: tries too hard to serve both experts and beginners).

F2.5 *Commentarii* – **Commentaries on the whole NT.**

3798 ᵀᴱ**Cola** S., GIROLAMO, Omelie sui vangeli e su varie ricorrenze liturgiche: TPatr 88. R 1990, Città Nuova. 244 p. Lit. 20.000. – ᴿAsprenas 38 (1991) 112s (L. *Fatica*).

3799 ᴱ**Delègue** Yves, ERASME, Les préfaces au NT 1990 ➤ 6,4578: ᴿBLitEc 92 (1991) 306 (H. *Hauser*); ColcT 60,3 (1990) 181s (R. *Bartnicki*, ❷); ÉTRel 66 (1991) 447s (H. *Bost*); RHPR 71 (1991) 399s (M. *Arnold*: unsatisfactory).

3800 **MacDonald** William, Believer's Bible Commentary (NT). Nv 1990, Nelson. 1205 p. – ᴿGraceTJ 11 (1990) 340 (D. *Rickards*: conservative, 'Darbyist').

3801 ᴱ**Reeve** A., *Screech* M. A., Erasmus' Annotations on the NT; Act Rom 2 Cor: StHistChrTht 42, 1990 ➤ 6,4578*b*: ᴿNRT 113 (1991) 424s (X. *Jacques*).

3802 **Sheppard** G. T., The Geneva Bible: NT 1602 Pilgrim Classic Commentaries: 1989, Pilgrim. 320 p. $30; pa. $15. 0-8298-0789-4; -5-3. – ᴿTorJT 7 (1991) 106s (P. J. *Fedwick*).

Sieben Hermann J., Kirchenväterhomilien zum Neuen Testament; ein Repertorium der Textausgaben und Übersetzungen [... Kommentare: Anhang]: Instrumenta Patristica 22, 1991 ➤ 1598.

> X. Evangelia

F2.6 **Evangelia Synoptica;** *textus, synopses, commentarii.*

3803 ᴱ**Hainz** J., Synopse zum Münchener NT ['as close to the Greek as possible']. Dü 1991, Patmos. 263 p. DM 40, pa. 30. 3-491-71093-6; -102-9 [NTAbs 36,263].

3804 *Lang* Marijke H. de, Jean GERSON's Harmony of the Gospels (1420): NedArchiefKG 71 (1991) 37-49 [< ZIT 91,598].

3805 **Lindsey** R. L., Comparative Greek concordance of the Synoptic Gospels, 1985-9. 3 vol. [NTAbs 36,172 sans publ.].

3806 **Neirynck** Frans, The minor agreements in a horizontal-line synopsis: StNTAux 15. Lv 1991, Univ./Peeters. 103 p. Fb 400. 90-6186-457-7 / 90-6831-347-9.

3806* *Oftestad* Bernt T., Harmonia evangelica; die Evangelienharmonie von Martin CHEMNITZ — theologische Ziele und methodologische Voraussetzungen: ST 45,1 (1991) 57-74.

3807 **Poppi** Angelico, Sinossi dei quattro Vangeli 1² 1990 → 6,4590: ᴿETL 67 (1991) 165 (F. *Neirynck*, duquel la nouvelle édition s'est servie: donne *chaque* Évangile en ordre avec les parallèles); Protestantesimo 46 (1991) 75 (P. *Tognina*, 2¹).

3808 **Sanders** E. P., *Davies* Margaret, Studying the Synoptic Gospels 1989 → 5,4289; 6,4591: ᴿScotJT 44 (1991) 243-5 (C. M. *Tuckett*: authors husband and wife; high quality).

F2.7   *Problema synopticum:* **The Synoptic Problem.**

3809 **Bergemann** Thomas, Das Verhältnis der Grundrede zur Logionquelle; Überlegungen zur Methode der Ausgrenzung des Q-Stoffes aus dem Mt/L-Gut: Diss. ᴰ*Hunzinger* C. Hamburg 1991s. - RTLv 23, p. 543.

3810 *Bivin* D., A new solution to the Synoptic problem [LINDSEY R. L.: Luke was used by Mark but Matthew did not know Lk]: Jerusalem Perspective 4,3 (1991) 3-5 [6-9, *Notley* R., on Lindsey's Concordance].

3811 ᴱ**Dungan** David, The interrelations of the Gospels; BOISMARD-symposium 1984/90 → 6,524: ᴿDowR 109 (1991) 75-77 (B. *Orchard*: a watershed); LvSt 16 (1991) 271s (R. F. *Collins*: worth the long wait); NT 33 (1991) 381s (J. K. *Elliott*).

3812 **Havener** Ivan, Q, the sayings of Jesus; with a reconstruction of Q by Athanasius *Polag*: GoodNewsSt 19. ColMn 1990, Liturgical. 176 p. 0-8146-5441-X.

3813 *a*) *Horsley* R., The Q people; renovation, not radicalism; – *b*) *Downing* F. G., Actuality versus abstraction; the Synoptic Gospel model: Continuum 1,3 (NY 1991) 49-63 / 104-120 [< NTAbs 36,171s].

3814 *a*) *Kloppenborg* John S., Literary convention, self-evidence, and the social history of the Q people; – *b*) *Vaage* Leif E., The Son of Man sayings in Q; stratigraphical location and significance; – *c*) *Seeley* David, Blessings and boundaries; interpretations of Jesus' death in Q; – *d*) *Catchpole* David R., The mission charge in Q: → 312, Semeia 55 (1991) 77-102 / 103-129 / 131-146 / 147-174.

3815 **New** David S., Old Testament quotations in the Synoptic Gospels, and the two-document hypothesis: diss. McMaster, ᴰ*Westerholm* S., 1990. 312 p. 0-315-60679-7 (DANN-60679). – DissA 52 (1991s) 3633-A.

3816 *Roberts* Richard H., HEGEL and the Synoptic Problem [Lectures on the Philosophy of Religion 1831, ᵀ*Hodgson* P. 1984]: JTS 42 (1991) 565-576.

3817 *Robinson* James M., The international Q project work session 16 November 1990: JBL 110 (1991) 494-8.

3818 **Sato** Migaku, Q und Prophetie; Studien zur Gattungs- und Traditionsgeschichte der Quelle Q: WUNT 2/29, 1988 → 4,4412; 6,4611: ᴿBiblica 72 (1991) 122-130 (F. G. *Downing*); JTS 42 (1991) 223-5 (D. *Catchpole*).

3819 *Scholer* David M., Q bibliography, supplement II, 1991: → 446, SBL sem. 30 (1991) 1-7 [108 items to add to *Lull* D., Sem 28,23-27; 29, 11-13].

3820 *a) Shepherd* Tom, Intercalation in Mark and the Synoptic Problem; – *b) Peabody* David B., Repeated language in Matthew; clues to the order and composition of Luke and Mark; – *c) Farmer* William R., The minor agreements of Matthew and Luke against Mark and the Two-Gospel hypothesis; a study of these agreements in their compositional context: → 446, SBL Sem 30 (1991) 687-697 / 647-686 / 773-815.

3821 *Wansbrough* H., The Synoptic Problem; a beginner's guide: PrPeo 5 (1991) 365-9 [< NTAbs 36,23].

Wenham John, Redating Matthew, Mark and Luke; a fresh assault on the Synoptic Problem 1991 → 3585.

F2.8 *Synoptica:* **themata.**

3822 **Glancy** Jennifer A., Satan in the Synoptic Gospels: diss. Columbia, ᴰ*Brown* R. E. NY 1990. 250 p. 91-18573. – DissA 52 (1991s) 569-A.

3823 *Henderson* Ian H., Gnomic quatrains in the Synoptics; an experiment in genre definition: NTS 37 (1991) 481-498.

3824 *Horn* Friedrich W., Christentum und Judentum in der Logienquelle: EvT 51 (1991) 344-364 [332-344, *Schottroff* L. → 8839].

3825 *Humphrey* Hugh M., Temptation and authority; sapiential narratives in Q [... KLOPPENBORG J.]: BibTB 21 (1991) 43-50.

3826 **Melbourne** Bertram L., Slow to understand; the disciples in Synoptic perspective [diss. Andrews, ᴰ*Terian* A.] 1988 → 5,4312; 6,4623: ᴿEvQ 63 (1991) 67s (T. *Dwyer:* several publications since 1984 affect the problem).

3827 **Orchard** B., *Riley* H., The order of the Synoptics 1987 → 3,4198 ... 6,4626: ᴿMilltSt 23 (1989) 122-8 (P. *Byrne*); ScripB 21 (1991) 24s (R. C. *Fuller*).

3828 **Piper** Ronald A., [Mt 7,7-11] Wisdom in the Q tradition; the aphoristic teaching of Jesus [< diss. L]: SNTS Mg 61, 1989 → 5,4518: ᴿBibTB 21 (1991) 127s (H. *Humphrey*); CBQ 53 (1991) 715s (H. T. *Fleddermann*); FgNt 4 (1991) 77-79 (S. E. *Porter*); JBL 110 (1991) 522-5 (J. D. *Crossan*); NBlackf 71 (1990) 516-8 (Morna D. *Hooker*); RelStT 10,2 (1990) 123s (M. G. *Steinhauser*); ScripB 21 (1989) 22s (J. K. *Elliot*, but *-tt* p. 24); TR 87 (1991) 474-7 (H. von *Lips*).

3828* **Raja** R. J., The Gospels with an Indian face [Mt: *jñāna*; Mk: *karma*; Lk: *bhakti*]: Vidyajyoti 55 (1991) 61-72 [121-141, applied to Mt 7,12; 5,3; 15,21; 17,24; Mk 1,35; 8,22 ...].

3829 *Segalla* Giuseppe, [30 brani sinottici] La triplice funzione dell'esperienza nell'etica sapienziale di Gesù: TItSett 16 (1991) 101-146.

3830 **Seung-Ku Yoon** Victor, Did the evangelist Luke use the canonical Gospel of Matthew?: Diss. Berkeley GTU 1986, ᴰ*Herzog* W. iii-187 p. – ᴿETL 67 (1991) 391-4 (T. A. *Friedrichsen*).

3831 **Theissen** Gerd, Lokalkolorit ... der synoptischen Tradition: NOrb 8, 1989 → 5,4317; 6,4632: ᴿBiblica 72 (1991) 421-5 (D. C. *Allison*); CBQ 53 (1991) 153s (D. E. *Oakman:* compelling); RechSR 79 (1991) 421-3 (J. *Guillet*).

3831* **Theissen** Gerd, The Gospels in context; social and political history in the Synoptic tradition, ᵀ*Maloney* Linda M. Mp 1991, Fortress. xx-298 p. $30 [RelStR 18,296, F. W. *Burnett* & G. A. *Phillips*].

3832 **Vouga** F.,   Jésus et la loi selon la tradition synoptique 1988 → 4,4575; 5,4320; 6,4636:   ᴿProtestantesimo 46 (1991) 214s (F. *Ferrario*).

F3.1   **Matthaei evangelium:** *textus, commentarii.*

3833 **Davies** W. D., *Allison* Dale C.,   Mt I ICC 1988 → 4,4439 ... 6,4642: ᴿBZ 35 (1991) 131-3 (R. *Schnackenburg*); CBQ 53 (1991) 697-9 (S. *McKnight*); Interpretation 45 (1991) 294-6 (M. A. *Powell*); JBL 110 (1991) 344-6 (J. D. *Kingsbury*).

3834 **Fornberg** Tord,   Matteusevangeliet 1-13. U 1989, 'EFS'. 260 p. – ᴿSvEx 56 (1991) 128s (Kari *Syreeni*).

3835 **Forte** Anthony J.,   A critical edition of a Hiberno-Latin commentary on Matthew 1-8 (Codex Vindobonensis 940), diss. UCLA 1991, ᴰ*Löfstedt* B. 269 p. 91-22717. – DissA 52 (1991s) 954-A.

3836 **Gardner** Richard B.,   Matthew: Believers Church Bible Commentary [third volume to appear (after Jeremiah, Genesis) in this Mennonite series, ᴱ*Martens* Elmer A., *Charles* Howard H.].   Scottdale PA 1991, Herald. 446 p. $18. 0-8361-3555-5.

3837 **Gnilka** Joachim,   Das Matthäusevangelium: HerdTK 2, 1988 → 4,4440 ... 6,4645: ᴿETL 67 (1991) 167-9 (F. *Neirynck*, 1s).

3837* **Gnilka** Joachim,   Il vangelo di Matteo, testo greco e traduzione [1986 → 2,3304; 1988 → 4,4440], ᵀ*Cavallini* S., ᴱ*Soffritti* O. 1986-8 → 6,4646; CommTeol NT 1/1s. Brescia 1990s, Paideia. 755 p.; 809 p. ... Lit. 100.000/-. 88-394-0437-6; -73-2. – ᴿAsprenas 38 (1991) 109-111 (S. *Cipriani*, 1); ÉTRel 66 (1991) 120s (É. *Cuvillier*, 1).

3838 **Harrington** D. J.,   The Gospel of Matthew: Sacra Pagina 1.   ColMn 1991, Liturgical.   xiii-429 p. $30. 0-8146-5803-2 [NTAbs 36,264].

3839 ᴱ**Löfstedt** B., SEDULIUS Scottus, Kommentar zum Ev. nach Matthäus, [1-11, 1989 → 6,4648]; 11,2 bis Schluss: VLatG 19. FrB 1991, Herder. iv + p. 307-706 [NRT 114,743, X. *Jacques*]. – ᴿCBQ 53 (1991) 333s (A. *Cody*: total lack of introduction unfortunate).

3840 ᵀᴱ**Longobardo** Luigi, ILARIO de Poitiers, Commentario a Matteo: TPatr 74. R 1988, Città Nuova. 326 p. – ᴿTeresianum 42 (1991) 640-6 (M. *Diego Sánchez*, con 3 biblici e 6 altri della collana).

3841 **Luz** Ulrich,   Matthew 1-7, a commentary: ᵀ*Linss* Wilhelm: Continental Commentaries 1989 → 5,4333; also 1990 → 6,4640: ᴿInterpretation 45 (1991) 294-6 (M. A. *Powell*); NBlackf 72 (1991) 346s (Meg *Davies*); Neotestamentica 25 (1991) 445s (H. J. B. *Combrink*); Pacifica 4 (1991) 346-350 (C. J. *Monaghan*); Vidyajyoti 55 (1991) 228-230 (P. M. *Meagher*); ZkT 113 (1991) 299s (R. *Oberforcher*).

3842 **Luz** Ulrich,   Das Evangelium nach Matthäus [I. 1-7, 1985 → 1,4213; Eng. 1989 → 5,4333], II. 8-17: EkK 1/2. Z/Neuk 1985, Benziger/Neuk. 550 p. DM 125; sb. 100. 3-7887-1334-8. – ᴿETL 67 (1991) 169-171 (F. *Neirynck*).

3843 **Maggioni** Bruno,   Il racconto di Matteo⁴ [¹1981]: Bibbia per tutti. Assisi 1990, Cittadella. 375 p. Lit . 20.000.

3844 **Mateos** Juan, *Camacho* F. Il vangelo di Matteo, lettura commentata [1981], ᵀ*Tosatti* Teodora: Bibbia per tutti. Assisi 1986, Cittadella. 407 p. Lit. 18.000.

3845 **Montague** George T.,   Companion God ... Mt comm. 1989 → 5,4334*; 6,4651: ᴿBibTB 21 (1991) 81s (D. M. *May*).

3846 **Mounce** Robert M.,   Matthew: NewInternatBC, 1. Peabody MA 1991 = 1985, Hendrickson. xiii-288 p. 0-943575-18-4.

3847 **Smith** Robert H., Mt Augsburg 1989 ➤ 5,4338; 6,4656: ^RCurrTMiss 18 (1991) 139s (F. W. *Danker*).

3848 **Tassin** C., L'évangile de Matthieu; commentaire pastoral. P 1991, Centurion/Novalis. 305 p. F 135 [NRT 114,941].

3849 ^{TE}**Vogt** Hermann J., ORIGENES, Der Kommentar zum Evangelium nach Matthäus [I. 1983 ➤ 64,4205]; II. libri 14-17 [Kap. 18-22]: Bibliothek der griechischen Literatur 30. Stu 1990, Hiersemann. ix-371 p. ➤ 6, 4658; DM 270. 3-7772-9011-4. – ^RRHPR 71 (1991) 375 (P. *Maraval*: 'un troisième volume sera consacré aux parties qui ne nous sont parvenues qu'en latin, de RUFIN').

F3.2 **Themata** de Matthaeo.

^E**Balch** David L., The social history of the Matthaean community 1989/91 ➤ 415*d*.

3850 **Bieber** Anneliese, J. BUGENHAGEN zwischen Reform und Reformation; die Entwicklung seiner frühen Theologie anhand des Matthäuskommentar und der Passions- und Auferstehungsharmonie: ev. Diss. Münster 1991, ^D*Hauschild*. – TR 87 (1991) 520.

3851 **Brooks** Stephenson H., Matthew's community ^D1987 ➤ 3,4233 ... 6,4663: ^RTLZ 116 (1991) 738s (U. *Luz*).

3852 **Casalini** N., Il Vangelo di Matteo come racconto teologico: analisi delle sequenze narrative: SBF Anal 30, 1990 ➤ 6,4664: ^RRechSR 79 (1991) 419s (J. *Guillet*); RivB 39 (1991) 59s (G. *De Virgilio*).

3853 *a) Comblin* José, As linhas básicas do Evangelho segundo Mateus / Justiça e lei; – *b) Galazzi* Sandro, O poder da morte não vai derrotá-la: EstudosB 26 (1990) 9-18. 19-27 / 34-42.

3853* *Deutsch* Celia, Torah, Jesus and discipleship in the Gospel of Matthew: SIDIC 24,2s (1991) 43-52.

3854 *Gollinger* Hildegard, Heil für die Heiden — Unheil für die Juden? Anmerkungen zu einem alten Problem mit dem Mt.-ev.: ➤ 46*, ^FEHRLICH E., 1991, 201-211.

3855 **Granger** John W., Matthew's use of apocalyptic: diss. Baptist Theol. Sem., ^D*Simmons* B. E. New Orleans 1990. 188 p. 91-17902. - DissA 52 (1991s) 185-A.

3855* *Hendrickx* H., Matthew's/Mark's community: Theology Annual 12 (Hong Kong 1990s) 141-143 / 124-140 [< NTAbs 36,332.340].

3856 *Hergesel* Tomasz, ❷ Matthew's salvation-history: RuBi 44 (1991) 25-36.

3857 **Howell** David B., Matthew's inclusive story: JStNt supp 42, ^D1990 ➤ 6,4674: ^RBiblica 72 (1991) 280-2 (J. D. *Kingsbury*); ExpTim 103 (1991s) 24s (G. *Stanton*: 'readers'? modern or early); JTS 42 (1991) 651-4 (H. B. *Green*); RExp 88 (1991) 267s (A. A. *Trites*); TTod 48 (1991s) 376s (D. R. *Bauer*).

3858 *a) Humphries-Brooks* Stephenson, Indicators of social organization and status in Matthew's Gospel; – *b) Powell* Mark A., Direct and indirect phraseology in the Gospel of Matthew; – *c) Wilkins* Michael J., Named and unnamed disciples in Matthew; a literary-theological study: ➤ 446, SBL Sem 30 (1991) 31-49 / 405-417 / 418-439.

3859 **Johne** Karin, Dein Wort wird mich verwandeln; das Matthäusevangelium meditieren. FrB 1991, Herder. 260 p. DM 29,80 [CBQ 54,403].

3860 **Kingsbury** J. D., Matthew as story² 1988 ➤ 5,4362; 6,4675: ^RRelStT 10,2 (1990) 113 (M. *Desjardins*).

3861 **Kynes** William L.,   A Christology of solidarity: Jesus as the representative of his people in Matthew. Lanham MD 1991, UPA. xiii-247 p. $27 [TR 88,251].

3862 **Lenz** E.,   Betrachtungen über das Matthäus-Evangelium; Studien zu Komposition und Initiation im ersten Evangelium. Stu 1990, Urach. 140 p. DM 32. 3-87838-628-1 [NTAbs 36,265: anthroposophist sectfounder].

3863 a) *Luz* Ulrich,   L'évangéliste Matthieu; un judéo-chrétien à la croisée des chemins; – b) *Strecker* Georg,   La conception de l'histoire chez Matthieu: → 30, ^FBONNARD F., Mémoire 1991, 77-92 / 93-111.

3864 a) *Luz* Ulrich,   Eine thetische Skizze der matthäischen Christologie [p. 6, Thesen zur Christologie des Matthäus]; – b) *Klein* Hans,   Christologie und Anthropologie in den Petruslegenden des matthäischen Sondergutes: → 72, ^FHAHN F., Anfänge 1991, 221-235 / 209-220.

3865 **Massaux** Édouard,   Influence... Mt avant IRÉNÉE 1986 = 1950 + bibliog. → 2,3327 ... 4,4473: ^RSecC 8 (1991) 246s (Pheme *Perkins*).

3866 **Massaux** Édouard,   The influence of the Gospel of Saint Matthew on Christian literature before Saint IRENAEUS, 1. The first ecclesiastical writers, ^T*Belval* Norman J., *Hecht* Suzanne; ^E*Bellinzoni* Arthur J. Lv/Macon GA 1990, Peeters/Mercer Univ. xxvi-1130 p. $25. 0-86554-377-1 [TDig 39,274].

3867 **Meier** John P.,   The vision of Matthew; Christ, church, and morality in the First Gospel. NY 1991 [= 1984 + introd.], Crossroad. viii-270 p. $17. 0-8245-1092-5 [TDig 39,74].

3868 **Mora** Vincent,   La symbolique de la création dans l'évangile de Matthieu: LDiv 144. P 1991, Cerf. 236 p. F 150 [TR 88,163]. 2-204-04132-7. – ^RArTGran 54 (1991) 376s (A. *Segovia*).

3869 **Neerakkal** Cyriac,   The concept of 'perfect' in the Gospel of Matthew; an exegetico-theological investigation: diss. Pont. Univ. Gregoriana, ^D*Stock* K. Roma 1991. 382 p.; extr. N° 3727, 109 p. – RTLv 23, p. 545 [< DissA-C].

3870 *Nepper-Christensen* Poul,   Apostlen Matthæus og Matthæusevangeliet: DanTTs 54 (1991) 95-112 [NTAbs 36,174].

3871 **Orton** David E.,   The understanding scribe; Matthew and the apocalyptic ideal: JStNT supp 25, 1989 → 5,4374; 6,4686: ^RBiblica 72 (1991) 119-123 (G. *Claudel*); BL (1991) 141s (C. J. A. *Hickling*); CBQ 53 (1991) 503s (B. F. *Meyer*); EvQ 63 (1991) 268-270 (J. *Nolland*); JBL 110 (1991) 527-9 (Amy-Jill *Levine*); JTS 42 (1991) 189-191 (C. J. A. *Hickling*: doubly ground-breaking, but unproved); RB 98 (1991) 626s (B. R. *Doyle*, Eng.)

3872 **Overman** J. Andrew,   Matthew's... social world ^D1990 → 6,4687: ^RExpTim 102 (1990s) 316 (S. C. *Barton*); RExp 88 (1991) 268s (A. A. *Trites*); TS 52 (1991) 388 (L. *Cope*).

3873 **Quesnel** Michel,   Jésus-Christ selon Saint Matthieu; synthèse théologique: JJC 47. P 1991, Desclée. 240 p. F 119. 2-7189-0494-1. – ^REspr-Vie 101 (1991) 253-5 (É. *Cothenet*).

3874 *Raja* Rao T. J.,   Proverbs Jesus used in the Gospel according to Matthew: Jeevadhara 20 (1990) 133-150.

3875 *Rodríguez Carmona* Antonio,   Leer a san Mateo en el Ciclo Litúrgico A/B: Proyección 37 (1990) 5-21 / 38 (1991) 19-30.

3876 **Sand** Alexander,   Das Matthäus-Evangelium: Erträge der Forschung 275. Da 1991, Wiss. viii-196 p. 3-534-10878-7 [TR 88,75].

3877 *Stenger* Werner,   'Hypokrisis' im Matthäusevangelium: → 398, Simulation 1989/91, 71-85.

3878 *Trainor* Michael, The begetting of wisdom; the teacher and the disciples in Matthew's community: Pacifica 4 (1991) 148-164 [< NTAbs 36,24].
3879 **Wainwright** Elaine M., Towards a feminist critical reading of the Gospel according to Matthew [< ᴰBrisbane]: BZNW 60. B 1991, de Gruyter. xxiii-410 p. DM 166. 3-11-012860-8 [TDig 39,252].
3880 **Wilkins** Michael J., The concept of disciple in Matthew's Gospel; NTSup 59, ᴰ1988 ➤ 4,4485 ... 6,4703: ᴿRB 98 (1991) 624-6 (B. R. *Doyle*, Eng.).
3881 **Wong Kun-Chun,** Juden und Heidenchristen im Matthäusevangelium; die interkulturelle Theologie des Mt.Evs. und seine bikulturelle Gemeinde: Diss. Heidelberg 1991, ᴰ*Theissen.* – TR 87 (1991) 519.

F3.3   *Mt 1s (Lc 1s* ➤ F7.5) *Infantia Jesu* – **Infancy Gospels.**

3881* *a) Ahirika* Edwin A., The theology of Matthew in the light of the Nativity story; – *b) Mangatt* George, The public ministry of Jesus in Mt; – *c) Kayalaparampil* Thomas, Passion and Resurrection in Mt: Bible Bhashyam 16 (1990) 5-19 / 20-40 / 41-51.
3882 *Allen* John L.,ᴶ, The Protevangelium of James as an Historia; the insufficiency of the Infancy Gospel category: ➤ 446, SBL Sem 30 (1991) 508-517.
3883 *Blomberg* Craig L., The liberation of illegitimacy; women and rulers in Matthew 1-2: BibTB 21 (1991) 145-150.
3884 *Burnett* Fred W., The undecidability of the proper name 'Jesus' in Matthew ['designed to educate the reader to construct a charade out of the name']: ➤ 311, Semeia 54 (1991) 123-144.
3885 *Canal* José M., Identificados dos textos pseudo-agustinianos citados por Pascasio RADBERTO en su 'De partu sanctae Mariae': Marianum [30 (1968) 53-160 y ahora *Matter* E. 1976, *Maloy* R. 1971] 53 (1991) 537-543.
3886 **Casalini** Nello, Libro dell'origine di Gesù Cristo; analisi letteraria e teologica di Matt 1-2: SBF Anal 28, 1990 ➤ 6,4706: ᴿRivB 39 (1991) 56-58 (G. *De Virgilio*); Salesianum 53 (1991) 578 (J. J. *Bartolomé*).
3887 *Chrostowski* Waldemar, ❷ Les évangiles de l'enfance de Jésus; histoire, légende, mystère: PrzPow 270,832 (1990) 357-375; français 376 [509-513, Ewangelie dzieciństwa, Tydzień biblijny Kraków 10-14.IX.1989].
3888 *Faucher* Alain, Les récits de l'enfance de Jésus; aimez-vous 'l'architexture'?: Appoint 24 (Montréal, Québec nov. 1991) 37-39.
3889 **Fernández y Avila** Gaspar, La infancia de Jesus-Christo: Pg. Granada 1987, Univ. 384 p. – ᴿScripTPamp 23 (1991) 366s (V. *Balaguer*).
3890 **Feuillet** A., Sauveur... Mt 1s/Lc 1s, 1990 ➤ 6,4709: ᴿSalesianum 53 (1991) 582s (J. J. *Bartolomé*).
3891 ᶠFINEGAN J.: Chronos... Nativity, ᴱ**Vardaman** J., *al.*, 1989 ➤ 5,58: ᴿRivB 39 (1991) 366-374 (A. *Valentini*: fondamentalismo sia letterario che astronomico).
3892 *Frasso* G., Un frammento di 'Vangelo dell'infanzia' in versi?: Italia Medioevale e Umanistica 31 (Padova 1988) 127-149; 2 pl. [< RHE 86,19*].
3893 **Pérez Rodríguez** Gabriel, La infancia de Jésus (Mt 1-2; Lc 1-2): Teología en diálogo 4. S 1990, Univ. 266 p. 84-7299-260-8. – ᴿSalmanticensis 38 (1991) 373s (S. *Muñoz Iglesias*).
3894 *Sicre* Jose L., Temas selectos de san Mateo, I. La infancia de Jesús; II. Tríptico introductorio; III. Sermón del Monte I: Proyección 38 (1991) 3-18 / 101-110 / 263-274.

3895 **Stichel** Rainer, Die Geburt Christi in der russischen Ikonenmalerei; Voraussetzungen in Glauben und Kunst des christlichen Ostens und Westens. Stu 1990, Steiner. 176 p.; 92 pl. DM 122. – ᴿIrénikon 64 (1991) 149s (E. *Lt.*).

3896 **Johnson** Marshall D., The purpose of the biblical genealogies ... of Jesus: SNTS Mg 8, 1969 ²1988 → 4,3022: ᴿScripB 21 (1991) 25 (S. *Greenhalgh*).

3897 *Muñoz Iglesias* Salvador [→ 4498*], Las mujeres en la genealogía de Jesús según san Mateo: → 421, Luso-Esp 1989/91, 347-360.

3898 — *Heil* John P., The narrative roles of the women in Matthew's genealogy: Biblica 72 (1991) 538-545.

3899 **Horsley** Richard A., The liberation of Christmas 1989 → 4,4500 ... 6,4711: ᴿAnnTh 5 (1991) 417-9 (B. *Estrada*); JBL 110 (1991) 159-162 (R. A. *Ramsaran*).

3900 *Nicolescu-Leordeni* Nicolăe (roum.), Contributions à l'éclaircissement de l'origine de la fête de Noël: STBuc 39,3s (1987) 21-78. 9-74; Eng. Summary 39,4, p. 75-78.

3901 *Mellor* Philip A., The Virgin Birth and the [BALTHASAR] theology of beauty: IrTQ 57 (1991) 196-208.

3902 **Segalla** G., Una storia annunciata ... Mt 1s, 1987 → 4,4509 ... 6,4722: ᴿMarianum 52 (1990) 228-234 (S. *Muñoz Iglesias*); Nicolaus 18 (1991) 398-405 (A. *Moda*).

3903 *Fernández* Domiciano, Jesús, el hijo de José; la virginidad de María en los recientes artículos de Uta RANKE-HEINEMANN: EphMar 38 (1988) 385-396.

3904 **Freitas Ferreira** José de, Conceição virginal de Jesus; análisi crítica da pesquisa liberal protestante desde a 'Declaração de Eisenach' até hoje, sobre o testemunho de Mt 1,18-25 e Lc 1,16-38; diss. R 1977 → 61,5616; ᴰGalot J.]: AnGreg 217. R 1980, Pont. Univ. Gregoriana. 535 p.

3904* *Olivera* F., Interpretación derásica de Mt 1,18-25: Mayéutica 17,44 (Marcilla 1991) 281-304 [< NTAbs 36,333].

Gibert P., Le récit biblique de rêve [Mt 1,20-25 ...] 1990 → 2063.

3905 *a) Brändle* Francisco, Jesús Nazareno, ¿por qué? El puesto de San José en el camino de la revelación; – *b) Bartina* Sebastián, Los sueños o éxtasis de San José; – *c) Stramare* Tarcisio, L'annunciazione a Giuseppe in Mt 1,18-25; analisi letteraria e significato teologico; – *d) Mercier* Gérard, Dom Augustin CALMET, O.S.B., sa pensée sur saint Joseph: → 480c, EstJos 45 (1991) 33-41 / 43-53 / 55-76 / 77-93.

3906 *Marín Heredia* F., Más allá de las apariencias; Mt 2,1-23: Carthaginensia 7 (1991) 319-330; Eng. 317.

3907 *Lockmann* Paulo, Do Egito chamei meu filho (Mt 2,13-23): EstudosB 26 (1990) 28-33.

3908 *Halleux* André de, L'adoration des Mages dans le commentaire syriaque du Diatessaron: Muséon 104 (1991) 251-264.

Martinetz Dieter, *al.*, Weihrauch und Myrrhe 1989 → e494.

3909 *Tupper* E. Frank, [Mt 2,16] The Bethlehem massacre — Christology against Providence?: RExp 88 (1991) 399-418.

3910 *Schilder* Klaas, The weeping of Rachel, Matthew 2:17,18, ᵀ*Jones* Stuart: Kerux 1,3 (1986) 4-16.

3911 *Mangatt* G., The family of Nazareth: Bible Bhashyam 17 (1991) 181-195.
3912 **Lorber** Jakob, Jezusova mladost (Jesus' youth). Ljubljana 1990, Izdelki D.O.O. 441 p. – ᴿBogVest 50 (1990) 461-3 (F. *Rozman*).

F3.4 *Mt 3 ... Baptismus Jesu,* **Beginning of the Public Life.**

3913 **Backhaus** Knut, Die 'Jüngerkreise' des Täufers Johannes [< *Álloi kekopiákasin...*, Diss. ᴰ*Ernst* J., Pd 1989 ➤ 6,4736]; eine Studie zu den religionsgeschichtlichen Ursprüngen des Christentums: PdTSt 19. Pd 1991, Schöningh. xviii-405 p. 3-506-76269-9.
3914 *Engemann* J., Johannes der Täufer: ➤ 681, LexMA 5 (1990) 529s (530, *Restle* M., Byzanz).
3915 **Ernst** Josef, Johannes der Täufer...: BZNW 53, 1989 ➤ 5,4433; 6,4740: ᴿCBQ 53 (1991) 141s (C. *Bernas* compares with LUPIERI E.); TRu 56 (1991) 206-8 (E. *Lohse*).
3916 *Hollingsworth* Mark, [Jesus and John Baptist] Opponents and brothers: BToday 28 (1990) 284-290.
3917 *Holtz* Traugott, Die Standespredigt Johannes des Täufers [< ᶠ*Fuchs* Emil 1964, 461-474]: ➤ 211, Geschichte 1991, 45-54.
Leloir Louis, Élie et Jean le Baptiste 1991 ➤ 2563.
3918 **Lupieri** Edmondo, Giovanni Battista fra storia e leggenda: BiblCuRel 53, 1988 ➤ 4,4537; 5,4743: ᴿEstE 66 (1991) 97s (J. *Alonso Díaz*); Salesianum 53 (1991) 770s (C. *Bissoli*); TLZ 116 (1991) 358s (C. *Wolff,* auch über GB/sinott. ➤ 4,4536).
3918* *a*) *Lupieri* Edmondo, G. Battista, fra i testi e la storia; – *b*) *Grech* Prospero, La pratica del battesimo ai tempi di Gesù; – *c*) *Ricca* Paolo, Il battesimo di Gesù nel Giordano; storia e teologia; – *d*) *Quesnel* Michel, Les premiers témoignages du baptême au nom de Jésus: ➤ 561*d*, Origini del battesimo 1989/91, 75-107 / 59-73 / 109-127 / 129-144.
3919 **Webb** Robert L., John the Baptizer and prophet, a socio-historical study: JStNT supp 62. Sheffield 1991, Academic. 446 p. £35; sb. £28. 1-85075-316-4.
3920 *Webb* Robert L., The activity of John the Baptist's expected figure at the threshing floor (Mt 3.12 = Lk 3.17): JStNT 43 (1991) 103-111.

3921 *Schmidt* Andreas, [Mt 3,16s] Der mögliche Text von P. Oxy. III 405, Z[eilen] 39-45: NTS 37 (1991) nur 160.
3922 *McVann* Mark, [Mt 4,1-11] Uno de los profetas; interpretación del relato de las tentaciones en Mateo como rito de iniciación: EstB 49 (1991) 191-208.
3923 *Mense* Josef, *a*) Die Versuchung Jesu, Mt 4,1-11: ZPraxRU 21 (Stu 1991) 143-6 [< ZIT 91,827]; – *b*) Die Versuchung Jesu (I); mehrdimensionale Auslegung und didaktische Anregungen zu Mt 4,1-11: KatBlätt 116,1 (Mü 1991) 28-39 [< ZIT 91,11]; – *c*) Die Versuching Jesu IIs. Künstgeschichtlicher Überblick / Didaktische Anregungen: KatBlätter 116 (Mü 1991) 184-192 [< ZIT 91,250].
3924 *Genuyt* F., Mt 4,12-7,29; 8-9,8; 9,9-26; 10,1-42: SémBib 62 (1991) 2-20; 63 (1991) 3-17; 64 (1991) 3-14; 65 (1992) 3-17.

3925 *Safrai* Chana, [Mt 4,19 ...] Jesus and his disciples; the beginnings of their organization; ᵀ*Chipman* Jonathan: ➤ 54, ᶠFLUSSER D., Immanuel 24s (1990) 95-108.

F3.5 **Mt 5 ... Sermon on the Mount** [... plain, Lk 6,17].

3926 *Betz* Hans D., The sermon on the mount; in defense of a hypothesis [responses *Saunders* Ernest W., *Snodgrass* Klyne]: BiRes 36 (1991) 74-80 [81-87, 88-94].

3927 *Davies* W. D., *Allison* Dale C.ᴶ, Reflections on the Sermon on the Mount: ScotJT 44 (1991) 283-309.

3928 **Deidenbach** Hans, Zur Psychologie der Bergpredigt. Fra 1990, Fischer. 251 p. DM 16,80 [TPQ 140,193, J. *Janda*].

3929 **Entrich** Manfred, Die Bergpredigt in der Matthäuspostille ALBERTs des Grossen als katechetischer Entwurf einer 'ratio formalis': kath. Diss. Salzburg 1991, ᴰ*Biesinger*. – TR 87 (1991) 514.

3930 *George* Martin, Die Heilige Schrift als Quelle gesellschaftlicher Reform; Johannes CHRYSOSTOMOS und die Bergpredigt: ➤ 558, Sola Scriptura 1990/1, 251-261.

3931 **Kühlwein** Klaus, Familienbeziehung und Bergpredigt-Weisungen: kath. Diss. Fra St-Georgen 1991, ᴰ*Lay*. – TR 87 (1991) 517.

3932 **Lapide** P., The Sermon on the Mount, ᵀ*Swidler* A. 1986 ➤ 2,3405 ... 4,4560: ᴿJDharma 14 (1989) 404s (J. *Akkara*).

3933 **Lohfink** G., Wem gilt die Bergpredigt? 1988 ➤ 4,4564; 5,4457: ᴿTR 87 (1991) 192-4 (T. *Söding*).

3934 **Lohfink** Gerhard, El sermón ... ¿ para quién? 1989 ➤ 6,4765: ᴿIter 2 (1991) 154s (J.-P. *Wyssenbach*); PerspT 22 (1990) 400-2 (J. *Vitório*).

3935 **Lohfink** Gerhard, Per chi vale il Discorso della montagna? Contributi per un'etica cristiana [1988 ➤ 4,4564],ᵀ: BtB 3. Brescia 1990, Queriniana. 229 p. – ᴿRivB 39 (1991) 61-63 (L. *Cilia*).

3936 *McCarthy* Carmel, Gospel exegesis from a Semitic church; EPHREM's commentary on the Sermon on the Mount: ➤ 17, ᶠBARTHÉLEMY D., Tradition 1991, 103-121.

3937 **Martini** Carlo M., Il vangelo alle sorgenti; meditando ad Assisi il Discorso della Montagna. Mi 1990, Àncora. 114 p. Lit. 10.000. – ᴿBenedictina 38 (1991) 527-9 (Annamaria *Valli*).

3938 *Mesters* Carlos, 'Ouvi o clamor do meu povo!' — Estudos bíblicos de Mat 5-9: EstudosB 26 (1990) 61-69.

3939 **Mokrosch** Reinhold, Die Bergpredigt im Alltag; Anregungen und Materialien für die Sekundarstufe I/II: Siebenstern 746. Gü 1991, Mohn. 192 p. DM 24,80 [TLZ 117,870, P. *Lehmann*].

3940 *Schweizer* Eduard, El sermón de la montaña [escrito en Baleares],ᵀ 1990 ➤ 6,4769: ᴿCarthaginensia 7 (1991) 259 (R. *Sanz Valdivieso*).

3941 **Schweizer** Eduard, Il discorso della montagna, Matteo cap. 5-7 [1982, ²1984], ᵀ*Fiorillo* Michele: PiccCollana Moderna 66. T 1991, Claudiana. 144 p. Lit. 16.000. 88-7016-139-0.

3942 **Stoll** Brigitta, De virtute in virtutem; zum Auslegungs- und Wirkungsgeschichte der Bergpredigt 1988 ➤ 4,4570 ... 6,4771: ᴿCritRR 4 (1991) 237-9 (H. D. *Betz*); RB 98 (1991) 629-632 (B. T. *Viviano*: valuable despite errors of biblical citation).

3943 **Syreeni** Kari, Making of the Sermon on the Mount I ᴰ1987 ➤ 3,4360

... 5,4463:   RÉTRel 66 (1991) 287s (Danielle *Ellul*); RBgPg 69 (1991) 203-5 (J. *Schamp*).

F3.6 Mt 5,3-11 (Lc 6,20-22) Beatitudines.

3944 *Gonella* G., [Mt 5,3-12] Song of the Beatitudes: Church 7,4 (NY 1991) 8-11 [< NTAbs 36,175].

3945 *Leske* Adrian M., The beatitudes; salt and light in Matthew and Luke: → 446, SBL Sem 30 (1991) 816-839.

3946 a) *Molari* Carlo, L'intreccio ideale delle Beatitudini; – b) *Rossi de Gasperis* Francesco, Le beatitudini del vangelo secondo Matteo; – c) *D'Agostino* Francesco, La povertà scandalo e beatitudine; – d) *Galot* Jean, Sofferenza e beatitudine; – e) *Balducci* Ernesto, Beati e miti perché erediteranno la terra: → 416, Beatitudini 1990/1, 5-20 / 21-38 / 39-47 /49-61 / 63-90.

3947 **Mugaruka-Ngabo** Richard, La traduction de la Bible comme moment d'inculturation du message révélé; application à la version shi des Béatitudes en Mt 5,1-12: diss: DPonthot J. Louvain-la-Neuve 1991. 411 p. – RTLv 22 (1991) 568; RTLv 23, p. 562.

3948 *Puech* Émile, 4Q525 et les péricopes des Béatitudes en Ben Sira et Matthieu: RB 98 (1991) 80-106; Eng. 80.

3949 a) *Martini* Carlo M., Beati i misericordiosi, perché troveranno misericordia; – b) *Scilligo* Pio, Beati i puri di cuore perché vedranno Dio; – c) *Vallauri* Luigi L., Beati i costruttori di pace: → 416, Beatitudini 1990/1, 111-131 / 133-145 / 147-156.

3950 *Lux* Rüdiger, Das Erbe der Gewaltlosen; Überlegungen zu Mt 5,5 und seiner Vorgeschichte: → 163, FWAGNER S., Gottesvolk 1991, 75-90.

3950* **Sicari** Antonio, a) [Mt 5,4] La consolazione degli afflitti; interpretazione cristologica della seconda beatitudine: → 346, Communio 119 (1991) 22-28; – b) [Mt 5,6] The hunger and thirst of Christ: CommND 18 (1991) 590-602 [< NTAbs 36,334].

3951 *Bovati* Pietro, Beati quelli che hanno fame e sete della giustizia, perché saranno saziati: → 416, Il mondo dell'uomo nascosto 1991, 91-109.

3952 *Vos* Geerhardus, [Mt 5,6] Hungering and thirsting after righteousness: Kerux 6,3 (1991) 3-18.

3953 *Maartens* Pieter J., Critical dialogue in theory and practice of literary interpretation; a study of semiotic relations in Matthew 5:11 and 12: LingBib 65 (1991) 5-24.

3954 *Derrett* J. D. M., The light and the city; Mt 5:14: ExpTim 103 (1991s) 174s.

3955 [*Fusako*] *Onishi* Immaculata, 'Je ne suis pas venu abroger mais accomplir' (Mt 5,17): Spiritus 32 (1991) 51-58.

3956 **Brown** Robert L., [Mt 5,17] Matthew's presentation of the Law in light of early Christian-Jewish dialogue: diss. Southern Baptist Theol. Sem. 1991, DGarland D. 219 p. 92-10175. – DissA 52 (1991s) 3632-A.

3957 *Casciaro* José M., Una búsqueda del alcance de las antítesis de Mt 5,21-48: → 421, Luso-Esp 1989/91, 409-423.

3958 **Ewald** G. R., [Mt 5,31...] Jesus and divorce; a biblical guide for ministry to divorced persons. Scottdale PA 1991, Herald. 176 p. $9.50 pa. 0-8361-3572-5 [NTAbs 36,282].

3959 **Riggs** Douglas L. [Mt 5,31 + 3 texts] A rhetorical-critical interpretation of the divorce and remarriage passages in the Synoptic Gospels:

diss. SW Baptist Theol. Sem. 1991, DUrrey T. 267 p. 91-35753. – DissA 52 (1991s) 2589-A.

3960 **Haraguchi** Takaaki, [Mt 5,33] The prohibition of oath-taking in the Gospel of Matthew: diss. Lutheran School of Theology, DLinss W. [Ch] 1991. 249 p. 91-29533. – DissA 52 (1991s) 1389-A.

3961 *Ito* Akio, The question of the authenticity of the ban on swearing (Mt 5,33-37): JStNT 43 (1991) 5-13.

3962 *Duling* Dennis C., '[Do not swear ...] by Jerusalem because it is the city of the Great King' (Matt 5:35): JBL 110 (1991) 291-309.

3963 *Gill* David, [Mt 5,38-48; Crito 47-49, Republic 331-6] Socrates and Jesus on non-retaliation and love of enemies: Horizons 18 (1991) 246-262.

3964 *Rathey* Markus, Talion im NT? Zu Mt 5,38-42: ZNW 82 (1991) 264-6.

3965 **Zerbe** Gordon M., [Mt 5,39] Non-retaliation in early Jewish and New Testament texts; ethical themes in social contexts: diss. Princeton Theol.Sem., DCharlesworth J. Princeton 1991. vi-403 p. 91-27021. – OIAc 2,30.

F3.7   *Mt 6,9-13 (Lc 11,2-4)* **Oratio Jesu,** Pater Noster, **Lord's Prayer** [➤ H1.4].

3966 **Clément** O., *Standaert* B., Pregare il Padre nostro. Magnano 1988, Qiqajon. 134 p. Lit. 9.000. – RAsprenas 38 (1991) 126s (L. *Medusa*).

EDeun P. Van, MAXIMI Confessoris, In orationem dominicam: CChrSG 23, 1991 ➤ 2848*.

3967 *a) Frye* Roland M., On praying 'Our Father'; the challenge of radical feminist language for God; – *b) McMichael* Ralph N.J, God-language and inclusive language liturgy: AnglTR 73 (1991) 388-402 / 430-445.

3968 *Härle* Wilfried, Den Mantel weit ausbreiten; theologische Überlegungen zum Gebet [Vaterunser, LUTHER]: NSys 33 (1991) 231-247; Eng. 247.

3969 *Hübsch* Bruno, Le Notre Père, quand la prière devient mémorial (Matthieu 5-7): ➤ 121, FRAMAROSON L., Ta parole 1991, 20-31.

3970 **Lapide** P., Das Vaterunser — ein jüdisches oder christliches Gebet?: Renovatio 47 (1991) 108-110 [< NTAbs 36,26].

3971 **Sabugal** S., Il Padrenostro nella catechesi antica e moderna² [¹1982],T 1985 ➤ 4,4610 ... 6,4821: RHoTheológos 9 (1991) 380-2 (A. *Cavadi*).

3972 **Stefani** Piero, Il Padrenostro: Le voci della preghiera 1. Genova 1991, Marietti. 104 p. 88-211-6945-6.

3973 **Stritzky** Maria-Barbara von, Studien zur Überlieferung und Interpretation des Vaterunsers D1989 ➤ 5,4503: RÉtClas 59 (1991) 282s (X. *Jacques*); TS 52 (1991) 178 (L. P. *Schrenk*).

3974 *Bindemann* Walther, Das Brot für morgen gib uns heute; sozialgeschichtliche Erwägungen zu den Wir-Bitten des Vaterunsers: BTZ 8 (1991) 199-215.

3975 *Ramaroson* Léonard, 'Notre part de nourriture' (Mt 6,11): ScEsp 43 (1991) 87-115.

3976 *Lapide* Pinchas, 'Eine tragfähige Brücke der Versöhnung'; das Vaterunser — ein jüdisches oder ein christliches Gebet?: Klerusblatt 71,1 (Mü 1991) 5-7 [< ZIT 91,120].

3977 *Genre* Ermanno, 'Dove c'è il tuo tesoro lì c'è anche il tuo cuore' Mt 6.19-21: Protestantesimo 46 (1991) 41-48.

3977* **Łach** J., ❷ 'Nul ne peut servir deux maîtres' (Mt 6,24): STWsz 28,2 (1990) 38-50 [< NTAbs 36,335].

3978 *Bartolomé* Juan J., Los pájaros y los lirios; una aproximación a la cuestión ecológica desde Mt 6,25-34: EstB 49 (1991) 165-190; Eng. 165.

3979 *Dillon* Richard J., Ravens, lilies, and the Kingdom of God (Matthew 6:25-33 / Luke 12:22-31): CBQ 53 (1991) 605-627.

3980 *Crampsey* J. L., [Mt 6,25-29] 'Look at the birds of the air...': Way 31 (1991) 286-294.

3980* *Irwin* M. E., [Mt 6,28-30] Considering the lilies: McMaster JTheol 2,2 (Hamilton ON 1991) 20-28 [1,2 (1990) 1-21 on Mt 18,3, *Hobbs* T. R., Crossing cultural bridges; the biblical world: < NTAbs 36,336s].

3981 *Crocker* P. T., [Mt 7,5] Nets, styli and ophthalmology... a mystery solved: Buried History 27 (1991) 59-63 [< NTAbs 36,177].

3982 *O'Callaghan* José, La variante antioquena 'los asemejaré' de Mt 7,24: ➤ 421, III Simposio Bíblico Español (I Luso-Espanhol) 1991, 135-138 [< AcPIB 9/8,657].

3983 *Romaniuk* Kazimierz, [Mt 8,18-22; Lc 9,57-60] ❷ De l'Imitation de Jésus: ColcT 60,1 (1990) 5-13; franç. 14.

3984 *Kiilunen* Jarmo, Der nachfolgewillige Schriftgelehrte; Matthäus 8.19-20 im Verständnis des Evangelisten: NTS 37 (1991) 268-279.

3985 **Hengel** Martin, Sequela e carisma; studio esegetico e di storia delle religioni su Mt 8,21s e la chiamata di Gesù alla sequela [1968], 1990 ➤ 6,4833 (TEGianotto Claudio): RAsprenas 38 (1991) 395s (S. *Cipriani*); CC 142 (1991,3) 448 (V. *Fusco*).

F4.1 *Mt 9-12; Miracula Jesu* – **The Gospel miracles.**

3986 *Aichele* GeorgeJ, Biblical miracle narratives as fantasy: AnglTR 73 (1991) 51-58.

3987 **Basinger** David & Randall, Philosophy and miracles; the contemporary debate: Problems in contemporary philosophy 2. Lewiston NY 1986, Mellen.... – REvQ 63 (1991) 90-92 (T. A. *Hart*: reserves).

3988 **Beckwith** F., D. HUME... against miracles 1989 ➤ 6,4837: RJRel 71 (1991) 434s (T. F. *Godlove*).

3989 *Billault* Alain, Les formes romanesques de l'héroïsation dans la Vie d'APOLLONIOS de Tyane par PHILOSTRATE: BBudé (1991) 267-274.

Blackburn B., *Theîos anēr* and the Markan miracle traditions 1991 ➤ 4284.

3990 *Cirillo* Antonio, Il valore rivelativo dei miracoli di Cristo in San TOMMASO: AnnTh 4 (1990) 151-173.

3991 **Fischbach** Stephanie, Totenerweckungen; zur Geschichte einer Gattung: kath. Diss. Würzburg 1991, DKlauck. – TR 87 (1991) 522.

3992 **Flynn** Leslie B., The [35] miracles of Jesus: Wheaton IL 1990, Victor. 168 p. $7. – RBS 148 (1991) 501s (R. P. *Lightner*, brief).

3993 **Goldingay** John, Signs, wonders and healing 1989 ➤ 6,4849: REvQ 63 (1991) 92-94 (G. A. *Houston*).

3994 **Greer** Rowan A., Fear of freedom... miracles 1989 ➤ 5,4546; 6,4851: RJRel 71 (1991) 430s (R. L. *Wilken*).

3995 **Habermas** Rebekka, Wallfahrt und Aufruhr; zur Geschichte des Wunderglaubens in der frühen Neuzeit: HistSt 5. Fra 1991, Campus. 235 p. DM 48 [TR 88,78].

3996 **Kee** Howard C., Medicine, miracle and magic in NT times 1986 ➤ 2,3468...6,4854: RBASOR 281 (1991) 88s (J. *Fossum*); Bijdragen 52

(1991) 330s (M. *Parmentier*, Eng.: curiously uninterested in charismatic 'inner healing'; *iatrós*, not *hiatrós*, occurs only 7 times in NT).

3997 **Koskenniemi** Erkki, Der philostrateische APOLLONIOS: CommHumLit 94. Helsinki 1991, Finnish Academy. 101 p. 951-653-234-9.

3998 **Latourelle** R., Miracles of Jesus and theology... 1988 ➤ 4,4652... 6,4855*a*: ᴿHeythJ 32 (1991) 395s (Mary E. *Mills*).

3999 **Latourelle** R., Miracoli 1987 ➤ 4,4651; 5,4555: ᴿAnnTh 5 (1991) 421-4 (A. *Cirillo*).

4000 **Latourelle** René, Milagros de Jesús y teología del milagro 1990 ➤ 6, 4855*b*: ᴿActuBbg 28 (1991) 77s (J. *Boada*: 'maximalista'); AugM 35 (1990) 396 (J. A. *Galindo*); Carthaginensia 7 (1991) 261 (R. *Sanz Valdivieso*); EfMex 9 (1991) 403s (M. *Ramírez* A.); NatGrac 38 (1991) 212s (A. *Villalmonte*); RTLim 25 (1991) 312s (J. M. *Carreras*).

4001 **Leeper** Elizabeth A., Exorcism in early Christianity: diss. Duke, ᴰ*Gregg* R. Durham ɴᴄ 1991. 400 p. 92-02489. – DissA 52 (1991s) 2957-A; RelStR 18,173.

4002 **McCready** William D., Signs of sanctity, miracles / GREGORY 1989 ➤ 5,4558; 6,4857: ᴿZkT 113 (1991) 342s (S. C. *Kessler*).

4003 **Mills** Mary E., Human agents of cosmic power...: JStNT supp 41, 1990 ➤ 6,4680*: ᴿCritRR 4 (1991) 215-7 (D. *Frankfurter*); HeythJ 32 (1991) 260 (Margaret *Barker*: about magic); TLZ 116 (1991) 431s (P. W. van der *Horst*: too flawed).

4004 **Mosetto** F., I miracoli... Celso/ORIGENE 1986 ➤ 2,3474... 6,4861: ᴿAugR 30 (1990) 191-3 (R. *Scognamiglio*).

4005 **Padilla** Carmen, Los milagros de la 'Vida de APOLONIO de Tiana'; morfología del relato de milagro y géneros afines: EstFgNt 4. Córdoba 1991, Almendro. 263 p. [TR 88,253]. 84-86077-93-1. – ᴿSFulg 1 (1991s) 170.

4006 *Reckinger* François, Fakten und ihre Bezeugung; neuere Veröffentlichungen zum Thema Wunder [NICHOLS T. ...]; ForumKT 7 (1991) 132-9.

4007 *Sansterre* J.-M., Apparitions et miracles à Menouthis; de l'incubation païenne à l'incubation chrétienne: ➤ 488, Apparitions 1991, 69-83.

4008 *Stock* Klemens, Die Machttäten Jesu; ihr Zeugnis in den synoptischen Evangelien: IkaZ 18 (1989) 195-206 > Le 'azioni potenti' di Gesù nella testimonianza dei Vangeli sinottici: Communio 107 (1989) 10-23.

4009 **Uth** David F., An eschatological interpretation of the Synoptic miracles in the mission and message of Jesus: diss. SW Baptist Theol. Sem. 1991. 252 p. 91-25072. – DissA 52 (1991s) 1374s-A.

4010 **Ward** Keith, Divine action [i. creation; ii. accepting evil; iii. miracles; iv. in Christ]. L 1990, Collins. v-274 p. £8 pa. – ᴿJTS 42 (1991) 797-9 (T. F. *Tracy*).

4011 **Weiss** Wolfgang, Zeichen und Wunder; eine Studie zu der Sprachtradition und ihrer Verwendung im Neuen Testament: ev. Hab.-Diss. Mainz 1991. – TR 87 (1991) 512.

4012 *Wilkinson* John, *a*) Physical healing and the Atonement; – *b*) The body in the OT [AV 57 times, RSV 139, NIV 127]: EvQ 63 (1991) 149-167 / 195-210.

4013 **Zakovich** Yair, The concept of miracle in the Bible: Broadcast Univ. TA 1991, ᴹᴼᴰ. 150 p. 965-05-0549-0 [OIAc 1,27].

4014 **Herrenbrück** Fritz, [Mt 9,10...] Jesus und die Zöllner...: WUNT 2/41, ᴰ1990 ➤ 6,4873: ᴿArTGran 54 (1991) 369s (A. *Segovia*); TsTNijm 31 (1991) 97 (P. J. *Farla*); TZBas 47 (1991) 183s (K.-F. *Ulrichs*).

4015 **Trummer** Peter, [Mt 9,20] Die blutende Frau; Wunderheilung im NT. FrB 1991, Herder. 184 p. DM 28. 3-451-22326-0. – [R]NRT 113 (1991) 796 (L.-J. *Renard*); TGL 81 (1991) 394 (J. *Ernst*).

4016 *Mullins* Terence Y., [Mt 9,27 ...] Jesus, the 'Son of David': AndrUnS 29 (1991) 117-126.

4017 **Weaver** Dorothy Jean, [Mt 9,35-11,1] Matthew's missionary discourse 1990 ➤ 6,4876 [< diss. Richmond, [D]*Kingsley* J.]: [R]ÉTRel 66 (1991) 288s (Danielle *Ellul*); Interpretation 45 (1991) 422.4 (A. *Terian*); JTS 42 (1991) 192s (J. C. *Fenton*); TLZ 116 (1991) 432s (C. *Kähler*).

4018 *Weder* H., Die Suche nach den Söhnen und Töchtern des Friedens; Auslegung der Botenrede der Logienquelle (Mt 10 par Lk 10); ZeichZt 44,2 (1991) 54-59 [< NTAbs 36,27].

4019 *Ridgway* John E., A correlation between healing and peace in Matt 10:1-16, Jesus' commission of the Twelve: ProcGLM 11 (1991) 104-115.

4020 **Levine** Amy-Jill, The social and ethnic dimensions of Matthean salvation-history, Mt 10,5: 1988 ➤ 4,4682; 6,4878: [R]TorJT 7 (1991) 130s (S. *Brown*).

4021 *Doignon* Jean, HILAIRE de Poitiers témoin latin le plus ancien d'un texte rare du logion 'Matthieu' 10,38: RBén 101 (1991) 28-31.

4022 **Kister** Menahem, [Mt 12,1-8] Plucking on the Sabbath and Christian-Jewish polemic: ➤ 54, [F]FLUSSER D., Immanuel 24 (1990) 35-51.

4023 *Faivre* A. & C., [Mt 12,33; 7,15; Rom 10,10] Genèse d'un texte et recours aux Écritures; IGNACE, Aux Ephésiens 14,1-16,2: RevSR 65 (1991) 173-196.

4024 *Sugirtharajah* R. S., [Mt 12,41-44] The widow's mites revalued: ExpTim 103 (1991s) 42s.

4025 **Grasso** Santi, Gesù e la fraternità nel vangelo di Matteo (Mt 12,46-50; 25,31-46; 28,1-10): diss. Pont. Ist. Biblico, [D]*Stock* K. R 1991. – AcPIB 9/8, 684 & 730s; RTLv 23, p. 544.

F4.3   Mt 13 ... Parabolae Jesu — the Parables.

4026 **Aerts** Lode, Gottesherrschaft als Gleichnis? Eine Untersuchung zur Auslegung der Gleichnisse Jesu nach Eberhard JÜNGEL: EurHS 22/403, 1990: ➤ 6,4890: [R]ActuBbg 20 (1991) 166s (J. *Boada*); TsTNijm 31 (1991) 204 (J. *Augustus*).

4027 *Aerts* Lode, Parabels van Jezus; openbaringen van Gods Rijk? Over de parabeltheorie van E. JÜNGEL: CollatVL 21 (1991) 341-363.

4028 *Archer* Keith M., Contexts and meaning; a practical experiment in parable interpretation: diss. [D]*Lindars* B. Manchester 1991. – RTLv 23, p. 542.

4029 **Baudler** Georg, Jesus erzählt von sich; die Gleichnisse als Ausdruck seiner Lebenserfahrung: Tb 1616. FrB 1989, Herder. 127 p. DM 9,90.

4030 **Baudler** Georg, A figura de Jesus nas parábolas [1986 ➤ 2,3504],[T]. Aparecida 1990, Santuario. 326 p.

4031 *Baumann* Rolf, Gleichnisse und 'Reich Gottes'; Gleichnisauslegung im Zeichen der kühnen lebendigen Metapher: KatBlätt 116 (Mü 1991) 396-404 [< ZIT 91,466].

4032 **Bomberg** Craig L., Interpreting the parables 1990 ➤ 6,4894: [R]Biblica 72 (1991) 582-5 (C. M. *Tuckett*: his claim that the parables cannot be reduced to single aphorisms deserves consideration).

4033 *Blomberg* Craig L., Interpreting the parables of Jesus; where are we and where do we go from here?: CBQ 53 (1991) 50-78.

4034 *Brosend* William F.[II], Parable, allegory and metaphor: ProcGLM 11 (1991) 191-9.

4035 **Bucher** Anton A., Gleichnisse verstehen lernen; strukturgenetische Untersuchungen zur Rezeption synoptischer Parabeln: Praktische Theologie im Dialog 5, 1990 ➤ 6,4898: [R]TPQ 139 (1991) 443 (J. *Janda*).

4036 **Bucher** Anton, Symbol — Symbolbildung — Symbolerziehung; ... Gleichnisse verstehen lernen; strukturgenetische Untersuchungen zur Rezeption synoptischer Parabeln; die Kenntnisse von Theologiestudenten über alttestamentliche Erzählungen ...: kath. Hab-Diss. Mainz, [D]*Stachel* 1991. – TR 87 (1991) 512.

4037 **Capon** R. F., The parables of the Kingdom. GR 1991 = 1985, Eerdmans. vi-174 p. $13. 0-8028-0605-8 [NTAbs 36,263].

4038 *Cuvillier* Elian [➤ 4288], *Parabolé* dans la tradition synoptique: ÉTRel 66 (1991) 25-44.

4040 [E]**Delorme** Jean, Les paraboles ... ACFÉB 1987/9 ➤ 5,576; 6,4901: [R]AnnTh 4 (1990) 440-2 (B. *Estrada*); IndTSt 27 (1990) 192s (L. *Legrand*: scientific and Christian openness contrasting with dry tabulating approach of American Jesus seminar); ScEsp 43 (1991) 243-6 (J.-Y. *Thériault*).

4041 **Donahue** John R., The Gospel in parable 1988 ➤ 4,4700 ... 6,4902: [R]AnnTh 5 (1991) 419-421 (B. *Estrada*); RRel 49 (1990) 309 (P. *Jurkowitz*).

4042 **Dschulnigg** Peter, Rabbinische Gleichnisse und das NT [D] 1988 ➤ 4,4700 ... 6,4903: [R]EvQ 63 (1991) 171 (D. *Wenham*).

4043 **Dutzmann** Martin, Gleichniserzählungen Jesu als Texte evangelischer Predigt [D]1990 ➤ 6,4904: [R]TLZ 116 (1991) 694-8 (H. *Hirschler*).

4044 **Fisher** Neal F., The parables of Jesus; glimpses of God's reign [= 1979 revised] 1990 ➤ 6,4906: [R]NewTR 4,3 (1991) 95-97 (D. P. *Reid*).

4045 *Gerhardsson* Birger, *a*) If we do not cut the parables out of their frames [45th SNTS presidential address, Milan 24.VII.1990]: NTS 37 (1991) 321-335; – *b*) Om vi inte skär ut liknelserna ur ramarna: SvEx 56 (1991) 29-44.

4046 **Harnisch** W., Las parábolas de Jesús [1985] [T]1989 ➤ 5,4621; 6,4907: [R]Iter 2 (1991) 127s (J.-P. *Wyssenbach*); Teresianum 42 (1991) 349s (V. *Pasquetto*).

Heininger Bernhard, Metaphorik ... Sondergutgleichnisse Lk 1991 ➤ 4463.

4047 *Heydebrand* Renate von, Parabel; Geschichte eines Begriffs zwischen Rhetorik, Poetik und Hermeneutik: ArBegG 34 (1991) 27-122.

4048 **Jeremías** Joachim, Las parábolas de Jesús[9] [= 1971; deutsch [1]1947, [3]1965], [T]*Calvo* Francisco J.: Buena noticia 4. Estella 1991, VDivino. 302 p. 84-7151-004-9.

4049 [E]**Kertelge** Karl, Metaphorik und Mythos im NT: QDisp 126, 1990 ➤ 6,350: [R]TR 87 (1991) 470-5 (F. *Mussner*, sehr eingehend; 4 Endbemerkungen); ZkT 113 (1991) 301s (R. *Oberforcher*).

4050 *King* James R., The parables of Jesus; a social psychological approach: JPsy&T 19 (1991) 257-267 [< NTAbs 36,172].

4051 *Kümmel* Werner G., Jesusforschung seit 1981, IV. Gleichnisse: TRu 56 (1991) 27-53.

4052 **McArthur** H., *Johnson* R., They also ... rabbinic parables 1990 ➤ 6, 4910: [R]AndrUnS 29 (1991) 178-180 (E. *Hilgert*).

4053 **Mack** Burton L., *Robbins* Vernon K., Patterns of persuasion 1989 ➤ 5,4628: [R]Interpretation 45 (1991) 326.328 (Dorothy Jean *Weaver*); JTS 42 (1991) 649-651 (R. A. *Burridge*); Paradigms 7,2 (1991s) 44s (D. A. *de Silva*).

4054 **Marguerat** Daniel, Parabole: CahÉv 75. P 1991, Cerf. 66 p. F 25. 0222-0714 [NTAbs 36,112].

4054* *Martini* Carlo M., a) Parlare oggi in parabole; – b) La comunicazione tra santi nella Chiesa: Ambrosius 67 (1991) 12-20 / 5-11 (217-235, intervista con *Babin* Pierre).

4055 **Mateos** Juan, *Camacho* Fernando, Vangelo; figure e simboli [1989 ↠ 5,4630], TDemarchi Enzo: Orizzonti biblici. Assisi 1991, Cittadella. 238 p. 88-308-0478-9.

4056 **Mohring** Ruth E., Interpreting the parables of Jesus with a contemporary congregation; diss. Drew, DDay Lala. Madison NJ 1991. 265 p. 91-36113. – DissA 52 (1991s) 2598-A.

4057 *Moskow* Ruth, The dialectics of biblical enigma, parable and typology, from Genesis to the Revelation of John; from Qumran, revelation and the teacher of righteousness: ↠ 420, Mogilany 1989-II, 23-46.

4058 **Rau** Eckhard, Reden in Vollmacht ... Gleichnisse Jesu: FRL 149, D1990 ↠ 6,4914: RBZ 35 (1991) 262-5 (B. *Heininger*); ExpTim 102 (1990s) 266s (E. *Best*); Neotestamentica 25 (1991) 430-2 (I. J. du *Plessis*: not user-friendly, but good); NRT 113 (1991) 430s (X. *Jacques*); RechSR 79 (1991) 427s (J. *Guillet*); TLZ 116 (1991) 506-8 (C. *Kähler*).

4059 *Salvatierra Ossorio* Aurora, Los Mesalim; parábolas de Mekilta de R. YISMAEL; ensayo literario sobre sus personajes: ↠ 421, Luso-Esp. 1989/91, 497-520.

4060 *Sandifer* D. Wayne, The humor of the absurd in the parables of Jesus: ↠ 446, SBLSem 30 (1991) 287-297.

4061 **Scott** B. B., Hear then the parable 1989 ↠ 5,4632; 6,4915: RInterpretation 45 (1991) 296-8 (K. A. *Plank*); JBL 110 (1991) 720-2 (C. L. *Blomberg*: a must despite five disconcerting presumptions).

Stern David, Parables in midrash 1991 ↠ a12 (p. 596 infra).

4062 EThoma C., *Wyschogrod* M., Parable and story in Judaism and Christianity [Lucerne 2-4.VI.1986]; 1989 ↠ 5,610: RCBQ 53 (1991) 529s (M. C. de *Boer*: tit. pp. comments); NewTR 4,2 (1991) 81s (H. G. *Perelmuter*); RivB 39 (1991) 81-83 (Anna *Passoni Dell'Acqua*).

4063 **Timmer** J., The Kingdom equation; a fresh look at the parables of Jesus. GR 1990, CRC. 102 p. $9. 0-930265-87-4 [NTAbs 36,271].

4064 **Tumbarello** Giacomo, Uso della parabola da Gesù: BbbOr 33 (fasc. 167, non 163 come copertina: 1991) 31-38.

4065 **Ulonska** Herbert, Der geschenkte Augenblick; ein Gleichnisbuch. Stu 1991, Quell. 144 p. DM 14,80. 3-7918-2266-7 [NTAbs 36,117].

4066 **Weder** Hans, Metafore del Regno; le parabole di Gesù, ricostruzione e interpretazione [1978, ³1984], TGarra Giovanni, EFusco Vittorio: BtCu-Rel 60. Brescia 1991, Paideia. 389 p. 88-394-0468-6.

4067 **Wenham** David, The parables of Jesus; pictures of revolution: Jesus Library, 1989 ↠ 6,4021: REvQ 63 (1991) 171-3 (J. F. *Maile*).

4068 **Westermann** Claus, The parables of Jesus in the light of the Old Testament 1990 ↠ 6,4922: RBL (1991) 149 (B. *Lindars*: mostly on OT, and notably skipping intertestamental); Pacifica 4 (1991) 350-2 (G. *Nicholson*: firmly not recommended); TLond 94 (1991) 222 (J. *Drury*).

4069 **Winton** Alan P., The proverbs of Jesus; issues of history and rhetoric: JStNT supp. 35, 1990 ↠ 6,4923: RBiblica 72 (1991) 580-2 (J. D. G. *Dunn*: promises well, disappoints repeatedly); JBL 110 (1991) 722s (J. G. *Williams*).

4070 **Young** Brad H., Jesus and his Jewish parables 1989 ↠ 5,4639; 6,4924: RAndrUnS 29 (1991) 110-2 (R. M. *Johnston*); BibTB 21 (1991) 84 (R. L.

Mowery); CBQ 53 (1991) 726s (D. M. *Sweetland*); CritRR 4 (1991) 254s (also R. M. *Johnston*); EvQ 63 (1991) 174-6 (R. A. *Piper*).

4071 **Zymner** Rüdiger, Uneigentlichkeit; Studien zu Semantik und Geschichte der Parabel: Explicatio. Pd 1991, Schöningh. 322 p. DM 48 [TR 88, 24, H.-J. *Klauck*].

4072 *Bernardi* Jean, 'Cent, soixante et trente', Matthieu 13,8: RB 98 (1991) 308-402; Eng. 308.

4073 **Casalis** Georges, Un semeur est sorti pour semer [reprints] 1988 ➤ 5,244: ᴿProtestantesimo 45 (1990) 75s (G. *Girardet*).

4074 *Lindemann* Andreas, Die Erzählung vom Sämann und der Saat (Mk 4,3-8) und ihre Auslegung als allegorisches Gleichnis: WDienst 21 (1991) 115-131.

4075 *Ford* Mary, [Mt 13,11-15] Seeing, but not perceiving; crisis and context in biblical studies: StVlad 35 (1991) 107-125.

4076 *New* David S., The occurrence of *autôn* in Matthew 13.15 and the process of text assimilation: NTS 37 (1991) 478-480.

4077 *Joosten* Jan, The text of Matthew 13.21a and parallels in the Syriac tradition: NTS 37 (1991) 153-9.

4078 **Kögler** Franz, [Mt 13,31s] Das Doppelgleichnis vom Senfkorn und vom Sauerteig 1988 ➤ 4,4733 ... 6,4929: ᴿTGegw 34 (1991) 153s (H. *Giesen*).

4079 **Grassi** Joseph A., [Mt 14,13-21 ...] Loaves and fishes; the Gospel feeding narratives: GlazierZc. ColMn 1991, Liturgical. 184 p. $7. 0-8146-5753-2 [TDig 39,265].

4080 *Demeulenaere* R., [Mt 14,25-28] Le sermon LXXVI de S. AUGUSTIN sur la marche de Jésus et de Pierre sur les eaux; édition critique: ➤ 18, ᶠBASTIAENSEN A., Eulogia 1991, 51-63.

F4.5   Mt 16 ... *Primatus promissus* – The promise to Peter.

4081 **Baumann** Richard, Was Christus dem Petrus verheisst; eine Entdeckung im Urtext von Mt 16. Stein-R 1988, Christiana. 112 p. – ᴿForumKT 7 (1991) 151s (L. *Scheffczyk*).

4082 **Caragounis** Chrys C., [Mt 16,18] Peter and the rock: BZNW 58, 1990 ➤ 5,4654; 6,4939: ᴿCBQ 53 (1991) 492s (J. P. *Meier*, severe); CritRR 4 (1991) 177s (F. W. *Burnett*); RechSR 79 (1991) 427 (J. *Guillet*: considère le titre 'à dessein provocant').

4082* *Cipriani* Settimio, La figura di Pietro nel Nuovo Testamento; ➤ 346, Communio 116 (1991) 8-23.

4083 **Claudel** Gérard, La confession de Pierre: EtBN 10, ᴰ1988 ➤ 4,4741; 6,4940: ᴿRechSR 79 (1991) 426s (J. *Guillet*).

4084 **Deproost** Paul-Augustin, L'apôtre Pierre dans une épopée du VIᵉ siècle; l'Historia apostolica d'ARATOR. P 1990, Inst. Ét. Aug. 345 p. F 480 [TR 87,527].

4085 *Fàbrega* Valenti, La pericopa de Cesarea de Filipo (Mc 8,27-33 y Mt 16,13-23) en la exégesis protestante alemana de las últimas décadas: ActuBbg 28 (1991) 149-153.

4086 *Feuillet* André, La primauté et l'humilité de Pierre: NVFr 66 (1991) 3-24.

4087 **Jeffers** James S., Conflict at Rome; social order and hierarchy in early Christianity [(1 Clemens, Hermas) ... led to claims of primacy]. Mp 1991, Fortress. viii-215 p. $15. 0-8006-2469-6 [TDig 39,67]. – ᴿTorJT 7 (1991) 249s (E. A. *Varos*).

4088 *Karavídopoulos* John, Ⓖ The role of Peter and his importance for the Church in the NT: DeltioVM 10,1 (1991) 47-66.

4088* *a) Knoch* Otto, Petrus im NT; – *b) Maccarrone* Michele, 'Sedes apostolica – Vicarius Petri'; la perpetuità del primato di Pietro nella sede e nel vescovo di Roma (secoli III-VIII); – *c) Horn* Stephan O., Die Stellung des Bischofs von Rom auf dem Konzil von Chalcedon: ⇥ 523, Primato 1989/91, 1-52 / 275-362 / 261-274.

4089 *Lülsdorff* Raimund, Vom Stein zum Felsen; Anmerkungen zur biblischen Begründung des Petrusamtes nach Mt 16,18: Catholica 44 (1990) 271-283.

4090 *Luz* U., Das Primatwort Matthäus 16.17-19 aus wirkungsgeschichtlicher Sicht [... 'most Catholic exegetes agree' (a) it is of post-Easter origin, not a 'direct and immediate' conferring of a primacy; (b) expresses a non-juridical leadership of Peter]: NTS 37 (1991) 415-433.

4091 *Luz* Ulrich, The primacy text (Mt 16:18); PrincSemB 12 (1991) 41-55 [< ZIT 91.282].

4092 *Ratzinger* Joseph, Il primato di Pietro e l'unità della Chiesa: EuntDoc 44 (1991) 157-176 [< NTAbs 36,215].

4093 **Schatz** Klaus, Der päpstliche Primat; seine Geschichte von den Ursprüngen bis zur Gegenwart 1990 ⇥ 6,4947: ᴿTPQ 139 (1991) 96 (R. *Zinnhobler*); ZkT 113 (1991) 339-341 (R. *Schwager*).

4094 *Tillard* J. M. R., The presence of Peter in the ministry of the Bishop of Rome: OneInC 27 (1991) 101-120.

4095 *Vos* Geerhardus, A sermon on Matthew 16:24,25: Kerux 3,3 (1988) 3-14 [Vos also leadoff of most of the preceding issues].

4096 **Coune** M., [Mt 17] *a)* Joie de ...; *b)* Grâce de la Transfiguration d'après les Pères d'Occident: Vie Monastique ../24, 288 p. F 97. Bellefontaine 1990, Abbaye. – ᴿEsprVie 101 (1991) 431 (P. *Jay*: les héritiers peuvent corriger parfois l'œuvre de leurs prédécesseurs).

4097 *Hengel* Martin, Traum und Wirklichkeit (Mt 17,1-8): TBeit 22 (Wu 1991) 113-7 [< ZIT 91,432].

4098 *Lamarche* Paul, Transfiguration du Seigneur: ⇥ 668, DictSpir 15 (1990s) 1148-51 [-60].

4099 **McGuckin** John A., The transfiguration 1986 ⇥ 2,1563; 5,4667: ᴿSTBuc 39,6 (1987) 121-8 (T. *Baconsky*, en roum.).

4100 *Paretsky* Albert, The transfiguration of Christ; its eschatological dimensions: NBlackf 72 (1991) 313-324.

4101 *Rodd* C. S., [Lk 9,28-36 Transfiguration]: ExpTim 103 (1991s) 149s.

4102 *Taylor* Justin, The coming of Elijah, Mt 17,10-13 and Mk 9,11-13; the development of the texts: RB 98 (1991) 107-119; franç. 107.

4103 *Willert* Niels, [Mt 17,22] Kristologien i Mattæus' passionsfortælling: DanTTs 54 (1991) 241-260 [< ZIT 92,4].

4104 *a) Stock* Klemens, I figli sono liberi, Mt 17,26; Lc 15,11-32; – *b) Zevini* Giorgio, Il Figlio vi renderà liberi, Gv 8,31-36; liberazione e libertà del credente in Giovanni; – *c) Bianchi* Enzo, Il Cristo e il sabato nei quattro vangeli: ⇥ 292a, ParSpV 23 (1991) 145-161 / 163-182 / 125-143.

4105 **Müller** Peter, [Mt 18,2] In der Mitte der Gemeinde; Kinder im Neuen Testament: ev. Hab.-Diss. München 1991, ᴰHahn F. – TR 87 (1991) 512; RTLv 23, p. 545.

4106 **Tellan** Sergio, La correzione fraterna nella chiesa di Matteo (Mt 16,15-20): diss. Pont. Univ. Gregoriana, ᴰRasco Emilio. R 1991s. – InfPUG 24/123, 11.

4107 *O'Callaghan* Josep, Reflexions sobre dues variants de Mt (18,20.25): Miscellània entorn de l'obra del pare Miquel BATLLORI (Barc 1991, Generalitat de Catalunya) 208-211 [< AcPIB 9/6,657].
4108 **Buckley** Thomas W., [Mt 18,22] Seventy times seven; sin, judgment, and forgiveness in Matthew: GlazierZc. ColMn 1991, Liturgical. 102 p. $7. 0-8146-5686-2.
4109 *Derrett* J. D. M., [Mt 18,28-34] Bankruptcy and the NT: DowR 109 (1991) 173-182.
4110 **Carter** Warren C., Discipleship, liminality and households; a literary-historical study of Matthew's Gospel with particular reference to Mt 19-20: diss. ᴰ*Marcus* J. Princeton 1991. 383 p. 91-27014. – DissA 52 (1991s) 1371s-A; RelStR 18,173.
4111 *Abela* Anthony, Jesus' reasoning on marriage and divorce in Mt 19, 1-12: Forum 2 (1991) 23-63.
4112 a) *Blomberg* Craig L., Marriage, divorce, remarriage, and celibacy; an exegesis of Matthew 19:3-12; – b) *Smith* David L., Divorce and remarriage from the early Church to John WESLEY; – c) *Heth* William A., The changing basis for permitting remarriage after divorce for adultery; the influence of R. H. CHARLES: TrinJ 11 (1990) 161-196 / 131-142 / 143-159.
4113 *Molldrem* Mark J., A hermeneutic of pastoral care and the Law/Gospel paradigm applied to the divorce texts of Scripture: Interpretation 45 (1991) 43-54.
4114 *Porter* Stanley E., *Buchanan* Paul, On the logical structure of Matt 19:9 [cannot solve the ambiguity]: JEvTs 34 (1991) 335-340 [< NTAbs 36,178].
4115 *Bartnik* Czesław S., [Mt 19,16-22 ...] 'Das ewige Leben erlangen' [JOHANNES PAUL II an die Jugend, 31.III.1985]: RoczTKan 37,2 (1991 für 1987) 5-16; deutsch 16.
4116 [ᴱ**Pizzolato** Luigi F., Mc 10,25; Mt 19,16-22] *Vissonà* G., Per foramen acus 1986 → 2,3572 ... 6,4964: ᴿMnemosyne 44 (1991) 237-9 (G. J. M. *Bartelink*).
4117 *Demeulenaere* R., [Mt 19,17] Le sermon 84 de saint AUGUSTIN sur l'invitation de Jésus au jeune homme riche; édition critique: → 130, ᶠSANDERS G., Aevum 1991, 67-73.

F4.8 **Mt 20** ... *Regnum eschatologicum* – **Kingdom eschatology**.

4118 *Ardizzoni* Anthos, I disoccupati dell'ultima ora (Riflessioni su Matteo 20,1-20): StTardAnt 8 (1989) 213-226.
4119 a) *Lowe* Malcolm, [Mt 20,1-16] A Hebraic approach to the parable of the laborers in the vineyard; – b) R. *Menahem zal., Epitropos/Paqîd* in the parable of the laborers in the vineyard, ᵀ*Levine* Edward: → 54, ᶠFLUSSER D., Immanuel 24s (1990) 109-117 / 118-131.
4120 *Grams* Rollin, The Temple conflict scene; a rhetorical analysis of Matthew 21-23: → 86, ᶠKENNEDY G., Persuasive 1991, 41-65.
4121 *Amphoux* C.-B., Les contextes de la parabole des deux fils (Matthieu 21,28-32): LOrA 3 (1991) 215-248.
4121* *Flusser* David, [... Mt 22,39] Jesus, his ancestry, and the commandment of love [< Jesus in Selbstzeugnissen 1968) 7-24.64-72]: → 294, Jesus' Jewishness 1991, 153-174 (-176, select Flusser bibliography).
4122 *Weinfeld* Moshe, The charge of hypocrisy in Matthew 23 and in Jewish sources: → 54, ᶠFLUSSER D., Immanuel 24s (1990) 52-57.

4123 **Becker** Hans-Jürgen, Auf der Kathedra des Mose; rabbinischtheologisches Denken und antirabbinische Polemik in Matthäus 23,1-12: ArbNTZ 4. B 1990, Inst. Kirche und Judentum. 267 p. – ᴿRB 98 (1991) 624 (B. T. *Viviano*, Eng.); SWJT 34,2 (1991s) 66 (E. E. *Ellis*).

4124 *Mason* Steve, Pharisaic dominance before 70 CE and the Gospels' hypocrisy charge (Matt 23:2-3): HarvTR 83 (1990) 363-381.

4126 *Winter* Bruce W., The Messiah as tutor; the meaning of *kathēgētēs* in Matthew 23:10: TyndB 42 (1991) 152-7.

4127 **Del Verme** Marcello, [Mt 23,23] Guidaismo e NT ... decime 1989 → 5,4687*; 6,4985: ᴿAsprenas 38 (1991) 244-6 (S. *Cipriani*); BibTB 21 (1991) 79s (B. J. *Malina*); CC 142 (1991,1) 632 (M. *Simone*); Henoch 13 (1991) 377-9 (P. *Capelli*); RasT 32 (1991) 103s (R. *Penna*); RivStoLR 27 (1991) 334s (V. *Fusco*); Sapienza 44 (1991) 99-101 (S. *Tanzarella*); Sefarad 51 (1991) 474s (V. *Fernández Marcos*); SMSR 57 (1991) 182-4 (Liliana *Rosso Ubigli*).

4128 *Del Verme* Marcello, Le decime giudaiche negli scritti di FLAVIO GIUSEPPE e nel NT: RivB 39 (1991) 175-191.

4128* **Reiser** Marius, [Mt 24s] Die Gerichtspredigt Jesu ...: NTAbh 23, ᴰ1990 → 6,4988: ᴿBZ 35 (1991) 257-9 (R. *Schnackenburg*).

4129 *Harrington* Daniel J., Polemical parables in Matthew 24-25: UnSemQ 44 (1991) 287-298 [< NTAbs 36,179].

4130 *Sours* Michael, [Mt 24] The prophecies of Jesus. Ox 1991, Oneworld. 223 p. $19. 1-85168-025-X [TDig 39,188].

4130* *Vorster* W. S., A reader-response approach to Matthew 24:3-28: HervTSt 47 (1991) 1099-1108 [< NTAbs 36,338].

4131 *Wong Kun-Chun* Eric, [Mt 24,20] The Matthaean understanding of the sabbath; a response to G. N. STANTON: JStNT [37 (1989) 17-30] 44 (1991) 3-18.

4132 *Manns* Frédéric, [Mt 25,14-30] La parabole des talents; Wirkungsgeschichte et racines juives: RevSR 65 (1991) 343-362.

4133 *a*) *Siniscalco* Paolo, 'Intra in gaudium Domini tui'; nota su una citazione di Matteo (25, 21 e 23) nelle Confessioni di AGOSTINO; esperienza mistica e beatitudine celeste; – *b*) *Waldschütz* Erwin, Probleme philosophischer Mystik am Beispiel Meister ECKHARTS: → 4*, ᶠALBERT K., Probleme 1991, 187-196 / 71-93.

4134 *Anderson* Ana Flora, *Gorgulho* Gilberto, *a*) Ovelhas e cabritos; discernimento e julgamento (Mt 25,31-46); – *b*) As parábolas nasceram da terra e do trabalho da Galiléia: EstudosB 26 (1990) 51-60 / 43-50.

4135 *Brandenburger* Egon, Gerichtskonzeptionen im Urchristentum und ihre Voraussetzungen: SUNT A-16 (1991) 5-54 [< ZIT 92,309].

4137 *Farahian* Edmond, Relire Matthieu 25,31-46 [jugement dernier]: Gregorianum 72 (1991) 437-457; Eng. 457.

4138 **Gray** Sherman W., The least of my brothers; Mt 25:31-46: SBL diss. 114, 1989 → 5,4702: ᴿCBQ 53 (1991) 336s (D. J. *Harrington*); CritRR 4 (1991) 195-7 (J. L. *Thompson*); TLZ 116 (1991) 828s (G. *Haufe*).

4139 *Hutter* Manfred, Mt 25:31-46 in der Deutung MANIS: NT 33 (1991) 276-282.

4140 *Sayer* J., 'Ich hatte Durst, und ihr gabt mir zu trinken'; zum Ansatz einer Theologie der menschlichen Grundbedürfnisse nach Mt 25,31ff im Rahmen der Pastoral der Befreiung: MüTZ 42 (1991) 151-167 [< NTAbs 36,29].

4141 **Kainz** Elisabeth, Die Salbungsgeschichte in den Evangelien; exegetische und traditionsgeschichtliche Untersuchungen zu Mk 14,3-9;

Mt 26,6-13; Joh 12,1-8; Lk 7,36-50: Diss. Graz 1991, ᴰ*Zeitlinger*. – TR 87 (1991) 513.
4142 *a) Sweet* J. P. M., [Mt 26,61, Mk 14,58] A house not made with hands; – *b) Catchpole* David R., Temple traditions in Q: ➤ 15, ᶠBAMMEL E., Templum 1991, 368-390 / 305-329.

F5.1   *Redemptio,* Mt 26, *Ultima coena;* The Eucharist [➤ H7.4].

4143 *Amaladoss* M., The Eucharist and the apostolate: IndTSt 27 (1990) 311-320.
4144 **Bätzing** Georg, Die Eucharistie als Opfer der Kirche nach H. U. von BALTHASAR: Kriterien 74, 1986 ➤ 2,3603; DM 24: ᴿZkT 113 (1991) 107s (L. *Lies*).
4145 **Barth** M., *a)* Rediscovering 1988 ➤ 4,4801: ᴿAsbTJ 46,2 (1991) 102 (D. R. *Bauer*). – *b)* Riscopriamo la Cena del Signore 1990 ➤ 6,4998*b*: ᴿHoTheológos 9 (1991) 252-9 (C. *Scordato*).
4146 **Bermejo** Luis M., Body broken and blood shed 1986 ➤ 3,4600 ... 6,5000: ᴿIndTSt 27 (1990) 362-5 (S. *Arulsamy*).
4147 *Bradshaw* P. F., Zebaḥ Todah and the origins of the Eucharist: EcOrans 8 (R 1991) 245-260 [< NTAbs 36,382].
4148 **Cabié** Robert, Histoire de la Messe des origines à nos jours: BtHistC 23. P 1990, Desclée. 144 p. – ᴿBLitEc 92 (1991) 153s (F. *Rausières*).
4149 *Carmichael* Deborah B., David DAUBE on the Eucharist and the Passover Seder: JStNT 42 (1991) 45-67.
4150 **Crockett** William R., Eucharist, symbol of transformation 1989 ➤ 5, 4710; 6,5006: ᴿEcuR 41 (1991) 147-9 (G. *Kelly*).
4151 **Croken** Robert C., LUTHER's first front; the Eucharist as sacrifice. Ottawa 1990, Univ. 171 p. $20 [TR 88,255].
4152 *Crownfield* David, The seminal trace; presence, difference, and transubstantiation: JAAR 59 (1991) 361-371.
4153 *De Zan* Renato, [Mt 26,28 ‖] 'Sangue versato in remissione dei peccati': RivLtg 78 (1991) 582-7.
4154 *a) FitzPatrick* P. J., On eucharistic sacrifice in the Middle Ages; – *b) McHugh* J. F., The sacrifice of the Mass at the council of Trent: ➤ 384, Sacrifice 1991, 129-156 / 157-181.
4155 *Fleischer* Barbara J., The Eucharist as parable [... moving away from Thomism]: IrTQ 57 (1991) 26-40.
4156 **Foley** Edward, From age to age; how Christians celebrated the Eucharist. Ch 1991, Liturgy Training. ix-206 p.; ill, (Faulkner R.). $16 pa. 0-929650-41-7 [TDig 39,152].
4157 *Galot* Jean, Pasto e presenza; l'Eucaristia fonte di vita: VConsacr 27 (1991) 3-15 [+ 9 art.].
4158 **Giraudo** Cesare, Eucaristia per la Chiesa 1989 ➤ 5,4714 ... 6,5011: ᴿBLitEc 92 (1991) 47-49 (R. *Cabié*); HumBr 46 (1991) 475s (A. *Biazzi*); RasT 32 (1991) 86-92 (M. *Arranz*) & 92-97 (P. J. *Rosato*); ScEsp 43 (1991) 257s (B. de *Margerie*).
4159 — *Giraudo* C. [AnBib 92 ➤ 62,4765 + Alois 22] réponse a J. BRIEND: Mais D [181 (1990) 155-8] 187 (1991) 155-9 [160 Briend: rien à modifier; l'analyse des textes reste le souci premier de l'exégète].
4160 *Goering* Joseph, The invention of transubstantiation: Traditio 46 (1991) 147-170 [< TR 88,430].
4161 **Heyer** C. J. den, De maaltijd van de Heer; exegetische en bijbeltheologische studie over Pascha en Avondmaal. Kampen 1990, Kok. 128 p. Fb. 470. – ᴿCollatVL 21 (1991) 315 (A. *Goossens*).

4162 **Kaufmann** Thomas, Die Abendmahlstheologie der Strassburger Reformatoren bis 1528: ev. Diss. Göttingen 1991, ^D*Moeller*. – TR 87 (1991) 517.

4163 **Keefe** Donald J., Covenantal theology; the Eucharistic order of history. Lanham MD 1991, UPA. xviii-553 p.; x-536 p. $63.50 each. 0-8181-8086-6; -7-4 [TDig 38,364: his 'radical critique of theological methods'].

4163* **Kodell** Jerome, Eucharist in NT 1988 → 5,4724; 6,5017: ^RVidyajyoti 55 (1991) 59s (G. *Gispert-Sauch*, also on STEVENSON K.).

4164 **Kollmann** Bernd, Ursprung und Gestalten der frühchristlichen Mahlfeier ^D1990 → 6,5018: ^RBZ 35 (1991) 265-8 (H.-J. *Klauck*); TLZ 116 (1991) 602s (K.-H. *Kandler*).

4165 **Léon-Dufour** X., Sharing the Eucharistic bread 1987 → 3,4620 ... 6,5019: ^RRRel 49 (1990) 147s (E. *Hensell*).

4166 **McAdoo** H. R., The Eucharistic theology of Jeremy TAYLOR ['Church of Ireland' bishop 19th cent.] today 1988 → 5,4729; 6,5020: ^RScotJT 44 (1991) 129-133 (K. *Stevenson*).

4167 *Magne* Jean, Les récits de la Cène et la date de la Passion: EphLtg 105 (1991) 145-236.

4168 **Margerie** Bertrand de, Vous ferez ceci en mémorial de moi ...: THist 80, 1989 → 5,4730; 6,5022: ^RArTGran 53 (1990) 299s (A. *Segovia*); BLitEc 92 (1991) 46s (R. *Cabié*); CiuD 203 (1990) 749 (J. M. *Ozaeta*); MélSR 48 (1991) 251-3 (B. *Rey*).

4169 **Marini** Angelo, La celebrazione eucaristica presieduta da sant'AGOSTINO; la partecipazione dei fedeli alla Liturgia della Parola e al Sacrificio Eucaristico 1989 → 5,g845: ^RMaisD 187 (1991) 151-3 (J.-P. *Bouhot*: pastorale, non archeologico).

4169* *Martín Ramos* Nicasio, La presencia eucarística según Edward SCHILLEBEECKX: CommSev 24 (1991) 19-56.

4170 **Meyer** Hans B., Eucharistie; Geschichte, Theologie, Pastoral: HbLtgW 4, 1989 → 6,5025: 602 p.; DM 68; sb. 62. – ^RColcT 60,3 (1990) 188-190 (L. *Balter*); NRT 113 (1991) 121s (A. *Toubeau*).

4171 **Moloney** F. J., A body broken for a broken people. Melbourne/SF 1991, Collins Dove / Harper. 143 p. $14. – ^RPacifica 4 (1991) 235-8 (J. *Thornhill*).

4172 **Morrison** Barry D., In spirit and in truth; the theology and spirituality of the Lord's Supper within the context of worship in the Baptist tradition: diss. Regis-Toronto 1988. 226 p. 0-315-63776-5 (DANN -63776). – DissA 52 (1991s) 3637-A.

4173 **Navarro Girón** M. Ángeles, La carne de Cristo; el misterio eucarístico a la luz de la controversia entre Pascasio RADBERTO, RATRAMNO, RABANO Mauro y GODESCALCO: Estudios 44, ^D1989 → 6,5027; ^RMiscCom 49 (1991) 303s (G. *Higuera Udías*; merece todas felicitaciones); NRT 113 (1991) 586s (L. *Renwart*).

4174 **O'Carroll** Michael, Corpus Christi, an encyclopedia of the Eucharist 1988 → 4,4832; 6,5028: ^RNewTR 4,1 (1991) 111-3 (G. *Ostdiek*).

4175 **O'Connor** J. T., The hidden manna; a theology of the Eucharist 1988 → 5,4735; 6,5029: ^RAnnTh 4 (1990) 463-5 (T. J. *McGovern*).

4176 *Paretsky* Albert, Proleptic recapitulation; Passover, Eucharist and God's saving acts: NBlackf 71 (1990) 541-7.

4177 **Power** D. N., The sacrifice we offer 1987 → 3,4625 ... 6,5032: ^RCrNSt 12 (1991) 215s (T. *Franke*); HeythJ 32 (1991) 92-94 (F. J. van *Beeck*); JAAR 59 (1991) 415-8 (J. F. *Puglisi*).

4178 **Rigaux** Dominique, À la table du Seigneur; l'Eucharistie chez les [peintres] Primitifs italiens (1250-1497) [< diss. Paris-IV Sorbonne 1985]. P 1989, Cerf. 319 p.; 120 fig. – ᴿRHPR 71 (1991) 385s (P. *Prigent*: l'iconographie chrétienne est rarement d'intention purement narrative).

4179 **Ronze** Bernard, Le dernier repas ou l'avènement du réel. P 1991, Centurion. 166 p. F 68. – ᴿÉtudes 375 (1991) 140 (P.-J. *Labarrière*).

4180 **Sanguineti** A. M., El Sacrificio eucaristico, Pascua de la Iglesia, estudio teológico a la luz del Magisterio de Pablo VI (dis. S. Croce). Buenos Aires 1990, Cedro. – ᴿAnnTh 5 (1991) 430s (J. *Brosa*).

4181 *Schulz* Frieder, Eucharistiegebet und Abendmahlsvermahnung; eine Relecture reformatorischer Abendmahlsordnungen im ökumenischen Zeitalter: ➤ 72*, ᶠHARNONCOURT P., Sursum corda 1991, 147-158.

4182 *Smith* B. D., The chronology of the Last Supper [... not a passover-meal]: WestTJ 53 (1991) 29-45 [< NTAbs 36,20].

4182* **Smith** Dennis E., *Taussig* Hal E., Many tables; the Eucharist in the NT and the liturgy today 1990 ➤ 6,5037: Vidyajyoti 59 (1991) 119s (G. *Gispert-Sauch*).

4183 **Stevenson** Kenneth, Accept this offer; the Eucharist as sacrifice today 1989 ➤ 5,4742: ᴿScotJT 44 (1991) 392s (C. *Buchanan*).

4184 *Szyszman* Simon, Une Pâque chrétienne célébrée mercredi au XIIIᵉ siècle? ➤ 17, ᶠBARTHÉLEMY D., Tradition 1991, 309-310.

4185 *Thornhill* John, The Eucharistic gesture of Jesus; what did it mean to those who shared his table fellowship?: AustralasCR 68 (1991) 395-405.

4186 a) *Wenham* David, How Jesus understood the Last Supper; a parable in action; – b) *Yates* John, Role of the Holy Spirit in the Lord's Supper: Churchman 105 (1991) 246-260 / 350-.. [< ZIT 94,71].

F5.3 **Mt 26,30** ... || *Passio Christi;* **Passion-narrative.**

4187 a) *Bartelmus* Rüdiger, Die Matthäuspassion J. S. BACHS als Symbol; Gedenken zu einem unerschöpflichen musikalisch-theologischen Werk [p. 44, '2.2.2.2.2 Rhetorik']; – b) *Sandberger* Jörg V., Theologische Existenz angesichts der Grenze und auf der Grenze; Karl BARTH über MOZART und Paul TILLICH über bildende Kunst: TZBas 47 (1991) 18-63 + 2 fig. / 66-86.

4188 **Cassidy** Sheila, Good Friday people [we have emasculated the biblical text, which is 'trapped like a fly in the honey of a beautiful liturgy']. L 1991, Darton-LT. 195 p. £7. 0-232-51921-8. – ᴿExpTim 103 (1991s) 87 (K. G. *Greet*).

4190 **Garland** David E., One hundred years of study on the Passion narratives: NABPR 3, 1989 ➤ 6,5051: ᴿRelStR 17 (1991) 363 (L. *Cope*).

4191 **Gourgues** Michel, Le crucifié; du scandale à l'exaltation: JJC 38, 1989 ➤ 5,4759: ᴿRTLv 22 (1991) 119s (R. *Guelluy*).

4192 **Grayston** Kenneth, Dying we live 1990 ➤ 6,5053: ᴿNBlackf 72 (1991) 498-501 (E. *Franklin*).

4193 **Guillet** Jacques, Jésus devant sa vie et sa mort²: Théologie. P 1991, D-Brouwer. vi-253 p. F 98. – ᴿNRT 113 (1991) 893s (L. *Renwart*).

4194 *Jonge* Marinus de, a) The use of *ho Christos* in the Passion narratives [< BtETL 40 (1975) 169-192]; – b) The earliest Christian use of *Christos*; some suggestions [< NTS 32 (1986) 321-343]; – c) The use of the expression *ho Christos* in the Apocalypse of John [< BtETL 53 (1980) 267-281]: ➤ 215, Jewish Eschatology 1991, 63-86 / 102-124 / 87-101.

4195 **Martin** Ernest L.,   Secrets of Golgotha 1988 ► 4,4864...6,5058:   ᴿCrit-
RR 4 (1991) 213-5 (J. D. *Tabor*: pioneering).

4196 *Möde* Erwin,   Der Passionsweg Jesu Christi; vom 'Hosianna' zum
'Kreuzige':   ForumKT 7 (1991) 61-72.

4197 **Myllykoski** Matti,   Die letzten Tage Jesu; Markus und Johannes, ihre
Traditionen und die historische Frage, I.: Annales B/256. Helsinki 1991,
Acad. Fennica.   250 p.   951-41-0624-0.

4198 *Neirynck* F.,   Note on Mark's chronology; the Holy Week [FEINDLER F.
on Mk 11]: ETL 67 (1991) 395-7.

4199 *Nicholas* Aidan,   St. Thomas AQUINAS on the Passion of Christ; a
reading of Summa Theologiae IIIa, q. 46: ScotJT 43 (1990) 447-459;
p. 457, Aquinas' 'only recorded [and unintended] joke': his Summa was
intended for beginners.

4200 **Rivkin** Ellis,   Wat kruisigde Jezus? De politieke executie van een cha-
rismaticus [1984 ► 64,4625], ᵀ.   Baarn 1988, Ten Have.   106 p. ƒ19,50.
90-2594-371-3 [NedTTs 45,68].

4201 *Schenk* Wolfgang,   Leidensgeschichte Jesu: ► 690,   TRE 20 (1990)
714-721.

4202 **Senior** D.,   La Passione di Gesù nel Vangelo di Matteo.   Mi 1990,
Àncora.   190 p. Lit. 18.000. – ᴿCiVit 46 (1991) 115s (Duccia *Camiciotti*).

4203 *a) Stegemann* Wolfgang,   Die Passionsgeschichten der Evangelien; – *b)*
Link Christian, 'Für uns gestorben nach der Schrift'; – *c) Konrad*
Johann-Friedrich,   Der Weg Jesu ans Kreuz aus der Sicht Maria
Magdalenas; ein Erzählvorschlag für die Grundschule: EvErz 43 (Fra
1991) 139-147 / 148-169 / 170-186 [< ZIT 91,248].

4204 **Stock** Klemens,   Il racconto della Passione nei vangeli sinottici.   R 1991,
Pont. Ist. Biblico.   158 + 137 p.

4205 *Stuhlmacher* Peter,   Zur Predigt an Karfreitag: ► 72, ᶠHAHN F.,
Anfänge 1991, 447-472.

4206 **Voorgang** Dietrich,   Die Passion Jesu Christi in der Gnosis: Diss.
Kassel 1991, ᴰ*Schottroff.* – TR 87 (1991) 519.

4207 **Gillabert** Émile,   [Mt 26,14] Judas traître ou initié: Mystiques et religions.   P 1989, Dervy.   203 p. F 120.   2-85076-307-1. – ᴿÉTRel 66
(1991) 128 (J.-D. *Dubois*: à la suite d'ouvrages sur Ev. Thomas/gnose).

4207* **Dieckmann** Bernhard,   Judas als Sündenbock; eine verhängnisvolle
Geschichte von Angst und Vergeltung.   Mü 1991, Kösel.   376 p. –
ᴿMiscFranc 91 (1991) 321s (J. *Imbach*).

4208 *Hughes* Kirk T.,   Framing Judas: ► 311, Semeia 54 (1991) 223-238;
1 fig.

4209 **McGlasson** Paul,   Jesus and Judas; biblical exegesis in BARTH: AAR 72.
Atlanta 1991, Scholars.   160 p. $15 pa.   1-55540-568-1 [Int 45,334].

4210 ᴱ**Niemann** Raul,   Judas, wer bist du?   Gü 1991, Mohn.   120 p.
DM 24,80 [TLZ 117,119].

4211 *Conard* Audrey,   The fate of Judas; Matthew 27; 3-10:   TorJT 7 (1991)
158-168.

4212 **Post** P. G. J.,   De haanscene 1984 ► 1,4702; 3,4684:   ᴿVigChr 45 (1991)
96-101 (P. C. J. van *Dael*).

4213 **Castello** Gaetano,   L'interrogatorio di Gesù davanti al Sinedrio;
contributo esegetico alla cristologia neotestamentaria: diss. Pont. Univ.
Gregoriana, ᴰ*Grech* P.   Roma 1991. 277 p. – RTLv 23, p. 568.

4214 *Fantuzzi* Virgilio, Una nuova rappresentazione [teatrale] del 'Processo a Gesù' di Diego FABBRI: CC [106 (1955,4) 397-408] 142 (1991,1) 62-66.

4215 ᴱ**Kertelge** Karl, Der Prozess gegen Jesus [Tagung Graz 1987]: QDisp 112, 1988 ➤ 4,491*; 6,5078: ᴿColcT 61,2 (1991) 188 (R. *Bartnicki*, ❷): TLZ 116 (1991) 187s (T. *Holtz*).

4216 *Kümmel* Werner G., Jesusforschung seit 1981, V. Der persönliche Anspruch sowie der Prozess und Kreuzestod Jesu: TRu 56 (1991) 390-420.

4217 *Matera* Frank J., The trial of Jesus; problems and proposals: Interpretation 45 (1991) 5-16.

4218 *Kinman* Brent, Pilate's Assize and the timing of Jesus' trial: TyndB 42 (1991) 282-295.

4219 *McGing* Brian C., Pontius Pilate and the sources: CBQ 53 (1991) 416-438.

4220 *Vicent Cernuda* Antonio, La condena inopinada de Jesús [I. Pesquisa sobre la identidad de Barrabás] II. La agresividad obtusa de Pilato y la política ignorada de Caifás: EstB [48 (1990) 375-422] 49 (1991) 49-96; Eng. 49.

4221 *Cargal* Timothy B., [Mt 27,24s] 'His blood be upon us and upon our children'; a Matthean double entendre?: NTS 37 (1991) 101-112.

4222 *Heil* John P., [Mt 27,25] The blood of Jesus in Matthew; a narrative-critical perspective: PerspRelSt 18 (1991) 117-124.

4223 *Vanhoye* Albert, Catechesi biblica sul sangue di Cristo: ➤ 563, ᴱ*Triacca* A., Il mistero del sangue di Cristo e la catechesi (1991) 17-35.

4224 *Karavidopoulos* John, L'heure de la crucifixion de Jésus selon St. Jean et les Synoptiques (Marc 15,25 par rapport à Jean 19,14-16) [Colloquium 39, Lv 7-9 août 1990]: TAth 62 (1991) 445-451; Eng. 930.

4225 *Kreitzer* Larry, The seven sayings of Jesus from the Gross: observations on the order and presentation in the NT, literature and cinema: NBlackf 72 (1991) 239-244 [< NTAbs 36,19].

4226 **Rossé** G., [Mt 27,46] The cry, ᵀ*Arndt* S.A. 1987 ➤ 4,4899 ... 6,5093: ᴿBibTB 21 (1991) 82 (M. *McVann*); RRel 49 (1990) 309-311 (M.R. *Tripole*); ScripB 21 (1991) 30 (R.C. *Fuller*).

4227 *Donaldson* Terence L., The mockers and the Son of God (Mt 27,37-44); two characters in Matthew's story of Jesus: JStNT 41 (1991) 3-18.

4228 **Green** Joel B., The death of Jesus: WUNT 2/33, ᴰ1988 ➤ 4,4856 ... 6,5054: ᴿCBQ 53 (1991) 327-9 (D. *Senior*); Salesianum 53 (1991) 767s (C. *Bissoli*).

4228* *Grudem* W., He did not descend into Hell; a plea for following Scripture instead of the [late insertion into the] Apostles' Creed: JEvTS 34 (1991) 103-113 [< NTAbs 36,72].

4229 **Zangara** Vincenza, Exeuntes de corpore; discussioni sulle apparizioni dei morti in epoca agostiniana: RivStLR Bt 1. F 1990, Olschki. xviii-225 p. Lit. 45.000 [TR 88,77].

4230 *Heil* John P., The narrative structure of Matthew 27:55-28:20: JBL 110 (1991) 419-438.

4231 *Schaeffer* Susan E., The guard at the tomb (Gos.Pet. 8:28-11:49 and Matt 27:2-66; 28:2-4, 11-16): a case of intertextuality?: ➤ 446, SBL Sem 30 (1991) 499-507.

F5.6 **Mt 28 ‖ : Resurrectio.**

4232 **Alves** M.I., Ressurreição e fé pascal: a) Fundamenta 8. Lisboa 1991, Didaskalia. 284 p. esc 2800. – b) Didaskalia 19,2 (1989) 277-537; franç 275 [NTAbs 36,327; 260].

4233 **Balthasar** Hans Urs von, Mysterium paschale [< Myst. Salutis 1969] [T]*Nichols* Aidan, 1990 ➤ 6,5099: [R]NBlackf 72 (1991) 246-8 (J. *O'Donnell*).

4234 *Beasley-Murray* George R., [1 Thes 1,9s] Resurrection and parousia of the Son of Man: TyndB 42 (1991) 296-309.

4235 *Brambilla* Franco G., Risurrezione di Gesù e fede dei discepoli: ScuolC 119 (1991) 547-617.

4236 [E]**Broer** Ingo, *Werbick* Jürgen, 'Der Herr ist wahrhaft auferstanden' (Lk 24,34): SBS 134, 1988 ➤ 4,4903; 5,4804: [R]TR 87 (1991) 105-7 (F. *Mussner*).

4236* *Contreras* E., Cristo ha resucitado; notas para leer la reflexión de los Padres sobre el mistero de Cristo (siglos I-V): NVZam 14 (1989) 189-235 [< RET 51,124].

4237 *Edwards* Denis, The relationship between the risen Christ and the material universe: Pacifica 4,1 (1991) 1-14.

4238 *Firinga* M., La Résurrection de Jésus, illustration de l'unité psycho-somatique de l'homme: ➤ 121, [F]RAMAROSON L. 1991, 82-99.

4239 *Geisler* N. L., In defense of the Resurrection; a reply to criticisms [HARRIS M.]: JEvTS 34 (1991) 243-261 [< NTAbs 36,20].

4240 **Guilbert** Pierre, Il ressuscita le troisième jour 1988 ➤ 5,4818; 6,5108: [R]Christus 37 (P 1990) 207s (C. *Flipo*).

4241 *Guilbert* P., Resurrection: ➤ 664, Catholicisme XII, 58 (1990) 995-1028 (col. 1025 ajoute une ligne à 1024) [-1032, iconographie, *David-Danel* M. L.].

4242 **Hirsch** Emanuel, Die Auferstehungsgeschichten und der christliche Glaube, [E]*Müller* Hans M. Tü 1988, Katzmann. 223 p. [TPQ 140,187, C. *Niemand*].

4243 *Jones* Stuart, The resurrection feud, a review article [GEISLER N. 1989; HARRIS M. 1990]: Kerux 6,2 (1991) 43-57.

4244 **Kessler** H., La resurrección de Jesús, [Sucht ²1987] 1989 ➤ 5,4824; 6,5113: [R]EfMex 9 (1991) 402s (J. A. *Díaz Pérez*); Teresianum 42 (1991) 350s (V. *Pasquetto*).

Klassen Franz J., Über das Bild des Auferstandenen [D]1989 ➤ b981*.

4245 *a) Krentz* Edgar, Images of the Resurrection in the NT; – *b) Delloff* Linda M., The Resurrection; link between faith and art: CurrTMiss 18,2 (1991) 98-108 / 92-97 [al., in art and music].

4246 **McDonald** J. I. H., The resurrection; narrative and belief 1989 ➤ 5, 4832; 6,5116: [R]JBL 110 (1991) 723-5 (J. G. *Janzen*); NBlackf 72 (1991) 354-6 (A. R. C. *Leaney*).

4247 **Marxsen** Willi, Jesus and Easter 1990 ➤ 6,5118: [R]Horizons 18 (1991) 318s (Pheme *Perkins*); Interpretation 45 (1991) 314 . 316 (J. L. *Bailey*).

4248 *Mauny* Michel de, Le symbolisme universel de l'œuf [... de Pâques: PeCa 251, 1991]: EsprVie 101 (1991) 587s (J. *Daoust*).

4249 **O'Collins** G., Interpreting the Resurrection 1989 ➤ 6,5125: [R]BibTB 21 (1991) 126s (A. J. *Tambasco*); DoctLife 41 (1991) 215s (D. *Flanagan*).

4250 **O'Collins** Gerald, Jesús resucitado 1988 ➤ 4,4931 ... 6,5124*b*: [R]CiuD 203 (1991) 245s (J. M. *Ozaeta*); ScripTPamp 23 (1991) 741s (L. F. *Mateo-Seco*).

4251 *O'Grady* John F., The Resurrection: ChSt 30 (1991) 220-234.

4252 *Sabugal* Santos, La resurrección de Jesús en el Evangelio de Mateo (Mt 28,1-20): Salesianum 53 (1991) 467-478.

4253 *Schurb* K., The Resurrection in Gospel proclamation: ConcordJ 18,1 (1992) 28-39 [< NTAbs 36,326].

4254 **Watson** Nigel M., Easter faith and witness. Thornbury 1990, Des-
books. 115 p. A$13. 0-949824-17-8. – RExpTim 102 (1990s) 279 (G. T.
Eddy); Pacifica 4 (1991) 238-240 (W. *Loader*).

4254* *Manus* C., 'King-Christology'; the result of a critical study of
Matt. 28:16-20 as an example of contextual exegesis in Africa: Scriptura 39 (1991) 25-42 [< NTAbs 36,339].
4255 *Coleman* R. E., [Mt 28,19s] The promise of the great commission: EvJ
9,2 (Myerstown 1991) 75-85 [< NTAbs 36,216].
4256 **Duck** Ruth C., Gender and the name of God; the trinitarian baptismal
formula. NY 1991, Pilgrim. 192 p. $17 [JAAR 59,887]. 0-8298-0894-9.

F6.1   **Evangelium Marci** – *Textus, commentarii.*

4257 **Aranda Pérez** G., El evangelio de S. Marcos en Copto sahidico 1988
→ 4,4954 ... 6,5145: RScripB 21 (1991) 29s (J. K. *Elliott*).
4258 **Beare** F. W., Il vangelo secondo Matteo [1981], T*Maresca* Bianca;
E*Valentino* Carlo. R 1990, Dehoniane. 646 p. Lit. 50.000. – RRasT 32
(1991) 109s (V. *Fusco*).
4259 **Brooks** J. A., Mark. New American Comm. 23. Nv 1991, Broadman.
288 p. $20. 0-8054-0123-7 [NTAbs 36,263].
4260 **Cole** R. A., Gospel according to Mark²: Tyndale NT comm 1989
→ 5,4856: RAsbTJ 46,2 (1991) 98s (D. L. *Thompson*).
4261 **Drewermann** Eugen, *a*) Das Markusevangelium, Bilder von Erlösung
1987 → 4,4956; 6,5148: RActuBbg 28 (1991) 42-50 (J. *Boada*: excelente, a
pesar de unos problemas); StiZt 208 (1990) 279-281 (L. *Wachinger*). – *b*)
Beelden van verlossing; toelichtingen op het evangelie van Marcus. Haag
1990, Meinema. 307 p. ƒ 39,50. 90-211-3550-7. – RTsTNijm 31 (1991)
97s (A. *Uleyn*).
4262 **Ernst** Josef, Il Vangelo secondo Marco, tradotto e commentato [1981],
T*Faini* Silvia: NT commentato. Brescia 1991, Morcelliana. I. (1-8) 367 p.;
II. p. 375-841. Lit. 80.000. 88-372-1425-1 both.
4263 **Fischer** B., Varianten zu Mk: VLatGesch 15, 1989 → 5,4858: RJTS 42
(1991) 281s (J. K. *Elliott*); RHE 86 (1991) 464 (P.-M. *Bogaert*: aussi zu
Lukas).
4264 **Funk** Robert W., (*Smith* Mahlon H.), The gospel of Mark, red [also
pink, gray, black] letter edition. Sonoma CA 1991, Polebridge. xxii-
250 p. $20 pa. 0-944344-09-7 [TDig 39,62: 'the aim is not historical truth,
but scholarly consensus', red that Jesus almost certainly said the saying,
black that he did not].
4265 **Georgeot** J. M., Évangile selon saint Marc 1988s → 5,4859; 6,5150:
RGregorianum 72 (1991) 142s (E. *Farahian*).
4266 **Guelich** Robert A., Mark 1 - 8:26: Word comm. 34A, 1989 → 5,4863;
6,5152: RAndrUnS 28 (1990) 261-3 (R. L. *Jolliffe*); CBQ 53 (1991) 703-5
(J. *Marcus*).
4267 **Hervieux** Jacques, L'Évangile de Marc, compagnon pastoral. P/Mon-
tréal 1991, Centurion/Novalis. 240 p. F 120. – REsprVie 101 (1991) 566
(É. *Cothenet*).
4268 **Hooker** Morna D., A commentary on the Gospel according to Saint
Mark: Black's NT Comm. L/Peabody MA 1991, Black/Hendrickson.
viii-424 p. / 1-56563-010-6.
4268* **Hurtado** Larry, Mark 1983/9 → 6,5154: RVidyajyoti 55 (1991) 228
(P. M. *Meagher*).

4269 **Iersel** Bas van, Reading Mark, ᵀ*Bisscheroux* W. H., 1989 ➤ 5,4865: ᴿScotJT 44 (1991) 383-5 (H. *Anderson*: a fresh commentary); ScripB 21 (1991) 28s (J. A. *McGuckin*: 'narratology' seems to bypass historico-critical research).

4270 **Kilgallen** John J., A brief commentary on the Gospel of Mark 1989 ➤ 6,5157: ᴿPerspRelSt 18 (1991) 185-7 (R. B. *Vinson*: 'devotional-theological': also on Paulist THOMPSON Mt and FITZMYER Lk).

4271 **Lührmann** Dieter, Das Markusevangelium: HbNT 3, 1987 ➤ 3,4750 ... 6,5158: ᴿSvEx 56 (1991) 129-135 (K. *Búason*).

4272 **Mann** C. S., Mark: AnchorB 27, 1986 ➤ 2,3736 ... 5,4870: ᴿAndrUnS 29 (1991) 94-96 (R. K. *McIver*).

4273 **Mason** S., *Robinson* T., An early Christian reader [NT in historical order plus 'first century documents' 1 Clement, Didache, Ignatius]. Toronto 1990, Canadian Scholars. xiii-605 p.; 5 maps. C$25. 0-921627-56-4 [NTAbs 36,256].

4274 **Senft** Christophe †, L'évangile selon Marc, non achevé, avec sa 'Théologie de Marc' 1976 (p. 91-103) et préf. de *Vouga* François: Essais Bibliques 19. Genève 1991, Labor et Fides. 107 p. Fs 22. 2-8309-0615-2 [Benedictina 39,479, S. *de Piccoli*].

4275 **Stock** Augustine, The method and message of Mark 1989 ➤ 5,4939; 6,5218: ᴿCBQ 53 (1991) 344-6 (Q. *Quesnell*: full-scale commentary); CritRR 4 (1991) 234-6 (M. R. *Mansfield*).

4276 **Strelan** R., Crossing the boundaries; a commentary on Mark: Chi Rho comm. Adelaide 1991, Lutheran. 233 p.; 2 maps. 0-85910-584-9 [NTAbs 36,270].

4277 **Zuurmond** Rochus, The Gospel of Mark [in Ge'ez]: ÄthFor 27 (1989 ➤ 6,1906: ᴿGregorianum 72 (1991) 395s (E. *Farahian*); JTS 42 (1991) 658-662 (J. N. *Birdsall*); ZDMG 141 (1991) 408-410 (E. *Wagner*).

F6.2 *Evangelium Marci*, **Themata.**

4278 *Arens* Eduardo, ¿Qué es evangelizar? La respuesta de Marcos: TVida 32 (1991) 259-271.

4279 **Balaguer** Vicente, Testimonio y tradición en San Marcos; narratología del Segundo Evangelio: Teológica 73, 1900 ➤ 6,5168: ᴿActuBbg 28 (1991) 161s (X. *Alegre*); AnnTh 5 (1991) 407-410 (B. *Estrada*); Scrip-TPamp 23 (1991) 695-702 (J. M. *Casciaro*: 'metodología novedosa').

4280 *Balaguer* Vicente, El sentido de la estructura de Marcos: ➤ 421, Luso-Esp 1989/91, 425-432.

4281 **Best** E., Disciples and discipleship according to Mark 1986 ➤ 2,132* ... 6,5170: ᴿRelStR 17 (1991) 12.14-16 (Joanna *Dewey*, also on D. VIA and Elizabeth MALBON).

4282 **Best** Ernst, The temptation and the Passion; the Markan soteriology² [= ¹1965 + 62 p. preface]. 1990 ➤ 6,5287: ᴿNBlackf 72 (1991) 536 (K. *Grayston*).

4283 **Black** C. Clifton, The disciples according to Mark: JStNT supp 27, ᴰ1989 ➤ 5,4885; 6,5173: ᴿBiblica 72 (1991) 123-7 (V. *Fusco*); CBQ 53 (1991) 314s (J. B. *Green*); CritRR 4 (1991) 169-171 (Adela Y. *Collins*); Interpretation 45 (1991) 82.84 (Elizabeth S. *Malbon*).

4284 **Blackburn** Barry, Theios aner and the Markan miracle traditions; a critique of the theios aner concept as an interpretative background of the miracle traditions used by Mark: WUNT 2/60. Tü 1991, Mohr. xii-334 p. DM 96. 3-16-145503-7. – ᴿArTGran 54 (1991) 352s (A. *Segovia*).

4285 *Botha* P.J.J., Mark's story as oral traditional literature; rethinking the transmission of some traditions about Jesus: HervTSt 47 (1991) 304-331 [< NTAbs 36,179].

4286 **Bravo** C., Galilea año 30; para leer el evangelio de Marcos: En torno al NT 12. Córdoba 1991, Almendro. 178 p. 84-86077-90-7 [NTAbs 36,108].

4286* *Breytenbach* C., Die debat rondom die Markaanse Christologie; die laaste tien jaar: SkrifKerk 12,2 (1991) 135-172 [< NTAbs 36,339].

4287 **Cotter** Wendy J., The Markan sea miracles; their history, formation, and function in the literary context of Greco-Roman antiquity: diss. St. Michael, ᴰ*Guenther* H. Toronto 1991. 516 p. – RTLv 23, p. 543.

4288 **Cuvillier** Elian, L'arrière-plan littéraire du terme 'parabolè' dans le second Évangile; sa signification dans le cadre de la rédaction marcienne; son utilisation dans la tradition de Jésus: diss. Montpellier 1991. 325 p. [< ÉtBN]. – RTLv 23, p. 543.

4289 **Dahm** Christof, Israel im Markusevangelium [Diss. Mainz, ᴰ*Schenke* L. ➔ 6,5180]: EurHS 23/420, Fra 1991, Lang. v-353 p., 9 fig. $62. 3-631-43657-2 [NTAbs 36,262].

4290 **Danove** Paul L., A failed story but a successful plot; an analysis of the plot of the Gospel of Mark as a guide to the narrative rhetoric: diss. Graduate Theological Union. Berkeley 1991. 435 p. 91-26303. — DissA 52 (1991s) 1774-A.

4291 *Dewey* Joanna, Mark as interwoven tapestry; forecasts and echoes for a listening audience: CBQ 53 (1991) 221-236.

4292 **Dillmann** Rainer, Christlich handeln in der Nachfolge Jesu ... Mk 1989 ➔ 6,5181: ᴿBiKi 46 (1991) 91s (M. *Helsper*).

4293 *Doty* M., 'Amazed' in Mark [7 nuanced Greek terms]: NotTr 4,2 (1990) 49-58 [< NTAbs 36,339].

4294 **Dunn** James D.G., Jesus, Paul and the Law; studies in Mark and Galatians. L 1990, SPCK. x-277 p. £15. – ᴿHorizons 18 (1991) 146s (P.G. *Henry*); Studies 80 (1991) 95-97 (W. *Harrington*).

4294* *Eck* E. van, Die ideologiese funksie van ruimte [space] in die Markus-vertelling; 'n verkenning [survey]: HervTSt 47 (1991) 1010-1041 [< NTAbs 36,340].

4295 *Ehrman* B.D., The text of Mark in the hands of the orthodox [i.e. early correctors of 1,1.3.10; 15,34]: LuthQ 5 (Milwaukee 1991) 143-156 [< NTAbs 36,30].

4296 **Ernst** Josef, Marco, un ritratto teologico 1990 ➔ 6,5184: ᴿCC 142 (1991,3) 449 (V. *Fusco*).

4297 **Fander** Monika, Die Stellung der Frau im Markusevangelium, unter besonderer Berücksichtigung kultur- und religionsgeschichtlicher Hintergründe: Münsteraner TA 8, ᴰ1989 ➔ 5,4896: ᴿBiKi 46 (1991) 136s (D. *Kosch*); BO 48 (1991) 673-7 (D. *Monshouwer*); JTS 42 (1991) 195-8 (Ruth B. *Edwards*); TLZ 116 (1991) 111-3 (D. *Lührmann*); TR 87 (1991) 107-9 (G. *Theissen*).

4298 **Fausti** Silvano, Ricorda e racconta il Vangelo; la catechesi narrativa di Marco: Parole di Vita. Mi 1990, Àncora. 557 p. Lit. 45.000. – ᴿBenedictina 38 (1991) 485-8 (A. *Ranzato*).

4299 **Fendler** Folkert, Studien zum Markusevangelium; zur Gattung, Chronologie, Messiasgesheimnistheorie und Überlieferung des zweiten Evangeliums [Diss. Giessen, ᴰ*Strecker* ➔ 6,5186]: GöTArb 49. Gö 1991, Vandenhoeck & R. 208 p. 3-525-87803-6.

4300 **Fowler** R. M., Let the reader understand; reader-response criticism and the Gospel of Mark. Mp 1991, Fortress. xiii-279 p. $22. 0-8006-2491-2 [NTAbs 36,263].

4301 **France** R. T., Divine government... Mk 1990 → 6,5187: ᴿTLond 94 (1991) 147s (Clare *Drury*).

4302 *Garofalo* Rob, The family of Jesus in Mark's Gospel: IrTQ 57 (1991) 265-276.

4303 *Graham* Susan L., Silent voices; women in the gospel of Mark: → 311, Semeia 54 (1991) 145-158.

Johnson David W., Mark, relation to Romans ᴰ1990 → 5278.

4304 **Kalajainen** Larry R., Speaking plainly, seeing clearly; the hermeneutical implications of the imagery of sight and hearing in the Gospel of Mark: diss. Drew, ᴰ*Day* Lala. Madison ɴᴊ, 1991. 259 p. 91-29308. – DissA 52 (1991s) 1391-A; RelStR 18,173 'Dey'.

4305 **Kelber** Werner, [Mc...] Tradition orale et Écriture, ᵀ*Prignaud* J.: LDiv145. P 1991, Cerf. 332 p. F 200. – ᴿEsprVie 101 (1991) 565s (É. *Cothenet*: chemins non battus qui risquent d'être des impasses).

4306 **Kingsbury** J. D., Conflict in Mark 1989 → 5,4908; 6,5194: ᴿScotJT 44 (1991) 415-7 (E. *Best*: lectures for pastors and students); TorJT 7 (1991) 117-9 (Wendy J. *Cotter*); Vidyajyoti 55 (1991) 227s (P. M. *Meagher*).

4307 **Kingsbury** Jack D., Conflicto en Marcos; Jesús, autoridades, discípulos, ᵀ*Godoy* Rufino: En torno al NT 10. Córdoba 1991, Almendro. 170 p. 84-8005-002-0.

4308 **Latour** Pascal, 'Lutron' concept in Mark [RTLv 23, p. 544] and its scriptural significance: diss. Inst. prot. Paris 1991. 607 p.

4309 **Mabongo** Daniel, Le nomadisme de Jésus dans l'Évangile de Marc: diss. prot. ᴰ*Trocmé* É. Strasbourg 1991. 275 p. – RTLv 23, p. 545.

4310 **Mack** B. L., 'A myth of innocence' [Mk → 4,4988...6,5199] at sea [i.e. defended against reviewers]: Continuum 1,2 (NY 1991) 140-157 [< NTAbs 36,30].

4311 *a) Mack* Burton L., Q and the gospel of Mark; revising Christian origins; – *b) Guenther* Heinz O., The sayings gospel Q and the quest for Aramaic sources; rethinking Christian origins; – *c) Horsley* Richard A., Q and Jesus; assumptions, approaches, and analyses: → 312, Semeia 55 (1991) 15-39 / 41-76 / 175-209.

4312 *McVann* Mark, Baptism, miracles, and boundary jumping in Mark: BibTB 21 (1991) 151-7.

4313 **Marín** Javier-José, The Christology of Mark; does Mark's Christology support the Chalcedonian formula 'truly man and truly God'? [diss. Z 1990, ᴰ*Weder* → 6,5201]: EurHS 23/417. Bern 1991, Lang. [lxxi-] 276 p. 3-261-04330-X.

4314 **Marshall** Christopher D., Faith as a theme in Mark's narrative [ᴰ1985, London] 1989 → 5,4920; 6,5202: ᴿBS 148 (1991) 375s (J. F. *Williams*); ÉTRel 66 (1991) 123 (É. *Cuvillier*); EvQ 63 (1991) 66s (T. *Dwyer*); JBL 110 (1991) 726-9 (C. C. *Black*); NBlackf 71 (1990) 463s (I. H. *Marshall*); RelStR 17 (1991) 261 (C. *Mercer*); TR 87 (1991) 281-3 (T. *Söding*).

4315 **Martini** Carlo M., The spiritual journey of the apostles; growth in the Gospel of Mark, ᵀ*Whitehead* K. D. Boston 1991, St. Paul. 105 p. $6 pa. 0-8198-6910-4 [TDig 39,274].

4316 **Martini** Carlo M., Was er euch sagt; Leben aus der Freude des [Mk.-] Evangeliums. FrB 1989, Herder. 160 p. DM 22,80 [TPQ 140,195, J. *Hörmandinger*].

4317 **Matera** F. J.,   What are they saying about Mark? 1987 ➤ 3,4795 ...
5,4921:   ᴿScripB 21 (1991) 21 (J. *McGuckin*).

4318 *Mearns* C. L.,   Parables, secrecy and eschatology in Mark's Gospel:
ScotJT 44 (1991) 423-442.

4319 **Miller** D. & P.,   Gospel of Mark as midrash 1990 ➤ 6,5205: ᴿTLZ 116
(1991) 429-431 (W. *Schmithals*); TsTNijm 31 (1991) 194s (H. van de
Sandt).

4320 *Minette de Tillesse* Caetano,   Marcos e o Evangelho: RCuBíb 14,55s
(1990) 44-60.

4321 *Minor* M.,   The women of the Gospel of Mark and contemporary
women's spirituality: SpTod 43 (St. Louis 1991) 134-141 [< NTAbs
36,30].

4322 **Myers** Ched,   Binding the strong man ... Mk 1988 ➤ 4,4994; 6,5207:
ᴿCBQ 53 (1991) 336-8 (D. M. *Rhoads*: courageously explores new approaches, but imposes his liberation-model everywhere).

4323 *Neirynck* F.,   The minor agreements and Proto-Mark, a response to H.
KOESTER: ETL 67 (1991) 82-94.

4324 **O'Mahoney** Gerald,   Praying St. Mark's Gospel.   L 1990, Chapman.
viii-138 p. £7. – ᴿNBlackf 72 (1991) 256 (H. *Wansbrough*).

4324* *Pérez Fernández* Miguel,   La herencia de la Biblia hebrea (II.) el
caso paradigmático del Evangelio de Marcos: ➤ 453, Orígenes 1989/91,
99-120.

4325 **Quintens** Werner,   Aan de hand von Marcus [B-cyclus homilieën].
Brugge 1990, Tabor. 181 p. – ᴿCollatVL 21 (1991) 316 (E. Vanden
Berghe).

4326 **Räisänen** Heikki,   The 'Messianic secret', ᵀ*Tuckett* Christopher 1990
➤ 6,5210: ᴿÉTRel 66 (1991) 435s (E. *Cuvillier*); ExpTim 102 (1990s) 346
(C. S. *Rodd*); JTS 42 (1991) 654-7 (Mary Ann *Beavis*); Pacifica 4 (1991)
344-346 (Dorothy A. *Lee-Pollard*); TLond 94 (1991) 223s (W. R. *Telford*:
a fine book from a distinguished scholar).

4327 **Riley** Harold,   Making of Mark 1989 ➤ 5,4930; 6,5212: ᴿAnglTR 73
(1991) 74-76 (H. H. *Graham*); JBL 110 (1991) 346-8 (W. O. *Walker*); JTS
42 (1991) 193-5 (C. M. *Tuckett*).

4328 **Robinson** James M.,   Messiasgeheimnis (1956) 1989 ➤ 5,4931: ᴿTLZ
116 (1991) 283s (P. *Pokorny*: inspirierend).

4329 **Rowe** Robert D.,   God's kingdom and God's son; a study in the
background to Mark's Christology with special reference to concepts of
kingship in the Psalms: diss. British Council/Awards. 1990. 449 p.
BRDX-93418. — DissA 52 (1991s) 1775-A.

4330 *Sahlin* H.   Haggada- och Midrash-inslag i Markusevangeliet: Religion
och Bibel 48 (Lund 1991) 38-54 [< NTAbs 36,180].

4331 **Sariola** Heikki,   Markus und das Gesetz: DissHumLitt 56. Helsinki
1990, Acad. 277 p.

4332 *Scholtissek* Klaus,   Nachfolge und Autorität nach dem Markusevangelium: TrierTZ 100 (1991) 56-74.

4333 **Schüling** Joachim,   Studien zum Verhältnis von Logienquelle und Markusevangelium [Diss. Giessen 1987, ᴰ*Dautzenberg* G.]: ForBi 65. Wü
1991, Echter. 252 p. DM 39. 3-429-01368-2 [TLZ 117,843, W. *Schenk*].

4334 **Shepherd** Tom,   The definition and function of Markan intercalation as
illustrated in a narrative analysis of six passages: diss. Andrews, ᴰ*Johnston*
R., Berrien Springs MI 1991. 440 p. 91-29722. — DissA 52 (1991s)
1773-A [not in 'Religion: Biblical Studies' section, though *Danove* is
p. 1774 (fasc. 5)].

4335 *Smith* S.H., 'Inside' and 'outside' in Mark's Gospel; a response: Exp-Tim [97 (1986s) 39-43, MOORE W.] 102 (1990s) 363-7.

4336 *Stock* Klemens, De camino con Jesús; los Ejercicios siguiendo el texto del Evangelio de S. Marco: ➤ 287, Emaús en Manresa 1991, 39-112.

4337 **Suh** J.S., Discipleship and community; Mark's Gospel in sociological perspective [diss. Boston Univ. 1986, ᴰ*Kee* H.C.]: Nexus Mg 1. Claremont CA 1991, Center for Asian-American Ministries. ix-175 p. [NTAbs 36,116].

4338 **Thompson** Mary R., Role of disbelief in Mark 1989 ➤ 5,4942: ᴿCrit-RR 4 (1991) 241-3 (M.R. *Mansfield*); ScripTPamp 23 (1991) 368 (V. *Balaguer*).

4339 **Tolbert** Mary Ann, Sowing the Gospel, Mark's world 1989 ➤ 5,4943: ᴿBibTB 21 (1991) 82s (R.L. *Mowery*); CritRR 4 (1991) 245-7 (Adela Y. *Collins*); Interpretation 45 (1991) 186s (F.J. *Matera*: 'reading Mark as an ancient novel'); LvSt 16 (1991) 72s (R.F. *Collins*); RelStR 17 (1991) 16-23 (V.K. *Robbins*, also on WAETJEN, MYERS, MACK); TS 52 (1991) 542-4 (B.B. *Scott*).

4340 **Waetjen** Herman C., A reordering of power; Mk 1989 ➤ 5,4948; 6,5225: ᴿAnglTR 73 (1991) 333s (Joanna *Dewey*, also on MYERS C. 1988); BibTB 21 (1991) 83s (C.C. *Black*); CBQ 53 (1991) 352-4 (R.J. *Miller*); CritRR 4 (1991) 249-251 (W. *Wink*).

4341 **Weiss** Wolfgang, 'Eine neue Lehre...' Mk: BZNW 52, 1989 ➤ 5,4951; 6,5226: ᴿCBQ 53 (1991) 156s (R. *Morton*); ÉTRel 66 (1991) 121s (M. *Schuster*).

4342 **Zwick** Reinhold, Montage im Markusevangelium; Studien zur narrativen Organisation der ältesten Jesuserzählung [kath. Diss. Rg 1988, ᴰ*Schmuttermayr* G.]: BoBB 18. Stu 1989, KBW. xvi-652 p. DM 39. ➤ 6,5226*; 3-460-00181-X. – ᴿNTAbs 35 (1991) 116 ('montage' = rapid succession of images to illustrate an association of ideas); TLZ 116 (1991) 285-7 (W. *Vogler*); TR 87 (1991) 16-18 (D. *Dormeyer*).

F6.3   **Evangelii Marci versiculi 1,1 ...**

4343 *Hess* H.H., Dynamics of the Greek noun phrase in Mark [1-6]: OPTAT 4 (Dallas 1990) 353-370 [< NTAbs 36,31].

4344 *Head* Peter M., A text-critical study of Mark 1.1, 'the beginning of the Gospel of Jesus Christ': NTS 37 (1991) 621-9.

4345 *Edwards* J.R., [Mk 1,9] The baptism of Jesus according to the Gospel of Mark: JEvTS 34 (1991) 43-57 [< NTAbs 36,31].

4346 *Ulansey* David [Mk 1,10; 15,38] The heavenly veil torn; Mark's cosmic inclusio: JBL 110 (1991) 123-5.

4347 *Monshouwer* Dirk, Die Beziehungen zwischen Markus [1,12f], Lukas [4.1-13] und dem TNK: DielB 26 (1989s) 125-136.

4348 **Kuthirakattel** Scaria, The beginning of Jesus' ministry according to Mark's Gospel (1,14-3,6), a redaction-critical study [diss. Pont. Ist. Biblico, ᴰ*La Potterie* I. de]: AnBib 123, 1990 ➤ 6,5231: ᴿExpTim 103 (1991s) 82s (R.S. *Barbour*).

4349 *Gutiérrez* Gustavo, Mark 1:14-15, expository: RExp 88 (1991) 427-431 [< The God of Life, ᵀ*O'Connell* M.].

4350 *Kollmann* Bernd, [Mk 1,25] Jesu Schweigegebote an die Dämonen: ZNW 82 (1991) 267-273.

Delorme Jean, [Mc 1,40-45; 2,1-13; 5,21-43; Lc 1,46-55; 10,25-37; Mt 25,14-30] Au risque de la Parole; lire les évangiles: Parole de Dieu, 1991 ➤ 195.

4351 **Roure** Damiá, Jesús y la figura de David en Mc 2,23-26 ...: AnBib 124,
ᴰ1990 ➤ 6,5238: ᴿArTGran 54 (1991) 384s (A. *Segovia*); BLitEc 92
(1991) 391s (M. *Delcor*); EstFranc 92 (1990) 556-8 (J. *Ferrer*); RThom 91
(1991) 707s (H. *Ponsot*); Salmanticensis 88 (1991) 376s (G. *Pérez*).

4352 *Dieterlé* Christiane, Le jeu entre l'espace et le temps en Marc 4,1-34:
➤ 30, ᶠBONNARD P., Mémoire 1991, 127-140.

4352* *a) Hartin* P.J., Disseminating the Word; a deconstructive reading
of Mark 4:1-9 and Mark 4:13-20; – *b) Maartens* P.J., 'Sign' and
'significance' in the theory and practice of ongoing literary critical
interpretation with reference to Mark 4:24 and 25; a study of semiotic
relations in the text: ➤ 307, Text 1991, 187-200 / 63-81.

Lindemann A., Mk 4,3-8: 1991 ➤ 4074.

4353 *Goulder* Michael D., Those outside (Mk. 4:10-12): NT 33 (1991) 289-302.

4354 **Beavis** Mary Ann, Mark's audience ... 4,11s ᴰ1989 ➤ 5,4975: ᴿÉTRel
66 (1991) 122 (É. *Cuvillier*); ExpTim 102 (1990s) 278 (J. *Muddiman*); JTS
42 (1991) 657s (H. *Anderson*); TLZ 116 (1991) 352-4 (J.-W. *Taeger*).

4355 *a) Lindemann* Andreas, Die Erzählung der Machttäten Jesu in Markus
4,35-6,6s; Erwägungen zum formgeschichtlichen und hermeneutischen
Problem; – *b) Breytenbach* Cilliers, Grundzüge markinischer Gottessohn-
Christologie: ➤ 72, ᶠHAHN F., Anfänge 1991, 185-207 / 169-184.

4356 **Selvidge** Marla J., Woman, cult, and miracle ... Mk 5,24-34, 1990
➤ 6,5254: ᴿCBQ 53 (1991) 506s (Judette M. *Kolasny*); RelStR 17 (1991)
364 (C. *Mercer*).

4357 *Janse* Mark, A note on the fibula praenestina [... invoking *tís mou
hēpsato* Mk 5,31 for *hēpsató moú tis* of Lk 8,46]: IndogF 95 (1990) 101-3.

4358 **Balembo** Buetubela, L'identité de Jésus et Jean-Baptiste en Mc 6,14-29:
Recherches Africaines de Théologie 12. Kinshasa 1991, Fac.Catholiques.
63 p.

4359 *Smit* J.A., *a)* Mark 7:8 & 9 in counter-determining context; – *b)* Theoretic perspectives; contextualisation as metaphoric activity: Neotestamentica 25,1 (1991) 17-28 / 1-15.

4360 *Cunningham* S., The healing of the deaf and dumb man (Mark 7:31-37)
with application to the African context: AfJEv 9,2 (Kenya 1990) 13-26
[< NTAbs 36,33].

4361 *Drury* John, [Mk 8,14-21] Understanding the bread; disruption and
aggregation, secrecy and revelation in Mark's gospel: ➤ 454b, Not in
Heaven 1989/91, 98-119 . 239.

4362 *Mateos* Juan, [Mc 8,24; 9,2; 10,46] Algunas notas sobre el evangelio de
Marcos (III): FgNt 4 (1991) 193-203.

4363 *Sugirtharajah* R.S., Men, trees and walking; a conjectural solution to
Mk 8:24: ExpTim 103 (1991s) 172-4.

4364 *Debergé* Pierre, 'Hacerse como niños ...', desafio para un cristiano;
reflexiones sobre Mc 9 y 10: ➤ 316, Reflexión 1990, 141-172.

4365 *Tilley* Terrence W., [Mk 9,23] 'Lord, I believe; help my unbelief'; prayer
without belief: ModT 7 (1990s) 239-247.

4366 *La Verdiere* E., [Mk 9,30 ...] Servant of all / Salted with fire: Emmanuel
97 (1991) 342-7 / 394-400.

4367 *Dumortier* Francis, Marc 10,1-12, Que l'homme ne sépare pas ce que
Dieu a uni: Masses Ouvrières 439 ('Des couples' 1991) 70-76.

4368 *La Verdiere* E., [Mk 10,1-12] The question of divorce: Emmanuel 97
(1991) 454-460 . 514-520 . 566-569 . 582-4 [< NTAbs 36,183].

4369 *Delorme* J., Royaume de Dieu, royaume d'enfance, Mc 10,13-16: ➤ 121,
ᶠRAMAROSON L., Ta parole 1991, 32-42.

4370 **Fusco** Vittorio,   Povertà e sequela; la pericope sinottica della chiamata del ricco (Mc 10,17-31): StBPaid 94. Brescia 1991, Paideia.   148 p. Lit. 18.000. – ᴿAsprenas 38 (1991) 523-8 (V. *Scippa*); LA 40 (1990!) 515-7 (A. M. *Buscemi*); StPatav 38 (1991) 184 (G. *Segalla*).

4371 *Fusco* Vittorio,   Povertà e sequela nell'episodio della chiamata del ricco (Mc 10,17-31): → 444*, Ricchezza 1989/91, 135-169.

4372 *Loessl* J.,   The ethical dimension of Mk 10:17-22:   Hekima Review 6 (Nairobi 1991) 57-82 [< NTAbs 36,183].

4373 *Vos* Geerhardus,   A sermon on Mark 10:45:   Kerux 6,1 (1991) 3-15.

4374 *Suggit* John N.,   Bartimaeus and Christian discipleship (Mark 10,46-52): JTSAf 74 (Braamfontein 1991) 57-63 [< ZIT 91,275].

4375 *Telford* William R.,   [Mk 11,12-20]   More fruit from a withered tree; Temple and fig-tree in Mark from a Graeco-Roman perspective: → 15, ᶠBAMMEL E.,   Templum 1991, 264-304.

4376 *Buchanan* George W.,   [Mk 11,15-19; Zech 14,21; Is 56,7; Jer 7,11] Symbolic money-changers in the Temple: NTS 37 (1991) 280-290.

4377 *a) Miller* Robert J.,   [Mk 11,15-17] The (a)historicity of Jesus' Temple demonstration; a test case in methodology; – *b) Evans* Craig A.,   In what sense blasphemy? Jesus before Caiaphas in Mark 14:61-64: → 446, SBL Sem 30 (1991) 235-252 / 215-234.

4378 **Dowd** Sharyn E.,   Prayer, power... Mk 11,22-25: ᴰ1988 → 4,5059... 6,5280:   ᴿCritRR 4 (1991) 187-9 (Elizabeth S. *Malbon*).

4379 *Schenker* Adrian,   Gleichnis eines gescheiterten Vergleichs?   Mk 12,1-9 par. [ineditum]: → 258, Text 1991, 263-271.

4380 **Florio** Giuseppe,   Interpretazione della pericope Mc 12,13-17 in questo secolo (Dio e Cesare): diss. Pont. Univ. Gregoriana, ᴰO'Collins G.   R 1991s – InfPUG 24/123, 9.

4381 **Kiilunen** Jarmo,   Das Doppelgebot der Liebe... Mk 12,28-34 par. 1989 → 5,5001:   ᴿETL 67 (1991) 432s (F. *Neirynck*); JTS 42 (1991) 664s (C. M. *Tuckett*).

4382 *Isheim* Reiner,   Evangelium und Gesetzlichkeit; eine homiletische Studie zu Mk 12,41-44 (Das Scherflein der Witwe): TBei 22,1 (Wu 1991) 21-31 [< ZIT 91,156].

4383 *Malbon* Elizabeth S.,   [Mk 12,41-44] The poor widow in Mark and her poor rich readers: CBQ 53 (1991) 589-604 [odd-page headings 'in Mark 12'].

4384 *Black* C. Clifton,   An oration at Olivet; some rhetorical dimensions of Mark 13: → 86, ᶠKENNEDY G., Persuasive 1991, 66-92.

4385 **Geddert** T.   Watchwords, Mk 13 [diss. Aberdeen 1986 → 2,3838; 550 p. BRDX-93928; – DissA 52 (1991s) 2588]: JStNT supp 26, 1989 → 5,5003: ᴿBiblica 72 (1991) 426s (L. *Gaston*); CBQ 53 (1991) 700s (L. W. *Hurtado*); ÉTRel 66 (1991) 123s (E. *Cuvillier*); ExpTim 102 (1990s) 278s (J. *Muddiman*); HeythJ 32 (1991) 545-7 (M. *Smith*); JTS 42 (1991) 198-201 (Morna D. *Hooker*).

4386 *Klappert* Bertold,   Zeichen des Sprossens der Erlösung; das Gleichnis vom sprossenden Feigenbaum (Mk 13,28-33): BTZ 8 (1991) 129-138.

4387 **Mussner** Franz,   [Mk 13,30] Dieses Geschlecht wird nicht vergehen; Judentum und Kirche. FrB 1991, Herder. 165 p. DM 39 [TLZ 117,184, W. *Wiefel*].

F6.8   **Passio secundum Marcum, 14,1 ... [→ F5.3].**

4388 **Broadhead** Edwin K.,   Prophet, Son, Messiah; narrative form and function in Mark 14-16: ev. Diss. Zürich 1991, ᴰWeder. – TR 87 (1991) 515.

4389 *Delorme* Jean, Parole, Évangile et mémoire (Marc 14,3-9): ↗ 30, F BONNARD P., Mémoire 1991, 113-125.
4390 **Jackson** Dalen C., The apocalyptic orientation of Mark 14:26-16:8: diss. Southern Baptist Theol. Sem., D*Garland* D. 1991. 257 p. 92-05759. – DissA 52 (1991s) 2956-A.
4391 **Lawrence** Walter S.III, Reader-response criticism for Markan narrative with a commentary on Mark 14:26-53: diss. St. Louis Univ., D*O'Toole* R. 348 p. 91-15510. — DissA 52 (1991s) 186-A.
4392 *Smith* Karen E., Mark 14:32-42, expository: RExp 88 (1991) 433-7.
4393 **Herron** R., [Mk 14,69-71] Mark's account of Peter's denial of Jesus. Lanham MD 1991, UPA. 212 p. $43.50; pa. $24.50 [TS 53,396].
4394 **Schreiber** Johannes, Der Kreuzigungsbericht Mk 15,20-41 ... nach W. WREDE [< diss Bonn 1959, D*Vielhauer* P.] BZNW 48, 1986 ↗ 2,3852 ... 6,5295: RRB 98 (1991) 627-9 (B. T. *Viviano*: an odd history, an odd appearance; a Lutheran thesis solid for its day, with unsatisfactory additions).
4395 **Magnolfi** Maria, Elōi Elōi lema sabachthani (Mc. 15,34), indagine esegetica e contributo all'interpretazione del grido di abbandono di Gesù: diss. Pont. Ist. Biblico, D*Grech* P. R 1990. – Biblica 72 (1991) 145; AcPIB 9,623-5; RTLv 23, p. 545.
4395* *Stockklausner* S. K., *Hole* C. A., Mark 15:39 and 16:6-7; a second look: McMasterJTheol 1,2 (Hamilton 1990) 34-44 [< NTAbs 36,343].
4396 *Bauckham* Richard, [Mk 15,40; 16,1] Salome the sister of Jesus, Salome the disciple of Jesus, and the Secret Gospel of Mark: NT 33 (1991) 245-275.
4397 **Cox** Steven L., [Mk 16,8.20] A history and critique of scholarship concerning the Markan endings; diss. Southern Baptist Theol. Sem. 1991. D*Blevins* J. 261 p. 91-25190. – DissA 52 (1991s) 954-A.

| XII. Opus Lucanum |

F7.1 *Opus Lucanum* – **Luke-Acts.**

4398 *Aarde* A. G. van, 'The Most High God does live in houses, but not houses built by men ...'. The relativity of the metaphor, temple, in Luke-Acts (Responses *Elliott* J. H., *Esler* P. F.): Neotestamentica 25,1 (1991) 51-64 (171s, 173s).
4399 **Bovon** F. L'œuvre de Luc 1987 ↗ 3,195 ... 5,5025: RETL 67 (1991) 429s (F. *Neirynck*).
4400 **Brawley** Robert L., Centering on God; method and message in Luke-Acts: Literary currents in biblical interpretation, 1990 ↗ 6,5304: RExpTim 103 (1991s) 53 (R. *Morgan*).
4401 **Buckwalter** H. Douglas, The character and purpose of Luke's Christology. diss. D*Marshall* I. Aberdeen 1991. 424 p. – RTLv 23, p. 542.
4402 *Dawsey* James M., The origin of Luke's positive perception of the Temple: PerspRelSt 18,1 (1991) 5,22.
4403 *Elliott* John H., Household and meals vs. Temple purity; replication patterns in Luke-Acts [10s]: BibTB 21 (1991) 102-8.
4404 *Elliott* J. H., Temple versus household in Luke-Acts; a contrast in social institutions: HervTSt 47 (1991) 88-120 [< NTAbs 36,35].
4405 a) *Elliott* John H., Temple versus household in Luke-Acts; a contrast in social institutions; – b) *Malina* Bruce J., Reading theory perspective;

reading Luke Acts: ➤ 450, Social world of Luke-Acts 1991, 211-240 / 3-23.

4406 **Fitzmyer** Joseph A., Luke the theologian; aspects of his teaching [1987 d'Arcy lectures; i. The authorship of Luke-Acts reconsidered (and upheld)] 1988 ➤ 5,5034; 6,5312: ᴿBibTB 21 (1991) 121s (J.S. *Siker*); CBQ 53 (1991) 699s (W.J. *Harrington*); EvQ 63 (1991) 176-8 (J.B. *Green*); Interpretation 45 (1991) 86.88 (G.E. *Witte*); JBL 110 (1991) 729-733 (Susan B. *Garrett*: lengthy analysis and high praise); NBlackf 72 (1991) 298-300 (M. *Turner*); RuBi 43 (1990) 176s (P. *Pietrusiak*).

4407 **Fitzmyer** Joseph A., Luca teologo; aspetti del suo insegnamento [1989], ᵀ*Gatti* E.: Biblioteca Biblica 6. Brescia 1991, Queriniana. 192 p. Lit. 22.000. – ᴿETL 67 (1991) 430s (F. *Neirynck*, surtout sur l'anglais).

Garrett Susan R., The demise of the devil ... Luke 1989 ➤ 1938 supra.

4408 *Gault* J.A., The discourse function of *kai egéneto* in Luke and Acts: OPTAT 4 (Dallas 1990) 388-399 [< NTAbs 36,35].

4409 **Gillman** John, Possessions and the life of faith; a reading of Luke-Acts: Glazier-Zacchaeus. ColMn 1991, Liturgical. 120 p. $7. 1-8146-5675-7 [TDig 38,392].

4410 **Gower** David B., Host, guest, enemy and friend; portraits of the Pharisees in Luke and Acts: Emory StEC 2. SF 1991, Lang. 405 p. DM 109 [TR 88,163]. 0-8204-1329-1.

4411 *a) Jervell* Jacob, Retrospect and prospect in Luke-Acts interpretation; – *b) Chance* J. Bradley, The Jewish people and the death of Jesus in Luke-Acts; some implications of an inconsistent narrative role; – *c) Carlson* Richard P., The role of the Jewish people in Luke's Passion theology: ➤ 446, SBL Sem 30 (1991) 383-404 / 50-81 / 82-102.

4412 **Klinghardt** Matthias, Gesetz und Volk Gottes ... Luk. ᴰ1988 ➤ 4,5098 ... 6,5317: ᴿJRel 71 (1991) 91s (E. *Krentz*).

4413 **Koet** Bart J., Five studies on interpretation of Scripture in Luke-Acts ᴰ1989 ➤ 5,5043; 6,5318: ᴿHeythJ 32 (1991) 394s (J.D.M. *Derrett*); RB 98 (1991) 453 (tit. pp.); SvEx 56 (1991) 135-7 (W. *Übelacker*).

ᴱ**Luomanen** Petri, Luke-Acts, Scandinavian perspectives 1991 ➤ 318.

4414 **Mainville** Odette, L'esprit dans l'œuvre de Luc [diss. Montréal, ᴰ*Myre* A. 1989]: Héritage et projet 45. St. Laurent QUE 1991, Fides. 378 p. 2-7621-1541-8.

4415 *Malina* Bruce J., *Neyrey* Jerome H., *a)* Honor and shame in Luke-Acts; pivotal values of the Mediterranean world; – *b)* First-century personality; dyadic, not individualistic; – *c)* Conflict in Luke-Acts; labelling and deviance theory: ➤ 450, Social world of Luke-Acts 1991, 25-65 / 67-96 / 97-122.

4416 *Marconi* Gilberto, La veste (esthēs) come categoria ermeneutica del 'vedere' e semantica del divino negli scritti lucani, ovvero l'estetica non-umana di Luca: RivB 39 (1991) 3-23.

4417 **Menzies** Robert P., The development of early Christian pneumatology, with special reference to Luke-Acts [diss. Aberdeen 1989 ➤ 6,5324]: JStNT supp 54. Sheffield 1991, Academic. 375 p.

4418 *a) Moxnes* Halvor, Patron-client relations and the new community in Luke-Acts; – *b) Robbins* Vernon K., The social location of the implied author of Luke-Acts; – *c) McVann* Mark, Rituals of status transformation in Luke-Acts; the case of Jesus the prophet: ➤ 450, Social world of Lk-Ac 1991, 241-268 / 305-332 / 333-360.

4419 *Neyrey* Jerome H., *a)* The symbolic universe of Luke-Acts; 'they turn the world upside down' [Act 17,6]; – *b)* Ceremonies in Luke-Acts; the case of meals and table-fellowship: → 450, Social World of Lk-Ac 1991, 271-304 / 361-387.

4420 *Ommeren* Nicholas M. van, Was Luke an accurate historian?: BS 148 (1991) 57-71.

4421 *a)* *O'Toole* Robert F., Poverty and wealth in Luke-Acts; – *b)* *Cunningham* Agnes, ... in Christian antiquity; ChSt 30 (1991) 29-41 / 43-57.

4422 **Plymale** Steven F., The prayer-texts of Luke-Acts [diss. Garrett, Evanston, ᴰ*Sundberg* A.]: AmerUnivSt 7/118. NY 1991, Lang. ix-134 p. $36. 0-8204-1658-4 [NTAbs 36,425].

4423 **Ray** Jerry L., Narrative irony in Luke-Acts: diss. Virginia, ᴰ*Gamble* H. 1991. 267 p. 92-08905. – DissA 52 (1991s) 4372-A; RelStR 18,173.

4424 *a)* *Robbins* Vernon K., Luke-Acts; a mixed population seeks a home in the Roman Empire; – *b)* *Edwards* Douglas R., Surviving the web of Roman power; religion and politics in the Acts of the Apostles, Jᴏsᴇᴘʜᴜs and Cʜᴀʀɪᴛᴏɴ's Chaereas and Callirhoe: → 412, Images of empire 1990/1, 202-221 / 179-201.

4425 **Sanders** Jack T., The Jews in Luke-Acts 1987 → 3,4930 ... 6,5382: ᴿJAAR 59 (1991) 619-621 (D. E. *Lewycky*).

ᶠSᴄʜɴᴇɪᴅᴇʀ Gerhard, Der Treue Gottes trauen; Beiträge zum Werk des Lukas, ᴱ**Bussmann** C., *Radl* W., 1991 → 135*a*.

4426 **Shelton** James B., Mighty in word and deed; the role of the Holy Spirit in Luke-Acts [diss. Stirling, ᴰ*Drane* J.] Peabody ᴍᴀ 1991, Hendrickson. xii-196 p. $12 pa. 0-943575-44-3 [NTAbs 36,270].

4427 **Stegemann** Wolfgang, Zwischen Synagoge und Obrigkeit; zur historischen Situation der lukanischen Christen [Hab.-Diss. Heidelberg 1983, ᴰ*Theissen* G.]: FRL 152. Gö 1991, Vandenhoeck & R. 304 p. [TR 87, 340; NRT 144,745s, X. *Jacques*].

4428 **Thornton** Claus-Jürgen, Der Zeuge des Zeugen; Lukas als Historiker der Paulusreisen [Diss. Tü 1989s, ᴰ*Hengel* M.]: WUNT 56. Tü 1991, Mohr. viii-430 p. DM 128. [RHE 86,280*].

4429 *Turner* Max, [Lk 4,18-21; Act 10,38] The Spirit and the power of Jesus' miracles in the Lucan conception: NT 33 (1991) 124-152.

4430 ᴱ**Tyson** Joseph B., Luke-Acts and the Jewish people 1988 → 4,5112; 6,5337: ᴿCBQ 53 (1991) 530-2 (Marie-Eloise *Rosenblatt*: tit. pp. comments); IndTSt 27 (1990) 355-7 (L. *Legrand*: not homogeneous).

4431 *Übelacker* Walter, Lukasskrifternas förhållande till Markusevangeliet: SvEx 56 (1991) 45-77.

4432 *Villegas* M. Beltrán, La evangelización en la teología lucana: TVid 32 (1991) 163-173.

4433 **Weatherly** Jon, Jewish responsibility for the Cross in Luke-Acts: diss. ᴰ*Marshall* I. Aberdeen 1991. 480 p.; extr. JStNT 42 (1991) 79-98. – RTLv 23, p. 547.

4434 *Wenham* John, The identification of Luke: EvQ 63 (1991) 3-44.

4435 *a)* *Williams* David S., On Tᴇʀᴛᴜʟʟɪᴀɴ's text of Luke; – *b)* *Petzer* Jacobus H., Tertullian's text of Acts: SecC 8 (1991) 193-9 / 201-215.

F7.3 **Evangelium Lucae** – *Textus, commentarii.*

4436 *Amphoux* Christian-B., Les premières éditions de Luc [...? Celse]; 1. Le texte de Luc 5: ETL 67 (1991) 312-327 ...

4437 **Bittleston** K., The Gospel of Luke. E 1990, Floris. 255 p. £4. 0-86315-097-7 [NTAbs 36,108: translation of the Gospel text].

4438 **Bovon** François, Das Evangelium nach Lukas I (1-9) 1989 ➤ 5,5057; 6,5340: ᴿCBQ 53 (1991) 695-7 (W. S. *Kurz*); TPhil 66 (1991) 575s (J. *Beutler*).

4439 **Bovon** François, L'Évangile selon saint Luc [1,1-9,50]: CommNT 3a. Genève 1991, Labor et Fides. 515 p. 2-8309-0617-9. – ᴿETL 67 (1991) 426-9 (F. *Neirynck*).

4440 — *Dupont* Jacques, Un important commentaire du troisième évangile [Bovon F. 1989–]: Biblica 72 (1991) 397-403.

4441 **Craddock** Fred B., Luke: Interpretation Comm 1990 ➤ 6,5341: ᴿMid-Stream 30 (1991) 174-6 (M. E. *Boring*); RExp 88 (1991) 461s (A. A. *Trites*).

4441* **Danker** F. W., Jesus & new age, comm Lk² 1988 ➤ 5,5059; 6,5342: ᴿVidyajyoti 55 (1991) 606s (P. M. *Meagher*).

4442 ᴱ**Elliott** J. K., Luke: NT in Greek, Ox 1984-7 ➤ 3,4941 ... 6,5343: ᴿCBQ 53 (1991) 322-5 (M. C. *Parsons*); JTS 42 (1991) 201-215 (Barbara *Aland*); ScotJT 43 (1990) 524-6 (C. D. *Osburn*: no ms. errors, but several patristic).

4443 **Evans** C. F., Saint Luke: TPI (ex-Pelican) comm. 1990 ➤ 6,5344: ᴿJTS 42 (1991) 215-8 (I. H. *Marshall*); NewTR 4,1 (1991) 109s (Barbara E. *Reid*).

4444 **Fischer** B., Varianten zu Lukas: VLat 17, 1990 ➤ 6,5362: ᴿJTS 42 (1991) 663s (J. K. *Elliott*).

4445 **Goulder** Michael D., Luke, a new paradigm ➤ 5,5066; 6,5347: ᴿCBQ 53 (1991) 325s (R. F. *O'Toole*: Luke composed from Mt & Mk on the table before him, with no Q); ETL 67 (1991) 434-6 (F. *Neirynck*); JBL 110 (1991) 162-4 (F. W. *Danker*: claims to drive the nails in Q's coffin).

4446 **Johnson** Luke T., The Gospel of Luke: Sacra Pagina 3. ColMn 1991, Liturgical. xiv-466 p. $30. 0-8146-5805-9 [NTAbs 36,265].

4447 **La Verdiere** Eugene, Luke: NTMessage 5. Dublin 1984 = 1980 (Glazier), Veritas. xlix-296 p. 0-86217-008-7.

4448 **Lindeboom** G. A., Dokter Lukas: Carillon. Amst 1988, Rodopi. 123 p. ƒ 19,50. 90-51830-64-5. – ᴿNedTTs 45 (1991) 68s (J. *Smit Sibinga*).

4449 **McBride** Denis, The Gospel of Luke; a reflective commentary. Dublin 1991, Dominican. xiii-324 p. £12 [TR 88,75].

4450 **Masini** M., Luca, il vangelo del discepolo: LoB 2.3, 1988 ➤ 4,5125 ... 6,5348: ᴿScuolC 118 (1990) 271-3 (G. *Betori*).

4451 **Nolland** J., Luke 1-9: Word comm. 35A, 1989 ➤ 5,5071; 6,5351: ᴿBiblica 72 (1991) 427-431 (A. *Weiser*); JTS 42 (1991) 218-222 (E. *Franklin*).

4452 ᵀᴱ**Sieben** H. J., Origenes, In Lucam homiliae, Homilien zum Lukasevangelium: Fontes Christiani 4/1. FrB 1991s, Herder. 275 p.; viii + p. 276-536; je DM 44 [TLZ 117,758, G. *Haendler*]. 3-451-22204-3; pa. –7.

4453 **Talbert** Charles H., Reading Luke: A New Commentary for Preachers. L 1990 [= 1982 ➤ 64,4881], SPCK. ix-246 p. £10 pa. – ᴿTLond 94 (1991) 219s (R. A. *Burridge*: many merits but).

4454 **Tiede** D. L., Luke: Augsburg comm. 1988 ➤ 4,5130 ... 6,5352: ᴿCritRR 4 (1991) 243-5 (F. W. *Danker*).

4456 **Wojcik** Jan, The road to Emmaus ... Lk 1989 ➤ 6,5354: ᴿCritRR 4 (1991) 253s (C. H. *Talbert*).

F7.4 *Lucae themata* – **Luke's Gospel, topics.**

4457 **Aletti** J.-N., L'art de raconter Jésus-Christ 1989 ➤ 5,5080; 6,5355: ᴿCritRR 4 (1991) 163-5 (R. C. *Tannehill* is pleased to find his own perspectives shared in Europe); Masses Ouvrières 438 (1991) 105s (J.-M. *Carrière*); RTLv 22 (1991) 82s (C. *Focant*); ScEsp 43 (1991) 356s (L. *Sabourin*).

4458 **Aletti** Jean-Noël, L'arte di raccontare Gesù Cristo; la scrittura narrativa del Vangelo di Luca: BtBiblica. R 1991, Queriniana. 228 p. [AcPIB 9/8,652].

4459 **Beck** Brian E., Christian character in the Gospel of Luke 1989 → 5, 5082; 6,5356: ᴿRExp 88 (1991) 95s (J. E. *Jones*: Methodist Conference secretary).

4460 *Cook* Cornelia, The sense of audience in Luke; a literary examination: NBlackf 72 (1991) 19-30.

4461 *a*) *Davies* Stevan, Women in the Third Gospel and the New Testament apocrypha; – *b*) *Reinhartz* Adele, [Lk 10,38-42...] From narrative to history; the resurrection of Mary and Martha: → 329, Women like this 1991, 185-197 / 161-184.

4462 **Ernst** Josef, Luca, un ritratto teologico [1985],ᵀ. Brescia 1988, Morcelliana. 255 p. – ᴿSalesianum 53 (1991) 767 (J. J. *Bartolomé*: en alemán ya Mc 1987, Mt 1989, Jn 1991).

4463 **Heininger** Bernhard, Metaphorik, Erzählstruktur und szenisch-dramatische Gestaltung in den Sondergutgleichnissen bei Lukas [< Diss. Würzburg, ᴰ*Klauck* H.]: NT Abh 24. Münster 1991, Aschendorff. vii-250 p. DM 56 [TR 88,163]. 3-402-04772-1.

4464 **Hensman,** C. Richard, Agenda for the poor claiming their inheritance; a Third World people's reading of Luke: Quest 109. Colombo 1990 [TContexto 2/2,137, G. *Evers*].

4465 *Jervell* Jacob, [Jesus in Lk] Der Sohn des Volkes: → 72, ᶠHAHN F., Anfänge 1991, 245-254.

4466 *Kilgallen* John J., A consideration of some of the women in the Gospel of Luke: StMiss 40 (1991) 27-55.

4467 **Kingsbury** Jack D., Conflict in Luke; Jesus, authorities, disciples. Ph 1991, Fortress. 180 p. $11. 0-8006-2472-6. – ᴿExpTim 103 (1991s) 153 (I. H. *Marshall*: Son of Man a technical term designating Jesus rather than a title).

4468 *Langkammer* Hugolin, ❷ Das Lukasevangelium; das Evangelium vom Erlöser und vom universalen Heil: RoczTK 36,1 (1989) 43-59; Eng. 59.

4469 **Meynet** Roland, Avez-vous lu Saint Luc? 1990 → 6,5368: ᴿEsprVie 101 (1991) 46s = 146 (L. *Walter*).

4470 **Meynet** Roland, L'Évangile selon saint Luc, analyse rhétorique I-II 1988 → 4,5126; 5,5069: ᴿBijdragen 52 (1991) 210s (H. *Welzen*: from 1986 Aix dissertation; the 'classic Reisebericht' loses its force).

4471 *Moore* Stephen D., [Luke] The gospel of the look: → 311, Semeia 54 (1991) 159-196.

4472 **Moxnes** H., Economy of... Luke's Gospel 1988 → 4,5141*... 6,5369: ᴿInterpretation 45 (1991) 84.86 (D. J. *Balch*).

4473 **Neale** David A., None but the sinners; religious categories in the Gospel of Luke [Diss. Sheffield, ᴰ*Alexander* I.]: JStNT supp 58. Sheffield 1991, Academic. 217 p. £22.50; pa £18.75. 1-85075-314-8.

4474 **Nebe** Gottfried, Prophetische Züge im Bilde Jesu bei Lukas: BW 127, ᴰ1989 → 5,5098; 6,5370: ᴿBZ 35 (1991) 133-5 (B. *Heininger*); JBL 110 (1991) 534-6 (D. P. *Moessner*); TLZ 116 (1991) 115-7 (J. *Ernst*); TPQ 139 (1991) 322s (B. *Pittner*).

4475 ᴱ**Neirynck** Frans, L'évangile de Luc²: BtETL 32, 1989 → 5,5099; 6,5371: ᴿNT 33 (1991) 283-5 (J. K. *Elliott*); RTLv 22 (1991) 533s (C. *Focant*).

4476 **Petzke** Gerd, Das Sondergut des Evangeliums nach Lukas: ZWerk-komm, 1990 → 6,5373: ᴿTLZ 116 (1991) 669-671 (M. *Rese*).

4477 **Pherigo** L.P., The great physician, Luke; the healing stories[2rev] [¹1983]: Lay Bible Studies. Nv 1991, Abingdon. viii-136 p. $6. 0-687-15788-9 [NTAbs 36,114].

4478 **Pittner** B., Studien zum lukanischen Sondergut; sprachliche, theologische und formkritische Untersuchungen zu Sonderguttexten in Lk 5-19 [< Diss. Erfurt 1988. ᴰ*Schürmann* H.]: ErfurtTSt 18. Lp 1991, St. Benno. xxviii-159 p. DM 49 pa. 3-7462-0538-7 [NTAbs 3,267].

4479 **Powell** M.A., What are they saying about Luke? 1989 → 5,5072; 0-8091-3111-0 [NTAbs 34,387]: ᴿInterpretation 45 (1991) 312 (W.E. *Pilgrim*).

4480 **Rius-Camps** J., El éxodo del hombre libre; catequesis sobre el Evangelio de Lucas [L'Éxode 1989]: En torno al NT 11. Córdoba 1991, Almendro. 364 p. 84-86077-87-9 [NTAbs 36,114].

4481 **Salo** Kalervo, Luke's treatment of the Law; a redaction-critical investigation [diss. Helsinki, ᴰ*Aejmelaeus* L.]: AnnAcad DissHum 57. Helsinki 1991, Acad. Fennica. 337 p. 951-41-0634-2.

4481* *a*) *Scheffler* E.H., Reading Luke from the perspective of liberation theology; – *b*) *Nortjé* S., On the road to Emmaus — a woman's experience: → 307, Text 1991, 281-298 / 271-280.

4482 **Segbroeck** Frans van, The Gospel of Luke, a cumulative bibliography 1973-1988: BtETL 88, 1989 → 5,5102; 6,5378: ᴿCBQ 53 (1991) 349s (Barbara E. *Reid*); LavalTP 47 (1991) 435s (P.-É. *Langevin*).

4483 **Somerville** James G., The reader's role in the realization of Luke's [Gospel] purpose: diss. Southern Baptist Theol. Sem. ᴰ*Culpepper* R.A. 1991. 308 p. 91-31514. – DissA 52 (1991s) 1776-A.

4484 **Stock** Klemens, Gesù la bontà di Dio; il messaggio di Luca [1984],ᵀ: Bibbia e Preghiera 10. R 1991, Apost. Preghiera. 184 p. Lit. 15.000. 88-7357-099-2.

4485 **Zedda** Silverio, Teologia della salvezza nel vangelo di Luca: StBDeh 18. Bo 1990, Dehoniane. 188 p. Lit. 18.000 [TR 87,525].

F7.5 *Infantia, cantica* – **Magnificat, Benedictus: Luc. 1-3.**

4486 **Ó Fearghail** Fearghus, The introduction to Luke-Acts; a study of the role of Lk 1,1 – 4,44 in the composition of Luke's two-volume work [diss. Pont. Biblical Inst. ᴰ*Lentzen-Deis* F. 1987 → 3,4976]: AnBib 126. R 1991, Pont. Ist. Biblico. xii-256 p. Lit. 38.500. [TDig 39,261]. 88-7653-126-2.

4487 **Gerber** Daniel, La préparation du salut d'après Luc 1-2; la signification sotériologique de la naissance de Jésus; diss. prot. ᴰ*Trocmé* É. Strasbourg 1991. 248 p. – RTLv 23, p. 544.

4488 *Kolden* M., The birth of Jesus never saved anyone; the Lucan Advent texts: Word + World 11 (1991) 415-421 [< NTAbs 36,184].

4489 **Panier** Louis, La naissance du Fils de Dieu; sémiotique et théologie discursive, lecture de Luc 1-2: CogF 164. P 1991, Cerf. 385 p. F 196. 2-204-04217-X [NTAbs 36,286].

4490 **Berlingieri** Giovanni, Il lieto annuncio della nascita e del concepimento del precursore di Gesù [Lc 1,5-23.24-25] nel quadro dell'opera lucana; uno studio tradizionale e redazionale [diss. Pont. Univ. Gregoriana, ᴰ*Rasco* E.]: AnGreg 258. R 1991, Pont. Univ. Gregoriana. xvii-185 p. Lit. 28.000 [TR 88,163]. 88-7652-636-6.

4491 **Chappuis-Juillard** I., Le temps des rencontres; quand Marie visite Élisabeth (Luc 1). Aubonne 1991, Moulin. 83 p. [NTAbs 36,262].

4492 *Pérès* Jacques-Noël, [Lc 1,19] Gabriel, qui se tient devant Dieu (note exégétique): PosLuth 39 (1991) 247–... [< ZIT 92,17].

4493 *Della Corte* Ernesto, *Kecharitōménē* (Lc 1,28); crux interpretum: Marianum 52 (1990) 101-148.

4494 *Cortés-Quirant* Juan B., [Lc 1,28] 'Bendita tu sobre todas las mujeres' ¿[dijo] Gabriel o Isabel?: EstB 49 (1991) 271-276 [Gabriel, repetido por Isabel].

4495 *Zedda* Silverio, L'Hóti di Lc 1,45; 'che' o 'perché'?; RivB 39 (1991) 193-9.

4496 **Bemile** Paul, The Magnificat... Lk 1:46-55: RgStT 34, 1986 ⇨ 2,3945; 4,5153: RMarianum 52 (1990) 399-404 (A. *Valentini*).

4496* *Carmignac* Jean †, Théologie du Magnificat: FolOr 27 (1990) 13-24.

4497 *Coste* René, 'El Magníficat' o la revolución de Dios [1987 ⇨ 3,4984],T. 1989. RTeresianum 42 (1991) 352s (V. *Pasquetto*: 'in chiave esclusivamente socio-politica').

4498 *Irigoin* Jean, La composition rythmique des cantiques de Luc: RB 98 (1991) 5-50; Eng. 5.

4498* **Muñoz Iglesias** Salvador, Los Evangelios de la Infancia I-IV, 1986-90 ⇨ 4,5151... 6,4714: RSalmanticensis 38 (1991) 374-6 (G. *Pérez*, 4); StPatav 38 (1991) 179-186 (G. *Segalla*).

4499 *Ghiberti* Giuseppe, Lc 1,48b: anche genere agiografico?: RivB 39 (1991) 133-143; Eng. 143.

4500 *a) Govaert* L., 'From henceforth all nations shall call Me blessed' (Lk 1,48); J. H. NEWMAN on our Lady; – *b) Stern* J., La Vierge Marie dans le chemin de foi parcouru par J. H. Newman: Marianum 53 (1991) 17-41 / 42-68.

4501 *a) Kerr* A. J., 'No room in the *katáluma*' ['guest-room' in *any* home, as Lk 22,11 last supper; no 'paid lodging' implications]: ExpTim 103 (1991s) 15s. – *b) Olley* John W., God on the move — a further look at *katáluma* in Luke [2,6]: ExpTim 103 (1922s) [15s, *Kerr* A.] 300s.

4502 *Stichel* Rainer, [Lc 2,8] Die musizierenden Hirten von Bethlehem [so p. 249; but at top of pages 'Die Bedeutung der slavischen Übersetzungsliteratur']: ⇨ 594, Lexicographica Byzantina 1989/91, 249-282.

4503 *[de Sousa] Schulz* Eduardo, O coração no A. T. como realidad parcial e total do homem; uma aplicação de Lc 2,19-51: RCuBíb 14,55s (1990) 74-80.

4504 *Marconi* Gilberto, [Lc 2,23] Il Bambino da vedere; l'estetica lucana nel cantico di Simeone e dintorni: Gregorianum 72 (1991) 629-653; Eng. 654.

4505 *Bruners* Wilhelm, Das lebenslange Lernen Jesu: KatBlätt 116 (Mü 1991) 270-2 [< ZIT 91,317].

4506 *Bauckham* Richard, [Lk 3,36] More on Kainam the son of Arpachshad in Luke's genealogy: ÉTL [65 (1989) 409-411, STEYN G.] 67 (1991) 95-103; rejoinder 103s.

F7.6 **Evangelium Lucae 4,1...**

4507 *a) Bovon* François, La funzione delle Scritture nella formazione dei racconti evangelici; le tentazioni di Gesù (Lc 4,1-13 e par) e la moltiplicazione dei pani (Lc 9,10-17 e par), TCorsani Mirella C.; – *b) Caba* José, Dalla parenesi lucana alla cristologia giovannea; studio comparato di Lc 9,23-24 e Gv 12,25-26, TCorsani: ⇨ 124, FRASCO E., Luca-Atti 1991, 38-45 / 72-104.

4508 **Kimball** Charles A. [III] [Lk 4,1-13 + 7 other passages] Jesus' exposition of the Old Testament in Luke's Gospel: diss SWBaptist Theol. Sem., [D]*Ellis* E. 1991. 300 p. 91-35751. – DissA 52 (1991s) 2589-A.

4509 *Giallanza* Joel, The ministry of Jesus: RRel 49 (1990) 499-508.

4510 **Schreck** Christopher J., Luke 4,16-50; the Nazareth pericope in modern exegesis: diss. Leuven 1990, [D]*Neirynck* F. xi-490 p. – LvSt 16 (1991) 347s.

4511 *Monshouwer* D., [Lk 4,16-30] The reading of the prophet in the synagogue at Nazareth: Biblica 72 (1991) 90-99.

4512 **Noorda** S., Historia vitae magistra; een beoordeling van de geschiedenis van de uitleg van Lucas 4,16-30 als bijdrage aan de hermeneutische discussie [diss. Utrecht 1989, [D]*Baarda* T.]. Amst 1989, Vrije Univ. 343 p. ƒ 69,50. 90-6256-790-8. – [R]NedTTs 45 (1991) 249s (H. W. *Hollander*).

4513 *a) Ghiberti* Giuseppe, La buona novella della liberazione, Lc 4,16-30; – *b) Valentini* Alberto, Libertà nel Nuovo Testamento; – *c) La Potterie* I. de, Libertà gnostica e libertà cristiana: → 292*a*, ParSpV 23 (1991) 105-124 / 91-103 / 239-251.

4514 *Gootjes* N. H., Luke 4:16 — redemptive-historical or exemplary?: Kerux 3,2 (1988) 20-26.

4515 *Vattioni* Francesco, Sangue in Edom; Lc 4,29 e la morte di Aronne e Mosè: → 565, Sangue 1989/91, 179-217.

4516 **Polich** James C., The call of the first disciples; a literary and redactional study of Luke 5:1-11: diss. Fordham, [D]*Dillon* R. NY 1991. – RelStR 18,173.

4517 *Bock* Darrell L., The Son of Man in Luke 5:24: BBRes 1 (1991) 109-121.

4518 *Tolsma* Cornelius, The raising of Levi, Luke 5:27,28: Kerux 2,2 (1987) 14-20.

4519 *Lee* J.A.L., A non-Aramaism in Luke 6:7: NT 33 (1991) 28-34.

4520 *Beutler* Johannes, Lk 6,16 [Judas, qui factus est traditor 17: et descendens cum illis stetit in loco plano ...; post v. 16]: Punkt [wie Nestle-Aland[26]] oder Komma? [besser, wie bis[25]]: BZ 35 (1991) 231-3.

4520* **Hahn** Paul D., Structure in rhetorical criticism and the structure of the Sermon on the Plain (Luke 6:20-49): diss. Marquette. Milwaukee 1990. 483 p. 91-17346. – DissA 52 (1991s) 569-A.

4521 *Beck* Edmund †, Der syrische Diatessaronkommentar zu der Perikope von der Sünderin, Luc. 7,36-50: OrChr 75 (1991) 1-15.

4522 *Kilgallen* John J., A proposal for interpreting Luke 7,36-50: Biblica 72 (1991) 305-330; franç. 330.

4523 *Resseguie* James L., Automatization and defamiliarization in Luke 7:36-50: LitTOx 5 (1991) 137-150 [< NTAbs 36,37].

4524 *Schaberg* J., [Lk 8,2 ...] Thinking back through the Madgalene: Continuum 1,2 (NY 1991) 71-90 [< NTAbs 36,18: Luke's misogynous artistry distorts].

4525 *Horton* W. D., [Lk 8,4-15] The prodigal sower [modern methods avoid such waste, but God's prodigality is not concerned with cost-effectiveness]: ExpTim 103 (1991s) 115s.

4526 *Westendorf* Craig, The parable of the sower (Luke 8:4-15) in the seventeenth century: Lutheran Quarterly NS 3 (Milwaukee 1989) 49-64 [< LuJb 58, p. 187].

4527 *Karris* Robert J., Luke 8:26-39; Jesus, the pigs, and human transformation: NewTR 4,3 (1991) 39-51.

4528 *Clark* David K., [Lk 9,23] Interpreting the biblical words for the self: JPsy&T 18 (1990) 309-317 [< BS 148 (1991) 358 (S. D. *Shores*)].

F7.7 *Iter hierosolymitanum – Lc 9,51 ... –* **Jerusalem journey.**

4529 **Moessner** David P., Lord of the... Lukan travel narrative 1989 ➤ 5,5153; 6,5421: ᴿEvQ 63 (1991) 270-3 (J. *Weatherly*); Interpretation 45 (1991) 196 (Marilyn *Salmon*); JBL 110 (1991) 165-7 (J. T. *Carroll*); ScotJT 44 (1991) 406s (I. H. *Marshall*: literary criticism rightly used as a bridge to history); TZBas 47 (1991) 366-8 (R. B. *Sloan*, Eng.).

4530 *O'Leary* Anthony, The role of possessions in the journey narrative of Luke 9:15–19:27: MilltSt 28 (1991) 41-60.

4530* **Schnackenburg** Rudolf, [Lc 9,51 ...] El camino de Jesús; meditaciones de un viaje escritas por san Lucas. Estella 1991, VDivino. 123 p. 84-7151-765-5 [RET 52,367, J. L. *Larrabe*].

4531 *Jarvis* Peter G., [Lk 9,58] 'Nowhere to lay his head' [a metaphorical way of saying 'my kind of life is hard'? or a dangerous political comment (Herod the fox and the Roman birds have dispossessed our nest), rather far-fetched in 'splendid' MANSON? or likelier a general comment on the human condition]: ExpTim 102 (1990s) 369s.

4532 *O'Toole* Robert F., The literary form of Luke 10:1-10 [favors TAN-NEHILL's furthering of BULTMANN on Zacchaeus]: JBL 110 (1991) 107-118.

4533 *Hale* David G., [Lk 10,30-37] 'The glose was gloriously writen'; the textuality of LANGLAND's Good Samaritan: PatrMedRen 14 (1989) 127-134 [< ZIT 91,368].

4534 *Burgos Nuñez* Miguel de, Una religión de muerte y una religión de vida; la parábola del Samaritano (Lc 10,25-37): ComSev 24 (1991) 333-354.

4534* *Gombrich* E. H., Archaeologists or Pharisees [Pope's rescue of Jove statue painted into Good Samaritan scene]: reflections on a painting by Maarten van Heemskerck: JWarb 54 (1991) 253-6.

4535 *Hoyer* Stepen, *McDaniel* Patrice, From Jericho to Jerusalem; the Good Samaritan from a different direction: JPsy&T 18 (1990) 326-333 [< ZIT 91,316].

4536 **Légasse** S. [Lc 10,25] Et qui ...? *agape* 1989 ➤ 5,5160; 6,5425: ᴿBLitEc 92 (1991) 145s (A. *Marchadour*); Carthaginensia 7 (1991) 517 (R. *Sanz Valdivieso*); RThom 91 (1991) 511s (L. *Devillers*).

4537 *Tumbarello* Giacomo, La parabola del buon Samaritano, lettura eti-co-morale: BbbOr 33 (1991) 223-231.

4538 *Thimmes* Pamela L., The language of community; metaphors, systems of convictions, ethnic and gender issues in Luke 10:25-37 and 10:38-42; ➤ 446, SBL Sem 30 (1991) 698-713.

4539 *Brutscheck* Jutta, La intención de Lucas en el relato de María y Marta (Lc 10,38-42) [< GeistL 62 (1989) 84-96], ᵀᴱ*Escrivá* M.-Dolores: SelT 30 (1991) 215-221.

4540 **Fornari Carbonell** Isabel M., La escucha del huesped; sentido de Lc 10,38-42; la hospitalidad en horizonte de la comunicación: diss. Pont. Ist. Biblico, ᴰ*Lentzen-Deis* F. Roma 1991. – AcPIB 9,621s; RTLv 23, p. 543.

4541 *Leipold* Heinrich, Bleiben unter dem Wort; Bibelarbeit zu Lukas 10,38-42: Im Lichte der Reformation 34 (Gö 1991) 34-41 [< ZIT 91,254].

4542 *Garrett* Susan R., 'Lest the light in you be darkness'; Luke 11:33-36 and the question of commitment: JBL 110 (1991) 93-105.

Stegemann W., [Lk 11,53-12,1...] Zwischen Synagoge und Obrigkeit; zur historischen Situation der lukanischen Christen [Hab.-Diss. Heidelberg 1983]: 1991 ⇒ 4427.

4544 *Wuellner* Wilhelm, The rhetorical genre of Jesus' sermon in Luke 12.1-13.9: ⇒ 86, ^FKENNEDY G., Persuasive 1991, 93-118.

4545 *Mora Paz* César, Necedad y cordura en la vida cristiana; una reflexión sobre Lc 12,13-34: ⇒ 316, Reflexión 1990, 93-139.

4546 **Spegne** Luca, 'Cercate piuttosto il Suo Regno e queste cose vi saranno date in aggiunta'; esegesi e teologia di Lc 12,22-34: diss. Pont. Univ. Gregoriana, ^D*Rasco* E. Roma 1991. 344 p. – RTLv 23, p. 547 [< DissA-C].

4547 **März** Claus-Peter, '...lasst eure Lampen brennen!' Studien zur Q-Vorlage von Lk 12,35-14,24: ErfurtTSt 20. Lp 1991, St. Benno. 134 p. DM 49. 3-7462-0544-1 [NTAbs 36,265].

4548 **Visonà** Giuseppe, Citazioni patristiche e critica testuale; il caso di Lc 12,49: AnBib 125, 1990 ⇒ 6,5435: ^RBLitEc 92 (1991) 293s (S. *Légasse*); Gregorianum 72 (1991) 769s (J. *Galot*).

4549 *Theissen* Gerd, The open door to life, a penitential sermon (Luke 13,23-30): ⇒ 269, The open door 1991, 79-86 + 24 other sermons.

4550 **York** John O., [Lk 13,30] The last shall be first; the rhetoric of reversal in Luke [diss. Emory, ^D*Robbins* V.]: JStNT supp 46. Sheffield 1991, JStOT. 209 p. £25. 1-85075-278-8 [TDig 39,91]. – ^RExpTim 103 (1991s) 52s (R. *Morgan*).

4551 **Staden** Piet van, Compassion — the essence of life; a social-scientific study of the religious symbolic universe reflected in the ideology/theology of Luke [ch. 14: diss. Pretoria, ^D*Aarde* A. van; HervTSt supp 4. – DissA 53 (1991s) 1398s-A]: Pretoria 1991, NDR Kerk. xi-274 p. 0-9583-2082-9.

4552 *Bregman* Marc, [Lk 14,13s] The parable of the lame and the blind; [Panarion 64,70.5-17] EPIPHANIUS' quotation from an apocryphon of Ezekiel: JTS 42 (1991) 125-138.

4553 *Vine* Victor E., Luke 14:15-24 and anti-Semitism: ExpTim 102 (1990s) 262s.

4554 *Trau* Jane M., [Lk 15,4-7] The lost sheep: BToday 28 (1990) 277-283.

4555 ^E**Galli** Giuseppe, Interpretazione e invenzione... Lc 15, 1986/7 ⇒ 3,543 ... 5,5182: ^RSalesianum 53 (1991) 584s (C. *Bissoli*); TR 87 (1991) 110s (J. *Kremer*).

4556 *Couffignal* Robert, Un père au coeur d'or; approches nouvelles de Luc 15,11-32: RThom 91 (1991) 95-111.

4557 *Ereiser* Christine, [Lk 15] Will the real Prodigal Son please stand up?: RRel 49 (1990) 289-295.

4558 *Niebuhr* Karl-Wilhelm, Kommunikationsebenen im Gleichnis vom verlorenen Sohn [< Hab. Vorlesung Halle]: TLZ 116 (1991) 481-494.

4559 *Landau* Rudolf, Vom gewinnenden Vater (Lk 15,11-32): TBei 22,1 (1991) 1-6 [< ZIT 91,156].

4560 **Ostaszewski** Andrzej, L'immagine di Dio presentata nelle tre parabole del cap. 15 del vangelo di Luca: diss. Pont. Univ. Gregoriana, ^D*Lentzen-Deis* Fritzleo. – InfPUG 24/123 (1991s) 11.

4561 **Du Plessis** I.J., 'n Kykie in die hart van God [...historical questions connected with the parable of the prodigal son]. Pretoria 1990 Kerk-B. 156 p. – ^RNedTTs 45 (1991) 340s (J. *Smit Sibinga*: gelijkenissen van Jezus); Neotestamentica 25 (1991) 188s (J.J. *Engelbrecht*).

4562 *Scobel* Gert, La parábola del hijo pródigo como texto metalingüístico; planteamientos en torno a la problemática de la comprehensión en Lucas 15: ➤ 316, Reflexión 1990, 47-92.

4563 **Robbins** Jill, Prodigal son / elder brother; interpretation and alterity in AUGUSTINE, PETRARCH, KAFKA, LEVINAS: Religion and Postmodernism. Ch 1991, Univ. viii-182 p. $25. 0-226-72110-8 [NTAbs 36,268].

4564 *Parrott* Douglas M., The dishonest steward (Luke 16.1-8s) and Luke's special parable collection [J. JEREMIAS after verse 8 in 3d person allots the praise to Jesus in 1st; 'there is no hint of the issues raised by DERRETT and FITZMYER in the parable itself']: NTS 37 (1991) 499-515.

4565 *Bauckham* Richard, [Lk 16,19-31] The rich man and Lazarus; the parable and the parallels [Setme and his son Si-Osiris overstressed since GRESSMANN H. 1918]: NTS 37 (1991) 235-246.

4566 **Hintzen** Johannes, Lukas und seine Leser; rezeptionsästhetische Analyse von Lk 16,19-31 im Rahmen des lukanischen Doppelwerkes: kath. Diss. Bonn, ᴰRitt 1991. – TR 87 (1991) 516.

4567 **Hintzen** J., Verkündigung und Wahrnehmung; über das Verhältnis von Evangelium und Leser am Beispiel Lk 16,19-31 im Rahmen des lukanischen Doppelwerkes [< kath. Diss. Bonn 1989, ᴰMerklein H.]: BoBB 81. Fra 1991, Hain. xiii-404 p. DM 98. 3-445-09144-7 [NTAbs 36,264].

4568 *Kreitzer* Larry, Luke 16:19-31 and 1 Enoch 22: ExpTim 103 (1991s) 139-142.

4569 **Dagron** Alain, Aux jours du Fils de l'homme; essai sur le service de la parole Luc XVII,1 à XVIII,8; lecture sémiotique et propositions théologiques. Profac Biblique 3. Lyon 1990, Fac. Théol. 124 p. – ᴿEsprVie 101 (1991) 563s (É. *Cothenet*: très hétérogène; intéressera ceux qui pratiquent l'analyse sémiotique).

4570 *Hicks* J.M., The parable of the persistent widow (Luke 18:1-8): RestQ 33 (1991) 209-223 [< NTAbs 36,187].

4571 *Ravens* D.A.S., [Lk 19,1-10] Zacchaeus; the final part of a Lucan triptych?: JStNT 41 (1991) 19-32.

4572 *Hamm* Dennis, [Lk 19,8] Zacchaeus revisited once more; a story of vindication or conversion?: Biblica 72 (1991) 249-252.

4573 *Mitchell* Alan C., The use of *sykophanteîn* in Luke 19,8: further evidence for Zacchaeus's defense: Biblica 72 (1991) 546s.

4574 *Codina* Víctor, [Lc 19,16] Parábolas de la mina y del lago; teologia desde la noche oscura: Pedal 202. S 1990, Sígueme. 270 p. – ᴿRLatAmT 23 (1991) 212s (R. *Sivatte*).

4575 *Puig i Tàrrech* Armand, La paràbola dels vinyaters homicides (Lc 20,9-19) en el context de Lc-Ac: RCatalT 16 (1991) 39-65; Eng. 65.

4576 *Radici Colace* Paola, [Lc 20,20-26] L'uomo = Nummus nella teologia AGOSTINIANA dell'imago Dei: StTardAnt 8 (1989) 401-417.

4577 *Fusco* Vittorio, Problemi di struttura nel discorso escatologico lucano (Lc 21,7-36): ➤ 124, ᶠRASCO E., Luca-Atti 1991, 105-134.

F7.8 **Passio** – *Lc 22*...

4578 *Petzer* [Ja-]Kobus, Style and text in the Lucan narrative of the institution of the Lord's Supper (Luke 22.19b-20): NTS 37 (1991) 113-129.

4579 **Neyrey** Jerome, The Passion according to Luke; a redaction study of Luke's soteriology 1985 ➤ 1,5054... 3,5067: ᴿGregorianum 72 (1991) 768s (E. *Farahian*: un certain flou de langage, 'juge jugé', 'sauveur sauvé').

4580 **Senior** Donald, The Passion... Luke 1989 → 5,5202; 6,5452: RCBQ 53 (1991) 149s (J. E. *Bruns*: too many compounds like 'faith-filled'; queries FITZMYER interpretation of Lk 22,36); CritRR 4 (1991) 229s (J. B. *Green*).

4581 **Soards** Marion L., The Passion... Luke 22: JStNT supp 14, 1987 → 3,5063... 6,5453: RCBQ 53 (1991) 150s (F. W. *Danker*: good).

4582 *Nelson* Peter K., The flow of thought in [apostles' quarrel related only in] Luke 22.24-27: JStNT 43 (1991) 113-123.

4583 *Plevnik* Joseph, Son of Man seated at the right hand of God; Luke 22,69 in Lucan Christology: Biblica 72 (1991) 331-347; franç. 347.

4584 *Heil* John P., Reader-response and the irony of the trial of Jesus in Luke 23:1-25: ScEsp 43 (1991) 175-186.

4585 *a) Evans* C. A., Is Luke's view of the Jewish rejection of Jesus anti-Semitic?; – *b) Moessner* D. P., The 'leaven of the Pharisees' and 'this generation'; Israel's rejection of Jesus according to Luke [more negative view than usually assumed]: → 4588 infra, Reimaging 1990, 29-56 / 79-107.

4586 *Untergassmair* Franz G., Der Spruch vom 'grünen und dürren Holz' (Lk 23,31): SNTU A-16 (1991) 55-88 [< ZIT 92,309].

4587 *a) Carroll* J. T., [Lk 23,33s] Luke's crucifixion scene; – *b) Danker* F. W., Imaged through beneficence: → 4588 infra, Reimaging 1990, 108-124 / 57-67.

4588 ESylva Dennis D., (p. 153-169, Death and life at the center of the world), Reimaging the death of the Lukan Jesus: BoBB 73, 1990 → 6,378: RCarthaginensia 7 (1991) 511s (R. *Sanz Valdivieso*); CBQ 53 (1991) 731s (J. A. *Darr*: tit. pp. comments).

4589 *a) Karris* R. J., Luke 23:47 and the Lucan view of Jesus' death [the centurion proclaimed him 'righteous', not 'innocent']; – *b) Green* J. B., The death of Jesus, God's Servant: → 4588 supra, Reimaging 1990, 68-78 / 1-28.

4590 *a) Green* Joel B., The death of Jesus and the rending of the Temple veil (Luke 23:44-49); a window into Luke's understanding of Jesus and the Temple; – *b) Mowery* Robert L., The divine hand and the divine plan in the Lukan Passion; – *c) Ehrman* Bart D., The cup, the bread, and the salvific effect of Jesus' death in Luke-Acts: → 446, SBL Sem 30 (1991) 543-557 / 558-575 / 576-591.

4591 *Amphoux* Christian B., Le chapitre 24 de Luc et l'origine de la tradition textuelle du codex de Bèze (D.05 du NT): FgNt 4,7 (1991) 21-48; Eng. 48s.

4591* **McBride** D., [Lk 24,13-35] Emmaus; the gracious visit of God according to Luke. Dublin 1991, Dominican. x-214 p. £10. 1-871552-18-4 [NTAbs 36,426].

4592 *Ordon* Hubert, Ⓟ Die letzte Rede des auferstandenen Christus (Lk 24,44-49): RoczTK 34,1 (1991 für 1987) 87-99; deutsch 100.

4593 *a) Rigato* Maria Luisa, Riflessioni su Lc 24,6c-8, 'Ricordatevi... e si ricordarono'; – *b) Betori* Giuseppe, Lc 24,47, Gerusalemme e gli inizi della predicazione ai pagani negli Atti degli Apostoli: → 124, FRASCO E., Luca-Atti 1991, 135-148 / 149-176.

XII. Actus Apostolorum

F8.1 **Acts** – *Text, commentary, topics.*

4594 *Balderas* G., La inculturación de la fe como apertura a los otros según los Hechos de los Apóstoles: Anámnesis 1,1 (México 1991) 79-90 [< NTAbs 36,43].

4595 *a) Barbi* Augusto, L'uso e il significato di '(hoi) Ioudaioi' negli Atti; – *b) Kilgallen* J. J., La persecuzione negli Atti degli Apostoli, ^T*Corsani Mirella* C.: ➤ 124, ^FRASCO E., Luca-Atti 1991, 178-203 / 204-233.

4596 *Barrett* C. K., *a)* Attitudes to the Temple in the Acts of the Apostles: ➤ 15, ^FBAMMEL E., Templum 1991, 345-367; – *b)* Submerged Christology in Acts: ➤ 72, ^FHAHN F., Anfänge 1991, 237-244.

4597 *Betori* Giuseppe, Strutturazione degli Atti e storiografia antica: CrNSt 12 (1991) 251-263; Eng. 263.

4598 **Boismard** M.-É., *Lamouille* A., Les Actes des deux Apôtres I-III, 1990 ➤ 6,5466: ^RÉTRel 66 (1991) 292s (Danielle *Ellul*); NRT 113 (1991) 431-3 (X. *Jacques*); RechSR 79 (1991) 430-2 (J. *Guillet*: conception artificielle du récit).

4599 *Boismard* M.-E., Atti degli Apostoli; aspetti letterario-teologici, ^T*Manfredi* Silvana: Ho Theológos 9 (1991) 7-17.

4600 **Brawley** Robert L., Luke-Acts and the Jews...: SBL Mg 33, 1987 ➤ 3,4902...5,5027: ^RBijdragen 52 (1991) 441s (B. J. *Koet*).

4601 **Brown** Margie, The art of dramatic monologue and its homiletical application illustrated in an original script based on the Acts of the Apostles: diss. Graduate Theological Union, ^D*Adams* D. Berkeley 1991. 101 p. 92-06901. – DissA 52 (1991s) 3320-A; RelStR 18,172.

4602 **Bruce** F. F., Acts^{3rev} [¹1951] 1990 ➤ 6,5469: ^RGraceTJ 12,1 (1991) 136s (H. A. *Kent*).

4603 **Campos Cabañas** Ángel, El modo narrativo en Hechos de los Apóstoles: diss. ^D*Balaguer* Bertrán V. Pamplona 1991. 413 p. – RTLv 23, p. 542.

4604 **Cassidy** R. J., Society and politics in Acts 1987 ➤ 3,5088...6,5471: ^RCiuD 203 (1990) 228s (J. *Gutiérrez*); IrTQ 57 (1991) 323 (M. *Hogan*); RelStT 9,2s (1989) 77-79 (B. *Przybylski*); TLZ 116 (1991) 186s (G. *Schille*).

4605 **Chance** J. Bradley, Jerusalem, the Temple, and the New Age in Luke-Acts 1988 ➤ 4,5087; 5,5029: ^RBijdragen 52 (1991) 442s (B. J. *Koet*, under Bradley, also ind.).

4606 **Coleman** R. E., The master plan of discipleship. Old Tappen NJ 1987, Revell. 156 p. $10. – ^RIndTSt 27 (1990) 196s (L. *Legrand*: a surface reading of Acts from the viewpoint of 'evangelical' voluntarism).

4607 **Colin Cruz F.** Armando, Los discursos kerigmáticos en Hechos de los Apóstoles y los diferentes auditorios a quienes van dirigidos (estudio retórico-teológico): dis. Pont. Univ. Gregoriana, ^D*Grech* P. 1991s. – InfPUG 24/123, 9.

4608 **Conzelmann** Hans, Acts of the Apostles [²1972], ^T*Limburg* James, *al.*, Hermeneia comm. 1987 ➤ 3,5089...5,5219: ^RHeythJ 32 (1991) 84s (Judith *Lieu*); Neotestamentica 25 (1991) 185s (J. L. de *Villiers*).

4609 *Dattler* Frederico, 'Lógos kyríou' nos Atos: RCuBíb 14,55s (1990) 61-67.

4610 **Delebecque** E., Les deux Actes 1986 ➤ 2,4028...5,5220: ^RRÉG 104 (1991) 659s (P. *Nautin*).

4611 **Dini** Averardo, I figli del vento [= gli Apostoli degli Atti]: Alle origini del nostro futuro. R 1990, Logos. 118 p. Lit. 14.000. – ^RBenedictina 38 (1991) 532-4 (Germana *Ganassini*).

4612 *Dukes* J. W., Introduction to Acts: TEdr 43 (New Orleans 1990) 49-61 [< NTAbs 36,195].

4613 **Estridge** Charles A., Suffering in contexts of the [26] speeches of Acts: diss. Baylor 1991. 308 p. 92-05389. – DissA 52 (1991s) 3319-A.

4614 *González Luis* José, Los discursos en los Hechos de los Apóstoles en la tradición historiográfica helenística-romana: ➤ 421, Luso 1989/91, 395-407.

4614* **Hargreaves** John, A guide to Acts: TEF Study Guide 1990 ➤ 6,5477: ᴿVidyajyoti 55 (1991) 364 (Lancy *D'Cauz*).

4615 **Hemer** Colin J. †, The book of Acts in the setting of Hellenistic history [republication of WUNT 49, 1989], ᴱ*Gempf* C. H. 1990 ➤ 5,5231; 6,5479: ᴿExpTim 102 (1990s) 379 (C. K. *Barrett*: useful but prompting severe questions); JTS 42 (1991) 227-230 (J. C. *Lentz*); SvTKv 66 (1990) 34-36 (E. *Lövestam*).

4616 **Kee** Howard C., Good news... theology of Acts 1990 ➤ 6,5480: ᴿExpTim 102 (1990s) 317 (M. *Goulder*: careful, but with some lapses, especially against BAUR cited only second hand); JTS 42 (1991) 670-2 (E. *Franklin*).

4617 **Kistemaker** Simon J., Exposition of the Acts of the Apostles: NT Comm. GR 1990, Baker. 1010 p. $30. – ᴿGraceTJ 12,1 (1991) 137s (H. A. *Kent*: excellent).

4618 **Kliesch** Klaus, Apostelgeschichte: StuKK 5, 1986 ➤ 2,4032*; 3,5099: ᴿTLZ 116 (1991) 34s (G. *Schille*).

4619 **Kliesch** Klaus, Gli Atti degli Apostoli [1986], ᵀ*Termini* Cristina, ᴱ*Del Bianco* Antonio: Bibbia per tutti. Assisi 1991, Cittadella. 285 p. 88-308-0482-7.

4620 **Lövestam** Evald, Apostlagärningarna. Falköping 1988, Verbum. 443 p. 91-526-1492-1. – ᴿSvEx 56 (1991) 141-3 (P. *Block*); SvTKv 66 (1990) 82-84 (T. *Fornberg*).

4621 *Lohse* Eduard, St. Peter's apostleship in the judgment of St. Paul, the Apostle to the Gentiles; an exegetical contribution to an ecumenical debate [Gregorian Univ. McCarthy lecture 1990]: Gregorianum 72 (1991) 419-433; franç. 433.

4622 **Lüdemann** Gerd, Das frühe Christentum nach... Apg, ein Kommentar 1987 ➤ 3,5102... 6,5483: ᴿBijdragen 52 (1991) 330s (M. *Parmentier*, Eng.); SvEx 56 (1991) 144 (E. *Larsson*).

4623 **Lüdemann** Gerd, Early Christianity according to the traditions in Acts, a commentary 1989 ➤ 5,5327; 6,5483*b*: ᴿAnglTR 73 (1991) 207-9 (F. W. *Hughes*).

4624 **Maloney** Linda M., 'All that God had done with them'; the narration of the works of God in the early Christian community as described in the Acts of the Apostles [diss. Tübingen 1988s, ᴰ*Lohfink* G. ➤ 4,5245]: AmerUnivSt 7/91. NY 1991, Lang. xiii-237 p. 0-8204-1410-7.

4625 **Marchesi** Giovanni, Il Vangelo da Gerusalemme a Roma; l'origine del cristianesimo negli Atti degli Apostoli. Mi 1991, Rizzoli. 293 p.; 2 pl. Lit. 12.000. 88-17-11543-6. – ᴿCC 142 (1991,3) 99s (F. *Quilici*).

4626 **Marshall** Michael, Great Expectations. ... 1991, Bible Reading Fellowship / Cowley. 143 p. £4. 0-900164-87-5 / 1-56101-033-2. – ᴿExpTim 103 (1991s) 60s (G. S. *Gibson*: six studies on Acts).

4627 *Mealand* David L., Hellenistic historians and the style of Acts: ZNW 82 (1991) 42-66.

4628 **Ocker** Christopher M., Interpretation, authority, and religious community in fourteenth-century Germany; the 'Postilla' of Johannes KLENKOK (c. 1310-1374) on the Acts of the Apostles in its cultural and intellectual contexts: diss. ᴰ*Froehlich* K. Princeton Theol. Sem. 1991. 644 p. 91-32189. – DissA 52 (1991s) 2174s-A; RelStR 18,173.

4629 *Osburn* Carroll D., The search for the original text of Acts; the international project on the text of Acts: JStNT 44 (1991) 39-55.

4630 **Pervo** Richard L., Luke's story of Paul [... whole of Acts]. Mp 1990, Fortress. 96 p. $7. – RNewTR 4,1 (1991) 11s (Barbara E. *Reid*).

4631 **Pesch** Rudolf, Die Apostelgeschichte 1:1-12:   EkK NT 5,1, 1986 ➤ 2,4037 ... 6,5491:   RZkT 113 (1991) 300s (R. *Oberforcher*).

4632 **Powell** Mark A., What are they saying about Acts? NY 1991, Paulist. ix-147 p. $7.

4633 *Powell* Mark A., *a*) Reading Acts as history: AsburyT 46,1 (1991) 39-62; – *b*) Luke's second volume; three basic issues in contemporary studies of Acts: TrinSemR 13,2 (Columbus 1991) 69-81 [< NTAbs 36,357].

4634 *Richard* E., Jesus' Passion and death in Acts: ➤ 4588 supra, Reimaging 1990, 125-152.

4635 **Richter-Reimer** Ivoni, Aufbruch und Erinnerung; eine sozialgeschichtliche Rekonstruktion der Lebenswirklichkeit von Frauen in der Apostelgeschichte des Lukas in feministisch-befreiungstheologischer Perspektive: Diss. Kassel, DSchottroff 1991. – TR 87 (1991) 519.

4636 **Rius Camps** J., De Jerusalén a Antioquía; génesis de la Iglesia cristiana... Hch 1-12 1989 ➤ 5,5246: RProyección 37 (1990) 235 (J. A. *Estrada*).

4637 *Sanders* Jack T., Who is a Jew and who is a Gentile in the Book of Acts?: NTS 37 (1991) 434-455.

4638 ESchenke Hans-Martin, Apg 1,1-15,3 im mittelägyptischen Dialekt des Koptischen (Codex Glazier): TU 137. B 1991, Akademie. xvi-251 p.; 18 pl. DM 128. 3-05-000563-7 [NTAbs 36,269].

4639 **Schneider** G., Atti 1986 ➤ 2,4040 ... 4,5251:   RAugM 35 (1990) 186s (J. A. *Galindo*).

4640 **Segalla** Giuseppe, Carisma e istituzione a servizio della carità negli Atti degli Apostoli: Communità degli uomini. Padova 1991, Gregoriana. 141 p. Lit. 15.000. 88-7706-097-2.

4641 **Tannehill** Robert C., The narrative unity of Luke-Acts... 2. Acts 1990 ➤ 6,5490: RBiblica 72 (1991) 589-591 (C. H. *Talbert*: 4 ways in which it is a commentary; 4 illustrations of method; 4 items outside the method); ComSev 24 (1991) 274s (M. de *Burgos*); ExpTim 102 (1990s) 316s (I. H. *Marshall*: stimulating but fails to draw the conclusions; JBL 110 (1991) 733-5 (Susan R. *Garrett*: almost a threat to the traditional commentary; not convincing on Stephen's speech); TLZ 116 (1991) 834-6 (J. *Roloff*); TS 52 (1991) 141-3 (D. *Juel*).

4642 *Vanhoye* Albert, Les Juifs selon les Actes des Apôtres et les Épîtres du Nouveau Testament: Biblica 72 (1991) 70-89: brotherhood, from initial good will to generalized opposition; but Paul from polemic to hope.

4643 *Williams* David J., Acts: New International Biblical Commentary 5. Peabody MA 1990, Hendrickson. xvi-493 p. 0-8146-5807-5.

4644 *Wills* Lawrence M., The depiction of the Jews in Acts: JBL 110 (1991) 631-654.

4645 *Wylie* Amanda B., The exegesis of history in John CHRYSOSTOM's Homilies on Acts: ➤ 58, FFROEHLICH K., Biblical hermeneutics 1991, 59-72.

F8.3 *Ecclesia primaeva Actuum:* **Die Urgemeinde.**

4647 **Brown** Raymond E., *Meier* John P., Antioche et Rome, berceaux du christianisme: LDiv 131, 1988 ➤ 4,5274; 6,5506: RRTLv 22 (1991) 244s (C. *Focant*).

4648 **Cwiekowski** Frederick J., The beginnings of the Church 1988 ➤ 4,5279 ... 6,5510: RScripTPamp 23 (1991) 1070s (G. *Aranda*).

4649 **Daniélou** Jean, La chiesa degli apostoli [1970], T*Lunghi* Pietro: Il cristianesimo delle origini. R 1991, Archeosofica. 127 p. Lit. 22.000.

4650 *Dumais* Marcel, La vie de la communauté chrétienne et sa portée missionnaire dans l'Église des temps apostoliques: NZMissW 46 (1990) 49-61.

4651 *Hartin* P. J., Jewish Christianity; focus on Antioch in the first century: Scriptura 36 (Stellenbosch 1991) 38-50 [< NTAbs 36,96].

4652 **Hoornaert** Eduardo, The memory of the Christian people 1988 ➤ 5, 5276: Ris^{REx}p 87 (1990) 350s (E. G. *Hinson*: informed objections).

4653 **Kirchschläger** Walter, Die Anfänge der Kirche; eine biblische Rückbesinnung 1990 ➤ 6,5221: RAtKap 117, 494 (1991) 148s (M. *Marczewski*); TGL 81 (1991) 391 (J. *Ernst*).

4653* *López Rivera* Francisco, La Iglesia de Lucas: Christus 57,9s (Méx 1991) 10-18.

4654 **MacDonald** Margaret Y., The Pauline churches D1988 ➤ 4,5296 ... 6,5524: RInterpretation 45 (1991) 90.92 (E. Elizabeth *Johnson*); NBlackf 71 (1990) 50s (J. *Ziesler*).

4656 *Meyer* B. F., The Church in earliest Christianity: Journal of Theology 2,2 (Hamilton ON 1991) 1-19 [< NTAbs 36,380].

4657 **Montserrat Torrents** J., La sinagoga cristiana; al gran conflicto religioso del Siglo I, 1989 ➤ 6,5526 ('Torrens'): REstFranc 92 (1991) 317-9 (E. *Cortès* en catalán).

Ralph Margaret N., Discovering the First Century Church 1991 ➤ 3549*.

4659 *a) Rook* J., Women in Acts; are they equal partners with men in the earliest Church?; – *b) Trites* A. A., Church growth: McMasterJT 2,2 (1991) 29-41 / 1,1 (1990) 1-18 [< NTAbs 36,357s].

4660 **Schenke** Ludger, Die Urgemeinde 1990 ➤ 6,5527: RExpTim 102 (1990s) 267 (E. *Best*); TLZ 116 (1991) 739-741 (E. *Lohse*); TsTNijm 31 (1991) 193s (W. H. *Berflo*).

4661 *Schoeps* Hans-Joachim, Was wurde aus den ersten Jüngern Jesu?: ➤ 13, FBAETKE W., 1966, 327-9.

4662 **Schwarz** Hans, Die Entstehung der Kirche [1]; 2. Die grossen Veränderungen; 3. Die Verheissung für die Zukunft: Die christliche Kirche. Gö 1986, Vandenhoeck & R. 135 p.; 140 p.; 131 p. ➤ 4,8988; pa. 3-525-61373-3; -3-1; -6-8. – RBijdragen 52 (1991) 212 (M. *Parmentier*).

4663 *Sesboüé* Bernard, Ecclesia ex circumcisione, Ecclesia ex gentibus: Istina 36 (1991) 182-201.

4664 *Strand* Kenneth A., Church organization in first-century Rome; a new look at the basic data ['dual leadership']: AndrUnS 29 (1991) 139-160.

4666 **Vögtle** Anton, Die Dynamik des Anfangs; Leben und Fragen der jungen Kirche 1988 ➤ 5,371: RColcT 61,2 (1991) 189s (R. *Bartnicki* ☻); Salesianum 53 (1991) 773s (J. J. *Bartolomé*).

4667 **Zettner** Christoph, Amt, Gemeinde und kirchliche Einheit in der Apostelgeschichte des Lukas [kath. Diss. Bochum 1991, D*Schneider* G. – TR 87 (1991) 516]: EurHS 23/423. Fra 1991, Lang. lviii-434 p. $65.80. 3-631-43818-4 [NTAbs 36,271].

F8.5   Ascensio, Pentecostes; ministerium Petri – *Act 1* ...

4668 **Pongutá Hurtado** Silvestre, Para que seáis mis testigos; una presentación de los Hechos de los Apóstoles; una lectura de Act 1-2: CuadBíb 2. Caracas 1991, Asn. Bíblica Salesiana. 150 p.

4669 *a) Horne* Brian, Beyond tragedy; – *b) Houlden* Leslie, Beyond belief: Preaching the Ascension I-II: TLond 94 (1991) 168-173-181.

4670 **Parsons** Mikeal C., [Lk 24,50-53; Acts 1,9-11] Departure of Jesus in Luke-Acts 1987 ⇒ 4,5321 ... 6,5540: ᴿRelStT 9,1 (1989) 54-56 (M. *Desjardins*).

4671 *Mussies* Gerard, [Acts 1,2-14; Lk 24,36-53] Variations in the Book of Acts: FgNt 4 (1991) 165-180 (cont.); español 180-2.

4672 *Mealand* David, 'After not many days' in Acts 1.5 and its Hellenistic context: JStNT 42 (1991) 67-77.

4673 *Ellis* E. Earle, 'The end of the earth' (Acts 1,18): BBRes 1 (1991) 123-132.

4673* **Wilcke** K., Christi Himmelfahrt; ihre Darstellung in der europäischen Literatur von der Spätantike bis zum ausgehenden Mittelalter: Beiträge zur älteren Literaturgeschichte. Heid 1991, Winter. 505 p. DM 125; pa 96. 5-333-04441-6; 0-8 [NTAbs 36,429].

4674 *Jáuregui* José A., [Hch 2,1-13] Pentecostes, fiesta de identidad cristiana: EstE 66 (1991) 369-396.

4675 *Schüngel-Straumann* Helen, Pfingstliche Geistkraft/Lebenskraft (*rûaḥ*); alttestamentliche Wurzeln einer bedrängten weiblichen Vorstellung: Diakonia 21 (Mainz 1990) 149-157 > TDig 38 (1991) 333-7, 'Ruach, pneuma and Pentecost', ᵀᴱ*Asen* B.A. [... ruach is maternal dispenser of life].

4676 *Tannehill* Robert C. [Acts 2 ...] The functions of Peter's mission speeches in the narrative of Acts: NTS 37 (1991) 400-414.

4677 *Schwartz* Daniel R., On some new and old wine in Peter's Pentecost speech (Acts 2): ⇒ 76, ᶠHILGERT E., StPhilonAn 3 (1991) 256-271.

4678 *Sloan* Robert, [Acts 2,14-40] 'Signs and wonders'; a rhetorical clue to the Pentecost discourse: EvQ 63 (1991) 225-240.

4679 **Phelps** Dennis L., [Act 2,17-36] Implications of Lucan-Peter's Pentecost homily for Christian preaching of the OT: diss. SW Baptist Theol. Sem. 1990. 251 p. 91-15310. – DissA 51 (1991s) 194-A.

4680 *a) Legrand* L., 'Celui qui invoquera le nom du Seigneur', Ac 2,17-21; – *b) Rafanambinana* J.R., 'Poieîn kaì didáskein'; activités de Jésus, activités des témoins dans les Actes des Apôtres: ⇒ 121, ᶠRAMAROSON L., Ta parole 1991, 61-72 / 50-60.

4681 *Koester* Helmut, [Acts 2,17-21; 1 Cor 12,7-10] Writings and the Spirit; authority and politics in ancient Christianity [... from the writings of Paul to the writings of bishops]: HarvTR 84 (1991) 353-372.

4682 *Panimolle* Salvatore A., La *koinōnía* della Chiesa alle sue origini (At 2,42): Sandalion 14 (1991) 103-146 [< RHE 87,192*].

4683 *a) O'Collins* Gerald, Luca sulla fine delle apparizioni pasquali, ᵀ*Corsani* Mirella C., – *b) Marconi* Gilberto, La storia come ermeneutica; interpretazione del confronto tra At 3,1-10 e 4,8-12; – *c) Prato* Gian Luigi, L'idolatria alla ricerca forzata dei suoi dèi; un singolare accordo tra la tradizione del testo e l'esegesi (Am 5,25-27 e At 7,42-43): ⇒ 124, ᶠRASCO E., Luca-Atti 1991, 234-242 / 243-263 / 264-292.

4684 **Prete** B., *Scaglioni* A., I miracoli degli apostoli nella Chiesa delle origini [Atti] 1989 ⇒ 4,5250 ... 6,5556: ᴿProtestantesimo 46 (1991) 215-7 (G. *Anziani*).

4685 *Messier* M., Restauration [*apokatástasis* Act 3,21]: ⇒ 664, Catholicisme 12,57 (1990) 971-8.

4686 *a) Le Roux* L.V., Style and the text of Acts 4:25(a); – *b) Petzer* J.H., St. AUGUSTINE and the Latin version of Acts: Neotestamentica 25,1 (1991) 29-32 / 33-50.

4687 **Tosco** Lorenzo, Pietro e Paolo ministri del giudizio di Dio ... At 5,1-11 e 13,4-12 [diss. PIB, Roma 1983]: RivB supp 19, 1989 → 5,5310: ᴿCBQ 53 (1991) 719-721 (C. *Bernas*: conclusions not really new but not superfluous); RivB 39 (1991) 64-68 (G. *Betori*).

4688 **Brakemeier** Gottfried, [Apg 5] Der 'Sozialismus' der Urchristenheit; Experiment und neue Herausforderung: KLReihe 1535, 1988 → 5,5302: ᴿTPQ 139 (1991) 327s (F. *Reisinger*: Scheitern des Projekts der Apg, p. 18).

4689 *a) Franco* Ettore, Povertà e solidarietà nella comunità primitiva; Atti degli Apostoli e giudaismo esseno-qumranico a confronto; – *b) Cipriani* Settimio, Povertà, annuncio, condivisione dei beni nelle lettere di S. Paolo: → 444*, Ricchezza 1989/91, 171-208 / 209-228.

4690 *Holtz* Traugott, Christus diakonos; zur christologischen Begründung der Diakonie in der nachösterlichen Gemeinde [< ᴱ*Schäfer* G. K., Diakonie, biblische Grundlagen und Orientierungen (Heid 1990, Univ.) 127-143]: → 211, Geschichte 1991, 399-416.

4691 *a) Donegani* Isabelle, Chronique d'un fanatisme dénoncé; Étienne relit l'histoire du salut, en Actes 6 à 7; – *b) Rouiller* Grégoire, Entre témoignage et fanatisme; l'exemple de Paul de Tarse; – *c) Badaud* George, L'inquisition; la violence au service de la foi?; – *d) Carron* Yves, De la tolérance à la liberté religieuse: Échos de Saint-Maurice 21,4 ('Fanatisme et intolérance' 1991) 271-284 / 285-298 / 253-263 / 264-269 [*al.*].

4692 **Seland** Torrey, [Acts 6,8ss; 21,15-36; 23,12-15] Jewish vigilantism [Rosenbaum H., Sederberg P. 1976] in the first century CE; a study of selected texts in Philo [spec 1,54-57.315-8; 2,252-4] and Luke on Jewish vigilante reactions against nonconformers to the Torah: diss. Trondheim 1991. 432 p. Nk 150. – ST 46,73.

4693 *Borchert* Gerald L., Acts 6:13, expository: RExp 88 (1991) 73-78.

4694 *Holtz* Traugott, Beobachtungen zur Stephanusrede Acta 7 [< ᶠ*Holtz* Gottfried 1965, 102-114]: → 211, Geschichte 1991, 106-120.

4695 *Sandt* Huub van de, Why is Amos 5,25-27 quoted in Acts 7,42f?: ZNW 82 (1991) 67-87. → 4683c.

4696 **Kelley** Shawn J., 'And your young will see visions'; a functionalist literary reading of the visions to Saul and Peter in Acts [9,1-22; 10,1-11,18]: diss. Vanderbilt, ᴰ*Tolbert* Mary Ann. Nv 1991. 324 p. 92-03336. – DissA 52 (1991s) 2956-A; RelStR 18,173 'Kelly'.

4697 *Scott* J. J. [Acts 10s] The Cornelius incident in the light of its Jewish setting: JEvTS 34 (1991) 475-484 [< NTAbs 36,359].

4698 *Schuppan* Christoph, Bewegung in Antiochia; eine narrative Exegese zu Apg 11,26: → 163, ᶠ*Wagner* S., Gottesvolk 1991, 125-135.

4699 **Rakocy** Waldemar, Trionfo del piano salvifico di Dio; uno studio letterario della narratività e della funzione di Atti 12,1-24: diss. Pont. Univ. Gregoriana, ᴰ*Lentzen-Deis* F. Roma 1991. 282 p. – InfPUG 121 (dic. 1991) 19; RTLv 23, p. 546.

4700 *Wall* Robert W., Successors to 'the Twelve' according to Acts 12:1-17: CBQ 53 (1991) 628-643.

F8.7   Act 13 ... *Itinera Pauli*, Paul's Journeys.

4701 *Molthagen* J., [Apg 13-28] Die ersten Konflikte der Christen in der griechisch-römischen Welt: Historia 40,1 (Stu 1991) 42-76 [< NTAbs 36,46: relativizes view of F. Vittinghoff that from the beginning Rome considered Christians criminals].

4702 **Pervo** R., Luke's story of Paul 1990 ➤ 6,5584: ᴿAnglTR 73 (1991) 77s (D. J. *Horton*).

4703 **Reck** Reinhold, Kommunikation und Gemeindeaufbau; eine Studie zu Entstehung, Leben und Wachstum paulinischer Gemeinden in den Kommunikationsstrukturen der Antike [Diss. Würzburg 1990, ᴰ*Klauck* H.]: SBB 22. Stu 1991, KBW. xii-354 p. DM 39 pa. 3-460-00221-2 [NTAbs 36,124]. – ᴿTR 87 (1991) 379s (E. *Arens*, with no indication of either Acts or Epistles focus).

4704 *Taylor* Justin, La estrategía de San Pablo en su primer viaje misionero (Actos 13-14), ᵀ*Maravi* Raúl: RTLim 25 (1991) 329-342.

4705 *Devreker* J., [Act 13,7] Les Sergii Paulli; problèmes généalogiques d'une famille supposée chrétienne: ➤ 130, ꟳSANDERS G., Aevum 1991, 109-119.
Trebilco Paul R., Jewish communities in Asia Minor 1991 ➤ e24.

4706 *a) Gratseas* G., ⊚ The Apostolic Council (Acts 15,1-15) and the councils of the Essenes; – *b) Adeyemi* M. E., A sociological approach to the background of Pauline Epistles; – *c) Karavidopoulos* J., The role of Peter and his importance for the Church in the NT: DeltioVM 20,10 (1991) 5-31; franc.31 / 32-46 / 47-66.

4707 **Taylor** Nicholas H., [Act 15...] Paul, Antioch and Jerusalem; a study in relationships and authority in earliest Christianity: diss. Durham 1991. – RTLv 23, p. 547.

4708 *Wilt* Timothy, on Acts 15,19-21: BTrans [41 (1990) 416-421, *Omanson* R.] 42 (1991) 234-6 (–240, reply).

4709 *Farahian* Edmond, La visione di Paolo a Troade (At 16,9-10): ➤ 124, ꟳRASCO E., Luca-Atti 1991, 293-308.

4710 **Wehnert** Jürgen, [Apg 16,10] Die Wir-Passagen...: GöTArb 40, ᴰ1989 ➤ 5,5333: 6,5595: ᴿJBL 110 (1991) 355-7 (C. R. *Matthews*); RivB 39 (1991) 231-9 (V. *Fusco*); TZBas 47 (1991) 93-95 (M. *Rese*).

4711 **Thornton** Claus-Jürgen, Der Zeuge des Zeugen; Lukas als Historiker der Paulusreisen [ᴰTü]: WUNT 56. Tü 1991, Mohr. viii-430 p. DM 120. 3-16-145737-4 [TR 88,163]. – ᴿArTGran 54 (1991) 390 (A. *Segovia*).

4712 *Slingerland* Dixon, Acts 18:1-18, the Gallio inscription, and absolute Pauline chronology: JBL 110 (1991) 439-449.

4713 *Hansen* Mogens H., *Pedersen* Lars, The size of the council of the Areopagos and its social composition in the fourth century B.C.: ClasMedK 41 (1990) 73-78.

4714 *Rapske* Brian M., [Acts 20...] The importance of helpers to the imprisoned Paul in the book of Acts: TyndB 42 (1991) 3-30.

4715 *Watson* Duane F., Paul's speech to the Ephesian elders (Acts 20,17-38); epideictic rhetoric of farewell: ➤ 86, ꟳKENNEDY G., Persuasive 1991, 184-208.

4716 **Yoo Sang-Hyeon**, Une étude sur le procès de Paul (Ac 21-28): diss. prot. ᴰ*Trocmé* É. Strasbourg 1991. 449 p. – RTLv 23, p. 547.

4717 **Tajra** H. W., Trial of St. Paul ᴰ1989 ➤ 5,5341; 6,5599: ᴿCritRR 4 (1991) 239-241 (Susan R. *Garrett*); JTS 42 (1991) 230s (C. K. *Barrett*); RivArCr 67 (1991) 487s (P. *Saint-Roch*); SvTKv 66 (1990) 81s (E. *Lövestam*); TLZ 116 (1991) 599s (G. *Schille*).

4718 *Rinaldi* Giancarlo, Procurator Felix; note prosopografiche in margine ad una rilettura di At 24: RivB 39 (1991) 423-465; Eng. 466.

4719 *Winter* Bruce, The importance of the *captatio benevolentiae* in the speeches of Tertullus and Paul in Acts 24:1-21: JTS 42 (1991) 505-531.

4720 *Schwank* Benedikt, [Act 27s] Also doch Malta [Besuch in Kefalonia 1989]: BiKi 45 (1990) 43-46.

4721 *Suhl* Alfred, [Act 27] Zum Seeweg Alexandrien-Rom [Malta war keine Station; WARNECKE H. ...]: TZBas 47 (1991) 208-213.

XIV. Johannes

G1 *Corpus Johanneum* .1 **John and his community.**

4722 *Black* David A., El grupo de Juan; Helenismo y Gnosis: → 453, Orígenes 1989/91, 303-323.

4723 **Bull** Klaus-Michael, Gemeinde zwischen Integration und Abgrenzung; ein Beitrag zur Frage nach dem Ort der johanneischen Gemeinde in der Geschichte des Urchristentums: Diss. Rostock 1991, ᴰ*Becker*. – TR 87,522.

4724 **Collins** Raymond F., John and his witness: GlazierZc. ColMn 1991, Liturgical. 112 p. $7. 0-8146-5670-6.

4725 **Hanson** Anthony T., The prophetic gospel [... by an early Christian prophet freely relating to the Jesus tradition]; a study of John and the OT. E 1991, Clark. 393 p. £27.50. 0-567-09583-5. – ᴿMonth 252 (1991) 539 (Mary E. *Mills*).

4726 *Hendrickx* Herman, The Johannine community: Theology Annual 12 (Hong Kong 1990s) 167-180 [< TContexto 2/2,40].

4727 ᴱ**Kaestli** Jean-Daniel, *Poffet* Jean-Michel, *Zumstein* Jean, La communauté johannique et son histoire; la trajectoire de l'évangile de Jean aux deux premiers siècles 1987/90 → 6,538*: ᴿAntonianum 66 (1991) 440s (M. *Nobile*); Gregorianum 72 (1991) 571-5 (H. *Pietras*); NRT 113 (1991) 106-8 (Y. *Simoens*); RechSR 79 (1991) 296-8 (X. *Léon-Dufour*: riches résultats); RHPR 71 (1991) 235s (F. *Grob*); RivStoLR 27 (1991) 334-340 (Giuliana *Iacopino*).

4728 *Klauck* H.-J., Gemeinde ohne Amt? Erfahrungen mit der Kirche in den johanneischen Schriften: TJb (Lp 90) 107-128 [< ZIT 91,654].

4729 *Logan* Alastair H.B., John and the Gnostics; the significance of the Apocryphon of John for the debate about the origins of the Johannine literature: JStNT 43 (1991) 41-69.

Painter John, The quest for the Messiah; ... Johannine community 1991 → 245.

4730 **Quast** Kevin [→ 4787], Peter and the Beloved Disciple; figures for a community in crisis: JStNT supp 32, 1989 → 5,5354; 6,5624*a*: ᴿCBQ 53 (1991) 716s (B.D. *Ehrman*: nothing new); CritRR 4 (1991) 218-220 (P.N. *Anderson*: title 'Kevin Quast'; 2d line 'Michael Quast').

4731 **Rensberger** David, [6,5625] Overcoming the world; politics and community in the Gospel of John. L 1989, SPCK. 168 p. £10. – ᴿCritRR 4 (1991) 222-4 (W. *Wink*); EvQ 63 (1991) 164s (R.B. *Edwards*).

4732 *Ruff* Pierre-Yves, La communauté johannique et son histoire [KAESTLI J., POFFET J., ZUMSTEIN J. 1990]: RTPhil 123 (1991) 79-92; Eng. 128.

4733 *Schnelle* Udo, Johanneische Ekklesiologie: NTS 37 (1991) 37-50.

4734 *a)* *Speigl* Jakob, Il Vangelo di Giovanni, la 'primizia' dei commenti neotestamentari d'ORIGENE; – *b)* *Mara* Maria Grazia, Presenza della tradizione giovannea nelle prime comunità cristiane; – *c)* *Studer* Basil, I 'Tractatus in Ioannem' di Sant'AGOSTINO: → 451, Efeso I, 1990/1, 129-134 / 111-127 / 135-146.

4735 **Stowasser** Martin A., Johannes der Täufer im vierten Evangelium; eine Untersuchung zu seine Bedeutung für die johanneische Gemeinde: kath. diss. ᴰ*Kremer*. Wien 1991. – TR 87,514.

4736 **Taeger** J.-W., Johannesapokalypse und johanneischer Kreis: BZNW 51, 1988 ➤ 5,5359; 6,5631: ᴿBijdragen 52 (1991) 99 (R. *Host*); CBQ 53 (1991) 151-3 (P. J. *Cahill*); CiuD 203 (1990) 743s (J. *Gutiérrez*); NedTTs 45 (1991) 340 (J. W. van *Henten*); RechSR 79 (1991) 295s (X. *Léon-Dufour*).

4737 **Wahlde** U. C. von, The Johannine commandments; 1 John and the struggle for the Johannine tradition 1990 ➤ 6,5633: ᴿNRT 113 (1991) 110s (Y. *Simoens*); PerspRelSt 18 (1991) 198-201 (F. S. *Spencer*); RechSR 79 (1991) 306-8 (X. *Léon-Dufour*); TLZ 116 (1991) 743-5 (K. *Wengst*).

G1.2   **Evangelium Johannis:** *textus, commentarii.*

4738 ᴱ**Backus** Irena, M. BUCER, Enarratio in Evangelium Johannis: Opera 2/2 1988 ➤ 6,5636: ᴿJTS 42 (1991) 766-770 (D. F. *Wright*; for 'enarratio' see K. HAGEN on 'commentarius' in ᴱBackus, Théorie et pratique de l'exégèse 1990).

4739 **Barrett** C. K., Das Evangelium nach Johannes 1955, ²1978 ᵀ*Bald* H.: KeK Sonderband, 1990 ➤ 6,5637; DM 128: ᴿBZ 35 (1991) 271s (H.-J. *Klauck*); ErbAuf 67 (1991) 74 (B. *Schwank*).

4740 ᵀᴱ**Berrouard** M. F., Œuvres de saint AUGUSTIN 73B, Homélies sur l'Évangile de saint Jean XLIV-LIV [ch. 9-12] 1989 ➤ 4,5411*...6,5638: ᴿRHPR 71 (1991) 378s (J. *Doignon*).

4741 **Blank** Josef, O Evangelho segundo João 4/1a (cap. 1-6), 4/1b (cap. 7-12); 4/3 (18...). Petrópolis 1990s, Vozes. 426 p. 352 p. 212 p. – ᴿREB 51 (1991) 237s (I. *Mazzarollo*) [51,511.754].

4742 **Calloud** Jean, **Genuyt** François, L'Évangile de Jean [analyse sémiotique]. L'Arbresle 1985-91, Centre Thomas More. II. ch. 7-12, 1987; vii-140 p.; – III. ch. 13-17, 1985; - IV. ch. 18-21, 1991, 109 p. 2-905600-02-0; -00-4; -13-6.

4743 **Carson** D. A., The Gospel according to John. Leicester / GR 1991, Inter-Varsity / Eerdmans. 715 p. 0-85111-749-X / GR 0-8028-3683-6 [NTAbs 35,238; RelStR 18,230, D. M. *Smith*: conservative, vigorous]. – ᴿSWJT 34,3 (1991s) 38 (G. L. *Munn*).

4744 ᵀᴱ(Sante) **Centi** Tito, Tommaso d'AQUINO, Commento al Vangelo di San Giovanni (cap. 1-6): Fonti Cristiane per il Terzo Millennio 5s. R 1990-, Città Nuova. 544 p.; Lit. 48.000 [Asprenas 39,439, V. *Scippa*]: II (cap. 7-14, 1992) 364 p. 88-311-1005-6; -6-3.

4745 ᵀᴱ**Delebecque** É., Ev. Jean 1987 ➤ 3,5250...6,5641: ᴿRBgPg 69 (1991) 205-7 (J. *Schamp*: superbe leçon de lecture).

4746 **Fatica** Luigi, [I commentari a Giovanni di TEODORO M e di CIRILLO A: StEphAug 29, 1988 ➤ 4,5418...6,5642: ᴿAugR 30 (1990) 198-203 (B. *Studer*); risposta 31 (1991) 459-464.

4746* ᵀᴱ**Fatica** L. TEODORO di Mopsuestia, Commentario al Vangelo di Giovanni apostolo libri I-VII: CuCrAnt. R 1991, Borla. 320 p. Lit. 30.000. – ᴿStPatav 38 (1991) 458s (G. *Segalla*).

4747 **Fischer** Bonifatius, Varianten zu Johannes: VLatGesch 18. FrB 1991, Herder. 48*-569 p. [RHE 86,280*; RB 99,612, P. *Henne*]. 3-451-21934-4.

4748 **Gabr** Manal Y., Philological studies on the Coptic versions of the Gospel of John: diss. Liverpool 1990. 173 p. BRDX-93171. – DissA 52 (1991s) 1305-A.

4749 **Léon-Dufour** X., Lecture...Jn 1-4, 1988 & 5-12, 1990 ➤ 3,5259; 6,5650*a*; ᴿAngelicum 68 (1991) 577-9 (S. *Jurić*, 2); ArTGran 54 (1991) 372s (A. *Segovia*, 2); Bijdragen 52 (1991) 330 & 440 (J. *Lambrecht*); BZ 35 (1991) 268-271 (R. *Schnackenburg*, 1s); Études 437 (1991) 426 (P. *Gibert*, 2);

RazF 223 (1991) 551s (M. *Matos*, 2); RechSR 79 (1991) 414-6 (É. *Cothenet*, 2); Salesianum 53 (1991) 770 (C. *Bissoli*: I. uscito in italiano); TLZ 116 (1991) 665-7 (W. *Wiefel*, 2); TsTNijm 31 (1991) 429s (L. *Grollenberg*, 2).

4750 **Léon-Dufour** Xavier, Lectura del Evangelio de Juan 1-4, 1989 ➤ 6, 5650*b*: ᴿCiTom 118 (1991) 415 (J. L. *Espinel*); ScripTPamp 23 (1991) 340-3 (A. *García-Moreno*); RTPhil 123 (1991) 116s (J. *Borel*); Teresianum 42 (1991) 351s (V. *Pasquetto*).

4751 ᵀᴱ**Livrea** Enrico, NONNO di Panopoli, Parafrasi del Vangelo di S. Giovanni, Canto XVIII: Speculum 9, 1989 ➤ 6,5651: ᴿByZ 83 (1991) 468s (K. *Treu*).

4752 **McPolin** James, John: NTMessage 6. Dublin 1984 = 1979 (Glazier) Veritas. 273 p. 0-86217-013-3.

4753 **Michaels** J. Ramsey, John: New International Biblical Commentary [cf. his Good News Comm. 1984, 390 p. ➤ 65,4765]. Peabody ᴹᴬ 1989, Hendrickson. xiii-386 p. 0-943575-14-1.

4754 **Morris** L., Reflections on the Gospel of John. GR 1986-8, Baker. 750 p. (4 vol.). 0-8010-6202-0. – ᴿAsbTJ 46,2 (1991) 100 (R. J. *Green*).

4755 *Oñate* Juan A., La mujer [7 veces] en el evangelio según san Juan: AnVal 4 (1990) 35-119.

4756 **Parmentier** Roger, L'Évangile selon Jean actualisé et réécrit à Montpellier; résonances actuelles du quatrième évangile. Montpellier 1989, Association Œcuménique A.C.T.U.E.L. xi-150 p. – ᴿRHPR 71 (1991) 239s (E. *Trocmé*: Dieu 'l'Indicible'; Jésus 'le Poète', mais la poésie est effacée — comme aussi tout le miraculeux).

4757 ᵀᴱ**Phillips** Jane E., ERASMUS, paraphrase on John: Works 46. Toronto 1991, Univ. xvi-371 p. $85. 0-8020-5859-0. $85. [RelStR 18,337, M. *Hoffmann*).

4758 **Porsch** Felix, Joh-ev: Stu KLKomm NT 4, 1988 ➤ 4,5443 ... 6,5653: ᴿTPQ 139 (1991) 335s (F. *Kogler*).

4759 **Quecke** Hans, Das Johannesevangelium saïdisch: PapyrCastroct 11, 1984 ➤ 65,4769 ... 5,5379: ᴿCdÉ 65 (1990) 373s (E. *Lucchesi*).

4760 *a*) *Vogt* Hermann J., Il 'Commento a Giovanni' di ORIGENE; – *b*) *Cremascoli* Giuseppe, I commenti al Vangelo di Giovanni in età carolingia: ➤ 423, Giovanni 1989/91, 121-135 / 137-154.

4761 **Wengert** Timothy J., Philip MELANCHTHON's Annotationes in Johannem in relation to its predecessors and contemporaries: TravHumRen 120, 1987 ➤ 3,5267; ... 5,5385: ᴿRelStR 17 (1991) 76 (J. B. *Payne*).

4762 **Zevini** Giorgio, Vangelo secondo Giovanni 11-21 ➤ 5,5386; 6,5659: ᴿAugM 35 (1990) 188s (J. A. *Galindo*).

G1.3 **Introductio** *in Evangelium Johannis.*

4763 *Arion* Leon, (en roum.) Le caractère historique et la valeur du IVᵉ Évangile: STBuc 39,3 (1987) 104-128.

4764 **Ashton** John, Understanding the Fourth Gospel. Ox 1991, Clarendon. 599 p. £65. 0-19-826461-5. – ᴿExpTim 103,1 2d-top choice (1991s) 2s (C. S. *Rodd*: splendid scholarship); Month 252 (1991) 502-5 (J. A. *Crampsey*).

4765 **Belle** Gilbert Van, Johannine bibliography 1966-1985: BtETL 82, 1988 ➤ 4,876 ... 6,5660: ᴿCBQ 53 (1991) 348s (F. J. *Moloney*: continues in 563 pages the 19 years since MALATESTA's 45 years in 205 pages); Laurentianum 32 (1991) 301-3 (L. *Martignani*).

4766 **Bjerkelund** C.J., Tauta egeneto ... Joh: WUNT 40, 1987 ➤ 3,5275 ...
5,5392: ᴿCrNSt 12 (1991) 183s (B. *Lindars*, Eng.); NedTTs 45 (1991) 348s
(M.J.J. *Menken*).

4767 **Booth** Steven C., A discourse analysis of certain peak marking features
in the Gospel of John: diss. SW Baptist Theol. Sem. ᴰ*Lacostemunn* G.
1991. 233 p. 92-13032. – DissA 52 (1991s) 4365s-A.

4768 *Botha* J. E., The case of Johannine irony reopened, 1. The problematic
current situation; 2. suggestions, alternative approaches: Neotestamentica
25 (1991) 209-220 . 221-232.

4769 *a) Carreira das Neves* Joaquim, O pronome pessoal *hēmeîs* como chave
hermenêutica do IV Evangelho; – *b) Morujão* Geraldo, Exemplos de
desenvolvimento deráxico no IV Evangelho: ➤ 422, Didaskalia 20,1
(1990) 43-65 / 83-92 = 421, Luso-Esp 1989/91, 361-383 / 385-394.

ᴱ**Ceresa-Gastaldo** Aldo, Lingua e stile del Vangelo di Giovanni 1989/91
➤ 423.

4770 **Collins** Raymond F., John and his witness: Glazier-Zacchaeus. ColMn
1991, Liturgical. 112 p. $7. 0-8146-5657-9 [TDig 38,392].

4771 *Cook* Cornelia, 'I gotta use words when I talk to you'; a literary
examination of John: NBlackf 72 (1991) 365-376.

4772 **Fortna** Robert T., The Fourth Gospel and its predecessor 1988 ➤ 4,
5454 ... 5,5395: ᴿBiblica 72 (1991) 283-6 (Kikuo *Matsunaga*); ScotJT 43
(1990) 526s (B. *Lindars*: a house of sand, but beautifully and sensitively
written); StPatav 38 (1991) 442-4 (G. *Segalla*).

4773 **Gądecki** Stanisław, ❷ Wstęp do pism Janowych (introduction to the
Johannine writings). Gniezno 1991, Gaudentinum. 199 p.

4774 *García-Moreno* Antonio, *a)* Aspectos eclesiológicos del IV Evangelio:
➤ 422, Luso-Esp 1989/91, 269-278; – *b)* Autenticidad e historicidad del IV
Evangelio: ScripTPamp 23 (1991) 13-66; lat. 66s; Eng. 67.

4775 **Grassi** Joseph A., The secret identity of the beloved disciple. NY 1990,
Paulist. iv-135 p. $8.

4777 **Hengel** Martin, The Johannine question 1989 ➤ 5,5397*; 6,5671: ᴿJBL
110 (1991) 536s (R. A. *Culpepper*: as dense as it is significant); JTS 42
(1991) 666-8 (E. *Bammel*); TLZ 116 (1991) 662-5 (F. *Neugebauer*).

4778 **Hinrichs** Boy, 'Ich bin' ... SBS 133, 1988 ➤ 4,5456 ... 6,5672: ᴿCBQ 53
(1991) 136s (M. *Kiley*); StPatav 38 (1991) 201s (G. *Segalla*).

4779 *Koester* Craig R., R. E. BROWN and J. L. MARTYN; Johannine studies in
retrospect: BibTB 21 (1991) 51-55.

4780 *a) La Potterie* Ignace de, Il discepolo che Gesù amava; – *b) Philippe*
Marie-Dominique, L'Évangile des rencontres personnelles: ➤ 451, Efeso
I, 1990/1, 33-55 / 57-74.

4781 *Léon-Dufour* Xavier, Bulletin d'exégèse du NT; l'Évangile de Jean:
RechSR 79 (1991) 291-315; 17 livres.

4782 **Lindars** Barnabas, John: NTGuides 1990 ➤ 6,5676: ᴿÉTRel 66 (1991)
593s (Isabelle *Parlier*).

4783 **Manns** Frédéric, L'Évangile de Jean à la lumière du Judaïsme: SBF Anal
33. J 1991, Franciscan. 548 p. $45 [NTAbs 36,112].

4784 ᴱ**Marchadour** Alain, Origines et postérité de l'Évangile de Jean; Actes de
l'ACFÉB [Association catholique française pour l'étude de la Bible] 13,
Toulouse sept. 1986: LDiv 143, 1990 ➤ 6,545*: ᴿAnnTh 5 (1991) 414-7
(B. *Estrada*); RechSR 79 (1991) 298s (X. *Léon-Dufour*); RHPR 71 (1991)
236-8 (F. *Grob*).

4785 **Mlakuzhyil** George, The Christocentric literary structure of the
Fourth Gospel 1987 ➤ 3,5286 ... 6,5680: ᴿKerux 5,1 (1990) 47-50

(J. T. *Dennison*: highly commended; a book which changes the course of things).

4786 *Østenstad* Gunnar, The structure of the Fourth Gospel; can it be defined objectively?: ST 45,1 (1991) 33-55.

4787 **Quast** Kevin [➤ 4730], Reading the Gospel of John; an introduction. NY 1991, Paulist. viii-165 p. $9. 0-8091-3297-4.

4788 **Rabanos Espinosa** R., *Muñoz León* D., Bibliografía joánica 1990 ➤ 6,5684: ᴿAngelicum 68 (1991) 580-2 (L. *de Santis*); CiTom 118 (1991) 416s (J. L. *Espinel*); Gregorianum 72 (1991) 570s (G. *Ferraro*); Marianum 53 (1991) 662-6 (M. *Masini*; p. 665 compara i pregi con questo Elenchus e NTAbs); StPatav 38 (1991) 200s (G. *Segalla*).

4789 **Rand** J. A. du, *a*) Johannese perspektiewe; inleiding tot die Johannese geskrifte; – *b*) An introduction to the Johannine writings. Pretoria 1990s, Orion. 313 p., r 46. – ᴿNeotestamentica 25 (1991) 186-8 (D. F. *Tolmie*, also on 1-3 Jn and Rev).

4790 **Ruckstuhl** Eugen, *Dschulnigg* Peter, Stilkritik und Verfasserfrage im Johannesevangelium; die johanneischen Sprachmerkmale auf dem Hintergrund des NTs und des zeitgenössischen hellenistischen Schrifttums: NOrb 17. FrS/Gö 1991, Univ./Vandenhoeck & R. 275 p. DM 69. [TLZ 117,917, U. *Schnelle*], 3-7278-0740-7 / 3-525-53918-5. – ᴿETL 67 (1991) 437-440 (F. *Neirynck*).

4791 **Schram** T., The logical structure of John's Gospel: NoTr 4,3 (Dallas 1990) 24-33 [< NTAbs 36,41].

4792 **Sloyan** Gerard S., What are they saying about John? NY 1991, Paulist. iii-125 p. $7. 0-8091-3238-9 [TDig 39,84].

4793 *Stibbe* M.W.G., The elusive Christ; a new reading of the Fourth Gospel: JStNT 44 (1991) 19-38.

4794 *Thielman* Frank, The style of the Fourth Gospel and ancient literary critical concepts of religious discourse: ➤ 86, ᶠKENNEDY G., Persuasive 1991, 169-183.

4795 **Thomas More** sr., [Jn 19,32-35; 1 Jn 5,6-8] His witness is true; John and his interpreters [diss. Drew 1988]: AmerUnivSt 7/42. NY 1989, Lang. vii-242 p. $43.50. – ᴿChH 59 (1990) 437s (T. J. *Wengert*).

4796 *a*) *Vanni* Ugo, Il 'Segno' in Giovanni; – *b*) *Valgiglio* Ernesto, Aspetti stilistici del quarto 'Vangelo': ➤ 423, Giovanni 1989/91, 39-58 / 59-119.

4797 **Voigt** Gottfried, Licht-Liebe-Leben; das Evangelium nach Johannes: Bib-theol. Schwerpunkte 6. Gö 1991, Vandenhoeck & R. 296 p. DM 38. 3-525-61287-7 [NTAbs 36,271].

4798 ᴱ**Wagner** Gunter, An exegetical bibliography of the NT, 3 [Jn-1-3 Jn] 1987 ➤ 3,985: ᴿAsbTJ 46,2 (1991) 101 (R. J. *Green*).

4799 **Wahlde** U. C. von [➤ 4737], The earliest version of John's Gospel 1989 ➤ 5,5410; 6,5692: ᴿBibTB 21 (1991) 130s (J. S. *Siker*).

G1.4   *Johannis themata,* **topics.**

4800 *Adamo* David T., The concept of sin in the Gospel of John: Bible Bhashyam 17 (1991) 45-59.

4801 *Backhaus* Knut, Praeparatio evangelii; die religionsgeschichtlichen Bezeichungen zwischen Täufer- und Jesus-Bewegung im Spiegel der sog. Semeia-Quelle des vierten Evangeliums: TGL 81 (1991) 202-215. ➤ 4873.

4802 *Ball* David M., 'My Lord and my God'; the implications of 'I am' sayings for religious pluralism: ➤ 485, One God 1991, 53-71.

4803 **Beasley-Murray** George, Gospel of life; theology in the Fourth Gospel [Fuller Payton lectures, Pasadena 1990]. Peabody MA 1991, Hendrickson. xii-131 p. $8 pa. 0-943575-76-1 [NTAbs 36,261].

4804 **Boismard** Marie-Émile, Moïse ou Jésus [essai de christologie johannique, + 3 reprints]: BtETL 84, 1988 ➤ 5,5416; 6,5698: ᴿCBQ 53 (1991) 693-5 (R. E. *Brown* clarifies his own revelance and qualified acceptance; and notes that the last 100 pages are reprints irrelevant to the title); NRT 113 (1991) 108s (Y. *Simoens*); RechSR 79 (1991) 303s (X. *Léon-Dufour*); RHPR 71 (1991) 238s (F. *Grob*); RivB 39 (1991) 71-74 (M. *Làconi*); TLZ 116 (1991) 184-6 (Anna Maria *Schwemer*).

4805 *Bratcher* Robert G., What does 'glory' mean in relation to Jesus? Translating *doxa* and *doxazo* in John: BTrans 42 (1991) 401-8.

4806 **Burkett** Delbert, The Son of Man in the Gospel of John [diss. Duke 1989, ᴰ*Smith* D. ➤ 5,5418]: JStNT supp 56. Sheffield 1991, Academic. 199 p. £39.50; sb £22.50. 1-85075-292-3.

4806* **Castellarín** Tomás A., El didaskein de Jesús; estudio exegético-teológico del término en el cuarto Evangelio: Diss. Pont. Univ. Gregoriana Nᵒ 6894, ᴰ*Caba* José. R 1991. – InfPUG 23/119 (1990s) 14.

4807 ᴱ**Charlesworth** James H., John & DSS 1972, 1990 reprint ➤ 6,5702: ᴿBA 54 (1991) 180 (J. R. *Michaels*); Interpretation 45 (1991) 426 (J. C. *Wilson*, also on 1968 Paul & DSS); JStJud 22 (1991) 125s (F. *Garcia-Martínez*, also on Paul reprint); Vidyajyoti 55 (1991) 174 (P. M. *Meagher*, Jn Paul).

Collins Raymond, These things have been written 1991 ➤ 193.

4808 *Cothenet* Édouard, Le témoignage selon saint Jean: EsprVie 101 (1991) 401-7.

4809 **Cuamatzi Montiel** Agustin, *chara/chaîrein*; estudio exegético-teológico del tema 'alegría' en el 'corpus joanneum': diss. Pont. Univ. Gregoriana, ᴰ*Caba* J. Roma 1991. 492 p. – RTLv 23, p. 543 [< DissA-C].

4810 *Delfini* Mario, Sul rapporto delle lettere di IGNAZIO di Antiochia con il Vangelo di Giovanni: ScuolC 119 (1991) 514-525.

4811 *Ernst* Joseph, Das Johannesevangelium — ein frühes Beispiel christlicher Mystik?: TGl 81 (1991) 323-338.

4812 *Filipović* Ana s. Thea, Život za prijatelje; teološki dometi terminologije prijateljstva u Ivanovim spisima– ➤ 67, ᶠGOLUB I., 1991, 71-86; 87, ital. Amicizia nel Vangelo e Lettere di Giovanni.

4812* *García-Moreno* A., Las fiestas en el IV evangelio: NVZam 16 (1991) 3-25.167-197 [< RET 52,390].

Hanson Anthony T., The prophetic Gospel; a study of John and the OT 1991 ➤ 4725.

4814 ᴱ**Hartman** L., *Olsson* B., Aspects on the Johannine literature 1986/7 ➤ 3,546 ... 5,5436: ᴿNedTTs 45 (1991) 338 (M.J.J. *Menken*).

4815 *a) Hengel* Martin, Reich Christi, Reich Gottes und Weltreich im Johannesevangelium; – *b) Merkel* Helmut, Die Gottesherrschaft in der Verkündigung Jesu; – *c) Müller* Klaus W., König und Vater; Streiflichter zur metaphorischen Rede über Gott in der Umwelt des NTs: ➤ 438, Königsherrschaft 1986/91, 163-184 / 119-161 / 21-43.

4816 *Hoeps* Reinhard, Die Herrlichkeit Gottes auf dem Antlitz Jesu Christi und die Verherrlichung des Sohnes; zum Realitätsgehalt der Christusikone und der johanneischen Doxa-Vorstellung: ➤ 398, Simulation 1989/91, 239-261.

4817 *Huerta* P. Eduardo, La realeza de Jesús en el Cuarto Evangelio: TVid 32 (1991) 213-220.

4818 *Johnson* William A., Anti-Semitism in St. John's Gospel: ➤ 56, [F]FOX M., 1 (1991) 149-170.

4819 *Juel* Donald, *Keifert* Patrick, 'I believe in God'; a Johannine perspective: ➤ 435, HorBT 12,2 (1990) 39-63.

4820 **Kaufman** Philip S., The beloved disciple; witness against anti-Semitism. ColMn 1991, Liturgical. 71 p. $6. 0-8146-2067-1 [TDig 39,171].

4821 **Keener** Craig S., The function of Johannine pneumatology in the context of late first century Judaism: diss. Duke, [D]*Smith* D.M. Durham NC 1991. 500 p. 92-02488. — DissA 52 (1991s) 2957-A; RelStR 18,173.

4822 **Kieffer** René, Le monde symbolique de Saint Jean: LDiv 137, 1989 ➤ 5,5540; 6,5721: [R]FgNt 4 (1991) 79-81 (J. *Mateos*); NRT 113 (1991) 105s (Y. *Simoens*); SvEx 56 (1991) 138-141 (H. *Riesenfeld*).

4823 *Landier* Jean, Les écrits johanniques sont-ils des fruits de la gnose?: Masses Ouvrières 437 (1991) 85-102.

4824 **Loader** William, The Christology of the Fourth Gospel: BeitBExT 23, 1989 ➤ 5,5446; 6,5730: [R]BZ 35 (1991) 135-7 (R. *Schnackenburg*); Interpretation 45 (1991) 197s (K. *Quast*); JBL 110 (1991) 537-9 (Marianne *Meye Thompson*); Pacifica 4 (1991) 108-110 (F.J. *Moloney*); RechSR 79 (1991) 300-3 (X. *Léon Dufour*: étude magistrale); TLZ 116 (1991) 667-9 (H.-M. *Schenke*).

4825 *Luzárraga* Jesús, La 'vita eterna' negli scritti di Giovanni, [T]*Pistocchi* Bruno: ➤ 346, Communio 115 (1991) 8-18.

4826 **McGann** Dairmuid, Journey within transcendence; a Jungian perspective on the Gospel of John 1988 ➤ 4,5461 [6,5677 title modified; 'Diarmuid' both; BIP 'Dairmuid']: [R]DocLife 40 (1990) 167s (sr. Josephine *Newman*).

4827 *Mannucci* Valerio, Il teo-finalismo nel quarto vangelo: VivH 1 (1990) 15-30.

4828 *a) Mara* Maria Grazia, Presenza della tradizione giovannea nelle prime comunità cristiane; – *b) Speigl* Jakob, Il Vangelo di Giovanni, la 'primizia' dei commenti neotestamentari d'ORIGENE; – *c) Studer* Basil, I 'Tractatus in Ioannem' di Sant'AGOSTINO: ➤ 451, Efeso I, 1990/1, 111-127 / 129-134 / 135-146.

4829 *Menken* M.J.J., De christologie van het vierde evangelie; een overzicht van resultaten van recent onderzoek: NedTTs 45 (1991) 16-33: Eng. 60.

4830 *Morgen* M., Les femmes dans l'évangile de Jean: Revue de Droit Canonique 40,1 ('Le mariage' 1989) 77-96 [97-115, *Heyer* M., Mariage et féminisme: < RSPT 75,166].

4831 **Morris** Leon, Jesus is the Christ; studies in the theology of John 1989 ➤ 5,5450; £9 pa.: [R]EvQ 63 (1991) 276 (I.H. *Marshall*).

4832 *Mourlon Beernaert* Pierre, La vérité au sens biblique; approche de saint Jean: LVitae 46 (1991) 287-300.

4833 *Muñoz León* Domingo, Evangelio de Juan y Targum; balance y nuevos horizontes: ➤ 421, Luso-Esp 1989/91, 299-328.

4834 **Neyrey** Jerome, An ideology of revolt; John's Christology 1989 ➤ 6, 5732: [R]BibTB 21 (1991) 125 (S. *Joubert*); LvSt 16 (1991) 73s (R.F. *Collins*).

4835 **Panimolle** Salvatore A., Gesù di Nazaret nell'ultimo evangelo e nei primi scritti dei Padri: StRB, 1990 ➤ 6,5739: [R]RivB 39 (1991) 491s (Clara *Burini*: rende pressoché inutile l'accostamento fra Gv e i testi patristici).

4836 **Pazdan** M.M., The Son of Man; a metaphor for Jesus in the Fourth Gospel: Glazier-Zaccheus. ColMn 1991, Liturgical. 87 p. $8. 0-8146-5677-3. [NTAbs 36,267].

4837 *Piñero* Antonio, Inspiración, canonicidad y cuarto evangelio; reflexiones en torno al encuadre ideológico del evangelio de Juan: ➤ 421, Luso-Esp 1989/91, 279-297.

4838 *Plantinga* Cornelius[J], The Fourth Gospel as trinitarian source then and now: ➤ 58, [F]FROEHLICH K., 1991, 303-321.

4839 *Pryor* John W., The Great Thanksgiving [Q Mt 11,25-27; Lk 10,21s] and the Fourth Gospel: BZ 35 (1991) 157-179.

4840 **Rodríguez Ruiz** Miguel, Missionsgedanke des Johannesevangeliums 1987 ➤ 3,5329 ... 6,5746: [R]CiuD 203 (1991) 492s (J. *Gutiérrez*); ColcT 60,4 (1990) 171s (R. *Bartnicki* ❷).

4841 **Röhl** Wolfgang G., Studien zur Frage nach der Rezeption des Johannesevangeliums in christlich-gnostischen Schriften aus Nag Hammadi [Diss. Kirchliche Hochschule Berlin, 1991, [D]Osten-Sacken P. von der. – TR 87 (1991) 515]: EurHS 23/428. Fra 1991, Lang. 232 p. 3-631-43860-5.

4842 **Schuchard** Bruce G., Scripture within Scripture; the interrelationship of form and function in the explicit Old Testament citations in the Gospel of John: diss. Union, [D]Rissi M. Richmond 1991. 307 p. 91-36878. – DissA 52 (1991s) 2589-A.

4843 **Sherry** Lee F., The hexameter 'Paraphrase of St. John' attributed to NONNUS of Panopolis; prolegomenon and translation: diss. Columbia, [D]Cameron A. NY 1991. 302 p. 91-27971. – DissA 52 (1991s) 1317-A.

4844 **Stimpfle** Alois, Blinde sehen; die Eschatologie im traditionsgeschichtlichen Prozess des Joh.-Evs [kath. Diss. Augsburg]: BZNW 57, 1990 ➤ 6,5753: [R]BZ 35 (1991) 137-9 (R. *Schnackenburg*); TLZ 116 (1991) 510-512 (S. *Vollenweider*: die Stärke: weckt viele Fragen und Einwände).

4845 *Thomas* John C., The Fourth Gospel and rabbinic Judaism: ZNW 82 (1991) 159-182.

4846 **[Meye] Thompson** Marianne, The humanity of Jesus 1988 ➤ 4,5523 ... 6,5755: [R]TorJT 7 (1991) 128s (A. M. *Osiander*).

4847 *[Meye] Thompson* Marianne, Signs and faith in the fourth gospel: BBRes 1 (1991) 89-108.

4848 **Tobler** Eva, Vom Missverstehen zur Glauben ... 4 Ev; EurHS 23/395, 1990 ➤ 6,5756: [R]TsTNijm 31 (1991) 195 (A. van *Diemen*).

4849 **Uglorz** Manfred, ❷ Obecność Boga ... The presence of God in the Christological reflexion of John the Evangelist. Wsz 1988, Akad Teol. 209 p. – [R]ColcT 61,2 (1991) 190s (S. C. *Napiórkowski*, ❷).

4850 *Waldstein* Michael, The mission of Jesus and the disciples in John: CommND 17 (1990) 311-334.

4851 *Weiss* Herold, The sabbath in the Fourth Gospel: JBL 110 (1991) 311-321.

4852 *a) Zumstein* Jean, Mémoire et relecture pascale dans l'Évangile selon Jean; – *b) Léon-Dufour* Xavier, Les deux mémoires du chrétien: ➤ 30, [F]BONNARD P., Mémoire 1991, 153-170 / 143-151.

G1.5 Johannis Prologus 1,1 ...

4853 **Wallace** Ronald S., The Gospel of John chapters 1-11; pastoral and theological studies including some sermons. E 1991, Scottish Academic. xviii-216 p. 0-7073-0700-7.

4854 *Letellier* Joël, Le Logos chez ORIGÈNE: RSPT 75 (1991) 587-611; Eng. 612.

4855 *Muñoz León* Domingo, Las fuentes y estadios de composición del Prólogo de Juan según P. HOFRICHTER [1986] (En torno a la 'Primitiva confesión cristiana del Logos'): EstB 49 (1991) 229-250; Eng. 229.

4856 *a) Nayak* Anand, Der Stellenwert des johanneischen Logos in indischer Theologie; – *b) Rordorf* Willy, Die Jakobsleiter; Gen 28,10ff und Joh 1,51 in der patristischen Exegese: ➤170, [F]ZUMSTEIN J., 1991, 9-38 / 39-46.

4857 *Pietras* Henryk, ⦿ Logos a początek stworzenia [et initium creationis secundum] według FILONA z Aleksandrii: Bobolanum 2 (1991) 86-98; franç. 158.

4858 *Scarpat* Giuseppe, Prologo di Giovanni e Sapienza di Salomone: ➤ 423, Giovanni 1989/91, 7-37.

4859 *Schoneveld* Jacobus, Torah in the flesh; a new reading of the prologue of the Gospel of John as a contribution to a Christology without anti-Judaism: ➤ 54, [F]FLUSSER D., Immanuel 24s (1990) 77-94.

4860 **Shehadeh** Imad N., A comparison and a contrast between the Prologue of John's Gospel and Qur'ānic Sūrah 5: diss. Dallas Theol. Sem., [D]*Toussaint* S. 1990. 497 p. 91-25348. – DissA 52 (1991s) 1790-A.

4861 *Sindima* Harvey J. [Jn 1,1-18] Moyo, fullness of life; a hermeneutic of the Logos in John's Prologue: AfChrSt 6,4 (1990) 50-62 [< NTAbs 36,191; TContexto 2/2,125].

4862 **Speyr** Adrienne Von, Jean [1,19-5], Le Verbe se fait chair [Das Wort wird Fleisch 1949], [T]*Steinmann* sr. Élisabeth, *Lépine* Madi. Namur 1990, Culture et Vérité. – [R]BLitEc 92 (1991) 227s (Jacqueline des *Rochettes*).

4863 *Stead* G. Christopher, Logos, [T]*Schäferdiek* Knut: ➤ 690, TRE 21 (1991) 432-444.

4864 **Theobald** Michael, Die Fleischwerdung des Logos: NTAbh 20, 1988 ➤ 4,5536... 6,5773: [R]JTS 42 (1991) 668s (R. *Morgan*); ZkT 113 (1991) 304s (M. *Hasitschka*).

4865 *Biedenkopf-Ziehner* Anneliese, Ostrakon BM 50466 (John 1,1-7): Enchoria 18 (1991) 1-11; pl. 1-2.

4866 *Miller* E.L., Salvation-history in the Prologue of John; the significance of [locating the punctuation between] John 1:3-4: NT supp. 60, 1989 ➤ 5,5490; 6,5775: [R]CBQ 53 (1991) 710s (F.F. *Segovia*); EvQ 63 (1991) 185-7 (G.R. *Beasley-Murray*); JTS 42 (1991) 225-7 (B. *Lindars*); RechSR 79 (1991) 308 (X. *Léon-Dufour*: sa 'révolution' était proposée par LACAN M. 1957, BOISMARD M.E. 1977).

4867 **Hofrichter** Peter, Wer ist... Joh 1.6? 1990 ➤ 6,5776: [R]CBQ 53 (1991) 499 (J.E. *Bruns*); Claretianum 31 (1991) 375 (B. *Proietti*); EstB 49 (1991) 285-7 (D. *Muñoz León*); JBL 110 (1991) 439-441 (J. *Goss*); MüTZ 42 (1991) 275s (L. *Wehr*); RHPR 71 (1991) 239 (F. *Grob*).

4868 *O'Neill* J.C., [Jn 1,14] The Word did not 'become' flesh [rather 'was born']: ZNW 82 (1991) 125-7.

4869 **Kuhn** Hans-Jürgen, Christology und Wunder... Joh 1,35-51: BibUnt 18, [D]1988 ➤ 4,5547...6,5787: [R]CiuD 203 (1990) 739s (J. *Gutiérrez*); Salesianum 53 (1991) 587 (C. *Bissoli*); TPhil 66 (1991) 244s (J. *Beutler*).

4870 **Ottilinger** Angelika, Vorläufer, Vorbild oder Zeuge? Zum Wandel des Täuferbildes im Johannesevangelium [Diss. München]: DissTheol 45. St. Ottilien 1991, EOS. vi-315 p. DM 33 [TR 87,339].

4871 *Sandy* D.B., [Jn 1,35] John the Baptist's 'Lamb of God' affirmation in its canonical and apocalyptic milieu: JEvTSoc 34 (1991) 447-459 [< NTAbs 36,353].

4872 *Markschies* Christoph, 'Hie ist das recht Osterlamm', Christentum und Lammsymbolik bei M. LUTHER und Lucas CRANACH: ZKG 102 (1991) 209-230.

4873 *Backhaus* Knut [➤ 4801], Täuferkreise als Gegenspieler jenseits des Textes; Erwägungen zu einer kriteriologischen Verlegenheit am Beispiel der Joh.-Forschung: TGL 81 (1991) 279-301.

4874 *a) Loader* William, John 1:50-51 and the 'greater things' of Johannine Christology; – *b) Schnackenburg* Rudolf, 'Der Vater, der mich gesandt hat'; zur johanneischen Christologie; – *c) Biser* Eugen, Was ist mit Diesem? Eine theologische Improvisation über das Thema des von Jesus geliebten Jüngers: ➤ 72, ᶠHAHN F., Anfänge 1991, 255-274 / 275-291 / 323-336.

4875 **Lütgehetmann** Walter, Die Hochzeit von Kana (Joh 2,1-11) ᴰ1990 ➤ 6,5796: ᴿActuBbg 28 (1991) 163 (X. *Alegre*); Claretianum 31 (1991) 378-380 (B. *Proietti*); MüTZ 42 (1991) 276-8 (L. *Wehr*); RechSR 79 (1991) 310-2 (X. *Léon-Dufour*); StPatav 38 (1991) 200s (G. *Segalla*); TPQ 139 (1991) 325 (A. *Fuchs*).

4876 *Moreira Azevedo* Carlos A., A manifestação epifánica de Cristo em Caná (Jo 2,1-11); patristica, liturgia e iconografia: ➤ 67, ᶠGOLUB I. 1991, 59-70; 70 sažetak (croat.).

4877 **Tognocchi** Eraldo, Le nozze di Cana; nuova alleanza nuziale tra Dio e l'umanità: Orizzonti Biblici. Assisi 1991, Cittadella. 194 p. Lit. 20.000 [Asprenas 39,110, A. *Rolla*]. 88-308-0470-3.

4878 **Serra** Aristide, [Gv 2,1] E c'era la madre di Gesù 1989 ➤ 5,5505; 6,5799: ᴿDivThom 94 (1991) 162s (J. *Stöhr*, ᵀ); NRT 113 (1991) 587s (V. *Roisel*); StPatav 38 (1991) 207 (G. *Segalla*); Teresianum 42 (1991) 344s (V. *Pasquetto*).

4879 *Ellul* Danielle, Les jarres de Cana; rhétorique et symbole: ➤ 140, ᶠSMYTH-FLORENTIN F. 1991, 237-244.

4880 *Serra* Aristide M., '...ma lo sapevano i servi che avevano attinto l'acqua'; Giovanni 2,9c e le tradizioni biblico-giudaiche sul pozzo di Beer (Num 21,16-20): Marianum 53 (1991) 435-506.

4881 *Clark* R. Scott, Jesus' spring house cleaning; John 2:13-22: Kerux 4,2 (1989) 22-32.

4882 *Wood* William P., John 2:13-22 [Temple cleansing], expository: Interpretation 45 (1991) 59-63.

4883 *Chilton* B. D., [Jn 2,15] *hōs phragéllion ek schoiniōn*: ➤ 15, ᶠBAMMEL E., Templum 1991, 330-344.

G1.6 Jn 3ss... Nicodemus, Samaritana.

4884 **Létourneau** Pierre, Jn 2,23-3,26: un exposé sommaire de la double christologie johannique; analyse de l'argumentation christologique de l'entretien avec Nicodème et du second témoignage de Jean-Baptiste: diss. Laval, 1990, ᴰ*Roberge* M. 572 p. 0-315-62611-9 (DANN-62611). – DissA 52 (1991s) 4374-A.

4885 *Gibbons* Debbie, Nicodemus; character development, irony and repetition in the Fourth Gospel: ProcGLM 11 (1991) 116-128.

4886 *Goulder* Michael, Nicodemus: ScotJT 44 (1991) 153-168.

4887 *Nicol* George G., Nicodemus: ExpTim 103 (1991s) 80s.

4888 *a) Pryor* John W., John 3.3,5; a study in the relation of John's Gospel to the Synoptic tradition; – *b) Painter* John, Quest stories in John 1-4: JStNT 41 (1991) 71-95 / 33-70.

4889 *Trudinger* P., Jesus' 'comfortable words' in John 3:16 [not from Jesus' lips but a displaced part of the Prologue]; a note of disappointment to some?; St. Mark's Review 2147 (Canberra 1991) 30s [< NTAbs 36,353].

4890 **Boers** Hendrikus, Neither on this mountain... Jn 4: 1988 → 4,5560; 6,5812: ᴿJBL 110 (1991) 167-9 (C. R. *Koester*); RelStT 10,2 (1990) 121s (D. A. *Carson*).

4891 **Botha** J. Eugene, Jesus and the Samaritan woman; a speech act reading of John 4:1-42 [diss. Unisa 1990, ᴰ*Vorster* W.]: NT supp 65. Leiden 1991, Brill. xii-220 p. *f*115. 90-04-09505-5 [NTAbs 36,418].

4892 *Link* Andrea, Kritische Bestandsaufnahme neuer methodischer Ansätze in der Exegese des Johannesevangeliums anhand von Joh 4 [OLSSON B., OKURE T., DREWERMANN E. ...]: TGL 81 (1991) 253-278.

4893 **Okure** Teresa, The Johannine approach to mission... 4:1-42: WUNT 2/31, ᴰ1988 → 4,5564 ... 6,5816: ᴿCBQ 53 (1991) 338s (D. *Senior*); Spiritus 32 (1991) 327-332 (J.-M. *Guillaume*); NZMissW 46 (1990) 149s (P. *Dschulnigg-Bucher*); RB 98 (1991) 290-2 (F. J. *Moloney*); RechSR 79 (1991) 304-6 (X. *Léon-Dufour*).

4894 *Rodríguez* José D., The challenge of [U.S.-] Hispanic ministry (reflections on John 4): CurrTMiss 18 (1991) 420-426.

4895 **Carmona** Paul, The Jewish Scriptures in the background of John 4:4-42, the Samaritan woman narrative: diss. Leuven 1990, ᴰ*Collins* R. F. xliii-291 p. – LvSt 16 (1991) 345s.

4896 *Garcia-Moreno* Antonio, [Jn 4,23] Adorar al Padre en espíritu y verdad: ScripTPamp 23 (1991) 785-835.

4897 *Kudasiewicz* Józef, ❷ Worshipping the Father in spirit and truth: RoczTK 36,1 (1989) 61-70; Eng. 70s.

4898 *Aarde* A. G. van, Narrative criticism applied to John 4:43-54: → 307, Text 1991, 101-128.

4899 *a*) *Borgen* Peder, The sabbath controversy in John 5:1-18 and analogous controversy reflected in PHILO's writings; – *b*) *Weiss* Herold, Philo on the Sabbath: → 76, ꟻHILGERT E., StPhilonAn 3 (1991) 209-221 / 83-105.

4900 *Rigato* Maria-Luisa, 'Era festa dei Giudei' (Gv 5,1); quale? [Pentecoste]: RivB 39 (1991) 25-29.

4901 **Morujão** Geraldo, Relações Pai-Filho em S. João; subsidios para a teologia trinitària a partir do estudo de sintagmas verbais grecos (Jo 5 e 17). Viseu 1989. 303 p. – ᴿScripTPamp 23 (1991) 343-5 (A. *Garcia-Moreno*).

4902 *Boring* M. Eugene, John 5:19-24, expository: Interpretation 45 (1991) 176-181.

G1.7 **Panis Vitae** – *Jn 6* ...

4903 *Nellithanam* Susy, [and her husband Ranjit, poetic-form], Meditations on the 'I am' sayings of Jesus [Jn 6,15]: Jeevadhara 21 (1991) 232-245.

4904 *Beutler* Johannes, Zur Struktur von Johannes 6: SNTU A-16 (Linz 1991) 89-104 [< ZIT 92,309].

4905 *Fenton* John, Eating people [Jn 6 not cannibalistic; the Jewish metaphor means hostility; R. E. BROWN holds the chapter misplaced from a Eucharist-institution account]: TLond 94 (1991) 414-423 (-425, *Morgan* Robert, response).

4906 *Valletta* Thomas R., The 'bread of life' discourse in the context of Exodus typology: ProcGLM 11 (1991) 129-143.

4907 *a*) *Zevini* Giorgio, Cafarnao; Giovanni rilegge e interpreta Mosè e Gesù (Gv 6,22-59); – *b*) *Fabris* Rinaldo, Gesù e la legge; compimento profetico; – *c*) *Panimolle* Salvatore A., Gesù 'exegeta' della Parola: → 292*b*, ParSpV 24 (1991) 145-162 / 113-127 / 129-143.

4908 *a) Rose* Martin, [Joh 6,31 ...] Manna; das Brot aus dem Himmel; – *b)*
Hammann Gottfried, Zwischen LUTHER und ZWINGLI; Martin BUCERS
theologische Eigenständigkeit im Lichte seiner Auslegung von Johannes 6
im Abendmahlsstreit: ➤ 170, ᶠZUMSTEIN J., 1991, 75-107 / 109-134; 1 fig.
4909 *Schweizer* Eduard, Joh 6,51c-58 – vom Evangelisten übernommene
Tradition? [zu LÉON-DUFOUR X.]: ZNW 82 (1991) nur 274.
4910 **Freeman** Clarence H., The function of polemic in John 7 and 8: diss.
Southern Baptist Theol. Sem., ᴰ*Borchert* G. 1991. 248 p. 91-31507. –
DissA 52 (1991s) 1775-A.
4911 *a) Bodi* Daniel, Der altorientalische Hintergrund des Themas der
'Ströme lebendigen Wassers' in Joh 7,38; – *b) Moser* Félix, Missver-
ständnis und Ironie in der johanneischen Argumentation und ihr Gebrauch in der heutigen pfarramtlichen Praxis: ➤ 170, ᶠZUMSTEIN J. 1991,
137-158 / 47-73.
4912 *a) Zizemer* Osmar, 'Este povo que não conhece a Lei, são uns malditos'
(Jo 7,49); – *b) Hoefelmann* Verner, A crítica de Jesus à Lei como opção
pelos marginalizados; – *c)* [Assis] *Lima* Cyzo, Os Samaritanos; os
oprimidos como primícias do Reino: EstudosB 27 (1990) 47-53 / 54-63 /
64-70.
4913 *Heil* John P., The story of Jesus and the adulteress (John 7,53-8,11)
reconsidered: Biblica 72 (1991) 182-191; franç. 191.
4914 *Minear* Paul S., Writing on the ground; the puzzle in John 8:1-11:
HorBT 13 (1991) 23-37.
4915 *Cottier* Georges [Jn 8,12.32; 18,37] Méditations sur l'Évangile de saint
Jean [< Retraite, à paraître]: NVFr 66 (1991) 161-176.
4916 *Heine* Ronald E., [Jn 8,19] A note on the text of ORIGEN, Commentary
on John, 19:III:16: JTS 42 (1991) 596-8.
4917 *Simonetti* Manlio, [Gv 8,20] ORIGENE e la povera vedova; commento a
Giovanni 19,7-10 (40-58): RivStoLR 27 (1991) 475-481.
4918 *a) Rodríguez Carballo* José, La verdad os hará libres (Jn 8,32); – *b)*
Mielgo Constantino, Cautiverio y libertad; experiencia bíblica; – *c) Salas*
Antonio, La comunidad primitiva; proceso y oferta de liberación: BibFe
51 (1991) 338-358 / 316-337 / 359-382 (... al.).
4919 **Brooks** Alan D., Responses to the light; sight and blindness in the
characters of John 9: diss. Baylor 1991. 269 p. 92-14709. – DissA 52
(1991s) 4365-A.
4920 *Roth* David L., Behold my servant; John 9: Kerux 1,2 (1986) 27-37.
4921 *Müller* Mogens, 'Have you faith in the Son of Man?' (John 9.35):
NTS 37 (1991) 291-4.
ᴱ**Beutler** J., *Fortna* R., Shepherd, John 10, 1985/91 ➤ 417.
4922 *Reinhardt* Klaus, Christus, der 'kleine' Hirte; pastorale Christologie bei
JOHANNES vom Kreuz and Luis de LEÓN: TrierTZ 100 (1991) 114-125.
4923 *a) Bottino* Adriana, La metafora della porta (Gv 10,7.9); – *b) Segalla*
Giuseppe, Gesù *anēr* e *anthrōpos* nel quarto vangelo: RivB 39 (1991)
207-215 / 201-6.
4924 *Skedros* J. C., The works of Jesus; a study of John 10:22-39: DeltioVM
10,2 (1991) 51-56; ⊕ 56s.
4925 *Treu* Kurt, [Joh 10,29s] P. Berol. 21315, Bibelorakel mit griechischer und
koptischer Hermeneia: ArPapF 37 (1991) 55-60.

4925* **Bridges** J. J., Structure and history in John 11; a methodological
study comparing structuralist and historical critical approaches [diss.
Graduate Theological Union, ᴰ*Boyle* J., Berkeley]: Distinguished Dis-

sertations 4. SF 1991, Mellen. viii-313 p. $50 pa. 0-7734-9942-3 [NTAbs 36,410].

4926 **Byrne** Brendan, Lazarus, a contemporary reading of John 11:1-46: GlazierZacchaeus. ColMn 1991, Liturgical. 94 p. $7 [TDig 38,392]. 0-8146-5657-9.

4927 *Dubied* Pierre-Luigi, Lazarus – Raskolnikow; eine Begegnung mit vielschichtigen Verwicklungen: ➤ 170, FZUMSTEIN J., 1991, 159-173.

4928 *Heffner* Blake R., Meister ECKHART and a millennium with Mary and Martha: ➤ 58, FFROEHLICH K., Biblical hermeneutics 1991, 117-130.

4929 **Kremer** J., Lazarus, Jn 11: 1985 ➤ 1,5340...4,5591: RCiuD 203 (1991) 493 (J. *Gutiérrez*).

4930 **Larder** Dale R., The role of the Lazarus story in the redaction of the Fourth Gospel: diss. Marquette, DHills J. V. Milwaukee 1991. 91-33798. – DissA 52 (1991s) 3322s-A.

4931 **Marchadour** A., Lazare 1988 ➤ 4,5592...6,5851: RCiuD 203 (1990) 740s (J. *Gutiérrez*).

4932 *Paschos* P. B., ☉ The righteous friend of Christ, Lazarus, in Byzantine hymnography: TAth 62 (1991) 91-103. 344-377; Eng. 928.

4933 **Wagner** Josef, Auferstehung... Joh 11, D1988 ➤ 4,5588b...6,5852: RCiuD 203 (1990) 741-3 (J. *Gutiérrez*); ColcT 61,1 (1991) 168-170 (J. *Łach* ☉); Gregorianum 72 (1991) 191s (G. *Ferraro*); RechSR 79 (1991) 314s (X. *León-Dufour*: 'modèle d'exploration archéologique du texte').

4934 *Wuellner* W., Rhetorical criticism and its theory in culture-critical perspective; the narrative rhetoric of John 11: ➤ 307, Text 1991, 171-185.

4935 *Rigato* Maria Luisa, [Gv 11,2...] Maria di Betania nella redazione giovannea: Antonianum 66 (1991) 203-226; Eng. 203.

4936 *Story* Cullen I. K., The mental attitude of Jesus at Bethany; John 11. 33,38: NTS 37 (1991) 51-66.

4937 *Trudinger* Paul, [Jn 12,12] Hosanna to the son of David; St John's perspective: DowR 109 (1991) 297-301.

4938 *Cachia* Nicholas, The servant in a fellowship of suffering and life with the Lord; an exegesis of John 12,26: MeliT 43,1 (1991) 39-60.

4939 **Bettan** Giorgio, Attirerò tutti a me (Gv 12,32): Cor Christi 11. R 1991, Apost. Preghiera. 150 p. Lit. 15.000.

4940 **Kühschelm** Roman G., Verstockung, Gericht und Heil; exegetische und bibeltheologische Untersuchung zum 'Dualismus' und 'Determinismus' in Joh 12,35-50 [kath. Hab-Diss. Wien 1990, DKremer] 1990 ➤ 6,5856: RRechSR 79 (1991) 291-3 (X. *Léon-Dufour*); TPQ 139 (1991) 323s (C.-P. *März*).

G1.8 Jn 13... Sermo sacerdotalis et Passio.

4941 *a) Tolmie* D. F., The function of focalization in John 13-17; – *b) Rand* J. A. du, Perspectives on Johannine discipleship according to the farewell discourses; – *c) Toit* B. A. du, The aspect of faith in the Gospel of John with special reference to the farewell discourses of Jesus; – *d) Domeris* W. R., The farewell discourse; an anthropological approach; – *e) Bammel* C. P., The farewell discourse in patristic exegesis: Neotestamentica 25 (1991) 273-287 / 311-325 / 327-340 / 233-250 / 193-207.

4942 *a) Lombard* H. A., *Oliver* W. H., A working supper in Jerusalem; John 13:1-38 introduces Jesus' farewell discourses; – *b) Oliver* W. H., *Aarde* A. G. van, The community of faith as dwelling-place of the Father;

basileía toû theoû as 'household of God' in the Johannine farewell discourse(s):   Neotestamentica 25 (1991) 357-378 / 379-400.

4943 **Thomas** John C.,   Footwashing in John 13 and the Johannine community: JStNT supp 61.   Sheffield 1991, Academic.   214 p. £22; sb. £18.75.

4944 *Moloney* Francis J.,   A sacramental reading of John 13:1-38:   CBQ 53 (1991) 237-256.

4945 **Kurz** William S., [Jn 13s, 15s, Acts 20, Lk 22] Farewell addresses in the New Testament: GlazierZc.   ColMn 1990, Liturgical.   134 p. $8 [RelStR 18,141, C. *Bernas*].

4946 *Léon-Dufour* Xavier,   Le cri de triomphe de Jésus, Jn 13,31-32: ➤ 121, ᶠRAMAROSON L., Ta parole 1991, 43-49.

4946* **McCaffrey** J.,   The house / Temple... Jn 14,2s: AnBib 114, ᴰ1988 ➤ 4, 5606; 5,5581: ᴿRAg 31 (1990) 289s (S. *Sabugal*).

4947 *La Potterie* Ignace de,   'Chi vede me vede il Padre' (Gv 14,9);   dalla storia al mistero: ➤ 504, L'ombra di Dio 1990/1, 53-71.

4948 *Slater* T. B., [Jn 14,16 ...] The Paraclete as advocate in the community of the Beloved Disciple: AfTJ 20,2 (Tanzania 1991) 101-8 [< NTAbs 36,354].

4949 **Breck** John,   Spirit of truth; the Holy Spirit in Johannine tradition, I. The origins of Johannine pneumatology.   Crestwood NY 1991, St. Vladimir.   xviii-188 p. $11.   0-88141-081-0 [TDig 39,152].

4950 *Tilborg* S. van,   Ideology and text; John 15 in the context of the farewell discourse: ➤ 307, Text 1991, 259-270.

4951 *a) Dettwiler* Andreas,   Umstrittene Ethik – Überlegungen zu Joh 15,1-17 [neither consistently ethical nor non-ethical]: – *b) Bühler* Pierre,   Ist Johannes eine Kreuzestheologie? Exegetisch-systematische Bemerkungen zu einer noch offenen Debatte: ➤ 170, ᶠZUMSTEIN J., 1991, 175-189 / 191-207.

4952 *a) Smidt* J. C. de,   A perspective on John 15:1-8; – *b) Hartin* P. J., Remain in me (John 15:5); the foundation of the ethical and its consequences in the farewell discourse: Neotestamentica 25 (1991) 251-272 / 341-356.

4953 *Laskey* Dennis A.,   LUTHER's exposition of John 17:   CurrTMiss 18 (1991) 204-8.

4954 *Livrea* Enrico, *a)* NONNO interprete in Ev. Jo. 18,4-7; – *b)* Towards a new edition of NONNUS' Paraphrase of St. John's Gospel: ➤ 223, Studia Hellenistica II (1991) 479-484 / 485-490.

4955 **Koen** Lars,   The saving Passion; incarnational and soteriological thought in CYRIL of Alexandria's commentary on the Gospel according to John [diss. Uppsala 1991]: AcU DocChr 31.   Sto 1991, Almqvist & W.   149 p.   91-554-2696-4. – ST 45 (1991) 175. – ᴿETL 67 (1991) 442-4 (A. de *Halleux*).

4956 *Koester* C. R.,   The Passion and Resurrection according to John: WWorld 11,1 (1991) 84-91 [< NTAbs 35,170].

4957 **La Potterie** I. de,   La Passion de Jésus selon l'Évangile de Jean, Texte et Esprit 1986 ➤ 2,4290 ... 5,5596: ᴿBrotéria 132 (1991) 477s (F. de *Sales Baptista*).

4958 **Senior** Donald,   The Passion of Jesus in the Gospel of John: Passion Series 4.   ColMn/Leominster 1991, Liturgical/Gracewing.   176 p. $11. 0-8146-5462-2 [TDig 39,187].

4959 *Natale* Giuseppe,   L'arresto di Gesù nel Quarto Vangelo; una vittoria della comunicazione: Sapienza della Croce 6,1 (1991) 15 ...

4960 *Gros* Jean, Voilà l'homme selon Jean, XVIII,1-XIX,16: Esprit 59,9 (P 1991) 64-75 [< NTAbs 36,193].

4961 **Panackel** Charles, Idou o Anthropos (Jn 19,5b): AnGreg 251, ᴰ1988 ⇸ 4,5621 ...6,5887: ᴿSalesianum 53 (1991) 771s (C. *Bissoli*).

4962 **Urbán** Ángel, El origen divino del poder; estudio teológico e historia de la interpretación de Jn 19,11a: EstFgNt 2, ᴰ1989 ⇸ 5,5602; 6,5888: ᴿFgNt [2,3 (1989) ⇸ 5,5602] 4 (1991) 222s (D. A. *Black*); NRT 113 (1991) 109s (Y. *Simoens*); RechSR 79 (1991) 313s (X. *Léon-Dufour*).

4963 *Trebolle Barrera* Julio, Posible substrato semítico del uso transitivo o intransitivo del verbo *ekáthisen* en Jn 19,13: FgNt 4,7 (1991) 51-54; Eng. 51.

4964 *Dennison* James T.ᴶ, Witnesses to the King; John 19:17-42: Kerux 5,2 (1990) 21-31.

4965 *Primentas* Nikolaos, ☯ [Jn 19,23] The tunic without seam; technological and hermeneutical approach: DeltioVM 10,2 (1991) 38-50; 5 fig.

4966 **Leone** Cosimo, La morte di Gesù e il dono dello Spirito (Gv 19,28-37: diss. Pont. Univ. Gregoriana, Teol. 6932, ᴰ*Rasco* E. R 1991s. - InfPUG 24/122,28.

4967 *Bruteau* Beatrice, [Jn 19,31] The great Sabbath: NBlackf 71 (1990) 132-147.

4968 *Schulz* Hans-Joachim, 'Der dies gesehen hat, legte Zeugnis dafür ab...' (Joh. 19,35); zeitgeschichtlich transparente Augenzeugenbürgschaft und liturgisch orientierte Christusanamnese im Johannesevangelium: ForumKT 7 (1991) 95-119.

4969 *Ducatillon* Jeanne, [Jn 19,40] Le linceul de Jésus d'après saint Jean: RThom 91 (1991) 421-4.

4970 *Visotzky* Burton L., [Jn 19,41; Ac. Thom] Three Syriac cruxes: JJS 42 (1991) 167-175.

4971 *Bernabé* Carmen, Trasfondo derásico de Jn 20: EstB 49 (1991) 209-228; Eng. 209.

4972 **Blanquart** Fabien, Le premier jour (Jn 20): LDiv 146. P 1991, Cerf. 177 p. F 112. 2-204-04401-6 [NTAbs 36,261].

4973 *Sabugal* Santos, [⇸ 4252] La resurrección de Jesús en el cuarto evangelio (Jn 20,1-29; 21,1-14): Salesianum 53 (1991) 649-667.

4974 *Derrett* J. D. M., Miriam and the Resurrection (John 20,16): BbbOr 33 (1991) 211-219 [34,56: missing accents inserted].

4975 *Rossum* Joost van, The 'Johannine Pentecost'; John 20:22 in modern exegesis and in Orthodox theology: StVlad 35 (1991) 149-167.

4976 *Perraymond* Myla, L'incredulità di Tommaso (Io. 20,25-29); iconografia e cenni patristici: SMSR 57 (1991) 21-41; 8 fig.

4977 *Hofrichter* Peter, Joh 21 im Makrotext des Vierten Evangeliums: TGL 81 (1991) 302-322.

G2.1 Epistulae Johannis.

4978 *Anderson* J., Cultural assumptions behind the First Epistle of John: NoTr 4,4 (1990) 39-44 (27-34 *en toútō, Larsen* I.) [< NTAbs 36,63].

4979 **Baur** Wolfgang, 1., 2. und 3. Johannesbrief: KLK NT 17. Stu 1991, KBW. 128 p. 3-460-15471-3.

4980 **Dalbesio** Anselmo, Quello che abbiamo udito e veduto; l'esperienza cristiana nella prima lettera di Giovanni: RivB supp 22, 1990 ⇸ 6,5912: ᴿLA 41 (1991) 576s (A. M. *Buscemi*); RTLv 22 (1991) 535 (J.-P. *Kaefer*).

4981 **Klauck** Hans-Josef, Der erste Johannesbrief: EkK NT 23/1. Z 1991, Benziger. xi-363 p. 3-545-23122-4 / Neuk 3-7887-1377-1.

4982 **Klauck** Hans-J., Die Johannesbriefe: Erträge der Forschung. Da 1991, Wiss. xix-186 p. [NTAbs 36,275]. 3-534-10008-5.

4983 *Klauck* Hans-Josef, Bekenntnis zu Jesus und Zeugnis Gottes; die christologische Linienführung im ersten Johannesbrief: → 72, FHAHN F., Anfänge 1991, 293-306.

4984 **Lieu** Judith M., The theology of the Johannine epistles: NTTheol. C 1991, Univ. xii-130 p. £22.50; pa. £8. 0-521-35246-0 [TDig 38,371]. – RExpTim 103 (1991s) 66 (C. S. *Rodd*).

4985 **Marshall** I. Howard, Las cartas de Juan [1978, TPadilla Washington I.], texto de la versión Reina Valera, revisión de 1960 con introducción, comentario i notas. Buenos Aires 1991, Nueva Creación. xv-275 p. 0-8028-0911-1.

4986 **Neufeld** Dietmar, Reconceiving texts as speech acts; an analysis of the First Epistle of John: diss. McGill, DWisse F. Montreal 1991. 248 p. DANN-67470. – DissA 53 (1992s) 344s-A; RTLv 23, p. 545.

4987 *Segalla* Giuseppe, Due recenti commenti alle lettere di Giovanni [STRECKER G. 1989; VOUGA F. 1990]: StPatav 38 (1991) 145-9.

4988 **Smith** D. M., 1-3 John: Interpretation comm. Louisville 1991, Knox. viii-164 p. $18. 0-8042-3147-8 [NTAbs 36,279].

4989 *Staden* P. J. van, The debate on the structure of 1 John: HervTSt 47 (1991) 487-502 [< NTAbs 36,210].

4990 **Strecker** Georg, Die Johannesbriefe: KeK NT 14, 1989 → 5,5623; 6,5909: RCBQ 53 (1991) 718s (P. J. *Cahill*); TPhil 66 (1991) 576 (J. *Beutler*).

4991 **Vouga** François, Die Johannesbriefe: HbNT 15/3, 1990 → 6,5910: RExpTim 102 (1990s) 269 (E. *Best*); JTS 42 (1991) 691s (Judith *Lieu*).

4992 *Washburn* David L., Third class conditions [eán + subj.] in First John: GraceTJ 11 (1990) 221-8.

4993 *Watson* Duane F., An epideictic strategy for increasing adherence to community values; 1 John 1:1 - 2:27: ProcGLM 11 (1991) 144-152.

4994 *George* Martin, [1 Jn 1,18] Die Fälschung der Wahrheit und des Guten; Gestalt und Wesen des Antichrist im 19. Jahrhundert [ev. Theologie]: ZKG 102 (1991) 76-103.

4995 **Jenks** Gregory C., The origins and early development of the Antichrist myth [term possibly coined by 1 John, but for a much earlier tradition including Dan 7, though not à la BOUSSET; diss. Queensland 1989]: BZNW 59. B 1991, de Gruyter. 416 p. DM 158. 3-11-012405-X. – RExpTim 103 (1991s) 182 (M. *Casey*); NT 33 (1991) 374-7 (L. J. *Lietaert Peerbolte*).

4996 *Breck* John, The function of *pâs* in 1 John 2:20: StVlad 35 (1991) 187-208.

4997 *Boer* Martinus C. de, The death of Jesus Christ and his coming in the flesh (1 John 4:2): NT 33 (1991) 326-346.

4998 **Breck** John [1 Jn 4,6] Spirit of truth; the origins of Johannine pneumatology. Crestwood NY 1991, St. Vladimir. 188 p. $11 [RelStR 18, 333, Joyce *Woolridge*].

4999 *Wendland* E. R., What is truth?... semantic density 2 Jn 1990 → 6,5919 = NoTr 5,2 (1991) 31-60 [< NTAbs 36,376].

5000 *Klauck* Hans J., [3 Joh 12...] Kirche als Freundesgemeinschaft? Auf Spurensuche im NT: MüTZ 42 (1991) 1-14.

G2.3 *Apocalypsis Johannis* – Revelation: text, introduction.

5001 **Blanchard** Robert, L'Apocalypse ou révélation de Jésus-Christ[2] abrégée. Mazaugues c. 1990, auct. F 135. – [R]EsprVie 101 (1991) 48 (É. *Cothenet*: 'universalisant', moralisant).

5002 **Boring** M. Eugene, Revelation: Interpretation Comm 1989 ➤ 5,5643; 6,5922: [R]CritRR 4 (1991) 173-5 (L. L. *Thompson*); Interpretation 45 (1991) 45 (1991) 187-9 (Adela Y. *Collins*: appreciating the Apocalypse as a whole).

5003 **Campo Hernández** Alberto del, Comentario al Apocalipsis de APRINGIO de Beja, texto latino y traducción: Inst. S. Jerónimo 25. Estella 1991, VDivino. 222 p. 84-7151-760-4.

5004 *Campo Hernández* Alberto del, Un exegeta lusitano del Apocalipsis, Apringio de Beja: ➤ 421, Luso-Esp 1989/91, 433-7.

5005 **Charlier** J.-P., Comprendre l'Apocalypse I-II: Lire la Bible 90. P 1991 Cerf. 582 p. (306 p., 284 p. F 109 chaque). 2-204-04191-2; -245-5. – [R]ArTGran 54 (1991) 357-360 (F. *Contreras*: no sólo comentario; método hermenéutico); EsprVie 101 (1991) 256 (É. *Cothenet*: hypothèses aventureuses à côté d'explications solidement fondées).

5006 [TE]**Courreau** Joël, L'Apocalypse expliquée par CÉSAIRE d'Arles + [TE]*Bouquet* Solanges, Scholies attribuées à ORIGÈNE; intr. *La Potterie* I. de, *Hamman* H.-G.: Les Pères dans la Foi 36, 1989 ➤ 5,5646; 6,5923: [R]StMonast 33 (1991) 174 (J. A. *Rocha*).

5007 **Foulkes** R., El Apocalipsis desde América Latina 1989 ➤ 5,5648; 6,5924: [R]Iter 2 (1991) 131s (J.-P. *Wyssenbach*).

5008 **Giblin** Charles H., The Book of Revelation; the open book of prophecy: Glazier Good News 34. ColMn 1991, Liturgical. 231 p. $15. 0-8146-5005-8 [TDig 39,62].

5009 **Guimond** John, The silencing of Babylon; a spiritual commentary on the Revelation of John. NY 1991, Paulist. iv-124 p. $9. 0-8091-3239-7.

5010 **Hartingsveld** L. van, Revelation, a practical commentary [T]1985 ➤ 2,4326; 3,5479: [R]RelStT 10,2 (1990) 124s (A. E. *Milton*).

5011 **Hughes** Philip E., [† May 1990], The book of Revelation, a commentary [➤ 6,5927]. Leicester/GR 1990, Inter-Varsity/Eerdmans. 242 p. $18. /0-8028-3684-4. – [R]RExp 88 (1991) 271s (A. A. *Trites*: fresh; no interaction with secondary literature).

5012 *Mazzaferri* Fred, Commentaries on Revelation — a translator's guide: BTrans 42 (1991) 133-9.

5013 **Minear** Paul S., Revelation: Interpretation Comm ...: [R]Mid-Stream 30 (1991) 92s (M. E. *Boring*).

5014 **Prévost** J.-P., Pour lire l'Apocalypse. Ottawa/P 1991, Novalis/Cerf. 160 p.; ill. [NRT 114,941, A. *Toubeau*].

5015 **Reiswitz** Wenzel von, Ich mache alles neu; das letzte Buch der Heiligen Schrift, Vorw. *Hennig* K. Metzingen 1991, Franz. 200 p. [TLZ 117,437].

5016 **Schmolinsky** Sabine, Der Apokalypsenkommentar des ALEXANDER Minorita; zur frühen Rezeption Joachims von FIORE in Deutschland [Diss. München]: MonGermHist ST 3. Hannover 1991, Hahn. xv-128 p. DM 40 [RHE 87,41*].

5017 **Schüssler Fiorenza** Elisabeth, Revelation; vision of a just world: Proclamation comm. Mp 1991, Fortress. x-150 p., map. $10. 0-8006-2510-2 [TDig 39,261].

5018 **Sweet** John, Revelation: TPI NT 1990 → 6,5934: [R]ÉTRel 66 (1991) 127 (E. *Cuvillier*).

5019 **Thompson** Leonard L., The book of Revelation; apocalypse and empire. NY 1990, Oxford-UP. 265 p. $30. − [R]AndrUnS 29 (1991) 188-190 (K. A. *Strand*); JBL 110 (1991) 748-790 (Adela Y. *Collins*).

5020 **Vanni** Ugo, L'Apocalisse; ermeneutica esegesi teologia: RivBSupp 17, 1988 → 4,5676... 6,5936: [R]Antonianum 66 (1991) 157s (M. *Nobile*); AugR 30 (1990) 217s (P. *Grech*); FgNt 4 (1991) 81s (J. *Mateos*); HeythJ 32 (1991) 401s (H. J. *Richards*: too leisurely); Salesianum 53 (1991) 589s (C. *Bissolì*).

5021 — *Uricchio* Francesco, [Apc 1,3] 'Beato chi legge e coloro che ascoltano' [VANNI U. 1988]: MiscFranc 91 (1991) 393-400.

5022 **Wall** Robert W., Revelation: New International [Version] Biblical Commentary 18. Peabody MA 1991, Hendrickson. xv-295 p. $10 pa. 0-943575-49-4 [NTAbs 36,279].

G2.4 *Apocalypsis,* **Revelation, topics.**

5023 *a*) *Aune* David E., Intertextuality and the genre of the Apocalypse; − *b*) *Linton* Gregory, Reading the Apocalypse as an apocalypse; − *c*) *Snyder* Barbara W., Triple-form and space/time transitions; literary structuring devices in the Apocalypse; − *d*) *Humphrey* Edith M., The sweet and the sour; epics of wrath and return in the Apocalypse; the Apocalypse as a macro-genre: → 446, SBL Sem 30 (1991) 142-160 / 161-186 / 440-450 / 451-460.

5025 *a*) *Buzzetti* Carlo, 'Sangue' nell'Apocalisse; semantica e traduzione; − *b*) *Bottino* Adriana, Il sangue di Cristo nel commento all'Apocalisse di Ambrogio AUTPERT: → 565, Sangue 1989/91, 313-326 / 975-983.

5027 *Clapp* R., Overdosing on the Apocalypse: ChrTod 35,12 (1991) 26-29 [< NTAbs 36,216].

5028 *Festa* Francesco Saverio, Apocalisse e storia [LA ROCCA T., Es ist Zeit, Apocalisse e storia ... MÜNTZER]: RasT 32 (1991) 532-6.

5029 *a*) *Ford* Josephine M., Persecution and martyrdom in the Book of Revelation; − *b*) *Osiek* Carolyn, Early Christian theology of martyrdom: BToday 28 (1990) 141-6 / 153-7.

5030 *Fredriksen* Paula, Apocalypse and redemption in early Christianity, from John of Patmos to AUGUSTINE of Hippo: VigChr 45 (1991) 151-183.

5031 *Groote* Marc De, Die *sýnopsis scholikē* aus dem Kommentar des OECUMENIUS zur Apokalypse [mit gr. Text]: SacrEr 32 (1991) 107-119.

5032 **Hill** Robert A., An examination and critique of the understanding of the relationship between apocalypticism and gnosticism in Johannine studies: diss. McGill, [D]*Wisse* F. Montreal 1991. − RTLv 23, p. 544; RelStR 18,173.

5033 *Holtz* Traugott, Gott in der Apokalypse [< BtETL 53 (1980) 247-265]: → 211, Geschichte 1991, 329-346.

5034 **Humphrey** Edith Mary, The ladies and the cities; transformation and apocalyptic identity in Joseph and Aseneth, IV Ezra, the Apocalypse and the Shepherd of Hermas: diss. McGill, [D]*Runnalls* D. Montreal 1991. 355 p. DANN-67760. − DissA 53 (1992s) 801-A; RelStR 18,173; RTLv 23, p. 544.

5035 TEIsaac Jean [O.P.], L'Apocalypse de Jésus Christ: les épreuves de l'Alliance et le sens de l'histoire. P 1991, Cerf. 109 p. 2-204-04329-X. – REsprVie 101 (1991) 523s (L. *Walter* ne recommande pas; 'aus yeux de Dieu Satan est par nature à la fois son chef-d'œuvre et son fils' ...).

5036 **Jones** Benny J., A study of the Son of Man in Revelation with special reference to the Suffering Servant motif: diss. Baptist Theol. Sem. D*Smith* B. K. New Orleans 1990. 91-17904. – DissA 52 (1991s) 185s-A.

5037 **Kamp** H. R. van de, Israël in Openbaring; een onderzoek naar de plaats van het joodse volk in het toekomstbeeld van de Openbaring van Johannes: diss. Kampen, Univ. Geref. Kerken, D*Bruggen* J. van. Kampen 1990, Kok. 380 p. ƒ60. 90-242-5112-5. – TsTNijm 31 (1991) 220; NTAbs 36,128.

5038 *a) Kuhn* Cynthia L., The fine line; the relevance of apocalyptic today; – *b) Witherup* Ronald D., Revelation and conversion; an analysis of Flannery O'CONNOR's 'Revelation': BToday 28 (1990) 267-9 / 270-276.

5039 *Liverziani* Filippo, Verso l'Apocalisse, dove si compie il destino dell'uomo. R 1991, Hermes. 180 p.

5040 **Lowery** Robert A., Holy living in an unholy world; the doctrine of the Christian life in the Book of Revelation: diss. D*Edwards* R. Aberdeen 1991. – RTLv 23, p. 545.

5041 **Lumpkin** Walter H., A comparative study of the concept of temple and its imagery in the writings of the Qumran community and in the Apocalypse: diss. Baptist Theol. Sem., D*Simmons* B. New Orleans 1991. 211 p. 91-37410. – DissA 52 (1991s) 2597-A.

5042 **Mazzaferri** Frederich D., Genre of Revelation ... [diss. Aberdeen D*Edwards* Ruth]: BZNW 54, 1989 ➤ 5,5683: RAndrUnS 29 (1991) 98-100 (J. *Paulien*); ArTGran 54 (1991) 361-6 (F. *Contreras*).

5043 *Peterson* E. H., Learning to worship from John's Revelation: ChrTod 35,12 (1991) 23-25 [< NTAbs 36,211].

5044 **Pousseur** R., *Montalembert* J. de, Le cri de l'Apocalypse. P 1990, Centurion; 162 p. F 90. 2-227-31089-8 [NTAbs 36,277: text in form of a drama]. – REsprVie 101 (1991) 523 (L. *Walter*: ...pas d'exégèse, bien que basé sur d'études sérieuses; visant les personnes cultivées attachées à leur Église même s'ils la critiquent beaucoup).

5045 *Raja* R. J., 'As it was in the beginning...' eco-spirituality in the Book of Revelation: Vidyajyoti 55 (1991) 681-697.

5046 *Rand* J. A. du, Twaalf honderd en sestig dae' lank in die krisis: Scriptura 36 (Stellenbosch 1991) 17-37 [< NTAbs 36,65].

5047 **Ranisavljevic** Daniel, Le témoignage de Jésus et celui des fidèles dans l'Apocalypse de Jean: diss. Inst. Cath., D*Cothenet* É. Paris 1991. 262 p. – RTLv 23, p. 546.

5048 **Ravasi** Gianfranco, Vieni, Signore Gesù; un invito alla speranza nel libro dell'Apocalisse: Frammenti di saggezza biblica 6. T 1990, Paoline. 199 p. Lit. 12.000 pa. 88-215-2044-7 [NTAbs 36,124].

5049 *Rosenau* Hartmut, Die 'masslose' Natur — apokalyptische Naturerfahrung im Ausgang von der Johannesoffenbarung: TPhil 66 (1991) 384-397.

5050 **Sand** Alexander, Jüdische und christliche Apokalyptik; exegetische Fragen und theologische Aspekte: Renovatio 45 (1989) 12-24 > TDig 38 (1991) 327-332, 'Apocalyptic and the Apocalypse', TE*Asen* B. A.

5051 *Satake* Akira, Christologie in der Johannesapokalypse im Zusammenhang mit dem Problem des Leidens der Christen: ➤ 72, FHAHN F., Anfänge 1991, 307-322.

5052 **Schiller** Gertrud, Ikonographie der christlichen Kunst 5/2, Die Apokalypse des Johannes, Bildteil. Gü 1991, Mohn. 1264 p. DM 990. 3-579-00262-7.

5053 *Schmidt* Daryl D., Semitisms and Septuagintalisms in the Book of Revelation: NTS 37 (1991) 592-603.

5054 *Sieg* Franciszek, ℗ Określenia chrześcijan [determination of the Christians] w Apokalipsie św. Jana 4-22: Bobolanum 1 (1990) 88-101.

5055 **Snyder** Barbara W., Combat myth in the Apocalypse; the liturgy of the day of the Lord and the dedication of the heavenly temple: diss. Univ/GTU, ᴰWuellner W. Berkeley 1991. 406 p. 91-26307. – DissA 52 (1991s) 1374-A; RelStR 18,173.

5056 *Strand* Kenneth A., 'Overcomer'; a study in the macrodynamic of theme development in the Book of Revelation: AndrUnS 28 (1990) 237-254.

5057 *Vanni* Ugo, *a)* L'Apocalisse e il Vangelo di Luca: ⇥ 124, ᶠRasco E., Luca-Atti 1991, 17-37; – *b)* La figura della donna nell'Apocalisse: StMiss 40 (1991) 57-94; – *c)* Liturgical dialogue as a literary form in the Book of Revelation: NTS 37 (1991) 348-372.

5058 *Wendland* E. R., 7 × 7 (× 7); a structural and thematic outline of John's Apocalypse: OPTAT 4 (1990) 371-387 [< NTAbs 36,65].

5059 *Witherup* Ronald D., Visions in the book of Revelation: BToday 28 (1990) 19-24; ill.

5060 **Woods** Deane J., STATIUS' 'Silvae' and John's 'Apocalypse', some [11 simultaneously] parallel and contrastive motifs: diss. Dallas Theol. Sem. 1990. 374 p. 91-25350. – DissA 52 (1991s) 1729-A.

5061 *Zager* Werner, Begriff und Wertung der Apokalyptik in der neutestamentlichen Forschung: EurHS 23/358. Fra 1989, Lang. 534 p. Fs. 79. 3-631-40885-4. – ᴿCarthaginensia 7 (1991) 262s (R. *Sanz Valdivieso*).

G2.5   *Apocalypsis,* **Revelation 1,1 ...**

5062 *a)* *Adinolfi* Marco, I cristiani 'sacerdoti' secondo Apc. 1,6; 5,10 e 20,6 nella interpretazione di TERTULLIANO; – *b)* *Corsini* Eugenio, Per una nuova lettura dell'Apocalisse; – *c)* *Rossano* Piero, Ipotesi di un 'corpus ephesinum Novi Testamenti': ⇥ 451, Efeso I, 1990/1, 99-109 / 75-97 / 17-32.

5063 *Michaels* J. Ramsey, Revelation 1.19 and the narrative voices of the Apocalypse: NTS 37 (1991) 604-620.

5064 *Smith* Christopher R., Revelation 1:19, an eschatologically escalated prophetic convention: JEvTS 461-6 [< ZIT 91,269].

5065 **Marcato** Giorgio, Le chiese dell'Apocalisse, storia e teologia: diss. Angelicum, ᴰSalguero J. R 1991, Univ. S. T. Aquinatis. 227 p.

5066 *Mottu* Henry, Apocalypse 2-3 comme modèle homilétique: BCentProt 43,1s (1991) 3-18 [19-35, *Bonhoeffer* D., (Apc 2,4-7) Prédication pour la fête de la Réformation; 25-35, *Ruff* Pierre-Yves].

5067 *Heiligenthal* Roman, [Apk 2,6.15] Wer waren die 'Nikolaiten'? Ein Beitrag zur Theologiegeschichte des frühen Christentums: ZNW 82 (1991) 133-7; skeptics.

5068 *Tarocchi* Stefano, Il ruolo del 'soggetto interpretante' nella lettera a Laodicea (Ap 3,14-21): VivH 1 (1990) 31-41.

5069 *Rand* J. A. du, Die narratiewe funksie van die liedere in Openbaring 4:1-5:15: SkrifKerk 12,1 (1991) 26-35 [< NTAbs 36,212].

5070 **Manna** Salvatore, [Apc 5,1] Il 'De septem sigillis' di BENEDETTO di Bari [1227] e la teologia fra XI e XIII secolo: Nicolaus 17,1s (1990) intero volume; xxiv-423 p.; ill.

5071 **Rosenthal** Marvin, [Rev 6,17...] The pre-wrath rapture of the Church. Nv 1990, Nelson. – RBS 148 (1991) 90-111 (G. B. *Stanton*: strange, often false).

5072 *Bauckham* Richard, The list of the tribes in Revelation 7 again: JStNT 42 (1991) 99-115.

5073 **Louis** Jeffrey, An expositional study of the 144,000 in the Book of the Revelation [7,1-17; 14,1-5]: diss. Dallas Theol. Sem., DPentecost J. D. 1990. 226 p. 91-25342. – DissA 52 (1991s) 967-A.

5074 **Ulfgard** Håkan, Feast and future, Rev 7:9-17 and the Feast of Tabernacles: ConBib NT 22, 1989 ➤ 5,5713 [6,5984 '*Håkan* U.']: RCBQ 53 (1991) 723s (L. L. *Thompson*); JBL 110 (1991) 551-3 (R. *Morton*); RechSR 79 (1991) 314s (X. *Léon-Dufour*); SvEx 56 (1991) 149-151 (J. H. *Ulrichsen*, svensk).

5075 *Wilcox* Max, 'Silence in heaven' (Rev 8:1) and early Jewish thought: ➤ 420, Mogilany 1989-II, 241-4.

5076 **Paulien** Jon, Decoding Revelation's trumpets; literary allusions and interpretations of Revelation 8:7-12: Diss. 11. Berrien Springs MI 1988, Andrews Univ. xi-497 p. $15 pa. – RAndrUnS 28 (1990) 269-271 (S. *Thompson*).

5077 **Brighton** Louis A., The angel of Revelation [10]; an angel of God and an icon of Jesus Christ: diss. DO'Toole R. St. Louis 1991. 249 p. 91-30981. – DissA 52 (1991s) 1783-A; RTLv 23, p. 542.

5078 *a) Combet-Galland* Corina, *Smyth-Florentin* François, Apocalypse 10 — l'urgence de la mémoire; – *b) Barthélemy* Dominique, L'intégration de l'espace et du temps dans la nouvelle Jérusalem: ➤ 30, FBONNARD P., Mémoire 1991, 171-7 / 179-190.

5079 **Min Byong-Seob** Paolo, I due testimoni di Apocalisse 11,1-13; storia, interpretazione, teologia: diss. Pont. Univ. Gregoriana, DVanni U. Roma 1991. 448 p. [No 3724, 463 p.: RTLv 23, p. 545].

5080 *Minear* Paul S., Far as the curse is found; the point of Revelation 12:15-16: NT 33 (1991) 71-77.

5081 *DeSilva* David A., The 'Image of the Beast' and the Christians in Asia Minor; escalation of sectarian tension in Revelation 13: TrinJ 12 (1991) 185-208.

5082 *Judge* Edwin A., The mark of the beast, Revelation 13:16: TyndB 42 (1991) 158-160.

5083 *Aune* David E., A Latinism in Revelation 15:2 [victory over (*ek*) the beast]: JBL 110 (1991) 691s.

5084 **Ruiz** Jean-Pierre, Ezekiel in Apc 16-19: EurUnivSt 23/376, D1989 ➤ 5,5718: RBLitEc 92 (1991) 148 (S. *Légasse*); JBL 110 (1991) 549-551 (J. *Paulien*).

5085 **Dyer** Charles H. (*Hunt* Angela E.), [Rev 17 & 18] The rise of Babylon. Wheaton IL 1991, Tyndale. 236 p. $9. – RBS 148 (1991) 363 (S. D. *Toussaint*).

5086 *a) Bauckham* Richard, The economic critique of Rome in Revelation 18; – *b) Griffin* Miriam, Urbs Roma, plebs and princeps; – *c) Mosley* D. J., Calgacus, clash of Roman and native: ➤ 412, Images of empire 1990/1, 47-90 / 19-46 / 107-121.

5087 [de Souza] **Nogueira** Paulo A., Der Widerstand gegen Rom in der Apokalypse des Johannes; eine Untersuchung zur Tradition des Falls von

Babylon in Apokalypse 18: Diss. Heidelberg 1991, ᴰ*Berger* K. – TR 87 (1991) 518; RTLv 23, p. 546.

G2.7 **Millenniarismus,** *Apc 20 ...*

5088 **Heid** Stefan, Chiliasmus und Antichrist-Mythos; eine frühchristliche Kontroverse um das Heilige Land: kath. Diss. Bonn, ᴰ*Dassmann,* 1991. – TR 87 (1991) 516.
5089 **Helms** C. R., The Apocalypse in the early Church; eschaton and millenium: diss. Oxford 1991. – RTLv 23, p. 544.
5090 *a) Tello Ingelmo* N., El milenarismo como exageración mesiánica; – *b) Metz* J.-B., Ante el peligro, meditación teológica sobre Lc 21 y el Apocalipsis de Juan; – *c) García Paredes* C. R., Recuperar el instinto escatológico y apocalíptico; – *d) Schillebeeckx* E., Mesianismo 'antimesiánico' de Jesús y los mesianismos exclusivamente humanos; – *e) Aparicio Rodríguez* A., Itinerario mesiánico del pueblo de Israel; – *f) Fernández* B., [*al.*] ¿Es mesiánica la vida religiosa?: Vida Religiosa 68,5 (1990) 351-362 / 347-350 / 322s / 337-346 / 324-336 / 363-370 [-399; < RET 52,261].
5090* *Moorhead* James H., Prophecy, millennialism, and biblical interpretation in nineteenth-century America: ➤ 58, ᶠFROEHLICH K., 1991, 291-302.
5091 **Rowland** C., Radical Christianity; a reading of recovery ['chiliastic mentality', MANNHEIM K...]. C/Ox 1988, Polity/Blackwell. vi-199 p. £8. 0-7456-0294-0. – ᴿTsTNijm 31 (1991) 327s (T. *Witvliet*).

5092 **Carlson** Stephen W., The relevance of apocalyptic numerology for the meaning of *chília été* in Revelation 20: diss. Mid-America Baptist Theol. Sem. 1990. 261 p. 91-18485. – DissA 52 (1991s) 190-A.
5093 **Adamson** James T., The concept of the millennium in Revelation 20:1-10; its origin and meaning: diss. Ottawa. 225 p. 0-315-60554-5 (DANN-60554). – DissA 52 (1991s) 3967-A.
5094 *Snyder* B. W., How millennial is the millennium? A study in the background of the 1000 years in Revelation 20: EvJ 9,2 (Myerstown PA 1991) 51-74 [< NTAbs 36,212].
5095 *Fritsch-Oppermann* Sybille, Das neue Jerusalem; Bibelarbeit zu Offenbarung 21,1-7: Diakonie (1991,2) 85-88 [< ZIT 91,383].
5096 *Hodges* J. C., [Rev 22,12] We believe in rewards: JGraceEv 4,2 (Roanoke TX 1991) 3-11 [< NTAbs 36,219].

XIII. Paulus

G3.1 **Pauli vita, stylus, chronologia.**

5097 **Amjad-Ali** Christine M., Paul's relation to non-Pauline Christianity; an examination of Paul's use of non-Pauline traditions: diss. Union, ᴰ*Scroggs* R. NY 1990. – RelStR 18,173.
5098 ᴱ**Babcock** William S., Paul and the legacies of Paul 1987/90 ➤ 6,510: ᴿCathHR 77 (1991) 492s (F. J. *Matera*); LvSt 16 (1991) 273s (R. F. *Collins*).
5099 **Barbaglio** Giuseppe, Pablo de Tarso y los orígenes cristianos [1985], ᵀ1989 ➤ 6,6005*b*: ᴿAugM 35 (1990) 396s (J. A. *Galindo*); CiTom 118 (1991) 183s (J. *Huarte*); TVida 32 (1991) 247s (B. *Villegas M.*).

5100 **Baslez** Marie-Françoise, Saint Paul. P 1991, Fayard. 440 p. F 150. 2-2130-2662-6. – ᴿÉtudes 375 (1991) 566s (J. *Thomas*); RAg 31 (1990) 973s (S. *Sabugal*).

5101 **Becker** Jürgen, Paulus, der Apostel der Völker 1989 ➤ 6,5739: ᴿExpTim 102 (1990s) 267s (E. *Best*); JTS 42 (1991) 672-5 (J. D. G. *Dunn*: first since BORNKAMM G. 1969); NT 33 (1991) 190-2 (J. S. *Vos*); RechSR 79 (1991) 40s (J.-N. *Aletti*); TLZ 116 (1991) 423s (H. *Räisänen*); TR 87 (1991) 18-21 (D. *Zeller*).

5102 **Beker** Johan Christiaan, Heirs of Paul; Paul's legacy in the New Testament and in the Church today. Mp 1991, Fortress. 146 p. $9. 0-8006-2525-0 [TDig 39,253; TS 53,601].

5103 **Beker** J. C., Paul the apostle; the triumph of God in his life and thought 1989 = 1980 ➤ 5,5740: ᴿNeotestamentica 25 (1991) 179s (P. J. *Gräbe*); ScotJT 44 (1991) 414s (E. *Best*).

5104 **Beker** J. Christiaan, The triumph of God; the essence of Paul's thought [abridgment and defense of 1980 Paul/triumph ➤ 61,6997], ᵀ*Stuckenbruck* Loren T., 1990 ➤ 6,6009: ᴿTS 52 (1991) 389 (B. *Fiore*).

5105 **Best** Ernest, Paul and his converts 1988 ➤ 4,5770 ... 6,6010: ᴿBibTB 21 (1991) 77s (A. J. *Tambasco*); HeythJ 32 (1991) 258 († F. F. *Bruce*); NBlackf 71 (1990) 149 (J. A. *Ziesler*); ScotJT 43 (1990) 527-9 (W. S. *Campbell*).

5106 **Blasi** A. J., Making charisma; the social construction of Paul's public image. New Brunswick 1991, Transaction. x-170 p. $30. 0-88738-400-5 [NTAbs 36,272].

5107 *Botermann* Helga, Paulus und das Urchristentum in der antiken Welt [BECKER J. 1989]: TRu 56 (1991) 296-305.

5108 **Callan** T., Psychological perspectives on the life of Paul; an application of the methodology of Gerd *Theissen*: StBeC 22. Lewiston NY 1990, Mellen. 161 p. $50. 0-88946-622-X. – ᴿTLZ 116 (1991) 593s (G. *Theissen*); TsTNijm 31 (1991) 99 (L. *Visschers*).

5109 **Campbell** William S., Paul's Gospel in an intercultural context. Fra 1991, Lang. 213 p. 3-631-42981-9 [ScotJT 44,549].

5110 **Castelli** Elizabeth A., Imitating Paul; a discourse of power [< diss. Claremont, ᴰ*Mack* B.]: Literary currents in biblical interpretation. Louisville 1991, W-Knox. 176 p. $16. 0-664-25234-6 [NTAbs 36,272].

5111 *Corsani* Bruno, Forza e debolezza nella vita e nel pensiero di Paolo: Benedictina 38 (1991) 5-17.

5112 **Ellis** E. Earle, Paul's use of the Old Testament: Twin Brooks. GR 1991 = 1957, Baker. xii-204 p. 0-8010-3368-3.

5113 *Ferrari* Leo C., AUGUSTINE's 'discovery' of Paul (Confessions 7.21.27): AugSt 22 (1991) 37-61.

5114 **Gerleman** G., Der Heidenapostel; ketzerische Erwägungen ... 1989 ➤ 5,5751 [NTAbs 36,120: what Paul calls 'solid food' means Greek myths]; – ᴿGymnasium 98 (1991) 286-8 (M. *Wolter*: maybe not a parody).

5115 **Gianantoni** Luigi, [➤ 6,6016 'Cianantoni'] La paternità apostolica di Paolo in rapporto al kerygma e alla paraklesi: diss. Pont. Univ. Gregoriana, ᴰ*Rasco* E. Roma 1991. 266 p. – RTLv 23, p. 544 [< DissA-C].

5116 *Giannarelli* E., Paolo, Tecla e la tradizione della Cilicia cristiana: Quaderni Storici 26 (Bo 1991) 185-203.

5117 *Gibson* George S., Go for the real [did Paul really 'hardly ever allow the real Jesus to get a word in' (JUNG)?]: ExpTim 103 (1991s) 76s.

5118 *a) Hengel* Martin, Der vorchristliche Paulus [➤ 6,6626]; – *b) Barrett* C. Kingsley, Paulus als Missionar und Theologe: ➤ 437, Paulus 1988/91, 177-291 (-3) / 1-15.

5119 **Hengel** Martin [*Deines* Roland: WUNT 1991], The pre-Christian Paul, ᵀ*Bowden* John. L/Ph 1991, SCM/Trinity. 162 p. £11.   0-334-02497-8 / Ph 1-36338-009-9. – ᴿExpTim 103 (1991s) 118 (D. *Catchpole*: agreeably lashing polemic against SCHMITHALS *al.*).

5120 **Hildebrandt** Dieter,   Saulo-Pablo, una doble vida [1989 ➤ 6,6028], ᵀ. Barc 1991, Herder.   454 p. – ᴿSFulg 1 (1991s) 172.

5122 **Holzner** Josef,   L'Apostolo Paolo [Tb. 1959], ᵀ*Dalmazio* Francesca, ᴱ*Bontempi* Franco.   Brescia 1987, Morcelliana.   333 p. Lit. 32.000.

5123 **Hubaut** Michel A.,   Paul de Tarse: BtHistChr 18, 1989 ➤ 5,5757; 6,6029: ᴿMélSR 48 (1991) 190-2 (L. *Derousseaux*); RTLv 22 (1991) 409s (J. *Ponthot*: < Catholicisme 10, 866-910 de 1985).

5124 **Hultgren** Arland J.,   The self-definition of Paul and his communities: SvEx 56 (1991) 78-100.

5125 **Ide** A. F.,   Battling with beasts; sex in the life and letters of St. Paul; the issue of homosexuality, heterosexuality and bisexuality.   Garland TX 1991, Tangelwüld.   121 p.; ill. $12.   0-934667-09-8 [NTAbs 36,275: Paul overreacts against his former homosexuality].

5126 **Krahe** Susanne,   Das riskierte ich; Paulus aus Tarsus; ein biografischer Roman.   Mü 1991, Kaiser.   266 p.   3-459-01888-7.

5127 **Laato** Timo,   Paulus und das Judentum; anthropologische Erwägungen.   Åbo 1991, Academy.   341 p.

5128 **Lapide** Pinchas, *Stuhlmacher* Peter,   Paulus – Rabbi en apostel; een joods-christelijke dialog.   Kampen 1988, Kok.   77 p. ƒ12,90.   90-242-4041-7. – ᴿBijdragen 52 (1991) (B. J. *Koet*).

5129 **Légasse** Simon,   Paul apôtre; essai de biographie critique.   P 1991, Cerf/Fides.   268 p.; 14 maps. F 150.   2-204-04267-6. – ᴿLA 41 (1991) 573s (A. M. *Buscemi*).

5130 **Lüdemann** G.,   Opposition to Paul in Jewish Christianity, ᵀ*Boring* M. 1989 ➤ 5,5765; 6,6034: ᴿInterpretation 45 (1991) 298-300 (R. *Scroggs*: the Jerusalem church versus Paul); SecC 8 (1991) 249-251 (Annewies van den *Hoek*).

5131 **Maccoby** Hyam,   The mythmaker 1986 ➤ 3,4437 (1990 UK): ᴿExpTim 103 (1991s) 26 (C. *Tuckett*).

5132 **Maccoby** Hyam,   Paul and Hellenism.   L 1991, SCM.   xii-222 p. £10 pa. [Tablet 245,547 adv.] 0-334-02485-4.

5133 *Maccoby* Hyam,   Paul and circumcision; a rejoinder: JQR [79 (1988s) 248-250, J. GAGER] 82 (1991s) 177-180.

5134 **Malherbe** Abraham J.,   Paul and the popular philosophers 1989 ➤ 5, 5768; 6,6036: ᴿAndrUnS 29 (1991) 93s (H. *Weiss*); AnglTR 73 (1991) 491s (A. K. M. *Adam*); CBQ 53 (1991) 526s (L. E. *Vaage*); Interpretation 45 (1991) 88 (F. W. *Danker*); Neotestamentica 25 (1991) 178s (J. C. *Thom*).

5135 **Martini** Carlo M.,   Pablo, en lo vivo del ministerio [1989 ➤ 6,6037*], ᵀ. Valencia 1991, Edicep.   120 p. – SFulg 1 (1991s) 169.

5136 **Messadié** Gérard,   L'incendiaire; vie de Saül, apôtre [... petit-fils d'Hérode le Grand par Antipater].   P 1991, Laffont. ➤ 3723 [BLitEc 92,292].

5137 *Michaels* J. Ramsey,   Paul and John the Baptist; an odd couple: TyndB 42 (1991) 245-260.

5138 *Mínguez* Dionisio,   Pablo de Tarso y el judaismo de la diáspora: ➤ 453, Orígenes 1989/91, 283-301.

5139 **Niebuhr** Karl-Wilhelm, Heidenapostel aus Israel; die jüdische Identität des Paulus nach ihrer Darstellung in seinen Briefen: Hab-Diss. Halle-Wittenberg 1991, ᴰ*Holtz*. – TR 87 (1991) 512.

5140 **Pak Yeong-Sik** James, Paul as missionary; a comparative study of missionary discourse in Paul's epistles and selected contemporary Jewish texts [diss. Pont. Ist. Biblico, ᴰ*Vanhoye* A., R 1990 → 6,6038]: EurUnivS 23/410. Fra 1991, Lang. vi-208 p. DM 63 [TR 88,164]. 3-631-43459-6. – ᴿNTAbs 35 (1991) 252 (D. J. *Harrington*).

5141 **Pastor Ramos** Federico, Pablo, un seducido por Cristo: El mundo de la Biblia. Estella 1991, VDivino. 202 p. 84-7151-741-8. – ᴿREspir 50 (1991) 707s (S. *Castro*).

5142 *Patterson* Stephen J., Paul and the Jesus tradition; it is time for another look: HarvTR 84 (1991) 23-41.

5143 *Penna* Romano, Problemi e natura della mistica paolina [< ᴱ*Ancilli* E., La mistica 1984, 181-221]: → 247, L'apostolo 1991, 630-675.

5144 **Plevnik** Joseph, What are they saying about Paul? 1986 → 2,4445 ... 5,5777: ᴿTLZ 116 (1991) 117 (J. *Rohde*).

5145 **Reck** Reinhold, Kommunikation und Gemeindeaufbau; eine Studie zur Entstehung, Leben und Wachstum paulinischer Gemeinden in den Kommunikationsstrukturen der Antike: SBB 22. Stu 1991, KBW. xii-354 p. DM 39 [TLZ 117,511, H. *Frankemölle*].

5146 **Riesner** Rainer, Die Frühzeit des Paulus; Studien zur Chronologie, Missionsstrategie und Theologie des Apostels bis zum ersten Thessalonicherbrief: ev. Hab.-Diss. Tübingen 1991, ᴰ*Stuhlmacher* P. – TR 87 (1991) 513; RTLv 23, p. 546.

5147 **Saffrey** H.-D., Histoire de l'apôtre Paul ou faire chrétien le monde [< MondeB 50-61]: Lire la Bible 91. P 1991, Cerf. 203 p. – ᴿEsprVie 101 (1991) 522s (L. *Walter*).

5148 **Sanders** E. P., Paul: Past Masters. Ox 1991, UP. 138 p. £5. 0-19-287679-1. – ᴿExpTim 103 (1991s) 61 (C. S. *Rodd*: invented dialogues tough but valuable); TLond 94 (1991) 224s (J. D. G. *Dunn*: very stimulating).

5149 **Sandnes** Karl Olav, Paul – one of the prophets? a contribution to the Apostle's self-understanding [diss. Oslo 1988 → 6,6046]: WUNT 2/43. Tü 1991, Mohr. vii-291 p. DM 84. 3-16-145557-6.

5150 **Segal** Alan F., Paul the convert 1990 → 6,6049: ᴿAmHR 96 (1991) 823s (F. F. *Bruce*); CritRR 4 (1991) 226-9 (Beverly R. *Gaventa*); JAAR 59 (1991) 418-420 (E. V. *Gallagher*); JJS 42 (1991) 269s (C. *Rowland*); NewTR 4,1 (1991) 110s (H. G. *Perelmuter*); VigChr 45 (1991) 203-5 (G. *Quispel*: 'by far the best book about Paul I have ever read; it revolutionizes Pauline studies').

5151 *Shillington* G., Paul's success in the conversion of Gentiles; dynamic center in cultural diversity: Direction 20,2 (1991) 125-134 [< NTAbs 36,198].

5152 **Tambasco** Anthony J., In the days of Paul; the social world and teaching of the Apostle. NY 1991, Paulist. vi-125 p.; ill.; maps. $7. 0-8091-3283-4.

5153 *Tuckett* Christopher M., Paul, tradition and freedom: TZBas 47 (1991) 307-325.

5154 *Vogüé* A. de, La Vita Pauli de S. Jérôme et sa datation; examen d'un passage-clé (ch. 6): → 18, ᶠBastiaensen A., Eulogia 1991, 395-406.

Vollenweider Samuel, ... Paulus-Mystik 1991 → a993.

5155 ᴱWedderburn A.J.M., Paul and Jesus 1989 ➤ 5,615; 6,6054: ᴿTLZ 116 (1991) 117s (K.T. *Kleinknecht*).

5156 *Wolff* Christian, Niedrigkeit und Verzicht in Wort und Weg Jesu und in der apostolischen Existenz des Paulus: TJb (Lp 1990) 129-140 [< ZIT 91,654].

5157 ᴱZincone Sergio, Giovanni CRISOSTOMO, Panegirici su san Paolo. R 1988, Città Nuova. 129 p. – ᴿAugR 30 (1990) 198 (O. *Pasquato*).

G3.2 Corpus paulinum; *introductio, commentarii.*

5158 ᴱAland Kurt, *al.*, Text und Textwert der griechischen Handschriften des NTs II. Die paulinischen Briefe: 1. Allgemeines, Römerbrief; 2. 1-2Kor.; 3. Gal bis Php; 4. Kol bis Heb: ArbNT Textf 16-19. B/NY 1991, de Gruyter. xvii-625 + 181* p. / 819 p. / 658 p. / 941 p. DM 280 + 280 + 228 + 318 [TR 88,372-6, J.K. *Elliott*].

5159 *Appleton* George, Paolo interprete di Cristo [1988], ᵀ*Vincenti* Francesco: Bibbia per tutti. Assisi 1991, Cittadella. 164 p. 88-308-0471-1.

5160 [ᴱArtola Antonio M.] Curso de exégesis sobre san Pablo, [I. Tes Gal Rom 1989 ➤ 5,5785*] II. Cor Caut Past Heb: Apuntes 'Teología Deusto', Manuales 5,8. Bilbao 1991, Deusto. 227 p.

5161 *Biffi* Inos, LANFRANCO esegeta di S. Paolo: ScuolC 118 (1990) 202-216 (217-230, convegno su Lanfranco, Pavia 21-24.IX.1989: *Marabelli* Costante).

5162 *Brown* John P., Inversion of social roles in Paul's letters: NT 33 (1991) 303-325.

5163 ᵀᴱCarena Carlo, San Paolo, Le lettere; testo a fronte; intr. *Luzi* Mario: I Millenni, 1990 ➤ 6,6058: ᴿRivStoLR 27 (1991) 519-523 (F. *Bolgiani*); StPatav 38 (1991) 202s (G. *Segalla*).

5164 **Clabeaux** J.J., Lost edition of the letters of Paul... MARCION: CBQ Mg 21, 1989 ➤ 5,5788; 6,6059: ᴿArTGran 53 (1990) 294s (A.S. *Muñoz*); CBQ 53 (1991) 320s (G.D. *Fee*).

5165 *Classen* Carl J., Paulus und die antike Rhetorik: ZNW 82 (1991) 1-33.

5166 *Cocchini* Francesca, Aspetti del paolinismo origeniano: AugR 31 (1991) 245-275.

5167 **Detering** Hermann, Paulus und die Paulusbriefe in der holländischen Radikalkritik: Diss. ᴰ*Schmithals* W. Berlin 1991. 552 p. [> Kontexte]. – RTLv 23, p. 543.

5168 **Fuerst** Norbert, Der Schriftsteller Paulus. Da 1989, Wiss. 138 p. DM 14,80. – ᴿCritRR 4 (1991) 192s (E.H. *Lovering*); TR 87 (1991) 376-9 (T. *Söding*).

5169 **Godet** F., Survol des épîtres de Paul: Réimpression 17. St. Léger 1991 = 1893, Emmaüs. 261 p. Fs 26 [NTAbs 36,275].

5170 **Hays** Richard B., Echoes of Scripture in the letters of Paul 1989 ➤ 5,5795; 6,6061: ᴿCBQ 53 (1991) 496-8 (Craig A. *Evans*: major); Interpretation 45 (1991) 88.90 (D.M. *Hay*); ModT 7 (1990s) 291s (D.B. *Martin*); TS 52 (1991) 732-4 (K.P. *Donfried*).

5172 **Keck** L.E., Paul and his letters² [= ¹1979 + 32 p. on Paul's theology in historical criticism]. Ph 1988, Fortress. x-164 p. – ᴿNeotestamentica 25 (1991) 181 (J.H. *Roberts*).

5173 **Locke** John, Paraphrase 1-2, ᴱ*Wainwright* A. 1987 ➤ 3,5634... 6,6062: ᴿSalesianum 53 (1991) 183 (G. *Abbà*).

5174 **Marrow** Stanley B., Paul, his letters and his theology 1986 → 2,4473 ...
5,5803: RGregorianum 72 (1991) 143s (E. *Farahian* regrette le caractère
'cours polycopié').

5175 **Neyrey** Jerome H., Paul, in other words 1990 → 6,6066: RAndrUnS 29
(1991) 180-2 (H. *Weiss*); Commonweal 118 (1991) 346 (L. S. *Cunningham*);
TS 52 (1991) 734-6 (L. T. *Johnson*); TTod 48 (1991s) 506s (J. J. *Pilch*).

5176 **Richards** E. Randolph, The secretary in the letters of Paul: WUNT
2/42. Tü 1991, Mohr. x-251 p. DM 98. 3-16-145575-4 [TDig 39,81]. –
RArTGran 54 (1991) 381s (A. *Segovia*).

5177 **Roetzel** Calvin J., The letters of Paul; conversations in context[2] [rev.
chiefly ch. 1]. Louisville 1991, W-Knox. 217 p. $15. 0-664-25201-X [TDig
39,185].

5178 **Schnider** Franz, *Stenger* Werner, Studien zum neutestamentlichen Briefformular: NT TSt 11, 1987 → 3,5629 ... 6,6074: RCBQ 53 (1991) 341s (J.
Gillman).

5179 **Schoon-Janssen** Johannes, Umstrittene 'Apologien' in Paulusbriefen: Diss.
DStrecker G. Göttingen 1989. 271 p. – NTAbs 36,125s; RTLv 23, p. 546.

5180 **Schreiner** Thomas R., Interpreting the Pauline epistles: Guides NTExeg.
1990 → 6,6075: RCritRR 4 (1991) 224-6 (M. L. *Soards*); GraceTJ 11
(1990) 107-9 (G. T. *Meadors*); RExp 88 (1991) 269s (J. E. *Jones*).

5181 *Stirewalt* Martin L.[J], The form and function of the Greek letter-essay
[ineditum]: → 298, EDonfried K., The Romans debate[2rev] 1991, 147-171.

5182 **Taatz** Irene, Frühjüdische Briefe; die paulinischen Briefe im Rahmen
der offiziellen religiösen Briefe des Frühjudentums [diss. Halle]: NOrb
16. FrS/Gö 1991, Univ./VR. 129 p. Fs 32. 3-7278-0700-8 / VR 3-525-
53917-7. – RRivB 39 (1991) 357s (A. *Bonora*).

5183 **Trobisch** David, Die Entstehung der Paulusbriefsammlung; Studien zu
den Anfängen christlicher Publizistik: NOrb 10, 1989 → 5,5810; 6,6081:
RCBQ 53 (1991) 721-3 (S. K. *Stowers*: new insights, some convincing);
ÉTRel 66 (1991) 290s (M. *Bouttier*); JBL 110 (1991) 736-8 (E. H. *Lovering*); JTS 42 (1991) 258s (R. *Beckwith*); RB 98 (1991) 145s (J. *Murphy-O'Connor*); RivB 39 (1991) 358-360 (M. *Làconi*).

5184 **Viciano** Alberto, Cristo el autor de nuestra salvación; estudio sobre
el comentario de TEODORETO de Ciro a las Epístolas paulinas 1990
→ 6,6082: RSalmanticensis 38 (1991) 249-252 (R. *Trevijano*); ScripT-
Pamp 23 (1991) 333-6 (D. *Ramos-Lissón*).

G3.3 Pauli theologia.

5185 **Arzt** Peter J., Christsein im Kontrast; zu Eigenart und Funktion escha-
tologischer bedrohlicher Propositionen in Protopaulinen: kath. Diss.
Salzburg 1991, DBeilner W. 477 p. – TR 87 (1991) 514; RTLv 23, p. 542.
EBassler Jouette M., Pauline theology 1991 → 290.

5186 *Bowers* Paul, Church and mission in Paul: JStNT 44 (1991) 89-111.

5187 **Breytenbach** Cilliers, Versöhnung; eine Studie zur paulinischen Soteriologie [Hab.-Diss. München 1985] WM 60, 1989 → 5,5814; 6,6088:
RCBQ 53 (1991) 491s (N. *McEleney*: carefully reasoned); CurrTMiss 18
(1991) 136s (F. W. *Danker*); JBL 110 (1991) 541-3 (F. W. *Hughes*).

5188 **Cousar** Charles B., Theology of the Cross ... Pauline: OvBT, 1990
→ 6,6094: RTS 52 (1991) 544-6 (R. J. *Dillon*).

5189 **Doohan** Helen, Paul's vision of Church: Good News Studies 32, 1989
→ 5,5817; 6,6097: RCBQ 53 (1991) 131 (V. P. *Branick*: inadequately-exe-
getical cheers for liberating views).

5190 *Dunn* J. D. G., Paul's understanding of the death of Jesus as sacrifice:
→ 384, Sacrifice 1991, 35-56.
5191 **Ellis** E. Earle, Pauline theology; ministry and society 1989 → 5,5819;
6,6099: ᴿCritRR 4 (1991) 189-191 (G. D. *Fee*); Interpretation 45 (1991)
200.202 (C. H. *Talbert*); StPatav 38 (1991) 203 (G. *Segalla*).
5192 **Fitzmyer** Joseph A., Paul and his theology² [< NJBC] 1989 → 4,5820;
6,6101: ᴿNBlackf 71 (1990) 50s (J. *Ziesler*); TR 87 (1991) 23s (T.
Söding).
5193 *Frankemölle* Hubert, ℗ Apostel Paulus und seine Interpretation des
Todes Jesu Christi, ᵀ*Bartnicki* Roman [Akad Wsz 27.III.1990]: ColcT
61,2 (1991) 5-16 [< NTAbs 36,361].
5194 **Georgi** Dieter, Theocracy in Paul's praxis and theology [< ᴱ*Taubes* J.,
Theokratie 1987], ᵀ*Green* David E. Mp 1991, Fortress. xi-112 p. $9 pa.
0-8006-2468-8 [NTAbs 36,274].
5195 *Guillet* Jacques, La foi du Christ, foi donnée et foi vécue, dans les
épîtres pauliniennes: → 121, ᶠRᴀᴍᴀʀᴏsᴏɴ L., Ta parole 1991, 73-81.
5196 a) *Hofius* Otfried, Wort Gottes und Glaube bei Paulus; – b) *Chester*
Andrew, Jewish messianic expectations and mediatorial figures and
Pauline Christology: → 437, Paulus 1988/91, 379-408 / 17-82; bibliog.
82-89.
5197 **Kaigama** Ignatius A., The Trinitarian implications of the Pauline
spirituality of communion: diss. Pont. Univ. Gregoriana, ᴰ*Martinez* E.
Rome 1991. 405 p.; excerpt n° 3733, 303 p. – RTLv 23, p. 545 [<
DissA-C].
5198 **Kertelge** K., 'Giustificazione' in Paolo; studi sulla struttura e sul significato del concetto paolino di giustificazione [1971, < kath. Diss.
Münster 1964], ᵀ*Chiavarino* R.: GLNT supp 5. Brescia 1991, Paideia.
389 p. Lit. 59.000 [NRT 114,752, X. *Jacques*]. 88-394-0456-2.
  Kertelge Karl, Grundthemen paulinischer Theologie 1991 → 217*.
5199 **Kreitzer** L. Joseph, Jesus and God in Paul's eschatology ᴰ1987 → 3,
5648 ... 6,6103: ᴿHeythJ 32 (1991) 83s († F. F. *Bruce*).
5200 *Lovely* R., Paul; the tortured doctrine of 'justification by faith':
Unitarian Universalist Christian 46,1s (Boston 1991) 12-26 [< NTAbs
36,198].
5201 a) *McLean* Bradley H., Christ as a *pharmakos* in Pauline soteriology; –
b) *Hays* Richard B., *Pistis* and Pauline Christology; what is at stake?; –
c) *Dunn* James D. G., Once more, *pistis Christou*: → 446, SBL Sem 30
(1991) 187-206 / 714-729 / 730-744.
5202 **Muller** Earl C., Trinity and marriage in Paul 1990 → 6,6108: ᴿNRT
113 (1991) 439-441 (X. *Jacques*); TS 52 (1991) 736s (R. *O'Toole*).
5203 **Oechslen** Rainer, Kronzeuge Paulus; paulinische Theologie im Spiegel
katholischer und evangelischer Exegese und die Möglichkeit ökumenischer
Verständigung [ᴰ1987]: BeitEvT 108, 1990 → 6,6109: ᴿCommSev 24
(1991) 275 (M. de *Burgos*); ExpTim 102 (1990s) 334 (G. *Wainwright*).
5204 **Pastor-Ramos** Federico, La salvación del hombre en la muerte y
resurrección de Cristo; ensayo de teología paulina: InstSJerón 24. Estella
1991, VDivino. 152 p. 84-7151-729-9.
5206 **Renwick** D. A., Paul, the Temple, and the presence of God [diss.
Richmond Union, ᴰ*Achtemeier* P.]: BrownJudSt 224. Atlanta 1991,
Scholars. xiv-179 p. $55. 1-55540-615-7 [NTAbs 36,278].
5207 **Schäfer** K., Gemeinde als 'Bruderschaft'; ein Beitrag zum Kirchenverständnis des Paulus ᴰ1989 → 6,6115: ᴿExpTim 103 (1991s) 57s (E.
Best); TsTNijm 31 (1991) 99s (J. *Smit*).

5208 **Seeley** David, The noble death ...: JStNT supp 28, ᴰ1990 ➤ 6,6116: ᴿJTS 42 (1991) 242-4 (F. G. *Downing*).

5209 **Tambasco** Anthony J., A theology of atonement and Paul's vision of Christianity: Glazier-Zacchaeus. ColMn 1991, Liturgical. 114 p. $7. 0-8146-5679-X [TDig 38,393].

5210 — [THEISSEN G.] *Lubomirski* M., Per un metodo in esegesi; Gerd Theissen, Psychologische Aspekte paulinischer Theologie [1983 ➤ 64,5591; Eng. 1987 ➤ 3,5658]: Gregorianum 72 (1991) 747-755.

5211 **Way** D., The lordship of Christ; Ernst KÄSEMANN's interpretation of Paul's theology [diss. Oxford 1987, ᴰ*Morgan* R.]: TMg. Ox 1991, Clarendon. xiv-336 p. $79. 0-19-826742-8 [NTAbs 36,280].

5212 **Wedderburn** A. J. M., Baptism and resurrection; studies in Pauline theology ...: WUNT 44, ᴰ1987 ➤ 3,5661 ... 6,6120: ᴿCiuD 203 (1991) 220s (J. *Gutiérrez*); Henoch 12 (1990) 386-8 (P. G. *Borbone*); HeythJ 32 (1991) 80s († F. F. *Bruce*); RechSR 79 (1991) 42-44 (J.-N. *Aletti*); Salesianum 53 (1991) 774s (J. *Heriban*).

5212* **Wright** N. T., The climax of the covenant; Christ and the Law in Pauline theology. E 1991, Clark. xiii-316 p. £20 [TR 88,340].

5213 **Yorke** Gosnell I. O. R., The Church as the Body of Christ in the Pauline corpus; a reexamination [diss. McGill, Montreal 1987]. Lanham 1991, UPA. xx-156 p. $42.50; pa. $23.50. 0-8191-8215-X; -6-8 [NTAbs 36,126].

5214 *Zahl* P. F. M., E. P. SANDERS's Paul vs. LUTHER's Paul; justification by faith in the aftermath of a scholarly crisis: StLuke 34,3 (1991) 33-40 [< NTAbs 36,50].

5215 *Ziesler* John, Justification by faith in the light of the 'New Perspective' [SANDERS E. 1977; WESTERHOLM S. 1988] on Paul: TLond 94 (1991) 188-192.

G3.4 **Themata paulina** [Israel & Lex/Law ➤ G4.6].

5216 *Álvarez Verdes* L., La ética del indicativo en S. Pablo: StMor 29,1 (1991) 3-26 [< ZIT 91,534]; franç. 25, Eng. 25s.

5217 *Bermúdez* Catalina, Predestinazione, grazia e libertà nei Commenti di san TOMMASO alle lettere di San Paolo: AnnTh 4 (1990) 399-421.

5218 **Byrne** Brendan, Inheriting the earth; the Pauline basis of a spirituality for our time. Homebush NSW/Staten Island NY 1991, St. Paul/Alba. xiv-100 p. $6. 0-8189-0603-0 [TDig 39,53]. – ᴿAustralasCR 68 (1991) 528s (J. *McSweeney*: A$9).

ᴱ**Charlesworth** J. H., Paul and the Dead Sea Scrolls reprint reviews ➤ 4807.

5219 *Chevallier* Max-A., La liberté chez Paul [inédit] ➤ 189, Souffle III, 1991, 141-155.

5220 *Colijn* B. B., Paul's use of the 'In Christ' formula: AshlandTJ 23 (1991) 9-26 [< NTAbs 36,360].

5221 **Cook** William F., A comparison of the Christ-Christian relationship in the Pauline and Johannine literature: diss. Baptist Theol. Sem.,ᴰ*Simmons* B. New Orleans 1990. 188 p. 91-17901. – DissA 52 (1991s) 964-A.

5222 **Cruz** H., Christological motives and motivated actions in Pauline paraenesis [Diss. Pont. Univ. Gregoriana, Roma 1982]: EurHS 23/396. Fra 1990, Lang. 484 p. 3-611-42857-X. – ᴿNRT 113 (1991) 436 (X. *Jacques*: limite à 'christologiques' les motivations déjà étudiées par NIEDER L. 1956, MERK O. 1968); TsTNijm 31 (1991) 430 (L. *Visschers*).

5223 **Ebner** Martin, *a)* Peristasenkataloge bei Paulus; Untersuchungen zu ihrer Form, ihren Motiven und ihrer brieflichen Funktion: kath. Diss.

Würzburg 1991, ᴰ*Klauck*. – TR 87 (1991) 522; – *b*) Leidenslisten und Apostelbrief; Untersuchungen zu Form, Motivik und Funktion der Peristasenkataloge bei Paulus: ForBi 66. Wü 1991, Echter. xvi-414 p. 3-429-01393-3. – ᴿArTGran 54 (1991) 368 (A. *Segovia*).

5224 **Gryziec** Piotr, ❷ Parakalein dans les Épîtres de s. Paul: diss. ᴰ*Langkammer* H. Lublin 1991. 262 p. – RTLv 23, p. 544.

5225 **[Gundry] Volf** Judith M., Paul and perseverance...: WUNT 2/37, ᴰ1990 ➤ 6,6131: ᴿEvQ 63 (1991) 273-5 (S. *Mosedale*); JBL 110 (1991) 738-740 (A. J. *Hultgren*); JTS 42 (1991) 236-240 (J. M. *Barclay*; reserves); NRT 113 (1991) 437s (X. *Jacques*); RB 98 (1991) 471s (J. *Murphy-O'Connor*: she distorts the texts and misses the point); TLZ 116 (1991) 36s (R. P. *Martin*, Eng.: justifies misgivings about I. H. MARSHALL's 1969 Kept by the power of God).

5226 **Heckel** Theo K. [RTLv 23, p. 544], Der 'innere Mensch'; die paulinische Verarbeitung eines platonischen Motivs: Diss. ᴰ*Roloff* J. Erlangen 1991. 239 p.

5227 *Helewa* Giovanni, Obbedire a Cristo Signore, un aspetto primario della fede secondo San Paolo: Teresianum 42 (1991) 381-412.

5228 *Hendrickx* Herman, The 'House Church' in Paul's letters: Theology Annual 12 (Hong Kong 1990s) 154-166 [< NTAbs 36,362].

5229 **Hofius** Otfried, Paulusstudien: WUNT 51, 1989 ➤ 5,280; 6,6134: ᴿArTGran 53 (1990) 301s (A. *Segovia*); JTS 42 (1989) 233-5 (A. J. M. *Wedderburn*); SvEx 56 (1991) 145-7 (L. *Aejmelaeus*).

5230 **Jones** F. Stanley, 'Freiheit' in... Paulus 1987 ➤ 3,5688...6,6137: ᴿSvTKv 66 (1990) 84-86 (H. *Gustafsson*).

Kertelge Karl, 'Giustificazione' in Paolo; studi sulla struttura e sul significato del concetto paolino di giustificazione 1991 ➤ 5198.

5231 **Kitzberger** Ingrid, Bau der Gemeinde... *oikodomē*... paulinisch: ForBi 53, 1986 ➤ 4,a682... 6,6139: ᴿColcT 60,4 (1990) 172-4 (R. *Bartnicki*, ❷).

5232 **Leonarda** Salvatore, La gioia nelle lettere di S. Paolo 1988 ➤ 4,6241 (5,5863*) 6,6572s: ᴿCritRR 4 (1991) 209s (L. *Tosco*); Salesianum 53 (1991) 769s (J. *Heriban*).

5233 *Loader* William, Hellenism and the abandonment of particularism in Jesus and Paul: Pacifica 4 (1991) 245-256.

5234 **Luque** Antonio, La relación promesa-ley en las epístolas de san Pablo según santo TOMÁS: diss. Santa Croce, ᴰ*Tábet* M. Roma 1986. 150 p. – RTLv 23, p. 545.

5235 *Meagher* Patrick M., Women in the Pauline letters: Jeevadhara 21 (1991) 150-160.

5236 *Mindling* J., Home is where your family is: BToday 29 (1991) 315-9 [< NTAbs 36,48].

5237 **O'Toole** Robert, Who is a Christian? a study in Pauline ethics 1990 ➤ 6,6158: ᴿBbbOr33 (1991) 233s (G. *De Virgilio*); NTAbs 35 (1991) 252 (D.J. *Harrington*); StPatav 28 (1991) 184s (G. *Segalla*: sua copia difettosa).

Radloff Matthias, Le ministère de la Parole de la femme; examen de textes pauliniens ᴰ1991 ➤ 8837.

5239 **Sampley** J. P., Walking between the times; Paul's moral reasoning. Mp 1991, Fortress. vi-122 p. $9. 0-8006-3479-3 [NTAbs 36,125].

5240 **Scott** James, Huiothesía; an exegetical investigation into the background of divine 'adoption as sons' in the Corpus Paulinum: diss. Tübingen 1989. – TLZ 116 (1991) 318s.

5241 *a*) *Soards* Marion L., Once again 'righteousness of God' in the writings of the Apostle Paul; – *b*) *Onunwa* Udobata R., Paul, social issues and future salvation; a challenge to the modern Church: Bible Bhashyam 17 (1991) 11-44 / 5-13.

5242 **Söding** Thomas, Das Liebesgebot bei Paulus; die Mahnung zur Agape im Rahmen der paulinischen Ethik: kath. Hab.-Diss. Münster 1991, ᴰ*Kertelge* K. – TR 87 (1991) 513.

5243 **Thorsell** Paul R., Spirit and law in the new age; a study of the Pauline conception of the New Covenant: diss. Dallas Theol. Sem. 1991, ᴰ*Burns* L. 438 p. 92-14492. – DissA 52 (1991s) 4376-A.

5244 *a*) *Toit* A. B. du, Faith and obedience in Paul; – *b*) *Lategan* B. C., Formulas in the language of Paul; a study of prepositional phrases in Galatians: Neotestamentica 25,1 (1991) 65-74 / 75-87.

5245 **Via** Dan O.ᴶ, Self-deception and wholeness in Paul and Matthew 1990 ➤ 6,6169: ᴿExpTim 102 (1990s) 346s (N. *Clark*: strange bedfellows, hint of human/NT predicament); Neotestamentica 25 (1991) 437s (L. *Floor*); NRT 113 (1991) 760s (X. *Jacques*); RExp 88 (1991) 492 (E. *Jones*); TS 52 (1991) 776 (K. A. *Barta*).

5246 **Vollenweider** Samuel, Freiheit... Paulus: FRL 147, ᴰ1989 ➤ 5,5880; 6,6170: ᴿCBQ 53 (1991) 510-2 (E. C. *Muller*); NedTTs 45 (1991) 64 (J. S. *Vos*); Protestantesimo 46 (1991) 151-3 (F. *Ferrario*); RechSR 79 (1991) 55 (J.-N. *Aletti*: sur l'*eleutheria*).

5247 **Wu** Julie Lee, Paul's use of prayer speech in his chief epistles; backgrounds and significance: diss. Fuller Theol. Sem. Pasadena 1991. 376 p. 92-11410. – DissA 52 (1991s) 4377-A.

5248 **Ziesler** John A., Pauline Christianity²ʳᵉᵛ [¹1983]: Oxford Bible Series. Ox 1991, Univ. Press. ix-166 p. 0-19-826460-7; pa. -59-3.

G4 Ad Romanos .1 Textus, commentarii.

5249 **Aland** Barbara, *Juckel* Andreas, Die paulinischen Briefe, 1. Römer und 1 Kor: NT syr. 2, ArbNtTextf 14. B 1991, de Gruyter. x-644 p. DM 410. – ᴿMuséon 104 (1991) 389-391 (A. de *Halleux*).

5250 ᵀᴱ**Buzzi** Franco, Martin LUTERO, La lettera ai Romani (1515-1516): Classici del pensiero cristiano 7. CinB 1991, Paoline. 794 p.

5251 **Cantalamessa** R., Life in the lordship of Christ; a spiritual commentary on the letter to the Romans for a new evangelization [La vita nella Signoria di C 1986], ᵀ*Villa* F. L. KC 1990, Sheed & W. xii-284 p. $15. 1-55612-350-7 [NTAbs 36,119].

5252 **Díaz Sánchez-Cid** José R., Justicia, pecado y filiación; sobre el comentario de ORÍGENES a los Romanos [dis. 1989, ᴰ*Orbe* A.; Roma, Inst. Patr. 'Augustinianum']. Toledo 1991, S. Ildefonso. xxii-354 p. [TR 88,253].

5253 **Dunn** James D. G., Romans 1-2; WordComm 38, 1988 ➤ 4,5904... 6,6178: ᴿAndrUnS 29 (1991) 85-87 (W. *Richardson*); CBQ 53 (1991) 494s (G. E. *Montague*, 1: balanced; meticulous bordering on repetitive); Interpretation 45 (1991) 92 (K. *Quast*, 1); JTS 42 (1991) 244-252 (F. *Watson*); PerspRelSt 18 (1991) 189s (C. H. *Talbert*).

5254 **Edwards** James R., Romans: New International [Version] Biblical Commentary 6. Peabody MA 1991, Hendrickson. xx-395 p. $10 pa. 0-943575-34-6.

5255 ᴱ**Fraenkel** P., *Perrotet* L., Théodore de BÈZE, Cours sur Rom/Heb 1988 ➤ 4,5905... 6,6179: ᴿRHPR 71 (1991) 396 (M. *Arnold*).

5256 **Grenholm** Cristina, Romans interpreted ᴰ1990 ➤ 6,6181: ᴿNRT 113 (1991) 767s (X. *Jacques*); TLZ 116 (1991) 282 (W. *Wiefel*).

5257 ᴱHammond Bammel Caroline P., Der Römerbriefkommentar des ORI-
GENES: RUFINS Buch 1-3; VLatGesch 16. FrB 1990, Herder. – ᴿJTS 42
(1991) 717-720 (A. *LeBoulluec*, franç.); NRT 113 (1991) 433s (X. *Jacques*).

5258 **Heil** John P., Paul's letter to the Romans, a reader-response commentary 1987 ⇥ 3,5729 ... 6,6184: ᴿTorJT 7 (1991) 124s (J. *Plevnik*: not
for scholars, nor on major issues).

5259 ᴱJunack K., *al.*, Das NT auf Papyrus II. Die paulinischen Briefe 1. Röm
1-2 Kor: ArbNtTextf 12. B/NY 1989, de Gruyter. lvi-418 p. DM 148
[TR 88,372, J. K. *Elliott*].

5260 **Kruijf** T. de, Paulus, Brief aan de Romeinen: Belichting. Boxtel/Brugge
1990, KBS/Tabor. 128 p. *f* 34,50 [dated 1986 ⇥ 2,4559]: ᴿCollatVL 21
(1991) 319 (H. *Hoet*).

5261 **Maly** Eugene H. † 1980, Romans: NTMessage [Wilmington 1979, Gla-
zier], also Dublin 1979, Veritas. xv-134 p.

5262 **Möhler** Johann A., Vorlesung zum Römerbrief, ᴱ*Rieger* Reinhold. Mü
1990, Wewel. 308 p. DM 48. – ᴿMüTZ 42 (1991) 190 (G. L. *Müller*).

5262* **Moo** D., Romans 1-8: Wycliffe exeg. comm. Ch 1991, Moody. xxxix-
591 p. $30. 0-8024-9263-0 [NTAbs 36,433].

5263 ᵀᴱ**Pani** Giancarlo, Martin LUTERO, Lezioni sulla lettera ai Romani
(1515-1516) I. (Rom 1-7) II (8-16): Ascolta, Israele! 7-. Genova 1991,
Marietti. 306 p.; x-352 p. 88-211-8457-9; -62-5.

5264 ᵀᴱ**Ring** Thomas G., AUGUSTINUS Aurelius, Die Auslegung einiger
Fragen aus dem Brief an die Römer: Schriften, Prolegomena 1, 1989
⇥ 6,6192; DM 59: ᴿTPQ 139 (1991) 215 (U. G. *Leinsle*).

5265 **Rolland** Philippe, À l'ećoute de l'épître aux Romains: Lire la Bible. P
1991, Cerf. 166 p. F 100. 2-204-04215-3. – ᴿNTAbs 35 (1991) 253 (D. J.
Harrington).

5266 **Stuhlmacher** Peter, Der Brief an die Römer: NTD 6, 1989 ⇥ 5,5901:
ᴿExpTim 102 (1990s) 268 (E. *Best*); TLZ 116 (1991) 359-361 (K.
Haacker).

5267 ᵀᴱ**Ugenti** Valerio, CIRILLO di Alessandria, Commento alla lettera ai Romani: Collana TPatr 95. R 1991, Città Nuova. 156 p. 88-311- 3095-1.

5268 *Wedderburn* A. J. M., 'Like an ever-rolling stream'; some recent commentaries on Romans [BLACK M., DUNN J.; SCHMITHALS W.; STUHL-
MACHER P.; ZIESLER J.]: ScotJT 44 (1991) 367-380.

5269 **Wilckens** Ulrich, La carta a los Romanos I (1-5): BtEstB 1989
⇥ 6,6195: ᴿCiTom 118 (1991) 188s (J. *Huarte Osacar*); EfMex 9 (1991)
139-141 (R. *Lugo*).

5270 **Ziesler** J., Paul's ... Rom: TPI 1989 ⇥ 5,5903; 6,6196: ᴿLvSt 16 (1991)
74-76 (R. F. *Collins*, comparing with *Heil* J. 1987); NBlackf 72 (1991) 202s
(Morna D. *Hooker*).

G4.2 *Ad Romanos: themata,* topics.

5271 **Aletti** Jean-Noël, Comment Dieu est-il juste? Clefs pour interpréter
l'épître aux Romains. P 1991 [⇥ 6,6197], Seuil. 286 p. F 130. 2-02-
012854-3. – ᴿÉtudes 375 (1991) (S. *Marrow*); StPatav 38 (1991) 186-9 (G.
Segalla).

5272 *Alison* James, Justification and the constitution of consciousness; a new
look at Romans and Galatians [... GIRARD R.]: NBlackf 71 (1990) 17-26.

5273 *Antonios* metrop., ☉ [Rom] The foundation of the conviction of
salvation on love: TAth 61 (1991) 537-552; Eng. 906.

ᴱ**Donfried** Karl P., The Romans debate²ʳᵉᵛ 1991 ⇥ 298.

5274 **Elliott** Neil, The rhetoric of Romans [diss. Princeton DBecker J.] 1990
➤ 5,5908; 6,6202; £35: RExpTim 102 (1990s) 279s (R. Morgan: stimu-
lated by E. P. SANDERS' paradigm shift).

5275 *Gestrich* C., Der Römerbrief des Paulus und wir heute; eine Einführung:
ZeichZt 45,3 (1991) 86-91 [< NTAbs 36,199].

5276 **Heither** Theresia, Translatio religionis; die Paulusdeutung des ORIGENES
in seinem Kommentar zum Römerbrief D1990 ➤ 6,6206: RBLitEc 92
(1991) 126s (H. *Crouzel*); Gregorianum 72 (1991) 789 (G. *Pelland*); TLZ
116 (1991) 836-840 (K. *Beyschlag*); TPhil 66 (1991) 583-5 (H. J. *Sieben*,
auch über Fontes Christiani 3, SCHMITZ J., AMBROSIUS); VigChr 45
(1991) 293s (J. C. M. van *Winden*).

Jeffers J. J., Conflict at Rome [1 Clement – Hermas 1991], but really concluding to origins of Primacy ➤ 4087.

5277 **Jervis** L. Ann, The purpose of Romans; a comparative letter structure
investigation: JStNT supp 55. Sheffield 1991, JStOT. 187 p. £25; sb.
£18.75. 1-85075-304-0. – RExpTim 103 (1991s) 154 (J. M. G. *Barclay*; a
fine study though not taking the body of the letter into account).

5278 **Johnson** David W., The conciliatory role for the Gospel of Mark in
relation to the background of the epistle to the Romans: diss. SW Baptist
Theol. Sem. 1990. 294 p. 91-15305. – DissA 52 (1991s) 185-A.

5279 *a*) *Klein* Günter, Paul's purpose in writing the Epistle to the Romans
[< Rekonstruktion 1969, 129-144], TDonfried K., Hoffman Jocher; – *b*)
Jervell Jacob, The letter to Jerusalem [< ST 25 (1971) 61-73]: ➤ 298,
EDonfried K., The Romans debate² 1991, 29-43 / 53-64.

5280 **Lombard** H. A., [Rom] Uit genade alleen?: HervTSt 47 (1991) 136-150
[< NTAbs 36,50].

5281 **Lyonnet** Stanislas, Études sur l'Épître aux Romains: AnBib 120, 1989
➤ 5,307; 6,6210: RColcT 61,2 (1991) 185-8 (J. *Za/ęski*, ❷); RTLv 22
(1991) 83 (J. *Ponthot*).

5282 **Martin** Lynn L., The righteousness of God in Romans; a study in
Paul's use of Jewish tradition: diss. Marquette, DStockhausen Carol.
Milwaukee 1991. 526 p. 92-00158. – DissA 52 (1991s) 2597-A.

5283 **Mullins** M., Called to be saints; Christians living in first-century Rome.
Dublin 1991, Veritas. 471 p. £20 [RHE 87,53*].

5284 *Penna* Romano, Ira e giustizia di Dio nella lettera ai Romani: ➤ 535,
Firmana 1 (1991s) 64-76.

5285 *Penna* Romano, Rom 1,18-2,29 / 3,(1-)8 / 6,1-11 / 8,32 / aspetti nar-
rativi / problema della Legge / Gli Ebrei a Roma [< RivB, Lateranum,
Biblica, *al.*]: ➤ 247, L'apostolo 1991, 126-134 / 77-110. 135-149 / 150-170
/ 171-199 / 496-518 / 33-76.

5286 **Ponsot** Hervé, Une introduction à la lettre aux Romains: Initiations,
1988 ➤ 4,5924; 5,5914: RRTLv 22 (1991) 408s (C. *Focant*).

5287 **Ruschitzka** Ernst, Der Weltbegriff des Apostels Paulus im Römerbrief:
kath. Diss. Innsbruck 1991, DHasitschka M. – TR 87 (1991) 513; ZkT
113,507; RTLv 23, p. 546.

5288 **Simonis** Walter, Der gefangene Paulus; die Entstehung des sogenannten Römerbriefs... in Rom 1990 ➤ 6,6216: RCBQ 53 (1991) 507s (R.
Morton: holds only 1-11 written by Paul, and not to Rome); NRT 113
(1991) 439s (X. *Jacques*); NT 33 (1991) 185-8 (J. A. D. *Weima*).

5289 *Sontag* Frederick, BARTH, Romans and feminist theology; the problem
of God's freedom: *a*) EvQ 63 (1991) 313-330; – *b*) RelStT 10,2 (1990)
42-56.

5290 **Vorster** Johannes N., The rhetorical situation of the letter to the Romans; an interactional approach: diss. Pretoria 1991, ᴰdu *Toit* A. – DissA 52 (1991s) 4376-A.

5291 **Vouga** François, Ce Dieu qui m'a trouvé; vingt lettres inédites [pseudonymes; de 'Philologus', Rom 6,15] sur l'Épître de Paul aux Romains. Aubonne 1990, Moulin. 94 p. Fs 12,80. – ᴿÉTRel 66 (1991) 438 (E. *Cuvillier*).

5292 **Walters** James C., Ethnic issues in Paul's letter to the Romans; an analysis in light of the changing self-definition of early Christianity in Rome: diss. ᴰ*Sampey* J. Boston Univ. 1991. 292 p. 91-13524. – DissA 51 (1990s) 4159s-A; RelStR 18,173.

5293 **Wedderburn** A. J. M., The reasons for Romans 1988 ➤ 4,5926 ... 6,6217: ᴿAnglTR 73 (1991) 76s (D. R. *Ruppe*); BibTB 21 (1991) 131s (J. S. *Siker*: good); IndTSt 27 (1990) 359-361 (L. *Legrand*); JBL 110 (1991) 169-171 (A. J. *Hultgren*); RechSR 79 (1991) 40 (J.-N. *Aletti*: insatisfaction).

5294 *Young* Frances M., Understanding Romans in the light of 2 Corinthians: ScotJT 43 (1990) 433-446.

G4.3   *Naturalis cognitio Dei* ... **Rom 1-4.**

5295 **Elorriaga** Carlos, [Rom 1-11] La fuerza del Evangelio: EstudiosB 6. M 1988, Paulinas. 172 p. – ᴿScripTPamp 23 (1991) 1067 (C. *Basevi*: borroso sobre el pecado original; no toma partido sobre 1,16s; 3,21-31; 5,12-19).

5296 **Longenecker** Bruce W., Eschatology and the Covenant; a comparison of 4 Ezra and Romans 1-11: Sheffield 1991, JStOT. 318 p. £35; sb. £26. 1-85075-305-9. – ᴿExpTim 103 (1991s) 118s (J. A. *Ziesler*).

5297 **Davies** Glenn N., Faith and obedience in ... Rom 1-4 ᴰ1990 ➤ 6,6219: ᴿJBL 110 (1991) 740-2 (F. S. *Thielman*); JTS 42 (1991) 675-680 (J. M. G. *Barclay*).

5298 *Wagner* Guy, [Rom 1,3] La filiation davidique de Jésus chez Paul, Marc et Matthieu: ÉTRel 66 (1991) 419-422.

5299 *Kušar* Stjepan, [Rom 1,18-23; Wis 13-19] On the practice of natural theology in the Bible: ObnŽiv 46 (1991) 432-445 (Croatian); Eng. 445.

5300 *Novak* David, [Rom 1,19-21] Before revelation; the Rabbis, Paul, and Karl Bᴀʀᴛʜ: JRel 71 (1991) 50-66.

5301 *Henriksen* J.-O., Naturen som norm? En drøfting av naturbegrepet i tilknytning til Rom 1,24-27; TsTKi 62 (1991) 95-112 [< NTAbs 36,364].

5302 **Stuart** G. H. C., Tweestrijd; strijd tussen goed en kwaad bij Paulus en zijn tijdgenoten. Kampen 1988, Kok. 143 p. ƒ 22,50. 90-242-4462-5. – ᴿBijdragen 52 (1991) 443 (B. J. *Koet* & J. R. de *Kwadsteniet*: 'Cohen Stuart' in title, text, index; not indicated as translation).

5303 **Garlington** Don B., The obedience of faith; a Pauline phrase in historical context [diss. ᴰ*Dunn* J., Durham 1987]: WUNT 2/38. Tü 1991, Mohr. xiv-337 p. DM 114. 3-16-145506-1.

5304 *Garlington* D. B., [Rom 2,13] The obedience of faith in the letter to the Romans, II. The obedience of faith and judgment by works: WestTJ 53,1 (1991) 47-72 [< NTAbs 36,50].

5305 *Walter* Nikolaus, Gottes Erbarmen mit 'allem Fleisch' (Röm 3,20 / Gal 2,16) — ein 'femininer' Zug im paulinischen Gottesbild?: BZ 35 (1991) 99-102.

5306 **Kraus** Wolfgang, Der Tod Jesu als Heiligtumsweihe; eine Untersuchung zum Umfeld der Sühnevorstellung in Römer 3,25-26a [Diss.

Erlangen-N. 1989s → 6,6229]: WM 66.   Neuk 1991.   x-342 p.   DM 72 [TR 88,163].   3-7887-1395-X.

5307 *Kraus* Wolfgang,   Der Jom Kippur, der Tod Jesu und die 'biblische Theologie'; ein Versuch, die jüdische Tradition in die Auslegung von Röm 3,25f einzubeziehen: → 390, JbBT 6 (1991) 155-172.

G4.4   *Peccatum originale; redemptio cosmica:* **Rom 5-8.**

5308 *a*) *Zabatiero* Júlio P.T.,   Reescrever a espiritualidade na vida — uma proposta para a leitura de Romanos 5-8; – *b*) *Lazier* Josué A.,   A espiritualidade de Paulo em 1 Coríntios: EstudosB 30 (1991) 67-73 / 59-66.

5309 *a*) *Cosby* Michael R.,   Paul's persuasive language in Romans 5; – *b*) *Jewett* Robert,   The rhetorical function of numerical sequences in Romans: → 86, [F]KENNEDY G., Persuasive 1991, 209-226 / 227-245.

5310 *Harrisville* Roy A.,   Romans 5:1-15:   Interpretation 45 (1991) 181-5.

5311 *Porter* Stanley E.,   [Rom 5,6] The argument of Romans 5; can a rhetorical question make a difference?:   JBL 110 (1991) 655-677.

5312 *Kertelge* K.,   Die Sünde Adams im Lichte der Erlösungstat Christi nach Röm 5,12-21: IkaZ 20 (1991) 305-314 = The sin of Adam in the light of Christ's redemptive act ... Rom: CommND 18 (1991) 502-513 [< NTAbs 36, p. 200.364].

5313 *Kertelge* Karl,   Adam und Christus; die Sünde Adams im Lichte der Erlösungstat Christi nach Röm 5,12-21: → 72, [F]HAHN F., Anfänge 1991, 141-153.

5314 **Mascellani** E.,   Prudens dispensator verbi; Rom 5,12-21 nell'esegesi di CLEMENTE A. e ORIGENE: MiFacLett 134.   F 1990, Nuova Italia. viii-153 p.   Lit. 29.700.   88-221-8811-6 [NTAbs 36,123].

5315 *Kline* M.G.,   Gospel until the Law: Rom 5:13-14 and the Old Covenant: JEvTS 34 (1991) 433-446 [< NTAbs 36,364].

5316 *Légasse* Simon,   Être baptisé dans la mort du Christ; étude de Romains 6,1-14:   RB 98 (1991) 544-559; Eng. 544.

5317 *Penna* Romano,   Battesimo e partecipazione alla morte di Cristo in Rom 6,1-11: → 561*d*, Origini 1989/91, 145-166.

5318 **Schlarb** Robert,   Wir sind mit Christus begraben ... Röm 6,1-11 [Diss. Wien 1987, [D]*Niederwimmer* K.]: BeitGbEx 31, 1990 → 6,6239:   [R]CritRR 4 (1991) 224 (J.A. *Burgess*); TLZ 116 (1991) 841-3 (W. *Schmithals*).

5319 *Basevi* Claudio,   Cinco sermones de san AGUSTÍN sobre Rom 7:   AugM 35 (1990) 127-161.

5320 *Garlington* D.B.,   Romans 7:14-25 and the creation theology of Paul: TrinJ 11 (1990) 197-235.

5321 *Holtz* Traugott, *a*) [Röm 8] Die Hoffnung der Kreatur nach Paulus [< ZeichZt 34 (1980) 96-103]; – *b*) Theo-logie und Christologie bei Paulus [< [F]*Kümmel* W. 1985, 105-121]: → 211, Geschichte 1991, 223-233 / 189-204.

5322 *Greene* M. Dwaine,   A note on Romans 8:3 ['as a sin-offering' better than 'for sin']:   BZ 35 (1991) 103-6.

5323 **Christoffersson** Olle,   The earnest expectation of the creature; the flood-tradition in Rom 8,18-27: ConBib NT 23, 1990 → 6,6347: [R]ExpTim 102 (1990s) 280 (C.J.A. *Hickling*); ÉTRel 66 (1991) 599 (B. *Coyault*); JTS 42 (1991) 253s (M. *Bockmuehl*); NRT 113 (1991) 768-770 (X. *Jacques*); RHPR 71 (1991) 240 (E. *Trocmé*: relevance to a flood tradition in Enoch and Jubilees as well as Genesis is as plausible as the alternatives).

5324 *Rossi* Benedetto, Struttura letteraria e teologia della creazione in Rm 8,18-25: LA 41 (1991) 87-124; Eng. 490.

5325 *Haacker* Klaus, Ratlos, aber getrost (Rö 8,26-28): TBeit 22 (1991) 289-292 [< ZIT 91,789].

5326 *Hiebert* Edmond, Romans 8:28-29 and the assurance of the believer: Bibliotheca Sacra 148 (1991) 170-183.

5327 *Breuning* W., Gott hat uns bestimmt, an Wesen und Gestalt seines Sohnes teilzuhaben (Röm 8,29): LebZeug 46 (1991) 277-288 [< ZIT 91,778].

G4.6   *Israel et Lex;*   **The Law and the Jews,** *Rom 9-11.*

5328 **Bell** Richard H., The origin and purpose of the jealousy motif in Romans 9-11; a case study in the theology and technique of Paul: ev. Diss. ᴰ*Stuhlmacher* P. Tübingen 1991. xix-359 p. – TLZ 117,395; RTLv 23, p. 542.

5329 **Campbell** William S., Paul's Gospel in an intercultural context; Jew and Gentile in the letter to the Romans [4 inedita + 7]: Studien zur interkulturellen Geschichte des Christentums 69. Fra 1991, Lang. xix-213 p. $46.80. 3-631-42981-9.

5330 **Cassirer** Heinz W., Grace and law, 1989 → 4,5959 ... 6,6255: ᴿScotJT 44 (1991) 242 (U. *Simon:* Kantian, refugee; 'a great scholar with a passionate heart').

5331 *Castellina* Paolo, La salvezza di Israele, Romani 9-11: STEv 3 (1991) 174-206 [249-259, colloquio di Willowbank 1989].

5332 *Cranfield* C. E. B., 'The works of the Law' in the epistle to the Romans: JStNT 43 (1991) 89-101.

5333 *Dalton* William, Once more Paul among Jews and Gentiles: Pacifica 4 (1991) 51-61.

5334 **Dunn** James D. G., Jesus, Paul and the law 1990 → 6,226: ᴿJTS 42 (1991) 231-3 (M. E. *Glasswell*); RExp 88 (1991) 95 (J. E. *Jones*).

5336 **Gaston** Lloyd, Paul and the Torah 1987 → 4,196 ... 6,6263: ᴿGrOrTR 35 (1990) 164 (G. C. *Papademetriou:* translates some Rom-Gal to fit his thesis); RechSR 79 (1991) 49-51 (J.-N. *Aletti*).

5337 **Johnson** E. Elizabeth, The function of apocalyptic and wisdom traditions in Romans 9-11: SBL diss. 109, 1989 → 5,5965; 6,6270: ᴿCBQ 53 (1991) 138-140 (J. P. *Heil*); JBL 110 (1991) 742-4 (J. M. *Scott*).

5338 *Katoppo* Pericles G., Translating *nomos* 'law' in Romans in simplified Indonesian; BTrans 42 (1991) 420-6.

5339 **Kaylor** R. David, Paul's covenant community; Jew and Gentile in Romans 1988 → 5,5966; 6,6271: ᴿCritRR 4 (1991) 207-9 (B. *Martin*).

5340 **Korsch** Dietrich, Glaubensgewissheit und Selbstbewusstsein; vier systematische Variationen über Gesetz und Evangelium: BeitHistT 76. Tü 1989, Mohr. x-290 p. 3-16-145455-3. – ᴿActuBbg 28 (1991) 173s (J. *Boada*).

5341 **Laato** Timo, Paulus und das Judentum; anthropologische Erwägungen: Diss. Åbo, ᴰ*Thurén* J. Åbo 1991, Akademis. [xvi-] 341 p. 951-9498-99-0.

5342 *a) Lichtenberger* Hermann, Paulus und das Gesetz; – *b) Aune* David E., Romans as a logos protreptikos in the context of ancient religious and philosophical propaganda: → 437, Paulus 1988/91, 361-374 (-8) / 91-121 (-4).

5343 **Lubking** Hans-Martin, Paulus und Israel im Römerbrief; eine Untersuchung zu Römer 8-11: Diss. ᴰ*Klein* G.: EurHS 23/260, 1986 ➤ 2,4622; 4,5967: ᴿRelStR 17 (1991) 69 (L. E. *Keck*).

5344 **Martin** Brice L., Christ and the law in Paul: NT supp 62, ᴰ1989 ➤ 6,6276: ᴿJBL 110 (1991) 349s (F. *Thielman*); TLZ 116 (1991) 913-916 (K.-W. *Niebuhr*, also on THIELMAN F. 1989).

5345 *Meeks* Wayne A., Om tilltron till en oförutsägbar Gud; en hermeneutisk meditation över Rom 9-11 [for honorary doctorate Uppsala 1990; a longer version in ᴱ*Meyer* P., Faith and history 1990]: SvEx 56 (1991) 101-117.

5346 **Motyer** Steve, [Rom 9-11] Israel in the plan of God 1989 ➤ 5,5970: ᴿScotBEvT 9 (1991) 73s (G. *Grogan*).

5346* **Panimolle** Salvatore A., La libertà cristiana... dalla legge 1988 ➤ 6, 6280: ᴿTeresianum 42 (1991) 345-7 (V. *Pasquetto*).

5347 **Räisänen** Heikki, Paul and the Law²: WUNT 29, 1987 ➤ 5,5976; 6,6282: ᴿHenoch 12 (1990) 389s (G. *Boccaccini*, also on his Torah and Christ).

5348 **Refoulé** F., Et ainsi... Rom 11,25s, 1984: ➤ 65,5281... 4,5991: ᴿNVFr 65 (1990) 77s (J. *Kaelin*).

5349 *Refoulé* François, Cohérence ou incohérence de Paul en Romains 9-11?: RB 98 (1991) 51-79; Eng. 51.

5350 *Reid* Daniel G., The misunderstood Apostle: ChrTod (July 16, 1990) 25-27 [< BS 148 (1991) 231s (E. E. *Johnson*)].

5351 **Richardson** Peter, *Westerholm* Stephen, Law in religious communities in the Roman period; the debate over Torah and Nomos in post-biblical Judaism and early Christianity: Studies in Christianity and Judaism 4. Waterloo 1991, W. Laurier Univ. x-164 p. $20 [C$17!].

5352 **Sanders** E. P., Paolo, la legge e il popolo giudaico 1989 ➤ 6,6285: ᴿHenoch 13 (1991) 121-3 (R. *Penna*).

5353 **Sanders** E. P., Paulo, a Lei e o povo judeu. São Paulo 1990, Paulinas. 348 p. [REB 51,245].

5354 *a) Schellong* Dieter, Paulus und das Gesetz nach dem Römerbrief; – *b) Mauser* Ulrich, Paulus als Theologe des Alten Testaments: ➤ 310, JbBT 6 (1991) 69-87 / 47-68.

5355 *Sloan* Robert B., Paul and the Law; why the Law cannot save: NT 33 (1991) 35-60.

5356 **Thielman** Frank, From plight to solution... Paul's view of the Law in Gal Rom: NT supp 61, 1989 ➤ 5,5979: ᴿJBL 110 (1991) 350-3 (E. Elizabeth *Johnson*); RB 98 (1991) 469 (J. *Murphy-O'Connor*); TorJT 7 (1991) 119-122 (D. *Seeley*).

5357 **Tomson** Peter J., Paul and the Jewish law; halakha in the letters of the Apostle to the Gentiles: CompJudNT 3/1. Assen/Mp 1990, Van Gorcum/Fortress. xix-327 p. $30. 90-232-2490-6 / Mp 0-8006-2467-X [TDig 39,190]. – ᴿJTS 42 (1991) 682-8 (M. *Bockmuehl*).

5358 **Tuck** Gary E., The purpose of the Law relative to sin in Pauline literature: diss. Dallas Theol. Sem. 1991. 288 p. 92-14493. – DissA 52 (1991s) 4376-A.

5359 *Versteeg* J. P., Kerk en Israël volgens Romeinen 9-11: TRef 34 (Woerden 1991) 151-... [< ZIT 91,432].

5360 **Watson** Francis, Paul, Judaism and the Gentiles: SNTS mg 56, 1986 ➤ 2,4634*... 6,6291: ᴿCBQ 53 (1991) 154-6 (F. W. *Burnett*); JAAR 59 (1991) 429s (S. G. *Wilson*).

5361 **Westerholm** Stephen, Israel's law and the Church's faith... 1988
➤ 4,3981 ... 6,6292: ᴿRechSR (1991) 52 (J.-N. *Aletti*); TLZ 116 (1991)
433-7 (H. *Hübner*: good, but the discussion is not finished).
5362 *Widmer* Gabriel-P., La mise en question des valeurs en théologie [...'le
paulinisme conteste radicalement la portée rédemptrice que le judaïsme et
l'hellénisme reconnaissent aux valeurs... Sa relecture...']: RTPhil 123
(1991) 131-146; Eng. 223 [147-178 *al.*, valeurs, transmission...].
5363 **Winger** [Joseph] Michael, [Rom 7,14-25; Gal 2,15-21] By what law?
The meaning of *nómos* in the letters of Paul [diss. Columbia, ᴰ*Scroggs*
R. 91-18664. – DissA 52 (1991s) 569-A]: SBL diss 128. Atlanta 1991,
Scholars. xiv-236 p. $45; sb./pa. $30. 1-55540-593-2 [NTAbs 36,435].
5364 **Wright** N. T., The climax of the Covenant; Christ and the law in
Pauline theology: diss. 1990 + varia. E 1991, Clark. xiii-316 p. 0-567-
09594-0; pa. -X.

5365 **Mesner** David E., The rhetoric of citations; Paul's use of Scripture in
Romans 9: diss. Northwestern, ᴰ*Jewett* R. Evanston IL 1991. 606 p.
91-29037. – DissA 52 (1991s) 1775-A.
5366 **Pattee** Stephen B., Stumbling stone or cornerstone; the structure
and meaning of Paul's argument in Romans 9:30-10:13: diss. Marquette,
ᴰ*Stockhausen* Carol. Milwaukee 1991. 371 p. 91-33805. – DissA 52
(1991s) 2182-A.
5367 *Schreiner* Thomas R., *a)* Israel's failure to attain righteousness in
Romans 9:30-10:3: TrinJ 12 (1991) 209-220; – *b)* 'Works of law' in Paul
[8 times]: NT 33 (1991) 217-244.
5368 *Tobin* Thomas H., Romans 10:4; Christ the goal of the Law: ➤ 76,
ᶠHILGERT E., StPhilonAn 3 (1991) 272-280.
5369 *Jegher-Bucher* Verena, Erwählung und Verwerfung im Römerbrief?
Eine Untersuchung von Röm 11,11-15: TZBas 47 (1991) 326-336.
5370 *a)* *Wolter* Michael, Evangelium und Tradition; Juden und Heiden
zwischen solus Christus und sola scriptura (Gal 1,11-24; Röm 11,25-36); –
b) *Koch* Dietrich-Alex, '... bezeugt durch das Gesetz und die Propheten';
zur Funktion der Schrift bei Paulus; – *c)* *Vouga* François, Apostolische
Briefe als 'scriptura'; die Rezeption des Paulus in den katholischen
Briefen: ➤ 558, Sola Scr. 1990/1, 180-193 / 169-179 / 194-210.

G4.8   Rom 12...

5371 *a)* *Frutiger* Simone, '... Afin de réveiller votre mémoire', Romains 12-15;
– *b)* *Collange* Jean-François, Écriture et histoire selon l'apôtre Paul:
➤ 30, ᶠBONNARD F., Mémoire 1991, 203-217 / 193-201.
5372 **Thompson** Michael, Clothed with Christ; the example and teaching of
Jesus in Romans 12.1 - 15.13 [diss. Cambridge]: JStNT supp 59. Sheffield
1991, Academic. 292 p. £30. 1-85075-309-1.
5373 *Smiga* George, Romans 12:1-2 and 15:30-32 and the occasion of the
letter to the Romans: CBQ 53 (1991) 257-273.
5374 **Wilson** Walter T., Love without pretense; Romans 12,9-21 and Hel-
lenistic-Jewish wisdom literature [diss. Chicago 1980, ᴰ*Betz* H.]: WUNT
2/46. Tü 1991, Mohr. xi-262 p. DM 74 pa. 3-16-14756-0 [NTAbs
36,280].
5375 *Lategan* B. C., Reception; theory and practice in reading Romans 13:
➤ 307, ᴱ*Hartin*, Text 1991, 145-169.

5376 **Ellul** Jacques, [Rom 13,1s... BARTH, MAILLOT] Anarchy and Christianity. GR 1981, Eerdmans. vi-105 p.

5377 *Bielecki* Stanisław, ✪ Röm 13,1-7 im Kontext der Heilsgeschichte: RoczTK 34,1 (1991 für 1987) 47-56; deutsch 56.

5378 **Schneider** Nelio, Die 'Schwachen' in der christlichen Gemeinde Roms ➤ 5,5918: eine historisch-exegetische Untersuchung zu Röm 14,1-15,13: Diss. ᴰ*Barth* G. Wuppertal 1989. – TLZ 116 (1991) 474-6.

5379 *Reichrath* Hans L., Juden und Christen — eine Frage von 'Ökumene'? Was uns Römer 15,7-13 dazu lehrt: ➤ 78, ᶠHRUBY K., Judaica 47,1 (1991) 22-30.

5380 *Porter* C.L., [Rom 15,14s] 'For the sake of the grace given me': Encounter 52 (Indianapolis 1991) 251-262 [< NTAbs 36,51].

5381 *a) Wiefel* Wolfgang, The Jewish community in ancient Rome and the origins of Roman Christianity [< Judaica 26 (1970) 65-88], ᵀwith *Hoffmann* Jochen]; – *b) Lampe* Peter, The Roman Christians in Romans 16 [ineditum < Stadtröm. Chr. 1987]: ➤ 298, ᴱ*Donfried* K., Romans debate²ʳᵉᵛ 1991, 85-101 / 216-230.

G5.1 **Epistulae ad Corinthios** (I vel I-II) – *textus, commentarii.*

5382 ᵀᴱ**Fatica** Luigi, AMBROSIASTER, 1 Cor 1989 ➤ 5,6007; 6,6318: ᴿCC 142 (1991,2) 298s (G. *Cremascoli*).

5383 **Fee** Gordon D., The First Epistle to the Corinthians: NICNT 1987 ➤ 3,5842... 6,6319: ᴿGraceTJ 11 (1990) 104-6 (G.T. *Meadors*); ScripTPamp 23 (1991) 1067 (C. *Basevi*: pentecostal y supone 1-2 Cor anteriores a Gal).

5384 *Kreitzer* Larry, Notations on First and Second Corinthians in Albert SCHWEITZER's 1929 New Testament: AndrUnS 28 (1990) 219-235; phot. 235.

5385 *Rossano* P., La prima lettera ai Corinzi; il Vangelo nella metropoli: Aquinas 33 (R 1990) 243-256 [< ZIT 91,307].

5386 **Schrage** Wolfgang, Der erste Brief an die Korinther I. 1 Kor 1,1-6,11: EkK NT 7/1. Z 1991, Benziger. x-436 p. DM 118. 3-545-23121-6 (Neuk 3-7887-1378-X) [NTAbs 36,279].

5387 **Senft** Christopher, La première épître aux Corinthiens²ʳᵉᵛ 1990 ➤ 6, 6322: ᴿComSev 24 (1991) 420-2 (M. de *Burgos*).

5388 **Talbert** Charles H., Reading Corinthians: a new commentary for preachers 1987 ➤ 3,5851... 6,6323; also (new subtitle) L 1990, SPCK. xxiii-188 p. £10. – ᴿTLond 94 (1991) 120s (R.A. *Burridge*: relies strongly on chiasms, also for identifying Paul's opponents).

G5.2 *1 & 1-2 ad Corinthios* – *themata,* topics.

5389 *Castelli* Elizabeth A., Interpretations of power in 1 Corinthians: ➤ 311, Semeia 54 (1991) 197-222.

5390 **Fuller** Ruth M., A Pauline understanding of rewards; its background and expression in First Corinthians: diss. Fuller, ᴰ*Hagner* D. Pasadena 1991. 400 p. 91-20004. – DissA 52 (1991s) 574-A.

5391 *Gerlin* Andrea, Comunidad y moralidad; prescripciones paulinas a los Corintios interpretadas en la Regla de san AGUSTÍN, ᵀ*Anoz* José: ➤ 540, AugM 36 (1991) 119-126.

5392 **Gooch** Paul W., [1 Cor 13,12] Partial knowledge; philosophical studies in Paul [1 Cor ...] 1987 ➤ 3,5857; 5,6112: ᴿPhoenix 45 (1991) 174-7 (Wendy E. *Helleman*).

5393 *Goulder* Michael D., Sophía in 1 Corinthians: NTS 37 (1991) 516-534.

5394 **Green** Michael, To Corinth with love 1988 ➤ 4,6023: ᴿNESTR 12 (1991) 37-40 (H. N. *Karjian*).

5395 *Hyldahl* Niels, The Corinthian 'parties' and the Corinthian crisis: ST 45,1 (1991) 19-32.

5396 *Klein* Thomas A. P., Eine Jungfrau aus Korinth am südlichen Nachthimmel im 'Ernestus' des Odo von Magdeburg?: Hermes 119 (1991) 127s.

5397 *La Serna* Eduardo de, Los orígenes de 1 Corintios: Biblica 72 (1991) 192-216; Eng. 216: basically answers to questions in writing (7,1; 8,1; 12,1; 16,1) to which are added reactions to oral information that the situation had worsened (1-6...).

5398 *Lindemann* Andreas, Paulus und die korinthische Eschatologie [1-2 Kor]; zur These von einer 'Entwicklung' im paulinischen Denken: NTS 37 (1991) 373-399.

5399 **Mitchell** Margaret M., Paul and the rhetoric of reconciliation; an exegetical investigation of the language and composition of 1 Corinthians [diss. Chicago 1989, ᴰ*Betz* H.]: HermUntT 28. Tü 1991, Mohr. xiii-380 p. [TR 88,164]. 3-16-145794-3.

5400 *Murphy-O'Connor* Jerome, Christ and ministry: Pacifica 4,2 (1991) 121-136 [< NTAbs 36,52].

5401 **Ott** Rudi, Dialogische Bibeldidaktik; korrelative Auslegung der Korintherbriefe in der Kolleg-/Studienstufe: EurHS .../406. Fra 1990, Lang. 553 p. – ᴿTrierTZ 100 (1991) 317-9 (J. *Theis*).

5402 *Pittner* Bertram, Das Entstehen eines christlichen Menschenbildes beobachtet am Beispiel des I. Korintherbriefes: ➤ 564, Erfurter 1989/90, 20-30.

5403 *Rubio Miralles* Francisco, Los signos de la predicación en I Corintios según San Juan Crisóstomo: Scripta Fulgentina 1 (Murcia 1991s) 95-126.

5404 **Voigt** Gottfried, [DDR] Paulus an die Korinther; [= BR] Gemeinsam glauben, hoffen, lieben, Kor 1. B 1989, Ev.-V. 128 p. ➤ 5,6031: ᴿTLZ 116 (1991) 35s (G. *Heintze*).

5405 *Willis* Wendell, Corinthusne deletus est? [or *deleta*? anyway the article is in English; most commentators hold the city was destroyed in 146 B.C.]: BZ 35 (1991) 233-241.

5406 **Wire** Antoinette C., The Corinthian women prophets 1990 ➤ 6,6329: ᴿExpTim 103 (1991s) 83 (Ruth B. *Edwards*: she reconstructs the part of a conversation which she does not hear).

G5.3   1 Cor 1-7: *sapientia crucis ... abusus matrimonii.*

5406* **Piguet** H., [1 Cor 1-4] La folie de Dieu; lettre de Paul aux chrétiens d'aujourd'hui. Aubonne 1991, Moulin. 91 p. – ᴿEsprVie 101 (1991) 524 (L. *Walter*).

5407 **Pogoloff** Stephen M., Logos and sophia; the rhetorical situation of 1 Corinthians 1-4 in the light of Greco-Roman rhetoric: diss. Duke, ᴰ*Smith* D. M. Durham NC 1990. 450 p. 91-19334. – DissA 52 (1991) 576-A (RelStR 18,173, without 'Logos and sophia' in title).

5408 **Theis** Joachim, Paulus als Weisheitslehrer; der Gekreuzigte und die Weisheit Gottes in 1 Kor 1-4 [Diss. Trier ➤ 6,6330]: BUnt 22. Rg 1991, Pustet. v-575 p. DM 58 [TLZ 117,360-3, G. *Sellin*]. 3-7917-1276-4.

5409 **Brown** Alexandra R., Paul's apocalyptic word of the cross; perception and transformation in 1 Corinthians 1-2: diss. Columbia. NY 1990. 305 p. 91-27823. – DissA 52 (1991s) 1386s-A.

5410 *Pfitzner* V. C., [1 Cor 1,1-3; 16,19-24] Proclaiming the name; cultic narrative and eucharistic proclamation in First Corinthians: LuthTJ 25,1 (Adelaide 1991) 15-25 [< NTAbs 36,53].

5411 *Gragg* Douglas L., Discourse analysis of 1 Corinthians 1:10 - 2:5: LingBib 65 (1991) 37-57.

5412 *Díaz Mateos* Manuel, 'Cristo no me llamó a bautizar sino a evangelizar' (1 Cor 1,17): RTLim 25 (1991) 343-367.

5413 *Marshall* Molly T., Forsaking a theology of glory; 1 Corinthians 1:18-31: ➤ 448c, ExAuditu 7 (1991) 101-4.

5414 *Trotti* John B., 1 Corinthians 1:18-31 [folly to the Greeks], expository: Interpretation 45 (1991) 63-66.

5415 *Penna* Romano, 1 Cor 1,18-25 / 7,29-31 / 13 / 15,45-49 / 2 Cor 4,7-5,10 / 10-13 [< RivB, Biblica, Lateranum, ᶠ*Cipriani* S., *al.*]: ➤ 247, L'Apostolo 1991, 200-212 / 213-222 / 223-239 / 240-268 / 269-298 / 299-331.

5416 *Montagnini* Felice, 'Videte vocationem vestram' (1 Cor 1,26): RivB 39 (1991) 217-221.

5417 **Bockmuehl** Markus N. A., [1 Cor 2,7-10] Revelation and mystery in ancient Judaism and Pauline Christianity: WUNT 2/36, ᴰ1990 ➤ 6,6334: ᴿJTS 42 (1991) 240-2 (A. J. M. *Wedderburn*); TrinJ 12 (1991) 106-112 (D. S. *Huffman*).

5418 *de Lacey* D. R. [1 Cor 3,16] *hoîtinés este hymeîs*; the function of a metaphor in St. Paul: ➤ 15, ᶠBAMMEL E., Templum 1991, 391-409.

5419 a) *Lassen* Eva Maria, The use of the father image in imperial propaganda and 1 Corinthians 4:14-21; – b) *Rosner* Brian S., Temple and holiness in 1 Cor 5; – c) *Clarke* Andrew D., Another Corinthian Erastus inscription [1960, beside 1929]: TyndB 42 (1991) 127-136 / 137-145 / 146-151.

5420 *Harris* Gerald, The beginnings of Church discipline; 1 Corinthians 5: NTS 37 (1991) 1-21.

5421 *Vos* Geerhardus, A sermon on 1 Corinthians 5:7: Kerux 5,3 (1990) 1-8.

5422 a) *Sellin* Gerhard, 1 Korinther 5-6 und der 'Vorbrief' nach Korinth; Indizien für eine Mehrschichtigkeit von Kommunikationsakten im ersten Korintherbrief; – b) *Winter* Bruce W., Civil litigation in secular Corinth and the Church; the forensic background to 1 Corinthians 6:1-8: NTS 37 (1991) 535-558 / 559-572.

5423 *Derrett* J. D. M., Judgement and 1 Corinthians 6: NTS 37 (1991) 22-36.

5424 *Rosner* Brian S., Moses appointing judges, an antecedent to 1 Cor 6,1-6?: ZNW 82 (1991) 275-8.

5425 *Porter* S. E., How should *kollōmenos* in 1 Cor 6,16.17 be translated [not just 'unites' but 'sells into bondage']: ETL 67 (1991) 105s.

5426 **Deming** Will, Paul on marriage and celibacy; the Hellenistic background of 1 Corinthians 7: diss. ᴰ*Betz* H. Chicago 1991. 418 p. – RTLv 23, p. 543.

5427 *Orge Ramírez* Manuel †, El propósito temático de 1 Corintios 7; un discernimiento sobre la puesta en práctica del ideal de la continencia sexual y el celibato: Claretianum [27 (1987) 5-125; 28 (1988) 5-114] 31 (1991) 125-152.

5428 *Callahan* A., A note on 1 Corinthians 7:21 [slave/freedman]: JIntdenomC 17,1s (Atlanta 1989s) 110-4 [➤ NTAbs 36,365].

5429 *Glenny* W. Edward,   1 Corinthians 7:29-31 and the teaching of continence in the Acts of Paul and Thecla: GraceTJ 11 (1990) 53-70.

G5.4   *Idolothyta ... Eucharistia:*   **1 Cor 8-11.**

5430 **Probst** Hermann,   Paulus und der Brief; die Rhetorik des antiken Briefes als Form der paulinischen Korintherkorrespondenz ['1 Kor 8-10', Diss. Erlangen 1985, ᴰ*Roloff* J.]:   WUNT 2/45.   Tü 1991, Mohr.   xii-407 p. DM 120 [TR 88,163; DM 99, NTAbs 36,277]. 3-16-145678-5.

5431 *Delobel* Joel, [1 Cor 8,6; Col 1,15...] Christ, the lord of creation, ᵀ*Koperski* Veronica: LvSt 16 (1991) 155-169.

   Martin Dale B., Slavery as salvation (1 Cor 9,19) ᴰ1990 ➤ 5647.

5432 *Barbaglio* Giuseppe,   'E tutti in Mosè sono stati battezzati nella nube e nel mare', 1 Cor 10,2: ➤ 561*d*, Origini del battesimo 1989/91, 167-191.

5433 **Alappat** Vincent,   Paul's contribution to an understanding of the Lord's Supper; an exegetico-theological study of 1 Cor 10,14-22 and 11,17-34: diss. Pont. Univ. Gregoriana, ᴰ*Grech* P.   R 1991s. – InfPUG 24/123, 9.

5434 *Vattioni* F.,   Calice del Signore, calice dei demoni; mensa del Signore, mensa dei demoni (1 Cor 10,21; Isa 65,11): ➤ 565, Sangue 1989/91, 261-311.

5435 *a) Schreiner* Thomas R.,   Head coverings, prophecies and the Trinity; 1 Cor 11:2-16; – *b) Carson* D. A., 'Silent in the churches'; on the role of women in 1 Cor 14:33b-36: ➤ 375, Recovering 1991, 124-139 . 485-7 / 149-153 . 487-490.

5436 *Corrington* Gail P.,   The 'headless woman'; Paul and the language of the body in 1 Cor 11:2-16:   PerspRelSt 18 (1991) 223-232.

5437 *Wilson* Kenneth T. [1 Cor 11,2-16] Should women wear headcoverings?: Bibliotheca Sacra 148 (1991) 442-462.

5438 *a) Engberg-Pedersen* T.,   Proclaiming the Lord's death; 1 Corinthians 11:7-34 and the forms of Paul's theological argument; – *b) Kraftchick* Steven J., [2 Cor] Death in us, life in you; the apostolic medium: ➤ 446, SBL Sem 30 (1991) 592-617 / 618-637.

5439 *Engberg-Pedersen* Troels,   1 Corinthians 11:16 and the character of Pauline exhortation: JBL 110 (1991) 679-689.

5440 *Lampe* Peter, *a)* Das korinthische Herrenmahl im Schnittpunkt hellenistisch-römischer Mahlpraxis und paulinischer Theologia Crucis (1 Kor 11,17-34); ZNW 82 (1991) 183-213; – *b)* The Corinthian Eucharistic dinner party; exegesis of a cultural context: Affirmation 4,2 (Richmond 1991) 1-15 (4/3, 17-25) [< NTAbs 36,203].

5441 *Campbell* R. Alastair, [1 Cor 11:21] Does Paul acquiesce in divisions at the Lord's Supper?:   NT 33 (1991) 61-70.

5442 *Maccoby* Hyam, [1 Cor 11,23-30] Paul and the Eucharist [< Paul and Hellenism, SCM 1991]: NTS 37 (1991) 247-267.

G5.5   **1 Cor 12s ... Glossolalia, charismata.**

5443 **Bentivegna** Giuseppe,   Effusione dello Spirito Santo e doni carismatici; la testimonianza di S. Agostino 1990 ➤ 6,6366: ᴿRasT 32 (1991) 219s (A. *Barruffo*).

5444 **Boring** M. Eugene,   The continuing voice of Jesus; Christian prophecy and the Gospel tradition. Louisville 1991, W-Knox.   303 p. $19 pa. 0-664-25184-6 [TDig 39,51].

5445 **Bridges** Carl B.,   Paul and the pneumatics; a study in social control: diss. Union Theol. Sem. Richmond 1990. 212 p. 91-17784. – DissA 52 (1991s) 189-A.

5446 **Crowe** Terrence R., Towards a common witness; a comparative study of the Assemblies of God and the Catholic charismatic renewal: diss. Marquette, ᴰ*Carey* P. Milwaukee 1991, 436 p. 91-33790. – DissA 52 (1991s) 1174-A.

5447 **Devailly** Anne, Les charismatiques. P 1990, Découverte. 260 p. F 109. – ᴿEsprVie 101 (1991) 635 (R. *Epp*); Études 374 (1991) 139s (J. *Thomas*).

5448 **Farnell** F. David, The NT prophetic gift; its nature and duration: diss. Dallas Theol. Sem. 1990. 434 p. 91-25339. – DissA 52 (1991s) 965-A.

5449 **Gerosa** Libero, Charisma und Recht; Kirchenrechtliche Überlegungen zum 'Urcharisma' der neuen Vereinigungsformen in der Kirche: Horizonte NF 27. Einsiedeln 1989, Johannes. 303 p. – ᴿTPhil 66 (1991) 309s (R. *Sebott*).

5450 **Giesriegl** Richard, Die Sprengkraft des Geistes; Charismen und apostolischer Dienst... 1 Kor 1989 ⮕ 5,6075; 6,6373: ᴿTLZ 116 (1991) 33s (C. *Wolff*).

5451 **Goff** James R.ᴶ, Fields white unto harvest; Charles F. PARHAM and the missionary origins of Pentecostalism. L 1988. 236 p. – ᴿZKG 102 (1991) 417-9 (W. J. *Hollenweger*).

5452 **Gowins** John J., A pastoral psychological study of glossolalia: diss. Iliff, ᴰ*Graham* L. Denver 1990. 221 p. 91-06646. – DissA 52 (1991s) 966-A.

5453 **Hocken** P., Rassemblés par l'Esprit; la grâce œcuménique du renouveau [One Lord 1987 ⮕ 5,6080], ᵀ. P 1989, D-Brouwer. 181 p. F 65. – ᴿNRT 113 (1991) 464 (L. *Volpe*).

5454 *a) Hoffmann* Paul, Das paulinische Konzept einer charismatischen Gemeinde; – *b) Suhl* Alfred, [Gal I.] Ein Konfliktlösungsmodell der Urkirche und seiner Geschichte; – *c) Oberlinner* Lorenz, Zwischen Anpassung und Konflikt: BiKi 45 (1990) 72-79 / 80-86 / 87-93.

5455 *a) Knoch* Otto, Erneuerung aus der Kraft des Geistes Gottes; die katholische Charismatische Gemeindeerneuerung; Werden, Wollen, Eigenart, Bedeutung; – *b) Niewiadomski* Józef, Die nachkonziliaren Traditionalisten: TPQ 139 (1991) 355-361 / 362-9.

5456 **Land** Steven J., A passion for the Kingdom; an analysis and revision of Pentecostal spirituality: diss. Emory, ᴰ*Saliers* E. Atlanta 1990. – RelStR 18,174.

5457 *Langella* Alfonso, *a)* Doni di guarigione e prodigi nei credenti secondo il NT; – *b)* La funzione terapeutica della salvezza nell'esperienza del movimento carismatico: Asprenas 38 (1991) 147-169 / 477-490.

5458 **Meistre** Savin, Gemeentebou in terme van die charismata: diss. *Pieterse* H. Pretoria 1991. 265 p. – RTLv 23, p. 565.

5459 *Minear* Paul S., Propheten Gottes; das Wesen ihrer Berufung [NT: 'Frauen und Männer']: ⮕ 160, ᶠVISCHER L., Ök. Theol. 1991, 175-191.

5460 **Nation** Garey D., The hermeneutics of Pentecostal-Charismatic restoration theology; a critical analysis: diss. SW Baptist Theol. Sem. 1990. 268 p. 91-15308. – DissA 52 (1991s) 193-A.

5461 **Neitz** Mary Jo, Charisma and community; a study of religious commitment within the charismatic renewal (new observations). New Brunswick 1987, Transaction. xxi-294 p. £24.50. – ᴿHeythJ 32 (1991) 266s (F. A. *Sullivan*: good insight of a sociologist-observer).

5462 *a) Nwahaghi* Felix N., Priesthood and prophecy in Judeo-Christian religion; – *b) Nereparampil* Lucius, Christ the prophet; – *c) Nesy* D., Hindu priesthood; – *d) Nooruddin* M., Prophets in Islam: JDharma 15 (1990) 5-17 / 18-27 / 28-39 / 40-44.

5463 *Parmentier* Martien, 'Heil und Heilung'; Erfahrungen mit einer erneuerten Praxis: IkiZ 82 (1992) 25-37.

5464 *Ruschitzka* E., Charisma zur Mündigkeit — Amt zur Disziplin? Der Apostel Paulus und sein Problem mit dem Selbstbewusstsein der Gemeinde in Korinth: ➤ 373, Mündigkeit 1989, 121-142.

5465 *Scippa* Vincenzo, I carismi per la vitalità della Chiesa; studio esegetico su 1 Cor 12-14; Rm 12,6-8; Ef 4,11-13; 1 Pt 4,10-11: Asprenas 38 (1991) 5-25.

5466 *Siniscalco* Paolo, Sognatori e visionari, veggenti e profeti dall'antichità ai tempi odierni [< ᴱ*Semeraro* S., Don Bosco e Brasilia 1988/-]: AugR 30 (1990) 127-143.

5467 *a)* *Theobald* Michael, 'Prophetenworte verachtet nicht!' (1 Thes 5,20); Paulinische Perspektiven gegen eine institutionelle Versuchung; – *b)* *Greinacher* Norbert, Apostel, Propheten und Lehrer — damals und heute; – *c)* *Siefer* Gregor, Prophetie versus Amtskirche? Die notwendige Spannung zwischen Inspiration und Institution in der verwalteten Welt der établierten Grosskirchen; – *d)* *Gross* Walter, Prophetie gegen Institution im alten Israel? Warnung vor vermeintlichen Gegensätzen: TüTQ 171 (1991) 30-47 / 48-63 / 2-15 / 15-30.

5468 *Vanhoye* Albert, Carismi: ➤ 669, DizTF (1990)...

_____

5469 *Paige* Terence, 1 Corinthians 12.2; a pagan *pompē*?: JStNT 44 (1991) 57-65.

5470 *Söding* Thomas, 'Ihr aber seid der Leib Christi' (1 Kor. 12,27); exegetische Beobachtungen an einem zentralen Motiv paulinischer Ekklesiologie: Catholica 45 (1991) 135-162.

5471 *Leipold* Heinrich, Der Weg des Glaubens unter dem Kriterium der Liebe; Bibelarbeit über 1 Kor 13: Im Lichte der Reformation 34 (Gö 1991) 25-33 [< ZIT 91,254].

5472 **Maillot** Alphonse, L'hymne à l'amour; éloge de la vie ordinaire selon 1 Corinthiens 13. Aubonne 1990, Moulin. 98 p. – ᴿProtestantesimo 46 (1991) 155 (B. *Subilia*: vivace pastore).

5473 *Smit* J., The genre of 1 Corinthians 13 in the light of classical rhetoric: NT 33 (1991) 193-216.

5474 *Stuart* Elizabeth, [1 Cor 13; 4,8-13] Love is... Paul: ExpTim 102 (1990s) 264-6.

5475 *Martin* Dale B., [1 Cor 13,1] Tongues of angels and other status indicators: JAAR 59 (1991) 547-580; bibliog. 581-9.

5476 *Johnson* Michael, [1 Cor 13,12] Face to face: ProcGLM 11 (1991) 222-237.

5477 *Maier* Walter A., An exegetical study of 1 Corinthians 14:33b-38: ConcordTQ 55 (1991) 81-104 [< NTAbs 36,55].

5478 *Gerberding* Kieth A., [1 Cor 14,34s] Women who toil in ministry, even as Paul: CurrTMiss 18 (1991) 285-291.

G5.6   **Resurrectio;** *1 Cor 15*... [➤ F5.6; H9].

5479 **Pyne** Robert A., The resurrection as restoration; a thematic study in Paul's theology: diss. Dallas Theol. Sem. 1990. 349 p. 91-25345. – DissA 52 (1991s) 969-A.

5480 *Lambrecht* Jan, Line of thought in 1 Cor 15,1-11: Gregorianum 72 (1991) 655-670; franç. 670, 'En dialogue avec G. CLAUDEL 1988'.

5481 *Zimmer* Christoph, Das argumentum resurrectionis in 1 Kor 15,12-20: LingBib 65 (1991) 25-35; Eng. 36.

5482 *a) Gubler* Maria-Louise, ... Nun aber ist Christus von den Toten auferweckt worden, als Erster der Entschlafenen (1 Kor 15,20); – *b) Woschitz* Karl M., Ostererscheinungen — Grundlage des Glaubens: Diakonia 22,1 (Mainz 1991) 1-5 / 6-16.

5483 **Teani** Maurizio, Corporeità e risurrezione; l'interpretazione di 1 Cor 15,35-49 nel Novecento: diss. Pont. Univ. Gregoriana, D*Vanni* Ugo. R 1991s. – InfPUG 24/123, 11.

5484 *Horn* Friedrich W., 1 Korinther 15,56 — ein exegetischer Stachel [Hab.-Vorlesung Göttingen 1990]: ZNW 82 (1991) 88-105.

G5.9 **Secunda epistula ad Corinthios.**

5485 **Aejmelaeus** Lars, Streit und Versöhnung; das Problem ... 2 Kor [1983] T*Trabant* K.-J. 1987 ➔ 3,5985; 4,6122: RTLZ 116 (1991) 31-33 (C. *Wolff*).

5486 *Bieringer* R., Der 2. Korintherbrief in den neuesten Kommentaren: ETL 67 (1991) 107-130.

5487 **Crafton** Jeffrey A., The agency of the Apostle; a dramatistic analysis of Paul's responses to conflict in 2 Corinthians [diss. 1989 ➔ 5,6130]: JStNT supp 51. Sheffield 1991, Academic. 188 p. £21. 1-85075-268-0. – RExpTim 103 (1991s) 53s (Margaret E. *Thrall*).

5488 **Danker** F. W., II Cor: Augsburg Comm. 1989 ➔ 5,6131: 6,6428: RCrit-RR 4 (1991) 185-7 (W. *Willis*); IndTSt 27 (1990) 357-9 (L. *Legrand*); JTS 42 (1991) 254s (C. J. A. *Hickling*); Neotestamentica 25 (1991) 177 (V. *Krüger*); RB 98 (1991) 148 (J. *Murphy-O'Connor*).

5489 **Klauck** H.-J. 1 Cor c. 1984 + 2 Cor c. 1986, NEchter. Lp 1990, St. Benno. 235 p. DM 30. 3-7462-0508-5 [NTAbs 36,276].

5490 **Murphy-O'Connor** Jerome, The theology of the second letter to the Corinthians: NTTheol. C 1991, Univ. xii-166 p. $30; pa. $11 [TDig 38,371]. 0-521-35379-3; -898-1. – RExpTim 103 (1991s) 66s (C. S. *Rodd* doubts that 'a theology' of any isolated book can be so given).

5491 *Simmons* B. E., Introduction to II Corinthians: TEdr 40 (1989) 59-65 (-143, *al.* on 2 Cor passages) [< NTAbs 36,204].

5492 *Taylor* N. H., The composition and chronology of Second Corinthians: JStNT 44 (1991) 67-87.

5493 **Wolff** Christian, Der zweite Brief des Paulus an die Korinther: ThHk NT 8, 1989 ➔ 6,6439: RRivB 39 (1991) 360s (G. *Segalla*); Salesianum 53 (1991) 775s (J. *Heriban*); TLZ 116 (1991) 512-4 (E. *Lohse*).

5494 **Young** Frances, *Ford* David F. Meaning and truth in 2 Cor 1987 ➔ 3,5999 ... 6,6440: RHeythJ 32 (1991) 81s († F. F. *Bruce*); JDharma 15 (1990) 357-9 (P. *Kalluveettil*); RB 98 (1991) 285-290 (J. *Murphy-O'Connor*).

5495 *a) Hughes* Frank W., The rhetoric of reconciliation; 2 Corinthians 1.1 - 2.13 and 7.5-8.24; – *b) Danker* Frederick W., Paul's debt to the De corona of Demosthenes; a study of rhetorical techniques in Second Corinthians: ➔ 86, FKENNEDY G., Persuasive 1991, 246-261 / 262-280.

5496 *Derrett* J. D. M., Nai (2 Cor 1:19-20): FgNt 4 (1991) 205-9.

5497 *Reed* Jeffrey T., [2 Cor 2,13; Act 18,28] The infinitive with two substantival accusatives; an ambiguous construction? [MOELLER H., KRAMER A.]: NT 33 (1991) 1-27.

5498 **Fredrickson** David E., Paul's bold speech in the argument of 2 Corinthians 2:14-7:16: Diss. Yale, ᴰ*Malherbe* A. NHv 1990. 358 p. 91-21100. – DissA 52 (1991s) 571-A; RelStR 18,173.

5499 **Jong** M. de, Paulus, struikeblok of toetsteen; een studie van 2 Korintiërs 2:12-4:6 als bijdrage in het gesprek met Israel [prot. diss. Bru, ᴰ*Nielsen* J.]. Kampen 1989, Mondiss. 235 p. ƒ37,50. 90-66511-04-4. – ᴿNedTTs 45 (1991) 146s (H. W. *Hollander*).

5500 *Breytenbach* Cilliers, [2 Kor 2,14-16; 4,7-15; Mk 8,34] Christologie, Nachfolge/Apostolat: BTZ 8 (1991) 183-196 + 3 fig.

5501 **Oliveira** Anacleto de, Die Diakonie der Gerechtigkeit und der Versöhnung in der Apologie des 2. Korintherbriefs [2,14-4,6; 5,11-6,10]: NTAbh NF 21, ᴰ1990 ➤ 6,6443: ᴿCritRR 4 (1991) 182-4 (F. W. *Danker*); JTS 42 (1991) 680s (Margaret E. *Thrall*); NRT 113 (1991) 434-6 (X. *Jacques*); RB 98 (1991) 468s (J. *Murphy-O'Connor*).

5501* **Renwick** David A., [2 Cor 2,14-3,18] Paul, the Temple, and the presence of God [diss. Union Richmond, ᴰ*Achtemeier* P.]: BrownJudSt 224. Atlanta 1991, Scholars. xiv-179 p. [TR 88,252]. 1-55540-615-7.

5502 *Duff* Paul B., Metaphor, motif, and meaning; the rhetorical strategy behind the image 'led in triumph' in 2 Corinthians 2:14: CBQ 53 (1991) 79-92.

5503 **Belleville** Linda L., Reflections of glory; Paul's polemical use of the Moses-doxa tradition in 2 Corinthians 3,1-10 [diss. Toronto, ᴰ*Longenecker* R.): JStNT supp 52. Sheffield 1991, JStOT. 351 p. £35 [TR 88, 163]. 1-85075-265-6.

5504 **Stockhausen** Carol K., Moses' veil 2 Cor 3,1-4,6: AnBib 116, ᴰ1989 ➤ 5,6148; 6,6449: ᴿJBL 110 (1991) 543-5 (J. S. *Siker*: uneven); RB 98 (1991) 148-150 (J. *Murphy-O'Connor*: eisegesis compounded, but useful); Salmanticensis 38 (1991) 377-9 (R. *Trevijano*, también sobre BELLEVILLE).

5505 *Duff* Paul B., Apostolic suffering and the language of processions in 2 Corinthians 4:7-10: BibTB 21 (1991) 158-165.

5506 **Pate** C. Marvin, Adam Christology as the exegetical substructure of 2 Corinthians 4:7-5:21 [diss. Marquette]. Lanham MD 1991, UPA. ix-174 p. $34.50. 0-8191-8188-9 [TDig 39,78: teaches at Ch Moody Inst.]. – ᴿExpTim 103 (1991s) 119 (Margaret E. *Thrall*, written Margart).

5507 *Chvala-Smith* Anthony J., The politics of reconciliation in 2 Corinthians 5: ProcGLM 11 (1991) 210-221.

5508 *a) Macky* Peter W., St. Paul's collage of metaphors in II Cor. 5:1-10; ornamental or exploratory?; – *b) Anderson* John T., The cosmological roots of Pauline metaphors; – *c) Fiore* Benjamin, Root metaphors in Paul — Pauline comings and goings; the travel image; – *d) Holland* Glenn S., The problem of the root; a response to the three papers: ProcGLM 11 (1991) 162-173 / 151-161 / 174-184 / 185-190.

5509 **Mell** Ulrich, [2 Cor 5,14-17; Gal 6,11-18] Neue Schöpfung; eine traditionsgeschichtliche und exegetische Studie zu einem soteriologischen Grundsatz paulinischer Theologie [diss. 1987s ➤ 3,5650*]: BZNW 56, 1989 ➤ 5,5826; 6,6106.6461: ᴿCBQ 53 (1991) 708s (B. *Fiore*); ÉTRel 66 (1991) 125s (G. *Wagner*); NedTTs 45 (1991) 147s (J. S. *Vos*); RechSR 79 (1991) 54s (J.-N. *Aletti*); RHPR 71 (1991) 242 (M. *Carrez*).

5510 **Webb** William J., New covenant and second Exodus/return theology as the contextual framework for 2 Corinthians 6:14-7:1: diss. Dallas Theol. Sem. 1990. 313 p. 91-25349. – DissA 52 (1991s) 1375s-A.

5511 *Lodge* John G., The Apostle's appeal and readers' response; 2 Corinthians 8 and 9: ChSt 30 (1991) 59-75.

5512 *Zeilinger* Franz, 2 Kor 9; Theologie des Klingelbeutels oder Manifest der Hoffnung?: ➤ 6,171, FSTÖGER A., Exeget 1990, 185-201.

5513 **Heckel** Ulrich, Kraft in Schwachheit; das Sich-Rühmen der Schwachheiten in 2 Kor 10-13 auf dem Hintergrund der paulinischen Theologie: Diss. D*Hengel* M. Tübingen 1991. 366 p. – TLZ 117,880; RTLv 23, p. 544.

5514 **Sumney** Jerry L., Identifying Paul's opponents... 2 Cor: JStNT supp 40, D1990 ➤ 6,6469: RBiblica 72 (1991) 431-5 (J. J. *Bartolomé*); BZ 35 (1991) 274s (B. *Heininger*); ÉTRel 66 (1991) 289 (M. *Carrez*); Interpretation 45 (1991) 424.6 (J. H. *Sieber*); Salmanticensis 38 (1991) 382-5 (R. *Trevijano*).

5515 **Sundermann** Hans-Georg, Der schwache Apostel und die Kraft der Rede; eine rhetorische Analyse von 2 Kor 10-13: Diss. D*Harnisch* W. Marburg 1991s. – RTLv 23, p. 547.

5516 *Eckert* Jost, 'Ich ermahne euch bei der Sanftmut und Milde des Christus' (2 Kor 10,1); zur pastoralen Strategie des Apostels Paulus: TrierTZ 100 (1991) 39-55.

5517 *Baumert* Norbert [2 Cor 10,2; 1 Thes 3,3...] Brüche im paulinischen Satzbau?: FgNt 4,7 (1991) 3-17; Eng. 17-20.

5518 *Loubser* J. A., Winning the struggle (or, How to treat heretics) (2 Cor 12:1-10): JTSAf 75 (1991) 75-83 [< NTAbs 36,56].

5519 *McCloskey* James, [2 Cor 12,1-10] The weakness gospel: BToday 28 (1990) 235-241.

5520 *a*) *Woods* Laurie, Opposition to a man and his message; Paul's 'thorn in the flesh' (2 Cor 12:7); – *b*) *Murphy-O'Connor* Jerome, The date of 2 Corinthians 10-13: AustralBR 39 (1991) 44-53 / 31-43 [NTAbs 36,367s].

G6.1 Ad Galatas.

5521 **Aland** K., Text und Textwert [1s, Röm Kor 1991 ➤ 5158] 3. Galaterbrief bis Philipperbrief / 4. Kolosserbrief bis Hebräerbrief: ArbNTTextf 18s. B 1991, De Gruyter. v-658 p. DM 228 / v-941 p. DM 318. 3-11-013444-6 / -5-4 [NTAbs 36,430].

5522 **Arnold** James P., Jewish Christianity in Galatians; a study of the teachers and their gospel: diss. Rice, D*Kelber* W. 1991. 367 p. 91-35993. – DissA 52 (1991s) 2592-A.

5523 **Barclay** John, Obeying the truth... Gal D1988 (Clark; also Mp 1991, Fortress): RCrítRR 4 (1991) 167-9 (D. J. *Lull*); HeythJ 32 (1991) 398s (F. F. *Bruce*); Interpretation 45 (1991) 94 (R. G. *Hall*); RechSR 79 (1991) 51s (J.-N. *Aletti*).

5524 **Corsani** Bruno, Lettera ai Galati: CommStoEseg 9, 1990 ➤ 6,6480: RÉTRel 66 (1991) 439s (A. *Moda*); Protestantesimo 46 (1991) 330-2 (Yann *Redalié*); STEv 2 (1990) 331s (N. *Ciniello*); StPatav 38 (1991) 147-150 (G. *Segalla*).

5525 **Cosgrove** Charles H., The cross and the Spirit... Gal D1988 ➤ 4,6170; 6,6481: RJBL 110 (1991) 171-3 (G. *Lyons*); JRel 71 (1991) 93s (D. J. *Lull*); TrinJ 11 (1990) 339-342 (D. A. *Carson*: unconvincing); TTod 48 (1991s) 374s (C. B. *Cousar*).

5526 **Crouch** James A., The scope and significance of deliverance from the present evil age in Galatians: diss. Baptist Theol. Sem., D*Dukes* J. New Orleans 1991. 239 p. 91-37411. – DissA 52 (1991s) 2588-A.

5527 **Dunnam** Maxie D., Galatians, Ephesians, Philippians; Colossians, Philemon: Communicator's Comm. 8. Waco 1982, Word. 420 p. 0-8499-0161-8 [-3808-2, de luxe].

5528 **Ebeling** Gerhard, La verità dell'evangelo; commento alla Lettera ai Galati, ᵀRizzi A.; introd. Corsani B.: Dabar 7. Genova 1989, Marietti. xviii-308 p. – ᴿAsprenas 38 (1991) 246s (V. Scippa); CrNSt 12 (1991) 184-8 (A. Gallas); RivB 39 (1991) 68-70 (G. Segalla); Salesianum 53 (1991) 766s (J. Heriban).

5529 **Fung** R.Y.K., The epistle to the Galatians: NICNT 1988 ➤ 4,6173 ... 6,6485: ᴿHeythJ 32 (1991) 397s (F. F. Bruce).

5530 **Giavini** Giovanni, Galati; libertà e legge nella Chiesa²ʳᵉᵛ [¹1983]: LoB 2.8. Brescia 1991, Queriniana. 109 p. 88-391-1584-2.

5531 **Gordon** B., Zurich and the Scottish Reformation; Rudolf GWALTHER's Homilies on Galatians of 1576: ➤ 35, ᶠCAMERON J., Humanism 1990, 207-219 [< RHE 87,48*].

5532 **Hong** I.-G., The perspective of Paul in Galatians: Scriptura 36 (Stellenbosch 1991) 1-16 [< NTAbs 36,56].

5533 **Howard** George, Paul; crisis in Galatia² 1990 [¹1979] ➤ 6,6487; £25: ᴿRB 98 (1991) 470s (J. Murphy-O'Connor).

5534 — Pitta Antonio, Paolo e la crisi in Galazia; una significativa seconda edizione (Howard G. 1990 ¹1979); Asprenas 38 (1991) 529-534.

5535 **Jegher-Bucher** Verena, Der Galaterbrief auf dem Hintergrund antiker Epistolographie und Rhetorik; ein anderes Paulusbild [Diss. Basel]: ATANT 78. Z 1991, Theol.-V. viii-214 p. 3-290-10817-1 [NTAbs 36,122].

5536 **Mussner** F., Lettera ai Galati 1987 ➤ 3,6047 ... 5,6179: ᴿCiuD 203 (1990) 229s (J. Gutiérrez).

5537 **Pitta** Antonio, Dal 'rhetorical criticism' alla 'retorica letteraria'; rilevanza della 'dispositio' nella lettera ai Galati: diss. Pont. Ist. Biblico, ᴰAletti J. R 1991. – AcPIB 9/8, 685. & 732s; RTLv 23, p. 546.

5538 **Rohde** J., Der Brief des Paulus an die Galater: Theologischer Handkommentar zum NT 9. B 1989, Ev.-V. xxiii-284 p. DM 32. 3-374-00464-4. [NTAbs 36,278].

5539 **Stott** John R. W. The message of Galatians; Only one way: The Bible Speaks Today. Leicester 1991 = 1968, Inter-Varsity. 191 p. 0-85110-7346 / US (ICF-Madison WI). 0-87784-288-4.

5540 Toit A. B. du, Analise van die opbouw, argumentatiegang en pragmatiek van die Galatebrief ... gedetailleerd: SkrifKerk 12 (1991) 214-241 [< NTAbs 36,368].

5541 **Zuurmond** R., God noch gebod; bijbelstheologische notities over de brief van Paulus aan de Galaten. Baarn 1990, Ten Have. 218 p. ƒ20. – ᴿCollatVL 21 (1991) 320 (H. Hoet).

5542 Fredriksen Paula, Judaism, the circumcision of Gentiles, and apocalyptic hope; another look at Galatians 1 and 2: JTS 42 (1991) 532-564.

5543 Hansen G.W., [Gal 1s] The basis of authority: TrinityTJ 2 (Singapore 1990) 42-54 [< NTAbs 36,56].

5544 a) Hester James D., Placing the blame; the presence of epideictic in Galatians 1 and 2; – b) Hall Robert G., Historical inference and rhetorical effect; another look at Galatians 1 and 2: ➤ 86, ᶠKENNEDY G., Persuasive 1991, 281-307 / 308-320.

5545 **Bartolomé** Juan J., El evangelio y su verdad ... Gal 2,5.14: BtScRel 82, ᴰ1988 ➤ 4,6188; 5,6191: ᴿAugM 35 (1990) 188 (J. A. *Galindo*); RechSR 79 (1991) 53s (J. N. *Aletti*); ScripTPamp 23 (1991) 1034-7 (C. *Basevi*).

5546 *a*) *McLean* Bradley H., Galatians 2.7-9 and the recognition of Paul's apostolic status at the Jerusalem conference; a critque of G. LUEDE-MANN's solution; – *b*) *Böttger* Paul C., Paulus und Petrus in Antiochien; zum Verständnis von Galater 2.11-21: NTS 37 (1991) 67-76 / 77-100.

5547 **Hennings** Ralph, Der Briefwechsel zwischen AUGUSTINUS und HIE-RONYMUS und ihr Streit um den Kanon und die Auslegung von Gal 2,11-14: Diss. ᴰ*Ritter* A. Heidelberg 1991s. – RTLv 23, p. 548.

5548 *a*) *McHugh* John, Galatians 2:11-14; was Peter right?; – *b*) *Dunn* James D. G., What was the issue between Paul and 'those of the circumcision'?: ➤ 437, Paulus 1988/91, 319-330 / 295-313 (-7).

5549 **Wechsler** Andreas, Geschichtsbild und Apostelstreit; eine forschungs-geschichtliche und exegetische Studie über den antiochenischen Zwi-schenfall (Gal 2,11-14) [ev. Diss. Erlangen-N 1991, ᴰ*Merk*. – TR 87 (1991) 516; RTLv 23, p. 547]: BZNW 62. B 1991, de Gruyter. xiii-425 p. 3-11-01339-7.

Winger Joseph M., [Gal 2,15-21] *Dià poiou nómou*? The meaning of *nómos* in the letters of Paul: ᴰ1990 ➤ 5363.

5551 *Lambrecht* Jan, Transgressor by nullifying God's grace; a study of Gal 2,18-21: Biblica 72 (1991) 217-236; franç. 238.

5552 **Farahian** Edmond, Le 'je' paulinien ... Gal 2,19-21: AnGreg 253, 1988 ➤ 4,6191 ... 6,6515: ᴿEstB 49 (1991) 143s (F. *Pastor-Ramos*); RB 98 (1991) 146-8 (J. *Murphy-O'Connor*: unconvincing); RechSR 79 (1991) 46s (J.-N. *Aletti*: thèse fragile); TLZ 116 (1991) 277-280 (H. *Hübner*: ignoriert wichtige Literatur).

5553 *Hamerton-Kelly* Robert, [Gal 2,20 ...] Allegory, typology, and sacred violence; sacrificial representation and the unity of the Bible in Paul and PHILO: ➤ 76, ᶠHILGERT E., StPhilonAn 3 (1991) 53-70.

5554 *Reinmuth* Eckart, [Gal 2,21 ...] 'Nicht vergeblich' bei Paulus und Pseu-do-PHILO, Liber antiquitatum biblicarum: NT 33 (1991) 97-123.

5555 **Hansen** G. W., Abraham in Galatians [3; 4,23-31] ᴰ1989 ➤ 5,6170; 6,6517: ᴿCBQ 53 (1991) 705-7 (B. S. *Crawford*); ÉTRel 66 (1991) 124s (É. *Cuvillier*); TLZ 116 (1991) 505s (G. *Haufe*).

5556 *Lambrecht* Jan, Vloek en zegen; een studie van Galaten 3,10-14: Col-latVL 21 (1991) 133-157.

5557 *Dalton* William J., The meaning of 'we' in Galatians [3,1-14 ..., pagan converts; but 2,15-17 Jewish evangelizers]: AustralBR 38 (1990) 33-44 [< NTAbs 36,368].

5558 *Braswell* Joseph P. 'The blessing of Abraham' versus 'the curse of the law'; another look at Gal 3:10-13: WestTJ 53 (1991) 73-91 [< BS 148 (1991) 489s (R. A. *Pyne*); NTAbs 36,57].

5559 *Hopko* Thomas, Galatians 3:28; an Orthodox interpretation: StVlad 35 (1991) 169-186.

5560 *Johnson* S. Lewis, Role distinctions in the Church; Gal 3:28: ➤ 375, Recovering 1991, 154-164. 490-2.

5561 *a*) *De Lorenzi* Lorenzo, 'Se voi siete di Cristo ...' (Gal 3,29); la crescita della Parola in Paolo; – *b*) *Corsani* Bruno, L'interpretazione tipologica della storia di Agar e Sara in Gal 4: ➤ 292*b*, ParSpV 24 (1991) 179-212 / 213-224.

5562 **Denton** Peter T.[J], [Gal 4,1-7; Rom 8,1-30] 'No longer a slave but a son[J]; a model for Pauline ethics: diss. Duke, [D]*Via* D. Durham NC 1991. 319 p. 91-30660. – DissA 52 (1991s) 1785-A; RelStR 18,173.

5563 *Bundrick* D. R. Tà stoicheîa toû kósmou (Gal 4:3): JEvTS 34 (1991) 353-364 [< NTAbs 36,206].

5564 *Schweizer* Eduard, [Gal 4,4s; Röm 8,3; Jn 3,16s; 1 Jn 4,9] Was meinen wir eigentlich, wenn wir sagen 'Gott sandte seinen Sohn...'?: NTS 37 (1991) 204-224.

5565 **Gouw** Rudolf G. M., Hagar and Isaac (Gal 4:21-31), an allegory around Jerusalem: diss. Pont. Univ. Gregoriana, [D]*Vanni* U. Roma 1991. 315 p. – RTLv 23, p. 544 [< DissA-C].

5566 *Wagner* Guy, Les enfants d'Abraham ou les chemins de la promesse et de la liberté; exégèse de Galates 4,21 à 31: RHPR 71 (1991) 285-295; Eng. 422.

5567 *Clausi* Benedetto, Letture antiche e medievali di Gal 4,24: ➤ 452, An-StoEseg 8,2 (1991) 385-404.

5568 **Russell** Walter B.[III], Paul's use of *sárx* and *pneûma* in Galatians 5-6 in light of the argument of Galatians: diss. Westminster Theol. Sem. 1991, [D]*Silva* Moisés. 309 p. 91-25536. – DissA 52 (1991s) 1396s-A.

5569 **Duvall** Jeffrey S., [Gal 5; Rom 6; Php 2] A synchronic analysis of the indicative-imperative structure of Pauline exhortation: diss. SWBaptist Theol. Sem. 1991. 372 p. 92-13033. – DissA 52 (1991s) 4365-A.

5570 *Blank* Josef, [Gal 5,1] ¿Qué libertad nos ha dado Cristo? Dimensión teológica de la libertad [< StiZt 207 (1989) 460-472], [TE]*Suñer* Pedro: SelT 30 (1991) 225-232.

5571 *a*) *De Lorenzi* Lorenzo, 'Liberati per restare liberi', Gal 5,1; – *b*) *Panimolle* Salvatore A., La libertà personale nei Vangeli e nella Lettera ai Romani; – *c*) *Vanni* Ugo, Filemone, un caso, una lezione; – *d*) *Gargano* Innocenzo, L'*apátheia* come libertà in ORIGENE: ➤ 292a, ParSpV 23 (1991) 199-224 / 183-198 / 225-236 / 253-266.

5572 *Garlington* D. B., Burden-bearing and the recovery of offending Christians (Galatians 6:1-5): TrinJ 12 (1991) 151-183.

5573 *Álvarez Verdes* Lorenzo, La ley de Cristo en Gal 6,2; convergencia semántica de los sintagmas *nómos Christoû* y *noûs Christoû*: ➤ 421, Luso-Esp 1989/91, 329-346.

5574 *Stagg* Frank, Galatians 6:7-10: RExp 88,3 (1991) 247-251.

G6.2 Ad Ephesios.

5575 **Arnold** Clinton E., Ephesians; power and magic: SNTS 63, [D]1989: ➤ 5,6213; 6,6524: [R]CBQ 53 (1991) 488s (R. A. *Wild*: rightly shows relevance of magic-texts to Eph 'power' but less-convincingly claims Ephesus was a magic-center); CritRR 4 (1991) 165-7 (W. *Wink*); HeythJ 32 (1991) 399s (Mary E. *Mills*); JStNT 42 (1991) 121s (T. *Klutz*).

5576 **Bouttier** Michel, L'épître de s. Paul aux Éphésiens: Comm NT 9b. Genève 1991, Labor et Fides. 316 p. – [R]ComSev 24 (1991) 422s (M. de *Burgos*); ÉTRel 66 (1991) 479 (*ipse*); Études 375 (1991) 566 (S. *Marrow*).

5577 **Cho Kyong Cheol** (Tscho ... Tscheol), Die ethischen Weisungen und ihre theologische Begründung im Epheserbrief: ev. Diss. [D]*Hofius* O. Tübingen 1991s. 354 p. – RTLv 23, p. 547; TLZ 117, 714.

5578 *Goulder* M. D., [Eph., genuine, to Laodicea] The visionaries of Laodicea: JStNT 43 (1991) 15-39.

5579 *Martin* Alain-G., Quelques remarques sur le texte syriaque de l'Épître aux Éphésiens: ÉTRel 66 (1991) 99-103.
5580 **Martin** Ralph P., Ephesians, Colossians, and Philemon: Interpretation comm. Louisville 1991, Knox. xiii-156 p. $18. 0-8042-3139-7 [NTAbs 36,433].
5581 a) *Moritz* Thorsten, 'Summing up all things'; religious pluralism and universalism in Ephesians; – b) *Winter* Bruce W., In public and in private; early Christian interactions with religious pluralism: → 485, One God 1991, 88-111 / 112-134.
5582 **Patzia** Arthur G., Ephesians [p. 119-295], Colossians [p. 3-102], Philemon [p. 103-117]: New International [NIV] Bible Commentary 10. Peabody MA 1990 = 1984, Hendrickson. xviii-311 p. 0-943575-19-2.
5583 **Penna** Romano, La lettera agli Efesini: Scritti delle origini cristiane 10, 1988 → 4,6206; 5,6223: ᴿCrNSt 12 (1991) 341-351; Eng. 351 (G. D. *Cova*); Gregorianum 72 (1991) 144-6 (E. *Farahian*).
5584 *Rossano* Piero, Ipotesi di un 'Corpus ephesinum Novi Testamenti': → 451, Efeso I, 1990/1, 17-31.
5585 **Schlier** Heinrich, La carta a los Efesios, comm., ᵀ*Ruiz-Garrido* C.: BtEstB 71. S 1991, Sígueme. 415 p. – ᴿNatGrac 38 (1991) 389s (F. *Ramos*); TVida 32 (1991) 326 (M. A. *Ferrando*).
5586 *Schnackenburg* Rudolf, Ephesians; a commentary [1982 → 63,6040], ᵀ*Heron* Helen. E 1991, Clark. 256 p. £25. 0-567-09556-8 [NTAbs 36,279].
5587 *Schnackenburg* Rudolf, Ephesus; Entwicklung einer Gemeinde von Paulus zu Johannes: BZ 35 (1991) 41-64.
5588 **Stockhausen** Carol L., Letters in the Pauline tradition...: Message BSp 13, 1989 → 5,6228: ᴿCBQ 53 (1991) 346s (J. *Winkler*).
5588* *Swain* Lionel, Ephesians: NTMessage. Wilmington/Dublin 1980, Glazier / Veritas. xii-114 p. £7. 0-86217-031-1.
Tscho Kyong Tscheol → 5577, Cho supra.

5589 *Vos* Geerhardus, The spiritual resurrection of believers; a sermon on Ephesians 2:4,5, ᵀ*Gaffin* Richard B.ᴶ: Kerux 5,1 (1990) 3-21.
5590 **Faust** Eberhard, Christus und der Kaiser stiften Frieden; gnoseologisches Heilsverständnis und politisch-soziales Zeitbezug in Eph 2,11-22, untersucht im Zusammenhang mit der Geschichte griechisch-jüdischer Konflikte und römischer Diasporapolitik in Kleinasien seit Caesar: Diss ᴰ*Theissen* G. Heidelberg 1991s. – RTLv 23, p. 543.
5591 *Klappert* Bertold, Miterben der Verheissung; Christologie und Ekklesiologie der Völkerwallfahrt zum Zion, Eph 2,11-22: → 46*, ᶠEHRLICH E., Israel 1991, 72-109.
5592 a) *Long* William R., Ephesians 2:11-22, a rescue mission; – b) *Jarvis* Cynthia A., Ephesians 3:14-21; – c) *Eckel* Paul T., Ephesians 6:10-20: Interpretation 45 (1991) 281-3 / 283-8 / 288-293.
5593 *Jiménez Castellano* J. I., [Eph 2,14-18] Cristo es nuestra paz, nos ha reconciliado: Mayéutica 16,42 (Murcilla 1990) 483-542 [< NTAbs 36,57].
5594 **Dockery** David S., Ephesians 4:1-6, expository: RExp 88 (1991) 79-82.
5595 **Harris** Walker H.ᴵᴵᴵ, The descent of Christ in Ephesians 4:7-11; an exegetical investigation with special reference to the influence of traditions about Moses associated with Psalm 68:19: diss. Sheffield 1988. 318 p. BRDX-94935. – DissA 52 (1991s) 3632-A.
5596 *Taylor* Richard A., The use of Psalm 68:18 in Ephesians 4:8 in light of the ancient versions: BS 148 (1991) 319-336.

5597 *a*) *Knight* George W.[III], Husbands and wives as analogues of Christ and the Church; Eph 5:21-33 and Col 3:18-19; – *b*) *Grudem* Wayne, [Eph 5,23] The meaning of *kephalē* ('head'); a response to recent studies: → 375, Recovering 1991, 165-178.492-5 / 425-468.534-541.

5598 — *Grudem* Wayne, [Eph 5,23; 1 Cor 11,3] The meaning of *kephalē* ('head'); a response to recent studies: TrinJ 11,1 (1990) 3-72.

5599 **Miletic** Stephen F., 'One flesh' Eph 5,29 [diss. [D]*Wild* R.]: AnBib 115, 1988 → 4,6221 ... 6,6546: [R]ScEsp 43 (1991) 118-121 (Y. *Guillemette*); TLZ 116 (1991) 114s (G. *Schille*: arge Druckfehler).

5600 *Kostenberger* Andreas J., [Eph 5,32] The mystery of Christ and the Church; head and body 'one flesh': TrinJ 12 (1991) 79-94.

5601 *Harris* W. Hall [III], [Eph 6,9-12...] 'The Heavenlies' reconsidered; *ouranós* and *epouránios* in Ephesians: BS 148 (1991) 72-89.

G6.3 Ad Philippenses.

5602 **Bruce** Frederick F., Philippians: New International Bible Commentary [NIV] 11. Peabody MA 1989 = 1983, Hendrickson. xvi-183 p. 0-943575-15-X. – [R]Vidyajyoti 55 (1991) 363 (P. M. *Meagher*, also on *Daalen*, Galatians).

5603 *Gillman* F. M., Early Christian women at Philippi: Journal of Gender in World Religions 1,1 (Montreal 1990) 59-79 [< NTAbs 36,58].

5604 *Marshall* I. Howard, Which is the best commentary? 12. Philippians: ExpTim 103 (1991s) 39-42: no answer attempted.

5605 **Melick** R. R., Philippians, Colossians, Philemon: New American (NIV) comm. Nv 1991, Broadman. 384 p. $23. 0-8054-0132-6 [NTAbs 36,277].

5606 **Motyer** J. A., The message of Philippians; Jesus our joy: The Bible speaks today. Leicester 1991 = 1984, Inter-Varsity. 234 p. 0-85110-710-9 / US 0-88784-310-4.

5607 **O'Brien** Peter T., The Epistle to the Philippians: NIGT. GR 1991, Eerdmans. xli-597 p. $40. 0-8028-2392-0 [TDig 39,279].

5608 **Portefaix** Lilian, Sisters rejoiee 1988 → 4,6228 ... 6,6256: [R]TR 87 (1991) 109s (R. *Pesch*).

5609 **Silva** Moisés, Philippians: [E]*Barker* K.,] Wycliffe Evangelical Commentary [first to appear]. Ch 1988, Moody. xxiii-255 p. $24. – [R]CritRR 4 (1991) 230-2 (C. E. *Arnold*); EvQ 63 (1991) 348s (I. H. *Marshall*).

5610 *McClendon* James W.[J], Philippians 2:5-11, expository: RExp 88 (1991) 439-444.

5611 **Fowl** Stephen E., [Phlp 2,6-11] The story of Christ in the ethics of Paul... hymnic material [D]1990 → 6,6564: [R]ÉTRel 66 (1991) 598 (M. *Bouttier*); TLZ 116 (1991) 908-912 (G. *Strecker*).

5612 **Hofius** Otfried, Der Christushymnus Philipper 2,6-11[2]; Untersuchungen zu Gestalt und Aussage eines urchristlichen Psalms [= [1]1976 + Supp. p. 103-136]: WUNT 17. Tü 1991, Mohr. ix-170 p. DM 78. 3-16-145672-6 [NTAbs 36,275].

5613 *Trudinger* P., A down-to-earth ascension; a note on Philippians 2:6-9; Faith & Freedom 44,3 (Ox 1991) 126-9 *harpagmós*, not 'up there' but (as with Jesus) in complete self-giving.

5614 *Kruse* H., ❶ 'At the name of Jesus all beings should bend their knees' (Phil 2:10): KatKenk 59 (1991) 39-56 [< NTAbs 36,58: kneeling was commoner than standing for prayer].

5615 *Reumann* John, Christology in Philippians, especially chapter 3: ➤ 72, ᶠHAHN F., Anfänge 1991, 131-140.
5616 *Greenlee* J. H., Saint Paul — perfect but not perfected; Php 3,12: NoTr 4,4 (1990) 53-55 [< NTAbs 36,58].
5617 *Bilde* Per, Eskatologi, soteriologi og kosmologi hos Paulus på grundlag av Fil. 3,20-21 og beslægtede tekster; et bidrag til debatten om GRONBECHS Paulus-bog: DanTTs 54 (1991) 209-227 [< ZNW 83,149].
5618 *Bugg* Charles, Philippians 4:4-13, expository: RExp 88,3 (1991) 253-7.
5619 *Allen* Ronald J., The partnership that makes all things possible — Philippians 4:10-20: RestQ 33 (1991) 169-...[< ZIT 91,645].
5620 *Peterman* Gerald W., 'Thankless thanks'; the epistolary social convention in Philippians 4: 10-20: TyndB 42 (1991) 261-270.

G6.4 Ad Colossenses.

5621 **Ghini** Emanuela, Lettera ai Colossesi, commento pastorale: LPast 21, 1990 ➤ 6,6578: ᴿProtestantesimo 46 (1991) 218 (L. *De Lorenzi*: un 'commento pastorale' è sempre una scommessa; qui riuscito); RivB 39 (1991) 372-7 (anche L. *De Lorenzi*).
5622 **Harris** Murray J., Colossians and Philemon: Exegetical Guide to the Greek NT [first of 20 projected volumes]. GR 1991, Eerdmans. xxix-310 p. $22 pa. 0-8028-0375-X [TDig 38,361].
5623 ᵀᴱ**Parker** David C., Philip MELANCHTHON, Paul's letter to the Colossians 1989 ➤ 6,6579: ᴿÉTRel 66 (1991) 131 (Marguerite *Soulié*); ScotJT 44 (1991) 385 (D. F. *Wright*: hopefully he will go on to translate M's commentary on Col, a completely different work).
5624 **Pokorný** Petr, Colossians, a commentary [ThK 10, 1987], ᵀ*Schatzmann* Siegfried S. Peabody MA 1991, Hendrickson. xxx-232 p. $20. 0-943575-38-9 [*Hodgson* R.: 'European evangelical theology at its best'; *Best* R., mainly theological].
5625 **Rogers** Patrick V., Colossians: NTMessage 15. Wilmington/Dublin 1980, Glazier/Veritas. xxii-98 p. £7. 0-86217-032-X.
5626 **Ryen** J. O., Hvem skrev Kolosserbrevet? [Paul or a disciple]: TKirk 62 (1991) 175-186 [< NTAbs 36,207].
5627 **Sappington** Thomas J., Revelation and redemption at Colossae. Sheffield 1991, JStOT. 266 p. £30. 1-85075-307-5. – ᴿExpTim 103 (1991s) 83s (D. S. *Russell*).
5628 **Talercio** Giuseppe, [Col. comm.] Nuove creature in Cristo; con Paolo alla scuola del Maestro. Mi 1990, Paoline. 186 p. Lit. 10.000. – ᴿCC 142 (1991,3) 450 (P. *Ferrari da Passano*).

5629 *Tripp* David, [Col 1,12-20] The Colossian 'hymn'; seeking a version to praise with: OneInC 26 (1990) 231-7.
5630 *Helyer* Larry R., Recent research on Colossians 1:15-20 (1980-1990): GraceTJ 12,1 (1991) 51-67.
5631 **Reid** Jennings B., [Col 1,15-20; Php 2,5-11], Jesus; God's emptiness, God's fullness; the Christology of St. Paul, 1990 ➤ 6,6113,8091: ᴿNRT 113 (1991) 441, (X. *Jacques*); ScripTPamp 23 (1991) 1066s (C. *Basevi*).
5632 *Perriman* Andrew, The pattern of Christ's sufferings; Colossians 1:24 and Philippians 3:10-11: TyndB 42 (1991) 62-79.

5633 **Radjagukguk** Robinson, *Tà stoicheîa toû kósmou* and life with Christ; an exegetical study of Col. 2:6-3:4: diss. Lutheran School of Theology, ᴰ*Krentz* E. 1991. 246 p. 91-29535. – DissA 52 (1991s) 2182-A.

5634 **De Maris** Richard E., [Col 2,8] The reconstruction of the Colossian philosophy: diss. Columbia, ᴰ*Scroggs* R. NY 1990. 195 p. 91-18551 – DissA 52 (1991s) 570-A.

5635 **Yates** Roy, Christ triumphant, a study of Colossians 2:13-15: diss. Manchester 1989. 289 p. BRD-92556. – DissA 52 (1991s) 577-A.

5636 *Yates* Roy, Colossians 2.15; Christ triumphant: NTS 37 (1991) 573-591.

5637 *Christopher* Gregory T., A discourse analysis of Colossians 2:16 -3:17: GraceTJ 11 (1990) 205-220.

5638 *Yates* Roy, The Christian way of life; the paraenetic material in Colossians 3:1-4:6: EvQ 63 (1991) 241-251 [< ᴰManchester Col 2,13-15].

5639 **Gielen** Marlies, [Col 3 ...] Tradition und Theologie neutestamentlicher Haustafelethik; ein Beitrag zur Frage einer christlichen Auseinanderstellung mit gesellschaftlichen Normen [ᴰ1988 Bonn, ᴰ*Merklein* H.]: Athenäum Mg. BoBB 75. Fra 1990, Hain. 600 p. – ᴿTPhil 66 (1991) 577s (H. *Engel*).

5640 *Roth* David, Colossians 3:1-18: Kerux 6,3 (1991) 27-37.

G6.5   *Ad Philemonem* – **Slavery in NT Background.**

5640* *Annequin* Jacques, L'esclavage antique [ForASkl; Servus ...]: DialHA 16,2 (1990) 323-340 [17,2 (1991) 199-214].

5641 **Bradley** Keith R., Slavery and rebellion in the Roman world 1989 → 5,6293; 6,6594: ᴿAmHR 96 (1991) 1516s (D. B. *Nagle*: likely to be the standard reference work for years to come); ClasPg 86 (1991) 252-8 (W. J. *Tatum*); ClasR 41 (1991) 146s (A. *Keaveney*); Gerión 9 (1991) 322 (P. *López Baria Q.*); JRS 81 (1991) 192s (Jane F. *Gardner*).

Callahan A., slave 1 Cor 7,21 → 5428.

5641* ᴱ**Capozza** Maria, Schiavitù, manumissione e classi dipendenti nel mondo antico [10 art., Padova 25-27 nov. 1976]: Univ. PublStoAnt 13. R 1979, Bretschneider. 203 p.

5642 *Dennison* James T.ᴶ, Paul, Philemon, Onesimus and the new creation in Christ Jesus: Kerux 6,3 (1991) 38-45.

5643 **Dumont** J.-C., Servus; Rome et l'esclavage: Coll. ÉcFR 103, 1987 → 5,6296; 6,6598: ᴿGerión 9 (1991) 329-333 (D. *Plácido*); RÉAnc 91,3s (1989s) 73-87 (Monique *Clavel-Lévêque*).

5644 **Klein** Richard, Die Sklaverei in der Sicht der Bischöfe AMBROSIUS und AUGUSTINUS 1988 → 4,6269 ... 6,6600: ᴿGnomon 63 (1991) 177s (G. *Gottlieb*); Mnemosyne 44 (1991) 240s (J. J. *Thierry*).

5645 *a) Lewis* Lloyd A., An African American appraisal of the Philemon-Paul-Onesimus triangle; – *b) Martin* Clarice J., The Haustafeln (household codes) in African American biblical interpretation; 'free slaves' and 'subordinate women': → 433, Stony the road 1986/91, 232-246 / 206-231.

5646 *Martin* Clarice J., The rhetorical function of commercial language in Paul's letter to Philemon (verse 18): → 86, ᶠKENNEDY G., Persuasive 1991, 321-337.

5647 **Martin** Dale B., Slavery as salvation ... [1 Cor 9,19] Pauline ᴰ1990 → 6,6602: ᴿTTod 48 (1991s) 492.494s (Beverly R. *Gaventa*: vitality).

5648 *Martin* Dale B., Ancient slavery, class, and early Christianity: Fides et Historia 23,2 (1991) 105-113 [< NTAbs 36,223].

5649 *Nordling* John G., Onesimus fugitivus; a defense of the runaway slave hypothesis in Philemon: JStNT 41 (1991) 97-119.

5650 *a) Rapske* B.M., [Phm 10] The prisoner Paul in the eyes of Onesimus; – *b) Barclay* John M.G., Paul, Philemon and the dilemma of Christian slave-ownership: NTS 37 (1991) 187-203 / 161-186.

5651 *Snyman* A.H., A semantic discourse analysis of the letter to Philemon: ➤ 307, Text 1991, 83-99.

5652 *Straus* Jean A., Sur la date de quelques contrats de vente d'esclave d'époque romaine conservés sur papyrus: ➤ 98*, [F]MEKHITARIAN A., CdÉ 66 (1991) 297-302.

5653 **Yavetz** Zvi, Slaves and slavery in ancient Rome. New Brunswick NJ 1991, Transaction. viii-182 p. 0-88738-128-6.

G6.6 Ad Thessalonicenses.

5654 **Adinolfi** Marco, La prima lettera ai Tessalonicesi nel mondo greco-romano 1990 ➤ 6,6606: [R]ArTGran 54 (1991) 350s (A. *Segovia*); Gregorianum 72 (1991) 575s (G. *Marconi*); LA 41 (1991) 574s (G.C. *Bottini*); NRT 113 (1991) 766s (X. *Jacques*).

5655 [E]**Collins** R.F., The Thessalonian correspondence 1988/90 ➤ 6,521: [R]JTS 42 (1991) 681s (M.D. *Hooker*); RivB 39 (1991) 493-500 (L. *De Lorenzi*); RThom 91 (1991) 515 (tit. pp.); TLZ 116 (1991) 905-8 (G. *Haufe*).

5656 *Collins* Raymond F., God in 1 Thes; Paul's earliest written appreciation of *ho theós*: LvSt 16 (1991) 137-154.

5657 *Holtz* Traugott, *a)* Traditionen im I. Thes.-brief [< [F]*Schweizer* E. 1983, 55-78]; – *b)* 'Euer Glaube an Gott'; zu Form und Inhalt von 1. Thess 1,9f [< [F]*Schürmann* H. 1977, 459-488]; – *c)* Der Apostel des Christus; der paulinische 'Apologie' 1. Thess 2,1-12 [< [F]*Krusche* W. 1982, 101-116]; – *d)* Das Gericht über die Juden und die Rettung ganz Israels (1. Thess 2,15f und Röm 11,25f): ➤ 211, Geschichte 1991, 246-269 / 270-296 / 297-312 / 313-325.

5658 **Malherbe** Abraham J., Paul and the Thessalonians 1987 ➤ 3,6178 ... 6,6611: [R]CurrTMiss 18 (1991) 137s (E. *Krentz*).

5659 **Marxsen** W., La prima lettera ai Tessalonicesi 1988 ➤ 4,6293 ... 6,6612: [R]RivB 39 (1991) 362s (R. *Fabris*).

5660 *a) Merk* Otto, Zur Christologie im 1. Thessalonicherbrief; – *b) Dietz-felbinger* Christian, Sohn und Gesetz; Überlegungen zur paulinischen Christologie [... Gal]: ➤ 72, [F]HAHN F., Anfänge 1991, 111-129.

5661 **Morris** Leon, 1-2 Thessalonians[2rev] [[1]1959]: NICNT. GR 1991, Eerdmans. xvi-278 p. $28. 0-8028-2168-5 [NTAbs 36,277].

5662 **Morris** Leon, 1,2 Thessalonians: Word **Themes** 1989 ➤ 5,6322: [R]EvQ 63 (1991) 275-7 (I.H. *Marshall*, also on MARTIN R. Cor. themes).

5663 *Pesch* Rudolf, La scoperta della più antica lettera [fuse in 1 Thes due lettere, una da Atene, altra da Corinto] 1987 ➤ 4,6295; 5,6324: [R]Protestantesimo 46 (1991) 217 (G. *Conte*).

5664 *Sánchez Bosch* Jorge, La chronologie de la première aux Thessaloniciens et les relations de Paul avec d'autres églises: NTS 37 (1991) 336-347.

5665 **Schoon-Janssen** J., Umstrittene 'Apologien' in den Paulusbriefen; Studien zur rhetorischen Situation des 1. Thessalonicherbriefes, des Galaterbriefes und des Philipperbriefes [ev. Diss. Göttingen 1988s]: GöTArb 45. Gö 1991, Vandenhoeck & R. 182 p. DM 40. 3-525-87399-9 [NTAbs 36,125].

5666 *Söding* Thomas, Der Erste Thessalonicherbrief und die frühe paulinische Evangeliumsverkündigung; zur Frage einer Entwicklung der paulinischen Theologie: BZ 35 (1991) 180-203.
5667 **Stott** John R. W., The message of Thessalonians; preparing for the coming King: The Bible speaks today. Leicester 1991, Inter-Varsity. 216 p.
5668 **Wanamaker** Charles A., The epistles to the Thessalonians: NIGT, 1990 ➤ 6,6621: ᴿCarthaginensia 7 (1991) 519 (M. *Álvarez Barredo*: 'Vanamaker', pero p. 577 'W–'); GraceTJ 12,1 (1991) 138s (R. A. *Young*).

5669 *Weatherly* Jon A., The authenticity of 1 Thessalonians 2.13-16; additional evidence: JStNT 42 (1991) 79-98.
5670 **Avotri** Solomon K., Possessing one's vessel in 1 Thess 4:4; marital or martial metaphor [*skeûos* for the male organ, but to inculcate celibacy]: diss. Iliff. Denver 1991. 111 p. 91-22244. – DissA 52 (1991s) 963-A.
5671 **Xavier** Aloysius, A study of 'theodídaktoi' (1 Thessalonians 4,9); source and theology: diss. Pont. Univ. Gregoriana, ᴰRasco E. Roma 1991. 273 p. – RTLv 23, p. 547 [< DissA-C].
5672 **Holland** G. S., The tradition ... 2 Thess: HermUnT 24, ᴰ1988 ➤ 4,6302 ... 6,6643: ᴿHeythJ 32 (1991) 256-8 († F. F. *Bruce*); RechSR 79 (1991) 45s (J.-N. *Aletti*).
5673 **Hughes** Frank W., Early Christian rhetoric and 2 Thessalonians: JStNT supp 30, 1989 ➤ 5,6331; 6,6644: ᴿAnglTR 73 (1991) 209-211 (R. I. *Pervo*); CBQ 53 (1991) 137s (D. F. *Watson*); CritRR 4 (1991) 203-5 (A. J. *Dewey*); RExp 88 (1991) 462s (C. A. *Loscalzo*).

G7 **Epistulae pastorales.**

5674 **Cothenet** E., Les épîtres pastorales 1990 ➤ 6,6651: ᴿEsprVie 101 (1991) 47s & 176 (L. *Walter*).
5675 **Fee** G. D., 1-2 Timothy Titus 1986 = 1984 ➤ 2,4912; 6,6653; also Peabody MA 1988, Hendrickson, 0-94-35751-09: ᴿCritRR 4 (1991) 191s (R. J. *Karris*, also on ODEN).
5676 **Fiore** Benjamin, Function of ... example, Socratic/Past: AnBib 105, ᴰ1986 ➤ 2,4913 ... 6,6654: ᴿTLZ 116 (1991) 280-2 (J. *Roloff*).
5677 **Knoch** O., 1. und 2. Timotheusbrief; Titusbrief 1988 ➤ 4,6311 ... 6,6657: ᴿRivB 39 (1991) 363s (R. *Fabris*).
5678 **McDermott** John S., The quest for community stabilization; a social science interpretation of the Pastoral Epistles: diss. Drew, ᴰDay Lala K. Madison NJ 1991. 231 p. 91-29311. – DissA 52 (1991s) 1381-A; RelStR 18,173, 'Dey'.
5679 **Merkel** Helmut, Die Pastoralbriefe, übersetzt und erklärt: NTD 9/1 [als ¹³*Jeremias* J.]. Gö 1991, Vandenhoeck & R. iv-114 p. DM 18 [TLZ 117,601, J. *Roloff*]. 3-525-51373-9.
5680 **Oden** Thomas C., First and Second Timothy and Titus [➤ 5,6343]; Interpretation comm. Louisville 1989, W-Knox. $17. 0-8042-3143-5. – ᴿInterpretation 45 (1991) 318 (C. E. *Brewster*).
5681 **Towner** Philip H., The goal of our instruction: JStNT supp 34, 1989 ➤ 5,6346; 6,6665: ᴿBiblica 72 (1991) 132-7 (R. *Schwarz*); ÉTRel 66 (1991) 126s (E. *Cuvillier*); Interpretation 45 (1991) 202 (N. *Elliott*); JTS 42 (1991) 256-8 (Frances M. *Young*); TLZ 116 (1991) 284s (A. *Weiser*).
5682 a) *Weiser* Alfons, Die Kirche in den Pastoralbriefen; Ordnung um jeden Preis? – b) *Roloff* Jürgen, Kampf gegen die Irrlehrer; – c) *Trummer* Peter, Gemeindeleiter ohne Gemeinden? – d) *Oberlinner* Lorenz, Ein ruhiges

Leben; ein Ideal für christliche Gemeinden?: BiKi 46 (1991) 107-113 / 114-120 / 121-6 / 98-106.
5683 **Wolfe** Benjamin P., The place and use of Scripture in the Pastoral Epistles: diss. Aberdeen 1991. – RTLv 23, p. 547.

G7.2 1-2 ad Timotheum.

5684 *Fee* Gordon D., *a)* The great watershed — intentionality and particularity/eternality; 1 Timothy 2: 8-15 [< Inerrancy and common sense (1980, Baker)]; – *b)* Hermeneutics and common sense; an exploratory essay on the hermeneutics of the Epistles [< *ibid.*]: ➤ 199, Gospel and Spirit 1991, 52-65 / 1-23.
5685 *Ferguson* Everett, *Tópos* in 1 Timothy 2:8: RestQ 33,2 (1991) 65-73 [< NTAbs 36,60].
5686 **Gritz** Sharon H., Paul, women teachers, and the mother goddess at Ephesus; a study of 1 Timothy 2:9-15 in light of the religious and cultural milieu of the first century [diss.]. Lanham MD 1991, UPA. xii-186 p. $37.50; pa. $18.75 [CBQ 53,735].
5687 *Kuske* D.P., An exegetical brief on 1 Timothy 2:12 (*oudè authenteîn andrós*): WisLuthQ 88,1 (1991) 64-67 [< NTAbs 36,373].
5688 *Grey* Mary, 'The woman will be saved through bearing children' (1 Tim 2.16); motherhood and the possibility of a contemporary discourse for women [*Kristeva* Julia ...]: Bijdragen 52 (1991) 58-69.
5689 *Reid* M.L., An exegesis of 1 Timothy 4:6-16: Faith and Mission 9,1 [Wake Forest NC 1991] 51-63 [< NTAbs 36,373].

5690 *Murphy-O'Connor* Jerome, 2 Timothy contrasted with 1 Timothy and Titus [differs on 30 points]: RB 98 (1991) 403-418.
5691 **Prior** Michael, Paul ... & 2 Tim: JStNT supp 23, 1989 ➤ 5,6356; 6,6680: ᴿCBQ 53 (1991) 339-341 (L. T. *Johnson*); DeltioVM 10,2 (1991) 58-61 (J. *Karavidopoulos* ⊖); HeythJ 32 (1991) 400s (F. F. *Bruce*).
5692 *Roloff* Jürgen, Der Weg Jesu als Lebensnorm (2 Tim 2,8-13); ein Beitrag zur Christologie der Pastoralbriefe: ➤ 72, ᶠHAHN F., Anfänge 1991, 155-167.
5693 *Moo* Douglas, [1 Tim 2,11-15] What does it mean not to teach or have authority over men?: ➤ 375, Recovering 1991, 179-193.495-9.
5694 *Pietersma* Albert, [2 Tim 3,8s] The apocryphon of Jannes and Jambres: ➤ 429, IOSOT 1989/91, 383-395.

5695 **Quinn** Jerome D. † (ᴱ*Boelter* Philip), The letter to Titus; a new translation with notes and commentary and an introduction to Titus, I and II Timothy, the Pastoral Epistles: AnchorB 35. NY 1990, Doubleday. xlviii-334 p. 0-385-05900-0.

G8 Epistula ad Hebraeos.

5696 **Attridge** Harold W., The epistle to the Hebrews: Hermeneia comm. 1989 ➤ 5,6362; 6,6683: ᴿBiblica 72 (1991) 286-290 (B. *Lindars*: a great commentary, a notable achievement); BibTB 21 (1991) 118 (J. N. *Neyrey*: magisterial); BR 7,5 (1991) 7.41 (B. A. *Pearson*); CBQ 53 (1991) 688s (M. L. *Soards*); JBL 110 (1991) 545-7 (C. R. *Koester*); TZBas 47 (1991) 368-370 (M. *Bachmann*).

5697 **Chay** Fred W., A strategy of motivation toward spiritual maturity in the book of Hebrews: diss. ᴰ*Reed* J. Dallas Theol. Sem. 1990. 147 p. 91-25335. – DissA 52 (1991s) 1784-A.

5698 *Chester* A. N., Hebrews; the final sacrifice: ➤ 384, Sacrifice 1991, 57-72.

5699 **Ellingworth** Paul, The epistle to the Hebrews. L 1991, Epworth. xiv-144 p. 0-7162-0474-6.

5700 **Frede** H. J., Vetus Latina 25/2 [Lfg 7s, 1990 ➤ 6,6693] Lfg 9, Heb 10,28-11,37; Lfg 10, Heb 11,37-13,10; Lfg 11, Heb 13,10 bis Schluss, Nachträge, Register. FrB 1991, Herder. p. 1477-1556 / 1557-1636 / 1637-1741. – ᴿRHE 86 (1991) 463 (P.-M. *Bogaert*, 7s); TR 87 (1991) 21-23 (G. D. *Kirkpatrick*, 3s; auch kurz über Colloque Frede Lv 1986/7).

5701 **Gooding** David, An unshakeable kingdom; the letter to the Hebrews for today ➤ 5,6373; Leicester/GR 1989, Inter-Varsity/Eerdmans, 255 p. /0-8028-0471-3. – ᴿEvQ 63 (1991) 350s (G. *Houston*).

5702 **Grässer** E., An die Hebräer I.; EkK 17/1, 1990 ➤ 6,6694: ᴿLA 41 (1991) 125-158 (N. *Casalini* si limita ai punti in cui l'esegesi non aiuta a chiarire il pensiero o spesso lo tradisce).

5703 *Grässer* Erich, Neue Kommentare zum Hebräerbrief: TRu 56 (1991) 113-139.

5704 **Guthrie** George H., The structure of Hebrews; a text-linguistic analysis: diss. SWBaptist Theol. Sem. 1991. 245 p. 92-13038. – DissA 52 (1991s) 4365-A.

5705 *Hegermann* Harald, Christologie im Hebräerbrief: ➤ 72, ᶠHAHN F., Anfänge 1991, 337-351.

5706 *Horak* Tomasz, ❷ Theologia fidei / Ecclesiologia in Epistola ad Hebraeos: ColcT 61,1 (1991) 49-62; lat. 62 / 61,2 (1991) 17-31; deutsch 31.

5707 **Josuttis** Manfred, Über alle Engel; politische Predigten zum Hebräerbrief. Mü 1990, Kaiser. 218 p. DM 34. 3-459-01860-7. – ᴿTsTNijm 31 (1991) 325 (F. *Peerlinck*).

5708 **Lane** William L., Hebrews 1-8 / 9-13: Word Comm. 47AB. Dallas 1991, Word. I. clvii-211 p., $25; II. xlvi + p. 213-617. 0-8499-0246-0; -935-X. [NTAbs 36,276].

5709 **Lehne** Susanne, The New Covenant in Hebrews: JStNT supp 44, ᴰ1990 ➤ 6,6700: ᴿBiblica 72 (1991) 592s (A. *Vanhoye*); ÉTRel 66 (1991) 440s (P. *Magne de la Croix*); JBL 110 (1991) 744-6 (C. R. *Koester*); JTS 42 (1991) 688-691 (A. S. *Browne*); RExp 88 (1991) 270 (J. E. *Jones*); TLZ 116 (1991) 912s (C. P. *März*).

5710 **Leschert** Dale F., Hermeneutical foundations of the Epistle to the Hebrews; a study in the validity of its interpretation of some core citations from the Psalms [45,6s; 8,4s; 95,7s]: diss. Fuller Theol. Sem., ᴰ*Fuller* D. Pasadena 1991. 385 p. 91-29273. – DissA 52 (1991s) 1373-A.

5711 **Lillie** D., Let us go on; studies in Hebrews 5 and 6; a handbook for disciples. Exeter 1991, Paternoster. viii-97 p. £3.50 pa. 0-85364-519-1. [NTAbs 36,433].

5712 **Lindars** Barnabas, The theology of the Letter to the Hebrews: NTTheol. C 1991, Univ. xiv-155 p. $30; pa. $11. 0-521-35487-0 [TDig 38,371]. – ᴿExpTim 103 (1991s) 65s (C. S. *Rodd*; but see his ➤ 5490ᴿ).

5713 *a*) *Lindars* Barnabas, Hebrews and the Second Temple; – *b*) *Gordon* Robert P., Better promises; two passages in Hebrews against the background of the OT cultus: ➤ 15, ᶠBAMMEL E., Templum 1991, 410-433 / 434-449.

5714 *Löhr* Hermut, Thronversammlung und preisender Tempel; Beobachtungen am himmlischen Heiligtum im Hebräerbrief und in den Sabbatopferliedern aus Qumran: → 438, Königsherrschaft 1986/91, 185-205.

5715 *MacLeod* David J., The present work of Christ in Hebrews: BS 148 (1991) 184-200.

5716 **Rissi** Mathias, Die Theologie des Hebräerbriefes ... : WUNT 41, 1987 → 3,6242 ... 5,6387: ᴿCrNSt 12 (1991) 183s (G. *Segalla*).

5717 **Schlossnikel** R. F., Der Brief an die Hebräer und das Corpus Paulinum; eine linguistische 'Bruchstelle' im Codex Claromontanus (P-BN grec 107 + 107a + 107b) und ihre Bedeutung im Rahmen von Text- und Kanongeschichte: VLatG 20. FrB 1991, Herder. 193 p. [NRT 114,754, X. *Jacques*]. 3-451-21936-0.

5718 **Scholer** John M., Proleptic priests; priesthood in the Epistle to the Hebrews ['project' supervision, *Longenecker* R.]: JStNT supp 49. Sheffield 1991, Academic. 243 p. £30. 1-85075-265-6.

5719 *Söding* Thomas, Zuversicht und Geduld im Schauen auf Jesus; zum Glaubensbegriff des Hebrärbriefes: ZNW 82 (1991) 214-239.

5720 **Strobel** August, Der Brief an die Hebräer, übersetzt und erklärt: NTD 9/2 [¹1975]. iv-202 p. 3-525-51374-7.

5721 *Szlaga* Jan, Die Eschatologie des Briefes an die Hebräer: RoczTK 34,1 (1991 für 1987) 73-85, auf deutsch, ᵀ*Ulrich* Herbert.

5722 **Vanhoye** Albert, Structure and message of the Epistle to the Hebrews², ᵀ*Swetnam* James H.: SubsBPont 12, 1989 → 5,6395: ᴿBTrans 42 (1991) 153 [P. *Ellingworth*, commending also 5 earlier volumes of the series].

5723 *Vanhoye* Albert, a) Hebraeos (carta a los); – b) Carisma; – c) Sacerdocio: → 683, NDizTB (1990) 4307 / 245-250 / 1387-98.

5724 *Vanhoye* Albert, Anamnèse historique et créativité théologique dans l'Épître aux Hébreux: → 30, ᶠBONNARD P., Mémoire 1991, 219-231.

5725 **Weiss** Hans-Friedrich, Der Brief an die Hebräer, übersetzt und erklärt¹ [= ¹⁵]: KeK NT 13. Gö 1991, Vandenhoeck & R. 901 p. 3-525-51625-8 [NTAbs 36,280].

5726 *Witherington* Benᴵᴵᴵ, The influence of Galatians on Hebrews: NTS 37 (1991) 146-152.

5727 **Übelacker** Walter G., Der Hebräerbrief als Appell I [1s; 13,22-25] ConBib NT 21, 1989 → 5,6397; 6,6710: ᴿBZ 35 (1991) 143-8 (F. *Laub*); JTS 42 (1991) 259-261 (R. *Williamson*); NedTTs 45 (1991) 253s (H. *Welzen*); RechSR 79 (1991) 47s (J.-N. *Aletti*).

5728 a) *Layton* Scott C., Christ over his house (Hebrews 3.6) and Hebrew ᵃšer 'al-ha-bayit; – b) *Nardoni* Enrique, Partakers in Christ (Hebrews 3.14): NTS 37 (1991) 473-7 / 456-472.

5729 a) *Gaffin* Richard B.ᴶ, [Heb 4:14] Christ, our High Priest in heaven; – b) *Baugh* Steven M., Firstborn over all; Colossians 1:15-20: Kerux 1,3 (1986) 17-27 / 28-34.

5730 *Miller* J. I. [Heb 5; Phm 6] Two Pauline Coptic fragments re-visited: ArPapF 37 (1991) 61-63.

5731 **Zesati Estrada** Carlos, Hebreos 5,7-8; estudio histórico-exegético [Diss. Pont. Ist. Biblico, ᴰ*Vanhoye* A.]: AnBib 113, 1990 → 6,6715: ᴿGregorianum 72 (1991) 770s (J. *Galot*); RivB 39 (1991) 377-9 (M. *Masini*).

5732 *Neyrey* Jerome H., 'Without beginning of days or end of life' (Hebrews 7:3); topos for a true deity: CBQ 53 (1991) 439-455.

5733 **Casalini** Nello, Dal simbolo alla realtà ... Ebr 9,1-14, 1989 ➤ 5,6408; 6,6718: ᴿCBQ 51 (1991) 318s (J. *Swetnam*: clearly reasoned and thoroughly usable dissertation, Paris Institut Catholique, including jury's reactions).

5734 *Laub* Franz, 'Ein fur allemal hineingegangen in das Allerheiligste' (Hebr 9,12) — Zum Verständnis des Kreuzestodes im Hebräerbrief: BZ 35 (1991) 65-85.

5735 *Jobes* Karen H., Rhetorical achievement in the Hebrews 10 'misquote' of Psalm 40: Biblica 72 (1991) 387-396.

5736 **Cosby** Michael R., The rhetorical composition and function of Hebrews 11 in light of example lists in antiquity [diss.] 1988 ➤ 4,6362; 6,6721: ᴿJBL 110 (1991) 548 (Mary Rose *D'Angelo*).

5737 ᴱ**Augustine** John H., William PERKINS, A commentary on Hebrews 11 (1609 edition): Classic Commentaries. NY 1991, Pilgrim. $35; pa. $20. 0-8298-0856-6; -7-4 [TDig 39,78 sans pp.].

5738 *Mende* Theresia, 'Wen der Herr liebhat, den züchtigt er' (Hebr 12,6); der alttestamentliche Hintergrund von Hebr 12,1-11; 1,1-4; 2,6-10: TrierTZ 100 (1991) 23-38.

5739 *Dennison* Charles G., The new heavens and the new earth; Hebrews 12:26-29: Kerux 5,1 (1990) 22-31.

5740 *Basevi* Claudio, La teología del matrimonio nell'Epistola agli Ebrei (Eb 13,4): AnnTh 4 (1990) 349-368.

5741 *Vos* Geerhardus, A sermon on Hebrews 13:8: Kerux 4,2 (1989) 12-21.

G9.1   1-2 Petri.

5742 *Adinolfi* Marco, Appunti ERODOTEI [11 volte in ATENAGORA] su Dio e l'uomo; un confronto con 1 Pt: RivB 39 (1991) 223-9.

5743 **Bosetti** Elena, Il Pastore; Cristo e la chiesa nella prima lettera di Pietro: RivB supp. 21, 1990 ➤ 6,6727: ᴿGregorianum 72 (1991) 613s (*ipsa*).

5744 **Cervantes Gabarrón** José, La Pasión de Jesucristo en la Primera Carta de Pedro; centro literario y teológico de la Carta [diss. Pont. Univ. Gregoriana (p. 9; non menzionato p. 6), ᴰ*Vanhoye* A. (Valencia 1991, Soler)]: Inst. S. Jerónimo 22. Estella 1991, VDivino. 434 p. 84-7151-745-0 [TR 88, 252].

5745 *Chin* Moses, A heavenly home for the homeless; aliens and strangers in 1 Peter: TyndB 42 (1991) 96-112.

5746 **Davids** Peter H., The First Epistle of Peter: NICNT, 1990 ➤ 6,6729: ᴿBTrans 42 (1991) 348-350 (D. C. *Arichea*); GraceTJ 11 (1990) 238-240 (H. A. *Kent*); RelStR 17 (1991) 365 (C. *Bernas*); RExp 88 (1991) 270 (J. E. *Jones*).

5747 **Elliott** J. H., A home for the homeless² [¹1981 ➤ 62,6815]. Mp 1990, Fortress. xxxvi-306 p. $17. 0-8006-2474-2 [NTAbs 36,120].

5748 **Feldmeier** Reinhard, Fremde in einer entfremdeten Welt; die Erschliessung christlichen Selbstverständnisses durch die Kategorie der Fremde im 1. Petrusbrief: ev. Diss. ᴰ*Hengel* M. Tübingen 1991s. – RTLv 23, p. 543.

5749 **Frankemölle** Hubert, 1-2 Petrusbrief, Judasbrief: NEchter 18/20, 1987 ➤ 3,6269 ... 6,6732: ᴿRivB 39 (1991) 365s (R. *Fabris*).

5750 **Grudem** W. A., 4,6369 ... 6,6734: 1 Peter 1988: ᴿGraceTJ 11 (1990) 106s (A. B. *Luter*).

5752 **Heimann** Peter, Der griechische Weg zu Christus; Elemente zum Verständnis des ersten Petrusbriefes. Stu 1991, Urachhaus. 115 p. 3-87838-915-9.

5753 **Knoch** Otto, Der erste und zweite Petrusbrief; der Judasbrief: RgNT, 1990 ➤ 6,6736: RArTGran 54 (1991) 371 (A. *Segovia*); ErbAuf 67 (1991) 406 (B. *Schwank*); TGL 81 (1991) 391s (J. *Ernst*).

5754 *Knoch* Otto B., Gab es eine Petrusschule in Rom?: SNTU A16 (1991) 105-127 [< ZIT 92].

5756 **Prostmeier** F.-R., Handlungsmodelle im ersten Petrusbrief: ForBi 61, 1990 ➤ 6,6743: RArTGran 54 (1991) 380s (A. *Segovia*); TsTNijm 31 (1991) 325 (G. *Manenschijn*).

5757 **Reichert** Angelika, Eine urchristliche Praeparatio ad Martyrium... 1 Pt: BeitBExT 22, D1989 ➤ 5,6426: RTLZ 116 (1991) 508-510 (J. *Rohde*).

5758 *Schlosser* Jacques, Le thème exodial dans la Prima Petri: ➤ 30, FBONNARD P., Mémoire 1991, 259-274.

5759 **Schutter** William L., Hermeneutic and composition in 1 Peter [diss. 1985, DLindars B.]: WUNT 2/30, 1989 ➤ 5,6428: RCBQ 53 (1991) 343 (J. H. *Elliott*); EvQ 63 (1991) 187s (I. H. *Marshall*); JBL 110 (1991) 357-9 (P. J. *Achtemeier*); JTS 42 (1991) 261-4 (E. *Best*).

5760 *a) Schweizer* Eduard, Zur Christologie des Ersten Petrusbriefs; – *b) Vögtle* Anton, Christo-logie und Theo-logie im Zweiten Petrusbrief: ➤ 30, FHAHN F., Anfänge 1991, 369-382 / 383-398.

5761 *Sywulka* P., El sufrimiento de Cristo como patrón para el creyente in 1 Pedro: Kairós 8 (Guatemala 1991) 53-66 [< NTAbs 36,62].

5762 **Thurén** Lauri, The rhetorical stategy of 1 Peter with special regard to ambiguous expressions: Åbo diss. 1990 ➤ 6,6746: RExpTim 102 (1990s) 317 (I. H. *Marshall*: lucid and insightful); JBL 110 (1991) 746-8 (D. F. *Watson*: forceful, despite Achilles' heel); SvEx 56 (1991) 148s (R. *Kieffer*, svensk).

5763 *Warden* D., Imperial persecution and the dating of 1 Peter and Revelation: JEvTS 34 (1991) 203-212 [< NTAbs 36,62].

5764 *Azzali Bernardelli* Giovanna, *a)* 1 Pt 1,18-19 e 1 Gv 1,7 nell'esegesi di EUSEBIO di Cesarea, di CIRILLO di Gerusalemme, di EPIFANIO; – *b)* Concezioni antropologiche nell'esegesi TERTULLIANEA dei passi vetero-testamentari con la parola *dām*: ➤ 565, Sangue 1989/91, 853-893 / 825-851.

5765 *McCartney* Dan G., Logikós in 1 Peter 2,2: ZNW 82 (1991) 128-132.

5765* *Lugo Rodriguez* Raúl, El verbo *hypotássein* y la parénesis social de 1 Pe 2,11-17: EfMex 9 (1991) 57-70.

5766 *Snyder* Scot, 1 Peter 2:17; a reconsideration [NEB and NIV rightly take first phrase as main clause, the other three as specifying]: FgNt 4 (1991) 211-5.

5766* *Grudem* Wayne, Wives like Sarah, and the husbands who honor them; 1 Peter 3:1-7: ➤ 375, Recovering 1991, 194-208. 499-503.

5767 **Dalton** William J., Christ's proclamation to the spirits; a study of 1 Peter 3:18², 1989 ➤ 5,6436 [not 6²]: RAustralasCR 68 (1991) 252s (W. *Hoekstra*: very technical; will enhance his already established reputation).

5768 *Sly* Dorothy J., 1 Peter 3:6b in the light of PHILO and JOSEPHUS: JBL 110 (1991) 126-9.

5769 *Staudinger* Ferdinand, Verantwortete Hoffnung (1 Petr 3,15): ➤ 6,171, FSTÖGER A., Exeget 1990, 113-122.

5770 *Volip* Isidoro, La definizione del battesimo secondo 1 Pt 3,20b-21: ➤ 561*d*, Origini del battesimo 1989/91, 193-241.

5771 *Cazeaux* Jacques, Liberté ou mémoire? La rhétorique dans la seconde épître de Pierre: → 76, ᶠHILGERT E., StPhilonAn 3 (1991) 222-255.

G9.4 **Epistula Jacobi** ... data on both apostles James.

5772 **Adamson** James B., James, the man and his message 1989 → 5,6442; 6,6764: ᴿBZ 34 (1991) 285-7 (H. *Frankemölle*); CritRR 4 (1991) 162s (J. S. *Kloppenborg*: sequel to his 1976 comm.); TLZ 116 (1991) 29-31 (W. *Popkes*: zu apologetisch); Vidyajyoti 55 (1991) 56s (P. M. *Meagher*).

5773 **Andriopoulou** Panayiotis, Ⓖ The epistle of James: NT History and Theology. Athena 1990. 233 p. – ᴿDeltioVM 10,2 (1991) 61-63 (S. *Agourides* Ⓖ).

5774 *Burchard* Christof, Zu einigen christologischen Stellen des Jakobusbriefes: → 72, ᶠHAHN F., Anfänge 1991, 353-368.

5775 **Cervantes** José, *al.*, Cartas judeocristianas (Santiago, 1a-2a San Pedro y San Judas, p. 1-92); p. 93-136, *Ramos* Felipe F., Cartas de San Juan; p. 137-259, *Contreras* Francisco, Apocalipsis: comentario: El Mensaje del NT. S 1990, Sígueme. 259 p. 84-301-1112-3 / LDiv 84-7151-6977.

5778 *Cornish* Alison, The Epistle of James in Inferno 26: Traditio 45 (1989s) 367-379.

5779 **Davids** Peter H., James: New [NIV] International Biblical Commentary 15. Peabody MA 1989 = 1983, Hendrickson. xvii-172 p. 0-943575-13-3.

5780 **García Araya** Alfonso, Santiago, il profeta; la tradición profética en la Carta de Santiago: diss. ᴰ*Fernández Ramos* F. Salamanca 1991. 605 p. – RTLv 23, p. 544.

5781 *Hann* Robert R., The Jewish Christianity of James bar Joseph; conflict and controversy in the first century: JRelSt 17 (Cleveland 1989) 56-66 [< ZIT 91,764].

5782 **Hartin** Patrick J., James and the Q sayings of Jesus [Catholic South-African dissertation]: JStNT supp 47. Sheffield 1991, JStOT. 266 p. 1-85075-267-2 [ÉTRel 67,110, B. *Coyault*].

5783 **Ludwig** Martina, Wort als Gesetz; eine Untersuchung zum Verständnis von 'Wort' und 'Gesetz' in israelitisch-frühjüdischen und neutestamentlichen Schriften; gleichzeitig ein Beitrag zur Theologie des Jakobusbriefes: Diss. Heidelberg 1991, ᴰ*Kuhn* H. 251 p. – TR 87 (1991) 518; RTLv 23, p. 545.

5784 **Marconi** Gilberto, La lettera di Giacomo, tr.comm. R 1990, Borla. 265 p. Lit. 35.000. 88-263-0787-3. – ᴿGregorianum 72 (1991) 405 (*ipse*).

5785 **Martin** Ralph P ..., James: Word Comm 48, 1988 → 4,4604; 6,6772: ᴿCBQ 53 (1991) 707s (D. R. *Bauer*); PerspRelSt 18 (1991) 189-191 (C. H. *Talbert*); ScotJT 44 (1991) 385-7 (Rosemary J. *Fletcher*: author is James the brother of Jesus).

5786 *Motyer* J. A., The message of James; the tests of faith: The Bible speaks today. Leicester 1990 = 1985, Inter-Varsity. 214 p. 0-85110-744-3.

5787 *Plötz* R., Jacobus (Maior): → 681, LexMA 5 (1990) 253s.

5788 **Pratscher** Wilhelm, Der Herrenbruder Jakobus und die Jakobustradition: FRL 139, ᴰ1987 → 3,6305 ... 6,6773: ᴿBijdragen 52 (1991) 210 (M. *Parmentier*, Eng.); TR 87 (1991) 194-7 (R. *Hoppe*).

5789 *Ruegg* Ulrich, À la recherche du temps de Jacques: → 30, ᶠBONNARD P., Mémoire 1991, 235-257.

5790 a) *Sato* M., Wozu wurde der Jakobusbrief geschrieben? eine mutmassliche Rekonstruktion; – b) *Shimada* K., Is 1 Peter dependent on Eph? ... C. L. MITTON: AnJapB 17 (1991) 55-76 / 77-106 [< NTAbs 36,374s].

5791 *Sivo* Vito, Il 'carmen de translatione' [in Galizia dopo il martirio a Gerusalemme] di san Giacomo il Maggiore (cod. Vindobonensis 898): VetChr 28 (1991) 103-140.

5792 *Tamez* Elsa, Elemente der Bibel, die den Weg der christlichen Gemeinde erhellen; eine hermeneutische Übung anhand des Jakobusbriefes [< RIBLa 1 (1988) 92-100]. ᵀ*Kessler* E.: EvT 51 (1991) 92-100.

5793 **Tamez** Elsa, The scandalous message of James; faith without works is dead. NY 1990, Crossroad. viii-102 p. $9. – ᴿNewTR 4,1 (1991) 108 (D. *Senior*).

5794 *Vanni* Ugo, Può il cristiano essere ricco? Ricchezza e povertà nella lettera di Giacomo: → 444*, Ricchezza 1989/91, 231-241.

5795 **Vries** Egbert de, De brief van Jakobus, dispositie en theologie: diss. Groningen, ᴰ*Klijn* A.F.J. Kampen 1991, Kok. xi-204 p. *f* 37,50. 90-242-3377-1. – TsTNijm 31 (1991) 319; RTLv 23, p. 543.

5796 *Wolmarans* J.L.P., Making sense out of suffering; James 1:2-4: HervTSt 47 (1991) 1109-1121.

5797 *Heide* Gale Z., The soteriology of James 2:14: GraceTJ 12,1 (1991) 69-97 (+ some missing words or lines).

5798 *Westhuizen* J.D.N. van der, Stylistic techniques and their functions in James 2:14-26: Neotestamentica 25,1 (1991) 89-107.

5799 *Meyendorff* John, [Jas 5,13-16] The anointing of the sick; some pastoral considerations: StVlad 35 (1991) 241-255.

G9.6 Epistula Judae.

5800 **Bauckham** Richard, Jude and the relatives of Jesus [*desposunoi*] in the early Church 1990 → 6,6788: ᴿExpTim 102 (1990s) 378s (S. H. *Travis*: significant); NRT 113 (1991) 442-4 (X. *Jacques*).

5801 *Buchegger* Jörg, Literatur zum Judasbrief: TRu 56 (1991) 210s (Nachtrag zu 56 (1986) 117].

5802 **Charles** J. Daryl, Literary strategy in the epistle of Jude: diss. Westminster Theol. Sem. 1991. 417 p. 91-25467. – DissA 52 (1991s) 1372-A.

5803 *Charles* J. Daryl, a) Jude's use of pseudepigraphical source-material as part of a literary strategy: NTS 37 (1991) 130-145; – b) Literary artifice in the Epistle of Jude: ZNW 82 (1991) 106-124.

5803* *Feuillet* André, Le péché évoqué aux chapitres 3 et 6,1-4 de la Genèse; le péché des anges de l'Épître de Jude et de la Seconde Épître de Pierre: Divinitas 35 (1991) 207-229.

5804 **Heiligenthal** Roman, Studien zum theologiegeschichtlichen Ort des Judasbriefes; eine Untersuchung zur Geschichte des frühen Christentums im syrisch-kleinasiatischen Raum: Hab.-Diss. Heidelberg 1991, ᴰ*Berger* K. – TR 87 (1991) 512; RTLv 23, p. 544.

5805 **Manton** Thomas, An exposition on the Epistle of Jude [1658]: Limited Classical Reprint Library. Mp 1978, Klock. [iv–] 376 p.

5806 *Merkelbach* R., [Judas 13; Plp 2,6] Zwei Beiträge zum NT: RheinMus 134 (1991) 346-351.

Non adhibentur hoc anno – Nº 5807-6999 – **not used this year.**

XV. Theologia Biblica

H1   **Biblical Theology**   .1 [OT] **God**

7001 **Birnbaum** David,   God and evil; a Jewish perspective 1989 ➤ 5,7001; 6, also 7001: ᴿAnglTR 73 (1991) 224s (S. L. *Jacobs*); ExpTim 102 (1990s) 80 (C.H. *Middleburgh*: excellent).

7002 **Bouyer** Louis,   *a)* Gnosis, la connaissance de Dieu dans l'Écriture 1988 ➤ 4,a662; 6,7003:   ᴿAngelicum 68 (1991) 136-8 (A. *Wilder*: one wonders if the rehabilitation of spiritual exegesis is so important to the health of Catholic theology). – *b)* Gnosis; la conoscenza di Dio nella Scrittura [1988 ➤ 4,a662],ᵀ Vaticano 1991, Editrice. 177 p. Lit. 24.000.

7003 **Buber** Martin,   La regalità di Dio [1932, per una prevista trilogia La fede biblica]: Radici, 1989 ➤ 5,7006:   ᴿRivB 39 (1991) 79s (P. *Stefani*).

7003* **Buckley** Michael J.,   At the origins of modern atheism 1987 ➤ 4,8010 ... 6,7004:   ᴿJRel 71 (1991) 440-2 (D. C. *Wilson*: pleasant journey but never arrives).

7004 *Cangh* Jean-Marie van,   Les origines d'Israël et de la foi monothéiste; apports de l'archéologie et de la critique littéraire: RTLv 22 (1991) 305-326.457-487.

7005 **Cazelles** Henri,   La Bible et son Dieu: JJC 40, 1989 ➤ 5,7010; 6,7005: ᴿCarthaginensia 7 (1991) 194 (R. *Sanz Valdivieso*); NRT 113 (1991) 95s (J.-L. *Ska*); RechSR 79 (1991) 285s (J.-M. *Carrière*: utile malgré fautes de présentation); RevSR 65 (1991) 135s (B. *Renaud*).

7006 **Farley** Wendy,   Tragic vision and divine compassion; a contemporary theodicy 1990 ➤ 6,7007:   ᴿJAAR 59 (1991) 829-831 (W. *McWilliams*); Thomist 55 (1991) 327-9 (P. C. *Phan*).

7006* **García-Murga Vázquez** José R.,   El Dios del amor y de la paz; tratado teológico de Dios desde la reflexión sobre su bondad: Comillas 3/12. M 1991, Univ. Pont. Comillas [NRT 114,108, L. *Renwart*].

7007 *Garrigues* Jean-Miguel,   Comment Dieu connaît-il le mal? [son 'Dieu sans idée du mal' 1982]: NVFr 65 (1990) 1-6.

7008 *Goldberg* Arnold,   Ist Gott allmächtig? Was die Rabbinen Hans JONAS antworten könnten: ➤ 78, ᶠHRUBY K., Judaica 47,1 (1991) 51-58.

7009 **Goldman** Ari L.,   The search for God at Harvard. NY 1991, Random. 283 p. $20. – ᴿTTod 48 (1991s) 338s (D. C. *Murchison*).

7010 **Hebblethwaite** Brian,   The ocean of truth 1988 ➤ 4,8020; 6,1010: ᴿScotJT 44 (1991) 535-7 (T. *Hart*).

7010* *Jiménez Ríos* Francisco J.,   Dios y la historia del tiempo; estudio de la cuestión De principio durationis rerum creatarum de S. TOMÁS (1,46), en diálogo con Stephen HAWKING: diss. 6940 Pont. Univ. Gregoriana, ᴰ*Lafont* G. R 1991s [InfPUG 24/122,28].

7011 **Kennedy** Philip,   'Deus humanissimus'; the knowability of God in the theology of R. SCHILLEBEECKX: diss. Laval, ᴰ*Vergauwen* G. Montreal 1991. – RTLv 23, p. 569.

7011* *Kooi* C. van der, Geheimnis; over de aard van Gods tegenwoordigheid volgens de theologie van Eberhard JÜNGEL: NedTTs 45 (1991) 120-133; Eng. 231.

7012 *Launderville* Dale, Human images of God; the OT: BToday 29 (1991) 79-86.

7013 **Lohfink** Norbert, Dio l'unico; sulla nascita del monoteismo in Israele [p. 9-53.115-192 < QDisp 1985], ᵀ*Tagliacarne* Pierfelice, ᴱ*Bellini* Alberto: QDisp. Brescia 1991, Morcelliana. 167 p.; Bibliog. 103-126. 88-372-1445-6. Anche *Braulik* G., *Scharbert* J., *Zenger* E.

7014 *Maccise* Camillo, L'esperienza di Dio nella Bibbia: RivVSp 43 (1989) 229-242.

7015 **McFague** Sallie, Models for God 1987 ↠ 3,6354 ... 6,7017: ᴿHeythJ 32 (1991) 89 (A. *Primavesi*: Cartesian).

7015* a) *McGrath* A.E., The biography of God: ChrTod 35,8 (1991) 22-24 [< NTAbs 36,7]. – b) *Mauser* U., One God alone; a pillar of biblical theology [different from the 'monotheisms' of our time]: PrincSemB 12 (1991) 255-265 [< NTAbs 36,220].

7016 **McLelland** Joseph C., Prometheus rebound; the irony of atheism. Waterloo 1988, W. Laurier Univ. 366 p. – ᴿTorJT 7 (1991) 211s (A.H. *Khan*) & 213-5 (J. *Newman*) & 216-9 (J. *Sohner*) & 220-5 (B. *Ward*) & 226-9 (J. *Webster*); reply 230-4.

7016* **Moor** J.C. de, Rise of Yahwism 1990 ↠ 6,7022: ᴿJRel 71 (1991) 572s (D. *Edelman*).

7017 **Neusner** Jacob, The incarnation of God; the character of divinity in formative Judaism 1988 ↠ 4,8033: ᴿCritRR 3 (1990) 352-5 (Z. *Garber*); ScotJT 44 (1991) 110-2 (R.P. *Carroll*: most interesting, unusually eirenic, basically valid).

7018 **Nipkow** K.E., Erwachsenwerden ohne Gott? Gotteserfahrung im Lebenslauf. Mü 1987 [Bijdragen 52,293: first cause of loss of faith is impossibility of reconciling problem of evil with an all-powerful good God (as M. WEBER ⁵1976); next three commonest causes: does God really 'explain' the world as it is?; is 'God' merely a symbol?; discrepancy between people's faith and their moral life].

7019 *Spieckermann* Hermann, 'Die ganze Erde ist seiner Herrlichkeit voll'; Pantheismus im Alten Testament? [Antrittsvorlesung Zürich 29.I.1990]; ZTK 87 (1990) 415-436.

7019* **Staton** Cecil P.ᴶ, 'And Yahweh appeared...'; a study of the motifs of 'seeing God' and of 'God's appearing' in Old Testament narratives: diss. Oxford 1988. 338 p. BRD-93958. – DissA 52 (1991s) A.

7020 *Stohr* Martin, Der befreiende Gott; zur biblischen Gottesvorstellung: Junge Kirche 52 (1991) 271-5 [< ZIT 91,342].

7021 *Théobald* Christoph, Quand on dit aujourd'hui: 'Dieu est juste': NRT 113 (1991) 161-184.

7022 **Thompson** Alden, Who's afraid of the OT God? 1989 ↠ 5,7035; 6,7028: ᴿAndrUnS 29 (1991) 105-7 (A.J. *Greig*).

7023 **Tilley** Terrence, The evils of theodicy. Wsh 1991, Georgetown Univ. xii-277 p. $30; pa. $16. – ᴿHorizons 18 (1991) 290-5 (K. *Surin*) & 296-300 (Alice L. *Laffey*) & 300-3 (J.P. *Burns*) & 300-6 (Morna *Joy*); response 306-312.

7024 *Vermeer* Paul, *Vossen* H., *Ven* J. van der, Theodicy and rationalization [WEBER M., NIPKOW K.E., ...]: Bijdragen 52 (1991) 293-316; Eng. 317.

7024* **Williams** Daniel D.†, The demonic and the divine, ᴱ*Evans* Stacy A. Mp 1990, Fortress. xi-100 p. 0-8006-2431-9.

7025 **Yu** Carver T.,   Being and relation; a theological critique of western dualism and individualism.   E 1987, Scottish Academic.   xxiv-239. £15. – RScotJT 44 (1991) 102s (A. *Thompson*: God not 'Being in himself', from Greek 'reality in itself', but 'Being with and for man').

H1.3   *Immutabilitas* –   **God's suffering; process theology.**

7025* **Beek** Abraham Van de,   Why? On suffering, guilt, and God, T*Vriend* John.   GR 1990, Eerdmans.   vii-349 p. $22. – RTS 52 (1991) 570s (J. H. *Wright*: continuing his 1980 book on the mutability and history of God).

7026 *Beardslee* W. A.,   Process thought on the borders between hermeneutics and theology: Process Studies 19 (Claremont 1990) 230-4 [< NTAbs 36,149].

7026* **Carroll** Denis,   A pilgrim God for a pilgrim people 1988 → 5,7041: RRExp 88 (1991) 488s (Molly *Marshall-Green*); ScotJT 44 (1991) 257s (J. P. *Mackey*: good).

7027 **Case-Winters** Anna,   God's power; traditional understandings and contemporary challenges,   Louisville 1990, W-Knox.   246 p. $20 pa. – RHorizons 18 (1991) 336s (J. A. *Bracken*).

7028 **Dodds** M.,   The unchanging God of love 1986 → 2,5074 ... 4,8049:   RLvSt 16 (1991) 178-180 (R. *Wielockx*: reformulates rather than answers the question).

7029 *Dodds* Michael J.,   Thomas AQUINAS, human suffering, and the unchanging God of love: TS 52 (1991) 330-344.

7030 **Fiddes** Paul S.,   The creative suffering of God 1988 → 4,8051 ... 6,7034: RHeythJ 32 (1991) 269s (J. *O'Donnell*).

7031 *Ford* Lewis S.,   Evangelical appraisals of process theism: ChrSchR 20 (1990) 149-163 [< ZIT 91,264].

7032 *Galot* Jean, ❷ Dieu souffre-t-il? [< CC (1990,1) 533-545], T*Schmidt* Grzegorz: PrzPow 271 (1991) 359-375; franç. 375.

7033 **Griffin** David R.,   God, power, and evil; a process theodicy. Lanham MD 1991, UPA.   336 p. $19.75. – RTTod 48 (1991s) 485. 488 (T. W. *Tilley*).

7033* **Hallman** Joseph M.,   The descent of God; divine suffering in history and theology.   Mp 1991, Fortress.   xvi-150 p. $13 pa. 0-8006-2485-8 [TDig 39,167].

7034 **Helm** Paul,   Eternal God, a study of God without time 1988 → 6,7041: RJRel 71 (1991) 591s (P. L. *Quinn*); NBlackf 71 (1990) 287-296 (B. *Davies*).

7035 **Kreuzer** Siegfried,   Der lebendige Gott: BW 116, 1983 → 64,6184 ... 5,7051: RWeltOr 22 (1991) 171-4 (T. *Podella*).

7036 **Lucas** George R.J,   The rehabilitation of WHITEHEAD; an analytic and historical assessment of process philosophy.   Albany 1989, SUNY.   261 p. $44.50; pa. $15. – RJAAR 59 (1991) 846-9 (N. F. *Gier*).

7037 *a) Luyten* Jos,   Het lijden van God volgens het Oude Testament; – *b)* *Steen* Marc,   Een God die met ons lijdt?:   CollatVL 21 (1991) 21-36 / 37-56.

7038 **Meessen** Frank,   Unveränderlichkeit und Menschwerdung Gottes [D1988 → 5,7053]: FreibTSt 140. FrB 1989, Herder.   xiii-562 p. DM 68.   3-451-21555-1. – RTR 87 (1991) 53-56 (M. *Kappens*).

7039 *Nash* Ronald,   Lewis FORD and the evangelical critique of process theology: ChrSchR 20 (1990) 286-... [< ZIT 91,336].

7040 **O'Hanlon** Gerard F.,   The immutability of God in the theology of H. U. von BALTHASAR 1990 ➤ 6,7048:   ᴿJTS 42 (1991) 787s (A. *Louth*); NBlackf 72 (1991) 399-401 (J. *O'Donnell*); RelStR 17 (1991) 339 (J. R. *Sachs*); ScotJT 44 (1991) 538-540 (Francesca *Murphy*); TPhil 66 (1991) 289s (W. *Löser*).

7040* **Olson** Ronald D.,   The immutability of God; the study of a contemporary theological dispute [BURRELL D. vs. HARTSHORNE C.] in light of the phenomenon of faith: diss. Vanderbilt, ᴰ*Farley* E. Nv 1991. 193 p. 91-25302. – DissA 52 (1991s) 969-A; RelStR 18,171.

7041 *Peel* David R.,   Is Schubert M. OGDEN's 'God' Christian?:   JRel 70 (1990) 147-166.

7042 *Pendergast* Richard J.,   A process theory of creation: ScEsp 43 (1991) 135-160.

7043 *Richard* Jean [➤ 7062],   Dieu tout-puissant et souffrant: LavalTP 47 (1991) 39-51.

7043* **Runzo** Joseph,   Reason, relativism and God 1986 ➤ 5,7166:   ᴿJAAR 59 (1991) 866-870 (C. D. *Hardwick*).

7044 *Steen* Marc,   Jürgen MOLTMANN's critical reception of K. BARTH's theopaschitism;   ETL 67 (1991) 278-311.

7044* **Suchocki** Marjorie H.,   God-Christ-Church; a practical guide to process theology 1989 ➤ 6,7056:   ᴿCurrTMiss 18 (1991) 381 (J. *Zell*).

7045 **Sullivan** John A.,   Explorations in Christology; the impact of process/relational thought.   NY 1987, P. Lang.   354 p. $28. – ᴿLvSt 15 (1990) 76s (T. J. van *Bavel*).

7045* **Ward** Keith, Divine action.   L 1990, Collins Flame.   vi-274 p. £8 pa. – ᴿTLond 94 (1991) 204-6 (C. *Crowder*, also on same title dealing with FARRER).

7046 *Wells* Paul,   Dieu et le changement; Jürgen MOLTMANN à la lumière du théisme réformé: Hokhma 43 (1990) 49-67.

7047 **Yates** John C.,   The timelessness of God.   Lanham MD 1990, UPA. vii-360 p. $49,25 [TR 87,434].

7048 **Zoffoli** Enrico,   Mistero della sofferenza di Dio; il pensiero di S. TOMMASO: StTom 34, 1988 ➤ 6,7060:   ᴿRThom 91 (1991) 404s (Louise-M. *Antoniotti*).

H1.4   *Femininum in Deo* – **God as father and as mother** [➤ F3.7; H8.8s].

7049 *Axmacher* Elke,   Feministisch von Gott reden? Eine Auseinandersetzung mit Rosemary R. RUETHERs Buch 'Sexismus und die Rede von Gott' [1985; Eng. ²1986]: ZevEth 35 (1991) 5-20.

7050 **Bergstrand** Göran,   Gud Fader; ett faderlöst samhälle.   Sto 1987, Verbum. – ᴿTsTKi 60 (1989) 148s (Astri *Hauge*).

7051 *Cross* Nancy M.,   Another view of the Bible's use of sexual language [masculine pronouns for God approved]: RRel 50 (1991) 839-848.

7051* *a) Dion* Michel,   Pour une interprétation féministe de l'idée chrétienne de Dieu: LavalTP 47 (1991) 169-184. – *b) Wagner* Walter,   Divine femaleness; two second century contributions: JRelSt 17 (Cleveland 1989) 19-43.

7052 **Dourley** John P.,   The goddess, mother of the Trinity; [ECKHART] a JUNGIAN implication 1990 ➤ 6,7063:   ᴿSR 20 (1991) 399 (Winnie *Tomm*).

7053 **Durrwell** F. X.,   Nuestro Padre; Dios en su misterio [1987],ᵀ 1990 ➤ 6,7064: ᴿCarthaginensia 7 (1991) 270 (P. *Martínez Fresneda*); EfMex 9

(1991) 145s (E. *Serraima Cirici*); Lumen-Vr 39 (1990) 537 (F. *Ortiz de Urtaran*); NatGrac 38 (1991) 208s (A. *Villalmonte*).

7053* **Foster** Ruth A., The role of feminine language and imagery for God in the development of a NT view of God: diss. SW Baptist Theol. Sem. 1989. 307 p. 91-15313. – DissA 52 (1991s) 191-A.

7054 *Kimel* Alvin F.^J, The God who likes his name; Holy Trinity, feminism, and the language of faith: Interpretation 45 (1991) 147-158.

7055 **Kinkel** Gary S., Our dear mother the Spirit; an investigation of Count ZINZENDORF's theology and praxis. Lanham MD 1990, UPA. 251 p. $39.50 [TR 87,529]. – ^RJTS 42 (1991) 776s (C. J. *Podmore*: he excluded women from the clergy).

7055* **McAvoy** Jane, From beyond God the Father to the Trinity; Christian feminist understanding of God. Chicago [? Univ. RTLv 23, 570] ^D1991.

7056 **Marazzi** Ugo, La Grande Madre in Siberia e Asia Centrale; aspetti del principio femminile nella religiosità arcaica: supp. 60 to AION 49,3 (1989). 47 p.

7057 **Matura** T., Dieu le Père très saint contemplé par FRANÇOIS d'Assise: Présence de SF 33. P 1990, Franciscaines. 139 p. F 69. – ^RNRT 113 (1991) 460 (G. *Navez*).

7058 **Miller** John W., Biblical faith and fathering 1989 ➤ 5,7087; 6,7075*: ^RLvSt 16 (1991) 188 (R. T. *Collins*); RivB 39 (1991) 93s (A. *Bonora*).

7058* *Moreschini* Claudio, La Persona del Padre nella teologia di GREGORIO Nazianzeno: VetChr 28 (1991) 77-102.

7059 **Nzuzi** Bibaki, Le Dieu-Mère chez les Yombe; l'inculturation et le discours 'proverbial' sur Dieu: diss. Pont. Univ. Gregoriana, ^D*Roest Crollius* A. Roma 1991. 363 p. – RTLv 23, p. 562 [< DissA-C].

7059* *Plaskow* Judith, Naar een God met duizend namen; feministisch anti-judaïsme en de christelijke God: Mara 2,2 (1990) 7-18 [19-24, *Dijk-Hennes* F. van, een nederlandse reaktie: < GerefTTs 90,124].

7060 **Pouilly** Jean, Dios nuestro Padre; la revelación de Dios Padre y el 'Padre nuestro': CuadBib 68. Estella 1990, VDivino. 66 p. – ^RIter 2 (1991) 155s (J.-P. *Wyssenbach*).

7061 *a)* *Raja* R. J., God as mother in the OT; – *b)* *Mary* Corona, Woman in creation story; – *c)* *Luke* G., Women and politics in ancient Israel: Jeevadhara 21 (1991) 107-117 / 95-106 / 133-149 [118-132 on Prov 31,10-13].

7062 **Richard** Jean [➤ 7043], Dieu [... père et mère; tout-puissant et souffrant]. Montréal 1990, Novalis. 196 p. – ^REsprVie 101 (1991) 303s (P. *Jay*).

7062* **Richardson** Jane E., *a)* Feminine imagery of the Holy Spirit in the hymns of St. EPHREM the Syrian: diss. ^D*Hayman* A. Edinburgh 1991. – Aram (1989,2) 307; RTLv 23, p. 549. – *b)* Ephrem and the ministries of women, Logos (1991,3).

7063 *Schenker* Adrian, Gott als Vater – Söhne Gottes; ein vernachlässigter Aspekt einer biblischen Metapher [< FreibZ 25 (1978) 3-55]: ➤ 258, Text 1991, 1-53.

7063* **Smiley** Pamela M., In the name of the Father; the effects of orthodoxy on Roman Catholic women authors: diss. Wisconsin, ^D*Friedman* Susan. Madison 1991. 293 p. 91-28938. – DissA 52 (1991s) 3278-A.

7064 **Strotmann** Angelika, 'Mein Vater bist du' (Sir 51,10); zur Bedeutung der Vaterschaft Gottes in kanonischen und nichtkanonischen frühjüdischen Schriften [Diss. Fra St. Georgen 1990, ^D*Beutler* J.]: FraTSt 39. Fra 1991, Knecht. xv-408 p. 3-7820-0625-9.

7065 *a*) ^E**Wacker** M.-T., *Zenger* E., Der eine Gott und die Göttin; Gottesvorstellungen des biblischen Israel im Horizont feministischer Theologie: QDisp 135. FrB 1991, Herder. 192 p.; DM 49 [NRT 114,938, L. J. *Renard*].
— *b*) **Widdicombe** P. J., The fatherhood of God in the thought of JUSTIN Martyr, ORIGEN and ATHANASIUS: diss. Oxford 1990. – RTLv 23, p. 549.
— *c*) ^E**Wodtke** V., Auf den Spuren der Weisheit; Sophia, Wegweiserin für ein neues Gottesbild: Frauenforum. FrB 1991, Herder. 199 p. DM 29,80 [NRT 114, 583s, P. *Evrard*].

7065* **Wren** Brian, What language shall I borrow 1989 ➤ 4,a864; 5,7098: ^REcuR 41 (1991) 483s (Nancy *Cocks*: wonderful and unsettling; 'evidence for a maternal instinct is rather flimsy'); Horizons 18 (1991) 165s (Janet *Walton*); Interpretation 45 (1991) 106.108 (N. C. *Theiss*); Worship 64 (1990) 180-2 (Gail *Ramshaw*).

7066 *Wüchelt* Agnes, Was ist die Frau, dass du ihrer (nicht) gedenkst? Weibliche Gottesbilder in der Bibel: KatBlätt 116 (Mü 1991) 389-395 [< ZIT 91,466].

H1.7   Revelatio.

7067 **Alonso Schökel** Luis, La Palabra de Dios en la historia de los hombres 1989 ➤ 952: ^E**Artola** A., Introducción 2: ^RTVida 32 (1991) 326s (M. A. *Ferrando*).

7068 **Beeck** Frans J. van, Divine revelation; intervention or self-communication?: TS 52 (1991) 199-226.

7069 *Blanco* Arturo, Parola, persona e storia nella Rivelazione divina: AnnTh 4 (1990) 263-282.

7070 **Bockmuehl** Klaus, Listening to the God who speaks. Colorado Springs 1990, Helmers & H. 164 p. $8 pa. 0-939443-18-X [ScotJT 44,548].

7071 **Bockmuehl** Markus N. A., Revelation and mystery in ancient Judaism and Pauline Christianity [^DC 1987]: WUNT 2/36, 1987 ➤ 6,7089: ^RArTGran 53 (1990) 292s (A. *Segovia*); NedTTs 45 (1991) 338-340 (R. A. *Bitter*).

7071* **Burton** Brian, The relationship between revelation and religion in the theology of Karl BARTH and his criticism: diss. ^D*Thompson*. Belfast 1991. – RTLv 23, p. 567.

7072 *Chirico* Peter, Revelation and Natural Law: TS 52 (1991) [57, *Sullivan* F. (*Betti* U.)] 539s.

7073 *Cottier* Georges, Les motifs de crédibilité de la Révélation selon saint THOMAS: NVFr 65 (1990) 161-9.

7074 ^E**Elders** Léon, La doctrine de la révélation divine de saint Thomas d'AQUIN, symposium Rolduc 1989/90 ➤ 6,607: ^RZkT 113 (1991) 101s (K. H. *Neufeld*).

7075 **Fisichella** Rino, La revelación, evento y credibilidad [1985 ➤ 2,5162; franç. 1989 ➤ 5,7108], ^T*Ortiz García* Alfonso: Lux Mundi 63. S 1989, Sígueme. 406 p. 84-301-1076-3. – ^RActuBbg 28 (1991) 74s (J. *Boada*); LumenVr 39 (1990) 92 (U. *Gil Ortega*: no 'Alfredo', no 'Fisiochella', también Índice); ETL 67 (1991) 452s (E. *Brito*); LavalTP 47 (1991) 130s (R. M. *Roberge*: manuel traditionnel).

7077 *Forte* Bruno [➤ b61], Rivelazione; parola, silenzio, incontro: Ho Theológos 9 (1991) 19-40.

7078 *Goldingay* J., Models for Scripture [A. DULLES' successful 1974 Models of the Church has a change in the meaning of 'model' in his 1983 Models of Revelation]: ScotJT 44 (1991) 19-37.

7079 **Gorringe** T.J., Discerning the Spirit; a theology of revelation. L/Ph 1990, SCM/Trinity. vi-144 p. £9. 0-334-02462-5. – ᴿTLond 94 (1991) 212 (A. *Marriage*); TsTNijm 31 (1991) 335 (A. *Brants*).

7080 **Haberman** Joshua O., Philosopher of revelation; the life and thought of S. L. STEINHEIM [1789-1866]. Ph 1990, Jewish Publication Soc. xv-332 p. $30. – ᴿRelStR 17 (1991) 266 (D. *Ellenson*).

7081 *Halivni* David W., On man's role in revelation: → 56, ꟳFOX M., 2 (1991) 29-49.

Haught John F., The revelation of God in history 1988 → b70.

7082 *Hereu* Josep, Bases para una teología cristiana de la revelación en el contexto del pensamiento moderno: CiTom 118 (1991) 473-495.

7083 *a) Jossua* Jean-Pierre, About the word 'revelation'; – *b) Radcliffe* Timothy, Time and telling; how to read biblical stories; – *c) McDermott* Thomas, Abraham's bedroom-slippers [claimed by WOOLLEY possibly found at Ur: arresting mélange of the transcendental and the everyday]: NBlackf 72,2 ('How *does* God "speak" to us'? 1992] 124-130 / 131-9 / 114-123.

7084 **Kraus** G., Gotteserkenntnis ohne Offenbarung; natürliche Theologie als ökumenisches Problem [diss. Rg.] 1987 → 3,6553.7833; 5,7112: ᴿDivThom 93 (1990) 160-3 (L. *Elders*).

7085 **Kuhn** Peter, Bat Qol, die Offenbarungsstimme in der rabbinischen Literatur; Sammlung, Übersetzung und Kurzkommentierung der Texte [von Offenbarungsstimmen im Antiken Judentum 425 p. DM 258 → 5,7113]: Eichstätter Materialien 13, Ph/Th 5. Rg 1989, Pustet. 110 p. DM 36 [TR 88,102, B. *Ego*]. – ᴿAntonianum 66 (1991) 441s (M. *Nobile*); AugM 35 (1990) 187s (J. L. *Sáenz*); CritRR 3 (1990) 350s (J. *Neusner*: if HENGEL and SCHÄFER accepted this, scholars no longer need to learn German); Salesianum 53 (1991) 181s (R. *Vicent*); TLZ 116 (1991) 502s (H.-J. *Becker*).

7086 **Kuhn** Peter, Offenbarungsstimmen im Antiken Judentum... Bat Qol 1989 → 5,7113: ᴿTLZ 115 (1990) 501-4 (H.-J. *Becker*).

7087 *Labbé* Yves, La théologie et la philosophie entrecroisées; révélation et langage: RSPT 75 (1991) 185-209; Eng. 210, 'Theology and philosophy interlaced; revelation versus argument'.

7088 *Lamont* John, The nature of revelation [... a set of propositions, after all]: NBlackf 72 (1991) 335-345.

7089 *Latourelle* R., Révélation: → 664, Catholicisme XII,58 (1990) 1046-1118.

7090 **Muis** J., Openbaring en interpretatie; het verstaan van de Heilige Schrift volgens K. BARTH en K. H. MISKOTTE. Haag 1989, Boeken-C. 556 p. *f* 65. – ᴿNedTTs 45 (1991) 345s (F. *Staudt*); TsTNijm 31 (1991) 202 (R. J. *Peeters*; diss. TsTNijm 30,85).

7091 *Myers* Christopher, The paradoxical character of revelation; a sympathetic essay on dialectical theism: Colloquium 23 (1990) 13-17 [< ZIT 91,75].

7092 **Nielsen** Bent F., Die Rationalität der Offenbarungstheologie; die Struktur des Theologieverständnisses von K. BARTH. Aarhus 1988, Univ. – ᴿTZBas 47 (1991) 184s (U. *Gerber*).

7093 **Niemann** Franz-J., Jesus der Offenbarer, I. Altertum bis Mittelalter; II. Frühe Neuzeit bis Gegenwart: Texte zur Theol. Fund. 5,1s. Graz 1990, Styria. 151 p. / 216 p. DM 29,80. – ᴿRPhil 66 (1991) 596s (T. *Hain-*

thaler); TPQ 139 (1991) 90 (J. *Singer*); TR 87 (1991) 490s (H. *Verweyen*); ZkT 113 (1991) 98 (W. *Kern*).

7094 **Oppenheim** Michael, What does Revelation mean for the modern Jew? Lewiston NY 1985, Mellen. 152 p. $50. 0-88946-708-0. – ᴿRelStT 9,1 (1989) 35s (R. *Firestone*).

7095 *Pattyn* Bart, Verlangen, ervaring en openbaring; het werkelijkheidsbegrip in het denken van A. VERGOTE: TsTNijm 31 (1991) 381-400; Eng. 400s.

7095* **Perlman** Laurence, Abraham HESCHEL's idea of revelation: Brown-JudSt 171, 1989 ⇥ 6,7099: ᴿJQR 82 (1991s) (D. J. *Moore*).

7096 **Ruiz Arenas** O., Teologia della Rivelazione [Jesús Epifanía 1987],ᵀ. CasM 1989, Piemme. 335 p. – ᴿAnnTh 5 (1991) 205s (A. *Blanco*).

7096* *a*) *Schenk* Wolfgang, 'Offenbarung' — eine Simulations-Kategorie? Offenbarung, die nichts offenbart; – *b*) *Zimmer* Christoph, Existenz-Simulation in den Gottesbeweisen: ⇥ 398, Simulation 1989/91, 107-142 / 86-106.

7097 **Schmitz** Josef, La revelación [Offenbarung 1988 ⇥ 4,8116], ᵀ*Ruiz-Garrido* Constantino: BtT 15. Barc 1990, Herder. 292 p. 84-254-1704-X. – ᴿActuBbg 28 (1991) 79s (J. *Boada*); BibFe 17,49 (1991) 142 (A. *Salas*); Carthaginensia 7 (1991) 268 (F. *Oliver Alcón*); NatGrac 38 (1991) 407 (A. *Villalmonte*).

7097* **Schmitz** J., La Rivelazione [1988]: GdT 206. Brescia 1991, Queriniana. 262 p. Lit. 25.000 [NRT 114, 898, A. *Toubeau*].

7098 *Schmitz* Josef, Das Vernehmen und Bezeugen des 'Wortes Gottes' nach dem Zweiten Vatikanischen Konzil: TrierTZ 100 (1991) 205-221.

7099 **Schnabel** Eckhard, Inspiration und Offenbarung; die Lehre vom Ursprung und Wesen der Bibel 1986 ⇥ 3,6492: ᴿCarthaginensia 7 (1991) 253 (R. *Sanz Valdivieso*).

7100 *Schwöbel* Christoph, Offenbarung und Erfahrung — Glaube und Lebenserfahrung: Marburger Jb Theologie 3 (1990) 68-... [< ZIT 90,675].

7101 *a*) *Sequeri* PierAngelo, La cattiva infinità della dialettica e la salutare finitezza della rivelazione; – *b*) *Bof* Giampiero, Gesù rivelatore di Dio: ⇥ 504, L'ombra di Dio 1990/1, 13-51 / 73-101.

7102 **Trembath** Kern R., Divine revelation; our moral relation with God. Ox 1991, UP. 230 p. $32.50 [JAAR 59,885].

7103 **Weidhas** Annette, 'Revelatio – traditio – ecclesia'; Versuch einer systematisch-theologischen Erörterung des Offenbarungsbegriffes und seiner ekklesiologischen Konsequenzen unter besonderer Berücksichtigung des traditio-Aspektes: Diss. Halle-W 1991, ᴰ*Müller*. – TR 87 (1991) 517.

Young Frances M., The art of performance; towards a theology of Holy Scripture 1990 ⇥ g16.

H1.8 Theologia fundamentalis.

7104 **Ansaldi** Jean, L'articulation de la foi, de la théologie et des écritures [correspond à celle que LACAN établit entre le réel, l'imaginaire et le symbolique]: CogF 163. P 1991, Cerf. 248 p. F 120. – ᴿÉtudes 348 (1991) 136s (R. *Marlé*).

7105 *Bonhoeffer* Thomas, Die Wurzeln des Begriffs Theologie: ArBegG 34 (1991) 7-26.

7106 **Brom** L. J. van den, Creatieve twijfel; een studie in de wijsgerige theologie. Kampen 1990, Kok. 152 p. *f*29,50. 90-242-2390-3. – ᴿTsT-Nijm 31 (1991) 205 (G. de *Grunt*).

7108 **Boureau** R., Dieu a des problèmes [plutôt toute la théologie, dans la culture actuelle]. P 1990, Cerf. 139 p. F 60. – ᴿNRT 113 (1991) 259 (G. *Navez*).

7109 **Dalferth** Ingolf U., Kombinatorische Theologie; Probleme theologischer Rationalität: QDisp 130. FrB 1991, Herder. 158 p. – ᴿZkT 113 (1991) 450-3 (E. *Runggaldier*: Spezialist über die Rede von Gott).

7110 **Dalferth** Ingolf U., Theology and philosophy: Signposts in Theology 1988 → 4,8136... 6,7115: ᴿTLZ 116 (1991) 56-58 (F. *Wagner*).

7111 **Dauer** Joachim, Glaubend Gott verstehen; der fundamentaltheologische Beitrag Eugen BISERs: diss. Pont. Univ. Gregoriana, ᴰ*Fisichella* R. Roma 1990, Nᵒ 6880 [InfPUG 23/119 (1990s) 14].

7112 *Delaney* Hubert, The theologian and foundations; on the road to general and special categories in theology [*Doran* R. 1990]: MilltSt 28 (1991) 102-131.

7113 *Dumont* C., Qui est théologien?: NRT 113 (1991) 185-204.

7114 **Engels** Dietrich, Religiösität im Theologiestudium. Stu 1990, Kohlhammer. 240 p. DM 59. – ᴿTLZ 116 (1991) 701-3 (G. *Wegner*, Rubrik 'Religions- und Kirchensoziologie').

7115 *Fisichella* Rino, Generi letterari in teologia fondamentale: Gregorianum 72 (1991) 543-556.

7116 **Forde** Gerhard O., Theology is for proclamation. Mp 1990, Augsburg-Fortress. 208 p. $11 pa. 0-8006-2425-4. – ᴿTLZ 116 (1991) 611s (K. *Schwarzwäller*).

7117 **Forte** Bruno, La teología como compañía, memoria y profecía [1987 → 3,6525],ᵀ. S 1990, Sígueme. 222 p. – ᴿCarthaginensia 7 (1991) 527s (F. *Martínez Fresneda*).

7117* *Goldingay* John, Modes of theological reflection in the Bible: TLond 94 (1991) 181-8.

7118 **Graf** Friedrich W., Theonomie; Fallstudien 1987 → 4,8145: ᴿTRu 56 (1991) 314-320 (D. *Korsch*: theologische Einheit pluraler Wirklichkeit?).

7119 *Gravem* Peder, Teologiens rasjonalitet; en vurdering av Ole HALLESBYs 'Principlære' [¹1920 ²1925]: TsTKi 60 (1989) 81-92; Eng. 93 [a good move even if out of date].

7120 **Haight** Roger, Dynamics of theology. NY 1990, Paulist. x-274 p. $13. – ᴿTLond 94 (1991) 361s (M. *Wiles*: good); TS 52 (1991) 573-5 (M. L. *Cook*).

7121 *a) Henriksen* Jan-Olav, Enhet og sannhet [unity and truth]; fundamentalteologiske overvejelser til temaet 'teologiens enhet'; – *b) Morland* Kjell A., Sannhet, bibeltekst og livstolkning [...GADAMER H.]; – *c) Hegstad* Harald, Bibelen og teologien; til spørsmålet om forholdet mellom eksegese og systematisk teologi: TsTKi 61 (1990) 81-96; Eng. 96 / 97-108; Eng. 108 / 131-144; Eng. 144.

7121* **Hoitenga** Dewey J.ᴶ, Faith and reason from Plato to Plantinga; an introduction to Reformed epistemology. Albany 1991, SUNY. xvii-263 p. $57.50; pa. $19. 0-7914-0590-7; -1-5 [TDig 39,169].

7122 *Hülser* Heinrich, Stellung und Aufgabe der Theologie im Zusammenhang mit der modernen Rationalitätskrise: NSys 33 (1991) 282-299; Eng. 299.

7122* **Jiménez Ortiz** A., Teología fundamental; la revelación y la fe en Heinrich FRIES [ᴰ1986 R, Salesianum]: BtSalm 106. S 1988, Univ. 517 p. 84-7299-213-6. – ᴿActuBbg 28 (1991) 76s (J. *Boada*).

7123 *Kannengiesser* Charles, Scripture interpreted; the definition of Catholic theology: → 470, Anselm 1989/91, 13-24 (25-31, response, *Connelly* J. J.).

7124 ᴱKern Walter, *al.*, Corso di teologia fondamentale I-IV [→ 6,846]. Brescia 1990, Queriniana. 274 p.; 332 p.; 346 p.; 667 p. Lit. 32.000; 35.000; 40.000; 70.000. – ᴿCC 142 (1991,4) 93-95 (F. *Ardusso*).

7125 **Lakeland** Paul, Theology and critical theory [... HABERMAS]; the discourse of the Church. Nv 1990, Abingdon. 320 p. $19 [RelStR 18, 39, J. K. *Downey*, high praise].

7126 **Lash** Nicholas, Easter in ordinary 1988 → 5,7019; 6,7130: ᴿHeythJ 32 (1991) 263s (H. *Meynell*: overreacts to DESCARTES); RExp 87 (1990) 358s (C. J. *Scalise*: a forest-prowl, not a forward march).

7127 **Léonard** André, Cohérence de la foi; essai de théologie fondamentale 1989 → 6,7132: ᴿRTLv 22 (1991) 90-92 (M. *Clairbois*).

7128 **McGrath** Alister E., The genesis of doctrine; a study in the foundations of doctrinal criticism [1990 Bampton Lectures]. Ox 1990, Blackwell. x-266 p. £35. 0-631-16658-0 [TDig 38,174]. – ᴿExpTim 102 (1990s) 249s (M. *Wiles*); NBlackf 72 (1991) 451s (G. *Hibbert*); TLond 94 (1991) 300-3 (P. *Avis*).

7129 *Maldamé* Jean-Michel, Renouveaux en théologie fondamentale (BEAU-CHAMP P. 1990; BELLET M. 1990): RThom 91 (1991) 651-665.

7130 **Migliore** Daniel L., Faith seeking understanding; an introduction to Christian theology. GR 1991, Eerdmans. xiv-312 p. $30; pa. $19 [Rel-StR 18, 128, P. C. *Hodgson*: Reformed; excellent, also as text for classroom].

7130* **Mitchell** Basil, How to play theological ping-pong, ᴱ*Abraham* W., *Prevost* R. L 1990, Hodder & S. 218 p. £9. – ᴿTLond 94 (1991) 136-8 (C. *Conti*: splendid, elegant, readable essays on faith and reason).

7131 **Moltmann** J., Theology today 1988 → 4,8161; 5,7149: ᴿRelStT 10,1 (1990) 62s (R. *Haight*).

7131* **Muller** Richard A., The study of theology; from biblical interpretation to contemporary formulation: Foundations of Contemporary Interpretation 7. GR 1991, Zondervan. 237 p. $13. 0-310-41001-0 [TDig 39,178].

7132 *Netland* Harold A., Apologetics, worldviews and the problem of neutral criteria: TrinJ 12 (1991) 39-58.

7133 **Noller** Gerhard, Metaphysik und theologische Realisation; das Ende der metaphysischen Grundstellung der Neuzeit und die Neubesinnung auf die theologische Wirklichkeit der Bibel. Z 1990, TVZ. 156 p.; 8 maps. Fs 22. – ᴿTLZ 116 (1991) 533-5 (G. *Keil*).

7134 **Ohlig** Karl-Heinz, Fundamentaltheologie im Spannungsfeld von Christentum und Kultur 1986 → 2,5639 ... 5,7160*: ᴿAugR 30 (1990) 205-212 (B. *Studer*).

7135 ᶠPANNENBERG Wolfhart, Vernunft des Glaubens, ᴱ**Rohls** J., *Wenz* Gunther, 1988 → 4,114: ᴿTR 87 (1991) 3-6 (E. *Sturm*).

7136 **Phillips** D. Z., Faith after foundationalism 1988 → 5,7161: ᴿJAAR 59 (1991) 855-8 (Kathryn E. *Tanner*: focuses RORTY, P. BERGER, G. LINDBECK, P. HOLMER).

7137 **Pié i Ninot** Salvador, Tratado de Teología Fundamental 1989 → 5,7162; 6,7144: ᴿScripTPamp 23 (1991) 737s (C. *Izquierdo*).

7137* **Prevost** Robert, Probability and theistic explanation [< diss.]. Ox 1990, Clarendon. 195 p. £25. – ᴿTLond 94 (1991) 390s (B. *Mitchell*).

7138 **Roberts** J. Deotis, A philosophical introduction to theology. L 1991, SCM. x-182 p. £10. – ᴿNBlackf 72 (1991) 503s (M. *Wynn*: 2000 years hastily, but one has to start somewhere).

7139 *Schmidinger* Heinrich M., Zur Geschichte des Begriffs 'christliche Philosophie' [ᴱ*Coreth* E. 1 (1987) 29-45]: ArBegG 34 (1991) 373s.

7140 *Schrimm-Heins* Andrea,   Gewissheit und Sicherheit; Geschichte und Bedeutungswandel der Begriffe certitudo und securitas I: ArBegG 34 (1991) 123-213.
7141 *Seckler* Max,   'Philosophia ancilla theologiae'; über die Ursprünge und den Sinn einer anstössig gewordenen Formel: TüTQ 171 (1991) 161-187.
7141* **Sölle** Dorothy,   Thinking about God; an introduction to theology, ᵀ*Bowden* John. L/Ph 1990, SCL/Trinity. 210 p. £10 pa. – ᴿTLond 94 (1991) 362s (Frances M. *Young*).
7142 **Stannard** Russell,   Grounds for reasonable belief. E 1989, Scottish Academic. xiv-361 p. £12.50. – ᴿScotJT 44 (1991) 240-2 (I. *Paul*).
7143 **Torrance** Thomas F.,   Science théologique, ᵀ*Lacoste* Jean-Yves: Théologiques. P 1990. PUF. vi-410 p. F 260. – ᴿZkT 113 (1991) 447-450 (K. H. *Neufeld*: seit 20 Jahren Standardwerk).
7144 **Traupe** Gert,   Studium der Theologie; Studienerfahrungen und Studienerwartungen. Stu 1990, Kohlhammer. xiv-289 p. DM 74. – ᴿTLZ 116 (1991) 262-5 (Roija *Weidhas*, auch über ᴱWOHLMUTH J. ⇒ 387, 'völlig unterschiedlich, unvergleichbar').
7145 **Verweyen** Hansjürgen,   Gottes letztes Wort; Grundriss der Fundamentaltheologie. Dü 1991, Patmos. 619 p. – ᴿMiscFranc 91 (1991) 525 (J. *Imbach*).
7146 ᴱ**Vresey** Godfrey,   The philosophy in Christianity: Royal Institute of Philosophy General Lecture series 1990 ⇒ 5,462*: ᴿJTS 42 (1991) 429-431 (D. *Brown* thinks he may be the only one ever to read through it).
7147 **Waldenfels** Hans,   Manuel de théologie fondamentale [1985 ⇒ 1,6448; ²1988], ᵀ*Depré* O., ᴱ*Geffré* C.: CogF 159. P 1990, Cerf. 868 p. F 239. 2-204-03119-4. – ᴿGregorianum 72 (1991) 609 (J. *Galot*); NRT 113 (1991) 615 (L. *Renwart*).
7147* **Wojtowicz** Marek,   Il compito della teologia fondamentale secondo Henri de LUBAC: diss. Teol. 6941, Pont. Univ. Gregoriana, ᴰ*Henrici* P.   R 1991 [InfPUG 121,19].

H2.1   **Anthropologia theologica** – VT & NT.

7148 **Álvarez Turienzo** Saturnino,   Regio media salutis; Imagen del hombre ... AGUSTIN, 1988 ⇒ 5,7173; 6,k233*: ᴿTR 87 (1991) 119s (A. *Zumkeller*).
7149 **d'Andia** Ysabel,   Homo vivens ... IRÉNÉE 1986 ⇒ 2,5248 ... 4,8195: ᴿRevSR 63 (1989) 156s (Mariette *Canévet*).
7150 *a) Ansaldi* J.,   Piste per una antropologia teologica, ᵀ*Corsani* Mirella; – *b) Bein Ricco* Elena, La crisi del soggetto tra modernità e postmodernità; – *c) Rostagno* Sergio, M. LUTERO, Le tesi de homine (1536): Protestantesimo 45,4 ('Persona' 1990) 282-9 / 294-305 / 306-317.
7151 *Ashbrook* James B.,   Making sense of soul and sabbath; brain processes and the making of meaning: Zygon 27 (1992) 31-49.
7152 *a) Bjornard* Reidar B.,   Beyond looks and appearances; the OT on the body; – *b) Bowe* Barbara,   'You are the body of Christ'; Paul's understanding of the human person; – *c) Anderson* Herbert,   The paradox of being bodies and having bodies; the pastoral care of body-souls: BToday 29 (1991) 133-8 / 139-144 / 145-9.
7153 *Bogliolo* Luigi,   Antropologia filosofica e teologica: Divinitas 33 (1989) 44-61.
7154 **Bokwa** Ignacy,   Christologie als Anfang und Ende der Anthropologie; Über das gegenseitige Verhältnis zwischen Christologie und Anthropologie bei Karl RAHNER [Diss. Pont. Univ. Gregoriana, Rom 1989 ⇒ 5,7174*]:

EurHS 23/381. Fra 1990, Lang. 367 p. Fs 85. – RTsTNijm 31 (1991) 332s (H.-E. *Mertens*); ZkT 113 (1991) 288-293 (A. *Batlogg*).

7155 EBühler Pierre, Humain à l'image de Dieu 1985/9 ➤ 5,447; 6,7160: RProtestantesimo 46 (1991) 234s (E. *Genre*); RTLv 22 (1991) 88s (A. de *Halleux*); RTPhil 123 (1991) 341s (F. *Gerber*).

7156 *a) Calkins* Arthur B., The tripartite biblical vision of man; a key to the Christian life; – *b) Saavedra* Alejandro, Perspectiva tomista para meta-antropología: DoctCom 43 (1990) 135-159 / 126-134.

7157 **Comblin** José, Being human; a Christian anthropology [1985 ➤ 2,5239], T*Barr* Robert R. L 1990, Burns & O. £10. – RTablet 244 (1990) 1230 (J. *Todd*).

7158 *Daubercies* P., Nature, personne et existence chrétienne: EsprVie [99 (1989) 193-200; 100 (1990) 17-24.33-39] 101 (1991) 33-43.65-76.81-90.97-106.

7159 **Ebeling** Gerhard, [LUTHER] Disputatio de homine [1. 1977; 2. 1982] 3. Die theologische Definition des Menschen; Kommentar zu These 20-40. Tü 1989, Mohr. xxiii-698 p. DM 178. 3-16-145493-6. – RGregorianum 72 (1991) 776-8 (J. E. *Vercruysse*); TsTNijm 31 (1991) 432 (B. L. de *Groot-Kopetzky*).

7160 **Farley** Edward, Good and evil; interpreting a human condition. Mp 1991, Fortress. xxi-295 p. [RelStR 18, 40, P. C. *Phan*: a theological anthropology].

7161 **Febrer** Mateo, Antropología del universo o lo que en el universo representa la existencia del hombre. Barc 1991, Inst. Teología y Humanismo. – RRCatalT 16 (1991) 200-2 (F. *Nicolau*).

7162 EFelici S., Crescita dell'uomo 1986/7 ➤ 4,562; 5,7184: RAugR 30 (1990) 213s (E. *dal Covolo*).

7163 **Fernández Ardanaz** Santiago, Genesis y anagennesis; fundamentos de la antropología cristiana según CLEMENTE de Alejandría [diss. Pont. Inst. St. Or., D*Ortiz de Urbina* I.]. Vitoria 1990, Eset. xxiv-411 p. 84-7167-123-9.

7164 *Fischer* Klaus-P., Gott als das Geheimnis des Menschen; Karl RAHNERs theologische Anthropologie – Aspekte und Anfragen: ZkT 113 (1991) 1-23.

7165 *Freyer* Thomas, Der Mensch 'unter dem Himmel auf der Erde'; zur 'Ontologie des Menschen' bei Karl BARTH: Catholica 45 (1991) 193-213.

7166 EHamman A., L'uomo immagine somigliante di Dio [1987 ➤ 3,6629], T*Pini* G., EGiannelli E. Mi 1991, Paoline. 310 p. – RAsprenas 38 (1991) 397-9 (B. *Forte*).

7167 **Hollenweger** Walter J., Geist und Materie [... eine 'Pneumatologie des Lebens']: Interkulturelle Theologie [I. 1979, Erfahrung der Leiblichkeit; II. 1982, Umgang mit Mythen]. Mü 1988, Kaiser. 415 p. DM 38. – RTR 87 (1991) 421-3 (W. *Schüssler*).

7168 **Kowalczyk** Stanisław, Dieu et homme dans la doctrine de S. AUGUSTIN. Wsz 1987, Studia i szkice. 276 p. – RAugM 35 (1990) 176 (T. *Madrid*: 'Kowalzyk').

7168* **Kowalski** Aleksy, ✪ Obraz człowieka... L'image de l'homme dans les 'Stromates' de CLÉMENT d'Alexandrie: diss. D*Drączkowski* F. Lublin 1991. 228 p. – RTLv 23, p. 548.

7169 *Leisch-Kiesl* Monika, Zur Anthropologie der Geschlechter [GÖSSMANN Elisabeth in FIMMOOS T. 1988; SCHÜNGEL-STRAUMANN H. 1989...]: Orientierung 55 (1991) 250s.

McDermott John M., La sofferenza umana nella Bibbia 1990 ➤ 1302.

Mannucci Valerio, Teologia biblica del lavoro 1991 ➤ 1303.

7171 ᴱMartin Jochen, *Zöpfel* Renate, Aufgaben, Rollen und Räume von Frau und Mann: Inst. Hist. Anthrop. 5/1s. FrB 1989, Alber. xii-441 p.; xii-p. 443-1013. 3-495-47554-0. – ᴿActuBbg 28 (1991) 187-9 (J. *Boada*).

7171* **Martín García-Alos** José Luis, El 'existencial sobrenatural', clave interpretativa de la antropología de Karl RAHNER: diss. ᴰ*Rovira* J. M. Barc 1991. 350 p. – RTLv 23, p. 570.

7172 *Matabosch* Antoni, 'Manuals' d'antropologia teològica en la dècada dels '80 [MONDIN B., ANCILLI E., BAZZICHI O., LADARIA L., SANNA I. ...]: RCatalT 16 (1991) 187-201.

7173 *a)* **Mondin** Battista, L'uomo libero. R 1982, Dino. 257 p. – *b) Derisi* Octavio, Una seria contribución al tema de la libertad: DoctCom 43 (1990) 176-181.

7174 **Moore** Henrietta L., Mensch und Frau sein; Perspektiven einer feministischen Anthropologie, ᵀ*Denzel* Sieglinde, *Naumann* Susanne; intr. *Pissarek-Hudelist* Herlinde: Tb-Siebenstern 483. Gü 1990, Mohn. 384 p. DM 40. 3-579-00483-2. – ᴿTLZ 116 (1991) 608s (U. *Gerber*).

7175 *Moreno* Fernando, La oposición entre naturaleza y cultura; un malentendido histórico: ScripTPamp 23 (1991) 255-265.

7176 *a) Müller* Gerhard L., Theologische Anmerkungen zum Thema 'Menschenbild'; – *b) Hartman* Fritz, Anthropologische Grenzen der Heilkunde – Menschenbilder in Schulmedizin und Alternativmedizin; – *c) Bierich* Jürgen R., Arzt und Kranker; Wandlungen des Menschenbildes in der Medizin: Arzt und Christ 17 (1991) 24-32 / 16-23 / 3-10.

7177 **Nellas** Panayotis, Le vivant divinisé 1989 ⮕ 5,7195; 6,7181: ᴿLavalTP 47 (1991) 461 (R.-M. *Roberge*).

7178 **Nellas** Panayotis, Deification in Christ; orthodox perspectives on the nature of the human person 1987 ⮕ 4,8230: ᴿAngelicum 68 (1991) 127s (A. *Wilder*); Gregorianum 72 (1991) 371s (J. *Galot*).

7179 **Otten** W., The anthropology of Johannes Scotus ERIUGENA [diss. Amst. 1989]: StIntelHist 20. Leiden 1991, Brill. viii-242 p. – ᴿRHE 87 (1991) 273 (E. *Gaziaux*).

7180 **Panteghini** Giacomo, L'uomo alla luce di Cristo; lineamenti di antropologia teologica: Strumenti di Scienze Religiose. Padova 1990, Messaggero. 253 p. Lit. 18.000 [TR 87,170].

7181 **Pattaro** Germano, La svolta antropologica; un momento forte della teologia contemporanea: Bo c. 1990, Dehoniane. 680 p. Lit. 38.000. Nuovi Saggi T. [RivB 39,166 adv.].

7182 **Pesch** Otto H., Frei sein aus Gnade; theol. Anthropologie 1983 ⮕ 65, 5909 ... 5,7198: ᴿTsTKi 60 (1989) 236-8 (I. *Asheim*).

7183 **Petterson** Alvyn, ATHANASIUS and the human body. Bedminster 1990, Bristol. vii-117 p. – ᴿJTS 42 (1991) 732-5 (C. *Stead*: too-consistently optimistic); NBlackf 72 (1991) 537s (A. *Louth*).

7184 **Ruiz de la Peña** J. L., *a)* Imagen de Dios antropología teológica fundamental: Presencia Teológica 49, 1988 ⮕ 4,8243; 6,7186*: ᴿDivThom 93 (1990) 148s (M. *Tábet*); RAg 31 (1990) 713-5 (G. *Tejerina Arias*). – *b)* El don de Dios; antropología teológica especial: Presencia Teológica 63. Sdr 1991, Sal Terrae. 412 p. [TR 88,171]. 84-293-0911-X.

7185 **Sachs** John R., The Christian vision of humanity; basic Christian anthropology: Glazier-Zacchaeus. Collegeville MN 1991, Liturgical. 112 p. $7 [CBQ 54,405].

7185* **Sayes** J. A., Antropología del hombre caído: Historia Salutis 2, BAC 514. M 1991, Católica. xx-393 p. [NRT 114,899, L. *Renwart*].

7186 *Scharbert* Josef [*Wolter* Michael] Leiden, AT [NT]: → 690, TRE 20 (1990) 670-2 [677-688-711, *al.*].

7187 **Schenk** R., Die Gnade vollendeter Endlichkeit; zur transzendental-theologischen Auslegung der thomanischen Anthropologie: FreibTSt 135. FrB 1989, Herder. 638 p. DM 98. 3-451-21153-X. – ᴿTsTNijm 31 (1991) 329s (P. *Valkenberg*: 'theomanischen'); TGL 81 (1991) 410s (K. *Hollmann*).

7188 **Schillebeeckx** Edward, *a*) Menschen; die Geschichte von Gott, ᵀ*Zulauf* Hugo. FrB 1990, Herder. 326 p. DM 69. – ᴿActuBbg 28 (1991) 182s (J. *Boada*); Carthaginensia 7 (1991) 529s (F. *Martínez Fresneda*); HerdKorr 45 (1991) 98 (U. *Ruh*); TGegw 34 (1991) 313-5 (H. *Schmied*). – *b*) Church, the human story of God → 7929; – *c*) Mensen als verhaal van God 1989 → 6,7190; 90-24415-31-4; ᴿNedTTs 45 (1991) 169s (M. E. *Brinkman*).

7189 ᴱ**Schneider** Theodor, Mann und Frau, Grundproblem theologischer Anthropologie: QDisp 121, 1989 → 5,513: ᴿSalesianum 52 (1990) 754s (M. *Midali*); TsTNijm 31 (1991) 439 (C. *Halkes*); ZkT 113 (1991) 323 (H. *Rotter*).

7190 **Schnelle** Udo, Neutestamentliche Anthropologie; Jesus-Paulus-Johannes: BTSt 18. Neuk 1991. ix-197. 3-7887-1394-1.

7190* *Schrey* Heinz-H., Leib/Leiblichkeit: → 690, TRE 20 (1990) 638-643 (-649, und Seele, *Gloy* Karen).

7191 *Sciattella* Marco, *a*) Antropologia e cristologia in S. IRENEO di Lione, Adversus Haereses V,1-2 analisi strutturale teologica e scritturistica del testo; – *b*) Dio, l'anima e l'uomo nell'antropologia teologica di S. AMBROGIO: Divinitas 33 (1989) 269-285 / 34 (1990) 172-8.

7191* *Seebass* Horst [*Dautzenberg* Gerhard], Leben AT [NT]: → 690, TRE 20 (1990) 520-4 [526-530] (-566, *al.*).

7192 *Seweryniak* Henryk, ❷ La genèse et les principes méthodologiques de l'anthropologie théologico-fondamentale de W. PANNENBERG: ColcT 60,2 (1990) 45-65; franç. 65.

7193 *Stagliano* Antonio, L'uomo e la natura; sull'antropocentrismo cristiano: RasT ForumATI 32 (1991) 198-205.

7194 *a*) *Stroumsa* Gedaliahu G., Caro salutis cardo; shaping the person in early Christian thought; – *b*) *Sullivan* Lawrence E., Body works; knowledge of the body in the study of religion [FÉHER M. Eng. 1989; CAMPORESI P. Eng. 1988...]: HistRel 30 (1990s) 25-50 / 86-99.

7194* **Telepneff** Gregory, The concept of the person [... human free will] in the Christian Hellenism of the Greek Church Fathers; a study of ORIGEN, St. GREGORY the Theologian, and St. MAXIMUS the Confessor: diss. Graduate Theological Union, ᴰ*Ludwig* E. Berkeley 1991. 436 p. 92-06905. – DissA 52 (1991s) 3324-A.

7195 **Theau** Jean, Le crépuscule de l'homme. Montréal 1986, Bellarmin. 161 p. $15. 2-89007-609-1. – ᴿBijdragen 52 (1991) 115s (L. *Anckaert*).

7196 **Torres Queiruga** Andrés, La revelación de Dios en la realización del hombre [A revelación, Vigo 1985]. M 1987, Cristiandad. 505 p. 84-7057-398-5. – ᴿGregorianum 72 (1991) 370s (F.-A. *Pastor*).

7197 *a*) *Cazelles* H., L'homme devant Dieu; – *b*) *Fauquet* Y., Un type d'homme selon les Psaumes; le 'hasid'; – *c*) *Cothenet* É., Corps psychique, corps spirituel: ᴱ**Triacca** A. M., *Pistoia* A., Liturgie et anthropologie, S.-Serge XXXVIᵉ Semaine d'Études Liturgiques 1989/90 → 6,702.

7198 *Zavalloni* Roberto, Linee di sviluppo nella concezione della 'corporeità' umana: Antonianum 65 (1990) 345-382; Eng. 385 [p. 346-353, nella visione biblica].

7199 **Zincone** Sergio, Studi sulla visione dell'uomo in ambito antiocheno 1988
   ➤ 5,7207: ᴿAugR 30 (1990) 197 (O. *Pasquato*).

H2.8 **Œcologia VT & NT** – saecularitas.

7200 **Albertz** R., Der Mensch als Hüter seiner Welt; alttestamentliche Bibelarbeiten zu den Themen des konziliaren Prozesses: Tb 16, 1990
   ➤ 6,7196: ᴿZAW 103 (1991) 443 (H.-C. *Schmitt*).

7201 *Anderlini* Gianpaolo, Bibbia e natura; appunti per una lettura ecologica
   della Bibbia: BbbOr 33 (1991) 193-209.

7202 *a) Angelhardt* Paulus, Konziliarer Prozess – Ende, Wende, Anfang?; –
   b) Duchrow Ulrich, *Liedke* Gerhard, Beichtspiegel im Konziliaren Prozess; – *c) Blasberg-Kuhnke* Martina, Wortgottesdienst für Gerechtigkeit,
   Frieden und Bewahrung der Schöpfung; – *d) Schneider* Gert, Konziliarer
   Prozess und Landpastoral: BLtg 63 (1990) 66-73 / 95s / 88-94 (Hymnen)
   / 99-108.

7202* *Arce Valentin* Reinerio, Die Schöpfung muss gerettet werden; aber für
   wen? Die ökologische Krise aus der Perspektive lateinamerikanischer
   Theologie: EvT 51 (1991) 565-577.

7203 **Austin** Richard C., Environmental theology; 1. Baptized into wilderness... John MUIR; – 2. Beauty of the Lord; – 3. Hope for the Land;
   nature in the Bible; – 4. Reclaiming America. Abingdon VA 1987-8-8
   (reprinted), 1990, Creekside. 103 p.; 225 p.; 262 p.; 243 p. $9.75; $13; $14;
   $14; pa.; all four $38. 0-8042-0869-7; -59-X; -61-1; vol. 4 0-962-831-0-3
   [TDig 38,250].

7204 **Barros Souza** M. de, *Caravias* J. Luis, Theologie der Erde [1989 ➤ 5,
   7214],ᵀ: BtT Befreiung. Dü 1990, Patmos. 240 p. DM 34,80. 3-491-
   77724-0. – ᴿTsTNijm 31 (1991) 340 (R. G. van *Rossum*).

7205 **Bartl** K., Theologie und Sekularität; die theologische Ansätze Friedrich
   GOGARTENs und Dietrich BONHOEFFERs zur Analyse und Reflexion der
   säkularisierten Welt: EurHS 23/393. Fra 1990, Lang. viii-262 p. Fs 73.
   3-631-42774-3. – ᴿActuBbg 28 (1991) 167s (J. *Boada*); TsTNijm 31 (1991)
   435s (A. *Brants*).

7206 *Bavel* Tarcisius van, The Creator and the integrity of Creation in the
   Fathers of the Church, especially in St. AUGUSTINE: AugSt 21 (Villanova
   1990) 1-34 [55-66, *Burt* D.; < ZIT 91,443].

7207 *a) Bergant* Dianne, Is the biblical world-view anthropocentric?: – *b)*
   Reilly William K., Theology and ecology; a confluence of interests; – *c)*
   French William C., Ecological dangers and Christian response; attending
   to creation: NewTR 4,2 (1991) 5-14 / 15-25 / 26-42.

7208 **Bhagat** S., Creation in crisis. Elgin IL 1991, Brethren. 173 p. $10 [TS
   52,601].

7209 *a) Birch* Charles, Der Gott aller Dinge; – *b) Moltmann* Jürgen, Komm
   Heiliger Geist — erneuere die ganze Schöpfung: ➤ 160, ᶠVISCHER L.
   1991, 311-7 / 318-331.

7209* **Büsser** Fritz, Das 'Buch der Natur'; vom Lob des Schöpfers zum
   Schutz der Schöpfung; grosse Theologen über Schöpfung und Natur.
   Stäfa 1990, Gut. 111 p. Fs 24 [TLZ 117,149].

7210 *Chang Hyung Kyung*, Komm, Heiliger Geist — erneuere die ganze
   Schöpfung: Junge Kirche (1991,3) 130-5 [< NSys 33 (1991) 316s].

7211 *Daoust* J., De la condition ouvrière à la création entière [LÉON XIII,
   Rerum novarum; É. *Poulat*, Revue des Deux Mondes, mai 1991]: EsprVie
   101 (1991) 585-7.

7211* ᴱDe Witt C. B., The environment and the Christian; what does the NT say about the environment? GR 1991, Baker. 156 p. $8. 0-8010-3006-4 [NTAbs 36,128 mentions five other contributors].

7212 *Di Sante* Carmine, Presenza del creato nella religione e nel culto d'Israele: RivLtg 77 (1990) 233-251.

7213 **Duchrow** U., *Liedke* G., Shalom, biblical perspectives on creation, justice and peace. Geneva 1989, WCC. 200 p. £9.50. 2-8254-0962-6. – ᴿProtestantesimo 46 (1991) 327 (P. *Ribet*).

7214 **Echlin** Edward P., *a*) The Christian Green heritage; world as creation: Nottingham 1990, Grove. – *b*) Let's re-enter God's creation now [... catholicity is insufficiently cosmic]: Month 252 (1991) 359-364.

7215 *a*) *Echlin* Edward P., Greenness in the NT; – *b*) *Arguile* Roger, A green theology: NBlackf 72 (1991) 278-281 / 517-525.

7216 *Eckensperger* Walter, Der Logos und die 'Logizität' der Natur; ein fundamentaltheologischer Beitrag zur Frage nach der Natur im Horizont der Umweltkrise: ZkT 113 (1991) 385-400.

7217 *a*) *Fantini* Bernardino, La biologia moderna e il posto dell'uomo nella natura; – *b*) *Bein Ricco* Elena, Modelli di pensabilità del rapporto uomo – natura; – *c*) *Bühler* Pierre, 'Sola gratia' una rivalutazione del naturale? Natura e grazia secondo i Riformatori; – *d*) *Comba* Pietro, Il rischio ambientale e la salvaguardia della vita umana; aspetti etici: Protestantesimo 46,4 (1991) 242-255 / 256-268 / 269-286 / 287-300.

7218 **Fedeli** P., La natura violata; ecologia e mondo romano. Palermo 1990, Sellerio. 223 p. – ᴿAufidus 11s (1990) 269-272 (Paola *Lisimberti*).

7218* *Fedeli* Paolo, Uomo e ambiente nel mondo romano: Aufidus 8 (1989) 7-50.

7219 **Fox** Matthew, *a*) Der grosse Segen; Umarmt von der Schöpfung [1983],ᵀ. Mü 1991, Claudius. 384 p. DM 36. – *b*) Vision vom kosmischen Christus; Aufbruch ins dritte Jahrtausend [1988 ⇒ 4,8510],ᵀ. Stu 1991, Kreuz. 400 p. DM 48. – ᴿTGL 81 (1991) 407-9 (K. *Hollmann*).

7219* *García Paredes* José C., Ecología y vida consagrada [< Diz./Dicc. Teol. Vita Consacrata/Vida Consagrada 1989]: Claretianum 31 (1991) 295-325.

7220 *a*) *Gorsky* Jonathan, Judaism and the environment; – *b*) *Oderberg* David S., A civilising influence – Basil WRIGHTON and animal rights: Month 252 (1991) 78-83 / 84-88.

7221 **Granberg-Michaelson** Wesley, Ecology and life 1988 ⇒ 5,7225*: ᴿScotJT 43 (1990) 518-520 (J. *Begbie*: by the president of a Montana institute 'for educating the Church in environmental issues').

7222 ᴱ**Granberg-Michaelson** Wesley, Tending the garden; essays on the Gospel and the earth 1987 ⇒ 3,636: ᴿJRelEth 19,1 (1991) 193s (T. *Derr*).

7223 *Granberg-Michaelson* Wesley, Renewing the whole creation: VerbumSVD 32 (1991) 45-59.

7224 *Gulick* Walter B., The Bible and ecological spirituality: TTod 48 (1991s) 182-194.

7225 **Guzzetti** G. B., Ecologia, popolazione e morale: Saggi di Teologia 32. T-Leumann 1988, LDC. 216 p. – ᴿAntonianum 65 (1990) 395 (P. G. *Pesce*).

7225* *Hagemann* L., Islam und ökologische Kultur: ⇒ 530, ᴱ*Mensen* B., Die Schöpfung in den Religionen 1990, 23-31.

7226 *a*) *Harskamp* Anton van, 'Processus conciliaire', analyse d'un terme, ᵀ*Braat* Anne; – *b*) *Coste* René, La dynamique œcuménique, 'Justice, paix, sauvegarde de la création'; – *c*) *Ganoczy* Alexandre, Perspectives écologiques dans la doctrine chrétienne de la création; – *d*) *Klinken* Johan van, Le troisième élément du processus JPIC; l'écologie entre théologie et science; ᵀ*Divault* André; – *e*) *Burggraeve* Roger, [Isa 66,22; Apc 21,1] Responsable d'un 'ciel nouveau' et d'une 'terre nouvelle' ᵀ*Braat* Anne; ⇥ 348, Concilium 236 (P 1991) 43-54 / 29-42 / 57-68 / 80-96 / 129-141.

7227 **Hösle** Vittorio, Philosophie der ökologischen Krise: Moskauer Vorträge. Mü 1991, Beck. 151 p. DM 16,80. – ᴿHerdKorr 45 (1991) 389s (U. *Ruh*).

7228 *Hoogstraten* H. D. van, Fundamenten voor een theologische milieu-ethiek; BONHOEFFER's 'ethische theologie' sociaal-ethisch bezien: TsTNijm 31 (1991) 42-63; Eng. 64.

7228* *Jenssen* Hans-Hinrich, 'Bewahrung der Schöpfung' ohne christliche Naturfrömmigkeit? Gedanken über die Notwendigkeit und Möglichkeiten einer zeitgemässen Naturpredigt: TLZ 116 (1991) 91-100.

7229 *Johannes Paul II*, 'Friede mit Gott, dem Schöpfer — Friede mit der ganzen Schöpfung', Weltfriedenstag 1990: HerdKorr 44 (1990) 75-79.

7229* **Jones** P., L'eschatologie et l'avenir de la création: RRéf 42,3 (1991) 43-70 [< NTAbs 36,73].

7230 **Kessler** H., Das Stöhnen der Natur; Plädoyer für eine Schöpfungsspiritualität und Schöpfungsethik. Dü 1990, Patmos. 140 p. DM 19,80. 3-491-77805-0. – ᴿTsTNijm 31 (1991) 210 (G. *Manenschijn*).

7230* **Kostelec** William A., The gardener in the garden; the creative capacity of the human creature in an ecological context: diss. Emory, ᴰ*Saliers* D. Atlanta 1991, 257 p. 91-27605. – DissA 52 (1991s) 1391s-A; RelStR 18,171.

7231 **Krolzik** Udo, Säkularisierung der Natur; Providentia-Dei-Lehre und Naturverständnis der Frühaufklärung 1988 ⇥ 5,7233; 6,7234: ᴿTLZ 116 (1991) 376-8 (M. *Petzoldt*).

7232 *a*) *Limouris* Gennadios, The integrity of creation in a world of change today; – *b*) *Economou* Elias B., An Orthodox view of the ecological crisis: TAth 61 (1990) 270-297 / 607-619.

7233 *Lucereau* Jérôme, *Joucla* Jean, L'animal de compagnie [16 million cats and dogs cost 4 (US) billion dollars annually]: Études 374 (1991) 193-200.

7233* **McDaniel** Jay B., *a*) Of God and pelicans. Louisville 1987, W-Knox. 168 p. $15. – *b*) Earth, sky, gods, and mortals; developing an ecological spirituality. Mystic CT 1990, Twenty-Third. 192 p. $12. 0-89622-412-0. – ᴿTorJT 7 (1991) 145s (M. *McIntyre*).

7234 **McDonagh** Sean, The greening of the Church 1990 ⇥ 6,7239; also Melbourne, Canterbury: ᴿAustralasCR 68 (1991) 118-120 (A. *Fisher*: 'more pink than green' against poverty); NewTR 4/3 (1991) 107 (P. J. *Wadell*); PrPeo 4 (1990) 383s (S. E. *Hall*); Tablet 245 (1991) 943s (A. *Lieven*); TS 52 (1991) 767s (Mary Ellen *Ross*).

7235 *Manenschijn* Gerrit, Christian ethics of peace and creation between Utopism and reality: LvSt 16 (1991) 41-58.

7236 *a*) *Martin* Alain-Georges, Le repos de la création; – *b*) *Jones* Peter, L'eschatologie et l'avenir de la création: RRéf 42 ('Écologie et création' 1991) 11-18 / 43-... [< ZIT 91,506].

7237 *a*) *Melchert* Charles F., Creation and justice among the sages; – *b*) *Rogers* Donald E., Lessons from the Exile for the instruction of the Church in ecological education: RelEdn 85 (Ch 1990) 368-381 / 412-423 [< ZIT 90,853].

7238 **Moltmann** Jürgen, Gerechtigkeit schafft Zukunft 1989 [⇥ 6,7247]: ᴿActuBbg 28 (1991) 31-35 (J. *Boada*).

7239 **Moltmann** Jürgen, Creating a just future 1989 ➤ 6,7248: ᴿLvSt 16 (1991) 83s (H.-E. *Mertens*); ScotJT 43 (1990) 503s (R. *Ambler*).

7240 **Moltmann** J., La giustizia crea futuro: GdT 193, 1990 ➤ 6,7247: ᴿAsprenas 38 (1991) 261s (G. *Mattai*).

7240* **Montefiore** Hugh, Reclaiming the high ground; a Christian response to secularism. L 1990, Macmillan. viii-154 p. £35; pa. £13. – ᴿTLond 94 (1991) 229s (J. *Habgood*).

7241 *Mousalimas* S. A., The divine in nature; animism or panentheism?: GrOrTR 35 (1990) 367-375.

7242 **Murphy** Charles M., At home on earth; foundations for a Catholic ethic of the environment 1989 ➤ 6,7251: ᴿNewTR 4,1 (1991) 114 (J. T. *Pawlikowski*).

7243 *Musfeldt* Klaus, Wird der Löwe Stroh fressen? A. SCHWEITZERs Ehrfurcht vor dem Leben und die gegenwärtigen Ansätze einer ökologischen Schöpfungsethik: NSys 33 (1991) 300-314; Eng. 315.

7243* *Norelli* Enrico, Paix, justice, intégrité de la création; IRÉNÉE de Lyon et ses adversaires: Irénikon 64 (1991) 1-42; Eng. 42s.

7244 **Oviedo Torró** Lluis, La secularización como problema: Valentina 25. Valencia 1990, Fac. T. Ferrer. 316 p. 84-86067-40-5. – ᴿActuBbg 28 (1991) 180s (J. *Boada*).

7245 *Pharantos* Megas L., Ⓖ Ideological currents and the ecological crisis: TAth 62 (1991) 312-343; Eng. 929.

7246 a) *Platten* Stephen, Authority and order in creation [MOLTMANN J.]; – b) *Soskice* Janet M., Creation and relation: TLond 94 (1991) 23-30 / 31-39.

7246* **Primavesi** Anne, From Apocalypse to Genesis; ecology, feminism and Christianity. Mp 1991, Fortress. xii-324 p. 0-8006-2522-6.

7247 *Quacquarelli* Antonio, L'ecologia nei riflessi del linguaggio simbolico dei Padri della Chiesa: VetChr 28 (1991) 5-24.

7248 **Regenstein** Lewis G., Replenish the earth; a history of organized religion's treatment of animals and nature – including the Bible's message of conservation and kindness toward animals. NY 1991, Crossroad. 304 p. $15 pa. 0-8245-1075-5 [TDig 38,375].

7249 *Rizzi* Marco, Una teologia verde?: ➤ 6,633*: La responsabilità ecologica 1989/90, 175-186 [... *al.*].

7250 a) *Rock* Martin, Elemente einer Umweltethik; – b) *Kirchhoff* Hermann, Mensch und Tier in der Heiligen Schrift; – c) *Gruber* Elmar, Gottbegegnung in der Schöpfung; – d) *Bumiller* Meinrad, Ökologische Lebensstil — wichtiges Element einer zeitgemässen Spiritualität: LebSeelsorge 42 (FrB 1991) 88-94 / 95-99 / 106-110 / 120-2 [< ZIT 91,318].

7251 *Rössler* Andreas [➤ 7286], Der kosmische Christus; die Offenbarung geht weiter: Deutsches Pfarrerblatt 91 (Essen 1991) 267s [< ZIT 91,536].

7252 **Rotsaert** M., *al.*, God in heel de schepping; jonge jezuïeten over de inspiratie van IGNATIUS van Loyola. Kapellen 1990, Pelckmans. 175 p. Fb 595. 90-289-1542-7. – ᴿTsTNijm 31 (1991) 213s (P. *Begheyn*).

7252* **Russell** David M., The 'new heavens and new earth'; hope for the creation in Jewish apocalyptic and the New Testament: diss. SW Baptist Theol. Sem. 1991, ᴰCorley B. 291 p. 92-13049. – DissA 52 (1991s) 4367-A.

7253 a) *Ryan* Tom, Ethics and the environment; has Catholic social teaching and moral theology anything to offer?; – b) *Walker* David, The

Christian and the environment; – c) *Green* Veronica, A Christian attitude to the environment: AustralasCR 68 (1991) 18-30 / 31-42 / 43-55.

7253* *Sánchez González* Miguel, Los derechos de los animales y el valor moral de los seres vivos: RazF 223 (1991) 272-284.

7254 *Schmidt* Leigh E., From Arbor Day to the environmental sabbath; nature, liturgy, and American Protestantism: HarvTR 84 (1991) 299-323.

7255 *Schreiner* Stefan, Die Verbesserung der Welt, oder die Aufgaben des Menschen als Partner Gottes nach jüdischer Tradition: Orientierung 55 (1991) 8-10.

7256 **Schreiner** Susan E., The theater of his glory; nature and the natural order in the thought of John CALVIN: StHistT 3. Durham 1991, Labyrinth. 164 p. [TR 88,167].

7257 **Schupp** Franz, *al.*, Schöpfung und Sünde; von der Verheissung einer wahren und gerechten Welt, vom Versagen der Menschen und vom Widerstand gegen die Zerstörung 1990 → 6,7267: ᴿTLZ 116 (1991) 692-4 (M. *Plathow*).

7258 *Selling* Joseph H., The 'conciliar process' ... [→ 6,7267*]: LvSt 14 (1989) 346-364.

7259 *a) Siegwalt* Gérard, The ecological crisis; challenge for Christians [< Sup (VSp) 169 (1989) 88-100]: – *b) Aubert* Jean-Marie, Justice, peace, creation [< Sup (VSp) 169 (1989) 101-110]; – *c) Sebahire* Mbonyinkebe, Saving the earth to save life; an African point of view [< Pro mundi vita studies 13 (Feb. 1990) 1-26], ᵀᴱ*Jermann* Rosemary: TDig 38 (1991) 123-5 / 119-122 / 128s.

7260 *a) Sivadas* S., A new gospel on nature; – *b) Therukattil* George, Towards a biblical eco-theology; – *c) Arokiasamy* S., Ecological ethics in a divided world: Jeevadhara 21 (1991) 421-433 / 465-483 / 484-498.

7261 *Strolz* Walter, Schöpfungsgeheimnis statt Weltbemächtigung; das Schöpfungsthema in der gegenwärtigen evangelischen Theologie: HerdKorr 45 (1991) 330-335.

7262 **Tanner** Kathryn, God and creation 1988 → 4,8928 (5,7652) 6,7270; ᴿThomist 55 (1991) 321-6 (B. D. *Marshall*).

7263 **Thiele** J., Visioen van een nieuwe aarde; een kleine theologie van de schepping. Baarn 1990, Ten Have. 123 p. *f*21,50. 90-259-4447-7. – ᴿCollatVL 21 (1991) 434s (W. Van *Soon*); TsTNijm 31 (1991) 306 (W. B. *Drees*).

7264 *Ulrich* Lothar, Bewahrung der Schöpfung; Versuch einer ökumenisch-theologischen Grundlegung: → 564, Erfurter 1989/90, 55-70.

7265 *Veken* J. Van der, Een kosmos om in te leven; een nieuw gesprek tussen kosmologie en geloof. Kapellen/Kampen 1990, Pelckmans/Kok. 127 p. *f*25. 90-289-1491-9 / 90-242-7706-X. – ᴿTsTNijm 31 (1991) 336s (W. B. *Drees*).

7266 *Wackenheim* Charles, Des religions aux idéologies; 'sécularisation' de l'intolérance: RevSR 63 (1989) 117-135.

7266* *Wainwright* E., A metaphorical walk through Scripture in an ecological age: Pacifica 4 (1991) 273-294 [< NTAbs 36,223].

7267 **Weeber** Karl-Wilhelm, Smog über Attika; Umweltverhalten im Altertum. Z 1990, Artemis. 223 p.

7268 **Wolf** Ursula, Das Tier in der Moral. Fra 1990, Klostermann. 169 p. – ᴿTPhil 66 (1991) 471-3 (M. *Bordt*).

7269 **Wrighton** Basil † 1988, Reason, religion and the animals. L 1987,

Catholic Animal Welfare.   101 p. – ^RNBlackf 72 (1991) 206-8 (D. S. *Oderberg*).

H3.1   *Foedus* – **the Covenant;** the Chosen People; Providence.

7270 *Badr* Habib,   Medium quiddam; 'the problematic relation of general election and individual salvation in CALVIN's theology': NesTR 10,1s (1989) 21-65 [< ZIT 91,19].

7271 **Craig** William L.,   The only wise God; the compatibility of divine foreknowledge and human freedom 1987 → 3,6389: ^RThemelios 15 (1989s) 106s (R. C. *Cook*).

7272 **Cypser** Cora,   Covenant and consensus: Kim Pathways. 264 p. $12 pa. [Interp 45,109].

7273 *Les Évêques de France*, Catechisme pour adultes — l'alliance de Dieu avec les hommes. P 1991. – ^RBrotéria 133 (1991) 519-527 (R. *Marlé*).

7273* **Goebel** H. T.,   Vom freien Wählen Gottes und des Menschen; Interpretationsübungen zur 'Analogie' nach Karl BARTHs Lehre von der Erwählung... Fra 1990, Lang. 378-xiii p. – ^RLaurentianum 32 (1991) 437s (B. de *Armellada*).

7274 *Kaiser* Walter C.^J,   God's promise plan and his gracious law: JEvTS 33 (1990) 289-302 [< ZAW 103,434].

7275 *Kaladzakis* Stauros E.,   ⊚ *Distagmos*... The uncertainty of the elect of the OT toward God's call: Epistemonike Epeteris Thessalonikes 29 (1988) 477-515 [< TAth 61 (1990) 331-3, P. *Simotas*].

7276 **Kaufmann** Yehezkel,   Christianity and Judaism, two covenants 1988 = 1929s → 6,7284: ^RTLZ 116 (1991) 271s (W. *Wiefel*).

7277 **Klein** William W.,   The new chosen people; a corporate view of election. GR 1990, Zondervan Academie. 314 p. $16.   0-310-51251-4 [TDig 39,69].

7278 **Krusche** Werner,   Verheissung und Verantwortung; Orientierung auf dem Weg der Kirche.   B 1990, Ev.-VA. 240 p. DM 24,80.   3-374-00969-7. – ^RTLZ 116 (1991) 577s (G. *Heintze*).

7278* **Le Roux** Petrus J.,   Verbond en gemeente; de betekenis van verbond vir kerk en kosmos: diss. ^D*König* A. Pretoria c. 1991. 320 p. – RTLv 23, p. 565.

7279 **Lohfink** Norbert,   The covenant never revoked; biblical reflections on Christian-Jewish dialogue [Der niemals gekündigte Bund 1989 → 5,7274], ^T*Scullion* John J.   NY 1991, Paulist. v-96 p. $8 pa.   0-8091-3228-1. – ^RLVitae 46 (1991) 351 (G. van *Hoomissen*); ZAW 103 (1991) 453.

7280 **Lohfink** Norbert,   L'alleanza mai revocata; riflessioni esegetiche per il dialogo tra cristiani ed ebrei [1989], ^T*Gillini* Gilberto. Brescia 1991, Queriniana. 101 p. Lit. 12.000. 88-399-0701-7. – ^RRivB 39 (1991) 500 (C. *Di Sante*).

7281 *Lohfink* Norbert,   *a)* Der Begriff 'Bund' in der biblischen Theologie: TPhil 66 (1991) 161-176; – *b*) Il concetto di 'alleanza' nella teologia biblica [TPhil 66 (1991) 161-176 meno alcune note]: CC 142 (1991,3) 353-367.

7282 *Morris* Kenneth R.,   The Puritan roots of American universalism [paradoxical, because Puritan Calvinism held the opposite of universal salvation]: ScotJT 44 (1991) 457-487.

7283 **Nicholson** E. N.,   God and his people; Covenant 1986 → 2,5342... 6,7292: ^RRB 98 (1991) 431-6 (M. *Weinfeld*); VT 41 (1991) 506s (R. P. *Gordon*).

7284 *Osten-Sacken* Peter van der,   Die Erwählung des jüdischen Volkes in ihrer Bedeutung für die Kirche: → 46*, ^FEHRLICH E., Israel 1991, 224-235.

Preuss Horst-Dietrich, JHWHs erwählendes und verpflichtendes Handeln: Theologie des ATs 1, 1991 → 7388.

7285 *Renaud* Bernard, Le concept biblique d'alliance à l'épreuve de l'exil babylonien: → 6,109*, ^FLAURENTIN R., Kecharitōménē 1990, 113-125.
7286 **Rössler** Andreas [→ 7251], Steht Gottes Himmel allen offen? Zum Symbol des kosmischen Christus. Stu 1990, Quell. 189 p. DM 29,90 pa. – ^RTLZ 116 (1991) 338s (P. *Heidrich*); TR 87 (1991) 330s (W. *Schüssler*).
7286* **Sanders** John, No other name; an investigation into the destiny of the unevangelized. GR 1991, Eerdmans. xviii-315 p. 0-8028-0615-5.
7287 **Sharp** Douglas R., The hermeneutics of election; the significance of the doctrine in BARTH's Church Dogmatics. Lanham MD 1990, UPA. xiii-246 p. $41.25; pa. $21.50. 0-8191-7944-2; -5-0 [TDig 38,187].
7288 **Sohn** S.T., The divine election of Israel. GR 1991, Eerdmans. 0-8028-0545-0 [BL 92,146].
7289 **Strehle** Stephen, Calvinism, Federalism and Scholasticism; a study of the Reformed doctrine of covenant: BaBSt 58. Bern 1988, Lang. viii-410 p. $53.60. 3-261-03886-1. – ^RJEH 42 (1991) 485s (E. *Cameron* dislikes both style and content).
7290 **Vermeylen** J., *a)* El Dios de la promesa y el Dios de la alianza [1986 → 2,5344],^T. Sdr 1990, Sal Terrae; 399 p. – ^RCarthaginensia 7 (1991) 527 (F. *Martínez Fresneda*). – *b)* Het geloof van Israël; theologie van het Oude Testament [Le Dieu de la promesse/alliance 1986 → 2,5344], ^T*Nederstigt* H.L. Brugge/Boxtel 1989, Tabor/KBS. 434 p. ƒ49,50. 90-65971-84-X / 90-61734-42-8. – ^RNedTTs 45 (1991) 143s (P.B. *Dirksen*).
7291 *a)* *Waschke* Ernst-J., Die Frage nach Israel als die Frage nach dem Bekenntnis seiner Erwählung; – *b)* *Osten-Sacken* Peter von der, Vom Gottesvolk zu den Gottesvölkern; zum neuen Lesen der alten Texte: → 163, ^FWAGNER S., Gottesvolk 1991, 11-28 / 209-223.
7292 **Watson** David L., God does not foreclose; the universal promise of salvation. Nv 1990, Abingdon. 160 p. $13. – ^RTTod 48 (1991s) 346.348 (J.P. *Wind*).

H3.3   *Fides in VT* –   **Old Testament faith.**

7292* *Fohrer* Georg, Basic structures of biblical faith [Fourth World Congress of Jewish studies 1 (1967) 161-166 + NedGerefT 7 (1966) 198-206) + Biblical Essays 1966s, 31-39]: → 200, Studien zum AT V (1991) 101-111-121-131.
7293 *Petuchowski* Jakob J., Glaube und Werke in der rabbinischen Literatur: Judaica 46 (1990) 12-21.
7293* *Wénin* André, Foi et justice sociale dans l'AT: LVitae 46 (1991) 380-392.

H3.5   *Liturgia, spiritualitas VT* –   **OT prayer.**

7294 **Arndt** Timotheus, Tora, Liturgie und Wohltätigkeit; Untersuchungen zu den Bibelzitaten in den Morgenbenediktionen der jüdischen Liturgie: Diss Kirchliche Hochschule Leipzig 1991, ^D*Seidel*. – TR 87 (1991) 519.
    Bradshaw Paul F., *Hoffman* Lawrence A., The making of Jewish and Christian worship: Two Liturgical Traditions 1, 1991 → 474.
7296 ^E**Cattani** Luigi, La preghiera quotidiana di Israele: [^E*Neri* U.] Le grandi preghiere, 1990 → 6,7299: ^RJStJud 22 (1991) 124 (J. *Maier*); RivB 39 (1991) 78s (M. *Perani*).
7297 **Di Sante** Carmine, Het gebed van Israël [1985 → 2,5358],^T. Hilversum/ Turnhout 1989, Goij/Brepols. 264 p. DM 90-304-0467-1. – ^RTsTNijm 31 (1991) 342 (A. *Scheer*).

7298 ^E**Fisher** Eugene J.,   The Jewish roots of Christian liturgy [< SIDIC]
1990 ➤ 6,7303:   ^RCCurr 41 (1991s) 264-7 (L. A. *Hoffman*: misnomer; flawed).

7298* **Frankiel** Tamar,   The voice of Sarah; feminine spirituality and traditional Judaism.   SF 1990, Harper.   xv-140 p. $19.   0-06-063016-7 [TDig 39,60].

7299 **Gammie** John G.,   Holiness in Israel 1989 ➤ 5,7297; 6,7305:   ^RBibTB 21 (1991) 122s (Betty Jane *Lillie*); CBQ 53 (1991) 468-470 (B. E. *Shafer*); CritRR 4 (1991) 136s (B. W. *Anderson*); JRel 71 (1991) 428s (D. P. *Wright*); ScotJT 44 (1991) 418-420 (R. *Mason*); TLZ 116 (1991) 897s (E.-J. *Waschke*); TorJT 7 (1991) 110s (D. E. *Burke*).

7300 ^E**Green** Arthur,   Jewish spirituality [to / from] 16th century: EWSp 13s 1986-9 ➤ 2,5361 ... 6,7307:   ^RRelStR 17 (1991) 121-3 (D. *Biale*) & 124-7 (C. E. *Vernoff*); RRel 49 (1990) 470-2 (H. G. *Perelmuter*).

7301 **Greenberg** Irving,   The Jewish way; living the holidays.   NY 1988, Summit.   480 p. $20. – ^RWorship 64 (1990) 89-91 (H. G. *Perelmuter*).

7301* *Hoffman* Lawrence A.,   Jüdische Liturgie, ^T*Schnitker* T.: ➤ 690, TRE 21 (1991) 377-383.

7302 *Kessler* Colette,   Les Psaumes dans la liturgie juive: LumièreV 40,202 (1991) 13-24.

7303 **Petuchowski** Jakob J., 'Dass wir ...' Sabbatmorgen 1988 ➤ 4,8345:   ^RBLtg 63 (1990) 122s (K. *Richter*).

7304 *Reif* Stefan,   ❶ On the earliest development of Jewish prayer: Tarbiz [59 (1989s) 397-441, *Fleischer* E.] 60 (1990s) 677-681 [683-8 rejoinder]; Eng. VIII.

7305 **Reventlow** Henning,   Gebet im AT 1986 ➤ 2,5374 ... 4,8346:   ^RTLZ 116 (1991) 824s (H. *Seidel*).

7306 *Sacchi* Paolo,   Considerazioni sulla spiritualità giudaica del Secondo Tempio [conferenza Modena 1990]: Henoch 13 (1991) 3-15; Eng. 16s.

7307 *Soleh* M. Z., ❶ Prayer in the Bible: BethM 36,127 (1990s) 358-367.

H3.7   *Theologia moralis VT* – **OT moral theology.**

7308 **Birch** Bruce C.,   Let justice roll down; the Old Testament, ethics, and Christian life.   Louisville 1991, W-Knox.   383 p. $20 [CBQ 54,401].

7308* **Ciechanover** Joseph,   Suicide in the Jewish tradition: diss. Boston Univ. 1991, ^D*Wiesel* E. 236 p. 91-22861. – DissA 52 (1991s) 951-A. Pardonable only for the deranged; a severe rule but applied leniently.

7309 **Cohn** Haim H.,   Human rights in the Bible and Talmud: Broadcast Univ.   TA 1989, MOD.   118 p. 965-05-0563-6 [OIAc 1,14].

7310 *De Young* J. B.,   The contribution of the Septuagint to biblical sanctions against homosexuality: JEvTS 34 (1991) 157-177 [< ZAW 104,270].

7310* *Dorsey* D. A.,   The law of Moses and the Christian; a compromise [all 613 stipulations are binding 'pedagogically' though not 'legally']: JEvTS 34 (1991) 321-334 [< NTAbs 36,218].

7311 *Fowl* Stephen E.,   Could Horace talk with the Hebrews? Translatability and moral disagreement in [Alasdair] MACINTYRE and [Jeffrey] STOUT: JRelEth 19,1 (1991) 1-20.

7312 *Frankfurter* Gershom, *Ulmer* Rivka,   Eine Anfrage über Homosexualität im jüdischen Gesetz: ZRGg 43 (1991) 49-68.

7313 **Goldstein** Sidney,   Suicide in rabbinic literature 1989 ➤ 6,7328:   ^RCritRR 4 (1991) 359s (J. D. *Tabor*).

7313* **Kuhn** J., Heilsame Begegnungen; Gotteserfahrungen im ANT. Stu 1991, Quell. 144 p. DM 12,80. 3-7918-2263-2 [NTAbs 36,129: ev. pastor].

7314 *Lasker* Judith N., *Parmet* Harriet L., Rabbinic and feminist approaches to reproductive technologies: JFemRel 6,1 (1990) 117-130 [< ZIT 90,794].

7315 *Lipiński* E., Marriage and divorce in the Judaism of the Persian period [Elephantine, Naḥal Ḥever]: TEuph 4 (1991) 63-71 [< ZAW 104,283].

7316 *Otto* E., a) Die Geburt des moralischen Bewusstseins; die Ethik der hebräischen Bibel; – b) Der Stand der alttestamentlichen Wissenschaft und ihre zukünftige Gestalt im Rahmen der theologischen Disziplinen: Orientalia Biblica et Christiana 1 ('Bibel und Christentum im Orient' 1991) 9-28 / 63-87 [< ZAW].

ᴱ**Richardson** Peter, *Westerholm* Stephen, Law in religious communities in the Roman period; the debate over Torah and Nomos in post-biblical Judaism and early Christianity: StChrJ 4, 1991 ⇢ 454.

7318 *Safran* Alexandre, Esquisse d'une éthique religieuse juive: ⇢ 78, ᶠHRUBY, Judaica 47,1 (1991) 38-50.

7319 **Sherwin** Byron L., In partnership with God; contemporary Jewish law and ethics. Syracuse NY, Univ. xiv-306 p. $45.

7320 **Soete** Annette, Ethos der Rettung / Normenbegründung AT ᴰ1987 ⇢ 6,7336: ᴿTRu 56 (1991) 205s (M. *Oeming*).

7321 *Tosato* Angelo, Le mariage dans l'AT, ᵀ*Carrière* Jean-Marie: Masses Ouvrières 439 ('Des couples' 1991) 25-34.

7322 *Wyschogrod* Edith, Works that 'faith'; the grammar of ethics in Judaism: CCurr 40,2 ('Faith that works' 1990) 176-193.

H3.8   *Bellum et pax VT-NT* –   **War and peace in the whole Bible.**

7323 *Alegre* Xavier, Violencia y NT; aporte exegético a una cuestión debatida: RLatAmT 23 (1991) 149-167.

7324 **Arens** Eduardo, La violencia y el Evangelio; ¿Cuál fue la actitud de Jesús ante la violencia?: Buena Nueva 3. La Florida, Chile 1988, Paulinas. 269 p. [CBQ 53,533].

7325 **Beestermöller** Gerhard, Thomas von AQUIN und der gerechte Krieg; Friedensethik im theologischen Kontext der Summa Theologiae. Köln 1990, Bachem. 260 p. DM 39. – ᴿTGL 81 (1991) 239-241 (H. *Gruss*).

7326 a) *Bergant* Dianne, [Gn 12,7; 26,3s; 28,13] 'Drive them out and destroy them'; – b) *Schmitt* John J., [Jer 7,7; Ezek 33,24; Amos...] The land is mine: BToday 29 (1991) 324-9 / 336-345.

7327 **Burggraeve** R., *Tavernier* J. De, Strijden op de weg van Jahwe, God, Allah!? De heilige oorlog in het OT, westers Christendom en Islam. Leuven 1989, Acco/VBS. 176 p. Fb. 395. – ᴿCollatVL 21 (1991) 220 (J.-P. *Vermassen*).

7328 *Calvez* Jean-Yves, La notion de 'guerre juste': Études 374 (1991) 181s (293-8, Golfe).

7329 **Dumézil** Georges, Le sorti del guerriero; aspetti della funzione guerriera presso gli Indoeuropei. Mi 1990, Adelphi. 213 p. Lit. 35.000. – ᴿCC 142 (1991,4) 204 (M. *Dhavamony*).

7330 **Durland** William, God or nations; radical theology for the religious peace movement. Baltimore 1989, Portkamp. xxi-309 p. $17 [TDig 38,57].

7330* **Feininger** Bernd, 'Denk ich...' (Ps 77,4); bibeltheologische Aufarbeitung, dogmatische Problemskizze und religionspädagogische Konkretion zum kriegerischen Gottesbild im AT im Rahmen seiner Hoffnung auf Gerechtigkeit und Frieden: Diss. FrB 1991, ᴰ*Deissler* A. 403 p. – TR 87 (1991) 517; RTLv 23, p. 539.

7331 *Hamerton-Kelly* R. G., Violent epiphany; nuclear deterrence and the sacred [... GIRARD R.]: JAAR 59 (1991) 481-509.

7332 **Herr** Édouard, La violence, nécessité ou liberté: Culture et Vérité. Turnhout 1990, Brépols. 144 p. Fb 780. – ᴿCC 142 (1991,1) 426s (J. *Joblin*).

7333 **Herr** Édouard, Sauver la paix: Chrétiens d'aujourd'hui NS 5. Namur 1991, Culture et Vérité. 146 p. Fb 600. – ᴿNRT 113 (1991) 744-8 (P. *Favraux*).

7334 **Hobbs** T. R., A time for war ... OT 1989 → 6,7352: ᴿBibTB 21 (1991) 123 (J. F. *Craghan*; extraordinarily good); CBQ 53 (1991) 671s (K. M. *Craig*); Interpretation 45 (1991) 196 (J. M. *Hamilton*: neither 'just war' nor pacifism; just a piece of military history); RExp 88,3 (1991) 266 (T. G. *Smothers*).

7335 **Joblin** Joseph, La Iglesia y la guerra; conciencia, violencia y poder, ᵀ*López de Castro* J. Barc 1990, Herder. 405 p. pt. 2358. 84-254-1710-4. – ᴿActuBbg 28 (1991) 321 (A. *Borràs*).

7336 **Joest** Wilfried, Der Friede Gottes und der Friede auf Erden; zur theologischen Grundlegung der Friedensethik. Neuk 1990. viii-153 p. DM 34. – ᴿTLZ 116 (1991) 538s (W. *Huber*).

7337 **Kang Sa-Moon**, Divine war in the OT ...: BZAW 177, 1989 → 5,7339*; 6,7354: ᴿCBQ 53 (1991) 288-290 (M. C. *Lind*); GerefTTs 90 (249s (C. *Houtman*); JBL 110 (1991) 131s (C. L. *Seow*: badly written and edited); RechSR 79 (1991) 270-2 (J.-M. *Carrière*); RivB 39 (1991) 344-8 (G. L. *Prato*); TR 87 (1991) 5-10 (H. M. *Niemann*: unannehmbar, dass das Y-Krieg-Konzept in der David-Zeit entwickelt sein muss).

7338 **Lana** Italo, Studi sull'idea della pace nel mondo antico: Ac T Mem. mor/fg 5/13/1s. T 1989, Accademia. 68 p. – ᴿGnomon 63 (1991) 647-9 (B. *Näf*).

7339 **Lingen** A. van der, Les guerres de Yahvé 1990 → 6,7359: ᴿBL (1991) 115 (R. A. *Mason*); Masses Ouvrières 438 (1991) 103-5 (D. *Noël*).

7339* a) *Lobo* George V., The Church's teaching on violence; – b) *Podimattam* Felix, Violence and struggle for justice: Jeevadhara 20 (1990) 461-480 / 497-510.

7340 **Lohfink** Norbert, Violencia y pacifismo en el Antiguo Testamento [sus dos artículos < Gewalt 1983 → 64,407*], ᵀ*Albizu* José Luis: Cristianismo y Sociedad. 111 p. 1100 pt. Bilbao 1990, D-Brouwer. 84-330-0818-8 [BL 92,108]. – ᴿProyección 38 (1991) 156 (J. L. *Sicre*).

7341 *Lohfink* Norbert, 'Holy war' and the 'ban' in the Bible [< IkaZ 18 (1989) 104-112], ᵀᴱ*Asen* B. A.: TDig 38 (1991) 109-114.

7342 *Lombardo* Gregory L., La doctrina de san Agustín sobre la guerra y la paz, ᵀ*Juango* J. M.: → 540, AugM 36 (1991) 173-9.

7343 a) *Martín Juárez* Miguel A., La paz, potencial liberador; Ant. Testamento; – b) *Salas* Antonio, ... realizador NT: BibFe 17,49 (1991) 5-28 / 29-56 [57-137, al.].

7344 *Martínez* Germán, Cómo construir la paz? Perspectivas eclesiológicas: BibFe 17 (1991) 121-137 [> TDig 38 (1991) 235-9, ᵀᴱ*Bonness* Mary Kay].

7345 *Mattai* Giuseppe, Guerre di ieri e di oggi e coscienza ecclesiale: RasT 32 (1991) 17-30.

7346 **Rad** Gerhard von, Holy war in ancient Israel [1951+introd.; bibliog.], ᵀ*Dawn* M. J., GR 1991, Eerdmans. vii-166 p. 0-8028-0528-0. – ᴿOTAbs 14 (1991) 363 (C. T. *Begg*).

7347 **Ricca** Paolo, Le chiese evangeliche e la pace. F 1989, Cultura della Pace. 196 p. Lit. 18.000. – ᴿProtestantesimo 45 (1990) 132-4 (Debora *Spini*).

7348 *Soggin* J. Alberto [*Hegermann* Harald], Krieg AT [NT]: → 690, TRE 20 (1990) 19-25 [-28] (-55, *Schrey* Heinz-H., historisch-ethisch).

7349 ᴱ**Stelmachowicz** Michael J., Peace and the just war tradition; Lutheran perspectives in the nuclear age. 119 p. – ᴿLutheran Quarterly 2 (Milwaukee 1988) 281-4 (J. T. *Pless*) [< LuJb 58, p. 148, with indication of 2 items there cited].

7350 ᴱ**Tambasco** A. J., Blessed are the peacemakers; biblical perspectives on peace 1989 → 5,609; 6,7376: ᴿLvSt 16 (1991) 85s (E. J. *Cooper*).

7351 **Vaillant** F., La non-violence; essai de morale fondamentale. P 1991, Cerf. 281 p. – ᴿArTGran 54 (1991) 418 (I. *Camacho*).

7351* *Venter* A. F., Biblical ethics and Christian response to violence: TEv 24,2 (Pretoria 1991) 25-39 [< NTAbs 36,75].

7352 *Vetter* D., Krieg und Frieden; Weisungen und Erwartungen im Judentum der talmudischen Zeit: → 6,473. *Binder* G., *Effe* B. Friede 1989, 123-149.

7353 ᴱ**Viaud** Pierre, Les religions et la guerre. P 1991, Cerf. 580 p. F 145. – ᴿEsprVie 101 (1991) 603-7 (F. *Mabille*).

7354 *Walker* Breifne, Official Roman Catholic teaching on revolutionary armed force; Pope Leo XIII to Vatican Instruction on liberation theology (1966): IrTQ 57 (1991) 41-79.

7355 *Weippert* Manfred, 'Heiliger Krieg' in Israel und Assyrien; kritische Anmerkungen zu G. von RAD 1951 [→ ZAW 84 (1972) 460-493]: → 321, WegF 633 (1991) 259-300.

7356 **Wengst** Klaus, Pax romana and the peace of Jesus 1987 → 3,3869 ... 6,7378: ᴿThemelios 15 (1989s) 34 (D. F. *Wright*).

7357 **Zsifkovits** Valentin, Ethik des Friedens, soziale Perspektiven I. Linz 1987, Veritas. 224 p. DM 29. [→ 5,8465: Politik ohne Moral? Soziale Perspektiven. Linz 1989, Veritas. 136 p.]. – ᴿBLtg 63 (1990) 119s (K. *Remele*).

H4.1 **Messianismus.**

7358 *Cano* María José, El mesianismo en el Sefer Šebet Yehudah de Šelomoh IBN VERGA: → 421, Luso-Esp 1989/91, 689-696.

7359 *Ellis* Marc H., Critical thought and messianic trust; reflections on a Jewish theology of liberation: EcuR 42 (1990) 35-47.

7359* *Festorazzi* Franco, Messianismo senza Messia? Ipotesi di lavoro sulla questione messianica: RivB 39 (1991) 157-165.

7360 **Feuillet** André, L'accomplissement des prophéties ou les Annonces convergentes du Sauveur Messianique dans l'AT. P 1991, Desclée. 181 p. F 119. – ᴿDivinitas 35 (1991) 292s (D. *Vibrac*).

7361 **Haacker** Klaus, Jesus – Messias Israels?: EvT 51 (1991) 444-457.
    Jossa Giorgio, Dal Messia al Cristo 1989 → 7416*.
    Karrer Martin, Der Gesalbte; die Grundlagen des Christustitels [Hab.-D. Erlangen ᴰ*Roloff* J., 1988s]: FRL 151, 1991 → 3662.

7362 ᴱ**Neusner** J., *al.*, Judaisms and their messiahs 1987 → 4,494; 5,7368: ᴿRelStT 9,2 (1989) 108-110 (S. S. *McGurty*).

7363 **Nussbaum** Chaim, Semblance and reality; Messianism in biblical perspective. Hoboken 1991, KTAV. x-156 p. $17. 0-88125-385-5.

7364 **Oegema** G. S., De messiaanse verwachtingen ten tijde van Jezus; een inleiding in de messiaanse verwachtingen en bewegingen gedurende de hellenistisch-romeinse tijd. Baarn 1991, Ten Have. 214 p. ƒ40. 90-259-4456-6. – ᴿTsTNijm 31 (1991) 428s (J. *Negenman*).

7364* *Sand* A., Ist Jesus der Messias — oder sollen wir auf einen anderen warten?: Renovatio 47 (Bonn 1991) 229-243 [< NTAbs 36,213].

7365 **Van Groningen** Gerard, Messianic revelation in the OT 1990 → 6,7388: ᴿSWJT 33,2 (1990s) 53 (R. L. *Smith*).

H4.3 *Eschatologia VT* – OT hope of future life.

7366 **Aalen** S., Heilsverlangen und Heilsverwirklichung; Studien zur Erwartung des Heils in der apokalyptischen Literatur des antiken Judentums und im ältesten Christentum [1974 Delitzsch lecture + Ezek 37; Isa. 24-27; 65s; ᴱ*Rengstorf* K. H.; on Aalen, *Baasland* S.]: ArbLHJ 21. Leiden 1990, Brill. xxi-70 p. ƒ55. 90-04-09527-9 [BL 92,122, M. A. *Knibb*: essentially on Resurrection belief].

7366* **Alonso Schökel** Luis, I miei occhi hanno visto la tua salvezza; meditazioni bibliche sulla speranza, ᵀ*Sembrano* Lucia. CasM 1991, Piemme. 357 p.

7367 **Bloch** Ernst, The principle of hope [1954-9], ᵀ*Plaice* Neville & Stephen, *Knight* Paul. CM 1986, MIT. xxxiv-1420 p. (3 vol.). – ᴿHistTheor 30 (1991) 221-232 (R. *Aronson*).

7367* *Dietrich* M., *Loretz* O., a) Zur Debatte [Tᴏᴏʀɴ K. van der 1991] über 'Funerary rituals and beatific afterlife in Ugaritic texts and in the Bible' [Sᴘʀᴏɴᴋ K. 1986]; Grabbeigaben für den verstorbenen König; – b) Bemerkungen zur Neuausgabe von RS 34.126 = KTU 1.161 [Bᴏʀᴅʀᴇᴜɪʟ P., Pᴀʀᴅᴇᴇ D.]: UF 23 (1991) 85-90 / 103-6.

7368 **Krieg** Matthias, Todesbilder im AT ᴰ1988 → 4,8411 ... 6,7395: ᴿÉTRel 66 (1991) 277s (T. *Römer*).

7369 **Martin-Achard** Robert, La mort en face selon la Bible hébraïque 1988 → 4,8414 ... 6,7397: ᴿBZ 35 (1991) 308s (Helga *Weippert*); RechSR 79 (1991) 286s (J.-M. *Carrière*).

7369* *Perani* Mauro, Mᴀɪᴍᴏɴɪᴅᴇ sull'escatologia; la risurrezione dei morti e l''olam ha-ba': RivB 39 (1991) 31-42.

7370 a) *Rebic* Adalbert, La Résurrection dans l'AT; – b) *Dagens* Claude, Notre corps promis à la Résurrection: Comm-P 15,1 (1990) 14-25 / 4-13.

7370* *Sabugal* Santos, El preanuncio sobre la resurrección de los muertos; anastasiología veterotestamentaria y judaica: RAg 29 (1988) 69-128; 30 (1989) 143-154.

7371 **Spronk** Klaas, Beatific afterlife in Ancient Israel and in the Ancient Near East [... Ugarit]: AOAT 219, 1986 → 2,5463 ... 4,8416: ᴿBO 48 (1991) 40-66 (K. van der *Toorn*).

7372 a) *Steck* Odil H., Zukunft des einzelnen – Zukunft des Gottesvolkes; Beobachtungen zur Annäherung von weisheitlichen und eschatologischen Lebensperspektiven im Israel der hellenistischen Zeit: → 126, ᶠRɪᴄʜᴛᴇʀ W., Text 1991, 471-482. – b) *Balzer* H. R., Eschatological elements as permanent qualities in the relationship between God and nation in the Minor Prophets: OTEssays 4 (1991) 408-414 [< ZAW 104,436].

7372* **Sysling** H., 'Techiyyat ha-metim', de opstanding van de doden in de Palestijnse targumim op de Pentateuch en overeenkomstige tradities in de klassieke rabbijnse bronnen: diss. Leiden, ᴰ*Mulder* M. Zutphen 1991, Terra. 347 p. 90-6355-482-2. – TsTNijm 32,87; RTLv 23, p. 540.

7373 *Vetter* D.,   Die Lehren vom Tod und von der 'kommenden Welt' im talmudischen Schrifttum ➤ 575, *Binder*-Tod 1991, 21-49.

H4.5 *Theologia totius VT* – **General Old Testament theology.**

7373* *Andrade* Carlos G.,   La experiencia teológica en el Antiguo Testamento: EphMar 38 (1988) 201-227.

7374 **Baumann** Rolf,   'Gottes Gerechtigkeit' — Verheissung und Herausforderung für diese Welt: Tb 1643, 1989 ➤ 5,7375*:   R TüTQ 171 (1991) 145s (D. *Mieth*).

7375 **Childs** Brevard S.,   Teologia dell'AT in un contesto canonico [1985 ➤ 1,6759],T.   CinB 1989, Paoline. 306 p. Lit. 20.000.   ➤ 5,7377:   R STEv 2 (1990) 230s (P. *Bolognesi*).

7376 — *Scippa* Vincenzo, Sulla teologia dell'AT, la proposta dell''approccio canonico' di B. CHILDS [it. 1989]: Asprenas 38 (1991) 93-98.

7377 **Gese** H.,   Sulla teologia biblica [AT Vorträge 1983 < 1977] T*Odasso* G.: BiblCuRel 54. Brescia 1989, Paideia. 286 p. Lit. 30.000. – R Asprenas 38 (1991) 248s (V. *Scippa*).

7378 **Girard** Marc,   Les symboles dans la Bible; essai de théologie biblique enracinée dans l'expérience humaine universelle: Recherches NS 26. Montréal/P 1991, Bellarmin/Cerf. 1023 p. 2-89007-021-2 / P 2-204-02548-8.

7379 **Gnuse** Robert,   Heilsgeschichte as a model for biblical theology 1989 ➤ 5,7382:   R BibTB 21 (1991) 168s (J. B. *Burns*); BL (1991) 111 (R. A. *Mason*); CBQ 53 (1991) 286s (R. S. *Boraas*); CritRR 3 (1990) 126 (J. J. M. *Roberts*); Interpretation 45 (1991) 194 (R. G. *Bowman*); JRel 71 (1991) 255s (J. *Kaminsky*).

7380 **Hasel** Gerhard F.,   Old Testament theology; basic issues in the current debate[4] [[1]1972, [3rev]1982]. GR 1991, Eerdmans. x-262 p. 0-8028-0537-X.

7381 **Høgenhaven** Jesper,   Problems and prospects of OT theology 1988 ➤ 5,7385; 6,7411*:   R ETL 67 (1991) 142-5 (M. *Vervenne*, Eng.).

7382 **Jelonek** T., ⊕ Biblical salvation history. Kraków 1987, Pol. Tow. Teologiczne. 215 p. – R RuBi 42 (1989) 151s (T. *Zaklukiewicz*).

7382* **Klassen** Alfred,   Heilsgeschichte bei Peter BRUNNER: ev. Diss. D*Beiler* F. Mainz 1991. – RTLv 23, p. 569.

7383 **Legrand** Lucien,   Le Dieu qui vient 1988 ➤ 4,8427; 6,7412:   R ZMissRW 74 (1990) 85s (J. *Kuhl*).

7383* *a) Levenson* Jon D.,   Warum Juden sich nicht für biblische Theologie interessieren [< E*Neusner* J., Judaic Perspectives 1987, 281-307], T*Rendtorff* R., *Henze* M.; – *b) Rendtorff* Rolf,   Wege zu einem gemeinsamen jüdisch-christlichen Umgang mit dem AT: EvT 51,5 ('Jüdisch-christliches Bibelgespräch' 1991) 402-430 / 431-444.

7384 **Mattioli** A.,   Dio e l'uomo nella Bibbia d'Israele; teologia dell'Antico Testamento 1981 ➤ 62,69ss... 65,6148:   R Protestantesimo 45 (1990) 139s (J. A. *Soggin*).

7385 **Mildenberger** Friedrich,   Eine biblische Theologie in dogmatischer Perspektive; Prolegomena, Verstehen und Geltung der Bibel: Biblische Dogmatik 1. Stu 1991, Kohlhammer. 281 p.

7386 *a) Nobile* Marco,   Teologie e teologia nella Bibbia; pluralismo di pensiero e sistema teologico; – *b) Colombo* Giuseppe,   Il pluralismo teologico: Antonianum 66 (1991) 469-481 / 482-496; Eng. 469, 482.

7387 **Oeming** M., Gesamtbiblische Theologien der Gegenwart; das Verhältnis von AT und NT in der hermeneutischen Diskussion seit G. von RAD 1985 ➤ 1,6777 ... 4,8430: RVT 41 (1991) 509s (G. I. *Davies*).

7388 **Preuss** Horst Dietrich, JHWHs erwählendes und verpflichtendes Handeln: Theologie des ATs 1. Stu 1991, Kohlhammer. viii-330 p. DM 36 pa. [CBQ 54,405]. 3-17-011074-8.

7389 **Ragaz** Leonhard, [EEhrlich E. L., *al.*] Die Bibel – eine Deutung: 1. Die Urgeschichte + Moses 1947; 2. Geschichte Israels 1948, Propheten 1949; 3. Jesus 1949; 4. Die Apostel + Johannes 1950. FrS 1990, Exodus. 1700 p. Fs 92. – ROrientierung 55 (1991) 68-71 (U. *Eigenmann*: 'ein biblischer Grundkurs des Glaubens').

7390 *Schreiner* Josef, Gottes Forderung zum Heil der Menschen: ZAW 103 (1991) 315-328.

7391 *Scobie* Charles H. H., *a*) The challenge... / *b*) The structure of biblical theology: TyndB 42 (1991) 31-61 / 163-194.

7392 *Tucker* Gene M., Old Testament theology and Israelite religion: Colloquium 22,2 (Sydney 1990) 1-11 [< ZIT 90,665].

Vermeylen J., Het geloof van Israël; theologie van het Oude Testament 1989 ➤ 7290*b*.

7393 **Weber** Ferdinand, Jüdische Theologie, auf Grund des Talmud und verwandter Schriften gemeinfasslich dargestellt[2rev], EDelitzsch Franz, *Schnedermann* Georg [[1]System der altsynagogalen palästinischen Theologie 1890]. Hildesheim 1975 = 1897, Olms. xl-427 p. 3-487-05739-5.

7394 **Werner** Wolfgang, Studien zur alttestamentlichen Vorstellung vom Plan Jahwes: BZAW 173, 1988 ➤ 5,7403; 6,7419*: RTR 87 (1991) 187-9 (O. *Loretz*).

H5.1 *Deus* – NT – **God** [as Father ➤ H1.4].

7395 *Altizer* Thomas J. J., HEGEL and the Christian God: JAAR 59 (1991) 71-91.

7396 **Chaunu** Pierre, Dieu: Apologétique. P 1990, D-Brouwer. 200 p. 2-220-03177-2. – RGregorianum 72 (1991) 773s (J. de *Finance*).

7397 *Harakas* Stanley S., Must God remain Greek?: EcuR 43 (1991) 194-9.

7398 **Hurtado** L. One God 1988 ➤ 4,8021 ... 6,7423: RNBlackf 71 (1990) 51s (Meg *Davies*); RExp 87 (1990) 493-5 (M. C. *Parsons*); ScripB 21 (1991) 21s (M. *McNamara*); SecC 8 (1991) 56s (N. *Elliott*).

7399 **Kelsey** Morton, Encounter with God; a theology of Christian experience[2]. NY 1987, Paulist. 282 p. – RRTLv 22 (1991) 537 (E. *Brito*).

7399* **Król** Mieczysław, Critique du monothéisme selon Jürgen MOLTMANN: diss. Inst. Cath. & Sorbonne, DGeffré C. Paris 1991. 1158 p. – RTLv 23, p. 570.

7400 **Marguerat** Daniel, Le Dieu des premiers chrétiens: Essais Bibliques 16, 1990 ➤ 6,7426; also P, Cerf [RHE 86,345*]: RBLitEc 92 (1991) 228s (L. *Monloubou*: sur la 'parole'; peu sur 'Dieu'); ÉTRel 66 (1991) 441s (E. *Cuvillier*); Études 374 (1991) 135s (R. *Marlé*) & 571 (P. *Gibert*); Protestantesimo 46 (1991) 219s (B. *Costabel*); RCatalT 16 (1991) 203-6 (M. *Taradach*).

7401 **Muñoz** Ronaldo, The God of Christians [... paradoxes: 1987 ➤ 5,7411], TBurns Paul: Theology and Liberation. Mkn 1990, Orbis. xv-192 p. $35; pa. $17. 0-88344-696-0 [NTAbs 36,130].

7402 *O'Donnell* John, PANNENBERG's doctrine of God: Gregorianum 72 (1991) 73-97; franç. 98.

7403 **Paulsen** David L.,   Early Christian belief in a corporeal deity; ORIGEN and AUGUSTINE as reluctant witnesses: HarvTR 83 (1990) 105-116.

7404 **Simonis** Walter,   Gott in Welt; Umrisse christlicher Gotteslehre 1988 ➤ 5,7414; 6,7431:   RTR 87 (1991) 56-59 (G. L. *Müller*: he polemically claims that Christology can no longer be simply a systematization of too-Greek developments of the early Church).

7405 **Stählin** Wilhelm,   Le mystère de Dieu [... dans sa révélation et dans son œuvre de grâce], TWolf R.: Théologies.   P 1991, Cerf.   170 p.   F 99. – RÉtudes 375 (1991) 713s (R. *Marlé*).

7406 **Torres Queiruga** Andrés,   Creo en Dios Padre; el Dios de Jesús como realización plena del hombre 1987 ➤ 3,6498; 5,7124* [Creo en Deus Pai; o Deus de Jesús e a autonomia humana, Vigo 1986]: PresT 34.   Sdr 1986, Sal terrae. 191 p. 84-293-0960-5. – RGregorianum 72 (1991) 370s (F.-A. *Pastor*).

7407 **Vives** Josep, 'Si oyerais su Voz...'; exploración cristiana del misterio de Dios: PresT 48, 1988 ➤ 5,7417:   RActuBbg 28 (1991) 67-70 (J. M. *Rovira Belloso*: acuerdos y discrepancias); Salmanticensis 38 (1991) 65s (A. *González Montes*).

7408 **Vorgrimler** H.,   Dottrina teologica su Dio [➤ 6,7432], TEFrancesconi G.: GdT 188.   Brescia 1989, Queriniana.   242 p. Lit. 22.000. – RAsprenas 38 (1991) 116s (A. *Langella*).

Zimmer C., 'Deus' 1991 ➤ 9133.

H5.2   Christologia ipsius NT.

7410 **Casey** Maurice,   From Jewish prophet to Gentile God; the origins and development of New Testament Christology.   C/Louisville 1991, Clarke/ W-Knox.   197 p. £22.50.   0-227-67920-2.

Cruz H.,   Christological motives and motivated actions in Pauline paraenesis [diss. Pont. Univ. Gregoriana, DRasco E.] 1990 ➤ 5222.

7411 EDupont Jacques,   Jésus aux origines de la christologie^{2rev} [¹1973]: BtETL 40, 1989 ➤ 5,7423; 6,7432*:   RScEsp 43 (1991) 355s (P.-É. *Langevin*); TR 87 (1991) 448-451 (H. *Giesen*, sehr detailliert).

7412 **Fitzmyer** Joseph A.,   A Christological catechism; New Testament answers^{2rev} [¹1982 ➤ 63,6563]. NY 1991, Paulist. viii-189 p. $10.   0-8091-3253-2.

7413 **Forte** Bruno,   Gesù di Nazareth, storia di Dio, Dio nella storia 1981 ➤ 62,7219... 65,6198: RRivLtg 77 (1990) 346s (G. *Gozzelino*).

7414 **Giesen** Heinz,   Der irdische Jesus — Ursprung der neutestamentlichen Christologie; neuere Literatur über Jesus und die Christologie des Neuen Testaments [BRAUN H. 1988; GNILKA J. 1990; Sammelwerke...]: TR 87 (1991) 441-460.

7415 **Habermann** Jürgen,   Präexistenzaussagen im NT [D1985] 1990 ➤ 6, 7434: RNRT 113 (1991) 426s (X. *Jacques*); TR 87 (1991) 577-9 (K. *Backhaus*); TsTNijm 31 (1991) 196 (L. *Visschers*).

7416 **Jankowski** Augustyn, ❷ Dopowiedzenia Chrystologii biblijnej. Poznań 1987, Ś. Wojciecha.   225 p. – RColcT 60,1 (1990) 167s (J. *Królikowski*, ❷).

7416* **Jossa** Giorgio,   Dal Messia al Cristo 1989 ➤ 5,7429:   RAntonianum 65 (1990) 665s (M. *Nobile*); CC 142 (1991,1) 425s (V. *Fusco*); Henoch 13 (1991) 118-120 (P. *Sacchi*).

7417 **Lemcio** Eugene E.,   The past of Jesus in the Gospels: SNTS Mg 68. C 1991, Univ. xiv-190 p. 0-521-40113-3.

7418 **Sabourin** Léopold, La cristologia a partire da testi chiave [1984 Eng.
➤ 65,6214; 1986 franç. ➤ 2,5537]: Testi 4. Brescia 1989, Queriniana.
235 p. Lit. 27.000. 88-399-1104-9. – ᴿAntonianum 65 (1990) 106s (V.
Battaglia).

7419 **Scroggs** Robin, The reality and revelation of God; Christology in Paul
and John 1988 ➤ 4,8461 ... 6,7443: ᴿGregorianum 72 (1991) 154 (J.
Dupuis); IrBSt 12 (1990) 150-2 (V. *Parkin*).

7420 *Seweryniak* Henryk, ❷ La révélation de Dieu en Jésus-Christ [... sa-
vait-il qu'il était Sauveur et Fils de Dieu?]: PrzPow 273 (1991) 397-412;
franç. 413.

7420* **Witherington** Ben, The Christology of Jesus 1990 ➤ 6,7448: ᴿHorBT
13 (1991) 177s (Arland J. *Hultgren*); TrinJ 12 (1991) 113-8 (C. A. *Evans*);
TS 52 (1991) 775s (A. C. *Mitchell*).

H5.3 *Christologia praemoderna* – patristic through Reformation.

7421 ᴱ**Balthasar** Hans Urs von, The scandal of the Incarnation; IRENAEUS,
Against the heresies [Irenäus, Gott im Fleisch und Blut 1981], ᵀ*Saward*
John. SF 1990, Ignatius. 111 p. $11 pa. 0-89870-315-8 [TDig 38,271].

7421* **Böhm** Thomas, Die Christologie des ARIUS; dogmengeschichtliche
Überlegungen unter besonderer Berücksichtigung der Hellenisierungsfra-
ge [kath. Diss. 'Arius, eine frühkirchliche Christologie im Rahmen der
Hellenisierungsthese', ᴰ*Müller*, München 1991: TR 87,520]: StTG 7. St.
Ottilien 1991, EOS. xi-413 p. DM 44 [TR 88,165].

7422 **Bruns** Peter, Das Christusbild des Aphrahats des Persischen Weisen
[kath. Diss. Bochum 1988]: Hereditas 4. Bonn 1990, Borengässer. xxiv-
243 p. DM 48. – ᴿArTGran 54 (1991) 392 (A. *Segovia*); ETL 67 (1991)
172s (A. de *Halleux*); NRT 113 (1991) 884s (L. *Renwart*); RHE 86 (1991)
180 (aussi A. de *Halleux*); TPhil 66 (1991) 587-9 (H. J. *Sieben*); TS 52
(1991) 739s (F. *McLeod*).

7422* *Butin* Phil, Two early Reformed catechisms, the threefold office, and
the shape of Karl BARTH's Christology: ScotJT 44 (1991) 195-214.

7423 *Contat* Alain, Destin de l'homme et Incarnation du Verbe selon S. T.
d'AQUIN: Divinitas 35 (1991) 159-176.

7424 *Cross* Richard, Nominalism and the Christology of William of
OCKHAM: RTAM 58 (1991) 126-156.

7425 *Crowley* Paul G., Instrumentum divinitatis in Thomas AQUINAS;
recovering the divinity of Christ: TS 52 (1991) 451-475.

7427 ᵀᴱ**Dattrino** Lorenzo, GIOVANNI CASSIANO, L'incarnazione del Signore:
TPatr 94. R 1991, Città Nuova. 314 p. 88-311-3094-3.

7428 *Elder* E. Rozanne, The Christology of WILLIAM of St. Thierry: RTAM
58 (1991) 79-112 [< RHE 86,349*].

7429 ᵀᴱ**Farrell** Joseph P., [➤ g185] MAXIMUS the Confessor, The disputation
with Pyrrhus [... Christology]. South Canaan PA c. 1990, St. Tikhon.
xxxvi-74 p. $10 [RelStR 18,16, Verna F. F. *Harrison*].

Ferrua Antonio, La polemica antiariana nei monumenti paleocristiani 1991
➤ e275.

7431 **Gisel** Pierre, Le Christ de CALVIN: JJC 44, 1990 ➤ 6,7461: ᴿÉTRel 66
(1991) 141s (A. *Gounelle*: remarquable).

7432 *González* Carlos Ignacio, Antecedentes de la cristología arriana en el
siglo III: Medellín 16 (1990) 315-361 [< TR 87,340].

7433 *Gori* Franco, La pericope cristologica del De Trinitate X. pseudata-
nasiano nel Libellus emendationis di LEPORIO: AugR 31 (1991) 361-386.

7434 **Grillmeier** Alois, *(Hainthaler* Theresia), Jesus der Christus im Glauben der Kirche, 2/2. Die Kirche von Konstantinopel im 6. Jahrhundert 1989 ⇒ 5,7459; 6,7463:   ᴿRTLv 22 (1991) 69-74 (A. de *Halleux*); TGʟ 81 (1991) 237s (W. *Beinert*, 1 & 2/4); TLZ 116 (1991) 601s (B. *Lohse*); TR 87 (1991) 24-26 & 286-8 (B. *Studer*, 2/2.4); Irénikon 64 (1991) 433s (E. *Lanne).*

7435 **Grillmeier** Alois, Le Christ dans la tradition chrétienne 2/1: CogF 154, 1990 ⇒ 6,7465: ᴿÉTRel 66 (1991) 245s (J.-D. *Dubois*, 2/1, chiffre dont la mention est absente sur la couverture); Gregorianum 72 (1991) 584s (C. I. *González).*

7435* **Grillmeier** Alois, Christ in Christian tradition 2/1, 1987 ⇒ 3,7001 ... 6,7464: ᴿOrChrPer 57 (1991) 454 (E. G. *Farrugia).*

7436 **Hanson** R. P. C., The search for the Christian doctrine of God; the Arian controversy 1988 ⇒ 4,8475; 6,7468: ᴿAnglTR 73 (1991) 211-4 (L. G. *Patterson*); CathHR 76 (1990) 579-583 (C. *Kannengiesser*); IrBSt 12 (1990) 86-94 (R. B. *Knox*); JAAR 59 (1991) 835-9 (R. A. *Greer*); JTS 41 (1990) 668-673 (C. *Stead*); Themelios 16 (1990s) 31 (G. *Keith*); TS 51 (1990) 334-7 (J. T. *Lienhard*).

7438 **Kannengiesser** Charles, Le Verbe de Dieu selon Aᴛʜᴀɴᴀѕᴇ d'Alexandrie: JJC 45. P 1990, Desclée. 200 p. F 125. – ᴿÉtudes 347 (1991) 857s (M. *Fédou*); NRT 113 (1991) 885s (L. *Renwart*); ScEsp 44 (1992) 234-7 (P. *Poirier*).

7439 **Ladaria** L. F., La cristología de Hɪʟᴀʀɪᴏ 1989 ⇒ 5,7466; 6,7471: ᴿCiuD 203 (1990) 503s (J. M. *Ozaeta*); OrChrPer 57 (1991) 455-7 (E. G. *Farrugia*); TPhil 66 (1991) 246-8 (H. J. *Sieben*); TR 87 (1991) 380-2 (M. *Figuera*).

7440 ᴱ**Leonardi** C., Il Cristo III. da Agostino ad Anselmo. Mi 1990, Mondadori. xxiii-648 p. Lit. 40.000. – ᴿAsprenas 38 (1991) 253s (L. *Fatica).*

Madec Goulven, La Patrie et la Voie; le Christ dans la vie et la pensée de saint Aᴜɢᴜѕᴛɪɴ 1989 ⇒ g227.

7441 *Mondin* Battista, Il pensiero cristologico di san Tᴏᴍᴍᴀѕᴏ: Sapienza 44 (1991) 241-263.

7442 *a) Nicolson* R. B., A logical defense of Chalcedon?; – *b) Moulder James*, Why we shouldn't expect too much from Jesus: JStRel 2,2 (Natal 1989) 37-45 . 48 / 46s [< TContext 7/2, 17].

7443 *Norris* Frederick W., Wonder, worship and writ; patristic Christology: ⇒ 448c, Ex Auditu 7 (1991) 59-72.

7443* ᴱ**Ohlig** Karl-Heinz, Christologie: Texte 4/1s, 1989s ⇒ 5,7518*; 6,7476: ᴿGregorianum 72 (1991) 158s (J. *Galot*: trop peu d'objectivité); TPhil 66 (1991) 254s (T. *Hainthaler).*

7444 **O'Keefe** John J., A historic-systematic study of the Christology of Nᴇѕᴛᴏʀɪᴜѕ; a reexamination based on a new evaluation of the literary remains in his Liber Heraclidis: kath. Diss. ᴰ*Garijo-Guembe* M., Münster 1987. viii-343 p. – ᴿTR 87 (1991) 112-6 (A. de *Halleux*, ᵀ*Gaukesbrink* M.).

7445 *Oldfield* John, J., Las dimensiones cristológicas de la interioridad Aɢᴜѕᴛɪɴɪᴀɴᴀ: AugM 34 (1989) 281-291.

7445* **Overbeck** Winfried, Menschwerdung; eine Untersuchung zur literarischen und theologischen Einheit des 5. Buches Adversus Haereses des Iʀᴇɴᴀ̈ᴜѕ von Lyon: ev. Diss. Münster 1991, ᴰ*Aland* B. – TR 87 (1991) 520; RTLv 23, p. 549.

7446 *Principe* Walter H., Some examples of Aᴜɢᴜѕᴛɪɴᴇ's influence on medieval Christology: ⇒ 6,13, ꟳBᴀᴠᴇʟ T. van, II., AugLv 41 (1991) 955-974.

7447 **Quacquarelli** A., *al.*, La Cristologia nei Padri della Chiesa: Bessarion. quad. 8. R 1990. 173 p. – ᴿRivArCr 67 (1991) 492-6 (Lucrezia *Spera*).

7448 **Sarrasin** Claude, Théologie de l'âme du Christ selon saint Thomas d'Aquin: kath. Diss. Fribourg/S 1991, ᴰ*Schönborn*. – TR 87 (1991) 515.

7449 **Selejdak** Ryszard, La tipologia cristologica nelle opere esegetiche di Sant'Ambrogio: diss. Inst. Patr. Augustinianum, ᴰ*Mara* Maria G. R 1991, Inst. Patristicum Augustinianum. 153 p. extr.

7450 *Siepierski* Paulo D., Nicaea and the marginalized [... the common people can hardly appropriate many elements: Faith and Order paper, Ch 1990, unabridged]: TDig 38 (1991) 23-29.

H5.4   (*Commentationes de*) *Christologia* **moderna.**

7451 **Auer** Johann, Jesucristo hijo de Dios e hijo de María 1989 ⇥ 6,7490: ᴿAugM 35 (1990) 189s (J. A. *Galindo*); REspir 50 (1991) 305s (S. *Guerra*).

7452 **Beaudin** Michel, Obéissance et solidarité... christologie; essai sur la christologie de H. U. v. Balthasar: Héritage et projét. Montréal 1989, Fides. 390 p. – ᴿScEsp 43 (1991) 136-8 (J.-G. *Pagé*).

7453 **Brambilla** Franco G., La cristologia di Schillebeeckx 1989 ⇥ 5,7487: ᴿCC 142 (1991,1) 630 (Z. *Alszeghy*: importante).

7453* **Brandy** Hans C., Die späte Christologie des Johannes Brenz: Diss. ᴰ*Baur* J. Göttingen 1989. 327 p. – RTLv 23, p. 568.

7454 *Bravo* Carlos, Una cristología abierta al Jesús histórico y su seguimiento: ⇥ 542, EfMex 9,2 (1991) 155-170.

7454* *Brinkman* D. R., On Christ and the Church; Macquarrie [J.], Schillebeeckx [E.] and Moltmann J., all 1990]: HeythJ 32 (1991) 539-543.

7455 ᴱ**Davis** Stephen T., Encountering Jesus; a debate on Christology [5 Claremont contributors]. Louisville 1988, Knox. 200 p. $14. ⇥ 4,548: ᴿCritRR 3 (1990) 427-9 (R. D. *Shofrer*); CurrTMiss 18 (1991) 131s (C. L. *Nessan*); JRel 70 (1990) 116s (P. *Schineller*).

7455* **De Marchi** Sergio, La cristologia italiana dalla Costituzione Apostolica 'Deus Scientiarum Dominus' (1931) alla CA 'Sapientia Christiana' 1979: diss. Pont. Univ. Gregoriana 1991s [Inf. PUG 24/122,27].

7456 *Dupuis* Jacques, Le débat christologique dans le contexte du pluralisme religieux [< Current Dialogue 19 (1991) 18-24]: NRT 113 (1991) 853-863.

7456* **Etukuri** Michael, Towards an Indian Christology of liberation; a critical analysis of the Christology of Jon Sobrino in a Gandhian perspective: diss. Leuven 1991, ᴰ*De Schrijver* Georges. xlix-434 p. – LvSt 16 (1991) 350s; RTLv 23, p. 569 [> 'The God-image in Sobrino and Gandhi'].

7457 *Ford* Mary, Towards the restoration of allegory; Christology, epistemology and narrative structure: StVlad 34 (1990) 161-195.

7458 **Gounelle** André, Le Christ et Jésus; trois christologies américaines... Tillich, Cobb, Altizer: JJC 41, 1990 ⇥ 6,7506: ᴿFoiVie 90,3 (1991) 153s (G. *Vahanian*); LavalTP 47 (1991) 446-452 (J. *Richard*).

7459 **Griffin** David, A process Christology. Lanham MD c. 1991, UPA. 273 p. $19.25 pa. [Interp 45,109].

7460 **Guggenberger** Engelbert, Karl Rahners Christologie und heutige Fundamentalmoral [Diss. Pont. Univ. Gregoriana]: InTSt 28. Innsbruck 1990, Tyrolia. 221 p. DM 50 [TR 87,347].

7461 **Hebblethwaite** Brian, The Incarnation 1987 ⇥ 3,235 ... 6,7512: ᴿHeythJ 32 (1991) 88 (J. P. *Galvin*).

7462 *Hefling* C.C., Reviving Adamic adoptionism; the example of John MACQUARRIE [➔ 7479]: TS 52 (1991) 476-494.

7463 **Hill** Brennan, Jesus the Christ, contemporary perspectives. Mystic CT 1991, Twenty-Third. xii-308 p. $15 [CBQ 54,402].

7464 *Hort* Bernard, Conscience de soi du Christ? Réflexions sur un thème-clef de l'œuvre de Marcel LÉGAUT: RTPhil 123 (1991) 395-409; Eng. 457.

7465 *Iammarrone* Luigi, Un nuovo saggio di cristologia [BORDONI M. 1982-6]: DivThom 94 (1991) 96-148.

7466 *Jaki* Stanley L., La cristologia e l'origine della scienza moderna: AnnTh 4 (1990) 333-347.

7467 **Johnson** Elizabeth A., Consider Jesus; waves of renewal in Christology 1990 ➔ 6,7516: RAnglTR 73 (1991) 343s (C.C. *Hefling*); Horizons 18 (1991) 154s (Mary T. *Rattigan*); RExp 88,2 (1991) 230s (Molly *Marshall-Green*); RRel 50 (1991) 782s (J.P. *Gaffney*); Thomist 55 (1991) 511-7 (T. *Weinandy*: basically reliable despite disappointments).

7468 *Kennedy* Philip, Human beings as the story of God [➔ 7188]; SCHILLEBEECKX's third Christology: NBlackf 71 (1990) 120-131.

7468* **Kereszty** R.A., Jesus Christ; fundamentals of Christology, EMaddox J.S. NY 1991, Alba. xix-439 p. $20. 0-8189-0621-9 [NTAbs 36,283].

7469 *Knaebel* Simon, 'Vrai Dieu et vrai homme'; perspectives actuelles d'une prise au sérieux intégrale de la divinité et de l'humanité de Jésus-Christ: RevSR 65 (1991) 109-133.

7470 *Kramer* Rolf, Die Fleischwerdung des ewigen Gottessohnes; Heinrich VOGELs Theologie der Stellvertretung: BTZ 8 (1991) 245-258.

7471 **Kraus** C. Norman, God our savior; theology in a Christological mode. Scottdale PA 1991, Herald. 272 p. $20 pa. 0-8361-3551-2.

7472 **Küng** Hans, The incarnation of God; an introduction to HEGEL's theological thought as prolegomena to a future Christology 1987 ➔ 3, 7061 ... 6,7519: REvangel 7,1 (1989) 21s (R. *Kearsley*: good despite misprints); HeythJ 32 (1991) 86-88 (B.O. *McDermott*); JTS 42 (1991) 403-6 (Rowan *Williams*: disappointing).

7473 **Kuschel** Karl-Josef, Geboren vor aller Zeit? Der Streit um Christi Ursprung [D1989, title somewhat different ➔ 6,7519*]. Mü 1990, Piper. 834 p. DM 98. 3-492-03374-1. – ROrientierung 55 (1991) 87s (K.-H. *Ohlig*).

7474 **Lage** Dietmar, Martin LUTHER's Christology and ethics: TStRel 45. Lewiston NY 1990, Mellen. x-175 p. – RTLZ 116 (1991) 680s (B. *Lohse*).

7475 **Lane** Dermot, Christ at the centre; selected issues in Christology 1990 ➔ 6,261: also NY 1991, Paulist; $9; 0-8091-3242-7. – RLvSt 16 (1991) 274s (H.E. *Mertens*); MilltSt 28 (1991) 160-2 (R. *Moloney*); Studies 80 (1991) 205-8 (G. *O'Hanlon*).

7476 *Leroy* Marie-Vincent, Chronique de christologie: RThom 91 (1991) 425-441: WÉBER E., MADEC G., SESBOÜÉ B.

7477 *a) Lips* Hermann von, Christus als Sophia? Weisheitliche Traditionen in der urchristlichen Christologie; – *b) Paulsen* Henning, Von der Unbestimmtheit des Anfangs; zur Entstehung von Theologie im Urchristentum; – *c) Gnilka* Joachim, Das theologische Problem der Rückfrage nach Jesus: ➔ 72, FHAHN F., Anfänge 1991, 75-95 / 25-41 / 13-24.

7478 *MacLeod* Donald, The doctrine of the Incarnation in Scottish theology; Edward IRVING [1828; deposal for heresy in 1833]; ScotBEvT 9 (1991) 40-50.

7479 **Macquarrie** John, Jesus Christ in modern thought [classical Christologies from the beginning to now] 1990 ➔ 6,7473: RCritRR 4 (1991)

447-9 (E. T. *Long*: completes a triology); Gregorianum 72 (1991) 582s (J. *O'Donnell*); JTS 42 (1991) 793-7 (R. *Bauckham*); NBlackf 72 (1991) 203s (H. P. *Owen*); ScotJT 44 (1991) 533s (A. *Thatcher*: 'MacQuarrie'); TLond 94 (1991) 211 (A. H. B. *Logan*); TS 52 (1991) 476-494 (C. C. *Hefling*: 'reviving Adamic adoptionism'); TsTNijm 31 (1991) 439s (A. *Willems*).

7480 **Madonia** Nicolò, Ermeneutica e Cristologia in W. KASPER [diss. Gregoriana, ᴰDUPUIS J.]: Theologia 2. Palermo 1990, Augustinus. 311 p. – ᴿCiuD 203 (1990) 750s (J. M. *Ozaeta*); ScripTPamp 23 (1991) 742s (L. F. *Mateo-Seco*); Teresianum 42 (1991) 677s (G. *Vallejo T.*).

7481 **Marquardt** Friedrich-W., Das christliche Bekenntnis zu Jesus, dem Juden, eine Christologie I. Mü 1990, Kaiser. 308 p. DM 96. – ᴿActuBbg 28 (1991) 54s (J. *Boada*); EvT 51 (1991) 482-9 (M. *Weinrich*); TGL 81 (1991) 498-500 (G. *Fuchs*, 1s); TLZ 116 (1991) 304-8 (R. *Slenczka*: nicht Entfaltung sondern Auflösung des christlichen Christusbekenntnisses); TsTNijm 31 (1991) 337 (W. *Logister*).

7482 *Mateo-Seco* Lucas F., Notas introductorias al estudio de la Cristología: ScripTPamp 23 (1991) 125-166; lat. 166s; Eng. 167.

7483 **Mesa** José M. de, *Wostyn* Lode, Doing Christology; the re-appropriation of a tradition. Quezon City 1989, Claretan. 351 p. – ᴿTContext 7,2 (1990) 121 (G. *Evers*).

7484 *a*) *Milano* Andreia, Aletheia; la 'concentrazione cristologica' della verità: FilT 4 (1990) 13-45. – *b*) *Milbank* J., The name of Jesus; incarnation, atonement, ecclesiology: ModT (1991) 311-333.

7484* **Moioli** Giovanni, Cristología, proposta sistematica [1979 'pro manuscripto'], ᴱ*Brambilla* F. G. Mi 1989, Glossa. 352 p. – ᴿETL 67 (1991) 468-470 (E. *Brito*).

7485 *Molnar* Paul D., Some dogmatic consequences of Paul F. KNITTER's 'unitarian theocentrism' [No other name; Horizons 13 (1986) 116-135]: Thomist 55 (1991) 449-495.

7486 **Moltmann** Jürgen, Der Weg Jesu Christi; Christologie in messianischen Dimensionen 1989 ⇢ 5,7515; 6,7529: ᴿActuBbg 28 (1991) 6-31 (J. *Boada*); TLZ 116 (1991) 455-8 (U. *Kühn*); Gregorianum 72 (1991) 157s (J. *O'Donnell*).

7487 **Moltmann** Jürgen, The way of Jesus Christ: Christology in messianic dimension, ᵀ*Kohl* Margaret. SF 1991, Harper. xx-388 p. $25. 0-06-065910-6 [TDig 38,370]. – ᴿExpTim 102 (1990s) 56 (G. *Newland* gives publishers as SCM/Trinity, 0-334-01758-0; third volume of his systematic theology, second on Christology); TLond 94 (1991) 296-8 (R. *Bauckham*).

7488 — *Bauckham* Richard J., Moltmann's Messianic Christology [1990, 3d volume of 5]: ScotJT 44 (1991) 519-531.

7489 **Oden** T. C., The Word of Life: SystT 2, 1989 ⇢ 6,7534: ᴿInterpretation 45 (1991) 300-2 (G. *Fackre*: a Christology that resists reductionism).

7490 **Ottati** Douglas F., Jesus Christ and Christian vision 1989 ⇢ 6,7536: ᴿInterpretation 45 (1991) 191-3 (R. B. *Miller*: a Christology of the heart).

7491 **Parent** Mark A., The Christology of T. T. SHIELDs; the irony of fundamentalism: diss. McGill, ᴰ*Hall* D. Montreal 1991. – RelStR 18,174; RTLv 23, p. 554.

7492 **Petzoldt** Matthias, Gottmensch und Gattung Mensch; Studien zur Christologiekritik Ludwig FEUERBACHs: TArb 47. B 1989, Ev.-VA. 184 p. M 13,50. – ᴿTLZ 116 (1991) 298-300 (G. *Keil*).

7493 **Pikaza** Xabier, El Evangelio, vida y pascua de Jesús: TBibCr 2/BtEstB 75. S 1990, Sígueme. 442 p. – ᴿNRT 113 (1991) 895 (L. *Renwart*: continue sa christologie de 1976).

7494 **Pokorný** Petr, The genesis of Christology 1987 → 3,6973; 4,8458: ᴿHeythJ 32 (1991) 85s (J. P. *Galvin*: good).

7495 *Rainbow* Paul A., Jewish monotheism as the matrix for NT Christology; a review article [HURTADO L. 1988]: NT 33 (1991) 78-91.

7496 *Renwart* Léon, Jésus de Nazareth, le Christ de Dieu; chronique de christologie [QUESNEL M.: PANIMOLLE S., DUPUY M., *al.*]: NRT 113 (1991) 882-899.

7497 **Rey** Bernard, Gesù il Cristo; Dio assume un volto [série Centurion 1988s], ᵀ*Sirboni* Silvano, ᴱ*Laurita* Roberto: Biblioteca di formazione cristiana 2. Brescia 1990, Queriniana, 134 p.; Lit. 15.000. – ᴿETL 67 (1991) 179s (A. de *Halleux*, mention de 4 volumes de la série).

7497* **Scherer** Odilo P., 'O justo sofredor', um estudo de cristologia fundamental a partir da teoria de E. SCHWEIZER sobre 'O caminho de Jesus e do discípulo': diss. Pont. Univ. Gregoriana, ᴰ*Pastor* F. A. Roma 1991. 544 p.; extr. Nº 3720, 211 p. – RTLv 23, p. 571.

7498 *Schoonenberg* Piet, De Christus 'van boven' en de christologie 'van beneden'; nadere overdenkingen rond de 'God van mensen' 1969; [kritiek van A. KAISER, Der christologische Neuansatz 1988]: TsTNijm 31 (1991) 3-27; Eng. 27.

7499 **Serenthà** M., Gesù Cristo ieri ... cristologia 1988 → 4,8545: ᴿRivLtg 77 (1990) 111 (C. *Collo*).

7500 *Siegwalt* Gérard, Le problème christologique dans les rapports entre l'Église chrétienne et le Judaïsme d'une part, l'Islam d'autre part, un obstacle ou un pont: FoiVie 90,6 = CahÉtJuives 24 (1991) 23-44 (-50, réaction de *Faessler* Marc, 'trois voix pour un seul Dieu?').

7501 **Sim Jong-Hyeok** Luke, Christological vision of the 'Spiritual Exercises' of St. Ignatius of LOYOLA and the hermeneutical principles of sincerity ('*ch'eng*') in the Confucian tradition: diss. Pont. Univ. Gregoriana, ᴰ*Dupuis* J. Roma 1991. 448 p.; Nº 3793, 311 p. – RTLv 23, p. 560 [< DissA-C].

7502 **Skarsaune** Oskar, Incarnation, myth or fact? ᵀ*Skarsten* Tryg & R.: Concordia scholarship today. St. Louis 1991, Concordia. 176 p. $15. 0-570-04547-9 [TDig 39,84].

7503 **Sloyan** Gerard S., Jesus, Redeemer and divine Word: Theology & Life. (Collegeville) 1989 → 5,7727: ᴿCBQ 53 (1991) 344 (M. *Cahill*: lively; on Redeemer *sí*; on Divine Word *no*); NewTR 4,1 (1991) 82-84 (D. W. *Buggert*); RExp 87 (not 88 as top) (1990) 497s (E. G. *Hinson*); Worship 64 (1990) 476-8 (L. S. *Cunningham*).

7505 **Soloviev** Vladimir, Leçons sur la divino-humanité: Patrimoines; Orthodoxie. P 1991, Cerf. 178 p. F 125. – ᴿEsprVie 101 (1991) 548 (P. *Jay*).

7506 *Sonneville* Jacques, De christelijke contemplatie in het moderne mensbeeld [...'het is niet in de evolutie zelf dat Christus verschijnt, maar in de medemens']: CollatVL 21 (1991) 57-71.

7506* **Stümke** Volker, 'Die positive Christologie Christian H. WEISSES', eine Untersuchung zur Hinwendung der Christologie zur Frage nach dem historischen Jesus als Antwort auf das 'Leben Jesu' von David F. STRAUSS: ev. Diss. Hamburg 1991, ᴰ*Koch* T. 260 p. – TR 87 (1991) 518; RTLv 23, p. 572.

7507 **Sturch** Richard, The Word and the Christ; an essay in analytic Christology. Ox 1991, Clarendon. viii-292 p. $79. 0-19-826198-5 [TDig 39,86].

7508 **Texeira da Cunha** Jorge, O evento do Filho, advento do homem ... DURRWELL 1989 → 6,7547: ᴿCiuD 203 (1990) 504s (J. M. *Ozaeta*).

7509 **Thatcher** Adrian, Truly a person, truly God; a post-mythical view of Jesus 1990 → 6,7547*: £10: ᴿScotJT 44 (1991) 534s (B. *Marshall*); TLond 94 (1991) 294s (D. F. *Ford*).

7510 **Thompson** William M., Christology and spirituality. NY 1991, Crossroad. 240 p. $27.50 [JAAR 59,885].

Tilliette Xavier, Le Christ de la philosophie; prolégomènes à une christologie philosophique 1990 → 3744.

7512 *Wacławski* Tomasz, **☉** Elementy chrystologii: Bt Pomocy Naukowych 2. Poznań 1988, Św. Wojciecha. 190 p. – ᴿColcT 60,1 (1990) 168s (J. *Królikowski*, **☉**).

7513 *Wesche* Kenneth P., Pastoral implications of orthodox Christology: StVlad 34 (1990) 281-304 (324-7, defense of an earlier article).

7514 *a) Wright* N.T., One God, one Lord, one people; incarnational Christology for a Church in a pagan environment; – *b) Brown* Colin, Trinity and Incarnation; in search of a contemporary Christology; – *c) Murphy* Larry, African American Christian perspectives on Christology and Incarnation: → 448c, Ex Auditu 7 (1991) 45-58 / 83-100 / 73-82.

7514* **Yu Suk-Sung**, Christologische Grundentscheidungen bei Dietrich BONHOEFFER: Diss. Tübingen 1990. 270 p. – TLZ 116 (1991) 477-9.

7515 *Zañartu* Sergio, Notas conclusivas a una docencia en cristología bíblica: TVida 32 (1991) 221-232.

7516 ᴱ**Zeller** Dieter, Menschwerdung 1988 → 5,769; 6,7551: ᴿBiKi 45 (1990) 166s (F. J. *Stendebach*); BZ 35 (1991) 148s (M. *Theobald*); NedTTs 45 (1991) 149s (P. W. van der *Horst*: Mainz Lezingencyclus 1986s).

H5.5 *Spiritus Sanctus; pneumatologia* – **The Holy Spirit.**

7517 **Anderson** J. B., A Vatican II pneumatology of the Paschal Mystery, AnGreg 250, ᴰ1988 → 4,8558 ... 6,7552: ᴿCrNSt 12 (1991) 460s (K. *Wittstadt*).

7518 **Aranda Lomeña** Antonio, Estudios de pneumatología 1985 → 2,5678; 3,7097: ᴿDivThom 93 (1990) 149s (B. *Ardura*).

7518* **Badcock** Gary, The doctrine of the Holy Spirit in contemporary trinitarian theology: diss. ᴰ*Mackey* J. Edinburgh 1991. 381 p. – RTLv 23, p. 568.

7519 *Bentivegna* Giuseppe, L'effusion de l'Esprit Saint chez les Pères grecs: NRT 113 (1991) 690-707.

7520 *Bolognesi* Pietro, Lo Spirito Santo nel tempo: BbbOr 33 (1991) 39-51.

7521 *Bray* Gerald, Recent trends in pneumatology: [CONGAR Y.; SMAIL T. ...]: Evangel 7,1 (1989) 12-15.

7522 *Breuning* Wilhelm, Trinitarische Theologie als Quelle einer Erneuerung des Glaubens; zum Beitrag H. SCHAUFs für die Lehre der Einwohnung des Heiligen Geistes: → 132, Gedenkschrift 1991, 167-180.

7523 **Chevallier** M.-A., Souffle de Dieu; le Saint-Esprit dans le NT 3., Études: PoinT 55. P 1991, Beauchesne. v-197 p. F 90. 2-7010-1219-8. – ᴿArTGran 54 (1991) 361 (A. *Segovia*); CC 142 (1991,4) 214s (L. *De Lorenzi*, 1s); EsprVie 101 (1991) 188-191 (E. *Cothenet*; 2: 'in memoriam', sans détails); ÉTRel 66 (1991) 437-8 (E. *Cuvillier*, 2); NRT 113 (1991) 756-8 (X. *Jacques*, 2s).

7524 **Comblin** José, The Holy Spirit and liberation 1989 → 5,7547; 6,7559: ᴿMid-Stream 29 (1990) 344-6 (P. M. *Morgan*).

7525 **Congar** Yves, Der Heilige Geist². FrB 1986, Herder. 510 p. – ᴿTsTKi 61 (1990) 155s (Ola *Tjørhom*).

7525* *a) Dąbek* T. M., ❷ *Eucharystia* ... and Holy Spirit; biblico-theological link: AnCracov 21s (1989s) 179-202 [< NTAbs 36,216]. – *b) Dalbesio* Anselmo, Lo Spirito Santo e l'Eucaristia second il Nuovo Testamento: Laurentianum 32 (1991) 167-220.

7526 **Estrada** H., El Espíritu Santo en la Biblia y en nuestra vida. Bogotá 1989, Paulinas. 109 p. – ᴿREspir 49 (1990) 152s (S. *Castro*).

7527 **Ferlay** Philippe, Dieu le Saint-Esprit. P 1990, D-Brouwer. 159 p. – ᴿAtKap 117,494 (1991) 154-7 (A. *Nowicki*).

7528 **Ferraro** Giuseppe, Lo Spirito Santo nel 'De Trinitate' di Sant'Aɢᴏsᴛɪɴᴏ 1987 ↠ 4,8567; 5,7550: ᴿAugM 35 (1990) 182s (J. *Ortali*).

7529 *Galot* Jean, L'Esprit Saint, milieu de vie [Cazelles H., SDB 11,129: *rûaḥ* 'espace atmosphérique entre ciel et terre', ambiance vitale, plutôt que 'vent, souffle']: Gregorianum 72 (1991) 671-688; Eng. 688.

7530 **Gelpi** Donald L., God breathes; the Spirit in the world 1988 ↠ 4,8570: ᴿHorizons 18 (1991) 156-8 (P. D. *Molnar*: awkward changes in language).

7531 **Granado** Carmelo, El Espíritu Santo en la teología patristica 1987 ↠ 3,7112; 5,7552: ᴿEstE 65 (1990) 87s (J. R. *García Murga*).

7531* *a) Guers* É., De l'Esprit promis à l'Esprit donné: RRéf 42,4 (1991) 11-22 [< NTAbs 36,218]. – *b) Horgan* Thaddeus D., Who is the Holy Spirit?: a biblical survey: OneInC 25 (1989) 322-332.

7532 *Ioniță* Viorel, Geist – Reich Gottes – Kirche aus pneumatologischer Perspektive: OstkSt 40 (1991) 3-17.

7533 **Kraus** H.-J. Heiliger Geist 1986 ↠ 3,7121: ᴿTsTKi 61 (1990) 154s (Ola *Tjørhom*).

7534 **Laplace** Ignacio, El Espíritu y la Iglesia; en las fuentes mismas de la vida espiritual. Sdr 1989, Sal Terrae. 189 p. – ᴿBibFe 16 (1990) 156 (M. *Sáenz Galache*).

7534* **Lin Hong Hsin,** *a)* Die Person des Heiligen Geistes als Thema der Pneumatologie in der reformierten Theologie: Diss. Tübingen 1990. 265 p. – TLZ 116 (1991) 550s. – *b)* 'Wer ist der Heilige Geist' in der Pneumatologie H. Bᴇʀᴋʜᴏғs?: EvT 51 (1991) 259-270.

7535 **Lison** Jacques, L'Esprit répandu; la pneumatologie de Grégoire Pᴀ-ʟᴀᴍᴀs: diss. ᴰHalleux A. de. Louvain-la-Neuve 1991. 530 p. – RTLv 23, p. 141s & TravauxD 13/6. > ScEsp 44, 67-76.

7536 **McDonnell** Kilian, *Montague* George T., Christian initiation and baptism in the Holy Spirit; evidence from the first eight centuries [in NT always includes water-baptism in Jesus]. Collegeville ᴍɴ 1991, Liturgical. xiv-354 p. $13. 0-8146-5009-0 [NTAbs 35,259]. – ᴿLvSt 16 (1991) 280s (Susan K. *Roll*).

7536* **Mackett** John K., Eusᴇʙɪus of Caesarea's theology of the Holy Spirit: diss. Marquette, ᴰLienhard J. Milwaukee 1990. 335 p. 91-17354. – DissA 52 (1991s) 193-A.

7537 **Marriage** Alwyn, Life-giving Spirit. L 1989, SPCK. 133 p. £8. 0-281-04430-9. – ᴿExpTim 102 (1990s) 91s (N. *Slee*).

7537* **Mullins** Patrick J., The teaching of 'Lumen gentium' on the Holy Spirit; the Holy Spirit was sent at Pentecost in order that he might continually sanctify the Church: diss. Pont. Univ. Gregoriana. Rome 1991. 697 p. 91-23574. – DissA 52 (1991s) 568-A.

7538 **O'Brien** Henry, The Holy Spirit in the catechetical writings of John Cᴀʟᴠɪɴ; a comparative study with other constructive presentations of Christian doctrine between 1529 and 1566: diss. Pont. Univ. Gregoriana, ᴰWicks J. Roma 1991. 593 p. – InfPUG (1991) 19; RTLv 23, p. 551 > DissA-C.

7538* **Paprocki** Henryk, La promesse du Père; l'expérience du Saint-Esprit dans l'Église orthodoxe, [T]*Lhoest* F.: Théologies. P 1990, Cerf. 151 p.; 10 fig. F 99. – [R]EsprVie 101 (1991) 175s (P. *Jay*); NRT 113 (1991) 593s (L. J. *Renard*).

7539 **Santos Ferreira** José M. dos, Teologia do Espírito Santo em AGOSTINHO [D]1987 → 5,7562; 6,7573: [R]AugM 35 (1990) 182 (J. *Oroz*).

7539* *Schreiner* Josef, Wirken des Geistes Gottes in alttestamentlicher Sicht [i. schafft Leben, Ezech 37,1-14; ii. Gaben, Jes 11; iii. prophetische Existenz Joel 3,1-5; Num 10,24-30]: TGL 81 (1991) 3-51.

7540 **Siebel** Wigand, Der Heilige Geist als Relation 1986 → 3,7129; 4,8582: [R]WissWeis 51 (1988) 225-8 (N. *Hartmann*).

7541 **Smail** Thomas A., The giving gift. L 1988, Hodder & S. £7. 0-340-39915-5.

7542 [E]**Vives** Josep, [T]*O'Callaghan* Josep, BASILI EL GRAN, Sobre l'Esperit Sant: Clàssics del Cristianisme 19. Barc 1991, Proa. 155 p. 84-7739-174-2.

7542* **White** John, When the Spirit comes with power. L 1989, Hodder & S. 251 p. £5. – [R]EvQ 63 (1991) 190-2 (G. *Houston*, also on *Eaton*'s LLOYD-JONES).

7543 *Wicks* Jared, Heiliger Geist – Kirche – Heiligung; Einsichten aus Luthers Glaubensunterricht [Vortrag ISERLOH E. Gb. 1990]: Catholica 45 (1991) 79-101.

7544 *Zauner* William, Wortloser Geist: Diakonia 21 (W/Mainz 1990) 175-78; > Eng. [TE]*Asen* B. A.: TDig 39,34s [the Spirit is called 'third' person but Christ became flesh 'through' the Holy Spirit].

H5.6 **Spirit-Christology;** Filioque.

7544* **Del Colle** Ralph G., Christ and the Spirit-Christology in trinitarian perspective: diss. Union, [D]*Morse* C. NY 1990. – RelStR 18,171.

7545 **Hawthorne** Gerald F., The presence and the power; the significance of the Holy Spirit in the life and ministry of Jesus. Dallas 1991, Word. xii-264 p. 0-8499-3220-3.

7546 *Kunzler* Michael, Die Florentiner Diskussion über das Filioque vom 14.3.1439 im Licht des Palamismus: AnHistConc 21 (Pd 1989) 334-352 [< ZIT 91,364].

7547 **Lampryllos** Cyriaque, La mystification fatale, étude orthodoxe sur le Filioque [1883, in French], [E]*Motte* L., *Ranson* P.: La Lumière du Thabor. Lausanne 1987, Âge d'homme. 138 p.

7548 *Limouris* G., Is the Filioque still a theological question?: Kleronomía 19 (1991 for 1987) 205-218 [< RHE 87,91*].

7548* *Rorem* Paul, The *Filioque* issue in Protestant-Orthodox dialogues: NesTR 12 (1991) 63-80.

7549 **Schoonenberg** Piet, De Geest, het Woord en de Zoon; theologische overdenkingen over Geest-christologie, Logos-christologie en drieëenheidsleer. Averbode 1991, Altiora. 258 p. [TR 88,434].

H5.7 *Ssma Trinitas* – **The Holy Trinity.**

7549* **Adams** David R., The doctrine of divine person considered both historically and in the contemporary theologies of Karl BARTH and Jürgen MOLTMANN; diss. Fuller Theol. Sem. Pasadena 1991. 287 p. 92-10343. – DissA 52 (1991s) 3972s-A.

7550 *Antinucci* Lucia, Cristologia e mistero trinitario; la riflessione cristo-logica di G. LAFONT e B. SESBOÜÉ: Asprenas 38 (1991) 461-475.

7551 *Aranda* Antonio, Las propuestas de Karl RAHNER para una teología trinitaria sistemática: ScripTPamp 23 (1991) 69-122; lat. 122; Eng. 123.

7552 **Axt-Piscalar** Christine, Der Grund des Glaubens; eine theologiege-schichtliche Untersuchung zum Verhältnis von Glaube und Trinität in der Theologie Isaak A. DORNERS [1809-1934; ev. Diss. München 1990]: BeitHistT 79. Tü 1990, Mohn. vii-264 p. – ᴿTR 87 (1991) 290s (G. *Wenz*).

7553 *a) Beauchamp* Paul, Chemins bibliques de la révélation trinitaire; – *b) Bobrinskoy* Boris, Expérience vecue et doctrines trinitaires en Orient et en Occident; – *c) Théobald* Christoph, La foi trinitaire des chrétiens et l'énigme du lien social: ➤ 481, Monothéisme et Trinité 1990/1, 15-40 / 41-59 / 99-137 [+ 2 al.].

7553* **Bergian** Silke-Petra, THEODORET von Cyrus und der Neunizänismus; Aspekte der altkirchlichen Trinitätslehre: ev. Diss. ᴰ*Kretschmar* G. München 1991s. – RTLv 23, p. 548.

7554 **Boff** Leonardo, Trinity and society 1988 ➤ 5,7584; 6,7581: ᴿMid-Stream 29 (1990) 197s (W. R. *Barr*).

7555 **Boff** Leonardo, Trinité et société [1986 ➤ 2,5734], ᵀ*Malley* P.: Li-bération. P 1990, Cerf. 297 p. F 165. – ᴿÉtudes 375 (1991) 569 (R. *Marlé*); NRT 113 (1991) 583 (L. *Renwart*).

7556 **Boff** Leonardo, *a)* Trinità; la migliore comunità. Assisi 1990, Cittadella. 185 p. – *b)* La Santisima Trinidad es la mejor comunidad: Caminos 4. M 1990, Paulinas. 150 p. – ᴿSalesianum 53 (1991) 776s (L. A. *Gallo*).

7556* **Boff** Leonardo, Kleine Trinitätslehre, ᵀ*Goldstein* H. Dü 1990, Patmos. 147 p. DM 19,80 [TLZ 117, 219, J. *Althausen*].

7557 **Bracken** Joseph A., Society and Spirit; a trinitarian cosmology. Se-linsgrove PA 1991, Susquehanna Univ. 194 p. $29.50. [JAAR 59,881].

7558 **Bradshaw** Timothy, Trinity and ontology... BARTH & PANNENBERG 1988 ➤ 6,7583: ᴿJTS 42 (1991) 788-790 (C. *Gunton*).

7559 *Brito* Emilio, La doctrine trinitaire d'après la 'Glaubenslehre' de SCHLEIERMACHER: RTLv 22 (1991) 327-342; 455 Eng.

7560 **Fatula** Mary Ann, The triune God of Christian faith: Zacchaeus. Collegeville MN 1990, Liturgical [RelStR 18, 128, J. R. *Sachs*].

7561 **Ferlay** Philippe, Dieu [... Trinité] sacrifice éternel: Méristème. P 1990, Nouvelle Cité. 238 p. F 190. – ᴿNRT 113 (1991) 894s (L. *Renwart*).

7562 **Ferrario** Fulvio, Il Dio unico nella teologia trinitaria di Karl BARTH: Protestantesimo 46 (1991) 162-174.

7562* **Forte** Bruno, The Trinity as history; saga of the Christian God [Trinità nella storia³] ᵀ. NY 1989, Alba. xi-250 p. $15. – ᴿDoctLife 41 (1991) 272s (T. *MacCarthy*: severe).

7563 **Gironés** Gonzalo, La divina arqueología (... Trinidad). Valencia 1991, Fac. Teol. Ferrar. 95 p. – ᴿETL 67 (1991) 464s (A. de *Halleux*).

7564 *Harrison* Verna, Perichoresis in the Greek Fathers: StVlad 35 (1991) 53-65.

7565 *Havrilak* Gregory, Karl RAHNER and the Greek Trinity: StVlad 34 (1990) 61-77.

7566 ᶠHEMMERLE K., Der dreieinige Gott 1989 ➤ 5,82: ᴿTPhil 66 (1991) 292 (H.-L. *Ollig*).

7567 **Hofmann** Peter, [Trinitarische] Glaubensbegründung; die Tranzenden-talphilosophie [APEL K.-O.] der Kommunikationsgemeinschaft in fun-damentaltheologischer Sicht [Diss. ᴰ*Splett* J., Frankfurt St-Georgen):

FraTSt 36. Fra 1988, Knecht. 352 p. DM 58. – ᴿTR 87 (1991) 46-48 (E. *Arens*).

Holmberg Bo, ISRAEL of Kashkar, *Risala*, a treatise on the unity and trinity of God 1989 ⇥ g333.

7568 Kelly Anthony, The trinity of love; a theology of the Christian God: Glazier New Theology 4, 1989 ⇥ 6,7595: ᴿCurrTMiss 18 (1991) 297s (J. *Zell*).

7568* MacLennan Ronald B., The doctrine of the Trinity in the theology of Paul TILLICH: diss. Lutheran School of Theology. [Ch] 1991. 658 p. 01-29534. – DissA 52 (1991s) 1392-A.

7569 *a*) *Maggioni* Bruno, La Trinità nel NT; – *b*) *Serenthà* Mario, La teologia trinitaria oggi: ScuolC 118 (1990) 7-30 / 90-116 [31-89 *al.*].

7570 *Marchesi* Giovanni, Trinità e mistica; il vertice dell'esperienza religiosa: CC 142 (1991,4) 361-375.

7570* Meuffels Hans O., Einbergung des Menschen in das Mysterium der dreieinigen Liebe; eine trinitarische Anthropologie nach Hans Urs von BALTHASAR: kath. Diss. Würzburg, ᴰ*Ganoczy* A., 1991. – TR 87 (1991) 522.

7571 Meyer Hans-Bernard, Eine trinitarische Theologie der Liturgie und der Sakramente: ZkT 113 (1991) 24-38.

7572 Moltmann Jürgen, In der Geschichte des dreieinigen Gottes; Beiträge zur trinitarischen Theologie. Mü 1991, Kaiser. 248 p. DM 69. 3-459-01883-6 [TsTNijm 32,107, H.-E. *Mertens*].

Muller Earl C., Trinity and marriage in Paul 1990 ⇥ 5202.

7572* Navone John, Self-giving and sharing; the Trinity and human fulfilment. ColMn 1989, Liturgical. x-161 p. £10.65. – ᴿDoctLife 41 (1991) 273s (T. *MacCarthy*).

7573 O'Donnell John J., The mystery of the Triune God 1988 ⇥ 4,8626... 6,7600: ᴿAustralasCR 67 (1990) 109s (J. *Foley*); NBlackf 71 (1990) 462s (M. J. *Dodds*); RRel 50 (1991) 942s (J. A. *Bracken*: BALTHASAR's rhetoric will not answer implication of RAHNER citation, 'God becomes').

7574 O'Donnell John J., Il mistero della Trinità 1989 ⇥ 5,7599; 6,7601: ᴿCiuD 203 (1991) 499s (J. M. *Ozaeta*: magnífico).

7575 Otto Randall E., The God of hope; the Trinitarian vision of Jürgen MOLTMANN: diss. Westminster Theol. Sem. ᴰ*Knudsen* R. 1990. 90-26394. – DissA 51 (1990s) 1663-A.

7576 *Pelikan* Jaroslav, Canonica regula; the trinitarian hermeneutics of AUGUSTINE: ⇥ 6,688*, Collectanea 1986/90, 329-343.

7577 *Pietras* Henryk, L'unità di Dio in ATANASIO di Alessandria; una descrizione dinamica della Trinità: RasT 32 (1991) 558-581.

7578 Pikaza Xabier, Dios como Espíritu y Persona... misterio trinitario 1989 ⇥ 6,7606: ᴿCarthaginensia 7 (1991) 270s (P. *Martínez Fresneda*: 'Xavier'); Teresianum 42 (1991) 675-7 (G. *Vallejo* T.).

7578* Pikaza Xabier, Trinidad y comunidad cristiana; el principio social del cristianismo. S 1989, Secr. Trinitario, 304 p. – ᴿRazF 222 (1990) 361 (R. de *Andrés*).

7579 Radlbeck Regina, Der Personbegriff / MOLTMANN, KASPER 1989 ⇥ 6, 7607: ᴿActuBbg 28 (1991) 89s (J. *Boada*); TGegw 34 (1991) 69s (S. *Hammer*); TLZ 116 (1991) 690s (W. *Krötke*); TsTNijm 31 (1991) 438 (H. *Rikhof*).

7580 Rovira Belloso Josep M., La humanidad de Dios, aproximación a la esencia del Cristianismo: Agape 6. S 1986, Secretariado Trinitario. 351 p. – ᴿZkT 113 (1991) 98s (W. *Kern*: 'Cristianesimo').

7581 *Savvatos* Chrysostomos, Ⓖ The trinitarian terminology of HIPPOLYTUS of Rome: TAth 61 (1990) 698-712; Eng. 908.

7582 **Schadel** Erwin, *al.*, Bibliotheca Trinitariorum 1,1984 ➤ 65,929; 2,1988 ➤ 4,1978: ᴿAugR 30 (1990) 203s (B. *Studer*, 2); ScotJT 44 (1991) 90s (I. R. *Torrance*, 1: 4712 authors); Symbolon 10 (1991) 153 (P. *Gerlitz*, 2); TRu 56 (1991) 210s (F. *Wagner*).

7583 *Schadel* Erwin, Trinität als Archetyp? Ontologische Anmerkungen an C. G. JUNGs Versuch einer psychologischen Deutung des Trinitätsdogma: Symbolon 10 (Fra 1991) 105-151.

7584 *Schoonenberg* Piet, The doctrine of the Trinity; empty dogma or fruitful theologoumenon, ᵀ*Merrigan* Terrence: LvSt 16 (1991) 195-206 [= TDig 39, 23-31].

7585 **Sesé** Alegre F. J., Trinidad... RUPERTO 1988 ➤ 6,7608: ᴿAnnTh 4 (1990) 175-7 (A. C. *Chacón*).

7586 *Simonetti* Manlio, Il concilio del 362 e l'origine della formula trinitaria: AugR 30 (1990) 353-360.

7587 **Spada** Domenico, Le formule trinitarie da Nicea a Costantinopoli 1988 ➤ 6,7612: ᴿBLitEc 92 (1991) 63 (H. *Crouzel*).

7588 ᵀᴱ **Spinelli** Mario, RICCARDO di S. Vittore, La Trinità. R 1990, Città Nuova. 272 p. Lit. 23.000. – ᴿCC 142 (1991,3) 315s (A. *Orazzo*).

7589 *Suermann* Harald, Trinität in der islamisch-christlichen Kontroverse nach ABŪ RĀTTA: ZMissRW 74 (1990) 219-229.

7590 **Tavard** Georges, La vision de la Trinité: Théologies, 1989 ➤ 6, 7614: ᴿCiuD 203 (1990) 749s (J. M. *Ozaeta*); RSPT 75 (1991) 182s (D. *Galtier*).

7590* **Theilemann** Christof, Die Frage nach Analogie, natürlicher Theologie und Personbegriff in der Trinitätslehre; eine vergleichende Untersuchung britischer und deutsch-sprachiger Trinitätstheologie: Diss. Berlin-Brandenburg k. Hochschule 1989. 381 p. – TLZ 116 (1991) 476s.

7591 *Thompson* John, Modern Trinitarian perspectives: ScotJT 44 (1991) 349-365.

7592 **Torrance** Thomas F., The Trinitarian faith 1988 ➤ 4,8640 ... 6,7615: ᴿJAAR 59 (1991) 428s (Mary Ann *Donovan*).

7592* **Ury** Meredith W., The role and meaning of 'person' in the doctrine of the Trinity; an historical investigation of a relational definition: diss. Drew, ᴰ*Pain* J. Madison NJ 1991. 368 p. 91-29318. – DissA 52 (1991s) 1399-A; RelStR 18,171.

7593 *Villalmonte* Alejandro, Persona y Cristología [AUG.: DROBNER H.]: AugM 34 (1989) 395-7.

7594 *a) Wainwright* Geoffrey, The doctrine of the Trinity; where the Church stands or falls; – *b) Thistlethwaite* Susan B., On the Trinity; – *c) Babcock* William S., A changing of the Christian God; the doctrine of the Trinity in the seventeenth century: Interpretation 45 (1991) 117-132 / 139-171 / 133-146.

7595 *Warner* Robert, RAHNER on the Unoriginate Father: Thomist 55 (1991) 569-593.

7596 **Willis** W. Waite, Theism... Trinity ... BARTH, MOLTMANN 1987 ➤ 3, 7191 ... 6,7618: ᴿCritRR 3 (1990) 460s (R. D. *Shofner*).

7596* *Wojtczak* Adam, Ⓟ Die trinitarische Genese der sozialen Eucharistie in der Sicht der katholischen Theologen in Polen nach dem Konzil: ColcT 60,4 (1990) 45-61; deutsch 62.

7597 *Zimmerling* Peter, ZINZENDORFs Trinitätslehre, eine Herausforderung und Bereicherung in systematisch-theologischen Überlegungen der Gegenwart: EvT 51 (1991) 224-245.

H5.8 *Regnum messianicum, Filius hominis* – **Messianic kingdom, Son of Man.**

7597* **Abbott** Stephen L., A critical analysis of the meaning of the Kingdom of God in the theology of the Christian Reconstructionist movement [claiming to be heirs of New England Puritan Calvinism]: diss. SW Baptist Theol. Sem. 1990. 282 p. 91-15297 – DissA 52 (1991s) 189-A.

7598 **Bejick** Urte, Basileia; Vorstellungen vom Königtum Gottes im Umfeld des NTs: Diss. Heidelberg 1991, DBerger. – TR 87 (1991) 518.

7598* **Bing** Charles C., Lordship salvation [to be saved, one must take Jesus as master of his/her life: alternative to 'Free grace' position, trust in Christ suffices]: a biblical evaluation and response: diss. Dallas Theol. Sem. 1991, DToussaint S. 381 p. 92-14483. – DissA 52 (1991s) 4373-A. ➤ 7603/5s.

7599 *a) Casey* Maurice, Method in our madness, and madness in their methods; some approaches to the Son of Man problem in recent scholarship: JStNT 42 (1991) 17-43. – *b) Davis* D., The semantic content of 'Son of Man': NoTr 4,3 (1990) 9-23.

7599* **Dupuy** Michel, La royauté du Christ, lumières sur le traditionnalisme chrétien: JJC 46. P 1990, Desclée. 176 p. F 95. – REsprVie 101 (1991) 255 (É. *Cothenet*: début du livre: LEFEBVRE, 'Ils l'ont découronné).

7600 **Franke** Thomas, Leben aus Gottes Fülle; zur trinitarischen Reich-Gottes-Theologie Hermann SCHELLS: StKGnZ 3. Wü 1990, Echter. 293 p. DM 39. – RTGL 81 (1991) 141-3 (W. *Sosna*).

7600* *Guillaume* P.-M., Royaume de Dieu: ➤ 664, Catholicisme XIII, 59 (1991) 175-184.

7601 **Hampel** Volker, Menschensohn und historischer Jesus 1990 ➤ 6,7624: RActuBbg 28 (1991) 56s (J. *Boada*); Biblica 72 (1991) 585-8 (E. *Lohse*: am Ende nichts gewonnen); BZ 35 (1991) 259-262 (J. *Roloff*).

7602 **Hare** Douglas R. A., The Son of Man tradition 1990 ➤ 6,7625: RHorBT 13 (1991) 91-94 (B. *Witherington*); JStNT 43 (1991) 124s (C. M. *Tuckett* = CHT p. 128?); Neotestamentica 25 (1991) 444 (L. J. *Prockter*); TDig 38 (1991) 268 (W. C. *Heiser*: the conclusion, 'modest self-reference, not a theological title'); TR 87 (1991) 458-460 (H. *Giesen*).

7603 *a) Hatfield* Stephen G., The lordship of Christ, a biblical analysis; – *b) Bloesch* Donald G., ... in theological history; – *c) Erickson* Millard J., Lordship theology; the current controversy [➤ 7598*]: SWJT 34,2 (1991s) 16-25 / 26-34 / 5-15 (35-49 *al.*).

7603* **Hell** Leonhard, Reich Gottes als Systemidee der Theologie; historisch-systematische Untersuchung zum theologischen Werk B. GALURAS und F. BRENNERS: kath. Diss. Tübingen 1991, DKasper W. – TR 87 (1991) 522.

EHengel Martin, *Schwemer* Anna Maria, Königsherrschaft Gottes und himmlischer Kult 1986/91 ➤ 438.

7604 **Heyer** C. J. den, De messianse weg, 2. Jezus van Nazareth 1986 ➤ 2, 3137 ... 4,8655: RNedTTs 43 (1989) 146s (M. de *Jonge*).

7604* **Hix** Alan D., A comparative analysis of the Christological titles Son of Man and High Priest as reflected in the humiliation, exaltation, and redemptive significance of Jesus' mission: diss. Baptist Theol. Sem. DStevens Gerald L. New Orleans 1990. 118 p. 91-19551. – DissA 52 (1991s) 567s.

7605 **Hodges** Zane C., Absolutely free! A biblical reply to Lordship Salvation. GR 1989, Zondervan. 238 p. $15. – RSWJT 33,1 (1990s) 63s (B.

Hunt, also on MACARTHUR J., whose 'Gospel according to Jesus' heated up and redirected the controversy); TrinJ 11 (1990) 242-7 (T. J. *Nettles*).

7606 **House** H. Wayne, *Ice* Thomas, Dominion theology, blessing or curse 1988 ➤ 5,7386: ᴿGraceTJ 11 (1990) 114s (R. A. *Young*: shown not biblical).

7607 **Jonge** M. de, Jezus als Messias; hoe hij zijn sending zag. Boxtel/Brugge 1990, KBS/Tabor. 128 p. *f* 32,90. 90-61730-460-6. – ᴿTsTNijm 31 (1991) 429 (L. *Grollenberg*).

7608 **Kearns** Rollin, Die Entchristologisierung des Menschensohnes 1988 ➤ 4,8657 ... 6,7626: ᴿCBQ 53 (1991) 331s (R. *Doran*); Gregorianum 72 (1991) 139-141 (G. L. *Prato*, sotto 'Judaica').

7608* ᶠKINGDON Robert M., Regnum, ᴱ**Friedman** J. 1987 ➤ 4,82: ᴿCrit-RR 2 (1989) 306s (Jeannine E. *Olson*: DONNELLY J. P. on POSSEVINO, RICHGELS Robert on BELLARMINE; no pp.).

7609 **Kosch** Daniel, Die eschatologische Tora des Menschensohnes... in Q: NOrb 12, 1989 ➤ 5,7626: ᴿBiKi 46 (1991) 90s (C.-P. *März*); JBL 110 (1991) 525-7 (J. S. *Kloppenborg*).

7610 **Kraybill** D. B., The upside-down kingdom². Scottdale PA 1990, Herald. 307 p. $15. 0-8361-3522-9 [NTAbs 35,243].

7611 **Lindars** B., Jesus, Son of Man 1983 ➤ 64,6853 ... 1,7118; ᴿRivLtg 77 (1990) 109s (G. *Crocetto*).

7611* *Luz* Ulrich, Jesus der Menschensohn zwischen Juden und Christen: ➤ 46*, ᶠEHRLICH E. 1991, 212-223.

7612 *MacKinnon* Donald M., Son of Man; a comment: ScotR 11 (Stirling 1990) 89-92 [< ZIT 90,868].

7613 *Marshall* C. D., Kingdom come; the Kingdom of God in the teaching of Jesus: Journal of the Christian Brethren Research Fellowship 120 (Wellington NZ 1990) 7-25 [NTAbs 35,153].

7614 *Marshall* I. Howard, The Son of Man and the Incarnation: ➤ 448c, ExAuditu 7 (1991) 29-43.

7614* *Riesenfeld* Harald, Le règne de Dieu, parmi vous ou en vous?: RB 98 (1991) 190-8; Eng. 190.

7615 **Ruppert** M., Het Rijk Gods en de wereld; over de verhouding... naar aanleiding van LUTHERS onderscheiding van het eeuwige Rijk van God en Gods tijdelijke wereldlijke regiment. Kampen 1987, Kok. 342 p. *f* 45. 90-242-4887-6. – ᴿBijdragen 52 (1991) 103s (T. *Bell*).

7616 **Way** David, The lordship of Christ; Ernst KÄSEMANN's interpretation of Paul's theology: TMg. Ox 1991, Clarendon. xiv-336 p. 0-19-866742-8.

7617 *Zimmermann* Gunter, Die Vereinigung mit Gott und das Reich Christi nach CALVINs Institutio: Zwingliana 18 (Z 1990) 183-212 [< ZIT 91,43].

H6.1   *Creatio, sabbatum NT* [➤ E3.5]; **The Creation** [➤ E1.6; H2.8].

7618 **Allen** Edward M., Rest as a spiritual discipline; the meaning and manner of Sabbath observance: diss. Fuller, ᴰ*Anderson* R. Pasadena 1991, 305 p. 91-22241. – DissA 52 (1991s) 949-A.

7619 **Ambrose** E. J., The mirror of Creation. E 1990, Scottish Academic. 238 p. £12.50. 0-7073-0575-6 [ScotJT 44,547].

7620 *Arnould* J., *Fantino* J., *al.*, Théologie de la création: RSPT 75 (1991) 651-665.

7621 [Struyker] **Boudier** C. E. M., Morgen is het Zondag, verkenningen in hedendaags scheppingsdenken. Kampen/Kapellen 1990, Kok/Pelckmans.

322 p. *f*45.   90-242-7670-5 / 90-289-1523-0. – ᴿTsTNijm 31 (1991) 336 (W. B. *Drees*).

7622 **Daly** Gabriel,   Creation and redemption 1988 ➤ 6,7644:   ᴿScotJT 44 (1991) 106s (J. B. *Taylor*: excellent).

7623 *Corsani* Bruno,   La 'nuova creazione' nel Nuovo Testamento: Protestantesimo 46 (1991) 309-315.

7623* **Cupitt** Don,   Creation out of nothing. L 1990, SCM.   £9. – ᴿTablet 245 (1991) 646 (R. B. *Brinkman*: God-talk); TLond 94 (1991) 206s (A. *Race*).

7624 *Davis* Edward B.,   God, man and nature; the problem of creation in Cartesian thought: ScotJT 44 (1991) 325-348.

7625 *Ebeling* Gerhard,   Dogmatica della fede cristiana I (Prolegomeni – La fede in Dio creatore del mondo).   Genova 1990, Marietti.   Lit. 65.000. – ᴿProtestantesimo 46 (1991) 327s (G. *Scuderi*).

7626 **Gabus** Jean-Paul,   L'amour fou de Dieu pour sa création; croire à un Dieu créateur et libérateur.   P 1991, Bergers/mages.   147 p.   F 105. – ᴿEsprVie 101 (1991) 571-3 (P. *Jay* est d'accord sur l'essentiel).

7627 **Gerardi** Renzo,   La creazione 1990 ➤ 6,7647:   ᴿCC 142 (1991,1) 99 (J. *Joblin*).

7628 *Gesché* Adolphe,   L'homme créé créateur [El hombre, creado-creador, Madrid juillet 1990]: RTLv 22 (1991) 153-184; Eng. 303.

7629 **Haag** Ernst, Vom Sabbat zum Sonntag; eine bibeltheologische Studie: TrierTSt 52.   Trier 1991, Paulinus.   viii-199 p.   DM 42 [ZAW 104, 296, H.-C. *Schmitt*].

7630 *Hilger* Peter,   'Kreatürlichkeit', ein Schlüssel zum theologischen Denken Hermann VOLKs: Catholica 44 (1990) 147-168.

7631 *Hoeps* Reinhard,   Die Schöpfung und ihre Kreaturen; transzendentaler Vorgriff und kategoriale Beobachtung in der Schöpfungstheologie: ➤ 85, ᶠJORISSEN H., Mit dem Rücken 1991, 225-248.

7632 **König** Adrio,   New and greater things; re-evaluating the biblical message on creation 1988 ➤ 4,8680:   ᴿCBQ 53 (1991) 674s (J. C. *Kesterson*: a systematic theologian, especially in ch. 3-4; 1-2 are exegetical); NedTTs 45 (1991) 65s (P. B. *Dirksen*).

7633 *Moe* Steinar, 'Foreningen ...' søndagsforståelse: TsTKi 61 (1990) 193-205; Eng. 205, 'The Norwegian 'Association for the promotion of the right use of the Sunday'; Swiss sister movement 1862.

7634 *Monloubou* Louis,   Pour une théologie biblique de la création: BLitEc 92 (1991) 137-144.

Neville Robert C.,   Behind the masks of God; an essay toward comparative theology [based on creation ex nihilo].   Albany 1991, SUNY ➤ a478. x-200 p. $44.50; pa. $15.   0-7914-0578-8; -9-6 [TDig 38,371].

7635 **Parker** K. L.,   The English Sabbath 1988 ➤ 5,7648; 6,7653:   ᴿEngHR 106 (1991) 1002s (N. *Tyacke*, also on KATZ D.).

7636 *Signorini* A.,   L'idea di creazione ex nihilo e la libertà nel pensiero di E. LÉVINAS: Giornale di Metafisica 11 (1989) 241-271 [< FilT 4,559].

7637 *Sonderegger* Katherine,   The doctrine of creation and the task of theology: HarvTR 84 (1991) 185-203.

7638 **Tanner** Kathryn,   God and creation in Christian theology 1988 ➤ 5, 7652; 6,7660:   ᴿHeythJ 32 (1991) 270s (H. *Meynell*).

7639 **Trigo** Pedro,   Schöpfung und Geschichte [Creación e historia 1988 ➤ 5,7653.8570*], ᵀ*Kuhlmann* J., *Ludwig* J.: BtTBefr.   Dü 1989, Patmos. 319 p. DM 45. – ᴿTLZ 116 (1991) 930-2 (J. *Althausen*).

7640 *Veldhuijsen* Peter van, Eeuwige schepping...: Bijdragen 52 (1991) 139-157; 157, Eternal creation and eternal production of the world according to BONAVENTURE.

7641 *Young* Frances, 'Creatio ex nihilo'; a context for the emergence of the Christian doctrine of creation: ScotJT 44 (1991) 139-151.

H6.3 *Fides, veritas in NT* – **Faith and truth.**

7642 **Ansaldi** Jean, L'articulation de la foi, de la théologie et des écritures. P 1991, Cerf. 247 p. F 120 [TR 87,434].

7642* *Avis* Paul, Faith and fantasy in the countryside [Archbishops' Commission report, Faith in the countryside 1990, £13]: TLond 94 (1991) 124-8: inevitable sequel to 1985 Faith in the city.

7643 **Axt-Piscalar** Christine, Der Grund des Glaubens; eine theologiegeschichtliche Untersuchung zum Verhältnis von Glauben und Trinität in der Theologie Isaak A. DORNERS [Diss. München, ᴰ*Pannenberg* W.]: BeitHistT 79. Tü 1990, Mohr. viii-264 p. DM 138 [TLZ 117,683, H. *Peiter*: hohes Niveau].

7643* **Barbaglio** Giuseppe, A laicidade do crente; interpretaçâo bíblica, ʸ*Gomes* João P. Aparecida 1991, Santuario. 120 p. – ᴿREB 51 (1991) 740s (J. *Clasen*).

7644 Belgische Bischöfe, Unser Glaube 1988 → 5,7656; 6,7663: ᴿZkT 113 (1991) 122 (G. *Bader*).

7644* *Benz* Franz, Glaube und Umwelt: ForumKT 7 (1991) 21-37.

7645 **Berkhof** Hendrikus, Christian faith [1973, ᵀ*Woudstra* S. 1979 =] GR c. 1990, Eerdmans. xii-572 p. $30. – ᴿIrTQ 57 (1991) 91s (G. *Daly*).

7646 ᴱ**Birmelé** André, *Lienhard* Marc, La foi des Églises luthériennes; confessions et catéchismes. P/Genève 1991, Cerf/Labor et Fides. 605 p. – ᴿRHE 86 (1991) 527s (C. *Soetens*); RHPR 71 (1991) 262s (*Birmelé*: comble una lacune étonnante).

7647 *a*) *Caputo* John D., Hermeneutics and Faith; response to Olthuis; – *b*) *Olthuis* James H., Undecidability and the Im/Possibility of faith, rejoinder: ChrSchR 20 (1990) 164-170 / 171 ... [< ZIT 91,264].

7648 *Carrière* Jean-Marie, Croire et agir; foi et justice dans la Bible: Études 374 (1991) 789-800.

7649 [Deutsche Katechisten 1980] Manuel de la foi; le Notre Père, le Credo, les Sacrements, les Commandements. P 1989, Cerf. 334 p.; ill. F 120. – ᴿCC 142 (1991,1) 98s (G. *Caprile*: non menziona la scomunica per l'aborto non ancora confermata nel 1980).

7650 *Doré* Joseph, La foi entre raison et religion: Bulletin de théologie fondamentale 3: RechSR 79 (1991) 99-132.

7651 **Ferlay** Philippe, Compendio de la fe católica; el camino de los cristianos [1986], ᵀ*Montes* Miguel. Valencia 1989, Edicep. 316 p. – ᴿLumenVr 39 (1990) 338s (U. *Gil Ortega*).

7652 **Giussani** Luigi [fondatore de Communion et Libération], Le défi de la foi chrétienne. P 1990, Fayard. 214 p. – ᴿEsprVie 101 (1991) 91s (P. *Jay*: exégèse douteuse; citations trop longues de lui-même et d'autres).

7652* **Hagemann** Ludwig, Was glauben Christen? Die Grundaussagen einer Weltreligion: Tb 1729. FrB 1991, Herder. 191 p. [TLZ 117,174].

7653 **Kerr** Hugh T., The simple gospel; reflections on Christian faith. Louisville 1991, W-Knox. 72 p. $8. – ᴿTTod 48 (1991s) 470.472 (F. *Buechner*).

7653* **Klöcker** Michael, Katholisch – von der Wiege bis zur Bahre; eine Lebensmacht im Zerfall? Mü 1991, Kösel. 520 p. DM 50 [TLZ 117, 793, H. *Kirchner*: sozialgeschichtliche 'kollektive Biographie'].

7654 *a) Knauer* Peter, Die Korrelation von Glaubensgegenstand und Glaubensakt; – *b) Knoch* Wendelin, 'Das Credo der Kirche – Ausdruck und Massstab christlichen Glaubens' [Knauer]: Catholica 44 (1990) 49-63 / 131-144.

7655 **Korsch** Dietrich, Glaubensgewissheit und Selbstbewusstsein; vier systematische Variationen über Gesetz und Evangelium: BeitHistT 76. Tü 1989, Mohr. x-290 p. DM 138. – ᴿTR 87 (1991) 48-50 (G. *Wenz*).

7656 **Kruhöffer** Gerald, Grundlinien des Glaubens; ein biblisch-theologischer Leitfaden [➤ 5,7665 (index!)]: Bib-T. Schwerpunkte 1. Gö 1989, Vandenhoeck & R. 326 p. DM 38. 3-525-61282-6. – ᴿLuthTKi 14 (1990) 45s (H. *Brandt*).

7657 *Laurenzi* Maria Cristina, 'Sub contraria specie'; che significa 'esperienza' nella fede biblica?: HumBr 46 (1991) 731-742.

7658 *Lønning* Per, Kristen tro; tradisjon og oppbrudd 1989 ➤ 6,7681: ᴿTsTKi 61 (1990) 75s (J.-O. *Henriksen*).

7659 *Lülsdorff* Raimund, Glauben an die Kirche? [SEMMELROTH O. 1959; HENGSBACH F. 1987...]: Catholica 45 (1991) 119-134.

7660 **McGrath** Alister E., Explaining your faith without losing your friends [for college students]. GR 1989, Zondervan Academie. 112 p. $5. 0-310-29741-9. – ᴿRExp 87 (1990) 150s (H. L. *Poe*).

7661 **Nelson** C. Ellis, How faith matures. Louisville 1989, W-Knox. 252 p. $14 pa. – ᴿAndrUnS 28 (1990) 267s (R. *Naden*); Horizons 18 (1991) 328-330 (K. *Scott*).

7662 **Niebuhr** H. Richard, Faith on earth; an inquiry into the structure of human faith [c. 1951, ineditum], ᴱ*Niebuhr* R. R. 1989 ➤ 6,7685: ᴿAnglTR 73 (1991) 498-501 (D. S. *Cunningham*); CritRR 4 (1991) 455s (R. M. *Keiser*); Horizons 18 (1991) 327s (J. W. *Fowler*); JTS 42 (1991) 424-6 (D. F. *Ford*); Mid-Stream 30 (1991) 292s (E. L. *Becker*); RelStR 17 (1991) 289-292 (Claude *Welch*) & 293-5 (R. H. *King*).

7663 ᴱ**Nipkow** Karl E., *Schweitzer* Friedrich, *Fowler* James W., Glaubensentwicklung und Erziehung²ʳᵉᵛ [¹1988]. Gü 1989, Mohn. 312 p. DM 58. 3-579-01747-0. – ᴿBijdragen 52 (1991) 344 (U. *Hemel*, deutsch).

7664 *Ogliari* Donato, La vérité comme principe herméneutique de la vie monastique [... Jean; Aug.]: ColcCist 53 (1991) 105-116.

7665 **Parenti** Sergio, La credibilità umana di Cristo in rapporto all'atto di fede: diss. Angelicum, ᴰ*Boschi* B. Roma 1986 [Bo 1991]. 156 p. – RTLv 23,567.

7666 **Pasco** Rowamme, *Redford* John, La foi vivant des catholiques, ᵀ; préf. card. *Decourtray*. P 1991, Centurion. 392 p. F 195. – ᴿÉtudes 375 (1991) 426 (J. *Thomas*: britannique pour les 'catechismes des épiscopats').

7667 **Phillips** Dewi Z., Faith after foundationalism [against PLANTINGA, RORTY, Peter BERGER; LINDBECK, HOLMER; but favoring Flannery O'CONNOR]. L 1988, Routledge. xviii-341 p. £40. – ᴿScotJT 44 (1991) 103-6 (S. *Williams*).

7668 ᴱ**Pöhlmann** Horst G., Unser Glaube; Die Bekenntnisschriften der evangelisch-lutherischen Kirche³ʳᵉᵛ; [¹1986]; Ausgabe für die Gemeinde VELKD: Siebenstern 1289. Gö 1991, Mohn. 928 p. – ᴿTR 87 (1991) 494s (G. *Wenz*).

7669 **Ritter** Werner H., Glaube und Erfahrung im religionspädagogischen Kontext; die Bedeutung von Erfahrung für den christlichen Glauben im religionspädagogischen Verwendungszusammenhang: ArbRelPäd 4. Gö 1989, Vandenhoeck & R. 340 p. DM 88. – ᴿTR 87 (1991) 502s (N. *Mette*).

7670 **Rousselot** Pierre † 1915, The eyes of faith, ᵀ*Donceel* Joseph; Answer to two attacks, ᵀ*Dulles* Avery. NY 1991, Fordham Univ. 117 p. $27.50. 0-8232-1288-2 [TDig 39,82].

7671 **Sabugal** S., Io credo; la fede della Chiesa; il simbolo della fede, storia e interpretazione [1986 ➤ 2,5852]: Bo 1990, Dehoniane. 1294 p. Lit. 100.000. 88-396-0268-2. – ᴿCC 142 (1991,1) 98s (G. *Ferraro*).

7672 **Schneider** Theodor, La nostra fede; una spiegazione del simbolo apostolico 1989 ➤ 6,7688: ᴿRivScR 4 (1990) 603-9 (A. *Resta*).

7673 **Schneider** Theodor, Lo que nosotros creemos; exposición del símbolo de los Apóstoles, ᵀ*Olasagasti* M. S 1991, Sígueme. 518 p. – ᴿNatGrac 38 (1991) 408s (M. *González del Blanco*).

7673* **Strunk** R., Tor ins Weite; vom Geheimnis des Glaubens. Stu 1981, Quell. 303 p. DM 38. 3-7918-1990-9 [NTAbs 36,287].

7674 *Vanni* Ugo, La vita come cammino in uno spazio di verità: CC 142 (1991,2) 534-542 [< NTAbs 36,75].

7674* *Wackenheim* C., La foi entre l'incroyance et la crédulité; repères théologiques: RevSR 64 (1990) 307-317.

7675 *Waldenfels* Hans, Die eine Wahrheit und die Freiheit des Glaubens: Saeculum 42 (1991) 184-198.

H6.6   *Peccatum NT* – **Sin, Evil** [➤ E1.9].

7676 **Alonso Schökel** Luis, Posturas bíblicas ante la realidad del mal: Cómo leer el AT. M 1991. Fundación S. María. 41 p. 84-348-3430-8.

7677 **Beek** A. van de, Why?; on suffering, guilt, and God, ᵀ*Vriend* John. GR 1990, Eerdmans. vii-349 p. $22 pa. 0-8028-0427-6 [TDig 38,251]. – ᴿGraceTJ 11 (1990) 253-5 (J. *Blair*).

7678 **Carson** D. A., How long, O Lord? Reflections on suffering and evil. GR 1990, Baker. 280 p. $14. 0-8010-2556-7. – ᴿAsbTJ 46,2 (1991) 103s (J. L. *Walls*).

7679 *Dalferth* Ingolf H., Gott und Sünde ['Kann denn Liebe Sünde sein?' d.h. 'Kann Gott sündigen?']: NSys 33 (1991) 1-22; Eng. 22.

7680 **Farley** Edward, Good and evil; interpreting a human condition. Mp 1990, Fortress. xxi-295 p. $20. – ᴿTS 52 (1991) 568s (M. R. *Tripole*).

7681 *Fédou* Michel, Le christianisme et le problème du mal: NRT 113 (1991) 824-838.

7682 *Galot* Jean, Le mystère de la souffrance; problème existentiel et problème théologique [...châtiment du péché selon l'AT; réaction de Jésus contre...; sens rédempteur de toute souffrance]: EsprVie 101 (1991) 257-265 [266-270, *Gire* P., Le mal – pourquoi?].

7683 **Gestrich** Christof, Die Wiederkehr des Glanzes in der Welt; die christliche Lehre von der Sünde und ihrer Vergebung in gegenwärtiger Verantwortung 1989 ➤ 6,7695: ᴿTLZ 116 (1991) 142s (M. *Plathow*).

7684 **Highfield** Ronald, BARTH/RAHNER... on sin and evil: AmerUnivSt 7/62, 1989 ➤ 6,7699: ᴿCritRR 4 (1991) 440-2 (B. L. *Whitney*).

7685 **Kim Sung-Bong**, Die Lehre von der Sünde und vom Versöhner; THO-LUCKs theologische Entwicklung in seiner Berliner Zeit: Diss. ᴰ*Neuser*. Münster 1991. 211 p. > EurHS. – RTLv 23, p. 569.

7686 *Martínez de Pisón* Ramón, Le Dieu qui est 'victime'; le problème du mal dans la pensée de Maurice ZUNDEL: ScEsp 43 (1991) 55-68.

7687 **Millás** José M., Sünde... BULTMANN: FraTSt 34, 1987 ➤ 3,7324...
6,1702: ᴿRTLim 25 (1991) 313s (P. E. *Jiménez*, español 1989 ➤ 6,7703);
TrierTZ 100 (1991) 78s (A. *Dahm*).

7687* **Ricœur** Paul, Die Fehlbarkeit des Menschen; Phänomenologie der
Schuld I². Fr 1989, Alber. DM 48 [TLZ 117, 58, B. *Hildebrandt*].

7688 *Römelt* Josef, Schulderfahrung als Krise; zur anthropologischen und
theologischen Hermeneutik menschlicher Schuld: TGL 81 (1991) 454-466.

7689 **Scanlan** Michael, (*Manney* James), The truth about trouble. AA 1989,
Servant. 162 p. – ᴿSalesianum 53 (1991) 795s (G. *Abbà*: alta lode).

H7   Soteriologia NT.

7690 *Bavaud* Georges, La controverse sur la certitude du salut en rapport
avec la justification: ÉchSM 21 (1991) 135-142.

7691 *Bayer* Oswald, Rechtfertigung; Grund und Grenze der Theologie [➤ 6,
7711]: TBeit 21 (Wu 1990) 230-243 [< ZIT 90,753].

7692 *Beinert* Wolfgang, Who can be saved? [< StiZt 115,264-78], II: TDig
38 (1991) 303-8 [ᵀᴱB. A. *Asen*].

7693 *Blocher* Henri, The scope of redemption and modern theology: Scot-
BEvT 9 (1991) 80-103.

7694 *Boismard* M.-E., Le titre de 'fils de Dieu' dans les évangiles; sa portée
salvifique: Biblica 72 (1991) 442-450.

7695 **Cessario** Romano, The godly image; Christ and salvation in Catholic
thought from Anselm to Aquinas: Studies in Historical Theology 6.
Petersham ME 1990, St. Bede. 212 p. – ᴿAngelicum 68 (1991) 557-560
(J. R. *Morris*: on AQUINAs' satisfaction-theory, not as subtitle suggests a
history of the various theories); ETL 67 (1991) 448s (A. *Vanneste*: correspond partiellement au titre).

7696 *Chazelle* Celia M., To whom did Christ pay the price? The soteriology
of ALCUIN's Epistola 307: PatrMedRen 14 (Villanova 1989) 43-62 [< ZIT
91,368].

7697 **Clifford** Alan C., Atonement and justification; English evangelical theology 1640-1790; an evaluation. Ox 1990, Clarendon. xvi-268 p. £30.
0-19-826195-0. – ᴿEvQ 63 (1991) 287s (A. S. *Wood*); JEH 42 (1991) 326s
(W. R. *Ward*); JTS 42 (1991) 397s (A. *McGrath*: merits serious consideration); TLond 94 (1991) 140s (J. A. *Newton*); TsTNijm 31 (1991) 200s
(C. P. van *Andel*).

7698 **Corkery** James, The relationship between human existence and Christian salvation in the theology of Joseph RATZINGER: diss. Catholic Univ.,
ᴰ*Galvin* J. Wsh 1991. – RTLv 23, p. 568.

7699 *a) Delorme* J., Salut (Synopt., Actes); *Carrez* M., *Cothenet* É. (Paul);
Morgen M. (Jean); – *b) Meeks* D., *al.* (pré-biblique); – *c) Beaucamp* E.
(VT): ➤ 686, SDB. 63 (1990) 584-689-720-740 / 486-516 / 516-553.

7700 *Edwards* Denis, What are they saying about salvation? 1986 ➤ 2,5891*
... 6,7716: ᴿIrTQ 57 (1991) 318s (B. *Cosgrave*).

7702 **Eyjolfsson** Sigurjan, Rechtfertigung und Schöpfung in der Theologie
Werner ELERTs: Diss. ᴰ*Wölfel* E. Kiel 1991. – RTLv 23, p. 569:
> AGTL 10.

7703 **Fiddes** Paul, Past event and present salvation; the Christian idea of
atonement 1989 ➤ 6,7718: ᴿJTS 42 (1991) 799-801 (V. *White*); NBlackf
71 (1990) 209s (C. *Gunton*); PrPeo 4 (1990) 35s (Sr. M. Cecily *Boulding*: no
closer than H. WADDELL's novel Abelard; she treats also GUNTON C.).

7704 *Fiedler* Peter, 'Beim Herrn ist die Huld, bei ihm die Erlösung in Fülle':
➤ 48, ᶠERLICH E., 1991, 184-200.
7705 *Galindo Rodrigo* José A., Justificación y liberación; diálogo con algunos
teólogos de la liberación: CiuD 203 (1990) 613-645.
7706 *Galot* Jean, L'unico Salvatore e l'attività missionaria della Chiesa: CC
142 (1991,3) 125-137.
7707 **Graafland** C., WOELDERINKs visie op belofte en rechtvaardiging in het
licht van de Nadere Reformatie: TRef 33 (Woerden 1990) 197-213 [< ZIT
90,751].
7708 **Gunton** Colin E., The actuality of atonement; a study of metaphor,
rationality and the Christian tradition 1989 ➤ 5,7707; 6,7720: ᴿGraceTJ
11 (1990) 112-4 (D. A. *Wacome*); Interpretation 45 (1991) 100.102 (R.
Hjelm); IrTQ 57 (1991) 82-84 (A. P. F. *Sell* compares with DRIVER J. 1986
➤ 3,7347); NBlackf 71 (1990) 206-8 (M. *Wiles*, admiringly unconvinced);
PrPeo 4 (1990) 35s (M. C. *Boulding*: beautiful prose); RExp 87 (1990) 344s
(H. L. *Poe*); TTod 48 (1991s) 476.478 (A. J. *McKelway*).
7709 ᴱ**Heinz** Hanspeter, *al.*, Versöhnung in der jüdischen und christlichen
Liturgie [Bronstein-Kolloquium Augsburg 1989]: QDisp 124, 1990 ➤ 6,
625*: ᴿZkT 113 (1991) 307s (R. *Oberforcher*).
7710 *Herik* N. J. van d., *Jong* K. W. de, Tot een volkomen verzoening van al
onze zonden?: GerefTTs 90 (1989) 146-158 [154, Greek terms].
7711 **Hoekema** Anthony A. †, Saved by grace 1989 ➤ 6,7723: ᴿInterpretation
45 (1991) 96.98 (D. W. *Hall*: his last book).
7712 **Hryniewicz** Wacław, ◉ Zarys... Sketch of Christian paschal theology, I.
Christ our Passover². [II. ◉ 1987 ➤ 4,4920]. Lublin 1987, KUL. 492 p. –
ᴿColcT 60,1 (1990) 172-4 (J. *Królikowski* ◉).
7713 **Joubert** Jacques, Le corps sauvé: CogF 161. P 1991, Cerf. 214 p. F 120.
– ᴿArTGran 34 (1991) 409s (A. S. *Muñoz*); Études 375 (1991) 426 (R.
Marlé: jeune audacieux).
7713* **Juárez** Armando, An evaluation of Edward HEPPENSTALL's [Adventist]
doctrine of redemption: diss. Andrews, ᴰ*La Rondelle* H. Berrien Springs
MI 1991. 308 p. 92-06263. – DissA 52 (1991s) 3322-A.
7714 *Kelly* Brian, Towards a theology of redemption: IrTQ 57 (1991) 173-184.
7715 **Kimme** August, Rechtfertigung und Heiligung in christologischer Sicht;
eine dogmatische Untersuchung 1989 ➤ 6,7726: ᴿTRu 56 (1991) 211-3
(R. *Saarinen*).
7715* **McGrath** Alister E., Iustitia Dei 1986 ➤ 3,7373... 6,7728: ᴿChH 59
(1990) 240s (J. R. *Sommerfeldt*); EvQ 63 (1991) 281-5 (T. *Lane*).
7716 **Mateljan** Ante, Il pensiero soteriologico nel primo ciclo teologico di
Jürgen MOLTMANN: diss. Pont. Univ. Gregoriana, ᴰ*O'Collins* G. Roma
1991. 422 p.; extr. Nᵒ 3788, 160 p. – RTLv 23, p. 554 [> DissA-C].
7717 *Müller* Gerhard L., Heiligung und Rechtfertigung: Catholica 40 (1990)
169-186.
7718 **Muller** Richard A., Christ and the decree; Christology and predes-
tination in Reformed theology from Calvin to Perkins 1986 ➤ 3,7378;
4,8756: ᴿJEH 42 (1991) 618-628 (P. *Lake* on 'Protestants, Puritans and
Laudians'); TR 87 (1991) 399s (W. H. *Neuser*).
7719 **Naduvilekut** James, Christus der Heilsweg; soteria als Theodrama in ...
BALTHASAR 1987 ➤ 4,8756*: ᴿActuBbg 28 (1991) 87s (J. *Boada*); ForumKT 7 (1991) 78s (M. *Lochbrunner*).
7720 **Pagenkemper** Karl E., An analysis of the rejection motif in the Synoptic
parables and its relationship to Pauline soteriology: diss. Dallas Theol.
Sem. 1990, ᴰ*Bock* D. 421 p. 91-25344. – DissA 52 (1991s) 969-A.

7721 *Remy* Gérard, La théologie de la médiation selon S. AUGUSTIN: RThom 91 (1991) 580-623.

7722 La salvezza oggi 1989 ➤ 5,735; 6,684: ᴿEstE 66 (1991) 92-96 (A. *Santos Hernández*).

Sanders John, No other name; an investigation into the destiny of the unevangelized 1991 ➤ 7286*.

7724 **Schwager** Raymund, Jesus im Heilsdrama; Entwurf einer biblischen Erlösungslehre 1990 ➤ 6,7742: ᴿREB 51 (1991) 987-9 (H. *Assmann*); TPQ 139 (1991) 311s (P. *Schäfer*, 'etwas unbefriedigt').

7725 **Sesboüé** Bernard, Jésus-Christ, l'unique Médiateur: JJC 33, 1988 ➤ 4, 8765 ... 6,7745: ᴿTLZ 116 (1991) 144-6 (R. *Schwager*).

7726 **Sesboüé** Bernard, Jesucristo, el único mediador; ensayos sobre la redención y la salvación, I. Problemática y relectura doctrinal [1988], ᵀ*Ortiz García* Alfonso: Koinonia 27. S 1990, Secr. Trinitario. 420 p. 84-85376-85-4. – ᴿActuBbg 28 (1991) 201s (J. *Boada*); Gregorianum 72 (1991) 774 (C. I. *González*); NRT 113 (1991) 891 (L. *Renwart*); ScripTPamp 23 (1991) 1015-8 (L. F. *Mateo-Seco*).

7727 **Steindl** Helmut, Genugtuung; biblisches Versöhnungsdenken – eine Quelle für ANSELMS Satisfaktionstheorie?: StFrib 71, 1989 ➤ 5,7729; 6,7747: ᴿETL 67 (1991) 185-7 (A. *Vanneste*).

7728 **Strong** Karen H., Redemption as a key to the nature of the Church and its social role in the theologies of Frederick D. MAURICE and William TEMPLE: diss. Drew, ᴰ*Pain* J. Madison NJ 1991. – RelStR 18,174.

7729 **Studer** Basil, Gott und unsere Erlösung 1985 ➤ 1,7290 ... 4,8768: ᴿBijdragen 52 (1991) 216 (M. *Parmentier*, Eng.).

7730 **Studer** B., Dieu sauveur [1985] ᵀ1989 ➤ 5,7731; 6,7748: ᴿÉTRel 66 (1991) 244s (J.-D. *Dubois*).

7731 **Swinburne** Richard, Responsibility and atonement 1989 ➤ 6,7749 (+ Ox, Clarendon, £27.50; pa. £10): ᴿJTS 42 (1991) 801-4 (C. *Gunton*: Anselmian assurance); Sapienza 44 (1991) 92-94 (G. *Turco*); Tablet 244 (1990) 112 (G. *Daly*, also on C. GUNTON, P. FIDDES).

Tambasco Anthony J., A theology of atonement and Paul's vision of Christianity 1991 ➤ 5209.

7732 **Tamez** Elsa, Contra toda condena; la justificación por la fe desde los excluidos. San José CR 1991, DEI. 196 p. – ᴿRLatAmT 8 (1991) 211s (X. *Alegre*).

7733 *Tamez* Elsa, Justificación por la fe y vida amenazada de los pobres; ensayo de reconstrucción teológica: RLatAmT 8 (1991) 71-89.

7733* *Templeton* Elizabeth, The Church's task in reconciliation: TLond 94 (1991) 327-332.

7734 *Trowitzsch* Michael, Gesetz, Evangelium und Rechtfertigung bei Albrecht PETERS: TRu 56 (1991) 185-191.

7735 *Ullrich* Lothar, ❷ Modele soteriologiczne w historii dogmatów, ᵀ*Humeński* Julian: Bobolanum 1 (1990) 102-121.

7736 **Werbick** Jürgen, Soteriologie: LeitfadenT 16. Dü 1990, Patmos. 277 p. DM 28,80. 3-491-77924-3. – ᴿHerdKorr 45 (1991) 145 (U. *Ruh*); TGL 81 (1991) 501 (W. *Beinert*); TsTNijm 31 (1991) 338 (N. *Schreurs*).

7737 **Wheeler** David L., A relational view of the atonement; prolegomenon to a reconstruction of the doctrine: AmerUnivSt 7/54, 1989; ᴿTsTNijm 31 (1991) 337s (N. *Schreurs*).

7738 **White** Vernon, Atonement and incarnation; an essay on universalism and particularity. C 1991, Univ. ix-134 p. $34.50; pa. $12. 0-521-40031-7 [TDig 39,89].

H7.2   *Crux, sacrificium;*   **The Cross; the nature of sacrifice.**

7739 **Antwi** Daniel J.,   Did Jesus consider his death to be an atoning sacrifice?:   Interpretation 45 (1991) 17-28.

7740 **Artola** A. M.,   El morir de Cristo y su participación mística; estudios sobre la espiritualidad de la Pasión.   Bilbao 1990, D-Brouwer. 260 p. – ᴿArTGran 54 (1991) 401s (E. *Moore*).

7741 **Ashby** Godfrey,   Sacrifice, its nature and purpose 1988 ➤ 5,7743; 6,7761: ᴿNBlackf 71 (1990) 155-7 (K. *Grayston*).

7742 **Bader** Günter,   Symbolik des Todes Jesu [ANSELM]: UntTheol 25, 1988 ➤ 5,7744: ᴿNedTTs 45 (1991) 250s (J. W. van *Henten*).

7743 **Balmary** Marie,   Il sacrificio interdetto; Freud e la Bibbia [1986 ➤ 3, 7413], ᵀ*Savoldi* Fausto: Nuovi Saggi.   Brescia 1991, Queriniana.   323 p. Lit. 30.000.   88-399-0956-7.

7744 **Barbaglio** Giuseppe,   *a*) Dio violento? Letture delle scritture ebraiche e cristiane: Comm StB NS.. Assisi 1991, Cittadella;   307 p. 88-308-0466-6. – *b*) Gesù il giusto e la violenza [... GIRARD R.]: ➤ 535, Firmana 1 (1991s) 50-63.

7745 **Battaglia** Vincenzo,   Gesù crocifisso, Figlio di Dio: Spicilegium 30.   R 1991, Pont. Athenaeum Antonianum.   226 p. Lit. 30.000. – ᴿNRT 113 (1991) 892s (L. *Renwart*).

7746 **Bourassa** François,   Redenzione e sacrificio.   Vaticano 1989, Editrice. 238 p. Lit. 36.000. – ᴿDivinitas 35 (1991) 295s (D. *Vibrac*).

7747 **Cousar** Charles B.,   A theology of the Cross; the death of Jesus in the Pauline letters: OvBT 1990 ➤ 6,7765: ᴿNeotestamentica 25 (1991) 442-4 (S. P. *Botha*).

7748 *a*) **Dalferth** Ingolf U.,   Die soteriologische Relevanz der Kategorie des Opfers; dogmatische Erwägungen im Anschluss an die gegenwärtige exegetische Diskussion ['eher versteckt als veröffentlicht' in ᶠ*Jüngel* E. 1984; über GESE H., HENGEL M...., GIRARD R., SCHENKER A., SCHWAGER R.]; – *b*) *Wassermann* Christoph, Biblische Sühnetheologie im Kontext eines Weltbildes der Modernen Physik [... GESE H., JANOWSKI B.]; – *c*) *Stuhlmacher* Peter, Cilliers BREYTENBACHs Sicht von Sühne und Versöhnung [WM 60,1989 ➤ 5,7696*]: ➤ 310, JbBT 6 (1991) 173-194 / 195-211 / 339-354.

7749 *Daly* Robert J.,   *a*) The power of sacrifice in ancient Judaism and Christianity: Journal of Ritual Studies 4,2 (Pittsburgh 1990) [< ZIT 91,131]; – *b*) Sacrificio en ORÍGENES y AGUSTÍN; semejanzas y diferencias, ᵀ*Anoz* José: ➤ 540, AugM 36 (1991) 67-73

7750 **Deneken** Michel,   Le salut par la croix dans la théologie contemporaine (1930-1985): Thèses, 1988 ➤ 6,7766: ᴿDivinitas 34 (1990) 297s (D. *Vibrac*: inacceptable; fond aberrant): ScEsp 43 (1991) 252-5 (M. *Gourgues*).

7751 *a*) **Dragas** George D.,   St. ATHANASIUS on Christ's sacrifice; – *b*) *Bonner* Gerald, The doctrine of sacrifice; AUGUSTINE and the Latin patristic tradition; – *c*) *Gelston* A., Sacrifice in the early East Syrian eucharistic tradition: ➤ 384, Sacrifice 1991, 73-100 / 101-117 / 118-125.

7751* **Galot** Jean,   Perché la croce?: CC 142 (1991,1) 549-559.

7752 **Girard** René,   A violência e o sagrado [1972 ➤ 58,7916], ᵀ1990, Paz e Terra / UNESP [REB 51,743].

7753 **Girard** R., Der Sündenbock [1982 ➤ 63,6898], ^T*Mainberger-Ruh* Elisabeth. Z 1988, Benziger. 303 p. – ^RLebZeug 44 (1989) 68 (J. *Splett*).

7754 **Girard** René, Wat vanaf het begin der tijden verborgen was (Mt 13,35) [1978 ➤ 58,7797],^T Kampen/Kapellen 1990, Kok/Pelckmans. 527 p. *f*95. 90-242-7633-0 / 90-289-1320-3. – ^RCollatVL 21 (1990) 322s (E. van *Waelderen*); TsTNijm 31 (1991) 114s (A. *Lascaris*).

7755 — *a*) The God of victims; René GIRARD and the future of religion: RelEdn 86,3 (1991) 399...; – *b*) **Dunne** John S., The peace of the present; an unviolent way of life [...conversation with R. GIRARD]. ND 1991, Univ. xii-140 p. $20 [RelStR 18,41, J. *Nilson*].

7756 *Giraudo* Cesare, La Croce e il 'Legno della relazione'; saggio di inculturazione teologica alla Costa-Est del Madagascar: RasT 32 (1991) 115-143.

7756* ^E**Grottanelli** C., *Parise* N. F., Sacrificio e società nel mondo antico 1983/8: ➤ 5,790*; 6,7773: ^RLatomus 50 (1991) 907-9 (Dominique *Briquel*).

7757 **Hengel** Martin, Crocifissione ed espiazione [1976 ➤ 58,6229], ^T. Brescia 1988, Paideia. 240 p. – ^RAsprenas 38 (1991) 249-251 (A. *Rolla*); Henoch 13 (1991) 120s (Ariella *Boffi*).

7758 *Hoegger* Martin, Le festin des noces de l'Agneau; éclairage biblique sur la notion de sacrifice: Hokhma 40 (1989) 3-16.

7759 **Hughes** Dennis D., Human sacrifice in ancient Greece [diss. 1985, Ohio State – OIAc 1,18]. L 1991, Routledge. xiv-301 p. 0-415-03483-3.

7760 *Jean-Nesmy* Claude, Américains et anglais [dans la littérature] devant le sacrifice: EsprVie 101 (1991) 593-602.

7760* *Jensen* Gordon A., D. J. HALL's use of LUTHER's Theologia crucis: TorJT 7 (1991) 196-210.

7761 **Kasirye-Musoke** Alex B., Ritual sacrifice among the Baganga; its meaning and implication for African Anglican eucharistic theology: diss. St. Michael, ^D*Slater* P. Toronto 1991. 323 p. – RTLv 23, p. 564.

7762 *Lathrop* Gordon W., JUSTIN, Eucharist and 'Sacrifice': a case of metaphor: Worship 64 (1990) 30-48.

7763 *a*) *Malieckal* Louis, Sacrifice, core of Vedic religion and Christianity; – *b*) *Thachil* Jose, Theology of religions and sacrifice: JDharma 14 (1989) 313-328 / 329-342.

7764 *Padovese* L., Lo scandalo de la Croce; la polemica anticristiana nei primi secoli 1988 ➤ 5,7768: ^REstFranc 91 (1990) 349s (F. *Raurell*).

7765 **Palaver** Wolfgang, Politik und Religion bei Thomas HOBBES; eine Kritik aus der Sicht der Theorie René GIRARDs: InnTSt 53. Innsbruck 1991, Tyrolia. 386 p. [RelStR 18,214, J. G. *Williams*].

7766 **Rey** Bernard, Nous prêchons un Messie crucifié 1989 ➤ 5,7769; 6,7788: ^RAngelicum 68 (1991) 561s (G. M. *Salvati*); Gregorianum 72 (1991) 581s (J. E. *Vercruysse*); MélSR 48 (1991) 189s (L. *Derousseaux*); NBlackf 71 (1990) 407s (L. G. *Walsh*); ScEsp 43 (1991) 247-9 identique à 357-9 (J.-Y. *Thériault*).

7767 *Restle* J., al., Kreuz..., -igung: ➤ 681, LexMA 5 (1991) 1489-1508 [N.B. 1506 'Kreuzweg' nur bivium (magisch); nichts über die Andacht].

7768 *Ries* J., *Mathon* G., Sacrifice: ➤ 664, Catholicisme XIII,96 (1991) 363-375 (373-5 sur GIRARD R.) -425.

7769 *Root* Michael, Alister MCGRATH on cross and justification: Thomist 54 (1990) 705-725.

7770 **Rulleau** Jean-Marc, Le sacrifice. Bulle, Suisse 1990, Tradiffusion. 69 p. – ^REsprVie 101 (1991) 302s (P. *Jay*).

7771 *Rupp* Walter, Zur Theologie der Passionsspiele: StiZt 208 (1990) 326-332.
7772 **Salvati** G. M., Teologia trinitaria della Croce. T 1987, Elle Di Ci. 216 p. – ᴿAnnTh 5 (1991) 207-212 (L. *Clavell*).
7773 **Schalkewijk** Harry van, Kruisen, een studie over het gebruik van kruistekens ['sign(s) of the cross'] in de ontwikkeling van het godsdienstig en maatschappelijk leven. Hilversum ᴰ1989, Gooi & S. 362 p. ƒ55. 90-304-0486-8. – ᴿBijdragen 52 (1991) 106 (J. G. *Hahn*: uiterst leesbaar).
7774 **Schwarzenau** Paul, Das Kreuz; die Geheimlehre Jesu. Stu 1990, Kreuz. 213 p. – ᴿTGL 81 (1991) 127-9 [R. *Geisen*: empfehlenswertes ev. Plädoyer für die alte Gnosis].
7775 **Song** C. S., Jesus, the crucified people: The Cross in the Lotus World 1. NY 1990, Crossroad. 239 p. $17 [RelStR 18,40, R. H. *Drummond*: good].
7776 *Stern* Jacob, Scapegoat narratives in HERODOTUS: Hermes 119 (1991) 304-311.
7777 **Surgy** Albert de, De l'universalité d'une forme africaine du sacrifice. P 1988, CNRS. 286 p. F 120. – ᴿHistRel 30 (1990s) 427-9 (V. *Valeri*).
7778 **Todd** Kenneth K., Sacrifice; its meaning and special problems, with particular reference to early Rabbinic, early Christian, and Greco-Roman traditions: diss. ᴰ*Bolle* K., UCLA 1991. 308 p. – DissA 52 (1991s) 1383-A.
7779 **Williams** James, The Bible, violence, and the sacred; liberation from the myth of sanctioned violence [p. 31 'to weave a tapestry of biblical texts' in support of GIRARD]. SF 1991, Harper & R. xiii-288 p. [Bulletin CoV&R 2, 8-10, R. G. *Hamerton-Kelly*].
7780 *Young* Brad, The Cross, Jesus and the Jewish people: → 54, ᶠFLUSSER D., Immanuel 24s (1990) 23-34.

H7.4 Sacramenta, Gratia.

7781 Baptism, Eucharist & Ministry [1982] 1990 F&Order 149. Geneva 1990, WCC. viii-160 p. Fs 16. – ᴿTLZ 116 (1991) 622s (C. *Hinz*).
7781* **Blanchette** Claude, Pénitence et eucharistie; dossier d'une question controversée: Recherches NS 21, 1989 → 5.7783; 6,7799: ᴿRTLv 22 (1991) 100-2 (A. *Haquin*).
7782 *Borgen* Ole E., No end without the means; John WESLEY and the sacraments: AsburyTJ 46,1 (1991) 63-85.
7783 **Brooks** Oscar S., The drama of decision; Baptism in the NT 1987 → 5,7785: ᴿCritRR 3 (1990) 189-191 (J. R. *Michaels*); SWJT 33,3 (1990s) 52 (D. K. *Trimble*).
7784 *Caspani* Pierpaolo, La confermazione nel BEM: ScuolC 118 (1990) 131-152 (-163, *Caprioli* Adriano).
7785 **Cenzon** Santos M. A., Baptismal ecclesiology of St. Augustine: diss. S. Croce. R 1990. xii-370 p. – ᴿAnnTh 5 (1771) 410-4 (F. *Mendoza Ruiz*).
7786 *Chauvet* Louis-Marie, Simbolo e sacramento; una rilettura sacramentale dell'esistenza cristiana [1987 → 4,8813],ᵀ. T-Leumann 1990, LDC. 390 p. Lit. 30.000. – ᴿCC 142 (1991,4) 201s (G. *Ferraro*).
7787 *Chauvet* L.-M., Sacrements: → 664, Catholicisme XIII,96 (1991) 326-361.
7788 *Clerck* Paul de, [*al.*], Un seul baptême? Le baptême des adultes et celui des petits enfants: Mais-D 185 (1991) 7-33 [-130].
7789 *Craycraft* Kenneth R., Sign and word; M. LUTHER's theology of the sacraments: RestQ 32 (Abilene 1990) 143-164 [< ZIT 90,602]. – ᴿTorJT 7 (1991) 252s (M. *Downey*) & 253 (J. *Wiseman*) & 254s (Joann *Wolski*); 255-7 reply.

7790 **Dreyer** Elizabeth,   Manifestations of grace: Glazier Theology & Life 29. Collegeville MN 1990, Liturgical.   viii-246 p. $16.   0-89453-759-8 [TDig 38,365].

7791 ᴱ**Dudley** Martin, *Rowell* Geoffrey,   Confession and absolution.   L 1990, SPCK.   212 p.   £10.   0-281-04442-2. – ᴿExpTim 102 (1990s) 157 (J. *Frederick*: biblical basis for proximately Anglican practice).

7792 *Elberti* Arturo,   Accipe signaculum doni Spiritus Sancti; la Confermazione fonte del sacerdozio regale dei fedeli?:   Gregorianum 72 (1991) 491-512; franç. 513.

7793 **Fugel** Adolf,   Tauflehre und Taufliturgie bei H. ZWINGLI: Diss. Fr[?S] 1989 ➤ 6,7816;   524 p.:   ᴿTZBas 47 (1991) 286s (A. *Ehrensperger*).

7794 **Gaboriau** Florent,   Chrétiens confirmés 1988 ➤ 4,8816*; 5,7798:   ᴿDivThom 93 (1990) 151-3 (B. *Ardura*).

7795 **Ganoczy** Alexandre,   Aus seiner Fülle... Gnadenlehre 1989 ➤ 5,7799; 6,7817:   ᴿBogVest 50 (1990) 340-3 (C. *Sorč*); ColcT 60,4 (1990) 183-5 (L. *Balter*, ❷).

7796 **Ganoczy** Alexandre,   De su plenitud todos hemos recibido; la doctrina de la gracia, ᵀ*Gancho* Claudio: BtHerderTF 192.   Barc 1991, Herder. 405 p.   pt. 2500.   84-254-1716-3. – ᴿActuBbg 28 (1991) 195s (J. *Boada*); ArTGran 54 (1991) 407s (C. *Granado*); NatGrac 38 (1991) 396 (A. *Villalmonte*); REspir 50 (1991) 699 (G. *Turiño*); TEspir 35 (1991) 498s (M. *Gelabert*); TVida 32 (1991) 343s (Anneliese *Meis*).

7797 **Groen** Basilius J.,   'Ter genezing van ziel en lichaam'; de viering van het oliesel in de Grieks-Orthodoxe Kerk: kath. Diss. Nijmegen, ᴰ*Aalst* A. J, van der. Kampen/Weinheim 1990, Kok/Dt.Stud.   xv-282 p. DM 54.   90-242-3220-1 / 3-89271-262-X [TR 87,347].

7798 **Holeton** David R.,   La communion des tout-petits enfants; étude du mouvement eucharistique en Bohème vers la fin du Moyen-Âge [diss. Sorbonne/Inst. Cath.]: EphLtg Subsidia 50.   R 1989, Centro Ltg. Vincenziano.   323 p. Lit. 50.000. – ᴿJTS 42 (1991) 387-9 (K. *Stevenson*).

7799 **Hotz** Robert,   Los sacramentos en nuevas perspectivas [... ortodoxa] 1986 ➤ 4,8822; 5,7804:   ᴿEstE 66 (1991) 337-344 (J. L. *Larrabe*, A. *Simon*: 'la riqueza sacramental de Oriente y Occidente').

7800 **Kavanagh** Aidan,   Confirmation 1988 ➤ 4,8825; 5,7806:   ᴿMaisD 185 (1991) 134s (P. De *Clerck*).

7801 **Klauck** Hans-J.,   Gemeinde – Amt – Sakrament 1989 ➤ 5,292; 6,7830: ᴿWissWeish 52 (1989) 86s (H. *Rusche*).

7802 **Kleinheyer** Bruno,   Die Feiern der Eingliederung in die Kirche: Gottesdienst der Kirche, Handbuch der Liturgiewissenschaft 7/1/1.   Rg 1989, Pustet.   266 p. – ᴿMaisD 185 (1991) 131-3 (P. de *Clerck*: prestigieuse collection, 5 volumes parus depuis 1983].

7803 **Kranemann** Benedikt,   Die Krankensalbung in der Zeit der Aufklärung; Ritualien und pastoralliturgische Studien im deutschen Sprachgebiet: LQF 72, ᴰ1990 ➤ 6,7831:   xl-440 p. – ᴿTLZ 116 (1991) 868s (H.-C. *Piper*); TR 87 (1991) 312-4 (M. *Probst*); TsTNijm 31 (1991) 200s (G. *Lukken*).

7804 *Lahidalga Aguirre* J. M. de,   Antropología científica y matrimonio cristiano: Lumen 39 (1990) 36-52.

7805 *Laporte* Jean-Marc,   Patience and power; grace for the First World. NY 1988, Paulist.   iv-297 p. $15 pa. – ᴿHorizons 18 (1991) 161s (M. J. *McGinniss*); TorJT 7 (1991) 141-3 (D. *Donovan*).

7806 *Larchet* Jean-Claude,   Le baptême selon Saint MAXIME le Confesseur: RevSR 65 (1991) 51-70.

7807 **Larrabe** J. L., Bautismo y confirmación, sacramentos de iniciación cristiana. M 1989, NS Covadonga. 382 p. – ᴿNRT 113 (1991) 587 (L. *Renwart*).

7808 **Lawler** Michael G., Symbol and sacrament 1987 ➤ 4,8827*... 6,7832: ᴿHeythJ 32 (1991) 90-92 (Mary *Grey*); IrTQ 57 (1991) 244s (E. *Cullinan*); ScotJT 44 (1991) 271s (D. J. *Kennedy*).

7809 *Leussen* Lambert, Confirmation; status quaestionis with an overview of the literature: QLtg 70 (1989) 1-21; franç. 21; bibliog. 23-28 [*al.* 29-125].

7810 **Lies** Lothar, Sakramententheologie; eine personale Sicht 1990 ➤ 6,7833: ᴿNRT 113 (1991) 262 (L. *Renwart*); TS 52 (1991) 361-3 (L. *Örsy*); ZkT 113 (1991) 321s (H. B. *Meyer*).

7811 **López-González** Pedro, Penitencia y reconciliación; estudio histórico-teológico de la 'res et sacramentum': Eunsa Teológica 64, 1990 ➤ 6,7836: ᴿScripTPamp 23 (1991) 320-3 (J. L. *Lorda*).

McDonnell Kilian, *Montague* George T., Christian initiation and baptism in the Holy Spirit; evidence from the first eight centuries 1991 ➤ 7536.

7813 **Mackin** Theodore, The marital sacrament: Marriage in the Catholic Church. NY 1989, Paulist. xi-701 p. $25. 0-8091-3055-6 – ᴿTLZ 116 (1991) 871-3 (H. *Kirchner*).

7814 **Malnati** Ettore, I segni della fede; teologia dei sacramenti. Trieste 1990, LINT. – ᴿCC 142 (1991,4) 627s (G. *Ferraro*).

7815 *Marafioti* Domenico, La grazia, rapporto tra Dio e l'uomo nell'amore: CC 142 (1991,3) 243-255.

7816 **Marlé** René, La Confirmation; devenir adulte dans la foi: Première BtRel. P 1990, Marne. 64 p. – ᴿRThom 91 (1991) 166s (G.-M. *Marty*).

7817 *Mertens* Herman-Emiel, *a)* Natur und Gnade; ihre Entwicklung in der katholischen Theologie des 20. Jahrhunderts: ZdialekT 6 (1990s) 21-40 [< ZIT 90,703]. – *b)* Nature and grace in twentieth-century Catholic theology: LvSt 16 (1991) 242-262.

7818 **Martos** Joseph, Doors to the sacred; a historical introduction to sacraments in the Catholic Church²ʳᵉᵛ [¹1981 ➤ 62,7714]. Tarrytown NY 1991, Triumph. xix-468 p. $16 pa. [CBQ 54,204].

7819 *Martos* Joseph, Sacraments in the 1980s; a review of the books in print: Horizons 18 (1991) 130-142.

7820 **Moos** Alois, Das Verhältnis von Wort und Sakrament in der deutschsprachigen katholischen Theologie des 20. Jahrhunderts: kath. Diss. Mainz 1991, ᴰ*Schneider*. – TR 87 (1991) 519.

7821 *Moysa* Stefan, ❷ O znaczeniu... Significance of frequent confession: Bobolanum 2 (1991) 7-27; franç. 157.

7822 *Nocent* Adrien, La confirmation; questions posées aux théologiens et aux pasteurs: Gregorianum 72 (1991) 689-703; Eng. 704.

7823 **Ofrasio** Timoteo José M., The baptismal font, a study of patristic and liturgical texts: diss. S. Anselmo, Nᵒ 149, ᴰ*Ghupungco* A. R 1990, Pont. Athenaeum S. Anselmi. x-186 p.

7824 **Osborne** Kenan B., Reconciliation and justification; the sacrament and its theology 1990 ➤ 6,7843: ᴿHorizons 18 (1991) 159s (M. G. *Lawler*); NewTR 4,1 (1991) 96 (M. R. *Francis*); TS 52 (1991) 363-5 (C. J. *Peter*).

7825 **Piolanti** Antonio, I sacramenti³ʳᵉᵛ Vaticano 1990 ➤ 6,7846; Lit. 45.000: ᴿDivinitas 34 (1990) 286-290 (R. M. *Schmitz*) & 35 (1991) 177-181 (M. L. *Ciappi*).

7826 **Saint-Roch** Patrick, La pénitence dans les Conciles et les lettres des papes des origines à la mort de GRÉGOIRE le Grand: StAntCr 46. R 1991, Pont. Ist. di Archeologia Cristiana. 182 p. 88-85991-04-1.

7827 **Salacha(s)** Demetrios, ☉ *Mystēria/myēseōs* ... The mysteries of Christian
initiation in the new R.C. Code, 1989 ➤ 6,7853: ᴿTAth 61 (1991)
329-331 (E.A. *Theodorou*, ☉).

7828 **Saraiva Martins** J., I sacramenti della Nuova Alleanza 1987 ➤ 3,7498 ...
6,7855: ᴿAnnTh 4 (1990) 184-6 = 5 (1991) 424-7 (A. *Blanco*).

7829 *Saxer* Victor, Les rites de l'initiation chrétienne du IIᵉ au VIᵉ siècle;
esquisse historique et signification d'après leurs principaux témoins: Studi
Alto Medioevo 7, 1988 ➤ 6,7856: ᴿMaisD 185 (1991) 133s (P. *De
Clerck*).

7830 *Schilson* Arno, Symbolwirklichkeit und Sakrament; ein Literaturbericht:
LtgJb 40 (1990) 26-52.

7831 ᵀᴱ**Schmitz** Josef, AMBROSIUS Mediolanensis, De sacramentis / De
mysteriis: Fontes Christiani 3. FrB 1990, Herder. 289 p. – ᴿColcT 61,4
(1991) 205-208 (W. *Myszor*, ❷).

7831* **Smith** Thomas A., De gratia; Faustus of RIEZ's treatise on grace and
its place in the history of theology. ND 1990, Univ. 254 p. – ᴿAugSt 22
(1991) 207-216 (Marianne *Djuth*: continues Gustav WEIGEL 1938 on
Gallic reaction to AUGUSTINE).

7832 *Sorč* Ciril, Baptism as new birth (in Slovene): BogVest 50 (1990)
367-383; Eng. 381.

7833 **Tambling** Jeremy, Confession, sexuality, sin, the subject. Manchester
1990, Univ. vii-215 p. £30; pa. £9. – ᴿTLond 94 (1991) 381s (Mary Ann
Coate).

7833* **Turner** Paul, The meaning and practice of confirmation: AmerUnivSt
7/31. NY 1987, Lang. 358 p. – ᴿIrénikon 64 (1991) 144 (E. *Lanne*).

7834 **Vianney** Peter J., Sacrament of Christian initiation, as Christ's saving act
made present in the ecclesial community... Sacrosanctum Concilium II
Vat.: diss. Fordham, ᴰ*Babos* S. NY 1991. – RelStR 18 (1991) 171.

7835 *Voicu* Sever J., Textes peu connus concernant l'onction prébaptismale:
Irénikon 64 (1991) 468-481, Eng. 482.

7836 **Vorgrimler** Herbert, Teología de los Sacramentos ᵀ 1989 ➤ 6,7863:
ᴿAugM 35 (1990) 194 (J.A. *Galindo*); LumenVr 39 (1990) 450s (U. *Gil
Ortega*).

7837 **Walsh** Liam, The sacraments of initiation: Theology Library 7. L 1988,
Chapman. xii-317 p. – ᴿMilltSt 28 (1991) 159s (R. *Moloney*).

7838 *Zappella* Luciano, 'Élaion-Myron'; l'olio dello Spirito Santo nelle
catechesi battesimali di Cirillo di Gerusalemme: CrNSt 11 (1990) 5-26;
Eng. 27.

H7.6   *Ecclesiologia, theologia missionis, laici –* **The Church.**

7839 **Alberigo** Giuseppe, La Chiesa nella storia: BtCuRel 51, 1988 ➤ 5,7836:
ᴿRHist 283 (1990) 125-8 (M. *Pagaut*).

7840 *Antón* Ángel, A eclesiologia católica nos séculos XIX e XX: Brotéria
131 (1990) 80-94.

7841 **Atkins** Robert A. ᴶ, Egalitarian community, ethnography & exegesis.
Tuscaloosa 1991, Univ. Alabama. xxi-259 p. $25 [CBQ 54,201].

7842 **Banazak** Gregory A., The ecclesiology of VASCO DE QUIROGA: diss.
Pont. Univ. Gregoriana, ᴰ*Füllenbach* J. Roma 1991. 497 p.; extr. Nº
3744, 152 p. – RTLv 23, p. 564 [> DissA-C].

7843 *Beinert* Wolfgang, *a)* Die alleinseligmachende Kirche, oder: Wer kann
gerettet werden?: StiZt 208 (1990) 75-85. 264-278; – *b)* Who can be
saved?, ᵀᴱ*Asen* B., TDig 38 (1991) 223-8. Extra ecclesiam nulla salus,

first with ORIGEN, more recently understood with CYPRIAN and BO-
NIFACE VIII.

7844 *Bellah* Robert N., The role of the Church in a changing society: Curr-
TMiss 17 (1990) 181-191.

7845 **Bermejo** Luis M., Church, conciliarity, and communion: Jesuit Theological Forum X, 4. Anand 1990, Gujarat-SP. xii-361 p. $12; pa. $10
[TDig 38,149].

7846 **Blanc** Philippe, L'Église, mystère trinitaire et sacrement du salut; étude de l'ecclésiologie de Charles JOURNET: diss. Pont. Univ. Gregoriana,
ᴰ*Antón* A. R 1991. 290 p. – RTLv 23, p. 565 [> DissA-C].

7846* **Blasetti** Lorenzo, La Chiesa immagine dell'uomo [... immagine di Dio];
Il massimo della diversità per il massimo della comunione. Assisi 1989,
Cittadella. 168 p. Lit. 16.000. – ᴿCC 142 (1991,1) 630s (P. *Vanzan*).

7847 **Blázquez** Ricardo, La Iglesia del Concilio Vaticano II, 1988 ➤ 5,7842;
6,7875*: ᴿLumenVr 39 (1990) 88s (U. *Gil Ortega*).

7848 *a) Blocher* Henri, L'essence de l'Église; – *b) Wells* Paul, L'unité vivante
de l'Église: RRéf 41,2 (1990) 9-16 / 17-30.

7849 **Bordas Belmonte** Antoni, La missio de l'esglesia segons J. BALMES
(1810-1848): diss. Fac. Teol. Catalunya, ᴰ*Pou* R. – Barc 1991. 190 p. –
RTLv 23, p. 568.

7850 *Borras* Alphonse, *a)* L'Église peut-elle encore punir?: NRT 113 (1991)
205-218; – *b)* Prêtres et laïcs dans une communauté à construire: EsprVie
101 (1991) 145-150.

7851 **Bosch** David J., Transforming mission; paradigm shifts in theology
of mission: AmSocMiss 16. Mkn 1991, Orbis. xix-587 p. $45; pa.
$25. 0-88344-744-4; -19-3 [TDig 38,349]. – ᴿMissiology 19 (1991) 153-
160 (J. A. *Scherer*); PrPeo 5 (1991) 478 (R. *Esteban*: high praise).

7852 ᶠBOSCH David J., 60th b., Symposium S. Afr. Miss. Soc. 1990, Mission in creative tension, ᴱKritzinger J. N. J., *Saayman* W. A. 1990
➤ 6,579: ᴿVerbumSVD 32 (1991) 207-210 (F. *Mansfield*).

7853 ᴱBost Hubert, Genèse et enjeux de la laïcité [Montpellier 2-3.III.1990]:
Le Champ Éthique 18. Genève 1990, Labor et Fides. 228 p. 2-8309-
0614-4. – ᴿGregorianum 72 (1991) 578s (J. *Joblin*).

7854 **Braxton** Edward K., The faith community; one, holy, catholic and apostolic. ND 1990, Ave Maria. 196 p. $8 pa. 0-87793-437-1 [TDig 38,151].

7855 *Brueggemann* Walter, Rethinking Church models through Scripture:
TTod 48 (1991s) 128-138.

7856 *a) Bux* Nicola, Unità e conciliaritá della chiesa universale nelle chiese
particolari; – *b) Tillard* Jean-Marie R., Rome dans la communion des
églises locales: ➤ 526, Nicolaus 1989/91, 161-174 / 117-139.

7857 ᴱCazelles Henri, Unité et diversité dans l'Église 1988/9 ➤ 6,520:
ᴿRTLv 22 (1991) 550s (A. de *Halleux*).

7858 *Chantraine* Georges, Synodalité, expression du sacerdoce commun et du
sacerdoce ministériel? [... glissement du terme collégialité à partir de
1970]: NRT 113 (1991) 340-362.

7858* ᴱChauvet P., *al.*, Sacerdoce des baptisés; sacerdoce des prêtres; textes
de l'antiquité chrétienne, de Tertullien à Pierre Damien: Les Pères dans la
foi 46. P 1991, Migne. 176 p. F 85 [NRT 114,783, A. *Harvengt*].

7859 *Chiesa e missioni* (Urbaniana) 1990 ➤ 6,588: ᴿEstE 66 (1991) 349-351
(J. *Alonso Díaz*).

7860 *Collet* Giancarlo, Mission und Kommunikation; zum Beitrag von Missionswissenschaft für die Gegenwärtigkeit der Theologie: ZMissRW 74
(1990) 1-19.

7861 *De Virgilio* Giuseppe, La *ekklēsía* come 'società alternativa'; ricezione dell'opera di G. LOHFINK [Wie hat Jesus Gemeinde gewollt? 1982]: RivB 39 (1991) 467-475.

7862 *Dhavamony* Mariasusai, La visione cristocentrica della missione nella 'Redemptoris missio': RasT 32 (1991) 347-368.

7862* **Donovan** Daniel, The Church as idea and fact: Zacchaeus 1988 ➤ 4,8900: ᴿHorizons 18 (1991) 156 (P. D. *Molnar*: excellent introduction); RExp 88 (1991) 487s (Molly *Marshall-Green*, also on the other first three books of the series).

7863 **Donovan** Vincent J., The Church in the midst of creation [... no longer just West-European, since RAHNER and Vatican II]. Mkn 1989, Orbis. xi-169 p. £8. – ᴿNBlackf 71 (1990) 511-3 (Cecily *Boulding*).

7863* *a*) *Duarte Castillo* Raúl, Razón formal de la existencia de la Iglesia como Pueblo; un aspecto social-eclesiológico; – *b*) *Gasperin* Mario de, Anotaciones sobre la eclesiología posconciliar: ➤ 542, EfMex 9,2 (1992) 171-180 / 195-202.

7864 **Dulles** Avery, The reshaping of Catholicism; current challenges to the theology of the Church 1988 ➤ 4,183; 5,7862: ᴿCritRR 4 (1991) 436-8 (F. C. *Kirkpatrick*: nothing about relevant CURRAN); RelStT 10,2 (1990) 75-77 (D. *Donovan*); Thomist 55 (1991) 156-160 (T. *Hughson*).

7865 *Dylus* Franciszek, ❷ Some aspects of the eschatology of the Church in the light of 'Lumen Gentium': RuBi 42 (1989) 349-358.

7866 **Edlinger** Franz, Ihr werdet mein Volk sein, und Ich werde euer Gott sein; für eine Kirche im Sinne des Evangeliums. Mattersburg-Katzelsdorf 1989, Tau. 119 p. Sch 140. – ᴿTPQ 139 (1991) 329s (F. *Kuntner*).

7867 **Elberti** Arturo, Il sacerdozio regale dei fedeli nei prodromi del Concilio Ecumenico Vaticano II (1903-1962) [diss. Pont. Ist. Liturgico, Roma]: AnGreg 254, 1989 ➤ 5,7864; 6,7885: ᴿWorship 64 (1990) 379-381 (T. A. *Krosnicki*).

7868 *Elliott* Mark, Methodism in the Soviet Union since World War II: AsburyTJ 46,1 (1991) 5-47.

7869 **Esselmann** Thomas E., The principle of functionality in ecclesiology [KÜNG, SCHILLEBEECKX, GUTIÉRREZ, MOLTMANN, RAHNER, GUSTAFSON]: diss. St. Michael's. Windsor 1990. 333 p. 0-315-60411-5 (DANN-60411). – DissA 52 (1991s) 3973-A.

7870 **Estrada** Juan Antonio, La identidad de los laicos; ensayo de eclesiología: BtT 2, 1990 ➤ 6,7686*. 84-285-1339-2. – ᴿActuBbg 28 (1991) 83 (J. I. *González Faus*).

7871 **Faivre** Alexandre, The emergence of the laity in the early Church 1990 ➤ 6,7887; ᴿPerspRelSt 18 (1991) 202s (E. G. *Hinson*).

7872 **Famerée** Joseph, Histoire et Église; l'ecclésiologie du Père CONGAR, de 'Chrétiens désunis' à l'annonce du Concile Vatican II (1937-1959): diss. ᴰ*Halleux* A. de. Louvain-la-Neuve 1991. xxxi-463 p. – ᴿTLv 22 (1991) 566s > RSPT 76,377-419.

7873 *a*) *Flanagan* Finbarr, Missionaries without Christ [?]; – *b*) *Kealy* Sean P., Is Jesus the future of mission?; – *c*) *Shorter* Aylward, Urbanization; today's missionary reality in Africa: AfER 32 (1990) 263-275 / 280-9 / 290-300.

7874 *a*) *Fowler* Bill G., The New Testament basis for the small church; – *b*) *Ray* David R., A theological biblical foundation for small churches: AmBapQ 9 (1990) 91-96 / 97-103 [< ZIT 90,586].

7875 **Gallo** Luis A., Una Chiesa a servizio degli uomini. T-Leumann 1982, LDC. 224 p. Lit. 15.000. 88-01-10172-5. – ᴿRivLtg 77 (1990) 213s (C. *Collo*).

7876 **Garijo-Guembe** Miguel M., Gemeinschaft der Heiligen; Grund, Wesen und Struktur der Kirche 1988 → 5,7871: ᴿColcT 60,4 (1990) 181-3 (L. *Balter*, ❷).

7877 *Giovanni Paolo II,* Lettera enciclica 'Redemptoris missio' circa la permanente validità del mandato missionario: CC 142 (1991,1) 255-284. 369-404. [441-443, ed. commento].

7878 *Glazik* Josef, Vor 25 Jahren, Missionsdekret 'Ad gentes'; Bemerkungen eines Augenzeugen des Konzils: ZMissRW 74 (1990) 257-274.

7879 *Görtz* Heinz-Jürgen, Das kirchliche Handeln des Laien; 'Christifideles Laici' im Kontext der 'Communio-Ekklesiologie' von 'Lumen Gentium': TPhil 66 (1991) 177-191.

7880 *Gräf* Hermann, Die Kirchenbezogenheit des christlichen Initiationsprozesses: VerbumSVD 32 (1991) 25-43 [3-24, The Church local and universal, RC-WCC document].

7880* **Grohs** Gerhard, *Czell* Gernot, Kirche in der Welt — Kirche der Laien? Fra 1990, Lembeck. 214 p. DM 28 [TLZ 117,780-2, W.-D. *Talkenberger*].

7881 ᴱ**Gunton** Colin E., *Hardy* Daniel W., On being the Church; essays on the Christian community 1989 → 5,468; 6,7896: ᴿRelStR 17 (1991) 145 (P. C. *Hodgson*: nothing on women).

7881* **Gurp** P. van, Kerk en zending in de theologie van Johannes C. HOEKENDIJK (1912-1975); een plaatsbepaling [diss.] Haarlem 1989, Aca Media. 367 p. ƒ39,50. 90-71646-04-1. – ᴿNedTTs 45 (1991) 157s (A. *Wind*).

7882 *Hammann* Gottfried, Les incidences ecclésiologiques de nos projets diaconaux: PosLuth 39 (1991) 102-111 [< ᴢɪᴛ 91,501].

Hammann Konrad, Ecclesia spiritualis 1989 → g481.

7882* **Hanson** Paul D., The people called 1986 → 2,6072 ... 6,7898: ᴿRRel 49 (1990) 635s (P. *Jurkowitz*).

7883 **Herbert** Karl, Kirche zwischen Aufbruch und Tradition; Entscheidungsjahre nach 1945. Stu 1989, Radius. 407 p. – ᴿEvT 50 (1990) 167-170 (W. *Kreck*).

7884 **Herbst** Michael, Missionarischer Gemeindeaufbau in der Volkskirche [→ 4,8866*]. Stu 1987, Calwer. 477 p. DM 48. – ᴿTZBas 47 (1991) 91s (W. *Neidhart*).

7885 *Hoffmann* Paul, Eine geschwisterliche Kirche [NT: Christliche Gemende/Kirche; das Zentrum von Verkündigung und Praxis Jesu ... Kritik an jedem sakral verstandenem Amt]: Orientierung 55 (1991) 165-7.

7887 **Hutchison** William R., Errand to the world 1987 → 4,8926; 5,7883: ᴿNesTR 12 (1991) 99-110 (H. *Badr*).

7888 *Jelenic* Josip, [Croatian] 'Redemptoris missio'; missionary activity of the Church and social changes in the world: ObnŽiv 46 (1991) 220-230; Eng. 230.

7889 *a) Joncheray* Jean, [Lc 10,50; 11,23 pour/contre] La diversité des rapports à l'Église; – *b) Vincent* Gilbert, Les marqueurs protestants de l'ecclésialité; – *c) Mottu* Henry, 'Christ existant comme communauté'; le sens de la formule du premier ouvrage de D. BONHOEFFER; – *d) Perrot* Charles, Des premières communautés aux églises constituées: → 535*, RechSR 79,2 (1991) 169-190 / 191-210 / 211-221 / 223-252; Eng. 166ss.

7890 **Kasper** Walter, Theology and Church 1989 → 6,255a: ᴿInterpretation 45 (1991) 210 (R. *Burke*).

7891 **Kasper** Walter, Teología y Iglesia 1989 → 6,7908: ᴿAugM 35 (1990) 400 (J. A. *Galindo*); LumenVr 39 (1990) 336 (A. M. *Navarro*).

7892 **Klein Goldewijk** B. M. J., Praktijk of principe; basisgemeenschappen en de ecclesiologie van Leonardo BOFF: diss. *DBieuwenhove* J. Van. Nijmegen 1991. 372 p. – TsTNijm 31,189; RTLv 23, p. 565.

7893 *Koch* Kurt, Communio und Missio; zur Mitverantwortung der Laien für die Kirche in ihrer Sendung: TPQ 139 (1991) 168-180.

7894 *Kolb* Erwin J., The primary mission of the Church and its detractors: ConcordTQ 54 (1990) 117-130 [< ZIT 91,136].

7894* **Koschorke** Klaus, Spuren der alten Liebe; Studien zum Kirchenbegriff des BASILIUS von Caesarea: Paradosis 32. FrS 1991, Univ. vii-403 p.

7895 **Kress** Robert, The Church; communion, sacrament, communication 1986 → 1,7494 ... 3,7633; $10. 0-8091-2663-X: *R*Gregorianum 72 (1991) 148s (J. *Dupuis*).

7896 **Laemmlin** Georg, Ekklesiologie als dogmatische Reflexion von Handlungssinn; SCHLEIERMACHERS 'Glaubenslehre' und die soziologische Modernisierung der protestantischen Dogmatik: Diss. *DHungar* K. Heidelberg 1990s. 285 p. – RTLv 23, p. 565.

7897 *La Soujeole* Benoit-Dominique de, L'Église comme société et l'Église comme communion au deuxième concile du Vatican: RThom 91 (1991) 219-258.

7898 **Legrand** Lucien, Unity and plurality; mission in the Bible, *TBarr* Robert R. Mkn 1990, Orbis. xv-189 p. $19. 0-88344-692-8 [TDig 38,366]. – *R*TTod 48 (1991s) 371 (M. *Arias*).

7899 **Leith** John H., The reformed imperative; what the Church has to say that no one else can say 1988 → 4,8943: *R*Interpretation 44 (1990) 211 (B. W. *Farley*); JRel 70 (1990) 647 (R. A. *Muller*).

7900 **Lennan** Richard, The dynamics of change; a study in the ecclesiology of Karl RAHNER: Diss. *DVass* G. Innsbruck 1991. 244 p. – RTLv 23, p. 565.

7901 *Liebster* Wolfram, Die Kirche als das Zwischenreich [EHRENBERG Hans 1920]: BTZ 8 (1991) 76-93.

7902 **Lienhard** Marc, L'Évangile et l'Église chez LUTHER 1989 → 5,7892 ['selon Luther']: *R*TZBas 47 (1991) 88s (K. *Hammer*).

7903 *Ludwisiak* Tomasz, ℗ Implikacje eklezjologiczne nauki o charyzmatach II Soboru Watykańskiego: Bobolanum 2 (1991) 45-53; franç. 157s.

7904 *Lynch* Patrick J., Servant ecclesiologies; a challenge to RAHNER's understanding of Church and world: IrTQ 57 (1991) 277-298.

7905 *McGrath* Alister E., Dogma und Gemeinde; zur sozialen Funktion des christlichen Dogmas: KerDo 37 (1991) 24-43; Eng. 43.

7906 **Manjaly** Antony, The ecclesiology of the St. Thomas Christians in India; a historico-theological study: diss. *DMichiels* R. Leuven 1990, xvii-363 p. – ETL 67 (1991) 213.

7907 *Marchesi* Giovanni, Cristo sì, chiesa no? Gesù, origine e fondamento della Chiesa: CC 142 (1991,3) 368-381.

7908 *Marranzini* Alfredo, Sulla genesi storica della 'Nota explicativa praevia' al cap. III della Costituzione sulla Chiesa [... diede ansa ad attacchi contro PAOLO VI nella stampa popolare; risposta chiesta dal Papa in CC 1965, *Caprile* G.]: RasT 32 (1991) 61-72.

7909 **Mask** E. Jeffrey, At liberty under God; a Baptist ecclesiology: diss. Emory, *DRunyon* T. Atlanta 1991. – RelStR 18,174.

7909* **Meier** Bertram, Die Kirche der wahren Christen; J. M. SAILERs Kirchenverständis zwischen Unmittelbarkeit und Vermittlung: MüKHSt 4. Stu 1990, Kohlhammer. 415 p. – *R*ExpTim 102 (1990s) 282 (P. N. *Brooks*); ForumKT 7 (1991) 79s (P. *Schäfer*).

7910 **Miller** Edward J., J.H. NEWMAN on the idea of Church 1987 ➤ 3,7653; 5,7899*: ᴿLvSt 15 (1990) 77-79 (T. *Merrigan*).

7911 **Moltmann** Jürgen, Kirche in Kraft des Geistes; ein Beitrag zur messianischen Ekklesiologie² [¹1975]. Mü 1989, Kaiser. – ᴿTsTKi 61 (1990) 231s (O. *Tjørhom*).

7911* **Monsegú** Bernardo, La Iglesia que Cristo quiso 1986 ➤ 3,7657 ... 6,7934: ᴿScripTPamp 23 (1991) 1064 (J.R. *Villar*).

7912 *Moody* Christopher, Apostolicity and the call of the Kingdom: TLond 94 (1991) 86-91.

7913 *Morris* Jeremy, Church and People [in an industrial city, WICKHAM E.] thirty-three years on; a historical critique: TLond 94 (1991) 92-101.

7913* **Muschalek** Georg, Kirche – noch heilsnotwendig? Über das Gewissen, die Empörung und das Verlangen² 1989 ➤ 6,7926: ᴿForumKT 7 (1991) 319s (L. *Scheffczyk*).

7914 *Nardi* G., Cristianesimo primitivo e realtà terrene; note per una teologia della laicità: Vivens Homo 2 (F 1991) 221-241.

7915 *Naurois* Louis de, Les équivoques de la laïcité; remarques d'un juriste français: BLitEc 92 (1991) 181-207; Eng. 208 [deals rather with the extension to 'sects' of the 'lay State's' non-interference in the domain of the 'Churches'].

7916 **Neckebrouck** V., De stomme duivelen; het anti-missionair syndroom in de westerse Kerk. Brugge 1990, Tabor. 211 p. Fb. 495. – ᴿCollatVL 21 (1991) 108s (H. *Hoet*).

7917 **Neuner** Peter, Der Laie und das Gottesvolk. Fra 1988, Knecht. 236 p. DM 32. – ᴿTR 87 (1991) 60s (K.J. *Lesch*).

7918 **Norman** Bruce R., Ecclesiology in dialogue; a critique of the understanding of the nature of the Church in the thought of G.C. BERKOUWER: diss. Andrews, ᴰ*Dederen* R. Berrien Springs MI 1991. 200 p. 92-06264. – DissA 52 (1991s) 3323-A.

7919 *Nuth* Joan M., Ecclesiology in NEWMAN's Apologia; a study in narrative theology: CCurr 40 (1990s) 228-255.

7920 **Nyquist** John W., The uses of the New Testament as illustrated in missiological themes within selected documents of the Second Vatican Council: diss. Trinity Evangelical Divinity School, ᴰ*Rommen* E. 1991. 240 p. 91-32989. – DissA 52 (1991s) 2172-A.

7921 **O'Connor** J.T., The gift of infallibility ... GASSER V. 1986 ➤ 2,6112: ᴿRelStR 16 (1990) 239 (J.T. *Ford*).

7921* **Pettifer** Julian, *Bradley* Richard, Missionaries. L 1990, BBC. 272 p. £17. – ᴿTLond 94 (1991) 51-53 (M.J. *Nazir-Ali*: a grand idea defectively realized).

7922 ᴱ**Pottmeyer** Hermann J., Kirche im Kontext der modernen Gesellschaft; zur Strukturfrage der römisch-katholischen Kirche 1988/9 ➤ 6,670*; DM 28: ᴿTPhil 66 (1991) 293 (R. *Sebott*); TPQ 139 (1991) 90s (J. *Singer*).

7922* *Poustooutov* Joseph, Point de vue orthodoxe sur la Mission aujourd'hui: Irénikon 64 (1991) 483-498; Eng. 498.

7923 **Raatz** Bettina, Kirche als Gestaltwerdung der Koinonia im Heiligen Geist; Aspekte einer ekklesiologischen Pneumatologie und deren Konsequenzen für einen geistlichen Gemeindeaufbau: Diss. Jena 1991, ᴰ*Seils*. – TLZ 117,233s; TR 87 (1991) 519.

7923* **Ratzinger** Joseph, Zur Gemeinschaft gerufen; Kirche heute verstehen. FrB 1991, Herder. 158 p. DM 22,80 [TLZ 117,796, H. *Kirchner*].

7924 ᴱ**Rémond** René, Nouveaux enjeux de la laïcité; 1989/90 ➤ 6,673: ᴿRTLv 22 (1991) 274 (G. *Thils*: POULAT montre la fabuleuse polysémie du terme 'laïcité').

7924* **Richard** Pablo, Death of Christendom and birth of the Church 1987 ➤ 3,7680: ᴿJeevadhara 21 (1991) 247 (J. B. *Chethimattam*).

7925 *Ritter* Adolf M., *Barth* Hans M., *Wintzer* Friedrich, Laie: ➤ 690, TRE 20 (1990) 378-385-393-399.

7926 *Rossignol* R., Evangelization is an ecclesial act: IndTSt 27 (1990) 321-332.

7927 **Sabra** George, Thomas AQUINAS, vision of the Church; fundamentals of an ecumenical ecclesiology: TüTSt 27. Mainz 1987, Grünewald. 206 p. – ᴿSalesianum 52 (1990) 908s (P. T. *Stella*).

7928 **Scanzillo** Ciriaco, La Chiesa sacramento di comunione; commento alla Lumen Gentium. N 1987, Dehoniane. 462 p. – ᴿDoctCom 42 (1989) 91s (L. *Bogliolo*).

7929 **Schillebeeckx** Edward, Church, the human story of God [neerl. etc. ➤ 7188], ᵀ*Bowden* J. NY 1991, Crossroad. xix-268 p. $23. – ᴿTablet 245 (1991) 645 (J. *Komonchak*); TLond 94 (1991) 458s (B. *Horne*); TS 52 (1991) 571-3 (F. M. *Jelly*).

7930 **Schneider** Johannes, In irdenen Gefässen; Auftrag und Amt der Kirche. Innsbruck 1989, Tyrolia. 152 p. DM 29. – ᴿTPQ 139 (1991) 91 (J. *Hörmandinger*).

7930* **Schönauer** Gerhard, Kirche lebt vor Ort; Wilhelm LÖHEs Gemeindeprinzip als Widerspruch gegen kirchliche Grossorganisation: TMg 16. Stu 1990, Calwer. 205 p. DM 68 [TLZ 117, 774-8, R. *Keller*].

7931 **Secondin** Bruno, I nuovi protagonisti; movimenti, associazioni, gruppi nella Chiesa. CinB 1991, Paoline. 254 p. [AtKap 118, 344, M. *Chmielewski*].

7932 **Sedgwick** Peter, Mission impossible? A theology of the local Church. L 1990, Collins Flame. 201 p. £7 pa. – ᴿTLond 94 (1991) 53s (W. *Carr*).

7933 **Senn** Felix, Orthopraktische Ekklesiologie? K. RAHNERs Offenbarungsverständnis und seine ekklesiologischen Konsequenzen im Kontext der neueren katholischen Theologiegeschichte [Diss. summa cum laude FrS 1988]: FreibZts ÖkBeih 19, 1989 ➤ 6,7946: ᴿActuBbg 28 (1991) 184s (J. *Boada*); Orientierung 55 (1991) 147s (K. *Fischer*).

7934 **Solomone** Kafoa A., The People of God in the Second Vatican Council; the biblical antecedents of the notion and its reception: diss. Leuven 1989, ᴰ*Schrijver* G. de. lv-533 p. – ETL 67 (1991) 213.

7935 *a) Song Choan-Seng,* Einen Ausweg aus der Sackgasse christlicher Mission finden; – *b) Houtepen* Anton, Die Einheit der Kirche als sakramentale Wirklichkeit; – *c) Hoedemaker* Bert, Einheit der Kirche im universalen Horizont: ➤ 160, ᶠVISCHER L., Ök. Theol. 1991, 92-113 / 256-275 / 291-310.

7935* **Sontag** A., La géographie des catholiques: Parcours. P 1991, Centurion/Paulines. 115 p. F 62 [NRT 114, 629, G. *Navez*].

7936 *Staikos* Michael, ⊖ Die Stellung der Laien in der Orthodoxen Kirche: TAth 61 (1990) 73-95; Eng. 903.

7937 **Sullivan** Francis A., The Church we believe in 1988 ➤ 5,7920; 6,7949: ᴿIrTQ 57 (1991) 323s (M. *Howlett*); PerspRelSt 18,1 (1991) 106 (W. T. *Walker*); ScotJT 44 (1991) 133s (D. W. D. *Shaw*: valuable); TR 87 (1991) 491s (W. *Beinert*).

7938 **Szafrański** Adam L., ❷ *Kairologia, Zarys ...* Abriss der Lehre von der Kirche in der Welt von heute. Lublin 1990, KUL. 478 p. – ᴿTR 87 (1991) 492s (S. *Rabiej*).

7939 **Thils** G., Primauté/ecclésiologie. 1989. – ᴿLvSt 16 (1991) 277s (L. *Kenis*).

7940 *Tinker* Melvin, Towards an evangelical ecclesiology II: Churchman 105 (L 1991) 139-147 [< zɪᴛ 91,484].

7941 *Tolhurst* James, NEWMAN's vision of the Church: PrPeo 4 (1990) 397-402.

7942 *Trapani* Giuseppe, Aspetti teologici del pensiero di Henri de LUBAC: Ho Theológos 7 (1989) 223-274.

7943 *Turner* Max, Ecclesiology in the major 'apostolic' restorationist churches in the United Kingdom: VoxEvca 19 (1989) 83-108.

7943* **Valadier** P., Lettres à un chrétien impatient: Découverte/Essai. P 1991, Dćouverte. 235 p. F 95 [NRT 114, 630, A. *Toubeau*].

7944 *Valenčic* Rafko, Man – path of the Church [JOHN PAUL II, Redemptor hominis] (in Slovene): BogVest 50 (1990) 385-397; Eng. 386.

7945 **Valentini** Donato, La teologia, aspetti innovatori ... ecclesiologia, mariologia 1988/9 ➔ 6,703: ᴿActuBbg 28 (1991) 202 (J. *Boada*).

7946 **Vance** John L., The ecclesiology of James Henley THORNWELL, an Old South Presbyterian theologian: diss. Drew, ᴰ*Pain* J. Madison ɴᴊ 1990. – RelStR 18,171.

7947 **Verucci** G., La Chiesa nella società contemporanea, dal primo dopoguerra al concilio Vaticano II. R 1988, Laterza. 494 p. Lit. 45.000. – ᴿRasT 32 (1991) 215 (G. *Mattai*: con stile scorrevole e grande padronanza di complesse vicende storiche mantiene discutibilmente che la ierocrazia rimane sempre un sistema scolastico-tridentino).

7948 **Villar** José R., Teología de la Iglesia particular 1989 ➔ 6,7958: ᴿEstE 66 (1991) 345s (A. *Tornos*); Gregorianum 72 (1991) 372-4 (A. *Antón*); Salesianum 53 (1991) 783 (L. A. *Gallo*).

7949 *a*) *Villar* José R., Iglesia universal e iglesia local; a propósito de unas conferencias del Cardenal RATZINGER en Brasil; – *b*) *Cattaneo* Arturo, Teologia de la Iglesia particular (reflexiones a proposito de ...) [Villar 1989]: ScripTPamp 23 (1991) 267-286 / 287-309.

7950 **Voss** Klaus P., Der Gedanke des allgemeinen Priester- und Prophetentums; seine gemeindetheologische Aktualisierung in der Reformationszeit: Diss. ᴰ*Kraus* H. Göttingen c. 1990. 302 p. – RTLv 23, p. 550.

7951 **Weinrich** Adele, Die Kirche in der Glaubenslehre SCHLEIERMACHERS: EurHS 23/398. Fra 1990, Lang. 272 p. DM 77. 3-631-42667-4. – ᴿTLZ 116 (1991) 933-5 (H. *Peiter*).

7952 **Weiss** Paul, Die Gemeindekirche — Ort des Glaubens; die Praxis als Fundament und als Konsequenz der Theologie. Graz 1989, Styria. 716 p. DM 90. – ᴿZkT 113 (1991) 62-65 (R. *Zerfass*).

7953 **White** Gavin, How the churches got to be the way they are. L 1990, SCM. vii-120 p. – ᴿNBlackf 72 (1991) 497s (J. *Kent*).

7954 **Wirsching** Johannes, Kirche und Pseudokirche; Konturen der Häresie. Gö 1990, Vandenhoeck & R. 282 p. DM 38 pa. 3-525-56177-6. – ᴿTLZ 116 (1991) 615s (M. *Plathow*).

7954* **Wolanin** A., Teologia della missione, temi scelti. CasM 1989, Piemme. 189 p. Lit. 25.000 [NRT 114, 469].

7955 **Zambon** Gaudenzio, Laicato e tipologie ecclesiali; ricerca storica sulla 'teologia del laicato' in Italia alla luce del Concilio Vaticano II

(1950-1980): diss. Pont. Univ. Gregoriana, ᴰ*Dupuis* J. Roma 1991. 728 p. – InfPUG (dic. 1991) 19; RTLv 23, p. 566.

H7.7 *Œcumenismus* – **The ecumenical movement.**

7956 **Adolph** Anneliese, Die Theologie der Einheit der Kirche nach CYPRIAN: kath. Diss. Tübingen 1991, ᴰ*Kasper* W. – TR 87 (1991) 522.

7957 *Alberigo* Giuseppe, L'unità dei cristiani alla luce del concilio di Ferrara-Firenze; fallimento e speranze: CrNSt 11 (1990) 61-81; Eng. 82.

7958 *Alemany* José J., Teología y ecumenismo: EstE 66 (1991) 273-293.

7959 *Arinze* Francis card.; *Tomko* Jozef card., Conseil pontifical pour le dialogue interreligieux / Congrégation pour l'évangélisation des peuples [19 mai 1991], a) Dialogue et annonce: EsprVie 101 (1991) 609-619. 625-632; – b) Dialogo e annuncio; riflessioni e orientamenti sul dialogo interreligioso e l'annuncio del Vangelo di Gesù Cristo (Pontificio Consiglio...): CC 142 (1991,3) 51-80.

7960 **Arx** Urs von, Koinonia auf altkirchlicher Basis... Gemeinsame Texte des orthodox-altkatholischen Dialogs 1975-87 deutsch. franç. Eng.: IkiZ 79 Beih. 4. Bern 1989, Stämpfli. 229 p. – ᴿTLZ 116 (1991) 71 (M. *Ulrich*).

7961 *Asendorf* Ulrich, Was ergibt sich aus LUTHERs Predigten zum Thema ökumenischer Grundkonsens bzw. Grunddissens?: KerDo 37 (1991) 97-115; Eng. 116.

7962 *Assis* X. de, Ecumenismo nos inicios de 1991 (preparando Canberra): Brotéria 132 (1991) 79-85.

7963 **Avis** Paul, Anglicanism and the Christian Church; theological resources in historical perspective 1989 ➤ 6,7967.m52: ᴿNBlackf 72 (1991) 351s (A. *Stacpoole*); ScotJT 44 (1991) 411-4 (M. *Santer*); TLond 94 (1991) 58s (S. W. *Sykes*).

7964 **Avis** Paul, Christians in communion. L 1990, Chapman/Mowbray. ix-150 p. £8 pa. – ᴿTLond 94 (1991) 303s (B. *Horne*).

7965 **Badger** Percy G., The Nestorians and their rituals. L 1987 = 1852, Darf. xxii-448 p.; xiii-426 p., map. £70 [RelStR 18, 143, Susan A. *Harvey*].

7966 **Barnes** Michael, Christian identity and religious pluralism; religions in conversation. Nv 1989, Abingdon. 256 p. $16. 0-687-07219-0. – ᴿRelStT 9,2s (1989) 66-68 (D. *Plaxton*).

7967 ᴱ*Barringer* Robert, Rome and Constantinople; essays in the dialogue of love [Sts. Peter and Andrew lectures (2 Orthodox, 2 Catholic)] 1984 ➤ 2,276: ᴿSalesianum 53 (1991) 418 (D. *Valentini*).

7968 **Barth** Hans-Martin, Einander Priester sein; allgemeines Priestertum in ökumenischer Perspektive: Kirche und Konfession 29, 1990 ➤ 6,7969: ᴿNRT 113 (1991) 261 (A. *Toubeau*); TAth 62 (1991) 915s (M. *Begzos*, ☉); TLZ 116 (1991) 445-7 (E. *Winkler*).

7969 **Baur** Jörg, Einig in Sachen Rechtfertigung? 1989 ➤ 6,7970: ᴿTS 52 (1991) 590 (C. J. *Peter*: for Göttingen evangelical faculty, serious deficiencies of LEHMANN-PANNENBERG 1986).

7970 *Bavaud* Georges, Pour un dialogue œcuménique sur l'action de la grâce divine dans le cœur de l'homme: CALVIN, PASCAL et saint Thomas d'AQUIN: NVFri 65 (1990) 296-307.

7971 a) *Beaupère* René, Catholicisme et orthodoxie; nouvelles tensions et ecclésiologie; – b) *Goltz* Hermann, Le protestantisme dans l'ancien 'Bloc de l'Est'; l'heure de la vérité, ᵀ*Luzsenszky* Guy: LumièreV 40,201 (1991) 5-19 / 21-31.

7972 **Bedouelle** G. T., *al.*, Être catholique ou réformé aujourd'hui, 1586-1986. Genève 1986, Labor et Fides. 67 p. – ᴿProtestantesimo 45 (1990) 79s (G. *Conti*: iniziativa dei colleghi J. *Chappuis*, P. de *Laubier*).

7973 *a) Beinert* Wolfgang, Die Katholizität als Eigenschaft der Kirche; – *b) Petri* Heinrich, Einheit in Katholizität — eine bleibende Spannung?; – *c) Beestermöller* Gerhard, Möglichkeiten und Grenzen einer ökumenischen Sozialethik; eine Tagungsnachlese [Berlin 1988]: Catholica 45 (1991) 238-264 / 265-282 / 296-308.

7974 **Bent** Ans van der, Vital ecumenical concerns; sixteen documentary surveys 1986 → 3,7748; 4,9015: ᴿMid-Stream 28 (1989) 137-141 (A. D. *Falconer*).

7974* *Bermejo* Luis M., The winter of ecumenism: Vidyajyoti 55 (1991) 23-37.

7975 *Bildstein* Walter, Protestant-Catholic engagement; the case of the [WCC] joint working group: EcuR 42 (1990) 24-34.

7976 **Bilheimer** Robert S., Breakthrough; the emergence of the ecumenical tradition 1989 → 6,7972: ᴿCCurr 40 (1990s) 412-4 (Carolyn M. *Craft*); RTLv 22 (1991) 425s (A. de *Halleux*); Tablet 244 (1990) 115 (Pauline *Webb*).

7977 **Birmelé** André, Sola gratia; le salut dans les dialogues œcuméniques 1986 → 2,6163 ... 5,7748: ᴿProtestantesimo 45 (1990) 334s (Milena *Beux*).

7978 **Blaser** Klauspeter, Une église, des confessions [→ 6,7974]; leur unité et désunion, leurs doctrines et pratiques, tableaux comparatifs. Genève 1990, Labor et Fides. 119 p. F 99. 2-8309-0602-0. – ᴿETL 67 (1991) 182 (A. de *Halleux*: met à jour P. Conord 1959); NRT 113 (1991) 138 (L. J. *Renard*).

7979 **Böcker** Tobias, Katholizismus und Konfessionalität; der Frühkatholizismus und die Einheit der Kirche [Diss. Regensburg ᴰ*Petri* H.]: Abh PhPsySozRÖk 44. Pd 1989, Schöningh. 224 p. DM 42 [TR 88, 137, G. *Hintzen*].

7980 **Borges de Pinho** J. E., O ministério de Pedro como problema ecuménico: Didaskalia 19 (1989) 135-179.

7981 *Bradshaw* Timothy, ARCIC 2, salvation and the Church — pastoral and spiritual implications: EvQ 63 (1991) 331-340.

7982 *Brattinga* Teije, Oecumene; stand van zaken; verleden en heden, vooral in relatie tot de katholieke kerk: TsTNijm 31 (1991) 65-83; Eng. 83s.

7983 *Bremer* Thomas, Der theologische Dialog zwischen der römisch-katholischen und der orthodoxen Kirche; Implikationen für die katholische Ekklesiologie: → 67, ᶠGolub I., 1991, 458-472; croat. 472.

7983* **Bria** I., The sense of ecumenical tradition; the ecumenical witness and vision of the Orthodox. Geneva 1991, WCC. vii-120 p. Fs 15 [NRT 114, 772, A. *Harvengt*].

7984 *Brogi* Marco, Aperture ecumeniche del Codex Canonum Ecclesiarum Orientalium: Antonianum 66 (1991) 455-468; Eng. 455.

7985 *Calivas* Alkiviadis C., The date of Pascha; the need to continue the debate: GrOrTR 35 (1990) 333-343.

ᴱ**Camps** A., Œcumenische inleiding in die Missiologie; teksten en konteksten van het wereldchristendom 1988 → 480.

7986 Centre d'Études Œcuméniques de Strasbourg, Prise de position 1990, *Communio/Koïnonia*, un concept du NT et de la chrétienté antique aujourd'hui repris; son sens et sa portée: FoiVie 90,3s (1991) 107-139.

7987 *a) Chadwick* Henry, 'Substantial agreement'; a problem in ecumenism; – *b) Gerwen* Jef Van, Christian faith and (in-)tolerance: LvSt 16 (1991) 207-219 / 220-241.

7988 Chronique religieuse I, relations entre les Communions; II. Chronique des Églises: Irénikon 64 (1991) 72-103.236-261.381-393.503-541 / 104-138.262-302.394-426.542-586.

7989 **Clément** Olivier, La Chiesa Ortodossa, 1989 → 5,7959: ᴿAsprenas 38 (1991) 89-104 (Diana *Pacelli*).

7990 **Clément** Olivier, Orient-Occident; deux pasteurs, Vladimir LOSSKY et Paul EVDOKIMOV: Perspective Orthodoxe 6. Genève 1985, Labor et Fides. 210 p. – ᴿSalesianum 53 (1991) 592s (D. *Valentini*).

7991 Commission Biblique Pontificale, Unité et diversité dans l'Église 1989 → 6,520: ᴿCC 142 (1991,1) 315s (J. *Luzarraga*).

7992 *Cowdin* Daniel M., Religious liberty, religious dissent and the Catholic tradition: HeythJ 32 (1991) 26-61.

7993 **Cross** Lawrence, Eastern Christianity; the Byzantine tradition, ... 1988, Dwyer. – ᴿAustralasCR 68 (1990) 371-3 (C. *Hill*).

7994 *Culbertson* Philip, Scriptural warrants for religious tolerance: NewTR 4,2 (1991) 62-70.

7995 **Cullmann** Oscar, Einheit durch Vielfalt^{2rev} + réaction aux réactions. Tü 1991, Mohr. 224 p. DM 34 [RHPR 70,461]. – ᴿTAth 62 (1991) 915 (M. P. *Begzos*, 'Mpegzos').

7996 *Dal Ferro* Giuseppe, Libertà religiosa e intransigenza delle Sette: StEcum 7 (1989) 9-23; Eng. 23s.

7997 *Delahoutre* Michel, Unité des religions ou dialogue?: EsprVie 101 (1991) 529-534.

7998 **Desseaux** E. Jacques, Twenty centuries of ecumenism [1983], ᵀ*O'Connell* Matthew J. NY c. 1990, Paulist. 103 p. – ᴿSalesianum 53 (1991) 422 (D. *Valentini*).

8000 *a*) *Díaz Moreno* José M., La libertad religiosa; consideraciones desde la Declaración Conciliar y la Declaración de los Derechos Humanos; – *b*) *Higuera Udías* Gonzalo, La 'libertas ecclesiae' como principio fundamental de las relaciones Iglesia-Estado; – *c*) *Otaduy* Jorge de, Los proyectos de acuerdo de cooperación con las iglesias evangélicas y las comunidades israelitas: EstE 66 (1991) 123-151 / 153-163 / 205-218.

8001 **Dick** John A., The Malines conversations revisited: BtETL 85, 1989 → 6, 7790: ᴿGregorianum 72 (1991) 174-6 (J. E. *Vercruysse*: several Jesuits involved had little sympathy); RTLv 22 (1991) 548s (A. de *Halleux*).

8002 **Dieten** Jan-Louis van, Der Streit in Byzanz um die Rezeption der Unio florentina: OstkSt 40 (1991) 160-180.

8003 **Dionne** J. Robert, The papacy and the Church; a study of praxis and reception in ecumenical perspective [< diss.] 1987 → 3,7776 ... 6,7992: ᴿDivThom 93 (1990) 159s (L. *Elders*: misses the point); RHE 86 (1991) 517 (P. H. *Daly*).

8004 *a*) *Döring* Heinrich, *Schmidt-Leukel* Perry, Interreligiöser Dialog als ökumenisches Problem; – *b*) *Fries* Heinrich, NEWMANs Bedeutung für ökumenische Probleme der Gegenwart; – *c*) *Schlüter* Richard, Evangelisatorische Erziehung — Grundpfeiler einer ökumenischen Gemeindepädagogik heute: Catholica 44 (1990) 221-241 / 242-259 / 260-273.

8005 [Dombes, groupe] Pour la conversion des Églises; identité et changement dans la dialectique de communion. P 1991, Centurion. 119 p. F 85. – ᴿEsprVie 101 (1991) 316-8 (P. *Jay*).

8006 **Duquoc** Christian, Chiese provvisorie; saggio di ecclesiologia ecumenica: GdT 160, 1985 → 5,7968: ᴿSalesianum 53 (1991) 422s (D. *Valentini*).

8007 *Eijk* A. H. C. van, The difference between the Old and the New Testament sacraments as an ecumenical issue: Bijdragen 52 (1991) 2-36.

8008 **Ellis** C. J. Together on the way; theology of ecumenism. L 1990, British Council of Churches. 150 p. £7. 0-85169-209-5. – ᴿPrPeo 4 (1990) 382s (M. Cecily *Boulding*).

8009 **Escaffre** François, L'épiscopat dans les documents des dialogues œcuméniques; réponses des Églises au BEM, accords bilatéraux: cath. diss. ᴰ*Schlick* J. Strasbourg 1991. 357 p. – RTLv 23, p. 565.

8009* *Evers* Georg, Schwierigkeiten beim Weltkirchewerden; Spannungen sind nicht auf Europa beschränkt [... Neue Zentralisierungstendenzen; der Fall MILINGO]: HerdKor 44 (1990) 129-135.

8010 **Feigel** Uwe, Das evangelische Deutschland und Armenien [Diss. Kiel 1988]: Kirche und Konfession 28. Gö 1989, Vandenhoeck & R. 344 p.; map. DM 82. – ᴿTLZ 116 (1991) 73-75 (Friederike *Stockmann-Köckert*: heikles Thema).

8011 **Felmy** Karl Christian, Die Orthodoxe Theologie der Gegenwart; eine Einführung. Da 1990, Wiss. 260 p.; 8 fig. – ᴿTAth 62 (1991) 916-9 (M. P. *Begzos*, Ⓖ).

8012 **Fleckenstein** Wolfgang, Aussenseiter als Thema und Realität des katholischen Religionsunterrichts... Gastarbeiter: StTheol 4. Wü 1989, Stephans. xii-651 p. DM 38. – ᴿZkT 113 (1991) 468-470 (R. *Brandl*: unter anderem, GIRARD-SCHWAGER).

8013 *Fleinert-Jensen* Flemming, Ecclesia crucis; Erwägungen zu einer Ekklesiologie des Kreuzes in ökumenischer Perspektive: KerDo 37 (1991) 172-189; Eng. 189.

8014 ᴱ**Flesseman-van Leer** E., La Bibbia, la sua autorità e interpretazione nel movimento ecumenico [1980 ➤ 61,488],ᵀ: Verso l'unità dei cristiani. T 1982, LDC/Claudiana. 102 p. – ᴿProtestantesimo 46 (1991) 209s (D. *Mazzarella*).

8015 *a*) *Forward* Martin, The reconciling spirit and mission in the context of religious pluralism; – *b*) *Keshishian* Aram, Unity and mission from a Middle Eastern perspective: IntRMiss 79 (1990) 461-9 / 445-452.

8016 *Foster* Stewart, Continuity, collegiality and the prospects for ecumenism: DowR 109 (1991) 235-258.

8017 *França Miranda* Mário de, A Igreja católica diante do pluralismo religioso no Brasil: REB 51 (1991) 292-308.

8018 *a*) *George* K. M., Some aspects of the ecclesiology of the Malankara Orthodox Syrian Church; – *b*) *Abraham* M. V., Mar Thoma Church; origin, growth and ecumenical involvement; – *c*) *Santram* Pritam B., The Church of North India; its history, vision and life: Jeevadhara 20 (1990) 255-264 / 265-274 / 275-285.

8019 **Girault** René, Construire l'Église une: PEncMod. P 1990, D-Brouwer. 218 p. F 55. – ᴿEsprVie 101 (1991) 95s (P. *Jay*: livre qui dans son genre atteint une rare perfection).

8020 ᴱ**Gort** Jerald, *al.*, Dialogue and syncretism; an interdisciplinary approach [➤ 6,621: Amsterdam Free Univ. symposium, May 1988]. GR/ Amst 1989, Eerdmans/Rodopi. vi-228 p. $62.50. /90-5183-148-X. 17 art. – ᴿGregorianum 72 (1991) 185s (J. *Dupuis*).

8020* **Griffiths** P. J., An apology for apologetics; a study in the logic of interreligious dialogue: Faith Meets Faith. Mkn 1991, Orbis. xii-113 p. $40; pa. $17 [NRT 114, 281, J. *Masson*].

8021 *Gross* Selwyn, Religious pluralism in struggles for justice: NBlackf 71 (1990) 377-386.

8022 *a*) *Guillou* André, L'orthodoxie byzantine; – *b*) *Konidaris* Jean, Les monastères dans l'Église orthodoxe en Grèce: ArchivScSocRel 75 (1991) 5-10 / 11-22.

8023 *Gunten* A. F. von, Les ordinations anglicanes; le problème affronté par LÉON XIII dans 'Apostolicae Curae': NVFri 65 (1990) 46-60.

8024 *Halleux* André de, Uniatisme et communion; le texte catholique-orthodoxe de Freising [VIᵉ, 6-15 juin 1990]: RTLv 22 (1991) 3-29; Eng. 151.

8025 *Halleux* André de, *a)* L'unité par la diversité selon Oscar CULLMANN: RTLv 22 (1991) 510-523; – *b)* Cullmann's Unity through diversity; a Catholic response [< 109 (1987) 870-883], ᵀᴱ*Jermann* Rosemary: TDig 38 (1991) 19-22.

8026 *a) Halleux* A. de, Orthodoxes orientaux en dialogue; – *b) Parys* Michel van, Les Églises orientales catholiques et l'œcuménisme: Irénikon 64 (1991) 332-357; Eng. 358 / 323-331; Eng. 331.

8027 **Hamel** Martin, Schriftverständnis und Schriftgebrauch als Problem der neueren ökumenischen Missionstheologie, unter besonderer Berücksichtigung der Weltmissionskonferenz Melbourne 1980: ev. Diss. ᴰ*Beyerhaus* P. Tübingen 1991s. – RTLv 23, p. 566.

8028 *Hammerschmidt* Ernst, Die orthodoxen Kirchen 101: IkiZ 80 (1990) 158-243.

8029 **Harire Seda** Kamel Mahomed, El Magisterio de Pablo VI sobre el pluralismo teológico; análisis lexicográfico y textual: diss. ᴰ*Illanes Mestre* J. Pamplona 1991. – ExcDissSTheol 20 (1991); RTLv 23, p. 566.

8030 **Haudel** Matthias, Die Bibel und die Einheit der Kirchen: Diss. ᴰ*Lessing* E. Münster 1991s. – RTLv 23, p. 566.

8031 *a) Hesselink* I. John, Calvinus oecumenicus; CALVIN's vision of the unity and catholicity of the Church; – *b) Brouwer* Arie R., The Church, the churches, and councils of churches; – *c) Hoeven* James W. Van, Renewing God's creation; an ecumenical challenge: RefR 44,2 ('The changing face of ecumenism' 1990) 97-122 / 123-136 / 137... [< ZIT 91,283].

8032 **Hillman** Eugene, Many paths 1989 ⇥ 5,7984: ᴿCritRR 4 (1991) 442s (J. T. *Ford*); Thomist 54 (1990) 741-4 (G. *D'Costa*).

8033 *Hintzen* Georg, Das gemeinsame Priestertum aller Gläubigen und das besondere Priestertum des Dienstes in der ökumenischen Diskussion: Catholica 45 (1991) 44-77.

8034 *a) Hoffman* Lawrence A., Jewish-Christian services — Babel or mixed multitude; – *b) Thornton* Karen, Interfaith worship on campus: CCurr 40 (1990s) 5-17.21 / 27-33.

8035 ᴱ*Houtepen* Anton, Die verscheidenheid verzoend? Actuele thema's uit het gesprek Rome-Reformatie toegelicht aan de hand van de thesen van H. FRIES en K, RAHNER 'Einigung... 1983': IIMO publ. 26. Leiden 1989, IIMO. 251 p. ƒ29,50. 90-6495-204-3. – ᴿTsTNijm 31 (1991) 107 (H. J. van *Hout*).

8036 *Houtepen* Anton, Verso una visione ecumenica della Chiesa, ᵀ*Voicu* S.: StEcum 7 (1989) 137-171.

8037 ᴱ*Hryniewicz* Wacław, *Koza* Stanisław J., Chrzest, Eucharystia, posługiwanie duchowne; Dokument z Limy 1982, tekst i komentarze: Teologia w dialogu 4. Lublin 1989, KUL. 331 p. – ᴿColcT 61,1 (1991) 187-9 (J. *Królikowski* ❼).

8038 *Hryniewicz* Wacław, Der 'Uniatismus' und die Zukunft des katholisch-orthodoxen Dialogs, ᵀ*Patock* C., *Tretter* H.: OstkSt 40 (1991) 219-221.

8039 *Jarlert* Anders, [svensk, På väg mot ...] Towards personalistic ecumenics; two theological programs in active working fellowship; Emil BRUNNER,

Arvid RUNESTAM and the Oxford Group Movement: Kyrkohistorisk Årsskrift 21 (Sto 1989) 133-148 [< ZIT 91,298].

8040 *Kasper* Walter, Zum gegenwärtigen Stand des ökumenischen Gesprächs zwischen den Reformatorischen Kirchen und der katholischen Kirche: Klerusblatt 71 (Mü 1991) 99-104 [< ZIT 91,386].

8041 **Keller** Carl-A., New age; entre nouveauté et redécouverte: Entrée libre 12. Genève 1990, Labor et Fides. 91 p. Fs 55. 2-8309-0623-3. – ᴿÉTRel 66 (1991) 577-580 (J.-M. *Prieur*: plutôt positif, un pont).

8042 **Kinnamon** Michael, Truth and community; diversity and its limits in the ecumenical movement 1988 ➔ 6,8022: ᴿMid-Stream 29 (1990) 105s (A. D. *Falconer*).

8043 **Klöckner** Stefan, 'Sakrament im Wort' — christologische Fundamentierung, eschatologische Ausrichtung und ekklesiale Vermittlung wortsakramentalen Geschehens als Gegenstand ökumenischer Konvergenzbestrebungen: kath. Diss. Tübingen 1991, ᴰ*Hünermann* P. 296 p. – TR 87 (1991) 522; RTLv 23, p. 569.

8044 **Küng** Hans, Theologie im Aufbruch 1987 ➔ 4,213; 5,7991: ᴿEstE 66 (1991) 100-2 (J. J. *Alemany*).

8045 *Kuschel* Karl-Josef, Cristologia e dialogo interreligioso; l'unicità di Cristo nel dialogo con le religioni mondiali [HICK J., KNITTER P.: < StiZt 6 (1991) 387-402], ᵀ*Colombi* Giulio: HumBr 46 (1991) 694-718.

8045* *Legrand* Hervé, Collégialité des évêques et communion des églises dans la réception de Vatican II: RSPT 75 (1991) 545-567; Eng. 568.

8046 **Leins** Curtis C., Lutherans and Catholics; first world impasse, third world community: diss. Temple, ᴰ*Sloyan* G. Ph 1991. – RelStR 18,173.

8047 **Lochhead** David, The dialogical imperative; a Christian reflection on interfaith encounter 1988 ➔ 5,7996; 6,8029: ᴿScotJT 44 (1991) 272s (R. S. *Sugirtharajah*: to polish BARTH's negative image).

8048 ᴱ**Lossky** Nicholas, al., Dictionary of the ecumenical movement. Geneva/GR 1991, WCC/Eerdmans. xvi-1196 p. $80. 2-8254-1025-X / 0-8028-2428-5 [TDig 38,354: 22 editors, 340 contributors, 50 p. index]. – ᴿChrCris 51 (1991s) 315s (Betty *Thompson*).

8049 **Lovsky** F., Un passé de division — une promesse d'unité. P 1990, Saint-Paul. – ᴿFoiVie 90,3 (1991) 144 (O. *Millet*, aussi sur ATGER D.).

8051 *a) Luise* Raffaele, Da Basilea a Seùl; l'ecumenismo protagonista della costruzione della nuova Europa e di un mondo nuovo; – *b) Spini* Debora, Dal diluvio all'arcobaleno... Seùl: Circolo Rosselli Quad 2s. Mi 1990, Angeli. 171 p., Lit. 14.000 / 185 p., Lit. 18.000. – ᴿProtestantesimo 46 (1991) 149s (B. *Gabrielli*).

8052 *McCann* Joseph, Centurions and prophets; ecumenical organisational structures: IrTQ 57 (1991) 105-121.

8053 **Maffeis** Angelo, Apostolicità della Chiesa e ministero nel dialogo ecumenico cattolico-lutherano: diss. Pont. Univ. Gregoriana, ᴰ*Vercruysse* J. Roma 1991. 625 p.; extr. Nᵒ 3790, 361 p. – RTLv 23, p. 567.

8054 **Manikas** Constantine I., ❻ The Church of Greece and the dialogue between Orthodoxy and Roman Catholicism according to the 1st and 2nd Panorthodox Conference of Rhodes: TAth 62 (1991) 163-176. 478-501; Eng. 929.

8055 *Marlé* René, ❿ La question du pluralisme en théologie; ᵀ*Ludwisiak* Tomasz: *a)* PrzPow 268,824 (1990) 200-9; – *b)* Bobolanum 2 (1991) 28-44; franç. 157.

8056 *Martini* Carlo M., ❿ La réunion œcuménique de Bâle, ᵀ*Schmidt* Grzegorz: PrzPow 267,822 (1990) 226-236.

8057 **Maskine** Matta el-, Prière, Esprit-Saint et unité chrétienne: Spiritualité Monastique 48. Begrolles-en-Mauges 1990, Bellefontaine. 205 p. F 85. – ᴿEsprVie 100 (1990) 489-491 (P. *Jay*).

8058 *Maskine* Matta el-, L'unité véritable, source d'inspiration pour le monde: Irénikon 64 (1991) 365-380; Eng. 358.

8059 **Metallinos** Georgios D., Leben im Leib Christi (Einführung in die Orthodoxie). Athenai 1990. 288 p. – ᴿTAth 62 (1991) 184s (E. A. *Theodorou*).

8060 *a) Minnerath* B., La liberté religieuse dans l'histoire de l'Église; – *b*) en Israel: → 490, Liberté religieuse 1989/91, 25-42.

8061 *Pacelli* Diana, Spirito Santo e movimento ecumenico: Asprenas 38 (1991) 204-214.

8061* **Panikkar** Raimon, Der neue religiöse Weg; im Dialog der Religionen leben [The intrareligious dialog], ᵀ*Tepe* Georg. 189 p. DM 36. – ᴿTPhil 66 (1991) 466s (R. *Funick*); TPQ 139 (1991) 341 (J. *Janda*).

8062 *a) Panikkar* Raimon, Begegnung der Religionen; das unvermeidliche Gespräch; – *b*) *Samartha* Stanley J., Christen im Verhältnis zu Gläubigen anderer Religionen; Entwicklungen und Perspektiven; – *c*) *Wigoder* Geoffrey, Interreligiöser Dialog; eine jüdische Perspektive: Dialog der Religionen 1,1 (Mü 1991) 9-38 / 39-50 / 50-57 [< TR 87,259].

8063 ᴱ**Pannenberg** W., Lehrverurteilungen III. Materialien zur Lehre von den Sakramenten und vom kirchlichen Amt: Dialog der Kirchen 6. FrB/Gö 1990, Herder/VR. 352 p. DM 48. – ᴿTPhil 66 (1991) 294-8 (W. *Löser*, auch über I-II, ᴱLEHMANN K. → 3,661); TPQ 139 (1991) 213.215 (H. *Petri*).

8064 — ᴱ**Lehmann** K., *Pannenberg* W., The condemnations of the Reformation era; do they still divide? 1990 → 5,7993: ᴿCurrTMiss 18 (1991) 374 (K. *Killinger*); RExp 87 (1990) 658s (W. L. *Allen*); ScotJT 44 (1991) 408-410 (J. *Atkinson*).

8065 — ... Les anathèmes du XVIᴱ siècle sont-ils encore actuels? 1989. 306 p. F 130. 2-204-04006-1. – ᴿÉTRel 66 (1991) 151-3 (J.-M. *Poirier*: no hint of ᴱ*Pannenberg* or whoever).

8065* *Peri* Vittorio, Le storie della Chiesa e il recupero della prospettiva ecumenica [MEYENDORFF J. 1989]: OrChrPer 57 (1991) 11-25.

8066 **Pickering** W. S. F., Anglo-Catholicism, a study in religious ambiguity 1989 → 6,8043: ᴿNBlackf 71 (1990) 518s (J. *Kent*); PrPeo 4 (1990) 339-341 (A. *Symondson*); ScotJT 44 (1991) 381s (G. S. *Wakefield*).

8066* **Raiser** Konrad, Ecumenism in transition; a paradigm shift in the ecumenical movement? [Ökumene im Übergang 1989 → 6,8047], ᵀ*Coates* T. Geneva 1991, WCC. viii-133 p. $10 [NRT 114,119 A. *Harvengt*].

8067 **Ramsey** Michael, The Gospel and the Catholic Church. L 1990 = ²1956 [¹1936], SPCK. 248 p. £9. – ᴿEcuR 41 (1991) 377s (K. *McDonald*).

8068 *Ricca* Paolo, *a*) Gli Ortodossi, il Consiglio Ecumenico e noi: Protestantesimo 46 (1991) 192-200; – *b*) Il papa e l'ecumene cristiana [discorso al Segretariato vaticano: AAS 59 (1967) 498]: Protestantesimo 46 (1991) 316-323; – *c*) Unità protestante: Protestantesimo 45 (1990) 173-8.

8069 **Roberson** Ronald G., The Eastern Christian Churches; a brief survey³ʳᵉᵛ: Anatolian Christian publications. Rome 1990. xi-429 p. – ᴿTAth 62 (1991) 586-8 (V. T. *Staphidis*, ⊝).

8070 *Rodríguez* Pedro, Der theologische Dialog der katholischen Kirche mit den orthodoxen Kirchen: ForumKT 7 (1991) 290-307.

8071 *Romo* Pablo, Penetración Protestante en Iberoamérica, apuntes históricos de actualidad: DiálEcum 24 (1989) 367-381.

8072 *Rostagno* S., [9] Tesi sul pluralismo religioso: Protestantesimo 46 (1991) 128s.

8073 *Rügger* Heinz, Innerevangelische Ökumene; Überlegungen zu einem vernachlässigten Bereich ökumenischer Arbeit: TZBas 47 (1991) 337-353.

8074 **Rüppel** Gert, Die Menschheit und ihre Einheit als Thema in der ökumenischen Diskussion zwischen 1910 und 1983; die Interaktion von Ökumene und Oikumene dargestellt an den Hauptkonferenzen der ökumenischen Bewegung: ev. Diss. ᴰ*Raiser* K. Bochum 1991s. – RTLv 23, p. 567.

8074* **Russalesi** Steven, The history of the Roman Catholic – United Methodist dialogue in the United States, 1966-1989; a theological appraisal: diss. Catholic Univ., ᴰ*Ford* J. Wsh 1991. – RTLv 23, p. 567.

8075 *Ryan* Thomas, Ecumenism, dead or alive? an unofficial investigation: OneInC 27 (1991) 121-133.

8075* **Sartori** Luigi, L'unità della Chiesa, un dibattito e un progetto 1989 ➤ 6,8054: ᴿTeresianum 42 (1991) 678-680 (G. *Blandino*).

8076 ᴱ**Schlemmer** Karl [➤ 357*], Gottesdienst — Weg zur Einheit; Impulse für die Ökumene: QDisp 122, 1988/9 ➤ 6,687: ᴿTR 87 (1991) 62s (Teresa *Berger* supplies the source of an unidentified quote p. 9: herself).

8077 **Schlink** Edmund, Ökumenische Dogmatik 1983 ➤ 65,6793... 4,9122: ᴿTsTKi 60 (1989) 152s (T. *Austad*).

8077* *Schreiner* Lothar, Ökumenische Feuerprobe theologischer Ausbildung; Kirchengemeinschaft im Schmelztiegel — Anfang einer neuen Ökumene? [ᴱ*Herzog* F., *Groscurth* R. 1989]: EvT 51 (1991) 202-5.

8078 **Schütte** Heinz, Kirche im ökumenischen Verständnis; Kirche des dreieinigen Gottes. Pd 1991, Bonifatius. 203 p. DM 19,80. – ᴿTPhil 66 (1991) 617s (W. *Löser*); TR 87 (1991) 493s (B. *Lohse*).

8079 **Schütte** H., Ziel Kirchengemeinschaft; zur ökumenischen Orientierung 1985 ➤ 1,7554... 3,7893: ᴿSalesianum 53 (1991) 426s (D. *Valentini*).

Sesboüé Bernard, Pour une théologie œcuménique; Église et sacrements, Eucharistie et ministères, La Vierge Marie: CogF 160, 1990 ➤ 263.

8081 **Skublics** Ernest, How Eastern Orthodoxy can contribute to Roman Catholic renewal; a theological and pastoral proposition: Roman Catholic Studies 4. Lewiston 1989, Mellen. 229 p. $60 [RelStR 18, 126, P. *Viscuso*: will displease all parties].

8082 *Smyth* Françoise, L'inter-religieux et la théologie aujourd'hui: ÉTRel 66 (1991) 345-357.

8082* **Stackhouse** Max, Creeds, society and human rights; a study in three cultures [Hindu beside 'Puritan/democratic' and 'Marxist shaped by East German BONHOEFFER'] 1984 ➤ 3,7901; $21. – ᴿRExp 87 (1990) 347-9 (G. *Stassen*).

8083 **Stănilaoë** Dumitru, Il genio dell'Ortodossia. Mi 1986, Jaca. – ᴿFilT 4 (1990) 232-7 (M. *Crociato*: Staniloaë in text and title).

8083* **Theodorou** Evangelos D., Der päpstliche Primat aus der Sicht der Orthodoxen Tradition [Ök. Symposion Rg Juli 1989]: TAth 62 (1991) 286-293. 427-444; Eng. 929: proves that the Bishop of Rome was indeed first in the order of hierarchs, but not with a primacy as in Vatican I.

8084 ᴱ**Thompson** Norma H., Religious pluralism and religious education. NHv 1988, RelEdn. 330 p. $15. 0-89135-061-6. – ᴿIrTQ 57 (1991) 250s (J. *McDonagh*).

8085 **Thurian** Max, intervista con *Ugenti* Antonio, Una vita per l'unità. CasM 1991, Piemme. 221 p. – ᴿAngelicum 68 (1991) 560 (R. *Hoeckman*).

8086 **Tillard** J.-M. R. Église d'églises 1987 ➤ 3,7911... 5,8036: ᴿMid-Stream

30 (1991) 87-89 (W. G. *Rusch*); RechSR 79 (1991) 438s (P. *Vallin*, avec 15 livres d'ecclésiologie).

8087 **Tillard** J.-M. R.   Chiesa di Chiese; l'ecclesiologia di comunione 1989 → 5,8037; 6,8069:   ᴿAnnTh 4 (1990) 177-184 (E. *Juliá*: giustamente 'commento su AUG. Sermo 138' – poi ...).

8088 *Tillard* Jean-Marie R.,   'Konziliare Gemeinschaft', 'versöhnte Verschiedenheit'; Communio-Ekklesiologie und Schwesterkirchen: → 63, ᶠGASSMANN G., Gemeinsamer Glaube 1991, 135-156.

8089 **Tracy** David,   Dialogue with the other. Lv/GR 1990 [RelStR 18,127, P. F. *Knitter*: good].

8090 **Turcotte** Paul-André,   Les chemins de la différence; pluralisme et aggiornamento dans l'après-concile. Montréal 1985, Bellarmin. 191 p. – ᴿSR 20 (1991) 249s (R. *Lapointe*).

8091 **Vignot** B.,   Les Églises parallèles ['marginales', auxquelles manque la succession apostolique]: Bref 39. P 1991, Cerf/Fides. 126 p. F 45. – ᴿNRT 113 (1991) 934 (A. *Harvengt*).

Waldenfels H.,   Begegnung der Religionen: TVers 1. 1990 → 275.

8093 **Wenz** Gunther,   Kontradiktorische Grunddifferenz? zum Ökumeneplädoyer von Eilert HERMS [1989]:   TLZ 116 (1991) 253-262.

8094 ᴱ**White** Ronald C.,   *Fisher* Eugene J.,   Partners in peace and education, RC-Presb./Ref 4, 1988 → 6,706:   ᴿRTLv 22 (1991) 547s (A. de *Halleux*).

8095 **Willebrands** Johannes,   *Mandatum unitatis*, Beiträge zur Ökumene 1989 → 5,373; 6,8079:   ᴿEcuR 41 (1991) 484-6 (E. *Fahlbusch*).

8096 *Willebrands* Johannes Kard.,   Der Päpstliche Rat für die Förderung der Einheit der Christen im Jahre 1989 /1990:   Catholica 44 (1990) 73-90 / 45 (1991) 163-180.

8097 *Williams* Preston N.,   An African-American perspective on the unity of the Church and the renewal of the human community: Mid-Stream 28 (1989) 336-346 (-368, responses).

8098 *Wingenbach* Gregory C.,   Improvement in Orthodox/Roman Catholic relations; issues of marriage and family life;   StVlad 35 (1991) 359-379 [327-350, *Guroian* Vigen, CHRYSOSTOM on family].

8100 **Zafris** Chrysostomos-G., ⊖ Towards the reunion of the ancient oriental non-Chalcedonian churches with the Orthodox Church: TAth 61 (1990) 7-72; Eng. 903.

8101 *a) Ziegenaus* Anton,   Konversion als Bekenntnis; zu einem wieder aktuellen Thema; – *b) Bäumer* Remigius,   Motiva conversionis ad fidem catholicam; Konversionsgrunde im Zeitalter der katholischen Reform; – *c) Walli* Peter, NEWMAN als Konvertit und Ratgeber der Konvertiten: ForumKT 7 (1991) 242-253 / 254-272 / 273-289.

8101* **Zielinsky** Vladimir,   Afin que le monde croie; méditations d'un croyant orthodoxe à propos du livre du cardinal RATZINGER, 'Entretiens sur la voie'.   P 1989, Nouvelle Cité.   158 p. F 78. – ᴿEsprVie 101 (1991) 175 (P. *Jay*: mérite examen).

8102 *Zissis* Theodore,   Uniatism; a problem in the dialogue between the Orthodox and Roman Catholics: GrOrTR 35 (1990) 23-31 (221-236, *Clapsis* V., 25 years after Vat. II).

H7.8   Amt – *Ministerium ecclesiasticum.*

8103 **Antón** Ángel, Conferencias episcopales 1989 → 5,8050; 6,8081:   ᴿRET 50 (1990) 107-111 (M. *Gesteira Garza*).

8104 **Areeplackal** Joseph, Spirit and ministries; perspectives of East and West [diss. Pont. Gregorian Univ., [D]*Rosato* P., Rome 1988]. Bangalore 1990, Dharmaram. ix-350 p. $15. – [R]JDharma 15 (1990) 273-5 (P. *Kalluveettil*).

8105 **Arnau-García** Ramón, El ministerio en la Iglesia. Valencia 1991, Fac. T. Ferrer. 242 p. – [R]ScripTPamp 23 (1991) 1062s (J. R. *Villar*).

8105* *Arnau* Ramón, Sobre la autoridad docente de las conferencias episcopales: AnVal 4 (1990) 147-150.

8106 **Balthasar** Hans Urs von, Der antirömische Affekt; wie lässt sich das Papsttum in der Gesamtkirche integrieren?[2rev]. Einsiedeln 1989, Johannes. 303 p. DM 35. – [R]TR 87 (1991) 142-4 (H. *Moll*: auf hohem Niveau, aber die polemischen Töne klingen bisweilen schrill).

8107 **Barbaini** Pietro, Il prete e la Chiesa; una crisi profetica nella storia del post-Concilio. T 1990, Tempo di fraternità. 188 p. Lit. 24.000. – [R]HumBr 46 (1991) 785 (T. *Goffi*).

8108 **Bourgeois** Daniel, L'un et l'autre sacerdoce. P 1991, Desclée. 244 p. F 89. – [R]Études 375 (1991) 568 (J. *Thomas*: 'Alors, Église en marge?').

8109 **Bradshaw** Paul F., Ordination rites of the ancient churches of East and West 1990 → 6,8088: [R]JTS 42 (1991) 353-5 (B. D. *Spinks*).

8110 *Burgess* Joseph A., What is a bishop?: Lutheran Quarterly NS 1 (Milwaukee 1987) 307-329 [< LuJb 58, p. 161].

8111 **Caprioli** Mario, Il decreto conciliare 'Presbyterorum ordinis'; storia – analisi – dottrina: StTheol 7, 1989s → 6,8091: [R]Gregorianum 72 (1991) 152 (G. *Rambaldi*).

8112 **Carrasco Rouco** Alfonso, Le primat de l'Évêque de Rome: StFrib 73, canonica 7. FrS 1990, Univ. 284 p. Fs 39. – [R]TGL 81 (1991) 144s (W. *Beinert*).

8112* *Cattaneo* Arturo, Der ekklesiologische Ort der römischen Kurie nach der Apostolischen Konstitution 'Pastor bonus': → 97*, [F]MAY G. 1991, 109-118.

8113 **Chalendar** Xavier de, Le prêtre; hier, aujourd'hui et pour demain: L'Horizon du croyant 7, 1989 → 5,8057; F 69. [R]NRT 113 (1991) 139s (P. E. G.); ScEsp 43 (1991) 360s (G. *Novotný*).

8114 *Cislo* Mieczysław, ⊕ Die Identität des dienenden Priestertums: RoczTK 37,2 (1991 für 1987) 63-78; deutsch 79.

8115 **Cochini** Christian, The apostolic origins of priestly celibacy [[D]1981 → 62,7855], [T]*Marans* Nelly. SF 1990, Ignatius. xxii-470 p. $30. – [R]TS 52 (1991) 738s (G. T. *Dennis*).

Collins John N., Diakonia; re-interpreting the ancient sources [... misconceptions are current] 1990 → 9508.

Culbertson Philip L., *Shippee* Arthur B., The pastor; readings from the patristic period 1990 → e974.

8117 **Demmer** Klaus, Zumutung aus dem Ewigen; Gedanken zum priesterlichen Zölibat. FrB 1991, Herder. 94 p. DM 19,80. – [R]TGL 81 (1991) 406s (H. *Gleixner*).

8118 **Drewermann** Eugen, Kleriker 1989 [6]1990 [TPQ 139,303] → 6,8101: [R]StiZt 208 (1990) 125-9 (U. *Niemann*: 'zur Anthropologie der geistlichen Berufe'); TLZ 116 (1991) 386-8 (G. M. *Martin*).

8119 — **Eicher** Peter, Der Klerikerstreit; die Auseinandersetzung um E. DREWERMANN[2] [[1]1990]. Mü 1990, Kösel. 37 p. DM 29,80. 3-466-20326-0. – [R]TGL 81 (1991) 145s (W. *Beinert*: dreifach Skandalös: 1. enthüllt die skandalösen Zustände des katholischen Klerus; 2. das Evangelium ist ein Skandalon für diese Kirche; 3. Religionkritik für

Umkehr der Kirche selbst); TsTNijm 31 (1991) 436s (P. *Vander-meersch*).

8120 — *Sudbrack* Josef, Die Kleriker [... DREWERMANN]: GeistL 63 (1990) 182-199.

8121 *Drobner* Hubertus R., Die 'Instruktion über das Studium der Kirchenväter in der Priesterausbildung' [10.XI.1989]: TGL 81 (1991) 190-201.

8122 **Dunn** Patrick J., Priesthood; a re-exan:nation of the Roman Catholic theology of the presbyterate 1990 ➤ 6,8103: ᴿAustralasCR 68 (1991) 532-4 (M. *Putney*: he favors GALOT over SCHILLEBEECKX).

8123 ᴱ**Eicher** Peter, Der Dienst der Gemeinde: Neue Summe Theologie 3 [< 1982 ➤ 64,335: 1.1988 ➤ 5,458*; 2] 1989 ➤ 6,902: ᴿColcT 61,1 (1991) 170-3 (L. *Balter*, ❷); TPQ 139 (1991) 217s (W. *Zauner*).

8124 **Evans** Gillian, Authority in the Church, a challenge for the Anglicans. Norwich 1990, Canterbury. xx-147 p. £10. 1-85311-017-5. – ᴿExpTim 102 (1990s) 250s (J. *Macquarrie*); TLond 94 (1991) 372s (C. *Hill*).

8125 *a*) *Fang* Mark, ❷ Priesthood in the OT and NT; – *b*) *Gutheinz* Luis, ❸ Views of Catholic and Protestant Churches on the priesthood: ➤ 561*a*, Theological worshop 1990, ColcFuJen 87 (1991) 101-116 / 117-135.

8126 *Farahat* Kamal, Le sacerdoce de N. S. Jésus Christ et le ministère sacramentel (roum.): STBuc 39,5 (1987) 57-72.

8127 **Favale** Agostino, Il Ministero presbiterale 1989 ➤ 5,8064*; 6,8106: ᴿAnnTh 5 (1991) 212-7 (E. *Juliá*); RuBi 44 (1991) 81 (A. *Durak*).

8128 **Forestell** J. Terence, As ministers of Christ; the Christological dimension of ministry in the New Testament; an exegetical and theological study. NY 1991, Paulist. viii-199 p. $15. 0-8091-3220-6 [TDig 39,60].

8129 *Freitag* Josef, Schwierigkeiten und Erfahrungen mit dem 'sacramentum ordinis' auf dem Konzil von Trient: ZkT 113 (1991) 39-51.

8130 **Garuti** Adriano, Il Papa patriarca d'Occidente? Studio storico dottrinale 1990 ➤ 6,234: ᴿAnnTh 4 (1990) 460-2 (E. *Juliá*); CC 142 (1991,1) 422s (J. *Servais*); NRT 113 (1991) 770s (L. *Volpe*: dépourvu de fondement historique); RasT 32 (1991) 434-6 (G. *Pozzo*).

8131 *a*) *Garuti* Adriano, Il Papa patriarca d'Occidente? Considerazioni dottrinali: Antonianum 65 (1990) 23-59; Eng. 23. – *b*) *Congar* Yves, The pope as patriarch of the West [< Istina 28 (1983) 374-390], ᵀᴱ*Jermann* Rosemary: TDig 38 (1991) 2-7.

8132 *a*) *Gerosa* Libero, Zur Diskussion über die Bischofskonferenzen, I. Das Kolloquium von Salamanca [ᴱLEGRAND H. 1988]; – *b*) *Lüdicke* Klaus, Studien zum 'Instrumentum laboris' der Kongregation für die Bischöfe [ᴱMÜLLER H. 1989]: TR 87 (1991) 89-94 / 95-98.

8132* *a*) **Gestrich** Reinhold, Hirten füreinander sein; Seelsorge in der Gemeinde. Stu 1990, Quell. 168 p. DM 24,80. 3-7918-1415-X. – ᴿTLZ 116 (1991) 617 (R. *Schmidt-Rost*).

— *b*) *Giessen* Heinz, Im Dienst der Einheit; die Funktion der Dienstämter im Zeugnis neutestamentlicher Schriften: SNTU 15-A (1990) 5-40.

— *c*) ᴱ*Gramick* Jeannine, Homosexuality in the priesthood and the religious life. NY 1989, Crossroad. 251 p. $15. – ᴿCommonweal 117 (1990) 56-58 (E. *Kennedy*, also on ᴱWOLF J.).

8133 **Granfield** Patrick, Limits of the papacy 1987 ➤ 3,4537... 5,8073: ᴿScripTPamp 22 (1990) 258-263 (J. R. *Villar*).

8134 *Gromada* Conrad T., Toward a theology of ministry; the Lima Document and Roman Catholic theology: LvSt 15 (1990) 353-369.

8135 *Gutiérrez* Alfonso, La sacramentalidad del ministerio sacerdotal y su espiritualidad: T-Iusi 7 (1991) 107-114.

8136 **Hamstra** Sam J, John W. NEVIA, The Christian ministry; diss. Marquette. Milwaukee 1990. 228 p. 91-17347. – DissA 52 (1991s) 192-A.

8136* *Hennessey* L. R., *Diakonía* and *diakonoi*; early Christian perspectives on service and the servants: NewTR 4,4 (1991) 5-23 [< NTAbs 36,214].

8137 **Hill** Edmund, Ministry and authority in the Catholic Church 1988 → 4,9171 ... 6,8123:   RNBlackf 71 (1990) 261s (B. *Hebblethwaite*).

8138 EHoffmann Paul, Priesterkirche 1987 → 4,370; 5,8081:   RBLtg 63 (1990) 62s (A. *Damblon*: not discouraging).

8138* *Hofrichter* P., Amt und Amtsverständnis in der Urkirche: HDienst 45,1s (Salzburg 1991) 4-19 [< NTAbs 36,69].

8139 **Houssiau** Albert, *Mondet* Jean-Pierre, Le sacerdoce du Christ et de ses serviteurs selon les Pères 1990 → 6,8125; Fb 700:   RDivThom 94 (1991) 166s (L. J. *Elders*); EsprVie 100 (1990) 675-7 (É. *Cothenet*); NRT 113 (1991) 776-8 (G. *Peters*); RSPT 75 (1991) 356s (S.).

8140 *Jacob* Christoph, Zur Amtsterminologie des Johannes CHRYSOSTOMUS; die *archē* des *hiereús* nach De sacerdotio: TrierZT 100 (1991) 307-315.

8141 **Jacobs** Michael, Holding in trust; the appraisal of ministry: New Library of Pastoral Care. L 1989, SPCK. 187 p. £7. – RPrPeo 4 (1990) 75s (B. *Kilroy*).

8142 *Jaeger* David-M. A., L'autorità del vescovo in prospettiva conciliare; dimensioni sacramentale e comunionale [*Radu* D., tensions; *Ricca* P., Riforma; *Joss* A., Sobornost]: → 526, Nicolaus 1989/91, 89-113 [277-304 / 175-182 / 183-275].

8142* *Klauck* H. J., Gemeindearbeit im Team; grundlegende Gesichtspunkte aus dem NT: LebSeelsorge 42 (Wü 1991) 317-322 [< NTAbs 36,380: team-ministry].

8143 **Laghi** Pio, Sinodo '90; figura e formazione del prete del 2000: RasT 32 (1991) 5-16.

8144 **Lawler** Michael G., A theology of ministry 1990 → 6,8131:   RHorizons 18 (1991) 166s (K. B. *Osborne*).

8145 *Lebacqz* Karen, *Barton* Ronald G., Sex, power and ministry; the case of the normal neurotic: QRMin 10 (1990) 36-48 [3-35, Roundtable, The ministerial covenant].

8146 *L'Huillier* Peter, Episcopal celibacy in the Orthodox tradition: StVlad 35 (1991) 271-300.

8147 **Maciel** M., La formación integral del sacerdote. M 1990, BAC. 258 p. – RArTGran 34 (1991) 410s (J. M. *Rodríguez-Izquierdo*); Teresianum 42 (1991) 638-640 (M. *Caprioli*).

8148 **McKay** Michael J., The theology of the episcopate in the consultation on church union: Diss. DFord J. Wsh 1991. – RTLv 23, p. 566.

8149 **Martelet** Gustave, Deux mille ans d'Église en question; théologie du Sacerdoce, I. 1984 → 65,6768; II s. 1990 → 6,8141:   RCiTom 118 (1991) 419s (A. *Osuna*, 1); EsprVie 101 (1991) 132-140 (C. *Bouchaud*, 3); NRT 113 (1991) 256-9 (L. *Renwart*, 3); RHPR 71 (1991) 494 (G. *Siegwalt*, 3); RTLv 22 (1991) 524-7 (A. de *Halleux*, 2 'aimable fantaisie' d'orthographe des noms propres; 3); Salmanticensis 38 (1991) 253s (F. *Martín Hernández*, 3).

8149* *a)* [*Martins*] *Terra* João E., Bíblia e episcopado; – *b)* *Amiot* F., O bispo na Sagrada Escritura; – *c)* *D'Almeida Trinidade* M., O episcopado na tradição cristã; – *d)* *Colson* J., O bispo na tradição patrística antenicena; – *e)* *Mucci* Giandomenico, As conferencias episcopais e a autoridade de magistério: RCuBíb 13,51s (São Paulo 1989) 3-7 / 8-10 / 11-18 / 19-28 / 78-88.

8150 *Mathon* G., Sacerdoce: → 664, Catholicisme XIII,95s (1991) 245-260.

8151 **Möbs** Ulrich, Das kirchliche Amt bei Karl Rahner; eine Untersuchung der Amtsstufen und ihrer Ausgestaltung: kath. Diss. Giessen 1991, DMayer C. 395 p. – TR 87 (1991) 517; RTLv 23, p. 566 ('1990').

8152 **Nilsen** Else-Britt, sr. Le ministère ordonné dans la tradition catholique et luthérienne: [mémoire de maîtrise Angers 1982, DLegrand H.]: Thèses, 1987 → 3,7992: 4,7189: RRTLv 22 (1991) 103s (A. de Halleux).

8152* **O'Grady** J. F., Disciples and leaders; the origins of Christian ministry in the NT. NY 1991, Paulist. vii-137 p. $10. 0-8091-3269-9 [NTAbs 36,284].

8153 Passicos Jean, À l'écoute des travaux du congrès national du diaconat permanent (Vichy, 8-11 mai 1991): EsprVie 101 (1991) (507-) 509-511.

8154 Peri Vittorio, La dénomination de patriarche dans la titulature ecclésiastique du IVe au XVIe siècle: Irénikon 64 (1991) 359-364.

8155 a) Pottmeyer Hermann J., Kirche als communio; – b) Fabry Heinz-J., AT und Priesterbild; – c) Vorgrimler Herbert [Merz Michael M.], Diakon und Diakonat; – d) Meyer-Wilmes Hedwig, Frauen und Amt: BLtg 63,1 (1990) 2-9 / 36-41 / 9-15 [-18] / 22-29.

8156 **Ratzinger** Joseph, Serviteurs de notre joie; méditations sur la spiritualité sacerdotale, TGuillaume B. P 1990, Fayard. 119 p. F 65. – RRTLv 22 (1990) 260s (G. Thils).

8157 Ratzinger Joseph, Biblical foundations of priesthood [Rome Synod Oct. 1, 1990], TPeter Carl C.: CommND 17 (1990) 617-627.

8158 Reumann John, A new way for reading confessional documents on bishops and ministry?: CurrTMiss 18 (1991) 245-255.

8159 **Rolland** Philippe, Les ambassadeurs du Christ; ministère pastoral et Nouveau Testament: Lire la Bible 92. P 1991, Cerf. iv-147 p. F 68. REsprVie 101 (1991) 525 (L. Walter).

8160 Ruh Ulrich, Brauchen wir einen anderen Klerus?: HerdKor 9 (1990) 397.

8161 Sanson Michael, So, what is a deacon?: Anvil 7 (Bristol 1990) 215-224 [< ZIT 90,732].

8161* ESchäfer Gerhard K., Strohm Theodor, Diakonie, biblische Grundlagen und Orientierung; ein Arbeitsbuch zur theologischen Verständigung über den diakonischen Auftrag: Univ. Diak/wiss 2. Heid 1990, Heid-VA. 425 p. DM 36 [TLZ 117,466, R. Turre].

Schatz Klaus, Der päpstliche Primat 1990 → 4093.

8162 Scheffczyk Leo, Christus Stern und Weg priesterlichen Seins: VerbumSVD 32 (1991) 199-202.

8162* Schwank Benedikt, Zur Zölibatsfrage in unserer Zeit [Beuroner Bibeltag 12.II.1991]: ErbAuf 67 (1991) 134-9.

8163 a) Sicari Antonio, Appartenance à l'Église, charismes, sacerdoce ministériel; – b) Armogathe Jean-Robert, Formation des prêtres et formation sacerdotale: CommP 15,6 (1990) 28-52 / 14-27.

8163* Siegert F., Prophetie und Diakonie; über das 'Amt' im NT, verglichen mit heutiger kirchlicher Praxis: TBeit 22,4 (1991) 174-194 [< NTAbs 36,70].

8164 **Sipe** A. W. Richard, A secret world; sexuality and the search for celibacy. NY 1990, Brunner/Mazel. – RTablet 245 (1991) 69s (Jack Dominian's more casual experience as practicing psychiatrist confirms the conclusion, based on 1500 people admittedly either in therapy or sexual partners of priests: '50% of priests in U.S. either temporarily or permanently not observing strict celibacy; 10-20% homosexual...'); TS 52 (1991) 770s (V. J. Genovesi).

8165 *Staats* Reinhart, Von der Konfessionskirche zur Bischofskirche; der schwedische Rapport 'Das Bischofsamt' aus patristischer Sicht [ᴱ*Andrén* Olof, *al.* (... *Stendahl* K., katolsk. *Crochet* R., *al.*), Biskopsämbetet (Sto 1988, Verbum) 170 p.]: TLZ 116 (1991) 321-338.

8166 **Tavard** George H., A review of Anglican orders; the problem and the solution: Theology and Life 31. Collegeville MN 1990, Liturgical [RelStR 18,69, T. *Hummel*].

8167 *Theodorou* Evangelos D., ⑤ The institution of deaconesses in the Orthodox Church and the possibility of its revival: TAth 62 (1991) 621-660; Eng. 931.

8168 **Thils** Gustave, Prêtres de toujours et prêtres d'aujourd'hui, à l'occasion du Synode de 1980: RTLv Cah 1990 → 6,8162: ᴿNRT 113 (1991) 474 (G. N).

8169 *Thompson* J., Ordination: IrBSt 12 (1990) 117-128.

8170 *Thornhill* John, The role of the ordained minister within the Christian community: AustralasCR 67 (1990) 187-206.

8171 *Vanhoye* Albert, ⑨ Kapłaństwo Chrystusa i kapłaństwo Chrześcijan, ᵀ*Halas* Stanisław [Wsz. Akad. Teol. 5.X.1990) RuBi 44 (1991) 4-18.

8172 *Voulgaris* Christos S., ⑤ *To mystērion tês hierosýnēs* ... The sacrament of the priesthood according to the NT: TAth 62 (1991) 661-693; Eng. 931.

8173 *Walf* Knut, Erzbischof WEAKLANDs Alarmruf; ein Hirtenbrief zur Not der priesterlosen Gemeinden [p. 89, Das Recht der Gemeinde auf Eucharistie]: Orientierung 55 (1991) 92-94. 256-8.

8174 **Wolf** J., Gay priests. SF 1989, Harper & R. 216 p. $18 [TS 51,575].

8175 **Whitehead** James D. & Evelyn E., The promise of partnership; leadership and ministry in an adult Church. SF 1990, Harper. xiv-226 p. $20 [CBQ 53,538].

H8 *Liturgia; oratio, vita spiritualis* – NT – **Prayer.**

8176 *Albertine* Richard, 'Theiosis' according to the Eastern Fathers, mirrored in the development of the epiclesis: EphLtg 105 (1991) 393-417.

8177 **Alonso Schökel** Luis, Riflessioni bibliche per Esercizi Spirituali: → 287*b*, Pregare con Ignazio [R 1991, Ap. Preghiera] 141-202.

8177* *a*) *Alonso-Schökel* L., I fondamenti metodologici; – *b*) *Vanni* U., *al.*, Il testo biblico nel contesto celebrativo: → 422*, Esegesi/celebrazione 1987/91, ...

8178 **Arnold** Pierre, La santità per l'uomo d'oggi; un itinerario di fede fra tradizione e modernità: Problemi del nostro tempo 80. Mi 1991, Massimo. 253 p. Lit. 25.000.

8178* **Baldovin** John E., The urban character of Christian worship 1987 → 3,8037 ... 6,8170: ᴿHeythJ 32 (1991) 138s (B. D. *Spinks*).

8179 **Barbaglio** G., La spiritualità del NT: StSp (Deh) 2, 1988 → 4,810: ᴿAsprenas 38 (1991) 123s (V. *Scippa*).

8180 **Basurko** Xabier, El canto cristiano en la tradición primitiva: Victoriensia 59. Vitoria 1991, Eset. 301 p. 84-7167-125-5.

8181 ᴱ**Bériou** Nicole, Prier au Moyen Âge; pratiques et expériences (Vᵉ-XVᵉ s.): Témoins de notre histoire. Turnhout 1991, Brepols. 349 p. Fb 850 [TR 87,348].

8182 **Bernard** Charles-André, Teologia spirituale, temi e problemi, dialogo con *Gioia* Mario: Saggi 29. R 1991, AVE. 293 p. Lit. 32.000.

8183 **Blasucci** A., *al.*, La spiritualità del medioevo: → 6,854* StSpG (Borla) 4, 1988; ᴿAsprenas 38 (1991) 125s (D. *Sorrentino*).

Bouyer Louis, The Christian mystery; from pagan myth to Christian mysticism 1990 → 9525.

8185 **Bovenmars** Jan G., A biblical spirituality of the heart. NY 1991, Alba. xxiv-205 p. $13. 0-8189-0584-0 [TDig 39,52].

8185* **Brändle Matesanz** Francisco, La Biblia en San Juan de la Cruz: Logos 39. M 1990, Ed. Espiritualidad. 123 p. – RTeresianum 42 (1991) 652 (M. *Diego Sánchez*; N. B. the entire first fascicle p. 1-340 is on the centenary of St. John of the Cross).

8186 **Cantalamessa** R., Gesù Cristo il Santo di Dio [Vatican Advent-meditations]: Dimensioni dello Spirito 23. T 1990, Paoline. 171 p. Lit. 20.000 pa. 88-215-1909-0 [NTAbs 36,281].

8186* **Caprioli** Mario, Spiritualità sacerdotale; valutazione della bibliografia 1965-90: Teresianum 42 (1991) 435-473.

8187 *Casciaro* José M., La oración de Jesús en los evangelios sinópticos: ScripTPamp 23 (1991) 215-227.

8187* **Cipriani** Settimio, La preghiera nel NT: Meditazioni bibliche 3, 1989 → 6,8185: RScripTPamp 23 (1991) 1048 (A. *García-Moreno*).

8188 ECongourdeau Marie-Hélène, Nicolas CABASILAS, La vie en Christ V-VII: SChr 361, → 6,8186. P 1990, Cerf. 247 p. F 155. – RNRT 113 (1991) 593s (A. *Harvengt*).

8189 ECorsato Celestino, *al.*, Oranti e preghiere, dalla Bibbia e dal mondo: Oggi. Padova 1991, Gregoriana. 136 p. Lit. 10.000.

8190 **Cothenet** Édouard, Exégèse et liturgie: LDiv 133, 1988 → 4,9233 ... 6,8187: RCrNSt 12 (1991) 407-410 (P. *Prigent*).

8191 **Crichton** J. D., The living Christ; 'in Christ' through Scripture and liturgy. L 1988, Collins. ix-133 p. £2,50. – RHeythJ 32 (1991) 267s (R. C. D. *Jasper*: a life-work).

8192 **Cusson** Gilles, Biblical theology and the Spiritual Exercises 1988 → 4,9235; 5,8146: RHeythJ 32 (1991) 262s (P. *Endean*).

8192* **Darricau** R., *Peyrous* B., Histoire de la spiritualité: Que sais-je? 2621. P 1991, PUF. 127 p. [NRT 114,460, A. *Toubeau*].

8193 **Donghi** Antonio, A lode della sua gloria; il mistero della liturgia. Mi 1988, Àncora. 204 p. Lit. 14.000. 88-7610-261-2. – RGregorianum 72 (1991) 159s (A. *Elberti*).

8193* **Doohan** Helen & Leonard, Prayer in the NT; make your requests known to God. Collegeville MN 1991, Liturgical. 143 p. 0-8146-5007-4.

8194 **Dupré** Louis, *Saliers* Don E., Christian spirituality, post-Reformation and modern: EWSp 18, 1989 → 5,8151; 6,8193: RHorizons 18 (1991) 342s (D. *Burton-Christie*); RRel 50 (1991) 463-5 (F. G. *McLeod*); TLond 94 (1991) 367s (D. *Lonsdale*).

8195 *Ellacuría* Ignacio, Lectura latinoamericana de los Ejercicios Espirituales de San Ignacio: RLatAmT 23 (1991) 111-147.

8196 **Empereur** James L., *Kiesling* Christopher G. [O.P.† 1986], The liturgy that does justice: Theology and Christian Life. Collegeville MN 1990, Ltg/Glazier. x-262 p. $17. 0-8146-5643-9 [TDig 38,158].

8197 **Faricy** Robert, *Rooney* Lucy, Groeien in gebed, een weg naar verdiept bidden als omgang met God. Haag 1990, Cip. 96 p. 90-71571-19-X. – RGregorianum 72 (1991) 408s (Faricy).

8198 *Faure* Pierre, La liturgie catholique: Études 437 (1991) 547-556.

8199 *Fomum* Zacharias T., The practice of intercession. NY 1991, Vantage. xi-313 p. $18 [CBQ 54,402].

8200 *Garofalo* Salvatore, Sacra Scrittura e vita spirituale: Divinitas 34 (1990) 3-16.

8201 *Gibert* Pierre, Le rapport à l'Écriture dans l'oraison; une naïveté seconde: Christus 37 (P 1990) 425-443.

8202 *Gilbert* Paul, Esercizi, Scrittura e sistema [FESSARD G., ...'quattro sensi' della Scrittura]: ScuolC 118 (1990) 407-431.

8203 *González Cougil* Ramiro, Adaptación litúrgica; principios que dimanan de la 'Sacrosanctum Concilium' completada por otros documentos conciliares; EphLtg [104 (1990) 265-298] 105 (1991) 3-29.

8204 **Gozier** André, La ténèbre lumineuse; un moine lit la Bible: Spiritualité. P/FrS 1990, S-Paul. 184 p. F 89. – ᴿEsprVie 101 (1991) 31s (É. *Ricaud*).

8205 **Gozzelino** Giorgio, Al cospetto di Dio; elementi di teologia della vita spirituale: Saggi di Teologia. T-Leumann 1989, Elle Di Ci. 255 p. Lit. 18.000. 88-01-10149-X. – ᴿGregorianum 72 (1991) 586s (A. *Queralt*: merece ser leido).

8206 *Greiner* Sebastian, La prière est-elle toujours exaucée?: NRT 113 (1991) 839-852.

8207 **Grelot** P., *al.*; La liturgie dans le Nouveau Testament: Introd. à la Bible 9. P 1991, Desclée. 364 p. F 185. – ᴿEsprVie 101 (1991) 561s (É. *Cothenet*).

8208 **Guillet** Jacques, Textes bibliques pour prier: coll. VieChr 70. P c. 1990, VieChr. 48 p. F 32.

8209 **Hamman** Adalbert G., La prière dans l'Église ancienne: Traditio Christiana 7, 1989 ⟶ 5,8170*: ᴿRFgIC 119 (1991) 221-3 (M. *Simonetti*); RHPR 71 (1991) 366s (P. *Maraval*).

8209* **Hamman** Adalbert G., Das Gebet in der Alten Kirche [144 Texte bis 500], ᵀ*Spoerri* A.: Traditio Christiana 7. Fra 1989, Lang. xlvii-234 p. Fs 99,20 [TLZ 117,284, H.-G. *Thümmel*].

8210 *Haręzga* Stanisław, ❂ The revival of [chiefly Guy II (ML 40) before 1188] Lectio Divina in today's Church: ColcT 61,4 (1991) 45-69; Eng. 69.

8211 **Hegger** H.J., Bijbelse elementen bij rooms-katholieke mystici. Kampen 1990, Kok. 98 p. ƒ 15 [TR 87,348].

8212 *Hingley* Chris J.H., Evangelicals and spirituality: Themelios 15 (1989s) 86-91.

8213 *Jetter* Werner, Glaubensüberlieferung und Frömmigkeitssprache — das Beispiel der Katechismuspredigt: ZTK 87 (1990) 376-414.

8213* **Johnson** Luke T., Faith's freedom; a classic spirituality for contemporary Christians, 1990 ⟶ 6,8210: ᴿTS 52 (1991) 768-770 (E.C. *Muller*).

8214 ᴱ**Jones** Cheslyn, *Wainwright* Geoffrey, *Yarnold* Edward, The study of spirituality 1986 ⟶ 3,420: ᴿCritRR 3 (1990) 291-4 (Janet *Ruffing*); JRel 70 (1990) 111s (G. *Cleve*).

8214* **Kavanaugh** J.F., Following Christ in a consumer society; the spirituality of cultural resistance² [¹1981]. Mkn 1991, Orbis. xxx-194 p. $13 [NRT 114,423, A. *Toubeau*].

8215 **Kilmartin** E.J., Systematic theology of liturgy. KC 1988, Sheed & W. xii-405 p. – ᴿMilltSt 28 (1991) 156-8 (R. *Moloney*).

8216 **Kolvenbach** Peter-Hans, Le chemin de Pâques [retraite du Vatican 1987] 1990 ⟶ 6,8215: ᴿChristus 37 (P 1990) 211.

8217 *Kunzler* Michael, Indumentum salutis; Überlegungen zum liturgischen Gewand: TGʟ 81 (1991) 52-78.

Lane Belden C., Landscapes of the sacred; geography and narrative in American spirituality 1988 ⟶ e306,

8218 **Langkammer** *Hugolin,* Ⓟ Biblijne podstawy duchowości... Biblical foundations of Christian spirituality. Wrocław 1987, Archidiecez. 287 p. – ᴿRuBi 42 (1989) 149-151 (M. *Arndt*).

8219 **Lattke** Michael, Hymnus; Materialien zu einer Geschichte der antiken Hymnologie: NOrb 19. FrS/Gö 1991, Univ./VR. xiv-505 p. Fs 130 [CBQ 54,403]. 3-7278-0751-2 / 3-525-53920-7.

8220 **Le Gall** R., La liturgie de l'Église; mystère, signes et figures. Chambray-les-Tours 1990, C.L.D. 207 p. F 165. – ᴿNRT 113 (1991) 454s (A. *Toubeau*).

8221 **Leniaud** Jean-Michel, Pour une théologie des objets de culte [... où commence l'idolâtrie?... les Puces de Vanves...comme des kleenex que l'on jette après usage]: MaisD 188 (1991) 87-107.

8222 ᴱ**Léthel** F.-M., Évangile/Venasque 1989/90 → 6,542: ᴿRThom 91 (1991) 168s (M.-É. *Lauzière*).

8223 **Lodi** Enzo, Il Credo ecumenico pregato nella liturgia bizantina e romana. Padova 1990, Messaggero. 478 p. Lit. 60.000. – ᴿCC 142 (1991,3) 334s (G. *Ferraro*).

8224 **Lohfink** N., Le nostre grandi feste, esegesi e liturgia. CasM 1990, Piemme. 92 p. Lit. 14.000. – ᴿAsprenas 38 (1991) 268 (A. *Petti*).

8225 **Luzarraga** Jesús, Orando con IGNACIO tras Jesús; método de oración siguiendo a Ignacio de Loyola; la oración de Jesús según el Nuevo Testamento: Espiritualidad ignaciana 13. Bilbao 1991, Mensajero. 236 p. [AcPIB 9/7 (1991) 550].

8226 **MacGregor** Alistair J., Fire and light in the Western Triduum; their use at Tenebrae and at the Paschal Vigil: diss. Durham. 418 p. BRD-92906. – DissA 52 (1991s) 1381-A.

8227 *a*) *Maier* Martin, La théologie des Exercices [de s. Ignace de LOYOLA] de Karl RAHNER; – *b*) *Baldé* Françoise, Relire Ignace après FREUD avec Louis BEIRNAERT; expérience spirituelle et acte éthique: RechSR 79 (1991) 535-560 / 561-584; Eng. 489s.

8228 *Margerie* B. de, Sacré-Cœur: → 664, Catholicisme XIII,96 (1991) 293-303.

8229 **Martini** Carlo M., Il Vangelo alle sorgenti. Mi 1990, Àncora. 114 p. Lit. 10.000. – ᴿCiVit 46 (1991) 118 (Duccia *Camiciotti*).

8230 *Martini* Carlo M., S. IGNAZIO e il Vaticano II; la 'lectio divina' nella vita del cristiano [Napoli 24.V.1991]: RasT 32 (1991) 547-557.

8230* *Martini* Carlo M., *a*) La nostra vita spirituale di fronte alle sfide di oggi (*Ambrosio* Gianni, commento); – *b*) Il programma pastorale 'comunicare'; – *c*) Uomini della comunicazione perché uniti al Crocifisso: Ambrosius 66 (1990) 5-17 (31-43) / 413-429 / 525-535.

8231 **Mazza** Enrico, La mistagogia, una teologia della liturgia in epoca patristica. R 1988, Liturgiche. 198 p. – ᴿRevSR 65 (1991) 137 (M. *Metzger*).

8232 **Mazza** Enrico, Mystagogy; a theology of liturgy in the patristic age, ᵀ*O'Connell* Matthew J. NY 1989, Pueblo. xii-228 p. $14.50 pa. – ᴿWorship 64 (1990) 381s (P. F. *Bradshaw*).

8233 **Mazza** Enrico, Le odierne preghiere eucaristiche: 1. Struttura, teologia, fonti; 2. Testi e documenti editi e inediti: Studi e Ricerche di Liturgia. Bo 1991, Dehoniane. 592 p. (2 vol.) Lit. 40.000 [RivB 39,175].

8234 *Metzger* Marcel, *a*) Liturgie, spiritualité et vie en Christ; Nicolas CABASILAS [† 1397] et Ignace de LOYOLA: RevSR 65 (1991) 227-239; – *b*) Liturgie, sacrements et théologie pastorale: RevSR 63 (1989) 85-115; i. La disgrace de la liturgie dans des publications récentes.

8235 **Miles** Margaret R., The image and practice of holiness; a critique of the classic manuals of devotion 1989 → 6,8225a: ᴿMilltSt 27 (1991) 146-9 (Teresa *Clements*).

8236 **Moore** Sebastian, Jesus the liberator of desire 1989 → 5,8184: ᴿHorizons 18 (1991) 93-112 (S. *Duffy*) & 112-9 (Elisabeth *Koenig*) & 119-123 (W. P. *Loewe*), response p. 123-9; RRel 50 (1991) 462s (C. *Cummings*).

8237 *Navone* John, *a)* Glenn TINDER's prophetic spirituality [of a political science prof.: Political Meaning of Christianity, Baton Rouge 1989]: MilltSt 28 (1991) 132-150; – *b)* Il mistero di Dio interpella l'uomo: CC 142 (1991,1) 23-32.

8238 *Nikolakopoulos* Konstantinos, Das Neue Testament als hymnologische Quelle in der Orthodoxen Kirche: TAth 61 (1990) 161-196; Eng. 903.

8239 *Oliana* Guido, La Chiesa, corpo di Cristo in crescita... nella Veglia Pasquale: EphLtg 105 (1991) 30-58.

8239* **Olst** E. H. van, The Bible and liturgy [Bijbel en...], ᵀ*Vriend* J. GR 1991, Eerdmans. xii-159 p. $14 pa. 0-8028-0306-7 [NTAbs 36,288].

8240 **Pablo Maroto** Daniel de, Historia de la espiritualidad cristiana. M 1990, Espiritualidad. 395 p. – ᴿBrotéria 133 (1991) 471s (F. de *Sales Baptista*).

8241 *Parker* David, Evangelical spirituality reviewed: EvQ 63 (1991) 123-148.

8241* **Power** David N., Worship, culture and theology. Wsh 1990, Pastoral. xii-283 p. $12 pa. [TLZ 117,464, G. A. *Krieg*].

8242 **Rahner** Karl, The practice of faith, a handbook of contemporary spirituality [anthology of short excerpts], ᴱ*Lehmann* Karl, *Raffelt* Albert, 1986 → 3,8105: ᴿCritRR 2 (1989) 451-4 (M. L. *Taylor*).

8243 **Roose-Evans** James, The inner stage; finding a center in prayer and ritual. CM 1990, Cowley. 216 p. $10 [RelStR 18,130, J. T. *Ford*].

8244 *Ruggieri* Vincenzo, *Douramani* Katherine, Tempio e mensa [Euchologia Bessarione Gamma-beta 1, per consacrazione di chiesa e altare]: RasT 32 (1991) 279-286; testo 287-300.

8245 ᴱ**Sargologos** E., Un traité de vie spirituelle et morale au XIᵉ siècle; le florilège sacro-profane du manuscrit 6 de Patmos. Saloniki 1990, Mélissa. 1027 p. F 590. – ᴿNRT 113 (1991) 458s (A. *Harvengt*).

8245* **Schmidt-Lauber** Hans-Christoph, Die Zukunft des Gottesdienstes; von der Notwendigkeit lebendiger Liturgie: TBt 19. Stu 1990, Calwer. 482 p. DM 38 [TLZ 117,628, G. *Möller*].

8246 **Špidlík** Tomáš, La spiritualité de l'Orient chrétien II. La prière: OrChrAnal 230, 1988 → 4,9288... 6,8244: ᴿRevSR 65 (1991) 139s (M. *Metzger*).

8247 *Stolle* Volker, Das Gebet der Gemeinde Jesu Christi nach dem NT: KerDo 37 (1991) 307-330; Eng. 331.

8248 **Subilia** Vittorio, La parola che brucia: Meditazioni bibliche. T 1991, Claudiana. 176 p. 88-7016-151-X.

8248* **Sudbrack** Josef, Was heisst christlich meditieren? Wege zu sich selbst und zu Gottes Du: Tb 1717. FrB 1990, Herder. 126 p. DM 10 [TLZ 117,64, G. *Bunners*].

8249 **Salzmann** Jorg Christian, Lehren und Ermahnen — zur Geschichte des christlichen Wortgottesdienstes in den ersten drei Jahrhunderten: Diss. Tübingen 1990. vi-313 p.; 230 p. – TLZ 116 (1991) 232s.

8250 *Swetnam* James, La Biblia y los ejercicios; algunas observaciones: → 287a, Emaús en Manresa 1991, 9-19.

8251 **Świerzawi** Wacław, ❷ Il mistero di Cristo e della Chiesa; mistica radicata nella liturgia. Kraków 1988, Apost. Modlitwy. – ᴿAntonianum 66 (1991) 588s (C. *Teklak*).

8252 **Taft** Robert, The liturgy of the hours in East and West 1986 → 2,6444 ... 6,8248: ᴿOrChr 74 (1990) 349-353 (G. *Winkler*).

8253 **Talbert** Charles H., Learning through suffering; the educational value of suffering in the NT and its milieu: Glazier-Zacchaeus. Collegeville MN 1991, Liturgical. 92 p. $7. 0-8146-5677-2 [TDig 38,393].

8254 **Talley** Thomas J., Aux origines de l'année liturgique, ᵀ*Davril* Anselme: Liturgie. P 1990, Cerf. 268 p. F 195. – ᴿEsprVie 101 (1991) 651s (P. *Rouillard*).

8255 **Thilo** Hans Joachim, Frömmigkeit; aus dem Reichtum der Traditionen schöpfen. Mü 1991, Kösel. 231 p.; 6 fig. – ᴿTLZ 116 (1991) 816s (M. *Haustein*).

8256 *Triacca* Achille M., Linee teologico-liturgiche della 'celebrazione' della Parola di Dio: Salesianum 53 (1991) 669-689.

8256* **Untergassmair** F.G., Im Namen Jesu beten; biblische Impulse zu christlichem Gebet. Stu 1990, KBW. 153 p. DM 24,80. – 3-460-32921-1 [NTAbs 36,132].

8257 **Vidal** J., L'Église et les religions ou le désir réorienté [retraite 1987 enregistrée]. P 1990, Albin Michel. 179 p. F 89. – ᴿNRT 113 (1991) 153 (A. *Toubeau*).

8258 **Viller** Marcel, *Rahner* Karl, Aszese und Mystik in der Väterzeit; ein Abriss der frühchristlichen Spiritualität, ᴱ*Neufeld* K.H. 1989 → 6,k22: ᴿTLZ 116 (1991) 131s (P. *Heidrich*: Viller français 1930, deutsch 1939 'fast ein Originalwerk des Bearbeiters'; heute wirken die Literaturangaben des damaligen Standes unbefriedigend).

8259 **White** James F., Protestant worship; traditions in transition. Louisville 1989, W-Knox. 288 p. $16. 0-664-25037-8. – ᴿÉTRel 66 (1991) 569-575 (B. *Reymond*).

8260 a) *Wolterstorff* Nicholas, Justice as a condition of authentic liturgy; – b) *Olson* Dennis T., Which comes first, justice or worship?: TTod 48 (1991s) 6-21 / 22-25 (-44, other responses).

H8.1 **Vocatio**, *vita religiosa communitatis* – *Sancti;* the Saints.

8261 **Battelli** Giovanni, Missione apostolica; breve storia, natura e scopo della vita consacrata nella Chiesa; riflessioni. Bo 1991, EMI. 199 p. Lit. 14.000.

8262 **Baumeister** Theofried, a) Genese und Entfaltung der altchristlichen Theologie des Martyriums: TrC 8. Bern 1991, Lang. xl-202 p. – b) Genèse et évolution de la théologie du martyre dans l'Église ancienne: Traditio Christiana 8. Bern 1991, Lang. xl-202 p. 3-261-04288-5; franç. -9-3.

8263 ᴱ**Beinert** Wolfgang, Die Heiligen heute ehren; eine theologisch-pastorale Handreichung. Lp 1988, St. Benno. 230 p. [LuJb 57 (1990) p. 319 with indication of four articles there cited].

8264 *Beyer* Jean, I consigli evangelici [... i riferimenti scritturistici nei testi del Concilio]: ... La pratica: VConsacr 26 (1990) 52-67 / 677-684.

8265 **Böhler** Heidemarie, La dottrina dei consigli evangelici dal Vaticano II ad oggi: diss. Pont. Univ. Gregoriana, ᴰ*Beyer* J. R 1991s [InfPUG 24/122, p. 27].

8266 **Boisvert** Laurent, Le célibat religieuse 1990 → 6,8258: ᴿScEsp 43 (1991) 131s (R. *Potvin*).

8267 **Brown** Peter, The body and society 1988 → 4,9307... 6,8261: ᴿJRel 70 (1990) 432-6 (Elizabeth A. *Clark*); JRS 81 (1991) 180-2 (Mary *Beard*); Laverna 2 (1991) 144-6 (T. *Pekáry*).

8267* **Brown** Peter, Die Heiligenverehrung; ihre Entstehung und Funktion in der lateinischen Christenheit [1978 Lectures, 1981 → 62,k910], ᵀ*Bernardt* J.†. Lp 1991, St. Benno. 156 p. DM 30 [TLZ 117,131s, H. *Holze*].

8268 *Ciardi* Fabio, Indicazioni metodologiche per l'ermeneutica del carisma dei Fondatori: Claretianum 30 (1990) 5-47.

8269 **Cole** Basil, *Conner* Paul, Christian totality; theology of the consecrated life. Bombay 1990, Saint Paul. 258 p. $5.50. – ᴿAngelicum 68 (1991) 562-4 (J. *Aumann*: fills a gap).

8270 *Congar* Yves, Communion of saints and memorial [< VSp 686 (1989) 593-6], ᵀᴱ*Jermann* Rosemary: TDig 38 (1991) 313-5.

8270* a) **da Spinetoli** Ortensio, I consigli evangelici; proposta e interpretazione. R 1990, Dehoniane. 198 p. – ᴿTeresianum 42 (1991) 343s (V. *Pasquetto*).

— b) **Delizy** B., sr., Appelé[e]s, rassemblés, envoyés [diss. cath. Strasbourg]: Maranatha 22. P/Montréal 1991, Médiaspaul/Paulines. 141 p. F 75 [NRT 114,604, L.-J. *Renard*].

— c) *Desprez* V., Christian asceticism between the NT and the beginning of monasticism; the second century / Africa 3d c.; / Egypt and the East:: AmBenR 42 (1991) 163-178. 334-344. 356-374.

8271 **Elliott** Alison G., Roads to Paradise; reading the lives of the early saints 1988 → 6,8267: ᴿAnzAltW 44 (1991) 22 (J.-B. *Bauer*); Helios 18,1 (1991) 83-87 (Gail P. *Corrington*).

8272 ᴱ**Favale** Agostino, Vocazione comune e vocazioni specifiche; aspetti biblici, teologici e psico-pedagogico-pastorali: BtScRel 44, 1981 → 62,394: ᴿRThom 91 (1991) 165 (J.-M. *Fabre*).

8273 **Felder** Thomas, Jungfräulichkeit als Anteilnahme am Geheimnis der Kirche nach Aᴜɢᴜsᴛɪɴᴜs: Diss. ᴰ*Sauser*. Innsbruck 1991. 200 p. – RTLv 23, p. 548.

8273* **Galot** Jean, Vivere con Maria nella vita consacrata 1987 → 4,9802 ('comunitaria'): ᴿMarianum 52 (1990) 445s (A. *Rum*).

8274 a) *Harrison* Verna, Poverty in the Orthodox tradition; – b) *Chryssavgis* John, Obedience – hierarchy and asceticism: StVlad 34 (1990) 15-47 / 49-60.

8275 **Harvey** Susan A., Asceticism and society in crisis; Jᴏʜɴ of Ephesus and the lives of the Eastern saints: TransfClasH 18. Berkeley 1990, Univ. California. xvi-226 p. $35. – ᴿJTS 42 (1991) 746-8 (G. *Gould*).

8276 **Heffernan** Thomas J., Sacred biography ; saints and their biographers in the Middle Ages, NY 1988, Oxford-UP. ix-333 p. – ᴿMilltSt 27 (1991) 149-152 (W. *Mathews*).

8277 **Hilpisch** S., Histoire du monachisme bénédictin. P 1989, Téqui. 421 p. F 235. – ᴿNRT 113 (1991) 141s (L. J. *Renard*).

8277* St. Iꜱᴀᴀᴄ of Nineveh on ascetical life. Crestwood ɴʏ 1989, St. Vladimir. 116 p. $6 pa. [TLZ 117,739, P. *Heidrich*].

8278 ᴱ**Kieckhefer** Richard, *Bond* George D., Sainthood; its manifestations in world religions 1988 → 5,480: ᴿCritRR 3 (1990) 251-3 (D. P. *Sheridan*); JRel 70 (1991) 669s (G. G. *Stroumsa*).

8278* **Metz** Johann B., *Peters* Tiemo R., Gottespassion; zur Ordensexistenz heute. FrB 1991, Herder. 103 p. DM 17,80 [TLZ 117,635, H. *Kirchner*].

8279 *Morales* José, La vocación cristiana en la primera patrística: ScripTPamp 23 (1991) 837-889.

8280 **Neal** sr. Marie Augusta, From nuns to sisters, an expanding vocation. Mystic CT 1989, Twenty-Third. $10 pa. – RCCurr 40 (1990s) 135-7 (Dody *Donnelly*).

8281 **Nürnberg** Rosemarie, Askese als sozialer Impuls D1988 → 6,8284: RTR 87 (1991) 121s (K. S. *Frank*).

8281* **O'Murchu** Diarmuid, Religious life; a prophetic vision; hope and promise for tomorrow. ND 1991, Ave Maria. 259 p. $10 pa. 0-87793-463-0 [TDig 39,180: social psychologist].

8282 **Panikkar** Raimon, Den Mönch in sich entdecken, T*Tepe* Georg. Mü 1989, Kösel. 204 p. – RZMissRW 74 (1990) 90s (H. *Waldenfels*).

8284 *Peloso* Flavio, Il culto dei santi: EphLtg 105 (1991) 237-262.418-448.

8285 **Pujol** Jaume, Les religieux aujourd'hui et pour demain, T*Chambert* J. P 1990, Desclée. 206 p. – REsprVie 101 (1991) 17-19 (G.-M. *Oury*).

8286 **Rausch** Thomas P., Radical Christian communities [religious life originating from Acts...]. Collegeville MN 1990, Liturgical. 216 p. $15 [RelStR 18,40, J. T. *Ford*: useful especially on recent FOUCAULD, Taizé, M. TERESA, Arche, base].

8287 **Sago** Athanase, The religious life according to Saint Augustine, T*Thabault* Paul C., NY 1990, New City. 240 p. $12 pa. [CBQ 53,537].

8288 **Scheuer** Manfred, Die evangelischen Räte... Strukturprinzip systematischer Theologie bei H. v. BALTHASAR, K. RAHNER, J.-B. METZ und in der Theologie der Befreiung: Stud. Syst. Spir. T. 1. Wü 1990, Echter. xiv-449 p. DM 58. 3-429-01296-1. – RTPhil 66 (1991) 228s (M. *Schneider*); TPQ 139 (1991) 313s (J. *Singer*); ZkT 113 (1991) 112-4 (K. H. *Neufeld*).

8289 *Scheuer* Manfred, IGNATIANA [12 Bücher] — zum 500-Jahr-Jubiläum der Jesuiten: TPQ 139 (1991) 421-7 [p. 436, *Rupp* Walter, Jesuiten-Spiegel, ein amüsantes Lesebuch (Graz 1990, Styria; 208 p.; Karikaturen, *Graw* Hans; DM 24,80) p. 63, 'Gesellschaft Jesu' war zunächst Ochs und Esel, später Zöllner und Dirnen, danach zwei Schächer; diese 'Gesellschaft Jesu' hat sich nicht bewährt... musste 1540 neu gegründet werden].

8290 *Serra* Rafael M., Vocazione profetica e religiosa: Claretianum 30 (1990) 115-173.

8291 **Tamburrino** Pio, Koinonia; aspetti ecclesiologici del cenobitismo PACOMIANO nel IV secolo: diss. Anselmianum, Theol. 244, D*Neunheuser* B. R 1989, Pont. Athenaeum Anselmianum. 109 p. (estratto).

8291* *Tavard* George H., The veneration of the Saints as an ecumenical question: OneInC 26 (1990) 40-50.

8292 *Tilley* Maureen A., The ascetic body [SUEDFELD E. 1990; SCARRY E. 1985, 1990] and the (un-)making of the world of the martyr: JAAR 59 (1991) 467-479.

8293 *Vogüé* Adalbert de, Histoire littéraire du mouvement monastique dans l'antiquité, I. Le monachisme latin, de la mort d'Antoine à la fin du séjour de Jérôme à Rome (356-385): Patrimoines Christianisme. P 1991, Cerf. 448 p. F 250. – REsprVie 101 (1991) 554 (G.-M. *Oury*).

8294 **Walter** Patricia F., Religious authority; a conflict of interpretations [on revising (women's) religious institutes after Vatican II]: diss. Graduate Theological Union, D*Stagaman* D. Berkeley 1991. 382 p. 92-06907. – DissA 52 (1991s) 3325-A.

8295 *Wegman* Herman, 'Een menigte getuigen' (Hebr 12,1); de verering van de heiligen; een ecclesiologisch paradigma 3 [= FTALLEY 1989, 221-241]: TsTNijm 31 (1991) 28-41; Eng. 41, 'the Successio Sanctorum'.

8296 a) *Wiefel* Wolfgang, Die Heiligen im NT; – b) *Seidel* Hans, Lobgesänge im Himmel und auf Erden: ➤ 163, [F]WAGNER S., Gottesvolk 1991, 29-42 / 114-124.
8297 [E]**Wimbush** V. L. Ascetic behaviour in Greco-Roman antiquity, a sourcebook [28 texts]: StAntChr. Mp 1990, Fortress. xxviii-514 p. $46. 0-8006-3105-6 [BL 92,133, N. de *Lange*].
8298 **Wyschogrod** Edith, Saints and postmodernism; revisioning moral philosophy. Ch 1990, Univ. xxvii-298 p. $40; pa. $20. – [R]TS 52 (1991) 582-4 (M. *Gareffa*: important).
8299 *Zanetti* Ugo, Les lettres de saint Antoine et la naissance du monachisme; à propos d'un ouvrage récent [LAVAUD B. 1943/79]: NRT 113 (1991) 87-93.
8300 *Zanzi* Luigi, Storicità e santità; questioni metodologiche: ScuolC 119,2s ('Agiografia' 1991) 135-182 [120-134 . 183-278 *al.*].

H8.2 **Theologia moralis NT.**

8300* *Álvarez Verdes* Lorenzo, Bulletin: La ética del Nuevo Testamento; panorámica actual: StMor 29 (1991) 421-454.
8301 **Arts** H., [une approche anthropologique et chrétienne] – Pourquoi se marier? Le mariage des chrétiens, [T]*Passelecq* G., *Wampach* N. P 1990, Duculot. 187 p. F 105. – [R]NRT 113 (1991) 449s (A. *Toubeau*).
8302 **Baltensweiler** Heinrich, Il matrimonio nel NT; ricerche esegetiche su celibato, matrimonio, divorzio 1981 ➤ 62,8032: [R]Protestantesimo 45 (1990) 219 (Eliana *Briante*).
8302* *Barilier* R., Le divorce; étude biblique et pastorale: RRéf 42,5 (1991) 5-43 [< NTAbs 36,216].
8303 **Beach** Waldo, Christian ethics in the Protestant tradition 1988 ➤ 5, 8253: [R]SWJT 23 (1990s) 67 (W. M. *Tillman*: quiet provocateur).
8304 **Beilner** Wolfgang, El Evangelio regla de vida, [T]*Ruiz-Garrido* Constantino, 1989 ➤ 6,8299*: Barc 1989, Herder. 258 p. – [R]LumenVr 39 (1990) 337s (U. *Gil Ortega*).
8305 a) *Bielas* Lucjan, ❷ The child before birth in the ancient pagan world; – b) *Chmiel* Jerzy, ... in the Bible and ancient Judaism; – c) *Staniek* Edward, ... in the Fathers: RuBi 44 (1991) 37-41 / 42-47 / 47-53.
8306 **Birch** Bruce C., *Rasmussen* Larry L., Bible and ethics in the Christian life[2] 1989 ➤ 5,8259: [R]NewTR 4,1 (1991) 100 (D. P. *Reid*); ScotJT 44 (1991) 136s (M. *Keeling*).
8307 **Blasi** Anthony J., Moral conflict and Christian religion: AmerUnivSt 7/35, 1988 ➤ 4,9342: [R]JAAR 59 (1991) 394-6 (Cynthia *Eller*: multiple agendas).
8308 *Böhler* Dietrich, Menschenwürde und Menschentötung; über Diskursethik und utilitaristische Ethik: ZevEth 35 (1991) 166-183; Eng. 183.
8309 **Boey** Koen, Wat heet vooruitgang? Filosofen beantwoorden de vraag naar onze hedendaagse maatschappelijke identiteit. Leuven 1989, Acco. 144 p. 90-334-2002-3. – [R]Bijdragen 52 (1991) 113-5 (P. *Meijs* & W. *Jansen*, four times as long as the usual review).
8310 *Bonhoeffer* Thomas, Zur Entstehung des Begriffs Seelsorge: ArBegG 33 (1990) 7-21.
8311 **Boswell** John, Cristianesimo, tolleranza, omosessualità; la Chiesa e gli omosessuali dalle origini al XIV secolo [1980 ➤ 62,8040; franç. 1985 ➤ 1,7835]. Mi 1989, Leonardo. 509 p. Lit. 42.000. – [R]CC 142 (1991,1) 96s (P. *Molinari*).

8312 **Boyle** Philip J., Paul RAMSEY's motif, 'Christ transforming the Natural Law' in light of its theological and philosophical influences: diss. St. Louis Univ. 1990, ᴰ*Magill* G. 305 p. 91-15490. – DissA 52 (1991s) 187-A.

8313 *Burke* Cormac, S. AGOSTINO e la sessualità coniugale: AnnTh 5 (1991) 183-204.

8314 *Butler* Brian, Sex and marriage in Puritan thought [... misunderstood]: Evangel 7,3 (1989) 14-19.

8315 **Carlotti** Paolo, Storicità e morale; un'indagine nel pensiero di A. AUER: BtScR 86, 1989 ➤ 6,8309: ᴿSalesianum 53 (1991) 591s (G. *Gatti*).

8316 **Chilton** B., *McDonald* J.I.H., Jesus and the ethics of the Kingdom 1987 ➤ 3,8176 ... 6,8312: ᴿNBlackf 71 (1990) 558s (D.V. *Way*, also on DUNN-MACKEY).

8317 *Christoffersen* Svein A., Church and theology in a Scandinavian perspective; the quest for ethics: ST 44 (1990) 95-105.

8318 **Church** F. Forrester, The seven deadly virtues; a guide to Purgatory [... here and now] for atheists and true believers. SF 1988, Harper & R. 104 p. $14. 0-06-061373-4. – ᴿRExp 87 (1990) 534s (H.L. *Poe*: some virtues repel, but so does his style).

8319 *Clark* Elizabeth A., Sex, shame, and rhetoric; en-gendering early Christian ethics: JAAR 59 (1991) 221-245.

8320 **Clemens** James T., What does the Bible say about suicide? 1990 ➤ 6,8314: ᴿSWJT 33,3 (1990s) 54 (G. *Greenfield*); TTod 42 (1991s) 262 (L.R. *Bailey*: base slender, replete with eisegesis; the real question is where we get our morality for crises not really envisioned in the Bible).

8321 **Countryman** L. William, Dirt, greed and sex; sexual ethics in the NT 1988 ➤ 4,9356 ... 6,8319: ᴿRelStT 10,2 (1990) 103s (J. *Sandys-Wunsch*).

8322 **Cupitt** Don, The new Christian ethics 1988 ➤ 5,8268: ᴿScotJT 44 (1991) 269s (N.P. *Harvey*: pillories 'non-historical absolutes' but his own absolutes are far more uncritical and unproved).

8323 **Curran** C.E., Toward an American Catholic moral theology 1987 ➤ 3,210; 4,9358: ᴿJRel 70 (1990) 122s (T. *Byrnes*).

8324 **Dacquino** P., Storia del matrimonio 2,1988 ➤ 5,8270; 6,8322: ᴿAnnTh 4 (1990) 191-9 (A. *Miralles*).

8325 *Demmer* Klaus, Das vergeistigte Glück; Gedanken zum christlichen Eudämonieverständnis: Gregorianum 72 (1991) 99-114; ital. 115.

8326 *De Virgilio* Giuseppe, Etica del Nuovo Testamento; lo stato della ricerca: BbbOr 33 (1991) 141-155.

8327 **Diehl** Douglas A., The significance of almsgiving in primitive Christianity as a means of understanding NT piety: diss. SW Baptist Theol. Sem. ᴰ*Gideon* V. 235 p. 91-35749. – DissA 52 (1991s) 2588-A.

8328 **Dumas** André, Les vertus... encore. P 1989, D-Brouwer. 239 p. F 92. – ᴿFoiVie 89,2 (1990) 94s (J. *Blondel*: 'si biblique donc si peu moralisateur').

8329 **Enichlmayer** Johann, Wiederverheiratet nach Scheidung 1986 ➤ 3,8198: 6,8328: ᴿRoczTK 34,6 (1987) 148-151 (A. *Stankiewicz*, ☻).

8330 *Feil* Ernst, Zur ursprünglichen Bedeutung von 'Theonomie' [1793; GRAF F. 1987]: ArBegG 34 (1991) 295-313.

8331 **Fowl** Stephen E. [➤ 5611], *Jones* L. Gregory, Reading in communion; Scripture and ethics in Christian life. GR 1991, Eerdmans. [ix-] 166 p. $12 pa. 0-8028-0597-3 [NTAbs 36,129: Loyola-Baltimore profs].

8332 **Frey** Christopher, Die Ethik des Protestantismus von der Reformation bis zur Gegenwart. Gü 1989, Mohn. 287 p. – ᴿColcT 60,1 (1990) 157-9 (A. *Marcol*, ☻).

8333 **Fuchs** Éric, L'éthique protestante; histoire et enjeux: Le Champ Éthique 19. Genève 1990, Labor et Fides. 142 p. F 100. – ᴿÉtudes 375 (1991) 138s (R. *Marlé*); FoiVie 90,1 (1991) 103s (J. *Blondel*); Gregorianum 72 (1991) 780s (J. T. *Bretzke*).

8334 **Fuchs** Éric, La morale selon Calvin 1986 → 3,8201; 4,9368: ᴿTR 87 (1991) 29s (A. *Ganoczy*).

8335 **Fuchs** Josef, Für eine menschliche Moral; Grundfragen der theologischen Ethik [1. 1988 → 5,263], 2. Ethische Konkretisierungen: St-TheolEthik 26, 1989 → 5,263; 6,8331: ᴿTPQ 139 (1991) 331s (J. *Janda*); ZkT 113 (1991) 327s (H. *Rotter*).

8336 **Fuchs** J., Christian morality; the word becomes flesh 1987 → 5,8284: ᴿCritRR 2 (1989) 270-2 (K. *Keulman*); HeythJ 32 (1991) 99-101 (M. *Reidy*).

8337 **García de Haro** Ramón, Cristo fundamento de la moral; los conceptos básicos de la vida moral en la perspectiva cristiana: Éhica y Sociedad 1. Barc 1990, Ediciones Internacionales Universitarias [EIUNSA (sic)]. 192 p. – ᴿSalesianum 53 (1991) 437s (G. *Abbà*).

8338 *García de Haro* Ramón, Il rapporto natura-grazia e il dinamismo dell'agire morale cristiano: AnnTh 5 (1991) 327-349.

8339 **Garland** Diana R. & David E., Marriage for better or worse: The Bible and Personal Crisis. Nv 1989, Broadman. 168 p. 0-8054-5439-X. – ᴿRExp 87 (1990) 640 (D. L. *Anderson*).

8339* **Gérard** Marie-Suzel, La volonté de Dieu dans le Nouveau Testament: L'Épiphanie 5. Kinshasa-Limete 1990, BP 724. 48 p. – ᴿEsprVie 101 (1991) 338-*jaune* (? M. *Noirot*).

8340 *Guroian* Vigen, Incarnate love, essays in Orthodox ethics. ND 1988, Univ. – ᴿGrOrTR 35 (1990) 71-81.

8341 *Guroian* Vigen, Bible and ethics; an ecclesial and liturgical interpretation: JRelEth 18 (Decatur GA 1990) 129-158 [< ZIT 90,703].

8342 **Habermas** J., Teoria dell'agire comunicativo, I. Razionalità nell'azione e razionalizzazione sociale; II. Critica della ragione funzionalistica, ᵀᴱ*Rusconi*. Bo 1986, Mulino. 1,135 p. Lit. 42.000 + 50.000. – ᴿCC [già 141 (1990,4) 142-9] 142 (1991,1) 153-162 (G. L. *Brena* riesamina permettendo una posizione più aperta).

8343 **Häring** Bernhard, No way out? [Ausweglos? 1989 → 6,8337]. Slough 1990, St. Paul. 90 p. £3.75. 0-85439-317-X. – ᴿExpTim 102 (1990s) 221 (D. G. *Deeks*: marvellously compassionate).

8344 *Häring* Bernhard, ¿Hay una salida? Pastoral para divorciados 1990 → 6,8338: ᴿCarthaginensia 7 (1991) 303s (J. L. *Parada Navas*).

8345 *Haight* Roger, *Langan* John, Recent Catholic social and ethical teaching in the light of the Social Gospel: JRelEth 18,1 (1990) 103-128 [< ZIT 90,703].

8346 **Hallett** Garth L., Christian neighbor-love; an assessment of six rival versions 1989 → 5,8299: ᴿJRelEth 19,1 (1991) 196 (S. G. *Post*).

8347 **Harvey** A. E., Strenuous commands; the ethic of Jesus. L/Ph 1990, SCM/Trinity. 248 p. £12.50. 0-334-02471-4. – ᴿExpTim 102,7 2d-top choice (1990s) 194s (C. S. *Rodd*); TLond 94 (1991) 307 (F. G. *Downing*); TrinJ 12 (1991) 224-8 (S. *McKnight*).

8348 **Harvey** Nicholas P., The morals of Jesus. L 1991, Darton-LT. xiii-112 p. £7. 0-232-51926-9. – ᴿMonth 252 (1991) 304s (P. *Edwards*).

8349 **Hauerwas** Stanley M., Christian existence today; essays on Church, world, and living in between 1988 → 5,277: ᴿTR 87 (1991) 419 (E. *Sturm*).

8350 **Hazelett** Richard, *Turner* Dean, Benevolent living; tracing the roots of motivation to God; pref. *Hartshorne* C. Pasadena 1990, Hope. xiv-429 p. $20 [TLZ 116,343].

8351 *Honecker* Martin, a) Paradigmenwechsel in der katholischen Moraltheologie [RHONHEIMER M.; GILLEN E.]; – b) Zur ethischen Diskussion der 80er Jahre: TRu 56 (1991) 437-445 / 54-97 [98-105, Rechtsgeschichte, *Campenhausen* Axel von].

8351* **Ide** A. F., Zoar and her sisters; homosexuality, the Bible, and Jesus Christ. Oak Cliff TX 1991, Minuteman. viii-234 p.; $15 pa. 0-926899-02-3 [NTAbs 36,129: no Bible veto].

8352 **Jonsen** Albert R., *Toulmin* Stephen, The abuse of casuistry; a history of moral reasoning. Berkeley 1988, Univ. California. vii-420 p. $45. – ᴿRelStR 17 (1991) 298-302 (Patricia B. *Jung*: they call for the resurrection of casuistry) & 302-5 (P. *Turner*).

8353 ᶠKAISER Matthias: Recht als Heilsdienst, 65 Gb. ᴱSchulz W. 1989 ➤ 5,104: ᴿTPhil 66 (1991) 310 (G. *Schmidt*).

8354 **Keener** Craig, And marries another; divorce and remarriage in the teaching of the NT. Peabody MA 1991, Hendrickson. xii-256 p. $10.

8355 *Kern* Udo, Barmherzigkeit als souveräne Daseinsgestaltung [... ii. biblisches Feld; iii. als Weisheit ...]: TZBas 47 (1991) 125-135.

8356 **Kirchschläger** Walter, Ehe und Ehescheidung im NT: Überlegungen und Anfragen zur Praxis der Kirche 1987 ➤ 3,8232 ... 6,8347: ᴿTLZ 116 (1991) 113s (H. *Schulz* †).

8356* *Kivunzi* T., Seven biblical exclusions for married life [defects to be avoided by spouses]: AfJEvT 9,2 (Kenya 1990) 27-32 [< NTAbs 36,73].

8357 **Kötting** Bernhard, Die Bewertung der Wiederverheiratung (der zweiten Ehe) in der Antike und in der frühen Kirche: Rh/Wf Akad, Vorträge G 292, 1988 ➤ 5,8316: ᴿRömQ 86 (1991) 279-281 (H. *Moll*).

8358 **Langa** Pedro, San AGUSTÍN y el progreso de la teología matrimonial. Toledo 1984, S. Ildefonso. 301 p. – ᴿAugR 30 (1990) 195s (H. *Crouzel*).

8358* *Lawler* Michael G., Faith, contract and sacrament in Christian marriage; a theological approach: TS 52 (1991) 712-731.

8359 **Le Bourgeois** Armand, Chrétiens divorcés remariés. P 1990, Desclée-de Brouwer. 192 p. F 90. – ᴿTüTQ 171 (1991) 74s (R. *Puza*).

8360 **Lohse** Eduard, Theological ethics of the New Testament [1988 ➤ 4, 9394 ... 6,8352], ᵀBoring M. Eugene. Mp 1991, Fortress. ix-236 p. 0-8006-2506-4.

8361 **Lohse** Eduard, Etica teologica del Nuovo Testamento, ᵀBressani Clara, ᴱSoffritti Omero: BtCuRel 57. Brescia 1991, Paideia. 235 p. 88-394-0462-7.

8362 *Lona* Horacio E., El problema de la sexualidad en el cristianismo antiguo: ProyectoCSE 3,7s (Buenos Aires 1991) 7-32.

8363 **MacIntyre** Alasdair, Three rival versions of moral inquiry 1990 ➤ 6, 8354: ᴿAmerica 164 (1991) 578-580 (J. B. *Benestad*); TTod 48 (1991s) 74-76 (Elizabeth *Bettenhausen*).

8364 **MacIntyre** Alasdair, Whose justice? which rationality? 1988 ➤ 6,8355: ᴿGregorianum 72 (1991) 183-5 (T. *Kennedy*).

8365 ᶠMACKINNON Donald, Christ, ethics and tragedy, ᴱSurin K., 1986/9 ➤ 5,701: ᴿHorizons 18 (1991) 331-3 (B. L. *Whitney*).

8366 **McQuilkin** Robertson, Biblical ethics, an introduction. Wheaton IL 1989, Tyndale. 547 p. $13 pa. – ᴿSWJT 33,1 (1990s) 67 (G. *Greenfield*).

8367 *Marcol* Alojzy, ⊕ Beichtvater und nichtsakramentale Ehen: ColcT 61,4 (1991) 107-117; deutsch 118.

8368 **Marra** Bruno, Etica della vita coniugale 1988 ➤ 6,8359: ᴿIrTQ 57 (1991) 86s (J. *McEvoy*).
8369 **Martin** Thomas M., The challenge of Christian marriage; marriage in Scripture, history and contemporary life. NY 1990, Paulist. viii-183 p. $10. 0-8091-3190-0 [TDig 38,280].
8370 **Martínez García** Francisco, He creído en el amor [... NT]: Barc 1989, Herder. 236 p. – ᴿNatGrac 38 (1991) 389 (E. *Montalvo*).
8371 **Marxsen** W., 'Christliche' und christliche Ethik im NT 1989 ➤ 5,8334; 6,8360: ᴿZkT 113 (1991) 284-6 (R. *Oberforcher*).
8372 **May** William, Principios de vida moral. Barc 1990, Ed. Int. Univ. 269 p. – ᴿAnthropotes (1991.1) 83-86 (T. *Kennedy*).
8373 **Moser** Antônio, *Leers* Bernardino, a) Teologia moral, impasses e alternativas. Petrópolis, Vozes. – b) Moral theology; dead ends and alternatives, ᵀ*Burns* Paul: Theology and Liberation. Mkn 1990, Orbis. xvi-240 p. $17. 0-88344-665-0. – ᴿGregorianum 72 (1991) 585s (J. T. *Bretzke*); NRT 113 (1991) 446s (A. *Harvengt*: basé sur l'Alliance et le NT).
8374 **Mouw** Richard J., The God who commands. ND 1990, Univ. viii-214 p. $25. 0-268-01019-6 [TDig 38,178]. – ᴿTTod 42 (1991s) 240.242s (T. D. *Kennedy*).
Muller Earl C., Trinity and marriage in Paul 1990 ➤ 5202.
8375 **Mullins** Michael, The catechesis of the Roman church; approaches to Christian morality in the city of Rome in the first Christian century: diss. Pont. Univ. S. Thomae (Angelicum), ᴰ*Parsons* S. R 1991. 471 p. 1-85390-177-6.
8376 **Munier** Charles, Matrimonio e verginità nella Chiesa antica [1987 ➤ 5,8342], ᵀ*Ramella* G. T 1990, SEI. lvi-300 p. Lit. 50.000. – ᴿHumBr 46 (1991) 785s (P. V. *Cova*).
8377 *Mynatty* Hormis, The concept of social sin: LvSt 16 (1991) 1-26.
8378 **Nagórny** Janusz K., ❷ Teologiczna interpretacja moralności Nowego Przymierza: Hab. Diss. Lublin 1990. KUL. 511 p. [NTAbs 36,130]. – ᴿRoczTK 37,3 (1990) 113-6 (I. *Mroczkowski*).
8379 **Oates** Wayne E., Temptation; a biblical and psychological approach. Louisville 1991, W-Knox. 105 p. $10 [RelStR 18,215, Lucinda A. *Huffaker*].
8380 *Palmquist* Stephen, Four perspectives on moral judgement; the rational principles of Jesus and KANT [Mt 7,1.12; 32,37]: HeythJ 32 (1991) 216-232.
8381 a) *Panikkar* R., The mythical origin of every human right; – b) *Amaladoss* M., Religions and human rights: Jeevadhara 21 (1991) 48-52 / 35-47.
8382 **Pinckaers** Servais T., [➤ 248] Les sources de la morale chrétienne 1985 ➤ 2,6548 ... 6,8373: ᴿRoczTK 37,3 (1990) 116-8 (A. F. *Dziuba*).
8383 **Pinckaers** Servais, La Parola e la coscienza: Morale [L'Évangile et la morale 1990], ᵀ*Pistocchi* Bruno. T 1991, SEI. x-230 p. 88-05-05212-4.
8383* *Pommereau* Xavier (psychiatre), Le suicide à travers les âges: FoiVie 90,2 (1991) 7-22 (-43, réponse à demandes).
8384 *Pope* Stephen J., The order of love and recent Catholic ethics; a constructive proposal: TS 52 (1991) 256-288.
8385 **Porter** Jean, The recovery of virtue; the relevance of AQUINAS for Christian ethics. Louisville 1990, W-Knox. 208 p. $25. – ᴿTS 52 (1991) 581s (G. S. *Harak*).
8386 *Power* David, Le sacrement de l'onction; questions ouvertes, ᵀ*Divault* André: ➤ 348, Concilium 234 (P 1991) 123-137.

8387 **Pozo Abejón** Gerardo del, Lex evangelica ... suareciana 1988 ➤ 5,8352: RTeresianum 42 (1991) 672s (E. *Pacho*).

8388 **Ranke-Heinemann** Uta, Eunuchs for the kingdom of God [1988 ➤ 5,8353]: RBiblTB 21 (1991) 121s (L. J. *White*); CathHR 77 (1991) 659s (Elisabeth C. *Gleason*: an unseated convert-Catholic theologian hostile and uncomprehending, against 'a folly that poses as religion ... but has distorted the consciences of countless people'); TLond 94 (1991) 312s (D. *Nineham*: cannot be ignored even if unfair); TS 52 (1991) 770-3 (V. J. *Genovesi*: disdain).

8389 *Reilly* Martin, A critical evaluation of James M. GUSTAFSON's theocentrism: IrTQ 57 (1991) 1-13 (299-310).

8390 **Richard** Lucien, Is there a Christian ethics? 1988 ➤ 5,8356; 6,8383: RGregorianum 72 (1991) 376s (K. *Demmer*).

8391 E**Richter** Klemens, Eheschliessung – mehr als ein rechtlich Ding?: QDisp 120. FrB 1989, Herder. 180 p. – RTPhil 66 (1991) 315s (G. *Schmidt*).

8392 **Rousselle** Aline, Porneia; on desire and the body in antiquity 1988 ➤ 4,b794; 6,8386: RHeythJ 32 (1991) 408s (J. *Ferguson*); JRS 81 (1991) 180-2 (Mary *Beard*: tries to show roots of Christian asceticism in pagan classicism, chiefly medical writings; enlivened by stories about fornication and castration, but insufficiently reflective).

8393 **Schnackenburg** R., Sittliche Botschaft NT 2,1988 ➤ 4,9422... 6,8388: RColcT 61,1 (1991) 167s (R. *Bartnicki*, ℗).

8394 **Schnackenburg** Rudolf, Il messaggio morale del NT I, Da Gesù alla Chiesa primitiva², 1989 ➤ 5,8361; 6,8389: RAntonianum 66 (1991) 438s (M. *Nobile*); CC 142 (1991,1) 626s (F. *Cultrera*); Helmantica 42,129* (1991) 396 (S. *García-Jalón*).

8395 **Schnackenburg** Rudolf, El mensaje moral del NT [I. 1989 ➤ 6,8390] 2. Los primeros predicadores cristianos, T*Villanueva* Marciano: BtHerder-SEscr 186. Barc 1991, Herder. 333 p. pt. 2300. – RActuBbg 28 (1991) 164s (J. *Boada*); LumenVr 39 (1990) 82s (J. *Querejazu*, 1); ScripTPamp 23 (1991) 1026-9 (A. *García-Moreno*, 1).

8396 F SCHNACKENBURG R., NT und Ethik, E**Merklein** H., 1989 ➤ 5,173: RÉTRel 66 (1991) 565-8 (D. *Müller*).

8397 *Seebass* Horst / *Neudecker* Reinhard / *Wischmeyer* Oda, Liebe AT / Judaismus / NT: ➤ 690, TRE 21 (1991) 128-133-138-146.

8398 **Segalla** G., Introduzione all'etica del NT 1989 ➤ 6,300: RAnnTh 4 (1990) 443-7 (B. *Estrada*); ScripTPamp 23 (1991) 1065s (C. *Basevi*); Teresianum 42 (1991) 358 (V. *Pasquetto*).

8399 [Marantonio] *Sguerzo* Elsa, Il Battesimo nella Chiesa primitiva; dalle origini agli inizi del II secolo: Monitor Ecclesiasticus 115 (R 1990) 112-123 [3-220 al. sul battesimo].

8400 **Sloyan** Gerard S., Catholic morality revisited; origins and contemporary challenges 1990 ➤ 6,8395: RDoctLife 41 (1991) 47s (V. *Boland*); Horizons 18 (1991) 178s (N. J. *Rigali*).

8401 *Šolić* Peytar, The theology of homosexuality: ObnŽiv 45 (1990) 44-77 (Croatian; Bible 46-49; celibates 73s). Eng. 77.

8402 *Spohn* William C., *al.*, Notes on moral theology 1990: TS 52 (1991) 69-87 (-127).

8403 **Stout** Jeffrey, Ethics after Babel; the languages of morals and their discontents 1988 ➤ 5,8368; 6,8400: RTLond 94 (1991) 149s (S. *Platten*).

8404 **Thévenot** Xavier, Omosessualità maschile e morale cristiana [Homosexualités masculines 1985 ➤ 1,7944], T*Caré* Mario: Saggi di Teologia. T-Leumann 1991, Elle Di Ci. 248 p. – ᴿStMor 29 (1991) 507-9 (J. S. *Botero*).

8405 **Valadier** P., Inévitable morale. P 1990, Seuil. 224 p. F 95. – ᴿNRT 113 (1991) 445s (T. *Macheron* ne note rien sur l'Écriture).

8406 **Vidal** Marciano, Il cammino dell'etica cristiana [→ 6,8404]. Brescia 1989, Queriniana. 127 p. Lit. 15.000. – ᴿCC 142 (1991,1) 206s (F. *Cultrera*).

8407 *Wiebe* Ben, Messianic ethics; response to the Kingdom of God: Interpretation 45 (1991) 29-42.

8408 **Wilkinson** John, Christian ethics in health care. E 1988, Handsel. xiv-510 p. £27.50. – ᴿScotJT 44 (1991) 239s (A. *Bird*, frankly 'irritated' notably at Greek 'ethics distinct from religion').

8409 *You* Alain, La loi de la gradualité... et non pas la gradualité de la loi [HÄRING B. et réponse du Vatican, DocCath 86 (1989) 243-5.246-8]: EsprVie 101 (1991) 120-7.

8410 *Zawadzka* sr. Anna, ☯ Normative character / anthropological assumptions of the Christian *powołania* [call, invitation] according to Enda MCDONAGH [1972]: ColcT 60,1 (1990) 47-60 / 15-33; Eng. 60s.33.

8411 **Zulehner** P. M., Pastoraltheologie 1. Fundamentalpastoral. Dü 1989, Patmos. 335 p. – ᴿColcT 60,3 (1990) 182-4 (R. *Kamiński*, ☯).

H8.4   *NT ipsum de reformatione sociali* – **Political action in Scripture.**

8412 *Alana* Olin E., Reconsidering the poor by Gospel norms: AfER 12 (1990) 193-200.

8413 *Alonso Schökel* Luis, Solidarietà umana e paternità divina: → 291*, Teologia e dottrina sociale; il dialogo ecclesiale in un mondo che cambia. CasM 1991, Piemme. 75-97.

8413* **Arens** Edmund, *al.*, Erinnerung – Befreiung – Solidarität; BENJAMIN, MARCUSE, HABERMAS und die politische Theologie [METZ J.-B.]. Dü 1991, Patmos. 200 p. DM 29,80 pa. [TLZ 117,690, H.-J. *Höhn*].

8414 **Bauckham** Richard, The Bible in politics 1989 → 6,8415: ᴿHorBT 13 (1991) 88-90 (W. M. *Swartley*); ScotJT 44 (1991) 540s (J. I. H. *McDonald*).

8415 *Bavel* T. J. van, Keuze voor de Armen bij AUGUSTINUS: CollatVL 21 (1991) 73-88.

8416 *Bellah* Robert, The role of the Church in a changing society: CurrTMiss 17 (1990) 181-191; p. 183 accuses Walnut Creek St. Luke's of yielding to pressures from market forces; response of pastor, *Dunfee* Scott J., 18 (1991) 45-48.

8416* *a) Cañellas* Gabriel, La justicia, ¿qué es?: Respuesta desde la tradición veterotestamentaria; – *b) Struik* Félix, Justicia integral, en mensaje de los profetas pre-exílicos; – *c) Salas* Antonio, Justicia y reino, en el mensaje social de Jesús; – *d) Sáenz Galache* Mercedes, Justicia de Dios – justicia del hombre; cristianización del concepto en la teología paulina: BibFe 50 (1991) 149-170 / 171-193 / 194-225 / 242-257 [... *al.*].

8417 ᴱ**Chewning** Richard C., *al.*, Business through the eyes of faith: Christian College Coalition for Enduring Values. SF 1990, Harper. xii-266 p. $10 [RelStR 18,136, J. *Moody*].

8418 **Chiavacci** E., Morale della vita economica, politica e di comunicazione: TMor 3/2. Assisi 1990, Cittadella. 369 p. Lit. 28.000. – ᴿRasT 32 (1991) 538s (G. *Mattai*).

8419 **Christophe** Paul, Les pauvres et la pauvreté des origines à nos jours: BtHistChr. 7012. P 1985-7. 152 p., 200 p. – RRHist 280 (1988) 549-551 (M. *Mollet*).

8420 *Cipriani* Settimio, La dimensione biblica nell'insegnamento sociale di Giovanni Paolo II, con particolare riferimento alla 'Centesimus Annus': Asprenas 38 (1991) 291-308 [309-342, *Bof* Giampiero; 375-381, *Marra* Bruno].

8421 **Codina** Víctor, Para comprender la eclesiología desde América Latina. Estella 1990, VDiv. 132 p. – RRLatAmT 23 (1991) 219s (J. A. E.).

8422 **Coulie** Bernard, Les richesses / GREG. NAZ. 1985 → 3,8325; 6,8424: RBijdragen 52 (1991) 334 (M. *Parmentier*).

8424 *Curran* Charles E., A century of Catholic social teaching: TTod 48 (1991s) 154-169.

8425 *Draulans* Veerle, Kroniekrecensie; Rerum Novarum als aanleiding: CollatVL 21 (1991) 417-423.

8426 **Dussel** Enrique, Éthique communautaire, TGuibal F.: Libération. P 1991, Cerf. 256 p. F 155. – RÉtudes 375 (1991) 566s (R. *Marlé*).

8427 **Elliott** Michael C., Freedom, justice and Christian counter-culture. L/Ph 1990, SCM/Trinity. xvii-222 p. £9.50. 0-334-02452-8. – RExpTim 102 (1990s) 220 (G. T. *Eddy*).

8428 **Ellul** Jacques, Jesus and Marx; from gospel to ideology → 4,9454, THanks Joyce M. GR 1988, Eerdmans. 187 p. $13. – RPerspRelSt 18,1 (1991) 79-82 (S. *Blakemore*).

8429 **Ellul** Jacques, Money and power [²1979]T, Basingstoke 1986, Marshall Pickering. 173 p. £7. 0-551-01392-3. – REvangel 7,3 (1989) 34 (S. *Williams*: excellent).

8430 *a) Falise* Michel, Une pratique chrétienne de l'économie. P 1985, Centurion. 119 p. – *b) Mandy* Paul, Réflexions d'un économiste sur 'Une pratique chrétienne de l'économie': RTLv 22 (1991) 370-397; Eng. 456.

8431 *Fears* J. Rufus, Optimus princeps – salus generis humani; the origins of Christian political theology: → 149, FSTRAUB J., 1989, 88-105.

8431* **Forrester** Duncan B., Beliefs, values and policies. Ox 1989, Clarendon. 110 p. £7 pa. – REvQ 63 (1991) 188-190 (A. *Main*).

8432 *Füssel* Kuno, Perspektiven einer theologischen Kapitalismuskritik: Orientierung 55 (1991) 169-176.

8432* *Furger* Franz, al., 1891-1991, cien años desde la encíclica 'Rerum novarum', TStrotmann N.: RTLim 25,1 (1991) 11-14 (-128).

8433 **González** J. L., Faith and wealth; a history of early Christian ideas on the origin, significance, and use of money 1990 → 6,8436: RCritRR 4 (1991) 300-2 (J. B. *Green*); NewTR 4,1 (1991) 112s (Carolyn *Osiek*); TsTNijm 31 (1991) 197 (A. *Lascaris*: not economic but patristic history).

8434 **Gordon** Barry, The economic problem [... 'the problem of scarcity'] in biblical and patristic thought: VigChr supp. 9. Leiden 1989, Brill. x-144 p. f 70. 90-04-09048-7. – RCritRR 4 (1991) 302s (J. B. *Green*); ExpTim 102 (1990s) 255; JTS 42 (1991) 266s (D. *Mealand*).

8435 *a) Hasitschka* M., Die Botschaft Jesu vom nahegekommenen Reich Gottes und die darin begründete soziale Wirklichkeit; – *b) Oesch* J.M., Königtum und Heil: → 373, Mündigkeit 1989, 143-153 / 172-192.

8436 *a) Haufe* Günter, Christ und Staat nach dem NT; – *b) Trilling* Wolfgang, Gottesvolk und Weltverantwortung im NT: → 163*, FWAGNER S., Gottesvolk 1991, 91-97 / 143-155.

8437 **Hay** Donald A.,   Economics today; a Christian critique. 1989 ➤ 6,8442; also Worcester 1989, Apollos.   320 p. [BIP: $18 pa.).   0-8028-0401-2 (Eerdmans)]:   ᴿTsTKi 61 (1990) 235 (A. *Smith*).

8438 **Hilton** Boyd,   The age of atonement; the influence of evangelicalism on social and economic thought 1795-1865 1988 ➤ 5,k303:   ᴿScotJT 44 (1991) 258s (G. *White*).

8439 **Hoffmann** Paul,   Das Erbe Jesu und die Macht in der Kirche; Rückbesinnung auf das Neue Testament [... *Drewermann* E.]: Topos-Tb 213.   Mainz 1991, Grünewald.   155 p. DM 9,80.   3-7867-1588-2 [NTAbs 36,282].

8440 *Hofrichter* Peter, Die Stellung der Christen zum Staatsdienst in vor- und nachkonstantinischer Zeit: TPQ 139 (1991) 181-191 (i. Die Anfänge im NT und in profanen Quellen].

8441 *Honecker* Martin,   Zur Wirtschaftsethik: TRu 56 (1991) 260-279.

8442 *Jackson* Robert,   Prosperity theology and the faith movement: Themelios 15 (1989s) 16-24.

8443 *Jennings* Theodore,   Good news to the poor; John WESLEY's evangelical economics.   Nv c. 1990, Abingdon. 234 p. [Int 45,333].

8444 **Kaufman** Peter I.,   Redeeming politics.   Princeton 1990, Univ.   xiii-209 p. $22.50. – ᴿTS 52 (1991) 553s (F. H. *Russell*: 'the long shadow of Constantine' ... 'the myth that God works through deputies' ... does title mean politics redeems, or is redeemed?).

8445 **Keulman** Kenneth,   The balance of consciousness; Eric VOEGELIN's political theory.   Univ. Park 1990, Penn State Univ.   xx-194 p. $28.50 [RelStR 18,214, J. *Carmody*: includes biblical views].

8446 **Klinger** Elmar,   Armut, eine Herausforderung Gottes; der Glaube des Konzils und die Befreiung des Menschen.   Z 1990, Benziger.   333 p. Fs 31. – ᴿZkT 113 (1991) 441-7 (E. *Schrofner*).

8447 **Koslowski** Peter,   Prinzipien der ethischen Ökonomie; Grundlegung der Wirtschaftsethik und der auf die Ökonomie bezogenen Ethik.   Tü 1988, Mohr.   ix-339 p. DM 89; pa. 49. – ᴿZkT 113 (1991) 335-7 (B. *Braun*).

8448 *Krocker* P. Travis,   Pluralism and policy monism; the political irrelevance of theology: TorJT 7 (1991) 35-43 [19-34, *Cormie* L., social ethics].

8449 *a*) *Kurien* C. T.,   Capitalism and socialism, a reconsideration; – *b*) *West* Charles C.,   Ecumenical social ethic beyond socialism and capitalism: EcuR 41 (1991) 308-317 / 329-340.

8450 **Laot** Laurent,   Catholicisme, politique, laïcité: Églises/Sociétés.   P 1990, Ouvrières.   187 p. – ᴿEsprVie 101 (1991) 158s (G. *Cholvy*).

8451 **Lohfink** Norbert F.,   Option for the poor; basic principles of liberation theology in the light of the Bible ➤ 3,8348 ... 6,8456:   ᴿIndTSt 27 (1990) 353s (M. *Devadass*: on Exodus, little on NT).

8452 *Lustig* B. Andrew,   Property and justice in the modern encyclical literature: HarvTR 83 (1990) 415-446.

8453 **McClelland** William R.,   Worldly spirituality; biblical reflections on money, politics, and sex.   St. Louis 1990, CBP.   158 p. $11. – ᴿMid-Stream 29 (1990) 444-6 (D. E. *Stevenson*).

8454 **Manning** Ian,   God and goods. Melbourne 1989, Council of Christian education.   80 p. – ᴿAustralasCR 68 (1991) 249-231 (A. *Fischer* compares to J. SCHALL 1990).

8454* *Manus* Chris U.,   NT theological foundations for Christian contribution to politics in Nigeria: BEcumT 2,1 (Nigeria 1989) 7-30 [< NTAbs 36,74].

8455 *Mason* John D., *Schaefer* Kurt C., The Bible, the State and the economy; a framework for analysis: ChrSchR 20,1 (1990) 45... [< ZIT 91,74].

8456 **Mateos** Juan, L'utopia di Gesù [M 1990, Almendro], ᵀ*Demarchi* Enzo: Vangelo e vita NS. Assisi 1991, Cittadella. 210 p. 88-308-0486-X.

8457 **Meeks** M. Douglas, God the Economist 1989 ➤ 5,8429; 6,8459: ᴿChrCent 107 (1990) 82s (Kathleen *Housley*); JRel 71 (1991) 453-5 (D. *Finn*); ScotJT 44 (1991) 396-8 (D. B. *Forrester*: creative); TS 51 (1990) 789 (W. J. *Byron*); TZBas 47 (1991) 190s (A. *Jäger*).

8458 *Miguez* Néstor O., The witness to justice and the renewal of the Church; a biblical approach: MidStream 28 (1989) 35-53.

8459 *Moberly* Walter, Political wellbeing in biblical perspective: StCEth 3,1 (E 1990) 14-29 (-32, response, *Parsons* Susan).

8461 **Nelson** Robert H., Reaching for heaven on earth; the theological meaning of economics. ... 1991, Rowman & L. 378 p. [JAAR 54,884].

8462 *Nessan* Craig L., How social is the Gospel? Some twentieth century answers: CurrTMiss 18 (1981) 166-175 [response 176-8, *Hess* Nancy A.].

8463 **Oakman** Douglas E., Jesus and the economic questions of his day 1986 ➤ 2,6627... 5,8437: ᴿChH 59 (1990) 222s (R. M. *Grant*); RB 98 (1991) 312s (J. *Murphy-O'Connor*: good within agrarian limits).

8464 *Ombres* Robert, The temporal possessions of the Church [... must be combined with witness to service and poverty]: PrPeo 4 (1990) 130-5.

8465 **Owensby** Walter L., Economics for prophets; a primer on concepts, realities, and values in our economic system. GR 1988, Eerdmans. 201 p. $10. – ᴿSWJT 33,1 (1990s) 66 (W. M. *Tillman*, also on WELLS Wm. W., The agony of affluence 1989).

8466 *Pangritz* Andreas, Il 'volto messianico' della società senza classi; il materialismo d'ispirazione teologica di Walter BENJAMIN: Protestantesimo 46 (1991) 175-186.

8467 *Potter* Philip, God's economy and the world's economy: Colloquium 23,1 (1990) 1-11 [< ZIT 91,75].

8468 **Regnier** Jérôme, Chrétiens dans la cité: Horizon du Croyant 11. P 1990, Desclée. 191 p. – ᴿMélSR 48 (1991) 192s (L. *Debarge*).

8469 **Rich** Arthur, Wirtschaftsethik II, Marktwirtschaft, Planwirtschaft, Wirtschaft aus sozialethischer Sicht. Gü 1990, Mohn. 375-xli p. – ᴿTZBas 47 (1991) 187-9 (A. *Jäger*).

8470 ᵀᴱ**Riley** Patrick, Jacques-Bénigne BOSSUET, Politics drawn from the very words of Holy Scripture [first six books before 1679 while he was tutor to the Dauphin; the rest taken up after 1700]: Texts in the History of Political Thought. C 1991, Univ. lxxix-415 p. $59.50. 0-521-36237-7 [TDig 39,51]. – ᴿRHR 208 (1991) 347s (J. *Le Brun*).

8471 *Robertson* O. Palmer, Reflections on NT testimony concerning civil disobedience: JEvTS 33 (1990) 331-352 [< ZIT 90,806].

8472 **Santa Ana** Julio de, Die politische Ökonomie des Heiligen Geistes [Eng.], ᵀ*Heider* M.: Junge Kirche (1990,12) ... 62 p. [TLZ 116,459].

8473 **Schall** James V., Religion, wealth and poverty. Vancouver 1990, Fraser. xx-202 p. $20. 0-88975-112-9. – ᴿGregorianum 72 (1991) 186-8 (J. *Joblin*: stimulant).

8474 *Schellong* Dieter, Carl SCHMITT als HOBBES-Interpret [1922]; Überlegungen zum Begriff der Politischen Theologie: BTZ 8 (1991) 94-112.

8475 **Schenkel** Albert F., The rich man and the kingdom; John D. ROCKEFELLER jr. and the Protestant establishment, 1900-1960: diss. Harvard. – HarvTR 83 (1990) 451: he gave away one billion dollars.

8476 *Schinella* Ignazio, La vita spirituale e l'impegno politico del credente: Asprenas 38 (1991) 26-41.

8477 **Schottroff** Luise, *Stegemann* W., Gesù di Nazareth, speranza dei poveri[2] [[1]1978 → 60,6692] 1988: [R]Salesianum 53 (1991) 772 (J. J. *Bartolomé*: 'Stegemann Wolfgang').

8478 *Semeraro* Cosimo, Prestito, usura e debito pubblico nella storia del cristianesimo: Salesianum 53 (1991) 383-400 [... Dt 23,19s; *Le Goff* J. 1982].

8479 [E]**Sheils** W. J., *Wood* Diana, The Church and wealth 1986/7 → 3,721; 5,8453: [R]CathHR 77 (1991) 89s (S. *Gilley*).

8480 **Soelle** Dorothee, The window of vulnerability: a political spirituality. Mp 1990, Fortress. 210 p. $16. – [R]TTod 48 (1991s) 472.474.476 (Linda A. *Mercadante*).

8481 *Sölle* Dorothee, Moses, Jesus und Marx – Utopien auf der Suche nach Gerechtigkeit: Junge Kirche 52 (1991) 261-5 [< ZIT 91,342].

8482 **Taylor** Michael, Good for the poor. L 1990, Mowbray. 114 p. £7. 0-264-67190-2. – [R]ExpTim 102 (1990s) 216s (R. G. *Jones*: brilliant).

8483 **Tinder** Glenn E., The political meaning of Christianity; the prophetic stance, an interpretation 1989 → 6,8484; also Harper: [R]Commonweal 117 (1990) 324-6 (R. W. *Fox*); Interpretation 45 (1991) 330.332 (J. H. *Adams*); Paradigms 7,2 (1991s) 42s (P. Y. *Clark*).

8484 *a*) *Villa-Vicencio* Charles, Centesimus annus, an alternative church reading [disapproves 'sexist' translation; and mentions prominently twice in the first paragraph 'John XIII']; – *b*) *Miguez Bonino* José, Social doctrine as a locus for ecumenical encounter: EcuR 41 (1991) 435-442 / 392-400.

8485 **Weber** H.-R., Power 1989 → 5,8463; 6,8489: [R]ÉTRel 66 (1991) 285s (J. *Rennes*); Mid-Stream 28 (1989) 442s (D. E. *Stevenson*); ScotJT 43 (1990) 521-3 (J. J. *Vincent*).

8486 **Wogaman** J. Philip, Christian perspectives on politics 1988 → 5,8464: [R]Salesianum 53 (1991) 192-4 (G. *Abbà*).

8487 **Yoder** John H., [G] The politics of Jesus [1984 → 1,262], [T]*Liau* Timothy. 1990. – [R]ColcFuJen 85 (1990) 423-433.

H8.5   **Theologia liberationis latino-americana.**

8488 **Alves** Rubem A., The poet, the warrior, the prophet [→ 173*b*]. L/Ph 1990, SCM/Trinity. 148 p. £9. 0-334-02475-7. – [R]ExpTim 102 (1990s) 252 (B. L. *Horne*: nonsense or poetic theology? anyway a reaction against reason).

8489 *a*) *Andreo García* Juan, De la América española a la América americana; consideraciones a un proceso frustrado; – *b*) *Borges* Pedro, Panorama de la evangelización hispanoamericana (1492-1824): Carthaginensia 7 (1991) 397-414 / 415-451.

8490 **Antoncich** Ricardo, Christians in the face of injustice; a Latin American reading of Catholic social teaching 1987 → 3,8402: [R]IntRMiss 79 (1990) 102-5 (Priscilla *Pope-Levison*, also on three cognate Catholic publications).

8491 *Antoniazzi* Alberto, Bigarrure religieuse du Brésil [traditions protestante, 'médiumnique', mysticisme écologique, œcuménique ...]: Études 374 (1991) 245-256.

8492 **Azzi** Riolando, A cristiandade colonial, mito e ideologia. Petrópolis 1987, Vozes. 152 p. – [R]REB 51 (1991) 1003-6 (Marilia *Mello de Vilhena*).

8493 **Baldwin** Deborah R., Protestants and the Mexican revolution; missionaries, ministers and social change 1990 ► 6,8495: ^RJAAR 59 (1991) 592-5 (T. Sue *Montgomery*).

8494 **Batstone** David B., From conquest to struggle; Jesus of Nazareth in Latin America. Albany 1991, SUNY. xiv-224 p. $44,50; pa. $15. 0-7914-0421-8; -2-6 [TDig 38,347]. – ^RTS 52 (1991) 787 (M. L. *Cook*); TZBas 47 (1991) 373s (T. *Lorenzen*).

8495 **Berryman** Phillip, Liberation theology 1987 ► 3,8406... 5,8475: ^RPr-Peo 4 (1990) 117s (P. *Fleetwood*).

8496 ^E**Beumer** J., Bevrijdingstheologie, vormen en varianten. Baarn 1990, Ten Have. 167 p. ƒ28,50. 90-259-4413-2. – ^RTsTNijm 31 (1991) 104s (E. *Borgman*).

8497 **Bigo** Pierre, Débat dans l'Église; théologie de la libération. Mareil-Marly 1990, Aide à l'Église en détresse. 177 p. – ^REsprVie 101 (1991) 300-2 (P. *Jay*: donne à penser).

8498 **Boff** C., *Pixley* G. V., Les pauvres, choix prioritaire: Libération 1, 1990 ► 6,8500: ^RLavalTP 47 (1991) 465s (G. *Chénard*); LumièreV 40,203 (1991) 91 (A. *Durand*).

8499 **Boff** Clodovis, *Pixley* George, The Bible, the Church and the poor. Mkn/Tunbridge Wells 1989, Orbis / Burns & Oates. 286 p. $30; pa. $15. 0-88344-614-6; -599-9. – ^REvQ 63 (1991) 373s (Ruth B. *Edwards*); NewTR 4,1 (1991) 110s (L. J. *Hoppe*).

8500 **Boff** Clodovis, Optie voor de armen [1986], ^T*Jonker* C. Averbode 1989, Altiora. 123 p. Fb 450. 90-317-0744-9. – ^RBijdragen 52 (1991) 452 (B. *Höfte*: J. *Pixley* indicated as co-author in text, 'Opção', but not in title 'Opçã').

8500* **Boff** Clodovis, Théorie et pratique; la méthode des théologies de la libération ^T(avec nouvelle préface): CogF 157. P 1990, Cerf. 408 p. F 239 [NRT 114,451, P. *Tihon*].

8501 *Boff* Clodovis M., O capitalismo triunfante na visão atual de João Paulo II (Leitura da 'Centesimus Annus' a partir do Terceiro Mundo): REB 51 (1991) 825-846 [771-921, *al.*].

8502 **Boff** L., When theology listens 1988 ► 4,9540; 6,8504: ^RCritRR 3 (1990) 422-4 (C. *Cadorette*).

8503 **Borgman** E., Sporen van de bevrijdende God; universitaire theologie in aansluiting op latijnamerikaanse bevrijdingstheologie, zwarte theologie en feministische theologie [kath. diss. Nijmegen, ^D*Häring* H. ► 6,8506*]. Kampen 1990, Kok. xviii-360 p. 90-242-6510-X. – ^RTsTNijm 31 (1991) 339s (R. G. van *Rossum*).

8504 **Cadorette** Curt, From the heart... G. GUTIÉRREZ 1988 ► 5,8486; 6,8508: ^RCritRR 3 (1990) 424-7 (D. *Brackley*).

8505 **Campbell** Howard D., The Cross of Christ ['a purely human, rather than a divine transaction; Jesus died because of his commitment to the cause of the poor'] in Latin American liberation theology: diss. Drew, ^D*Pain* J. Madison NJ 1991. 249 p. 92-13364. – DissA 52 (1991s) 4373-A.

8506 **Ciorra** Anthony J., Saint FRANCIS of Assisi and [SEGUNDO J.] liberation theology: diss. Fordham, ^D*Cousins* E. NY 1991. 361 p. 91-27025. – DissA 52 (1991s) 1387-A; RelStR 18,173.

8507 **Cohn-Sherbok** Dan, On earth as it is in heaven; Jews, Christians and liberation theology 1987 ► 3,8440... 5,8491; ^RIndTSt 27 (1990) 98-100 (M. D. *Ambrose*); IrTQ 57 (1991) 246-8 (J. *Littleton*).

8508 *Colombo* J. A., God as hidden, God as manifest; 'who is the subject of salvation in history in liberation theology?': JRel 71 (1991) 18-35.

8509 **Comblin** J.,   La forza della Parola [1986], pref. *Molari* Carlo.   Bo 1989, EMI.   xvi-463 p. Lit. 34.000. – ᴿDivThom 90 (1990) 176s (L. *Elders*: plan social plutôt que théologique; affirmations malencontreuses de Molari).

8510 **Cox** Harvey,   Silencing of L. Boff 1988 ➤ 5,8494; 6,8518: ᴿJRel 70 (1990) 651s (T. *Swanson*); PrPeo 4 (1990) 157 (S. E. *Hall*); ScotJT 44 (1991) 135s (G. *Markus*: shocking but unfair to Ratzinger; and 'A theologian in El Salvador told me I had no right to question his views on "the suffering of God" simply because he worked with refugees and I didn't. Who is silencing whom?').

8511 **Dussell** Enrique [➤ 6,8526],   Prophetie und Kritik; Entwurf einer Geschichte der Theologie in Lateinamerika [Bogotá 1986].   Fribourg 1989, Exodus.   187 p. – ᴿTContext 7,2 (1990) 121 (R. *Fornet-Betancourt*).

8512 **Dussel** Enrique,   Ethics and community, ᵀ*Barr* Robert R.: Liberation and theology 3.   Tunbridge Wells 1988, Burns & O.   xii-260 p. £9. – ᴿHeythJ 32 (1991) 444s (J. R. *Williams*).

8513 ᴱ**Ellacuría** I., *Sobrino* J.,   Mysterium liberationis; conceptos fundamentales de la Teología de la Liberación.   M 1990, Trotta.   642 p.; 689 p. – ᴿRazF 223 (1991) 218s (M. *Alcalá*).

8514 *Esquiza* Jesús,   Teología de la Liberación y dualismos de ayer y de hoy: LumenVr 39 (1990) 251-293.

8515 ᴱ**Ferm** Deane W.,   Liberation theology, North American style 1988 ➤ 5,461: ᴿJRel 70 (1990) 474s (B. *Stenger*).

8516 *Filipe* Thomaz Luis, *Oliveira e Costa* João Paulo,   A Bíblia e a expansão portuguesa: ➤ 422, Didaskalia 20,1 (1989/90) 223-240.

8517 **Fornet-Betancourt** Raúl,   Philosophie und Theologie der Befreiung 1988 ➤ 5,8505*; DM 21,80 pa.: ᴿZkT 113 (1991) 466s (M. *Maier*).

8518 **Galilea** Segundo,   The way of living faith. 1988: ᴿJRel 70 (1990) 118s(J. *Lara-Braud*).

8519 **Gomez** Fausto,   Liberation theology and Christian liberation.   Manila 1987, Social Research.   83 p. – ᴿColcT 60,4 (1990) 185s (A. F. *Dziuba*, ❷).

8520 *González Faus* José I.,   De la 'indiferencia' al 'tercer grado de humildad'; notas para una cristología de libertad: RLatAmT 8 (1991) 39-49.

8521 **Goodpasture** H. M., Cross and sword ... in Latin America 1989 ➤ 6,8535: ᴿETL 67 (1991) 465s (J. E. *Vercruysse*); Interpretation 45 (1991) 320 (T. Sue *Montgomery*).

8521* *a) Greinacher* Norbert,   Bekehrung durch Eroberung; kritische Reflexion auf die Kolonisations- und Missionsgeschichte in Lateinamerika; – *b) Richard* Pablo,   Die kirchlichen Basisgemeinden; die Zukunft der Kirche in Mittelamerika, ᵀ*Bruegman* Veit; – *c) Cook* Guillermo,   Entstehung und Praxis der evangelischen Basisgemeinden in Mittelamerika, ᵀ*Müller-Fahrenholz* Geiko: EvT 51,6 ('Lateinamerika 1492-1992' 1991) 504-519 / 532-543 / 543-9.

8522 *Grogan* Geoffrey,   Liberation and prosperity theologies: ScotBEvT 9 (1991) 118-132: both are biblical but subsidiary.

8523 **Gutiérrez** Gustavo,   Dios o el oro 1989 ➤ 5,8515; 6,8537: ᴿEfMex 9 (1991) 142s (E. *Serraima Cirici*); Gregorianum 72 (1991) 168 (J. *López-Gay*: no aportará luz ni paz); Iter 2 (1991) 134-6 (E. *Frades*); LumenVr 39 (1990) 91s (U. *Gil Ortega*); NewTR 4,1 (1991) 108-110 (J. *Gros*); VerbumSVD 32 (1991) 112-5 (H. *Dumont*).

8524 **Gutiérrez** G.,   Gott oder das Gold ... Las Casas 1990 ➤ 6,8538: ᴿTsTNijm 31 (1991) 433 (J. Van *Nieuwenhove*).

8525 **Gutiérrez** G.,   El Dios de la vida 1982 ²1989:   ᴿPerspT 22 (1990) 380-2 (F. *Taborda*).

8526 **Gutiérrez** Gustavo,   The truth shall make you free; confrontations 1990 ➤ 6,8541:   ᴿGregorianum 72 (1991) 377s (A. M. *Abela*).

8527 *Hanselmann* Johannes,   Justification, liberté et théologie de la libération: PosLuth 38 (1990) 179-189 [< zıт 90,817].

8528 ᴱ**Hennelly** Alfred T.,   Liberation theology; a documentary history 1989 ➤ 6,8544:   ᴿCritRR 4 (1991) 438-440 (M. R. *Candelaria*: a rich reservoir); Interpretation 45 (1991) 318-320 (R. P. *Roth*); ScripTPamp 23 (1991) 741 (L. F. *Mateo-Seco*, también sobre Mᴄ GOVERN A.); TS 52 (1991) 164-6 (J. P. *Hogan*).

8529 *Hennelly* Alfred T.,   Participating in the liberating spirit; bibliographical essay: IntRMiss 79 (1990) 379-386.

8530 **Herzog** Frederick,   God-walk; liberation shaping dogmatics 1988 ➤ 5,8520; 6,8547:   ᴿRExp 87 (1990) 145-7 (C. J. *Scalise*: all 'God-talk' originates in 'God-walk').

8531 **Hewitt** Marsha A.,   From theology to social theory; J. L. SEGUNDO and the theology of liberation [➤ 6,8547*]: AmerUnivSt 7/73. NY 1990, P. Lang. x-184 p. $42.   0-8204-1258-9 [TDig 38,165]. – ᴿTsTNijm 31 (1991) 208s (E. *Borgman*).

8531* **Hewitt** Warren E.,   Base Christian communities and social change in Brazil. Lincoln 1991, Univ. Nebraska. xvi-150 p. $25.   0-8032-2356-0 [TDig 39,168].

8532 **Hoornaert** Eduardo,   O cristianismo moreno do Brasil. Petrópolis 1991, Vozes. 182 p. – ᴿREB 51 (1991) 491-504 (E. D. B. de *Menezes*).

8533 **Hortelano** Antonio,   Comunidades de base; fracaso o base y futuro de la Iglesia?: Nueva Alianza 108. S 1987, Sígueme. 335 p. – ᴿLumenVr 39 (1990) 185-7 (U. *Gil Ortega*).

8534 **Hynes** Mary J.,   Gustavo GUTIÉRREZ's concepts and images of God [... less political than in Peru's first evangelizers]: diss. *Nichols* F. St. Louis 1991. 203 p. 91-31004. – DissA 52 (1991s) 1778s-A; RTLv 23, p. 569.

8535 **Ibáñez Langlois** J. M.,   Teología de la liberación y libertad cristiana. Santiago 1989, Univ. Cat. 126 p. – ᴿAnnTh 4 (1990) 474-8 (E. *Colom Costa*).

8536 **Jaén** Néstor,   Toward a liberation spirituality, ᵀ*Berryman* Phillip. Ch 1991, Loyola. xvii-123 p. $10 pa.   0-8294-0698-0 [TDig 39,67].

8537 **Kee** Alistair,   MARX and the failure of liberation theology 1990 ➤ 6,8552:   ᴿJTS 42 (1991) 436-441 (P. *Scott*); Tablet 244 (1990) 1443 (P. *Hebblethwaite*: paradoxical ironical defense); TS 52 (1991) 375-7 (A. F. *McGovern*).

8538 **Kern** Bruno,   Fundamentaltheologie im Horizont des Marxismus; zur Marxismusrezeption in der lateinamerikanischen Theologie der Befreiung: diss. Laval, ᴰ*Vergauwen* G. Sainte-Foi QUÉ 1991. – RTLv 23, p. 536.

8539 *Kerr* Susan A.,   Liberation and the liturgical year: RRel 49 (1990) 837-842.

8540 ᴱ**Kirkpatrick** Dow,   Faith born in the struggle for life; a re-reading of Protestant faith in Latin America today, ᵀ*McCoy* Lewistine. GR 1988, Eerdmans. 328 p. – ᴿJDharma 15 (1990) 359s (B. *Mukalel*).

8541 **Klinger** [➤ 8446] Elmar,   Armut; eine Herausförderung Gottes; der Glaube des Konzils und die Befreiung des Menschen. Z 1990, Benziger. 333 p. 3-545-24077-0. – ᴿActuBbg 28 (1991) 154s (J. *Boada*).

8541* **Koopmans** Jopp,   Das Leben umarmen; Befreiungstheologie in der Praxis, ᴱ*Bikuys* U., *Bubik* M. W-Mödling 1990, St. Gabriel/Südwind. 223 p. Sch 189 pa. [TLZ 117,531, J. *Althausen*].

8542 **Lamola Maleseza** John,   The poverty of a theology of the poor; an Althusserian exposure of the philosophical basis of Latin American theology of liberation: diss. ᴰ*Kee* A.   Edinburgh 1991. 329 p. – RTLv 23, p. 536.

8543 **Levi** Werner,   From alms to liberation; the Catholic Church, the theologians, poverty and politics.   NY 1989, Praeger. 175 p. $36. – ᴿJRel 71 (1991) 288s (A. T. *Hennelly*: insightful political scientist).

8544 **Löschke** Eberhard,   Auf dem Weg zur Religion des Lebens; Christen im Befreiungskampf Nicaraguas und die marxistische Religionstheorie. Bochum 1988, SWI.   377 p. – ᴿTLZ 116 (1991) 526s (M. *Petzoldt*).

8545 **Löwy** Michael,   Marxisme en bevrijdingstheologie.   Kampen 1989, Kok. 140 p. ƒ 32,75.   90-24248-71-X. – ᴿNedTTs 45 (1991) 169 (V. *Brümmer*: 'Löwy pleit voor een nieuwe marxistische interpretatie van het verschijnsel religie').

8546 *Löwy* Michael,   Modernité et critique de la modernité dans la théologie de la libération: ArchivScSocRel 35,71 (1990) 7-23 [ELLACURIA I. + 5 *al.*) 25-92].

8547 **Lynch** Edward A.,   Religion and politics in Latin America; liberation theology and Christian democracy.   NY 1991, Praeger. xi-200 p. [RelStR 18,220, R. F. *Wilson*].

8548 *MacDowell* João A.,   I Gesuiti in America Latina: CC 142 (1991,3) 403-414.

8549 **McGovern** Arthur F.,   Liberation theology and its critics 1989 → 6,8560: ᴿJRel 71 (1991) 450 (J. A. *Colombo*); TS 52 (1991) 164-6 (J. P. *Hogan*: copes with the 'red herring thicket' of Nicaragua-style 'people's Church'); Vidyajyoti 55 (1991) 300s (G. V. *Lobo*, also on GUTIÉRREZ G. 1990; BOERMA G. 1989).

8550 **McKelway** A. J.,   The freedom of God and human liberation.   L/Ph 1990, SCM/Trinity.   xvi-128 p.   0-334-02466-8. – ᴿTsTNijm 31 (1991) 441 (E. *Borgman*).

8551 **Marlé** René, Introduction à la TL 1988 → 4,9603... 6,8533:   ᴿGregorianum 72 (1991) 378s (A. *Angulo*).

8552 *Marlé* René, ❷ Dieu, le Christ et l'Église dans la théologie de la libération [< Cah. Actualité Rel. Soc. Supp 307], ᵀ*Opiela* Stanisław: PrzPow 267,822 (1990) 237-248.

8553 **Marson** Orioldo,   Il metodo della teologia della liberazione in G. GUTIÉRREZ, L. & C. BOFF, J. L. SEGUNDO: diss. Pont. Univ. Gregoriana, ᴰ*Dupuis* J.   Roma 1991. 545 p. – RTLv 23, p. 554 [< DissA-C].

8554 **Martin** David,   Tongues of fire; the explosion of Protestantism in Latin America.   Ox 1990, Blackwell.   352 p. $40. – ᴿAmerica 164 (1991) 475-7 (J. *Gros*); CritRR 4 (1991) 329s (Deborah *Baldwin*); TTod 48 (1991s) 102 . 104 . 106 (R. K. *Fenn*).

8555 **Martínez Morales** Victor M.,   Acceso a una lectura ético-social del Misterio Eucarístico en la teología post-conciliar: diss. Pont. Univ. Gregoriana, Nᵒ 6937, ᴰ*Rosato* P.   R 1991s. – InfPUG 121 (1991s) 19.

8556 ᴱ**Meier** Johannes,   Zur Geschichte des Christentums in Lateinamerika [Kath. Akad. Freiburg 1987] 1988 → 5,491: ᴿTR 87 (1991) 205 (N. *Borengässer*: tit. pp. Analysen).

8557 **Melo Magalhaes** Antonio C. de,   Christologie und Nachfolge; eine systematisch-ökumenische Untersuchung zur Befreiungstheologie bei Leonardo BOFF und Jon SOBRINO: ev. Diss. Hamburg 1991, ᴰ*Pesch*. – TR 87 (1991) 518.

8558 **Mertens** Herman-Emiel, Niet het kruis maar de Gekruisigde; Schets van een christelijke bevrijdingsleer 1990 ➤ 6,8566; 90-334-2194-1: ᴿETL 67 (1991) 470-2 (R. *Michiels*); LvSt 16 (1991) 189s (also R. *Michiels*); TsTNijm 31 (1991) 337s (M. Van *Tente*).

Miguez Bonino J., Faces of Jesus; Latin American Christologies 1984 ➤ 3617.

8559 **Min Kyongsuk** Anselm, Dialectic of salvation; issues in theology of liberation 1989 ➤ 6,8589: ᴿScotJT 44 (1991) 255s (R. S. *Sugirtharajah* finds chiefly interesting the mutual critique between Latin American and other Third World liberation theologies).

8560 **Mondin** Battista, ❷ Teologowie wyzwolenia, ᵀ*Borkowski* Rejmund. Wsz 1989, Pax. 181 p. – ᴿColcT 60,4 (1990) 186s (J. *Królikowski*).

8561 **Muñoz** Ronaldo, Dieu; 'J'ai vu la misère de mon peuple': Libération. P 1990, Cerf. iv-237 p. F 150. – ᴿLumièreV 40,203 (1991) 91s (A. *Durand*); NRT 113 (1991) 581s (L. *Volpe*).

8562 **Nessan** Craig L., Orthopraxis or heresy; the North American theological response to LAmLibT 1989 ➤ 6,8574: ᴿCritRR 4 (1991) 451-3 (Anselm *Min*).

8563 *Nichols* Aidan, al., The rise and fall of liberation theology: NBlackf 72 (1991) 408-423 (-450).

8564 **Nowak** Jutta, Theorie der Befreiung; Struktur, Bedingungen und Resultat 'theologischer Produktion' bei Clodovis BOFF: diss. ᴰ*Greshake* G. FrB 1991. 231 p. – RTLv 23, p. 537.

8565 *O'Hare* Padraic, *Klenicki* Leon, Liberation theology; romantic ideology? teacher of contempt?: CCurr 40 (1990s) 109-114-119 [422-6, letters by R. M. *Brown* and Mary E. *Hunt*].

8565* **Ojoy** V., Traces of humanist Marxism in G. GUTIÉRREZ's TL: diss. 1990 Lv, ᴰ*Schrijver* G. De. xxxiv-284 p. – TsTNijm 32,87.

8566 **O'Neill** Miceál, God hears the cry of the poor; the emerging spirituality in the Christian communities in Peru (1965-1986): diss. Pont. Univ. Gregoriana. R 1990. viii-320 p. – ᴿMilltSt 28 (1991) 162-7 (Teresa *Clements*).

8567 **Pasquetto** Virgilio, Mai più schiavi... 1988 ➤ 4,9613... 6,8580: ᴿSalesianum 53 (1991) 587s (C. *Bissoli*).

8568 *Petitdemange* Guy, ❷ Théologie(s) de la libération et marxisme [Cah. Actualité Rel. Soc.], ᵀ*Opiela* Stanisław: PrzPow 270,830 (1990) 40-56.

8569 **Piar** Carlos R., Jesus and liberation; a critical analysis of the Christology of L. BOFF, J. SOBRINO, and J. L. SEGUNDO [they challenge Christological narratives as having legitimated oppression, but they are eclectic and authoritarian, and should be more faithful to the people's and the NT understanding of Jesus' identity]: diss. So. Cal. 1991, ᴰ*Crossley* J. P. [Microfilm only from U.So. Cal. LA]. – DissA 52 (1991s) 2960s-A; RelStR 18,171.

8570 *Reinhardt* Heinrich, Die laute und die stille Hoffnung der Befreiungstheologie: WissWeis 52 (1989) 228-236.

8571 a) *Reinis* Austra, A Latvian perspective on liberation theology; – b) *Nessan* Craig L., Dynamics of polarization; North American critics versus Liberation Theology: CurrTMiss 18 (1991) 427-431 / 432-8.

8572 **Robbins** Bruce W., Costa Rican theological education today; a history of the Seminario Bíblico Latinoamericano San José 1922-90: diss. Southern Methodist Univ, ᴰ*Deschner* J. 1991. – RelStR 18,174.

8573 **Rowland** Christopher, *Corner* Mark, Liberating exegesis; the challenge of liberation theology to biblical studies: Biblical Foundations in Theology. L 1990, SPCK. ix-205 p. £11. 0-281-04437-6. – ᴿBL (1990) 113 (A. G. *Auld*: little on OT); REB 51 (1991) 745-9 (Henrique de *Ternay*); TTod 48 (1991s) 93s (R. D. *Witherup*).

8574 **Scannone** Juan Carlos, Teología de la liberación y doctrina social de la Iglesia 1987 ➤ 6,8593: ᴿPerspT 21 (1989) 123-6 (J. B. *Libânio*).

8575 *Scannone* Juan-Carlos, Begegnung der Kulturen und inkulturierte Philosophie in Lateinamerika: TPhil 66 (1991) 365-383.

8576 **Schipani** Daniel S., Religious education encounters liberation theology. Birmingham AL 1988, Rel. Edn. 276 p. $15. – ᴿIrTQ 57 (1991) 90s (P. M. *Devitt*).

8576* *a) Schwantes* Milton, Wege der biblischen Theologie in Lateinamerika; – *b) Ramírez F.* Dagoberto, Die Bibel in Chile heute; ein Erfahrungsbericht; – *c) Mesters* Carlos, Bibellektüre durch das Volk; – *d) Richard* Pablo, Bibellektüre durch das Volk in Lateinamerika; Hermeneutik der Befreiung: EvT 51,1 ('Lat.-Am. Exegese' 1991) 8-19 / 101-8 / 3-7 / 20-39. Translations of parts of published works.

8577 **Scott** Peter M., An epistemology for liberation; Marxist questions to liberation theology: diss. Bristol 1990. 402 p. BRDX-93861. – DissA 52 (1991s) 3599-A.

8578 **Shaull** Richard, The Reformation and liberation theology; insights for the challenges of today. Louisville 1991, W-Knox. 136 p. $12 [RelStR 18,220, D. R. *Janz*: ignores data that do not fit].

8579 ᴱ**Sievernich** Michael, Impulse der Befreiungstheologie für Europa; ein Lesebuch [➤ 5,8560 'Forum Politische Theologie 2; 1987']: Gesellschaft und Theologie 6. Mainz/Mü 1988, Grünewald/Kaiser. 195 p. DM 22,80. – ᴿTR 87 (1991) 490 (K. J. *Tossou*).

8580 *Sievernich* Michael, Théologie de la libération: ➤ 668, DictSpir 15,96ss (1990) 500-9.

8581 **Sigmund** Paul E., Liberation theology at the crossroads; democracy or revolution 1990 ➤ 6,8597: ᴿRLatAmT 23 (1991) 216-8 (D. B.); TLond 94 (1991) 459s (A. *Kee*); TS 52 (1991) 377-9 (A. T. *Hennelly*: lacks McGovern's balance).

8582 **Sobrino** Jon, Geist, der befreit; Anstösse zu einer neuen Spiritualität [verkürzte Aufsatzsammlung ➤? 5,8562s], ᵀ*Hermans* Karel, *Schmalen* Georg. FrB 1989, Herder. 191 p. DM 29,80. – ᴿOrientierung 55 (1991) 254-6 (M. *Maier*); TR 87 (1991) 336 (J. *Sudbrack*).

8583 **Sobrino** Jon, Bevrijding met geest, notities voor een nieuwe spiritualiteit ➤ 5,8563; ᵀ*Deelen* F. Kampen/Averbode 1988, Kok/Altiora. 240 p. ƒ 34,50. 90-242-0930-7 / 90-317-0667-1. – ᴿBijdragen 52 (1991) 108s (W. G. *Tillmans*, also on BRAS K., DUINTJER O.).

8584 **Sobrino** J., Jesus in Latin America 1987 ➤ 3,8546; 4,9634: ᴿTGL 81 (1991) 130 (Kossi J. *Tossou*).

8585 *Sontag* Frederick, Liberation theology and the interpretation of political violence: Thomist 55 (1991) 271-292.

8586 *Suess* Paulo, 500 Jahre Christentum in Lateinamerika; Herausforderung einer nachkolonialischen Evangelisierung: Orientierung 55 (1991) 207-211.

8587 *a) Trindade Liana* Salvia, La crisi del sistema schiavista brasiliano e le interpretazioni mitiche della realtà sociale; – *b) Mazzoleni* Gilberto, Lo sviluppo delle attese salvifico-apocalittiche nella società contemporanea [... Brasile]: SMSR 57 (1991) 131-141 / 143-150.

8588 *Trundle* Robert C.[J], The case for and against theological approaches to business ethics: LavalTP 47 (1991) 241-259.

8589 a) *Vaage* Leif E., Text, context, conquest, quest; the Bible and social struggle in Latin America; – b) *West* Gerald, *Draper* Jonathan A., The Bible and social transformation in South Africa; a work-in-progress report on the Institute for the Study of the Bible: → 446, SBL Sem 30 (1991) 357-365 / 366-382.

8590 ᴱ**Witvliet** J. T., Bevrijdingstheologie in de Derde Wereld; Teksten uit Azië, Afrika en Latijns-Amerika: Sleutelteksten in godsdienst 9. Haag 1990, Meinema. 310 p. *f* 39,90. 90-211-6108-7. – ᴿTsTNijm 31 (1991) 208 (R. G. van *Rossum*).

H8.6 *Theologiae emergentes* – 'Theologies of' emergent groups.

8591 ᴱ**Abraham** K. C., Third world theologies, commonalities and divergences 1986/90 → 6,565: ᴿEcuR 41 (1991) 378s (W. *Russell*); Gregorianum 72 (1991) 775s (J. *Dupuis*).

8592 **Akrong** Abraham A., An Akan Christian view of salvation from the perspective of John CALVIN's soteriology: diss. Lutheran School of Theology. [Ch] 1991. 287 p. 91-29531. – DissA 52 (1991s) 1386-A.

8593 *Amaladoss* M., Cross-inculturating Indian-African Christianity: AfER 12 (1990) 157-168.

8594 a) *Amaladoss* M., Hermeneutic of tradition and social change; – b) *England* John C., Towards the new humanity; some watershed figures in Asian theology: IndTSt 27 (1990) 113-132 / 155-174.

8595 *Anikuzhikattil* M., The penitential life of the St Thomas Christians of India: QLtg 71 (1990) 1-11 [70 (1989) 251-263, rites of reconciliation).

8596 **Ante** O. A., Contextual evangelization in the Philippines; a Filipino Franciscan experience; kath. diss. Nijmegen, ᴰ*Camps* P. Kampen 1991, Kok. viii-196 p. 90-242-3409-3. – TsTNijm 31 (1991) 321.

8597 **Arbuckle** Gerald A., Earthing the Gospel; an inculturation handbook for pastoral workers. L/Mkn 1990, Chapman/Orbis. 236 p. £15/$17. – ᴿMissiology 19 (1991) 103s (D. *Whiteman*); Pacifica 4 (1991) 341-4 (M. *Mason*); RRel 50 (1991) 786s (R. J. *Faley*).

8598 **Baur** John, The Catholic Church in Kenya, a centenary history 1990 → 6,8611; sh. 120: ᴿAfER 12 (1990) 245s (C. *McGarry*).

8599 ᴱ**Bertsch** Ludwig, Laien als Gemeindeleiter; Texte der Erzdiözese Kinshasa: Theologie der Dritten Welt 14. FrB 1990, Herder. 237 p. DM 38 pa. – ᴿTGL 81 (1991) 503s (Kossi J. *Tossou*).

8600 *Bianchi* Eugene C., Resources for a democratic Catholic Church: Horizons 18 (1991) 207-226.

8601 **Boothe** Hyacinth I., Gospel and culture — accommodation or tension? An inquiry into the priorities of the Gospel in the light of Jamaica's historico-cultural experience vis-à-vis western Christian civilization: diss. St. Andrews, 1988. 517 p. BRDX-94025. – DissA 52 (1991s) 2956-A.

8602 *Byrne* Andrew, Some ins and outs of inculturation: AnnTh 4 (1990) 109-149.

8603 *Carrier* Hervé, Évangélisation et développement des cultures: StSoc NS 4. R 1990, Pont. Univ. Gregoriana. 380 p. Lit. 32.000. 88-7652-631-5. – ᴿCC 142 (1991,1) 320 (G. *Salvini*); Gregorianum 72 (1991) 407s (*ipse*).

8603* **Castles** B. C., Hymns; the making and shaping of a theology for the whole people of God; a comparison of the four last things in some English and Zambian hymns in intercultural perspective: Studies in the

Intercultural History of Christianity 67. Fra 1990, Lang. xi-290 p.; 2 maps. Fs 85 [NRT 114,603, J. *Scheuer*].

8604 **Chenu** Bruno, Théologies chrétiennes des Tiers Mondes 1987 → 3,8594; 4,9658: RIndTSt 27 (1990) 103s (L. *Ray*: extension of his dissertation on Black American theology).

8605 **Chenu** Bruno, Teologías cristianas de los terceros mundos 1989 → 5, 8589; 6,8623: RAugM 35 (1990) 466 (J. A. *Galindo*).

8606 *a) Chilver* E. M., Thaumaturgy in contemporary traditional religion; the case of Nso' [Cameroon] in mid-century; – *b) Barnes* Sandra T., Religion, power, and outside knowledge; JRelAf 20 (1990) 226-247 / 248-268.

8607 **Christensen** Thomas, An African tree of life. Mkn 1989, Orbis. $20. – RCCurr 41 (1991s) 565s (Ann E. *Nielsen*: 'Why add Christianity?').

8608 **Coeurdoux** Gaston-Laurent, real author in 1777 of the Moeurs et Coutumes des Indiens [d'Inde], revised by N.-J. *Desvaulx* and presented after 1774 to Colonies Minister de Sartine as his work; the famous Hindu Manners, Customs, and Ceremonies published by Jean-Antoine DUBOIS was shown by Sylvie *Murr* [L'indologie du Père Coeurdoux (P 1987, ÉcFr d'Extrême Orient) 247 + 250 p.] to be based on an earlier original of Coeurdoux: IndTSt 27 (1990) 371-3 (R. *DeSmet*).

8609 **Cone** James H., A black theology of liberation 1990 (1986 = 1970 → 3,8601): RLvSt 16 (1991) 263-5 (D. *Rochford*).

8609* *Copher* C. B., The Bible and the African experience; the biblical period: JIntdenom 16,1s (1988s) 32-50 [< NTAbs 36,71].

8610 **Costas** Orlando E.†, Liberating news; a theology of contextual evangelization. GR 1989, Eerdmans. 182 p. $13. – RTTod 48 (1991s) 122s (M. *Arias*).

8611 **Davis** Cyprian, The history of Black Catholics in the United States 1990 → 6,8634: RCathHR 77 (1991) 712-5 (S. *Ochs*) [< RHE 87,156*]; Commonweal 118 (1991) 699 (L. C. *Cunningham*); RRel 50 (1991) 937 (J. J. *Mueller*).

8611* *Deist* F. E., South-Africanising biblical studies; an epistemological and hermeneutical inquiry; Scriptura 37 (1991) 32-50 [1-16, *Hartin* P. J.: < NTAbs 36,3.5].

8612 EDoré J., *Kabasélé* F., Chemins de la christologie africaine 1982/6 → 5,8596*: RMilltSt 23 (1989) 108-112 (R. *Moloney*: 'The tree of the huntsman').

8613 *Dupuis* Jacques, La missione in Asia negli anni 90: CC 142 (1991,4) 228-243.

8614 **Dyrness** William A., Learning about theology from the Third World. GR 1990, Zondervan Academie. 221 p. $13. 0-310-20971-4 [TDig 38, 157]. – RAndrUnS 29 (1991) 172s (J. L. *Dybdahl*).

8615 **Eckhardt** A. Roy, Black – Woman – Jew 1989 → 6,8638: RCritRR 4 (1991) 266-8 (A. T. *Hennelly*).

8616 **Ehusani** George O., An Afro-Christian vision, 'Ozovehe!' ['the human person is life' + imago Dei]; toward a more humanized world. Lanham MD 1991, UPA. xi-264 p. $39.75; pa. $24.50. 0-8191-8114-5; -5-3 [TDig 39,58].

8617 **Ejizu** Christopher I., Ofo, Igbu ritual symbol [< diss. Univ. Nigeria 1984]. Enugu 1987, Fourth Dimension. xxii-190 p. – RJDharma 15 (1990) 81s (F. N. *Nwahaghi*).

8618 *England* John C., Towards the charting of Asian theologies: Arasaradi 4,2 (1991) 49-58.

8619 *Evans* James H., Deconstructing the tradition; narrative strategies in nascent Black Theology: UnSemQ 44,1 (NY 1990) 101-121 [< ZIT 90,608].

ᴱ**Felder** Cain H., Stony the road we trod; African American biblical interpretation 1991. ➤ 431.

8620 *Frankl* P.J.L., The word for 'God' in Swahili: JRelAf 20 (1990) 269-275 [< ZIT 90,864].

8621 **Frostin** Per, Liberation theology in Tanzania and South Africa; a first world interpretation: STLund 42, 1988 ➤ 6,8648: ᴿJScStR 29 (1990) 406 (O. *Maduro*); TContext 8/2 (1991) 132 (H. *Janssen*); TLZ 116 (1991) 71-73 (J. *Althausen*); TZBas 47 (1991) 90s (K. *Blaser*).

8622 **Gelpi** Donald L., Inculturating North American theology 1988 ➤ 4, 9683; 5,8607: ᴿCritRR 3 (1990) 431-3 (C. *Davis*); JRel 71 (1991) 446s (R. *Schreiter*: challenges LONERGAN).

8623 **George** Francis E., Inculturation and ecclesial communion; culture and Church in the teaching of JOHN PAUL II. R 1990, Urbaniana Univ. 380 p. – ᴿLvSt 16 (1991) 278-280 (R. *Boudens*; some questions).

8624 ᴱ**Gilliland** Dean S., The Word among us; contextualizing theology for mission today 1989 ➤ 6,8650: ᴿTLZ 116 (1991) 228s (N.-P. *Moritzen*: an exciting development from *bibeltreu* Pasadena).

8625 *Görski* Jan, Zum Problem der kontextuellen Theologie: VerbumSVD 32 (1991) 61-63.

8625* **Grafe** H., History of Christianity in India, 4/2, Tamilnadu in the nineteenth and twentieth century. Bangalore 1990, Church History. xix-325 p. [NRT 114,620, J. *Masson*].

8626 **Gray** R., Black Christians and white missionaries. NHv 1990, Yale Univ. viii-134 p.; map. $30 [RHE 86,252*].

8627 **Hall** Douglas J., Thinking the faith; Christian theology in a North American context 1989 ➤ 5,8611; 6,8655: ᴿHeythJ 32 (1991) 561s (J.R. *Williams*).

8628 **Hastings** Adrian, African Catholicism; essays in discovery² 1989 ➤ 5, 276; 6,8658: ᴿCCurr 40 (1990s) 132s (P.H.K. *Gundani*); HeythJ 32 (1991) 562s (A. *Shorter*); JRelAf 21 (1991) 90-92 (J.D.Y. *Peel*); NBlackf 71 (1990) 554-6 (E. *Hill*); TContext 8/1 (1991) 130 (H. *Janssen*: still unresolved is the contrast between academic and popular religiosity).

8629 **Hastings** Adrian, The theology of a protestant Catholic 1990 ➤ 6,244: ᴿTLond 94 (1991) 61s (P. *Baelz*).

8630 **Heijke** J.P., Kameroense bevrijdingstheologie; Jean-Marc ELA, theologie van onder de boom: Kerk en theologie en context 6. Kampen 1990, Kok. 226 p. ƒ37,50. 90-242-5335-7. – ᴿTsTNijm 31 (1991) 209 (W. *Eggen*).

8631 *Hergesel* Tomasz, ❷ Bible reading in Africa: RuBi 43 (1990) 144-155: in the beginning was the tom-tom.

8631* **Hood** R.E., Must God remain Greek? Afro cultures and God-talk. Mp 1990, Fortress. xiii-273 p. [NRT 114,471].

8632 *Jenkins* David, Evangelization and culture: TLond 94 (1991) 5-10.

8632* **Jesudasan** Ignatius, Gandhian theology of liberation: Jesuit Theological Forum 3. Anand 1987, Gujarat-SP. xii-318 p. rs 48; pa. 45 ➤ 65,7339 ... 6,8666: ᴿIndTSt 27 (1990) 97s (R. *De Smet*: complete original of which the Maryknoll abridged edition appeared in 1984, also Italian, German; French, Spanish in process).

8633 **Johnson** Alonso, Good news for the disinherited; the meaning of Jesus of Nazareth in the writings of Howard THURMAN: diss. Union Theol. Sem. NY 1990. 247 p. 91-28444. – DissA 52 (1991s) 1390s-A.

8634 **Jones** Major J., The color of God ... Afro-American thought 1987
→ 3,8645: ᴿJRel 71 (1991) 111s (E. H. *Oglesby*).

8635 *a) Jung* I. Shannon, Why globalization? – *b) Benz* Frank L., Was
David's theologian [the Yahwist] concerned about mission?; – *c) Fish*
James, Teaching as we preach; education for the sake of mission:
CurrTMiss 18 (1991) 325-330 / 363-7 / 357-362.

8636 *Kasper* Walter, Postmodern dogmatics; toward a renewed discussion of
foundations in North America; ᵀ*Asselin* D., *Waldstein* M.: CommND 17
(1990) 181-191.

8637 **Kim Won-bae,** Die Revolution Gottes und Minjung; der Sitz und das
Paradigma der Minjung-Theologie: Diss. ᴰ*Lochman* J. Basel 1991. –
RTLv 23, p. 562.

8638 **Kirwen** Michael C., The missionary and the divine; contending theologies of Christian and African religions. Mkn 1987, Orbis. 134 p.
0-88344-585-9. – ᴿJeevadhara 20 (1990) 423-5 (J. B. *Chethimattam*);
JRelAf 20 (1990) 316s (M. *Schoffeleers*).

8639 **Kochuparampil** Xavier, Evangelization in India; a theological analysis
of the missionary role of the Syro-Malabar church: diss. ᴰ*Leijssen* L.
Leuven 1991. lvi-436 p. – RTLv 23, p. 565.

8640 **Kuriedath** Jose, Authority in the Catholic community in Kerala
[< Diss. Kerala]. Bangalore 1989, Dharmaram. xx-341 p. – ᴿJDharma
15 (1990) 77s (A. *Kariyil*: brilliant analysis of how participative Church
administration gradually disappeared).

8641 **Lee Sunbee,** Die Minjung-Theologie AHN BYUNGMUS von ihren Voraussetzungen her dargestellt: Diss. ᴰ*Sauter* G. Bonn 1991. 265 p. –
RTLv 23, p. 566 [> EurHS].

8642 **Lestringant** Frank, Le Huguenot et le Sauvage, l'Amérique et la controverse coloniale, en France, au temps des Guerres de Religion (1555-
1589). P 1990, Amateurs de Livres. xiii-374 p. – ᴿFoiVie 90,3 (1991)
147-151 (Marie-Dominique *Legrand*).

8643 **Losigo** Kulu Aimé, Perspectives ecclésiologiques en Afrique noire francophone; pour une théologie de l'église locale à la lumière du Synode de
1974: diss. Pont. Univ. Gregoriana, ᴰ*Dupuis* J. Roma 1991. 516 p.; extr.
n° 3791, 182 p. – InfPUG 121,18; RTLv 23, p. 565 [> DissA-C].

8643* **Loth** Heinz-Jürgen, Rastafari; Bibel und afrikanische Spiritualität:
Kölner Rel-G 20. Köln 1991, Böhlau. viii-128 p. DM 48 [TLZ 117,664,
S. *Uhlig*: superficial].

8644 **Luzbetak** Louis J., The Church and cultures; new perspectives in missiological anthropology 1989 [= 1963 revised] → 5,8627; 6,8676: ᴿAnthropos 86 (1991) 283s (F. A. *Salamone*); AustralasCR 67 (1990) 245-8
(T. D. *Carroll*).

8645 **Malieckal** Louis, Yajna and Eucharist; an inter-religious approach to
the theology of sacrifice [diss. Louvain]. Bangalore 1989, Dharmaram.
xxx-368 p. – ᴿJDharma 15 (1990) 275s (T. *Kadankavil*).

8646 *Manzone* Gino, La preparazione al sacerdozio in Madagascar; nota da
una nazione giovane: CC 142 (1991,3) 382-392.

8646* *Massimini* Fausto, *Delle Fave* Antonella, Religion and cultural evolution: Zygon 26 (1991) 27-47.

8647 *Masson* Joseph, Croyance et recours au Suprême dans la tradition
d'Afrique noire: NRT 113 (1991) 219-238.

8648 *Mazzoleni* Gilberto, Le radici storiche del Candomblé brasiliano [presso
intellettuali 'africanisti' divenuto strumento consolatorio per emarginati ed
ambiziosi (PRANDI R. 1991)]: SMSR 57 (1991) 289-300.

8649 a) *Mbefo* Luke Nnamdi, Theology and the African heritage; – b) *Edokobi* Alfred C., Adaptation in the post-centenary Catholic Church in Nigeria: Bigard Theological Studies 11 (1991) 4-20 / 42-50.

8650 **Mbiti** John S., Bibel und Theologie im afrikanischen Christentum: Theologie und Ökumene 22, 1987 ➤ 3,8664 ... 6,8680: ᴿLuthTKi 13 (1989) 124 (V. *Stolle*).

8651 a) *Mercado* Edwin E., a) Emerging images of the Asian Church; – b) *Mercado* Leonardo N., Inculturation and the biblical apostolate: Philippiniana Sacra 26,76 (1991) 77-94 [> TDig 39,143-6] / 37ss.

8652 *Mesters* Carlos, 'Écouter ce que l'Esprit dit aux Églises'; l'interprétation populaire de la Bible au Brésil, ᵀ*Dumont* Jacqueline: ➤ 348, Concilium 233 (P 1991) 133-145.

8653 **Metuh** Emefie I., Comparative studies of African traditional religions. Onitsha, Nigeria 1987, IMICO. xii-283 p. – ᴿJDharma 15 (1990) 79s (F. N. *Nwahaghi*).

8654 a) *Mookenthottam* Antony, Groundwork for an Indian Christian theology; – b) *Vinceth* V. F., Dialogue and theology of religious pluralism: JDharma 14 (1989) 343-352 / 376-396.

8655 **Moon** Cyrus H. S., A Korean Minjung theology – an OT perspective 19....: ᴿJDharma 15 (1990) 85s (P. *Kochalumkal*).

8656 *Mosothoane* Ephraim, John W. COLENSO, pioneer in the quest for an authentic African Christianity: ScotJT 44 (1991) 215-236.

8657 a) *Moti Lal* Pandit, The historico-religious development of the concept of guru; – b) *Cornille* Catherine, Who is the guru in Catholic ashrams?: IndTSt 27 (1990) 273-297 / 298-310.

8657* ᴱ**Mugambi** J. N. K., *Magesa* L., Jesus in African Christianity — experimentation and diversity in African Christology: Nairobi 1989, Initiative. 164 p. 100 Kenya shillings. – ᴿPrPeo 5 (1991) 35s (P. J. *Kerr*).

8658 a) *Nereparampil* Lucius, Biblical festivals and Hindu feasts; – b) *Canizares* Raul J., The Epiphany and the Cuban Santería; – c) *Ahirika* Edwin A., Egwu-Onicha, a religious festival in African tradition: JDharma 15 (1990) 289-308 / 309-313 / 324-340.

8659 a) *Newbigin* Lesslie, Mission in einer pluralistischen Gesellschaft; – b) *Wilson* Henry S., Die Geschichte des Christentums innerhalb der Geschichte der Menschheit: ➤ 160, ᶠVISCHER L., Ök. Theol. 1991, 66-91 / 140-152.

8660 **Mveng** Engelbert, Identità africana e cristianesimo. T 1990, SEI. 210 p. Lit. 28.000. – ᴿCC 142 (1991,4) 319s (G. *Bellucci*).

8661 **Nicholson** Ronald, A black future? Jesus and salvation in South Africa 1990 ➤ 6,8699*: ᴿCurrTMiss 18 (1991) 217s (D. *Rhoads*).

8661* *Nieuwenhove* Jacques Van, (Klein) *Goldewijk* Berma, Popular religion, liberation and contextual theology; exploring some questions: ➤ 480b, ᶠCAMPS A. congress 1990/91, 1-12 [... al.].

8662 a) *Noel* James A., Memory and hope; toward a hermeneutic of African American consciousness; – b) *Jordan* Brian A., Sources for African American Catholic spirituality: JRelTht 47,1 (Wsh 1990) 18-28 / 29-41 [< ZIT 90,672].

8663 **Nolan** Albert, God in South Africa 1988 ➤ 6,8700: ᴿCurrTMiss 18 (1991) 331-7 (P. L. *Kjeseth*: an invitation).

8664 **Obeng** J. Pashington, Asante Catholicism; ritual communication of the Catholic faith among the Akan of Ghana: diss. Boston Univ. 1991, ᴰ*Ruck* C. – RelStR 18,170.

8664* *Odumuyiwa* E. Ade, A historical note on Christianity and Jewish culture in the early century (AD 29-70): AsiaJT 5 (1991) 286-295 [< NTAbs 36,68].

8665 **Oduyoye** Mercy A., Hearing and knowing; theological reflections on Christianity in Africa 1986 ➤ 3,8692; 5,8650: ᴿTLZ 115 (1990) 553s (J. *Althausen*); ZMissRW 74 (1990) 87-89 (M. *Hakenes*).

8666 *Olson* Howard S., A seamless garment — African understandings of wholeness: CurrTMiss 18 (1991) 273-280.

8667 *Oosterom* L., Contemporary missionary thought in the Republic of Korea; three case-studies on the missionary thought of Presbyterian churches in Korea: IIMO 28. Utrecht 1990, Interuniv. Inst. van Missiologie en Oecumenica. viii-136 p. *f* 19,75. 90-6495-239-9. – ᴿTsTNijm 31 (1991) 442 (J. van *Lin*).

8668 *Ortegat* Xavier, L'annonce de l'Évangile aux cultures; vers une inculturation? Étude de documents du magistère 1962-1977: NRT 113 (1991) 864-881.

8669 *Panikkar* Raimondo, The new role of Christian universities in Asia [< Vidyajyoti 1990]: *a*) Month 252 (1991) 389-395; – *b*) CCurr 41 (1991s) 466-493.

8670 **Paris** Peter J., The social teaching of the Black Churches 1985 ➤ 1,8329: ᴿRTPhil 122 (1990) 573 (S. *Molla*).

8671 **Park Il-young**, Minjung 1988 ➤ 5,8652: ᴿZMissRW 74 (1990) 91s (H. *Waldenfels*).

8672 **Park Yong-Kyu**, Korean Presbyterianism and biblical authority; the role of Scripture in the shaping of Korean Presbyterianism, 1918-1953: diss. Trinity Ev., ᴰ*Woodbridge* J. 1991. 415 p. 91-32991. – DissA 52 (1991s) 2170-A.

8673 ᴱ**Parratt** John, A reader in African Christian theology 1987 ➤ 4,9735 ... 6,8703: £6.50. 0-281-04308-6. – ᴿJRelAf 20 (1990) 318s (M. *Schoffeleers*).

8674 **Partonadi** Sutarman S., Sadrach's community [c. 1900] and its contextual roots; a nineteenth century Javanese expression of Christianity: Currents of Encounter 3. Amst 1990, Rodopi. 317 p. *f* 90. 90-5183-094-7. – ᴿNedTTs 45 (1991) 343-5 (T. van den *End*); TLZ 116 (1991) 706s (T. *Ahrens*).

8675 **Peelman** Achiel, L'inculturation 1989 ➤ 5,8654*; 6,8704: ᴿScEsp 43 (1991) 118 (G. *Langevin*).

8676 **Pieris** Aloysius, An Asian theology of liberation 1988 ➤ 5,8655; 6,8705: ᴿJeevadhara 20 (1990) 333s (J. B. *Chethimattam*); ScotBEvT 9 (1991) 72s (W. G. *Young*: no! frankly syncretistic); ScotJT 43 (1990) 508s (R. S. *Sugirtharajah*: radically different from Latin American; concerns expressing faith in traditional and popular Asian forms).

8677 **Pieris** Aloysius, Une théologie asiatique de la libération 1990 ➤ 6,8706; 2-227-31572-5: ᴿNRT 113 (1991) 305 (J. *Masson*).

8678 **Pieris** Aloysius, El rostro asiático de Cristo; notas para una teología asiática de la liberación, ᵀᴱ*Sánchez-Rivera Peiró* Juan M.: Verdad e Imagen 119. S 1991, Sígueme. 219 p. 84-301-1130-1. – ᴿActuBbg 28 (1991) 89 (J. I. *González Faus*).

8679 *Pieris* Aloisius, Religionsgemeinschaften und Kommunalismus [50-Jahr Vidyajyoti New Delhi 1987], ᵀ*Faymonville* Ursula: ZMissRW 74 (1990) 106-123.

8680 ᴱ**Pirotte** Jean, *Soetens* Claude (*Cheza* Maurice), Évangélisation et cultures non européennes — guide du chercheur en Belgique francophone: RTLv Cah 22, 1989 ➤ 6,8707: ᴿRTLv 22 (1991) 280s (H. *Derroitte*).

8681 ᴱ**Pobee** John S., *Hallenkreutz* Carl F., Variations in Christian theology in Africa, 1986 ➤ 6,8708; sh. 60: ᴿIntRMiss 79 (1990) 106-8 (J. *Mbiti*, also on two cognate works).

8682 *Poupard* Paul card., Église et cultures; l'Évangile au cœur de l'homme et de l'humanité: EsprVie 101 (1991) 497-505.

8683 *a*) *Pula* A. L., Balimo [ancestor] veneration and Christianity; – *b*) *Osei-Bonsu* Joseph, Biblically/theologically based inculturation: AfER 12 (1990) 330-345 / 346-358.

8684 **Randrianasolo** Joseph, Christ and ancestors in the African context; a Lutheran perspective: diss. Lutheran School of Theology. 1991. 333 p. 91-29536. – DissA 52 (1991s) 1395-A.

8685 **Renck** Günther, Contextualization of Christianity and Christianization of language;... Papua/New Guinea: Mg Mission/Ök 5. Erlangen 1990, Ev.-Luth Mission. xvi-316 p.; 4 maps. DM 35. – ᴿTLZ 116 (1991) 707-9 (Hannes *Gänssbauer*).

8686 **Rubinstein** Murray A., The Protestant community on modern Taiwan; mission, seminary, and church: East Gate Taiwan in the modern world. Armonk NY 1991, Sharpe. xi-199 p. $40. 0-87332-6458-X [TDig 39,82: professor of history at CCNY Baruch College].

8687 ᴱ**Ruggieri** Giuseppe, Église et histoire l'Église en Afrique, Colloque de Bologne 1988 ➤ 6,681; 2-7010-1205-8: ᴿJRelAf 21 (1991) 181s (A. *Hastings*); ZkT 113 (1991) 317s (K. *Piskaty*).

8688 *a*) *Saoût* Yves, De bijbel bij de Mafa van Ouzal; – *b*) *Kolm* Gerrit J. van der, De bijbel in Babel; – *c*) *Kritzinger* Klippies, Ontmaskering en bemoediging; de bijbel in de preken von Allan BOESAK: Wereld en Zending 15 (Amst 1990) 206-8 / 245-8 / 240-4 [< ZIT 90,793].

8689 **Schaaf** Ype, Hij ging zijn weg met blijdschap; over de geschiedenis en de rol van de Bijbel in Afrika 1990 ➤ 6,8722: ᴿNedTTs 45 (1991) 259 (M. R. *Spindler*).

8690 *Schoffeleers* Matthew, Folk Christology in Africa; the dialectics of the Nganga paradigm: JRelAfr 19 (1989) 157-183.

8691 *Segovia* Fernando F., A new manifest destiny; the emerging theological voice of Hispanic Americans [ELIZONDO V., DECK A., *al.*]: RelStR 17 (1991) 101-9 [+ 145, J. *Ford* on H. RECINOS].

8692 ᴱ**Sheils** W. J., *Wood* Diana, The churches, Ireland and the Irish [Ecclesiastical History Society meeting, Maynooth 1987]: StChH 25, 1989 ➤ 5,747: ᴿIrTQ 57 (1991) 85s (F. M. *Jones*).

8693 **Shorter** Aylward, The Church in the African city. Mkn 1991, Orbis. vii-152 p. $20 [CBQ 54,206].

8694 **Shorter** Aylward, Toward a theology of inculturation 1988 ➤ 4,9753 ... 6,8731: ᴿCritRR 4 (1991) 468-471 (A. F. *Deck*: nothing on popular religiosity); NBlackf 71 (1990) 45s (W. S. F. *Pickering*); ZkT 113 (1991) 286-8 (H. B. *Meyer*).

8695 ᴱ*Simensen* Jarle, *Fuglestad* Finn, Norwegian missions in African history, 2. Madagascar. Oslo c. 1989, Norwegian Univ. – ᴿTsTKi 61 (1990) 237-9 (L. *Munthe*).

8696 **Song Choan-Seng**, Theologie des Dritten Auges; Asiatische Spiritualität und christliche Theologie [1979 ➤ 61,9284], ᵀ*Scherhans* Peter, *Oesterle* Annemarie: Theologie der Oekumene 19. Gö 1989, Vandenhoeck & R. 256 p. DM 38. 3-525-56322-1. – ᴿNZMissW 47 (1991) 172s (F. *Frei*); TLZ 116 (1991) 623s (U. *Link-Wieczorek*).

8697 **Sorge** G., *a*) Il cristianesimo in Giappone e il De Missione; – *b*) Il cristianesimo in Giappone e la Seconda Ambasceria Nipponica in Europa, introd. Keiichi *Takeuchi*. Bo 1988 / 1981, CLUEB. 115 p. / 118 p. – ᴿSMSR 57 (1991) 184-6 (Mariam de *Ghantuz Cubbe*).

8698 **Spijker** G. van 't, Les usages funéraires et la mission de l'Église; une étude anthropologique et théologique des rites funéraires au Rwanda: diss. Amst V.U. 1990, ᴰ*Wessels* A. x-262 p. Kampen 1990, Kok. 90-242-3320-8. – TsTNijm 31 (1991) 89.

8699 *Standaert* Nicolas, L'histoire d'un néologisme; le terme 'inculturation' dans les documents romains [NRT 110 (1988) 555-570]: ArBegG 34 (1991) 374.

8700 **Steffner** Hans, The significance of Jesus Christ in Asia. Anand 1985, Guj-SP. xvii-264 p. rs 35. – ᴿJDharma 14 (1989) 409 (V. *Kochuparambil*).

8701 **Sugirtharajah** R. S., Voices from the margin; interpreting the Bible in the Third World. L 1991, SPCK. ix-454 p. £15. 0-281-04506-2 [BL 92,112, D. B. *Forrester* notes approvingly E. *Cardenal* on Mt 26,5-13; C. *Boff*; Itumeleng *Mosala*; G. *Gutiérrez* on Job].

8702 **Sumartana** T., Mission at the crossroads; indigenous churches, European missionaries, Islamic associations and socio-religious change in Java 1812-1936: diss. Amsterdam VU 1991, ᴰ*Wessels* A. Lijderdorp 1991, De Zijlbedrijven. 408 p. – TsTNijm 31 (1991) 319.

8703 **Takenaka** Masao, *O'Grady* Ron, The Bible through Asian eyes. Auckland 1991, Pace. 199 p. (OT 15-71, NT 72-192); 93 color. phot. 0-9597-9710-6.

8704 **Tanko** Bauna Peter, The Christian Association of Nigeria and the challenge of the ecumenical imperative: diss. Angelicum, ᴰ*Angeli* C. Roma 1991. 236 p. – RTLv 23, p. 567.

8705 **Taylor** M. K., Remembering Esperanza; a cultural-political theology for North American praxis. Mkn 1990, Orbis. xii-292 p.; $30 [NRT 114,114, L. *Renwart*: Presbyterian against sexism, racism, and other prejudices].

8706 **ter Haar** G., Spirit of Africa; the healing ministry of Archbishop MILINGO of Zambia: diss. ᴰ*Schoffeleers* J. Utrecht 1991. 286 p. – TsTNijm 32,89; RTLv 23, p. 563 [publ. London, Hurst].

8707 *Tossou* Kossi J. K., Chancen und Schwierigkeiten der Inkulturation in Afrika: TPQ 139 (1991) 49-57 [... zu viele Apostel, aber zu wenige Propheten?... > Eng. ᵀᴱ*Asen* B. A., TDig 38 (1991) 317-322].

8708 Towards an Indian Christian theology of religious pluralism, Statement of the Indian Theological Association 13th annual meeting, Dec. 28-31, 1989: IndTSt 27 (1990) 333-345; 346-350, *Chethimattam* John B., objections.

8709 *Trigo* Pedro, Una mala fe; campaña de extirpación de idolatrías [... P. de Arriaga SJ 1621]: Iter 2 (1991) 81-126.

8710 *Vempeny* Ishanand, KRSNA and Christ in the light of some of the fundamental concepts and themes of the Bhagavad Gîtâ and the NT. Anand 1988, Guj-SP. xl-498 p. $20 – ᴿTDig 37 (1990) 292 (W. C. *Heiser*: 'Bundhu Ishanand' a Jesuit, compares flute and cross as symbols of attitude toward suffering).

8711 *Visca* Danila, Simon KIMBANGU, il *ngunza* [Congo/Zaire]; analisi storica di una qualificazione profetica: SMSR 57 (1991) 301-364.

8712 **Wan-Tatah** Victor, Emancipation in African theology; an inquiry on the relevance of Latin American revelation theology to Africa 1986 ➤ 6,8740; ᴿHeythJ 32 (1991) 563s (A. *Shorter*).

8713 **West** Gerald O., Biblical hermeneutics of liberation; modes of reading the Bible in the South African context: Mg 1. Pietermaritzburg 1991, Cluster. ix-274 p. $13 pa. [CBQ 54,206].

8714 **Widok** Norbert, ❷ Akomodacja... Accommodation de la mission dans la théorie et la pratique de CLÉMENT d'Alexandrie: diss. ᴰ*Drączkowski* F. Lublin 1991. 206 p. – RTLv 23, p. 549.

8715 **Williams** C.P., The idea of the self-governing Church; a study in Victorian missionary strategy: Studies in Christian Mission 1. Leiden 1990, Brill. xvii-293 p. *f* 148 [NRT 114,589, P. *Detienne*].

8715* *Williams* C. Peter, The necessity of a native clergy; the failure of Victorian missions to develop indigenous leadership [1990 Laing Lecture]: VoxEvca 21 (1991) 33-52.

8716 *Williams* David T., The appeal to follow Christ; the Bible, prosperity cult, and African Independent churches: Evangel 7,4 (1989) 14-21.

8717 ᴱ**Wilmore** Gayraud S., African American religious studies; an interdisciplinary anthology. Durham ɴᴄ 1989, Duke Univ. 468 p. $52.50; pa. $20. – ᴿCritRR 4 (1991) 63s (R. M. *Franklin*); RTPhil 123 (1991) 344 (S. *Molla*: first such since C. LINCOLN 1974).

8718 **Witvliet** Theo, The way of the black Messiah 1987 ➤ 3,8748... 5,8690: ᴿHeythJ 32 (1991) 130s (W. D. *Lindsey*).

8719 ᴱ**Yoshiki** Terazono, *Hamer* Heyo E., Brennpunkte in Kirche und Theologie Japans, Vorw. *Sundermeier* Theo. Neuk 1988, Neuk.-V. 235 p. – ᴿVerbumSVD 32 (1991) 97-102 (H.-J. *Marx*).

8719* ᴱ**Yuhaus** Cassian, The Catholic Church and American culture; pref. *Nesti* D.S. NY 1990, Paulist. xvi-115 p. [TLZ 117,875, J. *Langer*].

8720 **Zago** M., Volti della Chiesa in Asia: Dossier Chiese. CinB 1990, Paoline. 151 p. Lit. 14.000 [NRT 114,593, B. *Clarot*, non 'Cisinella'].

H8.7 *Mariologia* – The mother of Jesus in the NT.

8720* **Aldama** José A. de, María en la patrística de los siglos I y II: BAC 300, 197: ᴿArTGran 54 (1991) 261-280 (C. *Pozo*).

8721 **Auer** Johann, Jesus Christus – Heiland der Welt; Maria – Christi Mutter im Heilsplan Gottes 1988 ➤ 5,8693: ᴿTR 87 (1991) 51s (J. *Galot*, ᵀ*Gaukesbrink* M.).

8722 **Auer** J., Jesucristo salvador del mundo, María en el plan salvífico de Dios [completa J. hijo de Dios 1989 ➤ 5,7482; ᴿMarianum 52 (1990) 419-423 (J. *Stohr*, critical)] 1986, ᵀ*Gancho* C. Barc 1990, Herder. 602 p. – ᴿCarthaginensia 6 (1990) 383 (F. *Martínez Fresneda*); CiTom 118 (1991) 417s, también 634 (P. *Fernández*); CiuD 203 (1991) 240 (J. M. *Ozaeta*).

8723 ᴱ**Bäumer** R., *Scheffczyk* L., Marienlexikon I, 1988s ➤ 5,917*: ᴿForumKT 7 (1991) 76s (H.-A. *Klein*); TLZ 116 (1991) 544-7 (R. *Frieling*).

8724 **Basetti-Sani** Giulio, Maria e Gesù figlio di Maria nel Corano: Linea. Palermo-São Paolo 1989, Ila (Italoamericana) Palma. 218 p. Lit. 28.000. – ᴿOrChrPer 57 (1991) 217s (V. *Poggi*); RHE 87 (1991) 250s (J.-L. *Blanpain*: 'São Paolo').

8725 **Beinert** Wolfgang, Unsere Liebe Frau und die Frauen 1989 ➤ 5,8697; 6,8750: ᴿBogVest 50 (1990) 343-7 (V. *Dermota*).

8726 *a)* **Beinert** Wolfgang, Maria in der deutschen protestantischen Theologie der Gegenwart; – *b) Müller* Gerhard L., Prinzipien der katholischen Mariologie im Licht evangelischer Anfragen; – *c) Schulz* Hans-J., Prinzipien Orthodoxer Mariologie: Catholica 45 (1991) 1-35 / 181-192 / 283-295.

8727 **Berger** Pamela, The goddess obscured ... grain protectress to saint 1985
➤ 2,6994 ... 4,9774*: ᴿJAAR 59 (1991) 392-4 (Ursula *King*); Marianum
52 (1990) 473s (W. *Brennan*: respectful).

8728 **Biegger** C., 'De invocatione Beatae Mariae Virginis', PARACELSUS
[Theophrastus von Hohenheim 1493-1541] und die Marienverehrung:
Kosmosophie 6. Stu 1990, Steiner. 308 p. – ᴿArTGran 53 (1990) 364s
(A. *Segovia*: excelente).

8729 **Brennan** Walter T., The sacred memory of Mary 1988 ➤ 5,9780; 6,8752:
ᴿNBlackf 71 (1990) 520 (C. *O'Donnell*).

8729* *a*) *Brennan* Walter T., The issue of archetypes in Marian devotion; – *b*)
Hamman Adalbert G., Aux origines de la théologie mariale; – *c*) *Courth*
Franz, Maria im ökumenischen Dialog; erreichte Annäherungen und
verbliebene Gesprächspunkte; – *d*) Documenta *Ioannis Pauli II*: Marianum 52 (1990) 17-41 / 149-171 / 42-62 / 237-363.

8730 *Buckley* Gerald A., Mary, the alternative to feminism: HomPast 91,8
(1991) 11-17.

8731 **Cantalamessa** Raniero, Maria, uno specchio per la Chiesa 1990
➤ 6,8754: ᴿCC 142 (1991,1) 427s (E. *Sonzini*: 'dedicato ai fratelli
protestanti; può sembrare strano').

8732 *a*) *Caporale* Vincenzo, Nota sul Dogma dell'Immacolata Concezione
[... ᴿCC su Maria nostra sorella ➤ 8781]; – *b*) *Ricca* Paolo, Un dialogo
amichevole ma difficile: Protestantesimo 46 (1991) 66-69 / 69-72.

8733 **Carroll** Michael, Catholic cults and devotions; a psychological inquiry.
Kingston 1989, McGill/Queens. 258 p. $23. – ᴿCritRR 4 (1991) 406-8
(Mary *Neill*; his 'anal rosary' and 'flatulent Angelus' add nothing to the
recognition already in AUGUSTINE that 'everyone is born between urine
and faeces').

8734 **Casale** Umberto, Benedetta fra le donne; saggio teologico sulla mariologia e la questione femminile 1989 ➤ 6,8756: ᴿAntonianum 65
(1990) 388-390 (D. *Aračić*); Marianum 52 (1990) 428s (M. *Semeraro*).

8735 **Cipollone** Paolo, Maria alla luce della Trinità; studio sul capitolo VIII
della 'Lumen Gentium'. R 1990, Trinitari. 192 p. – ᴿAsprenas 38 (1991)
254s (A. *Terracciano*).

8736 **Clayton** Mary, The cult of the Virgin Mary in Anglo-Saxon England:
C 1990, Univ. xiii-299 p. $54.50 [RelStR 18,146, T. F. X. *Noble*].

8737 *Daoust* J., La dévotion mariale et l'archéologie [PICCIRILLO M., TerreS
nov. 1989, Ch(aîr)e Maria de Nazareth ...]: EsprVie 101 (1991) 183.

8737* **da Spinetoli** Ortensio, Maria nella Bibbia 1988 ➤ 4,9793: ᴿTeresianum
42 (1991) 342s (V. *Pasquetto*).

8738 **De Fiores** Stefano, María en la teología contemporánea [1978], ᵀ*Ortiz*
García A. S 1991, Sígueme. 603 p. – ᴿCarthaginensia 7 (1991) 530 (F.
Martínez Fresneda: ᵀrehecha casi completamente); NatGrac 38 (1991) 395s
(A. *Villalmonte*).

8739 ᴱ**Donnelly** Doris, Mary, woman of Nazareth 1990 ➤ 6,523: ᴿBibTB 21
(1991) 119s (B. *Buby*).

8740 **Dourley** John P., The Goddess, mother of the Trinity; a Jungian
implication: Studies in the psychology of religion 4. Lewiston 1990,
Mellen. 102 p. $50. 0-88946-244-5 [TDig 38,261].

8740* **Duggan** P. E., The Assumption dogma; some reactions and ecumenical
implications in the thought of English-speaking theologians [diss. Dayton/
Marianum-Roma]. Dayton 1989, Univ. vii-236 p. – ᴿNRT 113 (1991)
263 (L.-J. *Renard*).

8741 **Esquerda Bifet** Juan, Mariologia... missionaria 1988 → 4,9799; 5,8709: RAntonianum 65 (1990) 109s (D. *Aračić*); Marianum 52 (1990) 431s (A. *Rum*).

8742 E**Felici** S., Mariologia ...dei Padri 1988/9 → 5,8711; 6,8764: RAntonianum 65 (1990) 670-2 (D. *Aračić*); AugR 31 (1991) 486-8 E. *dal Covolo*).

8743 **Forte** Bruno, Maria, la donna icona² 1989 → 5,8712; 6,8766: RHumBr 46 (1991) 299s (A. *Biazzi*); RivScR 4 (1990) 584-7 (M. *Semeraro*).

8743* *Galot* Jean, Marie, modèle de la femme dans la théologie catholique: StMiss 40 (1991) 95-113.

8744 **Gambero** Luigi, Maria nel pensiero dei Padri della Chiesa. CinB 1991, Paoline. 406 p. Lit. 28.000. – RBbbOr 33 (1991) 237 (Christina *Vertua*).

8745 *Gargano* Giovanni P.M., Mariologia biblica [*Manelli* S. 1989]: Doct-Com 43 (1990) 76-78.

8746 **Gebara** Ivone, *Bingemer* Maria Clara, Mary, mother of God, mother of the poor 1989 → 6,8769: REvQ 63 (1991) 370-2 (Ruth B. *Edwards*: many insights, but poses six problems).

8747 **Gebara** Ivone, *al.* Maria/der Armen 1988 → 5,8721: RZMissRW 74 (1990) 86s (M. *Hakenes*).

8748 [*Gharib* G. 1s, 1889 → 5,8723], E**Gambero** L., Testi mariani del primo millennio, III. Padri e altri autori latini. R 1990, Città Nuova. 1018 p. Lit. 110.000 [NRT 114,430]. – RCC 142 (1991,3) 321s (G. *Cremascoli*); OrChrPer 57 (1991) 241s (G. *Capizzi*).

8749 **Gherardini** Brunero, La madre; Maria... → 6,8771: RDoctCom 43 (1990) 182-4 (N. *Lanzi*); Marianum 52 (1990) 423-6 (M. *Semeraro*).

8750 **Gherardini** B., LUTERO-Maria 1985 → 1,2960... 4,9807: RAsprenas 38 (1991) 257-9 (S. *Cipriani*).

8751 *Gherardini* Brunero, Sant'AGOSTINO e l'immacolata concezione / e la divina maternità di Maria. Divinitas 35 (1991) 114-133 / 230-243.

8752 E**Gössmann** Elisabeth, *Bauer* Dieter R., Maria – für alle Frauen oder über alle Frauen? [Tagung 1987] 1989 → 5,669; 6,8773: RTPQ 139 (1991) 223s (Roswitha *Unfried*); Marianum 53 (1991) 687s (S. *Neuhaus*).

8752* *Gómez de Cadiñanos* Aurelio, María, personificación del Espíritu Santo, según Leonardo BOFF: EphMar 38 (1988) 55-86.

8753 **González Dorado** Antonio, De María conquistadora a María liberadora 1988 → 4,9810; 5,8727: RMarianum 52 (1990) 426-8 (X. *Pikaza*).

8753* *Grassi* Joseph A., Mary, mother and disciple from the Scripture to the Council of Ephesus 1988 → 4,9812; 5,8729: RMarianum 58 (1990) 404-7 (B. *Buby*).

8754 *Grzybek* Stanisław, ℗ Biblijne inspiracje encykliki Jana Pawła II 'Redemptoris Mater': RuBi 42 (1989) 278-283.

8755 **Guardini** Romano, La madre del Signore [Mutter des Herrn 1942],T. Brescia 1989, Morcelliana. 86 p. Lit. 10.000.

8756 **Guarducci** Margherita, La più antica icone di Maria [→ 5,8730]; un prodigioso vincolo fra Oriente e Occidente. R 1989, Ist. Poligrafico. 100 p.; ill.

8757 *Hennessy* Anne, Marian mysteries in the public ministry of Jesus: RRel 50 (1991) 913-923.

8757* [**Holzherr** Georg], Maria, piccolo compendio di mariologia: La Donna Nuova 7. T 1989, Paoline. 146 p. – RMarianum 52 (1990) 414-6 (F. *Courth* says it is a pastoral of the Swiss bishops, of 85 pages, though by Einsiedeln Abbot Holzherr, 146 p. in title, and with no comment on its Italian connections) & 417-9 (P. *Sartor* in italiano).

8758 *Jordan* David R., Choliambs for Mary in a papyrus phylactery [P. Berol. inv. 21911]; HarvTR 45 (1991) 343-6.

8759 **Journet** Charles, Maria corredentrice. Mi 1989, Ares. 125 p. Lit. 18.000. – ᴿHumBr 46 (1991) 143s (A. *Biazzi*).

8760 *Kirchschläger* Walter, Die jungfräuliche Mutter des Herrn: ➤ 6,171, ꟳSTÖGER A., Exeget 1990, 87-101.

8761 **Kniazeff** Alexis, La Mère de Dieu dans l'Église orthodoxe: Théologies 1990 ➤ 6,8781; F 139: ᴿNRT 113 (1991) 618 (V. *Roisel*).

8761* ᴱ[? *Koehler* T. A.] **Thompson** T. A., Marian Studies 41. Dayton 1990, Marian Library. 203 p. $12 [TLZ 117,794-6, H. J. E. *Beintker*, auch über 39].

8762 *Kretschmar* Georg, 'natus ex Maria virgine'; Zur Konzeption und Theologie des Protevangeliums Jacobi: ➤ 72, ꟳHAHN F., Anfänge 1991, 417-428.

8763 *Królikowski* Janusz, ᴼ Marie – 'mère de l'Église' dans le kérygme pastoral du cardinal Stefan WYSZIŃSKI: ColcT 61,4 (1991) 81-105; franç. 105 [➤ b990].

8764 **La Potterie** I. de, Maria in het mysterie van het verbond²ʳᵉᵛ [¹1985]: Schrift en Liturgie 8, 1990 ➤ 6,8782: ᴿCollatVL 21 (1991) 320s (H. *Hoet*).

8765 **Laurentin** René, *a)* Breve Mariologia 1987 ➤ 5,8741*a*: ᴿMarianum 52 (1990) 434 (M. *Semeraro*); – *b)* Verso l'anno 2000 con Maria. Brescia 1990, Queriniana. 186 p. Lit. 20.000. – ᴿCC 142 (1991,2) 617s (G. *Caprile*).

8766 **López Melús** Francisco M., María de Nazareth, la verdadera discípula: Pastoral aplicada 162. M 1991, Promoción Popular Cristiana. 416 p.; pt. 2700. 84-288-1053-2.

8767 **Macquarrie** John, Mary for all Christians. L/GR 1991, Collins/Eerdmans. xiii-160 p. $13. .../0-8028-0543-4 [TDig 38,368]. – ᴿNBlackf 72 (1991) 402s (J. *Alison*); Tablet 245 (1991) 1182 (E. J. *Yarnold*).

8768 **Maeckelberghe** Els, Desperately seeking Mary; a feminist appropriation of a traditional religious symbol: diss. ᴰ*Hoedemaker* L. A. Groningen 1991 [Kampen, Kok]. 195 p. – TsTNijm 32, p. 86; RTLv 23, p. 536.

8769 **Magli** Ida, La Madonna 1987 ➤ 4,9839: ᴿProtestantesimo 45 (1990) 74s (Eliana *Briante*).

8770 **Maiaroli** Emilio, Vita di Maria. R 1991, Logos. 110 p. Lit. 14.000. – ᴿCiVit 46 (1991) 586 (Duccia *Camiciotti*).

8771 **Manelli** M. Stefano, Mariologia biblica, I. Antico Testamento. Frigento 1989, Casa Mariana. 430 p. – ᴿDivinitas 33 (1989) 314 (B. *Gherardini*); EphMar 38 (1988) 485 (D. *Fernández*: no brilla por su sentido crítico).

8772 **Martini** Carlo M., Seht die Frau; Lebenswege mit Maria ['die erste grosse Forscherin im... Reich der Frau']. FrB 1991, Herder. 144 p. DM 11,80 [TPQ 140,195, J. *Hörmandinger*].

8773 **Matrangolo** V., La venerazione a Maria nella tradizione della Chiesa bizantina; fondamenti teologici. Acireale 1990, Galatea. 72 p. – ᴿVetChr 28 (1991) 217s (B. *Degórski*).

8773* *a)* *Mimouni* S. C., Genèse et évolution des traditions sur le sort final de Marie; étude de la tradition littéraire copte; – *b)* *Serra* A. M., [GIOVANNI PAOLO II] La 'Mulieris dignitatem'; consensi e dissensi: Marianum 53 (1991) 69-143 / 144-182.

8774 *Mimouni* Simon, 'Transitus Mariae': ➤ 668, DictSpir 15 (1991) 1160-74.

8775 **Napiórkowski** Stanisław C., ᴼ *a)* Spór [debate] o Matke; Mariologia jako problem ekumeniczny: Teologia w dialogu 3. Lublin 1988, KUL.

188 p. – ᴿTR 87 (1991) 61s (S. *Rabiej*). – *b*) ❷ The mother of any Lord; problems, inquiries, perspectives. Opole 1988, S. Krzyża. 255 p. – ᴿColcT 61,2 (1991) 199-201 (J. *Królikowski*, ❷); Marianum 52 (1990) 429-431 (G. *Bartosik*).

8776 **Perry** N., *Echeverria* L., Under the heel of Mary 1988 ➤ 5,8760; 6,8809: ᴿJEH 42 (1991) 293s (Ann *Loades*: chiefly against apparitions); JRel 71 (1991) 448s (Sandra *Zimdars-Swartz*).

8777 ᴱ**Petri** Heinrich, Divergenzen in der Mariologie... ökum.: MarSt 7. Rg 1989 ➤ 5,723: ᴿColcT 60,4 (1990) 177s (S. C. *Napiórkowski*, ❷); TR 87 (1991) 145s (auch S. C. *Napiórkowski*).

8778 *Piétri* Charles, Les premières images de Marie en Occident: ➤ 52, ꟳFASOLA U., 1989, (II) 587-603.

8779 **Pikaza** Xavier, La madre de Jesús 1989 ➤ 6,8810: ᴿCarthaginensia 7 (1991) 273s (P. *Martínez Fresneda*: 'Xavier'); Marianum 52 (1990) 411-4 (M. *Semeraro*); Teresianum 42 (1991) 348s (V. *Pasquetto*).

8780 **Pozo** Cándido, María en la obra de la salvación: BAC. M 1991 = 1947, Católica. xxvi-385 p. [ScripTPamp 23,1060].

8781 **Rostagno** Sergio, *al.*, Maria nostra sorella [convegno Federazione ev./Fac. Valdese, Roma 12-13.III. 1988]. R 1988, Com/nuovi tempi. 128 p. – ᴿRasT 32 (1991) 206-210 (V. *Caporale*).

8782 **Salgado** Jean-Marie, La maternité spirituelle de la Très Sainte Vierge Marie: Studi Tomistici 36. Vaticano 1990, Libreria. 234 p. Lit. 32.000. – ᴿBenedictina 38 (1991) 507s (A. B. *Calkins*); Divinitas 34 (1990) 192-4 (D. *Vibrac*); DoctCom 43 (1990) 291-4 (A. B. *Calkins*).

8783 *a) Schummer* Léopold, Un Réformé parle de Marie; – *b) Jerdan* Diane, Les femmes dans l'Église: RRéf 41,3 (1990) 1-20 / 21-30 [< ZIT 90,604].

8783* **Scott** M. Philip, A virgin called woman; essays on NT texts 1986 ➤ 3,8829; 4,9868: ᴿMarianum 52 (1990) 410s (W. *Brennan*: far-fetched).

8784 **Serra** Aristide [➤ 4878.4880], Maria secondo il Vangelo 1987 ➤ 3,8831 (²1988): ᴿAntonianum 65 (1990) 110s (D. *Aračić*).

8785 *Šimić* Josip, Marianische Theologie – Andacht [Croatian: a crisis of Mariology and Marian piety culminated in 1970]: ObnŽiv 45 (1990) 317-330; deutsch 330s.

8786 **Spourlakou-Eutychiadou** Amalias, ❻ *He panagía Theotókos*, symbol of Christian holiness; summary of the Orthodox position regarding the Roman-Catholic dogmas related to the Immaculate Conception: diss. Athens Univ. Athenai 1990. 662 p. – ᴿTAth 62 (1991) 582-4 (E. A. *Theodorou*).

8787 **Stirnimann** Heinrich, Marjam; Marienrede an einer Wende 1989 ➤ 6, 8821: ᴿForumKT 7 (1981) 236s (L. *Scheffczyk*); Marianum 53 (1991) 273-5 (A. *Amato*); OstkSt 40 (1991) 224-7 (R. C. *Grill*); TLZ 116 (1991) 874-7 (H. *Kirchner*: nicht ein weiteres Glied in der langen Reihe).

8787* *Touron* Eliseo, La mariología veinticinco años después del Concilio: VerVid 48 (1990) 331-373.

8788 **Trettel** G., La Vergine Maria in S. CROMAZIO: Centro Friuli 21. Trieste 1991, Centro Studi Storico-Religiosi Friuli Venezia Giulia. 94 p.; indice biblico. – ᴿNRT 113 (1991) 468 (A. *Harvengt*).

8789 ᴱ*Uthemann* K.-H., Des Johannes von DAMASKUS Predigten In dormitionem B.M.V. in einer lateinischen Übersetzung des ix. Jahrhunderts; zum überlieferungsgeschichtlichen Ort der griechischen Vorlage: ➤ 18, ꟳBASTIAENSEN A., Eulogia 1991, 333-352.

8790 *Vázquez Janeiro* Isaac, El encomio mariano 'cunctas haereses sola interemisti'; origen de su sentido inmaculista: Antonianum 66 (1991) 497-531; Eng. 531.

8791 *Vergote* Antoine, Visions et apparitions; approche psychologique: RTLv 22 (1991) 202-225; Eng. 303.

8792 **Walch** Otto-Eugen, Maria im Heilsplan Gottes; eine theologische Untersuchung von evangelischen und katholischen Positionen der Mariologie in unserem Jahrhundert: kath. Diss. Innsbruck 1991, ᴰ*Lies* L. 369 p. - TR 87 (1991) 513; RTLv 23, p. 567.

8793 ᴱ**Wright** D. F., Chosen by God; Mary in evangelical perspective. 1989. - ᴿEvQ 63 (1991) 369s (Ruth B. *Edwards*).

8794 *Zappella* Marco, Le donne nel giudaismo e la figura di Maria nei vangeli; osservazioni ermeneutiche in margine a una recente opera [MAGGI A., Nostra signora degli eretici 1988]: RivB 39 (1991) 335-341 = Quaderni Monfortani 6 (1989) 135-153.

8795 **Zimdars-Swartz** Sandra L., Encountering Mary; from La Salette to Medjugorje. Princeton 1991, Univ. xv-342 p. 0-691-07371-6 [TDig 39,91].

H8.8   *Feminae NT* – **Women in the NT and early Church.**

8796 **Aspegren** Kerstin, The male woman, a feminine ideal in the early Church 1990 ➤ 6,8827: ᴿETL 67 (1991) 441s (A. de *Halleux*); NRT 113 (1991) 774s (V. *Roisel*); RHPR 71 (1991) 369s (C.-L. *Meyer*); TS 52 (1991) 778 (Carolyn *Osiek*).

8797 **Avis** Paul, Eros and the sacred 1989 ➤ 6,8828: ᴿScotJT 44 (1991) 388-390 (Linda *Woodhead*: greatest challenge to Christianity today: it is patriarchal but not irredeemably; the concept of eros that emerges is that 'it is everything positive that anyone has ever said about eros').

8798 **Aynard** Laure, La Bible au féminin; de l'ancienne tradition à un christianisme hellénisé: LDiv 138, 1990 ➤ 6,8829: ᴿCBQ 53 (1991) 690-2 (Alice L. *Laffey*); CritRR 4 (1991) 486-8 (Margaret *MacDonald*); EstB 49 (1991) 145-7 (F. *Elizondo*); NRT 113 (1991) 574s (V. *Roisel*); Salesianum 53 (1991) 576s (M. *Cimosa*).

8799 *Battista* Giuseppina, Olimpiade e Giovanni CRISOSTOMO; amicizia e collaborazione nel ministero pastorale: Claretianum 30 (1990) 335-383.

8800 *Bellenzier* Maria Teresa, Vai dai tuoi fratelli e di' loro: Presbyteri 24 (1990) 21-31.

8801 *a) Borland* James A., Women in the life and teaching of Jesus; – *b) Schreiner* Thomas R., The valuable ministries of women in the context of male leadership; a survey of ONT examples and teaching; – *c) Weinrich* William, Women in the history of the Church as learned and holy, but not pastors; – *d) Patterson* Dorothy, The high calling of wife and mother in biblical perspective: ➤ 375, Recovering 1991, 113-123 . 483-5 / 209-224 . 503-6 / 263-279 . 512-6 / 364-377 . 531s.

8802 *Boughton* Lynne C., From pious legend to feminist fantasy; distinguishing hagiographical license from apostolic practice in the Acts of Paul / Acts of Thecla: JRel 71 (1991) 382-4 [< TR 87,428].

8803 **Burrus** Virginia, The making of a heresy; authority, gender, and the Priscillianist controversy: diss. Graduate Theological Union, ᴰ*Lyman* R. Berkeley 1991. - RelStR 18,173.

8804 *Burrus* Virginia, The heretical woman as symbol in [bishop] Alexander, ATHANASIUS, EPIPHANIUS, and JEROME: HarvTR 84 (1991) 229-248.

8805 **Byrne** Brendan, Paul and the Christian women 1989 ➤ 5,8791; 6,8839: ᴿRB 98 (1991) 472s (J. *Murphy-O'Connor* disagrees in part).

8806 **Clark** Elizabeth, Ascetic piety and women's faith; essays on late ancient Christianity [13, 1977-85]: Studies in women and religion 20, 1986 ➔ 3,204 ... 5,8795: ᴿRevSR 65 (1991) 299-304 (Christine *Schenesse*).

8806* *Clark* E. A., Patrons, not priests; gender and power in late ancient Christianity: Gender and History 2,3 (Oxford 1990) 253-273 [< NTAbs 36,244].

8807 **Condren** Mary, The serpent and the goddess; women, religion, and power in Celtic Ireland. SF 1989, Harper & R. xxv-268 p. $14 pa. – ᴿHorizons 18 (1991) 148s (W. *Whelan*).

8808 **De Berg** Betty A., Ungodly women; gender and the first wave of American fundamentalism [antifeminist from the start]. Mp 1990, Fortress. 165 p. $10. – ᴿTTod 42 (1991s) 261 (J. H. *Moorhead*).

Fander Monika, Die Stellung der Frau im Mk-Ev 1989 ➔ 4297.

8809 **Faricy** Robert, The Lord's dealing; the primacy of the feminine 1988 ➔ 5,8805; 6,8848: ᴿLvSt 16 (1991) 90 (Mary T. *Burns*).

8810 *Fatum* L., Image of God and glory of man; women in the Pauline congregation: ➔ 472, Image/Gender 1991, 56-137.

8811 **Garzonio** M., Gesù e le donne. Mi 1990, Rizzoli. – ᴿScuolC 118 (1990) 386-391-397 (M. *Serenthà* & G. *Borgonovo*: notevolmente differenti).

8811* **Gentili** A., Si vous ne devenez comme des femmes; symboles religieux du féminin. Montréal/P 1991, Paulines/Médiaspaul. 200 p.; 17 fig. F 140 [NRT 114,58, L.-J. *Renard*: 'bien sûr Dieu contient *eminenter* tout ce qui est masculin ou féminin, ... mais à une époque où la foi aux vérités sûrement attestées a besoin d'être affermie, on préférerait une sobriété...'].

8812 **Grey** Mary, Feminism, redemption and the Christian tradition [= Redeeming the dream 1989 ➔ 6,8851]. Mystic CT 1990, Twenty-Third. vii-251 p. $17 pa. 0-89622-428-7 [TDig 38,267]. – ᴿTLond 94 (1991) 133s (Deborah F. *Sawyer*).

8813 *Grey* Mary, Has feminist theology a vision for [the] Christian Church?: LvSt 16 (1991) 27-40.

8814 **Heine** Susanne, Women and early Christianity 1988 ➔ 4,9902*; 6,8857: ᴿRelStT 9,2s (1989) 64s (Yvonne B. *Cross*: superb corrective).

8815 **Hourcade** J., L'Église est-elle misogyne? Une vocation féminine antique et nouvelle. P 1989, Téqui. 99 p. F 62. – ᴿNRT 112 (1990) 777 (A. *Toubeau*).

8816 **Ibarra Benlloch** Martin, Mulier fortis; la mujer en las fuentes cristianas (280-313): MgHistAnt 6. Zaragoza 1990, Univ. vii-396 p. – ᴿSalesianum 53 (1991) 760s (B. *Amata*); ScripTPamp 23 (1991) 711s (A. *Viciano*).

8817 **Kunz** Erhard, Maria von Magdala; Jesus, den Boten der Liebe Gottes finden: GeistL 63 (1990) 213-5.

8818 *a*) *Kušar* Stjepan, God created male and female (Gn 1,27); – *b*) *Mišić* Anto, Women in the works of early Christian writers; – *c*) *Ljumanovic* Azra, ... in Jesus' mission: ObnŽiv 45 (1990) 461-6 / 495-510 / 519-532 (Croatian); Eng. —; 511,533.

8819 *Lambropoulou* Anna, ⊙ Information about women stylites in Byzantium: TAth 61 (1991) 187-199; Eng. 904.

8820 *La Potterie* Ignace de, L'identità della donna e il mistero dell'Alleanza (Principi ermeneutici per l'interpretazione della visione biblica sulla donna): StMiss 40 (1991) 1-26.

8820* **Leonardi** Giovanni, Apostoli al femminile; le discepole del Signore nelle prime comunità cristiane. Padova 1991, Messaggero S. Antonio. 204 p. Lit. 18.000. 88-250-0104-5.

8821 **Lindboe** Inger Marie, Women in the NT, a select bibliography 1990 ⇥ 6,8864: [R]RTLv 22 (1991) 536s (Alice *Dermience*).

8822 *Lissner* Anneliese, Zur Situation von Frauen in Gesellschaft und Kirche; zehn Thesen katholischer Frauenbewegungen: Diakonia 22 (Mainz 1991) 81-98 > TDig 38 (1991) 339-343, [TE]*Asen* B.A., Women in society and church; ten theses.

8823 *Lockwood* Rose, Potens et factiosa femina; women, martyrs and schism in Roman North Africa: AugSt 20 (Villanova 1989) 165-182 [< ZIT 91,167].

8824 **Maillot** Alphonse, Marie, ma sœur; étude sur la femme dans le NT 1990 ⇥ 6,8866: [R]RechSR 79 (1991) 428-430 (J. *Guillet*).

8825 *a*) *Maloney* Linda, La thèse de la différence de la femme dans la philosophie classique et dans le christianisme antique, [T]*Divault* André (aussi *c.d.*); – *b*) *Gössmann* Elisabeth, La construction de la différence des femmes dans la tradition théologique chrétienne; – *c*) *Ruether* Rosemary R., Différence et égalité des droits des femmes dans l'Église; – *d*) *Johnson* Elizabeth, La masculinité du Christ: ⇥ 348, Concilium 238 ('La femme a-t-elle une nature spéciale?' 1991) 63-73 / 75-85 / 25-33 / 145-154.

8826 *a*) *Mangatt* George, Jesus' option for women; – *b*) *Meagher* P.M., Women in the Pauline letters: Jeevadhara 21 (1991) 161-175 / 150-160.

8827 *Martin* C.J., Womanist interpretations of the NT; the quest for holistic and inclusive translation and interpretation: JFemStRel 6,2 (1990) 41-61 [< NTAbs 35,147].

8828 **Mazzucco** Clementina, E fui fatta maschio 1989 ⇥ 6,8870: [R]Protestantesimo 46 (1991) 153s (Erika *Tomassone*).

8829 **Migliorino Miller** Monica M., Sexuality and authority in the Catholic Church: diss. Marquette, [D]*Keefe* D. Milwaukee 1991. 433 p. 91-33801. – DissA 52 (1991s) 2182-A.

8829* **Moloney** Francis J., La donna prima tra i credenti [Woman, first among the faithful 1984 ⇥ 1,8477 (also Melbourne, Collins Dove; US 1985],[T]: Religion. T 1989, SEI. 148 p. – [R]Marianum 52 (1990) 466-8 (A. M. *Maggi*).

8830 *Mroczkowski* Ireneusz, ⊘ The Christian dignity of women: RoczTK 37,3 (1990) 13-24; Eng. 24.

8831 **Neipp** Bernadette, Marie Madeleine femme et apôtre; curieuse histoire d'un malentendu [dû à GRÉGOIRE: les trois une]. Lausanne 1991, Moulin. 88 p. – [R]EsprVie 101 (1991) 118-jaune (P. *Cousin*).

8832 *a*) *O'Connor* Kathleen, The invitation of wisdom woman, a feminine image of God; – *b*) *Harris* Xavier J., Ministering women in the Gospels; Jesus' female disciples: BToday 29 (1991) 87-93 / 109-112.

8833 **Paletschek** Sylvia, Frauen und Dissens; Frauen im Deutschkatholizismus und in den freien Gemeinden 1841-1852 [Diss. Hamburg]: Kritische Studien zur Geschichtswissenschaft 84. Gö 1990, Vandenhoeck & R. 374 p. DM 78 [TR 87,431].

8833* *Pelletier* Anne-Marie, Le signe de la femme [... Gen 2s; Eph 5]: NRT 113 (1991) 665-689.

8834 **Pernoud** Régine, La femme au temps des Croisades [cf. ⇥ 6,8877]. P 1990, Stock. 408 p. F 145. – [R]Études 373 (1990) 129s (P. *Vallin*).

8835 *a*) (*Luzia*) *Petry* Zenilda, As mulheres, testemunhas do Reino; –

b) (Beise) *Ulrich* Claudete,   Marta e María; as mulheres dão sinais da vivência de uma nova espiritualidade: EstudosB 30 (1991) 44-51 / 52-59.

8836 *a*) *Pissarek* H.-A.,   'Viele kamen zum Glauben an Jesus auf das Wort der Frau hin ...' (Joh. 4,39); mündige Frauen in den Evangelien; Überlegungen zu einer veränderten Sichtweise; – *b*) *Frick-Pöder* R., 'Schweige, liebe Schwester...' (2 Sam 13,20) Ermutigung zum Schweigen? Mündigkeit als Raster für eine frauenorientierte alttestamentliche Suche: → 373, Mündigkeit 1989, 37-51 / 21-36.

8837 **Radloff** Matthias,   Le ministère de la Parole de la femme; examen de textes pauliniens: prot. diss. ᴰ*Collange* J.   Strasbourg 1991. 635 p. – RTLv 23, p. 546.

8838 ᴱ**Russell** Letty M.,   Interpretazione femminista della Bibbia [1985 → 1,307], ᵀ*Lanzarini* Liliana: Orizzonti biblici.   Assisi 1991, Cittadella. 223 p. 88-308-0475-4.

8839 **Salisbury** Joyce E.,   Church fathers, [conflict with] independent virgins. NY 1991, Verso.   vii-168 p. $35.   0-86091-293-0 [TDig 39,82].

8839* *Schottroff* Luise,   Wanderprophetinnen; eine feministische Analyse der Logienquelle: EvT 51 (1991) 332-344.

8840 **Schüssler Fiorenza** Elisabeth,   *a*) Zu ihrem Gedächtnis 1988 → 5,8836: ᴿEvT 51 (1991) 383-395 (W. *Stegemann*). – *b*) In memoria di lei, ᵀ*Corsani* Mirella C. 1990 → 6,8888:   ᴿProtestantesimo 46 (1991) 49-55 (Erika *Tomassone*) & 55-62 (Rosanna *Ciappa*).

8841 *Schultze* Harald,   Evangelische Frauen in der deutschen Aufklärung; Desiderate kirchengeschichtlicher Forschung: BTZ 8 (1991) 59-75.

8842 **Selvidge** Maria J.,   Daughters of Jerusalem.   Scottdale PA 1987, Herald. 172 p. $10 pa.   0-8361-3440-0. – ᴿJStNT 41 (1991) 121 (L. *Alexander*).

8843 ᴱ**Sheils** W.J., *Wood* Diana, Women in the Church [Eccl. Hist. Soc. conference(s)]: Studies in Church History 27, 1989/90 → 6,692*: ᴿJTS 42 (1991) 784 (G. R. *Evans*: refreshing absence of special pleading).

8844 ᴱ(**Martins**) **Terra** J. E.,   A mulher na Igreja = RCuB 14,53s (1990).   São Paulo 1990, Loyola.   175 p.

8845 **Thurston** Bonnie B.,   The widows 1989 → 6,8894:   ᴿAnglTR 73 (1991) 332s (R. I. *Pervo*); CritRR 4 (1991) 493s (Margaret Y. *MacDonald*); CBQ 53 (1991) 347s (S. *Davies*: uneven, too narrow).

8846 **Tucker** Cynthia G.,   Prophetic sisterhood; liberal women ministers of the frontier. Boston 1990, Beacon.   xii-298 p. $25.   0-8070-1608-X [TDig 38,192].

8847 **Valerio** Adriana,   Cristianesimo e femminile; donne protagoniste nella storia delle Chiese.   N 1990, D'Auria.   205 p. Lit. 30.000 [TR 87,346].

8848 *Verbeeck-Verhelst* Muriel,   Madeleine dans la littérature féminine au XVIIᵉ s.:   Foi-Vie 90,5 = CahB 30 (1991) 35-42.

8849 *Walcot* Peter,   On widows and their reputation in antiquity [p. 22, 1 Cor 7,9; TERTULLIAN...]: Symbolae Osloenses 66 (1991) 5-26.

8850 ᴱ**Wilson** Katharine M., *Makowski* Elizabeth M.,   Wykked wyves and the woes of marriage; misogamous literature from Juvenal [... JEROME] to Chaucer.   Albany c.1991, SUNY.   206 p. $13 [RelStR 18,147, Lynda L. *Coon*].

Wire Antoinette C.,   The Corinthian women prophets 1990 → 5406.

8851 **Witherington** B. [ᴱA.],   Women and the genesis of Christianity 1990 → 6,8897:   ᴿNRT 113 (1991) 605s (A. *Toubeau*).

8852 **Witherington** Ben,   Women in the earliest churches 1988 → 6,8898:

ᴿRelStT 9,2s (1989) 84s (Barry W. *Henaut*: with sins of omission defends status quo).

H8.9 *Theologia feminae* – **Feminist theology.**

8853 **Ahl** Ruth, Eure Töchter werden Prophetinnen sein ... Kleine Einführung in die feministische Theologie: Tb 1673. FrB 1990, Herder. 224 p. DM 12,90. – ᴿTPQ 139 (1991) 222s (Irmtraud *Fischer*).

8854 **Alexandre** Dolores, Mujeres en la hora undécima. M 1990, Fe y secularidad. 39 p. – ᴿREspir 50 (1991) 129s (G. *Turiño*).

8855 *Armour* Ellen T., Recent French feminist works [in English: IRIGARAY Luce 1985 (two), CIXOUS Hélène, CLÉMENT Catherine 1986]: RelStR 17 (1991) 205-8.

8856 *Ashe* Kaye, The feminist revolution and religious education: RelEdn 86,1 (Ch 1991) 99-105 [< ZIT 91,389].

8857 *Baker* Tony, Men, women, and the presbyterate; does Scripture speak clearly?: Churchman 104 (1990) 43-50 [< ZIT 90,447].

8858 **Bennett** Anne M., From woman-pain to woman-vision, ᴱ*Hunt* Mary E., 1989 ➤ 6,8905: ᴿHorizons 18 (1991) 334s (Christine E. *Gudorf*).

8859 **Borrowdale** Anne, Distorted images; Christian attitudes to women, men and sex. L 1991, SPCK. 152 p. £7. 0-281-04530-5 [ScotJT 44,548].

8860 **Brunelli** Delir, Libertação da mulher; um desafio para a Igreja e a Vida Religiosa da América Latina. Rio 1988, CRB. 109 p. – ᴿIter 2 (1991) 158s (Jesús de la *Torre*).

8861 *Bunge* Marcia, Modelle feministischer Bibelauslegung: ➤ 310, JbBT 6 (1991) 285-297.

8861* **Burke** Christine, Through a woman's eyes; encounters with Jesus. Melbourne 1989, CollinsDove. 73 p. A$10. – ᴿAustralasCR 68 (1991) 381s (Marie *Farrell*).

8862 **Carr** Anne E., Transforming grace 1988 ➤ 4,9957 ... 6,8918: ᴿInterpretation 45 (1991) 432.4 (T. W. *Currie*).

8862* **Carr** Anne E., Frauen verändern die Kirche; christliche Tradition und feministische Erfahrung, ᵀ*Reppekus* M.: Siebenstern 407. Gü 1990, Mohn. 330 p. DM 30 [TLZ 117,141, Gudrun *Althausen*].

8863 **Chopp** Rebecca, The power to speak; feminism, language, God 1989 ➤ 5,8866; 6,8922: ᴿCCurr 40 (1990s) 560-2 (Sonya A. *Quitslund*, also on MILES M.); ChrCent 107 (1990) 1070s (Susan R. *Briehl*); Interpretation 45 (1991) 324.6 (R. S. *Dietrich*: a mine of specificity and plurivocity); JRel 71 (1991) 594 (Mary Ellen *Ross*).

8864 **Christ** Carol P., Laughter of Aphrodite 1987 ➤ 4,9959; 6,8923: ᴿJRel 71 (1991) 290s (Elena *Vassallo*).

8865 ᴱ**Cooey** Paula M., *al.*, Embodied love 1988 ➤ 4,352; 5,8869: ᴿBibTB 21 (1991) 78s (E. Jane *Via*).

8866 **Costa** Denise de, Sprekende stiltes; een postmoderne lezing van het vrouwelijk schrift, IRIGARAY [Luce], KRISTEVA [Julia], LYOTARD [Jean-François]. Kampen 1989, Kok Agora. 144 p. ƒ25. 90-242-7634-9. – ᴿBijdragen 52 (1991) 105 (Freda *Dröes*).

8867 *Courtois* Luc, Vers l'admission des étudiantes à Louvain (octobre 1920); jalons pour une histoire des mentalités catholiques en matière de condition féminine: RHE 86 (1991) 324-346.

8868 *Curry* David, Inclusive language liturgies; the renunciation of revelation: Churchman 105 (1991) 54- ... [< ZIT 91,408].

8869 a) D'Souza Flavia D., Women live their faith in a sexist church; – b) Gnanadason Aruna, God knows why you women weep and weeps with you: Jeevadhara 20 (1990) 182-8 / 189-196.

8870 Edgar W., Le ministère pastoral féminin; pour mettre de l'ordre dans les idées: RRéf 41,1 (1990) 29-35 [< NTAbs 34,345].

8871 **Edwards** Ruth B., The case for women's ministry 1989 → 6,8943: ᴿJTS 42 (1991) 270-3 (Frances M. Young).

8872 **Ehrenreich** Barbara, English Deirdre, Por su propio bien. M 1990, Taurus. 405 p. – ᴿRazF 223 (1991) 435 (J. M. Vallarino cites: easier to admit that women are superior to men than that they are equal).

8873 a) Elliot Elizabeth, The essence of femininity; a personal perspective; – b) Dee Jepsen, Women in society; the challenge and the call; – c) Balasa Donald A., Is it legal for religious organizations to make distinctions on the basis of sex?; – d) Ayers David, The inevitability of failure; the assumptions and implementations of modern feminism: → 375, Recovering 1991, 349-9 / 388-393 / 332-341. 527-9 / 312-331. 523-7.

ᴱ**Fabella** Virginia, Park Sun Ai Lee, We dare to dream 1990 → 406.

8874 **Field-Bibb** Jacqueline, Women towards priesthood; ministerial politics and feminist praxis. NY 1991, Cambridge-UP. xiii-387 p. $49.50. 0-521-39283-7 [TDig 39,60].

8875 **Fischer** Kathleen, Women at the well; feminist perspectives on spiritual direction 1989 → 6,8949: ᴿTablet 244 (1990) 49 (Margaret Hebblethwaite).

8876 **Friemel** Franz G., Zur Stellung der Frau in der heutigen Kirche: → 564, Erfurter 1989/90, 107-119.

8877 Gärtner Heiderose, 'Die guten ins Kröpfchen; die schlechten ins Töpfchen'; Bemerkungen zu der Stellungnahme zu Fragen der feministischen Theologie: Deutsches Pfarrerblatt 91 (Essen 1991) 271-3 [< ZIT 91,536].

8878 **Gebara** Ivone, As incômodas filhas de Eva na Igreja de América Latina. Saõ Paulo 1989, Paulinas. 47 p. – ᴿPerspT 22 (1990) 131 (F. Taborda).

8878* Genest O., Does the NT resolve the question of women in ministry?: Ecumenism 26,103 (Montreal 1991) 25-38 [< NTAbs 36,214].

ᴱ**Glaz** Maxine, Stevenson Jeanne, Women in travail and transition; a new pastoral care 1991 → 355.

8879 Gleeson Gerald P., The ordination of women and the symbolism of priesthood: AustralasCR 67 (1990) 472-482; 68 (1991) 80-88.

8880 **Godel** Erika, 'Gegenreden'; Bibelarbeiten von Frauen auf deutschen evangelischen Kirchentagen: ev. Diss. Hamburg 1991, ᴰCornehl P. – TR 87 (1991) 518; RTLv 23, p. 539.

8881 ᴱ**Gössmann** E., EBERTI Johann C., Eröffnetes Cabinet Dess Gelehrten Frauen = Zimmers (1706) + Schlesiens Hoch = und Wohlgelehrtes Frauenzimmer (1727). Mü 1987 ²1990, Iudicium. – ᴿOrientierung 55 (1991) 61s (Helen Schüngel-Straumann).

8882 ᴱ**Gössmann** E., Moltmann-Wendel E., Pissarek-Hudelist H. al., Wörterbuch der feministischen Theologie. Gü 1991, Mohn. 476 p. DM 78 [TLZ 117,690, U. Gerber].

Grant Jacquelyn, White women's Christ and black women's Jesus 1989 → 3722.

8883 Greider Kathleen H., The authority of our ambivalence; women and priestly ministry: QRMin 10 (1990) 22-39.

8884 **Hampson** Daphne, Theology and feminism [...the rise of feminism exposes Christianity as both immoral and untrue] 1990 → 6,8960 [C. Rodd: 'not strident']: ᴿScotJT 43 (1990) 390-400 (Rosemary R. Ruether);

Tablet 244 (1990) 1227 (Janet M. *Soskice*: praise and disagreement); TLond 94 (1991) 132s (Sarah *Coakley*).
8885 **Hauke** Manfred, Women in the priesthood? 1988 ➤ 5,8896; 6,8963: ᴿMid-Stream 29 (1990) 187s (J. *Gros*, also on TRAPP J.).
8886 **Hauschild** Ingeborg, Die feministische Versuchung und die Antwort der christlichen Frau. Wu 1989, Brockhaus. 125 p. DM 18. 3-417-12428-X. – ᴿLuthTKi 13 (1989) 78s (Hilke *Junker*).
8887 *Henking* Susan E., The personal is the theological; autobiographical acts in contemporary feminist theology: JAAR 59 (1991) 511-525 (527-546, *Ross* Ellen M. on Margery KEMPE).
8888 *a) Hermisson* Hans-Jürgen, Zur 'feministischen' Exegese des ATs; – *b) Stuhlmacher* Peter, Feministische Theologie und die Auslegung des NTs; – *c) Köpf* Ulrich, Bemerkungen zur feministischen Auffassung der Kirchengeschichte; – *d) Schneider-Flume* Gunda, Systematisch-theologische Bemerkungen zur feministischen Theologie; – *e) Müller* Hans-Martin, Feministische Theologie und kirchliche Praxis; – *f) Beyer* Peter, Die feministische Theologie in religionswissenschaftlicher und missionstheologischer Sicht; – *g) Haacker* Klaus, Eine Herausforderung: TBeit 22,3 ('Tübinger Stellungnahme' 1991) 120-6 / 127-138 / 139s / 141-5 / 146-8 / 149-153 / 154 [< ZIT 91,432].
8889 **Heuser** Frederick J.ᴶ, Culture, feminism, and the Gospel; American Presbyterian women and foreign missions, 1870-1923: diss. Temple, ᴰ*Davis* A. Ph 1991. 337 p. 92-07863. — DissA 52 (1991s) 3455-A.
8889* *Hewitt* Marsha, Woman, nature and power; emancipatory themes in critical theory and feminist theology: SR 20 (1991) 267-279.
8890 ᴱ**Hojenski** Christine, Meine Seele sieht das Land der Freiheit; feministische Liturgien, Modelle für die Praxis; Vorw. *Meyer-Wilmes* Hedwig. Mü 1990, Liberación. 276 p. DM 29,80. – ᴿZkT 113 (1991) 295-9 (H.-A. *Pissarek*ᴶ).
8891 *Horoszewicz* Michał, ❷ Teologia feministyczna o macierzyństwie [motherhood; < Concilium français 226 (1989)]: ColcT 61,1 (1991) 152-160.
8891* *a) Hrdy* Sarah B., Raising DARWIN's consciousness; females and evolutionary theory; – *b) James* George A., The status of the anomaly in the feminist God-talk of Rosemary RUETHER; – *c) McDaniel* Jay, Six characteristics of a postpatriarchal Christianity: Zygon 25 (1990) 129-137 / 167-185 / 187-217.
8892 **Hull** Gretchen Gaebelein, Equal to serve; women and men in the church and home. Old Tappan NJ 1987, Revell. 302 p. $15. – ᴿSWJT 33,2 (1990s) 60 (G. *Greenfield*: daughter and granddaughter of noted conservative exegetes).
8892* *Hull* G. G., An exegetical case for the full participation of women and men in the Church: JBEq 3 (Lakewood CO 1991) 4-22 [< NTAbs 36,73].
8893 *a) Iriarte* Maria E., Mujer y ministerio, AT; – *b) Salas* Antonio, ... NT; – *c) Sáenz Galache* Mercedes, Mujer y estructura eclesial; análisis histórico y valoración crítica; – *d) Bellosillo* Pilar, Mujer y praxis ministerial, hoy; la respuesta del primer mundo; – *e) Pintos Cea-Naharro* Margarita, Mujer y sacerdocio; anotaciones—evaluación—perspectivas; – *f) Folgado Flórez* Segundo, Estructura ministerial de la Iglesia: BibFe 16,46 ('Mujer y ministerio, fundamento bíblico y praxis eclesial' 1990) 29-50 / 51-74 / 75-97 / 99-139 / 140-151 / 5-28.
8894 *Jansen* Gertrud, Keuschheit — (k)eine feministische Tugend?: WoAnt 31 (Mainz 1990) 163s [< ZIT 91,24].

8895 *a) Johnson* Gregg, The biological basis for gender-specific behavior; – *b) Rekers* George A., Psychological foundations for rearing masculine boys and feminine girls ➤ 375, Recovering 1991, 280-293. 516-8 / 294-311. 518-523.

8896 ᴱ**Joseph** Alison (f.), Through the devil's gateway; women, religion and taboo. L 1990, SPCK (TV-4 programs). vi-106 p. £8 pa. – ᴿTLond 94 (1991) 214s (Anne *Burrowdale*).

8897 *Keller* Catherine, 'To illuminate your trace'; self in late modern feminist theology: Listening 23 (1990) 211-224 [< ᴢɪᴛ 91,83].

8898 ᴱ**Loades** Ann, Feminist theology, a reader. L/Louisville 1990, SPCK/ W-Knox. ix-340 p. $17. 0-664-25129-3 [TDig 38,263]. – ᴿTLond 94 (1991) 213s (Susan F. *Parsons*).

8899 *Lowe* Stephen D., Rethinking the female status/function question; the Jew/Gentile relationship as paradigm: JEvTS 34 (1991) 59-76 [< ᴢɪᴛ 91,415].

8900 *McEwan* Dorothea, *Poole* Myra, Making the connections; the global agenda of feminist theology [Maryknoll summer 1989]: NBlackf 71 (1990) 229-243.

8901 **May** Melanie A., Bonds of unity; women, theology and the worldwide Church: AAR 65. Atlanta 1989, Scholars. x-175 p. $23; sb./pa. $15. – ᴿCritRR 4 (1991) 491-3 (Mary M. *Fulkerson*).

8902 **Meyer-Wilmes** Hedwig, Rebellion auf der Grenze; Ortsbestimmung feministischer Theologie: Frauenforum, 1990 ➤ 6,8987: ᴿTPQ 139 (1991) 222 (Herlinde-Anna *Pissarek*ᴶ); ZkT 113 (1991) 293-5 (R. *Frick-Pöder*: Nachfolgerin von Catherina HALKES in Nijmegen).

8902* *Miccoli* Paolo, 'La condición humana hoy; ser hombre, ser mujer'; prospectivas fenomenológicas sobre la sexualidad humana: RAg 30 (1989) 155-199.

8903 *Milne* Pamela J., Women and words; the use of non-sexist, inclusive language in the Academy: StRTo 18,1 (1989) 25-36 [< ᴢɪᴛ 89,636].

8904 *Ohler* Annemarie, Ich bin Gott und nicht ein Mann (Hos 11,9): Lebendige Seelsorge 41,5s ('Frauen und Männer in der Kirche' 1990) 284-291 [*al.*, 17 art. p. 267-359s: ᴢɪᴛ 90,713].

8905 **O'Neill** Maura, Women speaking, women listening 1990 ➤ 6,8997: ᴿTLond 94 (1991) 460s (Ursula *King*).

8906 *Parvey* Constance, Feministische Theologie; eine Avantgarde der Theologie: ➤ 160, ꜰVISCHER L., Ök. Theol. 1991, 114-139.

8907 **Pearson** Carol S., The hero within; six archetypes we live by [... feminist critique]. SF 1986, Harper & R. 176 p. $9. – ᴿRExp 87 (1990) 138s (E. E. *Thornton*).

8908 ᴱ**Plaskow** Judith, *Christ* Carol P., Weaving the visions 1989 ➤ 6,444: ᴿHorizons 18 (1991) 347s (Georgia M. *Keightley*).

8909 *a) Poythress* Vern S., The Church as family; why male leadership in the family requires male leadership in the Church; – *b) Knight* George W.ᴵᴵᴵ, The family and the Church; how should biblical manhood and womanhood work out in practice?: – *c) House* H. Wayne, Principles to use in establishing women in ministry; – *d) Patterson* Paige, The meaning of authority in the local church: ➤ 375, Recovering 1991, 233-262. 508-512 / 345-357. 529-531 / 358-363 / 248-259. 509-512.

Primavesi Anne, From Apocalypse to Genesis; ecology, feminism, and Christianity 1991 ➤ 7246*.

8911 **Procter-Smith** Marjorie, In her own rite; constructing feminist liturgical traditions 1990 ➤ 6,9003: ᴿRelStR 17 (1991) 237 (Susan A *Ross*).

8912 **Rabuzzi** Kathryn A., Motherself; a mythic analysis of motherhood. Bloomington 1988, Indiana Univ. 248 p. $37.50; pa. $13. – [R]CritRR 3 (1990) 448-450 (V. R. *Mollenkott*).

8913 *Raming* Ida, Die Frauen in der Kirche: StiZt 208 (1991) 415-426.

8914 **Rhodes** Lynn N., Co-creating; a feminist vision of ministry. Louisville 1987, W-Knox. 132 p. $10. 0-664-24032-1. – [R]Interpretation 45 (1991) 406-411 (J. L. *Allen*, amid five non-feminist books on ministry).

8915 *Ricca* Paolo, Donna e sacerdozio: che cosa dice la tradizione: Protestantesimo 45 (1990) 120-2 [LEGRAND H.: niente contro].

8916 **Riley** Maria, Transforming feminism. KC 1989, Sheed & W. xiv-112 p. $9 pa. – [R]Horizons 18 (1991) 336s (Sonya A. *Quitslund*).

8917 *Riley* Maria, La réception de l'enseignement social catholique chez les féministes chrétiennes, [T]*Divault* André: ➤ 348, Concilium 237 (P 1991) 141-9.

8918 **Ruether** R. R., Women-Church 1985 ➤ 2,7105...5,8939: [R]Bijdragen 52 (1991) 106 (Freda *Dröes*, under Radford).

8919 *a*) *Ruether* Rosemary R., Frauenkirche; feministische liturgische Gemeinschaften, Theologie und Praxis, [T]*Lungu* Renate; – *b*) *Jeggle-Merz* Birgit, Experiment Liturgie; das 'Experiment' feministische Liturgie; – *c*) *Merz* Michael B., Experiment Liturgie — ein neues Stichwort zur Frage der Inkulturation der Liturgie?: BLtg 63 (1990) 223-9 / 230-234 / 194-201.

8920 *Ruether* Rosemary R., Is feminism the end of Christianity? [*Hampson* D. 1990]: ScotJT 43 (1990) 390-400.

8921 **Russell** Letty M., Household of freedom 1987 ➤ 3,9018...5,8941: [R]CritRR 2 (1989) 461s (Sharon H. *Ringe*).

8922 **Scherzberg** Lucia, Sünde und Gnade in der feministischen Theologie [kath. Diss. Münster 1991, [D]*Lengsfeld*. – TR 87 (1991) 521]. Mainz 1991, Grünewald. 258 p. DM 36 [NRT 114,584, P. *Evrard*].

8923 **Schneiders** Sandra, Beyond patching; faith and feminism in the Catholic Church [1990 Edmonton Jordan lectures]. NY 1991, Paulist. viii-136 p. $7 pa. [Horizons 19,154s, Marie-Eloise *Rosenblatt*]. – [R]TTod 48 (1991s) 372s (Denise L. *Carmody*).

8924 *a*) *Schottroff* Luise, Feministisch-theologische Wissenschaft heute; – *b*) *Traitler* Reinhild, Ein Gespräch über feministische Literatur; – *c*) *Heine* Susanne, Probleme einer feministischen Hermeneutik: EvKomm 23 (1990) 347s / 348-353 / 354-6 [< ZIT 90,453].

8925 **Schüssler Fiorenza** Elisabeth, Bread not stone[2] [[1]1984 ➤ 1,8622... 6,9014]. E 1990, Clark. 182 p. £10. 0-567-29184-7. – [R]DoctLife 41 (1991) 385s (W. *Harrington*); ÉTRel 66 (1991) 459-461 (F. *Beydon*); TLond 94 (1991) 217s (N. *Slee*).

8926 *Scordato* Cosimo, Maddalena, ovverossia il sacerdozio alla donna?: Ho Theológos 9 (1991) 195-231.

8927 **Sjöö** Monica, *Mor* Barbara, The great cosmic mother; rediscovering the religion of the earth. SF 1991, Harper & R. ix-501 p. $17. – [R]HeythJ 32 (1991) 134s (C. *Walter*).

8928 **Solié** Pierre, Les Odyssées du Féminin. P 1990, Séveyrat. 208 p. F 140. – [R]Études 374 (1991) 704 (Cécile *Sales*: y compris 'le féminin en l'homme').

8929 *a*) *Sontag* Frederick, Crucifixion and realized eschatology; a critique of some proposals concerning feminist theology; – *b*) *Coyle* Kathleen, Tradition, theology, and women in the churches: AsiaJT 4,1 (1990) 66-73 / 212-224 [< ZIT 91,202].

8930 **Steichen** Donna,   Ungodly rage; the hidden face of Catholic feminism. SF 1991, Ignatius.   420 p. $16.   0-89870-348-4 [TDig 39,85: blow-by-blow account].

8930* *a) Strohm* Doris,   'Fur wen haltet ihr mich?' Einige historische und methodische Bemerkungen zu Grundfragen der Christologie; – *b) Hopkins* Julia,   Sind Christologie und Feminismus unvereinbar? Zur Debatte zwischen Daphne HAMPSON und R. R. RUETHER [... gegen die traditionelle Methode]; – *c) Schüssler Fiorenza* Elisabeth,   Zur Methodenproblematik einer feministischen Christologie des NTs; – *d) Strahm Bernet* Silvia,   Jesa Christa / Die grössten Unmenschlichkeiten ...; – *e) Kohn-Roelin* Johanna,   Antijudaismus — die Kehrseite jeder Christologie; – *f) Moltmann-Wendel* Elisabeth,   Beziehung — die vergessene Dimension der Christologie: → 383*, Chr/Fem 1991, 11-36 / 194-207. 37-51 / 129-147 / 172-191. 81-99 / 65-80 / 100-111.

8931 **Thistlethwaite** Susan,   Sex, race and God 1989 → 6,9020:   RHorizons 18 (1991) 339s (Jane *Kopas*); Interpretation 45 (1991) 214-6 (Marie-Eloise *Rosenblatt*); JRel 71 (1991) 595 (Delores *Williams*); NewTR 4,1 (1991) 90-92 (Ann O. *Graff*); TLond 94 (1991) 57s (Elaine *Edwards*); TTod 48 (1991s) 82.84s (Kelly D. *Brown*).

8932 *a) Thistlethwaite* Susan B., *Eugene* Toinette M.,   A survey of contemporary global feminist, womanist, and mujerista theologies; – *b) Anderson* Janice C.,   Mapping feminist biblical criticism; the American scene, 1983-1990; – *c) Morey* Ann-Janine,   Feminist perspectives on arts, literature, and religion: CritRR 4 (1991) 1-20 / 21-44 / 45-62; Morey footnotes omitted by error, supplied 5 (1992) 543s.

8933 **Thomsen** Elizabeth L.,   'The woman's Bible' [STANTON Elizabeth C.]; heritage and harbinger of hope for feminist biblical hermeneutics: diss. Graduate Theological Union,   DFischer Clare B. Berkeley 1991.   230 p. DissA 52 (1990s) 3455-A; RelStR 18,170.

8934 ETroch L.,   Nelle MORGAN, Mary DALY, Rosemary Radford REUTHER, Elisabeth SCHÜSSLER FIORENZA; een inleiding in haar denken [kursus Univ. Heerlen, sept. 1989]. Heerlen 1990, UTP. f6 [NedTTs 45,168]. – RTsTNijm 31 (1991) 308 (Hedwig *Meyer-Wilmes*).

8934* **Welch** Sharon D.,   A feminist ethic of risk 1990 → 6,9028:   RCurrTMiss 18 (1991) 125 (Ann M. *Pederson*).

8935 *Wright* R. K. M.,   [1 Tim 2; I Cor 11] Hierarchicalism unbiblical: JBEq 3 (1991) 57-66 [< NTAbs 36,76].

8935* **Young** Pamela D.,   Feminist theology / Christian theology; in search of method 1990 → 6,9030:   RHorizons 18 (1991) 335s (Sonya A. *Quitslund*).

H9   Eschatologia NT, *spes, hope.*

8936* *Albright* John R.,   The end of the world; a scientific view of Christian eschatology: Dialog 30 (1991) 279-382 [< TLZ 117,697].

8937 **Ancona** Giovanni,   Il significato escatologico cristiano della morte: Corona Lateranensis 38,   D1990 → 6,9032:   RRivScR 4 (1990) 577-9 (M. *Semeraro*); VetChr 28 (1991) 213-5 (S. *Bettocchi*).

8938 **Anderson** Ray S.,   Theology, death and dying.   Ox 1986, Blackwell. viii-170 p. $21. – RRelStT 9,1 (1989) 56-59 (D. W. *Atkinson*, compares GUALTIERI A.).

8939 **Aubert** J.-M.,   Et après... Vie ou néant? Essai sur l'au-delà. P 1991, D-Brouwer. 176 p. F 98 [NRT 114,586, C. *Verdonck*).

8939* ᴱBadham Paul & Linda, Death and immortality in the religions of the world 1987 ➤ 3,377 ... 6,9033: ᴿIndTSt 27 (1990) 205s (A. *Klencherry*).

8940 *Bayer* Oswald, Das Letzte Gericht als religionsphilosophisches Problem: ➤ 125, ᶠRATSCHOW C., NSys 33 (1991) 199-210; Eng. 210.

8941 *Berghe* Eric Van den, Kroniekrecensie; leven over de dood heen: CollatVL 21 (1991) 209-214.

8942 **Blank** Renold J., Nossa vida tem futuro: Escatologia cristã 1. São Paulo 1991, Paulinas. 240 p. [REB 51,1020].

8943 **Bowker** John, The meanings of death. C 1991, Univ. xii-243 p. £17. 0-521-39117-2 [TDig 39,52].

8944 *Bynum* Caroline W., Material continuity, personal survival, and the resurrection of the body; a scholastic discussion in its medieval and modern contexts: HistRel 30 (1990s) 51-85.

8944* *Cabrera Sánchez* C., Actitud ante la muerte y experiencia religiosa en las sociedades avanzadas: Almogaren 4 (1989) 59-75 [< RET 51,112].

8945 *Carle* Paul-Laurent, Saint IRENÉE de Lyon et les fins dernières: Divinitas 34 (1990) 53-72. 171.

8946 **Chanceaulme** J., Mourir, ultime tendresse: Psychologie et Sciences Humaines. Liège 1990, Mardaga. 156 p. Fb 750. – ᴿNRT 113 (1991) 450s (G. *Menin*).

8947 **Chung** Jae Hyun, Being and freedom; a problem in the interpretation of human death: diss. Emory, ᴰ*Runyon* T. Atlanta 1991. 340 p. 91-27585. — DissA 52 (1991s) 1384-A; RelStR 18,171; RTLv 23, p. 568.

8948 **Cooper** John W., Body, soul, and life everlasting 1989 ➤ 5,8984; 6,9047: ᴿThomist 55 (1991) 522-6 (P. *Blosser*).

8949 *Couture* André, [Réincarnation] L'accès aux vies antérieures selon Joan GRANT et Denys KELSEY et d'après les expériences de Denise DESJARDINS: LavalTP 47 (1991) 417-434.

8950 **Daley** Brian E., The hope of the early Church; a handbook of patristic eschatology. C 1991, Univ. xiv-300 p. £30 [TR 88,165]. 0-521-35258-4. – ᴿNRT 114 (1992) 585s (L. *Renwart*).

8951 **Deissler** A., Was wird am Ende der Tage geschehen? Biblische Visionen der Zukunft. FrB 1991, Herder. 112 p. DM 16. 3-451-22190-X [BL 92,104, J. *Goldingay*].

8952 *Dieterlé* Christiane, La mort comme un deuil; approche biblique: LumièreV 40,204 (1991) 81-94.

8953 *Disley* Emma, Degrees of glory; Protestant doctrine and the concept of rewards hereafter: JTS 42 (1991) 77-105.

8953* **Douglass** J.W., The nonviolent coming of God. Mkn 1991, Orbis. xvi-236 p. $14. 0-88344-753-3 [NTAbs 36,281].

8954 **Druet** François-X., Langage, images et visages de la mort chez Jean CHRYSOSTOME 1990 ➤ 6,9052: ᴿAnzAltW 44 (1991) 42 (J.-B. *Bauer*); RHPR 71 (1991) 378 (W. *Fick*).

8954* **Dubied** P.-L., L'angoisse et la mort: Entrée libre 13. Genève 1991, Labor et Fides. 96 p. Fs 13 [NRT 114,587, C. *Verdonck*].

8955 **Dunn** J., *Mackey* J., NT Theology in dialogue, Christology and ministry 1987 ➤ 3,9161 ... 5,9071: ᴿJRel 70 (1990) 654s (P. E. *Devenish*).

8955* **Durst** Michael, Die Eschatologie des HILARIUS 1987 ➤ 3,9069 ... 6,9053: ᴿForumKT 7 (1991) 143s (A. *Ziegenaus*).

8956 *Dylus* Franciszek, ❷ Eschatologischer Sinn der Idee der Pleromisation bei P. TEILHARD de Chardin: ColcT 60,4 (1990) 75-82; deutsch 82.

8957 **Felder** Angela, Reinkarnationshypothese in der New-Age-Bewegung. Nettetal 1991. 101 p. – ᴿForumKT 7 (1991) 238s (Elfi *Moder-Frei*).

8958 **Finger** Thomas N., Christian theology, an eschatological approach I, 1985 ➤ 2,7164; II, 1989 ➤ 6,9058: ᴿLvSt 16 (1991) 275s (H.-E. *Mertens*, 2); PerspRelSt 18,1 (1991) 71s (J. W. *McClendon*, 1s).

8959 **Fischer** Alfons, CALVINS Eschatologie in der Erstausgabe der 'Christianae religionis institutio' 1536: kath. Diss. Würzburg 1991, ᴰ*Ganoczy*. – TR 87 (1991) 522.

8960 *Flannery* Kevin, How to think about Hell [... BALTHASAR]: NBlackf 72 (1991) 469-481.

8961 *Gaffin* Richard B.ᴶ, The Holy Spirit and eschatology: Kerux 4,3 (1989) 14-29.

8962 *Gentile* Luigi, Tommaso d'AQUINO; finitudine dell'esistenza umana e immortalità: FilT 4 (1990) 295-304 (amid 12 articles on death in various religious traditions but none on the Bible).

8963 ᴱ**Gerhards** A., Die grössere Hoffnung der Christen; eschatologische Vorstellungen im Wandel: QDisp 127, 1990 ➤ 6,411*a*: ᴿNRT 113 (1991) 113s (A. *Toubeau*).

8964 **Gounelle** A., *Vouga* F., Après la mort qu'y a-t-il? Les discours chrétiens sur l'au-delà: Théologies. P 1990, Cerf. 190 p. F 93. – ᴿÉtudes 347 (1991) 282s (J. *Thomas*); NRT 113 (1991) 452s (C. *Verdonck*).

8965 **Harris** Murray J., Raised immortal 1983 ➤ 64,7722 ... 3,9089: ᴿRelStT 9,1 (1989) 44-46 (E. E. *Milton*: serious defects) = 10,2 (1990) 107s.

8966 **Hayes** Zachary, Visions of a future; study of Christian eschatology: New Theology 8, 1988 ➤ 6,9066: ᴿRelStR 17 (1991) 51 (N. *Kollar*).

8967 *Hennessey* Lawrence R., ORIGEN of Alexandria; the fate of the soul and the body after death: SecC 8 (1991) 163-178.

8968 **Hjelde** Sigurd, Das Eschaton und die Eschata ...: BeitEvT 102, 1987 ➤ 4,a88: ᴿBijdragen 52 (1991) 104 (H. J. *Adriaanse*).

8969 **Hockey** Jennifer, Experiences of death. E 1991, Univ. £30. – ᴿTablet 245 (1991) 1117 (Caroline *Miles*).

8970 **Hodgkinson** Liz, Reincarnation; the evidence, ... c. 1990, Piatkus. £13. – ᴿTablet 244 (1990) 50 (Renée *Haynes*).

8971 *Holzmüller* Thilo, 'Die endende Zeit'; eine Überlegung zum Verständnis von Tod und Auferstehung bei Karl BARTH: WDienst 21 (1991) 197-213.

8972 *Horvath* Tibor, Society, world and eternity ['Aeon' is alphabetically first of the 61 terms here given as basic to eschatology; and 'world' is last]: ScEsp 43 (1991) 319-337.

8973 *Hryniewicz* Wacław, ❷ Pascha mortis; man's death as a paschal event: RoczTK 37,2 (1991 for 1987) 17-38; Eng. 39.

8973* *a) Jahr* Hannelore, Vom Kairos zur heiligen Lehre; TILLICHs eschatologische Deutung der Gegenwart; – *b) Reimer* A. James, The Kingdom of God in the thought of Emanuel HIRSCH and P. Tillich; – *c) Keil* Günther, Kunjektur und Symbol als Sprache für das Letzte: CUES & Tillich: ➤ 515, New creation 1990/1, 3-25 / 44-56 / 107-194.

8974 *Jüngel* Eberhard, The Last Judgment as an act of grace: LvSt 15 (1990) 389-405.

8975 *Kehl* Medard, Wiedergeburt — Häresie oder Hoffnung?: GeistL 63 (1990) 445-457.

8976 **Kelly** Tony, Touching on the infinite; explorations in Christian hope. SF 1991, Harper Collins. viii-250 p. $16 pa. [CBQ 54,403].

8977 **Kirsch** Ulrich, Blaise PASCAL 'Pensées' (1656-1662); systematische 'Gedanken' über Tod, Vergänglichkeit und Glück: Symposion 88. Fr 1989, Alber. 390 p. – ᴿTPhil 66 (1991) 105-7 (J. *Splett*).

8978 **König** Adrio, The eclipse of Christ in eschatology 1989 ➤ 5,9008; 6,9074: ᴿGraceTJ 11 (1990) 115-7 (J.D. *Morrison*); TTod 48 (1991s) 116 (Catherine *Keller*).

8979 ᴱ**Lambrecht** J., *Kenis* L., Leven over de dood heen; verslagboek van een interdisciplinair Leuvens colloquium 1990 ➤ 6,638*; 90-334-2317-0. – ᴿTsTNijm 31 (1991) 440s (H.J.M. *Vossen*).

8980 *Lanne* Emmanuel, L'enseignement de l'Église catholique sur le purgatoire: Irénikon 64 (1991) 205-228; Eng. 229.

8981 **Lannert** Berthold, Die Wiederentdeckung der neutestamentlichen Eschatologie durch J. WEISS [ᴰ1988s ➤ 5,9011]: TArbNZ 2. Tü 1989, Francke. xiv-304 p. DM 68. 3-7720-1881-5. – ᴿSNTU A-15 (1990) 148s (A. *Fuchs*).

8982 **Lemasters** Philip, The import of eschatology in John H. YODER's critique of Constantinianism: diss. Duke, ᴰ*Smith* H. Durham ɴᴄ 1990. – RelStR 18,172.

8983 **Lohmann** Hans, Drohung und Verheissung; exegetische Untersuchungen zur Eschatologie bei den Apostolischen Vätern: BZNW 55, 1989 ➤ 5,9016; 6,9079: ᴿCritRR 4 (1991) 325-7 (W.R. *Schoedel*); ÉTRel 66 (1991) 247s (J.-D. *Dubois*); NedTTs 45 (1991) 153-5 (R. van den *Broek*).

8984 **Lorimer** David, Whole in one; the near-death experience and the ethic of interconnectedness. 1990, Arkana. 340 p. £7. 0-14-019258-1. – ᴿExpTim 102 (1990s) 253 (G.T. *Eddy*).

8985 **McDannell** C., *Lang* B., Heaven, a history 1988 ➤ 4,a106 ... 6,9082: ᴿSpeculum 66 (1991) 200-2 (A.E. *Bernstein*).

8986 *McDermott* Gerald R., Karma and rebirth as Christian pedagogy; Geddes MACGREGOR's attempt to synthesize reincarnation and Christianity: JRelSt 16 (Cleveland 1988) 157-173 [< ᴢɪᴛ 90,865].

8987 **McKeating** Colm, Eschatology in the Anglican sermons of John H. NEWMAN: diss. 6970 Pont. Univ. Gregoriana, ᴰ*Sharkey* M. R 1991s [InfPUG 30/92, 28].

8988 **Marcheselli-Casale** Cesare, Risorgeremo, ma come? 1988 ➤ 4,a110 ... 6,9086: ᴿAngelicum 68 (1991) 128-131 (J. *Garcia Trapiello*: ultimately seems based on inspired and canonical character of some apocalyptic writings).

Meer G. van der, Afscheid van het leven 1990 ➤ 233.

8989 **Micaelli** C., TERTULLIANO, La resurrezione dei morti: TestPatr 87, 1990 ➤ 6,9087: ᴿAsprenas 38 (1991) 251s (L. *Fatica*).

8990 **Miller-McLemore** Bonnie, Death, sin, and the moral life; contemporary cultural interpretations of death. Atlanta 1988, Scholars. 196 p. $30; pa./sb. $20. – ᴿCritRR 4 (1991) 415s (Lucy *Bregman*).

8991 *Müller* Hans M., Christliche Rede vom ewigen Leben: KerDo 37 (1991) 190-207; Eng. 208 'in Christian preaching'.

8992 *Murray* John, Structural strands in NT eschatology: Kerux 6,3 (1991) 19-26.

8992* **Nassehi** Armin, *Weber* Georg, Tod, Modernität und Gesellschaft; Entwurf einer Theorie der Todesverdrängung. Opladen 1989, Westd.-V. 483 p. DM 78 [TLZ 117,68, K. *Dirschauer*].

8993 *Osei-Bonsu* J., The intermediate state in the New Testament: ScotJT 44 (1991) 169-194.

8993* **Ott** L. †, ᴱ*Naab* E., Eschatologie in der Scholastik: HbDG 4/7b 1990 ➤ 6,9096: ᴿNRT 113 (1991) 263s (R. *Escol*).

8994 **Paxton** Frederick S., Christianizing death; the creation of a ritual process in medieval Europe. Ithaca ɴʏ 1990, Cornell Univ. xiv-229 p. $31.50 [RelStR 18,145, T.F.X. *Noble*: humane and eloquent].

8995 **Pfammatter** J., *Christen* E., Hoffnung über den Tod hinaus: TBer 19. Z 1990, Benziger. 224 p. DM 29,80. – ᴿTGL 81 (1991) 238s (W. *Beinert*).

8996 *Quinn* Patrick, The relationship between human transcendence and death in the philosophy of St. Thomas AQUINAS: MilltSt 25 (1990) 63-75.

8997 **Ratzinger** Joseph, Eschatologie — Tod und ewiges Leben⁶ [= ¹1977 ↠ 58,9367* + zwei Anhänge]: KLKDogm 9. Rg 1990, Pustet. 238 p. DM 29,80. – ᴿTR 87 (1991) 412 (H. *Vorgrimler*).

8997* ᴱ**Richter** Klemens, Der Umgang mit den Toten; Tod und Bestattung in der christlichen Gemeinde: QDisp 123. FrB 1990, Herder. 200 p. 3-451-02123-4; p. 132-152, *Zenger* E., Das atliche Israel und seine Toten.

8998 *Robbins* Jerry K., Christian thinking about life after death: CurrTMiss 18 (1991) 179-183.

Rössler Andreas, Steht Gottes Himmel allen offen? Zum Symbol des kosmischen Christus 1990 ↠ 7286; 7251.

9000 *Sachs* John R., Current eschatology; universal salvation and the problem of Hell: TS 52 (1991) 227-254.

9001 **Sanders** G., ᴱ*Donati* A., *al.*, 'Lapides memores'; païens et chrétiens face à la mort; le témoignage de l'épigraphie funéraire latine: Epigrafia e Antichità 11. Faenza 1991, Lega. 527 p. [RHE 86.271*].

9001* **Sanford** John A., Soul journey; a JUNGIAN analyst looks at reincarnation. NY 1991, Crossroad. xii-180 p. $17. 0-8245-1091-7 [TDig 39,187].

9002 **Schoenborn** Christoph, Risurrezione e reincarnazione. CasM 1990, Piemme. 93 p. Lit. 9.500. – ᴿProtestantesimo 46 (1991) 154s (G. *Scuderi*).

9003 *Schreurs* Nico, 'Keine festbegrenzte und wahrhaft anschauliche Vorstellung'; SCHLEIERMACHERS Schwierigkeiten mit dem Lehrstück von der Auferstehung des Fleisches, ᵀ*Akker* Yvonne van de: FreibZ 38 (1991) 27-56.

9004 *Scordato* Cosimo, Per una teologia della morte: Ho Theológos 7 (1989) 77-111.

9005 **Seed** Michael, I will see you in heaven [opinions of widely-different types of people]. Middlegreen, Slough 1991, St. Paul. £25 [Tablet 245, 1179 adv.].

9006 **Sesboüé** Bernard, La résurrection et la vie; petite catéchèse sur les choses de la fin: PEncModC, 1990 ↠ 6,9112: ᴿEsprVie 101 (1991) 431s (P. *Jay*); LavalTP 47 (1991) 285s (C. *Renauld*); NRT 113 (1991) 304 (A. *Toubeau*); ZkT 113 (1991) 112 (K. H. *Neufeld*).

9007 *a*) *Sia* Marian F. & Santiago, Death and the Christian: NBlackf 72 (1991) 172-7. – *b*) *Solignac* Aimé, Caelum ↠ 660, AugL 1,5s (1992) 698-704.

9008 *a*) *Sicari* Antonio, God enters into the flesh; the flesh enters into God; Incarnation and Resurrection; – *b*) *Schönborn* Christoph, 'Resurrection of the flesh' in the faith of the Church; – *c*) *Daley* Brian E., The ripening of salvation; hope for resurrection in the early Church: CommND 17 (1990) 4-7 / 8-26 / 27-49.

9009 *Skowronek* Alfons, ℗ Grands problèmes de l'eschatologie chrétienne contemporaine: PrzPow 270/831 (1990) 183-202; franç. 202.

9010 *Thomas* Joseph, Résurrection ou réincarnation?: Études 374 (1991) 235-243.

9011 **Tornos** Andrés, Escatología I, 1989 ↠ 5,9057; 6,9121: ᴿEstE 66 (1991) 87-89 (J. *Benavides*).

9012 **Tugwell** Simon, Human immortality and the redemption of death [Bristol Univ. lectures 1988]. L 1990, Darton-LT. 196 p. – ᴿAngelicum 68 (1991) 131-3 (J. *Henchey*); ExpTim 102 (1990s) 284 (S. R. L. *Clark*); NBlackf 72 (1991) 297s (K. *Ward*); TLond 94 (1991) 69s (P. *Carnley*).

9013 **Turner** Layne H., The use of eternal reward as a motivation in the NT: diss. Dallas Theol. Sem. 1991. 288 p. 92-14494. — DissA 52 (1991s) 4376-A.

9014 *Ubbiali* Sergio, L'evento e il definitivo; per una teologia dell'escatologico: ScuolC 118 (1990) 507-530.

9015 **Ulrich** Hans G., Eschatologie und Ethik; die theologische Theorie der Ethik in ihrer Beziehung auf die Rede von Gott seit F. SCHLEIERMACHER [Hab. 1991]: BeitEvT 104. Mü 1988, Kaiser. 329 p. - ᴿTsTKi 61 (1990) 303s (J.-O, *Henriksen*).

9016 *Verdière* Raoul, Le concept de la sensibilité après la mort chez les anciens: Latomus 50 (1991) 56-63.

9017 a) *Vorgrimler* Herbert, Der Tod als Thema der neueren Theologie; – b) *Kessler* Hans, Die Auferstehung Jesu Christi und unsere Auferstehung; – c) *Kehl* Medard, 'Bis du kommst in Herrlichkeit...'; neuere theologische Deutungen der 'Parusie Jesu'; – d) *Koch* Kurt, Weltende als Erfüllung und Vollendung der Schöpfung; – e) *Halter* Hans, Gericht und ethisches Handeln: TBer 19 (Z 1990) 13-64 / 65-94 / 95-138 / 139-180 / 181... [< ZIT 91,21].

9018 **Walther** Christian, Eschatologie als Theorie der Freiheit; Einführung in neuzeitliche Gestalten eschatologischen Denkens: TBtTöpelmann 48. B 1991, de Gruyter. xii-307 p. DM 128 [TR 87,259].

9019 *Webster* John, Eschatology, ontology and human action: TorJT 7 (1991) 4-18.

9020 *Weigert* Andrew J., Christian eschatological identities and the nuclear context: JScStR 27 (1988) 175-191.

9021 **Wheeler** Michael, Death and the future life in Victorian literature and theology. NY 1991, Cambridge-UP. $54.50. 0-521-30617-5 [TDig 39,89, sans pp.]. - ᴿTLond 94 (1991) 310-2 (S. *Prickett*).

9022 ᴱ**Xella** P., Archeologia dell'inferno 1987 ⇢ 3,844; 5,9064: ᴿÉtClas 59 (1991) 183s (P.-P. *Druet*).

9023 **Zaleski** Carol, Otherworld journeys... near-death 1987 ⇢ 3,9157; 4,a150: ᴿJRel 70 (1990) 507s (Sandra *Zimdars-Swartz*).

H9.5 *Theologia totius [V-] NT* – **[O-] NT theology.**

9024 **Adam** Andrew K. M., New Testament theology and the problem of modernity: diss. Duke, ᴰ*Via* D. Durham NC 1991. 296 p. 91-27518. — DissA 52 (1991s) 1385s-A; RelStR 18,173.

9025 **Beeck** Franz J. Van, God encountered, I. Understanding the Christian faith 1989 ⇢ 5,9067; 6,9131: ᴿCritRR 4 (1991) 472-4 (M. C. *Hilkert*); ETL 67 (1991) 451 (E. *Brito*: clair); JRel 71 (1991) 587s (J. *Carlson*); ScotJT 44 (1991) 97s (R. R. *Brinkman*: in pursuit of the catholicity with small *c* normative for all the churches).

9026 *Beilner* Wolfgang, Neutestamentliche Theologie aus dem Faktum 'Neues Testament': ⇢ 6,171, ᶠSTÖGER A., Exeget 1990, 37-58.

9027 **Casalini** Nello, I misteri della fede; teologia del Nuovo Testamento: SBF Anal 32. J 1991, Franciscan. 772 p. $65 pa. [CBQ 54,202].

9028 *Cholewiński* Alfred, † ☉ Teologia Nowego Przymierza [covenant] w NT, ᴱ*Sulowski* Julian: Bobolanum 1 (1990) 25-87.

9029 **Conzelmann** Hans, Teologia del Nuovo Testamento, [4rev]*Lindemann* Andreas [[1]1967, [3]1976], [T]*Zani* Antonio: BtTeol 5. Brescia 1991, Paideia. 492 p. 88-394-0470-8.

9030 **Dunning** H. Ray, Grace, faith, and holiness; a Wesleyan systematic theology [based on H. Orton WILEY's three volumes but interacting with other traditions]. KC 1988, Beacon Hill. 671 p. 0-83411-219-1. – [R]AsburyTJ 46,1 (1991) 121-3 (D. *Rightmire*) & 124s (R. T. *Leupp*).

9031 [E]**Eicher** Peter, Neue Summe Theologie, [1. 1988 ➤ 5,458*] 2. Die neue Schöpfung 1989 ➤ 6,902: [R]ColcT 60,2 (1990) 175 (L. *Balter*, ➊).

9032 **Garrett** James L., Systematic theology, biblical, historical, and evangelical I. GR 1990, Eerdmans. 658 p. $35. – [R]SWJT 33,3 (1990s) 42s (W. L. *Hendricks*).

9033 **Gnilka** Joachim, NTliche Theologie, ein Überblick 1989 ➤ 5,9073; 6,9135: [R]BLtg 63 (1990) 187-190 (W. *Beilner*).

9034 **Hübner** Hans, Biblische Theologie des NTs I. Prolegomena 1990 ➤ 6, 9138: [R]TLZ 116 (1991) 830-2 (K. *Niederwimmer*).

9035 **Kittel** Gisela, Der Name über alle Namen, Biblische Theologie, I. AT; II. NT, 1989s ➤ 6,9140: [R]TR 87 (1991) 464s (H. *Seebass*: Lob); ZkT 113 (1991) 89s (R. *Frick-Pöder*).

9036 **Klein** H., Leben neu entdecken; Entwurf einer Biblischen Theologie: TBt 23. Stu 1991, Calwer. 246 p. DM 30. 3-7668-3138-0 [BL 92,107, J. *Goldingay*: Rumanian].

9036* **Klöckner** Stefan, 'Sakrament im Wort'; christologische Fundamentierung, eschatologische Ausrichtung und ekklesiale Vermittlung wortsakramentalen Geschehens als Gegenstand ökumenischer Konvergenzbestrebungen [Inaug.-Diss. Tü [D]*Walter* P.]: Tü 1991. vi-279 + 17 p.

9037 **Ladd** G., Théologie du Nouveau Testament 1984 ➤ 1,8773; 2,7230: [R]Protestantesimo 46 (1991) 218s (Teodora *Tosatti*: mancanza di critica).

9038 *Langkammer* Hugolin, ➊ NT theology in Polish: RoczTK 34,1 (1991 for 1987) 101-115.

9039 **Lohse** Eduard, Théologie du NT [Grundriss 1974], [T]1987 ➤ 6,9143: [R]Antonianum 66 (1991) 156s (M. *Nobile*).

9040 **Lohse** E., Compendio di teologia del NT, [T]*Poletti* G., [E]*Masini* M. Brescia 1987, Queriniana. 248 p. Lit. 28.000. 88-399-1038-7. – [R]Protestantesimo 45 (1990) 326 (B. *Corsani*).

9041 **McKenzie** Peter, The Christians, their beliefs... 1988 ➤ 5,9081: [R]CritRR 3 (1990) 308-311 (S. R. *Gordy*: adaptation of Erscheinungsformen und Wesen der Religion, *Heiler* F. [2]1979); JRelHist 16 (1990s) 107-9 (E. J. *Sharpe*); Themelios 15 (1989s) 107 (D. *Hughes*).

9042 **Mildenberger** Friedrich, Biblische Dogmatik; eine biblische Theologie in dogmatischer Perspektive, I. Prolegomena; Verstehen und Geltung der Bibel. Stu 1991, Kohlhammer. 3-17-011081-0 [ZAW 104,451, H. C. *Schmitt*].

9043 *a) Mildenberger* Friedrich, Biblische Theologie versus Dogmatik? – *b) Daniels* Dwight R., Biblische Theologie in den USA; ein Forschung- und Tagungsbericht [... Okt. 1989]; – *c) Baldermann* Ingo, Elementare Theologie; zu Gisela KITTELS Entwurf einer Biblischen Theologie [Der Name 1989s ➤ 9035]: ➤ 310, JbBT 6 ('Altes Testament und christlicher Glaube' 1991) 269-281 / 299-309 / 333-7.

9044 **Oden** T. C., Word of life: SystT 2 (Christology) 1989 ➤ 6,7534: [R]JRel 71 (1991) 447 (J. E. *Burkhart*).

9045 **Pannenberg** Wolfhart, Systematic theology I, [T]*Bromiley* Geoffrey W. GR 1991, Eerdmans. 473 p. $40 [JAAR 59,884].

9046 **Räisänen** Heikki, Beyond NT theology; a story and a programme 1990
→ 6,9149: ᴿCritRR 4 (1991) 220-2 (R. H. *Fuller*); CurrTMiss 18 (1991)
378s (D. *Rhoads*); RExp 88 (1991) 97s (J. D. W. *Watts*).
9047 **Robinson** Donald, Faith's framework; the structure of New Testament
theology 1985 → 2,7238; 3,9176; £4.20 pa. 0-85364-317-2: ᴿEvangel 7,2
(1989) 23 (A. *Olu Igenoza*).
Schweizer Eduard, Theologische Einleitung in das NT 1988 → 3556.
9048 **Siegwalt** Gérard, Dogmatique pour la catholicité évangélique [I. 1986
→ 3,6581] 2/1, L'Église chrétienne dans la société humaine. Genève/P
1991, Labor et Fides / Cerf. 450 p. 2-8309-0633-0. – ᴿRHPR 71 (1991)
506 (*ipse*).
9049 — *Schüssler* Werner, Theologie der recapitulatio — zur Dogmatik
Gérard Sɪᴇɢᴡᴀʟᴛs [1986s]: TR 87 (1991) 1-4.
9050 ᴱ**Sucupira** L., Revista Biblica Brasileira 8,1-3. Fortaleza 1991, Nova
Jerusalém. 240 p. $25 [BL 92,24, J. M. *Dines*: launches a new venture,
theology of the whole Christian Bible, rejecting Liberation Theology
(p. 82-88); *Minette de Tillesse* adds Fᴀɴᴜʟɪ's defense of JEPD against
Wʜʏʙʀᴀʏ, p. 21-46 (-104)].
9051 **Van Buren** Paul, A theology of the Jewish-Christian reality, [Is, 1980
→ 61,k176] 3. Christ in context 1988 → 4,8436.8555 … 6,7418: ᴿRRel 49
(1990) 788s (J. M. *Ballweg*).
9052 **Van Roo** William A., Telling about God 1-3, 1987 → 2,3248 … 6,7418*:
ᴿDivThom 93 (1990) 145-7 (L. *Elders*: unusual, often attractive, sort of
retreat-book in a dogmatic and metaphysical garment).

XVI. Philologia biblica

ᴊ1 **Hebraica** .1 *grammatica.*

9053 **Barr** James, The variable spellings of the Hebrew Bible (Schweich
Lectures 1986) 1989 → 5,9095; 6,9154: ᴿCritRR 4 (1991) 121-6 (F. I. *Andersen*); General Linguistics 31,3s (1991) 185-90 (S. *Levin*); JAOS 111
(1991) 647-650 (Ziony *Zevit*); JStJud 22 (1991) 114-121 (D. N. *Freedman*:
ill-mannered attack on Aʟʙʀɪɢʜᴛ school).
9054 **Deiana** G., *Spreafico* A., Guida allo studio dell'Ebraico biblico 1990
→ 6,9156: ²1991; Lit. 35.000: ᴿAnStoEseg 8 (1991) 295 (M. *Pesce*); Salesianum 53 (1991) 579 (R. *Sabin*).
9055 **Eckhardt** W., Computergestützte Analyse althebräischer Texte …: AOtt
29, 1987 → 3,9193: ᴿCritRR 3 (1990) 118-121 (H. V. *Parunak*).
9056 **Eskhult** Mats, Studies in verbal aspect and narrative technique in
biblical Hebrew prose 1990 → 6,9158: ᴿBiblica 72 (1991) 575-580 (F. I.
Andersen); ZAW 103 (1991) 152s (H. W. *Hoffmann*).
9057 **Garr** W. Randall, Dialect geography of Syria-Palestine, 1000-586 B.C.E.
1985 → 1,8791*b* … 5,9100: ᴿJESHO 32 (1989) 109s (A. *Caquot*).
9058 *Givón* Talmy, The evolution of dependent clause morpho-syntax in
biblical Hebrew: → 409*, ᴱ**Traugott** Elizabeth C., *Heine* Bernd, Approaches to grammaticalization 2 (1991) 257-310.
9059 *Gordon* Constance W., Qᵉᵗûl nouns in clasical Hebrew: AbrNahrain 29
(1991) 83-86.
9060 *a*) *Gross* Walter, Satzfolge, Satzteilfolge und Satzart als Kriterien der
Subkategorisierung hebräischer Konjunktionalsätze, am Beispiel der
bî-Sätze untersucht; – *b*) *Wehrle* Joseph, Die PV *k' = m'aṭ* als Indikator

für den Satzmodus in Sprechakten: → 126, FRICHTER W. Text, 1989, 97-117 / 577-594.

9061 *a*) *Hospers* J.S., Some remarks about the so-called imperative use of the infinitive absolute in classical Hebrew; – *b*) *Tobin* Y., Process and result and the Hebrew infinitive; a study in linguistic isomorphism; – *c*) *Bekkum* Wout J. van, The status of the infinitive in early piyyut: → 77, FHOFTIJZER J. 1991, 97-102 / 194-209 / 1-13.

9062 *a*) *Jongeling* K., On the VSO character of classical Hebrew; – *b*) *Muraoka* Takamitsu, The biblical Hebrew nominal clause with a prepositional phrase; – *c*) *Goldenberg* G., On direct speech and the Hebrew Bible: → 77, FHOFTIJZER J. 1991, 103-111 / 143-151 / 79-96.

9063 **Joüon** Paul, A grammar of biblical Hebrew [1923, ²1947], TEMuraoka Takamitsu; I. Orthography and phonetics; II. Morphology; III. Syntax, Paradigms and Indices: SubsBPont 14. R 1991, Pont. Ist. Biblico. I-II, xlv-352 p.; III. p. 353-779. Lit. 53.000. 88-7653-595-0 [ZAW 104,297, H. W. *Hoffmann*].

9064 **Kittel** Bonnie P., †, EHoffer Vicki, *Wright* Rebecca A., Biblical Hebrew, a text and workbook 1989 → 5,9103; 6,9164: RCBQ 53 (1991) 291s (G. *Vall*: bombarding with too much information from the start causes discouragement); CritRR 4 (1991) 130s (E. C. *Hostetter*).

9065 **Köhn** Rosemarie, Hebraisk grammatikk³ [¹1971, ²1972]. Oslo 1988, Univ. 196 p. – RTsTKi 60 (1989) 55s (A. *Aschim*).

9065* *Kroeze* J. H., Die chaos van die 'genitief' in Bybelse Hebreeus: JSemit 3 (1991) 129-143; Eng. 129.

9066 **La Maisonneuve** Dominique de, L'hébreu biblique par les textes I, 1988 → 5,9105: RRechSR 79 (1991) 116s (J. *Miler*).

9067 **Lambdin** T.O., TESiebenthal H. von, Lehrbuch Bibel-Hebräisch 1990 → 6,9167: RErbeAuf 67 (1991) 241s (R. *Dietzfelbinger*); TLZ 116 (1991) 590s (G. *Begrich*).

9068 **Levi** Jaakov, Die Inkongruenz im biblischen Hebräisch [Inaug.-Diss. Heidelberg 1986] 1987 → 3,9209 ... 5,9106: RCBQ 53 (1991) 676-8 (G. J. *Hamilton* agrees there may be hundreds of examples, not just 88; but offers several reserves); VT 41 (1991) 382s (J. A. *Emerton*).

9068* *Merwe* C. H. J. van der, Applied linguistics and the teaching of Biblical Hebrew; not a bag of tricks, but a confrontation with basics in teaching a foreign language: JSemit 3 (1991) 167-187.

9069 *Millard* A. R., Variable spelling in Hebrew and other ancient texts [BARR J., does not treat 'Was the Bible exceptional?']: JTS 42 (1991) 106-115.

9070 *Müller* Hans-Peter, wa-, ha-, und das Imperfectum consecutivum: ZAHeb 4 (1991) 144-160.

9071 **Niccacci** Alviero, Lettura sintattica della prosa ebraico-biblica; principi e applicazioni: SBF Anal 31. J 1991, Franciscan. xi-264 p. $15 [BL 92,137, W. G. E. *Watson*: workbook for his Syntax].

9072 **Niccacci** Alviero, The syntax of the verb 1990 → 6,9173: RJTS 42 (1991) 625s (A. R. *Millard*); RExp 88 (1991) 96 (J. D. W. *Watts*: indispensable); TLZ 116 (1991) 823-5 (Jutta *Körner*: 127 S. > 218 S., italienischer Text beträchtlich erweitert); ZAW 103 (1991) 164s (H.W. *Hoffmann*).

9073 — *Eskhult* Mats, Text structure in focus [NICCACCI A. 1991]: OrSuec 40 (1991) 95-101.

9074 *Ramos* José A. M., *a*) O sufixo verbal não-acusativo em hebraico antigo; – *b*) Hifil interno e sufixo dativadival: → 422, Didaskalia 20,1 (1990) 67-82 / 211-222.

9075 **Retsö** J., Diathesis in the Semitic languages; a comparative morphological study: StSemLLing 14. Leiden 1989, Brill. xvii-254 p. ƒ96. 90-04-08818-0 [BL 92,138, J. *Barr*: a major intellectual achievement; will influence exegesis; 'diathesis' is the semantic relation between verb and its nouns].

9076 *Revell* E. J., First person imperfect forms with *waw* consecutive — addenda [R. Poswick could not only show why his computer had overlooked some occurrences, but add twelve others]: VT 41 (1991) 127s.

9077 **Ro Soon-Koo** David, Interrogative *ha-* sentences in the Deuteronomic History: Diss. Southern Baptist Theol. Sem. 1991, ᴰ*Kelley* P. 292 p. 91-25197. — DissA 52 (1991s) 903-A.

9078 **Seow** C. L., A grammar for biblical Hebrew 1987 ➤ 3,9224 … 6,9174: ᴿBTrans 41 (1990) 353s (T. D. *Gledhill*).

9079 **Siebesma** P. A., The function of the niphʿal in biblical Hebrew in relationship to other passive-reflective verbal stems and to the puʿal and hophʿal in particular: StSemNeerl. Assen 1991, Van Gorcum. ix-207 p. ƒ49.50. 90-232-2594-5 [BL 92,140, R. S. *Hess*].

9080 **Smith** Mark S., The origins and development of the waw-consecutive; Northwest Semitic evidence from Ugarit to Qumran: HarvSemSt 39. Atlanta 1991, Scholars. xiv-100 p. 1-55540-602-5.

9081 **Soden** Wolfram von, Gab es bereits im vorexilischen Hebräisch Aramaismen in der Bildung und der Verwendung von Verbalformen?: ZAHeb 4 (1991) 32-45.

9082 *a*) *Soden* Wolfram von, Tempus und Modus im älteren Semitischen [ineditum 1988]; – *b*) *Sarauw* Christian, Das altsemitische Tempussystem [< ᶠ*Thomsen* V. 1912, 59-69]; – *c*) *Landsberger* Benno, Prinzipienfragen der semitischen, speziell der hebräischen Grammatik [< OLZ 29 (1926) 967-976]: ➤ 321, WegF 633 (1991) 463-493 / 423-434 / 434-446.

9083 *a*) *Swiggers* P., Nominal sentence negation in biblical Hebrew; the grammatical status of *'ayn*; – *b*) *Talstra* E., Biblical Hebrew clause types and clause hierarchy; – *c*) *Davies* G. I., The use and non-use of the particle *'et* in Hebrew inscriptions: ➤ 77, ᶠHOFTIJZER J. 1991, 173-9 / 180-193 / 14-26.

9084 **Tirkel** Eliezer, L'ebraico è facile, ᵀ*Sciloni* Gaio. F 1990, Giuntina. 272 p. Lit. 30.000. – ᴿStCatt 34 (1990) 975 (U. de *Martino*).

9085 **Waldman** N. M., The recent study of Hebrew 1989 ➤ 5,9117; 6,9177: ᴿBL (1991) 156 (J. C. L. *Gibson*); BO 48 (1991) 612s (J. *Klener*); CritRR 4 (1991) 159 (Z. *Garber*).

9086 **Waltke** Bruce K., O'Connor M., An introduction to biblical Hebrew syntax 1990 ➤ 6,9178: ᴿAndrUnS 29 (1991) 107s (Leona G. *Running*); Biblica 72 (1991) 572-5 (A. *Gianto*); JSS 36 (1991) 331s (T. *Collins*: not elementary but midway toward GESENIUS-KAUTZSCH or JOÜON).

9087 *Young* Ian, The language of the judicial plea from Meṣad Ḥashavyahu: PEQ 122 (1990) 56-58.

9088 **Zohori** Menahem, ⊕ *Ha-Muḥlat* … The absolute infinitive and its uses in the Hebrew language. J 1990, Carmel. 183 p. 965-407-006-5 [OIAc 1,28].

J1.2 Lexica et inscriptiones hebraicae; later Hebrew.

9089 **Alonso Schökel** Luis, Diccionario bíblico hebreo-español 1990s ➤ 6, 9182. – ᴿBibFe 17,49 (1991) 138 (A. *Salas*); NRT 113 (1991) 578s (J.-L. *Ska*); Salesianum 53 (1991) 575s (R. *Sabin*).

9090 *Alonso Schökel* Luis, The Diccionario bíblico hebreo-español (DBHE): ZAHeb 4 (1991) 76-84.

9091 — *Alonso Schökel* Luis, Un sueño de la ciencia bíblica española: RazF 223 (1991) 644-650.

9092 *a) Alonso Schökel* Luis, Sobre diccionarios bilingües; – *b) Görg* Manfred, Der Name im Kontext; Zur Deutung männlicher Personennamen auf -*at* im AT: ➔ 126, ᶠRICHTER W., Text 1991, 1-10 / 81-95.

9093 **Andersen** F. I., *Forbes* A. D., Vocabulary of the OT 1989 ➔ 5,9120; 6,9184: ᴿBiblica 72 (1991) 290-2 (W. *Gross*); JTS 42 (1991) 624s (J. F. A. *Sawyer*: alongside meticulous technology, some old-fashioned outlooks).

9094 *Banitt* Menahem, Une vue d'ensemble sur les glossaires bibliques juifs en France au Moyen Âge: RÉJ 149 (1990) 475s.

9095 [*Baumgartner* W., *Koehler* L.] **Stamm** Johann J., Hebräisches und Aramäisches Lexikon zum AT³ʳᵉᵛ Lfg 4, Leiden 1990, Brill. p. 1081-1659. DM 300. – ᴿTüTQ 171 (1991) 225s (W. *Gross*: some 20 misprints); UF 23 (1991) 444s (M. *Dietrich*, O. *Loretz*: 20 Vorschläge).

9096 *Colless* Brian E., The proto-alphabetic inscriptions of Canaan: Abr-Nahrain 29 (1991) 18-66.

9097 **Davies** G. I., (*Bockmuehl* M. N. A., *al.*), Ancient Hebrew inscriptions; corpus and concordance. C 1991, Univ. xxxiv-535 p. £75. 0-521-40248-4 [BL 92,29, J. C. L. *Gibson*].

9098 *Den Exter Blokland* A. F., Clause-analysis in biblical Hebrew narrative; an explanation and a manual for compilation: TrinJ 11,1 (1990) 73-102.

9099 *Elman* Yaakov, Babylonian Baraitot in the Tosefta and the 'dialectology' of Middle Hebrew: AJS 16 (1991) 1-29.

9100 **Fohrer** Georg, *al.*, Hebräisches und aramäisches Wörterbuch zum AT² 1989 ➔ 5,9129: ᴿTAth 62 (1991) 187-9 (P. *Simotas*).

9101 **Fowler** Jeaneane D., Theophoric personal names ᴰ1980, 1988 ➔ 4,a221 ... 6,9194: ᴿJAOS 111 (1991) 817s (D. M. *Pike*).

9102 **Glinert** Lewis, The grammar of modern Hebrew 1989 ➔ 5,9132; 6,9195; £55: ᴿBO 48 (1991) 614-6 (J. *Klener*); ExpTim 102 (1990s) 26 (J. F. A. *Sawyer*: jargon not for learners: 'pro-words', 'truth disjuncts', 'focus-clefting').

9103 **Hazout** Ilan, Verbal nouns; Theta theoretic studies in [Modern] Hebrew and Arabic ['government and binding theory' 'head (nominalizer)-movement' invoked, but 'theta' not explained]: diss. Mass. 1991. 454 p. 91-32863. — DissA 52 (1991s) 2127-A.

9105 *Klaus* Nathan, ✡ Events of simultaneity in the Bible: BethM 36,127 (1990s) 382-8.

9106 *Kuyt* A., *Wesselius* J. W., The Yavne-Yam ostracon, an exercise in classical Hebrew prose: BO 48 (1991) 726-735.

9107 **Layton** S. C., Archaic features of Canaanite personal names in the Hebrew Bible [diss. 1987, ᴰ*Pardee* D.]: HarvSem Mg 47, 1990 ➔ 6,9202: xiii-299 p. $30 [ZAW, 104,300, I. *Kottsieper*].

9108 *Lübbe* John, Methodological implications in the early signs of a new dictionary of classical Hebrew [11 sample pages and some norms by D. *Clines*, Sheffield]: ZAHeb 4 (1991) 135-143 [a 'new' dictionary should group together words of related meaning, and cite number of occurrences of a particular meaning rather than of the root-form].

9109 *Margalit* Shlomoh, ✡ Name and description: BethM 36,126 (1990s) 223-5.

9110 *Meliṣ* Amram, ✡ Acrostic in the Bible: BethM 36,126 (1990s) 250-266.

9112 [*Gesenius* W.] **Meyer** R., *Donner* H., Hebräisches und aramäisches Handwörterbuch zum AT 1, 1987 ➤ 4,a232 ... 6,9204: ᴿWeltOr 22 (1991) 174-8 (T. *Podella*, many items in detail); WZKM 79 (1989) 305-7 (E. *Kutsch*).

9113 *Muraoka* Takamitsu, *Shavitsky* Ziva, A. IBN EZRA's biblical Hebrew lexicon; the minor prophets II: AbrNahrain 29 (1991) 106-128.

9114 **Murtonen** A., Hebrew in its West Semitic setting I-A 1986 ➤ 2,7036 ...6,9207: ᴿWZKM 79 (1989) 307-9 (S. *Segert*, I-A, Eng.).

9115 ᴱNir Raphael, *Neubach* Abigail, Teaching Hebrew language and literature at the academic level. J 1991, International Center for University Teaching of Jewish Civilization. 43 + ❺ 45 art. 965-222-232-1.

9116 ᴱNir Raphael, *Uval* Ezri, University teaching of modern Hebrew; workshop proceedings I. J 1985, Int.Center J.Civ. xiii p. + ❺ 119. 965-222-051-5. P. 1-6, ❺ *Azar* Moshe, A classification of the construct state; 80-85, ❺ *Schwarzwald* Ora, Feminine formation in Hebrew; 8 others, mostly on modern Hebrew.

9117 **Qimron** E., The Hebrew of the DSS 1986 ➤ 2,7262 ... 5,9112: ᴿJAOS 111 (1991) 137s (G. A. *Rendsburg*).

9118 **Rabin** Chaim, Die Entwicklung der hebräischen Sprache: Heid Hochschule für Jüdische Studien 2, 1988 ➤ 6,9212; DM 9,80: ᴿKratylos 36 (1991) 177-182 (F. *Rundgren*).

9119 *a*) **Rendsburg** Gary A., Diglossia in ancient Hebrew [diss. NYU 1980, 'Evidence for spoken Hebrew in biblical times', ᴰ*Gordon* C.]: AOS 72. NHv 1990, [J]AOS. xxi-233 p. 0-940490-72-2. – 'Diglossia' [< *Ferguson* A.] here means 'distinguishing *within* Hebrew a written and a spoken form'. – *b*) *Ólafsson* Sverrir, On diglossia in ancient Hebrew and its graphic representation: ➤ 41*c*, ᶠCZAPKIEWICZ A., FolOr 28 (1991) 193-205.

9120 **Reymond** Philippe, Dictionnaire d'Hébreu et d'Araméen bibliques. P 1991, Cerf / Soc. Biblique Française. 449 p. F 290. 2-204-04463-6 / SB 2-85300-713-8 [BL 92,139, J. A. *Emerton*: good despite compression].

9121 *Schneider* Wolfgang, Geisterformen [linguistic phantoms: Jos 5 and Jer 9 as proof of a media-waw passive participle]: BibNot 53 (1990) 28s.

9122 **Smelik** K. A. D., Writings from ancient Israel; a handbook of historical and religious documents [1984 ➤ 1,8859], ᵀ*Davies* G. I. E 1991, Clark. ix-191 p. £12.50. 0-567-29202-9 [BL 92,39, J. C. L. *Gibson*].

9123 *Smith* Mark S., *a*) Converted and unconverted perfect and imperfect forms in the literature of Qumran: BASOR 284 (1991) 1-17; – *b*) The *waw*-consecutive at Qumran: ZAHeb 4 (1991) 161-4.

9124 **Spradlin** Michael R., An investigation of conditional sentences in the Hebrew text of Isaiah: diss. Mid-America Baptist Theol. Sem. 1991. 184 p. 91-26375. — DissA 52 (1991s) 1374-A.

9126 *Stamm* Johann J., [➤ 9095] Bericht über den Stand der Arbeit an der 3. Auflage des hebräischen und aramäischen Wörterbuches von Ludwig KOEHLER und Walter BAUMGARTNER [< TZBas 45 (1989) 277-289]: ZAHeb 4 (1991) 85-94.

9127 *Sznol* Shifra, Notas lexicográficas sobre una lista de compuestos griegos en literatura rabínica (siglos I d. C. - X d. C.): Emerita 59 (1991) 327-342.

9128 **Zadok** Ran, The Pre-Hellenistic Israelite anthroponomy and prosopography: OrLovAn 28. Lv 1988, Peeters. xxv-465 p. Fb 4950. – ᴿKratylos 36 (1991) 174-6 (Rüdiger *Schmitt*).

9129 **Zilkha** Avraham, Modern Hebrew-English dictionary. NHv 1989, Yale Univ. vi-306 p. 0-300-04648-0.

9130 *Zurro Rodríguez* Eduardo,   Vocabulario hebreo y léxico ebláita: ➤ 421,
Luso-Esp 1989/91, 67-81.

9130* *Baumgarten* Juan,   Le yiddish: Que sais-je 2552, 1990 [JJS 42 (1991)
289].
9131 *Jacobs* Neil G.,   A reanalysis of the Hebrew status constructus in
Yiddish: HUCA 62 (1991) 305-327.
9132 ᴱ**Katz** David,   Dialects of the Yiddish language: Oxford Winter
Symposium 2. Ox 1988, Pergamon. [v-] 122 p. – ᴿBSO 53 (1990) 402 (L.
Glinert).

J1.3   **Voces** ordine alphabetico *consonantium* **hebraicarum.**

9133 *'dn* nell'onomastica postesilica: Henoch 13 (1991) 283-6 (F. *Israel*).
9134 *aḥk: Barkay* Gabriel,   'Your poor brother'; a note on an inscribed bowl
from Beth Shemesh: IsrEJ 41 (1991) 239-241; 2 fig.
9135 *'ak, raq* [Gn-2 Kgs]: *Merwe* H.J. van der,   The Old Hebrew 'particles'
~: ➤ 126, ᶠRICHTER W., Text 1991, 297-311.
9136 *āmar: Trumer* Penina, ❶ The infinitive constructus of the verb 'to say',
lēmor — a study of its syntactic, semantic and pragmatic usage in biblical
Hebrew: ➤ 303, Teuda 7 (1991) 75-93; Eng. X-XII.
9137 *Chilton* Bruce,   Recent and prospective discussion of *memra*: ➤ 56,
ᶠFOX M., 2 (1991) 119-137.
9138 *az: Mulder* M.J.,   Die Partikel *az* als Konjunktion und Interjektion im
biblischen Hebräisch: ➤ 77, ᶠHOFTIJZER J., 1991, 132-142.
9139 *eš: Morla Asensio* Víctor,   El fuego en el AT ᴰ1988 ➤ 4,a249 ... 6,9233:
ᴿBL (1991) 153 (D. *Clines*); CBQ 53 (1991) 111s (E. J. *Fisher*).
9140 *Bocher* Otto,   Licht und Feuer AT-NT: ➤ 690, TRE 21 (1991) 90-107.
9141 *'ašr* als Konjunktion — Überblick und Versuch einer Klassifikation
der Belege in Gen-2 Kön: ➤ 126, ᶠRICHTER W., Text 1991, 445-469 (T.
Seidl).
9141* *Knauf* Ernst A.,   *Aššur, Šuaḥ* und der stimmlose Sibilant des Assyrischen: BibNot 49 (1989) 13-16.
9142 *Althann* Robert,   Does *'et* (*'æt*) sometimes signify 'from' in the Hebrew
Bible [DAHOOD M., Sirach 16,14; Isa 7,17; Gn 6,11; Jer 29,3: possible]:
ZAW 103 (1991) 121-4.
9143 *Garr* W. Randall,   Affectedness, aspect, and biblical *'et*: ZAHeb 4 (1991)
119-134.
9144 *bdlh* ('Bdellium') — zur Etymologie: BibNot 48 (1989) 12-16 (M. *Görg*).
9145 *gᵉbîrâ: Ben-Barak* Zafrira,   The status and right of the *gᵉbîrâ*: JBL 110
(1991) 23-34.
9146 **Merwe** C.H.J. van der,   The Old Hebrew particle *'gam'* [diss. Stellenbosch 1988, ᴰClaassen W.]: AOtt 34, 1990 ➤ 6,9242: ᴿBL (1991) 153
(J.A. *Emerton*); TR 87 (1991) 280s (K. F. *Diethard Römbeld*).
9147 *dam: Cazelles* H., Sang: ➤ 686, SDB XI, 65 (1991) 1332-1353.
9148 *Cimosa* Mario,   L'uso e il significato di 'sangue' nel Rotolo del Tempio
(RT) e nella Torah biblica: ➤ 565, Sangue 1989/91, 329-337.
9149 *dᵉmût: Martínez Borobio* Emiliano,   DMWT', ṢLM, NṢB, 'Estatua' en la
epigrafía aramea: Sefarad 51 (1991) 85-97.
9150 *dr', drt, dry* ❶ *zrh* II: UF 23 (1991) 79-82 (M. *Dietrich, O. Loretz*).
9151 **ha-:** *Müller* Augustin R.,   Zu den Artikelfunktionen im Hebräischen:
➤ 126, ᶠRICHTER W., Text 1991, 313-329.

9152 *heder:* BethM 36,126 (1990s) 212-9 (D. *Rafel*).

hālak: **Ausín Olmos** Santiago, Moral y conducta en Qumran; estudio lexicográfico y semántico de los verbos de 'movimiento' en la literatura de Qumran: Coll.Teol. 1991 ➤ 9895.

9153* *hāmās:* **Swart** I., In search of the meaning of *hāmās* [wider than 'violence'; injustice of various kinds]; studying an OT word in context: JSemit 3 (1991) 156-166.

9154 *hesed:* **Goldin** Judah, ❷ Good kindness [... 'is there any other kind?']: Tarbiz 60 (1990s) 659-661; Eng. VI.

9155 *yd‘* II 'be humbled, humiliated'?: VT 41 (1991) 48-62 (W. *Johnston*, querying D. WINTON THOMAS); p. 145-163, further comments of J. A. *Emerton*.

9156 *yārā’:* **Costacurta** Bruna, La vita minacciata: AnBib 119, ᴰ1988 ➤ 4,a264 ... 6,9252: ᴿArTGran 53 (1990) 297s (J. L. *Sicre*); BZ 35 (1991) 292s (J. *Becker*); ETL 67 (1991) 148 (E. *Eynikel* uses male pronouns for the author); RechSR (1991) 284s (J.-M. *Carrière*).

9158 *yārad:* **Kuyt** Annelies, Once again: *yarad* [for ‘*alâ*, heavenly ascent] in the Hekhalot literature: FraJudBeit 18 (1990) 45-69 [< JStJud 22,267].

9159 *kᵉ:* **Jenni** Ernst, Zur Semantik der hebräischen Personen-, Tier- und Dingvergleiche: ZAHeb 3 (1990) 133-166.

9160 *kᵉbôd:* **Struppe** U. 1988: ➤ 4,a270; 5,9179: ᴿBZ 35 (1991) 295s (K. *Grünwaldt*).

9161 *kpr:* **Sanders** Todd K., 'Young lion' or [rather, as in all other Semitic languages] 'he forgives'; a note on the name *kpr*: AndrUnS 29 (1991) 71s.

9162 *lō’:* **Ognibeni** Bruno, Tradizioni orali *lo’/lô* 1989 ➤ 4,2547 ... 6,9257: ᴿBO 48 (1991) 240-4 (P. *Cassuto*); CBQ 53 (1991) 681s (W. J. *Fulco*).

9163 *ndr:* **Berlinerblau** Jacques, The Israelite vow; distress or daily life?: Biblica 72 (1991) 548-555.

9164 *noa‘:* **Jenni** Ernst, [*nô‘* + 11] Verba gesticulationis im Hebräischen: ➤ 126, ᶠRICHTER W., Text 1991, 191-203.

9164* *nāšaq:* **Ellington** John, Kissing in the Bible; form and meaning [... in many cultures, people never kiss; renditions like 'suck the jaw', 'lick the lips' miss the point altogether]: BTrans 41 (1990) 409-416.

9165 *smr:* **Lemaire** André: *smr* dans la petite inscription de Kilamuwa (Zencirli): Syria 67 (1990) 323-7; 1 fig. [= amulet].

9166 *‘ibrî:* **LaGrand** James, 'Hebrews' in the Tanak: ProcGLM 11 (1991) 1-8.

9167 *‘d:* **Wilson** E. Jan, Ugaritic *‘d* and an unusual use of Sumerian *id*: Akkadica 74s (1991) 48-53 [akin to *‘ēd* Jos 22,27 but also to Greek *hédos*].

9168 *‘ēdût:* **Lohfink** Norbert, *‘d(w)t* im Deuteronomium und im Königsbüchern: BZ 35 (1991) 86-93.

9169 [*zm...*] **Masson** Michel, Étude d'un parallélisme sémantique; 'tresser' / 'être fort': Semitica 40 (1991) 89-105 ...

9170 *‘am:* **Haas** Peter, The am ha'arets as literary character: ➤ 56, ᶠFOX M., 2 (1991) 139-153.

9171 *‘ānâh:* **Kessler** Rainer, Der antwortende Gott [*‘ānāh* 35 times in Psalms, usually too passively 'hear (or exaudire)' in both LXX and LUTHER]: WDienst 21 (1991) 43-57.

9172 *‘anāwâ:* **Dawes** Stephen B., *‘ānāwâ* in translation and tradition [Talmudic 'humility' also all 6 times in Bible]: VT 41 (1991) 38-48.

9173 *‘aqar, pispas:* **Qimron** Elisha, ❷ New texts from Qumran and their contribution to the Hebrew lexicon: Tarbiz 60 (1990s) 649-651; Eng. VI.

9174 *'ārab: Hoftijzer* J., *Soldt* W.H. van, Texts from Ugarit concerning security [pledge], and related Akkadian and West Semitic material: UF 23 (1991) 189-216.

9175 *'et: Gruber* Mayer J., The reality behind the Hebrew *k't ḥyh* [4 times: 'in this season next year' — as human gestation-period plus three menstrual cycles which normally precede]: ZAW 103 (1991) 271-4.

9176 **peger:** *Bodi* Daniel, Les expressions *pigre malkêhem* dans Ez 43,7b.9 et *pigrê gillûlêkem* dans Lv 26,30 à la lumière des termes akkadiens *pagrû(m)/pagrâ'u(m)* et *maliku* des textes de Mari: ⇥ 140, FSMYTH-FLORENTIN F. 1991, 87-101.

9177 **pḥd, phr,** ❿ *pḥd:* UF 23 (1991) 75-78 (M. *Dietrich,* O. *Loretz*).

9178 *pᵉlî'âh* etc., etymological notes: BethM 36,127 (1990s) 352-7 (J. *Hookerman*).

9179 **prz:** *Na'aman* Nadiv, Amarna *ālāni pu-ru-zi* (EA 137) and biblical *'ry hprzy/hprzwt* ('rural settlements'): ZAHeb 4 (1991) 72-75.

9180 **ṣedeq:** *Ho* Ahuva, Ṣedeq and ṣedaqah in the Hebrew Bible [LA Univ. Judaism, ᴰ*Zevit* Z.]: AmerUnivSt 7/78. NY 1991, P. Lang. [xii-] 212 p. [BL 92,106, J.G. *Snaith*]. 0-8204-1349-6.

9181 **Krašovec** Jože, La justice (ṣdq) de Dieu...: OBO 76, ᴰ1988 ⇥ 4,a307 ... 6,9278: ᴿAntonianum 65 (1990) 383s (M. *Nobile*).

9182 *Lang* F., Gesetz und Gerechtigkeit Gottes in biblisch-theologischer Sicht [Paulus: *tôrâ, ṣᵉdāqâ*]: TBeit 22 (1991) 195-207 [< ZAW 104,282; NTAbs 36,73].

9183 *Rebić* Adalbert, Der Gerechtigkeitsbegriff im AT: IkaZ 19 (1990) 390-6 [> Eng. ᵀᴱ*Asen* B., TDig 39,139-142].

9184 **ṣur:** 'Roc, rocher': ⇥ 664, Catholicisme XIII,95 (1991) 29s (G.-H. *Baudry*).

9186 *Deller* Karlheinz H., Neuassyrisch *qanū, qinītu* und *tidintu:* ⇥ 61, F*GARELLI* P., Marchands 1991, 345-356.

9187 **qara':** *Calder* Norman, The *Qurrā'* ['Qur'an reciters'... in politics] and the Arabic lexicographical tradition: JSS 36 (1991) 297-307.

9188 **qārab:** *Schweizer* Harald, Sprachkritik als Ideologiekritik; zur Grammatikrevision am Beispiel von QRB: [Textwissenschaft, Hermeneutik, Linguistik, Informatik] THLI 1. Tü 1991, Francke. xii-173 p. DM 68. 3-7720-1950-1 [ZAW 104,159, H.W. *Hoffmann*].

9189 **rûaḥ:** *Adamo* David T., Ruach in the OT: DeltioVM 10,2 (1991) 27-37 [TLZ 117,670].

9190 **Dreytza** Manfred, Der theologische Gebrauch von Ruah im AT; eine wort- und satzsemantische Studie [Diss. Basel, ᴰ*Jenni* E. 1989 ⇥ 5,9238]. Giessen 1990, Brunnen. 272 p. 3-7655-9358-3. – ᴿTLZ 116 (1991) 820-2 (J. *Heller*).

9191 **Koch** R., Der Geist Gottes im AT. Fra 1991, Lang. 147 p. Fs 15. 3-631-93885-0 [BL 92,107, J. *Goldingay*].

9192 **Sekki** Arthur E., The meaning of *ruah* at Qumran: SBL diss. 110, 1989 ⇥ 5,9239: ᴿCritRR 4 (1991) 383-5 (J. *Kampen*); TLZ 116 (1991) 502-4 (S. *Holm-Nielsen:* nach wie vor, unlösbar).

9193 RZḤ; **marzeaḥ** [from 1300 B.C.E. to 500 C.E. rabbinics, including Palmyra and Elephantine]: *McLaughlin* John L., The *marzeaḥ* at Ugarit: UF 23 (1991) 265-281 'an association of property-owners', with inference of banqueting not necessarily funereal.

9194 **rîb:** **Bovati** Pietro, Ristabilire la giustizia: AnBib 110, ᴰ1986 ⇥ 2,7458 ... 5,9240: ᴿCBQ 53 (1991) 279s (L. *Laberge:* to be a just person, it is not enough merely to act justly oneself; one must also act for justice denied by others; N. B. he objects that *pathaḥ furtivum* is not transliterated; but this was consistent with the system licitly adopted).

9195 *šûb:* *Willi-Plein* Ina, Šwb šbwt — eine Wiedererwägung: ZAHeb 4 (1991) 55-71.

9195* **Ramos** José A. M., Hifil interno e sufixo datival no tema teológico do regresso de Jave (*šub*): → 422, Didaskalia 20 (1990) 211-222 = → 421, Luso-Esp. 1, 1989/91, 139-149.

9196 *Tropper* Josef, Die hebräischen Verbalwurzeln *šuḥ*, *šḥh* und *šḥḥ*: ZAHeb 4 (1991) 46-54.

9197 *šāḥāh:* *Soden* Wolfram von, Ist im Alten Testament schon vom Schwimmen die Rede?: ZAHeb 4 (1991) 165-170 [Isa 25,11 vielmehr *šaḥāh* 'sich beugen'; auch Ps 6,7; Ezech 47,7 nicht 'schwimmen' in LXX; nie akkadisch oder hethitisch, obgleich ägyptisch schon).

9198 *šôḥad* [bribe, Ex 23,8]: BethM 36,126 (1990s) 220-2 (J. *Hookerman*).

9199 *šākam:* **Janowski** Bernd, Rettungsgewissheit... am Morgen I: WM 59, 1989 → 5,9245; 6,9365: ᴿBL (1991) 112 (J. R. *Porter*); TLZ 116 (1991) 172-4 (P. D. *Miller*: Eng.).

9200 *šamaʿ:* **Arambarri** J., Der Wortstamm 'hören' im AT; Semantik und Syntax eines hebräischen Verbs [kath. Diss. Mainz, ᴰ*Mosis* R.]: SBB 20, 1990 → 6,9362; DM 39: ᴿZAW 103 (1991) 291 (H.-C. *Schmitt*).

9201 *tmh:* *Eckhardt* Walter, *Riepl* Christian, Zur Grammatizität der Grammatik, am Beispiel der Basis G-TMH: → 126, ᴿRICHTER W., Text (1991) 41-55.

J1.5   *Phoenicia, ugaritica* – **North-West Semitic** [→ T5.4].

9202 **Aartun** Kjell, Studien zur ugaritischen Lexikographie, mit kultur- und religionsgeschichtlichen Parallelen, I. Bäume, Tiere, Gerüche, Götterepitheta, Götternamen, Verbalbegriffe. Wsb 1991, Harrassowitz. vii-218 p. DM 88. 3-447-03164-6. – ᴿUF 23 (1991) 439-443 (M. *Dietrich*, O. *Loretz*: praise with warnings).

9203 *Alfaro Asíns* Carmen, Epigrafía monetal púnica y neopúnica en Hispania; ensayo de síntesis: → 9, ᶠARSLAN E., Monetazione 1 (1991) 109-150 + pl. 32-37.

9204 **Aufrecht** Walter E., A corpus of Ammonite inscriptions 1989 → 6,9367: ᴿCBQ 53 (1991) 655s (J. W. *Betlyon*: not for clergy); CritRR 4 (1991) 100s (W. H. *Shea*).

9205 **Bordreuil** Pierre, *Pardee* Dennis, La trouvaille épigraphique de l'Ougarit, 1. Concordance: RS 5, 1989 → 6,9368: ᴿAbrNahrain 29 (1991) 129s (W. G. E. *Watson*); BL (1991) 27s (J. F. *Healey*); BO 48 (1991) 873-5 (W. H. van *Soldt*); CBQ 53 (1991) 457s (W. L. *Fulco*).

9206 *Bordreuil* Pierre, Recherches ougaritiques, 1. Où Baal a-t-il remporté la victoire contre Yam?; 2. La mention du mois d'Adara dans une lettre du roi de Tyr au roi d'Ougarit (RS 18.59, 1.14): Semitica 40 (1991) 17-27. 28-30.

9207 *Branden* A. Van den, Une bague magique [*Garbini* G., RStFen 17 (1989) 41]: BbbOr 33 (1991) 3-14; 1 fig.

9208 *Briquel-Chatonnet* F., Les derniers témoignages sur la langue phénicienne en Orient: RStFen 19 (1991) 3-31.

9209 **Caquot** André, *Tarragon* Jean-Michel de (*Cunchillos* Jesús-Luis), Textes religieux et rituels (Correspondance): Textes ougaritiques 2, LAPO 14, 1989 → 5,9253: ᴿBiblica 72 (1991) 292-7 (E. *Verreet*: zahlreiche Verbesserungen); BO 48 (1991) 605-8 (K. *Spronk*); CBQ 53 (1991) 96s (S.

Segert: a helpful tool; abbreviations from vol. 1 updated but not bibliographies); Orientalia 60 (1991) 128-131 (A. *Gianto*: numerous proposals).

9210 ᴱ**Dearman** Andrew, Studies in the Mesha inscription and Moab 1989 ⇥ 5,392.9256*; 6,9372: ᴿCBQ 53 (1991) 728-730 (S. H. *Horn*: tit. pp. analyses).

9211 *Dietrich* M., *Loretz* O., *a*) Mythen als Schultexte; KTU 1.133; 1.152 und die Vorlagen KTU 1.5 I 11-22; 1.15 IV 6-8; – *b*) Das Löwengesicht-Gefäss KTU 6.62 (RS 25.318): UF 23 (1991) 91-102 / 83s.

9212 *a*) *Fronzaroli* Pelio, La langue d'Ebla; – *b*) *Ḥamadeh* Ḥamîdû, ➋ Phonetic changes in the Ebla language: ⇥ 626, AnASyr 40 (1989/90) 56-63; ➌ 125-6 / ➊ 51-55.

9213 *Garbini* Giovanni, *a*) KAI 78 nella lettura di un filologo: RStFen 19 (1991) 83-88. – *b*) La letteratura dei Fenici: ⇥ 627, Fen. 2, 1987/91, 489-494.

9214 **Huehnergard** John, Ugaritic vocabulary in syllabic transcription: HarvSemSt 32, 1987 ⇥ 3,9468 ... 6,9377: ᴿJNES 50 (1991) 304-6 (D. *Pardee*); VT 41 (1991) 249 (J. A. *Emerton*: skilful).

9214* *a*) *Israel* Felice, Note ammonite III; problemi di epigrafia sigillare ammonita: ⇥ 630, Phoinikeia 1989/91, 201-213. – *b*) *Kaye* Alan S., Does Ugaritic go with Arabic in Semitic genealogical sub-classification?: ⇥ 41c, ᶠCZAPKIEWICZ A., FolOr 28 (1991) 115-128.

9215 *Kotansky* R., A magic gem inscribed in Greek and artificial Phoenician: ZPapEp 85 (1991) 237s; pl. Ibc.

9216 *Krebernik* Manfred, Gt- und tD-Stämme im Ugaritischen: ⇥ 126, ᶠRICHTER W., Text 1991, 227-270.

9217 **Levi della Vida** Giorgio, *Amadasi Guzzo* Maria Giulia, Iscrizioni puniche della Tripolitania (1927-1967): MgArchLibica 22, 1987 ⇥ 3,e371; Lit. 400.000: ᴿBO 48 (1991) 230-2 (E. *Lipiński*).

9218 *Long* Gary A., A kinsman-redeemer in the Phoenician inscription from Cebel Ires Daği: ZAW 103 (1991) 421-4.

9218* *a*) *McCarter* P. Kyle, The dialect of the DeirʿAlla texts ['archaic, local' rather than Aramaic]; – *b*) response, *Pardee* Dennis [Aramaic somewhat likelier]; – *c*) *Greenfield* Jonas C., Philological observations on the DeirʿAlla inscription [not Aramaic, as held in *Hoftijzer's* editio princeps]; (responses, *Davies* G. I., *Huehnergard* J., *Israel* F.) ⇥ 534, Balaam Text 1989/91, 87-89 / 100-5 / 109-120 (143-8; 282-293; 305-317).

9219 *Margalit* B., The Ugaritic poem of Aqht: BZAW 182, 1989 ⇥ 5,9267*; 6,9380: ᴿBO 48 (1991) 608-611 (W. *Herrmann*); JBL 110 (1991) 326s (D. *Pardee*); RB 98 (1991) 138s (J. M. de *Tarragon*); Syria 67 (1990) 752s (A. *Caquot*); ZkT 113 (1991) 75s (J. M. *Oesch*).

9220 *Mitchell* T. C., The Phoenician inscribed ivory box from Ur: PEQ 123 (1991) 119-128; 5 fig.

9221 *Moscati* Sabatino, *a*) Dalle stele votive alle stele funerarie; il 'laboratorio' del Sinis; – *b*) con *Uberti* M. L., La stele di Uras: RStFen 19 (1991) 145-7 / 23-26.

9222 **Müller** Hans-Peter, Die Sprache der Texte von Tell DeirʿAllā im Kontext der nordwestsemitischen Sprachen — mit einigen Erwägungen zum Zusammenhang der schwachen Verbklassen: ZAHeb 4,1 (1991) 1-31.

9223 *Naveh* J., The Phoenician Hundred-Sign: RStFen 19 (1991) 139-144; 10 fig.

9224 **Pardee** Dennis, Les textes para-mythologiques de la 24ᵉ campagne ... Ougarit 1988 ⇥ 4,a349 ... 6,9382: ᴿJAOS 111 (1991) 833-6 (A. *Cooper*: splendid, overcautious); BO 48 (1991) 601-5 (K. *Spronk*).

9225 *Pardee* Dennis, Ugaritic proper nouns: Personal names; month, divine, geographical names: AfO 36s (1989s) 390-513.

9226 **Parker** Simon B., The pre-biblical narrative tradition... Keret/Aqhat: SBL Resources 24, 1989 ➤ 5,9270; 6,9383: ᴿBiblica 72 (1991) 139-142 (G. del *Olmo Lete*); CBQ 53 (1991) 476-9 (S. *Sperling* compares with MARGALIT B.); JAOS 111 (1991) 190s (D. *Pardee*).

9227 *Säve-Söderbergh* Torgny, An alleged 'Canaanite' name [*P3-grgr* + *et, Holthoer* R. in ᶠLICHTHEIM M.]: OrSuec 40 (1991) 226s.

9228 *Shea* William H., The dedication on the Nora Stone [3d letter of last line is *n* rather than (*Cross, Peckham*) *m*]: VT 41 (1991) 241-5.

9229 **Tropper** Josef, Der Ugaritische Kausativstamm und die Kausativbildungen des Semitischen; eine morphologisch-semantische Untersuchung zum S-Stamm und zu den umstrittenen nichtsibilantischen Kausativstämmen des Ugaritischen: AbhLitAltSPal 2. Münster 1990, Ugarit. xii-229 p. 3-927120-06-5.

9230 *Tropper* Josef, *a*) Finale Sätze und *yqtla*-Modus im Ugaritischen; – *b*) Subjunktiv in ugaritischen Relativsätzen?; – *c*) '*rš* 'verlangen'; G-, D- oder N-Stamm: UF 23 (1991) 341-352 (Eng. 341) / 353-5 / 356-8.

J1.6 **Aramaica.**

9231 *Aggoula* Basile, Remarques sur les inscriptions Hatréennes [XIII-XIV] XV (*qšyš*); XVI, Nᵒˢ 388-405: Syria 65 (1988) 193-6 (197-216); 67 (1990) 397-421.

9232 **Arnold** Werner, Das Neuwestaramäische [I. 1989 ➤ 5,9284*b*] 2, Texte aus Ġubba'adin / 3, Volkskundliche Texte aus Ma'lūla / 5. Grammatik: Semitica viva 4. Wsb 1991, Harrassowitz. x-454 p.; xii-382 p.; xxi-410 p. DM je 112. 3-447-03051-8; -166-2; -099-2 [BL 92,133, J.F. *Healey*: another volume of Maalula texts awaited, and a dictionary].

9232* **Arnold** W., Lehrbuch des Neuwestaramäischen [...Ma'lûla] 1989 ➤ 5,9284*a*: ᴿZAW 103 (1991) 291 (H. *Bobzin*).

9233 *Avinery* Iddo, The Aramaic dialect of the Jews of Zakho. J 1988, Israel Acad. 261 p. + ❻ 6 p. – ᴿJAOS 111 (1991) 653-6 (Y. *Sabar*).

9234 *Caen* V.J.J. De, A revised bibliography for the Samalian dialect of Old Aramaic [400 items from 1891-1991]: NewsTarg 18,1 suppl. 6 (1991) [< ZAW 104,274].

9235 *Dempsey* Deirdre, The 'epistolary perfect' in Aramaic letters: BibNot 54 (1990) 7-11.

9236 *Florentin* Moshe, The object suffixes in Samaritan Aramaic and the modes of their attachment to the verb: AbrNahrain 29 (1991) 67-82.

9237 *a*) *Folmer* Margaretha L., Some remarks on the use of the finite verb form in the protasis of conditional sentences in Aramaic texts from the Achaemenid period; – *b*) *Meehan* C., Qal/Pe'al as the passive of Hif'il/Af'el in Mishnaic Hebrew and Middle Aramaic: ➤ 77, ᶠHOFTIJZER J. 1991, 56-78 / 112-131.

9238 *Fox* Samuel E., The phonology and morphology of the Jilu dialect of Neo-Aramaic: JAfAL 3 (1991s) 35-57.

9239 *Greenfield* Jonas C., Asylum at Aleppo; a note on Sfire III, 4-7: ➤ 150, ᶠTADMOR H., Ah Assyria 1991, 272-8.

9240 **Heinrichs** Wolfhart, Studies in Neo-Aramaic 1990 ➤ 6,9401: ᴿJAOS 111 (1991) 789s (S. *Hopkins*); JSS 36 (1991) 343-7 (R. *Macuch*).

9241 **Hoberman** Robert D., The syntax and the semantic of verb morphology in modern Aramaic; a Jewish dialect of Iraqi Kurdistan. NHv 1988,

Amer. Or. Soc. 226 p. – RJAOS 111 (1991) 138s (G. *Krotkoff*); JSS 36 (1991) 125-8 (B. *Poizat*: a modern Aramaic is spoken by some hundred thousand people).

9242 **Jastrow** Otto, Der neuaramäische Dialekt von Hertevin 1988 ➤ 4,a369; 6,9403: RJAfAL 3 (1991s) 77-81 (M. *Tosco*).

9243 *Kotansky* Roy, Two inscribed Jewish Aramaic amulets from Syria [Getty Museum]: IsrEJ 41 (1991) 267-281; 4 fig.

Kottsieper Ingo, Die Sprache der Ahiqarsprüche: BZAW 194, D1990 ➤ 2991.

9244 ELloyd Jones G. Robert WAKEFIELD, On the three languages [Arabic, Aramaic, Hebrew]: MedRenTSt 13. Binghamton 1989, SUNY. xii-260 p. $40 [BL 92,17s, R. *Loewe*]. – RJEH 42 (1991) 159 (R. *Rex* mentions only Greek and Hebrew); JSS 36 (1991) 145-7 (J. Enoch *Powell*: Reuchlin's successor in Tübingen for a year, then at Cambridge with this inaugural).

9245 **Maraqten** Mohammed, Die semitischen Personennamen in den alt- und reichsaramäischen Inschriften aus Vorderasien: TStOrientalistik 5, 1988 ➤ 4,a371*; 6,9404*: RAfO 36s (1989s) 183s (A. *Zaborski*); BO 48 (1991) 25-40 (R. *Zadok*).

9246 **Müller-Kessler** Christa, Grammatik des Christlich-palästinisch-Aramäischen, 1. Schriftlehre, Lautlehre, Formenlehre: TStOrientalistik 6/1. Hildesheim 1991, Olms. xxxiv-342 p.; XI pl. 3-487-09479-7.

9247 *Poizat* Bruno, Une bibliographie commentée sur le néo-araméen: GLECS 18-23 (1973-9) 347-414 [JSS 36,126].

9248 **Porten** B., *Yardeni* Ada, Textbook of Aramaic documents from ancient Egypt 1s, 1988/9 ➤ 2,7529 ... 6,9409: RJSS 36 (1991) 342s (S. P. *Brock*, 2).

9249 **Selby** G. R., Jesus, Aramaic and Greek ... ..., Brynmill. 120 p. £12 [Interp 45,224].

9250 **Sokoloff** Michael, A dictionary of Jewish Palestinian Aramaic of the Byzantine period 1990 ➤ 6,9414: RRÉJ 150 (1991) 484s (J. *Margain*); ZAW 103 (1991) 309 (I. *Kottsieper*).

9250* *Steiner* Richard C., The Aramaic text in demotic script; the liturgy of a New Year's festival imported from Bethel to Syene by exiles from Rash [or Arash, between Babylonia and Elam]: JAOS 111 (1991) 362s.

9251 *Voigt* Rainer, Die sog. Schreibfehler im Altaramäischen und ein bislang unerkannter Lautwandel: OrSuec 40 (1991) 236-245.

9252 EYadin Yigael, *Naveh* Joseph, [*Meshorer* Yaacov], The Aramaic and Hebrew Ostraca and jar inscriptions [Coins]: Masada Yadin Excavations 1963-5, I. J 1989, Israel Exploration Soc. – RJBL 110 (1991) 340-3 (J. J. *Collins*, also on II and Hever cave of letters).

J1.7 **Syriaca.**

9253 *Abou Assaf* Ali, Inscription syriaque au Musée de Ma'aret al No'man, TKhoury W.: ➤ 626, AnASyr 40 (1989/90) 161s.

9254 *Bobzin* Hartmut, Über eine bisher unbekannte europäische Bezeugung des Terminus 'Karsûnî' [NTSyrische Handschriften 1705] im 16. Jahrhundert: JSS 36 (1991) 259-261.

9255 *Briquel-Chatonnet* Françoise, Note sur l'origine du manuscrit syriaque 366 de la Bibliothèque Nationale de Paris: VT 41 (1991) 119-121.

9256 *Brock* Sebastian P., Syriac culture in the seventh century: Aram 1 (1989) 268-280.

Desreumaux Alain, Répertoire des ... manuscrits syriaques 1991 ➤ 890.

9257 **Gignoux** Philippe, Incantations magiques syriaques 1987 ➤ 3,9543 ...
6,9425: ᴿBO 48 (1991) 705-716 (J.W. *Wesselius*).

9258 *Goldenberg* Gideon, On predicative adjectives and Syriac syntax: BO
48 (1991) 716-726.

9259 **Kiraz** George A., Syriac primer ...: JStOT Manuals 5, 1989 ➤ 5,9322;
6,9427: ᴿCBQ 53 (1991) 290s (E.G. *Mathews*); VT 41 (1991) 252s (Erica
Hunter seems to want more rather than less of the same).

9260 *Maróth* Miklós, Eine unbekannte [syrische] Version der Georgios-Le-
gende aus Turfan: AltOrF 18 (1991) 86-108: text, translation, comment;
pl. I-IX.

9261 ᵀᴱ**Martikainen** Jouko, Johannes I. SEDRA (Patr. Antioch.), Einleitung,
Syrische Texte; Wörterverzeichnis: GöOrF 1/34. Wsb 1991, Harrassowitz. x-291 p. 3-447-03114-X.

9262 **Muraoka** Takamitsu, Classical Syriac for Hebraists 1987 ➤ 3,9550 ...
6,9428: ᴿJAfAL 3 (1991s) 76s (G. *Krotkoff*).

9263 *Polotsky* H.J., Modern Syriac conjugation [< ᶠ*Rundgren* F., OrSuec 33
(1986) 323-332], ᵀ*Hoberman* Robert D.: JSS 36 (1991) 263-277.

9264 *Rompay* Lucas van, Some reflections on the use of post-predicative *hwā*
in classical Syriac: ➤ 77, ᶠHOFTIJZER J. 1991, 210-9.

9265 ᵀᴱ**Selb** Walter, Sententiae syriacae; Glossar: Szb 567. W 1990.
Österr.Akad. 219 p. 3-7001-1798-1.

9265* ᴱ**Strothmann** Werner, Syrische Passionslieder: GöOrF 1/32, 1989
➤ 6,9432: ᴿBSO 54 (1991) 147 (S. *Brock*); JSS 36 (1991) 201-4 (also
S.P. *Brock*).

9266 *Zonta* Mauro, Nemesiana syriaca; new fragments from the missing
Syriac version of the De natura hominis: JSS 36 (1991) 223-258.

J2.1 **Akkadica** (sumerica).

9267 *Alster* Bendt, The instructions of Urninurta and related compositions
[Sumerian, with some proposed improvements on J. van DIJK 1955 and
1976]: Orientalia 60 (1991) 141-157.

9269 *Arnaud* Daniel, Une lettre de Kamid el-Loz [akk.; rapport avec
Amarna]: Semitica 40 (1991) 7-16; facsim; 5 phot.

9270 **Black** Jeremy A., Sumerian grammar in Babylonian theory²ʳᵉᵛ [¹1984
(diss. Oxford 1980) ➤ 6,7964]: StPohl 12. R 1991, Pont. Ist. Biblico.
xii-165 p.; ill. 88-7653-443-3. – ᴿWZKM 78 (1988) 282-5 (M. *Krebernik*,
¹1984).

9271 **Borger** Rykle, Assyrisch-babylonische Zeichenliste⁴: AOAT 33. Neuk/
Kevelaer 1988, Neuk./Butzon & B. x-452 p. DM 86 [Egb zu¹, 40 p.;
DM 4]. 3-7887-0668-6 [-9-4]. – ᴿJAOS 111 (1991) 836s (J.S. *Cooper*).

9272 **Borger** Rykle, Ein Brief Sîn-Iddinams von Larsa an den Sonnengott
sowie Bemerkungen über 'Joins' und das 'Joinen': NachGö ph/h 1991/2.
Gö 1991, Vandenhoeck & R. 45 p.; ill.

9273 **CAD**: The Chicago Assyrian Dictionary, ᴱ**Reiner** Erica, *Biggs* Robert
D., 15 'S' 1984 ➤ 65,758 ['Q' 1982 ➤ 63,784; 65,9329]: ᴿAfO 36s (1989s)
92-106 (Dominique *Charpin*, Q); BO 48 (1991) 154-7 (R. *Borger*, S); OLZ
86 (1991) 488-492 (W. von *Soden*, S, some 50 addenda); Orientalia 60
(1991) 109-116 (W. *Mayer*) 116-120 (W.H. van *Soldt*, S).

9274 **D'Agostino** Franco, Il sistema verbale sumerico nei testi lessicali di Ebla;
saggio di linguistica tassonomica: StSemit NS 7. R 1990, Univ. x-189 p.

9275 *Dietrich* M., *Meyer* W., Beiträge zum Hurritischen (I); Einzelfragen zu
Grammatik und Lexikon des Mitanni-Briefs: UF 23 (1991) 107-126.

9276 a) *Edzard* Dietz O., Sargon's report on Kish; a problem in Akkadian philology; – b) *Lambert* W. G., An unknown king in an unknown city; – c) *Moran* William L., Assurbanipal's message to the Babylonians (ABL 301), with an excursus on figurative *biltu*; – d) *Grayson* A. Kirk, Old and Middle Assyrian Royal Inscriptions — marginalia; – e) *Abusch* Tsvi, The ritual tablet and rubrics of Maqlû; toward the history of the series; – f) *Jacobson* Thorkild, Abstruse Sumerian; – g) *Cogan* Mordechai, A plaidoyer on behalf of the royal scribes: → 150, ᶠTADMOR H., Ah Assyria 1991, 258-263 / 314-9 / 320-331 / 264-6 / 233-253 / 279-291 / 121-8.

9277 **Gianto** A., Word order variation in the Akkadian of Byblos: StPohl 15, 1990 → 6,9448: ᴿRHPR 71 (1991) 201 (J.-G. *Heintz*, aussi sur la traduction de MORAN W. et compléments).

9277* a) *Hayes* John, Some thoughts on the Sumerian genitive; – b) *Watanabe* Kazuko, Segenswünsche für den assyrischen König in der 2. Person Sg.; – c) *Yoshikawa* Mamoru, Focalization in Sumerian verbs: AcSum 13 (1991) 185-194 / 347-387 / 389-417.

9278 **Hecker** K., Rückläufiges Wörterbuch des Akkadischen: Santag 1 (Arbeiten und Untersuchungen zur Keilschriftkunde). Wsb 1990, Harrassowitz. xii-316 p. DM 112. 3-447-02868-8 [BL 92,136, W. *Lambert*: not for Hebraists].

9279 **Huehnergard** John, The Akkadian of Ugarit 1989 → 5,5240; 6,9453: ᴿOLZ 86 (1991) 45-48 (W. von *Soden*); Syria 67 (1990) 753-5 (Florence *Malbran-Labat*).

9280 *Hummel* Siegbert, Beziehungen des Sumerischen zu einigen Sprachen im protoaltaischen Substrat: Anthropos 86 (1991) 174-184.

9281 *Huÿssteen* P. J. J. van, Assyrianisms in the Emar letters [*Arnaud* D.]: JSemit 3 (1991) 109-121.

9282 **Izre'el** Shlomo, Amurru Akkadian; a linguistic study [diss. TA 1985] + *Singer* Itamar, History of Amurru: HarvSemSt 40s. Atlanta 1991, Scholars. 387 p.; 253 p. 1-55540-633-5.

9283 *La Penna* Antonio, Un'altra favola esopica di origine babilonese: Maia 43 (1991) 163-5.

9283* **Lara Peinado** Federico, Himnos sumerios; estudio preliminar, traducción y notas. M 1988, Tecnos. – ᴿGerión 8 (1990) 305 (G. *Rueda Muñoz de S. Pedro*).

9284 **Longman** Tremper[III], Fictional Akkadian autobiography; a generic and comparative study. WL 1991, Eisenbrauns. xi-274 p. $29.50. 0-931464-41-2 [BL 92,118, W. G. *Lambert*: a biblical scholar but with Assyriological training and guidance of W. *Hallo*].

9285 **Oberhuber** Karl, Sumerisches Lexikon zu REISNER, Hymnen 1896 etc. 1990 → 6,9462: ᴿAfO 36s (1989s) 126-131 (R. *Borger*).

9286 *Römer* W. H. P., Zum sog. Gudam-Text: MiscSum 2: BO 48 (1991) 363-378.

9287 **Sigrist** Marcel, Messenger texts from the British Museum. Potomac MD 1990, Capital Decisions. 46 p. + 337. 0-962-0013-3-2.

9288 **Smet** W. de, 'Kashshû' in Old-Babylonian documents: Akkadica 68 (1990) 1-19.

9289 **Soden** Wolfram von, ⁴*Röllig* Wolfgang, Das akkadische Syllabar [¹1918; ²(*Röllig*) 1966]: AnOr 42. R 1991, Pont. Ist. Biblico. xli-76 + 21* p. 88-7653-257-9.

9290 **Soden** Wolfram von, Introduzione all'orientalistica antica 1989 → 5, 9857; 6,9467: ᴿSalesianum 53 (1991) 175 (R. *Sabin*).

9291 **Soden** W. von, Aus Sprache... Babyloniens, N 1989 → 5,360: ᴿOLZ 86 (1991) 511s (H. *Freydank*).
9292 **Soldt** Wilfred H. van, Studies in the Akkadian of Ugarit; dating and grammar: AOAT 40. Kevelaer/Neuk 1991, Butzon & B / Neuk.-V. xxiii-805 p. [TR 88,162]. 3-7666-9674-2 / Neuk 3-7887-1337-2. — Plan omitted from p. 142 and corrections supplied in UF 23 (1991) 339s; summary p. 452.
9293 *Vajman* A. A., Beiträge zur Entzifferung der archaischen Schriften Vorderasiens II. der proto-sumerischen Schrift *a-d*: BaghMit 21 (1990) 91-123.
9294 **Veldhuis** Niek, A cow of Sîn: Library of Oriental Texts 2. Groningen 1991, Styx. 70 p. 90-72371-28-3.
9295 **Yoshiwara** R. [= *Ahlberg* Roger], Sumerian and Japanese; a comparative language study. Chiba 1991, Japan English Service. vi-142 p. 4-915809-50-1 [OIAc 1,27].

ᴊ2.7 **Arabica.**

9295* *Ambros* Arne A. [→ a849], Syntaktische und stilistische Funktionen des Energikus im Koran: WZKM 79 (1989) 35-56.
9296 *Biondi Assali* Estela, Análisis de oraciones estativas en Arabe (II) [con *kāna*]: BAsEspOr 26 (1990) 285-293.
9297 **Blau** Joshua, Studies in Middle Arabic and its Judaeo-Arabic variety. J 1988, Magnes. 482 p. 28 art.; 1959-87. – ᴿJAfAL 3 (1991s) 67-71 (B. *Hary*).
9298 *Bloch* Ariel A., On attractional pronouns in classical Arabic; a contribution to general syntax: JAfAL 3 (1991s) 1-8.
9299 **Borg** Alexander, Cypriot Arabic 1985 → 2,7574 ... 4,a427: ᴿOLZ 86 (1991) 408s (H.-R. *Singer*).
9300 *Corré* Alan D., A 'dictionary' and chrestomathy of modern literary Judeo-Arabic [302 texts]. Milwaukee 1989, Univ. Wisconsin-M. 109 p.; 11 disks. – ᴿJAOS 111 (1991) 612s (B. *Hary*).
9301 *Durand* Olivier, L'affixe verbal -ta- et un archaïsme chamito-sémitique pré-flexif: RSO 64 (1990) 247-253.
9302 **Fischer** Wolfdietrich, Grammatik des klassischen Arabisch²ʳᵉᵛ [¹1972] 1987 → 6,9478: ᴿWZKM 79 (1989) 269 (A. A. *Ambros*).
9303 **Forstner** Martin, Materialien für den Arabischunterricht unter Berücksichtigung des Häufigkeitswortschatzes. Wsb 1988, Reichert. 304 p. DM 44. – ᴿWZKM 79 (1989) 279s (A. A. *Ambros*).
9304 **Gruber-Miller** Ann Marie, Internal developments in the loss of Arabic case-endings: diss. Ohio State 1991, ᴰ*Joseph* B. 237 p. 92-01670. – DissA 52 (1991s) 3257-A.
9305 **Harbi** Abdallah, Al-. A syntactic approach to Arabic verbal morphology: diss. Essex 1990. 369 p. BRD-93390. – DissA 52 (1991s) 1729-A.
9306 *a) Hatim* Basil, The pragmatics of argumentation in Arabic; the rise and fall of a text type; – *b) Teeffelen* Toiné van, Argumentation and the Arab voice in Western bestsellers: Text 11,2 (1991) 189-199 / 241-266.
9307 **Henninger** J., Arabica varia 1989 → 5,279: ᴿAnthropos 86 (1991) 361-3 (W. *Dostal*); WeltOr 22 (1991) 222s (Katharina *Hackstein*).
9308 **Hinds** Martin, *Badawi* El-Said, A dictionary of Egyptian Arabic: Arabic-English. Beirut 1986, Librairie du Liban. xviii-981 p. £45. – ᴿBO 48 (1991) 290-2 (A. J. *Gully*).
9309 ᴱ**Kay** Ernest, Arabic computer dictionary, English-Arabic, Arabic-English. NY 1986, Routledge-KP. 177 p. + ❹ 127 p. £30. – ᴿOLZ 86

(1991) 406-8 (E. *Schulz*: one of three on recent technical terms; not specified clearly as the 'military' and 'civil engineering' columns).

9310 **Krahl** Günther, *Gharieb* Gharieb M., Wörterbuch arabisch-deutsch 1984 ➤ 1,9148 ('Krehl', 'Charieb'): ᴿOLZ 86 (1991) 404-6 (W. *Vycichl*).

9311 *Macdonald* M.C.A., a) Epigraphic gleanings [J. MANKIN's 1932 Safaitic] from the archive of the PEF: PEQ 123 (1991) 109-116; 3 fig.; – b) HU 501 and the use of S³ in Taymanite: JSS 36 (1991) 11-35; 3 fig.

9312 **McGuire** Russell, Colloquial Arabic of Egypt. L 1986, Routledge-KP. 193 p. – ᴿJAOS 111 (1991) 199s (A.S. *Kaye*: *abadan* for never is a 'mistake' in Egypt; you have to say *'umur* + suff.).

9313 *Nebe* G.W., Eine spätsabäisch-jüdische Inschrift mit satzeinleitendem doppeltem Amen aus dem 4./6. Jahrundert nach Chr.?: JStJud 22 (1991) 235-253.

9314 **Osman** Mirghani E., On the communicative role of word-order in written Modern Standard Arabic; a contribution to functional linguistics: diss. Salford. 274 p. BRD-92725. – DissA 52 (1991s) 902s-A.

9315 **Owens** J., Foundations... medieval Arabic grammatical theory 1988 ➤ 6,9482: ᴿJAOS 111 (1991) 395-9 (M.G. *Carter*: numerous errors preclude confidence).

9316 *Owens* Jonathan, Models for interpreting the development of medieval Arabic grammatical theory: JAOS 111 (1991) 225-238 [239-259, *Sells* Michael, male-female in Sura 92,1s].

9317 *Pirenne* J., *al.*, Corpus des inscriptions et antiquités sud-arabes 1977-86 ➤ 3,9634*; 5,9382: ᴿRHPR 71 (1991) 209-214 (J.-G. *Heintz*).

9318 **Ricks** Stephen D., Lexicon of inscriptional Qatabanian: StPohl 14, 1989 ➤ 5,9385; 6,9484: ᴿJSS 36 (1991) 134-142 (A.F.L. *Beeston*: laborious compiling good; interpretation unoriginal); Orientalia 60 (1991) 131-3 (R. *Weipert*).

9319 **Schall** Anton, Elementa arabica 1988 ➤ 4,a443; 6,9488: ᴿWZKM 79 (1989) 274-6 (A.A. *Ambros*).

9320 **Sughayil** Khalil I al-, Aspects of comparative Jordanian and modern standard Arabic phonology: diss. Michigan State. East Lansing 1990. 275 p. 91-17788. — DissA 52 (1991s) 148-A.

9321 **Tarouti** Ahmed F. al-, Temporality [not aspect as traditionally held] in Arabic grammar and discourse: diss. UCLA 1991, ᴰ*Anderson* R. 397 p. 92-00915. — DissA 52 (1991s) 2524-A.

9322 **Ullmann** Manfred, Aufs Wasser schreiben 1989 ➤ 6,9493: ᴿOLZ 82 (1991) 56s (E. *Schulz*); WeltOr 22 (1991) 213s (A. *Heinen*).

9323 **Ullmann** Manfred, Das arabische Nomen generis [Kollektiva]: AbhGö ph/h 3/176. Gö 1989, Vandenhoeck & R. 111 p. DM 65 [OLZ 87,272, S. *Wittig*].

9324 a) *Veersteegh* Kees, Two conceptions of irreality in Arabic grammar; IBN HIŠĀM and IBN AL-ḤĀGIB on the particle *law*; – b) *Tarrier* Jean-Michel, À propos de sociolinguistique de l'arabe; présentation de quelques difficultés: BÉtOr 43 ('De la grammaire de l'arabe aux grammaires des Arabes' 1991) 77-92 / 1-15.

9325 **Voigt** Rainer M., Die infirmen Verbaltypen des Arabischen und das Biradikalismus-Problem: Mainz Or.-Komm. 39, 1988 ➤ 4,a448 ... 6,9494: ᴿJSS 36 (1991) 116-122 (W. von *Soden*).

J3 Aegyptia.

9326 **Barta** Winfried, a) Zur Mutilation tradierter Texte am Beispiel des Kannibalenhymnus; – b) Phonetische Substitutionen in den Handschriften

der Lebenslehre des Ani: ZäSpr 118 (1991) 10-20 / 103; – c) Die Le-
xikostatistik der Pyramidentexte des Unas (mit einem Nachtrag zu *jn* als
Pleneschreibung der Präposition *n*): GöMiszÄg 121 (1991) 25-30.

9327 a) *Barta* Winfried, Zu ungewöhnlicheren Verwendungsweisen des selb-
ständigen Personalpronomens im Alt- und Neuägyptischen; – b) *Seidl-
mayer* Stephan J., Weitere Überlegungen zu einem philologisch-pro-
sopographischen Texterschliessungssystem: GöMiszÄg 125 (1991) 7-13 /
53-111.

9328 *Beaux* Nathalie, Cultures et supports en Égypte ancienne; remarques
iconographiques et paléographiques autour du signe M 43: LOrA 3
(1991) 205-214.

9329 **Betrò** Maria Carmela, Racconti di viaggio e di avventura dell'antico
Egitto [Sinuhe, Bentresh]: Testi VO Antico. Brescia 1990, Paideia. 85 p.
Lit. 13.000 – ᴿArcheo 65 (1990) 137 (S. *Moscati*).

9330 *Boyaval* Bernard, 'Les âges' de Sakaon [lui-même varie de 10 ans]: CdÉ
65 (1990) 321s.

9331 *Brashear* William, *Hoogendijk* Francisca A. J., Corpus tabularum li-
gnearum ceratarumque aegyptiarum, Einleitung, Holzbretter als Schrift-
träger in Ägypten: Enchoria 17 (1990) 21-54.

9332 a) *Bresciani* Edda, L'amore per il paese natio nel mito egiziano del-
l' 'Occhio del Sole' in demotico; – b) *Cenival* Françoise de, Lettre de-
mandant la libération d'un prisonnier (P. dém. Lille 5), provenance
Ghoran (Fayoum); date 20 août 245 av.n.è.: ➤ 40, Mém. CLÈRE J. 1991,
35-38 / 39-46.

9333 **Broze** Michèle, La princesse de Bakhtan; essai d'analyse stylistique: Mg.
R. Élisabeth 6. Bru 1989, Fond. Ég. R. Élisabeth. 125 p. Fb 800. – ᴿBO
48 (1991) 456-9 (J. *Winand*); OLZ 86 (1991) 368s (K. A. *Kitchen*: a
fairy-tale about a Pharaoh composed of some names of Tuthmosis IV and
Ramesses II).

9334 **Brunner-Traut** Emma, Frühformen des Erkennens am Beispiel Altägyp-
tens. Da 1990, Wiss. xi-210 p. 3-534-08149-8.

9334* **Budge** E. A. Wallis, Egyptian language; easy lessons in Egyptian hiero-
glyphics with sign list. L 1989 = 1910 (1983 pa.), Routledge. viii-246 p.
0-415-04330-1.

9335 *Callender* V. G., A contribution to discussion on the title of *sšt nṯr*
['daughter of the god']: StAäK 18 (1991) 89-111.

9335* **Caluwe** Albert de, Un Livre des Morts sur bandelette de momie
(Bru Musées E. 6179): BtAeg 18. Bru 1991, Fond. Reine Élisabeth.
xxviii-40 p.

9336 **Cenival** Françoise de, Le mythe de l'œil du soleil; translitération et
traduction avec commentaire philologique: Demotische Studien 9.
Sommerhausen 1988, Zauzich. DM 96. – ᴿEnchoria 18 (1991) 205-215
(R. *Jasnow*: meets challenge of SPIEGELBERG 1917).

9337 **Champollion** Jean-François, Grammaire égyptienne ou principes gé-
néraux de l'écriture sacrée égyptienne appliquée à la représentation de la
langue parlée 1836 (1941), ᴱ*Ziegler* Christiane. P 1990, Institut de
l'Orient. 2-905304-00-6 [OIAc 1,13].

9337* a) *Collier* Mark, Constructions with *ḥ3* revisited: GöMiszÄg 120
(1991) 13-32.

— b) *Derchain* Philippe, Les hiéroglyphes à l'époque ptolémaïque: ➤ 630,
Phoinikeia 1989/91, 243-256.

9338 **Diop** Cheikh Anta, Nouvelles recherches sur l'égyptien ancien et les

langues négro-africaines modernes. P 1988, Présence Africaine. 221 p.
2-7087-0507-5 [OIAc 1,15].

9339 **Doret** Eric, The narrative verbal system of Old and Middle Egyptian
1986 → 2,7603 ... 6,9520: ᴿJNES 50 (1991) 56-59 (A. *Loprieno*); WZKM
79 (1989) 197-220 (H. *Satzinger*, also on LOPRIENO A. 1986).

9340 *a) Egberts* A., The chronology of the report of Wenamun; – *b) Collier*
Mark, The relative clause and the verb in Middle Egyptian; – *c) Depuydt*
Leo, Late Egyptian *'inn*, 'if', and the conditional clause in Egyptian:
JEA 77 (1991) 57-67 / 23-42 / 69-78.

9341 *Eichler* Eckhard, a) Untersuchungen zu den Königsbriefen des Alten
Reiches; – b) Untersuchungen zu den Wasserträgern von Deir el-Medineh
II: StAäK 18 (1991) 141-171 / 173-205.

9341* *a) Eyre* Christopher J., Was ancient Egyptian really a primitive
language?; – *b) Allen* James P., Form, function, and meaning in the
early Egyptian verb; – *c) Depuydt* Leo, On distinctive and isolating
emphasis in Egyptian and in general; – *d) Gilula* Mordechai, The King's
Egyptian; – *e) Loprieno* Antonio, Focus, mood, and negative forms;
Middle Egyptian syntactic paradigms and diachrony; – *f) Meltzer*
Edmund S., Participles, relative forms and gemination in Middle
Egyptian: → 620, LAeg 1990/1, 97-123 / 1-32 / 33-56 / 125-7 / 201-226 /
227-240.

9342 *a) Fecht* Gerhard, Die Belehrung des Ba und der 'Lebensmüde'; – *b)*
Westendorf Wolfhart, Die 'Löwenmöbelfolge' und die Himmels-Hie-
roglyphe: → 85*c*, ᶠKAISER W., MiDAI-K 47 (1991) 113-126 / 425-434;
9 fig.

9342* **Fischer** Henry G., L'écriture et l'art de l'Égypte ancienne; quatre
leçons sur la paléographie et l'épigraphie pharaoniques: Collège de
France, essais et conférences 1986 → 2,7606; 2-13-038788-8: BO 48
(1991) 110s (N. *Cherpion*: aussi sur le mobilier et sur différence d'ap-
préciation entre l'Europe et l'Amérique).

9343 **Fischer-Elfert** Hans-W., Literarische Ostraka der Ramessidenzeit 1986
→ 3,9674; 4,a472: ᴿJAOS 111 (1991) 832s (R. *Jasnow*).

9344 **Fischer-Elfert** Hans-Werner, Die satirische Streitschrift des Papyrus
Anastasi I; Übersetzung und Kommentar: ÄgAbh 44, 1986 → 6,9523;
3-447-02612-X: ᴿBO 48 (1991) 87-90 (J. *López*).

9345 *a) Foster* John L., Wordplay in The Eloquent Peasant, the eighth
complaint; – *b) Goelet* Ogden, The nature of the term pr-ˁ3 during
the Old Kingdom: → 135*, ᶠSCHULMAN A., BEgSem 10 (1989s) 61-76 /
77-90.

9345* ᴱ**Frandsen** Paul J. [*Zauzich* K.-T., *al.*], Demotic texts from the collection: Carlsberg Papyri 1 / Niebuhr Publ. 15. K 1991, Univ. vii-141 p.;
10 pl. 87-7289-361-0.

9346 *Goedicke* Hans, a) About an early use of the emphatic possessive
expression: VarAeg 6 (1990) 139-153 (–160); – b) About the hermeneutics
of pyramid texts; Pyr. Spell 439: StAäK 18 (1991) 215-232.

9346* *a) Goldwasser* Orly, On dynamic canonicity in Late-Egyptian; the
literary letter and the personal prayer; – *b) Israeli* Shlomit, Narrative in
the Medinet Habu war inscriptions: → 620, LAeg 1 (1990/1) 129-141 /
155-164.

9347 **Grenier** Jean-Claude, Les titulatures des empereurs romains dans la
documentation en langue égyptienne: PapyrBrux 22, 1989 → 5,9425:
ᴿAegyptus 71 (1991) 281s (S. *Pernigotti*); RÉG 104 (1991) 616-9; 1 fig.
(J.-L. *Fournet*).

9347* **Hannig** Rainer, Pseudopartizip und $sdm.n=f$; der Kernbereich des mittelägyptischen Verbalsystems II: HÄgBei 32. Hildesheim 1991, Gerstenberg. xxxvii-326 p. 3-8067-8123-0 [OLZ 87,517, W. *Schenkel*].

9348 **Janssen** Jac J., Late Ramesside letters and communications: Hieratic Papyri 6. L 1991, British Museum. 57 p., 109 pl. 0-7141-0957-6.

9348* **Johnson** Janet H., Thus wrote 'Onchsheshonqy: SAOC 45, 1986 → 2,7615 ... 5,9431: ᴿOLZ 86 (1991) 369s (U. *Kaplony-Heckel*).

9349 a) *Junge* Friedrich, How to study Egyptian grammar and to what purpose; a summary of sorts; – b) *Silverman* David P., Texts from the Amarna period and their position in the development of ancient Egyptian; – c) *Ray* John D., An approach to the $sdm-f$; forms and purposes; – d) *Doret* Éric, Cleft-sentence, substitutions et contraintes sémantiques en égyptien de la première phase (V-XVIII Dynastie); – e) *Ritter* Thomas, The distribution of past tense verbal forms in 18th dynasty non-literary texts from Kamose to Amenophis III: → 620, LAeg 1990/1, 389-426 / 301-314 / 243-258 / 57-96 / 259-292.

9349* *Kahl* Jochem, Von ẖ bis ḳ; Indizien für eine 'alphabetische' Reihenfolge einkonsonantiger Lautwerte in spätzeitlichen Papyri: GöMiszÄg 122 (1991) 33-45; 6 fig.; II pl.

9350 a) *Kammerzell* Frank, Augment, Stamm und Endung; zur morphologischen Entwicklung der Stativkonjugation; – b) *Groll* Sarah I., Semiotics, pragmatics and structuralism as a means to determine the degree of correctedness between utterances, I: p3-A versus Ø-A; – c) *Satzinger* Helmut, May themes follow on rhemes, and why might they do so?; – d) *Sweeney* Deborah, What's a rhetorical question?; – e) *Winand* Jean, Le verbe iy/iw; unité morphologique et sémantique; – f) *Vernus* Pascal, Le rhème marqué; typologie des emplois et effets de sens en Moyen Égyptien (temps seconds, cleft sentences et constructions apparentées dans les stratégies de l'énonciateur): → 620, LAeg 1 (1990/1) 165-199 / 143-153 / 293-300 / 315-331 / 357-387 / 333-355.

9350* a) *Klemm* Dietrich & Rosemarie, Calcit-Alabster oder Travertin? Bemerkungen zu Sinn und Unsinn petrographischer Bezeichnungen in der Ägyptologie: GöMiszÄg 122 (1991) 57-70; 2 fig.; – b) *Koenig* Yvan, Les ostraca hiératiques du Musée du Louvre: RÉgp 42 (1991) 95-116; facsimiles.

9351 a) *Loprieno* Antonio, The sign of literature in the Shipwrecked Sailor; – b) *Rössler-Köhler* Ursula, Bemerkungen zur Totenbuch-Tradierung während des Neuen Reiches und bis Spätzeitbeginn; – c) *Thissen* Heinz J., Ägyptologische Beiträge zu den griechischen magischen Papyri; – d) *Graefe* Erhart, Über die Verarbeitung von Pyramidentexten in den späten Tempeln [... Spruch 600, Umhangen des Halskragens]; – e) *Broze* Michele, 'Entretemps ...' 'ḥ'.n.f + pseudoparticipe dans une narration: → 43, ᶠDERCHAIN P., Religion 1991, 209-217 / 277-291 / 293-302 / 129-148 / 65-77.

9351* *Lorton* David, What was the pr-nsw and who managed it? Aspects of royal administration in [G. van den *Boorn*] 'The duties of the vizier': StAäK 18 (1991) 291-316.

9352 ᴱ**Lüddeckens** Erich, Ägyptische Handschriften, 3. (**Kaplony-Heckel** Ursula) 1986 → 2,7617*: ᴿOLZ 86 (1991) 267 (B. *Menu*).

9353 **Munro** Irmtraut, Untersuchungen zu den Totenbuch-Papyri der 18. Dynastie; Kriterien ihrer Datierung: StEg, 1988 → 6,9538; 0-7103-0288-6: ᴿBO 48 (1991) 90-93 (U. *Luft*); JEA 77 (1991) 212-5 (A. *Niwiński*).

9354 *Parkinson* R. B., The date of the 'Tale of the eloquent peasant' [late 12th dynasty]: RÉgp 42 (1991) 171-181.

9355 ᴱ**Pestman** P. W., Textes et études de papyrologie grecque, démotique et copte (P. Lug.-Bat. 23) Leiden 1985 ➤ 1,9214: ᴿOLZ 82 (1991) 18-21 (M. *Chauveau*).

9356 **Petraček** Karel, Altägyptisch, Hamitosemitisch und ihre Beziehungen zu einigen Sprachfamilien in Afrika und Asien 1985: Ac. Pg. Praha 1986. Praha 1988, Univ. 156 p. – ᴿJAOS 111 (1991) 382-4 (C. T. *Hodge*).

9357 ᶠPOLOTSKY H. J.: Essays on Egyptian grammar [symposium for his visit 1985], ᴱ**Simpson** W.: Yale Egyptological Studies 1, 1986 ➤ 4,711; 6,9541: ᴿEnchoria 18 (1991) 197-203 (H. *Satzinger*).

9358 *a) Quack* Joachim F., Über die mit *'nḫ* gebildeten Namenstypen und die Vokalisation einiger Verbalformen; – *b) Jansen-Winkel,* Karl, Der Ausdruck *w' z3 w';* – *c) Eichler* Eckhard, Zwei Bemerkungen zu den hieratischen Schriften des Alten Reiches; – *d) Goldwasser* Orly, *Laor* Nathaniel, The allure of the holy glyphs; a psycholinguistic perspective on the Egyptian script: GöMiszÄg 123 (1991) 91-100 / 53-56 / 21-26 / 37-50.

9358* *Quack* Joachim F., Die Konstruktion des Infinitivs in der Cleft Sentence: RÉgp 42 (1991) 189-206; Eng. 207.

9359 *Reineke* W. F., Gedanken zur Herkunft der altägyptischen Mathematik [WAERDEN B. L. van der 1983; BRUNNER-TRAUT E. 1990]: OLZ 86 (1991) 247-256.

9360 **Renaud** Odette, Le dialogue du désespéré avec son âme; une interprétation littéraire: Cah 1. Genève 1991, Soc. d'Égyptologie. 74 p. 2-940011-00-1. – ᴿGöMiszÄg 125 (1991) 17-19 (P. *Derchain*).

9361 ᴱ**Rosati** Gloria, Libro dei morti: Testi VOA 2, Eg. clas. 2. Brescia 1991, Paideia. 119 p. Lit. 18.000. 88-394-0466-X. [Antonianum 67, 148, M. *Nobile*].

9362 *Sadek* Abdel Aziz, Varia graffitica: VarAeg 6 (1990) 109-120.

9363 **Sadek** Abdul-Aziz F. Contribution à l'étude de l'Amduat: OBO 65, 1985 ➤ 1,a647*...6,9547: ᴿCdÉ 65 (1990) 261 (Annie *Gasse*).

9364 **Sambin** Chantal, L'offrande de la soi-disant 'Clepsydre'; le symbole *šbt* / *wnšb* / *wtt*: StÄg 11. Budapest 1988, Univ. 449 p. 96-34621-92-9.

9365 **Schenkel** Wolfgang, Materialien zur Vorlesung; Einführung in die altägyptische Sprachwissenschaft ¹1987 ²1989 ➤ 3,8694...6,9548 [cf. 9547!]: ᴿBO 47 (1990) 614-8 (E. *Doret*, ¹1987).

9366 **Schlott** Adelheid, Schrift und Schreiben im Alten Ägypten. 1989 ➤ 5,9446; DM 48: ᴿBO 48 (1991) 86s (V. *Wessetzky*); OLZ 86 (1991) 270s (W. *Helck*).

9367 *a) Schreiber* Silke, 'Keusch wie kaum ein anderes Volk' [*Brunner-Traut* E.]? Einige Anmerkungen zum Sexual-Vokabular der alten Ägypter; – *b) Loprieno* Antonio, Topics in Egyptian negations: ➤ 20c, ᶠBEHRENS P., Ägypten 1991, 213-235 / 315-335.

9368 **Smith** M., Catalogue of demotic papyri in the British Museum, 3., The mortuary texts of Papyrus BM 10507, 1987 ➤ 5,9448; 6,9550: ᴿEnchoria 17 (1990) 177s (H.-J. *Thissen*); WZKM 79 (1989) 258-262 (G. *Vittmann*).

9369 *Smith* Mark, Papyrus Harkness [some questions regarding the original extent and problematic passages of the edition which he has now ready to publish]: Enchoria 18 (1991) 95-105.

9370 *Spalinger* Anthony, An unexpected source in a [Greco-Roman Esna] festival calendar: RÉgp 42 (1991) 209-222 (New Kingdom calendar of Lucky and Unlucky days and goddesses of every day of the year].

9371 **Sturtewagen** Christian, The funerary papyrus Palau Rib. Nr. Inv. 450: Estudis Pap/FgB 1. Barc 1991, Institut de Teologia Fonamental. 37 p.; ill. 84-87843-00-X. – ᴿActuBbg 28 (1991) 231 (E. *Durban*).

9372 **Thompson** Stephen E., A lexicographic and iconographic analysis of anointing in ancient Egypt [14 hieroglyphic words used by translators, but in the Old Kingdom there was only *wrḥ*]: diss. Brown 1991. 290 p. 92-04969. – DissA 52 (1991s) 3257-A.

9372* *Tobin* Vincent A., A re-assessment of the Lebensmüde [Dispute between a man and his Ba, Pap. Berlin 3024]: BO 48 (1991) 341-363.

9373 **Valbelle** Dominique, L'égyptologie: Que sais-je? 1312. P 1991, PUF. 128 p. [Bibliog. p. 125 through 1990]. 2-13-043-562-9.

9374 [*Goyon* Jean-Claude, présente] Valeurs phonétiques des signes hiéroglyphiques d'époque gréco-romaine: Publ. Recherche. Montpellier 1988–, Univ. I. 291 p. (709 items) + indices. – II. p. 292-432 (732 items) + indices. – III. 1990, p. 433-654 (615 items) + indices.

9375 **Vernus** Pascal, Future at issue; tense, mood and aspect in Middle Egyptian; studies in syntax and semantics: YaleEgSt 4. NHv 1990, Yale Univ. vii-228 p. $35. 0-912532-21-1.

9376 ᴱ**Vleeming** S. P., Aspects of demotic lexicography 1984/7 ➤ 4,715; 5,9455: ᴿJEA 77 (1991) 225-7 (C. J. *Martin*); JNES 50 (1991) 155-8 (J. G. *Manning*); OLZ 86 (1991) 278s (U. *Kaplony-Heckel*).

9377 **Wente** E. F., *McItzer* F. S., [350] Letters from ancient Egypt: SBL Writings 1990 ➤ 6,9559: ᴿZAW 103 (1991) 313 (K.F.D. *Römheld*).

9379 **Browne** Gerald M., Old Nubian texts from Qaṣr Ibrim [I. 1986; II. 1989 ➤ 5,9463] III: TExc Mem 12. L 1991, Egypt Expl. Soc. xii-155 p.; 8 pl. 0-85698-114-1. – ᴿJEA 77 (1991) 234s (J. D. *Ray*, 2).

9380 **Browne** Gerald M., Introduction to Old Nubian 1989 ➤ 5,9462: ᴿBO 48 (1991) 824-6 (W. *Vycichl*).

9381 *Browne* Gerald M., Old Nubian studies; past, present and future: ➤ 635, Egypt and Africa 1991, 286-293.

9382 **Rouchdy** Aleya, Nubians and the Nubian language in contemporary Egypt; a case of cultural and linguistic contact: StSemLLing 15. Leiden 1991, Brill. xiv-84 p.; map. 90-04-09197-1.

J3.4 Coptica.

9383 **Biedenkopf-Ziehner** A., Untersuchungen zum koptischen Briefformular 1983 ➤ 64,8229 ... 4,a522: ᴿWZKM 78 (1988) 211-8 (W. *Brunsch*).

9384 **Brunsch** Wolfgang, Kleine Chrestomathie nichtliterarischer koptischer Texte 1987 ➤ 3,9709; 4,a525: ᴿJEA 77 (1991) 231s (M. *Green*).

9385 *Brunsch* Wolfgang, Bemerkungen zu koptischen und griechischen Inschriften aus Kairo [alles scheinbar koptisch; nur korrigierter Text zu Kᴀᴍᴇʟ I., Coptic Funerary Stelae 1987]: Orientalia 60 (1991) 92-108; pl. I-XXVI.

9386 **Elanskaya** A. I., Coptic literary texts of the Pushkin State Fine Arts museum in Moscow: StÄg 13. Budapest 1991, Univ. 307 p. 963-462-542-8.

9387 *Funk* W.-P., Formen und Funktionen des interlokutiven Nominalsatzes in den koptischen Dialekten I: LOrA 3 (1991) 1-75.

9388 **Green** Michael, The Coptic *share* pattern 1987 ➤ 3,9713; 6,9570: ᴿBO 48 (1991) 144-8 (H. *Satzinger*).

9389 ᴿHasitzka Monika R. M., Koptische Texte: Corpus Papyrorum Raineri 12, 1987 ➤ 3,9714; 6,9569: ᴿJEA 77 (1991) 230s (M. *Green*).

9389* ᴱHasitzka Monika R. M. (*Harrauer* Hermann), Neue Texte und Dokumentation zum Koptisch-Unterricht: Pap. Rainer 18. W 1990, Hollinek. Textband p. 343 + vol. of 143 pl. 3-85119-241-9.

9390 *Kuhn* K. H., *Tait* W. J., Two leaves from a [Coptic homily] codex from Qasr Ibrim: JEA 77 (1991) 145-9; pl. XIII-XIV.

9391 **Mattar** Nabil, A study in Bohairic Coptic. Pasadena 1990, Hope. vi-641 p. $27: pa. $20. 0-932727-42-5; –1–7 [TDig 38,176].

9392 **Polotsky** Hans J., Grundlagen des koptischen Satzbaus [1. 1987 ➤ 4,a536] 2: AmerStPapyr [27.] 29. Atlanta 1990, Scholars. [xi-168 p.] p. 169-272. 1-55540-076-0.

9392* *Polotsky* Hans J., 'Article' and 'determinative pronoun' in Coptic: ➤ 620, LAeg 1 (1990/1) 241s.

9393 *a) Quecke* Hans, Zur direkten und indirekten Rede im Koptischen; – *b) Layton* Bentley, The Coptic determinator syntagm and its constituents; – *c) Kasser* Rodolphe, Marius CHAÎNE et la thèse d'une relation phonologique privilégiée entre les langues coptes saïdique et bohaïrique (+ A standard system of sigla for referring to the dialects of Coptic): JCopt 1 (1990) 129-135 / 79-97 / 73-77 (141-151).

9394 *Säve-Söderbergh* Torgny, [Coptic] Papyrus Thorburn: OrSuec 40 (1991) 228-235; phot.; facsim.

9395 *Schenke* Hans-Martin, Bemerkungen zum P. Hamb. Bil. 1, und zum altfayumischen Dialekt der koptischen Sprache: Enchoria 18 (1991) 69-93.

9396 **Shisha-Halevy** Ariel, Coptic grammatical categories 1986 ➤ 2,7652 ... 4,a538: ᴿOLZ 86 (1991) 154-9 (H. M. *Schenke*).

9397 **Tattam** Henry, A Coptic-Latin lexicon. Beirut 1991 = 1835, Librairie du Liban. vii-958 p.

9399 *Vliet* J. van der, Varia magica coptica [en français]: Aegyptus 71 (1991) 217-242.

9400 **Vycichl** Werner, Dictionnaire étymologique de la langue copte 1983 ➤ 64,8250 ... 5,9480: ᴿCdÉ 65 (1990) 377s (H. De *Meulenaere*).

J3.8 Æthiopica.

9400* **Bernand** E., *al.*, Recueil des inscriptions de l'Éthiopie des périodes pré-Axoumite et Axoumite: AIBL. P 1991, de Boccard. 540 p.; vol. of 233 pl. [OLZ 87, 408s, J. *Oelsner*].

9401 **Haile** Getatchew, *Amare* Misrak, Beauty of the creation [Amharic text]: JSS Mg 16. Manchester 1991, Univ. xiv-87 p. 0-9516124-3-3.

9401* **Haile** G. *Macomber* W. F., Catalogue of Ethiopian ms 7-9, 1983/5/7 ➤ 57,1009 ... 6,9582: ᴿMuséon 104 (1991) 403s (U. *Zanetti*).

9402 *Lamberti* Marcello, Cushitic and its classifications: Anthropos 86 (1991) 552-561.

9402* **Leslau** Wolf, Arabic loanwords in Ethiopian Semitic. Wsb 1990, Harrassowitz. xvii-373 p. DM 98. – ᴿMuséon 104 (1991) 214-6 (Y. *Gruntfest*).

9403 **Leslau** Wolf, Comparative dictionary of Ge'ez 1987 ➤ 3,9734 ... 5,9488: ᴿAfO 36s (1989s) 188-190 (Renate *Richter*); WZKM 79 (1989) 295-7 (H. *Eisenstein*).

9403* **Neugebauer** Otto † 19.II.1990, *a)* Chronography in Ethiopic sources: Szb ph/h 512. W 1989, Österr.Ak. ➤ 5,9486: ᴿAfO 36s (1989s) 100-2 (E.

Hammerschmidt); BSO 54 (1991) 589s (A. K. *Irvine*). – *b*) ABU SHAKER's 'Chronography'... in Ethiopic: Szb 498, W 1988 ⇒ 4,a547: ᴿBSO 54 (1991) 589 (A. K. *Irvine*); ZDMG 141 (1991) 433 (E. *Hammerschmidt*).

9404 **Raineri** Osvaldo, Il sangue nel codice etiopico Comboniani A1 (tetraevangelo del XV sec.) della Vaticana: ⇒ 565, Sangue 1989/91, 225-260.

9405 **Richter** Renate, Lehrbuch der amharischen Sprache 1987 ⇒ 3,9740 ... 5,9488: ᴿWZKM 79 (1989) 297-9 (W. *Leslau*, Eng).

9406 ᴱ**Tafla** Bairu, Aṣma Giyorgis and his work; history of the Gallā and the kingdom of Sawā; ÄthFor 18. Stu 1987, Steiner. 1053 p. DM 288 [OLZ 87, 270-2, S. *Uhlig*].

9407 *Uhlig* Siegbert, Der Äthiopier Ṣagā ZAʿAB und der portugiesische Humanist Damian de GOIS: eine äthiopisch-europäische Kulturbegegnung im 16. Jahrhundert und ihre Bedeutung: ⇒ 322, Bibel im Orient 1991, 29-61.

9408 **Uhlig** Siegbert, Äthiopische Paläographie 1988 ⇒ 4,a550; 6,9588: ᴿJSS 36 (1991) 128-134 (E. *Ullendorff*); ZDMG 141 (1991) 405-8 (M. A. *Knibb*).

9409 **Ullendorff** Edward, Studia aethiopica et semitica: ÄthF 24, 1987 ⇒ 3, 313; 5,9489a: ᴿBSO 53 (1990) 188s (D. L. *Appleyard*).

9410 **Ullendorff** Edward, From the Bible to E. Cerulli: AthF 32, 1990 ⇒ 6,313: ᴿOrChrPer 57 (1991) 435s (O. *Raineri*).

J4 Anatolica.

9411 **Alp** Sedat, Hethitische Briefe aus Maşat-Höyük: Yayınları 6/35. Ankara 1991, Türk Tarih Kurumu. xv-465 p.; 13 pl.; map. 975-16-0338-2.

9412 *Carruba* O., À propos du sceau ... 'A new seal in hieroglyphic Luvian': Akkadica [62 (1989) 21-23, *Poetto* M., *al.*] 68 (1990) 20-24 [25 datation, *Mora* C.].

9413 **Catsanicos** Jean, Recherches sur le vocabulaire de la faute [*waš-tul*]; apports du Hittite à l'étude de la phraséologie indo-européenne: NABU Cah 2. P 1991, SEPOA [Soc.Ét.Pr.Or.Anc.] x-103 p. 0989-5671.

9414 **Cotticelli-Kurras** Paola [⇒ 9419], Das hethitische Verbum 'sein'; syntaktische Untersuchungen: Texte der Hethiter 18. Heid 1991, Winter. xv-224 p.

9415 **Friedrich** Johannes, *Kammenhuber* Annelies, Hethitisches Wörterbuch²ʳᵉᵛ Lfg 8s, 10, 1984/8 ⇒ 6,9595*: ᴿBO 48 (1991) 210-5 (G. *Beckman*); BSLP 85 (1990) 90-94 (F. *Bader*).

9416 *Garrett* Andrew, Hittite enclitic subjects and transitive verbs: JCS 42 (1990) 227-242.

9416* **Greppin** John A. C., The survival of ancient Anatolian and Mesopotamian vocabulary until the present: JNES 50 (1991) 203-7.

9417 **Güterbock** Hans G., *Hout* Theo P. van den, The Hittite instruction for the royal bodyguard: Assyriological Studies 24. Ch 1991, Univ. Or. Inst. xvi-99 p. 0-918986-70-2.

9417* **Hagenbuchner** Albertine, Die Korrespondenz der Hethiter: Texte 15s, ᴰ1989 ⇒ 5,9498; 6,9600: ᴿZDMG 141 (1991) 394-9 (J. *Tischler*).

9418 **Held** Warren H., *al.*, Beginning Hittite 1988 ⇒ 6,9601: ᴿJAOS 111 (1991) 658s (G. *Beckman*).

9419 **Kammenhuber** A., Materialen zu einem hethitischen Thesaurus, Lfg. 11 [*Cotticelli* Paola: *ḫandaí*] 1989 ⇒ 5,9502: ᴿBO 48 (1991) 215-222 (Franca *Pecchioli-Daddi*); IndogF 96 (1991) 302-310 (H. *Otten*, 10s); ZDMG 141 (1991) 175s (O. *Soysal*).

9420 *Kammenhuber* Annelies,   Nochmals; der hethitische König trinkt Gott
NN: ➤ 126, ᶠRICHTER W., Text 1991, 221-6.
9421 **Kronasser** Heinz,   Etymologie der hethitischen Sprache 2, **Neu** W.
Indices 1987 ➤ 3,9775 ... 6,9603:   ᴿIndogF 95 (1990) 256s (J. *Tischler*).
9421* — *a*) *Neu* Erich,   Hethitische Etymologien aus dem Nachlass Heinz
KRONASSERS; – *b*) *Puhvel* Jan,   Verba delendi; Pentagonese in Hittite:
➤ 167, Mem. WINDEKENS A. van, 1991, 201-210 / 221-3.
9422 *Mora* Clelia, Sull'origine della scrittura geroglifica anatolica: Kadmos
30 (1991) 1-28; 1 pl.
9423 *Oshiro* Terumasa,   Hieroglyphic Luwian *nini-* [son, child] and congeners:
AltOrF 18 (1991) 67-72.
9424 ᶠOTTEN H.,   Documentum Asiae Minoris antiquae ᴱ**Neu** E. 1988
➤ 4,112*:   ᴿIndogF 96 (1991) 281-295 (J. *Catsanicos*).
9425 **Rüster** Christel, *Neu* Erich,   Hethitisches Zeichenlexikon; Inventar und
Interpretation der Keilschriftzeichen aus den Boğazköy-Texten: StBoğT
Beih. 2, 1989 ➤ 5,9510; 6,9612:   ᴿAfO 36s (1989s) 175-7 (M. *Popko*);
Kratylos 36 (1991) 122-6 (H. C. *Melchert*: 'a grievous disappointment').
9426 **Starke** F.,   Die keilschrift-luwischen Texte in Umschrift: StBoğT 30,
1985 ➤ 1,9277 ... 5,9511:   ᴿWZKM 78 (1988) 274-280 (J. D. *Hawkins*,
Eng.).
9427 *Umar* Bilge,   The close affinity between the Iron Age language of Luvian
origin in Anatolia and the first Iranian languages: ➤ 634, 2d Anatolian
Iron Age 1987/91, 113-6.
9428 **Werner** Rudolf, (*Luscher* Barbara),   Kleine Einführung ins Hieroglyphen-
Luwische: OBO 106.   FrS / Gö 1991, Univ. / VR.   xii-101 p. Fs 34.
3-7278-0749-0 / VR 3-525-53739-5 [BL 92,121, K. A. *Kitchen*].
9429 **Yoshida** Daisuke,   Die Syntax des althethischen substantivischen Ge-
nitivs 1987 ➤ 3,9764 ... 6,9617:   ᴿBO 48 (1991) 222-5 (A.A.M. *Prins*).

9430 **Hazai** György,   Handbuch der türkischen Sprachwissenschaft 1: BtOr-
Hung 31.   Budapest 1990, Akad.   493 p. ft 850. – ᴿOLZ 86 (1991)
414-421 (S. *Kleinmichel*).
9431 *Saraçgil* Ayşe,   La lingua turca tra riforma e rivoluzione: AION 50
(1990) 249-278.

J4.4   **Phrygia, Lydia, Lycia.**

9432 *Bakir* Tomris, *Gusmani* Roberto,   Eine neue phrygische Inschrift aus
Daskyleion: EpAnat 18 (1991) 157-164; pl. 19; ❶ 164.
9433 **Brixhe** Claude, *Lejeune* Michel,   Corpus des inscriptions paléo-phry-
giennes 1984 ➤ 1,9258 ... 3,9765:   ᴿRÉAnc 92 (1990) 166-8 (R. *Hodot*).
9434 *Carruba* Onofrio,   Valvel e Rkalil monetazione arcaica della Lidia;
problemi e considerazioni linguistiche: ➤ 9, ᶠARSLAN E., Monetazione 1
(1991) 13-21; pl. I-II.
9435 **Diakonoff** I. M., *Neroznak* V. P.,   Phrygian: Anatolian and Caucasian
Studies 1985 ➤ 3,9767;   0-88206-042-2:   ᴿAfO 36s (1989s) 182s (M.
Mayrhofer); BO 48 (1991) 225-230 (A. *Lubotsky*: goal unattainable).
9436 *Durnford* Stephen,   An instance of the Lycian name for Xanthos in
Carian script: Kadmos 30 (1991) 90-92; 1 fig.
9437 *Garrett* Andrew,   The Lycian nasalized preterite: MüStSprW 52 (1991)
15-26.

9438 **Gusmani** Roberto, Lydisches Wörterbuch Lfg. 3, 1986 → 2,7679, 3,9769: ᴿIndogF 95 (1990) 258-261 (A. *Heubeck* †).

9439 **Hodot** René, Le dialecte éolien d'Asie; la langue des inscriptions, VIIᵉ s.a.C. – IVᵉ s.p.C.: RCiv Mém 88. P 1990, ADPF. 325 p. 2-86535-207-5. – ᴿRÉG 104 (1991) 623s (L. *Dubois*).

9440 *Martin* Cary J., Carians in Egypt – the demotic evidence: Kadmos 30 (1991) 173s.

9441 *Melchert* H. Craig, The Lydian emphasizing and reflexive particle -*ś/is*: Kadmos 30 (1991) 131-142.

9442 **Neumann** Günther, Phrygisch und griechisch 1988 → 4,a575; 5,9523: ᴿRBgPg 69 (1991) 194s (Y. *Duhoux*).

J4.8 **Armena, georgica.**

9442* *Bolognesi* G., Langues en contact; syriaque, iranien, arménien [2 exemples arméniens]: → 167, Mem. WINDEKENS A. van, Studia etymologica 1991, 39-46.

9443 **Garsoïan** Nina G., Epic histories... BUZAND 1989 → 5,9529: ᴿJAOS 111 (1991) 398s (R. W. *Thomson*).

9443* **Nichanian** Marc, Âges et usages de la langue arménienne: Langues en péril. P 1990, Entente. 432 p. 2-7266-0081-1. – ᴿRSO 64 (1990) 403-5 (G. *Traina*).

9444 *Stempel* Reinhard, Die Entwicklung von auslautendem **m* und das Problem sekundärer *n*-Stämme im Armenischen: IndogF 95 (1990) 38-62.

9445 *Salvini* Mirjo, Una nuova iscrizione urartea: Orientalia 60 (1991) 344-6; pl. CVII.

9445* *Fähnrich* Hans, Kartwelische Wurzelmorpheme der Struktur CVC: ZDMG 141 (1991) 83-87.

J5 **Graeca** .1 *grammatica, onomastica* [inscriptiones → J5.4].

9446 *Acosta Méndez* Eduardo, Notas lexicográficas herculanenses: Emerita 59 (1991) 279-296.

9447 [*Bauer* Walter], ⁶ʳᵉᵛAland Kurt & Barbara, Griechisch-deutsches Wörterbuch zu den Schriften des NTs 1988 → 4,a579...6,9633: ᴿRHE 86 (1991) 178 (J.-C. *Haelewyck*).

9448 — *Rehkopf* Friedrich, Walter BAUER und Bauer/Aland, Wörterbuch zum NT: TRu 56 (1991) 428-436.

9449 — *Strecker* Georg, Walter BAUERS Wörterbuch zum Neuen Testament in neuer Auflage [ALAND K. & B. 1988]: TLZ 116 (1991) 81-92.

9450 **Bauer** W.,... *Danker* F., Greek-English lexicon of the NT 1979 → 60,a603 ...: ᴿNeotestamentica 25 (1991) 438-440 (J. G. van der *Watt*: reviewed now to show it is still valuable if used with awareness of some later developments).

9451 **Bergren** Theodore A., A Latin-Greek index of the Vulgate NT, based on Alfred SCHMOLLER's Handkonkordanz zum griechischen NT: SBL Res 26. Atlanta 1991, Scholars. xiii-207 p. $40 pa; sb. $25.

9452 **Biville** F., Les emprunts du latin au grec; approche phonétique, 1. Introduction et consonantisme: Bt Information Grammaticale 19. Lv 1990, Peeters. 399 p. Fb 2100. 2-904685-18-9 [JRS 81,254].

9453 **Bottin** L., *Quaglia* S., Corso di lingua greca I-II. Bergamo 1990, Minerva. 558+478 p. – RAufidus 11s (1990) 264 (Anna Maria *Belardinelli*).

9454 *Boyer* James L., Adverbial clauses; statistical studies: GraceTJ 11 (1990) 71-96.

9454* **Bubeník** Vít, Hellenistic and Roman Greece as a sociolinguistic area: Current Issues in Linguistic Theory 57. Amst 1989. xv-331 p. – RBSLP 85 (1990) 124-7 (C. *Brixhe*: fragile).

9455 **Buzzetti** Carlo, Dizionario base del NT greco-italiano 1989 → 5,9547: RHenoch 13 (1991) 117s (J. A. *Soggin*); Protestantesimo 45 (1990) 66s (B. *Corsani*).

9456 **Delaunois** Marcel, Essai de syntaxe grecque classique; réflexions et recherches: Fac.Univ. S. Louis 44, 1988 → 4,a596; 6,9651: RAntClas 60 (1991) 228-244 (A. *Cheyne*: 'de la concentration sémantique à la diversité des nuances').

9457 *Devine* A. M., *Stephens* Laurence D., The Greek phonological phrase: GrRByz 31 (1990) 421-446.

9459 **Efird** J., Grammar 1990 → 6,9658: RAndrUnS 29 (1991) 173-5 (S. *Kubo*).

9460 **Fanning** Buist M., Verbal aspect in New Testament Greek: Theol.Mg., 1990→ 6,9659; 0-19-826729-0; RClasR 41 (1991) 504s (J. A. *McIntyre*); FgNt 4 (1991) 217-222 (J. *Mateos*); JStNT 43 (1991) 127s (S. E. *Porter*: 'linguistically unprincipled').

9461 EFraser Peter M., *Matthews* Elaine, A lexicon of Greek personal names I, 1987 → 3,9805 ... 6,9660: RKratylos 36 (1991) 127-9 (J. *Untermann*); VDI 196 (1991) 198-200 (S. R. *Tokhtasyev*).

9462 **Glover** Carl W., Kairós and composition; modern perspectives on an ancient idea [Greek/OT]: diss. Louisville 1990, DRickey Mary Ellen. 155 p. 91-23907. – DissA 52 (1991s) 895-A.

9463 *Herweg* Michael, A critical examination of two classical approaches to aspect: JSemant 8 (1991) 363-402.

9463* **Horstmann** Axel, Materialien für griechische Sprachkurse an theologischen Ausbildungsstätten; Kurzgrammatik und Lehrbuch³rev [¹1978]: Forum Linguisticum 16. Fra 1991, Lang. viii-112 p. DM 29 pa. [TLZ 117, 228, S. *Kratsch*].

9464 **Jacquinod** Bernard, Le double accusatif en grec d'Homère à la fin du Vᵉ siècle av. J.-C. LvN 1989, Peeters. 305 p. [RÉG 104,679].

9465 **Jeanne d'Arc** sr., Petite initiation au grec des Évangiles. P 1990, BLettres. 96 p. – RSalesianum 53 (1991) 768s (C. *Buzzetti*).

9466 **Lamberterie** Charles de, Les adjectifs grecs en –ýs; sémantique et comparison: BCILL. LvN 1990, Peeters. 524 p.; p. 525-1036. – RRÉG 104 (1991) 279-281 (F. *Skoda*); RPg 64 (1990) 197-200 (J. L. *Perpillou*).

9468 **Lillo** Antonio, The ancient Greek numeral system; a study of some problematic forms. Bonn 1990, Habelt. vii-66 p. – RRFgIC 119 (1991) 381s (Donatella *Fogazzo*).

9469 **Lloyd-Jones** Hugh, Greek in a cold climate. L 1991, Duckworth. 236 p. [RÉG 104,680].

9470 ELouw Johannes P., *Nida* Eugene A., Greek-English lexicon of the NT based on semantic domains 1988 → 4,2617; 5,9572: RCBQ 53 (1991) 334-6 (F. T. *Gignac*); JTS 41 (1990) 198-201 (K. *Grayston*: raises questions fundamental to lexicography); Kerux 5,3 (1990) 39-58 (S. M. *Baugh*).

9471 **Metzger** Bruce M., Lexical aids for students of NT Greek³rev 1990 → 6,9780: RCarthaginensia 7 (1991) 555 (R. *Sanz Valdivieso*).

9472 *Moszyński* Leszek, ❷ Greek constructions of the type *páter hēmôn ho en toîs ouranoîs* in the Cyril-Methodius exemplar of the Gospels: ➤ 68, ᶠGRACIOTTI S. 1990, 47-54.

9473 *Navarrete Orcera* Antonio R., Confección de un léxico jurídico griego: Emerita 59 (1991) 351-7.

9474 *New* David S., The injunctive future and existential injunctions in the NT: JStNT 44 (1991) 113-127.

9475 **North** M.A., *Hillard* A.E., Greek prose composition for schools. L 1991, Duckworth. viii-272 p.

9476 *Padilla* Carmen, Ensayo de clasificación de la especie semántica atributo en el Nuevo Testamento (letra alpha) [Contribuciones al DGENT (diccionario griego-español del Nuevo Testamento)]: FgNt 4,7 (1991) (59–) 61-72; Eng. 61.

9477 **Palmer** Michael M., Levels of constituent structure in NT Greek: diss. Southern Baptist Theol. Sem. 1991, ᴰ*Culpepper* R.A. 162 p. 91-25196, – DissA 52 (1991s) 896-A ('Micheal').

9478 *Perdicoyianni* Hélène, Le nom de personne en Chypre ancienne: ÉtClas 59 (1991) 101-7.

9479 ᴱ**Perschbacher** W.J. [< *Wigram* G. 1852], The new analytical Greek lexicon. Peabody MA 1990, Hendrickson. lv-449 p. $30. 0-943575-33-8 [NTAbs 35,235].

9480 *Plooy* G.P.V. du, Aspect and biblical exegesis: Neotestamentica 25,1 (1991) 157-170.

9481 **Porter** Stanley E., Verbal aspect in the Greek of the New Testament, with reference to tense and mood: Studies in Biblical Greek 1, 1989 ➤ 5,9581; 6,9692: ᴿBTrans 42 (1991) 345-8 (Ruth B. *Edwards*); FgNt 4 (1991) 73-76 (J. *Mateos*).

9482 *Porter* Stanley E., *Reed* Jeffrey T., Greek grammar since BDF [BLASS F. 1896, ⁴*Debrunner* A. 1913, ᵀ*Funk* R. 1961 (¹⁶*Rehkopf* F. 1984)]; a retrospective and prospective analysis: FgNt 4 (1991) 143-163; español 163s.

9483 *Quarg* Gunter, Buchstaben als Zahlen: Symbolon 10 (1991) 43-50.

9484 **Rehkopf** Friedrich, Septuaginta-Vokabular 1989 ➤ 5,9584; 6,9694: ᴿBijdragen 52 (1991) 436 (E. *Eynikel*); CBQ 53 (1991) 480s (B.G. *Wright*: all words in Greek alphabetical order, thus a compact updated HATCH-REDPATH, which still must be consulted for all words occurring over 20 times); TAth 61 (1990) 890s (P. *Simotas* ❷).

9485 *Sakkos* Stergios N., ❷ The preparation of a new dictionary of the NT [Sydney Macquarie Univ.]: TAth 62 (1991) 452-477; Eng. 930.

9486 **Schawaller** Doris, Fortbewegungsverben im griechischen NT und ihre altkirchenslavische Übersetzung [Diss. Köln 1989, ᴰ*Untermann* J.]: EurHS 21/88. Fra 1990, Lang. xv-241 p. 3-631-43171-6.

9487 *Skoda* Françoise, Les adjectifs grecs en -*sos* traduisant des particularités ou des défauts physiques; un micro-système lexical: RÉG 104 (1991) 367-393.

9488 **Spicq** Ceslas, Lexique théologique du NT [= Notes 1978 ... ➤ 60,368 ... 63,8325], trois volumes en un. FrS/P 1991, Univ./Cerf. 1668 p. F 290 [NRT 114, 739, X. *Jacques*].

9489 **Spicq** Ceslas, Note di lessicografia neotestamentaria I. 1988 ➤ 4,a640 ... 6,9702. ᴿAntonianum 65 (1990) 387s (M. *Nobile*).

9490 **Thackeray** Henry S., A grammar of the OT in Greek 1987 = 1909: ᴿScripTPamp 23 (1991) 345-350 (K. *Limburg*).

9491 **Van Voorst** Robert E., Building your NT Greek vocabulary 1990
➤ 6,9707: ᴿGraceTJ 11 (1990) 241s (T. R. *Edgar*); RExp 88 (1991) 272s
(A. A. *Trites*).

9492 **Vincenzi** Giuseppe C., Il greco; preistoria e storia di una lingua indoeuropea. Bo 1991, CLUEB. 125 p.; maps. Lit. 15.000.

9493 *Wathelet* Paul, Les datifs analogiques en -*essi* dans la tradition épique:
RÉG 104 (1991) 1-14.

9494 **Windekens** A. J. van, Dictionnaire étymologique complémentaire de la
langue grecque; nouvelles contributions à l'interprétation historique et
comparée du vocabulaire. Lv 1986, Peeters. xii-286 p. – ᴿRÉAnc 92
(1990) 145s (A. *Christol*: compléments à *Chantraine* P. – *Frisk* H., comme
Jucquois G. 1977; conclusion: Cratyle 'sans le scepticisme amusé de Alain
Christol').

9495 **Windham** Neal, New Testament Greek for preachers and teachers; five
areas of application. Lanham MD 1991, UPA, [xvi–] 247 p. $39,50; pa.
$19.50 [CBQ 54,406].

9496 **Zuntz** Günther, Griechischer Lehrgang²ʳᵉᵛ [¹1983]: StAltW 15. Gö
1991, Vandenhoeck & R. I. 295 p.; 10 fig. – II. 272 p. – III. 317 p.
3-525-25320-6 all.

J5.2 **Voces graecae** (*ordine alphabetico* **graeco**).

9497 *agallíasis:* *Langis* Dean, Joy; a scriptural and patristic understanding:
GrOrTR 35 (1990) 47-57.

9498 *Graffigna* Paola, Un hapax di FILONE d'Alessandria, **agalmatophoreúō:**
Maia 43 (1991) 143-9.

agápē: **Légasse** S., 'Et qui...' agape: LDiv 136, 1989 ➤ 4536.

9499 *aiōn:* **Zuntz** Günther, Aiōn im Römerreich; die archäologischen
Zeugnisse: AbhHeid ph/h 1991/3. Heid 1991, Winter. 45 p.

9500 *hamartia:* *Steenbergen* Gerrit van, Translating 'sin' in Pökoot [Kenya;
relation to *shalom* and *eirene*]: BTrans 42 (1991) 431-7.

9501 *anánkē:* **Ostwald** Martin, Anankē in THUCYDIDES: AmerClasSt 18, 1988
➤ 5,9601; 6,9720: ᴿPhoenix 45 (Toronto 1991) 356-8 (J. R. *Wilson*:
good).

9502 *Rodríguez* Isidoro, Las preposiciones griegas vehículos del dogma (*antí,
diá, perí, hypér*; Jn 1,16]: Scripta Fulgentina 1 (1991s) 127-139.

9502* *apeithéō:* **Thibaut** Andre, L'infidélité 1988 ➤ 4,a657: ᴿGnomon 63
(1991) 200-5 (W. *Thiele*).

9503 *apeleútheroi* im ptolemäischen Ägypten (?): ArPapF 36 (1990) 39-42 (R.
Scholl).

9504 *auxánō:* *Adrados* F. R., Morfología de griego *aéxō, auxánō, auxéō,
aúxō:* ➤ 167, Mem. WINDEKENS A. van 1991, 13-20.

9505 *acheiropoiētos* [3 times NT, not used for God]: *Horst* P. W. van der, 'De
waarachtige en niet met handen gemaakte God' [*Brixhe* C., *Hodot* R.,
L'Asie Mineure 1988 p. 124: Belkis in Pamphylia]: NedTTs 45 (1991)
177-182; Eng... 241 (from a God-fearer).

9505* **Dale** J. W., Judaic baptism; **baptízō,** an inquiry into the meaning of
the word as determined by the usage of Jewish and patristic writers.
Wauconda IL/Phillipsburg NJ 1991 = 1869, Bolchazy-C/Presb/Ref.
400 p. 0-86516-247-6 / 0-87552-231-9 [NTAbs 36,291].

9506 *geláō:* **Arnould** Dominique, Le rire et les larmes dans la littérature
grecque d'Homère à Platon [diss. Sorbonne 1987]. P 1990, BLettres.
293 p. – ᴿRÉG 104 (1991) 628-630 (Yvonne *Boudon*).

9507 *deûro: Eyníkel* E., *Lust* J., The use of *deûro* and *deúte* in the LXX: ETL 67 (1991) 57-68 ['go' as often as 'come', unlike classical usage].

9508 *diakonía:* **Collins** John N., *Diakonia*; [Mk 10,45] reinterpreting the ancient sources 1990 ➤ 6,9729: RBibTB 21 (1991) 166s (J.H. *Neyrey*); CritRR 4 (1991) 181s (F.W. *Danker*); TLond 94 (1991) 464-6 (W.H.C. *Frend*).

9509 *diōkō: Buth* Randall, Pursuing righteousness: Jerusalem Perspective 4,3 (1991) 11s.

9509* *doûlos: Kisembo* Benezeri T., Translating 'servant' words into Runyoro-Rutooro [Uganda]: BTrans 42 (1991) 426-431.

9510 *dýnamis:* **Gräbe** Petrus J., *Dýnamis* in the sense of power in the main Pauline letters: diss. DDuToit A. Pretoria 1990. – DissA 52 (1991) 1379-A.

9511 *eulogeîn: Dukiel* Zbigniew, ❷ *Znaczenie...* Meaning of *eulogein* and related roots in the Septuagint: RuBi 43 (1990) 131-5.

9512 *eusebēs, asebēs* (Platon): RBgPg 69 (1991) 44-74 (A. *Cheyns*).

9513 *Roberts* J.H., **Thaumázō;** an expression of perplexity in some examples from papyri letters: Neotestamentica 25,1 (1991) 109-122.

9514 *thymós:* **Caswell** Caroline P., A study of *thumos* in early Greek epic: Mnemosyne 114. Leiden 1990, Brill. ix-85 p. *f* 48. – RÉtClas 59 (1991) 291s (D. *Donnet*).

9515 *kainós: Wainwright* G., Renewal as a trinitarian and traditional event: LexTQ 26,3s (1991) 117-124 [< NTAbs 36,215].

9516 *Kathōs* and *hōsper* in the NT: FgNt 4,7 (1991) 55-58 (J.K. *Elliott*, from notes left by G.D. *Kilpatrick*).

9517 *kairós:* **Gallet** Bernard, Recherches sur *kairós* et l'ambiguité dans la poésie de PINDARE. Bordeaux 1990, Univ. 404 p. – RRÉAnc 93 (1991) 417s (J.-C. *Carrière*: richesse éclatante); RÉG 104 (1991) 284s (J. *Bompaire*).

9518 *kertoméō: Knobloch* Johann, Gr. *kertoméō* 'verspotte' und gr. *skerbóllō* 'lästere' und ihr ethnolinguistischer Hintergrund: IndogF 95 (1990) 49s.

9519 *loidoría: Harding* Philip, All pigs are animals, but are all animals pigs? [against Virginia HUNTER on *loidoria* / gossip in Phoenix 44 (1990) 299-325 ignoring his 1987 article there]: AncHB 5 (1991) 145-8.

9520 *Dehandschutter* B., **'Martyr** – Martyrium'; quelques observations à propos d'un christianisme sémantique: ➤ 18, FBASTIAENSEN A., Eulogia 1991, 33-39.

9521 *Ellingworth* Paul, '(Y)Our father(s)' in the Greek NT: BTrans 41 (1990) 135-8 [–9, closing of the *martyr*ᶜ*a* debate].

9522 *maûros: Rizakis* Athanase, Les Maurétaniens et la couleur du bronze de Corinthe: Karthago 22 (1990) 55-62 + 1 pl.

9523 *metánoia:* **Fink-Dendorfer** Elisabeth, Conversio; Motive und Motivierung zur Bekehrung in der Alten Kirche 1986 ➤ 3,7352*.9903: RSalesianum 53 (1991) 423s (G. *Meinholf*).

9524 *misthós: Winter* Martin, Lohn NT: ➤ 690, TRE 21 (1991) 447-9 (-453 ethisch, *Huber* W.).

9525 *mystērion:* **Bouyer** L., The Christian mystery; from pagan myth... 1990 ➤ 6,9750: RDowR 109 (1991) 304-8 (A. *Louth*); TLond 94 (1991) 138s (G. *Gould*).

9526 *nomárchēs: Hébal* Suzanne, Deux équivalents démotiques du titre *nomárchēs*: CdÉ 65 (1990) 304-320.

9527 *ólbos: Schmiel* Robert, The *ólbos, kóros, hýbris, atē* sequence [genealogy of evil]: Traditio 45 (1989s) 343-6.

9528 *orgē:* ᵀᴱ**Indelli** Giovanni, FILODEMO, l'ira: Scuola d'Epicuro (Ercolano) 5. N 1988, Bibliopolis. 273 p. – ᴿBASP 28 (1991) 79-89 (D. *Obbink*).

9529 *Riel* Marijana, *Hósios* kai *díkaios* [*Robert* L. (? annoncé? pour ÉPR)]; I. Catalogue des inscriptions: EpAnat 18 (1991) 1-50; maps 51-53; 55-70, 16 pl.

9530 *parabolē: Uytfanghe* M. Van, Du grec et du latin bibliques aux langues romanes; un réexamen du cas de 'parabole' parole et de 'parabolare' parler: ⇥ 18, ᶠBASTIAENSEN A., Eulogia 1991, 385-393.

9531 *paraskeuē:* **Allison** June W., Power and preparedness in THUCYDIDES: AJPg Mg 5. Baltimore 1989, Johns Hopkins Univ. iii-168 p. – ᴿPhoenix 45 (Toronto 1991) 358s (J. R. *Wilson*: unsatisfactory).

9531* *pelargós: Kaczor* Idaliana, *Witczak* Krzysztof T., Grec pelārgós, 'cicogne, ciconia alba' et indo-européen *sr̥g̑ós*, même sens: ⇥ 167, Mem. WINDEKENS A. van, 1991, 151-3.

9532 *pístis:* **Lindsay** Ray D., Pistis und pisteuein als Glaubensbegriffe in den Schriften des Flavius JOSEPHUS und im Neuen Testament: ev. Diss. Tübingen 1991, ᴰ*Betz*. O. 243 p. – TR 87 (1991) 522; RTLv 23, p. 545 'Dennis *Ray*'.

9534 *polý: Lamberterie* Charles de, La préhistoire des composés en *polu*: RÉG 103,2 (1990) XIII-XIV.

9535 *prosélytos: Donaldson* Terence L., Proselytes or 'righteous gentiles'? The status of Gentiles in eschatological pilgrimage patterns of thought: JPseud 7 (1990) 3-27.

9536 *proskynéō: Jobes* Karen H., Distinguishing the meaning of Greek verbs in the semantic domain [of the eight different terms used] for worship: FgNt 4 (1991) 183-191; 1 fig.

9536* *pōléō: Drexhage* Hans-J., [⇥ e763] Die Komposita mit *-pōlēs* und *-prátēs* im hellenistischen Ägypten: MünstHand 10,2 (1991) 1-17; Eng. franç. 17.

9537 *Baldwin* Barry, Notes on the word *rhóga* [cash allowance; *rhogeúō* commoner]: Eranos 89 (1991) 121s.

9538 *syngéneia / oikeiótēs:* **Elwyn** Susan F., The use of kinship terminology in Hellenistic diplomatic documents: diss. Pennsylvania, ᴰ*Graham* A. J.   Ph 1991. 398 p. 92-00333. – DissA 52 (1991s) 2674-A.

9539 *syngnōmē:* **Metzler** Karin, Der griechische Begriff des Verzeihens, untersucht am Wortstamm syggnōmē von den ersten Belegen bis zum vierten Jahrhundert n. Chr. [Diss. Zürich 1990, ᴰ*Burkert* W.]: WUNT 2/44. Tü 1991, Mohr. vii-352 p. 3-16-145671-8 [NTAbs 36,138].

9540 *sōzō:* **Cowen** Gerald, Salvation; word studies from the Greek New Testament. Nv 1990, Broadman. 159 p. $8. 0-8054-1035-X [TDig 38,257].

9540* *téssares: Shields* Kennethᴶ, The Indo-European numeral '4'; a new etymology ['those ones in pairs together', < *kwe* + collective-markers]: ⇥ 167, Mem. WINDEKENS A. van, 1991, 265-272 [305-311, *Weber* Dieter, Ordinalzahlen des Ossetischen].

9541 *hýpsistos: Paz de Hoz* María, Theos hypsistos in Hierokaisareia [Teyenli, Lydia]: EpAnat 18 (1991) 75-77; pl. 1.

9542 *phthonerós* [DEMOSTHÈNE Leptine 20.140.164: pingre/stingy, not jealous]: RÉAnc 92 (1990) 45-58; Eng. 45 (B. *Gallet*).

9543 *phýlarchos: Mayerson* Philip, The use of the term *phylarchus* in the Roman-Byzantine East: ZPapEp 88 (1991) 291-5.

chará, **Cumatzi Montiel** A. ⇥ 4809.

9544 *chárisma: Baumert* Norbert, 'Charisma' – Versuch einer Sprachregelung: TPhil 66 (1991) 21-48.

9545 **chílios:** Rix Helmut, Urindogermanisch *$\bar{g}^h$eslo-* in den südindoger-
manischen Ausdrücken für '1000': → 167, Mem. WINDEKENS A. van,
1991, 225-231.

9546 **chráomai:** Falus R.†, Zu den Derivatbildungen des Stammes chrē:
AcAntH 32 (1989) 273-282.

9547 Edwards M.J., **Chrēstos** in a magical papyrus ['not a vulgar orthographic
variant, but the key to the identity of the group']: ZPapEp 85 (1991)
323-6.

9547* **phōnē:** Martin García José A., El campo semántico del sonido y la voz
en la Biblia griega de los LXX: Analecta Malacitana, Anejos 3, 1986
→ 3,9935: ᴿRAg 29 (1988) 289 (S. Sabugal).

9548 **psychē,** thymós: Jahn Thomas, Zum Wortfeld 'Seele-Geist' in der
Sprache HOMERS: Zetemata 83, 1987 → 5,9644: ᴿEos 59 (1991) 109-111
(H. Wojtowicz); Helmantica 42,129* (1991) 325 (J. Mazas); Mnemosyne
44 (1991) 440-5 (S. van der Mije).

j5.4   Papyri et inscriptiones graecae – Greek epigraphy.

9549 Bousquet Jean, Corpus des inscriptions de Delphes 2 (1989), addenda et
corrigenda: BCH 115 (1991) 595s.

9549* Bowersock G.W., The Babatha papyri, Masada, and Rome: JRom-
Arch 4 (AA 1991) 336-344 [< NTAbs 36,83].

9550 **Boyaval** Bernard, Album de papyrus documentaires de Lille 1990
→ 6,9640*: ᴿCdÉ 65 (1990) 353-4 (W. Clarysse).

9551 ᴱ**Clarysse** W. al., Konkordanz und Supplement zu Berichtigungs-
liste...Papyrusurkunden Band I-VII 1989 → 6,9646: ᴿBASP 28 (1991)
77s (Deborah W. Hobson).

Clarysse W., Zenon, een Grieks 1990 → b117; **Orrieux** C. → e796.

9552 **Cotton** Hannah M., Geiger J., Masada II, Latin and Greek documents
1989 → 5,9552; 6,9648: ᴿBL (1991) 28 (J.R. Bartlett); ClasR 41 (1991)
458s (Margaret M. Roxan); JJS 72 (1991) 129s (M. Goodman).

9553 **Cuvigny** H., Wagner G., Les ostraca grecs de Douch [I, 1986 → 2,7705]
II, 1988 → 4,a595...6,9649: ᴿBO 48 (1991) 536-9 (M. Lauretta Moioli, 2).

9554 ᴱ**Daniel** Robert W., Two Greek magical papyri in the National
Museum of Antiquities in Leiden; a photographic edition of J 384 and
J 395: PapyrColon 19. Opladen 1991, Westdeutscher-V. xxvii-96 p.
3-531-09929-9.

9555 **Daris** Sergio, Il lessico latino nel greco d'Egitto² [¹1971]. Barc 1991,
Inst. Teol. Fonamental, Sem. Papir. 117 p. 84-87843-01-8. – ᴿRCatalT 16
(1991) 214s (J. Fábregas i Baqué).

9556 **Dubois** Laurent, Inscriptions grecques dialectales de Sicile; contribution
à l'étude du vocabulaire grec colonial; préf. Masson O.: Coll. Éc.Fr. 119,
1989 → 5,9557: ᴿRÉG 104 (1991) 624s (Catherine Dobias-Lalou).

9557 ᴱ**Fantoni** Georgina, Corpus papyrorum Raineri 14/10, 1989 → 5,9559
('15/10'): ᴿAegyptus 71 (1991) 292-6 (Carla Salvaterra).

9558 **Felle** Antonio E., Concordanze delle Inscriptiones graecae christianae
veteres Occidentis: InscrChrIt sub. 2. Bari 1991, Edipuglia. [vi–] 143 p.
88-7228-090-7.

9559 **Frösén** Jaakko, al., Ptolemäische Urkunden: Papyri Helsingienses I:
Comm. Hum. Lit. 80, 1986 → 3,9806; 5,9561*; 951-653-145-8: ᴿBO 48
(1991) 841-4 (E. Van 't Dack: mummy-wrappings).

9560 Gauthier P., al., Bulletin épigraphique: RÉG 104 (1991) 434-55: 763
items, 3 supra [→ e100, Sardis].

9561 *Goodman* Martin, Babatha's story [Yadin papyri ᴱ*Lewis* N. 1989
➤ 9574 infra]: JRS 81 (1991) 169-175.
9562 **Gronewald** Michael, *al.*, Kölner Papyri [Band 6 ➤ 4,a606]; Band 5/7:
PapyrolColon 7. Opladen 1985 / 1991, Westd.-V. xv-349 p. / xiii-200 p.
–/3-531-09931-0. – ᴿCdÉ 65 (1990) 344-351 (J. *Lenaerts*, 6).
9563 **Guarducci** Margherita, L'epigrafia greca dalle origini al tardo impero
1987 ➤ 3,9809; 6,9665: ᴿVDI 197 (1991) 229-232 (Yu. B. *Vinogradov* ❸).
9564 **Harrauer** Herrmann, Corpus papyrorum Raineri 13/9, 1987 ➤ 4,h473:
ᴿAegyptus 71 (1991) 289-292 (Eddy *Lanciers*).
9565 **Haslam** M. W. *al.*, Oxyrhynchus Papyri 57, Mem. 77. L 1990,
Eg.Expl.Soc. X-154 p 8 pl. 0-85698-111-7. [BO 48,983] – ᴿBASP 28
(1991) 201-8 (Kathleen *McNamee*).
9566 **Herrmann** Peter (*Keil* J.) Tituli Lydiae 2: TAsMin 5, 1989 ➤ 6,9671:
ᴿBonnJbb 191 (1991) 820-4 (W. *Eck*).
9567 **Immerwahr** Henry R., Attic script, a survey: Oxford Monographs on
Classical Archaeology. Ox 1990, Clarendon. xxiii-215 p.; 42 pl. 0-19-
813223-9. ➤ J8.4.
9568 **Iplikçioğlu** Bülent, *al.*, Epigraphische Forschungen in Germessos und
seinem Territorium I: Szb ph/h 575. W 1991, Österr. Akad. 53 p.
9569 *Katzoff* Ranon, Papyrus Yadin 18 again; a rejoinder: JQR [80 (1989s)
93-103, A. WASSERSTEIN] 82 (1991s) 171-6.
9570 *Kotansky* Roy, An inscribed [Greek] copper amulet from ʿEvron [W.
Galilee, 1621.2656]: ʿAtiqot 20 (1991) 81-87; 2 fig.
9571 **Kramer** Bärbel, *Shelton* John C., Das Archiv des Nepheros [14 gr. 2
kopt. Papyri] und verwandte Texte 1987 ➤ 4,8482: ᴿJEA 77 (1991)
227-230 (Alanna M. *Nobbs*).
9572 *Lajtar* Adam, Two Greek inscriptions from Tell Kadesh (Upper
Galilee): ZPapEp 89 (1991) 155-7.
9573 *Lejeune* Michel, Ambiguités du texte [ionien, du plomb] de Pech-Maho:
RÉG 104 (1991) 311-329.
9574 **Lewis** Naphtali, *a*) Greek papyri [Yadin]: JDSt 2, 1989 ➤ 6,9678:
ᴿJStJud 22 (1991) 130s (M. *Mach*). – *b*) The world of P. Yadin
[WASSERSTEIN A., JQR 80 (1989) 93-130] BASP 28 (1991) 35-41.
9574* *MacCoull* Leslie S. B., *philotimía* in Byzantine papyrus documents:
Tyche 5 (1990) 63-66.
9575 **Migliardi Zingale** Livia, Papiri dell'Università di Genova 3: Papyrologica Florentina 20. F 1991, Gonnelli. viii-93 p.; 36 pl.
9576 *Obbink* Dirk, Bilingual literacy and Syrian Greek [P. Yadin]: BASP 28
(1991) 51-57.
9578 **Petzl** G., Die Inschriften von Smyrna II, 1, 1987 ➤ 5,9580*: ᴿMnemosyne 44 (1991) 290-3 (H. W. *Pleket*).
9579 ᴱ**Pintaudi** Rosario, *al.*, Papyri graecae Wessely Pragenses (PPrag I):
PapyrolFlor 16, 1988 ➤ 4,a632: ᴿBySlav 51 (1990) 59s (G. *Poethke*);
Tyche 5 (1990) 199-202 (P. *Palme*).
9580 *Salamé-Sarkis* Ḥassān, Syria grammata kai agalmata: Syria 66 (1989)
313-330; 12 fig.
9581 **Schwartz** Jacques *al.*, Papyrus grecs de la Bibiothèque N/U de
Strasbourg, Nos 881-900: Publ. 9/5. Strasbourg 1989, Bibliothèque N/U.
p. 127-151. – ᴿGnomon 63 (1991) 641s (J. D. *Thomas*).
9581* **Shelton** John C., Greek ostraca in the Ashmolean .. 1988 ➤ 4,a639:
ᴿCdÉ 65 (1990) 354-6 (J. *Bingen*).
9582 **Sirivianou** M. G., The Oxyrhynchus Papyri 56: Memoir 76. L 1989
➤ 6,9700*: ᴿTyche 6 (1991) 253-6 (B. *Palme*).

9583 *Wachter* Rudolph, Abbreviated writing [in Greek inscriptions]: Kadmos 30 (1991) 49-80.
9584 **Wessel** Karl †, ᴱ*Ferrua* A. *Carletti* C., Inscriptiones graecae christianae veteres Occidentis 1989 ➤ 6,9711: ᴿCC 142 (1991,1) 438s (*Ferrua*); Salesianum 53 (1991) 161s (R. *Della Casa*).
9584* **Wouters** Alfonso, Beatty Codex Ac 1499, Pauline epp., Greek grammar 1988 ➤ 4,2657... 6,9715: ᴿBO 48 (1991) 523-7 (K. *Versteegh*).

J5.5 **Cypro-Minoa** [➤ T 9.1-4].

9585 *a)* *Baurain* Claude, L'écriture syllabique à Chypre; – *b)* *Perna* Massimo, Alcune considerazioni sulla tavoletta di Enkomi n. 1885; – *c)* *Collombier* Anne-Marie, Écritures et sociétés à Chypre à l'Âge de Fer; – *d)* *Palaima* Thomas G., The advent of the Greek alphabet on Cyprus; a competition of scripts: ➤ 630, Phoinikeia 1989/91, 389-424 / 473-8 + 2 fig. / 425-447 / 449-468 + 3 pl.
9585* **Bile** Monique, Le dialecte crétois ancien 1988 ➤ 5,9648: ᴿBSLP 85 (1990) 120-4 (A. *Blanc*).
9586 *Bruce* William C., *a)* Notes on Linear A: V. The legibility of the account tablets; VI. Hieroglyphic antecedents of Linear signs; – *b)* Notes on the inscriptions from Mallia Quarter Mu; IV. The clay bar from Knossos P 116: Kadmos 30 (1991) 42-46-48; 2 fig. / 93-100-104, 6+5 fig. – With this issue Bruce passes the editorship of Kadmos to Wolfgang *Blümel* of Köln.
9587 ᶠCHADWICK John: Studies in Mycenaean... ᴱ**Killen** J... 1987 ➤ 3,37; 5,9652: ᴿRPg 64 (1990) 204-9 (N. *Maurice*).
9588 *Dürr* Friedrich, A thread leading out of the VENTRISIAN labyrinth; remarks on Minoan Linear B: BibNot 54 (1990) 42-59.
9589 *Duhoux* Yves, *a)* La situation du yod en grec mycénien: BSLP 85 (1990) 359-365; – *b)* Observations sur l'œnochoé du Dipylon: Kadmos 30 (1991) 153-169; 1 fig.
9590 *Godart* Louis, *Tzedakis* Yannis, Les nouveaux textes en Linéaire A de La Canée: RFgIC 119 (1991) 129-149; 2 pl.
9591 *Haecker* Hans-Joachim, Zur Frage der 'internen Analyse' der Schrift auf dem Diskos von Phaistos: Kadmos 30 (1991) 29-33; 2 fig.
9592 *Hallager* Erik, *al.*, New... Linear A documents from Kastelli, Khania: Kadmos 30 (1991) 34-41; 2 pl.
9593 *Hooker* James T., Mycenology in the 1980's: Kratylos 36 (1991) 32-72.
9594 **Melena** José L., *Olivier* Jean-Pierre, Tithemy; the tablets and nodules in Linear B from Tiryns, Thebes and Mycenae: Minos supp. 12. Salamanca / Lejona 1991, Univ. Salamanca / País Vasco. 97 p.
9595 *Morandi* Alessandro, Die Goldbleche von Pyrgi, Indizien für eine neue Lesung: AntWelt 22 (1991) 119-126; 13 fig.
9596 *Owens* Gareth, A Linear B tablet at University College, London: BInstClas 37 (1990) 95-98.
9597 *Palmer* Ruth, Linear A and the Minoan wine trade: ➤ 627*, AJA 95 (1991) 325s, summary.
9598 *Perna* Massimo, À propos de la fonction des rondelles minoennes: Kadmos 30 (1991) 105-112.
9598* *a)* *Risch* Ernst, La contribution de la langue mycénienne au problème de la transition du palais à la cité; – *b)* *Brixhe* Claude, Du mycénien aux dialectes du Iᵉʳ millénaire; quelques aspects de la problématique: ➤ 649, Transizione 1988/91, 231-240 / 251-272.

9599 *Schmitt* Rüdiger, Eine neue kyprische Gefässinschrift: Kadmos 30 (1991) 128-130; 2 pl.

9599* *Varias García* Carlos, La metodología actual en el estudio de los textos micénicos; un ejemplo práctico [KN Ln 1568]: Faventia 12s (1990s) 353-365.

J6 Indo-Iranica.

9600 ᴱ**Caillat** Colette, Dialectes dans les littératures indo-aryennes; Actes du Colloque CNRS 16-18 sept. 1986. P 1989, Institut de Civilisation Indienne [de Boccard]. xv-579 p. – ᴿBSO 54 (1991) 387-9 (Rachel *Dwyer*).

9600* ᴱ**Camps** Arnulf, *Muller* Jean-Claude, The Sanskrit grammar and manuscripts of Father Heinrich Roth S.J. 1988 ➔ 4,a709; 5,9678: ᴿBSLP 85 (1990) 101-4 (P.-S. *Filliozat*); ZMissRW 75 (1991) 81s (H.-W. *Gensichen*).

9601 **Chari** V.K., Sanskrit [poetics] criticism. Honolulu 1990, Univ. xii-302 p. $35. – ᴿJAOS 111 (1991) 593-6 (R.E. *Goodwin*: consummately intelligent).

9602 **Gignoux** Philippe, Noms propres sassanides en moyen-perse épigraphique 1986 ➔ 5,9681; 6,9787: ᴿOrientalia 60 (1991) 379-387 (S. *Shaked*); WZKM 79 (1989) 301s (O. *Klima* †).

9603 **Grillot-Susini** Françoise, (*Roche* C.), Éléments de grammaire élamite 1987 ➔ 5,9682; 6,9788: ᴿAfO 36s (1989s) 180-2 (Heidemarie *Koch*); Syria 67 (1990) 759-761 (Florence *Malbran-Labat*).

9604 **Kellens** Jean, *Pirart* Eric, Les textes vieil-avestiques, 1. Wsb 1988, Reichert. 195 p. – ᴿJAOS 111 (1991) 659-662 (P.O. *Skjaervo*).

9605 *Malbran-Labat* Florence, *a*) Les briques inscrites de Suse (époque pre-achéménide): Syria 66 (1989) 281-301; 17 fig. – *b*) Système pronominal et système verbal en élamite achéménide: BSLP 85 (1900) 61-90; Eng. 376; deutsch 377.

9606 ᴱ**Schmitt** Rüdiger, Compendium linguarum iranicarum. Wsb 1989, Reichert. xiv-529 p. DM 280. – ᴿBSO 54 (1991) 172-7 (D.N. *MacKenzie*); OLZ 86 (1991) 423-7 (M. *Lorenz*).

9607 **Tikkanen** Bertil, The Sanskrit gerund 1987 ➔ 4,a717: ᴿIndogF 95 (1990) 262-5 (Annemarie *Etter*).

9608 *Zimmer* Stefan, Zur sprachlichen Deutung sasanidischer Personennamen: AltOrF 18 (1991) 109-150.

J6.5 Latina.

9609 *a*) *Carvalho* Paulo de, Structure morpho-syntactique de l'adjectif latin; la présence de l'absent; – *b*) *Kircher-Durand* Chantal, Syntax, morphology and semantics in the structuring of the Latin lexicon, as illustrated in the *-lis* derivatives: ➔ 580, ᴱ*Coleman* R., 4th Latin Linguistics 1987/91, 251-267 / 111-127.

9610 *Castillo* Carmen, El progreso de la epigrafía romana en Hispania (1983-1987); Emerita 59 (1991) 225-273.

9611 *a*) *Drinka* Bridget, LACHMANN's law; a phonological solution [... why *pango* > *pactus* but *pungo* > *punctus*?]; – *b*) *Stephens* Laurence D., On the modal semantics of the Latin construction *fore/futurum (esse) ut(i)*: IndogF 96 (1991) 52-74 / 75-95.

9612 **Gaide** Françoise, Les substantifs latins en *-i(ō)*, *-(i)ōnis*. Lv/P 1988, 'B.I.G.' 373 p. – ᴿRPg 64 (1990) 232-6 (J. *Daude*).

9613 **Haverling** G., Studies on [Latin] SYMMACHUS' language and style: Ac, GLat 49. Göteborg 1988, Univ. 295 p. – REmerita 59 (1991) 383s (J. M. *Díaz de Bustamante*).

9614 **Salomies** Olli, Die römischen Vornamen 1987 → 5,9685*; 6,9795: RBeiNam 26 (1991) 89-91 (H. *Rix*); Gnomon 63 (1991) 33-36 (I. *Di Stefano Manzella*).

9615 **Schulze** Wilhelm, Zur Geschichte latenischer Eigennamen (1904), ESalomies Olli. Z 1991, Weidmann. [vi–] 650 p. 3-615-00061-7.

J8.1 Philologia generalis.

9615* **Buck** Carl D., A dictionary of selected synonyms in the principal Indo-European languages; a contribution to the history of ideas (1949). Ch 1988, Univ. xix-1515 p. $36. – RBSLP 85 (1990) 69-71 (P. *Swiggers:* unique).

Hölscher Tonio, Römische Bildsprache als semantisches System 1987 → b923.

9616 EKleiber Georges, *Roques* Gilles, Travaux de Linguistique et de Philologie ['de Littérature' jusqu'à 1988] 25,1 / 27. Strasbourg 1987/9. 385 p. / 283 p. – RBSLP 85 (1990) 212-6 (P. *Swiggers*).

9617 **Köbler** Gerhard, Gotisches Wörterbuch. Leiden 1989, Brill. xlvi-716 p. 90-04-09128-9.

9618 **Lehmann** Winfred P., [< *Fust* Sigmund ³1939] A Gothic etymological dictionary. Leiden 1986, Brill. [iv–] [xix–] 712 p. 90-04-08176-3.

9619 *Louw* Johannes P., How do words mean – if they do?: FgNt 4 (1991) 125-141; español 141s.

9620 **Oberhuber** Karl, Linguistisch-philologische Prolegomena zur altorientalischen Religionsgeschichte: InBeitSprW Vortr 53. Innsbruck 1991, Univ. Inst. SprW. 39 p. 3-85124-624-1.

9622 **Salvadore** Marcello, Il nome, la persona; saggio sull'etimologia antica: ArchFgClas 110. Genova 1987, Univ. Fac. Lettere. 131 p. – RJHS 111 (1991) 230s (S. *Halliwell*); ParPass 257 (1991) 158-160 (L. *Spina*).

9623 **Siewerska** Anna, Word order rules: Ling. Series. L 1988, Croom Helm. [xiv–] 304 p. 0-7099-4484-5.

J8.2 Grammatica comparata.

9624 *Adrados* Francisco R., El formante –*n* y el origen de la flexión heteroclítica del Indoeuropeo: Emerita 59,1 (1991) 5-21.

9625 EBechert Johannes, *al.*, Toward a typology of European languages: Empirical approaches to language typology 8. B 1990, Mouton de Gruyter. x-388 p. 3-11-012108-5. 17 art.

9625* *a*) *Bomhard* A. R., Lexical parallels between Proto-Indo-European and other languages [477 examples]; – *b*) *Levet* Jean-Pierre, Étymologie et formation du verbe proto-indo-européen; remarques sur les désinences –*ṣ* et –*s* du tokharien A [*Lindeman* F. O., laryngeals]; – *c*) *Merlingen* Weriand, Etymologie und Sprachgeschichte; – *d*) *Swiggers* Pierre, Forme et sens en étymologie; Antoine THOMAS et Hugo SCHUCHARDT: → 167, Mem. WINDEKENS A. van 1991, 47-106 / 161-176 [177s] / 187-199; 8 tables / 285-294.

9626 **Durand** Olivier, Précédents chamito-sémitiques en hébreu; études d'histoire linguistique: StSemit NS 8. R 1991, Univ. vii-150 p.

9627 *Durand* Olivier, *a*) L'affixe verbal *-ta-* et un archaïsme cha-mito-sémitique pré-flexif: RSO 64 (1990) 247-253; – *b*) Une réflexion sur les Begadkefat en langue chamito-sémitique. OrAnt 28 (1989) 217-225.

9628 *Ellegård* Alvar, The Indo-European question reconsidered: Fornvännen 85 (1990) 128-132.

9628* *Gamkrelidze* T.V., *Ivanov* V.V., Les premiers Indo-Européens de l'histoire; les ancêtres des Tokhariens en Asie Mineure ancienne: ➤ 48*, ᶠEsenç T., RÉtGéorg 6s (1990s) 265-296.

9629 *Jucquois* Guy, Langues anciennes et grammaire comparée: ÉtClas 59 (1991) 205-229.

9630 **Khan** G., Studies in Semitic syntax (ᴰ1984L) 1988 ➤ 4,9757; 5,9140: ᴿJAOS 111 (1991) 135-7 (A.S. *Kaye*); JSS 36 (1991) 122-5 (A.F.L. *Beeston*, on the Arabic part a few minor flaws).

9631 **Markey** T.L., *Greppin* John A., When worlds collide; Indo-Europeans and pre-Indo-Europeans; the Bellagria papers: Linguistica Extranea 19. AA 1990, Karoma. 395 p. 0-89720-090-X [Antiquity 66, 251, R. *Crossland*: when specialists collide].

9632 **Meid** Wolfgang, Archäologie und Sprachwissenschaft; Kritisches zu neueren Hypothesen der Ausbreitung der Indogermanen: InBeitSprW 43, 1989 ➤ 5,594: ᴿKratylos 36 (1991) 95-98 (A. *Häusler*).

9633 *Müller* Hans-Peter, Zur Theorie der historisch vergleichenden Grammatik dargestellt am sprachgeschichtlichen Kontext des Althebräischen: ➤ 281, *Wolf* L., Semitic Studies II (1991) 1100-1117.

9634 **Renfrew** Colin, Archaeology and language 1987 ➤ 5,9730: ᴿAct-ArchH 43 (1991) 437-9 (J. *Makkay*); SovArch (1991,2) 279-283 (A.D. *Rezepkin*).

9635 **Retsö** Jan, Diathesis 1989 ➤ 5,9731: ᴿJAOS 111 (1991) 650-3 (S. *Lieberman*).

9636 ᶠRísch Ernst, o-o-pe-ro-si, 75. Gb., ᴱ**Etter** A. 1986 ➤ 2,95: ᴿIndogF 95 (1990) 248-256 (T. *Krisch*).

9637 *Robb* John, Random causes with directed effects; the Indo-European language spread and the stochastic loss of lineages: Antiquity 65 (1991) 287-291.

9638 **Rosén** Haiim B., L'hébreu et ses rapports avec le monde classique; essai d'évaluation culturelle: Ét.Cham.-Sém. supp. 7, 1979 ➤ 60,a880 ... 62,8724: ᴿEos 59 (1991) 271-3 (T. *Polański*, ❸).

9639 **Soden** Wolfram von, *a*) Zur Einteilung der semitischen Sprachen [< WZKM 56 (1960) 177-181 = BibelAO, BZAW 163 (1985) 36-50]. – *b*) Tempus und Modus im älteren Semitischen [ineditum 1988]: ➤ 321, WegF 633 (1991) 447-462 / 463-494.

9640 **Svenbro** Jesper, Phrasikleia, anthropologie de la lecture en Grèce ancienne 1988 ➤ 5,9701*: ᴿRÉAnc 92 (1990) 399-401 (Colette *Jourdain-Annequin*: Phrasikleia n'est que le nom d'une jeune fille dont la statue funéraire fut découverte au sud de Marathon en 1972).

9641 **Szemerényi** Oswald, Einführung in die vergleichende Sprachwissenschaft3ʳᵉᵛ 1989 ➤ 5,9733; DM 62; sb. 49: ᴿIndogF 96 (1991) 261-6 (E. *Eggers*).

9642 *Tischler* Johann, Hundert Jahre *kentum-satem* Theorie [Solta G.R.]: IndogF 95 (1990) 63-98.

9643 *a*) *Vine* Brent, Indo-European and nostratic; – *b*) *Euler* Wolfram, Die Frage nach der Entstehung der indogermanischen Genera im Lichte der relativen Chronologie: IndogF 96 (1991) 9-35 / 36-45.

9644 *Wilson* E.J., Sibilant rivalry [interchange of sibilants in Semitic languages]: Akkadica 70 (1990) 28-40.

J8.3 Linguistica generalis.

9644* Actes du XIVᵉ colloque international de linguistique fonctionnelle (Elseneur 29.VI-4.VII. 1987): Cah 14,1s. LvN 1988, Inst. Linguistique. 295 p. – ᴿBSLP 85 (1990) 52s (X. *Mignot*).

9645 a) *Andersen* Henning, Markedness theory – the first 150 years; – b) *Gvozdanović* Jadranka, Defining markedness: → 607, Markedness 1986/9, 11-46 / 47-66.

9645* ᴱ**Auroux** S., Antoine MEILLET et la linguistique de son temps: Histoire, épistémologie, langage 10,2 (P 1988). 348 p. – ᴿBSLP 85 (1990) 61-3 (M. *Bile*).

9646 **Black** David A., Linguistics for students of NT Greek 1988 → 4,a766; 5,9740: ᴿCritRR 4 (1991) 172s (S. E. *Porter*).

9646* *Botha* J.E., The potential of speech act theory for New Testament exegesis: HervTSt 47 (1991) 277-293.

9647 **Bynon** Theodora, Historische Linguistik [1977, amplified], ᵀ*Abraham* W. [adapted], 1981 → 64,8531: ᴿIndogF 96 (1991) 258-261 (J. *Udolph*).

9648 **Corbett** Greville G., Gender: Textbooks in Linguistics. C 1991, Univ. xix-363 p. 0-521-32939-6; pa. –3845-X.

9649 **Cotterell** Peter, *Turner* Max, Linguistics and biblical interpretation 1989 → 5,9746; 6,9837: ᴿBTrans 42 (1991) 139-144 (Lynell *Zogbo*); CritRR 4 (1991) 77-79 (S. E. *Porter*); Evangel 8,3 (1990) 22s (F. F. *Bruce*).

9650 *Davidson* Iain, The archaeology of language origins – a review: Antiquity 65 (1991) 39-45.

9651 *Fludernik* Monika, Shifters [chiefly Ist-2d person pronouns] and deixis; some reflections on JAKOBSON, JESPERSEN, and reference: Semiotica 86 (1991) 193-230.

9651* ᴱ**Gessinger** Joachim, *Rahden* Wolfert von, Theorien vom Ursprung der Sprache 1989 → 5,541: ᴿDLZ 112 (1991) 724-9 (W. *Bahner*).

9652 *Haarmann* Harald, 'Basic' vocabulary and language contacts; the disillusion of glottochronology: IndogF 95 (1990) 1-37.

9652* **Harris** R., *Taylor* T.J., Landmarks in linguistic thought; the western tradition from Socrates to SAUSSURE. L 1989, Routledge. xviii-199 p. – ᴿBSLP 85 (1990) 57-61 (P. *Swiggers*).

9653 **Hock** Hans H., Principles of historical linguistics: TrendsL 34, 1986 → 2,7858: ᴿIndogF 95 (1990) 232-7 (B. *Künzle*).

9654 **Keller** Rudi, Sprachwandel; von der unsichtbaren Hand in der Sprache: Uni-Tb 1567. Tü 1990, Francke. 218 p. DM 24,80. – ᴿDLZ 112 (1991) 18-20 (E. *Albrecht*).

9655 ᴱ**Lazzeroni** Romano, Linguistica storica 1987 → 5,9759: ᴿIndogF 95 (1990) 237-241 (E. *Blasco Ferrer*).

9656 ᴱ**Lepschy** G.C., Storia della linguistica I. Bo 1990, Mulino. 310 p. 88-15-02483-2. – ᴿHenoch 13 (1991) 395s (G. *Tamani*).

9658 **Lindeman** Fredrik O., Introduction to the 'Laryngeal Theory' [1970, expanded],ᵀ: Kulturforskning B-75, 1987 → 4,a781: ᴿIndogF 96 (1991) 269-274 (H. *Rix*); Kratylos 36 (1991) 92-95 (M. *Mayrhofer*).

9658* **McCray** Stanley, Advanced principles of historical linguistics: AmerUnivSt 13/6. NY 1988, Lang. xii-262 p. $46. – ᴿIndogF 96 (1991) 251-8 (E. *Eggers*).

9659 **Malmberg** Bertil, Histoire de la linguistique de Sumer à Saussure. P 1991, PUF. 496 p. – ᴿOrSuec 40 (1991) 290s (T. *Kronholm*).

9660 ᴱ**Malmkjaer** Kirsten, (*Anderson* James M.), The linguistic encyclopedia. L 1991, Routledge. xx-575 p. 0-415-02942-2.

9661 *Marty* François, [➤ 2031] Le langage ou la patience: Études 375 (1991) 351-363.

9662 *Mazaudon* Martine, *Lowe* John B., Du bon usage de l'informatique en linguistique historique: BSLP 86 (1991) 49-87.

9663 *Mignot* Xavier, Ordre des mots, linéarité du langage et structures syntaxiques: BSLP 86 (1991) 1-17.

9664 *a*) *Nesher* Dan, Understanding sign semiosis as cognition and as self-conscious process; a reconstruction of some basic concepts in PEIRCE's semiotics; – *b*) *Staat* Wim, Interactive meaning representation of audiovisual texts; a Peircean approach: Semiotica 79 (1990) 1-49 / 51-78.

9665 **Noppen** Jean-Pierre van, *Hols* Edith, Metaphor II, a classified bibliography of publications 1985 to 1900: Library and Information Sources in Linguistics 5/20, Amst/Ph 1990, Benjamins. 350 p. *f* 140. – ᴿRBgPg 69 (1991) 665-7 (Dragan *Momirović*; superbly usable but not likely to be adequately used).

9666 *Petrilli* Susan, For a semiotic narration of semiotics [ᴱHERZFELD M., *Melazzo* L., Semiotic theory and practice, Palermo 1984/8]: Semiotica 87 (1991) 119-146.

9667 ᶠPOLOME Edgar C., Languages and cultures, ᴱ**Jazayery** M. A., *Winter* W. 1988 ➤ 5,153: ᴿRBgPg 69 (1991) 644-6 (Francine *Mawet*).

9668 **Raible** Wolfgang, Die Semiotik der Textgestalt; Erscheinungsformen und Folgen eines kulturellen Evolutionsprozesses: Abh Heid ph/h 1991/1. Heid 1991, Winter. 44 p.

9669 ᴱ**Schröder** Hartmut, Subject-oriented texts; languages for special purposes and text theory: Research in Text Theory 16. B 1991, de Gruyter. viii-322 p. 3-11-012568-4.

9670 **Sebeok** Thomas A., Semiotics in the United States: Advances in Semiotics. Bloomington 1991, Indiana Univ. [viii–] 173 p. 0-253-35134-0.

9672 **Simone** Raffaele, Fondamenti di linguistica: Manuali Laterza 9. R 1990, Laterza. xvi-584 p. 88-420-3499-1. – ᴿSalesianum 53 (1991) 803s (R. *Della Casa*).

9672* **Sotiropoulos** Dimitris, ⓖ *Hē glōssología kaì ho* Noam CHOMSKY. Athenai 1988, Pneumatikē Zōē. 72 p. – ᴿBSLP 85 (1990) 138s (A. *Panayotou*, C. *Brixhe*).

9673 ᴱ**Taylor** Daniel J., The history of linguistics in the classical period 1987 ➤ 6,9856: ᴿEos 59 (1991) 269-271 (W. *Stefański*, Eng.).

9673* **Tovar** Antonio, El lingüista español Lorenzo HERVÁS [y PANDURO 1735-1809]; estudio y selección de obras básicas; I. Catálogo delle lingue [sic]. M ..., Soc. Librerᶜa. 366 p. – ᴿBSLP 85 (1990) 284-8 (P. *Swiggers*).

9674 *a*) *Veggel* Rob J. van, [*Charles* S.] PEIRCE's semiosis, MORRIS's semiosis, and studies of reference; – *b*) *Peirce* Jeremy H., Signs as information: Semiotica 87 (1991) 95-117 / 83-94.

J8.4   *Origines artis scribendi* – **The origin of writing.**

9674* *a*) *Bisi* Anna Maria †, Les plus anciens objets inscrits en phénicien et en araméen retrouvés en Grèce; leur typologie et leur rôle; : *b*) *Isserlin* J.B.S., The transfer of the alphabet to the Greeks; the state of documentation; – c) *Amadasi Guzzo* M. G., 'The shadow line'; réflexions sur l'introduction de l'alphabet en Grèce; – d) *Brixhe* C., De la phonologie à l'écriture; quelques aspects de l'adaptation de l'alphabet cananéen en grec: ➤ 630, Phoinikeia 1989/91, 277-282 / 283-291 / 293-309; 1 fig. / 313-356.

9675 a) *Cavallo* Guglielmo, Metodi di descrizione delle scritture in paleografia greca; – b) *Marazzi* Massimiliano; Il cosiddetto geroglifico anatolico; spunti e riflessioni per una sua definizione; – c) *Crisci* Edoardo, Scritture greche palestinesi e mesopotamiche (III s.a.C.-III s.d.C.); – d) *Roccati* Alessandro, Scrittura e testo nell'antico Egitto: ScrCiv 15 (1991) 21-30 / 31-77 + 42 fig. / 125-179 + 77 fig., XXVI pl. / 307-316.

9675* a) *Delcor* Mathias, L'alphabet phénicien; son origine et sa diffusion, de Samuel BOCHART à Emmanuel de ROUGÉ; trois siècles de recherches, XVIIᵉ-XIXᵉ s.; – b) *Millar* A. R., The uses of the early alphabets; – c) *Puech* É., La tablette cunéiforme de Beth Shemesh, premier témoin de la séquence des lettres en sud-sémitique; – d) *Dietrich* M., *Loretz* O., Die Keilalphabete aus Ugarit: ➤ 630, Phoinikeia 1989/91, 21-32 / 101-114 / 33-46; 2 fig. / 49-67.

9676 **Desbordes** Françoise, Idées romaines sur l'écriture. Lille 1990, Presses Universitaires. 295 p. 2-85939-369-2.

9677 ᴱ**Detienne** Marcel, Les savoirs de l'écriture en Grèce ancienne 1988 ➤ 5,9799; 6,9864: ᴿRÉAnc 93 (1991) 153s (M. M. *Mactoux*).

9679 **Godart** Louis, Le pouvoir de l'Écrit: Néreïdes 1990 ➤ 6,9865*: ᴿÉTRel 66 (1991) 269 (J. *Argaud*: l'écriture est née d'un 'pouvoir des palais' et demeure longtemps son apanage); RFgIC 119 (1991) 457-461 (M. *Del Freo*).

9680 a) *Haarmann* Harald, Pre-Indo-European writing in Old Europe as a challenge to the Indo-European intruders: IndogF 96 (1991) 1-8; – b) *Curto* S., Il progresso della Scrittura dall'Antico Egitto alla Fenicia: ➤ 627, Fen. II, 1987/91, 475-8.

9681 **Harris** W. V., Ancient literacy 1989 ➤ 6,9869; ᴿClasR 41 (1991) 168s (E. J. *Kenney*); JHS 111 (1991) 240s (Carol G. *Thomas*); JRS 81 (1991) 182s (R. *Thomas*: Rome's élite rarely and barely needed to read and write; that was taken care of for them by slaves).

9682 **Healey** John F., The early alphabet: Reading the past 9. L/Berkeley 1991, British Museum/Univ. California. 64 p.; 40 fig. [BAR-W 17/6,4]. 0-520-07309-6.

9683 **Hinüber** Oskar v., Der Beginn der Schrift und frühe Schriftlichkeit in Indien: Abh Mainz g/soz 1989/11. Stu 1990, Steiner. 75 p. 3-515-05627-0.

9684 **Jeffery** L. H., The local scripts of archaic Greece; a study of the origin of the Greek alphabet and its development from the eighth to the fifth centuries B.C., ²*Johnston* A. W. [¹1961] 1990 ➤ 6,9873: ᴿClasR 41 (1991) 265s (D. M. *Lewis*); RÉG 104 (1991) 434s (L. D.) ➤ 9567.

9685 *Naveh* Joseph, Semitic epigraphy and the antiquity of the Greek alphabet: Kadmos 30 (1991) 143-152.

9686 **Powell** Barry B., HOMER and the origin of the Greek alphabet. C 1991, Univ. xxv-280. 0-521-37157-0 [RÉG 104,682].

9686* a) *Powell* Barry B., The origins of alphabetic literacy among the Greeks; – b) *Baslez* Marie-Françoise, *Briquel-Chatonnet* Françoise, De l'oral à l'écrit; le bilinguisme des Phéniciens en Grèce; – c) *Lemaire* André, L'écriture phénicienne en Cilicie et la diffusion des écritures alphabétiques: ➤ 630, Phoinikeia 1989/91, 357-370 / 371-386 / 133-171.

9687 *Rocchi* Maria,   L'invenzione della scrittura nel mito: Seminari SMEA (1988) 45-51.
9687* *a) Sacconi* Anna,   I sistemi grafici del mondo egeo tra la fine del II e l'inizio del I millennio a.C.; – *b) Bennett* Emmett L.[J], The end of the Mycenaean script; the case of the missing heirs: ➤ 649, Transizione 1988/91, 43-52 / 563-571.
9688 **Sass** Benjamin,   Studia alphabetica; on the origin and early history of the Northwest Semitic, South Semitic and Greek alphabets: OBO 102, FrS/Gö 1991, Univ./VR. viii-124 p. Fs 39, 3-7278-0729-6 / VR 3-525-0729-6 – [R]OTAbs 14 (1991) 349 (C. T. *Begg*).
9689 *Sass* Benjamin,   The Beth Shemesh tablet and the early history of the Proto-Canaanite, Cuneiform and South Semitic alphabets: UF 23 (1991) 315-325 + 3 fig.
9690 *Schwink* Frederick W.,   The writing of ancient Greek consonant clusters [*ks/ps* also in Linear B and Cypriote]: Kadmos 30 (1991) 113-127.
9691 **Senner** W.,   Origins of writing 1989 ➤ 5,9790; 6,9875: [R]JAOS 111 (1991) 826s (M. *Bernal*).
9692 *Strohmaier* Gotthard,   Die Erfindung der Vokalbuchstaben durch die Griechen: Pg 135 (1991) 38-44.

J9.1   Analysis linguistica loquelae de Deo – God-talk.

9694 **Babin** Pierre,   The new era in religious communication, [T]*Smith* David.   Mp 1991, Fortress. xii-235 p. [CBQ 53,733].
9695 *a) Bavel* T. J. van,   SCHOONENBERG's paradoxaal spreken over God; – *b)* *Schreurs* Nico,   Oneindig ver en oneindig dichtbij; God ter sprake gebracht in zijn handelen; – *c) Häring* Hermann,   Eerlijk voor God? [ROBINSON J. 1962]; over de resultaten van een voortgaande discussie; – *d) Harskamp* Anton van,   Behoefte aan religie of verlangen naar God?: TsTNijm 31 ('Voor Piet Schoonenberg' 1991) 246-264; Eng. 264 / 265-284; 284 / 285-314; 314s / 223-244; 244s.
9696 *a) Bottani* Livio,   'Parole come fiori'; metafora e ontologia in Paul RICŒUR; – *b) Prini* P.,   Sull'esperienza del sacro e la civiltà tecnica; dialogo con A. NESTI: Religioni e Società 5,9 ('Linguaggi del sacro' 1990) 9-24 / 87-94 [< FilT 5,566].
9697 **Bryant** David J.,   Faith and the play of imagination: Studies in American Biblical Hermeneutics 5. Macon GA 1989, Mercer Univ. 165 p. $25; pa. $17. 0-86554-319-4; 49-6. – [R]HeythJ 32 (1991) 550 (D. *Jasper*).
9698 **Cooke** Bernard,   The distancing of God 1990 ➤ 6,9884:   [R]CathHR 77 (1991) 660-2 (D. N. *Power*); CCurr 41 (1991s) 420s (R. *Grigg*); Commonweal 118 (1991) 376s (L. T. *Johnson*); NRT 113 (1991) 581 (J. *Masson*); RelStT 10,2 (1990) 68s (P. J. *Cahill*); TS 52 (1991) 755-7 (J. M. *Powers*).
9698* **Crabtree** Harriet,   The Christian life; traditional metaphors and contemporary theologies [diss. [D]*Niebuhr* Richard]: HarvDissRel. Mp 1991, Fortress. xxxvii-190 p. $14 pa. [TDig 39,257].
9699 *a) Crowley* Paul,   Technology, truth and language; the crisis of theological discourse; – *b) Carter* Alan, The real meaning of 'meaning'; HeythJ 32 (1991) 323-339 / 355-368.
9700 *Cunningham* David S.,   Theology as rhetoric ['Half the controversies in the world are verbal ones', NEWMAN]: TS 52 (1991) 407-430.
9701 *Cupitt* Don [➤ 7623],   The long-legged fly 1987 ➤ 4,a821:   [R]HeythJ 32 (1991) 97 (P. *Vardy*: compulsory reading).

9702 **Ellul** Jacques, What I believe, ᵀ*Bromiley* Geoffrey W. GR/L 1989, Eerdmans/Marshall-MS. viii-223 p. $20. – ᴿTS 52 (1991) 593s (D. W. *Gill*).

9703 *Fischer* Johannes, Behaupten oder Bezeugen? Zum Modus der Wahrheitsanspruchs christlicher Rede von Gott: ZTK 87 (1990) 224-244.

9704 *Forrest* Peter, How can we speak of God? How can we speak of anything?: IntJPhilosR 29 (Dordrecht 1991) 33-52 [< TR 87,170].

9706 **Franck** Olof, The criteriological problem; a critical study with special regard to theories presented by Antony FLEW, D. Z. PHILLIPS, John HICK, Basil MITCHELL, Anders JEFFNER and Hans HOF [diss. Uppsala 1989]: Studia Philosophiae Religionis 15. Sto 1988, Almqvist & W. 287 p. 91-22012-47-8. – ᴿNedTTs 45 (1991) 172s (L. J. Van den *Brom*).

9707 **Green** Garrett, Imagining God 1989 → 6,9890: ᴿHorizons 18 (1991) 324-6 (J. V. *Apczynski*); JRel 71 (1991) 597 (C. *Welch*).

9708 **Griffiss** James E., Naming the mystery; how our words shape prayer and belief. CM 1990, Cowley. xv-204 p. $12 pa. 1-56101-016-2 [TDig 38,267]. – ᴿAnglTR 73 (1991) 347s (A. *Jones*); Worship 65 (1991) 555s (Gail *Ramshaw*).

9708* **Hansson** Mats J., Understanding an act of God; an essay in philosophical theology: AcU DocChr 33. Sto 1991, Almqvist & W. 158 p. Sk 132 [TLZ 117, 933, E. *Holze*].

9709 **Hilberath** Bernd J., Der dreieinige Gott und die Gemeinschaft der Menschen; Orientierungen zur christlichen Rede von Gott. Mainz 1990, Grünewald. 117 p. DM 19,80 [TLZ 116,308].

9710 **Hofmeister** Heimo E. M., Truth and belief; interpretation and critique of the [FLEW-HARE-BRAITHWAITE linguistic] analytical theory of religion: StPhRel 14. Boston 1990, Kluwer. 253 p. $92. 0-7923-0976-6 [TDig 38,362: the original English, previously published in German].

9710* a) *Jansen* Gerd, Metaphorisches Handeln als Zeichen für Simulation in der weltanschaulichen Praxis; – b) *Röller* Dirk, Simulation und Fiktion als semiotisches Problem im Religionsunterricht angesichts der Informations- und Kommunikationstechniken; – c) *Schmitz* H. Walter, Simulatio und dissimulatio in ritualisierter Kommunikation; – d) *Juchem* Johann G., Kommunikation als Simulation; – e) *Magass* Walter, Die Simulation im Insgesamt der Zeicheninventare: → 398, Simulation 1989/91, 262-276 / 225-238 / 187-205 / 171-186 / 206-215.

9711 **Jeanrond** Werner G., Text and interpretation as categories of theological thinking 1988 → 2,7910 ... 6,9894: ᴿScotJT 43 (1990) 520s (D. F. *Ford*).

9711* **Koch** Walter A., Gott und die Welt; Semiogenese und Theogenese: BeitSemiotik 32. Bochum 1991, Brockmeyer. ix-92 p.; ill.; 11 foldouts. DM 24,80 [TLZ 117, 859, W. *Schenk*].

9712 *Kolvenbach* Peter-Hans, Langage et anthropologie; le Journal spirituel de saint IGNACE: Gregorianum 72,2 (1991) 211-221; Eng. 221 [223-364 sur S. Ignace; 317-347, *Tilliette* Xavier, FESSARD et les Exercices].

9713 **Long** Charles, Significations ... in religion 1986 → 2,187 ... 5,9818: ᴿRelStT 9,2s (1989) 79-81 (P. *Gose*).

9714 a) *Loose* Donald, Voor een theologie van de metafoor; – b) *Soskice* Janet M., 'By a new notation no facts of geography are changed' (WITTGENSTEIN); some comments on metaphor and linguistic change in religion: RBgPg 68 (1990) 576-596 / 597-607 [527-679 al., from 'How to do things with metaphor' Bru 10.III. 1990].

9715 *Meckenstock* Günter, Über die Schwierigkeit, von Gott zu reden: NSys 33 (1991) 217-230; Eng. 230.

9716 *Miles* Margaret B., [Image as insight defense against J. W. Dixon review: JAAR [56 (1988)] 59 (1991) 149-151; Dixon rejoinder, 151-3.

9717 **Miller** David L., Hells and holy ghosts 1989 ➤ 6,7682: RCritRR 4 (1991) 450s (J. R. *Sibley:* a demystifying theopoetics).

9717* **Morin** Dominique, Para decir Dios. Estella 1990, VDivino. 143 p. – REfMex 9 (1991) 128s (B. *González*).

9718 **Müller** W. W.   Das Symbol in der dogmatischen Theologie... K. RAHNER, P. TILLICH, P. RICŒUR, J. LACAN [Diss. 1989 ➤ 5,9825]. Fra 1990, Lang. 455 p. – RLaurentianum 32 (1991) 435-7 (B. de *Armellada*).

9719 **Noppen** Jean-Pierre van, Erinnern... Metapher 1988 ➤ 4,a848; 5,9826: RCritRR 3 (1990) 470s (E. J. *Epp*).

9720 *Pandharipande* [dh. p. 182 & 282; d. p. 185] Rajeshwari, Metaphor in the language of religion: JDharma 15 (1990) 185-203.

9721 *Pannenberg* Wolfhart, Eine philosophisch-historische Hermeneutik des Christentums [... 'Gott' im Mund]: TPhil 66 (1991) 481-492.

9722 **Ricœur** Paul, Soi-même comme un autre [E 1986 Gifford Lectures, 'On Selfhood; the question of personal identity', revised]: L'ordre philosophique. P 1990, Seuil, 424 p. 2-02-011458-5. – RTsTNijm 31 (1991) 446 (J. Van den *Hengel*).

9723 *Saint-Germain* Christian, Le mot Dieu de Karl RAHNER à Edmond JABÈS; la tradition interrogée: LavalTP 47 (1991) 161-7.

9724 **Schaeffler** Richard, Das Gebet und das Argument; zwei Weisen des Sprechens von Gott; eine Einführung in die Theorie der religiösen Sprache: BeiTRelW, 1989 ➤ 6,9910: REstE 66 (1991) 361s (J. *Pardo*); TR 87 (1991) 47s (R. *Miggelbrink*).

9725 ESCharlemann Robert P., *Oguto* Gilbert E. M., God in language [Seoul 1984]. NY 1987. Paragon. XI-224 p. – RJRel 70 (1990) 134s (Mary *Gerhart*).

9726 **Schilling** Klaus, Symbole erleben; Glauben erfahren mit Hand, Kopf und Herz: Tb 7. Stu 1991, KBW. 160 p. 3-460-11007-4.

9727 **Soskice** Janet M., Metaphor and religious language 1985 ➤ 1,9626... 5,9831: RCurrTMiss 17 (1990) 299s (J. K. *Robbins*); NedTTs 43 (1989) 171 (L. J. van den *Brom*).

9728 **Tracy** David, Plurality and ambiguity 1977 ➤ 3,a117.a997... 6,9913: RModT 7 (1990s) 483-7 (G. *Loughlin*); RelStT 10,2 (1990) 115-7 (J. *McCarthy*).

9729 *Tracy* David, The hermeneutics of naming God: IrTQ 57 (1991) 253-264.

9730 **Vahanian** Gabriel, Dieu anonyme, ou la peur des mots 1989 ➤ 5,9815; 6,9914: RÉTRel 66 (1991) 141 (A. *Gounelle*); FoiVie 89,5 (1990) 101-3 (A. *Dumas*: attaque frontale menée sans cesse contre la notion de salut, devenue pour lui totalement incompréhensible aujourd'hui).

9731 *Wallace* Mark I., Can God be named without being known? The problem of revelation in THIEMANN, OGDEN, and RICŒUR: JAAR 59 (1991) 281-308.

9732 **Watts** Fraser, *Williams* Mark, The psychology of religious knowing [... are doctrinal statements verifiable?]. C 1988, Univ. x-169 p. £19.50. – RScotJT 43 (1990) 529-531 (A. *Millar*).

9733 **Zimmer** Christoph, 'Deus'; logische Syntax und Semantik: Forum

Theologie Linguisticae 20. Bonn 1991, Linguistica Biblica. 105 p. DM
19 pa. 3-87797-030-3. – ᴿZkT 113 (1991) 464s (E. *Runggaldier*).

J9.2 *Hermeneutica paratheologica* – **wider linguistic analysis.**

9734 **Bayer** Oswald, Autorität und Kritik, zu Hermeneutik und Wissen-
schaftstheorie. Tü 1991, Mohr. x-225 p. 3-16-145742-0.
9735 *Beuchot* Mauricio, Nombres proprios, sujetos y predicados en la
semántica tomista y en la actual: Angelicum 68 (1991) 255-279.
9736 **Coffa** J. Alberto, ᴱ*Wessels* Linda, The semantic tradition from Kant
to Carnap: To the Vienna Station. C 1991, Univ. xi-445 p. 0-521-
37429-4.
9737 **Edwards** James C., The authority of language; HEIDEGGER, WITT-
GENSTEIN, and the threat of philosophical nihilism. Tampa 1990, Univ.
S. Florida. – ᴿPerspRelSt 18 (1991) 171-180 (C. J. *Kinlaw*).
9738 **Gadamer** Hans-Georg, Truth and method⁴, 1975 (Sheed/Seabury)
translation revised by *Weinsheimer* Joel, *Marshall* Donald G. L 1989,
Sheed & W. xxxviii-594 p. £37.50. 0-7220-9280-6. – ᴿGregorianum 72
(1991) 194 (J. *Wicks*).
9739 *a) Grondin* J., L'universalisation de l'herméneutique chez H.-G.
GADAMER [liée à une conception dialogale du langage]; – *b) Margolis* J.,
Les trois sortes d'universalité dans l'herméneutique de H.-G. Gadamer; –
c) Rockmore T., Herméneutique et épistémologie; Gadamer entre Heidegger et Hegel: Archives de Philosophie 53 (P 1990) 531-545 / 559-571 /
547-557 [< RSPT 75,517].
ᴱ**Güttgemanns** Erhardt, Das Phänomen der 'Simulation'; Beiträge zu einem
semiotischen Kolloquium: Forum Theologiae Linguisticae 17, 1991
➤ 591c.
9741 *Krieg* G. A., Das Andere und die Zeichen: TLZ 116 (1991) 561-578.
9742 *Moltmann* Jürgen, Die Entdeckung der Anderen; zur Theorie des
kommunikativen Erkennens: EvT 50 (1990) 401-414.
9743 *a)* **Morgan** George Allen, Speech and society; the Christian linguistic
social philosophy of Eugen ROSENSTOCK-HUESSY. Gainesville 1987,
Florida Univ. 209 p. – *b)* **Voorsluis** Bart, Taal en relationaliteit; over de
scheppende en verbindende kracht van taal volgens Eugen Rosenstock-Huessy: Bezinningscentrum V. U. 16. Kampen 1988, Kok. 256 p.
f 54. 90-24232-64-3. – ᴿNedTTs 45 (1991) 87s (A. F. de *Jong*, both).
9744 **Müller** Denis, L'accueil de l'autre et le souci de soi [RICŒUR ...]: RTPhil
123 (1991) 195-212; Eng. 224.
9745 *Müller* Hans-Peter, Zur Wechselbeziehung von Wirklichkeitswahrnahme
und Sprache: ➤ 240, Mythos-Kerygma-Wahrheit 1991, 264-309 [no prior
publication indicated p. ix].
9746 **Ong** Walter J., Oralità e scrittura (le tecnologie della parola) [1982]ᵀ.
Bo 1986, Mulino [StCatt 34,530].
9747 **Ong** Walter J., *a)* Interfaces of the Word. Ithaca NY 1989, Cornell
Univ. – *b)* Interfacce della parola,ᵀ. Bo 1989, Mulino. – ᴿStCatt 34
(1990) 528-530 (A. *Fumagalli*).
9748 ᴱ**Plett** Heinrich F., Intertextuality [coined 1967 by Julia KRISTEVA]:
Research in Text Theory 15. B 1991, de Gruyter. viii-268 p. 3-11-
011637-5. 13 art.
9749 *Reix* André, Des mots comme non étants; topographie critique du
cheminement WITTGENSTEINIEN [REGAL E., NICOLET D.; Actes 1988/
90 ...]: RThom 91 (1991) 468-486.

9750 **Saint-Fleur** Joseph P., Logiques de la représentation; essai d'épistémologie wittgensteinienne. LvN 1988, Academia. – ᴿScEsp 42 (1990) 103-109 (M. *Maesschalck*).

9750* ᴱ**Wachterhauser** B. R., Hermeneutics and modern philosophy [16 reprints of Gadamer and others] 1986 → 3,368: ᴿSWJT 23,1 (1990s) 64s (E. E. *Ellis*: 'Hardcover $14.50; paper, $16,95').

9751 *Żak* Adam, ❷ L'actualité de la pensée d'Eugeniusz ROSENSTOCK-HUESSY: PrzPow 271 (1991) 250-6; franç. 257.

J9.4 Structuralismus, deconstructio.

9752 **Hart** Kevin, The trespass of the sign [Dante P-26]; deconstruction, theology and philosophy 1989 → 6,9939: ᴿHorizons 18 (1991) 340s (Irena *Makarushka*); TorJT 7 (1991) 153s (Pamela J. *Reeve*); TS 52 (1991) 166-8 (M. J. *Kerlin*).

9753 **Poster** Mark, Critical theory and poststructuralism; in search of a context. Ithaca 1989, Cornell Univ. – ᴿPoetics Today 12 (Duke Univ. 1991) (K. *Racevskis*).

9754 *Tilborg* Sjef van, Uitstel van betekenis; het dekonstruktie-projekt in de literatuurwetenschappen: Bijdragen 52 (1991) 271-292; Eng. 292.

9755 *a) Toporov* V. N., A few remarks on PROPP's Morphology of the folktale; – *b) Brown* Edward J., Soviet structuralism; a semiotic approach: → 48, ᶠERLICH V., 1985, 252-271 / 114-129.

J9.6 *Analysis narrationis* – Narrative-analysis.

9755* **Donaldson** Mara E., Holy places are dark places... LEWIS, RICŒUR on narrative transformation 1988 → 5,9876: ᴿCritRR 4 (1991) 66-68 (Ann-Janine *Morey*).

9756 **Ledbetter** Mark, Virtuous intentions; the religious dimension of narrative 1989 → 6,9949: ᴿJAAR 59 (1991) 409s (Ann-Janine *Morey*).

9757 **McCully** Robert S., The enigma of symbols in fairy tales; ZIMMER's dialogue renewed: Studies in comparative literature 14. Lewiston NY 1991, Mellen. [xiii-] 105 p. 0-88946-498-7.

9758 *Mitchell* Pamela, Why care about stories? A theory of narrative art: RelEdn 86,1 (Ch 1991) 30-43 [< ZIT 91,389].

9759 *Preus* J. Samuel, Secularizing divination; spiritual biography and the invention of the novel: JAAR 59 (1991) 441-466.

9760 **Stanzel** Franz K., A theory of narrative [Gö 1979 ²1982], ᵀ*Goedsche* Charlotte. C 1988, Univ. xvi-308 p. 0-521-24719-5; pa. –31063-6.

J9.8 *Theologia narrativa* – Story-theology.

9761 *Aichele* George, Literary fantasy and postmodern [... also narrative] theology: JAAR 59 (1991) 323-337.

9762 *Carr* Dhyanchand, Theology through story: Arasaradi 4,1 (1991) 25-29; 4,2 (1991) 59-63.

9762* ᴱ**Hauerwas** Stanley, *Jones* L. Gregory, Why narrative? Readings in narrative theology. GR 1989 Eerdmans. 329 p. $30; pa. $20 0-8028-3668-2; -0439-X. – ᴿCritRR 4 (1991) 480-2 (Rebecca B. *Prichard*); Interpretation 45 (1991) 210 (J. O. *Duke*); TS 52 (1991) 373-5 (W. R. *Herzog*).

9763 **Navone** John J., Seeking God in story. Collegeville MN 1990, Liturgical. xvi-335 p. $12. 0-8146-1919-3 [TDig 38,370]. – ᴿTLond 95 (1992) 379s (A. *Race*: featured prominently, before CUPITT, but with reserves).

9763* **Stegner** William R., Narrative theology in early Jewish Christianity. Louisville 1990, W-Knox. 141 p. $12. – ᴿChrCent 107 (1990) 576s (J.D. *Kingsbury*).

| **(IV). Postbiblica** |

κ1   **Pseudepigrapha** [= catholicis 'Apocrypha'] .1 *VT, generalia.*

9764 *a) Amsler* Samuel, La Bible judéo-chrétienne en tous ses états; – *b) Dubois* Jean-Daniel, Une lecture chrétienne des 'Écrits intertestamentaires': FoiVie 89,5 = Cahier Biblique 29 ('Tiers-Testament; diversité des écrits intertestamentaires' 1990) 29-38 / 11-19.

9765 *Beckwith* Roger, Intertestamental Judaism, its literature and its significance: Themelios 15 (1989s) 77-81.

9765* **Boccaccini** G., Middle Judaism; Jewish thought, 300 B.C.E. to 200 C.E. Mp 1991, Fortress. xxvii-289 p. $25. 0-8006-2493-9 [NTAbs 36,289].

9766 *Bundy* David, Pseudepigrapha in Syriac literature: → 446, SBL Sem 30 (1991) 745-765.

9767 **Cavalletti** Sofia, Il giudaismo intertestamentario: LoB 3.14. Brescia 1991, Queriniana. 110 p. 88-399-1694-6.

9768 **Charlesworth** J.H., Gli pseudepigrafi dell'AT e il NT, prolegomena allo studio delle origini cristiane, ᵀᴱ*Boccaccini* G.: StBPaid 91, 1990 → 6,9956: ᴿAntonianum 65 (1990) 664s (M. *Nobile*); Asprenas 38 (1991) 395s (A. *Rolla*); Helmantica 42, 129* (1991) 397 (S. *García-Jalón*); Henoch 13 (1991) 244-6 (E. *Lupieri*: rimaneggiamento, bibliografia aggiornata).

9769 **Denis** A.-M., Concordance grecque des pseudépigraphes 1987 → 3,a212 ... 6,9957: ᴿCBQ 53 (1991) 463-5 (G.W.E. *Nickelsburg*); CrNSt 11 (1990) 373-6 (N. *Walter*).

9769* *Guelich* R.A., Spiritual warfare; Jesus, Paul and PERETTI [F., novel 'This present darkness' 1986, fits Jewish apocalypticism better than NT]: Pneuma 13,1 (Gaithersburg MD 1991) 33-64 [< NTAbs 36,72].

9770 **Lechner-Schmidt** W., Wortindex der lateinisch erhaltenen Pseudepigraphen zum AT: NZ 3. Tü 1990, Francke. xi-241 p. DM 98. 3-7720-1882-3 [NTAbs 35,266].

9771 **Maier** Johann, Zwischen den Testamenten; Geschichte und Religion in der Zeit des Zweiten Tempels: NEchter ATEgb 3. Wü 1990, Echter. 320 p. DM 48. 3-429-01292-9. – ᴿJStJud 22 (1991) 150s (F. *García Martínez*).

9772 *Müller* Karlheinz, Die Pseudepigraphie im Schrifttum der frühjüdischen Apokalyptik [= Die Propheten sind schlafen gegangen, syr Bar 85,3, BZ 26 (1982) 179-207]: → 241, Studien 1991, 195-227.

9772* ᴱ**Pfabigan** A., Die andere Bibel [pseudepigrapha] mit Altem und Neuen Testament. Fra 1991, Eichborn. 384 p. DM 36. 3-8218-4413-2 [NTAbs 36,140].

9773 **Rubinkiewicz** Ryszard, ❷ Wprowadzenie ... Introduction to the OT Apocrypha 1987 → 3,a220; 5,9891: ᴿRoczTK 36,1 (1989) 91s (J. *Homerski*).

9774 ᴱ**Sacchi** Paolo, Apocrifi dell'AT 2, 1989 → 5,9893; 6,9962: ᴿAugR 30 (1990) 505s (A. *Camplani*); RHR 208 (1991) 73-75 (P. *Piovanelli*); Salesianum 53 (1991) 177s (R. *Vicent*).

9775 **Turdeanu** E., Apocryphes slaves et roumains de l'Ancien Testament: Studia in VT Pseudepigrapha 5. Leiden 1981, Brill. 465 p. – ᴿBySlav 50 (1989) 76-78 (Zoe *Hauptová*).

к1.2 Henoch.

9776 **Barker** Margaret, [1 Enoch] The lost prophet 1988 ⟶ 4,a947; 5,9898: ᴿScotJT 43 (1990) 523 (D. C. *Parker*).

9777 **Böttrich** Christfried, Weltweisheit — Menschheit — Urkult; Studien zum slavischen Henochbuch: Diss. Kirchliche Hochschule Leipzig 1991, ᴰ*Kähler*. – TR 87 (1991) 519.

9778 *Idel* Moshe, Enoch is Metatron [< ᴱ*Dan*, Early Jewish Mysticism 1987 ⓗ 151-170], ᵀ*Levine* Edward: ⟶ 54, ᶠFLUSSER D., Immanuel 24s (1990) 220-240.

9779 *Nickelsburg* George W. E., The apocalyptic construction of reality in I Enoch: ⟶ 425, Mysteries 1989/91, 51-64.

9780 *a*) *Nickelsburg* George W. E., The Qumran fragments of 1 Enoch and other apocryphal works; implications for the understanding of early Judaism and Christian origins; – *b*) *Charlesworth* James H., Qumran in relation to the Apocrypha, rabbinic Judaism, and nascent Christianity; impacts on university teaching of Jewish civilization in the Hellenistic-Roman period: ⟶ 458, Jewish-Hellenistic 1986/91, 191-195 / 168-180.

9781 **Tiller** Patrick A., A commentary on the Animal Apocalypse (1 Enoch 85-90): diss. Harvard, ᴰ*Strugnell* J. CM 1991. 562 p. 91-22230. – HarvTR 84 (1991) 477s; DissA 52 (1991s) 955s-A; RelStR 18,174.

к1.3 Testamenta.

9782 *Jonge* Marinus de, Testaments des douze Patriarches: ⟶ 668, DictSpir 15 (1990s) 300-8.

9783 *Jonge* M. de, Robert GROSSETESTE and the Testaments of the Twelve Patriarchs: JTS 42 (1991) 115-125.

9784 *Jonge* M. de, Two Messiahs in the Testaments of the Twelve Patriarchs? [< ᶠ*Lebram* 1986, 150-162]: ⟶ 215, GesAufs 1991, 191-203.

9785 **Ulrichsen** Jarl H., Diathêkai ... Die Grundschrift der Testamente der zwölf Patriarchen; eine Untersuchung zu Umfang, Inhalt und Eigenart der ursprünglichen Schrift: AcU HistRel 10. U 1991, Almqvist & W. 368 p. Sk 195. 91-554-2833-9.

9786 **Schmidt** Francis, Le testament grec d'Abraham 1986 ⟶ 2,8055 ... 6,9970: ᴿRuBi 42 (1989) 314s (M. *Wittlieb*).

9787 ᴱ**Knibb** M. A., *Horst* P. W. van der, Studies on the Testament of Job 1986/9 ⟶ 5,9908; 6,9971: ᴿAugR 31 (1991) 484s (P. *Grech*); BL (1991) 138 (C.F.R. *Hayward*); JTS 42 (1991) 182-4 (R. *Bauckham*); TLZ 116 (1991) 428s (H.-M. *Schenke*); VT 41 (1991) 381 (W. *Horbury*).

9788 *a*) *Grelot* Pierre, Le coutumier sacerdotal ancien dans le Testament araméen de Lévi; – *b*) *García Martínez* Florentino, Traditions communes dans le IVᵉ Esdras et dans les MSS de Qumran: ⟶ 145, ᶠSTARCKY J., RQum 15 (1991) 253-263 / 287-301.

9789 *a*) *Cousin* Hugues, Le Testament de Moïse; présentation; – *b*) *Ellul* Danielle, Le Testament d'Abraham; mémoire et source d'imaginaire, la pesée des âmes [-Bibliographie]; – c) *Balestier-Stengel* Guy, Un aperçu sur les Jubilés; le personnage d'Abram: FoiVie 89,5 = CahB 29 (1990) 39-48 / 73-82; 8 fig. [93-97] / 61-71.

K1.5   **Salomonis psalmi** et odae.

9790 *Laperrousaz* Ernest-Marie, Le milieu d'origine du 17ᵉ des Psaumes (apocryphes) de Salomon: RÉJ 150 (1991) 557-564.

9791 **Azar Saqat** Éphrem, La figure du Christ selon les Odes de Salomon: diss. Inst. Cath. & Sorbonne, ᴰ*Perrot* C. Paris 1991. 633 p. – RTLv 23, p. 542.

9792 *Cameron* Peter, a) The crux in Ode of Solomon 19:6; a new solution: JTS 42 (1991) 588-596; – b) The 'sanctuary' in the fourth ode of Solomon: > 15, ᶠBAMMEL E., Templum 1991, 450-463.

9793 **Franzmann** Majella, The Odes of Solomon; an analysis of the poetical structure and form: NOrb 20. FrS/Gö 1991, Univ./VR. xxvii-456 p. Fs 125. 3-7278-0780-6 / VR 3-525-53921-5.

9794 *Lattke* Michael, Die Oden Salomos 1986 ➤ 2,8069 ... 6,9972: ᴿTLZ 116 (1991) 190s (H.-M. *Schenke*).

9795 *Lattke* Michael, Die Messias-Stellen der Oden Salomos: ➤ 72, ᶠHAHN F., Anfänge 1991, 429-445.

K1.6   **Jubilaea, Adam, Aḥiqar, Asenet.**

9795* *Rook* John, The names of the wives from Adam to Abraham in the Book of Jubilees: JPseud 7 (1990) 105-117.

9796 *VanderKam* J.C., *Milik* J.T., The first Jubilees manuscript from Qumran cave 4; a preliminary publication: JBL 110 (1991) 243-270.

9797 ᵀᴱ**VanderKam** J.C., The Book of Jubilees, a critical text, new edition / translation: CSCOr 510s, Aethiopici 87s [➤ 5,9919]. Lv 1989, Peeters. xviii-301 p.; xxxviii-369 p. Fb 4750 + 4830. 0070-0398. – ᴿBL (1991) 43, with haplography corrected in 92,6 (M.A. *Knibb*: unusually thorough).

9797* a) *Zuurmond* Rochus, Asshur in Jubilees 13.1?; – b) *Carroll* Scott, A preliminary analysis of the Epistle to Rehoboam: JPseud 4 (1989) 87-89 / 91-103 [< TR 87,74].

9798 a) *Pervo* Richard I., Aseneth and her sisters; women in Jewish narrative and in the Greek novels; – b) *Chesnutt* Randall D., Revelatory experiences attributed to biblical women in early Jewish literature [Jubilees, Testament of Job, Joseph and Aseneth]; – c) *Lefkowitz* Mary R., Did ancient women write novels?: ➤ 329, Women like this 1991, 145-160 / 107-125 / 199-219.

9798* *Eshel* Hanan, ⊕ The prayer of Joseph; a papyrus from Masada and the Samaritan Temple on *Argarizin*: Zion 56 (1991) 125-136; Eng. 137.

K1.7   **Apocalypses, ascensiones.**

9799 *Himmelfarb* Martha, Revelation and rapture; the transformation of the visionary in the Ascent apocalypses: ➤ 425, Mysteries 1989/91, 79-90.

9800 **Rubinkiewicz** R., L'Apocalypse d'Abraham en vieux slave ᴰ1978/87 ➤ 3,a262; 6,9979: ᴿRoczTK 36,1 (1989) 89s (J. *Homerski*).

9801 Leemhuis F., *al.*, The Arabic text of the Apocalypse of Baruch 1986 → 2,8079; 3,a263: ᴿBSO 52 (1990) 118 (S. *Brock*).

9802 Acerbi Antonio, L''Ascensione d'Isaia'; cristologia e profetismo in Siria nei primi decenni del II secolo 1989 → 5,9929; 6,9984: ᴿRHE 86 (1991) 267 (A. de *Halleux*).

9803 *Piovanelli* Pierluigi, Un nouveau témoin éthiopien de l'Ascension d'Isaïe et de la Vie de Jérémie (Paris, BN Abb. 195): Henoch 12 (1990) 347-363.

9804 Schalit Abraham [d. 1979], Untersuchung zur Assumptio Mosis [only ch. 1, the first 286 p. of his 506 p. manuscript on ch. 1-4 left uncompleted], ᴱ*Schreckenberg* H., *al.*: ArbLGJ 17, 1989 → 6,9982: ᴿBL (1991) 144 (M. A. *Knibb*); BLitEc 92 (1991) 146 (M. *Delcor*); CritRR 4 (1991) 381-3 (T. A. *Bergren*: thorough and definitive); ZAW 103 (1991) 457 (D. *Lührmann*); ZDMG 141 (1991) 428 (K. *Rudolph*).

к2.1 Philo judaeus alexandrinus.

9805 *a*) *Bailey* Jon N., *Metanoia* in the writings of Philo Judaeus; – *b*) *Sly* Dorothy L., Philo's practical application of *dikaiosýnē*; – *c*) *Martens* John W., Philo and the higher law; – *d*) *Jastram* David N., Philo's concept of generic virtue: → 446, SBL Sem 30 (1991) 135-141 / 298-308 / 309-322 / 323-347.

9806 *Barker* Margaret, Temple imagery in Philo; an indication of the origin of the Logos?: → 15, ᶠBAMMEL E., Templum 1991, 70-102.

9807 Borgen Peder, Philo, John and Paul 1987 → 4,167: ᴿStPhilonAn 2 (1990) 217-220 (K. G. *Sandelin*).

9808 Burkhardt Helmut, Inspiration/Philo 1988 → 4,1405...6,9987: ᴿSt-PhilonAn 2 (1990) 204-8 (F. *Siegert*).

9809 Cazeaux Jacques, La trame et la chaîne 2. Le cycle de Noé dans Philon d'Alexandrie: ALGJ 20, 1989 → 5,2217: ᴿCritRR 4 (1991) 351-5 (G. E. *Sterling*).

9810 Conley Thomas M., Philo's rhetoric; studies in style, composition and exegesis: CHS Mg 1, 1987 → 3,a270: ᴿStPhilonAn 2 (1990) 209-211 (D. T. *Runia*).

9811 Daniel-Naṭaf S., ❶ Philo of Alexandria, Writings, I. Historical, apologetical. J 1988, Bialik / Israel Academy. xxxviii-326 p. – ᴿStPhilonAn 2 (1990) 182-4 (D. *Satran*).

9812 *Decharneux* Baudouin, Interdits sexuels dans l'œuvre de Philon d'Alexandrie dit 'le Juif': ProbHistRel [non = ProbHistChr]. Bru 1 (1990) 17-32 [< ᴢɪᴛ 91,330].

9813 *Diéterlé* Christiane, Le livre des Antiquités Bibliques [Pseudo-Philon]; regard sur quelques textes: FoiVie 89,5 = CahB 29 (1990) 49-60.

9814 Grabbe Lester S., Etymology... in Philo 1988 → 5,9938; 6,9991: ᴿJAOS 111 (1991) 815s (A. *Kamesar*).

9815 *a*) *Hilgert* Earle, A review of previous research on Philo's De virtutibus; – *b*) *Runia* David T., Underneath COHN and COLSON; the text of Philo's De virtutibus: → 446, SBL Sem 30 (1991) 103-115 / 116-134.

9815* *a*) *Mack* Burton L., Wisdom and apocalyptic in Philo; – *b*) *Hay* David M., Philo's view of himself as an exegete; inspired, but not authoritative; – *c*) *Laporte* Jean, The High Priest in Philo of Alexandria; – *d*) *Winston* David, Aspects of Philo's linguistic theory; – *e*) *Radice* Roberto, Observations on the theory of the Ideas as the thoughts of God in Philo of Alexandria; – *f*) *Alexandre* Manuelᴶ, The art of periodic composition in Philo of Alexandria: ➤ 76, ᶠHILGERT E., StPhilonAn 3 (1991) 21-39 / 40-52 / 71-82 / 109-125 / 126-134 / 135-150.

9816 **Martín** José Pablo, Filón de Alejandría y la génesis de la cultura occidental 1986 ➤ 3,a276 ... 5,9943 [Marin!]: ᴿRevSR 65 (1991) 294s (Mariette *Canévet*).

9817 **Ménard** Jacques, La gnose de Philon d'Alexandrie [class-notes circulating for 12 years under the title 'Introduction à l'anthropologie religieuse de PA'] 1987 ➤ 3,a277 ... 6,9996: ᴿBO 48 (1991) 152s (P.-H. *Poirier*); TR 87 (1991) 111s (Manuela *Wüsteney* empfiehlt).

9818 **Mendelson** Alan, Philo's Jewish identity: BrownJudSt 161, 1988 ➤ 5, 9947: ᴿAbrNahr 29 (1991) 138s (E. *Osborn*); CritRR 4 (1991) 371s (G. E. *Sterling*); JQR 81 (1990s) 449-452 (L. H. *Feldman*).

9818* **Piñero** Antonio, A Mediterranean view of prophetic inspiration; on the concept of inspiration in the Liber Antiquitatum Biblicarum by Pseudo-Philo: MeditHR 6,1 (L 1991) 5-34 [< NTAbs 36,237].

9819 **Radice** R., *Runia* D. T., Philo bibliography 1988 ➤ 4,a933 ... 6,9899: ᴿJQR 81 (1990s) 494s (D. *Winston* adds a score); RÉJ 150 (1991) 481s (Madeleine *Petit*).

9820 *Riaud* Jean, Les Thérapeutes d'Alexandrie et l'idéal lévitique [< Sagesse et Religion 1976-9, 105-125]: ➤ 420, Mogilany 1989-II, 221-240.

9821 **Riedweg** Christoph, Mysterienterminologie bei PLATON, Philon und KLEMENS A.: UntALG 26, 1987 ➤ 3,a284 ... 5,9953: ᴿStPhilonAn 2 (1990) 214-7 (D. *Zeller*).

9822 **Royse** James R., The spurious texts of Philo of Alexandria; a study of textual transmission and corruption with indexes to the major collections of Greek fragments: ArbLGJ 22. Leiden 1991, Brill. xiii-252 p. 90-04-09511-X.

9823 **Runia** David T., Philo and the Timaeus of Plato 1986 ➤ 3,a285 ... 6,a1: ᴿStPhilonAn 2 (1990) 195-201 (B. *Rosenstock*).

9824 **Runia** D. T., *Radice* R., *Cathey* P., Philo of Alexandria, an annotated bibliography 1987-8 [+ provisional 1989-91]: ➤ 76, ᶠHILGERT E., StPhilonAn 3 (1991) 347-368, with lengthy summaries [369-374, titles only].

9824* **Siegert** Folker, PHILON, Über ... 'Feuer': WUNT 46, 1988 ➤ 3,a987; 5,9957: ᴿMuséon 104 (1991) 212s (B. *Coulie*).

9825 **Sly** Dorothy, Philo's perception of women [diss. McMaster]: Brown JudSt 219. Atlanta 1990, Scholars. vii-258 p. $60 [TR 87,526].

9825* *Umemoto* Naoto, Die Königsherrschaft Gottes bei Philon: ➤ 438, Königsherrschaft 1986/91, 207-256.

9826 *a*) *Wegner* Judith R., Philo's portrayal of women — Hebraic or Hellenic?; – *b*) *Halpern-Amaru* Betsy, Portraits of women in Pseudo-Philo's Biblical Antiquities: ➤ 329, Women like this 1991, 41-66 / 83-106.

9826* *Weinberg* Joanna, The quest for Philo in sixteenth-century Jewish historiography: ➤ 4, ᶠABRAMSKY C., Jewish history 1988, 163-187.

9827 **Williamson** Ronald, Jews in the Hellenistic World, Philo: CamCW 1/2, 1989 ➤ 6,a6: ᴿBO 48 (1991) 977-9 (J. A. *Loader*); JRel 71 (1991) 295s (D. *Winston*); StPhilonAn 2 (1990) 186s (D. M. *Hay*).

K2.4   *Evangelia apocrypha* – **Apocryphal Gospels.**

9828 *Junod* Éric, La littérature apocryphe chrétienne constitue-t-elle un objet d'études?: RÉAnc 93 (1991) 397-414; (p. 407) 'un ensemble hétérogène et inclassable'; pourtant (p. 414) 'renferme des ouvrages curieux et de qualité'.

9829 **Langkammer** Hugolin, ❷ Apokryfy NT. Katowice 1989, Jacka. 96 p. – ᴿRuBi 43 (1990) 178s (Jolanta *Wlodarczyk*).

9830 ᴱ**Puig** Armand, Apòcrifs del Nou Testament: Clàssics del Cristianisme 17. Barc 1990, Proa. 396 p. 84-7739-137-8.

9831 ᴱ**Ramos** Lincoln, Fragmentos de los Evangelhos apócrifos: Col.BApocr. Petrópolis 1989, Vozes. 212 p. – ᴿRLatAmT 23 (1991) 226s (R. S.: de 'dos' Ev.A.).

9832 **Schneemelcher** Wilhelm, Neutestamentliche Apokryphen I⁵ 1987 ➤ 3, a298* (I⁶ 1990 ➤ 6,a10); II⁵ 1988 ➤ 5,417: ᴿAntonianum 66 (1991) 586-8 (M. *Nobile*, II⁵); NRT 113 (1991) 444s (X. *Jacques*, I⁶, II⁵); SNTU A-15 (1990) 215-7 (A. *Fuchs*, I⁶); TPQ 39 (1991) 328 (F. *Kogler*, II⁵); ZkT 113 (1991) 303 (R. *Oberforcher*).

9833 **Schneemelcher** Wilhelm, New Testament apocrypha, I. Gospels and related writings², ᵀ*Wilson* R. M. C/Louisville 1991, Clarke/W-Knox. vii-560 p. £30 [RHE 86,281*]. 0-227-67915-6 / Knox 0-664-21878-4.

9834 **Schaeffer** Susan E., The 'Gospel of Peter', the canonical gospels, and oral tradition: diss. Union, ᴰ*Brown* R. E. NY 1991. 280 p. 91-28448. – DissA 52 (1991s) 1374-A; RelStR 18,173.

9835 **Crossan** J.D., The Cross that spoke [Gospel of Peter] 1988 ➤ 5,9983; 6,a15: ᴿInterpretation 45 (1991) 71s (R. H. *Fuller*: useful but unproved).; JAAR 59 (1991) 159-162 (G.W.F. *Nickelsburg*: apocr. Peter reflects canonical Gospels more than Crossan suggests).

9836 *Demoen* Kristoffel, S. Pierre se régalant de lupins; à propos de quelques traces d'apocryphes concernant Pierre dans l'œuvre de GRÉGOIRE de Nazianze: SacrEr 32 (1991) 95-106 [< RHE 87,30*].

9836* ᴱ**Giustolisi** E., *Rizzardi* G., Il Vangelo di Barnaba; un vangelo per i musulmani?: TFStR. Mi 1991, Ist.Prop.Libr. vii-805 p. Lit. 64.000. 88-7836-344-8 [NTAbs 36,292].

9837 **Moraldi** Luigi, Vangelo arabo apocrifo dell'Apostolo Giovanni, da un manoscritto nella Biblioteca Ambrosiana: Di fronte e attraverso 285. Mi 1991, Jaca. 218 p. Lit. 29.000. 88-16-40285-7. – ᴿCiVit 46 (1991) 487 (Duccia *Camiciotti*).

K2.7 Alia apocrypha NT.

9838 ᴱ**Prieur** Jean-Marc, Acta Andreae [diss. ᴰ*Bovon* F.]: CCApocr 5s, 1989 ➤ 5,9975; 6,a21: ᴿGregorianum 72 (1991) 795s (J. *Janssens*); JTS 42 (1991) 334-6 (H. *Chadwick*); NT 33 (1991) 377-381 (J. K. *Elliott*, also on MACDONALD D.).

9839 *a) Gallagher* Eugene V., Conversion and salvation in the apocryphal Acts of the Apostles; – *b) MacDonald* Dennis R., Andrew and the ant people: SecC 8 (1991) 13-30 / 43-49.

9840 **MacDonald** Dennis R., The Acts of Andrew and 'The Acts of Andrew and Matthias in the city of the cannibals' [with reasons for his decision to include it]: SBL TTr 33. Atlanta 1990, Scholars. xvii-460 p. $40; sb./pa. $25. 1-55540-492-8; -3-6 [TDig 38,279].

9841 **Van Voorst** Robert E., The Ascents of James...: SBL diss 112, 1989 ➤ 5,9976; 6,a26: ᴿCBQ 53 (1991) 724s (D. H. *Little*: a source of the Pseudo-Clementine Recognitions); CritRR 4 (1991) 344-6 (F. S. *Jones*); Salmanticensis 38 (1991) 245-7 (R. *Trevijano*).

9842 ᴱJunod Eric, *Kaestli* Jean-Daniel, Acta Iohannis I-II 1983 ➤ 64,8746 ...
4,b13: ᴿMilltSt 28 (1991) 152-6 (M. *McNamara*).

9843 **Onuki** Takashi, Gnosis und Stoa ... ApokrJoh: NOrb 9, 1989 ➤ 5,9978:
ᴿBiblica 72 (1991) 435-441 (H. *Neitzel*); CBQ 53 (1991) 145-7 (Janet *Timbie*).

9844 *Schneider* Paul G., A perfect fit; the major interpolation in the Acts of
John: ➤ 446, SBL sem 30 (1991) 518-532 [533-543, *Riley* G., Acts of
Thomas ➤ a308; 348-356, *Wagener* K., Acts of Andrew ➤ 1982; 508-517;
Allen J., Protevangelium of James ➤ 3882].

9845 *Hills* Julian V., Parables, pretenders, and prophecies; translation and
interpretation in the Apocalypse of Peter 2 [*Buchholz* D. 1988]: RB 98
(1991) 560-573; franç. 560.

9846 *Hilhorst* A., The Epistola Anne ad Senecam, Jewish or Christian? with
a new edition of the text: ➤ 18, ᶠBASTIAENSEN A., Eulogia 1991, 147-161.

9847 *Stichel* Rainer, L' 'Epistola laodicena' attribuita all'eretico Fedor Ku-
RICYN, uno scritto di epoca paleocristiana in ᴱ**Graciotti** Sante, Il battesimo delle terre russe [F 1991, Olschki] p. 213-231.

9848 **Johnston** Sarah I., Hekate soteira; a study of Hekate's roles in the
Chaldean Oracles and related literature: AmClasSt 21. Atlanta 1990,
Scholars. viii-192 p.

9849 *Chester* Andrew, The Sibyl and the temple [Sibylline Oracles 3 (c. 150
B.C.) and 5 (c. 100 A.D.); Egypt]: ➤ 15, ᶠBAMMEL E., Templum 1991,
37-69.

9851 *Krǎstev* G., Vita Petri; origin and problems of: ÉBalk 27 (1991) 105-111
[< RHE 87,29*].

9852 **Leloir** Louis, Écrits apocryphes ... armén. I. Pierre ... Jean: CCApc 3,
1986 ➤ 2,8117 ... 5,9973: ᴿMilltSt 28 (1991) 151s (M. *McNamara*).

9853 **Herbert** Maire, *McNamara* Martin, Irish biblical apocrypha 1989
➤ 6,a28: ᴿCritRR 4 (1991) 89-91 (M. *Cahill*); IrBSt 12 (1990) 101-4 (I.
Herbison); IrTQ 57 (1991) 171s (P. Ó *Fiannachta*), ScotJT 44 (1991) 247
(D. C. *Parker*: 20 NT + 9 OT texts translated from Gaelic manuscripts by
Herbert); ScripB 21 (1991) 17 (M. *Prior*).

K3 **Qumran** .1 *generalia*.

9854 **Baigent** Michael, *Leigh* Richard, The Dead Sea Scrolls deception.
L 1991, Cape. £15. – ᴿTablet 245 (1991) 1254 (N. *King*: silly and thin
claim of 'dirty tricks at the École Biblique').

9855 — *a) Shanks* Hershel, Is the Vatican suppressing the Dead Sea Scrolls?
[*Baigent* M., *Leigh* R., 1991: 'badly flawed, ludicrous']: BAR-W 17,6
(1991) 66-71. – *b) Murphy-O'Connor,* Jerome, Were we deceived about
the Dead Sea Scrolls? A claim rebutted [BAIGENT M., LEIGH R. 1991]:
DocLife 41 (1991) 451-7 [< NTAbs 36,230].

9855* **Baigent** M., *Leigh* R., Verschlusssache Jesus; die Qumranrollen und die
Wahrheit über das frühe Christentum, ᵀ*Dachs* Paul S., *Neumeister-Taroni*
Brigitte. Mü 1991, Droemer Knaur. 319 p. DM 40 [ZAW 104, 442,
Ulrike *Schorn*]. 3-426-26557-5.

9856 *a) Bonani* G., *al.*, Radiocarbon dating of the Dead Sea Scrolls: 'Atiqot
20 (1991) 27-32: map. – *b) Goranson* S., Radiocarbon dating of the Dead
Sea Scrolls: BA 54 (1991) 172.

9857 **Charlesworth** James H. [➤ 9780*b*], (*Whitaker* R. E., *al.*), Graphic Concordance to the Dead Sea Scrolls: Princeton DSS Project 5. Tü/Louisville

1991, Mohr/W-Knox. xxxi-529 p. DM 248. 3-16-145797-8 [BL 92, 134, J.C.L. *Gibson* explains many things but not why 'graphic'].

9859 **Fitzmyer** J.A., *a*) DSS major publications ²1990 ➤ 6,a33: ᴿJStJud 22 (1991) 265s (A.S. van der *Woude:* indispensable but bypasses Hodayot). – *b*) The concordance, the computer and the battle for the Dead Sea Scrolls: America 165 (1991) 270-2.

9859* *Laperrousaz* Ernest-Marie, Qoumrân 40 ans après: DialHA 16,1 (1990) 131-158.

9860 **Mitchell** James R., The riddle of the Dead Sea Scrolls, two 50-minute video films. NY 1990, Cinema Guild, 1697 Broadway. $250 each ($395 both); rental $100. – ᴿArchaeology 44,1 (1991) 72s (P.S. *Allen*).

9861 *Paul* A., Qumran: ➤ 664, Catholicisme XII, 56 (1990) 405-410.

9862 *Reed* Stephen A., Survey of the Dead Sea Scrolls fragments and photographs at the Rockefeller Museum: BA 54 (1991) 44-51 [110-111, *Goranson* S., publications in progress.

9863 *Shanks* Hershel, Carbon-14 tests substantiate scroll dates [though M. *Broshi* refused to release the lab report ('Why should we give it to you when you taunt us?'); likewise I. *Carmi*]: BAR-W 17,6 (1991) 72 (information provided by G. *Bonani* of Zurich laboratory).

9864 *a*) *Strugnell* John, The Qumran scrolls; a report on work in progress; – *b*) *Talmon* Shemaryahu, Between the Bible and the Mishnah; Qumran from within: ➤ 458, Jewish-Hellenistic 1986/91, 94-106 / (16-44) 214-257.

9865 — *a*) *Katzman* Avi, interview with J. STRUGNELL: BAR-W 17,1 (1991) 64-67. – *b*) Letters on J. Strugnell and anti-Semitism, BAR-W 17,4 (1991) 16-20; strong (mostly Jewish) reactions, 17/6 (1991) 8.10s.

9866 **Talmon** S., The world of Qumran 1989 ➤ 5,365: ᴿJJS 42 (1991) 127-9 (G. *Vermes*).

9866* *Vermes* Geza, New life for the Dead Sea Scrolls; questions that full publication may help to answer: (London Times Literary Supplement (20.XII.1991) 5s [< NTAbs 36,231].

9867 **Wacholder** Ben Zion, *Abegg* Martin G., A preliminary edition of the unpublished Dead Sea Scrolls — the Hebrew and Aramaic texts from Cave 4 [reconstructed from the concordance made in 1958 by R. *Brown*, J. *Fitzmyer*, W. *Oxtoby*, J. *Teixidor*, and published in 1988]. Wsh 1991, Biblical Archaeology Society. I. 118 p. $25 [BAR-W 17/5, p.4; 17/6, 62-65].

9868 *Woude* A.S. van der, Fünfzig Jahre (cont.): Lieder Cave 4, Sabbatopfer; DJD 6s; Hebr.Bible texts, TRu 55 (1990) ... 245-307 ... long bibliog.:

к3.4 *Qumran,* **Libri biblici [➤ singuli] et pseudo-biblici.**

9869 **Burgmann** Hans, Der 'Sitz im Leben' in den Josuafluch-Texten [Jos 6,26] in 4Q 379 22 II und 4 Q Testimonia: Qumranica Mogilanensia 1 ['Moglanensia', cover & p.13]. Kraków-Offenburg 1990. 53 p.; P p.54; 3-6.56-61, *Kapera* Z.J., pref & Burgmann-Bibliog.

9870 *a*) *Caquot* André, 4QMessAr 1 i 8-11; – *b*) *White* Sidnie A., Special features of four biblical manuscripts from Cave IV, Qumran; 4QDtᵃ, 4QDtᶜ, 4QDtᵈ, and 4QDtᵍ; – *c*) *Catastini* Alessandro, Da Qumran al testo masoretico dell'AT; spunti metodologici per la valutazione di varianti: ➤ 145, ꟳSTARCKY J., RQum 15 (1991) 145-155 / 157-167 / 303-313.

9871 *Eshel* Esther & Hanan, *Yardeni* Ada, [4Q448] ✪ A scroll from Qumran which includes part of Psalm 154 and a prayer for King Jonathan and his kingdom: Tarbiz 60 (1990s) 295-325; 4 fig.; Eng. I.

9872 *García Martínez* Florentino, *a)* Las fronteras de 'lo bíblico' [... textos de Qumran]: ScripTPamp 23 (1991) 759-784; – *b)* 4QSecond Ezekiel y las tradiciones apocalípticas: → 421, Luso-Esp 1989/91, 477-488.

9873 *Huggins* Ronald V., A canonical 'Book of Periods' [postulated by Milik for chronology of apocalypses] at Qumran?: 145, FSTARCKY J. 15 (1991s) 421-436.

9873* EKapera Z.J., Qumran Cave Four and MMT special report [= QChron 1/2s (1991)] 120 p. XII pl. Kraków 1991, Enigma. [tit. pp. in ZAW 104,456]. [MMT = *Miqsar ma'aśê ha-Torah*, Anchor BD 4,843].

9874 *Puech* Émile, Le Testament de Qahat en araméen de la grotte 4 (4QTQah): → 145, FSTARCKY J., I. RQum 15 (1991) 23-54; 2 pl. [rectification of R. *Eisenmann*, BAR 17,6 (1991) 64s].

9875 *Schwemer* A.M., Gott als König und seine Königsherrschaft in den Sabbatliedern aus Qumran: → 438, Königsherrschaft 1991, 45-118.

9876 **Steudel** Annette, Der Midrasch zur Eschatologie aus der Qumrangemeinde (4Q MidrEschat[a,b]); materielle Rekonstruktion, Textbestand, Gattung und traditionsgeschichtliche Einordnung des durch 4Q174 ('Florilegium') und 4Q177 ('Catena A') repräsentierten Werkes aus den Qumranfunden: ev. Diss. Göttingen 1991, DStegemann H. – TR 87 (1991) 517; RTLv 23, p. 542.

Tov Emanuel, The Greek minor prophets scroll from Nahal Ḥever 1990 → 3380.

9877 *Vegas Montaner* Luis, Nuevos textos bíblicos procedentes de Qumrán; implicaciones exegéticas: → 421, Luso-Esp 1989/91, 151-9.

9878 *Yardeni* Ada, The paleography of 4QJer[a] – a comparative study: Text 15 (1990) 233-268; ✪ 12s.

K3.5 *Rotulus Templi et alii* – **The Temple Scroll, al.**

9879 EBrooke George J., Temple Scroll studies 1987/9 → 5,568; 6,a58: RÉTRel 66 (1991) 113s (K. *Smyth*); JSS 36 (1991) 191-5 (Devorah *Dimant*).

9880 *Milgrom* Jacob, Deviations from Scripture in the purity laws of the Temple Scroll; → 458, Jewish-Hellenistic 1986/91, 159-167.

9881 *Schiffman* Lawrence H., Architecture and laws; the Temple and its courtyards in the Temple Scroll: → 56, FFox M. 1 (1991) 267-284.

9882 EVivian Angelo, Rotolo del Tempio 1990 → 6,a65: RAntonianum 65 (1990) 663s (M. *Nobile*); Archeo 65 (1990) 127 (S. *Moscati*); BL (1991) 148 (P.R. *Davies*); CC 142 (1991,4) 415s (G.L. *Prato*); ÉTRel 66 (1991) 589 (Françoise *Smyth*: 'Rotolo du Templio'); Helmantica 42, 129* (1991) 395 (S. *García-Jalón*); RBén 101 (1991) 211s (P.-M. *Bogaert*).

9883 *Wacholder* Ben Zion, The fragmentary remains of 11Q Torah (Temple Scroll), 11Q Torah[b] and 11Q Torah[c] plus 4Qpara Torah integrated with 11Q Torah: HUCA 62 (1991) 1-110 + VI pl.

9883* *Wilk* R., ✪ JOSEPHUS and the Temple Scroll [11QTemp 51,17 is like Ap 2,207]: Sinai 106 (1990s) 281-3 (< JStJud 22,318].

9884 **Wise** M.O., A critical study of the Temple Scroll from Qumran Cave 11 [< diss. Chicago, DGolb N.]: SAOC 49, 1990 → 6,a66: RBL (1991) 150 (P.S. *Alexander:* such clinical dissection can hardly convince completely); JStJud 22 (1991) 155-161 (F. *García Martínez*).

9885 — *García Martínez* Florentino, Sources et rédaction du Rouleau du Temple [WISE M. 1990]: Henoch 13 (1991) 219-252.

9886 a) *Wise* Michael O., The Temple Scroll and the teacher of righteousness; – b) *Tyloch* Witold, Le maître de justice dans les documents de Qumran: ➤ 420, Mogilany 1989-II, 121-147 / 119s.

9887 **Yadin** Y., The Temple Scroll 1983-7 ➤ 65,8615...6,a68: ᴿQadmoniot 24 (1991) 64s (H. *Eshel*).

9888 **Schiffman** Lawrence H., The eschatological community of the DSS; a study of the Rule of the Congregation 1989 ➤ 5,a30; 6,a69: ᴿCBQ 53 (1991) 307s (N. J. *Fujita*); JBL 110 (1991) 147s (B. Z. *Wacholder*); ᴿTLZ 116 (1991) 272s (J. *Kampen*).

9889 a) *Delcor* Mathias, La fête des Huttes dans le Rouleau du Temple et dans le livre des Jubilés; – b) *Schiffman* L. H., The law of vows and oaths (Num 30,3-16) in the Zadokite fragments and the Temple Scroll: ➤ 145, ᶠSTARCKY J., RQum 15 (1991) 181-198 / 199-214.

9890 *García Martínez Florentino*, a) Algunas aportaciones al conocimiento del judaísmo del segundo templo de los textos no-bíblicos de Qumrán recientemente publicados: ➤ 421, Luso-Esp 1989/91, 161-8; – b) Nuevos [1987-9] textos no bíblicos procedentes de Qumran (I): EstB 49 (1991) 97-134.

9891 **Wacholder** Ben Zion, *Abegg* Martin G., Qumran; a preliminary edition of the unpublished Dead Sea Scrolls; the Hebrew and Aramaic texts from Cave Four, 1. Wsh 1991, BA(R) Society. xiii-118 p. 0-9613089-9-0.

9891* a) *Qimron* Elisha, ◐ A preliminary publication of 4QSᵈ VII-VIII: Tarbiz 60 (1990s) 435s + photo; – b) *Vermes* Geza, Preliminary remarks on [4QSᵈ·ᵇ]: JJS 42 (1991) 250-5; 2 phot.

9892 a) *Smith* Mark S., 4Q462 (Narrative) Fragment 1; a preliminary edition; – b) *Baumgarten* J. M., On the nature of the seductress in 4Q184; – c) *Wise* M. O., 4QFlorilegium and the Temple of Adam: ➤ 145, ᶠSTARCKY J., RQum 15 (1991) 55-77, pl. 4 / 133-143 / 103-132.

9892* *Talmon* Shemaryahu, *Knohl* Israel, ◐ A calendrical scroll from Qumran Cave IV — Miš Ba (4Q321): Tarbiz 60 (1990s) 505-521; Eng. I-II.

к3.6 Qumran et NT.

9893 **Daniélou** Jean, I manoscritti del Mar Morto e le origini del cristianesimo [1957], ᵀ*Palamidessi* Silvestre. R 1990, Archeosofica. 109 p. Lit. 20.000.

9893* *Shavit* Yaakob, 'Ex Qumran lux?' Notas históricas y literarias sobre los manuscritos del Mar Muerto y los orígenes del cristianismo: ➤ 453, Orígenes 1989/91, 135-174.

9894 *Stegemann* Hartmut, The 'Teacher of Righteousness' and Jesus; two types of religious leadership in Judaism at the turn of the era: ➤ 458, Jewish-Hellenistic 1986/91, 196-213.

9894* *Thiede* Carsten P., Il più antico manoscritto dei Vangeli?... Marco 1987 ➤ 3,a358: ᴿRAg 30 (1989) 275 (S. *Sabugal*).

к3.8 Historia et doctrinae Qumran.

9895 **Ausín Olmos** Santiago, Moral, y conducta en Qumrân; estudio lexicográfico y semántico de los verbos de 'movimiento' en la literatura de Qumran [Mem. Lic. Complutense, ᴰ*Vegas Montaner* L.]: Teológica

74. Pamplona 1991, Univ. Navarra. 171 p. 84-313-1111-8. – ᴿActuBbg 28 (1911) 161 (J. *Boada*); ScripTPamp 23 (1991) 1071s (J. M. *Casciaro*).

9896 *a) Bauckham* Richard, A quotation from 4QSecond Ezekiel in the Apocalypse of Peter; – *b) Chazon* Esther G., 4QDibHam, liturgy or literature?; – *c) Beckwith* Roger T., The Essene calendar and the moon; a reconsideration; – *d) Greenfield* Jonas C., The 'defension clause' in some documents from Naḥal Ḥever and Naḥal Ṣe'elim: ➤ 145, ᶠSTARCKY J., RQum 15 (1991s) 437-445 / 447-455 / 457-466 / 467-471.

9897 *Bronznick* Nahum M., ❿ The meaning of *dôrᵉšê halᵉqût* ('expounders of empty things', Qumran taunt of Pharisees]: Tarbiz 60 (1990s) 653-7; Eng. VI.

9897* **Burgmann** Hans, Vorgeschichte und Frühgeschichte ... Qumran/Damaskus 1987 ➤ 3,a363; 4,b63: ᴿSefarad 51 (1991) 203s (F. *Sen*).

9898 **Callaway** Phillip R., The history of the Qumran community ᴰ1988 ➤ 4,b64 ... 6,a82: ᴿBZ 35 (1991) 301s (J. *Maier:* recht mager); HeythJ 32 (1991) 403s (Sarah *Pearce*); Sefarad 51 (1991) 204 (F. *Sen*).

9899 *a) Davies* P. R., Communities at Qumran and the case of the missing 'Teacher'; – *b) Laperrousaz* E.-M., A propos du Maître de justice et du Temple de Jérusalem; deux problèmes de nombre: ➤ 145, ᶠSTARCKY J., RQum 15 (1991) 275-286 / 265-274.

9900 *a) Denis* Albert-Marie, La place de la Loi de Moïse à Qumrân et dans le Judaïsme du Deuxième Temple; – *b) Fröhlich* Ida, Jewish literary tradition and the Qumran tradition; – *c) Nitzan* Bilha, The *Pesher* and other methods of instruction; – *d) Eisenman* Robert, Playing on and transmuting words; interpreting 'abeit-galuto' in the Habakkuk Pesher: ➤ 420, Mogilany 1989-II, 149-175 / 207 / 209-220 / 177-196.

9901 *Geyer* Thomas W., Zölibat am Toten Meer [*Qimron* E., Rockefeller-Museum-Vortrag 13.I.1991]: ErbAuf 67 (1991) 140.

9902 *a) Gluskina* Lea N. [his wife], The teacher of righteousness in Joseph AMUSSIN's studies; – *b) Schiffman* Ilja, The teacher of righteousness in the Soviet Qumran studies; – *c) Schweitzer* Frederick M., The teacher of righteousness; – *d) Thiering* Barbara, Can the Hasmonean dating of the teacher of righteousness be sustained?: ➤ 420, Mogilany 1989-II, 7-21 / 47-52 / 53-98 / 99-118.

9903 **Hanson** Kenneth L., Reflections of early Halakha in the Dead Sea Scrolls: diss. Texas, ᴰ*Liebowitz* H. Austin 1991. 364 p. 92-00632. — DissA 52 (1991s) 2571-A.

9904 *Nickelsburg* George W. E., The Qumran radicalizing and anthropologizing of an eschatological tradition; IQH 4:29-40: ➤ 87, ᶠKOCH K., Ernten 1991, 423-435.

Smith Mark S., Converted and unconverted perfect and imperfect forms in the literature of Qumran 1991 ➤ 9123*a*.

K4.1 **Esseni, Zelotae.**

9905 **Beall** T. S., JOSEPHUS ... Essenes ... Scrolls 1988 ➤ 4,b72; 6,a95: ᴿEvQ 63 (1991) 262-4 (J. N. *Birdsall*); NedTTs 45 (1991) 71s (P. W. van der *Horst*).

9906 *Bohrmann* Monette, La pureté rituelle; une approche de la communauté des esséniens: Dialogues d'histoire ancienne 17,1 (Besançon 1991) 307-331.

9907 *Du Buit* M., Sadducéens: ➤ 664, Catholícisme XIII, 96 (1991) 427-430 (432s, Sadoq).

9908 **Burgmann** Hans, Die essenischen Gemeinden von Qumran und Damaskus in der Zeit der Hasmonäer und Herodier (130 ante-68 post): ArbNJ 8, 1988 ➤ (3,a163) 6,a96:   ᴿCBQ 53 (1991) 317s (J.C. *VanderKam*: implausible); JStJud 22 (1991) 255-9 (A.S. van der *Woude*, auch über seine Vorgeschichte 1987).

9909 **Burgmann** Hans, Die Geschichte der Essener von Qumran und 'Damaskus': Qumranica Mogilensia 5. Kraków 1990, auct. 180 p.; ill.

9910 **Hengel** Martin, The Zealots 1989 ➤ 5,a59; 6,a97:   ᴿInterpretation 45 (1991) 82 (W.R. *Farmer*); IsrEJ 41 (1991) 219-221 (D.R. *Schwartz*); NedTTs 45 (1991) 254s (P.W. van der *Horst*).

9911 **Laperrousaz** E.-M., Gli Esseni 1988 ➤ 4,b76; 5,a60:   ᴿHenoch 13 (1991) 112-4 (E. *Jucci*, mostly additions to the bibliography).

9912 *Riaud* Jean, Quelques réflexions sur les Thérapeutes d'Alexandrie à la lumière de De Vita Mosis II, 67: ➤ 76, ᶠHILGERT E., StPhilonAn 3 (1991) 184-191.

9913 **Stemberger** Günter, Pharisäer, Sadduzäer, Essener: SBS 144. Stu 1991, KBW. 144 p. 3-460-04441-1 [NTAbs 36,143].

9914 ᴱ**Vermes** Geza, *Goodman* Martin D., The Essenes 1989 ➤ 5,a63; 6,a100: ᴿCBQ 53 (1991) 509s (J.R. *Mueller*); JAOS 111 (1991) 134s (A. *Kamesar*).

9915 **Welburn** Andrew, The beginnings of Christianity; Essene mystery, Gnostic revelation, and the Christian vision. E 1991, Floris. 351 p. $20. [Gnosis 23, 64, S.A. *Hoeller*].

κ4.3   Samaritani.

9916 *Baillet* M., Samaritains: ➤ 686, SDB XI, 63s (1990) 773-1047.

9917 **Ben-Ḥayyim** Z., ⊕ *Tibat Marqê*, a collection of Samaritan midrashim 1988 ➤ 5,a64; 6,a101:   ᴿJQR 82 (1991s) 515-8 (A.D. *Crown*); RB 98 (1991) 605-7 (J. *Margain*).

9918 **Boid** Iain R.M., Principles of Samaritan Halachah 1989 ➤ 5,a65: ᴿJQR 82 (1991s) 496s (J.M. *Baumgarten*); ZDMG 141 (1991) 172-5 (R. *Macuch*).

9919 *Cabezon* Agripino, Les Samaritains [d'aujourd'hui...TerreS janv. 1991]: EsprVie 101 (1991) 326-8 (J. *Daoust*).

9920 ᴱ**Crown** Alan D., The Samaritans 1989 ➤ 5,389; 6,a103:   ᴿCritRR 4 (1991) 355-7 (D.J. *Harrington*); CrNSt 12 (1991) 179-182 (R. *Le Déaut*); HeythJ 32 (1991) 405s (M.J. *Walsh*); NedTTs 45 (1991) 341s (P.W. van der *Horst*).

9921 **Egger** Rita, JOSEPHUS F. & die Samaritaner NOrb 4, ᴰ1986 ➤ 2,8195 ...6,a106:   ᴿTPhil 66 (1991) 581-3 (K.S. *Krieger*).

9922 *Horst* Pieter Van der, The Samaritan diaspora in antiquity [< NedTTs 42 (1988) 133-144, rev.]ᵀ: ➤ 212, NOrb 14 (1990) 136-147.

9923 *Poliakov* L., Aux origines du monothéisme, les Samaritains [*Crown* A. 1989]: RHDroit 68 (1990) 391-3 [< RSPT 75,343].

9924 **Pummer** R., Samaritans: IconRel 23/5, 1987 ➤ 3,a399...6,a108: ᴿBAnglsr 10 (1990s) 95s (Joan E. *Taylor*).

9925 *Thornton* T.C.G., The Samaritan calendar, a source of friction in NT times: JTS 42 (1991) 577-580.

κ4.5   Ṣadoqitae, Qaraitae – **Cairo Genizah; Zadokites, Karaites.**

9925* *a) Brooke* G.J., The Messiah of Aaron in the Damascus Document; – *b) Maier* Johann, Von Eleazar bis Zadok: CD V,2-5; – *c) Knibb*

Michael A., The interpretation of Damascus Document VII,95 – VIII,2a and XIX,5b-14: ⇒ 145, ᶠSTARCKY J., RQum 15 (1991) 215-230 / 231-241 / 243-251.

9926 *a)* *Burgmann* Hans, Die Nordemigration hat stattgefunden [Zadokite document was to justify migration from the Holy Land toward Damascus]; – *b)* *Harviainen* Tapani, Abraham FIRKOVITSH, Karaites in Hīt, and the provenance of Karaite transcriptions of biblical Hebrew texts into Arabic script: ⇒ 41*, ᶠCZAPKIEWICZ A., FolOr 28 (1991) 157-178; Eng. 178 / 179-191.

9926* *Coulot* Claude, La Nouvelle Alliance au pays de Damas: RevSR 65 (1991) 1-9.

9927 *Erder* Yoram, The first date in Megillat Ta'anit in light of the Karaite commentary on the Tabernacle dedication [... reflects Pharisee controversy with Qumran sect, not with Sadducees]: JQR 82 (1991s) 263-283.

9928 *Genot* Jacqueline, La création dans l'alliance de Damas: ⇒ 140, ᶠSMYTH-FLORENTIN F. 1991, 245-261.

9929 **Goitein** S. D., A Mediterranean society 5, 1988 ⇒ 4,b95; 6,a114: ᴿJESHO 34 (1991) 369-371 (J.-C. *Garcin*).

9929* **Khan** Geoffrey, Karaite Bible manuscripts of the Cairo Genizah: Genizah 9, 1990 ⇒ 6,a116: ᴿBSO 54 (1991) 576s (J. *Blau*); ExpTim 102 (1990s) 314 (W. *Johnstone*).

9930 *Nemoy* Leon, Israel al-MAGHRIBI's [Karaite] tract on ritual slaughtering: Henoch 13 (1991) 195-208; Eng. 208; 209-218 facsimile of Arabic text.

9931 *Noja* Sergio, Notice sur quelques manuscrits de QIRQISANI: Henoch 12 (1990) 365s; Eng. 366.

9932 ᴱ**Reif** S. C., Published material from the Cambridge Genizah collections 1988 ⇒ 6,a121: ᴿCritRR 4 (1991) 350s (J. J. *Collins*); NedTTs 45 (1991) 70s (P. W. van der *Horst*); Salesianum 53 (1991) 588s (R. *Vicent*).

9933 *Swartz* Michael D., Scribal magic and its rhetoric; formal patterns in medieval Hebrew and Aramaic incantation texts from the Cairo Genizah: HarvTR 83 (1990) 163-180.

K5   **Judaismus prior vel totus.**

9934 **Alba** Amparo, Cuentos de los rabinos: Estudios de cultura hebrea 12. Córdoba 1991, Almendro. 260 p. 84-86077-88-5.

9935 **Baker** Menachem, ⊕ *Parperaot Latora* [Torah crumbs]. J 1983-6, Omen. I. 264 p.; map; 2. 245 p.; map; 3. 278 p.; map, all 1983; – 4. 322 p.; 1985; – 5. 351 p.; map, 1986. All have photos of some scholars.

9936 *Capelli* Piero, Sullo status quaestionis nella ricerca sulla 'letteratura' rabbinica; riflessioni metodologiche in margine ad una polemica recente [SCHÄFER P., JJS 37 (1986) 139-152; 40 (1989) 89-94; MILIKOWSKY C., 39 (1988) 201-211]: Henoch 13 (1991) 349-363; solo casualmente p. 350, J. NEUSNER, metodo form-analysis dopo 1985; metodo biografico prima, fallito (ma non pienamente, Capelli p. 352).

9937 **Chapin** Richard S., Mesopotamian [... Nisibis] scholasticism; a comparison of the Jewish and Christian 'schools': diss. HUC. Cincinnati 1990. 281 p. 91-14090. – DissA 52 (1991s) 187s-A.

9938 **Chouraqui** André, Il pensiero ebraico 1989 ⇒ 5,a36; 6,a126; Lit. 15.000: ᴿCC 141 (1990,4) 628s (... M. *Katunarich*).

9938* **Cohen** Shaye J. D., From the Maccabees to the Mishnah 1987 ⇒ 3,a413 ... 6,a126*: ᴿTorJT 7 (1991) 114s (A. E. *Milton*: important on canonicity).

9939 *Colafemmina* Cesare, Le regole ermeneutiche di Hillel: ➤452, An-StoEseg 8,2 (1990/1) 443-454.

9940 *Díez Merino* Luis, Exculpación-inculpación, principio de exégesis targúmica desconocido en la hermenéutica judía oficial: ➤421, Luso-Exp 1989/91, 411-476.

9941 **Ego** Beate, Im Himmel wie auf Erden...: WUNT 2/34, 1989 ➤ 5,a90; 6,a128: ᴿÉTRel 66 (1991) 284s (M. *Bouttier*); NedTTs 45 (1991) 150s (P. W. van der *Horst*); RechSR 79 (1991) 433s (J. *Guillet*).

9941* *Ego* Beate, a) Gottes Weltherrschaft und die Einzigkeit seines Namens; eine Untersuchung zur Rezeption der Königsmetapher in der Mekhilta de R. YISHMAʼEL; – b) Der Diener im Palast des himmlischen Königs; zur Interpretation einer priesterlichen Tradition im rabbinischen Judentum: ➤ 438, Königsherrschaft 1986/91, 257-283 / 361-384.

9942 *Figueras* Pau, Epigraphic evidence for proselytism in ancient Judaism: ➤ 54, ᶠFLUSSER D., Immanuel 24s (1990) 194-206.

9942* a) *Goldberg* Arnold, Formen und Funktionen von Schriftauslegung in der frührabbinischen Literatur (1.Jh.v.Chr. bis 8.Jh.n.Chr.); – b) *Güttgemanns* Erhardt, Gêmatriyyaʼ und Lᵉchĕshbôn: LingBib 64 (1990) 5-22 / 23-52; Eng. 21 / 52.

9943 a) *Goodman* Martin, Opponents of Rome; Jews and others; – b) *Alexander* Philip S., The family of Caesar and the family of God; the image of the emperor in the Heikhalot literature: ➤412, Images 1990/1, 222-238 / 276-297.

9943* a) *Hayman* Peter, Monotheism a misused word in Jewish studies?; – b) *Hirshman* Marc, The preacher and his public in third-century Palestine: JJS 42 (1991) 1-15 / 108-114.

9944 *Heinsohn* Gunnar, Was ist Judentum? Altisraelitentum/Christentum und jüdischer Monotheismus; Differenz und Konflikt: ZRGg 43 (1991) 333-344.

9945 **Hengel** Martin, The 'Hellenization' of Judaism [Zum Problem der 'Hellenisierung' Judäas im 1.Jh.v. Chr. 1989], ᵀ*Bowden* John. L/Ph 1989, SCM/Trinity. 0-334-00602-3. – ᴿJStJud 22 (1991) 142-4 (L. H. *Feldman*).

9946 ᴱ**Henten** J. W. van, Die Entstehung der jüdischen Martyrologie [workshop Leiden 6.-8.IX. 1984]: StPostB 38, 1989 ➤ 5,a99; 6,533: ᴿBL (1991) 137 (L. L. *Grabbe*); BO 48 (1991) 645-7 (P. *Höffken*); BZ 35 (1991) 147 (H.-J. *Klauck*).

9947 **Johnson** Paul, A history of the Jews. NY 1987, Harper & R. 644 p. – ᴿJRel 71 (1991) 124s (L. A. *Segal*).

9947* *Lehnhardt* Thomas, Der Gott der Welt ist unser König; zur Vorstellung von der Königsherrschaft Gottes im Shema und seinen Benedictionen: ➤ 438, Königsherrschaft 1986/91, 285-307.

9948 *Lenhardt* Pierre, *Osten-Sacken* Peter von der, Rabbi AKIVA: ArbNTJud 1, 1987 ➤ 4,b119; 5,a103: ᴿBijdragen 52 (1991) 444 (M. *Poorthuis*).

9949 **Levine** Lee I., The rabbinic class of Roman Palestine in late antiquity (ⓓ 1985) 1989 ➤ 5,a103*: ᴿJJS 42 (1991) 271-3 (M. *Goodman*); JRS 81 (1991) 241s (S. *Stern*); JTS 42 (1991) 275s (F. *Millar*: readable but superficial).

9950 **Licht** Chaim, Ten legends of the sages; the image of the sage in rabbinic literature. Hoboken 1991, KTAV. 221 p. [JAAR 59,883].

9951 **Maccoby** Hyam, Early rabbinic writings 1988 ➤ 4,b122; 5,a105: ᴿCritRR 4 (1991) 368-370 (T. *Zahavy* does not recommend).

9952 **Maccoby** H., Judaism in the first century: Religious Studies 1989 ➤ 5,a106; 6,a139: ᴿFaventia 12s (1990s) 481-4 (G. *Fernández*).

9953 **McKnight S.**, A light among the Gentiles; Jewish missionary activity in the Second Temple period. Mp 1991, Fortress. x-205 p. $13. 0-8006-2452-1 [BL 92,125, J. R. *Bartlett*].

9954 **Maier Johann**, Il giudaismo del Secondo Tempio; storia e religione, ᵀ*Chiesa* Bruno: BtCuRel 59. Brescia 1991, Paideia. 380 p. Lit. 49.000. 88-394-0465-1 [Antonianum 67, 145, M. *Nobile*].

9955 **Mandelbaum Bernard**, Pesikta de-Rav KAHANA²ʳᵉᵛ [¹1962]. NY 1987, Jewish Theol. Sem. I. 331 p. II. p. 333-559 + Eng. XXIV. 0-87334-043-4.

9956 *Martola K.*, Rabbinatet i historiskt perspektiv: NorJud 10 (1989) 11-26 [< JStJud 22,315].

9957 *Massonet J.*, Sanhédrin: ➤ 686, SDB XI, 64 (1991) 1353-1413.

9958 **Neusner J.**, Ecology of religion 1989 ➤ 6,a147: ᴿRelStT 9,2s (1989) 66 (S. S. *McGurty*).

9959 **Neusner** Jacob, An introduction to Judaism; a textbook and reader. Louisville 1991, W-Knox. 0-664-25348-2 [BL 92,145].

9960 **Neusner J.**, Judaism and its social metaphors; Israel ... 1989 ➤ 5,a114; 6,a149: ᴿCritRR 4 (1991) 373-5 (G. G. *Porton*); JAAR 59 (1991) 190-3 (A. J. *Saldarini*); JScStR 29 (1990) 272s (B. *Beit-Hallahmi*); JSS 36 (1991) 188s (Sacha *Stern*: disappointingly limited in scope).

9960* **Neusner** Jacob, Das pharisäische und talmudische Judentum 1984 ➤ 65,8719 ... 3,a499: ᴿProtestantesimo 45 (1990) 142 (J. A. *Soggin*).

9961 **Neusner J.**, Studying classical Judaism; a primer. Louisville 1991, W-Knox. 208 p. $16. 0-664-25136-6 [NTAbs 36,139: 'traces the paradigm shift ... from critical historical positivism to concern with a religious understanding of the sacred books on their own terms'].

9961* **Neusner** Jacob, Symbol and theology in early Judaism. Mp 1991, Fortress. xxi-242 p. $15 pa. 0-8006-2456-4 [NTAbs 36,139].

9962 **Neusner** Jacob, Torah through the ages; a short history of Judaism 1990 ➤ 6,a150: ᴿBL (1991) 140 (A. P. *Hayman*); PrPeo 4 (1990) 456s (B. *Robinson*).

9963 **Neusner J.**, Green W. S., Writing with Scripture; the authority and uses of the Hebrew Bible in the Torah of formative Judaism 1989 ➤ 5,a118; 6,a153: ᴿBL (1991) 141 (N. de *Lange*); Gregorianum 72 (1991) 559s (G. L. *Prato*); JRel 71 (1991) 569-571 (D. *Kraemer*); SecC 8 (1991) 59-61 (A. *Saldarini*).

9964 **Neusner J.**, Grondslagen van het Jodendom (Tora, Misjna, Messias) [Foundations 1983-5],ᵀ. Boxtel/Brugge 1990, KBS / Tabor. 158 p. ƒ39,50. – ᴿCollatVL 21 (1991) 316s (H. *Hoet*).

9965 *a*) *Neusner* Jacob, From philosophy to religion; – *b*) *Borowitz* Eugene, A theological response to orthodoxies; – *c*) *Morris* Paul, The quest for a Jewish theology and a non-fundamentalist Halakhah: ➤ 82, ᶠJACOBS L., A traditional quest 1991, 9-23 / 24-41 / 194-216.

9966 **Newby** Gordon D., A history of the Jews of Arabia ... to Islam 1988 ➤ 4,b138: ᴿCritRR 3 (1990) 355s (J. *Neusner:* of some value); JAOS 111 (1991) 814-6 (W. M. *Brinner*); JQR 82 (1991s) 543-4 (Haya *Lazarus-Yafeh*).

9967 **Otzen** Benedikt, Judaism in antiquity 1990 ➤ 6,a155. b733*b*: ᴿCBQ 53 (1991) 713 (L. J. *Hoppe:* appreciative stance toward the religion); ÉTRel 66 (1991) 116s (Jeanne-Marie *Léonard*); JJS 42 (1991) 126s (J. G. *Campbell*); JSS 36 (1991) 351s (L. L. *Grabbe*, unfavoring in every way); JTS 42 (1991) 187s (Meg *Davies:* a feast of well-digested learning); ZAW 103 (1991) 306 (I. *Kottsieper*).

9967* **Peláez del Rosal** J., La sinagoga: EstCuHebr 7. Córdoba 1990, Almendro. 180 p. 84-86077-63-X [NTAbs 36,139].

9968 **Sager** Stephen, Studies in three 'pisqaot' of 'Pesiqta de Rab KAHANA': diss. Duke, ^D*Meyers* E. Durham NC 1989. – RTLv 23, p. 541.

9968* *Samely* Alexander, Between Scripture and its rewording; towards a classification of rabbinic exegesis: JJS 42 (1991) 39-67.

9969 **Schaefer** Peter, Histoire des Juifs dans l'antiquité, ^T*Schulte* Pascale: Patrimoines Judaïsme. P 1990, Cerf. 280 p. F 139. – ^RÉtudes 437 (1991) 426s (P. *Gibert*).

9970 **Schiffman** Lawrence H., From text to tradition; a history of Second Temple and rabbinic Judaism. Hoboken 1991, KTAV. xvi-299 p.; ill. $39.50; pa. $17. 0-88125-371-5; –2-3 [BL 92,129, L. L. *Grabbe*: his views are sound but he fails to show why].

9970* **Schwarzwald** Ora (Rodrigue), ⊕ The Ladino translations of Pirke Aboth: Hebrew Language Traditions 13. J 1989, Hebrew Univ. vii-518 p. – ^RBSO 54 (1991) 358s (A. *Sáenz-Badillos*).

9971 **Sigal** P., Judaism 1988 → 5,a131; 6,a164: ^RCritRR 3 (1990) 332s (J. *Neusner:* Sigal recognizes and ignores that there is no single 4000-year Judaism).

9972 ^{TE}**Smilévitch** Éric, MAÏMONIDE, RACHI, *al.*, Commentaires du Traité des Pères (Pirké Avot): Les Dix Paroles, 1990 → 6,a165: ^RRTPhil 123 (1991) 455s (J. *Borel*).

9973 ^E**Stemberger** Günter, Die Juden, ein historisches Lesebuch 1990 → 6,a166: ^RZDMG 141 (1991) 427s (L. *Prijs*).

9973* *Stemberger* Günter, La relation à la Bible dans le Judaïsme; ^T*Guého* Marie-Thérèse: → 348, Concilium 233 (P 1991) 55-65.

9974 **Trautner-Kromann** Hanne, Jødedommen. K 1983, Politikens. 320 p. – ^RTsTKi 60 (1989) 57s (D. *Rian*).

9974* *Visotsky* B. L., Reading with the Rabbis; making the Bible a timeless text: ChrCent 108 (1991) 932-5 [< NTAbs 36,240: the rabbis believed that everything is in the Bible].

9975 **Wylen** Stephen M., Settings of silver; an introduction to Judaism 1989 → 6,a171: ^RSalesianum 53 (1991) 188 (R. *Vicent:* con todo, útil).

K6 **Mišna**, *tosepta; Tannaim.*

9975* ^{TE}**Correns** D., Gittin, Scheidebriefe: Mischna 3/5. B 1991, de Gruyter. x-188 p. DM 158 [NRT 114,775, X. *Jacques*].

9976 *Elman* Yaakov, Babylonian Baraitot in the Tosefta and the 'dialectology' of Middle Hebrew: AJS 16 (1991) 1-29.

9977 *a) Flesher* Paul V. M., Are women property in the system of the Mishnah? – *b) Wolfson* Elliot, Female imaging of the Torah; from literary metaphor to religious symbol: → 56, ^FFOX M., (1991) 1,219-231 / 2,271-307.

9978 **Kaufmann** Asher S., ⊕ *Massekah Middot* according to the manuscripts and the earliest printed texts: Miqdaš Jerusalem 1. J c.1990, auct. viii-102 p.; 10 fig. $45. 965-379-000-5; -1-3.

9979 *Neusner* Jacob, Making the classics in Judaism; the three stages of literary formation: Brown JudSt 180, 1989 → 5,a149: ^RBL (1991) 140 (P. R. *Davies*).

9980 **Neusner** Jacob, Judaism as philosophy; the method and message of the Mishnah. Columbia 1991, Univ. S. Carolina. 301 p. $40. 0-87249-736-4 [BL 92,127, P. R. *Davies*].

9981 **Neusner** Jacob, Judaism without Christianity; an introduction to the system of the Mishnah. Hoboken 1991, KTAV. xxi-138 p. $17. 0-88125-333-2 [BL 92,145].

9982 **Neusner** Jacob, The philosophical Mishnah: BrownJudSt 163s [➤ 5, a150].168.172. Atlanta 1988s, Scholars. xi-236 p.; xv-303 p.; xv-344 p.; xv-200 p. $219; sb. $141. – ᴿRelStR (1991) 176 (P. *Ochs*).

9983 **Neusner** Jacob, Mekhilta according to Rabbi *Ishmael*, 1: Brown JudSt 148. Atlanta 1988, Scholars. xiv-268 p. – ᴿJAOS 111 (1991) 391-5 (E. A. *Goldman*: significant approach).

9985 **Neusner** Jacob, Rabbinic political theory; religion and politics in the Mishnah: ChStHistJudaism. Ch 1991, Univ. xxii-262 p. $57.50; pa. $30. 0-226-57650-7; -1-5 [BL 92,127, A. P. *Hayman*; NTAbs 36,139].

9986 *a) Neusner* Jacob, The Mishnah's philosophical method; the Judaism of hierarchical classification in Greco-Roman context; – *b) Grabbe* Lester L., Philo and Aggada; a response to B. J. BAMBERGER [HUCA 48 (1977) 153-185]: ➤ 76, ᶠHILGERT E., StPhilonAn 3 (1991) 192-206 / 153-166.

9986* *Neusner* Jacob, After forty years; epilogue to a career: RelStT 10,1 (1990) 19-42 [49s, transfer to S. Florida].

K6.5 Talmud; midraš.

9987 **Aminoah** Noah, ❺ *'Arikat* ... The redaction of the tractate Sukkah and Moed Katan in the Babylonian Talmud compilation. TA 1988. 407 p. – ᴿJQR 82 (1991s) 218-220 (J. *Hauptman*); TLZ 115 (1990) 444s (H. M. *Schenke*).

9987* **Bergler** Siegfried, Talmud für Anfänger, ein Werkbuch: Schalom 1. Hannover 1991, Luther. 145 p. DM 16,80 [TLZ 117,502, M. *Morgenstern*].

9988 **Boyarin** Daniel, *a)* Intertextuality and the reading of midrash: Indiana Studies in Biblical Literature. Bloomington 1990, Indiana Univ. xiii-161 p. – ᴿJQR 81 (1991) 427-434 (H. W. *Basser*: 'serious annoyances hamper the struggle to understand this book'). – *b)* Intertextuality and the reading of Midrash: JQR 82 (1991s) 451-9, defense against *Basser*.

9989 *Chico* G., El valor hermenéutico del Midrash: Anamnesis 1,1 (1991) 67-77 [< ZNW 82,280].

9990 *Friedman* Mordechai A., ❺ 'He planted eternal life in our midst' – in the past; 'may he plant his Torah in our heats' – in the future: Tarbiz 60 (1990s) 265-8; Eng. IV.

9990* ᴱ**Friedman** S. Y., ❺ bBava Meziʿa VI [on hiring craftsmen]; Talmud Arukh. NY 1990, Jewish Theol. Sem. v-423 p. $25. 0-87334-066-3 [NTAbs 36,135].

9991 **Gafni** I. M., ❺ The Jews of Babylonia in the Talmudic era. J 1991, Shazar. – ᴿZion 56 (1991) 209-212 (J. *Schwartz*).

9992 **Garsiel** Moshe, Biblical names; a literary study of midrashic derivations and puns. Ramat-Gan 1991, Bar-Ilan Univ. 296 p. $30. 965-226-115-7.

9993 **Garsiel** Moshe, Midrashic name-derivations in the Bible 1987 ➤ 3,9252: ᴿCBQ 53 (1991) 100-2 (Z. *Garber*).

9994 *Goldberg* Arnold, *a)* Midraschsatz; Vorschläge für die descriptive Terminologie der Formalanalyse rabbinischer Texte: FraJBeit 17 (1989) 45-56 [< TLZ 117,185]; – *b)* Die paraphrasierenden Midraschsätzen: FraJud-Beit 18 (1990) 1-22 [< JStJud 22,266].

9995 *Kalmin* Richard, Collegial interaction in the Babylonian Talmud: JQR 82 (1991s) 383-415.

9996 **Kraemer** David, The mind of the Talmud; an intellectual history of the Bavli. NY 1990, Oxford-UP. xv-217 p. 0-19-506290-6.

9996* **Krasilschikov** Itzchak I., ⓪ The Jerusalem Talmud with previously published commentaries, textual emendations and two new commentaries Toledot Itzchak and Tevunah (1954, Moskva). J 1981-, Mutzal Me'esh. 0-914787-05-5...

9997 **Kuyt** A., *al.*, Variety of forms; Dutch studies in midrash. Amst 1990, Univ. Library Palache Inst. 133 p. 90-71396-05-3. – ᴿJStJud 22 (1991) 268s (A. S. van der *Woude*).

9998 ᵀᴱ**Loopik** Marcus van, The ways of the Sages and the way of the world; the minor tractates of the Babylonian Talmud, Derekh Eretz Rabbah, Derekh Eretz Zuta; Pereq ha-Shalom: TStAJud 26. Tü 1991, Mohr. xiii-389 p. 3-16-145644-0.

9999 **Manns** Frédéric, Le Midrash, approche et commentaire. Strasbourg 1990, Commissariat de TS. 162 p. – ᴿRHPR 71 (1991) 232 p. (B. *Keller*).

a1 **Morag** Shelomo, Vocalised Talmudic manuscripts in the Cambridge Genizah collection 1, 1988 ⇒ 4,b189; 5,a179*: ᴿJSS 36 (1991) 347-351 (B. *Chiesa*, also on ʀᴇɪғ S. bibliog.).

a2 *a)* *Moskovitz* Leib, ⓪ Parallel *sugiot* and the text-tradition of the Yerushalmi; – *b)* *Rosenthal* David, ⓪ 'The Talmudists jumped to raise an objection into the Baraita' – Bavli Ketubot 77a-b: Tarbiz 60 (1990s) 523-549 / 551-576; Eng. II / III.

a3 **Nelson** David N., Responses to the destruction of the Second Temple in the tannaitic midrashim: diss. NYU 1991, ᴰ*Schiffman* L. 386 p. 92-13267. – DissA 52 (1991s) 4346-A.

a4 **Neusner** Jacob, The canonical history of ideas; the place of the so-called Tannaite Midrashim: StHistJud 4. Atlanta 1990, Scholars. xvi-224 p. $55 [RelStR 18,156, M. S. *Jaffee*].

a5 **Neusner** Jacob, Language as taxonomy; the rules for using Hebrew and Aramaic in the Babylonian Talmud: SFlorJud 12. Atlanta 1990, Scholars. xvi-237 p. $60 [TR 87,524]. 1-55540-538-X.

a6 *a)* *Neusner* Jacob, Did the Talmud's authorship utilize prior 'sources'? A response to ʜᴀʟɪᴠɴɪ's Sources and traditions; – *b)* *Goldenberg* Robert, The problem of originality in talmudic thought; – *c)* *Goldblatt* Harold, The rabbis of the Babylonian Talmud, a statistical analysis: ⇒ 56, ᶠᶠᴏx M. 2 (1991) 53-79 / 19-27 / 81-94.

a6* ᵀᴱ**Salzer** Israël, Le Talmud, traité ḥaguiga, traduction de l'araméen et de l'hébreu: Les Dix Paroles. Lagrasse 1991, Verdier. 213 p. F 150. 2-86432-131-9.

a7 *Sawyer* Deborah F., Heterodoxy and censorship; some critical remarks on ᴡᴇʀᴛʜᴇɪᴍᴇʀ's edition of Midrash Aleph Beth: JJS 42 (1991) 115-121.

a7* ᴱ**Schäfer** Peter, *Becker* Hans-Jürgen (*Reeg* Gottfried), Synopse zum Talmud Yerushalmi, I/1; Zeraim Berakhot, Pe'a: TStAJud 31. Tü 1991, Mohr. xvi-401 p. 3-16-145849-4.

a8 **Steinsaltz** Adin, Talmud Bava Metzia 1989 ⇒ 5,a190; 6,a227: ᴿBSO 54 (1991) 149s (L. *Glinert*: 'a supernoval event').

a9 **Stemberger** G., Midrasch... 1989 ⇒ 5,a193: ᴿBL (1991) 147 (N. de *Lange*).

a9* [*Strack* Hermann †], **Stemberger** Günther [since 1982], The Talmud, introduction to Talmud and Midrash, ᵀ*Bockmuehl* M. E 1991, Clark. 324 p. £25. 0-567-09509-6 [RB 99,622, B. T. *Viviano*]. – ᴿTsTNijm 31 (1991) 327 (M. *Poorthuis*).

a10 [**Strack** H.], *Stemberger* G., Introducción a la literatura talmúdica y midrásica, ᵀ: BtMidrasica 3. Valencia 1988, Inst. S. Jerónimo. 492 p. – ᴿCiuD 203 (1991) 486 (J. *Gutiérrez*).

a11 **Stemberger** Günter, Il Talmud; introduzione, [selezione di] testi, commenti: Studi Religiosi. Bo 1989, Dehoniane. Lit 50.000 [RivB 39,222 adv.]. – ᴿAsprenas 38 (1991) 108s (V. *Scippa*); STEv 2 (1990) 117 (G. *Emetti*).

a12 **Stern** David, Parables in midrash; narrative and exegesis in rabbinic literature. CM 1991, Harvard Univ. xxi-347 p. $35. 0-674-65447-1 [NTAbs 36,304].

a13 **Taradach** Madeleine, Le Midrash; introduction à la littérature midrashique (*drš* dans la Bible, les Targumim, les Midrasim): MondeB 22, 1990 ➤ 6,a232: ᴿArTGran 54 (1991) 389 (I. *Vilchez*); JStJud 22 (1991) 286-292 (R. *Le Déaut*: beaucoup de choses à corriger ou discuter); Laurentianum 32 (1991) 235-243 (F. *Raurell*, ed. catalán ➤ 6,a231).

a14 **Touati** Charles, Prophètes, talmudistes, philosophes: Patrimoines Judaïsme 1990 ➤ 6,311: ᴿRÉJ 150 (1991) 479s (G. *Nahon*); Salesianum 53 (1991) 589 (R. *Vicent*).

a15 ᵀᴱ**Townsend** John T., Midrash Tanhuma 1989 ➤ 6,a234: ᴿTLZ 116 (1991) 276s (S. *Schreiner*).

a16 **Visotsky** Burton L., Midraš mišlê, a critical edition based on Vatican MS Ebr. 44, with variants from all known manuscripts and early editions. NY 1990, Jewish Theol. Sem. 0-87334-044-2 [NTAbs 36,145].

a16* *Zalcman* Lawrence, Christians, noṣerim [not Christians but Babylonian sun-worshipers in bAboda Zara 6a.7b], and Nebuchadnezzar's daughter: JQR 81 (1990s) 411-426.

a17 **Zegdun** Jehudà, Il mondo del midrash: Cultura Ebraica 15. R 1989, Carucci. 123 p. 88-85027-29-6.

K7.1 Judaismus mediaevalis, *generalia.*

a17* *Alexander-Frizer* Tamar, The pious sinner; ethics and aesthetics in the medieval Hasidic narrative: TStMedJud 5. Tü 1991, Mohr. xi-180 p.

a18 *Carrete Parrondo* Carlos, Nostalgia for the past (and for the future?) among Castilian Judeoconversos: MeditHR 6 (1991) 25-43.

a19 *Dahan* G., Juifs et Chrétiens en Occident médiévale; la rencontre autour de la Bible (XIIᵉ-XIVᵉ s.): Revue de Synthèse 110 (1989) 3-30 [< FilT 4,565].

a20 *Danzig* Neil, The first discovered leaves of Sefer Ḥefes: JQR 82 (1991s) 51-136 + 8 loose facsimiles.

ᴱ**Ebenbauer** A., Die Juden in ihrer mittelalterlichen Umwelt 1991 ➤ 350c.

a21 *Goetschel* R., Nature et miracle dans la pensée juive du moyen âge: ➤ 488, Apparitions 1991, 167-183.

a22 **Hayoun** Maurice-Ruben, La philosophie médiévale juive: Que sais-je? 2595. P 1991, PUF. 128 p. 2-130-43826-7.

a23 **Heide** A. van der, *Voolen* E. van, ❶ The *Amsterdam Mahzor* 1989 ➤ 5,1672: ᴿBO 48 (1991) 647-9 (J. *Klener*).

a24 **Jordan** William C., The French monarchy and the Jews, from Philip Augustus [1179] to the last Capetians: Middle Ages Series. Ph 1989, Univ. Pennsylvania. xi-369 p. – ᴿJQR 81 (1990s) 441-6 (B. *Chilton*).

a25 *Kellner* M., Dogma in medieval Jewish thought; from Maimonides to Abravanel 1986 ➤ 3,a524: ᴿCritRR 3 (1990) 365-9 (Chava *Tirosh-Rothschild*).

a26 **Levy** Ze'ev, Between Yafeth and Shem; on the relationship between Jewish and general philosophy 1987 ➤ 5,a206*: ᴿJQR 81 (1990s) 482-8 (N. M. *Samuelson*).

a27 *Lotter* Friedrich, Talmudisches Recht in den Judenprivilegien Heinrichs IV.? Zu Ausbildung und Entwicklung des Marktschutzrechts im frühen und hohen Mittelalter: ArKulturG 72 (1990) 23-61.

a28 **Newby** G. D., A history of the Jews of Arabia. Columbia 1988, Univ. S. Carolina. 177 p. – ᴿHenoch 13 (1991) 382-4 (R. *Tottoli*: fragile).

a29 ᵀᴱ**Pearl** Chaim [< *Bialik* H. N., *Rawnitzky* Y. H., Sefer ha-Aggadah], Stories of the Sages. TA 1991, Dvir. 366 p.

a30 *Rodrigues* M. A., A cultura judaica medieval e os incunábulos hebraicos: ➤ 475, Braga Sé 1990, 231-261.

a31 *Rothschild* Jean-Pierre, Listes de livres hébreux en Italie; nouveaux documents pour une typologie: RHistText 19 (1989) 291-339.

a32 **Simon** H. & M., ⊕ Filozofia żydowska [1984 ➤ 65,8732], ᵀ*Pszczółkowski* Tomasz G. Wsz 1990, Wiedza Powszechna. 195 p. – ᴿColcT 61,3 (1991) 208-210 (sr. Anna *Zawadska*); PrzPow 831 (1990) 334-6 (Małgorzata *Jantos*).

K7.2 Maimonides.

a33 **Ben-Or** Ehud Z., A concept of prayer; a study of prayer in Maimonides and his sources: diss. Harvard, ᴰ*Putnam* H. CM 1991. 262 p. 92-11768. – DissA 52 (1991s) 3972-A; RelStR 18,174.

a33* ᴱ**Buijs** Joseph A., Maimonides; a collection of [14] critical essays. ND 1988, Univ. vii-317 p. – ᴿJJS 42 (1991) 132s (D. *Frank*: tit. pp.).

a34 ᴱ**Dana** Nissim, ⊕ Abraham MAIMUNI, Kifāyat al-ʿĀbidīn. Ramat-Gan 1989, Bar-Ilan Univ. 346 p. – ᴿJQR 82 (1991s) 194-206 (P. R. *Fenton*).

a35 *David* Abraham, An unknown autographic genizah fragment of Maimonides' Code (*Mishneh Torah*) in the JRUL of Manchester: BJRyL 73,1 (1991) 3-5.

a36 **Fox** Marvin, Interpreting Maimonides; studies in methodology, metaphysics and moral philosophy 1990 ➤ 6,a259: ᴿJAAR 59 (1991) 599s (I. *Robinson*); JRel 71 (1991) 627s (R. *Lerner*).

a37 **Hoffmann** Daniel, Die Erkenntnis auf dem Weg zur Vollkommenheit; Wunderwissen und Gotteserkenntnis in Maimonides' 'More Nebuchim'. Mü 1991, Fink. 117 p. DM 48 [TR 87,169].

a38 ᴱ**Hyman** Arthur, Maimonidean studies 1 (1990). NY 1990, Yeshiva Univ. 222 p. + ⊕ 42. 0-88125-358-8. $35 [➤ 6,a262: '398-8']. – ᴿÉTRel 66 (1991) 591s (Jeanne-M. *Léonard*: plans to be annual, ISSN 1050-1636).

a39 *Imbach* Ruedi, Ut ait Rabbi Moyses; Maimonidische Philosopheme bei Thomas von AQUIN und Meister ECKHART: ColcFran 60 (1990) 99-115.

a40 **Kellner** Menachem M., Maimonides on human perfection: BrownJudSt 202. Atlanta 1990, Scholars. xiv-100 p. $55; sb. $35. 1-55540-437-5 [TDig 38,274].

a40* ᴱ**Lazar** Moshe, Maimonides, Guide for the perplexed, a 15th century Spanish translation by Pedro de TOLEDO (ms. 10289, B.N. Madrid): Sephardic Classical Library 2. Culver City CA 1989, Labyrinthos. xviii-370 p. – ᴿJQR 82 (1991s) 555s (N. *Roth*: also on the other first 3 volumes of the series).

a41 ᴱ**Peláez del Rosal** Jesús, Sobre la vida y obra de Maimonides, I congreso internacional, Córdoba 1985. Córdoba 1991, Almendro. 605 p.; ill. 84-86077-97-4. 46 art.

a41* ᵀᴱ**Rosner** Fred, The existence and unity of God; three treatises attributed to Moses Maimonides; bibliog. *Dienstag* Jacob I. Northvale NJ 1990, Aronson. xiii-247 p. 0-87668-805-9.

a42 *Shifman* Yair, ❶ Ibn Bājja as a source of Maimonides [; FALAQUERA] commentary to the Guide III, 51,54: Tarbiz 60 (1990s) 225-236.

a43 **Strauss** Leo, Philosophy and law; essays toward the understanding of Maimonides and his predecessors, ᵀ*Baumann* Fred. Ph 1987, Jewish Publ. 120 p. $19. 0-8276-0273-1. – ᴿJAAR 59 (1991) 426-8 (N. M. *Samuelson*).

a44 *Turner* Masha, ❶ The structure of the lexicographic chapters in the Moreh Nevukhim: HUCA 62 (1991) ❶ 29-61.

a45 *a) Twersky* Isadore, Aspects of Maimonidean epistemology; halakah and science; – *b) Kreisel* Howard, Intellectual perfection and the role of the Law in the philosophy of Maimonides: ➤ 56, ᶠFox M. 3 (1991) 3-23 / 25-46 [+ 3 on Maimonides p. 57-77-89-107].

K7.3   Alii magistri Judaismi mediaevalis.

a46 RASHI: **Fogel** Dov I., Rashi's commentary to Tractate Bava Metria; selected parts, introductory chapters: diss. Bar-Ilan. Ramat-Gan c. 1991. 289 p. [? ❶ RTLv 23, p. 541].

a46* ᴱ**Kapach** Joseph D., SAADIAH (Ben Joseph) Gaon, ❶ Perušei al ha-Torah. J 1984. 205 p.

a47 ᵀᴱ*Perani* Mauro, NAHMANIDE (Ramban), La legge del Signore è perfetta; omelia rabbinica sulla perfezione della Tora: CuEbr 27. R 1989, Caracci. 158 p. – ᴿHenoch 13 (1991) 250s (P. *Capelli*).

a48 *Perani* Mauro, La terminologia esegetica nel commento alla Torah di Nahmanide; il SOD e l'interpretazione cabalistica: ➤ 452, AnStoEseg 8,2 (1990/1) 421-441.

a49 **Brin** Gershon, Studies in the biblical exegesis of R. Joseph QARA. TA 1990, Univ. Rosenberg School. 179 p. – ᴿBSO 54 (1991) 578s (A. *Sáenz-Badillos*).

a50 ᵀᴱ*Ginsburg* Elliot K., Sod ha-Shabbat < Meir IBN GABBAI 1988 ➤ 5,a252; SUNY; vii-264 p. $50. – ᴿCritRR 4 (1991) 386-9 (K. P. *Bland*).

a50* *Wolfson* Elliot R., HAI Gaon's letter and commentary on ʿAleynu; further evidence of Moses de LEÓN's pseudepigraphic activity [in title; in text 'forgery']: JQR 81 (1990s) 365-410.

a51 **Alba Cecilia** A., Midrás de los diez Mandamientos y [NISSIM b. Yaʿaqob 1038] Libro precioso de la salvación: BtMidrásica 7. Valencia 1990, Inst. S. Jerónimo. 298 p. – ᴿArTGran 54 (1991) 455-8 (F. *Contreras*).

a52 **Perry** T. A., The moral proverbs of SANTOB [Shem Tov] de Carrón; Jewish wisdom in Christian Spain. Princeton 1987, Univ. ix-198 p. $26. – ᴿCritRR 2 (1989) 388-391 (M. *McGaha*).

a53 ABULAFIA: **Idel** Moshe, The mystical experience in Abraham Abulafia ❶, ᵀ*Chipman* J. Albany 1988, SUNY. x-246 p. – ᴿJQR 82 (1991s) 207-214 (E. K. *Ginsburg*).

a54 FALAQUERA [1223-91]: **Jospe** Raphael. Torah and Sophia... Falaquera 1988: ᴿJAAR 58 (1991) 180s (N. M. *Samuelsson*); JRel 71 (1991) 628s (C. *Raffel*); Tarbiz 60 (1990s) 689-695 (Y. *Shifman*, ❶; Eng. IX).

a54* **Harvey** Steven, FALAQUERA's Epistle of the Debate; an introduction to Jewish philosophy. CM 1987, Harvard. xvi-155 p. – ᴿTarbiz 60 (1990s) 465-7 (D. J. *Lasker*, ❶).

a55 *Lockshin* Martin I., Tradition or context; two exegetes struggle with *peshat* [*Rashbam* (S. BEN-MEIR) and A. BEN EZRA]: ➤ 56, FFOX M. 2 (1991) 173-186.

a56 *Horst* Pieter van der, The measurement of the body, a chapter in the history of ancient Jewish mysticism [Shiur QomahT < EPlas J. van der, Effigies Dei (L 1987) 56-68]: ➤ 212, Essays, NOrb 14 (1990) 123-135.

K7.4 Qabbalâ, Zohar, Merkabâ – Jewish mysticism.

a57 **Brody** Seth L., Human hands dwell in heavenly heights; worship and mystical experience in thirteenth-century Kabbalah: diss. Pennsylvania, DGreen A. Ph 1991. 717p. 92-11913. – DissA 52 (1991s) 3968s-A; RelStR 18,174.

a58 *Chaze* Micheline, De l'identification des patriarches au char divin ['les Patriarches sont la Merkaba']; recherches du sens d'un enseignement rabbinique dans le midrash et dans la kabbale prézoharique et ses sources: RÉJ 149 (1990) 5-75.

a59 **Gruenwald** I., From apocalypticism to gnosticism; studies in apocalypticism, Merkavah mysticism and Gnosticism: BeitErfAJ 14, 1988 ➤ 5,a253: RBL (1991) 137 (J. F. A. *Sawyer*); OTAbs 14 (1991) 363s (M. S. *Smith*).

a59* TEHansel Joëlle, Rabbi Moïse Hayyim LUZZATTO, Le philosophe et le cabaliste; exposition d'un débat: Les Dix Paroles. Lagrasse 1991, Verdier. 185p. 2-86432-137-8.

a60 **Idel** Moshe, Kabbalah, new perspectives 1988 ➤ 4,b248... 6,a304: RJQR 82 (1991s) 224-6 (R. C. *Kiener*).

a61 **Idel** Moshe, Studies in ecstatic Kabbalah. Albany 1988, SUNY. xiv-178p. – RJQR 82 (1991s) 525-7 (P. B. *Fenton*).

a62 — *Tirosh-Rothschild* Hava, Continuity and revision in the study of Kabbalah [*Idel* M. 1988]: AJS 16 (1991) 161-192.

a63 **Janowitz** N., Poetics of ascent 1989 ➤ 5,a205; 6,a306: RAJS 16 (1991) 218-221 (M. D. *Swartz*); SecC 8 (1991) 61s (Adela Y. *Collins*).

a64 *a*) *Morray-Jones* C. R. A., Hekhalot literature and talmudic tradition; [P. S.] ALEXANDER's three test cases; – *b*) *Fauth* Wolfgang, Ṭaṭrosjah-Ṭoṭrosjah und Meṭaṭron in der jüdischen Merkabah-Mystik: JStJud [18 (1987) 40-68] 22 (1991) 1-39 / 40-87.

a64* **Schäfer** Peter, Konkordanz zur Hekhalot-Literatur 1986-8 ➤ 2,8361... 6,a316: RJudaica 46 (1990) 50 (S. *Schreiner*).

a65 **Schäfer** Peter, al., Übersetzung der Hekhalot-Literatur 3s §335-597/ 598-985: TStAJ 22,29, 1989 ➤ 5,a268: [vol. 4, xlv-208p.; 3-16-145745-5]. – RNumen 38 (1991) 134-6 (J. *Dan*); Salesianum 53 (1991) 187s (R. *Vicent*).

a66 **Schäfer** Peter, Der verborgene und offenbare Gott; Hauptthemen der frühen jüdischen Mystik. Tü 1991, Mohr. xii-186p. 3-16-145812-5; pa. -05-2.

a66* **Scholem** Gershom, Origins of the Kabbalah, TArkush Allan, EWerblowski R. J. Zwi 1987 ➤ 3,2596... 5,a270: RCritRR 3 (1990) 370-2 (R. C. *Kiener*); RelStR 17 (1991) 313-321 (L. *Fine* & E. *Wolfson*, comparing IDEL M.).

a67 — *a*) **Dan** Joseph, G. SCHOLEM and the mystical dimension of Jewish history 1987 ➤ 3,a578: RJQR 81 (1990s) 489s (P. *Schäfer*). – *b*) *Galas* Michał, ⊕ G. SCHOLEM's method of aphorism; or the relation of contemporary philosophy to the Kabbala: RuBi 42 (1989) 139-141. –

c) Idel M., Rabbinism versus Kabbalism; on G. SCHOLEM's phenomenology of Judaism: Modern Judaism 11 (Baltimore 1991) 281-296 [< NTAbs 36,235].

a67* *Schwemer* Anna Maria, Irdischer und himmlischer König; Beobachtungen zur sogenannten David-Apokalypse in Hekhalot Rabbati 122-126: → 438, Königsherrschaft 1986/91, 309-359.

K7.5 Judaismus saec. 14-18.

a68 **Alexander-Friezer** Tamar, The pious sinner; ethics and aesthetics in the medieval Hasidic narrative: TStMedJ 5. Tü 1991, Mohr. x-180 p. 3-16-145656-4.

a68* **Askof** Yitzhak, ❺ The laws and customs in 'Ḥem'at ha-Ḥemda' [13 cent. Aleppo Pentateuch/Haftarot commentary, mostly Hebrew, some Arabic]: diss. NYU, ᴰ*Schiffman* L. 1991, 284 p. 92-13215. – DissA 52 (1991s) 4370s-A.

a69 **Bowman** Steven P., The Jews of Byzantium, 1204-1453: 1985 → 2,8731... 6,a321: ᴿSpeculum 66 (1991) 383-6 (N. *Golb*).

a70 **Hayoun** Maurice-Ruben, La philosophie et la theólogie de MOÏSE de Narbonne (1300-1362): TStMJ 4. Tü 1989, Mohr. xxi-320 p. DM 168. – ᴿAJS 16 (1991) 223-6 (K.P. *Bland*); JQR 82 (1991s) 541s (D.J. *Lasker*); Judaica 46 (1990) 58s (S. *Schreiner*); RTPhil 123 (1991) 339 (J. *Borel*).

a71 **Hayoun** Maurice, Moshe NARBONI [1300-62]: Texts and Studies in Medieval and Early Modern Judaism 1. Tü 1986, Mohr. 184 p. – ᴿJQR 81 (1990s) 161-5 (L.E. *Goodman*: French translation and text of part I of commentary on Maimonides by 'the keenest Averroist of his day').

a72 **Frank** Daniel, The religious philosophy of Karaite Aaron BEN ELIJAH [Istanbul c. 1350]; the problem of divine justice: diss. Harvard, ᴰ*Twersky* I. CM 1991. 360 p. 91-23056. – DissA 52 (1991s) 936-A.

a73 ᴱ**Lasker** Daniel J., r. Hasdai CRESCAS, ❺ *Sefer Biṭṭûl*, Réfutation des principes des Chrétiens 1398. Ramat-Gan 1990, Univ. Bar-Ilan. 112 p. 965-226-111-4. – ᴿRÉJ 150 (1991) 457s (J.-C. *Attias*).

a74 **Attias** Jean-Christophe, Le commentaire biblique; Mordekhai KOMTINO ou l'herméneutique du dialogue: Patrimoines Judaïsme. P 1991, Cerf. 204 p. F 120. 2-204-04261-7 [BL 92,123: N. de *Lange*: or Khomatiano, 1402-1482].

a74* *a) Fuencisla García Casar* María, Jewish participation in Castilian fairs; the example of Medina del Campo in the fifteenth century: → 533, MeditHR 6 (1991) 12-24.

a75 ᵀᴱ**Ruderman** David B., A valley of vision; the heavenly journey of Abraham ben Hananiah YAGEL [16th cent.] 1990 → 6,a330: ᴿTarbiz 60 (1990s) 469-476 (E. *Horowitz*, ❺, also on his 1988 Kabbalah; Eng. IX).

a76 **Ruderman** David B., [YAGEL Abraham, 1553-1623] Kabbalah... magic and science... physician 1988 → 6,a329: ᴿAJS 16 (1991) 229-231 (H. *Adelman*).

a77 ᵀᴱ*Jacobs* Louis, Rabbi Moses CORDOVERO [1522-1570]. The Palm Tree of Deborah [1588]. NY 1981, Sepher-Hermon. 133 p. 0-87203-097-0.

a78 **Israel** Jonathan I., European Jewry in the age of mercantilism, 1550-1750: 1985 → 4,b267; 5,a285: ᴿRHR 207 (1990) 320-2 (S. *Schwarzfuchs*).

a79 **Toaff** Ariel, Il Ghetto di Roma nel Cinquecento; conflitti etnici e problemi socioecomici. Ramat-Gan 1984, Bar-Ilan. xvii-99 p. 965-226-0479.

a80 **Segal** Lester A., Historical consciousness and religious tradition in [1511-77] Azariah de' Rossi's [1573] Me'or 'Einayim. Ph 1989, Jewish Publ. 194 p. $23. – ᴿJAAR 59 (1991) 873s (A. M. *Lesley*); JSS 36 (1991) 168-170 (Joanna *Weinberg*).

a81 **Kaplan** Yosef, From Christianity to Judaism; the story of Isaac Orobio de CASTRO [1617-87], (1982), ᵀ*Loewe* R.: Littman Library. Ox 1989, UP. xxviii-531 p.; 8 pl.; 4 maps. £45. 0-19-710060-0. – ᴿJEH 42 (1991) 321-3 (A. *MacKay*); JRelHist 16 (1990s) 497-9 (Rachael *Kohn*: Spain's crypto-Judaism).

a82 **[Basch] Moreen** Vera, Iranian Jewry's hour of peril and heroism... Bahai IBN LUṬF 1617-62: 1987 → 5,a290: ᴿRÉJ 150 (1991) 462-5 (P. *Fenton*).

K7.7 Hasidismus et Judaismus saeculi XIX.

a82* **Breuer** Mordechai, Jüdische Orthodoxie im Deutschen Reich, 1871-1918; die Sozialgeschichte einer religiösen Minderheit. Fra 1986, Athenäum. 525 p. – ᴿRHR 208 (1991) 105, (S. *Schwarzfuchs*).

a83 **Carlebach** Elisheva, Two Amens that delayed the redemption; Jewish messianism and popular spirituality in the post-Sabbatian century [Y. Leib (of) Zelechow, witness of the messianic failure 1666]: JQR 82 (1991s) 241-261.

a84 **Grégoire,** abbé, Essai sur la régénération physique, morale et politique des Juifs. P c. 1991, Stock = Metz 1887, Société Royale des Sciences. – ᴿFoiVie 90,6 (1991) 110-2 [?*Giniewski* Paul: une nouvelle lecture est opportune].

a85 ᵀᴱ**Gross** Benjamin, Hayyim Ben Isaac VOLOZHINER, L'âme de la vie, *Nefesh Haḥayyim*: Les Dix Paroles. Lagrasse 1986, Verdier. lxxii-404 p. 2-86432- 046-0.

a86 *Guetta* Alessandro, Un Kabbaliste à l'heure du progrès; le cas d'Élie BENAMOZEGH: RHR 208 (1991) 415-436; Eng. 415.

a87 **Krassen** Miles A., Mystical consciousness and radical self-effacement in early Hasidism; the religious tracts of R. Meshullam FREIBUSH of Zbarazh: diss. Pennsylvania, ᴰ*Green* A. Ph 1990. – RTLv 23, p. 541.

a88 **Malka** Victor, Ainsi parlait le hassidisme: Toledot/Judaïsmes. 1991. 174 p. F 99. – ᴿÉtudes 375 (1991) 140 (G. *Petitdemange*: sans éditrice).

a89 **Mintz** Alan, 'Banished from their father's table'; loss of faith in [19th century] Hebrew autobiography. Bloomington 1989, Indiana Univ. 234 p. $37.50. 0-253-33857-1. – ᴿJAAR 59 (1991) 612-5 (E. *Spicehandler*); JJS 42 (1991) 136s (Glenda *Abramson*).

a90 ᵀᴱ**Newman** Louis I., (*Spitz* Samuel), The Hasidic anthology; tales and teachings of the Hasidim. Northvale NJ 1987, Aronson. xc-715 p. 0-87668-968-3.

a91 **Robberechts** Édouard, Les Hassidim: Fils d'Abraham 1990 → 6,a342*: ᴿEsprVie 101 (1991) 535s (M. *Delahoutre*).

K7.8 Judaismus contemporaneus.

a91* ᴱ**Abramson** Glenda, The Blackwell companion to Jewish culture 1989 → 5,a298; £50; ᴿBSO 54 (1991) 150 (L. *Glinert*).

a92 *Adriaanse* H. J., Hermann COHEN, joods filosoof: NedTTs 45 (1991) 293-309; Eng. 329.

a92* **Borowitz** Eugene B., A theology for the postmodern Jew. Ph 1991, Jewish Publ. xiv-319 p. $25. 0-8276-0400-9 [TDig 39,255].

a93 **Cohn-Sherbok** Dan, The Jewish heritage 1988 → 5,a314: ᴿCritRR 4 (1991) 347-9 (C. E. *Vernoff*); JRelHist 16 (1990s) 91-93 (A. D. *Crown*).

a94 **Danzger** M. Herbert, Returning to tradition; the contemporary revival of Orthodox Judaism. NHv 1989, Yale Univ. x-374 p. $30. 0-300-03947-6 [TDig 37,356]. – ᴿJRel 71 (1991) 126s (C. *Liebman*).

a95 **Davidman** Lynn, Tradition in a rootless world; women turn to orthodox Judaism. Berkeley 1991, Univ. California. 254 p. [JAAR 59,882].

a96 **Deshen** Schlomo, The Mellah society; Jewish community life in Sherifian Morocco: Ch Studies in the History of Judaism. Ch 1989, Univ. xi-152 p. $34.50; pa. $13.75. 0-226-14339-2; pa. -40-9. – ᴿBijdragen 52 (1991) 211s (H. *Goddijn*).

a97 **Ellis** Marc H., *a*) Toward a Jewish theology of liberation 1987 → 3,a620 ... 6,a346: ᴿJJS 42 (1991) 287-9 (J. G. *Campbell*). – *b*) Hacia una teología judía de la liberación [1987 → 3,a620], ᵀ*Knoblauch* Diana M. D. de: HistIglT. San José 1988, DEI. 168 p. – ᴿPerspT 21 (1989) 126-8 (J. B. *Libânio*). '9977-904-60-X'.

a98 *Ellis* Marc H., Critical thought and messianic trust; reflections on a Jewish theology of liberation: EcuR 42 (1990) 33-47 [< TLZ 116,277].

a99 **Fackenheim** Emil L., What is Judaism? An interpretation for the present age 1987 → 6,a348: ᴿJRel 70 (1990) 127s (P. *Mendes-Flohr*).

a100 **Fiorentino** Luca, L'ebreo senza qualità ovvero identità e mizwoth (terzomillennio) [... risente di E. FROMM, Voi sarete come dèi ...]. Genova 1989, Marietti. Lit. 17.000. ix-137 p. – ᴿProtestantesimo 46 (1991) 150s (M. *Abbà*).

a100* *Fishbane* S., Structure and form in halakhic literature; a different approach to the study of modern Jewish law: MethTRel 2,1 (Toronto 1990) 72-90 [< NTAbs 36,234].

a101 **Gillman** Neil, Sacred fragments; recovering theology for the modern Jew. Ph 1990, Jewish Publ. xxvii-289 p. $20. 0-8276-0352-5 [TDig 38,60].

a102 **Greenberg** Simon, A Jewish philosophy and pattern of life: Moreshet 9. NY 1981, Jewish Theol. Sem. xix-550 p. 0-87334-012-4.

a102* *Haberman* Jacob, Abraham WOLF [1876-1948, disciple of SPINOZA], a forgotten Jewish Reform thinker: JQR 81 (1990s) 267-304.

a103 *Hayoun* Maurice-Ruben, Réflexions critiques sur l'existence d'un 'intégrisme' juif: FoiVie 89,1 (1990) 11-19.

a104 **Hertzberg** Arthur, The Jews in America, four centuries of an uneasy encounter; a history. NY 1990, Simon & S. $23. – ᴿCCurr 40 (1990s) 406-410 (L. A. *Hoffman*: 'American Judaism; challenging the myth').

a105 **Jacobs** Louis, God, Torah, Israel; traditionalism without fundamentalism [1989 Efroymson lectures]. Cincinnati 1990, HUC. $18 [RelStR 18,150, M. H. *Vogel*].

a106 **Katz** Jacob, The 'Shabbes Goy' 1989 → 5,a302: ᴿJRel 71 (1991) 630s (L. A. *Segal*).

a107 *Klein* Judith, Literatur des Exils und der Erinnerung; die zeitgenössische jüdisch-maghrebinische Literatur in französischer Sprache: Judaica 46 (1990) 225-239.

Kraus Hans J., Rückkehr zu Israel 1991 → 221.

a108 *Lasker* Daniel J., Judah HALEVI and Karaism: → 56, ᶠFOX M., 3 (1991) 111-125 [127-156, *Jospe* Raphael].

a108* *a*) *Lerner* Stephen C., Conservative Judaism's academy, Jewish Theological Seminary, combining scholarship and practice; – *b*) *Gillman* Neil, Judaism's fragile center; JTS and the Conservative movement: ChrCris 51 (1991s) 195-8 / 198-202.

a109 **Lessing** Théodore, La haine de soi, le refus d'être juif [c. 1930], [T]*Hayoun* Maurice-R. P 1990, Berg. – [R]RÉJ 150 (1991) 471-4 (F. *Kaplan*).

a110 **Lévinas** Emmanuel, Difficult freedom; essays on Judaism, [T]*Hand* Séan. Baltimore 1990, Johns Hopkins Univ. 320 p. $30 [RelStR 18,150, Annette *Aronowicz*].

a111 *a) Lévy* Michel-Louis, Démographie, généalogie et Torah; existe-t-il un peuple juif?; – *b) Rashi* Yehoshua, Religion, laïcité, société et politique dans le judaïsme israélien: FoiVie 90,6 = CahÉtJuives 24 (1990) 57-67 / 69-88.

a112 [E]**Loewenberg** Robert J., *Alexander* Edward, The Israeli fate of Jewish liberalism. Lanham MD 1988, UPA. xii-146 p. $14.50 [RelStR 18,152, L. E. *Newman*].

a113 **Löwy** Michel, Rédemption et Utopie; le judaïsme libertaire en Europe centrale [XX s.], une étude d'affinité élective: Sociologie d'aujourd'hui. P 1988, PUF. 258 p. F 150. – [R]TR 87 (1991) 44s (E. *Arens*).

a114 **Loth** Heinz-Jürgen, Judentum. Gö 1989, VR. – [R]Protestantesimo 46 (1991) 220s (R. *Casonato*).

a115 **Lubarsky** Sandra B., Tolerance and transformation; Jewish approaches to religious pluralism. Cincinnati 1990, HUC. 149 p. $25 [RelStR 18,239, N. M. *Samuelson*].

a116 **Meyer** Michael A., Jewish identity in the modern world. Seattle 1990, Univ. Washington. $17.50. – [R]CCurr 41 (1991s) 555-7 (M. *Polner*: A. SCHINDLER called defining Jewishness around Israel and the Holocaust a 'kidney machine').

a117 **Meyer** Michael A., A response to modernity; a history of the Reform movement in Judaism 1988 → 4,b286 ... 6,a360: [R]JRel 70 (1990) 129s (T. *Endelman*); RHR 208 (1991) 106s (S. *Schwarzfuchs*).

a118 **Mittleman** Alan L., Between Kant and Kabbalah ... I. BREUER [1883-1996] 1990 → 6,a362: [R]JAAR 59 (1991) 184-6 (W. *Klubock*).

a118* **Panonzi** (Ponzian) Giuseppe, L'ebreo attraverso i secoli e nelle questioni sociali dell'età moderna [Treviso 1898]. Sala Bolognese 1991, Forni. v-481 p.

a119 **Prell** Riv-Ellen, Prayer and community; the Havurah in American Judaism. Detroit 1989, Wayne State Univ. 335 p. $16.50. – [R]JAAR 59 (1991) 860-2 (H. *Eilberg-Schwartz*: superb on why American Jews of the 1970s rejected their parents' Judaism).

a120 **Raphael** Marc L., Abba Hillel SILVER, a profile in American Judaism. 1989, Holmes & M. $49.50. – [R]CCurr 40 (1990s) 278-280 (R. B. *Garrison*: attributes to W. N. EWER, not Ogden Nash, 'How odd / of God / to choose / the Jews, and adds anonymous 'But not so odd / as those who choose / the Jewish God / and spurn the Jews').

a121 *Schäfer* Peter, Judaistik — jüdische Wissenschaft in Deutschland heute; historische Identität und Nationalität: Saeculum 42 (1991) 199-216.

a122 *Scheel* Heinrich, Ein jüdischer Lehrer an seinen einstigen Schüler; Briefe Hans GAERTNERs aus den Jahren 1946-1950: ZRGg 43 (1991) 18-29.

a123 **Schwartz** Howard, Lilith's cave [... legends] 1988 → 4,k292: [R]CritRR 3 (1990) 330-2 (J. *Zwelling*).

a124 **Shmueli** Efraim [d. 1988], Seven Jewish cultures; a reinterpretation of Jewish history and thought, [T]*Shmueli* Gila, 1990 → 6,a163: [R]BL (1991) 147 (S. C. *Reif*); TLond 94 (1991) 309s (M. *Braybrooke*); TS 52 (1991) 577-9 (J. T. *Pawlikowski*).

a125 *Sierra* Sergio J., Apporto degli Ebrei all'interpretazione della Bibbia (l'età moderna): HumBr 46 (1991) 335-364.

a126 ᴱSobel Zvi, *Beit-Hallahmi* Benjamin, Tradition, innovation, conflict; Jewishness and Judaism in contemporary Israel. Albany 1991, SUNY. viii-316 p. $18. 11 art. on how Jewish religion is lived [RelStR 18,159, C. S. *Liebman*, high praise].

a127 **Weiler** Gershon, Jewish theocracy 1988 ➤ 5,b332: ᴿJQR 82 (1991s) 498-501 (G. J. *Blidstein*).

a128 ᴱ**Wertheimer** Jack, The American synagogue, a sanctuary transformed 1987 ➤ 4,329; 5,a345: ᴿCritRR 3 (1990) 374-6 (Laura *Levitt*); RelStR 17 (1991) 197-204 (S. C. *Heilman* & E. B. *Holifield*); RHR 208 (1991) 108s (S. *Schwarzfuchs*).

a129 *Yaffe* Martin D., Leo STRAUSS as Judaic thinker; some first notions: RelStR 17 (1991) 33.35.37-41.

ᴋ8 *Philosemitismus* – **Judeo-Christian rapprochement.**

a130 *Agursky* Mikhail, *Segal* Dmitry, Jews and the Russian Orthodox Church; a common legacy, a common hope: StVlad 35 (1991) 21-32.

a131 **Arnoldi** Udo, Pro Judaeis; die Gutachten der hallischen Theologen im 18. Jahrhundert zu Fragen der Judentoleranz: ev. Diss. Bochum 1991, ᴰ*Wallmann* J. – TR 87 (1991) 516; RTLv 23, p. 541.

a132 **Barromi** Joel, L'antisemitismo moderno [corso alla Gregoriana] 1988 ➤ 5,a349*: ᴿProtestantesimo 46 (1991) 237s (M. *Abbà*).

a133 **Beeck** Frans J. van, Loving the Torah more than God? Towards a Catholic appreciation of Judaism 1989 ➤ 6,a375: ᴿGregorianum 72 (1991) 778s (J. *Galot*).

a134 **Ben-Chorin** Schalom, Weil wir Brüder sind; zum christlich-jüdischen Dialog heute. Gerlingen 1989, Bleicher. 238 p. – ᴿColcT 61,3 (1991) 204-6 (P. *Gajewski*, ❶).

a134* *a) Ben-Shalom* Ram, ❶ The disputation of Tortosa; Vincente FERRER and the problem of the conversos according to the testimony of Isaac NATHAN: – *b) Shapiro* Alexander M., ❶ An anti-Christian polemic of the twelfth century: Zion 56 (1991) 21-45; Eng. VIs / 72-85; Eng. VIII.

a135 **Berti-Anker** Christine, Das theologische Verständnis des Judentums in der deutschsprachigen katholischen Dogmatik des 20. Jahrhunderts: Diss. ᴰ*Schwager* R. Innsbruck 1991. 248 p. – RTLv 23, p. 541; ZkT 114,499.

a136 *Bobertz* Charles A., 'For the vineyard of the Lord of Hosts was the house of Israel'; CYPRIAN of Carthage and the Jews: JQR 82 (1991s) 1-15.

a137 *Bons* Eberhard, Die Ursprünge der Judenfeindschaft [... 'Urdrama', den Juden angelastet ... was vermag Bibelkritik gegen Vorurteile?]: Orientierung 55 (1991) 20s.

a138 **Bowler** Maurice, Claude MONTEFIORE and Christianity: BrownJudSt 157, 1988 ➤ 5,a357: ᴿJQR 82 (1991s) 569s (J. B. *Stein*).

a139 *a) Boys* Mary C., An educational perspective on interreligious dialogue; a Catholic's view; – *b) Lee* Sara S., Jewish view; – *c) Athans* Mary C., Teaching about Judaism in a Christian seminary: RelEdn 86 (Ch 1991) 171-183 / 184-196 / 197-207 [< ᴢɪᴛ 91,470].

a140 ᴱ**Brakelmann** Günter, *Rosowski* Martin, Antisemitismus: V-Reihe 1547, 1989 ➤ 6,a377: ᴿJudaica 46 (1990) 185s (E. *Bons*).

a141 ᴱ**Bunte** Wolfgang, Religionsgespräche zwischen Christen und Juden in den Niederlanden (1100-1500): JudUmw 27. Fra 1990, Lang. 812 p. – ᴿRHE 86 (1991) 183s (Bat-Sheva *Albert*).

a142 ᴱ**Charlesworth** J. H., *al.*, Jews and Christians I, 1990 ➤ 6,396: ᴿAnStoEseg 8 (1991) 710 (M. *Pesce*); Henoch 13 (1991) 247-250 (P. *Sacchi*).

a143 **Chazan** Robert, Daggers of faith 1989 ↝ 5,a363; 6,a381: ᴿJJS 42 (1991) 281-6 (D. *Frank*); JQR 81 (1990s) 464-6 (D. J. *Lasker*).

a143* *Chazan* Robert, The Christian position in Jacob BEN REUBEN's Milhamot ha-Shem: ↝ 56, ᶠFOX M., 2 (1991) 157-170.

a144 ᴱ**Chrostowski** W., *Rubinkiewicz* R., ↝ a215, ☻ Żydzi i judaizm w dokumentach Kościoła i nauczaniu Jana Pawła II (1965-1989). Wsz 1990, Akad. Teol. Kat. 254 p. – ᴿColcT 61,3 (1991) 191-6 (M. *Horoszewicz*, ☻); PrzPow 271 (1991) 521-3 (Maria M. *Matusiak* ☻).

a145 *Chrostowski* Waldemar, The Church, Jews and Judaism [Symposium Warszawa 5-6.VI.1989]: ColcT 60,3 (1990) 107-111; + ☻ 19-30 [11-106, 7 art.; 113-8 bibliografia polskojęzyczna].

a146 *Chrostowski* Waldemar, ☻ Dylematy chrześcijańsko-żydowskiego dialoga: PrzPow 267,821 (1990) 39-53; franç. 53.

a147 *Chrostowski* Waldemar, ☻ 'Nostra aetate' vue de la perspective d'un quart de siècle: PrzPow 270,830 (1990) 75-92; franç. 92.

a148 *Chrostowski* Waldemar, ☻ Les Chrétiens et les Juifs dans la nouvelle Europe de l'est: PrzPow 271 (1991) 54-72; franç. 72.

a149 *Cohn-Sherbok* Dan, Transcending Christian anti-Semitism: Month 252 (1991) 382-8.

a150 **Colpe** C., Das Siegel der Propheten 1990 ↝ 6,214: ᴿRÉJ 150 (1991) 441s (S. *Mimouni*).

a151 **Czermak** Gerhard, Christen gegen Juden; Geschichte einer Verfolgung. Nördlingen 1989, Greno. 429 p. DM 44. – ᴿColcT 61,3 (1991) 206-8 (Ewa *Jóźwiak*, ☻); Judaica 46 (1990) 184s (U. *Mazura*).

a152 *Dagron* G., Le traité de GRÉGOIRE de Nicée sur le baptême des Juifs: Travaux et mémoires 11 (1991) 313-357 [RHE 87,40* 'Nicée'].

a153 *Dagron* G., *Déroche* V., Juifs et Chrétiens dans l'Orient du VIIᵉ s. [Doctrina Jacobi nuper baptizati]: Travaux et mémoires 11 (1991) 17-273 [! < RHE 87,30*].

a154 **Dahan** Gilbert, Les intellectuels chrétiens et les juifs au Moyen Âge: Patrimoines, Judaïsme. P 1990. – ᴿRBén 101 (1991) 202s (P.-M. *Bogaert*).

a155 *Del Valle* Carlos, El 'De comprobatione sextae aetatis' [polémica antijudía 724] de JULIÁN de Toledo y el judaismo español: EstB 49 (1991) 251-263.

a156 *Dreyer* Michael, Judenhass und Antisemitismus bei Constantin FRANTZ: HistJb 111,1 (Mü 1991) 155-173 [< ZIT 91,525].

a157 *a*) *Dubois* Marcel, Thomas AQUINAS on the place of the Jews in the divine plan; – *b*) *Stöhr* Martin, Learning step by step in the Jewish-Christian dialogue, ᵀ*Naftali* Miryam; – *c*) *Mussner* Franz, Catholic-Jewish dialogue since 1945; survey and observations [< 1988 Cologne inter-German symposium]: ↝ 54, ᶠFLUSSER D., Immanuel 24s (1990) 241-266 / 267-279 / 280-291.

a157* ᴱ**Dundes** Alan, The blood libel legend; a case-book in anti-Semitic folklore. Madison 1991, Univ. Wisconsin. ix-385 p. $42.50; pa. $17.50. 0-299-13110-6; -4-9 [TDig 39,254].

a158 *Duponcheele* Joseph, Quelle philosophie pour le judaïsme et le christianisme?: Bijdragen 52 (1991) 37-56; Eng. 56s.

a159 **Edwards** John, The Jews in Christian Europe, 1400-1700: Christianity and Society in the Modern World, 1988 ↝ 5,a377; 6,a391: ᴿJSS 36 (1991) 186-8 (B. *Pullan*); Speculum 66 (1991) 149s (J. *Cohen*).

a160 *Ehrlich* Ernst L., Christen und Juden auf meinem Weg: Judaica 46 (1990) 1-11 [5s, BEA A. ...].

a161 *Ellis* Marc, Jewish-Christian impasse: Tablet 244 (1990) 68.70; p. 213, reply by *Keimach* B.

a162 **Fisher** Eugene J., *Klenicki* Leon, In our time; the flowering of Jewish-Catholic dialogue: StJudChr. NY 1990, Paulist. vi-161 p. $7 pa. 0-8091-3196-X [TDig 38,271].

a163 **Fornberg** Tord, Jewish-Christian dialogue and biblical exegesis 1988 ⮞ 4,b328 ... 6,a397: ᴿIndTSt 27 (1990) 361s (L. *Legrand*).

a164 **Friedrich** Martin, Zwischen Abwehr und Bekehrung ... ev. Theol./Judentum ᴰ1988 ⮞ 5,a384: ᴿHistJb 110 (1990) 215-7 (M. *Agethen*); JRel 71 (1991) 263s (Jane *Strohl*).

a164* *Friedrich* Martin, Vom christlichen Antijudaismus zum modernen Antisemitismus: ZKG 102 (1991) 319-347.

a165 ᴱ**Frohnhofen** Herbert, Christlicher Antijudaismus und jüdischer Antipaganismus 1990 ⮞ 6,335*: ᴿColcT 61,3 (1991) 198-201 (W. *Chrostowski*, ❷).

a166 *Fubini* G., Ebraismo e cristianesimo; la parabola del figliol prodigo [Baeck L., Buber M., Benamozegh E., et tous sauf Freud insistent sur la priorité permanente du judaïsme et la dépendance du christianisme]: Rivista di Filosofia 81 (1990) 429-455 [< RSPT 75,345].

a167 *a) Fumagalli* Pier Francesco, Chiesa e popolo ebraico venticinque anni dopo il Concilio Vaticano II [conferenza Ṭanṭur 1991]: RasT 32 (1991) 369-388.

— *b) Gossmann* Hans-Christoph, Die Verbindung von jüdischer Kultur und hebräischer Sprache und ihre Rezeption in der antijüdischen Literatur: LingBib 64 (1990) 96-99.

a167* **Gutwirth** Jacques, Les Judéo-Chrétiens d'aujourd'hui. P 1987, Cerf. 293 p. – ᴿJQR 81 (1990s) 477-480 (L. *Podselver*: un outil précieux pour l'anthropologie urbaine).

a168 **Harrelson** Walter, *Falk* Randall M., Jews and Christians, a troubled family. Nv 1990, Abingdon. 208 p. $14. 0-687-20332-5 [TDig 38,263 unclearly puts Falk first].

a169 ᴱ**Heinonen** Reijo E., *Illman* Karl-Johan, *Toivanen* Arne, Religionsunterricht und Dialog zwischen Judentum und Christentum. Åbo 1988, Akademisk. 207 p. [LuJb 57 (1990) p. 319 with indication of three articles there cited].

a170 *Hendrix* Scott H., Toleration of the Jews in the German Reformation; Urbanus Rhegius and Braunschweig (1533-1540): ArRefG 81 (1990) 189-208; deutsch 209; Rhegius letter, 209-215.

a171 **Hood** John Y. B.ᴵᴵ, Aquinas and the Jews: diss. Kansas. 1991. 284 p. 92-10058. – DissA 52 (1991s) 4048-A.

a172 ᴱ**Hostens** M., Anon. ... Dissertatio contra Iudaeos: CCG 14, 1986 ⮞ 2,8457 ... 4,b349: ᴿHenoch 12 (1990) 390s (B. *Chiesa*); JbÖstByz 40 (1990) 460s (W. *Lackner*).

a173 **Hsia** Po-Chia R., The myth of ritual murder; Jews and magic in Reformation Germany 1988 ⮞ 6,a406: ᴿCritRR 4 (1991) 393-5 (S. G. *Burnett*); JQR 82 (1991s) 538-540 (G. J. *Langmuir*); JRel 70 (1990) 455s (M. U. *Edwards*).

a174 **Iber** Harald, Christlicher Glaube oder rassischer Mythus, A. Rosenberg: EurHS 33/286. Fra 1987, Lang. 374 p. Fs 71. — ᴿTR 86 (1990) 307s (K. *Meier*).

a175 *a) Jansen* Reiner, Christliche Kirche und Judentum von den Kirchenvätern bis zu den Reformatoren; – *b) Reichrath* Hans L., Die

'Judenfrage' im Lichte der Evang. Sonnttagsblätter der Pfalz im 3. Reich: Judaica 46 (1990) 134-163 / 164-181.

a176 **Juden:** Luther-Bibliographie: LuJb 57 (1990) p. 350, N° 723-742; 58 (1991) p. 181, N° 871-880.

a177 **Jung** Martin, Die württgembergische Kirche und die Juden in der Zeit des Pietismus (1675-1780): Diss. Tübingen 1989. vi-425 p. – TLZ 116 (1991) 158s.

a179 **Kirchberg** Julie, Theo-logie in der Anrede als Weg zur Verständigung zwischen Juden und Christen [Diss. Bochum]: InnsbTSt 31. Innsbruck 1991, Tyrolia. 568 p. DM 48 [TR 87,259].

a180 **Kirn** Hans-Martin, Das Bild vom Juden im Deutschland des frühen 16. Jahrhunderts, dargestellt an den Schriften Johannes PFEFFERKORNs [< Diss. Tübingen 1983s]: TStMJ 3. Tü 1989, Mohr. viii-253 p. DM 118. – ᴿJudaica 46 (1990) 57s (S. *Schreiner*).

a181 **Kjær-Hansen** Kai, Josef RABINOWITSCH og den messianske bevægelse: Dansk. Israelsmission. Århus 1988, OKAY/Savanne. 270 p. – ᴿTsTKi 61 (1990) 311 (Terje *Stordalen*).

a182 *Knoch-Mund* Gaby, Das Judenbild in der erzählenden Geschichte des Mittelalters: BTZ 8 (1991) 31-50.

a182* **Kohler-Spiegel** Helga, Juden und Christen, Geschwister im Glauben; ein Beitrag zur Lehrplantheorie am Beispiel Verhältnis Christentum Judentum [Diss.]: LehrprozessCJ 6. FrB 1991, Herder. x-398 p. DM 78.

a183 **Korbonski** Stefan, The Jews and the Poles in World War II. NY 1989, Hippocrene. viii-136 p. $15. – ᴿCathHR 77 (1991) 128s (A. A. *Hetnal*).

Kraus Hans-Joachim, Rückkehr zu Israel; Beiträge zum christlich-jüdischen Dialog 1991 ⇥ 221.

a184 *Kraus* H. J., Fragen des Judentums an die Kirche in der Theologie K. H. MISKOTTES: ZdialekT 5,1 (Kampen 1989) 65-80 [< Judaica 46,191].

a185 *a)* *Kroplewski* Zdzisław, ℗ Religious beliefs as the source of anti-Semitism; – *b)* *Zuberbier* Andrzej, ℗ Jesus and Judaism in the teaching of JOHN PAUL II during pilgrimages to the homeland; – *c)* *Dylus* Franciszek, Jesus Christ in the writings of M. BUBER: ⇥ 483, ColcT 61,3 (1990/1) 127-9 / 109-112 / 131-5 [*al.* 81-125].

a186 **Kuikman** Jacoba H., Christology in the context of Jewish-Christian relations; unresolved issues and the theology of E. SCHILLEBEECKX: TorJT 7 (1991) 76-91.

a187 *a)* *Kula* Marcin, ℗ Une affaire délicate; les relations polono-juives de 1918 à 1989; – *b)* *Chrostowski* Waldemar, ℗ État et perspectives du dialogue catholico-judaïque en Pologne: PrzPow 269,827s (1990) 71-94, franç. 94 / 95-115, franç. 115.

a188 **Kusche** Ulrich, Die unterlegene Religion; das Judentum im Urteil deutscher Alttestamentler; zur Kritik theologischer Geschichtsschreibung [< Diss. Heidelberg 1982, ᴰ*Rendtorff* R.]: StKirche/Israel 12. B 1991, Inst. Kirche und Judentum. 209 p. DM 24,80. 3-923095-63-5 [ZAW 104,298, H.-C. *Schmitt*].

a189 **Langmuir** Gavin J. [⇥ 222*a*], History, religion, and antisemitism 1990 ⇥ 6,a420: ᴿAmHR 96 (1991) 1489s (D. *Berger*).

a190 *a)* *Leplay* Michel, PÉGUY et les Juifs; – *b)* [document de Sigtuna] Les Églises et le peuple juif; vers une entente nouvelle: FoiVie 89,1 (1990) 51-63 / 65-70.

a191 *Letellier* J., Les Juifs chez les chrétiens; vingt siècles de déraison. P 1991, Centurion. 219 p. F 120 [RHE 86,343*].

Lohfink Norbert, The covenant never revoked; biblical reflections on Christian-Jewish dialogue 1991 ➤ 7279.

a192 *Lollini* Fabrizio, Una possibile connotazione antiebraica della 'Flagellazione' di Piero DELLA FRANCESCA: BArteR 77/65 (1991) 1-28; 12 fig. + 1 color.

a193 **Lubac** Henri de, Christian resistance to anti-Semitism; memories from 1940-1944 [1988 ➤ 4,b363], ᵀ*Englund* sr. Elizabeth. SF 1990, Ignatius. 261 p. $16 pa. 0-89870-291-7 [TDig 38,173].

ᴱ**McMichael** C., Was Jesus of Nazareth the Messiah? [against the Jews:] ESPINOSA Alphonso de, Isaiah comm. in 'Fortalitium Fidei' c. 1464: ᴰ1991s ➤ 3145.

a193* *Maslin* Simeon J., A new day for Jewish-Christian partnership: ChrCent 107 (1990) 247s . 250.

a194 **Miller** Ronald H., Dialogue and disagreement, F. ROSENZWEIG's relevance... 1989 ➤ 5,a414; 6,a434: ᴿJRel 71 (1991) 631-3 (D. *Novak*).

Mussner Franz, Dieses Geschlecht wird nicht vergehen; Judentum und Kirche 1991 ➤ 242.

a195 **Neudecker** Reinhard, I vari volti del Dio unico; cristiani ed ebrei in dialogo 1990 ➤ 6,a436: ᴿCC 142 (1991,3) 160-4 (F. *Rossi de Gasperis*); RasT 32 (1991) 334s (L. *Sembrano*).

a196 **Neunzeit** Paul, Juden und Christen auf neuen Wegen zum Gespräch; Ziele, Themen, Lernprozesse 1990 ➤ 6,a437: ᴿActuBbg 28 (1991) 178s (J. *Boada*); ZkT 113 (1991) 308s (R. *Oberforcher*).

Neusner Jacob, Jews and Christians; the myth of a common tradition 1991 ➤ 3673.

a198 *Niewöhner* Friedrich, Anmerkungen zum Begriff eines 'jüdischen Humanismus' [Judentum ist theozentrisch, unhuman; Christentum anthropozentrisch]: ArBegG 34 (1991) 214-224.

a199 **Novak** David, Jewish-Christian dialogue 1989 ➤ 5,a419; 6,a441: ᴿCCurr 40 (1990s) 548-552 (G. B. *Pepper*).

a200 **Orfali** M., JERÓNIMO de Santa Fe, El tratado 'De iudaicis erroribus in Talmut' 1987 ➤ 6,a443: ᴿCiuD 203 (1991) 238s (J. *Gutiérrez*).

a201 *Osten-Sacken* Peter von der, Der Wille zur Erneuerung des christlich-jüdischen Verhältnisses in seiner Bedeutung für biblische Exegese und Theologie: ➤ 310, JbBT 6 (1991) 243-267.

a202 **Pakter** Walter, Medieval Canon Law and the Jews [diss. 1974, Hopkins]: Abh. RechtsWissGrForsch 68. Ebelsbach 1988, Gremer. xiv-379 p. DM 128. – ᴿHZ 253 (1991) 428-430 (F. *Lotter*); Speculum 66 (1991) 221-3 (J. A. *Brundage*).

a203 ᴱ**Pallière** Aimé [cristiano divenuto ebreo, comprimendo in francese 1914 il manoscritto incompiuto di più di 2000 pagine lasciato da] Elia BENAMOZEGH, Israele e l'umanità; studio sul problema della religione universale, ᵀ. Genova 1990, Marietti. 290 p. Lit. 39.000. – ᴿCC 142 (1991,3) 329s (S. M. *Katunarich*: pagine spesso ispirate).

a204 **Papademetriou** George C., Essays on Orthodox Christian - Jewish relations. Bristol IN 1990, Wyndham Hall. 133 p. $15 [TR 87,347].

a205 **Petuchowski** J., *Thoma* C., Lexikon der jüdisch-christlichen Begegnung 1989 ➤ 5,a421; 6,a446: ᴿBLtg 63 (1990) 184-6 (L. *Schwienhorst-Schönberger*); Judaica 46 (1990) 240s (S. *Schreiner*); ScripTPamp 23 (1991) 368s (K. *Limburg*: se dirige a la parte cristiana del diálogo); ZRGg 43 (1991) 374s (S. *Ben-Chorin*).

a206 ᴱ**Petuchowski** J., When Jews and Christians meet 1988 ➤ 4,625: ᴿCritRR 3 (1990) 463-5 (A. *La Cocque*).

a207 **Reck** U., Das Judentum im katholischen Religionsunterricht; Wandel und Neuentwicklung [Diss. FrB]. FrB 1990, Herder. viii-264 p. DM 48. 3-451-21535-7. – ᴿTLZ 116 (1991) 314-6 (K. *Wegenast*: gut); TsTNijm 31 (1991) 214 (L. van der *Tuin*); ZkT 113 (1991) 118s (H. *Pissarek-Hudelist*).

a208 **Reichrath** Hans, Katholische Kirche und Juden – 'quo vadis?': Pfälzisches Pfarrerblatt 79,10 (Kaiserslautern 1989) 207-210 [80,1 (1990) 13-15, Nazi-Zeit; < Judaica 46,63].

a209 **Richardson** F., *Granskou* D., Anti-Judaism in early Christianity 1986 ➤ 2,398... 4,b382: ᴿCrNSt 11 (1990) 210-3 (G. *Barbaglio*); RelStT 10,2 (1990) 83-85 (R. K. *MacKenzie*).

a210 ᵀᴱ**Robles Sierra** Adolfo, Capistrum Iudaeorum [1267, fuente de Pugio Fidei], I. Texto crítico y traducción: WüForMissRelW 3/1. Wü/Altenberge 1990, Echter/Telos. 345 p. DM 65. – ᴿRTLv 22 (1991) 427 (P. M. *Bogaert*); ZkT 113 (1991) 315s (K. H. *Neufeld*: typos; zu wenig Hintergrund besonders islamisch).

a211 **Röhm** Eberhard, *Thierfelder* Jörg, Juden, Christen, Deutsche 1933-1945; 1. [aus 4] 1933 bis 1935: TBt 8. Stu 1990, Calwer. 451 p.; ill. DM 24,80. – ᴿTLZ 116 (1991) 442-5 (Elke *Wolgast*).

a212 *Rokéaḥ* David, A note on the philological aspect of Paul's theory of faith [< The 'chosen people' conflict of Jews and Christians, Mg in preparation, J Hebrew Univ.]: TZBas 47 (1991) 299-306.

a213 *Rossi de Gasperis* Francesco, Un nuovo giudeo-cristianesimo e la sua possibile rilevanza ecclesiale: CrNSt 12 (1991) 119-161; Eng. 161s.

a214 ᴱ**Rothschild** Fritz A., Jewish perspectives on Christianity 1990 ➤ 6,449: ᴿCurrTMiss 18 (1991) 138 (Jay C. *Rochelle*); RExp 88 (1991) 481 (E. G. *Hinson*).

a215 *a) Rubinkiewicz* Ryszard, ❷ Jews and Judaism in the teaching of John Paul II; – *b) Chrostowski* Waldemar, ❷ Fundamental aspects of the Church's reorientation toward Jews and Judaism: ColcT 90,3 (Symposium Wsz 1989) 11-18 / 19-30; Eng. 107-111. ➤ a144.

a216 **Rufeisen** D. O, [mit *Corbach* Dieter], [Karmeliterpater] Daniel Oswald Rufeisen, der Mann aus der Löwengrube [the Jewish-born Carmelite Father who in 1962 lost his suit before the Israel Supreme Court to be acknowledged as Israeli citizen by right of birth; he obtained citizenship on other grounds]: Spurensuche jüdischen Wirkens 3. Köln 1989, Scriba. 59 p.; ill. – ᴿJudaica 46 (1990) 182s (H. L. *Reichrath*).

a217 *Sawyer* John F. A., Combating prejudices about the Bible and Judaism: TLond 94 (1991) 269-278.

a218 SCHREIBER Alexander mem., Occident and Orient, ᴱ**Dán** R. 1988 ➤ 4,130: ᴿBO 48 (1991) 960s (S. C. *Reif*).

a219 **Schöppner** Lothar, Empirische Analyse des Würzburger Lernprojekts Juden-Christen: kath. Diss. Würzburg 1991, ᴰ*Neuenzeit*. – TR 87 (1991) 522.

a220 **Schottroff** Willy, Das Reich Gottes und der Menschen; Studien über das Verhältnis der christlichen Theologie zum Judentum: AbhChrJüdDialog 19. Mü 1991, Kaiser. 235 p.; ill. DM 78 pa. 3-459-01881-X [NTAbs 36,267; TR 87,259]. 6 art.

a221 **Schreckenberg** Heinz, Die christlichen Adversus-Judaeos-Texte 1988 ➤ 4,b389; 6,a456: ᴿAntonianum 66 (1991) 442-4 (M. *Nobile*); DLZ 112 (1991) 90-93 (G. *Haendler*); ForumKT 6 (1990) 316s (A. *Frenken*); Judaica 46 (1990) 53-55 (P. *Maser*).

a222 *a) Seim* Jürgen, Zur christlichen Identität im christlich-jüdischen Gespräch; – *b) Friedlander* Albert H., Die Erklärung der Rheinischen

Landessynode von 1980 und ein Rabbiner; – *c*) *Huber* Wolfgang, Sechs Überlegungen zum Verhältnis von Juden und Christen: EvT 51 (1991) 458-467 / 469-473 / 473-8.

a223 [ᴱ*Seltzer* Robert M., Essential papers on ... (Jewish studies):] *a*) ᴱ**Cohen** Jeremy, ... on Judaism and Christianity in conflict, from late antiquity to the Reformation; – *b*) ᴱ**Cohen** Naomi W., ... on Jewish-Christian relations in the U.S., imagery and reality; – *c*) ᴱ**Greenspahn** Frederick E., ... on Israel and the Ancient Near East; – *d*) ᴱ**Hundert** Gershon D., ... on Hasidism. NY 1990s, NYU. xiv-578 p.; ... p.; xvii-464 p.; xi-546 p. Each vol. $55, pa. $25. 0-8147-1442-0, -3-9; -1445-5, -6-3; -3037-X, -8-8; -3469-3, -70-7 [TDig 38,356].

a224 **Setzer** Claudia J., Jewish responses to early Christians (30-150 B.C.) [Celsus to Eusebius; but also earlier 'materials' not specified as NT]: diss. Columbia. NY 1990. 485 p. 91-18643. — DissA 52 (1991s) 571s-A.

a224* *Setzer* C., 'You invent a Christ!' Christological claims as points of Jewish-Christian dispute: UnSemQ 44 (1991) 315-328 [< NTAbs 36,213].

a225 *a*) *Shanks* Hershel, Silence, anti-Semitism and the Scrolls; – *b*) *Fisher* Eugene J., The Church's teaching on supersessionism [since 1965 it is impossible to hold that the Christian Church has superseded or replaced Israel as God's chosen people]: BAR-W 17,2 (1991) 54-57.59s [and p. 15, remarks on defense of J. *Strugnell* signed by 85 prominent Jewish and other scholars] / p. 58 only; 17/5,16, Fisher reply to J. *Treacy*.

a225* *Shaw* Stanford J., Christian anti-Semitism in the Ottoman Empire: Belleten 54,211 (1990) 1073-1149.

a226 **Shermis** M., *Zannoni* A. E., Introduction to Jewish-Christian relations. NY 1991, Paulist. v-275 p. $14 pa. 0-8091-3261-3 [NTAbs 36,287]. 10 art.

a227 *Sherwin* Byron L., rabbi, ⊕ Le dialogue catholique-juif en Pologne, ᵀ*Chrostowski* Waldemar: PrzPow 272,1 (1991) 51-61 . 279-293.

a228 **Simonsohn** Shlomo, The Apostolic See and the Jews [1s. 1988s ↠ 6, a459] 3. 1464-1521. Toronto 1990., Pont. Inst. Mediaeval St. p. 1333-1624. C$49. 0-88844-099-5. – ᴿArHPont 28 (1990) 393-6 (P. *Rabikauskas*); JEH 42 (1991) 158 (P. N. R. *Zutshi*); JQR 82 (1991s) 571s (K. *Stow*).

a229 **Smid** Marikje, Deutscher Protestantismus und Judentum 1932-1933: Heid. Unters. Judenverfolgung 2. Mü 1990, Kaiser. xxx-551 p. DM 110. 3-456-01808-9. – ᴿTLZ 116 (1991) 293-5 (K. *Meier*).

a230 **Stern** David N., Messianic Jewish manifesto. J 1988, Jewish NT Publ. 281 p. – ᴿTsTKi 61 (1990) 312 (H. *Hegstad*).

a231 *Tobin* Gary, Ideology of antisemitism; the American Jewish view: ↠ 56, ᶠFox M., 4 (1991) 189-327.

a232 *a*) *Townsend* John T., The New Testament, the early Church, and Anti-Semitism; – *b*) *MacLennan* Robert, Four Christian writers on Jews and Judaism in the second century [BARNABAS, MELITO, JUSTIN, TERTULLIAN]: ↠ 56, ᶠFox M. 1 (1991) 171-186 / 187-202.

a233 **Wigoder** G., Jewish-Christian relations 1988 ↠ 5,a451: ᴿCritRR 3 (1990) 376-9 (S. P. *Haynes*).

a234 **Williams** Janice, Conceptual change and religious practice with special reference to Jews in Britain and Israel. Aldershot 1987, Avebury. x-323 p. £22.50. – ᴿHeythJ 32 (1991) 124s (C. *Davies*).

a234* **Williamson** Clark M., When Jews and Christians meet [not ↠ a206]; a guide for Christian preaching and teaching. St. Louis 1989, CBP. 125 p. $10. – ᴿMid-Stream 30 (1991) 98s (J. T. *Rock*).

a235 **Williamson** C., *Allen* R., Interpreting difficult texts; anti-Judaism and Christian preaching 1989 ➤ 5,1446*: ᴿCritRR 4 (1991) 251-3 (T. L. *Donaldson*).

a235* **Yardeni** Myriam, Anti-Jewish mentalities in early modern Europe. Lanham MD 1990, UPA. xv-297 p. $42. 0-8191-7559-5 [TDig 38,392].

a236 **Yohanan** frère, Juifs et chrétiens d'hier à demain: Foi vivante 258. P 1990, Cerf. 116 p. – ᴿEsprVie 101 (1991) 117s-*jaune* (L. *Barbey*); RThom 91 (1991) 516s (D. C.).

a237 **Zacour** Norman, Jews and Saracens in the Consilia of OLDRADUS de Ponte [14th c.]: StT 100. Toronto 1990, Pont. Inst. Med. St. x-114 p. $18. – ᴿSpeculum 66 (1991) 253s (I. *Robinson*).

a238 *Żak* Adam, Aufgeschobene Begegnung — Franz ROSENZWEIGS Konzeption der Beziehung zwischen Judentum und Christentum, ᵀ*Schreiner* Stefan: Judaica 46 (1990) 195-207.

a239 **Ziegler** Josef G., Das Oberammergauer Passionsspiel; Erbe und Auftrag. St. Ottilien 1990, EOS. 128 p. DM 9,80. – ᴿTPQ 139 (1991) 227 (H. *Dobisch*).

XVII.3 Religiones parabiblicae

M1.1   **Gnosticismus classicus.**

a240 **Alt** Karin, Philosophie gegen Gnosis; PLOTINs Polemik in seiner Schrift II 9: Abh Mainz, g/soz 1990/7. Mainz 1990, Akad. 74 p. 3-515-05810-9.

a241 **Benelli** Gian Carlo, La Gnosi, il volto oscuro della storia: uomini e religioni. Mi 1991, Mondadori. 388 p. Lit. 14.000. 88-04-34354-0 [NTAbs 36,289].

a242 **Böhlig** A., Gnosis und Synkretismus Ges. Aufätze I: WUNT 47, 1989 ➤ 5,236: ᴿArTGran 53 (1990) 321s (A. S. *Muñoz*); JAOS 111 (1991) 829-831 (Jorunn J. *Buckley*); OrChr 75 (1991) 267 (W. *Gessel*).

a243 **Churton** T., The Gnostics. L 1990, Weidenfeld & N. xi-187 p.; 8 pl. £7. 0-297-81104-5 [NTAbs 36,133].

a244 **Filoramo** Giovanni, A history of Gnosticism, ᵀ*Alcock* Anthony, 1990 ➤ 6,a474: ᴿRExp 88 (1991) 467 (E. G. *Hinson*: splendid, but rather on its theology); TLond 94 (1991) 226s (Frances M. *Young*: 'phenomenology' rather).

a245 *Glazer* Brian, The goddess with a fiery breath; the Epyptian derivation of a Gnostic mythologoumenon: NT 33 (1991) 92-94.

a246 ᶠGUILLAUMONT Antoine de, Mélanges 1988 ➤ 4,59: BO 48 (1991) 962-972 (J. *Helderman*).

a247 ᴱ**Guillaumont** A. & C., ÉVAGRE, Le Gnostique: SChr 356, 1989 ➤ 5, a159: ᴿHelmantica 42,129* (1991) 319s (Mᵃ *Jiménez*); RÉAnc 93 (1991) 162s (A. Le *Boulluec*).

a248 **MacRae** George, Studies in the NT & Gnosticism 1987 ➤ 5,g466: ᴿBibTB 21 (1991) 124s (Karen L. *King*).

a249 ᴱ**Pearson** Birger A., *Goehring* James E., The roots of Egyptian Christianity 1986 ➤ 2,484... 4,b418: ᴿSecC 8 (1991) 62-64 (P. C. *Finney*).

a250 **Pétrement** Simone, A separate God [Le Dieu séparé 1984 ➤ 65,8901], ᵀ*Harrison* C. SF 1990, Harper Collins. viii-542 p. $35. 0-06-066501-7 [NTAbs 35,268].

a251 **Rudolph** Kurt, Die Gnosis[3] [[1]1978 ➤ 61,k263]. Gö 1990 VR. 451 p. –
[R]EWest 41 (1991) 355-8 (G. *Gnoli*: Rudolph informed him that [2]pp.
294-393, pp. 275-366 of the 1984 English edition, were published by
Cariscript in French 1986 with J. MÉNARD given as author, and that
Cariscript has now put out a new edition in Rudolph's name).

a252 *Scopello* Maddalena, Le renard symbole de l'hérésie dans les polémiques
patristiques contre les gnostiques: ➤ 22, [F]BENOÎT A., RHPR 71 (1991)
73-88; Eng. 126.

a253 *Simonetti* Manlio, Alcune riflessioni sul rapporto tra gnosticismo e cristianesimo: VetChr 28 (1991) 337-374.

a254 **Slavenburg** J., Gnosis; de esoterische traditie van het oude weten: Her-
mesreeks 1. Deventer 1990, Ankh-Hermes. 160 p. *f* 29,50. 90-202-
1026-2. – [R]TsTNijm 31 (1991) 431 (M. *Lamberigts*).

a255 **Valantasis** Richard, Spiritual guides of the third century; a semiotic
study of the guide-disciple relationship in Christianity, Neoplatonism,
Hermetism, and Gnosticism: HarvDissRel 27. Mp 1991, Fortress. xi-
155 p. [RelStR 18,59, Gail P. *Corrington*].

a256 *Vogt* K., 'Becoming male', a Gnostic and early Christian metaphor:
➤ 341, Image/gender 1991, 172-187.

M1.2 **Valentinus** – *Pistis sophia,* Elchasai.

a257 **Desjardins** M. R. Sin in Valentinianism [D]1990 ➤ 6,a496: [R]ETL 67
(1991) 172 (A. de *Halleux*); JAAR 59 (1991) 162-4 (Karen L. *King*);
Salmanticensis 38 (1991) 247-9 (R. *Trevijano*); SR 20 (1991) 361s (G.
Vallée).

a258 **Ménard** Jacques E., L'exposé valentinien... (NH XI,2): BCNH-T 14,
1985 ➤ 2,8573; 3,a788: [R]BO 48 (1991) 149-152 (W. P. *Funk*).

a258* *Reeves* John C., The 'Elchasaite' Sanhedrin of the Cologne Mani
Codex, in light of Second Temple Jewish sectarian sources: JJS 42 (1991)
68-91.

a259 *Ries* J., Le rite baptismale elchasaïte et le symbolisme manichéen de
l'eau: ➤ 130, [F]SANDERS G., Aevum 1991, 367-378.

a260 **Strutwolf** Holgar, Gnosis als System; zur Rezeption der valentiniani-
schen Gnosis bei ORIGENES: Diss. Heidelberg 1991, [D]*Ritter* A. – TR 87
(1991) 519; RTLv 23, p. 549 ('Holger').

M1.3 **Corpus hermeticum; Orphismus.**

a260* *Anemoyannis-Sinanidis* Spyrodimos, Le symbolisme de l'œuf dans les
cosmogonies orphiques: Kernos 4 (1991) 83-90.

a261 **Bader** Françoise, La langue des dieux, ou l'hermétisme des poètes
indo-européens: Testi Linguistici 14. Pisa 1989, Giardini. 308 p. Lit.
90.000. – [R]BSLP 85 (1990) 72-75 (A. *Blanc*).

a262 *Brisson* Luc, Orphée et l'Orphisme à l'époque impériale; témoignages et
interprétations philosophiques, de Plutarque à Jamblique: ➤ 659, ANRW
36,4 (1990) 2867-2931; 1 pl.

a263 **Büchli** J., Poimandres 1987 ➤ 3,a793... 5,491: [R]CritRR 3 (1990) 263-5
(W. C. *Grese*).

a264 *Ghidini* Maria T., *McClintock* Giuliana S., Aletheia nel pensiero Orfico:
FilT 4 (1990) 73-83.

a265 *Luck* Georg, The doctrine of salvation in the Hermetic writings: SecC 8
(1991) 31-41.

a266 *Paramelle* J., *Mahé* J.-P., Extraits hermétiques inédits dans un manuscript d'Oxford [Bodl. Clarke 11]: RÉG 104 (1991) 109-139.
a267 **Matthews** Caitlin, Sophia, goddess of wisdom; the divine feminine from
black goddess to world soul. NY 1991, Harper/Collins. 375 p. $28. ‒
ᴿGnosis 23 (SF 1992) 65s (Joan *Ohanneson*).
a268 **Scott** Thomas [McAllister], Egyptian elements in Hermetic literature:
diss. [1987]. 271 p. 91-22229. ‒ DissA 52 (1991s) 955-A.

M1.5   **Mani,** *dualismus;* **Mandaei.**

a269 **Beausobre** M. de, Histoire critique de Manichée et du Manichéisme.
Amst 1988, Gieben. lxxvi-594 p. xxxiv-806 p. ‒ ᴿAugM 34 (1989) 191s (J.
Ortali).
a270 **Couliano** Ioan P., I miti dei dualismi occidentali; dai sistemi gnostici al
mondo moderno. Mi 1989, Jaca. 326 p. Lit. 40.000. ‒ ᴿCC 142 (1991,3)
350s (C. *Capizzi*).
a270* *Coyle* J. Kevin, Mary Magdalene in Manichaeism?: Muséon 104 (1991)
39-55.
a271 *Decret* François, Le traité d'Evodius Contre les Manichéens; un
compendium à l'usage du parfait controversiste: AugR 31 (1991)
387-409.
a272 **Eksell** Kerstin, Semantic notes on Mandaic poetry: OrSuec 40 (1991)
87-94.
a273 **Hutter** Manfred, Mani und die Sasaniden; der iranisch-gnostische Synkretismus einer Weltreligion: Scientia 12, 1988 ⇥ 4,b449; 6,a517: ᴿEWest
41 (1991) 399-403 (G. *Gnoli*).
a274 *Hutter* Manfred, Manis Umgang mit anderen Religionen im Spannungsfeld zwischen Absolutheitsanspruch, Inklusivismus und Synkretismus: ZRGg 43 (1991) 289-304.
a275 **Klimkeit** Hans J., Hymnen und Gebete der... Manichäer 1989 ⇥ 5,
a511*: ᴿZRGg 43 (1991) 86 (H.-P. *Hasenfratz*).
a276 *Maalouf* Amin, Les jardins de lumière [vie de Mani]. 1991, Lattès
[BLitEc 92,293].
a277 ᴱRies J., Les études manichéennes 1988 ⇥ 4,b456; 6,a525: ᴿEWest 41
(1991) 403-5 (G. *Gnoli*); RHPR 71 (1991) 344s (M. *Scopello*).
a278 *Ries* Julien, Dieux cosmiques et Dieu biblique dans la religion de Mani:
⇥ 6,13, ᶠBAVEL T. van, AugLv 41 (1990s) 757-772.
a279 **Sims-Williams** Nicholas, The Christian Sogdian manuscript C2; Berliner
Turfantexte 12. B 1985, Akademie. 250 p.; 95 pl. ‒ ᴿZRGg 43 (1991)
189s (H.-J. *Klimkeit*).
a280 *Smagina* Eugenia B., Some words with unknown meaning in Coptic
Manichaean texts: Enchoria 17 (1990) 115-122.
a281 *Tardieu* Michel, La nisba de Sisinnios [Mar Sīsīn, successeur de Mani]:
AltOrF 18 (1991) 3-8.
a282 *Tongerloo* Alois van, Manicheism in recent studies [RIES J. 1988]: ETL
67 (1991) 204-212.
a283 *Vannier* M.A., Manichéisme et pensée augustinienne de la création:
⇥ 6,688*, Collectanea 1986/90, 421-431.

M2.1   **Nag Ḥammadi,** *generalia.*

a284 **Robinson** J.M., NH Library in English³ 1988 ⇥ 4,b460; 6,a533: ᴿBO
48 (1991) 550-2 (W. *Myszor*).

a285 ᴱHedrick C. W., NH Codices XI, XII, XIII 1990 ➤ 6,a534: ᴿNRT 113 (1991) 915s (X. *Jacques*).

a286 ᴱLayton B., *al.*, Nag Hammadi Codex VIII [*Sieber* John H., Zostrianus; *Meyer* Marvin W. Letter of Peter to Philip]: NHS 31. Leiden 1991, Brill. xxxv-301 p. 90-04-09477-6.

a287 ᴱParrott Douglas M., Nag Hammadi Codices III,3-4 and V,1 with Papyrus Berolinensis 8502,3 and Oxyrhynchus Papyrus 1081 Eugnostos and The Sophia of Jesus Christ: NHS 27. Leiden 1991, Brill. xxiii-216 p. 90-04-08366-9.

a288 **Arthur** Rose H., The wisdom goddess... NH 1984 ➤ 1,a220... 6,a515: ᴿOLZ 86 (1991) 273-5 (D. *Kirchner*).

a289 *Daoust* J., Les manuscrits de Nag Hammadi [< *Kuntzmann* Raymond, MondeB 63, mars 1990]: EsprVie 100 (1990) 440-2.

a290 *Gianotto* Claudio, *Iacopino* Giuliana, I generi letterari in alcuni testi di Nag Hammadi: ➤ 452, AnStoEseg 8,2 (1990/1) 455-484.

a291 ᴱHedrick C., *Hodgson* R., NH... Gnosticism, and early Christianity 1983/6 ➤ 2,374... 6,a539: ᴿJAOS 111 (1991) 384s (D. M. *Scholer*).

a292 **Hosroev** Aleksander L., ❸ Aleksandrijskoe christianstvo... Alexandrian Christianity in the data of Nag Hammadi texts (II,7; VII,4; IX,3). Moskva 1991, Nauka. 276 p. 5-02-017257-X.

a293 ᵀᴱJanssens Yvonne, Évangiles gnostiques dans le Corpus de Berlin et dans la Bibliothèque Copte de Nag Hammadi; préf. Ries Julien: Homo Religiosus 15. LvN 1991, Centre Hist. Rel. 301 p.

a294 **Scholten** Clemens, Martyrium und Sophiamythos im Gnostizismus nach den Texten von NH: JbAC Egb 14, 1987 ➤ 4,b463; 6,a542: ᴿBO 48 (1991) 975-7 (J. *Helderman*).

a294* *Tröger* Karl-Wolfgang, [➤ 6,a543] 'Sie haben ihn nicht getötet...'; koptische Schriften von Nag Hammadi als Auslegungshintergrund von Sure 4,157: Carl-Schmidt-Kolloquium an der Martin-Luther Univ. 1988 (Halle 1990) 221-233 [> Jesus, the Koran and Nag Hammadi: TDig 38 (1991) 213-8, ᵀᴱ*Asen* B.].

a295 *Yamauchi* Edwin M., Gnosticism; has Nag-Hammadi changed our view?: Evangel 8,2 (1990) 4-7.

M2.2   *Evangelium etc. Thomae* – **The Gospel** (etc.) **of Thomas.**

a296 *Abou Zayd* Shafiq, The Acts of Thomas and the unity of the dualistic world in the Syrian Orient: Aram 1 (1989) 217-252.

a297 **Alcalá** Manuel, El evangelio copto de Tomás; palabras ocultas de Jesús 1989 ➤ 5,a530; 6,a545: ᴿBibFe 16,46 (1990) 152 (A. *Salas*).

a298 *Baarda* Tjitze, 'Chose' or 'collected'; concerning an Aramaism in Logion 8 of the Gospel of Thomas and the question of independence: HarvTR 84 (1991) 373-397.

a299 *Callan* Terrance, The sayings of Jesus in Gos. Thom. 22 / 2Clem 12 / Gos. Eg. 5: JRelSt 16,1 (Cleveland 1988) 46-64 [< ᴢɪᴛ 90,865].

a300 ᵀᴱCoune M., Woorden van Jezus volgens Tomas; een apocriefevangelie van de tweede eeuw. Brugge 1989, Zevenkerken. 44 p. – ᴿCollatVL 21 (1991) 331 (L. *Lemmens*).

a301 ᵀᴱCuvelier F., Jezus mysticus; naar het heromdekte Thomas-evangelie. Kapellen/Haarlem 1990, Pelckmans/Gottmer. 190 p. 90-389-1543-5 / 90-257-2332-2. – ᴿCollatVL 21 (1991) 106 (H. *Hoet*); TsTNijm 31 (1991) 430 (M. *Lamberigts*).

a302 **Fieger** Michael, Das Thomasevangelium; Einleitung, Kommentar und Systematik [kath. Diss. Mü 1989, ᴰGnilka J.]: NTAbh NS 22. Münster 1991, Aschendorff. 296 p. DM 98 [RHE 86,41*]. 3-402-04770-5. – ᴿJTS 42 (1991) 696-9 (R. M. *Wilson*).

a303 *Gierth* Brigitte, Un apophtegme commun à la Pistis Sophia et à l'Evangile selon Thomas [111]?: RevSR 64 (1990) 245-9.

a304 **Kuntzmann** Raymond, *Dubois* Jean-Daniel, Nag Hammadi, O Evangelho de Tomá. São Paulo 1990, Paulistas, 182 p. [REB 51,245].

a305 ᴱ**Layton** B., NH Codex 2 (Thomas etc.) 1989 ➤ 6,a551: ᴿJAOS 111 (1991) 668s (D. *Good*).

a306 **Lelyveld** Margaretha, Les logia de la vie dans l'Évangile selon Thomas; à la recherche d'une tradition et d'une rédaction [diss. ᴰMénard, Strasbourg]: NHS 34, 1987 ➤ 3,a842 ... 5,a535: ᴿJBL 110 (1991) 359-361 (H. W. *Attridge*: often quite critical of Menard).

a307 *Onuki* Takashi, Traditionsgeschichte von Thomas 17 und ihre christologische Relevanz: ➤ 72, ᶠHAHN F., Anfänge 1991, 399-415.

a308 *Riley* Gregory J., Thomas tradition and the Acts of Thomas: ➤ 446, SBL Sem 30 (1991) 533-542.

a309 **Ross** Hugh M., Thirty essays on the Gospel of Thomas. Shaftsbury 1990, Element. vi-169 p. 1-85230-183-X.

a310 ᴱ**Schenke** Hans-M., Das Thomas-Buch, NH II,7; TU 138, 1989 ➤ 5, a452: ᴿJTS 42 (1991) 327s (M. *Smith*).

a311 *Tuckett* Christopher M., Q and Thomas; evidence of a primitive 'Wisdom Gospel'?; a response to H. KOESTER [Ancient Christian Gospels 1990]: ETL 67 (1991) 346-360.

M2.3 *Singula scripta* – Nag' Hammadi, various titles.

a312 ᴱ**Kirchner** Dankwart, Epistula Jacobi apocrypha NHC I,2: TU 136, 1989 ➤ 5,a553: ᴿCritRR 4 (1991) 273-5 (R. *Cameron*); JTS 42 (1991) 325s (R. M. *Wilson*).

a313 **Rouleau** Donald, L'Épitre apocryphe de Jacques [NH 1,2], + *Roy* Louise, L'Acte de Pierre: BCNH-T 4, 1988 ➤ 3,a855 ... 6,a559: ᴿJAOS 111 (1991) 667s (Deirdre *Good*); SecC 8 (1991) 55s (R. I. *Pervo*).

a314 *Schoedel* William R., A Gnostic interpretation of the fall of Jerusalem; the first Apocalypse of James: NT 33 (1991) 153-178.

a315 **Veilleux** Armand, 1-2 Apocalypse de Jacques 1986 ➤ 3,a856 ... 6,a560: ᴿCdÉ 65 (1990) 375-7 (C. *Cannuyer*); JAOS 111 (1991) 668s (Deirdre *Good*).

a316 ᴱ**Gianotto** Claudio, La testimonianza veritiera [NHC IX,3]: TestiVOA. Brescia 1990, Paideia. 111 p. Lit. 30.000. 88-394-0453-8.

a317 **Williams** Jacqueline A., Biblical interpretations in the Gnostic Gospel of Truth ... NH ᴰ1988 ➤ 4,b494 ... 6,a568: ᴿCritRR 4 (1991) 280s (H. W. *Attridge*).

a318 **Schenke** Gesine, Die dreigestaltige Protennoia (NHC XIII) 1984 ➤ 65,8982 ... 3,a863: ᴿOLZ 86 (1991) 485-8 (J. *Helderman*).

a319 ᴱ**Thomassen** Einar (ᵀ with *Painchaud* Louis), Le traité tripartite (NH I,5): BCNH-T 19, 1989 ➤ 6,a569: ᴿCBQ 53 (1991) 350-2 (Pheme *Perkins*: 'La traité'; also on 17s); JAOS 111 (1991) 665s (Deirdre *Good*); JTS 42 (1991) 328-330 (M. *Smith*); TLZ 116 (1991) 101-4 (H.-M. *Schenke*).

a321 *Hills* Julian V., The three 'Matthean' aphorisms in the Dialogue of the Savior [NHC 3,5] 53: HarvTR 84 (1991) 45-58.

a322 **Linder** Per-Arne, The Apocalypse of Adam; Nag Hammadi Codex V,5 considered from its Egyptian background: LundStAfAsRel 7. Ödeshög 1991. 165 p.

a323 *Painchaud* Louis, The redactions of The Writing without Title (CG II,5): SecC 8 (1991) 217-234.

a324 **Zandee** J., The teachings of Sylvanus (NHC VII,4): EgUitg 6. Leiden 1991, Ned. Inst. NO. iv-601 p. ƒ110. 90-6258-206-0 [BO 48,984].

M3.1   *Quid est religio? Inquisitiones speculativae.* – **What is religion?**

a325 **Adler** Mortimer J., Truth in religion; the plurality of religions and the unity of truth; an essay in the philosophy of religion. NY 1990, Macmillan. xi-162 p. $19. 0-02-500225-2 [TDig 38,147].

a325* **Baird** Robert D., Category formation and the history of religions[2] [new pref.]: Religion and Reason 1. B/NY 1991, Mouton de Gruyter. xi-178 p. DM 48 [TLZ 117,895, N.-P. *Moritzen*].

a326 **Barnes** Michael H.[J], In the presence of mystery[2] ... 1990 ⇥ 6,a574: ᴿRelStT 10,1 (1990) 56s (D. *Kinsley*).

a327 *Barua* Archana, A re-examination of the nature of religion: JDharma 15 (1990) 212-222.

a328 **Bataille** Georges, Theory of religion, ᵀ*Hurley* Robert 1989 ⇥ 5,a572: ᴿCritRR 4 (1991) 476-8 (G. *Weekman*: not a scrap of evidence, but makes you think).

a329 **Bourgeois** Patrick L., The religious within experience and existence; a phenomenological investigation 1990 ⇥ 6,a578; pa. $15: ᴿTS 52 (1991) 393 (D. L. *Gelpi*).

a330 **Byrne** Peter, Natural religion and the nature of religion 1989 ⇥ 6,a582: ᴿNBlackf 72 (1991) 303s (H. F. G. *Swanston*); NedTTs 45 (1991) 170s (V. *Brümmer*); ScotJT 44 (1991) 390s (D. A. *Pailin*).

a331 **Carmody** Denise L. & John T., The republic of many mansions; foundations of American religious thought. NY 1990, Paragon. 244 p. $23. – ᴿTTod 48 (1991s) 480.482 (R. G. *White*).

a332 **Carrier** H., Psico-sociologia dell'appartenenza religiosa. T 1988, Elle DiCi. 288 p. Lit. 19.000 [Antonianum 67,160, T. *Larrañaga*).

a333 *Carrier* Hervé, Lo studio psicosociale dell'identità religiosa [... che cosa significa appartenere a una religione?]: CC 142 (1991,2) 154-162.

a333* *a*) *Crosson* Frederick J., The analogy of religion; – *b*) *Schmitz* Kenneth L., Natural religion, morality and LESSING's ditch; – *c*) *Godfrey* Joseph J., Trust, the heart of religion; – *d*) *Lauder* Robert E., Religious story, religious truth, religious pluralism; a prolegomenon to religious faith: ProcAmCathPhilos 65 (1991) 1-15 / 57-73 / 157-167 / 123-132.

a334 **Curletto** Silvio, La norma e il suo rovescio; coppie di opposti nel mondo religioso antico. Genova 1990, ECIG. 333 p. – ᴿRHR 202 (1991) 440-2 (R. *Turcan*).

a335 ᴱ**Daiber** Karl-Fritz, Religion und Konfession; Studien zu politischen, ethischen und religiösen Einstellungen von Katholiken, Protestanten und Konfessionslosen in der Bundesrepublik Deutschland und in den Niederlanden. Hannover 1989, Luther. 155 p. DM 24,80 [TLZ 117,227, H. *Grote*].

a336 **Davis** Caroline F., The evidential force of religious experience. Ox 1989, Clarendon. xii-268 p. $50. – ᴿTS 51 (1990) 519s (J. A. *Colombo*).

a337 *Di Censo* James, Religion as illusion; reversing the FREUDIAN hermeneutic: JRel 71 (1991) 167-179.

a338 *Dijk* A. M. G. van, Het ethos van de beoefenaar van de godsdienstwetenschap ten aanzien van nieuwe religieuze bewegingen: NedTTs 45 (1991) 265-278; Eng. 329.

a338* **Driver** Tom F., The magic of ritual; our need for liberating rites that transform our lives and our communities. SF 1991, Harper. x-270 p. $20. 0-06-062096-X [TDig 39,259].

a339 *a) Dubuisson* Daniel, Contribution à une épistémologie dumézilienne; l'idéologie; – *b) Demoule* Jean-Paul, Réalité des Indo-Européens; les diverses apories du modèle arborescent; – *c) Charachidzé* Georges, Hypothèse indo-européenne et modes de comparaison: RHR 208 (1991) 123-140 / 159-202 / 203-228.

a341 *Forward* Martin, Evangelism and people of other faiths: ExpTim 102 (1990s) 197-200.

a342 **Fraas** Hans-Jürgen, Die Religiosität des Menschen; ein Grundriss der Religionspsychologie: Uni-Tb 1578. Gö 1990, Vandenheock & R. 336 p. DM 35 [TLZ 117,222, H.-J. *Thilo*].

a343 **Harrison** Peter, 'Religion' and the religions in the English Enlightenment. C 1990, Univ. ix-227 p. £30. – [R]ScripTPamp 23 (1991) 1047 (María D. *Odero*).

a344 **Haught** John F., What is religion? 1990 ➤ 6,a589*: [R]Horizons 18 (1991) 179s (S. *Casey*).

a345 **Hay** David, Religious experience today; studying the facts. L 1990, Mowbray. 114 p. – [R]NBlackf 72 (1991) 398s (R. *Woods*).

a346 **Herrmann** Eberhard, The rationality of ideologies and religions [lectures Utrecht 1990]: NedTTs 45 (1991) 223-238.

a347 **Hick** John, An interpretation of religion; human responses to the transcendent (Gifford Lectures 1986s) 1989 ➤ 5,a631; 6,a640: [R]AnglTR 73 (1991) 501-4 (O. C. *Thomas*); JRel 70 (1990) 269s (C. *Gillis*); [T]Lond 94 (1991) 152s (A. *Race*); Zygon 26 (1991) 328-333 (B. *Heblethwaite*).

a348 **Karafin** Brian, Prophecy, ideology, and utopia; towards a critical theory of religion: diss. [D]*Winquist* C. Syracuse NY 1991 [RelStR 18,170].

a349 **Kimminich** Otto, Religionsfreiheit als Menschenrecht; Untersuchungen zum gegenwärtigen Stand des Völkerrechts: Entwicklung and Frieden 52. Mainz/Mü 1990, Grünewald/Kaiser. 231 p. DM 29,80 pa. – [R]TGL 81 (1991) 241s (W. *Beinert*).

a350 **Lawson** E. Thomas, *McCauley* Robert N., Rethinking religion; connecting cognition and culture. C 1990, Univ. ix-194 p. $42.50. 0-521-37370-0 [TDig 38,365].

a351 **Lott** Eric J., Vision, tradition, interpretation; theology, religion and the study of religion: Religion and Reason 35, 1988 ➤ 4,b560; 5,a659: [R]JRel 71 (1991) 127s (R. F. *Campany*); TsTKi 60 (1989) 222-4 (N. O. *Breivik*, also on H. GRESCHAT, F. STOLZ).

McKenzie P., The Christians 1988 < **Heiler** F., Erscheinungsformen der Religionen [2]1979 ➤ 9041.

a353 *Maesschalck* Marc, Les modernes et la liberté de penser en religion: RTLv 22 (1991) 488-509.

a353* **Magnani** Giovanni, Introduzione storico-fenomenologica allo studio della religione, 1. Preistoria e storia, metodo, teorie e realtà [codice scuola]. R 1989, Pont. Univ. Gregoriana. 116 p.

a354 [*Mathon* G., Religion et religions:] *a*) *Geffre* C., Théologie de la religion et du dialogue interreligieux; – *b*) *Ries* Julién, L'histoire des religions de Benjamin CONSTANT (1767-1830) à Mircea ELIADE (1907-1986); – *c*) *Debarge* L., Religions de guérison; – *d*) *Daubercies* P., Vertu de religion; – *e*) *Lauwers* M., Religion populaire: ► 664, Catholicisme XII,57 (1990) 783-803-813-826-835-849.

a355 *a*) *Matthes* Joachim, Wie erforscht man heute Religion?; – *b*) *Stock* Konrad, Die evangelische Form religiöser Erfahrung; – *c*) *Sparn* Walter, Religion: GLern 5 (Gö 1990) 125-135 / 112-124 / 101-111 [< ZIT 91,56].

a356 *Orlando* Pasquale, La vera logica della religione: DoctComm 42 (1989) 137-154.

a357 **Pandian** Jacob, Culture, religion, and the sacred self; a critical introduction to the anthropological study of religion. ENJ 1991, Prentice Hall. xiii-226 p. 0-13-194226-3.

a358 **Pfleiderer** Georg, Theologie als Wirklichkeitswissenschaft; Studien zum Religionsbegriff bei G. WOBBERMIN, R. OTTO, H. SCHOLZ und M. SCHELER: ev. Diss. München 1991, ᴰ*Rendtorff*. – TR 87 (1991) 520.

a359 **Pieper** Josef, In search of the sacred; contributions to an answer, ᵀ*Krauth* Lothar. SF 1991, Ignatius. 136 p. $10. 0-89870-301-8 [TDig 39,79].

a360 **Preus** J. Samuel, Explaining religion 1987 ► 3,a971 ... 5,a680: ᴿJRel 71 (1991) 242-254 (T. W. *Tilley*: 'polemics and politics').

a361 **Richards** Glyn, Towards a theology of religions. L 1989, Routledge-CH. xi-179 p. $55. – ᴿJRel 71 (1991) 592s (T. M. *Vial*); NBlackf 71 (1990) 513s (G. *D'Costa*).

a362 *Ries* J., Sacré: ► 664, Catholicisme XIII,96 (1991) 271-293.

a363 **Rusecki** Marian, ⊕ Istota [essence] i geneza religii 1989 ► 6,a595: ᴿAntonianum 65 (1990) 390-2 (C. *Teklak*).

a364 *Sachot* Maurice, 'Religio / superstitio'; historique d'une subversion et d'un retournement: RHR 208 (1991) 355-394; Eng. 355: Christians reversed their meaning.

a364* *a*) *Schlette* Friedrich, *Kirschke* Siegfried, Religion und Kult in der frühen Menschengeschichte; – *b*) *Gediga* Boguslaw, Methodische Probleme bei der Auswertung archäologischer Quellen für die Rekonstruktion urgeschichtlicher Religionen: ► 656, Religion 1985/9, 11-24 / 211-7.

a365 **Schmitz** Bertram, Der Religionsbegriff im Denken von Paul TILLICH und Karl JASPERS: ev. Diss. Marburg 1991, ᴰ*Keil*. – TR 87 (1991) 520.

a366 **Schüssler** Werner, Jenseits von Religion und Nicht-Religion; der Religionsbegriff im Werk Paul TILLICHs: MgTheol 4. Fra 1989, Athenäum. 264 p. DM 78. – ᴿTLZ 116 (1991) 686-8 (E. *Sturm*).

a367 *a*) *Sharpe* Eric J., The study of religion [Judaism, *Cohn* R.; Islam, *Antes* P.] in the Encyclopedia of Religion; – *b*) *Bouchard* Larry D., The arts and the study of religion: JRel 70 (1990) 340-352 [392-402 / 403-411] / 353-367.

a368 **Tessier** Robert, Le sacré: Bref 34. P 1991, Cerf. 124 p. F 45. – ᴿEspr-Vie 101 (1991) 196-*jaune* (L. *Debarge*).

a369 *Thils* G., La 'religion' dans un État démocratique pluraliste: NRT 113 (1991) 728-743.

a370 *Track* Joachim, Begriff und Thema der Religion: TRu 56 (1991) 176-184.

a371 **Vallet** Odon, Culture religieuse: Concours Culture. P 1989, Masson. 208 p. F 130. 2-225-81979-3. – ᴿÉTRel 66 (1991) 118s (D. *Lys*).

a372 *a) Versnel* H., Some reflections on the relationship Magic-Religion; – *b) Leertouwer* Lammert, Primitive religion in Dutch religious studies: Numen 38 (1991) 177-197 / 198-213.
a373 **Vroom** Hendrik M., *a)* Religies en de waarheid. Kampen 1988, Kok. 334 p. ƒ59,50. 90-24233-14-3. – ᴿNedTTs 45 (1991) 82s (L. J. van den *Brom*). – *b)* Religions and the truth, ᵀ*Revel* J. W. GR 1990, Eerdmans. 338 p. – ᴿScripTPamp 23 (1991) 1086 (F. *Conesa*).
a375 **Waardenburg** Jacques, Religionen und Religion; systematische Einführung in die Religionswissenschaft: Göschen 2228, 1986 ➤ 2,8772... 4,b610: ᴿTR 87 (1991) 507 (G. *Girschek*).
a376 *Wagner* Falk, Religionsphilosophie und Theorie des Absoluten: NSys 31 (1989) 43-61; Eng. 61.
a377 *Waldenfels* Hans, ❷ Vers la théologie de la religion [< Ignatianisch 1990, 624-639], ᵀ*Pronobis* Tadeusz: PrzPow 270,832 (1990) 431-452.
a377* **Wuchterl** Kurt, Analyse und Kritik der religiösen Vernunft; Grundzüge einer paradigmenbezogenen Religiosphilosophie. Bern 1989, Haupt. 309 p. – ᴿPrzPow 273 (1991) 172-4 (J. *Machnacz*).

M3.2 Historia comparationis religionum: *centra, scholae.*

a378 **Baird** Robert D., Category formation and the history of religions² [= ¹1979 + new pref.]: Religion and Reason 1. B 1991, Mouton de Gruyter. [xii-] 178 p. 3-11-012821-7 / NY 0-89925-809-3.
a379 *Breivik* N. O., Religionsfenomenologi igår og idag; orientering i et problemfylt fagområde: TsTKi 60 (1990) 125-139.
a380 *a) Burkert* Walter, HERODOT als Historiker fremder Religionen; – *b) Bondi* Sandro F., I Fenici in Erodoto; – *c) Lloyd* Alan B., Herodotus on Egyptians and Libyans: ➤ 592, Hérodote / non-grecs 1988/90, 1-32(-39 discussion) / 255-286(-300) / 215-244(-253).
a381 **Godlove** Terry F.ᴶ, Religion, interpretation, and diversity of belief; the framework model from Kant to Durkheim to [Donald] DAVIDSON. C 1989, Univ. 207 p. $34.50. – ᴿJAAR 59 (1991) 831-5 (M. L. *Morgan*).
a382 *Greenwood* Susan F., Émile DURKHEIM and C. G. JUNG; structuring a transpersonal sociology of religion: JScStR 29 (1990) 482-495.
a383 *Kantzenbach* Friedrich W., Tendenzwende in der Religionskritik?: ZRGg 43 (1991) 324-332.
a384 **Penner** Hans, Impasse and resolution; a critique of the study of religion. NY 1989, P. Lang. 239 p. $39. 0-8204-0976-6. – ᴿNumen 38 (1991) 261-5 (E. T. *Lawson*: 'dispatches from the methodological wars', also on BOYER P. Tradition 1990).
a385 *Pinnock* Clark H., Toward an Evangelical theology of religions: JEvTS 33 (1990) 359-368 [< ZIT 90,806].
a386 **Ries** J., Les chemins du sacré dans l'histoire [... d'abord les approches: DURKHEIM, MAUSS; OTTO, van der LEEUW; ELIADE]: Présence et pensée, [1981] 1985 ➤ 1,a354... 4,b588: ᴿNRT 113 (1991) 281 (J. *Scheuer*).
a387 **Siebert** Rudolf J., The critical theory of religion; the Frankfurt school 1985 ➤ 1,a370... 4,b599: ᴿNedTTs 45 (1991) 78-80 (H. *Manschot*); TPhil 66 (1991) 464-6 (B. *Groth*).

M3.3 Individui conspicui *in investigatione religionum.*

a388 **ApRoberts** Ruth, The ancient dialect; T. CARLYLE and comparative religion. Berkeley 1988, Univ. California. $20. 0-520-06116-0, – ᴿJRel 71 (1991) 635s (W. *Woodfield*).

a389 *Arroyo Arrayas* Luis M., Antropodicea y antropokatadicea, la religión como afirmación y negación del hombre, en FEUERBACH y SCHOPEN-HAUER: CiuD 203 (1990) 305-331.
E Assmann Jan, Das Fest und das Heilige 1991 → 338.

a390 **Belier** Wouter W., Decayed gods; origin and development of Georges DUMÉZIL's 'Idéologie tripartite' [so in text; 'tripartie' in title]: StGr-RomRel 7. Leiden 1991, Brill. xv-254 p. 90-04-09487-3.

a391 *Belier* Wouter, DUMÉZIL's 'Idéologie tripartite'; from revolutionary paradigm to 'normal' science [PUHVEL J. 1989]: BO 48 (1991) 66-84.

a391* **Biallas** Leonard J., World religions; a story approach. Mystic CT 1991, Twenty-Third. $15 pa. 0-89622-493-7 [TDig 39,253].

a392 *Bieri* Anton, *Calder* William M.ᴵᴵᴵ, Instinct against proof; the correspondence between Ulrich von WILAMOWITZ-MOELLENDORFF and Martin P. NILSSON on Religionsgeschichte: Eranos 89 (1991) 73-99.

a393 ᴱBorgeaud Philippe, La mémoire des religions 1986/8 → 5,635: ᴿRHR 208 (1991) 437-440 (Jocelyne *Dakhlia*).

a394 **Colpe** Carsten, Über das Heilige; Versuch, seiner Verkennung kritisch vorzubeugen. Fra 1990, Hain. 93 p. DM 20. – ᴿZkT 113 (1991) 462s (B. *Braun*).

a395 **Cornwell** John, Powers of darkness, powers of light. L 1991, Viking. £17. – ᴿTablet 245 (1991) 1218 (P. *Birrell*: even more readable than William JAMES' 'wonderful monument' Varieties of Religious Experience 1902).

a396 **Cox** Harvey, Göttliche Spiele 1989 → 6,216: ᴿGeistL 63 (1990) 78s (A. *Raffelt*); NRT 113 (1991) 281 (J. *Masson*); ZMissRW 74 (1990) 507-9 (L. *Hagemann*).

a396* **Dawson** Lorne L., Reason, freedom and religion; closing the gap between the humanistic and scientific study of religion: Toronto StRel 6. NY 1988, Lang. 247 p. $47. 0-8204-0600-7. – ᴿRelStT 10,2 (1990) 94s (T. *Olson*).

a397 *D'Sousa* Felix, Independent evidence of religion [WHITEHEAD A., ...]: Bijdragen 52 (1991) 122-138.

a398 **Dupré** Wilhelm, Einführung in die Religionsphilosophie 1985 → 1,a288; 2,8672: ᴿNedTTs 43 (1989) 164s (A. F. de *Jong*).

a398* [**Eliade** Mircea 1907-1986; *Couliano* Ioan P.† 1991] ᴱ*Wiesner* Hillary, The Eliade guide to world religions [his 3-volume history abridged, with items from the 16-vol. EncRel]. SF 1991, Harper. xiii-301 p. $23. 0-06-062145-1 [TDig 39,260].

a399 **Finegan** Jack, Myth and mystery... pagan religions 1989 → 5,a610; 0-8010-3555-4: ᴿAndrUnS 29 (1991) 89-91 (M. M. *Kent*); BA 54 (1991) 178s (K. N. *Schoville*); BR 7,6 (1991) 8 (J. *Brashler*); CritRR 4 (1991) 256s (R. *Hodgson*); JAOS 111 (1991) 828s (J. C. *Reeves*); RExp 88 (1991) 274 (E. G. *Hinson*); TS 52 (1991) 345-7 (J. A. *Fitzmyer*: very fine; a bit to add on Mithraism).

a399* *Geffré* C., *Ries* J., Théologie/histoire des religions: → 664, Catholicisme 12,57 (1990) 784-802-812.

a400 **Gimbutas** Marija [→ a616], The civilization of the goddess, ᴱ*Marles* Jean [religion and way of life of 7th-3d millennium Europe]. SF 1991, Harper. xi-529 p. $60. 0-06-250368-5 [TDig 39,164].

a401 **Gregersen** Niels H., Gud og universet; W. PANNENBERGs religionsfilosofi. K 1989, Gad. 164 p. – ᴿTsTKi 61 (1990) 306s (J.-O. *Henriksen*).

a402 **Griffiths** J. Gwyn, The divine verdict; a study of divine judgement in the ancient religions: Numen supp. 52. Leiden 1991, Brill. xviii-410 p. ƒ180. 90-04-09231-5 [BL 92,116, N. *Wyatt*].

Hick John, An interpretation of religion 1989 → a347.

a403 **Hofmeister** Heimo E. M., Truth and belief; interpretation and critique of the analytical theory of religions [1978; his own translation]. Dordrecht 1990, Kluwer. 233 p. – ᴿScripTPamp 23 (1991) 1045 (F. *Conesa*).

a403* **Hutchison** John A., Paths of faith⁴ [¹1969, ²1975, ³1981: beginner's guide to the world's religions]. NY 1991, McGraw-Hill. xx-629 p. $37. 0-07-031543-4 [TDig 39,267].

a404 **Jaeschke** Walter, Die Vernunft in der Religion; Studien zur Grundlegung der Religionsphilosophie HEGELs [Hab.-D.]: Spekulation und Erfahrung 2.4, 1986 ➤ 3,a925; DM 147: ᴿJRel 70 (1990) 478s (B. E. *Hinze*); ZkT 113 (1991) 435-441 (W. *Kern*).

a405 **Kitagawa** Joseph M., The quest for human unity; a religious history [< 1985 Evanston Hale lectures]. Mp 1990, Fortress. xiv-289 p. $17 pa. 0-8006-2422-X [TDig 38,170]. – ᴿNumen 38 (1991) 278-280 (Ursula *King*); TTod 48 (1991s) 356.358 (Jane I. *Smith*).

a406 **Kušar** Stjepan, Dem göttlichen Gott entgegen denken... B. WELTE (1906-1983) 1986 ➤ 2,8712: ᴿTLZ 115 (1990) 908-910 (U. *Kern*).

a407 **Lenz** Hubert, Mut zum Nichts als Weg zu Gott; Bernhard WELTES religionsphilosophische Anstösse zur Erneuerung des Glaubens [Diss.]: FreibTSt 139. FrB 1989, Herder. xii-339 p. 3-451-31476-8. – ᴿActuBbg 28 (1991) 175 (J. *Boada*).

a407* **Lewis** James F., *Travis* William G., Religious traditions of the world. GR 1991, Zondervan. 422 p. $30. 0-310-51900-4 [TDig 39,272: concluding chapter on HICK, RAHNER, NEWBIGIN; Lewis lived in India and traveled in China].

a408 **Lotz** Johannes B., Vom Sein zum Heiligen; metaphysisches Denken nach HEIDEGGER. Fra 1990, Knecht. 140 p. DM 24. – ᴿTLZ 116 (1991) 52s (G. *Wenz*).

McKenzie P., [< HEILER F., Phenomenology of religion] 1988 ➤ 9041.

a409 *Makrakis* Michael K., ⊚ The philosophy of religion in Greece today; the contribution of Evangelos D. THEODOROU: TAth 62 (1991) 694-717; Eng. 931.

a410 *a) Murphy* Tim, Is a psychology of religion possible? A critique of William JAMES' taxonomy of religion in The varieties of religious experience; – *b) Kille* D. Andrew, Word and psyche; intersections of the psychology of religion and the Bible: Paradigms 7,2 (1991s) 1-10 / 11-19.

a411 **Nicole** J.-M., Précis d'histoire des religions. Nogent-sur-Marne 1990, 'Institut Biblique'. 175 p.; map. F 68 [RHE 86,120*].

a412 *Nowak* Kurt, Romanticism – religion – Utopia; SCHLEIERMACHER's and CHATEAUBRIAND's interpretation of religion about 1800: NSys 33 (1991) 44-58; deutsch 58.

a413 **Pollack** Detlef, Religiöse Chiffrierung und soziologische Aufklärung; die Religionstheorie Niklas LUHMANNs im Rahmen ihrer systematischen Voraussetzungen: EurHS 22/322. Fra 1988, Lang. 291 p. – ᴿTPhil 66 (1991) 119s (H.-J. *Höhn*).

a414 **Raposa** Michael L., [1839-1914, Charles S.] PEIRCE's philosophy of religion: Peirce Studies 5. Bloomington 1989, Indiana Univ. x-180 p. $25. – ᴿJRel 71 (1991) 452 (C. *Raschke*); Semiotica 87 (1991) 147-166 (C. *Hookway*, 'On reading God's great poem'); TLZ 116 (1991) 300-303 (M. *Grünewald*: 'Lw. 25.—').

a415 **Rennie** Bryan, Mircea ELIADE; making sense of religion: diss. ᴰWhaling F. Edinburgh 1991. 460 p. – RTLv 23, p. 564.

a416 ᴱ**Ries** Julien, *a)* I simboli nelle grandi religioni; – *b)* I riti di iniziazione. Mi 1988s, Jaca. 272 p. / 252 p. – ᴿStCatt 34 (1990) 418-420.

a417 ᴱRies Julien, Trattato di antropologia del sacro. I. Le origini e il problema dell'homo religiosus. Mi 1989, Jaca/Massimo. 326 p. Lit. 52.000. – ᴿArcheo 64 (1990) 128 (S. *Moscati*: 'Rice'); StCattMi 34 (1990) 418-420.

a418 **Ryba** Thomas, The essence of phenomenology and its meaning for the scientific study of religion. NY 1991, P. Lang. 268 p. $48 [JAAR 59,884].

a419 **Scharfenberg** Joachim, Sigmund FREUD and his critique of religion [1968], ᵀ*Dean* O. C., 1988 ➤ 4,b594: ᴿJRel 71 (1991) 285 (C. J. *Steckel*).

a420 **Siebrand** H. J., SPINOZA and the Netherlanders; an inquiry into the early reception of his philosophy of religion ᴰ1988 ➤ 4,b600; *f* 69,50: ᴿNedTTs 45 (1991) 90s (W. *Klever*).

a421 *Stekeler-Weithofer* Pirmin, Religionsphilosophie nach William JAMES: NSys 33 (1991) 74-87; Eng. 87.

a422 ᴱ**Sutherland** S., *al.*, The world's religions 1988 ➤ 4,418; 5,a709: ᴿCritRR 3 (1990) 467-470 (C. M. *Brown*); HeythJ 32 (1991) 125s (M. *Barnes*).

a423 *Taylor* Mark K.., Religion, cultural plurality, and liberating praxis; in conversation with the work of Langdon GILKEY: JRel 71 (1991) 145-166.

a424 *Ven* J. A. van der, Religieuze variaties; religie in een geseculariseerde en multiculturele samenleving: TsTNijm 31 (1991) 163-181; Eng. 181s.

a424* ᴱ**Wilson** Andrew [Moon Sun Myung International Religious Foundation], World scripture, a comparative anthology of sacred texts; pref. *Smart* Ninian. NY 1991, Paragon. xiv-914 p. $30. 0-89226-129-3 [TDig 39,194].

M3.4   **Religiones mundi** *inter se comparatae*.

a425 ᴱ**Akoun** André, L'Europe; le monothéisme...: mythes et traditions 1990 ➤ a501.

a426 **Bryant** David J., Faith and the play of imagination; on the role of imagination in religion. Macon GA 1989, Mercer Univ. xiii-217 p. 0-86554-319-4; pa. -49-6.

a427 *Camporesi* Piero, The incorruptible flesh; bodily mutation and mortification in religion and folklore [essays...], ᵀ*Croft-Murray* Tania. C 1988, Univ. x-286 p. $44.50. – ᴿCritRR 3 (1990) 249-251 (E. V. *Gallagher*).

a428 **Cupitt** Don, What is a story? [...(religious) truth is the story on top at present]. L 1991, SCM. £9. – ᴿTablet 245 (1991) 1546 (D. *Edwards*: 'he may know the questions, but beware of his answers').

a429 **De Falco Marotta** M., Le grandi religioni oggi; storia, dottrina, culto, etica, libri sacri; complemento ai testi di religione. T-Leumann 1989, LDC. 227 p. Lit. 18.000. – ᴿProtestantesimo 45 (1990) 78 (G. *Girardet*: unilaterale).

a430 *Dijk* Alphons van, Prostitution in Lehre, Sozialethik und Praxis der grossen Weltreligionen und der Stammesreligionen: ZMissRW 74 (1990) 35-52; Eng. 52s.

a431 **Ellwood** Robert, The history and future of faith; religions past, present and to come. NY 1988, Crossroad. viii-184 p. $19. – ᴿCurrTMiss 17 (1990) 300 (J. K. *Robbins*).

a432 **Fisher** Mary Pat, *Luyster* Robert, Living religions. ENJ 1991, Prentice Hall. 367 p. $29 pa. 0-13-538560-3 [TDig 38,357].

a433 **Fraas** H.-J., Die Religiosität des Menschen; ein Grundriss der Religionspsychologie: UniTb 1578. Gö 1990, Vandenhoeck & R.

336 p. DM 40. 3-525-03274-9. – ᴿTsTNijm 31 (1991) 447s (P. *Vandermeersch*).

a434 **Gollnick** James, Dreams in the psychology of religion. Lewiston NY 1987, Mellen. 183 p. $38.50. – ᴿCritRR 3 (1990) 405-9 (L. W. *Bailey*).

a435 **Goodman** Felicitas D., Ecstasy, ritual, and alternate reality; religion in a pluralistic world 1988 ➤ 5,a620: ᴿJScStR 29 (1990) 544s (S. D. *Glazier*).

a436 **Guerra** M., Storia delle religioni 1989 ➤ 5,a628: ᴿAnnTh 5 (1991) 468-473 (A. *Cirillo*).

a437 **Harrison** Peter, 'Religion' and the religions in the English enlightenment. C 1990, Univ. ix-277 p. $49.50. 0-521-38530-X [TDig 39,64].

a438 *a) Hultkrantz* Åke, The application of the method of ecology of religion in prehistory; the case of the goddess; – *b) Müller-Beck* Hansjürgen, Zur inhaltlichen Interpretation früher paläolithischer plastischer Darstellungen: ➤ 6,128, Saeculum 42 (1991, ᶠNARR K. Teil 2) 71-81 / 56-70; 2 fig.

a439 *Keller* Carl-A., Approche de la mystique [comparée]. Lausanne 1989, Ouverture. 229 p.; 255 p. [RelStR 18,124, D. *Blumenthal*].

a440 ᴱ**Limet** H., *Ries* J., L'expérience de prière dans les grandes religions 1978/80 ➤ 61,797 ... 64,9287: ᴿNRT 113 (1991) 283s (J. *Scheuer*).

a441 **Paden** William E., *a)* Religious worlds; the comparative study of religion 1988 ➤ 5,a672: ᴿCritRR 4 (1991) 260s (D. A. *Pittman*); RelStR17 (1991) 42 (J. W. *Laine*). – *b)* Am Anfang war Religion; die Einheit in der Vielfalt, ᵀ*Kipp* Günther & Hilde: Siebenstern 787. Gü 1990, Mohn. 224 p. DM 30. 3-579-00787-4. – ᴿTLZ 116 (1991) 587s (N.-P. *Moritzen*).

a442 *Papathomas* Gregory, La question de l'hénothéisme; contribution à l'étude du problème de l'origine des religions, I. II [Hindou; Anatolie] / III. (Hellénique-romaine)...: TAth 62 (1991) 502-527. 820-837 ...; Eng. 930.

a443 **Poupard** P., Las religiones 1989 ➤ 5,a678; ᵀ*Colom de Llopis* María: ᴿLumenVr 39 (1990) 184s (U. *Gil Ortega*: '1928').

a444 *Riccardi* Andrea, Du monde aux religions [malgré leur vitalité et leurs divisions, et sans syncrétisme, l'esprit d'Assise (prière unie)]: NRT 113 (1991) 321-339.

a445 ᴱ**Ries** J. [➤ a416s], Expression du Sacré 2. asianique...; 3. Mazdéisme, NT, 1983/6 ➤ 2,493; 3,a978 (!4,b589): ᴿNRT 113 (1991) 282s (J. *Scheuer*).

a446 *a) Schlesier* Renate, Prolegomena to Jane HARRISON's interpretation of ancient Greek religion; – *b) Fowler* Robert L., Four (five) stages of Greek religion; – *c) Smith* Morton, William Robertson SMITH; – *d) Jones* Robert A., La genèse du système? The origins of DURKHEIM's sociology of religion: ➤ 479, Cambridge Ritualists 1989/91, 185-226 [21-59 *al.*] / 79-95 / 251-261 / 97-121.

a447 ᴱ**Seltzer** Robert M., Religions of antiquity [< EncRel ➤ 674] 1989 ➤ 6,a671*: ᴿRelStR 17 (1991) 63 (E. *Rowell*).

a448 **Smith** Wilfred C., Towards a world theology 1989 [reprint of 1981 ➤ 61,k678 ... 4,b602]: ᴿLavalTP 47 (1991) 132s (A. *Couture*); LvSt 16 (1991) 286s (Catherine *Cornille*).

a449 **Terrin** Aldo N., Introduzione allo studio comparato delle religioni: Guide di cultura. Brescia 1991, Morcelliana. 282 p.

a450 **Turner** Victor W., Le phénomène rituel, structure et contre-structure: Ethnologies. P 1990, PUF. 208 p. F 148. 2-13-042805-3. – ᴿÉTRel 66 (1991) 581 (J. *Argaud*).

a451 **Wright** G. R. H., As on the first day; essays in religious constants 1987
→ 3,321: ᴿJPrehRel 3s (1989s) 69s (J. van *Leuven*: liberating).

M3.5 **Religiones mundi ex conspectu christianismi.**

a452 **Anderson** Brian D., The locus and effect of divine revelation among
non-Christian religions; a critical analysis of the views of K. BARTH, K.
RAHNER and W. C. SMITH: diss. SW Baptist Theol. Sem. 1991. 303 p.
91-35745. – DissA 52 (1991s) 2595-A.

a453 **Barnes** Michael [→ 6,a574], Religions in conversation; Christian
identity and religious pluralism 1989 → 6,a676: ᴿHeythJ 32 (1991) 126s
(G. *Loughlin*: intelligent).

a454 *Beeck* Frans J. van, Professing the creed among the world religions:
Thomist 55 (1991) 539-568.

a455 **Bernhardt** R., Der Absolutheitsanspruch des Christentum; von der
Aufklärung bis zur pluralistischen Religionstheologie [Diss. Heidelberg,
ᴰ*Ritschl*]. Gü 1990, Mohn.   263 p. DM 58.   3-579-00274-0. – ᴿTsTNijm
31 (1991) 215 (H. *Stoks*).

a456 *Bucher* Gérard, Des religions du Verbe [... de l'idolâtrie (Égypte) aux
'théo-logies du Verbe dans l'optique de l'hypothèse loganalytique sur
l'origine du sens et du sacré']: RHPR (1991) 169-182.

a457 **Carruthers** Gregory H., The uniqueness of Jesus Christ in the
theocentric model of the Christian theology of world religions; an
elaboration and evaluation of the position of John HICK.   Lanham MD
1990, UPA.   xii-363 p. $42.50.   0-8191-7889-6 [TDig 38,255].

a458 *a) Chethimattam* John B., The Christian hermeneusis and other
religions; – *b) Verstraaten* J., Christian approach to other religions from
a sociologist's perspective; – *c) Strotmann* Norberto, Theology and social
thought; the challenge of particular sociologies: Jeevadhara 21 (1991)
339-364 / 380-3 / 396-401.

a459 ᴱ**Clarke** Andrew D., *Winter* Bruce W., One God, one Lord in a world
of religious pluralism. C 1991, Tyndale.   200 p.

a459* *a) Cook* E. David, Truth, mystery and justice; HICK and the myth of
Christian uniqueness; – *b) Demarest* Bruce A., General and special
revelation; epistemological foundations of religious pluralism; – *c)
Bradshaw* Tim, Grace and mercy; Protestant approaches to religious
pluralism; – *d) Wright* David, The watershed of Vatican II; Catholic
attitudes towards other religions: → 485, One God 1991, 182-191 /
135-152 / 172-181 / 153-171.

a460 **Cunningham** Richard B., The Christian faith and its contemporary rivals
[atheism... world religions].   Nv 1988, Broadman.   205 p. $10. 0-8054-
6705-X. – ᴿRExp 87 (1990) 123s (J. P. *Newport*).

a461 ᴱ**D'Costa** Gavin, Christian uniqueness reconsidered; the myth of a
pluralistic theology of religions: Faith Meets Faith. Mkn 1990, Orbis.
xii-218 p.   0-88344-686-3. – ᴿGregorianum 72 (1991) 787s (J. *Dupuis*);
LvSt 16 (1991) 267-9 (Catherine *Cornille*); ScripTPamp 23 (1991) 1045s
(J. M. *Odero*); TLond 94 (1991) 298-300 (G. *Loughlin*).

a461* *Dumont* Heinrich, Theologie der Religionen? Zum Problem des wach-
senden religiösen Pluralismus: TGegw 34 (1991) 27-36 [260-8 *Geffré* C.].

a462 **Dupuis** Jacques, Jésus-Christ à la rencontre des religions: JJC 39, 1989
→ 6,a68a: ᴿScEsp 43 (1991) 233-242 (P. *Pellettier*); Vidyajyoti 55 (1991)
174-6 (G. *Gispert-Sauch*).

a463 **Dupuis** J., Gesù Cristo incontro alle religioni 1989 → 6,a684b: ᴿDiv-
Thom 93 (1990) 264-7 (L. *Iammarrone*).

a464 **Dupuis** Jacques,   Jesus Christ at the encounter of world religions, ᵀ*Barr* Robert R.: Faith Meets Faith.   Mkn 1991, Orbis.   xi-301 p. $40; pa. $19. 0-88344-724-X; -3-1 [TDig 39,58].

a465 **Euler** Walter A.,   Unitas et pax; Religionsvergleich bei Raimundus LULLUS und Nikolaus von KUES [Diss. Fr 1989]: WüFor MissRW 15. Wü/Altenberge 1990, Echter/Telos.   296 p.   DM 44. – ᴿTLZ 116 (1991) 811-4 (K.-H. *Kandler*: Absolutheitsanspruch des Christentums).

a466 *Fédou* Michel,   Le christianisme parmi les religions: Études 375 (1991) 525-535.

a467 ᴱ**Fu Wei-hsun** Charles, *Spiegler* Gerhard E.,   Religious issues and interreligious dialogue; an analysis and sourcebook of developments since 1945. NY 1989, Greenwood.   x-693 p. $95. – ᴿCritRR 4 (1991) 258 (D. A. *Pittman*).

a468 *Geffré* Claude,   Christian faith and religious pluralism [< VSp 143 (1989) 805-815], ᵀᴱ*Jermann* R.:   TDig 38 (1991) 15-18.

a469 **Gira** D.,   Les religions: Parcours.   P 1991, Centurion/Paulines.   119 p. F 62 [NRT 114,472].

a469* **Griener** George E.,   Ernst TROELTSCH and Herman SCHELL [on 'Absolutheit des Christentums']; Christianity and the world religions; an ecumenical contribution to the history of apologetics [kath. Diss. Tübingen 1988]: EurHS 23/375.   Fra 1990, Lang.   349 p. [NRT 114,774s, J. *Scheuer*; TLZ 117,660-3, F. W. *Graf*].

a470 ᴱ**Griffiths** Paul J.,   *a*) Christianity through non-Christian eyes [texts]: Faith meets Faith 1990 ➤ 6,a689; $30; $15.   0-88344-661-8. – ᴿGregorianum 72 (1991) 786s (J. *Dupuis*); Missiology 19 (1991) 241s (A. *Zahniser*). – *b*) Doctrines and the virtue of doctrine; the problem of religious plurality: Proc.Amer.Cath.Phil.Soc. 65 (1991) 29-44.

a471 ᵀᴱ**Holtrop** P. N., *Minnema* L.,   Voor Hem een ander? Ontwerpen voor een pluralistische theologie der religies [< ᴱHICK J., KNITTER P., Myth of Christian uniqueness 1086/7 ➤ 4,b546].   Haag 1990, Meinema.   150 p. *f* 27.50.   90-211-3541-8. – ᴿTsTNijm 31 (1991) 209s (H. *Stoks*).

a472 **Kimminich** O.,   Religionsfreiheit als Menschenrecht: Untersuchung zum gegenwärtigen Stand des Völkerrechts: Entwicklung und Frieden 52. Mainz/Mü 1990, Grünewald/Kaiser.   231 p. DM 29,80.   3-7867-1517-3 / 3-459-01878-X. – ᴿTsTNijm 31 (1991) 216 (P. *Stevens*).

a473 **Knitter** Paul F.,   Ein Gott – viele Religionen; Gegen den Absolutheitsanspruch des Christentums [1985 ➤ 1,a319], ᵀ*Wimmer* J., 1988 ➤ 4,b411; 5,a648:   ᴿTR 87 (1991) 234-240 (A. *Kolping*: Fragen).

a474 **Knitter** Paul F.,   Nessun altro nome?   Un esame critico degli atteggiamenti cristiani verso le religioni mondiali [1985 ➤ 1,a319],ᵀ: GdT 207.   Brescia 1991, Queriniana.   278 p. Lit. 26.000 [NRT 114,279, J. *Masson*].

a475 **Krieger** David J.,   The new universalism; foundations for a global theology [... based on R. PANIKKAR]: Faith Meets Faith.   Mkn 1991, Orbis.   ix-219 p. $40; pa. $17.   0-88344-728-2; -7-4 [TDig 39,70].

a476 **Matthey** Jacques,   Non-chrétiens mes frères; le Nouveau Testament ouvre le dialogue avec les autres religions.   Aubonne 1991, Moulin. – ᴿEsprVie 101 (1991) 550 (P. *Jay*).

a476* *Monnot* Guy,   ABŪ QURRA [Théodore, évêque melkite c. 820] et la pluralité des religions: RHR 208 (1991) 49-71; Eng. 49.

a477 **Netland** Harold H. [➤ 7132] Dissonant voices; religious pluralism and the question of truth.   GR/Leicester 1991, Eerdmans/Apollos.   xii-323 p. $18.   0-8028-0602-3 / .

a478 **Neville** Robert C., Behind the masks of God; an essay toward comparative theology [... Christian, Buddhist, Tao]. Albany 1991, SUNY. x-200 p. $15. 0-7914-0578-8; -9-6 [TDig 38,371]. – ᴿTS 52 (1991) 598s (J. A. *Bracken*).

a479 **Newbigin** Lesslie, The Gospel in a pluralist society [Glasgow Univ. lectures]. GR/L 1989, Eerdmans/SPCK. xi-244 p. $9. ↠ 6,a697: ᴿEvQ 63 (1991) 368s (P. *Ellingworth*).

a480 **Okoro** Kieran C., The contemporary official Catholic position on non-Christian religions: diss. Fordham, ᴰ*Hennelly* A. NY 1991. 238 p. 91-37206. – DissA 52 (1991s) 2598-A; RelStR 18,171.

a480* **Panikkar** Raimon, Der neue religiöse Weg; im Dialog der Religionen leben [The intrareligious dialog], ᵀ*Tepe* Georg. Mü 1990, Kösel. 189 p. – ᴿTPhil 66 (1991) 466s (R. *Funiok*).

a481 *Phan* Peter C., Gott als heiliges Mysterium und die Suche nach 'Gottes-Äquivalenten' im interreligiösen Dialog, ᵀ*Molinski* Waldemar; ZMiss-RW 74 (1990) 161-175; Eng. 175.

a482 **Reinhold** Bernhard, Der Absolutheitsanspruch des Christentums, von der Aufklärung bis zur pluralistischen Religionstheologie. Gü 1990, Mohn. 202 p. DM 58. – ᴿTGL 81 (1991) 132s (W. *Beinert*).

a484 **Runia** K., Het evangelie en de vele religies: Kamper Cah. 71. Kampen 1990, Kok. 78 p. ƒ10. – ᴿNedTTs 45 (1991) 349 (L. J. van den *Brom*).

a485 **Smart** Ninian, *Konstantine* Steven, Christian systematic theology in a world context. Mp 1991, Fortress. 466 p. $18 [TDig 39,188].

a486 **Smith** Jonathan Z., Drudgery divine; on the comparison of early Christianities and the religions of late antiquity (Jordan Lectures 4) 1990 ↠ 6,a706: ᴿAsbTJ 46,2 (1991) 105-7 (D. *Bundy*); BSO 54 (1991) 575s (A. *Cameron*); JTS 42 (1991) 703-5 (F. G. *Downing*); TS 52 (1991) 777s (D. G. *Hunter*).

a487 **Swidler** Leonard J., After the absolute; the dialogical future of religious reflection: Mp 1990, Fortress. xvi-248 p. $15. 0-8006-2423-8 [TDig 38,190]. – ᴿCurrTMiss 18 (1991) 223 (R. H. *Bliese*).

a487* **Terrin** Aldo N., Introduzione allo studio comparato delle religioni [raccolta di saggi]: Guide di Cultura. Brescia 1991, Morcelliana. 282 p. 88-372-1438-3.

a488 **Tracy** David, Dialogue with the other; the inter-religious dialogue [Leuven Dondeyne lectures 1988]: TheolPastMg 1. Lv/GR 1991, Peeters/ Eerdmans. xii-123 p. $13 pa. /0-8028-0562-0 [TDig 39,87].

a489 *a) Twiss* Sumner B., The philosophy of religious pluralism; a critical appraisal of HICK and his critics; – *b) Stinnett* Timothy R., John Hick's pluralistic theory of religion: JRel 70 (1990) 533-568 / 569-588.

a490 *Vergottini* Marco, Singolarità del cristianesimo e pluralismo religioso: TItSett 16 (1991) 306-315.

a491 *Weiser* Alfons, Die vielen Religionen und der 'einzige Mittler'; neutestamentliche Aspekte: ↠ a994, Christus in Afrika 1991, 40-66.

a492 **Wong** Joseph H. P., Christ and world religions; towards a pneumatological Christocentrism: Landas 5,1 (Manila 1991) 3-45 [< ZIT 91,493].

M3.6 **Sectae.**

a492* **Bull** Malcolm, *Lockhart* Keith, Seeking a sanctuary; Seventh-Day Adventism and the American dream. SF 1989, Harper & R. xi-319 p. $26. – ᴿAndrUnS 28 (1990) 255s (B. E. *Strayer*).

a493 **Gasper** Hans, *al.*, Lexikon der Sekten. FrB 1990, Herder. viii-1210 p. DM 98. – ᴿTGL 81 (1991) 128 (W. *Beinert*).

a494 **Greeley** Andrew, God in popular culture. Ch 1988, T. More. 207 p. $15. 0-88347-234-1. – ᴿRExp 87 (1990) 139s (B. *Leonard*: pop fringing blasphemy, but justifiably).

a495 **Samuel** Albert, Para comprender las religiones en nuestro tiempo [... Les religions aujourd'hui], ᵀ*Ortiz* Alfonso. Estella 1989, VDivino. 218 p.; ill. 84-7151-633-0. – ᴿActuBbg 28 (1991) 114 (J. *Boada*).

a496 **Wilson** Bryan B., The social dimensions of sectarianism; sects and new religious movements in contemporary society. Ox 1990, Clarendon. xii-299 p. $32.50. – ᴿTLond 94 (1991) 54s (G. *Howes*).

a497 **Zananiri** G., Des sectes au Nouvel Âge: EsprVie 101 (1991) 331-5.

M3.8 **Mythologia.**

a499 *Ackermann* Erich, Theriomorphie in Mythos und Märchen der Antike: ➤ 146, ᶠSTEINMETZ P., Pratum 1990, 57-73.

a500 *Aiken* D. Wyatt, History, truth and the rational mind; why it is impossible to separate myth from history: TZBas 47 (1991) 226-253.

a501 ᴱ**Akoun** André, I. L'Europe / II. Le monothéisme [Babylone, Judaïsme, Chrétienté, Islam, Égypte, Iran...]: Mythes et traditions. P/Turnhout 1990, Lidis/Brepols. 486 p. / 476 p.; color. ill. 2-503-82375-0; -6-9.

a501* ᴱ**Akoun** André, Mythes et croyances du monde entier. P/Turnhout 1985s, Lidis/Brepols. I. L'Asie, 1991; 492 p.; – II. L'occident contemporain, 1991; 524 p. (color.) ill. 2-503-50072-2; -1-4.

a502 **Austin** Norman, Meaning and being in myth 1990 ➤ 6,a722: ᴿClasR 41 (1991) 155-7 (S. *Goldhill*); Phoenix 45 (Toronto 1991) 268s (A. *Rawn*: lively but bewildering).

a503 *Baum* Klaus, Die Transzendierung des Mythos; zur Philosophie und Ästhetik SCHELLINGS und ADORNOS: Epistemata 38, 1988 ➤ 6,a723: ᴿDLZ 112 (1991) 712-4 (G. *Kleinstück*).

a505 **Benoist** Luc, Signes, symboles et mythes⁶ [¹1975]: Que sais-je? 1605. P 1991, PUF. 128 p. 2-13-044285-4.

a506 **Breslauer** S. Daniel, Martin BUBER on myth, an introduction: Theorists of Myth 3. NY 1990, Garland. 395 p. $44 [TR 87,530; RelStR 18,150, M. *Friedman*]. 0-8240-3721-9.

a507 *Carazzali* Giulia, Mito e filosofia del mito: HumBr 46 (1991) 237-246.

a508 **Eliade** Mircea, Mythos und Wirklichkeit [Aspects du mythe 1963], ᵀ*Moldenhauer* Evan. Fra 1988, Insel. – ᴿOrientierung 55 (1991) 83-87 (J. *Mohn*).

a509 **Golan** Ariel, Myth and symbol; symbolism in prehistoric religions. J 1991, auct. (150/44 Derek Hebron). 346 p.; ill. $50 [Antiquity 66,534, T. *Taylor*: undisciplined and thoroughly illustrated romp].

a510 **Isermann** Gerhard, Revitalisierung der Mythen? Gegen den Missbrauch alter Geschichten für neue Interessen: Vorlagen NF 10. Hannover 1990, Luther. 144 p. DM 12,80 [TR 87,256].

ᴱ**Kahil** Lilly, Linant de Bellefonds Pascal, Religion, mythologie, iconographie 1991 ➤ 594*b*.

a512 **Kajanto** Iiro, Humanism in a Christian society, I. The attitude to classical mythology and religion in Finland 1640-1713: 1989 ➤ 5,a738: ᴿBStLat 21 (1991) 82 (Teresa *Piscitelli*).

a513 **Kulikowski** Mark, A bibliography of Slavic mythology. Columbus 1989, Slavica. 137 p. 0-89357-203-9.

a514 *Lattanzi* Anna Rita, Recenti studi sul trickster [CULIANO I., I miti dei dualismi occidentali 1987, ital. 1989]: SMSR 57 (1991) 205-220.

a515 **Leick** Gwendolyn, A dictionary of ancient Near Eastern mythology [... based mainly on excavated tablets]. NY 1991, Routledge.   xiii-199 p.; 44 pl. $60.   0-415-00762-3 [TDig 39,71; RelStR 18,224, J. M. *Sasson*].

a516 ᴱ**Limet** H., *Ries* J., Le mythe, son langage et son message; Actes du Colloque de Liège et LvN 1981: Homo Religiosus 9 1983 ➤ 64,513 ... 2,8797:   ᴿNRT 113 (1991) 284 (J. *Scheuer*).

a517 **Mascioni** Grytzko, Mare degli immortali; miti del Mediterraneo europeo: Oscar narrativa 1165.   Mi 1991, Mondadori.   267 p.   Lit. 11.000. 88-04-34790-2.

a518 *Mezzadri* Bernard, Jason ou le retour du pécheur; esquisse de mythologie argonautique [... *Dubuisson* D., Indra]: RHR 208 (1991) 273-301; Eng. 273.

a519 *Okpewho* Isidore, Myth in Africa; a study of its aesthetic and cultural relevance.   C 1983, Univ. 305 p. 0-521-24544-0. – ᴿJRelAf 19 (1989) 86-88 (O. U. *Kalu*).

a520 **Opie** Iona, *Tatem* Moira, A dictionary of superstitions.   Ox 1990, Univ. xv-494 p. – ᴿSalesianum 53 (1991) 800s (R. *Sabin*).

a521 **Pernety** Antonio G. [1713-1801], Le favole egizie e greche, svelate e riportate ad un unico fondamento, con la spiegazione dei geroglifici jeratici e della guerra di Troia, ᵀ*Catinella* Giacomo: Classici del Pensiero Magico. Genova 1988, ECIG. xvi-413 p. 88-7545-116-8.

a522 Il potere del mito [ᴱ*Mecozzi* Maurizio]: Quaderni di Avallon 25.   R 1991, Cerchio.   136 p.   Lit. 18.000.

a523 **Pozzi** Dora C., *Wickersham* John M., Myth and the Polis.   Ithaca NY 1991, Cornell Univ.   ix-232 p. [RÉG 104,682].

a524 *Puhvel* Jaan, Comparative mythology. Baltimore 1987 ➤ 4,8649; 5,a750; pa. 1989, Johns Hopkins Univ.   302 p. $43; pa. $15. 0-8018-3413-9; -938-6. – ᴿBO 48 (1991) 66-84 (W. *Belier* on DUMÉZIL); ClasR 41 (1991) 111-3 (K. *Dowden*); Phoenix 45 (1991) 76-81 (H. J. *Westra*).

a525 ᴱ**Reynolds** Frank E., *Tracy* Daniel, Myth and philosophy. Albany 1990, SUNY. 382 p. $20 [RelStR 18,38, K. *Surin*].

a526 **Strenski** Ivan, Four theories of myth in twentieth-century history; CASSIRER, ELIADE, LÉVI-STRAUSS and MALINOWSKI 1987 ➤ 4,b651; 6,a746: ᴿJAAR 59 (1991) 874-7 (D. *Allen*: bold, challenging; with flair claims there is no such real 'thing' as myth; means everything and nothing, scholars of myth just pretend they are referring to the same 'object').

a527 *Ström* Åke V., *Hermisson* Hans-J., Märchen [... und Mythos; ... in der Bibel?]: ➤ 690, TRE 21 (1991) 668-672-677.

a527* *Tarrant* H. A. S., Myth as a tool of persuasion in PLATO: Antichthon 24 (1990) 19-31.

a528 **Triomphe** Robert, Le lion, la vierge et le miel [cycle des saisons]: Vérité des mythes 3, 1989 ➤ 6,a47: ᴿRÉG 104 (1991) 263s (F. *Jouan*); Salesianum 53 (1991) 764 (R. *Della Casa*).

a529 *Vycinas* Vincent, The great goddess and the Aistian [oldest Indo-European] mythical world: AmerUnivSt 5/91. NY 1990, P. Lang. xi-275 p. 0-8204-1264-3.

a530 *a*) *Weder* Hans, Mythos und Metaphor – Überlegungen zur Sachinterpretation mythischen Redens im NT; – *b*) *Beisser* Friedrich, Mythos und christliche Theologie: ➤ 442, Bibel und Mythos 1991, 38-73 / 74-89.

a530* **White** David G., Myths of the dog-man. Ch 1991, Univ. xix-334 p.; 14 pl. 0-226-89508-4; pa. -9-2.

a531 *Zippert* T., Religion im Märchen und das Märchen in der Religion: Pastoraltheologie 79 (Gö 1990) 270-284 [< ZIT 90,497].

M4 Religio romana.

a532 *Andreoni Fontecedro* Emanuela, Le espressioni del fato nella scrittura di SENECA: Aufidus 11s (1990) 127-140.

a533 *Auvray-Assayas* Clara, Le livre I du De natura deorum [CICERO] et le traité De signis de PHILODÈME; problèmes de théologie et de logique: RÉLat 69 (1991) 51-69.

a534 **Baistrocchi** M., Arcana Urbis; considerazioni su alcuni rituali arcaici di Roma. Genova 1987, ECIG. 342 p. – ᴿGerión 8 (1990) 317-9 (S. *Montero*: consul en Madrid).

a535 *Baldus* Hans R., Zur Aufnahme des Sol Elagabalus-Kultes in Rom, 219 n.Chr.: Chiron 21 (1991) 175-8.

a535* ᴱ**Beard** Mary, **North** John, Pagan priests 1990 ↠ 6,389: ᴿClasR 41 (1991) 118-120 (J. *Liebeschuetz*).

a536 *Becher* Ilse †, Der Kult der Magna Mater in augusteischer Zeit: Klio 73 (1991) 157-170.

a537 *Bowersock* G.W., The pontificate of Augustus: ↠ b344, Between Republic and Empire 1987/90, 380-394.

a538 **Bremmer** J.N., **Horsfall** N.M., Roman myth and mythography 1987 ↠ 3,b48*... 6,a751: ᴿGnomon 63 (1991) 166-8 (T. *Köves-Zulauf*).

a539 **Champeaux** Jacqueline, Fortuna 1987 ↠ 5,a760; 6,a755: ᴿRÉAnc 92 (1990) 429-431 (R. *Turcan*).

a540 *Classen* C. Joachim, Virtutes imperatoriae: Arctos 25 (1991) 17-39.

a541 **D'Aversa** Arnaldo, La divinazione nella cultura etrusca e romana; antologia. Brescia 1989, Paideia. 128 p. – ᴿSalesianum 53 (1991) 155s (R. *Sabin*).

a542 **Donner** Herbert, Völker und Staaten des Alten Orients [< Geschichte 2 (1986) 287-303 . 359-369]: ↠ 321, WegF 633 (1991) 33-62.

a543 **Eingartner** Johannes, Isis und ihre Dienerinnen in der Kunst der römischen Kaiserzeit: Mnemosyne supp. 115. Leiden 1991, Brill. xii-199 p.; XCVIII pl. 90-04-09312-5.

a544 **Feo** Giovanni, Dei della terra; il mondo sotterraneo degli Etruschi: Nuova Atlantide. Genova 1991, ECIG. 187 p. 88-7545-455-8.

a545 **Fishwick** Duncan, The imperial cult in the Latin West 1: ÉPR 108, 1987 ↠ 3,b57... 6,a671: ᴿAmJPg 112 (1991) 424-7 (R. *Mellor*).

a545* ᵀᴱ**Gallo** Italo, *al.*, PLUTARCO, Moralia. N 1988-90, D'Auria. I. 1988, 209 p.; II. 1988, 177 p.; III. 1989; IV. 1989, 137 p.; V. 1990, 251 p. III.-V. 88-7092-0038-0; -39-9; -46-1.

a546 *García Bellido* María Paz, Las religiones orientales en la península ibérica; documentos numismáticos, I: ArEspArg 64 (1991) 37-81; 10 fig.

a547 **Giancotti** F., 'Religio, natura, voluptas'; studi su LUCREZIO, con un'antologia di testi annotati e tradotti. Bo 1989, Pàtron. 551 p. – ᴿRPg 64 (1990) 252s (J.-M. *André*).

a547* *Gill* David W.J., Behind the classical façade; local religions of the Roman Empire: ↠ 485, One God 1991, 72-87.

a548 **Grimal** Pierre, Marc Aurèle. P 1991, Fayard. 449 p., map. F 150. 2-2130-2763-0.

a549 **Gruen** E. S., Studies in Greek culture and Roman policy [manipulating it, i. Advent of the Magna Mater; ii. The Bacchanalian affair...]: Cincinnati Classical Studies 7. Leiden 1990, Brill. x-209 p. *f* 75. 90-04-09051-5. – ᴿJRS 81 (1991) 190s (Emma *Dench*).

a550 **Heim** François, Virtus; idéologie politique et croyances religieuses au IVᵉ siècle: EurHS 15/49. Bern 1991, Lang. 378 p. 3-261-04329-6.

a551 ᴱ**Hinard** F., La mort... l'au-delà dans le monde romain 1985/7 ➤ 5, a773: ᴿMnemosyne 44 (1991) 507-9 (A. J. L. van *Hooff*).

a552 **Hörig** M., *Schwertheim* E., Corpus cultus Iovis Dolicheni: ÉPR 106, 1987 ➤ 3,b64; 5,a774: ᴿMnemosyne 44 (1991) 295-8 (G. *Mussies*).

a553 **Hooff** Anton J. L. van, From autothanasia to suicide; self-killing in classical antiquity [960 recorded cases]. L 1990, Routledge. 306-xv p.; 13 fig. $55 [RelStR 18,228, W. G. *Rusch*].

a554 *Hutchinson* V. J., The cult of Dionysos/Bacchus in the Graeco-Roman world; new light from archaeological studies: JRomArch 4 (1991) 222-230 [< NTAbs 36,79].

a555 *Janon* Michel, De Judée en Narbonnaise, reconnaissance de quelques sanctuaires du pouvoir: MÉF-A 103 (1991) 735-783; 12 fig.

a556 *Kahil* Lilly, Le sacrifice d'Iphigénie: MÉF-A 103 (1991) 183-196; 10 fig.

a557 *Krumme* Michael, Isis in Praeneste; zur Rekonstruktion des unteren Heiligtums: JbDAI 105 (1990) 155-165; 2 fig.

a557* **Lane** E. N., Corpus cultus Iovis Sabazii 3: ÉPR 100, 1989 ➤ 5,a778; 6,a773: ᴿClasR 41 (1991) 124-6 (K. *Dowden*).

a558 *Lee* Peter, bp. Worship, ancient and modern [(Greek and) Roman cults]: ExpTim 102 (1990s) 105-9.

a559 ᴱ*Lévêque* Pierre [➤ 748], Les rites de passage dans l'Antiquité [colloque Rome, Univ. – ÉcFr. – Univ. Besançon] = MÉF-A 102,1 (1990) 1-138.

a560 **Luck** Georg, Magie und andere Geheimlehren in der Antike: Tb 489. Stu 1990, Kröner. xvii-499 p. [112 Quellentexte ᵀ].

a561 ᵀᴱ**Majercik** Ruth, The Chaldean oracles: StGrRomRel 5. Leiden 1989, Brill. xiv-247 p. $60 pa. 90-04-09043-6. – ᴿJRS 81 (1991) 225-7 (D. *Potter*); TPhil 66 (1991) 101s (F. *Ricken*).

a561* *a*) *Menuet-Guilbaud* E., 'Lᴜᴄʀᴇᴛɪ poemata...', une lecture ironique du jugement de Cɪᴄᴇ́ʀᴏɴ; – *b*) *Gély* Suzanne, La religion de l'Antique de Cicéron à Chateaubriand; le signe et le sens: BBudé (1991) 6-18 / 76-88.

a562 *Méthy* Nicole, Réflexions sur le thème de la divinité de Rome; à propos de l'Éloge de Rome d'Aelius Aʀɪsᴛɪᴅᴇ: Latomus 50 (1991) 660-8.

a563 **Montanari** Enrico, Identità culturale e conflitti religiosi nella Roma repubblicana: Filologia e Critica 54, 1988 ➤ 4,b683; 5,a783: ᴿGnomon 63 (1991) 173-5 (C. *Ulf*).

a564 **Moore** Timothy J., Artistry and ideology; Lɪᴠʏ's vocabulary of virtue 1989 ➤ 6,a778: ᴿAnJPg 112 (1991) 276-9 (T. J. *Luce*).

a565 ᵀᴱ**Nickel** Rainer, Marc Aᴜʀᴇʟ, Wege zu sich selbst. Mü 1990, Artemis. 392 p. – ᴿTyche 6 (1991) 239-241 (G. *Dobesch*).

a566 **Önnerfors** Alf, Antike Zaubersprüche, zweisprachig: Univ.-Bibl. 8686. Stu 1991, Reclam. 72 p. – ᴿWienerSt 104 (1991) 289s (Christine *Harrauer*: grossenteil latein).

a567 **Paladino** Ida, Fratres arvales; storia di un collegio sacerdotale romano 1988 ➤ 5,a785: ᴿMnemosyne 44 (1991) 278-280 (H. *Freis*).

a568 **Parke** H. W., Sibyls and Sibylline prophecy in classical antiquity 1988 ➤ 4,b685; 6,a784: ᴿMnemosyne 44 (1991) 269-271 (D. *Holwerda*).

a569 **Pötscher** Walter, Hᴏʀᴀᴢ, carm. 1,34 und die persönliche Religiosität des Autors: Latomus 50 (1991) 822-839.

a570 **Porte** Danielle, Les donneurs du sacré; le prêtre à Rome 1989 ⇸ 5,2789; 6,a786: ᴿGnomon 63 (1991) 124-7 (G. *Radke*); RPg 64 (1990) 271-3 (Jacqueline *Champeaux*).

a571 **Potter** D.S., Prophecy and history in the crisis of the Roman empire; a historical commentary on the thirteenth Sibylline oracle: Clas. Mg. Ox 1990, U.P. XIX-443 p.; 27 fig.; 2 maps. £50. – ᴿGreeceR 38 (1991) 253 (T. *Wiedemann*).

a572 *Radke* Gerhard, Nouveaux points de vue sur la mentalité religieuse des Romains: Kernos 4 (1991) 31-46.

a572* *Reis* P., The [Pompeii] Villa of Mysteries; initiation into woman's midlife passage: Continuum 1,3 (NY 1991) 64-91 [< NTAbs 36,242].

a573 **Rüpke** Jörg, Domi militiae; die religiöse Konstruktion des Krieges in Rom. Stu 1990, Steiner. 312 p. – ᴿWienerSt 104 (1991) 397-9 (Christine *Harrauer*).

a574 **Rutherford** R.B., The meditations of Marcus Aurelius: *a*) ᵀpartly by *Farquharson* A.S.L. Ox 1989, UP. xxvii-195 p. £25. – *b*) a study: ClasMg 1989 ⇸ 6.a789: ᴿClasR 41 (1991) 42-44 (Miriam *Griffin*); JHS 111 (1991) 228s (M.B. *Trapp*).

a575 *Sajkowski* Ryszard, ✆ De divi Augusti cultu Tiberii principis temporibus propagato: Meander 46 (1991) 29-42.

a576 *Santi* Claudia, A proposito della 'vocazione solare' degli Aurelii: SMSR 57 (1991) 5-19.

a577 **Scheid** John, La religione a Roma 1983 [cf. Religion et piété à Rome 1985 ⇸ 1,a451 = 3,b77]: Mondo degli antichi 7/2. R 1983, Laterza. vii-180 p. – ᴿHelmantica 38 (1987) 447s (M.A. *Marcos Casquero*).

a577* *Scheid* John, Rituel et rituel à Rome: ⇸ 470*, Rituel 2 (1988/90) 1-15.

a578 **Schön** Dorit, Orientalische Kulte im römischen Österreich 1988 ⇸ 4, b690: ᴿOLZ 86 (1991) 12-14 (K. *Parlasca*).

a579 **Segal** Charles, Lucretius on death and anxiety; poetry and philosophy in De rerum natura 1990 ⇸ 6,a793: ᴿBStLat 21 (1991) 333-5 (L. *Perelli*).

a580 **Simon** Erika, Die Götter der Römer. Mü 1990, Hirmer. 319 p.; 332 fig. DM 98. – ᴿErbAuf 67 (1991) 159s (Elisabeth *Bitter*).

a581 **Turcan** Robert, Les cultes orientaux du monde romain 1989 ⇸ 5,a797 ['dans le']: ᴿRÉG 104 (1991) 607s (Hélène *Cassimatis*).

a582 **Turcan** Robert, Religion romaine 1. Les dieux; 2. Le culte: IconRel 17,1, 1988 ⇸ 4,b694 ... 6,a796: ᴿClasR 41 (1991) 247s (Glenys *Davies*); RHPR 71 (1991) 243s (P. *Prigent*).

a583 **Vanggaard** Jens H., The flamen 1988 ⇸ 5,a597*; 6,a797: ᴿClasR 41 (1991) 117s (J. *Liebeschuetz*); Gnomon 63 (1991) 333-6 (C. *Ulf*); Latomus 50 (1991) 477s (G. *Freyburger*).

a584 *Wlosok* Antonie, Römischer Religions- und Gottesbegriff in heidnischer und christlicher Zeit [< AntAb 16 (1970) 39-53]: ⇸ 280, Res humanae 1990, 15-34.

M4.5   **Mithraismus.**

a585 *Behn* Friedrich, Der reitende Mithras: ⇸ 13, ꟳBAETKE W., 1966, 46-49; 5 fig.

a586 *Bivar* A.D.H., ✆ Mithra and Sarapis, ᵀ*Kulandi* C.V.: VDI 198 (1991) 52-63; Eng. 63.

a587 **Clauss** M., Mithras 1990 ⇸ 6,a802 ['Claus']: ᴿGymnasium 98 (1991) 285s (H. *Opelt*).

a588 *Rosenqvist* Jan O., The hagiographical evidence of Mithraism in Trebizond; local tradition or learned design?: Eranos 89 (1991) 107-120.

a589 *Swerdlow* N. M., On the cosmical mysteries of Mithras [acceptance of ULANSEY D. requires faith rather than reason]: ClasPg 86,1 (1991) 48-63 [< NTAbs 36,77].

a590 *Turcan* Robert, Les autels du culte mithriaque: → 587, L'espace sacrificiel 1988/91, 217-225.

a591 **Ulansey** David, The origins of the Mithraic mysteries; cosmology and salvation 1989 → 5,a808; 6,a811: ᴿClasR 41 (1991) 122-4 (J. G. *Griffiths*); CritRR 4 (1991) 277-280 (L. J. *Alderink*); RelStR 17 (1991) 66 (A. T. *Kraebel*: 'Mythraic' in title).

a592 *Vollkommer* Rainer, Mithras tauroctonus – Studien zu einer Typologie der Stieropferszene auf Mithrasbildwerken: MÉF-A 103 (1991) 265-275 + 12 fig.

a593 *Will* Ernest, Mithra et les astres: Syria 67 (1990) 427-433.

M5.1   *Divinitates Graeciae* – **Greek gods and goddesses.**

a594 **Alroth** Brita, Greek gods and figurines; aspects of the anthropomorphic dedications 1989 → 6,a813: ᴿAnzAltW 44 (1991) 227-9 (W. *Pötscher*); Gnomon 63 (1991) 241-4 (Mary E. *Voyatzis*, Eng.).

a595 **Arlen** Shelley, The Cambridge ritualists; an annotated bibliography of the works by and about Jane Ellen HARRISON, Gilbert MURRAY, Francis M. CORNFORD, and Arthur B. COOK. Metuchen NJ 1990, Scarecrow. x-414 p.

a596 *a) Aubriot* Danièle, Formulations possibles du serment et conceptions religieuses en Grèce ancienne; – *b) Calame* Claude, 'Mythe' et 'rite' en Grèce; des catégories indigènes?: Kernos 4 (1991) 91-103 / 179-204.

a597 *Avagianou* Aphrodite A., ⓖ Ancient Greek religion; the anthropological-biological phenomenon of civilizational problematics [BURKERT W.]: TAth 62 (1991) 813-9; Eng. 932.

a598 *Bader* Françoise, Autobiographie et héritage dans la langue des dieux, d'Homère à Hésiode et Pindare. II: RÉG 104 (1991) 330-345.

a599 *Barringer* Judith M., Europa and the Nereids; wedding or funeral?: AJA 95 (1991) 657-667; 2 fig.

Belier Wouter W., Decayed gods; origins and development of Georges DUMÉZIL's 'Idéologie tripartite'': StudiesGrRRel 7, 1991 → a390.

a600 *Billot* M.-F., Apollon Pythéen et l'Argolide archaïque; histoire et mythos: Archaiognosia 6 (1990) 35-98; ⓖ 99s.

a601 *Bremer* Dieter, Prometheus-Variationen; ein Mythos in der Renaissance und die Renaissance eines Mythos: WienerSt 104 (1991) 261-284.

a602 **Burkert** Walter, Wilder Ursprung; Opferritual und Mythos bei den Griechen: KL.Kulturw.B 22. B 1990, Wagenbach. 95 p.

a602* *Burkert* Walter, Typen griechischer Mythen auf dem Hintergrund mykenischer und orientalischer Tradition: → 649, Transizione 1988/91, 527-536; 537s, *Brenk* Frederick E., comment on bird-epiphanies.

a603 **Burn** L., Greek myths: The legendary past. L 1990, British Museum. 80 p.; 50 fig. (map). £6. 0-7141-2061-8 [JRS 81,254].

a604 **Caldwell** Richard, The origin of the gods; a psychoanalytic study of Greek theogonic myth 1989 → 6,a825: ᴿÉtClas 59 (1991) 359 (Corinne *Bonnet*).

a605 **Clarke** Larry R., The return of the gods; transformations of the Greek gods [from their violent sacrificial origins] in nineteenth and twentieth century literature: diss. ᴰ*Casillo* R. Miami Univ. 1991. 516 p. 91-36474. – DissA 52 (1991s) 2559s-A.

a606 **Clay** Jenny S., The politics of Olympus; form and meaning in the major Homeric Hymns. Princeton 1989, Univ. xii-291 p. $37.50. – ᴿClasR 41 = 105 (1991) 12s (R. *Janko*).

a607 **Deforge** Bernard, Le commencement est un dieu ['le miracle (de la culture) grec(que)']: Vérité des Mythes. P 1990, BLettres. 189 p. – ᴿRÉG 103 (1990) 710s (Yvonne *Vernière*).

a608 **Desautels** Jacques, Dieux et mythes de la Grèce ancienne; la mythologie gréco-romaine 1988 → 6,a831: ᴿPhoenix 45 (Toronto 1991) 371-3 (M. *Lebel*).

a609 **Diel** P., El simbolismo en la mitología griega [1966], ᵀ*Satz* Mario: Labor NS 1. Barc 1991, Labor. 241 p. – ᴿArTGran 54 (1991) 461 (A. *Segovia*).

a610 **Durand** J.-L., Sacrifice et labour en Grèce ancienne 1986 → 3,b118: ᴿRÉAnc 92 (1990) 196-8 (Colette *Annequin*). → 7759.

a611 ᴱ**Edmunds** Lowell, Approaches to Greek myth 1990 → 6,a834: ᴿPhoenix 45 (Toronto 1991) 263-8 (A. *Rawn*: good).

a612 **Feeney** D. C., The gods in epic; poets and critics of the classical tradition. Ox 1991, Clarendon. xii-449 p. 0-19-814055-X.

a613 **Ferguson** John, Among the gods; an archaeological exploration of ancient Greek religion 1989 → 6,a836: ᴿAJA 95 (1991) 175s (C. G. *Simon*); JHS 111 (1991) 236s (R. *Garland*: deficiencies 'aimiably' admitted).

a614 **Forbes** Irving P. M. C., Metamorphosis in Greek myth. Ox 1990, Clarendon. 396 p. – ᴿRÉG 104 (1991) 264s (Y. *Vernière*).

a615 **Frontisi-Ducroux** Françoise, Le dieu-masque; une figure de Dionysos d'Athènes: Images à l'appui 4. P 1991, Découverte. 288 p.; 120 fig. F 270. 2-7071-2039-1.

a616 **Gimbutas** Marija [→ a399], The language of the goddess [picture-symbols as script]. L 1989, Thames & H. xxiii-387 p.; 492 fig.; 24 pl.; 13 maps. £30. – ᴿGreeceR 38 (1991) 115s (P. *Walcot*: illustrations largely from Cyclades and Crete); PrPreh Soc 57,2 (1991) 222s (C. *Renfrew*).

a616* **Goodison** Lucy, Death, women, and the sun; symbolism of regeneration in early Aegean religion; L Clas.Inst. Bulletin Supp. 53, 1989 → 6,a839: ᴿJField 18 (1991) 498-501 (Tracey *Cullen*).

a617 ᴱ**Halperin** David M., *al.*, Before sexuality; the construction of erotic experience in the ancient Greek world. 1990 → 6,487; 13 art. (including *Vernant* and Peter *Brown*; 6 inedita). – ᴿClasR 41 (1991) 159-161 (S. *Goldhill*).

a618 *Hedrick* Charles W., Phratry shrines of Attica and Athens: Hesperia 60 (1991) 241-268; 4 fig.; pl. 80.

a619 **Hernández Lucas** María Teresa, Mitología clásica; teoría y práctica docente. M 1990, Ed. Clásicas. 172 p. – ᴿGerión 9 (1991) 302s (D. *Plácido*).

a620 **Jost** Madeleine, Sanctuaires et cultes d'Arcadie 1985 → 3,b136: ᴿGnomon 63 (1991) 147-150 (U. *Sinn*).

a621 *Jourdain Annequin* Colette, Héraclès aux portes du soir; mythe et histoire: Ann. Besançon 402, HistAnc 89. Besançon/Paris 1989. 729 p. – ᴿSMSR 57 (1991) 383-6 (C. *Bonnet*).

a622 *Kahil* Lilly, Artemis, Dionysos et Pan à Athènes: Hesperia 60 (1991) 511-523; 5 fig.

a623 *a) Konstan* David, What is Greek about Greek mythology?; – *b) Rudhardt* Jean, Comprendre la religion grecque: Kernos 4 (1991) 11-30 / 47-59.

a624 *Lafond* Yves, Artémis en Achaïe: RÉG 104 (1991) 410-433.

a625 ᴱ**Linders** Tullia, *Nordquist* Gullóg, Gifts to the gods 1985/7 ► 3,866; 5,a658: ᴿJNES 50 (1991) 144-7 (G. W. *Ahlström*); RÉAnc 92 (1990) 193-5 (P. *Lévêque*).

a626 **Long** Charlotte R., The twelve gods of Greece and Rome: ÉPR 107, 1987 ► 3,b143; 6,a847: ᴿGnomon 63 (1991) 46-50 (E. *Simon*).

a627 *Mavleev* Eugen, Antike Mythologie; Sankt Petersburg und die staatliche Ermitage: MÉF-A 103 (1991) 213-222; 8 fig.

a628 **Morrison** James B., Homeric Prayers: Hermes 119 (1991) 145-157.

a629 **Müller** Claudia, Kindheit und Jugend in der griechischen Frühzeit E. Studie zur pädagogischen Bedeutung von Riten und Kulten [diss. Giessen 1988]. Giessen 1990, Focus. 189 p.

a630 **Nagy** Gregory, Greek mythology and poetics. Ithaca NY 1990, Cornell Univ. xii-363 p. 0-8014-1985-9.

a631 **Neils** Jenifer, The youthful deeds of Theseus. R 1987, Bretschneider. xii-190 p.; 17 pl.: ᴿRBgPg 69 (1991) 247s (R. *Turcan*).

a632 *Picard* Olivier, Images des dieux sur les monnaies grecques: MÉF-A 103 (1991) 223-233; 6 fig.

a632* *Pirenne-Delforge* Vinciane, Le culte de la persuasion; Peithô en Grèce ancienne: RHR 208 (1991) 395-413; Eng. 395, Peithô was a goddess in some city-states.

a633 **Pötscher** Walter, Aspekte und Probleme der minoischen Religion; ein Versuch: RelWTSt 4. Hildesheim 1990, Olms. 282 p.

a634 **Pyykkö** Vappu, Die griechischen Mythen bei den grossen Kappadokiern und Johannes CHRYSOSTOMOS: Ann. Univ. B-193. Turku 1991, Akatemin. 188 p. – ᴿWienerSt 104 (1991) 297 (H. *Schwabl*).

a635 *Ridgway* Brunilde S., Archaic architectural sculpture and travel myths: DialHistAnc 17,2 (1991) 95-112.

a636 *a)* **Robbins** Miriam, Whence the goddessses; a source book. xi-280 p. $47.50; pa. $19. – *b) Orenstein* Gloria F., The reflowering of the goddess. xxii-211 p. $47,50; pa. $18. Athens Series, NY 1990, Pergamon. 0-08-037279-1; pa. -81-3 / 0-08-035179-4; pa. -8-6 [TDig 38,148].

a637 *Roberts* Louis, The unutterable symbols of *gē-themis* reconsidered: ► 446, SBL Sem 30 (1991) 207-214.

a638 *Robertson* Noel, Some recent work in Greek religion and mythology: ÉchMClas 35 (1990) 419-442; 36 (1991) 57-79.

a639 **Rupp** David, Blazing altars; the depiction of altars in Attic vase painting: ► 587, L'espace sacrificiel 1988/91, 57-60 + 6 fig.

a640 *Rutkowski* Bogdan, Prayer (adoration) gestures in prehistoric Greece: ArchWsz 41 (1990) 9-20; 30 fig.

a641 *Salvadori Baldascino* Lina, Rileggendo P. Cornell 55; un elenco di ieromnemoni mitici?: Aegyptus 70 (1990) 205-210; 1 pl.

a642 *Sautel* Jacques-Hubert, La genèse de l'acte volontaire chez le héros homérique; les syntagmes d'incitation à l'action: RÉG 104 (1991) 346-366.

a643 **Schmitt** Arbogast, Selbständigkeit und Abhängigkeit menschlichen Handelns bei Homer; hermeneutische Untersuchungen zur Psychologie Homers: Abh Mainz g/soz 1990/5. Mainz 1990, Akad. 328 p. 3-515-05726-9.

a644 **Sihvola** Julia, Decay, progress, the good life? [Greek myths]. Helsinki 1989. – ᴿRPg 64 (1990) 226-8 (A. *Machin*).

a644* *Simon* S., The functions of priestesses in Greek society: ClasB 67,2 (1991) 9-13 [< NTAbs 36,243].

a645 **Sissa** Giulia, Greek virginity (1987), ᵀ*Goldhammer* Arthur, 1990 ➔ 6, a946; £20: ᴿClasR 41 (1991) 162-4 (Gillian *Clark*).

a645* **Sourvinou-Inwood** Christiane, 'Reading' Greek culture; texts and images, rituals and myths [7 reprints restructured]. Ox 1991, Clarendon. viii-315 p.; 17 fig. 0-19-814750-3.

a646 *Soverini* Luca, Il 'commercio nel tempio'; osservazioni sul regolamento dei *kápēloi* a Samo (SEG XXVIII, 545): Opus 9s (1990s) 59-121.

a646* *Stock* Klemens, Heilige Orte der Griechen: Entschluss 46 (1991) 16-18.

a647 **Tyrrell** William B., *Brown* Frieda S., Athenian myths and institutions; words in action. NY 1991, Oxford-UP. ix-229 p. 0-19-506719-3.

a648 *Walcot* Peter, The Homeric Hymn to Aphrodite; a literary appraisal: GreeceR 38 (1991) 137-155.

a649 **Weglage** Matthias, Leid und Erkenntnis; zum Zeus-Hymnus im aischyleischen 'Agamemnon': Hermes 119 (1991) 265-281.

a650 **Weiss** Carina, Griechische Flussgottheiten in vorhellenistischer Zeit; Ikonographie und Bedeutung: BeitArchäologie 17. Wü 1984, Triltsch. 256 p.; 16 pl. 3-87825-040-1. – ᴿBabesch 66 (1991) 191s (R. W. M. *Schumacher*).

a651 [Bruit-]**Zaidman** Louise, *Schmitt-Pantel* Pauline, La religion grecque: Cursus 1989 ➔ 6,a823: ᴿKernos 4 (1991) 331-3 (Annie *Verbanck- Piérard*); RBgPg 69 (1991) 229s (E. *Guillaume*); RÉAnc 93 (1991) 201s (M. M. *Mactoux*).

M5.2   *Philosophorum critica religionis;*   **Greek philosopher-religion.**

a653 *Ballabriga* Alain, L'anthropologie de la Grèce ancienne entre l'histoire et la structure: ArScSocR 35,70s (1990) 177-184 [< ZIT 90,863].

a654 **Barnes** Jonathan, The toils of scepticism. C 1990, Univ. 161 p. – ᴿElenchos 12 (1991) 342-9 (A. *Alberti*).

a655 *Bennahmias* [p. 261; Bennhamias 264 & iv] Richard, La *stoa*, une religion pour le XXIᵉ siècle? [DARAKI Maria, Une religiosité sans Dieu... et AUGUSTIN 1989]: ÉTRel 66 (1991) 261-4.

a656 *Blanchard* Alain, ÉPICURE, 'sentence vaticane' 14; Épicure ou Métrodore?: RÉG 104 (1991) 394-409.

a657 **Bortolotti** Arrigo, La religione nel pensiero di Platone [I. dai primi dialoghi al Fedro 1986], II. dalla Repubblica agli ultimi scritti: Accad. Toscana Studi 114. F 1991, Olschki. 297 p. 88-222[3664-6]-3834-6.

a658 *a)* *Brenk* Frederick E., Tempo come struttura nel dialogo 'Sul *daimonion* di Socrate' di Plutarco ['*daimonion* è mondo dei daímones']; – *b)* *Fernández Delgado* José Antonio, Los proverbios en los 'Moralia' de Plutarco: ➔ 585, Strutture di Plutarco (1989/91) 69-82 / 195-212.

a659 ᴱ**Broek** R. van den, *al.*, Knowledge of God in the Graeco-Roman world: ÉPR 112, 1988 ➔ 4,b712; 5,a882: ᴿNedTTs 45 (1991) 61s (J. J. W. *Drijvers*).

a660 **Desjardins** Rosemary, The rational enterprise; *logos* in PLATO's Theaetetus. Albany 1990, SUNY. x-275 p. $45; pa. $17 [RelStR 18,229, J. P. *Hershbell*].

a661 ᵀᴱ**Dillon** John, *Hershbell* Jackson, IAMBLICHUS, On the Pythagorean way of life: SBL TTr 29, GrR 11. Atlanta 1991, Scholars. ix-285 p. 1-55540-522-3.

a661* **Engberg-Pedersen** T., The Stoic theory of *oikeiosis*; moral development and social interaction in early Stoic philosophy: StHellenCiv 2. Aarhus 1990, Univ. 278 p. Dk 162. 87-7288-323-5 [NTAbs 36,292].

a662 ᴱ**Everson** Stephen, Companions to ancient thought, 1. Epistemology; 2. Psychology. C 1990s, Univ. 288 p.; 269 p. £11 (each). – ᴿArctos 25 (1991) 206s (R. *Westman*, deutsch).

a663 *Fago* Angelica, Mito esiodeo delle razze e *logos* platonico della *psyché*; una comparazione storico-religiosa: SMSR 57 (1989) 221-251.

a664 *Garrison* Elise P., Attitudes toward suicide in ancient Greece: AmPgTr 121 (1991) 1-34.

a665 **Gerson** L. P., God and Greek philosophy; studies in the early history of natural theology. L 1990, Routledge. xi-340 p. 0-415-03486-8.

a666 ᴱ**Giannantoni** Gabriele, Socratis et Socraticorum reliquiae: Elenchos 18/1-4. N 1990, Bibliopolis. I. biographica, xi-521 p.; II. Socratici, xi-632 p.; III. indice 301 p.; IV. 56 note, ix-609 p. 88-7088-215-2 all.

a667 **Hossenfelder** Malte, Epikur: BsR 520. Mü 1991, Beck. 177 p. 3-406-34632-4.

a668 **Irwin** Terence, Classical thought: History of western philosophy 1. Ox 1989, UP. xii-206 p. – ᴿRÉG 104 (1991) 630 (A. *Laks*).

a669 *Jedrkiewicz* Stefano, Alterità e saggezza; un aspetto dell'intellettuale nel mondo greco: Clio 25 (R 1989) 199-209.

a670 **Long** Antony A., La filosofia ellenistica; stoici, epucurei e scettici [1974, ²1986], ᵀ*Calzolari* Alessandro: Univ.-pa. 232. Bo 1991, Mulino. [vi-] 355 p. 88-15-03253-3.

a671 **Loraux** Nicole, Il femminile e l'uomo greco [Expériences de Térésias], ᵀ*Guidobaldi* Maria P. (cap. 5s, *Botteri* Paola): Coll. Storica. R 1981, Laterza. xxvi-380 p. 88-420-3840-7.

a671* *Places* Édouard, Chronique de la philosophie religieuse des Grecs (1987-1991): BBudé (1991) 414-429.

a672 **Prior** William J., Virtue and knowledge; an introduction to ancient Greek ethics. L 1991, Routledge. xi-240 p. 0-415-02490-6.

a673 *Rămureanu* Ioan, La conception platonicienne de l'âme: STBuc 39,4 (1987) 27-43 (roum.).

a674 ᴱ**Russell** D. A., ☺ An anthology of Greek prose. Ox 1991, Clarendon. xxxviii-289 p. 0-19-814498-9; pa. -72122-6.

a675 **Saffrey** H. D., Recherches sur le néoplatonisme après PLOTIN: Hist. Doct. Ant. Clas. 14, 1990 ⊁ 6,a921*; F 210: ᴿRSPT 75 (1991) 180s (J.-P. *Jossua*).

a677 *Schmoll* Edward A., The manuscript tradition of XENOPHON's Apologia Socratis: GrRByz 31 (1990) 313-321.

a678 **Spiegel** Nathan, War and peace in classical Greek literature. J 1990, Magnes. 288 p. – ᴿRÉG 104 (1991) 632 (Yvonne *Vernière*: not erudition but plea for brotherhood).

a679 *Splett* Jörg, Die Wahrheit und das Gute; Sokrates und die Geburt der Metaphysik: TPhil 66 (1991) 216-225.

a680 **Vegetti** M., L'etica degli antichi [... Omero a Plotino]. Bari 1989. 321 p. Lit. 30.000. – ᴿProtestantesimo 46 (1991) 156-8 (Elena *Bein Ricco*).

a681 **Vernant** Jean-Pierre, L'individu, la mort, l'amour; soi-même et l'autre en Grèce ancienne. P 1989, Gallimard. 232 p. – ᴿRÉG 103 (1990) 711-3 (Hélène *Cassimatis*).

a681* ᴱ**Voelke** André-Jean, Le scepticisme antique 1989/90 ⊁ 6,771: ᴿRPg 64 (1990) 220-3 (D. *Babut*).

a682 ᴱWalzer R. R., *Mingay* J. M., ARISTOTELIS Ethica Eudemia: ScrClas-BtOxon. Ox 1991, Clarendon. xx-162 p. 0-19-814575-6.
a683 **Winkler** John J., The constraints of desire; the anthropology of sex and gender in ancient Greece. NY 1990, Routledge. x-269 p. $47.50; pa. $25. – ᴿAmHR 96 (1991) 1174s (Eva C. *Keuls*).

M5.3 Mysteria Eleusinia; Hellenistica; Mysteries, Hellenistic cults.

a684 *Ammermatt* Rebecca M., The religious context of Hellenistic terracotta figurines: ➤ 154, Coroplast 1990, 37-46; fig. 26-36.
a685 **Avagianou** Aphrodite, Sacred marriage in the rituals of Greek religion [diss. Zurich, ᴰ*Burkert* W., 1991]: EurHS 15/54. Bern 1991, Lang. xv-280 p. 3-261-04432-2.
a686 *Brown* Christopher G., *a*) Honoring the goddess; PHILICUS, hymn to Demeter: Aegyptus 70 (1990) 173-189; – *b*) The prayers of the Corinthian women (SIMONIDES, Ep. 15 Page FGE): GrRByz 32 (1991) 5-14.
a687 **Burkert** Walter, Ancient mystery cults 1987 ➤ 3,b103 ... 6,a934*: ᴿRÉG 104 (1991) 605s (J.-F. *Balaudé*).
a688 **Burkert** Walter, Antichi culti misterici, ᵀ*Falivene* Maria R.: BtUniv. Bari 1991, Laterza. viii-227 p. 88-420-3720-6.
a688* *a*) *Burkert* Walter, Antike Mysterien, eine Einführung; – *b*) *März* Claus-Peter, Initiation und Initiationsriten; – *c*) *Zeller* Dieter, Sterbende Götter als Identifikationsfiguren; – *d*) *Söding* Thomas, Eucharistie und Mysterien; – *e*) *Bauer* Dieter, Mithras: BiKi 45 (1990) 118-124 / 125-131 / 132-9 / 140-5 / 146-158; ill.
a689 **Colli** Giorgio † 1979, La sagesse grecque I. Dionysos, Apollon, Eleusis, Orphée, Musée, Hyperboréens, Énigme [1977], ᵀ*Tramuta* Marie-José. P 1990, Éclat. 462 p. F 250. – ᴿÉtudes 347 (1991) 280 (A. *Jeannière*: + 2 autres volumes + 8 inachevés; pour ne pas privilégier le courant pré-socratique).
a690 **Daniel** Robert W., *Maltomini* Franco, Supplementum magicum I [zu *Preisendanz* K.]: PapyrColon 16,1. Opladen 1990, Westdeutscher-V. xxiv-213 p.; VIII pl. – ᴿWienerSt 104 (1991) 289 (Christine *Harrauer*).
a691 **Dörrie** Heinrich, †, ᴱ*Baltes* Matthias, *al.*, Der hellenistische Rahmen des kaiserzeitlichen Platonismus: Bausteine 36-72. Stu-Bad Cannstatt 1990, Frommann-Holzboog. xvi-531 p. DM 550. – ᴿDLZ 112 (1991) 165 (F. *Jürss*); TPhil 66 (1991) 103-5 (E. *Ricken*).
a692 *Dowden* Ken, Death and the maiden 1989 ➤ 6,a937: ᴿHZ 253 (1991) 697-9 (F. *Graf*).
a693 *Downing* C., Only the wounded healer heals; the testimony of Greek mythology: Soundings 73 (Nv 1990) 551-573 [< NTAbs 36,92].
a693* **Erskine** Andrew, The Hellenistic stoa; political thought and action. L 1990, Duckworth. xii-233 p. £30. – ᴿClasR 41 (1991) 105s (P. *Cartledge*).
ᴱ**Faraone** Christopher A., Magika hiera 1991 ➤ 392.
a694 **Freyburger-Galland** Marie-Laure, *al.*, Sectes religieuses en Grèce et à Rome dans l'antiquité 1986 ➤ 2,8877 ... 5,a843: ᴿWienerSt 104 (1991) 295-7 (Christine *Harrauer*).
a695 *Funck* Bernd, Herrscherkult der Seleukiden – Religion einer Elite oder Reichsideologie? Einige Bemerkungen zur Fragestellung: Klio 73 (1991) 402-7.
a696 **Gill** David, Greek cult tables [diss. Harvard 1964]: Harvard Diss. Clas. NY 1991, Garland. xvi-91 p.; 37 fig.; 35 pl. 0-8153-0448-X.

a697 *Hedreen* Guy, The cult of Achilles in the Euxine [to 200 A.D.]: Hesperia 60 (1991) 313-330.

a698 **Hopfner** Theodor. PLUTARCHUS... über Isis und Osiris, I. Die Sage; II. Die Deutung der Sage. Hildesheim 1991 (= Praha 1940s), Olms. xiv-313 p.; ill.; map. 3-487-05051-X.

a699 *Kloos* John, The phallus-bearing winnow and initiation into the Dionysiac mysteries: JRelSt 16 (Cleveland 1988) 65-75 [< ZIT 90,865].

a700 **Malkin** Irad, Religion and colonization in ancient Greece 1987 ➤ 4, b762; 5,a866: ᴿRÉAnc 92 (1990) 194-6 (C. *Mossé*).

a701 **Martin** Luther H., Hellenistic religions, an introduction 1987 ➤ 3,b151 ... 5,a870: ᴿCritRR 4 (1991) 275-7 (J. D. *Tabor*).

a701* ᴱ**Merkelbach** Reinhold, *Totti* Maria, Abrasax; ausgewählte Papyri religiösen und magischen Inhalts 1. Gebete, 1990 ➤ 6,a945: ᴿClasR 41 (1991) 378s (J. G. *Griffiths*).

a702 **Nasemann** Beate, Theurgie und Philosophie in JAMBLICHs De mysteriis: BeitAltK 11. Stu 1991, Teubner. 320 p. 3-519-07460-5.

a702* ᴱ**Places** E. des, JAMBLIQUE, Protreptique 1989 ➤ 6,a912: ᴿRÉAnc 93 (1991) 161s (Jeannie *Carlier*).

a703 *Rămureanu* Ioan, La religion solaire de l'empereur Julien l'Apostat [en roum.]: STBuc 396 (1987) 38-60.

a704 *Ribichini* Sergio, La magia nel mondo antico: Archeo 54 (1989) 45-91.

a706 **Sfameni Gasparro** Giulia, Misteri e culti mistici di Demetra: Storia delle Religioni 3. R 1986, Bretschneider. 371 p. – ᴿTR 87 (1991) 199 (Maria-B. von *Stritzky*: 'DM 0.00').

a707 *Verrycken* Koenraad, La psychologie platonicienne dans l'œuvre de Philopon [490-570]: RSPT 75 (1991) 211-234; Eng. 234.

a708 ᴱ**Winiarczyk** Marcus, EUHEMERI Messenii reliqviae: BtScrGR. Stu 1991, Teubner. xxxvii-76 p. 3-8154-1957-3.

M5.5   **Religiones anatolicae.**

a709 *Badalì* Enrico, Il concetto di sangue presso gli Ittiti II; riflessioni alla luce dei testi religioso-cultuali e mitologici: ➤ 565, Sangue 1989/91, 429-471.

a710 *Cole* Susan G., Dionysiac mysteries in Phrygia in the imperial period: EpAnat 17 (1991) 41-49: ⏺ 49.

a711 *Gočeva* Zlatozara, Le culte des Cabires et des nymphes en Asie Mineure et en Thrace: Eos 79 (1991) 199-202.

a712 **Hoffner** Harry A.ᴶ, [22] Hittite myths: SBL Writings 2, 1990 ➤ 6,a960; $20; sb./pa. $13. 1-55540-481-2; pa. -2-0: ᴿOTAbs 14 (1991) 341 (R. E. *Murphy*).

a712* *Hout* Theo P.J. van den, A tale of Tiššaruli(ya); a dramatic interlude in the Hittite KI.LAM festival: JNES 50 (1991) 193-202.

a713 **Hutter** M., Behexung, Entsühnung...: OBO 82, 1988 ➤ 4,b815 ... 6,a961: ᴿWeltOr 22 (1991) 202-7 (J. *Klinger*).

a714 *Hutter* Manfred, Bemerkungen zur Verwendung magischer Rituale in mittelhethitischer Zeit: AltOrF 18 (1991) 32-43.

a715 **Jakob-Rost** Liane, Hethitische Rituale ➤ 5,a926; 6,a963: ᴿOrientalia 60 (1991) 124-7 (M. *Popko*: zahlreiche Vorschläge).

a716 **McMahon** Gregory, The Hittite state cult of the tutelary deities: Assyriological Studies 25. Ch 1991, Univ. Oriental Inst. xxi-302 p. 0-918986-69-9.

a717 **Masson** Émilia, Le combat pour l'immortalité; héritage indo-européen dans la mythologie anatolienne: Ethnologies. P 1991, PUF. ii-318 p.; 20 pl. F 198. 2-13-043775-3 [BO 48,985].

a718 **Masson** Émilia, Les douze dieux de l'immortalité... Yazilikaya 1989 ➤ 5,a928: ᴿRÉG 104 (1991) 262s (F. *Jouan*); Syria 67 (1990) 531-4 (J. *Freu*).

a720 **Popko** M., Hethitische Rituale 1988 ➤ 4,b824; 6,a966: ᴿAfO 36s (1989s) 174s (J. *Tischler*); BO 48 (1991) 579-585 (T. van den *Hout*).

a721 *Roller* Lynn E., The Great Mother at Gordion; the Hellenization of an Anatolian cult: JHS 111 (1991) 128-143.

a722 **Wegner** Ilse, *Salvini* Mirjo, Die hethitisch-hurritischen Ritualtafeln des (ḫ)išuwa-Festes: CorpusHurrit 1/4. R 1991 Multigrafica. xix-319 p. [OIAc 1,27].

a722* *Yoshida* Daisuke, Ein Hethitisches Ritual gegen Behexung (KUB XXIV) und der Gott Zilipuri/Zalipura: ➤ 402, Anatolia 1991, 45-61.

M6 **Religio canaanaea, syra.**

a723 *Albertz* Rainer, Magie AT: ➤ 690, TRE 21 (1991) 691-5.

a724 *Amadasi Guzzo* Maria Giulia, Tanit-ʿŠTRT e Milk-ʿŠTRT; ipotesi: Orientalia 60,2 (1991) 82-91.

a725 **Anderson** Gary A., A time to mourn, a time to dance; the expression of grief and joy in Israelite religion. Univ. Park 1991, Penn State Univ. xvii-139 p. $28.50. 0-271-00729-X.

a726 **Barker** Margaret, The older testament 1987 ➤ 3,b327... 6,a970: ᴿBib-TB 21 (1991) 76s (L. E. *Frizzell*).

a727 **Baudler** Georg, Erlösung vom Stiergott; Christliche Gotteserfahrung im Dialog mit Mythen und Religionen 1989 ➤ 6,a971: ᴿTLZ 116 (1991) 99-101 (P. *Heidrich*); TR 87 (1991) 241s (H. *Waldenfels*).

a728 **Beltz** Walter, Gott und die Götter; biblische Mythologie⁶ [¹1975]: Dokumentation, Essayistik, Literaturwissenschaft. B 1990, Aufbau. 323 p. 3-351-00976-3.

a729 **Block** Daniel J., The gods of the nations; studies in Ancient Near Eastern national theology [... Yahweh as a national deity committed to a people and a territory]: [J]EvTS Mg 2, 1988 ➤ 5,a939; 6,a973: ᴿBL (1991) 124 (N. *Wyatt*: aims to be fair); CritRR 4 (1991) 105-7 (R. K. *Gnuse*); VT 41 (1991) 488s (J. *Day*, caveats).

a730 **Bonnet** Corinne, Melqart 1988 ➤ 4,b839... 6,a974: ᴿJNES 50 (1991) 303s (D. *Pardee*); RArchéol (1991) 130s (Susan B. *Downey*, Eng.: healthily 'reductive'); RÉAnc 92 (1990) 446-9 (C. *Jourdain-Annequin*); SMSR 57 (1991) 178-182 (Maria G. *Amadasi Guzzo*).

a731 *Bonnet* Corinne, Tinnit, sœur cadette d'Astarté? À propos des cultes de Deir el-Qalʿa près de Beyrouth: WeltOr 22 (1991) 73-84.

a732 *Bordreuil* Pierre, *Gatier* Pierre-Louis, Le relief du prêtre Philôtas: Syria 67 (1990) 329-338; 3 fig.

a732* *a) Braulik* Georg, Die Ablehnung der Göttin Aschera in Israel; war sie erst deuteronomistisch, diente sie der Unterdrückung der Frauen; – *b)* Antwort, *Wacker* Marie-T.; – *c) Jüngling* Hans-W., Bemerkungen zur Wechselwirkung zwischen den Auffassungen von der Frau und der Darstellung von Göttinnen; – *d) Schüngel-Straumann* Helen, Weibliche Dimensionen in mesopotamischen und alttestamentlichen Schöpfungsaussagen und ihre feministische Kritik; – *e) Schroer* Silvia, Die göttliche Weisheit und der nachexilische Monotheismus [Antwort *Vanoni* Gottfried]: ➤ 385c, Gott/Göttin 1991, 106-136 / 137-150 (17-48) / 82-105 / 49-81 / 151-182 (-190).

a733 ᴱCaquot A., Tarragon J.-M. de, Textes ougaritiques II. Textes religieux et rituels; correspondance: LAPO 14, 1989 ➤ 5,a944; 6,a979: ᴿAbr-Nahrain 29 (1991) 130-5 (W. G. E. Watson); NRT 113 (1991) 101s (J.-L. Ska).

a734 ᶠCROSS Frank M., Ancient Israelite religion, ᴱMiller P. D., al., 1987 ➤ 3,42... 6,a981: ᴿHenoch 12 (1990) 371-5 (B. Chiesa: tit. pp. commenti).

a735 Day J., Molech 1989 ➤ 5,a948: ᴿBL (1991) 108 (W. G. E. Watson); BSO 54 (1991) 358 (J. D. Martin); JJS 42 (1991) 261-3 (J. Hughes); NedTTs 45 (1991) 337 K. A. D. Smelik); TLZ 116 (1991) 348-350 (E. Otto: 4-mal im AT: Lev 18,21; 20,2-5; Jer 32,35; 2K 23,10); ZAW 103 (1991) 294 (O. Kaiser).

a736 Eilbert-Schwartz Howard, The savage in... Israelite religion 1990 ➤ 6,a985: ᴿJStJud 22 (1991) 131-4 (H. Maccoby).

a737 a) Good Robert M., On RS 24.252 [Rapi'u]; – b) Fleming D., The voice of the Ugaritic incantation priest (RIH 78/20); – c) Gordon Robert P., [Mi 5,4s] K/kȋ/ky in incantational incipits; UF 23 (1991) 155-160 / 141-154 / 161-3.

a738 Hadley J. M., a) Yahweh's Asherah in the light of recent discovery: diss. Cambridge 1989. – ZAHeb 5, 22 n. 17; – b) Some drawings and inscriptions on two pithoi from Kuntillet ʿAjrud: VT 37 (1987) 180-211.

a738* a) Hess Richard S., Yahweh and his Asherah? Epigraphic evidence for religious pluralism in OT times; – b) Goldingay John E., Wright Christopher J. H., 'Yahweh our God Yahweh one'; the OT and religious pluralism: ➤ 485, One God 1991, 5-33 / 34-52.

a739 Hestrin Ruth, Understanding Asherah; exploring Semitic iconography: BAR-W 17,5 (1991) 50-59; (color.) ill.

a740 Houston George W., The altar from Rome with inscriptions to Sol and Malakbel: Syria 67 (1990) 189-193.

a741 Hvidberg-Hansen F. O., Kanaʿanæiske myter og legender: ᴿRStFen 19 (1991) 131s (P. Xella).

a742 Jaramillo M., Julio, La experiencia religiosa de Israel I: Medellín 17,66 (1991) 149 ...

a743 a) Katzenstein H. J., Phoenician deities worshipped in Israel and Judah during the time of the First Temple; – b) Lust J., Molek and Archōn; ➤ 445, Phoenicia 1990/1, 187-191 / 193-208.

a744 Korpel M. C. A., A rift in the clouds; Ugaritic and Hebrew descriptions of the divine ᴰ1990 ➤ 6,a995: ᴿBL (1991) 113 (W. G. E. Watson); ETL 67 (1991) 160s (W. A. M. Beuken); RHPR 71 (1991) 221 (J. G. Heintz); ZAW 103 (1991) 300 (H. Wahl).

a746 Lambert W. G., Metal-working and its patron deities in the early Levant [Dalley S., Rep Cypr (1987) 61-66]: Levant 23 (1991) 183-6; 187, Dalley response.

a747 Lewis Theodore J., Cults of the dead in ancient Israel and Ugarit: HarvSemMg 39, 1989 ➤ 5,a961: ᴿBO 48 (1991) 234-240 (K. Spronk: nevertheless useful); CBQ 53 (1991) 108-110 (J. W. Betlyon); JBL 110 (1991) 327-330 (Elizabeth M. Bloch-Smith); Syria 67 (1990) 755s (A. Caquot); VT 41 (1991) 383s (J. A. Emerton).

a748 Moor Johannes C. De, The rise of Yahwism; the roots of Israelite monotheism: BtETL 91, 1990 ➤ 6,7022: ᴿBiblica 72 (1991) 103-7 (S. Norin); CBQ 53 (1991) 297-301 (M. S. Smith, at length in accord with the book's challenging complexity); RHPR 71 (1991) 251-7 (J.-G. *Heintz*); VT 41 (1991) 502s (A. *Lemaire*).

a749 **Moor** Johannes C. De, An anthology of religious texts from Ugarit: NISABA 16, 1987 → 3,b265*a*... 6,b1: ᴿOLZ 86 (1991) 391-3 (W. *Herrmann*).

a750 **Moor** J. De, *Spronk* K., A cuneiform anthology of religious texts from Ugarit 1987 → 3,b265... 6,b2: ᴿAfO 36s (1989s) 177-9 (D. *Pardee*: ventures some restorations); OLZ 86 (1991) 502s (W. *Herrmann*).

a751 *Muchiki* Yoshi, The unidentified god *Pmy* in Phoenician texts: JSS 36 (1991) 7-10: a lion-god.

a752 **Niehr** Herbert, Der höchste Gott; alttestamentlicher JHWH-Glaube im Kontext syrisch-kanaanäischer Religion des 1. Jahrtausends v.Chr [Hab.-Diss. Würzburg 1989]: BZAW 190, 1990 → 6,b3: ᴿJBL 110 (1991) 698-701 (D. R. *Daniels*); ZAW 103 (1991) 165 (H.-C. *Schmitt*).

a753 **Olyan** Saul M., Ashera &... Y. 1988 → 4,b871... 6,b5: ᴿRelStT 9,2 (1989) 105s (Yvonne B. *Cross*, 'Oylan').

a754 **Page** Hugh R.ᴶ, [Gn 6,1-4; Isa 14,4-20; Ezek 28,1-19; Ps 82; Dan 11,21-45; Ugarit Athtar] The astral revolt; a study of its reflexes in Canaanite and Hebrew literature: diss. Harvard. CM 1990. 250 p. 91-13246 – HarvTR 84 (1991) 474; DissA 51 (1990s) 4104-A.

a755 **Patai** Raphael, The Hebrew goddess³ʳᵉᵛ [¹1967]: Jewish Folklore and Anthropology. Detroit 1990, Wayne State Univ. 368 p. 0-8143-2221-2; pa. -71-9.

a756 **Pettey** Richard J., Asherah, Goddess of Israel: AmerUnivSt 7/74. NY 1990, Lang. x-231 p. 0-8204-1306-2.

a757 **Pike** Dana M., Israelite theophoric personal names in the Bible and their implications for religious history: diss. Pennsylvania, ᴰ*Tigay* J. Ph 1990. 448 p. – 91-12609. – DissA 51 (1990s) 4159-A.

a759 *Provera* Mario, Il culto lunare nella tradizione biblica e profana: BbbOr 33 (1991) 65-68.

a759* *Rendtorff* Rolf, Die Entwicklung des altisraelitischen Festkalenders: → 338, ᴱ*Assmann* J., Fest 1988/91, 185-205 [206-233 *Klinghardt* Matthias, Sabbat].

a760 *Schenker* Adrian, Elemente volkstümlicher Religion im Alten Testament [< ᴱ*Baumgartner* J., Wiederentdeckung der Volksreligiosität 1979, 11-23]: → 258, Text 1991, 55-67.

a761 **Smith** Mark S., The early history of God; Yahweh and the other deities in ancient Israel 1990 → 6,b11: ᴿCurrTMiss 18 (1991) 141 (R. W. *Klein*); JBL 110 (1991) 693-8 (D. N. *Freedman*, in comparing with De Moor, sees 'provisionally established that Yahweh had a consort'); OTAbs 14 (1991) 105s (A. *Cody*); TS 52 (1991) 347-9 (M. D. *Guinan*).

a762 **Stähli** Hans-Peter, Solare Elemente im Jahweglauben des ATs: OBO 66, 1985 → 1,6266... 4,b877: ᴿJAOS 111 (1991) 128-130 (J. G. *Taylor*: poor use of the evidence); TorJT 7 (1991) 248 (also J. G. *Taylor*).

a763 *Stolz* Fritz, Probleme westsemitischer und israelitischer Religionsgeschichte: TRu 56 (1991) 1-26.

a764 **Tigay** J., You shall have no other gods 1986 → 3,b276... 6,b14: ᴿIsrEJ 41 (1991) 224-6 (A. *Millard*).

a765 **Walls** Neal H.ᴶ, The goddess Anat in Ugaritic myth: diss. Johns Hopkins. Baltimore 1991. 331 p. 91-32747. – DissA 52 (1991s) 2176-A.

a766 *a*) *Wiggins* Steve A., The myth of Asherah; lion lady and serpent goddess; – *b*) *Izre'el* Shlomo, A god Rib(b)ān in Ugarit?; – *c*) *West* David R., Some Minoan and Hellenic goddesses of Semitic origin / Gello and Lamia, two Hellenic daemons of Semitic origin: UF 23 (1991) 381-393 + 3 fig. / 217s / 369-381 . 361-8.

a767 **Xella** Paolo, Baal Hammon; recherches sur l'identité et l'histoire d'un dieu phénico-punique: CollStFen 32. R 1991, Cons.Naz.Ric. 248 p.; XII pl. – ᴿRHR 208 (1991) 442-4 (A. *Caquot*); UF 23 (1991) 453s (O. *Loretz*).

a768 *Yon* M., *Gachet* J., Une statuette du dieu El à Ougarit: Syria 66 (1989) 349; phot.

a769 *Zangenberg* Jürgen, Religion der Nabatäer / Bestattungssitten: ➤ d511, ᴱ**Lindner** M. Petra 1991, 26-36 / 79-82.

a770 *Zevit* Ziony, Yahweh worship and worshippers in 8th-century Syria: VT 41 (1991) 363-6.

M6.5 **Religio aegyptia.**

a771 **Assmann** Jan, Maat; l'Égypte pharaonique et l'idée de justice sociale [➤ 6,b20],ᵀ. P 1989, Julliard. 172 p. 2-260-00671-X. – ᴿBO 48 (1991) 479-481 (V. A. *Tobin*).

a771* *a) Attiatallah* Hazim, Der Monotheismus vor Echnatons Zeit; – *b) McFarlane* Ann, Titles of *sm3* + god and *ḫt* + god; dynasties 2 to 10: GöMiszÄg 121 (1991) 19-24 / 77-101.

a772 *a) Aubert* Jean-Jacques, The appointment of temple personnel in the second century A.D.; P. Col. Inv. 438: BASP 28 (1991) 101-120. – *b) Baines* John, Egyptian myth and discourse; myth, gods, and the early written and iconographic record: JNES 50 (1991) 81-105.

a773 *a) Baines* John, On the symbolic content of the principal hieroglyph for 'god'; – *b) Quaegebeur* Jan, Les quatre dieux Min; – *c) Traunecker* Claude. De l'hiérophanie au temple; quelques réflexions; – *d) Boochs* Wolfgang, Religiöse Strafen: ➤ 43, ᶠDᴇʀᴄʜᴀɪɴ P., Religion 1991, 29-45; 7 fig. (captions p. 45) / 253-265 + 3 pl. / 303-317 / 57-64.

a773* *a) Banna* Essam el-, Une stèle inédite d'un prêtre-*ouab* d'Hathor-Nébet-Hétépet: GöMiszÄg 124 (1991) 7-18 + 2 fig. – *b) Barta* Winfried; Zur Überlieferung des Opferrituals der Pyramidentexte auf Privatsärgen des Mittleren Reiches: GöMiszÄg 120 (1991) 7-12.

a774 *a) Barta* Winfried, Zur grammatischen Bedeutung synkretistisch verbundener Götternamen am Beispiel der Namen von Re und Amun; – *b) Felber* H. M., Augustus *Zeùs eleuthérios* im Demotischen und die Etymologie von RM2E; – *c) Tooley* Angela M. J., Child's toy or ritual object?: GöMiszÄg 123 (1991) 7-10 / 27-36 / 101-111.

Beinlich Horst, Das Buch vom Fayum; zum religiösen Eigenverständnis einer ägyptischen Landschaft: ÄgAbh 51, 1991 ➤ d953.

a775 *a) Bickel* Susanne, L'iconographie du dieu Khnoum; – *b) Cauville* Sylvie, Dieux et prêtres à Dendéra au I s. av.J.C.: BIFAO 91 (1991) 55-67; 13 fig. / 69-97; 3 fig.; pl. XXXII.

a775* *Bolshakov* Andrey O., The moment of the establishment of the tomb-cult in ancient Egypt: AltOrF 18 (1991) 204-218.

a776 **Bomann** Ann H., The private chapel in ancient Egypt; a study of the chapels in the workmen's village at El Amarna with special reference to Deir el Medina and other sites [diss. Birmingham 1987]. L 1991, Kegan Paul. xiv-144 p.; 84 fig. 0-7103-0346-7.

a777 *Bresciani* Edda, L'Egitto antico e il problema della morte: FilT 4 (1990) 260-270.

a778 **Brunner** Hellmut, Altägyptische Religion [¹1983; ²1988]: Grundzüge. Da 1989, Wiss. vii-159 p. ...-08424-1.

a779 **Brunner** H., Das hörende Herz 1988 ➤ 4,169: ᴿJAOS 111 (1991) 185s (A. R. *Schulman*).

a780 *Daszewski* Wiktor A., The gods of the north-west coast of Egypt in the Graeco-Roman period: MÉF-A 103 (1991) 91-104; 10 fig.

a781 ᴱ**Delvaux** Luc, *Warmenbol* Eugène, Les divins chats d'Égypte; un air subtil, un dangereux parfum. Lv 1991, Peeters. ix-185 p.; 73 fig. 90-6831-362-2.

a782 **Derchain-Urtel** M.-T., Priester im Tempel... Edfu, Dendera 1989 ➤ 5,a996: ᴿBL (1991) 125 (K. A. *Kitchen*: full but fragile); OLZ 86 (1991) 271s (J. *Hallof*).

a783 **Dunand** Françoise, *Zivie-Coche* Christiane, Dieux et hommes en Égypte 3000 av.J.-C. - 395 apr.J.-C.; anthropologie religieuse. P 1991, Colin. 367 p. map.

a784 **Eingartner** Johannes, Isis und ihre Dienerinnen in der Kunst der römischen Kaiserzeit: Mnemosyne supp. 15. Leiden 1991, Brill. xi-197 p.; 99 pl. *f* 140. 90-04-09312-5 [JRS 81,257].

a785 ᴱ**Englund** Gertie, The religion of the ancient Egyptians 1988 ➤ 5,842: ᴿBO 48 (1991) 474-8 (L. *Kákosy*).

a786 **Fazzini** Richard A., Egypt dynasty XXII-XXV: IconRel 16/10, 1988 ➤ 4,b901 ... 6,b37: ᴿJEA 77 (1991) 222s (J. G. *Griffiths*).

a787 *Fitzenreiter* M., *Schrammek* N., Tempel am Nil, Struktur und Funktion: [Tagung] Univ. Berlin 22.-25.X.1990: Orientalia 60 (1991) 347-9.

a788 **Gasse** Annie, Données nouvelles administratives et sacerdotales sur l'organisation du Domaine d'Amon, XXᵉ-XXIᵉ Dynastie, à la lumière des papyrus Prachov, Reinhardt et Grundbuch (avec édition princeps des papyrus Louvre AF 6345 et 6346-7): IFAO BÉt 104, 1988 ➤ 5,b7: ᴿEnchoria 18 (1991) 217-227 (S. P. *Vleeming*).

a788* *Goedicke* Hans, The prayers of Wakh-ʿAnkh-Antef-ʿAa: JNES 50 (1991) 235-253.

a789 **Guglielmi** Waltraud, Die Göttin Mr.t; Entstehung und Verehrung einer Personifikation: ProbÄg 7. Leiden 1991, Brill. xi-346 p.; XVI pl. 90-04-08814-8 [BO 48,982].

a790 *Guglielmi* Waltraud, Zur Bedeutung von Symbolen der persönlichen Frömmigkeit: die verschiedenfarbigen Ohren und das Ka-Zeichen: Zäg-Spr 118 (1991) 116-127; 4 fig.

a791 **Hart** George, A dictionary of Egyptian gods and goddesses. L 1990 [= 1986 ➤ 2,9024]. Routledge. xv-229 p.; ill.; maps. 0-415-05909-7.

a792 ᴱ**Helck** W., Tempel und Kult 1986/7 ➤ 3,818.b313 ... 6,b43: ᴿWeltOr 22 (1991) 178-180 (Malte *Römer*).

a792* *Helck* Wolfgang, Ein früher Beleg für eine Kultgenossenschaft: StAäK 18 (1991) 233-8 + 2 Faksim.

a793 *a) Helck* Wolfgang, Zu Ptah und Sokar; – *b) Altenmüller* Hartwig, Ihy beim Durchtrieb durch die Furt — Bemerkungen zu Gestalt und Person eines Gottes; – *c) Doetsch-Amerberger* Ellen, Bes auf der Blüte; – *d) Cenival* Françoise de, Individualisme et désenchantement; une tradition de la pensée égyptienne; – *e) Zandee* Jan †, Religion und philosophie in der alexandrinischen Theologie, besonders in JUSTINUS Martyr, KLEMENS von Alexandria, ORIGENES und 'Die Lehre des Silvanus'; ➤ 43, ᶠDER-CHAIN P., Religion 1991, 159-164 / 17-27 / 123-7 + 2 fig. / 79-91 / 375-397.

a793* *a) Helck* Wolfgang, Maat — Ideologie und Machtwerkzeug; – *b) Altenmüller* Hartwig, Zum möglichen religiösen Gehalt von Grabdarstellungen des Alten Reiches: ➤ 87, ᶠKOCH K., Ernten 1991, 11-19 / 21-35.

a794 **Hermsen** Edmund, Die zwei Wege des Jenseits; das altägyptische Zweiwegebuch und seine Topographie: OBO 112. FrS/Gö 1991, Univ./ VR. xii-282 p.; color front.; map; Eng. summary 289s. 3-7278-0784-9 / VR 3-525-53746-8 [TR 88,525].

a795 **Hibbs** Vivian A., The Mendes maze; a libation table for the inundation of the Nile 1985 → 4,b909:   RCdÉ 65 (1990) 276-9 (France *Le Corsu*).

a796 **Hoffmeier** James K.,   Sacred ... Egypt, *dsr:* OBO 59, 1985 → 1,a623 ... 6,b44:   RJEA 77 (1991) 199-202 (D. *Meeks*).

a797 **Hornung** Erik, *al.*, Der ägyptische Mythos von der Himmelskuh[2rev] [= ¹1982 → 63,9342]: OBO 46. FrS/Gö 1991, Univ./VR. 133 p.   3-7278-0262-0 / VR 3-525-53737-9.

a798 **Hornung** Erik, Les dieux de l'Égypte: l'Un et le Multiple [Der Eine 1971 → 52,6240],[T]: Civilisation et Tradition. Monaco 1987, Rocker. 310 p.; 20 fig. 2-268-00549-6.

a799 **Hornung** Erik, Die Nachtfahrt der Sonne, eine altägyptische Beschreibung des Jenseits. Z 1991, Artemis & W. 238 p. 3-7608-1036-5.

a800 **Johnson** Sally B., The cobra goddesses of ancient Egypt; predynastic, Early Dynastic, and Old Kingdom periods. L 1990, Kegan Paul. xxv-276 p. [BO 48,311].

a801 *Kákosy* László, From fertility to cosmic symbolism; outlines of the history of the cult of Apis: AcClasDebrecen 26 (1990) 3-7.

a802 **Koch** Klaus, Das Wesen altägyptischer Religion im Spiegel altägyptischer Forschung 1989 → 5,h21; 6,b54:   RBO 48 (1991) 477s (V. A. *Tobin*).

a803 **Kruchten** Jean-Marie, Les annales des prêtres de Karnak (XXIe-XXXIIImes dynasties) et autres textes contemporains relatifs à l'initiation des prêtres d'Amon; *Zimmer* Thierry, archéol.: OrLovAnal 32. Lv 1989, Dept. Orientalistiek. viii-306; 32 pl. Fb. 1980. 90-6831-170-0. – RBO 48 (1991) 765-771 (K. *Jansen-Winkeln*); OLZ 86 (1991) 482s (W. *Helck*).

a804 **Kruchten** Jean-Marie, Le grand texte oraculaire de Djéhoutymose, intendant du domaine d'Amon sous le pontificat de Pinedjem II 1986 → 2,9032; 6,b57:   RJEA 76 (1990) 242-4 (K. *Jansen-Winkeln*, deutsch).

a805 *Lanciers* Eddy, Die ägyptischer Priester des ptolemäischen Königskultes: RÉgp 42 (1991) 117-144; pl. 2; Eng. p. 145.

a806 **Luckert** Karl W., Egyptian light and Hebrew fire; theological and philosophical roots of Christendom in evolutionary perspective: SUNY series in religion studies. Albany 1991, SUNY. viii-347 p.; 11 fig. 0-7914-0967-8; pa. -8-6.

a807 *Menu* Bernadette, 'Maât fille de Re': → 140, FSMYTH-FLORENTIN F., 1991, 55-60.

a808 **Milde** H., The vignettes in the Book of the Dead of Neferrenpet: Eg.Uitgaven 7. Leiden 1991, Ned.Inst.NO. ix-284 p.; 73 fig.; 48 pl. 90-6258-207-9.

a809 *a)* *Miosi* Frank (Terry), Some aspects of Geb in the pyramid texts; – *b)* *Millet* N. B., A representation of the Deir el-Bahri shrines: → 136*, FSCHULMAN A., BEgSem 10 (1989s) 101-7 / 95-98 + 2 pl.

a809* **O'Callaghan** José, Las raíces religiosas del hombre; el alma del antiguo Egipto [... papiros] 1990 → 6,b63:   RRTLim 25 (1991) 489s (R. *Espejo Reese*).

a810 *Pamminger* Peter, Das Trinken von Überschwemmungswasser — eine Form der jährlichen Regeneration des Verstorbenen: GöMiszÄg 122 (1991) 71-75.

Saunders Nicholas J., The cult of the cat 1991 → e475.

a811 **Schumacher** Inke W., Der Gott Sopdu – der Herr der Fremdländer: OBO 79, ᴰ1988 ➤ 5,b141: ᴿBO 48 (1991) 98-100 (A. R. *Schulman*).

a811* *Seyfried* Karl-J., Stellenverzeichnis zu: J. Assmann, Ägyptische Hymnen und Gebete (ÄHG), Bibliothek der Alten Welt, Zürich-München 1975; GöMiszÄg 120 (1991) 85-93.

a812 ᴱ**Shafer** Byron E., Religion in ancient Egypt; gods, myths, and personal practice 1991 ➤ 625: Art. by *Silverman* D., *Lesko* L., *Baines* J.

a813 *Spalinger* Anthony, Remarks on an Egyptian feast calendar of foreign origin: StAäK 18 (1991) 349-373.

a814 **Tobin** Vincent A., Theological principles of Egyptian religion: AmerUnivSt 7/59, 1989 ➤ 5,b47: ᴿBL (1991) 131 (N. *Wyatt*: useful and needed; key-term 'mytho-theology'); SR 20 (1991) 359s (Sarah *Israelit-Groll*).

a815 **Žabkar** Louis V., Hymns to Isis in her temple at Philae 1988 ➤ 4,b940; 6,b75: ᴿBO 48 (1991) 467-471 (D. *Kurth*).

a815* ꟳZandee Jan: Studies in Egyptian religion, ᴱ**Heerma van Voss** M., *al.*, 1982 ➤ 63,171; 65,153*: ᴿJNES 50 (1991) 209-212 (R. K. *Ritner*).

---

a816 **Griggs** C. Wilfred, Early Egyptian Christianity; from its origins to 451 C.E.: Coptic Studies 2. Leiden 1990, Brill. vii-276 p. ƒ140. 90-04-09159-9. – ᴿJEH 42 (1991) 466s (W. H. C. *Frend*); JRS 81 (1991) 228s (D. *Kyrtatas*).

M7 **Religio mesopotamica.**

a817 **Abusch** I. Tsvi, Babylonian witchcraft literature; case studies: BrownJudSt 132, 1987 ➤ 4,b941: ᴿBO 48 (1991) 159-163 (W. *Schramm*).

a818 **Bottéro** J., *Kramer* S. N., Lorsque les dieux faisaient l'homme; mythologie mésopotamienne 1989 ➤ 5,b64: ᴿOrientalia 60 (1991) 354-362 (M.-J. *Seux*); RHPR 71 (1991) 195-7 (J.-G. *Heintz*).

a819 **Bottéro** Jean, Mesopotamia; la scrittura, la mentalità e gli dèi [1987 ➤ 3,194], ᵀ*Matthiae* Claudio: Saggi 744. T 1991, Einaudi. xxxvi-351 p.; 36 fig. 88-06-12264-9. – ᴿLetture 46 (1991) 661s (G. *Ravasi*).

a820 **Braun-Holzinger** Eva A., Mesopotamische Weihgaben der frühdynastischen bis altbabylonischen Zeit: HeidStAO. Heid 1991, Orient-V. xii-406 p.; 24 pl. DM 169. 3-927552-02-X [OIAc 2,15].

a821 *Cagni* Luigi, La morte e i morti nel mondo mesopotamico: FilT 4 (1990) 253-9.

a822 *Castel* Corinne, Temples à l'époque néo-babylonienne; une même conception de l'espace sacré: RAss 85 (1991) 169-182 + 5 pl. of plans.

a823 **Colbow** Gudrun, Die kriegerische Ištar; zu den Erscheinungsformen bewaffneter Gottheiten zwischen der Mitte des 3. und der Mitte des 2. Jahrtausends: MüVorderasSt 8. Mü 1991, Profil. 526 p.; 32 pl.; 6 maps. DM 148. 3-89018-280-7 [BO 48,989].

a824 **Farber** N., Schlaf, Kindlein ... Rituale 1989 ➤ 5,b69; 6,b80: ᴿAfO 36s (1989s) 132-4 (M. J. *Geller*, 'Kindchen').

a825 **Haas** Volkert, *Wegner* Ilse, Die Rituale der Beschwörerinnen ˢᴬᴸŠU.GI: Hurritisch/Boğazköy 5/1. R 1988, Multigrafica. I. Texte, xx-510 p.; II. Glossar iv-285 p. – ᴿBO 48 (1991) 585-9 (G. *Beckman*); Orientalia 60 (1991) 372-9 (E. *Neu*).

a826 *Harris* Rivkah, Inanna-Ishtar as paradox and as coincidence of opposites: HistRel 30 (1990s) 261-278.
a827 **Jeyes** Ulla, Old Babylonian extispicy 1989 ➤ 5,b77: ᴿBO 48 (1991) 175-9 (I. *Starr*).
a828 **Kraus** F. R., The role of temples from the third dynasty of Ur to the first dynasty of Babylon, ᵀ*Foster* Benjamin R.: MgANE 2/4. Malibu 1990, Undena. 20 p. 0-89003-240-8 [OIAc 1,19].
a829 **Maul** Stefan M., 'Herzberuhigungsklagen'... Eršaḫunga-Gebete 1988 ➤ 6,b91: ᴿAfO 36s (1989s) 124-6 (J. A. *Black*).
a830 *Maul* Stefan M., 'Wenn der Held (zum Kampfe) auszieht...'; ein Ninurta-Eršemma: Orientalia 60 (1991) 312-331 + 9 facsimiles.
a831 **Meyer** Jan-Waalke, Untersuchungen zu den Tonleber-Modellen aus dem Alten Orient: AOAT 39, 1987 ➤ 3,b382: ᴿBO 48 (1991) 247-250 (L. B. van der *Meer*).
a832 **Michel** Cécile, Innāya dans les tablettes paléo-assyriennes: P 1991, RCiv. I. Analyse, 290 p.; II. Textes, 436 p. 2-86538-221-4; -2-2.
a833 **Pettinato** Giovanni, *Chiodi* Silvia, Gli dèi di Babilonia. T 1991, RAI. 227 p.; 12 pl.; 2 maps. Lit. 15.000. 88-397-0644-5.
a834 **Pomponio** Francesco, Formule di maledizione della Mesopotamia antica 1990 ➤ 6,b97 ['Mesop. preclassica']. – ᴿArcheo 65 (1990) 127 (S. *Moscati*).
a835 *Pomponio* Francesco, L'umorismo di Enki-Ea; alcune considerazioni su una Summa mitologica di recente edizione [*Bottéro* J., *Kramer* S., 1989]: RSO 64 (1990) 235-246.
a836 **Ringgren** Helmer, Le religioni dell'Oriente Antico [1979], ᵀ*Alberti* Amedeo: BtCuBib 58. Brescia 1991, Paideia. 285 p. 88-394-0463-5.
a837 **Rochberg-Halton** Francesca, Aspects of Babylonian celestial divination; the lunar eclipse tablets of Enūma Anu Enlil: AfO Beih 22. Horn 1988, Berger. 296 p. – ᴿOLZ 86 (1991) 378-384 (A. R. *George*, Eng.: Sch 1980).
a838 *Scurlock* J. A., Was there a 'love-hungry' *Ēntu*-priestess named Eṭirtum?: AfO 36s (1989s) 107-112.
a839 **Seidl** Ursula, Die babylonischen Kudurru-Reliefs, Symbole mesopotamischer Gottheiten: OBO 87, 1989 ➤ 5,b89: ᴿOLZ 86 (1991) 50s (J. *Börker-Klähn*).
a840 *Soden* Wolfram von, (*Oelsner* Joachim), Ein spät-altbabylonisches *pārum*-Preislied für Ištar: Orientalia 60 (1991) 339-343.
a841 *Spaey* J., Some notes on KÙ.BABBAR / *nebiḫ kezēr(t)i(m)* [...religious duties of women]: Akkadica 67 (1990) 1-9.
a842 *a) Wilhelm* Gernot, Zur hurritischen Gebetsliteratur; – *b) Dietrich* Manfried, Die Tötung einer Gottheit in der Eridu-Babylon-Mythologie: ➤ 87, ᶠKOCH K., Ernten 1991, 37-47 / 49-73.

M7.4   **Religio persiana,** *Iran.*

a842* *a)* **Boyce** M., *Grenet* F., Zoroastrianism under Macedonian and Roman rule: HistZ 3/HbOr 1/8/1/2/2. Leiden 1991, Brill. xix-596 p.; 3 maps. *f* 380. 90-04-09271-4 [NTAbs 36,133]. – *b) Boyce* Mary, *Pādyāb* and *nērang*; two Pahlavi terms [for purity (-ritual)]: BSO 54 (1991) 281-291.
a843 **Choksy** Jamsheed K., Purity and pollution in Zoroastrianism 1989 ➤ 5,b100; 6,b111: ᴿJAOS 111 (1991) 411 (W. W. *Malandra*: updates 1922 MODI J. but gives more); JRel 71 (1991) 461s (C. S. *Anderson*).

a844 **Russell** James R., Zoroastrianism in Armenia 1988 ➤ 4,b979: ᴿJAOS 111 (1991) 151s (J. P. *Asmussen*: outstanding, unrivaled).
a845 *Trokay* M., Les origines du dieu élamite au serpent: ➤ 621, Rencontre 36, 1989/91, 153-160 + 19 fig.
a846 **Waldmann** Helmut, Der Kommagenische Mazdaismus: IstMit Beih 37. Tü 1991, Wasmuth. 237 p.; 8 pl.; 2 plans. – ᴿWienerSt 104 (1991) 291 (H. *Schwabl*).

M8.1 *Religio proto-arabica* – **Early Arabic religious graffiti.**

a846* *a) Bashear* Suliman, ʿĀshūrā an early Muslim fast: ZDMG 141 (1991) 281-316; – *b) Firestone* Reuven, Abraham's association with the Meccan sanctuary and the pilgrimage in the pre-Islamic and early Islamic periods: Muséon 104 (1991) 359-387; *c) Beeston* A. F. L., Sabaean graffiti from the Wadi al-Ḥār; – *d) Thaeb* S. al-, A new Minaean inscription from North Arabia: ArabArchEp 1 (1990) 16-19; 2 fig. / 20-23; 1 fig.
a847 ᴱ**Fahd** T., L'Arabie préislamique et son environnement historique et culturel 1987/9 ➤ 5,816: ᴿZDMG 141 (1991) 218 (W. W. *Müller*).
a847* **Lecker** Michael, The [also pre-Islamic] Banū Sulaym; a contribution to the study of early Islam: Schloessinger Mg 4. J 1989, Hebrew Univ. xiii-269 p. – ᴿBSO 54 (1991) 359-362 (G. R. *Hawting*); JESHO 34 (1991) 366s (R. T. *Mortel*).
a848 *Rowson* Everett K., The effeminates [transvestite marriage-brokers usually not known to be homosexual] of early Medina: JAOS 111 (1991) 671-693.

M8.2 *Muḥammad et asseclae* – **Qur'ān and early diffusion of Islam.**

a848* **Abdullah** M. S., Geschichte des Islams in Deutschland: Islam und westliche Welt 5. Graz 1981, Styria. 220 p. – ᴿWZKM 79 (1989) 331-4 (M. *Köhbach*).
a849 *Ambros* Arne A., Die Divergenzen zwischen dem [1834, Gustav] FLÜGEL- und dem Azhar-Koran: WZKM 78 (1988) 9-21.
a849* *Athar* Ali M., The Islamic background to Indian history; an interpretation of the Islamic past: JESHO 32 (1989) 335-345.
a851 *Bashear* Suliman, Riding beasts on divine missions; an examination of the ass and camel traditions [in Arabic, like Zech 9,9; Mt 21,1-6 ...]: JSS 36 (1991) 37-75.
a852 *Bruck* Gabriele vom, Heiratspolitik der 'Prophetennachfahren': Saeculum 40 (1989) 272-295.
a853 **Crone** Patricia, Meccan trade 1987 ➤ 6,b127: ᴿSpeculum 66 (1991) 137-9 (R. *Schick*).
a854 **Dabashi** Hamid, Authority in Islam from the rise of Muhammad to the establishment of the Umayyads. New Brunswick 1989, Transaction. 158 p. – ᴿMuslimW 81 (1991) 168s (S. P. *Blackburn*).
a855 **Dall'Oglio** P., Speranza nell'Islam; interpretazione della prospettiva escatologica di Corano XVIII: diss. Pont. Univ. Gregoriana, ᴰ*Roest Crollius* A. Roma 1990. 362 p. – RTLv 22, p. 613.
a856 *Debarge* Louis, La caverne des Sept Dormants [... Éphèse]; une légende chrétienne dans le Coran: EsprVie 101 (1991) 227-9-*jaune*.
a857 **Gimaret** D., Les noms divins en Islam 1988 ➤ 4,b997 ... 6,b136; F 295; 2-204-02828-2: ᴿJSS 36 (1991) 356-9 (J. *Burton*: witty); OLZ 86 (1991) 181-2 (T. *Nagel*).

a858 ^E**Haarmann** Ulrich, Geschichte der arabischen Welt 1987 ➤ 4,b998: ^ROLZ 86 (1991) 178-181 (G. *Höpp*); WZKM 79 (1989) 289-291 (H. *Eisenstein*).

a859 **Hagemann** Ludwig, *Glei* Reinhold, Nicolai de CUSA, Cribratio Alkorani, Sichtung des Korans 1, 1989 ➤ 6,b139: ^RZRGg 43 (1991) 84s (W. *Beltz*). – II. Ha 1990, Meiner. viii-111 p. DM 28. – ^RTLZ 116 (1991) 919s (K.-H. *Kandler*).

a859* *Hagemann* L., Islam und ökologische Kultur: ➤ 530. Schöpfung 1989/ 90, 21-31.

a860 **Hourani** Albert, The history of the Arab peoples [chiefly Islamic]. C 1991, Univ. xx-551 p. $25 [RelStR 18,74, A. *Nanji*].

a861 *Kelsay* John, Religion, morality, and the governance of war; the case of classical Islam: JRelEth 18,2 (1990) 123-139.

a862 **Khoury** Adel T., Wer war Muhammad? Lebensgeschichte und prophetischer Anspruch. FrB 1990, Herder. 126 p. DM 10,90. – ^RTPQ 139 (1991) 339s (J. *Janda*).

a863 ^E**Khoury** Adel T., *al.*, Islam-Lexikon; Geschichte – Ideen – Gestalten. FrB 1991, Herder. 941 p. (3 vol.). – ^RMiscFran 91 (1991) 524 (J. *Imbach*).

a864 ^{TE}**Khoury** Adel T., Der Koran, arabisch-deutsch 1. Sure 1,1 - 2,74; 2. Sure 2,75 - 2,212. Gü 1990s, Mohn ... p.; 384 p. – ^RTR 87 (1991) 157-9 . 506s (P. *Heine*: Kommentar zu seiner Übersetzung 1987 ➤ 4,d8).

a865 ^T**Khoury** Adel T., Der Koran 1987 ➤ 4,d8; 6,b147: ^RWZKM 79 (1989) 272-4 (A. A. *Ambros*).

a866 **Khoury** Adel T., Was sagt der Koran zum Heiligen Krieg?: Siebenstern 789. Gü 1991, Mohn. 95 p. DM 12,80 [TLZ 117,174].

a867 *Kister* M. J., Land property and *jihad*, a study of some early traditions: JESHO 34 (1991) 270-311.

a868 *Mir* Mustansir, Humor in the Qur'an: Muslim World 81 (1991) 179-193.

a869 *Neuwirth* Angelika & Karl, Sūrat al-Fātiḥa – 'Eröffnung' des Text-Corpus Koran oder 'Introitus' der Gebetsliturgie?: ➤ 126, ^FRICHTER W., Text 1991, 331-357.

a870 *a) O'Shaughnessy* Thomas J., The Qur'ānic view of youth and old age; – *b) Versteegh* Kees, Greek translations of the Qur'ān in Christian polemics (9th century A.D.): ZDMG 141 (1991) 33-51 / 52-68.

a871 *Richter-Bernburg* L., Islam: ➤ 681, LexMA 5 (1990) 680-6 (-8, *Brisch* K., Kunst).

a872 ^E**Rippin** Andrew, Approaches to the history of the interpretation of the Qur'ān 1985/8 ➤ 6,780: ^RJAOS 111 (1991) 155-7 (B. G. *Weis*: title wrongly suggests a contents less heterogeneous than is par for meetings); RelStT 10,2 (1990) 90s (S. *McDonough*).

a873 **Rippin** Andrew, Muslims, their religious beliefs and practices, I. The formative period. L 1990, Routledge-CH. $14. 0-415-04519-3. – ^RRSPT 74 (1990) 480-2 (G. *Gilliot*).

a874 *Rudolph* Kurt, Die Anfänge Moḥammeds im Lichte der Religionsgeschichte: ➤ 13, ^FBAETKE W. (Weimar 1966, Böhlau) 298-326.

a875 **Simon** Róbert, Meccan trade and Islam; problems of origins and structure [⑩ 1975]: BtOrH 32. Budapest 1989, Akad. 205 p. – ^RJAOS 111 (1991) 794s (F. M. *Donner*); JESHO 34 (1991) 367s (R. T. *Mortel*: really pre-Islamic Meccan trade).

a876 **Wessels** Anton, De Koran verstaan; een kennismaking met het boek

van de Islam.   Kampen 1986, Kok.   196 p. – RBijdragen 52 (1991) 445s
(M. *Parmentier*).

M8.3   Islam, *evolutio recentior* – later history and practice.

a877 **Ashmawy** M. S. al-,   L'Islamisme contre l'Islam; TE*Jacquement* Richard,
P/Caire 1989, Découverte/Fikr.   108 p. F 69. – RÉtudes 374 (1991) 572s
(H. *Loucel*).

a878 **Balić** Smail,   Ruf vom Minarett; Weltislam heute – Renaissance oder
Rückfall? Eine Selbstdarstellung.   Ha 1984, Rissen.   272 p. – RTR 87
(1991) 423 (G. *Girschek*).

a879 *Barbato* Antonio,   Conquista e presenza arabo-islamica a Malta: AION
50 (1990) 233-247.

a879* **Bürgel** Johann C.,   The feather of Simurgh; the 'licit magic' of the arts
in medieval Islam 1988 → 4,b989; 6,b169: ROLZ 86 (1991) 5-12 (G.
Strohmaier: 'SPENGLER redivivus?').

a880 E**Burrell** R. M.,   Islamic fundamentalism [4 art. 1988]: Royal Asiatic
Sem. 1.   L 1989, Royal Asiatic Soc.   86 p. £8. – RBSO 54 (1991) 367s (N.
Calder).

a880* **Campo** Juan E.,   The other sides of Paradise; explorations into the
religious meanings of domestic space in Islam [house-construction familiar
to his Egyptian wife Magda].   Columbia 1991, Univ. S. Carolina.   xvi-
246 p. $50.   0-87249-738-0 [TDig 39,153].

a881 *Debarge* Louis,   Mysticisme islamique et modernité: MélSR 48 (1991)
135-152; Eng. 152.

a882 **Fakhry** Majid,   Histoire de la philosophie islamique [Eng. ¹1970 ²1983],
T*Nasr* Marwan: Patrimoines.   P 1989, Cerf.   416 p. F 250. – RLavalTP 47
(1991) 283 (R. *Bodéüs*); RHR 208 (1991) 89-92 (G. *Monnot*).

a883 *Giladi* Avner,   Concepts of childhood and attitudes towards children in
medieval Islam; a preliminary study with special reference to reactions to
infant and child mortality [ARIES P., L'enfant et la vie familiale; Eng.
Centuries of childhood 1986, p. 36 '... one had several children in order to
keep just a few (surviving)']: JESHO 32 (1989) 122-132.

a884 **Gilliot** Claude,   Exégèse, langue et théologie en Islam; l'exégèse co-
ranique de ṬABARĪ: ÉtMusulmanes 32.   P 1990, Vrin.   320 p. – RJSS 36
(1991) 353-5 (A. *Rippin*: excellent).

a885 *Jomier* Jacques,   Penseurs et textes musulmans [GIMARET D. + 6]:
RThom 91 (1991) 160-4.

a886 *Kennedy* Hugh,   Change and continuity in Syria and Palestine at the
time of the Moslem Conquest: Aram 1 (1989) 258-267.

a887 E**Kepel** Gilles, *Richard* Yann,   Intellectuels et militants de l'Islam
contemporain.   P 1990, Seuil.   290 p. F 160. – RÉtudes 347 (1991) 853s
(H. *Loucel*).

a888 *Kohlbrugge* Hanna,   Tawhid, das Herz der islamischen Theologie: EvT
51 (1991) 271-295.

a889 **Lambton** Ann K. S.,   State and government in medieval Islam: London
Or. 36.   Ox 1982, UP. $52.   0-19-713600-1. – RJESHO 32 (1989) 110-4
(T. *Bianquis*).

a890 **Lapidus** I. M.,   A history of Muslim society 1988 → 6,b190 ['societies']:
RJESHO 34 (1991) 246-253 (J.-C. *Garcin*: supplément à The Cambridge
History of Islam 1970).

a890* *Micheau* F., *al.*,   Le monde arabo-musulman au moyen age: → g340*,
E*Balard* M., L'histoire médiévale en France 1991, 363-379.

a891 **Nasr** Seyyed H.,   Islamic spirituality [I. Foundations, 1987 → 3,b460...
6,b149], II. Manifestations [Sufism]:   EWSp 20.   NY 1991, Crossroad.
xxviii-548 p. $49.50.   0-8245-0768-1 [TDig 38,272]. – ᴿHeythJ 32 (1991)
133s (I. R. *Netton*, I: satisfying).

a892 **Netton** Ian R.,   Allāh transcendent; studies in the structure and semiotics
of Islamic philosophy, theology and cosmology: Exeter Arabic and Islamic
Series. L 1989, Routledge-CH.   xiv-384 p. £45.   0-415-01893-5. – ᴿBO 48
(1991) 931-3 (J. van *Ess*); ZDMG 141 (1991) 179-183 (U. *Rudolph*).

a893 **Piamenta** M.,   The Muslim conception of God and human welfare, as
reflected in everyday Arabic speech 1983 → 1,9159:   ᴿRSO 64 (1990) 412s
(A. *Scarabel*).

a894 *Pulsfort* Ernst,   Die indischen Muslime zwischen Säkularismus und Fundamentalismus;   ZMissRW 74 (1990) 193-204.

a895 ᴱ**Robbe** Martin,   Welt des Islam, Geschichte und Alltag einer Religion.
B 1988, ²1991 aktualisiert, Urania.   240 p.; 62 (color.) pl. ²304 p. DM 38.
– ᴿOLZ 86 (1991) 532-4 (Monika *Gronke*).

a896 **Sabbagh** Abdulkarim,   Frauen im Islam 1986 → 5,b208:   ᴿOLZ 86
(1991) 413s (R. *Schulze*).

a897 ᴱ**Schimmel** Annemarie, *al.*,   Der Islam, 3. Islamische Kultur – Zeitgenössische Strömungen – Volksfrömmigkeit: Religionen der Menschheit
25/3.   Stu 1990, Kohlhammer.   xii-486 p. DM 132. – ᴿTLZ 116 (1991)
339-343 (T. *Lohmann*).

a897* ᵀ**Smith** Jane I., AL-GHAZZALI, The precious pearl: Studies in World
Religions 1. (Atlanta) 1979, Scholars. viii-120 p. 0-89130-278-6; pa. -303-7.

a898 *Tröger* Karl-Wolfgang,   Peace and Islam, in theory and practice [*jihad* is
part of Muslim tradition (but) Koran sanctions defensive, not offensive
war; both Mohammed and the Koran searched for reconciliation with
Jews & Christians: < Islam and Christian-Muslim Relations 1,1 (June
1990) 17-24], ᵀ*Walpole* Michael, ᴱ*Asen* B. A.: TDig 38 (1991) 115-8.

a899 **Watt** W. M.,   Islamic fundamentalism and modernity 1988 → 5,b223;
6,b206:   ᴿJSS 36 (1991) 362-4 (A. *Rippin*).

a900 ᴱ**Young** M. J. L., *al.*,   Religion, learning, and science in the ʿAbbasid
period.   C 1991, Univ.   587 p. $95 [JAAR 59,886].

a902 *Zeggaf* Abdeljamid,   L'écriture hagiographique dans l'Islam mahgrébin:
BLitEc 92 (1991) 83-91; Eng. 91.

a903 *Zirker* Hans,   Das Heil des Menschen im Islam: GeistL 63 (1990)
293-304.

M8.4   *Alter philosemitismus* – **Islamic-Christian rapprochement.**

a904 *Amjad-Ali* Charles,   Not so much a threat as a challenge; acknowledging
the religio-cultural heritage of others: NBlackf 71,2 ('The world of Islam'
1990) [55-] 94-103.

a905 *Anawati* Georges C.,   La rencontre de deux cultures, en occident, au
Moyen-Âge; dialogue islamo-chrétien et activité missionnaire [congrès
Lull, Majorque 1976]: EstLul 29 (1989) 155-178.

a906 **Arnaldez** Roger,   Réflexions chrétiennes sur la mystique musulmane:
Lumière des peuples 1989 → 6,b210:   ᴿRTPhil 123 (1991) 123 (J. *Borel*).

a907 *a*) *Balic* Smail,   Worüber können wir sprechen? Theologische Inhalte
eines Dialogs zwischen Christen und Muslimen; – *b*) *Shivamurti* Shi-
vacharya,   Hoffnungen und Enttäuschungen des interreligiösen Dialogs;
Erfahrungsbericht eines Hindu: Dialog der Religionen 1 (1991) 57-73 /
73-82 [< TR 87,259].

a908 **Basetti-Sani** Giulio, Dal Corano al Vangelo [... esegesi; alcune conversioni]. Spino d'Adda 1991, Grafica. 202 p. – ᴿOrChrPer 57 (1991) 450 (V. *Poggi*).

a909 **Borrmans** Maurice, Guidelines for dialogue between Christians and Muslims [1970, ²1981], ᵀ*Speight* R. Marston: Pontifical Council for Interreligious Dialogue. NY 1990, Paulist. vi-132 p. $13. 0-8091-3181-1 [TDig 38,253].

a909* *Bottignolo* Bruno, Christian-Muslim dialogue in the Philippines: EAPast 27 (1990) 165-177.

a910 **Bouman** Johan, Die Theologie al-GHAZALIS und AUGUSTINS im Vergleich: Glaubenskrise und Glaubensgewissheit im Christentum und im Islam 2 / MgStudB 351. Giessen 1990, Brunnen. vii-364 p. DM 44 [TR 87,427]. – ᴿTLZ 116 (1991) 337s (H.-J. *Diesner*).

a911 ᴱ**Brown** Stuart E., Meeting in faith... Christian/Muslim 1989 ➤ 5,641: ᴿTsTKi 61 (1990) 239s (J. *Opsal*).

a912 **Busse** Heribert, Die theologischen Beziehungen des Islams zu Judentum und Christentum, Grundlagen des Dialogs im Koran und die gegenwärtige Situation 1988 ➤ 6,b213; 3-534-06394-5: ᴿEstE 66 (1991) 473 (J. J. *Alemany*).

a913 **Caspar** Robert, Pour un regard chrétien sur l'Islam: Religions en dialogue 1990 ➤ 6,b214; F 135; 2-227-36303-7: ᴿÉTRel 66 (1991) 311 (J.-P. *Gabus*).

a914 **Cassen** Karl, Aus einem Licht; Christentum, Islam, Judentum; Versuch eines ökumenischen Dialogs. Koblenz 1990, Fölbach. 197 p. DM 19,80 [TR 87,348].

a915 *Clément* Nicolas, Islam; pour une théologie de la liberté et de la raison: Études 375 (1991) 391-401.

a916 *a)* *Danecki* Janusz, ☯ À l'origine des élans et des décadences de l'Islam contemporain; – *b)* *Kolvenbach* Peter-Hans, ☯ Le difficile dialogue avec l'Islam [< ᴱ*Giacomelli* Renzo, Fedeli a Dio e all'uomo 1990], ᵀ*Schmidt* Grzegorz: PrzPow 270,832 (1990) 377-392; franç. 392 / 393-5.

a917 *Dodge* John, What has Jerusalem to do with Mecca?: ChrSchR 20 (1991) 401-... [< ZIT 91,484].

a918 **Gaudeul** J.-M., Appelés par le Christ, ils viennent d'Islam [témoignages de musulmans venus au christianisme]: L'histoire à vif. P 1991, Cerf. 346 p. F 125 [NRT 114,603, L.-J. *Renard*].

a919 *a)* *González* Fidel, ¿Es posible el diálogo con el Islam?; – *b)* *Martínez Montavez* Pedro, Europa y el Islam: RazF 223 (1991) 518-528 / 224 (1991) 24-33.

a921 *Hamès* Constant, *al.*, L'Islam en France et en Europe: ArchivScSocRel 68,1 (1989) 5-7 (-91).

a922 **Hourani** A., Islam in European thought. C 1991, Univ. xi-199 p. £25 [NRT 114,475, J. *Scheuer*].

a923 **Kepel** Gilles, Die Rache Gottes; radikale Moslems, Christen und Juden auf dem Vormarsch, ᵀ*Schmidt* T. Mü 1991, Piper. 316 p. [TLZ 117,403, H. *Zahrnt*].

a924 *Khodr* Georges, La comunicación del mensaje en tierras del Islam [< ÉTRel 64 (1989) 373-391], ᵀᴱ*Rocafiguera* José M.: SelT 30 (1991) 57-64.

Khoury Adel T., Was ist los in der islamischen Welt? 1991 ➤ e934.

a925 *a)* *Khoury* Adel T., Islam, theocracy and tolerance [< UnSa 45 (1990) 14-19], ᵀᴱ*Asen* B.; – *b)* *Nispen tot Sevenaer* Christian van, Christian-Muslim encounter [< Christus 38 (P 1991) 181-192]; ᵀᴱ*Jermann* Rosemary; – c) *Basetti-Sani* Giulio, Mohammed's authentic prophetic mission [< StPatav 36 (1989) 121-7], ᵀᴱ*Lavender* Earl D.: TDig 38 (1991) 203-6 / 207-211 / 219-221.

a926 *Khoury* Adel T., Die islamische Welt heute; Strömungen – Organisationen – Probleme: HerdKorr 45 (1991) 258-263 [451-3, 'G.E.'; 481-6 *Heine* P., Algérien].

a927 **Kimball** Charles, Striving together; a way forward in Christian-Muslim relations. Mkn 1991, Orbis. xv-132 p. $9. – ᴿCurrTMiss 18 (1991) 296s (F. *Nelson*); TLond 94 (1991) 461s (Harriet *Crabtree*: omits AYOUB).

a928 *Leveau* Rémy, Musulmans en France [nombre non donné (3 millions?), pour la plupart désireux de s'intégrer sans disparaître; les Français acceptent à condition de se convertir à la laïcité de la société française]: Études 374 (1991) 323-332.

a929 *a) Lewis* Philip J., Christian-Muslim relations in a cold climate; – *b) Johnstone* Penelope, The mosque and the market; views of a new Europe: Month 252 (1991) 405-411 / 412-5.

a930 **Longton** J., Uit Abraham geboren [1987 ➛ 5,b178]; Jodendom, Christendom, Islam en hun vertakkingen. Turnhout 1990, Brepols. 273 p. Fb 495. – ᴿCollatVL 21 (1991) 107 (E. Van *Waelderen*).

a931 **McAuliffe** Jane D., Qur'anic Christians; an analysis of classical and modern exegesis. C 1991, Univ. xii-340 p. 0-521-36470-1 [... iv. followers of the Qur'anic Jesus ... viii. Christians as pre-Islamic Muslims].

a932 *Michel* Thomas F., ❷ Le monde arabe face à la guerre du Golfe [< CC 1991,1], ᵀ*Schmidt* Grzegorz: PrzPow 272,2 (1991) 100-111.

a932* **Mooren** Thomas, Macht und Einsamkeit Gottes; Dialog mit dem islamischen Radikal-Monotheismus: ForMRelW 17. Wü/Altenberge 1991, Echter/Oros. 409 p. DM 60 [TLZ 117,897-900, R. *Kirste*].

a933 *O'Shaughnessy* Thomas J., *a)* The spiritual life as faith-commitment in the Qur'ān; – *b)* The Qur'anic view of man's sojourn on earth: Landas 3 (Manila 1989) 25-31 / 237-... [< ZIT 91,343].

a934 **Sanson** Henri, Dialogue intérieur avec l'Islam: Religions en dialogue, 1990 ➛ 6,b228: 2-227-36302-9: ᴿÉTRel 66 (1991) 312 (J.-P. *Gabus*).

a934* *a) Schoen* Ulrich, Das Schriftprinzip im Islam; – *b) Becken* Hans-J., Schrift und Tradition in den Afrikanischen Unabhängigen Kirchen; – *c) Nürnberger* Klaus, Der realsoteriologische Ansatz in Drittwelttheologien als Herausforderung an das protestantische Schriftprinzip: ➛ 454c, Sola Scriptura 1990/1, 363/372 / 337-347 / 348-362.

a935 **Schuon** F., Das Islam verstehen 1988 ➛ 5,b212: ᴿEstE 66 (1991) 100 (J. J. *Alemany*).

a936 *Teissier* Henri, Le chrétien questionné par l'Islam; un effort chrétien de compréhension de l'Islam: NRT 113 (1991) 801-823.

a937 **Thyen** Johann-D., Bibel und Koran; eine Synopse gemeinsamer Überlieferungen 1989 ➛ 5,b219: ᴿHenoch 13 (1991) 381s (R. *Tottoli*).

a938 *Vázquez Janeiro* Isaac, I Francescani e il dialogo con gli Ebrei e i Saraceni nei secoli XIII-XV: ➛ Libertà = Antonianum 65 (1990) 533-549.

a939 ᴱ**Waardenburg** Jacques [inaugurale 1988], ᴱ*Gisel* Pierre, L'Islam, une religion ... Quels types d'approches requiert le phénomène religieux? 1989 ➛ 5,b222: ᴿFoiVie 89,2 (1990) 93s (J.-D. *Dubois*); RTPhil 123 (1991) 123 (J.-C. *Basset*).

a939* **Watt** William M., Muslim-Christian encounters; perceptions and misconceptions. NY 1991, Routledge. 164 p. $50; pa. $15. 0-415- 05410-9; -1-7 [TDig 39,192].

a940 **Wingate** Andrew, Encounter in the Spirit; Muslim-Christian meetings in Birmingham. L 1988, British Council of Churches. 86 p. £3.50. – ᴿScotJT 44 (1991) 138 (J. *Hick*).

a941 *Zananiri* Gaston, Spiritual Semitism: NBlackf 72 (1991) 508-517.

a942 **Zirker** Hans, Christentum und Islam; theologische Verwandtschaft und Konkurrenz 1989 ➤ 5,b227, DM 29,80; 3-491-77784-4: ᴿEstE 66 (1991) 473 (J. J. *Alemany*); GeistL 63 (1990) 231s (R. *Kirste*); HerdKor 44 (1990) 46 (U. *Ruh*).

M8.5   **Religiones Indiae** *et variae.*

a943 *Argaud* Jacky (*al.*), Le Bouddhisme en situation... et à grands traits: ÉTRel 66 (1991) 45.47-52 (-98).

a943* **Bartholomeusz** Tessa J., Women under the bo tree: diss. Virginia, ᴰ*Lang* K. 1991. – RelStR 18,174.

a944 **Carmody** Denise L. & John T., Stories of Eastern religions. Mountain View CA 1991, Mayfield. xiii-242 p. $18 pa. 1-55934-054-1 [TDig 38,350].

a945 ᴱ**Carruthers** Michel, *Humphrey* Caroline, The assembly of listeners; Jains in society [influential out of proportion to their 0.5% of India's population; colloquium Cambridge, June 1985]. C 1991, Univ. xiii-328 p. $54.50. 0-521-36508-X. 17 art. [TDig 39,47].

a945* **De Bary** William T., The trouble with Confucianism. CM 1991, Harvard Univ. xiv-132 p. $20. 0-674-91015-X [TDig 59,156].

a946 **Delahoutre** Michel, Les Sikhs: Fils d'Abraham. Turnhout 1990, Brepols. 2-503-50081-5. – ᴿEsprVie 101 (1991) 536s (R. *Smet*, aussi sur son anthologie avec H. SINGH, 1985).

a947 **Gombrich** Richard, *Obeyesekere* Gananath, Buddhism transformed; religious change in Sri Lanka. Princeton 1988, Univ. xvi-484 p. $60; pa. $17. – ᴿRelStR 17 (1991) 307-312 (J. C. *Holt*).

a948 **Halbfass** Wilhelm, Tradition and reflection; explorations in [Asiatic] Indian thought. Albany 1991, SUNY [TLZ 117,169, M. v. *Brück*].

a949 **Han Sang-Woo,** Die Suche nach dem Himmel im Denken Koreas; eine religionswissenschaftliche und -philosophische Untersuchung zur Hermeneutik des Menschen zwischen Himmel und Erde [Diss. Rg.]: EurHS 23/325. Fra 1988, Lang. 512 p. – ᴿZMissRW 74 (1990) 93 (H. *Waldenfels*).

a951 *a) Jacob* Plamthodathil S., Soteriological perspectives in Hindu religion; – *b) Feys* J., Sanskrit derived terminology in the philosophy of God: IndTSt 27 (1990) 46-62 / 73-95.

a952 **Kalliath** Anthony, Self-awakening; an analytico-critical study of the religious experience of Swami Abhishiktananda (Dom Henri LE SAUX O.S.B.) in the context of Hindu-Christian meeting: diss. Theol. 6924, Pont. Univ. Gregoriana, ᴰ*Dupuis* J. R 1991 [InfPUG 121,18].

a953 **Küng** Hans, *a)* (met *Bechert* Heinz) Boeddhisme; – *b)* (met *Stietencron* Heinrich von) Hindoeïsme; – *c)* (met *Ess* Josef van) Islam: Christendom en wereldgodsdiensten 3/2/1, all ᵀ*Groot* Ger. Hilversum 1987/7/6, Gooi & S. 232 p.; 224 p.; 207 p. ƒ37,50 each. 90-304-0374-8; -72-1; -58-6. – ᴿBijdragen 52 (1991) 460 (J. G. *Hahn*).

a953* **Laine** James W., Visions of God; narratives of theophany in the Mahābhārata: De Nobili Research Library 16. W 1989 [Brill etc.]. – ᴿBSO 54 (1991) 382s (P. *Schreiner*).

a954 *Le Manchec* Claude, Mircea ELIADE, le chamanisme et la littérature: RHR 208 (1991) 27-48; Eng. 27.

a955 ᴱMinor Robert, Modern Indian interpreters of the Bhagavad Gita. Albany 1986, SUNY. 278 p. – ᴿJDharma 14 (1989) 407 (A. *Njaliampuzha*).

a956 **Nandi** R. N., Social roots of religion in ancient India. Calcutta 1986, Bagchi. rs. 125. 81-7074-009-6. – ᴿJESHO 32 (1989) 346-9 (G. *Berkemer*).

a957 **Panikkar** Raimundo, The silence of God; the answer of the Buddha 1989 ⇒ 5,b269; 6,b261: ᴿHorizons 18 (1991) 181s (D. P. *Sheridan*); JRel 71 (1991) 612 (J. R. *Timm*).

a958 **Robinet** I., Histoire du taoïsme, des origines au XIVᵉ siècle: Patrimoines. P 1991, Cerf. 269 p. F 147 [NRT 114,599, J. *Scheuer*].

a959 **Rothermundt** Gottfried, Buddhismus für die moderne Welt; die Religionsphilosophie K. N. JAYATILLEKEs: TMg C4. Stu 1979, Calwer. 190 p. – ᴿTRu 56 (1991) 215-9 (H. *Bechert*).

a960 **Schneider** Ulrich, Einführung in den Hinduismus. Da 1989, Wiss. 257 p. [OLZ 87,303, E. *Ritschl*).

a961 **Smith** Brian, Reflections on resemblance, ritual and religion [Hinduism]. NY 1989, Oxford-UP. 280 p. $32.50. – ᴿCritRR 3 (1990) 276-8 (A. *Sharma*).

a962 *Swamy* M. Sivakumara, Neo-revivalist movements in Hinduism and their challenges to Hindu fundamentalism: JDharma 15 (1990) 135-147 [148-167, *Thadavanal* Jose; 168-178, *George* Dominic].

a963 *Taylor* Rodney L., The religious dimensions of Confucianism. Albany 1990, SUNY. xii-198 p. $44.50; pa. $15. 0-7914-0311-4; -2-2 [TDig 38,291].

a964 *Weinberger-Thomas* Catherine, Cendres d'immortalité, la crémation des veuves en Inde [recently revived]: ArchivScSocRel 67,1 ('Twists and turns of religion in India' 1989) 9-51 [al. 53-124].

a965 **Wiltshire** M. G., Ascetic figures before and in early Buddhism; the emergence of Gautama as the Buddha: Religion and Reason 30. B 1990, Mouton de Gruyter. xxxvi-338 p. DM 168 [NRT 114,595, J. *Masson*].

M8.7 *Interactio cum religione orientali;* **Christian dialogue with the East.**

a966 *Ariarajah* S. Wesley, Hindus and Christians, a century of Protestant ecumenical thought: Currents of Encounter 5. Amst/GR 1991, Rodopi/Eerdmans. x-244 p. $22. -/0-8028-0504-3 [TDig 39,46: the author is a Sri Lanka Methodist minister].

a966* **Brück** Michael von, The unity of reality; God, God-experience and meditation in the Hindu-Christian dialogue, ᵀ*Zeitz* James V. NY 1991, Paulist. vi-340 p. $20 pa. 0-8091-3214-1 [TDig 39,255].

a967 **Ching** Julia, Konfuzianismus und Christentum 1989 ⇒ 6,b268: ᴿTR 87 (1991) 242-7 (W. *Promper*: thorough; notes English and French 'Ancestors' 1988 of her brother Frank).

ᴱCobb J., *Ives* C., The emptying God; a Buddhist-Jewish-Christian conversation 1990 ⇒ 6,398.

a969 **Cornille** Catherine, The Guru in Indian Catholicism; ambiguity or opportunity of inculturation?: TPastMg 6. Lv 1991, Peeters. 214 p. Fb 695 [NRT 114,593, J. *Masson*].

a970 ᴱ**Coward** Harold, Hindu-Christian dialogue; perspectives and encounters. Mkn 1989, Orbis. xix-281 p. $30; pa. $15. 0-88344-634-0; pa. -3-2. – ᴿHorizons 18 (1991) 353s (D. P. *Sheridan*); LvSt 16 (1991) 389-391 (Catherine *Cornille*).

a971 **Dharmasiri** Gunapala,   A Buddhist critique of the Christian concept of God 1988 → 5,b242:   [R]CurrTMiss 18 (1991) 292-5 (J. C. *Rochelle*).

a972 **Dumoulin** Heinrich,   Begegnung mit dem Buddhismus, eine Einführung[2rev] [[1]1978]: Tb 1732.   FrB 1991, Herder.   205 p.   DM 15,80 [TLZ 117,417, M. *Baumann*].

a973 *Favaro* Gaetano,   'Dio, mondo e natura nelle religioni orientali' [Brescia 20-22.VI.1991; 7 compendi nutriti]: RasT ForumATI 32 (1991) 420-6.

a974 **Griffiths** Bede, A new vision of reality, [E]*Edwards* Felicity 1989 → 6,b278: [R]TLond 94 (1991) 56s (U. *King*).

a975 **Hardy** Gilbert G.,   Monastic quest and interreligious dialogue [Zen, DÔGEN]. NY 1990, Lang.   x-285 p. $52.   0-8204-1207-4 [TDig 39,167].

a976 **Healy** Kathleen,   Christ as common ground; a study of Christianity and Hinduism.   Pittsburgh 1990, Duquesne Univ.   xiv-218 p. $25.   0-8207-0227-7 [TDig 38,165].

a977 **Henderson** John B.,   Scripture, canon, and commentary; a comparison of Confucian and Western exegesis.   Princeton 1991, Univ.   xii-247 p.   0-691-06832-1 [TDig 38,361].

a978 [E]**Hiltebeitel** Alf,   Criminal gods and demon devotees... Hinduism 1985/9 → 6,b279:   [R]Anthropos 86 (1991) 365s (Aditya *Malik*); JAOS 111 (1991) 737-767 (R. P. *Das*).

a979 **Ingram** P., *Streng* F.,   The modern Buddhist-Christian dialogue 1986 → 5,b250:   [R]ZMissRW 74 (1990) 309s (H. *Waldenfels*).

a980 **Jang Wang Shik,**   Faith as the ground of freedom in the teaching of WHITEHEAD and WONHYO; a comparative study between Whtehead's metaphysics and Hua-yen Buddhism: diss. [D]*Cobb* J.   Claremont 1991 [RelStR 18,170; there also **Kang Sungdo** on POJO].

a981 *a) Jensen* Debra J.,   Soteriology from a Christian and Hindu perspective; – *b) Adamo* David T.,   Soteriological dialogue between Wesleyan Christian and Pure Land Sect Buddhism: JDharma 14 (1989) 353-365 / 366-375.

a982 **Kaiser** Rudolf,   Gott schläft im Stein; [asiat.] indianische und abendländische Weltansichten im Widerstreit.   Mü 1990, Kösel.   175 p. – [R]ZkT 113 (1991) 498 (K. H. *Neufeld*).

a983 **Minnema** L.,   Bespiegelingen aan het venster; anthropologische bouwstenen voor een vergelijkend-godsdienstwetenschappelijke verheldering van de interreligieuze dialoog naar aanleiding van K. NISHITANI's boeddhistische en K. RAHNER's christelijke godsdienstwijsbegeerte: geref. diss. Kampen, [D]*Holtrop* P.   Kampen 1990, Mondiss.   343 p. 90- 5337-007-2. – TsTNijm 31 (1991) 90.

a983* *Okumura* Ichiro,   Bouddhisme-Zen et mystique chrétienne: Teresianum 42 (1991) 475-510.

a984 **Paul** G. S.,   Aspect of Confucianism; a study of the relationship between rationality and humanness.   Fra 1990, Lang.   203 p. Fs 60 [NRT 114,595, J. *Scheuer*].

a985 **Pieris** Aloysius,   Love meets wisdom 1988 → 5,b272; 6,b291:   [R]Tablet 245 (1991) 75s (M. *Barnes*).

a986 **Pieris** Aloysius,   Liebe und Weisheit; Begegnung von Christentum und Buddhismus 1989 → 5,b273; 6,b291:   [R]MiscFranc 91 (1991) 525s (J. *Imbach*).

a987 **Puttanil** Thomas,   A comparative study on the theological methodology of IRENAEUS of Lyon and SANKARACHARYA [Vedanta-philosopher 800 A.D.; diss. München]: RelW 4.   Fra 1990, Lang.   xii-379 p. – [R]TLZ 116 (1991) 814-6 (M. von *Brück*).

a987* *Sin* Jaime L., Situación de la Iglesia en Asia y el diálogo con las religiones no-cristianas: Studium 31 (M 1991) 99-109.

a988 *Sobrino* Jon, Eastern religions and liberation: Horizons 18 (1991) 78-92.

a989 **Staffner** Hans, Jesus Christ and the Hindu community... synthesis? 1988 ➤ 5,b280; 6,b297: ᴿETL 67 (1991) 461-3 (V. *Neckebrouck*, also on *Vempeny* I. and ᴱ*Coward* H.).

a990 **Standaert** N., YANG TINGYUN, Confucian and Christian in late Ming China; his life and thought: Sinica Leidensia 19, ᴰ1988 ➤ 5,b281: 90-04-08127-5. – ᴿGregorianum 72 (1991) 379-381 (A. *Wolanin*).

a991 *Steyn* H.C., The influence of Buddhism on Thomas MERTON: JStRel 3,2 (1990) 3-14 [< ZIT 91,130].

a992 **Thomas** M.M., Christus im Neuen Indien; Reform-Hinduismus und Christentum [c. 1965, verkürzt], ᵀ*Gensichen* A. & H.-W.: TÖk 23. Gö 1989, Vandenhoeck & R. 204 p. DM 40 [TLZ 117,172, M. v. *Brück*].

a993 *Vollenweider* Samuel, Grosser Tod und grosses Leben; ein Beitrag zum buddhistisch-christlichen Gespräch im Blick auf die Mystik des Paulus: EvT 51 (1991) 365-382.

M8.9 **Religiones Africae** (maxime ➤ H8.6) **et Amerindiae.**

a994 ᴱ**Hering** Wolfgang, Christus in Afrika; Zur Inkulturation des Glaubens im schwarzen Kontinent: Glaube-Wissen-Wirken 15. Limburg/L 1991, Lahn. 168 p. DM 25. 3-7840-2017-8.

a995 **Leon-Portilla** Miguel, Native Mesoamerican spirituality; ancient myths, discourses, stories...: Classics of Western Spirituality. NY 1980, Paulist. xx-300 p. 0-8091-2231-6.

a996 *a) Lewis* James R., Images of traditional African religions in surveys of world religions; – *b) Baum* Robert M., Graven images; scholarly representations of African religions: Religion 20 (L 1990) 311-322 / 355-360 [< ZIT 90,866].

a997 *Martin* Joel W., Before and beyond the Sioux ghost dance; native American prophetic movements and the study of religion: JAAR 59 (1991) 677-701.

a998 **Monaco** Emanuela, Manitu e Sindigo; visione e antropofagia tra gli Algonchini: 'Chi siamo' 20. R 1990, Bulzoni. 215 p. – ᴿSMSR 57 (1991) 187-193 (P. *Taviani*).

a999 **Parkin** David, Sacred void; spatial images of work and ritual among the Giriama of Kenya. C 1991, Univ. 259 p. $54.50 [JAAR 59,884].

b1 **Ridington** Robin, Trail to heaven; knowledge and narrative in a Northern [British Columbia Indian] native community. Iowa City 1988, Univ. 304 p. $27.50. – ᴿJAAR 55 (1991) 864-6 (W.C. *James*).

XVIII,1. Historia Medii Orientis Biblici

Q1 *Syria prae-islamica, Canaan,* **Israel Veteris Testamenti.**

b2 **Ahlström** Gösta W., Who were the Israelites? 1986 ➤ 2,9202. b811... 6,b306: ᴿIsrEJ 41 (1991) 297-300 (Gloria S. *Merker*).

b3 **Alt** Albrecht, Essays on OT history and religion [1953/64], ᵀ*Wilson* R.A. 1989 ➤ 5,225: ᴿETL 67 (1991) 131-3 (M. *Vervenne*, Eng.).

b3* *Bietak* Manfred, Zur Landnahme Palästinas durch die Seevölker und zum Ende der ägyptischen Provinz Kana'an: ➤ 85c, [F]KAISER W., MiDAI-K 47 (1991) 35-50; 4 fig.

b4 **Bock** Sebastian, Kleine Geschichte des Volkes Israel — von den Anfängen bis in die Zeit des NTes; Einl. *Lohfink* N.: Tb 1642, 1989 ➤ 5,b291; 6,b311: [R]BL (1991) 35 (A. *Mayes*: popularization of the best sort); TLZ 116 (1991) 106-8 (D. *Conrad*); TPhil 66 (1991) 239s (H. *Engel*, auch 240-2 über GUNNEWEG A., beide unter Rubrik 'Biblische Theologie').

b5 **Castel** François, The history of Israel and Judah in OT times 1985 ➤ 1,a904... 5,b292: [R]BZ 35 (1991) 282s (D. *Kinet*).

b6 **Clauss** Manfred, Geschichte Israels 1986 ➤ 2,9210... 6,b314: [R]CiuD 203 (1991) 485 (J. *Gutiérrez*).

   Coote Robert B., Early Israel 1990 ➤ 2362.

b7 *Crown* Alan D., Redating the schism between the Judaeans and the Samaritans [3d cent. C.E.]: JQR 82 (1991s) 17-50.

b8 **Egan** J. M., The fullness of time; essays in biblical chronology. Elmira NY 1990, Sator. iv-388 p. $17 [RB 99,565, J. J. *Taylor*].

b9 **Galbiati** Enrico, A história da salvação no Antigo Testamento,[T]. Petrópolis 1988, Vozes. 552 p. – [R]Brotéria 132 (1991) 89 (F. *Pires Lopes*).

b10 **Giardina** Andrea, *al.*, Palestine, histoire d'une terre [1987 ➤ 3,b570], [T]*Vallée* Mireille, [E]*Bontems* Claude. P 1990, Harmattan. 224 p.

b11 **Glatt** David A., Chronological displacement in biblical and related literatures: diss. Pennsylvania, [D]*Tigay* J. Ph 1991. 354 p. 92-11936. – DissA 52 (1991s) 3967s-A.

b12 **Hughes** Jeremy, Secrets of the times; myth and history in biblical chronology [D]1990 ➤ 6,b322: [R]ÉTRel 66 (1991) 280s (D. *Lys*); Henoch 13 (1991) 239-242 (P. *Sacchi*); JTS 42 (1991) 155-7 (G. H. *Jones*); TLZ 116 (1991) 269-271 (P. *Mommer*: Alternativ zu JEPSEN).

b13 **Kessler** Rainer, Staat und Gesellschaft im vorexilischen Juda: ev. Hab.– Diss. Bethel 1991, [D]*Crüsemann* F. – TR 87 (1991) 511.

b14 **Knauf** Ernst A., Ismael[2] 1989 ➤ 4,d97; 6,b327: [R]OrAnt 28 (1989) 275-7 (G. *Garbini*).

b15 **Kreuzer** Siegfried, Die Frühgeschichte Israels: BZAW 178, [D]1989 ➤ 5, b304; 6,b328: [R]TRu 56 (1991) 202-5 (A. H. J. *Gunneweg*).

   [E]**Laperrousaz** E. M., La protohistoire d'Israël; de l'exode à la monarchie 1990 ➤ 2371.

b17 **Lemche** Niels P., [➤ 2372s] The Canaanites and their land; the tradition of the Canaanites: JStOT supp 110. Sheffield 1991, Academic. 191 p. 1-85075-310-5.

b18 **Mazzinghi** Luca, Storia di Israele: Manuali di base. CasM 1991, Piemme. 199 p.; map.

b19 *a*) *Mazzoni* Stefania, Ebla e la formazione della cultura urbana in Siria; – *b*) *Archi* Alfonso, Ebla; la formazione di uno Stato del III millennio a.C.: ParPass 46,258ss (1991) 163-184 + 9 fig. / 195-219. ➤ d609s.

b20 **Mijolla** Joseph de, *Warnier* Philippe, Histoire de la foi: C'est-à-dire. P 1990, Centurion. 131 p. F 54. – [R]EsprVie 101 (1991) 93s (P. *Jay*: nouvelle Histoire Sainte, lisible, mais pour qui?).

b21 *a*) *Miller* J. Maxwell, Is it possible to write a history of Israel without relying on the Hebrew Bible?; – *b*) *Thompson* Thomas L., Text, context and referent in Israelite historiography; – *c*) *Knauf* Ernst A., From history to interpretation: ➤ 428, Fabric 1989/91, 93-102 / 65-92 / 26-64.

b22 **Nibbi** A., Canaan and Canaanite in ancient Egypt 1989 ➤ 5,b314; 6,b333*: [R]VT 41 (1991) 506 (J. D. *Ray*).

b23 **Oorschot** Jürgen, Von Babel zum Zion: Hab.-Diss. Marburg 1991s. – RTLv 23, p. 540.
b24 **Pixley** Jorge, *a)* A história de Israel a partir dos pobres[2], ᵀ*Mincato* Ramiro. Petrópolis 1990, Vozes. – ᴿEstudosB 29 (1991) 96-102 & REB 51 (1991) 486-491 (N. *Brasil Pereira*). – *b)* Historia sagrada, historia popular; historia de Israel desde los pobres (1220 a.C. a 135 d.C.). San José CR 1989, DEI. 125 p. – ᴿEfMex 9 (1991) 120-2 (M. *Villalobos*).
b25 **Quinzio** S., *al.*, Israele e le genti 1991 ➤ 5,b325a.
b27 **Sarigiannis** Chrysanthos G., ❻ *Synoptikē historía tês epochês tês P.D.* Cyprus 1990. 466 p. – ᴿTAth 29 (1990) 528-532 (P. *Simotas*).
b28 **Schäfer** Peter, Histoire des Juifs dans l'antiquité, ᵀ*Schulte* Pascale 1989 ➤ 5,b320; 6,b337: ᴿÉTRel 66 (1991) 117s (Marianne *Seckel*).
b29 ᴱ**Shanks** Hershel, Ancient Israel 1989 ➤ 4,326; 5,b322; 6,b338: ᴿEvangel 7,2 (1989) 21 (K. A. *Kitchen*: outdated); EvQ 63 (1991) 347s (R. P. *Gordon*: MᶜCARTER on patriarchs up-to-date but constructive); PrzPow 268,824 (1990) 141-4 (W. *Chrostowski*, ❼); Themelios 15 (1989s) 25-28 (also K. A. *Kitchen*: unfavoring, especially on the Egypt chapter) & 28s (R. S. *Hess*: touches recent developments).
b30 **Sharkansky** Ira, Ancient and modern Israel; an exploration of political parallels. Albany c. 1991 SUNY. xi-194 p. $11 [RelStR 18,243, J. *Teitelbaum*].
b31 **Smelik** Klaas A. D., Writings from ancient Israel; a handbook of historical and religious documents [1984/7 ➤ 3,b592], ᵀ*Davies* G. I. E 1991, Clark. ix-191 p. maps. 0-567-29202-9.
b32 *Smelik* Klaas A. D., Het Oude Testament en de geschiedenis van Oud-Israel; CollatVL 21 (1991) 251-270.
b32* **Soggin** J. A., Einführung in die Geschichte Israels und Judas, von den Ursprüngen bis zum Aufstand Bar Kochbas. Da 1991, Wiss. xv-295 p. DM 45 [ZAW 104,460, H.-C. *Schmitt*].
b33 **Stioui** R., Le calendrier hébraïque, *yᵉsôd ha'ibbûr*. P 1988, Colbo. 259 p. – ᴿHenoch 12 (1990) 379s (B. *Chiesa*: 'un singolare e riuscitissimo esempio di connubio tra tradizione e innovazione' in comparazione con le 'tante belle ipotesi' di HAYES-HOOKER).
b34 ṬABARĪ: The immense history, including Palestine and early biblical data, is being translated in two simultaneous projects, of which we have noted these volumes in their respective geographical area: **SUNY** project: vol. **1**, 1989 ➤ 5,1974; 6,2131; – **4**. 1987 ➤ 5,b481; 6,b517; – **6**. 1988 ➤ 5,b225; 6,b158; – **18**. ➤ 6,b517a (BO); **26**. 1989 ➤ 6,b182; **27**. ➤ 6,b517a (BO); **30**. 1989 (➤ 6,b160); **32**. 1987 ➤ 5,b125a; **37**. 1987 ➤ 5,b125b; **38**. ➤ b517a (BO); add now **9**. ᴿRelStR 18,243 (G. *Newby*); **13**. ᴱ**Juynboll** Gautier H. A., The conquest of Iraq 1989; ᴿJSS 36 (1991) 172-181 (R. *Kimbar*, rectifications); **20**. ᴱ**Hawting** G., 1989, ᴿJSS 36 (1991) 365-8 (D. *Jackson*; 368-70, A. *Elal* on vol. 30); – In the **Cambridge** project, only **1**s. 1989 ➤ 6,b160; now **23**. ᴱ**Hinds** Martin, 1990: ᴿBSO 54 (1991) 579s (L. A. J. *Okhman*).
b35 **Talmon** Shemaryahu, King, cult and calendar in ancient Israel 1986 ➤ 2,227: ᴿBijdragen 52 (1991) 96s (F. De *Meyer*).
b36 *Thompson* Thomas L., 'From the Stone Age to Israel': ProcGLM 11 (1991) 9-32; p. 9 accepting J. M. MAXWELL abandons his 'former erroneous objection ... that the tradition was irrelevant to a history of Israel's origins'.
b36* **Vogt** K., Piccola storia di Israele [Wann ihr 1985, ᵀ*Poletti* Gianni], 1989 ➤ 6,b343: ᴿAntonianum 66 (1991) 583 (M. *Nobile*).

b37 *Weippert* Manfred & Helga,   Die Vorgeschichte Israels in neuem Licht: TRu 56 (1991) 341-390 [MENDENHALL G., FINKELSTEIN I. ...].

b38 *a) Wenning* Robert,   Nachrichten über Griechen in Palästina in der Eisenzeit; – *b) Rey-Coquais* Jean-Paul,   Les Grecs en Syrie du IVème s. avant J.-C. au IVème s. après J.-C.; – *c) Hegyi* Dolores,   Greek cults in Syria in the archaic age: ➤ 588, Diaspora 1988/91, 207-219 / 185-197 / 199-206.

b39 *a) Westermann* Claus,   Kirchengeschichte und Geschichte Israels; – *b) Stiewe* Martin,   Altes Testament und Studienreform: ➤ 75, [F]HERRMANN S., Prophetie 1991, 425-8 / 376-384.

Q2   **Historiographia** – *theologia historiae.*

b40 **Adler** William,   Time immemorial; archaic history and its sources in Christian chronography 1989 ➤ 6,b344; $19.50. – [R]AmHR 96 (1991) 488s (C. *Frazee*); BSO 54 (1991) 147s (A. *Cameron*); ByZ 83 (1991) 469s (F. *Winkelmann*); CritRR 4 (1991) 98-100 (B. Z. *Wacholder*); JAOS 111 (1991) 664s (A. A. *Mosshammer*); RÉByz 49 (1991) 293s (A. *Failler*); Speculum 66 (1991) 112-4 (B. *Baldwin*).

b41 *Baget Bozzo* Giovanni,   La teología de la historia en la Ciudad de Dios: AugM 35 (1990) 31-80. 321-367.

b42 *Bogliolo* Luigi,   Il concetto di storia in S. TOMMASO: DoctCom 43 (1990) 266-276.

b43 **Boschi** Bernardo G.,   Le origini di Israele nella Bibbia fra storia e teologia; la questione del metodo e la sfida storiografica 1989 ➤ 5,b337: [R]Carthaginensia 7 (1991) 251s (R. *Sanz Valdivieso*).

b44 **Boucher** David,   The social and political thought of R. G. COL-LINGWOOD.   C 1989, Univ.   xi-300 p. $44.50. – [R]AmHR 96 (1991) 127s (W. M. *Johnston*).

b45 **Breese** Dave,   Seven men who rule the world from the grave.   Ch 1990, Moody.   237 p. $15 [CBQ 53,532].

b45* *a) Brezzi* P.,   Chroniques universelles du moyen âge et histoire du salut; – *b) Nelson* J. L.,   Gender and genre in woman historians of the Early Middle Ages: ➤ 590*, [E]*Genet* J., Historiographie 1989/91, 235-245 / 149-163.

b46 [E]**Cameron** Averil,   History as text; the writing of ancient history. L 1989, Duckworth.   viii-208. £17.   0-7156-2240-4. – [R]JRS 81 (1991) 176s (D. F. *Kennedy*).

b47 **Carena** Omar,   History of the Near Eastern historiography and its problems, 1852-1985: AOAT 218/1, 1989 ➤ 5,b340:   [R]Protestantesimo 46 (1991) 214 (J. A. *Soggin*).

b48 *Cazelles* Henri,   Historiographies bibliques et prébibliques: RB 98 (1991) 481-512; Eng. 481.

b49 **Cesana** Andreas,   Geschichte als Entwicklung? Zur Kritik des geschichtsphilosophischen Entwicklungsdenkens.   B 1988, de Gruyter.   xii-406 p. – [R]HistTheor 30 (1991) 115s (*ipse*).

b50 [E]**Clarke** Graeme, *al.*,   Reading the past in late antiquity [meeting 1988, follow-up to 1983 History & historians].   0-08-034407-0. 1990 ➤ 6,479: [R]JRS 81 (1981) 233 (J. *Liebeschuetz*); Prudentia 23 (1991) 55-62 (A. D. *Lee*); RHPR 71 (1991) 367s (P. *Maraval*).

b52 **Colombo** Joseph A.,   An essay on theology and history; studies in PANNENBERG, METZ, and the Frankfurt School: [J]AAR StR 61. Atlanta

1990, Scholars.   xiv-264 p. $45; pa. $30.   1-55540-540-1; -1-X [TDig 38,352: treats also M. HORKHEIMER and T. ADORNO].

b53 *Derisi* Octavio, Filosofia de la historia; historia y conocimiento histórico: DoctCom 43 (1990) 16-25.

b54 *Díaz Mateos* Manuel, The Word in history: Jeevadhara 21 (1991) 391-5.

b55 **Dilthey** Wilhelm, L'édification du monde historique dans les sciences de l'esprit [1910], TE*Mesure* Sylvie: Œuvres 3. P 1988, Cerf. 144 p. – RBrotéria 132 (1991) 352 (F. *Pires Lopes*).

b56 **Doran** Robert M., Theology and the dialectics of history 1900 ➤ 6,b361: RMilltSt 27 (1991) 155-8 (H. *Delaney*) [+ 28 (1991) 102-131]; SR 20 (1991) 369 (H. *Meynell*); TorJT 7 (1991) 257-263 (C. C. *Hefling*).

b56* *Douglass* Jane D., Marie DENTIÈRE's use of Scripture in her theology of history: ➤ 58, FFROEHLICH K. 1991, 227-244.

b57 **Dray** William H., On history and philosophers of history [2 inedita + 8 since 1967] 1989 ➤ 6,224: RHistTheor 30 (1991) 90-95 (A. *Donaghan*).

b58 **Dunkel** Achim, Christlicher Glaube und historische Vernunft; eine interdisziplinäre Untersuchung über die Notwendigkeit eines theologischen Geschichtsverständnisses: ForSystÖ 57, D1989 ➤ 6,b362: RTsTKi 61 (1990) 304s (J.-O. *Henriksen*).

b59 **Elton** G. R., Return to essentials; some reflections on the present state of historical study. C 1991, Univ. ix-128 p. £17 [RHE 86,256*].

b60 *Fischer* Hermann, Storia e metafisica; le radici religiose della filosofia della storia di Ernst TROELTSCH, T*Cantillo* Giuseppe, *Sorrentino* Sergio: RasT 32 (1991) 144-159.

b61 **Forte** Bruno, Teologia della storia; saggio sulla rivelazione, l'inizio e il compimento: Simbolica ecclesiale 7. Mi 1991, Paoline. 376 p. Lit. 25.000. – RAsprenas 38 (1991) 215-228 (A. *Russo*); RasT 32 (1991) 427-432 (P. *Coda*).

b62 **Garbini** Giovanni, History and ideology in ancient Israel 1988 ➤ 4, d131 ... 6,b366: RBZ 35 (1991) 115s (D. *Kinet*); HeythJ 32 (1991) 256 (B. P. *Robinson*: refreshing, irritating); NBlackf 71 (1990) 43s (W. *Harrington*: Italy's James BARR).

b63 *Garsiel* Moshe, Between history & historiography: Teuda 4 (c. 1988) ...

b64 **Góźdź** Krzysztof, Jesus Christus als Sinn der Geschichte bei W. PANNENBERG [DEichstätt 1986] 1988 ➤ 6,b370: RArTGran 53 (1990) 246s (R. *Franco*); ColcT 60,4 (1990) 179-181 (C. S. *Bartnik*, ●).

b65 *Gruber* J. [*al.*], Historiographie, Antike: ➤ 681, LexMA 5 (1990) 45s [-54].

b66 **Guerra Pratas** Maria H. da, El valor revelador de la historia según santo Tomás de AQUINO: diss. Santa Croce, DCirillo A. Roma 1989. 787 p. – RTLv 23, p. 567.

b67 **Haga** Tsutomi, Theologie und Geschichtstheologie; ein Versuch der Überwindung der Problematik des deutschen Idealismus bei K. BARTH: ForSysÖkT 59. Gö 1991, Vandenhoeck & R. 289 p. 3-525-56266-7. – RActuBbg 28 (1991) 170s (J. *Boada*).

b68 **Hall** Robert G., Revealed histories; techniques for ancient Jewish and Christian historiography: JPseud supp 6. Sheffield 1991, Academic. 276 p. £35; pa. £26.25. 1-85075-249-4.

b69 *Hardtwig* Wolfgang, Geschichtsreligion — Wissenschaft als Arbeit — Objektivität; der Historismus in neuer Sicht: HZ 252 (1991) 1-32.

b70 **Haught** John F., The revelation of God in history 1988 ➤ 4,8107: RHorizons 17 (1990) 340-3 (P. D. *Molnar*).

b70* *Herrmann* Siegfried, Die Abwertung des ATs als Geschichtsquelle; Bemerkungen zu einem geistesgeschichtlichen Problem: ➤ 454c, Sola Scriptura 1990/1, 156-165.

b71 **Hodgson** Peter C., God in history; shapes of freedom 1989 ➤ 5,b359: RJRel 70 (1990) 266s (B. E. *Hinze*); ScotJT 44 (1991) 538 (R. *Morgan*).

b72 *Laak* Dirk van, 'Am Anfang war das Wort'; über die Theorien zum Beginn von Geschichte: Sæculum 40 (1989) 296-312.

b73 **Laudizi** G., SILIO Italico; il passato tra mito e restaurazione etica. Galatina 1989, Congedo. 187 p. – RAufidus 11s (1990) 274s (Paola *L-isimberti*).

b74 ELe **Goff** Jacques, *al.*, Die Rückeroberung des historischen Denkens... T*Kaiser* Wolfgang. Fra 1990, Fischer-Tb. 287 p. DM 48. – RHZ [233 (1981) 106-129] 253 (1991) 675s (L. *Raphael*).

b75 **Lettieri** Gaetano, Il senso della storia in Agostino 1988 ➤ 5,b364: RAugM 35 (1990) 384-6 (J. *Oroz*); AugR 30 (1990) 193-5 (P. *Miccoli*).

b76 **McNeill** William H., Arnold K. TOYNBEE, a life. Ox 1989, UP. viii-346 p. – RHistTheor 30 (1991) 381-4 (G. *Muller*: a historian who undeservedly fell into oblivion so soon after his death).

b77 **Maffeis** Gustavo, Il piano di Dio nella storia. T-Leumann 1989, Elle Di Ci. 334 p. – RScuolC 118 (1990) 268s (E. *Galbiati*).

b78 **Manno** A. G., Lo storicismo di W. DILTHEY [1833-1911]. N 1990, Loffredo. 350 p. Lit. 40.000. – RDoctCom 43 (1990) 193-6 (A. *Capuano*).

b80 **Miccoli** P., *al.*, Il problema della storia: Filosofia per problemi. Palermo 1988, Augustinus. 170 p. Lit. 13.000. – RDivThom 93 (1990) 186-190 (J. J. *Sanguineti*); Protestantesimo 45 (1990) 236s (Elena *Bein Ricco*).

b81 *Müller* Karlheinz, Abschied von der 'Heilsgeschichte' [< EMaier J., Lit. Rel. Früh.-J. 1973, 73-92]: ➤ 241, Studien 1991, 175-193.

b82 **Muhlack** U., Geschichtswissenschaft im Humanismus und in der Aufklärung; die Vorgeschichte des Historismus. Mü 1991, Beck. 460 p. DM 98 [RHE 86,256*].

b83 *Neusner* Jacob, The historical event as a cultural indicator; the case of Judaism: HistTheor 30 (1991) 136-152.

b84 *Nobbs* Alanna M., PHILOSTORGIUS' Ecclesiastical History; an alternative ideology: TyndB 42 (1991) 271-281.

b85 *Noort* Edward, Klio und die Welt des ATs: ➤ 87, FKOCH K., Ernten 1991, 533-560.

b86 *Penco* Gregorio, Chiesa, cristianesimo, cristianità nella riflessione storiografica moderna: HumB 46 (1991) 719-730.

b87 **Plass** Paul, Wit and the writing of history; the rhetoric of historiography in imperial Rome. Studies in Classics, 1988 ➤ 5,b373; 6,b392: RAmJPg 112 (1991) 417-420 (Elizabeth *Keitel*); Phoenix 44 (Toronto 1990) 393-7 (J. *Griffin*); RÉAnc 92 (1990) 410s (Lucienne *Deschamps*); RFgIC 119 (1991) 358s (N. *Horsfall*: mancanze 'perdonabili' notate da lui come già da A. *Woodman*, ClasR 1990, 312; H. *Benario*, AmerHR 1990, 361).

b88 **Ratzinger** Joseph, La théologie de l'histoire de s. BONAVENTURE [D1957-9] TGivord R. 1988 ➤ 5,b374; 6,b395: RLavalTP 47 (1991) 129s (J.-C. *Petit*).

b89 *a*) *Reisch* George A., Chaos, history, and narrative; – *b*) *McCloskey* Donald N., History, differential equations and the problem of narration: HistTheor 30 (1991) 1-20 / 21-36.

b90 *Russell* Peter A. Eric VOEGELIN; an eschatological direction in history?: Fides et historia 22,3 (1990) 3-15 [< ZIT 91,100].

b91 *Russo* Adolfo, Teologia della storia e crisi di senso [FORTE B. 1991]: Asprenas 38 (1991) 215-228.

b92 *Schepens* Guido, Oorlog en beschaving; beschouwingen bij het antieke geschiedenisbegrip: RBgPg 69 (1991) 7-32.

b93 ᴱ**Sebeok** Thomas A., *Umiker-Sebeok* J., Recent developments in theory and history; the semiotic web 1990: Approaches to Semiotics 100. B 1991, Mouton de Gruyter. xi-554 p.; portraits. 3-11-012796-2. 21 art.

b94 *Siegele-Wenschkewitz* Leonore, Ist Ethik eine Kategorie der Historiographie?: EvT 51 (1991) 155-168.

b95 *Tavernier* Johan de, L'histoire humaine dite 'profane', véhicule de l'histoire du salut et du malheur; 'hors du monde, point de salut': ᵀ*Braat* Anne: → 348, Concilium 236 (P 1991) 13-28.

Thompson Thomas L., Text, context and referent in Israelite historiography; *Knauf* E.; *Miller* J., 1989/91 → b21 supra.

b96 *Vansina* Jan, Oral tradition as history. L 1988, Currey. xviii-258 p. 0-85255-006-5; pa. -7-3.

b97 *Viciano* Alberto, Dos visiones de la historia en la antigüedad; Tito Livio y Agustín de Hipona: CiuD 203 (1990) 583-592.

b98 *Vinke* Ramón, El Dr. Mario Briceño-Iragorry y la interpretación cristiana de la historia: T-Iusi 7 (1991) 79-90.

b99 *Weichel* Erich, Hegels Geschichtsphilosophie: NSys 33 (1991) 23-43; Eng. 43.

b100 **Wells** Ronald A., History through the eyes of faith [→ 6,b403]; Western civilization and the Kingdom of God: Christian College Coalition. SF 1989, Harper & R. 262 p. $10 pa. – ᴿInterpretation 45 (1991) 102.104 (T. J. *Wengert* compares Dean W. 1988).

b101 **Wilcox** Donald J., The measure of times past; pre-Newtonian chronologies and the rhetoric of relative time. Ch 1987, Univ. 292 p. – ᴿEngHR 106 (1991) 425s (G. *Leff*: straw man; what does he expect of the writing of history?).

Q3 *Historia Ægypti* – Egypt.

b102 *Allam* Schafik, *a*) Egyptian law-courts in Pharaonic and Hellenistic times: JEA 77 (1991) 109-127; – *b*) Note sur le mariage par deux contrats dans l'Égypte gréco-romaine: CdÉ 65 (1990) 323-333; – *c*) Women as holders of rights in ancient Egypt (during the late period): JESHO 33 (1990) 1-34.

b103 *Andrassy* P., Zur Struktur der Verwaltung des Alten Reichs: ZäSpr 118 (1991) 1-10.

b104 *a*) *Arnold* Felix, The High Stewards of the early Middle Kingdom; – *b*) *Smith* Stuart T., A model for Egyptian imperialism in Nubia: GöMiszÄg 122 (1991) 7-14 / 77-102; 5 fig.

b105 *Bagnall* Roger S., The beginnings of the Roman Census in Egypt: GrRByz 32 (1991) 255-265; 1 pl.

b106 *Beaux* Nathalie, Ennemis étrangers et malfaiteurs égyptiens; la signification du châtiment au pilori: BIFAO 91 (1991) 33-53; 9 fig.

b106* *a*) *Beckerath* Jürgen von, Gedanken zu den Daten der Sed-Feste; – *b*) *Hornung* Erik, Sedfest und Geschichte; – *c*) *Seeher* Jürgen, Gedanken zur Rolle Unterägyptens bei der Herausbildung des Pharaonenreiches; – *d*) *Simpson* William K., Mentuhotep, vizier of Sesostris I, patron of art and architecture [largely at Karnak]: → 85c, ᶠKaiser W., MiDAI-K 47 (1991) 29-33 / 169-171 / 313-8; 2 fig. / 331-340; 1 fig.; pl. 45.

b107 ᶠBIEZUŃSKA-MALOWIST Iza: ℗ *Świat antyczny*... Le monde antique; rapports sociaux, idéologie et politique, religion, ᴱBravo Benedetto, *al.* 1988 ↠ 5,29: ᴿCdÉ 65 (1990) 371s (G. *Nachtergael*).

b108 **Bonhême** Marie-Ange, *Forgeau* Annie, Pharaon, les secrets du pouvoir 1988; 2-200-97120-9 ↠ 4,d175 (non 2-200-37129-9). – ᴿBO 48 (1991) 751-6 (M. *Malaise*).

b109 **Boorn** G.P.F. van den, The duties of the vizier; civil administration in the early New Kingdom: StEg 1988 ↠ 4,d177; 6,b414; £45: ᴿBO 48 (1991) 821-831; 1 fig. (J.-M. *Kruchten*: mise à jour de FARINA 1916).

b110 **Brambach** Joachim, Kleopatra und ihre Zeit; Legende und Wirklichkeit. Mü 1991, Calwey. 352 p.; 6 pl. 3-7667-0998-4 [OIAc 1,12].

b111 **Brunner**-Traut Emma, Kleine Ägyptenkunde, von den Pharaonen bis heute [³ʳᵉᵛ + *Jacobi* Renate, Islam]. Stu 1991, Kohlhammer. 302 p. DM 40.

b112 **Bryan** Betsy M., The reign of Thutmose IV [< diss. Yale 1980]. Baltimore 1991, Johns Hopkins Univ. 390 p.; 19 pl. 0-8018-4202-6 [OIAc F91].

b113 *Canducci* Daniela, I 6475 cateci [? property–owners] greci dell'Arsinoite: Aegyptus 71 (1991) 121-216.

b114 *Cesaretti* Maria Pia, Nerone e l'Egitto; messaggio politico e continuità culturale: StStoAnt 12. Bo 1989, CLUEB. 120 p.; 12 plans. Lit. 18.000. – ᴿCdÉ 65 (1990) 359-361 (J.C. *Grenier*).

b115 *Chauveau* Michel, a) Montouhotep et les Babyloniens; – b) Un contrat de 'hiérodule', le P. Dém. Fouad 2; – c) Étiquettes de momies: BIFAO 91 (1991) 147-153 / 119-127 / 135-146, pl. 38-45 / 155-9, pl. 46-47.

b116 *Cifola* Barbara, The terminology of Ramses III's historical records, with a formal analysis of the war scenes: Orientalia 60,2 (1991) 9-57.

b117 **Clarysse** Willy, *Vandorpe* Katelijn, Zenon, een Grieks manager in de schaduw van de piramiden [15 km van Meidoem, omslag-foto]. Leuven 1990, auct. 112 p.; color. ill.

b117* **Der Manuelian** Peter, Studies in the reign of Amenophis II, 1987 ↠ 3,b667: ᴿJNES 50 (1991) 213-5 (W.A. *Ward*).

b118 a) *Endrödi* J., 'Figurative discourse' and 'communication' in the emerging state of [early] Egypt; – b) *Guksch* Christian E., Ethnological models and processes of state formation; chiefdom survivals in the Old Kingdom: GöMiszÄg 125 (1991) 21-36 / 37-50.

b119 *Goedicke* Hans, Egyptian military actions in 'Asia' in the Middle Kingdom: RÉgp 42 (1991) 89-94.

b120 **Grenier** Jean-Claude, Les titulatures des empereurs romaines dans les documents en langue égyptienne: PapyrolBrux 22, 1989 ↠ 5,9425: ᴿArPapF 37 (1991) 73 (J. *Hallof*).

b121 **Grimal** Nicolas, Storia dell'antico Egitto. Bari 1990, Laterza. 619 p.; ill. Lit. 60.000. – ᴿArcheo 70 (1990) 128 (S. *Pernigotti*).

b122 **Grimal** N.-C., Les termes de la propagande royale égyptienne... 1986 ↠ 4,d196: ᴿVDI 198 (1991) 197-203 (T.A. *Delneka* ℗).

b123 **Helck** Wolfgang, Untersuchungen zur Thinitenzeit 1987 ↠ 3,b681; 6,b434: ᴿBO 48 (1991) 13-23 (G. *Godron*); OLZ 86 (1991) 145-150 (E. *Endesfelder*).

b124 **Hornung** Erik, Geist der Pharaonenzeit. Z 1990, Artemis. 224 p. 3-7608-1005-5. – ᴿBO 48 (1991) 747-751 (Gertie *Englund*).

b125 **James** T.G.H., Ancient Egypt; the land and its legacy 1988 ↠ 4,d201; 5,b406: ᴿJNES 50 (1991) 53s (W.A. *Ward*).

b126 *Jansen-Winkeln* Karl, Das Attentat auf Amenemhet I. und die erste ägyptische Koregentschaft: StAäK 18 (1991) 241-264.

b127 **Kambitsis** Sophie, Le papyrus Thmouis I, col. 68-160, 1985 ➤ 2,9331 ... 5,b408: ᴿBO 48 (1991) 527-9 (A. *Lukaszewicz*).

b128 *Kanawati* Naguib, The governors of the *w3ḏt*-Nome in the Old Kingdom: GöMiszÄg 121 (1991) 57-67.

b129 **Kemp** B., Ancient Egypt 1989 ➤ 5,b409: ᴿPhoenixEOL 37,1 (1991) 63s (L. *Zonhoven*).

b130 **Kitchen** K. A., Ramesside inscriptions 8,3-9. Ox c.1990, Blackwell. – ᴿOLZ 86 (1991) 267s (J. von *Beckerath*).

b131 **Lewis** N. La mémoire des sables 1988 ➤ 6,b441: ᴿCdÉ 65 (1990) 358s (J. *Lenaerts*); Syria 67 (1990) 763s (M. *Pezin*).

b132 **Lichtheim** Miriam, Ancient Egyptian autobiographies 1988 ➤ 4,d210*; 6,b442: ᴿArOr 59 (1991) 79s (Jana *Pečírková*); BO 48 (1991) 760-4 (R. B. *Parkinson*); OLZ 86 (1991) 364-7 (K. *Jansen-Winkeln*).

b133 **Lloyd** Alan B., *a*) Herodotus Book II 99-182: ÉPH 43, 1988 ➤ 4,d363; 5,b422: ᴿJEA 77 (1991) 223-5 (C. J. *Eyre*); – *b*) ERODOTO 2/2, L'Egitto: Fond. Valla. Mi 1989, Mondadori. lxxxii-410 p.; 13 maps. Lit. 45.000. – ᴿClasR 41 (1991) 309s (D. *Fehling*).

b134 *Maderna-Sieben* Claudia, Der historische Abschnitt des Papyrus Harris I [über Ramesses III]: GöMiszÄg 123 (1991) 57-90.

b135 **Manniche** Lise, Liebe und Sexualität im alten Ägypten; eine Text- und Bilddokumentation [Sexual life 1987 ➤ 3,b697]. Z 1988, Artemis. 193 p. Fs 36,80. 3-7608-0994-4. – ᴿBO 48 (1991) 756-9 (Lana *Troy*).

b136 **Müller-Wollermann** Renate, Krisenfaktoren im ägyptischen Staat des ausgehenden Alten Reichs. Tü 1986. viii-266 p. – ᴿBO 48 (1991) 93-97 (N. *Strudwick*).

b137 **Obsomer** Claude, Les campagnes de Sésostris dans HÉRODOTE ... à la lumière des réalités égyptiennes 1989 ➤ 5,b432; Fb 1000: ᴿRBgPg 69 (1991) 198-202 (M. *Malaise*); RÉG 104 (1991) 287s (G. *Lachenaud*).

b138 **Palme** B., Das Amt des apaitētēs: MPER 20. W 1989, Hollinek. 279 p.; 15 fig. – ᴿAegyptus 71 (1991) 296-9 (Carla *Salvaterra*): ᴿCdÉ 65 (1990) 366-9 (J. D. *Thomas*).

b138* **Pernigotti** Sergio, Siria e Palestina nella politica estera della XXVI dinastia: ➤ 627, Fen. 2, 1987/91, 187-192.

b139 **Piacentini** Patrizia, L'autobiografia di Uni, principe e governatore dell'Alto Egitto. Pisa 1990, Giardini. 107 p.

b140 **Quirke** Stephen, Who were the Pharaohs? 1990 ➤ 6,b451: ᴿPhoenixEOL 37,1 (1991) 65 (L. *Zonhoven*).

b141 **Redford** Donald B., Pharaonic king-lists, annals and day books; a contribution to the study of the Egyptian sense of history [< seminar partly in Orientalia 41 (1980)] 1986 ➤ 4,d219* ... 6,b455: ᴿBASOR 284 (1991) 92s (J. *Baines*: vast evidence not as clear as HORNUNG and OTTO); JNES 50 (1991) 51-53 (W. A. *Ward*).

b142 *Roehrig* Catherine, Royal nurses and tutors of Dynasty XVIII: News-AmEg 145 (1999) 4-6.

b143 **Rössler-Köhler** Ursula, Individuelle Haltungen zum ägyptischen Königtum der Spätzeit; private Quellen und ihre Königswertungen im Spannungsfeld zwischen Erwartung und Erfahrung: GöOrF 4/21. Wsb 1991, Harrassowitz. xiv-448 p. 3-447-03149-2.

b144 **Roth** Ann M., Egyptian phyles in the Old Kingdom; the evolution of a system of social organization: SAOC 48. Ch 1991, Univ. Or. Inst. xxvi-243 p.; ill. 0-918986-68-0.

b145 **Samuel** Alan E.,   The shifting sands of history; interpretations of Ptolemaic Egypt: AsnAncHistorians 2, 1989 → 6,b460:   ᴿPhoenix 45 (Toronto 1991) 361-5 (P. *Green*).

b146 *a*) *Simpson* William K.,   The political background of the Eloquent Peasant; – *b*) *Dodson* Aidan,   On the internal chronology of the seventeenth dynasty: GöMiszÄg 120 (1991) 95-99 / 33-38.

b147 **Sonnabend** Holger,   Fremdenbild und Politik; Vorstellungen der Römer von Ägypten und dem Partherreich in der späten Republik und frühen Kaiserzeit: EurHS 3/286, 1986 → 2,9619 ... 5,b440:   ᴿLatomus 50 (1991) 465-7 (A. *Valvo*).

b148 *Topozada* Zakeya,   Une stèle de Horemheb [Daressy 1917] retrouvée au Musée du Caire: BIFAO 91 (1991) 249-254; pl. 71-74.

b148* **Trigger** B. G., *al.*,   Storia sociale dell'antico Egitto,ᵀ.   Bari 1989, Laterza. 517 p. Lit. 55.000. – ᴿArcheo 62 (1990) 127 (S. *Pernigotti*).

b149 **Valbelle** D.,   Les neufs arcs — L'Égyptien et les étrangers de la préhistoire à la conquête d'Alexandre. P 1990, Colin. 316 p.; 6 maps. – ᴿRHPR 71 (1991) 209 (J.-G. *Heintz*).

b150 *Vercoutter* Jean,   La prédynastie égyptienne; anciens et nouveaux concepts: → 40, Mém. CLÈRE J. 1991, 137-146.

b151 *Wessetzky* Vilmos,   Fragen zum Verhalten der mit Persern zusammenarbeitenden Ägypter: GöMiszÄg 124 (1991) 83-89.

Q4   Historia Mesopotamiae.

b152 ᴱ**Aurenche** Olivier, *al.*,   Chronologies du Proche-Orient 1986/7 → 4,719: ᴿBO 48 (1991) 438-442 (Patty Jo *Watson*).

b153 **Barrelet** M.-T.,   Problèmes concernant les Hurrites II 1984 → 65,d31; 3,f677:   ᴿSyria 66 (1989) 365-7 (D. *Beyer*).

b154 **Beaulieu** Paul-Alain,   The reign of Nabonidus king of Babylon 556-539 B.C. [diss. 1985]; NERes 10, 1989 → 5,b452:   ᴿBL (1991) 35 (W. G. *Lambert*); CritRR 4 (1991) 103-5 (D. *Weisberg*).

b155 **Bengtson** Hermann,   Geschichte der Alten Welt. Fra 1989, Fischer Tb. 240 p.; 9 maps. – ᴿHispania Antiqua 15 (1991) 349s (J. *Díez Asensio*).

b156 **Crawford** Harriet,   Sumer and the Sumerians. C 1991, Univ. x-182 p.; 87 fig. 0-521-381754; pa. -8503. – ᴿMesop-T 26 (1991) 235s (A. *Invernizzi*).

b157 ᴱ**Deissmann** Marieluise,   Daten zur antiken Chronologie und Geschichte: Universal-Bibliothek 8628,3. Stu 1990, Reclam. 213 p.

b158 **Diakonoff** Igor M. [p. 87-97; and Palestine p. 286-308], *al.*,   Early antiquity, ᵀ*Kirjanov* Alexander. Ch 1991, Univ. xxiii-461 p.; maps. 0-226-14465-8.

b159 ᴱ**Durand** J.-M.,   La femme dans le Proche-Orient antique [Rencontre Assyr. 33, 1986] 1987 → 3,779:   ᴿOLZ 86 (1991) 276-283 (A. *Livingstone*).

b160 *a*) *Fales* Frederick M.,   Narrative and ideological variations in the account of Sargon's eighth campaign; – *b*) *Hallo* William W.,   The death of kings; traditional historiography in contextual perspective; – *c*) *Millard* Alan R.,   Large numbers in the Assyrian royal inscriptions; – *d*) *Lipiński* E.,   The Cypriot vassals of Esarhaddon; – *e*) *Leichty* Erle,   Esarhaddon's 'Letter to the gods'; → 150, ᶠTADMOR H., Ah Assyria 1991, 129-147 / 148-165 / 213-222 / 58-64 / 52-57.

b161 **Freydank** Helmut,   Beiträge zur mittelassyrischen Chronologie und Geschichte: SchrGKuAO 21. B 1991, Akademie. 227 p. 3-05-001814-3.

b162 *Freydank* Helmut,   Zum mittelassyrischen Königsbrief KBo XXVIII 61-64 [Tukultī-Ninurta I]: AltOrF 18 (1991) 23-31.

b164 **Grayson** A. Kirk,   Assyrian rulers of the early first millennium BC (1114-859): RIMA Periods 2, 1987 ➤ 3,b736 ... 6,b492:   ᴿAfO 36s (1989s) 120-4 (W. *Schramm*); OLZ 86 (1991) 38-41 (H. *Freydank*).

b165 **Harrak** Amir,   Assyria and Hanigalbat 1987 ➤ 3,b738 ... 6,b493:   ᴿAfO 36s (1989s) 140-3 (H. D. *Galter*); BO 48 (1991) 865-870 (W. H. van *Soldt*).

b166 **Healy** Mark,   The ancient Assyrians: Elite 39. L 1991, Osprey. 63 p.; colour. ill. (*McBride* A.).   1-85332-163-7.

b167 **Hrouda** Barthel (+ *Bottéro* Jean, *al.*),   Der Alte Orient; Geschichte und Kultur des alten Vorderasien. Mü 1991, Bertelsmann. 464 p.; (color.) ill. 3-570-08578-3.

b168 ᴱ**Klengel** Horst,   Kulturgeschichte des alten Vorderasien 1989 ➤ 6,b498: ᴿOLZ 86 (1991) 503-511 (M. *Liverani*).

b169 **Knapp** A. Bernard,   The history and culture of ancient Western Asia and Egypt 1988 ➤ 4,d248; 5,b471:   ᴿBA 54 (1991) 118-120 (K. A. *Kitchen*); JAOS 111 (1991) 139 (M. A. *Powell*).

b170 **Kraus** F. R.,   Königliche Verfügungen in altbabylonischer Zeit: StDJA 11, 1984 ➤ 65,9700 ... 5,b472:   ᴿJESHO 34 (1991) 116-122 (W. F. *Leemans*).

b171 **Kromholz** Alfred H.,   [➤ 4,d249]: *Sigrist* Marcel,   Concordance of the Isin-Larsa year-names 1986:   ᴿBO 48 (1991) 861s (Tina *Breckwoldt*).

b172 **Longman** Tremperᴵᴵᴵ,   Fictional Akkadian autobiography; a generic and comparative study. WL 1991, Eisenbrauns. xi-274 p. 0-931464-41-2.

b173 **Margueron** Jean-Claude,   Les Mésopotamiens: Civilisations. P 1991, Colin.   I. Le temps et l'espace, 231 p. – II. Le cadre de vie et la pensée. 233 p.; map. F 150.   2-200371-73-9; -4-6.

ᴱ**Müller** Hans-P.,   Babylonien und Israel: WegFor 633, 1991 ➤ 321.

b174 ᶠNAGEL W.,   Altvorderasien, ᴱ**Jacobs** B. 1988 ➤ 4,234:   ᴿAfO 36s (1989s) 145-8 (P. *Amiet*).

b175 **Nissen** Hans J.,   Protostoria del Vicino Oriente [1983 ➤ 64,a95], ᵀᴱ*Liverani* Mario. Bari 1990, Laterza. 264 p. Lit. 32.000.   88-420-3647-1.

b177 **Oelsner** Joachim,   Materialien zur babylonischen Gesellschaft und Kultur in hellenistischer Zeit 1986 ➤ 3,b745; 4,d255:   ᴿAfOr 36s (1989s) 136-8 (L. E. *Pearce*); BSO 53 (1990) 326s (R. J. van der *Spek*).

b178 **Parpola** Simo, *Watanabe* Kazuko, Neo-Assyrian treaties 1988 ➤ 4,d256: ᴿOLZ 86 (1981) 286s (Jana *Pečírková*).

b179 **Questa** C.,   Semiramide redenta [➤ 6,b513]; archetipi, fonti classiche, censure antropologiche nel melodramma: Lettura e antropologia.   Urbino 1989.   405 p. – ᴿAufidus 11s (1990) 279-281 (Rosalba *Dimundo*).

b180 **Saggs** H. W. F.,   Civilization before Greece 1989 ➤ 5,b488:   ᴿBAR-W 17,6 (1991) 4 (Diana *Edelman*); JAOS 111 (1991) 828 (T. B. *Jones*).

b181 **Saporetti** Claudio,   La terra tra i due fiumi. T 1989, Castalia.   37 p.; Lit. 16.000. – ᴿArcheo 64 (1990) 128 (S. F. *Bondi*).

b182 **Schmitt Pantel** Pauline,   Storia delle donne in occidente [ᴱ*Duby* G.], 1: l'antichità. Bari 1990, Laterza. xvii-598 p.; ill. Lit. 45.000. – ᴿEikasmos 2 (1991) 359-365 (Elena *Colla*).

b183 **Schneider** Tammi J.,   A new analysis of the royal annals of Shalmaneser III: diss. Pennsylvania, ᴰ*Leichty* E. Ph 1991. 285 p. 92-00385. – DissA 52 (1991s) 2674s-A.

b184 **Sigrist** Marcel,   Larsa year names: Assyr. 3. Berrien Springs MI 1990, Andrews Univ. [iv-] 87 p. 0-943872-54-5.

b185 **Starr** Chester G.,   A history of the ancient world⁴ [¹1965].   NY 1991, Oxford-UP. xviii-742 p.; 32 pl.; 20 maps. 0-19-506628-6; pa. -9-4.

b186 **Tinney** Stephen J.,   The Nippur Lament; ancient Sumerian literature and politics in the reign of Ishme-Dagan of Isin (1953-1935 B.C.): diss. Michigan, ᴰ*Michalowski* P. AA 1991. 283 p. 91-35707. – DissA 52 (1991s) 2675-A.

b188 **Wilhelm** G.,   The Hurriansᵀ + *Stein* Diana, Hurrian architecture, 1989 ➤ 5,b497; 6,b521*:   ᴿBInstArch 27 (1990) 253s (C. O. *Lange*).

b189 *Young* Dwight W.,   The incredible regnal spans of Kish I in the Sumerian King List: JNES 50 (1991) 23-35.

Q4.5   *Historia Persiae* – **Iran.**

b190 **Balcer** Jack M.,   HERODOTUS and Bisitun 1987 ➤ 3,b765 … 6,b528: ᴿMnemosyne 44 (1991) 469 (H. T. *Wallinga*).

b191 *Cardascia* Guillaume,   La ceinture de Parysatis; une Morgengabe chez les Achéménides?: ➤ 61, ᶠGARELLI P.,   Marchands 1991, 363-370.

b192 **Cassin-Scott** Jack,   The Greek and Persian wars: Men-at-Arms 69. L 1991, Osprey. 40 p.; 34 (colour.) ill. 0-85045-271-6.

b193 **Curtis** John,   Ancient Persia. L 1989, British Museum.   72 p.; 85 (colour.) fig.; map. £7. 0-7141-2046-4.

b194 **Dandamaev** M. A., *Lukonin* V. G.,   The culture and social institutions of ancient Iran 1989 ➤ 5,b504:   ᴿAmHR 96 (1991) 922 (W. L. *Hanaway*); BSO 54 (1991) 374-6 (P. *Briant*, français).

b195 **Dodgeon** M. H.,   *Lieu* S. N. C.,   The Roman Eastern frontier and the Persian wars, A.D. 226-263; a documentary history. L 1991, Routledge. xxviii-430 p. – ᴿEWest 41 (1991) 393-5 (G. *Gnoli*).

b196 **Petit** Thierry,   Satrapes et satrapies dans l'empire achéménide de Cyrus le Grand à Xerxes Iᵉʳ [diss. Liège, ᴰ*Limet* H.]: Univ. Liège, BtPhLett 254. Genève 1990, Droz. 304 p.; map. 2-251-67214-1; pa. -6254-5.

b197 **Schippmann** Klaus,   Grundzüge der parthischen Geschichte 1980 ➤ 61, q604 … 63,9763 …:   ᴿWZKM 78 (1988) 297-9 (B. G. *Fragner*).

b198 *Shrimpton* Gordon,   Persian strategy against Egypt and the date for the battle of Citium [387/6 B.C.]: Phoenix 45 (Toronto 1991) 1-20.

b199 *Wheeler* Brannon M.,   Imagining the Sasanian capture of Jerusalem; the 'Prophecy and dream of Zorobabel' [Edessa] and Antiochos Strategos's 'Capture of Jerusalem': OrChrPer 57 (1991) 69-85.

b200 **Yamauchi** Edwin M.,   Persia and the Bible 1990 ➤ 6,b553:   ᴿAndrUnS 29 (1991) 108-110 (L. A. *Willis*); BA 54 (1991) 115s (K. G. *Hoglund*); BS 53 (1991) 491s (E. H. *Merrill*); CurrTMiss 18 (1991) 140s (R. W. *Klein*: unconvincingly conservative); JStJud 22 (1991) 295-8 (L. L. *Grabbe*: takes biblical data uncritically, and Persian data either irrelevantly much or too little); SWJT 33,3 (1990s) 49s (T. V. *Brisco*); TS 52 (1991) 176 (J. A. *Fitzmyer*).

Q5   *Historia Anatoliae:* **Asia Minor, Hittites** [➤ T8.2], **Armenia** [➤ T8.9].

b201 **Astour** Michael C.,   Hittite history and absolute chronology of the Bronze Age: SIMA pocket 1989 ➤ 5,b523; Sk 150:   ᴿOLZ 86 (1991) 469-477 (G. *Wilhelm*).

b202 *Cline* Erik,   A possible Hittite embargo against the Mycenaeans: Historia 40 (1991) 1-9.

b203 *Darnell* John C., Supposed depictions of Hittites in the Amarna period: StAäK 18 (1991) 113-140.

b204 *a) De Martino* Stefano, I Hurriti nei testi ittiti dell'antico regno; – *b) Treuil* René, L'Atlantide à Santorin? L'éruption du volcan de Théra au II millénaire...: Seminari SMEA (1990) 71-83 / 165-172.

b205 **Desideri** Paolo, *Jasink* Anna M., Cilicia, dall'età di Kizzuwatna alla conquista macedone: T Univ. Fond. Parini-Chirio, Storia 1, 1990 ↠ 6,b556: ᴿClasR 41 (1991) 397s (J. M. *Cook*: good, erudite); RFgIC 119 (1991) 503s (J. *Thornton*).

b206 *Gindin* L. A., ⊕ The Trojan War and the Aḫḫijawa of the cuneiform Hittite sources: VDI 198 (1991) 28-51; Eng. 51 (a 20-year Achaean invasion).

b207 *Klengel* Horst, Tutḫalija IV. von Ḫatti; prolegomena zu einer Biographie: AltOrF 18 (1991) 224-238.

b208 *Rémy* Bernard, L'activité des fonctionnaires sénatoriaux dans la province de Galatie au Haut-Empire d'après les inscriptions: RÉAnc 92 (1990) 85-108.

b209 *Shaw* Brent D., Bandit highlands and lowland peace; the mountains of Isauria-Cilicia [... XENOPHON, CICERO]: JESHO 33 (1990) 199-233 . 237-270.

b210 *Singer* Itamar, The 'land of Amurru' and the 'lands of Amurru' in the Šaušgamuwa treaty: Iraq 53 (1991) 69-74.

b211 *Singer* Itamar, The title 'Great Princess' in the Hittite Empire: UF 23 (1991) 327-338.

b212 *Staltmayr* Maria, Aischylos und die Phrygier: Hermes 119 (1991) 367-374.

b213 *Wilhelm* Gernot, Probleme der hethitischen Chronologie [ASTOUR M. 1989]: OLZ 86 (1991) 469-477.

Q6.1   **Historia Graeciae classicae.**

b214 **Bengtson** Hermann † 2.XI.1989, Geschichte der Alten Welt. Fra 1989, Fischer-Tb. 240 p. DM 16,80. – ᴿHZ 253 (1991) 155s (D. *Vollmer*).

b214* **Bernal** Martin, Black Athena; the Afroasiatic roots of classical civilization [**I.** 1987 ↠ 3,b809; 5,b589; 6,b570*]: ᴿGerión 9 (1991) 309-315 (J. L. *López Castro*). – **II.** The archaeological and documentary evidence. L 1991, Free Association/Rutgers. xxxiv-736 p.; 17 maps. £40. 1-85343-053-6 / 0-8135-1583-1; -4-X ($50/16). – ᴿAntiquity 65 (1991) 981 (T. *Taylor*: often right for the wrong reason).

b215 **Blázquez** José M., *López Melero* Raquel, *Sayas* Juan J., Historia de Grecia antigua. M 1989, Cátedra. 1131 p.; 84 fig.; 18 mapas. – ᴿGerión 9 (1991) 303s (M. P. *García-Gelabert*).

b216 **Bogdanov** Bogdan, Histoire de la culture grecque ancienne (en bulgare). Sofia 1989, Science et art. 287 p. – ᴿRHR 208 (1991) 80-83 (Nadina *Radeva*).

b217 *Brodersen* Kai, Heiliger Krieg und heiliger Friede in der frühgriechischen Geschichte: Gymnasium 98 (1991) 1-14.

b218 **Bubel** Frank, Herodot-Bibliographie 1980-1988: AltWTSt 20. Hildesheim 1991, Olms. [vi-] 63 p. 3-487-09507-6.

b219 *Bultrighini* Umberto, Il 'pacifismo' di Archidamo; TUCIDIDE e i suoi interpreti: RCuClasMed 23 (1990) 5-28.

b220 **Capriglione** Jolanda C., La passione amorosa nella città 'senza' donne, etica e prassi politica. N 1990, Tempi Moderni. 225 p. – ᴿRÉG

104 (1991) 295 (Yvonne *Vernière*: la 'race des femmes' comme terrible fléau).

b221 **Carter** L. B.,   The quiet Athenian ᴰ1986 ➤ 3,b817; 4,d323: ᴿMnemosyne 44 (1991) 251-4 (J. A. E. *Bons*).

b222 *Ceauşescu* G.,   Un topos de la littérature antique; l'éternelle guerre entre l'Europe et l'Asie [... HÉRODOTE]:   Latomus 50 (1991) 327-341.

b222* **Chaniotis** Angelos,   Historie und Historiker in den griechischen Inschriften; epigraphische Beiträge zur griechischen Historiographie [Diss.]: HeidAlth 4.   Stu 1988, Steiner.   426 p.   DM 58.   – ᴿClasR 41 (1991) 195s (E. E. *Rice*: excellent, though badly printed).

b223 **Christ** Karl,   Neue Profile der Alten Geschichte.   Da 1990, Wiss.   378 p.   DM 49.   – ᴿHZ 253 (1991) 693-6 (H. *Kloft*).

b224 **Drews** Robert,   The coming of the Greeks; Indo-European conquests in the Aegean and the Near East 1988 ➤ 4,d330 ... 6,b579:   ᴿAntiquity 64 (1990) 167-9 (M. *Bernal*); ArchWsz 41 (1990) 159s (P. *Taracha*, Eng.); ClasR 41 (1991) 132s (D. F. *Easton*); Gnomon 62 (1991) 703-6 (F. *Kiechle*); RÉG 103 (1990) 718-720 (Hélène *Cassimatis*).

b225 **Erbse** Hartmut,   Fiktion und Wahrheit im Werke HERODOTs: NachGö ph/h 1991/4.   Gö 1991, Vandenhoeck & R.   22 p.

b226 **Erbse** Hartmut, ᴱ*Bühler* Winfried von, *al.*,   THUKYDIDES-Interpretationen: UntAntLitG 33.   B 1989, de Gruyter.   xiii-192 p.   DM 98.   3-11-012126-3.   – ᴿAmJPg 112 (1991) 135s (W. C. *West*).

b227 **Farrar** Cynthia,   The origins of democratic thinking; the invention of politics in classical Athens 1988 ➤ 5,b557:   ᴿÉchMClas 36 (1991) 81-89 (J. *Ober*; also on R. SINCLAIR; E. WOOD).

b228 **Flory** Stewart,   The archaic smile of Herodotus 1987 ➤ 4,d335 ... 6,b583: ᴿRFgIC 119 (1991) 126s (P. *Vannicelli*).

b229 **Garland** R.,   The Greek way of life; from conception to old age 1990 ➤ 6,b584:   ᴿClasR 41 (1991) 164-6 (Jane F. *Gardner*); JHS 111 (1991) 239 (Helen *King*).

b230 **Golden** Mark,   Children and childhood in classical Athens: Ancient society and history.   Baltimore 1990, Johns Hopkins Univ.   xix-268 p.

b231 *a*) *Griffin* Jasper,   Die Ursprünge der Historien HERODOTS; – *b*) *Nickau* Klaus,   Mythos und Logos bei Herodot: ➤ 39, ᶠCLASSEN C., Memoria 1990, 51-82 / 83-100.

b232 ᵀᴱ**Guzman Guerra** Antonio,   TUCÍDIDES, Historia de la guerra del Peloponeso: LBolsillo 1385.   M 1989, Alianza.   695 p.   – ᴿGerión 8 (1990) 306-8 (D. *Plácido*).

b233 *Halliwell* Stephen,   The uses of laughter in Greek culture: ClasQ 41 (1991) 279-296.

b234 **Halperin** David M.,   One hundred years of homosexuality, and other essays on Greek love.   NY 1990, Routledge.   x-229 p.   – ᴿClasR 41 (1991) 161s (K. J. *Dover*); Helios 18 (1991, not 1992 as top of page 147) 154-9 (R. J. *Hexter*).

b235 **Hartog** François,   The mirror of HERODOTUS, ᵀ*Lloyd* Janet 1988 ➤ 6, b592: ᴿJRel 70 (1990) 136-8 (D. *Grene*).

b236 **Jones** Nicholas F.,   Public organization in ancient Greece 1987 ➤ 5,b584; 6,b596:   ᴿAnzAltW 44 (1991) 197-9 (Ingomar *Weiler*); Gymnasium 98 (1991) 90s (K.-W. *Welwei*); Phoenix 45 (1991) 71-76 (P. J. *Rhodes*).

b237 **Koliadis** Manolis G.,   Die Jugend im Athen der klassischen Zeit; Ansätze zu einer historischen Jugendforschung: EurHS 11/353.   Fra 1988, Lang.   – ᴿMünstHand 10,2 (1991) 124-130 (J. *Engels*).

b238 **Kondylis** Panajotis, MARX und die griechische Antike. Heid 1987, Manutius. 92 p. – ᴿHZ 253 (1991) 642s (W. *Schuller*).

b239 **Lateiner** Donald, The historical method of HERODOTUS: Phoenix supp 23, 1988 ⇥ 6,b600: ᴿClasR 41 (1991) 23-25 (Stephanie *West*); GreeceR 38 (1991) 97s (P. J. *Rhodes*); Phoenix 45 (1991) 68-71 (J. M. *Bigwood*).

b240 *Lefèvre* François, Remarques sur le calendrier des réunions de l'amphictionie pyléo-delphique: BCH 115 (1991) 579-594.

b241 **Leo** Friedrich [1851-1914], Die griechisch-römische Biographie nach ihrer literarischen Form [¹1901]. Hildesheim 1990, Olms. [x-] 329 p. 3-487-00986-2.

b242 **Lévêque** Pierre, La naissance de la Grèce; des rois aux cités. P 1990, Gallimard. 176 p.; ill.

b243 **Levi** Mario A., Il mondo dei Greci e dei Romani. Padova 1987, Píccin. 222 p.

b244 *a) Londey* Peter, Greek colonists and Delphi; – *b) Rapin* C., Greeks in Afghanistan; Ai Khanoum; – *c) Barrett* D. S., Ancient Hellenism and the Jews; a study in attitudes and acculturation: ⇥ 5,196, ᶠTRENDALL Arthur D., Proceedings of the first Australian congress of classical archaeology, Sydney 9-14.VII.1985, ᴱDescœudres Jean-Paul (Canberra/Oxford 1990; 0-19-814969-0) 117-127 / 329-342 / 543-550 [plus 42 almost equally relevant articles].

b245 *López Eire* Antonio, La revolución en el pensamiento político de TUCIDIDES, I: Gerión 8 (1990) 89-114.

b246 *Meier* Christian, Die Rolle des Kriegs im klassischen Athen: HZ 251 (1990) 555-605.

b246* **Meister** Klaus, Die griechische Geschichtsschreibung, von den Anfängen bis zum Ende des Hellenismus. Stu 1990, Kohlhammer. 240 p. DM 45. 3-17-010264-8. – ᴿClasR 41 (1991) 497 (J. M. *Alonso-Núñez*).

b247 **Musti** Domenico, Storia greca, linee di sviluppo dall'età micenea all'età romana. R 1989 ²1990, Laterza. xiv-942 p.; 100 fig. Lit. 65.000. – ᴿGnomon 63 (1991) 177-181 (W. *Schuller*: high praise; merits Verdeutschung).

b248 **Ober** Josiah, Mass and elite in democratic Athens; rhetoric, ideology and the power of the people 1989 ⇥ 6,b607: ᴿClasPg 86 (1991) 67-74 (H. *Yunis*).

b249 **Osborne** Robin, Demos, the discovery of classical Attika 1985 ⇥ 2,9464 ... 6,b608: ᴿRÉG 104 (1991) 268s (A. *Laronde*).

b250 **Otkupszczikow** Jurij W., ⊕ Dogrieczieskij substrat. Leningrad 1988. 264 p. – ᴿEos 59 (1991) 265-8 (E. *Konik* ⊕).

b251 *Packman* Zola Marie, The incredible and the incredulous; vocabulary of disbelief in HERODOTUS, THUCYDIDES and XENOPHON: Hermes 119 (1991) 399-414.

b252 *Pecorella Longo* Chiara, Gli arconti; iterabilità della carica e accesso all'Areopago: AtenR 36 (1991) 169-180.

b253 **Raaflaub** K., Entdeckung der Freiheit 1985 ⇥ 3,b851* ... 5,b605: ᴿGymnasium 98 (1991) 91-93 (Elle *Stein-Hölkeskamp*).

b254 **Reinsberg** Carola, Ehe, Hetärentum und Knabenliebe in antiken Griechenland 1989 ⇥ 6,b614: ᴿDLZ 112 (1991) 282-4 (Verena *Paul-Zinserling*).

b255 *a) Rösler* Wolfgang, Die 'Selbsthistorisierung' des Autors; zur Stellung HERODOTS zwischen Mündlichkeit und Schriftlichkeit; – *b) Gočeva* Zlatozara, Mündliche und schriftliche Tradition über Thrakien im Geschichtswerk des Herodot: Pg 135 (1991) 215-220 / 221-234.

b256 **Romilly** Jacqueline de, La construction de la vérité chez THUCYDIDE: Collège de France, Conférences-Essais. P 1990, Julliard. 156 p.; maps. – ᴿBBudé (1991) 211s (Valérie *Fromentin*); RÉG 104 (1991) 295s (Dominique *Arnould*).

b257 *Romilly* Jacqueline de, Les prévisions non vérifiées dans l'œuvre de THUCYDIDE: RÉG 103 (1990) 370-382.

b258 ᴱ**Rosén** H. B., HERODOTUS, Historiae I (1-4) 1987 → 3,b854 ... 6,b616: ᴿGGA 243 (1991) 23-44 (R. *Renehan*); RÉG 104 (1991) 286s (G. *Liberman*: more disposed than McNEAL 1986 to make available dubious variants).

b259 *Rubincam* Catherine, Casualty figures in the battle descriptions of THUCYDIDES [relatively but limitedly objective]: AmPgTr 121 (1991) 181-198.

b260 *Ruzé* Françoise, Le conseil et l'assemblée dans la grande Rhètra de Sparte [Plut.Lyc. 6,1.8]: RÉG 104 (1991) 15-30.

b261 **Sakellariou** M. B., Between memory and oblivion; the transmission of early Greek historical traditions: Meletemata 12. Athens/P 1990, De Boccard. 267 p. 960-7094-76-X.

b262 **Samuel** Alan E., The promise of the West; the Greek world, Rome and Judaism 1988 → 4,d384; 5,b611: ᴿRBgPg 69 (1991) 224-5 (P. *Salmon*).

b263 *Sanders* Lionel J., Dionysius I of Syracuse and the origins of the ruler cult in the Greek world: Historia 40 (1991) 274-287.

b264 **Sawliwich** Lynn M., The reception of HERODOTUS from Cicero ['father of history'] to PLUTARCH ['De malignitate Herodoti']: diss. Harvard, ᴰ*Nancy* G. CM 1991. 119 p. 91-32033. – DissA 52 (1991s) 1737-A.

b265 **Shimron** Binyamin, Politics and belief in Herodotus: Historia Einz. 58, 1989 → 6,b620: ᴿGnomon 63 (1991) 146-8 (M. *Stahl*); JHS 111 (1991) 241s (C. W. *Fornara*).

b266 **Shrimpton** Gordon S., THEOPOMPUS the historian [now mostly lost]. Montreal 1991, McGill-Queens Univ. xviii-346 p. A$50. – ᴿPrudentia 23 (1991) 60-62 (V. J. *Gray*); RÉAnc 93 (1991) 418s (P. *Brun*).

b267 **Specht** Edith, Schön zu sein und gut zu sein; Mädchenbildung und Frauensozialisation im antiken Griechenland: Frauenforschung 9. W 1989, Frauenverlag. 190 p.; 17 fig. – ᴿGymnasium 98 (1991) 343-351 (Gisela *Wickert-Micknat*: 'Frauen im archaischen und klassischen Griechenland').

b267* **Starr** C. G., The birth of Athenian democracy. Ox 1990, UP. ix-86 p. £13. – ᴿClasR 41 (1991) 388-390 (S. *Hornblower*).

b268 **Stockton** David, The classical Athenian democracy. Ox 1990, U.P. xiv-210 p.; 12 pl.; map. £25. – ᴿGreeceR 38 (1991) 99 (P. J. *Rhodes*).

b269 **Thomas** Rosalind, Oral tradition and written record in classical Athens 1989 → 5,b618; 6,b625: ᴿGnomon 62 (1991) 673-7 (Ø. *Andersen*).

b270 **Traill** J., Demos and Trittys 1986 → 4,d401; 5,b619: ᴿGnomon 63 (1991) 25-30 (G. R. *Stanton*).

b271 **Vandiver** Elisabeth, Heroes in HERODOTOS; the interaction of myth and history: StKlasPg 56. Fra 1991, Lang. 288 p. – ᴿWienerSt 104 (1991) 311s (H. *Schwabl*).

b272 **Wallace** Robert W., The Areopagos council to 307 BC, 1989 → 6,b630: ᴿAmHR 96 (1991) 487 (R. *Garner*).

b273 **Winkler** John J., The constraints of desire; the anthropology of sex [&] gender in ancient Greece. NY 1990, Routledge. x-269 p. £10. –

RClasR 41 (1991) 424-6 (Gillian *Clark*); Helios 18 (1991) 147-152 (R. J. *Hexter*).

Q6.5   **Alexander, Seleucidae; historia Hellenismi.**

b274 **Badi** Amir M., D'Alexandre à Mithridate: Les grecs et les barbares 6. P 1991, Geuthner. I. 214 p.; II. 192 p.; III. 214 p.; IV. 150 p.; V. 200 p. 2-7053-0644-7 (I + II); -8-X; -4-7 (aussi IV); -8-X (aussi V) [OIAc 1,11].

b274* **Badi** Amir M., La paix du roi: Les grecs et les barbares 5. Lausanne 1984, Payot. I. 430 p.; II. 379 p.; III. 321 p.; IV. 453 p. (+ index 32 p.). 2-601-09821-X; -2-8; -3-6; -4-4 [OIAc 1,11].

b275 **Bengtson** Hermann, Die Diadochen 1987 ➤ 4,d311 ... 6,b636: RZSavR 106 (1989) 730-2 (L. *Schumacher*).

b276 **Bichler** Reinhold, 'Hellenismus'; Geschichte und Problematik eines Epochenbegriffs: ImpulsF 41, 1983 ➤ 65,9762 ... 3,b890: RKlio 73 (1991) 315-324 (B. *Funck*); WienerSt 104 (1991) 291s (H. *Bonnert*).

b277 **Billows** Richard A., Antigonus the one-eyed and the creation of the Hellenistic state. Berkeley 1990, Univ. California. xix-515 p.; maps. 0-520-06378-3. – RAmHR 96 (1991) 1173s (F. L. *Holt*).

b278 E**Bommelaer** Bibiane, DIODORE de Sicile, Bibliothèque historique III: Coll. Budé. P 1989, BLettres. liii-150 (d.) p.; map. – RClasR 41 (1991) 37-39 (N. G. L. *Hammond*).

b279 **Bosworth** A. B., Conquest and empire ... Alexander 1988 ➤ 5,b546; 6,b643: RHZ 252 (1991) 133-5 (J. *Seibert*).

b280 **Bowersock** G. W., Hellenism in late antiquity [lectures AmerAcad/ Rome] 1990 ➤ 6,b645: RRÉG 104 (1991) 303s (A. *Billault*).

b282 *a*) *Casevitz* Michel, *Hellenismós*; formation et fonction des verbes en *-ízō* et leurs dérivés; – *b*) *Lévy* Edmond, Apparition des notions de Grèce et des Grecs; – *c*) *Trédé* Monique, Quelques définitions de l'hellénisme au IVᵉ siècle avant J.-C. et leurs implications politiques; – *d*) *Frézouls* Edmond, L'hellénisme dans l'épigraphie de l'Asie Mineure romaine; – *e*) *Bowie* E. L., Hellenes and Hellenism in writers of the early Second Sophistic: ➤ 602, Hellenismos 1989/91, 9-16 / 49-69 / 71-80 / 125-147 / 183-204.

b282* **Cunliffe** Barry, Greeks, Romans and barbarians 1988 ➤ 4,d580 ... 6,b647: RBonnJbb 191 (1991) 730-4 (W. *Schmitz*).

b283 **Droysen** Johann Gustav [1833, franç. 1934; 1877, franç. 1880],T (or rather 'psychological transposition' in partly-acknowledged dependence on the 1880 French) *Apostolidis* Renos I., ❻ Historía tou megálou Alexándrou. Athenai 1988. xxxviii-890 p. (2 vol.), 3 maps. – RRÉG 104 (1991) 614 (J. *Schneider*: searching comments on the translator's sources or changes and their effects).

b284 R**Duggan** Hoyt T., *Turville-Petre* Thorlac, The wars of Alexander, [5800 surviving out of] 6300-line Middle English poem: Early English Text Society 10. Ox 1989, Univ. lx-397 p.; front. $58. – RSpeculum 66 (1991) 858-862 (R. *Hanna*).

b285 **Errington** Malcolm, Geschichte Makedoniens 1986 ➤ 3,d333: RHZ 253 (1991) 668-670 (H.-J. *Gehrke*, auch über HAMMOND-WALBANK 3).

b286 TE**Foulon** Éric, *Weil* Raymond, POLYBE, Histoires X-XI. P 1990, BLettres. 194 (d.) p. 2-251-00401-0. – RClasR 41 (1991) 35-37 (F. J. *Walbank*).

b287 **Gehrke** Hans-J., Geschichte des Hellenismus: Grundriss der Geschichte 1A. Mü 1990, Oldenbourg. 285 p. – RTyche 6 (1991) 245s (G. *Dobesch*).

b288 **Grainger** John D., Seleukos Nikator; constructing a Hellenistic kingdom. L 1990, Routledge. 268 p.

b289 **Green** Peter, Alexander of Macedon 356-323 B.C., a historical biography[2rev] [[1]1974 Pelican]. Berkeley 1991, Univ. California. xxxvii-617 p.; maps. 0-520-07165-4 [OIAc 1,17].

b290 **Green** Peter, Alexander to Actium; the ... Hellenistic age 1990 ➤ 6,b653: [R]GreeceR 38 (1991) 250 (P. J. *Rhodes*: a marvellous achievement).

b291 **Grzybek** E., Du calendrier macédonien au calendrier ptolémaïque; problèmes de chronologie hellénistique: SchwBeitAltW 20. Ba 1990. 212 p. – [R]Aegyptus 71 (1991) 282-9 (L. *Criscuolo*: base di discussione); RÉG 104 (1991) 459s (P. *Gauthier*).

b292 **Hammond** N. G. L., *Walbank* F. W. A history of Macedonia 3, 1988 ➤ 5,b569; 6,b657: [R]AmHR 96 (1991) 1172s (D. *Engels*).

b293 **Hammond** N. G. L., The Macedonian state 1989 ➤ 5,b570: [R]HZ 253 (1991) 701-3 (M. *Errington*).

b294 *a) Irmscher* Johannes, Die griechische Diaspora / Der Diasporabegriff in der Antike; – *b) Sakellaríou* Mikhaíl B., La typologie de la diaspora grecque; – *c) Fossey* John M., Relations between diaspora and Greece proper in Hellenistic / Roman times: ➤ 588, Diaspora 1988/91, 1-9. 11-14 / 15-24 / 73-80.

b295 **Jones** C. P., Culture and society in LUCIAN: CM 1986, Harvard. xvi-195 p. £22.50. – [R]ClasR 41 (1991) 40-42 (G. *Anderson*).

b296 [E]**Kuhrt** Amélie, *Sherwin-White* Susan, Hellenism in the East 1984/7 ➤ 4,d358 ... 6,b660: [R]RÉAnc 92 (1990) 176 (P. *Briant*).

b297 *Kuhrt* Amélie, *Sherwin-White* Susan, Aspects of Seleucid royal ideology [i.e. governing policy]; the cylinder of Antiochus I from Borsippa: JHS 111 (1991) 71-86; pl. II.

b298 **Samsaris** D. K., Ⓖ Historikē geographía tēs Romaïkēs enarchías Makedonías. Thessaloniki 1989. 328 p.; 36 pl. – [R]RÉG 104 (1991) 615s (J.-N. *Corvisier*; comble un trou important).

b299 **Schmitt** Hatto H., *Vogt* Ernst, Kleines Wörterbuch des Hellenismus 1988 ➤ 6,937: [R]Klio 73 (1991) 693s (C. *Mileta*).

b300 *Tsetskhladze* Gocha R., Colchis and Greek culture; a problem of Hellenization: Mesop-T 26 (1991) 119-139.

[E]**Walker** Susan, *Cameron* Averil, The Greek renaissance in the Roman Empire; papers from the tenth British Museum classical colloquium [1986]; 1989 ➤ 610.

b301 **Warry** John, Alexander 334-323 B.C., conquest of the Persian empire: Campaign Series 7. L 1991, Osprey. 96 p.; ill.; maps. 1-85532-110-6.

Q7 **Josephus Flavius.**

b302 **Bohrmann** Monette, F. Josèphe, les zélotes et Yavné ... Guerre des Juifs 1989 ➤ 5,b628; 6,b675: DM 50. 3-261-03942-6. – [R]ActuBbg 28 (1991) 71 (J. *Vives*).

b303 *Fauth* Wolfgang, 'Zeichen und Wunder' im Alten Testament und bei Josephus: ➤ 39, [F]CLASSEN C., Memoria 1990, 9-31.

b304 **Feldman** L. H., *Hata* G., Josephus, the Bible, and history. Leiden 1989, Brill. 473 p. *f* 150 [continuation of 1987 ➤ 3,338]. – [R]ClasR 41 (1991) 39s (Margaret H. *Williams*: patchy, and not much on the Bible); JTS 42 (1991) 636-641 (P. R. *Davies*).

b304* *Gilbert* G., The making of a Jew; 'God-fearer' or convert in the story of Izates [A 20,34-48]: UnSemQ 44 (1991) 299-313 [< NTAbs 36,234].

b305 *Golan* David, Der Besuch Alexanders in Jerusalem [A 11,340]: BTZ 8 (1991) 19-30.

b306 **Gray** R. N., Prophetic figures in late Second Temple Jewish Palestine; the evidence from Josephus: diss. Oxford 1990. – RTLv 23, p. 541.

b307 **Hadas-Lebel** Mireille, Flavius J., le Juif de Rome 1989 ➤ 5,b635; 6,b685: ᴿJTS 42 (1991) 273-5 (R. *Williamson*); LavalTP 47 (1991) 459s (Esther *Benaim-Ouaknin*); RÉJ 150 (1991) 443s (C. *Touati*); RHR 208 (1991) 338s (A. *Lemaire*).

b308 *Hadas-Lebel* Mireille, VOLTAIRE lecteur de Flavius J.: RÉJ 150 (1991) 529-534.

b309 **Hardwick** Michael E., Josephus as an historical source in patristic literature through Eusebius: BrownJudS 128. Atlanta 1989, Scholars. xi-137 p. $45; pa./sb. $30. 1-55540-311-5/. – ᴿAbrNahrain 29 (1991) 144s (G. W. *Clarke*); CritRR 4 (1991) 310s (S. *Mason*: grammar-errors); JRS 81 (1991) 227s (N. *Kokkinos*).

b311 *Jonge* Marinus de, Josephus und die Zukunftserwartungen seines Volkes [< ᶠ*Michel* O. 1974, 205-219]: ➤ 215, Ges. Aufs. 1991, 48-62.

b312 **Krieger** Klaus-Stefan, Geschichtsschreibung als Apologetik und Polemik; F. Josephus' Darstellung römischer Machtsübung und jüdischer Reaktionen in Palästina 6-70 n.Chr.: kath. Diss. Regensburg 1991, ᴰ*Ritt*. – TR 87 (1991) 521.

b313 **Lémonon** Jean-Pierre, *al.*, Flavius Josèphe, un témoin juif de la Palestine au temps des Apôtres: Documents autour de la Bible. P 1988, Cerf. 101 p. 2-204-03006-6.

b314 **Mason** Steve, Flavius Josephus on the Pharisees; a composition-critical study [diss. Toronto, ᴰ*Longenecker*]: StPostB 39. L 1991, Brill. xv-424 p. *f* 55. 90-04-09181-5 [NTAbs 35,267].

b315 **Nodet** Étienne, *al.*, Flavius Josèphe, Les antiquités juives I-III 1990 ➤ 6,b692: ᴿÉTRel 66 (1991) 116 (E. *Cuvillier*); JStJud 22 (1991) 88-113 (L. H. *Feldman*: 3,291, Moses as inventor of silver trumpet, *bykáně*, made comparable to Hermes/lyre and Athena/oboe); RTLv 22 (1991) 242s (J. *Ponthot*); Salesianum 53 (1991) 583s (R. *Vicent*).

b316 **Paul** André, Le Judaïsme ancien 1987 ➤ 3,b893 ... 6,b693: ᴿCiuD 203 (1990) 735 (J. *Gutiérrez*); CritRR 4 (1991) 375s (S. D. *Robertson*).

b317 *Price* J.J., The enigma of Philip Ben Jakimos [officer of Agrippa II, inconsistently in Josephus]: Historia 40,1 (Stu 1991) 77-94 [< NTAbs 36,89].

b318 **Rajak** Tessa, Friends, Romans, subjects; Agrippa II's speech in Josephus's Jewish War [2,345-401]: ➤ 412, Images 1990/1, 122-124.

b319 *Saulnier* Christiane, Flavius Josèphe et la propagande flavienne: RB [96 (1989) 545-562] 98 (1991) 199-221; Eng. 199.

b320 **Schwartz** Seth, Josephus and Judaean politics 1990 ➤ 6,b695: ᴿJStJud 22 (1991) 283-5 (H. *Schreckenberg*).

b321 *Villalba i Varneda* Père, Flavius Josephus; graeca [A 3,172] et latina [A 1,156; conjecturae]: Faventia 12s (1990s) 433-5.

Q8.1　*Roma Pompeii et Caesaris* – **Hyrcanus to Herod.**

b323 **Alexander** M. C., Trials in the late Roman Republic, 149 B.C. to 50 B.C.: Phoenix supp 26. Toronto 1990, Univ. xviii-233 p. $50. 0-8020-5787-X [JRS 81,253].

b324 **Bleicken** J., Zwischen Republik und Prinzipat; zum Charakter des Zweiten Triumvirats: AbhGö pg/h 3/185. Gö 1990, Vandenhoeck & R. 122 p. DM 54. 3-525-82471-8 [JRS 81,254].

b325 *Boatwright* Mary T.,   The imperial women of the early second century
A.C. [after Christ]:   AmJPg 112 (1991) 513-540.

b326 **Burckhardt** L. A.,   Politische Strategien der Optimaten in der späten
römischen Republik: Historia Einz 57, ᴰ1988 ➤ 6,b703:   ᴿMnemosyne 44
(1991) 497-500 (P. *Vanderbroeck*).

b327 *a) Burian* Jan,   Die Errichtung des Prinzipats und der Tatenbericht des
Augustus; – *b) Korpanty* Józef,   Römische Ideale und Werte im augusteischen Prinzipat: Klio 73 (1991) 420-432 / 432-447.

b328 *Buschmann* Kai,   Motiv und Ziel des Aelius-Gallus-Zuges nach
Südarabien [25 v.Chr.]:   WeltOr 22 (1991) 85-92 + map.

b329 **Cate** Robert L. [➤ b358],   A history of the Bible lands in the in-
terbiblical period [330 BC- AD 135] 1989 ➤ 5,b655 [not B.L.]:   ᴿBA 54
(1991) 57 (R. *Hodgson*); RExp 87 (1990) 341 (J. D. W. *Watts*: HENGER,
NEUSNER bypassed].

b330 **Chamoux** François,   Marcus Antonius; der letzte Herrscher des griechischen Orients [1986] ➤ 5,b655*: ᵀ*Kügler* W.   Gernsbach 1989, Katz.
399 p. – ᴿAnzAltW 44 (1991) 220-2 (G. *Dobesch*).

b331 **Duplá Ansuategui** A.,   Videant consules; las medidas de excepción en la
crisis de la República romana: Humanidades 12.   Zaragoza 1990, Univ.
306 p.   84-7733-148-0 [JRS 81,257].

b332 **Ferrary** Jean-Louis,   Philhellénisme et impérialisme; aspects idéologiques
de la conquête romaine...: BÉF 271; R 1988, Éc. Franç. – ᴿAmJPg 112
(1991) 132-5 (A.-M. *Eckstein*); Gnomon 63 (1991) 119-124 (R. M.
Errington); RPg 64 (1990) 268-271 (Mireille *Corbier*); TopO 1 (1991) 132-5
(E. *Will*).

b333 *a) Girardet* Klaus M.,   Die Entmachtung des Konsulates im Übergang von der Republik zur Monarchie und die Rechtsgrundlagen des
Augusteischen Prinzipats; – *b) Koster* Severin,   VERGIL und Augustus:
➤ 146, ᶠSTEINMETZ P., Pratum 1990, 89-126 / 127-146.

b333* *Heubner* F.,   Formelemente und Funktion in der römischen Geschichtsschreibung des I. Jh. v.u.Z.: ➤ 591*e*, ActAntH 33 (1990s) 83-92.

b334 **Jacques** François, *Scheid* John,   Rome et l'intégration de l'Empire (44
av. J.-C. - 260 ap. J.-C.) 1. Les structures de l'Empire romain: NClio. P
1990, PUF. liv-412 p.; maps. F 198   2-13-043010-4. – ᴿMasses Ouvrières
(1992) 445 (T. *Dumortier*).

b335 **Kasher** A.,   Jews, Idumaeans, and ancient Arabs 1988 ➤ 4,h295; 5,b690;
6,g571:   ᴿHenoch 13 (1991) 115-7 (L. *Troiani*).

b335* *Kasher* Aryeh,   Political and national connections between the Jews of
Ptolemaic Egypt and their brethren in the Eretz Israel ➤ 449, Eretz/
Diaspora 1988/91 ...

b336 **Keppie** Lawrence,   Understanding Roman inscriptions. L 1991, Batsford. 158 p.; 82 fig. 0-7134-5693-0; pa. -3-2.

b337 *Le Glay* Marcel,   Rome, grandeur et déclin de la République; préf.
Chaunu Pierre: Histoire et décadence. P 1990, Perrin. vii-401 p.

b338 *Levi* Mario A.,   Appunti su Roma arcaica [c. 30 a.C.]: ParPass 257
(1991) 121-134.

b339 **McLaren** James S.,   Power and politics in Palestine; the Jews and the
governing of their land 100 BC- AD 70 [diss. Oxford 1990 ➤ 6,b723]: JStNT
supp 63. Sheffield 1991, JStOT. 244 p.   1-85075-319-9 [BL 92,144].

b339* *MacMullen* Ramsay,   Hellenizing the Romans (2d century B.C.): Historia 40 (1991) 419-438.

b340 **Maier** J.,   Zwischen den Testamenten; Geschichte und Religion in der
Zeit des Zweiten Tempels: NEchter AT Egb 3, 1990 ➤ 6,b724:   ᴿArT-

Gran 54 (1991) 375 (A. *Segovia*); TPQ 139 (1991) 320 (G. *Stemberger*); ZAW 103 (1991) 303 (O. *Kaiser*).

b341 **Martin** Paul M., Antoine et Cléopatra, la fin d'un rêve. P 1990, A. Michel. 285 p. F 120. – ᴿÉtClas 59 (1991) 99s (A. *Wankenne*).

b342 *Nagy* T., Die Okkupation Pannoniens durch die Römer in der Zeit des Augustus: AcArchH 43 (1991) 57-85.

Otzen Benedikt, Judaism in antiquity 1990 ➤ 9967.

b343 ᴱ**Pelling** C. B. R., PLUTARCH, Life of Antony 1988 ➤ 5,b707; 6,b734: ᴿAmJPg 112 (1991) 420-4 (A. J. *Podlecki*).

b343* **Podes** S., Die Dependenz des hellenistischen Ostens von Rom zur Zeit der römischen Weltreichsbildung: EurHS 3/310, 1986 ➤ 4,d517: ᴿClasR 41 (1991) 253s (M. *Crawford*).

b344 ᴱ**Raaflaub** K. A., *Toher* M., Between republic and empire [... SYME R.]: Brown Univ. 1987/90 ➤ 6,764: ᴿJRS 81 (1991) 201s (J. *Carter*).

b345 **Reinhold** Meyer, From republic to principate, an historical commentary on CASSIUS DIO's 'Roman History', Books 49-52. Atlanta 1988, Scholars. xxii-261 p. – ᴿAmJPg 112 (1991) 413-7 (B. *Manuwald*).

b346 ᴱ**Reynolds** L. D., Quintus SALLUSTIUS Crispus, Catilina, Ivgvrtha, Historiarvm Fragmenta: Scriptorum Classicorum Bibliotheca Oxoniensis. Ox 1991, Clarendon. xxix-249 p. 0-19-814667-1.

b347 **Schmidt** M. G., Caesar und Cleopatra; philologischer und historischer Kommentar zu LUCAN 10,1-171: StKlasPg 25. Fra 1986, Lang. xii-258 p. Fs 61. 3-8204-8383-7. – ᴿJRS 81 (1991) 198s (C. *Pelling* compares with ᴱTOWNSEND C. 1986).

b348 **Simon** M., *Benoit* A., Le judaïsme et le christianisme antique d'Antiochus Épiphane à Constantin³ [¹1968, ²1985 + bibliog.]: NClio. P 1991, PUF. xvii-360 p. F 148 [NRT 114,779, J. *Bernard*].

b349 *Sohlberg* David, Militärtribunen und verwandte Probleme der frühen römischen Republik: Historia 40 (1991) 257-274.

b350 *Stanley* Farland H.ᴶ, Roman education; observations on the Iberian experience ['dense network of schools' (MARROU, BONNEX)]: RÉAnc 93 (1991) 299-319; map 320; résumé français 299.

b351 **Sullivan** R. D., Near Eastern royalty and Rome, 100-30 BC, 1990: ➤ 6,b741: ᴿPEQ 123 (1991) 73s (D. M. *Jacobson*).

b352 **Thommen** L., Das Volkstribunat der [klassischen 1955] späten römischen Republik: HistEinz 59. Stu 1989, Steiner. 287 p. DM 66. – ᴿMnemosyne 44 (1991) 501-4 (P. *Vanderbroeck*).

b353 **Vollmer** Dankward, Symploke; das Übergreifen der römischen Expansion auf den griechischen Osten; Untersuchungen zur römischen Aussenpolitik am Ende des 3. Jh. v.Chr.: Hermes Einz 54. Stu 1990, Steiner. xi-183 p.; 2 maps. DM 68. – ᴿDLZ 112 (1991) 457-9 (Barbara *Kühnert*); GreeceR 38 (1991) 103 (T. *Wiedemann*); Tyche 6 (1991) 252s (G. *Dobesch*).

b354 **Will** Wolfgang, Der römische Mob; soziale Konflikte in der späten Republik. Da 1991, Wiss. vii-280 p.

Q8.4 Zeitalter Jesu Christi: particular/general.

b355 *Alföldy* Géza, Augustus und die Inschriften; Tradition und Innovation; die Geburt der imperialen Epigraphik: Gymnasium 98 (1991) 289-324.

b356 ^E**Binder** Gerhard, Saeculum Augustum, I. Herrschaft und Gesellschaft; II. Religion und Literatur, 1987s ➤ 3,483; 4,e436: ^RLatomus 50 (1991) 206-8 (J.-M. *André*).

b357 **Blázquez Martínez** J. M., El nacimiento del cristianismo. M 1990, Historia Universal 16. 192 p. – ^RGerión 9 (1991) 334-6 (Guadalupe *López Monteagudo*).

b358 **Cate** Robert L., A history of the New Testament and its times. Nv 1991, Broadman. 348 p. $20. 0-8054-1325-1 [TDig 39,153; NTAbs 46,133] ➤ b329, interbiblical period, 1989.

b359 *Cizek* Eugen, La poétique de l'histoire chez TACITE: RÉLat 69 (1991) 136-146.

b359* *Cogitore* Isabelle, La *potentia* chez TACITE, accusation indirecte du Principat: BBude (1991) 158-171.

b360 *Feldman* Louis H., Pro-Jewish intimations in TACITUS' account [*six* accounts] of Jewish origins: RÉJ 150 (1991) 331-363.

b361 **Grimal** Pierre, TACITE, Œuvres complètes: Pléiade 361. P 1990, NRF. lx-180 p. – ^RRPg 64 (1990) 260s (P. *Flobert*).

b362 **Grimal** Pierre, TACITE. P 1990, Fayard. 404 p. – ^RLatomus 50 (1961) 493-5 (R. *Chevallier*).

b363 *Heilig* Ernst, Towards a new hermeneutic analysis? Prolegomena to a text-structural analysis of Latin texts, illustrated from TACITUS' Germania: ➤ 580, 4th Latin 1987/91, 467-474.

b364 a) *Hellegouarc'h* Joseph, Le style de TACITE; bilan et perspectives; – b) *Borzsak* Stefan, Tacitus – ein Manierist? – c) *Aubrion* Étienne, L'*eloquentia* de Tacite et sa *fides* d'historien; – d) *Tanner* R. G., The development of thought and style in Tacitus; – c) *Billerbeck* Margarethe, Die dramatische Kunst des Tacitus: ➤ 659, ANRW 33,4 (1991) 2385-2453 / 2581-2596 / 2597-2688 / 2689-2751 / 2752-2771.

b365 **Hengel** Martin, (*Markschies* Christoph), The Hellenization of Judaea in the first century after Christ [1989], ^T*Bowden* John, 1989 ➤ 6,b673: ^RCritRR 4 (1991) 363-6 (S. *Mason*); CurrTMiss 18 (1991) 130s (D. *Rhoads*); ErbAuf 67 (1991) 153s (B. *Schwank*); JJS 42 (1991) 266-8 (C. R. A. *Murray-Jones*).

b366 *Hickson* Frances V., Augustus triumphator; manipulation of the triumphal theme in the political program of Augustus: Latomus 50 (1991) 124-138.

b367 a) *Horbury* William, Herod's Temple and 'Herod's days'; – b) *Davies* G. I., The presence of God in the Second Temple and rabbinic doctrine; – c) *Draper* J. A., 'Korah' and the Second Temple; – d) *Rowland* C. C., The Second Temple; focus of ideological struggle; – e) *Bockmuehl* Markus N. A., 'The trumpet shall sound'; Shofar symbolism and its reception in early Christianity: ➤ 15, ^FBAMMEL E., Temple 1991, 103-149 / 32-36 / 150-174 / 175-198 / 199-225.

b368 **Horsley** G. R. H., New documents illustrating early Christianity, 5. Linguistic essays; Index to vol. 1-5 (*Swinn* S. P.) 1989 ➤ 5,401: ^RRB 98 (1991) 607-615 (J. *Taylor*).

b369 *Ilan* Tal, Julia Crispina, daughter of a Herodian princess in the Babatha archive [YADIN: DJD]. A case study in historical identification: JQR 82 (1991s) 361-381.

b370 [Mastellone] **Iovane** Eugenia, Paura e angoscia in TACITO; implicazioni ideologiche e politiche. N 1989, Loffredo. 175 p. – ^RClasR 41 (1991) 789s (R. H. *Martin*); RPg 64 (1990) 261s (P. *Jal*).

b371 **Jossa** Giorgio, I cristiani e l'impero Romano da Tiberio a Marco Aurelio: StGiudCA 2. N 1991, D'Auria. 286 p. 88-7092-075-5.

b372 *a*) *Keitel* Elizabeth, The structure and function of speeches in TACITUS' Histories I-III; – *b*) *Giua* Maria Antonietta, Paesaggio, natura, ambiente come elementi strutturali nella storiografia di Tacito; – *c*) *Luce* T.J., Tacitus on 'history's highest function', *praecipuum munus annalium* (3.65); – *d*) *Rouveret* Agnès, Tacite et les monuments: → 659, ARNW 33,4 (1991) 2772-94 / 2879-2902 / 2904-27 / 3007-50 / 3051-99.

b373 **Keresztes** Paul, Imperial Rome and the Christians 1989 → 6,b753: RJEH 42 (1991) 146 (S.G. *Hall*); JTS 42 (1991) 314-6 (T.D. *Barnes*: largely repeats his ANRW).

b374 T**Le Bonniec** H., TACITE, Histoires, livres [I. 1987 → 4,d566], II et III, E*Hellegouarc'h* J. P 1989, BLettres. xvi-326 p., map. – RLatomus 50 (1991) 422-6 (S. *Borzsák*, deutsch).

b375 E**Martin** R.H., *Woodman* A.J., TACITUS, Annals, Book IV [...Tiberius]: GrLatClas. C 1989, Univ. viii-283 p. £30; pa. £12. 0-521-30504-7; -1543-3. – RClasR 41 (1991) 341-5 (S.P. *Oakley*: high praise); Gymnasium 98 (1991) 281-3 (S. *Borzsák*); JRS 81 (1991) 209s (M. *Comber*).

b376 **Martin** Ronald, TACITUS. L 1989 pa. = 1981, Batsford. 288 p. – RGnomon 63 (1991) 655s (R. *Urban*); Latomus 50 (1991) 442-4 (E. *Cizek*).

b377 **Nippel** Wilfried, Aufruhr und 'Polizei' in der römischen Republik 1988 → 5,b701: RGGA 243 (1991) 172-184 (K. *Bringmann*); JRS 81 (1991) 193-5 (J.W. *Rich*).

b378 **Niswonger** Richard L., New Testament history 1988 → 6,b674; $20: RGraceTJ 11 (1990) 97 (D.S. *Dockery*: fine conservative text for beginners).

b379 **Penna** Romano, L'ambiente storico culturale delle origini cristiane[2rev] 1986 → 3,b998; 4,d515: RSefarad 50 (1990) 218s (F. *Sen*).

b380 *Richardson* I.S., Imperium romanum; empire and the language of power: JRS 81 (1991) 1-9.

b381 **Sartre** M., L'Orient romain; provinces et sociétés provinciales en Méditerranée orientale d'Auguste aux Sévères (31 av.J.-C. - ap.J.-C.). P 1991. 638 p. [LA 40,478]. – RMasses Ouvrières 445 (1992) 106 (F. *Dumortier*).

b382 **Saulnier** Christiane, Histoire d'Israël 3, 1985 → 1,a940... 5,b717: RBZ 35 (1991) 279 (D. *Kinet*).

b383 **Schwartz** Daniel R., Agrippa I, the last king of Judea: TStAJud 23. Tü 1990, Mohr. xviii-233 p. DM 138. 3-16-145341-7. – RBL (1991) 146 (Tessa *Rajak*); TLZ 116 (1991) 742s (W. *Wiefel*).

b384 **Shotter** D.C.A., TACITUS, Annals IV, 1989 → 5,b730*a*: RGnomon 63 (1991) 21-25 (S. *Borzsák*).

b385 *Toher* M., Augustus and the evolution of Roman historiography: → 599*, Between Republic and Empire 1987/90, 139-154.

b386 [*Schürer* E.] E**Vermes** Geza, *al.*, History of the Jewish people in the age of Jesus Christ 1973-1986 → 55,6676... 6,b772: RBijdragen 52 (1991) 99s (M. *Poorthuis*, 3,1-2).

b387 E**Wellesley** Kenneth, C. TACITUS 2/1, Historiae. Lp 1989, Teubner. xxii-222 p. – RClasR 41 (1991) 74s (R.H. *Martin*: in almost half the cases where he differs from HUEBNER he prints conjectures: others', his own, or both combined); RPg 64 (1990) 250-2 (P. *Jal*).

b388 *a*) *Wellesley* K., TACITUS, 'Histories'; a textual survey, 1939-1989; – *b*) *Murison* C.L., The historical value of Tacitus' 'Histories'; – *c*) *Römer*

Franz, Kritischer Problem- und Forschungsbericht zur Überlieferung der taciteischen Schriften: → 659, ANRW 33,3 (1991) 1651-1685 / 1686-1713 / 2299-2339.

Q8.7   *Roma et Oriens,* **prima decennia post Christum.**

b389 **Ayaso Martínez** José R., Iudaea capta; la Palestina romana entre las dos guerras judías (70-132 d.C.): BtMidrásica 10. Estella 1990, VDivino. 348 p.; map. 84-85873-07-6.

b389* **Barrett** A. A., Caligula 1989 → 6,b781: [R]ClasR 41 (1991) 406-8 (C. *Edwards*).

b390 [E]**Blagg** T., *Millett* M., The early Roman Empire in the West. Ox 1990, Oxbow. vi-250 p.; ill. £18. 0-946897-22-0 [JRS 81,254].

b391 *Braund* David, Hadrian and Pharasmanes [difficult ruler in Georgia]: Klio 73 (1991) 208-219.

b391* **Demougin** Ségolène, L'Ordre équestre sous les Julio-Claudiens: Coll-ÉcF 108. R 1988, École Française. iv-923 p.; 6 pl. – [R]ClasR 41 (1991) 153s (T. J. *Cadoux*).

b392 **Ferrill** A., Caligula, Emperor of Rome. L 1991, Thames & H. 184 p.; 8 pl.; map. £13. 0-500-25112-6 [JRS 81,257].

b393 *a) Galand-Hallyn* Perrine, Bibliographie suétonienne (Les 'Vies des XII Césars') 1950-1988; vers une réhabilitation; – *b) Lewis* R. G., SUETONIUS' 'Caesares' and their literary antecedents; – *c) Coninck* Luc De, Les sources documentaires de Suétone 1900-1990; – *d) Bradley* K. R., The imperial ideal in Suetonius' 'Caesares': → 659. ANRW 33,5 (1991) 3576-3622 / 3623-74 / 3675-3700 / 3701-32.

b394 *a) Gina* Maria A., Una lettura della biografia svetoniana di Tiberio; – *b) Lounsbury* R. C., Inter quos et Sporus erat; the making of SUETONIUS' 'Nero'; – *c) Murphy* John P., The anecdote in Suetonius' Flavian 'Lives': → 659, ANRW 33,5 (1991) 3733-47 / 3748-79 / 3780-93.

b395 **Goodman** Martin, The ruling class of Judaea 1987 → 4,d472... 6,b791: [R]PEQ 122 (1990) 75 (M. *Casey*).

b395* **Gutsfeld** A., Römische Herrschaft und einheimischer Widerstand in Nordafrika; militärische Auseinandersetzungen Roms mit den Nomaden: HeidAltHBeit 8. Stu 1989, Steiner. 215 p.; map. DM 48 [Gymnasium 99,184, D. *Schmitz*].

b396 **Hadas-Lebel** Mireille, Jérusalem contre Rome: Patrimoines Judaïsme 1990 → 6,b792: [R]ArTGran 54 (1991) 428s (A. *Segovia*).

b397 *Harris* B. F., DIO of Prusa; a survey of recent work: → 659, ARNW 33,5 (1991) 3853-81 [3882-3959 *Desideri* P.].

b398 *a) Idinopulos* Thomas A., Religious and national factors in Israel's war with Rome; – *b) Rappaport* Uriel, The material culture of the Jews in the Hellenistic-Roman period; – *c) Blidstein* Gerald J., The import of early rabbinic writings for an understanding of Judaism in the Hellenistic-Roman period; – *d) Dimant* Devorah, Literary typologies and biblical interpretation in the Hellenistic-Roman period; – *e) Baumgarten* Joseph M., Recent Qumran discoveries and Halakhah in the Hellenistic-Roman period: → 458, Jewish-Hellenistic 1986/91, 50-63 / 44-49 / 64-72 / 73-80 / 147-158.

b399 **Lambrecht** Ulrich, Herrscherbild und Prinzipatsidee in SUETONs Kaiserbiographien 1984 → 2,9584; 3,b966: [R]Klio 73 (1991) 324-7 (K.-P. *Johne*).

b400 **Levick** Barbara, Claudius 1990 → 6,b794*: [R]ClasR 41 (1991) 150s (R. *Seager*); GreeceR 38 (1991) 101 (T. *Wiedemann*).

b401 *Mélèze-Modrzejewski* J., ⒽComptabilité domaniale et législation impériale; Hadrien et les Juifs d'Égypte: VDI 196 (1991) 117-135; franç. 135s.

b402 **Paltiel** Eliezer, Vassals and rebels in the Roman Empire; Julio-Claudian policies in Judaea and the kingdoms of the East: Coll. Latomus 212. Bru 1991. 352 p.

b402* *Pitcher* R. A., The emperor and his virtues [MARTIAL book 9]; the qualities of Domitian: Antichthon 24 (1990) 86-95.

b403 *Poignault* Rémy, Images de l'empereur Hadrien d'après l'Histoire Auguste relue par Marguerite YOURCENAR: RÉLat 69 (1991) 203-218.

b404 **Schwier** Helmut, Tempel und Tempelzerstörung: NOrb 11, 1989 ↦ 5, b723; 6,b810: ᴿTR 87 (1991) 197-9 (R. *Wenning*).

b405 *a) Shotter* D. C. A., TACITUS' view of emperors and the Principate; – *b) Benario* Herbert W., Tacitus' view of the Empire and the Pax Romana; – *c) Wallace* K. Gilmartin, Women in Tacitus, 1903-1986: ↦ 659, ANRW 33,5 (1991) 3263-3331 / 3332-53 / 3556-74.

b405* *Stefan* Alexandra, Dédicace de Tomi en l'honneur de Trajan (ISM II, 38 et 42): RÉG 104 (1991) 574-583; 2 pl.

b406 *Swain* Simon, PLUTARCH, Hadrian, and Delphi: Historia 40 (1991) 318-330.

b407 **Wellesley** Kenneth, The long year A.D. 69 ²[notes p. 223-7]. Bristol 1989, Classical. xvi-238 p. – ᴿHZ 253 (1991) 419s (K. *Strobel*).

b407* **Wiedemann** Thomas, The Julio-Claudian emperors 1989 ↦ 6,b814: ᴿClasR 41 (1991) 254s (J. S. *Richardson*).

b408 ᵀᴱ**Williams** Wynne, PLINY, Correspondence with Trajan from Bithynia (Epistles X) 1990 ↦ 6,b816: ᴿGnomon 63 (1991) 643-5 (W. A. *Krenkel*); GreeceR 38 (1991) 104 (T. *Wiedemann*).

b409 *Yamauchi* E., Christians and the Jewish revolts against Rome: Fides et Historia 23,2 (GR 1991) 11-30 [< NTAbs 36,225].

Q9.1 *Historia Romae generalis et* **post-christiana.**

b410 **Albrecht** Michael von, Rom, Spiegel Europas; Texte und Themen: Weltliteratur 2/1. Heid 1988, L. Schneider. 671 p.; 14 fig. – ᴿGnomon 63 (1991) 581-5 (J. *Griffin*).

b411 **Alföldy** Geza, Histoire sociale de Rome [¹1975], ᵀÉvrard Étienne. P 1991, Picard. 220 p. F 250. – ᴿÉtClas 59 (1991) 377 (A. *Wankenne*).

b412 **Alföldy** G., Die Krise des römischen Reiches: Habes 5 (HeidAlthist Beitr&EpigrSt). Stu 1989, Steiner. 541 p. – ᴿGerión 8 (1990) 328-330 (G. *Bravo*).

b413 **Benko** Stephen, Pagan Rome and the early Christians 1985 ↦ 1,b254... 4,d443: ᴿBInstArch 27 (1990) 188s (L. A. *Foley*).

b414 **Bertrand-Dagenbach** C., Alexandre Sévère et l'Histoire Auguste: Coll. Latomus 208. Bru 1990, Latomus. 216 p. Fb 1000. 2-87031-148-6 [JRS 81,254].

b415 **Bommelaer** Bibiane, DIODORE de Sicile, Bibliothèque historique III: Coll. Budé. P 1989, BLettres lxxi-150 p. – ᴿRPg 64 (1990) 211s (M. *Casevitz*).

b416 **Dal Covolo** Enrico, I Severi e il cristianesimo 1989 ↦ 5,b659; 6,b825: ᴿAugR 31 (1991) 485s (V. *Grossi*); BLitEc 92 (1991) 229s (H. *Crouzel*); Nicolaus 18 (1991) 387s (S. *Manna*); Sileno 17 (1991) 370s (Franca Ela *Consolino*).

b417 **Dodds** E. R., Pagan and Christian in an age of anxiety; some aspects of religious experience from Marcus Aurelius to Constantine [Belfast Queen's Univ. Wiles lectures 1963]. C 1990, Univ. xv-144 p. £9 pa. 0-521- 38599-7 [JRS 81,257].

b418 ᴱ**Duby** G., *Perrot* M., Histoire des femmes en Occident, 1. [➤ b182] L'antiquité, ᴱ*Pantel Schmitt* P. P 1991, Plon. 590 p.; 50 fig.; 21 pl. 2-259-02326-6 [JRS 81,257].

b418* *Feldman* Louis H., Abba Kolon [Ct Rabbah 1.6.4] and the founding of 'Rome[-Babylon]': JQR 81 (1990s) 239-266.

b419 **Frey** Martin, Untersuchungen zur Religion und zur Religionspolitik des Kaisers Elagabal [proclaimed emperor at 14 in 218]: HistEinz 62, 1989 ➤ 6,b832: ᴿAnzAltW 44 (1991) 217-9 (G. *Radke*); BO (1991) 268-270 (P. W. van der *Horst*: informative on pantheon of Emesa); Gerión 8 (1990) 324s (S. *Montero*).

b420 ᵀᴱ**Freyburger** Marie-Laure, **Roddaz** Jean-Michel, Dɪᴏɴ Cᴀssɪᴜs, Histoire romaine, livres 50 et 51: Coll. Budé. P 1991, BLettres. xcix-176 [doubles] p.; maps. 2-251-00416-5.

b421 ᴱ**González Blanco** Antonino, *Blázquez Martínez* José M., Cristianismo y aculturación en tiempo del Imperio Romano: Antigüedad y cristianismo 7. Murcia 1990, Univ. 667 p.; ill. 22 art.; p. 73-89, *Alonso Díaz* J., Espiritualización del 'Reino'.

b421* **Gottlieb** Gunther, Christentum und Kirche in den ersten Jahrhunderten: Heid StHAltW. Heidelberg 1991, Winter. vi-118 p. DM 20 [TR 88,252].

b422 **Haehling** Raban von, Zeitbezüge des T. Livius in der ersten Dekade seines Geschichtswerkes: nec vitia nostra nec remedia pati possumus: Historia Einz. 61, 1989 ➤ 6,b836: ᴿGnomon 63 (1991) 585-592 (E. *Mensching*); Tyche 5 (1990) 193s (G. *Dobesch*).

b423 **Hamel** G., Poverty and charity in Roman Palestine, first three centuries ᴄ.ᴇ.: NE Studies 23. Berkeley 1990, Univ. California. xiii-290 p.; 2 maps [RHE 86,408*].

Jacques François, *Scheid* John, Rome et l'intégration de l'Empire (44 av.J.-C. - 200 ap.J.-C.), 1. Les structures 1990 ➤ b334.

b425 ᵀᴱ**Jal** Paul, Tɪᴛᴇ-Lɪᴠᴇ XI livre XXI: Coll. Budé. P 1988 ➤ 6,b837*: ᴿClasR 41 (1991) 336-8 (S. P. *Oakley*); Gnomon 63 (1991) 17-21 (E. *Burck*).

b426 **Johnson** Stephen, Rome and its empire: The Experience of Archaeology. L 1989, Routledge. viii-167 p.; 39 fig. £20. 0-415-03267-9. – ᴿBInstArch 27 (1990) 212s (K. R. *Dark*).

b427 **Kearney** James T., Aᴍᴍɪᴀɴᴜs Marcellinus and his Roman audience: diss. Michigan, ᴰ*Potter* D. AA 1991. 271 p. 91-24032. – DissA 52 (1991s) 895s-A.

b428 **Laudizi** G., Sɪʟɪᴏ Italico, il passato tra mito e restaurazione etica 1989 ➤ 6,b840: ᴿRÉAnc 93 (1991) 422-4 (M. *Martin*).

b429 **MacMullen** Ramsay, Christianizing the Roman Empire 1984 ➤ 65,9961 ... 4,d607: ᴿEos 59 (1991) 277s (M. *Żyromski*, ❷).

b430 **MacMullen** Ramsay, Corruption and the decline of Rome 1988 ➤ 4, d609 ... 6,b841: ᴿÉtClas 59 (1991) 100 (J. A. *Straus*); Phoenix 45 (1991) 85-87 (R. J. A. *Talbert*).

b430* **MacMullen** Ramsay, *a)* 'What difference did Christianity make?' [< Historia 1986]; – *b)* Two types of conversion to early Christianity [< VigChr 1983]: ➤ 227, Changes 1990, 142-155 . 327-335 / 130-141 . 322-7.

b431 **Matthews** John, The Roman Empire of AMMIANUS 1989 ➤ 6,b842:
ᴿAmJPg 112 (1991) 137-141 (Hagith S. *Sivan*: to continue TACITUS);
ClasR 91 (1991) 84s (J. F. *Drinkwater*).

b432 **Pallottino** Massimo, A history of earliest Italy [1984], ᵀ*Ryle* Martin,
Soper Kate. L 1991, Routledge. x-206 p.; ill.; maps. 0-415-05469-9.

b433 *Piette* Isabelle, Tite-LIVE traduit en français; une bibliographie: ÉtClas
59 (1991) 147-164.

b434 **Ridley** Ronald T., History of Rome; a documented analysis: Prob-
RicStoAnt 8. R 1987, Bretschneider. 696 p.; 15 fig. – ᴿGerión 8 (1990)
311s (J. *Martínez-Pinna*); Gnomon 63 (1991) 329-333 (L. *Burckhardt*).

b435 **Sartre** M., *Tranoy* A., La Méditerranée antique, IVs.av.J.-C. III
ap.J.-C. P 1990, Colin. 190 p. – ᴿLatomus 50 (1991) 499-501 (R.
Chevallier: formation de l'Empire romain).

b436 **Saunders** Randall T., A biography of the emperor Aurelian (A.D.
270-275): diss. ᴰ*Sage* M. Cincinnati Univ. 1991. 507 p. 92-00460. –
DissA 52 (1991s) 2674-A.

b437 **Schuller** Wolfgang, Frauen in der römischen Geschichte 1987 ➤ 3,d16
... 5,b721: ᴿKlio 73 (1991) 665-8 (Isolde *Stark*).

b438 **Segal** Alan F., Rebecca's children; Judaism and Christianity in the
Roman world 1989 = 1986 ➤ 2,9613 ... 5,b724: ᴿJEH 42 (1991) 87-90
(Judith M. *Lieu*); JJS 42 (1991) 122s (M. *Goodman*).

b439 **Sordi** Marta, Los cristianos y el imperio romano 1988 ➤ 6,b854:
ᴿCiuD 203 (1991) 496 (J. *Gutiérrez*).

b440 *Stark* R., Christianizing the urban empire; an analysis based on
22 Greco-Roman cities: Sociological Analysis 52,1 (Wsh 1991) 77-88
[< NTAbs 36,224].

b441 **Thomasson** Bengt E., Legatus; Beiträge zur römischen Verwaltungsge-
schichte: Svensk Inst. Rom 8/17. Sto 1991, Åström. 173 p. 91-7042-140-4.

b442 *Timonen* Asko, Prejudices against provincials in the Historia Augusti
[N.B. it starts only with Hadrian]: Arctos 25 (1991) 183-197: Aegyptii,
Galli, Syri the most slandered.

b443 **Veyne** P., Geschichte des privaten Lebens [I. 1985; Eng. 1987 ➤ 3,d113],
ᵀ*Fliessbach* H. Fra 1989, Fischer. 621 p.; 490 fig. DM 88. – ᴿGymnasium
98 (1991) 381-3 (I. *Stahlman*).

b444 **Wallinger** Elisabeth, Die Frauen in der Historia Augusta: Althist.
Epig.Stud. 2. W 1990, Österr. Ges. Archäologie. 162 p.

b445 **Walsh** Michael, Christen und Caesaren; die Geschichte des frühen
Christentums, ᵀ*Wollmann* Gabriele, 1988 ➤ 5,b803: ᴿZkT 113 (1991) 341
(H. B. *Meyer*: fine though a bit trigger-happy with the word 'magic').

b446 *Warrior* Valerie M., Notes on intercalation: Latomus 50 (1991) 80-87.

b446* **Whittaker** C. R., Les frontières de l'Empire Romain 1989 ➤ 6,b858:
ᴿArchaiognosia 6 (1990) 203s (R. N. *Doukellis*); Gerión 9 (1991) 325s
(M. *Ribagorda*) ➤ e370.

b447 *Wlosok* Antonie, a) Die Rechtsgrundlagen der Christenverfolgungen der
ersten zwei Jahrhunderte [< Gymnasium 66 (1959) 14-32]; – b) Christliche
Apologetik gegenüber kaiserlicher Politik bis zu Konstantin [< ᴱ*Frohnes*
H., Die alte Kirche 1974, 147-165]: ➤ 280, Res humanae 1990, 116-136 /
137-156.

Q9.5   **Constantinus**, Julianus, **Imperium Byzantinum.**

b448 *a)* *Azarnoush* Massoud, La mort de Julien l'Apostat selon les sources
iraniennes; – *b)* *Meulder* Marcel, Julien l'Apostat contre les Parthes, un

guerrier impie: → 62, Mém. GARITTE G., Byzantion 61 (1991) 322-9 / 458-495.

b448* **Chuvin** Pierre, *a*) Chronique des derniers païens 1990 → 6,b864: ᴿBBudé (1991) 91s (Danièle *Berranger*). – *b*) A chronicle of the last pagans 1990 → 6,b865: ᴿClasR 41 (1991) 258s (M. *Whitby*).

b449 **Fassina** Giuseppe, Teodosio [379-395], i teodosiani e la rivoluzione cristiana. Bari 1989, De Donato. 406 p. Lit. 48.000. – ᴿCC 142 (1991,3) 104s (G. *Capizzi*).

b450 *Fikhman* I. H., ❷ Late Roman Colonat: a myth created by historians?; some notes on articles by J.-M. CARRIÉ [Opus 1982s]: VDI 196 (1991) 27-44; Eng. 45 (no, it really existed).

b451 *Gliściński* Jan, ❷ Antichristliche Schulgesetzgebung von Julian Apostata: ColcT 61,2 (1991) 47-53; deutsch 53.

b452 **Haldon** J. F., Byzantium in the seventh century. C 1991, Univ. £45. – ᴿTablet 245 (1991) 1219 (D. *Barchard*: basically New Left Marxist, but raises big questions).

b453 **Herrin** Judith, The formation of Christendom 1987 → 3,d81... 6,b873: ᴿJRelHist 16 (1990s) 494s (Lynette *Olson*).

b454 *Klein* R., Konstantin: → 681, LexMA 5 (1991) 1372-5.

b455 *Kuhoff* Wolfgang, Ein Mythos in der römischen Geschichte; der Sieg Konstantins des Grossen über Maxentius vor den Toren Roms am 28. Oktober 312 n.Chr.: Chiron 21 (1991) 129-174; 8 fig.

b456 **Lane Fox** Robin, Pagans and Christians 1987 → 3,d87... 6,b879: ᴿCurrTMiss 18 (1991) 135s (F. W. *Danker*).

b456* **Liebeschuetz** J. M. W. G., Barbarians and bishops... age of Chrysostom 1990 → 6,b882: ᴿClasR 41 (1991) 417-9 (E. D. *Hunt*); JTS 42 (1991) 346-8 (R. Van *Dam*).

b457 ᴱLieu Samuel N. C., The emperor Julian, panegyric [MAMERTINUS C.] and polemic [CHRYSOSTOM, EPHREM]: Translated Texts for Historians, Greek 1, 1986 → 2,9673... 4,d604: ᴿBijdragen 52 (1991) 213s (M. *Parmentier*, Eng.); Latomus 50 (1991) 922s (E. *Pack*).

b458 **Lim** Richard, Public disputation [Manichaeans,Anomoeans; NAZIANZEN, CHRYSOSTOM], power, and social order in late antiquity: diss. ᴰ*Brown* P. Princeton 1991. 359 p. 92-07640. – DissA 52 (1991s) 3321-A; RelStR 18,173.

b459 ᵀᴱMasaracchia Emanuela, Giuliano imperatore, Contra Galilaeos. R 1990, Ateneo. 398 p. – ᴿAntClas 60 (1991) 221-7 (G. *Giangrande*: un monument); RÉG 104 (1991) 666s (P. *Nautin*); RFgIC 119 (1991) 86-88 (H. Van *Looy*).

b460 **Mazal** Otto, Handbuch der Byzantinistik 1989 → 6,b886: ᴿOLZ 86 (1991) 261s (H. *Köpstein*).

b461 **Meyendorff** John, Imperial unity and Christian divisions 1989 → 6, b887: ᴿAngelicum 68 (1991) 141-4 (A. *Wilder*); DoctLife 41 (1991) 441s (H. *Peel*); JTS 42 (1991) 348-350 (A. *Louth*); Mid-Stream 30 (1991) 171-4 (J. *Gros*); StVlad 35 (1991) 400-4 (J. *Jorgenson*).

b461* **Näsström** Britt-Mari, O mother of the gods and men; some aspects of the religious thoughts in Emperor JULIAN's discourse on the mother of the gods [diss. Göteborg]: Lund Studies in African and Asian Religions 6. Lund 1990, Plus Ultra. 142 p. [TR 88,81].

b462 **Obolensky** Dimitri, Six Byzantine portraits. Ox 1988, Clarendon. xii-228 p.; 8 pl.; 5 maps. £27.50. – ᴿJTS 42 (1991) 350-3 (S. *Hackel*).

b463 **Pabst** Angela, Divisio regni ᴰ1986 → 5,b780: ᴿLatomus 49 (1990) 223 (R. *Delmaire*).

b463* ᴱPrato C., *Micalella* D., GIULIANO, Contro i cinici 1988 → 5,b785; 6,b889: ᴿRBgPg 69 (1991) 207s (É. des *Places*).
b464 **Rabello** Alfredo M., GIUSTINIANO, Ebrei e Samaritani 1987s → 5,b787: ᴿByzantion 61 (1991) 562-5 (Rivkah *Fishman-Duker*, Eng.); Ivra 39 (1988) 183-5 (D. *Piattelli*).
b465 ᵀᴱSchamp Jacques, PHOTIUS, Bibliothèque Tome IX: Coll. Budé. P 1991, BLettres. 525 (d.) p. 2-251-00424-6.
b466 **Schreiner** Peter, Byzanz: Grundriss der Geschichte 22, 1986 → 3,d105: ᴿByzantion 61 (1991) 560s (J. M. *Alonso-Núñez*).
b467 **Shahid** Irfan, Byzantium and the Arabs [1984 → 65,9974...6,b892] = 1989: ᴿAmHR 96 (1991) 1179s (C. E. *Bosworth*); BO 48 (1991) 921-9 (W. W. *Müller*: Standardwerk trotz marginaler Einwände); JRS 81 (1991) 243s (R. *Browning*); JSS 36 (1991) 182-4 (M. *Sartre* presumably wrote 'indispensable' malgré tout); RHR 208 (1991) 340-342 (G. *Troupeau*).
b468 **Sotiroudis** Panagiotis, Untersuchungen zum Geschichtswerk des JO-HANNES von Antiocheia [byz. Diss. Hamburg ᴰ*Kambylis* A.]. Thessaloniki 1989, Univ. Wiss. Zts. xvi-224 p. – ᴿGnomon 63 (1991) 148-150 (P. *Schreiner*).
b469 **Stemberger** Günther, Juden und Christen im Heiligen Land... Konstantin 1987 → 3,d110...6,b893: ᴿHZ 252 (1991) 144s (Helga *Botermann*); Judaica 46 (1990) 48s (S. *Schreiner*); TrierTZ 100 (1991) 156 (E. *Sauser*).
b470 *Testa* Emmanuele, Legislazione contro il paganesimo e cristianizzazione dei templi (sec. IV-VI): LA 41 (1991) 311-326; Eng. 492.

XVIII. Archaeologia terrae biblicae

T1.1 **General biblical-area archeologies.**

b471 **Adkins** L. & R. A., Talking archaeology; a handbook for lecturers and organizers: Practical handbooks in archaeology 9. L 1990, Council for British Archaeology. vi-42 p.; 2 pl. £3. 0-906780-87-X [JRS 81,253].
b472 *Arata Mantovani* Piera, L'archeologia siro-palestinese e la storia di Israele, rassegna 6: Henoch 13 (1991) 337-347.
b473 ᴱ**Ben-Tor** Ammon, The archaeology of ancient Israel [= Mabô lᵉ-, revised], ᵀ*Greenberg* R. NHv/J 1991, Yale Univ./Israel Open Univ. xxi-398 p.: ill.; 20 maps. 0-300-04768-1.
b474 **Bienert** Wolfgang A., *Koch* Guntram, Christliche Archäologie: KG 1 / Urban-TB 423, Stu 1989, Kohlhammer. 124 + 16 p.; 23 fig. DM 20. 3-17-010555-8. – ᴿGregorianum 72 (1991) 171s (J. *Janssens*); Protestantesimo 46 (1991) 155s (U. *Eckert*); TLZ 116 (1991) 120s (Gerlinde *Strohmaier-Wiederanders*); TPQ 139 (1991) 95 (G. *Feige*).
b475 **Binford** Lewis R., Debating archaeology. San Diego 1989, Academic. xvi-534 p.; 87 fig. £36. 0-12-100045-1. – ᴿAntClas 60 (1991) 287-294 (F. *Verhaege*); BAR-W 17,2 (1991) 8.10s (J. C. H. *Laughlin*: p. 3 claims we study only artifacts, not human behavior); JField 18 (1991) 383-7 (I. *Hodder*).
b476 **Bintliff** John, The Annales [-ÉSC] school and archaeology. L 1991, Leicester Univ. viii-127 p.; 21 fig. £35. 0-7185-1354-1 [Antiquity 66,539, Catherine D. *Smith*].
b477 *Chapman* Rupert L., The three ages [Stone-Bronze-Iron] revisited; a critical study of Levantine usage; II. The proposal ['CLARKE's Taxonomy', named by subcultures of local sites]: PEQ 122 (1990) 1-20.

b478 ᴱ**Clayton** Peter A., *Price* Martin J., Die sieben Weltwunder, ᵀ*Oeser* Hans-C. Stu 1990, Reclam. 240 p.; 88 fig.; map. – ᴿWienerSt 104 (1991) 323 (Angelika *Huber*).

b479 **Courbin** Paul, What is archaeology? [... against BINFORD L.] 1988 ➤ 6,b906: ᴿHistTheor 30 (1991) 246-261 (J. *Moreland*).

b480 **Dever** W. G., Recent archaeological discoveries ... 1990 ➤ 6,b908: ᴿBA 54 (1991) 58s (P. J. *King*); CritRR 4 (1991) 112s (Suzanna *Richard*).

b481 *a)* **Dever** William G., Archaeology, material culture and the early monarchical period in Israel; – *b)* **Ahlström** Gösta W., The role of archaeological and literary remains in reconstructing Israel's history: ➤ 428, Fabric 1986/91, 103-115 / 116-141.

b482 ᴱ**Duval** N., Actes du XIᵉ congrès d'Archéologie Chrétienne, Lyon etc. 21-28 sept. 1986: 1989 ➤ 5,827: ᴿBInstArch 27 (1990) 177-9 (B. *Reece*: good); JEH 42 (1991) 297-300 (W. H. C. *Frend*: was it worthwhile?).

ᴱ**Edelman** Diana V., The fabric of history; text, artifact and Israel's past 1991 ➤ 428.

b483 *Elia* Ricardo J., Popular archaeology and the antiquities market [Minerva, the international review of ancient art and archaeology 1/1 Jan. 1990 GB: rebaptized Archaeology Today, but attempts to navigate a safe course between responsible archaeology and the illicit antiquities market 'dirty money']: JField 14 (1991) 95s.

b484 **Fagan** Brian M., L'aventure de l'archéologie [1985 ➤ 2,9713], ᵀ*Dispa* M.-Fr. Bru 1988, Bordas. 368 p.; 289 color. ill. Fb 1843. – ᴿRBgPg 69 (1991) 240s (R. *Lambrechts*: most beautiful ever).

Finkelstein Israel, The archaeology of the Israelite settlement 1988 ➤ 2366.

b485 **Fritz** Volkmar, Introduzione all'archeologia biblica [1985 ➤ 1,b421], ᵀ*Calabrese* Maria V.: BtStoStoriogBib 7. Brescia 1991, Paideia. 253 p.; 45 fig. Lit. 43.000. 88-394-0460-0. – ᴿLA 41 (1991) 579-581 (M. *Piccirillo*).

b486 **Grant** Michael, The visible past; Greek and Roman history from archaeology 1960-1990: 1990 ➤ 6,b912: ᴿGreeceR 38 (1991) 254 (B. A. *Sparkes*).

b486* **Guimier-Sorbets** Anne-Marie, Les bases de données en archéologie; conception et mise en œuvre. P 1990, CNRS. 272 p. 2-222-04481-2 [OIAc 2,20].

b487 **Hodder** Ian, Reading the past 1986 ➤ 2,9722; 3,d139: ᴿBInstArch 27 (1990) 207s (T. *Watkins*).

b488 [Israel] 1991 excavation opportunities: BAR-W 17,1 (1991) 24-33.

b489 *Joukowsky* Martha S., Ethics in archaeology; an American perspective: Berytus 39 (1991) 11-20.

b490 **Kenyon** Kathleen, ᴱ*Moorey* P. R. S., The Bible and recent archaeology 1987 [Atlanta, Knox] ➤ 3,d143; 4,d645: ᴿAfO 36s (1989s) 187s (S. *Kreuzer*); RelStT 9,2 (1989) 91-93 (L. G. *Herr*); SWJT 33,3 (1990s) 49 (T. V. *Brisco*).

b491 **Kroll** Gerhard, Auf den Spuren Jesu¹⁰. Lp 1988, KBW. 470 p. – ᴿJudaica 46 (1990) 51 (C. *Locher*: gegen 'galiläischer, Spätjudentum' von Dura-Europos p. 142); ScripTPamp 23 (1991) 708 (K. *Limburg*).

b492 **Lance** H. Darrell, Archéologie et Ancien Testament 1990 ➤ 6,b923: ᴿCiuD 203 (1990) 731s (F. *Diez*, bajo 'Darrell'); ÉTRel 66 (1991) 281s (Françoise *Smyth*: Eng. title better, The OT and the archeologist); RechSR 79 (1991) 289 (J. *Briend*); RHPR 71 (1991) 189s (J.-G. *Heintz*).

b493 ᴱ**Layton** R., Who needs the past? Indigenous values and archaeology [Southampton 1986]: One World Archaeology 5. L 1989, Unwin Hyman.

xv-215 p. £28.   0-04-445020-6. – ᴿAntiquity 66 (1992) 260 (Isabel *McBryde*, also on his OneW 8 and S. SHENNAN's 5).

b494 *McDonald* William A.,   Archaeology in the 21st century; six modest recommendations: Antiquity 65 (1991) 829-839.

b495 **McRay** John,   Archaeology and the New Testament. GR 1991, Baker. 432 p. $40.   0-8010-6267-5 (TDig 39,72: professor at Wheaton).

b496 **Masom** Caroline, *al.*, ➋ Świat biblijny; miejsca, odkrycia, najważniejsze wydarzenia (The biblical world), ᵀ*Mierzejewska* Bozena.   Wsz 1991, Arkady.   192 p. – ᴿColcT 61,3 (1991) 210-212 (Anna *Kuźmirek*, ➋).

b497 **Mazar** Amihai,   Archaeology in the land of the Bible 1990 ➤ 6,b927: ᴿAJA 95 (1991) 546 (W. G. *Dever*; some reserves); AndrUnS 29 (1991) 96-98 (R. W. *Younker*); BA 54 (1991) 114s (J. D. *Seger*); Biblica 72 (1991) 137-9 (R. *North*); BL (1991) 31s (A. G. *Auld*: on the whole good; bland); CritRR 4 (1991) 110-112 (Suzanne *Richard*); ÉTRel 66 (1991) 282s (Françoise *Smyth*); Interpretation 45 (1991) 305s (J. A. *Dearman*); IrTQ 57 (1991) 121s (M. *Drennan*); JJS 42 (1991) 260s (P. R. S. *Moorey*); NRT 113 (1991) 780s (X. *Jacques*); RechSR 79 (1991) 288s (J. *Briend*); ZAW 103 (1991) 160s (Ulrike *Schorn*).

b498 **Millard** Alan,   Discoveries from the time of Jesus. Ox 1990, Lion. 188 p. $23. – ᴿBA 54 (1991) 55s (J. F. *Wilson*).

b499 **Millard** A.,   Trésors des temps évangéliques 1990 ➤ 6,b930: ᴿArTGran 54 (1991) 375s (A. *Segovia*).

b499* **Moorey** P. R. S.,   A century of biblical archaeology. C 1991, Lutterworth. xvii-189 p. £10. – ᴿBAngIsr 11 (1991s) 29-31 (W. G. *Dever*: his failure to distinguish the 'sacred' and the 'secular' streams obscures the fact that only one survives today as an academic enterprise); ExpTim 103 (1991s) 182 (C. S. *Rodd*: his account of the 'new archaeology' since 1970 will be useful to the many of us who have been brought up on ALBRIGHT and WRIGHT).

ᴱ**Negev** Avraham,   Archäologisches Bibel-Lexikon 1991 ➤ 706, also Eng.

b500 **Renfrew** Colin, *Bahn* Paul,   Archaeology; theories, methods and practice. L 1991, Thames & H.   543 p.; 500 + fig. £19.   0-500-27605-6 [Antiquity 66,272, W. A. *Turnbaugh*: excellent classroom text].

b500* ᴱ**Schiffer** Michael B.,   Archaeological method and theory 1 [series replacing Advances in... ➤ 5,551]. Tucson 1989, Univ. Arizona. xii-273 p. $35.   1043-1691. – ᴿBInstArch 27 (1990) 154s (L. *Copeland*: K. L. *Kvamme* on computers, D. *Rindos* on DARWIN, + 3).

b501 **Shanks** Michael, *Tilley* Christopher,   Re-constructing archaeology, theory and practice: New Studies in Archaeology, 1987 ➤ 4,d660; 5,b844: ᴿPraehZ 66 (1991) 235s (J. *Löning*).

b502 **Silberman** Neil A.,   Between past and present; archaeology, ideology, and nationalism in the modern Middle East 1989 ➤ 6,b946: ᴿAJA 95 (1991) 173s (B. E. *McConnell*); BA 54 (1991) 116s (K. M. *Yates*: a guided tour).

b503 *Silberman* Neil A.,   Desolation and restoration; the impact of a biblical concept on Near Eastern archaeology: BA 54 (1991) 76-87.

b504 ᴱ**Tilley** Christopher,   Reading material culture; structuralism, hermeneutics, and post-structuralism [LÉVI-STRAUSS, RICŒUR, BARTHES, DERRIDA...]. Ox c. 1990, Blackwell. 335 p. $46; pa. $14.   0-631-16081-7. – ᴿJField 18 (1991) 397-404 (R. A. *Watson*).

b505 **Trigger** Bruce G.,   A history of archaeological thought 1989 ➤ 5,b852; 6,b950: $49.50; pa. $18: ᴿJField 14 (1991) 106-9 (G. R. *Willey*) & 109-111 (S. *Piggott*); PrPrehSoc 57,2 (1991) 211s (J. C. *Barrett*).

b506 **Vorhees** Duane L., The 'Jewish science' of Immanuel VELIKOVSKY; culture and biography as ideational determinants: Diss. Bowling Green State University 1991, ᴰ*Tweney* Ryan D. ix-1069 p. 91-07813. – OIAc 1,26.

T1.2   Musea, organismi, expositiones.

b507 *Affholder-Gérard* Brigitte, *Cornic* Marie-Jeanne, Angers musée Pincé, collections égyptiennes: Inventaire des collections publiques françaises 35. P 1990, Réunion Musées Nat. 216 p. F 180. 2-7118-2293-1 [BO 48,310].

b508 **Albertson** Fred C., Catalogue of the Cypriote sculptures and terracottas in the Kelsey Museum of Archaeology AA: SIMA 20,14. Jonsered 1991, Åström. 44 p.; 22 pl.

b508* ᴱ**Allen** Marti Lu, *Dix* T. Keith, The beginning of understanding; writing in the ancient world, Exhibition, Kelsey Museum. AA 1991, Univ. vii-158 p. [OIAc 2,13, excerpted].

b509 ᴱ**Amandry** Michel, *Brissaud* Philippe, Tanis; les Pharaons de l'incertitude: Cabinet des médailles, Exposition mai-octobre 1991. P 1991, Librairie d'Égyptologie. 32 p. [OIAc 1,10].

b510 ᴱ**Balbi de Caro** Silvana, *al.*, Geld aus dem antiken Rom: Ausstellung Karmeliterkloster Fra 1991. Fra 1991, Museum VFG. 77 p.

b511 ᴱ**Barqué-Gramont** J.-L., *al.*, Anatolie antique; fouilles françaises en Turquie, catalogue de l'exposition, Bib. Nat. Cab. Médailles 1989s. P 1989, Inst. Fr. Ét. Anatoliennes. 106 p.; ill.

b512 ᴱ**Beck** H., *al.*, Polyklet, der Bildhauer der griechischen Klassik; Ausstellung im Liebighaus, Fra 1990s, Katalog. Mainz 1990, von Zabern. 678 p.; ill.

b513 ᴱ**Bienkowski** P., The art of Jordan [exhibition 'Jordan, treasures from an ancient land', Liverpool Museum 1991]. Liverpool 1991, Merseyside Museums. xii-178 p.; 200 fig. £8 [BL 92,26, W. G. E. *Watson*] (US, Sutton: BAR-W 17/6,4]. – ᴿLA 41 (1991) 531s (P. *Kaswalder*: di valore scientifico).

b514 ᴱ**Boeck** Juliette De, *Rassart-Debergh* Marguerite, Arts tardifs et chrétiens d'Égypte, exposition Louvain-la-Neuve 6.IX-23.X.1988: Monde Copte 14s. Limoges 1988, Monte Copte. 108 p.

b515 **Bothmer** Bernard V., [Eg.] *al.*, Antiquities from the collection of Christos G. Bastis → 4,d674; 6,b960: ᴿJEA 77 (1991) 202-4 (B. *Bryan*).

b516 **Bourriau** Janine, Pharaohs and mortals; Egyptian art in the Middle Kingdom: Cambridge Fitzwilliam Museum exposition catalogue 1988 → 5,e297: ᴿJEA 77 (1991) 209-212 (D. *Franke*, deutsch).

b517 ᴱ**Cantilena** Renata, *Rubino* Paola, La collezione egiziana del Museo Archeologico Nazionale di Napoli. N 1989, Arte Tipografica. vi-316 p.; 18 pl. + 26 color.

b518 **Caubet** Annie, Aux sources du monde arabe... Louvre 1990 → 6,b965: ᴿAfO 36s (1989s) 171-3 (D. T. *Potts*).

CLÉDAT Jean: L'Égypte en Périgord, 1991 → b528*.

b519 *Colaert* Maurice, À travers cent cinquante années d'histoire de la Société Royale de Numismatique de Belgique: RBgNum 137 (1991) III-XL (-LXXVI, anciens membres).

b520 DAI Jahresbericht 1990: ArchAnz (1991) 611-689.

b522 *a*) *Donadoni Roveri* Anna Maria, Il Museo Egizio di Torino; – *b*) *James* T. G. H., The development of the Egyptian collection in the British

Museum; – c) *Leospo* Enrichetta, Atanasio KIRCHER e l'Egitto; il formarsi di una collezione egizia nel museo del Collegio Romano [*Nota* Maresita, Barracco]; – d) *Satzinger* Helmut, Der Werdegang der Ägyptisch-Orientalischen Sammlung des Kunsthistorischen Museums in Wien; – e) *Del Francia* Pier Roberto, I Lorena e la nascita del Museo Egizio fiorentino: ➤ 618, Egitto fuori Egitto 1990/1, 191-7 / 255-265 + 4 fig. / 269-2 + 6 fig. [283-7 + 15 fig.] / 367-382 / 159-185 + 5 fig.

b522* **Drenkhahn** Rosemarie, Ägyptische Reliefs. Hannover 1989 ➤ 5,b861*a*: ᴿBO 48 (1991) 504-7 (J. *Malek*).

b523 ᴱ**Ewigleben** Cornelia, *al.*, Götter, Gräber und Grotesken; Tonfiguren aus dem Alltagsleben im römischen Ägypten: Ausstellung Hamburg 15.III.-12.V.1991: Bilderheft 25. Ha 1991, Museum für Kunst und Gewerbe. 109 p.

b524 **Feucht** Erika, Vom Nil zum Neckar; Kunstschätze Ägyptens... Heidelberg 1986 ➤ 3,d188: ᴿBO 48 (1991) 136-8 (J. H. *Taylor*).

b525 ᴱ**Geominy** Wilfred, H. SCHLIEMANN, Ausstellung. Bonn 1991, Univ. 87 p.

b526 Die Gesellschaft Jesu und ihr Wirken im Erzbistum Trier; für Gott und die Menschen ; Katalog-Handbuch zur Ausstellung im bischöflichen Dom- und Diözesanmuseum Trier, Sept-Okt. 1991: QAbh MrhKG 66. Mainz 1991, Mittelrheinische KG. 574 p.; ill. [RHE 87,150*].

b527 **Greenfield** Jeanette, The return of cultural treasures. C 1989, Univ. xviii-361 p.; 88 fig. $44.50. – ᴿAJA 95 (1991) 344 (O. W. *Muscarella*).

b528 ᴱ**Homès-Fredericq** Denyse, *Franken* Hendrik J., Pottery and potters, past and present; 7000 years of ceramic art in Jordan: Ausstellungskataloge 20, 1986 ➤ 6,b973: ᴿZDPV 107 (1991) 193s (J. *Kamlah*).

b528* **Leclant** J., [présent] L'Egypte en Périgord: Dans les pas de Jean CLÉDAT = Catalogue raisonné de l'exposition; Musée du Périgord 16 mai - 15 septembre 1991. – Paris-Louvain 1991, Peeters. (6) 121 p. (Cahiers de la Bibliothèque Copte, 7).

b529 **Maruéjol** Florence, Œuvres choisies; l'art égyptien au Louvre. P 1991, Scala. 125 p.; ill. 2-866560-078-7 [OIAc 2,23].

b529* ᴱ**Merhav** Rivka, Urartu, a metalworking centre in the first millennium B.C.E. [exposition May-Oct. 1991]: Museum Catalogue 324. J 1991, Israel Museum. xii-364 p.; (color.) ill. [OIAc 1,21].

b530 *Meyer* Laure, Faux? L'art de la tromperie [exposition British Museum]: Archéologie 259 (1990) 52-59; ill.

b530* **Mitchell** T. C., The Bible and the British Museum; interpreting the evidence 1988 ➤ 4,d696; 6,b986: ᴿSyria 67 (1990) 528s (P. *Amiet*).

b531 **Patch** Diana C., Reflections of greatness; ancient Egypt at the Carnegie Museum of Natural History. Pittsburgh 1990. x-118 p.; 115 fig. 0-911239-14-6. $25. – ᴿBO 48 (1991) 817-9 (H. J. A. De *Meulenaere*).

b531* ᴱ**Priese** Karl-Heinz, Ägyptisches Museum und Papyrussammlung: Staatliche Museen zu Berlin, Stiftung Preussischer Kulturbesitz. Mainz 1991, von Zabern. cxii-288 p.; 176 phot. 3-8053-1184-2; pa. -30-X.

b532 Rediscovering Pompeii: exhibition by IBM-Italia; NY IBM Gallery of Science and Art 1990. R 1990, Ministero Beni CA/Bretschneider. xvii-287 p.; 197 (color.) fig. Lit. 110.000 [Gymnasium 99,276, Agnes *Allrogen-Bedel*].

b532* **Reinking** Gudrun, Forum der Völker; völkerkundliches Museum der Franziskaner; Babylonien, Ägypten... Katalog. Werl 1989, Coelde. 214 p.; 220 fig.; 50 color. pl. 3-87163-174-4 [OIAc 2,25].

b533 **Riis** P. J., *al.*, Catalogue of ancient sculptures, I. Aegean, Cypriote and Graeco-Phoenician. K 1989, National Museum. 116 p.; ill. – ᴿRArchéol (1991) 133s (A. *Hermary* singles out some of the 70 Cyprus and 16 others).

b534 ᴱ**Sievernich** Gereon, *Budde* Hendrik, Europa und der Orient 800-1900 [Ausstellung Berlin 1989]. B/Mü 1989, Festspiele/Bertelsmann. 923 p.; ill. DM 78 [OLZ 87,418, D. *Sturm*].

b535 ᴱ**Temple** Richard, Early Christian and Byzantine art; textiles, metalwork, frescoes, manuscripts [catalogue of an unidentified exhibition presumably at London Temple Gallery]. Longmead 1990, Element/Haber. 120 p.; (colour.) ill. £15 [RelStR 18,231, J. J. *Yiannias*].

b536 ᶠ**THOMPSON** Dorothy B. [→ 154], 90th b; her bibliog. p. 170s: ᴱ**Uhlenbrock** Jaimee P., The coroplast's art; Greek terracottas of the Hellenistic world; catalog of an exhibition. SUNY, New Paltz Art Gallery. New Rochelle 1990, Caratzas. 175 p. 0-89241-496-0; pa. 5-2. 12 essays + catalog, 52 fig.

b537 **Tzachou-Alexandri** Olga, Ⓖ Tò pneûma kaì tò sôma; hoi athlētikoì agônes stēn archaían Elláda: Ethnikò Archaiologiko Mouseîo, 1989s. Athenai 1989, ICOM. 348 p.; 235 pl. dr. 3000. – ᴿNikephoros 3 (1990) 275-282 (W. *Decker*).

b538 *Van Siclen* Charles C., An illustrated checklist for Mummies, myths and magic [1989s San Antonio display, the whole catalog]: VarAeg 6 (1990) 27-74.

b539 ᴱ**Vergo** Peter, The new museology. L 1989, Reaktion. 224 p.; ill. £23; pa £9. 0-948462-04-3; -3-5. – ᴿBInstArch 27 (1990) 251-3 (A. *Hatton*).

b540 *Villedieu* Françoise, *al.*, Activités de l'École Française de Rome, section antiquité: MÉF-A 103 (1991) 313-367; 32 fig.

b540* *Viviano* Benedict T., École Biblique et Archéologique Française de Jérusalem: BA 54 (1991) 160-177.

b541 [*Strommenger* Eva, *al.*] Wiedererstehendes Babylon; eine antike Weltstadt im Blick der Forschung; Ausstellung, Museum für Vor- und Frühgeschichte. B 1991, Staatliche Museen Preussischer Kulturbesitz. 95 p.; 78 fig.

b542 ᴱ**Zatelli** Ida, La Bibbia a stampa da Gutenberg a Bodoni [esposizione Laurenziana/Biblia 1991]. F 1991, Edifimi. 222 p.; (color.) ill. [ZAW 104,292].

b543 **Zemmer-Plank** Liselotte, Herrscher, Krieger und Geliebte; antike Götter und ihr Himmel: Ausstellung 1989. Innsbruck 1989, Tiroler Landesmuseum. 95 p.; ill.

b544 **Zimmermann** Jean-Louis, Ancient art from the Barbier-Mueller museum, ᵀ*Michelsen* Leonor. NY 1991, Abrams. 183 p.; 52 ill. (phot. Ferrazini Pierre-Alain). 0-8109-1904-4 [OIAc 2,30].

T1.3 *Methodi,* Science in archeology.

b545 **Aitken** M. J., Science-based dating in archaeology 1990 → 6,d7: ᴿBInstArch 27 (1990) 149s (K. E. *Jenny* < Minerva 1/8, 1990).

b546 *Akkermans* Peter, New radiocarbon dates from the Later Neolithic in northern Syria: Paléorient 17,1 (1991) 121-5.

b547 **Alvisi** Giovanna, La fotografia aerea nell'indagine archeologica: NISarch 11. R 1989, Nuova Italia Scientifica. 190 p.; 52 fig. Lit. 29.000.

b547* *Biger* Gideon, *Liphschitz* Nili, Regional dendrohistory and timber analysis; the use of wood in the buildings of nineteenth-century Jaffa: MeditHR 6 (1991) 86-98 + 6 pl.

b548 **Cronyn** J. M., The elements of archaeological conservation (marine: *Robinson* W. S.). L 1990 Routledge. xx-326 p.; ill. £50; pa. £17. 0-415-01206-6; -7-... – RBInstArch 27 (1990) 181 (W. A. *Oddy* < Minerva 1/8, 1990: too technical for claimed users).

b548* **Ehrenreich** Robert M., *a*) Archaeometallurgy and archaeology; widening the scope: ⇥ 639*, EGlumac P., Masca 8,1 (1991) 55-61; – *b*) Metals in society: ⇥ 636c, Masca 8,2 (1991) 5s.

b549 *Eiteljorg* Harrison II, Reconstructing with computers: BAR-W 17,4 (1991) 60-63; ill.

b550 *a*) *Graham* Ian, Computer recording of archaeological excavations; – *b*) *Lahanier* Christian, *Malfoy* Jean-Michel, Data-processing systems for the analysis of archaeological finds: ⇥ 636b, PACT 16 (1987) 75-83 / 155-176.

b551 **Griffiths** Nick, *Jenner* Anne, Drawing archaeological finds. L Univ. College. Occ. Paper 13. L 1990, Archetype. IV-120 p.; 86 fig.

b551* *a*) *Jones* R. E., *Vagnetti* L., Traders and craftsmen in the central Mediterranean; archaeological evidence and archaeometric research; – *b*) *Cherry* J. F., *Knapp* A. B., Quantitative provenance studies and Bronze Age trade in the Mediterranean; some preliminary reflections: ⇥ 637, Bronze Age Trade 1989/91, 127-148 / 92-120.

b552 **Kiesow** Gottfried, Einführung in die Denkmalpflege²rev. Da 1989, Wiss. vii-221 p. DM 39. – RTLZ 116 (1991) 522-4 (W. *Velten*).

b553 **Leach** Peter E., Surveying of archaeological sites. L 1988, Institute of Archaeology, 52 p. 0-905853-19-9.

b554 ELeonard R. D., *Jones* G. T., Quantifying diversity in archaeology. C 1989, Univ. 160 p.; 66 fig. – RAJA 95 (1991) 341s (A. J. *Ammerman*).

b555 *Le Roux* C., 'The answers lie beneath the waves' — assessing the value of underwater archaeology for the study of biblical archaeology: TEv 24,1 (Pretoria 1991) 39-48 [< NTAbs 36,80].

b555* **Leute** Ulrich, Archaeometry, an introduction to physical methods in archaeology and the history of art 1988 ⇥ 4,d724; 5,b896; 0-89573-612-8: RPraehZts 67 (1992) 115s (Anette *Rother*).

b556 **McMillon** Bill, The archaeology handbook; a field manual and resource guide. NY 1991, Wiley. xii-260 p.; ill. $17. 0-471-53051-4. – RAntiquity 65 (1991) 977s (T. *Taylor*: very bad).

b557 **Moussa** Ali Helmi, *Dolphin* Lambert T., *Mokhtar* Gamal, Applications of modern sensing techniques to Egyptology, 1977 experiments. Menlo Park CA 1991, SRI. xvii-173 p. [OIAc 1,21].

b558 *Rosen* Arlene M., Microartifacts and the [microscopic] study of ancient societies [Miqne-Ekron]: BA 54 (1991) 97-103.

T1.4   *Exploratores* – **Excavators, pioneers.**

b558* **Angelomatis-Tsougarakis** Helen, The eve of the Greek revival; British travellers' perceptions of early nineteenth-century Greece. L 1990, Routledge. xvii-289 p.; 6 maps. £35. – RClasR 41 (1991) 463-5 (G. P. *Henderson*).

b559 **Aufrère** Sydney H., La momie et la tempête; Nicolas-Claude FABRI DE PIERESC et la curiosité égyptienne en Provence au début du XVIIe siècle. Avignon 1990, Barthélemy. 356 p.; 32 pl. 2-003-044-78-3 [OIAc 1,10].

b560 AVI-YONAH Michael mem., Eretz-Israel 19, 1987 ⇥ 3,13: ROLZ 86 (1991) 396-9 (G. *Pfeifer*: tit. pp. comments).

b561 *a*) *Barbanti Tizzi* Alessandra, Sul valore fonetico dei geroglifici; dall'Italia una lettera gnomica di CHAMPOLLION a Stanisław KOSSAKOWSKI;

– *b*) *Cesaretti* Maria Pia, Ippolito ROSELLINI e Bologna; – *c*) *Curto* Silvio, Il collezionismo di cose egizie e Bernardino DROVETTI; – *d*) *Finzi* Claudio, Leon Battista ALBERTI, geroglifici e gloria: ≻ 618, Egitto fuori Egitto 1990/91, 13-31; 4 fig. / 69-82 / 97-101 / 205-8.

b561* **Beaucour** Fernand É., La campagne d'Égypte (1798-1801). Levallois 1983, Château Pont-de-Briques. 228 p.; 63 pl. (*Dejuin* Noël, dessins inédits). 2-900348-19-6 [OIAc 2,14].

b562 *Ben-Artzi* Yossi, Unbekannte Pläne und Landkarten von Gottlieb SCHUMACHER: ZDPV 107 (1991) 176-192; pl. 5-10 + portr. pl. 4.

b563 **Berchem** Denis von, L'égyptologue genevois Édouard NAVILLE; années d'études et premiers voyages en Égypte 1862-1870: 1989 ≻ 5,b914: ᴿAnzAltW 44 (1991) 255 (P. W. *Heider*); BO 48 (1991) 744-7 (Elisabeth *Staehelin*).

b564 **Chauvet** Michael, Frédéric CALLIAUD; les aventures d'un naturaliste en Égypte et au Soudan 1815-1822; intr. *Dewachter* Michel. S. Sebastien/Loire 1989, ACL-Crocus. 374 p. F 295. 2-86723-034-2. – ᴿBO 48 (1991) 743s (P. A. *Clayton*).

b565 ᴱ**Christophe** Louis-A., G. BELZONI, Voyages en Égypte et en Nubie: Les grandes aventures de l'archéologie. P 1979, Pygmalion. 332 p.; 8 pl. 2-85704-316-3 [OIAc 1,12].

b566 ᴱ**Curto** Silvio, *Donatelli* Laura, Bernardino DROVETTI [Egyptian consul of France under Napoleon], Epistolario [largely arranged and edited 1940 by Giovanni MARRO]. Mi 1985, Cisalpino. ix-776 p.; 46 pl. Lit. 70.000. 88-205-0513-4. – ᴿJEA 77 (1991) 237-241 (R. T. *Ridley*: errors abound).

b567 *Descœudres* J. P., Contributions de l'Australie et de la Nouvelle-Zélande à l'archéologie du monde méditerranéen, étude préliminaire: ≻ 5,196, ᶠTRENDALL A. = MeditArch 2 (1989) [A. *Laronde*, RÉG 104,255 sans pp.: V. Gordon CHILDE got a doctorate at Sydney University in 1914].

b568 **Dörner** Karl F. & Eleonore, Von Pergamon zum Nemrud Dağ; die archäologischen Entdeckungen Carl HUMANNs [geb. 1839]: KgAW 40, 1989 ≻ 5,b922: ᴿAJA 95 (1991) 178s (E. E. *Rice*); Gymnasium 98 (1991) 77s (W. *Orth*).

b569 *Dyck* Andrew T., SCHLIEMANN on the excavation of Troy; three unpublished letters: GrRByz 31 (1990) 323-337.

b570 **Ehrenberg** Margaret, Women in prehistory. L/Norman 1989, British Museum/Univ. Oklahoma. 192 p.; 52 fig. £10. 0-8061-2223-4; pa. -7-4. – ᴿJField 18 (1991) 501-5 (Alison *Wylie*); PrPrehSoc 57,2 (1991) 213s (Barbara *Bender*).

b571 ᴱ**Fales** F. M., *Hickey* B. J., A. H. LAYARD tra l'Oriente e Venezia 1983/7 ≻ 5,849: ᴿRArchéol (1991) 354s (A. *Caubet*).

b572 ᴱ**Gibson** Margaret, *Wright* Susan M., Joseph MAYER [museum-donor] of Liverpool 1803-1866: OccP NS 11. L 1988, Soc. Antiquaries. xiii-244 p. £18. 0-85431-349-8. – ᴿBO 48 (1991) 136.

b573 **Gran-Aymeric** Ève & Jean, [biographie de J. DIEULAFOY, célèbre par son exploration de la Perse et ses fouilles de Suse]. P 1990, Perrin. 300 p.; 8 pl.; map. – ᴿCRAI (1991) 83-86 (J. *Heurgon*).

b574 **Huhn** Ingeborg, Der Orientalist Johann G. WETZSTEIN als preussischer Konsul in Damaskus (1849-1861) dargestellt nach seinen hinterlassenen Papieren: IslamkUnt 136. B 1989, Schwarz. ix-465 p.; front.; 7 fig.; 6 maps; 6 documents. 3-922-96889-9. – ᴿBSO 54 (1991) 438s (P. M. *Holt*); ZDPV 107 (1991) 201s (E. A. *Knauf*).

b575 **Korres** George S., H. SCHLIEMANN, ein Leben für die Wissenschaft; Beiträge zur Bibliographie. B 1990, Nicolai. 104 p.; ill.

b576 *a) Kröger* Jens, Carl Johann LAMM (1902-1981), ein Beitrag zur Forschungsgeschichte islamischer Kunst; – *b) Hillmann* Reinhard, Otto EISSFELDT und die orientalische Religionsgeschichte: Oriens 32 (1990) 250-9 / 260-292.

b577 *a) Leclant* Jean, Torino, CHAMPOLLION e l'egittologia italiana; – *b) Bresciani* Edda, Ippolito ROSELLINI e l'egittologia italiana: Archeo 79 (1991) 6-16 / 36-44.

b578 **Lipman** Vivian D., Americans and the Holy Land through British eyes 1820-1917; a documentary history. L 1989, Self-Publishing Asn. 320 p. £15. – ᴿPEQ 122 (1990) 62 (M. *Hannam*: begins with Lt. LYNCH exploring the Jordan).

b579 **Moscati** Sabatino, [autobiog.] Sulle vie del passato; cinquant'anni di studi, incontri, scoperte: Arte storia archeologia 3. Mi 1990, Jaca. 183 p.; ill. 88-16-66003-1. – ᴿArcheo 73 (1991) 125 (S.F. *Bondi*); Letture 46 (1991) 387 (Carla *Castelli*).

b580 **Rastegar** N., **Slaje** W., Uto von MELZER (1881-1981); Werk und Nachlass eines österreichischen Iranisten: Szb 477 p/h, Iran. Komm. 20. W 1987, Österr. Akad. 113 p.; ill. DM 24. – ᴿIndogF 96 (1991) 311s (D. *Weber*); OLZ 86 (1991) 427-9 (B. *Fragner*).

b581 **Raven** Maarten J., Willem de FAMARS TESTAS, Reisschetsen uit Egypte 1858-1860 naar ongepubliceerde handschriften. Haag 1988, G. Schwartz. 232 p. 90-6179-070-0. – ᴿBO 48 (1991) 84-86 (C. *Cannuyer*).

b582 **Rice** Edward, Captain Sir Richard Francis BURTON. NY 1990, Scribner's. xx-522 p. $35 [BA 55,160, M.P. *Graham*: latest of several biographies of him].

b582* *a) Rinsveld* Bernard Van, Une égyptomanie anti-bonapartiste; le journaliste Jean-Gabriel PELTIER [*Denon* D.V. 1802]; – *b) Ridley* Ronald T., CHAMPOLLION in the tomb of Seti I; an unpublished letter; – *c) Cockle* Walter E.H., A.H. SAYCE at Elkab: ⇥ 98*, ᶠMEKHITARIAN A., CdÉ 66 (1991) 5-22; 5 fig. / 23-30 / 31-38.

b583 **Roller** Duane W., Early travellers in eastern Boiotia: McGill Univ Mg Clas 8. Amst 1989, Gieben. 211 p. $44. 90-5063-006-5. – ᴿRBgPg 69 (1991) 228 (R. *Chevallier*).

b584 *a) Scandone* Matthiae Gabriella, L'Egitto antico nell'opera del Canonico Giovanni SPANO; – *b) D'Amicone* Elvira, La riscoperta dell'Egitto antico nei fondi della Biblioteca Reale di Torino; il viaggio di Vitaliano DONATI in Oriente (1759-1762); – *c) De Salvia* Fulvio, Cataldo JANNELLI e gli studi di egittologia a Napoli nella prima metà del secolo XIX: ⇥ 618, Egitto fuori Egitto, 1990/1, 383-390 / 101-6 / 107-119.

b585 **Siebler** Michael, Troia, HOMER, SCHLIEMANN; Mythos und Wahrheit: KuGaW 46. Mainz 1990, von Zabern. 248 p.; ill.

b586 *Stannikow* Sergei, Otto Friedrich von RICHTER und Ägypten [1815]: AltOrF 18 (1991) 195-203; pl. I.

b586* *Volke* Klaus, [Thomas] YOUNG oder CHAMPOLLION? eine kritische Betrachtung: AntWelt 22 (1991) 63-66; 5 fig.

b587 ᴱ**Van Beek** Gus W., Scholarship of W.F. ALBRIGHT 1984/9 ⇥ 5,613: ᴿBO 48 (1991) 877-9 (R. *Smend*).

T1.5   *Materiae primae* – **metals, glass.**

b588 **Aufrère** Sydney, L'univers minéral dans la pensée égyptienne: BtÉt. Cairo 1991, IFAO. 835 p. (2 vol.); 25 loose p. index. 2-7247-0102-X [OIAc 1,10].

b589 *Capanelli* Daniele,   La explotación de las minas ibéricas y el comercio de metales en la época romana: Gerión 8 (1990) 227-239.
b590 **Alum:** *Kaczmarczyk* Alexander,   The identity of *wšbt* alum [cobalt-bearing, from Dakhla and Karga]:   JEA 77 (1991) 1095.

b591 **Argentum,** SILVER: *Conophagos* Constantin E.,   The ancient Athenian silvermines: ➤ 632, Ancient Technology 1987/90, 11s + 17 fig.
b592 [Pirzio] **Biroli Stefanelli** L., Argento/Bronzo dei Romani 1990s ➤ b687s.

b593 **Aurum,** GOLD: *Derchain* Philippe,   L'Atelier des Orfèvres à Dendara et les origines de l'alchimie: CdÉ 65, 130 (1990) 219-242.
b594 ᴱ**Descat** Raymond,   L'or perse 1989/9 ➤ 5,782*: ᴿNumChr 151 (1991) 229s (I. A. *Carradice*).
b595 **Gopher** Avi, *Tsuk* Tsvika,   Ancient gold; rare finds from the Nahal Qanah cave: Israel Museum Catalogues 321.   J 1991, Israel Museum. xxxvi-36 p.; color. ill.   965-278-118-X [OIAc 1,17].
b596 *Montero* Ignacio, *Rovira* Salvador,   El oro ... prerromano: ArEspArq 64 (1991) 7-21.

b597 **Cuprum,** COPPER: **Knapp** A. B.,   Copper production and divine protection ... Cyprus; SIMA pocket 42, 1986 ➤ 2,9859; 6,d64: ᴿPEQ 122 (1990) 75s (G. *Philip*).
b597* a) *Gale* N. H.,   Copper oxhide ingots; their origin and their place in the Bronze Age metals trade in the Mediterranean; – b) *Stos-Gale* Z. A., *Macdonald* C. F.,   Sources of metals and trade in the Bronze Age Aegean; – c) *Rehren* T.,   Selenium and tellurium in Mediterranean copper ingots; – d) *Muhly* J. D.,   The development of copper metallurgy in Late Bronze Age Cyprus: ➤ 637, Bronze Age Trade 1989/91, 197-239 / 249-288; 12 fig. / 240-8 / 180-196.

b598 **Lapis Lazuli:** *Degraeve* Ann,   Je t'écris au sujet d'une pierre [... noms akkadiens de lapis lazuli etc.]: Akkadica 74s (1991) 1-18.
b598* OBSIDIAN: a) *Henrion* G., *al.*,   Herkunftsnachweise von Obsidianartefakten mittels multivariater Klassifizierung von Spurenelementanalysen; – b) *Schneider* Gerwulf,   Herkunft von Obsidianartefakten in Uruk: BaghMit 21 (1990) 73-90 / 67-72.
b599 **Saxum,** STONE: *Harrell* James A.,   An inventory of ancient Egyptian quarries: NewsAmEg 146 (1989) 1-7; map.

b600 **Stannum,** TIN: *Belli* Oktay,   The problem of tin deposits in Anatolia and its need for tin, according to the written sources; – b) *Lightfoot* C. S., Glass in the Iron Age: ➤ 634, 2d Anatolian Iron Age 1987/91, 1-9 / 67-74.
b601 *Joannès* F.,   L'étain, d'Élam à Mari: ➤ 621, Rencontre 36, 1989/91, 67-76.

b602 **Vitrum,** GLASS: **Barag** D.,   Catalogue of Western Asiatic glass in the British Museum 1, 1985 ➤ 1,b607 ... 4,d807: ᴿBO 48 (1991) 907s (D. *Whitehouse*: good); IsrEJ 41 (1991) 215-9 (Yael *Israeli*).
b603 Checklist of recently published articles and books on glass: JGlass 33 (1991) 124-182.

b604 *Dussart* O., *Velde* B., La composition du verre hellénistique en Jordanie et Syrie du Sud: Syria 67 (1990) 687-693; 3 fig.
b605 *Freestone* I. C., Technical examination of Neo-Assyrian glazed wall plaques: Iraq 53 (1991) 55-58; pl. XI.
b606 **Grose** David F., Early ancient glass; core-formed, rod-formed and cast vessels and objects from the Late Bronze Age to the early Roman Empire, 1600 B.C. to A.D. 50: Toledo Museum 1989 ➤ 6,d70: [R]AJA 95 (1991) 174s (M. C. *McClellan*); TopO 1 (1991) 76-79 (Marie-D. *Nenna*).
b608 **Herrmann** Christian, Formen für ägyptische Fayencen 1985 ➤ 1,b615; 2,9871: [R]CdÉ 65 (1990) 275s (A. *Rammant-Peeters*).
b609 [E]**Newby** Martine, *Painter* Kenneth, Roman glass; two centuries of art and invention: Occ.P. 13. L 1991, Soc. Antiquaries. xxix-177 p.; ill.

T1.6 *Silex, os:* **'Prehistory' flint and bone industries.**

b610 *a) Bar-Yosef* O., The search for lithic variability among Levantine epi-palaeolithic industries; – *b) Phillips* J. L., Refitting, edge-ware, and *chaînes opératoires*; a case study from Sinai: ➤ 651, 25 ans 1990/1, 319-335; 6 pl. / 305-317.
b611 **Calley** S., Technologie du débitage à Mureybet, Syrie 9e-8e millénaire: BAR-Int 312. Ox 1986. 437 p.; 160 fig. £22. – [R]PEQ 122 (1990) 74 (Loraine *Copeland*).
b612 **Clark** Grahame, Prehistory at Cambridge and beyond 1989 ➤ 6,d78: [R]BInstArch 27 (1990) 173s (F. R. *Hodson*); JField 18 (1991) 222-4 (G. R. *Willey*).
b613 **Eichmann** Ricardo, Aspekte prähistorischer Grundrissgestaltung in Vorderasien; Beiträge zum Verständnis bestimmter Grundrissmerkmale in ausgewählten neolithischen und chalkolithischen Siedlungen des 9.-4. Jahrtausends v.Chr.: BaghFo 12. Mainz 1991, von Zabern. xxiv-113 p.; 74 pl. 3-8053-3283-0.
b614 **Fagan** Brian, Journey from Eden; the peopling of our world. L 1991, Thames & H. 256 p.; 96 fig. £13. 0-500-05057-0. – [R]Antiquity 65 (1991) 981 (T. *Taylor*: good).
b615 **Fagan** Brian M., Aufbruch aus dem Paradies; Ursprung und frühe Geschichte des Menschen, [TE]*Müller* Wolfgang. Mü 1991, Beck. 274 p.; 45 fig. DM 48 [DLZ 113,420, J. *Herrmann*].
b616 **Feder** Kenneth L., *Park* Michael A., Human antiquity; an introduction to physical anthropology and archaeology. Mountain View 1989, Mayfield. xvi-412 p.; 227 fig. – [R]BonnJbb 191 (1991) 709-712 (Ulrike *Sommer*).
b617 [E]**Foster** Mary L., *Botscharow* Lucy J., The life of symbols. Boulder 1990, Westview. ix-318 p.; ill. 0-8133-7841-9 [Antiquity 66,534s, T. *Taylor*: Stone Age, remarkably little illustrated by the symbols it discusses].
b618 **Goren-Inbar** N., Quneitra, a Mousterian site on the Golan Heights: Qedem 31. J 1990, Hebrew Univ. 239 p. – [R]Paléorient 17,1 (1991) 169s (E. *Boeda*).
b619 **Henry** Donald O., From foraging to agriculture 1989 ➤ 6,d87: [R]PEQ 122 (1990) 69s (J. *Mellaart*).
b620 *Jensen* Helle J., *al.*, Understanding the Late Palaeolithic tools with lustrous edges from the lower Nile valley [Qadan: siliceous sheen not 'sickle gloss' of a precociously early cereal-culture]: Antiquity 65 (1991) 122-8; 5 fig.

b621 **Klein** Richard G., The human career; human biological and cultural origins. Ch 1989, Univ. 524 p.; 171 fig. – ^RPrPrehSoc 57,2 (1991) 217s (C. *Gamble*).

b622 *Lawson* A. J., Proceedings of the conference on palaeolithic art held in Oxford 1989: ProcPrehSoc 57,1 (C 1991) 1s (3-174, 12 art. on Europe).

b623 ^E**Mellars** Paul, The emergence of modern humans; an archaeological perspective. E/Ithaca 1991, Univ./Cornell. xii-555 p.; 125 fig. £50. 0-85224-0130-9. – ^RAntiquity 65 (1991) 412-7 (C. *Gamble*).

b624 ^E**Mellars** Paul, *Stringer* Chris, The human revolution; behavioural and biological perspectives on the origins of modern humans 1989 → 6,d92*: ^RJField 18 (1991) 111-6 (L. R. *Binford*); PrPrehSoc 57,2 (1991) 216s (Jill *Cook*).

b625 **Mithen** Steven J., Thoughtful foragers; a study of prehistoric decision making 1990 → 6,d93: ^RAntiquity 65 (1991) 158 (P. G. *Bahn*); PrPrehSoc 57,2 (1991) 218s (P. C. *Woodman*).

b626 *Mithen* Steven J., 'A cybernetic wasteland'? Rationality, emotion and mesolithic foraging: PrPrehSoc [54 (1988) 59-66] 57s (1991) 9-14; 15-20, *Thomas* Julian rejoinder, 'The hollow men?'

b627 **Olszewski** Deborah L., The North Syrian late epipaleolithic; the earliest occupation at Tell Abu Hureyra in the context of the Levantine late epipaleolithic: BAR-Int 309, 1986 → 3,d314*b*: ^RPEQ 122 (1990) 72s (Loraine *Copeland*).

b628 **Roodenberg** J. J., Le mobilier en pierre de Bouqras 1988 → 2,9888 ... 6,d101: ^RSyria 67 (1990) 522s (H. de *Contenson*).

b630 *Simmons* Alan H., Humans, island colonization and pleistocene extinctions in the Mediterranean; the view from Akrotiri Aetokremnos, Cyprus: Antiquity 65 (1991) 857-869; 3 fig. [670-8, date for first human settlement ± 12,000; *Manning* S. W.].

b631 **Spencer** Frank, *a*) Piltdown, a scientific forgery. – *b*) The Piltdown papers. NY 1990, Oxford-UP. 272 p./282 p. – ^RArchaeology 44,3 (1991) 58-60 (B. *Fagan*).

b632 **Tomsky** Jan, Das Mittelpaläolithikum im Vorderen Orient: TAVO B-25. Wsb 1991, Reichert. 332 p.; VIII pl. 3-88226-215-X.

b633 ^E**Torrence** Robin, Time, energy and stone tools (Minneapolis meeting 1982): New directions in archaeology. C 1989, Univ. viii-124 p. £27.50. 0-521-25350-0. – ^RBInstArch 27 (1990) 249-251 (J. *Chapman*); PrPrehSoc 57,2 (1991) 215s (A. *Saville*).

b634 **Unger-Hamilton** Romana, Method in microwear analysis; prehistoric sickles and other stone tools from Arjoune, Syria: BAR-Int 435. Ox 1988. 331 p.; 45 fig.; 29 pl. £20. – ^RBInstArch 27 (1990) 251 (R. *Willis*).

b635 *Wapnish* Paula, Beauty and utility in bone [Persian era Ashkelon; also Byzantine and Islamic prominent there; and some MB; elsewhere from before 5000]: BAR-W 17,4 (1991) 54-57. 72; (color.) ill.

b636 *Welinder* Stig, The word *förhistorisk*, 'prehistoric', in Swedish [... before written records]: Antiquity 65 (1991) 295s.

b637 ^E**Yon** Marguerite, Arts et industries de la pierre: RS-Ougarit 6. P 1991. 410 p. 2-86538-218-0 [UF 23,454].

T1.7 Technologia antiqua.

b638 **Allad** James W., Persian metal technology, 700-1300 A.D. L 1979, Ithaca. x-179 p. £12.50. 0-903729-47-4. – ^RBO 48 (1991) 270-2 (D. *Whitehouse*).

b639 **Domergue** Claude, Les mines de la péninsule ibérique dans l'antiquité romaine. R 1990, École Française. 626 p. – ᴿTopO 1 (1991) 136-8 (J. *Andreau*).

b640 *Gorelick* L., *Gwinnett* A. J., Technical 'mutations' in drilling: Akkadica 74s (1991) 37-40 + 13 fig.

b640* **Klein** Michael J., Untersuchungen zu den kaiserlichen Steinbrüchen ... in der östlichen Wüste Ägyptens: DissAG 26, 1988 ➤ 5,b995: ᴿBO 48 (1991) 845-7 (A. *Bülow-Jacobsen*: outdated at birth by ongoing excavations there).

b641 *Mattusch* Carol C., Corinthian metalworking: *a*) the gymnasium bronze foundry; – *b*) an inlaid fulcrum panel: Hesperia 60 (1991) 383-395; 5 fig.; pl. 101-106 / 525-8; 1 fig.; pl. 135-136.

b642 *Philip* Graham, *a*) Cypriot bronzework in the Levantine world; conservatism, innovation and social change: JMeditArch 4 (1991) 59-107; – *b*) Tin, arsenic, lead; alloying practices in Syria-Palestine around 2000 B.C.: Levant 23 (1991) 93-104; 4 fig.

b643 ᴱ**Rothenberg** Beno, Researches in the Arabah, 1959-1984, II. The ancient metallurgy of copper – archaeology, experiment, theory. L 1990, Inst. Archaeo-Metallurgical S. 191 p.; 167 fig.; 7 pl. – ᴿQadmoniot 24 (1991) 62 (S. *Shalev* ☻).

b644 *Schiøler* Thorkild, *García-Diego* José A., Bronze Roman piston-pumps: ➤ 632, Ancient technology 1987/90, 46-67; 17 (some double) fig.

b645 *Steinmann* Frank, Untersuchungen zu den in der handwerklich-künstlerischen Produktion beschäftigten Personen und Berufsgruppen des Neuen Reichs, V. Bemerkungen zur sozialen Stellung und materiellen Lage; 1. Sozialer Rang: ZägSpr 118 (1991) 149-151.

b646 **Tallon** Françoise, *al.*, Métallurgie susienne I. De la fondation de Suse au XVIIIᵉ siècle avant J.-C.: NotesDocMusFr 15, 1987 ➤ 3,e674: ᴿSyria 66 (1989) 356-8 (P. de *Miroschedji*).

b647 **Wartke** Ralf-B., *a*) Handwerk und Technologie im Alten Orient; ein Beitrag zur Geschichte der Technik des Altertums; Sonderausstellung des Vorderasiatischen Museums 1990s. B 1990, Staatliche Museen. 48 p.; ill. [OIAc 1,26]. – *b*) Handwerk und Technologie im Alten Orient, 1. Ver- und Bearbeitung von Ton und Stein; 2. ... von Metall und Glas; Antike Reparaturen: AntWelt 22 (1991) 35-47; 21 (color.) fig. / 82-96; 26 fig.

b648 *Zawadzki* Stefan, Ironsmiths, bronzesmiths and goldsmiths in the neo-Babylonian texts from Sippar: WeltOr 22 (1991) 21-47.

T1.8   **Architectura.**

b648* *Abeele* Barbara Van Den, Comparison of the Roman domus with the domus of Ostia: AcArchLov 28s (1989s) 49-53 + 17 fig.

b649 **Adam** Jean-Pierre, La construction romaine, matériaux et techniques 1984 ➤ 65,a200 ... 3,d335: ᴿHelmantica 42,129* (1991) 374 (F. J. *Udaondo Puerto*).

b650 **Altekamp** Stefan, Zu griechischen Architekturornamentik im sechsten und fünften Jahrhundert ... Auswertung der nicht-dorischen Blattornamentik [Diss. Münster 1989]: EurHS 38/37. Fra 1991, Lang. xiii-586 p.

b651 **Arnold** Dieter, Building in Egypt; Pharaonic stone masonry. NY 1991, Oxford-UP. ix-316 p. 0-19-506350-3 [OIAc F91,1; BAR-W 17/5, 10].

b652 *a*) *Aurenche* Olivier, Le dessin d'architecte dans le Proche-Orient des origines au milieu du IVᵉ millénaire; – *b*) *Callot* Olivier, Rôle et méthode des constructeurs de maisons à Ras Shamra-Ougarit; – *c*) *Margueron* Jean,

Y a-t-il un tracé régulateur dans les palais mésopotamiens du IIe millénaire?; – *d*) *Schmid* Martin E., Esquisse du tracé d'un ensemble architectural de l'époque minoenne; Malia, le quartier Mu: → 631, ^E*Bommelaer* J., Dessin 1984/5, 9-14 + 9 fig. / 19-28; 6 fig. / 29-45; 5 fig. / 63-73; 11 fig.

b652* ^E**Bazzana** A., *al.*, Habitats fortifiés et organisation de l'espace en Méditérranée médiévale: Table Ronde 4-5 mai 1982. Lyon 1983, Maison de l'Orient. 219 p. 2-903264-33-3 [OIAc 2,14].

b653 *Billot* Marie-Françoise, Terres cuites architecturales d'Argolide: RArchéol (1991) 199-209; 13 fig.

b654 **Bretschneider** Joachim, Architekturmodelle in Vorderasien und der östlichen Ägäis vom Neolithikum bis in das 1. Jahrtausend; Phänomene in der Kleinkunst an Beispielen aus Mesopotamien, dem Iran, Anatolien, Syrien, der Levante und dem ägäischen Raum, unter besonderer Berücksichtigung der bau- und religionsgeschichtlichen Aspekte [Diss. Münster 1990, ^D*Mayer-Opificius* Ruth]: AOAT 229. Neuk/Kevelaer 1991, Neuk-V./Butzon & B. x-261 p. 157 pl. 3-7887-1883-6 / BB 3-7666-9765-X.

b655 **Brödner** Erika, Wohnen in der Antike. Da 1989, Wiss. x-341 p.; 149 fig. – ^RKlio 73 (1991) 704-6 (Gerda von *Bülow*).

b656 **Cooper** Nancy K., The development of roof-revetment in the Peloponnese [diss. 1983]: SIMA pocket 88. Jonsered 1988, Åström. viii-136 p.; 58 pl. – ^RRArchéol (1991) 375-8 (Marie-Françoise *Billot*).

b656* **Creswell** K. A. C. [1932, ²1969] ³rev*Allan* James W., A short account of early Muslim architecture. Aldershot 1989, Scholar. xx-435 p. £47.50. – ^RBSO 54 (1991) 580-3 (G. *Fehérvári*).

b657 **Danner** Peter, Griechische Akrotere der archaischen und klassischen Zeit [< Diss. 1986, Salzburg]: RivArch supp. 5. R 1989, Bretschneider. 96 p.; 32 pl. – ^RRArchéol (1991) 374s (Marie-Françoise *Billot*); RBgPg 69 (1991) 253-5 (P. *Gros*); RÉG 104 (1991) 256 (Mary-Anne *Zagdoun*).

b658 *Dentzer-Feydy* J., Les chapiteaux ioniques de Syrie méridionale: Syria 67 (1990) 143-181; 57 fig. [633-663; 26 fig.: corinthiens normaux I].

Eichmann R., Aspekte prähistorischer Grundrissgestaltung 1991 → b613.

b659 **Fischer** Moshe L., *a*) Das korinthische Kapitell im alten Israel in der hellenistischen und römischen Periode: Studien zur Geschichte der Baudekoration im Nahen Osten. 134 p.; 51 pl. – ^RPEQ 123 (1991) 136s (D. M. *Jacobson*). – *b*) Figured capitals in Roman Palestine; marble imports and local stones; some aspects of imperial and 'provincial' art: ArchAnz (1991) 119-144; 11 fig. (map).

b660 **Fleury** Philippe, VITRUVE, De l'architecture I. P 1990, BLettres. cxviii-208 (d.) p., 4 pl. 2-251-01349-0. – ^RLatomus 50 (1991) 698-700 (L. *Callebat*).

b661 — **Gros** P., VITRUVE, De l'architecture III. P 1990, BLettres. xcii-223 p. 43 fig. 2-251-01350-4. – ^RRArchéol (1991) 389s (C. *Le Roy*).

b662 **Freyberger** K. S., Stadtrömische Kapitelle aus der Zeit von Domitien bis Alexander Severus; zur Arbeitsweise und Organisation stadtrömischer Werkstätten der Kaiserzeit. Mainz 1990, von Zabern. xii-143 p.; 61 pl. DM 98. 3-8053-1078-1 [JRS 81,258]. – ^RTGL 81 (1991) 414s (W. *Knoch*).

b663 **Ganschow** Thomas, Untersuchungen zur Baugeschichte in Herculaneum: Antiquitas 3/30, 1989 → 6,d149: ^RBonnJbb 191 (1991) 795-800 (V. *Kockel*).

b664 ^E**Henig** M., Architecture and architectural sculpture in the Roman Empire: Mg 29. Ox 1990, Univ. Committee for Archaeology [distr. Oxbow]. viii-163 p.; ill.; maps. £30. 0-947816-29-1 [JRS 81,258].

b664* **Hiesel** Gerhard, Spälthelladische Hausarchitektur; Studien zur Architekturgeschichte des griechischen Festlandes in der späten Bronzezeit. Mainz 1989, von Zabern. ix-269 p.; 172 fig.; 8 pl.; map. DM 115. – RClasR 41 (1991) 435s (R. A. *Tomlinson*).

b665 **Johnson** Lora L., [cf. ➤ 1,b688] The Hellenistic and Roman library; studies pertaining to their architectural form: diss. Brown. Providence 1984. 282 p.

b666 *Jones* Mark W., Designing the Roman Corinthian capital: PapBritSR 59 (1991) 89-150; 27 fig.

b667 **Klein** Nancy L., The origin of the Doric order on the mainland of Greece; form and function of the geison in the archaic period: diss. Bryn Mawr, DWright J. Ph 1991. 266 p. 91-28580. – DissA 52 (1991s) 1403-A.

b668 *Kleiner* Fred S., a) The sanctuary of the matronae aufaniae in Bonn and the tradition of votive arches in the Roman world: BonnJbb 191 (1991) 149-224; 10 fig.; – b) The trophy on the bridge and the Roman triumph over nature: AntClas 60 (1991) 182-192.

b669 **Kleiss** Wolfram, Die Entwicklung von Palästen und palastartigen Wohnbauten in Iran: Szb W p/h 524, Komm. Iranistik 22, 1989 ➤ 5,d40: ROLZ 86 (1991) 195s (A. D. N. *Bivar*, Eng.).

Lackenbacher Sylvie, Le palais sans rival; le récit de construction en Assyrie 1990 ➤ d701.

b671 **Maguire** Eunice & H., *Duncan-Flowers* M., Art and holy powers in the early Christian house: ILByzSt II. Urbana 1990, Univ. Illinois. 251 p. $25. 0-252-06095-4. – ROrChrPer 57 (1991) 438s (V. *Ruggieri*).

b672 **Martin** Susan D., The Roman jurists and the organization of private building in the late Republic and early Empire: Coll. Latomus 204. Bru 1989. 157 p. Fb 750. 2-87031-144-3. – RGnomon 63 (1991) 514-6 (R. A. *Bauman*); JRS 45 (1991) 184s (M. T. *Boatwright*: valuable).

b673 *Matthiae* Paolo, Architettura e urbanistica di Ebla paleosiriana: ParPass 46,258ss (1991) 304-345 + 21 fig.

b674 **Milburn** Robert, Early Christian art and architecture. Berkeley 1991, Univ. California. 336 p.; 194 fig.; 4 maps. – RScripTPamp 23 (1991) 1082s (A. de *Silva*).

b675 a) *Moretti* J.-C., L'architecture des théâtres en Grèce [ancienne; chronique 1980-1989]; b) *Étienne* Robert, Architecture et democratie: Topoi Orient-Occident 1 (1991) 7-38 / 39-47.

b676 **Müller-Wiener** Wolfgang, Griechisches Bauwesen in der Antike 1988 ➤ 5,d60; 6,d170: RGnomon 63 (1991) 71-73 (H. *Knell*).

b677 **Nielsen** I., Thermae et balnea; the architecture and cultural history of Roman public baths. Århus 1990, Univ. xiii-194 p.; 212 p. + 260 fig. Dk 408. 87-7288-212-3 [JRS 81,260].

b678 *Pisani Sartorio* Giuseppina, (*Steinby* Eva M.), Costruire l'impero; materiali tecniche e arte edilizia dei Romani: Archeo 56 (1989) 53-97.

Richardson L., Pompeii, an architectural history 1988 ➤ e289.

b679 **Ruggieri** Vincenzo, Byzantine religious architecture (582-867); its history and structural elements [< diss. Oxford, DMango C.]: OrChrAnal 237. R 1991, Pont. Inst. St. Orientalium. xli-287 p.; 51 fig.; 22 pl. [Muséon 105,208, A. *Boonen*]. 88-7210-284-7.

b680 *Schaar* Kenneth W., An architectural theory for the origin of the four-room house: ➤ 428*, ScandJOT (1991,2) 75-98.

b680* **Segal** Arthur, ✪ & Eng., *Teatron we-Teatriyût* ... Architecture and the theatre in Eretz-Israel during the Roman and Byzantine periods: Catalogue 7. Haifa 1991, Hecht Museum. 47 p.; 39 fig. [OIAc 2,26].

b681 **Thornton** M. K. & R. L., Julio-Claudian building programs... 1989
➤ 6,d185: ᴿClasR 41 (1991) 255s (T. P. *Wiseman*); Gnomon 63 (1991)
131-5 (P. *Herz*).

b682 **Tomlinson** R. A., Greek architecture: Classical World. Bristol 1989,
Classical. viii-104 p.; 44 fig. – ᴿClasR 41 (1991) 259s (J. E. *Jones*);
Gnomon 63 (1991) 626-9 (D. *Wannagat*).

b682* **Vemi** Vassiliki, Les chapiteaux ioniques à imposte de Grèce à l'époque
paléochrétienne; BCH supp. 17, 1989 ➤ 5,d71: ᴿRivArCr 67 (1991)
195-7 (Monica *Faita*).

b683 *Waele* Jos de, Le dessin d'architecture du temple grec au début de
l'époque classique: ➤ 631, Dessin 1984/5, 87-102; 12 fig.

b684 **White** Michael L., Building God's house 1990 ➤ 6,d189: ᴿGreeceR 38
(1991) 109 (B. A. *Sparkes*); SecC 8 (1989) 253-5 (D. E. *Smith*).

b685 ᴱ**Winter** Nancy A., Greek architectural terracottas [2-4.XII.1988]: Hesperia 59,1 (1990). – ᴿAJA 95 (1991) 746s (Gloria S. *Merker*); ArchWsz
42 (1991) 156s (S. *Parnicki-Pudelko*, ❷).

T1.9   *Supellex;* furniture; objects of daily life.

b686 *Anabolu* Mükerrem, ❶ Efes Müzesinde... table-legs: Türk Ark 29 (1991)
71-74 + 19 fig.

b687 [Pirzio] **Biroli Stefanelli** L., L'argento dei Romani; vasellame da tavola e
d'apparato: Il metallo. R 1991, Bretschneider. xii-329 p.; 89 fig.; 16
pl. + 141 color.; map. Lit. 200.000. 88-7062-702-0 [JRS 81,254].

b688 ᴱ[Pirzio] **Biroli Stefanelli** L., Il bronzo dei Romani; arredo e supellettile:
Il metallo, mito e fortuna nel mondo antico. R 1990, Bretschneider.
xii-299 p.; 68 fig.; 12 pl. + 141 color.; 4 maps. 88-7062-675-X [JRS
81,254]. – ᴿAJA 95 (1991) 355s (E. *Dwyer*).

b689 **Gardner** J. F., *Wiedemann* T., The Roman household; a sourcebook. L
1991, Routledge. xviii-210 p.; 12 pl. £11. 0-415-04421-9 [JRS 81,258].
0-415-04421-9.

b690 *González Echegaray* Joaquín, Mesas domésticas del siglo I en Jerusalén,
y altares cristianos: ➤ 421, Luso-Esp 1989/91, 23-29 + 6 fig.

b691 **Gubel** E., Phoenician furniture 1987 ➤ 4,d915... 6,d193: ᴿSyria 67
(1990) 210-215 (Hélène *Benichou-Safar*).

b692 *Kaplony-Heckel* Ursula, Niltal und Oasen; ägyptischer Alltag nach
demotischen Ostraka: ZägSpr 118 (1991) 127-141.

b692* **Klengel** Horst, König Hammurapi und der Alltag Babylons [= Ham-
murabi⁴ 1980 völlig neu überarbeitet]. Z 1991, Artemis & W. 280 p.
3-7608-1057-8 [OIAc 2,22].

b693 **Matthews** Victor H., Manners and customs in the Bible²ʳᵉᵛ [¹1988].
Peabody ᴹᴬ 1991, Hendrickson. xxviii-283 p.; ill.; maps. 0-943575-
77-X; -81-8.

b693* *Oikonomides* Nikolas, The contents of the Byzantine house from the
eleventh to the fifteenth century: ➤ 647*, Byzantine Family 1989, DumbO
44 (1990) 205-214.

b694 *Olson* S. Douglas, Firewood and charcoal in classical Athens: Hesperia
60 (1991) 411-420.

T2.1   *Res militaris;* weapons, army activities.

b694* ᴱ**Adam** Anne-Marie, *Rouveret* Agnès, Guerre et sociétés en Italie aux
Vᵉ et IVᵉ siècles avant J.-C.; les indices fournis par l'armement et les

techniques de combat: Table Ronde CNRS 5 mai 1984: 1986 → 5,828 ('et société'): ᴿRArchéol (1991) 175s (Christine *Delplace*).

b695 *Betlyon* John W., Archaeological evidence of military operations in southern Judah during the Early Hellenistic period: BA 54 (1991) 36-43.

b696 **Bottini** Angelo, *al.*, Antike Helme, Sammlung Lipperheide Berlin: Mg. 4. Mainz 1988, Röm.-German. Zentralmuseum. ix-500 p.; 814 fig.; 7 pl.; 2 foldouts. – ᴿGnomon 63 (1991) 566-8 (J. *Borchhardt*).

b697 *Bowman* Alan K., *Thomas* J. David, A military strength report from Vinolanda [1988 excav., 'most important military document ever discovered in Britain']: JRS 81 (1991) 62-73; pl. VIII.

b698 *Brizzi* Giovanni, La guerra nell'impero romano: Archeo 52 (1989) 46-97.

b698* **Cernenko** E. V., The Scythians 700-300 B.C.: Men-at-Arms 137. L 1991, Osprey. 40 p.; 8 colour drawings (*McBride* Angus). 0-85045-478-6.

b699 *Chevereau* Pierre-Marie, Contribution à la prosopographie des cadres militaires du Moyen Empire: RÉgp 42 (1991) 43-88; Eng. 88.

b700 **Dack** E. Van't, Ptolemaica selecta, études sur l'armée 1988 → 5,250: ᴿGnomon 63 (1991) 115-8 (R. *Scholl*).

b701 **Davison** David P., The barracks of the Roman army... BAR-Int 472, 1988 → 5,d588; 6,d214: ᴿBSAA 57 (1991) 546-9 (S. *Carretero Vaquero*).

b702 **Devijver** Hubert, The equestrian officers of the Roman imperial army: Mavors 6. Amst 1989, Gieben. xii-474 p. – ᴿSalesianum 53 (1991) 156 (R. *Della Casa*).

b703 *Dezső* Tamás, *Curtis* John, Assyrian iron helmets from Nimrud now in the British Museum: Iraq 53 (1991) 105-126; 22 fig.; pl. XV-XX.

b704 **Dintsis** Petros, Hellenistische Helme 1986 → 6,d216: ᴿAcArchH 43 (1991) 455-7 (M. *Szabó*).

b705 *Esayan* S. A., Schutzwaffen aus Armenien: BVgArch 9s (1990) 83-100 + 10 fig.

b706 *Fortenberry* Diane, Single greaves in the Late Helladic period: AJA 95 (1991) 623-7; 4 fig.

b707 **Franzoni** C., Habitus atque habitudo militis 1987 → 5,d93; 6,d221: ᴿGymnasium 98 (1991) 88-90 (M. *Donderer*).

b708 ᴱ**Freeman** Philip, *Kennedy* David, The defence of the Roman and Byzantine East: BAR-Int 297, 1986 → 3,813; 4,d936: ᴿGnomon 63 (1991) 259-263 (H.-P. *Kuhnen*).

b709 *a*) *Fuentes* N., The mule of a soldier [really about shovels and similar heavy equipment]; – *b*) *Coulston* J. C. N., The 'draco' standard: JRomMil 2 (1991) 65-100; 24 fig. / 101-114; 15 fig.

b710 *Gichon* Mordechai, *Vitale* Michaela, Arrow-heads from Ḥorvat 'Eqed [1507.1382]: IsrEJ 41 (1991) 242-7; 19 fig.

b711 **Hanson** Victor D., Hoplites, the classical Greek battle experience. L 1991, Routledge. xvi-286 p. [RÉG 104,679].

b711* **Hanson** Victor D., L'arte occidentale della guerra; descrizione di una battaglia nella Grecia classica [PLUTARCO: Pidna; The western way...], ᵀ*Panzeri* Davide. Mi 1990, Mondadori. 267 p. Lit. 30.000. – ᴿLetture 46 (1991) 284-6 (Carla *Castelli*).

b712 *Hoffmann* Friedhelm, 'Schlinge des Kampfes' (*ḥgy n sḏy*) [vielmehr 'Kampfplatz' (für Sport oder Krieg)]: Enchoria 18 (1991) 183-6.

b713 **Isaac** Benjamin, The limits of empire; the Roman army in the east. Ox 1990, U.P. xiv-492 p.; 13 fig.; 5 maps. £50. – ᴿBInstArch 27 (1990) 211 (R. M. J. *Isserlin*); ClasR 41 (1991) 411-3 (A. R. *Birley*); 103 (T. *Wiedemann*); JStJud 22 (1991) 147-150 (M. *Goodman*); RÉAnc 93 (1991) 199-201 (M. *Sartre*).

b714 **Junkelmann** Marcus, Die Legionen des Augustus; der römische Soldat im archäologischen Experiment: KuAW 33. Mainz 1986, von Zabern. 313 p.; 24 fig.; 64 pl. + 16 color. – RAJA 95 (1991) 563s (C. M. *Wells*: how eight men dressed and armed like legionaries marched from Verona to Augsburg: admirable).

b714* **Kolbus** Suzanne, Zur Funktion der frühbronzezeitlichen umwallten Plätze Palästinas: Diss. Münster 1990. – ArchAnz (1991) 147.

b715 **Kolias** Taxiarchis G., Byzantinische Waffen 1988 → 5,d95*; 6,d228: RByzantion 61 (1991) 575-8 (P. *Colman*, P. *Joris*); Klio 73 (1991) 669-675 (M. *Springer*).

b716 **Künzl** Ernst, Der römische Triumph; Siegesfeiern im antiken Rom: BArchBt 1988 → 5,b692; DM 38: RAJA 95 (1991) 353-5 (Laetitia *La Follette*).

b717 **Le Bohec** Yann, La troisième légion Auguste (diss. d'État 1982): Ét. Antiq. Africaines. P 1989, CNRS. 632 p.; ill. – RRÉAnc 93 (1991) 196-8 (J. *Peyras*).

b718 **Le Bohec** Yann, Les unités auxiliaires de l'armée romaine en Afrique proconsulaire et Numidie sous le Haut Empire: ÉtAntAfr. P 1989, CNRS. 220 p.; 16 fig. F 190. 2-222-04239-9. – RJRS 81 (1991) 218-220 (D. J. *Mattingly*, also on his Légion Auguste); RÉAnc 93 (1991) 198s (J. *Peyras*).

b719 ELeriche Pierre, *Tréziny* Henri, La fortification dans l'histoire du monde grec 1982/6 → 5,d97: RRÉG 104 (1991) 273 (A. *Laronde*).

b720 **Levi** Mario A., L'impiego tattico della cavalleria in Roma antica: ParPass 46,256 (1991) 16-32.

b721 **Link** Stefan, Konzepte der Privilegierung römischer Veteranen. Stu 1989, Steiner. 168 p. DM 48. – RLatomus 50 (1991) 204s (Y. *Le Bohec*).

b722 **Lissarague** François, L'autre guerrier; archers, peltastes, cavaliers dans l'imagerie attique: Images à l'appui 3. P/R 1990, Découverte/Éc. Française. 326 p.; 130 fig. – RRArchéol (1991) 365-7 (Marie-Christine *Villanueva-Puig*: '130 photos et dessins' mais 'un millier d'images' ... '700 scènes d'archer scythe').

b723 **Müller** Hans W., Der 'Armreif' ... 1989 → 6,d232: RBO 48 (1991) 502-4 (R. H. *Wilkinson*).

b724 **Roth** Jonathan, The logistics of the Roman army in the Jewish War: diss. Columbia, DHarris W. NY 1991. 509 p. 92-09887. – DissA 52 (1991s) 4046s-A.

b725 **Rüpke** Georg, Domi militiae; die religiöse Konstruktion des Krieges in Rom [Diss. Tübingen]: FrB Militärgeschichtliches Forschungsamt. Stu 1990, Steiner. 312 p. DM 64 [TR 87,433].

b726 *Russell* James, A Roman military diploma from eastern Pamphylia [Cebel Ires; now in Alanya museum]: AJA 95 (1991) 469-488; 5 fig. (map).

b727 **Sekunda** Nick, The ancient Greeks; armies of classical Greece, 5th and 4th centuries B.C.: Elite 7. L 1990, Osprey. 64 p.; ill.; 12 colour. drawings (McBride A.). 0-85045-086-X.

b728 **Shatzman** Israel, The armies of the Hasmonaeans and Herod; from Hellenistic to Roman frameworks: TStAJud 25. Tü 1991, Mohr. xv-354 p. DM 178. 3-16-145617-3 [BL 92,130, L. L. *Grabbe*].

b729 *Shatzman* Israel, ⊕ Ballistra stones from Tel Dor and the artillery of the Greco-Roman world: Qadmoniot 24 (1991) 94-104; ill. [105-113, *Sharon* Ilun].

b729* **Simkins** Michael, The Roman army from Caesar to Trajan / From Hadrian to Constantine: Men-at-Arms 46/93. L 1991, Osprey. each

40 p. with 8 colour drawings by *Embleton* Ronald.   0-85045-528-6;
-333-X.

b730 *Taracha* Piotr,   On the ancestry of Aegean type E daggers; ArchWsz 41
(1990) 21-27; 2 multiple plates.

b731 *Tarragon* J.-M. de,   La pointe de flèche inscrite ['flèche (d') Adônišuʿa ']
des Pères Blancs de Jérusalem: RB 98 (1991) 244-251; 2 fig.; pl. II.

b732 **Treviño** Rafael,   Rome's enemies, 4: Spanish armies 218 BC-19 BC:
Men-at-Arms 180.   L 1990, Osprey.   48 p.; maps.   8 drawings (A.
McBride).   0-85045-701-7.

b732* *Völling* Thomas,   Plumbata – mattiobarbulus – *martzobarboulon*?
Bemerkungen zu einem Waffenfund aus Olympia: ArchAnz (1991)
287-298; 4 fig.

b733 *Vutiropulos* Nikos,   The sling in the Aegean Bronze Age: Antiquity 65
(1991) 279-286; 4 fig. (map).

b734 ᵀᴱ**Whitehead** David,   AENEAS the tactician; how to survive under siege.
Ox 1990, U.P.   xxi-214 p. £27.50; pa. £11. – ᴿGreeceR 38 (1991) 99 (P. J.
Rhodes).

b735 **Wise** Terence,   *a*) Ancient armies of the Middle East; – *b*) Armies of the
Carthaginian wars 265-146 BC: Men-at-Arms 109.121.   L 1991, Osprey.
each 40 p., 8 drawings (A. *McBride*). 0-85045-384-4; -430-1.

b735* *Zorn* Jeffrey,   LÚ-*pa-ma-ḫa-a* in EA(marna) 162:74 and the role of the
mhr in Egypt and Ugarit [a type of military personnel]: JNES 50 (1991)
129-138.

т2.2   *Vehicula,*   **transportation.**

b736 *Anthony* David W.,   **Brown** Dorcas R.,   The origins of horseback riding
[the bit leaves traces on the horse's teeth: Ukraine 4000 B.C. – pre-dating
the wheel]: Antiquity 65 (1991) 22-38; 11 fig. [119-122, *Littauer* M.,
Crouwel J., on harness].

b737 **Liebowitz** Harold,   Terra cotta figurines and model vehicles... Se-
lenkahiye, Syria 1988 ➤ 5,d114; 6,d246:   ᴿWeltOr 22 (1991) 227-9 (R.
Mayer-Opificius).

b737* *Littauer* Mary A., *al.*,   Ein spätbronzezeitliches Speichenrad vom Lidar
Höyük in der Südost-Türkei: ArchAnz (1991) 349-358; 5 fig.

b738 *Littauer* M.A.,   *Crouwel* J.H.,   Assyrian Trigas and Russian Dvoikas:
Iraq 53 (1991) 97-99; 1 fig.; pl. XIV.

b738* *Owen* David I.,   The 'first' equestrian; an Ur III glyptic scene: AcSum
13 (1991) 259-269; 7 fig.

т2.3   **Nautica.**

b739 *a*) *Adam* P.A.,   À la recherche d'une permanence dans la construction
navale antique; – *b*) *Pomey* P.,   Principes et méthodes de construction en
architecture navale antique; – *c*) *Nieto* J.,   Cargamento principal y
cargamento secundario: ➤ 128, ᶠROUGÉ J. Navires 1988, 255-270 /
397-412 / 379-395.

b740 *Artzy* Michal,   ❶ The Bronze Age anchorage site of Tel Nami:
Qadmoniot 24 (1991) 31-38; ill.

b741 *Bakr* Mohammed I.,   **Nibbi** Alessandra,   Three stone anchors from Tell
Basta: RÉgp 42 (1991) 3-10; 1 fig.; 1 pl.

b742 **Basch** Lucien,   Le musée imaginaire de la marine antique 1987 ➤ 4,
d967:   ᴿTopO 1 (1991) 83-88 (F. *Richard*).

b743 **Beike** Manfred, Kriegsflotten und Seekriege der Antike[2] [[1]1987]. B 1990, Brandenburg. 179 p.; ill. 3-327-00289-4.

b744 **Beurdeley** Cécile, L'archéologie sous-marine; l'odyssée des trésors. P 1991, Bibliothèque des Arts. 222 p. 2-85047-160-7.

b745 *Black* Eve, *Samuel* David, What were sails made of? [Jon 1,4; Egypt...]: Mariner's Mirror 77 (1991) 217-226; 7 fig.

b746 **Casson** Lionel, The ancient mariners; seafarers and sea fighters of the Mediterranean in ancient times[2] [[1]1959]. Princeton 1991, Univ. xviii-246 p.; 7 fig.; 54 pl.; 4 maps. 0-691-06836-4; pa. -1477-9.

b747 **Eiseman** Cynthia, *Ridgway* Brunilde S., The Porticello shipwreck 1987 ➤ 3,d430*... 5,d133: [R]VDI 197 (1991) 233-8 (L. M. *Korotkikh*, ❽).

b748 *Fellmeth* Ulrich, Die Häfen von Ostia und ihre wirtschaftliche Bedeutung für die Stadt Rom: MünstHand 10,1 (1991) 1-31; Eng. 31; franç. 32.

b749 **Garland** Robert, The Piraeus 1987 ➤ 4,d973; 6,d263: [R]Gnomon 62 (1991) 706-710 (K.-V. von *Eickstedt*).

b750 *Gibbins* D. J. L., The Roman wreck of c. AD 200 at Plemmirio, near Siracusa (Sicily), third interim report; the domestic assemblage, 2. kitchen and table pottery, glass, and fishing weights: IntJNaut 20 (1991) 227-246; 11 fig.

b751 **Green** Jeremy, Maritime archaeology; a technical handbook. L 1990, Academic. 282 p.; 128 fig. £27. 0-12-298630-X. – [R]JField 18 (1991) 246-9 (R. A. *Gould*); IntJNaut 20 (1991) 175s (J. *Adams*) & 176s (F. *Hocker*).

b752 **Jundziłł** Juliusz, ❽ Rzymianie a morze... The Romans and the sea. Bydgoszcz 1991. 182 p.; ill.; Eng. deutsch résumé.

b753 *Linder* Elisha, ❽ The Ma'agan Mikhael shipwreck excavations: Qadmoniot 24 (1991) 39-46; ill.

b754 *Longerstay* Monique, Représentations de navires archaïques en Tunisie du Nord; contribution à la chronologie des Haouanet: Karthago 22 (1990) 33-44 + XVI pl.; map p. 32.

McCann Anna M., *al.*, The Roman port of Cosa 1987 ➤ e781.

b755 **McGrail** Seán, Ancient boats in N.W. Europe; the archaeology of water transport to A.D. 1500: 1987 ➤ 3,d443... 5,d145: [R]RBgPg 69 (1991) 514s (Stéphane *Lebecq*).

b755* a) *McGrail* Seán, Bronze Age seafaring in the Mediterranean; a view from northwest Europe; – b) *Bass* George F., Evidence of trade from Bronze Age shipwrecks: ➤ 637, Bronze Age Trade 1989/91, 83-91 / 69-82.

b756 *Mark* Samuel E., Odyssey 5.234-53 and Homeric ship construction; a reappraisal: AJA 95 (1991) 441-5.

b757 **Meijer** Fik, A history of seafaring in the classical world 1986 ➤ 4,d990... 6,d273: [R]RÉAnc 92 (1990) 174s (J. *Dumont*).

b758 [E]**Morrison** J. S., *Coates* J. F., An Athenian trireme reconstructed: BAR-Int 485, 1989 [? not = 1987 ➤ 2,a18... 5,d150]: [R]Fornvännen 86 (1991) 215-7 (C. O. *Cederlund*).

b759 *Morrison* J. S., The Greek ships at Salamis and the *diekplous*: JHS [108 (1988) 250, J. F. *Coates* criticism] 111 (1991) 196-200.

b760 *Mosca* Annapaola, Caratteri della navigazione nell'area benacense in età romana [Lago di Garda]: Latomus 50 (1991) 269-284; map.

b761 *Nibbi* Alessandra, Five stone anchors from Alexandria: IntJNaut 20 (1991) 185-194; 13 fig.

b762 *Raveh* Kurt, *Kingsley* Sean A., The status of Dor in late antiquity; a maritime perspective [... not overshadowed by Caesarea harbor]: BA 54 (1991) 198-207; ill.

b762* *Riesner* Rainer, Neue Funde in Israel; grosse und kleine Boote auf dem See Gennesaret: BiKi 46 (1991) 181-3.

b763 *Rougé* Jean, Trois textes d'époque impériale sur le navire: Latomus 50 (1991) 669-676.

b764 *Schubert* Paul, Ordre de mise à disposition d'un bateau: ZPapEp 86 (1991) 233-6.

b765 **Starr** Chester G., The influence of sea power on ancient history 1989 ⇥ 5,d163; 6,d285: ᴿHZ 253 (1991) 409s (O. *Höckmann*).

b766 *Tooley* A. M. J., Boat deck plans and hollow hulled models: ZäSpr 118 (1991) 68-75.

b767 **Wachsman** Shelley, *al.*, The excavations of an ancient boat in the Sea of Galilee 1990 ⇥ 6,d288: ᴿIntJNaut 20 (1991) 181s (Honor *Frost*).

T2.4 *Athletica,* **sport, games.**

b768 *a*) [Angeli] *Bernardini* Paolo, Proposte per un lessico dell'agonistica sportiva della Grecia antica; – *b*) *Zumbo* Antonino, Per un lessico greco della pesca; ⇥ 579, Lessici Tecnici 1990/1, 329-339 / 281-290.

b769 *Calcani* Giuliano, Magia del gioco; come facevano? [giocattoli, musei Atene e Roma]: Archeo 70 (1990) 118-121.

b770 *Crowther* Nigel B., Old age, exercise and athletics in the ancient world: Stadion 16 (1990) 171-183.

b771 *Decker* Wolfgang [⇥ 905], *a*) Olympiasieger aus Ägypten: ⇥ 43, ꟻDERCHAIN P., Religion 1991, 93-104 + 1 fig. – *b*) Ägyptischer Sport und Afrika: ⇥ 20c, ꟻBEHRENS P. 1991, 95-108.

b772 **Di Donato** Michele, *Teja* Angela, Agonistica e ginnastica nella Grecia antica 1989 ⇥ 5,d175: ᴿArcheo 71 (1991) 128 (Giovanna *Quattrocchi*).

b773 **Facchini** Sandra, I luoghi dello sport nella Roma antica e moderna. R 1990, Ist. Poligrafico. – ᴿStRom 39 (1991) 321 (Flaminia *Verga*).

b774 *Faraone* Christopher A., The agonistic context of early Greek binding spells: ⇥ 392, Magika hiera 1991, 3-32.

b775 **Golvin** J.-C., *Landes* C., Amphithéâtres et gladiateurs. P 1990, CNRS. 238 p.; (color.) ill.; plans. F 490. 2-87682-046-3 [JRS 81,258].

b776 **Golvin** Jean-Claude, L'amphithéâtre romain 1988 ⇥ 5,d30; 6,d316: ᴿNikephoros 3 (1990) 287-291 (J.-P. *Thuillier*).

b777 *Gregori* Gian Luca, Tra epigrafia e filologia; un gladiatore di nome Rutumanna: Arctos 25 (Helsinki 1991) 45-50 + 2 fig.

b778 *Griffith* R.D. & Gloria D., Il gioco della 'chelichelōnē': Maia 43 (1991) 83-88.

b779 *Heikkilä* Kai, 'Now I have the mind to dance'; the references of the chorus to their own dancing in Sophocles' tragedies: Arctos 25 (1991) 51-68.

b780 **Humphrey** John H., Roman circuses; arenas for chariot racing 1986 ⇥ 2,a44... 5,e27; £50; 0-7134-2116-9: ᴿAntiqJ 70 (1990) 487-9 (T. F. C. *Blagg*).

b780* *Khanoussi* Mustapha, Ein römisches Mosaik aus Tunesien mit der Darstellung eines agonistischen Wettkampfes: AntWelt 22 (1991) 146-153; 17 (color.) fig.

b781 *Kilmer* Anne D., An oration on Babylon [LANDSBERGER B. 'children's games', but more; not satirical; possibly (to be spoken) by Ištar; the reverse may show faint traces of a seal impression, perhaps of an animal-circus or carnival]: AltOrF 18 (1991) 9-22.

b782 **Kolmer** Hans, Vorformen sportlicher Aktivitäten in prähistorischen Felsbildern. W 1989, Bundesverlag. 80 p.; 7 color pl. Sch 228. – ᴿNikephoros 3 (1990) 263s (T. *Lenssen-Erz*).

b783 *Laffey* Alice S., Humour and play [including victory-celebrations, music, feast-meals, story-telling]: Way 31 (1991) 187-195 [< NTAbs 36,73].

b784 ᴱ**Landes** Christine, *al.*, Le cirque et les courses de chars Rome-Byzance: catalogue de l'exposition [Montpellier-Lattes juin-oct. 1990]. Lattes 1990, Imago. 391 p.; 10 color. pl. F 180. 2-9501586-5-X. – ᴿNikephoros 3 (1990) 292-6 (W. *Decker*).

b785 *Ley* Anne, Atalante – von der Athletin zur Liebhaberin: Nikephoros 3 (1990) 31-72.

b786 *Liberati Silverio* Anna Maria, *al.*, Lo sport nel mondo romano: Archeo 65 (1990) 62-109; ill.

b787 *McDonnell* Myles, The introduction of athletic nudity [not before 730; general after 550]: THUCYDIDES, PLATO, and the vases: JHS 111 (1991) 182-192.

b788 [Alighiero] *Manacorda* Mario, Lo sport a Roma ieri e oggi: StRom 38 (1990) 34-52.

b789 **Maul-Mandelartz** Elsbeth, Griechische Reiterdarstellungen in agonistischem Zusammenhang [Diss. Bochum 1989]: EurHS 38/32. Fra 1990, Lang. 280 p.

b790 *Milner* N. P., Victors in the Meleagria and the Balbouran élite: AnSt 41 (1991) 23-62; 5 fig.; pl. I-VIII.

b791 **Morgan** Catherine, Athletes and oracles; the transformation of Olympia and Delphi in the eighth century B.C. 1990 → 6,d329: ᴿClasR 41 (1991) 439s (R. *Osborne*); ÉtClas 59 (1991) 97s (H. *Leclercq*); RÉG 104 (1991) 265s (Valérie *Visa*).

b792 *Morgan* M. G., Politics, religion and the games in Rome, 200-150 B.C.: Pg 134 (1990) 14-36.

b793 *Mouratidis* John, Anachronism in the Homeric games and sports: Nikephoros 3 (1990) 11-22.

b794 *Mura Sommella* Anna, *Talamo* Emilia, Lo sport nel mondo antico: Archeo 47 (1989) 49-93.

b795 *Pietilä-Castrén* Leena, L. Mummius' contributions to the agonistic life in the mid second century B.C.: Arctos 25 (1991) 97-106.

b796 **Poliakoff** Michael B., Kampfsport in der Antike; das Spiel um Leben und Tod [1987 → 3,d477],ᵀ. Z 1989, Artemis. 260 p.; 97 fig. DM 40. – ᴿHZ 252 (1991) 130s (Ingomar *Weiler*); RBgPg 69 (1991) 238 (R. *Chevallier*).

b797 ᴱ**Raschke** Wendy J., The archeology of the Olympics 1984/8 → 4,767 ... 6,d338: ᴿRÉAnc 92 (1990) 425s (P. *Lévêque*: some quite interesting items, but his own numerous contributions are ignored; FUSTEL appears as Coulanges; and some of the authors cite only themselves).

b798 *Scanlon* Thomas F., Race or chase at the Arkteia of Attica? [Brauron vases, KAHIL L.]: Nikephoros 3 (1990) 73-120; 9 pl.

b799 *Shanks* H., Buzz or button? [VAN BEÉK G., BASOR 275 (1989) 53]: BAR-W 17,3 (1991) 62s.

b800 **Sijpesteijn** P. J., Nouvelle liste des gymnasiarques des métropoles de l'Égypte romaine: StAmstEpig 28. Zutphen 1986, Terra. ix-131 p. *f*65. 90-6255-282-X. – ᴿBO 48 (1991) 141s (Marie *Drew-Bear*).

b801 **Sweet** Waldo E., Sport and recreation in ancient Greece; a source-book with translations 1987 → 3,d483*; 6,d346: ᴿÉtClas 59 (1991) 96s (H. *Leclercq*); Mnemosyne 44 (1991) 265-8 (A. van *Hooff*).

b802 **Thuillier** Jean-Paul,   Les jeux athlétiques dans la civilisation étrusque 1985 → 2,a59 ... 4,e44:   ᴿLatomus 50 (1991) 462s (P. *Defosse*).

b803 *Tracy* Stephen V.,   *Habicht* Christian,   New and old Panathenaic victor-lists: Hesperia 60 (1991) 187-236; 1 fig.; pl. 71-76.

b803* *Valavanis* Panos,   *Tēnella kallinikē*, Prozessionen von Panathenäensiegern auf der Akropolis: ArchAnz (1991) 487-498; 4 fig.

b804 *Wistrand* Magnus,   Violence and entertainment in SENECA the Younger: Eranos 88 (1990) 31-46 [< ÉtClas 59,279].

b805 *Yiannakis* Thomas,   The relationship between the underground-chthonian world and the sacred Panhellenic games: Nikephoros 3 (1990) 23-30.

T2.5 **Musica.**

b806 **Badali** Enrico,   Strumenti musicali, musici e musica nella celebrazione delle feste ittite I: Texte der Hethiter 14/1.   Heid 1991, Winter. xxxii-387 p. DM 175, pa. 150.   3-533-04380-0; -79-7 [BO 48,985].

b807 ᵀ**Barker** Andrew,   Greek musical writings [I. 1984 → a333], II. Harmonic and acoustic theory: Readings in the History of Music.   C 1989, Univ.   viii-581 p. £55. – ᴿClasR 41 (1991) 45s (M. L. *West*).

b807* **Benzoor** Nina, ☉ & Eng.,   Kᵉlê nᵉgînâ... Musical instruments in biblical Israel. Haifa ... Museum of Music and Ethnology.   70 p. [OIAc 2,14].

b808 *Beschi* Luigi,   La prospettiva della musica greca: MÉF-A 103 (1991) 35-50; 6 fig.

b808* *Careddu* Giorgio,   L'art musical dans l'Égypte ancienne: → 98*, ᶠMEKHITARIAN A., CdÉ 66 (1991) 39-59; 9 fig.

b809 *Delattre* Daniel,   Philodème, De la musique IV: CronErc 19 (1989) 49-143 [< Gnomon 63,481].

b810 *Dyk* P. J. van, Music in OT times: OTEssays 4 (1991) 373-380 [< ZAW 104,436].

b811 **Flammer** A.,   *Tordjman* G.,   El violín [orígenes; repertorio antiguo ...]. Barc 1991, Labor.   92 p. – ᴿArTGran 54 (1991) 461 (E. M. C.).

b812 ᴱ**Gentili** B.,   *Pretagostini* R.,   La musica in Grecia 1985/8 → 5,d218; 6,d364:   ᴿWienerSt 104 (1991) 299s (H. *Bannert*).

b813 **Haik-Vantoura** S.,   The music of the Bible revealed; the deciphering of a millenary notation [¹1976, ²1978 → 60,3916], ᵀ*Weber* D., ᴱ*Wheeler* J. Berkeley/SF 1991, BIBAL/King David's Harp.   xviii-557 p. $30 pa.   0-941037-10-X [BL 92,16, J. H. *Eaton*: bold but all we have].

b814 ᴱ**Jan** Karl [Lp ¹1985], ²*Zanoncelli* Luisa,   La manualistica musicale greca; [Euclide] Cleonide, Nicomaco ... Bacchio, Gaudenzio, Alipio: Ricerche.   Mi 1990, Guerini.   508 p. – ᴿRÉG 104 (1991) 610-2 (Annie *Bélis*: even for the French far more usable than 'calamitous' C. RUELLE 1985); WienerSt 104 (1991) 301s (G. *Danek*: Jan-Text einschliesslich Druckfehler).

b814* *Jordan* William,   AUGUSTINE on music: Grace → 367* 1990, 123-134.

b815 **Kotsidu** Haritini,   Die musischen Agone der Panathenäen in archaischer und klassischer Zeit [Diss. Fra 1990 ᴰ*Steuben* H. v.]: QFantW 8.   Mü 1991, TUDUV. 293 p. + Katalog.; 12 fig.; 20 pl. 3-88073-418-6.

b816 **Krieg** Gustav A.,   Die gottesdienstliche Musik als theologisches Problem: EvGesLTgF 22.   Gö 1990, Vandenhoeck & R.   346 p. DM 88 [TR 88,143, E. *Jaschinski*].

b817 *Krispijn* T. J. H.,   Beiträge zur altorientalischen Musikforschung 1. Sulgi und Musik: Akkadica 70 (1990) 1-27; 2 fig.

b818 *Lawergren* Bo, The ancient harp from Pazyryk [Leningrad Hermitage]: BeitAVgArch 9s (1990) 111-118; pl. 57-61.

b819 **Liavas** Lambros, Catalogue des archives du fonds ethnomusicologique Samuel Baud-Bovy [grec: antique 44 titres p. 66-69; Byz-mod. 300). Genève 1989, Conservatoire. 186 p. – ᴿRÉG 104 (1991) 612 (Annie *Bélis*).

b820 **Maas** Martha, *Snyder* Jane M., Stringed instruments of ancient Greece 1989 ➤ 3,d222*: ᴿAmJPg 112 (1991) 273-6 (M. *West*: valuable); Gnomon 62 (1991) 739s (Annie *Bélis*: hitherto treated only in Helen Roberts' Reading Univ. diss.).

b821 *Neubecker* Annemarie J., Altgriechische Musik 1958-1986: Lustrum 32 (Gö 1990) 99-176.

b822 **Pass** David B., Music and the Church. Nv 1989, Broadman. 131 p. $10. 0-8054-6814-5. – ᴿRExp 87 (1990) 163-5 (P. A. *Richardson*: 'a theology of church music' subtitle only on dust-jacket).

b823 ᴱPizzani Ubaldo, *Milanese* Guido, Agostino d'Ippona, De musica, commento: Settimana Agostiniana Pavese 5. Palermo 1990, Augustinus. 89 p. Lit. 16.000. – ᴿBenedictina 38 (1991) 231s (B. *Ferretti*); CC 142 (1991,2) 200s (G. *Cremascoli*).

b824 ᴱPöhlmann Egert, Beiträge zur antiken und neueren Musikgeschichte 1988 ➤ 6,d373: ᴿWienerSt 104 (1991) 301 (G. *Danek*).

b825 **Ravasi** Gianfranco, Il canto delle rane; musica [...danza] e teologia nella Bibbia, CasM 1990, Piemme. 170 p. Lit. 40.000. – ᴿAsprenas 38 (1991) 382-8 (V. *Scippa*); Letture 46 (1991) 179s (P. *Sequeri*).

b826 *Restani* Donatella, Dionysos tra *aulós* e *kithára*; un percorso di iconografia musicale: ➤ 573, Dionysos 1989/91, 379-391 + 12 fig.

b827 **Rispoli** Gioia Maria, Il primo libro del *Perì mousikḗs* di Filodemo: Ricerche sui Papiri Ercolanesi 1 (ᴱ*Sbordone* F.). N 1989, Giannini. – p. 23-286. – ᴿGnomon 63 (1991) 481-6 (E. *Pöhlmann*, auch über ᴱNeubecker A. 1986).

b828 **Rouget** G., La musique et la transe; esquisse d'une théorie générale des relations de la musique et de la possession²ʳᵉᵛ, préf. *Leiris* M. P 1990, Gallimard. 621 p. – ᴿRÉG 104 (1991) 609s (P. *Brunet*).

b829 *Safrien* Volker, Vom Totentanz zum Reigen der Seligen; eine christliche Kulturgeschichte des Tanzes: BTZ 8 (1991) 2-18.

b830 *Schafter* Debra, Musical victories in early classical vase painting: ➤ 627*, AJA 95 (1991) 333s, summary.

b831 **Seidel** Hans, Musik in Altisrael [< Hab.-Diss. Lp 1970] 1989 ➤ 6,d379: ᴿOTAbs 14 (1991) 350 (M. P. *Graham*).

b832 *Sophocleous* S., *Georghiou* T., Cypriot terracotta figurines of the sixth and fifth centuries in the Pierides Foundation Museum [i. Musician with tambourine ...]: TEuph 4 (1991) 45-49 [< ZAW 104,283].

b833 *Taplin* Oliver, Auletai and auletrides in Greek comedy and comic vase painting: Numismata AntClas 20 (Lugano 1991) 31-44 + 3 pl.

T2.6 **Textilia**, *vestis,* clothing.

b834 **Archi** A., Testi... metalli, tessuti: ARET 7, 1988 ➤ 4,e77: ᴿJAOS 111 (1991) 390s (J. H. *Platt*); StEpL 7 (1990) 133s (F. *Pomponio*).

b835 **Atalay** Erol †, Weibliche Gewandstatuen des 2. Jh. n.Chr. aus ephesischen Werkstätten: Denks. ph/h 206. W 1989, Österr. Akad. 128 p.; 106 fig. – ᴿRÉAnc 93 (1991) 210 (J. *Marcadé*).

b836 **Barber** E. J. W., Prehistoric textiles; the development of cloth in the Neolithic and Bronze Ages with special reference to the Aegean. Princeton 1991, Univ. xxxi-471 p.; 134 fig.; 86 pl. + colour; 4 maps. $69.50. 0-691-035970 [Antiquity 66,271, Helen H. *Brock*].

b837 *Barber* Elizabeth, Aegean textiles and textile trade: ➤ 627*, AJA 95 (1991) 326, summary.

b838 *Dalley* Stephanie, Ancient Assyrian textiles and the origins of carpet design: Iran 29 (1991) 117-135; 24 fig.

b838* **Gazda** Elaine K., al., The art of the ancient weaver; textiles from Egypt (4th-12th century A.D.); Kelsey Museum exhibition. AA 1980, Univ. 35 p. [OIAc 2,19].

b839 *Lohuizen-Mulder* Mab van, Two Coptic artefacts; a weaver's comb and a water jug stand: Babesch 66 (1991) 145-151; 6 + 8 fig.

b840 **Losfeld** Georges, Essai sur le costume grec; préf. *Chamoux* François. P 1991, de Boccard. 415 p.; 8 pl. 2-7018-0058-7. – ᴿRÉG 104 (1991) 259s (A. *Wartelle*: vast erudition, exquisite clarity, no abbreviations for periodicals).

b841 *Maes* Annemie, Le costume phénicien des stèles d'Umm el-ʿAmed: ➤ 445, Phoenicia 1990/1, 209-230.

b841* *Maguire* Henry, Garments pleasing to God; the significance of domestic textile designs in the early Byzantine period: ➤ 647*, Byz. Family 1989, DumbO 44 (1990) 215-224; 36 fig.

b842 *Martiniani-Reber* Marielle, Tissus façonnés d'Achmim (Égypte): Genava 37 (1989) 19-28; 8 fig.

b843 **Nauerth** Claudia, Die koptischen Textilien der Sammlung Wilhelm Rautenstrauch im Simeonstift. Trier 1989, Städtisches Museum. 190 p.; 62 pl.

b844 **Pekridou-Gorecki** Anastasia, Mode im antiken Griechenland; Textile-Fertigung und Kleidung: Archäol. Bibliothek. Mü 1989, Beck. 159 p.; 76 fig. DM 38. – ᴿDLZ 112 (1991) 374-6 (Verena *Paul-Zinserling*).

b845 *Prestiani Giallombardo* Anna Maria, Per un lessico greco dell'abbigliamento; copricapi come segni di potere; la kausia: ➤ 579, Lessici tecnici 1990/1, 165-187; 6 fig.

b846 *a)* **Rajab** Jehan S., Palestinian costume [Kuwait museum]. L 1989, Kegan Paul. 160 p. £35. – *b)* **Weir** Shelagh, Palestinian costume [L Museum of Mankind]. L 1989, British Museum. 288 p. £15. – ᴿPEQ 123 (1991) 139s (Katharina *Hackstein*).

b847 **Renner-Volbach** Dorothée, Die koptischen Textilien im Museo Missionario Etnologico der Vatikanischen Museen. Wsb 1988, Harrassowitz. – ᴿBO 48 (1991) 848-851 (P. *Cauderlier*: suite du volume 1982 Pinacoteca Vat.).

b847* *Rittig* Dessa, Das Fürstengewand des Jariris, des tarwanis von Karkamis: AcPraeh 22 (1990) 139-147; 5 fig.

b848 **Rutschowskaya** Marie-Hélène, Tissus coptes. P 1990, Biro. 159 p.; (color.) ill. 2-87660-064-1 [OIAc 1,23].

b849 *Sheffer* Avigail, *Tidhar* Amalia, Textiles and basketry at Kuntillet ʿAjrud; Atiqot 20 (1991) 1-26; 22 fig.; 2 color. phot.

b850 *Utzschneider* Helmut, Die 'Realia' und die Wirklichkeit; Prolegomenazu einer Sozial- und Kulturgeschichte des Alten Israel am Modell der Handweberei in Israel und seiner Umwelt: WDienst 21 (1991) 59-80.

b851 **Walters** E. J., Attic grave reliefs that represent women in the dress of Isis: Hesperia supp 22, 1988 ➤ 5,d543: ᴿRÉG 104 (1991) 258s (Mary-Anne *Zagdoun*).

b852 *Watson* W. G. E., Two Ugaritic terms concerning textiles [*az, all*]: AulaO 8 (1990) 138-140.

b852* **Wild** John P., Textiles in archaeology; Shire. Aylesbury 1988. 68 p. 45 fig. £2.50. – ᴿAcPraeh 22 (1990) 202 (Annelies *Goldmann*).

T2.7 *Ornamenta corporis*, jewelry, mirrors.

b853 **Albert** Jean-Pierre, Odeurs de sainteté; la mythologie chrétienne des aromates: Rech.Hist.Sc.Soc. 42. P 1990 ÉPHÉ. 375 p.

b854 **Andrews** Carol, Ancient Egyptian jewellery. L 1990, British Museum. 208 p.; ill.

b855 Aphrodite's scents; aromatic journey through experimental archaeology: exhibition 1985 [*Bisogno* Paolo, on PLINY, DIOSKORIDES]. F 1984, Vision. 40 p.; ill.

b856 *Bisi* Anna Maria, I gioielli nel mondo antico: Archeo 58 (1989) 50-101; 72-75 [65 (1990)] Siria e Palestina (... Gaza-Ajjûl).

b857 **Dayagi-Mendels** Michal, Perfumes and cosmetics in the ancient world 1989 ➤ 6,d409: ᴿPEQ 123 (1991) 136 (F. N. *Hepper*).

b858 *de Grummond* Nancy T., Mirrors and *manteia*; themes of prophecy on Etruscan mirrors: AJA 95 (1991) 301s (summary, also of four other papers in the AIA 91 workshop 'Etruscan Mirrors' ➤ 627*).

b859 **Devoto** Guido, *Molayem* Albert, Archeogemmologia; pietre antiche, glittica magia e litoterapia. R 1990, Meridiana. 247 p.; ill. Lit. 120.000. – ᴿAntRArch 16 (1991) 71 (A. *Cremonesi*).

b860 *Gwinnett* A. John, *Gorelick* Leonard, Bead manufacture at Hajar ar-Rayhani, Yemen: BA 54 (1991) 186-196; color. ill.

b861 **Hasson** Rachel, Early / Later Islamic jewellery. J 1987, Mayer Institute for Islamic Art. 111 p. / 160 p. [OIAc 1,18].

b861* *Ilani* Zvi, *al.*, Diamonds and gemstones in Judaica; a selective anthology from the Scriptures, the Mishna, the Talmud, Midrashim, and Responsa literature. Ramat Gan ... Bar-Ilan Univ. 253 p. [OIAc 2,21].

b862 **Kellner** Hans-Jörg, Gürtelbleche aus Urartu: PrähBronz 12/3. Stu 1991, Steiner. ix-87 p.; ill. 3-515-05526-6.

b863 *Laux* Friedrich, Die 'Christus'-Schnalle von Wegeleben ['Christian' symbols on belt-buckle]: ➤ 79, ᶠHÜBENER W. 1989, 157-161; 6 fig.

b864 *Liberati Silverio* Anna Maria, L'impero della seduzione [cosmetici; mostra Roma, Musei Capitolini]: Archeo 65 (1990) 48-61; ill.

b865 **Megow** Wolf-Rüdiger, Kameen von Augustus bis Alexander Severus [diss. Bonn 1974] 1987 ➤ 5,d259; 6,d420: ᴿGnomon 63 (1991) 255-9 (D. *Boschung*); Latomus 50 (1991) 488s (J.-M. *Doyen*).

b866 *Philip* Hanna, Mira et magica, Gemmen 1986 ➤ 3,d539 ... 6,d426: ᴿAcArchH 43 (1991) 472-4 (T. *Gesztelyi*).

b867 *Rossi Osmida* Gabriele, La scoperta della vanità; profumi e cosmetici nel mondo antico: Archeo 58 (1989) 62-111; 84-87, gli Ebrei.

b868 **Schoske** Sylvia, Schönheit, Abglanz der Gottlichkeit; Kosmetik im alten Ägypten... Ausstellung, Katalog. Mü 1990, Äg. Sammlung. 173 p.; ill.

b869 *Shoemaker* Michael T., Herod's lady's earring? [found June 1989 by Dan *Rodriguez*, Puerto Rico pastor]: BAR-W 17,4 (1991) 58s.

b870 **Speidel** M. Alexander, Die Friseure des ägyptischen Alten Reiches; eine historisch-prosopographische Untersuchung zu Amt und Titel. Konstanz 1990, Hartung-Gorre. 244 p.; ill.

T2.8 **Utensilia.**

b871 *Albenda* Pauline, Decorated Assyrian knob-plates in the British Museum: Iraq 53 (1991) 43-53; 7 fig.; pl. I-X.

b872 *Bilgi* Önder, Metal objects from Ikiztepe, Turkey: BAVgArch 9s (1990) 119-301 + 20 fig. (2 foldout).

b873 **Dresken-Welland** Jutta, Reliefierte Tischplatten aus theodosianischer Zeit [Diss. Bonn 1990, ᴰ*Himmelmann* N.]: StAntCr 44. R 1991, Pont. Ist. Archeologia Cristiana. xviii-365 p.; 112 pl.

b873* **Hayes** John W., Ancient metal axes and other tools in the Royal Ontario museum; European and Mediterranean types. Toronto 1991, Museum. xii-105 p. 0-88854-393-X [OIAc 2,21].

b874 *Healey* John F., A Nabataean sundial from Madā'in Saliḥ [Ḥegrā]: Syria 66 (1989) 331-6; II pl.

b875 *Henne* W., Bemerkungen zur altägyptischen Streiflicht-Uhr: ZäSpr 118 (1991) 21-31.

b876 **Kunisch** Norbert, Griechische Fischteller; Natur und Bild 1989 ⇢ 6, d440; 150 p.; 23 fig.; 17 color. pl.: ᴿGymnasium 98 (1991) 79s (Magdalene *Söldner*).

b877 *Malek* Jaromir, Trumpets and [*šnb* on Tahurqa stela rather] kohl-tubes: JEA 77 (1991) 185s; 2 fig.

b878 **Muscarella** O. W., Bronze and iron 1988 ⇢ 5,d281*; 6,d444: ᴿAfO 36s (1989s) 173 (R. M. *Boehmer*).

b879 *a*) *Payton* Robert, The Ulu Burun writing-board set; – *b*) *Warnock* Peter, *Pendleton* Michael, The wood of the Ulu Burun diptych; – *c*) *Symington* Dorit, Late Bronze Age writing boards and their uses; textual evidence from Anatolia and Syria: AnSt 41 (1991) 99-106; 4 fig. / 107-110 / 111-123; pl. XVII-XIX.

b880 **Riz** Anna E., Bronzegefässe in der römisch-pompejanischen Wandmalerei: DAI-R Sonderschriften 7. Mainz 1990, von Zabern. xviii-115 p.; 14 pl. + 53 color. DM 135. 3-8053-1121-4 [JRS 81,261]. – ᴿArctos 25 (1991) 217-220 (A. *Tammisto*).

b881 *Schön* Werner, *Holter* Uta, Grinding implements from the Neolithic and recent times in desert areas in Egypt and Sudan: BAVgArch 9s (1990) 359-379; 4 fig. (map) pl. 96-97.

b882 *Sparks* Rachael, A series of Middle Bronze Age bowls with ram's-head handles from the Jordan Valley: MeditArch 4 (1991) 45-54; 4 fig.

b883 *Villard* Laurence, (*Blondé* Francine, essais de reconstitution) À propos de deux vases (le trublion [marmite, pot] et l'oxybaphe [jarre de vinaigre]); l'apport de la Collection Hippocratique: RÉG 104 (1991) 202-222 (-231, 3 fig.).

T2.9   *Pondera et mensurae*   – **Weights and measures.**

b883* *Bankel* Hansgeorg, Akropolis-Fussmasse: ArchAnz (1991) 151-163; 5 fig.

b884 *Boskamp* Anton, Die minoischen Masseinheiten; Korrekturen zu Kadmos 21 (1982) 15-25: Kadmos 30 (1991) 85-87.

b885 *Dekoulakou-Sideris* Ifigenia, A metrological relief from Salamis [now in Piraeus museum]: AJA 94 (1990) 445-451.

b886 *Di Segni* Leah, The systems of weights in Palestine, including N. AVIGAD's Taanach stone [IsrEJ 18 (1968) 211, frontispiece here, but now generally dismissed as a fake [IsrEJ 41 (1991) 306]: ➤ 443, Commerce in Palestine 1980/90, 202-220.

b887 *Elayi* Josette, Quelques poids nord-ouest sémitiques inédits: Semitica 40 (1991) 31-38.

b888 *Englund* Robert K., Archaic dairy metrology [*sila* = 1 litre]: Iraq 53 (1991) 101-4; 1 fig.

b889 *Lejeune* Michel, 'Un huitième' dans le lexique métrologique grec: RÉG 104 (1991) 198-201.

b890 *Mengoli* Pierangelo, La clessidra di Karnak; l'orologio ad acqua di Amenophis III: OrAnt 28 (1989) 227-271; 8 fig.; pl. XXVIII-XXXVII.

b891 *Mittmann* Siegfried, 'Königliches *bat*' und '*ṭēt*-Symbol', mit einem Beitrag zu Micha 1,14b und 1 Chronik 3,21-23: ZDPV 107 (1991) 59-76; 5 fig.; pl. 1.

b892 *Morrison* John, Ancient Greek measures of length in nautical contexts: Antiquity 65 (1991) 298-305; 2 fig.

b893 *Parise* Nicola F., Dai pesi egei per la lana alla mina Dudu: Numismata e Antichità Classiche 20 (Lugano 1991) 13s.

b893* *a)* *Rottländer* Rolf C.A., Metrologische Untersuchungen an Umriss-zeichnungen von Füssen im ägyptischen Theben; – *b)* *Sonntagbauer* Wolfgang, Ein Spiel zwischen Fünf und Sieben; zum Kanon des Polyklet [männlicher Körper]: JhÖsW 61-B (1991s) 57-66; 1 fig. / 69-124; 15 fig.

T3.0 **Ars antiqua,** *motiva, picturae* [icones ➤ T3.1 infra].

b894 **Ahlberg-Cornell** Gudrun, Herakles and the sea-monster in Attic black-figure vase painting 1984 ➤ 1,b965; 3,d578: RRÉG 103 (1990) 707s (L. *Gourmelen*).

b895 **Arafat** K.W., Classical Zeus, a study in art and literature 1990 ➤ 6, d471: RAJA 95 (1991) 747s (H.A. *Shapiro*).

b896 *Azarpay* Guitty, A canon of proportions in the art of the Ancient Near East: ➤ 641, Artistic 1988/90, 93-103; 11 fig.

b897 **Beach** Eleanor F., Image and word; iconology in the interpretation of Hebrew scriptures [KEEL; GOODENOUGH; others use artifacts out of context]: diss. Claremont 1991, DKnierim R. 372 p. 91-23639. – DissA 52 (1991s) 949-A.

b898 **Belting** Hans, Bild und Kult; eine Geschichte des Bildes vor dem Zeitalter der Kunst 1990 ➤ 6,d478: RKlio 73 (1991) 678-685 (P. *Speck*).

b899 *Bergamini* Giovanni, Neo-Sumerian 'vignettes'; a methodological approach: Mesop-T 26 (1991) 101-118.

b900 *Bianchi* Raffaella, A proposito del simbolo nella teoria di E. GOODENOUGH: SMSR 57 (1991) 365-377; 13 fig.

b901 **Blocher** Felix, Untersuchungen zum Motiv der nackten Frau 1987 ➤ 3,d586; 5,d315: ROrientalia 60 (1991) 369-372 (Agnès *Spycket*, aussi sur COLBOW G., en texte Golbow: tous deux basés sur marché de fouilles clandestines).

b902 *Brown* L.B., *Moore* A.C., Art and the structure of religion: JEmpirT 3,2 (1990) 51... [< ZIT 91,119].

b903 **Carpenter** Thomas H., Art and myth in ancient Greece; a handbook: World of Art. L 1991, Thames & H. 256 p.; 370 fig. £7. – RClasR 41 (1991) 444s (R. *Hannah*); GreeceR 38 (1991) 255 (B.A. *Sparkes*: fills a long-felt want).

b904 **Chenis** Carlo, Fondamenti teorici dell'arte sacra; magistero post-conciliare [i. La Bibbia e l'arte sacra ...]: BibScRel 94. R 1990, LAS. 220 p. Lit. 25.000 [Salesianum 53, p. 466e].

b906 *Dagron* Gilbert, Holy image and likeness [... image of Christ]: DumbO 45 (1991) 23-33.

b907 **Davis** Whitney, The canonical tradition in ancient Egyptian art. C 1989, Univ. xx-272 p.; 106 fig. £40. 0-521-36590-2. – ᴿAntiquity 65 (1991) 170 (J. *Baines*).

b908 *a) De Angeli* Stefano, Problemi di iconografia romana; dalle Moire alle Parche; – *b) Delivorrias* Angelos, Problèmes de conséquence méthodologique et d'ambiguité iconographique: MÉF-A 103 (1991) 105-128; 11 fig. / 129-157; 37 fig.

b909 *Delplace* Christiane, Publications récentes sur la peinture murale antique III: RBgPg 69 (1991) 167-181.

ᴱ**Dohmen** Christoph, *Sternberg* Thomas, '... kein Bildnis machen', Kunst und Theologie im Gespräch 1987 ➤ 2210.

b910 *Dolinska* Monika, Red and blue figures of Amun: VarAeg 6 (1990) 3-7.

b911 *Donato* Maria M., Hercules and David in the early decoration of the [Firenze] Palazzo Vecchio; manuscript evidence: JWarb 54 (1991) 83-98.

b912 *Dulaey* M., 'Virga virtutis tuae, virga oris tui'; le bâton du Christ dans le christianisme ancien: ➤ 52, ᶠFASOLA U. 1989, 235-245.

b913 **Ehrhardt** Wolfgang, Stilgeschichtliche Untersuchungen an römischen Wandmalereien von der späten Republik bis zur Zeit Neros 1987 ➤ 5,d327; 6,d504: ᴿLatomus 50 (1991) 215-221 (S. *De Maria*).

b914 **Fowler** Barbara H., The Hellenistic aesthetic. Madison 1989, Univ. Wisconsin. xix-213 p.; 127 fig. – ᴿAJA 95 (1991) 176s (J. J. *Pollitt*: stronger on poetry than on art).

b915 *Gesztelyi* Tamás, Über die gesellschaftliche Rolle der römischen Kunst: AcClasDebrecen 26 (1990) 63-75; 8 fig.

b916 *Ghedini* Francesca, Adriano; l'arte e il potere: Archeo 49 (1989) 47-92.

b917 **Goldman** Bernard, The ancient arts of western and central Asia: Asia Institute Bulletin Supp. Univ. Ames 1991, Iowa State Univ. ix-303; p. 103-9 Fs, 153-7 series; otherwise mostly by areas. 0-8138-0597-X.

b918 **Goldmann** Christoph, Message biblique Marc Chagall – der Bildmidrasch eines jüdischen Malers zur hebräischen Bibel: Diss. Heidelberg, ᴰ*Rendtorff* R. 1991. – TR 87 (1991) 518.

b919 *Guillaud* Jacqueline & Maurice, La peinture à fresque au temps de Pompei. P 1990, Guillaud. 255 p.; ill.

b920 **Hachlili** Rachel, Ancient Jewish art ...: HbOr 7/1/2/B4, 1988 ➤ 4,e193; 6,d516: ᴿCritRR 4 (1991) 360-3 (Jo *Milgrom*); IsrEJ 41 (1991) 212-5 (L. I. *Levine*: updates GOODENOUGH); JQR 82 (1991s) 502-6 (B. *Brenk*, deutsch); JStJud 22 (1991) 136-142 (K. J. H. *Vriezen*).

b921 **Hall** Emma S., The Pharaoh smites 1986 ➤ 2,a179 ... 5,d334: ᴿCdÉ 65 (1990) 267s (J.-C. *Degardin*).

b922 **Haussperger** Martha, Die Einführungsszene; Entwicklung eines mesopotamischen Motivs von der altakkadischen bis zum Ende der altbabylonischen Zeit [Diss. Mü 1989]: Mü Univ. Vorderas. St. 11. Mü 1991, Profil. 301 p.; 92 fig. 3-89019-272-6.

b923 **Hölscher** Tonio, Römische Bildsprache als semantisches System [... Eigenart römischer Kunst]: AbhHeid 1987/2 (➤ 3,9983). Heid 1987, Winter. 78 p.; 16 pl. – ᴿGnomon 62 (1991) 722-9 (B. *Fehr*); GrazBeit 17 (1990) 258-261 (P. *Felten*).

b924 **Holtzmann** Bernard, La Grèce [art; sculpture]: Vent des siècles. P 1989, Citadelles. 252 p., 115 fig. + 108 color.; map. – RRArchéol (1991) 135s (J. *Marcadé*: fautes non de l'auteur).

b925 **Immerwahr** Sara A., Aegean painting in the Bronze Age 1990 ➤ 6,d519: RClasR 41 (1991) 429-431 (R. L. N. *Barber*); Phoenix 45 (Toronto 1991) 375-7 (Maria C. *Shaw*).

b926 **Isager** Jacob, PLINY on art and society; the elder Pliny's chapters on the history of art. L 1991, Routledge. 255 p.

b927 **Jacobs** Bruno, Griechische und persische Elemente in der Grabkunst Lykiens zur Zeit der Achämenidenherrschaft: SIMA 78, 1987 ➤ 6,d522: RGnomon 63 (1991) 244-7 (W. A. P. *Childs*, Eng.).

b928 *Jung* Michael, *a*) Bronze Age rock pictures in North Yemen: EWest 41 (1991) 47-78; 27 fig.; – *b*) Rock art of North Yemen: RSO 64 (1990) 255-273; 16 fig.

b929 **Koch-Harnack** Gundel, Erotische Symbole; Lotosblüte und gemeinsamer Mantel auf antiken Vasen 1988 ➤ 5,d338: RDLZ 112 (1991) 684 (B. *Brentjes*); Gnomon 63 (1991) 539-542 (Gloria *Ferrari*: some weaknesses); Hephaistos 10 (1991) 147-150 (Eva C. *Keuls*, Eng.).

b930 *a*) *Kötzsche* Dietrich, Eine verschollene Evangelisten-Serie; – *b*) *Plotzek* Joachim M., Die Taufe Christi als Brautbad der Ecclesia: ➤ 27, FBLOCH P. 1990, 45-54; 7 fig. / 55-64; 7 fig.

b931 *Kraemer* Ross S., Jewish tuna and Christian fish [Frey CIS 653a]; identifying religions in epigraphic sources: HarvTR 84 (1991) 141-162.

b932 **Kultermann** Udo, Geschichte der Kunstgeschichte; der Weg einer Wissenschaft. Mü 1990, Prestel. 272 p.; 149 fig. – RDLZ 112 (1991) 583-5 (E. *Ullmann*).

b933 *Kuryluk* Ewa, Veronica and her cloth; history, symbolism and structure of a 'true' image. Ox 1991, Blackwell. xvi-272 p.; ill. [TR 88,164].

b934 **Laag** Heinrich, Kleines Wörterbuch der frühchristlichen Kunst und Archäologie: Universal-Bibliothek 8633,4. Stu 1990, Reclam. 275 p.; 100 fig.

b935 **Lange** Günter, al., Kunst zur Bibel; 32 Bildinterpretationen 1988 ➤ 5, d341: RRuBi 44 (1991) 80 (J. *Chmiel*).

b936 **Leach** Eleanor W., The rhetoric of space; literary and artistic representations of landscape in Republican and Augustan Rome. Princeton 1988, Univ. 493 p.; 45 fig. – RAJA 95 (1991) 179-181 (Bettina *Bergmann*); ClasPg 86 (1991) 158-163 (Ann J. *Adams*); Phoenix 45 (Toronto 1991) 278-282 (Ann *Kuttner*).

b937 *Lebessi* Angheliki, Flagellation ou autoflagellation [... spartiate]; données iconographiques pour une tentative d'interprétation: BCH 115,1 (1991) 99-123; 11 fig.

b938 **MacCormack** Sabine G., Art and ceremony in late antiquity: Transformation of the Classical Heritage 1. Berkeley 1990, Univ. California. xvi-417 p.; ill. 0-520-06966-8.

b939 **Martin** James A.,J Beauty and holiness; the dialogue between aesthetics and religion. Princeton 1990, Univ. ix-222 p. $27.50. – RTLond 94 (1991) 438-445 (G. *Howes*, amid seven books on religion and art).

b940 **Mekhitarian** Arpag, Ägyptische Malerei. Genf 1989 = 1954, Skira. 165 p. 3-8030-3113-3 [OIAc 2,23].

b941 **Milde** H., The vignettes in the Book of the Dead of Neferrenpet [a comparative iconographical study, D1988 ➤ 4,e214]: Egyptologische Uitgaven 7. Leiden 1991, Nederlands Instituut voor het Nabije Oosten. ix-284 p.; 48 pl. 90-6258-207-9 [OIAc 1,21].

b942 **Morgan** Lyvia,   The miniature wall-paintings of Thera 1988 ➤ 5,d353; 6,d540:   ᴿPhoenix 45 (Toronto 1991) 372-5 (Maria C. *Shaw*).

b943 **Moscati** S., L'arte dei Fenici. Mi 1990, Fabbri. 232 p.; ill. – ᴿRStFen 19 (1991) 239-242 (G. *Garbini*).

b944 **Naissance** des arts chrétiens; la pénétration du christianisme en France du 2. au 8. siècle. P 1991, Impr. Nat. 432 p. F 890 [TR 88,165].

b945 *Nauerth* Claudia, '... und verhüllte sein Angesicht' [Christliche Früh-sarkophage]: ➤ 140, ᶠSMYTH-FLORENTIN F. 1991, 103-9 + 4 phot.

b946 **Nunn** Astrid,   Die Wandmalerei und der glasierte Wandschmuck im Alten Orient; HbOrientalistik 7/1/2/B6, 1988 ➤ 5,d256:   ᴿWeltOr 22 (1991) 144-8 (E. A. *Braun-Holzinger*).

b947 *a) Otranto* Giorgio,   Alle origini dell'arte cristiana precostantinia-na; interpretazione simbolica o storica?; – *b) Carletti* Carlo, Origine, committenza e fruizione delle scene bibliche nella produzione figurativa romana del III secolo: ➤ 419, AnStoEseg 7,2 (1989/90) 437-454 / 455-466.

b948 **Paglia** Camille,   Sexual personae; art and decadence from Nefertiti to Emily Dickinson. NHv 1990, Yale Univ. xiv-718 p. $35. – ᴿAmHR 96 (1991) 1499s (Valerie *Steele*).

b948* **Patrich** Joseph,   The formation of Nabatean art 1990 ➤ 6,2666:   ᴿLA 41 (1991) 541s (M. *Piccirillo*).

b949 **Pfeiffer** Heinrich,   Gottes Wort im Bild; Christusdarstellungen 1986 ➤ 2,a201 ... 6,d546:   ᴿCathHR 77 (1991) 283s (A. A. *Zinn*).

b950 **Pfisterer-Haas** Susanne, Darstellungen alter Frauen in der griechischen Kunst: EurHS 38/21. Fra 1989, Lang. xii-237 p. 173 fig. – ᴿAJA 95 (1991) 552s (Eva C. *Keuls*).

b951 **Pipili** Maria,   Laconian iconography of the sixth century B.C.: Mg 12, ᴰ1987 ➤ 5,d359:   ᴿGnomon 63 (1991) 340-3 (H. von *Steuben*).

b952 **Poulitt** J.J.,   The art of ancient Greece, sources and documents. C 1990, Univ. xiv-298 p. [RÉG 104,682].

b953 **Prigent** Pierre [abrégé de ➤ 2211] L'image dans le judaïsme du IIᵉ au VIᵉ siècles: MondeB 24. Genève 1991, Labor et Fides. 236 p.; 61 fig.; VIII (color.) pl. 2-8309-0632-2 [NTAbs 36,301].

b954 *Prigent* Pierre,   Du bon usage de l'image dans l'Église ancienne [... malgré les sévères condemnations des premiers siècles patristiques]: ➤ 22, ᶠBENOÎT A., RHPR 71 (1991) 61-72; Eng. 126.

b955 **Ramage** Nancy H. & Andrew,   The Cambridge illustrated history of Roman art. C 1991, Univ. 304 p.; ill.

b956 **Rouveret** Agnès,   Histoire et imaginaire de la peinture ancienne (Vᵉ s. av. - Iᵉ s. ap.J.-C.). 1989 ➤ 6,d552; 2-728-30174-3. – ᴿClasR 41 (1991) 181-3 (R. *Ling*); Latomus 50 (1991) 221-3 (L. *Foucher*); RArchéol (1991) 367 (A. *Barbet*); RÉAnc 93 (1991) 207s (aussi A. *Barbet*); RPg 64 (1990) 274s (H. *Lavagne*).

b957 *Schmitt* J.-C., *Baschet* J.,   La 'sexualité' du Christ: AnECS 46 (1991) 337-346 [< RHE 86,179*].

b958 **Seymour** Howard,   Antiquity restored; essays on the afterlife of the antique. W 1990, Irsa. 344 p. – ᴿRHPR 71 (1991) 246 (P. *Prigent*: 'Restaured', 'Vienna').

b959 *Shapiro* H. A.,   The iconography of mourning in Athenian art: AJA 95 (1991) 629-656; 26 fig.

b960 **Tilley** Christopher,   Material culture and text; the art of ambiguity [... meanings for rock-carvings]. L 1991, Routledge. xiv-192 p.; 52 fig. £35. 0-415-05588-1. – ᴿAntiquity 65 (1991) 992-4 (K. *Helskog*).

b961 **Walberg** Gisela, Tradition and innovation; essays in Minoan art 1986
→ 4,g743: RGnomon 63 (1991) 237-241 (W *Müller*).

b962 **Weitzmann** K., *Kessler* H. L., The frescoes of the Dura Synagogue and
Christian art: DumbOSt 28. Wsh 1990. 202 p.; 202 fig. – ROrChr 75
(1991) 277s (W. *Gessel*).

b963 **Wolff** Walther, The origins of western art; Egypt, Mesopotamia, the
Aegean: Universe History of Art and Architecture. NY 1989, Universe.
207 p.; 182 (color.) ill. 0-87663-757-8 [OIAc 1,27].

b964 **Xenaki-Sakellariou** A., *Chatziliou* Christos, 'Peinture en métal' à
l'époque mycénienne; Incrustation – Damasquinage – Niellure. Athe-
nai/P 1989, Ekd. Athēnôn/de Boccard. 39 p.; 16 pl. – RGnomon 63
(1991) 280-2 (W. *Schiering*); RArchéol (1991) 134s (C. *Rolley*: clair et
sobre).

b965 **Zanker** Paul, Augusto e il potere delle immagini. T 1989, Einaudi.
391 p.; ill. Lit. 65.000. – RArcheo 67 (1990) 128 (A. M. *Steiner*); ClasR 41
(1991) 186-9 (G. B. *Waywell*).

T3.1 *Theologia iconis,* ars postbiblica.

b966 *Anagnostopoulos* Basil N., Ⓖ The seventh oecumenical council of
Nicaea on the veneration of icons and the unity of the Church: TAth 61
(1990) 417-442; Eng. 905.

b967 *Aussermair* Josef, Zum theologischen Verständnis der Ikone: TPQ 139
(1991) 58-66.

b968 **Babolin** Sante, Icona e conoscenza, preliminari d'una teologia iconica:
StT 24. Padova 1990, Gregoriana. 379 p. Lit. 45.000. 88-7706-072-7. –
RAsprenas 38 (1991) 256s (C. N. *Ho*); Gregorianum 72 (1991) 406s (*ipse*);
HumBr 46 (1991) 146 (Maria *Donadeo*); RasT 32 (1991) 213 (N.
Galantino).

b969 **Baggley** John, Doors of perception; icons and their spiritual significance
1988 → 4,e169: RDocLife 40 (1990) 48s (H. *Pyle*); RTLv 22 (1991) 106 (A.
de *Halleux*).

b970 **Boespflug** F., *Lossky* N., Nicée II, 787-1987; douze siècles d'images
religieuses 1986/7 → 3,592... 5,d317: RBijdragen 52 (1991) 224 (M.
Parmentier, Eng.: very rich).

b971 *Broscareǎnu* René, [en roum.] Aspects dogmatiques de la dispute entre
les orthodoxes pour ou contre la vénération des icones: STBuc 39,6 (1987)
22-37.

b972 *Carle* P. L., Le mystère de Dieu et le culte des images dans la liturgie de
la Nouvelle Alliance; l'enseignement conciliaire; le Concile de Trente:
DivThom 94 (1991) 67-95.

b973 **Cormack** Robin, Writing in gold; Byzantine society and its icons 1985
→ 2,a166; 3,d591: RAmHR 96 (1991) 146s (G. P. *Majeska*).

b974 *Cornarakis* Constantine J., Ⓖ Hosios NEILOS' position concerning the
sacred icons: TAth 61 (1991) 311-325; Eng. 904.

b975 **Cottin** Jérôme, Jésus-Christ en écriture d'images; premières représenta-
tions chrétiennes. Genève 1990, Labor et fides. 155 p. FF 99. – RÉT-
Rel 66 (1991) 129 (J. L. *Klein*) & 247 (J.-D. *Dubois*) [2-8309- 06404-7!?];
RHPR 71 (1991) 247-9 (P. *Prigent*: heureuse originalité).

b976 *Di Cristina* Salvatore, Iconodulia e iconoclastia nei sinodi dell'VIII
secolo; l'appello alla tradizione: Ho Theológos 9 (1991) 41-60.

b977 **Feld** Helmut, Der Ikonoklasmus des Westens: StudHistChrThought 41.
Leiden 1990, Brill. 344 p. – RRHPR 71 (1991) 353 (P. *Prigent*).

b978 **Fischer** Helmut, Die Ikone; Ursprung – Sinn – Gestalt. FrB 1989, Herder. 255 p.; ill. – ᴿOstkSt 39 (1990) 64 (H. M. *Biedermann*); TLZ 116 (1991) 297s (K. *Onasch*).

b979 **Hart** Russell M., The icon through Western eyes. Springfield IL 1991, Templegate. 164 p. $17 pa. 0-87243-186-4 [TDig 39,168].

b980 **Jung-Inglessis** E.-M., Römische Madonnen; über die Entwicklung der Marienbilder in Rom von den Anfängen bis in die Gegenwart. St. Ottilien 1989, EOS. 211 p.; 65 color. fig. DM 30. – ᴿTLZ 116 (1991) 134s (Gerlinde *Strohmaier-Wiederanders*).

b980* **Kari** Daven M., Finding a face for the triune God; Christian iconography in stained glass: diss. Southern Baptist Theol. Sem. 1991, ᴰ*Hendricks* W. 345 p. 91-33436. – DissA 52 (1991s) 2179s-A.

b981 ᴱ**Kasack** Wolfgang, Die geistlichen Grundlagen der Ikone: Arbeiten und Texte zur Slawistik 45. Mü 1989, Sagner. 201 p.; ill. DM 28. – ᴿTLZ 116 (1991) 135 (K. *Onasch*) [137: 16 Zts-Titel zur Kunst].

b981* **Klassen** Franz J., Über das Bild des Auferstandenen und seinen Verlust in der Geschichte der deutschen Kunst [Diss. FrB 1989, ᴰ*Lehmann* K.]: EurHS 23/383. Fra 1991, Lang. 295 p. DM 84 [TR 88,247, A. *Stock*].

b982 **Lafontaine-Dosogne** Jacqueline, Histoire de l'art byzantin 1987 ⮞ 4, e204 ... 6,d538: ᴿTRu 56 (1991) 447s (R. *Warland*).

b983 *Maderakis* Stavros N., ❸ Themes from the iconographic tradition of Crete; the Holy Trinity – the throne of grace [IV (conclusion)]: TAth 62 (1991) 104-162; Eng. 929.

b984 *Magnarella* Paul J., A Christian Armenian's contribution to Islamic art: MuslimW 81 (1991) 262-6.

b985 *Meinardus* Otto F. A., Law and Gospel in iconography: LuthQ 4 (Ridgefield NJ 1990) 143-160 [< ZIT 91,345].

b986 **Mennekes** Friedhelm, *a*) BEUYS zu Christus; eine Position im Gespräch [+ English (title only?)]. Stu 1989, KBW. 151 p.; ill. DM 19,80. 3-460-32861-4. – ᴿLuthTKi 14 (1990) 94 (V. *Stolle*: Mennekes ist SJ 'Kunst-Pfarrer in Köln'; Interview 1984 mit Joseph Beuys 1921-86, bedeutendem bildendem Künstler). – *b*) La provocazione dell'immagine di Cristo; le relazioni tra religione e mondo moderno: CC 142 (1991,1) 56-61.

b987 **Menozzi** Daniele, Les images; l'Église et les arts visuels, ᵀᴱ*Baillet* P. (*Vial* F.): Textes en main. P 1991, Cerf. 305 p. – ᴿArTGran 54 (1991) 429s (A. *Segovia*); BLitEc 92 (1991) 285-9 (J. *Rocacher*); EsprVie 101 (1991) 74-77-*jaune* (aussi J. *Rocacher*); RHPR 71 (1991) 247 (P. *Prigent*).

b988 **Muzj** Maria Giovanna, Transfiguration; introduction to the contemplation of icons, ᵀ*Whitehead* Kenneth D. Boston 1991, St. Paul. 179 p.; 32 color. pl. $20. 0-8198-7350-0 [TDig 39,75].

b989 **Muzj** Maria Giovanna, Ganz Auge, ganz Licht, ganz Geist; Einführung in die Betrachtung der Ikonen, ᵀ*Gäde* Gerhard. Wü 1989, Echter. 155 p. – ᴿOstkSt 39 (1990) 66 (H. M. *Biedermann*).

b990 *Napiórkowski* Stanisław C., ❷ A Polish theology of the icon? the problem of the presence of Mary among us in the light of the experiences of peregrination [in documents of S. WYSZYNSKI and (Kraków bishop) K. WOJTYŁA]: ColcT 61,4 (1991) 23-42; Eng. 42s: Orthodox term or usage 'theology of icon' not mentioned; 'Presence of Mary' can often but not always be due to poetic/homiletic style; no 'proofs' from Cana (Wyszynski) or Last Supper (Wojtyła); both leave the question of 'proof' to the theologians; but 'there are evident theological slips in the pastoral materials disseminated by the diocesan curia'.

b991 **Pelikan** Jaroslav, Imago Dei, the Byzantine apologia for icons; Mellon Lectures 1987: Bollingen 35/36, 1990 ➤ 6,d544; 0-691-09970-7: ^RAmerica 165 (1991) 149 (D. *McNally*); ExpTim 102 (1990s) 281 (J. *Frederick*: splendid); TTod 48 (1991s) 222.224.226 (J. W. *Cook*).

b992 *Pfeiffer* Heinrich W., Gemalte Theologie in der Sixtinischen Kapelle, I. Die Szenen des Alten und Neuen Testaments ausgeführt unter Sixtus IV: AnHPont 28 (1990) 99-159 + 12 fig.

b992* *Pressouyre* L., Histoire de l'art et iconographie: ➤ g340*, ^E*Balard* M., Histoire 1991, 247-268.

b993 **Quenot** Michel, L'icona, finestra sull'Assoluto, ^T. CinB 1991, Paoline. 218 p. Lit. 15.000. – ^RBbbOr 33 (1991) 234s (Cristina *Vertua*).

b994 *Rigaux* Dominique, À la table du Seigneur; l'Eucharistie chez les Primitifs italiens (1250-1497) [< diss. P-IV Sorbonne 1985], préf. *Vauchez* André. P 1989, Cerf. 320 p. 120 fig.; 7 pl.; 5 maps. F 130. – ^RBLitEc 92 (1991) 43-45 (J. *Rocacher*); EsprVie 101 (1991) 654s (P. *Rouillard*).

b995 *Ronig* Franz, Zwei Darstellungen des Gekreuzigten im Trierer Codex Egberti: TrierTZ 100 (1991) 161s; 2 color. fig.

b995* **Rudolph** Conrad, Artistic change at St-Denis; Abbot Suger's program and the early twelfth-century controversy over art. Princeton 1990, Univ. 119 p.; 14 fig. $21.50 [TR 88,392, Ursula *Nilgen*].

b996 *Saradi-Mendelovici* Helen, Christian attitudes toward pagan monuments in late antiquity and their legacy in later Byzantine centuries: DumbO 44 (1990) 47-61.

b996* *Sauser* Ekkart, Zur Geschichte und Ikonographie zweier Typen von Christusikonen: TrierTZ 100 (1991) 81-90; 2 color. fig.

b997 *Soskice* Janet M., Voir la vérité; peinture et théologie, ^T*Blancy* Édouard: LumièreV 40,203 (1991) 51-66.

b998 *Spatharakis* I., The left-handed Evagelist[s portrayed so]; a contribution to Palaeologan iconography. L 1988, Pindar. iii-120 p.; 135 fig. – ^RByZ 83 (1990) 504-6 (Kathleen *Maxwell*).

b998* a) *Stichel* Rainer, Gab es eine Illustration der jüdischen Heiligen Schrift in der Antike?; – b) *Koenen* Ulrike, Spätantike Vertreibungsbilder; zur unterschiedlichen Darstellung von Gen. 3.23 und 3.24; – c) *Dassmann* Ernst, Zu den Davidzyklen im Apollon-Kloster von Bawit; – d) *Wisskirchen* Rotraut, *Held* Stefan, Der Prototyp des Lämmerfrieses in Alt.-St. Peter; Ikonographie und Ikonologie: ➤ 47*, ^FENGEMANN J., Tesserae 1991, 93-111 / 112-125; pl. 12-14 / 126-137; plan; pl. 15-17 / 138-160; 4 fig.; pl. 18.

b999 **Stock** A., Gesicht bekannt und fremd; neue Wege zu Christus durch Bilder des 19. und 20. Jahrhunderts. Mü 1990, Kösel. 160 p. DM 38. 3-466-36192-3. – ^RTsTNijm 31 (1991) 103 (L. *Goosen*).

d1 **Temple** Richard, Icons and the mystical origins of Christianity. Longmead 1991, Element. x-198 p.; 56 fig. £10 [RelStR 18,231, J. J. *Yiannias*].

d2 **Thümmel** Hans Georg, Bilderlehre und Bilderstreit; Arbeiten zur Auseinandersetzung über die Ikone und ihre Begründung vornehmlich im 8. und 9. Jahrhundert [reprints]: Das östliche Christentum NF 40. Wü 1991, Augustinus. 186 p. DM 106 [TLZ 117,878, K. *Onasch*].

d3 *Thümmel* Hans Georg, Die Theorie der Ikone; die ostkirchliche Bilderlehre [*Belting* H., ...]: TLZ 116 (1991) 641-650.

d4 **Warland** Rainer, Das Brustbild Christi [alle nicht ganzfigurige Darstellungen]; Studien zu spätantiker und frühbyzantinischer Bildgeschichte: RömQ Supp 41, 1986 ➤ 4,e324: ^RByZ 83 (1991) 498-504 (Christa *Belting-Ihm*).

d5 **Weinhold** Gertrud, Der Friedefürst; Leiden, Kreuzestod und Ostersieg des Herrn Jesus Christus im Zeugnis der universalen Volkskunst. B 1985, Wichern. 213 p. DM 78. 3-88981-013-6. – ^RÉTRel 66 (1991) 317s (J. *Cottin*).

d6 **Wilson** Jan, Holy faces, secret places; an amazing quest for the face of Jesus. NY 1991, Doubleday. xvii-238 p.; 22 fig.; 32 phot. $26. 0-385-26105-5 [TDig 39,193].

T3.2 Sculptura.

d7 *Ammerman* Rebecca M., The naked standing goddess; a group of archaic terracotta figurines from Paestum: AJA 95 (1991) 203-230; 23 fig. (maps).

d8 **Anderson** Maxwell L., *Nista* Leila, Radiance in stone; sculptures in colored marble from the Museo Nazionale Romano. R 1989, De Luca. 115 p.; 33 fig. – ^RAJA 95 (1991) 354s (Frances Van *Keuren*, N. *Herz*).

d9 **Andreae** Bernard, Laokoon und die Gründung Roms 1988 → 4,e254*; 6,d575: ^RGGA 243 (1991) 52-67 (Angelika *Geyer*); Gnomon 63 (1991) 351-8 (R. R. R. *Smith*, Eng.).

d10 *a*) *Aston* D. A., Two Osiris figures of the Third Intermediate period; – *b*) *Quinn* Sarah, A New Kingdom stela in Girton College showing Amenophis I wearing the *hprš*; – *c*) *Malek* Jaromir, A stela of the draughtsman Pashed I of Deir el-Medina; – *d*) *Bailey* Donald M., *Craddock* Paul T., A portrait of an early Ptolemy; – *e*) *Abdalla* Aly, A Graeco-Roman statue of unusual character from Dendera: JEA 77 (1991) 95-107; 4 fig.; pl. V-VIII / 169-175; 1 fig.; pl. XVI,2 / 176-9; 1 fig. / 186-8; pl. XVIII-XIX / 189-193; pl. XX-XXI.

d11 **Baines** John, Fecundity figures; Egyptian personification and the iconology of a genre, 1985 → 3,d661 ... 6,d578; ^RAcArchH 43 (1991) 434-7 (U. *Luft*); CdÉ 65,130 (1990) 257-261 (J. C. *Goyon*).

d12 **Bergemann** Johannes, Römische Reiterstatuen; Ehrendenkmäler im öffentlichen Bereich [Diss. München 1987]: DAI Beit. Skulptur/Architektur 11. Mainz 1990, von Zabern. 196 p.; 96 pl.

d13 *a*) *Bianchi* Robert S., Ramesside art as reflected by a dated faience statuette identifying Ramesses II with Horus, the falcon-god; – *b*) *Redford* Donald B., A Ramesside stela from East Karnak: → 134*, ^FSCHULMAN A., BEgSem 10 (1989s) 17-22 + 2 fig. / 129-132 + 3 fig.

d14 *Bretschneider* J., *a*) Zu einer Flügelsonne im ethnologischen Museum von Adana; – *b*) Götter in Schreinen; eine Untersuchung zu den syrischen und levantinischen Tempelmodellen, ihrer Bauplastik und ihren Götterbildern: UF 23 (1991) 9s + 5 fig. / 14-26 + 17 fig.

d15 **Broman Morales** Vivian, Figurines and other clay objects from Sarab and Cayönü: OIComm. 25. Ch 1990, Univ. 92 p.; 30 pl.; map. – ^RPaléorient 17,1 (1991) 170-2 (C. *Jarrige*).

d16 *a*) *Caubet* Annie, Ivoires de Cappadoce; – *b*) *Bachelot* Luc, La fonction politique des reliefs néo-assyriens: → 61, ^FGARELLI P., Marchands 1991, 223-6 / 109-128.

d17 **Chappaz** J. L., Les figurines funéraires égyptiennes... Genève 1984 = AegHelv 10 (1982). – ^RWZKM 78 (1988) 219-221 (E. *Haslauer*: 20 suggestions).

d18 *Cohen* Beth, Perikles' portrait and the Riace bronzes; new evidence for 'schinocephaly' [disproportionately long 'squill-shaped' head]: Hesperia 60 (1991) 465-502; pl. 113-126.

d19 **Colbow** Gudrun,   Zur Rundplastik des Gudea 1987 ➤ 3,d670; 5,d397: ᴿBO 48 (1991) 899-904 (Jutta *Börker-Klähn*: 'inkompetent-genialisch').

d20 *Dareggi* Gianna,   Le groupe en bronze de Ṭarṭūs avec la Tyché et le trophée: ➤ 445, Phoenicians 1990/1, 231-241; 2 fig.

d21 *D'Ercole* Maria C.,   Voti d'argilla [1500 ex-votos from Apulia]: Archeo 56 (1989) 112-5.

d21* *Donderer* Michael,   Irreversible Deponierung von Grossplastik bei Griechen, Etruskern und Römern: JhÖsW 61-B (1991s) 193-276; 19 fig.

d22 **Donohue** Alice A.,   Xoana and the origins of Greek sculpture 1988 ➤ 5,d401; 6,d591:   ᴿAnzAltW 44 (1991) 236-240 (R. *Fleischer*); Gnomon 63 (1991) 372-4 (H.-V. *Herrmann*).

d23 *Elsner* John,   Cult and sculpture; sacrifice in the Ara Pacis Augustae: JRS 81 (1991) 50-61; 1 fig.; 7 pl.

d24 **Evers** Cécile,   Remarques sur l'iconographie de Constantin; à propos du remploi de portraits des 'bons empereurs':   MÉF 103 (1991) 785-802; 9 fig.

d24* *Fittschen* Klaus,   Pathossteigerung und Pathosdämpfung; Bemerkungen zu griechischen und römischen Porträts des 2. und 1. Jahrhunderts v.Chr.: ArchAnz (1991) 253-270; 18 fig. [219-252, *Stähli* Adrian, Karneades].

d25 **Floren** Josef,   Die geometrische und archaische Plastik: Die griechische Plastik I.   Mü 1987, Beck.   xxi-482 p.; 11 fig.; 40 pl. – ᴿGnomon 63 (1991) 529-538 (A. H. *Borbein*).

d26 **Fridh-Haneson** Britt-Marie,   Le manteau symbolique [2 sous 1] 1983 ➤ 64,a899; 2,a238:   ᴿRArchéol (1991) 144s (Simone *Besques*).

d27 **Fullerton** Mark D.,   The archaistic style in Roman statuary: Mnemosyne supp. 110, 1990 ➤ 6,d597:   ᴿRArchéol (1991) 415s (Mary-Anne *Zagdoun*).

d28 *Gauer* Werner,   Penelope, Hellas und der Perserkönig; ein hermeneutisches Problem: JbDAI 105 (1990) 31-65; 12 fig.

d29 *Gergel* Richard A.,   The Tel Shalem Hadrian reconsidered ['one of the finest bronze imperial portraits to survive from antiquity']: AJA 95 (1991) 231-251; 15 fig.

d30 *Ghedini* Francesca, *Bejor* Giorgio,   La scultura greca, dalle origini all'età classica: Archeo 72 (1991) 50-104.

d31 *Goring* E.,   Pottery figurines; the development of a coroplastic art in chalcolithic Cyprus: BASOR 282s (1991) 153-161.

d31* a) *Hawass* Zahi,   The statue of the dwarf Pr-n(j)-ʿnḫ(w) recently discovered at Giza; – b) *Sourouzian* Hourig,   La statue d'Amenhotep fils de Hapou, âgé [80 ans], un chef-d'œuvre de la XVIIIᵉ dynastie: ➤ 85c, ᶠKAISER W., MiDAI-K 47 (1991) 157-162; p. 12-14 / 341-355; 4 fig.; pl. 46-52.

d32 **Himmelmann** Nikolaus,   Herrscher und Athlet; die Bronzen vom Quirinal. Mi 1989, Olivetti/Mondadori.   248 p.; ill. – ᴿRArchéol (1991) 380-2 (F. *Queyrel*).

d33 *Hintzen-Bohlen* Brigitte,   Die Familiengruppe – ein Mittel zur Selbstdarstellung hellenistischer Herrscher: JbDAI 105 (1990) 129-154; 5 fig.

d34 *Holtzmann* Bernard,   Une sphinge archaïque de Thasos ['tête Wix' de Copenhague]: BCH 115,1 (1991) 125-165; 20 fig.

d35 *Işık* Fahri,   Zur Entstehung der tönernen Verkleidungsplatten in Anatolien: AnSt 41 (1991) 63-86; pl. IX-XVI.

d36 *Jacoby* Ruth,   The representation and identification of cities on Assyrian reliefs: IsrEJ 41 (1991) 112-131; 18 fig.

d37 **Kreikenbom** Detlev,   Bildwerke nach Polyklet; kopienkritische Untersuchungen zu den männlichen statuarischen Typen nach polykletischen

Vorbildern; 'Diskophoros', Hermes, Doryphoros, Herakles, Diadumenos. B 1990, Mann. 140 p.; Katalog (Fra 1990s) 143-228; 348 pl. DM 198. – RNikephoros 3 (1990) 283-6 (Renate *Thomas*).

d38 EKyrieleis H., Archaische/Klassische griechische Plastik 1985/6 → 3,794 ... 5,d418: RMnemosyne 44 (1991) 512-525 (J. M. *Hemelrijk*).

d39 Maderna Caterina, Archäologie and Geschichte, I. Iuppiter Diomedes und Merkur als Vorbilder für römische Bildnisstatuen ... 1988 → 5,d421; 6,d313*: RRArchéol (1991) 416s (F. *Queyrel*).

d40 *Madigan* Brian, A transposed head [found 1916 at Aigeira and linked via other fragments with Eukleides]: Hesperia 60 (1991) 503-510; pl. 127-128.

d41 *Magou* E., *Pernot* M., Bronzes orientaux et orientalisants, analyses complémentaires: BCH 115 (1991) 561-577.

d42 Malbon Elizabeth S., The iconography of the sarcophagus of Junius Bassus [359, in Vatican Museum; 10 main and 6 minor biblical scenes]. Princeton 1990, Univ. xxi-256 p. $47.50. – RRExp 88 (1991) 469 (E. G. *Hinson*); TS 52 (1991) 587s (B. *Ramsey*).

d43 *Marinescu-Nicolajsen* Liliana, Un fragment de statue héroïque de Trajan au musée Rodin: RArchéol (1990) 387-404; 21 fig.

d44 Mattusch Carol C., Greek bronze statuary 1988 → 5,d424; 8,d618: RPhoenix 44 (Toronto 1990) 388-392 (M. F. *Kilmer*).

d45 *Melucco Vaccaro* Alessandra, I grandi bronzi: Archeo 60 (1990) 53-103.

d46 *Moormann* Eric M., La pittura ... per la scultura 1988 → 5,d425; 6,d619: RLatomus 50 (1991) 742-4 (Christiane *Delplace*).

d47 *Myśliwiec* K., Royal portraiture of the Dynasties XXI-XXX 1988 → 5,d426: RBO 48 (1991) 122-6 (H. *De Meulenaere*).

d48 Pekáry Thomas, Das römische Kaiserbildnis in Staat, Kult und Gesellschaft, dargestellt anhand der Schriftquellen: Das Römische Herrscherbild 3/5, 1985 → 5,d428: RBonnJbb 191 (1991) 768-772 (R. H. W. *Stichel*).

d49 *Pernigotti* Sergio, La scultura nell'antico Egitto: Archeo 50 (1989) 46-93.

d50 *Pfanner* Michael, Über das Herstellen von Porträts; ein Beitrag zu Rationalisierungsmassnahmen und Produktionsmechanismen von Massenware im späten Hellenismus und in der römischen Kaiserzeit: JbDAI 104 (1989) 157-257; 52 fig.

d51 Pfrommer Michael, Studien / Toreutik 1987 → 5,d429; 6,d323: RAcArchH 43 (1991) 219s (M. *Szabó*); Babesch 66 (1991) 193s (L. *Byvanck-Quarles van Ufford*); RArchéol (1991) 147-9 (Fabienne *Burkhalter*).

d52 Ridgway Brunilde S., Hellenistic Sculpture I. The styles of ca. 331-200 B.C. 1990 → 6,d628: RAJA 95 (1991) 554s (M. D. *Stansbury-O'Donnell*).

d53 Riis P. J., *al.*, Catalogue of ancient sculpture, 1. Aegean, Cypriote and Graeco-Phoenician. K 1989, National Museum. 115 p.; 149 pl. Dk 200. – RClasR 41 (1991) 433s (Veronica *Tatton-Brown*).

d54 *Rolley* Claude, Les bronzes grecs et romains; recherches récentes: RArchéol (1991) 281-296; 5 fig.

d55 *Romano* James F., A Sed-Festival statuette of Pepy II in the Brooklyn Museum: GöMiszÄg 120 (1991) 73-80 + 6 fig.

d56 *Schmidt* Heike, Zur Determination und Ikonographie der sogenannten Ersatzköpfe: StAäK 18 (1991) 331-348.

d57 *Schneider* Rolf M., Augustus und der frühe römische Triumph: JbDAI 105 (1990) 167-205; 27 fig.

d58 Schröder Stephan F., Römische Bacchusbilder in der Tradition des Apollon Lykeios ...; Archaeologia 77, 1989 → 6,d634*: RLatomus 50 (1991) 919-921 (R. *Turcan*); RBgPg 69 (1991) 348 (R. *Chevallier*).

d59 **Schulman** Alan R., Ceremonial execution and public rewards...: OBO 75, 1988 ➤ 6,d635: ᴿBASOR 281 (1991) 91-93 (J. *Baines*); IsrEJ 41 (1991) 301-5 (S. *Ahituv*).

d60 **Seidl** Ursula, Die babylonischen Kudurru-Reliefs 1989 ➤ 5,d442: ᴿWelt-Or 22 (1991) 142-4 (T. *Podella*).

d61 *Sève* Michel, Note sur la date du sculpteur Thoinias de Sicyone [c. 180 av. J.-C.]: RÉG 104 (1991) 232-5.

Sinn Friederike, Die Grabdenkmäler 1. Reliefs, Altäre, Urnen: Vaticano, Museo Gregoriano, Katalog der Skulpturen 1,1: 1991 ➤ d212.

d62 **Smith** R. R. R., Hellenistic royal portraits 1988 ➤ 4,e315; ... 6,d639: ᴿRNum 32 (1990) 295s (F. *Queyrel*); TopO 1 (1991) 122-7 (Marie-F. *Boussac*).

d63 **Spanel** Donald, Through ancient eyes; Egyptian portraiture: Birmingham Museum exhibition 1988 ➤ 4,d704; 5,d372: ᴿBO 48 (1991) 117-9 (R. *Tefnin*: price in dollars the only hint whether Alabama or England).

d65 **Stewart** Andrew, Greek Sculpture; an exploration ['a personal selection of the most significant works' but declared not intended to succeed RICHTER]. NHv 1990, Yale Univ. xiii-380 p.; 35 fig.; maps; – vol. of 881 pl. $95. – ᴿAJA 95 (1991) 349-351 (Carol C. *Mattusch*); GreeceR 38 (1991) 106s (B. A. *Sparkes*: replacement, not revision, of Gisela Richter's four editions 1929-1970).

d66 *Talalay* Lauren E., Body imagery of the ancient Aegean [Kephala cemetery figurines]: Archaeology 44,4 (1991) 46-49; ill.

d67 *Vitto* Fanny, Two marble heads of goddesses from Tel Naharon-Scythopolis: ʿAtiqot 20 (1991) 33-45; 10 fig. [46-48 *al.* Marble source: Thasos Cape Vathi].

d68 *Walter-Karydi* Elena, Poseidons Delphin; der Poseidon Loeb und die Darstellungen des Meergottes im Hellenismus: JbDAI 106 (1991) 243-259; 4 fig.; pl. 57-64.

d69 **Wheeler** Mortimer, Archéologie, la voie de la terre [1954]. Aix-en-Provence c. 1990, Edisud. 256 p. – ᴿRArchéol (1991) 129s (Michèle *Vallerin*: translated into German, Italian, Spanish; but the 1981 Payot venture was abandoned in the second proofs).

d70 *Zagdoun* Mary-Anne, Bulletin archéologique [449 publications], La sculpture; la ronde-bosse hellénistique (1960-1987): RÉG 104 (1991) 140-197.

d71 **Zagdoun** Mary-Anne, La sculpture archaïsante... BÉF 269, 1989 ➤ 6, d850: ᴿRArchéol (1991) 148s (F. *Queyrel*).

d72 **Zimmermann** Jean-Louis, Les chevaux de bronze dans l'art géométrique grec: Univ. Genève, Éd. archéologiques. Mainz 1989, von Zabern. viii-380 p.; 557 fig.; 80 pl. DM 156. – ᴿAJA 95 (1991) 348s (Susan *Langdon*); ClasR 41 (1991) 173-5 (P. *Cartledge*); Gnomon 63 (1991) 658-660 (W. D. *Heilmeyer*).

T3.3 *Glyptica:* **stamp and cylinder seals,** scarabs, amulets.

d73 *Antonova* E. V., ❸ Towards an interpretation of the anthropomorphic images that appear on Iranian and Mesopotamian seals: VDI 197 (1991) 3-17; 14 fig.; Eng. 17s.

d74 *Auerbach* E., Heirloom seals and political legitimacy in Late Bronze Age Syria [... Alalaḫ]: Akkadica 74s (1991) 19-33 + 5 fig.

d75 **Avigad** Nahman, Hebrew bullae [255 from an antiquities dealer] 1986 ➤ 2,a264 ... 5,d453: ᴿJNES 50 (1991) 222-4 (D. *Pardee* approves).

d76 **Ben-Tor** Daphna,   The scarab, a reflection of ancient Egypt [display 1989 based on 4000 scarabs donated 1973 by will of London collector Kurt STERN].   J 1989, Israel Museum.   84 p.; ill.   965-278-083-9 [BO 48 (1991) 138].

d77 E*Bordreuil* P., *Gubel* E., BAALIM (Bulletin d'antiquités archéologiques du Levant inédites ou méconnues): Syria 66 (1989) 437-456; 29 fig. / 67 (1990) 483-520; 40 fig.

d78 **Buchanan** B.†, *Moorey* P., Iron Age stamp seals 1988 ➤ 5,d549; 6,d660: E*JAOS 111 (1991) 628-630 (Michelle J. *Marcus*).

d79 *Carruba* Onofrio,   The name of the scribe [two Boğazköy seals with both cuneiform and hieroglyphic]: JCS 42 (1990) 243-252.

d80 *Cheynet* J.-C.,   Les sceaux du musée d'Iznik: RÉByz 49 (1991) 219-235; 18 fig. [< RHE 86,267*].

d81 **Collon** Dominique,   Near Eastern Seals BM 1990 ➤ 6,d662; also Berkeley, Univ. California;   64 p.; 45 fig. /0-520-07308-8: R*OLZ 86 (1991) 395s (E. *Bleibtreu*).

d82 **Courtois** J.-C., *Webb* Jennifer M., Les cylindres-sceaux d'Enkomi 1987 ➤ 3,d741 ... 6,d664: R*Syria 66 (1989) 371-3 (P. *Amiet*).

d83 *Dijkstra* Meindert,   The weather-god on two mountains [Dab'a 1979 cylinder seal]:   UF 23 (1991) 127-137 + 3 pl.

d84 *During Caspers* Elisabeth C. L.,   The Indus Valley 'Unicorn' [stamp seals] — a Near Eastern connection: JESHO 34 (1991) 312-350.

d85 **Gasse** Annie,   Catalogue des ostraca figurés de Deir el-Médineh n⁰ 3100-3372 (5ᵉ fasc.) 1986 ➤ 3,d744 ... 5,d466: R*CdÉ 65 (1990) 268s (Lise *Manniche*).

d86 **Gignoux** Philippe, *Gyselen* Rika,   Bulles et sceaux sassanides 1987 ➤ 3,d745 ... 6,d672: R*DLZ 112 (1991) 297s (B. *Brentjes*); JAOS 111 (1991) 381s (T. S. *Kawami*).

d87 **Giveon** Raphael, Egyptian scarabs ... British Museum: OBO arch. 3, 1985 ➤ 1,d140 ... 5,d470: R*BASOR 281 (1991) 81-83 (J. *Weinstein*); CdÉ 65 (1990) 272-5 (E. *Gubel*).

d88 **Giveon** Raphael, *al.*, Scarabs from recent excavations in Israel: OBO 83, 1988 ➤ 4,e356 ... 6,d674: R*WeltOr 22 (1991) 149s (Helga *Weippert*).

d89 **Giveon** R.†, E*Kertesz* Trude,   Egyptian scarabs and seals in Acco 1986 ➤ 2,a286; 4,e355: R*JNES 50 (1991) 55s (S. H. *Horn*).

d90 **Joshi** Jagat P., *Parpola* A.,   Corpus of Indus seals and inscriptions: Annales B-239, Helsinki 1987 ➤ 6,d680: R*JESHO 34 (1991) 125s (W. F. *Leemans*).

d91 **Keel** Othmar, *Uehlinger* Christoph,   Altorientalische Miniaturkunst; die ältesten visuellen Massenkommunikationsmittel [Sammlungen Univ. FrS] 1990 ➤ 6,d683: R*BiKi 46 (1991) 90s (W. *Zwickel*); RB 91 (1991) 293 (F. *Langlamet*).

d92 **Keel** Othmar, *Shuval* Menakhem, *Uehlinger* Christoph,   Studien zu den Stempelsiegeln aus Palästina/Israel, 3. Die frühe Eisenzeit; ein Workshop: OBO 100, 1990 ➤ 6,d682: R*ArOr 59 (1991) 439s (Jana *Pečírková*); PEQ 123 (1991) 71s (B. *Teissier*); RB 98 (1991) 602-5 (É. *Puech*).

d93 **Keel** O., *Schroer* S., Studien ... Stempelsiegeln: OBO 67, 1985 ➤ 1,d152 ... 5,d474: R*WZKM 78 (1988) 281s (K. *Jaroš*).

d94 **Keel-Leu** Hildi, (*Keel* Othmar),   Vorderasiatische Stempelsiegel; die Sammlung des Biblischen Instituts der Universität Freiburg Schweiz: OBO 110.   FrS/Gö 1991, Univ./VR.   169 p.; 187 fig.   3-7278-0785-7 / VR 3-525-53743-3.

d95 **Kjærum** Poul,   Stamp and cylinder seals: Failaka 1/1,1983 → 64,a933 ...
   3,e638:   ᴿBInstArch 27 (1990) 186s (D. *Collon*).
d96 *Kotansky* Roy, Incantations and prayers for salvation on inscribed Greek
   amulets: → 392, Magika 1991, 107-137 [188-213, *Graf* F.; 244-259, papyri,
   Betz H. D.].
d97 *Lapp* Nancy L., Some cylinder seals and impressions from the Dead Sea
   plain [Bab/Ḍra] and the Early Bronze Age in the Eastern Mediterranean:
   ProcGLM 11 (1991) 37-50; 4 fig.
d98 *Layton* Scott C., A new interpretation of an Edomite seal impression
   [Buseirah 1972: name Mlkl with ʿb left over (from following ʿbd) by
   scribal error]: JNES 50 (1991) 37-43.
d99 **Lumsden** Stephen P., Symbols of power; Hittite royal iconography in
   seals: diss. California, ᴰ*Stronach* D. Berkeley 1990, 352 p. 91-26677. –
   DissA 52 (1991s) 1403s-A; OIAc 2,23.
d100 **Martin** Geoffrey T., Scarabs, cylinders and other ancient Egyptian
   seals; a checklist of publications 1985 → 3,d763: ᴿCdÉ 65 (1990) 269-272
   (W. A. *Ward*).
d101 *Matthews* Donald, Middle Assyrian glyptic from Tell Billa: Iraq 53
   (1991) 17-34 + 44 fig. [147-158 Brak].
d103 *Meltzer* Edmund S., The commemorative scarab; a 'gem' of a text:
   → 133*, ꟻSCHULMAN A., BEgSem 10 (1989s) 91-93; facsim. 94.
d104 *Miranda* Elena, Una gemma 'gnostica' dalle catacombe di S. Gennaro
   [Napoli]: RivArCr 67 (1991) 115-124; 2 fig.
d105 *a) Parayre* Dominique, Les cachets ouest-sémitiques à travers l'image
   du disque solaire ailé (perspective iconographique); – *b) Salvini* Mirjo,
   Un sceau original de la reine hittite Ašmunikal: Syria 67 (1990) 269-
   304 + XIII pl. / 257-268; 6 fig.
d106 **Pini** Ingo, Corpus der minoischen und mykenischen Siegel Beih 3,
   Symposium (ᴱ*Müller* W.) 1985/9 → 651*.
d107 *a) Rainey* Anson, Rejoinder to the Eliakim Naʿar Yokan seal impressions; – *b) Albenda* Pauline, To Sumerian bats: BA 54,1 (1991) inside
   back cover (to BA 53,74, *Garfinkel* Y.; and 53,142 *Goldsmith* N.).
d107* **Root** Margaret C., The art of seals; aesthetic and social dynamics of
   the impressed image from antiquity to the present. AA 1984, Univ.
   Kelsey Museum. 48 p. [OIAc 2,26].
d108 **Salje** Beate, Der 'common style' der Mitanni-Glyptik und die Glyptik
   der Levante und Zyperns in der späten Bronzezeit [Diss. Berlin 1989]
   BaghFor 11. Mainz 1990, von Zabern. xxxii-336 p.; 32 pl.
d109 *Salvini* Mirjo, Autour du sceau de Muršili II (RS 14.202): Syria 67
   (1990) 423-6; 2 fig. [735-741, *Hawkins* J. D. doubts authenticity; 743-7
   reply; support from *Amiet* P. 749s].
d110 *Sass* Benjamin, The Queen Alia airport seal – proto–Arabic [KNAUF] or
   Gnostic?: Levant 23 (1991) 187-190; fig. 4-8.
d110* *Sax* M., Techniques used to decorate the perforations of some
   Akkadian rock crystal cylinder seals: Iraq 53 (1991) 91-95; 1 fig.; pl.
   XII-XIII.
d111 *Schneider* Tsvi, Six biblical signatures; seals and seal impressions of six
   biblical personages recovered: BAR-W 17,4 (1991) 26-33 [four by
   AVIGAD, after he had declared in 1978 that not one of the hundreds of
   known seals could be attributed to a Bible person].
d112 *Verter* Bradford, Gem index to Studies in magical amulets by Campbell
   BONNER [AA 1950]: HarvTR 83 (1990) 207-211.

d113 *Voet* Gabriella, Het Ur-Utu archief; evolutie in het zegelpraxis: Akkadica 72 (1991) 20-30 + 30 fig.

d114 *Weingarten* Judith, A royal Egyptian 'nodulus' from Canaan [Tel Michal]: Kadmos 30 (1991) 87-89; 1 fig.

d115 **Werr** Lamia al-Gailani, Studies in ... cylinder seals 1988 ➤ 4,e383: ᴿOrientalia 60 (1991) 366-9 (D. *Collon*).

d116 **Wiese** André, Zum Bild des Königs auf ägyptischen Siegelamuletten: OBO 96, 1990 ➤ 6,d702: ᴿRStFen 19 (1991) 133s (Gabriella *Scandone Matthiae*); TüTQ 171 (1991) 137 (W. *Gross*); ZAW 103 (1991) 461 (Brigitte *Michallik*).

T3.4 Mosaica.

d117 *a*) *Álvarez Martínez* J.M., La iconografía de Orfeo en los mosaicos hispanorromanos; – *b*) *Torres Carro* Mercedes, Iconografía marina: ➤ 628, Mém. BALIL Illana A. 1990, 29-50 + 2 fig.; 8 pl. / 107-134.

d118 **Balmelle** C., *al.*, Le decór géométrique de la mosaïque romaine 1985 ➤ 2,a325 ... 4,e387: ᴿBonnJbb 191 (1991) 792-4 (Gisela *Hellenkemper Salies*).

d119 *Balty* Janine, Notes d'iconographie dionysiaque; la mosaïque de Sarrîn (Osrhoène): MÉF-A 103 (1991) 19-33; 9 fig.

d120 ᴱ**Bertelli** Carlo, Die Mosaiken; ein Handbuch der musivischen Kunst von den Anfängen bis zur Gegenwart 1989 ➤ 6,d708 [ital.], ᵀ*Wolf* Gabriele: ᴿTrierTZ 100 (1991) 319s (E. *Sauer*).

d120* **Campbell** Sheila, The mosaics of Antioch 1988 ➤ 5,d497; 6,d712: ᴿSpeculum 66 (1991) 130s (R. E. *Kolarik*).

d121 **Donderer** M., Die Mosaizisten der Antike und ihre wirtschaftliche und soziale Stellung; eine Quellenstudie: Erlanger Forschungen A-48. Erlangen 1989, Univ.-Bt. 183 p. 74 pl. DM 79. 3-9221-3564-1 [JRS 81,257].

d122 **Donderer** M., Chronologie der römischen Mosaiken in Venetien ... 1986 ➤ 3,d789*: ᴿGnomon 63 (1991) 73-75 (Gisela H. *Salies*).

d123 **Geir** Hellemo, Adventus Domini; eschatological thought in 4th-century apses and catecheses [diss. Oslo 1985],ᵀ: VigChr supp. 5. Leiden 1989, Brill. 309 p.; 47 pl. – ᴿRHPR 71 (1991) 350-2 (P. *Prigent*: admirable, though it is not shown which of the images correspond to which of the varying outlooks of the catecheses).

d124 *Ghedini* Francesca, Il mosaico greco e romano: Archeo 62 (1990) 58-107; ill.

d125 *Hunt* Lucy-Anne, Art and colonialism; the mosaics of the Church of the Nativity in Bethlehem (1169) and the problem of 'Crusader' art: DumbO 45 (1991) 69-85; 13 fig.

Khanoussi Mustapha, Mosaik ... Wettkampfes 1991 ➤ b780*.

d126 *Koranda* Christian, Geometrische Gliederungsschemata frühchristlicher Mosaiken in Bulgarien: JhÖsA 61-H (1991) 83-141; 29 fig.; III pl.

d127 **Lavagne** Henri, La mosaïque: Que sais-je? 2361. P 1987, PUF. 125 p.

d128 *a*) *López* Guadalupe, La caza en el mosaico romano; iconografía y simbolismo; – *b*) *Neira Jiménez* Luz, Acerca de las representaciones del thiasos marino en los mosaicos romanos tardo-antiguos de Hispania: ➤ 25, ꟳBLÁZQUEZ MARTÍNEZ J. 1991, 497-505 + 14 fig. / 513-534 + 9 fig.

d129 *Moormann* Eric M., Imperial Roman mosaics from Melos and İzmir at Leiden: OMRO 71 (1991) 97-107 + 8 pl.

Ovadiah Asher, *al.*, The mosaic pavements of Sheikh Zouède in northern Sinai 1991 ➤ d992*.

d130 *Ovadiah* A., *al.*, ❸ A new look at the mosaic floor from Sheikh Zuweid in the Ismailiya museum: Qadmoniot 24 (1991) 122-6; 7 phot.

d131 *Saliou* Catherine, Léda callipyge au pays d'Aphrodite; remarques sur l'organisation, la fonction et l'iconographie d'une mosaïque de Palaepaphos (Chypre): Syria 67 (1990) 369-375; 6 fig.

d132 *Tancke* Karin, Wagenrennen; ein Friesthema der aristokratischen Repräsentationskunst spätklassisch-frühhellenistischer Zeit: JbDAI 105 (1990) 95-127; 18 fig.

d133 **Wisskirchen** Rotraut, Das Mosaikprogramm von S. Prassede in Rom; Ikonographie und Ikonologie: JbAC Egb 17. Münster 1990, Aschendorff. 156 p.; 28 pl.

d134 *Zaqzuq* Abd ar-Rifâq, ❹ Holy scenes in mosaics discovered in the Hama region: ↠ 626, AnASyr 40 (1989/90) ❹ 81-85 + 12 pl., imposing peacock, birds, deer, Adam, church.

T3.5 *Ceramica,* **pottery** [↠ *singuli situs*, infra].

d135 **Amyx** D. A., Corinthian vase-painting of the archaic period 1988 ↠ 5,d516... 6,d729: ᴿGnomon 63 (1991) 630-4 (M. *Tiverios*).

d136 *Arias* Paolo E., La ceramica greca: Archeo 80 (1991) 57-107; ill.

d136* *Åström* Paul, Canaanite jars from Hala Sultan Tekke: ↠ 637, Bronze Age Trade 1989/91, 149-151 [-161, *Fischer* P. M., ion mass spectrometry].

d137 ᴱ**Barrelet** Marie-Thérèse, *Gardin* Jean-Claude, À propos des interprétations archéologiques de la poterie 1984/6 ↠ 2,a335; 4,e406: ᴿJAOS 111 (1991) 185 (Carol *Kramer*: fresh despite production-defects); WZKM 78 (1988) 290s (Jane *Moon*).

d138 **Beltrán Lloris** Miguel, Guía de la cerámica romana. Zaragoza 1990, Pórtico. 373 p.; ill.

d139 **Boardman** John, Vasi ateniesi a figure nere; un manuale. Mi 1990, Rusconi. 271 p.; 319 fig. Lit. 25.000. – ᴿArcheo 68 (1990) 128s (P. E. *Arias*).

d140 *Bolger* D., Evolution of the chalcolithic painted style: BASOR 282s (1991) 81-93.

d141 *a) Bottini* Angelo, Da Atene alla Daunia; ceramica ed acculturazione; – *b) Stea* Giuliana, La ceramica grigia del VII sec. a.C., dall'Incoronata di Metaponto: MÉF-A 103 (1991) 443-455; 9 fig. / 405-442; 19 fig.

d142 **Bourgeois** Brigitte, La conservation des céramiques archéologiques... chypriotes 1987 ↠ 4,e413: ᴿSyria 67 (1990) 758s (Liliane *Courtois*).

d143 *Bouzek* Jan, Studies of Greek pottery in the Black Sea area. Praha 1990, Univ. 200 p. [diss. Åström (Partille)]. – ᴿDialogues Hist. Anc. 17,1 (1991) 445s (P. *Lévêque*).

d144 *Bowden* Hugh, The chronology of Greek painted pottery; some observations: Hephaistos 10 (1991) 49-53 + 6 fig.; bibliog. p. 59.

d145 *Bruneau* Philippe, La céramique pergaménienne à reliefs appliqués de Délos: BCH 115 (1991) 588-610; 4 fig.; catalogue 611-666, ill.

d146 **Burow** Johannes, Die Antimenesmaler: Kerameus 7. 1989 ↠ 6,d737: ᴿAJA 95 (1991) 551s (Marjorie S. *Venit*); RArchéol (1991) 362 (H. *Metzger*).

d147 *Crée* F. De, The black-on-red or Cypro-Phoenician ware: ↠ 445, Phoenicians 1990/1, 95-102.

d147* *Crouwel* Joost H., Mycenaean pictorial pottery in Göttingen: Arch-Anz (1991) 1-9; 9 fig.

d148 *Danali-Giole* K., Dionysus and Peleus; problems of interpretation in Athenian black-figure vases: Archaiognosia 6 (1990) 109-118; ❼ 119.

d148* *Esse* Douglas L., The collared store jar; scholarly ideology and ceramic typology: → 428*, ScandJOT (1991,2) 99-116.

d149 **Ettlinger** Elisabeth, *al.*, Conspectus formarum terrae sigillatae italico modo confectae: Materialien zur Römisch-Germanischen Keramik 10. Bonn 1990, Habelt. 210 p.; 2 foldouts.

d150 *a) Franken* H. J., 'Form is the essence of a ceramic vessel' (FRENDO A. 1988); – *b) As* A. van, *Wijnen* M.-H., Neolithic and early chalcolithic pottery from Ilipinar; – *c*) The pottery from Örnekköy (Turkey) – some observations: NewsPot 7s (1989s) 1-7 / 21-68 / 69-74.

d151 *Frifelt* Karen, A third millennium kiln from the Oman Peninsula: ArabArchEp 1 (1990) 4-15; 16 fig.

d152 **Gibson** Alex, **Woods** Ann, [British] Prehistoric pottery for the archaeologist. Leicester 1990, Univ. 293 p.; 239 ill. £60. 0-7185-1274-X. – ᴿAntiquity 65 (1991) 978 (T. *Taylor*: Prudence *Rice* 1987 is far cheaper and better).

d153 *Gill* D. W. J., Pots and trade; spacefillers or objets d'art? [i.e. was (decorated) pottery valued or tolerated as cargo?]: JHS 111 (1991) 29-47.

d154 *Gill* David W. J., *Vickers* Michael, Reflected glory; pottery and precious metal in classical Greece: JbDAI 105 (1990) 1-30; 5 fig.

d154* **Guidotti** Maria Cristina, Firenze, Museo Egizio; vasi dall'epoca protodinastica al Nuovo Regno: Cataloghi Musei d'Italia NS 3. R 1991, Libreria dello Stato. I. x-361 p.; ill.

d155 *Gunneweg* Jan, *al.*, The origin, classification and chronology of Nabatean painted fine ware: Jb des Römisch-Germanischen Zentralmuseums Mainz 35 (1988) 315-345.

d156 **Hope** Colin, Egyptian pottery 1987 → 3,d837: ᴿJEA 77 (1991) 199 (P. *French*).

d157 *a) Humbert* J.-B., Essai de classification des amphores dites 'à anse de panier' [basket-handles]; – *b) Gunneweg* J., *Perlman* I., The origin of 'loop-handled jars' from Tell Keisan: RB 98 (1991) 574-590; Eng. 574 / 591-9; franç. 591.

d158 **Iacovou** Maria, The pictorial pottery of eleventh century B.C. Cyprus [diss. Cincinnati 1984]: SIMA 79 [not 78 as printed] 1988 → 4,g637; 6,d747: ᴿBO 48 (1991) 909-911 (S. *Hood*); Gnomon 63 (1991) 181s (H. *Matthäus*); JHS 111 (1991) 246 (Elizabeth *Goring*: disentangles much confusion).

d159 **Jircik** Nancy R., The Pisticci and Amykos painters; the beginnings of red-figured vase painting in ancient Lucania: diss. Texas. Austin 1990. 382 p.

d160 **Kearsley** R., The pendent semi-circle skyphos; a study of its development and chronology and an examination of its evidence for Euboean activity at al-Mina [Orontes-mouth, not Ugarit]: Bull. Supp. 44. L 1989, Univ. Inst. Clas. xviii-220 p.; 9 pl. [Gymnasium 99,283, H. *Matthäus*].

d161 **Lezzi-Hafter** Adrienne, Der Eretria-Maler, Werke und Weggefährten: Kerameus 6, 1988 → 6,d752: ᴿRArchéol (1991) 364 (H. *Metzger*).

d161* **London** Gloria, *al.*, Töpferei auf Zypern damals-heute [Traditional pottery], ᵀ*Krull* Karin. Mainz 1989, von Zabern. 88 p.; front. 3-8053-1028-5. – ᴿBO 48 (1991) 917-9 (A. van *As*).

d162 *Malaise* Michel, Harpocrate au pot [with a jar]: → 43, ᶠDERCHAIN P., Religion 1991, 219-232.

d163 **Oakley** John H., The Phiale painter 1990 → 6,d758: ᴿAJA 95 (1991) 748-750 (Susan B. *Matheson*); ClasR 41 (1991) 447-9 (Elizabeth *Moignard*, also on BUROW); RArchéol (1991) 362s (H. *Metzger*).

d164 *Pape* A., Keramik – eine schwierige Quelle; interdisziplinäre Methoden ihrer Erforschung: ZäSpr 118 (1991) 54-68.

d165 **Peleg** Michal, A bibliography of Roman, Byzantine and early Arab pottery from Israel and neighbouring countries (excluding glazed ware). J 1990, Israel Antiquities Authority.

d166 *Pfrommer* Michael, Ein achämenidisches Amphorenrhyton mit ägyptischem Dekor: ArchMIran 23 (1990) 191-209; 7 fig.; pl. 36-44.

d167 *Picon* Maurice, L'analyse par activation neutronique est-elle la meilleure méthode que l'on puisse employer pour déterminer l'origine des céramiques?: RArchéom 15 (1991) 95-101; 4 fig.

d168 ᴱ**Rosati** Roberto, La ceramica attica nel Mediterraneo, analisi computerizzata della diffusione; le fasi iniziali (630-560 a.C.). Bo 1989, Coop. Univ. x-370 p.; 19 fig. Lit. 50.000. – ᴿAJA 95 (1991) 550s (M. M. *Eisman:* 'has taken all of BEAZLEY's distinctions and ignored them' e.g. combining Nettos and Chimera painter).

d169 *Rotroff* Susan I., Attic west slope vase painting: Hesperia 60 (1991) 59-102; 32 fig.; pl. 14-46.

d170 **Rottländer** Rolf C. A., Verwitterungserscheinung an Keramik [; II.] Silices und Knochen. Tü 1989, Archaeologica Venatoria. 139 p. [176 p.]. – ᴿBonnJbb 191 (1991) 703-8 (H. *Mommsen*).

d171 *Schauenburg* Konrad, *a)* Zu Grabvasen des Baltimoremalers; – *b)* Der Varresmaler [so A. D. TRENDALL, *lebes* im Genfer Kunsthandel, seit 1981] in Kiel: JbDAI 105 (1990) 67-94; 40 fig. / 106 (1991) 183-197; pl. 35.

d172 **Sinopoli** Carla M., Approaches to archaeological ceramics. NY 1991, Plenum. xiii-237 p.; 65 fig. $39.50; pa. $24. 0-306-43852-6; -575-6 [Antiquity 66,550-3, Karen D. *Vitelli*].

d173 **Spivey** Nigel J., The Micali painter and his followers 1987 ➤ 4,e453; 5,d555: ᴿAJA 95 (1991) 179 (F. *Gilotta*).

d174 *Stern* E. Marianne, The workshop of the floating handles [one end not attached]: ➤ 147, ᶠSTIBBE C. 1991, 199-204 + 5 fig.

d175 **Trendall** A. D., Red-figure vases of South Italy and Sicily, a handbook. L 1989, Thames & H. 288 p.; 596 fig. – ᴿToposO 1 (1991) 89-97 (Hélène *Cassimatis*).

d176 *Watson* P. M., Jerash bowls; study of a provincial group of Byzantine decorated fine ware [> diss. Sydney]: Syria 66 (1989) 223-261; 14 fig.

d177 *Wenning* R., Attische Keramik in Palästina; ein Zwischenbericht: ➤ 636*, TEuph 2 (1989/90) 157-166, bibliographical; map 167.

T3.6 **Lampas.**

d178 *Bailey* Donald M., *a)* Aegina, Aphaia-Tempel [sic in title; in text Temple], XIV. The lamps: ArchAnz (1991) 31-68; 58 fig. – *b)* [27] Lamps metal, lamps clay; a decade of publication: JRomArch 4 (AA 1991) 51-62 [< NTAbs 36,78].

d179 *Bakalakis* G., Les *Kernoi* éleusiniens: Kernos 4 (1991) 105-113 + 6 fig.

d180 *a)* *Carretero Vaquero* Santiago, Lucernas romanas con paisaje de influencia alejandrina; temas marítimos; – *b)* *Puya García de Leaniz* Miguel, Lucernas romanas del Museo Arqueológico de Sevilla, A; – *c)* *Modrzewska* Iwona, Lucernas romanas inéditas en los Museos Arqueológico Nacional y de Barcelona, ᵀ*Rgawek* Jolanta: BSAA 57 (1991) 193-211 + 22 fig. / 215-236 + 33 fig. + V pl. / 245-9; 3 fig.

d181 **Loffreda** Stanislao, Lucerne bizantine in TS 1989 ⇥ 5,d571; 6,d787:
ᴱOrChrPer 57 (1991) 439s (R. M. *Mackowski*); TAth 62 (1989) 920s (J. E.
Meïmaris).

d182 *Magness* Jodi, Inscribed Byzantine oil lamps from Jerusalem: ⇥ 627*,
AJA 95 (1991) 334, summary.

т3.7 **Cultica** [⇥ м4-7 et singuli situs].

d183 *a) Barrett* John C., Towards an archaeology of ritual; – *b) Garwood*
Paul, Ritual tradition and the reconstitution of society: ⇥ 639, Sacred
and profane, 1989/91, 1-9 / 10-32.

d184 **Broek** R. van den, *al.*, Kerk en kerken in Romeins-Byzantijns Palestina;
archeologie en geschiedenis: Palaestina antiqua 6. Kampen 1988, Kok.
232 p. ƒ 36. 90-242-4889-2. – ᴿBijdragen 52 (1991) 447s (M. *Parmentier*).

d185 *D'Andria* Francesca, *Lombardo* Mario, I grandi santuari dell'antica
Grecia: Archeo 51 (1989) 55-99.

d186 **Donceel-Voûte** Pauline, Les pavements des églises byzantines de Syrie et
du Liban; décor, archéologie et liturgie: HistArtArch 69. LvN 1988,
Univ. I. 585 p.; 433 fig.; 13 pl.; vol. II of plates.

d187 *Goodman* M., Synagogue and Temple in late antiquity: BAngIsr 10
(1990s) 104s (lecture summary).

d188 **Lawlor** John I., The Esbous North church in its stratigraphic and
historical contexts; diss. Drew, ᴰ*Bull* B. Madison ɴᴊ 1990. – RTLv 23,
p. 558.

d189 *Kaminski* Gabriele, Thesauros; Untersuchungen zum antiken Opfer-
stock [Altar, aus Stein]: JbDAI 106 (1991) 63-181; 35 fig.; pl. 27-34.

d190 *Margueron* J., Sanctuaires sémitiques [Canaan, *Mazar* A.; juifs, *Delcor*
M.]: ⇥ 686, SDB XI (1991) 1104-1258 [-1286-1329].

d191 **Norman** Edward, Das Haus Gottes; die Geschichte der christlichen
Kirchen [i. Palästina. ii. Byzanz...], ᵀ*Summerer* Siglinde, *Kurz* Gerda. Stu
1990, Kohlhammer. 312 p.; 306 pl. + 80 color. DM 128. – ᴿZkT 113
(1991) 488-490 (H. B. *Meyer*).

d192 **Ottosson** Magnus, Temples and cult places in Palestine 1980 ⇥ 61,s602
... 4,e497: ᴿGymnasium 98 (1991) 87s (P. *Grossmann*).

d193 **Stähli** Hans-Peter, Antike Synagogenkunst 1988 ⇥ 5,d595: ᴿTLZ 116
(1991) 136s (H. G. *Thümmel*).

т3.8 **Funeraria;** *Sindon,* **the Shroud.**

d194 *a) Bolshakov* Andrey O., The Old Kingdom representations of funeral
procession; – *b) Kruchten* Jean-Marie, Une adaptation 'libyenne' de la
formule in *s3.f šnḫ rn.f* (Chambre III du Tombeau d'Osorkon III à
Tanis): GöMiszÄg 121 (1991) 31-54 / 69-75 + 1 fig. [à suivre... non 1991].

d195 **Boschung** Dietrich, Antike Grabaltäre aus den Nekropolen Roms 1987
⇥ 4,e496; 5,d603: ᴿLatomus 50 (1991) 214s (L. *Foucher*).

d196 **Bulst** Werner, Betrug am Turiner Grabtuch; der manipulierte Car-
bontest 1990 ⇥ 6,d814: ᴿTPQ 139 (1991) 226 (J. *Hörmandinger*).

d197 **Caillet** Jean-Pierre, *Loose* Helmuth N., La vie d'éternité; la sculpture
funéraire dans l'Antiquité chrétienne. P/Genève 1990, Cerf/Tricorne.
147 p. – ᴿRHPR 71 (1991) 249s (P. *Prigent*); RivArCr 67 (1991) 181s
(Palmira M. *Barbini*).

d198 *Feig* Nurit, *al.*, Tombs: ʿAtiqot 20 (1991) 119-128 (-165), ill.; 180 = Ⓗ
27*-30*.

d198* *Gramaglia* Pier Angelo, Ancora la sindone di Torino ['spietata campagna denigratoria' dopo l'esame radiocarbonico; ... PETROSILLO O., BAIMA BOLLONE P., BONNET-EYMARD B.]: RivStoLR 27 (1991) 85-114.

d199 **Haffner** Alfred, *al.*, Gräber, Spiegel des Lebens; Totenbrauchtum der Kelten und Römer: RhMusTrier. Mainz 1989, von Zabern. 447 p.; 336 fig. + 54 color. – ᴿAJA 95 (1991) 360s (P. S. *Wells*).

d200 ᶠHEERMA VAN VOSS M., Funerary symbols and religion, ᴱ**Kamstra** J., *al.* 1988 → 5,78: ᴿBO 48 (1991) 450-6 (W. *Helck*).

d200* **Hodel-Hoenes** Sigrid, Leben und Tod im Alten Ägypten; thebanische Privatgräber des Neuen Reiches. Da 1991, Wiss. 256 p. 3-534-11011-9 [OIAc 2,21].

d201 **Horst** Pieter W. van der, Ancient Jewish epitaphs; an introductory survey of a millennium of Jewish funerary epigraphy (300 B.C.E.-700 C.E.): ContrBExT 2. Kampen 1991, Kok Pharos. 179 p. 90-242-3307-0.

d202 **Kleiner** Diana E. E., Roman imperial funerary altars with portraits: Archaeologica 62, 1987 → 3,d921 ... 6,d831: ᴿRBgPg 69 (1991) 261s (P. *Gros*: toil and expense disproportionate to the awaited diffusion).

d203 ᴱ**Laffineur** R., Thanatos 1986/7 → 4,752; 5,d619: ᴿKernos 4 (1991) 343-6 (P. *Warren*, Eng.).

d204 **Longerstay** Monique, Les tombes rupestres à auge du Maghreb antique: AION supp. 69 al vol. 49,4 (1989). 53 p.; III pl.

d205 *McCane* Byron R., Bones of contention? Ossuaries and reliquaries in early Judaism and Christianity: SecC 8 (1991) 235-246.

d206 *Neri* P., La sindone [il volto è quello immaginato da coloro che hanno guardato la sindone]: BbbOr 33 (1991) 52.

d207 **Petrosillo** Orazio, *Marinelli* Emanuela, La Sindone, un enigma alla prova della scienza² 1990 → 6,d839: ᴿCC 142 (1991,1) 94s (P. *Vanzan*: per dirla con MESSORI, cattolici 'genefluttendosi [sic] in modo acritico ... davanti a Santa Madre Scienza e al figlioletto suo, San Carbonio 14').

d208 *Pilón* José M., La inaceptabilidad del C-14 para la Santa Sábana de Turín: RazF 222 (1990) 228-234.

d209 **Reiser-Haslauer** Elfriede, Die Kanopen I-II: Corpus Ant. Äg 1989 → 5,d633: ᴿBO 48 (1991) 819-821 (Jeannot *Kettel*).

d210 *Sartre* A., Obbé fille de Sachamelos; un buste funéraire syrien: Syria 67 (1990) 675-685; 6 fig.

d211 **Schlögl** Hermann A., *Brodbeck* Andreas, Ägyptische Totenfiguren ... der Schweiz: OBO arch. 7. FrS/Gö 1990, Univ./VR. 354 p.; ill.

d212 **Sinn** Friederike, Die Grabdenkmäler 1. Reliefs, Altäre, Urnen: Museo Vaticano Gregoriano Profano, Katalog der Skulpturen 1/1. Mainz 1991, von Zabern. 252 p.; 333 fig. 3-8053-1057-9.

d213 **Tooley** Angela M. J., Middle Kingdom burial customs; a study of wooden models and related material: diss. ᴰ*Shore* A. Liverpool 1989. xix-435 p.; vol. of 106 pl. BRDX-92226. – OIAc 1,26; DissA. 51 (1991s) 102-A.

d214 **Walker** Susan, Catalogue of Roman sarcophagi in the British Museum: Corpus Signorum Imperii Romani 11/2. L 1990, British Museum. 120 p.; ill.

d215 **Weber** Thomas, Syrisch-römische Sarkophagbeschläge; orientalische Bronzewerkstätten in römischer Zeit: DamaszF 2. Mainz 1989, von Zabern. viii-86 p.; 51 fig.; 62 pl. – ᴿBonnJbb 191 (1991) 812-4 (G. *Koch*).

d216 *Wöhrle* Georg, 'Eine sehr hübsche Mahn-Mumie...' Zur Rezeption eines HERODOTeischen Motivs: Hermes 118 (1990) 292-301.

d217 *Wrede* Henning, Die opera de' Pili von 1542 und das Berliner Sarkophagcorpus; zur Geschichte der Sarkophagforschung, Hermeneutik und klassischer Archäologie: JbDAI 104 (1989) 373-414; 11 fig.

T3.9 *Numismatica,* **coins.**

d218 **Alföldi** Andreas & Elisabeth [c. 1940] ²ʳᵉᵛ[*Cameron* Alan, *al.*], Die Kontorniat-Medaillons [I. c. 1976] II, Text: AMUGS 6/2. B 1990, de Gruyter. xxiii-455 p.; 64 pl. DM 348. – ᴿAJA 95 (1991) 755s (W. E. *Metcalf*: Nero-portraits, 4th-5th century Zeitgeist...).

d219 **Alteri** Giancarlo, Tipologia delle monete della Repubblica di Roma (con particolare riferimento al denario); Catalogo della Mostra, Salone Sistino 21.IV-30.IX. 1990: ST 337. Vaticano 1990, Biblioteca. xiv-344 p.; CXXVI pl. + 8 color. 88-210-0623-9.

d220 **Amandry** Michel, Le monnayage des duovirs corinthiens 1988 ⇥ 4,e537; 5,d650: ᴿGnomon 63 (1991) 30-33 (Marieluise *Deissmann*).

d221 **Aulock** Hans von, Münzen und Stätte Phrygiens II: IstMitt 27, 1987 ⇥ 4,e542; 5,d653: ᴿAJA 95 (1991) 358-360 (Barbara *Burrell*: in press 1980 when he died in an accident; also reviews TOURATSOGLOU I. 1988).

d222 *Baldus* Hans R., Wankt die karthagische Münzchronologie des 3. Jahrhunderts v.Chr. ? : Chiron 21 (1991) 179-184.

d222* *Barag* Dan P., Gleanings of Jewish art from the coins of Bar Kokhba: BAngIsr 11 (1991s) 44s (lecture summary).

d223 *Bisi* A. M. Quelques remarques sur la coroplastie palestinienne à l'époque perse; tradition locale et emprunts étrangers: ⇥ 636*, Syrie perse 1989, TEuph 3 (1990) 75-84.

d224 *Bland* Roger, Six hoards of Syrian tetradrachms of the third century A.D.; NumC 151 (1991) 1-33; pl. 1-12.

d225 **Burnett** Andrew, Coins. L/Berkeley 1991, British Museum [BAR-W 17/6,4].

d226 **Buttrey** T. V., *al.*, Morgantina [Serra Orlando, Sicilia] studies, II. The coins. Princeton 1989. – ᴿRitNum 93 (1991) 246 (D. *Foraboschi*).

d227 *Caccamo Caltabiano* Maria, *Radici Colace* Paola, Lessico monetale greco: ⇥ 579, Lessici tecnici 1990/1, 139-157 (-163, liste, *Rao* Maria).

d228 **Carson** R. A. G., Coins of the Roman Empire 1990 ⇥ 6,d867; Routledge; 0-415-01591-X: ᴿNumC 151 (1991) 247-250 (H. B. *Mattingly*).

d229 **Cellini** Giuseppina A., *Calabria* Patrizia, L'influsso dei prototipi greci nelle monete romane; proposte per uno studio tipologico. R 1991, Univ. 102 p.; 17 pl.

d230 **Christiansen** E., The Roman coins of Alexandria 1988 ⇥ 4,e554... 6,d870: ᴿActa Numismàtica 19 (Barc 1989) 207s (L. *Villaronga*); Gnomon 62 (1991) 753-5 (Alessandra *Gara*).

d231 *Colenko* V. K., ❸ Coin weight dualism under Seleucus I: VDI 196 (1991) 100-116; Eng. 116-7.

d232 *Coltelloni-Trannoy*, Le monnayage des rois Juba II et Ptolomée de Maurétanie; image d'une adhésion réiterée à la politique romaine: Karthago 22 (1990) 45-53.

d233 *Consolo Langher* Sebastiana Nerina, Oriente persiano-ellenistico e Sicilia; trasmissione e circolazione di un messaggio ideologico attraverso i documenti numismatici: RÉAnc 92 (1990) 30-44; 2 pl.; franç. 29, Eng. 30.

d234 **Davesne** A., *Le Rider* G., Le trésor de Meydancikkale (Cilicie Trachée, 1980), Gülnar II, 1989 ⇥ 6,d874: ᴿPhoenix 45 (1991) 177-180 (L. *Mi-*

geotte); RitNum 93 (1991) 245s (D. *Foraboschi*); RNum 33 (1991) 289-291 (M. *Amandry*); TopO 1 (1991) 108-121 (F. *Planet*).

d235 *Draganov* Dimitar,   An unknown gold medallion of Julian the Apostate: NumC 151 (1991) 215s.

d236 *Elayi* Josette,   Remarques méthodologiques sur l'étude paléographique des légendes monétaires phéniciennes: → 630, Phoinikeia 1989/91, 187-200; 1 pl.

d237 *Elayi* Josette & Alain G.,   Trésor d'époque perse de la région d'Arwad: RNum 32 (1990) 7-17.

d238 *Fischer* Thomas,   Literaturüberblicke der griechischen Numismatik: Estudis numismàtics valencíans 5.   Valencia 1990, Generalitat.   165 p.; 5 pl. Seleukiden (Nachtrag 1984-89): Chiron 21 (1991) 425-464.

d239 **García Bellido** M. P.,   El tesoro de Mogente y su entorno monetal: RRStFen 19 (1991) 135-7 (L.-J. *Manfredi*).

d240 *García Garrido* M.,   El hallazgo de Villarrubia de los Ojos (Segunda guerra púnica, final siglo III a.C.): AcNum 20 (1990) 37-78; 152 fig.

d241 **Hare** K. W.,   Civic coins and civic politics in the Roman East 1987 → 5,d669:   RFaventia 12s (1990s) 465s (F. *Gascó*); RNum 33 (1991) 297-9 (F. *Rebuffat*).

d242 *Hatamleh* M. M., ❹ [comments on] Coinage of the ancient and Islamic world;   ADAJ 35 (1991) 31-36; 4 pl. [❹ 41-48, 4 pl. *Goussous* N.].

d243 **Hill** P. V.,   The monuments of ancient Rome as coin types 1989 → 6,d883:   RJRS 81 (1991) 211s (R. H. *Darwall-Smith*, also on EBARTON I. 1989; THORNTON M. & R. 1989).

d244 *Houghton* Arthur,   Some Alexander coinages of Seleucus I with anchors: MeditArch 4 (1991) 99-117; pl. 3-5.

d245 **Johnston** Ann,   The coinage of Metapontum 3: NumNMg 164.   NY 1990, American Numismatic Soc.   ix-102 p.; 21 pl. [RÉG 104,679].

d246 **Jones** John M., A dictionary of ancient Roman coins. L 1990 [? Seaby]. – RNumC 151 (1991) 250s (R. *Bland*).

d247 **Kaenel** Hans-Markus von,   Münzprägung und Münzbildnis des Claudius: AntMünzen 9, 1986 → 3,d970... 5,d676:   RNumC 151 (1991) 257-260 (C. L. *Clay*: 'a new era in our knowledge of Claudius' coinage').

d248 *Karbach* Franz-B.,   Die Münzprägung der Stadt Augusta in Kilikien [Saros/Şeyhan Ostufer], I: JbNumG 40 (1990) 35-68; 130 fig.

d249 *Karwiese* Stefan,   The Artemisium coin-hoard and the first coins of Ephesus: RBgNum 137 (1991) 1-28.

d250 **Klose** Dietrich O.,   Die Münzprägung von Smyrna D1987 → 4,e577; 6,d887:   RRNum 33 (1991) 299s (F. *Rebuffat*).

d251 *Koch* Heidemarie,   A hoard of coins from Eastern Parthia: NumNMg 165.   NY/Malibu 1990. 64 p.; 12 pl. – RJbNumG 40 (1990) 122 (D. O. A. *Klose*).

d252 KRAAY Colin M., MØRKHOLM Otto, mem., Numismatic Studies, ELe Rider G., *al.*: NumLov 10, 1989 → 5,113:   RRNum 33 (1991) 282-8 (M. *Amandry*).

d253 *a*) *Kutaisov* V. A., ❽ Kerkinitidian [now Eupatoria] coins of the fifth century B.C. [NW Black Sea]; – *b*) *Anfimov* I. N., ❽ A hoard of Pantikapaion copper coins of the early third century B.C. from the eastern littoral of the sea of Azov: VDI 196 (1991) 40-68; 6 fig.; Eng. 68 / 70-77; 5 fig.; Eng. 77.

d254 **Lahusen** Götz,   Die Bildnismünzen der römischen Republik 1989 → 6, d889:   RSalesianum 53 (1991) 165s (R. *Gottlieb*).

d255 *Lemaire* André, *Elayi* Josette, Les monnaies de Byblos au sphinx et au faucon; nouveaux documents et essai de classement: RBgNum 137 (1991) 29-37; pl. I.

d256 *Levante* Edoardo, Cilician coinage [Trajan to Gallienus; 3 centers]: NumC 151 (1991) 205-215.

d257 *Levy* Abraham H., The making of coin dies [150 publications on the subject never mention the lost-wax method, used exclusively for non-ferrous coins, from 4th millennium B.C.E. (!) to 1700 C.E.]: → 14*, BALOG P., mem., IsrNumJ 10 (1988s) 137-141; pl. 22, 1-5.

d258 *Liampi* Katerini, Ein numismatisches Zeugnis für den Bund der perrhaibischen Tripolis [Pythion ... Thermaischer Golf] im zweiten Viertel des 4. Jh. v.Chr.: JbNumG 40 (1990) 11-22; 1 pl.

d259 **Lindgren** Henry C., Ancient Greek bronze coins, European mints. San Mateo 1989, Chrysopylon. xx-89 p.; 89 pl. – ᴿNumC 151 (1991) 230-2 (J. *Morcom*, Jennifer *Warren*).

d260 [*Schwabacher* Willy, catalog] ᴱ**Lorber** Catharine C., Amphipolis; the civic coinage in silver and gold. LA 1990, Numismatic Fine Arts. iv-196 p.; 31 pl. $87.50. 0-9626-9870-9 [Schweiz. Numism. Rundschau 71, 210-3, Dominique *Gerin*]. – ᴿJbNumG 40 (1990) 117-120 (D. O. A. *Klose*).

d261 **Martin** Thomas H., Sovereignty and coinage in classical Greece 1985 → 2,a479 ... 5,d681: ᴿRNum 33 (1991) 292-5 (D. *Gerin*).

d262 *a*) *Masson* Olivier, Notes de numismatique chypriote; – *b*) *Le Rider* Georges, Les trouvailles monétaires dans le temple d'Artémis à Sardes (IGCH 1299 et 1300); – *c*) *Sweeney* William B., *Visonà* Paolo, A hoard of Antoniniani from the Mount of Olives: RNum 33 (1991) 60-70; 4 fig.; pl. IX-X / 71-88; 3 fig. / 263-8; 1 fig.; pl. XVIII.

d263 *Medas* S., Monete puniche da Ravenna: RStFen 19 (1991) 27-32.

d264 *Mildenberg* L., Gaza mint authorities in Persian time; preliminary studies of the local coinage in the fifth Persian satrapy [1. ᶠ*Thompson* M. 1979, 183-196; 2. ErIsr 19 (1987) 29-35; 3. awaited]; 4: → 636*, Syrie Perse 1989, TEuph 2 (1990) 137-146; pl. IV-VII.

d265 **Mørkholm** Otto †, ᴱ*Grierson* Philip, *Westermark* Ulla, Early Hellenistic Coinage; from the accession of Alexander to the Peace of Apamea (336-188 B.C.). C 1991, Univ. xxii-273 p.; 638 fig.; end-maps. 0-521-39504-6.

d266 **Münsterberg** [not Münsterberger as → 3,d984] Rudolf, Die Beamtennamen auf den griechischen Münzen, geographisch und alphabetisch geordnet: SubsEpig 3. Hildesheim 1985 = 1911-27, Olms. 274 + 81 p. 3-487-05059-5.

d267 *a*) *Naster* Paul, Remarque complémentaire concernant les carrés creux des monnaies de Zancle; – *b*) *Elayi* Josette & *Alain* G., Un trésor de monnaies séleucides de la Trouée de Homs: → 9, ᶠARSLAN E., Monetazione 1 (1991) 25-34 / 157-162 + pl. 38-39.

d267* **Nicolaou** Ino, The [839] coins of the house of Dionysos [+ 122 from Odeion, Gymnasion, Asklepieion]: Paphos 2. Nicosia 1900, Dept. Antiquities. xi-227 p.; XVI pl. 99-6336-415-2 [RBgNum 138,182, P. *Naster*].

d268 *Oddy* Andrew, Arab imagery on early Umayyad coins in Syria and Palestine; evidence for falconry: NumC 151 (1991) 59-66; pl. 19-20.

d269 *Picozzi* Vittorio, Considerazioni su una rara moneta d'oro di Costantino I coniata ad Aquileia: RitNum 93 (1991) 135-142.

d270 **Potts** D. T., The pre-Islamic coinage of eastern Arabia; appendix *Boucharlat* Rémy, *Drieux* Monique: C. Niebuhr Publ. 14. K 1991, Univ. 119 p.; ill. 87-7289-156-4.

d270* *Potts* D. T., Pre-Alexandrine Phoenician staters from northern Arabia: ArabArchEp 2 (1991) 24-30.

d271 *Preda* Constantin. Prämonetäre Zahlungsmittel in Form von Pfeil-spitzen an der West- und Nordküste des Schwarzen Meeres: Klio 73 (1991) 20-27; 18 fig.

d271* ᴱR(adnoti)-**Alföldi** M., Methoden der antiken Numismatik: WegFor 529, 406 p.; 53 pl. DM 98; sb. 79 [Gymnasium 99,78, T. *Fischer*].

d272 **Sutherland** C. H. V., Roman history and coinage 44 B.C. - A.D. 69; fifty points of relation from Julius Caesar to Vespasian 1987 ➤ 3,d995... 5,d699: ᴿHZ 253 (1991) 416-8 (M. *R.-Alföldi*).

d272* **Thompson** Margaret † 29.II.1992, Alexander's drachm mints, II: Lampsacus and Abydus: NumSt 19. NY 1991, Amer. Numism. Soc. 77 p., 34 pl. $35. 0-89722-241-5 [RBgNum 138,181, F. de *Callatay*].

d273 **Touratsoglu** Ioannis, Die Münzstätte von Thessaloniki in der römischen Kaiserzeit (32/31 v.Chr. bis 268 n.Chr.): DAI Ant. Münz. 12, 1988 ➤ 6,d902: ᴿAnzAltW 44 (1991) 112-5 (W. *Szaivert*); RNum 33 (1991) 301s (F. *Rebuffat*).

d274 **Turcan** R., Nigra moneta 1987 ➤ 6,d903: ᴿLatomus 50 (1991) 241 (B. *Remy*).

d275 *Vanni* Franca Maria, Alcuni aspetti dell'iconografia di Dioniso nella monetazione di Leptis Magna: ➤ 573, Dionysos 1989/91, 217-222 + 8 fig.

d276 *Vermeeren* Thierry, Le type legio dans le monnayage de Septime Sévère: RBgNum 137 (1991) 65-94; pl. IV.

d277 *Villaronga* L., *Assaig-balanç* dels volums de les emissions monetàries de bronze a la Península Ibèrica d'abans [avant] d'August: AcNum 20 (1990) 19-35.

d278 **Vismara** Novella, Monetazione arcaica della Lycia I-II: StudRNum 2s. Mi 1989, Ennerre. 155 p.; 360 p. – ᴿNumC 151 (1991) 232-7 (J. *Spier*).

d279 *a) Westermark* Ulla, Bronze coins of Pergamon; – *b) Le Rider* Georges, Ephèse [drachmes] et Arados au IIᵉ siècle avant notre ère: Numismata AntClas 20 (Lugano 1991) 147-157 + 2 pl. / 193-210 + 2 pl.

Yadin Y. (*Meshorer* Y.) Masada coins 1989 ➤ d378.

d280 **Ziegler** Ruprecht, Münzen Kilikiens aus kleineren deutschen Samm-lungen: Vestigia 42. Mü 1989, Beck. 202 p.; 72 pl. – ᴿAnzAltW 44 (1991) 109s (W. *Szaivert*).

T4 *Situs, excavation-sites* .1 *Chronica, bulletins.*

d281 ᴱ*Aurenche* Olivier, Chronique archéologique; Syrie, Jordanie: Syria 67 (1990) 435-470 / 471-482; ill.; index.

d282 ᶠCORBO V., Christian archaeology in the Holy Land; new discoveries, ᴱ**Bottini** G. C., *al.* 1990 ➤ 6,39: ᴿRB 98 (1991) 615-7 (J. *Murphy-O'Connor*).

d283 Excavations and surveys [signed, infra]: IsrEJ 41 (1991) 176-205; map. *Piccirillo* M., 1991 ➤ d465; *de Vries* B. 1991 ➤ d462.

T4.2 *Situs effossi,* **syntheses.**

d284 ᴱ**Åström** Paul, High, middle or low? chronology 1987/9 ➤ 5,831*: ᴿBO 48 (1991) 911-7 (R. S. *Merrillees*: also on other SIMA projects, all with high praise).

d285 *a) Ben-Tor* Amnon, [En-Beşor] New light on the relations between Egypt and southern Palestine during the Early Bronze Age; – *b) Bietak* Manfred, Egypt and Canaan in the Middle Bronze Age: BASOR 281 (1991) 3-10 [11-26, *Ward* William A., comments] / 27-72 [73-79, *Dever* William G., rejoinder]; ClasR 41 (1991) 426-9 (Diane L. *Bolger*).

d286 **Cree** Fernand-J. de, 'Mutatis mutandis'; Egyptian relations with Palestine in the Chalcolithic and Early Bronze Age I-IV: GöMiszÄg 124 (1991) 21-42.

d287 **Earle** Timothy J., The wars of the Philistines in the Early Iron Age: diss. Golden Gate Baptist Theol. Sem., ᴰ*Eakins* J.K. Mill Valley 1990. 256 p. 91-22775. – DissA 1039-A.

d288 **Ehrlich** Carl S., From defeat to conquest; a history of the Philistines in decline [ca. 1000 - ca. 730 B.C. (until defeated by Tiglath-Pileser III)]: diss. Harvard, ᴰ*Cross* F. CM 1991. 381 p. 91-32084. – HarvTR 84 (1991) 471s; DissA 52 (1991s) 1851-A.

d289 **Esse** Douglas L., Subsistence, trade, and social change in Early Bronze Age Palestine [< diss. Chicago 1982, ᴰ*Stager* L.]: SAOC 50. Ch 1991, Univ. Oriental Inst. xvii-219 p.; 36 fig.; 9 pl. 0-918986-66-4 [OIAc F91,7].

Finkelstein Israel, The archaeology of the Israelite settlement 1988 (➤ 4, e629; 6,d921) ➤ 2366.

d290 *Finkelstein* Israel, The central hill country in the Intermediate Bronze Age: IsrEJ 41 (1991) 19-45; 15 fig.

d290* **Gal** Zvi, Lower Galilee during the Iron Age [diss. TA 1982], ᵀ*Josephy* Martha R.: ASOR diss. 8. WL 1992, Eisenbrauns. ix-118 p. 0-931464-69-2 [OIAc 2,19].

d291 *Geus* C.H.J. de, The material culture of Phoenicia and Israel: ➤ 445, Phoenicia 1990/1, 11-16.

d292 **Hanbury-Tenison** J.W., Late Chalcolithic-EBI transition in Palestine and Transjordan 1986 ➤ 5,d984 (Jerash/Mutawwah): ᴿPEQ 123 (1991) 137s (K. *Prag*).

d293 **James** Peter, *al.*, Centuries of darkness; a challenge to the conventional chronology of Old World archaeology [all that archeologists ascribe to the years 1200-950 never really existed; *Renfrew* preface accepts]. L 1991, J. Cape. xxii-434 p. £20. 0-224-02647-X. – ᴿBAngIsr 11 (1991s) 35-38 (J. *Mellaart*: just the fact that evidence so far available is unsatisfactory does not justify thus theorizing without evidence); CamArchJ 1,2 (1991) 227-253 (James + *Kitchen* K., *Kemp* B., *Postgate* N., *Snodgrass* A., *Sherratt* A. & P.).

d294 **Joffe** Alexander H., Settlement and society in Early Bronze I and II Canaan: diss. Arizona, ᴰ*Dever* W. 1991. 559 p. 91-25460. – DissA 52 (1991s) 1402s-A.

d295 *Joffe* Alexander H., Early Bronze I and the evolution of social complexity in the southern Levant: JMeditArch 4 (1991) 3-58.

d296 **Kuhnen** Hans-Peter, Palästina in griechisch-römischer Zeit 1990 ➤ 6, d926: ᴿDLZ 112 (1991) 204s (B. *Brentjes*).

d296* **Liverani** Mario, Prestige and interest; international relations in the Near East ca. 1600-1100 B.C. Padova 1990. – ᴿVT 41 (1991) 493s (Joan *Oates*).

d297 *Mazzoni* Stefania, Tell Afis and the chronology of Iron Age in Syria: ➤ AnASyr 40 (1989/90) 76-83 + 12 fig.; ❹ 149-151.

d298 **Palumbo** Gaetano, The Early Bronze Age IV in the southern Levant; settlement patterns, economy, and material culture of a 'Dark Age':

CMatAr 3 (1990). R 1991, Univ. 243 p. + 68 fig.; 12 pl.; 63 maps + finder-maps. Lit. 60.000.

d299 **Randsborg** Klaus, The first millennium A.D. in Europe and the Mediterranean; an archaeological essay. C 1991, Univ. xvi-230 p.; 83 fig.; 9 pl. 0-521-38401-X; pa. -787-6.

d300 *Weinstein* James, Egypt and the MB II / LB IA transition in Palestine: Levant [21 (1989) 181-193, J. *Hoffmeier*] 23 (1991) 105-115; 116-124, Hoffmeier rejoinder.

d301 **Weippert** Helga, Palästina in vorhellenistischer Zeit 1988 ➤ 4,e639... 6,d929: ᴿBLtg 63 (1990) 245s (L. *Schwienhorst-Schönberger*); JAOS 111 (1991) 645-8 (W. G. *Dever*); Orientalia 60 (1991) 135 (A. J. *Frendo*); RB 98 (1991) 439-442 (R. *Donceel*).

d302 *Weippert* Helga, Metallzeitalter und Kulturepochen: ZDPV 107 (1991) 1-23: die palästinische Archäologie erhielt 1890 das chronologische Gerüst, das sie bis heute trägt.

d303 *Wood* Bryant G., The Philistines enter Canaan; were they Egyptian lackeys or invading conquerors?: BAR-W 17/6 (1991) 44-52.89; (color.) ill.

T4.3 **Jerusalem,** *archaeologia et historia.*

d304 ᴱ**Asali** K. J., Jerusalem in history 1989 ➤ 6,d933: ᴿRB 98 (1991) 632 (J. *Murphy-O'Connor*); RelStR 17 (1991) 134 (I. J. *Boullata*). ➤ d319.

d304* **Avigad** N., The Herodian quarter in Jerusalem: Wohl Archaeological Museum. J 1991, Keter. 80 p.; (color) ill.

d305 **Bahat** Dan, (*Rubenstein* Chaim T.), The illustrated atlas of Jerusalem 1990 ➤ 6,d934; pref. *Mazar* B.; *Meyers* E.; ᵀ*Ketko* Shlomo: ᴿBA 54 (1991) 113s (J. D. *Purvis*); BAR-W 17,5 (1991) 4 (O. *Borowski*); Qadmoniot 24 (1991) 62-64 (H. *Geva* ❿); TS 52 (1991) 586s (K. G. *O'Connell*).

d306 *a) Bahat* Dan, The Western Wall tunnels: Ariel 94 (J 1991) 54-84; color foldout. – *b) King* Philip J., Exploring the valleys of Jerusalem: BR 7,2 (1991) 28-33.52.

d307 **Ben-Arieh** Y., Jerusalem in the nineteenth century [1. 1984 ➤ 1,d418], 2. Emergence of the New City. NY 1986, St. Martin's. xiii-509 p.; 60 fig.; 30 maps. £25. – ᴿPEQ 122 (1990) 73s (M. *Hannam*).

d308 **Blok** H., *Steiner* M., De onderste steen boven; opgravingen in Jerusalem. Kampen 1991, Kok. 154 p. 90-242-3170-1 [BL 92,27, J. *Day*].

d309 **Borgehammar** Stephan, How the Holy Cross was found; from event to medieval legend: BtTPr 47. Sto 1991, Almqvist & W. viii-326 p. [TR 88,165]. 91-22-01432-2.

d310 *Cahill* Jane, *al.,* Scientists examine remains of ancient bathroom [Jerusalem city of David]: BAR-W 17,3 (1991) 64-69; ill.

d311 **Cardini** Franco, Gerusalemme d'oro, di rame, di luce; pellegrini, crociati, sognatori d'Oriente fra XI e XV secolo: La Cultura. Mi 1991, Saggiatore. xi-402 p.

d312 **Cohen** Amnon, Economic life in Ottoman Jerusalem 1989 ➤ 6,d940: ᴿJAOS 111 (1991) 603s (A.-K. *Rafeq*); JESHO 34 (1991) 372-6 (Suraiya *Faroqhi*, also on GERBER H., Bursa).

d313 *Daoust* J., L'histoire de Jérusalem à la citadelle [I. Routes bibliques...] II: EsprVie 101 (1991) 438-440.

d314 **Durst** Stefan, Der Status von Jerusalem als ökumenisches Problem im 20. Jahrhundert: ev. Diss. ᴰ*Raiser* K. Bochum 1991s. – RTLv 23, p. 566.

d315 *Eibeschitz* A., ⊕ The great court and the gates: Sinai 105,1 (1990) 1-21 [< JStJud 22,192].

d315* **Elon** Amos, Jerusalem, city of mirrors. Boston 1989, Little, Brown. $20. 0-316-23389-9. – ᴿChrCent 107 (1990) 575 (M. *Krupnick*).

d316 **Fleckenstein** K.-H., *Müller* W., Jérusalem, ville sainte des trois monothéismes 1989 ⇒ 6,d948; F 245: ᴿChristus 37 (P 1990) 210s (Brigitte *Haviland*).

d316* **Fleckenstein** Karl-Heinz, Wanderer, kommst du nach Jerusalem? [150] Anekdoten und Geschichten aus der Heiligen Stadt. FrB 1990, Herder. 208 p.; 16 color. pl. [RB 98,634].

d317 **Foerster** Frank, Mission im Heiligen Land; der Jerusalems-Verein zu Berlin 1852-1945: MissWFor 25. Gü 1991, Mohn. 286 p. [TR 88,79].

d318 **Franken** H. J., *Steiner* M. L., Excavations in Jerusalem 1961-7, II. The Iron Age extramural quarter on the south-east hill 1990 ⇒ 6,d949: ᴿBAR-W 17,4 (1991) 4.6.9s (H. *Shanks*).

d319 *a*) *Franken* H. J., Jerusalem in the Bronze Age, 3000-1000 B.C.; – *b*) *Mendenhall* G. E., ... 1000-63 B.C.; – *c*) *Wilkinson* J., ... Rome/Byz; – *d*) *Duri* A., ... Islamic; – *e*) *Hiyari* M. A., ... Crusader; + al.: ⇒ d304 supra, ᴱ*Asali* K. J., Jerusalem in history 1989 ...

Galambush Julie, Jerusalem in the Book of Ezekiel; the city as Yahweh's wife, ᴰ1991 ⇒ 3520.

d320 *Greenhut* Zvi, Discovery of the Caiaphas family tomb [Jerusalem Talpiyyot Peace Forest, loculus IV, ossuary 3]: Jerusalem Perspective 4, 4s (1991) 6.11 (13-21, the ossuary inscriptions, *Reich* Ronny; 23-28, Caiaphas, *Flusser* David). ⇒ d337.

d321 **Idinopulos** Thomas A., Jerusalem blessed, Jerusalem cursed; Jews, Christians, and Muslims in the Holy City from David's time to our own. ... 1991, Ivan R. Dee. 368 p. $30 [JAAR 59,882]. – ᴿChrCent 108 (1991) 1170 (D. *Peretz*).

d322 **Jeremias** Joachim, Gerusalemme al tempo di Gesù 1989 ⇒ 5,d746; 6,d951: ᴿProtestantesimo 46 (1991) 76s (G. *Scuderi*: appendice sulla situazione sociale della donna); Teresianum 42 (1991) 341s (V. *Pasquetto*).

d323 *a*) *Kaufhold* Hubert, Der Ehrentitel 'Jerusalempilger' (syrisch *maqd-šaya*, arabisch *maqdisî*, armenisch *mahtesi*); – *b*) *Palmer* Andrew, The history of the Syrian Orthodox in Jerusalem [I]: OrChr 75 (1991) 44-61 / 16-43.

d323* **Kaufmann** H. G., *al.*, Wege der Sehnsucht – Jerusalem. Mü 1990, Süddeutscher. 192 p. DM 78. – ᴿTGegw 34 (1991) 68s (J. *Romelt*).

d324 *a*) *Kloner* Amos, *Stark* Harley, A burial cave on Mount Scopus, Jerusalem; – *b*) *Nadelman* Yonatan, Vessels from a *Favissa* of the First Temple: BAngIsr 11 (1991s) 7-17; 9 fig. / 18-21; 1 fig.

d325 ᴱ**Küchler** M. [ᶠKEEL O. & H.], Jerusalem; Texte-Bilder-Steine: NOrb 6, 1987 ⇒ 3,e48; 4,e667: ᴿNedTTs 45 (1991) 251s (P. W. van der *Horst*).

d325* *a*) *Küchler* Max, Moscheen und Kalifenpaläste Jerusalems nach der Aphrodito-Papyri; – *b*) *Busse* Heribert, Zur Geschichte und Deutung der frühislamischen Ḥaram bauten in Jerusalem: ZDPV 107 (1991) 120-143 / 144-154.

d326 *Laperrousaz* E.-M., Quelques remarques sur le tracé de l'enceinte de la ville et du temple de Jérusalem à l'époque perse: Syria 67 (1990) 609-631; 11 fig.

d327 *Magness* Jodi, The walls of Jerusalem in the Early Islamic period [... more Umayyad activity than was previously thought]: BA 54 (1991) 208-217; ill.

d328 **Meinardus** Otto, Die Heilige Woche in Jerusalem; ein Tagebuch eines Reiseleiters. Wü 1988, Catholica Unio. 365 p.

d328* *Na'aman* Nadav, ✪ The boundaries of the kingdom of Jerusalem in the second millennium B.C.E.: Zion 56 (1991) 361-380.

d329 *a) Niccacci* Alviero, The city of Yahweh; Jerusalem in prophetic tradition; – *b) Schoenstene* Robert, An image of the Promised Land; Jerusalem in Isaiah; – *c) Hoppe* Leslie J., 'Remember Zion and the law'; the fall of Jerusalem according to Baruch 15; – *d) Reid* Barbara, The centerpiece of salvation-history; Jerusalem in the Gospel of Luke; – *e) Sharkey* Sarah A., A vision of hope; the new Jerusalem in the book of Revelation: BToday 29 (1991) 5-7 / 9-13 / 15-19 / 20-24 / 25-31.

d331 **Pellistrandi** Christine, Jérusalem, épouse et mère 1989 ➤ 5,d766; 6,d964: ᴿRevSR 65 (1991) 389s (B. *Renaud*).

d332 **Peters** F.E., Jerusalem and Mecca 1986 ➤ 2,a564... 6,d964*: ᴿBO 48 (1991) 933-5 (G.R. *Hawting*).

d333 **Prag** K., Jerusalem: Blue Guide 1989. ➤ 5,d768; 6,d967: ᴿPEQ 122 (1990) 62s (M. *Hannam*: excellent; very minor reserves).

d334 *Prag* Kay, An early Middle Bronze Age burial in Jerusalem: PEQ 123 (1991) 129-132; 1 fig.

d335 *Pringle* D., Crusader Jerusalem: BAngIsr 10 (1990s) 105-113.

d336 **Purvis** James D., Jerusalem, the Holy City; a bibliography, II [adds 4500 entries to the 5800 of vol. I, 1988 ➤ 4,e680]: ATLA. Metuchen 1991, Scarecrow. 525 p. $49.50 [BA 55,161; TDig 39,282].

d337 *Riesner* Rainer, Wurde das Familiengrab des Hohenpriesters Kajaphas entdeckt?: BiKi 46 (1991) 82-84.

d337* *Ritmeyer* Leen, The early development of the Temple mount in Jerusalem: BAngIsr 11 (1991s) 46 + plan (lecture summary).

d338 **Rosen-Ayalon** Myriam, The Early Islamic monuments of al-Ḥaram: Qedem 28, 1989 ➤ 5,d777; 6,d971: ᴿAJA 95 (1991) 188s (J.M. *Bloom*); CritRR 4 (1991) 346s (R. *Schick*); PEQ 123 (1991) 133-5 (F.B. *Flood*).

d339 [**Rustaveli** Čofa] ✪ Les peintures murales de la Sainte Croix à Jérusalem. Tbilisi 1973, Mezniereba. 82 p.; 29 fig.

d340 *Sass* Benjamin, Arabs and Greeks in late First Temple Jerusalem: PEQ 122 (1990) 59-61; 3 fig.

d341 *Schein* S., Jerusalem: ➤ 681, LexMA 5 (1990) 351-6 [-59, *Riley-Smith* J., Königreich/Patriarchat].

d342 **Schütz** Christiane, Preussen in Jerusalem (1800-1861); Karl Friedrich SCHINKELs Entwurf der Grabeskirche und die Jerusalempläne Friedrich Wilhelms IV: Bauwerke von Berlin Beih 19. B 1988, Mann. 192 p.; 77 fig. DM 88. – ᴿHZ 252 (1991) 179s (W. *Elz*).

d343 *Schwartz* Joshua, Once more on the Nicanor Gate: HUCA 62 (1991) 245-281 + 2 plans.

d344 **Shanks** Hershel, Please return the Siloam inscription [from İstanbul] to Jerusalem: BAR-W 17,3 (1991) 58-60.

d345 *Siebecke* Horst, Die Grabeskirche im Osterrummel: EvKom 24 (1991) 228... [< ZIT 91,269].

d346 *Sordi* Marta, La tradizione dell'Inventio crucis in AMBROGIO e in RUFINO: Rivista di Storia della Chiesa in Italia 44 (1990) 1-9 [< RSPT 75,171].

d347 *Strange* J., Jerusalems topografi i hasmonæisk tid; Akra-problemet: DanTTs 54 (1991) 81-94 [< NTAbs 36,228].

d348 *Swanton* Michael, A further manuscript of the siege of Jerusalem [Titus; Middle English romance]: Scriptorium 44 (Bru 1990) 103s.

d348* *Taylor* Joan E., The Jerusalem ship [drawn recently, not by a 4th century pilgrim; in the Armenian part of] the Church of the Holy Sepulchre: BAngIsr 11 (1991s) 54 (summary of lecture at the Society of Antiquaries, March 1991).

d349 ᴱTrotta Giuseppe, Gerusalemme: Attendendo l'aurora. Brescia 1990, Morcelliana. 208 p. 88-372-1404-9. 12 art.: *Hussar* B., *Sonnet* J., *Rossi de Gasperis* F., *al.*

d350 **Walker** P.W.L., Holy city, holy places? Christian attitudes to Jerusalem and the Holy Land in the fourth century: Early Christian Studies. Ox 1990, Clarendon. xix-438 p. £45. – ᴿBAngIsr 11 (1991s) 40-42 (Joan *Taylor*); JEH 42 (1991) 300-2 (R.A. *Markus*, also on Oosterhout); JRS 81 (1991) 242s (E.D. *Hunt*); JTS 42 (1991) 720-3 (E.J. *Yarnold*); RB 98 (1991) 632-4 (J. *Murphy-O'Connor*: convincingly claims Eusebius downgraded Jerusalem).

d351 ᴱ**Wilson** Eliane, Jerusalem – reflections of eternity. ... c. 1990, Shepheard-Walwyn; paintings by Motke Blum. £29. – ᴿTablet 245 (1991) 78 (J. *Taylor*).

d352 **Yarden** Leon, The spoils of Jerusalem on the Arch of Titus, a re-investigation: Rome Swedish Institute Acta 8/16. Sto 1991, Åström. 137 p.; 134 fig. 91-7042-138-2.

d353 ᴱ**Zarzecki** Anabel, Arqueología de Jerusalén, desde los inicios de la ciudad hasta el período musulmano temprano [reprints]. J 1990, Escuela de estudiantes extranjeros. iv-140 p. [OIAc 1,28].

---

d354 **Arnold** Patrick M., Gibeah...: JStOT supp. 79, 1990 ⇒ 6,d988: ᴿJBL 110 (1991) 701-3 (Diana *Edelman*: witty; < 1986 Emory diss. ᴰ*Miller* J.M.); JTS 42 (1991) 158-160 (B.A. *Mastin*).

T4.4 *Situs alphabetice:* **Judaea, Negeb.**

d355 ʿ**Abda**: *Negev* Avraham, The temple of Obodas; excavations at Oboda in July 1989: IsrEJ 41 (1991) 62-80; 15 fig.

d356 ᴱ**Marks** Anthony, Prehistory and paleoenvironments in the Central Negev, Israel, 1/1-3, The Avdat/Aqev area. Dallas 1976/77/83, Institute for the Study of Earth and Man. viii-383 p.; x-356 p.; xv-349 p. – ᴿBASOR 281 (1991) 85-88 (G.A. *Clark*).

d357 **Negev** A., The late Hellenistic and early Roman pottery of Nabatean Oboda: Qedem 22, 1986 ⇒ 2,a620; 4,e702: ᴿJNES 50 (1991) 66-69 (Z.T. *Fiema*); OLZ 86 (1991) 175-8 (H.M. *Niemann*).

d358 **Arîš**: *Tuell* Steven S., The southern and eastern borders of Abar-Nahara [wadi Arîš and Jordan River, in Herodotus and Pseudo-Scylax as Nm 17; Ezek 47]: BASOR 284 (1991) 51-57.

d358* *Verhoeven* Ursula, Eine Vergewaltigung? Vom Umgang mit einer Textstelle des Naos von El Arish (Tefnut-Studien I); ⇒ 43, ᶠDerchain P., Religion 1991, 319-330.

d359 *Ascalon*: *Stager* Lawrence E., *a)* When Canaanites and Philistines ruled Ashkelon; – *b)* Why were hundreds of dogs buried at Ashkelon? – *c)* Eroticism and infanticide at Ashkelon: BAR-W (1991) 17/2, 24-43; 17/3, 26-42; 17/4, 34-53. 78; all with (color.) ill.; letters 17/4, 66s; 17/6, 12.14 (18, response).

d360 *Batash* (Timnah) 3d 1984-9: ⇒ 407. ASOR 1982/91, 47-67 (G. *Kelm*).

d361 *Beersheba*: **Shereshevski** Joseph, Byzantine urban settlements in the
Negev desert: Beer-Sheva 5. Beersheba 1991, Univ. Negev. 277 p.; 70 pl.; 7
loose maps.

d361* **Commenge-Pellerin** Catherine, La poterie de Safadie (Beershéva) au
IVᵉ millénaire avant l'ère chrétienne; introd. *Perrot* Jean: Cah. Rech.
Franç. J, 5. P 1990, Paléorient. xxiii-261 p.; ill. [0243-0258: OIAc 2,16].

d362 *Gaza*: *Gatier* P. L., Le commerce de Gaza au 6ᵉ siècle: ➤ 128, ᶠRouGÉ
J., Navires 1988, 361-370.

d363 *Halif,* Iron Age cemetery: Qadmoniot 24 (1991) 89-91; ill. (O. *Borowski*, ❸).

d364 *Haror* (Gerar, 6 seasons): Qadmoniot 24 (1991) 2-18 (Eliezer *Oren, al.*
❸); 19, hieratic ostracon (O. *Goldwasser*).

d365 *Hebron*: *Magen* Yiṣhaq, ❸ Elonei Mamre – Herodian cult site:
Qadmoniot 24 (1991) 46-55.

d366 *Herodium*: **Corbo** V. C., Herodion 1989 ➤ 5,d804; 6,e15: ᴿPEQ 122
(1990) 68s (D. M. *Jacobson*: obliquely acknowledges improvements due to
Israelis).

d367 *Ḥorša* (Qadîs) 1980, EB: ʿAtiqot 20 (1991) 177s (M. *Haiman*; ❸ 1*-12*;
flints 169-176, S. *Rosen*).

d368 *'Ira*: *Beit-Arieh* Itzhaq, An Early Bronze Age III settlement at Tel 'Ira
in the northern Negev: IsrEJ 41 (1991) 1-17; 8 fig. (map).

d369 *Jannaba* / taḥta, 1975s Byz.: ʿAtiqot 20 (1991) 111-7; 4 fig. (C.
Dauphin).

d370 *Jericho*: **Bienkowski** Piotr, Jericho LB 1986 ➤ 2,a608 ... 4,e716: ᴿBO
48 (1991) 649-651 (Margaret *Steiner*).

d371 *Daoust* J., Promenade dans Jéricho [*Brossier* François, MondeB 69,
1991; J. *Briend* ajoute que la conquête de Jéricho n'est pas forcément
historique, mais laisse ouverte une lecture religieuse ou liturgique]: Espr-
Vie 101 (1991) 520s.

d372 **Hirschfeld** Yishar, The Judean desert monasteries in the Byzantine
period [50, of which 12 discovered by him]. NHv 1992 [➤ vol. 8], Yale
Univ. xix-305 p. $45. 0-300-04977-3 [TDig 39,169].

d373 *Hirschfeld* Yizhar, Gerasimus and his laura in the Jordan valley: RB
98 (1991) 419-430; 7 fig.; franç. 419.

d374 *Rosenthal* Eliezer S., ❸ Baʿra [Berešit Rabba 76,10; Josephus B,63; a
place named Yarden, for a river (read kᵉnaḥal)]: Tarbis 60 (1990s)
325-353; Eng. I-II.

d375 *Lachish*: *Bleibtreu* Erika, Grisly Assyrian record of torture and death
[Nineveh frieze]: BAR-W 17,1 (1991) 52-61. 75; (color.) ill.

d376 *Mampsis*: **Negev** Avraham, The architecture of Mampsis 1s: Qedem 26,
1988 ➤ 3,d838; 6,e34: ᴿBO 48 (1991) 267 (J. *Wilkinson*).

d377 *Maresha*: Qadmoniot 24 (1991) 70-85; ill. (A. *Kloner*, ❸).

d378 *Masada* I, ᴱ**Yadin** Y. *Naveh* J., The Aramaic coins (*Meshorer* Y.) 1989
➤ 5,9316: ᴿJJS 42 (1991) 271 (G. *Vermes*); JStJud 22 (1991) 269-273 (M.
Mach, also on II ᴱCoTTON H.).

d379 **Netzer** Ehud, Masada III, the Y. Yadin excavations 1963-5, final
reports: The Buildings, Stratigraphy and Architecture. J 1991, Israel
Exploration Society. xxviii-655 p.; 945 fig.; 74 plans (6 foldout). 965-
221-012-9.

d380 *Netzer* Ehud, The last days and hours at Masada: BAR-W 17,6 (1991)
19-32; (color.) ill.

d381 *Miqne*/Ekron, 8th 1990; 11th cent.: ➤ 627*, AJA 95 (1991) 513, fig.
22-27 (T. *Dothan*, S. *Gitin*).

d382 *Smit* E.J., The Saqqara letter; historical implications: JSem 2 (Pretoria 1990) 57-71 [< OTAbs 14,275: from Philistine Ekron; dating under Nebukadnezzar remains more probable than Sennacherib].

d383 *Negeb:* **Rubin** Rehav, ⊕ The Negev as a settled land [Byzantine period] < diss. Hebr. Univ. J 1990. 200 p. – ᴿIsrEJ 41 (1991) 305s (Hannah *Katzenstein*).

d384 **Sharon** M., *Halloun* Moïn, Ancient rock inscriptions. Nafha 1990.

d385 *Nessana:* BAngIsr 10 (1990s) 103s (D. *Urman*, lecture summary).

d386 *Qitmit: Beit-Arieh* I., The Edomite shrine at Horvat Qitmit in the Judean Negev: TAJ 18 (1991) 93-116; ill. [< ZAW 18 (1991) 282].

d387 *Radum ḥ* (Negeb): Qadmoniot 24 (1991) 86-89 (I. *Beit-Arieh*, ⊕).

d388 *Rehovot* (Negeb): **Tsafrir** Yoram, Excavations at Rehovot I., N. Church: Qedem 25, 1988 → 4,e737: ᴿAJA 95 (1991) 186-8 (Claudine M. *Dauphin*); CritRR 4 (1991) 342-4 (R. *Schick*).

d389 *Shiqmim* 1987: → 407, ᴱ*Rast* W., ASOR 1982/91, 29-46 (T. *Levy, al.*).

d390 *Timna:* **Rothenberg** Beno, *al.*, The Egyptian mining temple at Timna I 1988 → 4,e742: ᴿJEA 77 (1991) 207s (S. R. *Snape*).

d390* *'Uza: Beit-Arieh* Itzhak, *Cresson* Bruce C., Ḥorvat 'Uza, a fortified outpost on the eastern Negev border: BA 54 (1991) 126-135 (-145, *Tatum* Lynn, King Manasseh).

d391 *Yarmut* 7th/8th 1989s, EB: IsrEJ 41 (1991) 200-205 / 286-292; 4 fig. (P. de *Miroschedji*).

d392 **Miroschedji** P. de, Yarmouth I. 1988 → 4,e744*; 5,d857: ᴿBO 48 (1991) 651-3 (U. *Hübner*); Syria 67 (1990) 323s (H. de *Contenson*).

T4.5 Samaria, Sharon.

d393 *Aphek* (Ras al-'Ayn): **Kokhavi** Moshe, Aphek in Canaan; the Egyptian governor's residence and its finds. J 1990, Israel Museum. xxix-43 p.; ill.; maps. 965-278-081-2.

d393* *Apollonia:* **Roll** Israel: *Ayalon* Eitan, ⊕ Apollonia... TA 1989, Meuchad. 354 p. [OIAc 2,26].

d394 *Caesarea M.* 10th 1982: → 407, ASOR 1982/91, 69-94 (R.J. *Bull, al.*).

d395 *Gersht* Rivka, Dionysiac sarcophagi from Caesarea Maritima: IsrEJ 41 (1991) 145-156; 13 fig.

d396 *Hirschfeld* Y., *Birger-Calderon* R., Early Roman and Byzantine estates near Caesarea: IsrEJ 41 (1991) 81-111; 29 fig. (map).

d397 **Holum** K.G., King Herod's dream, Caesarea... 1988 → 4,e753: ᴿPEQ 122 (1990) 67s (D. M. *Jacobson*).

d398 **Holum** Kenneth A., From the director's chair; starting a new dig: BAR-W 17,1 (1991) 34-39.

d399 *Labbé* Gilbert, Ponce Pilate et la munificence de Tibère; l'inscription de Césarée: RÉAnc 93 (1991) 277-297; Eng. 277; still undeciphered; [munu]s Tiberieum is likeliest, probably referring to the gift of a library.

d400 *Vann* Robert L., *a)* The Drusion, a candidate for Herod's lighthouse at Caesarea Maritima: IntJNaut 20 (1991) 123-139; 21 fig. – *b)* Underwater excavations in Herod's harbor at Caesarea Maritima: ArchNews 16 (Athens GA 1991) 61-70; 12 fig.

d401 *Carmelus:* **Kuhnen** Hans-P., NW-Palästina hellen.-röm. ... Karmelgebiet 1987 → 3,e160 ... 5,d869: ᴿJAOS 111 (1991) 140s (E. M. *Meyers*, D. J. *Drake*).

d402 *Dor* 1988s: IsrEJ 41 (1991) 46-61; 5 fig. (E. *Stern, al.*).

d403 *Stern* E., The Dor province in the Persian period in the light of recent excavations at Dor: ⇥ 636*, TEuph 2 (1989/90) 147-153; franç. 147.

d404 *Stern* Ephraim, Phoenicians, Sikils [a tribe of Sea Peoples] and Israelites in the light of recent excavations at Tel Dor: ⇥ 445, Phoenicians 1990/1, 85-94; 3 fig.

d405 *Gera* Dov, *Cotton* Hannah M., A dedication from Dor to a governor of Syria [in Greek]: IsrEJ 41 (1991) 258-266.

d406 *Farʿah-N*: **Mallet** Joël, Tell el-Farah II. Le Bronze Moyen 1988 ⇥ 4,a763; 6,e80 (1987): ᴿSyria 67 (1990) 524s (P. *Amiet*).

d407 *Gezer* 1990 (continuing 1984), 'Solomonic gate' in fact twelfth century: IsrEJ 41 (1991) 280-6; 4 fig.; map (W. *Dever*, R. *Younker*) despite FIN-KELSTEIN, *al.* in BASOR 277s (1990).

d408 *Gezer* 1990, Outer Wall, 'Solomonic' gate; AndrUnS 29 (1991) 19-33 + 19 pl. (R. W. *Younker*).

d409 **Gitin** Seymour, A ceramic typology of the Late Iron II, Persian and Hellenistic periods at Tell Gezer: Gezer 3 / HUC Annual 3, 1990 ⇥ 6,a86: ᴿBAR-W 17,2 (1991) 9.

d410 *Ḥiraf*: **Hirschfeld** Y., Khirbet Khiraf, a 2nd-c. fort in the Jordan valley [near mid-Jericho-BethShan road]: JRomArch 4 (AA 1991) 170-183 [< NTAbs 36,78].

d411 *Izbet Ṣarṭa*: **Finkelstein** Israel, Izbet Sarṭa... BAR-Int 299, 1986 ⇥ 4,e766*: ᴿBASOR 184 (1991) 77-90 (W. G. *Dever*, also on his 1988 Settlement).

d412 *Jaffa*: ⇥ 681, LexMA 5 (1990) 269s (S. *Schein*).

d413 *Kaplan* Haya R., Parallelism between Naḥal Lākīs and the sites in the Yarqōn valley: ZDPV 107 (1991) 24-27.

d413* *Michal*: ᴱHerzog Ze'ev, *al.*, Excavations at Tel Michal. TA/Mp 1988 / Univ. 462 p. – ᴿBAR-W 17,3 (1991) 4.6 (J. D. *Seger*).

d414 *Netiv Hagdud*, early neolithic village site in the Jordan Valley: JField 18 (1991) 405-4; 13 fig. (O. *Bar-Yosef, al.*).

d415 *Ono* (Lydda): *Sapin* J., *a*) Recherches sur les ressources et les fonctions économiques du secteur d'Ono à l'époque perse: TEuph 4 (1991) 51-62 [< ZAW 104,283]. – *b*) Sur le statut politique du secteur d'Ono à l'époque perse: ⇥ 140, ᶠSMYTH-FLORENTIN F. 1991, 31-42; map 43.

d416 *Qanah* (W. Samaria): cave, 'treasures' [sickle-flints, (incised-) decorated jars shown]: Qadmoniot 24 (1991) 23-31 (Z. *Tsuk*, A. *Gopher* Ⓗ).

d417 *Qatzin*: *Killebrew* Ann, *Fine* Steven, Qatzin; reconstructing village life in Talmudic times: BAR-W 17,3 (1991) 44-56.

d419 *Ramla*: *Singer* Amy, The countryside of Ramle in the sixteenth century; a study of villages with computer assistance [sic]: JESHO 33 (1990) 51-79.

d420 *Samaria*: *Briend* J., Samarie [*Lemaire* A., ostraca]; ⇥ 686, SDB XI,63s (1990) 740-756 [-762].

d421 **Dar** Shimon, Landscape and pattern... Samaria: BAR-Int 308, 1986 ⇥ 3,e175... 6,e99: ᴿBASOR 284 (1991) 91s (W. R. *Kotter*).

d422 *Šekem*: *a) Anderson* Robert T., The elusive Samaritan temple [archaeology has failed to find any on Gerizim]: BA 54 (1991) 104-107. – *b) Brändle* Rudolf, Das Tempelneubauprojekt Julians: ⇥ 46*, ᶠEHRLICH E., Israel 1991, 168-183.

d423 **Campbell** Edward F., Shechem II, portrait of a hill country vale; the Shechem regional survey, Tell Balatah Shechem archaeological excavations: ASOR Report 2. Atlanta 1991, Scholars. xii-123 p.; 95 fig.; 3 foldouts. 1-55540-842-4.

d423* ᴱJacoby David, *Tsafrir* Joram, ❻ Jews, Samaritans and Christians in Byzantine Palestine 1988 ➤ 6,e62: ᴿLA 41 (1991) 586s (M. *Pazzini*).

d424 *Vilar Hueso* Vicente, Santuarios de Tel Balata (Siquén): ➤ 421, Luso-Esp 1989/91, 17-22.

d425 *Šiloh*: Schley Donald G., Shiloh 1989 ➤ 5,d886: ᴿBS 148 (1991) 245s (M. F. *Rooker*); CBQ 53 (1991) 120s (V. H. *Matthews*); JBL 110 (1991) 134-6 (C. D. *Evans*); JTS 42 (1991) 157s (G. I. *Davies*); OLZ 86 (1991) 402-4 (H. *Seidel*).

d426 *Zeror* (10 k Caesarea-M): *Ogawa* Hideo, Bronze industry remains at Tel Zeror [Japanese excavations 1964ss, 1974]: ➤ 102c, ᶠPrince MIKASA 1991, 267-277 + plan.

т4.6   **Galilaea; pro tempore** *Golan.*

d427 *Banyas*: *Daoudal* Yves, 'Et sur ce roc...' [Mt 16,....]: PeCa 250 (1991)...: EsprVie 101 (1991) 434-6 (J. *Daoust*).

d428 *Bethsaida* 1989: IsrEJ 41 (1991) 184s (R. *Arav*).

d429 *Arav* Rami, *Rousseau* John J., Elusive Bethsaida recovered [et-Tell is not only Bethsaida-Julias; el-Araj 5 k S cannot be a Gospel-era Bethsaida: The Fourth R (Religious History) 4,1 (Sonoma CA 1991) 1-4.

d430 *Beth-Shan*: Yadin Y., *Geva* Shulamit, Investigations at Beth Shean: Qedem 33, 1986 ➤ 2,a658 ... 4,e788: ᴿOLZ 86 (1991) 194s (E. *Otto*).

d430* *Arnould* Caroline, Scythopolis, capitale de la Décapole: Archéologia 268 (1991) 20-25; color. ill.

d431 *a) Raban* Avner, The Philistines in the western Jezreel valley; – *b) Gál* Zvi, A note on the settlement pattern of the MB II Jezreel and Beth-Shan valleys: BASOR 284 (1991) 17-27; 3 fig. / 29-31; 2 fig.

d431* *Bir'am*: *Ohel* Milla, Prehistoric survey of the Baram plateau: PEQ 123 (1991) 32-47; 7 fig.

d432 *Capharnaum*: *Tzaferis* Vassilios, Excavations at Capernaum 1978-87, I: 1989 ➤ 6,e122: ᴿJAOS 111 (1991) 376s (E. M. *Meyers*).

d433 *Dabiyye* [Golan 3 k NE Qaṣrin], *Ma'oz* Zvi U., Excavations in the ancient synagogue at Dabiyye: 'Atiqot 20 (1991) 49-65; 12 fig. (66-73, 2 fig., *Killebrew* Ann, pottery; 74-80, 1 fig. *Ariel* Donald T., coins).

d434 *Dan*: *Ilan* David, 'Stepped-rim' juglets from Tel Dan and the 'MB I-II (MB II A-B) transitional period': IsrEJ 41 (1991) 229-238; 7 fig.

d435 *Biran* A., The tale of two cities — Israelite Dan and Canaanite Laish: BAngIsr 10 (1990s) 104 (lecture summary).

d435* *Gamla*, Golan heights: BAngIsr 11 (1991s) 43s (D. *Goran*, lecture summary).

d436 *Guš Ḥalav* (Jîš): Meyers Eric M. & Carol L., Excavations at the ancient synagogue of Gush Halav: Meiron 5, ASOR. WL 1991, Eisenbrauns. xx-292 p.; 50 fig.; 32 pl. 0-931464-59-5.

d437 *Haifa*: *a) Briend* J., L'occupation de la Galilée occidentale à l'époque perse; – *b) Balensi* J., al., Le niveau perse à Tell Abu Hawam, résultats récents et signification dans le contexte régional côtier: TEuph 2 (1990) 109-122 + map / 125-130 + 7 plans.

d438 *Hananya* (Ïnan): IsrEJ 41 (1991) 186-8 (D. *Adan-Bayewitz*).

d439 *Hazor*: ᴱBen-Tor Amnon, *Geva* Shulamit, Hazor III-IV 1989➤ 5,d915: ᴿBL (1991) 27 (H. G. M. *Williamson*); JBL 110 (1991) 499-501 (R. S. *Boraas*).

d439* Geva Shulamit, Hazor, Israel, an urban community of the 8th century B.C.E.: BAR-Int 543. Ox 1989. v-180 p.; 55 fig. [TR 88,360-3, R. *Wenning*: not a reprise of Yadin 1976 but a new approach].

d440 *Milson* David, On the chronology and design of 'Ahab's citadel' at Hazor: ZDPV 107 (1991) 39-47; 5 fig.

d441 *Jalamé* (W. Galilee): ᴱWeinberg Gladys D., Excavations at Jalamé, site of a glass factory in Late Roman Palestine. Columbia 1987, Univ. Missouri. 404 p. $85. 0-8262-0409-0. – ᴿTopO 1 (1991) 79-82 (Marie-D. *Nenna*).

d442 *Jezreel*: *Williamson* H. G. M., Jezreel in the biblical texts: TAJ 18 (1991) 72-92 [< ZAW 104,282].

d443 *Raban* Avner, The Philistines in the western Jezreel valley: BASOR 184 (1991) 17-28 [29-31, *Gâl* Z].

d444 *Kabri* (N. Akko): IsrEJ 41 (1991) 188-194; 5 fig. (A. *Kempinski*, W.-D. *Niemeier*).

d444* **Kempinski** Aharon, *Niemeier* W.-D., ❺ Excavations at Kabri, preliminary report [1.-3. 1986-8] 4. 1989s. TA 1990, Univ. 53 p. + LII Eng. + 23 fig.

d445 *Kinneret*: **Fritz** Volkmar, *al.*, Kinneret 1982-5: AbhDPV 15. Wsb 1990, Harrassowitz. xviii-393 p.; 30 fig.; 120 pl., 22 plans. – ᴿRHPR 71 (1991) 190-3 (J.-G. *Heintz*).

d446 *Megiddo*: *Currid* John D., The re-stratification of Megiddo during the United Monarchy: ZDPV 107 (1991) 28-38.

d447 **Kempinski** A., Megiddo 1989 ➤ 5,d927; 6,e146: ᴿLevant 23 (1991) 193s (*G. I. Davies*).

d447* *Alexander* Robert L., Saušga and the Hittite ivory from Megiddo: JNES 50 (1991) 161-182; 9 fig.

d448 *Naffakh* (Golan) 2194.2742; etc.: IsrEJ 41 (1991) 176-9 (Claudine M. *Dauphin*, Shimon *Gibson*).

d449 *Nahariya*: **Dauphin** C., *Edelstein* G., L'église byzantine de Nahariya 1984 ➤ 3,e218 ... 6,e151: ᴿLevant 23 (1991) 194s (D. *Pringle*).

d451 *Nazareth*: **Pritz** Ray A., Nazarene Jewish Christianity 1988 ➤ 4,e781; 6,e156: ᴿJQR 82 (1991s) 573s (G. S. *Stroumsa*).

d452 **Santarelli** Giuseppe, La Santa Casa di Loreto, tradizione e ipotesi; Collana del centenario [1294] 7. Loreto 1988, Santa Casa. 399 p. – ᴿLaurentianum 32 (1991) 293-5 (T. *Jansen*).

d453 *Sepphoris*: Qadmoniot 24 (1991) 113-121 (Z. *Weiss*, E. *Netzer* ❺).

d454 *Folda* Jaroslav, The Church of St. Anne [Sepphoris]: BA 54 (1991) 88-96; ill.

d455 Mona Lisa [Sepphoris mosaic] of the Galilee, 42-Min. video tape. Durham NJ c. 1990, Duke Univ. $37. – ᴿBAR-W 17/2 (1991) 9s (Charlotte *Anker*).

d456 **Batey** Richard A., Jesus and the forgotten city; new light on Sepphoris and the urban world of Jesus. GR 1991, Baker. 234 p. $25. 0-8010-1016-0 [TDig 39,252].

d457 *Sussita*: Epstein Claire, *Tzaferis* Vassilios, The baptistery at Sussita-Hippos: ʿAtiqot 20 (1991) 89-94; 5 fig.

d457* *Taʿanach*: **Taha** Hamdan, Die Bestattungssitten im bronzezeitlichen Palästina mit besonderer Berücksichtigung der Unter-Fussboden-Bestattungen von Tell Taanek: Diss. Freie Univ. Berlin 1990. – ArchAnz (1991) 149.

d458 *Tabor*: *Briand* Jean M., L'histoire du Mont Thabor: TerreS nov. 1990 [EsprVie 101 (1991) 252s, 325s (J. *Daoust*)].

d459 *Tiberias*, church, ? theater: *a*) BA 54 (1991) 170s (Y. *Hirschfeld*); – *b*) *Hirschfeld* Yizhar, Tiberias; preview of coming attractions: BAR-W 17,2 (1991) 44-51; (color.) ill.

d459* **Dudman** Helga, *Ballhorn* Elisheva, Tiberias. J 1988, Carta. 240 p. $40. – ᴿBA 54 (1991) 174 (W. *Wegner*).

d460 *Nadel* Dani, ❹ Historical and prehistorical sites on the shores of the Sea of Galilee: Qadmoniot 24 (1991) 20-23.

T4.8   *Transjordania:* **East-Jordan.**

Bartlett J., Edom 1989 ➤ e615.

Bienkowski Piotr, The art of Jordan 1991 ➤ b513.

d461 **Boling** Robert G., The early biblical community in Transjordan 1988 ➤ 4,e823*... 6,e172: ᴿBA 54 (1991) 60 (G. M. *Landes*).

d462 *De Vries* Bert, Archaeology in Jordan: AJA 95 (1991) 253-280; 28 fig. [24 reports; to continue annually].

d463 **Khouri** Rami G., *a)* The antiquities of the Jordan Rift valley. Amman/Sebastopol CA 1988, Kutba/Solipsist. 157 p. $23. – ᴿBA 54 (1991) 175s (G. L. *Mattingly*); BAR-W 17,3 (1991) 4 (L. G. *Herr*). – *b)* **Khouri** Rami, *Whitcomb* Donald, Palestine on the China Sea. Amman c. 1990, Kutba. 36 p. $5. – ᴿBA 54 (1991) 173 (J. *McRay*).

d464 **MacAdam** Henry J., Studies in the history of the Roman province of Arabia, the northern sector [Hauran]: BAR-Int 295. Ox 1986. xv-420 p.; 11 fig.; 15 pl. £25. – ᴿPEQ 122 (1990) 65s (J. *Bowsher*); VDI 198 (1991) 215-9 (A. G. *Grushevoi* ❽).

d465 *Piccirillo* Michele, *a)* Archaeological expeditions to Jordan in 1991 (*Hamid* Basmah; 32 sites); – *b)* 12 signed reports; – *c)* Bibliografia, recensioni gran parte di P. *Kaswalder*: LA 41 (1991) 499s; map. / 500-530 / 531-546.

d465* *Piccirillo* Michele, Scoperte e problemi di archeologia cristiana in Giordania: RivArCr 67 (1991) 160s (sommario).

d466 ᴱ**Thompson** Henry O., Archaeology in Jordan 1989 ➤ 6,502: ᴿKlio 73 (1991) 688s (H. *Klengel*).

d467 **Timm** Stefan, Moab zwischen den Mächten; Studien zu historischen Denkmälern und Texten: ÄgAT 17, 1989 ➤ 5,d963: ᴿCritRR 4 (1991) 113-6 (J. A. *Dearman*); Henoch 13 (1991) 100s (J. A. *Soggin*); RHPR 71 (1991) 193-5 (J.-G. *Heintz*).

d467* *a)* **Worschech** Udo, Das Land jenseits des Jordan; biblische Archäologie in Jordanien: StBAZ 1. Wu/Ha 1991, Brockhaus/Saatkorn. 240 p.; 149 fig.; 24 color. pl. DM 30 [TR 88,187, R. *Wenning*].

— *b)* **Zwickel** Wolfgang, [1335] Eisenzeitliche Ortslagen im Ostjordanland: TAVO B-81. Wsb 1990, Reichert. 416 p. DM 74 [TR 88,189, R. *Wenning*].

---

d468 *Abila* 5th 1988, Bronze through Arab: ADAJ 35 (1991) 203-220; 12 fig.; 1 pl. (W. H. *Mare*).

d469 *Winter* Willard W., Christian evidences from Abila of the Decapolis; finds in the 1990 season: ProcGLM 11 (1991) 92-103; 2 plans.

d470 *Amman* area, 1988 survey: ADAJ 35 (1991) 361-395; 9 fig. (A. S. *Abu Dayyah, al.*).

d470* Amman, Citadelle troisième terrasse 1991: LA 41 (1991) 502-6 (J.-B. *Humbert*, F. *Zayadine*).

d471 **Hübner** Ulrich, Die Ammoniter; Untersuchungen zur Geschichte, Kultur und Religion eines transjordanischen Volkes im 1. Jahrtausend v.Chr.: Diss. Heidelberg 1991, ᴰ*Weippert* M. 430 p. – TR 87 (1991) 518; RTLv 23, p. 539.

d472 *'Amr* Abd el-Jalil, Hand-made Umayyad bowls with excised decoration from Rujm al-Kursi [near Amman]: Berytus 38 (1990) 171-8; 2 fig.; II pl.

d473 *Gatier* P.-L., *Vérilhac* A.-M., Les colombes de Déméter à Philadelphie-Amman: Syria 66 (1989) 337-348; 4 fig.

d474 *Kletter* Raz, The Rujm El-Malfuf buildings and the Assyrian vassal state of Ammon: BASOR 284 (1991) 33-50; 10 fig.

d475 *Najjar* Mohammad, A new Middle Bronze Age tomb at the citadel of Amman: ADAJ 35 (1991) 105-130; 16 fig. (Laressa Najjar); IV pl.

d476 *Shea* William H., The architectural layout of the Amman citadel temple inscription: PEQ 123 (1991) 62-66; 1 fig.

d477 *Aqaba* W, pre-Islamic 1990: ADAJ 35 (1991) 397-414; 4 fig. (J. L. *Meloy*).

d478 *Azraq*: *Copeland* Lorraine, The Late Acheulian knapping-floor at C-spring, Azraq Oasis, Jordan: Levant 23 (1991) 1-6; 3 fig.

d479 **Bab eḏ-Ḏra**: **Schaub** R. Thomas, *Rast* Walter E., Bab edh-Dhra excavations... P. W. LAPP 1965-7; Reports DS Plain 1, 1989 → 5,d974: RAJA 95 (1991) 744s (E. *Braun*).

d480 *Baq'ah*: **McGovern** Patrick E., *al.*, LB-EI... Baq'ah 1986 → 3,e267; 4,e847: RJAOS 111 (1991) 188-190 (H. A. *Leibowitz*: 'the data is well presented'); JNES 50 (1991) 219-221 (D. L. *Esse*).

d481 *Basṭa* 1988, dubiously Neolithic: ADAJ 35 (1991) 13-34; 6 fig.; VI pl. (H. J. *Nissen, al.*).

d482 *Deir 'Alla*: *Wenning* Robert, *Zenger* Erich, Heiligtum ohne Stadt — Stadt ohne Heiligtum? Anmerkungen zum archäologischen Befund des Tell Dēr 'Alla: ZAHeb 4 (1991) 171-193.

d483 *a*) *Franken* H. J., Deir 'Alla revisited; – *b*) *Ibrahim* Moawiyah M., *Kooij* G. van der, The archaeology of Deir 'Alla Phase IX: → 534, Balaam text 1989/91, 3-15 / 16-29.

d484 *Dibon*: EDearman A., Studies in Mesha/Moab 1989 → 5,392; 9256*... 6,e191: RJAOS 111 (1991) 187s (W. H, *Shea*: chiefly informative on W. MORTON's 1955-65 Dhiban excavation); LA 41 (1991) 535-541 (P. *Kaswalder*).

d485 *Dohaleh al-N'aymeh* 1st 1990: ADAJ 35 (1991s) ❹ 5-14; 11 fig.; 2 pl. (S. *Sari*).

d486 *Feinan*: two miner's tools; ADAJ 35 (1991) 195-8; 1 fig.; 3 pl. (A. *Hauptmann, al.*).

d487 *Fuḥar* (10 k NE Irbid) 1st, 1990: LA 41 (1991) 500-2; pl. 61 (M. *Ottosson*).

d488 *Gadara* 4th, 1990, Byz...: ADAJ 35 (1991) 223-231; 3 fig.; IV pl. (T. *Weber*).

d489 *Dvoretski* Esti, *Last* Rosa, Gadara – colony or colline tribe; another suggested reading of the Byblos [1864 tombstone] inscription: IsrEJ 41 (1991) 157-162.

d490 *Politis* Konstantinos D., El-Kabu [2 k E Umm Qeis 'with wider Corinthian columns'] 100 years after SCHUMACHER's discovery: PEQ 122 (1990) 53-55; 2 fig.

d490* *Ġazal* 'ain, 1988: → 407, ASOR 1982/91, 95-116 (G. *Rollefson, al.*).

d491 *Gerasa*: **Hackstein** Katharina, Ethnizität und Situation; Ġaraš – eine vorderorientalische Kleinstadt: TAVO B-94, 1989 → 5,d982: RZDPV 107 (1991) 299s (E. A. *Knauf*).

d492 Jerash international project: santuario d'Artemide (*Parapetti* Roberto; iscrizioni *Lazzarini* M.-L.); The hippodrome (*Ostrasz* A. A.; inscriptions, *Borkowski* Z., lamps, *Kehrberg* L.); monuments disparus (*Seigne* J.); fabrique de céramique (*Braemer* P.); macellum (*Martin-Bueno* M.): Syria 66 (1989) 1-39; 19 fig. (41-49; 4 fig.) / 51-77; 7 fig. (79-83; 85-97) / 99-116; 16 fig. / 153-167; 13 fig. / 177-199; 16 fig.

d493 Jerash, 1985-90 hippodrome restoration: ADAJ 35 (1991) 237-246; 4 fig.; IV pl. (A. A. *Ostrasz*).

d494 *Ḥaraz* 1989 (w. Yabis, S Fahil) EB-LB-Iron: ADAJ 35 (1991) 67-101; 15 fig.; III pl. (P. M. *Fischer*).

d495 *Hešbon*: ᴱGeraty L. T., *al.*, Hesban 3, Historical foundations 1989 → 5,d988: ᴿBL (1991) (J. R. *Bartlett*: 'mere antiquity guarantees nothing').

d496 *Prag* Kay, A walk in the wadi Hesban: PEQ 123 (1991) 48-61; 7 fig.

d497 *Horonaim*: *Dearman* J. Andrew, The Moabite sites of Horonaim and Luhith: PEQ 122 (1990) 41-46.

d498 *Ḥumeima*, Nabatean hydraulic system: ADAJ 35 (1991) ❹ 17-22; 1 fig.; 8 pl. (S. *Farajat*).

d499 *Iktanu*, Hammam 1990: Levant 23 (1991) 55-66; 10 fig. (Kay *Prag*).

d500 *Kerak*: ᴱMiller J. Maxwell (*Pinkerton* Jack M.), Archaeological survey of the Kerak plateau 1987-82: ASOR arch. report 1. Atlanta 1991, Scholars. [x-] 343 p.; 424 fig.; 2 foldouts. 1-55540-642-4.

d501 **Worschech** Udo, Die Beziehungen Moabs zu Israel und Ägypten in der Eisenzeit: ÄgAT 18, 1990 → 6,e208: ᴿOTAbs 14 (1991) 353 (A. *Fitzgerald*).

d502 *Kir Harešet*: *Jones* Brian C., [2 Kgs 3: not Kerak; nearer Hešbon] In search of Kir Hareseth; a case study in site identification: JStOT 52 (1991) 3-24.

d503 *Limes Arabicus* 1989: → 407, ASOR 1982/91, 117-154 (S. T. *Parker*).

d504 *Madaba*: **Piccirillo** Michele, Madaba; le chiese e i mosaici 1989 → 6, e214: ᴿBO 48 (1991) 908s (J. *Wilkinson*: uniquely successful and well illustrated); RivB 39 (1991) 86s (A. *Rolla*).

d504* Madaba since 1982, chiesa della Vergine, Medaglione del Mare: LA 41 (1991) 518-522 (M. *Piccirillo*, A. *Michel*).

d505 *Maḥanajim*: → 690, TRE 21 (1991) 703s (V. *Fritz*).

d506 *Nebo*: **Piccirillo** Michele, *Alliata* Eugenio, La chiesa del monastero di Kaianos alle 'Ayoun Mousa' sul monte Nebo: → 52, ᶠFASOLA U., 1989, (II) 561-586; 11 fig.

d507 *Pella*: **Smith** Robert H., *Day* Leslie P., Pella 2, 1989 → 5,e4: ᴿCBQ 53 (1991) 684 (R. S. *Boraas*).

d508 *Petra*-Zantur 2d 1989: ADAJ 35 (1991) 251-267; 5 fig.; VI pl. (R. A. *Stucky*, not Stuckey as pl.-headings) [275-295; 14 fig., XVI pl., Petra and Beida, F. *Zayadine*, S. *Farajat*; 313-321, Zurrabah pottery workshop, Khairieh ʿ*Amr*].

d508* *Augé* Christian, *Linant de Bellefonds* Pascale, Deux Français à Pétra en 1828: [Léon de] LABORDE et [Maurice] LINANT DE BELLEFONDS: Archéologia 262 (1990) 48-59; ill.

d509 **Byrd** B., Excavations at Beidha, I. The Natufian encampment: Jutland Archaeol. Soc. Publ. 23/1, 1989 → 6,e230: ᴿLA 41 (1991) 533s (P. *Kaswalder*); Levant 23 (1991) 191 (Lorraine *Copeland*).

d510 **Khairy** Nabil I., The 1981 Petra excavations: AbhDPV 13. Wsb 1990, Harrassowitz. xiv-162 p. DM 128 [RB 99,456, J. M. de *Tarragon*].

d511 ᴱLindner Manfred, *Zeitler* John P., Petra, Königin der Weihrauchstrasse: Katalog, Nürnberg. Fürth 1991, VKA. 220 p.; ill. 3-94099-001-9. 24 art. (mit zahlreichen Korrekturen für I. *Parlasca* Terrakotten).

d512 ᴱ**Lindner** Manfred, Petra und das Königreich der Nabatäer⁵ 1989 ➤ 5,e8: ᴿLevant 23 (1991) 194-7 (Judith *McKenzie*, also on his 1968 and Tsafrir Y., Rehovot I); WeltOr 22 (1991) 155-8 (E. A. *Knauf*).

d513 *Lindner* Manfred, Neue archäologische Erkundigungen und Grabungen der Naturhistorischen Gesellschaft Nürnberg, in Südjordanien 1986-90: AfO 36s (1989s) 354-361.

d514 *Macdonald* M. C. A., Was the Nabataean Kingdom a 'bedouin state'? [*Knauf* E. A., 13 art.]: ZDPV 107 (1991) 102-119.

d515 *Matthiae* Karl, Die nabatäische Felsarchitektur in Petra [500 Grab-fassaden]: Klio 73 (1991) 226-278; 28 fig.

d516 **Negev** Avraham, Nabataean archaeology today 1986 ➤ 3,e316 ... 5,e9*: ᴿBASOR 281 (1991) 89s (P. C. *Hammond*); IsrEJ 41 (1991) 221-4 (A. *Ovadiah*).

d517 *Oleson* John P., Nabataean hydraulic engineering: ➤ 627*, AJA 95 (1991) 330, summary (with four other items on Petra area).

d517* *Potts* D. T., Nabatean finds from Thaj and Qatif: ArabArchEp 2 (1991) 138-144; 7 fig.

d518 *Roche* Marie-Jeanne, Bustes fragmentaires trouvés à Pétra: Syria 67 (1990) 377-395; 12 fig.

d519 **Wenning** Robert, Die Nabatäer 1987 ➤ 3,e317 ... 6,e239: ᴿGnomon 63 (1991) 154-7 (H. P. *Kuhnen*).

d520 *Zayadine* Fawzi, L'iconographie d'Isis à Pétra: MÉF-A 103 (1991) 283-306; 20 fig.

d521 *Qurma: Knauf* Ernst A., More notes on Ġabal Qurma, Minaeans and Safaites: ZDPV [104 (1988) 127, *Jamme* A., 'too far from common sense to warrant a reply'] 107 (1991) 92-104; 1 fig.; pl. 3.

d522 *Quweisma* church 1989: ADAJ 35 (1991) 325-335; 7 fig.; V pl. (R. *Schick*, E. *Suleiman*).

d523 *Sa'idiyeh* 5th 1990, Iron Age: ADAJ 35 (1991) 181-190; 2 fig.; IV pl.

d524 Sa'idiyeh 5th 1990, Hellenistic-Persian: Levant 23 (1991) 67-86; 18 fig. (J. N. *Tubb*, P. G. *Dorrell*).

d525 *Samra: Fernández Tresguerres* Juan, Grabados sobre roca en la zona de Khirbet es-Samra (Jordania): ➤ 421, Luso-Esp 1989/91, 53-61 + 8 fig.

d525* Samra 1991: LA 41 (1991) 509-514; pl. 68 (J.-B. *Humbert*).

d526 *Taylor* Justin, Khirbet es-Samra dans l'histoire, ᵀ*Lozier* Pierre: RB 98 (1981) 222-243.

d527 *Sresleh* [15 k E. Amman] 1990, chalco/EB1, MB2; Umayyad: ADAJ 35 (1991) 41-62; 10 fig.; III pl. (Gunnar *Lehmann, al.*).

d528 *Umeiri* 3d 1989, late Iron II: ADAJ 35 (1991) 155-174; 11 fig.; V pl. (L. *Herr, al.*).

d528* *Umm Raṣāṣ:* a) 6th 1991: LA 41 (1991) 522-6 (M. *Piccirillo*); – b) *Piccirillo* Michele, Il complesso di Santo Stefano a Umm al-Rasas – Kastron Mefaa in Giordania (1986-1991): LA 41 (1991) 327-364; 23 fig.; pl. 1-38; 2 foldout plans (ceramica 365-422; 27 fig.; pl. 39-44, *Alliata* E., inscriptions 423-8, *Macdonald* M. C. A.); Eng. 493.

d529 *Yaşileh* 8 k E Irbid, Rom.-Byz. tombs: ADAJ 35 (1991) 341-4; 3 fig.; II pl. (Z. Al-*Muheisin*).

т5.1 **Phoenicia** – *Libanus*, **Lebanon.**

d530 **Botto** Massimo, Studi storici sulla Fenicia l'VIII e il VII secolo a.C.: Quad. Orientalistica Pisana I. Pisa 1990, Univ. 261 p.

d531 **Elayi** Josette, Économie des cités phéniciennes sous l'empire perse: AION supp. 62 au fasc. 50/1 (1989). N 1991, Ist. Universitario Orientale. viii-104 p. [OIAc 2,18].

d531* **Elayi** Josette, Pénétration grecque en Phénicie 1988 ➤ 4,e911 ... 6,e253: ᴿAbr Nahrain 29 (1991) 143-6 (G. *Bunnens*).

d532 *a*) ᴱ**Gehrig** Ulrich, *Niemeyer* Hans G., Die Phönizier im Zeitalter Homers, Katalog der Ausstellung 1990, Hannover Kestner-Mus., *al.* Mainz 1990, von Zabern. 260 p.; ill.; – *b*) *Niemeyer* Hans G., I Fenici al tempo di Omero: Archeo 71 (1991) 56-63; le foto dalla mostra di Hannover.

d533 **Grainger** John D., Hellenistic Phoenicia. Ox 1991, Clarendon. ix-228 p.; 7 maps. 0-19-814770-8.

d534 *Khoury* Raif G., Libanon: ➤ 690, TRE 21 (1991) 40-47.

d535 *Morschauser* Scott N., 'Crying to the Lebanon'; a note on Wenamun 2, 13-14: StAäK 18 (1991) 317-330.

d536 ᴱ**Moscati** S., Les Phéniciens [I Fenicei, Mi 1986, Bompiani], franç. préf. *Amiet* P. P 1989, Belfond. 591 p. (color.) ill. F 870. – ᴿRB 98 (1991) 436-9 (É. *Puech*).

d537 ᴱ**Moscati** S., Phoenicians 1988 ➤ 5,e59: ᴿJAOS 111 (1991) 811-4 (S. *Segert*).

d538 *Salles* Jean-François, Du bon et du mauvais usage des Phéniciens [ELAYI J. 1988; GRAS Michel, *al.* 1989]; TopO 1 (1991) 48-70.

d539 *Tsyrkin* Yu. B., *a*) ⊕ Some problems of Phoenicia's socio-political structure: VDI 199 (1991) 3-13; Eng. 13; – *b*) Socio-political structure of Phoenicia: Gerión 8 (1990) 29-43.

---

d539* ʿ*Arqa*: **Thalmann** Jean-Paul, L'âge du bronze à Tell ʿArqa (Liban); bilan et perspectives (1981-1991): Berytus 39 (1991) 21-38; 6 fig.

d540 *Baʿalbek*: **Hajjar** Youssef, La triade d'Héliopolis-Baalbek 1977 ➤ 58, b431 ... 6,e258; défense contre J. *Greenfield*: Numen [37 (1990) 280-3] 38 (1991) 267-271; 271-3, rejoinder.

d540* *Rumscheid* Frank, Architekturproben aus Baalbek ... Göttingen: Arch-Anz (1991) 527-558; 49 fig.

d541 *Byblos*: **Nibbi** Alessandra, Ancient Byblos reconsidered 1985 ➤ 1,d729 ... 5,e35: ᴿWZKM 78 (1988) 280s (K. *Jaroš*).

d541* **Nibbi** Alessandra, Wenamun and Alashiya reconsidered 1985 ➤ 1,e388 ... 4,e926: ᴿWZKM 78 (1988) 224-6 (G. *Vittmann*).

d542 *a*) *Puech* Émile, Les premières émissions byblites et les rois de Byblos à la fin du Vᵉ siècle av. J.-C.; – *b*) *Scandone Matthiae* Gabriella, Hathor signora di Biblo e la Baalat Gebal: ➤ 627, Fen. 2, 1987/91, 287-298 / 401-6.

d543 *Labrique* Françoise, La chevelure des servantes de la reine de Byblos; un rite égyptien en filigrane? (PLUTARQUE, De Iside et Osiride, 15) [< diss. 1991]: ➤ 43, ᶠDERCHAIN P., Religion 1991, 203-7.

d544 *Ribichini* Sergio, Taautos et l'invention de l'écriture chez PHILON de Byblos: ➤ 630, Phoinikeia 1989/91, 201-213.

d545 *Kamīd/Loz*: **Metzer** M., 20 Jahre Ausgrabungen auf dem Tell Kamid el-Loz 1964-1984. Kiel 1988 [< Christiana Albertina 6 (1977) + Nachtrag]. 54 p.; 12 pl. – ᴿVT 41 (1991) 500 (G. I. *Davies*).

d546 *Sarafand:* **Anderson** W., *al.* Sarepta I-IV 1985-8 ➤ 6,e264: ᴿSyria 67 (1990) 525-7 (H. de *Contenson*).

d547 **Pritchard** J.-B., Sarepta IV, 1988 ➤ 5,e38: ᴿPEQ 122 (1990) 70-72 (S. *Bourke*).

d548 *Briend* J., *Thalmann* J.P., Sarepta: ➤ 686, SDB XI,64s (1991) 1414-1420.

d549 **Sidon: Elayi** Josette, Sidon, cité autonome de l'Empire Perse[2] [¹1989 ➤ 5,e40]. P 1990, Idéophane. 321 p.; ill.

d550 *Isaac* Benjamin, A Seleucid inscription from Jamnia-on-the-Sea; Antiochus V Eupator and the Sidonians: IsrEJ 41 (1991) 132-144; 1 fig.

d551 **Stucky** R., Tribune d'Echmoun 1984 ➤ 65,b13... 6,e266: ᴿRÉG 103 (1990) 704 (Mary-Anne *Zagdoun*).

d552 *Tarablus: Elayi* J., Tripoli (Liban) à l'époque perse: ➤ 636*, Syrie perse 1989, TEuph 2 (1990) 59-70; map.

d553 **Tyrus:** *a) Seeden* Helga, A tophet in Tyre?; – *b) Conheeny* Janice, *Pipe* Alan, Note on some cremated bone; – *c) Ward* William A., The scarabs, scaraboid and amulet-plaque from Tyrian cinerary urns; – *d)* Sader Helen, Phoenician stelae from Tyre: Berytus 39 (1991) 39-82; 68 fig. / 83-87; fig. 70-73 / 89-99; 12 fig. / 101-126; 21 fig.

d553* *Lemaire* André, Le royaume de Tyr dans la seconde moitié du IVᵉ siècle av. J.-C.: ➤ 627, Fen 2, 1987/91, 131-150.

d554 **Schmeling** Gareth, Historia Apollonii regis Tyri 1988 ➤ 4,e942... 6,e268: ᴿHelmantica 42,129* (1991) 360 (S. *García-Jalon*).

d554* *Kortekaas* G.A.A., The Historia Apollonii regis Tyri and ancient astrology; a possible link between Apollonius and *katochē*: ZPapEp 85 (1991) 71-85.

d555 *Holcroft* Alison, Riddles and prudentia in the Historia Apollonii regis Tyri: Prudentia 23 (1991) 45-54.

T5.2   Situs mediterranei **phoenicei et punici.**

d556 **Bernal** Martin, Cadmean letters [Semitic-Egyptian influences in forming Greek culture]. WL 1990, Eisenbrauns. xiii-156 p. $19.50. – ᴿAndrUnS 29 (1991) 167s (J.E. *Miller*).

d557 **Delz** J., Sɪʟɪᴜs Italicus, Punica 1987 ➤ 5,e49; 6,e271: ᴿEmerita 59,1 (1991) 187 (A. *Ramírez de Verger*); GGA 243 (1991) 102-113 (W. *Ehlers*); RBgPg 69 (1991) 214 (H. *Bardon*).

d558 — **Spaltenstein** François, Commentaire des Punica de Silius Italicus (livres 9 à 17]: Lausanne Fac. Lett. 28*b*. Genève 1990, Droz. 527 p. Fs. 55. – ᴿClasR 41 (1991) 485s (D.W. *Vessey*).

d559 **Gras** M., *al.*, L'univers phenicien 1989 ➤ 5,e51; 6,e273: ᴿAION 50 (1990) 335-340 (F. *Vattioni*); RHR 208 (1991) 76-80 (M. *Delcor*); StEpL 7 (1990) 136-9 (Corinne *Bonnet*).

d559* — *Gras* Michel L., The Phoenicians and death [Les Phéniciens et la mort, chap, 6 de L'univers phénicien 1989], ᵀSeeden Helga: Berytus 39 (1991) 127-176; 16 fig.

d560 ᴱMazza F., *al.*, Fonti classiche per la civiltà fenicia e punica, I. Fonti letterarie greche dalle origini alla fine dell'età classica: Coll.StFen 27, R 1988, ➤ 5,e55; 6,e276: ᴿWienerSt 104 (1991) 290 (H. *Schwabl*).

d561 **Moscati** Sabatino, L'ancora d'argento; colonie e commerci fenici tra Oriente e Occidente: Arte, storia, archeologia 2. Mi 1989, Jaca. 241 p.; ill.

d562 **Moscati** Sabatino, Techne; studi sull'artigianato fenicio: StPunica 6. R 1990, Univ. 91 p.; 29 pl. [OIAc 1,21].

d563 *a*) *Moscati* Sabatino, Les Phéniciens reconsidérés; – *b*) *Bonnet* Corinne, Les scribes phénico-puniques; – *c*) *Swiggers* P., Linguistic considerations on Phoenician orthography; – *d*) *Hoz* Javier de, The Phoenician origin of the early Spanish scripts; – *e*) *Wagner* Carlos G., Writing and problems of acculturation in Tartessos: ➤ 630, Phoinikeia 1989/91, 3-17 / 147-169 / 115-132 / 669-678 + 4 pl. (map) / 683-9.

d564 *Dor*: **Stern** E., Phoenician finds from Tel Dor, Israel: RStFen 19 (1991) 97-105.

d565 *Hispania*: **Blázquez** J. M., Panorama general del desarrollo histórico de la cultura tartésica desde finales de la Edad del Bronce, s. VIII a.c., hasta los orígenes de las culturas turdetana e ibérica; los influjos fenicios: RStFen 19 (1991) 33-48.

d566 *Guerrero* V. M., El palacio-santuario de Cancho Roano (Badajoz) y la comercialización de ánforas fenicias indígenas: RStFen 19 (1991) 49-82.

d567 *a*) *Júdice-Gamito* Teresa, Greeks and Phoenicians in south west Iberia — who were the first? Aspects of archaeological and epigraphic evidence; – *b*) *Domínguez* Adolfo J., New perspectives on the Greek presence in the Iberian Peninsula: ➤ 588, Diaspora 1988/91, 81-108 / 109-161.

d568 *López Pardo* Fernando, Sobre la expansión fenicio-púnica en Marruecos; algunas precisiones a la documentación arqueológica: ArEspArq 63 (1990) 7-41.

d569 **Perdigones Moreno** Lorenzo, *al.*, La necrópolis fenicio-púnica de Cádiz, siglos VI-IV a. de C.: StPunica 7. R 1990, Univ. 90 p.; 38 fig.; XV pl. [OIAc 1,22].

d570 *Rouillard* Pierre, Péninsule ibérique – Phéniciens et puniques III, publications 1983-1987: Karthago 22 (1990) 69-81.

d571 *Bisi* Anna Maria, La Spagna prima di Roma [... La civiltà tartessica; Fenici e Cartaginesi]: Archeo 74 (1991) 58-102.

d572 *Melita*: **Hölbl** Günther, Ägyptisches Kulturgut... Malta, Gozo phoen./ pun. 1989 ➤ 5,e74: ᴿOrientalia 60 (1991) 387-9 (A. J. *Frendo*).

d573 *Sardinia*: **Fadda** M. A., *Madau* M., Scavi a Nurdòle (Nuora): RStFen 19 (1991) 107-129.

d574 **Regoli** Paola, I bruciaprofumi a testa femminile dal nuraghe Lugherras (Paulilatino): StPunica 8. R 1991, Univ. 233 p.; XXVIII pl.

d575 Gli insediamenti fenici e punici in Italia: Itinerari 1. R 1988, Libreria dello Stato. 126 p. ill.

d576 *Guido* Francesco, Un ripostiglio monetale punico da Riola Sardo (Oristano): ➤, ᶠARSLAN E., Monetazione 1 (1991) 97-102 + pl. 26-31.

d577 *S. Antioco* 1983-6: RStFen 19 (1990) 37-123; ill. (P. *Bartoloni, al.*).

d578 **Porru** Leone, *al.*, Sant'Antioco; le catacombe, la chiesa martyrium, i frammenti scultorei. Cagliari 1989, STEF. 197 p. – ᴿGregorianum 72 (1991) 174 (J. *Janssens*).

d579 *Sicilia*: **Bisi** Anna Maria, La Sicilia antica: Archeo 64 (1990) 58-106; 71-76 L'età fenicia e cartaginese.

d580 *Tharros*: **Acquaro** E., *al.*, XVII (1990): RStFen 19 (1991) 159-163 (-237).

d581 ᴱ**Barnett** R. D., *Mendelson* C., Tharros 1987 ➤ 3,e391 ... 6,e287: ᴿSyria 66 (1989) 367-371 (Hélène *Benichou-Safar*).

T5.3 **Carthago.**

d582 *Alonso-Núñez* J. M., Trogue-Pompée sur Carthage: Karthago 22 (1990) 11-19 (5-9, digression sur Cyrène).

d583 **Barceló** P. A., Karthago und die Iberische Halbinsel vor den Barkiden; Studien zur karthagischen Präsenz im westlichen Mittelmeerraum vor der Gründung von Ebusus (VII Jh. v.Chr.) bis zum Übergang Hamilkars nach Hispanien (237 v.Chr.) 1988 ➤ 5,e91; 6,e288: ᴿGerión 8 (1990) 340-2 (Carlos G. *Wagner*); GGA 243 (1991) 6-12 (M. *Koch*); Latomus 50 (1991) 901-3 (E. *Lipiński*).

d584 **Bertrandy** François, *al.*, Les stèles puniques de Constantine 1987 ➤ 3,e397: ᴿStEpL 7 (1990) 140s (Maria Giulia *Amadasi Guzzo*); Syria 67 (1990) 764s (F. *Bron*).

d585 *a) Bron* François, *Briquel-Chatonnet* Françoise, Notes sur quelques stèles provenant du Tophet de Carthage; – *b) Sznycer* Maurice, Un texte carthaginois relatif aux constructions (C.I.S. 1,5523): Semitica 40 (1991) 55-60 + 41 phot. / 69-81; 1 fig.

d586 **Brown** Shelby, Late Carthaginian child sacrifice and sacrificial monuments in their Mediterranean context: JStOT/ASOR Mg 3. Sheffield 1991, Academic. 335 p.; ill. 1-85075-240-0.

d587 *Christol* Michel, Remarques sur une inscription de Thugga; le pagus dans la colonie de Carthage au Iᵉʳ siècle ap. J.-C.: ➤ 583, Mem. DE-GRASSI A., Epigrafia 1988/91, 607-628.

d588 **Clover** F. M., **Humphreys** R. S., Tradition and innovation in late antiquity 1989 ➤ 5,781; 6,e292: ᴿJRS 81 (1991) 232s (J. *Liebeschuetz*).

d589 **Holst** J., *al.*, Die deutschen Ausgrabungen in Karthago: DAI-Karthago [ᴱ*Rakob* F.] 1. Mainz 1991, von Zabern. x-279 p.; 112 fig.; iv-21 p. + 41 foldout plans. DM 198. 3-8053-0985-6 [JRS 81,255].

d590 **Humphrey** John H., The circus and a Byzantine cemetery at Carthage. AA 1988, Univ. Michigan. xi-594 p.; 287 fig.; 16 pl. 0-472-10113-7. – ᴿAJA 95 (1991) 564-6 (C. M. *Wells*: good despite jargon, prolixity).

d591 **Huss** Werner, Die Karthager. Mü 1990, Beck. xii-438 p. DM 45. 3-406-34385-6. – ᴿDLZ 112 (1991) 163-5 (Friederike *Heubner*).

d592 *Krings* Véronique, Les lettres grecques à Carthage: ➤ 630, Phoinikeia 1989/91, 649-668.

d593 **Lipiński** E., Carthago: StPhoen 6, OrLovAnal 26, 1986/8 ➤ 4,752; 6,e296: ᴿLatomus 50 (1991) 460-2 (J. *Desanges*: Lipiński/Stager important on 4th century infant sacrifices, voluntary and up to 4 years, instead of only firstborn infant often replaced by lamb or goat).

d594 *Mariotti* Maria Giovanna, Templi e sacerdoti a Cartagine: ➤ 565, Sangue 1989/91, 713-736.

d595 ᴱ**Mastino** A., L'Africa romana 1988/9 ➤ 5,856: ᴿRivArCr 67 (1991) 213-220 (Laura *Saladino*) & 220-7 (Maria Carla *Somma*).

d596 *Nicolet* Claude, *Beschaouch* Azedine, Nouvelles observations sur 'La mosaïque des chevaux' et son édifice à Carthage: CRAI (1991) 472-507; 22 fig.

d597 *Paskoff* Roland, *al.*, Le littoral de la Tunisie dans l'antiquité; cinq ans de recherches géoarchéologiques: CRAI (1991) 515-546; 12 fig.

d598 **Ros** Karen E., The Roman theater at Carthage: diss. Michigan, ᴰ*Gazda* Elaine K. AA 1990. 360 p. 91-16289. – DissA 51 (1991s) 201-A.

d599 **Schmitz** Philip C., Epigraphic contributions to a history of Carthage in the fifth century B.C.: diss. Michigan, ᴰ*Krahmalkov* C. AA 1991. x-325 p. 90-23633. – OIAc Ja91.

d599* *a) Suder* W., Tophet à Carthage; quelques remarques sur le site funéraire et les problèmes démographiques; – *b) Wagner* C. G., El sacrificio del Moloch en Fenicia; una respuesta cultural adaptativa a la presión demográfica: ➤ 627, Fen. 2, 1987/91, 407-410 / 411-6.

T5.4 Ugarit – *Ras Šamra.*

d600 ᴱBordreuil Pierre, *al.,* Une bibliothèque au sud de la ville; les textes de la 34ᵉ campagne (1973): RS-Ougarit 7. P 1991, RCiv. 208 p. 2-86538-219-2 [UF 23,449].

Bordreuil P., *Pardee* D., La trouvaille épigraphique de l'Ougarit I, 1989; Caquot A., *al.,* Textes ougaritiques 2, 1989 ➤ 9205; 9209.

d601 *a) Calvet* Yves, Les bassins du palais royal d'Ougarit; – *b) Courtois* Jacques-Claude, Yabninu et le palais sud d'Ougarit; Syria 67 (1990) 31-42; 10 fig. / 103-142; 6 fig.

d602 *Hunt* Patrick N., Mount Saphon in myth and fact: ➤ 445, Phoenicia 1990/1, 103-115; 5 fig.

Pardee D., Les textes para-mythologiques 1988 ➤ 9224.

d604 *a) Xella* Paolo, Tradition orale et rédaction écrite au Proche-Orient ancien; le cas des textes mythologiques d'Ugarit; – *b) Teixidor* J., Lire et entendre en ouest-sémitique: ➤ 630, Phoinikeia 1989/91, 69-89 / 91-97.

d605 **Yon** Marguerite, Arts et industries de la pierre: Ras Shamra-Ougarit 6. P 1991, RCiv. 410 p. 70 fig.; 53 pl. 2-86538-218-0.

d606 *a) Yon* M., *al.,* Fouilles de la 48ᵉ campagne (1988) à Ras Shamra-Ougarit; – *b) Mallet* Joël, Stratigraphie des vestiges du Bronze Moyen II exhumés de 1979 à 1988 (39ᵉ, 40ᵉ, 41ᵉ, 43ᵉ et 48ᵉ campagnes): Syria 67 (1990) 1-29; 23 fig. / 43-81; 5 fig.; + XVIII pl.; plan.

d607 **Yon** Marguerite, Ras Shamra-Ugarit 38th-46th, 1978-86: ➤ d627, AfO 36s (1989s) 287-293; fig. 100-104.

d608 *Yon* Marguerite, Ras Shamra 'last five years': ➤ d630, AJA 95 (1991) 723-7; fig. 26s.

T5.5 Ebla.

d609 ᴱArchi A., Eblaite personal names 1985/8 ➤ 4,718: ᴿBO 48 (1991) 590-600 (P. J. J. van *Huÿssteen*); OLZ 86 (1991) 159-162 (W. *Sommerfeld*).

d610 *Biga* Maria Giovanna, *Pomponio* Francesco, Elements for a chronological division of the administrative documentation of Ebla: JCS 42 (1990) 179-203.

d611 *a) Bonechi* Marco, ga-šurᵏⁱ dans les tablettes d'Ebla; – *b) Baldacci* Massimo, ÉxPAP and the Eblaite administrative terminology: WeltOr 22 (1991) 5-9 / 10-20.

d612 *a) Buccellatti* George, The Ebla electronic corpus, graphemic analysis; – *b) Platt* James H., *Pagan* Joseph M., Orthography and onomastics computer applications in Ebla language study: ➤ 626, AnASyr 40 (1989/90) 8-26, 161-6 / 27-38, ❹ 155-160.

d613 ᴱConti G., Miscellanea eblaitica 3: QuadSemit 17. F 1990, Univ. Dip. Linguistica. viii-220 p. [BL 92,135, W. G. E. *Watson*: 'These are (or ? there are) four sources for the Sumerian-Eblaite bilinguals ... The fourth of these is examined'; on the same page, comments on Quad-Semit 16, ᴱ*Fronzaroli* P. ➤ 5,e114].

d613* *D'Agostino* Franco, The study of Sumerian grammar at Ebla, I: AcSum 13 (1991) 157-180.

d614 *a) Dolce* Rita, La produzione artistica e il Palazzo di Ebla nella cultura urbana della Siria del III millennio a.c.; – *b) Scandone Matthiae* Gabriella, Una testa paleosiriana in avorio con corona atef: ParPass 46, 258ss (1991) 237-257 + 15 fig. / 372-387 + 6 fig.

d615 *a) Fronzaroli* Pelio, Lingua e testo negli archivi di Ebla; – *b) Biga* Maria Giovanna, Donne alla corte di Ebla; – *c) Baffi Guardata* Francesca, Il culto praticato ad Ebla paleosiriana: ParPass 46,258ss (1991) 220-235 / 285-303 / 394-409 + 7 fig.

d616 *Khayyata* M. W., ◐ Ebla between historical reality and biblical [Torah] interpretation: ➤ 626, AnASys 40 (1989/90) 27-30.

d617 *Matthiae* Paolo, Mardikh/Ebla: ➤ d630, AJA 95 (1991) 707-9; fig. 16s.

d618 *Matthiae* Paolo, Tall Mardīḫ-Ebla 1986s: ➤ d627, AfO 36s (1989s) 260-3; fig. 65-67.

d619 *Matthiae* Paolo, A new monumental temple of M.B. II at Ebla and the unity of architectural tradition in Syria-Palestine; – *b) Scandone Matthiae* Gabriella, Egyptianizing ivory inlays from Palace P at Ebla: ➤ 626, AnASyr 40 (1989/90) 111-116 + 5 pl.; ◐ 119-123 / 146-150 + 20 fig.; ◐ 127-9.

d620 *a) Mazzoni* Stefania, La période perse à Tell Mardikh et dans sa région dans le cadre de l'Âge de Fer en Syrie; – *b) Cagni* L., Considérations sur les textes babyloniens de Neirab près d'Alep: ➤ 636*, REuph 2 (1989/90) 187-196 + 3 fig. / 169-185.

d621 **Pettinato** Giovanni, Ebla, a new look at history, ᵀ*Richardson* C. Faith. Baltimore 1991, Johns Hopkins University. x-290 p.; ill. 0-8018-4150-X.

d622 **Waetzoldt** H., *Hauptmann* H., Wirtschaft und Gesellschaft von Ebla 1986/8 ➤ 4,707; 6,e133*: ᴿAnOr 59 (1991) 326-8 (B. *Hruška*); BO 48 (1991) 870-3 (B. R. *Foster*: what exactly was a 'palace' in which 1500 people lived? what language did the Eblaites speak?... This is a 'second' volume to which there will never be a 'first').

T5.8 **Situs effossi Syriae in ordine alphabetico.**

d623 *Adshead* S. A. M. & K., Topography and sanctity in the North Syrian corridor [TCHALENKO G.; THEODORET, Philotheos]: OrChr 75 (1991) 113-122.

d623* **Arnaud** Daniel, Textes [cunéiformes] syriens de l'âge du Bronze Récent (*Gonnat* Hatice, Sceaux hiéroglyphiques anatoliens de Syrie): AulaO supp. 1. Barc 1991, AUSA. 221 p. (1*-17* hiéroglyphes); 106 facsim.; VII pl. sceaux. 0212-5730.

d624 ᴱ**Dentzer** J.-M., *Orthmann* W., Archéologie et histoire de la Syrie II, 1989 ➤ 6,481: ᴿMesop-T 26 (1991) 239-244 (A. *Allara*); OLZ 86 (1991) 258-260 (H. *Klengel*); RÉByz 49 (1991) 325s (J.-C. *Cheynet*); RivArCr 67 (1991) 229-235 (Lucrezia *Spera*).

d625 *Elayi* Josette, Réflexion sur la place de l'histoire dans la recherche sur la Transeuphratène achéménide: TEuph 4 (1991) 73-80 [81-102, bibliographie].

d626 **Grainger** John D., The cities of Seleukid Syria 1990 ➤ 6,e335; £27.50: ᴿGreeceR 38 (1991) 98 (P. J. *Rhodes*).

Kennedy D., *Riley* D., Rome's desert frontier from the air 1990 ➤ e370.

d627 ᴱ*Kühne* Hartmut, Archäologische Forschungen in Syrien (4): AfO 36s (1989s) 202-353 [signed articles]; 165 fig.

d628 **Meijer** Diederich J. W., A survey in northeastern Syria [1976s, 1979], ᴰ1986 ➤ 6,e337: ᴿSyria 66 (1989) 373s (J.-Y. *Monchambert*).

d629 *Millard* A. R., Archaeology and ancient Syria [Palmyra, Khabuba Kabira, Ugarit ...]: ➤ 402, Anatolia 1991, 195-202.

d630 ᴱ*Weiss* Harvey, Archaeology in Syria: AJA 95 (1991) 683-740; 37 fig.; intended biennial.

---

d631 *Afis:* ➤ d630, AJA 95 (1991) 729-732; fig. 30-31 (Stefania *Mazzoni*).

d632 *Aḥmar:* *Bunnens* G., Melbourne university excavations at Tell Aḥmar, 1988 season: ➤ 621, Rencontre 36, 1989/91, 163-6 + 6 fig.

d633 *Aḥmar* [Til Barsip excavated c. 1930 by F. *Thureau-Dangin*]: **Bunnens** G., *al.*, Tell Aḥmar, 1988 season: Melbourne Expedition 1. Lv 1990, Peeters. x-151 p. 90-6831-322-3 [BL 92, 27, H. G. M. *Williamson*].

d634 *A'la:* **Peña** I., *Castellana* P., *Fernández* R., Inventaire du Jebel el-A'la; recherches archéologiques dans la région des Villes Mortes de la Syrie du Nord: SBF min. 31, 1990 ➤ 6,e342; $25: ᴿRB 98 (1991) 457s (J. M. de *Tarragon*).

d635 *Aleppo:* *Salati* M., Note in margine alla storiografia musulmana su Aleppo; una lista di Naqîb al-Ashrâf del XVI e XVII secolo: RSO 64 (1990) 381-7.

d635* *Apameia:* *Brenk* Beat, Die Umwandlung der Synagoge von Apamea in eine Kirche; eine mentalitätsgeschichtliche Studie: ➤ 47*, ᶠENGEMANN J., 1991, 1-25; 9 fig.; pl. 1-3.

d636 *'Arqa:* a) *Thalmann* J.-P., Teil 'Arqa (S trouée de Homs], de la conquête assyrienne à l'époque perse; – b) *Sapin* J., Essai sur les structures géographiques de la toponymie araméenne dans la Trouée de Homs (Liban-Syrie) et sur leur signification historique: ➤ 636*, Syrie perse 1989, TEuph 2 (1990) 51-56; 2 fig.; pl. III / 73-98 + 7 maps.

d637 *Aruda:* *Driel* G. van, Een reconstructie van de tempels op de Jebel Aruda [Euphrat/Habuba]: PhoenixEOL 37,2 (1991) 21-31; 4 fig.

d638 *Atij* 2/3, Gudeda 1/2 (Khabour) 1987: Syria 67 (1990) 219-256; 32 fig. / 525-577; 46 fig. (M. *Fortin*).

d639 *Bi'a* 1985, 1987: ➤ d627, AfO 36s (1989s) 221-7; fig. 26-30 (Eva *Strommenger*).

d640 Bi'a 1990, Byz, Early Dyn: MDOG 123 (1991) 7-34 (E. *Strommenger*) 41-70, Schrifturkunden (M. *Krebernik*).

d641 *Strommenger* Eva, Ergebnisse der Palastgrabung in Tell Bia bis 1987: ➤ 626*, AnASyr 40 (1989/90) 100-110; ❹ 175-7.

d642 *Bderi* 1985-7: ➤ d627, AfO 36s (1989s) 212-221; fig. 15-25 (P. *Pfälzner*).

d643 *Boṣra:* *Mougdad* Ryad al-, *al.*; Un amphithéâtre à Boṣra?: Syria 67 (1990) 201-4; 3 fig.

d644 *Brak* 1990s: Iraq 53 (1991) 127-145; 8 fig.; pl. XXI-XXXI (D. & Joan *Oates*); 147-148 glyptic (D. *Matthews*); 159-168, fig. 1, A Hurrian letter (G. *Wilhelm*).

d645 Brak, 9th 1987: ➤ d627, AfO 36s (1989s) 227-231; fig. 31-33 (D. *Oates*).

d646 *Burkuš:* *Freyberger* Klaus S., Zur Architekturdekoration der Tempelanlage von Burkush [SE Mt. Hermon, c. 10 B.C. - 10 A.D.]: Berytus 38 (1990) 155-162 + 6 pl.

d648 *Damascus:* *Dodinet* M., *al.*, Le paysage antique en Syrie; l'exemple de Damas: Syria 67 (1990) 341-355 + 12 pl.

d649 **Pitard** Wayne T., Ancient Damascus 1987 ➤ 3,e466... 6,e354: ᴿJNES 50 (1951) 147-150 (G.W. *Ahlström*); RÉAnc 92 (1990) 166 (M. *Sartre*); Syria 67 (1990) 527s (J. *Teixidor*).

d650 **Sack** Dorothée, Damaskus; Entwicklung und Struktur einer orientalisch-islamischen Stadt 1989 ➤ 5,e128*; 6,e356: ᴿBonnJbb 191 (1991) 891-4 (Annegret *Nippa*).

d651 *Dara, ain:* **Abu ʿAssāf** ʿAlī, Der Tempel von ʿAin Dārā [40 k NW Aleppo]: DAI-DamFor 3, 1990 ➤ 6,e358; DM 88: ᴿOLZ 86 (1991) 512-5 (R.-B. *Wartke*).

d651* *Derʿa:* **Kettenhofen** Erich, Zur Geschichte der Stadt Derʿā in Syrien: ZDPV 107 (1991) 77-91; map; pl. 2, coins.

d652 *Dura-Europos* since 1986: ➤ d630, AJA 95 (1991) 736-8; fig. 34s (P. *Leriche*).

d653 **Weitzmann** Kurt, *Kessler* Herbert L., The frescoes of the Dura synagogue and Christian art: DumbO 28. Wsh 1990. 292 p. $68. 0-88402-182-3. – ᴿAJA 95 (1991) 566s (Caroline J. *Hemans*).

d654 *Ḥama:* **Thuesen** I., Hama I. pre-/protohistoric 1988 ➤ 4,g45: ᴿSyria 67 (1990) 512s (H. de *Contenson*).

d655 *Hammam/Turkman:* ➤ d630, AJA 95 (1991) 719-723; 1 fig. (D.J.W. *Meijer*).

d656 Hammam Turkman 3d 1984, 4th 1986: ➤ d627, AfO 36s (1989s) 251-8; fig. 54-60 (M. van *Loon*, D.J.W. *Meijer*).

d657 *Ḥuwayra* / Chuera, 1986: ➤ d627, AfO 36s (1989s) 232s (W. *Orthmann*).

d658 **Orthmann** W., L'architecture religieuse de Tell Chuera: Akkadica 69 (1990) 1-18; 9 fig.

d659 *Ḥwes,* Ḥabur, 1986s: Berytus 38 (1990) 125-136; 4 fig.; 2 pl (Sophie *Berthier*), 137-154, Keramik, Hurri-Mitannisch / Neuassyrisch (P. *Pfälzner*).

d660 *Idlib:* **Klengel** Horst, The region of Idlib in Bronze Age: ➤ 626, AnASyr 40 (1989/90) 93-99; ◑ 169-174.

d661 *Kazel* -Syria, N Nahr al-Kabîr], 1985-7: Berytus 38 (1990) 10-124; 55 fig.; IX plans (Leila *Badre, al.*).

d662 **Stieglitz** Robert R., The city of Amurru: JNES 50 (1991) 45-48, map [Kazel or Simiriyan N of Nahr al Kabir].

d663 *a) Lund* J., The northern coastline of Syria in the Persian period; a survey of the archaeological evidence; – *b) Gubel* E., Tell Kazel (Ṣumur/Simyra) [S. Amrit] à l'époque perse; résultats préliminaires de trois premières campagnes de fouilles de l'Université américaine de Beyrouth (1985-1987): ➤ 636*, Syrie perse 1989, TEuph 2 (1990) 13-32 + 4 maps; pl. I / 38-46 + 3 fig. (old maps); pl. II.

d664 *Kerma:* **Saghieh** M., The Lebanese University recent excavations at Tell Kerma; a salvage operation on the Middle Khabur, N.E. Syria: ➤ 621, Rencontre 36, 1989/91, 171-5 + 10 fig.

d665 *Kowm:* **Dornemann** Rudolph H., A neolithic village at Tell el Kowm...: SAOC 43, 1986 ➤ 2,a875... 6,e376*: ᴿBASOR 281 (1991) 90s (A.M.T. *Moore*).

d666 *Leilan:* AJA 95 (1991) 703-7; fig. 14s (H. *Weiss*).

d667 *Eidem* Jasper, The Tell Leilan archives 1987: RAss 85 (1991) 109-135; français 135.

d668 *Mari* 28th 1990: ➤ 627*, AJA 95 (1991) 709-711; fig. 18s (J.-C. *Margueron*).

d669 **Anbar** Moshé, Les tribus amurrites de Mari: OBO 108. FrS/Gö 1991, Univ./VR. 248 p. DM 96 [TR 87,433]. 3-7278-0750-4 / 3-525-53741-7.

d669* *Cavigneaux* Antoine, *Ismail* Bahija K., Die Statthalter von Suḫu und Mari im 8. Jh. v. Chr. anhand neuer Texte aus den irakischen Grabungen im Staugebiet des Qadissiya-Damms: BaghMit 21 (1990) 321-410, 2 fig.; p. 411-456 facsimiles; pl. 35-38.

d670 **Durand** Jean-Marie [1], *Charpin* Dominique, *al.* [2], Archives épistolaires de Mari: ARM 26, 1988 ➤ 4,g55; 6,e383: ᴿJAOS 111 (1991) 626-8 (M. *Stol*).

d671 *Durand* Jean-Marie, Précurseurs syriens aux protocoles néo-assyriens; considérations sur la vie politique aux Bords-de-l'Euphrate: ➤ 61, ᶠGA-RELLI P., Marchands 1991, 13-71; 35 phot. (tablettes).

d672 *a) Gates* Marie-Henriette, Artisans and art in Old Babylonian Mari; – *b) Sasson* Jack M., Artisans... Artists; documentary perspectives from Mari: ➤ 641, Artistic 1988/90, 29-37; 4 fig. / 21-27.

d673 *a) Kupper* Jean-R., Zimri-Lim et ses vassaux; – *b) Charpin* Dominique, Le traité entre Ibāl-pi-El II d'Enunna et Zimri-Lim de Mari; – *c) Joannès* Francis, Le traité de vassalité d'Atamrum d'Andarig envers Zimri-Lim de Mari: ➤ 61, ᶠGARELLI P., Marchands 1991, 179-184 / 139-166 / 167-178.

d674 **Limet** Henri, Textes administratifs relatifs aux métaux: ARM 25. P 1986, RCiv. viii-291 p.; ill. – ᴿSyria 66 (1989) 362s (J. *Eidem*).

d675 **Malamat** Abraham, Mari and the early Israelite experience 1984/9 ➤ 5,b307; 6,b329*: ᴿBO 48 (1991) 862-5 (M. *Stol*); VT 41 (1991) 495s (J. N. *Postgate*).

d675* *a) Nakata* Ichiro, On the official pantheon of the Old Babylonian city of Mari as reflected in the records of issuance of sacrificial animals; – *b) Alster* Bendt, Incantation to Utu [OrAnt 8 (1969) 1-57]: AcSum 13 (1991) 249-258 / 27-96.

d676 **Talon** Philippe, Textes administratifs 'Y', 'Z': ARM 24, 1985 ➤ 1,d986 ... 4,g53: ᴿWZKM 78 (1988) 285-290 (M. Van de *Mieroop*, Eng., also on ARM 22s).

d678 *Mastuma:* AnASyr 40 (1990) ⊕ 167s (Namio *Ikami*, ᵀKhalid *as-Saʿad*).

d679 *Mozan* 5th 1988, 6th 1990, 3d-millennium immediately below surface: ➤ d630, AJA 95 (1991) 712-4, 1 fig. (G. & M. *Buccellati*).

d680 **Buccellati** G. & M., Mozan I 1988 ➤ 4,g57; 6,e389: ᴿWeltOr 22 (1991) 150-5 (J. *Waalke-Meyer*).

d681 *Munbāqa* 1989: MDOG 123 (1991) 71-93 (D. *Machule*).

d681* *Musmiye:* *Maʿoz* Z. Uri, The 'praetorium' at Musmiye, again [Phaene, erected before 169 A.D., now known only from 1875 recording]: DumbO 44 (1990) 41-46 [< JStJud 22,308].

d682 *Palmyra: a) Gawlikowski* Michel, Les *principia* de Dioclétien à Palmyre; projet et réalisation; – *b) Will* Ernest, La maquette de l'adyton du Temple A de Niha (Beqa): ➤ 691, Dessin 1984/5, 283-290; 2 fig. / 276-281; 3 fig.

d683 ᶠ**Ruprechtsberger** Erwin M., Palmyra; Geschichte, Kunst und Kultur der syrischen Oasenstadt: Ausstellung Linz 1987, Stadtmuseum. 274 p.; Katalog 275-357. – ᴿAnzAltW 44 (1991) 240-2 (Astrid *Larcher*).

d684 **Teixidor** Javier, Un port romain du désert: Semitica 34, 1984 ➤ 1,f253 ... 3,f891: ᴿJNES 50 (1991) 73-76 (D. *Kennedy*).

d685 **Qadbûn: Bounni** Adnan, La stèle de Qaḍboun [Baal combattant Qad-mous-Masyaf]: MÉF-A 103 (1991) 51-55; 1 fig.

d686 **Sabi Abyad: Akkermans** Peter, **Rossmeisl** Inge, Excavations at Tell Sabi Abyad, northern Syria, a regional centre on the Assyrian frontier: Akkadica 66 (1990) 13-43 + 17 fig. (map) [two name-lists, *Jas* E., 67 (1990) 33-39].

d687 **Šēḫ Ḥamad** 1985-7: ➤ d627, AfO 36s (1989s) 308-321; fig. 119-138 (H. *Kühne*).

d688 **Šenef: Bartl** K., Khirbet esh-Shenef, a Late Bronze Age settlement in the Balikh valley, Northern Syria: Akkadica 67 (1990) 10-22 + pl. (map).

d689 **Sūkās: Buhl** M., Sukas VII, 1983 ➤ 64,b702; 65, b162: ᴿPEQ 123 (1991) 67-70 (S. *Bourke*, also on *Lund* VIII).

d690 **Lund** J., Sūkās VIII, 1986 ➤ 3,e527... 5,e172: ᴿJNES 50 (1991) 153-5 (H. I. *MacAdam*).

d691 **Oldenburg** Evelyn, Sūkās IX, the chalcolithic and Early Bronze Age periods: Carlsberg Phoenicia 11 / Dansk Vid Selsk h/f 14. K 1991, Munksgaard. 63 p. + 65-125 = fig. 1-59; pl. I-IV apart. 87-7304-218-8.

d692 **Terqa** (Collège de France 1987-9): ➤ d630, AJA 95 (1991) 727-9; plan (O. *Rouault*).

d693 **Tûqân: Baffi Guardata** Francesca, Tell Touqan, une ville paléosyrienne: ➤ 626, AnASyr 40 (1989/90) 64-69 + 6 pl.; ❹ 137-9.

d693* **Wreide: Orthmann** Winfried, **Rova** Elena, Gräber des 3. Jahrtausends v.Chr. im syrischen Euphrattal, 2. Ausgrabungen in Wreide: Saarb-VorderasA 2. Saarbrücken 1991, S-Druckerei. 179 p.; 48 fig. 3-925036-47-4 [OIAc 2,25].

T6.1 Mesopotamia: Generalia.

d694 *a) Cooper* Jerrold S., Mesopotamian historical consciousness and the production of monumental art in the third millennium B.C.; – *b) Michalowski* Piotr, Early Mesopotamian comunicative systems; art, literature and writing: ➤ 641, Artistic 1988/90, 39-51; 14 fig. / 53-69.

d694* **Crawford** Harriet, Sumer and the Sumerians. C 1991, Univ. x-182 p. £27.50; pa. £11. 0-521-38175-4; pa. -850-3. – ᴿExpTim 103 (1991s) 22 (W. G. *Lambert*: really on Mesopotamian archaeology 4000-2000 with no input from Sumerian writings).

d695 *Daoust* J., L'Irak, ancienne Mésopotamie [DOROZYNSKI Alexandre, Science et Vie 883, avril 1991]: EsprVie 101 (1991) 516-8.

Echegaray J., El Creciente Fertil y la Biblia 1991 ➤ e302.

d697 *Englund* Robert A., Hard work – where will it get you? Labor management in Ur III Mesopotamia [Erlenmeyer collection auctioned London 1988, Nº 155]: JNES 50 (1991) 255-280; 5 fig.

d698 [**Gelb** Ignace J.,] *Steinkeller* Piotr, Earliest land tenure systems in the Near East; ancient kudurrus: OIP 104. Ch 1989-91, Univ. Oriental Institute. I. xviii-303 p.; 29 fig. – II. 166 pl. 0-918986-56-7.

d699 [*Hawkins* J. D., *al.*] Excavations in Iraq 1989-90: Iraq 53 (1991) 169-182; map.

d700 ᴱ**Henrickson** E. F., *Thuesen* I., Upon this foundation; the 'Ubaid reconsidered 1988/9 ➤ 6,804: ᴿMesop-T 26 (1991) 225-230 (P. *Mollo*).

d701 **Lackenbacher** Sylvie, Le palais sans rival; le récit de construction en
Assyrie: Textes à l'appui. P 1990, Découverte. 224 p.; 12 fig. 2-7071-
1972-5 [OIAc 1,19]. – [R]RÉAnc 93 (1991) 205s (S. *Ribichini*).

d701* *Lipiński* E., Phéniciens en Assyrie; l'eponyme Milkiram et la sur-
intendante Amat-Ashtart: ➤ 627, Fen. 2, 1987/91, 151-4.

d702 [E]*Meyer* L. De, (largely by) **Gasche** H.: Northern Akkad project reports:
Mesopotamian history and environment 1/1-7. Ghent 1987-91, Univ. 1.
(Sippar wall) 1987, 52 p. – 2. (Ṣaḫr) 1989, 70 p. – 3. (Dēr...) 1989, 61 p., 9
pl. – 4. (Abu Qubur) 1989, 43 p., 13 pl. – 5. (also Abu Qubur) 1991, 69 p.
– 6 (Dēr) 1991, 94 p. – 7. (Abu Qubur) 1991, 91 p.

d703 **Reade** Julian, Mesopotamia. L 1991, British Museum. 77 p.; ill.; map.
£6. 0-7141-2078-2 [BL 92,38, D. J. *Wiseman*).

d704 [F]SACHS Abraham, A scientific humanist, [E]**Leichty** E., *al.* 1988 ➤ 5,166:
[R]JAOS 111 (1991) 148-150 (Stephen J. *Lieberman*).

d705 *Sanlaville* P., Pays et paysages du Tigre et de l'Euphrate; réflexions sur
la Mésopotamie antique: Akkadica 66 (1990) 1-8; 4 maps.

T6.3 *Mesopotamia, scripta effossa* – **Excavated Tablets.**

d706 *Bauer* Josef, Altsumerische Wirtschaftsurkunden in Leningrad: AfO
36s (1989s) 76-91.

d707 **Cooper** Jerrold S., Sumerian and Akkadian royal inscriptions, 1. Pre-
sargonic 1986 ➤ 2,a914... 4,g91: [R]OLZ 86 (1991) 492-8 (H. *Neumann*:
zahlreiche Addenda).

d708 **Dalley** Stephanie, *Yoffee* Norman, Old Babylonian texts in the
Ashmolean Museum; texts from Kish and elsewhere: CuneifT 13. Ox
1991, Clarendon. (iv-) 290 p.; (288) facsim. 0-19-814479-2.

d709 **Donbaz** Veysel, Keilschrifttexte... Stamboul, II. 1989 ➤ 5,e184; 6,e434:
[R]BO 48 (1991) 179-183 (J. G. *Dercksen*).

d710 **Englund** Robert K., *Grégoire* Jean-Pierre, The Proto-Cuneiform texts
from Jemdet Nasr, I. Copies, transliterations and glossary: MSVO 1. B
1991, Mann. 220 p.; 91 + XII pl. 3-7861-1646-6.

d711 **Ferwerda** G. T., ... Isin craft archive: Tabulae Böhl 5. Leiden 1985,
Ned. Inst. Nab. Oosten. ix-63 p. 90-6258-127-7. – [R]BO 48 (1991) 565-7
(H. *Neumann*).

d711* *Friberg* Jöran, *al.*, 'Seed and reeds', a metro-mathematical topic text
from Late Babylonian Uruk: BaghMit 21 (1990) 483.553; 554-7
facsimile with facing-page transliteration on tablet facsimile; pl. 46-48.

d712 **Gelb** I. J.†, *Kienart* B., Die altakkadischen Königsinschriften... 1990
➤ 6,e443: [R]Orientalia 60 (1991) 351-4 (W. H. P. *Römer*: Beobachtungen).

d713 *George* A. R., Babylonian texts from the folios of Sidney SMITH [I. ...]
II. Prognostic and diagnostic omens, Tablet I: RAss [82 (1988) 139-162]
85 (1991) 137-169.

d713* **Gomi** Tohru, *Sato* Susumu, Selected Neo-Sumerian administrative
texts from the British Museum. Abiko 1990, Chuo-Gakuin Univ. 334 p.
(autographs of 258 texts). [OIAc 2,19].

d714 **Gurney** O. R., Literary and miscellaneous texts in the Ashmolean Mu-
seum: OxCuneif 11, 1989 ➤ 5,e188*a*; 6,e444: [R]AfO 36s (1989s) 118-120
(W. von *Soden*); BO 48 (1991) 852-860 (S. M. *Maul*); BSO 54 (1991) 234
(M. J. *Geller*); OLZ 82 (1991) 35-38 (E. v. *Weiher*).

d715 **Gurney** O. R., The Middle Babylonian legal and economic texts from
Ur, 1983 ➤ 65,b193... 2,a928: [R]JESHO 33 (1990) 117-124 (W. F. *Leemans*, franç.).

d716 *Hruška* Blahoslav, Die altsumerischen Nikolskij-Texte aus der Leningrader Eremitage: ArOr 59 (1991) 414-426.

d717 **Hunger** Hermann, *Pingree* David, MUL.APIN; an astronomical compendium in cuneiform: AfO Beih 24, 1989 ➤ 5,9341; 6,e445; Sch 495: ᴿOLZ 86 (1991) 165-8 (J. *Oelsner*); WeltOr 22 (1991) 183-8 (J. *Koch*).

d718 **Joannès** Francis, Archives de Borsippa; la famille Ea-ilûta-bâni 1989 ➤ 5,e190; 6,e447: ᴿWeltOr 22 (1991) 195-7 (R. *Zadok*).

d719 **Kessler** Karlheinz, Uruk; Urkunden aus Privathäusern; die Wohnhäuser westlich des Eanna-Tempelbereichs, I. Die Archive der Söhne des Bēl-Ušallim, des Nabû-Ušallim und des Bēl-Supê-Muhur: Uruk Endberichte 8. Mainz 1991, von Zabern. xxi-202 p.; 24 pl.; 3 plans. 3-8053-1229-6 [OIAc 1,19].

d720 **Kutscher** R., Royal inscriptions... Brockmon 1989 ➤ 5,e191; 6,e452: ᴿJAOS 111 (1991) 630s (B. R. *Foster*); StEpL 7 (1990) 134s (F. *Pomponio*).

d721 — *Frayne* Douglas R., Historical texts in Haifa; notes on R. KUTSCHER's 'Brockmon Tablets': BO 48 (1991) 378-409.

d721* *Horowitz* Wayne, *Watson* Philip J., Further notes on [Watson 1986] Birmingham Cuneiform Tablets volume 1: AcSum 13 (1991) 409-416 (417, 10 brief facsimiles).

d722 **Kwasman** Theodore, Neo-Assyrian legal documents in the Kouyunjik collection of the British Museum: StPohl 14, 1988 ➤ 4,g101; 6,e453: ᴿAfO 36s (1989s) 135s (A. R. *George*); Orientalia 60 (1991) 123s (J. N. *Postgate*).

d723 **Kwasman** Theodore, *Parpola* Simo, Legal transactions of the royal court of Niniveh, 1. Tiglath-Pileser III through Esarhaddon: SAA 6. Helsinki 1991. Univ. xliv-369 p.; 30 fig.; II pl. 951-570-093-0; pa. -2-2.

d724 **Lacheman** E. R., *Maidman* M. P., Nuzi 7 (texts), 1989 ➤ 5,e192: ᴿBO 48 (1991) 574s (W. von *Soden*).

d725 **Leichty** Erle, *al.*, Tablets from Sippar I-III: BM Catalogue 6-8, 1986-8 ➤ 4,g103... 6,e435; £35 + ? + 50; 0-7141-1115-5; -22-8; -24-4: ᴿBO 48 (1991) 202-210 (F. *Joannès*).

d726 **Lerberghe** Karel Van, Sippa – Amnānum; the Ur-Utu archive, 1: MesopHistEnv 3/1. Ghent 1991, Univ. xii-193 p.; 82 pl.

d727 **Marchant** Anne J., Old Babylonian tablets from Larsa in the [Berkeley] Lowie Museum of Anthropology: diss. California 1990, ᴰ*Kilmer* Anne. 310 p. 91-26688. – DissA 52 (1991s) 1477-A.

d728 **Mieroop** Marc Van de, ... Sumerian... documents... Išbi-Erra, Šu-ilušu 1987 ➤ 3,e572: ᴿJAOS 111 (1991) 366-372 (Maria D. *Ellis*); JNES 50 (1991) 65s (H. *Behrens*).

d729 *Milano* Lucio, Mozan 2 [➤ d679]; the epigraphic finds of the sixth season: SyrMes 5/1. Malibu CA 1991, Undena. 34 p.; 8 fig.; 4 pl. 0-89003-276-9.

d730 *Neumann* Hans, Zu einer Kopie der Inschrift Narāmsīn 2 aus Babylon: JCS 42 (1990) 202-210.

d731 **Owen** David I., Neo-Sumerian texts from American collections: Materiali per il vocabolario neosumerico 15. R 1991, Multigrafica. xiii-177 p.; 63 pl. (384 facsimiles); XXVI photos [OIAc 1,21].

d732 **Parpola** Simo, The correspondence of Sargon II, 1. Letters from Assyria and the West 1987 ➤ 3,e570... 6,e459: ᴿBO 48 (1991) 183-202 (K. *Watanabe*); JNES 50 (1991) 62s (R. D. *Biggs*).

d733 **Parpola** S., *Watanabe* K., Neo-Assyrian treaties SAA 2, 1988 ➤ 6,e460: ᴿWeltOr 22 (1991) 188-195 (W. v. *Soden*, also on SAA 3).

d734 **Postgate** J. N.,   The archive of Urad-Šerūa and his family; a Middle Assyrian household in government service: Analisi elettronica del cuneiforme 1988 ➤ 6,e461:   ᴿOLZ 86 (1991) 162-5 (O. *Pedersén*).

d735 **Sachs** A. J.†,   ᴱ*Hunger* H.,   Astronomical diaries and related texts from Babylonia 1, 1988 ➤ 4,g110; 5,e200:   ᴿJAOS 111 (1991) 323-332 (F. *Rochberg-Halton*); JNES 50 (1991) 63-65 (R. D. *Biggs*); OLZ 86 (1991) 499-502 (J. *Oelsner*).

d736 **Selz** Gebhard J.,   Altsumerische Verwaltungstexte aus Lagaš I, 1989 ➤ 5,e202:   ᴿJAOS 111 (1991) 147s (J. N. *Postgate*); JESHO 34 (1991) 241-3 (B. R. *Foster*).

d736* **Sigrist** Marcel,   Documents from the tablet collections in Rochester NY. Bethesda 1991, CDL.   124 p.; 32 pl.   0-9620013-8-4 [OIAc 2,27].

d737 **Sigrist** Marcel,   Textes économiques néo-sumeriens de ... Syracuse: RCiv 29, 1983 ➤ 64,b733 ... 5,e203:   ᴿJESHO 32 (1989) 104-6 (W. F. *Leemans*, also on RCiv 61, LAFONT B., Tello).

d738 **Sigrist** Marcel,   Old Babylonian account texts in the Horn Archaeological Museum: Assyriol. 7.   Berrien Springs MI 1990, Andrews Univ. v-138 p.   0-943872-53-7.

d738* **Sigrist** Marcel, *Gomi* Tohru,   The comprehensive catalogue of published Ur III tablets.   Bethesda MD 1991, CDL.   382 p.   0-9620013-8-4 [OIAc 2,27].

d739 **Spar** Ira,   Cuneiform texts in the Metropolitan Museum of Art, I. Tablets, cones and bricks 1988 ➤ 4,g112 ... 6,e466:   ᴿBO 48 (1991) 163-175 (Caroline *Janssen*, with extensive concordances).

d739* **Steinkeller** Piotr,   Sale documents of the Ur-III-period ᴰ1989 ➤ 5,e207; 6,e467:   ᴿJESHO 34 (1991) 243-6 (B. *Lafont*).

d740 **Stolper** Matthew W.,   Late Achaemenid legal texts from Uruk and Larsa: BaghMit 21 (1990) 559-599; 600-622, facsimiles; pl. 49-51.

d740* **Tsukimoto** Akio,   Akkadian tablets in the Hirayama collection (II): AcSum 13 (1991) 275-311 (-333 facsimiles; 335-345, six Euphrates fragments).

d741 **Weiher** Egbert von,   Spätbabylonische Texte aus Uruk 3, 1988 ➤ 4, g117:   ᴿOLZ 82 (1991) 41-45 (J. *Oelsner*).

d742 **Weisberg** David B.,   The Late Babylonian texts of the Oriental Institute collection: BtMesop 24.   Malibu CA 1991, Undena.   xiii-87 p.; 131 pl. 0-89003-303-1; pa. -0-5.

d743 **Whiting** Robert ᴶ,   Old Babylonian letters from Tell Asmar 1987 ➤ 4,g118 ... 6,e471:   ᴿJAOS 111 (1991) 145-7 (S. *Greengus*).

d744 **Wilhelm** S.,   Archiv Silwa-teššup, 3. Rationenlisten II.   Wsb 1985, Harrassowitz.   213 p.; x pl. – ᴿOrAnt 28 (1989) 273-5 (Paola *Negri Scafa*).

d745 **Yıldız** F., Gomi T.,   Puzriš-Dagan Texte 1988 ➤ 4,g119; 6,e472:   ᴿBO 48 (1991) 556-8 (H. *Limet*); JAOS 111 (1991) 380s (W. *Heimpel*); OLZ 87 (1992) 524-6 (F. *Pomponio*); WeltOr 22 (1991) 180-3 (D. I. *Owen*).

d746 **Yıldız** F., *Waetzoldt* H., *Renner* H., Umma-Texte 1988 ➤ 5,e215:   ᴿBO 48 (1991) 558-565 (W. H. P. *Römer*).

T6.5 **Situs effossi 'Iraq** *in ordine alphabetico.*

d747 *Agadé*: **Glassner** Jean-J.,   La chute d'Akkadé 1984 ➤ 6,e475:   ᴿSyria 67 (1990) 208-210 (P. *Amiet*).

d748 *'Ana*: **Northedge** A.,   Excavations at 'Ana, Qal'a Island: Iraq (British School/Directorate of Antiquities) Archaeological Reports 1. Wmr 1988,

Aris & P. xi-145 p.; 6 fig.; 41 pl.; 26 plans. £30. 0-85668-425-2 [JRS 81,253].

d749 **Asmar:** *Meyer* Carol, al., From Zanzibar to Zagros; a copal pendant from Eshnunna [i.e. a cigar-shaped object with a suspension-loop found at Asmar, dated c. 2400 B.C., formerly believed to be amber, but here claimed to be of a material (from the Mozambique area) called copal]: JNES 50 (1991) 289-298; 4 fig.

d750 **Aššur** 1990: MDOG 123 (1991) 95-109 (B. *Hrouda*), 111-4, Texte (K. *Hecker*), 115-122 topog. Neuaufnahme (M. *Stephani*); 123-131 magnetische Prospektion (H. *Becker*).

d750* *Miglus* Peter A., Auf dem Suche nach dem 'EKUR' in Assur: BaghMit 21 (1990).

d751 **Pedersén** Olof, Archives... Assur 1985s ➤ 1,d981 ... 5,e217: ᴿJAOS 111 (1991) 372-4 (J.A. *Brinkman*, also on ᴱVEENHOF K. 1986); JSS 36 (1991) 147-9 (Stephanie *Dalley*).

d751* **Babylon:** [*Faton* Andrée] *Zamora* Raoul, Babylone reconstruite par Saddam Hussein: Archéologia 266 (1991) 26-39.

d752 **Dūr Yaḫdun-Lim:** *Safren* Jonathan D., Dūr Yaḫdun-Lim – raison d'être of an ancient Mesopotamian fortress-city: JESHO 32 (1989) 1-48.

d753 **Fara:** **Martin** Harriet P., Fara... Shuruppak 1988 ➤ 6,e485: ᴿAJA 95 (1991) 170-173 (Edith *Porada*); Orientalia 60 (1991) 362-6 (Eva A. *Braun-Holzinger*).

d754 **Matthews** R.J., Fragments of officialdom from Fara: Iraq 53 (1991) 1-15; 9 fig.

d755 **Hassan** (Iraqi Hamrin basin): *Breniquet* Catherine, Une maison tripartite halafienne à Tell Hassan?: Mesop-T 26 (1991) 23-34; 5 fig.; map.

d756 **Isin** 11, 1989: ➤ 621, Rencontre 36, 1989/91, 185-7 + 12 fig. (B. *Hrouda*).

d757 **Karrana** (N Mossul): *Wilhelm* Gernot, *Zaccagnini* Carlo, Excavations at Tell Karrana 3 (1985 and 1986): Mesop-T 26 (1991) 5-14 (-22 pottery, *Rova* Elena); fig. 1-18.

d758 **Kar-Tukulti-Ninurta:** **Eickhoff** Tilman, Kar Tukulti Ninurta, eine mittelassyrische Kult- und Residenzstadt: AbhDOG 21. B 1985, Mann. DM 99. 3-7861-1384-X. – ᴿJAOS 111 (1991) 625s (M. van de *Mieroop*).

d759 **Khorsabad:** **Albenda** Pauline, The palace of Sargon... Dur-Sharrukin BOTTA-FLANDIN drawings 1843s: 1986 ➤ 2,a969 ... 5,e227: ᴿBO 48 (1991) 259-262 (R.P. *Sobolewski*); JNES 50 (1991) 151 (Ann C. *Gunter*).

d760 **Larsa:** *Beaulieu* Paul-Alain, Neo-Babylonian Larsa, a preliminary study: Orientalia 60,2 (1991) 58-81.

d761 ᴱ**Huot** Jean-Louis, Larsa 8-9, 1978-81, et Oueili 2-3, 1978 & 81, 1983 ➤ 64,b761; 65,b229: ᴿAcPraeh 22 (1990) 191-4 (B. *Jacobs*).

d762 **Huot** J.-L., Les travaux français à Tell el 'Oueili et Larsa, un bilan provisoire: Akkadica 72 (1991) 1-16 + 23 fig.

d762* ᴱ**Huot** Jean-Louis, 'Oueli, travaux de 1985: Mém. 89. P 1991, RCiv. 343 p. + ❹ 57. 2-86538-212-1 [OIAc 2,21].

d763 **Mohammed Arab:** **Bolt** Dianna G., Burial in an ancient northern Mesopotamian town; the evidence from Tell-MA: diss. California, ᴰ*Stronach* D. Berkeley 1991. 220 p. 92-03498. – DissA 52 (1991s) 2963s-A.

d764 **Mohammed Diyab:** ᴱ**Durand** Jean-Marie, Tell Mohammed Diyab, campagnes 1987 et 1988: CahNABU. P 1990, SEPOA. vi-122 p.; 8 pl. [OIAc 1,15].

d765 **Nimrud:** *Curtis* John, Excavations at Nimrud, Balawat and other Assyrian sites: BAngIsr 11 (1991s) 51-53 (lecture summary).

d766 **Herrmann** Georgina, Ivories from Nimrud 4/1s, Room SW 37, 1986
➤ 2,a973 ... 5,e231: ᴿAfO 36s (1989s) 156s (J. *Borchhardt*); BO 48 (1991)
250-8 (E. *Gubel*).

d767 *Nineveh* 1990: ➤ 627*, AJA 95 (1991) 313 (D. *Stronach*, S. *Lumsden*).

d767* **Russell** John M., Sennacherib's palace without rival at Nineveh
[< diss. 1985, Philadelphia]. Ch 1991, Univ. xii-342 p.; 137 fig.; 4 pl.,
map. 0-226-73175-8 [OIAc 2,26].

d768 *Nippur:* Kramer Samuel N.,† Lamentation over the destruction of
Nippur: AcSum 13 (1991) 1-26.

d768* *Nuzi:* ᴱ**Owen** D.I., *Morrison* Martha A., Studies Nuzi/Hurrians
2, 1987 ➤ 3,505.e566; 6,e513: ᴿWeltOr 22 (1991) 199-202 (Jeanette
Fincke).

d769 *Rudeidbeh* or Rubeidbeh: ᴱ**Killick** R.G., Tell Rudeidbeh, an Uruk
village in the Jebel Hamrin. Wmr 1988, British School Iraq. 182 p.; 55
fig.; 10 pl.; ◑ 21 p. – ᴿMesop-T 26 (1991) 230s (P. *Fiorina*).

d770 *Salabiḫ,* Uruk-mound, 1990: Iraq 53 (1991) 59-68; 5 fig. (Susan *Pollock, al.*).

d771 **Moon** Jane, Catalogue of Early Dynastic pottery 4: Abu Salabikh 3,
1987 ➤ 5,e242; 6,e516: ᴿAfO 36s (1989s) 148-155 (D. *Sürenhagen*).

d772 *Samarra: Breniquet* Catherine, Tell es-Sawwan [près de Samarra], réalités et problèmes: Iraq 53 (1991) 75-90; 10 fig.

d773 *Seleucia: Invernizzi* Antonio, Séleucie du Tigre, métropole grecque
d'Asie: RArchéol (1991) 180-5; 8 fig.

d774 *Šemšāra: Læssøe* Jørgen, *Jacobsen* Thorkild, Šikšabbum again [person
mentioned in Tell Šemšāra letters, Orientalia 54 (1985) 182-8]: JCS 42
(1990) 127-178.

d774* *Udannu: Beaulieu* Paul-Alain, Ubara (Ezenₓkaskal)ᵏⁱ = Kissik, not as
F. JOANNÈS Udannu: AcSum 13 (1991) 97-109.

d775 *Warka:* **Boehmer** Rainer M., Uruk 1985: Endberichte I, 1987 ➤ 6,
e525: ᴿBO 48 (1991) 904-6 (Ö. *Tunca*).

d776 **Eichmann** Ricardo, Uruk, die Stratigraphie: Endb. 3, 1989 ➤ 6,e526:
ᴿBSO 54 (1991) 357s (Harriet *Crawford*); Mesop-T 26 (1991) 232-5 (A.
Invernizzi).

d776* **Finkbeiner** Uwe, *al.*, Kampagne 35-37, 1982-1984; die archäologische
Oberflächenuntersuchung (Survey): Uruk-Warka Endberichte 4. Mainz
1991, von Zabern. xi-277 p.; x-278 pl., 32 foldout plans. 3-8053-1116-8
[OIAc 2,18, excerpted].

d777 *a) Hermansen* Bo D., Ubaid–pottery from Warka, Eanna XVIII-XVII;
– *b) Boehmer* Rainer M., Zur Funktion des Steinstifttempels in Uruk nach
Befunden der Kampagne 39; – *c) Sanati-Müller* Shirin, Texte aus dem
Sinkašid-Palast, III. Metalltexte; – *d) Wrede* Nadja, Katalog der Terrakotten der archäologischen Oberflächenuntersuchungen (Survey) des
Stadtgebietes von Uruk: BaghMitt 21 (1990) 1-31 + 16 fig. / 49-65; 13
fig.; pl. 1-6 / 131-213 / 216-301; pl. 7-34.

T6.7 Arabia.

d778 **Denton** (Branwen) Elizabeth, The late second millennium B.C. in the
Arab/Iranian gulf: diss. Bryn Mawr, ᴰEllis R. Ph 1991. 338 p. 92-12994.
– DissA 52 (1991s) 4380-A.

d779 ᴱ**Fahd** T., L'Arabie préislamique 1987/9 ➤ 5,816: ᴿBO 48 (1991) 653-7
(M. *Stol*); JAOS 111 (1991) 598-600 (P. *Mayerson*); OLZ 86 (1991) 292-6
(W.W. *Müller*).

Henninger Josef, Arabica varia: OBO 90, 1989 ≽ 9307: ᴿWeltOr 22 (1991) 222s (Katharina *Hackstein*).

d781 *Knauf* E., The Persian administration in Arabia: ≽ 636*, TEuph 2 (1989/90) 201-206; franç. 201.

d782 **Parker** S. Thomas, Romans and Saracens ᴰ1986 ≽ 2,a987... 5,e254: ᴿJNES 50 (1991) 151-3 (D. F. *Graf*: one-dimensional).

d783 **Potts** D. T., The Arabian Gulf in antiquity, I. From prehistory to the fall of the Achaemenid Empire. Ox 1990, Clarendon. xxii-419 p.; 44 fig.; 12 pl. £50. 0-19-814390-7. – ᴿAntiqJ 70 (1990) 484-6 (Beatrice de *Cardi*: good); BAngIsr 11 (1991s) 31-33 (Y. *Nini*).

d784 **Rice** M., Search for the Promised Land... Arabian Gulf. L 1985, Longman. vi-298 p.; 16 colour pl. £30. 0-582-75664-2. – ᴿBO 48 (1991) 277s (Elisabeth C. L. *During Caspers*).

d785 ᴱ**Salles** J. F., L'Arabie et ses mers 1, 1988 ≽ 5,822: ᴿBO 48 (1991) 657s (M. *Stol*).

Shahid Irfan, Byzantium and the Arabs 1984/9 ≽ b467.

d786 **Tabachnik** Stephen E., Explorations in [1888 Charles] DOUGHTY's Arabia Deserta. Athens GA 1987, Univ. Georgia. xii-275 p. $35. – ᴿJAOS 111 (1991) 791s (M. *Sells*).

---

d787 *Abraq*: **Potts** D. T., A prehistoric mound in the emirate of Umm al-Qaiwain; excavations at Tell Abraq in 1989. K 1990, Munksgaard. 157 p.; ill. – ᴿDLZ 112 (1991) 495-7 (B. *Brentjes*).

d787* *Bahrain*: **Killick** R. G., al., London–Bahrain 1990 excavations at Saar: ArabArchEp 2 (1991) 107-137; 22 fig.

d788 *Dhayab* (Ras Ḥayma UAE): ≽ 46, Mem. DRIEHAUS J. 1990, 339-378 (J. *Kastner*, J. *Häser*, C. *Velde*).

d789 *Dilmun–Failaka*: **Calvet** Yves, *Gachet* Jacqueline, Failaka. Lyon 1990, Maison de l'Orient. 377 p.; 4 pl. – ᴿMesop-T 26 (1991) 245-7 (E. *Valtz*).

d790 a) *MacAdam* Henry I., Dilmun revisited: ArabArchEp 1 (1990) 49-87; – b) *Bernard* Vincent, *Callot* Olivier, *Salles* Jean-François, L'église d'al-Qousoun, Failaka, Ière 1989: ArabArchEp 2 (1991) 145-181; 20 fig.

d790* **Jeppesen** Kirsten, Failaka... sacred enclosure. Aarhus 1989, Moesgard. 125 p.; 110 fig. – ᴿMesop-T 26 (1991) 248-250 (A. *Invernizzi*).

Kjaerum P., Dilmun 1/1, Stamp and cylinder seals 1983 ≽ d95.

d791 *Dur* (Umm al-Qaiwain, U.A.E.) 2d, 1988: ArabArchEp 2 (1991) 31-60; 43 fig. (E. *Haerinck*, al.).

d792 *Shabwa* (Yemen): **Pirenne** Jacqueline, Fouilles de Shabwa I, Les témoins écrits de la région de Shabwa et l'histoire: IFAO BAH 134. P 1990, Geuthner. [vi-] 161 p.; 34 fig.; LXXXIII pl. 2-7053-066-8.

d793 *Tayma*: **Potts** Daniel T., Tayma and the Assyrian empire: Arabian Archaeology and Epigraphy 2,1 (1991) 10-23.

d794 **Jung** Michael, Research on rock art in North Yemen: supp. 66 to AION 51,1 (1991). N 1991, Ist. Univ. Orientale. viii-59 p.; ill.

d794* *Jung* Michael, Rock art of North Yemen: RSO 64 (1990) 255-273; 16 fig.

T6.9   **Iran, *Persia;*   Asia centralis.**

d795 **Carter** Elizabeth, *Stolper* Matthew W., Elam 1984 ≽ 1,419... 3,b768: ᴿJESHO 32 (1989) 106-8 (W. F. *Leemans*).

d796 **Curtis** John, Ancient Persia, British Museum guide. L 1989. 72 p., ill.
    – ᴿBSO 54 (1991) 376 (A. D. H. *Bivar*).
d797 **Dittmann** Reinhard, Betrachtungen zur Frühzeit des Südwest-Iran; re-
    gionale Entwicklungen vom 6. bis zum frühen 3. vorchristlichen Jahr-
    tausend: BBeitVO 4. B 1986, Reimer. I. xxviii-487 p. – II. v + p. 489-
    645 (fig.; 2 maps). 3-496-00883-0.
d799 ᴱ**Ferrier** Ronald W., The arts of Persia 1989 ➤ 5,539: ᴿJAOS 111
    (1991) 400s (G. D. *Lowry*: lavish but unsatisfactory).
d800 **Gall** Hubertus von, Das Reiterkampfbild in der iranischen und iranisch
    beeinflussten Kunst parthischer und sasanidischer Zeit: TehFor 6. B
    1990, Mann. 113 p.; 24 pl.; 2 foldouts. 3-7861-1511-7 [OIAc 1,16].
d801 ᴱ**Hole** Frank, The archaeology of Western Iran; settlement and so-
    ciety from prehistory to the Islamic conquest (Hole ch. 1-3; ch. 4-6
    Susiana, *Johnson* G., *Wright* H., *Alden* J. ...): Archaeological Inquiry,
    1987 ➤ 4,744.g197; 5,e268: ᴿAfO 36s (1989s) 166-170 (R. *Bernbeck*);
    AJA 95 (1991) 546 (W. M. *Sumner*).
d802 *Joannès* F., Pouvoirs locaux et organisation du territoire en Babylonie
    achéménide; – *b*) *Lecoq* P., Observations sur le sens du mot *dahyu*
    [(lawless) mob, populace]: ➤ 636*, TEuph 3 (1989/90) 173-195 / 131-140.
d803 *a*) *Stève* M.-J., Élam – histoire continue ou discontinue?; – *b*) *Oates* J.,
    Babylonia and Elam in prehistory; – *c*) *Selz* G. J., 'Elam' und 'Sumer' –
    Skizze einer Nachbarschaft nach inschriftlichen Quellen der vorsar-
    gonischen Zeit; – *d*) *Uchitel* A., Foreign workers in the [Persepolis]
    fortification archive: ➤ 621, Rencontre 36, 1989/91, 1-9 / 23-26 / 27-43 /
    127-135.
d804 **Schippmann** Klaus, Grundzüge der Geschichte des sasanidischen Rei-
    ches. Da 1990, Wiss. 155 p.
    Yamauchi Edwin M., Persia and the Bible 1900 ➤ b200.

---

d805 *Bisitun*: **Schmitt** Rüdiger, Epigraphisch-exegetische Noten zu Dareios'
    Bisutun-Inschriften: Szb ph/h 561. W 1990, Österr. Akad. 88 p.; 12 pl.
    3-7001-1770-1 [AIOc 1,24].
d806 *Dinkha*: *Rubinson* Karen S., A mid-second millennium tomb at Dinkha
    Tepe (Iran, Azarbaijan): AJA 95 (1991) 373-394; 29 fig. [395, glass beads,
    McGovern P. E., al.].
d807 *Haft*: **Negahban** Ezat O., Excavations at Haft Tepe, Iran: Mg 70. Ph
    1991, Univ. Museum. xxix-156 p.; 62 fig.; 58 pl. + 4 color.; 8 maps.
    0-934718-89-X. – ᴿMesop-T 26 (1991) 237-9 (B. *Carruba*).
d808 *Marlik*: **Negahban** Ezzat O., Marlik, a prehistoric Persian civilization.
    1991, Mage. 0-934211-23-X.
d809 *Luristan*: *Moorey* P. R. S., The decorated ironwork of the Early Iron
    Age attributed to Luristan in western Iran: Iran 29 (1991) 1-12 (13-19,
    Rehder J. E.); pl. I-III.
d810 *Malyan* [46 k from Shiraz]: *Wasilewska* E., To be or not to be a
    temple? the possible identification of a Banesh period temple at Tall-i
    Malyan, Iran: ➤ 621, Rencontre 36, 1989/91, 143-9 + 7 fig.
d811 **Nicholas** Ilene M., The proto-elamite settlement at ᴛᴜᴠ, Malyan I. Ph
    1990, Univ. Museum. xiv-166 p.; 38 fig.; 37 pl. – ᴿMesop-T 26 (1991)
    236s (B. *Carruba*).
d812 *Nišapur*: **Wilkinson** Charles K., Nishapur... early Islamic decoration
    [*Upton* J. excavations 1935-40]. NY 1986, Metropolitan Museum of Art.

328 p.; 500 fig. $75. – ᴿJAOS 111 (1991) 153s (A. S. *Shahbazi*: magnificent).

d813 *Naqš-i Rustam*: **Seidl** Ursula, Die elamischen Felsreliefs ... Naqš-i Rustam 1986 ⇥ 4,g206* ... 6,e547: ᴿSyria 66 (1989) 358-362 (P. de *Miroschedji*).

d814 *Persepolis*: a) *Roaf* Michael, Sculptors and designers at Persepolis; – b) *Root* Margaret C., Circles of artistic programming; strategies for studying creative process at Persepolis: ⇥ 641, Artistic 1988/90, 105-114; 10 fig. / 115-139; 15 fig.

d815 *Byvanck-Quarles van Ufford*, L., 'Achämenidischer Becher' ou 'bol ionien à panse arrondie' [Persépolis etc.]: Babesch 66 (1991) 159-162; 5 fig.

d816 *Sirjan:* **Allan** James, **Roberts** Caroline, Syria and Iran; three studies in medieval ceramics [mostly on N. Iran Sirjan excavation of Andrew *Williamson*]. Ox 1987, UP. 220 p.; 68 fig.; 41 pl. £37.50; pa. £25. 0-19-728007-2; -0. – ᴿAntiqJ 70 (1990) 492-4 (D. *Whitehouse*).

d817 *Susa:* **Amiet** Pierre, Suse, 6000 ans d'histoire 1988 ⇥ 4,g213: ᴿSyria 66 (1989) 355s (P. de *Miroschedji*).

d818 a) *Lambert* W. G., The Akkadianization of Susiana under the Sukkalmaḫs; – b) *Charpin* D., *Durand* J.-M., La suzeraineté de l'empereur (Sukkalmaḫ) d'Élam sur la Mésopotamie et le 'nationalisme' amorrite; – c) *Glassner* J. J., Les textes de Haft Tépé, la Susiane et l'Élam au 2ème millénaire: ⇥ 621, Rencontre 36, 1989/91, 53-57 / 59-66 / 109-126.

d819 *Ṭāq-i Bustan*: *Meyer* Marion, Die Felsbilder Shapurs I: JbDAI 105 (1990) 237-302; 45 fig.

d820 *Bejuk-Emili*: *Brentjes* Burchard, Kirche oder iranischer Tempel? [Kilisadag Bejuk-Emili, like Mamkrukh and Lekit]: ArchMIran 23 (1990) 229s; 3 fig.

d821 **Kohl** Philip L., Central Asia; paleolithic beginnings to the Iron Age: Synthèse 14. P 1984, RCiv/ADPF. 282 p.; 24 fig.; 23 maps. – ᴿAJA 95 (1991) 167-170 (Elizabeth *Carter*: western Turkestan).

d821* **Goldman** Bernard, The ancient arts of Western and Central Asia; a guide to the literature. Ames 1991, Iowa State Univ. ix-303 p. 0-8138-0597-X [OIAc 2,19].

d822 *Harappa*: **Possehl** Gregory L., **Raval** M. H., Harappan civilization and Rojdi [100 k SW Rangpur]. New Delhi 1989, IBH/American Institute of Indian Studies. 197 p.; 85 fig.; 46 pl. rs 225. – ᴿJAOS 111 (1991) 108-113 (W. A. *Fairservis*).

d823 **Chakrabarti** Dilip K., A history of Indian archaeology from the beginning to 1947. New Delhi 1988, Manoharlal. 262 p. – ᴿJESHO 34 (1991) 376-8 (E. C. L. *During Caspers*).

d824 ᴱGhosh A., An encyclopaedia of Indian archaeology 1. Subjects; 2. Sites. Leiden 1990, Brill. xvi-413 p.; 470 p. *f* 400 [OLZ 87,573, C. *Wessels-Mevissen*].

T7.1 **Aegyptus**, *generalia*.

d825 **Adams** Barbara, Predynastic Egypt: Shire Egyptology 7. ... 1988, Shire. 76 p.; 47 fig. 0-85263-938-4. – ᴿFolOr 27 (1990) 263s (K. M. *Ciałowicz*).

d826 [E]Assmann Jan, *al.*, Problems and priorities in Egyptian archaeology 1985/7 ➤ 3,796: [R]BO 48 (1991) 100-110 (M. *Bietak*).

d827 **Assmann** Jan, Stein und Zeit; Mensch und Gesellschaft im alten Ägypten. Mü 1991, Fink. 334 p.; 39 fig. 3-7705-2681-3 [OIAc 1,10].

d828 **Aufrère** Sydney, *al.*, L'Égypte restituée; sites et temples de la Haute Égypte (1650 av. J.-C. - 300 ap. J.-C.). P 1991, Errance. 270 p.; (color.) ill. 2-87772-063-2.

d829 *Blumenthal* Elke, Ein Leipziger Grabdenkmal im ägyptischen Stil und die Anfänge der Ägyptologie in Deutschland: ➤ 75, [F]HERRMANN S., Prophetie 1991, 9-28.

d830 [Boddens] **Hosang** F. J. E., De Egyptische verzameling van Baron von Westreenen / The Egyptian collection...: Mg Museum van het Boek 4. Haag 1989, SDU. 104 p.; 57 fig.

Bothmer Bernard V. [C.C. Bastis Egyptian] Antiquities... 1987 ➤ b515.

d832 **Caputo** Robert, Viaggio lungo il Nilo dal Delta alle sorgenti. Novara 1989, De Agostini. 164 p.; ill. (color.) Lit. 55.000. – [R]Archeo 69 (1990) 128 (S. *Pernigotti*).

d833 **Der Manuelian** Peter, Studies in archaism of the Egyptian twenty-sixth dynasty: diss. Chicago 1990, [D]*Baer* K. xxxi-659 p. (3 vol.). – OIAc 1,20.

d834 *Donadoni* Sergio, La classicità dell'arte egizia: ➤ 618, Egitto fuori Egitto 1990/1, 3-11.

d835 **France** Peter, The rape of Egypt; how the Europeans stripped Egypt of its heritage. L 1991, Barrie & J. vii-240 p.; 10 pl. 0-7126-2102-4.

d836 *Grimal* Nicolas, Travaux de l'IFAO en 1990-1991; chantiers archéologiques et programmes de recherche: BIFAO 91 (1991) 265-345.

d837 **Günther** Peter, *Wellauer* Rudolf, [185 untraceable] Ägyptische Steingefässe der Sammlung R. Schmidt: Äg. Hefte 2. Z 1988, Univ. Or. Sem. x-82 p.; 38 pl. – [R]BO 48 (1991) 812s (S. *Hendrickx*: unenthusiastic).

d838 **Harpur** Yvonne, Decoration in Egyptian tombs of the Old Kingdom 1987 ➤ 3,d607: [R]JEA 77 (1991) 208s (R. *Freed*).

d839 **Hobson** Christine, Exploring the world of the Pharaohs 1987 ➤ 3,e703; 4,g243: [R]JNES 50 (1991) 159s (W. J. *Murnane*: pleasurable but with far too many mistakes).

d840 **Hoffman** Michael A., Egypt before the Pharaohs; the prehistoric foundations of Egyptian civilization. Austin 1991 [= 1979 ➤ 61,t419 + Addendum], Univ. Texas. xxi-409 p.; 84 fig. 0-292-72073-4 [OIAc 1,18].

James P., *al.*, Centuries of darkness; a challenge to the conventional chronology of Old World archeology [events assigned since PETRIE to the years 1200-950 must be relocated and the gap closed] 1991 ➤ d293.

d842 *Kamil* Jill, Coptic Egypt, history and guide 1987 ➤ 4,d206: [R]JAOS 111 (1991) 378s (D. B. *Spanel*).

d843 *Kitchen* Kenneth A., Ancient Egypt and the Old Testament: BAnglsr 11 (1991s) 48-51; 2 fig. (lecture summary).

d844 **Leclant** Jean, *Clerc* Gisèle, Fouilles et travaux en Égypte [99 sites] et au Soudan [34], 1989-1990: Orientalia 60 (1991) 159-273; pl. XXVII-CV.

d844* a) **Leclant** Jean, Les Phéniciens et l'Égypte; – b) *Nibbi* Alessandra, The Canaan in Egypt: ➤ 627, Fen. 2, 1987/91, 7-17 / 169-178.

d845 [F]MOKHTAR Gamal Eddin, Mélanges, [E]**Posener-Kriéger** Paule. 1985 ➤ 2,77: [R]CdÉ 65,130 (1990) 243-6 (N. *Strudwick*).

d846 *Ogdon* Jorge R., Some reflections on the 'megalit[h]ic' cultural expressions in ancient Egypt (with reference to the symbolism of the stone): VarAeg 6 (1990) 17-22.

d847 ᶠPARKER Richard A., Egyptological Studies, ᴱLesko L. 1986 ➤ 3,126; 5,e311: ᴿCdÉ 65,130 (1990) 246-252 (D. *Devauchelle*, détaillé).

d848 **Payne** Willis E., Ancient Egyptian ethnicity; a case of obscurantism: anthropology M.A. thesis, California State Univ., ᴰ*Bates* Eleanor H. Long Beach 1988. iv-43 p. 13-35091. – OIAc 1,22.

d848* *Pernigotti* Sergio, Le 'arti minori' nell'antico Egitto: Archeo 71 (Novara 1991) 64-107.

d849 **Prisse d'Avennes** E., Atlas de l'art égyptien. Cairo 1991 = 1868-78, Zeitouna. xix-405 p.; 159 pl. 977-5170-00-1 [OIAc 1,23].

d850 **Russmann** Edna R., Egyptian sculpture, Cairo and Luxor 1989 ➤ 6, e590: ᴿVarAeg 6 (1990) 96s (R. H. *Wilkinson*).

d851 *Sidebotham* Steven E., *al.*, Survey of the ʿAbu Shaʿar (Coptos-on)-Nile road: AJA 95 (1991) 571-622; 39 fig.

d852 *Smits* J., Het oude Egypte als voorbeeld? Een dromerige oratie van prof. Johannes BRAUN (1692) in Groningen: Phoenix-EOL 37,2 (1991) 12-20.

d853 *Strudwick* Nigel, An objective colour-measuring system for the recording of Egyptian tomb-paintings: JEA 77 (1991) 43-56; 2 fig.; pl. IV,1.

d854 **Syriani** Samuel al-, *Habib* Badri, Guide to ancient Coptic churches and monasteries in Upper Egypt 1990 ➤ 6,e594: ᴿOstkSt 39 (1990) 224s (O. *Meinardus*).

d855 *Verner* M., ⊕ Unearthing ancient Egypt; thirty years of explorations of the Czechoslovak Institute of Egyptology in Egypt: VDI 196 (1991) 138-165; 14 fig.

d856 **Wildung** Dietrich, Die Kunst des alten Ägypten 1988 ➤ 5,e322: ᴿBO 48 (1991) 774-9 (Maya *Müller*).

т7.2 **Luxor,** *Karnak* [East Bank] – **Thebae** [West Bank].

d857 **Gammal** Maged H., Luxor, Egypt; balancing archaeological preservation and economic development; a policy analysis using computer transportation and land use simulation models: diss. Pennsylvania, ᴰ*Putman* S. [20-year developer of this model]. Ph 1991. 458 p. 92-00332. – DissA 52 (1991s) 2727-A.

d860 **Portman** Ian, Luxor; a guide to the temples and tombs of ancient Thebes. Cairo 1989, American Univ. 96 p.

---

d861 **Golvin** J.-C., *Goyon* J., Karnak, Ägypten; Anatomie eines Tempels [1987], ᵀ1990 ➤ 6,e598: ᴿKlio 73 (1991) 687s (J. *Hallof*).

d862 **Jacquet-Gordon** Helen, Karnak-Nord VI: Fouilles 32. Le Caire 1988, IFAO. vi-302 p., 3 pl.; vol. of xiv + 74 pl. 2-7247-0073-2. – ᴿBO 48 (1991) 482 (W. J. *Murnane*: exemplary).

d863 *Kruchten* Jean-Marie, Le 'Maître des dieux' de Karnak: ➤ 43, ᶠDERCHAIN P., Religion 1991, 179-187.

d864 *Letellier* Bernadette, Thoutmosis IV à Karnak; hommage tardif rendu à un bâtisseur malchanceux: BSocFrÉg 122 (1991) 36-52; 4 fig.

d864* *Rainey* Anson, Challenge [to YURCO's 'Israelites' at Karnak] BAR-W 17,6 (1991) 60; 18,2 (1992) 21 . 72, Diana *Edelman* protests ignoring of alternatives in her article (with G. W. *Ahlström*) in JNES 44 (1985) 59-61.

d865 *Van Siclen* Charles C., Preliminary report on epigraphic work done in the edifice of Amenhotep II [Karnak], seasons of 1988-89 and 1989-90: VarAeg 6 (1990) 75-90 (-95).

---

d865* **Hornung** Erik, *a*) The valley of the kings [1982 ➤ 63,d426], ᵀ*Warburton* David, 1990 ➤ 6,e617: ᴿAntiquity 65 (1991) 135 (T. *Taylor*). – *b*) The tomb of Pharaoh Seti I. Mü 1991, Artemis. 263 p.; 243 fig. (Burton H.) 243 p. DM 198. – ᴿErbAuf 67 (1991) 488 (B. *Schwank*).

d866 **Abitz** Friedrich, Ramses III. in den Gräbern seiner Söhne: OBO 72, 1986 ➤ 5,e339; 6,e605: ᴿBO 48 (1991) 471-4 (T. *Podgórski*); WZKM 79 (1989) 262-4 (E. *Winter*).

d867 **Abitz** Friedrich, Baugeschichte und Dekoration des Grabes Ramses' VI. 1989 ➤ 5,e338; 6,e606: ᴿOLZ 86 (1991) 150-2 (W. *Barta*).

d868 **Assmann** Jan, Das Grab des Amenemope, TT 41: Theben 3. Mainz 1991, von Zabern. x-299 p.; 11 fig.; vol. of 76 + LXXXIV pl. 3-8053-1091-9.

d869 **Beinlich** Horst, **Saleh** Mohamed, Corpus der hieroglyphischen Inschriften aus dem Grab des Tutanchamun 1989 ➤ 5,e342; £45: ᴿBO 48 (1991) 764s (H. A. *Schlögl*).

d869* — *a*) **Reeves** Nicholas, The complete Tutankhamun; the king, the tomb, the royal treasure 1990 ➤ 6,e627: ᴿAntiquity 65 (1991) 135 (T. *Taylor*). – *b*) **Winstone** H. V. F., Howard CARTER and the discovery of the tomb of Tutankhamun. L 1991, Constable. 333 p.; 24 pl. 0-09-469900-3.

d870 **Beinlich-Seeber** Christine, *Shedid* Abdel G., Das Grab des Userhat (TT 56): DAI-K ArchVeröff 50, 1987 ➤ 3,e742: ᴿBO 48 (1991) 790-3 (P. *Der Manuelian*); JEA 77 (1991) 215-8 (N. *Strudwick*).

d871 **Dorman** Peter, The tombs of Senenmut; the architecture and decoration of [Thebes] tombs 71 and 353: Publ. Eg. Exped. 24. NY 1991, Metropolitan. 181 p.; 96 (color.) pl.; map. 0-87099-620-7.

d871* ᴱ**Sayfried** Karl-Joachim, Das Grab des Paenkhemenu (TT 68) und die Anlage TT 227: Theben 6. Mainz 1991, von Zabern. viii-149 p.; 13 pl. + 8 color. + 13 foldout. 3-8053-1233-4 [OIAc 2,27].

---

d872 *Eaton-Krauss* Marianne, [Dra Abu l-Naga] The coffins of Queen Ahhotep, consort of Seqeni-en-Re and mother of Ahmose: CdÉ 65,130 (1990) 195-205.

d873 **Eigner** Diethelm, Die monumentalen Grabbauten der Spätzeit der thebanischen Nekropole 1984 ➤ 65,b332; 1,e116: ᴿBO 48 (1991) 491-6 (J. *Assmann*).

d874 *Gundlach* Rolf, *al.*, Sennefer; die Grabkammer des Bürgermeisters von Theben. Mainz 1991, von Zabern. 104 p.; 69 (color.) fig. 3-8053-1022-6.

d876 *Leblanc* Christian, *Abdel-Rahman* Ibrahim, Remarques relatives à la tombe de la reine Douatentipet: RÉgp 42 (1991) 147-169; 5 fig. + facsimiles; pl. 3-10.

d877 *Kitchen* Kenneth A., Building the Ramesseum: ➤ 40, Mém. CLÈRE J. 1991, 85-93.

d879 **Krzyzanowski** Lech, *al.*, The temple of Queen Hatshepsut, 4: report of the Polish-Egyptian archaeological and preservation mission, Deir el-Bahari 1980-1988. Wsz 1991, PKZ. 96 p.; ill.; maps. 83-85044-20-5.

d880 **Manniche** Lise, Wall decoration 1988 ➤ 4,g278; 6,e623:   ᴿBO 48 (1991) 785s (N. *Cherpion*); OLZ 82 (1991) 27-30 (F. *Kampp*).

d881 **Mekhitarian** A., *al.*, Passage vers l'éternité; peintures de la nécropole thébaine. P/Knocke 1989, Ozalid/Mappamundi. 194 p. 2-905904-02-X. – ᴿBO 48 (1991) 779-781 (E. *Dziobek*).

d884 Tomb 32, 5th 1988 / 6th 1989: AcArchH 43 (1991) 3-14 / 15-34, 8 fig. (L. *Kákosy*).

d885 **Wachsmann** Shelley, Aegeans in the Theban tombs [all from two Minoan delegations under Hatshepsut and Thutmosis III] 1987 ➤ 3, e746... 5,e363: ᴿJEA 77 (1991) 218s (K. A. *Kitchen*); JMeditArch 4 (1991) 235-247 (J. D. *Muhly*, mostly on S. MANNING's chronology; 249-262, Manning's reply).

d886 **Thissen** Heinz J., Die demotischen Graffiti von Medinet Habu; Zeugnisse zu Tempel und Kult im ptolemäischen Ägypten: Demotische Studien 10, 1989 ➤ 5,b46: ᴿBO 48 (1991) 465-7 (H. De *Meulenaere*).

d887 **Ventura** R., Living in a city of the dead 1986 ➤ 3,e752... 6,e634: ᴿVDI 196 (1991) 188-198 (E. S. *Bogoslovsky* †, also on GUTGESELL M. 1981; BIERBRIER M. 1984; VALBELLE D. 1985).

d888 **Burkard** Günter, Die Papyrusfunde: Asasif 3, 1986 ➤ 2,b147; 6,e637: ᴿJNES 50 (1991) 54 (E. S. *Meltzer*).

T7.3   **Amarna.**

d888* **Aldred** Cyril, Akhenaten, King 1988 ➤ 4,g290... 6,e638;   also L 1991, Thames & H.: ᴿAmHR 96 (1991) 142 (D. B. *Redford*); JAOS 111 (1991) 388-390 (W. J. *Murnane*: good but controvertible).

d889 *a) Altenmüller* Hartwig, Papyrusdickicht und Wüste; Überlegungen zu zwei Statuen-ensembles des Tutanchamun; – *b) Junge* Friedrich, Ein Bruchstück vom Kopf einer Achenaten-Statue aus Elephantine; – *c) Munro* Peter, Anmerkungen zu zwei Königsplastiken der Amarna-Zeit: ➤ 85c, ᶠKAISER W., MiDAI-K 47 (1991) 11-19 / 191-4; pl. 18 / 255-262; 7 fig.; pl. 32-33.

Beinlich H., *Saleh* M., Inschriften... Grab des Tutanchamun 1989 ➤ d869; **Reeves** N., The complete Tutankhamun 1990; ➤ d869*.

d889* **Bell** Martha R., The Tutankhamun burnt group from Gurob, Egypt; bases for the absolute chronology of LH III A and B: diss. Pennsylvania, ᴰ*DeVries* Keith. Ph 1991. xiii-551 p. 91-25590. – OIAc 2,14.

Bomann Ann H., Private chapel... workmen's village, Amarna ᴰ1987: 1981 ➤ a776.

d890 *Eaton-Krauss* Marianne, Neue Forschungen zum Schatz des Tutanchamun: AntWelt 22 (1991) 97-105; 16 fig.

d891 *Fritz* Walter, Bemerkungen zum Datierungsvermerk auf der Amarnatafel Kn 27: StAäK 18 (1991) 207-214; pl. 7.

d892 *a) Hess* R. S., The operation of case vowels in the personal names of the Amarna texts; – *b) Izre'el* S., Some thoughts on the Amarna version of Adapa: ➤ 621, Rencontre 36, 1989/91, 201-210 / 211-230.

d893 **Jacq** Christian, Nefertiti et Akhénaten; le couple solaire. P 1990, Perrin. 256 p.; 8 pl. 2-262-00802-7 [OIAc 1,18].

d894 *Jones* Michael, The early Christian sites at Tell el-Amarna and Sheikh Said: JEA 77 (1991) 129-144; 4 fig.; pl. IX-XII.

d895 **Kemp** Barry J., Amarna reports: *a*) 3s, 1986s ➤ 2,b87; 3,e762: ᴿOLZ 86 (1991) 376-8 (M. *Mode*); – *b*) 5, 1989 ➤ 5,e378: ᴿBO 48 (1991) 786-9 (M. *Eaton-Krauss*).

d896 *Krauss* Rolf, Einige Kleinfunde mit Namen von Amarnaherrschern: CdÉ 65,130 (1990) 206-218; 3 fig.

d897 *Lagrange* M.-J., *a*) The pretended monotheism of Amenophis IV (1911); – *b*) The Jewish military colony of Elephantine under the Persians (1907): ➤ g864: Exégète 1991, 145-160 / 129-144.

d898 **Martin** Geoffrey T., A bibliography of the Amarna Period and its aftermath; the reigns of Akhenaten, Smenkhkare, Tutankhamun and Ay (c. 1350-1321 B.C.). L 1991, Kegan Paul. 136 p. £30. 0-7103-0413-7 [Antiquity 65,409].

d899 **Moran** William L., *al.*, Les lettres d'El-Amarna...: LAPO 13, 1987 ➤ 3,e766 ... 6,e647: ᴿAbrNahrain 29 (1991) 139-142 (G. *Bunnens*).

d900 — *Rainey* A. F., A new translation of the Amarna letters — after 100 years [MORAN W. 1987]: AfO 36s (1989s) 56-75.

d901 **Müller** Maya, Die Kunst Amenophis' III und Echnatons 1988 ➤ 4, g309; Fs 108: ᴿBO 48 (1991) 119-122 (R. *Tefnin*).

d902 *Muntingh* L. M., Syro-Palestinian problems in the light of the Amarna letters: ➤ 402, Anatolia 1991, 155-194.

d903 **Redford** Donald B., Akhenaten 1984 ➤ 65,b351 ... 5,e383: ᴿWZKM 78 (1988) 233-5 (L. M. *Young*, Eng.).

T7.4 **Memphis,** *Ṣaqqāra* – **Pyramides,** *Giza* (Cairo).

d904 *Altenmüller* Hartwig, *Moussa* Akhmed M., Die Inschrift Amenemhets II. aus dem Ptah-Tempel von Memphis, Vorbericht: StAäK 18 (1991) 1-48.

d905 **Betrò** Maria Carmela, I testi solari del portale di Pascerientaisu (Bn2): Saqqara 3. Pisa 1990, Giardini. 143 p.; 9 fig.; 4 pl. [OIAc 2,14].

d906 **Cherpion** Nadine, Mastabas et hypogées de l'Ancien Empire 1989 ➤ 5,e387: ᴿOLZ 86 (1991) 370-6 (E. *Martin-Pardey*). ➤ d926.

d907 *Gohary* Said, The tomb-chapel of the royal scribe Amenemone at Saqqâra: BIFAO 91 (1991) 195-205; pl. 49-60.

d908 **Lauer** Jean-Philippe, The pyramids of Sakkara / Les pyramides de Sakkaraᶜʳᵉᵛ (French and English on facing pages). Cairo 1991, IFAO. 145 p.; 90 fig. 2-7247-009-6 ...

d909 **Martin** Geoffrey, Corpus of reliefs... Memphite Necropolis I, 1987 ➤ 4,g329; 5,e393: ᴿBO 48 (1991) 781-5 (A. *Zivie*); JEA 77 (1991) 219s (E. *Bleiberg*); JNES 50 (1991) 306 (W. J. *Murnane*).

d910 **Martin** Geoffrey T., The hidden tombs of Memphis; new discoveries from the time of Tutankhamun and Ramesses the Great. L 1991, Thames & H. 216 p.; 129 fig. + 11 colour. £30. 0-500-39026-6 [Antiquity 65,409].

d911 **Martin** Geoffrey T., The tomb-chapels of Paser and Raᵓia at Saqqara 1985 ➤ 1,e163 ... 6,e661: ᴿBO 48 (1991) 482-8 (J. *Berlandini*, franç.).

d912 *Martin* G. T., ❸ The rediscovery of the tomb of Maya, Tutankhamun's treasurer, in the Memphite necropolis: VDI 198 (1991) 159-165.

d913 **Raven** Maarten J., The tomb of Iurudef, a Memphite official in the reign of Ramesses II: ExcMem 57. Leiden/L 1991, National Museum of Antiquities/Egypt Expl. Soc. xvii-83 p.; 55 pl. /0-85698-119-2.

d914 *a*) *Schneider* Hans D., *al.*, The tomb of Maya and Meryt; preliminary report on the Saqqara excavations, 1990-1; – *b*) *Giddy* Lisa L., *Jeffreys*

D. G., Memphis, 1990: JEA 77 (1991) 7-21; 4 fig., pl. II-III / 1-6; 1 fig. (pl. I left blank).

d915 **Thompson** Dorothy J., Memphis under the Ptolemies 1988 → 4,g340 ... 6,e663: RHZ 253 (1991) 704s (H. *Sonnabend*); TopO 1 (1991) 105-7 (Françoise *Dunand*).

d915* **Wietheger** Cäcilia, Das Jeremias-Kloster zu Saqqara unter besonderer Berücksichtigung der Inschriften [D1991 Münster]. Altenberge 1991, Oros. xvi-509 p.; 51 fig.; 4 pl.; foldout plan [OIAc 2,29]

d916 *Willems* Harco, The end of Seankhenptah's household ([Saqqara] Letter to the Dead, Cairo JDE 25975): JNES 50 (1991) 183-191.

d916* *a)* *Arnold* Dieter, Zur Zerstörungsgeschichte der Pyramiden; – *b)* *Verner* Miroslav, Remarks on the pyramid of Neferirkare [Abusir]: → 85c, FKAISER W., MiDAI-K 47 (1991) 21-27 / 411-8; 4 fig.; pl. 61-63.

d917 FEDWARDS I., Pyramid Studies, EBaines J., 1988 → 4,41; 6,e672: ROLZ 86 (1991) 477-482 (P. *Janosi*: tit. pp. + Beobachtungen).

d918 **Lauer** Jean-Philippe, Le mystère des Pyramides²ʳᵉᵛ [¹1974 < Problème 1948], préf. *Leclant* J., 1988 → 6,e676: ROrientalia 60 (1991) 121-3 (R. *Stadelmann*).

d919 **Lepre** J. P., The Egyptian pyramids; a comprehensive illustrated reference 1990 → 6,e679: RAntiqJ 70 (1990) 479 (A. J. *Spencer*: altogether unsatisfactory; full of errors; outdated chronology and nomenclature).

d920 *Neumann* Claudio, The sarcophagus in Khephren's pyramid — its design and construction: VarAeg 6 (1990) 11-16; 5 fig.

d921 *a)* *Pitlik* Herbert, Baustelle Cheops-Pyramide (Auszug Mass- und Teilungssystem-Winkel) [+ (p. 3) Höhere Mathematik, oder nur ein Stück Schnur]; – *b)* *Legon* John A. R., The Giza site plan revisited: GöMiszÄg 124 (1991) 79-82 / 69-78; 3 fig.

d922 **Stadelmann** Rainer, Die ägyptischen Pyramiden 1985 → 1,e169 ... 6,e685: RBO 48 (1991) 112-4 (J. *Dorner*).

d923 *Cherpion* Nadine, En reconsidérant le grand sphinx du Louvre A 23 [début de l'Ancien Empire plutôt que sous Amenemhat II]: RÉgp 42 (1991) 25-40; 20 fig.; Eng. 41.

d924 **Zivie-Coche** Christiane M., Giza au premier millénaire; autour du Temple d'Isis dame des pyramides. Boston 1991, Museum of Fine Arts. xx-331 p.; 18 fig.; 47 pl. 0-87846-343-7.

d925 *Fischer* Henry G., Some Old Kingdom names reconsidered [25 from S. HASSAN, Excavations at Giza + 32 others]: Orientalia 60 (1991) 289-311.

d926 **Kromer** Karl, Nezlet Betran, eine Mastaba aus dem Alten Reich bei Giseh (Ägypten); österreichische Ausgrabungen 1981-1983: Österr. Arch-InstKairo. W 1991, Österr. Akad. 68 p.; 15 fig.; 45 pl.; 2 foldout plans. 3-7001-1905-4.

d927 **Kubiak** Władysław B., Al-Fustat, its foundation and early development 1987 → 5,e419; 6,e690: RBSO 54 (1991) 151-3 (G. R. D. *King*); JEA 77 (1991) 236s (J. M. *Rogers*).

d928 EKrzyżanowski Lech, Mausoleum of Qurqumas in Cairo, results of the investigations and conservation works 1984-1988, 3. Wsz 1991, PKZ. 71 p.; ill. 83-85044- 19-1.

d929 *Bareš* Ladislav, The necropolis at Abusir south field in the Middle Kingdom: ZäSpr 118 (1991) 89-96; 1 fig.

d930 *Verner* Miroslav, Excavations at Abusir, season 1988/9, preliminary report: ZäSpr 118 (1991) 162-168; 3 fig.; pl. V-VI.

T7.5 Delta Nili.

d931 *Nibbi* Alessandra, ⊕ The importance of the Egyptian Delta to our understanding of Pharaonic history, ᵀ*Golovinoi* V. A.: VDI 198 (1991) 93-110; 12 fig.; Eng. 110s.

d932 *Alexandria*: **Kiss** Zsolt, Sculptures des fouilles polonaises à Kôm el-Dikka [Alexandrie]. Wsz 1988, Éd. Scientifiques. 73 p.; 62 pl. 83-01-06530-3. – ᴿArchWsz 41 (1990) 160s (A. *Sadurka* ⊕); BO 48 (1991) 142-4 (K. *Parlasca*).

d933 ᶠMONDÉSERT Claude, Alexandrina 1987 ↠ 3,117: ᴿOLZ 86 (1991) 256-8 (J. *Irmscher*).

d934 Alexandria, the journal of the Western cosmological traditions 1. GR 1991, Pharos. 378 p. $15. 0-933999-95-X [NTAbs 36,288 notes 6 of the 15 authors/topics].

d935 **Canfora** Luciano, La biblioteca scomparsa [franç. 1980 ↠ 5,e424; 6,e697]. Palermo 1990, Sellerio. 203 p. Lit. 10.000. – ᴿArcheo 69 (1990) 128 (P. G. *Guzzo*).

d936 *Farkha*: a) *Chlodnicki* M., *al.*, Italian excavations in the Nile Delta [Farkha, S Mansura]; fresh data and new hypotheses in the 4th millennium cultural development of Egyptian prehistory; – b) *Salvatori* Sandro, *Usai* Donatella, Chipped stone industries: RivArch 15 (1991) 5-33; 18 fig. / 34-45; 7 fig.

d937 *Naucratis*: **Venit** Marjorie S., Greek painted pottery from Naukratis in Egyptian museums 1988 ↠ 4,e457: ᴿBO 48 (1991) 814s (E. *Simon*).

d938 *Omari*: **Debono** F., *Mortensen* B., El Omari, a neolithic settlement, and other sites in the vicinity of Wadi Hof, Helwan: DAI-K 82. Mainz 1990. 154 p.; ill. – ᴿArchWroc 42 (1991) 153 (M. *Kobusiewicz* ⊕).

d939 *Qanṭîr*, Dabʿa 1988/1900s: JbÖsArch 59-BG (1989) 3-s & 61-BG (1991s) 1-3 (J. *Dörner*).

d940 **Bietak** Manfred, *al.*, Tell el-Dabʿa V, ein Friedhofsbezirk der mittleren Bronzezeitkultur mit Totentempel und Siedlungsschichten, I: Denks 9. W 1991, Österr. Akad. 339 p.; 297 fig.; 8 foldout plans. 3-7001-1884-8.

d941 **Winkler** Elke-Meinrad, *Wilfing* Harald, Tell el-Dabʿa VI, anthropologische Untersuchungen an den Skelettresten der Kampagnen 1966-69, 1975-80, 1985: UntÖAI-K 9 / Denks 10. W 1991, Österr. Akad. 172 p.; 21 pl. 3-7001-1703-3 [OIAc 1,27].

d942 *Tanis*: ᴱBrissaud Philippe, Cahiers de Tanis 1, 1987 ↠ 4,g380; 6,e714: JEA 77 (1991) 220-2 (S. *Snape*).
ᴱAmandry M., *Brissaud* P., Tanis, exposition 1991 ↠ b509.

d943 *Zagazig*: ᴱFrösén Jaako, *Hagedorn* Dieter, Die verkohlten Papyri aus Bubastos 1990 ↠ 6,e705: ᴿClasR 41 (1991) 460s (A. *Bülow-Jacobsen*).

T7.6 Alii situs Aegypti **alphabetice**.

d943* *Abū Mīnā*, Kirchen 1984-6: ArchAnz (1991) 457-486; 28 fig.; foldout plan (P. *Grossmann*).

d944 *Abydos*: *Sawi* Ahmed El-, a) Some variations of writing of the name of Seti I at Abydos; – b) Some sacred emblems employed as substitutes for figures of deities; – c) A newly discovered statue of a priest of Min from Akhmim: ASAE supp. (1987) to 70 (1984s) 653-63 / 29-52 / 79-88; – d) *Dreyer* Günter, Zur Rekonstruktion der Oberbauten der Königsgräber der 1. Dynastie in Abydos; – e) *Stadelmann* Rainer, Das Dreikammersystem der Königsgräber der Frühzeit und des Alten Reiches [Abydos, Saqqara]: → 85c, FKAISER W., MiDAI-K 47 (1991) 93-103, pl 4-5 / 373-388.

d944* *Meulenaere* Herman de, Meskhénet à Abydos: → 43, FDERCHAIN P., Religion 1991, 243-9 + 2 pl.

d945 *Adaïma* 2d, 1990, prédynastique: BIFAO 91 (1991) 231-247; pl. 63-70 (Béatrix *Midant-Reynes, al.*); p. 244-7, restes végétaux (C. de *Vartavan*).

d945* *Akoris:* EKawanishi Hiroyuki, *Tsujimura* Sumiyo, Preliminary report; eighth season of the excavation of the site of Akoris, Egypt, 1988. Kyoto 1989, Paleological Asn. v-56 p.; 2 pl. [OIAc 2,22].

d946 *Alamein,* Marina: EKrzyżanowski Lech, Marina El Alamein, archaeological background and conservation problems 1988, 1. Wsz 1991, PKZ. 56 p.; ill. 83-85044-22-1.

Aphrodito (upper Egypt), **MacCoull** Leslie S.B., Dioscorus of Aphrodito: TransfClasHer 16 1988 → g321.

d948 *Aswan: Andraschko* Frank M., *al.*, Terminologie, Klassifikation und computergestützte Bearbeitung der Keramik des 1. Jahrtausends v.Chr. vom Westkôm auf Elephantine, Oberägypten: → 46, Mem. DRIEHAUS J. 1990, 327-338; 10 fig.

d949 *Kellermann* Diether & Mechthild, YHW-Tempel und Sabbatfeier auf Elephantine?: → 137, FSINGER H.-R., 1991, 433-452.

d949* *Dendera:* Castel G., *al.*, Dendera, Fontaines 1984 → 5,e459: RBO 48 (1991) 501s (A. *Lukaszewicz*).

d950 *Cauville* Sylvie, Le temple de Dendera, guide archéologique: Bt générale 12. Le Caire 1990, IFAO. [viii-] 104 p.; ill. 2-7247-0095-3.

d951 *Quaegebeur* Jan, Cléopâtre VII et le temple de Dendara: GöMiszÄg 120 (1991) 49-68 + 6 fig.

d952 *Esna: Derchain-Urtel* Maria-Theresia, Das Bildprogramm von Esna – eine Rettungsaktion: → 43, FDERCHAIN P., Religion 1991, 107-121.

d953 *Fayûm:* **Beinlich** Horst, Das Buch vom Fayum; zum religiösen Eigenverständnis einer ägyptischen Landschaft: ÄgAbh 51. Wsb 1991, Harrassowitz. 367 p.; vol. of 45 pl., 2 foldouts. 3-447-03117-4 [OIAc 1,12].

d953* *Hawawish* (Ahmim): **Kanawati** Naguib [→ 4,g390] A mountain speaks; the first Australian excavation in Egypt. Sydney 1988, Macquarie Univ. 96 p.; color. ill. (*Scannell* R.). 0-85837-633-4.

d954 *Heracleopolis:* **Thomas** Thelma K., Niche decorations from the tombs of Byzantine Egypt (Heracleopolis Magna and Oxyrhynchus, A.D. 300-500); visions of the afterlife: diss. NYU 1990, DMathews T. xxiii-299 p.; 252 p., 88 pl. 90-25149.

d955 *Hermopolis:* **Snape** Steven, *Bailey* Donald, The great portico et Hermopolis Magna 1988 → 5,e469: RBO 48 (1991) 115-7 (Marie *Drew- Bear*).

d956 *Hierakonpolis:* **Quibell** J.E., *Green* F.W., Hierakonpolis II [L 1902] L c. 1990, History and Mysteries of Man. $75. Also Starnberg c. 1990, LTR. DM 380. – RVarAeg 6 (H.G. *Fischer:* London reprint *far* superior).

d957 *Idfu: Kurth* Dieter, Über den Ursprung des Tempels von Edfu: → 43, FDERCHAIN P., Religion 1991, 189-200 + 5 fig.

d958 *El-Kab:* **Bingen** J., *Clarysse* W., Elkab III, Les ostraca grecs. Bru 1989, Fond. Reine Élisabeth. 155 p.; 14 fig.; 20 pl.; 2 maps. – RCdÉ 65 (1990) 356s (P. *Heilporn*).

d959 **Kom Ombo**: **Wettengel** Wolfgang, *Winter* Erich, Der Text der Kom Ombo-Szene von der Fahrt im Papyrusdickicht: ➤ 43, ᶠDERCHAIN P., Religion 1991, 363-370 + 4 fig.

d960 **Lisht**: **Arnold** Felix, *al.*, The control notes and team marks: South Cemeteries of Lisht 2. NY 1990, Metropolitan Museum. 188 p.; 14 pl. 0-87099-551-0.

d961 *Arnold* Dieter, El-Lischt: AntWelt 22 (1991) 154-160; 15 (color.) fig.

d962 **Mašayiḫ**: **Ockinga** Boyo G., *Masri* Yahya al-, Two Ramesside tombs at El Mashayikh, 1. Sydney 1988, Macquarie Univ. Anc. Hist. I. v-79 p.; 66 pl. – II (1990) vii-74 p.; 71 pl. 0-85837-632-6; -712-8.

d963 **Meidum**: *Bolshakov* Andrey O., Some observations on the early chronology of Meidum: GöMiszÄg 123 (1991) 11-20.

d964 **Krüger** Julian, *Oxyrhynchus* in der Kaiserzeit; Studien zur Topographie und Literaturrezeption: EurHS 3/341, 1990 ➤ 6,e749; ᴿErbAuf 67 (1991) 332-4 (Elisabeth *Bitter*).

d965 **Philae**: **Vassilika** Eleni, Ptolemaic Philae 1989 ➤ 5,e483: ᴿBO 48 (1991) 496-500 (D. *Kurth*).

d966 **Samalūṭ**: **Gomaà** Farouk, *al.*, Mittelägypten zwischen Samalūṭ und dem Gabal Abū Ṣīr: TAVO B-69. Wsb 1991, Reichert. xx-287 p.; 97 fig.; XCV pl. + 5 color.; 2 maps. 3-88226-467-5.

d967 **Silsila**: *Peden* A. J., The quarrying inscription of Ramesses V at West Silsila: Orientalia 60 (1991) 335-8.

d968 **Siwa**: **Kuhlmann** Klaus P., Das Ammoneion... Siwa 1988 ➤ 4,b820; 6,e751: ᴿBO 48 (1991) 794-801 (P. *Derchain*).

d969 **Tuna**: *a) Thissen* Heinz-Josef, Demotische Inschriften aus den Ibisgallerien in Tuna el-Gebel; ein Vorbericht; – *b) Vandorpe* Katelijn, Les villages des Ibis dans la toponymie tardive; – *c) Vittmann* Günter, Eine demotische Erwähnung des Ibi [sic]?: Enchoria 18 (1991) 107-111; pl. 14-21 / 115-122 / 123-9.

T7.7   **Antiquitates Nubiae et alibi.**

d970 **Hein** Irmgard, Die ramessidische Bautätigkeit in Nubien: GöOrF 4/22. Wsb 1991, Harrassowitz. xiv-200 p.; 21 pl.; maps. 3-447-03080-1.

d971 *Pernigotti* Sergio, L'Egitto fuori dell'Egitto; Archeo 79 (1991) 55-89.

d972 **Säve-Söderbergh** Torgny, *Troy* Lana, New Kingdom Pharaonic sites; the finds and the sites: Scandinavian Joint Expedition 5/2s. U 1991, Almqvist & W. I. xvi-327 p.; ii. p. 81; 226 (color.) pl. 91-7081-030-3; -2-X.

d973 ᴱ**Säve-Söderbergh** Torgny, Temples and tombs of ancient Nubia 1987 ➤ 3,e876: ᴿJNES 50 (1991) 60s (B. *Williams*).

d974 **Taylor** John H., Egypt and Nubia. L 1991, British Museum. 72 p.; 94 fig. 0-7141-2077-4.

---

d975 **Berenice**: *Castiglioni* Alfredo & Angela, *Negro* Giancarlo, À la recherche de Bérénice Pancrisia [ville] dans le désert oriental nubien: BSocFrÉg 121 (1991) 5-24; 10 fig.

d976 **Cyrene**: **Laronde** André, Cyrène et la Libye hellénistique 1987 ➤ 6, e781: ᴿGnomon 63 (1991) 223-6 (Gabriella *Bevilacqua*).

d977 **Dongola**: *Godlewski* Wlodimierz, Old Dongola 1988s, house PCH 1/1990, fortifications: ANilM 5 (1991) 79-96 + 5 pl. / 103-123; 11 fig., 3 pl.

d978 *Kerma*: *Bourriau* Janine, Relations between Egypt and Kerma during the Middle and New Kingdoms: ➤ 635, Egypt and Africa 1991, 129-144.

d979 *Leptis*: **Caputo** Giacomo, Il teatro augusteo di Leptis Magna. R 1987, Bretschneider. 148 p.; 158 + 39 fig. – ᴿAJA 95 (1991) 562s (W. E. *Mierse*); Gymnasium 98 (1991) 85-87 (G. *Zimmer*).

d980 *Melita*: **Hölbl** Günther, Ägyptisches Kulturgut / Malta 1989 ➤ 5,e74: ᴿAfO 36s (1989s) 175s (Ingrid *Gamer-Wallert*).

d981 *Meroe*: **Hofmann** Inge, Steine für die Ewigkeit; meroitische Opfertafeln und Totenstelen: BeitSud Beih 6. W-Mödling 1991, Univ. Inst. Afrikanistik. 259 p.; XV pl.

d982 *Moya*: *Caneva* Isabella, Jebel Moya [S. Sudan] revisited; a settlement of the 5th millennium B.C. in the middle Nile basin: Antiquity 65 (1991) 262-8; 3 fig. (maps).

d983 *Nubia*: **Deichmann** F. W., *Grossmann* P., Nubische Forschungen 1988 ➤ 4,g437: ᴿOLZ 86 (1991) 25s (I. *Hofmann*).

d983* **Gratien** Brigitte, Prosopographie des Nubiens et des Égyptiens en Nubie avant le Nouvel Empire: Lille CahPapÉg supp. 3. Lille 1991, Univ-III. 194 p. 2-9504764-1-4 [OIAc 2,20].

d984 ᴱ**Krause** Martin, Nubische Studien 1982/6 ➤ 4,750: ᴿJNES 50 (1991) 59s (B. *Williams*).

d985 *Qustul*: **Williams** Bruce B., Meroitic remains from Qustul cemetery B, and a Ballana settlement: OINub 8. Ch 1991, Univ. xlviii-458 p.; xiv-293 p., 114 pl. [OLZ 87,241, I. *Hofmann*].

d986 **Williams** B., Noubadian X-group remains from royal complexes in cemeteries Q and 219 and from private cemeteries Q, R. V. W, B, J, and M at Qustul and Ballana: OINub 9. Ch 1991, Univ. xxxix-409 p.; 145 fig.; 83 pl. 0-918986-74-5.

d987 *Sabratha*: **Dore** John, *Kray* Nina, Excavations at Sabratha 1948-1951, II/1, Amphorae, coarse pottery and building materials. Tripoli 1989, Department of Antiquities. xi-298 p.; 72 fig.; ❹ summary. – ᴿAJA 95 (1991) 364s (Virginia R. *Anderson-Stojanović*).

d987* *Soba*: **Welsby** D. A., *Daniels* C. M., al., Soba; archaeological research at a medieval capital on the Blue Nile [Nubian kingdom of Alwa or Alodia]. L 1991, Royal Geographical Soc. [Thames & H.]. xvii-363 p.; 201 fig.; 55 pl.; foldout map. £40. 1-872566-02-2. – ᴿAntiqJ 70 (1990) 494s (G. S. P. *Freeman-Grenville*).

т7.9   Sinai.

d988 *Bergoffen* Celia J., Overland trade in northern Sinai; the evidence of the Late Cypriot pottery: BASOR 284 (1991) 59-75; 13 fig.

d989 *a*) *Carrez-Maratray* J.-Y., Les relations entre l'épigraphie pélusienne et le Nord-Sinai; – *b*) *Maksoud* M. A., Excavations on 'The ways of Horus', Tell Heboua, North Sinai, 1986-7: ➤ 5,859, ᴱ*Nibbi* A., Delta 1988/9, 53-60 / 173-192.

d990 *Hinz* Walter, Zu den Sinai-Inschriften: ZDMG 141 (1991) 16-32; facsimiles.

d991 *Leb* Ioan-Vasile, (en roum.) Les relations des roumains avec le Monastère Ste. Catherine du Sinai: STBuc 39,4 (1987) 97-106.

d992 *Macchi* Jean-Daniel, Aurait-on perdu les Shosou yahwistes du Sinaï: ➤ 140, ꜰSMYTH-FLORENTIN F. 1991, 45-53.

d992* *Ovadiah* Asher, *al.*, [→ d130] The mosaic pavements of Sheikh Zouède in northern Sinai [excavated by J. CLÉDAT in 1913; now in Ismailiya Museum]: → 47*, [F]ENGEMANN J., Tesserae 1991, 181-191; pl. 22-27.

d993 [E]**Rainey** Anson F., Egypt, Israel, Sinai 1982/7 → 3,834... 6,e803: [R]JEA 77 (1991) 204-6 (K. A. *Kitchen*: BIETAK better than REDFORD on Exodus; 'VAN SETERS/THOMPSON chorus-line to downgrade respectable narratives'); WeltOr 22 (1991) 207-212 (Helga *Weippert*).

d994 **Solzbacher** Rudolf, Mönche, Pilger und Sarazenen... Sinai 1989 → 5,e20: [R]RÉG 104 (1991) 553 (D. *Feissel*); TPhil 66 (1991) 250s (H. J. *Sieben*).

d995 *a*) *Stewart* Frank H., Notes on the arrival of the Bedouin tribes in Sinai [C. BAILEY's use of St. Catherine manuscripts]: JESHO [28 (1985) 20-49] 34 (1991) 97-110 [-115 rejoinder: criticism is fine but Stewart's is unfounded]. – *b*) **Bailey** Clinton, Bedouin poetry from Sinai and the Negev; mirror of a culture. NY 1991, Oxford-UP. 512 p.; ill. $125. 0-19-826547-6. – [R]BR 7,4 (1991) 8s (S. *Cohen*).

d996 **Weitzmann** Kurt, *Galavaris* George, The monastery of St. Catherine at Mount Sinai; the illuminated Greek manuscripts, I. 9-12 cent. Princeton 1990, Univ. ...; 198 pl.

T8.1   **Anatolia**, *generalia.*

d997 **Akurgal** Ekrem, Griechische und römische Kunst in der Türkei 1987 → 3,e905: [R]Gnomon 63 (1991) 336-340 (Y. *Boysal*).

d998 *Baronowski* Donald W., The status of the Greek cities of Asia Minor after 190 B.C.: Hermes 119 (1991) 450-463.

d999 **Belke** Klaus, *Mersich* Norbert, Phrygien und Pisidien: Tabula Imperii Byzantini 7. W 1990, Österr. Akad. 462 p.; 161 pl., 2 foldout maps. Sch 1800. – [R]Klio 73 (1991) 675-8 (W. *Brandes*); RÉtByz 49 (1991) 295s (J.-C. *Cheynet*).

e1 *Černyh* E. N., *al.*, The circumpontic metallurgical province as a system: EWest 41 (1991) 11-45; 20 fig.

e2 **Cox** C. W. M., *al.*, Monuments from the Aezanitis: MonAsMinAnt 9. L 1988, JRS. lxix-209 p.; 48 pl. £40. 0-907764-10-X. – [R]JRS 81 (1991) 223-5 (G. W. *Bowersock* tenderly calls the series 'MAMA').

e3 **Durugönül** Serra, Die Felsreliefs im Rauhen Kilikien: BAR-Int 511, 1989 → 5,e525: [R]BonnJbb 191 (1991) 814-6 (Guntram *Koch*).

e4 **Eid** Volker, Ost-Türkei, Völker und Kulturen zwischen Taurus und Ararat: Kunst-Reiseführer 1990 → 6,e811: [R]ByZ 83 (1991) 496-8 (Nicole *Thierry*).

e5 **Elsner** Jacques, Sites antiques du sud-ouest de l'Anatolie[2] [[1]1987 → 5,e 527]. Bodrum 1991, Yachting Loisirs Bleus. 272 p. [OIAc 2,18].

e6 **Francovich** Géza de, Santuari e tombe rupestri dell'Antica Frigia, e un'indagine sulle tombe della Licia: Mediaevalia 3. R 1990, Bretschneider. xviii-207 p.; vol. of 188 pl., 2 plans, map. Lit. 350.000. 88-7062-683-0 [JRS 81,258].

e7 *a*) *Frangipane* Marcella, Arslantepe-Malatya; sviluppo di un centro locale tra Anatolia e mondo siro-mesopotamico; – *b*) *Imparati* Fiorella, Significato politico della successione dei testimoni nel trattato di Tuthaliya IV con Kurunta; – *c*) *Voza* Giuseppe, Thapsos [Siracusa]; – *d*) *Benzi* Mario, Rodi in età micenea: Seminari Cons. Naz. Ric. Ist. SMEA (1991) 13-28 + 22 fig. / 59-86 / 43-50 + 10 fig. / 5-11.

e8 *a*) *Frei* P., Zentralgewalt und Lokalautonomie im achämenidischen Kleinasien; – *b*) *Lemaire* A., *Lozachmeur* H., La Cilicie à l'époque perse;

recherches sur les pouvoirs locaux et l'organisation du territoire: ➤ 636*, TEuph 3 (1989/90) 157-171 / 143-144 + map.; pl. XI.

e9 **Hild** F., *Hellenkamper* M., Tabula Imperii Byzantini, 5. Kilikien und Isaurien. W 1990, Österr. Akad. 465 p.; 96 p., 402 fig., maps [RÉG 104,683].

e10 **Kaspar** Elke & Hans-Dieter, Phrygien, ein sagenumwobenes Königreich in Anatolien; ein Reisehandbuch. Hausen 1990, Korient. 116 p.

e11 **Koenigs** Wolf, Westtürkei, von Troia bis Knidos[5rev] [⁴1988]. Mü 1991, Artemis. 284 p.; ill.

e12 *Lightfoot* C. S., *Healey* J. F., A Roman veteran on the Tigris [Tilli / Çattepe altar now in Diyarbakır museum]: EpAnat 17 (1991) 1-7; pl. 1; ❶ 7.

e13 **Lloyd** Seton, Ancient Turkey 1989 ➤ 5,e533; 6,e815: ᴿBSO 54 (1991) 236 (Caroline *Finkel*).

e14 **Loon** Maurits N. van, Anatolia in the earlier first millennium B.C.: IconRel 15/13. L 1991, Brill. xiii-49 p.; 48 pl.

ᴱ**Lordkipanidze** Otar, *Lévêque* Pierre, Le Pont-Euxin vu par les grecs 1987/90 ➤ 596.

e16 ᶠMELLINK Machteld, Ancient Anatolia, ᴱ**Canby** Jeanny V., *al.*, 1987 ➤ 2,71 ... 6,e816: ᴿMnemosyne 44 (1991) 300-4 (M. van *Loon*); OLZ 82 (1991) 33-35 (E. *Klengel-Brandt*).

e17 *Mellink* Machteld J., Archaeology in Anatolia [1989]: AJA 95 (1991) 123-153; 32 fig.; map.

e18 *Mellink* M., Anatolian contacts with chalcolithic Cyprus: ➤ 657, BASOR 282s (1991) 167-175.

ᴱ**Mikasa** T., Essays on Anatolian [Keban dam, Kaman-Kalehöyük] 1988 ➤ 402.

e19 *Mitchell* Stephen, The Hellenization of Pisidia: MeditArch 4 (1991) 119-145; pl. 6-19.

e20 *a) Özgüç* Tahsin, Kültepe-Kanis 1988; – *b) Özgüç* Nimet, Acemhöyük 1988; – *c) Alp* Sedat, Konya-Karahöyük 1988; – *d) Bilgi* Önder, İkiztepe 1988; – *e) Çambel* Halet, *al.*, Karatepe, Aslantaş; Domuztepe; – *f) Bakır* Güven, Klazomenai 1988; – *g) Abbasoğlu* Haluk, Perga 1988: Höyük 1 (1988: Ankara 1991) 11-13 / 17-19 / 21-23 / 25-27 / 43-49 / 85-96 / 121-5: all (color.) ill.

e21 **Şahin** Sencer, Forschungen in Kommagene, I. Epigraphik; II. Topographie; III. Archäologie (*Jacobs* B.), EpAnat 18 (1991) 99-111; ❶ 112; map 113; pl. 10-13 / 114-131; ❶ 132; 5 fig.; pl. 14-17 / 133-9; ❶ 140; pl. 15-17.

e22 **Sinclair** T. A., Eastern Turkey 1987/9 ➤ 3,e920; 5,e359; 6,e825. – ᴿBInstArch 27 (1990) 244s (C. *Burney*, 1); JSS 36 (1991) 191 (S. P. *Brock*, 2).

e23 *Taeuber* Hans, Die syrisch-kilikische Grenze während der Prinzipatszeit: Tyche 6 (1991) 201-210.

e24 **Trebilco** P. R., Jewish communities in Asia Minor: Mg 69. C 1991, Univ. xv-330 p. £30. 0-521-40120-8. – ᴿExpTim 103 (1991s) 84 (W. *Horbury*); JStJud 22 (1991) 292-5 (P. W. van der *Horst*: outflanking T. KRAABEL's awaited ᴰ1968); TsTNijm 31 (1991) 429 (J. *Negenman*).

e25 Turchia, crocevia di culture e religioni [colloquio Iskenderun sept. 1989]: Turchia, la Chiesa e la sua storia 1, 1990 ➤ 6,559*: ᴿAnStoEseg 8 (1991) 714-7 (M. *Pesce*); NRT 113 (1991) 604s (L.-J. *Renard*).

e26 *a) Ünal* Ahmet, Two peoples on both sides of the Aegean Sea; did the Achaeans and the Hittites know each other?; – *b) Emre* Kutlu,

Cemeteries of second millennium B.C. in central Anatolia: ➤ 402, Anatolia 1991, 16-44 / 1-8 + 11 fig. (map).

e26* **Yakar** Jak,   Prehistoric Anatolia; the neolithic transformations and the early Chalcolithic period: Nadler Mg 9.   TA 1991, Univ. Inst. Archaeology. x-361 p.   965-550-000-6 [OIAc 2,29].

T8.2 Boğazköy, *Hethaei* – The Hittites.

e27 **Boehmer** Rainer M., *Güterbock* Hans G.,   Glyptik aus dem Stadgebiet: Boğazköy-Hattuša 14, 1987 ➤ 3,e926:   ᴿAfO 36s (1989s) 157-160 (Dominique *Collon*); BO 48 (1991) 262-4 (Hatice *Gonnet*); OLZ 86 (1991) 393-5 (E. *Klengel-Brandt*).

e28 *Meijer* D. J. W.,   Opgravingskroniek van West-Azie [Boğazkoy; Nevalı Çorı; Irak, Syrië]:   PhoenixEOL 37,2 (1991) 42-47; 1 fig.

e28* *Neve* Peter,   Die Ausgrabungen in Boğazköy-Hattuša 1990:   ArchAnz (1991) 299-345; 49 fig. (345-8, *Otten* H., Landschenksurkunden).

e29 **Otten** Heinrich,   Die Bronzetafel Wsb 1988 / Innsbruck 1989 ➤ 4,g514; 5,e351; 6,e835:   ᴿIndogF 96 (1991) 295-300 (G. *Neumann*).

e30 **Otten** Heinrich, *Rüster* Christel,   Keilschrifttexte aus Boghazköi 32, Die hurritisch-hethitische Bilingue: AkWissKommAO. B 1990, Mann. xvi-56 p.; plan. DM 54. – ᴿOLZ 86 (1991) 384-391 (V. *Haas*, I. *Wegner*).

e31 **Otten** Heinrich, *Rüster* Christel,   Hethitische Texte vorwiegend von Büyükkale Gebäude A: KaB 34.   Berlin 1991, Mann. xviii-50 p.   3-7861-1663-6.

e32 **Wilhelm** Gernot,   Literarische Texte in sumerischer und akkadischer Sprache: KaB 36. B 1991, Mann. xiii-29 p.   3-7861-1664-4.

e33 *Willemaers* N.,   Les 'enseignes' d'Alaca Hüyük: Akkadica 69 (1990) 19-26 + 3 pl.

T8.3 Ephesus.

e34 *Alföldy* Géza,   Epigraphische Notizen aus Kleinasien I. Ein beneficium des Augustus in Ephesos: ZPapEp 87 (1991) 157-162; 1 fig.

e35 **Aurenhammer** M.,   Die Skulpturen ... 1. Bildwerke aus Stein; Idealplastik: Forschungen in Ephesos 10/1.   W 1990, Österr. Akad. 204 p.; 128 pl.; 2 foldout plans. DM 100. 3-7001-1757-4 [JRS 81,257].

e36 *Bammer* Anton,   *a)* Multikulturelle Aspekte der frühen Kunst im Artemision von Ephesos: JhÖsW 61-B (1991s) 17-54; 45 fig. – *b)* Les sanctuaires du VIIIᵉ et VIIᵉ siècles à l'Artémision d'Éphèse: RArchéol (1991) 63-84; 33 fig.

e37 *Büyükkolancı* M., *Engelmann* H.,   Inschriften aus Ephesos: ZPapEp 86 (1991) 137-143.

e38 *Daoust* J.,   Centenaire de la 'Maison de la Vierge' à Éphèse: EsprVie 101 (1991) 440s.

e39 **Karwiese** Stefan,   Erster vorläufiger Grabungsbericht über die Wiederaufnahme der archäologischen Untersuchung der Marienkirche in Ephesos: Denkschr. p/h 200. W 1989, Österr. Akad. 48 p.; 78 fig. – ᴿGnomon 63 (1991) 374-6 (W. *Müller-Wiener*).

e40 *Knibbe* Dieter, *al.*,   Neue Inschriften aus Ephesos XI: JhÖsArch 59-B (1989) 162-238.

e41 *a) Knibbe* Dieter, *Büyükkolancı* Mustafa, Zur Bauinschrift der Basilica auf dem sog. Staatsmarkt von Ephesos; – *b) Lang-Auinger* Claudia,   Opus sectile – Boden aus den Hanghäusern I und II in Ephesos: JhÖsArch 59-H (1989) 43-46 / 47-54.

e41* *Langmann* Gerhard, Ephesos 1990s: JhÖsA 61-B-Grabungen (1991) 4-15.

e42 *Nicolet* Claude, Le monumentum ephesenum et les dîmes d'Asie: BCH 115,1 (1991) 465-480.

e43 **Oster** Richard E., A bibliography of ancient Ephesus: ATLA 19, 1987 ➤ 6,e842*: ᴿBijdragen 52 (1991) 446s (M. *Parmentier*, Eng., also on ATLA 17, 20, 23); JNES 50 (1991) 160 (Eleanor *Guralnick*).

e43* **Outschar** Ulrike, Römische Architekturornamente in Ephesos: Diss. Wien 1990. – ArchAnz (1991) 148.

e44 **Rogers** Guy M., The sacred identity of Ephesos; foundation myths of a Roman city. L 1991, Routledge. xviii-209 p.; 11 fig. 0-415-05530-X.

e45 *Rudolf* Ernst, Attische Sarkophage aus Ephesos: Denks 209. W 1989, Österr. Akad. 60 p.; 32 pl. – ᴿBonnJbb 191 (1991) 816-9 (Guntram *Koch*).

e45* *Schädler* Ulrich, Die Säulenhöhe des archaischen Artemisions bei PLINIUS und VITRUV: ArchAnz (1991) 107-110.

e46 **Thür** Hilke, Das Hadrianstor: ForEphesos 11/1, 1989 ➤ 6,e843: ᴿAJA 95 (1991) 754s (Shelley C. *Stone*: just SW of Celsus library); ArchWsz 41 (1990) 166 (S. *Parnicki-Pudelko* ❷); RArchéol (1991) 169s (P. *Gros*).

T8.4 Pergamum.

e47 **Andreae** Bernard, Laokoon und die Kunst von Pergamon; die Hybris der Giganten. Fra 1991, Fischer-Tb. 96 p.; ill. [JRS 81,253].

e48 **Andreae** B., *al.*, Phyromachos-Probleme; mit einem Anhang zur Datierung des grossen Altars von Pergamon: MiDAI-R Egb 31. Mainz 1990, von Zabern. 72 p.; 4 fig.; 96 pl.; 3 plans. DM 135. 3-8053-1126-5 [JRS 81,253].

e49 **Filgis** M. N., *Radt* W., Das Heroon: Altertümer von Pergamon 15/1, 1986 ➤ 3,e951 ... 6,e845: ᴿJHS 111 (1991) 251s (R. A. *Tomlinson*).

e49* *Kertész* I., Pergamon und die Strategie des römischen Imperialismus: ➤ 591e, AcAntH 33 (1990s) 247-253.

e50 *Kunze* Max, Neue Forschungen zum Pergamonaltar: ➤ 587, L'espace sacrificiel 1988/91, 135-140; pl. XXXIX.

e51 **Mandel** Ursula, Kleinasiatische Reliefkeramik: PergFor 5, 1988 ➤ 5,e565: ᴿArchWsz 41 (1990) 166s (H. *Meyza*, Eng.).

e51* *Meyer* Laure, Le grand autel de Zeus à Pergame: Archéologia 268 (1991) 56-65; color. ill. (réconstruction à Berlin).

e52 **Meyer-Schlichtmann** Carsten, Die pergamenische Sigillata 1988 ➤ 5,e566: ᴿGnomon 63 (1991) 150-4 (Kathleen W. *Slane*).

e53 *a*) *Nohlen* Klaus, La conception d'un projet et son évolution; l'exemple du Trajaneum de Pergame, ᵀ*Lugger* Émile; – *b*) *Coulton* J. J., Incomplete preliminary planning in Greek architecture, some new evidence: ➤ 631, Dessin 1984/5, 269-276; 7 fig. / 103-121.

e54 *Radt* Wolfgang, Pergamon, Geschichte und Bauten 1988 ➤ 5,e570; 6,e850: ᴿAJA 95 (1991) 177s (E. E. *Rice*); RArchéol (1991) 386s (C. *Le Roy*).

e55 *Radt* Wolfgang, Pergamon, Vorbericht über die Kampagne 1989: *a*) TürkArk 29 (1991) 85-109 + 10 fig.; ❶ 111; – *b*) AJA 95 (1991) 148s [➤ e17, ᴱ*Mellink*].

e55* *a*) *Radt* Wolfgang, Pergamon, Vorbericht über die Kampagne 1990; – *b*) *Hoepfner* Wolfram, Bauliche Details am Pergamonaltar; – *c*) *Jones* Christopher P., Aelius ARISTIDES, 'On the water in Pergamon': Arch-

Anz (1991) 399-432; 30 fig. [433-456, *Salzmann* Dieter, Mosaiken und Pavimente] / 189-202; 6 fig. / 111-7; 3 fig.
e56 **Rheidt** Klaus, Die byzantinische Wohnstadt; Altertümer von Pergamon 15/2. 1991.

T8.6   *Situs Anatoliae,* **Turkey sites** in alphabetical order.

e57 *Adrassus:* **Alföldi-Rosenbaum** Elisabeth, *al.*, The necropolis of Adrassus (Balabolu) in Rough Cilicia (Isauria) 1980 ➤ 63,d545: ᴿPhoenix 45 (Toronto 1991) 180-2 (H. *Williams*).
e58 *Alabanda* [80 k SE Ephesus] und seine antike Wasserversorgung: AntWelt 22 (1991) 106-113; 26 (color.) fig.
e59 *Amorium* 3d 1990: AnSt 41 (1991) 215-229; 7 fig.; pl. XLIII-XLIV (R. M. *Harrison*).
e60 *Anemurium:* **Williams** Caroline, Anemurium, the Roman and early Byzantine pottery: SubsMediaev 16. Toronto 1989, Pont. Inst. Medv. St. 125 p.; 63 fig.; 24 pl. – ᴿAJA 95 (1991) 185s (Virginia R. *Anderson-Stojanović*).
e61 *Antakya: Cabouret* Bernadette, L'iconographie de la source Castalie de Daphne (Syrie): Karthago 22 (1990) 63-68 + 8 fig.

e62 *Aphrodisias* 1989: AJA 95 (1991) 143s [K. *Erim* ➤ e17].
e63 *Chaisemartin* N. de, Le 'portique de Tibère' à Aphrodisias; problèmes d'identification et de fonction; RÉAnc 91,3s (1989) 23-45; 10 fig.; Eng. 23.
e64 **Reynolds** Joyce, *Tannenbaum* Robert, Jews and Godfearers at Aphrodisias 1987 ➤ 2,b236... 5,e584: ᴿGnomon 63 (1991) 559-561 (J. *Linderski*); Mnemosyne 44 (1991) 293-5 (G. *Mussies*).

e65 *Ariassos* 1990: AnSt 41 (1991) 159-172; 9 fig.; pl. XXXI-XXXII (S. *Mitchell*).
e66 *Aşıklı:* *Esin* Ufuk, ✪ Aşıklı Höyük (E Aksaray): TürkArk 29 (1991) 1-10 + 34 fig.; map.
e67 *Büyüktepe* [or İkiztepe, near Çiftetaş/Trabzon], 1st 1990: AnSt 41 (1991) 145-158; 8 fig.; pl. XXIX-XXX (A. *Sagona, al.*).
e68 *Caria: Varinlioğlu* Ender, *al.*, Une inscription de Pladasa en Carie: RÉAnc 92 (1990) 59-78; 4 fig.
e68* *Çayönü:* **Morales** Vivian B., Figurines and other clay objects from Sarab and Çayönü; OIComm 25. Ch 1990, Univ. xv-92 p.; 30 pl. $19.80 [PraehZts 67,245, J. *Seeher*].
e69 *Demirci:* **Korfmann** M., Demircihüyük 2d, 1987 ➤ 5,e588: ᴿSovArch (1991,1) 275-282 (Sh. *Amirov*, T. *Mishina*).

e70 *Didyma:* **Pülz** Stefan, Untersuchungen zur kaiserzeitlichen Bauornamentik von Didyma: IstMitt Beih 35. Tü 1989, Wasmuth. xviii-178 p.; 36 pl. – ᴿRArchéol (1991) 167s (M.-C. *Hellmann*).
e71 **Tuchelt** Klaus, Branchidai-Didyma: AntWelt 22 Sond. (1991). 63 p. 86 (color.) fig.
e72 *a)* **Tuchelt** Klaus, Drei Heiligtümer von Didyma and ihre Grundzüge; – *b)* **Haselberger** Lothar, Aspekte der Bauzeichnungen von Didyma: RArchéol (1991) 85-98; 9 fig. / 99-113; 13 fig.
e73 **Fontenrose** Joseph, Didyma; Apollo's oracle, cult and companions 1988 ➤ 5,e591: ᴿArchNews 16 (1991) 98s (Alice S. *Riginos*); Gnomon 63 (1991) 604-9 (W. *Günther*).

e74 *Rodríguez Somolinos* Juan, Le plus ancien oracle d'Apollon Didymien: EpAnat 17 (1991) 69-71; ❶ 71.

e74* *Haselberger* Lothar, *Seybold* Hans, Seilkurve oder Ellipse? Zur Herstellung antiker Kurvaturen nach dem Zeugnis der didymeischen Kurvenkonstruktion: ArchAnz (1991) 165-188; 15 fig.

e75 **Gordion** 1989: AJA 95 (1991) 140s [< M. *Voigt* ➤ e17].

e76 **Gülpinar** (Assos): *Bingöl* Orhan, Die problematischen Bauglieder des Smintheion: RArchéol (1991) 115-128; 6 fig.

e77 **Hierapolis**: **Sayar** Mustafa, *al*., Inschriften aus Hierapolis-Kastabala [Ost-Kilikien, nicht Pamukkale oder andere in Phrygien]: Szb ph/h 547. W 1989, Österr. Akad. 40 p.; 20 pl. – ᴿKlio 73 (1991) 338s (J. *Hallof*).

e78 **İstanbul**: *Fowden* Garth, Constantine's porphyry column; the earliest literary allusion [Life of Elagabalus]: JRS 81 (1991) 119-131; pl. IX.

e79 **Harrison** R. M., Excavations at Saraçhane I, 1986 ➤ 3,e998; 4,g579: ᴿJRS 81 (1991) 237-9 (C. *Mango*: also on his Temple for Byzantium 1989).

e80 **Harrison** Martin, A temple for Byzantium 1989 ➤ 6,e878: ᴿAJA 95 (1991) 188 (F. P. *Hemans*); JField 18 (1991) 245s (T. E. *Gregory*); JHS 111 (1991) 252s (S. *Hill*: puts some life into 1986 Saraçhane).

e81 **Connor** Carolyn L., Art and miracles in medieval Byzantium; the crypt at Hosios Loukas and its frescoes. Princeton 1991, Univ. [BAR-W 17/6,4].

e82 *Bassett* Sarah G., The antiquities in the [4th cent.] hippodrome of Constantinople: DumbO 45 (1991) 87-96; 1 pl.

e83 *Giatsis* Sotiris G., ❸ Ho megálos Ippódromos — the great hippodrome of Constantinople as place of Byzantine diplomacy: Nikephoros 3 (1990) 209-223.

e84 **Downey** Glanville, Constantinople in the age of Justinian. NY 1991, Dorset. ix-181 p.; maps. 0-88029-620-8.

e85 **Kaman-Kalehöyük**, Survey 1985, 1st 1986: ➤ 402, Anatolia 1991, 62-69 + 8 fig.; 4 pl. / 87-101; 15 fig.; 5 pl. ➤ 402.

e86 **Karakaya**: **Ökse** Tuba, Mitteleisenzeitliche Keramik Zentral-ostanatoliens, mit dem Schwerpunkt Karakaya-Stauseegebiet am Euphrat: BBeit-VO 9. xxii-301 p.; pottery drawings + 15 pl., 7 plans. 3-496-00993-4.

e86* **Kayseri**: *Eskioğlu* Mehmet, ❶ Kaisareia'da ... Byzantine church: Türk-Ark 29 (1991) 133-9 + 2 plans; 20 fig.

e87 **Kültepe** Kaniš 1989: AJA 95 (1991) 129s [T. *Özgüç* ➤ e17].

e88 *a) Özgüç* Tahsin, The newly discovered cult objects from the Karum of Kanesh; – *b) Özgüç* Nimet, The composite creatures in Anatolian art during the period of Assyrian trading colonies; – *c) Kammenhuber* Annelies, Die hethitische Getreidegottheit Ḫalki/Nisaba: ➤ 102c, ᶠPrince MIKASA 1991, 319-334; 12 fig. / 293-312; 38 fig. + 14 phot. / 143-160.

e89 *a) Na'aman* N., ❹ The Assyrian colonies in Anatolia and the Assyrian commerce in the early second millennium; – *b) Eilath* M., International commerce in Eretz Israel under Assyrian rule: ➤ 443, Commerce in Palestine 1980/90, 21-41 / 67-88.

e90 **Dittmann** Reinhard, Eisenzeit I und II in West- und Nordwest-Iran zeitgleich zur Karum-Zeit Anatoliens?: ArchMIran 23 (1990) 105-138; 11 fig.; pl. 21.

e91 *Donbaz* Veysel, A small archive of Innāya — an Assyrian merchant [Kültepe]: RAss 85 (1991) 101-8.

e91* *Kaunos* 1988/9: *Schmaltz* Bernhard, Aktivitäten der deutschen Mitarbeiter: Belleten 55,212 (1991) 121-177 + 20 fig.; 10 pl.

e92 *Kurban*: a) **Wilkinson** T. J., Settlement and land use at Kurban Höyük and other sites in the lower Karababa Basin; – b) ᴱ**Algaze** G., The stratigraphic sequence of Kurban Höyük: OIP 109s/Town and country in southeastern Anatolia 1s. Ch 1990, Univ. Or. Inst.

e93 *Labraunda*: *Hellström* Pontus, The architectural layout of Hecatomnid Labraunda: RArchéol (1991) 297-308; 5 fig.

e94 *Limyra*: *Borchhardt* Jürgen, Ein Ptolemaion in Limyra: RArchéol (1991) 309-322; 16 fig.

e94* *Borchhardt* Jürgen, *al.*, Grabungen und Forschungen in Limyra aus den Jahren 1984-90: JhÖsA 61-B (1991s) 125-192; 23 fig.

e95 *Marksteiner* Thomas, Das Südtor von Limyra mit Berücksichtigung von Toranlagen und Wehrarchitektur in Lykien: JhÖsArch 59-B (1989) 41-110.

e96 *Sagalassos*: a) 1989: AcArchLov 28s (1989s) 75-82 + 17 fig., IV pl. (M. *Waelkens, al.*); – b) 1990: AnSt 41 (1991) 197-213; 12 fig.; pl. XXXVII-XLII (M. *Waelkens, al.*).

e97 *Sardis* 1987 ⇥ 407, ASOR 1982/91, 1-28 (C. H. *Greenewalt*).

e98 **Hanfmann** G. M. A., Sardis from prehistoric to Roman times 1983 ⇥ 64,d74 ... 5,e615: ᴿBASOR 281 (1991) 83-85 (Pamela *Gaber*).

e99 *Chaumont* M.-L., Un nouveau gouverneur de Sardes à l'époque achéménide d'après une inscription récemment découverte [fouilles de Sardes 1974; CRAI 1975, 306-330, *Robert* L.]: Syria 67 (1991) 579-608.

e100 **Gauthier** Philippe, Nouvelles inscriptions de Sardes [I. (*Robert* L.) 1964] II 1989 ⇥ 6,9662: ᴿGnomon 63 (1991) 609-613 (J. H. M. *Strubbe*).

e101 **Vann** Robert L., The unexcavated buildings of Sardis: BAR-Int. 538. Ox 1989. ix-253 p.

e102 *Toprakkale*: **Wartke** Rolf-B., Toprakkale 1990 ⇥ 6,e907: ᴿAfO 36s (1989s) 164-6 (P. R. S. *Moorey*).

e103 *Troja*: Heinrich Schliemann, the rediscovery of Troy: 26-minute color film. Princeton 1990, Films for the Humanities, P.O.B. 2053. $149 video; rental $75. – ᴿArchaeology 44,4 (1991) 68 (P. S. *Allen*).

e104 **Schliemann** Heinrich, Bericht über die Ausgrabungen in Troja in den Jahren 1871-1873, ᴱ*Korfmann* M. Mü 1990, Artemis. 311 p.; 70 fig. + 48 < 'Atlas trojanischer Alterthümer'.

e105 *Ottaway* James H., New assault on Troy [*Korfmann* M. 1982-7]: Archaeology 44,5 (1991) 54-59; ill.

e106 *Siehler* Michael, Das Gold von Troia; neue Rätsel um den 'Schatz des Priamos': AntWelt 22 (1991) 134s; 4 fig. [auch p. 195-206, *Goldmann* Klaus].

e107 *Assael* Jacqueline, L'image de la submersion de Troie dans les Troyennes d'Euripide: RÉAnc 92 (1990) 17-28; Eng. 17.

e108 **Korfmann** M. [1-35 (-39) < 1988s], *al.*, Studia Troica 1. Mainz 1991, von Zabern. 182 p. [101-9, *Easton* D., *al.*, From Seewulf to Schliemann; 111-129, *Hertel* D., *al.*; 131-180, *Schliemann* H., *al.*].

e109 a) *Piejko* Francis, Antiochus III and Ilium: ArPapF 37 (1991) 9-50. –
b) *Bradley* Dennis R., Troy revisited [against rehabilitation of Dares
Phrygius 'De excidio Troiae' in 1969]: Hermes 119 (1991) 232-246.

e110 *Ṭūr Abdīn*: *Macuch* Rudolf, Ṭūr ʿAbdīn through the ages [PALMER A.
1990]: AbrNahrain 29 (1991) 87-105.

e111 **Palmer** Andrew, Monk and mason on the Tigris frontier; the early
history of Tur Abdin 1990 ⇥ 6,e915:   ᴿJRS 81 (1991) 239-241 (I.G.
Tompkins, also on HARVEY S. 1990); RHE 86 (1991) 259s (D. *Bradley*).

e112 *Turlu* (45 k E Gaziantep): *Breniquet* Catherine, Un site halafien en
Turquie méridionale, Tell Turlu; rapport sur la campagne de fouilles de
1962: Akkadica 71 (1991) 1-19 + XVI pl. (map) [faune, *Ducos* P., 72
(1991) 1-19].

e113 **Xanthos**: *Bryce* Trevor R., Tombs and the social hierarchy in ancient
Lycia: AltOrF 18 (1991) 73-85.

e114 **Childs** William A. P., *al.*, Le monument des Néréides, le décor sculpté:
Fouilles de Xanthos 8, 1989 ⇥ 6,e916:   ᴿRArchéol (1991) 137-140 (J.
Marcadé).

e115 a) *Hansen* Erik, Le temple de Létô ou Létôon de Xanthos; – b) *Le Roy*
Christian, Le développement monumental du Létôon: RArchéol (1991)
323-340; 16 fig. / 341-351; 4 fig.

T8.9   **Armenia, Urarṭu.**

e115* **Aydın** Nafiz, ❂ Inscription ourartéenne de Güzelhisar: Belleten 55,213
(1991) 323-9; + phot., facsimile; map.

e116 **Chahin** M., The kingdom of Armenia 1987 ⇥ 4,g624; 5.e622: ᴿBijdragen 52 (1991) 448s (M. *Parmentier*, Eng.; there is a chapter on religion
in the Urartu part and an unsatisfactory one in the Armenia part).

e117 **Diakonoff** Igor M., The prehistory of the Armenian people, ᵀ*Jennings*
Lori, 1984 ⇥ 65,h535; 3,f43: ᴿAfO 36s (1989s) 138-140 (R. *Kessler*).

e118 *Greppin* John A.C., Some effects of the Hurro-Urartian people and
their languages upon the earliest Armenians: JAOS 111 (1991) 720-6 (-8,
Diakonoff I.M. comments; 728-730, bibliog.).

Merhav Rivka, Urartu, exposition 1991 ⇥ b529*.

e119 a) *Salvini* Mirjo, Le cretule [sealings] iscritte del regno di Urartu come
documenti storici; – b) *Aravantinos* Vassilis L., Le cretule iscritte di Tebe
nel quadro dell'amministrazione micenea: Seminari SMEA (1989) 81-
87 + 3 fig. / 5-18.

e120 a) *Sevin* Veli, The southwestward expansion of Urartu; new observations; – b) *Ussishkin* David, On the architectural origin of the
Urartian standard temples: ⇥ 634, 2d Anatolian Iron Age 1987/91, 97-112
/ 117-130.

e120* **Zimansky** Paul E., Ecology and empire; the structure of the Urartian
state 1985 ⇥ 1,e371 ... 5,e628: ᴿBelleten 54,211 (1990) 1277-80 (K. *Kő-
roğlu*, ❂).

e121 *Bastam*: **Kleiss** W., *al.*, Bastam II, 1988 ⇥ 4,g630: ᴿJAOS 111 (1991)
141-5 (O.W. *Muscarella*).

──────────

e122 **Lordkipanidse** Otar, Archäologie in Georgien von der Altsteinzeit zum

Mittelalter: QFors 5. Weinhaim 1991, VCH. ix-284 p.; 58 p. 3-527-17531-8 [OIAc 1,20].

T9.1 Cyprus.

e123 **Albertson** Fred C., Catalogue of the Cypriote Sculptures and Terracottas in the Kelsey Museum, Univ., Ann Arbor: SIMA 20/14. Jonsered 1991, Åström. vii-158 p. [OIAc 2,13].

e124 **di Cesnola** Louis Palma, Cyprus, its ancient cities, tombs, and temples [²1878], [E]*Swiny* Stuart. Limassol 1991, Bendon. 5 + xix-456 p. 99-637624-6-8 [OIAc 2,16].

e125 *Collombier* A.-M., Organisation du territoire et pouvoirs locaux dans l'île de Chypre à l'époque perse: TEuph 4 (1991) 21-43.

e125* **Hermary** A., Louvre... Chypre, sculptures 1989 → 6,e928: [R]RÉG 103 (1990) 701s (B. *Holtzmann*).

e126 *a) Mazar* Amihai, Comments on the nature of the relations between Cyprus and Palestine during the 12th-11th centuries B.C.; – *b) Theodorou* Athanasios J., An attempt to delineate the sea-routes between Crete and Cyprus during the Bronze Age: → 645*, Aegean 1989, 95-104; pl. 20-22 / 32-56; pl. 4-9.

e126* **Niklasson** Karin, Early prehistoric burials in Cyprus: SIMA 96. Jonsered 1991, Åström. vii-258 p.; 101 fig. 91-7981-021-4 [OIAc 2,24].

e127 *Papagéorghiou* Athanassios, Chronique des fouilles et découvertes archéologiques à Chypre en 1990: BCH 115 (1991) 751-833; 58 fig. [Paphos 820-7].

e128 [E]**Peltenburg** Edgar J., Early society in Cyprus 1988/9 → 5,861; 6,e932; £30: [R]BInstArch 27 (1990) 234-6 (D. *Baird*); ClasR 41 (1991) 171-3 (Veronica *Tatton-Brown*).

e129 [E]**Tatton-Brown** Veronica A., Cyprus... Iron Age colloquium 1988/9 → 5,871; 6,e834: AJA 95 (1991) 745s (D. W. *Rupp*).

---

e130 *Alasia*: **Lagarce** J. & E., Alasia IV, 1985 → 2,b309: [R]Syria 67 (1990) 207s (J.-C. *Courtois*).

e131 **Merrillees** Robert, Alashia revisited 1987 → 3,f64... 6,e938: [R]RB 98 (1991) 600-2 (É. *Puech*: not clear whether he would still locate Alasia on the North-Syrian coast).

e132 *Amathous*: Amathonte 1988s, 'palais': TEuph 4 (1991) 9-20 [< ZAW 104,283].

e132* Amathous / Kourion / Katō Paphos: RepCyp (1990) 48-51 / 51-53 / 55-61 (63-66 Kouklia).

e133 *Bouetiez* Emmanuelle Du, *al.*, Rapport sur les travaux de l'École française à Amathonte de Chypre en 1990: BCH 115 (1991) 751-787; 50 fig.

e134 **Clerc** Gisèle (Aegyptiaca p. 1-157) *al.*, La nécropole d'Amathonte, tombes 110-385 [→ e138]: Ét. Chypriotes 13. Nicosie 1991, Service Ant. / Éc. Franç. d'Athènes, p. 159-170, seals, *Boardman* J.; 171-209, coins and inscriptions, *Picard* O., *Nicolaou* I.; ill. 99-63560-15-6 / 2-86958-01-01.

e135 **Karageorghis** V., *al.*, La nécropole d'Amathonte 3, 1987 → 5,e641: [R]Syria 67 (1990) 761-3 (J.-C. *Courtois*).

e136 *Karageorghis* V., a) Notes on some terracotta masks from Amathus now in the British Museum: RStFen 18,1 (1990) 3-15; pl. I-III. – b) Amathus

between the Greeks and the Phoenicians: → 627, Fen. 2, 1987/91. (3,)
959-968.

e137 *Petit* Thierry, Syllabaire et alphabet au 'palais' d'Amathonte de Chypre
vers 300 avant notre ère: → 630, Phoinikeia 1989/91, 481-490 + 23 fig.
→ 9585.

e138 **Tytgat** Christiane, Les nécropoles sud-ouest et sud-est d'Amathonte I,
Les tombes 110-385 [→ e134]: ÉtChypr 11. Nicosie/P 1989, Leventis/de
Boccard. viii-203 p. – [R]Gnomon 63 (1991) 565s (F. *Canciani*); RÉG 104
(1991) 257s (O. *Masson*: some proposals for completion).

e139 *Golgoi*: **Bakalakis** Georgios,' ⊝ *Anaskaphē... Gorkoi* (= Golgoi, NE
Athēainou, centre de Chypre): Bibliothèque fasc. 108. Athènes, 1988,
Soc. Archéologique. xv-160 p.; 94 pl., 2 plans. – [R]RÉG 104 (1991) 256s
(O. *Masson*: 4th century syllabic script as already published by him in
Kadmos 1989).

e140 *Kissonerga*: **Peltenburg** Edgar, A ceremonial area at Kissonerga: Lem-
ba Archaeological Project [I. 1985 → 1,e398]. II/2; SIMA 70/3. Göteborg
1991, Åström. xii-117 p.; 16 pl. 91-7081-011-7.

e141 *Paphos*: **Karageorghis** V., *Demas* M., Excavations at Maa-Palaeokastro
1988 → 6,e950: [R]AJA 95 (1991s) 547 (I. A. *Todd*).

e142 **Karageorghis** Vassos, Tombs at Palaepaphos, 1. Teratsoudhia; 2.
Eliomylia. Nicosia 1990, Leventis. viii-167 p.; LXXXIX pl. [RÉG 104,
679].

e142* *Soloi* (N-Chypre): **Ginouvès** René, Soloi, dix campagnes de fouilles
(1964-1974) II. La 'ville basse'. Laval 1989, Univ. viii-152 p.; 42 fig. –
[R]RArchéol (1991) 131s (A. *Hermary*).

T9.3   *Graecia,* **Greece** – mainland sites in alphabetical order.

e143 *Bloedow* Edmund F., The 'aceramic' noelithic phase in Greece reconsidered: MeditArch 4 (1991) 1-43.

e144 **Étienne** Roland & Françoise, La Grèce antique; archéologie d'une
découverte [+ 'collection 1986']. P 1990, Gallimard. 176 p.; ill. –
[R]RArchéol (1991) 358s (M.-C. *Hellmann*: secoue les idées reçues; s'oppose
aux fouilles).

e145 **Hackens** Tony, *al.*, La Grèce et le monde égéen de la période néolithique à la fin de la période mycénienne; choix de documents graphiques:
DocTravail 25. Lv 1990, Univ. Catholique. 163 p.; dessins.

e146 *Morgan* Catherine, *Whitelaw* Todd, Pots and politics; ceramic evidence
for the rise of the Argive state: AJA 95 (1991) 79-108; 10 fig.

e147 *Pariente* Anne, Chronique des fouilles et découvertes archéologiques en
Grèce en 1990: BCH 115 (1991) 835-946; 153 fig. [Corinthe p. 855];
947-957, index.

---

e148 *Argos* 1990: BCH 115 (1991) 667-686; 30 fig. (M. *Piérart, al.*).

e149 **Dietz** Soren, The Argolid at the transition to the Mycenaean age;
studies in the chronology and cultural development in the shaft grave
period. K 1991, National Museum. 336 p.; 92 fig. 87-7288-501-7.

---

e150 *Athenae*: **Aleshire** Sara B., The Athenian Asklepieion; the people, their
dedications, and the inventories 1989 → 6,e957: [R]ClasR 41 (1991) 441s
(Susan E. *Alcock*).

e151 **Harris** Diane, The inventory lists of the Parthenon treasures: diss. Princeton 1991. 540 p. 91-12941. – DissA 51 (1990s) 4241-A.

e152 **Heatley** Ernest, *Widdess* Margaret, Athens, city and empire. C 1989, Univ. 80 p. £4.50; teacher's handbook 37 p., also £4.50. – ᴿClasR 41 (1991) 506s (D. H. *Smith*: good).

e153 **Kovacsovics** Wilfried K., Kerameikos 14. Die Eckterrasse. B 1990, de Gruyter. xii-177 p.; 82 fig.; 65 pl.; 4 end-plans. – ᴿAJA 95 (1991) 750s (I. *Morris*).

e153* — *Knigge* Ursula, *al.*, Die Ausgrabungen im Kerameikos 1988/89: ArchAnz (1991) 371-388; 26 fig. [389-398, *Goette* H. R., zwei Relief-fragmente].

e154 *Goette* Hans R., Restaurierungen und Forschungen auf der Akropolis von Athen: AntWelt 22 (1991) 165-176; 21 (color.) fig.

e155 *McNeal* Richard A., Archaeology and the destruction of the later Athenian acropolis: Antiquity 65 (1991) 49-63; 11 fig.

e156 **Lang** Mabel L., Ostraka: Athenian Agora 25. Princeton 1990, American School Athens. xvi-188 p. $55. 0-87661-611-2. – ᴿArchWsz 42 (1991) 157-9 (B. *Bravo*, franç.).

e157 **Pallas** D. I., Ⓖ Atene negli anni di transizione dal culto antico a quello cristiano [< Epist. Epeterio Ath. 28 (1989) 851-830]. Athēnai 1989. 86 p.; 27 fig. – ᴿRivArCr 67 (1991) 186-8 (Eugenia *Chalkia*).

e158 *Rottländer* Rolf C. A., *al.*, Untersuchungen am Turm der Winde in Athen: JbÖsArch 59-H (1989) 57-92.

e159 **Schneider** Lambert, *Höcker* Christoph, Die Akropolis von Athen, antikes Heiligtum und modernes Reiseziel. Köln 1990, DuMont. 312 p.; 150 fig.; 32 pl.; 2 maps. – ᴿAntWelt 22 (1991) 71 (P. *Zazoff*); ClasR 41 (1991) 441 (Susan E. *Alcock*); RArchéol (1991) 369-372 (B. *Holtzmann*: bon).

e160 *Spaeth* Barbette S., Athenians and Eleusinians in the west pediment of the Parthenon: Hesperia 60 (1991) 331-362; 1 fig.; pl. 95.

e161 *Touloupa* Evi, Recherches archéologiques sur l'Acropole; bilan des cinq dernières années: RArchéol (1991) 210-220; 8 fig.

e162 **Willers** Dietrich, Hadrians panhellenisches Programm; archäologische Beiträge zur Neugestaltung Athens durch Hadrian: Antike Kunst Beih. 16. Basel 1990, Univ. Archäol. Sem. 107 p.; 28 fig.; 15 pl. Fs 120. 3-909064-16-7 [DLZ 113,408, M. *Oppermann*].

e163 *Beroea*: **Tataki** Argyro B., Ancient Beroea; prosopography and society: Meletemata 8, 1988 → 5,e683: ᴿClasR 41 (1991) 142-4 (E. E. *Rice*).

e164 *Corinthus*: **Engels** Donald, Roman Corinth; an alternative model for the classical city. Ch 1990, Univ. 264 p.; 16 pl.; 11 maps. 0-226-20870-2. – ᴿClasPg 86 (1991) 351-7 (R. P. *Saller*); GreeceR 38 (1991) 252 (T. *Wiedemann*); JRS 81 (1991) 221 (Mary E. *Hoskins-Walbank*).

e165 **Lambropoulou** Anastasia, The Middle Helladic period in the Corinthia and the Argolid; on archaeological survey: diss. Bryn Mawr, ᴰ*Wright* J. Ph 1991. 489 p. 91-28582. – DissA 52 (1991s) 1403-A.

e166 **Pemberton** Elizabeth G., The sanctuary of Demeter and Kore; the Greek pottery: Corinth 18. Princeton 1989, American School at Athens. xix-236 p.; 38 fig.; 61 pl.; 2 plans. – ᴿClasR 41 (1991) 178-180 (A. *Johnston*).

e167 *Williams* Charles K.[II], [*Zervos* Orestes H., coins] Corinth 1990; southeast corner of Temenos E: Hesperia 60 (1991) 1-40 [41-58]; 6 fig.; pl. 1-13.

e168 *Winter* Frederick E.,   The chronology of the ancient defenses of Acrocorinth, a reconsideration: AJA 95 (1991) 109-121; 12 fig.

e169 *Delphes* 1990: BCH 115 (1991) 686-711; 29 fig. (P. *Amandry, al.*).

e170 Guide de Delphes; le musée (*Bommelaer* Jean François), le site. P 1991, De Boccard. 278 p.; 117 fig. / 263 p.; ill. 2-86958-037-1; -8-X.

e171 **Arnush** Michael F., 'The chronology of Delphi in the late fourth and early third centuries B.C.; an epigraphic and historical analysis: diss. Pennsylvania, [D]*Graham* A.J. Ph 1991. 420 p. 91-25585. – DissA 52 (1991s) 1039-A.

e172 *Lacroix* Léon,   Pausanias et les origines mythologiques de Delphes: éponymes, généalogies, spéculations: Kernos 4 (1991) 265-276.

e173 *Epidauros*: *Käppel* Lutz,   Das Theater von Epidauros; die mathematische Grundidee des Gesamtentwurfs und ihr möglicher Sinn: JbDAI 104 (1989) 83-106; 13 fig.

e173* **Tomlinson** R.A.,   Epidauros: Archaeological sites 1983 ⇒ 64,d155; 2,b340: [R]RÉG 104 (1991) 266s (A. *Laronde*).

e174 *Kraynak* Lynn,   The *Katagogion* at Epidauros; a revised plan: Arch-News 16 (Athens GA 1991) 1-8; 6 fig.

e174* *Posch* Walter,   Die *typoi* des Timotheos [200 (Athen- und) Epidauros-Fragmente]: ArchAnz (1991) 69-73.

e175 *Mycenae*: Åkerström Å.,   Berbati 2. The pictorial pottery: SkrAth 36/2, 1987 ⇒ 4,g684: [R]AJA 95 (1991) 548s (Gisela *Walberg*: important for pictorial Mycenaean vases found in Cypriot tombs).

e176 *Graziadio* Giampaolo,   The process of social stratification at Mycenae in the Shaft Grave period; a comparative examination of the evidence: AJA 95 (1991) 403-440.

e177 **Lewartowski** Kazimierz,   The decline of the Mycenaean civilization; an archaeological study of events in the Greek mainland: Archiwum Filologiczne 43. Wrocław 1989, Akad. Nauk. 228 p.; 32 fig.

e178 **McDonald** William A., [2rev]*Thomas* Carol G.,   Progress into the past; the rediscovery of Mycenaean civilization [[1]1967]. Bloomington 1990, Indiana Univ. xxiv-534 p.; 122 fig. – [R]RArchéol (1991) 357s (Josette *Renard*).

e178* *a*) *Peltenburg* Edgar,   Greeting gifts and luxury faience; a context for orientalising trends in Late Mycenaean Greece; – *b*) *French* Elizabeth B., Tracing exports of Mycenaean pottery; the Manchester contribution: ⇒ 637, Bronze Age Trade 1989/91, 162-179 / 121-6.

e179 *Vagnetti* Lucia,   La civiltà micenea: Archeo 70 (1990) 52-103; ill.

e180 *Hiller* Stefan,   Österreich und die mykenisch-mitteleuropäischen Kulturbeziehungen: JhÖsA 61-H (1991) 1-19.

e181 *Nemea*: [E]**Miller** Stephen G.,   Nemea; a guide to the site and museum. Berkeley 1990, Univ. California. xiv-214 p.; 69 fig. $30; pa. $11. – [R]ClasR 41 (1991) 260 (R. L. N. *Barber*); RArchéol (1991) 372s (Marie-Françoise *Billot*).

e182 *Alcock* Susan E.,   Urban survey and the *polis* of Phlius [Nemea, NE Peloponnese]: Hesperia 60 (1991) 421-463; 20 fig. (map).

e183 *Olympia*: Hitzl Konrad,   Die kaiserzeitliche Statuenausstattung des Metroon: DAI OlympischeF 19. B 1991, de Gruyter. 131 p.; 45 pl. – [R]RArchéol (1991) 382s (F. *Queyrel*).

Morgan Catherine, Athletes and oracles 1990 ➤ b791.
e184 *Pella:* *Lilibaki-Akamati* Maria, Ⓖ New Pella inscriptions: Makedonika 26 (1987s) 51-62.
e185 *Philippes* 1990: BCH 115 (1991) 711s; 2 fig.
e186 *Pylos:* **Ball** William, Pylos, a colour filmstrip with commentary. Congleton, Cheshire 1990, Old Vicarage. 52 p.; 57 frames. £9.75. – ᴿClasR 41 (1991) 250s (D. H. *Smith*: delightful); GreeceR 38 (1991) 80s (A. *Powell*).
e187 *Sparta:* **Cartledge** P., *Spawforth* A., Hellenistic and Roman Sparta 1989 ➤ 6,e988: ᴿAmHR 96 (1991) 487s (C. D. *Hamilton*); ClasR 41 (1991) 398-401 (G. *Shipley*); Gnomon 63 (1991) 652-654 (M. *Clauss*); JRS 81 (1991) 221-3 (G. M. *Rogers*).
e188 **Rawson** Elizabeth † 1988, The Spartan tradition in European thought. Ox 1991 pa. [= 1969], Clarendon. x-390 p.; 6 fig. 0-19-814733-3.
e188* *Stylis:* *Dakoronia* Phanouria, Elemente der Haus- und Stadtplanung von Stylis [Hafenplatz für Lamia, c. 50 k N Delphi] im 4. Jh. v.Chr.: ArchAnz (1991) 75-88; 14 fig.
e189 *Tanagra* (20 k S Thebae-Boeotia): **Higgins** Reynold, Tanagra and the figurines 1986 ➤ 4,e382; 5,d410: ᴿRArchéol (1991) 143s (Simone *Besques*).
e190 *Camp* John M.ᴵᴵ, Notes on the towers and borders of classical Boiotia: AJA 95 (1991) 193-202; 8 fig. (maps).
e191 *Torone* (Chalkidike) 1989: MeditArch 4 (1991) 147-171; 29 fig.; pl. 20-25 (A. *Cambitoglou, J. K. Papadopoulos*).

T9.4   **Creta.**

e192 *Bloedow* Edmund F., Evidence for an early date for the cult of Cretan Zeus: Kernos 4 (1991) 139-171 + 8 fig.
e193 *Branigan* K., Social security and the state in MBA Crete: Aegaeum 2 (Liège 1988)... [RÉG 104,599].
e194 *Broodbank* Cyprian, *Strasser* Thomas F., Migrant farmers [cattle, ovicaprine, pig domesticates found] and the Neolithic colonization of Crete: Antiquity 65 (1991) 233-245; map.
e195 *Empereur* Jean-Yves, *al.,* Les centres de fabrication d'amphores en Crète centrale: BCH 115,1 (1991) 481-523; 58 fig.
e196 **Kirsten** Ernst, Die Insel Kreta in vier Jahrtausenden, Ges. Aufs. 1938-1974. Amst 1990, Hakkert. 126 p.
e196* **Mastorakis** M., *Effenterre* M. Van, Les Minoens, l'âge d'or de la Crète. P 1991, Errance. 197 p. [RÉG 104,680].
e197 *Warren* Peter, The destruction of the palace of Knossos: ➤ 645*, Aegaan 1989, 23-37.
e197* *a) Warren* P. M., A merchant class in Bronze Age Crete? The evidence of Egyptian stone vessels from the city of Knossos; – *b) Weingarten* J., Late Bronze Age trade within Crete; the evidence of seals and sealing; – *c) Wiener* Malcolm H., The nature and control of Minoan foreign trade: ➤ 673, Bronze Age Trade 1989/91, 295-302 / 303-324 / 325-350.
e198 *Watrous* L. Vance, The origin and iconography of the Late Minoan painted larnax ['chest (i.e. box)-shaped' coffin standard in Crete after 1300 B.C.]: Hesperia 60 (1991) 285-307; pl. 81-93.
e198* **Weingarten** Judith, The transformation of the Egyptian Taweret into the Minoan Genius; a study in cultural transmission in the Middle Bronze

Age: SIMA 88. Jonsered 1991, Åström. 24 p.; 10 fig.; 22 pl. 91-7981-028-1 [OIAc 2,29].

---

e199 *Aghia Triada*: *Laffineur* Robert, À propos du sarcophage d'Aghia triada; un rituel de nécromancie à l'époque protohistorique?: Kernos 4 (1991) 277-285.

e200 *Soles* Jeffrey S., The Gournia palace: AJA 95 (1991) 17-78; 75 (foldout) fig.

e201 *Kavousi* 1988: Hesperia 60 (1991) 145-177; 13 fig.; pl. 57-70 (Geraldine C. *Gesell, al.*) [179-86 fauna ➤ e453].

e202 *Knossos*: **Niemeier** Wolf Dieter, Die Palaststilkeramik von Knossos; Stil, Chronologie und historischer Kontext: ArchäolF 13. Berlin 1985, Mann. xiv-271 p.; 27 fig.; 29 pl. – ᴿBonnJbb 191 (1991) 718s (Karola *Czernohaus*).

e203 **Popham** M. R., *al.*, The Minoan unexplored mansion 1984 ➤ 65,b636... 5,e714: ᴿBInstArch 27 (1990) 237s (G. A. *Owens*).

e204 *Press* Ludwika, On the creators of the Minoan places of worship: Klio 73 (1991) 5-19; 8 fig.

e205 *Malia* 1990: BCH 115 (1991) 726-750; 54 fig. (O. *Pelon, al.*).

e206 *a) Farnoux* Alexandre, Malia à la fin du Bronze récent; – *b) Driesser* Jan, The proliferation of Minoan palatial architectural style, I. Crete: AcArchLov 28s (1989s) 25-33; 19 fig. / 3-23; 14 fig.

e207 *Vrocastro*: *Hayden* Barbara J., Terracotta figures, figurines, and vase attachments from Vrocastro, Crete: Hesperia 60 (1991) 103-144; 13 fig.; pl. 47-56.

T9.5   Insulae graecae.

e208 ᴱ**Acquaro** E., *al.*, Momenti precoloniali nel Mediterraneo antico: St. Fen. coll. 28, 1985/8 ➤ 5,811: ᴿJSS 36 (1991) 149s (Vronwy *Hankey*); WienerSt 104 (1991) 285s (H. *Schwabl*).

e209 *Åström* Paul, Early relations between the East Mediterranean and Italy: ➤ 595, Munuscula 1988/91, 9-15; 7 fig.

e210 **Cline** Eric H., Orientalia in the Late Bronze Age Aegean; a catalogue and analysis of trade and contacts between the Aegean and Egypt, Anatolia and the Near East: diss. Pennsylvania, ᴰ*Muhly* J. Ph 1991. 718 p. 91-25617. – DissA 52 (1991s) 1039-A.

e211 *Cline* Eric H., [23] Hittite objects in the Bronze Age Aegean: AnSt 41 (1991) 133-143.

e212 **Crowley** Janice L., The Aegean and the East: SIMA pocket 51, 1989 ➤ 5,d321: ᴿAJA 95 (1991) 347s (Karen P. *Foster*); ClasR 41 (1991) 431-3 (P. M. *Warren*).

e213 **Treuil** René, *al.*, Les civilisations égéennes du Néolithique et de l'Âge de Bronze: NClio 1, 1989 ➤ 6,503: ᴿAJA 95 (1991) 742s (J. E. *Rexine*).

e214 *Vagnetti* Lucia, Ricerche recenti sulle relazioni fra l'Egeo e l'occidente mediterraneo: Seminari SMEA (1988) 29-44.

e215 **Vanschoonwinkel** Jacques, L'Égée et la Méditerranée orientale à la fin du deuxième millénaire; témoignages archéologiques et sources écrites [< diss. 1987 ➤ 6,g21]: HistArtArch 66 / Archaeologia Transatlantica 9. LvN 1991, Univ. 590 p.; 11 fig.; 11 maps.

e216 **Warren** F., *Hankey* V., Aegean Bronze Age chronology 1989 ➤ 5,d723; £24: ᴿAcPraeh 22 (1990) 179-186 (J. *Maran*).

---

e217 *Cyclades*: **Délos** 1990: BCH 115 (1991) 720-5; 7 fig. (A. *Farnoux*).
e218 *Nenna* Marie-Dominique, La verrerie à l'époque hellénistique; l'exemple délien: RÉG 103,2 (1990) XIV-XVI.
e219 **Fitton** J. Lesley, Cycladic Art [< exhibition 1983 + symposium]. L 1989, British Museum. 72 p.; 50 fig. + 40 colour. £5. 0-7141-1293-3. – ᴿGreeceR 38 (1991) 105s (B. A. *Sparkes*).
e220 **Papagiannopoulou** Angelia G., The influence of Middle Minoan pottery on the Cyclades: SIMA pocket 96. Göteborg 1991, Åström. 377 p.; ill.
e221 **Renfrew** Colin, The Cycladic spirit; masterpieces from the N.P. Goulandris collection. L 1991, Thames & H. 208 p. 41 fig. + 142 colour. £32. 0-500-01527-9 [Antiquity 66,542, C. *Broodbank*].
e222 *a)* **Sampson** A., Early Helladic contacts with the Cyclades during the EBA 2; – *b)* *Melas* M., Minoans overseas; alternative models of interpretation: Aegaeum 2, Annales d'archéologie égéenne de l'Université de Liège 1988 [135 p.; XL pl.: RÉG 104,599, Hélène *Cassimatis*, avec 6 titres encore, sans pp.].
e223 *Tradalidou* Katerina, Ⓖ Eine neue prähistorische Stätte auf Mykonos; der 'Grabhügel' von Phteliá – Grab des Aias (?): Archaiognosia 6 (1990) 121-134; deutsch 135s.

e224 *Keos*: **Overbeck** John C., Ayia Irini 4/1: Keos 7, 1989 ➤ 5,e734: ᴿClasR 41 (1991) 169-171 (M. J. *Alden*).
e225 *Lesbos*: **Brun** Patrice, Les Lagides à Lesbos; essai de chronologie: ZPapEp 85 (1991) 99-113.
e226 *Paros*: **Schuller** Manfred, Der Artemistempel im Delion auf Paros: DAI-Architektur 18,1. B 1991. 140 p.; 58 fig.; 102 pl. – ᴿArchWsz 112 (1991) 155s (S. *Parnicki-Pudełko*, Ⓟ).
e227 *Rhodus*: **Goodlett** Virginia C., Rhodian sculpture workshops: AJA 95 (1991) 669-681; 4 fig.
e228 *Samos*: **Felsch** R. S. C., Samos II, Das Kastro Tigani; die spätneolithische und chalkolithische Siedlung: DAI. Mainz 1988, von Zabern. xii-261 p.; 92 fig.; 3 foldouts. – ᴿAJA 95 (1991) 344s (N. *Efstratou*).
e229 *Vilatte* Sylvie, Idéologie et action tyranniques à Samos; le territoire; les hommes: RÉAnc 92 (1990) 3-15; Eng. 3.
e230 *Simossi* Angeliki, Underwater excavation research in the ancient harbour of Samos, Sept.-Oct. 1988: IntJNaut 20 (1991) 281-298; 47 (foldout) fig.
e231 *Tenos*: **Roland** Étienne, Ténos 2: BÉF 263 bis, 1990 [N.B. Tenos I, 1986 ➤ 3,f171; 5,e742 sous Étienne]. – ᴿRArchéol (1991) 387-9 (C. *Vial*).
e232 *Teos*: **Piejko** Francis, Antiochus III and Teos reconsidered [HERR-MANN P. 1965]: Belleten 55/212 (1991) 13-69.
e233 *Thasos* 1990: BCH 115 (1991) 712-720; 12 fig. (J.-Y. *Empereur*, Angéliki *Simossi*).
e234 *Holtzmann* Bernard, À propos d'une sphinge archaïque recomposée [musée de Thasos 1987]: CRAI (1991) 89-97; 4 fig. (97-102, observations de Jean *Marcadé*, Pierre *Amandry*).
e235 *Thera*: **Doumas** Christos G., High art from the time of Abraham: BAR-W 17,1 (1991) 41-51; (color.) ill.

[E]**Hardy** D.A.,   Thera and the Aegean world: 3d internat. congress, Santorini 3-9.IX.1989:   1990 → 642.

T9.6   Urbs Roma.

e237 *Alfano* Carla,   Pyramids in Rome: GöMiszÄg 121 (1991) 7-17.

e238 *Alföldy* Géza,   Zwei augusteische Monumente in der Area Sacra des Largo Argentina in Rom: → 583, Mem. DEGRASSI A. Epigrafia 1988/91, 667-690; 7 fig.

e239 **Boatwright** Mary T.,   Hadrian and the city of Rome 1987 → 3,f178 ... 6,g46:   [R]Archaeology 44,2 (1991) 58s (S. *Brown*).

e240 *Branigan* Keith,   Images – or mirages – of empire? An archaeological approach to the problem: → 412, Images 1990/1, 91-105.

e241 **Cattabiani** Alfredo,   Simboli, miti e misteri di Roma.   R 1990, Newton Compton.   251 p.; ill.   Lit. 28.000. – [R]CC 142 (1991,4) 634 (A. *Ferrua*).

e242 **Coarelli** Filippo,   Il Foro Boario 1988 → 5,e753; 6,g49:   [R]Gnomon 62 (1991) 730-4; 3 fig. (T.P. *Wiseman*).

e243 *Cristofani* Mauro, *al.*,   La grande Roma dei Tarquini: Archeo 63 (1990) 60-109; ill.

e244 **De Maria** Sandro,   Gli archi onorari di Roma e dell'Italia romana 1988 → 5,e755:   [R]Latomus 50 (1991) 481-4 (J. *Debergh*).

e245 **Falbo** Giovanni,   Il primato della Chiesa di Roma alla luce dei primi quattro secoli 1989 → 6,4943:   [R]CC 142 (1991,2) 97s (G. *Cremasoli*).

e246 **Guarducci** Margherita,   Il primato della Chiesa di Roma; documenti, riflessioni, conferme.   Mi 1991, Rusconi.   180 p.   Lit. 25.000. – [R]Archeo 80 (1991) 128s (S. *Moscati*).

e247 **Guidobaldi** Federico, *al.*,   La Basilica e l'area archeologica di S. Clemente in Roma; guida grafica ai 3 livelli. R 1990. 3 plans.

e248 **Lefèvre** Eckard,   Das Bild-Programm des Apollo-Tempels auf dem Palatin: Xenia 24, 1989 → 6,g56:   [R]Gymnasium 98 (1991) 84s (Helga von *Heintze*); WienerSt 104 (1991) 323s (Christine *Harrauer*).

e249 **Lepper** F., *Frere* S.,   Trajan's column ... Cichorius plates 1988 → 4,g799; 5,e761:   [R]Gnomon 63 (1991) 135-9 (H. *Halfmann*).

e250 — *Baumer* Lorenz E., *al.*,   Narrative Systematik und politisches Konzept in den Reliefs der Traianssäule; drei Fallstudien: JbDAI 63 (1991) 261-295; 2 fig.

e251 — *Koeppel* Gerhard M.,   Die historischen Reliefs der römischen Kaiserzeit VIII. Der Fries der Trajanssäule in Rom, 1. Der erste dakische Krieg, Szenen I-LXXVIII: BonnJbb 191 (1991) 135-199; 55 fig.

e252 — *Settis* Salvatore,   La colonne trajane; l'empereur et son public: RArchéol (1991) 186-198; 7 fig.

e253 *Lorenzetti* Sandro,   Vicende del Tempio di Venere a Roma nel medioevo e nel Rinascimento: RINASA 13 (1990) 119-138; 6 fig.

e254 *Luce* T.J.,   LIVY, Augustus, and the Forum Augustum: → 599*, Between Republic and Empire 1987/90, 123-138.

e255 *Mathon* G., Rome: → 664, Catholicisme XIII,59 (1991) 87-90.

e256 **Neumeister** Christoff,   Das antike Rom; ein literarischer Stadtführer. Mü 1991, Beck. 328 p.; 77 fig. [GrazBeit 18,296, W. *Pötscher*].

e257 **Palmer** Robert E.A.,   Studies of the northern Campus Martius in ancient Rome: AmPhTr 80/2. Ph 1990. vii-64 p.

e258 *Rodríguez-Almeida* Emilio,   Tra epigrafia, filologia, storia e topografia urbana; quattro ipotesi: MÉF-A 103 (1991) 529-550.

e259 *Staccioli* Romolo A.,   Le terme dei Romani: Archeo 68 (1990) 64-107.

e260 *Turcan* Robert, Les *fondi* [médaillons] d'Hadrien sur l'arc de Constantin: CRAI (1991) 53-82; 15 fig.

T9.7 *Roma,* **Catacumbae.**

e261 [Perez] **Bargebuhr** Frederick, The paintings of the 'New' catacomb of the Via Latina and the struggle of Christianity against paganism: Abh Ak Heid ph/h 1991/2. Heid 1991, Winter. 107 p.

e262 **Baruffa** Antonio, Le catacombe di San Callisto; storia, archeologia, fede. T-Leumann ²1989, ¹1988 ➤ 6,g65: ᴿDivinitas 34 (1990) 291-3 (L. *Bogliolo*); RivArCr 67 (1991) 212s (D. *Mazzoleni*).

e263 *Carletti* C., *al.,* Attività della P[ont.]C[om.] di Arte Sacra nelle catacombe fuori Roma: RivArCr 67 (1991) 143-160.

e264 **Duval** Yvette, Auprès des saints, corps et âme 1988 ➤ 5,e774: ᴿBonn-Jbb 191 (1991) 767s (N. *Gauthier*).

e265 **Farmer** W.R., *Kereszty* Roch, Peter and Paul in the church of Rome 1990 ➤ 6,g52: ᴿLvSt 16 (1991) 187s (B. *Dehandschutter*); PerspRelSt 18 (1991) 202s (E.G. *Hinson*: Farmer is a Catholic former Methodist; Kereszty a Cistercian).

e266 **Ferrua** Antonio, La basilica e la catacomba di S. Sebastiano². Vaticano 1990, Pontificia Commissione di Arte Sacra. 80 p. Lit. 10.000. – ᴿArcheo 74 (1991) 128 (D. *Mazzoleni*); CC 142 (1991,3) 339s (C. *Capizzi*).

e267 *Guarducci* Margherita, La chiocciola [snail, circular staircase] cristiana: RFgIC 119 (1991) 447-456; 3 fig.

e268 *Guerrieri Borsoi* Maria B., L'attività di Stefano e Giuseppe POZZI [dal 1756] nella Basilica di San Pietro: StRom 39 (1991) 252-266.

e268* **Guyon** J., La cimetière 'Aux deux lauriers' 1987 ➤ 4,g814...6,g72: ᴿChH 59 (1990) 79s (G.T. *Armstrong*: magisterial).

e269 **Jordan** Wilhelm, Das Apostelgrab, der sakrale Grundstein der Vatikanischen Basilika: Schr. 5. Trier 1990, Rheinisches Landesmuseum. vii-116 p.

d269* **Konikoff** Adia, Sarcophagi from the Jewish catacombs of ancient Rome, a catalogue raisonné²ʳᵉᵛ [¹1986 ➤ 2,b437... 6,g73]. Stu 1990, Steiner. 59 p.; 16 pl.; map. 3-515-06773-0.

e270 **Reekmans** Louis, Le complexe cémétérial du Pape Gaius dans la Catacombe de Callixte 1988 ➤ 4,g818; Lit. 170.000 [< Het Gaiuscomplex 1987 ➤ 5,e782*]: ᴿGregorianum 72 (1991) 172-4 (J. *Janssens*); RivArCr 67 (1991) 235-8 (F. *Tolotti*).

T9.8 *Roma,* **Ars palaeochristiana.**

e271 **Arbeiter** Achim, Alt-St. Peter 1988 ➤ 4,g822... 6,g80: ᴿRömQ 86 (1991) 282-5 (G. *Mietke*).

e272 ᴱ**Binazzi** Gianfranco, Inscriptiones christianae Italiae septimo saeculo antiquiores; Bari 1989, Edipuglia. 256 p. – ᴿSMSR 57 (1991) 159-169 (D. *Mazzoleni*).

e273 **Duval** Yvette, Loca sanctorum Africae 1982 ➤ 1,e543; 4,g825: ᴿByZ 83 (1991) 482s (P. *Grossmann*).

e274 **Ferrua** Antonio, Note e giunte alle iscrizioni cristiane antiche della Sicilia [➤ 6,g85]: Sussidi allo Studio delle Antichità Cristiane 8. Vaticano 1989. 155 p. – ᴿRivArCr 67 (1991) 347-352 (M. *Griesheimer*).

e275 **Ferrua** Antonio, La polemica antiariana nei monumenti paleocristiani: StAntCr 43. Vaticano 1991, Ist. Arch. Cr. 313 p. – ᴿCC 142 (1991,2) 610s (G. *Capizzi*); SMSR 57 (1991) 169-172 (D. *Mazzoleni*).

e276 *Finch* Margaret, The cantharus and pigna at Old St. Peter's: Gesta, medieval art 30,1 (NY Cloisters 1991) 16-26; 9 fig.

e277 **Korol** Dieter, Die frühchristlichen Wandmalereien aus den Grabbauten in Cimitile/Nola; zur Entstehung und Ikonographie alttestamentlicher Darstellung: JbAC Egbd 13, 1987 ➤ 3,f227 [Cimitele]. 6,g86: ᴿTR 87 (1991) 479-482 (W. *Gessel*).

Malbon Elizabeth S., The iconography of the sarcophagus of Junius Bassus Neofitus [4th cent.] *iit ad Deum.* 1990 ➤ d42.

e279 *Mazzoleni* Danilo, *al.*, L'arte delle antiche chiese: Archeo 59 (1990) 52-109; ill.

e280 *Melograni* Anna, Le pitture del VI e VIII secolo nella basilica inferiore di S. Crisogono in Trastevere: RINASA 13 (1990) 139-178; 46 fig.

e281 *Petricioli* Ivo, Pavimenti musivi paleocristiani della Cattedrale di Zara: Atti Soc. Istriana Arch. 91 (Trieste 1991) 7-16; 6 fig.

e282 *Rizzi* Vivina, Sul restauro della facciata della Chiesa dei Ss. Vincenzo e Anastasio [Fontana Trevi]: StRom 39 (1991) 286-9; pl. XXV-XXVIII.

e283 *Russo* Eugenio, Una fronte frammentaria d'altare paleocristiano rinvenuta nella Cattedrale di Parma: RivArCr 67 (1991) 383-404; 14 fig.

T9.9 *(Roma) Imperium occidentale,* **Europa.**

e284 **d'Ambrosio** A., *Boriello* M., Le terrecotte figurate di Pompei: Cataloghi 4. R 1990, Bretschneider. 121 p.; 261 fig. + 12 color. Lit. 150.000 [Gymnasium 99,378, T. *Fröhlich*].

e285 **Andrén** Arvin, Capri, dall'età paleolitica all'età turistica. R 1991, Finanziaria Agricola del Mezzogiorno. 200 p.; 30 fig. – ᴿArcheo 82 (1991) 128 (S. *Moscati*).

e286 *Bonfante* Larissa, [Fifty] recent books from Italy on the Etruscans: AJA 95 (1991) 157-164.

e287 *Eschebach* Liselotte, Die Forumsthermen in Pompeji, Regio VII, insula 5: AntWelt 22 (1991) 257-287; 69 (color.) fig.

e288 — **Koloski** Ostrow A., The Sarno bath complex: Soprintendenza Pompei Mg. 4. R 1990, Bretschneider. xxviii-137 p.; 125 fig. Lit. 150.000 [Gymnasium 99,376, T. *Fröhlich*].

e289 — **Richardson** L.ᴶ, Pompeii, an architectural history 1988 ➤ 5,e804; 6,g100: ᴿAmHR 96 (1991) 143 (R. E. A. *Palmer*); JRS 81 (1991) 213s (W. *Jongman*, 'long-felt need'; also on 'elegant' ZANKER W. 1987); Latomus 50 (1991) 740-2 (P. *Gros*).

e290 — a) *Richardson* L.ᴶ, Innovations in domestic architecture at Pompeii, A.D. 62-79; – b) *Vos* Mariette de, Paving techniques at Pompeii, ᵀ*Thompson* David L.: ArchNews 16 (1991) 21-35; 8 fig. / 36-60; 31 fig.

e291 *Steingräber* Stephan, Zu Entstehung, Verbreitung und architektonischem Kontext der unteritalischen Grabmalerei: JbDAI 106 (1991) 1-36; map; foldout; 36 pl.

e292 **Tran Tam Tinh**, La casa dei cervi a Herculanum. R 1988, Bretschneider. xii-168 p., 242 fig.; 20 pl. Lit. 460.000. – ᴿAJA 95 (1991) 356s (C. *Parslow*).

e293 — *Kind* Richard de, The study of houses at Herculanum [TRAN TAM TINH, La casa dei cervi (R 1988, Bretschneider); GANSCHOW T., Untersuchungen zur Baugeschichte in H. (Bonn 1989, Habelt)]: Babesch 66 (1991) 175-185; 1 fig.

e294 *Giuntella* A. M., *al.*, Recenti indagini nella catacomba di Castelvecchio subequo (Aq): RivArCr 67 (1991) 249-321; 44 fig.; V foldouts.

e295 **Otranto** Giorgio, Italia meridionale e Puglia paleocristiana, saggi storici: Scavi e ricerche 5. Bari 1991, Edipuglia. vii-330 p.; ill. 88-7228-079-6 [AnBoll 110,178, U. *Zanetti*].

e296 **Pedley** John G., Paestum; Greeks and Romans in southern Italy: New Aspects of Antiquity. L 1990, Thames & H. 184 p.; 124 fig.; 11 color. pl. £20. – ᴿAJA 95 (1991) 555s (Frances *Van Keuren*); ClasR 41 (1991) 442-4 (T. W. *Potter*); GreeceR 38 (1991) 107 (B. A. *Sparkes*); JField 18 (1991) 513-5 (Elizabeth R. *Gebhard*).

e297 *Warren* John, The first church of San Marco in Venice [c. 830]: AntiqJ 70 (1990) 327-359; 12 fig.; pl. XXIX-XXXVI.

e298 **Wilson** Roger J. A., Sicily under the Roman Empire; the archaeology of a Roman province, 36 B.C. - A.D. 535: Archaeologists' guide to the Roman Empire. Wmr 1990, Aris & P. ix-452 p.; 290 fig. 0-85668-552-6; pa. -160-1.

XIX. Geographia biblica

ul **Geographies.**

e299 **Adamec** Ludwig W., Historical gazetteer of Iran, 4. Zahidan and southeastern Iran. Graz 1988, Akad. x-480 p. DM 370. – ᴿBSO [41 (1978) 426 vol. 1; 47 (1984) 203 vol. 2] 54 (1991) 593 (A. K. S. *Lambton*).

e300 **Crée** F.-J. de, Beyond existence; gazetteer of Early Bronze Age Palestine. Bru 1990, MIRI. ix-732 p. (4 vol.) + 11 loose plans [OIAc 1,14].

e301 **Gal** Z., ⊕ The lower Galilee; historical geography in the biblical period [< TAJ 9 & 15 + ZDPV 101]: TA Univ. TA 1990, Meuchad [ZAW 104,294, V. *Fritz*].

e302 **González Echegaray** Joaquín, El creciente fértil y la Biblia. Estella 1991, VDivino. 311 p.; maps. 84-7151-698-5 [TS 52,600].

e303 **Govrin** Yehuda, Maps of Naḥal Yattir [⊕] (139): Archaeological Survey / Antiquities Authority. J 1991. 173* p., photos [in Hebrew text p. 1-169] listed p. 24*-28*.

e304 **Hütteroth** Wolf-Dieter, Türkei: Wiss. Landurkunden 21, 1982 → 63,d739 ... 65,b716: ᴿWZKM 78 (1988) 313s (S. von *Gnielinski*).

e305 **Huntingford** G. W. B., The historical geography of Ethiopia from the first century A.D. to 1704; Fontes Historiae Africanae 1989 → 6,g106: ᴿZDMG 141 (1991) 175s (P. J. L. *Frankl*).

e306 **Lane** Belden C., Landscapes of the sacred; geography and narrative in American spirituality 1988 → 4,g860*: ᴿCritRR 4 (1991) 322s (Martha E. *Stortz*); JRel 71 (1991) 476s (Catherine L. *Albanese*).

e308 **Miquel** André, La géographie humaine du monde musulman jusqu'au milieu du 11ᵉ siècle, 4. Les travaux et les jours: Civilisations et sociétés 78, 1988 → 6,g109; F 280: ᴿHZ 252 (1991) 145s (Hannes *Möhring*).

e309 **Prontera** Francesco, Geografia storica della Grecia antica. R 1991, Laterza. vii-294 p. [RÉG 104,682].

ᴱ**Scott** J., *Simpson-Housley* P., Sacred places... geographies of Judaism, Christianity, and Islam 1991 → 328*.

e310 **Sitwell** O. F. G., A human geographer looks at religion; RelStT 10,2 (1990) 23-41.

e311 **Sondag** Antoine, La géographie des Catholiques [... entre 1900 et 2000, passés de 3% à 46% de la population en Afrique]. P/Montréal 1991,

Centurion/Paulines. 116 p. F 62. – ᴿEsprVie 101 (1991) 527s (L. *Barbey* dit '3%, 46% ').
e312 *Vallat* F., La géographie de l'Élam d'après quelques textes méso-potamiens: → 621, Rencontre 36, 1989/91, 11-17 + 7 maps.
e313 **Wilson** Robert T. O., Gazetteer of historical north-west Yemen in the Islamic period to 1650 [< diss. Cambridge], pref. *Serjeant* R. B.: Arabistische TSt 3. Hildesheim 1989, Olms. xii-374 p. DM 39,80. 3-487-09195-X. – ᴿZDMG 141 (1991) 223s (W. W. *Müller*).

Ul.2 Historia geographiae.

e314 *Albert* Michel, Les cartes dans les Bibles du XVIᵉ siècle [DELANO-SMITH C. 1990]: EsprVie 101 (1991) 37s-*jaune.*
e315 ᵀᴱ**Baladié** Raoul, STRABON, Géographie tome 4 (Livre VII) 1989 → 5, e818*; 6,g113: ᴿRÉG 103 (1990) 746s (P. *Cabanes*).
Belke Klaus, *Mersich* Norbert, Phrygien und Pisidien: Tabula Imperii Byzantini 7, 1990 → d999.
e317 *Ben-Arieh* Yehoshua, ❿ The character of Hebrew geographic literature about Eretz-Israel during the nineteenth century and until World War I: → 5, ꜰAMIRAN D., Eretz-Israel 22 (1991) 36-44; Eng. 34*.
e318 ᵀᴱ**Burstein** Stanley M., AGATHARCHIDES of Cnidus, On the Erythraean Sea: Hakluyt 2/172. L 1989, Hakluyt. xii-202 p.; map. £17.50. – ᴿCdÉ 65 (1990) 362-4 (J. *Desanges*).
e319 ᵀᴱ**Casson** L., The Periplus Maris Erythraei 1989 → 5,e819*: ᴿArchéonautica 10 (1990) 265-269 (J. *Rougé*); BO 48 (1991) 972-5 (E. Van der *Vliet*); IntJNaut 20 (1991) 264s (D. *Gibbins*).
e320 *Chroust* Anton-Hermann, Did the ancient Greeks ever see America or set foot on American soil? [PLUTARCH neither proves (as ORTELIUS and KEPLER suggest) nor disproves]: Serta Philologica Aenipontana 3 / InnsBeitKuW 20 (1979) 9-15.
e320* [Gautier] Daiché P., La 'descriptio mappe mundi' de HUGUES S. V. 1988 → 5,e821; 6,g120: ᴿRHist 284 (1990) 468-470 (J. *Verger*).
e321 **Delano-Smith** C., *Ingram* E. M., Maps in Bibles, 1500-1600; an illustrated catalogue: TravHumRen 256. Genève 1991, Droz. xxxviii-202 p.; 72 fig. [RHE 87,18*].
e322 ᴱ**Fusillo** M., Antonio DIOGENE, Le incredibili avventure al di là di Thule; testo greco, italiano di fronte, ᵀ(latina) *Schottus* Andreas (1606, p. 97-107): La città antica 4. Palermo 1990, Sellerio. 111 p. Lit. 18.000 [Gymnasium 99,349, O. *Schönberger*].
e323 *Gehrke* Hans-Joachim, Zur historischen Landeskunde des antiken Griechenland: HZ 251 (1990) 89-101.
e324 **Guzmán** Carmen, *Pérez* Miguel E., Concordantia in libros POMPONII Melae De chorographia: Alpha-O A-56. Hildesheim 1989, Olms. 610 p. – ᴿAnzAltW 44 (1991) 122 (H. *Schmeja*).
e324* **Habicht** Christian, PAUSANIAS's Guide to ancient Greece 1985 → 4, g878: ᴿMeditHR 6 (1991) 112-4 (S. *Perlman*).
e325 **Harley** J., *Woodward* D., History of cartography I, 1987 → 3,496 ... 6,g124: ᴿRÉAnc 93 (1991) 155-7 (P. *Arnaud*: manque d'esprit critique).
e326 *Herkenhoff* M., Der dunkle Kontinent; das Afrikabild im Mittelalter bis zum XII. Jht.: Weltbild und Kulturbegegnung 2. Pfaffenweiler 1990, Centaurus. x-213 p. [RHE 86,268*].
e327 **Hübner** Wolfgang, Die Begriffe 'Astrologie' und 'Astronomie' in der Antike; Wortgeschichte und Wissenschaftssystematik, mit einer Hypothese

zum Terminus 'Quadrivium': Abh g/soz 1989/7. Mainz 1990, Akad. 82 p. 3-515-05590-8. **Hunger** H., *Pingree* D., MUL.APIN, an astronomical compendium 1989 ➤ d717.

e329 — *Koch* Johannes, Der Mardukstern Nēberu: WeltOr 22 (1991) 48-72 [183-8, (further) ᴿof HUNGER-PINGREE 1989].

e330 **Jacob** Christian, La description de la terre habitée de DENYS d'Alexandrie ou la leçon de géographie, préf. *Détienne* Marcel. P 1990, Michel. 265 p. – ᴿRÉAnc 93 (1991) 157 (P. *Arnaud*); RÉG 104 (1991) 663 (P. *Nautin:* sous Hadrien 117-138).

e330* **Kennedy** E. S., *a)* Ibn al-HAYTHAM's determination of the meridian from one solar altitude; – *b)* Two topics from an astrological manuscript; Sindhind dyas and planetary latitudes [Indian influences in a chronological table beginning with the Flood]: Zeitschrift für Geschichte der arabisch-islamischen Wissenschaft [3 (1986) *Sezgin* F.] 5 (1989) 141-4 / 6 (1990) 167-178 [< OLZ 87,218].

e331 **Kliege** H., Weltbild und Darstellungspraxis hochmittelalterlicher Weltkarten. Münster 1991, Nodus. 213 p.; 17 fig. [RHE 86,268*].

e332 *Kolendo* Jerzy, Les 'déserts' dans les pays barbares; représentation et réalités: Dialogues d'histoire ancienne 17,1 (1991) 35-60.

e333 **Kunitzsch** Paul, C. PTOLEMÄUS, Der Sternkatalog des Almagest; die arabisch-mittelalterliche Tradition I 1986 ➤ 4,g884; 5,e835: ᴿOLZ 86 (1991) 183-5 (G. *Strohmaier*).

e334 *Kupfer* Marcia, The lost mappamundi at Chalivoy-Milor: Speculum 66 (1991) 540-571; 17 fig. [prototype for Hereford 1290; destroyed 1885; no copy but two descriptions survive].

e334* ᵀᴱ**Langermann** V. Tzvi, Ibn al-HAYTHAM's On the configuration of the world [< diss. Harvard 1979]. NY 1990. iv-280 p. + Ⓐ 97 p. [ZDMG 142,381s, P. *Kunitzsch*].

e335 **Leitz** Christian, Studien zur ägyptischen Astronomie: ÄgAbh 49, 1989 ➤ 5,e837; 6,g127: ᴿZDMG 141 (1991) 387-391 (J. von *Beckerath*).

e336 *Lindgren* U., Karte, Kartographie: ➤ 681, LexMA 5 (1990) 1021-4.

e337 *Lloyd* Andrew, Early atlases and printed books from the Manchester Geography Society collection; a catalogue: BJRyL 73,2 (1991) 37-157.

e338 **Maguire** Henry, Earth and ocean; the terrestrial world in early Byzantine art 1987 ➤ 3,f276... 6,g129: ᴿRivArCr 67 (1991) 484s (T. *Mivasaka*).

e339 **Musti** Domenico, PAUSANIA, Guida della Graecia: I. Attica, con *Beschi* L., 1982, 445 p. – II. Corinzia-Argolide, con *Torelli* M. 1986, lxxxvii-385 p. – [III. Laconia] IV. Messenia, con *Torelli* M., 1991, lix-305 p. – Mi, Mondadori; Gk.-It. on facing pages.

e340 **Nicolet** Claude, L'inventario del mondo; geografia e politica alle origini dell'impero romano [1988 ➤ 4,g892], ᵀ. Bari 1989, Laterza. 282 p. Lit. 44.000. – ᴿArcheo 63 (1990) 129 (S. *Rinaldi Tufi*).

e341 PLINIUS: **König** Roderich, (*Winkler* Gerhard) C. Plinius d. Ä., Naturkunde, Lat.-dt. Buch XXXIII, Metallurgie. Mü 1984, Artemis. 226 p.; 2 pl. Fs 46. – ᴿGnomon 63 (1991) 107-110 (P. *Rosumek*).

e342 — *Zehnacker* Hubert, Pline l'Ancien, Histoire naturelle, Livre XXXIII: Coll. Budé, 1983 ➤ 64,d320; F 100: ᴿGnomon 63 (1991) 107-9 (P. *Rosumek*).

e343 ᴱ**Prontera** Francesco, Geografia e geografi nel mondo antico; guida storica e critica. Bari 1990, Laterza. xxxiii-277 p. Lit. 28.000. – ᴿArcheo 72 (1991) 128 (C. *Zaccagnini*).

e344 *Radt* S. L., Eine neue STRABONausgabe [HOLWERDA D., *al.*, 1982 begonnen]: Mnemosyne 44 (1991) 305-326.

e345 *Rochberg-Halton* F., Between observation and theory in Babylonian astronomical texts: JNES 50 (1991) 107-120.

e346 ᴱRöllig Wolfgang, Von der Quelle zur Karte; Abschlussbuch des Sonderforschungsbereichs 'Tübinger Atlas des Vorderen Orients'. Weinheim 1991, VCH. xiii-286 p.; 2 loose maps. 3-527-17027-8 [OIAc 1,23: ch. 16 includes a listing of all existing and projected TAVO publications].

e347 *Rubin* Rehav, ⊕ Original maps and their copies; cartogenealogy of the early maps of Jerusalem, from the 15th to the 18th century: ⇥ 5, ᶠAMIRAN D., ErIsr 22 (1991) 166-183; Eng. 40*.

e348 *Smith* Catherine D., Geography or Christianity? Maps of the Holy Land before A.D. 1000: JTS 42 (1991) 143-152.

e349 ᴱTihon Anne, Le 'Grand commentaire' de THÉON d'Alexandrie aux Tables faciles de PTOLÉMÉE: ST 315; 340. Vaticano 1985, 1981, Bt.

e350 **Tsavari** Isabelle O., Histoire du texte de la Description de la terre de DENYS le Périégète [1186 hexamètres]: Epistem. Epiteris Parartema 28. Joannina 1990, Univ. 456 p.; 11 pl. + 1 foldout. – ᴿAnzAltW 44 (1991) 122 (W. *Lackner*); Ellinika 41 (1990) 411-422 (Beate *Noack*, deutsch); RÉAnc 93 (1991) 365-371 (P. *Counillon*).

e351 **Tzifopoulos** Ioannes Z., ...as *stēloskópos*; an epigraphical commentary of PAUSANIAS *Eliakōn* A and B: diss. Ohio State, ᴰ*Tracy* S. 1991. 499 p. 92-11238. – DissA 52 (1991s) 3915-A.

U1.4 **Atlas – maps.**

e351* **Aharoni** Yohanan, Avi-Yonah Michael, La Bible par les cartes [Macmillan ²1977 ⇥ 60,u402], première édition française, ᵀ*Langton* J., *Poswick* R. Turnhout 1991, Brepols. 185 p.; maps. 2-503-50057-9.

e352 ᴱBaladier Charles, Le grand atlas des religions. P 1989, Encyclopaedia Universalis. 413 p. – ᴿZMissRW 75 (1991) 232 (P. *Antes*).

e352* ᴱBlake Gerald, *al.*, The Cambridge atlas of the Middle East and North Africa 1987 ⇥ 5,e839; 6,g140: ᴿHZ 253 (1991) 692s (H. *Mejcher*).

e353 **Brossier** François, Atlante della storia biblica [1987], ᵀ1989 ⇥ 5,e860; 6,g141: ᴿAsprenas 38 (1991) 106s (V. *Scippa*).

e354 **Chadwick** H., *Evans* G. R., Atlas of the Christian Church 1990 [= 1987 ⇥ 3,f291]: ᴿMonth 252 (1991) 167 (F. X. *Walker*).

e355 **Dowley** T., Brunnen Bibelatlas [Student BA 1989],ᵀ. Giessen 1991, Brunnen. 32 p., 30 maps. 3-7655-5730-7 [NTAbs 36,292].

e356 **Friesel** Evyatar, Atlas of modern Jewish history [⊕ 1983ʳᵉᵛ]. NY 1990, Oxford-UP. 159 p. £25. – ᴿJJS 42 (1991) 133 (N. *Lucas*).

e357 **Galbiati** Enrico R., *Aletti* Aldo, Atlas histórico da Bíblia e do Antigo Oriente; da pré-historia à queda de Jerusalém no ano de 70 dC, ᵀ*Angonese* Antonio. Petrópolis 1991, Vozes. 272 p.; maps. 85-326-0036-0. – ᴿEstudosB 32 (1991) 107-9 (V. da *Silva*).

e358 **Gilbert** Martin [maps², ¹1970], text *Bakon* Josephine, The illustrated atlas of Jewish civilization; 4000 years of Jewish history. NY 1990, Macmillan. 224 p. $35. 0-02-543415-2 [TDig 38,161].

e358* **Haiman** Mordechai, ⊕ & Eng., Map of Mizpé Ramon Southwest (200): Archaeological Survey of Israel. J 1991, Antiquities Authority. 144 + 107 p. 965-406-003-5 [OIAc 2,20].

e359 **Hartmann** Karl, Atlas-Tafel-Werk zur Geschichte der Weltreligionen [1. 1987; 2. 1988], 3. Die Geschichte des Judentums. Stu 1990, Quell.

240 p. DM 56. 3-7918-3211-5. – ᴿTLZ 116 (1991) 583s (G. *Kehn-scherper*).

e360 **Hinkel** Friedrich W., The archaeological map of the Sudan, 2. The area of the South Libyan Desert; 6. The area of the Red Sea Coast and Northern Ethiopian frontier. B 1991s, Akademie. vii-160 p.; 28 fig. DM 148 / xii-365 p.; 72 fig.; 10 maps. DM 320. 3-05-001393-1; -845-3 [OLZ 87,491 adv.].

e361 **Jedin** H., *al.*, Atlas d'histoire de l'Église; les Églises chrétiennes hier et aujourd'hui 1990 ➤ 6,g149: ᴿÉtudes 374 (1991) 137 (P. *Vallin*).

e362 ᴱ**Pritchard** James B., The Harper concise atlas of the Bible [= 1987 (➤ 3,e869) Harper/Times Atlas compressed]. NY 1991, Harper-Collins. 151 p. $30. 0-06-270029-4 [TDig 38,360].

e363 ᴱ**Pritchard** J., Harper Atlas 1987 ➤ 3,e869; 6,g153: ᴿJAOS 111 (1991) 386-8 (J. *Coleson*: good but too many errors).

e364 **Riley-Smith** Jonathan, Atlas of the Crusades. NY 1991, Facts on file [BAR-W 17/5, 10].

e365 **Roaf** Michael, Cultural atlas of Mesopotamia and the Ancient Near East 1990 ➤ 6,g156; $45: ᴿBAR-W 17/4 (1991) 4 (Marie-H. *Gates*).

e366 **Roaf** Michael, Atlas de la Mésopotamie et du Proche-Orient ancien, ᵀ*Talon* Philippe. Turnhout 1991, Brepols. 237 p.; (color.) ill.; 48 maps.

e367 TAVO: B 1 Steinzeit, 4. Vorderer Orient, Jungpaläolithikum 1990; 18, Das iranische Hochland im Chalkolithikum 1990.

U1.5 Photographiae.

e368 **Balensiefen** Lilian, Index der antiken Kunst und Architektur [Begleit-band]; Denkmäler des griechisch-römischen Altertums in der Photo-sammlung des DAI-R. Mü 1991, Saur. 420 p.

Ball William, Pylos: colour filmstrip (57 views) 1990 ➤ e186.

e369 **Campbell** Richard H., **Pitts** Michael R., The Bible on film; a check-list 1897-1980. Metuchen NJ 1981, Scarecrow. ix-214 p. 0-8108-1473-0 [OIAc 2,16].

e369* ᴱ**Hrouda** Barthel, Der alte Orient; Geschichte und Kultur des alten Vorderasien. Mü 1991, Bertelsmann. 464 p.; ill. 3-570-08578-3 [OIAc 2,21, excerpted].

e370 **Kennedy** David, *Riley* Derrick, Rome's desert frontier from the air 1990 ➤ 6,g164: ᴿClasR 41 (1991) 189-191 (F. *Millar*); Gerión 9 (1991) 324s (M. *Ribagorda*); JField 18 (1991) 243-5 (G. S. *Maxwell*); LA 41 (1991) 543-6 (M. *Piccirillo*); Mesop-T 26 (1991) 253-5 (A. *Invernizzi*).

e371 **Le Coq** Albert von, Bilderatlas zur Kunst und Kulturgeschichte Mit-tel-Asiens [... Turfan Buddhist caves]. Graz 1977, Akad.-VA. 107 p. 3-201-01019-7. – ᴿBO 48 (1991) 284s (J. *Teske*).

e371* **Mayer** Fred, *Bruin* Paul, Terre sainte [Hier hat Gott gelebt, 1987], ᵀ*Baillet* Philippe. P 1991, Desclée. 271 p., mostly color photos. 2-7189-0548-4.

e372 *Müller-Kaspar* Ulricke, Franz CAUCIGs Aufnahmen antiker Skulpturen in Rom: JhÖsA 61-H (1991) 113-127; 17 pl.

e372* **Perring** Stefania & Dominic, Then and now ['the wonders of the ancient world brought to life in vivid see-through reconstructions']. NY 1991, Macmillan. 144 p. 0-02-599461-1 [OIAc 2,25].

e373 ᴱ**Racanicchi** Pietro, *al.*, Fotografi in terra d'Egitto; immagini dal-l'archivio storico della Soprintendenza al Museo delle Antichità Egizie di Torino. T 1991, PAS Informazione. 154 p.; 94 fig.

e374 *Raven* Maarten J., [J. H.] INSINGER and early photography in Egypt: OMRO 71 (1991) 13-25 + 2 pl.

e375 **Stephens** William H., The Old Testament world in pictures. Nv 1987, Broadman. 187 p. $30. – ᴿBA 54 (1991) 56 (J. F. *Wilson*).

e376 **Taylor** Jane, Jordanien, Luftaufnahmen: Biblische Stätten im Luftbild,ᵀ 1990 → 6,g169*b*: ᴿErbAuf 67 (1991) 161s (B. *Schwank*).

e377 **Willeman** René, *al.*, Passage to eternity [Egypt]. Knokke 1989, Mappamundi. 191 fig.; 160 colour pl. (*Mekhitarian* A.) 90-6958-008-X [JEA 78,340, N. *Strudwick*].

U1.6   **Guide books,** *Führer.*

e377* **Brodersen** Kai, PHILON von Byzanz, Reiseführer zu den Sieben Weltwundern. Fra 1992 [74ss: Neuedition aller Weltwunderlisten: ArchMIran 24 (1991) 53].

e378 **Caselli** Giovanni, Egitto: Guide Culturali Argos. F 1990, Caselli Giunti Gruppo Editoriale. 252 p. 88-09-20148-5 [OIAc 1,13].

e379 **Díez Fernández** F., Guía de Tierra Santa 1990 → 6,g175: ᴿCiuD 203 (1990) 732-4 (J. *Gutiérrez*).

e380 **Gonen** Rivka, Biblical Holy Places, an illustrated guide 1987 → 3,f322... 5,e896: ᴿBAR-W 17,1 (1991) 6 (A. *Neustadter*).

e381 **Hotz** Walter, Die Mittelmeerküsten Anatoliens; Handbuch der Kunstdenkmäler. Da 1989, Wiss. x-294 p. DM 76. – ᴿHZ 253 (1991) 682s (P. *Herrmann*).

e382 **Khouri** R. G., Pella. Amman 1988, Kutba Guides. 32 p. £3. – ᴿPEQ 122 (1990) 63-65 (J. *Bowsher*, also on his 4 cognate guides and M. ABU HAMDAN, Crafts of Jordan 1989).

e383 **Scheck** Frank R., Jordanien, Völker und Kulturen zwischen Jordan und Rotem Meer³ʳᵉᵛ. Köln 1988, DuMont. 495 p.; 142 fig.; 13 + 79 pl. + 41 color.; 2 end-maps. 3-7701-1573-2. – ᴿZDPV 107 (1991) 196-8 (E. A. *Knauf*).

U1.7   **Onomastica.**

e384 *a) Cornil* P., Liste des noms géographiques des textes hittites; – *b) Forlanini* M., Uda, un cas probable d'homonymie: Hethitica 10 (1990) 7-108 / 109-127 [< OLZ 86,293].

e385 **Eilers** Wilhelm, Iranische Ortsnamenstudien: Szb W p/h 465, 1987 → 3,f345... 6,g188: ᴿBeiNam 26 (1991) 83-85 (N. *Oettinger*).

e385* *Görg* Manfred, Name und Identität der 'Insel Swrws': GöMiszÄg 122 (1991) 31s.

e386 *Israel* Felice, Note di onomastica semitica 7/1, rassegna critico-bibliografica ed epigrafica su alcune onomastiche palestinesi; Israel e Giuda, la regione filistea: StEpL 8 (1991) 119-140 ....

e386* **Isserlin** B., Arabic place name types of the Islamic period; their derivation and distribution: Masāq 2 (1989) 9-14 [< JSS 37,137].

e387 **Nashef** Khaled, Répertoire géographique des textes cunéiformes IV. Die Orts- und Gewässernamen der altassyrischen Zeit: TAVO B-7/4. Wsb 1991, Reichert. xliv-160 p.; map. 3-88226-465-9.

e387* **Reeg** Gottfried, Die Ortsnamen Israels nach der rabbinischen Literatur: TAVO B-51, 1989 → 5,e915; 6,g196: ᴿSefarad 51 (1991) 212s (M. *Pérez Fernández*).

e388 *Scheepers* Anne, Anthroponymes et toponymes du récit d'Ounamon: ⇥ 445, Phoenicia 1990/1, 17-83.

e389 **Thompson** T., *al.*, Topographie palestinienne, Acre... 1988 ⇥ 4,g963 ... 6,g198: ᴿOLZ 82 (1991) 51-53 (W. *Herrmann*).

e390 *Worp* K. A., Observations on some military camps and place names in lower Egypt [... Babylon = Old Cairo; Heronpolis = Maskhuta-Pithoum: E. *Kettenhofen*, OrLovPer 20 (1989) 75-97]: ZPapEp 87 (1991) 291-5.

U2.1   *Geologia:*   **soils, mountains, volcanoes, earthquakes.**

e391 *Balty* Janine, L'épigraphie de la Syrie du Nord et le sisme de 458 de notre ère: ⇥ 626, AnASyr 40 (1989/90) 176-183; ❹ 179-181.

e392 ᴱ**Gratzl** Karl, Die heiligsten Berge der Welt [... Sinai, *Marböck* J.; Athos, *Hunger* H.]. Graz 1990, Verlag für Sammler. 160 p. Sch 680. – ᴿTPQ 139 (1991) 340s (J. *Janda*).

e393 **Guidoboni** Emanuele, I terremoti prima del mille in Italia e nell'area mediterranea. Bo 1989, Storia Geofisica Ambiente. 765 p.

e394 — *Biancofiore* Franco, Sismologia e archeologia [GUIDOBONI E. 1989]: Origini 15 (R 1990s) 35-56; Eng. 56.

e394* **Hatzor** Yossef, ❺ The geology of the Gilboa region [1988 M. Soc. diss. Jerusalem, Hebrew Univ.]. J 1991, Ministry of Energy. 107 p. + Eng. 11 p. [OIAc 2,20].

e395 *Helal* Hani M., *al.*, Geotechnical phenomena and their impacts on the stability of Alexander the Great temple at Siwa Oasis: ASAE supp. (1987) to 70 (1984s) 5-26; 7 fig.

e396 *Kalokyrē* Konstantinos D., ❻ Athos 963-1963, themata archaiologias kai technēs. Athenai 1963, Papademetriou. 358 p., ill.

e397 *Neubauer* Wolfgang, Geophysikalische Prospektion in der Archäologie: MitAntW 120 (1990) 1-60; 27 fig.

e397* **Shaliv** Gaby, ❺ Stages in the tectonic and volcanic history of the neogene basin in the Lower Galilee and the valleys: Geological Survey of Israel, Report. J 1991, Ministry of Energy. 94 p., 9 p. Eng. [OIAc 2,27].

e398 **Shazly** E. M. El-, *al.*, Sinai peninsula; Landsat imagery interpretation maps, 1:250.000. Cairo 1980, Remote Sensing Research Project. 11 maps [OIAc 1,16, with six other items of the same author and project].

U2.2   *Hydrographia:* **rivers, seas, salt.**

e399 *Andersson* Espen B., *a)* Fountains and the Roman dwelling; Casa del Torello in Pompeii: JbDAI 105 (1990) 207-236; 19 fig.; – *b)* Metamorphoses in water: Latomus 50 (1991) 544-562.

e400 *Atzler* Michael, Zu einigen [hydrologischen] Problemen der Herausbildung ägyptischer Kultur: ⇥ 40, Mém. CLÈRE J. 1991, 25-32; Eng. 32s.

e401 *Avitsur* Samuel, ❼ Water of affliction [Isa 30,20: water consumption in Israel increased from 5 million cu/m per year in 1870 to 25 million 1914, 500 million 1947, 2 billion 1990, with 14-fold increase in the energy required for pumping]: ⇥ 5, ᶠAMIRAN D., Eretz-Israel 22 (1991) 1-6; Eng. 33*.

e402 **Bergier** Jean-François, Die Geschichte vom Salz, ᵀ*Grube* Jochen. Fra 1989, Campus. 255 p.; 203 fig. DM 78. – ᴿHZ 253 (1991) 138s (F.-J. *Kos*).

e403 *Bonneau* Danielle, Le cycle du Nil; aspect administratif à l'époque gréco-romaine: BSocFrÉg 120 (1991) 7-21; 6 fig.; 3 pl.

e403* *Carroué* François, À la recherche de l'Euphrate au IIIe millénaire: AcSum 13 (1991) 111-156; map.

e404 *Casini* Maria, La valle del Nilo e il Sahara; la rappresentazione, l'ambiente, i rapporti reciproci: Origini 15 (R 1990s) 321-336; 5 fig.

e405 **Caulier** Brigitte, L'eau et le sacré; les cultes thérapeutiques autour des fontaines en France du Moyen Âge à nos jours. P/Laval 1990, Beauchesne/Univ. 176 p. F 126. – ^REsprVie 101 (1991) 528 (L. *Barbey:* 'Ce que nous appellerions superstition constitue à ses yeux une manière tout à fait respectable de rendre hommage au sacré').

e406 *Eshel* Hanan, *Amit* David, ❂ The Second Temple period water supply system of Horvat Kefira (N Abu Goš): Qadmoniot 24 (1991) 56-59; ill.

e407 *Faiz* Mohammed El-, Salinité et histoire de l'Irak pré-islamique: JESHO 33 (1990) 105-116.

e408 **Giddy** Lisa L., Egyptian oases ^D1986 → 3,f389... 5,e931: ^RBO 48 (1991) 132-5 (A. J. *Mills*).

e409 *Krüger* Julian, Terminologie der künstlichen Wasserläufe in den Papyri des griechisch-römischen Ägypten: MünstHand 10,2 (1991) 18-27; Eng. franç. 27.

e410 *Kuss* Werner, Die Quellen des Nils [STRABO 17,786]: CdÉ 65 (1990) 334-343; 3 fig.

e411 *Lohrmann* Dietrich, Bedarf und Angebot von Wasserkraft in frühen Siedlungen und Städten: → 643*, Saeculum 42,3s (1990/1) 262-5.

e412 **Ngan Lai Ling** Elizabeth, Water in ancient Israelite society during the period of the monarchy; substance and symbol: diss. Golden Gate Theol. Sem. 1991, ^DEakins J. K. 471 p. 92-11890. – DissA 52 (1991s) 4382-A.

e413 *Owens* E. J., The Kremna aqueduct and water supply in Roman cities: GreeceR 38 (1991) 41-58; 6 pl.

e414 *Quilici* Lorenzo, Acquedotti di Roma: Archeo 53 (1989) 50-97; ill.

e415 *Reimers* Pontus, Roman sewers and sewerage networks — neglected areas of study: → 595, Munuscula 1988/91, 111-6.

e416 **Tölle-Kastenbein** Renate, Antike Wasserkultur. Mü 1990, Beck. 231 p.; 132 fig.; 6 pl. – ^RRArchéol (1991) 353s (G. *Argoud*).

e416* *Tölle-Kastenbein* Renate, Entlüftung antiker Wasserleitungsrohre: ArchAnz (1991) 25-30; 8 fig.

e417 *a) Wikander* Örjon, Water-power and technical progress in classical antiquity; – *b) Sleeswyk* André W., Archimedes' (h)odometer [VITRUVIUS] and waterclock: → 632, Ancient technology 1987/90, 68-84; 10 fig. / 23-37; 9 fig.

U2.3   Clima, pluvia.

e418 *Flohn* H., *Kapala* A., Seasonal variations and climatic trends in the Southern Red Sea, Gulf of Aden and adjacent parts of the Indian Ocean: → 5, ^FAMIRAN D. ErIsr 22 (1991) 12*-24*.

e419 *Goldreich* Yair, *Gadoth* Gil, ❂ Temporal and spatial changes in the center of the rainfall map of Israel: → 5, ^FAMIRAN D., ErIsr 22 (1991) 52-60; Eng. 35*.

e420 **Libby** Leona M., Past climates; tree thermometers, commodities and people 1983 → 1,e738: ^RBInstArch 27 (1990) 220 (L. *Copeland*).

e421 *Panessa* Giangiacomo, Fonti greche e latine per la storia dell'ambiente e del clima nel mondo greco: Pubb. Lat/Fil 8s. Pisa 1991, Scuola Normale Superiore. I. lvi-541 p. – II. p. 543-1024 + 5 maps. 88-7642-021-5; -2-3.

e422 *Yasuda* Yoshinori, Climatic change at 5000 years B.P. and the birth of ancient civilizations: → 402, Anatolia 1991, 203-211 + 7 fig.

U2.5 *Fauna;* Animals.

e423 *Balicka-Witakowska* Ewa, L'oiseau dans la cage; exemple éthiopien: OrSuec 40 (1991) 53-71 14 fig. + 4 color.

e424 *Bartelink* G. J. M., AUGUSTINUS über die minuta animalia... 'eminet in minimis maximus ipse Deus': → 130, ᶠSANDERS G., Aevum 1991, 11-19.

e425 **Beavis** Ian C., Insects and other invertebrates in classical antiquity 1988 → 5,e951; 6,g240: ᴿBInstArch 27 (1990) 157s (R. G. *Adams*, D. B. *Pinninger*); Latomus 50 (1991) 893-8 (Liliane *Bodson*); RÉG 104 (1991) 281s (J.-L. *Perpillou*: sufficiently different from the independent M. DAVIES, J. KATHIRITHAMBY, Greek insects, L 1986, which treats also bees).

e426 *Beck* William, Dogs, dwellings, and masters; ensemble and symbol in the Odyssey: Hermes 119 (1991) 158-167.

e427 **Behrmann** Almuth, Nilpferd 1989 → 5,e952: ᴿBO 48 (1991) 509-511 (J. *Śliwa*).

e428 *Boardman* J., A monstrous pet [female quadruped with human head on Boston vase]: → 147, ᶠSTIBBE C. 1991, 7s + 2 fig.

e429 ᴱ**Bodson** Liliane, [Anthropozoologica;] L'animal dans l'alimentation humaine 1986/8 → 4,723... 6,341: ᴿAntiquity 65 (1991) 423. 426 (D. *Serjeantson*).

e430 **Boessneck** Joachim, Die Tierwelt des Alten Ägypten 1988 → 4,h8... 6,g244: ᴿAcArchH 43 (1991) 213s (S. *Bökönyi*); BO 48 (1991) 507-9 (C. S. *Churcher*); Nikephoros 3 (1990) 265-9 (M. *Herb*).

e431 *Borthwick* E. Kerk, Bee imagery in PLUTARCH: ClasQ 95=41 (1991) 560-2.

e431* *Brentjes* Burchard, Eine Tierkampfszene in Bronze: ArchMIran 24 (1991) 1 (nur); pl. 1.

e432 **Brewer** Douglas J., Fishermen, hunters and herders; Zooarchaeology in the Fayum, Egypt (ca. 8200-500 BP): BAR-Int 478, 1989 → 5,e956: ᴿBO 48 (1991) 129s (A. *Gautier*).

e433 **Brewer** Douglas J., *Friedman* Renée F., Fish and fishing in ancient Egypt 1989 → 5,e957: ᴿBInstArch 27 (1990) 162s (J. M. *Filer*); BO 48 (1991) 129-131 (I. *Gamer-Wallert*).

e434 *Campana* D., *Crabtree* P. [Communal hunting, Natuf Social-Econom. JMeditArch 3 (1990) 223-243 → 6,g251], comment of *Edwards* Phillip C. & *Rowley-Conwy* Peter: 4 (1991) 109-120 / 121-3; reply 125-138.

e435 **Capponi** Filippo, Natura aquatilium (PLIN. Nat. hist. IX): D.AR.FI.CL.ET 131. Genova 1990, Univ. Fg. Clas. 252 p.

e436 *Capponi* Filippo, PLINIO e la terminologia zoologica: → 579, Lessici Tecnici 1990/1, 225-241.

e437 **Charbonneau-Lassay** Louis, The bestiary of Christ [1975 → 6,g252*], ᵀᴱ*Dooling* D. M. NY 1991, Parabola [BAR-W 17/5, 10].

e438 **Chouliara-Raïos** Hélène, L'abeille et le miel en Égypte d'après les papyrus grecs: Dodone 30, 1989 → 6,g255: ᴿBO 48 (1991) 837-841 (Marie-Hélène *Marganne* adds cataract-medicine, honey mixed with hyena-bile); ÉtClas 59 (1991) 376 (B. *Rochette*).

e439 *Ciccarese* Maria Pia, *a*) Il simbolismo antropologico degli animali nell'esegesi cristiana antica; criteri e contenuti ermeneutici: → 419, An-StoEseg 7,2 (1989/90) 529-567; – *b*) 'Formam Christi gerere'; osservazioni sul simbolismo cristiano degli animali: ➤ 452, AnStoEseg 8,2 (1990/1) 565-587.

e441 *Collins* Billie Jean, The puppy in Hittite ritual: JCS 42 (1990) 211-226.

e442 *Croft* P., Man and beast in chalcolithic Cyprus: ➤ 657, BASOR 282s (1991) 63-79.

e443 **Domagalski** Bernhard, Der Hirsch in spätantiker Literatur und Kunst [Diss. Bonn 1988, ᴰ*Dassmann* ➤ 5,e967]: JbAC Egb. 15. Münster 1990, Aschendorff. 198 p.; 93 fig. DM 98; pa. 88. 3-402-08527-5; -6-7. – ᴿNRT 113 (1991) 775 (A. *Harvengt*: 'in spätantike'); TLZ 116 (1991) 296s (Gerlinde *Strohmaier-Wiederanders*).

e444 *a*) *Griffiths* J. Gwyn, The accusing animals; – *b*) *Vernus* Pascal, Ménès et Achtoès, l'hippopotame et le crocodile; lecture structurale de l'historiographie égyptienne; – *c*) *Meeks* Dimitri, Oiseaux des carrières et des cavernes; – *d*) *Herb* Michael, Das durch die Luft wirbelnde Wurfholz in den Bildern der Vogeljagd der fürstlichen Grabherrn; ➤ 43, ᶠDᴇʀᴄʜᴀɪɴ P., Religion 1991, 149-154 / 331-339 + pl. / 233-241 / 165-7.

e445 *Hanson* A. E., *Sijpesteijn* P. J., P. Oxy. XVI 1919 and mule-breeding: ZPapEp 87 (1991) 268-274.

e446 *Harrison* E. L., Homeric wonder-horses: Hermes 119 (1991) 252-4.

e447 *a*) *Hodjasch* Swetlana, Zum Motiv *tilapia* [eine Art Fisch] auf altägyptischen Kunstwerken in den Museen der Sowjetunion; – *b*) *Steinmann* Frank, Noch einmal zum 'Geflügelhirt': GöMiszÄg 120 (1991) 39-44 + 11 fig. / 101-7.

e448 *Hope* Edward R., *a*) Animals in the Old Testament; anybody's guess?; – *b*) Lions... Problems of interpretation in Amos 3,4: BTrans 42 (1991) 128-132 / 201-5.

e449 **Houlihan** Patrick F., The birds of ancient Egypt 1986 ➤ 2,b640... 6,g287: ᴿJNES 50 (1991) 54s (E. & T. *Meltzer*).

e450 **Hübner** Wolfgang, Zodiacus christianus 1983 ➤ 64,d458... 2,b641: ᴿHenoch 12 (1990) 391s (M. *Zonta*).

e451 *a*) *Ikram* Salima, Animal mating motifs in Egyptian funerary representations; – *b*) *Eissa* Ahmed, Zum Lepidotos-Fisch als eine Erscheinungsform des Osiris: GöMiszÄg 124 (1991) 51-63 + 23 fig. / 43-46 + 4 fig.

e452 *Kessler* Dieter, Hᴇʀᴏᴅᴏᴛ über heilige Tiere in Bubastis: StAäK 18 (1991) 265-289.

e453 *Klippel* Walter E., *Snyder* Lynn M., Dark-age fauna from Kavousi, Crete: Hesperia 60 (1991) 179-186; 1 fig.

e454 **Leone** Aurora, Gli animali da trasporto 1988 ➤ 4,h54; 6,g299: ᴿArPapF 37 (1991) 71 (G. *Poethke*); Emerita 59,1 (1991) 208s (J. A. *Berenguer*); RPg 64 (1990) 273s (Geneviève *Husson*: réserves).

e455 *Lepiksaar* Johannes, Die Tierreste vom Tell es-Salihiyeh [Damaskus] in Südsyrien: ➤ 144, ᶠSᴛᴀᴍᴘꜰʟɪ H. 1990, 115-120; 3 fig.

e456 *Lévêque* Pierre, Du roi-serpent de l'Acropole aux ourseries de Brauron: RÉAnc 91,3s (1989) 55-64; ill.; Eng. 45.

e457 *a*) *Lieberman* Daniel E., Seasonality and gazelle hunting at Hayonim Cave; new evidence for 'sedentism' during the Natufian; – *b*) *Becker* Cornelia, The analysis of mammalian bones from Basta, a pre-pottery neolithic site in Jordan; problems and potential: Paléorient 17,1 (1991) 47-57 / 59-75.

e458 **Lonsdale** Steven H., Creatures of speech; lion, herding and hunting similes in the Iliad: BeitAltK 5. Stu 1990, Teubner. vi-160 p. DM 38. – ᴿClasR 41 (1991) 293-5 (J. *Griffin*).

e459 *Loos-Dietz* Elizabeth P. de, Un échassier [wading-bird] avec un serpent [sur bols en argent]: Babesch 66 (1991) 133-144; 13 fig.

e460 *López Monteagudo* Guadalupe, Escenas de uenatio en mosaicos hispanorromanos: Gerión 9 (1991) 245-262; 15 fig.

e461 **Majut** Rudolf, Über hippologische Bezeichnungen; Tiernamen und ein gotischer Pflanzenname: ZtsDtPg Beih. Mü 1972. – ᴿBSLP 85 (1990) 171 (J. *Amsler*: mention pudique du 'buisson ardent').

e462 *Malaise* Michel, Harpocrate, la tortue et le chien [index p. 1 'Les animaux et le pot d'Harpocrate']; contribution à l'iconographie du fils d'Isis: BSocFrÉg 122 (1991) 13-35.

e463 *Metzger* Henri, Les images de faune aquatique et marine dans l'art grec [DELORME J., ROUX C. 1987; MCPHEE I., TRENDALL A., 1987]: RÉG 103 (1990) 673-683.

e464 *Micheli* Maria Elisa, Mensae marmoree istoriate con cacce e teorie di animali: BArteR 77/65 (1991) 79-112; 35 fig.

e465 a) *Müller* Hans-Peter, Die Funktion divinatorischen Redens und die Tierbezeichnungen der Inschrift von Tell Deir'Allā; – b) *Hoftijzer* J., What did the gods say? remarks on the first combination of the Deir'Alla plaster texts [... lists of birds]: ⇒ 534, Balaam text 1989/91, 185-205 / 121-142 [294-304, *Wolters* A.].

e466 ᴱNitecki Matthew H. & Doris V., The evolution of human hunting 1986/8 ⇒ 5,860; 0-306-42821-0: ᴿBInstArch 27 (1990) 232s (L. *Copeland*).

e467 ᴱOrbán Árpád P., Konrad von MURE, De naturis animalium [1194 Distichen < ISIDOR von Sevilla Etym. 12; 130 Tiere]: Ed. Heid. 23. Heid 1989, Winter. 180 p. – ᴿGnomon 62 (1991) 699-703 (D. *Schaller*).

e468 *Osten-Sacken* Elisabeth von der, Hürden und Netze [Jagddarstellungen Uruk- bis Akkad. Zeit]: MDOG 123 (1991) 133-148.

e469 *Palma* Ricardo L., Ancient head-lice on a wooden comb from Antinoe, Egypt: JEA 77 (1991) 194; pl. XXI,2.

e470 *Porada* Edith, Animal subjects of the Ancient Near Eastern artist: ⇒ 641, Artistic 1988/90, 71-79; 10 fig.

e471 ᴱPuschmann Wolfgang, Zootiere [zoo animals]. Lp 1989, VEB. 462 p.; 143 fig.; 193 pl. + 48 color. – ᴿSalesianum 53 (1991) 452 (R. *Bratky*).

e472 **Reimbold** Ernst T., Der Pfau, Mythologie und Symbolik. Mü 1983, Callwey. 198 p.; ill.

e473 **Rommelaere** Catherine, Les chevaux du Nouvel Empire égyptien; origines, races, harnachement: Étude 3. Bru 1991, Connaissance de l'Égypte ancienne. 278 p.; 8 color. pl. 2-87268-002-0 [OIAc 1,23].

e474 a) *Rosén* Haiim B., *Ekwos* et l''hippologie' cananéenne; réflexions étymologiques; – b) *Knobloch* Johann, Der Mensch – und die indogermanische Jägersprache: ⇒ 167, Mem. WINDEKENS A. van, Studia etymologica 1991, 233-7 / 155-9.

e475 **Saunders** Nicholas J., The cult of the cat. L 1991, Thames & H. 96 p.; 130 fig. 0-500-81036-2 [OIAc 1,24].

e476 **Sauneron** Serge, Un traité égyptien d'ophiologie; papyrus du Brooklyn Museum Nᵒˢ 47, 218, 48, 85 [Nachlass, ᴱ*Sauneron* Nadine, *Posener-Kriéger* Paule]: Bibliothèque Générale 11. P 1989, IFAO. 243 p.; pl. DM 200. – ᴿEnchoria 18 (1991) 229-234 (H.-W. *Fischer-Elfert*).

e477 *Schumacher* Meinolf, Die Sprünge der Fische; eine Speisevorschrift in Metaphorik und Allegorese [Lv 11,9; Dt 14,9]: ZKG 102 (1991) 307-312.

e478 *Sergent* Bernard, Ethnozoonymes indo-européens [...? totémisme]: Dialogues d'Histoire Ancienne 17,2 (1991) 9-55.

e479 ᵀᴱTerian Abraham, PHILON, Alexandre... bruta animalia 1988 ➤ 4,h64
... 6,g327: ᴿRBgPg 69 (1991) 203s (J. *Schamp*).

e480 *a)* *Tripodi* Bruno, Il fregio della caccia della II tomba reale di Vergina e
le caccie funerarie d'Oriente; – *b)* *Briant* Pierre, Chasses royales ma-
cédoniennes et chasses royales perses; le thème de la chasse au lion sur la
chasse de Vergina; – *c)* *Prestianni Giallombardo* Anna Maria, Recenti
testimonianze iconografiche sulla kausia in Macedonia e la datazione del
fregio della caccia della II tomba reale di Vergina: DialoguesHistAnc 17,1
(1991) 143-209 / 211-255 / 257-304.

e481 *Watson* Wilfred G. E., Two [pre-falconry hawk] similes in Aqht: UF 23
(1991) 359s.

e482 *Whitehouse* Helen, The elephant and its keepers; a postscript on P.
Mich. inv. 4290: ZPapEp 85 (1991) 277s.

Zeder Melinda A., Feeding cities; specialized animal economies 1991
➤ e552.

U2.7 **Flora;** *plantae biblicae et antiquae.*

e483 ᵀᴱ**Amigues** Suzanne, THÉOPHRASTE, Recherches sur les plantes 1s, 1988s
➤ 6,g335: ᴿGnomon 63 (1991) 293-300 (B. *Herzhoff*); Helmantica 42,
129* (1991) 305s (J. *Mazas*, I).

e484 **André** Jacques, Les noms de plantes dans la Rome antique 1985
➤ 1,e833 ... 3,f485: ᴿHelmantica 38 (1987) 451s (J. *Oroz*).

e484* **Bauer** Thomas, Das Pflanzenbuch des ABŪ ḤANIFA ad-Dinawarī
[† 895]; Inhalt, Aufbau, Quellen Diss. Erlangen]. Wsb 1988, Harrassowitz. viii-290 p. DM 58. 3-447-02822-X [ZDMG 142,381, T. *Sei-
densticker*].

e485 *Baum* Nathalie, Quelques idées sur l'arbre à cheveux *ḫt n šn*: RÉgp 42
(1991) 11-24; 18 fig.; Eng. 24.

e486 *Behlmer-Loprieno* Heike, Ein hapax legomenon in CRUMs Coptic Dictionary [*kon*, 'peach blossom']: GöMiszÄg 125 (1991) 15s.

e487 *Biger* Gideon, *Liphschitz* Nili, Historical geography and botany; timber
in the nineteenth-century Old City of Jerusalem: PEQ 123 (1991) 4-18; 12
fig.; map.

e488 *Evans* Jane D., The sacred figs in Rome: Latomus 50 (1991) 798-808; 1
fig(ure).

e489 **Germer** Renate, Katalog der altägyptischen Pflanzenreste... Berlin 1988
➤ 1,e843 ... 6,g345: ᴿBO 48 (1991) 511-5 (Wilma *Wetterstrom*, Eng.).

e490 **Germer** Renate, Die Pflanzenmaterialien aus dem Grab des Tutanchamun 1989 ➤ 5,g45; 6,g346: ᴿBO 48 (1991) 131s (F. N. *Hepper*).

e491 **Hugonot** Jean-Claude, Le jardin dans l'Égypte ancienne 1989 ➤ 5,
g46; 6,g355: ᴿBO 48 (1990) 515s (Lise *Manniche*: enjoyable and informative).

e492 *Janssen* Jac J., Requisitions [vegetables, cattle, garments, metals] from
Upper Egyptian temples [P. BM 10401]: JEA 77 (1991) 79-94.

e492* *a)* *Knapp* A. Bernard, Spice, drugs, grain and grog; organic goods in
Bronze Age East Mediterranean trade; – *b)* *Evans* John, Organic traces
and their contribution to the understanding of trade: ➤ 637, Bronze Age
Trade 1989/91, 21-68 / 289-294.

e493 *Liphshitz* Nili, *Biger* Gideon, Cedar of Lebanon (*Cedrus libani*) in Israel
during antiquity: IsrEJ 41 (1991) 167-175; map.

e494 **Martinetz** [sic] Dieter, *al.*, Weihrauch und Myrrhe; Kulturgeschichte und
wirtschaftliche Bedeutung; Botanik, Chemie, Medizin. Stu 1989, Wiss.

VG. 236 p. DM 48. 3-8047-1019-0. – ᴿBO 48 (1991) 442-6 (W. W. *Müller*).

e495 **Piperno** Dolores R., Phytolith analysis; an archaeological and geological perspective 1989 ➤ 4,h127: ᴿAJA 95 (1991) 741 (S. W. *Green*).

e496 *Rapisarda* Grazia, Il simbolismo delle piante nella patristica latina e nell'età carolingia; esegesi biblica e cura del corpo e dell'anima: ➤ 419, AnStoEseg 7,2 (1989/90) 569-592.

e497 *Salza Prina Ricotti* Eugenia, I giardini nell'antichità: Archeo 69 (1990) 50-97; ill.

e498 *Tortzen* C. Gorm, Male and female in peripatetic botany: ClasMedK 42 (1991) 81-110.

e499 *Willerding* Ulrich, Zur Rekonstruktion der Vegetation im Umkreis früher Siedlungen: ➤ 46, Mem. DRIEHAUS J. 1990, 97-129 + pl. 17-20.

U2.8   **Agricultura, alimentatio.**

e500 ᵀᴱ**André** Jacques, COLUMELLE, De l'agriculture XII (De l'intendante). 1988 ➤ 4,h144; 6,g378: ᴿClasR 41 (1991) 70-72 (K. D. *White*).

e500* *a) Aravantinos* Vassilis L., Agricultural production and subsistence economy in Cyprus during the Late Cypriot II period; – *b) Schäfer* Jörg, The role of gardens in Minoan civilization: ➤ 645*, Aegean 1989, 57-65 / 85-88.

e501 *Archi* Alfonso, Culture de l'olive et production de l'huile à Ebla: ➤ 61, ᶠGARELLI P., Marchands 1991, 211-222.

e502 *a) Archi* Alfonso, Agricultural production in the Ebla region; – *b) Dolce* Rita, Les magasins et les lieux de traitement des denrées alimentaires à Ebla au IIIème et au IIème millénaire: ➤ 626, AnASyr 40 (1989/90) 50-55, ➊ 141 / 122-145, ➊ 143-7.

e503 *Badler* Virginia R., *al.*, Drink and be merry; infrared spectroscopy and Ancient Near Eastern wine [Godin Tepe; Gebel Adda]: Masca 7 ('Organic contents of ancient vessels' 1990) 25-36; 9 fig.; 7 color pl.

e504 *Bakhuizen* S. C., Torcula graecanica; a note on the archaeology of olive and grape pressing: ➤ 147, ᶠSTIBBE C. 1991, 1-5 + 3 fig.

e505 **Battaglia** Emanuela, 'Artos', il lessico della panificazione nei papiri greci 1989 ➤ 5,g716; 6,g380: ᴿBO 48 (1991) 139s (J. *Diethart*); Byzantion 61 (1991) 578-580 (A. *Touwaide*); ClasR 41 (1991) 520 (J. D. *Thomas*); Salesianum 53 (1991) 197s (R. *Della Casa*).

e506 *Bazell* Diane, Christian diet; a case study using Arnald of VILLANOVA's De esu carnium: diss. Harvard, ᴰ*Murdoch* J. CM 1991. – RelStR 18,173.
ᴱ**Bodson** L., L'animal dans l'alimentation 1986/8 ➤ e429; ᴱ**Clutton-Brock** J., The walking larder, 1986/9 ➤ e816.

e507 *Bordreuil* Pierre, À propos de la topographie économique de l'Ougarit; jardins du midi et pâturages du nord [... tablette 1983]: Syria 66 (1989) 263-274; 6 fig. (275-9, le mont Nanou).

e508 *a) Burkert* Walter, Oriental symposia; contrasts and parallels; – *b) Miller* Margaret, Foreigners at the Greek symposium?; – *c) Dunbabin* Katherine M. D., Triclinium and stibadium: ➤ 656c, Dining in a classical context 1989/91, 7-24 / 59-81; 27 fig. / 121-148; 36 fig.

e509 *Cenival* Françoise de, Deux textes démotiques du Fonds Jouguet relatifs aux cultures de blé; P. dém. Lille 121 (Inv. Sorbonne 539): Enchoria 18 (1991) 13-22; pl. 3-6.

e510 **Chouquer** G., *al.*, Structures agraires en Italie centro-méridionale [5 siècles classiques]; cadastres et paysages ruraux: CÉF 100. R 1987, École

Française. vii-414 p.; 163 fig. F 600. 3-7283-0115-8. – ᴿJRS 81 (1991) 215 (J. R. *Patterson*).

e511 *Dauphin* Claudine, Man makes his landscape ('l'anthropisation du milieu') [ᴱ*Guilaine* J., Pour une archéologie agraire 1991 ⮞ 397*]: BAngIsr 11 (1991s) 22-28; bibliog.

e512 *Davis* Jack L., Contributions to a Mediterranean rural archaeology; historical case studies from the Ottoman Cyclades: JMeditArch 4 (1991) 131-216.

e513 *Docter* Roald F., Athena vs. Dionysos; reconsidering the contents of SOS amphorae [only oil in 8th cent.; sometimes wine from 7th, notably the Florence Françoise Dionysiac vase]: Babesch 66 (1991) 45-49 + 3fig.

e514 **Dolce** R., *Zaccagnini* C., Il pane del re 1989 ⮞ 5,841.g41; 6,g194: ᴿArcheo 65 (1990) 123 (C. *Saporetti*); ArOr 59 (1991) 328s (B. *Hruška*); JESHO 34 (1991) 239-241 (C. *Michel*); OLZ 86 (1991) 290s (H. *Freydank*).

e515 *Faltings* Dina, Die Bierbrauerei im Alten Reich: ZäSpr 118 (1991) 104-116; 15 fig.

e516 *Fischer-Elfert* Hans-Werner, Bemerkungen zum Felderinventar [Felderverwaltung und deren Produktivität] des Papyrus Louvre AP 6345 und der Griffith Fragments: Enchoria 18 (1991) 27-36.

e517 **Flach** Dieter, Römische Agrargeschichte: HbAltW 3/9. Mü 1990, Beck. xiii-347 p.; 14 pl. DM 145. – ᴿAmHR 96 (1991) 145 (J. *Bintliff*); DLZ 112 (1991) 455-7 (R. *Günther*).

e518 **Garnsey** Peter, Famine and food supply 1988 ⮞ 4,h164... 6,g399: ᴿAmHR 96 (1991) 145 (J. *Bintliff*).

e519 *Gras* Michel, De la céramique à la cuisine; le mangeur d'Olbia [*Bats* M. 1988]: RÉAnc 91,3s (1989s) 65-71; Eng. 65.

e520 ᴱ**Harris** D.R., *Hillman* G.C., Foraging and farming; the evolution of plant exploitation [partly from Southampton 1986]: One World Arch. 13, 1989 ⮞ 5,g102: ᴿAJA 95 (1991) 541-3 (Julie *Hansen*).

e521 *Hayward* R., The vine and its products as theological symbols in first century Palestinian Judaism: Durham Univ. Journal 92 (1990) 9-18 [< RHE 87,81*].

e522 *Helck* Wolfgang, Zur ägyptischen Küche: GöMiszÄg 125 (1991) nur 51: mice included, as all over the world.

e523 *Herz* P., Studien zur... Lebensmittelversorgung: Hist Einz 55, 1988 ⮞ 5,g107; 6,g414: ᴿClasR 41 (1991) 151s (K.D. *White*).

e524 *Hjelmqvist* Hakon, Über die Zusammensetzung einiger prähistorischer Brote: Fornvännen 85 (1990) 9-21; 5 fig.; svensk 20s; Eng. 9 (one piece of pre-Roman bread, 30 somewhat later).

e525 **Hopkins** David C., The highlands of Canaan... agricultural: SocWB 3, 1985 ⮞ 2,b773... 6,g417: ᴿETL 67 (1991) 133-5 (M. *Vervenne*, Eng.); VT 41 (1991) 248 (G.I. *Davies*).

e526 *Kaplony-Heckel* Ursula, Das Acker-Amt in Theben-West von 151 bis 141 v.Chr.; die zwanzig Acker-Amt-Quittungen des Sesostris, Sohn des Anchoapis (übersichtlich beschrieben und aufgelistet): Enchoria 18 (1991) 55-67; pl. 12-13.

e527 **Katary** Sally L.D., Land tenure in the Ramesside period 1989 ⮞ 5, g112; ᴿBO 48 (1991) 821-4 (S. *Allam*: Wilbour papyrus well suited for computer-patterns).

e528 **Kehoe** D.P., The economics of agriculture... N. Africa 1988 ⮞ 4,h176 ... 6,g420: ᴿMnemosyne 44 (1989) 280-8 († P.W. de *Neeve*).

e529 *Krüger* Julian, Terminologie der Landbezeichnungen in der Landwirtschaft des griechisch-römischen Ägypten: Laverna 2 (1991) 1-26.

e530 **Laubenheimer** Fanette, Le temps des amphores en Gaule; vins, huiles et sauces: Hespérides. P 1990, Errance. 181 p.; ill.

e531 *Laubenheimer* Fanette, Le vin Gaulois [bartered for metal or slaves in Roman times]: RÉAnc 91,3s (1989) 5-22; 7 fig.; Eng. 5.

e532 *a) Lefèvre* F., Vin et viticulture en pays rème [Rheims] à l'époque romaine; – *b) Braemer* F., L'iconographie de la grappe de raisin; – *c) Jalmain* D., L'amphore, le fût et l'outre: ➤ 633, Archéologie de la vigne 1988/90, 163-173 / 71-75 / 149-153.

e533 *Liverani* Mario, Il rendimento dei cereali durante la III dinastia di Ur; contributo ad un approccio realistico: Origini 15 (R 1990s) 359-368.

e533* *Maekawa* Kazuya, The agricultural texts of Ur III Lagash of the British Museum (VII): AcSum 13 (1991) 195-221 (-235, facsimiles).

e534 *Magoulias* Harry J., The lives of the saints as sources for the Byzantine agrarian life in the sixth and seventh centuries: GrOrTR 35 (1990) 59-70.

e535 *Miller* R. L., Counting calories in Egyptian ration texts: JESHO 34 (1991) 257-269.

e536 *Morgan* Gareth, 'Nourishing foods', HERODOTUS 2.77 [*trephóntōn* rather 'solidifying']: Mnemosyne 44 (1991) 415-7.

e537 [E]**Murray** Oswyn, Sympotica; a symposium on the symposium 1990 ➤ 6,758*: [R]Eikasmos 2 (1991) 407-411 (Elena *Fabbro*); RÉG 104 (1991) 619-621 (Hélène *Cassimatis* says the title perfectly reflects the contents of the volume, but it is about banquets, not about 'The' symposium; PLATO is barely mentioned; B. *Fehr* discusses intriguingly the acceptance of the uninvited guest).

e538 *Nazzaro* Antonio V., Metafore e immagini agricole del De uiduis di AMBROGIO: VetChr 28 (1991) 277-289.

e539 **Ponsich** Michel, Aceite... pescado 1988 ➤ 6,g445: [R]MünstHand 10,2 (1991) 119s (P. *Barcel*').

e540 *Rahmani* L. Y., Two Byzantine winepresses in Jerusalem: ʿAtiqot 20 (1991) 95-110; 15 fig.

e541 *a) Rammant-Peeters* A., De bereiding van bier en wijn bij de oude Egyptenaren; – *b) Stol* M., De Babyloniers dronken bier; – *c) Spronk* K., De wijn als troost in leven en in sterven; enkele gedachten over de wijn en de Marzeach in Syrië en Palestina; – *d) Driel* G. van, Spijkers met koppen, II.; Maskan-šapir, een begin bij de Tigris: PhoenixEOL 37,1 (1991) 6-23; 6 fig. / 24-39; 2 fig. / 40-54 / 55s.

e542 *Salza Prina Ricotti* Eugenia, L'arte del bere nell'antichità: Archeo 81 (1991) 63-105; color. ill.

e543 *[Salza Prina] Ricotti* Eugenia, *a)* L'alimentazione nel mondo greco; – *b)* Cibi e banchetti nell'antica Roma: Archeo 44 (1988) 49-91; ill. / 46 (1988) 52-97; ill.

e544 *Simpson* St. John, Iron Age crop storage and ceramic manufacture in rural Mesopotamia: BInstArch 27 (L 1990) 119-140.

e545 **Sirks** Boudewijn, Food for Rome; the legal structure of the transportation and processing of supplies for the imperial distributions in Rome and Constantinople: StAmstEpig 31. Amst 1991, Gieben. vi-446 p. 90-5063-069-3.

e546 *Small* Jocelyn P., The Tarquins and Servius Tullius at banquet [really on costume, which in Roman art was always contemporary to the artist]: MÉF-A 103 (1991) 247-264; 4 fig.

e547 *Smit* E.J., The Tell Siran inscription; linguistic and historical implications [in Ammonite, praise of king for agriculture; || Qoh 2]: JSem 1 (Pretoria 1989) 108-117 [< OTAbs 14,274].

e548 **Spurr** M.S., Arable cultivation in Roman Italy 1986 → 4,h197 ... 6,g456: RJRS 45 (1991) 185-7 (D.J. *Mattingly*).

e549 *Steen* Eveline J. van der, The Iron Age bread ovens from Tell Deir 'Alla: ADAJ 35 (1991) 135-152; 16 fig.; 1 pl.

e550 *a) Strobel* Karl, Landwirtschaft und agrarische Gesellschaft Palästinas im 3. Jh. n.Chr.; – *b) Bounegru* Octavian, Aspekte der Romanisierung der ländlichen Bevölkerung in Scythia Minor (2.-3. Jh. n. Chr.): Münst-Hand 10,2 (1991) 47-85 / 89-116; Eng. 87/117s; franç. 88/118.

e550* **Verdult** Philip A., P. Erasmianae 2, parts of the archive of an Arsinoite *sitologos* from the middle of the second century B.C: StAmstIusPap 32. Amst 1991, Gieben. vii-176 p.; 37 pl. 90-5063-033-2 [OIAc 2,28].

e551 **Whittaker** C.R., Pastoral economics in classical antiquity [9th Congress Bern]: Proc. Supp. 14, 1988 → 5,807: RAnzAltW 44 (1991) 212-6 (H. *Grassl*).

e552 **Zeder** Melinda A., Feeding cities; specialized animal economies in the Ancient Near East [< diss. Michigan, AA 1985]: ArchInquiry. Wsh 1991, Smithsonian Institution. xvii-280 p. 0-87474-996-4 [OIAc 1,28].

U2.9 **Medicina** *biblica et antiqua.*

e553 **Adinolfi** Marco, *Geraci* Paola, Bibbia e ginecologia a confronto 1989 → 5,g152: RCBQ 53 (1991) 275s (J.J. *Pilch*: valuable, though the authors do not interact with or beyond each other).

Aleshire Sara B., Asklepios at Athens... healing cults [no really relevant title] 1991 → 172.

e554 *Allan* Nigel, Christian Mesopotamia and Greek medicine: Hermathena 145 (1988) 39-58 [Greek science was preserved in Edessa: AnPg 60, p. 734].

e555 **Armelagos** George J., *Coppa* Alfredo, Alla scoperta delle malattie antiche: Archeo 72 (1991) 116-8 [73 (1991) 122-4].

e556 **Artaud** Medhanada & Yvonne, Der Weg des Horus; Bilder des inneren Weges im Alten Ägypten: Therapeutische Konzepte der Analytischen Psychologie Jung 8. Fellbach 1991, Bonz. 297 p. 3-87089-314-1 [OIAc 2,13].

e557 **Avalos** Hector I., Illness and health care in ancient Israel; a comparative study of the role of the Temple: diss. Harvard, DCross F. CM 1991. 405 p. 91-33078. – HarvTR 84 (1991) 467s; DissA 52 (1991s) 1774-A [interaction with Greek Asclepius and Mesopotamian Gula).

e558 **Bliquez** Lawrence J., Roman surgical instruments and minor objects in the University of Mississippi: SIMA pocket 58, 1988 → 4,h212: RLatomus 50 (1991) 471s (Danielle *Gourévitch*: possibly some counterfeits).

e559 *Bonner* Gerald, Sickness, death and sin in the early Church: Milltown Studies 27 (1991) 38-61.

e560 **Breasted** James H., The Edwin Smith surgical papyrus published in facsimile and hieroglyphic transliteration with translation and commentary: OIP 3s. Ch 1991 = 1930 + revisions, Univ. Or. Institute. xxiv-596 p.; 8 pl. + vol. of xiii + 22 facsimiles. 0-918986-73-7 [OIAc 2,15].

e560* *Byl* Simon, Le vocabulaire HIPPOCRATIQUE dans les comédies d'ARISTOPHANE et particulièrement dans les deux dernières: RPg 64 (1990) 151-162.

e561 *Capasso* Luigi, I Romani in farmacia: Archeo 57 (1989) 55-99.

e562 **Curtis** Robert I., Garum and salsamenta; [fermented and salted fish]; production and commerce in materia medica: Studies in ancient medicine 3. Leiden 1991, Brill. xv-226 p.; xv-226 p. (141-6 Palestine); 10 fig.; 8 pl. 90-04-09423-7.

e563 *Dion* Paul E., Medical personnel in the Ancient Near East; *asû* and *āšipu* in Aramaic garb: Aram 1 (1989) 206-216.

e564 *Durand* P., Sur la construction du Livre II du *Peri antidótōn* de GALIEN: RÉAnc 93 (1991) 99-108.

e565 *Eijk* P. J. van der, 'Air, waters, places,' and 'On the sacred disease' [? HIPPOCRATES]; two different religiosities: Hermes 119 (1991) 168-176.

e566 **Estes** J. Worth, The medical skills of ancient Egypt 1989 → 5,g161 [not 'skulls'; but g170 should have been skulls, not skills; the correction was made in the wrong skull]: ᴿBO 48 (1991) 516 (K. S. *Kolta*: klar, angenehm); Orientalia 60 (1991) 350s (Irene *Vincentelli*).

e567 *Finch* Charles S., The African background to medical science, essays on African history, science, and civilization [< Journal of African Civilizations]. L 1990, Karnak. 212 p. 0-907015-43-3 [OIAc 1,16].

e568 *Gero* Stephen, GALEN on Christians; a reappraisal of the Arabic evidence: OrChrPer 56 (1990) 371-411.

e569 **Grmek** Mirko D., Diseases in the ancient Greek world 1989 → 4,h286; 5,g178: ᴿAmHR 96 (1991) 143s (J. M. *Riddle*: 'a brilliant demonstration of the best in medical historical writing'); ClasPg 86 (1991) 74-76 (I. *Morris*: erudite but does not attain its stated goal, interconnections between diseases).

e570 ᴱ**Hankinson** R. I., Method, medicine and metaphysics; studies in the philosophy of ancient science [Montreal McGill Univ. Oct. 2-3, 1986]: Apeiron 21. Alberta 1988. 194 p. 5 art. – ᴿElenchos 10 (1989) 461-4 (L. *Simeoni*).

e571 *Hankinson* R. J., GALEN's anatomy of the soul: Phronesis 36 (1991) 197-233.

e572 **Harakas** Stanley S., Health and medicine in the Eastern Orthodox tradition 1990 → 6,g500: ᴿGrOrTR 35 (1990) 159-161 (D. J. *Constantelos*).

e573 **Holden** Lynn, Forms of deformity [OT-Talmud; diss. Edinburgh 1988, ᴰ*MacQueen* J.]: JStOT supp. 131. Sheffield 1991, Academic. 370 p. 1-85075-327-X [OIAc 1,18].

e574 **Jacquart** Danielle, *Micheau* Françoise, La médecine arabe et l'occident médiéval: Islam-Occident 7. P 1990, Maisonneuve & L. 271 p.; 8 pl. – ᴿJSS 36 (1991) 199-201 (O. *Kahl*, deutsch).

e575 ᵀᴱ**Jouanna** Jacques, HIPPOCRATE, De l'ancienne médecine: Œuvres 2, 1990 → 6,g513: ᴿClasR 41 (1991) 25s (V. *Nutton*); RÉG 104 (1991) 290s (P. *Demont*).

e576 *Jouanna* Jacques, *a*) Un nouveau témoin sur le traité hippocratique des Airs, Eaux, Lieux; le Parisinus Gr. 2047 A., fo. 85ʳ·ᵛ et fol. 120ʳ: RÉG 104 (1991) 85-108; – *b*) Le role des Glossaires dans la transmission et l'édition des textes hippocratiques: RHText 19 (1989) 1-17.

e577 **Kudlien** Fridolf, Die Stellung des Arztes in der römischen Gesellschaft 1986 → 2,b781 ... 6,g516: ᴿRBgPg 69 (1991) 237s (J. A. *Straus*).

e578 **Langholf** V., Medical theories in HIPPOCRATES; early texts and the 'Epidemics': UntAntLitG 34. B 1990, de Gruyter. 285 p. – ᴿRÉG 104 (1991) 641 (J.-N. *Corvisier*: dense and rich).

e579 *Langslow* David, The formation of Latin technical vocabulary with special reference to medicine: → 580, 4th Latin 1987/91, 187-200.

e580 **Lloyd** G. E. R., Methods and problems in Greek science. C 1991 Univ. xiv-457 p. [RÉG 104,680].

e580* *MacCoull* L. S. B., Biblical disease imagery in the (14th c. Coptic) Triadon: Orientalia 60 (1991) 1s.

e581 **Mangie** Evelyn D., A comparative study of the perception of illness in New Kingdom Egypt and Mesopotamia in the early first millennium [both saw it as caused by supernatural forces, but differently]: diss. *D*Oller* G. Akron 1991. 166 p. 92-03425. – DissA 52 (1991s) 3034-A.

e582 **Mazzini** Innocenzo, Introduzione alla terminologia medica [latina, secondo radice (... greca)]. Bo 1988, Pàtron. 222 p. – *R*RPg 64 (1990) 240s (J. *André*).

e583 *Montserrat* Dominic, Mallocouria and Therapeuteria; rituals of transition in a mixed society?: BASP 28 (1991) 43-49.

e584 *Murray* Jacqueline, Sexuality and spirituality; the intersection of medieval theology and medicine: Fides et Historia 23,1 (Longview TX 1991) 20-36 [< ZIT 91,524].

e585 *Mustakallio* Kimmo K., Ancient Greek medicine and skin diseases: ➤ 6,724*, Ancient and popular healing 1986/9, 39-42.

e586 **Nickel** Diethard, Untersuchungen zur Embryologie GALENS: SchrGK-Ant 27, 1989 ➤ 6,g524*: *R*AnzAltW 44 (1991) 121s (V. *Langholf*).

e587 *E***Palmer** Bernard, Medicine and the Bible 1986 ➤ 3,f640... 5,g206: *R*ScripB 21 (1991) 24s (D. G. *Scott*).

e588 *Papayiannopoulos* Ioannis G., *G* a) Information (plerophoriai) in the OT concerning bodily pain; – b) Historical elements within the OT relating to skin-diseases: TAth 61 (1990) 390-5 / 641-8; Eng. 905/7.

e589 **Penso** Giuseppe, Lexicon plantarum medicinalium; vocabula vernacula latina, anglica, gallica, germanica, hispanica, italica, russica. Mi 1991, Medico-Farmaceutica. xvii-193 p. 88-7076-061-8.

e589* *Pilch* John J., Sickness and healing in Luke-Acts: ➤ 450, Social world of Lk-Ac 1991, 181-209.

e590 *TE***Potter** Paul, HIPPOCRATES V and VI: Loeb, CM/L 1988 ➤ 6,g533: *R*ClasR 41 (1991) 225 (J. *Longrigg*); Phoenix 45 (Toronto 1991) 172-4 (J. R. *Pinault*).

e591 *Pugliese Carratelli* Giovanni, La scuola medica di PARMENIDE a Velia [< ParPass 18 (1963) 385s + 25 (1970) 245-8 + 40 (1985) 34-38 + 41 (1986) 108-111]: ➤ 250, Tra Cadmo e Orfeo 1991, 269-280.

e592 *Qimron* E., Notes on the 4Q Zadokite Fragment on skin disease: JJS 42 (1991) 256-9.

e593 *Rémy* Bernard, Les inscriptions de médecins dans les provinces romaines de la péninsule ibérique [17 men, 2 women, from 50 to 500 A.D.]: RÉAnc 93 (1991) 321-354 + 17 fig. (map).

e594 *Scarborough* John, The pharmacology of sacred plants, herbs, and roots: ➤ 392, Magika 1991, 138-174.

e595 *Schultz* Michael, Erkrankungen des Kindesalters bei der frühbronzezeitlichen Population von İkiztepe (Türkei), Vorbericht 1988: ➤ 46, Mem. DRIEHAUS J. 1990, 83-90; Eng. 83; pl. 13-16 + 1 color.

e596 *TE***Smith** Wesley D., HIPPOCRATES' pseudepigraphic writings; letters, embassy speech from the altar, decree. NY 1990, Brill. ix-133 p. [RelStR 18,140, Antonía *Tripolitis*].

e597 *Staden* Heinrich von, Matière et signification; rituel, sexe et pharmacologie dans le corpus hippocratique: AntClas 60 (1991) 42-61.

e598 **Stetter** Cornelius, Denn alles steht seit Ewigkeit geschrieben; die

geheime Medizin der Pharaonen. Mü 1990, Quintessenz. – ᴿGöMiszÄg
122 (1991) 103-111 (W. *Westendorf*: kritiklos, journalistisch).

e598* ᴱ**Sullivan** Lawrence E.,   Healing and restoring; health and medicine in
the world's religious traditions.   NY 1990, Macmillan.   468 p. $35 [15
essays, mostly outside the biblical (era) purview]. – ᴿChrCent 107 (1990)
942s (H. B. *Partin*).

e599 **Temkin** Owsei,   Hɪᴘᴘᴏᴄʀᴀᴛᴇꜱ in a world of pagans and Christians
[... Christian response to pagan and Jewish healing traditions].   Bal-
timore 1991, Johns Hopkins Univ.   xiv-315 p. $40 [RelStR 18,232, D. C.
Aune].

e600 **Vitrac** Bernard,   Médecine et philosophie au temps d'Hɪᴘᴘᴏᴄʀᴀᴛᴇ: Histoires de Science.   Saint-Denis 1989, Presses Univ. de Vincennes.   190 p.
F 80. 2-903981-52-3. – ᴿÉTRel 66 (1991) 105 (J. *Argaud*).

e601 *Waarsenburg* D. J.,   Auro dentes iuncti; an inquiry into the study of the
Etruscan dental prosthesis: → 147, ꜰSᴛɪʙʙᴇ C. 1991, 241-6 + 2 fig.

e602 **Wöhrle** Georg,   Studien zur Theorie der antiken Gesundheitslehre:
Hermes Einz 56.   Stu 1990, Steiner.   295 p.   DM 84 [Gymnasium 99,73, V.
Langholf].

e603 *Zias* J.,   Death and disease in ancient Israel: BA 54 (1991) 146-159.

U3   *Duodecim Tribus:* **Israel Tribes;** Land-Ideology.

e604 *a*) *Azria* Régine,   La Terre comme projet utopique dans les représentations religieuses et politiques juives; – *b*) *Dieckhoff* Alain,   Terre
rêvée, terre convoitée, Israël; – *c*) *Nederveen Pieterse* Jan,   The history of
a metaphor; Christian Zionism and the politics of apocalypse: Archiv-
ScSocRel 75 (1991) 55-67 / 69-73 / 75-99.

Boorer Suzanne,   The promise of the land as oath ᴰ1991 → 1690.

e605 *Da Spinetoli* Ortensio,   Le dodici tribù di Israele: → 418, Biblia gen.
1990, 155-185.

e606 *Garrone* Daniele,   Il tema della terra promessa nella Bibbia ebraica;
considerazioni esegetiche e teologiche [prolusione Fac. Valdese, Roma
1991; per il 65° compleanno di J. A. Sᴏɢɢɪɴ]: Protestantesimo 46 (1991)
82-102.

e607 ᴱ**Hallamish** *Moshe, Ravitzky* Aviezer, ❼ The land of Israel in medieval
Jewish thought [14 art.]. J 1991, Yad Ben-Zvi.   viii-356 [RelStR 18,72, M.
Kellner].

e608 *Herrera* M. Dolores,   El territorio de Aser en los inicios del I milenio
a.C. a la luz de la arqueología; fenicios e israelitas: → 421, Luso-Esp
1989/91, 33-49 + 5 planes.

e609 ᴱ**Hoffman** Lawrence A.,   The land of Israel; Jewish perspectives 1986
→ 2,b818; 5. g232: ᴿCritRR 4 (1991) 349s (S. B. *Reid*).

e610 *Jacob* Edmond,   La promesse de la terre: FoiVie = CahÉtJuives [71/15
(1972) *Weber* H. R.] 90/24 (1990) 51-56.

e611 **Kallai** Z.,   Historical geography... tribal territories 1986 → 4,h284:
ᴿJNES 50 (1991) 69-73 (Diana *Edelman*: weak on comparative literary data); VT 41 (1991) 250s (G. I. *Davies*: tribes rather than historical
geography).

e612 *a*) *Lemaire* A., Asher et le royaume de Tyr; – *b*) *Lipiński* E.,   The
territory of Tyre and the tribe of Asher: → 445, Phoenicia 1990/1, 135-152
/ 153-166 (1-9).

e613 *Tuell* Steven S.,   The southern and eastern borders of Abar-Nahara
[Kedar border S; Jordan rather than East-Jordan E; N Posideium at or

near Basit; W Phoenicia as in HERODOTUS, but hardly Cyprus]: BASOR 184 (1991) 51-57.

e614 **Wright** C. J. H.,   God's people in God's land; family, land and property in the OT [< diss. Cambridge 1977]. GR/Exeter 1990, Eerdmans/Paternoster. xx-284 p. $17.   0-8028-0321-0 / UK 0-85364-396-2 [BL 92,115, C. S. *Rodd*].

U4   *Limitrophi*, **adjacent lands.**

e615 **Bartlett** John R., Edom ...: JStOT supp 77, 1989 ➤ 5,g242; 6,g566: [R]BA 54 (1991) 58 (B. C. *Creason*); CBQ 53 (1991) 658 (T. H. *Matthews*: information welcome but suggests more is needed from excavation); ETL 67 (1991) 147s (J. *Lust*); CritRR 4 (1991) 101-3 (C. D. *Evans*); RB 98 (1991) 140s (J.-M. de *Tarragon*).

e616 *Brooke* George J.,   The Kittim in the Qumran pesharim: ➤ 412, Images 1990/1, 135-158.

e617 **Cabanes** Pierre,   Les Illyriens de Bardylis à Genthios (IVe-IIe siècles avant J.-C.: Regards sur l'histoire anc. 6. P 1988, Sedes. 342 p. – Gnomon 63 (1991) 510-4 (M. *Zahrnt*).

e617* *Gamq'relize* Tamaz,   On the history of the tribal names of ancient Colchis: ➤ 48*, [E]ESENÇ T., RÉtGeorg 6s (1990s) 237-245 [247-263, critique by *Hewitt* B. G.].

e618 *Gozalbes* Enrique,   La imagen de los Mauri en Roma: Latomus 50 (1991) 38-55.

e619 **Kasher** Aryeh,   Jews, Idumaeans, and ancient Arabs 1988 ➤ 4,h295; 6,g571: [R]Judaica 46 (1990) 47s (S. *Schreiner*); VT 41 (1991) 251s (W. *Horbury*).

e620 (Gade) **Kristensen** Anne K.,   Who were the Cimmerians? [➤ 6,b499]: Med h/fil 57.   K 1988, Danish Acad. 141 p. Dk 200. – [R]AfO 36s (1989s) 143-5 (A. *Kuhrt*); Gnomon 63 (1991) 507-510 (R. *Hachmann*).

e621 **Moscati** Sabatino,   Le civiltà periferiche del Vicino Oriente antico. T 1989, UTET. 270 p.; ill. – [R]Archeo 66 (1990) 127 (S. F. *Bondì*).

e622 *Raban* Avner, *Stieglitz* Robert W.,   The sea peoples and their contributions to civilization: BAR-W 17,6 (1991) 34-42.92; (color.) ill.

e623 *Reho* Maria, *al.*, I Traci: Archeo 67 (1990) 51-111; ill.

e624 *Rosén* Haiim B.,   Eine andere Antwort auf die *Ahhiyawa*-Frage [Iás = Ionia]: IndogF 96 (1991) 46-51.

e625 *Singer* Itamar,   The 'land of Amurru' and the 'lands of Amurru' in the Šaušgamuwa treaty: Iraq 53 (1991) 69-74.

e625* **Soustal** P.,   Thrakien (*Thrakē, Rodopē* und *Haimimontos*): Tabula Imperii Byzantini 6. W 1991, Österr. Akad. 579 p.; 2 detached maps. Sch 1960 [RHE 87,180*].

e626 **Strange** John.   Caphtor-Keftiu 1980 ➤ 61,3591 ... 65,d50: [R]FolOr 27 (1990) 257-9 (L. *Hellbing*).

e626* **Wilhelm** G., The Hurrians 1989 ➤ 6,g575: [R]BA 54 (1991) 177s (D. W. *Young*); PEQ 122 (1990) 66s (M. S. *Drower*).

U4.5   *Viae* – **Routes, roads.**

e627 *Beitzel* Barry J.,   The Via Maris in literary and cartographic sources [a century-old error (QUARESMIUS-SCHUMACHER) corrected; it linked merely Acco-Capernaum, not Babylon-Egypt]: BA 54 (1991) 64-75.

e628 *Boltrik* Y.V., Ⓡ Land routes of Scythia: SovArch (1990,4) 30-44; Eng. 44.

e629 **Dorsey** David A., The roads and highways of ancient Israel: ASOR library. Baltimore 1991, Johns Hopkins Univ. xx-300 p.; 15 maps. £28.50. 0-8018-3898-3 [BL 92,30, K. W. *Whitelam*].

e630 *Fischer* Henry G., Sur les routes de l'Ancien Empire: ⇥ 40, Mém. CLÈRE J. 1991, 59-64.

e631 **French** D., Roman roads and milestones of Asia Minor, 2. An interim catalogue of milestones 1988 ⇥ 5,g266: ᴿBInstArch 27 (1990) 187s (R. L. *Story*).

e632 *Har-El* Menashe, Jews and the great silk road: Ariel ['A review of arts and letters in Israel', quarterly in English, French, German, Russian and Spanish; 0004-1343]: 84 (1991) 4-18; (color) ill.

e633 **Kase** E. W., *al.*, The great Isthmian corridor route; explorations of the Phokis-Doris expedition. Dubuque 1991, K. Hunt. xvi-202 p.; ill. [RÉG 104,679].

e634 **Klimkeit** H. J., Die Seidenstrasse 1988 ⇥ 5,g272; 6,g581: ᴿOLZ 82 (1991) 99-101 (E. *Raschmann*).

e635 *Müller* Sylvie, Routes minoennes en relation avec le site de Malia: BCH 115 (1991) 545-560; 20 fig.

e636 *Petersen* Andrew D., Two forts on the medieval Hajj route in Jordan [Zarqa, Jīzeh]: ADAJ 35 (1990) 347-357; 4 fig.; II pl.

e637 **Pritchett** W. Kendrick, Studies in ancient Greek topography [... iii. Roads; iv. Passes]; app. *Vanderpool* Eugene, Berkeley 1989 [= CLSt 4; 22; 28; 31, 33], Univ. California. iii: 0-520-09635-5. – 7, 1991s, x-228; 9 fig., 173 pl.; 8, 1992, xxi-163 p.; 116 pl., maps. 90-5063-071-5.

e638 *Retsö* Jan, The domestication of the camel and the establishment of the frankincense road from South Arabia: OrSuec 40 (1991) 187-219.

e639 *Safrai* Z., ❷ The rural road system in Palestine at the time of the Mishnah and Talmud: ⇥ 443, Commerce in Palestine 1980/90, 159-180.

e639* *Sidebotham* Steven E., Römische Strassen in der ägyptischen Wüste: AntWelt 22 (1991) 177-182; 23 (color.) fig. (map).

e640 *Zertal* Adam, The Roman road Caesarea-Ginae and the location of Capercotani: PEQ 122 (1990) 21-33; 8 fig. (maps).

U5   *Ethnographia,* **Sociologia** [servitus ⇥ E3.5; G6.5].

e641 *Adeyemi* M. E., A sociological approach to the background of Pauline Epistles: DeltioVM 10,1 (1991) 32-42.

e642 *Ahern* Annette, Towards an academic praxis in religious studies; BER-GER's dual-citizenship approach: SR 20 (1991) 333-344.

e643 *Alexeev* V. P., ❷ Ancient societies; their interaction with environment, culture and history: SovArch (1991,1) 5-19; Eng. 19.

e644 *Arens* Eduardo, Los Evangelios en la perspectiva sociológica: Páginas 15,104 (1990) 71-87.

e644* **Atkins** R.A., Egalitarian community; ethnography and exegesis [< diss. Evanston, ᴰ*Jewett* R.]: Tuscaloosa 1991, Univ. Alabama. xix-254 p.; 7 fig. $25 pa. 0-8173-0513-0 [NTAbs 36,118].

e645 *Bechtel* Lyn M., Shame as a sanction of social control in biblical Israel; judicial, political, and social shaming: JStOT 49 (1991) 47-76.

e646 *Benjamin* Don C., An anthropology of prophecy: BibTB 21 (1991) 135-144.

Bernal Martin, Black Athena, the Afroasiatic roots of classical civilization [I. 1987] II. 1991 ⇥ b214*.

e646* *Billy* Ginette, La population de l'île de Saï au Kerma ancien: ANilM (1991) 13-20; Eng. 7: morphological features of 55 individuals [p. 21-29, Kerma in relation to Nubia].

e647 **Blasi** Anthony J., Early Christianity as a social movement: Toronto Studies in Religion 5, 1988 ➤ 6,g593: ᴿJAAR 59 (1991) 157s (J.H. *Elliott* queries some renditions, like 'party' for 'banquet'); RelStR 17 (1990) 260 (H.C. *Kee*); TorJT 7 (1991) 131-3 (J.S. *Kloppenborg*).

e647* *Bol'shakov* A.O., *Sushchevskij* A.G., ⊕ The hero and society in ancient Egypt: VDI 198 (1991) 3-27; Eng. 27s.

e648 *Borobio* Dionisio, Lo social en la liturgía y los sacramentos: doctrina y 'recepción': Salmanticensis 38 (1991) 33-64; Eng. 64.

e648* **Brandewie** Ernest, When giants walked the earth; the life and times of Wilhelm SCHMIDT: Anthropos Studia 44. FrS 1990, Univ. 357 p. – ᴿNZMissW 47 (1991) 326-9 (J. *Baumgartner*); VerbumSVD 32 (1991) 210-2 (A. *Quack*).

e649 *Calmeyer* Peter, Zur Darstellung von Standesunterschieden in Persepolis: ArchMIran 24 (1991) 35-41; 5 fig.; pl. 11-18.

e649* *Cascajero* Juan, Lucha de clases e ideología en la tardía República: Gerión 8 (1990) 115-139.

e650 **Champion** Françoise, *Hervieu-Léger* Danièle, L'émotion en religion: Religion et modernité. P 1990, Centurion. 253 p. F 125. 2-227-31571-7. – ᴿÉTRel 66 (1991) 146-8 (P. *Keller*).

e651 ᴱ**Clements** R.E., World of ancient Israel 1989 ➤ 5,387; 6,g607: ᴿNBlackf 72 (1991) 104-6 (A. *Paretsky*); RelStT 10,2 (1990) 119s (D.A. *Aycock*).

e652 **Colliot-Thélène** Catherine, Max WEBER et l'histoire. P 1990, PUF. 121 p. F 34. 2-13-043133-X. – ᴿÉTRel 66 (1991) 307s (J.-M. *Prieur*).

e652* **Coote** R. & M., Power, politics, and the making of the Bible 1990 ➤ 6,g608: ᴿBibTB 21 (1991) 79 (D.E. *Oakman*).

e653 **Dassen** P.G.C., 'Gestolde geest'; rationaliteit en rationalisering in Max WEBERs visie op de westerse geschiedenis: Theoretische geschiedenis 18 (Amst 1991) 285-311 [< RHE 86,256*].

e654 *Del Verme* Marcello, In margine al prossimo convegno del The context group [team di Bruce MALINA, Creighton Univ. Omaha / 1991 Napoli] (Madrid, 5-8 maggio 1991) e in preparazione a quello futuro (Napoli, nel 1993) ['quasi certamente']: RivB 39 (1991) 118-121.

e655 *Derda* Tomasz, Necropolis workers in Graeco-Roman Egypt in the light of the Greek papyri: JJurPap 21 (1991) 37-51.

e656 **Dixon** Suzanne, The Roman mother 1988 (pa. 1990) ➤ 4,h340... 6,g614: ᴿQuadUrb 68 (1991) 153-5 (R. *Scuderi*).

e656* *Domeris* W.R., *a*) Sociological and social historical investigations; – *b*) Marxism; historical materialist exegesis; ➤ 3756, Text 1991, 215-233 / 299-311.

e657 **Douglas** Mary, How institutions think 1986 ➤ 4,h340*; 5,g295: ᴿRelStR 17 (1991) 24.26-32 (J.A. *Donahue*, also on 7 cognate works).

e658 *Dutcher-Walls* Patricia, [...Jer 26; 36] The social location of the Deuteronomists; a sociological study of factional politics in late pre-exilic Judah: JStOT 52 (1991) 77-94.

e659 **Ebertz** Michael N., Das Charisma des Gekreuzigten; zur Soziologie der Jesusbewegung: WUNT 45, 1987 ➤ 3,f773... 6,g617: ᴿJTS 42 (1991) 188s (R. *Morgan*); NedTTs 44 (1990) 162s (P.W. van der *Horst*); RechSR 79 (1991) 421s (J. *Guillet*: disciple de M. WEBER).

e660 *a*) *Endesfelder* Erika,   Die Formierung der altägyptischen Klassengesellschaft; Probleme und Beobachtungen; – *b*) *Verner* Miroslav,   Zur Organisierung der Arbeitskräfte auf den Grossbaustellen der Alten-Reichs-Nekropolen; – *c*) *Vachala* Břetislav,   Zur Frage der Kriegsgefangenen in Ägypten; Überlegungen anhand der schriftlichen Quellen des Alten Reichs; – *d*) *Andrassy* Petra,   Die Beziehungen Ägyptens zu Vorderasien bis zum Ende des Alten Reichs: ➤ 616, Probleme 1991, 5-61 / 63-91 / 93-101 / 103-152.

Esse Douglas L., Subsistence, trade, and social change in Early Bronze Age Palestine, ᴰ1982/91 ➤ d289.

e661 **Forster** Peter G.,   T. Callen YOUNG, missionary and anthropologist. Hull 1989, Univ. xvii-251 p.; ill.; maps. £8. – ᴿAnthropos 86 (1991) 283s (F. A. *Salamone*).

e662 *a*) *Flanagan* James W., [➤ 2488] Technology and the constructs of social world studies; – *b*) *Levin* Miriam R.,   Artist/technologist; Eiffel's tower, technology and the social construction of meaning; – *c*) *Wood* Richard A., The use and significance of models for historical reconstruction: ➤ 446, SBL Sem 30 (1991) 461-481 / 482-7 / 488-498.

e663 *Frost* P.,   Attitudes toward Blacks in the early Christian era: SecC 8,1 (1991) 1-11 [< NTAbs 36,76].

e664 **Gibson** M., *Biggs* R.,   Organization of power 1983/7 ➤ 3,781... 6,g628: ᴿJAOS 111 (1991) 637-641, 2 facsimiles (H. *Waetzoldt*).

e665 *Garland* R.,   Juvenile delinquency in the Graeco-Roman world: History Today 41,10 (L 1991) 12-19 [< NTAbs 36,242].

e666 **Gill** Robin,   Competing convictions [...can theology and sociology be partners?]. L 1989, SCM.   180 p. £8 [HeythJ 33,233, J. *Sweeney*].

e667 ᴱ**Gill** R., Theology and sociology 1987 ➤ 4,h358; 6,g629: ᴿRelStT 9,1 (1989) 30s (Rachael L. E. *Kohn*: 'implications for biblical studies' by GOTTWALD N., RODD C. on WEBER, SCROGGS R.).

e668 *Gnuse* Robert K.,   Contemporary evolutionary theory as a new heuristic model for the socioscientific method in biblical studies: Zygon 25 (1990) 405-431.

e669 **Greeley** Andrew M.,   The Catholic myth; the behavior and beliefs of American Catholics. NY 1990, Scribner's.   322 p. $22. – ᴿCommonweal 117 (1990) 323s (D. *Wyclif*); TTod 48 (1991s) 98s (J. A. *Coleman*: very informative if you can take in stride that he considers fools all bishops and most priests and intellectuals).

e669* *Grecley* A. M.,   *a*) Protestant and Catholic; is the analogical imagination extinct?: American Sociological Review 54 (1989) 485-502; – *b*) Theology and sociology; on validating David TRACY: JAAR 59 (1991) 643-652.

e670 *Green* Henry A.,   Power and knowledge; a study in the social development of early Christianity [...Jesus movement... Nag-Hammadi]: SR 20 (1991) 217-231.

e671 **Hamel** Gildas,   Poverty and charity in Roman Palestine, three centuries C.E.: NE Studies 27.   Berkeley 1990, Univ. California.   304 p. $31. 0-520-09715-7. – ᴿJTS 42 (1991) 297-301 (M. *Goodman*).

Harris Gerald,   Church discipline 1 Cor 5 [...'sociological concepts and models'] 1991 ➤ 5420.

e672 **Holmberg** Bengt,   Sociology and the NT 1990 ➤ 6,g639: ᴿBibTB 21 (1991) 169s (E. L. *Bode*); CritRR 4 (1991) 197-9 (D. B. *Martin*); ExpTim 102 (1990s) 280s (S. C. *Barton*); Neotestamentica 25 (1991) 441s (P. F. *Craffert*: for 'sociology' read 'social science models'); TLond 94 (1991)

145s (L. *Houlden*); TLZ 116 (1991) 703-6 (G. *Theissen*); TorJT 7 (1991) 125-7 (M. P. *Knowles*); TS 52 (1991) 177 (A. C. *Mitchell*: restricts himself to sociology, leaving anthropology aside).

e673 **Horsley** Richard, Sociology and the Jesus movement. NY 1989, Crossroad. vii-178 p. $23 [BA 55,157s, D. M. *May*: chiefly a blunt critique of THEISSEN's 'vagueness and abstraction' and conservative functionalism]. – ᴿBibTB 21 (1991) 123s (D. C. *Duling*); CBQ 53 (1991) 329-331 (Carolyn *Osiek*); CritRR 4 (1991) 200-3 (J. L. *Jaquette*); Horizons 18 (1991) 317s (G. S. *Sloyan*); Interpretation 45 (1991) 198 (Jouette M. *Bassler*); RelStT 10,1 (1990) 59-61 (B. W. *Henaut*).

e673* *a*) *Hoyt* Thomasᴶ, Interpreting biblical' scholarship for the Black Church tradition; – *b*) *Wimbush* Vincent L., The Bible and African Americans; an outline of an interpretative history; – *c*) *Weems* Renita J., Reading *Her Way* through the struggle; African American women and the Bible: → 433, Stony the road 1986/91, 17-39 / 81-97 / 57-77.

e674 **Ingold** Tim, Evolution and social life. C 1986, Univ. xv-431 p. £35; pa. £12.50. 0-521-24778-0; -8955-6. – ᴿBInstArch 27 (1990) 208 (H. *Mytum*).

e675 *Ingravalle* F., Su Max WEBER e il problema della secolarizzazione: Fenomenologia e società 12,2 (1989) 39-52 [< FilT 4,558].

e676 **Jamieson-Drake** David W., Scribes and schools in monarchic Judah; a socio-archaeological approach [diss. Duke 1988, ᴰ*Meyers* Carol → 6, 9163*]: JStOT supp 109, Social World 9. Sheffield 1991, Almond. 240 p. £30. 1-85075-275-3. – ᴿExpTim 103 (1991s) (A. D. H. *Mayes*); TLZ 116 (1991) 898-900 (W. *Thiel*).

e677 *Jeffers* J., Conflict at Rome; social order and hierarchy in early Christianity. Mp 1991, Fortress. viii-215 p.; 12 fig. [NRT 114,613, A. *Harvengt*: LEUTZSCH non cité].

e678 *Joubert* S., 'n Verruimde invalshoek [broadened perspective] tot die verlede? Die sosiaal-wetenskaplike benadering tot die Nuwe Testament: HervTSt 47 (1991) 39-54 [< NTAbs 36,5].

e679 **Just** Roger, Women in Athenian law and life [< diss. Oxford 1976] 1989 → 6,g642: ᴿJHS 111 (1991) 237-9 (M. *Gagarin*); RÉG 104 (1991) 613 (Véronique *Boudon*: colorful and precise).

e680 **Kaster** R. A., Guardians of language 1988 → 5,g321; 6,g643: ᴿClasR 41 (1991) 97-101 (J. N. *Adams*); JRS 81 (1991) 246-8 (V. *Law*); Mnemosyne 44 (1991) 271-3 (D. M. *Schenkeveld*); RBgPg 69 (1991) 187-194 (P. *Hamblenne*).

e681 **Kee** Howard C., Knowing the truth; a sociological approach to NT interpretation 1989 → 5,g322; 6,g644: ᴿCBQ 53 (1991) 140s (Carolyn *Osiek*: comes down hard on MALINA-ELLIOTT-NEYREY use of Mary DOUGLAS' group-grid, and ultimately rejects rather than uses social-science method); Pacifica 4 (1991) 240-2 (R. *Fopp*).

e682 ᶠKEE Howard C., The social world of formative Christianity and Judaism, ᴱ**Neusner** Jacob, *al.*, 1988 → 4,77: ᴿGregorianum 72 (1991) 557-9 (G. L. *Prato*).

e683 *Keenan* J. G., The 'new papyrology' and ancient social history: AncHB 5 (Calgary 1991) 159-169 [< NTAbs 36,242].

e684 *Klees* Hans, Zur Beurteilung der Helotie im historischen und politischen Denken der Griechen im 5. und 4. Jh. v.Chr.: Laverna, Wirtschafts/ Sozialgeschichte 2 (St. Katharinen 1991) 27-52.

e685 **Kleijwegt** Marc, Ancient youth; the ambiguity of youth and the absence of adolescence in Greco-Roman society: Dutch Mg Arch 8. Amst 1991, Gieben. xvi-401 p. 90-5063-063-4.

e686 ᴱLevine Molly M., *Peradotto* J., The challenge of (BERNAL M.) 'Black Athena', 1989 ➤ 3,b809; 5,b589: ᴿClasR 41 (1991) 166s (Jane F. *Gardner*).

e687 **Lightstone** Jack N., Society, the sacred, and Scripture in ancient Judaism 1988 ➤ 4,h384; 6,g655: ᴿJRel 71 (1991) 123 (B. L. *Visotzky*: importantly canonizes sociological approach).

e688 **Love** J. R., Antiquity and capitalism; Max WEBER and the sociological foundations of Roman civilisation. L 1991, Routledge. x-336 p. £40. 0-415-04750-1 [JRS 81,259].

e689 *Malina* Bruce J. Scienze sociali e interpretazione storica; la questione della retrodizione [conferenza Napoli 22.I.1991; italiano riveduto da *Del Verme* M.]: RivB 39 (1991) 305-323.

e690 **Mayes** A. D. H., The Old Testament in sociological perspective 1989 ➤ 5,g337; £11: ᴿBL (1991) 38 (G. H. *Jones*); TLond 94 (1991) 66 (R. *Coggins*); VT 41 (1991) 487s (J. A. *Emerton*); ZAW 103 (1991) 160 (H.-C. *Schmitt*).

e691 **Meeks** W., The moral world of the first Christians 1987 ➤ 2,b908 ... 6,g662: ᴿColcT 61,4 (1991) 204s (M. *Wojciechowski*, ☉).

e692 *Mehring* Reinhard, Max WEBERs Werk in der Rekonstruktion W. SCHLUCHTERs (1988): ZRGg 43 (1991) 72-76.

e693 **Milbank** John, Theology and social theory; beyond secular reason. Ox 1990, Blackwell. x-443 p. £45. – ᴿTLond 94 (1991) 377 (R. *Preston*: 'A theological critique of the social sciences is certainly needed').

e694 **Mommsen** Wolfgang J., The political and social theory of Max WEBER. Ch 1989, Univ. xiv-226 p. – ᴿHistTheor 30 (1991) 79-89 (L. *McLemore*).

e695 ᴱMommsen Wolfgang J., *Schwentker* Wolfgang. Max WEBER und seine Zeitgenossen: DHistInst London 21, 1988 ➤ 5,546; 6,g664: ᴿZRGg 43 (1991) 376-8 (H.-C. *Kraus*).

e695* — *Swatos* William H.ᴶ, *Kivisto* Peter, Max WEBER as 'Christian sociologist': JScStR 30 (1991) 347-362 [< ᴢɪᴛ 92,137].

e696 **Mrozek** Stanisław, Lohnarbeit 1989 ➤ 6,g666: ᴿHZ 253 (1991) 411 (W. *Backhaus*).

e697 **Neesen** Lutz, Demiourgoi und Artifices; Studien zur Stellung freier Handwerker in antiken Städten [Hab.-Diss. Bochum]: EurHS 3/403. Fra 1989, Lang. 331 p. – ᴿKlio 73 (1991) 690-3 (Claudia *Rieck*).

e698 **Nippel** Wilfried, Griechen, Barbaren und 'Wilde'; alte Geschichte und Sozialanthropologie: Tb 4429/1680. Fra 1990, Fischer. 218 p. [Graz-Beit 18,276-9, I. *Weiler*].

e699 **O'Leary** Brendan, The Asiatic mode of production; oriental despotism, historical materialism and Indian history: Explorations in Social Structures. Ox 1989, Blackwell. xiv-394 p. 0-631-16766-9. – ᴿJESHO 34 (1991) 364s (P. W. *Klein*).

e700 **Orywal** Erwin, (*Hackstein* Katharina), Ethnische Gruppen des Vorderen Orients; Quellen und Kommentare zur Übersichtskarte A-VIII-13: TAVO B-91. Wsb 1991, Reichert. 110 p. 3-88226-528-0.

e701 **Overholt** Thomas W. [➤ 3116], Prophecy in cross-cultural [... anthropological] perspective 1986 ➤ 8,2603 ... 4,3619: ᴿRelStT 9,1 (1989) 37s (Ruth E. *Caldwell*).

e702 **Pailin** David A., The anthropological character of theology; conditioning theological understanding. C 1990, Univ. xi-290 p. £30. 0-521-39069-9 [TDig 38,181]. – ᴿExpTim 102 (1990s) 284s (D. R. *Peel*); JTS 42 (1991) 804-7 (H. *Oppenheimer*); NBlackf 72 (1991) 452-4 (M. *Durrant*); TLond 94 (1991) 210 (J. *Macquarrie*); TS 52 (1991) 753-5 (M. J. *Scanlon*).

e703 *Passakos* Dimitris, Ⓖ Prolegomena to the sociological interpretation of the NT: DeltioVM 10,2 (1991) 15-26.

e703* **Pedersen** Johannes, Israel, its life and culture I, ^E*Strange* James: SFlorida Studies in the History of Judaism 28. Atlanta 1991 = 1926-40, Scholars. x-578 p. 1-55540-643-2 [OIAc 2,25].

e704 ^E**Powell** Marvin A., Labor in the ANE 1978/87 ⇒ 3,786; 5,g352: ^RJAOS 111 (1991) 631-7 (H. *Neumann*).

e705 *a) Prades* José A., Sacré et société; – *b) Derczansky* Alexandre, Note sur la judéité de DURKHEIM; ArchivScSocRel 69 ('Relire Durkheim' 1990) 7s (55-68) / 157-160 [9-156, 10 al.].

e706 ^E**Rawson** Beryl, The family in ancient Rome; new perspectives [3-day seminar, Canberra National University, June 1981] 1986 ⇒ 3,507.f787... 6,g675: ^RKlio 73 (1991) 700s (Jana *Kepartová*).

e707 *Reed* Rosslyn, Calvinism, the WEBER thesis, and entrepreneurial behaviour; the case of David SYME: JRelHist 16 (1990s) 292-303.

e708 ^E**Rehbinder** Manfred, *Tieck* Klaus-Peter, Max WEBER als Rechtssoziologe: RSoz 63. B 1987... 187 p. DM 68. – ^RZEvEth 35 (1991) 72s (F. W. *Graf*).

e709 **Reviv** Hanoch, The elders in ancient Israel 1989 ⇒ 5,g356; ^T*Plitmann* Lucy: ^RBiblica 72 (1991) 100-4 (J. *Buchholz*); JBL 110 (1991) 132-4 (L. J. *Hoppe*).

e710 **Rilinger** Rolf, Humiliores – honestiores; zu einer sozialen Dichotomie im Strafrecht der römischen Kaiserzeit 1988 ⇒ 6,g676: ^RGnomon 63 (1991) 127-131 (J.-U. *Krause*); Gymnasium 98 (1991) 383s (A. *Poláček*); Latomus 50 (1989) 472s (R. *Delmaire*).

e711 **Saldarini** Anthony J., Pharisees... sociological 1988 ⇒ 4,h410*; 6,g680: ^RBL (1991) 143 (T. *Rajak*); CBQ 53 (1991) 147-9 (J. C. *VanderKam*); CritRR 4 (1991) 379-381 (G. G. *Porton*); JAOS 111 (1991) 133s (J. *Neusner*: starting point for all future study); NedTTs 45 (1991) 256s (P. J. *Tomson*); Neotestamentica 25 (1991) 191s (P. J. J. *Botha*); ScripB 21 (1991) 30s (H. *Wansbrough*: not so sociological); TLond 94 (1991) 67s (S. *Freyne*).

e712 *a) Saller* Richard, Corporal punishment, authority, and obedience in the Roman household; – *b) Dixon* Suzanne, The sentimental ideal of the Roman family; – *c) Eyben* Emiel, Fathers and sons: ⇒ 600, ^E*Rawson* B., Marriage 1988/91, 144-165 / 99-113 / 114-143.

e713 **Salzman** Michele R., On Roman time; the codex-calendar of 354 and the rhythms of urban life in late antiquity: Transformation of the Classical Heritage 17. Berkeley 1991, Univ. California. xxii-315 p.; 107 fig. 0-520-06566-2.

e714 *Sancho Rocher* Laura, Isonomía kaì dēmokratía: RÉAnc 93 (1991) 237-261; Eng. 237.

e715 **Scaff** Lawrence A., Fleeing the iron cage; culture, politics, and modernity in the thought of Max WEBER 1988 ⇒ 6,g681: ^RHistTheor 30 (1991) 79-89 (L. *McLemore*).

e716 *Schäfer-Lichtenberger* Christa, The pariah; some thoughts on the genesis and presuppositions of Max WEBER's Ancient Judaism: JStOT 51 (1991) 85-113.

e717 **Schmeller** Thomas, Brechungen; Urchristliche Wandercharismatiker im Prisma soziologisch orientierter Exegese: SBS 136, 1989 ⇒ 5,g359; 6,g685: ^RIndTSt 27 (1990) 105-7 (L. *Legrand*: post-THEISSENIAN).

e718 **Sealey** Raphael, Women and law in classical Greece. Chapel Hill 1990, Univ. NC. xi-202 p. $27.45; pa. $12.05. – ^RClasR 41 (1991) 128s (D. *MacDowell*); JHS 111 (1991) 237s (M. *Gagarin*).

e719 *Séguy* Jean, Lire WEBER et TROELTSCH [*Tribe* K., *Colliot-Thelène* C. ... *Vermeil* E.]: ArchivScSocRel 74 (1991) 187-202.

e720 **Sharashenidze** Dzh. H., ❻ Formy ekspluatatsii — Forms of labor utilization in the state economy of Sumer [2500-2000 B.C.]. Tbilisi 1986, Metsniereva. 173 p. – ᴿJAOS 111 (1991) 837s (D. C. *Snell*).

e721 ᴱ**Sigrist** Christian, *Neu* Rainer, Ethnologische Texte zum AT 1; Vor- und Frühgeschichte Israels 1989 ➤ 5,g365; 6,g689: ᴿBiKi 45 (1990) 164 (F. J. *Stendebach*).

e722 *a) Silva Airton* J. da, Leitura sociológica da Bíblia; – *b) Amaral da Costa* Julieta, Leitura espontânea da Bíblia a partir dos fatos de vida; – *c) Lara* Tiago, Leitura bíblica e leitura de nossa história — uma experiência de formação de agentes populares; – *d) Gruen* Wolfgang, Leitura libertadora também de textos não-libertadores da Bíblia: ➤ 99, ᶠMESTERS C., EstudosB 32 (1991) 74-84 / 24-26 / 33-38 / 85-88.

Smith Daniel L., The religion of the landless 1989 ➤ 1620.

e724 **Snowden** F. M., Before color prejudice; the ancient view of blacks. CM 1991 (pa. = 1983), Harvard Univ. ix-164 p.; 47 pl.; 3 maps. $13. 0-674-06381-5 [NTAbs 36,143].

e725 **Sourvinou-Inwood** Christiane, Studies in girls' transitions 1988 ➤ 6,g693: ᴿRÉG 104 (1991) 606s (Hélène *Cassimatis*).

e726 *Spickard* James V., A revised functionalism in the sociology of religion; Mary DOUGLAS's recent work: Religion 21 (L 1991) 141-164 [< ZIT 91,401].

e726* *Staden* P. van, *Aarde* A. G. van, Social description or social-scientific interpretation? A survey of modern scholarship: HervTSt 47,1 (1991) 55-87 [< NTAbs 36,9].

e727 **Synnove des Bouvrie** ..., Women in Greek tragedy, an anthropological approach: SymbOsl supp. 27. Ox 1990, UP. 394 p. – ᴿRÉG 104 (1991) 642s (Yvonne *Vernière*).

e728 **Tagliaferri** Maurizio, L'unità cattolica; studio di una mentalità: diss. Pont. Univ. Gregoriana, ᴰ*Martina* G. Roma 1991. 649 p. – RTLv 23, p. 566 [< DissA-C].

e729 **Tainter** Joseph A., The collapse of complex societies 1988 ➤ 4,h419; 5,g371: ᴿJField 18 (1991) 119-121 (G. W. *Bowersock*).

Tambasco Anthony J., In the days of Paul; the social world ... 1991 ➤ 5152.

e730 **Theissen** Gerd, Sociologia do movimento de Jesus, ᵀ*Fuchs* Werner, *Höhn* Annemarie 1989 ➤ 6,g700: ᴿEstudosB 26 (1990) 70-72 (L. *Garmus*).

e731 **Theissen** Gerd, *a)* The social setting of Pauline Christianity 1982 ➤ 63,270; 64,d746: ᴿNeotestamentica 25 (1991) 435-7 (J. C. *Latham*: four of the five essays are on Corinth). – *b)* The Gospels in context; social and political history in the Synoptic tradition [Lokalkolorit], ᵀ*Maloney* L. M. Mp 1991, Fortress. xvi-320 p.; 6 fig. $30. 0-8006-2499-8 [NTAbs 36,270].

e731* *Theissen* Gerd, Judentum und Christentum bei Paulus; sozialgeschichtliche Überlegungen zu einem beginnenden Schisma: ➤ 437, Paulus 1988/ 91, 331-356 (-9).

e732 *Thistlethwaite* Susan B., Great white fathers [five c. 1990 books on the 'Men's Movement' [BLY R.; MOORE R., NELSON J., KEEN S., GILMORE D.]: ChrCris 51 (1991s) 416-8.

e732* *Thompson* Lloyd A., Romans and Blacks 1989 ➤ 5,g375; 6,g703: ᴿAmHR 96 (1991) 1517s (A. R. *Birley*); Gnomon 63 (1991) 563-5 (H. *Sonnebend*); JRS 81 (1991) 183s (T. *Wiedemann*).

e733 *Tilley* Maureen A.,   Scripture as an element of social control; two martyr stories of Christian North Africa: HarvTR 83 (1990) 383-397.

e734 **Treggiari** Susan,   Roman marriage; iusti coniuges from the time of Cicero to the time of Ulpian.   Ox 1991, Clarendon.   xvi-578 p.   0-19- 814890-9.

e735 **Ulf** Christoph,   Die homerische Gesellschaft; Materialien zur analytischen Beschreibung and historischen Lokalisierung: Vestigia 43.   Mü 1990, Beck.   xi-285 p.

e736 *Vaillancourt* Jean-Guy,   Religion et société; une approche sociologique: SR 20 (1991) 137-150 (-199 *al.*).

e737 **Veyne** P.,   Bread and circuses; historical sociology and political pluralism [Le pain 1976 abridged by *Murray* Oswyn], [T]*Pearce* B.   L 1990, Lane. xxiii-492 p. £20. – [R]JHS 111 (1991) 239 (R. *Garland*); JRS 81 (1991) 164-8 (P. *Garnsey*).

e738 **Veyne** Paul,   Brot und Spiele; gesellschaftliche Macht und politische Herrschaft in der Antike [1976], [T]*Laermann* Klaus, *Brittnacher* Hans R.: Theorie und Gesellschaft 11.   Fra 1988, Campus.   698 p. DM 128. – [R]HZ 252 (1991) 128-130 (A. *Winterling*).

e739 *Vilatte* Sylvie,   La nourrice grecque; une question d'histoire sociale et religieuse: AntClas 60 (1991) 5-28.

e740 **Waldstein** Wolfgang,   Operae libertorum; Untersuchungen zur Dienstpflicht freigelassener Sklaven: ForAntSkl 19, 1986 ➤ 6,g709:   [R]Gnomon 63 (1991) 230-3 (W. *Nippel*).

e741 *Watkins* Clare,   Organizing the people of God; social-science theories of organization in ecclesiology: TS 52 (1991) 689-711.

e742 **Welwei** Karl-W.,   Unfreie im antiken Kriegsdienst, 3, 1988 ➤ 5,g380: [R]Gnomon 63 (1991) 36-39 (W. *Günther*); Klio 73 (1991) 327-331 (M. *Springer*); Latomus 50 (1991) 201-4 (J. *Annequin*).

e743 *Wessels* G. F., *Smit* D. J.,   Howard C. KEE's 'interrogating the text' [and J. H. ELLIOTT's critique of it]; a case-study [i.e. transferred from biblical to modern South Africa documents] in 'sociological interpretation':   Neotestamentica 25 (1991) 401-427.

e744 **Whale** Sheila,   The family in the 19th dynasty of Egypt; a study of the representation of the family in private tombs; Australian Centre for Egyptology 1.   Sydney 1989, La Haule.   xiv-305 p.; 13 pl.   0-85837-670-9 [BO 48,313].

e744* *Whitley* James,   Social diversity in Bronze Age Greece [not 'Crete' as p. ix]: AnBritAth 86 (1991) 341-365.

e745 **Wiedemann** Thomas,   Adults and children in the Roman empire 1989 ➤ 5,g383; 6,g713:   [R]AmHR 96 (1991) 952s (Beryl *Rawson*); ClasPg 86 (1991) 258-263 (K. *Bradley*); Gnomon 63 (1991) 517-521 (R. *Rilinger*: one of the many by-products of Philippe ARIE's 1960 History of Childhood); JRS 81 (1991) 178-180 (R. *Van Bremen*: unsatisfactory in comparison with DIXON S. 1988; RAWSON B. 1986); Phoenix 45 (Toronto 1991) 380s (Jacqueline *Tinson*).

e746 *Wlosok* Antonie,   *a*) Nihil nisi ruborem; über die Rolle der Scham in der römischen Rechtskultur [< GrazerB 9 (1930) 155-172]; – *b*) Vater und Vatervorstellungen in der römischen Kultur [< [E]*Tellenbach* H., Vaterbild 1978, 18-54. 192-200]: ➤ 280, Res humanae 1990, 84-100 / 35-83.

U5.3   **Commercium, oeconomica.**

e747 *Alvar* Jaime,   El contacto intercultural en los procesos de cambio: Gerión 8 (1990) 11-27.

e748 Amphores romaines et histoire économique: Actes du colloque de Sienne, 1986. R 1989, École Française. 660 p. 2-72830180-3/9. – ᴿLatomus 50 (1991) 730-2 (P. *Desy*).

e749 **Andreau** J., La vie financière dans le monde romain 1987 ⇥ 4,h437 ... 6,g718: ᴿMnemosyne 44 (1991) 490-7 (L. de *Ligt*).

e750 **Aubert** Jean-Jacques, Business managers in ancient Rome (200 B.C.- A.D. 250): diss. Columbia, ᴰ*Harris* W. NY 1991. 563 p. 92-09784. – DissA 52 (1991s) 4046-A.

e751 *Auld* Sylvia, The Mamluks and the Venetians; commercial exchange; the visual evidence: PEQ 123 (1991) 84-102; 8 fig.

e752 *Bagnall* Roger S., A trick a day to keep the tax man at bay? The prostitute tax in Roman Egypt: BASP 28 (1991) 5-12; pl. 1 [*McGinn* T., Helios 16 (1989) 79-110].

e753 *Ben-Tor* A., ◑ The commerce of Eretz-Israel in the Early Bronze Age: ⇥ 443, Commerce in Palestine 1980/90, 3-20 [cf. Eng. JJS 33 (1982) 3-18].

e754 *Bergoffen* Celia J., Overland trade in northern Sinai; the evidence of the late Cypriot pottery [< ᴰNYU 1989]: BASOR 184 (1991) 59-76.

e754* *Bisi* Anna Maria †, L'economia fenicia tra Oriente e Occidente: ⇥ 627, Fen. 2, 1987/91, 241-258.

e755 **Bousquet** Jean, Les comptes du quatrième et du troisième siècle: Corpus des Inscriptions de Delphes 2. P 1989, de Boccard. [vi-] 325 p.; XXIV pl. 2-86958-028-2.

e756 *a*) *Catling* H.W., Bronze Age trade in the Mediterranean, a view; – *b*) *Melas* Manolis, Mediterranean trade in the Bronze Age; a theoretical perspective; – *c*) *Snodgrass* A. M., Bronze Age exchange; a minimalist position; – *d*) *Sherratt* A. & S., From luxuries to commodities; the nature of Mediterranean Bronze Age trading systems: ⇥ 637, Bronze Age Trade 1989/91, 1-14 / 387-398 / 15-20 / 351-386.

e757 **Cozzo** Andrea, Kerdos 1988 ⇥ 4,h435 ... 6,g730: ᴿÉtClas 59 (1991) 78 (M. *Mund-Dopchie*); RBgPg 69 (1991) 195s (M. *Leroy*).

e758 **Csapo** Eric, An international community of traders in late 8th-7th c. B.C. Kommos in southern Crete: ZPapEp 88 (1991) 211-6.

e759 *Dan* Y., ◑ *a*) Internal and foreign trade in Palestine during the period of the Second Temple; – *b*) Economic life in Palestine during the Byzantine period: ⇥ 443, Commerce in Palestine 1980/90, 91-107 / 181-194.

e760 **de Martino** F., Wirtschaftsgeschichte des alten Rom [1979s], ᵀ1985 ⇥ 1,f190 ... 5,g400: ᴿMnemosyne 44 (1991) 273-7 (H. W. *Pleket*).

e761 **Depeyrot** G., Crises et inflation entre antiquité et Moyen Âge. P 1991. – ᴿRitNum 93 (1991) 247s (D. *Foraboschi*).

e762 *Drexhage* Hans-J. [⇥ 9656* *pōlēs*] Einige Bemerkungen zu den *émpora* und *kápēla* im römischen Ägypten (1.-3. Jh. n.C.): MünstHand 10,2 (1991) 28-46; Eng. franç. 46.

e763 **Drexhage** Raphaela, Untersuchungen zum römischen Osthandel 1988 ⇥ 5,g403; 6,g733: ᴿLatomus 50 (1991) 729s (L. de *Blois*); Tyche 6 (1991) 256-9 (W. *Scheidel*).

e764 **Duncan-Jones** Richard, Structure and scale in the Roman economy 1990 ⇥ 6,g734: ᴿGreeceR 38 (1991) 104 (T. *Wiedemann*).

e765 *Edens* Christopher, *Bawden* Garth, History of Taymā' and Hejazi trade during the first millennium B.C.: JESHO 32 (1989) 48-94; bibliog. 94-103; 3 fig. (map).

Elayi Josette, Économie des cités phéniciennes sous l'empire perse 1991 ⇥ d531.

e766 *French* A., Economic conditions in fourth-century Athens: GreeceR 38 (1991) 24-40.

e767 **Garlan** Yvon, Guerre et économie en Grèce ancienne 1989 → 5,g405; 6,g740:   ᴿAmHR 96 (1991) 1172 (I. *Morris*); RBgPg 69 (1991) 226 (P. *Salmon*); RFgIC 119 (1991) 63-69 (F. *Guizzi*).

e768 *Gentet* Didier, *Maucourant* Jérôme, Une étude critique de la hausse des prix à l'ère ramesside: Dialogues d'histoire ancienne 17,1 (Besançon 1991) 13-31.

e769 **Goldsmith** Raymond W., Premodern financial systems; a historical comparative study 1987 → 5,g407; 6,g745:   ᴿEngHR 106 (1991) 429s (H. van der *Wee*).

e770 **Gordon** Barry, The economic problem 1989 → 5,g408:   ᴿBL (1991) 15 (A. *Mayes*).

e771 **Gras** Michel, Trafics tyrrhéniens archaïques [diss. d'État]: BÉF 258, 1985 → 2,b970 ... 5,g409:   ᴿParPass 257 (1991) 154-8 (G. *Maddoli*).

e771* *Günbattı* Cahit, ❶ Certaines vues sur la destination de la terre publique et du Timar à l'époque babylonienne: Belleten 55,212 (1991) 1-12.

e772 ᴱ**Halstead** Paul, *O'Shea* John, Bad year economics; cultural responses to risk and uncertainty [anthropology, mostly archeology]. C 1989, Univ. x-145 p.; 40 fig. – ᴿAJA 95 (1991) 166s (P. *Bogucki*).

e773 *Hankel* Wilhelm, Rom – Weltstaat ohne Währungsgrenzen; vom *Aureus* über den Euro-Dollar zum ECH; Parallelen für heute: → 584, Kongress 1990, Gymnasium 98 (1991) 193-206.

e774 **Hatzopoulos** M. B., Actes de vente d'Amphipolis: Meletemata 14. P 1991, De Boccard. 111 p.; 19 fig. 960-7094-79-4.

e775 **Jongman** Willem, The economy and society of Pompeii: DutchMgHist 4, 1988 → 1988 5,g416; 6,g752:   ᴿHZ 252 (1991) 137s (H. *Halfmann*).

e776 **Katary** Sally L. D., Land tenure in the Ramesside period 1989 → 5, g112; £55:   ᴿBInstArch 27 (1990) 215-7 (E. P. *Uphill*).

e777 *a) Kayser* François, Un reçu bancaire thébain pour la taxe sur le natron; – *b) Zaghloul* El-Hussein, An agreement for sale from the reign of Ptolemy IX Sôter II in the museum of Mallawi: BIFAO 91 (1991) 219-223; 1 phot. / 255-263, pl. 75-76 avec facsimile en face.

e778 *Kirschenbaum* Aaron, Sons, slaves and freedmen in Roman commerce ᴰ1987 → 6,g257:   ᴿMünstHand 10,2 (1991) 121-3 (Raphaela *Czech-Schneider*).

e779 *Lewis* Naphtali, The governor's edict at Aizanoi [on prices; inaccurately reproduced from JRS in AnÉpig]: Ellinika 42 (1991) 15-20.

e780 *Ligt* L. de, The Roman peasantry; demand, supply, distribution between town and countryside, II. Supply, distribution and a comparative perspective: MünstHand 10,1 (1991) 33-76; deutsch 76s; franç. 77.

e781 **McCann** Anna M., *al.*, The Roman port and fishery of Cosa, a center of ancient trade 1987 → 3,f863 ... 6,g763:   ᴿIntJNaut 20 (1991) 177-180 (D. *Blackman*).

e782 **Mastrocinque** Attilio, L'ambra e l'Eridano [= Po] (studi sulla letteratura e sul commercio dell'ambra in età preromana): Univ. Trento fil/sto 3. Este 1991, Zielo. 163 p.; 85 fig.

e782* *Mazza* Mario, I modi della trasformazione; morte e trasfigurazione dell'economia nell'impero romano: RCuClasM 33 (1991) 115-141.

e783 *a) Michel* Cécile, Durhumid, son commerce et ses marchands; – *b) Lafont* Bernard, Un homme d'affaires à Karkemiš; – *c) Veenhof* Klaas R., Assyrian commercial activities in Old Babylonian Sippar; some new evidence: → 61, ᶠGARELLI P., Marchands 1991, 253-274 / 275-286 / 287-304.

e784 **Millett** Paul, Lending and borrowing in ancient Athens. C 1991, Univ. N 1989, d'Auria. 354 p. [RÉG 104,681].

e785 *Mirković* Miroslava, Flucht der Bauern, Fiskal- und Privatschulden: ➤ 149, ᶠSTRAUB J., 1989, 147-155.
e786 *Montgomery* Hugo, Old wine in new bottles? Some views of the economy of the early Church: Symbolae Osloenses 66 (1991) 187-201.
e787 *Mortel* Richard T., Prices in Mecca during the Mamlūk period: JESHO 32 (1989) 279-334.
e788 **Moscati** Sabatino, L'ancora d'argento; colonie e commerci fenici tra Oriente e Occidente: Arte storia archeologia 2. Mi 1989, Jaca. 241 p.; 83 fot.; maps. 88-16-66002-3.
e789 **Moxnes** Halvor, The economy of the Kingdom... Luke: OvBT 1988 ➤ 6,g767: ᴿCBQ 53 (1991) 144s (J. *Topel*: error-free).
e790 *a*) *Mutawally* Nawala al-, Economical texts from Išān-Mazyad; – *b*) *Janssen* C., *E'iltam paṭārum* [...debt, sin]; *awat ḫadê!*: ➤ 621, Rencontre 36, 1989/91, 45s / 77-107.
e791 **Nadjo** Léon, L'argent et les affaires à Rome des origines au IIᵉ siècle avant J.-C.; étude d'un vocabulaire technique. Lv/P 1989, Peeters/BIG. 544 p. – ᴿLatomus 50 (1991) 719-721 (Monique *Crampon*); RFgIC 119 (1991) 467-9 (A. *Traina*); RPg 64 (1990) 236-8 (Françoise *Gaide*).
e792 **Neusner** Jacob, The economics of the Mishnah 1990 ➤ 6,g768: ᴿTimes-LitSupp (L 14.VI.1991) 12 (H. *Maccoby*: omits or distorts the evidence) [< NTAbs 36,88].
e793 **Nicolet** Claude, Rendre à César; économie et société dans la Rome antique: Bibliothèque des histoires, 1988 ➤ 5,g429; 6,g770: ᴿGnomon 63 (1991) 175s (L. *Neesen*); Latomus 50 (1991) 726-8 (P. *Salmon*); TopO 1 (1991) 128-131 (J.-L. *Ferrary*); VDI 199 (1991) 182-6 (E. M. *Shtaerman* ❸).
e794 **Nissen** Hans J., *al.*, Frühe Schrift und Techniken der Wirtschaftsverwaltung im alten Vorderen Orient; Informationsspeicherung und -verarbeitung vor 5000 Jahren: Ausstellung [B 1990, Vorderasiatisches Museum] und Katalog. Bad Salzdetfurth 1991, Franzbecker. xii-222 p.; ill. 3-88120-110-6.
e795 *Oakman* Douglas E., The ancient economy in the Bible [... POLANYI K., WEBER M.]: BibTB 21 (1991) 34-39.
e796 **Orrieux** Claude, ZÉNON de Caunos 1985 ➤ 4,e627.f873; 5,g430: ᴿKlio 73 (1991) 647-9 (G. *Poethke*).
e797 **Pankiewicz** Ryszard, Fluctuations de valeur des métaux monétaires dans l'Antiquité romaine: PUnivEur 3/384. Fra 1989, Lang. 196 p. Fs 45. – ᴿGnomon 63 (1991) 561-3 (L. *Wierschowski*).
e798 *Peltenburg* E., Local exchange in prehistoric Cyprus; an initial assessment of picrolite: BASOR 282s (1991) 107-126 (17-35, his Kissonerga) [127-138, *Xenophontes* C. on picrolite].
e799 **Pinnock** Frances, *a*) Considerazioni sul sistema commerciale di Ebla protosiriana: ParPass 46,258ss (1991) 270-284; – *b*) Patterns of trade at Ebla in the third millennium B.C.: ➤ 626, AnASyr 40 (1989/90) 39-49; ❹ 131-5.
e800 *Radici Colace* Paola, Moneta, linguaggio e pensiero nei Padri della Chiesa tra tradizione pagana ed esegesi biblica: AugR 30 (1990) 405-421.
e801 *Rosivach* Vincent J., Some Athenian presuppositions about 'the poor': GreeceR 38 (1991) 189-198.
e802 *Roth* Martha T., *a*) The material composition of the Neo-Babylonian dowry: AfO 36s (1989s) 1-55; – *b*) The dowries of women of the Itti-Marduk-balāṭu family [250 economic transactions in Babylon 520 B.C.]: JAOS 111 (1991) 19-37.

e803 *a) Safrai* Z., **⊕** Trade in Palestine during the Roman period; – *b) Broshi* M., **⊕** Some methodical notes on commerce in antiquity; – *c) Dinur* Y., **⊕** Taxes on foreign and internal trade in Eretz Israel at the time of the Mishnah and Talmud: → 443, Commerce in Palestine 1980/90, 108-139 / 195-201 / 140-158.

e804 *Salomon* Richard, Epigraphic remains of Indian traders in Egypt: JAOS 111 (1991) 731-6.

e805 **Samons** Loren J.[III], Tribute and Athenian finance, 478 to 421 B.C.: diss. Brown. Providence 1991. 173 p. 92-04950. – DissA 52 (1991s) 3391-A.

e806 **Schmitz** Winfried, Wirtschaftliche Prosperität, soziale Integration und die Seebundpolitik Athens: QForAntW 1, 1988 → 4,h499; 5,g440: [R]ClasR 41 (1991) 137s (P. *Millett*).

e807 *Snell* Daniel C., Marketless trading [in Mesopotamian studies; A. OPPENHEIM & K. VEENHOF against K. POLANYI] in our time: JESHO 34 (1991) 129-141.

e807* **Sperberg** Daniel, Roman Palestine 200-400; money and prices[2] [= supp. + [1] 1974]: StNELangCu. Ramat-Gan 1991, Bar-Ilan Univ. 401 p.; ill. 965-226-147-5.

e808 **Stöver** Hans D., Macht und Geld im alten Rom 1989 → 5,g447: [R]HZ 253 (1991) 705s (T. *Pekáry*).

e808* **Stöver** Hans Dieter, Potere e denaro nella Roma antica [Macht 1989], [T]*Donati* Maurizio. Mi 1991, Rusconi. 212 p. Lit. 33.000. – [R]Letture 46 (1991) 569s (Carla *Castelli*).

e809 [F]TRÉHEUX Jacques, Comptes et inventaires dans la cité grecque, colloque [E]**Knoepfler** D. 1986/8 → 4,698; 5,g451: [R]RNum 33 (1991) 295s (D. *Gerin*).

e810 *Wachsmann* S., **⊕** The Syro-Canaanite maritime trade: → 443, Commerce in Palestine, 1980/90, 42-66 [Eng. awaited].

e811 *Warburton* D. A., KEYNES'sche Überlegungen zur altägyptischen Wirtschaft: ZäSpr 118 (1991) 76-85.

e812 *Wassink* Alfred, Inflation and financial policy under the Roman empire to the price edict of 301 A.D.: Historia 40 (1991) 465-493.

e813 *Wente* Edward F., A taxing problem: → 133*, [F]SCHULMAN A., BEgSem 10 (1989s) 169-174 + 2 pl.

e814 *Westhuizen* J. P. van der, Once again Turam-Ili [MIEROOP M. van de 1986]; an Ur III merchant?: JSemit 3 (1991) 122-8.

e815 *Zeeb* Frank, *a)* Studien zu den altbabylonischen Texten aus Alalaḫ I: Schuldscheine; – *b)* Tell Leilan und die Gründung des altbabylonischen Alalaḫ: UF 23 (1991) 405-434 + 4 pl. / 401-4.

U5.7 **Nomadismus;** ecology.

e816 [E]**Clutton-Brock** Juliet, The walking larder; patterns of domestication, pastoralism, and predation 1986/9 → 6,794: [R]Antiquity 65 (1991) 147-151 (A. J. *Legge*); BInstArch 27 (1990) 175s (L. *Copeland*).

e817 **Cribb** R., Nomads in archaeology: New Studies in Archaeology. C 1991, Univ. xiv-253 p. £35. 0-521-32881-0 [BL 92,27].

e818 **Fedeli** Paolo, La natura violata; ecologia e mondo romano: Prisma 125. Palermo 1990, Sellerio. 223 p. – [R]RFgIC 119 (1991) 346-8 (O. *Longo*).

e819 **Kent** Susan, Farmers as hunters, the implications of sedentism 1989 → 6,g788: [R]JField 18 (1991) 230-2 (R. W. *Preucel*); PrPrehSoc 57,2 (1991) 221s (F. *Pryor*).

e820 *McKenzie* Judith, The Beduin at Petra; the historical sources: Levant 23 (1991) 139-145 [-180, *Bienkowski* P., *Chlebik* B.].

e820* **Sadr** Karim, The development of nomadism in ancient northeast Africa [< diss. Southern Methodist 1988]. Ph 1991, Univ. Pennsylvania. xvi-180 p. [OIAc 2,26].

e821 **Sallares** Robert, The ecology of the ancient Greek world. L/Ithaca 1991, Duckworth/Cornell Univ. 588 p. £42. 0-7156-2339-7 /. – ᴿRÉG 104 (1991) 270s (J.-N. *Corvisier*).

e822 **Staubli** Thomas, Das Image der Nomaden im alten Israel und in der Ikonographie seiner sesshaften Nachbarn: OBO 107. FrS/Gö 1991, Univ./VR. xii-308 p.; ill. Fs 98. 3-7278-0769-5 / 3-525-53740-9 [BL 92,146].

U5.8 **Urbanismus.**

e823 **Abascal** Juan Manuel, *Espinosa* Urbano, La ciudad hispano-romana, privilegio y poder; pról. *Caro Baroja* Julio. Logroño 1989, Aparejadores. 254 p.; 21 fig. – ᴿGnomon 63 (1991) 613-7 (H. *Galsterer*).

e824 *Alcock* Susan E., Tomb cult and the post-classical polis: AJA 95 (1991) 447-467; 3 fig.

e824* *Bridge* J. David, The Pastor's patch, 3. Ministry in the suburbs [really on religious people's irrational retention of hymns like 'we plough the fields and scatter / The good seed on the land' and similar biblical images (though we never actually do these things); also Harvest Festivals in preference to any church mention of 'the joys of the town']: ExpTim 102 (1990s) 356-9 [but note 367s, *Bates* James B., The seed growing on its own; a family service for harvest-tide].

e825 **Demont** Paul, La cité grecque archaïque et classique et l'idéal de tranquillité: ÉtAnc, 1990 ➤ 6,g805: ᴿRÉG 104 (1991) 298s (A. *Wartelle*).

e825* ᴱ**Dogan** Mattei, *Kasarda* John D., The metropolis era. Newbury Park CA 1989, Sage. 716 p. (2 vol.) $45. 0-8039-3789-X; -90-3. – ᴿRExp 88 (1991) 283s (R. D. *Cochran*).

e826 *Ferrary* Jean-Louis, Le statut des cités libres dans l'Empire romain à la lumière des inscriptions de Claros: CRAI (1991) 557-577.

e827 **Fritz** Volkmar, Die Stadt im alten Israel: ArchäolBt, 1990 ➤ 6,g807; 3-406-34578-6: ᴿZDPV 107 (1991) 194-6 (R. *Schäfer*: some typos).

e828 **Frolov** Eduard, Ⓑ Roždenie grečeskogo polisa... Griechische Politogenese. Leningrad 1988, Univ. 230 p. – ᴿKlio 73 (1991) 689s (Simona *Preller*).

e829 **Grainger** John D., The cities of Seleukid Syria. Ox 1990, Clarendon. xi-253 p.; maps. 0-19-014694-9.

e830 **Gros** Pierre, *Torelli* Mario, Storia dell'urbanistica; il mondo romano 1988 ➤ 6,g809: ᴿLatomus 50 (1991) 915-9 (J. *Le Gall*).

e831 **Jacques** François, Les cités de l'Occident romain du Iᵉʳ siècle avant J.-C. au VIᵉ siècle après J.-C.; documents traduits et commentés: La roue à livres. P 1990, BLettres. 261 p. F 128. – ᴿGnomon 63 (1991) 367-9 (Helga *Botermann*).

e832 **Kasher** Aryeh, Jews and Hellenistic cities in Eretz Israel; relations of the Jews with the Hellenistic cities during the Second Temple period: Texte zum Antiken Judentum 21. Tü 1990, Mohr. 400 p. DM 110. 3-16-145241-0. – ᴿBAnglsr 11 (1990) 33s (D. M. *Jacobson*); JBL 111 (1992) 137-9 (D. J. *Harrington*: plenty of information; but Israel English typeset in Singapore).

e833 **Lampe** Peter, Die stadtrömischen Christen[2] 1989 [= [1]1987 + 15 p.]
➤ 3,f759 ... 6,g816: [R]RHPR 71 (1991) 241s (P. *Prigent*); Salesianum 53
(1991) 413s (E. *Fontana*); ZKG 102 (1991) 111-3 (R. *Klein*).
Baldovin John E., The urban character of Christian worship 1987
➤ 6,8170.

e834 **Levi** Mario A., La città antica; morfologia e biografia della ag-
gregazione urbana nell'antichità: ProbRicStoAnt 12, 1989 ➤ 6,g817; Lit.
230.000. 88-7062-649-0: [R]Gerión 8 (1990) 303s (J. L. *Riestra Rodríguez*);
JRS 81 (1991) 213-5 (W. *Jongman*: 100 brief descriptions of cities including Rome, China, pre-America, but virtually ignoring Ostia, Ephesos,
Pompeii); RÉAnc 92 (1990) 424s (J. *Annequin*).

e834* *a)* *Lotze* D., Die sogenannte Polis [GAWANTHA W. 1985]; – *b)*
Golubtsowa Ye., Polis et monarchie à l'époque des Séleucides: ➤ 591*e*,
ActAntH 33 (1990s) 237-242 / 243-6.

e835 **McKechnie** Paul, Outsiders in the Greek cities in the fourth century B.C.
L 1989, Routledge. viii-231 p. $45. 0-415-00340-7. – [R]ÉchMClas 35
(1991) 354-9 (V. D. *Hanson*).

e836 **Maisels** Charles K., The emergence of civilization; from hunting and
gathering to agriculture; cities and the State in the Near East. L 1990,
Routledge. xx-395 p.; ill.; maps. £45. 0-415-00168-4. – [R]BInstArch 27
(1990) 224s (H. *Crawford*: ambitious wide-ranging attempt); RAss 85
(1991) 189s (J.-L. *Huot*: reprend un titre de RENFREW).

e837 *Mar* Ricardo, La formazione dello spazio urbano nella città di Ostia:
MiDAI-R 98 (1991) 81-109; 12 fig.

e838 *Moggi* Mauro, Processi di urbanizzazione nel libro di PAUSANIA sul-
l'Arcadia: RFgIC 119 (1991) 46-62.

e839 *Morwood* James, Aeneas, Augustus, and the theme of the city: Greece-
R 38 (1991) 212-223.

e840 [E]**Murray** Oswyn, Price Simon, The Greek city 1990 ➤ 6,759: [R]ClasR
41 (1991) 387s (E. J. *Owens*); VDI 2199 (1991) 166-9 (S. G. *Karpyuk* ⊕).

e841 *Murray* Oswyn, History and reason in the ancient city: PapBritR 59
(1991) 1-14.

e842 **Niemann** Hermann M., Stadt, Land und Herrschaft — Skizzen und
Materialien zur Sozialgeschichte im monarchischen Israel: Hab.-Diss.
Rostock 1991, [D]*Schunck*. – TR 87 (1991) 513.

e843 *a)* *Nixon* Lucia, Price Simon, The size and resources of Greek cities; –
b) *Jameson* Michael, Private space and the Greek city; – *c)* *Lewis* David,
Public property in the city; – *d)* *Sourvinou-Inwood* Christiane, What is
Polis religion?: ➤ 403, The Greek city 1991, 137-170 / 171-195; 19 fig. /
245-263 / 295-322.

e844 **Owens** E. J., The city in the Greek and Roman world. L 1991, Routledge. xii-210 p.; 54 fig.; map. £30. – [R]GreeceR 38 (1991) 228 (W. H.
Manning).

e845 **Patch** Diana C., The origin and early development of urbanism in
ancient Egypt; a regional study: diss. Pennsylvania, [D]*O'Connor* D. Ph
1991. 611 p. 92-00380. – DissA 52 (1991s) 2604-A.

e846 **Polignac** François de, La nascita della città greca; culti, spazio e società
nei secoli VIII e VII a.C. Mi 1991, Jaca. 200 p. Lit. 25.000. – [R]Archeo
82 (1991) 128s (P. G. *Guzzo*).

e847 *a)* *Quirke* Stephen, 'Townsmen' in the Middle Kingdom; on the term
s n niwt in the Lahun Temple accounts; – *b)* *Müller-Wollermann*
R., Präliminierungen zur ägyptischen Stadt: ZäSpr 118 (1991) 141-9 /
48-54.

e848 **Regnier** Jérôme, Chrétiens dans la cité [... la culture]: L'horizon du croyant 11. P 1990, Desclée. 192 p. – ᴿEsprVie 101 (1991) 270s (L. *Debarge*).

e849 *Rohrbaugh* Richard L., The city in the Second Testament: BibTB 21 (1991) 67-75.

e849* *a) Rohrbaugh* Richard L., The pre-industrial city in Luke-Acts; urban social relations; – *b) Oakman* Douglas E., The countryside in Luke-Acts: → 450, Social World of Luke-Acts 1991, 125-149 / 151-179.

e850 **Sakellariou** M. B., The polis-state, definition and origin 1989 → 5,g505 ['origins']: ᴿClasR 41 (1991) 133-5 (A. M. *Snodgrass*); RÉG 104 (1991) 269s (G. *Liberman*).

e851 *Sancho* Laura, *Tò metéchein tês póleōs*; reflexiones acerca de las condiciones de pertenencia ciudadana entre Solón y Periclés: Gerión 9 (1991) 59-86.

e852 *Sarigiannis* G., ⑥ *Phyletikes hypodiaireseis kai poleodomikes ennoies...* Tribal divisions and urban planning for the ancient Hebrews according to the Hebrew Vorlage and the LXX tradition: DeltioVM (1989) 49-87 [< TAth 61 (1990) 333-5, P. *Simotas*].

e853 *Schofield* Malcolm, The Stoic idea of the city. C 1991, Univ. xii-164 p. 0-521-39470-8.

e854 **Segal** Arthur, Town planning and architecture in Provincia Arabia; the cities along the Via Traiana Nova in the 1st-3d centuries [Philadelphia, Gerasa... diss.]: BAR-Int 4. Ox 1988. 127 p.; 176 fig. – ᴿGnomon 63 (1991) 283-6 (K. S. *Freyburger*).

e855 *a) Snodgrass* A. M., Archaeology and the study of the Greek city; – *b) Rihll* T. E., *Wilson* A. G., Modelling settlement structures in ancient Greece; new approaches to the polis; – *c) Millett* Martin, Roman towns and their territories; an archaeological perspective; – *d) Wallace-Hadrill* Andrew, Elites and trade in the Roman town: → 601, City 1986/91, 1-23 / 59-95 / 169-189 / 241-272.

e856 **Stambaugh** John E., The ancient Roman city 1988 → 4,h557... 6,g832: ᴿÉchMClas 36 (1991) 126-9 (J.-P. *Thuillier*); Mnemosyne 44 (1991) 289s (H. W. *Pleket*).

e857 **Stein-Hölkeskamp** Elka, Adelskultur und Polisgesellschaft; Studien zum griechischen Adel in archaischer und klassischer Zeit. Stu 1989, Steiner. 272 p. DM 66. – ᴿClasR 41 (1991) 135s (Lorna *Hardwick*).

e858 **Todd** Stephen R., Citizenry divisions in ancient Greek *poleis*; military aspects of their origin and development: diss. Vanderbilt, ᴰ*Drews* R. Nv 1991. 258 p. 91-25318. – DissA 52 (1991s) 1039-A.

e858* **Uphill** Eric P., Egyptian towns and cities: Shire Egyptology 8, 1988 → 6,g835: ᴿFolOr 27 (1990) 264s (J. *Śliwa*).

e859 ᴱ**Weiss** Harvey, Origins of cities in dry-farming Syria and Mesopotamia 1984/6 → 2,d69... 6,g836: ᴿSyria 67 (1990) 751s (J.-Y. *Monchambert*).

U5.9 *Demographia*, **population-statistics.**

e860 *Brulé* Pierre, Enquête démographique sur la famille grecque antique; étude de listes de politographie d'Asie mineure d'époque hellénistique (Milet et Ilion): RÉAnc 92 (1990) 233-258.

e861 *Finkelstein* Israel, A few notes on demographic data from recent generations and ethnoarchaeology: PEQ 122 (1990) 47-52.

e862 **Gallo** Luigi, Alimentazione e demografia della Grecia antica; pref. *Nen-*

ci G. 1984 → 1,f301... 4,h163: [R]RÉG 104 (1991) 619 (F. *Hinard*: conférences 1984, Éc. Française de Rome).

e863 **Hansen** Mogens H., Three studies on Athenian demography 1988 → 4,h574: [R]Mnemosyne 44 (1991) 487-9 (F. *Naerebout*).

e864 **Rösler** Roland, Der Menschen Zahl oder Das zerstörte Sodom ist Euer Land (Jes 1,7). Stein/Rh 1989, Christiana. 335 p. – [R]ForumKT 6 (1990) 80s (Sabine *Düren*).

e865 **Sgarlata** Mariarita, Ricerche di demografia storica; le iscrizioni tardo-imperiali di Siracusa: Studi di Antichità Cristiana 45. R 1991, Pontificio Istituto di Archeologia Cristiana. 156 p.; 10 fig.

U6 **Narrationes peregrinorum et exploratorum;** *Loca sancta.*

e866 **Amman** Ludwig, Östliche Spiegel; Ansichten vom Orient im Zeitalter seiner Entdeckung durch den deutschen Leser 1800-1850: Germanistische TStud 32. Hildesheim 1989. 178 p. DM 29,80. – [R]WeltOr 22 (1991) 158s (H. *Fähndrich*).

e867 *Baldauf* Ingeborg, Mahmud XŮǦA BEHBUDIJ in Palästina; der Reisebericht eines Ğadidisten aus Samarkand (1914): ZDPV 107 (1991) 155-175.

e868 [TE]**Busi** Giulio, 'Ovadyah Yare da BERTINORO, Lettere dalla Terra Santa [1487-9]: Gli Erranti 3. Rimini 1991, Luisè. 103 p. 88-85050-56-5.

e869 [E]**Cassuto Salzmann** M., *Cassuto* D., Diario di un viaggio in Terra Santa di Moisè Vita CAFSUTO da Firenze 1734, estratto da un manoscritto italiano inedito, ☯ [T]*Rofé* J. J 1983, Kedem Yad Leyakkirenu. – [R]Henoch 12 (1990) 396s (B. *Chiesa*: memorial for Nathan Cassuto, b. 1909, chief rabbi of Florence, along with a volume of his writings [E]*Carpi* D. 1986).

e870 **De Sandoli** S., [cf. → 6,g890 ital.] The peaceful liberation of the Holy Places in the XIVth cent.; the third return of the Frankish or Latin clergy to the custody and service of the Holy Places through official negotiations in 1333: StOrChrMg 3. Cairo 1990, Franciscan Center. 99 p.; 4 plans [RHE 86,92*].

e871 [E]**Eade** John, *Sallnow* Michael J., Contesting the sacred; the anthropology of Christian pilgrimage [6 papers from 1988 Roehampton 'new agenda' for evaluating pilgrimages as 'a realm of competing discourses']. NY 1991, Routledge. xi-158 p. $50; pa. $18. 0-415-04360-3; pa. -1-1 [TDig 39,155].

e871* *Gessel* Wilhelm M., Frau Egeria als Pilgerin im Heiligen Land: Klerusblatt 71 (Mü 1991) 209-218 [< ZIT 91,680].

e872 *Graboïs* A., Les pèlerins occidentaux en Terre Sainte au Moyen Âge; une minorité étrangère dans sa patrie spirituelle: StMedv 30 (1989) 15-48 [< RSPT 75,171].

e873 **Guérin Dalle Mese** Jeannine, Égypte; la mémoire et le rêve, itinéraires d'un voyage, 1320-1601: Archivum Romanicum Bt 1/237. F 1991, Olschki. 657 p. 88-222-3822-2.

e874 [TE]*Iwaszkiewicz* Piotr, ☯ Itinerarium Burdigalense [Jerusalem usque] enarratur atque in linguam polonam transfertur: Meander 46 (1991) 63-75.

e874* **Jackson** Bernard, Pilgrim in the Holy Land. L 1991, Chapman. £8. – [R]Tablet 245 (1991) 1186 (D. *Forrester* briefly: up-to-date and easy for first-time pilgrims).

e875 ᵀᴱNatalucci Nicoletta, Egeria, Pellegrinaggio in Terra Santa: Bt Patrist. F 1991, Nardini. 333 p. 88-404-2017-7.

e875* ᴱSancisi-Weerdenburg Heleen, Drijvers Jan W., Through traveller's eyes; European travellers on the Iranian monuments: Achaemenid History 7. Leiden 1991, NedInstNabOosten. xi-223 p. 90-6258-407-1 [OIAc 2,26].

e876 Shaw J. M., The pilgrim people of God; recovering a biblical motif. Mp 1990, Augsburg. ix-245 p. $20. 0-8066-2471-X [NTAbs 36,131].

e877 a) Soares Sebastião A. G., Vieira de Mello Agostinha, A romaria dos pobres de Deus – leitura do Salmo 124; – b) Comblin José, A romaria no Novo Testamento; – c) Araújo Luis C., A Igreja peregrina: EstudosB 28 ('Romeiros de ontem e de hoje; peregrinação e romaria na Bíblia' 1990) 17-32 / 33-41 / 63-68.

e877* Stratkötter Rita, Von Kairo nach Mekka – Sozial- und Wirtschafts-geschichte der Pilgerfahrt nach den Berichten des Ibrāhīm RIFᴬT BĀŠĀ 1901-3-4-8]. B 1991, Schwarz. viii-392 p. [ZDMG 142,384, S. Fliedner].

e878 Tangban O. E., The Hajj and the Nigerian economy 1960-1981: JRelAf 21 (1991) 241-255.

e878* Tardieu Michel, Les paysages reliques; routes et haltes syriennes d'Isi-dore à Simplicius: Bt ÉPHÉR 94. Lv 1990, Peeters. 209 p.; ill. [TR 88,77].

e879 Theodorou Evangelos D., ⊚ ETHERIA's 'Itinerary' and its significance for liturgics: TAth ... 61 (1990) 129-143; Eng. 903.

e880 Väänänen Veikko, Le journal-épître d'Égérie 1987 ↠ 3,f964 ... 5,g539: ᴿRBgPg 69 (1991) 216-222 (P. Hamblenne).

e881 Vikan Gary, 'Guiden by land and sea'; pilgrim art and pilgrim travel in early Byzantium: ↠ 47*, ᶠENGEMANN J., Tesserae 1991, 74-92; pl. 8-11.

Walker P. W. L., Holy city, holy places? 1990 ↠ d350.

e882 Werbner Richard P., Ritual passage, sacred journey; the form, process, and organization of religious movement. Wsh/Manchester 1989, Smith-sonian/Univ. 396 p. $32.50. 0-87474-976-X. – ᴿJRelAfr 21 (1991) 86-88 (W. MacGaffey).

e883 Wilkinson J., Jerusalem pilgrimage 1099-1185: 1988 ↠ 5,g563; 6,g898: ᴿPEQ 122 (1990) 77 (J. Taylor).

u7   Crucigeri – The Crusades.

e883* Balard Michel, Les Croisades; les noms, les thèmes, les lieux: 1988 ↠ 5,g567: ᴿMeditHR 6 (1991) 116s (B. Arbel: a small encyclopedia).

e884 Barz Wolf-Dieter, Der Malteserorden als Landesherr auf Rhodos und Malta im Licht seiner strafrechtlichen Quellen aus dem 14. und 16. Jt.: QFor 5. B 1990, Schmidt. 210 p. – ᴿTPhil 66 (1991) 598s (R. Sebott).

e885 Breuil Paul du, La chevalerie et l'Orient; l'influence de l'Orient sur la naissance et l'évolution de la chevalerie européenne au Moyen Âge. P 1990, Maisnie. 192 p. 2-85707-415-8 [OIAc 2,17].

e886 Chazan Robert, The facticity of medieval narrative; a case study of the Hebrew First Crusade narratives: AJS 16 (1991) 31-56.

e887 Cole Penny J., The preaching of the crusades to the Holy Land, 1095-1270: Medieval Academy 98. CM 1991, Med. Acad. of America. xiv-281 p. $35 [RHE 86,349*]. – ᴿCathHR 77 (1991) 674-6 (J. M. Powell).

e888 Daoust J., L'Église latine à Jérusalem [liée aux Croisades: Dalmais I., MondeB 68, 1991]: EsprVie 101 (1991) 372-4.

e889 **Edbury** Peter W., The kingdom of Cyprus and the Crusades. C 1991, Univ. xviii-241 p.; ill.; maps. £27,50 [TR 88,166].

e890 **Efthimiou** M. B., Greeks and Latins on Cyprus [... Fourth Crusade] 1988 ➤ 5,g601: ᴿMid-Stream 28 (1989) 330s (J. *Gros*).

e890* *Forey* A. J., The military orders and the ransoming of captives from Islam (twelfth to early fourteenth centuries): StMonast 33 (Montserrat 1991) 259-279.

e891 *Grosse* R., Überlegungen zum Kreuzzugsaufruf Eugens III. von 1145-46: Francia 18,1 (1991) 85-92 [< RHE 87,21*].

e891* ᴱ**Hazard** H., *Zacour* N., Impact of the Crusades on Europe: Crusades 6. Madison 1990, Univ. Wisconsin. xxiv-703 p. $40. – ᴿCathHR 77 (1991) 298s (A. *Luttrell*).

e892 **Hillenbrand** Carole, [IBN EL-AZRAQ, Chronik], A Muslim principality in Crusader times, the early Artuqid state: Uitg. Ned. Inst. 86. İstanbul 1990. xiv-260 p. *f*89 [OLZ 87,416, W. *Madelung*].

e893 *Hoveida* Fereydoun, Le complexe de Saladin [plutôt 'le syndrome': devenu héros mythique pour avoir libéré la Palestine et la Syrie...: Revue des Deux Mondes, janv. 1991]: EsprVie 101 (1991) 328-330 (J.*Daoust*).

e894 **Irwin** Robert, The Middle East in the Middle Ages; the early Mamluk Sultanate 1250-1382. L 1986, Croom Helm. 180 p. – ᴿJESHO 32 (1989) 119s (C. *Cahen*, also on HOLT P. 1986).

e895 **Lawrence** T. H. [of Arabia], Crusader castles [visited in England 1906, France 1907; published 1936], ᴱ*Pringle* Denys 1988 ➤ 5,g880; 6,g915: ᴿSpeculum 66 (1991) 187-9 (J. *Rosser*).

e896 **Lewis** Archibald R., Nomads and Crusaders A.D. 1000-1368 [also China, India]. Bloomington 1988, Indiana Univ. x-213 p.; map. – ᴿByZ 83 (1991) 484s (R.-J. *Lilie*); ChH 59 (1990) 396-8 (J. A. *Brundage*); Speculum 66 (1991) 663-5 (Angeliki E. *Laiou*).

e897 *Linder* A., The liturgy of the liberation of Jerusalem [July 15, 1099: London BL addit. 8027ff, 134r-135r]: MedvSt 52 (1990) 110-131 [< RSPT 75,161].

e898 **Lloyd** Simon, English society and the Crusade 1216-1307: 1988 ➤ 6, g920; £30: ᴿHeythJ 32 (1991) 409-411 (B. *Hamilton*).

e898* **Mayer** H. E., The Crusades²ʳᵉᵛ [¹1965 ᵀ1972 also by *Gillingham* J.] 1988 ➤ 4,h612...6,g922: ᴿChH 59 (1990) 232-4 (J. E. *Lynch*).

e899 *Mayer* Hans Eberhard, *a*) Fontevrault und Bethanien; kirchliches Leben in Anjou und Jerusalem im 12. Jahrhundert: ZKG 102 (1991) 14-44; – *b*) Die antiochenische Regentschaft Balduins II. von Jerusalem im Spiegel der Urkunden: DtArchivErfMA 42 (Köln 1991) 559-... [< ZIT 92,313].

e900 **Pernoud** Régine, La femme au temps des croisades. P 1990, Stock. – ᴿEsprVie 101 (1991) 53-55 (J. *Daoust*: 'quand la femme n'avait pas besoin d'être féministe').

e901 **Powell** James M., Anatomy of a crusade, 1213-1221: 1986 ➤ 3,g13; 6,g924: ᴿJAAR 59 (1991) 413-5 (J. H. *Lynch*).

e902 **Powell** James M., Muslims under Latin rule, 1100-1300. Princeton 1990, Univ. viii-221 p. $30. – ᴿCathHR 77 (1991) 676s (J. *Muldoon*).

e903 *Prawer* Joshua, The history of the Jews in the Latin Kingdom 1988 ➤ 5,g585; 6,g924: ᴿEngHR 106 (1991) 977 (J. *Riley-Smith*).

e904 *Pringle* Denis, Survey of castles in the Crusader kingdom of Jerusalem 1989; a preliminary report: Levant 23 (1991) 87-91; map.

e904* *a*) *Pringle* D. P., Pottery as evidence of trade in the crusader states [< ᴱ*Airaldi* G., I Comuni italiani nel Regno crociato di Gerusalemme 1986, 449-475]: – *b*) *Prior* J., ● The export of food provisions and armaments from the Kingdom of Sicily to the Kingdom of Jerusalem [< AsAfrSt 22 (1988) 127-146]: ➤ 443, Commerce in Palestine 1980/90, 239-259 / 260-279.

e905 **Rheinheimer** Martin, Das Kreuzfahrerfürstentum Galiläa: Kieler Werkstücke C1. Fra 1990, Lang. 299 p.; 3 maps. DM 89 [DLZ 113,80, B. *Brentjes*].

e906 **Riley-Smith** Jonathan, Les Croisades [1990 ➤ 6,g929],^{T}. P 1990, Pygmalion. 329 p. [RHE 87,55*]. − ^{R}RHist 284 (1990) 470s (J. *Richard*).

e907 *Riley-Smith* J., Johanniter / Kreuzzüge: ➤ 681, LexMA 5 (1990) 613-5 / 1508-19.

e909 *Sarnowsky* Jürgen, Die Johanniter und Smyrna 1344-1402 (1. Teil): RömQ 86 (1991) 215-251.

e910 *Savigni* R., 'Militia Christi' e crociata nei secoli XI-XII [Semaine XIᵉ 28.VIII-1.IX.1989]: Rivista di Storia della Chiesa in Italia 44 (1990) 257-267 [< RSPT 75,171].

e911 **Schein** S., *a)* 'Fideles crucis'; the papacy, the West, and the recovery of the Holy Land, 1274-1314. Ox 1991, Clarendon. x-310 p. [RHE 86,91*]; − *b)* Die Kreuzzüge als volkstümlich-messianische Bewegungen; − *c) Mayer* Hans-Eberhard, Zur Geschichte der Johanniter im 12. Jahrhundert: DtAErMA 47 (1991) 119-138 / 139-160 [< zıт 91,806].

e911* ᴱWienand Adam, *al.*, Der Johanniterorden, der Malteserorden³ʳᵉᵛ [¹1969]. Köln 1988, Wienand. 704 p. − ^{R}HistJb 111 (1991) 497 (U. *Knefelkamp*).

U8 *Communitates Terrae Sanctae* − **The Status Quo.**

e912 **Abu Nowar** Maʿan, The history of the Hashemite Kingdom of Jordan, I. The creation and development of Transjordan [diss. St. Antony's 1987]: St. Antony's Middle East Monographs 21. Ox 1989, Ithaca press. [xii-] 313 p. £24. − ^{R}BSO 54 (1991) 163 (J. *Rudd*: informative, tendentious, badly edited).

e913 **Aronson** Ran, ❽ *Ha-Baron wᵉha-Mošabôt*, Baron Rothschild and the Jewish colonies in Erez-Israel 1882-1890. J 1990, Yad Ben-Zvi. 322 p. − ^{R}Zion 56 (1991) 349-351 (D. *Gilead* ❽).

e914 **Ateek** Naim S., *a)* Justice and only justice 1989 ➤ 5,g595; 6,g941: ^{R}Vidyajyoti 55 (1991) 208 (S. *Arokiasamy*). − *b)* La giustizia e solo la giustizia seguirai; una teologia per la riconciliazione nel conflitto israelo-palestinese ᵀ; contributi di *Cavallotto* Stefano. Assisi 1991, Cittadella. 406 p. Lit. 30.000. − ^{R}RasT 32 (1991) 625 (G. *Mattai*: pastore anglicano).

e915 *Balta* Paul, La naissance des États modernes [au Proche-Orient: Notre Histoire, Spécial Golfe 80, 1991]: EsprVie 101 (1991) 645-7 (J. *Daoust*).

e916 **Betts** Robert B., The Druze 1988 ➤ 4,h624; $22.50: ^{R}AmHR 96 (1991) 222s (P. S. *Khoury*).

e917 *Boujamra* John L., Christianity in Greater Syria after Islam: StVlad 35 (1991) 223-239.

e918 *a)* **Briquel-Chatonnet** Françoise, Rôle de la langue et de l'écriture syriaques dans l'affirmation de l'identité chrétienne au Proche-Orient; − *b) Hadas-Lebel* Mireille, L'Hébreu; écriture et culture: ➤ 630, Phoinikeia 1989/91, 257-274 / 717-725.

e919 **Cannuyer** Christian, Les Coptes: Fils d'Abraham, 1990 ➤ 6,g943: ^{R}EsprVie 101 (1991) 536 (M. *Delahoutre*); RHE 86 (1991) 477 (C. *Soetens*).

e920 *Caprile* Giovanni, La Santa Sede e lo Stato d'Israele: CC 142 (1991,1) 352-360.

e921 *Carey* John J., [Arab/Israeli] Jerusalem; old myths and new realities: TTod 48 (1991s) 195-201.

e922 **Caspi** Joshua, Policing the Holy Land, 1918-1957; the transition from a colonial to a national model of policing and changing conceptions of police accountability: diss. CityU NY 1991, ᴰ*Price* Barbara. 133 p. 91-19616. – DissA 52 (1991s) 649s.

e923 *Cohen* Avraham, ❻ The 'Alliance Israélite Universelle' and the Iranian Zionist movement: HUCA 62 (1991) ❻ 1-27.

e924 **Cohen** Mitchell, De la rêve sioniste à la réalité israélienne, ᵀ*Grasset* Jean-B. P 1990, Découverte. 403 p. – ᴿRÉJ 150 (1991) 474-7 (A. *Boyer*).

e925 *Cragg* Kenneth, The Arab Christian; a history in the Middle East. Louisville 1991, W-Knox. $30. 0-664-21945-4 [TDig 39,257].

e926 **Dann** Uriel, King Hussein and the challenge of Arab radicalism; Jordan, 1955-1967: Studies in ME History. NY 1989, Ox-UP. x-206 p. $30. – ᴿAmHR 96 (1991) 574s (J. *Jankowski*).

e927 *a*) *Fiey* J., Juifs et chrétiens dans l'Orient syriaque; – *b*) *Suárez Fernández* L., Iglesia y Judíos en España durante la Edad Media: Hispania Sacra 40,82 ('Judíos y cristianos en la cuenca mediterránea' 1988) 933-954 / 893-910 [< Judaica 46,188].

e928 *Gertz* Nurith, Changes in [modern Israel] ideological models: Semiotica 86 (1991) 247-255.

e929 **Hajjar** Joseph, L'Europe et les destinées du Proche-Orient (1815-1946). Damas, I-III jusqu'à 1883; IV 1908-14 en cours d'impression: Tlass. – ᴿEsprVie 101 (1991) 640 (J.-C. *Meyer*).

e930 **Hamada** Louis B., Understanding the Arab world. Nv 1990, Nelson. xvi-216 p. $13 pa. – ᴿBS 148 (1991) 373s (E. H. *Merrill*: useful and factual but too often inaccurate).

e931 **Jafari** Walid A. al-, The Palestinian national movements inside Israel; a study of their emergence, structure and objectives: diss. Exeter 1991. 398 p. BRDX-94505. – DissA 52 (1991s) 3399-A.

e932 **Jarrah** Dina I., Palestinian women; the status and roles of Palestinian women on the West Bank: diss. Golden Gate Univ. 319 p. 91-25537. – DissA 52 (1991s) 1546s-A.

e933 *Katz* Yossi, ❻ The formulation of the Jewish Agency's proposal for the boundaries of the partition, 1937-1938: Zion 56 (1991) 401-439; 4 maps.

e934 **Khoury** Adel T., Was ist los in der islamischen Welt? Die Konflikte verstehen. FrB 1991, Herder. 156 p. DM 16,80. – ᴿOLZ 86 (1991) 540-2 (F. *Steppat*); ZkT 113 (1991) 497 (K. H. *Neufeld*).

e935 **Kolsky** Thomas A., Jews against Zionism; the American Council for Judaism, 1942-1948. Ph 1990, Temple Univ. vi-269 p. $40. 0-87722-694-6 [TDig 39,70].

e936 **Konzelmann** Gerhard, Der Golf; vom Garten Eden zur Weltkrisen-region. Ha 1991, Hoffmann & K. 476 p. 3-455-08396-X [OIAc 2,22].

e937 **Krämer** Gudrun, The Jews in modern Egypt, 1914-1952 [< 1982 Wsb] 1989 → 6,g961: ᴿAJS 16 (1991) 199-210 (M. M. *Laskier*); JAOS 111 (1991) 170s (D. M. *Reid*).

e938 *Küng* Hans, A vision of peace for the Middle East [... possible only if there is peace among religions]: Tablet 145 (1991) 260-2.4 (294s, Sharing the Holy City).

e939 ᴱ**Kushner** David, Palestine in the Late Ottoman period 1986 → 4,h641: ᴿOLZ 86 (1991) 536-9 (G. *Höpp*).

e939* **Landau** J. M., ❻ *Toledot*... The Jews in Ottoman Egypt, 1517-1914. J 1988, Misgav Yerušalayim. 670 p. [RHE 87,320*].

e940 *Laurens* Henry, France et Liban; panorama historique: Revue des Deux Mondes (sept. 1990) [< EsprVie 101 (1991) 51-53 (J. *Daoust*)].

e941 **McKiddy** Gary E., The Arabs of the modern Middle East; a primer for teachers; diss. Illinois State 1990, ^D*McBride* Lawrence W. 575 p. 91-01121. – DissA 52 (1991s) 295-A.

e942 **Minerbi** Sergio I., The Vatican and Zionism; conflict in the Holy Land, 1895-1925 ✪, ^T*Schwarz* Arnold: Studies in Jewish History. NY 1990, Oxford-UP. xiv-253 p. $25. 0-19-505892-5 [TDig 39,74].

e943 *Müller* C. D. G., Kopten: → 681, LexMA 5 (1991) 1438-41.

e944 *Nicholl* Donald, Night thoughts in East Jerusalem, 2. The angel's challenge [... 'In some respects the Palestinians are suffering worse oppression than was endured by opponents of the regime ruling Germany between 1933 and 1938' (ed.)]: Tablet 245 (1991) 1104s; letters 1146s...

e945 **Pawel** Ernst, The labyrinth of exile; a life of Theodore HERZL. NY 1989, Farrar-SG. 665 p. $30. – ^RCritRR 4 (1991) 395-7 (J. *Neusner*; far inferior to A. ELON on 'the most important Jew of the nineteenth century').

e945* **Polish** David, 'Give us a king...' Legal-religious sources of Jewish sovereignty. Hoboken 1990, KTAV. 180 p. $20. 0-88125-309-X. – ^RExpTim 102 (1990s) 348s (Julia *Neuberger*: right questions but no answers; should moral values be abandoned for Israel-security? how does Jewish law view the Palestinians?).

e946 **Raheb** Mitri, Das reformatorische Erbe unter den Palästinensern; zur Entstehung der evangelisch-lutherischen Kirche in Jordanien: LuthKGGestalten 11. Gü 1990, Mohn. 317 p. DM 36 [TR 88,404, W. *Schwaigert*].

e946* **Rosenzweig** Rafael N., The economic consequences of Zionism. Leiden 1989, Brill. xiii-260 p. – ^RZion 56 (1991) 455-8 (E. *Kleiman*).

e947 ^E**Ruether** Rosemary, *Ellis* Marc, Beyond occupation; American Jewish, Christian and Palestinian voices for peace. Boston 1990, Beacon. $25. – ^RCCurr 40 (1990s) 552-5 (G. B. *Pepper*).

e948 **Ruether** R. R. & H. J., The wrath of Jonah 1989 → 5,g612; 6,g973*: ^RJQR 81 (1990s) 467-470 (F. H. *Littell*); JRel 71 (1991) 459-461 (S. *Sandler*: one-sided and inaccurate).

e949 *Sélis* Claude, Les Syriens orthodoxes et catholiques: Fils d'Abraham 1988 → 5,g616; 6,g978: ^RAngelicum 68 (1991) 135s (G. *Grasso*).

e950 *Shaham* Ron, Christian and Jewish *waqf* in Palestine during the late Ottoman period: BSO 54 (1991) 460-472.

e951 ^E**Shamir** Shimon, The Jews of Egypt; a Mediterranean society in modern times. Boulder 1987, Westview. xxi-304 p. – ^RJQR 82 (1991s) 566-8 (Rachel *Simon*).

e952 **Sokolowicz** J., Israeliani e Palestinesi; le radici, i fatti, le prospettive del conflitto mediorientale. Mi 1989, Garzanti. 141 p. Lit. 18.000 pa. – ^RProtestantesimo 46 (1991) 205-8 (J. A. *Soggin*, anche su CHANCOUR E. 1990); 325, commento di *Rochat* G.

e953 *a) Stein* Kenneth W., A historiographic review of literature on the origins of the Arab-Israeli conflict; – *b) Khalidi* Rashid, Arab nationalism; historical problems in the literature; – *c) Reich* Bernard, Themes in the history of the state of Israel: AmHR 96 (1991) 1450-1465 / 1363-1373 / 1466-1478.

e954 **Stillman** Norman A., The Jews of Arab lands in modern times. Ph 1991, Jewish Publication. xxviii-604 p.; ill. [RelStR 18,158, Rachel *Simon*].

e955 **Stoffregen-Pedersen** Kirsten, Les Éthiopiens: Fils d'Abraham. Turnhout 1990, Brepols. 201 p.; 32 fig.; map. Fb 750. – RisprVie 101 (1991) 535 (M. *Delahoutre*); RHE 86 (1991) 477 (A. de *Halleux*).

e956 **Timm** Stefan, Das christlich-koptische Ägypten in arabischer Zeit [I. 1984 → 65.d376; 4.1988 → 4,h654], 5. (Q-S): TAVO B-41/5. Wsb 1991, Reichert. p. 2086-2427. 3-88226-212-5 [OIAc 1,26].

e957 *White* Patrick, [Linda BRAYER,] An Israeli champion of the Palestinians: Tablet 245 (1991) 156s.

e958 **Wilson** Mary C., King Abdullah 1988 → 6,g981: RJAOS 111 (1991) 606s (P. *Sluglett*).

e959 *Zananiri* G., [Le monde arabe et les chrétiens] La migration des chrétiens du Moyen-Orient: EsprVie [100 (1990)] 101 (1991) 620-4.

e960 **Zarley** Kermit, Palestine [1. (2. Babylon; 3. Christ)] is coming; the revival of ancient Philistia [i.e. Palestinians should be relocated from West Bank to Gaza area]. Hannibal MO 1990. 269 p. $13. – RBS 148 (1991) 241s (J. F. *Walvoord*: dubious).

XX. Historia Scientiae Biblicae

Y1 **History of Exegesis** 1. **General.**

e961 **Alkier** Stefan, Urchristentum; Geschichte und Theologie einer exegetischen Disziplin: Diss. DSchrage W. Bonn 1991s. – RTLv 23, p. 542.

e962 **Altaner** Berthold, *Stuiber* Alfred, ● Patrologia [⁸1978], TPachciarek P. Wsz 1990, Pax. 733 p. – RTLZ 116 (1991) 515s (J. *Rohde*: stark erweiterte Indices).

e963 **Balthasar** H. U. v., Les grands textes sur le Christ: JJC 50. P 1991, Desclée. 322 p. F 149 [NRT 114,582, R. *Escol*].

e964 *a) Beatrice* Pier Franco, L'intolleranza cristiana nei confronti dei pagani; un problema storiografico; – *b) Gaudemet* Jean, La législation anti-païenne de Constantin à Justinien; – *c) Frend* W. H. C., Monks and the end of Greco-Roman paganism in Syria and Egypt: CrNSt 11 (1990) 441-7; Eng. 447 / 449-467; Eng. 468 / 469-484.

e965 **Beatrice** Pier Franco, Storia della Chiesa antica; i primi sei secoli: Manuali di base 5. CasM 1991, Piemme. 127 p.

e966 **Bernardi** J., I primi secoli della Chiesa [1987 → 4,h659], T: Strumenti 46. Brescia 1989, Queriniana. 138 p. [RHE 86,80*].

e967 **Bibbia alle origini** [< BTT] 1990 → 6,k147: RProtestantesimo 46 (1991) 210s (E. *Noffke*).

e968 **Blázquez Martínez** José María, El nacimiento del cristianismo: Historia universal antigua 16. M 1990, Síntesis. 192 p. 84-7738-085-6 [AnBoll 110,207, R. de *Fenoyl*].

e969 EBosio Guido, Introduzione ai Padri³ [¹1963s, ²1965-9] 1990 → 6,g987: RAntonianum 66 (1991) 444-6 & AugR 31 (1991) 483s (F. *Bergamelli*); CC 142 (1991,4) 533 (A. *Ferrua*); RasT 32 (1991) 104-6 (F. *Bergamelli*).

e969* **Brown** Colin, Christianity and western thought; a history of philosophers, ideas and movements, 1. From the ancient world to the age of enlightenment. L 1990, Apollos. 447 p. 0-85111-763-5. – RExpTim 102 (1990s) 285 (D. A. *Pailin*: a committed Christian surveys preconceptions that have influenced thought about religion).

e970 EBurini Clara, Epistolari greci e latini (secc. I-III), repertorio bibliografico [2. lat. sec. 4s, EAsdrubali Pentini Giovanna, *Spadoni Cerroni*

Maria Carla; 3. grec. sec. 4s, ᴱ*Silliti* Francesca]. R 1990, Benedictina. xxviii-129 p. [xxi-164 p.; xxi-206 p.]. – ᴿArTGran 54 (A. *Segovia*).

e971 **Cameron** A., Christianity and the rhetoric of empire; the development of Christian discourse [Sather Lectures 55]. Berkeley 1991, Univ. California. xv-261 p.; 16 fig. $40. 0-520-07160-3 [NTAbs 36,290].

e972 **Clévenot** M., Geschichte des Christentums, 1. Von Jerusalem nach Rom; 2. Der Triumph des Kreuzes 4.-5. Jh. ᵀ. FrS 1987s, Exodus. 193 p.; map, Fs 33 / 234 p. [RHE 86,79*s].

e973 **Contreras** Enrique, *Peña* Roberto, Introducción al estudio de los Padres, período pre-niceno. Azul ARG 1991, NS-Ángeles. xxxi-325 p. 950-99640-0-X [NRT 114,764s, V. *Roisel*]. – ᴿTVida 32 (1991) 323 (Anneliese *Meis*).

e974 ᴱ**Culbertson** Philip L., *Shippee* Arthur B., The pastor [not specially Hermas]; reading from the patristic period. Mp 1990, Fortress. 237 p. $17. 0-8006-2429-7 [TDig 38,156]. – ᴿRExp 88 (1991) 468 (E. G. *Hinson*); SecC 8 (1991) 124s (F. W. *Norris*).

e975 *a) Dal Covolo* Enrico, Sulla natura degli studi patristici e i loro obiettivi; – *b) Bergamelli* Ferdinando, Il metodo nello studio dei Padri; problemi, orientamenti e prospettive; – *c) Pasquato* Ottorino, Studi patristici e discipline storiche; – *d) Amato* Angelo, Studio dei Padri e teologia dogmatica; – *e) Iacoangeli* Roberto, Humanitas classica 'praenuntia aurora' all'insegnamento dei Padri; – *f) Felici* Sergio, Rilevanza degli studi filologici e letterari all'approccio ai Padri; Salesianum 53 (1991) [= ➤ 426*, ᴱ*Dal Covolo* E. 1991] 7-17 / 19-43 / 45-88 / 89-100 / 101-131 / 133-148.

e976 **Dassmann** E., Kirchengeschichte 1. Ausbreitung, Leben und Lehre der Kirche in den ersten drei Jahrhunderten: StudBTh 10. Stu 1991, Kohlhammer. 284 p. DM 29,80. 3-17-010620-1 [NTAbs 36,292].

e977 **Denzinger** H., ³⁷**Hünermann** P., (*Hoping* Helmut), Enchiridion symbolorum... Kompendium der Glaubensbekenntnisse und kirchlicher Lehrentscheidungen. FrB 1991, Herder. xxxvii-1706 p. DM 158 [NRT 114,580, A. *Toubeau*: now finally half in German, and with 300 p. on Vatican II].

e978 *Desjardins* Michel, BAUER and beyond; on recent scholarly discussions of *hairesis* in the early Christian era: SecC 8 (1991) 65-82 [< NTAbs 36,46].

e978* **Droge** Arthur J., Homer or Moses; early Christian interpretations of the history of culture 1989 ➤ 5,g629; 6,g995: ᴿAugR 30 (1990) 499s (E. *Peretto*); CritRR 4 (1991) 293-5 (W. R. *Schoedel*); CrNSt 11 (1990) 621-3 (P. F. *Beatrice*); Gregorianum 72 (1991) 365-9 (G. L. *Prato*); HeythJ 32 (1991) 551s (L. W. *Barnard*); JAAR 59 (1991) 166-9 (J. E. *Rexine*); JRel 70 (1990) 627s (E. V. *Gallagher*).

e979 **Eno** Robert B., The rise of the papacy: Theology and life 32. Wilmington 1990, Glazier. 184 p. $13. 0-89453-902-0. – ᴿRExp 88,2 (1991) 223 (E. G. *Hinson*: 'conservative Catholics will probably wish that this study had come out more unambiguously in support of the papacy').

e979* *a) Frank* G. L. C., The council of Constantinople II [553] as a model reconciliation council: TS 52 (1991) 636-650.

— *b) Froehlich* Karlfried, Church History and the Bible: LuthQ 5 (Ridgefield NJ 1991) 127-142.

ᶠFREND W., Early Christianity 1991 ➤ 57.

e980 *a) Gnilka* Christian, La conversione della cultura antica vista dai Padri della Chiesa [... MINUCIO Felice], ᵀ*Tateo* Giovanni; – *b) Irmscher* Johannes,   La politica religiosa dell'Imperatore Giustiniano: CrNSt 11 (1990) 593-615; Eng. 615 / 579-592; Eng. 592.

e981 **Hadot** Jean,   La formation du dogme chrétien 1990 → 6,g999:   ᴿRHPR 71 (1991) 368s (T. *Ziegler*).

e982 *Haendler* Gert,   Fontes christiani und Sources chrétiennes [Deutsche werden die Franzosen beneiden...]: TLZ 117, 407-417; 414 Euseb, Praep. SChr 369.

e983 **Hall** Stuart,   Doctrine and practice in the early Church.   L 1991, SPCK. x-262 p. £15 [TR 87,427].

e984 **Hamell** P. J.,   Handbook of patrology.   NY 1991 = 1968, Alba.   170 p. $7.   0-8189-0057-1 [NTAbs 36,186].

e985 **Hanson** Richard,   Studies in Christian antiquity [reprints] 1985 → 1,183; 2,168:   ᴿSecC 8 (1991) 51-55 (C. *Bobertz*).

e986 *Kannengiesser* Charles,   *a*) The future of patristics [presidential address, Patristics Society Chicago 25.V.1990]: TS 52 (1991) 128-139; – *b*) La Bible dans l'Église ancienne; nature et présupposés de l'exégèse patristique: → 348, Concilium 233 (P 1991) 45-54.

e986* **Kelly** John N. D.,   I simboli di fede della chiesa antica [→ 4,h675]; nascita, evoluzione, uso del credo. [¹1950]. N 1987, Dehoniane.   467 p. – ᴿSTEv 2 (1990) 121 (P. *Bolognesi*).

e987 **Kinzig** Wolfram,   'Novitas christiana'; die Idee des Fortschritts in der Alten Kirche bis Eusebius: Hab.-Diss. ᴰ*Ritter* A.   Heidelberg 1991. – RTLv 23, p. 548.

e988 *Kraemer* Ross S.,   Women's authorship of Jewish and Christian literature in the Greco-Roman period: → 329, Women like this 1991, 221-242.

e989 **Kraft** Heinrich,   Einführung in die Patrologie: Die Theologie.   Da 1991, Wiss.   vii-257 p, DM 40. 3-534-02441-9 [TR 88,76].

e990 ᴱ**Lenzenweger** Joseph, *al.*,   *a*) Geschichte der katholischen Kirche [1986 → 3,430; 4,h577].   Graz 1990, Styria.   584 p. DM 50.   3-222-11894-9; – *b*) Historia de la Iglesia Católica, ᵀ*Martínez de Lapera* Abelardo.   Barc 1989, Herder.   730 p. – ᴿScripTPamp 23 (1991) 693-5 (A. *Viciano*).

e991 [**Liébart** Jacques]   **Spanneut** Michel,   Les Pères de l'Église, [I. Iᵉ-IVᵉ s. → 2,d215; 3,g99] / 2. Vᵉ-VIIIᵉ s.: BtHistChr 10.22.   P [1986] 1990, Desclée.   190 p.; 357 p. – ᴿMélSR 48 (1991) 249s (G.-H. *Baudry*); RHPR 71 (1991) 365 (P. *Maraval*).

e992 ᴱ**Livingstone** Elizabeth A.,   Studia Patristica 22, 1987/9 → 5,696:   ᴿRHR 208 (1991) 83-89 (J. *Doignon*).

e993 **McGrath** Alister E.,   A cloud of witnesses; ten great Christians thinkers. GR 1990, Zondervan.   141 p. [RelStR 18,143, S. *Duffy*: well selected, except maybe C. S. Lᴇᴡɪs, and readable].

e994 *Matter* E. Ann,   Bible in all ages (BTT 1-8): JRel 71 (1991) 79-90.

e995 *Nardi* Carlo,   Il primo quinquennio della 'Biblioteca Patristica' [ᴱ**Naldini** Mario, *Simonetti* Manlio; Firenze, Nardini 1984-8]: VivH 1 (1990) 237-255.

e996 **Nouailhat** René, La genèse du christianisme; de Jérusalem à Chalcédoine. Besançon 1991, Centre Régional de Documentation Pédagogique. 150 fiches. – ᴿDialogues d'Hist. Anc. 17,1 (1991) 462-5 (S. *Breton*).

e997 **Panagopoulos** Ioannes: ⑥ *Hē hermēneia*... Patristic interpretation of Holy Scripture; the first three centuries and the Alexandrian exegetical tradition to the fifth, 1: Orthodoxē Martyría 38. Athēna 1991, Akritas. 428 p.

e998 **Perrone** Lorenzo,   L'iniziazione alla Bibbia nella letteratura patristica: CrNSt 12 (1991) 1-26; Eng. 27.

e998* **Pierrard** Pierre, L'église et l'histoire. P 1991, D-Brouwer. 260 p. [TR 88,428].

e999 **Pritz** Ray A., Nazarene Jewish Christianity, from the end of the NT period until its disappearance in the fourth century: Studia Post-Biblica 37, 1988 ➤ 4,781: ᴿBijdragen 52 (1991) 331s (M. *Parmentier*, Eng.: overlooks LUTTIKUIZEN's 'Elxai', BROCK's ᶠVööbus, and virtually LÜDEMANN).

g1 ᴱ**Quacquarelli** Antonio, Complementi interdisciplinari di Patrologia 1989 ➤ 5,503; 6,k9: ᴿAnnTh 5 (1991) 230-3 (V. *Reale*); Gregorianum 72 (1991) 592-5 (G. *Pelland*: 'fra patristica e patrologia', parfois embarrassant); JTS 42 (1991) 699s (A. *Louth*); RivArCr 67 (1991) 188-195 (L. *Dattrino*); ScuolC 118 (1990) 486-491 (M. *Delfini*); TüTQ 171 (1991) 139s (H. J. *Vogt*).

g2 **Reventlow** Henning, Epochen der Bibelauslegung I. Vom Alten Testament bis Origenes 1990 ➤ 6,k10: ᴿActuBbg 28 (1991) 163s (J. *Boada*); DLZ 112 (1991) 491-3 (G. *Haendler*); HerdKorr 45 (1991) 146 (U. *Ruh*).

Rinaldi Giancarlo, Biblia Gentium... citazioni negli autori pagani 1989 ➤ 1680.

g3 **Saxer** V., Bible et hagiographie 1986 ➤ 3,g115... 5,g650: ᴿCrNSt 11 (1990) 381s (R. *Grégoire*).

g4 *Saxer* Victor, Parler des martyrs une Bible à la main; l'usage de la Bible dans les Passions des martyrs d'Agaune: ÉchSM 21 (1991) 80-115.

g5 **Schneemelcher** Wilhelm, Il cristianesimo delle origini [Urchristentum 1981 ➤ 63,5200], ᵀ: UnivPa 201, 1987 ➤ 6,k14: ᴿScripTPamp 23 (1991) 1068s (G. *Aranda*).

g6 ᴱ**Sevrin** Jean-Marie, The Bible in early Christianity / La réception des écrits néotestamentaires dans le Christianisme primitif 1986/9 ➤ 5,606; 6,4227: ᴿRThom 91 (1991) 510 (L. *Devillers*).

g7 **Sieben** Hermann J., Kirchenväterhomilien zum NT; ein Repertorium der Textausgaben und Übersetzungen: InstrPatr 22. Haag 1991, Nijhoff. 202 p. Fb 1950. – ᴿGregorianum 72 (1991) 790s (L. F. *Ladaria*).

g8 **Sieben** Hermann J., Konzilsdarstellungen – Konzilsvorstellungen; 1000 Jahre Konzilsikonographie aus Handschriften und Druckwerken. Wü 1990, Echter. 88 p.; photos Nowicki (12 color.). – ᴿTPhil 66 (1991) 611s (F. *Mennekes*).

g9 *a)* *Slusser* Michael, Diversity, communion and catholicity in the early Church; – *b)* *Coleman* John A., Inculturation and evangelization in the North American context; – *c)* *Donders* Joseph G., Inculturation and catholicity in relation to the worldwide church; – *d)* *Patrick* Anne E., Presidential address [San Francisco June 6-9], Inculturation, catholicity and social justice: PrCathTheolAm 45 (1990) 1-14 / 15-29 / 30-40 / 41-54.

g10 **Stalter-Fouilloy** Danielle, Histoire et violence; essai sur la liberté humaine dans les premiers écrits chrétiens. P 1990, PUF. 160 p. F 150. 2-13-042684-0. – ᴿÉTRel 66 (1991) 446s (P.-Y. *Ruff*).

g11 *Starowieyski* Marek, ● Narodziny ['naissance, quel mot magnifique'] poezji chrześcijańskiej: Bobolanum 2 (1991) 99-110; franç. 158s.

Stuhlhofer Franz, Der Gebrauch der Bibel von Jesus bis Euseb... Kanongeschichte ➤ 1286*.

g12 **Tanner** Norman P., Decrees of the ecumenical councils 1990 (Sheed & Georgetown Univ. 0-87340-490-2) ➤ 6,k18: ᴿCommonweal 117 (1990) 590s (L. S. *Cunningham*); Gregorianum 72 (1991) 771s (J. *Dupuis*); HeythJ 32 (1991) 553s (G. *Vass*: ALBERIGO's 1973 text Jesuit-translated on facing pages); JTS 42 (1991) 737-8 (H. *Chadwick*: from a Latin text made to help

Vat. II); Month 252 (1991) 252s (J. N. D. *Kelly*); PrPeo 5 (1991) 118 (M. *Evans*); TS 52 (1991) 549-553 (J. A. *Komonchak*).

g12* **Vessey** Mark, Patristics and literary history: LitTOx 5 (1991) 341-354 [< ZIT 91,779].

g13 **Vilanova** Evangelista, Historia de la Teología cristiana I. hasta 1400: 1987 ➔ 3,g125... 6,k21: ᴿFilT 4 (1990) 222s (A. *Benlloch Poveda*).

g14 **Vielhauer** Philipp, Historia de la literatura cristiana primitiva, ᵀ*Olasagasti* M., *al.* S 1991, Sígueme. 865 p. – ᴿNatGrac 38 (1991) 391s (F. *Ramos*).

g14* *Walsh* Joseph J., On Christian atheism: VigChr 45 (1991) 355-377.

g15 **Wirsching** Johannes, Kirche und Pseudokirche; Konturen der Häresie. Gü 1990, Vandenhoeck & R. 282 p. – ᴿTRu 56 (1991) 321-6 (K. *Schwarzwäller*).

g16 **Young** Frances, The art of performance; towards a theology of Holy Scripture. L 1990, Darton-LT. ix-198 p. £10. – ᴿScotJT 44 (1991) 542-4 (Morna D. *Hooker*: how the Fathers formed and interpreted Scripture, and our interpretation compared with the performance of a musical work).

g17 **Young** Frances M., The making of the creeds. L/Ph 1991, SCM/Trinity. xii-115 p. $11 pa. 0-334-02488-9 [TDig 39,91: successor to A. *Richardson* 1935]. – ᴿExpTim 102/9 1st choice (1990s) 257s (C. S. *Rodd*); TLond 94 (1991) 362s (C. *Stead*).

Y1.4   *Patres apostolici et saeculi II* – **First two centuries.**

g18 **Battles** F. L., The apologists: Study Outline 1. Allison Park PA 1991, Pickwick. iii-51 p. $8. 1-55635-013-9 [NTAbs 36,132].

g19 **Fernández-Ardánaz** Santiago, El mito del 'hombre nuevo' en el siglo II; el diálogo cristianismo-elenismo. M 1991, Fundación Universitaria. 296 p. [Antonianum 67,163, F. *Uribe*].

g20 **Grant** R. M., Greek Apologists 2d C. 1988 ➔ 4,h708... 6,k26: ᴿJAAR 59 (1991) 177-180 (W. E. *Fahey*); NBlackf 71 (1990) 314-6 (A. *Louth*).

g21 **Grant** Robert M., Jesus after the Gospels... 2d cent. 1990 ➔ 6,k25: ᴿCritRR (1991) 306-8 (L. W. *Hurtado*); RExp 88,2 (1991) 222 (E. G. *Hinson*).

Grelot Pierre, Homélies... à l'époque apostolique 1989 ➔ 3526.

g22 *MacLennan* R. S., Were the second-century Adversus Judaeos preachers anti-Jewish?: Explorations 5,2 (Ph 1991) 1.4 [< NTAbs 36,246].

g23 **Neymeyr** Ulrich, Die christlichen Lehrer im zweiten Jahrhundert; ihre Lehrtätigkeit, ihr Selbstverständnis und ihre Geschichte: VigChr supp. 4, ᴰ1989 ➔ 6,k30: ᴿJTS 42 (1991) 701s (S. G. *Hall*); TLZ 116 (1991) 923s (F. *Winkelmann*); TR 87 (1991) 479 (Maria-Barbara von *Stritzky*); VigChr 45 (1991) 94-96 (G. J. M. *Bartelink*).

g24 **Orbe** Antonio, Introducción a la teología de los siglos II y III: AnGreg 248, 1987 ➔ 3,g128... 6,k31: ᴿAugR 30 (1990) 214-6 (E. *Peretto*).

g25 **Pilhofer** Peter, *Presbýteron kreîtton* ᴰ1990 ➔ 6,k32: ᴿSecC 8 (1991) 188-190 (R. M. *Grant*); TLZ 116 (1991) 832-4 (W. *Wiefel*); VigChr 45 (1991) 412s (J. C. M. van *Winden*).

g26 **Tugwell** Simon, The apostolic fathers 1990 ➔ 6,k35: ᴿNBlackf 72 (1991) 300s (A. *Louth*).

g27 ATHENAGORAS: ᴱ**Marcovich** Miroslav, Athenagoras, Legatio: PatrTSt

31, 1990 ➤ 6,k37: ᴿJTS 42 (1991) 714s (L. W. *Barnard*); VigChr 45 (1991) 399-403 (D. T. *Runia*, also on his Ps-Justinus).

g28 **Pouderon** Bernard, Athénagore: THist 82, ᴰ1989 ➤ 5,g667; 6,k38: ᴿRÉG 104 (1991) 306 (A. *Wartelle*); RHE 86 (1991) 382-7 (Nicole *Zeegers-Vander Vorst*); RTLv 22 (1991) 249-251 (A. de *Halleux*); RTPhil 123 (1991) 335 (É. *Junod*); TS 52 (1991) 145-7 (R. *Wilken*).

g29 BARNABAS: *Carleton Paget* J. N. B., Barnabas 9:4; a peculiar verse on circumcision: VigChr 45 (1991) 242-254.

g30 CLEMENS A.: ᵀᴱ**Ferguson** John, Clement of Alexandria, Stromateis I-III: Fathers of the Church 85. Wsh 1991, Catholic University of America. xiv-354 p. 0-8132-0085-7.

g31 *Mouraviev* Serge, [Clem. Strom. 3,3,21,1] Le dossier du Fr.B. 21 *Diels-Kranz* d'HÉRACLITE d'Éphèse: RÉG 104 (1991) 52-84.

g32 **Rzodkiewicz** Leopold, ❷ Le Christ prêché aux Hellènes dans les écrits de Clément d'Alexandrie: diss. ᴰ*Drączkowski* F. Lublin 1991. 258 p. – RTLv 23, p. 549.

g33 CLEMENS R.: **Bowe** Barbara E., A church in crisis ... Clement R. ᴰ1988 ➤ 4,h716; 6,k50: ᴿCBQ 53 (1991) 490s (T. M. *Finn*); JEH 42 (1991) 147s (S. G. *Hall*).

g34 *Dekkers* E., La lettre de Clément de Rome aux Corinthiens; sa 'réception' en Occident au Moyen Âge: ➤ 18, ᶠBASTIAENSEN A., Eulogia 1991, 41-49.

g35 **Hofmann** Johannes, Die historisch untersuchte Biographie des hl. Bischofs Klemens von Rom und seine Synaxarnotiz im gegenwärtigen griechisch-orthodoxen Menaion: Kath. Hab.-Diss. Passau 1991, ᴰ*Leidl*. – TR 87 (1991) 513.

Jeffers J. J., Conflict at Rome [1Cl-Hermas] 1991 ➤ 4087.

g37 ᴱ**Jambet** Christian (ᵀ*Siouville* André 1933), Les Homélies clémentines. P 1991, Verdier (PUF). xii-116 p. [RHE 87,224-7, É. *Poulat*: Jambet 'ignore tout' sur Siouville, pseudonyme de l'abbé Auguste LELONG, 'nicodémiste' du modernisme]. – ᴿÉtudes 348 (1991) 136s (M. *Fédou*).

g38 **Snowden** Joe, The redactions of the Pseudo-Clementines in the Tripolis Discourses: diss. Harvard. – HarvTR 83 (1990) 453s.

g39 DIDACHE: *Del Verme* Marcello, Didachè e Giudaismo; la *aparchē* di Did. 13,3-7: VetChr 28 (1991) 253-265.

g40 *Draper* J. A., Torah and troublesome apostles in the Didache community: NT 33 (1991) 347-372.

g41 **Niederwimmer** Kurt, Die Didache 1989 ➤ 6,k62: ᴿCBQ 53 (1991) 501-3 (J. S. *Kloppenborg*).

g42 ᵀᴱ**Schöllgen** Georg, Didache; Zwölf-Apostel-Lehre / *Geerlings* Wilhelm, Traditio apostolica; apostolische Überlieferung: Fontes Christiani 1. FrB 1991, Herder. 358 p. DM 53 [RHE 87,29*]. 3-451-22201-9; pa. -101-2.

g43 **Jefford** Clayton N., The sayings of Jesus in the Teaching of the Twelve Apostles [diss. ᴰ*Robinson* J., Claremont 1988]: VigChr supp. 11, 1990 ➤ 6,k61: ᴿCritRR 4 (1991) 318-320 (E. M. *Boring*).

g44 AD DIOGNETUM: *Cattaneo* Enrico, L'enigma dell'Ad Diognetum [RIZZI M. 1989]: RasT 32 (1991) 327-332.

g45 **Rizzi** Marco, La questione dell'unità dell''Ad Diognetum' 1989 ➤ 5, g681; 6,k65: ᴿCC 142 (1991,4) 535 (A. *Ferrua*); JTS 42 (1991) 330-4 (W. *Kinzig*); VigChr 45 (1991) 184s (G. J. M. *Bartelink*); SecC 8 (1991) 251s (Pamela *Bright*).

g46 HERMAS: **Brox** Norbert, Der Hirt des Hermas: KommApV 7. Gö 1991, Vandenhoeck & R. 589 p. DM 168. 3-525-51674-6 [NTAbs 36,290].

g47 ᴱ**Carlini** A., (*Giaccone* L., *al.*), Papyrus Bodmer 38, Erma, il Pastore (Ia-IIIa visione). Genève-Cologny 1991, Fondation M. Bodmer. 128 p.; 22 pl. Fs 74 [RHE 86,281*]. 3-85682-025-6.

g47* *Outtier* Bernard, La version géorgienne du Pasteur d'Hermas: ➤ 48*, ᶠESENÇ T., RÉtGéorg 6s (1990s) 211-5.

g48 **Henne** Philippe, *a*) La pénitence et la rédaction du Pasteur d'Hermas: RB 98 (1991) 358-397; Eng. 358; – *b*) Hermas en Égypte: CrNSt 11 (1990) 237-256 [< ZIT 91,37].

g49 **Leutzsch** Martin, Die Wahrnehmung sozialer Wirklichkeit im 'Hirten des Hermas': FRL 150, 1989 ➤ 5,g686; 6,k69: ᴿCritRR 4 (1991) 323-5 (W. R. *Schoedel*); TLZ 116 (1991) 516-8 (A. *Lindemann*); TsTNijm 31 (1991) 101 (F. van de *Paverd*).

g50 **Maier** Harry G., The social setting of the ministry as reflected in the writings of Hermas, CLEMENT and IGNATIUS [diss. Oxford, ᴰ*Wiles* M.]: Diss. SR 1. Waterloo ON, 1991, W. Laurier Univ. viii-230 p. 0-88920-995-2.

g51 IGNATIUS A.: ᴱ**Ayán Calvo** J.J., Ignacio de Antioquía, Cartas; POLICARPO de Esmirna, Carta; Carta de la Iglesia de Esmirna a la Iglesia de Filomelio: Fuentes Patrísticas 1. M 1991, Ciudad Nueva. 302 p. – ᴿNRT 113 (1991) 594s (A. *Harvengt*); Salmanticensis 38 (1991) 243-5 (R. *Trevijano*); ScripTPamp 23 (1991) 1029-33 (A. *Viciano*).

g52 *Brent* Allen, The relations between Ignatius and the Didascalia: SecC 8 (1991) 129-156 [< NTAbs 36,95].

g53 *Grego* Igino, S. Ignazio di Antiochia, testimone della fede e guida spirituale: Asprenas 38 (1991) 170-190.

g53* *Lawyer* John E., Eucharist and martyrdom in the letters of Ignatius of Antioch: AnglTR 73 (1991) 280-296.

g54 *Petterson* Alvyn, The laity – bishop's pawn? Ignatius of Antioch on the obedient Christian: ScotJT 44 (1991) 39-56.

g55 *Rius-Camps* Josep, Die echten Briefe des Ignatius von Antiochien: RCatalT 16 (1991) 67-103; Eng. 103.

g56 IRENAEUS: *Faivre* Alexandre, Irénée, premier théologien 'systématique'?: RevSR 65 (1991) 11-32.

g57 *a*) *Manzone* Gino, Exégèse gnostique et principe d'unité dans l'Adversus Haereses d'Irénée; – *b*) *Martelet* Gustave, L'évolution comme 'économie' de la création à la lumière de Saint Irénée: ➤ 121, ᶠRAMAROSON 1991, 100-115 / 116-124.

g58 **Orbe** Antonio, Espiritualidad de San Ireneo: AnGreg 256, 1989 ➤ 5,g698; 6,k80: ᴿAugR 30 (1990) 500-2 (E. *Peretto*).

g59 **Torisu** Yoshifumi, Gott und Welt, eine Untersuchung zur Gotteslehre des Irenäus von Lyon [kath. Diss. Wien]: StVDiv 52. Nettetal 1991, Steyler. 268 p. DM 55 [TLZ 117,919s, H.-J. *Jaschke*: Gewinn trotz sprachlicher Unbeholfenheit].

g60 *Tripp* David H., The original sequence of Irenaeus 'Adversus haereses' I, a suggestion: SecC 8 (1991) 157-162.

g61 JUSTINUS: **Chandler** William J., A comparison of the concept of Logos in the teaching of Justin Martyr and the Gnostics [Justin is not anti-Gnostic in his Apologies but becomes such in his Dialogue]: diss. Southern Baptist Theol. Sem. 1991, ᴰ*Hinson* E. G. 228 p. 92-05766. – DissA 52 (1991s) 2956s-A.

g62 *Edwards* M. J., On the Platonic schooling of Justin Martyr: JTS 42 (1991) 17-34.

g62* *a) Gallicet* Ezio, Sermo humilis, convinzione o convenzione? Osservazioni su due passi di Giustino; – *b) Otranto* Giorgio, Note sull'itinerario spirituale di Giustino; fede e cultura in Dialogo 1-9: StTardAnt 8 (1989) 11-22 / 227-244.

g63 **Marcovich** Miroslav, Pseudo-Iustinus, Cohortatio etc. 1990 ➤ 6,k85: ᴿJTS 42 (1991) 715-7 (H. *Chadwick*); TPhil 66 (1991) 245s (H. J. *Sieben*).

g64 **Otranto** Giorgio, Esegesi biblica e storia in Giustino (Dial. 63-84) 1979 ➤ 60,y532a; 61,u692: ᴿRÉJ 150 (1991) 482s (S. *Mimouni*).

g65 *Panimolle* Salvatore A., Storicità dell'incarnazione del Verbo e Vangelo dell'Infanzia nel 'Dialogo con Trifone' di san Giustino: Marianum 52 (1990) 63-85.

g66 **Robillard** Edmond, Justin, l'itinéraire philosophique: Recherches NS 23. Montréal/P 1989, Bellarmin/Cerf. 172 p. – ᴿRTLv 22 (1991) 251s (A. de *Halleux*: remet en valeur la grandeur d'un 'platonisme' des Pères); SR 20 (1991) 360s (P.-H. *Poirier*).

g67 Papias: *Dubois* Jean-Daniel, Remarques sur le fragment de Papias cité par Irénée: ➤ 22, ᶠBenoît A., RHPR 71 (1991) 3-10; Eng. 125.

g68 *Zuntz* Günther, Papiana A. Der Tod der Söhne Zebedaei; B. Über die Evangelien: ZNW 82 (1991) 242-263.

Y1.6 Origenes.

g69 *Boumis* Panagiotis I., Ⓖ For the lifting of the anathema against Origen: TAth 61 (1990) 620-630; Eng. 907.

g69* *Clark* Elizabeth A., *a)* From Origenism to Pelagianism; elusive issues in an ancient debate: PrincSemS 12 (1991) 283-303 [< ᴢɪᴛ 91,783]; – *b)* New perspectives on the Origenist controversy; human embodiment and ascetic strategies: ChH 59 (1990) 145-162.

g70 **Crouzel** H., Origen, the life and thought 1989 ➤ 5,g707; 6,k97: ᴿAmHR 96 (1991) 146s (R. A. *Krupp*); BO 48 (1991) 955-960 (K.-H. *Uthemann*); CathHR 77 (1991) 666s (R. J. *Daly*); HeythJ 32 (1991) 406s (A. *Meredith*: refreshing); IndTSt 27 (1990) 197s (B. J. *Francis*); ScotJT 44 (1991) 112-6 (R. *Heine*: predictably high quality, but ignores Trigg, justifies surprising statements with reference to Crouzel and not Origen; and defense of Origen's orthodoxy is both a merit and a source of demerits).

g71 *Crouzel* Henri [Guibert Bernard de, p. 131s sur Crouzel, Fins dernières], Chronique origénienne: BLitEc 92 (1991) 122-131.

g72 *Dal Covolo* Enrico, Morte e martirio in Origene: FilT 4 (1990) 287-294.

g73 **Daniélou** Jean, Origène, il genio del cristianesimo: I grandi della fede [1948], ᵀ*Palamidessi* Silvestra. R 1991, Archeosofica. 374 p.

g74 **Fédou** Michel, Christianisme et religions païennes dans le Contre Celse d'Origène: THist 81, 1989 ➤ 5,g708; 6,k102: ᴿAugM 36 (1991) 388s (J. *Oroz*); CrNSt 12 (1991) 411-3 (R. M. *Grant*); ÉTRel 66 (1991) 251-3 (J.-D. *Dubois*); RTLv 22 (1991) 85-87 (A. de *Halleux*); SR 20 (1991) 256 (L. *Painchaud*).

g75 **Fernández Lago** José, El monte en las homilías de Orígenes: diss. Pont. Univ. Gregoriana ᴰ*Orbe* A. R 1991s. – InfPUG 24/123, 9.

g76 **Grossi** Vittorino, La presenza in filigrana di Origine [sic in titolo, ma testo e testatine 'Origene'] nell'ultimo AGOSTINO (426-430): AugR 30 (1990) 423-440.

g77 **Hauck** Robert J., The more divine proof; prophecy and inspiration in Celsus and Origen 1989 ⇒ 5,g708: RCritRR 4 (1991) 312s (B. E. *Daley*).

g78 *Heither* Theresia, 'Glaube' in der Theologie des Origenes: ErbeAuf 67 (1990) 255-265.

g79 EKannengiesser C., *Petersen* W., Origen 1986/8 ⇒ 5,683; 6,k108: RSecC 8 (1989) 252s (G. C. *Berthold*: typos on 50 indicated pages).

g79* ELies Lothar, Origeniana quarta 1985/7 ⇒ 3,664b... 6,k111: RChH 59 (1990) 71s (J. W. *Trigg*).

g80 **Meis Wörmer** Anneliese, El problema del mal en Orígenes 1988 ⇒ 5,g713; 6,k113: RForumKT 6 (1990) 158s (M. *Hauke*).

g81 [Monaci] **Castagno** A., Origene predicatore e il suo pubblico: Univ. Dip. Storia 3, 1987 ⇒ 4,h759... 6,k114: RCrNSt 11 (1990) 382-4 (D. *Pazzini*).

g82 **Neuschäfer** Bernhard, Origenes als Philologe 1987 ⇒ 3,g177... 6,k115: RCrNSt 11 (1990) 214s (P. F. *Beatrice*); RÉG 104 (1991) 665 (A. *Laks*).

g83 *Orbe* Antonio, Orígenes y los Monarquianos: Gregorianum 72 (1991) 39-71; franç. 72.

g84 **Pace** Nicola, Ricerche sulla traduzione di RUFINO del De principiis di Origene: MiLett/fil 133. F 1990, Nuova Italia. xviii-222 p. Lit. 50.700. – RJTS 42 (1991) 744s (H. *Chadwick*: an indispensable tool for assessing the unreliability of our access to one of Origen's most exciting works).

g85 *a*) *Perrone* Lorenzo, Sulla preistoria delle 'quaestiones' nella letteratura patristica [Origene ...]; presupposti e sviluppi del genere letterario fino al IV secolo; – *b*) *Simonetti* Manlio, Ancora su allegoria e termini affini in alcuni scrittori greci [... cristiani, Filone]: ⇒ 452, AnStoEseg 8,2 (1990/1) 485-505 / 363-384.

g86 **Rubenson** Samuel, The letters of St. ANTHONY; Origenist theology, monastic tradition and the making of a saint: BtHistEcLund 24. Lund 1990, Univ. 222 p. – RJTS 42 (1991) 723-732 (T. D. *Barnes*); VigChr 45 (1991) 185s (G. J. M. *Bartelink*).

g87 **Schockenhoff** Eberhard, Zum Fest der Freiheit; Theologie des christlichen Handelns bei Origenes: TüThSt 33. Mainz 1990, Grünewald. 352 p. – RBLitEc 92 (1991) 128-130 (H. *Crouzel*); TPhil 66 (1991) 585-7 (H. J. *Sieben*).

g88 **Scott** Alan, *a*) Origen and the life of the stars; a history of an idea: Early Christian Studies. Ox 1991, Clarendon. xvi-189 p. 0-19-826462- 3. – *b*) Origen's use of XENOCRATES of Ephesus: VigChr 45 (1991) 278-285.

g88* ESgherri Giuseppe, Origene, Sulla Pasqua; il papiro di Tura 1989 ⇒ 6,k118: RVigChr 45 (1991) 91s (G. J. M. *Bartelink*).

g89 **Sträuli** Robert, Origenes der Diamantene. Z 1987, ABZ. 475 p. Fs 58. – RJTS 42 (1991) 336s (R. *Williams*: Harnackian, ignores CROUZEL, NAUTIN, HARL, VOGT, LIES).

g90 *Trigg* Joseph W., The angel of great counsel; Christ and the angelic hierarchy in Origen's theology: JTS 42 (1991) 35-51.

Y1.8 Tertullianus.

g91 *Azzali Bernardelli* Giovanna, Quomodo et scriptum est (Scorp. II, 5); nota su ermeneutica e tradizione apostolica in Tertulliano montanista: AugR 30 (1990) 221-257.

g92 ᵀᴱ**Braun** R., Tertullien contre Marcion [I ➤ 6,k122]: II: SChr 365.368. P 1990s, Cerf. 235 p. 2-204-04343-5. – ᴿETL 67 (1991) 442 (A. de *Halleux*).

g92* *Braun* René, *al.*, Chronica tertullianea et cyprianea 1990: RÉAug 37 (1991) 339-368.

g93 **Deakle** David W., The Fathers against Marcionism; a study of the methods and motives in the developing patristic anti-Marcionite polemic: diss. ᴰ*Greeley* Dolores. St. Louis 1991. 285 p. 91-30991. – DissA 52 (1991s) 1785-A.

g94 **González** Justo L., Christian thought revisited; three types of theology [Tertullian...] 1989 ➤ 5,g729: ᴿCurrTMiss 18 (1991) 375s (J.D. *Rodríguez*).

g95 *Guerra* Anthony J., Polemical Christianity; Tertullian's search for certitude: SecC 8 (1991) 109-123.

g96 **Hagendahl** Harald, Cristianesimo latino e cultura classica, da Tertulliano a Cassiodoro [Von Tertullian, Göteborg 1983; ANRW]ᵀ; introd. *Siniscalco* P.; CuCrAnt, 1988 ➤ 5,g869: ᴿAugR 30 (1990) 189-191 (Elena *Cavalcanti*: titolo italiano indica l'ottica del traduttore non nominato).

g97 *Hamman* A.G., La typologie biblique et sa formulation chez Tertullien: ➤ 18, ᶠBASTIAENSEN A., Eulogia 1991, 137-146.

g97* **Harnack** Adolf von, Marcion, the Gospel of the alien God [²1924], ᵀ*Steely* John E., *Bierma* Lyle D. Durham ɴᴄ 1990, Labyrinth. 265 p. 0-939464-16-0. – ᴿRExp 88 (1991) 466s (A.A. *Trites*).

g98 **Heine** Ronald E., The Montanist oracles and testimonia 1989 ➤ 5,g732; 6,k130: ᴿSecC 8 (1991) 57-59 (D.H. *Williams*).

g99 *Jacob* Christoph, Zur Krise der Mystagogie in der Alten Kirche: TPhil 66 (1991) 75-89.

g100 **MacLennan** Robert S., [Tertullian *al.*,] Early Christian texts on Jews and Judaism: BrownJudSt 194. Atlanta 1990, Scholars. xxv-203 p. $56; sb. $37. 1-55540-414-6 [TDig 38,279].

g101 ᵀᴱ**Mattéi** Paul, Tertullien, Le mariage unique (De monogamia): SChr 343, 1988 ➤ 4,h769; 5,g735: ᴿBijdragen 52 (1991) 212s (M. *Parmentier*, Eng.: T, was 'progressively obsessed with the problem of sexuality'); MélSR 48 (1991) 247s (M. *Spanneut*).

g102 *Munier* Charles, 'Ianua' chez Tertullien: RevSR 65 (1991) 197-211.

g103 *Orbe* Antonio, Marcionitica: AugR 31 (1991) 196-244.

g104 ᴱ**Pollman** Karla, Das Carmen adversus Marcionitas: Hypomnemata 96. Gö 1991, Vandenhoeck & R. 220 p.

Y2   *Patres graeci* – The Greek Fathers.

g105 *Beatrice* Pier Franco, Le traité de PORPHYRE contre les chrétiens; l'état de la question: Kernos 4 (1991) 119-138.

g106 ᶠCHADWICK Henry, The making of orthodoxy, ᴱ**Williams** Rowan 1989 ➤ 5,38*: ᴿJTS 42 (1991) 708-714 (P.M. *Parvis*: detailed analyses).

g107 **Geyer** Carl-Friedrich, Religion und Diskurs; die Hellenisierung des Christentums aus der Perspektive der Religionsphilosophie ᴰ1990 ➤ 6, k140: ᴿZkT 113 (1991) 102 (K.H. *Neufeld*).

g108 **Hadot** J., La formation du dogme chrétien des origines à la fin du IVᵉ s.: Cah. Fac. Religion et Laïcité 3. Charleroi 1990, Centre Univ. 167 p. [RHE 86,313]. – ᴿRTLv 22 (1991) 247-9 (A. de *Halleux*: lacunes répercutant sur des jugements).

g109 **Ivánka** Endre von, Plato christianus; la réception critique du platonisme chez les Pères de l'Église [1964], [T]*Kessler* Élisabeth: Théologiques. P 1990, PUF. 469 p. F 265. – [R]Études 347 (1991) 716 (M. *Fédou*); RHPR 71 (1991) 370s (J.-C. *Larchet*: excellente traduction); TS 52 (1992) 740-2 (M. A. *Schatkin*).

g110 *Markschies* Christoph, Platons König oder Vater Jesu Christi? Drei Beispiele für die Rezeption eines griechischen Gottesepithetons bei den Christen in den ersten Jahrhunderten und deren Vorgeschichte: → 438, Königsherrschaft 1986/91, 385-439.

g111 *Mühlenberg* Ekkehard, Griechische Patristik: TRu 56 (1991) 140-175.

g112 **Murphy** Francis X., *Sherwood* Polycarp, Konstantinopel II und III [1974, Orante], [T]: Geschichte der Ökumenischen Konzilien 3.   Mainz 1990, Grünewald. 403 p. DM 64 [TR 88,32, G. *Bausenhart*].

g113 **Polka** Brayton, The dialectic of biblical critique; interpretation and existence. NY 1986, St. Martin's. 190 p. $25. – [R]JAAR 59 (1991) 858-860 (D. E. *Klemm*: 'dazzling harangue against Greek texts ... carried into modernity by SPINOZA, KANT, HEGEL, KIERKEGAARD ... Outrageous conclusions from questionable premises, but with passion and intelligence ... no scholarly works cited').

g114 *Sandherr* Susanne, Die Bibel und die Griechen; Emmanuel LÉVINAS' 'Humanismus des anderen Menschen' [[T]*Wenzler* Ludwig. Ha 1989, Meiner. 150 p. DM 38]: StiZt 208 (1990) 67-69.

g115 **Stead** Christopher, Philosophie und Theologie 1. Die Zeit der Alten Kirche, [T]*Wildberg* C.: TWiss 14/4. Stu 1990, Kohlhammer. 182 p. DM 36 [TLZ 117,197, G. *Feige*].

g115* **Tsirpanlis** Constantine N., Introduction to Eastern patristic thought and Orthodox theology: Theology and Life 30. Collegeville MN 1991, Liturgical. viii-277 p. $17 [TR 88, 77].

g116 **Weltin** E. G., Athens and Jerusalem 1987 → 3,g212* ... 5,g754: [R]RelStT 10,2 (1990) 79-81 (B. H. *Henaut*).

g117 APOLLINARIUS: **Spoerl** Kelley M., A study of *Kata meros pistis* by Apollinarius of Laodicea: diss. Toronto 1990, [D]*Sinkewicz* R. – RelStR 18,173.

g118 **Hübner** Reinhard M., Die Schrift des Apolinarius [sic] 1989 → 5,g756: [R]ChH 66 (1990) 540s (J. T. *Lienhard*); JTS 42 (1991) 337-341 (L. R. *Wickham*: important).

g119 ARIUS: *Ritter* Adolf M., Arius in der neueren Forschung: → 67, [F]GOLUB I., 1991, 425-439; croat. 439.

g120 **Williams** Rowan, Arius, heresy and tradition 1987 → 3,g216 ... 5,g759: [R]Faventia 12s (1990s) 479s (G. *Fernández*).

g121 ARTEMIDORUS: *Martin* Luther H., Artemidorus; dream theory in late antiquity: SecC 8 (1991) 97-108.

g122 ATHANASIUS: **Arnold** Duane W., The early episcopal career of Athanasius of Alexandria [< diss. Durham 1989 → 6,k163]: Christianity and Judaism in Antiquity 6. ND 1991, Univ. xvi-235 p. $25. 0-268- 00925-2 [TDig 39,46].

g123 **Camplani** A., Le lettere festali di Atanasio di Alessandria; studio storico-critico 1989 → 6,k164: [R]BO 48 (1991) 547-550 (R.-G. *Coquin*); RasT 32 (1991) 313-5 (E. *Cattaneo*).

g124 *La Paz Rojas* Pedro F., La divinización del hombre en Atanasio de Alejandria: TVid 32 (1991) 175-183.

g125 **Meyer** John R., Saint Athanasius on divinization: diss. [D]*Mateo-Seco* L. Pamplona 1991. RTLv 23, p. 570 [> ExcDissSTh].

g126 *Meijering* E.P., Struktur und Zusammenhang des apologetischen Werkes von Athanasius: VigChr 45 (1991) 313-326.

Petterson Alvyn, Athanasius and the human body, ... 1990 ➤ 7183.

g127 **Szymusiak** Jan M., Athanase d'Alexandrie, Deux apologies; à l'empereur Constance pour sa fuite[2rev] [[1]1956]: SChr 56 bis. P 1987, Cerf. 267 p. 2-204-02695-6.

g128 ATHENOGENES: [TE]**Maraval** Pierre, La passion inédite de S. Athénogène de Pédachthoé en Cappadoce (BHG 197b): SubsHag 75. Bru 1990, Bollandistes. [viii-] 120 p.; maps. 2-87365-000-1.

g129 BASILIUS: **Backus** Iréna, Lectures humanistes de Basile de Césarée, traductions latines (1439-1618) [Prot. Hab.-Diss. Berne 1988]: ÉtAug Coll. Ant. 125. P 1990, Inst. ÉtAug (Brepols). 306 p. 2-85121-104-8. – [R]ETL 67 (1991) 444s (A. de *Halleux*); RHPR 71 (1991) 375s (P. *Maraval*: passionnant pour qui s'intéresse à l'histoire de la culture).

g130 **Barrois** Georges A., The Fathers speak: BASIL, G. NAZ., G. NYSS. 1986 ➤ 2,d327: [R]OrChrPer 57 (1991) 244s (E.G. *Farrugia*).

g131 [TE]**Ducatillon** Jeanne, BASILE de Césarée, Sur le baptême: SChr 357, 1989 ➤ 6,k169: [R]JTS 42 (1991) 341-3 (E. J. *Yarnold*).

g132 *Gliściński* Jan, ❾ Kirchliche Politik des hl. Basilius von Caesarea: ColcT 61,4 (1991) 71-78; Eng. 79.

g133 *Limberis* Vasiliki, The eyes infected by evil; Basil of Caesarea's homily, On envy: HarvTR 84 (1991) 163-184.

g134 *Testa Bappenheim* Italo, Attualità socio-antropologica di Basilio il Grande [... proprietà privata]: BbbOr 33 (1991) 69-91. 157-186.

g135 CHRYSOSTOMUS: *Houssiau* A. [introd. p. 7-48], **Mondet** J.-P., Le sacerdoce du Christ et de ses serviteurs selon les Pères de l'Église [Diss. 1986 sur Chrysostome, Comm. Hébr.]: Coll. Cerfaux-Lefort 8. LvN 1990, Centre Hist. Rel. viii-267 p. – [R]RTLv 22 (1991) 415-7 (A. *Haquin*).

g136 *Jackson* Pamela, John Chrysostom's use of Scripture as initiatory preaching: GrOrTR 35 (1990) 345-366.

g137 **Klasvogt** Peter, Leben zur Verherrlichung Gottes; Botschaft des Johannes Chrysostomos, ein Beitrag zur Geschichte der Pastoral: kath. Diss. Augsburg 1991, [D]*Heinz*. – TR 87 (1991) 515.

Liebeschuetz J., Barbarians and bishops... age of Chrysostom 1990 ➤ b456*.

g138 **Malingrey** Anne-Marie, PALLADIOS, Vita Chrysostomi: SChr 341s, 1988 ➤ 4,h812; 5,g770: [R]ChH 59 (1990) 72s (P.J. *Gorday*); ScEsp 43 (1991) 127 (G. *Pelland*).

g138* *Nardi* Carlo, *a)* Le idee antropologiche, morali e pedagogiche di Giovanni Crisostomo e la filosofia popolare; – *b)* L'ideale di felicità in Giovanni Crisostomo e la filosofia popolare; spunti epicurei: VivH 1 (Firenze 1990) 59-78 / 2 (1991) 29-68.

g139 **Nassif** Bradley L., Antiochene *theōria* in John Chrysostom's exegesis: diss. Fordham, [D]*Meyendorff* J. NY 1991. 356 p. 91-18841. – DissA 52 (1991s) 960-A (RelStR 18,173 omits 'Antiochene' and adds to title 'a study in biblical hermeneutics and the spiritual life').

g140 **Paverd** Frans van de, St. John Chrysostom, The homilies on the statues; an introduction: OrChrAn 239. R 1991, Pont. Inst. Stud. Orientalium. xxxi-395 p. 88-7210-286-3.

g141 **Piédagnel** Auguste, (*Doutreleau* L.), Jean Chrysostome, Trois catéchèses baptismales: SChr 366, 1990 ➤ 6,k176: ᴿBLitEc 92 (1991) 298s (R. *Cabié*); ETL 67 (1991) 173s (A. de *Halleux*); JTS 42 (1991) 745s (E.J. *Yarnold*); RHPR 71 (1991) 377s (P. *Maraval*).

g141* **Pyykkö** Vappu, Die griechischen Mythen bei den grossen Kappadokiern und bei J. Chrysostomos: TY-B 193. Turku [= Åbo] 1991, Turun Yliopisto. 188 p. [TR 88,77].

g142 **Schatkin** Margaret A., Jean Chrysostome, Discours sur Babylas: SChr 562, 1990 ➤ 6,k178: ᴿVigChr 45 (1991) 187s (J.C.M. von *Winden*).

g142* **Taft** Robert F., The diptychs; a history of the liturgy of St. John Chrysostom IV.: OrChrAn 238. R 1991, Pont. Inst. Stud. Orientalium. xxxiv-214 p. 88-7210-285-5.

g143 **Wenk** Wolfgang, Zur Sammlung der 38 Homilien des Chrysostomus Latinus (mit Edition der Nr. 6, 8, 27, 32 und 33). W 1988, Österr. Akad. 214 p. Sch. 420. – ᴿLatomus 50 (1991) 429s (P. *Hamblenne*).

g144 *Heid* Stefan, ISIDOR von Pelusium und die Schrift 'Über das Priestertum' des J. Chrysostomos: ForumKT 7 (1991) 196-210.

g145 CYRILLUS A.: ᵀᴱÉvieux Pierre, *al.*, Cyrille d'Alexandrie, Lettres festales (I-VI): SChr 372. P 1991, Cerf. 423 p. F 268 [TLZ 117,921]. 2-204-04274-9.

g146 *Rougé* Jean, La politique de Cyrille d'Alexandrie et le meurtre d'Hypatie: CrNSt 11 (1990) 485-503; Eng. 504.

g147 CYRILLUS H.: *Jackson* Pamela, Cyril of Jerusalem's use of Scripture in catechesis: TS 52 (1991) 431-450.

g148 DAMASCENUS: *Biedermann* H.M., J. Damaskenos: ➤ 681, LexMA 5 (1990) 566s.

g149 DAMASCIUS: ᴱWesterink Leendert G., ᵀ*Combes* Joseph, Damascius, Traité des premiers principes II. P 1989, BLettres. lxxvii-291 (doubles) p. F 250. – ᴿRBgPg 69 (1991) 208 (É. des *Places*).

g149* — ᶠWESTERINK Leendert G.: Gonimos; Neoplatonic and Byzantine studies, 75th b., 1988 ➤ 5,211: ᴿClasR 40 (1990) 138s (L. *Siorvanes*).

g150 DIONYSIUS ALEX.: *Pietras* Henryk, L'unità di Dio in Dionigi di Alessandria: Gregorianum 72 (1991) 459-489; Eng. 489s.

g151 DIONYSIUS PSEUD.-AREOP.: **Suchla** B.R., Ps-D. Areopagita, De divinis nominibus: PatrTSt 33, 1990 ➤ 6,k190*b*: ᴿArTGran 54 (1991) 393 (A. *Segovia*); AugR 31 (1991) 431-458 (S. *Lilla*).

g151* ᴱGozier André, Pseudo-Denys, La théologie mystique, lettres: Les Pères dans la foi. P 1991, Migne. 133 p.

g152 **Heil** Günter [† 25.VIII.1990], *Ritter* A.M., Ps-Dionysius Areop. De coelesti hierarchia, de ecclesiastica hierarchia, de mystica theologia, epistulae: PatrTSt 36. B 1991, de Gruyter. xv-300 p. – ᴿArTGran 54 (1991) 393s (A. *Segovia*).

g153 **Louth** Andrew, Denys the Areopagite 1989 ➤ 5,k16: ᴿHeythJ 32 (1991) 552s (J. *O'Donnell*); NBlackf 71 (1990) 556s (A. *Meredith*); Carthaginensia 7 (1991) 524 (F. *Martínez Fresneda*).

g154 ᵀᴱMartín Teodoro H., Pseudo Dionisio Areopagita, Obras completas: BAC 511. M 1990, Católica. xix-418 p. – ᴿArTGran 54 (1991) 413s (A. *Segovia*).

g155 EPIPHANIUS: **Dechow** Jon F., Dogma ... Epiphanius/Origen 1988 ➤ 5, g782; 6,k195: ᴿSecC 8 (1991) 181-6 (R. I. *Pervo*).

g155* *Riggi* Calogero, La paideia escatologica di Epifanio e la sua prima polemica contro l'ellenismo di ORIGENE: StTardAnt 8 (1989) 419-439.

g156 **Stewart** Columba, 'Working the earth of the heart'; the [Epiphanius, *al*.] Messalian controversy in history, texts, and language to A.D. 431: TheolMg. Ox 1991, Clarendon. xi-340 p. 0-19-826736-3.

g157 EUSEBIUS: *Elliott* T. G., Eusebian frauds in the Vita Constantini: Phoenix 45 (Toronto 1991) 162-171.

g158 ᴱ**Winkelmann** Friedhelm, Über das Leben des Kaisers Konstantin[2] [¹1975 + p. 267-270]: GCS Eusebius Werke 1/1. B 1991, Akademie. lxx-270 p. [TLZ 117,920, G. *Haendler*].

g159 **Christensen** Torben, RUFINUS and Eusebius Hist 8s 1989 ➤ 5,g793; 6,k197: ᴿZKG 102 (1991) 115s (M. *Wünsche*).

g160 ᵀᴱ(**Schroeder** Guy), **Places** Édouard des, Eusèbe, La préparation évangélique, livres VIII.X [IX des Places seul]: SChr 369. P 1991, Cerf. 510 p. 2-204-04429-6.

g161 ᴱ**Places** Édouard des, Eusèbe, La préparation évangélique XIV-XV: SChr 338, 1987 ➤ 3,g240 ... 6,k199: ᴿAugM 34 (1989) 190 (J. *Oroz*); ÉTRel 66 (1991) 254s (J.-D. *Dubois*).

g162 ᵀ**Williamson** G. A. (1965), ²*Louth* Andrew, EUSEBIUS, History of the Church from Christ to Constantine 1989 ➤ 6,k207; 0-14-044535-8: ᴿJEH 42 (1991) 149 (G. *Bonner*).

g163 **Verheyden** Jozef, De vlucht van de christenen naar Pella 1988 ➤ 4,h833 ... 6,k204: ᴿRHE 86 (1991) 379-382 (C. *Laga*); SecC 8 (1991) 186-8 (W. L. *Petersen*).

g164 — **Wehnert** Jürgen, Die Auswanderung der Jerusalemer Christen nach Pella — historisches Faktum oder theologische Konstruktion? [VER- HEYDEN J. 1988]: ZKG 102 (1991) 231-255.

g165 EUSEBIUS EMESINUS: *Novotný* Jiři A., Les fragments exégétiques sur les livres de l'Ancien Testament d'Eusèbe d'Émèse: OrChrPer 57 (1991) 27-67.

g166 EVAGRIUS: *Driscoll* Jeremy, A key for reading the Ad monachos of Evagrius Ponticus: AugR 30 (1990) 361-382 [383-404, *Elm* Susanna].

g167 GREGORIUS NAZ.: ᴱ**Kurmann** Alois, Gregor von Nazianz, Oratio 4. gegen Julian; ein Kommentar: SchweizBeitAltW 19, 1988 ➤ 4,h834*: ᴿTR 87 (1991) 116-8 (M. *Kertsch*); VigChr 45 (1991) 89-91 (J. den *Boeft*).

g167* *a*) *Foti* Maria B., Un palinsesto di Gregorio di Nazianzo; – *b*) *Lucà* Santo, Una presunta omilia di Gregorio di Nazianzo, Perì zōês aiōníou: StTardAnt 8 (1989) 23-40: fot. 41 / 43-53 + 4 pl.

g168 ᴱ**Norris** Frederick W., Faith gives fullness to reasoning; the five theological orations of Gregory Nazianzen [ᵀ*Wickham* L., *Williams* F.], introduction and commentary: VigChr supp. 13. Leiden 1991, Brill. xii-314 p. 90-04-09253-6.

g169 *Špidlík* Tomáš, La théologie et la poésie selon Grégoire de Nazianze: ➤ 67, ᶠGOLUB I., 1991, 97-111; 111 sažetak (Croat.).

g170 GREGORIUS NYSS.: *a*) *Hanriot-Coustet* Annie, Qui est l'auteur du Discours 35 transmis parmi les œuvres de Grégoire de Nazianze? [ré- ponse: Grégoire de Nysse]: – *b*) *Maraval* Pierre, Grégoire de Nysse pasteur; la lettre canonique a Létoios: ➤ 22, ᶠBENOîT A., RHPR 71 (1991) 101-114.

g171 **Altenburger** M., *Mann* F., Bibliographie zu Gregor von Nyssa 1988 ➤ 4,h838 ... 6,k215: ᴿNRT 113 (1991) 296s (B. *Pottier*).

g172 **Borrego-Pimentel** Enrique M., De Plotino a Gregorio de Nisa: diss. ᴰ*Navas-Gutiérrez* A. Granada 1991. 579 p. – RTLv 23, p. 548.

g173 ᴱ**Downing** J. Kenneth, *al.*, G. Nysseni Opera dogmatica minora II 1987 ➤ 5,g801: ᴿAugR 31 (1991) 465-474 (A. *De Nicola*).

Drobner H. R., Bibelindex ... Gregors von Nyssa 1988 ➤ 1592.

g174 ᵀᴱ**Lozza** Giuseppe, Gregorio di Nissa, Discorso sui defunti: Corona Patrum 13. T 1991, SEI. 213 p. 88-05-05196-9.

g175 ᵀᴱ**Maraval** Pierre, Grégoire de Nysse, Lettres: SChr 363, 1990 ➤ 6, k219; 2-204-04195-5: ᴿOrChrPer 57 (1991) 452-4 (V. *Ruggieri*); VigChr 45 (1991) 189s (J. C. M. van *Winden*).

g176 **Mateo-Seco** Lucas F., *Bastero* J., El 'Contra Eunomium I' ... Nisa 1988 ➤ 5,g805: ᴿIrTQ 57 (1991) 84s (B. *McNamara*).

g177 ᴱ**Spira** Andreas, The biographical works of Gregory of Nyssa, Mainz 1982/4 ➤ 3,723: ᴿBijdragen 52 (1991) 214s (M. *Parmentier*, Eng., also on MATEO-SECO L. and ALTENBURGER M.).

g178 *Vogt* Hermann J., Die Schrift 'Ex communibus notionibus' des Gregor von Nyssa; Übersetzung des kritischen Textes mit Kommentar: TüTQ 171 (1991) 204-218.

g179 HESYCHIUS: *Leanza* Sandro, Uno scoliaste del V secolo; Esichio di Gerusalemme: ➤ 452, AnStoEseg 8,2 (1990/1) 519-533.

g179* JOHANNES CLIMACUS: **Chryssavgis** John, Ascent to heaven; the theology of the human person according to St. John of the Ladder. Brookline MA 1989, Holy Cross Orthodox. 267 p. – ᴿPacifica 4 (1991) 358-361 (L. *Cross*).

g180 LEONTIUS B., *Evans* David B., Leontius von Byzanz (ca. 500-543), ᵀ*Schnitker* Thaddäus: ➤ 690, TRE 21 (1991) 5-10.

g181 MARCELLUS A.: **Seibt** Klaus, Markell von Ankyra als Reichstheologe: Diss. Tübingen 1990. 446 p. – TLZ 117,476.

g182 **Feige** Gerhard, Die Lehre Markells von Ankyra in der Darstellung seiner Gegner: ErfurtTSt 58. Lp 1991, St. Benno. xix-269 p. [TR 88,77]. 3-7462-0388-0.

MAXIMUS C.: ᴱ**Deun** Peter van, Maximi Confessoris opera exegetica duo: CCG 23. 1991 ➤ 2848*.

g183 *Dupont* Véronique L., Le dynamisme de l'action liturgique; une étude de la Mystagogie de saint Maxime le Confesseur: RevSR 65 (1991) 363-388.

g184 [Mariani] *Puerari* Milena, Per un'ermeneutica dei tempi e delle feste liturgiche nella Chiesa torinese tra il IV e il V secolo secondo i 'Sermones' del vescovo San Massimo: ScuolC 119 (1991) 60-96 . 476-513.

g185 **Farrell** Joseph P. [➤ 7429], Free choice in St. Maximus the Confessor [diss. Oxford]. South Canaan PA 1989, St. Tikhon. 252 p. $12 [RelStR 18,61, Verna F. F. *Harrison*].

g185* *Sfameni Gasparro* Giulia, Aspetti di 'doppia creazione' nell'antropologia di Massimo il Confessore: StTardAnt 8 (1989) 461-501.

g186 MELITO S.: ᵀᴱ*Hawthorne* Gerald F., Melito of Sardis, On the Passover [< ᶠTENNEY M. 1975]: Kerux 4,1 (1989) 2-35.

g187 PAMPHILUS: ᴱ**Declerck** J. J., Pamphili theologi opus; – ᴱ*Allen* P., EUSTATHII monachi opus: Diversorum Postchalcedonensium auctorum

collectanea 1: CCG 19. Turnhout/Lv 1989, Brepols/Univ. 476 p.
Fb 6350. – ᴿTLZ 116 (1991) 840s (F. *Winkelmann*).

g188 ROMANOS: **Petersen** W. L., Diatessaron, EPHREM ... Romanos M. 1985
➤ 65,d585 ... 5,g925: ᴿSecC 8 (1991) 179-81 (D. *Bundy*).

g189 SOPHRONIUS: ᵀᴱ**Gallico** Antonino, Sofronio di Gerusalemme, Le omelie: Collana TPatr 92. R 1991, Città Nuova. 229 p. 88-311-3092-7.

g190 SYNESIUS: **Roos** B. A., Synesius of Cyrene, a study in his personality:
StGrLat 2. Lund 1991, Univ. xvii-157 p. – ᴿRPg 64 (1990!) 213-5 (D.
Roques).

g191 **Roques** Denis, Études sur la correspondance de Synésios de Cyrène: Coll. Latomus 205. Bru 1989. 274 p.; 3 foldout maps. Fb 1300. –
ᴿClasPg 86 (1991) 357-364 (Jacqueline *Long*).

g191* **Garzya** A., Sinesio [di Cirene], Epistole, operette, inni: Classici Greci,
1989 ➤ 5,g814: ᴿRivStoLR 27 (1991) 192-7 (Rita *Lizzi*).

g192 TATIANUS: *Solignac* Aimé, Tatien: ➤ 668, DictSpir 15 (1991) 52-58.

g193 THEODORETUS C.: *Azéma* Yvan, Théodoret de Cyr: ➤ 668, DictSpir
15 (1991) 418-435.

g194 THEODORUS M.: *Lera* Jose M., Théodore de Mopsueste: ➤ 668, Dict-
Spir 15 (1990s) 385-400.

g195 *Petit* Françoise, Les fragments grecs d'EUSÈBE d'Emèse et de Théodore de Mopsueste; l'apport de PROCOPE de Gaza: Muséon 104 (1991)
349-354.

g196 **Zaharopoulos** Dimitri, Theodore of Mopsuestia on the Bible 1989
➤ 5,g818; 6,k232: ᴿAnglTR 73 (1991) 73s (Rowan A. *Greer*); DeltioVM
10,1 (1991) 67-69 (S. *Agourides,* ⑤); RExp 88 (1991) 99 (E. G. *Hinson*).

g196* ᵀᴱ**Touraille** Jacques, [*Bobrinskoy* Boris], Philocalie des Pères Neptiques
[18ᵉ s,], fasc. [1, 1977-] 11. Bellefontaine 1991, Abbaye. 312 p. – ᴿSt-
Monast 33 (1991) 406 (J. M. *Soler i Canals*).

Y2.4 Augustinus.

g197 *Adamo* David P., An African bishop, Augustine of Hippo, and his
concept of Church and State relationship: IndTSt 27 (1990) 133-150.

g198 **Azkoul** Michael, The influence of Augustine of Hippo on the Orthodox Church [i.e. on separating it from western Christendom]: TSt-
Rel 56. Lewiston NY 1990, Mellen. iv-299 p. $70. 0-88946-733-1 [TDig
39,47].

g199 *Barclift* Philip L., In controversy with Saint Augustine; JULIAN of
Eclanum on the nature of sin: RTAM 58 (1991) 5-20.

g200 *Bauer* Johannes B., Aurelius Augustinus, De divinatione daemonum —
vom Vorwissen der Dämonen: ➤ 6,171, ᶠSTÖGER A., Exeget 1990, 23-36.

g201 *Boyle* Marjorie O., Augustine in the garden of Zeus; lust, love and
language: HarvTR 83 (1990) 117-139.

g202 **Bright** Pamela, Book of Rules / TYCONIUS 1988 ➤ 5,g819: ᴿJRel 70
(1990) 629s (Maureen A. *Tilley*).

g203 — *Mandolfo* Carmela, Le Regole di TICONIO e le 'Quaestiones et
responsiones' di EUCHERIO di Lione: ➤ 452, AntStoEseg 8,2 (1990/1)
535-546.

g204 **Campodonico** Angelo, Salvezza e verità; saggio su Agostino: Ricerche
Filosofia 1. Genova 1989, Marietti. 215 p. Lit. 35.000. 88-211-9980-0. –
ᴿGregorianum 72 (1991) 596s (J. de *Finance*).

g205 ᴱ**Caprioli** A., *al.*, Agostino *a*) la conversione 1986 [*b*) opera letteraria 1987]: Augustiniana 1, 1987 ➤ 4,518: ᴿRThom 91 (1991) 681-4 (G.-H. *Masson*).

g206 **Ceiotti** G.,   La pastorale delle vocazioni in S. Agostino.   Palermo 1991, Augustinus. 152 p. Lit. 19.000 [TR 88,77].

g207 *a*) *Chadwick* Henry T. [*Finn* Thomas], History and symbolism in the garden at Milan; – *b*) *Clark* Mary T., Augustine the Christian thinker; – *c*) *Armstrong* A. H., Apophatic-kataphatic tensions in religious thought from the third to the sixth century A.D.: a background for Augustine and ERIUGENA; – *d*) *O'Daly* Gerard J. P., Hierarchies in Augustine's thought: ➤ 111, ᶠO'MEARA J. 1991, 42-55 [77-91] / 56-65 / 12-21 / 143-154.

g208 *Cipriani* Nello,   La morale pelagiana e la retorica: AugR 31 (1991) 309-327.

g209 **Cooper** Rodney H.,   Concordantia in libros XIII Confessionum... a concordance to the 1969 Skutella edition.   Hildesheim 1991, Olms-Weidmann. I. A-M, xi-614 p.; II. p. 617-1191. 3-487-09490-9; -1-6.

g210 **Daraki** Maria,   Une religiosité sans Dieu... Stoïciens/Augustin 1989 ➤ 6,k246: ᴿKernos 4 (1991) 334-6 (A. *Motte*).

g211 *Deproost* Paul-Augustin,   Miscellanées augustiniennes [conversion 1986, baptême 1987; 9 écrits]: RTLv 22 (1991) 41-59; Eng. 151.

g212 *Doignon* Jean, 'La vie heureuse' ou 'Sur la bonheur'? Comment comprendre le titre du 'De beata vita' de saint Augustin [défend son titre 'La vie heureuse?' contre FREDOUILLE J.]; Hermes 119 (1991) 502-5.

g213 *Donnelly* Dorothy F., *Sherman* Mark A.,   Augustine's De civitate Dei; an annotated bibliography of modern criticism, 1960-1990.   NY 1991, Lang. x-109 p. DM 49 [TR 88,253].

g214 *Doucet* Dominique,   Sol[iloquia] I. 14,24 - 15,30 et le médecin complaisant: RevSR 65 (1991) 33-50.

g214* *a*) *Fredriksen* Paula,   Vile bodies; Paul and Augustine on the resurrection of the flesh; – *b*) *Bernard* Robert W.,   The rhetoric of God in the figurative exegesis of Augustine; – *c*) *Johnson* David W.,   The myth of the Augustinian synthesis: ➤ 58, ᶠFROEHLICH K., Biblical hermeneutics 1991, 75-87 / 88-99 / 100-114.

g215 *Frend* William H. C.,   Augustine and OROSIUS; on the end of the ancient world: AugSt 20 (Villanova 1989) 1-38 [< ZIT 91,166].

g216 *Gasbarro* Nicola,   La *religio* di Agostino; per una lettura storico-comparativa del 'De vera religione':   SMSR 57 (1991) 43-129.

g216* ᴱ*Giomini* Remo,   A. Augustinus, 'De rhetorica': StLatIt 4 (1990) 7-82: testo latino, indici.

g217 *a*) *Hamilton* Gordon J.,   Augustine's methods of biblical interpretation; – *b*) *Westra* Haijo J.,   Augustine and poetic exegesis; – *c*) *Coward* Harold G.,   Memory and Scripture in the conversion of Augustine: ➤ 367*, ᴱ*Meynell* H., Grace, politics and desire 1990, 103-119 / 87-100 / 19-30.

g218 *Hamman* Adalbert G.,   Saint Augustin, la Bible et la théologie spirituelle [ᶠBAVEL T. van, AugLv 41 (1991) 773-782] ➤ 6,13.k240*c*.

g219 **Hensellek** Werner, *Schilling* Peter,   Specimina eines Lexicon Augustinianum CSEL 1987-9 ➤ 5,k255: ᴿTR 87 (1991) 285 (C. *Mayer*).

g220 **Kirwan** Christopher,   Augustine 1989 ➤ 5,g836: ᴿJRel 70 (1990) 628s (J. C. *Cavadini*); JTS 42 (1991) 343-6 (H. *Chadwick*: important).

g221 **Kowalczyk** Stanisław, ❷ Człowiek i Bóg... Man and God in the teaching of St. Augustine. Wsz 1988, Ośrodek Dokumentacji. 276 p. – ᴿColcT 60,1 (1990) 170s (J. *Królikowski*, ❷).

g222 **Kriegbaum** B., Kirche der Traditoren...? Donatismus 1986 ➤ 3,g286...
6,k259: ᴿMilltSt 23 (1989) 113s (F. *O'Donoghue*).

g223 **Lange van Ravenswaay** J.M.J., Augustinus totus noster; das Augustinverständnis bei J. CALVIN. Gö 1990, Vandenhoeck & R. 203 p.
DM 46 pa. – ᴿTLZ 116 (1991) 753-5 (H.-U. *Delius*); TZBas 47 (1991) 371 (G. *Zimmermann*).

g224 *Lanzi* Nicola, I Sermones di Sant'Agostino nell'edizione bilingue: Divinitas 35 (1991) 185-194.

g225 **Lavender** Earl D., The development of Pelagius' thought within a late fourth-century ascetic movement in Rome: diss. ᴰGreeley Dolores. St. Louis 1991. 199 p. 91-31009. – DissA 52 (1991s) 1780-A; RTLv 23, p. 548.

g225* *Lawless* George, Augustine of Hippo, an annotated reading list: Listening 26 (1991) 173-188 [< ZIT 91,778].

g226 ᵀᴱ**Lombardo** Gregory J., St. Augustine, On faith and works: Ancient Christian Writers 48. NY 1988, Newman. viii-112 p. – ᴿLatomus 50 (1991) 704s (J.P. *Weiss*).

g227 **Madec** Goulven, La Patrie et la voie: JJC 36, 1989 ➤ 5,g841; 6,k263: ᴿAugM 35 (1990) 179s (T. *Madrid*); CrNSt 12 (1991) 190s (J.J. *O'Meara*, Eng.); RAg 31 (1990) 282-4 (P. *Sahelices*).

g227* *Madec* G., Bulletin augustinien pour 1990/1: RÉAug 37 (1991) 369-439.

g228 **Madec** G., *al.*, De libero arbitrio di Agostino d'Ippona: Lectio Augustini 6. Palermo 1990, Augustinus. 88 p. Lit. 15.000. – ᴿETL 67 (1991) 446s (A. *Vanneste*).

g228* **Mader** Johann, Aurelius Augustinus, Philosophie und Christentum. St. Pölten 1991, Niederösterr. 447 p. Sch 345 [TR 88,77].

g229 **Maier** J.-L., Dossier du Donatisme I-II, 1987-9 ➤ 4,h864; 5,g842s; 6,k365: ᴿAugM 35 (1990) 185s (J.A. *Galindo*); CathHR 77 (1991) 95s (T.D. *Barnes*: like KRIEGBAUM can scarcely escape bias of religious commitment); CrNSt 12 (1991) 188-190 (Marcella *Forlin Patrucco*); JEH 42 (1991) 90s (W.H.C. *Frend*).

g230 *a) Martín* José P., PHILO and Augustine, De civitate Dei XIV 28 and XV; some preliminary observations; – *b) Runia* David T., PHILO of Alexandria in five letters of ISIDORE of Pelusium: ➤ 76, ᶠHILGERT E., StPhilonAn 3 (1991) 283-294 / 295-319.

g230* *Milbank* John, 'Postmodern critical Augustinianism'; a short *summa* in forty-two responses to unasked questions: ModT 7 (1990s) 225-237.

g231 **Mohler** James A., Late have I loved you; an interpretation of St. Augustine on human and divine relationships. Brooklyn 1991, NY City. 189 p. $9 [TR 88,77].

g231* **Mondin** Battista, Il pensiero di S. Agostino 1988 ➤ 4,h867; 6,k268: ᴿDivThom 54 (1991) 173-7 (L. *Clavell*).

g232 **Ocker** Christopher, Augustine, episcopal interests, and the papacy in late Roman Africa: JEH 42 (1991) 179-201.

g233 *O'Donnell* James J., The authority of Augustine (1991 Villanova Univ. lecture): AugSt 22 (1991) 7-35.

g234 **Oort** Johannes Van, Jerusalem and Babylon; a study into Augustine's City of God and the sources of his doctrine of the two cities: VigChr supp. 14. Leiden 1991, Brill. xi-427 p. 90-04-09323-0. – ᴿVigChr 45 (1991) 298-302 (W.H.C. *Frend*).

g235 **Oort** J. van, Augustinus [6 reprints]; facetten van leven en werk 1989 ➤ 6,k271; 90-242-4815-9: ᴿBijdragen 52 (1991) 450 (T.J. van *Bavel*).

g236 ^e**Oroz Reta** José, San Agustín, meditación de un centenario [1-2 apr. 1987]: BtSalmEst 99. S 1987, Univ. Pontificia. 215 p. – ^RTR 87 (1991) 118s (A. *Zumkeller*).

g237 *Pettineo* Alberta, Estetismo greco e estetica agostiniana: Atti Palermo 5/9/2 (1988s) 277-306.

g238 ^{TE}*Piscitelli Carpino* Teresa, PAOLINO di Nola, Epistole ad Agostino: Strenae Nolanae 2. N 1989, Redenzione. 317 p. Lit. 30.000. – ^RMaia 43 (1991) 61s (Rosanna *Rocca*).

g239 ^E**Pizzolato** Luigi F., Agostino a Milano; il battesimo 1987. Palermo 1988. Augustinus. 111 p. Lit. 28.000. – ^RLatomus 50 (1991) 448s (J. *Wankenne*); Gregorianum 72 (1991) 165s (F.-A. *Pastor*).

g240 **Rees** B. R., PELAGIUS, a reluctant heretic 1988 ⇥ 4,b873 ... 6,k280: ^RChH 59 (1990) 223s (E. *Te Selle*); HeythJ 32 (1991) 407s (T. J. *Ferguson*); ScotJT 44 (1991) 273-8 (G. *Bonner*: '1981'); VigChr 45 (1991) 87-89 (J. den *Boeft*).

g241 *Remy* Gérard, La théologie de la médiation selon S. Augustin; son actualité: RThom 91 (1991) 580-623 [681-5, Augustiniana varia, ^R*Masson* G.].

g242 *Starnes* Colin, La exégesis bíblica agustiniana y los orígenes de la ciencia moderna, ^T*Eguílar* Miguel A.: ⇥ 540, AugM 36 (1991) 295-304.

g242* *Steinhauser* Kenneth B., Augustine's autobiographical covenant; a contemporary reading of his Confessions: PerspRelSt 18 (1991) 233-240.

g243 *Stoll* Brigitta, Die Vita Augustini des POSSIDIUS als hagiographischer Text: ZKG 102 (1991) 1-13.

g244 *a*) *Thelamon* Françoise, Destruction du paganisme et construction du royaume de Dieu d'après RUFIN et Augustin; – *b*) *Barnard* Leslie W., L'intolleranza negli apologisti cristiani con speciale riguardo a FIRMICO Materno; – *c*) *Paschoud* François, L'intolérance chrétienne vue et jugée par les païens: CrNSt 11 (1990) 523-544; Eng. 544 / 505-521; Eng. 521 / 545-576; Eng. 577.

^FTRAPP D., Via Augustini, ^EOberman H., *James* F. 1991 ⇥ 155.

g245 *Zumkeller* A., Der Gebrauch der Termini famulus Dei, servus Dei, famula Dei und ancilla Dei bei Augustinus: ⇥ 18, ^FBASTIAENSEN A., Eulogia 1991, 437-445.

Y2.5   Hieronymus.

g246 *Adkin* Neil, TERTULLIAN's 'De ieiunio' and Jerome's 'Libellus de virginitate servanda' (epist. 22): WienerSt 104 (1991) 149-161.

g247 *Blázquez* José M., Aspectos de la sociedad romana del Bajo Imperio en las cartas de San Jerónimo: Gerión 9 (1991) 263-288.

g248 **Donalson** Malcolm D., Jerome's 'Chronicon' [translation and continuation of EUSEBIUS], a translation and commentary ['first in English']: diss. Florida State, ^D*Levenson* D. 181 p. 91-26977. – DissA 52 (1991s) 1305-A.

g249 ^E**Duval** Yves-Marie, Jéröme 1986/8 ⇥ 5,e577*; 6,k304: ^RScripTPamp 23 (1991) 713s (A. *Viciano*).

g250 *a*) *Fanning* Steven, Jerome's concept of empire; – *b*) *Clark* Gillian, Let every soul be subject; the Fathers and the Empire: ⇥ 412, Images of empire 1990/1, 219-250 / 251-275.

g250* *Feichtinger* Barbara, Der Traum des Hieronymus — ein Psychogramm: VigChr 45 (1991) 54-77.

g251 *Fontanier* J.-M., Sur une image hiéronymienne; le visage sidéral de Jésus [Ep 65,8 sur Ps 44: quiddam sidereum, une beauté dans son visage et dans ses yeux qui attira les disciples; AUGUSTIN et les autres pères considéraient oiseuse la question de sa beauté]: RSPT 75 (1991) 251-6.

g252 **Gorce** Denys, La Lectio Divina nell'ambiente ascetico di s. Girolamo [S. Jérôme... dans le milieu ascétique romain], ᵀ*Pedrazzi* Angelo: Cammini dello Spirito. Bo 1990, Dehoniane. 384 p. Lit. 34.000 [RivB 39,192 adv.]. – ᴿLetture 46 (1991) 474-6 (G. *Ravasi*).

g253 *Mišić* Anto, The elements of priestly spirituality in St. Jerome's letters: ObnŽiv 45 (1990) 219-231 (Croatian); Eng. 232.

g254 ᴱ**Moreschini** C., S. Hieronymi presbyteri Dialogus adversus Pelagianos: CCL 80. Turnhout 1990, Brepols. xxxi-137 p. – ᴿRHE 86 (1991) 347s (R. *Gryson*).

g254* *Nardi* Carlo, In compagnia di Girolamo; un eterno adolescente? [CERESA GASTALDO A. 1988, MORESCHINI C. 1989, LARBAUD V. 1946, it. 1989].

g255 **Oberhelman** Steven M., Rhetoric and homiletics in fourth-century Christian literature; prose rhythm, oratorical style, and preaching in the works of AMBROSE, Jerome, and AUGUSTINE: AmClasSt 26. Atlanta 1991, Scholars. [vi-] 199 p. 1-55540-617-3; pa. -8-7.

g256 **Rebenich** Stefan, Hieronymus und sein Kreis; prosopographische und sozialgeschichtliche Untersuchungen: Diss. Mannheim 1990. – Chiron 21 (1991) 466.

g257 *Schmid* H., Hieronymus: ➤ 681, LexMA 5 (1990) 2-4.

Y2.6   **Patres latini** *in ordine alphabetico.*

g257* **Chuvin** Pierre, A chronicle of the last pagans, ᵀ*Archer* B. A.: Revealing Antiquity. CM 1990, Harvard Univ. 188 p. $29.25 [RHE 87,568, P.-A. *Deproost*].

g258 **Fitzgerald** Allan, Conversion through penance in the Italian church of the fourth and fifth centuries; new approaches to the experience of conversion from sin: StBeC 15, Lewiston NY 1989, Mellen. 565 p. $80 [Horizons 19,134, J. C. *Cavadini*].

g259 **Margerie** Bertrand de, Introduction à l'histoire de l'exégèse, 4. L'Occident latin de León le Grand à Bernard de Clairvaux; préf. *Leclercq* J.; postf. *Vogüé* Adalbert de. P 1990, Cerf. vi-286 p. F 188. 2-204-04003-7 ➤ 6,k312: ᴿBL (1991) 84 (J. M. *Dines*: he traces with great skill the continuities and the new developments); ScripTPamp 23 (1991) 713 (A. *Viciano*).

Markus Robert, The end of ancient Christianity 1991 ➤ g379.

g260 *Parmentier* Martin [Martien], Trying to unravel [J. L.] JACOBI's unknown creed (CPL 1752) [Latin, published 1884, dated 600 or as late as 900]: Bijdragen 52 (1991) 354-378; – *b*) The creed of the Statuta ecclesiae antiqua (CPL 1776) in direct speech, as found on the last two pages of ms Berlin 32 (Phillips 1681): Bijdragen 52 (1991) 318-327.

g261 *Testard* Maurice, La Passion des saintes Perpétue et Félicité; témoignages sur le monde antique et le christianisme: BBudé (1991) 56-75.

---

g262 AMBROSIUS: **Banterle** Gabriele, Le fonti latine su Sant'Ambrogio: Opere, sussidi 24,2. Mi 1991, Bt Ambrosiana. 280 p. 88-311-9173-X.

g263 **Jacob** Christoph, 'Arkandisziplin', Allegorese, Mystagogie; ein neuer Zugang zur Theologie des Ambrosius von Mailand [diss. Bonn. ᴰ*Dassmann* E.]: Theophaneia 32, 1990 ➤ 6,k314; DM 98: ᴿTsTNijm 31 (1991) 431 (T. J. van *Bavel*); ZkT 113 (1991) 360s (H. B. *Meyer*: verdient Beachtung).

g264 *Labrique* Marie-Pierre, Ambroise de Milan et Sénèque; à propos du De excessu fratris II: Latomus 50 (1991) 409-418.

g265 **Mazzarino** Santo, Storia sociale del vescovo Ambrogio 1989 ➤ 6,k316: ᴿGerión 8 (1990) 326-8 (Rosa *Sanz Serrano*).

g266 ᴱ**Pasini** Cesare, Le fonti greche su sant'Ambrogio 1990 ➤ 6,k317; Lit. 60.000: ᴿCC 142 (1991,4) 96s (E. *Cattaneo*).

g266* **Schmitz** Josef, Ambrosius, De sacramentis / De mysteriis: Fontes christiani 3. FrB 1990, Herder. 279 p. – ᴿVigChr 45 (1991) 294-7 (J. C. M. van *Winden*).

g267 **Williams** Daniel H., Nicene Christianity and its opponents in northern Italy; an examination of late 4th century anti-Arian polemics and politics with particular emphasis on the early career of Ambrose of Milan: diss. Toronto 1991, ᴰ*Barnes* T. – RelStR 18,174.

g267* Arator [c. 550]: **Angelucci** Paolo, *a*) Centralità della Chiesa e primato romano in Aratore; – *b*) La tecnica poetica di Aratore. R 1990, Herder. [iv-] 133 p. / 344 p.

g268 Boethius: **Lluch-Baixauli** Miguel, La teología de Boecio [† 524] en la transición del mundo clásico al mundo medieval [diss. Navarra 1988]: Teológica 69. Pamplona 1990, Univ. Navarra. 350 p. pt 3250. 84-313-1096-0. – ᴿActuBbg 28 (1991) 213 (J. *Boada*); RTLv 22 (1991) 412s (A. de *Halleux*).

g268* **Chadwick** Henry, Boethius, The consolations of music, logic, theology, and philosophy: Clarendon Paperbacks [= 1981]. Ox 1990, Clarendon. xv-313 p. 0-19-826549-2. – ᴿRHPR 71 (1991) 380s (P. *Maraval*).

g269 Cassiodorus: **Macpherson** Robin, Rome in involution; Cassiodorus' Varia in their literary and historical setting: FgKlasyczna 14, 1989 ➤ 6,k321: ᴿClasR 41 (1991) 86s (M. *Whitby*); Gerión 8 (1990) 330-3 (F. J. *Moreno*); Gnomon 63 (1991) 196-9 (Gunhild *Vidén*).

g270 Chromatius: *Cuscito* Giuseppe, Cultural and religious environment of Chromatius' age in the light of recent historiography (in Slovene), ᵀ*Butković* Drago: BogVest 50 (1990) 443-454; Eng. 451.

g271 *Nauroy* G., Chromace, disciple critique de l'exégèse d'Ambroise; réalité et limites de l'influence de l'In Lucam sur les Tractatus in Matthaeum: Antichità altoadriatiche 34 (Udine 1989) 117-149 [< RHE 87,32*].

g272 Pseudo-Cyprianus: *Carroll* Scott T., An Early Church sermon against gambling (CPL 60) [Pseudo-Cyprian, De aleatoribus]: SecC 8 (1991) 83-95.

g273 Gaudentius: ᵀᴱ**Banterle** Gabriele, San Gaudenzio di Brescia; delle varie eresie: Scriptores circa Ambrosium 2. Mi 1991, Bt Ambrosiana. 520 p. 88-311-9196-9.

g273* Gregorius Agrig.: *Leanza* Sandro, Sul metodo esegetico di Gregorio di Agrigento: StTardAnt 8 (1989) 269-280.

g274 Gregorius M.: **Baasten** Matthew, Pride according to Gregory the Great; a study of the Moralia: StBeC 7, 1986 ➤ 4,h899: ᴿJAAR 59 (1991) 591s (C. *Kannengiesser*).

g274* *Bruzzone* Antonella, Sulla lingua dei Dialogi di Gregorio Magno: StLatIt 5 (1991) 195-280: a glossary.

g275 *Giordano* Lisania, La metafora nelle Omelie sui Vangeli di Gregorio Magno: ➤ 452, AnStoEseg 8,2 (1990/1) 599-613.

g276 **Godding** R., Bibliografia di Gregorio Magno (1890-1989): Opere, complemento 1, 1990 ➤ 6,k333: ᴿNRT 113 (1991) 297 (V. *Roisel*); StMonast 33 (1991) 156 (A. *Olivar*); TPhil 66 (1991) 594-6 (S. *Kessler*).

g277 ᵀᴱ**Hurst** D., Gregory the Great, Forty Gospel homilies: Cistercian Studies 123. Kalamazoo 1990, Cistercian. [iv-] 389 p. [RHE 86,48*].

g277* *Kampen* Lieuwe van, Acta Andreae and Gregory's De miraculis Andreae: VigChr 45 (1991) 18-26.

McCready William D., Signs of sanctity, miracles... in Gregory 1989 ➤ 4002.

g278 [ᵀ*Norberg* D. †1988], ᴱ**Minard** P. †, Grégoire le Grand, Registre des lettres 1s: SChr 370s. P 1991, Cerf. 541 p., map. F 191 + 170 [NRT 114,761, A. *Harvengt*]. 2-204-04150-5 both.

g279 **Modesto** Johannes, Gregor der Grosse, Nachfolger Petri und Universalprimat: StTheol&Gesch 1. St. Ottilien 1989, EOS. 412 p. – ᴿForumKT 6 (1990) 154s (W. *Gessel*); TPhil 66 (1991) 251-4 (S. C. *Kessler*).

g280 *Modesto* Johannes, Papst [590] Gregor der Grosse; eine ökumenische Integrationsfigur: Catholica 44 (1990) 284-307.

g280* *a*) *Calati* Benedetto, 'Scriptura crescit cum legente' nelle omelie di s. Gregorio Magno; – *b*) *Burini* Clara, 'Fede e carità' radice della catechesi patristica; – *c*) *Falchini* Cecilia, L'interpretazione delle Scritture in GUGLIELMO di Saint-Thierry: ➤ 292*b*, ParSpV 24 (1991) 249-270 / 237-248 / 271-286.

g281 **Portalupi** Enzo, Studi sulla presenza di Gregorio Magno in Tommaso d'AQUINO: Dokimion 10. FrS 1991, Univ. 125 p. [TR 88,78].

g282 **Straw** Carole E., Gregory / perfection in imperfection 1988 ➤ 5,g888; 6,k336: ᴿZkT 113 (1991) 343s (S. C. *Kessler*: the title is from the Moralia in Job).

g283 *Wilkins* Walter J., 'Submitting the neck of your mind'; Gregory the Great and women of power [p. 585, his 'efforts to identify with and empower women are found in both his historical and spiritual exegesis of Scripture']: CathHR 77 (1991) 583-594.

g284 *Wyrwa* Dietmar, Der persönliche Zugang in der Bibelauslegung Gregors des Grossen; ➤ 558, Sola Scr. 1990/1, 262-278.

g285 HILARIUS P.: *Pelland* Gilles, Gloriam ex conspectu gloriae (Hilaire, Tr. ps. 118, heth 8): Gregorianum 72 (1991) 757-763.

g286 *Williams* D. H., A reassessment of the early career and exile [356] of Hilary of Poitiers: JEH 42 (1991) 202-217.

g287 HIPPOLYTUS: **Botte** Bernard, Tradition apostolique de S. Hippolyte 1989 ➤ 6,k343: ᴿHeythJ 32 (1991) 136-8 (K. *Stevenson*).

g288 *Martimort* Aimé G., Encore Hippolyte et la 'Tradition apostolique': BLitEc 92 (1991) 133-7.

g289 **Visonà** G., Pseudo Ippolito, In sanctum Pascha 1988 ➤ 4,h918*... 6,k350: ᴿAugR 30 (1990) 490-2 (M. *Simonetti*); RHPR 71 (1991) 373 (P. *Maraval*); VigChr 45 (1991) 413-5 (G. J. M. *Bartelink*).

g290 LACTANTIUS: *Wlosok* Antonie, Lactantius, L. Caelius Firmianus (ca. 250-325): ➤ 690, TRE 20 (1990) 370-4.

g291 LEO M.: **Blümer** W., Rerum eloquentia; christliche Nutzung antiker Stilkunst bei St. Leo Magnus [Diss.]: EurHS 15/51. Fra 1991, Lang. [v-] 195 p. [RHE 86,270*].

g292 *a) Da Campione* A., Sulla presenza della Scrittura nelle epistole dei papi prima di Leone Magno; – *b) Marin* M., Le Sententiae LXXXVII episcoporum [Cartagine 256]: in margine al problema del rapporto tra Sacra Scrittura e Concili; – *c) Felle* Antonio E., Sacra Scrittura ed epigrafia cristiana a Roma fra III e VII secolo: ► 419, AnStoEseg 7,2 (1989/90) 467-483 / 501-527 / 485-500.

g293 LIBERATUS C.: ᵀᴱ**Carcione** Filippo, Liberato di Cartagine, Breve storia della controversia nestoriana ed eutichiana. Anagni 1989, Pont. Collegio Leoniano. 142 p. – ᴿCC 142 (1991,2) 202s (C. *Capizzi*).

g294 PALLADIUS: *McLynn* Neil, The 'Apology' of Palladius; nature and purpose [GRYSON R., Arian scholia; Aquileia council]: JTS 42 (1991) 52-76.

g295 PRUDENTIUS: **Kah** Marianne, 'Die Welt der Römer mit der Seele suchend ...'; die Religiosität des Prudentius im Spannungsfeld zwischen 'pietas christiana' und 'pietas romana': Hereditas 3, 1990 ► 6,k359: ᴿNRT 113 (1991) 779s (A. *Harvengt*); RömQ 86 (1991) 385-7 (B. *Stubenrauch*); RTLv 22 (1991) 412 (A. de *Halleux*).

g296 **Malamud** Martha A., A poetics of transformation; Prudentius and classical mythology 1989 ► 6,k360: ᴿJRS 81 (1991) 245s (Anne-Marie *Palmer*); Latomus 50 (1991) 446s (J. L. *Charlet*).

g296* *Starowieyski* Marek, Le origini della poesia cristiana: ► 582. AION-clas. 12 (1990) 239-255.

Y2.8 Documenta orientalia.

g297 **Agémian** Sylvia, Manuscrits arméniens enluminés du Catholicossat de Cilicie. Antélias 1991, Catholicossat. xx-137 p.; 98 pl. + 24 color. [Muséon 105,393, B. *Coulie*].

g298 **Breydy** Michael, Études maronites [... DUAYHY E., Apologie]: OrBibChr 2. Glückstadt 1991, Augustin. 140 p. 3-87030-151-1.

g299 *a) Brock* Sebastian, Syriac dispute poems; the various types; – *b) Drijvers* Han J. W., Body and soul; a perennial problem; – *c) Reinink* Gerrit J., Ein syrisches Streitgespräch zwischen Tod und Satan: ► 622, Dispute poems 1989/91, 109-119 / 121-134 / 135-152 with Syriac text.

g300 *Camplani* Alberto, In margine alla storia dei Meliziani [Alessandria c. 750 p.C.]: AugR 30 (1990) 313-351.

g301 *Cowe* S. Peter, The significance of the Persian War (572-591) in the Narratio de rebus Armeniae: Muséon 104 (1991) 265-276.

g302 **Cuming** Geoffrey J. †, The liturgy of St. Mark: OrChrAn 234, 1990 ► 6,k365: ᴿJTS 42 (1991) 355-8 (B. D. *Spinks*).

g303 [ᴱ*Depuydt* L.] ᴱ**Brakke** David, al., Homiletica from the Pierpont Morgan Library; seven Coptic homilies attributed to BASIL the Great, John CHRYSOSTOM, and EUODIUS of Rome: CSCOr 524s, Coptici 43s. Lv 1991, Peeters. I. xxi-123 p. Coptic text; II. xxiv-123, Eng. 0070-0428.

g304 **Gardner** Iain, Coptic theological papyri II 1988 ► 5,9467: ᴿBO 48 (1991) 544-6 (Albertyne *Dembska*).

g305 ᴱ**Haile** Getatchew, Misrak Amare, Beauty of the creation: JSS Mg 16. Manchester 1991, Univ. x-87 p. £25.

g306 **Haile** Getatchew, Haymanot Mäsiḥawit ... The faith of the Unctionists in the Ethiopian Church: CSCOr 517s, aeth. 91s. Lv 1990, Peeters. I. text 37 p.; II. tr. 36 p. 0070-0398.

g307 *Haile-Selassie* Sergew, An early Ethiopian manuscript, EMML 8509 [c. 1100, 57 homilies]: OstkSt 40 (1991) 64-80.

g308 **Isaac** Jacques, *Taksā*... Rite de pardon...: OrChrAn 233, 1989 ► 5, g904; 6,k369: ᴿJTS 42 (1991) 358-361 (B.D. *Spinks*).

g309 **Kannookadan** Pauly, The East Syrian lectionary; an historico-liturgical study [diss. Pont. Inst. Or., ᴰ*Taft* R. Roma 1991. 26 + 333 p. – RTLv 23, p. 559]. R 1991, Mar Thoma Yogam. xxxvi-215 p. [Muséon 105,197s, A, de *Halleux*].

g310 **Nasrallah** Joseph, (*Haddad* Rachid), Histoire du mouvement littéraire dans l'Église melchite 2/2, 1988 ► 5,g907: ᴿMuséon 104 (1991) 401s (J. *Grand'Henry*).

g311 ᵀᴱ**Selb** Walter, Sententiae syriacae: Szb ph./h. 567. W 1990, Österr. Akad. 219 p. – ᴿMuséon 104 (1991) 210s (A. de *Halleux*).

g312 **Stuart** Columba, 'Working the earth of the heart'; the Messalian controversy in history, texts and language to A.D. 431: OxTMg 10. Ox 1991, Clarendon. xi-340 p. £40 [Muséon 105,198, A. de *Halleux*].

g314 **Zanetti** Ugo, Les manuscrits de Deir Abû Maqâr; inventaire: Cah-Orientalisme 11. Genève 1986, Cramer. 100 p. Fs 75. – ᴿCdÉ 65 (1990) 374s (L. S. B. *MacCoull*).

---

g315 APHRAATES: ᵀᴱ**Bruns** Peter, Aphrahat, Unterweisungen 1: Fontes Christiani 5. FrB 1991, Herder. I, 279 p. 3-451-22206-X; pa. -106-3.

g316 **Bruns** Peter, Das Christusbild Aphrahats ᴰ1990 ► 6,k181: ᴿJTS 42 (1991) 738-740 (S. *Brock*).

g317 **Pierre** Marie-Joseph, Aphraate, Les Exposés I-II [► 6,k81]: SChr 349.359, 1988s ► 4,h935; 5,g912: ᴿGregorianum 72 (1991) 396s (J. *Janssens*); RBén 101 (1991) 401-3 (P.-M. *Bogaert*); RÉByz 48 (1990) 291 (J. *Wolinski*, 1); RHE 86 (1991) 115-7 (J.-M. *Fiey*); RTLv 22 (1991) 410s (A. de *Halleux*, II).

g318 BARSANUPHIUS: ᵀᴱ**Lovato** M. Francesca Teresa, *Mortar* Luciana, Barsanufio e GIOVANNI di Gaza, Epistolario: Collana TPatr 93. R 1991, Città Nuova. 650 p. 88-311-3093-5.

g319 CYRILLUS S.: ᵀ**Price** R. M., ᴱ*Binns* John, Cyril of Scythopolis [c. 524-558], Lives of the monks of Palestine. Kalamazoo 1991, Cistercian. lii-306 p. 0-87907-714-X; pa. -914-2.

g320 *Witakowski* Witold, Sources of Pseudo-DIONYSIUS [TM] for the third part of his Chronicle: OrSuec 40 (1991) 252-275.

g321 DIOSCORUS A.: **MacCoull** Leslie S. B., Dioscorus of Aphrodito, his works and his world: TransfClasH 16. Berkeley 1988, Univ. California. xvii-174 p. $30. 0-520-06226-4. – ᴿBO 48 (1991) 529-536 (Eva *Wipszycka*); StVlad 34 (1990) 101-4 (D. J. *Constantelos*).

g322 *MacCoull* Leslie S. B., A Coptic monastic letter to Dioscorus of Aphrodito: Enchoria 18 (1991) 23-25; pl. 7.

g322* ELIAS N.: *Khalil Samir*, Un traité nouveau d'Élie de Nisibe sur le sens des mots Kiyān et Ilāh: ParOr 14 (1987) 109-154 (263-288, Bulletin) [< ZIT 92,135].

g323 EPHRAEM: **Brock** Sebastian, L'œil de lumière, la vision spirituelle de S. Éphrem [10 conférences], ᵀ*Rance* D., + La harpe de l'Ésprit, florilège de poèmes: Spiritualité orientale 50. Bégrolles-en-Mauge 1991, Bellefontaine. 368 p. – ᴿEsprVie 101 (1991) 548-550 (P. *Jay*).

g323* *Bou Mansour* T., Étude de la terminologie symbolique chez Saint Éphrem: ParOr 14 (1987) 221-262 [< ZIT 92,135].

g324 *Griffith* Sidney H., Images of Ephraem; the Syrian holy man and his church: Traditio 45 (Fordham 1989s) 7-33.

g325 *Pattie* T. S., Ephraem's On repentance and the translation of the Greek text into other languages: British Library Journal 16 (1990) 174-185 [< RHE 87,34*].

g326 **Rouwhorst** G. A. M., Les hymnes pascales d'Éphrem de Nisibe; analyse théologique et recherche sur l'évolution de la fête pascale chrétienne à Nisibe et à Édesse et dans quelques églises voisines: VigChr supp. 7. Leiden 1989, Brill. I. Étude, xiii-224 p.; II. Textes (en français) 139 p. 90-04-08840-7; -1-5. – ᴿJTS 42 (1991) 741-4 (S. *Brock*: not the last word); RTLv 22 (1991) 398-401 (A. de *Halleux*).

g327 **Leloir** Louis, Saint Éphrem, commentaire de l'Évangile concordant, texte syriaque: Beatty 709, Mg 8. Lv 1990, Peeters. xxiv-157 p. – ᴿMuséon 104 (1991) 392-6 (A. de *Halleux*).

g328 EUSTATHIUS: **Tenšek** Tomislav Z., L'ascetismo nel Concilio di Gangra; Eustazio di Sebaste nell'ambiente ascetico siriaco dell'Asia Minore nel IV secolo: diss. Pont. Univ. Gregoriana, ᴰ*Špidlík* T. R 1991. 119 p. (excerpt.).

g329 HIPPOLYTE de Rome, Traité de l'Antéchrist, traduit de l'éthiopien: Semitica 40 (1991) 107-139.

g330 ISAACUS N.: ᵀᴱ**Bettiolo** Paolo, Isaaco di Ninive, Discorsi spirituali, capitoli sulla conoscenza, preghiere, contemplazione sull'argomento della gehenna, altri opuscoli²ʳᵉᵛ: Padri Orientali. Magnano 1990, Qiqajon. 266 p. 88-85227-21-X.

g331 St. Isaac of Nineveh, On ascetical life. Crestwood 1989, St. Vladimir. 116 p. 0-88141-077-2.

g332 IŠOˁ BAR NUN: **Molenberg** Cornelia, The interpreter interpreted; Išoˁ bar Nun's selected questions on the OT: diss. Groningen 1990. xviii-563 p. – ᴿMuséon 104 (1991) 208-210 (A. de *Halleux*).

g333 ISRAEL K.: **Holmberg** Bo, ❹ *Risala*... A treatise on the unity and trinity of God by Israel of Kashkar (d. 872): Lund Studies in African and Asian Religions 3. Lund 1989, Plus Ultra. 168 p. + ❹ 120 p.; 6 pl. – ᴿBSO 54 (1991) 438 (S. P. *Brock*); JSS 36 (1991) 167s (D. *Thomas*: good); Muséon 104 (1991) 402s (P. *Hanjoul*); ZDMG 141 (1991) 401s (H. *Daiber*).

g334 JACOBUS S.: *Hurst* Thomas R., The 'Transitus of Mary' in a homily of Jacob of Sarug: Marianum 52 (1990) 86-100.

g334* AL-JAḤIZ [siro-persiano]: ᵀᴱ**Caruso** Antonella, Il Libro dei moniti e della riflessione; un testo 'apocrifo' jahiziano: Asiatici min. 38. N 1991, Ist. Univ. Orientale. xiii-204 p.

g335 JOHANNES D.: **Beulay** Robert, L'enseignement spirituel de Jean de Dalyatha, mystique syro-oriental du VIIIe siècle: THist 83, 1990 → 6,k403: ᴿIrénikon 64 (1991) 141s (E. Lt.).

g336 JOHANNES S.: ᵀᴱ**Martikainen** Jouko, Johannes I. Sedra... syrische Texte, Worterverzeichnis: GöOrF 1/34. Wsb 1991, Harrassowitz. x-291 p. [Muséon 105,201, A. de *Halleux*].

g337 NARSAI: ᵀᴱ*Frishman* Judith, The ways and means of the divine economy... six biblical homilies by Narsai: diss. Leiden 1991. 18 + 116 + 4 + 124 + 18 + 193 p. [Muséon 105,388, A. de *Halleux*].

g337* PALLADIUS: a) *Vogüé* A. de, *Bunge* Gabriel, Palladiana 3. La version copte de l'histoire Lausiaque; – b) *Fisher* Arthur L., Women and gender in Palladius' Lausiac History: StMonast 33 (1991) 7-21 / 23-50.

g338 *Outtier* B., *Thierry* M., [MOVSĒS XORENACˈI] Histoire des saintes hripsimiennes: Syria 67 (1990) 695-733.

g338* THEODORUS AQ: *Griffith* S.H., Free will in Christian kalām; the doctrine of Theodore Abū Qurrah: ParOr 14 (1987) 79-108 [< ZIT 92,135].

g339 ZAR'A: ᵀᴱHaile Getatchew, The epistle of humanity of Emperor Zārʿa Yaʿaqob, *Tomarā Tesbeʿt*: CSCOr 522s, aeth. 95s. Lv 1991, Peeters. I. text vi-123 p.; II. Eng. xv-105 p. 0070-0398.

Y3 Medium aevum, generalia.

g340 **Angenendt** Arnold, Das Frühmittelalter; die abendländische Christenheit von 400 bis 900. Stu 1990, Kohlhammer. 499 p.; 89 fig. DM 69 pa. – ᴿTPhil 66 (1991) 258-260 (K. *Schatz*: standard reference).

g340* ᴱ**Balard** M., L'histoire médiévale en France; bilan et perspectives [textes]. P 1991, Seuil. 572 p. [RHE 87,169* < RNord 74,180, A. *Derville*].

g341 *Bataillon* Louis-Jacques, Le père M.-D. Chenu et la théologie du Moyen Âge; – b) Bulletin d'histoire des doctrines médiévales; ► 38, ᶠCHENU, RSPT 75 (1991) 449-456; Eng. 456 / 505-515.

g342 **Berschin** Walter, Greek letters and the Latin Middle Ages, from Jerome to Nicholas of Cusa²ʳᵉᵛ [1980 ► 63,b698], ᵀ*Frakes* J.C. Wsh 1988, Catholic Univ. xiv-415 p.; 2 fig. – ᴿByZ 83 (1991) 490-3 (F.J. *Thomson*: the 'revision' claimed by the translator is limited to corrections and minor additions).

g343 **Berschin** W., Medioevo greco-latino, da Gerolamo a Niccolò Cusano [1980 ► 63,b698], ᵀᴱ*Livrea* Enrico. N 1989, Liguori. Lit. 55.000. 88-207-1548-1. – ᴿFaventia 12s (1990s) 489-491 (J. *Martínez Gázquez*).

g344 ᴱ**Bertini** Ferruccio, Medioevo al femminile [... EGERIA, ELOISA]. R 1989, Laterza. xxvi-200 p.; ill. Lit. 28.000. – ᴿCC 142 (1991,1) 202s (P. *Vanzan*).

g344* **Beyer** Rolf, Die andere Offenbarung; Mystikerinnen des Mittelalters. ... 1989, Lübbe. 368 p.; 18 fig. DM 42. 3-7857-0449-6. – ᴿTLZ 116 (1991) 605s (J *Rüpke*).

g345 *Bliese* John R.E., The just war as concept and motive in the central Middle Ages: MedHum 17 (1991) 1-26.

g346 **Bot** P., Tussen verering en verachting; de rol van de vrouw in de middeleeuwse samenleving 500-1500. Kampen/Kapellen 1990, Kok/Pelckmans. 286 p. ƒ 49,50. 90-242-7687-X / 90-289-1554-0. – ᴿTsTNijm 31 (1991) 199 (M. van *Baest*).

g347 **Brundage** James A., Law, sex and Christian society in medieval Europe 1988 ► 4,h959; 5,g947: ᴿHeythJ 32 (1991) 142s (B.E. *Ferme*); Salesianum 53 (1991) 401s (G. *Gentileschi*).

g348 **Brunhölzl** F., Histoire de la littérature latine du Moyen Âge, I. De Cassiodore à la fin de la renaissance carolingienne, 1. L'époque mérovingienne [1975], ᵀ*Rochais* H.: Œuv.Réf.Médiév. LvN 1990, Inst. Ét. Médiév./Brepols. 327 p. Fb 2450. – ᴿNRT 113 (1991) 781 (S. *Hilaire* = 114,766).

g349 **Burrow** J.A., The ages of man; a study in medieval writing and thought 1986 ► 6,k425a: ᴿSalesianum 53 (1991) 403 (E. *Fontana*).

g350 **Bynum** Caroline W., Fragmentation and redemption; essays on gender and the human body in medieval religion. NY 1991, Zone. 426 p. £22.50 [TR 88,166 sub Walker].

Caulier B., L'eau et le sacré... en France du Moyen Âge à nos jours 1990 ► e405.

g351 **Cobban** Alan B., The medieval English universities 1988 ➤ 5,g649: ᴿScriptorium 44 (Bru 1990) 330 (Hilde de *Ridder-Symoens*].

g352 **Collins** R., Early medieval Europe, 300-1000. NY/Basingstoke 1991, St. Martin's/Macmillan. xxix-453 p. $45; pa. $17 [RHE 87,54*].

g353 *Cunningham* Lawrence S., The classics of western spirituality; some recent volumes [Paulist Press 1986-8; ALBERT & AQUINAS, ECKHART, BERNARD, PSEUDO-DIONYSIUS, ROLLE]: RelStR 17 (1991) 130-3.

g354 **Dahan** Gilbert, Les intellectuels chrétiens et les juifs au moyen âge [XIIᵉ-XIVᵉ s.] 1990 ➤ 6,k430; F 240: ᴿÉTRel 66 (1991) 604s (Dominique *Viaux*); Études 374 (1991) 410s (P. *Vallin*).

g355 **D'Ambrosio** Marcellino G., Henri de LUBAC and the recovery of the traditional hermeneutic: diss. Catholic University of America, ᴰ*Dulles* A. Wsh 1991. xxiv-388 p. – 91-23092.

g356 **Dekkers** E., Pour une histoire de la bibliographie chrétienne dans l'Antiquité et au Moyen Âge: ➤ 130, ᶠSANDERS G., Aevum 1991, 53-65.

g357 *a) Delcorno* Carlo, Bibbia e generi letterari del Medio Evo; – *b) Pani* Giancarlo, La tradizione esegetica dei quattro sensi biblici tra Medio Evo ed Età Moderna; – *c) Savigni* Raffaele, Uso della Scrittura e 'societas christiana' carolingia in GIONA d'Orléans [818-842]: ➤ 452, AnStoEseg 8,2 (1990/1) 547-564 / 657-676 / 631-655.

g358 ᴱ**Delègue** Yves, Les machines du sens [vastes constructions théoriques pour exposer, fonder, justifier et contrôler l'interprétation des Livres saints]; fragments d'une sémiologie médiévale; textes de HUGUES de Saint-Victor, Thomas d'AQUIN et Nicolas de LYRE. P 1987, Cendres. F 120. – ᴿRTLv 22 (1991) 89s (Marie *Hendrickx*).

g359 ᴱ**Dinzelbacher** Peter, *Bauer* Dieter R., Religiöse Frauenbewegung und mystische Frömmigkeit im Mittelalter: ArKuG Beih 28, 1986/8 ➤ 5,653: ᴿZKG 102 (1991) 135s (Martina *Wehrli-Johns*).

g360 **D'Onofrio** Giulio, Theological ideas and the idea of theology in the early Middle Ages: FreibZ 38 (1991) 273-297.

g360* **Duby** G., Wirklichkeit und höfischer Traum; zur Kultur des Mittelalters [franç.]ᵀ. Fra 1990, Fischer-Tb. 175 p. DM 14,80 [RHE 87,54*].

g361 **Ennen** Edith, The medieval woman. Ox 1989, Blackwell. 288 p. $35. 0-631-16166-X. – ᴿExpTim 102 (1990s) 287 (A. K. *McHardy*: well researched); JEH 42 (1991) 97s (Shulamith *Shahar*).

Fälschungen im Mittelalter 1986/8 ➤ 1464.

g361* ᴱ**Farrugia** E. G., *Taft* R. F., *Piovesana* G. K., Christianity among the Slavs [Rome Oct. 8-11, 1985]: OrChrAnal 231, 1988 ➤ 5,659: ᴿSpeculum 66 (1991) 494s (tit. pp.).

g362 **Fuhrmann** Horst, Einleitung ins Mittelalter 1987 ➤ 6,k436: ᴿSalesianum 53 (1991) 406 (G. *Gentileschi*).

g363 **Gaybba** B. P., Aspects of the medieval history of theology, 12th to 14th century: Studia Originalia 7, 1988 ➤ 6,k438; $22.75. 0-86981-563-6: ᴿSpeculum 66 (1991) 410-412 (G. *Marcil*); TsTNijm 31 (1991) 199s (P. *Valkenberg*).

g364 **Gies** Frances & Joseph, Marriage and the family in the Middle Ages 1987 ➤ 4,h967: ᴿSalesianum 53 (1991) 407s (G. *Gentileschi*).

g365 *Gliściński* Jan, ⊕ Der Arianismus als nationale Religion der Germanen [... WULFILAS]: ColcT 61,1 (1991) 81-87; deutsch 87.

g366 **Gonnet** Giovanni, Il grano e le zizzanie; tra eresia e riforme (secoli XII-XVI) 1989 ➤ 6,k440: ᴿProtestantesimo 46 (1991) 158s (D. *Maselli*).

g367 *Gonnet* Giovanni, La 'prima Riforma' [movimenti anteriori alla 'Seconda riforma' gregoriana ... Wiclif, Hus ... Mennoniti]: Protestantesimo 46 (1991) 187-191.

g368 **Herbert** Máire, Iona, Kells, and Derry; the history and hagiography of the monastic *familia* of Columba [< diss. Cambridge]. Ox 1988, Clarendon. 327 p. £35. 0-19-820114-1. – ᴿBijdragen 52 (1991) 218s (M. *Schneiders*).

g369 ᴱ**Humphreys** K. W., The friars' libraries; corpus of British medieval library catalogues. L 1990, British Library. xxxv-281 p.; 6 pl. – ᴿJTS 42 (1991) 381s (G. R. *Evans* speaks of 'the books' not obviously distinct from the 550 manuscripts).

g370 ᴱ**Iogna-Prat** Dominique, *Picard* Jean-Charles, Religion et culture autour de l'An Mil, royaume capétien et Lotharingie; Actes du colloque Hugues Capet, [couronné] 987-1987 (Auxerre/Metz 1987). P 1990, Picard. 352 p.; ill. – ᴿBén 101 (1991) 212-4 (D. *Misonne*).

g370* **Johnson** Penelope D., Equal in monastic profession; religious women in medieval France: Women in Culture and Society. Ch 1991, Univ. xv-294 p. $40. 0-226-40185-5 [TDig 39,67].

g371 *Keefer* S. L., *Burrows* D. R., Hebrew and the *Hebraicum* in late Anglo-Saxon England: in ᴱ**Lapidge** M., *al.*, Anglo-Saxon England 19 (C 1990, Univ.) 67-80 [< RHE 86,289*].

g372 **Kieckhefer** Richard, Magic in the Middle Ages. C 1990, Univ. x-219 p. £20; pa. £7 [HeythJ 33,213s, Mary E. *Mills*].

g373 **Leader** Damian R., A history of the university of Cambridge, I. to 1546, 1989 → 6,k452: ᴿScripB 21 (1991) 24 (C. *Harper-Bill*).

g374 **Leclercq** J., L'amour des lettres et le désir de Dieu; initiation aux auteurs monastiques du Moyen Âge³ [= ¹1957]. P 1990, Cerf. 272 p. [NRT 114,889, C. *Dumont*]. – ᴿÉtudes 375 (1991) 139 (J. *Thomas*).

g375 **Le Goff** Jacques, *al.*, El hombre medieval. M 1990, Alianza. 388 p. – ᴿRazF 223 (1991) 331 (J. *Fernández Sanz*).

g375* **Le Goff** Jacques, La borsa e la vita; dall'usuraio al banchiere. R 1987, Laterza. 124 p. Lit. 15.000 [Eng. 1988 → 5,9013]: ᴿCC 142 (1991,1) 302s (P. *Vanzan*); ChH 59 (1990) 401-3 (J. *Van Engen*, on the Eng.).

g376 *a)* ᴱ**Mackey** James P., An introduction to Celtic Christianity 1989 → 6,428: ᴿDocLife 40 (1990) 553-6 (H. *Pritchard Jones*); – *b)* *McNamara* Martin, Celtic Christianity, creation and apocalypse, Christ and Antichrist: MilltSt 23 (1989) 5-39.

g377 **Maisonneuve** Henri, L'inquisition. P/Ottawa 1989, D-Brouwer/Novalis. 170 p. F 120. – ᴿTüTQ 171 (1991) 150-2 (R. *Puza*).

g378 **Malcar** Linda A., The chalice at the Cross; a study of the Grail motif in medieval Europe: diss. UCLA 1991, ᴰ*Puhvel* J. 466 p. 91-26908. – DissA 52 (1991s) 1472s-A.

g379 **Markus** Robert A., The end of ancient Christianity. C 1990, Univ. xvii-258 p. £27.50; pa. £9 [TR 87,428]. 0-521-32716-4; -3949-9. – ᴿCathHR 77 (1991) 494s (J. J. *O'Donnell*); ExpTim 102 (1990s) 318s (W. H. C. *Frend*); Prudentia 23 (1991) 62-67 (P. *Rousseau*); TS 52 (1991) 742-4 (P. I. *Kaufman*).

g380 **Martin** H., Le métier de prédicateur à la fin du Moyen Âge (1350-1520). P 1990, Cerf. 720 p.; 14 pl. – ᴿCrNSt 11 (1990) 626-8 (G. M. *Cantarella*).

g381 *Meek* Donald, Celtic Christianity; what is it, and when was it? [Mackey J. 1989]: ScotBEvT 9 (1991) 13-21. → g376.

g381* *Menzel* Michael, Predigt und Predigtorganisation im Mittelalter: HistJb 111 (1991) 337-384.

g382 **Meyer** Heinz, *Suntrup* Rudolf, Lexikon der mittelalterlichen Zahlen-bedeutungen: Münsterische MA-Schriften 56. München 1987, Fink. xliv-1016 col. – RSalesianum 53 (1991) 167s (P. *Canaccini*).

g383 **Moulin** Léo, La vie des étudiants au Moyen Âge. P 1991, A. Michel. 300 p. F 120. – RÉtudes 375 (1991) 703 (P. *Vallin*).

g385 ENi **Chatáin** Próinséas, *Richter* Michael, Irland... / Ireland and Christendom, the Bible and the missions [1984 meeting, Dublin]: Tü Europa-Zentrum. Stu 1987, Klett-Cotta. xii-523 p. DM 64. 3-608-91441-2. – RBijdragen 52 (1991) 219s (M. *Schneiders*).

g386 *Oexle* O.G., Das Andere, die Unterschiede, das Ganze; Jacques LE GOFFS Bild des europäischen Mittelalters: Francia 17,1 (1990) 141-158 [< RHE 86,7*].

g387 *Pelikan* Jaroslav. The excellent empire 1987 → 4,h989... 6,k461: RJRel 71 (1991) 94s (R. *Saller*).

g388 *Penco* Gregorio, I secoli XI-XII, apogeo o crisi del monachesimo?: Benedictina 38 (1991) 351-363 [287-306, bibliografia Penco 1948-91].

g389 *Peters* Edward, Inquisition 1988 → 5,g982; 6,k462: RBogVest 50 (1990) 465s (B. *Kolar*); JRelHist 16 (1990s) 354-6 (G.B. *Harrison*).

g390 *Pilvousek* Josef, Zur Mentalität des mittelalterlichen Menschen: → 564, Erfurter 1989/90, 31-42.

g391 *Quacquarelli* Antonio, Esegesi biblica fra tardo-antico ed alto medioevo: VetChr 28 (1991) 223-252.

g391* *Ranft* Patricia, [The biblical concept of] Witness and the eleventh-century monastic renewal: JRelHist 16 (1990s) 361-373.

g392 *Reeves* Marjorie, The Bible and literary authorship in the Middle Ages: → 324, Reading the text 1991, 12-63.

g392* **Richards** Jeffrey, Sex, dissidence and damnation; minority groups in the Middle Ages. L 1991, Routledge. xii-179 p.; 34 pl. [RHE 87,583, D. *Bradley*].

g393 **Riché** Pierre, École et enseignement dans le Haut Moyen Age [Ve-XIe s.] 1989 → 6,k470: RScripTPamp 23 (1991) 1080s (M. *Lluch-Baixauli*).

g394 **Rubin** Miri, Corpus Christi; the Eucharist in late medieval culture. C 1991, Univ. xvi-300 p. £37.50. 0-521-25605-9. – REphLtg 105 (1991) 481-6 (A. *Ward*: worthwhile despite renderings of Latin).

g395 *Ruhe* Doris, Savoir des doctes et pratique pastorale à la fin du moyen âge; le cas du Second Lucidaire: CrNSt 11 (1990) 29-59; Eng. 60.

g396 [*Schneyer* Johannes B. †] **Lohr** Charles, *al.*, Repertorium der lateinischen Sermones des Mittelalters 10, Index der Textanfänge A-L/M-Z 1989s → 5,g987: RETL 67 (1991) 170s (R. *Wielockx*).

g397 *Sotomayor* Manuel, Enculturación y aculturación en la Andalucía tardoromana: Proyección 38 (1991) 295-308 [219-233, en la evangelización de los Jesuitas].

g398 **Spiridonakis** B.G., Grecs, occidentaux et Turcs de 1054 à 1453; quatre siècles d'histoire de relations internationales. Thessalonique 1990, Institute for Balkan Studies. 291 p. [RHE 87,55*].

g399 **Stürner** W., Peccatum und potestas; der Sündenfall und die Entstehung der herrscherlichen Gewalt im mittelalterlichen Staatsdenken: BeitGMA 11. Sigmaringen 1987, Thorbecke. 276 p. – RCrNSt 11 (1990) 386s (A.M. *Dubarle*).

ETennis H.B., *al.*, Kerstening... geestelijken en leken in de hoge middeleeuwen 1991 → 384*.

g400 *Valkenberg* Pim, *a*) Lecteurs de l'Écriture et auditeurs de la Parole dans l'Église du Moyen Âge, TBraat Anne: → 348, Concilium 233 (P 1991)

67-79; – *b*) Readers of Scripture and hearers of the Word in the mediaeval Church: ⇥ 347, Concilium (1991,1) 47-57.

g401 **Vauchez** André, Les laïcs au Moyen Âge; pratique et expériences religieuses. P 1987, Cerf. 309 p. [ital. 1989 ⇥ 6,k479]: ᴿSalesianum 53 (1991) 174s (E. *Fontana*).

g401* **Vernet** André, La Bible au moyen âge; bibliographie 1989 ⇥ 5,g996: ᴿHelmantica 42,129* (1991) 402 (S. *García-Jalón*).

g402 *Viciano* Alberto, Über die Priesterausbildung in der Spätantike: ForumKT 6 (1990) 260-7.

g403 **Weber** Alison, TERESA of Avila and the rhetoric of femininity. Princeton 1990, Univ. xi-183 p. $22.50 [RelStR 18,66, D. D. *Martin*: total unawareness of medieval monastic context].

g404 **Weijers** Olga, *a*) Dictionnaires et répertoires au Moyen Âge; une étude de vocabulaire: CIVICIMA 4. Turnhout 1991, Brepols. 212 p. Fb 1750 [TR 88,164]; – *b*) Méthodes et instruments de travail intellectuel au moyen âge; études sur le vocabulaire: CIVICIMA 3. Turnhout 1990, Brepols. 252 p. [RHE 87,167*].

g405 **Zerbi** Piero, Il Medioevo come categoria storiografica negli ultimi 50 anni; nascita d'Europa? Mi 1989, CUSI. 210 p. – ᴿCC 142 (1991,1) 201 (F. *Molinari*).

g406 *Zimmer* Christoph, Negation und via negationis: LingBib 64 (1990) 53-91; Eng. 91.

Y3.4 **Exegetae mediaevales** [hebraei ⇥ K7].

g407 ABELARDUS: **Allegro** Giuseppe, La teologia di Pietro Abelardo fra letture e pregiudizi: Scrinium 9. Palermo 1990, Studi Medievali. 159 p. Lit. 20.000. – ᴿBenedictina 38 (1991) 514s (S. *De Piccoli*: un grande pensatore da rivalutare).

g408 AEGIDIUS R.: **Luna** Concetta, *al.*, Medioevo 14 (volume intero su Egidio Romano, 1988). Padova 1990, Antenore. 438 p. Lit. 45.000. – ᴿETL 67 (1991) 447s (R. *Wielockx* ne mentionne pas l'Écriture).

g409 ALCUIN: **Forthomme-Nicholson** M., Pélage et Alcuin: ÉtClas 59 (1991) 43-51.

g410 ANDREAS SV: **Berndt** Rainer, André de Saint-Victor († 1175); exégète et théologien: Bibliotheca Victorina 2. Turnhout 1991, Brepols. 403 p. 2-503-50067-6.

g411 ANGELOMUS: **Cantelli** Silvia, Angelomo e la scuola esegetica di Luxeuil: Bt Medioevo Latino 1. Spoleto 1990, Centro Alto Medioevo. vi-530 p.; xxiv-250 pl. + 22*. Lit. 150.000.

g412 ANSELMUS: ᵀᴱ**Corbin** Michel, *al.*, Anselme de Cantorbéry 4. La conception virginale et le péché originel [⇥ 6,k484]; la procession du Saint-Esprit; lettres sur les sacrements de l'Église; Du pouvoir et de l'impuissance: Œuvres 4. P 1990, Cerf. 461 p. F 170. – ᴿRTLv 22 (1991) 253 (R. *Guelluy*).

g413 **Evans** G. R., Anselm 1989 ⇥ 5,g999: ᴿNBlackf 71 (1990) 316 (D. P. *Henry*).

g414 **Gilbert** Paul, Le Proslogion de S. Anselme; silence de Dieu et joie de l'homme. R 1990, Pont. Univ. Gregoriana. 284 p. Lit. 33.000. – ᴿCC 142 (1991,4) 92s (A. *Orazzo*).

g415 *a*) *Leclercq* Jean, Faith seeking understanding through images; – *b*) *Griffith* Sydney H., ... in the thought of St. EPHRAEM the Syrian: ⇥ 470, Anselm 1989/91, 5-12 / 35-55.

g416 **Southern** R.W., Saint Anselm, a portrait in a landscape. C 1990, Univ. xxx-493 p. £40. – RNBlackf 72 (1991) 245s (G.R. *Evans*: a plum-cake); RHE 86 (1991) 400s (P. *Brady*).

g417 AQUINAS: **Aartsen** Jan, Nature and creature; Thomas Aquinas's way of thought: StTGgMA 21. Leiden 1988, Brill. xiii-413 p. *f*142. – RTR 87 (1991) 392-6 (W.J. *Hoye*).

g418 **Brito** E., Dieu et l'être d'après Thomas d'Aquin et HÉGEL: Théologiques. P 1991, PUF. 422 p. F 245 [NRT 114,577-9, A. *Chapelle*: 'le véritable partenaire de Thomas n'est ni Descartes ni Kant, mais Hegel'].

g419 **Farthing** John L., Thomas Aquinas and Gabriel BIEL 1988 → 5,k110: RJAAR 59 (1991) 173-6 (W.J. *Courtenay*); Speculum 66 (1991) 150-2 (R. *McInerny*); Thomist 55 (1991) 149-156 (J. *Wawrykow*).

g420 **Geisler** Norman L., Thomas Aquinas, an evangelical appraisal. GR 1991, Baker. 195 p. $13 pa. 0-8010-3844-8 [TDig 39,164].

g421 *McGuckin* Terence, St. Thomas Aquinas and theological exegesis of Sacred Scripture: LvSt 16 (1991) 99-120.

g422 *Romaniuk* Kazimierz, L'esegesi dei passi neotestamentari sul sangue di Cristo in S. Tommaso d'Aquino: → 565, Sangue 1989/91, 1111-1124.

g423 **Tugwell** Simon, ALBERT & Thomas 1988 → 6,k489: RNBlackf 72 (1991) 199s (A. *Louth*: a delight).

g424 **Janz** Dennis R., LUTHER on Thomas Aquinas; the Angelic Doctor in the thought of the Reformer: Mainz Eur. Gesch. 140, 1989 → 5,k65; 3-515-05434-0: RJEH 42 (1991) 649-652 (R. *Rex*, also on LIENHARD 1989); JTS 42 (1991) 390-2 (A. *McGrath*: promises much, delivers little); Thomist 55 (1991) 145-8 (A.S. *Tune*).

g425 AVA: **Moehs** Teta E., The Gospel of Jesus according to Mistress Ava [Eng-German]. NY 1986, Senda Nueva. $13. 0-918454-53-0. – RJEH 42 (1991) 337 (Henrietta *Leyser*).

g426 BEDA: **Ward** Benedicta, The venerable Bede. L 1990, Chapman. xii-148 p. £19; pa. £9. 0-225-66542-5; -74-3. – RExpTim 102 (1990s) 352 (C.S. *Rodd*: superb); NBlackf 72 (1991) 348 (G.R. *Evans*).

g427 BERNARDUS C.: **Heller** Dagmar, Schriftauslegung und geistliche Erfahrung bei Bernhard von Clairvaux: Studien zur systematischen und spirituellen Theologie 2. Wü 1990, Echter. 228 p. DM 42; sb. 34. – RErbAuf 67 (1991) 147 ('V.A.' fehlt p. 506); TR 87 (1991) 382s (J. *Sudbrack*).

g428 **Leclercq** Jean, Bernhard von Clairvaux, ein Mann prägt seine Zeit [1989 → 6,k499], TBenning H.J.: Grosse Gestalten der Christenheit. Mü 1990, Neue Stadt. 198 p. DM 28. – RTLZ 116 (1991) 917-9 (H. *Holtze*).

g428* *Pérès* Jacques-Noël, Où il est question de source et de rivière; saint Bernard et Martin LUTHER à propos du rapport de l'Église à l'Écriture: → 91, FLECLERCQ J., ColcCist 52 (1990) 299-306.

g429 *Stercal* Claudio, Note su orientamenti e metodi degli studi su san Bernardo di Chiaravalle: TItSett 16 (1991) 236-251; Eng. 251.

g430 CUSANUS N.: *Boyle* Marjorie O., Cusanus at sea; the topicality of illuminative discourse: JRel 71 (1991) 180-201.

g431 **Haubst** Rudolf, Streifzüge in die cusanische Theologie: Cus.-Ges. Münster 1991, Aschendorff. xviii-633 p.; 2 fig. [TLZ 117,128, K.-H. *Kandler*].

g432 **Heinemann** Wolfgang, Einheit in Verschiedenheit; das Konzept eines intellektuellen Religionsfriedens in der Schrift 'De pace fidei' des Nikolaus von Kues [kath. Liz.-Diss. Tü 1986]: Studien 10. Altenberge 1987, CIS. 192 p. – ᴿTLZ 116 (1991) 194s (K.-H. *Kandler* würdigt nicht positiv; relativiert den Glauben, wie NK nicht).

g433 **Lentzen-Deis** Wolfgang, Den Glauben Christi teilen; Ansätze einer Verkündigungsdidaktik im Werk des Nikolaus von Kues unter besonderer Berücksichtigung ausgewählter Sermones: kath. Hab.-Diss. Bonn 1991, ᴰ*Bitter*. – TR 87 (1991) 511.

g433* DHOUDA: ᴱRiché Pierre, ᵀ*Vregille* Bernard de, *Mondésert* Claude, Dhouda, Manuel pour mon fils² [841 A.D.; ¹1975]: SChr 225 bis. P 1991, Cerf. 400 p. 2-204-04244-7.

g434 ECKHART: *Siena* Robertomaria, Eresia e ortodossia nella teologia di Meister Eckhart: Sapienza 44 (1991) 193-201.

g435 ERIUGENA: *Beierwaltes* Werner, Eriugena's fascination: → 111, ᶠO'MEARA J., 1991, 22-41.

g435* **Madec** Goulven, Jean Scot et ses auteurs: Annotationes Érigéniennes. P 1988, ÉtAug. 191 p. [TR 88,299, J. *Sudbrack*].

g436 **Jeauneau** Édouard, Études érigéniennes 1988 → 5,k21; 6,k514*: ᴿN-Blackf 71 (1990) 154s (P. L. *Reynolds*).

g436* **Klünker** Wolf-Ulrich, J. S. Eriugena; Denken im Gespräch mit dem Engel: Beiträge zur Bewusstseinsgeschichte 2. Stu 1988, Freies Geistesleben. 357 p.; 13 fig. DM 58 [TR 88,300, J. *Sudbrack*].

g437 **O'Meara** J. J., Eriugena 1988 → 4,k23 ... 6,k515: ᴿIrTQ 57 (1991) 328-330 (B. *McNamara*).

g438 **Otten** Willemien, The anthropology of Johannes Scottus Eriugena [Diss. Amsterdam]: StIntelH 20. Leiden 1991, Brill. viii-242 p. *f* 90 [TR 88,430].

g438* *Otten* Willemien, The dialectic of the return in Eriugenas's Periphyseon ['most original work in the history of Christian thought between Augustine and Anselm']: HarvTR 84 (1991) 399-421.

g439 **Rudnick** Ulrich, Das System des J. S. Eriugena; eine theologisch-philosophische Studie zu seinem Werk [Diss. Saarbrücken]: SaarbTF 2. Bern 1990, Lang. viii-412 p. DM 108 [TR 88,300, J. *Sudbrack*].

g439* *Schrimpf* G., J. Scot(t)us (Eriugena): → 681, LexMA 5 (1990) 602-5.

g440 EUCHERIUS L.: *Mandolfo* Carmela, Per una nuova edizione delle opere maggiori di Eucherio di Lione [Formulae spiritalis intellegentiae; Instructiones]: → 419, AnStoEseg 7,2 (1990) 647-657.

g441 GERSON: **Burger** Christoph, Aedificatio ... Gerson: BeitHistT 70, 1986 → 4,k24; 6,k519: ᴿBijdragen 52 (1991) 336s (B. *Leurink*).

g442 **Burrows** Mark S., Jean Gerson and De consolatione theologiae (1418); the consolation of a biblical and reforming theology for a disordered age [< diss. Princeton]: BeitHistT 78. Tü 1991, Mohr. xiii-312 p. DM 148. 3-16-145600-9 [TDig 39,152].

g442* *a)* *Burrows* Mark S., Jean Gerson on the 'traditional sense' of Scripture as an argument for an ecclesial hermeneutic; – *b)* *Ocker* Christopher, The fusion of papal ideology and biblical exegesis in the fourteenth century: → 58, ᶠFROEHLICH K. 1991, 152-172 / 131-151.

g443 GREGORIUS TUR.: **Nie** Giselle de, Views from a many-windowed tower; studies of imagination in the works of Gregory of Tours: StClasAnt 7. Amst 1987, Rodopi. 347 p. *f* 90. 90-6203-719-4. – ᴿArKulturG 72 (1990) 233-5 (Rosamund *McKitterick*, Eng.: good); Bijdragen 52 (1991) 217s

(M. *Parmentier*, Eng.: its much-needed empathy has been praised and even compared to Peter BROWN).

g444 GULIELMUS ST: **Piazzoni** A. M., Guglielmo di Saint-Thierry; il declino dell'ideale monastico nel secolo XII: Studi Storici 182s. R 1988, Ist. Medio Evo. 229 p. – ᴿCrNSt 11 (1990) 218s (Glauco M. *Cantarella*).

g445 HILDEGARD: *a*) *Inzolia* Santa, Esegesi biblica nell'epistolario di Ildegarda di Bingen; – *b*) *Giordano* Lisania, Figure dell'ascesi monastica in GUIGO I [certosino 12° sec.]; note sulle Consuetudines: ➤ 419, AnStoExeg 7,2 (1989/90) 659-668 / 669-684.

g446 HRABANUS M.: *Albert* Bat-Sheva, Raban Maur, l'unité de l'Empire et ses relations avec les Carolingiens [F. SULLIVAN 1989...]: RHE 86 (1991) 5-44.

g447 *Kottje* R., Hrabanus Maurus: ➤ 681, LexMA 5 (1990) 144-7.

g448 HUGO SV: *Ehlers* J., Hugo von S. Victor † 1141 = 681, LexMA 5 (1990) 177s.

g449 **Illich** I., Du lisible au visible; la naissance du texte, un commentaire du Didascalicon de Hugues de Saint-Victor, ᵀ*Mignon* J. P 1991, Cerf. 150 p. F 130 [NRT 114,768, S. *Hilaire*: 'du lisible au visible' means 'transit from monastic to scholastic reading'].

g450 **Sicard** P., Hugues de Saint-Victor et son École: Témoins de notre histoire. Turnhout 1991, Brepols. 288 p.; 6 pl. Fb 689 [NRT 114,767, A. *Harvengt*].

g451 ISIDORUS H.: *Fontaine* J., Isidor von Sevilla: ➤ 681, LexMA 5 (1990) 677-680.

g452 JOACHIM F.: ᴱ**Lee** Harold, *al.*, Western Mediterranean prophecy, Joachim 1987 ➤ 3,g448 ... 6,k528: ᴿJEH 42 (1991) 109s (R. E. *Lerner*); Speculum 66 (1991) 189s (D. *Burr*).

g452* *Pásztor* E., Joachim von Fiore: ➤ 681, LexMA 5 (1990) 485-7.

g453 JULIANA N.: **Jantzen** Grace M., Julian of Norwich 1987 ➤ 4,k31 ... 6,k531: ᴿChH 59 (1990) 81 (Ellen L. *Babinsky*); IrTQ 57 (1991) 349 (Deirdre *Carabine*); PerspRelSt 18 (1991) 203-6 (S. *Boyd*).

g453* **Nuth** Joan M., Wisdom's daughter; the theology of Julian of Norwich. NY c. 1991, Crossroad. 217 p. $25. 0-8245-1132-8 [TDig 39,279].

g454 **Pelphrey** Grant, Christ our mother; Julian 1989 ➤ 6,k532: ᴿNBlackf 71 (1990) 414-6 (J. P. H. *Clark*).

g455 LULLIUS R.: **Johnston** M. D., The spiritual logic of Ramón Llull [1232-1316; < diss. Baltimore 1977]. Ox 1987, Clarendon. xii-336 p. – ᴿCrNSt 11 (1990) 219s (F. *Santi*).

g456 ᴱ[Soria] **Flores** Abraham, *al.*, Raimundus Lullus, Opera latina 208-212: CCMed 80 / CETEDOC. Turnhout 1991, Brepols. 30 p.; 4 microfiches. 2-503-63802-3.

g457 MANETTI G.: **Dröge** Christoph, Giannozzo Manetti [1396-1459] als Denker und Hebraist [Diss. Bonn 1983]: JudUmw 20. Fra 1987, Lang. v-234 p. – ᴿJudaica 46 (1990) 55-57 (E. *Bons*).

g458 MARSH: *Lawrence* C. H., The letters of Adam Marsh [1241-59] and the Franciscan school at Oxford: JEH 42 (1991) 218-238.

g459 OCKHAM: *Kilcullen* John, Ockham and infallibility [... he fled with the Franciscan general from the Pope's court in 1328]: JRelHist 16 (1990s) 387-409.

g459* PEREGRINUS: ᴱ**Seyfarth** Jutta, Peregrinus, Speculum virginum: CCMed 5. Turnhout 1991, Brepols. 100 p.; 10 microfiches. 2-503-63052-9.

g460 PETRUS DAMIANUS: **Reindel** Kurt, Die Briefe des Petrus Damiani, 4. der deutschen Kaiserzeit 1-3. Mü 1983-8-9. vii-509 p.; xxx-557 p. [RHE 87,162s, P. *Riché*].

g461 PROSPER: *Tibiletti* Carlo, Nota sulla teologia del Carmen de providentia Dei [972 versi, attribuito a Prospero ML 51,615]: AugR 30 (1990) 453-476.

g462 RAMPEGOLUS: *Saak* E. L., The Figurae Bibliorum of Antonius Rampegolus O.E.S.A. (ca. 1360-ca. 1422): MS Uppsala C 162: ➤ 155, ᶠTRAPP D., Via Augustini 1991, 19-41.

g463 RUPERTUS T.: *Holze* Heinrich, Schriftauslegung aus monastischer Theologie bei Rupert von Deutz: ➤ 558, Sola Scriptura 1990/1, 229-239.

g464 *Silvestre* D., Rupert de Deutz (ca. 1075-1129): ➤ 664, Catholicisme XIII,95 (1991) 211-7.

g465 SALISBURY J.: ᴱHall J. B., Ioannes Saresberiensis, Metalogicon: CCMed 98 / CETEDOC. Turnhout 1991, Brepols. 61 p.; 6 microfiches. 2-503-63982-8.

SCOTUS: **Wolter** Allan B., Philosophical theology of Scotus 1990 ➤ 282.

g466 SEDULIUS: ᴱ**Meyers** I., Sedulius Scottus [† 854], Carmina: CCMed 117. Turnhout 1991, Brepols. li-192 p. 2-503-04171-2; pa. -2-8.

Y4.1 Luther.

g467 *Andersson* Bo, Luther's tower experience; the case for a rhetorical approach: Lutheran Quarterly NS 1 (1987) 205-213 [< LuJb 58, p. 165].

g468 **Asendorf** Ulrich, Die Theologie M. Luthers nach seinen Predigten 1988 ➤ 5,k44; 6,k548: ᴿGregorianum 72 (1991) 579-581 (J. E. *Vercruysse*).

g469 **Beck** Nestor, Igreja, sociedade e educação; estudos em torno de Lutero. Porto Alegre 1988, Concordia. 144 p. [LuJb 57 (1990) p. 320, with indication of six items there cited].

g470 ᴱ**Besch** Werner, *Wegera* Klaus P., Frühneuhochdeutsch; zum Stand der sprachwissenschaftlichen Forschung = Zts für deutsche Philologie 106 Sonderheft (1987). B 1987, Schmidt. 293 p. [LuJb 57 (1990) p. 321, with indication of four items there cited].

g471 **Beutel** Albrecht, In dem Anfang war das Wort; Studien zu Luthers Sprachverständnis: HermUnT 27. Tü 1991, Mohr. xviii-530 p. 3-16-145709-9.

g472 **Bluhm** Heinz, Studies in Luther / Lutherstudien. Fra 1987, Lang. 269 p. [LuJb 57 (1990) p. 322, with indication of 17 items there cited].

g473 **Brecht** Martin, Luther als Schriftsteller; Zeugnisse seines dichterischen Gestaltens. Stu 1990, Calwer. 127 p. [RelStR 18,63, D. R. *Janz*].

g474 **Brecht** Martin, Luther, shaping and defining the reformation, 1521-1532, ᵀ*Schaaf* James L. Mp 1990, Fortress. xvi-543 p. $40. 0-8006-2463-7. – ᴿTDig 38 (1991) 349 (W. C. *Heiser*: first of two volumes to continue his successful M. L.: road to reformation, Eng. 1985).

g475 *Brecht* Martin / *zur Mühlen* Karl-Heinz / *Mostert* Walter, Luther, Martin (1483-1546) Leben / Theologie / Wirtkungsgeschichte: ➤ 690, TRE 21 (1991) 513-530-567-594 (-620 *al.*, Ausgaben, Kirchen).

g476 **Brendler** Gerhard, Martin Luther, theology and revolution [c. 1983], ᵀ*Foster* Claude R. Ox 1991, UP. 383 p. $30. 0-19-505112-2 [TDig 39,52]. – ᴿSWJT 34,3 (1991s) 40s (W. R. *Estep*).

g477 **Delhaas** Sieth, Een protestantse non, Katharina von Bora [= ²Mevrouw Luther 1983]. Kampen 1989, Kok. 177 p. ƒ24,50. 90-24249-11-2. – ᴿNedTTs 45 (1991) 155 (R. van den *Broek*: onjuist).

g478 ᴱ**Dreher** Martin N., Reflexões em torno de Lutero 3. São Leopoldo 1988, Sinodal. 154 p. [LuJb 57 (1990) p. 320, with indication of five items there cited].

g479 **Emme** Dietrich, Martin Luthers Weg ins Kloster; eine wissenschaftliche Untersuchung in Aufsätzen. Rg 1991, auct. 219 p.; ill. DM 38 [TR 88,166].

g480 ᴱ**Fabisch** Peter, *Iserloh* Erwin, Dokumente zur Causa Lutheri [1. 1988 ➤ 4,k50; 5,k56; 2.] (1517-1521): CCath 41s. Münster 1991, Aschendorff. xv-558 p. 3-402-0345[5-7] -6-5.

g480* *Gritsch* Eric W., Luther's humor as a tool for interpreting Scripture: ➤ 58, ᶠFROEHLICH K. 1991, 187-197.

g481 **Hammann** Konrad, Ecclesia spiritualis... Luther, *al.* 1989 ➤ 6,k554*: ᴿTLZ 116 (1991) 678-680 (J. *Rogge*).

g482 ᴱ**Hutter** Ulrich, *Parplies* Hans-Günther, M. Luther und die Reformation in Ostdeutschland und Südosteuropa; Wirkungen und Wechselwirkungen: Jb SchlesKG Beih 8. Sigmaringen 1991, Thorbecke. 136 p.; 5 fig.; 4 pl. 9 art. [TLZ 117,203, S. *Bräuer*, tit. pp.].

Janz Dennis R., Luther on Thomas AQUINAS 1989 ➤ g424 supra.

g483 **Jüngel** Eberhard, The freedom of a Christian; Luther's significance for contemporary theology, ᵀ*Harrisville* Roy A., 1988 ➤ 5,k66: ᴿInterpretation 45 (1991) 206 (R. D. *Zimany*).

g484 *a) Kessler* Martin, Genealogische Beziehungen M. Luthers zu seinem Mansfelder Freundenkreis; – *b) Krodel* Gottfried G., Luther and the opposition to Roman Law in Germany: LuJb 58 (1991) 7-12 / 13-42.

g485 **Kittelson** James M., Luther the Reformer 1986 ➤ 3,g484... 6,k559; also Leicester 1989, Inter-Varsity. 300 p. + notes. £8. – ᴿScotJT 44 (1991) 266s (K. *Davies*).

g486 **Lienhard** Marc, Au cœur de la foi de Luther, Jésus-Christ: JJC 48. P 1991, Desclée. 348 p. F 159. – ᴿEsprVie 101 (1991) 551-3 (P. *Jay*).

g487 **Lienhard** Marc, L'Évangile et l'Église chez Luther 1989 ➤ 5,k75; 6,k562: ᴿNewTR 4,1 (1991) 89s (J. *Gros*); ScotJT 44 (1991) 410s (J. *Atkinson*).

g488 Lutero ayer y hoy. Buenos Aires 1984, Aurora. 331 p. [LuJb 57 (1990) p. 319 with indication of 11 articles there cited].

g489 Luthers Werke 64, Lateinisches Sachregister zu 1-60, A-C. Weimar 1990, Böhlau. xvii-667 p. – ᴿLuJb 58 (1991) 121-4 (H. *Junghans*; p. 64-70 über *ü*).

g490 **Lutz** Jürgen, Unio und communio; zum Verhältnis von Rechtfertigungslehre und Kirchenverständnis bei M. Luther; eine Untersuchung zu ekklesiologisch relevanten Texten der Jahre 1519-1528: KkKSt 55. Pd 1990, Bonifatius. 311 p. DM 48. – ᴿForumKT 7 (1991) 317s (A. *Schmidt*); MüTZ 42 (1991) 285-7 (M. *Hardt*); TR 87 (1991) 285-7 (M. *Hardt*).

g491 **McGoldrick** James E., Luther's Scottish connection 1989 ➤ 6,k565: ᴿJEH 42 (1991) 160 (M. *Lynch*).

g492 **Moda** Aldo, Martin Luthero, un decennio di studi (1975/76-1986/87) attorno ad un centenario (1483-1983) O odigos quad. 1989 ➤ 5,k83* (non 'Mora'): ᴿAsprenas 38 (1991) 260s (P. *Cacciapunti*); Divinitas 35 (1991) 100-2 (B. *Gherardini*); RHPR 71 (1991) 391 (M. *Arnold*).

g493 *Muesse* Mark W., Scripture as proclamation in the theology of Martin Luther: Arasaradi 4.2 (1991) 32-48.

g494 **Oberman** Heiko, Luther, man between God and the devil 1989 ➤ 6,k572: ᴿCommonweal 117 (1990) 161 (L. S. *Cunningham*); SWJT 34,3 (1991s) 38s (W. R. *Estep*).

Pérès Jacques-Noël, Où il est question... Bernard et Luther 1990 ➤ g428*.

g495 ᴱPeura S., *Raunio* A., Luther und Theosis 1989/90 → 6,669*: ᴿTR 87 (1991) 201s (G. *Wenz*).

g496 ᴱRonchi de Michelis Laura, Martin Lutero, Replica ad Ambrogio Catarino sull'Anticristo; antitesi illustrata della vita di Cristo e dell'Anticristo: Opere Scelte 3, 1989 → 6,k575; 88-7016-100-5: ᴿActuBbg 28 (1991) 83s (H. *Vall*).

g496* *Russell* William R., The Smalcald articles, Luther's theological testament: LuthQ 5 (Ridgefield 1991) 277-296. 469-492 [< ᴢɪᴛ 92,80].

g497 Saarinen Risto, Gottes Wirken auf uns; die transzendentale Deutung des Gegenwart-Christi-Motivs in der Lutherforschung [Diss.]: Mainz-EurGR 137. Stu 1989, Steiner. x-241 p. – ᴿForumKT 6 (1990) 156-8 (A. *Schmidt*); LuJb 58 (1991) 126-9 (H. *Junghans*).

g498 *Steinacker* Peter, Luther und das Böse; theologische Bemerkungen im Anschluss an Luthers Schrift 'De servo arbitrio' (1525): → 125, ᶠRAT-SCHOW C., NSys 33 (1991) 139-151; Eng. 151.

Y4.3   Exegesis et controversia saeculi XVI.

g499 Allison A. F., *Rogers* D. M., The contemporary printed literature of the English counter-reformation I, 1989 → 5,k98: ᴿEphLtg 105 (1991) 182s (A. *Ward*).

g500 *Allister* Donald, The English Reformers' teaching on salvation: Churchman 105 (1991) 148-165 [< ᴢɪᴛ 91,484].

g501 Arnold Martin, Handwerker als theologische Schriftsteller; Studien zu Flugschriften der frühen Reformation (1523-1525): Diss. Gö. Gö 1990, Vandenhoeck & R. x-383 p.; 5 fig. – ᴿLuJb 58 (1991) 137-9 (H. *Junghans*); ZtsBayerische Landesgeschichte 53 (Mü 1990) 805s (D. *Wölfel*) [< RHE 86,307*].

g502 *Augustijn* Cornelis, *a)* Les Réformateurs du XVIᵉ siècle et la Bible, ᵀ*Braat* Anne: → 348, Concilium 233 (P 1991) 81-93; – *b)* The sixteenth century Reformers and the Bible: → 347, Concilium (1991,1) 58-68.

g503 Bagchi David V. N., Luther's earliest opponents; Catholic controversialists, 1518-1525. Mp 1991, Fortress. xiii-305 p. $25. 0-8006-2517-X [TDig 39,252].

g503* Bauer Barbara, Jesuitische 'ars rhetorica' im Zeitalter der Glaubenskämpfe 1986 → 2,d678 (Index!); ᴿPrzPow 271 163-7 (S. *Obirek*, ❶).

g504 ᴱBedouelle Guy, *Roussel* Bernard, Le temps des Réformés et la Bible: BTT 5, 1989 → 5,k101; 6,k582: ᴿCathHR 77 (1991) 107s (J. H. *Bentley*); CiuD 203 (1990) 744s (J. *Gutiérrez*); IndTSt 27 (1990) 100-2 (L. *Legrand* would have preferred more on John of the Cross to the kabbalistic speculations of Luis de León); RTPhil 123 (1991) 118s (M. *Engammare*).

g504* *Biagetti* Stefania, Emilio Comba (1839-1904), storico della Riforma italiana e del movimento valdese medievale. T 1989, Claudiana. 127 p. – ᴿSTEv 2 (1990) 236 [non firmata; p. 243 indica come recensente P. *Guccini*, ma come autore S. Biagini].

g505 Birmelé A., *Lienhard* M., La foi des églises luthériennes; confessions et catéchismes P/Genève 1991, Cerf / Labor et Fides. 605 p. – ᴿProtestantesimo 46 (1991) 227 (B. *Corsani*).

g505* Böttcher Diethelm, Ungehorsam oder Widerstand? Zum Fortleben des mittelalterlichen Widerstandsrechtes in der Reformationszeit (1529-1530): HistF 46. B 1991, Duncker & H. [TR 88,343].

g506 **Buck** August, Humanismus; seine europäische Entwicklung in Dokumenten und Darstellungen: Orbis Academicus 1/16. Fr 1987, Alber. 583 p. – RSalesianum 53 (1991) 402 (G. *Gentileschi*).

g507 **Bujanda** J. M. de, Index des livres interdits, 7. Anvers 1569, 1570, 1571: 1988 ➤ 6,k589: RZKG 102 (1991) 265s (R. *Bäumer*).

g508 *Burian* Ilja, Die Gegenreformation in den tschechischen Ländern: JbGProtÖsterr 106 (1990) 19-61 [< ZIT 91,297].

g509 **Campi** Emilio, Protestantesimo nei secoli 15 e 16, fonti e documenti. T 1991, Claudiana. 474 p.; 89 fig. Lit. 48.000 [TR 88,255].

g510 EChaunu Pierre, The Reformation [➤ L'aventure... Calvin 1986 ➤ 2, 283],T. Gloucester 1989, Sutton. 296 p. £30. – REvQ 63 (1991) 286s (A. S. *Wood*).

g511 **Collinson** Patrick, The birthpangs of Protestant England; religious and cultural change in the sixteenth and seventeenth centuries [Kent Amsley Lectures 1986]. xiii-188 p. £30. – REvQ 63 (1991) 361s (A. G. *Newell*).

g512 **Dmitriev** Michail V., ❹ Pravoslavie... L'Église orthodoxe et la Réforme; les mouvements réformés dans les pays slaves orientaux de la République polonaise dans la seconde moitié du XVIe siècle. Moskva 1990, Univ. 134 p. – RRHR 208 (1991) 450-452 (J. *Tazbir*: already extensively treated, as shown by the author).

g514 *Dyl* Janusz, ❹ Bibeln und biblische Kommentare, die in Polnischen Offizinen etwa in den Jahren 1475-1550 gedruckt worden sind: RoczTK 37,4 (1991 für 1987) 5-21 (-25, Katalog); deutsch 26.

g515 EEvans Gillian R., *Wright* J. Robert, The Anglican tradition, a handbook of sources [120 pre-Anglican + 486 selections since 16th cent.]. L/Mp 1991, SPCK/Fortress. xx-620 p. $30. -/0-8006-2483-1 [TDig 39,45].

g516 **Evans** Gillian R., The language and logic of the Bible; the road to Reformation 1985 ➤ 1,f811 ... 4,k97: RRB 98 (1991) 151s (B. T. *Viviano*).

g517 *Frost* F., Réforme: ➤ 664, Catholicisme XII,56 (1990) 591-641.

g518 *Gäbler* Ulrich, Die Basler Reformation: TZBas 47 (1991) 7-17.

g519 **Ganzer** Klaus, Aspekte der katholischen Reformbewegungen im 16. Jahrhundert: AbhMainz g/soz 1991/13. Stu 1991, Steiner. 36 p. [TR 88,166].

g519* *García Oro* J., La Iglesia de Toledo en tiempo del Cardenal Cisneros (1495-1517): VerVid 49 (194s entero, 1991) 135-398.

g520 **George** Timothy, Theology of the Reformers 1988 ➤ 4,k102... 6,k606: RMid-Stream 28 (1989) 142-4 (A. P. F. *Sell*); RExp 88 (1991) 480 (W. L. *Allen*).

g521 EGilmont J.-F., La Réforme et le livre 1990 ➤ 6,411*: RBibHumRen 53 (1991) 203s (Monique *Droin-Bridel*); FoiVie 89,6 (1990) 114s (P. *Grojeanne*); Protestantesimo 46 (1991) 62-65 (G. *Gonnet*, con lista delle traduzioni bibliche citate); RHR 208 (1991) 447-450 (G. *Audisio*); TLZ 116 (1991) 125s (J. *Rogge*: blurb, 'The Reformation is GUTENBERG's daughter').

g522 *Higman* Francis, Les usages de l'histoire ecclésiastique [...CALVIN, VIRET]: RTPhil 123 (1991) 49-58; Eng. 127.

g523 EHudson Anne, *Wilks* Michael, From Ockham to Wyclif [Oxford 15-19.IV.1985] 1987 ➤ 5,473: RSalesianum 53 (1991) 189s (P. T. *Stella:* tit. pp.).

g524 EIserloh Erwin, Katholische Theologen der Reformationszeit 1-5, 1984-7 ➤ 1,362... 6,k614: RTrierTZ 100 (1991) 75s (A. *Dahm*, 3).

g525 **Iserloh** Erwin, Compendio di storia e teologia della riforma. Brescia 1990, Morcelliana. 308 p. Lit. 30.000. – RCC 142 (1991,1) 520-2 (J. *Wicks*).

g526 **Kantzenbach** Friedrich W., Geist und Religion der Neuzeit, 1. Transformation des Reformatorischen, von Luther bis Herder: Schriften zur Internationalen Kultur- und Geisteswelt 9. Saarbrücken-Scheidt 1991, Dadder. 457 p. DM 60 [TR 87,343].

g526* *Kaplan* Benjamin J., Dutch particularism and the Calvinist quest for 'holy uniformity': ArRefG 82 (1991) 239-256.

g527 **Kick** R., Au service de l'Église et de la Couronne; l'imprimerie durant la Réforme en Suède-Finlande: Kyrkhist. Årsbok (1991) 83-91 [en suédois, < RHE 87,277*].

g528 **Kirk** James, Patterns of Reform; continuity and change in the Reformation Kirk 1989 → 5,k120: ᴿRHPR 71 (1991) 394s (M. *Arnold*).

g529 **McGrath** Alister E., Reformation thought 1988 → 4,k107*... 6,k621: ᴿJRelHist 16 (1990s) 223-5 (B. E. *Mansfield*).

g530 **McGrath** Alister E., Il pensiero della Riforma; Lutero-Zwingli-Calvin-Bucero; una introduzione [Reformation thought 1988 → 4,k107*]ᵀ. T 1991, Claudiana. 224 p. Lit. 24.000. – ᴿHoTheológos 9 (1991) 246-252 (C. *Scordato*).

g531 *Menke* Karl-Heinz, Das Unfehlbarkeitsverständnis der 'gegenreformatorischen Konzilstraktate': Catholica 45 (1991) 102-118.

g532 ᴱ**Meuthen** Erich, Reichstage und Kirche [15.-16. Jh.]: Bayer. Akad. Hist. Komm. 42, Kolloquium 9.III.1990. Gö 1991, Vandenhoeck & R. 272 p. DM 78 [TR 88,167, tit. pp.].

g533 *Mies* Françoise [p. 456 Française], Faust et la révélation: RTLv 22 (1991) 343-369; Eng. 456 'The Faustbuch (1587), an anonymous Lutheran work, which opened the great Faustian mythical tradition'.

g534 *Miethke* Jürgen, Die mittelalterlichen Universitäten und das gesprochene Wort: HZ 251 (1990) 1-44.

g535 **Oelke** Harry, Die Konfessionsbildung des 16. Jahrhunderts im Spiegel illustrierter Flugblätter: ev. Diss. Kiel 1991, ᴰMaron. – TR 87 (1991) 519.

g536 **Olin** John C., Catholic reform; from Cardinal Ximenez to the Council of Trent, 1495-1563. NY 1991, Fordham Univ. 152 p. $35. – ᴿAmerica 164 (1991) 499s (J. W. *O'Malley*).

g538 *Seibrich* Wolfgang, Gegenreformation als Restauration; die restaurativen Bemühungen der alten Orden im deutschen Reich von 1580 bis 1648: BeitGBen 38. Münster 1991, Aschendorff. xlii-729 p. DM 230 [TLZ 117, 845-9, E. *Koch*: 'Standardwerk'].

Shaull Richard, The Reformation and liberation theology; insights for the challenges of today. 1991 → 8578.

g539 *Skowronek* Alfons, ❶ An der Abgrenzung der Häresie; das 16. Jahrhundert und heute: ColcT 61,1 (1991) 33-47; deutsch 48.

g540 *Snyder* Arnold, Biblical text and social context; Anabaptist anticlericalism in Reformation Zürich: MennoniteQR 65 (1991) 169-191 [< ZIT 91,396].

g541 **Vilanova** Evangelista, Historia de la teología cristiana, II. Pre-reforma, reformas, contra-reforma 1986 → 3,g553... 6,k641: ᴿCiuD 203 (1991) 243s (J. M. *Ozaeta*); TVida 32 (1991) 324s (Anneliese *Meis*).

g542 *Vinay* Valdo, La Riforma; chiese e sette protestanti: < ᴱFirpo Luigi, Storia delle idee politiche, economiche e sociali 3 (T 1987, UTET) 299-410. – ᴿRHPR 71 (1991) 388 (A. *Moda*).

g543 **Voss** Klaus P., Der Gedanke des allgemeinen Priester- und Prophetentums; seine gemeindetheologische Aktualisierung in der Reformationszeit: MgStB. Wu 1990, Brockhaus. 302 p. [TLZ 117,679-683, J. *Rogge*].

g544 **Weir** David A., The origins of the federal theology in sixteenth-century Reformation thought 1990 → 6,k643: ᴿJRelHist 16 (1990s) 495-7 (R. D. *Linder*).

g545 ᴱ**Wilson** Katharina M., Women writers of the Renaissance and Reformation. Athens GA 1987, Univ. xi-638 p. [LuJb 57 (1990) p. 322, citing only 2 items].

g545* *Wright* William J., Mainz versus Rome; two responses to Luther in the 1520s: ArRefG 82 (1991) 83-106 [< ZIT 91,661].

g546 *Zeeden* Ernst W., [Nachtridentinische] Visitationsforschung und Kirchengeschichtsschreibung: TR 87 (1991) 353-366 [365-7, H. *Molitor*, Repertorium der Kirchenvisitationsakten ᴱZeeden, 1-3, 1982-7].

g547 *Ziegler* Walter, Reformation als Gemeindereformation? [BLICKLE P. 1984 ²1987]: ArKulturG 72 (1990) 441-453.

g547* *Zim* Rivkah, The Reformation; the trial of God's word: → 324*, Reading the text 1991, 64-135.

Y4.4   Periti aetatis reformatoriae.

g548 ANDREAE: ᵀᴱ**Ehmer** H., Leben des Jakob Andreae, Doktor der Theologie, von ihm selbst mit grosser Treue und Aufrichtigkeit beschrieben, bis auf das Jahr 1562 [¹1630]: QForWürtKG 10. Stu 1991, Calwer. 146 p.; 1 pl. [TLZ 117,922, E. *Koch*].

g549 ARMINIUS: **Muller** Richard A., God, creation, and Providence in the thought of Jacob Arminius; sources and directions of scholastic Protestantism in the era of early orthodoxy. GR 1991, Baker. x-309 p. $16 pa. 0-8010-6279-9 [TDig 39,178].

g550 *Muller* Richard A., The Christological problem in the thought of Jacobus Arminius: NedArchiefKG 68 (1988) 145-163 [< ZIT 91,299].

g551 AZOR: **Dziuba** Andrzej F., ❷ Jan Azor teolog moralista [† 1603]. Wsz 1988, Archidiecezja. xxix-346 p. [español 337-346]. – ᴿColcT 61,1 (1991) 183-6 (J. *Lewandowski* ❷); Teresianum 42 (1991) 359 (S. T. *Praskiewicz*).

g552 BARRADAS: *a*) *Marques Gonçalves* Manuel, A noemática bíblica em Sebastião de Barradas (1543-1615); – *b*) *Coelho Matias* Jose, Manuel de SÁ (1531-1596), precursor do método histórico-crítico: → 422, Didaskalia 20,1 (1990) 85-123 / 125-142.

g553 BELLARMINO: **Biersack** Manfred, Initia Bellarminiana; die Prädestinationslehre bei Robert Bellarmin bis zu seinen Löwener Vorlesungen 1570-1576 [Diss. Tü 1980, ᴰ*Oberman* H.]: Hist, Forsch. 15. Stu 1989, Steiner. 550 p. [LuJb 58,186].

g554 ᴱ**Donnelly** John P., *Teske* Roland J., Robert Bellarmine, Spiritual writings 1989 → 5,k148; 6,k651: ᴿCathHR 77 (1991) 111s (D. C. *Nugent*: splendid).

g554* BEZA: *Summen* Kirk M., Theodore Beza's classical library and Christian humanism; ArRefG 82 (1991) 193-208 [< ZIT 91,662].

g555 BODENSTEIN: **Hasse** Hans-Peter, 'Gelassenheit ist besser denn Haben'; die Motive 'Gelassenheit', 'Kreuz' und 'Leiden' in der Theologie des Andreas Bodenstein von Karlstadt: Diss. Leipzig 1991, ᴰ*Junghans*. – TR 87 (1991) 519.

g556 BOLLANI: *Donvito* Luigi, Disciplinamento e storiografia; il volume di D. MONTANARI [Bo 1987] sul vescovo Bollani [Domenico, 1559-78]: CrNSt, fascicolo di 16 p. fornito col fasc. 2 per sostituire il testo 'mutilo' di CrNSt 11,1 (1990) 187-195; Eng. 196.

g557 BUCER: **Greschat** Martin, Martin Bucer. Mü 1990, Beck. 308 p.
DM 78. – ᴿDLZ 112 (1991) 578-580 (G. *Wendelborn*); JEH 42 (1991) 652s
(A. *McGrath*).

g557* *a) Hamman* Gottfried, Vivre autrement! Le message de Martin Bucer
pour notre temps: PosLuth 39 (1991) 211-230 [< ZIT 92,17]; – *b)*
Kaufmann Thomas, Bucers Bericht von der Heidelberger Disputation:
ArRefG 82 (1991) 147-170 [< ZIT 91,662].

g558 BUDNY, *al.*: **Pietrzyk** Zdzisław, Szymon Budny (1530-1593); *Wijaczka*
Jacek, Christian FRANCKEN (1552-1602); *Matuszewski* Adam, Pierre
STATORUS [† 1568], Antitrinitaires polonais: Bt. dissidentium 13 / Bt-
BibliogAureliana 129. Baden-Baden 1991, Koerner. 204 p. – ᴿRHE 87
(1991) 241 (J.-F. *Gilmont*).

g559 BULLINGER: *Biel* Pamela, Bullinger against the Donatists; St.
AUGUSTINE to the defence of the Zurich Reformed Church: JRelHist
16 (1990s) 237-246.

g560 **Blanke** Fritz, *Leuschner* Immanuel, Heinrich Bullinger, Vater der reformierten Kirche. Z 1990, Theol.-V. 334 p.; ill. Fs 19. – ᴿTLZ 116
(1991) 197-9 (E. *Koch*).

g561 **McCoy** Charles S., *Baker* J. Wayne, Fountainhead of federalism; Heinrich Bullinger and the covenantal tradition + ᵀDe testamento 1534.
Louisville 1991, W-Knox. 180 p. $25. 0-664-21938-1 [TDig 39,273].

g562 CALVIN: **Bouwsma** William J., John Calvin, a sixteenth-century portrait 1988 ➤ 4,k141; 5,k156: ᴿEcuR 41 (1991) 146s (Jill *Schaeffer*);
EngHR 106 (1991) 991s (F. M. *Higman*); RRel 49 (1990) 628s (J. *Gros*:
Roman Catholic spirituality has been more influenced by WESLEY and
LUTHER); Salesianum 53 (1991) 188s (E. *Fontana*: extraordinarily attractive, by a real expert, though in his bibliography his own name
appears only once); TrinJ 12 (1991) 102s (M. I. *Klauber*).

g563 **Coats** Catharine R., Subverting the system [... BÈZE overstressing
Scripture at the expense of selfhood; 1552-1630 Agrippa] d'AUBIGNÉ and
Calvinism: SixtC ESt 14. Kirksville MO 1990, SixtC. vii-214 p. $35
[RelStR 18,64, D. K. *McKim*].

g564 **Denniston** John J., An examination of Calvin's theory of knowledge in
his theology and exegesis: diss. Fordham, ᴰ*Viladesau* R. NY 1991. 284 p.
91-27029. – DissA 52 (1991s) 1387-A; RelStR 18,171.

g565 ᴱ**Furcha** E. J., In honor of J. Calvin 1986/7 ➤ 3,597*; 4,k143: ᴿJEH
42 (1991) 665s (Gillian *Lewis*: without reaction to BOUWSMA, does not
reflect any alleged 'lively debate').

g566 [Gallicet] **Calvetti** Carla, Sebastiano CASTELLION, il riformato umanista
contro il riformatore Calvino. Mi 1989, Univ. Cattolica. 424 p. Lit.
60.000. 88-343-1762-9. – ᴿCC 142 (1991,2) 300s (P. *Molinari*); RHPR 71
(1991) 400 (M. *Chevallier*).

g567 ᴱ**George** Timothy, John Calvin and the Church; a prism of reform
[Davidson College colloquia 1982-8] 1990 ➤ 6,616*: ᴿPerspRelSt 18
(1991) 193-7 (G. A. *Hewitt*: also on George 1988; and preferring
BOUWSMA W. 1989).

g568 *Hallett* Adrian, The theology of John Calvin, I., The Christian's conflict
with the world; II. with the flesh; III. with the Devil: Churchman 105 (L
1991) 102-138 . 197-245 . 293-325 [< ZIT 91,484; 92,71]..

g569 **Hamersveld** Michael D. van, The concept of 'suspensio' in Calvin's
interpretation of the Gospel: diss. ᴰ*Torrence* J. B. – RTLv 23, p. 553,
'Torrence'.

g570 **Leith** John H., John Calvin's Doctrine of the Christian life 1989 ➤ 5,k161; 6,k664: ᴿInterpretation 45 (1991) 67s (Elsie A. *McKee*).

g571 **McGrath** Alister E., A life of John Calvin; a study in the shaping of western culture 1990 ➤ 6,k666: ᴿÉTRel 66 (1991) 295s (H. *Bost*: destined to be standard reference); JEH 42 (1991) 653s (Gillian *Lewis*); TLond 94 (1991) 366s (P. N. *Brooks*); TS 52 (1991) 746-8 (Jeannine E. *Olson*).

g572 **Oberman** Heiko A., De erfenis van Calvijn, grootheid en grenzen [1986 Kuyper-lectures]. Kampen 1988, Kok. 57 p. ƒ14.90. 90-24233-42-9. – ᴿNedTTs 45 (1991) 72s (C. *Graafland*).

g573 ᴱ**Prestwick** Menna, *al.*, International Calvinism, 1541-1715; 1985 ➤ 3, 448; 5.k154: ᴿRHR 208 (1991) 101-3 (G. *Audisio*).

g574 **Scheld** Stefan, Media salutis; zur Heilsvermittlung bei Calvin 1989 ➤ 5,k166: ᴿTLZ 116 (1991) 40s (J. *Rogge*).

g574* *a) Steinmetz* David C., Calvin among the Thomists; – *b) McKee* Elsie Anne, Some reflections on relating Calvin's exegesis and theology: ➤ 58, ᶠFROEHLICH K. 1991, 196-214 / 215-226.

g575 **Wallace** Ronald S., Calvin, Geneva, and the Reformation 1988 ➤ 4, k153...6,k675: ᴿScotJT 44 (1991) 116 (W. P. *Stephens*, with brief praise for GANOCZY's now over 20-year-old Young Calvin).

g576 *Zimmermann* Gunter, Die Vereinigung mit Gott und das Reich Christi nach Calvins 'Institutio': Zwingliana 18,3 (1990) 193-212.

g577 CRANMER: *Clifford* Alan C., Cranmer as Reformer: EvQ 63 (1991) 99-122.

g577* **Brooks** P. N., Cranmer in context 1989 ➤ 4,k683: ᴿRExp 88 (1991) 105s (Karen E. *Smith*).

g578 ECK: ᴱ**Iserloh** E., J. Eck im Streit 1986/8 ➤ 5,k177; 6,k687: ᴿJEH 42 (1991) 518 (P. *Slack*); TLZ 116 (1991) 37-39 (S. *Bräuer*).

g579 ERASMUS: *González* Ignazio, Literatura y moral; la literatura erasmista (I): Moralia 13 (Madrid 1991) 33-58 [< ZIT 91,178].

g579* **Augustijn** Cornelis, Erasmus; his life, works, and influence: Erasmus Studies 10. Toronto 1991, Univ. x-239 p. [TR 88,431].

g580 **De Molen** Richard L., The spirituality of Erasmus 1987 ➤ 4,k156... 6,k689: ᴿOnsGErf 65 (1991) 82-84 (G. de *Baere*).

g581 **Halkin** Léon E., Érasme parmi nous 1988 ➤ 5,k181: ᴿScripTPamp 23 (1991) 336-340 (M. *Lluch-Baixauli*).

g582 *Klein* J. W. E., New light on the Gouda Erasmiana manuscripts: Quaerendo 18 (1988) 87-95; 4 facsimiles [< RHE 86,20*].

g582* *Lawrence* J. David, Erasmus' theological models: Fides et Historia 23,2 (1991) 31-39 [< ZIT 91,806].

g583 **McConica** James, Erasmus: Past Masters. Ox 1991, UP. 106 p. £5. 0-19-287599-X. – ᴿExpTim 103 (1991s) 61 (C. S. *Rodd*: a delight); NBlackf 72 (1991) 541s (A. *McGrath*).

g584 **McVitty** John D., Erasmus and the rhetorical tradition: diss. Califotnia. Berkeley 1991. 321 p. 92-03643. – DissA 52 (1991s) 2912-A.

g585 *Margolin* J.-C., Érasme, Guillaume BRIÇONNET [➤ 2792] et les débuts de la Réforme en France: Revue d'Histoire de l'Église de France 77 (1991) 13-28 [< RSPT 75,680].

g585* **Rummel** Erika, Erasmus and his Catholic critics 1989 ➤ 6,k693: ᴿCathHR 77 (1991) 685-7 (D. *Sheerin*).

g586 **Schoeck** R. J., Erasmus grandescens 1988 ➤ 5,k183: ᴿChH 59 (1990) 86-88 (A. *Rabil*).

g586* **Tinkler** John F., Erasmus' conversation with Luther: ArRefG 82 (1991) 59-82 [< ZIT 91,661].

g587 **Walter** Peter, Theologie aus dem Geist der Rhetorik; zur Schriftauslegung des Erasmus von Rotterdam: TüStTPh 1. Mainz 1991, Grünewald. 313 p. [RömQ 87,339, A. *Schmid*].

g588 ᴱ**Weiland** J. Sperna, *Frijhoff* W. T. M., Erasmus 1986/8 ➤ 5,k188; 6,k698: ᴿTLZ 116 (1991) 924s (C. *Augustijn*).

g589 FISHER: **Rex** R., The theology of John Fisher. C 1991, Univ. xii-293 p. £30 [NRT 114,929, P. *Evrard*].

g589* *Dowling* Maria, John Fisher and the preaching ministry: ArRefG 82 (1991) 287-310 [< ZIT 91,662].

g590 HOFFMAN: **Deppermann** Klaus, Melchior Hoffman; social unrest and apocalyptic visions in the age of Reformation [1979], ᵀ*Wren* Malcolm 1987 ➤ 3,g600 ... 5,k191: ᴿHeythJ 32 (1991) 143s (A. *Hamilton*).

g591 HUBMAIER: *a*) ᴱ**Pipkin** H. Wayne, *Yoder* John H., Balthasar Hubmaier, theologian of Anabaptism [major writings translated]. Scottdale PA 1989, Herald. 608 p. $40. 0-8361-3103-7. – ᴿRExp 88,2 (1991) 225s (Karen E. *Smith*); – *b*) *Weaver* J. Denny, Hubmaier versus [Hans] Hut on the work of Christ; the fifth Nicolsburg article: ArRefG 82 (1991) 171-192 [< ZIT 91,662].

g591* HUS: **Werner** Ernst, Jan Hus [1370-1415], Welt und Umwelt eines Prager Frühreformators: ForMAG 34. Weimar 1991, Böhlau. 256 p. DM 68. – ᴿArTGran 54 (1991) 443s (A. *Segovia*).

g592 JORIS: **Waite** Gary K., David Joris and Dutch Anabaptism, 1524-1543 [< diss. Waterloo]. Waterloo ON 1990, Laurier Univ. xi-235 p. $32.50, 0-88920-992-8 [TDig 38,387].

g593 KLINGE: **Rickauer** Hans-Christian, Rechtfertigung und Heil; die Vermittlung von Glaube und Heilshandeln in der Auseinanderstzung mit der reformatorischen Lehre bei Konrad Klinge (1483/4-1556): ErfurterTSt 53, 1986 ➤ 5,7722: ᴿTrierTZ 100 (1991) 77s (A. *Dahm*).

g594 KNOX: **Dawson** Jane E. A., The two John Knoxes; England, Scotland and the 1558 tracts: JEH 42 (1991) 555-576.

g595 *Kyle* Richard G., The Christian commonwealth; John Knox's vision for Scotland: JRelHist 16 (1990s) 247-259.

g596 LA PALUD: **Dunbabin** Jean, A hound of God; Pierre de la Palud and the fourteenth-century Church. Ox 1991, Clarendon. xi-211 p. [TR 88,78].

g597 LAYNEZ: *Vercruysse* Jos E., Lainez, Jakob/Diego (1512-1565) [... Konzil von Trient]: ➤ 690, TRE 20 (1990) 399-404.

g598 LEDESMA: *Aranci* Gilberto, Le 'Dottrine' di Giacomo Ledesma S.J. (1524-1575): Salesianum 53 (1991) 315-383.

g599 MARULIĆ: *Šimundza* Drago, Marko Marulić [1450-1524], father of Croatian biblical and theological studies: ➤ 67, ᶠGOLUB I., 1991, 88-95 (Croatian); 96 Eng.

g600 MELANCHTHON: ᴱ**Scheible** H., (*Thüringer* W.), Melanchthon's Briefwechsel 5. Regesten 4530-5707 (1547-1549) 1987 ➤ 4,k178: ᴿProtestantesimo 46 (1991) 77-79 (P. *Ricca*).

g601 *Scheible* Heinz, Luther and Melanchthon: LuthQ 4 (Ridgefield NJ 1990) 317-340 [< ZIT 91,425].

g602 *a*) *Burigana* Riccardo, De discrimine Veteris et Novi Testamenti nelle dispute di Melantone; – *b*) *De Michelis Pintacuda* Fiorella, Storia sacra e storia profana tra ERASMO e Lutero; – *c*) *Miegge* Mario, 'Foedus operatum' e 'foedus gratiae'; la teologia del patto di Johannes COCCEJUS (1603-1669) alla luce della critica di Karl BARTH: AnStoEseg 8 (1991) 39-54 / 9-37 / 105-123.

g603 MOLLER: **Axmacher** Elke, Praxis Evangeliorum; Theologie und Frömmigkeit bei Martin Moller (1547-1606): ForKDG 43, 1986 ➤ 5,k195: RBTZ 8 (1991) 139-146 (T. *Koch*).

g604 MORE: **Baumann** Eduard H. L., Der Konsensbegriff bei Thomas More als formales Glaubenskriterium im Spiegel der polemischen Auseinandersetzung mit M. Luther; eine theologiegeschichtliche Analyse der 'Responsio ad Lutherum' von 1523: Diss. *DPetri* H. Regensburg 1991. 241 p. – RTLv 23, p. 567.

g605 MÜNTZER: E**Bentzinger** R., *Hoyer* S. [neuhochdeutsch] T. Müntzer, Schriften, liturgische Texte, Briefe. B 1990, Union. 319 p. DM 18. – RTLZ 116 (1991) 39s (H.-J. *Goertz*).

g606 E**Bräuer** Siegfried, *Junghans* Helmar, Der Theologe Thomas Müntzer; Untersuchungen zu seiner Entwicklung und Lehre 1989 ➤ 6,k722: RTLZ 116 (1991) 122-5 (P. *Matheson*: 2000 Anmerkungen).

g607 **Bubenheimer** U., T. Müntzer 1989 ➤ 6,k723: RJEH 42 (1991) 314s (T. *Scott*).

g608 **Friesen** Abraham, Thomas Muentzer, a destroyer of the godless; the making of a sixteenth-century religious revolutionary. Berkeley 1990, Univ. California. xiv-331 p. $40. – RCathHR 77 (1991) 691s (E. W. *Gritsch*).

g609 **Goertz** Hans-Jürgen, Thomas Müntzer 1989 ➤ 6,k727: RDLZ 112 (1991) 353s (S. *Hoyer*).

g610 **Gritsch** E. W., T. Müntzer, a tragedy of errors 1989 ➤ 5,k197; 6,k728: RCritRR 4 (1991) 303-6 (G. *Strauss*, also on FRIESEN A. 1990).

g610* a) *Junghans* Helmar, Die Theologie Thomas Müntzers; die Bibel als Spiegel der Zeit: ArRefG 82 (1991) 107-122 [< ZIT 91,661]; – b) *Junghans* Reinhard, The rise and decline of Thomas Müntzer: LuthQ 5 (Ridgefield 1991) 247-276 [< ZIT 92,80].

g611 a) *La Rocca* Tommaso, Modernità di Thomas Müntzer; – b) *Miegge* Mario, La riattivazione del 'sensus historicus' della Bibbia nelle ermeneutiche riformate: AnStoEseg 7,1 (1990) 133-7 / 113-131.

g612 *Matheson* P., Christianity as insurrection [...T. Müntzer and peasants' war]: ScotJT 44 (1991) 311-324.

g613 *Mehring* Reinhard, Nachlese zum Müntzerjahr 1989: ZRGg 43 (1991) 69-72.

g613* **Rowland** Christopher, Radical Christianity, a reading of recovery [Müntzer < Fiore]. Mkn 1988, Orbis. 250 p. $30; pa. $15. 0-88344-370-8; -69-4. – RModT 7 (1990s) 296-8 (R. S. *Goizueta*).

g614 **Scott** Tom, Thomas Müntzer; theology and revolution in the German Reformation. L 1989, Macmillan. xix-203 p.; 8 maps. $35. 0-0333-46498-2. – RHeythJ 32 (1991) 576-8 (B. *Scribner*); JEH 42 (1991) 124-6 (E. *Cameron*, also on GRITSCH E.).

g615 **Seebass** Gottfried, Reich Gottes und Apokalyptik bei Thomas Müntzer: LuJb 58 (1991) 75-99.

g616 OETINGER: **Weyer-Menkhof** Martin, Christus, das Heil der Natur ... F. Oetinger 1990 ➤ 6,k738: RActuBbg 28 (1991) 203s (J. *Boada*).

g617 PFLUG J.: E**Neuss** Elmar, *Pollet* J. V., Pflugiana 1985/90 ➤ 6,670: RTLZ 116 (1991) 745s (S. *Bräuer*).

g618 REUCHLIN: **Erdmann-Pandžić** Elisabeth, *Pandžić* Basilius, Juraj DRA-
GIŠIĆ und Johannes Reuchlin; eine Untersuchungen zum Kampf für die
jüdischen Bücher mit einem Nachdruck der 'Defensio praestantissimi viri
Joannis Reuchlin' (1517) von Georgius Benignus (Juraj Dragašić): Quellen kroat. KuG 1. Bamberg 1989, Bayerische VA. 145 + 50 p. DM 48.
– ᴿAngelicum 68 (1991) 572-4 (S. *Krasić*).

g618* SCHATZGEYER Kasper, Von der waren Christlichen und Evangelischen
freyheit (1543), ᴱSchäfer P.: CCath 40, 1987 ➤ 4,k180; 5,k201: ᴿTLZ
116 (1991) 128-130 (S. *Bräuer*).

g619 SERVETUS: **Kinder** A. G., Michael Servetus: Bibliotheca dissidentium
10: BtBibliog Aureliana 116. Baden-Baden 1989, Koerner. 167 p.; ill.
DM 100 [RHE 86,15*].

g620 SOZZINI: ᴱ**Rotondo** Antonio, Lelio Sozzini, Opere 1986 ➤ 6,k743: ᴿCr-
NSt 11 (1990) 222-5 (U. *Mazzone*).

g621 SPEE: **Nigg** Walter, Friedrich von Spee; ein Jesuit kämpft gegen den
Hexenwahn. Pd 1991, Bonifatius. 106 p. DM 19,80. – ᴿTPQ 139 (1991)
434 (R. *Zinnhobler*).

g622 *Winkler* Gerhard B., Friedrich Spee von Langenfeld (1591-1635) [S.J. ab
1610]; ein Leben im Kampf gegen den Hexenwahn: TPQ 139 (1991)
387-395.

g623 STAUPITZ: **Wetzel** Richard, Johann von Staupitz, Lateinische Schriften
1. Tübinger Predigten: Sämtliche Schriften 1/1, 1987 ➤ 6,k747: ᴿTR 87
(1991) 27-29 (J. *Wicks,* ᵀ*Woestmann* Annegret).

g624 (& TREGER): *a) Zumkeller* Adolar, The Augustinian theologian Konrad Treger ca. 1480-1542 and his disputation theses of May 5,1521; –
b) Graf zu Dohna Lothar, STAUPITZ and Luther; continuity and
breakthrough at the beginning of the Reformation; – *c) Steinmetz* David
C., CALVIN and the natural knowledge of God: ➤ 155, ᶠTRAPP D., Via
Augustini 1991, 130-141 / 116-129 / 142-156.

g625 TYNDALE W.: *a) Richardson* A., Scripture as evidence in Tyndale's
The obedience of a Christian man; – *b) Clark* J. A., The Bible, his
tory, and authority in Tyndale's The practice of prelates; – *c) O'Donnell*
A. M., Scripture versus Church in Tyndale's Answer unto Sir Thomas
MORE's Dialogue; – *d) Day* J. T., Proper guidance in reading the Bible;
Tyndale's A pathway into the Holy Scripture; – *e) Millus* D. J., 'Howe
diligently wrote he to them'; Tyndale's own letter, The exposition of the
first epistle of St. John; – *f) O'Donnell* A. M., Philology, typology and
rhetoric in Tyndale's Exposition upon the V.VI.VII. chapters of Matthew:
Moreana 28,106s (1991) 83-104 / 105-117 / 119-130 / 131-143 / 145-153 /
155-164.

g626 VALDÉS: *Fanlo y Cortes* Teodoro, Juan de Valdés Riformatore in
Spagna e Italia: Protestantesimo 46 (1991) 103-115: non ha potuto usare
FIRPO M. 1990; ma NIETO J. 1970 supera la tesi di DOMINGO de S. Teresa
1957 facendo di Valdés un riformatore cattolico.

g627 VERGERIO: **Jacobson** Anne S., Pier Paolo Vergerio e la riforma a
Venezia 1498-1549, ᵀ*Cappelletti* V., *Fabbrini* A. M., R 1988, Il Veltro.
488 p.; 16 pl. – ᴿSalesianum 53 (1991) 414s (C. *Semeraro*).

g628 VERMIGLI: *Anderson* Marvin W., Vista tigurina; Peter Martyr [Ver-
migli] and European reform (1556-1562): HarvTR 83 (1990) 181-206.

g629 **Donnelly** J. P., *Kingdon* R. M., A bibliography of the works of Peter
Martyr Vermigli; correspondence, *Anderson* M. W.: Essays 13. Kirksville
MO 1990, SixtC. xvi-215 p.; ill. $50 [RHE 86,16*]. – ᴿRHE 87 (1991)
296s (J.-F. *Gilmont*: très grand service, malgré l'index pas assez complet).

g630 VIRET: **Bavaud** G., Le Réformateur Pierre Viret 1986 ➤ 2,d667...
5,k208: ᴿCrNSt 12 (1991) 213-5 (E. *Campi*).

g631 WYCLIF: **Hudson** Anne, The premature Reformation; Wycliffite texts
and Lollard history 1988 ➤ 4,k188*: ᴿCrNSt 11 (1990) 393s (Gloria
Cigman: she declares she regards 'Wycliffite' and 'Lollard' as synony-
mous).

g632 **Wey** Thomas G., Wyclif's doctrine of Scripture within the context of his
doctrinal and social ideas: diss. Vanderbilt, ᴰ*Te Selle* E. Nv 1991. 262 p.
91-25301. – DissA 52 (1991s) 968-A; RelStR 18,174.

g633 ZWINGLI: *Backus* Irene, Randbemerkungen Zwinglis in den Werken von
Giovanni Pico della MIRANDOLA: Zwingliana 18,4s (1990s) 291-309.

g633* *Bächtold* Hans U., *Haag* Hans J., Literatur zur zwinglischen Reformation: Zwingliana 18 (1990s) 393-406 [< ZIT 91,737].

g634 ᵀᴱ**Courvoisier** Jacques, Huldrych Zwingli, De la parole de Dieu [1522
avant la rupture, pour des dominicaines], 1989 ➤ 6,k759; 71 p. F 60.
2-7010-1192-2: ᴱÉTRel 66 (1991) 295 (A. *Gounelle*).

g635 ᴱ[*Egli* E., *al.* †] **Pfister** R., *Büsser* F., Zwingli Huldreich, Sämtliche
Werke VI, 4 & 5 [1530s / 1531]: Corpus Reformatorum 93/4. Z 1990s,
Theol.-V. xx-191 p.; xx-463 p. Fs 180 + 190 [TLZ 117,614, E. *Koch*].

g636 **Hamm** Berndt, Zwinglis Reformation der Freiheit 1988 ➤ 5,k215;
6,k760: ᴿZwingliana 18,3 (1990) 278-280 (E. *Saxer*).

g637 *Lienhard* Max, Aus der Arbeit an Zwinglis Exegetica zum Neuen
Testament; zu den Quellen der Schriftauslegung: Zwingliana 18 (1990s)
310-328 [< RHE 87,48*].

g638 **Pollet** J. V., Huldrych Zwingli et le Zwinglianisme [➤ 5,k216a]; essai de
synthèse historique et théologique mis à jour d'après les recherches
récentes [après son art. DTC 1951]. P 1988, Vrin. x-444 p. F 210. – ᴿTLZ
116 (1991) 200s (U. *Gäbler*); TR 86 (1990) 473s (R. C. *Walton*);
Zwingliana 18,4s (1990s) 415-7 (Irena *Backus*).

g639 **Stephens** W. P., The theology of Huldrych Zwingli 1986 ➤ 2,d674...
5,k217: ᴿJAAR 59 (1991) 625-7 (T. *George*).

g640 **Wandel** Lee P., Always among us; images of the poor in Zwingli's
Zurich. C 1990, Univ. vii-199 p. £27.50 [TR 88,79]. – ᴿJTS 42 (1991)
771-3 (W. P. *Stephens*).

Y4.5 *Exegesis post-reformatoria* – Historical criticism to 1800.

g641 ᴱ**Armogathe** Jean-R., Le grand siècle [XVII] et la Bible; BTT 6, 1989
➤ 6,k767: ᴿBrotéria 132 (1991) 476s (F. de *Sales Baptista*); JEH 42
(1991) 127-9 (W. *Ward*: LAPLANCHE best).

g642 *Armogathe* Jean-Robert, *a)* Les études bibliques au XVIIIᵉ siècle [des
Lumières BTT 7; lui-même ᴱLe grand siècle (XVIIᵉ) BTT 6]; de la lettre à
la figure: ➤ 348, Concilium 233 (P 1991) 95-103; – *b)* Biblical studies in
the eighteenth century; from the letter to the figure: ➤ 347, Concilium
(1991,1) 69-76.

g643 **Baumann** Thomas, Zwischen Weltveränderung und Weltflucht; zum
Wandel der pietistischen Utopie im 17. und 18. Jahrhundert [Diss. Fr].
Lah 1991, St.-Johannis. 247 p. DM 29,80 [TLZ 117,934, P. *Schicketanz*].

g644 **Bradley** James E., Religion, revolution and English radicalism;
nonconformity in eighteenth century politics and society. C 1990,
Univ. xxi-473 p. £35. 0-521-38010-3. – ᴿExpTim 103 (1991s) 28
(H. D. *Rack*).

g645 **Brüdermann** Stefan, Göttinger Studenten und akademische Gerichtsbarkeit im 18. Jahrhundert: Gö [250. Jubiläum 1987] Univ.-Schr. A-15. Gö 1990, Vandenhoeck & R. 592 p. DM 48. – ᴿTLZ 116 (1991) 15s (Inge *Mager*).

g646 **Butler** Jon, [U.S.] Awash in a sea of faith 1990 ➤ 6,k770: ᴿCommonweal 118 (1991) 269 (L. S. *Cunningham*); Horizons 18 (1991) 322 (J. P. *Dolan*); TTod 42 (1991s) 244.246 (J. R. *Fitzmier*).

g647 **Carmody** Denise L. & John T., The republic of many mansions; foundations of American religious thought. NY 1990, Paragon. ix-244 p. $23; pa. $17 [Horizons 19,316, Phyllis H. *Kaminski*].

Clifford Alan C., Atonement and justification; English evangelical theology, 1640-1790 – an evaluation 1990 ➤ 7697.

Cottret Bernard, Le Christ des lumières... 1660-1760: Jésus depuis Jésus 1990 ➤ 3717.

g648 *Deconinck-Brossard* Françoise, England and France in the eighteenth century: ➤ 324*, Reading the text 1991, 136-181.

g649 **Dompnier** Bernard, Le venin de l'hérésie; image du protestantisme et combat catholique au XVIIᵉ siècle 1985 ➤ 2,d681: ᴿCrNSt 11 (1990) 419-426 (L. *Donvito*).

g650 **Drury** John, Critics of the Bible 1724-1873: 1989 ➤ 5,k224: ᴿCritRR 4 (1991) 79s (W. *Baird*).

g651 *Feil* Ernst, Die Deisten als Gegner der Trinität; zur ursprünglichen Bedeutung und speziellen Verwendung des Begriffs 'Deistae' für die Sozinianer: ArBegG 33 (1990) 115-124.

g652 **Gross** Hans, Rome in the age of enlightenment; the post-Tridentine syndrome and the ancien régime. C 1990, Univ. x-109 p.; 12 pl.; 2 maps. £35. – ᴿRHE 86 (1991) 265s (D. *Bradley*).

g653 **Hanimann** Thomas, Zürcher Nonkonformisten im 18. Jahrhundert; eine Untersuchung zur Geschichte der freien christlichen Gemeinde im Ancien Régime [Diss. Zürich]. Z 1990, Theol.-V. viii-343 p. Fs 38 pa. [TLZ 117,925, E. *Koch*].

g654 *Hudson* Elizabeth K., The Catholic challenge to Puritan piety [... MᶜGʀᴀᴛʜ P. 1967]: CathHR 77 (1991) 1-20.

g655 **Jonge** H. J. de, Van Erasmus tot Reimarus; ontwikkelingen in de bijbelwetenschap van 1500 tot 1800: Voordracht 27.IV.1991. Leiden 1991, Rijks Universiteit. 24 p.

g656 **Lake** Peter, Anglicans and Puritans; Presbyterianism and English conformist thought from Whitgift to Hooker. L 1988, Allen & U. 262 p. $55. 0-04-942207-3. – ᴿJRelHist 16 (1990s) 95-98 (G. *Yule*).

g657 ᴱ**Leaver** Robin A., J. S. Bach [and Scripture 1985?] as Preacher; his Passion and music in worship. ... 1985, Concordia. 56 p. $5.25. 0-570-01332-1. – ᴿTLZ 116 (1991) 524-6 (M. *Petzoldt*).

g658 **Morgan** John, Godly learning; Puritan attitudes towards reason, learning, and education 1560-1640. C 1986, Univ. x-366 p. $35. – ᴿEvQ 63 (1991) 81-83 (A. G. *Newell*).

g659 *a*) *Nicastro* Onofrio, Una voce pacata e sommessa; William Wᴀʟᴡʏɴ [1647]: – *b*) *Bianchi* Daniela, A holy commonwealth; il modello teocratico di Richard Bᴀxᴛᴇʀ [1659]; – *c*) *Marchignoli* Saverio, La Bibbia come progetto; esplosione del canone, nuova mitologia, orientalismo in Friedrich Sᴄʜʟᴇɢᴇʟ e nella 'Frühromantik' (1798-1801): AnStoEseg 8 (1991) 125-143 / 145-168 / 169-191.

g660 *Noonkester* Myron C., Gɪʙʙᴏɴ and the clergy; private virtues, public vices: HarvTR 83 (1990) 399-414.

g661 **Pelikan** Jaroslav, Christian doctrine and modern culture [since 1700]; The Christian Tradition 5, 1989 ➤ 5,k235; 6,k850: ᴿGraceTJ 11 (1990) 124-6 (J.D. *Morrison*); Interpretation 45 (1991) 68-70 (D. *Jodock*).

g662 **Reinhardt** Klaus, Bibelkommentare spanischer Autoren (1500-1700), A-LL: MedHum 5, 1990 ➤ 6,k783: ᴿArTGran 54 (1991) 382s (A. *Segovia*); RHE 86 (1991) 500 (R. *Aubert*).

g662* **Rivers** Isabel, Reason, grace, and sentiment; a study of the language of religion and ethics in England, 1600-1780, I. Whichoote to Wesley: Studies 10th Cent. Lit. C 1991, Univ. xiii-277p. $50. 0-521-38340-4 [TDig 39,284].

g663 **Rupp** Ernest G., Religion in England 1688-1791: 1986 ➤ 3,g635; 6,k784: ᴿJAAR 59 (1991) 870-3 (A. *Rabil*).

g664 **Sáenz-Badillos** Ángel, La filología bíblica en los primeros helenistas de Alcalá [... políglota complutense; < ᴰ1972]: JerónMg 18. Estella 1990, VDivino. 84-7151-708-6. – ᴿFgNt 4 (1991) 84 (J. *Mateos*); Helmantica 42,129* (1991) 303 (C. *Carrete Parrondo*).

g665 *Scholder* Klaus, [† 1985], The birth of modern critical theology [1966 ... Descartes] ᵀ1990 ➤ 6,k785: ᴿExpTim 102 (1990s) 382 (J.A. *Newton*); JTS 42 (1991) 398-400 (R. *Morgan*); LvSt 16 (1991) 185s (R.F. *Collins*).

g666 **Schwarke** Christian, Jesus kam nach Washington; die Legitimation der amerikanischen Demokratie aus dem Geist des Protestantismus [Diss. München 1990]. Gü 1991, Mohn. 230p. DM 78 [TLZ 117,281,J. *Langer*].

g667 **Wallmann** Johannes, Der Pietismus: Die Kirche in ihrer Geschichte 4. Gö 1990, Vandenhoeck & R. v-143p. DM 48 [TLZ 117,765, P. *Schicketanz*].

g668 *Weaver* E., The Bible and Port-Royal: Citeaux 41 (1990) 66-97 [< RHE 86,39*].

---

g669 ARNOLD: **Erb** Peter C., Pietists, Protestants, and mysticism; the use of late medieval spiritual texts in the works of Gottfried Arnold (1666-1714): Pietist and Wesleyan Studies 2. Metuchen NJ 1989, Scarecrow. 329p. 0-8108-2281-4. – ᴿAsburyTJ 46,1 (1991) 129-131 (J.D. *Nelson*).

g669* BUNYAN: **Hill** Christopher, A tinker 1989 ➤ 5,k241*b*: ᴿRExp 88 (1991) 109s (H.L. *Poe*). ➤ 1375.

g670 DE ROSSI: *Allison* Gregg, Giovanni Bernardo de Rossi (1742-1831); a sketch of his life and works, with particular attention given to his contribution to the field of biblical criticism: TrinJ 12 (1991) 15-38.

g671 EDWARDS: **Jenson** Robert W., America's theologian... J. Edwards 1988 ➤ 4,k216... 6,k799: ᴿScotJT 44 (1991) 127-9 (Alasdair *Heron*: excellent, but 'worth nothing' for 'worth noting' p. 137 is only one of the many typos).

g671* **Morris** William S., The young Jonathan Edwards, a reconstruction: Chicago Studies in the History of American Religion. Brooklyn 1991, Carlson. xvi-688p. $125. 0-926019-50-3 [TDig 39,278].

g672 ᴱWilson John F., Jonathan Edwards, A history of the work of redemption; Works 9. NHv 1989, Yale Univ. 594p. $65. – ᴿJRel 71 (1991) 99-101 (C.C. *Goen*: a marvel of editing).

g673 FOX: **Gwyn** Douglas, Apocalypse of the Word; the life and message of George Fox (1624-1691). ...-... Friends United Press. 241p. $15. – ᴿJAAR 59 (1991) 399-401 (J.V. *Spickard*).

g674 **Sharman** Cecil W., George Fox [† 1691] and the Quakers. L 1991, Quaker Home Service. 255 p. £9. 0-85245-230-6. – RExpTim 103 (1991s) 64 [C. S. *Rodd*].

g675 HAMANN: **Baur** Wolfgang-Dieter, Johann G. Hamann alz Publizist; zum Verhältnis von Öffentlichkeit und Verkündigung: Diss. Tübingen 1989. 258 p. – TLZ 116 (1991) 711.

g676 **Bayer** Oswald, Zeitgenosse im Widerspruch; Johann G. Hamann [† 1878] als radikaler Aufklärer. Mü 1988, Piper. 275 p. DM 22,80. – RTLZ 116 (1991) 683-6 (M. *Seils*).

g677 HEBEL: **Wunderlich** Reinhard, J. P. Hebels 'Biblische Geschichten', eine Bibeldichtung zwischen Spätaufklärung und Biedermeier: päd./psych. Diss. Bamberg 1991, DLachmann. – TR 87 (1991) 515.

g678 HERBERT: *Hodgkins* Christopher, The Church legible; George Herbert [The Temple 1633] and the externals of worship: JRel 71 (1991) 217-241.

g679 JANSENIUS: **Albert** Marcel, Nuntius Fabio CHIGI und die Anfänge des Jansenismus 1639-1651; ein römischer Diplomat in theologischen Auseinandersetzungen: RömQ 44, Supp. Fr 1988, Herder. 301 p. – RTR 87 (1991) 488s (K. *Ganzer*).

g680 *Corts i Blay* Ramon, El Jansenisme en el pensament de Fèlix AMAT (1750-1824), arquebisbe de Palmira [in partibus; confesor de Carles IV]: RCatalT 16 (1991) 169-185; Eng. 186.

g681 EEijl J. M. van, L'image de C. Jansenius 1985/7 ⇒ 4,557 … 6,k808: RHPR 71 (1991) 405s (M. *Chevallier*).

g682 **Orcibal** Jean, Jansenius d'Ypres (1585-1638) 1989 ⇒ 6,k810; ÉtAug. 358 p. Fb 455: RJTS 42 (1991) 773-6 (J. *McManners*: rather 'of Louvain').

g683 **Wiel** C. Van de, Jansenistica te Mechelen; het archief van het Aartsbisdom [2076 pièces analysées]: Annua Nuntia Lovaniensia 28. Lv 1988, Univ./Peeters. 250 p. – RRHE 86 (1991) 196 (R. *Aubert*).

g684 LAW: *Thomann* Günther, Die Lehre von der Wiedergeburt bei William Law (1686-1761): ZRGg 43 (1991) 305-323.

g685 L'EMPEREUR: **Rooden** Peter T. Van, Theology, biblical scholarship, and rabbinical studies …, C. L'Empereur (1591-1648), TGrayson J. 1989 ⇒ 5,k267: RBL (1991) 22 (J. W. *Rogerson*: severe); RÉJ 150 (1991) 494s (B. E. *Schwarzbach*).

g686 LESSING: *Hornig* Gottfried, Lessing, Gotthold Ephraim (1729-1781): ⇒ 690, TRE 21 (1991) 20-33.

g687 ESchilson A., Gotthold E. Lessing, Werke 1774-8: Werke und Briefe, [EBarner W., al.] 8. Fra 1989, Deutsche Klassiker Vg. 1188 p. – RTLZ 116 (1991) 291-3 (H. *Schultze*: kath. Hg., auch für Band 9s; Fragen über 'Deismus': Lessings Hochschätzung der mündlichen Tradition stand näher der Kath. Bibelwissenschaft als der Prot.).

g688 LOCKE: *Schouls* Peter A., John Locke and the rise of western fundamentalism; a hypothesis: RelStT 10,2 (1990) 9-22.

g689 MORGAN: *Berg* Jan Van den, Thomas Morgan [Moral Philosopher 1737] versus William WARBURTON; a conflict the other way round [REVENTLOW, Authority 1985, 396 supports a long but wrong tradition that Warburton wrote against Morgan]: JEH 42 (1991) 82-85.

g690 MÜHLENBERG: EAland Kurt, Die Korrespondenz Heinrich M. Mühlenbergs; aus der Anfangszeit des deutschen Luthertums in Nordamerika [Is. 1986s], III. 1763-1768. B/NY 1990, de Gruyter. xiii-715 p. – RTLZ [113 (1988) 126] 116 (1991) 844s (H. *Winde*).

g691 NICODIM: *Karaisaridis* Konstantinos, Sfîntul Nicodim Aghioritul [diss.]: STBuc 39,1s (1987) 6-68 . 6-80.

g692 PASCAL: EMesnard Jean, Blaise Pascal, Œuvres complètes 1-4. Bruges 1964-91, Desclée-B. 3-220-03192-6. – RÉTRel 66 (1991) 607-9 (A. *Gounelle*: Les Provinciales sera vol. 5).

g693 *Vieillard-Baron* J.-L., al., Le Dieu de la foi et le Dieu de la raison; DESCARTES et Pascal: RSPT 75,1 (1991) 3-5 (-95).

g694 RÖELL: **Sluis** J. van, Herman Alexander Röell [Diss. Groningen, DKnetsch F.] ... 1988, Fryske Akademy 696. 258 p. ƒ59. 90-61716-96-9. – RNedTTs 45 (1991) 73s (A. de *Groot*).ʲ

g695 SEMLER: *Hornig* Gottfried, Wahrheit und Historisierung in Semlers kritischer Theologie [200. Todesjahr]: TLZ 116 (1991) 721-730.

g696 **Schulz** Hartmut H.R., J.S. Semlers Wesensbestimmung des Christentums 1988 → 5,k274: RTLZ 116 (1991) 755s (Susanne *Ehrhardt-Rein*).

g697 *Sommer* Wolfgang, Ein frommer Aufklärer; Erinnerung an Johann Salomo Semler: DtPfarrbl 91 (1991) 364-8 [< TLZ 117,449].

g698 SIMON: *a) Beaude* Pierre-Marie, Richard Simon, critique et théologie; – *b) Wrenn* Michael J., Contemporary Catholic biblical scholarship; certitudes or hypothèses?; – *c) Grelot* Pierre, Le langage symbolique dans la Bible; note méthodologique: → 6,109*, FLAURENTIN M., *Kecharitōménē* 1990, 71-84 / 85-101 / 53-69.

g699 SPINOZA: *Cuzzani* Paola de, Spinoza et les Spinozismes; de Oldenburg à Hegel, l'histoire d'une répudiation: RHPR 71 (1991) 349-364; Eng. 422, 'Spinoza and his apologists'.

g700 EPopkin R.H., *Signer* M.A., Spinoza's earliest publication? TFell. Assen 1987, van Gorcum. x-106 p. ƒ49,50. 90-232-2223-7. – RNedTTs 43 (1989) 340s (P.W. van der *Horst*).

g700* Yovel Yirmiyahu, Spinoza and other heretics: Princeton c. 1990. 244 + 225 p. $45. – RCommonweal 117 (1990) 227s (M. *Wyschogrod*).

g701 TAYLOR: ECarroll Thomas K., Jeremy Taylor, selected works: Classics of Western Spirituality. NY 1990, Paulist. x-526 p. $18. – RTS 52 (1991) 558s (P.J. *Korshin*: shortens even short items).

g702 WESLEY: *Cooper* Austin, John Wesley and the quest for catholicity: AustralasCR 68 (1991) 352-359.

g702* **Collins** Kenneth J., Wesley on salvation; a study in the Standard Sermons [5 vols. 1746-71]. GR 1989, Zondervan-Asbury. 142 p. $8. 0-310-75421-6. – RRExp 88 (1991) 274s (B.J. *Leonard*).

g703 **Pollock** John, John Wesley 1703-1791. L 1989, Hodder & S. 256 p. £13. – REvQ 63 (1991) 357-9 (A.S. *Wood*, also on RACK H.).

g704 **Rack** Henry C., Reasonable enthusiast; Wesley 1989 → 6,k828: RAndrUnS 29 (1991) 183-5 (R.L. *Staples*); AsburyTJ 46,1 (1991) 131-3 (K.C. *Kinghorn*); JTS 42 (1991) 400-2 (V.H.H. *Green*: splendid).

g705 **Rataboul** Louis J., John Wesley, un anglican sans frontières – 1703-1791. Nancy 1991, Pr. Univ. 239 p. F 160. 2-86480-459-X. – RRHPR 71 (1991) 402 (M. *Chevallier*).

Y5 *Saeculum XIX* – **Exegesis – 19th Century.**

g706 **Addinall** Peter, Philosophy and biblical interpretation; a study in nineteenth-century conflict [diss. Sheffield, DRogerson J.]. C 1991, Univ. xii-330 p. £35. 0-521-40423-1.

g707 **Bebbington** D. W., Evangelicalism 1730-1980: 1988 ↠ 5,k292; 6,k831: ᴿEvQ 63 (1991) 360s (A. S. *Wood*).

g708 **Berman** David, A history of atheism in Britain from Hobbes to Russell. L 1988, Croom Helm; also Routledge 1990 pa. 253 p. £10. 0-7099-3271-5 / 0-415-04727-7. – ᴿExpTim 102 (1990s) 285 (D. A. *Pailin*: exemplifies POPPER's 'understanding advances more by examining adverse than confirmatory arguments').

g708* **Bull** Malcolm, **Lockhart** Keith, Seeking a sanctuary; Seventh-Day Adventism and the American dream. SF 1989, Harper & R. 319 p. $26. 0-06-... – ᴿRExp 88 (1991) 277 (B. J. *Leonard*).

g709 **Cashdollar** Charles D., The transformation of theology 1830-90: 1989 ↠ 5,k295; 6,k835: ᴿChH 59 (1990) 577s (J. M. *Mulder*); JRel 71 (1991) 437s (Ellen K. *Wondra*).

g710 **Dyrness** William A., How does America hear the Gospels? [Puritans to present]. GR 1990, Eerdmans. xi-164 p. $12 pa. 0-8028-0437-3 [TDig 38,261].

g711 **Fogarty** Gerald P., American Catholic biblical scholarship 1989 ↠ 4, k245 ... 6,k839: ᴿBS 148 (1991) 503 (J. A. *Witmer*); CathHR 77 (1991) 531s (R. *Trisco*); CBQ 53 (1991) 133s (G. S. *Sloyan* gives important agreements and qualifications); ChH 59 (1990) 431s (D. G. *Schultenover*); CritRR 4 (1991) 83-85 (J. *Reumann*); GraceTJ 11 (1990) 120-2 (R. *Fisher*); JEH 42 (1991) 524 (B. L. *Horne*); RRel 49 (1990) 469s (P. *Jurkowitz*).

g712 ᴱ**Frerichs** E. S., The Bible/s in America 1988 ↠ 4,300; 5,k300: ᴿJRel 70 (1990) 110s (M. A. *Noll*).

g713 **Gastaldi** Ugo, I movimenti di risveglio nel mondo protestante; dal 'Great Awakening' (1720) ai 'revivals' del nostro secolo. T 1989, Claudiana. 200 p. Lit. 18.000. – ᴿProtestantesimo 46 (1991) 229 (Jean *Elliott*).

g714 **Hylson-Smith** Kenneth, Evangelicals in the Church of England, 1734-1984: 1989 ↠ 6,k844: ᴿCritRR 4 (1991) 317s (D. M. *Lewis*); EvQ 63 (1991) 85-87 (D. W. *Bebbington*).

g715 *Kenis* Leo, The Louvain faculty of theology and its professors, 1834-1889 [< diss. 1989 ↠ 6,k846]: ETL 67 (1991) 398-414.

g716 *Kustermann* Abraham P., La prima generazione della 'Katholische Tübinger Schule' tra rivoluzione e restaurazione: CrNSt 12 (1991) 489-525; Eng. 525.

g717 ᴱ**Leimgruber** S., **Schoch** M., Gegen die Gottvergessenheit; Schweizer Theologen im 19. und 20. Jh. 1990 ↠ 6,m71: ᴿRHPR 71 (1991) 410s (M. *Arnold*); TsTNijm 31 (1991) 433 (A. *Willems*).

g718 **Murtorinne** Eino, The history of Finnish theology, 1828-1918: History of Learning and Science in Finland, 1. Helsinki 1988, Soc. Scientiarum Fennica. 251 p. – ᴿRHE 86 (1991) 437-444 (H. R. *Boudin*).

g718* **O'Neill** J. C., The Bible's authority; a portrait gallery of [21] thinkers from Lessing to Bultmann. E 1991, Clark. ix-323 p. £12.50 [TR 88,161; BL 92,21, J. W. *Rogerson*]. 0-567-29189-8. – ᴿExpTim 103 (1991s) 84 (J. L. *Houlden*: all German, others being thought unworthy; their God was dead, excluded from practical reality in human affairs).

g719 *Prickett* Stephen, Romantics and Victorians; from typology to symbolism: ↠ 324*, Reading the text 1991, 182-224.

g719* *Sacquin* Michèle, Les divisions protestantes vues par l'opinion catholique sous le Second Empire: BSHistProt 137 (1991) 387-418 [< ZIT 91,665].

g720 **Schnabel** Wolfgang, Grundwissen zur Theologie und Kirchengeschichte; eine Quellenkunde 4. Die Neuzeit [REIMARUS... SCHLEIERMACHER...

TROELTSCH]. Gü 1990, Mohn. 195 p. DM 45 pa. [TLZ 117,280, K. *Nowak*].

g721 **Smend** Rudolf, Deutsche Alttestamentler in drei Jahrhunderten 1989 ➤ 5,358; 6,k852: ᴿAnnTh 5 (1991) 405s (K. *Limburg*: hervorragend); ScripTPamp 23 (1991) 707s + 1074s (K. *Limburg*); TGʟ 81 (1991) 232s (J. *Gamberoni*); TLZ 116 (1991) 499s (E.-J. *Waschke*); TRu 56 (1991) 326-330 (O. *Kaiser*: vom Nutzen der Wissenschaftsgeschichte für den Exegeten).

g721* **Tise** Larry E., Proslavery; a history of the defense of slavery in America 1701-1840. Athens 1987, Univ. Georgia. 362 p. $40. 0-8203-0927-3. – ᴿRExp 88 (1991) 110s (B. J. *Leonard*).

g722 **Vilanova** Evangelista, Història de la teología cristiana 3. Segles XVIII, XIX i XX: S. Pacià 41, 1989 ➤ 6,k854; 84-86065-17-8: ᴿActuBbg 28 (1991) 64-67 (E. *Colomer*).

g723 **Worrall** B. G., The making of the modern Church; Christianity in England since 1800. L 1988, SPCK. viii-312 p. £10. – ᴿEvQ 63 (1991) 87s (D. W. *Bebbington*); NBlackf 71 (1990) 48s (J. *Kent*).

---

g724 BAUR: *Sorrentino* Sergio, Geschichte und Zeitlichkeit in der Auseinandersetzung zwischen F. Ch. Baur und SCHLEIERMACHER: ArBegG 33 (1990) 247-269.

Andrae Christian, F. C. Baur als Prediger ᴰ1991 ➤ 1198.

g724* **Harris** Horton, The Tübingen school. GR 1990 = 1975, Baker. 262 p. 0-8010-4344-1. – ᴿRExp 88 (1991) 484s (A. A. *Trites*).

g725 BEECHER: **Harding** Vincent, A certain magnificence; Lyman Beecher and the transformation of American Protestantism, 1775-1863 [diss. Chicago 1965]: Chicago Studies in the History of American Religion 6. Brooklyn 1991, Carlson. xxix-573 p. $75. 0-926019-43-0 [TDig 39,266].

g726 BRIGGS: **Massa** Mark S., Charles A. Briggs [1841-1913] and the crisis of historical criticism: HarvDissRel 25. Mp 1990, Fortress. xii-220 p. $17. 0-8006-7079-5 [TDig 38,280].

g726* *Christensen* R. L., Charles A. Briggs; critical scholarship and the unity of the Church: American Presbyterian 69,3 (Ph 1991) 149-161 [< NTAbs 36,163].

g727 DREY: **Kustermann** Abraham P., Die Apologetik J. S. Dreys ᴰ1988 ➤ 5,k314: ᴿJRel 70 (1990) 260s (B. E. *Hinze*); TR 87 (1991) 34-37 (K.-H. *Menke*).

g728 **Tiefensee** Eberhard, Die religiöse Anlage und ihre Entwicklung; der religionsphilosophische Ansatz J. S. Dreys (1777-1853): ErfurtTSt TSt 56, 1988 ➤ 5,k316; 6,k864: ᴿTLZ 116 (1991) 216s (U. *Kern*); TR 87 (1991) 37-39 (K.-H. *Menke*).

g729 EMERSON: **Gelpi** Donald L., Endless seeker; the religious quest of Ralph W. Emerson. Lanham MD 1991, UPA. 169 p.; $48.50; pa. $26.25. 0-8191-7938-8; -9-6. – ᴿTS 52 (1991) 592 (W. C. *Spohn*).

g730 **Grusin** Richard A., [Emerson] Transcendentalist hermeneutics; institutional authority and the higher criticism: Post-contemporary interventions. Durham NC 1991, Duke Univ. vii-194 p. $32.50. 0-8223-1059-7 [TDig 38,360].

g731 FEUERBACH: **Meyer** Matthias, Feuerbach und ZINZENDORF; Lutherus redivivus und die Selbstauflösung der Religionskritik: ev. Diss. Tübingen 1991, ᴰ*Moltmann*. – TR 87 (1991) 522.

g732 FICHTE: *Radrizzani* Ives, Quelques réflexions sur le statut de l'histoire dans le système Fichtéen: RTPhil 123,3 (1991) 293-304; Eng. 352 [l'entier fascicule p. 225-332 est dédié au bicentenaire 1993 de l'Essai d'une critique de toute révélation anonyme – de Fichte mais universellement attribué à Kant: démenti de celui-ci (lettre à F. A. Weisshuhn) ici p. 229-248, ᴱ*Philonenko* Alexis].

g733 FINNEY: **Hardman** Keith J.,   Charles G. Finney 1987 ➤ 5,k318; 6,k865: ᴿAsbTJ 46,2 (1991) 111-3 (D. *Bundy*).

g733* ᴱ**Dupuis** Richard A. G., *Rosell* Garth,   The memoirs of Charles G. Finney, the complete restored text [with passages censored from J. H. FAIRCHILD edition]. GR 1989, Zondervan. 736 p. $23. 0-310-45920-6. – ᴿChH 59 (1990) 572-4 (J. E. *Johnson*); RExp 88 (1991) 227 (B. J. *Leonard*).

g734 **Hewitt** Glenn A.,   Regeneration and morality; a study of Charles Finney, Charles HODGE, John W. NEVIN, and Horace BUSHNELL [< diss. Chicago 1986]: Chicago Studies in the History of American Thought 7. Brooklyn 1991, Carlson. xix-210 p. $50. 0-926019-44-9 [TDig 39,267].

g735 FRANZELIN: *Massimino* Domenico, *a)* Franzelin e l'ecclesiologia del Vaticano I; – *b)* L'apporto alla stesura della Pastor aeternus e al dibattito sull'infallibilità; – *c)* Manoscritto, risposta al discorso del Card. F. M. GUIDI: Ho Theológos 9 (1991) 61-100 / 157-194 / 353-361; 4 fot.

g736 HASE: **Jaeger** Bernd,   Karl von Hase als Dogmatiker [⁶1870]: Luth-GeschGestalten 12.   Gü 1990, Mohn.   228 p. DM 24 [TLZ 117,141, U. *Kern*].

g737 HEGEL: *Borrego* Enrique M.,   Una 'Vida de Jesús' de G. W. F. Hegel [ᵀ*González Noriega* S., 1975]: Proyección 38 (1991) 325-339.

g738 **Fessard** Gaston † 1978, ᴱ*Sales* Michel,   Hegel, le Christianisme et l'histoire 1990 ➤ 6,k873:   ᴿBLitEc 92 (1991) 235s (A. *Dartigues*); Gregorianum 72 (1991) 397 (P. *Gilbert*).

g739 **Hegel** Georg W. F.,   Frühe Schriften [Jugendschriften bis 1800] ᴱ*Nicolin* Friedhelm, *Schüler* Gisela: GesSchr 1.   Ha 1989, Meiner.   656 p. DM 342. – ᴿRTLv 22 (1991) 401-4 (E. *Brito*).

g740 *Luc* Laurent-Paul,   La Vie de Jésus du jeune Hegel [harmonie des évangiles juin 1795]: ScEsp 43 (1991) 283-318.

g741 *Perkins* Mary Anne,   Logic and Logos — the search for unity in Hegel and COLERIDGE; I. Alienation and the logocentric response; II. The 'otherness' of God; III. A 'different' Logos: HeythJ 32 (1991) 1-25. 192-215. 340-354.

g742 *Stepelevich* Lawrence S.,   From Tübingen to Rome; the first Catholic response to Hegel [STAUDENMEIER F.]: HeythJ 32 (1991) 477-492.

g743 KIERKEGAARD: *Crouter* Richard,   Revolution and the religious imagination in Kierkegaard's Two ages: NSys 33 (1991) 58-72; deutsch 73.

g744 **Gouwens** David J.,   Kierkegaard's dialectic of the imagination. NY 1989, P. Lang.   viii-304 p. $38.50. – ᴿJAAR 44 (1991) 176s (R. E. *Hustwit*); ScotJT 44 (1991) 245-7 (G. *Pattison*).

g745 *Guerrero* Luis,   Fe luterana y fe católica en el pensamiento de Kierkegaard: ScripTPamp 23 (1991) 983-992.

g746 **Hartshorne** M. H.,   Kierkegaard, godly deceiver; the nature and meaning of his pseudonymous writings. NY 1990, Columbia Univ. xvii-112 p. [TR 87,431].

g747 KUENEN: *Kooij* A. van der,   Abraham Kuenen (1828-1891); de Pentateuch en de Godsdienst van Israël: NedTTs 45 (1991) 279-292; Eng. 329.

g748 LAMARTINE: *Jossua* Jean-Pierre, Sur le 'déisme' de Lamartine: RSPT 75 (1991) 569-585; Eng. 586.

g749 LIGHTFOOT: *Glasswell* Mark E., Lightfoot, Joseph Butler (1828-1899), ᵀ*Balz* Horst R. ⇢ 690, TRE 21 (1991) 196-9.

g750 MIGNE: ᴱ**Mandouze** A., *Fouilheron* J., Migne et le renouveau des études patristiques 1975/85 ⇢ 1,611 ... 4,k282: ᴿAugM 35 (1990) 191s (J. *Oroz*).

g751 MÖHLER: *Van Roo* William, Möhler's earlier symbolism [... spirit-body relationship]: Gregorianum 72 (1991) 129-138.

g752 NIETZSCHE: **Ahlsdorf** Michael, Nietzsches Juden; die philosophische Vereinnahmung des alttestamentlichen Judentums und der Einfluss von Julius WELLHAUSEN bei (in) Nietzsches Spätwerk: ev. Diss. FU Berlin 1991, ᴰ*Marquardt*. – TR 87 (1991) 515.

g753 **Anglet** Kurt, Zur Phantasmagorie der Tradition; Nietzsches Philosophie zwischen Historismus und Beschwörung. Wü 1989, Echter. 261 p. – ᴿTPhil 66 (1991) 440s (U. *Willers*).

g754 *Kienzler* Klaus, 'Nietzsche im christlichen Denken — am Beispiel Bernhard WELTES': TPhil 66 (1991) 398-410.

g755 **Valadier** Paul, Nietzsche e la critica radicale del cristianesimo. Palermo 1991, Augustinus. 554 p. [TR 88,79].

g756 ORR: **Scorgie** Glen G., A call for continuity; the theological contribution of James Orr [1844-1913] 1988 ⇢ 6,k896; £25. – ᴿEvQ 63 (1991) 88s (I. H. *Marshall*); ScotJT 44 (1991) 247-9 (J. G. *Levack*).

g757 OVERBECK: ᴱ**Patzer** Andreas, Franz Overbeck [1837-1905] – Erwin ROHDE, Briefwechsel; Einf. *Hölscher* U.; SuppNietzsche 1. B 1990, de Gruyter. xxxviii-645 p. DM 214 [TLZ 117,313, H. *Timm*].

g758 PALMER: **White** Charles E., The beauty of holiness; Phoebe Palmer [1807-1874] ⇢ 4,k288: ᴿJAAR 58 (1990) 319-321 (Carolyn D. *Gifford*).

g759 REUSS: *a*) *Jacob* Edmond, Édouard Reuss [Strasbourg 1804-1891], un théologien indépendant; – *b*) *Caquot* André, Reuss et RENAN; – *c*) *Heintz* Jean-Georges, E. Reuss, Karl H. GRAF et le Pentateuque; – *d*) *Westphal* Werner, É. Reuss, Directeur du Gymnase Protestant (1859-1865): RHPR 71 (1991) 427-435; phot. / 437-442 / 443-457 / 459-471.

g760 **Vincent** Jean Marcel, Leben und Werk des frühen Eduard Reuss [1804-1891; Heb.-Diss. Bochum 1985]: BeitEvT 106, 1990 ⇢ 6,k897; 3-459-01842-9: ᴿCritRR 4 (1991) 155 (M. P. *Graham*); OTAbs 14 (1991) 351 (C. T. *Begg*).

g761 RITSCHL 1822-1899: **McCulloh** Gerald W., Christ's person and life-work in the theology of Albrecht Ritschl with special attention to the *munus triplex*. Lanham 1990, UPA. 228 p. $44.50. 0-8191-7885-3 [TDig 38,278].

g761* **Gisel** Pierre, *al.*, Albrecht Ritschl, la théologie en modernité; entre religion, morale et positivité historique. Genève 1991, Labor et Fides. 224 p. [RHE 87,516, A. *Encrevé*].

g762 *a*) *Jacobs* Manfred, Liberale Theologie [Ritschl, HARNACK, TROELTSCH ...]: ⇢ 690, TRE 21 (1991) 47-68 [-73, *Konzemius* Victor, im Katholizismus]; – *b*) *Reynolds* Terrence, Ritschl's appropriation of LUTHER; a reappraisal: ConcordTQ 55 (1991) 105-... [< ZIT 92,74].

g762* ROBINSON E.: **Dearman** J. A., Edward Robinson, scholar and Presbyterian educator: American Presbyterian 69,3 (1991) 163-174 [< NTAbs 36,163].

g763 SAILER: *Gelébart* V.-C., Sailer (Johann Michael) 1751-1832: ⇢ 664, Catholicisme XIII,96 (1991) 448s.

g764 M. J. SCHEEBEN, teologo cattolico d'ispirazione tomista 1987/8 ⇒ 4, k398*b* ... 6,k898: ᴿRHE 86 (1991) 453-7 (R. *Aubert*).

g765 SCHELL: *a*) *Berning* Vincent, Konservatismus und Fortschritt; Erwägungen über das Statische und Dynamische in der Kirche im Anschluss an Herman Schell (1850-1906); – *b*) *Neufeld* Karl-Heinz, Zur 'Römischen Schule' im deutschen Sprachraum: ⇒ 132, Mem. SCHAUF H., Geist und Kirche 1991, 491-523 / 323-340.

g766 *Reinhardt* Rudolf, Exegese in Tübingen; Paul SCHANZ und Paul Wilhelm KEPPLER; ein Brief Anton HENLES an Hermann Schell (1886): Rottenburger JbKG 10 (Sigmaringen 1991) 197-202 [< ZIT 92].

g767 SCHLEIERMACHER: *Brito* Emilio, Nature, surnaturel, grâce chez Schleiermacher: ScEsp 43 (1991) 251-281.

g768 **Clements** Keith W., F. Schleiermacher, pioneer of modern theology 1987 ⇒ 3,g731 ... 5,k339: ᴿParadigms 7,2 (1991s) 36 (N. S. *Murrell*).

g769 ᵀᴱ**Crouter** Richard C., Schleiermacher, On religion; speeches to its cultured despisers 1988 ⇒ 5,k340: ᴿJRel 70 (1990) 259s (Dawn *De Vries*).

g770 **Junker** Maureen, Das Urbild des Gottesbewusstseins; zur Entwicklung der Religionstheorie und Christologie Schleiermachers von der 1. zur 2. Aufl. der Glaubenslehre [< Diss. Münster]: Schleiermacher-Archiv 8. B 1990, de Gruyter. xi-236 p. DM 84 [TR 87,431].

g771 **Ohst** Martin, Schleiermacher und die Bekenntnisschriften; eine Untersuchung zu seiner Reformations- und Protestantismusdeutung: BeitHistT 77. Tü 1989, Mohr. xi-283 p. 3-16-145480-4. – ᴿActuBbg 28 (1991) 179s (J. *Boada*).

g771* **Ottati** Douglas F., [Schleiermacher] Jesus Christ and the Christian vision 1989 ⇒ 6,7536: ᴿJRel 71 (1991) 274s (C. A. *Wilson*).

g772 STRAUSS: **Madges** William, The core of Christian faith; D. F. Strauss and his Catholic critics: AmerUnivSt 7/38, 1987 ⇒ 4,k298: ᴿChH 59 (1990) 103s (D. *Jodock*).

g772* THALHOFER: *Naab* Erich, Das Opfer Christi und die Kirche bei Valentin Thalhofer [1825-17.IX.1891]: Klerusblatt 71 (München 1991) 199-202 [< ZIT 91,679].

g773 WELCH Claude, The problem of a history of nineteenth century theology; Welch [1972] reconsidered: JRel 70 (1990) 606-617 (-624, *Madges* W., response).

Y5.5 *Crisis modernistica* – **The Modernist era.**

g774 **Barthélemy** Dominique, Études et documents sur l'histoire de l'Université de Fribourg, 1. Idéologie et fondation [...Crise moderniste]. FrS 1990, Univ. xxvi-266 p. – ᴿRThom 91 (1991) 676s (B. *Montagnes*).

g775 **Botti** Alfonso, La Spagna e la crisi modernista; cultura, società civile e religiosa tra Otto e Novecento 1987 ⇒ 4,k303; Lit. 22.000: ᴿCrNSt 11 (1990) 634-6 (A. *Zambarbieri*).

g776 *Cárcel Ortí* V., San Pío X, los jesuitas y los integristas españoles: ArHistPont 27 (1989) 349-355 [RHE 86,276, R. *Aubert*: *Razón y fe* contre *El siglo futuro*, ...ils avaient compris qu'un ralliement aux institutions modernes était inévitable].

g777 **Dante** Francesco, Storia della 'Civiltà Cattolica' (1850-1891); il laboratorio del Papa. R 1990, Studium. 287 p. Lit. 28.000. – ᴿCC 142 (1991,3) 549s (G. *Mucci*).

g778 ᴱFitzer Joseph, Romance and the Rock; nineteenth-century Catholics on faith and reason 1989 ➤ 6,k919: ᴿCritRR 4 (1991) 297s (J. E. *Thiel*).

g779 *a) Langlois* Claude, Le catholicisme au XIXᵉ siècle entre modernité et modernisation; – *b) Audinet* Jacques, Émergence de l'Église; ➤ 535*, RechSR 79,3 (1991) 325-336 / 337-351; Eng. 322.

g780 *Vibrac* Dominique, Le Dieu du modernisme: Divinitas 34 (1990) 272-285.

g781 O'Gara Margaret, Triumph in defeat 1988 ➤ 4,k310 ... 6,k922: ᴿMid-Stream 30 (1991) 89-91 (D. M. *Thompson*).

g782 *Schatz* Klaus, Die französischen Minoritätsbischöfe auf dem I. Vatikanum: TPhil 66 (1991) 1-20.

---

g783 BLONDEL: **Izquierdo** Cesar, Blondel y la crisis modernista; análisis de 'Historia y dogma', pref. *Troisfontaines* Claude: Teológica 71. Pamplona 1990, Univ. Navarra. 396 p. – ᴿRHE 86 (1991) 155-8 (É. *Poulat*); ScripTPamp 23 (1991) 356-9 (J. L. *Illanes*).

g784 **Theobald** Christoph, Maurice Blondel und das Problem der Modernität 1988 ➤ 5,k368; 6,k931: ᴿGregorianum 72 (1991) 147s (R. *Fisichella*).

g785 DÖLLINGER: *a)* **Neuner** Peter, Stationen ... Döllinger 1990 ➤ 6,k934: ᴿTPhil 66 (1991) 284-6 (K. *Schatz*); – *b) Parmentier* M. F. G., Ignaz von Döllinger und Vinzenz von LÉRINS [< Döllinger-Symposium, Salzburg 29. Sept. 1990]: IkiZ 81 (1991) 41-58.

g785* *Weiss* Otto, Döllinger und die Redemptoristen: Beiträge zur altbayerischen Kirchengeschichte 40 (1991) 7-54 [< zit 92,245].

g786 *a) Conzemius* Victor, Éduard HERZOG (1841-1924), exégète, premier Évêque catholique-chrétien de Suisse; – *b) Moll* Arnold, Eine Freundschaft unter Bischöfen; Joseph H. REINKENS und Eduard Herzog; – *c) Aldenhoven* Herwig, É. Herzog: IkiZ 81 (1991) 149-157 / 158-169 / 142-8.

g786* *Schatz* Klaus, Kirchengeschichte der Neuzeit II. Dü 1989, Patmos. DM 24,80. – ᴿIkiZ 81 (1991) 75s (E. *Kessler*: typisch ist die Darstellung der beiden vatikanischen Konzils ... der Machinationen von MANNING und SENESTREY ...].

g787 VON HÜGEL: *a) Rambaldi* G., Una memoria inedita del Barone Friedrich von Hügel sull'unione tra cattolici e anglicani: ArHistPont 27 (1989) 419-432; – *b)* **Zurzi** Giuseppe, Auf der Suche nach der verlorenen Katholizität; die Briefe Friedrich von Hügels an Giovanni SEMERIA: TüStTPh 3. Mainz 1991, Grünewald. 618 p. (2 vol.). DM 98 [TR 88,256].

g788 LEO XIII: *Aubert* Roger, Leo XIII, ᵀ*Schäferdiek* Knut: ➤ 690, TRE 20 (1990) 748-753.

g789 **Marini** Franco, La questione sociale a 100 anni dalla 'Rerum Novarum'; riflessioni dal sindacato. R 1991, Ministero per il Lavoro. 43 p.

g790 **Talamo** Salvatore [ispiratore dell'Æterni Patris ➤ 4,k301], Il rinnovamento del pensiero tomistico 4 [²1878], pref. *Piolanti* A.: Classici del Tomismo. Vaticano 1986, Accademia S. Tommaso. 134 p. – ᴿETL 67 (1991) 178 (R. *Wielockx*).

g791 LOISY: *Neuner* Peter, Loisy, Alfred (1857-1940): ➤ 690, TRE 21 (1991) 453-6.

g791* ᴱ**Hoffman** R. Joseph, Alfred Firmin Loisy, The Gospel and the Church [1902]: Classics of biblical criticism. Buffalo 1988, Prometheus.

388 p. $21. – RChC 59 (1990) 119s (D. G. *Schultenover*: Hoffman inadequate).

g792 *Forni* G., BERGSONISMO e modernismo; A. Loisy e la critica del cristianesimo: CrNSt 12 (1991) 85-118; Eng. 118.

g793 **Talar** C. J. T., Metaphor and modernist ... Loisy 1988 ⮕ 6,k946: RNBlackf 71 (1990) 150s (H. F. G. *Swanston*).

g794 *Talar* C. J. T., Reading Loisy: LitTOx 5,1 (1991) 49-67 [< ZIT 91,211].

g795 NEWMAN, OXFORD MOVEMENT: *a) Biemer* Günter, 'Sie müssen warten, bis sich das Auge der Seele in Ihnen gebildet hat'; Newmans Leben und Werk als Suche nach der Wahrheit; – *b) Kuld* Lothar, 'Die Religion des Tages'; Newmans Auseinandersetzung mit dem religiösen Liberalismus: RUntHö 33,6 (Newman 1990) 352-363 / 364-370 (-400, *al.*).

g796 **Biemer** Günter, J. H. Newman 1989 ⮕ 5,k378; 6,k949: RZkT 113 (1991) 347s (R. *Siebenrock*).

g797 **Britt** John, J. H. Newman's rhetoric: AmerUnivSt 21/-. NY 1989, Lang. viii-218 p. – RLvSt 16 (1991) 276s (T. *Merrigan*: incoherent).
EBrown David, Newman, a man for our time 1990 ⮕ 476c.

g798 **Chadwick** Owen, The spirit of the Oxford Movement 1990 ⮕ 6,211: RCathHR 77 (1991) 313s (J. R. *Griffin*: many sentences questionable or wrong); ÉTRel 66 (1991) 455 (L. *Gambarotto*); NRT 113 (1991) 610s (N. *Plumat*); RHE 86 (1991) 444-6 (M. *Tylor*); TLond 94 (1991) 371s (P. *Butler*); TLZ 116 (1991) 946-8 (J. *Mann*).

g799 *a) Coulson* John, Was Newman a modernist?; – *b) Daly* Gabriel, LABERTHONNIÈRE and Newman; – *c) Wansbrough* Henry, Newman, the modernists and biblical inspiration; – *d) Walgrave* J. H., 'Real' and 'notional' in BLONDEL and Newman: ⮕ 515, Newman and modernism 1990, 74-84 / 41-55 / 105-117 / 142-156.

g800 *Chitarin* Luigi, J. H. Newman nella controversia sulla giustificazione per fede: HumBr 46 (1991) 365-383.

g801 **Forrester** David, Young Dr. PUSEY 1989 ⮕ 6,k962: RNBlackf 71 (1990) 257s (R. *Strange*).

g802 — *Bedouelle* G., Pusey (Edward B., 1800-1882) ⮕ 664, Catholicisme XII,56 (1990) 320-2.

g803 *Gaffney* James, Discipline and influence; Newman on teaching and learning: Horizons 18 (1991) 48-56.

g804 *Gauthier* Pierre, L'attitude pastorale de Newman à l'Université: RevSR 65 (1991) 241-257.

g805 **Gilley** Sheridan, Newman and his age 1990 ⮕ k966: RCathHR 77 (1991) 520s (J. J. *Hughes*); Month 252 (1991) 26s (K. *Flannery*).

g806 *a) Gilley* Sheridan, Newman, conservatism and orthodoxy; – *b) Confessore* Ornella, L'americanismo; conservazione o innovazione: CrNSt 12 (1991) 613-622 / 623-638; Eng. 638.

g807 **Giorgini** Fabiano, (BÀRBERI) Domenico della Madre di Dio [beato], Lettera ai professori di Oxford; relazioni con Newman e i suoi amici: Ricerche di storia e spiritualità passionista 45. R 1990, C.Ip.I. 110 p. – RSalesianum 53 (1991) 156s (C. *Semeraro*).

g808 **Honoré** Jean, Newman, sa vie et sa pensée: BiblHistChr 17, 1988 ⮕ 5,k384: RScEsp 43 (1991) 138s (R. *Marcotte*).

g809 EJaki Stanley L., Newman today; proceedings of the Wethersfield Institute 1988 ➛ 5,632: ᴿPrPeo 4 (1990) 240-3 (P. *Hodgson*); ScripTPamp 23 (1991) 395 (J. *Morales*).

ᴱJenkins A., Newman and Modernism 1990 ➛ 516.

g809* *Kenedy* Finola, Newman, the man and his legacy: Studies 79 (1990) 343-352 [-376, al.].

g810 **Ker** I., J. H. Newman biog. 1988 ➛ 5,k385; 6,k972: ᴿAnnTh 4 (1990) 489-493 (R. A. P. *Stork*); HZ 253 (1991) 466s (P. *Alter*); NBlackf 71 (1990) 205s (P. *Parvis*); Thomist 55 (1991) 337-342 (E. J. *Miller*).

g811 **Ker** Ian, The achievement of J. H. Newman 1990 ➛ 6,k973; £15: ᴿTablet 245 (1991) 18 (Joyce *Sugg*, also on his 1991 Reader; both better than B. MARTIN 1991 = 1982).

g812 **Ker** I., Genius of Newman; selections 1989 ➛ 5,k385*: ᴿCathHR 77 (1991) 314s (J. T. *Ford*).

g813 **Ker** Ian, Newman; on being a Christian. ND 1990, Univ. 187 p. [RelStR 18,41, P. *Crowley*: completes a trilogy].

g814 ᴱ**Ker** Ian, *Hill* Alan G., Newman after a hundred years [22 art.] 1990 ➛ 6,422*: ᴿJTS 42 (1991) 407-9 (G. *Rowell*).

g815 **McRedmond** Louis, Thrown among strangers... Newman in Ireland 1990 ➛ 6,k973: ᴿDoctLife 41 (1991) 275s (G. *Slevin*) [40 (1990) 227-238, McRedmond's Prologue]; ScripTPamp 23 (1991) 729s (J. *Morales*).

g816 *Magill* Gerard, Imaginative moral discernment; Newman on the tension between reason and religion: HeythJ 32 (1991) 493-510.

g817 **Martin** Brian, J. H. Newman, his life and times. Homebush NSW 1990, St. Paul. 160 p. A$17. – ᴿAustralasCR 68 (1990) 308 (A. *Cooper*); RExp 88 (1991) 103s (E. G. *Hinson*).

g818 **Merrigan** Terrence, Clear heads and holy hearts; the religious and theological ideal of J. H. Newman: LvTPMg 7. 1991, Peeters. xvi-272 p. [TR 88,431].

g818* *Merrigan* T., Theologische publicaties rond J. H. Newman [KER I., BOUDENS R., GRAVE S., CHADWICK O.]: TsTNijm 31 (1991) 433-5.

g819 **Morales** José, Newman (1801-1890): Forjadores de Historia. M 1990, Rialp. 375 p. – ᴿSalesianum 53 (1991) 573 (G. *Abbà*); ScripTPamp 23 (1991) 324-6 (J. L. *Lorda*).

g819* **Murphy** Martin, Blanco WHITE, self-banished Spaniard [Oriel, Oxford; Letters from Spain...]. NHv 1989, Yale Univ. 270 p. $30. 0-300-04458-5. – ᴿRExp 88 (1991) 275s (B. J. *Leonard*).

g820 *Murray* Scott, LUTHER in Newman's 'Lectures on justification': ConcordTQ 54 (1990) 155-178 [< ZIT 91,137].

g821 ᴱ**Nicholls** David, *Kerr* Fergus, J. H. Newman; reason, rhetoric and romanticism. Carbondale 1991, Southern Illinois Univ. 257 p. $27.50. 0-8093-1758-3 [TDig 39,171]. 9 art.

g822 *O'Loughlin* Thomas, Newman, VINCENT of Lerins and development: IrTQ 57 (1991) 147-166.

g823 **Page** John Robert, What will Dr. Newman do? J. H. Newman and the definition of papal infallibility, 1865-1875: diss. Georgetown, ᴰ*Ford* J. Wsh 1990. 622 p. 91-35869. – DissA 52 (1991s) 2245-A.

g824 *Pattison* Robert, The great dissent; J. H. Newman and the liberal heresy. Ox 1991, UP. 231 p. $30 [JAAR 59,884].

g825 *Potvin* Thomas R., Le changement, condition de la fidélité selon J. H. card. Newman: SR 20 (1991) 281-298.

g826 *a)* *Powell* Geoffrey, J. H. Newman in ecumenical perspective; – *b)* *Simons* Robert G., Newman on revelation: AustralasCR 67,3 (Newman centenary, 1990) 259-272 / 288-298 [273-287 . 299-308, *al.*].

g827 *Rollmann* Hans, Franz X. KRAUS and J.H. Newman: DowR 109 (1991) 44-51 [16-34, *Jaki* L. ➤ 1870].
Runcie R., *Cossiga* F., *Chadwick* H., *al.*, Newman, a man for our time 1990 ➤ 476c.

g827* ᴱSvaglic Martin J., J.H. Newman, Apologia pro vita sua; being a history of his religious opinions. Ox 1990 = 1967, Clarendon. lx-603 p. $135. 0-19-811840-6 [TDig 39,278].

g828 **Thomas** Stephen, Newman and heresy; the Anglican years. C 1991, Univ. xiv-335 p. £35 [NRT 114,911, P. *Detienne*].

g828* *Torres Queiruga* Andrés, J.H. Newman, fe y razón en una época de crisis: RET 51 (1991) 5-42.

---

g829 PIUS IX: **Martina** Giacomo, Pio IX [III.] 1867-1878: 1990 ➤ 6,k985: ᴿCathHR 77 (1991) 706s (F.J. *Coppa*); CC 142 (1991,3) 31-42 (G. *Salvini*); HumBr 46 (1991) 787s (A. *Nassini*); TPhil 66 (1991) 280-3 (K. *Schatz*).

g830 *Croce* G.M., Una fonte importante per la storia del pontificato di Pio IX e del Concilio Vaticano I; i manoscritti inediti di Vincenzo TIZZANI: ArchHistPont 23 (1985) 372-375; 25 (1987) 263-364 [R 1985-7, 310 p. con indice: < CrNSt 11 (1990) 231-3, A. *Melloni*].

g831 RENAN: **Mercury** François, Renan. P 1990, Orban. 418 p. F 150 [Études 437,420].

g832 *Fraisse* S., Renan (Ernest) [1823-1892]: ➤ 664, Catholicisme XII,57 (1990) 879-882.

g833 *Fusco* Vittorio, *a*) Baldassarre Labanca [1829-1913] e gli studi neotestamentari [... Renan, LOISY] in Italia; – *b*) Convegno su 'B. LABANCA nella cultura italiana ed europea tra '800 e '900' (Agnone 14s.XII.1990): ➤ 452, AnStoEseg 8,2 (1990/1) 677-705 / 719s.

g833* SCHELL: *a*) *Rivinius* Karl J., Integralismmus und Reformkatholizismus; die Kontroverse um Herman Schell; – *b*) *Leugers-Scherzberg* August-H., Die Modernisierung des Katholizismus; das Beispiel Felix PORSCH: ➤ 363c, ᴱLoth W., Deutscher Katholizismus im Umbruch zur Moderne 1991, 199-218 / 219-235.

g834 TYRRELL: *Daly* Gabriel, Tyrrell (George) 1861-1909: ➤ 668, DictSpir 15 (1991) 1372-83.

g835 **Sagovsky** N., On God's side Tyrrell 1990 ➤ 6,k996: ᴿCathHR 77 (1991) 318s (L. *Barmann*); JEH 42 (1991) 141s (O. *Chadwick*: a hierarchy afraid and sometimes in panic); JTS 42 (1991) 409-411 (G. *Daly*: rectifies PETRE with SCHULTENOVER); Tablet 245 (1991) 50 (D. *Schultenover*: not intense like Maude PETRE's); TS 52 (1991) 781 (C.J. *Healy*).

g836 **McCarthy** Thomas A., A study of George Tyrrell's final position on dogmatic development in the light of modern Catholic theology: diss. Fordham 1991, ᴰ*Kilian* S. 189 p. 91-18839. – DissA 52 (1991s) 575-A: 'valuable but not acceptable'; – RelStR 18,171.

g837 **Tyrrell** George, Traditions and the critical spirit; Catholic modernist writings, ᴱ*Livingstone* J.C.: TextsModT. Mp 1990, Fortress. xl-205 p. [NRT 114,932, L.-J. *Renard*: 'chief Catholic theologian of the century after Newman', in a series with SCHLEIERMACHER, TROELTSCH, BULTMANN].

g838 **Leonard** Ellen, Unresting transformation; the theology and spirituality of Maude PETRE. Lanham MD 1991, UPA. viii-244 p. $46.50; pa. $26.50. 0-8191-8220-6; -1-4 [TDig 39,172].

Y6 *Saeculum XX* – **20th Century Exegesis.**

g839 *a) Aune* David E., The history of the Chicago society of biblical research [founded 1891]; – *b) Grant* Robert M., Is there a future for biblical research?: BiRes 36 (Centennial Issue, 1991) 98s [100, past presidents; 102-4 roster] / 95-97.

g840 **Epp** Eldon J., *MacRae* George W., The New Testament and its modern interpreters 1989 ➤ 5,394; 6,m2: ᴿBibTB 21 (1991) 120s (D.M. *Sweetland*); Gregorianum 72 (1991) 568-570 (E. *Rasco*).

ᴱ**Felder** Cain H., Stony the path we trod; African American Bible interpretation 1991 ➤ 431.

g840* *Gros* Jeffrey, Discerning the Gospel; dialogue in the Catholic Church: ChrCent 107 (1990) 460-3.

g841 BARR: *France* R.T., James Barr and evangelical scholarship: Anvil 8,1 (Bristol 1991) 51-... [< ZIT 91,202].

g842 BEA: **Schmidt** S., A. Bea, il cardinale dell'unità 1987 ➤ 3,g812 ... 6,m5: ᴿCrNSt 12 (1991) 463-6 (A. *Melloni*); RTLv 22 (1990) 279s (G. *Thils*).

g843 **Schmidt** Stjepan, A. Bea, der Kardinal der Einheit 1989 ➤ 5,k408; 6,m6: ᴿNRT 113 (1991) 294s (J. *Masson*: une discrétion toute romaine); StiZt 208 (1990) 569-572 (H. *Fries*); TrierTZ 100 (1991) 239s (H. *Schützeichel*).

g844 BENJAMIN: *Ruster* Thomas, Auslegung vergangener Hoffnung; Versuche einer benjaminischen Lektüre der Bibel [Benjamin (Walter), † 27.IX.1940]: Orientierung 55 (1991) 265-7.

g845 BLOCH: **Puthur** Bosco, From the principle of hope to the theology of hope [Bloch, MOLTMANN]: Publ. 47. Alwaye 1987, Pontifical Institute. xvi-322 p. rs 45. – ᴿIndTSt 27 (1990) 198s (B.J. *Francis*).

g845* ᴱ**Cacciatore** Giuseppe, Figure dell'utopia; saggi su Ernest Bloch; introd. *Tessitore* Fulvio. Avellino 1989, Redi. 464 p. Lit. 38.000. – ᴿRasT 32 (1991) 98s (F. *Miano*).

g846 **Schmidt** Burghart, Ernst Bloch: Realien zur Literatur D. Literaturgeschichte. Stu 1985, Metzler. vii-180 p. DM 19,80. – ᴿRBgPg 69 (1991) 770s (L. *Abicht*).

g847 BORNKAMM: *Theissen* Gerd, Theologie und Exegese in den neutestamentlichen Arbeiten von Günther Bornkamm: EvT 51 (1991) 308-332.

g848 BUBER: *Shapira* Avraham, Political messianism in Buber's conception of redemption: JJS 42 (1991) 92-107.

g849 **Friedman** Maurice, Encounter on the narrow ridge; a life of Martin Buber. NY 1991, Paragon. $32 [JAAR 59,882].

g850 **Silberstein** Lawrence J., Martin Buber's social and religious thought; alienation and the quest for meaning. Albany 1989, SUNY. 358 p. $40. – ᴿJAAR 59 (1991) 197-9 (M. *Friedman*).

g851 BULTMANN: **Bockmuehl** K., The unreal God ... Bultmann, BARTH 1988 ➤ 5,k420; 6,m11: ᴿJRel 71 (1991) 107 (M.I. *Wallace*).

g852 *a) Hübner* Hans, Was ist existentiale Interpretation?; – *b) Stoevesandt* Hinrich, Basel-Marburg, ein (un)erledigter Konflikt? – *c) Kaiser* Otto, Abschied von der existentialen Interpretation? Bericht und Rechenschaft: ➤ 442, Bibel und Mythos ... nach Bultmann 1991, 9-37 / 91-113 / 114-126.

g853 **Johnson** Roger, R. Bultmann; interpreting faith for the modern era 1987 ➤ 4,k567 ... 6,m17: ᴿCurrTMiss 18 (1991) 218s (W. C. *Linss*).

g854 *Kay* James F., Bultmann's 'New Testament and Mythology' [1941 Alpirsbach lecture] turns fifty: TTod 48 (1991s) 326-332.

g855 **Jones** Gareth, Bultmann; towards a critical theology. C/CM 1991, Polity. viii-219 p. $45. 0-7456-0697-0 [TDig 38,363].

g856 **Sinn** Gunnar, Christologie und Existenz; Rudolf Bultmanns Interpretation des paulinischen Christuszeugnisses: TANZ 4. Tü 1991, Francke. xiii-306 p. 3-7720-1883-1.

g857 **Trocholepczy** Bernd, Rechtfertigung und Seinsfrage; Anknüpfung und Widerspruch in der HEIDEGGER-Rezeption Bultmanns [Diss. ᴰ*Lehmann* K.]: FreibTSt 146. FrB 1991, Herder. 170 p. – ᴿTGL 81 (1991) 500s (B. *Dieckmann*).

g858 *Wassmann* Harry, Der 'Fall Bultmann' in Württemberg (1941-1953); der Alpirsbacher Mythologievertrag im Spannungsfeld von Kirchenleitung und Universitätstheologie: TüUnivG 4 / WerkschrArchivs 1/14 (1989) 137-177 [< ZKG 102 (1991) 278s (W. *Schmithals*)].

g858* CULLMANN: **Dorman** T. M., The hermeneutics of Oscar Cullmann [diss. Fuller ᴰ*Fuller* D., Pasadena 1983]. SF 1991, Mellen Univ. xii-184 p. $30 pa. 0-7734-9953-9 [NTAbs 36,252].

g859 HAAG Herbert, Mein Weg mit der Kirche. Basel 1991, Vetter. 224 p. Fs 30. [Orientierung 55,57 adv.].

g860 HESCHEL: ᴱ**Kasimow** Harold, *Sherwin* Byron L., No religion is an island; Abraham J. Heschel and interreligious dialogue. Mkn 1991, Orbis. xxv-205 p. (with Heschel bibliog.). $17 pa. 0-88344-769-X [TDig 39,179].

g861 JEREMIAS: *Meyer* Ben F., A caricature of Joachim Jeremias and his scholarly work [E. P. SANDERS' 'increasingly reckless campaign of misrepresentation' culminating in 1987 ꟳ*Farmer* W., 225-239]: JBL 110 (1991) 451-462; Sanders response 463-477.

g862 KAUFMANN: **Krapf** Thomas, Y. Kaufmann; Ein Lebens- und Erkenntnisweg zur Theologie der hebräischen Bibel 1990 ➤ 6,m31: ᴿRB 98 (1991) 466s (B. T. *Viviano*).

g863 LAGRANGE: ᴱ**Gilbert** Maurice, M.-J. Lagrange, L'écriture en Église; choix de portraits et d'exégèse spirituelle (1890-1937): LDiv 142, 1990 ➤ 6,m35: ᴿCiTom 118 (1991) 185s (M. *García Cordero*); NRT 113 (1991) 464s (A. *Toubeau*); RB 98 (1991) 674 (R. J. *Tournay*); RevSR 65 (1991) 389 (B. *Renaud*); RTLv 22 (1991) 243 (J. *Ponthot*).

g864 ᴱ**Gilbert** Maurice, Marie-Joseph Lagrange, Exégète à Jérusalem, nouveaux mélanges d'histoire religieuse (1890-1939): CahRB 29. P 1991, Gabalda. 260 p. F 370. 2-85021-047-1 [ZAW 104,299, tit. pp.]. – ᴿEspr-Vie 101 (1991) 562s (É. *Cothenet*); OTAbs 14 (1991) 343 (C. T. *Begg*: tit. pp. date); RThom 91 (1991) 675s (B. *Montagnes*).

g865 **Montagnes** B., Exégèse et obéissance; correspondance CORMIER-Lagrange 1989 ➤ 5,k444; 6,m37: ᴿAngelicum 68 (1991) 584-7 (J. *García Trapiello*); Biblica 72 (1991) 122-4 (M. *Gilbert*); RB 98 (1991) 125-134 (L.-M. *Dewailly*).

g866 LIETZMANN: *Schneemelcher* Wilhelm, Lietzmann, Hans Karl Alexander (1875-1942): ➤ 690, TRE 21 (1991) 191-8.

g867 LOHMEYER: *Haufe* Günter, Lohmeyer, Ernst (1890-1946): ➤ 690, TRE 21 (1991) 444-7.

g868 MARGOLIS: **Greenspoon** Leonard, Max I. Margolis 1987 ➤ 3,g836; 5,k445: ᴿJQR 82 (1991s) 257s (N. M. *Sarna*).

g869 MARTINI Carlo Maria, *a*) Comunicare nella Chiesa e nella società; lettere, discorsi e interventi 1990. Bo 1991, Dehoniane. 672 p. Lit. 37.000 [RivB 39,200 adv.]; – *b*) Dem Leben Richtung geben; Perspektiven für junge Menschen. Mü 1991, Neue Stadt. 87 p. DM 12,80 [ErbAuf 67,487].

g870 ROBINSON J. A.: **Taylor** T. F., J. Armitage Robinson [Ephesians commentary]. C 1991, Clarke. 139 p. £19.50. 0-227-67913-X. – ᴿExpTim 102 (1990s) 384 (C. S. *Rodd*).

g871 ROBINSON J. A. T.: *Dayras* S., Robinson. John A. T. 1919-1983: ➤ 664, Catholicisme XIII,59 (1991) 26-28.

g872 **Kee** Alistair, The roots of Christian freedom... J. A. T. Robinson 1988 ➤ 4.k380... 6,m46*: ᴿNBlackf 71 (1990) 46-48 (R. J. *Taylor*: 'dissatisfying'); ScotJT 43 (1990) 509-511 (W. M. *Jacob*).

g873 ROSENZWEIG: **Bauer** Anna, Rosenzweigs Sprachdenken im 'Stern der Erlösung' und in einer Korrespondenz mit Martin BUBER zur Verdeutschung der Schrift: Diss. FrB 1991, ᴰ*Casper*. 463 p. – TR 87 (1991) 517; RTLv 23, p. 541.

g874 *a*) *Bonola* Gianfranco, La peculiarità irriducibile; la Scrittura nella disputa su cristianesimo ed ebraismo tra F. Rosenzweig e E. ROSENSTOCK-HUESSY [1916]; – *b*) *Gaeta* Giancarlo, Verità e linguaggio; sull'ermeneutica religiosa di Simone WEIL; – *c*) *Bori* Pier Cesare, Antico Testamento, Evangelo, Legge eterna in Lev TOLSTOJ esegeta [1880]: AnStoEseg 8 (1991) 235-276 / 277-293 / 193-234.

g875 SANDAY, SANDERS: *Whybray* R. N., *a*) Sanday (William 1843-1930); – *b*) Sanders (Henry A. 1868-1956): ➤ 686, SDB XI,64 (1991) 1329-31 / 1331s.

g876 SCHLATTER: *Stuhlmacher* Peter, Adolf Schlatter als Paulusausleger — ein Versuch: ➤ 437, Paulus, Tübingen-Durham-Symposium im Gedenken an den 50. Todestag Adolf Schlatters († 19. Mai 1938) 409-424.

g877 SCHWEITZER: ᴱ**Günzler** Claus, *al.*, Albert Schweitzer heute; Brennpunkte seines Denkens [17 art.]: [Mainz], Beit. Schweitzer-Forschung 1. Tü 1990, Katzmann. 384 p.; map. DM 48 [TLZ 117,54, H. H. *Jenssen*].

g878 **Schweitzer** Albert, Gespräche über das Neue Testament [Strassburg 1901-4], ᴱ*Dobertin* Winfried. Mü 1988, Esslingen. 215 p. – ᴿZKG 102 (1991) 415s (E. *Grässer*).

g879 **Schweitzer** Albert, Out of my life and thought [1931], ᵀ*Lemke* A. B. NY 1990, Holt. xii-272 p. $25. 0-8050-1467-5 [NTAbs 36,105].

g879* WARFIELD: **Letis** T. P., B. B. Warfield [1851-1921]; common-sense philosophy and biblical [NT textual] criticism: American Presbyterian 69,3 (Ph 1991) 175-190 [< NTAbs 36,164].

g880 WINTON THOMAS: *Emerton* J. A., The work of David Winton Thomas [† 18.VI.1970] as a Hebrew scholar: VT 41 (1991) 287-303.

g881 ZAHN: **Zwarat** Uwe, Alte Kirche und Neues Testament; Theodor Zahn als Patristiker: MbStB 342. Wu 1991, Brockhaus. xiv-578 p. 3-417-29342-1.

Y6.4 **Theologi influentes** *in exegesim saeculi XX.*

g882 **Ahme** Michael, Der Reformversuch der E[vangelischen] K[irche] D[eutschlands] 1970-1976 [Diss. 1989]. Stu 1990, Kohlhammer. 207 p. DM 50. – ᴿTLZ 116 (1991) 731s (F. *Winter*).

g882* **Alberigo** Giuseppe, Il cristianesimo in Italia: Quadrante 25. R 1989, Laterza. 155 p. – ᴿHistJb 111 (1991) 215 (R. *Lill*).

g883 **Altermatt** Urs, Katholizismus und Moderne; Studien zur Sozialgeschichte der Schweizer Katholiken im 19. und 20. Jahrhundert²*rev*. Z 1990, Benziger. 470 p. Fs 48. 3-545- 25076-8. – ᴿHistJb 111 (1991) 508-511 (H. *Hürten*); IkiZ 81 (1991) 68-74 (P. *Hersche*); TLZ 116 (1991) 869-871 (F. *Stolz*).

Avis Paul, Anglicanism 1989 ➤ 7963.

g884 **Barlow** Philip L., Mormons and the Bible; the place of the Latter-day Saints in American religion: RelAmer. NY 1991, Oxford-UP. xxxix-251 p. 0-19-506233-7.

g885 **Bauman** Michael, Roundtable; conversations with European theologians. GR 1990, Baker. 142 p. $9 pa. 0-8010-0986-3 [TDig 39,49].

g886 **Bloom** Allan, The closing of the American mind. ... 1988, Touchstone. $9. 0-671-65715-1. – ᴿHomP 91,3 (1990s) 1-20 (J. V. *Schall*: an important book for Catholics).

g887 ᴱ**Bradbury** M. L., *Gilbert* James B., Transforming faith; the sacred and secular in modern American history [1987 conference, Univ. of Maryland; 12 art. including *Marty* M., *Cox* H.]: ContrStRel 23. Westport CT 1989, Greenwood. xi-197 p. $40 [RelStR 18,162, J. L. *Price*].

g887* **Coalter** Milton J., *al.*, The diversity of discipleship; the Presbyterians and the twentieth-century Christian witness. Louisville 1991, W-Knox. 402 p. $17 pa. [JAAR 59,886].

g888 **Ford** David E., The modern theologians 1989 ➤ 5,k461; 6,m65: ᴿJRel 71 (1991) 272s (T. *Peters*); TR 87 (1991) 292s (E. *Sturm*).

g889 **Gauly** Thomas M., Katholiken, Machtanspruch und Machtverlust 1991 ➤ 6,m66*b*: ᴿActuBbg 28 (1991) 219-221 (J. *Boada*).

g889* **Greeley** Andrew M., Religious change in America 1989 ➤ 6,m68: ᴿAnglTR 73 (1991) 88s (S. W. *Martin*).

g890 **Grigg** Richard, Theology as a way of thinking [... norms admitting RUETHER and CONE, also RAHNER and WHITEHEAD, but not BARTH]: AAR-SBL Ventures in Religion 1. Atlanta 1990, Scholars. xiv-129 p. [RelStR 18,39, J. R. *Sachs*].

g891 *Gros* Jeffrey, The vision of Christian unity; some aspects of faith and order in the context of United States culture: Mid-Stream 30 (1991) 1-19.

g892 *Haendler* Gert, Der Reichsbischof und die Theologischen Fakultäten [... Rostock] 1933/34: TLZ 116 (1991) 1-16.

g893 **Hastings** Adrian, A history of English Christianity 1920-1990 [1987 ➤ 6,m68*: reissue with 'Afterthoughts; the 1980s']. L/Ph 1991, SCM/Trinity. xxix-720 p. £17.50. 0-334-02496-X [ExpTim 103,63].

g894 **Hatch** Nathan O., The democratization of American Christianity 1989 ➤ 6,m69: ᴿAndrUnS 29 (1991) 175-7 (G. R. *Knight*: superb); JEH 42 (1991) 134s (R. *Carwardine*).

g895 *Henry* Carl F. H., The uneasy conscience revisited [< Twilight of a great civilization 1988]: Evangel 8,3 (1990) 13-20.

g895* **Herbert** Karl, Kirche zwischen Aufbruch und Tradition; Entscheidungsjahre nach 1945. Stu 1989, Radius. 407 p. DM 29. – ᴿTLZ 116 (1991) 42-44 (M. *Greschat*).

g896 **Hornsby-Smith** Michael P., Roman Catholic beliefs in England; customary Catholicism and transformations of religious authority. C 1991, Univ. 265 p. £27. 0-521-36327-6. – ᴿExpTim 102 (1990s) 290s (C. S. *Rodd*'s published pre-1970 researches enable him to query these interview–sociology too–comfortable conclusions).

g897 **Hummel** Gert,   Die Begegnungen zwischen Philosophie und evangelischer Theologie im 20. Jh.: Die philosophischen Bemühungen des 20. Jh.s, 1989 → 6,m70:   ᴿTR 87 (1991) 293 (W. *Schüssler*).

g898 ᴱ**Hutchison** W.,   Between the times – Protestant 1900-60 1989 → 5,679: ᴿJRel 71 (1991) 581s (J. W. *Lewis*).

g898* **Jorstad** Erling,   Holding fast / pressing on; religion in America in the 1980's.   Westport CT 1989, Greenwood.   216 p. $15.   0-275-93607-4. – ᴿRExp 88 (1991) 280s (B. J. *Leonard*).

g899 **Komonchak** Joseph A.,   What they said before the Council; how the U. S. bishops envisioned Vatican II: Commonweal 117 (1990) 714-7.

g900 **Launay** M.,   Les catholiques des États-Unis: BtHistChr 25.   P 1991, Desclée.   206 p.   F 119 [NRT 114,619, J. *Bernard*].

g901 ᴱ**Lutz** D.,   Altered landscapes; Christianity in America 1935-1985.   GR 1989, Eerdmans.   xi-387 p. $28; pa. $18. – ᴿAndrUnS 29 (1991) 177s (G. *Land*).

g902 **Marty** Martin E.,   Modern American religion [1. 1986 → 2,d739], 2. The noise of conflict, 1919-1941.   Ch 1991, Univ.   466 p. $27.50. – ᴿAmerica 165 (1991) 171.173s (J. *McShane*); Commonweal 118 (1991) 344s (L. S. *Cunningham*); TTod 48 (1991s) 371 (E. B. *Holifield*).

g902* *a) Marty* Martin E.,   Protestantism and the American way of life / America and the Protestant way of life; – *b) Winters* Charles L.,   The Episcopal Church and the 'American way of life'; – *c) Berzonsky* Vladimir,   An Orthodox Christian view of American values; – *d) Sunshine* Edward R., *Pierce* Joanne,   Catholicism in America: ChSt 30 (1991) 161-175 / 176-188 / 189-202 / 203-219.

g903 **Ormerod** Neil,   Introducing contemporary theologies; the what and the who of theology today.   Sydney 1990, Dwyer [Wilton CT, Morehouse].   180 p. $10.   0-85574-268-2 [TDig 38,372]. – ᴿAustralasCR 68 (1991) 534s (J. *Thornhill*: important); Pacifica 4 (1991) 233-5 (Margaret *Jenkins*).

g903* *a)* **Packer** J. I.,   Laid-back religion? A penetrating look at Christianity today.   Leicester 1989, Inter-Varsity.   158 p. – ᴿSTEv 2 (1990) 121s (M. *Clemente*).

— *b)* **Pinnock** Clark H.,   Tracking the maze; finding our way through modern theology from an evangelical perspective 1990 → 6,m74;   0-06-066581-5: ᴿChrCent 107 (1990) 1071s (J. G. *Stackhouse*); RExp 88 (1991) 102 (J. D. W. *Watts*).

g904 **Reher** Margaret M.,   Catholic intellectual life in America 1989 → 5,k468; 6,m75:   ᴿHorizons 18 (1991) 149s (R. V. *Allen*).

g905 **Rendtorff** Trutz,   Theologie in der Moderne; über Religion im Prozess der Aufklärung: Troeltsch-Studien 5.   Gü 1991, Mohn.   340 p.   DM 78 [TR 87,425].

g905* *Roberts* J. Deotis,   The status of black Catholics: JRelTht 48 (1991) 73-... [< ZIT 92,12].

g906 **Rogers** D. J.,   The American empirical movement in theology [diss. Northwestern]: AmerUnivSt 7/70.   NY 1990, Lang.   viii-246 p.   Fs 66,30.   0-8204-1218-X. – ᴿTsTNijm 31 (1991) 204 (J. A. van der *Ven*).

g906* **Sample** Rex,   U.S. lifestyles and the mainline churches.   Louisville 1990, W-Knox.   156 p. $13.   0-664-25099-8. – ᴿRExp 88 (1991) 281s (D. F. *D'Amico*: sociological).

g907 *a)* **Scherffig** W.,   Junge Theologen im 'Dritten Reich'; Dokumente, Briefe, Erfahrungen, 1. 'Es begann mit einem Nein' 1933-1935.   Neuk

1989. xvi-224 p. DM 24,80. 3-7887-1304-6. – ᴿTsTNijm 31 (1991) 103 (Bärbel de *Groot-Kopetzky*).

— *b*) ᴱ**Wall** James M., *Heim* David, How my mind has changed [essays < ChrCent by E. *Schüssler Fiorenza*, J. *Sobrino*, G. *Lindbeck*, R. *McCormick*, E. *Jüngel*, D. *Tracy*, P. *Berger* + 9]. GR 1991, Eerdmans. $9. 0-8028-0533-7 [ChrCent 108,1006 adv.].

g907* *a*) **Watt** David H., A transforming faith; explorations of twentieth-century American evangelicalism. New Brunswick NJ 1991, Rutgers Univ. ix-213 p. $30; pa. $13. 0-8135-1716-8; -7-6 [TDig 39,293].

— *b*) **Wentz** Richard E., Religion in the New World; the shaping of religious traditions in the United States. Mp 1990, Fortress. xiii-370 p. $20. – ᴿAnglTR 73 (1991) 487-9 (C. *Cherry*: very fine).

g908 **White** Gavin, How the Churches got to be the way they are. L/Ph 1990, SCM/Trinity. 120 p. £6. 0-334-03487-0 [C. S. *Rodd*: too arch for the uninitiated for whom its wit is intended].

g909 **Wuthnow** Robert, *a*) The restructuring of American religion 1988 ↠ 5,k724: ᴿJAAR 58 (1990) 321-4 (W. H. *Swatos*); – *b*) The struggle for America's soul; evangelicals, liberals, and secularism. GR 1989, Eerdmans. 208 p. $23; pa. $15. 0-8028-3669-0; -0469-1. – ᴿRExp 88 (1991) 112 (B. J. *Leonard*).

---

g910 ADAM: **Kreidler** Hans, Eine Theologie des Lebens; Grundzüge im theologischen Denken Karl Adams: TüThSt 29, 1988 ↠ 6,m79: ᴿForumKT 7 (1991) 152s (P. *Schäfer*); Gregorianum 72 (1991) 152s (J. J. *O'Donnell*).

g911 BALTHASAR Hans Urs von, The glory of the Lord [1s. 1982s ↠ 64, e259], 5. The realm of metaphysics in the modern age; 6. Theology, the old covenant, ᵀ*Meneil* Brian, *Leiva-Merikakis* Erasmo. SF/E 1991, Ignatius/Clark. 666 p.; 443 p. $40 each. 0-89870-247-X; -8-8 [TDig 38, 346] / 0-567-09577-0 (Clark vol. 6). – ᴿDocLife 41 (1991) 108s (G. *Daly*, 7); DowR 109 (1991) 302-4 (Francesca *Murphy*, 6); ExpTim 102 (1990s) 349s (P. S. *Fiddes*, 7) & 103 (1991s) 52 (R. E. *Clements*, 6: stimulating though rather strongly Christianizing); JTS 42 (1991) 417-9 (D. M. *MacKinnon*, 4; 7); Tablet 245 (1991) 1179s (J. *Riches*, 5-7).

g912 **Balthasar** Hans Urs von, Teodramática, I. Prolegómenos. M 1990, Encuentro. 645 p. – ᴿCarthaginensia 7 (1991) 526s (F. *Martínez Fresneda*).

g913 **Balthasar** H. U. v., Credo; meditations on the Apostles' Creed, ᵀ*Kipp* David. NY 1990, Crossroad. 105 p. $12 [RelStR 18,40, J. R. *Sachs* does not recommend].

g914 **Balthasar** H. U. von, Mysterium paschale (Eng.), ᵀ*Nichols* A. 1990 ↠ 6,7491; £20. 0-567-09534-7. – ᴿExpTim 102 (1990s) 283s (M. J. *Townsend*); ScotBEvT 9 (1991) 150-2 (R. *Bauckham*: a theologian of Barth-Rahner stature).

g915 **Balthasar** Hans U. von, Theologie der drei Tage [= 1969 Mysterium paschale]. Einsiedeln 1990, Johannes. 272 p. DM 42. – ᴿMüTZ 42 (1991) 280-2 (M. *Tiator*).

g916 **Guerriero** Elio, Hans Urs von Balthasar. CinB 1991, Paoline. 432 p. [VivH 3,424, A. *Bellandi*].

g917 **Krenski** Thomas R., Passio caritatis; trinitarische Passiologie im Werk H. U. v. Balthasars: [Diss.]: Horizonte NF 28. Fr 1990, Johannes. 406 p. DM 58. – ᴿMüTZ 42 (1991) 183-6 (M. *Schulz*).

g918 ᴱLehmann Karl, *Kasper* Walter, H. U. v. Balthasar, Gestalt und Werk 1990 ➤ 6,10: ᴿGregorianum 72 (1991) 374s (R. *Fisichella*: apparirà presto in diverse traduzioni).

g919 *Moda* Aldo, Struttura e fondamento della logica teologica secondo H. U. von Balthasar II: RasT [31 (1990) 548-566] 32 (1991) 31-60.

g920 **Saward** John, The mysteries of March ... Balthasar 1990 ➤ 6,7541: ᴿPrPeo 4 (1991) 381s (J. *Tolhurst*).

g921 **Spangenberg** Volker, Herrlichkeit des Neuen Bundes; die Bestimmung des biblischen Begriffs der Herrlichkeit bei Hans Urs von Balthasar: ev. Diss. Tübingen 1991, ᴰ*Jüngel* E. 363 p. – TLZ 117,233; TR 87 (1991) 522; RTLv 23, p. 572.

g922 **Topić** Franjo, L'uomo di fronte alla rivelazione di Dio nel pensiero di H. U. v. Balthasar: diss. Pont. Univ. Gregoriana. Münster 1990, Cramer. xv-248 p. – TR 87 (1991) 530.

g923 BARTH: *Alemany* José J., Karl Barth, commentarista de la 'Dei Verbum': EstE 66 (1991) 53-66.

g924 **Anzinger** Herbert, Glaube und kommunikative Praxis; eine Studie zur 'vordialektischen' Theologie Karl Barths [➤ Diss. Heidelberg]: BeitEvT 110. Mü 1991, Kaiser. xiii-291 p. DM 78 [TR 88,80].

g925 **Bächli** Otto, Das AT in ... Barth 1987 ➤ 3,g868 ... 5,k489: ᴿTrierTZ 100 (1991) 157s (A. *Dahm*).

g926 **Barth** Karl, The Göttingen dogmatics; instruction in the Christian religion [1924s], I., ᴱ*Reiffen* Hannelotte; ᵀ*Bromiley* Geoffrey W. GR 1991, Eerdmans. lxii-490 p. $40. 0-8026-2421-8 [TDig 39,149].

g927 **Barth** Karl, Homiletics, ᵀ*Bromiley* Geoffrey W., *Daniels* Donald E. Louisville 1991, W-Knox. 136 p. $11 pa. 0-664-25158-7 [TDig 39,149].

g928 **Barth** K., Introduzione alla teologia evangelica ... appendice autobiografica, ᴱ*Bof* G. Mi 1990, Paoline. 382 p. – ᴿAsprenas 38 (1991) 114-6 (B. *Forte*).

g929 ᴱ**Biggar** Nigel, Reckoning with Barth 1988 ➤ 5,18c; 6,m92: ᴿScotJT 44 (1991) 237s (S. *Wigley*: this centenary volume, unlike that of J. THOMPSON 1987, aims to attract Anglo-Saxons who appreciate Barth insufficiently; but for that goal it costs too much).

g930 **Boer** D., Een fantastisch verhaal; theologie en ideologische strijd [diss.: MARX en Barth]. Voorburg 1988, Prot. Stichting Bibliotheekw. 218 p. 90-64951-67-5. – ᴿNedTTs 45 (1991) 155s (W. van den *Bercken*).

g931 [*Busch* E. über Barth] 'Quousque tandem ...?' Zum evangelischen Kirchenverständnis in diesem Jahrhundert: Kirchliche Zeitgeschichte 2,2 (Gö 1989, DM 38; 0932-9951). p. 393-572 [< TsTNijm 31 (1991) 203 (H. *Witte*)].

g932 ᴱ**Duke** James O., *Streetman* Robert F., Barth and SCHLEIERMACHER; beyond the impasse? 1988 ➤ 5,458; 6,m93*: ᴿScotJT 44 (1991) 260-4 (B. L. *McCormack*).

g933 **Emery** Gregory, Postmodern philosophical theology; the Barthian and Heideggerian origins of the hermeneutic dimension in the contemporary religious thoughts of TAYLOR and CAPERTE: diss. Temple, ᴰ*Dean* T. Ph 1991. – RelStR 18,171.

g934 **Fisher** Simon, Revelatory positivism? ... Barth 1988 ➤ 4,k424; 6,m96: ᴿJTS 42 (1991) 412-2 (C. *Gunton*); ModT (1990s) 493 (R. *Osborn*); ScotJT 43 (1990) 504-8 (B. L. *McCormack*).

g935 **Frey** Christofer, Die Theologie K. Barths, eine Einführung 1988 ➤ 4,k424*; 6,m97: ᴿTZBas 47 (1991) 185-7 (H. *Beintker*).

g936 ᴱGreen Clifford E., K. Barth, theologian of freedom [anthology] 1989
→ 5,k492: ᴿCommonweal 117 (1990) 60 (L. S. *Cunningham*).

g937 **Gundlach** Thies, Christozentrik und Pluralität; Studien zur Neuzeitlich-
keit der Theologie Barths am Beispiel der Offenbarungs- und Er-
wählungslehre in der Kirchlichen Dogmatik: ev. Diss. Hamburg 1991,
ᴰ*Fischer*. – TR 87 (1991) 518.

g938 **Haynes** Stephen R., Prospects for post-holocaust theology [diss. Emory:
Barth, MOLTMANN, VAN BUREN]: AAR 77. Atlanta 1991, Scholars.
vii-309 p. $20; sb. $15 [TDig 39,266].

g939 **Hunsinger** George, How to read Karl Barth; the shape of his theology
1990 → 6,m100*: ᴿCommonweal 118 (1991) 618s (G. *Green*); ExpTim
103 (1991s) 348s (P. S. *Fiddes*); TS 52 (1991) 565-8 (R. W. *Palmer*).

g940 **Jüngel** Eberhard, Karl Barth, a theological legacy, ᵀ*Paul* G. E. 1986
→ 2,d934... 6,m101: ᴿTLZ 116 (1991) 614s (H. *Fischer*).

g941 **Klimek** Nicolaus, Der Begriff 'Mystik' in der Theologie Karl Barths
[kath. Diss. Bochum 1989]: KkKSt 56. Pd 1990, Bonifatius. 294 p.
DM 48. – ᴿTLZ 116 (1991) 857s (J. *Fangmeier*).

g942 **Köbler** Renate, In the shadow of Karl Barth, Charlotte von KIRSCH-
BAUM, ᵀ*Crim* Keith. Louisville 1989, W-Knox. 156 p. $11 pa. – ᴿCurr-
TMiss 18 (1991) 126s (R. *Hütter*: unconventional but deserving of honor
wherever the Church Dogmatics is valued); JAAR 59 (1991) 840-3 (Mary
K. *Cunningham*: aims mainly to show her own theological achievements
and her contribution to Barth's *Church Dogmatics* by research and discussion; but notes she moved into his family home in 1929, unconventional arrangement difficult especially for Barth's wife Nelly; but 'his
marriage was not dissolved'; all struggled to maintain their dignity).

g943 **Krauss** Reinhard, Gottes Offenbarung und menschliche Religion; eine
Analyse des Religionsbegriffs in Karl Barths 'Kirchlicher Dogmatik' mit
besonderer Berücksichtigung F. D. E. SCHLEIERMACHERs [whom he really
follows despite terminological dissent]: Diss. St. Andrews, 1990, ᴰ*Shaw* D.
277 p. 91-23681. – DissA 52 (1991s) 967-A.

g943* *a*) *Krötke* W., Die Ekklesiologie Karl Barths | im Kontext der
Aktualität; – *b*) *Gräb* W., ... im Kontext der Problemgeschichte des
neuzeitlichen Kirchenverständnisses; – *c*) *Neven* G. W., ... unter der
Voraussetzung der Aufhebung der Geschichte; – *d*) *Logister* W., ... im
Kontext der heutigen katholischen Theologie: ZdialekT 7,1 (Diebergen
1991) 11-28 / 29-46 / 47-66 / 67-90 [< ZIT 91,605].

g944 **Leslie** Benjamin C., Trinitarian hermeneutics; the hermeneutical
significance of Karl Barth's doctrine of the Trinity: AmerUnivSt 7/66. NY
1991, Lang. 286 p. DM 82 [TD 82,256].

g945 *McCormack* Bruce, Historical criticism and dogmatic interest in Karl
Barth's theological exegesis of the New Testament: *a*) → 58, ᶠFROEH-
LICH K., 1991, 322-338; – *b*) LuthQuart 5 (Milwaukee 1991) 211-225
[< NTAbs 36,7].

g946 **McCormick** Frances R., The task of the theologian in the thought of
Karl Barth: diss. Drew, ᴰ*Pain* J. Madison ɴJ 1990. – RelStR 18,171.

g947 **MacGlasson** Paul, Jesus and Judas; biblical exegesis in Barth: AAR
72. Atlanta 1991, Scholars. viii-160 p.; $25; pa. $15 [TR 87,432].
1-55540-567-3; -8-1.

g948 **Macken** John, The autonomy theme... Barth 1990 → 6,m104: ᴿJTS 42
(1991) 414-7 (T. *Gorringe*); TsTNijm 31 (1991) 332 (R. J. *Peeters*).

g949 **Matheny** Paul D., Dogmatics and ethics; the theological realism and
ethics of Karl Barth's Church Dogmatics [diss. Heidelberg]: Studies in the

intercultural history of Christianity 63. NY 1990, P. Lang. vi-264 p. $45.80. 3-631-42324-1 [TDig 39,176].

g950 *Mueller* David L., Foundation of Karl Barth's doctrine of reconciliation, Jesus Christ crucified and risen. Lewiston NY 1990, Mellen. 504 p. [TR 88,256].

g951 *O'Donovan* Oliver, Karl Barth and RAMSEY's 'Uses of Power': JRelEth 19,2 (1991) 1-30 [-237, al. on Paul Ramsey].

g952 **Riessen** J.P. van, Nihilisme op de grens van filosofie en theologie; een onderzoek naar de reflektie op het praktisch nihilisme bij WEISCHEDEL, TILLICH en Barth: diss. Groningen, *DHensen* R. Kampen 1991, Kok. 234 p. 90-242-6133-3. – TsTNijm 31 (1991) 319.

g953 **Torrance** Thomas F., Karl Barth, biblical and evangelical theologian [reprints, not a sequel to his 1962 Barth] 1990 ⇒ 6,m109a: RExpTim 103 (1991s) 28s (K.W. *Clements*, also on SHARP 1990).

g954 *Vanzan* Piersandro, Karl Barth; strutture della fede e incidenza politica della teologia [...pubblicazioni del centenario della nascita]: CC 142 (1991,2) 244-256.

g955 **Wallace** Mark I., The second naivete; Barth, RICŒUR and the New Yale theology. Macon GA 1990, Mercer Univ. 195 p. $25; pa. $17. 0-86554-357-7; -80-1. – RTS 52 (1991) 776s (Marie-Eloise *Rosenblatt*); TTod 48 (1991s) 482.484s (C.M. *Wood*).

g956 **BERKHOF** H., Two hundred years 1989 ⇒ 6,m109*: RTTod 42 (1991s) 252,254 (E. *Simmons*).

g957 BOEGNER: **Mehl** L., Le pasteur M. Boegner 1987 ⇒ 5,k510: RRTLv 22 (1991) 108s (A. de *Halleux*).

g958 BONHOEFFER: **Kodalle** K.M., D. Bonhoeffer; zur Kritik seiner Theologie. Gü 1991, Mohn. 206 p. DM 58 [TR 88,79].

g959 **Abromeit** Hans-Jürgen, Das Geheimnis Christi; D. Bonhoeffers erfahrungsbezogene Christologie [< Diss. Münster]: BeitSys 8. Neuk 1991. xi-386 p. DM 58 [TR 88,168].

g960 *Demarest* Bruce A., Devotion, doctrine, and duty in Dietrich Bonhoeffer [... grave theological flaws]: BS 148 (1991) 399-408.

g961 *McFadyen* A.I., The call to discipleship; reflections on Bonhoeffer's theme 50 years on: ScotJT 43 (1990) 461-483.

g962 **Rasmussen** Larry (*Bethge* Renate), Dietrich Bonhoeffer, his significance for North Americans. Mp 1990, Fortress. 198 p. $13. – RCritRR 4 (1991) 461s (J.D. *Godsey*).

g963 **Reynolds** Terrence, The coherence of life without God before God; the problem of earthly desires in the later theology of D. Bonhoeffer [diss. ⇒ 5,k516]. Lanham MD 1989, UPA. 190 p. $23.50. – RHeythJ 32 (1991) 436 (J. *Wilcken*); RelStR 17 (1991) 146 (C.J. *Brannen*, inadequate college text).

g964 **Robertson** Edwin, Bonhoeffer's heritage [⇒ 6,m117]; the Christian way in a world without religion. L 1989, Hodder & S. 232 p. £9 pa. – RTLond 93 (1990) 155s (K. *Clements*).

g965 **Robertson** E., The shame and the sacrifice 1987 ⇒ 5,k517: RCommonweal 117 (1990) 59s (L.S. *Cunningham*).

g966 **Schnübbe** Otto, Christus und die mündig gewordene Welt; D. Bonhoeffers letzte Denkphase und ihre Bedeutung für die Verkündigung heute. Hannover 1990, Luther. 103 p. DM 28,80 [TLZ 117,299, E. *Feil*].

g967 CHENU: **Biffi** Inos [medievalista], *Colombo* Giuseppe, Presenza e influsso di Marie-Dominique Chenu in Italia: TItSett 16 (1991) 198-220-234; Eng. 235.

g968 **Leprieur** F., Quand Rome condamne ... Chenu 1989 ➤ 6,m122: ᴿNBlackf 72 (1991) 200s (P. *Hebblethwaite*).

g969 *Potworowski* Christophe, Dechristianization, socialization and incarnation in M.-D. Chenu: ScEsp 43 (1991) 17-54.

g970 CHESTERTON: ᴱ**Macdonald** Michael H., *Tadie* Andrew A., G. K. Chesterton and C. S. LEWIS, the Riddle of Joy [Seattle Pacific Univ. conference 1987] 1989 ➤ 6,649; $19. 0-8028-3665-8. – ᴿRExp 87 (1990) 506s (H. L. *Poe*).

g971 CONGAR: **Nichols** A., Y. Congar 1989 ➤ 5,k529; 6,m123: ᴿNBlackf 71 (1990) 255-7 (J. *O'Donnell*); PrPeo 4 (1990) 201s (P. *McPartlan*: also on ANSELM and DENIS volumes).

g972 **Nichols** Aidan, From Newman to Congar; the idea of doctrinal development from the Victorians to the Second Vatican Council. E 1990, Clark. 290 p. £10. 0-567-29189-2. – ᴿTablet 145 (1991) 165s (G. *Daly*); TsTNijm 31 (1991) 201 (P. van *Leeuwen*).

g973 **Henn** Wm., Hierarchy of truths... Congar: AnGreg 246, 1987 ➤ 3,7276; ... 6,m121: ᴿETL 67 (1991) 456s (J. E. *Vercruysse*).

g974 *Meini* Mario, I riferimenti fondamentali del pensiero teologico di Yves Congar: VivH 1 (1990) 79-100.

g975 *Sicouly* Pablo, Yves Congar und Johann Adam MÖHLER; ein theologisches Gespräch zwischen den Zeiten: Catholica 45 (1991) 36-43.

g976 CUPITT: **Cowdell** Scott, Atheist priest? D. Cupitt 1988 ➤ 5,k531; 0-334-0000-3-3: ᴿNBlackf 71 (1990) 258-260 (M. *Durrant*).

g977 DELP Alfred [† 2.II.1945], Gesammelte Schriften, ᴱ*Bleistein* Roman. Fra 1982-8, Knecht. 304 p.; 500 p.; 499 p.; 463 p.; 360 p. DM 240 + (Band 5) 54 [TR 88,52, S. *Kleymann*; 51 über Bleisteins Delp-Biographie 1989].

g978 EBELING: **Schlögl** Herbert, Nicht moralisch, sondern theologisch; zum Gewissensverständnis von Gerhard Ebeling: WalberbergerSt 15. Mainz 1991, Grünewald. xxix-240 p. [TR 88,233, F. *Furger*].

g978* *a*) FARRER Austin † 1968, Faith and speculation; an essay in philosophical theology. E 1988 = 1967, Clark. 175 p. 0-567-29141-3. – ᴿRExp 88 (1991) 102s (C. J. *Scalise*: insight and wit, but with 'untenable voluntaristic personalism'); – *b*) *Conti* Charles, Farrer's Christian humanism: ModT 7 (1990s) 403-434.

g979 FEENEY L.: *Massa* Mark, On the uses of heresy; Leonard Feeney, Mary DOUGLAS [doctrine as an idiom of control], and the Notre Dame football team: HarvTR 34 (1991) 325-343.

g979* FLOROVSKY: **Künkel** Christoph, Totus Christus; die Theologie Georges V. Florovskys [Diss. Erlangen.-N]: ForSysÖkT 62. Gö 1991, Vandenhoeck & R. 469 p. DM 98 [TR 88,432].

g980 GOGARTEN Friedrich, [100. Gb.] Gehören und Verantworten, Ausgewählte Aufsätze, ᴱ*Göckeritz* H. G. (*Bultmann* M.). Tü 1988, Mohr. xvi-352 p. DM 89. – ᴿTLZ 116 (1991) 531-3 (H. *Fischer*).

g981 GUARDINI: *Farrugia* Mario, L'incontro; realtà fondante nel pensiero di Romano Guardini: RasT 32 (1991) 582-604.

g981* *Vloet* J. van der, Romano Guardinis theologische Kritik des modernen Zeitalters: Bijdragen 52 (1991) 159-184; Eng. 184.

g982 ᴱ**Zucal** S., La Weltanschauung cristiana di Romano Guardini [12 auct.]: Trento IstScR Pubbl. 13, 1988 ➤ 5,k543: ᴿNRT 113 (1991) 293 (S. *Hilaire*).

g983 HABERMAS: *Soosten* Joachim von, Zur theologischen Rezeption von Jürgen Habermas' 'Theorie des kommunikativen Handelns': ZevEth 34 (1990) 129-141.

g984 HÄRING Bernhard, Mi experiencia con la Iglesia [1989 ➤ 5,1375.k546; 6,m134], ᵀ. M 1990, Perpetuo Soccorro. 172 p. ➤ 6,m135: ᴿCarthaginensia 7 (1991) 301s (J. L. *Parada Navas*; 'el libro-testimonio del año').

g984* **Häring** B., (*Licheri* Gianni) Fede, storia, morale. R 1989, Borla. 303 p. ➤ 5,1375: ᴿDoctLife 41 (1991) 45-47 (S. *Fagan*).

g985 HARNACK: ᴱ**Rumscheidt** Martin, Adolph von Harnack; liberal theology at its height [selections]. L ... Collins. 329 p. $20. – ᴿCommonweal 117 (1990) 59 (L. S. *Cunningham*).

g986 HEIDEGGER: **Farias** Victor, Heidegger and Nazism [FrB Univ. Rector May 1933, resigned June 1934], ᴱ*Margolis* Joseph, *Rockmore* Tom. Ph 1989, Temple. xxi-349. $30. – ᴿAmHR 96 (1991) 472s (H. *Alderman*: wrongly finds Heidegger's philosophy compatible or suffused with Nazism; expects him to have known in 1933 what was clear only in 1945).

g986* **Puthenpurackal** Johnson J., Heidegger; through authentic totality to total authenticity; a unitary approach to his thought in two phases. Lv 1987, Leuven-UP. xviii-342 p. Fb 1000. – ᴿIndTSt 27 (1990) 367s (A. *Kolencherry*).

g987 *Vedder* Ben, Heideggers 'laatste God': Bijdragen 52 (1991) 238-252; 253 'The final God of Heidegger'.

g988 HICK: **Gillis** Chester, A question of final belief; John Hick's pluralistic theory of salvation. NY 1989, St. Martin's. 186 p. $40. – ᴿJRel 70 (1990) 269s (P. *Knitter*).

g988* **Mesle** C. Robert, John Hick's theodicy; a process humanist critique. NY 1991, St. Martins. 175 p. $45 [TR 88,433].

g989 IRELAND J.: **O'Connell** Marvin R., John Ireland [1838-1918] and the American Catholic Church. St Paul 1988, Minnesota Historical Soc. xii-610 p. $35. – ᴿChH 59 (1990) 260s (J. T. *Connelly*); JRel 71 (1991) 105-7 (S. *Appleby*).

g990 JENKINS David [as told through his daughter Rebecca], Free to believe. L 1991, BBC. £6. – ᴿTLond 94 (1991) 449-454 (M. *Northcott*).

g991 JOHANNES PAULUS II: *Calvez* Jean-Yves, [Giovanni Paolo II], 'Centesimus Annus': RasT 32 (1991) 227-232.

g992 *Coste* René, La nouvelle encyclique sociale de Jean-Paul II, Centesimus annus: EsprVie 101 (1991) 289-299 . 305-315.

g993 *Giovanni Paolo II,* Lettera enciclica 'Centesimus annus' [1.V.1991]: CC 142 (1991,2) 330-383.

g994 *Jean-Paul II.,* Lettre encyclique Redemptoris Missio, 7.XII.1990 [passages essentiels]: EsprVie 101 (1991) 209-219 (E. *Vauthier*).

g995 **Juan Pablo II,** Cartas a los sacerdotes; hacia una renovación sacerdotal, ᵀ*Molinero* Jorge. M 1990, Palabra. 234 p. – ᴿScripTPamp 23 (1991) 1050s (E. de la *Lama*).

g996 *Ploeg* Johann P. M. van der, Das philosophische Hauptwerk Kardinal Wojtyłas – eine kritische Analyse: Una Voce Korrespondenz 21,4 (Köln 1991) 195-210.

g997 *Repges* Walter, Der Beitrag von Papst Johannes Paul II. zur Befreiung Ost- und Mitteleuropas: Renovatio 46 (Köln 1990) 105-118 [< ZIT 91,88].

g998 **Woznicki** Andrew N., The dignity of man as a person [in] John Paul II. SF 1987, Society of Christ. xv-170 p. $5. – [R]Gregorianum 72 (1991) 149s (J. M. *McDermott*: not entirely faithful to the Pope's thought).

g999 **KASPER** Walter, Theology and Church [< 1987] 1990 ➤ 6,255a: [R]Horizons 18 (1991) 333s (F. J. *Parrella*).

k1 KING: **Baker-Fletcher** Garth, Somebodiness; resources for a theory of dignity in the thought of Martin Luther King [J] : diss. Harvard, [D]*Williams* P. CM 1990. – RelStR 18,171.

k1* **Cone** J. H., Martin and Malcolm and America; a dream or a nightmare? Mkn 1991, Orbis. 351 p. $23. – [R]ChrCent 108 (1991) 1031-4 (T. *Mikelson*); ChrCris 51 (1991s) 362-5 (Emilie M. *Townes*).

k2 *Mikelson* Thomas J. S., Cosmic companionship; the place of God in the moral reasoning of Martin Luther King jr.: JRelEth 18,2 (1990) 1-14 (-105, *al.*, on King).

k3 KÜNG Hans, Projekt Weltethos. Mü 1990, Piper. 192 p. DM 19,80. – [R]AnVal 4 (1990) 214 (F. T.); HerdKorr 45 (1991) 49 (U. *Ruh*).

k4 **Küng** Hans, Global responsibility; in search of a new world ethic, [T]*Bowden* John. L 1991, SCM. xx-158 p. £13. – [R]ExpTim 102,12 2d-top choice (1990s) 354s (C. S. *Rodd*); NBlackf 72 (1991) 534-6 (G. *Loughlin*).

k5 LEFEBVRE: [E]**Ahlers** Reinhild, *Krämer* Peter, Das Bleibende im Wandel; theologische Beiträge zum Schisma von Marcel Lefebvre. Pd 1990, Bonifatius. 148 p. DM 24,80. 3-87088-622-6. – [R]TPhil 66 (1991) 313-5 (R. *Sebott*); TsTNijm 91 (1991) 217 (F. *Haarsma*).

k6 *Fisher* Anthony, Lefebvrism–Jansenism revisited?: NBlackf 71 (1990) 274-286.

k7 LEWIS [➤ g970 supra]: [TE]**Moynihan** Martin, Letters, C. S. Lewis – Don Giovanni CALABRIA; a study in friendship. AA 1988, Servant. 126 p. – [R]Salesianum 53 (1991) 166 (G. *Abbà*).

k7* *a*) **Duriez** Colin, The C. S. Lewis handbook. GR 1990, Baker. 255 p. 0-8010-3001-3. – [R]RExp 88 (1991) 490 (H. L. *Poe*).

— *b*) **Lindeskoog** Kathryn, C. S. Lewis, mere Christian[2rev] [< diss. praised by Lewis]. Wheaton IL 1987, Shaw. 260 p. 0-87788-543-5. – [R]RExp 88 (1991) 490s (H. L. *Poe*).

k8 **Wilson** A. N., C. S. Lewis, a biography. NY 1990, Norton. 334 p. $22.50. 0393-02813-5. – [R]RExp 88 (1991) 111 (H. L. *Poe*: smashes every image).

k8* *Wilson* John, An appraisal of C. S. Lewis and his influence on modern evangelicalism: ScotBEvT 9 (1991) 22-39.

k9 LINDBECK G.: [E]**Marshall** Bruce D. [+ 9 *al.*], Theology and dialogue; essays in conversation with George Lindbeck. ND 1990, Univ. 302 p. $30. – [R]TTod 48 (1991s) 340.344 (Ellen T. *Charry*).

k10 LLOYD-JONES D.: **Murray** Iain H., David M. Lloyd-Jones [biography, II] The fight of faith 1939-1981. E 1990, Banner of Truth. xxiv-831 p. £16. – [R]EvQ 63 (1991) 68-71 (F. F. *Bruce* †); TrinJ 12 (1991) 95-99 (J. H. *Armstrong*).

k11 **LOCHMAN** Jan M., Christ and Prometheus? A quest for theological identity 1988 ➤ 4,219: [R]RTLv 22 (1991) 423-5 (A. de *Halleux*).

k12 LONERGAN: *Lamb* Matthew, Lonergan, Bernard (1904-1984), [T]*Schwöbel* Christoph: ➤ 690, TRE 21 (1991) 459-463.

k13 **Lonergan** Bernard, Método en teología [²1973], ᵀ*Remolina* Gerardo: Verdad e Imagen 106; 1988 ➤ 5,k587; 84-301-1053-4. – ᴿActuBbg 28 (1991) 177s (J. *Boada*).

k14 **Mooney** Hilary Anne Marie, The liberation of consciousness; Bernard Lonergan's fundamental theology in dialogue with the theological aesthetics of Hans Urs von BALTHASAR: diss. St. Georgen, ᴰ*Löser* W. Fra 1991. 307 p. [> FraTSt, subtitle slightly changed]. – RTLv 23, p. 537.

k15 **Rende** Michael L., Lonergan on conversion; the development of a notion. Lanham MD 1991, UPA. xi-225 p. $40.50. – ᴿTS 52 (1991) 595s (L. *Örsy*).

k16 *Reynolds* Terrence, Method divorced from content in theology? An assessment of Lonergan's Method in theology: Thomist 55 (1991) 245-269.

k17 DE LUBAC: **Berzosa Martínez** Raul, La teología del sobrenatural en los escritos de Henri de Lubac; estudio histórico-teológico (1931-1980) [< dis.]: FacNEsp 58. Burgos 1991, Aldecoa. 212 p. pt 1275 [TR 87,432]. – ᴿArTGran 54 (1991) 403s (R. *Franco*); DivThom 157s (L. *Elders*).

k18 *Chantraine* Georges, Lubac, Henri Marie-Joseph Sonier de (1896-1991), ᵀ*Schnitker* Thaddäus: ➤ 690, TRE 21 (1991) 471-3.

k19 *Lubac* Henri de, Mémoire sur l'occasion de mes écrits 1989 ➤ 5,k594: ᴿBLitEc 92 (1991) 67s (B. de *Guibert*); IndTSt 27 (1990) 373-5 (R. *DeSmet*); TR 87 (1991) 406-9 (H. *Vorgrimler*).

k20 **McCool** Gerald A., From unity to pluralism; the internal evolution of Thomism 1989 ➤ 6,m174: ᴿGregorianum 72 (1991) 150s (J. M. *McDermott*); HeythJ 32 (1991) 558-560 (R. A. *Brinkman*).

k21 — *Lauder* Robert E., On being or not being a Thomist [McCOOL G.]: Thomist 55 (1991) 301-319.

k22 **Russo** Antonio, H. de Lubac, teologia... influsso di BLONDEL 1990 ➤ 6,m175: ᴿCiVit 46 (1991) 586s (G. *Micheli*).

k23 *Trapani* Giuseppe, L'umanesimo ateo nel pensiero di H. de Lubac: Ho Theológos 9 (1991) 311-351.

k24 LUSTIGER Jean-Marie, Choosing God – chosen by God, conversations ᴱ*Missika* Jean-Louis, *Wolton* Dominique, ᵀ*Balinski* Rebecca H. SF 1991, Ignatius. 423 p. $20 pa. 0-89870-230-5 [TDig 39,72].

k24* *McCORMICK* Richard A., Changing my mind about the changeable Church: ChrCent 107 (1990) 732-6.

NIEBUHR, H. Richard, the legacy of, ᴱ**Thiemann** R. 1988/91 ➤ 561c.

k25 NOORDMANS: **Sonderen** J. H., De kerk en het leven; een bijdrage tot het onderzoek van de geschriften van dr. O. Noordmans. Kampen 1990, Kok. 111 p. *f* 22,50. 90-242-2109-9. – ᴿTsTNijm 31 (1991) 435 (H. *Rikhof*).

k26 ONG: *Cargas* Harry J., The Christian as scholar, the humanist as Christian; an interview with Walter Ong: CCurr 40 (1990s) 96-108.

k27 PANNENBERG: **Greiner** S., Die Theologie W. Pannenbergs 1988 ➤ 5, k611: ᴿArTGran 53 (1990) 349 (R. *Franco*).

k28 **Grenz** Stanley J., Reason for hope... Pannenberg 1989 ➤ 6,m185: ᴿJTS 42 (1991) 419-421 (A. D. *Galloway*).

k29 *Grenz* Stanley J., Pannenberg and evangelical theology; sympathy and caution: ChrSchR 20 (1990) 272-285 [< ZIT 91,336].

k30 **Pannenberg** W., Metaphysics and the idea of God, ᵀ*Clayton* Philip. GR 1990, Eerdmans. 170 p. $22. – ᴿAnglTR 73 (1991) 217-220 (J. R. *Schorn*); GraceTJ 11 (1990) 248-250 (D. H. *Wacome*).

k31 *a) Pannenberg* W., The Church today / The Christian vision of God; the new discussion as the Trinitarian doctrine; – *b) Wood* Lawrence W., Pannenberg's eschatologicalism as a replacement for supernaturalism; – *c) Grenz* Stanley, W. Pannenberg; reason, hope and transcendence: AsbTJ 46,2 (1991) 7-16 . 27-36 / 43-72 [17-25] / 73-90.

k32 **Polk** David P., On the way to God... Pannenberg 1989 → 5,k612; 6,m187: ᴿCritRR 4 (1991) 456-8 (Elizabeth A. *Johnson*); ScotJT 44 (1991) 98s (A. *McGrath*, 'thoroughly dissatisfied').

k33 Paolo VI: **Colombo** Giovanni, Ricordando G. B. Montini, arcivescovo e Papa. Brescia/R 1989, Ist. Paolo VI / Studium. 210 p.; ill. Lit. 25.000. – ᴿCC 142 (1991,1) 103s (G. *Caprile*).

k34 **Cremona** Carlo, Paolo VI. Mi 1991, Rusconi. 294 p.; ill. Lit. 32.000. – ᴿCC 142 (1991,3) 443s (G. *Mucci*: giornalista, piacevole).

k35 **Paoletti** Domenico, La testimonianza cristiana nel mondo contemporaneo di Papa Montini [diss. Fac. S. Bonaventura, ᴰ*Iammarrone* G., Roma]. Assisi 1991, CEFA. 422 p. Lit. 50.000. – ᴿCC 142 (1991,4) 200s (G. *Mucci*).

k36 **Peck** M. Scott, The road less traveled [popular theology, 7 million copies sold]. NY 1978, Simon & S. – ᴿTTod 48 (1991s) 279-288 (W. *Wink*); Peck's reply p. 288s.

k37 Pius XII: *Müller* Paul-Gerhard, Die Bedeutung Pius' XII. für die Bibelwissenschaft, in ᴱ**Heinze** A., *al.*, Pius XII (Schwerte, Kath. Akad.) p. 11-32 [< TLZ 117,496].

k38 **Zizola** Giancarlo, Il microfono di Dio; Pio XII, Padre Lombardi e i cattolici italiani. Mi 1990, Mondadori. 577 p. Lit. 37.000. – ᴿCC 142 (1991,1) 33-44 (G. *Martina*: una biografia del P. Riccardo Lombardi).

k38* Przywara Erich, Analogia entis [1932], *Secrétan* Philibert: Théologiques. P 1990, PUF. 191 p. – ᴿRTPhil 123 (1991) 442 (J. *Borel*).

k39 Rahner: **Athappilly** Sebastian, Glaube und Welt; eine Studie über das Wohl-Heil-Verhältnis bei Karl Rahner [< Diss. Graz]. Graz 1987, Technische Univ. 318 p. – ᴿRTLv 22 (1991) 92s (E. *Brito*).

k40 **Bonsor** Jack A., Rahner, Heidegger and truth; Karl Rahner's notion of truth 1987 → 5,k620; 6,m196: ᴿScripTPamp 23 (1991) 1046 (J. M. *Odero* continues the subtitle 'the influence of Christian Heidegger').

k41 **Rahner** Karl, Theological investigations [posthumous], 21. L 1988, Darton-LT. 279 p. £25. – ᴿScotJT 44 (1991) 251-3 (P. *Avis*: subtly relativises the magisterium, which cannot operate without a particular, European, theology).

k42 **Doré** J., Rahner K.: → 664, Catholicisme XII,56 (1990) 445-456 [- Hugo 444s, *Baudry* G.].

k43 **Vorgrimler** Herbert, Karl Rahner, Sehnsucht nach dem geheimnisvollen Gott; Profil – Bilder – Texte [Ergänzung zu 1985 ²1988]. FrB 1990, Herder. 194 p.; 17 phot. DM 29,80. – ᴿZkT 113 (1991) 114s (A. *Batlogg*).

k44 *Tallon* Andrew, Rahner bibliography supplement: TDig [36,4; 37,1 (1989s)] 38 (1991) 131-140.

k45 Ramsey Michael, The Gospel and the Catholic Church. 1990 = 1936, Anglican Classics./Cowley. 234 p. $20; pa. $15. 1-56101-006-5/0-936384-

91-3. – ᴿTLond 94 (1991) 141s (D. *Nineham*: no one today would so use the NT).
k45* **Chadwick** Owen, Michael Ramsey 1990 ➤ 6,m202*: ᴿMid-Stream 30 (1991) 400-2 (P. *Crow*).
k46 RATZINGER: **Nichols** Aidan, Theology of J. Ratzinger 1988 ➤ 4,k538... 6,m204: ᴿCritRR 4 (1991) 454s (J. A. *Komonchak*); HeythJ 32 (1991) 264-6 (J. *O'Donnell*).
k47 RAUSCHENBUSCH: *Duke* David N., Theology converses with the biographical narrative of W. Rauschenbusch: PerspRelSt 18 (1991) 143-158.
k48 **Minus** Paul M., W. Rauschenbusch 1988 ➤ 4,k540*... 6,m206: ᴿChH 59 (1990) 579 (P. D. *Jordan*); CritRR 4 (1991) 330-3 (S. C. *Mott*); RExp 88 (1991) 100 (Karen E. *Smith*).
k48* *Smith* Gary S., To reconstruct the world; W. Rauschenbusch and social change: Fides et Historia 23,2 (1991) 40-63 [< ZIT 91,806].
k49 RICŒUR: **Chiodi** Maurizio, Il cammino della libertà; fenomenologia, ermeneutica, ontologia della libertà nella ricerca filosofica di Paul Ricœur [diss. Alfonsiana, Roma, ᴰ*Vendrame* G.]: préf. Ricœur. Brescia 1990, Morcelliana. xx-604 p. Lit. 70.000. – ᴿCC 142 (1991,3) 323s (G. *Lorizio*).
k50 RUFFINI: *Stabile* Francesco M., Il Cardinal [Ernesto] Ruffini e il Vaticano II; le lettere di un 'intransigente': CrNSt 11 (1990) 83-112; Eng. 113; le lettere 114-176.
k51 RUNCIE: **Hastings** Adrian, Robert Runcie. L 1991, Mowbray. 221 p. £16. – ᴿDoctLife 41 (1991) 270-2 (M. *Carey*); Studies 80 (1991) 323-5 (J. D. *May*); TLond 94 (1991) 375 (R. *Chartres*: themes of his archiepiscopate).
k52 SAUER: *Bowers* Russell H.ᴶ, Dispensational motifs in the writings of Erich Sauer [1937; Wiedenest school in Germany for what is considered an Anglo-American phenomenon]: BS 148 (1991) 259-273.
k53 SCHILLEBEECKX: *Schoof* Ted, E. Schillebeeckx; 25 years in Nijmegen [< Meedenken 1983, p. 11-39],ᵀ: TDig 37 (1990) 37-41; 38 (1991) 31-44.
k53* *Conway* Pádraic, The human story of God; the spirituality of E. Schillebeeckx: DocLife 41 (1991) 523-530.
k54 ᴱ**Schreiter** R., *Hilbert* M. C., The praxis of Christian experience... Schillebeeckx 1989 ➤ 5,514: ᴿNBlackf 72 (1990) 106-8 (G. *D'Costa*).
k55 SCHLATTER: **Dintaman** Stephen F., Creative grace; faith and history in the theology of Adolf Schlatter: diss. Princeton Theol. Sem. 1991, ᴰ*Willis-Watkins* E. – RelStR 18,171.
k56 SCHMIDT K.: *a*) *Cullmann* Oscar, Karl Ludwig Schmidt zum 100. Gb. am 5.II.1991; – *b*) *Moessner* David P., K. L. Schmidt (1891-1956) [< ᴱ*Hayes* J., Dictionary of Biblical Interpretation; Eng.], Gründer: TZBas 47 (1991) 1s / 3-6, bibliog.
k57 *Schweizer* Eduard, Karl Ludwig Schmidt — Abschied von Illusionen über Jesus und die Kirche: TZBas 47 (1991) 193-207.
k58 SCHOLZ: **Molendijk** A. L., Aus dem Dunkeln ins Helle; Wissenschaft und Theologie im Denken von Heinrich Scholz, mit unveröffentlichten Thesenreihen von H. S. und Karl BARTH: Diss. Leiden, ᴰ*Adriaanse* H. Amst 1990, Rodopi. 390 p. 90-5183-247-8. – TsTNijm 31 (1991) 188.
k59 STÄHLIN Wilhelm: **Kellner** Hans E., Das theologische Denken W. Stählins: EurHS 23/439. Fra 1991. xii-709 p. DM 139 [TR 88,256].
k60 TEILHARD: *Noir* Pierre, Teilhard de Chardin: ➤ 668, DictSpir 15 (1991) 115-126.
k61 ᴱ**Schiwy** Günther, Pierre Teilhard de Chardin, Briefe an Frauen. FrB 1988, Herder. 167 p. DM 22,80 [TR 88,305, K. J. *Tossou*].

k62 **Schiwy** Günther, Der kosmische Christus; Spuren Gottes ins Neue Zeitalter [... Teilhard]. Mü 1990, Kösel. 176 p. DM 28 [TR 88,317, H. *Wagner*].

k63 TILLICH: **Bertinetti** Ilse, Paul Tillich: Biographien zur KG. B 1990, Union. 186 p. DM 14,80. – ᴿTLZ 116 (1991) 759 (U. *Müller*).

k64 ᴱ**Despland** Michel, *al.*, Religion et culture... centenaire Tillich 1986/7 ➤ 5,651: ᴿRTLv 22 (1990) 254s (E. *Brito*).

k65 **Gilkey** [Langdon] on Tillich 1990 ➤ 6,236: ᴿAmerica 164 (1991) 430 (D. S. *Cunningham*).

k66 **Kelsey** David H., Tillich's doctrine of *analogia imaginis* and the authority of Scripture in theological argument: diss. Yale. NHv 1964! 442 p. 91-14966. – DissA 52 (1991s) 967-A.

k67 **Reimer** A. James, The Emanuel HIRSCH and Paul Tillich debate; a study in the political ramifications of theology: TorStT 42. Lewiston NY 1990, Mellen. xv-384 p. $80. 0-88946-991-1. – ᴿTLZ 116 (1991) 845-7 (J. H. *Schørring*); TsTNijm 31 (1991) 104 (T. *Brattinga*).

k68 TROELTSCH: **Coakley** Sarah, Christ without absolutes... Troeltsch 1988 ➤ 5,7492; 6,m223: ᴿBijdragen 52 (1991) 222s (W. *Logister*); HeythJ 32 (1991) 423s (P. *Hebblethwaite*); JRel 71 (1991) 270-2 (B. A. *Gerrish*); ModT 7 (1990s) 490-3 (B. E. *Starr*).

k68* **Troeltsch** Ernst, Religion in history; essays, ᵀ*Adams* James L., *Bense* Walter F.: Texts in modern theology. Mp 1991, Fortress. x-386 p. $25 pa. 0-8006-3208-7 [TDig 39,191].

k69 **Rubanowice** Robert J., Crisis in consciousness; the thought of Ernst Troeltsch 1983 ➤ 1,f974 [RelStR 17 (1991) 323-7, also on COAKLEY S. and 3 others; p. 327-330 others, by R. *Morgan*].

k69* *Starr* Bradley E., Individualism and reform in Troeltsch's view of the Church: ModT 7 (1990s) 447-463.

k70 *a)* ᴱ**Tétaz** J.-M., Ernst Troeltsch, Religion et histoire, [5] esquisses philosophiques et théologiques: Lieux Théologiques 18. Genève 1990, Labor et Fides. 312 p. – ᴿZkT 113 (1991) 310s (K. H. *Neufeld*)..

— *b)* **Vermeil** Edmond, La pensée religieuse de Troeltsch [< RHPR 1921], ᴱ*Ruddies* Hartmut, préf. *Gisel* Pierre: Histoire et Société 18. Genève 1990, Labor et Fides. 105 p. – ᴿZkT 113 (1991) 310s (K. H. *Neufeld*).

k70* ᴱ**Le Fort** Gertrud (student notes), Troeltsch, The Christian faith [Heidelberg 1912s], ᵀ*Paul* Garrett E.: Texts in Modern Theology. Mp 1991, Fortress. xli-310 p. $20. 0-8006-3209-5 [TDig 39,291].

k71 VAN TIL: **Frame** John, [Cornelius] Van Til, le théologien: RRéf 62,1 (1991) 7-42 [3-6, *Edgar* W.].

k72 WELTE [➤ g754]: **Lenz** Hubert, Mut zum Nichts als Weg zu Gott; Bernhard Weltes religionsphilosophische Anstösse zur Erneuerung des Glaubens 1989 ➤ 5,k661*b*: ᴿMüTZ 42 (1991) 90-92 (S. *Antoni*).

k73 WHITEHEAD: **Lowe** Victor, Alfred N. Whitehead, the man and his work II. Baltimore 1990, Johns Hopkins Univ. xi-389 p. $39. – ᴿTorJT 7 (1991) 143-5 (R. T. *McCutcheon*).

k74 WITTGENSTEIN: **Kerr** Fergus, La théologie après Wittgenstein; une introduction à la lecture [1986 ➤ 2,e102], ᵀ*Letourneau* Alain. P 1991, Cerf. 217 p. – ᴿScripTPamp 23 (1991) 1043s (P. *Conesa*).

k75 *Martin* Michael, Wittgenstein's lectures on religious belief [C 1938, published from student notes 1966]: HeythJ 32 (1991) 369-382.

Y6.8 *Tendentiae exeuntis saeculi XX* – **Late 20th Century Movements.**

k76 **Abbruzzese** Salvatore, Comunione e liberazione; identité catholique et disqualification du monde; préf. *Séguy* Jean: Sciences humaines et religions. P 1989, Cerf. 253 p. – [R]RThom 91 (1991) 155-9 (G.-M. *Marty*); RTLv 22 (1991) 116-8 (G. *Thils*; peu de dialogue; GIUSSANI 1990, 'L'université est l'expression critique et systématique d'une expérience de société athée contraire au Christ').

k76* **Alegre X.** *al.*, Iglesia, ¿de dónde vienes? ¿a dónde vas? 1989 ➤ 6,m227: [R]RTLim 25 (1991) 400s (G. *Sánchez Rojas*).

k77 **Allen** Diogenes, Christian belief in a postmodern world; the full wealth of conviction 1989 ➤ 5,k667; 6,m228: [R]AndrUnS 29 (1991) 165s (F. *Canale*); SWJT 34,2 (1991s) 53 (Y. *Woodfin*).

k78 **Arbuckle** Gerald A., Earthing the Gospel; an inculturation handbook for pastoral workers. L 1990, Chapman. 236 p. £12. – [R]Month 252 (1991) 27s (R. *Darwen*).

k79 *Bartnik* Czesław S., ◉ The crisis of contemporary Catholic theology: ColcT 61,4 (1991) 7-22; Eng. 22.

k80 **Bermejo** Luis M., Church, conciliarity and communion. Anand c. 1991, Gujarat-SP. – [R]PrPeo 5 (1991) 289s (J. *Tolhurst*); Tablet 145 (1991) 306s (A. *Hastings*: 'How infallible is the dogma of infallibility?').

k81 **Boberski** Heiner, Das Engelwerk; ein Geheimbund in der katholischen Kirche? Salzburg 1990, Müller. 288 p. Sch 238. – [R]TPQ 139 (1991) 375-386 (J. *Singer*).

k82 **Boys** M. C., Educating in faith 1989 ➤ 6,m55: [R]Interpretation 45 (1991) 328.330 (C. F. *Melchert*).

k83 **Bühlmann** W., The Church of the future 1986 ➤ 2,e112... 5,k577: [R]JDharma 14 (1989) 409s (G. *Kulangara*).

k84 **Bühlmann** Walbert, *a)* Wer Augen hat zu sehen... Was Gott heute mit uns Christen vorhat. Graz 1989, Styria. 271 p. – [R]ZMissRW 75 (1991) 232s (M. *Hakenes*). – *b)* Ojos para ver... Los cristianos ante el tercer milenio. Barc 1990, Herder. 270 p. – [R]RTLim 25 (1991) 496s (J. *Pourrias*).

k84* **Bühlmann** Walbert, With eyes to see; Church and world in the third millennium, 1990 ➤ 6,m235*: [R]Missiology 19 (1991) 86 (A. *Nealy*); Tablet 245 (1991) 649 (J. *Wijngaards*).

k85 [E]**Burnham** Frederic B., Postmodern theology; Christian faith in a pluralist world [Trinity Institute conference] 1984/9 ➤ 6,584: [R]AnglTR 73 (1991) 81-83 (A. K. M. *Adam*); CurrTMiss 18 (1991) 219s (Clara E. *Wong*); JAAR 59 (1991) 396-8 (J. C. *Pugh*); Paradigms 7,2 (1991s) 41s (C. T. *Hawkins*).

k86 **Centore** F. F., Being and becoming; a critique of post-modernism: Contributions in philosophy 44. NY 1991, Greenwood. xiv-282 p. $47.50. 0-313-27616-1 [TDig 39,154].

k87 **Chrysostomos** ep. [*Zafeiris* Gerasimos S.], Quo vadis Helladikē Orthodoxía? Athenai 1988. 414 p. – [R]TAth 62 (1991) 198s (D. J. *Constantelos*, Eng., does not specify whether the 'courageous' book is in Greek).

k87* [E]**Coalter** Milton J., *al.*, The Presbyterian predicament; six perspectives. Louisville 1990, W-Knox. 180 p. $13. 0-664-25097-1. – [R]RExp 88 (1991) 278s (B. J. *Leonard*).

k88 **Cotterell** Peter, The decade of evangelism, 5. But what *is* evangelism?: ExpTim 102 (1990s) 259-262.

k89 *Cowdell* Scott, Radical theology, postmodernity and Christian life in the void: HeythJ 32 (1991) 62-71.

k90 **Cupitt** Don, Radicals and the future of the Church 1989 ➤ 6,m238: ᴿTLond 94 (1991) 60s (D. *Jenkins* agrees with most of the criticisms as it now is, but not with his simple-minded deconstruction).

k91 *Daiber* Karl-Fritz, Theologiestudium und religiös-kirchlicher Wandel: TZBas 47 (1991) 254-274 [275-285, *Gerber* Uwe].

k92 Deuxième Conc. Vat.: CollÉcFrR 113, 1989 ➤ 5,652; 6,m239: ᴿÉTRel 66 (1991) 299s (L. *Gambarotto* regrets absence of a Protestant Italian voice).

k93 **Duch** Lluis, Temps de tardor, entre modernitat i postmodernitat: Sauri 99. Montserrat 1990, Abadía. 326 p. – ᴿRCatalT 16 (1991) 217s (J. *Castnyé*).

k93* *Ebaugh* Helen R., The revitalization movement in the Catholic Church; the institutional dilemma of power: Sociological Analysis/Religion 52,1 (1991) 1-12 [< ᴢɪᴛ 91,401s].

k94 **Enebral Casares** A. M., Cómo interpretar el Concilio Vaticano II. M 1986, Palestra. 299 p. 84-86444-02-0. – ᴿActuBbg 28 (1991) 82s (F. de P. *Solá* no sabe si los profesores de Comillas estarán muy conformes con su discípula).

k95 Équipes Résurrection [19 auteurs nés après 1961], Le Concile en 75 questions. P 1990, Desclée. 282 p. F 120 [NRT 114,113, L.-J. *Renard*].

k96 **Famerée** J., Concile Vatican II et Église contemporaine, 2. Inventaires des Fonds A. Prignon et H. Wagnon, Archives de LvN: Cah RTLv 24. LvN 1991, Fac. Théol. 115 p. – ᴿRHE 86 (1991) 475 (C. *Soetens*).

k96* *Flood* Edmund [from bishops' answers, plus five bishops' articles], The Catholic Church in the 21st century: ChSt 30 (1991) 308-315 [255-307].

k97 **Fox** Matthew, Vision vom Kosmischen Christus; Aufbruch ins dritte Jahrtausend [The coming of... 1988], ᵀ*Wichmann* Jörg. Stu 1991, Kreuz. 400 p. DM 48 [TR 88,305-310, Barbara *Hallensleben*].

k98 **Griffin** David R., *Smith* Huston, Primordial truth and postmodern theology 1990 ➤ 5,k680: ᴿAnglTR 73 (1991) 83-85 (O. C. *Thomas*).

k99 a) *Gritsch* Eric W., Back to the future; manifest destiny and Lutheran identity [response, *Martin* John H.]; – b) *Strohl* Jane, Lutheranism's call to action amidst ambiguity [response, *Olson* Jeannine E.; – c) *Lull* Timothy F., Luther's voice within the confessions; – d) *Peters* Ted, Identifying with the Gospel: ➤ 29*, ᶠBᴏᴇꜱᴇʀ R., CurrTM 18 (1991) 17-24 [25s] / 27-33 [34-37] / 12-16 / 38-44.

k100 **Hastings** Adrian, Modern Catholicism; Vatican II and after. Oxford 1991, UP (also SPCK). 473 p. $23. – ᴿAmerica 165 (1991) 252 (J. R. *Connolly*); Studies 80 (1991) 414-6 (D. *Stevens*); Tablet 145 (1991) 272 (D. *Worlock*).

k101 *Hinze* Bradford E., The end of salvation history [postmodern approaches broader]: Horizons 18 (1991) 227-245.

k103 ᴱ**Johnson** Roger A., Critical issues in modern religion² [= ¹1973 + feminism & Catholica]. ENJ 1990, Prentice Hall. vii-436 p. – ᴿRelStT 10,1 (1990) 51-53 (J. C. *Hoffman*).

k104 *Kee* J. M., 'Postmodern' thinking and the status of the religions [... *Culler* J.]: Religion & Literature 22,2s (ND 1990) 47-60 [< NTAbs 36,6].

k105 **Klöcker** Michael, Katholisch von der Wiege bis zur Bahre; eine Lebensmacht im Zerfall? Mü 1991, Kösel. 520 p. DM 50 [TR 88,216, W. *Damberg*].

k106 **Kobler** John F., Vatican II, theophany and the phenomenon of man; the Council's pastoral servant leader theology for the third millennium:

AmerUnivSt 7/100. NY 1991, Lang. xvii-347 p. $49. 0-8204-1492-1 [TDig 39,271].

k107 ᴱKüng H., *Tracy* D., Paradigm change in theology, a symposium for the future, ᵀ*Köhl* Margaret. E 1989, Clarke. xvi-488 p. £20. – ᴿAnglTR 73 (1991) 336-8 (O. C. *Thomas*); IndTSt 27 (1990) 199s (B. J. *Francis*); PrPeo 5 (1991) 65-67 (M. Cecily *Boulding*); ScotJT 44 (1991) 394-6 (J. *Begbie*).

k108 **Küng** H., Reforming the Church today – keeping hope alive [➤ 221*]. 1990. – ᴿPrPeo 5 (1991) 118s (S. E. *Hall*: enlightening); RExp 88 (1991) 485 (E. G. *Hinson*).

k109 **Küng** H., Theology for the third millennium. L 1991, Harper Collins. xxiii-316 p. £25. – ᴿStudies 80 (1991) 446-8 (G. *Theissen*).

k111 *La Potterie* Ignace de, *a)* Il Concilio Vaticano II e la Bibbia, ᵀ*Costantini* V. M.; – *b)* L'esegesi biblica, scienza della fede, ᵀ*Tosolini* Fabrizio: ➤ 323, L'esegesi 1991, 19-42 / 127-165.

k112 *Larentzakis* Grigorios, Das Vaticanum II nach 25 Jahren aus dem Blickwinkel eines Orthodoxen Theologen: Catholica 45 (1991) 214-235.

k113 **Latourelle** René, Vatican II Assessment 1988s ➤ 5,k697; 6,m261: ᴿNewTR 4,1 (1991) 68-75 (J. *Linnan*).

k114 ᴱ**Latourelle** René, Vatican II, bilan 1988 ➤ 4,379; 5,k696: ᴿSR 20 (1991) 245-8 (C. *Ménard*) + 248s (P. J. *Cahill*, Eng. ed.).

k115 *Laux* Bernhard, Moderner als die Moderne; zur Zukunftsfähigkeit des Christentums: StiZt 208 (1990) 482-496.

k115* *Lebeau* Paul, Vers une théologie 'postmoderne'; un point de vue nord-américain: NRT 113 (1991) 386-399.

k116 *Liechty* Daniel D., Theology in a postliberal perspective. L/Ph 1990, SCM/Trinity. xiii-114 p. £8. 0-334-02481-1. – ᴿTLond 94 (1991) 456s (D. *Hart*); TsTNijm 31 (1991) 441 (E. *Borgman*).

k117 **Lohmann** Michael, Christliche Perspektiven; Bestandsaufnahme für eine Kirche von morgen. Pd 1990, Schöningh. 190 p. DM 28,80. – ᴿTPQ 39 (1991) 329 (R. *Zinnhobler*).

k118 *a)* *Lustiger* Jean-Marie, La nouveauté du Christ et la post-modernité [➤ 6,m267]; – *b)* *Chantraine* Georges, Sur quoi mésure-t-on le temps de l'Église; propos sur la sécularité; – *c)* *Landes* Serge, Le ringard [qui, ayant voulu se mettre à la mode, ne l'est plus] et le quèque [hors du coup mais sans prétentions]: CommP 15,2 (1990) 12-23 / 43-55 / 56-63.

k119 *Martini* Carlo M., Chrétiens en Europe [... 'le chrétien peut vivre à l'aise dans l'Europe sécularisée']: Études 437 (1991) 527-538.

k120 **Meagher** John C., The truing of Christianity; visions of life and thought for the future 1990 ➤ 6,m269: ᴿAmerica 164 (1991) 500s (T. J. *Mulry*); CCurr 41 (1991s) 267-9 (Carol *Ochs*).

k121 *a)* *Millman* Thomas S., The religion of law and the law of religion [... What is happening to the clergy and to the laity?]; – *b)* *O'Connell* Colin, An interview with Heinrich OTT [BARTH's successor at Basel]: RelStT 10,1 (1990) 9-18 / 43-48.

k122 *Morris* John R., St. Thomas in contemporary thought; is there a future? [against *Di Noia* A. J., Thomist 54 (1990) 499-518]: Angelicum 68 (1991) 503-533.

k123 **Neuhaus** Richard J., The Catholic moment 1987 ➤ 3,h74 ... 5,k707; 6,m276 (when the author was a Lutheran; he became a Catholic in September 1990). SF 1990 paperback, Harper. 292 p. $13. – ᴿBS 148 (1991) 503s (J. A. *Witmer*); RelStT 9,1 (1989) 51s (P. B. *Riley*); RExp 88 (1991) 104s (E. G. *Hinson*).

k124 *Neuhaus* John H., The future of the Reformation: America 164 (1991) 78-82.

k125 *Pagano* Maurizio, *Guglielminetti* Enrico, Filosofia e teologia in Europa; situazione e prospettive: FilT 4 (1990) 413-454 (dibattito *Geffré* C.).

k125* *a) Pathil* Kuncheria, The vision of an ecumenical Church; – *b) Panikkar* Raimond, Christendom, Christianity, Christianness: Jeevadhara 21 (1991) 316-323 / 324-330.

k126 *Poupard* Paul, L'Église et les défis des cultures européennes au seuil de l'an 2000: EsprVie 101 (1991) 1-8.

k126* *Principe* Walter H., Catholic theology and the retrieval of its intellectual tradition; problems and possibilities: PrCathTheolAm 46 (1991) 75-94 (presidential address, Atlanta June 12-15); 95-97-107 responses, *Donovan* Mary Ann, *Lamb* Matthew L.

k127 *a) Puthanangady* Paul, Worship in the third millennium; – *b) Wilfred* Felix, Liberating leadership; towards Christian leadership of tomorrow: Jeevadhara 21 (1991) 300-315 / 282-299.

k127* *Quinzá* Xavier, Leer los signos de Dios en la posmodernidad: RET 51 (1991) 429-473.

k128 ᴱ*Richard* Lucien, *al.*, Vatican II, the unfinished agenda 1987 ► 3,h81... 5,k711: ᴿGregorianum 72 (1991) 169s (J. *Dupuis*); RRel 49 (1990) 150s (M. J. *Lapierre*).

k129 *Shattuck* Gardiner H.ᴶ, Should the Episcopal Church disappear? Reflections on the decade of evangelism: AnglTR 73 (1991) 177-187.

k129* *Stott* J., Le chrétien et les défis de la vie moderne: Alliance. P 1987, Sator. 270 p. – ᴿSTEv 2 (1990) 122s (G. *Corradini*).

k130 **Timm** Hermann, Das ästhetische Jahrzehnt; zur Postmodernisierung der Religion. Gü 1990, Mohn. 192 p.; 3 fig. + 1 color. DM 58. – ᴿTLZ 116 (1991) 143s (U. *Gerber*).

k131 *a) Tornos* Andrés, La nueva teología de la cultura; los cambios de lenguaje de los documentos oficiales de la Iglesia, a partir del Vaticano II; – *b) Revuelta González* Manuel, Actitudes integristas e impulsos renovadores entre los jesuitas del siglo XIX; la residencia de Santander: EstE 66 (1991) 3-26 / 27-51.

k132 *a) Triacca* Achille M., L'uso dei 'loci' patristici nei documenti del Concilio Vaticano II; – *b) Maritano* Mario, La situazione degli studi patristici nel secolo XIX: Salesianum 53 (1991) 219-253 / 255-272.

k133 **Upton** Julia, A Church for the next generation; the sacraments in transition. Collegeville MN 1991, Liturgical. 136 p. £5.50. – ᴿPrPeo 5 (1991) 435s (sr. Pauline *Clarke*).

k133* *Wagner* Harald, Conciliarity and continuity: OneInC 25 (1989) 255-272.

k134 **Ward** Keith, A vision to pursue; beyond the crisis in Christianity. L 1991, SCM. xi-226 p. £10. – ᴿExpTim 103,6 top choice (1991s) 161-4 (C. S. *Rodd*).

k135 *Weakland* Rembert G., *a)* The Vatican II achievement; a new openness to the world: *b)* Church reform; what remains to be done: DoctLife 41 (1991) 116-123 / 170-8.

k136 **Welsch** W., *a)* Unsere postmoderne Moderne. Weinheit 1987,4; – *b)* Postmoderne-Pluralität als ethischer und politischer Wert. Köln 1988. – ᴿTPhil 66 (1991) 338-364 (H.-L. *Ollig*, auch über P. *Koslowski*).

k137 *a) Westphal* Merold, The ostrich and the bogeyman, placing postmodernism; – *b) Percesepe* Gary J., The unbearable lightness of being postmodern; – *c) Tollefson* Ken, *Steele* Les, College as an effective rite of passage: ChrSchR 20 (1990) 114-7 / 118-135 / 136-148 [< zit 91,264].

k137* **Winling** Raymond, La teología del siglo XX 1987 ➤ 3,h100; 5,k723: RAugM 34 (1989) 407s (J. A. *Galindo*).

Y7 (*Acta*) *Congressuum* .2 *biblica:* **nuntii,** rapports, Berichte.

k138 *Bertoletti* Ilario, Il sabato; un convegno a Ferrara [2-3.II.1991]: HumBr 46 (1991) 284-6.

k139 *Bogaert* Pierre-Maurice, Le livre de Daniel; colloquium biblicum lovaniense XL [20-22 août 1991]: RTLv 22 (1991) 564-6.

k140 *Borgonovo* Giannantonio, L'epoca di Ezechia; alle origini della letteratura religiosa d'Israele; VII convegno interdisciplinare sull'AT, Perugia, 9-11 sett. 1991: ScuolC 119 (1991) 657-666.

k141 *Burchard* Chr., Internationales Symposium; die Bibel in der armenischen Kultur [Heidelberg 16.-19. Juli 1990]: OrChr 75 (1991) 255-7.

k142 *Chrostowski* Waldemar, ❷ XIII Kongres międzynarodowej organizacji studiów Starego Testamentu, Leuven 27 VIII - 1 IX 1989: ColcT 60,4 (1990) 166-8.

k143 *del Agua* Agustín, 45.ᵃ Asamblea general de la SNTS, Univ. Cattolica, Milano 23-27 Julio 1990: EstB 49 (1991) 135-142.

k144 *Denaux* Adelbert, John and the Synoptics, Colloquium Biblicum Lovaniense XXXIX (1990): ETL 67 (1991) 196-203.

k144* *García Martínez* F., Resultados y tendencias; Congreso internacional sobre los manuscritos del Mar Muerto [19-23 marzo, Escorial]: Sefarad 51 (1991) 417-435.

k145 *Janssen* Hermann, 'The Bible in the new evangelization in Africa', BICAM Seminar (Catholic Biblical Centre for Africa and Madagascar), Nairobi 17-25.I.1990: TContext 8 (1991) 145s [< Biblical Pastoral Bulletin 10 (1990) 3-78].

k146 *Klauck* Hans-Josef, 45. Meeting der Studiorum Novi Testamenti Societas vom 23.-27. Juli 1990 in Mailand: BZ 35 (1991) 150s.

k147 *Laurenzi* M. Cristina, Sugli incontri di Biblia 1990; la Bibbia tra linguaggio e fede: Protestantesimo 46 (1991) 145s.

k148 *Matras* Tadeusz, ❷ XXVIII spotkanie sekcji biblistów polskich (Warszawa 1990): RuBi 44 (1991) 70s [71s, addresses of the 54 participants].

k149 *Mosetto* Francesco, Il profetismo da Gesù di Nazaret al Montanismo; IV Convegno Nazionale di Studi Neotestamentari e Anticocristiani, Perugia, 12-14 sett. 1991: ScuolC 119 (1991) 667-670.

k150 *Neirynck* F., A symposium on the Minor Agreements [Göttingen (STRECKER G.) 26-27.VII.1991]: ETL 67 (1991) 361-372 ['massive presence of the "Farmer school" (DUNGAN: "Griesbach Mafia")'; ORCHARD not mentioned]; p. 373-394, *Friedrichsen* T.A., New dissertations on the Minor Agreements.

k151 *Neufeld* Karl H., Schrift und Situation; Anmerkungen zum VII. Europäischen Theologenkongress Dresden 24.-28. September 1990: ZkT 113 (1991) 278-283.

k151* *Pilch* John J., First international meeting on the Social Sciences and New Testament interpretation, Medina del Campo May 6-8, 1981: Sefarad 51 (1991) 497-9.

k152 SBL 1991 international meeting, Rome July 14-17: *a*) Program; – *b*) Abstracts of [some of the] papers. Atlanta 1991, Scholars press. 48 p. / 72 p.

k153 *Shanks* H., Scholars, popularizers, ALBRIGHT and me [Baltimore Johns Hopkins Univ. commemoration of 100th birthday]: BAR-W 17,5 (1991) 70s.

k154 *Söding* Thomas, Tagung der deutschsprachigen katholischen Neutestamentler in Luzern vom 18. bis 22. März 1991: BZ 35 (1991) 311s.

k155 *a)* *Testa* Giuseppe, Il 45° congresso della SNTS all'università cattolica del Sacro Cuore (Milano 23-27 luglio 1990); – *b)* *Perani* Mauro, Congresso internazionale dell'Associazione italiana per lo studio del Giudaismo sul tema 'Il giudaismo palestinese dal I secolo a.C. al I. secolo d.C.; – *c)* *Danieli* Giuseppe, La quarta assemblea mondiale della Federazione Biblica Cattolica [Bogotá 27.VI–6.VII.1990]: RivB 39 (1991) 95-107 / 107-115 / 115-118.

k156 *Trebolle Barrera* Julio, Congreso internacional sobre los Manuscritos del Mar Muerto [Madrid-Escorial 17-22.III.1991]: *a)* EstB 49 (1991) 277-283; – *b)* FgNt 4 (1991) 246-251.

k157 *Tremolada* Pierantonio, XXXI Settimana Biblica Nazionale [10-14.IX. 1990, Roma], I Vangeli dell'Infanzia: ScuolC 118 (1990) 479-485.

k158 *Tuckett* C. M., Studiorum Novi Testamenti Societas, the forty-fifth general meeting 23-27 July 1990: NTS 37 (1991) 295-7 [298-320, entire membership-list with addresses].

k159 *Vanzan* Piersandro, Quale coabitazione fra religioni e laicità nel Mediterraneo? Diritti umani e sentieri d'Isaia (24-26 aprile 1991) [Centro Studi 'Storia Uomini Religioni']: CC 142 (1991,4) 49-59.

k160 *Walsh* Jerome T., Report of the fifty-fourth general meeting of the Catholic Biblical Association of America, Los Angeles Loyola-Marymount Aug. 10-13, 1991; CBQ 53 (1991) 645-650; 650-2, names only of participants; p. 649s, life-membership conferred on Michael GLAZIER, David STANLEY, and Roderick MACKENZIE.

Y7.4 *(Acta) theologica:* **nuntii.**

k161 *Arens* Edmund, Befreiungsethik als Herausforderung [Mexiko-Tagung ... *Apel* Karl-Otto, *Dussel* Enrique; *Fornet-Betancourt* R., Ethik und Befreiung, Aachen 1990]: Orientierung 55 (1991) 193-6.

k161* *Arx* Urs von, Zwischen Krise und Stabilität; Bericht über die Anglikanisch-Altkatholischen Theologiekonferenzen in Toronto 1987 und Morschach 1990: IkiZ 81 (1991) 1-40.

k162 *a)* *Avilés Pérez* A., 'De la América española a la América americana'; simposio América V Centenario (1492-1992), Murcia 26-29.XI.1990; – *b)* *Parada Navas* J. L., 'La adolescencia de los hijos y la familia'; II Jornadas de estudio sobre la Familia, Murcia 15-16.III.1991: Carthaginensia 7 (1991) 241-5 / 247-250.

k163 *Bertsch* Ludwig, 'African Theology', Seventeenth theological week, Kinshasa 2-8.IV.1989: TContext 8 (1991) 144 < RAfT 13 (1989) 223-6.

k164 *Bonandi* Alberto, La teologia alla XLIª Settimana Sociale dei Cattolici Italiani: TItSett 16 (1991) 95-100.

k165 *Camacho* Ildefonso, Paz y justicia para toda la creación; encuentro ecuménico de Basilea 1989: Proyección 37 (1990) 109-122.

k166 *Capizzi* Carmelo, Un istituto di studi e un nuovo convegno in onore di CASSIODORO a Squillace [21-27 ott. 1990]: CC 142 (1991,2) 48-52.

k167 *a)* *Carroll* Eamon R., The 41st annual convention of the Mariological Society of America (Rhode Island, May 30-31, 1990); – *b)* *Molette* Charles, 47ème session de la Société Française d'Études Mariales (Blois, 4-6 sept. 1990); – *c)* *Calvo Moralejo* Gaspar, XLIV semana de estudios marianos de la Sociedad Mariológica Española; 50 años de historia (1940-1990) (Zaragoza, 12-15 de septiembre 1990); – *d)* *Meaolo* Gaetano,

XXVI convegno dei rettori dei santuari d'Italia sul tema 'Il santuario luogo di proposta vocazionale' (Assisi, 20-23 nov. 1990): Marianum 52 (1990) 379s / 381-9 / 390-5 / 396s.

k167* a) *Carroll* Eamon R., The 42d annual convention of the Mariological Society of America (Chicago, May 29-30, 1991) [*al.* < Marian Library Newsletter 23,3s]; – b) *Bossard* Alphonse, 48ème session de la Société Française d'Études Mariales (ND-Trois Épis 3-5 sept. 1991]; – c) *Calcagno* Gianfranco, 'Maria in san Bernardo', R 21-24 ott. 1991; – d) *Meaolo* Gaetano, XIX convegno mariano nazionale, 'Maria di Nazareth', Assisi 18-21 luglio 1991; – e) *Valentini* Alberto, I Convegno dell'Associazione Mariologica Interdisciplinare Italiana, L'Aquila 9-12 ott. 1991: Marianum 53 (1991) 261s [635-7] / 638-644 / 645-7 / 649s (653s) / 649-652.

k168 *Chéza* Maurice, Le 12e colloque du CREDIC [Centre de recherches et d'échanges sur la diffusion et l'inculturation du christianisme, Vérone 26-30 août 1991] — Enseignement des sciences de la mission et formation missionnaire au XXe siècle: RTLv 22 (1991) 561-4.

k169 *Chéza* Maurice, Les semaines théologiques de Kinshasa [1964... 2.-IV.1989]: RTLv 22 (1991) 60-66; Eng. 152.

k170 *Chrostowski* Waldemar, a) ❷ Kościół a Żydzi i Judaizm (II Sympozjum Teologiczne, Warszawa 3-4.IV.1990): PrzPow 270,830 (1990) 158-160; – b) Znaczenie Szoah... Kraków 7-10.IV.1991: PrzPow 273 (1991) 150-5.

k171 *Chrostowski* Waldemar, ❷ a) Żydzi – Polacy; przeszłość-teraźniejszość, sympozjum KUL 20-21.II.1991; – b) Znaczenie Szoah dla chr.-żydow. myśli teologicznej, sympozjum Kraków 7-10.IV.1991: ColcT 61,4 (1991) 187-190 / 191-6.

k172 *Corral* Carlos, Iglesia y Estado en el Oriente Cristiano (IX Congreso Internacional de la Sociedad para el Derecho de las Iglesias Orientales): EstE 66 (1991) 295-305.

k172* a) *Crow* Paul A.ᴶ, The Canberra assembly as hope and struggle; – b) *Deschner* John, Canberra's Church unity statement in a 'restless' ecumenical movement: Mid-Stream 30 (1991) 181-190 / 191-8.

k173 *Dal Covolo* Enrico, Laici e teologia nei Padri della Chiesa; il XIV Convegno di Catechesi Patristica [Roma 14-15.III.1991]: a) Salesianum 53 (1991) 729-739; – b) VetChr 28 (1991) 181-193.

k174 *Denaux* Adelbert, De bischoppensynode over de priesteropleiding (okt. 1990) [i. Hoe verliep de b.; ii. welke klemtonen...]: CollatVL 21 (1991) 89-100.

k175 *Ferretti* Taddei, Un incontro ecumenico sul problema del ministero della donna [Palermo 17-19.XI.1989; Acta ᴱMilitello C. 1991]: RasT 32 (1991) 188-197.

k176 *Giuliani* Massimo, Ebrei e cristiani, oggi (Milano 16.X.1990): HumBr 46 (1991) 276-283.

k177 *Jossua* Jean-Pierre, Bilan du Congress de Louvain 1990 [sept., de Concilium, (de 200 membres et 700 'observateurs' à Bruxelles 1970)] → 348, Concilium 233 (P 1991) I-X.

k178 *Krakowiak* Czesław, ❷ Inkulturacja liturgii (XII Kongres 'Societas Liturgica' 1989) [York, 14-19.VIII]: RuBi 44 (1991) 65-70.

k179 *Mertens* Herman-Emiel, SCHOONENBERG-colloquium te Leuven [30.VIII - 2.IX.1991]: TsTNijm 31 (1991) 421.

k180 a) *Moda* Aldo, La cristologia contemporanea [Europa]; – b) *Iammarrone* Giovanni, ... Spagna, America Latina; – c) *Dupuis* Jacques, ... anglofona; – d) *Muratore* Saturnino, Tavola rotonda; ... Italia: RasT ForumATI [3-4.I.1990] 32 (1991) 77-79 / 79-81 / 81-83 / 83-85.

k181 *Nientiedt* Klaus, Vielfältig und widersprüchlich; der 24. Deutsche Evangelische Kirchentag im Ruhrgebiet [3.-4. Juni]: HerdKorr 45 (1991) 306-311.

k182 *Niewiadomski* Józef, Report on the symposium 'Dramatische Erlösungslehre im Lichte der Theorie GIRARDS' in Innsbruck (September 25-28, 1991): CoV&R [Bulletin of the Colloquium on Violence and Religion, Stanford/Innsbruck] 2, 11s.

k183 *Putney* Michael E., Come, Holy Spirit, renew the whole creation; seventh assembly of the World Council of Churches [Canberra Feb. 7-20, 1991]: TS 52 (1991) 607-635.

k184 Reports about theological conferences: TContext 8,2 (1991) 146-154 [also 9,1; also in TKontext, TContexto].

k185 *Ricca* Paolo, Echi di Canberra [WCC 7-20.II.1991, 'in Italia scandalosamente ignorato dai mass media']: Protestantesimo 46 (1991) 136-141.

k186 *Romita* Angelo, Il convegno mondiale delle chiese sulla giustizia, la pace e la tutela dell'ambiente [Seoul, 5-12.III.1990]: Nicolaus 18 (1991) 339-352.

k187 *Schiller* Karl E., Der neue Mensch, sein Werden und Sein, seine Krankheiten, seine Heilkunst; 2. Internationaler Christus Medicus-Kongress, Bad Ischl 5.-9.VI.1990: ArztC 17 (1991) 142.

k188 *Soetens* Claude, *a)* Second colloque international sur les Conférences épiscopales, Salamanque 2-7 avril 1991: RHE 86 (1991) 226-9, détaillé; – *b)* Le colloque de Salamanque sur les Églises locales et la catholicité [2-7.IV.1991]: Irénikon 64 (1991) 230-5; – *c)* Colloque sur l'Histoire du concile Vatican II [I, LvN oct. 1989], II, Houston, 12-15.I.1991: RHE 86 (1991) 332-4, détaillé.

k189 *Stacpoole* Alberic, Symposium Vaticanum Secundum LvN 22- 25.X. 1989: PrPeo 4 (1990) 19-28.

k190 *Tillard* J.-M.R., L'Esprit-Saint était-il à Canberra? [WCC Assembly ...]: Irénikon 64 (1991) 163-204; Eng. 204.

k191 *Velati* Mauro, *a)* Christianity and Churches on the eve of Vatican II (Houston Jan. 12-15, 1991): CrNSt 12 (1991) 165-175; – *b)* Symposium Vaticanum II [Lv 23-25 ott. 1989]: CrNSt 11 (1990) 197-205; Eng. 205.

k192 *Vesci* Uma Marina, Il tempo; echi di un convegno [Nuova Delhi nov. 1990]: SMSR 57 (1991) 151-7.

Y7.6 *Acta congressuum philologica:* **nuntii.**

k194 *Davaras* Costas, The Wace and Blegen [memorial] conference in Athens, 1989 [Dec. 2-3, British School, 'Pottery as evidence for trade in the Aegean Bronze Age': Kadmos 30 (1991) 81s.

k195 *Touwaide* Alain, *a)* Tradizione e ecdotica dei testi medici tardoantichi e bizantini [Capri 29-31.X.1990, Univ. N]; – *b)* Testi medici greci in versione orientale [Sem. internaz. 1990 (dove?), Ist. italiano per gli studi filosofici]: Byzantion 61 (1991) 586s.

Y7.8 *Acta congressuum orientalistica et archaeologica:* **nuntii.**

k196 *Bintliff* John, Post-modernism, rhetoric and scholasticism at TAG [Theoretical Archaeology Group, Lampeter Univ. Dec. 1990]: the current state of British archaeological theory: Antiquity 65 (1991) 274-8.

k197 *Bouzek* Jan, *Wasowicz* Aleksandra, Le Pont dans l'épopée et dans l'archéologie; 6ᵉ colloque sur l'histoire ancienne de la mer Noire [22-29.IX.1990, Vani, Géorgie]: Dialogues Hist. Anc. 17,1 (1991) 431-443.

k198 *Decker* Wolfgang, Kolloquium 'Le cirque et ses spectacles', Lattes 5.-7.X.1990: Nikephoros 3 (1990) 299-306.

k199 *Drew-Bear* Marie, XIXᵉ Congrès international de Papyrologie [Le Caire, Univ. Ain-Shems, 2-9.IX.1989]: TopO 1 (1991) 139s.

k200 *Gibbins* David, The maritime archaeology of Greece — London conference, 23 March 1991: IntNaut 20 (1991) 353-6.

k201 *Karathanasis* Athanasios E., ⊜ Two scientific [epistēmoniká] symposia on Christian Thessaloniki: TAth 62 (1991) 177-183; Eng. 929.

k202 *Loeben* Christian E., After Tutankamun; international conference on the Valley of the Kings, [Newbury] Highclere Castle 15-17 June 1990: Orientalia 60 (1991) 3-6.

k203 ᴱ*Pergole* Philippe, Seminari di archeologia cristiana (Archeologia e cultura della tarda antichità e dell'alto medioevo), Resoconto delle sedute dell'anno accademico 1990-1: RivArCr 67 (1991) 441-472 [451s, S. Cecilia in Trastevere].

k204 *Shanks* Hershel, When 5,613 scholars get together in one place; the annual [AAR-SBL-ASOR] meeting, 1990 [New Orleans]: BAR-W 17,2 (1991) 62-68.

k205 *Taracha* Piotr, ⊕ Archaeology and Heinrich SCHLIEMANN, a century after his death: Athens 17-21.IV.1990: ArchWsz 41 (1990) 127s.

k206 *Virduzzo* Francine, La Siria degli Umayyadi, un importante convegno internazionale [Lyon CNRS]: Studium 87 (R 1991) 421-433.

k207 *Volanakis* John B., ⊜ The Xth international conference on Christian archaeology: TAth 62 (1991) 866-873.

Y8   *Periti,* Scholars, Personalia, organizations.

k208 Acta Pontificii Instituti Biblici [in italiano eccetto alcuni titoli] 9/8 (1991s) 628-748; dissertationes 684s, summaria 728-734; in progress 685s; p. 706, Jerusalem Hebrew University program for students of the Pontifical Biblical Institute.

k209 Annuaire du Collège de France 1989-1990; résumé des cours et travaux. P 1990. 830 p.; p. 577-698 Égyptologie, Assyriologie... textes grecs; Rome; théorie linguistique. F 100. 0069-5580.

k210 **Arnold** Matthieu, La Faculté de théologie protestante de l'Université de Strasbourg, de 1919 à 1945: préf. *Lienhard* Marc; postf. *Cullmann* Oscar: Trav. Fac. 2. Strasbourg 1990, Fac. 321 p. - ᴿRHE 86 (1991) 169s (É. *Goichot*); TLZ 116 (1991) 672-4 (P. *François*: 321 p., 'leicht abgeänderte Fassung' einer vorgetragenen Arbeit).

k211 *a)* Bibelen i Norge: Det Norske Bibelskap. Oslo 1991. 384 p.; ill. 17 art. [BL 92,8, G. W. *Anderson*: thorough indication of contents without tit. pp.]. - *b) Grözinger* Karl E., Judaistik vid Lunds universitet, ᵀ*Jansson* Eva-M.: SvTKv 66 (1990) 1-6.

k212 *Broise* Henri, *al.*, Activités de l'École française de Rome, section antiquité: MÉF-A 102,1 (1990) 443-504.

k212* *Charlesworth* James H., The centenary of the École Biblique: Princ-SemB 12 (1991) 56ss.

k213 *a) Coreth* Emerich, Das Jesuitenkolleg Innsbruck; Grundzüge seiner Geschichte; – *b) Beneder* Emmerich, Aus der Geschichte der Innsbrucker Jesuitenbibliothek: ZkT 113 (1991) 140-213 / 214-221.

k214 *Dulles* Avery, Jesuits and theology, yesterday and today [opening Boston Public Library exhibit 'Jesuits in New England']: TS (1991) 524-538.

k214* *García Cordero* Maximiliano, Centenario de 'l'École Biblique' de Jerusalén: Salmanticensis 38 (1991) 225-236.

k215 *Hart* Ray L., Religious and theological studies in American higher education; a pilot study: JAAR 59 (1991) 715-792 [777, internationalization; 778-783, what is and should be the relation between study and practice of religion]; 793-827, statistical appendices.

k215* *Leavitt* Robert F., Bicentennial reflections [cover: St Mary's (Sulpician) Seminary, Baltimore; America's first seminary; two hundred years of impact]: The Priest 47,10 (1991) 14-16.

k216 **Murphy-O'Connor** Jerome, (*Taylor* Justin), The École Biblique and the NT, a century of scholarship 1990 ➤ 6,m401: ᴿCBQ 53 (1991) 501 (Barbara E. *Reid*); DoctLife 41 (1991) 387-9 (J. *Neill*); ETL 67 (1991) 440s (F. *Neirynck*); Pacifica 4 (1991) 352s (B. R. *Doyle*); RivB 39 (1991) 249s (A. *Bonora*).

k216* ᴱNeuser Wilhelm H., Die evangelisch-theologische Fakultät Münster, 1914 bis 1989: Unio und Confessio 15. Bielefeld 1991, Luther. 133 p. DM 28 [TR 88,432].

k217 *Selling* Joseph A., Chronicles [K. U. Leuven activities]: LvSt 16 (1991) 331-344; 344-354, doctoral defenses.

k218 ᴱSinclair R. K., Past, Present and Future; ancient world studies in Australia, 25th anniversary Antichthon. 1990, Australian Society for Classical Studies. 125 p. A$10. – ᴿPrudentia 23 (1991) 55-58 (T. R. *Stevenson*).

k219 *Viganò* Egidio, *al.*, Il 50º dell'Ateneo Salesiano: Salesianum 53 (1991) 209-217.

k220 [*Schalück* Hermann], *Conti* Martino, rettore, Chronica: Inizio dell'anno accademico 1991-2: Antonianum 66 (1991) 169-197... 595-622; 623 in memoriam (*Bagatti* B., *Corbo* V., *al.*).

Y8.5   *Periti,* **in memoriam.**

k221 Obituaries: AntiqJ 70 (1990) 516-528; – Necrologia: REB 51 (1991) 229-236.473-485.735-742.976-986; – Nécrologies RHE 86 (1991) 175*s.388*s.

k222 Allgrove (McDowell), Joan, 18.XII.1928-15.II.1991; textiles: Iran 29 (1991) vi.

k223 Alszeghy, Zoltan, † 19.V.91: RasT ForumATI 32 (1991) 324-6 (S. *Muratore*).

k224 Amalorpavadas, D. S., aet. 58, 25.V.1990 [road accident]; co-editor: IndTSt 27 (1990) 213-6.

k224* Angershausen, Julius, Bischof, 3.I.1911-22.VIII.1990: ZMissRW 75 (1991) 147s (H. *Waldenfels*).

k225 Apollonj Ghetti, Bruno M. [➤ 5,k833; 6,m415] 7.X.1905-23.V.1989: Byzantina 16 (1991) 439 (K. *Charalabidis,* Ⓖ).

k226 Arrupe, Pedro, s.J., 14.XI.1907-5.II.1991, generale dei Gesuiti: AcPIB 9/7 (1991) 616-8; America 164 (1991) 139 & 142-6.182 (V. *O'Keefe*) & 152.4s (P. R. *Divaekar*) & 156-163.186 (P. *Hebblethwaite*) & 166-173 (H. *Madelin*) & 174-8 (F. X. *Murphy*); CC 142 (1991,1) 327-340 (S. *Decloux*);

Manresa 62,243 (1990) 97-246: 10 art. (25º de elección); Orientierung 55 (1991) 37-40 (L. *Kaufmann*); MiscCom 49 (1991) 291-9 (I. *Iglesias*); Proyección 38 (1991) 91s; 93-100 su homilia S. Ignacio Manila 1981; RazF 223 (1991) 231; 294-300 (L. *González*); REB 51 (1991) 456-9; Tablet 145 (1991) 182 (R. *Rush*, V. *O'Keefe*); TXav 41 (1991) 199-209 (E. *Briceño*).

k227 Atalay, Erol, [➤ 6,m417] 13.XI.1935-5.IX.1989: JhÖsW-BG 59-Grabungen (1989) 1 (Maria *Aurenhammer*).

k228 Audiat, Jean, 9.XI.1903-16.IV.1991, directeur: RÉAnc 93 (1991) 5-9 (J. *Marcadé*; bibliog.).

k229 Bachellery, Édouard, 6.X.1907-11.VIII.1988; Études Celtiques: BSLP 85 (1990) ii. (P.-Y. *Lambert*).

k230 Bagatti, Bellarmino, OFM [➤ 6,m421] 11.XI.1905-7.X.1990: scavatore di Nazareth; ADAJ 35 (1991) 9-11; phot.; BToday 29 (1991) 113s (F. *Manns*); ParVi 36 (1991) 294-6 (G.C. *Bottini*, A. *Niccacci*); RivArCr 67 (1991) 125-7 (D. *Mazzoleni*); REB 51 (1991) 213-5; RivB 39 (1991) 122-4 (A. *Niccacci*).

k231 Balthasar, Hans Urs von [➤ 5,k837], 12.VIII.1905-16.VI.1989: DoctLife 41 (1991) 401-7 (G. *O'Hanlon*); TLZ 116 (1991) 401-416 (T. *Vogel*. 'Die Herrlichkeit des Gekreuzigten, eine theologische Erinnerung').

k232 Barbu, Francis J.J.M., 4.V.1914-16.III.1991; évêque de Quimper; licence Pont. Ist. Biblico 1942: AcPIB 9/7 (1991) 619.

k233 Barón Mora-Figueroa, Enrique, S.J.; 27.III.1922-7.V.1991, director 1968-76: Proyección 38 (1991) 175s.

k234 Beck, Edmond, 6.XI.1902-12.VI.1991; Éphrem; Koran: OrChr 75 (1991) 262 (J. *Assfalg*); RHE 86 (1991) 469 (L. *Leloir*).

k235 Belli, Carlo, 1903-... Studi Magna Grecia: StRom 39 (1991) 310s, fot. (M. *Barberito*).

k236 Beonio-Brocchieri, Paolo, 1934-1991, Japanese studies: EWest 41 (1991) 389s (G. *Gnoli*, L. *Lanciotti*).

k237 Bischoff, Bernhard, 20.XII.1906-17.IX.1991; latin médiéval: CRAI (1991) 511 (F. *Chamoux*).

k238 Bittel, Kurt, 5.VII.1907-30.I.1991: BaghMit 22 (1991) nur frontispiece; CRAI (1991) 167s (F. *Chamoux*); Ausgrabung Boğazköy: Gnomon 63 (1991) 663-5 (R. *Naumann*).

k239 Blanckenhagen, Peter Heinrich von, 21.III.1909-6.III.1990; NY Fine Arts Institute, classical archeology and art: AJA 95 (1991) 155s (Evelyn B. *Harrison*).

k240 Blanco Freijeiro, A., 6.IX.1923-6.I.1991: ArEspArq 63 (1990) 3-6 (Pilar *León*).

k241 Blank, Josef, [➤ 6,m432] 8.IX.1926-2.X.1989; Johannes, Paulus: BZ 35 (1991) 153 (R. *Schnackenburg*).

k242 Bogoslovsky, Eugeni Stepanovich, 21.VIII.1941-21.VII.1990: VDI 196 (1991) 234-6.

k243 Bollnow, Otto Friedrich, 14.III.1903-7.II.1991: ZRGg 43 (1991) 183 (J.H. *Schoeps*).

k244 Borkowski, Zbigniew, 13.XI.1936-19.VII.1991: ArchWsz 42 (1991) 171 (K. *Winnicki*).

k244* Bornkamm, Günther, 8.X.1905-18.II.1990: JbWfKG 85 (1991) 284-6 (D. *Lührmann*) [< ZIT 91,811].

k245 Bruce, Frederick F., [➤ 6,m442] 12.X.1910-11.IX.1990; editor 1957-71: PEQ 123 (1991) 25 (J.P. *Kane*); Churchman 105 (1991) 41 (J. *Wenham*); Manchester exegesis prof.: JSS 36 (1991) 1-6 (A.R. *Millard*).

k246 Brusselmans, Christiane, d. 1991: LvSt 16 (1991) 142s.

k247 Butz, Kilian, 12.III.1943-22.V.1990; Assyriologe: AfO 36s (1989s) 193s, phot. (H. *Waetzoldt*).

k248 Calver, Gordon A., 1921-21.IV.1990: Iran 29 (1991) v (D. *Wright*).

k249 Carettoni, Gianfilippo, 17.II.1912-6.XII.1990: ricerche sul Palatino: StRom 39 (1991) 308s, fot. (C. *Pietrangeli*).

k250 Chenu, Marie-Dominique (Marcel) O.P., [➤ 6,m450] 7.I.1895-11.II.1990: Commonweal 117 (1990) 252.254 (J. A. *Komonchak*); DocLife 40 (1990) 206-8 (Marie-Humbert *Kennedy*).

k251 Chevallier, Max-Alain, † 28.III.1991: EsprVie 101,188.567.

k251* Chtaerman, Elena Mikhaïlovna, 1914-22.X.1991: romaniste: VDI 196 (1991) 2; Dialogues d'histoire ancienne 18,1 (1992) 7-9 (Monique *Clavel-Lévêque*, ᵀJacqueline *Gaudey*).

k252 Collins, John J., 1900-8.VIII.1991: first editor: NTAbs 36 (1992) 1 (D. J. *Harrington*, C. R. *Matthews*).

k253 Colombo, Carlo, mons., 13.IV.1909-11.II.1991, collab.: ScuolaC 119 (1991) 115.283-300 (A. *Rimoldi*, bibliog.); TItSett 16 (1991) 3-8.26-30 (G. *Colombo*) & 9-25 (anche A. *Rimoldi*, bibliog.).

k253* Corbo, Virgilio, OFM: LA 41 (1991) insert.

k254 Corti, Gaetano, msgr., 19.I.1910-18.XI.1989: ScuolC 118 (1990) 264s (A. *Rimoldi*: biografia attesa dal suo successore *Cuscito* Giuseppe).

k255 Courtois, Jacques-Claude, 1931-18.III.1991, collaborateur d'Ugarit et Enkomi: Paléorient 17,1 (1991) 173 (H. de *Contenson*).

k256 Czapkiewicz, Andrzej, 3.VII.1924-1.III.1990; Arabist: FolOr 28 (1991) 5s.

k257 Darrouzès, Jean, père [➤ 6,m457] 3.IV.1912-26.VI.1990: RÉByz 49 (1991) 337-347, phot. (A. *Failler*; bibliog.).

k258 Delebecque, Édouard, 1910-c.1990: ᴿRÉG 103,2 (1990) xxvii-xxix (J. *Jouanna*).

k259 Della Corte, Francesco, † 24.IX.1991: dir.: Maia 43 (1991) 161 [44...]; Sileno 17 (1991) 359-362 (Giuseppina *Barabino*).

k260 Demus, Otto, 1902-17.XI.1990; byzantinologue, mosaïques de Venise: CRAI (1991) 512 (F. *Chamoux*); DumbO 45 (1991) vi-xi; phot. (H. *Belting*).

k261 di Giura, Giovanni, 6.I.1893-30.I.1989; diplomatico: StRom 38 (1990) 113, fot. (Fernanda *Roscetti*).

k262 Dimitrios I, patriarche de Constantinople, † 3.X.1991: Irénikon 64 (1991) 321s.

k263 Dirks, Walter, 1901-1991: kritischer Theoretiker politischer Theologie: Orientierung 55 (1991) 125 (N. *Klein*).

k264 Dohrn, Tobias, 23.XII.1910-29.III.1990: klass. Kunst: Gnomon 63 (1991) 286s (H. *Blanck*).

k265 Dubois, Jacques, O.S.B., 10.XI.1919-8.XII.1991; hagiographie [RHE 87,327, J. *Avril*].

k266 Dugmore, Clifford [➤ 6,m461] 1910-25.X.1990; editor 1950-79: JEH 42 (1991) 175-7 (P. *Collinson*).

k267 Edgar, Peter, O.P. provincial: aet. 67, 12.IV.1990: NBlackf 71 (1990) 243.

k268 Efimova, Aleksandra Mikhailovna, 1903-12.I.1990: SovArch (1991,2) 300 (N. A. *Kokorina, al.* ☉).

k269 Egermann, Franz [➤ 6,m464], 13.II.1905-9.VII.1989; klas. Pg.: Gnomon 62 (1991) 755-7 (J. *Dalfen*).

k270 Eilers, Wilhelm, [➤ 5,k871, 6,m465] 27.IX.1906-3.VII.1989; Iranist: ZDMG 141 (1991) 1-6; portr. (W. *Hinz*).

k271 Erdmann, Karl Dietrich, 29.IV.1910-23.VI.1990: HZ 252 (1991) 529-539 (E. *Jäckel*).

k272 Erim, Kenan Tevfik [➤ 6,m468], 13.II.1929-3.XI.1990; Aphrodisias excavator: AJA 95 (1991) 281-3 (G.W. *Bowersock*).

k273 Evelpidis-Argyropoulou, Réna, 1910 -27.VIII.1990: RBgNum 137 (1991) 253-5 (T. *Hackens*; surnames inverted p. 255).

k274 Fasola, Umberto M., 1917-1989; Barnabit. Stud. 6 (R 1989) 231-271 (V. *Colciago*, G. *Cagni*); Byzantina 16 (1991) 440 (K. *Charalabidis* ☺); RAC 65 (1989) 5-17 (V. *Fiocchi Nicolai*, bibliog.).

k275 Février, Paul-Albert, 1931 -10.IV.1991: RÉAug 37 (1991) 8; RivArCr 67 (1991) 435-440 (V. *Saxer*); MÉF-A 103 (1991) 307-312; phot. (J. *Guyon*).

k276 Flint, Hildebrand, O.S.B., 1921 -10.I.1991; ed. Pax: EphLtg 105 (1991) 180.

k277 Fonseca, Aloysius, S.J., 16.I.1915-25.X.1991: collaboratore: CC 142 (1991,4) 376-9.

k278 Frye, Northrop, 1912 -22.I.1991: America 165 (1991) 14s (J.P. *McIntyre*); ETL 67 (1991) 216 (R.F. *Collins*).

k278* Fuchs, Johannes Georg, 1926-1990: ZSav-R 108 (1991) 671s (P. *Simonius*).

k279 Gedye, Ione 1907-XI.1990: Conservation dept. pioneer: BInstArch 27 (L 1990) 1-5; portr. (H. *Hodges*) & 7-15 (Elizabeth *Pye*) & 17-25 (C. *Price*).

k280 Gill, Joseph, S.J., 8.IX.1901-15.X.1989: ed. Acts, Council of Florence; Rector Pont. Inst. Or.: OrChrPer 57 (1991) 5-9 (J.A. *Munitiz*).

k281 Gluskina, Ilya Mendelevna, 27.VI.1914-6.II.1991: VDI 198 (1991) 253 (G.P. *Zharkova, al.*).

k281* Goen, Clarence C., [or laudatio] Church historian: AmBapQ 10 (1991) 246 (M.S. *Burrows*; 355s bibliog.), 256-265 (M. *Marty, al.*).

k282 Göransson, Sven, 1910 -23.XI.1989: SvTKv 66 (1990) 45-47 (Ingun *Montgomery*).

k282* Golterman, Willem Frederik, 1898-28.VII.1990: liturgie, oecumenisme: NedTTs 45 (1991) 134s (H.B. *Kossen*).

k283 Graaf, Johannes de, 14.VII.1911-24.IV.1991: vrede, dialoog: NedTTs 45 (1991) 326-8 (A. van den *Beld*).

k284 Grabar, André, [➤ 6,m486] 1896 -5.X.1990: DumbO 45 (1991) xii-xv; photo (H. *Maguire*); Cah. Archéol. 39 (1991) 4-6, phot. (Tania *Velmans*).

k285 Greene, Graham, 1904-1991: America 164 (1991) 520 (J.J. *Feeney*).

k286 Grosvenor, Mary, † 5.IV.1991: Oxford Patristic Greek Lexicon; TE*Zerwick* M., Analysis philologica NT: AcPIB 9/7 (1991) 619.

k287 Guelich, Robert A., 20.VI.1939-3.VII.1991; editor: Ex Auditu 7 (1991) iv-v, phot.

k287* Gunneweg, Anton H.J., aet. 69, 17.VI.1990: Gnomon 64,384.

k288 Haimerl Franz Xaver, 11.III.1904-5.IX.1988: HistJb 110 (1990) 287s (E. *Buxbaum*).

k289 Halqin, Abraham S.: Lešonenu 53 (1988s) 153.

k290 Hamp, Vinzenz, 4.V.1907-3.I.1991; AT-Redaktor 1957-77: BZ 35 (1991) 314 (J. *Schreiner*); MüTZ 42 (1991) 269s (M. *Görg*).

k291 Haugan, Ireneo, O.S.B., 1937 -12.V.1991: Benedictina 38 (1991) 465s (S. *Baiocchi*).

k292 Hauret, Charles, mgr. 13.IV.1907-3.I.1991; introd. S. Écr.; Psaumes: RevSR 65 (1991) 153-6 (B. *Renaud*).

k293 Heidenreich, Robert, 8.IX.1899-20.XI.1990, altor. Kunst: Gnomon 63 (1991) 573-5 (G. *Heres*).

k294 Hengsbach, Franz, card. † 24.VI.1991: ETL 67 (1991) 497 (G. *Thils*).

k294* Henninger, Joseph, S.V.D., 1906 -4.V.1991: NZMissW 47 (1991) 224 (F. *Kollbrunner*).

k295 Holmqvist, Wilhelm, † 9.VIII.1989: Fornvännen 85 (1990) 183; phot. (P. *Lundström*); bibliog. 183-5 (J. P. *Lamm*).

k296 Jankuhn, Herbert, 8.VIII.1905-30.IV.1990: HZ 252 (1991) 216-9 (R. von *Uslar*).

k297 Jonker, Hendrik, 28.III.1917 -1990: liturgie: NedTTs 45 (1991) 136s (J. H. van de *Bank*).

k297* Källstad, Thorvald: SvTKv 66 (1990) 95s (O. *Wikstrom*, no dates).

k298 Kambitsis, Ioannis, 1938 -7.VIII.1990: Archaiognosia 6 (1990) 207-211 (N. *Petrocheilos*).

k299 Kaufmann, Ludwig, s.J., 20.X.1918-8.VII.1991: Redakteur: Orientierung 55 (1991) 150-4, phot. (P. *Selvatico*); Tablet 245 (1991) 950 (–: editor of Orientierung and part-author of its fine coverage of Vatican II) & 940 ('outstripped the solemn Stimmen der Zeit').

k300 Kazakevich (Grace), Emilia Lvovna 1911-1986: VDI 199 (1991) 227s ⊕.

k301 Klíma, Josef, 16.II.1909-30.II.1989; Keilschriftforscher: AfO 36s (1991s) 194-7, phot. (R. *Haase*).

k302 Kloiber, Ämilian J., 1910-1989: MitAntW 120 (1990) 231 (E. M. *Ruprechtsberger*).

k303 Kluke, Paul, 31.VII.1908-18.IV.1990: HZ 252 (1991) 212-5 (H. *Seier*).

k304 Kniazeff, Alexis, 1913-8.II.1991 'dernier' (? 1991): recteur S.-Serge 25 ans: MaisD 187 (1991) 93-95 (P.-M. *Gy*).

k304* Konstantinidis, Athanasios I., 1924 -23.VIII.1988: Makedonika 26 (1987s) xv-s (K. A. *Vavouskos*, ⊕).

k305 Kramer, Samuel Noah, 12.IX.1897-26.XI.1990; Assyriologist: AcSum 13 (1991) v-vi, 3 phot. (M. *Civil*); 'the grand old man of Sumerian': AfO 36s (1989s) 197s, phot. (T. *Jacobsen*); Belleten 54,211 (1990) 1283s, 4 phot. (M. I. *Çiğ*).

k306 Kraus, Fritz Rudolf, 21.III.1910-19.I.1991; Assyriologe, Leiden: BO 48 (1991) 331-5, portr. (M. *Stol*, bibliog.); PhoenixEOL 37,1 (1991) 4 (W. H. van *Soldt*); ZAss 81 (1991) 1-3 (D. O. *Edzard*) & 3-6 (Annette *Ganter*, lexicalische Beiträge).

k307 Kübler, Karl, 4.VII.1897-10.V.1990: Kerameikos-Grabung: Gnomon 63 (1991) 380-3 (W. *Schiering*).

k308 Kuss, Otto, 6.I.1905-...: MüTZ 42 (1991) 271-3 (J. *Gnilka*).

k308* Labrinos, Christos Evangelou, 1917-24.III.1988: Makedonika 26 (1987s) ix-xi, phot. (K. A. *Vavouskos*, ⊕).

k309 Laroche, Emmanuel, 11.VII.1914-16.VI.1991; Anatolien, grammaire comparée: RAss 85 (1991) 97-100 (J.-M. *Durand*).

k310 Lasserre, François [➤ 6,m518] 14.IX.1919-22.XII.1989: Gnomon 63 (1991) 76s (C. *Calame*).

k311 Leemans, Wilhelmus François, 1912 -28.VI.1981, collab.: JESHO 34,3 (1991) ii-v, phot. (K. R. *Veenhof*).

k312 Lefebvre, Marcel, 1905-25.III.1991: TPQ 139 (1991) 419s (J. *Gelmi*).

k313 Lemerle, Paul [➤ 6,m525] 22.IV.1903-17.VII.1989: Travaux et Mémoires 11 (1991) 1-15 [< RHE 87,116*]; RÉG 103,2 (1990) xxv-xxvii (J. *Jouanna*).

k314 Leroy, Maurice: Annuaire de l'Académie royale de Belgique (1991) 111-144 (J. *Bingen*) [< Byzantion 61 (1991) 5 avec photo mais sans dates].

k315 Levi, Doro, 1.VI.1898-3.VII.1991; scavatore Levante: Sileno 17 (1991) 349-358 (V. *La Rosa*).

k316 Lindars, Barnabas, JStNT 44 (1991) 56 (C. *Tuckett*).

k317 de Lubac, Henri, card. 1896 -4.IX.1991; Exégèse médiévale: America 165 (1991) 180-2 (A. *Dulles*); CC 142 (1991,4) 39-48, intervista; ComND

18 (1991) 297-304 (G.C. *Chantraine*); EsprVie 101 (1991) 101-jaune (E. *Vauthier*); EstE 66 (1991) 327-335 (A. *Santos Hernández*, bibliog.); Études 375 (1991) 371-8 (J.-Y. *Calvez*, 'Relire Catholicisme' 1938); RazF 224 (1991) 393-7 (X. *Tilliette*); Studium 87 (R 1991) 639-649 (A. *Russo*).

k318 Lyonnet, Stanislas, S.J. [➤ 2,e417; 3,h388], 23.VIII.1902-8.VI.1986: ColcT 61,2 (1991) 175-7 (W. *Chrostowski,* ❷).

k319 McHugh, William P., 3.I.1932 -1989: NewsAmEg 146 (1989) 20s (J. *McCauley*).

k320 McKenzie, John L., 9.X.1910-2.III.1991: BToday 29 (1991) 178-180 (L.J. *Hoppe*); Critic 45,4 (Ch 1991) 14-23; phot. (C. *Stuhlmueller, al.*).

k321 Maden, Meir: Lešonenu 53 (1988s) 149.

k322 Mandelli, Federico, 20.XI.1900-10.IX.1990, aiutante redattore 1926-38: ScuolC 119 (1991) 543s (A. *Rimoldi*, bibliog.).

k323 [Gonçalvez] Martins, Mario, S.J., aet. 82, 30.VI.1990; literatura medieval: RHE 86 (1991) 229 (R. *Aubert*).

k324 Maury, Pierre [† 13.I.1956], Les combats de ∼: FoiVie 90,3s (1991) 1-11 [-53] (A. *Dumas, al.*).

k325 Meo, Salvatore M., 1927 -7.VI.1990: Marianum 52 (1990) 7-16 (I.M. *Calabuig*).

k326 Meyer, Rudolf, 8.IX.1909-2.IV.1991; Semitistik und AT in: OLZ 86 (1991) 245.

k327 Mohrmann, Christine A.E.M., [➤ 4,k849] 1.VIII.1903-13.VII.1988: SacrEr 32 (1991) 13-22 (L.J. *Engels*: Une vie de savant) [< RHE 87,116*]; 1-62, G. *Bartelink*. A.A.R. *Bastiaensen*; p. 61s, thèses dirigées par C.M.

k328 Molnár, Amedeo [➤ 6,m544], aet. 67, 27.I.1990: histoire des dogmes, Praha: RHE 86 (1991) 618s (R. *Aubert*).

k328* Mondésert, Claude, S.J., aet. 85, 12.IX.1990; dir. Sources Chrétiennes: RHE 87,623, R. *Aubert*.

k329 Moss, Rosalind Louisa Beaufort [➤ 6,m548], 21.IX.1890-22.IV.1990; bibliographer: JEA 77 (1991) 150-5, 2 phot. (T.G.H. *James*).

k330 Müller-Wiener, Wolfgang, 17.V.1923-25.III.1991: Ausgrabung Resafa; Dir. DAI-Istanbul: ByZ 83 (1991) 762-4 (O. *Feld*).

k331 Murani, Ottorino, 23.VIII.1910-17.I.1991: RitNum 93 (1991) 258-262 fot. (A. *Rinaldi*: bibliog.).

k332 Nell-Breuning, Oswald von, S.J., 1890 -21.VIII.1991: CC 142 (1991,4) 491-6 (B. *Kuppler*); Orientierung 55 (1991) 183s (W. *Schroeder*).

k333 Neugebauer, Otto, 26.V.1899-19.II.1990; babylonische Mathematik: AfO 36s (1989s) 199, phot. (H. *Hunger*).

k334 Nikolajević, Ivanka, 1921-1990: RivArCr 67 (1991) 129-131 (N. *Duval*); 132-8 bibliog.

k335 Orge Ramírez, Manuel, 6.II.1931-27.V.1991; licenza Pont. Ist. Biblico 1958; collaboratore: Claretianum 31 (1991) 152s; bibliog.; Proyección 38 (1991) 176s.

k336 Palmieri, Alba, † 10.IV.1990; Malatya-Arslantepe excavator: AJA 95 (1991) 123 (Machteld J. *Mellink*).

k337 Passerin d'Entrèves, Ettore, 26.XII.1914-2.III.1990; jansénisme toscane...: RHE 86 (1991) 605 (R. *Aubert*).

k338 Pavan, Massimiliano, 30.VIII.1920-17.I.1991, 'Grecità politica': StRom 39 (1991) 119s, fot. (G. *Vitucci*); Atti Soc. Istriana Arch. 91 (Trieste 1991) 317-322 (G. *Rosada*).

k339 Perret, Jacques, † 1991: RÉLat 69 (1991) 34s (A. *Michel*).

k340 Petit, François, 20.VI.1894-28.VIII.1990; ét. prémontrées [RHE 87,326]; AnPraem 67 (1991) 120-137.

k341 Petuchowski, Jakob J., 1925 -12.XI.1991: Orientierung 55 (1991) 241-3 (R. *Walter*).

k342 Piétri, Charles, 19.IV.1932-7.VIII.1991; directeur de l'École française de Rome: MÉF 103 (1991) 369-376; phot. (J. *Guyon*); CRAI (1991) 512s (F. *Chamoux*); Rome chrétienne: RÉAug 37 (1991) 193-5 (C. *Lepelley*); RÉLat 69 (1991) 24 (A. *Michel*); RHE 86 (1991) 549 (J.-M. *Hannick*); RivArCr 67 (1991) 429-434 (N. *Duval*).

k343 Piotrovsky, Boris Borisovich, 14.II.1908-15.X.1990: SovArch (1991,3) 108-114, phot. (A.D. *Stolyar, al.* ⑧).

k344 Pisani, Vittore, 23.II.1899-22.XII.1990: Kratylos 36 (1991) 216-220 (G. *Bolognesi*).

k345 Pleijel, Hilding, in mem.: Kyrkohistorisk Årsskrift 21 (Sto 1989) 9ss (I. *Brohed*) [< ZIT 91,297].

k346 Pollet, Jacques Vincent, O.P. (aet. 85) 1905 -28.IX.1990 [RHE 87,623 'Vincent-Marie']: Zwingliana 18,4s (1990s) 407-410 (F. *Büsser*).

k347 Polotsky, Hans Jakob, 1905 -10.VIII.1991: RasEtiop 34 (1990!) 115-125 (S. *Hopkins*).

k348 Preneel, L., 26.V.1935-14.IV.1991, hist. eccl.: RHE 86 (1991) 499 (E. *Lamberts*).

k348* Raab, Heribert, 16.III.1923-7.VI.1990: RHE 87,608, R. *Aubert*.

k349 Rasker, Albert Jan, aet. 84, 23.VI.1990: history of Netherlands theology: NedTTs 45 (1991) 239s (K. E. *Biezeveld*).

k350 Ratto, Mario, 6.VIII.1906-8.I.1990: grande commerciante di monete: RitNum 92 (1990) 347s, fot. (C. *Crippa*).

k351 Reese, James M., O.S.F.S. [➤ 4,k947; 6,m572], 25.V.1926-3.XII.1989: BToday 28 (1990) 69 (C. *Stuhlmueller*).

k352 Renard, Marcel, [➤ 6,m573, d. 14.V] 3.III.1909-9.V.1990: Latomus 50 (1991) 3-13, portr. (Jacqueline *Dumortier-Bibauw*; bibliog. p. 14-16).

k353 Roguet, Aimon-Marie, O.P., 23.VII.1906-2.V.1991: MaisD 187 (1991) 97-125!(A. G. *Martimort*, bibliog. 125-136).

k354 Rossano, Pietro, Vescovo, 25.IV.1923-15.VI.1991; licenza PIB 1951; segretario della Commissione per la Neo-Volgata; Rettore della Pont. Univ. Lateranense: AcPIB 9/7 (1991) 620; ETL 67 (1991) 500; StMor 29 (1991) 325s (S. *Cannon*).

k355 Rougé, Jean, aet. 78, 1.VIII.1991: Archéonautica 10 (1990) 269; RÉAug 37 (1991) 196-8 (F. *Richard*).

k356 Rubinstein, Eliezer: Lešonenu 53 (1988s) 147.

Rüger, Hans Peter, aet. 57, 2.X.1990 ➤ 3002.

k357 Russo, Francesco, M.S.C., † 1991; Chiesa di Calabria [RHE 87,332].

k357* Schafer, Edward Hetzel, 25.VIII.1913-9.II.1991; Sinologist: JAOS 111 (1991) 441-3 (P. W. *Kroll*).

k358 Schuler, Einar von, 28.X.1930-14.II.1990: Hethitologe: AfO 36s (1989s) 200s, phot. (G. *Wilhelm*).

k359 Schultze, Bernhard, S.J. [➤ 6,m586], 19.I.1902-30.I.1990: OrChrPer 56 (1990) 269-282 (E. G. *Farrugia*).

k360 Schwarz, Klaus Peter, 1943 -2.VII.1989; Osmanist: ZDMG 141 (1991) 5-15; portr. (H. R. *Roemer*; Bibliog.).

k360* Sdan, Dov: Lešonenu 53 (1988s) 151.

k361 Setale, Eugenio (Francesco), 8.XII.1925-9.IX.1991: Benedictina 38 (1991) 466s (M. *Lapponi*).

k362 Singer, Isaac Bashevis 1904-1991; Nobel 1978: Orientierung 55 (1991) 176-9 (L. *Wachinger*).

k363 Skinner B. F., [➤ 6,m590] 20.III.1904-18.VIII.1990: major psychologist: Zygon 26 (1991) 189-193.

k364 Smith, Morton, aet. 76, 11.VII.1991: BAR-W 17,6 (1991) 6 [H. *Shanks*].

k365 Solmsen, Friedrich, 4.II.1904-30.I.1989: ILClasSt 16 (1991) vii; phot.

k368 Starcky, Jean, [➤ 4,k897] 3.II.1909-9.X.1988: Syria 66 (1989) 364s; phot. (E. *Will*).

k369 Stenger, Werner, 14.XI.1938-7.VI.1990: Christushymnus; Besteuerung: BZ 35 (1991) 155s (P.-G. *Müller*); LingBib 65 (1991) 117-129 (W. *Schenk*; 130-4 Bibliog.).

k370 Stenico, Arturo, Rei cretariae Acta 31s (1990/2) 19-24 (C. *Saletti*) & 25-30 (H. *Comfort*); 11-13 bibliog.; 5 fot.

k371 Stephanou, Pelopida, S.J., 25.XII.1911-13.VI.1989: OrChrPer 56 (1990) 265-8 (C. *Capizzi*).

k372 Stroheker, Karl Friedrich, 23.VIII.1914-12.XII.1988: Gnomon 63 (1991) 187-190 (J. A. *Schlumberger*).

k373 Syme, Ronald [➤ 5,k980; 6,m599]; 1903 -4.IX.1989: StRom 38 (1990) 117s (M. *Pavan*); VDI 196 (1991) 237-240 (V. I. *Kuzishchin*, E. M. *Shtaerman*).

k374 Taracha, Malgorzata, 16.XII.1959-1,XII.1989: ArchWsz 41 (1990) 169s, phot. (A. *Wąsowicz*, bibliog.).

k374* Taylour, William, lord, 1904-1989: AnBritAth 86 (1991) ii-v, portr. (I. *Stewart*).

k375 Testini, Pasquale, 17.V.1924-17.X.1989; archeologia cristiana: StRom 38 (1990) 114-6, fot. (Letizia Pani *Ermini*); Byzantina 16 (1991) 440s (K. *Charalabidis*, Ⓖ).

k375* [B.] Thomas, Edit, 10.III.1923-3.III.1988: FolAr 40 (1989) (E. *Tóth*).

k376 Titov, Valeri Sergeevich [➤ 6,m605], 16.X.1932-17.I.1990: SovArch (1990,4) 296s, phot. (V. I. *Markovich*).

k377 Treu, Kurt, 15.IX.1928-6.VI.1991: Tyche 6 (1991) 1s (U. *Treu*); FgNt 4 (1991) 245.

Tsori, Nehemia, ➤ k388 infra.

k378 Urbach, Ephraim E., 1912-2.VII.1991; Rome doctorate; a world leader in Rabbinic studies: IsrEJ 41 (1991) 295s (J. S.).

k379 Vidler, Alec, 1899-1991; 1939-64 editor: TLond 94 (1991) 325.

k380 Vinay, Valdo, 10.VIII.1906-25.XI.1990; prof. valdese; collaboratore: Protestantesimo 46 (1991) 2-40 (P. *Ricca*) [147s, laurea honoris causa di S. Anselmo, M. *Löhrer*]; 323-5, C. *Papini*, 'La chiesa, le chiese II fu rifiutato dalla Claudiana per il suo spirito ecumenico'.

k381 Vivian, Angelo, 31.XII.1942-20.IX.1991: giudaismo. lessicografia: Henoch 13 (1991) 131s, fot. (P. *Sacchi*).

k382 Vööbus, Arthur [➤ 5,k989] 28.IV.1909-25.IX.1988: Aram 1 (1989) 290-3 (M. *Hollerich*) & 294-6 (S. *Brock*; 297-9, Syriac bibliog.).

k383 Waszink, Jan Hendrik [➤ 6,m617], 27.X.1908-5.X.1990; VigChr: Gnomon 63 (1991) 660-2, portr. (Jan den *Boeft*); RÉAug 37 (1991) 6s (R. *Braun*).

k384 West, Edward Nason, 1909 -3.I.1990; NY Episcopal cathedral canon: StVlad 34 (1990) 237-9 (V. *Kesich*).

k385 Westerink, Leendert Gerritt, 2.XI.1913-24.I.1990; Plato: Gnomon 63 (1991) 76-78 (H. D. *Saffrey*).

k386 Zandee, Jan, 9.IX.1914-23.I.1991: Ägyptologie: BO 48 (1991) 697-700; portr. (J. *Helderman*); PhoenixEOL 37,1 (1991) 4s (M. *Heerma van Voss*).
k387 Zinn, Ernst, 26.I.1910-24.II.1990: Gnomon 63 (1990) 78-80; portr. (M. von *Albrecht*).
k388 Zori, Nehemya, 1902 -26.I.1991, Galilee explorer: Qadmoniot 24 (1991) 68 (H. *Katzenstein*); IsrEJ 41 (1991) 206.

Index Alphabeticus: Auctores – *Situs (omisso al-., tel, abu etc.)*
Ddiss./dir. Eeditor FFestschrift Mmentio, de eo Rrecensio Ttranslator † in mem.

Aalen S 7366
Aalst A van de D7797
Aarde A van 1065 4398
   4898   4942*b*   e726*
   D4551 M1435*
Aartsen J g417
Aartun K 9202
Abadie P 2603 2652
Abar-Nahara e613
Abascal J e823
Abbà   G   8337   8338
   R5173 7689 8486 g819
   k7 M Ra100 a 132
Abbasoğlu H e20*g*
Abbott S D7597*
Abbruzzese S k76
'Abda d355-d357
Abdalla A d10*e*
Abdel-Rahman I d878
Abdullah M a848*
Abeele B van den b648*
Abegg M 9867 9891
Abegunde S 2097
Abel O 1004*a*
Abela A 2037 2038 4111
   R1649 8526
Abelardus P M1944 g407
Abesamis C 1005
Abicht L Rg846
Abila d468 d469
Abitz F d866 d867
Abou Assaf 9253
Abou Zayd S a296
Abrabanel I M2131*ab*
Abraham K E8591 M
   8018*b* W E7130* T9647
Abrahams S 1930
Abramowiczównia Z F3
Abramsky C F4

Abramson G Ea91* Ra89
Abraq d787
Abromeit H Dg959
Abu 'Assāf 'A d651 E626
Aby Dayyah A d470
Abu Hamdan M Me382R
Abu Ḥanifa e484*
Abulafia Ma53
Abu Mina d943*
Abu Nowar M De912
Abu Qubur d702
Abu Qurra T Ma476*
   g338*
Abū Rātta M7589
Abusch T 2240 9276*e*
   a817
Abu Shaker 9403*b
Abusir d916*b
Abydos   d272*   d944
   d944*
Acconci A R1593
Acem e20*b*
Acerbi A 9802
Achenbach R D2342
Achtemeier E 1197 P
   416* 5759 D5206 5501*
Ackerman J R1346 1830
   S 2077 D3458 R3109
Ackermann E a499
Ackermans G E90*c*
Ackroyd P 2604 M2611R
AcNum Index 901
Acosta Méndez E 9446
Acquaro E 887 d580
   E627 e208
   Acre e389 → 'Akko
Acta Pontificii Instituti
   Biblici k208
– ÉtGrecques 569

Actes. Ling. Fonctions
   9644*
Adaïma d945
Adam   A   1341*   9024
   E694* R3712 5134 k85
   J b649 K Mg910 P
   b739*a*
Adamec L e299
Adamo   D   4800   9189
   a981*b* g197
Adams A Rb936 B d825
   D   D4601   7549*   H
   D1373 R1216 J R8483
   b751 e680 Tk68* M
   E282 R Re425
Adamson J 5772 D5093
Adan-Bayewitz D d438
Adda mons e503
Addinall P 916* 1006
   Dg706
Adelman H Ra76
Adeyemi M 4706*b* e641
Adinolfi M 171 5062*a*
   5742 e553
Adkin N g246
Adkins L b471
Adler G R1103 M a325
   S 2544 W 3670 b40
Adolph A D7956
Adorno T Ma503 b52
Adrados F 9504 9624
Adrassus e57
Adriaanse H a92 Dk58
   R1053 8968
Adshead S d623
Aegidius R Mg408
Aegyptus 9327-9400 a771-
   a816 b102-b151 b521
   b838* d300 d825-d969

ᴰdiss./dir. ᴱeditor ᶠFestschrift ᴹmentio, de eo ᴿrecensio ᵀtranslator † in mem.
Sub **de**, **van** etc.: cognomina *americana* (post 1979) et *italiana* (post 1984); **non** reliqua.

ᴰdiss./dir. ᴱeditor ᶠFestschrift ᴹmentio, de eo ᴿrecensio ᵀtranslator † in mem.
Sub de, van etc.: cognomina *americana* (post 1979) et *italiana* (post 1984); non reliqua.

Cognomina **italiana** et **americana** *sola* sub praefixo separato *da* etc.

Cognomina **italiana** et **americana** *sola* sub praefixo separato *da* etc.

Cognomina **italiana** et **americana** *sola* sub praefixo separato *da* etc.

Cognomina **italiana** et **americana** *sola* sub praefixo separato *da* etc.

Cognomina **italiana** et **americana** *sola* sub praefixo separato *da* etc.

Cognomina **italiana** et **americana** *sola* sub praefixo separato *da* etc.

Cognomina **italiana** et **americana** *sola* sub praefixo separato *da* etc.

ᴰdiss./dir. ᴱeditor ᶠFestschrift ᴹmentio, de eo ᴿrecensio ᵀtranslator † in mem.
Sub de, van etc.: cognomina americana (post 1979) et italiana (post 1984); non reliqua.

ᴰdiss./dir. ᴱeditor ᶠFestschrift ᴹmentio, de eo ᴿrecensio ᵀtranslator † in mem.
Sub **de, van** etc.: cognomina *americana* (post 1979) et *italiana* (post 1984); **non** reliqua.

ᴰdiss./dir. ᴱeditor ᶠFestschrift ᴹmentio, de eo ᴿrecensio ᵀtranslator † in mem.
Sub **de, van** etc.: cognomina *americana* (post 1979) et *italiana* (post 1984); **non** reliqua.

ᴰdiss./dir. ᴱeditor ᶠFestschrift ᴹmentio, de eo ᴿrecensio ᵀtranslator † in mem.
Sub **de, van** etc.: cognomina *americana* (post 1979) et *italiana* (post 1984); **non** reliqua.

Ddiss./dir. Eeditor FFestschrift Mmentio, de eo Rrecensio Ttranslator † in mem.
Sub de, van etc.: cognomina *americana* (post 1979) et *italiana* (post 1984); non reliqua.

Ddiss./dir. Eeditor FFestschrift Mmentio, de eo Rrecensio Ttranslator † in mem.
Sub de, van etc.: cognomina *americana* (post 1979) et *italiana* (post 1984); **non** reliqua.

ᴰdiss./dir. ᴱeditor ꟳFestschrift ᴹmentio, de eo ᴿrecensio ᵀtranslator † in mem.
Sub **de, van** etc.: cognomina *americana* (post 1979) et *italiana* (post 1984); **non** reliqua.

ᴰdiss./dir. ᴱeditor ᶠFestschrift ᴹmentio, de eo ᴿrecensio ᵀtranslator † in mem.
Sub **de, van** etc.: cognomina *americana* (post 1979) et *italiana* (post 1984); **non** reliqua.

ᴰdiss./dir. ᴱeditor ᶠFestschrift ᴹmentio, de eo ᴿrecensio ᵀtranslator † in mem.
Sub de, van etc.: cognomina americana (post 1979) et italiana (post 1984); non reliqua.

Ddiss./dir. Eeditor FFestschrift Mmentio, de eo Rrecensio Ttranslator † in mem.
Sub de, van etc.: cognomina americana (post 1979) et italiana (post 1984); non reliqua.

Ddiss./dir. Eeditor FFestschrift Mmentio, de eo Rrecensio Ttranslator † in mem.
Sub de, van etc.: cognomina americana (post 1979) et italiana (post 1984); non reliqua.

FINIS – Elenchus of Biblica 7, 1991 – END OF INDEX

Finito di stampare il 20 maggio 1994
Tipografia Poliglotta della Pontificia Università Gregoriana
Piazza della Pilotta, 4 – 00187 Roma

PONTIFICIO ISTITUTO BIBLICO
EDIZIONI 1993

NOVITÀ

ANALECTA BIBLICA

129. LENCHAK Timothy A.: *Choose Life! A Rhetorical-Critical Investigation of Deuteronomy 28,69-30,20.*
    pp. XII-308.   ISBN 88-7653-129-7.   Lit. 40.000

BIBLICA ET ORIENTALIA

44. DOBBS-ALLSOPP F.W.: *Weep, O Daughter of Zion: A Study of the City-Lament Genre in the Hebrew Bible.*
    pp. XIV-230.   ISBN 88-7653-346-X.   Lit. 30.000

STUDIA POHL: SERIES MAIOR

16. DI VITO Robert A.: *Studies in Third Millennium Sumerian and Akkadian Personal Names. The Designation and Conception of the Personal God.*
    pp. XII-328.   ISBN 88-7653-601-9.   Lit. 25.000

FUORI COLLANA

NORTH Robert (a cura di): *Elenchus of Biblica.* Vol. 6/1990.
    pp. 1.172.   ISBN 88-7653-599-3.   Lit. 170.000

RISTAMPE

Studia Pohl: Series Maior

4. Černý Jaroslav – Groll Sarah I., assisted by Eyre Christopher: *A Late Egyptian Grammar*. 4ᵃ edizione. pp. LXXXIV-620. ISBN 88-7653-435-0. Lit. 65.000

Subsidia Biblica

9. Joüon Paul: *Ruth. Commentaire philologique et exégétique*. pp. VIII-100. ISBN 88-7653-586-1. Lit. 13.000

14. Joüon Paul – Muraoka T.: *A Grammar of Biblical Hebrew*. Part One: *Orthography of Biblical Hebrew*. Part. Two: *Morphology*. Part. Three: *Syntax. Paradigms and Indices*. 2 volumi indivisibili. 2ᵃ edizione riveduta e corretta. pp. XLVI-780. ISBN 88-7653-595-0. Lit. 69.000

Fuori Collana

Zerwick Max – Grosvenor Mary: *A Grammatical Analysis of the Greek New Testament*. 4ᵃ edizione riveduta e corretta. pp. XXXVIII-778-16*. ISBN 88-7653-588-8. Lit. 35.000

È possibile sottoscrivere ordini in continuazione.

It is possible to subscribe standing orders.

Ordini e pagamenti a:

Orders and payments to:

AMMINISTRAZIONE PUBBLICAZIONI PIB/PUG
Piazza della Pilotta, 35 – 00187 Roma – Italia
Tel. 06/678.15.67 – Telefax 06/678.05.88

Conto Corrente Postale n. 34903005 – Compte Postal n. 34903005
Monte dei Paschi di Siena – Sede di Roma – c/c n. 54795.37

ISBN 88-7653-602-7